Encyclopedia
of the Arts

Encyclopedia
of the Arts

edited by
DAGOBERT D. RUNES
and
HARRY G. SCHRICKEL

PHILOSOPHICAL LIBRARY
New York

Printed in the United States of America

PREFACE

For several years there has been need for some compact, authoritative encyclopedic work in English dealing with the arts. Small art dictionaries, as have been published abroad for some time were not making available the definitive technical and critical information sought by the increasing audiences of the arts. Teachers and students of the arts, amateur and professional aestheticians, museum workers, and artists have been wanting some concise source of information dealing with the various aspects of their respective fields of artistic activity and appreciation. The present work is an answer to that demand.

While many subjects are covered by the *Encyclopedia* it is by necessity incomplete; a complete account of the arts could hardly be less than a comprehensive explanation of human nature and its history. Selection having been made, it became necessary to find those persons who would be most competent to speak authoritatively upon the subjects chosen. That we succeeded on this score can hardly be questioned by any who examine our roster of contributors. With regard to these contributors no praise is too high for their efforts to make the *Encyclopedia* a success. Without exception they worked with the greatest of care and enthusiasm, often under unusual circumstances brought about by World War II.

These war conditions multiplied what would normally have been a host of problems involved in the planning and carrying out of the *Encyclopedia* project. Yet it was judged better to go on to publication rather than postpone the project indefinitely, perhaps forever. The best argument for "seeing the thing through" lies in the fact that as we approach the termination of hostilities and are ever more aware of the post-war problems of reconstruction we realize the need for such a work as this in the cultural renaissance which shall and must come if we are to have a lasting peace and a better world in which to live.

We wish to extend our thanks to Dr. Thomas Munro of the Cleveland Museum of Art and Dr. Max Schoen of Carnegie Institute of Technology for their sustaining interest and valuable advice. Special thanks go to Miss Prudence Myer of the Cleveland Museum of Art for her assistance in reading of page proofs. As for the contributors themselves, their research and writing for the *Encyclopedia* was in most instances merely the beginning of their contributions; their suggestions, corrections and continued interest constituted the *élan vital* of the entire project from start to finish.

CONTRIBUTING EDITORS

Listed below, in alphabetical order, are the initials of the authors contributing to the *Encyclopedia*. These initials appear at the end of each contribution and the reader may identify the author by referring to this list. Note that the listing is an alphabetical arrangement of initials rather than surnames, the former system having been judged to be of greater convenience to the reader.

A. J. S.—Alois J. Schardt, Los Angeles
A. K. C.—Ananda K. Coomaraswamy, Museum of Fine Art, Boston
A. N.—Alfred Neumeyer, Mills College
A. P. B.—Achille P. Bragers, New York City
A. P. D.—Arthur P. Davis, Virginia Union University
A. V. B.—Arthur V. Berger, New York City

A. W. M.—Amy Woller McClelland, University of Southern California
A. W. O.—Anna Wetherill Olmsted, Syracuse Museum of Fine Arts

B. A. B.—B. A. Botkin, Library of Congress
B. G.—Balcomb Greene, Carnegie Institute of Technology
B. J.—Bernice Jamieson, Rhode Island School of Design
B. L-H.—Betty Lark-Horovitz, Purdue University
B. R.—Benjamin Rowland, Jr., U. S. Naval Reserve

C. A. M.—Clarence A. Manning, Columbia University
C. B. S.—Carter B. Storr, Ottowa, Ontario
C. C. P.—Carroll C. Pratt, Rutgers University
C. D. L.—Clark D. Lamberton, Western Reserve University
C. E. S.—Carl E. Seashore, State University of Iowa
C. L. S.—Carl L. Schmitz, New York City
C. M.—Clara Macgowan, Northwestern University
C. M. D.—Charles M. Diserens, University of Cincinnati
C. T.—Carl Thurston, Pasadena, California
C. W.—Charmion Wiegand, New York City
C. W. H.—Charles W. Hughes, Hunter College

D. H. P.—DeWitt H. Parker, University of Michigan
D. N. S.—Donald N. Ferguson, University of Minnesota
D. W. G.—D. W. Gotshalk, University of Illinois

E. C. H.—Eugene Clay Holmes, Howard University
E. F. D.—Ernst F. Detterer, Newberry Library, Chicago
E. K.—Ernst Krenek, Hamline University
E. N.—Eugen Neuhaus, University of California, Berkeley
E. N-S.—E. Neale-Silva, University of Wisconsin
E. S.—Eric Schroeder, Fogg Museum of Art, Harvard University
E. S.—Ernst Scheyer, Wayne University
E. S. B.—Edward S. Bordin, University of Minnesota

F. D.—Frederick Dorian, Carnegie Institute of Technology
F. F.—Finley Foster, Western Reserve University

G. A.—George Amberg, Museum of Modern Art
G. B. L.—G. B. Ladner, Pontifical Institute of Mediaeval Studies, Canada
G. C. V.—George C. Vaillant, University of Pennsylvania Museum
G. H.—Glen Haydon, University of North Carolina
G. K.—Gyorgy Kepes, School of Design in Chicago
G. L. M. M.—Grace L. McCann Morley, San Francisco Museum of Art
G. L. S.—George L. Stout, Fogg Museum of Art, Harvard University
G. M. A. H.—George M. A. Haufmann, Fogg Museum of Art, Harvard University
G. W. R.—Grace W. Ripley, Rhode Island School of Design

H. E. L-H.—Helmut E. Lehmann-Haupt, Columbia University
H. E. S.—Homer E. Sterling, Carnegie Institute of Technology
H. F. K.—H. Felix Kraus, Museum of Non-Objective Art, New York City
H. G.—Helen Gardner, School of the Art Institute of Chicago
H. G. S.—H. G. Schrickel, Carnegie Institute of Technology
H. Gu.—Hermann Gundersheimer, Temple University
H. H.—Helmut Hungerland, Piedmont, California
H. K.—Helmut Kuhn, University of North Carolina
H. M.—Henri Marceau, Philadelphia Museum of Art
Ho. H.—Howard Hollis, Cleveland Museum of Art
H. P. E.—Henry Purmort Eames, Scripps College and Claremont Graduate Colleges,
        California
H. R.—Herman Reichenbach, New York City
H. R. W.—Harry W. Warfel, University of Maryland

I. B.—Iris Barry, Museum of Modern Art
I. J.—Iredell Jenkins, Tulane University
I. L.—Irene Lewisohn, Museum of Costume Art, New York City
I. P.—Irena Piotrowska, New York City

J. A.—Joseph Aronson, New York City
J. A. M.—J. Arthur MacLean, Toledo Museum of Art
J. A. P.—James A. Porter, Howard University
J. C.—James Chillman, Jr., Museum of Fine Arts of Houston
J. F. M.—John F. Matthews, New York City
J. G.—Jennie Grainger, University of Wisconsin
J. G. V.—James Grote van Derpool, University of Illinois
J. M.—Jermayne Macagy, California Palace of the Legion of Honor, San
          Francisco
J. McA.—John McAndrew, Instituto Nacional de Anthropologia, México, D. F.
J. M. M.—J. Marshall Miller, Columbia University
J. R. T.—John R. Tuttle, Elmira College
J. V. H.—J. Vincent Higginson, Brooklyn, New York

K. E. G.—Katherine E. Gilbert, Duke University
K. F. B.—Kenneth F. Bates, Cleveland School of Art
K. J. C.—Kenneth J. Conant, Harvard University
K. K.—Kalman Kubinyi, Lakewood, Ohio

L. C. E.—L. C. Everard, American Association of Museums, Washington
          (deceased)
L. D. L.—Lester D. Longman, State University of Iowa
L. H.—Lawrence Hill, Washington University, St. Louis
L. K.—Lincoln Kirstein, American Ballet Caravan, New York City
L. L.—Leopold Levis, Cleveland Museum of Art
L. L. W.—Leon L. Winslow, Public Schools, Baltimore, Maryland
L. M-N.—L. Moholy-Nagy, School of Design in Chicago
L. P-E.—Lotte Pulvermacher-Egers, New York City
L. S.—Lawrence Schmeckebier, University of Minnesota
L. T. S.—Lucy T. Shoe, Mount Holyoke College

M. B.—Marion Bauer, New York City
M. C. G.—Merry Cartwright Gray, Los Angeles, California
M. E.—Mildred Eakes, Cincinnati Conservatory of Music
M. F. M.—Margaret Fairbanks Marcus, Cleveland Museum of Art
M. H.—Max Horkeimer, New School for Social Research, New York City
M. L.—Marie Lien, University of Minnesota
M. M.—Myra Miller, New York City
M. N. H'D.—Margaret N. H'Doubler, University of Wisconsin
M. R.—Maurice Ries, Office of the Coordinator of Inter-American Affairs
M. S.—Max Schoen, Carnegie Institute of Technology
M. S. F.—Milton S. Fox, Cleveland Museum of Art

N. C. M.—Norman C. Meier, State University of Iowa
N. L.—Nathan Lerner, School Design in Chicago
N. M.—Norman Macleod, Briarcliff Junior College
N. P.—Norman Pietan, New York City

O. B.—Otto Benesch, Fogg Museum of Art, Harvard University
O. M. S.—Oliver M. Stone, Case School of Applied Science
O. O.—Otto Ortmann, Baltimore, Maryland

P. A.—Phyllis Ackerman, New York City
P. C. B.—Philip C. Beam, Bowdoin Museum of Fine Arts
P. W.—Polaire Weissman, Museum of Costume Art, New York City
P. Z.—Paul Zucker, Cooper Union, New York City

R. A.—Rudolf Arnheim, Guggenheim Foundation, New York City
R. A. F.—Raymond A. Fisher, Carnegie Institute of Technology
R. B.—Richard Bernheimer, Bryn Mawr College
R. B. W.—Ralph B. Winn, College of City of New York
R. C. S.—Robert C. Smith, Library of Congress
R. D. W.—R. D. Welch, Princeton University
R. F. P.—R. F. Piper, Syracuse University
R. J. N.—Richard J. Neutra, Los Angeles
R. K.—Richard Krautheimer, Vassar College

R. L. W.—Ralph L. Wickiser, Louisiana State University
R. M.—Ralph Mayer, New York City
R. T.—Ramsay Traquair, Guysborough, Nova Scotia
R. W. C.—Ralph W. Church, Cornell University
R. W. Y.—Robert W. Young

S. C.—Schuyler Van R. Cammann, Washington, D. C.
S. C. P.—Stephen C. Pepper, University of Calfornia, Berkeley
S. M. W.—S. Macdonald Wright, University of Southern California
S. Z.—Sidney Zink, New York City

T. A. H.—Theodore Allen Heinrich, Berkeley, California
T. E. F.—Thomas E. French, Ohio State University
T. F.—Theodore Finney, University of Pittsburgh
T. I. C.—Theron I. Cain, Massachusetts School of Art
T. M.—Thomas Munro, Cleveland Museum of Art
T. W.—Thomas Wilfred, West Nyack, New York
T. W. A.—T. W. Adorno, New York City

V. A.—Vincent Aita, Hunter College
V. K. B.—Victoria K. Ball, Western Reserve University
V. M.—Valentine Muller, Bryn Mawr College
V. M. A.—Van Meter Ames, University of Cincinnati
V. N.—Virginia Nepodal, Cleveland School of Art
V. S.—Viktor Schreckengost, Cleveland, Ohio

W. A.—Walter Abell, Michigan State College
W. A. K.—W. A. Kerr, U. S. Naval Reserve
W. A. S.—William A. Strong, Cleveland, Ohio
W. C.—Walter Cerf, Brooklyn College, New York
W. C. H.—W. C. Handy, New York City
W. G. W.—William G. Whitford, University of Chicago
W. R. A.—Walter R. Agard, University of Wisconsin
W. R. H.—Walter R. Hovey, University of Pittsburgh
W. S.—Wolfgang Stechow, Oberlin College
W. S. R.—W. S. Rusk, Wells College
W. T. C.—Wing-tsit Chan, University of Hawaii

Y. K.—Yasuo Kuniyoshi, New York City

TOPICAL SUGGESTIONS

Listed below, under general headings, are some of the major articles and definitions to be found in the ENCYCLOPEDIA. The list is by no means exhaustive; e.g., no mention is made of several important articles on etching, photography, clavilux, prints and print processes, poetry, the novel, and others. The reader should not take this topical outline as indicative of the scope of the ENCYCLOPEDIA but, rather, should regard the suggestions given as a cross reference aid to his casual reading of the pages that follow.

AESTHETICS: AESTHETIC INQUIRY, current types of; AESTHETICS; AESTHETICS, recent trends in; ART; art criticism; ARTIST, PSYCHOLOGY OF THE; art tests; beauty; classification of the arts; design; engineering, aesthetics of; equilibrium; form; formalism; idealism; imagination; impressionism; inspiration; linear; LITERARY CRITICISM; materialism; naturalism; organic; painterly; participation; PHILOSOPHY OF ART; PSYCHOLOGY OF ART; rationalism; realism; regionalism; socialist realism; sociology of art; style; symmetry; TASTE AND ITS EDUCATION; unity; variety in unity.

ARCHITECTURE: ARCHITECTURE; balloon framing; Bauhaus; Brazil, The Colonial Architecture of; bridge; BYZANTINE ARCHITECTURE; CANADA, ARCHITECTURE OF; Carolingian architecture; castle; CIVIC PLANNING; Cluniac architecture; color in architecture; domestic architecture; EARLY CHRISTIAN ARCHITECTURE; functional architecture; GREAT BRITAIN, ARCHITECTURE OF; house; housing; INTERIOR ARCHITECTURE AND DECORATION (INTERIOR DESIGN); international architecture; LANDSCAPE ARCHITECTURE; Lombard architecture; Mexico, post-Conquest architecture of; monastic architecture; Neo-classic architecture; NEW ATTITUDES FOR THE FUTURE OF ARCHITECTURE; Queen Anne architecture; Romanesque architecture; synagogues.

ART EDUCATION: ART EDUCATION; art tests; CHILDREN'S ART; educational dance; genius.

CERAMICS AND POTTERY: Aegean vases; black-figured vases; CERAMICS I; CERAMICS II; Corinthian vases; Ionian vases.

CRAFTS: BOOK ILLUSTRATION; calligraphy; carpet; Cosmati; COSTUME ART; DRESS, EUROPEAN; EARLY BOOKBINDING AND FINE BINDING; edition binding; ENAMELLING ON METAL; FLOWER ARRANGEMENT; FURNITURE; GLASS AND GLASSMAKING; HERALDRY; INTERIOR ARCHITECTURE AND DECORATION (INTERIOR DESIGN); JEWELRY, HISTORY OF; lace; lettering; metalwork; ornament engraving; rebinding; Silk; STAINED GLASS; TAPESTRY; writing.

DANCE: absolute dance; adagio; aesthetic dance; ballet; bourrée; boutrade; character dance; chorovody; cracoviac; DANCE; dance of death; educational dance; farandole; galliard; gigue; hora; Irish jig; kinesthetic sense; morris dance; opposition; passepied; pavane.

DRAMA: AMERICAN NEGRO THEATRE; MODERN STAGESETTING; RADIO DRAMA; STAGESETTING; THEATRE.

EASTERN ART: Australian Aboriginal Art; Australian Contemporary Art; BYZANTINE ARCHITECTURE; BYZANTINE ART; CENTRAL ASIAN ART (TURKESTAN); CHINESE ARTS; EGYPTIAN ART; INDIAN ART; ISLAMIC ART; JAPANESE ART; Maori carving; MESOPOTAMIAN ART; OCEANIA, ARTS OF; PERSIAN ART; SOUTH-EASTERN ASIATIC ART; SYMBOLISM IN FAR EASTERN ART.

EUROPEAN ART: AUSTRALIAN ART; Bulgaria, art of; Carolingian art; Celtic art; CZECHOSLOVAKIA, ART OF; ENGLISH ART; Estonia, art of; ETRUSCAN ART; FLEMISH ART; FRENCH ART; GERMAN ART; HELLENIC ART; ISLAMIC ART; ITALIAN ART; JEWISH ART; LATE ANTIQUE ART; Latvia, art of; Lithuanian art; NETHERLANDISH ART; POLISH ART; ROMAN ART; RUSSIAN ARTS; RUSSIA, RELIGIOUS PAINTING IN; Salian art; SCANDINAVIAN ART; SPAIN, ART OF; Yugoslavia, art of.

HISTORY OF ART: academicism; Antwerp school; ARCHAEOLOGY, AESTHETIC ASPECTS OF; art nouveau; Arts and Crafts movement; baroque; Biedermeier; Blaue Reiter, the; chinoiserie; Chios, school of; cinquecento; classical style; classicism; Counter-Reformation; Cretan-Minoan; "degenerate" art; Deutscher Werkbund; Düsseldorf, school of; eclecticism; Expressionismus; Florentine school; formalism; futurism; Gothic; Hohenstaufen art; illusionism; impressionism; japonism; Jugendstil; LATE ANTIQUE ART; machine art; Mannerism; Meldrum, school of; Nazarenes, the; Neo-classicism; new objectivity; Nuremberg, school of; Renaissance; rococo; Romanticism; Siena, school of; surrealism; universal artwork.

MUSIC: acoustics; acoustics, terminology in; gallant style; gestalt psychology and music; Greek music, ancient; harmony; hymn; idiom; INDUSTRIAL MUSIC RESEARCH; In Nomine; interval; jazz; JEWISH MUSIC; key; Latin American music; mechanical instruments (musical); MEDIEVAL MUSIC; modes, ecclesiastical; MUSICAL INSTRUMENTS; MUSICAL PERFORMANCE, MAIN TRENDS IN; music appreciation; music-culture; music education; MUSIC HISTORY, PERIODS IN; musicology; music, origins of; music printng and engraving; OPERA; oratorio; ORIENTAL MUSIC; overture; performance score; phonophotography; polyphony.

MUSIC: AMERICAN NEGRO MUSIC; broadcasting of music, the; Byzantine music; chamber music; clef; comic element in music, the; counterpoint; dance music; eastern chants; electrical instruments (musical); EXPERIMENTAL PSYCHOLOGY OF MUSIC; Fancy, Fantasia; fauxbourdon; psychology of tone; radio and music; scales and modes, sequence; sonance; sonata; SONG; street music; symphony; timbre; tone quality; tremolo; twelve-tone technique; vibrato.

PAINTING: collage; COLOR; cubism; Dadaism; encaustic painting; FORGERIES IN PAINTINGS; frame; mural painting; non-objective painting; PAINTING; post-impressionism; PSYCHOLOGY OF DRAWING AND PAINTING; purism; RESTORATION OF PAINTINGS; RUSSIA, RELIGIOUS PAINTINGS IN; sand painting; tempera; water color.

PRIMITIVE ART: AFRICAN NEGRO ART; AMERICAN ABORIGINAL ART, Central and South America; Australian Aboriginal Art; Eastern North American Aboriginal Art; ESKIMO ART; PREHISTORIC ART; PRIMITIVE ART.

RELIGIOUS ART: altar; altarpiece; aureole and mandorla; ciborium; Cosmati; EARLY CHRISTIAN ARCHITECTURE; EARLY CHRISTIAN ART; Evangeliar; JEWISH ART; monastic architecture; nimbus; Resurrection; RUSSIA, RELIGIOUS PAINTING IN; synagogues; tiara, papal.

SCULPTURE: canon, sculptural; Chios, school of; Cosmati; negative carving; relief sculpture; SCULPTURE; terra cotta sculpture, direct method.

UNITED STATES, ART OF THE: Adena Culture; American folk forms, in literature; American folk forms, in music; AMERICAN NEGRO ART; AMERICAN NEGRO LITERATURE; AMERICAN NEGRO MUSIC; AMERICAN NEGRO THEATRE; California Indian art; EARLY AMERICAN ART; Eastern North American aboriginal art; Hohokam art; Hopi art; Mimbres art; POST-REVOLUTIONARY ARCHITECTURE AND DECORATIVE ARTS IN THE U. S. A.; POST-REVOLUTIONARY PAINTING AND SCULPTURE IN THE U. S. A.; Pueblo art; U. S. A., LITERATURE OF THE.

WESTERN HEMISPHERE ART: AMERICAN ABORIGINAL ART, Central and South America; Brazil, The Colonial Architecture of; CANADA, ARCHITECTURE OF; CANADA, ART OF; Eastern North American aboriginal art; HISPANIC AMERICAN LITERATURE; history of art; LATIN AMERICAN ART; Maya art; Mexican art, ancient; Mexican painting, contemporary; Navaho art; Northwest Coast Indian art;. Plains Indian art; SPANISH ARCHITECTURE IN THE NEW WORLD.

Encyclopedia
of the Arts

A

a. See NOTATION; ACOUSTICS.

Aaklae weaving. See SCANDINAVIAN ART.

Aaron Ha-Kodesch. See synagogues.

aba (Ar.). A coat. See COSTUME ART.

abacus. A slab forming the uppermost member or division of a capital.

abat-jour (F.). A device to regulate the quality of daylight by throwing the light downward as it enters a window. The effect is obtained by the use of a screen or skylight. —R.L.W.

Abbasid art. See ISLAMIC ART.

abbey. Large-sized monastery, Benedictine, Cluniac, Cistercian. Their plans, possibly derived from late antique villas, show a cloister south of the church, enclosed by dormitory and chapterhouse (east), refectory (south) and cellar (west). This nucleus may be surrounded by workshops, agricultural buildings, hospital, garden, schoolhouse, abbot's residence and guest house (parchment plan of St. Gall, ca. 820; description of Farfa, 1038-49; Montecassino, 1075; Cluny 980 and 1085 resp.). See Viollet-le-Duc, *Dictionnaire raisonné,* 1858, s.v. *architecture monastique;* Schlosser, *Die abendlaendische Klosteranlage,* 1899. —R.K.

abbozzo (It.). Sketch or preliminary draft of a work of art.

Abhaya mudra (Skr.). Mystic gesture symbolizing protection, fearlessness. Right hand, shoulder high, all fingers extended, palm outward. See mudra. —J.A.M.

absidiole. See apsidiole.

absolute art. (1) Art for art's sake (q.v.). (2) Abstract painting and sculpture, the music of forms and colors (see post-impressionism). (3) Schelling's conception of art as developed in his *System of Transcendental Idealism* (1800)—though Schelling himself does not use the term "absolute art". According to Schelling, Philosophy's main task is to explain knowledge, either by beginning on the side of the object and showing how the subject (intelligence, consciousness) is added to it—this is done in the Philosophy of Nature—or else by taking the subject as the primary principle and explaining the object in terms of the subject—this is the task of the Philosophy of Transcendence. The latter has, in turn, two branches, viz., theoretical philosophy which assumes that ideas can be determined by objects existing independently of them; and practical philosophy which assumes the opposite, i.e., that our ideas can influence the objective order. These two assumptions are contradictory and their conflict engenders the highest problem in the philosophy of transcendence, the problem of how ideas can be dependent upon objects and at the same time objects dependent upon ideas. This problem can be solved only if there is a pre-established harmony between the world of the objects (nature, the unconscious) and the world of the subject (ideas, intelligence, consciousness). The world of the object must be the unconscious product of the same activity that consciously produces the world of ideas.

But where can an activity be found that in itself guarantees the union of unconsciousness and consciousness, of objectivity and subjectivity, and thus denotes the point upon which the whole philosophy of transcendence hinges? The activity is to be found in the sphere of the subject itself: it is the aesthetic activity of the genius. Every true work of art bears witness to the identity of the conscious and unconscious activity in the subject. However skilful, prudent and deliberate the genius may be, "with respect to the properly objective side in his production he seems to stay under the influence of a power which separates him from all other beings and forces him to utter or represent things which are not completely transparent to him and whose meaning is infinite." (*System of Transc. Ideal.* p. 291). Art is the objective "revelation of the holy of holies" (op. cit., p. 302), of the absolute; it shows the union of the subjective and the objective, and philosophy of art, in which theoretical and practical philosophy are united is the keystone of the whole philosophical edifice.

Swept along by the artistic enthusiasm of German romanticism, Schelling thus assigned to art—the only objective revelation of the absolute—a place superior to philosophy and religion. Nowhere before or since has philosophy so readily yielded its primacy to art—a role, however, which art held only for a moment. Schelling himself, in his lectures on the *Philosophy of Art* (1802-3), was soon to achieve a juster, more balanced view.

—W.C.

absolute dance. A type of dance in which movement relies solely upon its own power to arouse emotive forces. It is not concerned with specific happenings or descriptions, nor does it depend upon extraneous aid, such as costume, stage setting, lighting, or music for its communication. Its movements are organized into a composition for no other reason than to be expressive of whatever beauty and meaning is embodied in them, and for the satisfaction of their being given form.

Although the movements of absolute dance are composed primarily to communicate feeling of motor origin, and not as motor symbols expressive of feeling states, they have the power to appeal to the intellectual, imaginative, and emotional natures and thus they may afford a very complete and satisfying aesthetic experience. Such dances may have any flavor from the comic to the tragic and may suggest a complete picture of gaiety, hope, despair, awe, or tranquility. Their expressive and communicative qualities, however, depend upon the spontaneous inspiration of the dancer. Meaning is immediate and seems to emerge spontaneously from the movements. Without this element such dances would exist as a series of well executed calisthenics and have little value as art. Absolute dance, like absolute music, may be thought of as dance in its purest form.

—M.N.H'D.

absolute music. (1) Music without words. (2) Music void of extra-musical content or subject matter.

absolute pitch. *Mus.* (1) The pitch of a tone when regarded or defined physically or acoustically or when referred to a standard thus established; opposed to relative pitch. (2) Aural recognition of the pitch name (C, Eb, etc.) of a single tone, irrespective of other tones.

abstract. See abstraction.

abstract cinematograph. See PHOTOGRAPHY.

abstraction. (1) In art, a design in a graphic or plastic medium which is non-representational in purpose, is ordinarily more or less geometric, but occasionally amorphous or vaguely biomorphic, and which presumes to have at least decorative beauty and may have cultural meaning and associations. It may be derived or abstracted from natural forms, may intend to portray the essential geometric structure of such forms, or may be entirely the product of aesthetic ingenuity, invention, and intuitive imagination without reference to natural forms. The free invention of designs is sometimes spoken of as 'non-objectivism' (q.v.) or 'pure-abstraction', and titles are generally numbered "Compositions" or "Improvisations" as in music. Designs derived from natural forms, particularly if any visible likeness to these forms survives the transformation, are spoken of as near-abstractions. Cubist painting (q.v.), however, is ordinarily too strongly suggestive of recognizable natural forms even to be called near-abstraction, but may be classified as semi-abstraction.

From a formal point of view, abstraction is the extreme opposite of naturalism (q.v.) in that it stresses the abstract (Universals) rather than the concrete (Particulars); but it is not necessary to the concept of abstraction that the form shall coincide with the essential structure of natural forms as in idealism. Instead it may be either largely or entirely a matter of the artist's self-expression.

(2) Abstraction is also used in the sense of abstractionism in reference to a principle or doctrine favoring the painting or carving of abstractions. As such it is a modern movement which flourished from the first world war to about 1930 and is still followed by numerous adherents in France, England, and America.

Little *abstract sculpture* has been produced

in the history of art, but modern abstract artists occasionally recall paleolithic and neolithic and some African primitive precedents. Since it is difficult to produce purely abstract sculpture of originality and aesthetic merit, most modern exponents are near-abstractionists or semi-abstractionists. Such sculptors include Archipenko, Brancusi, Belling (frequently), Lipschitz, Laurens, Duchamp-Villon, Picasso (occasionally), Henry Moore, Nicholson, Hepworth, Gabo, Pevsner, Rodchenko, Giacometti, Arp, Vantongerloo, Schwitters, Calder, and Robus.

Abstract painting is more popular than sculpture. Arising out of cubism in the early 1910's, it took many forms, most of which, like many of Picasso's paintings, are only semi-abstract or near abstract. It became 'Purism' (q.v.) at the hands of Ozenfant and Le Corbusier; 'Synchromism' (q.v.) with Russell and Wright; 'Orphism' (q.v.) with Delaunay, and Kupka; 'Futurism' (q.v.) with Severini, Russolo, Balla, Carra, and Boccioni; 'Dadaism' or 'Surrealism' (qq.v.), and usually amorphic or biomorphic rather than geometric, with Arp, Ernst, Picabia, Miro, Masson, et al.; and amorphous expressionism with Kandinsky and Klee. It was applied to photography and films by Man Ray, Moholy-Nagy, Leger, and Richter. And it became completely abstract and geometric with the Dutch 'de Stijl' group and 'Neo-plasticists' (qq.v.), e.g. Mondrian, Domela, and Van Doesburg; with the Russian 'Suprematists' and 'Constructivists' (qq.v.), Gabo, Pevsner, Malevich, and Rodchenko and the Hungarian 'Constructivist' Moholy-Nagy; with the English abstractionists Wadsworth and Nicholson; with the French "Abstraction-creationist" (q.v.) Hélion and with the American abstract artists, e.g. Feininger, Dove, Marin, Stuart Davis, Xceron, and 'non-objectivist' Bauer. See A. H. Barr, Jr., *Cubism and Abstract Art*, 1936. —L.D.L.

(3) Dance activity, as all art activity, lies in the realm of *abstraction*. The artist focuses his attention upon the essential nature of an experience and emphasizes that essence by every means in his power that he may express and communicate in movement his idea of it. Abstraction in movement is accomplished by the dancer searching within the movements commonly associated with an idea or feeling for movements that are more directly related to the basic material, or the essences, of his experience. He then consciously magnifies or distorts (see distortion) that particular movement or phase of a movement which is most nearly synonymous with the essentials as he perceives them. Although abstraction is the antithesis of realism, it nevertheless has its roots in reality. It is when abstraction is carried beyond any reference to reality that confusion and lack of communication results. —M.N.H'D.

Abstraction-Création group. A group of geometric-abstract painters and sculptors in Paris in the early 1930's, led by Piet Mondrian, including Jean Helion. —L.D.L.

abstractionism. A little-used term synonymous with the doctrine of *abstraction* (q.v.).

abstract music. See absolute music (2).

abstract painting and photography. See PHOTOGRAPHY.

abstract seeing. See PHOTOGRAPHY.

abutment. That which receives the end of, and gives support to, anything having a tendency to spread out, or to thrust out; a supporting or buttressing structure, as at the end of a wall. —J.M.M.

abutter. See CIVIC PLANNING.

academicism. As applied to art creation and appreciation, the term, academicism, is used in a classical period or in one where art is a means to an end other than aesthetic, as one of approval; in a romantic period or in any "modern" period it connotes the force of tradition. Academicism stresses formal relationships as contrasted with vital expression; its locale is the studio, if not the study, rather than the world of nature and man. Yet time and again the significant artists of a time are found to be builders on academic foundations. Even a Cezanne expresses a desire to paint as the old masters in the museums did, as well as to, or rather, in order to, "realize" objects in nature.

The prototype of all learned academies, with their resulting influence called academicism, was Plato's Academy in the groves beside the Cephissus outside Athens. The most noteworthy modern one is the Academy of Fine Arts in Paris, a section of the French Academy, founded by Louis XIV in 1648. From its members is chosen the Director of the French Academy in Rome. The training in the École des Beaux-Arts in Paris and in the Villa Medici at Rome has had a strong influence on French art and taste. In so far as Paris became the art center of the western world in the nineteenth century this influence affected art throughout the western hemisphere, even if it was negatively so, as the twentieth century approached. In the United States generations of painters have time and again marked their advent by "seceding" from the National Academy of Art until maturity or senility, as it is variously interpreted, lead them to synthesize the new with the old.

In some civilizations the academic point of view has been so completely shaped by the artist that room has been found in a strait jacket. True, the confining garment has been amply proportioned. Egypt and China and Byzantium are cases in point. The breakdown on occasion of conventional forms did not in the long run add stature to the Egyptian achievement. When they created within the limits of their millenial conventions, they radiated. Again, the traditions of Chinese craftsmanship, where artisan and artist are one, are not often honored by ignoring them. And one recalls that Byzantine tradition served medieval symbolism well and was vital enough after a thousand years to restrain Giotto, to inspire Duccio, and to inform Abbot Desiderius of Monte Cassino. On the other hand, the late or academic phase of Greek art was not always helpful to Roman or to Hindu. The Renaissance florescence all too soon ran into academic correctness which justified, if it did not occasion, baroque extravagances. As neo-classism, it encouraged the substitution of taste for expression and produced Canova and Thorsvaldsen as well as David and Ingres. Yet even here such continuities as Palladio-Inigo Jones-Wren-Latrobe and Rubens-Reynolds-Stuart produced notable results which still arouse admiration. A recent example of academicism triumphant is found in the flourishing American Academy at Rome where archaeology and art are taught to selected youth in storied settings. It inspires and conditions, and may also cramp, future creation. Paul Manship comes to mind.

Academicism has found expression in the art theories of practising artists and in the aesthetic theories of historians and critics. The former are often helpful to those who would appreciate works of other times and places; the latter to those who would understand historical and philosophical trends, and on occasion they are sufficiently suggestive to cause the reader to rethink and classify his own standards of judgment.

As an example of the former one might instance the evolution of the academic ideals of painting in the Italian Renaissance. Leonardo pointed out that modelling is the first purpose of the painter and that movement is a sure means of suggesting emotion. He urged selective imitation. He would illuminate pleasantly, counterpoise easily, compose freely. By the later 16th cent. the "Grand Style" was forming. Vasari, calling it the "modern" style and naming Leonardo as its initiator, points out that Fra Bartolommeo and Giorgione by graduation of color attained "force, relief, sweetness, and grace". Raphael reached complete perfection, he thinks, comparable to that attained by Apelles and Zeuxis in ancient times. Andrea del Sarto produced works sweeter and less bold, but "free from errors". Thus the stage is set for the eclectic to become the academic, and the critic to replace the master. In the early 18th cent. Lodovico Dolce showed how Titian combined the grandeur and terribleness of Michelangelo, the pleasantness and grace of Raphael, with the coloring "proper to nature", and, late in the century Sir Joshua Reynolds strikes the true classical note when he urges the embodiment of the abstract idea back of individualities. Beauty, simplicity, and nobility were the ends to be sought. As late as the early 20th cent. Kenyon Cox was still writing that the classic (academic?) point of view seeks "the essential rather than the accidental, the eternal rather than the momentary — loves impersonality rather than personality . . . to steep itself in tradition."

But the story of academicism in the 17th to the 20th cent. is also illustrated in works of art criticism and art history—Winckelmann, Goethe, Ruskin, Burckhardt, Woelfflin, Wilenski. In only a few cases in these years has an artist, Adolf Hildebrand, for example, successfully rationalized his creative ideas. The dangers of such a divorce as is here suggested between art and life are recalled by the successive clichés which have confused as well as clarified—"the sublime and the beautiful", "feeling is everything", "the lamp of truth", "art for art's sake", "significant form", "flowing space". Yet the intelligent layman is grateful for Woelfflin's analysis of Renaissance design into its linear, planar and recessive, closed and open, multiple and unified, and clear and unclear aspects. He is also grateful to Geoffrey Scott for his "fallacies" — biological, mechanical, romantic, and ethical — of architectural criticism; to Wilenski for his insistence that the artist alone is qualified to act as critic of his work; and to Panofsky for his iconographical interpretations of works of art. He is grateful if for no other reason than the stimulating one of disagreement. From

William Morris to Walter Gropius the academic approach has shown itself capable of possessing rejuvenating power, which suggests that tradition is not necessarily enslaving, that craftsmanship and artistry are not necessarily opposed, and that academicism and creation have much in common. See A. Hildebrand, *The Problem of Form,* 1907; Leonardo da Vinci, *Notebooks,* edited by Edward McCurdy, 1938; E. Panofsky, *Studies in Iconology,* 1939; S. Giedion, *Time, Space, and Architecture,* 1941; G. Scott, *The Architecture of Humanism,* 1924; F. P. Chambers, *History of Taste,* 1932; A. Blunt, *Artistic Theory in Italy 1450-1600,* 1940; L. Venturi, *History of Art Criticism,* 1936; L. Venturi, *Art Criticism Now,* 1941; R. H. Wilenski, *The Modern Movement in Art,* 1927; H. Woelfflin, *Principles of Art History,* 1932; N. Pevsner, *Academies of Art,* 1940.   —W.S.R.

academy. An institution devoted to the disinterested furtherance of some desirable nonreligious activity above the level of political and economic needs. The name 'Academy' is derived from a district in Athens in which Plato used to converse with his pupils and to teach them his philosophy. The name was revived by idealistic humanist circles during the early Italian Renaissance of which the most influential was the group gathered around Lorenzo de' Medici in Florence. It then used to designate the informal meeting of cultured and learned men to discuss in congenial surroundings problems of philosophy and science. Even the academy of Leonardo da Vinci referred to in inscriptions in some of his engravings seems to have been of that kind. In the 16th cent. the use of the word spread to cover almost any regular gathering for almost any ideal or recreational end.

Academies of art fall from the beginning into two distinct groups. Studio academies are gatherings of mature and incipient artists in somebody's private workshop for the purpose of drawing after sculptural or living models. Such was the academy of B. Bandinelli (1531), the earliest artistic enterprise known under that name, and that of the Caracci in Bologna (after 1590); the latter affected some of the pretensions of contemporary official institutions. Although, particularly in Italy, private studio academies were never quite discontinued even in time of severest institutionalization, their heyday dawned in 19th cent. France, owing to the initiative of J. L. David who transplanted the Italian type to Paris while adopting some

of the strict pedagogical routine of the official institutions.

From the beginning official academies differed from the private by their wider aims and their higher pretensions. They were designed to lift the artist from the level of the medieval craftsman to that of the creator by freeing him from the jurisdiction of the guilds. In order to achieve this, the founders usually invoked the protectorate of the absolute monarch, a device which in many cases resulted in the subservience of the freshly emancipated artist to the crown. Moreover they found it feasible to give to the institution a clearly defined representational function enhanced often by high sounding names and titles. The pedagogical aims of the academy, although not much emphasized in the early foundations, came more and more to the fore in a development which culminated in the 19th cent. monopoly of academies and related institutions in all matters of artistic education. Until then the artist had received his elementary education in the workshop of his master (see *bottega*) and the academy had attempted no more than to raise him to the demands of the grand style (q.v.) by perfecting his knowledge of design. It is only in the 19th cent. that academies added instruction in the actual technique of painting to their classes in drawing first after drawings, then after plaster casts and living models.

All official academies trace their origin back to the *Academia del Disegno* founded in 1563 by G. Vasari. Its immediate offspring was the *Academia di San Luca* in Rome (1593), the organization of which became the prototype of Lebrun's and Colbert's *Academie Royale de Peinture et de Sculpture.* The latter in turn, with its elaborate order of precedence, its mode of training, its artistic doctrines, its prizes and its affiliate institution in Rome, was the model for similar enterprises throughout the 17th and 18th cent. Even its close dependence on the court seemed worthy of imitation as long as there were absolute princes eager to engage art in the service of their cause. A new upsurge in the foundation of academies occurred in the second part of the 18th cent. owing to the belief of local potentates that academic education of taste among craftsmen would redound to the economic advantage of their country, — an argument narrowly utilitarian, but timely at a period when the abolition of guilds and the beginnings of the industrial revolution were undermining the hitherto solid foundations of European craftsmanship. The academies, however, failed to educate the craftsman and later saw that task relegated to schools of industrial arts. Instead of following the 19th cent. trends toward machine production and bourgeois realism they conservatively proclaimed their stewardship of the grand style thereby laying themselves open to criticism, since that style had lost its social justification after the end of absolutistic rule. The battle between independent progressive artists and the academies fills the annals of the 19th cent. That battle was lost by the artists socially, since their emancipation became a more and more bitter isolation; but it was won by them artistically, since the academies had to give up their tenets one by one to come to terms with modern modes of expression. See N. Pevsner, *Academies of Art,* 1940.   **—R.B.**

academy board. During the 19th cent. this material came into use as a support for painting. Usually it was a piece of pasteboard about ⅛ in. thick and with a pale gray or white ground of lead pigment mixed with oil, and with various other ingredients. The name probably came from its wide use in art schools where it furnished a cheaper support than wooden panels or stretched canvas. A somewhat similar material has the pasteboard as a secondary support and over it is attached a piece of canvas with the usual painting ground. This goes by the name, "canvas board." Probably such materials were not economical before the manufacture of pasteboard from wood-pulp toward the end of the 18th cent. The commercial manufacture of these boards goes back at least to 1819.
—G.L.S.

acanthus (Gr.). Architectural decoration, based on a conventionalization of the large dentate leaves of the acanthus plant. The most notable use has been on Corinthian capitals. The first known examples are on the interior columns of the temple of Apollo at Bassae in Southern Greece, dating about 420 B.C.; two girdles of modest acanthus leaves spring from the lower part of the capital. As the Corinthian style increased in favor, esp. in Roman times, the acanthus leaves became larger, projected further, and were more deeply undercut, becoming a luxuriant growth, the chief element of the capital. On Byzantine and Romanesque capitals they often appear, but the earlier exuberance is checked and the leaves are kept close to the block. The motif has also been used for other decorative purposes: girdling the great column supporting three dancing

maidens and a tripod at Delphi; as a finial on the Choragic Monument of Lysicrates at Athens; and as relief decoration on the side of the Ara Pacis and on Roman and Renaissance pilasters and borders, where curving tendrils unite with the acanthus to form the popular rinceau pattern. In Oriental art this motif is similar to the Greek and Roman form.
—W.R.A.

a capella. Unaccompanied choral music; in chapel style.

acca. A fabric of silk and gold made during the Middle Ages, probably in Syria.

accent. Dynamic stress put on a musical element, either because of its placement in a pre-established metrical pattern (*systematical accent*: see rhythm, meter, idiom B), or for the sake of phrase articulation (*phrase accent*: see phrase, articulation). In tonal music both kinds of accents are used; in modal and atonal music phrase accent prevails (see idiom).
—E.K.

Accentualists. See MEDIEVAL MUSIC.

accentus, concentus. Those parts of the liturgy such as the Collects, the Epistle and Gospel, the Preface, etc., which are recited in a monotone with occasional inflections and cadences by the priest, deacon or subdeacon are styled *accentus.* The *accentus* may not be accompanied. Those parts of liturgical song which are performed by the choir (or two or three singers) such as the divisions of Ordinary of the Mass and Proper of the Mass are styled *concentus.* See Mass.   **—V.A.**

accessory use. See CIVIC PLANNING.

accidental. See NOTATION.

accidental vanishing point. See PERSPECTIVE.

accompaniment. That which supports a musical composition.

accordatura. In stringed instruments óf the lute- and viol-classes, the regular or usual series of pitches to which the strings are tuned.

accordion. See MUSICAL INSTRUMENTS.

acerra (L.). A container for incense.

acetate rayon. Fiber, yarn or material made by the acetate process, a process in which the product is not reconverted cellulose but an ester of cellulose, i.e. cellulose-acetate.

acetone. Used occasionally as a solvent for painters' varnishes, particularly those derived from synthetic resins and plastics, acetone is more widely used in removing varnishes than in compounding them. Chemically, it is a dimethyl ketone. It has the unusual property of being miscible with water, oils, and most other solvents. Its action on resin is rapid and, if solution is not complete, it is apt to leave a white mark where the resin film is blanched on rapid cooling and condensation. Acetone is fairly safe so far as toxicity is concerned, but its vapors are highly flammable. —G.L.S.

Achaemenid art. See PERSIAN ART.

achievement. See HERALDRY.

Achilles. The leading warrior of the Greek tribal expeditionary force in the siege of Troy, hero of Homer's *Iliad*. His exploits were a favorite subject of Greek vase painters and gem cutters; one of the most famous portrayals is in Brygus' *Priam Ransoming the Body of Hector*. In post-classical sculpture he was represented by Thorvaldsen, Dannecker, Bissen, Westmacott and Herter.   —W.R.A.

achromatic color. A color without hue. See COLOR.

ACOUSTICS. Literally the science of hearing, is here taken to include the physical means by which music is produced, the media through which the vibrations may be transmitted and the circumstances under which the sound is received.

The **pitch** of a sound as perceived by the ear is largely determined by the **frequency of vibration**: that is, the number of to-and-fro motions completed by the vibrating body per unit time. The **loudness** depends upon the **amplitude** (one-half the total extent of vibration), and the **tone-quality** upon the **waveform**. Any complex form of vibration may be built up by the superposition of simple vibrations of different frequencies, and these components are called **partials**. Pitch, loudness and quality are the three subjective attributes which primarily correspond to the three physical characteristics, but they are all somewhat interrelated. For example, when the loudness of a simple tone in the neighborhood of middle C is increased, the pitch decreases even though the frequency is kept constant.

A musical instrument consists of the vibration producer proper, usually a **resonator** for selecting, modifying and/or assisting the transmission of sound to the surrounding air, and

mechanism for controlling same. In addition to the voice, **vibrators** now commonly used to initiate sounds for musical purposes are as follows, the name of a typical instrument being given in parentheses:

(a) **bar** or **plate** (xylophone), struck, bowed or blown;

(b) **membrane** under tension (drum);

(c) **string** under tension (violin), plucked, bowed, struck or blown;

(d) **air jet** (flute);

(e) **cane reed** (clarinet), either single or double;

(f) **lip reed** (cornet), meaning the vibrating lips in a **cupped mouthpiece**;

(g) **electric oscillation** (Novachord).

The first three produce vibrations of fixed frequency, determined by the size, density, tension or elasticity of the vibrator, whereas the next three are really means of producing pulses of air at a rate primarily determined by the associated resonator. Sound producer (d) leaves the end of the resonator to which it is attached relatively open to the surrounding air, whereas (e) and (f) behave as if to close the resonators to which they are attached. The electric oscillations of predetermined frequency, after being amplified electrically, are converted into sound by a loud speaker.

The resonator is of particular importance to the tuning of a wind instrument, since it largely determines the pitches which may be obtained. The air in a cylindrical tube open at both ends (example: flute) vibrates best in those ways, or modes, whose frequencies are to each other approximately as 1, 2, 3, 4, 5, etc. Frequencies which are exactly in these relations are called **harmonics**. Starting with the **fundamental**, which is that **mode of vibration** which provides the lowest frequency, the next is an **octave** higher (2/1 ratio), and the next a **twelfth** (3/1) above the fundamental. These modes of vibration should not be confused with the **partials** which make up the complex sound associated with any one mode of vibration, for the frequencies of the two are not always identical. Usually the partials from a wind instrument are harmonic, but the modes of vibration often depart somewhat from the simple 1, 2, 3, 4, 5 series.

The **normal modes of vibration** in the air of a cylindrical tube closed at one end (example: clarinet) have frequencies which are to each other approximately as 1, 3, 5, 7, etc. The fact that the gap between the lowest and the next lowest mode of vibration is a twelfth (ratio 3/1) necessitates **key mechanism** and tone holes on clarinet to bridge the gap of 19 semitones, whereas the mechanism of an octave instrument such as the flute needs only to fill in the gap of 12 semitones.

The tapered tube resonator may take a variety of forms ranging from the near conical shape of the oboe to the rapidly flaring French horn. A cone open at the large end and complete to its apex, terminated by either an open or closed end, theoretically sustains a full series of harmonic modes of vibration. A cone with small end closed, but not at the apex, gives rise to modes of vibration which are inharmonic. Since the mouthpiece cannot be attached quite at the apex (notice saxophone) the conical bore must be modified somewhat to restore approximately the harmonic relationship. In the course of years the shape of brass instruments has evolved such that the modes of vibration are nearly in the ratios of 2, 3, 4, 5, 6, even if the lips do in effect close the small end.

When a wind instrument emits a musical tone, the air inside it does not vibrate at the same amplitude throughout. At some spots (such as open ends) the air vibrates vigorously, and these places are called antinodes. At others (such as closed ends) there is a minimum of motion and these places of "no motion" are nodes. For different modes of vibration these nodes and antinodes appear in different positions throughout the tube. A reduction in cross section near an antinode lowers the frequency of that particular mode of vibration; a constriction near a node has a sharpening effect. By such modifications in the bore the "open" tones of a cornet, for example, may be tuned with respect to each other.

Sound is propagated through any medium at a speed which depends upon the density and elasticity of that medium. For free air at ordinary temperatures, this is about 1100 ft/sec. Now, the characteristic frequencies of a resonator are proportional to the velocity of sound in the contained air. Inasmuch as the density of air becomes less as the temperature rises, the velocity of sound increases, and a wind instrument becomes sharper in pitch as the air within it is warmed.

A musical scale (see scales and modes) is often defined as a series of tones ascending or descending in frequency by definite intervals (q.v.) suitable for musical purposes. However, some contend that each tone of this scale is subject to slight "mutation" in pitch depending upon the other tones with which it may be sounded. The so-called just scale, built from intervals found in the harmonic series, has

intervals which are not equal. As a consequence, a keyboard instrument, such as the piano, having only 12 tones to the octave, cannot be tuned to produce just scales in all keys. The compromise commonly accepted today is equal temperament wherein the 12 intervals to the octave are equal, i.e. each successive frequency bears the same ratio to the one preceding.

The range of the organ usually extends an octave above that of the piano and often down to $C_o = 16.35$ cycles/sec. The subscript notation here employed to identify the octave in which a tone lies is one of several used by different groups of musicians. Among the advantages of this method over others are the uniformity of characters (capital letters and subscripts only), subscripts fitted nicely into the musical range and requiring ordinarily but one digit, and the significance of the subscript in giving the number of octaves from C_o, which has a frequency approximately at the lower limit of hearing.

The A of 440 cycles/sec., which is now American standard pitch, seems likely to become international pitch. The history of music shows that during the past century standard pitch has fluctuated over considerably more than a semitone from below to above this value. Particularly since the prevalent use of wind instruments the insidious tendency has existed to raise the pitch standard, but evidently no lasting benefit has been gained from the higher pitches, and twice a costly return to a lower standard has been necessary.

The auditorium in which music reaches the listener modifies the actual sound which reaches his ears. When the sound starts from the stage part of it passes directly to the listener, while another part may travel a longer path and reach him via reflection from the ceiling. If the reflected part sounds like a distinct repetition of the original it is called an echo. Usually, however, multiple reflections occur such that the ear is unable to separate the individual returns as distinct sound, so that even after the sound source has ceased a mass of sound of decreasing intensity exists within the room, resulting in reverberation.

This overlapping of sounds frequently becomes a menace to understanding of speech and, to a lesser degree, to the satisfactory reception of music. A remedy lies in reducing the intensity of the reflected sound by the use of sound absorbing materials appropriately placed on walls, floor and ceiling. Reverberation is desirable when it constitutes reënforcement of the direct sound, but the problem is

to eliminate those sounds which arrive noticeably late after traversing devious paths, greater than that of the direct sound by more than about 70 ft. Sometimes the shape of the auditorium is such that curved surfaces focus the sound to certain spots to the detriment of others. In the famed tabernacle at Salt Lake City sound is transmitted well to the most distant part of the balcony, yet there are positions near the center of the main floor at which it is difficult to understand speech. See E. H. Barton, *A Text Book on Sound,* 1926; A. Carse, *Musical Wind Instruments,* 1939; J. A. Jeans, *Science and Music,* 1937; A. T. Jones, *Sound,* 1937; V. O. Knudsen, *Architectural Acoustics,* 1932; E. G. Richardson, *Acoustics of Orchestral Instruments,* 1929.
—R.W.Y.

acoustics, terminology in. (*Physical vs. Mental in acoustic correlates for music and speech*). Sound has a physical aspect and an approximately parallel mental aspect. For each of these, we have standardized terminology, but in most situations in music and speech we refer to both the physical and the mental. We, therefore, have three series of correlates in acoustic phenomena: the physical, the mental, and the integrated or total references.

The terminology for the physical aspect is based objectively on the physical attributes of sound waves; namely, **frequency, amplitude duration** of a sequence of waves, and **wave form.** Those represent the **tonal,** the **dynamic,** the **temporal,** and the **qualitative aspects** of the physical sound. Since all music exists directly or indirectly as sound waves; and, since sound waves have no other primary attribute than those mentioned, every element of the physical aspect of musical sounds may be accounted for in these four categories, their complex forms or derivatives. By combination of the four basic elements, endless varieties of melody, harmony, rhythm, volume, and tone quality may be represented. Each of these is defined in terms of units of energy, physical or electrical. For each of the four basic attributes, the physicist has also devised terms available for specific purposes; such as frequency modulation, energy, power, harmonic composition, or spectrum.

The terminology of the mental aspect roughly parallels the physical terminology in the naming of each category; namely, **pitch, loudness, time** and **timbre** as representing the **tonal,** the **dynamic,** the **temporal,** and the **qualitative aspects** of tones. For many artistic and for most scientific purposes it is essential

that the distinction between the physical and the mental aspects, respectively, be adhered to logically and consistently and that there be no slip-shod or dodging shift from one to the other for the evading of clarity or to cover ignorance. The two are rarely exactly parallel. *Frequency,* for example, has many times the range of *pitch.* We seldom hear a tone as a true copy of the physical tone; the ratio of the physical to the mental is rarely 1:1. The pitch for a standard physical frequency of 440 may vary under a variety of environmental, physiological, psychophysical, and psychological conditions. A tone of 60 decibel energy level may vary widely in loudness in hearing; a one-second duration may seem much longer or shorter; the timbre correlated with a specific structure of partials may vary widely in hearing. We recognize these divergencies as normal illusions; some due to the limitations of the human organism or the instrument, others to artistic demands, conventions or training. Without many of these illusions there could be no good music. In defining the mental terms, we relate them to the physical aspect and, when necessary, indicate essential deviations of the mental from the physical parallelism.

But in conventional treatment of musical sounds, we are most frequently thinking of the total or integrated situation involving both objective and subjective factors and concerned with physical, physiological, and mental aspects. That is what music is; and for this we have the well established usage of employing the mental terminology, as when we speak of concert pitch, staccato or legato movements a *major key, poor phrasing, vibrato, accent, resolution,* or harmony. Thus, whenever we speak or think of actual music or speech, we have the total situation in mind. The very words music and speech are exhibits of this. Unfortunately, that leaves us in the poverty of using the terms *pitch, intensity, time,* and *timbre* in two distinct meanings, that of the mental aspect specifically and that of the integrated situation in music and speech. We are here forced to depend upon the context or the universe of discourse to determine which of the two connotations is intended.

The Acoustical Society of America has a committee on terminology which publishes definitions from time to time in its Journal as clarification develops through experiment. In these, emphasis is rightly laid on consistent distinction between the mental and physical terminology; but only slight attention is given to artistic and common sense usage pertaining to what I have here distinguished as the total situation. But the history of music, musical criticism, and much of the psychology of music deals with this integrated situation without any reason for making the acoustic distinctions between the physical and the mental. Psychology is not ordinarily concerned with the historical "body and mind" situation but rather with the functions of the integrated organism.

Psychological usage, in terms of which musical organization must be built, sometimes brings us into verbal conflicts. This is exemplified in the use of the terms *intensity* and *loudness*. *Loudness* is an appropriate synonym for *intensity* but *intensity* is an attribute of all sensation; for example, *intensity of taste, odor, color, pressure, pain,* and *sound*. Therefore, scientists have historically preferred the word *intensity* when the reference is dominantly to the total situation, and favor the term *loudness* for a purely mental aspect of experience and behavior.   —C.E.S.

acrolith. A statue with trunk usually of wood and with extremities of stone; trunk often covered with drapery or metal.

acropolis (Gr. *akro'polis,* from *akro,* topmost, or peak, and *pólis,* city, the elevated part of a Greek city). The term refers to the summit of the crag or hill on and around which Greek cities were most commonly built, from the earliest period of established settlement. It is applied indiscriminately to this portion of a Greek city, whether its function be that of fortress or of temple area, as in the most famous example, the Acropolis of Athens. From its natural security, easily implemented by walls and redoubts to a condition of impregnability, this area was originally reserved to the chief of the community for his residence, and was maintained as a popular refuge in time of danger. In classic times, when the temple came to · be conceived as the actual home of the god, and the chief's megaron was taken as its architectural prototype, the acropolis generally was transformed into a temple precinct, walled not so much for security against attack as to emphasize its ritual separation from the mundane life of the city. When prefixed by *the,* acropolis always refers to the celebrated templed crag of Athens. Elsewhere the term is used with an identifying prefix, which establishes its specific connotation of citadel or elevated temple area. Notable examples of the citadel-acropolis are Tiryns, Mycenae, Argos, Gortys and Daulia; of the temple-area acropolis, Athens, Thebes, Corinth and Silenus.   —T.A.H.

acroterium. Over the three angles of the pediment of a Greek temple decorative statues or abstract designs, such as palmette, were often placed on pedestal blocks. They were called *acroteria* (topmost parts). On 6th cent. B.C., buildings they were often made of terra cotta; later ones were usually of marble.   —W.R.A.

acrylic resins. See resins, acrylic.

Actaeon. A Greek hunter who was slain by Artemis when he saw her bathing. The subject was treated by 5th cent. B.C., Athenian vase painters, notably the Pan Painter. In modern sculpture a spirited representation is Paul Manship's group in the Metropolitan Museum, New York.   —W.R.A.

action. *Mus.* In keyboard-instruments, the general term for the entire mechanism whereby the muscular acts of the performer are translated into motions and adjustments within the instrument so as to cause the desired tone-production.

action current. An electrical impulse generated by the flow of the nerve impulse and generally employed as a measure of the nerve impulse in sensory motor and central neural processes. See brain waves.   —C.E.S.

adagio (It. *ad agio,* at ease or at leisure). (1) A type of academic exercise in classic ballet training, calculated to develop large, sustained movements, to the accompaniment of music in slow tempo. The first section of the daily classic ballet lesson is known as *allegro* (It., quick or rapid); the second, *adagio,* featuring held extensions of the legs, with deliberate arm positions to balance the body supported on a single foot. (2) Portions of a ballet or divertissement, in which male dancers support female partners, either on toe point, or by lifts through the air, covering floor space impossible to negotiate unaided. The so-called **grand adagio** is the emotional climax of the traditional classic repertory, performed by soloists as a stylized love-duet, ornamented by brilliant turns, held poses, lifts and foot work, in which the cavalier effaces himself to display the grace and technique of his lady. (3) A term borrowed by variety, circus and ball-room artists from the above to describe acts or numbers of acrobatic virtuosity, in which the female partner is tossed or swung by arm or leg in the air, in spectacular muscular feats, which are not, strictly speaking, dancing.   —L.K.

Ada Group, school of the. See Carolingian art.

Adam style. A term derived from the fashion created by the English architect and furniture designer, Robert Adam, who about 1760 led the reaction against the excessively curvilinear and feminine rococo designs of Chippendale and others. Actually he shared in a general trend toward a stricter imitation of Roman antiquity, made possible and stimulated by the archeological recreations of ancient sites, notably Herculaneum and Pompeii. The style aimed at a correct Roman impressiveness, with accessories by Wedgwood and furniture in harmony, but Adam's personal sensitivity to exquisite decoration in stucco gave his designs a delicate and coherent distinction. See INTERIOR ARCHITECTURE AND DECORATION; FURNITURE.   —P.C.B.

adaptation. See RADIO DRAMA.

additive color mixing. See COLOR.

addorsed. *Her.* Turned or set back to back.

Adena Culture. An aboriginal American culture centering in southern Ohio near the Hopewell sites and extending into Kentucky, West Virginia, Pennsylvania and southern Indiana. It takes its name from the estate of an early governor of Ohio, where the first mound containing its artifacts was discovered. Far too little is known of the Adena type to determine its relation to the Hopewell, of which some authorities believe it is a phase. See Eastern North American aboriginal art.   —II.G.

ad libitum (abbrev. *ad lib.*). *Mus.* In a concerted passage or piece, an indication that a part for voice or instrument is suggested, but not absolutely required for the intended effect.

adobe (Sp. Am. from Sp. *adobar,* to daub, to plaster; traceable through the Arabic term *attuba* or *attob* to an Egyptian hieroglyph meaning "brick"). Unburnt, sun-dried clay or mud mortar, sometimes made with straw, and often in brick form.   —J.M.M.

Adonay Malach mode. See JEWISH MUSIC.

Adonis. The Asiatic lover of Aphrodite, slain by a wild boar and bitterly mourned by the goddess of love. The myth personifies the death of vegetation. In sculpture Adonis has been portrayed by Vincenzo de' Rossi, de Vries, Canova and Thorvaldsen.   —W.R.A.

advancing colors. See COLOR.

Aegean architecture. The generic term for the buildings of the stone and bronze ages, e.g. the pre-Hellenic architecture, of the Aegean basin, which is understood in this reference to include the mainland of Greece, Crete, the Aegean islands, and the Aegean littoral of Asia Minor; its period extends through the bronze age to the decay and extinction of the Mycenean civilization in the Dorian invasions sometime between 1200 and 1000 B.C. Its Cretan phase, extending roughly from 2500 to 1200 B.C., is called Minoan; its mainland phases are called Mycenean and Helladic; and its expression in the Aegean islands Cycladic. Each of these phases has been subdivided for convenience into three, or multiples of three, periods corresponding to rise and development, climax, and decadence, or, Early, Middle and Late. This culture is not uniform throughout the area in either its development or specific expression, but certain characteristics are common to all of its buildings and periods. Building materials were simple: timber, stone, plaster, and sun-dried brick. Structural methods were, with a few conspicuous exceptions, relatively haphazard, crudities were simply hidden with plaster, and it was common practise to support heavy stone walls with timber beams. **Minoan architecture** reflects the refinement of a peaceful maritime people who had contact with Egypt but had great inventive ability and made their borrowings distinctly their own. The climactic expression of their architectural skill is found in the great palaces of Knossos, Phaistos and Gournia, each a vast complex of halls, chambers, courts, monumental stairways and open ceremonial places on various levels and functionally divided into well-defined areas. The ceilings of the large halls were supported on pillars and the walls were lavishly decorated with frescoes of remarkable quality; in these the life and ceremonies of court and people are vividly depicted; decorative and abstract patterns were drawn largely from the inhabitants of the sea, though flowers were also widely used for this purpose. The Cretan towns, haphazard in plan and unprotected by walls, were made up of closely built but comfortable flat-roofed houses, often of two or three stories and sometimes built around a courtyard; with mullioned and transomed windows and regular facades, these houses are quite modern in appearance and had sanitary conveniences of a practicability and luxury not again found in the ancient world until their re-invention by the Romans. Tombs were of four types: cist and pit graves, chamber and beehive tombs, the latter two of architectural significance because of their vaulted roofs.

Religious architecture was largely confined to modest and simple walled shrines. On the mainland the most striking difference is seen in the massive megalithic fortifications with which the palaces of Mycenae, Tiryns, Troy and other cities were protected, but the most significant difference lies in the palace plans. The mainland palaces were centered on a large pillared hall with an open hearth at the center, the approach being through a porch *in antis* (q.v.) and a vestibule: the side walls of porch, vestibule and hall are continuous and the unit is called a **megaron**. This is not a Mediterranean type and is associated with primitive northern Europe, though its place of origin is still in dispute. In the larger palaces there are also subsidiary *megara,* presumably composing the quarters of the women of the chieftain's family and approachable only through the principal *megaron.* Decorative methods and details are the same as those in Crete, and in considerable part may have been executed by Cretan painters and craftsmen. The finest beehive tombs or **tholoi** are found on the mainland, notably at Mycenae and Orchomenos, where the masonry, carving and vaulting are of extraordinary refinement; except in these tombs, Mycenean stone work is generally megalithic, and ashlar masonry is found only in the latest levels at Troy.

—T.A.H.

Aegean vases. From the 4th to the 2nd millenium B.C., Crete was the center of a great commercial and artistic civilization (see Cretan-Minoan), in which the vases played an important part, both as objects of export and for local enjoyment. In the early Minoan period (3400-2100), small vase shapes of eggshell thinness, with lovely brown and white and gray and white veining, were produced. The potter's wheel appeared in the Middle Minoan period (2100-1580). In this period the most important product was **Kamares ware,** graceful copies of metal vases, decorated with bold geometric and stylized floral patterns in a range of colors: white, maroon red, yellow and black. Three successive types of vases mark the Late Minoan (1580-1200); first, the finest ware produced in Crete, in which multitudes of naturalistic floral and marine forms were painted in dark glaze to give gay and spirited decoration to finely shaped vases; vases of the "Palace Style", in which the spontaneity and verve of the former period were supplanted by formalized patterns, which nevertheless have dignity and monumental character; and finally, after a disaster preceding the final downfall of Crete, inferior ware with crude geometric patterns. To Crete the Greeks were indebted for the potter's wheel, the lustrous black glaze which was the stock-in-trade of later potters, and decorative designs from the world of nature which were never surpassed in later times. Crete also produced carved stone vases during the early Late-Minoan period which are masterpieces of bas-relief, notably the Harvester Vase, picturing a happy harvest-home, and the Boxer Vase, with friezes of boxers and bull-fighters. These were carved in steatite and covered with gold leaf. Influenced by Cretan ware were potters and metal smiths in the Cyclades, notably Syros, Melos, Thera, and Rhodes, who carried on the Cretan tradition of decorative painting.   —W.R.A.

Aeginetan art. During the fifty years preceding the conquest of Aegina by Athens (457 B.C.), that island was a center of art, which culminated in the temple of Aphaia (c. 500-480 B.C.). It was distinguished by skillful grouping of the human figure in pedimental decoration and by lithe, nervously energetic sculptural forms.   —W.R.A.

aegis. The shield of Zeus and protective cloak of Athena were called by this name. In Greek sculpture and vase painting Athena was usually represented wearing a breast covering of this sort, decorated with a Gorgon's head in the center and serpents on the border. — W.R.A.

aeolian harp. A mechanical device in which moving air produces tonal effects from a set of stretched strings.

Aeolian mode. See idiom A(2).

aerial perspective. See PERSPECTIVE.

aerial photo sketch. See military sketch.

aerial representation. In East Asiatic art, especially painting, it is commonly used; a bird's-eye view.   —J.A.M.

aerugo. See verdigris.

aesthetic dance. The name "aesthetic dance" was given to that style of dance taught in many professional studios and introduced into physical education curricula during the period from 1910 to approximately 1925. Aesthetic dance technique was a mixture of classical ballet technique and national dance steps all arranged in a formal and rigid system, to be taught with the discipline of formal gymnastics. This hybrid form was the result of efforts to modify and enrich the system of classic ballet. These efforts probably grew out of the beginning reaction to ballet rigidity, and the need for a dance form acceptable in general education.   —J.G.

aesthetic form. See form; form: a philosophical analysis.

AESTHETIC INQUIRY, current types of.

Traditionally, aesthetics was that branch of philosophy dealing with beauty (q.v.) or the beautiful, especially in art, and with taste (q.v.) and standards of value in judging art; also, a theory or consistent attitude on such matters. Aesthetics is now achieving a more independent status as the subject (whether it is or can be a "science" is a disputed issue) which studies (a) works of art, (b) the processes of producing and experiencing art, and (c) certain aspects of nature and human production outside the field of art — especially those which can be considered as beautiful or ugly in regard to form and sensory qualities. (E.g., sunsets, flowers, human beings, machines.)

While not abandoning its interest in beauty, artistic value, and other normative concepts, recent aesthetics has tended to lay increasing emphasis on a descriptive, factual approach to the phenomena of art and aesthetic experience. It is by no means restricted to the question of what is good or beautiful in art. On the other hand, it differs from *art history,* archeology, and cultural history in stressing a theoretical organization of materials in terms of recurrent types and tendencies, rather than a chronological or genetic one. It differs from *general psychology* in focusing upon certain selected phases in psychophysical activity, and on their application to certain types of objects and situations, especially those of art. It investigates the forms and characteristics of art, which psychology does not do. It differs from *art criticism* (q.v.) in seeking a more general, theoretical understanding of the arts than is usual in that subject, and in attempting a more consistently objective, impersonal attitude. It maintains a philosophic breadth in comparing examples of all the arts, and in assembling data and hypotheses from many sources, including philosophy, psychology, cultural history, and the social sciences. But it is departing from traditional conceptions of *philosophy* in that writing labelled "aesthetics" now often includes much detailed, empirical study of particular phenomena.

Overlapping among all the above-mentioned fields is inevitable, as well as great difference in approach among individual writers. Some of these stress the nature and varieties of form in art, with attention to historic types and styles, such as romanticism, the baroque, etc., and in studying their evolution adopt the historian's viewpoint to some extent. Some stress the psychology of aesthetic experience; of artistic creation, taste, and imagination.

The progress of aesthetics toward scientific status is being slowly made along many lines, through increasing use of an objective and logical approach instead of a dogmatic or personal one, and through bringing the results of other sciences to bear on aesthetic problems. Recent years have seen a vast increase in the amount and variety of artistic data available for the aesthetician, as a result of anthropological and archeological research and excavation, diversified museum collections, improved reproductions, translations, and phonograph records.

It is misleading to use such terms as "experimental aesthetics", "comparative aesthetics", etc., as if they stood for distinct subjects or distinct divisions of aesthetics. They stand rather for somewhat different approaches to the same general field, for the choice of different special problems within that field, or for different emphases in dealing with them. All these differences are in degree only, and there is much overlapping. As a result of departmental specialization in universities, they are often magnified into wide gulfs in educational presentation, through the fact that courses, teachers, and professional organizations concerned with various phases of art and aesthetics have little relation to each other. With this in mind, we may distinguish the chief present emphases in aesthetics as follows:

(1) In **philosophical aesthetics,** stress is laid on basic and central problems of theory; especially on such traditional questions as the nature of beauty, artistic value, aesthetic experience, sublimity, etc., and on the relation of beauty to truth and moral goodness. Basic assumptions of past and present aesthetic theory are analyzed and criticized as to their internal consistency, apparent reasonableness, and consistency with current hypotheses in other branches of philosophy and science. Abstract dialectic or speculative generalization is often the principal method, with great concern for proper definition of basic categories, and with comparatively little direct examination of concrete data. Writing on aesthetics can, of course, embrace large amounts of concrete data and still be philosophical if these data come from varied sources, and if the aim is to

coordinate them. Recent philosophical aesthetics has shown a trend in this direction.

(2) In **comparative aesthetics,** stress is laid on the results of observation, especially of works of art. Periods, styles, individual artists, and particular works of art are systematically compared, so as to bring out significant resemblances and differences, recurrent traits, trends, and causal connections. Approximately the same field and approach are called in German *allgemeine Kunstwissenschaft,* or 'general science of art'. But this term has not become current in English-speaking usage, partly from fear of exaggerating the scientific status of present ideas on the subject. As distinguished from the "aesthetics of music", "aesthetics of poetry", "aesthetics of sculpture", etc. (which are concerned with theoretical issues in some particular art), *comparative* aesthetics involves comparison of the arts with each other, and study of types and factors entering into more than one art. (See form; presentation; suggestion; component; composition.)

(3) **Psychological aesthetics** is an approach to aesthetic problems from the standpoint of psychology. It emphasizes the nature of aesthetic experience; of human behavior toward works of art; the processes involved in artistic production and appreciation, especially perception, imagination, and emotion; the phenomena of taste and preference; the nature and determinants of special art ability; the growth of art ability (creative and appreciative) in children. It considers the application to art of special psychological theories such as empathy and psychoanalysis. In addition, it studies the forms of art from a psychological standpoint; their nature and varieties; the genesis of styles —all with emphasis on how these factors operate as expressions of human nature and as stimuli to human experience. The terms **aesthetic psychology** and **psychology of art** (q.v.) are sometimes used as equivalents for this approach or some phase of it.

(4) The term **experimental aesthetics** has been applied to a special type of psychological approach: namely, that which restricts itself to quantitative measurement, laboratory and statistical procedure. It follows the lead of Fechner, whose studies of aesthetic preference in 1876 helped to inaugurate modern experimental psychology as well as the empirical approach to aesthetics. It has dealt less with works of art than with preference for various arbitrary, simplified linear shapes, color-combinations and tone-combinations. This approach has also led to attempted scales and tests for measuring ability to create and appreciate art,

especially in children. Broadly speaking, the term "experimental" applies to many other approaches and procedures in aesthetics, and this one could be more exactly described as **quantitative aesthetics.**

(5) **Sociological aesthetics** stresses the relation of art to social, political, and economic factors; to collective rather than individual behavior. It has been strongly influenced by Marx's theory of the economic determination of history, and sometimes by later socialism and communism; sometimes by fascism; but it is not necessarily prejudiced by any special belief or partisan spirit. It has emphasized the ways in which styles and tastes in art, and the characters and products of particular artists, are influenced by class and other socio-economic interests (see sociology of art).—T.M.

aesthetic judgment. See TASTE; AESTHETICS; art tests.

aesthetic language. See AESTHETICS.

aesthetic psychology. See PSYCHOLOGY OF ART; AESTHETIC INQUIRY (3).

AESTHETICS (Gr. *aesthetikos,* perceptive). The purpose of aesthetics is to discover the generic characterics of fine or beautiful art, and to determine the relation of art to other phases of culture, such as science, industry, morality, philosophy and religion. Understood in this way, aesthetics is sharply distinguished from the historical study of art, which is concerned, not with the essence of art, but with the filiation and development of styles and schools. Sometimes the scope of aesthetics is broadened to include the beautiful in nature and human life, but when this is done, it tends to lose definiteness of content, owing to the subjectivity of beauty in these fields; and, at all events, the preëminence of art as an embodiment of beauty is generally recognized. The term *aesthetics* was first used with its present meaning by Alexander Gottlieb Baumgarten in 1735, in his treatise *Meditationes philosophicae de nonnullis ad poema pertinentibus,* and later, in 1750, as the title of a book, *Aesthetica;* being derived from the Greek word *aistheta,* which means objects of sensuous as opposed to intellectual knowledge. The subject has been pursued chiefly by philosophers, but some of the most important insights have been contributed by poets and artists, such as Shelley, Goethe and Schiller, who have reflected on their own experience of creation and appreciation.

Two disciplines closely related to aesthetics in content and history are the psychology of art and art criticism (qq.v.). The former, originating in the 18th cent. in connexion with British empiricism, is an investigation of the elements, pattern and context of the experience offered by the works of art. Since works of art become alive and actual only as they are experienced, the philosophy and the psychology of art overlap and have often been identified; yet the division of labor between them is clear; for the one is interested in the detailed analysis of the aesthetic experience for its own sake, while the other uses this information only so far as it contributes to a general conception or definition of the nature and purpose of art. For an adequate discussion of the problems and methods of the psychology of art see PSYCHOLOGY OF ART and the works cited in the bibliography given below. Here I would merely note that the study of the process called *Einfühlung* or empathy (q.v.) —the objectification of feeling and meaning into the colors, lines, shapes, tones, words and the like, which make up the sensuous media or 'surface' of works of art; and the study of the total state of mind during appreciation, yielding such concepts as 'aesthetic distance' and 'aesthetic repose', have been of especial value for aesthetics.[1] No less important has been the activity of art criticism, including its literary and musical species. Interest in a work of art seldom ends with lonely appreciation, but goes on to conversation with friends or written discussion concerning its comparative merit as judged by some implicit or formulated principle or expectation. Aesthetic judgments, esp. those of connoisseurs (q.v.), constitute, therefore, a material of primary relevance for aesthetics. The critics pass judgments on individual works of art; the aestheticians investigate their nature and validity; and, viewed from this angle, aesthetics is essentially a criticism of criticism.

Three general conceptions of art have dominated the history of aesthetics: **imitation, imagination**, and **expression** or **language**. The first was the gift of Plato and Aristotle, and has always found a naive, popular acceptance. It fits best the drama, painting and sculpture, where we seem to have before our eyes an image of visible nature and human action, as in a mirror. The Greeks, however, conceived of it so broadly as to cover even music, the rhythm and harmony of which, they felt, imitates moral character and other states of the soul.[2] But obviously in the practice of no one of the arts is exact or full imitation either possible or desirable. In order to be useful, therefore, the concept of imitation must be understood in some refined, philosophical sense. Historically, in fact, two chief revisions have been made. The earlier one was already introduced by Aristotle and was accepted by most Renaissance writers, according to whom art seeks to imitate, not all aspects, but only the general aspects of nature. This was significant because it gave to art the value of truth— philosophical, scientific or religious, according to the prevailing theory of reality. The later revision proposed that art imitates only the beautiful aspects of nature. Yet neither of these modifications of the concept of imitation suffices to save it from difficulty, for the universal applicability of each is questionable. There are, to be sure, works of art which express the generic aspects of existence; but there have been whole movements which, by contrast, have tried to express the unique, the momentary, even the pathological. Moreover, some works of art express 'truth', but not all. "Golden lads and girls all must / As chimney sweepers come to dust" does so; but "Hark, hark, the lark at heaven's gate sings" utters not truth, but the urgency of passion. And when art does express truth, it never expresses bare truth, but includes its feeling tones for the artist, as in the quotation from *Cymbaline;* never the mere concept, but the 'lure' of the concept. In other words, this reformed concept of imitation neglects the factor of personality, essential to art, and so fails to distinguish art from science. With regard to the beautiful in nature as the object of imitation, we may well ask with Diderot[3], "What is beautiful nature?" Is it, for example, an Italian landscape à la Poussin, or one such as a Brueghel painted? Is it the same as the noble, the aristocratic, or may it pertain to what is bourgeois, or of the peasant or workingman? If, on the other hand, as some have thought, the beautiful is a mere form or pattern, the artist can freely construct that without looking to nature for a model.

The shortcomings of the concept of imitation were already recognized in antiquity, most forthrightly perhaps by Philostratus, who asked how, if art be imitation, the sculptor can represent the Gods, whom no man has seen?[4] Does he perchance ascend to Olympus? That is to say, the artist is a creator, not an imitator; and for the capacity to construct novel forms, the term in general use since Philostratus employed it, has been imagination. Thus a rival view of **art as imagination** was born out of the problem of religious art. Very early in modern times, as early at least as Huarte, Bacon and Pallavicino,[5] in the late

16th and early 17th cents., certain important characteristics of imagination were noted: its kinship with dream; its contrast, nay opposition to reason. Eventually also it has been seen that those products of imagination which we call works of art constitute little worlds by themselves, with their own space and time, different from that of nature; with their own typical structure of organic unity, rhythm, contrast and climax, recurrence and variation of theme; full of their own values or satisfactions, derived indeed from the same springs as those of action, yet independent of action— a realm not of reality, but of appearance, of play. A one-sided emphasis on the make-believe character of art leads to the doctrine of art for art's sake (q.v.); its corrective lies in the acknowledgment of the element of truth in the theory of imitation—that imagination ceases to interest us permanently if it fails to concern itself with the problems of real life.

However, that art cannot be adequately defined in terms of imagination is clear by reason of the social character of the former and the private character of the latter. Art is in truth a dream, but a dream that can be shared. The outstanding merit of the concept of **art as language or expression** is that it takes care of its communicable nature. To say just when and through whom this view arose, is difficult. One can perhaps trace it to the studies instituted by the Greek rhetoricians, for we find in Aristotle the crucial distinction between descriptive and emotional expression, under which art was destined to be classed. Among modern thinkers, Condillac, Vico and Herder had definitely the conception of art as a species of language, and one hundred and fifty years later, Véron was to give this theory unequivocal statement.[7] For the purpose of defining art, three types of language may be distinguished — descriptive or propositional, practical and lyrical. The first is illustrated by a scientific treatise, the aim of which is the record and conveyance of information; the second by a command or entreaty, a sermon or a tract, the intention of which is directly to stimulate or inhibit action; the third is illustrated by a poem or musical composition, the end of which is the induction of a mood. But only music or the abstractionist painting of a Bracque or Picasso is purely lyrical; the language of the other arts is descriptive as well. Thus in poetry the words used, besides expressing feelings, designate objects or express generalizations, and in traditional painting the colored shapes have their meanings, as of houses or trees or the human form. Neverthe-

less in art the descriptive function of language is not separate from the lyrical; for in indicating objects or in expressing universals, the artist gives definition and communication to feelings which otherwise would be formless and dumb. Cézanne could not express his feeling towards Mont Sainte Victoire without representing it; Frost could not express his feeling towards the 'passage' of the good without telling us definitely that "Nothing good can stay." In this connexion it is interesting to note that the difference between what Charles Peirce called 'iconic' and conventional languages is relevant to aesthetics; poetry being an illustration of the latter; painting, sculpture and drama, since they mean objects by offering likenesses of them, illustrating the former. Iconic languages have a sensuousness and easy intelligibility lacking in the conventional, to compensate which, verbal language resorts to metaphor and other figures of speech. On the other hand, verbal language is better able to express generalizations (thoughts).

While the conception of art as lyrical language is enough to establish the genus, it does not suffice to establish the differentia of art. Two distinguishing characteristics of **aesthetic language** may be cited. First, in contrast with ordinary language, where the signs or symbols are transparent, attention centering on their meanings only; in art, they are opaque, attention lingering lovingly in them, because they are directly expressive on their own account. In poetry the words themselves, as mere sounds, related through rhythm, assonance, rime and melody; in painting and architecture, colored shapes, repeated, contrasted, balanced, rhythmically disposed, are expressive of vague moods, as music is. Without this music of the mere medium, there is no beautiful art, no matter how significant be the meanings attached. This is the fact expressed by Pater in his well-known statement that all art tends towards the status of music. It is also the ground of the doctrine known as formalism, according to which the form, or patterned sensuous surface, is the sole bearer of aesthetic value.[8] Yet this theory is certainly in error, for in our experience of art, form and content, surface and underlying meanings, interpenetrate, and to this entire structure, not to one factor only, beauty belongs.

A second distinguishing characteristic of aesthetic language is suggestiveness, the paradoxical property, noticed by Kant,[9] of permitting a plurality of meanings, without however incurring ambiguity. In ordinary language, on the other hand, an expression aims to have a single meaning only, an ideal which it realizes perhaps in mathematics alone, but so far as it does not, is condemned. This contrast has been well put by saying that the ordinary expression is a 'unisign', while the aesthetic symbol is a 'plurisign'.[10] Of great importance in the case of art is the combination of a 'first' with a 'second' meaning, or as I would phrase it, of a 'surface' with a 'depth' meaning. Thus in the quotation from Frost, the word "gold" besides its obvious 'first' meaning, has the 'depth' meaning of valuable, and the entire phrase has the 'second' meaning, "nothing good abides". In such a poetic line as "The soul of Adonais like a star / Beacons from the above where the eternal are", the meanings are numerous, meaning beneath meaning. Every figure of speech is an example of a plurisign. Yet there is no ambiguity here, for all the meanings are relevant to the communication of the complex emotion of the poet, which requires them all for its definition. One might easily suppose that iconic languages were naturally unsignificant, but that is not so in the case of art. The representation of the shepherd and sheep, familiar in early Christian art, is evidently a plurisign, for besides its surface meaning it has also as depth meaning, a whole theory of the relation between God and man. And beneath the surface even of great landscape paintings and portraits, and of statues devoid of allegory, lie many layers of meaning for each spectator.

But although the conception of art as imagination needs to be supplemented by the conception of art as language, there is no contradiction between the two. For lyrical language induces in the artist and in his audience a state of mind akin to the dream, possessed of all the characteristics noted as pertaining to imagination. As a dream communicated, waywardness gives place to order and the assuagement of obscure desires fuses with the satisfaction of intelligible purposes. The best short definition of art remains therefore Shelley's, "the expression of the imagination", which unites the two points of view—of communication or language, and of the dream, self-sufficing and detached.

The approach to aesthetics by way of criticism belongs to modern times and has developed out of the prolific controversies of the critics, yet the seeds of later discussions may be found in Plato's *Phaedrus* and *Ion*, and subsequently in Horace, Plutarch, and Longinus. In his *Critique of the Aesthetical Judgment*, Kant was, I believe, the first to base aesthetic theory definitely on the aesthetic

judgment rather than on the aesthetic experience. The problems have been two: whether aesthetic judgment or 'taste' is intuitive, a sort of 'sixth sense',[11] or rational, an affair of rules; and what constitutes the beauty or value of works of art to be appraised. The two problems are, however, clearly interconnected, for if beauty be a sort of unique flavor, a *'je ne sais quoi'*, it would not be susceptible of formulation, but only of immediate apprehension; while if, on the contrary, it be no different in kind from other values, it would be as capable of rational estimation as they are. Considering the tenacity with which each of these alternatives has been maintained by critics with large experience in the arts, it would be strange if there were not some truth in both. For, on the one hand, the fact that a work of art is an imaginative creation implies a surprising uniqueness defying rationalization in terms of any traditional or other scheme. Every original artist has claimed this, and the history of all the arts is a series of revolts. On the other hand, it is yet to be proved that the satisfactions derived from art are generically different from those of ordinary experience. If they are of the same kind, criticism will concern itself with two things: one, the interrelations of the elements of the work of art, of form and of content, with reference to the contribution of each to the total communicable value, yielding a strictly internal, or 'artistic', standard of perfection; and two, the importance of this value in the light of an accepted philosophy of values. Some students of aesthetics have contended that only the first type of scrutiny is relevant, but by far the larger proportion have recognized that since art is of man and for man, it cannot be held exempt from criticism according to the principles by which other activities are judged. If the religious or metaphysical values are the highest, then those works of art which give them expression in perfect intelligible form, are the greatest. Hence although the narrowly artistic is a necessary, it is not a sufficient criterion of excellence; and if the validity of a second, philosophical criterion is admitted, aesthetic criticism becomes an application of the general theory of value to works of art. See AESTHETICS, recent trends in and AESTHETIC INQUIRY, current types of.

1. See E. Bullough, *Psychical Distance, British Journal of Psychology*, pp. 87-118; and Ethel Puffer, *Psychology of Beauty*, Chapter 3.
2. Aristotle, *Problems*, XIX.
3. D. Diderot, *Lettre sur les sourds et les muets*, 1757, in answer to C. Batteux, *Les beaux arts réduits a un meme principe*, 1746. For imitation under the limitation of the beautiful conceived as a form, see L. B. Alberti, *Della Pittura*, Bk. 3, 1435.

4. *In Life of Appolonius of Tyana*, VI. 19.
5. J. Huarte, *Examen de ingenios para les ciencias*, 1557; F. Bacon, *Advancement of Learning*, Bk. 2, 1605; Sforza Pallavicino, *Del Bene*, 1644.
6. *De Interpretatione*, 4, 17a, 1-5.
7. E. B. de Condillac, *Essai sur l'origine des connaisances humaines*, 2 ième partie, 1707; Giambattista Vico, *Scienza Nuova*, 1725; J. G. Herder, *Kritische Waelder*, 4 tes Waeldchen, 1769; Eugène Véron, *Esthétique*.
8. For what was perhaps the first clear-cut statement of formalism, see J. F. Herder, *Einleitung in die Philosophie*; for a contemporary statement, see Clive Bell, *Art*.
9. See Kant's discussion of the "aesthetical idea", in the *Critique of the Aesthetical Judgment*, 49.
10. This useful term has been coined by Philip Wheelwright.
11. For taste as a sixth sense, see J. B. Du Bos, *Reflexions critiques sur la poesie et sur la peinture*, pp 340-342, 1719; for the *Je ne sais quoi*, see Dominique Bouhours, *Les entretiens d'Ariste et d'Eugène*, passim, 1617.
BIBLIOG. L. Abercrombie, *Towards a Theory of Art*, 1926; H. Bergson, *Le Rire*, 1909; B. Bosanquet, *History of Aesthetics*, 1898 and *Three Lectures on Aesthetics*, 1915; B. Croce, *Aesthetic*, 2nd Ed., 1922 and *Essence of Aesthetic*, 1913; H. Delacroix, *Psychologie de l'art*, 1927; C. J. Ducasse, *Philosophy of Art*, 1929, K. Fiedler, *Ursprung der künstlerischen Taetigkeit*, 1889; G. Gentile, *Filosofia del Arte*, 1931; T. M. Greene, *The Arts and the Art of Criticism*, 1940; H. M. Guyau, *Les problèmes de l'esthétique contemporaine*, 1884; Hegel, *Vorlesungen ueber Aesthetik*, 1918; Kant, *Critique of Judgment*, Part I., 1790; V. Lee, *The Beautiful*, 1913; T. Lipps, *Aesthetik*, 2 vols., 1903, 1906; J. Maritain, *Art and Scholasticism*, 1920; H. Muensterberg, *The Principles of Art Education*, 1905; S. Pepper, *Aesthetic Quality*, 1937; E. Puffer, *Psychology of Beauty*, 1905; G. Santayana, *The Sense of Beauty*, 1896 and *Reason in Art*, 1906; F. Schiller, *Letters on the Aesthetic Education of Man*, 1793-'95; Schopenhauer, *The World as Will and Idea*, 1819; P. Souriau, *La reverie esthetique*, 1906; L. Tolstoi, *What is Art?* 1896; E. Veron, *Esthétique*, 1878; J. Volkelt, *System der Aesthetik*, 1905-1914.   —D.H.P.

aesthetics of children's art. See CHILDREN'S ART.

aesthetics of content. See form: a philosophical analysis.

AESTHETICS, recent trends in. Croce's theory of lyrical intuition was the reigning aesthetic at the turn of the century and for some years after. His trenchant negations, setting off the peculiar value of art from those often confused with it, and his positive conception of the poetical imagination, still operate in the writings of men able to revise and apply freshly those insights: In *Principles of Art* (1938), R. G. Collingwood, the philosopher and archaeologist of Roman Britain, reveals the distance he has gone since his early Crocean *Outlines of a Philosophy of Art* (1925). Lionello Venturi (*History of Art Criticism*, 1936; *Art Criticism Now*, 1941) uses Croce's general definition of art as the postulate of his own specific art criticism and his evaluations of criticisms by others. Edgar F. Carritt has compiled an historical anthology of aesthetic theories (*Philosophies of Beauty*, 1931), and takes his own largely historical

way of stating Crocean doctrine in *The Theory of Beauty* (4th ed. 1931) and then in the compact *What Is Beauty* (1932).

Sciences of signs and symbols have replaced Croceanism in the focus of attention. Three main directions have been taken: (1) **semantics**, the study of sign-situations, especially of verbal signs; (2) the psychological study of the sublimated dreams of art, the aftermath for aesthetics of Freud and Jung; (3) historical researches into icons as the most revealing manifestations of successive cultures.

(1) The chief writers under the first head are Messrs. Charles Ogden and I. A. Richards, and the scriptures of the school their *The Meaning of Meaning* (1st ed. 1923; begun in 1910; parts published in periodicals from 1920-1922). The wider purpose of the semanticists is to aid the process of verbal communication by producing awareness of the "frames of reference" during the act of meanings oriented in respect to each other. The uses of the school for aesthetics proper are illustrated by *The Foundations of Aesthetics* (Ogden, Richards, and Wood, 1922), in which sixteen different conceptions of beauty are fanned out, paralleled with pictures, and prepared for comparison by a statement of their respective frames of reference; also by the many chapters on the emotive use of language and on metaphor, and in the series of books on literary criticism by I. A. Richards: *Principles of Literary Criticism* (1925); *Practical Criticism* (1929); *Coleridge on the Imagination* (1934); *The Philosophy of Rhetoric* (1936); "The Interactions of Words," in *The Language of Poetry* (1942).

This first doctrine of signs and symbols is congruent with the favor now widely felt for rationalistic analysis and the relative disinclination for feeling and wholeness. D. W. Prall (*Aesthetic Judgment*, 1929, and *Aesthetic Analysis*, 1936) examines the basic orders in nature which "frame" the qualities of color and sound; C. J. Ducasse (*Philosophy of Art*, 1929) defines aesthetics as the science of the definitions of critical terms; R. W. Church (*An Essay on Critical Appreciation*, 1938) inquires into the meaning of the term beauty and defends intellectual criticism. Many writers on art, of a more technical sort, have followed the same trend. A large number of monographs have been written on the spatial frames, systems of perspective—or "rationalizations of sight"—implied or consciously devised by painters, sculptors, and architects, at various periods, e.g., Erwin Panofsky, *Die Perspektive als Symbolische Form* (1927); G. M. A.

Richter, *Perspective, Ancient, Medieval and Renaissance* (1937) ; S. Giedion, *Space, Time, and Architecture* (1941) : M. Bunim, *Space in Medieval Painting and the Forerunners of Perspective* (1940). In proportion as these frames and orders have been envisaged with measurable exactitude, there has been harmony with a tendency toward **mathematical aesthetics.** The latter is illustrated by the essays on *Dynamic Symmetry* by Jay Hambidge (1920) and by George Birkhoff's *Aesthetic Measure* (1933).

(2) But the terms sign and symbol have also had lately a markedly irrational connotation. Psychoanalysis focusses on emotion and content rather than on architectonic forms and definition-tracks; and on the creative process of the artist (Leonardo da Vinci; Goethe) rather than on the critical appreciative response. The artist is discovered to possess a soul peculiarly beset by archetypal human conflicts, e.g., those relating to sex and family rivalries, also those involving the trauma of birth (Otto Rank: *The Trauma of Birth,* 1924; *Art and the Artist,* 1932). Carl G. Jung (*The Theory of Psychoanalysis,* 1915; *Two Essays on Analytical Psychoanalysis,* 1926; *Psychology and the Unconscious,* 1916; *The Integration of Personality,* 1939) himself identified many symbols as dark psychic substitutes for a disturbing situation: water for the fluid depths of the soul; the world of Olympus, the myths of Œdipus, Narcissicism, the Sphynx, Prometheus, the Minotaur, Harpies, the gestures and postures of figures in statues and paintings for this or that biological fact D. H. Lawrence (*Psychoanalysis and the Unconscious,* 1921, and *Fantasia of the Unconscious,* 1930) develops the doctrine in an imaginative rather than scientific fashion.

(3) The third exploration of the meaning of symbols has found expression in the large scholarly output of the Warburg Institute (23 German, 14 English volumes of "studies"; 9 volumes of "lectures"; and *The Journal of the Warburg Institute,* 1937-). Ernst Cassirer's volumes on the meaning of symbolic form, Erwin Panofsky's studies in Neo-Platonic backgrounds and of the evolution of the concept *Idea* in art-history, and Edgar Wind's inquiry into the relation of eighteenth-century portraiture to the philosophy of the period may be mentioned as typical. The postulates of this group include the repudiation of the opposition of "inner" and "outer" approaches to art and history; the claim that the best analysis is historical; and the contention that man's expression of his psychic energies and habits in artistic symbols can only be understood by a recognition of the interplay of religious, social, scientific, and artistic elements in any epoch.

As the Warburg scholars call themselves "humanists" in the Renaissance sense, a group of recent American writers sympathetic with John Dewey have also taken the title. They wish to "recover the continuity of aesthetic experience with the normal processes of living." But they lean rather on biology and direct observation of experience than on scholarly reconstructions (John Dewey, *Art as Experience,* 1934; Laurence Buermeyer, *The Aesthetic Experience,* 1924; Irwin Edman, *The World, the Arts, and the Artist,* 1928; Albert C. Barnes, *The Art in Painting,* 1928).

The first article in *The Journal of the Warburg Institute* "Sign and Symbol" was written by the Neo-Thomist Jacques Maritain. He and the English Catholic, Eric Gill, have presented an aesthetic theory in which rational and irrational elements are neatly fused. The dark base of creative activity is shifted from Freudian embryology to the energy of the Divine Being working in the souls of poets and all makers. St. Thomas's definition of art as craftsmanship — the right rule of things made — is used to explain the conscious part of the work of the artist.

The philosopher and psychologist Samuel Alexander developed in *Beauty and Other Forms of Value* (1933) a view of artistic creativity as rooted in the constructive instinct, the organic impulse becoming planned craftsmanship on the human level, and "fine art" through the joy of contemplation. Helge Lundholm's recent *Aesthetic Sentiment* (1941) acknowledges the influence of Alexander but replaces the constructive impulse by the sentiment of curiosity.

A rich crop of monographs on the history of taste (Beverly Sprague Allen, *Tides in English Taste, 1619-1800,* 1937; Frank P. Chambers, *The History of Taste,* 1932) ; and of general aesthetic texts (De Witt Parker, *Principles of Aesthetics,* 1920 and *The Analysis of Art,* 1926; Max Schoen, *Art and Beauty,* 1932; Louis Flaccus, *The Spirit and Substance of Art,* 3rd ed. 1941; Katharine Gilbert and Helmut Kuhn, *A History of Esthetics,* 1939) ; a general bibliography (William A. Hammond, *A Bibliography of Aesthetics and of the Philosophy of the Fine Arts from 1900 to 1932,* 2nd ed. 1934) ; and the inauguration of a *Journal of Aesthetics and Art Criticism* (ed. Dagobert D. Runes, 1942) testify to the present liveliness of aesthetic interest.—K.E.G.

Africanism. See AFRICAN NEGRO ART;
AMERICAN NEGRO ART.

AFRICAN NEGRO ART. The controversy
as to whether African Negro art was first
appreciated by the ethnologist or the artist
has raged since the beginning of this century
in the literature of modern art. It is now an
academic question; and the contention of the
scientists that the appreciation of primitives
only began after ethnological collections had
been published in Europe seems of small significance against the fact that primitive styles
of art have contributed more than the historical
styles to the most modern aspects of contemporary art.

This controversy has installed two points of
view, respecting the study of primitive art,
which intermingle only at certain points. The
ethnologist now maintains that African Negro
art cannot be understood without first hand
knowledge of its social, traditional and psychological backgrounds; while the art critic
insists that first hand knowledge of the material culture and the primitive economy can
have but little effect upon our responses to the
admittedly great aesthetic appeal of the art
itself. In general, ethnography treats art as
one aspect of the *Kulturkreis* or social-cultural complex, following very closely the
nature and distribution of industrial production. This approach has served well to distinguish the various important centers of production and to catalog their various phenomenal differences.

Art criticism, recognizing the present difficulties that beset scientific effort to arrive at
some exact knowledge of the tribal cultures,
takes the high ground of sensitive aesthetic
appreciation and of psychoanalysis in determining the values and the place of African
art in the general picture of world art. The
chief drawback of this point of view is that
its practitioners are sometimes led into half-
mystical modes or attitudes of apperception
when confronted with the necessity for explaining a work of art in terms of its function
(see Ernst Fuhrmann, *Afrika,* 1922). It is
thus difficult for art criticism, where it fails
to make use of the findings of ethnology, to
avoid the charge of reading into the artifacts
of the primitives meanings and intentions that
cannot be objectively demonstrated.

The archaeological approach. While archaeological method has its own ends and develops
to some extent its own results, in respect to
African art it stands as arbiter between ethnology and art criticism. The general contributions to our knowledge of African art have
come through archaeological excursions in
Africa. In the area of pre-history these excursions have been somewhat delimited in
their results first by uncertainty as to the age
and original locus of Negro man in Africa,
and second, by the fact that archaeological
investigation has been restricted largely to
discovery and study of remains above ground.

Paleolithic and neolithic remains found in
Libya, Southern Egypt and the Eastern Sudan,
however, point to the possibility of an active
proto-history for the Negro. In this connection
the discoveries and observations of Leakey,
Frobenius, Talbot, and Breuil are important;
for they have introduced momentous possibilities into the general outline of the earliest
beginnings and earliest true maturation of
African Negro art. A line of emergence has
been traced from the pictographic art of
African neolithic times through the prevailing
patterns and formal bias of certain proto-
dynastic arts in Egypt, ancient Libya and the
early African Atlantic settlements. Connection
has likewise been made between ancient Zim-
babwe in Southern Rhodesia and the early
material culture of the Negroid Bantus of
Southeast Africa. Frobenius has further traced
the relation of early Sudanic and West Coast
cultures to the ever-expanding influences and
widely distributed products of the old Mediterranean civilizations; and he actually proves
Greco-Phoenecian influence by the remains
of stone altars, burial urns, and polychromed
statuary, found throughout the so-called *Clay-
complex* among the Ibibio and other tribal
cultures in Nigeria.

Origination and chronology. Most of the
African Negro art now in European and
American collections is of comparatively recent origin, although the greater part undoubtedly bespeaks a group of continuous traditions extending backward in time as far as
the first millienium, B. C. But very little is
known of the true history of Negro Africa
prior to the 15th cent., when both the West
and East Coast districts were to some degree
explored by Portuguese sailors. From some
of their reports and from reports made by
Dutch and later English explorers and trades-
men in the 17th, 18th and 19th cents., the
Western world has gradually learned something of the Negro and his history. For periods
prior to the 15th cent. in African art we must
rely upon archaeological testimony bolstered
by the historical writings of the Arab, Greek,
Roman and Abyssinian travellers and historians who knew something at least of the

movements and settlements of peoples on the Mediterranean coasts of North Africa as well as in those fertile lands which lie contiguous to the Sahara.

It is certain that the main artistic traditions of Negro Africa go back as far as the 12th cent. A.D. if not to an earlier period. Frobenius sees in the highly developed art of the Ifé-Yoruba complex a beginning in the first millenium B.C.; for he postulates a definite culture contact between the Greco-Phoenecian and the Egypto-Sudanese-Hyllaean worlds in the archaic times of Greek civilization. If this be merely a fantastic theory, it is at least undeniable that the art of **Yoruba** and of **Great Benin** was well advanced as early as the 13th cent. A.D. On the basis of local traditions, Burton, who visited the Kingdom of Benin in 1862, dated the foundation of the dynasty at about 1150. Struck's chronology for Benin permits some systematic review of its art. He has assigned a series of round bells and a grotesque man to the *Archaic period;* to the so-called *Early period* belong some figured bases, a plaster head now in the Rushmore Museum, England, and a few bronze heads; while the *Golden Age* of Benin art (roughly between 1500-1702) brings into existence some excellent examples of bronze relief-work, some of which carry the figures of Europeans. To this period belong also some truly magnificent stylised portraits of young women. A further stylistic classification brings us down to 1650, when the decline of the Golden Age sets in, as is indicated not only by the adulteration of technical means but also by the greater coarseness in conception exhibited in the portraits and commemorative plaques of the period. To the *Late period* (1700-1800) of Benin art are assigned some wooden figures with brass-covered heads. These are clearly imitations of the bronze heads and plaques of a more luxurious day. From this is but a step to the poorly conceived and poorly executed work of the 19th cent. which fell under the influence of European naturalism and brought the wonderful technics of Benin bronze and brass casting to a very low level.

Ethnologists divide the Negro peoples of Africa into two groups: The Negroes proper and the Bantus. The former are characterized by physical similarity, although they speak different languages; the latter speak a common language with little variation, but show great physical variety. The mode of life of these two ethnic groups is in most respects the same; yet in its broad controlling patterns contains wide variations as regards the dominance of herding, hunting, agriculture or trade in the culture of the group. Similarly, the main artistic traditions of the Negro peoples are in certain of their aspects indistinguishable from one another; but we are able to locate their centers of production and to describe them as well with some reference to their antiquity so far as known.

The centers of production of African Negro art may be classified for purposes convenient for study into Guinea, including Liberia and Sierra-Leone and the Bissagos Islands; the Sudan; the Ivory Coast; Yoruba and Benin; Cameroon and Gaboon; the Gold Coast; and the Congo.

From the West and inner Sudan districts we have the art work of the **Bagafore,** the **Banmana,** the **Senoufo, Habbé** and **Mossi.** Here, the influence of ancient and modern Egypt is traceable in certain features of the masks and statuettes. No extant work from this region, unless of stone, is more than 100 years old. The exceeding dryness of the Sudanese climate has been cited as one cause contributing to the early decay of works executed in wood. The neighboring region, French Guinea, lies between the Sudan and the Atlantic Ocean. It supports the highly artistic and very productive tribes of the Baga and the Kissi. The former, posessing an art of extraordinary formal consistency, have not been indigenous to the region more than 200 years. The subjects as well as the forms that they employ, do antedate, however, the Mohammedan infiltration of the early 19th cent. The Kissi are credited with a special type of statuette made of steatite which serves the double purpose of ancestral image and heroic memorial to a dead tribesman. Of very crude facture, it strongly resembles in type and in function those carved wood monuments erected by the Konso peoples of Abyssinia (sometimes called Galla) whose use of similar commemorative statuettes has been traced 35 generations within a single locality.

Since we have already characterized the art of Yoruba and Benin, the **Ivory Coast** will follow by geographical position as the next center of production. The impressive Ivory Coast work is distributed among the **Baoulé,** the **Gouro, Dan** and other lesser tribes. Among these, the Baoulé who are a branch of the **Ashanti** peoples on the **Gold Coast** are the most advanced artistically. In point of execution as well as tasteful composition, their work is only equalled by that of the Banmana in the Sudan. Present specimens of Ivory

Coast work cannot be said to antedate the mid-18th cent. Characteristics of older Baoulé work are the carrying of the arms pinned to the sides of the body, elongation of the torso and exaggeration of the abdominal eminence. The representation of tribal scarification and the attachment of an artificial beard are other characteristics.

Many varieties of art work are found in the **Cameroon** which touches the southern border of the Sudan. Wood, brass, ivory and ceramics are found; and everything of this nature is produced by the men. The women are permitted to help with the house building. Drums, pipes, stools, drinking cups, basketry, masks and statuary are produced; and from the **Cross River** (s.w. Cameroon) come masks of strikingly realistic and distinctive quality which are said to represent the native conception of the male and female elements or sky-father and earth-mother.

Originally, the Cameroon cultures derived from that of the Yoruba-Benin complex situated to the West; but in the use of certain other types of decoration, such as strips of embroidered beadwork, is evidenced likewise a relationship with the Congo.

Among the **Ashanti** of the Gold Coast has arisen an interesting custom of making small brass weights for the measuring of gold dust. These weights, which are miniature sculptures translated into permanent material through the "lost-wax" process, are given many different and curious forms, illustrating proverbs and folk tales. This art reached its highest development among the Ashanti in the 17th cent.

In wood-carving the Ashanti have produced some very fine examples of maternity fetishes and stools which are employed by these people as the insignia of rank or class.

The antiquity of **Congo art** has virtually been settled by Torday and Joyce who have made a thorough study of the culture, economy and political organization of the Bushongo nation which dominates the Kasai administrative region of the Congo. The only Bushongo portrait statues known are 7 statues of chiefs which were created following a custom said to have been instituted by King Shamba Bolongongo, the national hero (ca. 1600). All these statues conform to a definite type, i.e., all are seated with legs crossed. They wear shoulder, arm and wrist bracelets and belts of cowries and fibre. Each carries his attribute (drum, anvil) before him. Individual, facial and bodily characteristics vary and the features are so designed as to compliment the general

mass of the head. Possibly the only art of the Bushongo which antedates that of the sculptures is weaving, since the prevailing surface decoration of the plastic creations of this people obviously derives from textile designs.

The **Bushongo** nation itself has had its period of truly great efflorescence in modern times. The Bushongo were immigrants from the Ubangi-Shari region of Africa. They founded an empire which achieved ascendancy over a great area of Central Africa in the 18th cent. There are no other peoples in the Congo whose art can be referred to an earlier period than that of the Bushongo, nor is there any other type or form of sculpture among them that may be regarded as superior to their own.

Varieties of art produced. The corpus of African Negro art presents a limited repertory of subjects but an extensive vocabulary of styles and a great variety of technics. African art arises chiefly out of the religious customs of its producers, but runs a relatively long gamut of skills: It includes examples of monumental stone and wood and ivory carving, and also extends to the decoration of household and ceremonial utensils, notable in the art of the Bushongo tribes.

Clay-modelling, bronze, gold and brass casting reach in African art a truly magesterial splendor. The related technics of metalworking are also a skilled phase of native production; while bead, shell and other forms of ornamental embroidery, together with bark and raffia weaving, constitute a group of singular industrial arts among the Central African and West Coast tribes. In these several technics the Negro has made mask, figures, decorative and historical bas-reliefs, household and ceremonial utensils such as head-rests, stools, beds, king's sceptres and the batons of the chiefs, pottery of many kinds, weapons and gold assayers' weights, musical instruments, tobacco pipes, etc.

In architecture, however, little worthy of note may be attributed to the initiative of the Negro. In general, native African houses are of the simplest types and construction, the only exceptions being found in the now non-existent city of Benin where, wood, clay and metal were ingeniously used in the building of virtual palaces provided with terraces and elaborate colonnades. In Dahomey, the well-constructed clay-walled palaces of the kings resemble the shadowy low-roofed dwellings of the Fellaheen in Egypt. Ashantiland on the Gold Coast also contains some interesting specimens of native architecture. The best examples in this region recall in their total .

effect and interior decoration the Greco-Roman houses of Pompeii of the so-called architectural style. The interior and exterior walls of the Ashanti dwellings sometimes carry geometric designs in relief which closely resemble Arabian fret-work of a geometrical order in wood.

Portraitive qualities in African sculpture. The true portrait rarely occurs in good African Negro art; but where it does occur it is of the greatest historical and iconographic importance for the reason that the actual documents of African Negro cultural history are few. If the portrait represents a known human being who once held high place in the tribal society, it may be of invaluable effect in determining the antiquity or age of the originating tribal culture, or, if not so much as that, at least the possible age of works of art. Thus, from the Bakuba in the West Congo region have come no less than nine portraits which have been identified as the portraits of different kings who at some time held powerful sway over the Bushongo nation.

The remarkable terra cotta and bronze heads of Ifé are evidently portraits of great princes and princesses who in their personalities were also regarded as divine by their subjects. Portraits of princely personages likewise come from Benin and Dahomey except that in the latter state they are treated in so symbolical a manner as to be devoid of actual traits of likeness. Portraits of Europeans appearing in African art enable us, where other substantiation is lacking, to identify more certainly the date and place of origin of those specimens of art work on which the portraits appear. For example, the portraits of Portuguese sailors on the bronze plaques of Benin allow us to determine the approximate date of their production by the Bini craftsmen.

By and large the portraitive quality in African art, even when it appears in identifiable portrait monuments, is formally generalizing rather than directly individualising in artistic intent; so that the tinge of realism that we have learned to look for in modern Western traditions of direct portraiture is usually absent from African sculpture which places unity of design and of mass above truth to individual expression.

Plastic imagination and fantasy. One of the most stimulating aspects of African art is its boldness in juxtaposing abnormal, grotesque or strikingly irregular shapes and forms to forms normally perceived and logically developed. This phenomenon is the basis of that

ingenuity of presentation which we recognize as superior plastic imagination combined with primordial aesthetic feeling in the best primitive art. Various attempts have been made to explain these effects of African artistry on the basis of the interdependence of art and religion in the tribal spiritual life as well as on the more dubious ground of pre-logical mentality. To be sure, some of it can be thus accounted for, taking into consideration the greater or lesser vitality of totemism, animism and other primitive beliefs and practices among the art-producing cultures.

Theories proceeding on these primary assumptions usually fail to explain the use of grotesque or fantastic masks and statuettes in connection with ceremonies that have purely practical connotation with reference to the social structure of the tribe. Among the Baluba, the Bayake and the Mendi, there are war dances requiring the use of masks which so caricature the human features as to reach extremes of grotesque fantasy. But the motive for their creation was more practical than spiritual. Nor are the plastically rich and subjectively varied patterns of the Angola tobacco pipes to be accounted for merely on grounds of religious fantasy and pre-logical imagination. It is also true that some Negro tribes exhibit greater plastic imagination in their art than other tribes of the race. Yet, it is certain that the best traditions of African art are those which developed in areas where the tribal power and customs were sufficiently stable to exert formative influence on the artist. The rest was left to the artist's instinctive realization of the all-important truth that no effect of art is impressive which does not radically transform the object.

Influence on Modern Western Art. About 1904 African Negro art became known to several artists working in Paris. The revolutionary trend in European art initiated by the painting of Cezanne, of Gauguin and of van Gogh had prepared the artist for the reception and appreciation of African art as one of the major traditions of world art. For a generation or longer there had been working in the collective mind of the progressive spirits of artistic Europe a movement of reaction in favor of primitive feeling and modes of vision. It was therefore what African art (regarded by them as "primitive") could do to help clear the way for ideationally free and technically unfettered expression that was valued in its discovery by the artists of France and Germany.

The specific relationships of African art

to the art movements of the 20th cent. can be studied in the earlier phases of French Fauvism (q.v.) and cubism (q.v.) and in German expressionism (q.v.). After the discovery of Negro sculpture in Paris by Maurice de Vlaminck in 1904-05, the primitivistic trend in European art became more aggressive. It was taken up by André Derain and Pablo Picasso. The latter knew Ivory Coast masks and figural sculpture, and in his early cubist phase the influence of this region is most apparent. Henri Matisse, Georges Bracque, Modigliani, Constantin Brancusi (Hungarian sculptor), and Jacques Lipschitz (Russian sculptor), were all more or less influenced by examples of African art.

In Dresden, Germany, under the compelling leadership of Ernst Ludwig Kirchner, certain painters, now conveniently represented in the history of art under the generic term "Expressionists" (cf. Ernst Ludwig Kirchner, *Chronik der Brücke,* privately printed, 1916), introduced forms and effects of color into their painting (1906-1915) which convey the plastic yearnings of civilized humanity.

The general aesthetic yield of this extraordinary contact with African art must be considered in relation to the return of modern artists to those essentials of representation and design which may be regarded as fundamental to all artistic expression. Such terms as "instantaneousness", "intensity" and "dynamic forms" as used by these artists are indicative of the new aesthetic objectives which African art helped to release into the stream of organic Western art. In short, the progressives of the 20th cent. had set out to recover all that which academicism (q.v.) had tried to smother under many layers of outworn classico-romantic subject matter and technical recipes of the studio. See P. Guillaume and T. Munro, *Primitive Negro Sculpture,* 1926; L. Frobenius, *Das Unbekannte Afrika,* 1923; A. Basler, Opinions Récentes sur l'Art et la Psychologie Nègre, *Mercure de France,* CCVII (1928), pp. 593-610; O. Jones, *The Grammar of Ornament,* 1868; J. J. Sweeney, *African Negro Art,* 1935; C. Kjersmeier, *Centres de Style de la Sculpture Nègre Africaine,* (1935), I, II, III, IV; E. Vatter, *Religioese Plastik der Naturvoelker,* 1926; M. J. Herskovits, *Dahomey, an Ancient West African Kingdom,* 1938. —J.A.P.

after-image. See COLOR.

agalma. The common Greek term for a piece of sculpture; sometimes also applied to a painting, esp. a portrait.

Agamemnon. King of Argos, leader of the Greek expeditionary force against Troy as described in Homer's *Iliad.* The story of his tragic home-coming is told in Aeschylus' *Agamemnon.* In ancient art Agamemnon was pictured in vase paintings. —W.R.A.

Agano yaki (Jap). Pottery made in Yuzen province.

Age of Manners. See ENGLISH ART.

Age of Oak. See Jacobean.

Age of Romanticism. See POST-REVOLUTIONARY ARCHITECTURE AND DECORATIVE ARTS IN THE U.S.A.

Aghkand ware. See PERSIAN ART.

Aghlabid style. See ISLAMIC ART.

aging. Process of allowing clay to age, accelerating colloidal degeneration. See CERAMICS I.

Agni (Skr. fire). Vedic god of fire; most important of Vedic gods, represented by color red and conceived of as having two heads, each containing a split tongue.

Agnus Dei. The last division of the musical Mass (q.v.).

agoge. *Mus.* The rules of melodic succession.

agoge rhythmica. The succession of tones with reference to accent and rhythm.

agogic accent. *Mus.* A sign over a note denoting the slight prolongation of its value required to mark the measure-motive's culminating point.

agogics. *Mus.* Slight duration variations in tone-duration, other than note-values; equivalent to dynamic variations in tone intensity. Modifying strict tempo to bring out the full expression of a musical phrase.

agora. The Greek and Roman name for a marketplace. In Hellenistic and Roman times it was often enclosed partially or wholly by porticos. The most famous agora of ancient times, that of Athens, has been excavated since 1927 by American archaeologists; important architectural remains, sculpture, coins and inscriptions have been found there. —W.R.A.

agrèmens. *Mus.* French term for graces, ornaments. See embellishments.

Agrigentum. This Sicilian site (called Akragas by the Greeks) was a center of culture in the

5th cent. B.C., famous esp. for its Doric temples, of which the most important were the temples of "Herakles" (c. 510 B.C.), Zeus Olympios (c. 470 B.C.), "Juno" (c. 470 B.C.), "Concord" (c. 440 B.C.), and the Dioscuri (c. 250 B.C.). —W.R.A.

Ahavah Rabbah mode. See JEWISH MUSIC.

Ahriman (Per.). In Zoroastrianism, the evil spirit.

Ahura-Mazda. See Ormazd.

air. A tune, melody, song. A rhythmical, melodious series of single tones in a metrical group.

air-jet. See ACOUSTICS; MUSICAL INSTRUMENTS.

Ajax. A Greek hero in the Trojan War, famous for his great strength and tragic suicide. The Italian sculptor Canova included him among his portrayals of mythological subjects. —W.R.A.

Akahada pottery (Jap.). Pottery made in the province of Yamato.

Akkadian art. See MESOPOTAMIAN ART.

Akogi yaki (Jap.). Pottery made in Ise province.

Akragas. See Agrigentum.

akroterion. See acroterium.

alabastron. A small Greek perfume vase, with delicately curved sides and a bottom rounded so that it had to be supported to stand upright. —W.R.A.

à la Grecque (Fr.). In the Greek style. Having the character of Greek art due to strong Grecian influence.

à la mode (Fr.). Pertaining to the current style or fashion.

alba. See MEDIEVAL MUSIC.

albarium (Lat.). A thin stucco, white.

Alberti bass. Accompaniment for the left hand after the style of Domenico Alberti of Venice.

Albumblatt, album-leaf. A short lyrical instrumental piece.

album paintings. Paintings and graphic prints were sometimes made small in size to mount in albums; picture albums. —J.A.M.

alcarazza (Sp.). A porous earthenware receptacle.

alcazar (Sp.). Fortress; also palace.

alcohol. Either as the pure spirit, made by distillation of grains or fruits, or as a distillate of vegetable waste, particularly wood, alcohol has a limited use in the arts as a solvent for resins and as a general cleaning agent. It is found in some quantity in a few of the picture varnishes and almost as the sole agent for those materials used as fixatives for drawings. There it is combined with a soft resin or, in some cases, with a synthetic resin. Alcohol has been known probably since the 9th cent. but any extensive use of it in the arts has been during comparatively modern times. —G.L.S.

Alcora pottery. See SPAIN, ART OF.

alcove (Sp. *alcoba,* bed-chamber). A covered recess connected with, opening into, or at the side of a larger room. —J.M.M.

Alexander the Great. King of Macedon (356-323 B.C.) and "world-conqueror." His court sculptor was Lysippus, chosen because he succeeded best in portraying Alexander's "masculine and leonine appearance." Several extant busts of Alexander are doubtless copies or adaptations of Lysippus' work, notably the Azara bust in the Louvre and one in the British Museum. Perhaps more trustworthy representations are those on Macedonian coins of the period. W.R.A.

Alexander the Great, sarcophagus of. A sarcophagus found at Sidon, and now in Constantinople. It is perhaps the most beautiful of all classical sarcophagi, as well as an outstanding work of 4th cent. B.C., relief sculpture. Its top is in the form of a temple roof, and the reliefs on the sides are framed by exquisite carved mouldings. The sculpture, embellished with delicate red, blue and yellow color, represents dramatic battle and hunting scenes, with Alexander the Great playing a prominent role. H. Bey and T. Reinach, *Une necropole royale à Sidon.* —W.R.A.

Alexandrian art. See HELLENISTIC ART; EARLY CHRISTIAN ART.

alhambra. Usually a counterpane fabric, with fine warp and coarse filling threads. Jacquard figuring. This fabric resembles the hand loom woven bed covers made in New England in the 18th cent. —G.W.R.

alizarin. One of the coloring materials in the pigment madder, alizarin has been isolated and synthesized since 1868 when C. Grave and C. Lieberman reported its discovery. Since that time it has largely replaced as a pigment the naturally derived coloring matter from the madder root. It is a deep crimson and varies somewhat in hue according to its manufacture. It is one of the lake pigments, being a soluble dye precipitated on a base, usually aluminum hydrate. Like all such lake colors, it is highly transparent. In its reaction to light it is more stable than the natural madder.　　—G.L.S.

alkaline glass. See GLASS AND GLASS-MAKING.

alla-breve. See NOTATION .

alla prima (It.). In painting, the process of laying on all the pigments "at once"; i.e., a single application of the pigments rather than several in layers.

allée couverte (Fr.). A covered passage. A tunnellike entrance to an ancient tomb.

allegory. The use of images to represent abstract concepts and their relations, provided that to represent means "to stand for and instead of", not merely "to illustrate and to confirm". Such use is a reversal of ordinary mental processes in which images accompany and exemplify relationships of meaning operative on the basis of words and valid even without help of images. To speak of love, of its causes and its manifestations is to speak in terms of ordinary discourse, which emphasizes the relations of ideas; to speak of "lady love", her fate and her exploits, as medieval poets did, is to speak in terms of allegory, which emphasizes the relations of the sensuous embodiments of ideas.

Legitimate means of allegory are: (1) *personification,* such as the replacement of "love" by "lady love" or of "justice" by a blindfolded lady with a balance in her hand; (2) *exemplification,* such as the replacement of "justice" by a judge in the act of dispensing justice or by a judge well known in history such as king Solomon. Both methods are frequently used conjointly, which is all the more desirable, since no personification can act as such without some attribute, special character or inscription to confer upon it its identity.

Allegory claims the virtue of being able to invite the mind to contemplate metaphysical essences such as love and justice in their objective being apart from whatever relation they may possess to individual human experience. Therein lies its pedagogical value for those not trained in abstract thought as well as its danger for the pursuance of such thought. For allegory can only summarily point to abstract concepts without providing the tools for unraveling them. The task of allegory is to isolate universal concepts; it therefore is not its proper business to render as art does the complexities of individual experience which it could only imperfectly approximate by accumulating universal referents. Its range is further restricted by its being able to act as a visual substitute only for disconnected nouns, not for the verbs and predicates which we use as signs for relationships between nouns. The numerous and necessary relations between allegorical terms can consequently not be allegorical. The actions and gestures of allegorical figures (such as the battle between vices and virtues) are all symbolical and so are those spatial relationships which indicate their relative place in the hierarchy of concepts (such as the relation of "above" and "below" to indicate rank, or of "center" to "periphery" to indicate importance). It must finally be pointed out that the legitimacy of the claim of personification that it "represents" abstract concepts is open to question. If, as we assumed, to "represent" means to "stand for or instead of", then it is clear that no attribute can make the figure of a woman stand for or instead of a metaphysical principle.

Historically allegory is an invention of the ancient Greeks and a mode of representation exclusive to European civilization. It arose when Greek rationalism began to interpret the ancient mythological figures as embodiments of philosophical truths. It gained ground when Christian monotheism abolished the ancient divinities only to readmit part of them in the guise of allegorical personifications. Its permanent establishment is due to the so-called "realism" in medieval philosophy which upheld the reality, distinctness and separate existence of universal concepts. Under the influence of such philosophy the medieval mind was not only able to create novel allegorical entities, but it implanted the use of allegory so firmly in the European mentality, that no subsequent change in philosophy was able to dislodge it.　　—R.B.

allegro. Rapid tempo. See adagio (1).

alleluia. In church-music, an acclamation added to the end of a psalm or other item in the ritual. See Mass; MEDIEVAL MUSIC.

allemande. One of the *pre-classic* dance forms; was an ancient dance of the German people which found its way into 16th cent. French court life and thence to the rest of the Continent and to England. Its popularity must have been great, since its name and general style survive today in certain English and American square and round dances. The earliest allemande was done in slow, heavy, 4/4 meter and with simple movement. Its characteristic figures, danced with hands joined or arms linked throughout, produced an intertwining flow of motion. Court dancers exaggerated this quality to an over-graceful sentimentality. The court form was divided into three parts with couples moving in a column. An unusual feature was the pause for conversation between the first and second parts. The 3d part became much lighter and livelier than it had been in the ancient dance. German composers substituted the allemande music for that of the pavane as the opening piece in the instrumental suites based upon the court dances, and this substitution later became accepted in general suite composition (see pavane). —J.G.

allgemeine Kunstwissenschaft. See AESTHETIC INQUIRY (2).

allotments. See CIVIC PLANNING.

allusive arms. See HERALDRY.

almemar. Platform in the Jewish synagogue (q.v.) on which is located a reading desk.

Almohad art. See ISLAMIC ART.

Almoravid art. See ISLAMIC ART.

alms bowl. See SYMBOLISM IN FAR EASTERN ART.

Alpaca cloth. A thin cloth usually made of mohair.

alpaca yarn. Often used to refer to yarn used in rayon alpaca cloth. Misnomer.

alpenhorn. A wooden trumpet used by Swiss shepherds.

alpha and omega. The first and last letters of the Greek alphabet. (Rev. I, 8; XXI, 6; XXII, 13.) Frequently used in art as symbols of omnipotence. —L.L.

alphabet notation. See NOTATION.

alt, altissimo. *Mus.* High, highest. *Alt* notes begin with the g above the treble staff; altissimo notes are an octave higher.

Altamira art. See PREHISTORIC ART.

altar (Lat. *altare,* from *altus,* high). A high place, that is, a place of highest honor; more precisely, a pedestal (fixed or movable) used for supplication, invocation of, or sacrifice to a deity, deified hero, or saint. As supplication and sacrifices are common to most religions, the altar has been used generally by nations and peoples throughout the world.

The altar has always been closely associated with the actual presence or manifestation of the deity or saint, the place in which he abides, upon which he stands, which holds his relics, or which stands before his abode.

Earliest altars seem to have been mounds or platforms of sunbaked earth or large stones; however the development into more ornamental forms was rapid. Altars of various forms and materials were used in Egypt and Mesopotamia from the earliest times. In Assyria limestone and alabaster were used, while in Egypt basaltic rock and polished granite were the chief materials.

At Knossos, Crete, an altar was found consisting of a slab of black steatite supported by four legs at the corners. This was placed as a cover for a sacred stone (*omphalos*).

The early altars of the Hebrews were of the simplest material. This was required by priestly regulation (Exodus xx. 24). Later, two forms were recognized, the first for burnt-offerings, the second for incense. The **Altar of Burnt-Offering** was placed in the center of the temple (tabernacle) court, and was made of acacia wood covered with copper or brass. The corners were decorated with protruding forms called "horns." (Exodus xxvii. 1-8; I Kings i. 50; I Kings ii. 28.) (Similar forms are seen in the altars of Assyria and Crete.) The **altar of incense** stood in the holy place of the temple. Likewise it seems to have been made of wood, possibly cedar, smaller than the altar for burnt-offering, and also covered with metal, probably gold.

In classic Greece and Rome two types appeared, dependent upon use. The first type included those placed within temples before the image of the god. They were small low pedestals or platforms upon which the worshiper could kneel. The second type was larger, in the form of a table or pedestal, and was designed for offerings or burnt sacrifice. This type was placed in the open air, and if used in connection with temple worship, it stood before the principal entrance (in Greece, the east front). The size, shape, material, and decoration varied greatly, but the usual altar was of modest dimension, round or rectangular in plan, and built of marble. Notable exceptions in size are the altar of the Temple of Zeus and Athena at Pergamon, built by Eumenes II in the first half of the 2d cent. B.C., and the heroic altar of Augustan Pace in Rome, dedicated in 9 B.C.

The first Christian meeting places seem to have had no altars (probably because of pagan association). The communion or Eucharistic Feast probably was celebrated on a movable wooden table. The table-like tombs of the catacombs may have served this purpose, but the fact is not established, though the decree of Pope Felix I (A.D. 269-274) requiring that the mass be celebrated above the tombs of the martyrs strengthens the supposition. By the end of the 3d cent., however, the altar was being used. In western Europe and England wooden altars were customary until the 11th cent., although stone and marble were used in the Mediterranean countries as early as the beginning of the 4th cent. There are records of altars of gold or silver, probably referring to the use of these metals to form a decorative covering for the surfaces either in whole or in part. The *altar cover* (*palliotto*) given in A.D. 835 by Archbishop Engelbert to the Basilica of Sant' Ambrogio, Milan, is an existing example. It covers the four vertical faces of the altar and is made of sheets of gold, silver, and silver gilt with designs in engraving and relief, with added decoration of enamels, cameos, and precious stones.

The developed altar of the medieval church consisted of (1) the table (*mensa*), which was usually a stone slab generally marked with five crosses as a sign of its consecration; (2) the support (*stipes*), a solid mass of material or a series of piers or columns (usually four); and (3) the altar cavity (*sepulchrum*), which contained the relics, a practice probably developed from the aforementioned decree of Felix I. The step or base (*predella*) on which the altar stands often is considered a part of the altar. This is in accord with the use of the altar as a platform upon which the supplicant kneels. The decree that the mass should be celebrated above the tombs of the martyrs may have led to the multiplication and placing of the altars. If several martyrs were buried in close proximity, each would have an altar. This practice led to the side altars dedicated to various saints.

When a church has more than one altar, the principal one is called the **high altar**. This may be placed against the rear wall of the chancel or isolated in the body of the church. (The position of the isolated high altar varies, dependent upon local and national ritualistic custom.) The general practice in the Italian cathedral church with developed transepts places the high altar at the crossing (that is, the intersection of nave and transepts); in the French cathedral, toward the rear of the choir; in the Spanish cathedral, toward the rear of the nave, the front portion being occupied by the choir. There are many exceptions, however. The rules and practices relating to the use and decoration of the altar are complex and vary at different times, but its primary purpose is to provide a place for the consecration of the Eucharist and the celebration of the Eucharistic feast, and in the Roman Catholic Church it should contain a holy relic.

Movable or **portable altars** have been used commonly. The description of the Hebrew altar of burnt offering speaks of rings on its sides through which staves may be passed in order to transport it. (Exodus xxvii. 1-8) Small blocks of limestone bearing dedications to deities have been found in the classic lands and Mesopotamia. The use of **"pocket" altars** still prevails in India. Since the 7th cent. A.D. portable altars have been used in Christian worship. These altars are usually slabs of hard stone which are consecrated and marked with the five crosses. They may be set upon any material available at the place where use of the altar is desired. Since late Gothic times portable altars have also been formed by altarpieces removed for the occasion, or by a painted panel in the form of an altarpiece (q.v.). This form was preferred because of its light weight and relatively small mass, enabling ease of transportation.

In the ancient civilizations of the Americas the altar was of the usual table-like form, either round or square, and usually decorated with symbolic sculptural relief or inscriptions in the form of glyphs. Sizes varied, but the altar stones were relatively low. At Piedras Negras, Guatemala, a square altar measures 6 by 6 ft.; at Cobá, Mexico, a round altar has a diameter of 4 ft. Both altars are only 18 inches high. Dates are uncertain. See R. A. S. Macalister, Altar, *Encyclopaedia Britannica*, 11th ed.; Sir A. Evans, *Palace of Minos at Knossos*, 1923; S. G. Morley, *Inscriptions of Peten;* Thompson and Pollock, *Preliminary Study of the Ruins of Cobá*, Carnegie Institution of Washington, D. C.; G. M. A. Richter, *Sculpture and Sculptors of the Greeks*, 1929.
—J.C.

In southwestern archaeology: Sometimes termed the "deflector" or "fire screen". (Some archaeologists believe the "ventilator" served to conduct air into the chamber and that the "screen" or "deflector" was constructed or placed to prevent the incoming current of air from blowing directly onto the fire. Others are of the belief that the so-called "ventilator" was thought to be the entrance and exit of the spirit beings and that the so-called "deflector" was an "altar").   **—J.M.M.**

altarpiece. A decorated screen, panel, or series of panels, movable or fixed, placed upon or to the rear of an altar, generally incorporating paintings or sculpture in relief. (See also reredos; retable.)

The altarpiece as it is generally understood is peculiar to the Christian Church, though its counterpart may be seen in the wall carvings and painted banners at the shrines of the Buddhist and related faiths.

Few altarpieces are recorded prior to the 11th cent.; yet the elaborate design and technique of such examples as the "Palo d'Oro" of San Marco, Venice (11th cent., later restored and added to) indicate an earlier development, at least in the Eastern Roman Empire (Byzantine). The altarpiece of the Gothic period (13th and 14th cent.) was usually a group of hinged panels, a **triptych** of three panels or a **polyptych** of five or more panels, so arranged that the outer sections or wings would fold over the inner sections. The panels were pictorially treated, the principal subject appearing on the face of the inner panel or panels, related subjects or a continuation of the principal subject appearing on the outer panels. The back of the panels might also be painted, depending upon the placing and nature of the altarpiece. When this was done, the panels usually were divided into a series of smaller pictures. Where the panels were fixed rather than hinged, the same formal appearance was retained. The major panels usually were mounted, or appeared to be mounted, upon a step or base called the *predella* in the manner of the altar (q.v., movable) and itself decorated by a series of small paintings or carvings usually related in subject to that of the main panels. The *predella* was often included in the design of the frame and thus became an integral part of the altarpiece rather than a base supporting it. Frames were as elaborate as conditions permitted, usually of wood carved and gilded. Spaces upon the frame formed by the carved design were often treated with supplementary painting. Examples: single panel, *San Trinita Madonna* (13th cent.) by Cimabue, Uffizi, Flor-

ence; *Majesta* (14th cent.) by Duccio, Opera del Duomo, Siena; triptych form, *San Ansiano Annunciation* (14th cent.) by Simone Martini, Uffizi, Florence.

During the 15th cent. the Gothic forms were replaced gradually by the more typical Renaissance form of a single main panel, divided, however, into three (triptych form), under which in the base of the frame were the *predella* pictures. Examples: multiple panel, folding wings, St. Bavon (Ghent) altarpiece, *Adoration of the Lamb* by Hubert and Jan van Eyck; triptych form, San Zeno altarpiece by Mantegna, San Zeno, Verona, and the Frari altarpiece by Giovanni Bellini, I Frari, Venice; single panel with *predella, Coronation of the Virgin* by Fra Angelico, Louvre, Paris; single panel, *Nativity* by D. Ghirlandaio, Chapel, S. Trinita, Florence.

The altarpiece of the 16th cent. and later more often was a single picture attached to a wall behind the altar or set into an architectural frame. These altarpieces became quite elaborate in the Baroque era, often combining in extravagant design architecture, painting, and sculpture. Examples: *Sistine Madonna* by Raphael, Dresden Art Gallery; *Assumption of the Virgin* by Titian, Frari, Venice; Altar of San Ignazio, Gesu, Rome.

Special forms of the altarpiece are seen in the **reredos** and **retable**. In Gothic England and Spain these forms, usually combining architecture and sculpture, reached huge proportions, sometimes filling the entire rear wall of the chancel. This form, using both painting and sculpture, is typical of the late Renaissance in Spain and its colonial empire in the Americas. Examples: Capilla de los Reyes, Cathedral of Puebla, Mexico, and the Seminario de San Martín at Tepozotlan, Mexico. See Spanish Architecture in the New World.   **—J.C**

alteration. See MEDIEVAL MUSIC.

altered chord. Chord formed by chromatic alteration of one or more tones of a major or minor triad.

alternating coursed. Term applied to masonry in which two heights of stone alternate in regular manner.

alto. See alt.

alto clarinet, flute. See MUSICAL INSTRUMENTS.

alto-rilievo (It.). High relief; sculpture in high relief. See relief; relief sculpture.

aluminum. In painting, sheets of aluminum have occasionally been used as panel supports, more in the practice of restoration than elsewhere. It is a relatively modern metal in any general use, large-scale production having come in only during the early years of the 20th cent. As a leaf or powder mixed with a suitable medium, aluminum has been applied to the backs and edges of panels as a protective coating. —G.L.S.

amalaka (Skt.). An ornament, bulbous or melon-like in shape, which tops the turrets (shikharas) of medieval Indian temples. See INDIAN ART.

amalthea. A horn of plenty, so-called from the name of the goat which suckled Zeus, from whose horn flowed whatever the possessor wished.

Amarāvatī school. See SOUTHEASTERN ASIATIC ART.

Amazon River culture. See AMERICAN ABORIGINAL ART.

Amazons. In Greek mythology, the female warriors of Asia Minor against whom the Greeks fought at various times under the leadership of the heroes Theseus and Achilles; represented in art in short girt chiton and helmet, armed with shield, spear, bow and axe, and usually mounted. —L.T.S.

ambo. Pulpit and reading desk of large size; found in early Christian and Eastern churches. See EARLY CHRISTIAN ARCHITECTURE.

Ambrosian chant. See MEDIEVAL MUSIC.

ambry (L.). (1) A depository for goods, food, or valuables. (2) In ecclesiastical architecture: A place or closet for depositing sacred vessels, etc. —J.M.M.

ambulatory. A sheltered passageway or aisle, as around the apse of a church.

Amen, Amon, Amen-Ra. Ancient Egyptian god originating in Thebes; had varied history as god of reproduction, of creation, etc.

amenities. See CIVIC PLANNING.

Amenti. In ancient Egyptian religion, the realm of the dead.

AMERICAN ABORIGINAL ART, Central and South America. The art of the American Indians was a highly diversified one made by many different tribes and many different tradi-

tions and with many different purposes in view. A summary cannot do justice to its complexity. The subject may be best discussed in terms of the divisions used in current western culture, namely, architecture, sculpture, painting, jewelry, pottery, and applied design. Prominence in any one of these fields is not necessarily correlated with general cultural advancement. The technical horizon of the American Indian was Neolithic. His art was comparable to that of Bronze and Iron Age developments in the Old World.

The study of American Indian architecture in its highest manifestations depends on archaeological research, which in turn rests on the amount of damage done by nature, time, and man. The houses of various tribes, made of skin, birchbark, wood, adobe, thatch, or stone, often attained forms and shapes which are interesting to our modern eyes. Their buildings were usually utilitarian, however. In the Southwestern United States communal buildings of several stories often suggest a long-range planning ability influenced perhaps by principles of balance and harmony of plan. In Mexico in some of the ancient towns like Tenochtitlan the streets were so arranged that one emerged upon the central plaza where the important ceremonial buildings were located. In Peru city planning existed from very early times and enormous towns made of adobe and stone were laid out in an orderly plan. Few of these great cities have been extensively excavated because of prohibitive costs.

The utmost was achieved in the ceremonial architecture of Middle America. A set principle was involved since the concept was developed of having an altar set on a platform to dramatize and focus the religious acts. In time the altars came to be larger and developed into temples. Usually the temple and the platform were designed as a unit, and as time went on the platforms were made larger and higher and the temples were ornamented with increasing luxuriance. As religion in Middle America came to dominate and absorb the surplus energy of the people more and more immense ceremonial centers were created. Sometimes the temples were laid out in terms of a plan, and at other times and in other localities the ceremonial buildings were erected without much heed for orderly spacing. Usually when a ceremonial center was created there were subsidiary dwellings for the priesthood, some of which in size and elegance rivalled the temples themselves. Materials used in building were stone, plaster, adobe, wood, and thatch. Mechanical and technical developments were relatively rudimentary. Temples and houses were roofed with a pitched thatch or a roof of beams. Sometimes to get a high and soaring roof a beam cribwork served as an armature for plaster. The Maya of Yucatan and Guatemala made extensive use of the corbelled arch, encasing the tails of the stones in a monolithic structure of mortar. In Peru there are reports of an occasional tau keystone, used in vaulting a room or doorway.

Sculpture had a long historical development in the Americas, and it seems to have been religious rather than purely aesthetic. The earliest sculpture tradition may be observed in baked clay. Owing to its perishability we do not have much of this. At the beginning clay sculpture seems to have been representational, often used to make little female figures of clay, perhaps in illustrative association to a female goddess so often associated with agricultural peoples. Great emphasis was laid on anatomical details. As the cultural and technical development of the people increased and their theology was ramified, more sophistication came in. In Middle America where a polytheism held sway many gods and goddesses had to be defined ritualistically. Some divinities were thought to be more like human beings and here we find expression of a lively naturalism. Baked clay, even up to the time of the Conquest, apparently was considered a worthy medium for sculpture, and, just as in early China, no study is complete without strong emphasis on the work in clay.

Stone sculpture, to judge from the archaeological evidence, came in several centuries after the clay modelling had been in vogue. Since the sculptors had only stone tools to work with, contours rather than basic anatomical details tended to be emphasized. Free-standing monumental sculpture was to be found in the great images of the gods. Adorning the inner and outer walls of the temples relief sculpture was extensively used. The aim was representation, but always in the composition of American Indian sculpture was a strong sense of harmonious and balanced disposal of elements. There is considerable evidence among the Maya that they took their first steps in sculpture in clay, then shifted to carving the lime-plaster of their temples, and when lime-plaster gave way to dressed limestone they had already perfected the principles of their art.

Size does not seem to have had an effect in direct proportion to excellence of artistic presentation. There are small exquisitely carved jades that have all the sense of monumentality of presentation which can be found on the major figures of the temples. A very striking feature of American Indian sculpture in general is its perfect balance and harmony, no matter what its size.

Sculpture in wood is rarely found, but the surviving examples from Mexico give every indication that it closely paralleled work in stone.

There are several regions and tribes distinguished for their sculpture: the 19th cent. Indians of the Northwest coast for their work in wood; the burial mound builders of Southern Ohio for their naturalistic sculpture, made perhaps in the 11th to 12th centuries; the temple mound builders of the Southeastern United States for their work in pottery and in stone, made perhaps in the 14th to 16th centuries; the pre-Conquest Aztecs for lively naturalism in clay; the inhabitants of the Valley of Mexico from the 2d cent. B.C. to the Conquest for long-range evolution in sculpture in clay and stone; the tribes of the Vera Cruz region, and Olmec, for monumental and small size sculpture in porphyry, jade, and allied stones; Maya groups of central America for stone and plaster carving in the round as especially developed at Copan in the east, carving in relief on the west in the Usumacinta Valley; in Costa Rica a less developed carving in stone; in Peru stone work is important in the early periods but does not attain the great sophistication of Central America—in later times the plastic art is expressed more in clay; in Bolivia the important monumental sculpture in stone is inferior in technique.

Painting does not seem to have been the important vehicle for artistic expression that it has been in the western world. On the other hand, the materials and surfaces used by painters are very perishable. In general, painting was used to express ceremonial concepts or to tell some sort of a story. There was relatively little development of perspective and tones were flat. Frescoes showing considerable ability in design and of value as a record of human activity have been recovered at Teotihuacan, Mexico; others of ritualistic character have been found in several Aztec sites in the same country. A number of manuscripts dating from before and just after the Conquest reveal a lively pictorial sense. A few Maya frescoes have been recovered at Chichen Itza. These describe scenes of native life and warfare. The three Maya books surviving are ritualistic, so it is hard to judge of excellence in draftsmanship from them. However, in the bas-reliefs of the western Maya country one can see in the outlines of the figures evidence of excellent draftsmanship. This is borne out by the vases from the Alta Verapaz area, which take top rank in examples of Indian craftsmanship.

Little has survived further south. In Péru, however, potters of the Early Chimu period decorated their vases with lively naturalistic scenes. In the later Nazca periods naturalistic elements drawn and painted with rich colors attest to skill of a high order.

Jewelry was a highly developed craft in ancient America. Stones such as jade, turquoise, amethyst, moonstone, obsidian, and other varieties were used to make necklaces, amulets, earrings and mosaics. There was also some use of metals including gold, copper, gold plating, and, rather sporadically, silver. Metals were cold hammered and also cast. Outstanding jade work comes from southeastern Mexico. Mosaic work is prominent in the same area, and, while well executed gold jewelry was created in southern Mexico, the great bulk comes from a belt along the Pacific range from Costa Rica to Peru. The Spaniards found that the native jewelry rivalled the products of contemporary Spain.

The pottery of the American Indians reached the level of a fine art. The forms in general tended to be squat and broad, following almost architectonic principles, since they were built up by strips of clay. Since the potters' wheel was unknown, the graceful elongations created by this process were not obtained. The variety in form is astonishing. Each tribe, each region, each era, is distinguished by characteristic methods of shaping and decorating vessels. Decoration was achieved by many methods including painting, modelling, incision, and polishing. Effigy forms were likewise made. Some of these naturalistic vessels come under the head of sculpture. Glazing was virtually unknown. A lead glaze paint was occasionally used along the Rio Grande River after the 13th cent. A.D., and in Central America there is a highly burnished ware that approaches a glaze.

In terms of shape, excellence of clay, painting, and variety of form of ceramics Peruvian peoples are preëminent. Less for ability than imagination in combining form and design, Middle American ceramics stand out.

One of the old, old arts of the Americas is weaving. While many of the textiles are lost, in Middle America we can reconstruct patterns and designs from the sculptures. On the coast of Peru, however, the absence of rain has preserved many burial mounds and there is a rich harvest for the student of weaving.

Virtually every process known to the Old World was employed by the ancient Peruvians. Furthermore, most of the dyeing processes known today were known also to those masters of the weaving art. There is evidence that weaving was mastered considerably before other fields of design were developed, and a tendency to abstract handling of design visible throughout Indian art of the two Americas may well be due to the tremendous influence exerted by textile design.

Craftsmanship raised almost to the level of an art extended to the manufacture of almost every implement, since to manufacture any implement by hand calls into being the best of craftsmanship. Thus, a weight for a spindle may be a beautiful carved and burnished clay disk, a wooden throwing stick for propelling a javelin may be exquisitely carved in a ceremonial design. A dress for a priest or chieftain called into play the arts of the weaver, the jeweler, the sculptor in the preparation of a mask, and often the services of one of the great American crafts, that of feather work, used not only in clothing, but also in exquisite mosaics applied to shields and banners. Mirrors are sometimes a mosaic of iron pyrites. One or two examples exist of pyrites mirrors which have been ground to enlarge the image.

Whistles, flutes, and other instruments often bearing sculptured designs and made for use in temple services, also show excellent craftsmanship.

Art for art's sake apparently did not exist among the American Indians, nor are there words in their languages which have the same significance as our terms "art" and "aesthetics". There was a definite recognition, however, of superior things. The finest work in any new medium was almost always directed toward religious use. In that religious and civil life went hand in hand, the tribal leaders had access to the fruits of the craftsmanship directed to religion. In countries like Mexico, Guatemala, and Peru the outlet offered by the evangelists of the country after the Conquest continued in a different form the ancient tradition of craftsmanship. Today in outlying districts their handmade and homemade implements and utensils are still used and many of the old techniques persist. However, few of the ancient designs have been brought down. Usually there is a Spanish colonial background slightly altered by the ancient techniques. Given an outlet there is a latent force ready to spring into action today. See A. Caso, *Thirteen Masterpieces of Mexican Archaeology*, 1938; A. Caso and others, *Twenty Centuries of*

Mexican Art, 1940; H. Cahill, *American Sources of Modern Art,* 1933; W. H. Holmes, *Masterpieces of Aboriginal American Art* (*Art and Archaeology,* vol. 1, pp. 1-12, 91-102, 242-55; vol. 3, pp. 70-85; vol. 4, pp. 267-78; vol. 5, pp. 38-49; vol. 8, pp. 348-60), 1914-19; I. Marquina, *Estudio Arquietectonico Comparative de los Monumentos Arqueologicos de Mexico,* 1928; *Escultura Mexicana Antigua,* 1934; H. J. Spinden, *A Study of Maya Art,* 1913; G. O. Totten, *Maya Architecture,* 1926; G. C. Vaillant, *Artists and Craftsmen in Ancient Central America,* 1935; W. Lehman, and H. Doering, *Kunstgeschichte des Alten Peru,* 1924; E. Nordenskiold, *L'Archeologie du Bassin de l'Amazone,* 1930   —G.C.V.

American Empire style. See Duncan Phyfe; FURNITURE; INTERIOR ARCHITECTURE AND DECORATION.

American folk forms, in literature. As a result of the acculturation process, folklore in America has developed certain distinctive forms and traits that are American in history if not in origin. Many of these are variations in time as well as in place. Such, for example, is **tall talk,** which flourished South by West in the period of national expansion after the War of 1812. As a form of "backwoods eloquence" or strong language constantly striving to outdo itself, tall talk suited the frontier mood of reckless energy, boundless optimism, and outrageous confidence. It is further related to the national habit of boasting and boosting and has its political counterpart in stump-speech and spread-eagle oratory.

In the plays, fiction, and sketches of the time (James K. Paulding's *Lion of the West* and *Westward Ho!,* Robert Montgomery Bird's *Nick of the Woods,* the Mike Fink legends and the Davy Crockett almanacs), backwoodsmen and rivermen of the "half-horse, half-alligator" or "ringtailed roarer" type were represented as speaking fantastic strings of gab compounded of coined epithets and expletives, exaggerated comparisons, and animal allusions. This literary dialect culminated in boasts and "bad man yells," whose lineage may be traced to the epic brags and flytings of the Middle Ages but whose accents are distinctly American:

I'm that same David Crockett, fresh from the backwoods, half-horse half-alligator, a little touched with the snapping turtle; can wade the Mississippi, leap the Ohio, ride upon a streak of lightning, and slip without

a scratch down a honey locust; can whip my weight in wild cats. . . .

As their language was tall talk, so the deeds of the "tall men" of the woods and the rivers were **tall tales.** Many tall tales originate in competitive bragging which degenerates into competitive lying. The parent type is the **yarn,** a long, extravagant, amusing tale of invention, which in its rambling structure and leisurely pace resembles the "humorous story" described by Mark Twain in "How to Tell a Story" as the distinctive development of story-telling in America and best illustrated by his own yarn, "The Celebrated Jumping Frog of Calaveras County." As the vehicle of Southwest humorists in the 1830's, the mock-oral yarn was a droll story of local customs and characters, which simulated the manner of spoken narrative.

When incredibility rather than drollness is the main element of the yarn, it becomes a **tall story** (*tall:* remarkable, prodigious). The term "tall tale" is generally reserved for the traditional tall story as distinguished from the ordinary tall story, which is an individual invention.

Tall stories are known variously as windies or big windies (from the manner of telling); fish stories (from a common tall-story theme); bunkhouse, bunkroom, barroom, or grocery store stories (from the place of telling); sailor's or traveler's yarns (from the person who tells them); and whoppers or big lies (from the chief ingredient).

Although the yarn or droll tale is sometimes referred to as a tall tale (as in Franklin J. Meine's *Tall Tales of the Southwest*), the tall tale takes three typical forms: (1) the pranking or hoaxing tale, told to "take in" the newcomer and entertain the old-timers; (2) the whopper or lying tale, told in the spirit of competitive lying as at Liars' Clubs and in Liars' Contests or from the Liars' Bench (an actual or figurative seat for story-tellers) or on the Deacon's Seat of logging camps; and (3) the cycle of tales growing up around the marvelous feats and mythical companions of a superman of the Paul Bunyan type.

The themes of tall tales are the perennial ones of boosters and knockers — freaks of weather, climate, soil; insect pests; marvelous hunts; feats of skill and strength; and "fearsome critters" (which are also attracted into the Paul Bunyan cycle).

Perhaps it is because our folk story-tellers are mainly jesters that we have no great body of **hero legends** outside of the Paul Bunyan type (variously assigned to Pecos Bill, Tony

Beaver, and Febold Feboldson, the last two of whom are manifestly literary inventions). Most of our historical heroes are of the "success story" or Horatio Alger variety and have been taken over by the popular literature of edification or entertainment. In contrast to our comic demigods, our "bad men" have given rise to ballads rather than tales; while in between is a body of picaresque and "adventure" folk literature concerned with scouts, trappers, hunters, explorers, and other frontier characters, one of the best of whom is Big-Foot Wallace.

Many Western heroes, like Jim Bridger and Jim Beckwourth, were windjammers in their own right. But the greatest of our folk heroes who was also our greatest practical storyteller is Lincoln. His vehicle was the **anecdote** or story with a point, in which Bret Harte saw the origin of the American short story and which is admirably suited to the practical purposes of politics, religion, and business, as indicated by the innumerable collections of anecdotes for speakers. The humorous anecdote or *joke* in America rings the changes on human folly and meanness. Favorite themes of gags and wisecracks (q.v.) are the absent-minded professor, the tight Scotchman, the *enfant terrible* (Little Audrey), and the moron (the heir of the "so-dumb" lines).

The cruelty of these verbal jests reflects the sadism of **practical jokes,** the practicalness of which consists in the fact that something is done rather than said. These range from April Fool jokes and riddling tricks and catches ending in a "sell" to cheating tricks of swapping and trading (as in the many stories of horse-trading) through all the hoaxes perpetrated on strangers, such as sending a new hand in search of an impossible object, snipe hunts, badger fights, and the "whizzers" of the gold diggings.

Akin to the practical story-teller in his combination of horse sense and humor, with the addition of eccentric orthography and grammar, is the **crackerbox philosopher,** who has given us a long line of homespun humorists from Seba Smith's character, Jack Downing, to Will Rogers. Next to the newspaper letter, the favorite medium of the cracker box philosopher is the **humorous travelog,** a form which has been employed by literary comedians and vaudevillians of the "Slow Train through Arkansaw" type to point up local and regional differences. In countless place names and nicknames, phrases, sayings, allusions, rhymes, songs, and other **floating material** or "stuff that travels" American folklore reflects the restlessness and diversity of the American scene. See *American Humor,* by Constance Rourke, 1931; *Ring-Tailed Roarers,* by V. L. O. Chittick, 1941; *David Crockett, American Comic Legend,* by Richard M. Dorson, 1939; *Mike Fink, King of Mississippi Keelboatmen,* by Walter Blair and Franklin J. Meine, 1933; *Tall Tales of the Southwest,* by Franklin J. Meine, 1930; *Tall Tales from Texas,* by Mody C. Boatright, 1934; *Humor of the Old Deep South,* by Arthur Palmer Hudson, 1936; *Tall Tales,* by Lowell Thomas, 1931; *Paul Bunyan,* by Esther Shephard, 1924; *Crackerbox Philosophers in American Humor and Satire,* by Jennette Tandy, 1925; *Horse Sense in American Humor,* by Walter Blair, 1942; *The People, Yes,* by Carl Sandburg, 1936; *A Treasury of American Folklore,* by B. A. Botkin, 1944.
—B.A.B.

American folk forms, in music. Recent trends in the study of folk music in America have broadened its scope beyond the narrower limits of vocal music, especially balladry, to include the whole range of traditional musical idiom and taste. This is conceived in terms of social functions and group activities, such as work, play, the dance, and religion.

Thus in the field of the **country dance,** the distinctive American development from British sources has been the **square dance, quadrille,** or **cotillion,** in contrast to the English *contradance* or *longways dance,* which still persists in New England. In the U.S.A. the term *square dance* has come to stand for old-time set dancing generally, whether of the square, longways, or circle formation. In the Southern Appalachians there has survived an older English form of country dance, which, like many of the ballads, has been more or less forgotten in the mother country. This was dubbed by Cecil J. Sharp the **running set,** from the characteristic running step of the dancers—a fast glide, free and easy in its execution, with certain flourishes such as the clog, shuffle, two-step, hoe down, and buck dance. Its figures are square dance figures, in circle formation, without fixed order or the courtesy movements that the English country dance acquired under French influence.

The two most important persons at a country dance are the *fiddler* and the *caller.* Although the guitar and the banjo are used to accompany the fiddle at dances, as well as to accompany the folk singer, the fiddle is the American folk musical instrument par excellence. 'ts portability and adaptability made it the musical voice of backwoods and frontier

America and the country fiddler one of the most picturesque of pioneer folk characters. Another minstrel type is the square-dance caller or prompter, who, in a mixture of rhythmic prose and doggerel made up of "calls" interspersed with patter, intones and (in the Northeast and Southwest) sings or half-sings the directions.

Because of religious prejudice against dancing and especially the fiddle, as the instrument of the devil, the young people of rural America developed an alternative form known as the *play-party game* (q.v.), which substituted singing for instrumental accompaniment. A cross between dancing and the traditional singing games of children, the play-party retains the best features of both. To the courtship and other dramatic devices of the game, such as choosing and stealing partners, the play-party adds certain square dance movements and figures, in which, however, partners are swung by the hands instead of by the waist. The leader combines the functions of caller and floor-manager; and like the caller he is something of a folk-poet, with the gift of improvisation.

On the sacred side the old-time *country singing* keeps alive the church and singing-school tradition of unaccompanied three- and four-part singing. Throughout the rural South organizations like the United Sacred Harp Musical Association and their many state affiliates hold "little singings" of the "all-day-singing-and-dinner-on-the-grounds" type and annual "big singing" conventions during "laying-by" time. From the four or seven shape-note systems employed in their tune-books the singers are known as "fasola" or "dorayme" singers. The use of shape-notes, based on the older solmization, goes back to about 1800 when it was introduced by William Little and William Smith or by Andrew Law to make sight-reading easier by associating each note with a certain shape. The custom of solmization is a distinctive feature of shape-note singing, since, after the leader has given the page and the key, the group sings the song through once by notes, followed by one or more stanzas (often "lined out").

The songs are known as **white spirituals**, a mixture of "folk" and "art" hymns, anthems, and fuguing songs (the last traceable largely to William Billings' influence), with a variety of sources, including Isaac Watts hymns, ballad and dance tunes, and camp-meeting songs. White spiritual tune-book compiler-publishers, singing-teachers, and leaders have kept up a steady flow of composition and promotion,

amounting to our major "folk song" industry.

What distinguishes these country singings from the related gospel hymn singing of revivals, protracted meetings, baptizings, footwashings, and the like is the fact that here, without loss of religious faith, singing becomes its own reward.

Sacred harp singing has also penetrated to the Negro churches; and the question of the mutual indebtedness of white and Negro spirituals (q.v.) has stirred considerable controversy. By way of the Holiness Church, with its motto, "Enjoy your religion," musical instruments of the jazz-band type have been brought into the church, along with jazz singing and the "holy dance" (a variant of which is the ring-shout). "Folk quartets" in Negro churches also show the hybridizing influence of radio and commercial phonograph record techniques.

In contrast to square dancing and country singing, which have survived the competition of canned music, **work songs** tend to disappear with the displacement of hand by machine labor, symbolized in the greatest of American Negro occupational ballads and work songs, *John Henry*. The last refuge of Negro work songs of the choral type, accompanying group hand labor on roads, railroads, and levees and in the woods and fields, is the Southern prison, where forced labor creates a counterpart of the older plantation or slave songs. Even closer to the latter are the **field calls** and **hollers** or individual work songs of the "blues" type. In this connection it is worth noting that, outside of sea shanties and cowboy songs, our white "work songs," including lumberjack, canaller, and miners' songs, are occupational and labor songs rather than songs to accompany work.

Folk music is no longer a pure but a very hybrid activity, in which "folk," "art," and commercial influences mingle in a dynamic process of survival and revival. Increased popular interest in folk music, from true country music to the "hillbilly" variety, has been stimulated by **folk festivals** and contests (e.g., fiddlers' and dance contests at Galax, Va., and Asheville, N. C.; folk song festivals at White Top, Va., and Ashland, Ky.; and the National Folk Festival) as well as by organizations such as the American Square Dance Group. See *Research in Primitive and Folk Music in the United States,* by George Herzog, 1936; *The Country Dance Book,* V, by Cecil J. Sharp, 1918; *American Country Dances,* by Elizabeth Burchenal, 1918; *Traditional Music of America,* by Ira W. Ford,

1940; *Cowboy Dances,* by Lloyd Shaw, 1939; *Dances of Our Pioneers,* by Grace L. Ryan, 1939; *The American Play-Party Song,* by B. A. Botkin, 1937.; *White Spirituals in the Southern Uplands,* by George Pullen Jackson, 1933; *Our Singing Country,* edited by John A. and Alan Lomax and Ruth Crawford Seeger, 1941; *Folk Music of the United States from Records in the Archive of American Folk Song,* Albums I-V, edited by Alan Lomax, 1942; Album VI, edited by William N. Fenton, 1942; Albums V-VII, edited by B. A. Botkin, 1943; Album XI, edited by George Pullen Jackson, 1943.   —B.A.B.

American glass. See GLASS AND GLASS-MAKING.

AMERICAN NEGRO ART. *Colonial industry.* The beginnings of Negro art in America are found among the colonial crafts and industries of the 18th cent. Negroes brought from Africa and the West Indies to assist with the arduous tasks of farming and homesteading and to supply labor to a growing export trade soon became equally indispensable to various domestic industries such as spinning and weaving, iron manufacture, carriage-making, carpentry, woodblock-printing, gold and silversmithing and metalcasting. Induction into these skilled trades proceeded through the medium of the apprenticeship system; and while this was not an aspect of free labor, it did help to establish the Negro in a productive capacity in Colonial America by supplying many Negro members to the professional class of master artisans.

Servile production. Probably the outstanding instance of servile production in the field of the decorative arts is to be found in the city of New Orleans, where, legend as well as archaeological testimony has it, the greater part of the wrought iron in *Le Vieux Carré* originated in foundries completely manned by Negro slaves. This ornamental iron is undoubtedly the production of Negro blacksmiths of two different groups: There were those who emigrated to Louisiana territory from Santo Domingo and those who were born of slaves brought directly into the American colonies by the slave traffic.

The extant domestic architecture in North Carolina, Virginia and New York State also preserves identifiable traces of servile craftsmanship of distinguished quality. In North Carolina, the important vestiges of such skilfull functioning by Negro slaves can be observed in much of the brickwork that appears in several buildings of Dutch and Georgian colonial styles. For certain outstanding examples, however, of excellent construction and interior work see The Chapel of the Cross, Chapel Hill, Orange County (1835), and the Jansen House, Walkill Valley, New York State (1724).

In addition to the foregoing, the extant servile products of the early Negro craftsman and artist comprise fourteen portraits, thirteen of them in oil and one in pastel, one steel engraving and several blockprints of very good quality. There are also carved interior cabinet work *in situ,* and numerous items of iron work in the form of household utensils, hinges and locks which have been ascribed to the independent workmanship of the Negro slave.

Free craftsmen and artists. "Occasional" artists and craftsmen were those free or manumitted Negroes of the first half of the 19th cent. who were able to pursue their art only upon occasion of rare leisure or special assignment. Into this general classification fall such individuals as had actual workshop or studio training in one or more of the crafts or representational skills of the day. A certain number of Negro artists fulfill the terms of this grouping.

Patrick Reason (1813-18 ?) of New York City left a considerable body of steel-engravings and lithographs which were of an "occasional" or "commissioned" nature. Like the work of Robert Douglass (1805-1885) and J. W. Chaplin, Negro artists of Philadelphia, it grew out of race needs as well as the propagandistic efforts of the Anti-Slavery societies; but irregularity of employment together with the dispersal of the artists' energies in other channels of abolitionist work made actual production a sporadic affair. It is easily understood why the primary objectives of this early work became illustration and exposition rather than the capture of aesthetic appeal.

The best examples of Reason's work are his portraits of Granville Sharpe, DeWitt Clinton, James Williams and Henry Bibb. Reason is said to have copperplate-engraved a number of illustrations for Bayard Taylor's *History of America.*

Over against the work of these men was that of David B. Bowser and Vidal of Philadelphia, Robert S. Duncanson (1821-1876) of Cincinnati, and Primus of Boston. These painters, whose subjects and whose methods of work were more personal and far less concerned with popular movements, represent the persistent strain of individualism in American

Negro art at its earliest bloom. Paintings by Bowser ran to landscapes and a few figure pieces; the work of Duncanson consisted largely of panoramic landscapes of great size done in a semi-classical style, and reminiscent of Claude Lorrain. His paintings are owned by several public galleries in the State of Ohio and by Glasgow art gallery in Scotland. Primus was interested mainly in the illustration of biblical lore. Of this free-lance group, Duncanson was the only thoroughly trained artist. The rest were in the main self taught painters whose works strike us today as rather naive.

The Portraiture of Abolition and Emancipation. For a decade preceding and following the Civil War the American Negro artist found his subjects almost exclusively among the leading personages and the concrete objectives of abolition and emancipation. Excepting Robert Duncanson and Primus, who were interested respectively in heroic landscape and devotional painting, the outstanding Negro artists of the 1850's and later were committed to a rather prosaic if honest kind of portraiture. While the social and political emphases were different, the tradition was largely the same as that stemming from the work of Joshua Johnston, the Negro slave of Baltimore, Maryland, whose talent won him the privilege of devoting his entire time to portrait painting as early as 1800.

In the 1860's, Edmonia Lewis (1845-1890), first Negro woman sculptor, modelled the features of Henry Wadsworth Longfellow, James McCune Smith, Robert Gould Shaw and William Lloyd Garrison. William Simpson (ca. 1820-1878) painted portraits of Jeremiah Loguen and his wife Caroline Loguen; while A. B. Wilson of Philadelphia made the likenesses of various leaders of the militant Negro Church, using the mediums of oil and lithography. All this shows a curious parallelism with the trend in abolitionist literature to eulogize anti-slavery character and to stress the heroic act as the mark of a convinced radical.

The climactic art achievement of mid-century was Edmonia Lewis' plastic group entitled "Forever Free" which she intended as proclaiming in advance the effect of emancipation to the New World. Although neo-classical in style and naturalistic in conception this and other later works by the same hand compare favorably with the statuary of Harriet Hosmer, Hiram Powers and other American sculptors of neo-classical persuasion. Credit for advancing the interest of American artists in direct emotional reactions to the things of nature is accorded by Henry Tuckerman, famous American art critic of the last century to Edmonia Lewis and to Edward M. Bannister (1828-1901), a Negro landscape painter of Providence, Rhode Island. Owing largely to Bannister's efforts the Providence Art Club was formed, which in turn became the nucleus of the present Rhode Island School of Design located at Providence.

The Professional Tradition and the American School. Turning away from the more general and popular traditions of hero-painting and romantic landscape, the Negro artist about 1876 began to re-examine both the technics and the content of art upon the impetus of racial drives toward better economic status. The period of Reconstruction had brought stimulating experiences to the race as a whole; but the artist was at first completely overwhelmed by the rapid movement of events. Increased educational opportunity and the growing political consciousness of the Negro minority helped to dispel, in the course of time, the artist's sense of confusion. Negro art then gravitated towards the union of professional artistic tradition with the new experiences on the one hand and the direct experiential contact with the world of events on the other. The first reaction represented the crystallization of the Negro artist's sense of his profession as a calling and a responsible field of endeavor; the second was that of the new generation of Negro artists to the immediate variety and flavor of the life around them.

The results of this new orientation can be seen in the expanded repertory of subjects in Negro art between 1870 and 1915. In line with the professional tradition of the new period was the work of Henry O. Tanner (1859-1937) who chose the religious and historical *milieu* of the Palestinian East for his specialty, and in the supple painting of William H. Harper (1875-1910), a gifted painter of landscape who worked not only in the middle Western States but also in France and Mexico. In sculpture, the professional tradition found its chief exponent in Meta Vaux Warrick (1876-) who used the human figure to give tortured but eloquent expression to her belief that humanity suffers from spiritual frailty and immemorial greed.

The native Negro "American School" should be compared in its objects if not in its results with the Philadelphia group of white American painters; that is, with George Luks, William Glackens, Robert Henri, Everett Shinn and others who, at the beginning of this century, sought to document objectively their immediate surroundings, and for their pains were roundly scored by reactionaries and derisively termed the **Ashcan School** of American Art. Henry O. Tanner at first identified himself with similar interests, as witness "the Banjo Lesson" now at Hampton Institute, Hampton, Va. Vanquished, however, by American racial prejudice and the veniality of late 19th cent. American taste, he along with other American supporters of the professional tradition (Duveneck, Chase, Sargent, Whistler, *et al.*) took refuge in the broader sympathies and warmer taste of European art patronage.

The great fame and artistic success which Tanner finally achieved were denied the lesser talents whom he left behind to adapt their art to the untamed aspects of the American scene. Clinton DeVillis, W. O. Thompson, Samuel Collins (1880-1932), May Howard Jackson (1877-1931) and Richard Lonsdale Brown (1886-1915) provided some effectual lessons of creative contact with local American *genre* and practical idealism. DeVillis recorded brilliantly some scenes of boating and horseracing. Thompson evoked the native strain of mysticism in the Negro in several deftly brushed cosmic landscapes. A certain poetic naïveté developed in Brown's landscapes of Virginia hills. May Howard Jackson showed an aggressive spirit in her various well-modelled portrait-busts of Negro educators, and writers.

The New Negro Movement. From crucial post-War economic conditions directly affecting the physical mobility and labor status of the Negro masses developed the so-called **New Negro Movement** (sometimes referred to as the **Negro Renaissance**). More specifically, it arose in response to a widely felt need to interpret, to illustrate and to control the social and cultural by-products of the changed status of the Negro following World War I.

The most important cultural developments of the movement were localized in New York City; but there were significant correlative expressions in the District of Columbia, in Chicago, Boston and Indianapolis. The chief characteristics of Negro art within the movement of the 1920's were two: Subjectivity of expression and eclecticism of form. Subjectivity of expression governed the racial and social attitudes of the artist, aiding him in the selection of the materials of experience. But the eclectic training and cultural background of the Negro artist caused him to make use of various traditional forms in seeking to communicate his experience in fluent terms.

Evidence of the first characteristic is present in the work of nearly all the participating artists, but especially in the work of William E. Scott, Archibald Motley, Aaron Douglas, Malvin Gray Johnson (1898-1935), Hale Woodruff, James L. Wells, Sargent Johnson, and Elizabeth Prophet. With each artist the subjective element received a different adumbration. Of special interest as reflecting the folk pattern of the New Negro Movement are the paintings of Aaron Douglas and Hale Woodruff. For the documentation of Negro types and character one should consult the portraits of Laura Wheeler Waring, E. A. Harleston (1889-1934), and Malvin Gray Johnson.

Modernistic and Populist Developments. Towards the end of the third decade of this century another aspect of creative vision began to find prominent place in Negro art. For a while, a self-conscious modernism attributable to the influence of certain modern French painters of this century took actual vogue. This trend involved a short-lived academicism through imitation of African Negro sculpture as well as a serious application of Frenchified intellectualism to plastic and pictorial problems. **Negro Cubism** as exemplified in the experimental painting of Hale Woodruff and **Africanism** as shown in Malvin Gray Johnson's middle-period art, J. L. Wells woodcuts and Sargent Johnson's sculpture were direct outcomes. For a while, it was believed that this modernistic trend would completely alter the course of Negro art.

The reaction to this drift came indirectly to painting through scientific and literary channels. Anthropological, sociological and psychological and fictional studies of the southern Negro aroused an interest in the Negro folk as a repository of certain supposed original instincts and primordial virtues of the Negro peasant. There followed what may aptly be termed an interval of populist painting tinged with radical social meaning. The latter movement emphasized the work of Archibald Motley of Chicago, Richmond Barthé and Malvin Gray Johnson of New York City, Hale Woodruff of Atlanta, Georgia, Leslie G. Bolling, woodcarver, of Richmond, Va.

Federal Patronage of the Negro Artist. In contradistinction to the aims of the subsidized white artist the aims of the black artist sponsored by Federal Art Projects never wavered from self-expressional interests. Without altogether ignoring the growth of Regionalism in American art the Negro continued to portray his reaction to the segregated existence of his minority, taking care to stress the crude emotional values thereof above the painful down-to-earth facts. In mural painting this attitude had a retarding effect upon skilfull, deliberate and clear execution, except in the case of Aaron Douglas who rapidly developed a formula for decorative mural painting.

Since 1934, Negro art has gained enormously in technical facility and expediency and in that fluent presentation of ideas which implies both inspiration and reflection. There has been wide experimentation in new or revived mediums. For instance, in Philadelphia Dox Thrash under the sponsorship of the W. P. A., has discovered the application of carborundum to artistic print-making. At the same time, there has been developed a closer articulation of process with significant expression throughout the production of the second generation of Negro talents; so that a genuine and typical American thoroughness combined with a pioneering spirit marks the production of such painters as Charles White, Samuel Brown, Eldzier Cortor, Charles Alston, and Jacob Lawrence and of sculptors like Henry Bannern, William Crump, Alice Catlett, William Artis and Sargent Johnson. See B. Brawley, *The Negro Genius,* 1936; C. T. MacChesney, *A Poet Painter of Palestine, Intern'l Studio* (July, 1913) ; J. A. Porter, Versatile Interests of the Early Artists, *Art in America* (Jan. 1936) ; Locke, *The Negro in Art,* 1940; J. A. Porter, Four Problems in the History of Negro Art, *Journal of Negro History* (Jan 1942).　　　　　　　　　　　—J.A.P.

AMERICAN NEGRO LITERATURE is a segment of American literature. Although its subject-matter is predominantly concerned with the Negro's struggle for equality, it does not constitute a unique cultural pattern. It must not be thought of merely as "Negro literature," a tradition apart from the main stream of American literary development. The Negro writer is American; his work is American literature.

18th Cent. Beginnings. The first known publication by an American Negro was *An Evening Thought: Salvation by Christ with Penitential Cries.* Appearing in 1760, it was written by Jupiter Hammon (c. 1720-c. 1800), a slave of Queen's Village, Long Island. Obviously influenced by Methodist hymnody, the poem has historical significance only. It does show, however, the early influence of the evangelical churches on the slave mind, an influence reflected with greatest art in the spirituals.

The second 18th cent. poet, Phillis Wheatley (c. 1753-84), like Hammon was influenced by the religious forces of the Great Awakening, but unlike him was a writer of unusual talent. Born in Africa and captured by slavers when she was about seven, Phillis Wheatley acquired in an incredibly short time both the literary and the religious culture of her Boston masters. Her first publication, *A Poem by Phillis, a Negro Girl in Boston, on the Death of the Reverend George Whitefield,* appeared in 1770. *Poems on Various Subjects, Religious and Moral,* her only volume of collected verse, was published in London in 1773. Her best known poem is probably that dedicated to George Washington on his appointment as Commander-in-chief of the Colonial Army. Writing in the strictest of Neo-classic styles, Phillis Wheatley has little or no self-revelation in her poetry. A typical New Englander of the late 18th cent., she recorded as deftly as any of her contemporaries the moral and pious thoughts of the Boston Puritans of her day.

The first known prose publication by an American Negro was *A Narrative of the Uncommon Sufferings and Surprising Deliverances of Briton Hammon, a Negro* (1760). The two Hammons—Briton and Jupiter—are not related. Having no conspicuous literary merit, the *Narrative* is of significance only as the first of a long line of autobiographical works by American Negroes.

The **folk contribution** of the American Negro has been far better known and far more influential than his conscious art. The Negro's most important cultural gift to America has been the **spiritual**, the religious folk song of the slave. In recent years there has been much controversy concerning, first, the interpretation of these songs, and, second, their origin—i.e., whether their musical background is predominantly African or European. Whatever the origin, practically all scholars now agree that the spiritual itself is the Negro's own and is stamped with his originality.

Along with the spirituals go the **slave seculars**—dance songs, children's play songs, and humorous songs. In some the Negro sang ironically of his master and irreverently of his own religion. Whether **cornfield hollers** or **jigtunes**, these songs dealt realistically with the humorous or seamier side of life. They are a foil, as it were, to the noble mood of the spiritual. Ignored by the first New England

collectors because of their frivolity and realism, they were nevertheless early appropriated
by black-face minstrelsy and patternized.
Thomas W. Talley's *Negro Folk Rhymes*
(1922) was the first collection of these songs.

Collectors have found in Negro folk material variants of several well-known English
and Scottish ballads. Considering the social
and cultural isolation of the Southern Negro,
this is perfectly understandable. But the Negro
not only preserved and altered European ballads; he has made many vigorous ones of his
own, narrating the exploits of his own heroes
and bad men like "Stakalee", "Uncle Bud",
"Railroad Bill", "Po' Lazarus", "John Henry",
and others. The best known folk hero among
Negroes is John Henry. Like Paul Bunyan
but far more colorful, John Henry by his
strength, courage, and endurance symbolizes
the Negro workman's way of life. The Negro
ballad generally tells a story with economy,
without sentimentality, and with the tragic
sense of life so often characteristic of the best
ballad literature.

Among Negro folk songs the blues are second in importance only to the spiritual. The
latter is intended for group singing, the blues
to express the feelings (usually sorrowful) of
an individual singer. These feelings are expressed, however, in an idiom so familiar to
the singer's audience that they, too, can share
his feeling. "Blues" has become a part of the
American vocabulary. As songs they are internationally known.

The folk contribution of the Negro includes
also work songs, songs of protest, aphorisms,
folk tales and folk sermons. The most widely
known examples of folk tales have been those
told by Joel Chandler Harris' Uncle Remus.
The first substantial collection of these tales
by a Negro is *Mules and Men* (1935) by Zora
Neale Hurston. There are many collections of
work songs, but the first collection of Negro
songs of protest was made by Lawrence Gellert in 1936. The folk sermon has been often
burlesqued; Roark Bradford's *Ol' Man Adam
and His Chillun* from which *Green Pastures*
was derived is a good example. But James
Weldon Johnson in *God's Trombones* (1927)
has captured the essential dignity, eloquence,
and poetry of these sermons.

Anti-Slavery Writings (1800-65). By the early
years of the 19th cent. the larger Northern
cities had acquired sizable colonies of free
Negroes. Feeling the pressure of a steadily
rising prejudice, they were forced to form
their own social and religious organizations.
In 1816 Richard Allen founded the African

Methodist Episcopal church and became its
first bishop. Individual churches of other de-
nominations sprang up in the various cities.
The first Negro periodical, *Freedom's Journal,*
was founded by Samuel E. Cornish and John
B. Russwurm in 1827, and before 1855 over
one hundred journalistic ventures—successful
and unsuccessful—had been started by Negroes. The churches, literary clubs, social
organizations, and the journals of Northern
Negroes became increasingly articulate on the
subject of slavery and the chorus of protest
swelled.

The outstanding and most sensational attack
upon slavery prior to 1840 was the *Appeal,* a
pamphlet written after the model of the Constitution by David Walker (1785-1830), a
Boston Negro who had been born free in
Wilmington, N. C. The *Appeal* was so in-
cendiary in nature that it caused consternation
among the Southern slavocracy. Many planters
tried to attribute Nat Turner's Rebellion
(1831) to the inflammatory influence of
Walker's work.

Walker was the first and outstanding member of a group of protest writers of the period.
Among his best known and most powerful
successors and followers were David Ruggles,
Henry Highland Garnet, Martin R. Delany,
Samuel Ringgold Ward, James McCune Smith,
and William C. Nell (who was associated
with Garrison on the *Liberator*). These men
in pamphlet, speech, and periodical waged a
relentless propaganda war against the institution of slavery, and they worked hand in
hand with Garrison and other white aboli-
tionists.

William C. Nell was also the first Negro to
make a serious attempt at writing the history
of his own people. At the suggestion of
Whittier, Nell published in 1851 *Services of
Colored Americans in the Wars of 1776 and
1812.* In 1855 he brought out a larger work,
*The Colored Patriots of the American Revo-
lution.* James McCune Smith, William Wells
Brown, William T. Catto, William Douglas,
and J. W. C. Pennington were among the
others who attempted to write the history—
secular or church—of the Negro. They all,
of course, considered history good abolition
propaganda. But it was not until after the
Civil War that creditable work in the field
was accomplished by the Negro author.

The poetry of this period echoed the anti-
slavery sentiments of the prose writers; it
also echoed the strains of classic English and
American writers. Though too highly imitative, too highly oratorical, and too monotonous

in theme, this anti-slavery poetry showed at least that the Negro writer was mastering the medium in which he worked. Daniel Payne (1811-93), James M. Whitefield (1830-70), Charles L. Reason (1818-c.1898), George B. Vashon (? - 1878), James Madison Bell (1826-1902), and Frances E. W. Harper (1825-1911) were the outstanding poets of the period. With scorn and denunciation of all halfway measures, these writers demanded of America full democracy. For them poetry was primarily another vehicle for anti-slavery propaganda.

One poet of this age, George Moses Horton (1797-c.1883), deserves special mention. He was a slave (the others were free Northerners), and he was the first of the group in point of time. Born in North Carolina, Horton though a slave was allowed to hire himself out to the University president at Chapel Hill. There he learned to read and write and became a campus 'character", writing love lyrics for the students. His first volume, *The Hope of Liberty,* appeared in 1829, the second, *Naked Genius,* in 1865. Unlike his predecessors and contemporaries, Horton had a generous vein of humor in his make-up and could in his later work laugh at "Jefferson in a Tight Place." Even though his protest was conventional, he was the first Negro poet to write against slavery.

Another type of writing from this period is unique and little known to historians of American literature. It is the **slave narrative** —the story of an escaped slave, either written by himself or dictated to some agent of the various abolition groups and used by them for propaganda purposes. This new type of literature sprang into popularity during the thirties. Among the best known slave narratives were those by Henry Bibb, Samuel R. Ward, William Wells Brown, Frederick Douglass, and Josiah Henson. The last named person met Mrs. Harriet Beecher Stowe and is supposed to be the prototype of Uncle Tom.

William Wells Brown (c.1815-1884) and Frederick Douglass (c.1817-95) were the two outstanding writers of the period. Born a slave in Lexington, Ky., Brown escaped to freedom by way of a Mississippi river steamboat to Cincinnati. There he was helped through the Underground by a Quaker named Wells Brown whose name he took. As a boy of twelve, Brown was office-boy for Elijah P. Lovejoy. In 1847 he became an agent of the Mass. Anti-Slavery Society. A pioneer in several fields, Brown was the first American Negro to publish a book of travel, *Three Years*

in Europe (1852) ; the first to publish a drama, *The Escape, or A Leap to Freedom* (1858), and the first to publish a novel, *Clotel, or the President's Daughter* (London, 1853). He was also an early historian, short story writer, essayist, and the first biographer of note. Though often crude and inept, Brown deserves great credit when his background is considered.

Douglass, one of the great men of the Abolition Movement and one of the great orators of American history, was born a slave in Maryland. The story of his life is an American odyssey of success over almost insuperable odds. Twenty-four years a slave and three years a day laborer in Massachusetts, he rose to become the greatest Negro leader of the era. His literary fame rests upon his editorship of *The North Star, Frederick Douglass' Paper,* and *Douglass' Monthly;* his speeches; and his autobiography, *The Life and Times of Frederick Douglass* (1881, enlarged, 1882). The last named work is the best work of its type yet written by an American Negro.

Reconstruction and Transition (1865-1925). During the Reconstruction Period, there arose a strong school of Southern white "local color" (q.v.) sectional apologists who seized upon the "Negro question" and the Negro character as a means of propagandizing America concerning the Old South and its glories. Their works were peopled with indelible stereotypes of the plantation Negro—docile, contented, and comic. Their delineation and approach gave the Negro writer a nice problem : to deny the stereotype by setting up an opposite as the "true" Negro or to use the stereotype but deepen the characterization by sympathetic realism. Both ways were pursued by the Negro writer.

Albery A. Whitman (1851-1902) took the first means. In *Not a Man and Yet a Man,* the longest poem written by a Negro, he portrays the highly idealized slave. *The Rape of Florida* treats in a similar manner the Seminoles and their Negro friends and kinsmen. Whitman's militancy is pronounced in these and other poems.

A poet of much greater ability, Paul Laurence Dunbar (1872-1906) took the second way, displacing comic posters with sympathetic photography. A humorous observer and not a reformer, Dunbar wrote in the genre of Russell and Page about the Old South and after the pastoral manner of Riley and Will Carleton about his own times. Praised by William Dean Howells, as the first American Negro poet to "feel the Negro life aesthetically and to express it lyrically", Dunbar in his best dialect verse has written with a great deal of talent. His picture of rural life though idyllic is peopled not with caricatures but with likeable human beings. The most popular Negro author of his day, Dunbar was also short story writer and novelist. His work in these fields, however, was inferior to that in poetry.

Naturally, there were other Negro poets in both camps, but the dialect school had the larger following. On the other hand, there was also a third way of reacting to the conditions of the age—the way of escape. Choosing to ignore the race problem several Negro poets sought refuge in the ivory tower of "literary" poetry. Outstanding among these was William Stanley Braithwaite, whose finished and mystical verses fail to touch the question of race. A noted critic, Braithwaite is now better known as the editor of the *Anthology of Magazine Verse* (issued annually from 1913 to 1929) than as a poet.

The prose writers of the era also adopted two opposing attitudes. With the increase in mob-violence and the almost total disfranchisement of the Southern Negro by 1902, there arose among the colored leaders two schools of thought with reference to the "way out". The first was the way of appeasement, and its most highly gifted exponent was Booker T. Washington (1858-1915). Seasoning bitterness with good humor, Washington in his numerous speeches and works advocated patience, compromise, and interracial cooperation. His most popular work, *Up from Slavery* (1900), shows this conciliatory approach. It is a classic American autobiography and, with the probable exception of *Native Son,* the best known work by an American Negro.

Opposition to Washington's attitude was naturally most articulate among Northern Negroes. Chief among the militant writers of the period were William Monroe Trotter, Boston journalist; Kelly Miller, Dean of Howard University; and Dr. W. E. B. DuBois, able and uncompromising editor of the *Crisis*. With varying degrees of militancy, these men demanded justice from America.

Though DuBois' career carries over into the next period, much of his finest work was done before 1925. *Souls of Black Folk* (1902), *The Quest of the Silver Fleece* (1911), *Dark Water* (1921), *The Gift of Black Folk* (1924), and some of his best historical and sociological studies were all written during this period. In scholarship, in style, and in sheer power

DuBois has few peers. As a writer of protest he is unequalled.

After the Civil War several writers chose history as a means of justifying and vindicating the Negro's new position in American life. In 1883 George Washington Williams wrote *The History of the Negro Race in America from 1619-1880* to show that the Colored American has always "displayed matchless courage and incomparable heroism". In 1888 he published *A History of the Negro Troops in the War of Rebellion.* The same year saw Joseph T. Wilson's *Black Phalanx.* But the first scientific history written by a Negro was DuBois' *The Suppression of the African Slave Trade to the United States of America, 1638-1870* (1898), also the first monograph of the Harvard Historical Series.

Biography was also called upon to prove the black man's worth. Using as models the works of Henri Gregoire and Lydia Maria Child, William Wells Brown published the *Rising Son* (1874), a series of sketches of famous Negroes. Brown's work had originally appeared in 1863. William Still published in 1872 the *Underground Railroad Records,* a fascinating and unusual work, giving firsthand portraits of escaped Negroes. The first scholarly biographer, however, was Archibald H. Grimké, whose works, *William Lloyd Garrison, the Abolitionist* (1891) and *The Life of Charles Sumner, the Scholar in Politics* (1892), are distinguished studies. Charles W. Chesnutt's *Frederick Douglass* (1899) is also an able work.

The works of Charles W. Chesnutt (1858-1932) belong in the main to the protest school of American Negro writing. The best fiction writer of the period, Chesnutt in one volume of short stories, *The Wife of His Youth* (1899), and in three novels, *The House Behind the Cedars* (1900), *The Marrow of Tradition* (1901), and *The Colonel's Dream* (1905), has given us bitter but unforgettable pictures of conflicts along the "Color Line". In *The Conjure Woman* (1899), he made use of Negro folk material, creating in his character, Uncle Julius, a much more realistic raconteur than Uncle Remus. A sincere work of art, *The Conjure Woman* compares favorably with similar though better-known works by Harris and Page. Chesnutt, Dunbar, and Grimké were the three Negroes who in the nineties gained recognition as men of letters irrespective of race.

James Weldon Johnson (1871-1938) is a transitional figure. Teacher, lawyer, actor, musical comedy writer, diplomatist, organizer, novelist, and poet, Johnson in his varied and colorful career probably influenced the literature of the American Negro more than any other man of his generation. *The Book of American Negro Poetry* (1922) was a pioneer effort in anthologies, and it served both as an interpreter of Negro artistic achievement and as a stimulus to young writers. *The Autobiography of an Ex-Coloured Man* (1912), a novel of passing, anticipated several later works. Johnson has a place among the major Negro poets; his autobiography, *Along This Way* (1933), is an important American book. At his death, Johnson was the most successful interpreter of the Negro creative artist to America at large.

The New Negro to the Present (*1925-42*). During World War I and in the days immediately following, many social forces conspired to alter the general contour of Negro life in America. Chief among these were the extensive migrations of Southern Negroes to large Northern cities. As a result there arose among Negroes a new consciousness of the power and rights of labor and a growing awareness of the importance of organization, generally on the basis of race, though a few advanced thinkers saw the Negro problem as essentially proletarian. There arose among them greater self-respect, fostered both by Garveyite oratory and sober scholarship, and increased militancy. In the nation at large, post-war liberalism sponsored more than ever before the Negro's cause.

The Negro writer reflected these changes. Harlem became the most articulate center of this expression. Under the sponsorship of DuBois of the *Crisis* and Charles S. Johnson of *Opportunity*, the leaven of this new spiritual and literary awareness became more productive. Alain Locke supplied the name to the movement—New Negro—and his work, *The New Negro* (1925), not only interpreted the spirit of this minor renaissance but is now its landmark.

The forces that produced the New Negro poets were at work, of course, before 1925. Writing under the influence of the New Poetry Movement of Harriet Monroe, Fenton Johnson was the first of the new voices. His later work, modelled on Sandbury and Masters, exceeded in realism any earlier poetry and foretokened the work of Hughes and Brown. Claude McKay's *Harlem Shadows* (1922) with its trenchant poems of social and economic injustice and protest, written in classical verse, heralded a new and powerful poetic voice. In 1924 Jean Toomer's few but startling poems in *Cane* (1923) presaged much which unfortunately failed to materialize.

Among the New Negro poets Countee Cullen and Langston Hughes stand supreme. In *Color* (1925), *Copper Sun* (1927), and *The Black Christ* (1929), Cullen displayed technical mastery and lyrical gifts unequalled among Negro writers. In later years he has applied these talents to sophisticated children's verse. Although practically of the same age and emerging as poets at the same time, Cullen and Hughes are in many respects opposites. Much more unconventional than Cullen, Langston Hughes is an experimenter in subject-matter as well as in verse form. In *The Weary Blues* (1926), *Fine Clothes to the Jew* (1927), *A New Song* (1938), and in more recent works, he has written on all manner of themes: cabaret life, racialism, protest, jazz, blues, ballads, and the class struggle. Hughes has been a highly influential figure in poetry as well as in other fields.

Among the minor poets of the New Negro Movement are Georgia Douglass Johnson, Angelina Grimké, Lewis Alexander, Jessie Fauset, Helene Johnson, Gwendolyn Bennett, Anne Spencer, and Arna Bontemps. Mrs. Spencer, the ablest of the women writers, is a modern metaphysical poet who writes outside of a school. Bontemps is a finished craftsman and able writer who unfortunately abandoned poetry for other fields. Like Cullen and Hughes, all of these writers except Mrs. Spencer expressed ideas cardinal to the New Negro Movement: the celebration of brown beauty, the delineation of a romantic and idealized Africa, and the mystical power of black inheritance.

Since 1925 several new poets of promise have been heard. Sterling A. Brown in *Southern Road* (1932) and subsequent poems proves himself an able representative of the new regionalism in American literature. Social protest and regionalism characterize his later works. Frank Marshall Davis has published two volumes of powerful social criticism in *Black Man's Verse* (1935) and *I Am the American Negro* (1937). Robert Hayden's first work, *Heart Shape in the Dust* (1940), combines technical aptitude with trenchant social criticism and is a work of great promise. M. B. Tolson, Richard Wright, and Margaret Walker are also social critics of great insight. Miss Walker's *For My People* (1942) is a book of deep sincerity written in a style both startling and prophetic.

Though the experiences of the Negro has been the material for several of America's best known plays, the Negro playwright so far has contributed little to the drama. The Negro's place on the American stage has been rigidly limited to a few stereotypes. If the Negro dramatist did not conform, he found no audience. The serious Negro playwright has thus been denied the kind of apprenticeship in the theatre necessary to beget authorship. Except for musical comedies, he has made few appearances on Broadway. Forced to take to the tributary streets of the "Little" and experimental theatre, in recent years he has made some advances there.

In spite of a few sporadic attempts prior to 1925, the Negro playwright for all practical purposes began his career during the New Negro period. Encouraged by the spirit of the movement, expressed notably in the prize contests of *Opportunity* and the *Crisis,* and influenced by the new realism of Ridgely Torrence, Paul Green, and O'Neill, the Negro dramatist turned largely to one-act folk drama. Of the new playwrights the plays of the following have been most often acted by Little Theatre groups: Frank Wilson, Georgia Douglass Johnson, May Miller, Eulalie Spence, James W. Butcher, John F. Matheus, and Zora Neale Hurston. One of the most influential figures in the creation of a body of Negro plays and in building a Negro audience has been Randolph Edmonds. Wallace Thurman and William Rapp, a white writer, co-produced *Harlem* in 1929, a highly sensational melodrama which enjoyed Broadway success. Hall Johnson's *Run, Little Chillun* (1933), part opera, part ballet, part drama was another Broadway success. Langston Hughes, the most versatile of Negro dramatists, produced (in collaboration with Martin Jones) *Mulatto* (1935), a crudely effective dramatization of inter-racial mixture and violence in the Deep South. It, too, enjoyed Broadway success. The last play of part-Negro authorship to be successful in New York was *Native Son* by Richard Wright and Paul Green. It was considered one of the finer plays of the 1941 season.

In more recent years a new and promising crop of young dramatists has sprung up. Some are the products of the Federal Theatre Project, others of the Little Theatre movement throughout the country and especially in Negro colleges. Their themes have dealt with folk material and social criticism. Among them are Hughes Allison (*The Trial of Dr. Beck*), J. A. Smith and Peter Morell (*Turpentine*), Theodore Brown (*Natural Man*), Theodore Ward (*Big White Fog*), Abram Hill (*On Strivers' Row*), Thomas D. Pawley (*Judgement Day*), Arthur Clifton Lamb (*Black Woman in White*) and Owen Dodson (*Divine Comedy*).

With but few exceptions, the novels by Negroes since 1925 have dealt either directly or obliquely with American injustice. Two themes have come in for a disproportionate share of attention: lynching and "passing". Among the better known novelists are. Jessie Fauset (*There is Confusion,* 1924; *Plum Bun,* 1929; *The Chinaberry Tree,* 1932; and *Comedy, American Style,* 1933); Walter White (*Fire in the Flint,* 1925; *Flight,* 1928); W. E. B. DuBois (*Dark Princess,* 1928); Nella Larsen (*Quicksand,* 1928; *Passing,* 1930); Claude McKay (*Home to Harlem,* 1928; *Banjo,* 1929; *Banana Bottom,* 1933); Rudolph Fisher (*Walls of Jericho,* 1928; *The Conjure Man Dies,* 1930); Countee Cullen (*One Way to Heaven,* 1932); George Schuyler (*Black No More,* 1931); Wallace Thurman (*The Blacker the Berry,* 1929; *Infants of the Spring,* 1932); Langston Hughes (*Not Without Laughter,* 1930); George Wylie Henderson (*Ollie Miss,* 1935); George Lee (*River George,* 1936); Zora Neale Hurston (*Jonah's Gourd Vine,* 1934; *Their Eyes Were Watching God,* 1937); Arna Bontemps (*God Sends Sunday,* 1931; *Black Thunder,* 1936; *Drums at Dusk,* 1939); Waters E. Turpin (*These Low Grounds,* 1937; *O Canaan,* 1939); William Attaway (*Let Me Breathe Thunder,* 1939; *Blood on the Forge,* 1941); and Richard Wright (*Native Son,* 1940).

Pioneering in the effort, Jessie Fauset has delineated the middle class Negro in her novels. Writing in the *Nigger Heaven* vein, Claude McKay and Thurman have painted realistic portraits of Harlem's low class and Bohemian life. Zora Neale Hurston has written more fully than any other Negro of rural Southern life, making excellent use of her knowledge of Negro folkways and speech. Bontemp's *Black Thunder* and *Drums at Dusk* apply the technique of the historical novel to Negro heroes. *The Conjure Man Dies* by Fisher is the first detective story written by an American Negro. Written under the Steinbeck influence, Attaway's *Let Me·Breathe Thunder* is unique in that it deals principally with white characters. *Native Son,* the most widely discussed novel yet written by a Negro, is in all probability also the best. Fisher, Hughes, and Wright have also written excellent short stories.

Negro biographical works since 1925 have not been outstanding. In those that have appeared with but few exceptions, the development of race pride rather than the revealing of personality has seemed the primary object. Benjamin Brawley has done more work in this field than any other Negro writer.

Early Negro American autobiography like biographical writing tended largely to racial edification. The works have been not only success stories, but also reflectors of the social conditions confronting the Negro. In this group belong Washington's *Up from Slavery* (1900), Robert Russa Moton's *Finding a Way Out* (1920), William Pickens' *Bursting Bonds* (1923), Benjamin Brawley's *The Lower Rungs of the Ladder* (1925), and A. Clayton Powell's *Against the Tide* (1939).

But the various new trends in recent autobiographical writing have touched some of the contemporary Negro writers. Johnson's *Along This Way* is in large part social commentary. DuBois' *Dusk of Dawn* (1940) traces ideas concerning racial concepts. McKay's *A Long Way from Home* (1937) and Langston Hughes' *Big Sea* (1940) are personal records of world travelers. Angelo Herndon's *Let Me Live* (1937) is a leftist attack on Georgia and capitalist injustice. W. C. Handy's *Father of the Blues* (1941) tells much about Tin Pan Alley as well as the personal history of the author.

As the educational stature of the American Negro has increased, he has become a more versatile literary person. Within the past decade numerous well-equipped scholars in practically all of the major fields—science, sociology, education, music, history, economics—have analyzed and interpreted the Negro to himself and to America at large. Though their activities lie beyond the scope of this résumé, these scientific essays appearing in both Negro and white journals add greatly to the quality of American Negro literature.

The present day Negro writers excel their predecessors in scholarship, in objectivity, and in literary ability. Less inclined to be sentimental or oratorical and no longer propagandists except in a finer sense, they are still handicapped by the injustices of American life. As a consequence, they are still forced as honest artists and scholars to devote too much of their creative energy to the theme of protest. See F. W. Bond, *The Negro and the Drama*, 1940; B. Brawley, *Negro in Literature and Art*, 1929, *Early Negro American Writers*, 1935; S. A. Brown, *Negro in American Fiction*, 1937, *Negro Poetry and Drama*, 1937; S. A. Brown, A. P. Davis, and U. Lee (eds.), *The Negro Caravan*, 1941; J. W.

Johnson, (ed.), *The Book of American Negro Poetry*, 1931; A. L. Locke, (ed.), *The New Negro*, 1925; A. L. Locke and M. Gregory (eds.), *Plays of Negro Life*, 1927; V. Loggins, *The Negro Author*, 1931; C. G. Woodson, (ed.), *Negro Orators and their Orations*, 1925; R. N. Dett, *Religious Folk Songs of the Negro*, 1927; L. Gellert, *Negro Songs of Protest*, 1936; W. C. Handy, *Blues, An Anthology*, 1926; Z. N. Hurston, *Mules and Men*, 1935; G. B. Johnson, *John Henry*, 1929, *Folk Culture on St. Helena Island*, 1930; H. E. Kriehbrel, *Afro-American Folk Songs*, 1914; J. A. Lomax and A. Lomax, *American Ballads and Folk Songs*, 1938, *Negro Folk Songs as Sung by Lead Belly*, 1936; H. Odum, and G. B. Johnson, *The Negro and His Songs*, 1925; D. Scarborough, *On the Trail of Negro Folk Songs*, 1928; T. Talley, *Negro Folk Rhymes*, 1922; N. I. White, *American Negro Folk Songs*, 1928; J. W. Work, *American Negro Folk Songs*, 1940.   —A.P.D.

AMERICAN NEGRO MUSIC. In common form, what is called "Negro music"? Spirituals, shouts, work-songs, plantation numbers, minstrel melodies, rag-time and blues are all blended in a polyglot answer.

But what are the characteristics of Negro music? Syncopation (rhythm), the pentatonic scale and the blue note; the latter being extensively employed in the modern *jazz* and *swing*, which are not musical forms, but a method of expressing certain types of music.

The somewhat mysterious **blue note** (flatted 7th and minor third), first introduced in "The Memphis Blues" can now be traced back to the Negro's imposition of the five tone scale on the white man's hymns: common, short and long metres. Here it is heard in the colorful "wording out" of "long metres" by unsophisticated and backwoods preachers who intoned the lines.

The Fisk Jubilee Singers, immediately after the Civil War, were the first to introduce the spirituals in their concert tours of America and Europe. And, in their book—"The Story of the Jubilee Singers" (with their songs included), is an important example — "Roll, Jordan, Roll," which as a spiritual carries the flatted 7th in the third measure and elsewhere, but this has been deleted or changed to a 6th in subsequent arrangements by white harmonists and many Negro composers, influenced by the music of the Caucasians.

The five string **banjo**, a Negro creation, was used to accompany the plantation and minstrel songs until the piano became a fixture in his home. His love of syncopation on the banjo was transferred to the piano, and since the five black notes of the piano keyboard represent a five tone scale, it is understandable how rag-time songs came into being, and were made popular in the last decade of the 19th cent.

The chorus of "Under The Bamboo Tree," a popular song by Bob Cole and J. Rosamond Johnson, is a five tone scale, influenced by the melodic and rhythmic values in such spirituals as "Nobody Knows The Trouble I See."

At the turn of the 20th cent., the Negro's technique on the piano was expanding so as to permit the creation of difficult instrumentals and tricky rhythms usually played on the black keys and too difficult for the white pianists. Composers of both races transposed and orchestrated these instrumentals into practical keys, and rag-time became more popular. **Ragtime** was exaggerated rhythm with less melody and no blue note. Almost every city had its Negro composer of rag-time. It flourished while many of its songs held the race up to ridicule, and fell into disrepute because of this innovation.

However, it remained for the dark skinned Scott Joplin to assert his mastery in "Maple Leaf Rag," "Euphonic Sounds" and other instrumentals too full of syncopation for musicians of his day and time, and for the matchless Irving Berlin to redeem this catchy rhythm and apt song style with his "Alexander's Rag-time Band." Upon examination it will be seen that the melody of "Alexander's Rag-time Band" discarded the syncope (less Negroid). Rag-time is only reflected in the broken tempos, scattered rhythms and catchy words of its general composition.

While America was glorifying rag-time, and Europe was glorifying America because of it, the blue note was budding in the folk life and lore of the South's Black Belt. Wails about the 'boll-weevil' became the song of the plantation replacing James Bland's 'corn and taters' in "Carry Me Back To Ol' Virginny."

"O, De Mississippi River's So Deep and Wide" was the fore-runner of a Negro form emphasizing "All The World Is Sad and Dreary" — Foster's "Swanee River." The prisons, chain-gangs, bar-rooms, levees and honky-tonks were groaning beneath the weight of a new song that was to temper the hearts of the world because of suffering.

The **spirituals** were born of suffering, and that is why the great baritone and composer of "Deep River," Harry T. Burleigh, called the spirituals "first cousins" of the blues.

In our homes are phonograph records by Bessie Smith, queen of the **blues**; Ma Rainey, mother of the blues; Mamie Smith, the first of her race to record the blues; and the ever popular Ethel Waters and Louis Armstrong. Who taught them how to sing the blues? There was no school other than the white man's "long metres" on which for every single written note they had sung from five to nine notes of the pentatonic scale. They had heard the preaching of the Elders, and the wording of the Hymn. That 'blue' note was instinctive and inborn. The rhythm of the shout is in their blood. They speak their mother's tongue.

American culture has felt the influence of music and song derived from and inspired by folk dances like "Jump Jim Crow," "Juba," "Pasamala," "The Cake Walk," "Jennicoula," "Walking the Dog," "Ballin' the Jack," 'The Shimmy," "Charleston," "Black Bottom," "Eagle Rock," "Buzzin' 'Round," "Trucking" and the "Lindy Hop" which introduced "Jitterbug and Jive."

Since 1820 these dances and this music have been heard in a type of shows now known theatrically as 'Musical Comedies.' There are still living those who remember Billy Kersand's "Minstrels," Isham's "Octoroons," Sam T. Jack's "Creoles" and Black Patti's "Troubadours." In the late 90's, Negro producers with their productions set a new tempo. These were: S. H. Dudley's "Smart Set;" Ernest Hogan's "Rufus Rastus" with Joe Jordan collaborating; Cole and Johnson's "A Trip to Coontown" and Williams and Walker's "Sons of Ham." The current century ushered in Rogers and Shipp's "Bandana Land;" Williams and Walker's "In Dahomey" music by Will Marion Cook; "Runnin' Wild" Jimmy Johnson and R. C. McPherson; "Shuffle Along" music by Noble Sissle and Eubie Blake, starring Florence Mills, and "Hot Chocolates" music by Thomas "Fats" Waller and Andy Razaf.

Today the radio and talking pictures have replaced vaudeville and musical productions of yesterday, but the swing bands, white and black, bring the beat of the African jungle-drums into every home.

No longer do we travel to the cotton fields of the south to hear the spirituals and their singers. They can be heard and seen in moving pictures like "Hallelujah," "Green Pastures," "Cabin In The Sky" and "Stormy Weather."

More than a hundred and fifty years ago, an African slave girl, Phillis Wheatley, the first American poet of her race wrote these lines:

" 'Twas mercy brought me from my
　Pagan land,
Taught my benighted soul to understand
That there is God, that there's a Savior
　too;
Once I redemption neither sought nor
　knew."

In his newly found Christianity, influenced
by Bible stories, the African adapted them to
his folk forms, and gave us the **spirituals,**
which are being kept alive today by such
great artists as Marion Anderson, Roland
Hayes, Hall Johnson's Choir, Dorothy Maynor,
Abbie Mitchell, Paul Robeson and the South-
ernaires.

Behind these and other great singers are
works of recognized composers and arrangers:
Burleigh, Boatner, Cook, Dawson, Dett,
Dorsey, The Johnsons, Florence Price, Ryder,
Still, Stor, White and the Work Brothers;
and back of all of this, a music publishing
company founded by W. C. Handy, dedicated
to the proposition of preserving all forms of
music with which his race is credited.

Anton Dvorak, Coleridge Taylor, N. Clark
Smith and H. Lawrence Freeman pointed the
way, which the genius of George Gershwin
has lighted with rays, from jazz idioms of
the James Reece Europes, the Dixieland Jazz
Bands, the Cab Calloways and the Duke
Ellingtons. Gershwin took a drama based on
lowly Negro life—"Porgy and Bess" and developed an opera "Porgy" which reflected the
tempo of America, and expressed this in a
score that only Negro voices can interpret.

From the vast reservoir of this folk music
which James Weldon Johnson called the
greatest in the world, may be drawn all the
material which any composer needs from
symphony to swing.　　　　　—W.C.H.

AMERICAN NEGRO THEATRE. *The beginnings.* The story of the Negro in the
American theatre is an integral part of the
history of the American theatre. The earliest
colonizers and those who settled the West had
little time for entertainment involving mimicry
and impersonation; their energies were devoted to the development of the country. Lacking an indigenous theatre which could serve
as an object of imitation, neither the Negro
slave nor the free Negro had a model on
which to draw. The Negro's dramatic talents
could not be developed in such an atmosphere
and it was not until a flourishing theatre tradition took root in urban centers that the Negro
theatre emerged. The political and economic
factors of slavery loom large in the beginnings

of the Negro theatre, since the early American
theatre as a medium of entertainment was
molded by New York merchant interests and
the requirements of Southern plantation life.
Slavery and Emancipation. Throughout the
history of the Negro theatre can be seen a
stage on which the players were not all
Negroes. In the earliest American drama, the
Negro occupied the unenviable roles of slave,
servant or entertainer, usually to create comic
relief. The content of this early drama was
fashioned by the ideology of the slave-owning
class. Up to 1800 there were only two plays—
Yorker's Stratagem and *The Fall of British
Tyranny*—which depicted the Negro as anything but an acquiescent slave. All other
American drama describing Negro character
was designed for cheap entertainment. This
sterile environment precluded the development
of Negro actors or dramatists until for such
time as the patron producing class could
transfer its support.

The first legitimate Negro theatres mark a
slow progress through many hardships, for
they were attempts by Negroes in the North
to eradicate the comic relief and to come out
as actors in a worthy tradition. The African
Free Company organized in 1821 in New York
was perhaps the first Negro company; the
company played Shakespeare and other classics
under the leadership of James Hewlett the
principal actor. Ire Aldridge, one of the
greatest Shakespearean actors of all times,
as a young man in this company played Rolla
in Sheridan's *Pizzaro*. Aldridge also played
Othello to the Iago of Edmund Kean all over
the European continent, and was made a
Chevalier by the King of Prussia. The free
Negroes of New Orleans had their own theatre
in this southern center of antebellum culture.
The *Diegarias* of Victor Sejour (1817-1874),
who was one of the greatest dramatists of his
day, was the opening drama (1844) of Le
Théâtre Francais. Sejour's *Chute de Sejan*
(1844), *Richard III,* and *Andre Gerard* were
successful plays. His *Les Volontiers de 1814,*
a drama of five acts with an American setting
featuring the volunteers against the British in
the Battle of New Orleans, was presented in
1862. Virginia Girardeau, a celebrated Creole
actress, played tragic roles in the 1830's at
the Théâtre de la Renaissance and is said to
have toured America.

Up to the Emancipation Proclamation the
interest which centered around the Negro
theatre was owing largely to the influence of
the Abolitionist movement. The first Negro
dramatist, William Wells Brown (1816-1834)

wrote *The Escape or a Leap From Freedom* (1858), a shoddy piece of dramaturgy. Plays which directly reflected the slavery issue were Harriet Beecher Stowe's *Uncle Tom's Cabin* and *Dred,* Mrs. Swayze's *Ossawatomi Brown* and Boucicaults' *The Octoroon.* This theatre had a function which it performed, even though it retained the vestiges of stereotyped Negro character comic, namely, faithful slave and tragic mulatto. The *Emancipation Proclamation* and the consequent change in American society brought about changes in the function of American drama.

Negro dramatists and actors continued their contributions to the New Orleans Theatre. *Lydia,* a three act drama by Adolphe Duhart was presented in 1866 at the Théâtre d'Orleans. There were also plays by Edmond Dede, Samuel Snaër, Charles Veque, Eugene Macarty during the Reconstruction period. These were lengthy plays, usually for benefits and lasted far into the night.

Minstrelsy and Musicals 1890-1915. Blackfaced minstrelsy, an indigenous product, was the reflection of the treatment of a class considered inferior. The patron-artist relationship had not yet developed in this society, so that it was not possible for Negroes to have dignified roles. Blackface comedy and minstrelsy dominated the American theatre scene for a long period and many Negro performers followed in the wake of the white minstrels who monopolized this field. The source of the minstrelsy was the Negro folk; and the later Negro companies with blacked faces exploited this vein of theatre for many years. The Georgia Minstrels and Callender's Consolidated had Billy Kersands, Sam Lucas and the best known of them all, James Bland, composer of *Carry Me Back to Ole Virginny* and *Pretty Little South Carolina Rose.*

This later period reflected the Negro's reactions to his understanding of the dramatic forms and of the varying functions of the stage. In the plays of Steele Mackaye, Negroes were treated as human beings; in those of Edward Harrigan, they were pictured as buffoons; in the minstrel troupe and in the Negro musical show, the Negro himself carried forward ante-bellum blackface tradition. The patron class determined both the function and the actual material which the dramatist and actors employed.

The Negro show became the vehicle for Negro dramatic talent. Paul Laurence Dunbar, Will Marion Cook, Ernest Hogan, J. Rosamond Johnson, Will Vodery, Miller and Lyles wrote the words and music for these shows from 1890 to 1915, a period in which the cake walk, the coon song, the Jonah Man and the beginnings of jazz were dominant. One of the greatest performers was Bert Williams of whom W. C. Fields said, "he was the funniest man I ever saw and the saddest man I ever knew." George Walker, Bob Cole, Ernest Hogan, S. H. Dudley, other great artists, felt compelled to cork their faces, soft-shoe dance and clown before white audiences. The first New York show was the *Creole Show* from the Chicago World's Fair. *Oriental America* was the first Broadway Negro show. Ernest Hogan's *Rufus Rastus,* Bob Cole's and J. Rosamond Johnson's *A Trip to Coontown* played Worth's Museum. *Abysinnia,* by Bert Williams and George Walker, broke records at Koster and Bial's. The function of the theatre in this period was to entertain an affluent class, hence the Negro show kept closely to the blackface caricature of malapropisms and dice-playing.

The Negro Producing Theatre, 1915-1925. Barred from participation in a flourishing American theatre and without their own playwrights, Negroes sought devices and turned to their own producing shows. The first Negro theatres in the new century were stock-producing companies designed to counteract the race-baiting dramas of Thomas Dixon, to provide employment and to show Negro audiences an array of thespian ability. The repertory of Chicago's Pekin Theatre, Mrs. Sherwood Anderson's Ethiopian Art Players, the Anita Bush Company and the New York Lafayette players gave rise only to imitativeness and reflected the individualism of middle class culture. These plays, *The Count of Monte Cristo, The 13th Chair, Madame X, On Trial, Dr. Jekyll and Mr. Hyde* had no relation to Negro life, but they gave opportunities and they served as an apprentice home for such distinguished actors as Frank Wilson, Charles Gilpin, Rose McClendon, Evelyn Preer, Abbie Mitchell and Edna Thomas. Negro drama did not come of age until later, when the artistic period between 1920-1930 had developed an integrated style and a language which were more attuned to the times.

Transition in American Drama, 1920-1930. Negro theatre workers, actors and producers, together with the white dramatists who realistically explored Negro life, constituted a transitional phase in Negro drama. White dramatist-poets, such as Ridgely Torrence, who wrote *The Rider of Dreams, Granny Maumee,* Paul Green, who wrote *No Count Boy, In Abraham's Bosom,* Eugene O'Neill, who wrote *Emperor Jones, All God's Chillun Got Wings,* represented emergence from a folk art period. Plays by white writers who were concerned with social justice—James K. Millen's *Never No More,* Peters' and Sklar's *Stevedore,* Wexley's *They Shall Not Die,* Paul Green's *Hymn to the Rising Sun* — overshadowed the miracle dramaturgy of Roark Bradford's *Green Pastures* and the folk dramatization of Dubose and Dorothy Heyward's *Porgy* (1928). Distinguished actors like Opal Cooper (*The Rider of Dreams*), Frank Wilson, Rose McClendon, Abbie Mitchell (*In Abraham's Bosom*), Charles Gilpin (*Emperor Jones*), Paul Robeson (*All God's Chilluns Got Wings*), Leigh Whipper, Rex Ingram, Georgette Harvey, Jack Carter, Edna Thomas (*Stevedore*), Richard B. Harrison (*Green Pastures*), performed in these plays.

Negro playwrights in the 1920's became more articulate and concerned with the realism of Negro life in the American scene. The tone of this writing was racialistic, a result of the failures and disappointments suffered by Negroes in a post-war world. Poets, novelists, musicians and musical comedy writers, some of whom belonged to what Alain Locke called the *New Negro Movement,* emerged to express the disillusionments of post-war Negro life. *Shuffle Along* (1921) did not display any such dejection. A success from the start, it was written, produced, directed and acted by Negroes, giving the inimitable Florence Mills her first starring role. *Blackbirds, Running Wild, Brown Buddies, Choco-'ate Dandies,* written and composed by Noble Sissle and Eubie Blake appeared in the 1920's and featured such stars as Aida Ward, Adelaide Hall, Johnny Hudgins, Inez Clough and the unforgettable danseuse, Josephine Baker.

The social protest drama of white dramatists encouraged Negro playwrights to write straight forwardly of the plight of Negroes. Frank Wilson's *Sugar Cane* (1925), Willis Richardson's *Broken Banjo* (1925), sought to place on the stage the emotional realities of Negro life. The only plays written by Negroes to reach Broadway with any success were Wallace Thurman's *Harlem* (with William Jourdan Rapp), a lurid melodrama (1929), Hall Johnson's *Run Little Children* (1933), a highly successful treatment of Negro religious and folk life and Langston Hughes' *Mulatto* (1935), a tragic and sometimes heavy account of the realities of miscegenation.

The Little Theatre, 1920-1942. Growing up with the national drama consciousness of the 1920's and along with the post-war **New Negro Movement,** was the Negro Little Theatre. The appearance of the Negro Little Theatre was coincident with the flourishing Little Theatre Movement. This movement affirmed the relationship of patron and artist in a changing middle-class society and determined the functions and material forms taken by the theatre workers. The first of these groups, the Krigwa Players, sponsored by W. E. B. DuBois as part of the *Crisis* program, did not survive long. Other groups in Washington (the Howard Players organized in 1922 by Alain Locke and Montgomery Gregory) Boston, Philadelphia and Chicago, were more successful, but short-lived. Only the Gilpin players in Cleveland, under Rowena Jelliffe, dared to act plays of Negro life; elsewhere the content of the "drama" was dependent on the whims of the patron class. Later, the Negro theatre movement spread into the Negro colleges, propelled by Sterling Brown (Howard University) and Randolph Edmonds (Dillard University) who founded the Negro Intercollegiate Drama Association. Negro instructors, Owen Dodson (Hampton), Anne Cook (Atlanta), M. Ross (Fisk), James Butcher (Howard), realizing the possibilities of a Negro theatre, wrote their own plays, with much success. The late 1930's and the present period saw the continued development of the Negro Theatre Movement with such groups as the Bucket Theatre (near Tuskegee), the Rose McClendon Players (New York), the Negro Playwrights Company (New York), the American Negro Theatre (New York) and the Harlem Suitcase Theatre, which point to 'hope ahead' in a healthy direction.

Federal Subsidy, 1935-1939. The Federal Theatre Project, begun in 1935 as a result of the serious disruptions caused in the theatre world, moved in the direction of a genuine People's Theatre. The expressed purpose of the project was to give 'to the people access to the arts and tools of a civilization which they themselves are helping to make.' The project, a great boon to a depressed Negro theatre, gave employment and encouragement to Negro artists in every field, and 'a special program for Negro companies.' No other project or endeavor aided the Negro theatre as the Project did. Units were set up in Seattle, San Francisco, Los Angeles, Chicago, Birmingham, Raleigh, Hartford, Boston, Newark and New York. The plays of Negro authors—Frank Wilson's *Brother Mose,* Smith and Morell's *Turpentine,* Ward's *Natural Man* and *Big White Fog,* Bontemps and Cullen's *The Conjure Man Dies*—were acted before thousands all over the country. There were musicals, dance groups, mobile shows, puppet groups, well-known classics and modern plays. *Haiti* by William Du Bois, was highly successful; *Macbeth,* directed by Orson Welles and John Houseman, was colorful, different and unforgettable. *The Swing Mikado,* a Chicago version with modern trappings, played to millions. The demise of the Federal Theatre Project brought to an end what had begun as the richest promise of the Negro theatre.

The Present and the Promise. Negro writing in the 1930's followed the general trend of white proletarian literature and the direction of left-wing drama. Most of the Negro creative writers had been poets and novelists, working in forms well suited to middle-class life. Now the drama came to be influenced by the novel, expressing the complex desires, fears and struggles of the undifferentiated Negro masses. Class-conscious writers turned to the blunted and frustrated forms of Negro life and explored the inner facets of Negro experience. Langston Hughes' later work, especially his *Don't You Want to be Free,* expressed the desire of people for real freedom. Theodore Ward's *Big White Fog,* went down into the depths of Negro working class ambitions and experience. *Native Son,* a searing and gripping dramatization (Paul Green and Richard Wright) of the Wright novel about the slum-bred Bigger Thomas, brought to a focus the essence of Negro experience. The moving principle of *Native Son* was the source of its tragedy, its beauty and its creative power. *Native Son* regarded the Negro proletarian as part of a class-system, it revealed stark tragedy; but it also promised freedom, it trumpeted a call to action and it expressed the consciousness of the Negro people.

Shakespeare's universal appeal and message can be noted in the Negro theatre from the time when Ira Aldridge played Shylock until 1930 and 1942 when Paul Robeson enacted Othello. The Shakespeare Tercentenary of 1916 included Edward Wright's Shakespearean repertory at the New York Lafayette Theatre. Not since 1826 had an American Negro in an American production played Othello. In 1930, under Maurice Browne (who played Iago) Robeson gave a matchless London performance. In 1942, Robeson appeared under the great Shakespearean director, Margaret Webster (who played Emilia) in the role of Othello at Brattle Hall, Cambridge, Massachusetts and at Princeton University. His

Othello was played with a fiery spirit and a strength of interpretation which showed the black Moor moving with dignity, towering above the petty jealousies of Venetian life. Paul Robeson, as a great actor, played the main role of a universally valuable work, in a mixed cast and proved that Shakespeare was universal in more ways than one. Robeson's Othello was a plea for equal rights in every walk of life and a clarion call for the honor of American Negroes. This production was a landmark, a triumph for the Negro in the American theatre and a herald of a great future in the annals of the theatre. See S. A. Brown, *Negro Poetry and Drama,* 1937 and *The Negro Caravan* (with A. P. Davis and Ulysses Lee), 1941; R. Edmonds, *Seven Plays for a Negro Theatre,* 19 ; H. Flanagan, *Arena,* 1941; J. W. Johnson, *Black Manhattan,* 1930; A. Locke, *The New Negro,* 1926; the Negro Drama and Broadway, *Theatre Arts* (Oct., 1941); *Theatre Arts* (Aug. 1942); R. Torrence, *Three Plays for a Negro Theatre,* 1917. *Louisiana,* A State Guide, 1941.—E.C.H.

American organ. *Mus.* A reed organ in which the sound is produced by air sucked through the reeds by a bellows.

American Scene movement. See regionalism.

American standard pitch. See ACOUSTICS.

American ware. See CERAMICS II.

ammonia. Because of its alkaline character, ammonia, usually as ammonium hydroxide, is frequently used for general and destructive cleaning of oil paint. In some form it may have been an ingredient of cleaning agents for pictures since the Renaissance.   —G.L.S.

Amor. Cupid.

amorino (It.). An infant cupid; common in Italian 16th cent. sculpture and painting.

amphitheatre (L. *amphitheatrum,* from Gr. *amphi,* on both sides—*theatron,* a theatre, the term compounded by the Romans despite the lack of any precedent in Greek architecture for these buildings). An unroofed oval or circular building with seats rising in tiers continuously around an open space or arena for the exhibition of gladiatorial and mimic naval combats, fights between wild animals, and other forms of spectacular public entertainment during the period of the Roman Empire. Amphitheatres existed in every Roman town of the slightest importance, from the Near East to Spain, from North Africa to

Britain, and those which still stand are the most monumental examples of Roman architecture: the Colosseum of Rome (72-80 A.D.), the amphitheatres of El-Djem (Tunisia), Verona, Pola, Nimes, Pompeii, Capua and Cassano (Sicily) are the most complete and noteworthy. The amphitheatre was generally oval in plan, with gates opening onto the arena at either end of the major axis, which reached an extreme length of 626'6" at Pozzuoli. The arena itself, covered with sand, was frequently pierced with trap-doors to facilitate the display of illusions; it was often capable of being flooded for the presentation of naval battles, *naumachia;* while in some cases extensive substructures contained dressing rooms for gladiators and cages for wild animals. The surrounding *visorium,* at first built of wood or simply a terraced hillside from which the arena had been excavated (as at Sutri), was from the 1st cent. onward constructed of brick or stone. The moat which had surrounded the arena for the protection of the spectators was replaced by a wall or *podium,* so that the first row of seats was elevated ten or twelve feet above the arena. The *visorium,* supported partly on a solid substructure and partly on a complex of arcades, was at Rome divided into distinct stories, the lowermost reserved for the Emperor (who had a raised loge, *pulvinar*), the Senators and the Vestal Virgins; the next level was reserved for priests, knights, and the lesser magistracy; above them sat ordinary citizens, the *popularia,* with a special section for women; while the slaves were allowed to stand on the roof of the colonnade girdling the uppermost story. The Colosseum could accommodate nearly 50,000 spectators, though 15,000-20,000 was the average for the larger provincial amphitheatres. Access to the *visorium* was in all amphitheatres provided through *vomitoria* which occurred in every third or fourth arch in the outer wall; the seats, usually faced with marble, were divided into wedge-shaped sections by stairs. On the outside of the attic wall of the Colosseum, 157' above the ground, are consoles and stone rings for the support of the *velarium* or awning which in case of rain or overhot sun could be stretched across the whole theatre by sailors of the fleet who were always in attendance for this purpose. The outer arcaded walls of the amphitheatres, of noble beauty in even their present despoiled condition, were customarily faced with marble and ornamented with statues and superimposed engaged columns of the Doric, Ionic and Corinthian orders, or with square buttresses. These stu-

pendous monuments served throughout the Middle Ages and in Rome until so late as 1750 as convenient stone quarries, hence the high mortality and often total disappearance of the great majority of these buildings so substantial and once so numerous. The Roman amphitheatre is the direct inspiration of numerous modern athletic stadia in Europe and America and of the bull-rings of Spain. The designation of modern open-air theatres on the Greek model as amphitheatres is improper.
—T.A.H.

amphora. A large Greek jar with two handles, used for storing wine, grain, oil, etc. This is one of the earliest known vases, found all over the Greek world. Among the most interesting types are the geometrically decorated Dipylon vases (q.v.) found in Athens; the seventh-century amphorae with long, eggshaped bodies; the Panathenaic amphorae, decorated with a picture of the warrior-goddess Athena on the side, given as prizes to winners at the great Athenian festival; the elegant Nolan vases with their slim, long neck; the Apulian, egg-shaped, with thick mouths and the neck merging into the shoulder; and the twisted-handled Campanian amphorae. Many of the most prominent vase painters decorated these vases, including Nikosthenes in late 6th cent. Athens, whose amphorae were notable for their crisp, metallic shapes and band-handles.

In Oriental art the term is applied to vase forms that approach the Greek original in shape. —W.R.A.

amplitude. See ACOUSTICS.

amulet. A charm case or propitious ornament, generally worn around the neck; greatly varying in forms and in material. See JEWELRY.

amure (Fr. *amure,* armor). A textile with rep or twill background. The pattern is made of warp threads floated on the surface. Small patterns usually made on a Jacquard loom.

amusia. A condition in an individual marked by inability to follow or to appreciate music. Sometimes called tone-deafness.

amyl acetate. Distinguished by its penetrating sweet odor which gives it the common name, banana oil, amyl acetate is well known as a solvent for the synthetic resins. —G.L.S.

an (Ch.). A bronze box or casket for small objects.

anadem. A wreath; garland.

anaglypta. See relief.

analogous color scheme. See COLOR.

analytical cubism. See cubism.

ānanda laharī. See MUSICAL INSTRUMENTS.

Ananta (Skr.). In Hindu mythology the infinite, the endless.

Anasazi (Navaho, ancient ones). A term applied to the Basket Maker—Pueblo peoples. See Pueblo Art.

anchor. The dart of an egg-and-dart molding. In heraldry, used as an emblem of hope.

ancient modes. See scales and modes.

aṇḍa (Skr.). See stupa.

Andhra art. See INDIAN ART.

anecdote. See American folk forms in literature.

angelic hymn. The hymn sung by the angels at Chirst's birth (*Gloria in excelsis*).

anglaise (Fr.). A lively country-dance in "English" style, in 2/4 or 3/4 time.

angle shaft. A corner bead, often enriched and sometimes with capital and base.

Angora cloth. A variety of cloths made from Angora wool or from mohair and similar fibres.

angular perspective. See PERSPECTIVE.

animism. See PRIMITIVE ART.

ankh. A T-shaped or tau cross with a loop at the top; symbol of life in ancient Egypt.

annam. See SOUTHEASTERN ASIATIC ART.

Anna Selbdritt. German for "St. Anne with Two Others", the two others being Mary and the Infant.

annealing. See GLASS AND GLASS-MAKING.

annular vault. A vaulted enclosure with its plan having the form of an arc of a circle.

anonymous. (1) Nameless; or of unknown name (1601). (2) Of unknown authorship (1676). (3) Illegitimate or specious; *rare* (1881).   —R.W.C.

answer. The reply given in a fugue (q.v.) by the second voice to the antecedent of the first voice.

anta. A pilaster or pier terminating a wall and usually having a capital and base. A portico having columns between the antae is said to be *in antis.*   —O.M.S.

Antaeus. In Greek mythology, a giant of invincible strength as long as he remained in contact with his mother, Ge (Earth); overcome by Herakles who lifted him from the earth and crushed him in the air.   —L.T.S.

antecedent. The theme of a fugue or canon (q.v.), as proposed by the first part of any motive which is later imitated.

antechamber. A small room or vestibule usually between the outer entrance and an interior doorway to a larger chamber.

antefix (Lat. *ante,* before + *fixus,* fixed). In classical architecture, the upright decorative termination, at the cornice, of the covering tiles of the roof; usually in the form of a palmette, sometimes in the form of a human or satyr's head.   —L.T.S.

antetemple. The vestibule or narthex of a temple or church.

anthem. A piece of sacred music usually founded on biblical words, with or without instrumental accompaniment and having various forms: (1) Anthems for double choir, the choirs frequently answering each other. (2) Full anthems, consisting wholly of chorus, accompanied or not. (3) Full anthem with verses, certain parts of which are sung by solo voices, although beginning and closing are choruses and the chorus predominates throughout. (4) Verse anthems, in which the verses predominate the choruses. (5) Solo anthems, in which the solo part predominates, although the chorus always concludes them. (6) Instrumental anthems, those accompanied by instruments other than the organ. The anthem is essentially an English product.   —F.M.G.

anthemion. See palmette; lotus and palmette.

antimony pigments. The best known of these historically is Naples yellow or antimony yellow, which is a lead antimoniate. Its color runs from an orange to a pale, almost greenyellow. Its history is long. As a glaze in ceramics, it has been found in the ruins of Babylonia and Assyria, and Egyptian glass of the 19th dynasty is known to have contained this combination of elements. To what extent antimony was used in pigments for painting has not been generally decided because of the difficulty of distinguishing analytically between this and the closely related lead oxide known as massicot. There is evidence, however, that a yellow lead antimoniate figured in the color of pictures at least from the late Renaissance. A few modern paints are also derived from this element. One is an antimony oxide, a white pigment used industrially but not introduced to the artist's palette. A somewhat similar position is taken by antimony sulphide, a substitute for mercuric sulphide, or vermilion.   —G.L.S.

antinode. See ACOUSTICS.

antiphon. See psalmody.

antiphonal psalmody. See psalmody.

antiphonarius cento. See MEDIEVAL MUSIC.

antiphonary. See MEDIEVAL MUSIC.

antiphony. Responsive singing by two voices, choirs or a divided choir.

antiquarium. A building or room in which antiques are displayed. Also a cabinet or case containing antiques.

Antwerp blue. See Prussian blue.

Antwerp school. A school of art that developed in Antwerp. From 1480 to 1505 a group of painters came to Antwerp from Cologne, Westphalia, the lower Rhine and Bruges. It succeeded Bruges as the center of Flemish art. Among the artists who practised there were Quentin Massys, Mabuse, Joachim Patinir, Hendrik Bles, Pieter Breughel, Jan Massys, Antonio Moro, Rubens, Van Dyck, Frans Snyders, Gerard Seghers and many lesser known artists.   —R.L.W.

Anubis. Egyptian jackal god of the dead.

Apache art. The Apache (possibly Zuñi *apachu,* enemy), like the Navaho, were Athapascan nomad hunters who entered the Southwest from Alaska and Canada six or seven hundred years ago. Unlike the Navaho, they were non-assimilative and continued to be rovers and raiders, especially after the introduction of the horse. They never coalesced into a geographic unit but remained divided in small bands of warlike expert horsemen who roamed over Arizona, New Mexico and western Texas. Though some of them cultivated a limited amount of corn, for a large part of their food they depended upon native game and plants. Hence it is not surprising that their chief art was basketry, and that,

too, restricted to the women. The function of the baskets was to supply containers and carriers for a roving people for whom pottery was impracticable. Cottonwood, willow and yucca furnished the materials. Their coiled bowls and jars show a simple vigor of shape and design that seems consistent with the tribal character. Though the styles vary somewhat among the different bands, in general the bowls show a design boldly set forth in angular geometric patterns which frequently radiate or spiral outward from the center. Small figures of highly conventionalized men and animals are scattered almost at random over the surface like repeat patterns within the geometric framework. In their ceremonials the Apache reveal a boldly dramatic quality; and the Mescalero group, in the costumes and movements of the dance of the four nights' puberty rites of Apache girls, made the same use of straight line and angularity as is seen in the baskets. See F. H. Douglas, *Apache Indian Coiled Basketry,* Denver Art Museum Leaflet No. 64, 1934; O. T. Mason, *Aboriginal American Basketry,* U. S. National Museum, Annual Report, 1932; C. Wissler, *The American Indian,* 1938.   —H.G.

apadana. *Persian arch.* A columned hall supporting wooden roof of heavy timbers and wattling, combining the judgment-hall and the audience hall of the king.

Apelles. A Greek 4th cent. B.C., painter, famous, according to ancient writers, for the realism of his pictures. None of his work survives.   —W.R.A.

Aphrodite (L. *Venus*). The Greek and Roman goddess of love and beauty, favorite subject of Greek sculptors and vase painters. Among the most famous statues of her were Praxiteles' Aphrodite of Cnidus, of which a copy is in the Vatican; there are many Hellenistic variations of the type, including the Aphrodite of Melos in the Louvre and the Aphrodite of Cyrene in the Terme Museum, Rome. She has been popular as a subject in European painting, as in Botticelli's *Birth of Venus* and pictures by Giovanni Bellini, Raphael, Correggio, Giorgione, Rubens and Bouguereau. Scores of sculptors from Sansovino to Maillol and Manship have likewise given this title to their representations of attractive female figures. She has often been accompanied in art by her son, Eros (Cupid).   —W.R.A.

Apis. Sacred bull worshiped by the ancient Egyptians.

Apollo. One of the most important of Greek and Roman gods, the divinity of light and healing, music, athletics and prophecy. His chief attributes were the lyre, bow, laurel wreath and tripod. He was a favorite subject of Greek sculptors and vase painters, who represented him usually either as a vigorous young athlete or in more lyric fashion as a graceful musician, leader of the Muses. Outstanding sculptural representations are the majestic Apollo from the pediment of the Temple of Zeus at Olympia, the Apollo Slaying a Lizard by Praxiteles, and the Hellenistic Apollo Belvedere. By European painters he has frequently been pictured as the guiding spirit of music and poetry, as in Raphael's Parnassus, in the Sistine Chapel, Rome. The Apollo and Daphne story was illustrated by Giorgione. Among sculptors, Sansovino, Bernini, Thorvaldsen, and Flaxman represented him as a graceful youth; but Michelangelo realized his strength of body and spirit, and in modern times Barye, Rodin and Bourdelle have recaptured something of the vigorous personality of the early classical Apollo.
—W.R.A.

Apollonian and Dionysian. A distinction made by Nietzsche in *The Birth of Tragedy* between the two ways of artistic self-revelation that nature makes of itself. He refers to the Apollonian art-world of *dreams* and the Dionysian art-world of *drunkenness,* these characterizations of existence being analogous to the experience of nature as appearance, order, Being, on the one hand, and as reality, chaos, Becoming, on the other. The human artist is to be regarded as an imitator of these two and is thus the producer of either type of art; only the tragedian combines the two—as was the case in Attic tragedy. In his later thought, which is less Schopenhauerian, Nietzsche develops a psychology of art in which dreams are regarded as foreshadowing aesthetic intuition and aesthetic orgy. On this basis he regards dramatics, music, lyrical poetry, and dancing as Dionysian art, and sculpture, epic poetry, and painting as Apollonian art—architecture, being a product of pure will, is excluded from this distinction. By transcending the *principium individuationis,* the ordered aspect of nature (the Apollonian), the artist, in aesthetic mystical ecstasy, becomes one with the Heraclitean flux, the true reality (the Dionysian). Only the rhapsodic experience of the Dionysian aspect of existence makes the latter bearable. Truth, which is to be found in the Apollonian (rational) aspect

of existence, is destructive of living in its deepest sense.   —H.G.S.

apollonicon. An orchestrion (automatic organ) of large size and with five or six keyboards.

apotheosis. The act of deification; elevation of a man to the rank of an immortal. First introduced into art by the Romans in connection with emperor worship; reintroduced in 16th cent. Italy and later in 17th cent. France as a metaphorical celebration of the absolute prince. Spread from France to other European countries.   —R.B.

apotropaic eyes. In Greek art, a human eye with lids and eyebrow painted on objects, especially vases and prows of ships, to ward off evil.

apotropaic imagery. Any abstract or representational configuration designed to ward off evil influences and to frighten away ghosts; often takes the form of human or animal faces and of their staring eyes (relation to hypnotism). A magical device, apotropaic representation is based on the assumption that an image has the power of what it represents and that demons are combatted best by their own visible likeness. Universal in all primitive art.   —R.B.

apotygma. See wool.

Apoxyomenos. (Gr. *apo* + *xyo,* to scrape off). Name given to a statue in the Vatican. It is presumed to be a copy of a famous statue by the Greek sculptor Lysippos. It represents a young athlete in the act of scraping himself with the so-called *xystris* or *strigil* after a contest. The statue is frequently used to illustrate the change of style in the beginning of the Hellenistic epoch. Illustrated in: Gisela M. A. Richter, *The Sculpture and the Sculptors of the Greeks,* 1929, Figs. 739, 742, 743.
—L.L.

apparent color. See COLOR.

apple green. A special color, generally applied to Chinese monochrome porcelain, suggesting the color of a green apple.

applied art. The term applied art has had many different connotations. It may imply the application to or embellishment of more basic forms. In this sense it is essentially ornament. It may also seek to isolate the more useful object from the more aesthetically significant, and refer to productions of the craftsman rather than to those of the artist. In this sense applied art is analogous to applied science, stressing the practical rather than the theoretical, and is conceived as similar to one of the minor arts. Two other ideas are still current, although datable. One is the usage in many 19th cent. schools where the mechanic arts and the applied arts included all the crafts and trades whose techniques were taught. The other is seen in the contrast often made between applied art and fine art during discussions of machine art; a distinction, in fact, surviving from Renaissance times. In ancient and medieval times craft applied to both types of art. The term "fine" has latterly connoted academic art, or, as Herbert Read has it, "humanistic art", whereas applied art connotes useful art. (See classification of the arts.)

To list the chief categories of applied art is to name the main types of craftsmanship now practised. Those forms which have such a close relationship to painting that dividing lines are blurred include mosaics and murals. Modelling is often indistinguishable from sculpture; interior decoration, from architectural forms, as well as from theatre ensembles. Ceramics, wood, glass, and metal work; textiles, rugs, embroidery, and needlework; leatherwork, illumination, enamel, and jewelry are all included. And in many ways the industrial and the commercial arts should be cited as well. The world of pottery and glass are clearly capable of both fine and applied art design. Textiles, whether from natural or synthetic materials, provide another field for the artist of the applied arts. In fact, each survey of the field of applied art is likely to lead the student to wonder how the artist and the craftsman ever parted company.—W.S.R.

applied decoration. The application of decorative ornament to any object, as applying carving to a piece of furniture, or decalcomania designs to a household article. See applied design. Whitford and Winslow in *Dictionary of Education.*

applied design. A pattern used to decorate an object as differentiated from the structural planning of the object itself. (Thus a piece of pottery may be embellished by the application of ornament through painting, incising, or modeling.) See applied decoration. Whitford and, Winslow in *Dictionary of Education.*

applied order. Decorative column and entablature fixed to a wall or pier; non-structural in function.

applied psychology of music. See EXPERIMENTAL PSYCHOLOGY OF MUSIC.

appliqué. Ornament or ornaments of one material applied to another to form a design or pattern.

appogiatura. A grace which is followed by the main note. *Vorschlag* in German, *port de voix* in French. Numerous variations in the execution of the appogiatura are demonstrated in historic treatises on interpretation.   —F.D.

appuie-main. See mahlstick.

Apsaras. *Hindu myth.* A divine water nymph or dancer of the heaven of Indra. See INDIAN ART.

apse. Projecting part of a building, esp. a church; semicircular or polygonal recess covered with a half-dome or other vault.

apsidiole. Secondary apse where central apses are present in a church; usually found in number as small apse-like projections from the ambulatory and transepts.

apsis. See apse.

aqua fortis. A method of etching involving use of nitric acid as a mordant.

aquarelle. A water color drawing, esp. transparent water color. Printed plates colored with water color using stencils.

aquatint, an intaglio process (Lat. *aqua,* water, and *tincta,* dyed). The aquatint graphic process is a method of biting tones instead of lines, thus producing rich, deep, velvety, dark tones as well as delicate transparent tints. The tones resemble water color washes which accounts for the name, aqua, or water, tint.

The process differs from line etching or soft ground in that the ground laid does not protect the plate entirely from the acid. The method usually used for obtaining this porous ground is to raise an asphaltum or resin dust in a confined space, and then allowing it to settle on the surface of the plate. Specially constructed dust boxes are used for this purpose. After the plate is dusted it is placed over a heater which melts the particles of dust until they adhere firmly to the copper plate.

If the grounded plate were placed in the bath without stopping out, the acid would attack the metal between the protecting particles of ground, forming solid tone, the depth of which would depend on the depth of the biting. It follows then, that if one wanted a pure white it must be stopped out before the first immersion in the acid.

The next lightest tone is stopped out and it is put into the acid bath again. Dipping in the acid and stopping out is alternated until all tones on the plate are accommodated. Aquatint, rarely used by itself, is often combined with soft ground, etching, drypoint, pen process, and other intaglio mediums. See PRINTS AND PRINT PROCESSES.

—K.K.

aquatint, colored. A monochrome print tinted with water colors after printing.

aquatint, crayon method. A method of biting aquatint tones wherein stopping out gives the print the character of a drawing with white chalk on a black blackground.   —K.K.

aquatint, crayon method (an intaglio process). The aquatint crayon method is a variation on the aquatint process. In this method the plate is cleaned and a regular porous aquatint ground is laid on the plate. A drawing is made on the plate with a cheap paraffin wax crayon. Wherever the wax protects the plate from the action of the acid it will leave a white crayon-textured line on the plate. Usually, in actual practice, the pure whites only are drawn before the plate is immersed for a short bite; each subsequent drawing and biting produces a darker crayon-textured line.

The crayon method is sometimes used all by itself to produce an interesting, coarse, white, crayon-textured print; at other times it is used in combination with etching, soft ground, pen process, and other intaglio processes.   —K.K.

aquatint in color. An aquatint using more than one color, produced in either of two ways: (1) printing from one plate on which all the colored inks have been applied, or (2) multiple plate printing, in which each color is applied to a separate plate.   —K.K.

aquatint mezzotint. The plate is prepared by biting a solid tone of aquatint. The design is scraped and burnished by using the mezzotint method, the result being a great deal like mezzotint.   —K.K.

aquatint, pen process. A method of making aquatints that has the quality of a pen or brush line.

aquatint, three plate color (an intaglio process). The making of a three plate color aquatint is necessarily very complicated. The greatest care must be taken in timing the

exposures to the acid, as the slightest variation will materially change the colors. The problems of registry, shrinking of the damp paper, are considerable also. The most practical color chart developed shows 216 different combinations of the three primary colors: red, yellow and blue.

There are two methods of producing aquatints in color: (1) rubbing different colors on one plate, and (2) preparing a separate plate for each color, thereby producing innumerable additional variations by overlapping different color values on the color plates. The latter is the process described here.

The blue plate is made first, using one or more of the intaglio processes, usually soft ground or pen process. A tiny dent is put at either end of the plate for a register mark. A proof is pulled, dusted with powdered cobalt blue, and an offset is made from this proof to the red plate which has been aquatint grounded. The red plate is now bitten. Using a specially consructed chart, a trial proof is marked, showing how many minutes to bite the red plate at any given spot to produce the desired color.

The yellow plate is the last one to be made. Both the red and blue proofs are dusted with corresponding colors and offset to the aquatint grounded yellow plate. At this stage one should have a record on the yellow plate of all the work that has been done so far on the blue and red plates. Using this specially constructed chart and a marked proof of the blue plate as a guide, the yellow plate is now bitten to varying depths to produce various color combinations.

Tones of aquatint are now added to the blue plate in order to complete the color combinations, and the three plates are ready for printing.

The yellow plate is printed first with cadmium yellow ink. A pin hole is made in the paper at each of the two registry marks. The red plate is now inked with cadmium red, and two pins with sticks for handles are put through the registry pin holes in the back of the yellow proof, the points resting in the register dents of the red plate. The paper is allowed to slide down the pins to register with the red plate. The pins are withdrawn and the plate is printed. A similar procedure is followed for printing the final plate, which is ultra-marine blue.   —K.K.

aqueduct. Any conduit or channel used for the transmission of water; often supported on masonry arches.

arabesque (from Fr. *arabesque;* synonyms: It., *arabesco, rabesco;* Sp., *arabesco;* Ger., *arabeske* or *laubwerk*). (1) Literally whether used as an adj. or n., *arabesque* means Arabian or in the Arabian manner. In all European languages, the term is understood to mean mural or surface decoration in color or low relief composed of flowing lines and patterns of flowers, leaves, branches and scroll-work fancifully intertwined. The derivation would suggest an actual Arabic origin or influence for all decoration of this sort, which is not the case. The term actually refers to any decorative work of a capricious nature containing arbitrarily intertwined foliage, tendrils and flowers and scrollwork; in addition human figures, birds, beasts, fishes, reptiles, insects, and bits of fantastic edifices may be introduced. This grottesque (not *grotesque*) system of decoration was inherited by Renaissance artists, not from the Mohammedans, but from Graeco-Roman work, found in abundance and highest quality in the *thermae* of Titus and on the walls of numerous Pompeiian villas. Raphael (the Vatican *loggie*) and Giulio Romano (Palazzo del Te, Mantua) were notable practitioners of this art. The decorations of medieval illuminated manuscripts are in part properly called arabesques. In modern usage, any fantastic decoration based on flowing lines may be called arabesque, whether or not it contains representations of living animals; Moorish and Arabic work is now usually distinguished as Moorish arabesque, or **mauresque**. —T.A.H.
(2) A position in the classic academic ballet vocabulary, in which the dancer's body is supported on one foot, either straight or half-bent, with the other extended in the air, at right angles to it, the arms arranged to create the longest possible line from fingertips to toes. —L.K.
(3) A brilliant musical piece in rondo form; also a musical embellishment.

Aralu. *Bab. myth.* Gloomy abode of the dead.

Arapaho art. See Plains Indian art.

arcade. A series of arches supported by piers or columns.

arch. A semicircular or pointed structural device formed of separate truncated wedge-shaped solids, arranged with their joints at right angles to the curve, to span an opening.

ARCHAEOLOGY, AESTHETIC ASPECTS OF.
In Greek usage the word *archaiologia*

means "knowledge of old things, ancient history" (Josephus; Dionyisus of Halicarnassus). It may mean also "study of early legendary human culture" (Plato, *Hippias Maior, 285*). In modern scholarship the term *archaiologia* was first used by Jacques Spon (1647-85) to describe investigation concerned with the monuments rather than the literary remains of Classical antiquity. In relation to the modern field of archaeology as it has emerged within the last hundred years we may distinguish three definitions of progressively wider scope: (1) archaeology is not an academic discipline but a technique to which recourse is had when other lines of evidence fail to provide solutions for historical problems. (G. Kubler, *Art. Bull.* XXIV, 1942, p. 181). Here archaeology is conceived as a technique which through excavations and exploration detects, describes, restores, and makes accessible new material for historical research of all kinds. The study of art *qua* art is obviously considered outside the province of the archaeology in this definition.
(2) Archaeology is a study of the material remains of the human past which aims to reconstruct the historical environment and the civilization of a given period (D. E. Hogarth, *Authority and Archaeology,* 1899). Though this definition is usually rejected by Classical archaeologists, it represents the actual direction of research in many archaeological disciplines, especially those associated with geology, paleontology, anthropology, and ethnology. The development of human society in relation to its environment is seen as the focal point and art is treated as a social function or as a historical source (an example: W. B. Dinsmoor, in *Studies W. G. Leland,* 1942). Many students of Prehistoric and primitive archaeology feel that art cannot be treated as an autonomous phenomenon in primitive societies and that any aesthetic evaluation represents an illegitimate projection of a modern point of view. Another definition, formulated for medieval archaeology, concedes to archaeologists the privilege of studying all material remains as historical expressions of human activities or ideas, but leaves to art historians the stylistic analysis of art as an aesthetic expression to be judged by specific laws that are universal and timeless. The study of iconography and iconology is a branch of archaeology according to this definition. (G. de Jerphanion, *La voix de monuments,* 1930, Ch.i.).
(3) "Archaeology is a study of history in its material manifestations"; "archaeology of

art" is the most distinguished part of this historical field (C. T. Newton, *Essays on Art and Archaeology,* 1850 (1880) and E. Buschor, *Handb. Archaeol.* 1938, Ch. 1). This definition originated in Classical archaeology of the Romantic period. The archaeologist is here conceived as an investigator who starts from the material object in contrast to the philologist who starts from the written source. His proper domain included the study of the style and content of art in antiquity, the Middle Ages and the Renaissance. The increase of excavations and the influence of the natural sciences which dealt impartially with each object made it axiomatic that an ideal archaeologist must be able to interpret in every respect all objects of ancient civilization. The aesthetic interpretation of art is as much part of this encyclopedic task as the scientific interpretation of ancient technology. Theoretically this comprehensive ideal is still defended by many archaeologists. Practically, however, the growing diversity of methods and the increase of material has resulted in greater specialization. There are indications that histories of ancient art, science, material culture, and ancient religions are emerging as independent branches of scholarship, even though all of them employ the same archaeological material.

Aesthetic contributions of archaeology may be classified under three heads: the contribution of new artistic material, that of techniques in preservation, restoration, and description of art, and the contribution of new methods and ideas in dealing with art. If we regard the search for monuments of the past by the amateur and the profiteer as archaeology, Egyptian grave-robbers, Roman soldiers who plundered Greek tombs in Corinth, and treasure-hunters of all times may be classified as archaeologists. But archaeology conceived as a discipline determined by a search for knowledge is a product of the nineteenth century. Only isolated instances of historical conclusions drawn from archaeological evidence are reported from Classical antiquity. (Thucydides, I, 8 and Plutarch. Cf. R. Carpenter, *Humanistic Value of Archaeology,* 1933). The enthusiastic researches of the Renaissance, the Baroque, and the Rococo, while unquestionably determined by a desire for knowledge, did not provide an adequate excavating technique and failed to develop a systematic approach to the aesthetic aspects of ancient art.

Because they widen our horizon of aesthetic experience, archaeological discoveries have ex-

ercised an important influence upon our ideas of art. The idea of "Classical" art underwent progressive changes with the discovery of Greek originals, with the separation of Greek art from Etruscan, and with the subsequent periodization of Greek, Etruscan, and Roman art. The growth of archaeology is responsible also for making known the arts of Egypt, Mesopotamia, Mycenae, Crete, and India; as well as the arts of the Prehistoric, Far Eastern, Celto-Germanic, American, Oceanic, and Pacific cultures. These discoveries brought before European artistic circles types of expression hitherto undreamt of. Archaeologists may fail to show sufficient understanding of the artistic aspect of their own finds; artists and art critics may not understand the elements of these arts conditioned by environment, but the new artistic products become living values for our culture and are comprehended with greater depth and intensity when modern taste moves in their direction. (For archaeological discoveries cf. A. Michaelis, *A Century of Archaeological Discoveries,* 1909. P. Gardner, *New Chapters in Greek Art,* 1926. Th. Wiegand, *Handb. Archaeol.* I. 1938, 82 ff. *Antiquity* I, 1927 and following vols.) To investigate the influence of archaeological discoveries upon modern art and modern art criticism is an aim of the history of taste. Here we may recall the close relation of archaeological research and Neo-Classicism, the rise of Prehistoric and medieval archaeology promoted by Romanticism (*Antiquity* 1937, 3i), the influence exercised by the growing knowledge of Oriental and primitive art upon the exoticism in the later nineteenth century. Similarly the appreciation shown to Minoan and Tell-Amarna art by the period of art nouveau and Impressionism, the discovery of archaic, Egyptian, Sumerian, and Negro art by the artists and art critics of post-Impressionism, and the importance of Indian archaeological remains for the modern Mexican school of painting, reveal the stimulus of archaeological discoveries upon modern art. The aesthetic appreciation of the archaeological material shown by artists and art critics has often induced archaeologists to treat the art of their special fields as an artistic phenomenon. And in several fields, for instance in Prehistoric (Scheltema, Menghin, Kuhn), Egyptian (Worringger, Kaschnitz, G. Krahmer, E. B. Smith, D. Curtius, H. Evers vs. H. Schaefer, J. Capart, G. Reisner, A. Scharff, N. Davies, W. S. Smith), Sumerian (R. Fry, vs. H. Frankfort and W. Andrae)—and the art of the **American Indian** (*Cat. Mus. Modern*

Art) it is evident that the study of art as a separate discipline emerges from the controversy between "outsiders" (artists, art critics, art historians, anthropologists, psychologists) and archaeologists.

Techniques. Classical and Near Eastern archaeology has led the way in developing systematic techniques of excavation, preservation, and description of works of art. The development of scientific techniques of excavation and preservation have made incredible strides since the days of the "scavatori" in the Renaissance, or even since the days of Schliemann (E. Petrie, *Methods and Aims in Archaeology,* 1904. Th. Wiegand. *Hand. Archaeol.* I. 1938. W. F. Albright "So live the Works of Man", *70 Anniversary of E. H. Hewett,* 1939). With the aid of natural sciences the archaeological detectives have celebrated their greatest triumphs in the study of non-literate Prehistoric and primitive cultures. Excavation and preservation, however, have only a subsidiary significance for the aesthetic aspect of art although they make a vital contribution in recording any changes which may distinguish a work of art in its reconstructed form from its original condition.

The methodical description of a work of art is of great aesthetic significance: it was developed to a considerable degree in the archaeological fields. The archaeological description is not a uniform enumeration of surface appearances, but seizes upon the salient features of the object described. The object is thereby placed within a context and given a preliminary position within the system of our knowledge. Furthermore, any description of a work of art must attempt to express intelligibly the "unique" quality of a work of art: the description therefore touches upon the great secret of artistic creation. J. Winckelmann (1717-1768) was the first to insist upon the precedence of the visual impression over the subject matter. He was also the first to lay down a system of description according to formal criteria (beauty of concept or subject; beauty of expression; unity of composition and proportion; beauty of detail [anatomy]). W's method was influenced by the scientific classification of Linnaeus. His descriptions were often unsystematic and contained elements which are usually omitted in modern archaeological descriptions (broad concepts such as beauty and truth; literary anecdotes, antiquarian excursions), but other elements remain valid (aesthetic judgments, aesthetic categories, verbal imagery). Above all, he laid the foundation for the study of art

as a rational discipline. The archaeological descriptions were later perfected by G. Zoega, O. Jahn, H. Brunn and many others and influenced the early phases of art history.

Ideas. Ideas contributed to aesthetics by archaeology include modern art theory of the Renaissance, the Baroque, and the Rococo (cf. A. Blunt, *Artistic Theory in Italy,* 1940. E. Panofsky, *Idea,* 1924. R. Lee, *Art. Bull.* 1940, 197), but this discussion is confined to the treatment of aesthetic problems in modern archaeology. Winckelmann was the first theorist of Classical archaeology, although important elements of his art theory had been anticipated (e.g. "style" in visual arts as a phenomenon dependent on time and race, by de Caylus, 1692-1765). W. postulated that ancient art should be discussed "in a philosophic spirit and with a well-grounded expression of the truly beautiful". He was first to give a rational chronological sequence of Classical art thus making the study of art an historical discipline. He shared the naturalistic concept of eighteenth century historians (cf. Montesquieu and Gibbon) who regarded the development of art as a cycle of youth, growth, and decay. Superimposed upon this historical system is a Platonic metaphysic system: historically Classic Greek art is the high point of a cycle; philosophically it is the highest revelation of Beauty, Truth, and God, a consummate, eternally valid statement of absolute ideals of humanity. Students of ancient art have spent the last hundred and fifty years challenging and modifying W's view, but the cause, meaning and effect of Classicism still remain the central problems of the study of ancient art. The early nineteenth century elaborated W's theories and modified them in accordance with the increasing knowledge of Greek originals, but no systematic advance was made in the development of stylistic methods. C. T. Newton (*Essays on Art and Archaeology,* 1820-1850) sees "thought" and "noble motif" (iconography) as the essential stylistic qualities. The influence of philology caused archaeologists to consider the interpretation of subject matter as the supreme objective. Literary sources still constituted the historical framework, which was illustrated by works of art. Archaeologists of the Romantic period placed foremost the relationship of art to the individual, to the race, or to the nation. (F. Gerhardt, C. O. Mueller, G. Welcker, O. Jahn, C. T. Newton). Scientific historicism of the mid-nineteenth century shifted toward an Darwinian elaboration of developmental factors (typological method) and chronological sequences, and a new emphasis on the factual data (*Corpus* enterprises) which led to a systematic collection and publication of archaeological objects. Scientific observation of detail was also responsible for the rise of Morelli's comparative method, which seeks to recognize the work of individual artists, regions, and periods by the study of characteristic details. This method inaugurated the emphasis on visual form and helped to clarify the difference between the analysis of visual form and the interpretation of subject matter (Brunn, Furtwängler). The influence of philology weakened, but paleographic investigation of archtypes and copies supplied the method for differentiating Greek originals and Roman copies (Helbig, Furtwängler). The idealistic conception of art with its concomitant value judgment was gradually abandoned in the later nineteenth century in favor of a materialistic interpretation of art forms. They were thought to be determined by exigencies of technique, and by biological, physiological, social, economic, or political factors (Semper, Löwy, Milchhöfer, Kalkman). W. Pater still treats Greek art as an expression of Greek ideals, but its "sensuous form" is conceived as a result of techniques and materials, not of stylistic categories. In a modified form this point of view is accepted by Carpenter. He combines the materialistic interpretation of the development of art with the physiological theory of "empathy" which maintains that the enjoyment of art is conditioned by psycho-physical responses (*The Aesthetic Basis of Greek Sculpture*, 1929). The rebellion against the persistent Classicism of the Winckelmann variety originated with "objective historicists" who desired to reconstruct the meaning of each art for its own period (Carpenter) and from "philosophical historicists" (Riegl) who regarded history of art as a continuum (not as a cycle), in which new types of human experience manifest themselves in novel and different forms, all of equal value.

The appreciation of Roman and late antique art inaugurated by Wickhoff and Riegl presents an example of the new relativism. Riegl's categories of optic and haptic art were still based on physiology (cf. Hildebrandt), while Wickhoff's emphasis on representation of light, space, and movement is grounded in the aesthetic theories of Impressionism. The important distinction between conceptual and visual (optic) art was borrowed from psychology (H. Schäfer, R. Carpenter). The anti-Classical reaction was further strengthened

by the discovery of the primitive mind (anthropology, psychology) and by the non-objective ("expressionistic") trend of modern art theory. In Classical archaeology this glorification of the "primitive, strong, mythical, pre-logical" mind has resulted in an intensive study of the archaic, Orientalizing, and Geometric periods of Greek art (E. Buschor, H. Payne), while the idealistic creed of expressionism has produced a positive valuation of the late antique "primitivism" (Kaschnitz, Castelfranco). The new idealism, sharpened by experiences of World War I, is reflected in M. Dvorak's "history of ideas" (*Essay on Early Christian Art*). The general changes of human spirit rather than a specifically artistic "will" (Riegl) account for the changes in artistic expression. The study of cultural types initiated by Burckhardt (cf. also Ruskin, Pater, and the anthropological theories of types and cycles) has also contributed to this approach. The value judgment (absent in Dvorak) re-appears in archaeologists influenced by the "Third Humanism". They claim a special quality for Classical Greek art, not because it is Winckelmann's embodiment of transcendental ideas, but because it formulated for the first time in visual form the ideals of rational humanism fundamental for the European-American tradition. (B. Schweitzer, Dickinson, Rodenwaldt). The non-historical manner of the early 19th cent. Neo-Classicists, who expected to attain an art absolute solely through imitation of its external forms must be abandoned. But the general trend of our time toward fundamentalism indicates that Classical civilization and Classical art may again become symbolic of general human values.

Archaeologists maintained a lead in recognizing problems of artistic form, until the mid-nineteenth century when the leadership passed to historians of art. Ruskin, Semper, Hildebrandt, K. Fiedler, R. Norton, W. Pater, K. Lange, B. Berenson exercised considerable influence upon archaeology. The decisive step in the investigation of independent visual form came about 1900, when the historical growth of forms was shown by Wickhoff, Riegl, and Wölfflin to be capable of methodical analysis. Another group of investigators proceeded from a non-historical systematic treatment of categories of visual art toward an association of these categories with historical forms of art. This movement, too, had its influence upon the study of ancient art (D. Ross, J. Hambidge, A. Pope, cf. L. D. Caskey, *The Geometry of Greek Vases,* and many investigations of proportion, order, and "refinements" in ancient architecture). As a natural reaction against the emphasis on the iconographic and psychological elements these categories were at first confined to formal aspects of art, but later definitions of "form" and "structure" include psychological, emotional, and spiritual determinants as well as visual elements, and recognize the interdependent unity of these various aspects in a work of art. Ancient art has been discussed from this point of view by Kaschnitz, usually with the aim of isolating racial or national types of art, while the followers of Croce (R. Bianchi-Bandinelli, *Critica d'art*, 1935) insisted upon the importance of the creative individual and the unique quality of each work of art.

The present state of aesthetic problems in the various archaeological fields. Visual art is an historical phenomenon conditioned by environmental factors; but it is also a self-sufficient expression of human ideas and emotions, comparable to language or music. An ideal investigation of the aesthetic problems of art should recognize the varying relation of these two aspects. Hence the position of aesthetic research in archaeological fields is dependent upon the amount of historical information available. In fields where the historical framework remains to be created or is only vaguely outlined (Prehistoric, South American Indian) the study of art is frequently used for the solution of historical problems of "cultures", races, migrations, trade, diffusion, etc. Even if stylistic criticism is brought to bear, the autonomous values of art are neglected. Conversely, art critics sometimes treat the art of these fields on the basis of modern *l'art-pour-l'art* interpretation of artistic forms, omitting environmental elements which are essential to a complete comprehension. The gap between the historical and aesthetic approach can probably never be closed in the study of the arts of non-literate cultures except on the uncertain ground of parallels drawn from the study of the art of primitives of our time. In cultures whose historical background is known, the two aspects may be synthesized. Such synthesis has been achieved in the study of Greek and Roman art and this approach is being recognized by students of the arts of Egypt and the ancient Near East.

The direction of the study of art within the framework of the different archaeologies is in part dependent upon the completeness of material. Thus many of the Prehistoric and primitive archaeologies and, in a measure, the archaeology of early Egypt, early Near East,

and Asia are in a stage in which collection of new data is of decisive importance, whereas in Classical, late antique, medieval, and Byzantine archaeology revolutionary discoveries are less frequent and the problems of synthesis are of paramount importance. In Classical archaeology many smaller problems of chronology and grouping remain to be solved, especially in Minoan, Geometric, Hellenistic, Roman art and in the arts of borderlands exposed to Classical culture. But the major problems are those of "research in depth", the closer analysis of visual and formal vocabulary (e.g. M. Bunim, *Perspective Ancient and Medieval*, 1940), correlation of the visual arts within various periods, relation of form and content, systematic analysis of quality, relation of individual, school, and period, and the interpretation of visual art in relation to the culture of the different periods (T. B. L. Webster, *Greek Literature and Art*, 1936. L. Curtis, *Griech. Kunst*, 1938, E. Buschor). The views of ancient writers on art must be re-interpreted (Panofsky, *Idea*, 1924, B. Schweitzer, *Xenokrates*, 1932. E. Pernice, *Handb. Archaeol.* I, 1938, 239 ff.) not as sources for factual information or as foundations for absolute aesthetic systems, but as valuable clues to the artistic aims of a period whose meaning can be clarified by comparison with the visual remains of their time. The value of Classical art for our cultural tradition (*Jour. Warburg Inst.*) and for our own time must be presented under the wide perspective of the creation of human values in the historical development of man (F. Taylor, *Pennsylvania Centennial*, 1941).

In Egyptian archaeology, an integrated interpretation of art is a recent development. H. Schäfer has elucidated some of the specifically Egyptian forms and concepts and his work has been continued and elaborated (G. Scharff, H. Frankfort, W. S. Smith, *Hist. of Egypt. Painting and Sculpture in the Old Kingdom*). Appraisals of the entire Egyptian art by "outsiders" (Curtius, Worringer, Evers, Krahmer, Kaschnitz, E. B. Smith) have lacked the authoritative knowledge of the historical background. Better understanding of stylistic criticism, continued investigation of specifically Egyptian forms, and a closer integration of historical factors (psychology, ideas) with aesthetic criticism will present great opportunities for the future historians of Egyptian art.

In Near Eastern archaeology, too, art has been interpreted historically rather than aesthetically, but much work in stylistic correlation has been done (Christian, Woolley,

Moortgat, H. Frankfort). The more formal type of stylistic interpretation has been employed by V. Mueller. W. Andrae has interpreted Near Eastern art as a symbolic art oriented toward the essence of existence, providing an impressive synthesis of historical and aesthetic elements. The premises of this theory may be challenged, but it will certainly form the basis for future discussion (*Handb. Archaeol.* I, 1938, 747 ff.). The additions of new artistic material in this field have been more extensive and important than in other ancient fields and much work remains to be done on the organization and interpretation of art on all levels of aesthetic criticism.

In early Prehistoric archaeology, the origin of art in its relation to the development of early man is a problem intimately connected with the fundamental investigation into the nature of artistic creation. There results a close connection with psychological studies of artistic activity (comparison with the art of children and modern primitives). Social and economic interpretation of art as well as racial theories have also figured prominently in modern interpretation of Prehistoric art (Menghin, *Weltgeschichte der Steinzeit*, H. Read, *Art and Society*, 1936, with references). —G.M.A.H.

archaic Greek. Greek sculpture from its beginning in the 6th cent. B.C. up to about 480 B.C., termed archaic, is characterized by certain conventions which were due partly to the sculptors' technical inexperience, partly to the influence of work from Asia Minor and Egypt, and partly to their own predilections. Unable to portray the human form realistically, novices in the mastery of their limited number of tools, they showed nevertheless a keen delight in elements of formal design, and fresh and buoyant vitality in their pioneer experiments in representing human and animal forms. In the Naxian Sphinx at Delphi (c. 550 B.C.) an Oriental type was invested with nervous vitality and decorative neatness typical of the Greek mentality. The frieze on the Siphnian Treasury at Delphi (525 B.C.) introduced popular Greek themes: the assembly of the gods, wars of gods against giants, battles around Troy, and represented them in scenes of vigorous action and clearly-defined patterns. The pediments of the temple of Aphaia at Aegina at the close of this period were organized on a basis of the human figure assuming sharp geometric designs, yet naturalistically enough so that there is no lack of vitality. It is this combination of human bodies rendered with increasing naturalism, yet still held firmly in the grip of formal design, which characterizes archaic Greek sculpture. The best examples in free sculpture are the votive statues of youths (*kouroi*) and girls (*korai*), reminiscent of Egyptian sculpture in their rigidity of pose, standing without any twist of the body to disturb the perfect median symmetry, with the youths' torso muscles geometrically patterned quite as definitely as the maidens' zig-zag bordered Ionic garments, yet winsome in their variety of facial expression and human charm. See HELLENIC ART. —W.R.A.

archaistic Greek. Following the overpowering variety of sensuous, realistic, and dramatic sculpture done by able technicians in Hellenistic times, there came a reaction in favor of the simplicity and formal design of the archaic work of 6th cent. Greece. In consequence Graeco-Roman sculptors attempted to imitate the archaic types, producing figures simple in pose, with severely stylized faces and drapery. The resemblance is only superficial; the drapery is mechanically similar, but is hard and dry, lacking the subtlety of finish which the early Greek sculptors lovingly worked out with their emery stone; the faces likewise are monotonously regular, without the fresh bloom of the prototypes. They are also betrayed by certain technical details unattained in the earlier work, notably the sophisticated cutting of the eyes and the corners of the mouth. The result must be described as arid antiquarianism. —W.R.A.

archisynagogos. See synagogues.

architectural control. See CIVIC PLANNING.

architectural design. The disposition of the elements of a building or structure in accordance with the principles of architecture, particularly with reference to beauty of form, proportion, and function. —O.M.S.

architectural drawing. The delineation or representation by lines of architectural forms.

architectural education. See NEW ATTITUDES FOR THE FUTURE OF ARCHITECTURE.

architectural form. Term first employed by the critic R. H. Wilenski to describe the sense of formal order and unity desirable in painting and sculpture. Similar to such essentially synonymous terms as 'plastic orchestration', 'significant form', and 'plastic form', used by Cheney, Bell, Barnes and others to describe the expressive values inherent in well-ordered and original design in painting or sculpture, most clearly illustrated by analogy with architecture or music, where, because of the nature of the media, ideological connotations of forms must be minimized. See R. H. Wilenski, *The Modern Movement in Art,* 1935.   —L.D.L.

architectural ornamentation. The adornment or embellishment of a structure with the aim of enhancing its appearance.

architectural rendering. An architectural rendering, strictly defined, refers to the general representation of a building as a designer envisions it and as he wishes it to appear to a spectator. Contrasted with the carefully ruled and measured plans and elevations which serve as practical guides for engineers and contractors, a rendering presents a building as a product of design, and employs all of the devices of painting, drawing, and perspective which appeal to the artistic sense. Various media have been employed, but the most popular are those which combine subtle or dramatic effects of chiaroscuro with minute detail. For the former effect, charcoal, water-color, and various crayons are serviceable; for the latter, pencil, pen, and etching needle are popular for their accuracy. Defined freely, architectural rendering would include the work of artists, archaeologists, and scholars, as well as designers, who have made notable representations of buildings which have dramatized the architectural art. Among them would certainly be included the work of Piranesi, Meryon, Turner, Canaletto, and Whistler in past times, and, more recently, the work of Eliel Saarinen, Frank Lloyd Wright, Hugh Ferris, John Taylor Arms, Bertram Goodhue, and Kenneth Conant. Without sacrificing accuracy, each of these has fostered the prime requisite of an architectural rendering — namely, that it emphasizes the beauty and impressiveness of a building as distinct from its utility and durability.   —P.C.B.

architectural sculpture. In the greatest periods of architecture and sculpture the two arts have worked in intimate association with each other, sculpture indicating the social purpose of buildings, helping to suggest functional relationships, and enriching the surface; architecture giving its sister art increased dignity and power by virtue of the alliance. Such cooperation is natural, for both arts use similar materials and organize them into three-dimensional designs. To be successful, however, it demands the closest sympathy, understanding and collaboration between architect and sculptor; and, like architecture, the sculpture must adapt itself to the demands of physical surroundings, function, and aesthetic construction.

This was achieved in Egypt, in the low reliefs at Sakkara and Abydos, and the incised reliefs of the Empire at Luxor and Karnak; with a fine sense of scale, effective filling of space, crisp contours and rhythmic grace, the sculptors decorated the walls of the mastabas and temples with scenes of the everyday life about them. Assyrian sculptors used severe geometric stylization, befitting the austere and smooth-walled buildings. Mayan sculptors also employed a geometric type of carving. In the Persian palace at Persepolis the rhythms were more flexible and gracious; and the sculptors of the Cambodian temples in Indo-China covered their walls and towers with a riotous melange of figures in the most intricate compositions, but in very low relief which enriches rather than detracts from the monumental mass of the temples. Never has the relationship been more fruitful than in 5th cent. B.C. Greece; there architecture and sculpture united in achieving harmonious composition, logical arrangement of space, and coordinating rhythm. Later, in the Hellenistic period, the sculptors demanded too great attention for their work, which, dealing with melodramatic themes, protruded in high relief from the buildings. This error was avoided in Romanesque churches and early Gothic cathedrals, in which the relief was kept low and well adapted to the surface of the buildings; in later Gothic buildings, when the architectural surface became broken up into strong lights and shadows, the sculpture became increasingly assertive, sometimes detracting from the structural mass. Renaissance and later European sculptural decoration followed for the most part the Hellenic or Hellenistic tradition. In modern times a new type of building for a machine age emphasizes structural asceticism and stripped surfaces, with ornament reduced to a minimum. Architectural sculpture has therefore been relegated chiefly to churches which are adaptations of Romanesque, Gothic or classical types, or public buildings which follow classical patterns. But some sculptors are now beginning to work hand in hand with architects of the new order, creating sculpture in incised or low relief, sometimes geometric in style, more often of the human figure slightly stylized as in the archaic Greek and

Gothic, which harmonizes with geometric modern buildings. Among such sculptors have been Bourdelle and the Martel brothers in France, Franz Metzner in Austria, Ivan Mestrovic in Yugoslavia, Josef Wackerle and Hans Panzer in Germany, Eric Gill and Jacob Epstein in England, and Lee Lawrie, Alfonzo Iannelli, Rene Chambellan and Gaston Lachaise in America. An outstanding example of the collaboration of modern architects and sculptors may be seen in the State Capitol at Lincoln, Nebraska.　　　　　—W.R.A.

architectural stage. See MODERN STAGE-SETTING.

ARCHITECTURE (L., *architecture,* the act of building; Gr., *archi,* chief and *tecton,* artificer—hence, a masterwork). From the derivation of the term it is evident that the ancient conception of architecture was a kind of super-craftsmanship, and indeed until the close of the Middle Ages, it may be considered as an adaptation of materials to use, partly through the operation of tradition and partly through the gradual expansion of structural processes. The invariable accompaniment of ornamental embellishment was symbolic, commemorative or dialectic in character and formed an inseparable complement to the structural masses.

Throughout this long period all styles revolved about the fundamental problem of covering a unit of space. Two universal methods prevail: (a) the **trabeated system,** or post and lintel construction, embracing the ancient Egyptian, Minoan, Persian, Greek and recurring in the reinforced concrete, truss and steel skeleton construction of our day; (b) **the arcuated system,** including the derivatives of the arch, e.g., the various types of vault and dome construction which constitute the dominant units of the Roman, Byzantine, Romanesque and Gothic styles.

Initially the choice of one or the other of these methods was a consequence of the presence or absence of stone. In Egypt, Crete and Greece the trabeated system was adopted without compromise. In Mesopotamia, where stone was scarce, it was necessary to evolve a method of spanning voids by combining small units of perishable sun-dried brick into arches and barrel vaults. The Egyptians, while conversant with both methods, specifically isolated them according to use or material. Secular architecture was arcuated in brick; religious and mortuary architecture with negligible exceptions was executed in stone and trabeated.

The Greeks also were familiar with both systems, but definitely rejected the arch and vault in favor of the static majesty and simplicity of the column and lintel.

To the Romans is due the discovery of the structural possibilities in increased spans of the arcuated system when executed in concrete. In their hands, spans of 60 feet were attained by the intersection of barrel vaults and of 140 feet by the use of the dome. Nevertheless, inasmuch as these were executed in concrete, once the material had set the structure became static or monolithic, that is, the loads were vertical and vaults ultimately constituted little more than vast lintels in vaulted form.

It remained for the Middle Ages, first in the dome on pendentives of the Byzantine builders, so nobly exemplified in the Church of Hagia Sophia and eight centuries later in the balanced skeleton construction of the Gothic Cathedrals, to demonstrate the extraordinary possibilities of the arcuated system.

A second broad classification may be made, less noticed than the first but of far-reaching consequences, i.e., a differentiation based upon the manner of assembling walls. In this again, there are two types under which practically all styles may be grouped.

In countries where stone was abundant, such as Egypt, Greece, Syria and France, we find the wall built throughout of one material which is left in evidence both on the outside and inside of the structure, q.v., the Cathedrals, the Greek Temples. This may be broadly classified as **ashlar architecture.**

In countries such as Mesopotamia and Persia where the sun-dried brick which formed the heart of the wall was too perishable to leave exposed, it was customary to protect it by a coating of ceramic tile, or within, by decorative slabs of carved alabaster. In like manner, the Romans and Italians throughout their history habitually covered their walls of brick or concrete with slabs of varicolored marble or limestone or sheathed them in hard plaster (stucco duro). This is what is known as **veneered** or **revetted architecture.**

The Renaissance is, as its name signifies, usually considered as a rebirth of Classic forms. It had its origin in Italy and from there radiated throughout Europe. The French Renaissance is usually considered as a derivative of the Italian which superficially is the case. A profound difference, however, resulting from the foregoing distinction in materials, underlies the two, a difference which has powerfully affected our interpretive methods.

The **revetted system,** so obvious in the

Italian architecture, led to a differentiation in idea as well as in material, of the wall surface from its substance; and inferentially, a like distinction between the outer and inner faces and their functional relation. To the Italian, the wall was intended to mask the spatial areas behind it. In France, on the contrary, where limestone construction prevailed, the content of the wall was one with its surfaces and inferentially, the wall was integrated with the contained areas. Out of this habitual association evolved the basic theory of the French Renaissance, that of articulation of plan with function and its scrupulous expression in facade. The contemporary so-called "International" style (q.v.) introduces a third interpretation which leans rather to the Italian conception than it does to the French, but offers an interesting variant to both in this respect that it omits the wall as a mass and preserves the veneer. The building becomes fluid space within a skeleton of verticals of steel or concrete sustaining the slabs of the floors and roof and the walls become merely a protective shell around the whole.

In addition to these structural concepts, architecture embodies many elements, forces and traditions in which climate, materials, social and economic conditions, as well as geographic and ethnological influences play their part.

For the past four centuries its freedom has been hampered by the intrusion of a variety of doctrinal forms and dogmatic adherence to types. The revolutionary tendencies of our day are to be interpreted partly as a revulsion against the constriction of established types, partly as the effort to find a contemporary interpretation consistent with the technological character of modern life. It is to be regarded as in a state of fermentation from which a new and vital expression may be anticipated. In this, the inclusion of mass housing and the correlation of architecture to city and regional planning is to be noted.   —L.H.

architrave. The lintel or horizontal beam, lowest member of the entablature in the classic orders; a horizontal beam resting across two upright columns.

archivolt. An ornamental moulding following the outer curve of the voussoirs or wedge-shaped blocks forming an arch.

archlute, archilute. See MUSICAL INSTRUMENTS.

arcosolium. Cell in a Roman catacomb; arched.

arcuated. Curved like a bow. See ARCHITECTURE.

Ares (L., *Mars*). The Greek and Roman god of war, not a very popular figure in either classical literature or art. The most famous statues of him represent him clad in armor and usually seated in a nonchalant pose, as on the Parthenon frieze and in the Ludovisi Ares. In postclassical sculpture he has been represented by Guillaume Coustou II, Canova, Thorvaldsen and Dannecker. Iannelli's Mars on the Adler Planetarium, Chicago, realizes better than most of these the sterner quality of the god of war.   —W.R.A.

argent. *Her.* Silver.

Argentine tango. See tango.

argillite carvings. See CANADA, ART OF.

Argos, school of. Famous for its athletic tradition and canon of masculine proportions was the Argive School of Greek sculpture. The earliest examples are the 6th cent. B.C. twin kouroi at Delphi, signed by Polymedes (or Agamedes); these figures are of robust youths stiffly standing in a symmetrically frontal position. The greatest Argive sculptor was Polyclitus (fl. 450-420 B.C.), whose bronze statues of athletes were made according to his system of ideal proportions known as the Canon. Judged by Roman copies of his Doryphorus, this was a stocky, squarely-built type, measuring approximately the same in length of lower leg, thigh, and from the navel to the ear, and with a head about one-seventh of the total height. Although his figures were freely poised in an attitude suggesting movement, his modeling was rather austere and emphasized the formal character of the human body. In statues of youths he softened the planes of the body and the expression of the face, and worked out a lovely pattern of tousled hair. These figures inspired many later sculptors, among them the artist of the well-known Idolino in Florence. Polyclitus also made the ivory and gold cult statue of Hera for her temple near Argos. Argive sculpture in the 4th cent. B.C. followed the Polyclitan tradition, but introduced greater variety and charm; notable among products of the school were statues of boys scraping themselves, of which a bronze from Ephesus is probably a copy.   —W.R.A.

aria, aria da capa, aria parlante. See OPERA.

Ariadne. The Cretan princess who made it possible for Theseus to slay the Minotaur and escape from the Labyrinth. On his way back to Athens he deserted her on the island of Naxos, where she was comforted by Dionysus. This scene is best known in art by the paintings of Titian and Tintoretto, representing Dionysus blithely coming to console her. —W.R.A.

arioso. (1) Short aria. (2) A portion of melody ending a recitative (see OPERA). (3) A cantabile in instrumental music.

Aristion, stele of. A stele in the National Museum, Athens, dating about 510 B.C. It represents a warrior standing in profile. Archaic in rigid pose and patterned detail, it has the crispness and clarity of design characteristic of its period. Traces of the original color remain: red on the background and blue on the cuirass. —W.R.A.

Aristotelian form. See form: a philosophical analysis.

Arita yaki (Jap.). Ceramic ware made in Hizen province.

armarium. See ambry.

armature. A skeleton or framework upon which sculpture may be modeled; in small works it is usually made of stiff wire; for heavy pieces iron pipe, wire mesh, etc., are used. —R.M.

Armenian dragon-carpets. See ISLAMIC ART.

armes parlantes. See HERALDRY.

armorial bearings. See HERALDRY.

armorial-pictorial. See ex libris.

Armory Show. See POST-REVOLUTIONARY PAINTING AND SCULPTURE IN THE U.S.A.

army drum. See MUSICAL INSTRUMENTS.

aron hakodesch. See synagogues.

around the corner room. See MESOPOTAMIAN ART.

arpeggio. *Mus.* A broken chord, in harp style.

Arretine ceramics. A distinctive creation of Roman potters, Arretine ware was made of fine red clay and decorated with designs in low relief stamped on the outside and covered with red glaze. For this purpose molds were used in which the design had been cut. The shapes of the bowls were graceful, and the designs of delicate figures were nicely spaced. See CERAMICS II. —W.R.A.

arriccio (It.). The rough first coat of plastering in fresco painting.

arris. The sharp ridge formed by the meeting of two surfaces, as the edge between two flutes of a Doric shaft.

ars antiqua. See MEDIEVAL MUSIC.

ars mensurabilis. See MEDIEVAL MUSIC.

ars nova. See MEDIEVAL MUSIC.

art. (1) "Art" designates any activity that is at once spontaneous and controlled. In this general sense of the term, Art is distinguished from and contrasted with the processes of nature: Art is any intelligent method by which nature is controlled. The history of art, in this abstract sense of 'Art' would be the history of human ingenuity and contrivance; it would cover the range of human enterprise, in handicrafts and architecture, industry and medicine, government and law, religion and education. Art is controlled ingenuity that is aware of its objective. An art may be merely accidental in its inception; as was the Chinamen's discovery of how to roast pig. Yet unless a fortuitous event arouses interest in us, so that the conditions of its repetition are sought out and understood in practise, any such happening remains no more than a fortuitous event. An art arises whenever the conditions of a process are understood and made stable by practise.

(2) In aesthetics and in social theory, a distinction is usually drawn between the fine and the useful arts. The fine arts serve no ulterior purpose: their products are valued in and for themselves. The useful arts serve an ulterior purpose lying beyond those artefacts themselves. The artefacts of the fine arts are end-values, those of the useful arts are means to ends. A painting in egg-tempera is valued in and for itself: a sable hair brush is valued as a means to the end of a painting in egg-tempera. The useful or servile arts comprise all forms of instrumental manufacture, ranging from the relatively simple handicrafts to the highest complex technologies and techniques of modern industry. Many artefacts of the useful arts such as shipbuilding, are at once valuable as means to ulterior ends, and

delightful in and by themselves. And many artefacts of the fine arts are at once beautiful, or valued in and for themselves, and also useful; as is, for example, a Greek vase.

(3) There is no Art *as such*. There are only arts *such as* the fine art of painting, the useful art of rug-weaving, the fine art of music, the useful art of engineering. The connotation of the term art in any case of its use will derive from a description of the spontaneous and controlled activities the term Art is then used to designate. That description will describe the respects in which the art in question is spontaneous in energy and controlled in practise. Like any other abstract noun or adjective (such as "spontaneous" or "controlled") : "Art as such" is a term verbal whose connotation derives from its context. See classification of the arts.   —R.W.C.

art activities, school. Activities of a creative or appreciational sort dealing with art expression, carried on with or without teacher direction, and intended to afford emotional release and to offer training in the use and appreciation of art mediums. Whitford and Winslow in *Dictionary of Education.*

art administration. Management of the art education program in a school or community educational system. Whitford and Winslow in *Dictionary of Education.*

art appreciation. The effort to perceive vividly the content and quality of works of fine art, and to evaluate these works comparatively or in terms of an abstract standard.—D.W.G.

art as expression, as imagination, as imitation, as language. See AESTHETICS.

art commission. See CIVIC PLANNING.

art criticism. This term is used in a number of senses, some of which overlap and some of which are quite distinct from one another. A few of the more common or important senses are here explained:

(1) The commonest, and for many the fundamental, meaning of "art criticism" is a judgment of the aesthetic value of a work of art in accordance with some standard or criterion of aesthetic value or in accordance with some method of reaching an aesthetic evaluation. There are as many types of art criticism in this sense as there are proposed standards of aesthetic criticism or methods of aesthetic evaluation. These range from practical standards of technique in schools of art practice, through conceptions of what consti-

tutes the classics in an art, or conceptions of what constitute the high points or touchstones of aesthetic achievement, to standards philosophically supported or argued for on either *a priori* or empirical grounds. At the one extreme is the art-school teacher or master artist who is in possession of a set of rules of technique developed out of his personal experience or inherited from his own teachers, which he assumes without much reflection are well grounded because of the experience behind them. At the other extreme is the philosopher intent upon the definition and validation of aesthetic criteria, giving careful consideration to the grounds for accepting criteria of criticism but often lacking in the experience to give these detailed application. It is one of the problems of aesthetics to assay these proposed aesthetic criteria, and to attempt to distinguish those which are justifiable from those which are not. A history of aesthetics is essentially the narrative of this undertaking for as long as men have been interested in this problem.

(2) In another sense, art criticism is equated with the personal expression of a writer's appreciation or reaction to a work of art, supposedly without any standards of judgment. This is often called **impressionistic** or **expressionistic criticism.** It amounts to a complete skepticism regarding the possibility of establishing justifiable standards of criticism and it regards itself as frank and disillusioned in recognizing that writings about works of art are simply the statements of impressions and are not authoritative in any sense at all.

(3) In a third sense, art criticism is sometimes equated with the historical study of works of art especially where stress is laid upon their social significance in the culture of an epoch. In criticism of this sort the emphasis is upon scholarship and insight into distinctive traits of style and into art trends.

(4) A fourth sense of art criticism, overlapping some of the previous ones, identifies it with a study of the character and total work of individual artists. This permits of a wide range of approach from a methodical psychological or psychoanalytical study of the artist to an intuitive grasp and reconstruction of his personality. There may or may not be some suggestion of an ethical or aesthetic criterion for judging the greatness of a personality.

(5) In a fifth sense, art criticism is occasionally identified with expertizing. The aim here is to reach a judgment of the genuineness of a work of art, or, if the work has a complex authorship, or has been tampered with

in various ways, to unravel what happened to it and describe in detail how it reached its present state.

In the history of criticism there has been some rather unrewarding debate as to whether certain of these meanings were not the "real" meaning of the word. There seems to be no profitable way of controlling usage. What one can control, however, is the clarity of one's own distinctions in one's own uses of a word. Though the term, "art criticism" is ambiguous, a careful writer can employ the various senses of "art criticism" without ever being ambiguous, and can reserve his efforts to examining the degree of achievement under each one of these uses of the term. —S.C.P.

ART EDUCATION has two fundamental aspects, namely, subject matter and educative processes. Traditionally, its subject matter would be the so-called arts of design, painting, drawing, architecture and sculpture; its educative process would be described as academic. Modern art education has a much larger meaning. In its broadest sense, considering the first aspect, it is that area of education in which all achievements in the visual arts made by man in the past and all opportunities for continued art activity and cultural development through it at the present are so related for presentation and study as to provide students at all ages in school and out with a basic understanding of the place of art in modern life and with an experimental basis for individual expression and understanding in all media. In this statement the visual arts likewise are given the widest meaning. They include not only the traditional subjects, as has been noted, painting, drawing, architecture and sculpture, but as well crafts, decorative arts, and all the materials of nature and industry which can be utilized for individual or collective art expression.

The main aims, therefore, of art education, thus conceived are these:

(1) To give each individual a basis for making art judgments in the selection of clothing, practical everyday articles for his home, in planting and arranging a garden, etc.

(2) To develop a citizen who can share both the responsibilities and satisfactions involved in fine community and city planning, (public buildings, parks, highways, etc.) and who would understand that vital art is profoundly social.

(3) To make it possible for a layman to be sensitive and able to evaluate various works of art, historic and contemporary, to have an interest in critical discussion about these and, in general, to look upon the whole realm of visual arts as a source of unending curiosity, a stimulation for study, larger understanding and enjoyment. Such a person would be in a position to have an open-mindedness toward the arts of all peoples, as Chinese art of today or the art of the primitive peoples of Africa.

(4) To discover and develop artists, those who have been endowed with deep feeling and imaginative minds so that they can create new things in two or three dimensional forms, depending upon the availability of materials in terms of functions or use and expression of individual feeling.

(5) To develop teachers in the visual arts who would be creative in some medium and who would be motivated in guidance and instruction by a philosophy of this larger conception of art education.

Art education as an educative process has been generally characterized by two practices. One of these may be described as academic. Variously used as "academic" has been, historically it covered, first, the training of artists alone and, second, it was a well defined, most often dogmatic, method of instruction. Moreover, academic art education was, and in the main still is, interested in two dimensional work, painting and drawing; sculpture three dimensional, was of course included. The result of this was "studio art" and academies of art. Most of this was in the professional field.

Over one hundred years ago, with the rise of public schools, however, academic art education was introduced into the curriculum of these. Here again the emphasis as a method of instruction was placed on routine exercises, imitation, representation and technical proficiency or skills. It was aimed at the gifted student rather than all students. Academic art teachers made and make such instruction a communication of knowledge, hard-and-fast principles and information rather than a problem of guidance for individual growth. The result was and still is wherever the practice obtains, stereotyped, dull and unimaginative art.

Technical proficiency, the skill "to draw accurately" to execute work according to "established formulas," was regarded as a great virtue, not only in America but throughout the western world, especially where industrialism had developed. Even in 1944 many art schools, chiefly commercial art schools, and many art teachers in public schools, stress and insist upon this.

Another development of the philosophy and practice of academic art education was the art historian, who, especially previous to the present generation, most often held that the way to understand and enjoy art was mainly, if not solely, through scholarship and literary criticism. Academicians and historians of this sort worshipped the Old Masters and not infrequently despised contemporary developments or dismissed them as inconsequential.

A second educative process in art education is perhaps best designated as "Progressive Art Education." This is a 20th century development in the main, having for its pioneers, the modern artists in the professional field and like Cizek of Vienna and Dow of New York in public and private schools. The emphasis here is that art education, as the late Dean Melvin S. Haggerty most aptly phrased it, is "a way of life," meaning by that, all experiences which are involved in the transformation and perception of materials and media should be enjoyed and understood as a part of total living and not esoteric experiences which make for "art for art's sake."

Viewed as an educative process, then, progressive art education holds, first, that art experiences and expression are normal to and needed by all individuals; second, that the whole visual and contactual world, the materials of nature and products of industry, is its subject matter, not only canvas and colors paper and crayons, stone or wood and tools, etc.; and third, it is the growth of the individual with respect to his needs and the appropriate use of available materials that is vitally important, not the accuracy of representational drawings, nor great skill in techniques. Here too, the teacher guides the student rather than imparts information. The educational philosophy is to achieve the integrated development of the whole personality and, as a result, to make possible the realization of the educational aims stated above.

Another aspect of art education today is the development of a program of experimental research. Instead of accepting without question traditional practices and methods, art educators today have begun and completed many experimental studies in instructional procedures and in the psychology of art expression. Notable work has been done by individual Germans and Austrians and in the Bauhaus School of Europe previous to the Second World War and in America by such men as John Dewey, Thomas Munro, Melvin S. Haggerty, Ray Faulkner and others in the Owatonna Art Project, Norman C. Meier,

Lydia B. Powell, Betty Lark Horovitz and many others. A large body of information has been gathered, the utilization of which has made possible more effective teaching. There is yet much to be done in this field.

Art education, as a 20th century concept, is concerned with the entire world of visual arts and has as its chief aim the development of all individuals who will not only understand, create in or enjoy the arts but who also will understand that expression in these media is the expression of insights and sensitivities of others to the world in which they live.
—C.M.

Artemis (L., *Diana*). The sister of Apollo, virgin huntress and protector of maidens and matrons, moon goddess. Her attributes were the bow, deer, hound, and crescent moon. In art she has usually been represented as a sturdy, athletic young woman engaged in the hunt; as such she appears in Greek and Roman sculpture, and later sculptors, including Goujon, Houdon, Falguière, St. Gaudens, Anna Huntington, Milles and Manship followed this tradition. Correggio and Boucher painted pictures of her.   —W.R.A.

artemisia. See SYMBOLISM IN FAR EASTERN ART.

arterial street, highway, etc. See CIVIC PLANNING.

art exhibition. A display of two- or three-dimensional art products, or of reproductions of them, whether in the form of a showcase display, a wall display, or a demonstration Syn. *art exhibit.* Whitford and Winslow in *Dictionary of Education.*

art expression. Emotional release through art; the result of one's feelings and thoughts made manifest in a work of art. Whitford and Winslow in *Dictionary of Education.*

art, fine and industrial. A designation used for the organization of the study of art in public elementary and secondary schools, according to which both pure and applied arts are studied from the point of view of common elements; may include the study of painting, sculpture, arcitecture, commercial art, industrial design, and other phases. Whitford and Winslow in *Dictionary of Education.*

art for art's sake. Art executed primarily to appeal to aesthetic sensibilities, through exploitation of material, form, and expression, for their own sakes. Contrasts with *art for* *propaganda* (q.v.). The term may be applied to all art whose first purpose is to give aesthetic pleasure rather than to persuade to some conviction or course of action.

While in practice most works of historic art have combined the two purposes in a single aim, or at least have accomplished both objectives without conflict, such artists as Whistler, Inness, Cezanne, Picasso, Maillol, and Marin, and the art of the first third of the 20th cent. in general as contrasted with the art of Egypt or the Middle Ages, may be said to represent rather the doctrine of "art for art's sake" than "art for propaganda". Similarly, modern critics of the formal aspects of art, like Clive Bell, Roger Fry, Walter Pater, R. H. Wilenski, and Sheldon Cheney, contrast with such 18th and 19th cent. ideological writers as Diderot, Tolstoy, and Ruskin on this issue.   —L.D.L.

art for goods. See SCANDINAVIAN ART.

art form. (1) An expression of art, such as a picture, a statue, a poem, or a play; (2) a technique of art expression; thus etching and blank verse are both *art forms;* (3) the entire formation of a work of art, including consideration of design, medium, and construction. See form. Whitford and Winslow in *Dictionary of Education.*

art for propaganda. Ideological art, executed primarily to persuade the spectator in favor of a literary idea, a philosophical opinion a religious conviction, a political, social or economic doctrine, or any specific or general course of action. The term is not applied unless the aesthetic merit of the work was, in the mind of the artist, clearly a secondary consideration as contrasted with the propaganda value. Contrasts with 'art for art's sake' (q.v.), but most works of art throughout history have been neither clearly 'art for art's sake' nor 'art for propaganda'. The strongest contrasts exist today in the aesthetic approach of the French artists from the impressionists to the present on the one hand, and the ideological prejudices of the nationally controlled arts of Nazi Germany on the other.—L.D.L.

art guidance. (1) Provision for educational and vocational experience through observation of and participation in various phases of art; (2) direction of student interest into art, or into active participation in art activities. Whitford and Winslow in *Dictionary of Education.*

art history. See history of art.

articulation. *Mus.* Devices of composition aiming at clarity of design; purposeful arrangement of musical elements according to the functions which they have to fulfill in the context, esp. with a view to properly balancing their metrical weights; phrase construction.
—E.K.

art impulse. The urge to create or to appreciate art. Whitford and Winslow in *Dictionary of Education.*

art industry. An industry in which materials are transformed with the end in view of producing an art product; as for example: textiles, costumes jewelry, silverware, furniture, ceramics, printing. Whitford and Winslow in *Dictionary of Education.*

art interpretation. A specialized study of art objects with a view to developing habits of good taste and critical judgment in artistic matters. Whitford and Winslow in *Dictionary of Education.*

artisan. A person skilled in the techniques of an art or mechanical pursuit, but whose work does not demand creation, invention, or originality; dist. f. *artist.* (Thus, the sculptor, who makes a model for a statue in clay, is an *artist;* the stonecutter, who reproduces the clay model in marble, is an *artisan.*) Whitford and Winslow in *Dictionary of Education.*

artist. A person skilled in the practice of an art in which creative activity is dependent upon aesthetic judgment, imagination, and originality. (Different types of artists are architects, sculptors, painters, draftsmen, interior decorators, cartoonists, designers, and commercial artists.) Whitford and Winslow in *Dictionary of Education.*

artistic ability, art ability. Special aptitude or native talent and developed skill in the creative arts, as applied to drawing, painting, design, modeling, and other forms of art expression. See art tests. Whitford and Winslow in *Dictionary of Education.*

artistic ability of children. See CHILDREN'S ART.

artistic form. See form: a philosophical analysis.

artistic inspiration. See inspiration.

artistic myth. See myth.

artistic stimulation. See inspiration.

ARTIST, PSYCHOLOGY OF THE. In accord with all other human psychological phenomena, art represents an interaction of the person with an object (or other person). In most human behavior two aspects can be distinguished, a locomotion and a method of locomotion. It is his attention to the latter aspect which seems to distinguish the artist from the non-artist. In more commonly used terms, the artist is expressive and sets a satisfying mode of expression as his goal—no matter what other goals may move him.

By the classification the *psychology of the artist,* we mean that the artist, rather than the art object, forms the focus of our analysis. It would be futile to assume that by this emphasis we can remove from consideration the art object, or for that matter, any other factors in the situation. To avoid sterility, analysis must proceed from and never be far removed from the interactional setting from which it has been abstracted. Thus, the understanding of the psychology of the artist is furthered by a consideration of the significance of his artistic behavior—the art products—in his life history. Mursell expresses this view when he says, "The art of music is a creation of the mind of man. All its characteristics and organizing principles depend upon the action of the mind. All its effects upon us when we listen to it, all that we do when we perform it or create it, are determined by the laws of the mind.

All persons exhibit artistic behavior at some time, i.e., partake in interactions in which the locomotion is an end in itself. However, the term artist is used to describe individuals who habitually exhibit artistic behavior because it forms a persistent part of their life histories. A doorman may derive pleasure from opening a door with especial flourish and rhythm or an executive may delight in signing his name with graceful flowing strokes, but these are not the usual referents of the word artist. In social psychological and sociological terms, the word artist refers to specific sets of interactions involving specific types of objects and motives. Though the point of demarcation may be blurred, such behaviors as those involving music, theatre, various manipulations of visual stimuli, e.g., painting, sculpture, and language are referred to as artistic. Individuals who habitually participate in these behaviors to produce art objects are called artists. The behavior of these individuals is not dependent upon a different set of principles than the artistic behavior of non-artists. Indeed, each

may contribute to a better understanding of the other.

This, then, is our focus in the psychology of the artist. We are concerned with the artist and his life history as distinguished from other individuals. Also, we are concerned with determining the degree to which his present behavior patterns, other than the formal artistic ones, differ from those of other individuals. Though we are not concerned with applying some standard of value to his art products, we are concerned with comparing his interactions with art objects to those of non-artists. In other words, we attempt to determine whether the artist can be distinguished from the non-artist in any other terms than the fact that he habitually produces some type of art object. Our emphasis is upon what the artist does which includes what he says he does. Earlier in this field of inquiry, research has been largely confined to studies of autobiographies. This is certainly an important source of data, but the direct observation and analysis of the artist's behavior should not be neglected. In recent years the latter methods have received more attention.

In analyzing his behavior, the various roles of the artist should be considered. First and foremost, the artist is a member of a social group or one might say a member of a number of social groups. His special social group is the one defined by the artistic culture. The nature of this social group, its instituted ways of behaving are a rich source of data for both social psychologist and sociologist. In this connection would be included studies to determine the degree to which the "artistic personality" is defined by artistic group instituted behaviors and the degree to which these behaviors are idiosyncratic. Other similar problems for investigation would be a comparison of the degrees of idiosyncracy in the behavior of artists and non-artists, in the behavior of artists of one medium and another. Of great interest is the question of how the goals of the artist are influenced by his interactions with the other members of the artistic social group.

The artist plays roles in other cultural subgroups which are contained in our society. He has attitudes toward social and political questions. He has ways of approaching the group problems. Analysis of the artist is concerned with describing his modes of action in these social contexts. It concerns the questions of whether his solutions to social problems are different from non-artists; whether his modes of attack are different. It is also concerned with the way in which the goals related to these social interactions are reflected in his goals as an artist. In essence, the problem has two statements: 1. Can the artist be recognized in his larger social context? 2. Can the larger social context be recognized in the artist?

Obviously, the most important single role of the artist is that of a creator. This is his most specific role in that it is most quickly recognized. However, it is also a role which is not easily analyzed. For example, take the process of creation. Much of the behavior involved is implicit and therefore not easily accessible to the outside observer. At the same time, the demands of the creative process leave little opportunity for self-analysis. What self-analysis and observation there is comes as a reconstruction of the process after the fact. As such it is subject to the influence of social or personal stereotypes, meaning that the artist may report what he *thinks an* artist does rather than what he recalls that *he* did. Such a report is a valuable datum, but is not an evidence of what the artist did in the creative process. Other types of evidence that are available are preliminary sketches of final paintings, rough drafts of preliminary manuscripts of musical works and the like. As interim stations in the progress toward the final object, these data are of value only in so far as they lead to reconstruction of the creative behavior pattern.

Through observation it is possible to follow the work habits of the artist to gain some understanding of the specific stimulations to creative activity. There is a considerable body of dogma as to how the artist works. Some are inclined to believe that, once engulfed in the creative process, the artist must work until released. But others will claim that the artist operates in much the same fashion as any other worker of his level of complexity, following a fairly fixed routine. Observation can reveal the degree to which any description as to work habits can be generalized for artists exclusively.

Of special interest to the personnel psychologist is the question of what physiological functions and behavioral experiences make the artist able to perform his particular type of creative activities. It seems certain that a color blind individual will not become a painter, but what mechanical and motor skills must he possess; what verbal intellectual skills? Will experiences that develop certain ways of viewing his environment and certain ways of expressing his reactions exert a greater influence than organic and physio-

logical characteristics? These are the questions the personnel psychologist must answer to be of aid to the individual trying to come to a decision about a professional career. The acceptance of his work will be the final criterion for the professional artist, but it is expensive to delay one's occupational decision that long.

Closely linked with his role as a creator is the artist's role as an appreciator. Creation and appreciation can be viewed as Siamese twin processes, organically related but not congruent. As a creator, the artist is interacting with other objects to produce an expression of a feeling. In appreciation, he is interacting with an expression of a feeling. In so far as he recognizes and accepts the expressions contained in the artistic work, he reacts favorably to the art object.

There is much to be gained in studying the artist as an appreciator. From a study of the sensitivity of his reactions, it is possible to gain greater insight into his reactions as a creator. In studying the sensitivity of artists one would attempt to test many of the common claims of artists. For example, it is common for painters and sculptors to assert that they can tell the difference between original creative works and reproductive paintings of these works or between original oils and collotype reproductions, even when the factor of difference in reflective surfaces is ruled out. Musicians claim to be able to discriminate the playing of one symphony orchestra from another, the interpretations of one conductor from another, or the playing of one virtuoso from another. That some of these discriminations can be made is an undoubted fact. Whether all of them can be made is a topic for experimental inquiry. In such experiments it would be valuable to study differences in sensitivities of artists as related to their particular phases of operation in their media. For example, how would the commercial artist compare with the so-called fine artist, the purely instrumental musician with the composer, the poet with the novelist, etc. Comparisons of the sensitivities of artists and non-artists would also be in order.

In studying the artist as an appreciator, we are interested in the aspects of the art object to which he reacts. One kind of evidence on this question would be to ask a group of artists after having viewed a painting for the first time, to then retire to their studios and attempt to reproduce the painting. One can assume that those aspects of the painting that do not appear in the reproduction are aspects which had little effect upon the artist's reactions to the painting. From his handling of the subject it would be possible to develop ideas as to his modes of reaction in the creative processes. In one case in the writer's experience, this was done with art students. The results, which showed that one part of the group approached the reproduction in a highly enumerative way, that others emphasized certain relations to the exclusion of details and that still others made their reproductions into expanded close-ups of the most striking part of the original, were all very revealing to the instructor.

Another phase of observation of the artist as an appreciator is the gathering of evidence of the feelings and meanings derived from his interaction with the art objects. Presumably creation and appreciation are emotional experiences. The appreciative behavior of artists and non-artists can be analyzed to find some indices of the emotional reactions. Through mechanical devices it is possible to record physiological changes that might be linked to emotional reactions, but the use of such devices may introduce so much artificiality into the observations that their value would be destroyed.

It is somewhat easier to study the meanings of art objects for artists. Various art media are used to convey meanings to people. Advertising and propaganda are very dependent upon the assumption that certain types of expression convey meanings common to large numbers of people. In Russia, musicians are censured when their works reflect "bourgeois or counter-revolutionary sentiments." Two questions may be stated: 1. What does the artist's production mean to other artists? 2. What does the artist's production mean to non-artists? It is obvious that the different media can be distinguished in the degree to which they express ideas and to which they are purely expressive of feelings.

In summary, our discussion has delineated the areas of interest within the artist-object interactional matrix which are a part of the *psychology of the artist*. We have pointed out that the *psychology of the artist* is concerned with the artist in relation to his social contexts. It is concerned with describing the ways in which the artist can be differentiated from his fellow artists and from non-artists. Also, it is concerned with describing the ways in which the artist is like his fellow artists and like non-artists. See *Art in American Life and Education*, Fortieth Yearbook of the National Society for the Study of Education, 1941; Hevner, K., "Aesthetics", Chap. XXI in *Fields*

of Psychology, J. P. Guilford, ed., 1940; Meier, N. C., *Art in Human Affairs*, New York, 1942; Mursell, J. L., *The Psychology of Music*, 1937.   —E.S.B.

artist workman. See artisan.

art motivation. (1) The incentive or vitalizing drive that leads to art activity; (2) the stimulation of other school activity through contact with art experiences. Whitford and Winslow in *Dictionary of Education*.

art museum, school. A place set aside for the preservation and display of works of art for the purpose of appreciative recreation and education. Whitford and Winslow in *Dictionary of Education*.

art nouveau. Name given to a new style in art flourishing between 1890 and 1905, in France, Belgium, Germany, Austria, and sporadically in England, Spain, Holland, Italy and the U.S.A. The name is accidental, coming from the fact that the art dealer, S. Bing, who carried examples of the work, called his gallery, "Art Nouveau" (opened 1895-96). The style was variously named: in France, "modern style," "Style—1900," (E. de Goncourt called it "Yachting style"), in Germany "Jugendstil" (q.v.) (from the contemporary magazine, *Jugend*), in Italy, "Stile Liberty" (from the English store of that name carrying textiles, jewelry and small decorative arts). In Belgium, the art is associated with a group called *Les XXs*, later *La Libre Esthetique*, in Vienna with the *Sezessionists*. It found its expression in architecture, sculpture, painting, the graphic arts, furniture, wall paper, stained glass, textiles, glass, silver and other metals, ceramics, and jewelry. Its leaders aimed to break with old traditions and to create a new style. Their watchwords were spontaneity, naturalism, simplicity, good craftsmanship. Specifically they urged the use of new materials, cement, iron, steel, and glass, and frank expression in construction. One of its leaders, Henry van de Velde (Belgian) said "we need a logical structure of products, uncompromising logic in the use of materials, proud and frank exhibition of working processes." That forms like those of Art Nouveau evolved out of such aims as these is due to several factors. In spite of voices like van de Velde's there was during these years a general confusion and lack of confidence in the face of the machine. Furthermore, Japanese art was a compelling force (see Japonism). Again, both social and political factors, contributed their influence.

The style appeared fully fledged with the architecture of the Belgian Victor Horta in 1893, and had from its first appearance outstanding and unique characteristics in the contours of its forms, its line, and decorative details. It turned to nature, in her gentlest aspects, and sought inspiration from a definite and restricted group of natural forms: forms immature, but growing, whose functional structure was now familiar to the eye through microscopic analysis and micro-photography, (hence appear a host of foetuses in the graphic arts, and shapes that suggest cross sections of seeds and flowers in the decorative arts); and forms distinguished for grace, delicacy, and tenuous charm: trees like the elm; vines; unfurling fronds; sea weed and lily pads; flowers such as roses and lilies, heavy tulips, waving and bending on their stems; spiraling shells, sleek fish (and sirens); insects with frail wings and long antennae; sparrow hawks, goldfinches, doves, and peacocks with long sweeping tails. Stimulated by this range of material the art forms evolved were sinuous and flexible. The line, used decoratively on flat surfaces, and in the designing of metal balustrades and screens, was long, free-flowing, and supple, ending in a characteristic flick, well termed "whip lash". Supplementing the long line was a wealth of detail: shorter swirls (called in Germany *schnörkels,* or flourishes) suggesting the waving antennae of insects, flower stamens, filaments swept by the wind or the sea; or clusters of naturalistically rendered flowers, fruit, leaves, and tendrils, tiny birds and insects. Special effects in surface design, (on walls, or screens) in the work of Horta and Whistler are very reminiscent of Japanese art in their assymmetrical balance. The wealth of detail seems to grow naturally out of the structural points where it is concentrated, while long flexible lines lead the eye to wide open areas. Assymmetrical balance is not universal, however, as some artists prefer to balance the whip lash line symmetrically, making flower-like or spread-eagle cartouches and panels. Contours in architecture and furniture were curvilinear, in some cases tense and wiry, in others as svelt as the outline of a lily, or the contour of a pear. In fact, individual artists show a wide range of variation in their handling of these basic components. Horta's work, best seen in the stairway of his Brussels house at 12 Rue de Turin (Pevsner, figs. 23, 24) is luxurious and leisurely to the point of languor, while the decoration of the German August Endell (Atelier Elvira, Munich, Pevsner, fig.

64) is defiant in its boldness and energy. While some artists, like the German J. M. Olbrich, use a wealth of ornament, men like van de Velde eliminate all naturalistic detail and work with austere simplicity. Aubrey Beardsley and Leon Bakst evolve in their graphic art an intricacy and fineness of detail and technique in sharp contrast to the large, tranquil forms of the German Otto Eckmann in the same field. Leon Bakst's work is quite different in its brilliant color from the favorite Art Nouveau color schemes, which are pale, dull, misty and muddy: greys, mauves, blues, sea-greens, and dusty yellows.

Art Nouveau found its expression in various art forms. A study of its buildings, exteriors and interiors alike, reveals originality and definite predilections in the treatment of planes, line, doors, windows, and interior space. Planes of facades have often one or several double curves, and projecting balconies; roof lines slope with a slight S-curve. There is a preference for domes, dome-shaped and vaulted rooms. Entrance doors and windows are curvate, without frames or pediments, sometimes with hood-like projections over them. Endell's architecture, however, in spite of his extravagant ornament, is as straight and severe as the modern International style. Guimard, J. M. Olbrich and Otto Wagner use exuberant detail, the typical Art Nouveau line and clusters of ornament, on the exteriors of their Metropolitan Railways (Paris and Vienna) while Horta, van de Velde and the Spaniard A. Gaudi use little interior ornament confining it to the metal balustrades at window. German architects liked color, introduced by glazed tiles. The Rookwood pottery in the U.S.A. turned out architectural tiles for fireplaces and walls in soft pastel shades; flowers, vines and birds predominate. (It is interesting that they had a Japanese potter on their staff.) Rooms, whether or not domed or vaulted, often have curvate walls. Ornament here is sometimes theatrical in its extravagance (Peter Behrens). Some of the finest creations of the style are found in the nervously delicate iron balustrades (Edgar Brandt, Horta). At their worst these interiors give an unpleasant sense of over-weaning effort and their wavering contours are unstable in effect. This can not be said of the securely controlled work of Renet Binet's interior for the Magasins du Printemps in Paris where the sweeping lines of the style sing with breathtaking confidence and grace. One of the real contributions of the style to architecture is its sense of the flexibility of the new materials.

Sculpture, painting, and the graphic arts bring up the matter of representation, choice of subject matter, and its interpretation. The visual components, and modes of composition remain the same. Subject matter tends toward obscure symbolism, allegory, myth, legend, and emotional or psychic experiences that have to do with man in the modern world: loneliness in, and fear of the city (E. Munch) religious doubt, etc. Either these matters or a rather dreamy, vacuous, decorative treatment of subject matter at hand, as in the work of John Alexander, Aman-Jean and others. The most original figure, in the field of sculpture, is the German Max Klinger. He used various colored stones, combined with white marble and bronze, encrusted with jewels, metal and ivory. No complex symbolism or remote expression was too obscure for him to undertake. His figure of Beethoven is a superb example of the style in the medium of sculpture. The portrait of Princess Baratinsky by the Russian Troubetzkoi is a good example of the style at its dullest, as is the work of Falguiére and the figurines of A. Léonard. There is an abundance of architectural sculpture in relief, tombs, monuments, drinking fountains, and garden pieces (Constantin Meunier, Hermann Obrist, et al). On the whole American sculptors were busy assimilating earlier European styles. Daniel Chester French comes the nearest to Art Nouveau in his Melvin Memorial in Concord, Massachusetts.

In painting there is much work that tends to be ingenuous, unsophisticated and naive: paintings filled with women in flowing, preferably white, styleless robes, characterized by idealistic faces and yearning gestures, like a child's image of his mother, or having a slight tinge of the "belle dame sans merci"; male figures, when they appear, are knights in armor, with their dream-filled eyes on far places. Outstanding figures are Burne-Jones in his mosaic the *Tree of Life* in Rome, Ferdinand Hodler and Jan Toorop (Dutch), Fernand Khnoopf (Flemish), Von Giovanni Segantini (Italian), Franz Stuck, Max Klinger, Edvard Munch (German), Gustav Glimt (Austrian), Aman-Jean, Besnard, Menard (French), Frank Brangwyn, James Shannon (English), Blashfield, John Alexander, Abbot Thayer, Edwin Abbey, Whistler (American), José Maria Sert (Spanish).

There is an abundance of material in the graphic arts and the art of the book: bindings, illustrations, posters, and in the format of title pages, frontispieces, theatre programs, and sheet music covers. A host of art journals, and other magazines sprang up championing the new trends and their pages are filled with excellent examples of Art Nouveau: *Pan, Jugend, Simplicissimus, Deutsche Kunst und Dekoration, Dekorative Kunst* (Germany), *The Studio, The Yellow Book* (England), *Art et Décoration, L'Art Décoratif, Revue des Arts Décoratifs* (France), *Ver Sacrum* (Vienna Sezession), to mention a few. Masters of book illustration, William Morris, Eckmann, Klimt, Aubrey Beardsley, Max Klinger, and Walter Crane, tend to frame their pages with borders of swaying flowers or figures. The illustrations themselves are flat, distinguished for their linear grace. (Max Klinger is the exception here. He was a devotee of Goya, and introduces depth and modelling with a fine stippling technique.) When color is used it is laid on in flat areas, or drawings are tinted as with Walter Crane. The illustrations of Howard Pyle and Charles Dana Gibson, and the work of the Roycroft Press should be mentioned to represent briefly the U.S.A. In posters Cheret, E. Grasset and the Austrian, Mucha, distinguished themselves. With printing types there is a good deal of experiment and confusion. The best efforts show the influence of Morris's Golden Type (while the influence of his Gothic is not so good). Goudy had begun his work, but the main text of most publications was set up in Bodoni type and its like.

Art Nouveau furniture and decorative arts were presented to the public on the Continent in a continuous series of exhibitions from about 1892 forward, and its mannerisms are observable in the work of Follot, Dufresne, Brandt, and Ruhlmann as late as the Paris Exhibition of 1925. (Its peculiar linear characteristics are not the only ones observable in furniture. As early as 1898, however, there is a marked tendency towards straight line in the work of Adolf Loos in Austria, and of Charles Mackintosh in England.) The work grows out of arts and crafts movements (q.v.) appearing all over Europe, influenced often by the English Arts and Crafts Societies, and the missionary zeal of William Morris. The Vienna Sezession was such a movement and there was a similar German group. Looking into a fine Art Nouveau room, designed by Colonna, Guimard, Plumet, de Feure, or van de Velde one is impressed by the subdued color, with perhaps an iridescent glow from some piece of opaque glass, and by a certain nervous tautness in the lines of the furniture. But looking into a room of one of the extravagant interpreters of the style like Gaillard, one is apprehensive. The furniture, like great winged bats, or swollen-jointed grasshoppers, looks as though it might come alive; the chandelier of metal might fly about the room, the glass bowl moulded like a pair of mating doves might dart about, the cricket crawling up the pottery bowl, hop off. The idea of function seems to have been interpreted to mean: able to move, and everything looks capable of that. Some pieces among the decorative arts are moulded to *suggest* animate forms: pottery vases like folded petals (Gruby, Cowan, U.S.A.); glass like lilies (Tiffany), while others exactly imitate them; doves in glass (Lalique); butterflies in jewelry (Lalique). There is a marked preference for texture and moulded surfaces: Wallpaper, like velvet and leather, is embossed; pottery has thick, opaque, runny glazes (Delaherbe, is an outstanding figure in this field); glass has a frosty surface; stained glass is thick, and full of gummy, mixed colors; textiles are embroidered, couched, or if flat, are dyed or block-printed to take on heavy atmospheric effects (sun-set, sunrise, and aquarium iridescences). Notable in the field of textiles and wallpapers are Morris, Felix Aubert, Obrist and Voysey. The best work (Gallé in glass, Delaherbe in pottery, Obrist in textiles, E. Robert in iron) will rarely be excelled.

Last, but not least, it is to be observed that the contour of women's figures from tip to toe was moulded on Art Nouveau lines: hair swept up in pompadours like the calyxes of open flowers; hats were laden with flowers, preferably full blown roses, or with darting birds or sweeping ostrich plumes; "leg-of-mutton" sleeves have the typical line; the waist tapered and the contour of the long skirt was like a lily. Witness the Gibson girl, and the portraits, of Sert, Lavery, Boldini, Sargent, Helleu, Howard Chandler Christy, Alexander and others. Details of costume, Lalique and "Arts and Crafts" jewelry, Liberty silks, chiffon scarfs and veils were, of course, concrete products of the style.

In all of its manifestations and in spite of its brief duration Art Nouveau stands as a distinct style. The time has not yet come for its final evaluation. Its development, sensed by some critics today as a Romantic throwback, is too closely woven with the development of the modern movement to so dismiss it. Some of the leaders of the architectural style developed as creative leaders of modern architecture (Obrich and others) yet its forms are too naturalistic and its attitude too ingenuous for us to feel at home with it. Adolescent,

defiant, and naive it yet has tinges of fatigue and exhaustion which defy the objective analysis we, so near the scene of its nascence, endeavor to give it. See Andre Michel, *Histoire de L'Art,* vol. VIII, parts 2 and 3, Paris,1929, under direction of Leon Deshairs; *L'Art des Origines a Nos Jours,* vol. II, Paris, 1933; Anton Springer, *Kunstgeschichte,* vol. V., Leipzig, 1925; Nikolaus Pevsner, *Pioneers of the Modern Movement,* 1936; Platz, *Die Baukunst der Neuesten Zeit,* Berlin, 1930; Le Corbusier, *L'Art Decoratif d'Aujourd'hui,* Paris, 1925; Ernst Michalski, Article on the Jugendstil in *Repertorium für Kunstwissenschaft,* vol. 46, 1925.   —M.F.M.

art of the iron brush. See CHINESE ARTS.

art principles. See design principles.

art program, fused. See art program, integrated (2).

art program, integrated. (1) A school art program in which art functions as an integral part of the total curriculum, thereby contributing its share to the integration of pupil personality; (2) a program in which several areas of the fine arts are fused together or integrated for purposes of study; for example, music, literature, painting, sculpture, and architecture may be studied together, without regard for subject matter boundaries, stressing basic principles, forms, or types of expression common to all. Syn. *fused art program.* Whitford and Winslow in *Dictionary of Education.*

Arts and Crafts movement. Refers to the movements in England and America which followed, perhaps superficially, the ideas inherent in the Pre-Raphaelite movement and William Morris' doctrines in the latter part of the last century. Many of the fundamental ideas of Rossetti and Burne-Jones as well as the dicta of Morris found expression only in the 20th cent., while the efforts of the leaders of the Arts and Crafts movement resulted in the embellishment of the "house beautiful." A late phase of this same cult guided the early efforts of city planners who argued that the "city beautiful" and garden cities were ends to be sought. In both cases good was doubtless accomplished, but the dangerous dichotomy of art and life was not avoided. It has latterly been acknowledyed that beauty is not something to be added to the practical, and that city planning is intimately concerned with the sociological needs of the whole man and his wise use of land.

The Arts and Crafts movement gathered force about 1875. By 1888 the Arts and Crafts Exhibition Society held its first exhibition in London. In a land where neo-medievalism was flourishing, where the sound craftsmanship principles of pre-Raphaelite and Ruskin and Morris were widely current, and where the appalling dangers of the industrial revolution were most apparent such a movement had brighter prospects of success than on the continent; America was likewise a more fertile field than the Far East. The movement urgently stressed the simplification, humanization, beautification of everything with which one was surrounded. The personality of the craftsman was emphasized, as was frequently the idea that the material, the technique and the purpose of the object must find expression in the design.

The Arts and Crafts movement is a transitional movement. Through it, the powerful forces which since the 1840's had been active in combating the industrial revolution as a way of life were transmitted to the next century, though the movement itself petered out in America in "mission" furniture and the activities of the amateur. One has only to recall the work in architecture and interior decoration of the Pugins and of Norman Shaw, of Webb, Butterfield, and G. E. Street, or the healthy insistence of the pre-Raphaelites on the importance of color and soundness of technique in design to be reminded of the worthy beginnings of the movement. When Morris' workshop undertook in inlays and textiles, in printing and furniture designing, to preach the lessons of simplicity and truth to function, the movement gained survival value. Ruskin's intoxicating prose, Rossetti's and Morris' hypnotic poetry, and in a burst of activity the superficiality of amateur disciples, were not enough to destroy it. Pattern was rediscovered by Lewis Day, pottery was recreated by William de Morgan, jewelry, gold and silversmithy, enamels, book-binding, and needle-work were all revitalized as the century closed.

One has only to glance through such an historical review as Pevsner's to see clearly the continuing influence of this movement in the 20th cent. Through it William Morris contacts the world of Walter Gropius. C. F. Annesley Voysey in his wallpapers and glass and furniture, Walter Crane and Frank Brangwyn in the arts of design, are all seen waking from the medieval dream and eager to relate art to life once more. Ernest Gimson at the turn of the century was already designing furniture which was honestly and simply traditional, yet modern in feeling, while Ambrose Heal caught the spirit of modernism in his inlay and designs marked by a limited use of curves. Even in the work of Charles R. Mackintosh, despite his enthusiasm for the decorative formulas of Art Nouveau, one senses the modern feeling in space relations, use of materials, attention to function, notably in his Glasgow Art School, 1898-1899. And it is in this period that garden cities began to become practical as greenbelt cities.

In America, the feeling of the amateur and of the superimposition of ornament was never entirely absent from "arts and crafts" products. The scope of the interest is indicated in the files of The Craftsman, which ran its course from 1901-1916; "an illustrated monthly magazine in the interest of better art, better work, and a better and more reasonable way of living." The first World War shifted the emphasis and this phase of American design had chiefly historical interest when the postwar prosperity arrived. It was rather the Armory Show of 1913, Alfred Stieglitz and his studio at "291" Fifth Avenue, and the Museum of Modern Art, New York City, which has latterly provided the ideology for the minor arts, checked by the practical American sense and feeling for the mechanics of the problem. Even the Decorative Arts Exposition in Paris in 1925 did not wholly change the course. The fundamentals of design and soundness of craftsmanship preached by Morris and expressed now and again by the Arts and Crafts enthusiasts, the frankly accepted machine, and a growing social awareness are being integrated with notable results, in a world of Machine Art, but prophetic of a world of Human Art. See CIVIC PLANNING; GREAT BRITAIN, ARCHITECTURE OF; also for Morris and his influence, cf. L. F. Day, Of William Morris and his work, 1939, and N. Pevsner, Pioneers of the Modern Movement, 1937. For more general discussions of the place of the minor arts in modern life, cf. S. Giedion, Time, Space, and Architecture, 1941; W. C. Behrendt, Modern Building, 1937; R. Faulkner, E. Ziegfeld, and G. Hill, Art Today, 1941; S. and M. Cheney, Art and the Machine, 1936.   —W.S.R.

art song. See song.

art supplies. The materials employed in the visual and space arts that go into the product and are used up in the process of transformation of materials; for example, pastels, paper, canvas, clay, paints, etc. Whitford and Winslow in *Dictionary of Education.*

art talent. Innate aptitude for creative expression through such mediums as drawing, painting, designing, modeling, or any other form of artistic expression; ability to appreciate works of art and to produce art forms. Whitford and Winslow in *Dictionary of Education.*

art tests. (1) General art tests have centered upon **aesthetic judgment** as the most significant single factor in aptitude. It is measured by responses to sets of pictorial materials prepared in from two to five variations, one being regarded as superior in aesthetic quality. The subject either chooses one of two or ranks four or five in order of merit as judged. The criterion is either survival (recognized as good over period of time, as masterpieces) or statistically established by consensus of competent judges, or by a combination of both. The two best known tests are the *McAdory Art Test* (1929) and the *Meier Art Judgment Test* (1929). The former makes use of miscellaneous subject-matter (rug-design, textiles, furniture), while the latter uses graphic material only (paintings, etchings). These tests are also regarded as tests of appreciation. (2) *Tests of psychological capacities and skills* feature such items as memory for color and form, simple design facility, and simple imagination. The subject is shown a jumbled pattern of color strips and then by turning the page is required to select from a larger array of colors only the ones just seen; or having viewed for five seconds a complex assembly of objects to identify it on the next page whereon appear five similar assemblies all slightly different. Exercises are also required touching upon rhythm problems and simple design. The assumption is implied that such capacities are expected in the artist. The *Varnum Selective Art Aptitude Test* (1940) is the single example of the type. (3) *Tests of learning and elementary skills.* These, represented by the *Lewerenz Test of Fundamental Abilities* (1927) and the *Knauber Art Test* (1932) attempt to measure the results of learning and elementary imagination, as in the drawing of simple expression of concepts, such as Santa Claus or "the homeless dog." Featured in both are problems concerned with the detection of common errors in drawing relative to proportion, perspective, light and shade. The tests include art terms and art information (art history), tested by the mul-

tiple-choice method. The *Lewerenz* test is adapted primarily to the junior and high school level; the *Knauber,* senior high school and junior college level. (4) The *scale,* the best known being the *Kline-Carey,* is a device for assigning a numerical value to a given product of specified nature. It is hence confined to given subject-matter, such as a drawing of a boy running, a house, or the little red school-house. The scale itself consists of a long sheet on which appear drawings from crude examples to progressively better and better ones, with a numerical value under each. The child's product is hence evaluated by matching it with the example on the scale most like it. (5) *Tests of creative imagination.* Elementary aspects of imagination are touched upon in several tests (*Varnum, Knauber*) but for complex creative imagination and perceptual capacity no tests are yet published but on the basis of research now completed the forthcoming *Meier Art Tests: II Creative Imagination and III Perceptual Facility* are designed toward that end. The traits are measured by problems taken through progressive stages of interpretation, by variations of multiple choice methods with differential weighing of responses; and by leading the subject through progressive stages in perceptual identification, with the degree of adequacy of response assigned at each stage. —N.C.M.

art unit. An art experience or series of experiences having unity through being organized around some theme, activity, or concept. Whitford and Winslow in *Dictionary of Education.*

Arundel marbles. The collection of ancient Greek sculptures and inscriptions collected by Thomas Howard, 2d Earl of Arundel, in the 17th cent., presented to the Ashmolean Museum, Oxford University; includes the Parian Chronicle, an inscription recording events in Greek history. —L.T.S.

Ashanti art. See AFRICAN NEGRO ART.

Ash can school. See AMERICAN NEGRO ART; POST-REVOLUTIONARY PAINTING AND SCULPTURE IN THE U.S.A.

ashide-e (Jap.). A design which combines written characters with other motives.

Ashikaga art. See JAPANESE ART.

ashlar. (1) Term applied to masonry in which the stones are dressed, hewn, or squared to permit laying with uniformly thick horizontal joints of one-half inch or less. (2) Dressed stone as distinguished from natural, roughly tooled, or rubble.   —J.M.M.

asphaltum. The chief use in the arts of this tarry compound has been as a painter's pigment. Its general utility has been known from ancient times and it had a good deal to do with the Egyptian processes of mummification. There is little sign of it, however, as a painting material until the late Renaissance, and it was probably most used in the 18th cent. The color is neutral brown and, since the material itself, a natural mixture of hydrocarbons with other elements, is a kind of liquid, it dissolves to some extent in the oil medium. As a glazing material, it was much favored for this reason and because of its warm, neutral tone. As an oil paint, however, it never becomes thoroughly dry and is always subject to further softening from heat. It tends to crawl and flow like tar in a heavy film and has undoubtedly been the cause of much of the breaking and crackling found in dark passages of oil paintings since the 17th cent.   —G.L.S.

Assyrian art. See MESOPOTAMIAN ART.

Astarte. In Phoenician religion, goddess of sexual love and fertility; western Semitic form of the goddess Ishtar.

asterisk. An object shaped like a star.

astragal (Gr. *astragalos,* ankle bone). A small moulding of single convex curve in the form of a half circle; in classical architecture usually ornamented with the bead and reel pattern.

astrakhan. A grade of karakul lambskins, less lustrous, with longer hair and more open curl than the best grade of karakul which are termed Persian lambskins. Astrakhan also applied to imitations of the natural "fur" in' fabric for coatings.   —G.W.R.

Asturian architecture. See SPAIN, ART OF.

asymmetry. Asymmetry in art does not mean simply want of symmetry and is not, therefore, the negating antonym of symmetry. It means that a symmetrical arrangement is avoided for certain artistic reasons. To the artist, for instance, who supposes that perfection or harmony is an unknown value, to be achieved only by infinite permutations, symmetrical order is of no sense, because symmetry starts from the belief that perfection is

the known value of a central ideal, standing before or above all particular things. Each artist therefore, who expresses himself asymmetrically considers his work as a part or a kind of segment of movement, the center of which lies beyond all particular things in infinity. In doing so he faces the highly interesting problem of balance without conspicuous equilibrium, since balance is the main attribute of every work of art. He may accomplish this by placing the axis on one side of the work so that the whole picture pivots upon that axis. The sowing of figures upon the canvas, as for instance in the picture by Peter Brueghel, *The Blind Leading The Blind,* may be another solution of asymmetrical arrangement. The northern artists tried to solve this problem in many different ways. It is one of the most interesting of historical problems.
                                        —A.J.S.

atelier. A studio; a workshop.

Aten. *Egypt. relig.* The solar disk.

at gaze. See HERALDRY.

Athena (L. *Minerva*). Goddess of administrative sagacity, including warfare as well as statesmanship, and of women's arts, especially weaving. She was patron goddess of Athens. Her attributes were the owl, the aegis, the olive, and a suit of armor. She was often pictured on Greek vases, fighting the giants or sponsoring Theseus, the favorite hero of Athens; in sculpture she was usually represented as a warrior. The most famous statue of her was Phidias' great chryselephantine figure in the Parthenon. Phidias' Lemnian Athena was of a more gracious type. Roman Minervas were colder in character. In later European and American sculpture she was pictured by Cellini, Sansovino, Permoser, Thorvaldsen, and Roy Sheldon.   —W.R.A.

Athletic school. See POST-REVOLUTIONARY PAINTING AND SCULPTURE IN THE U.S.A.

atlante. Male of caryatid (q.v.).

Atlas. One of the Titans, whose duty it was to bear the world on his shoulders. The most famous classical illustration is a metope at Olympia, which pictures him offering the apples of the Hesperides to Heracles. In modern art he has been represented by Lee Lawrie in a mammoth bronze statue at Radio City, New York.   —W.R.A.

atlatl. The throwing stick of ancient Mexico.

atmospheric perspective. See PERSPECTIVE.

Aton. Var. of Aten (q.v.).

atonal idiom. See twelve-tone technique.

atonality. See idiom (c) ; key.

atonal music. See twelve-tone technique.

atrio. Large walled forecourt of Mexican churches (rarely elsewhere in Latin America). In 16th cent. monasteries it was also in a sense the church of the Indians, for here they stood to witness the celebration of mass in the *open chapel* (q.v.), here they were taught catechism, singing, etc. Without *posas* (q.v.) and open chapel, it became a regular adjunct of later parish churches, retaining its central stone cross ornamental gateways and battlemented or crested wall. —J.Mc.

atrium. (1) The chief room of an ancient Roman house, an open court usually surrounded by a roofed gallery. (2) The open court before the narthex of a Christian church or basilica. See EARLY CHRISTIAN ARCHITECTURE.

Attabi. See ISLAMIC ART.

attack. In vocal music, the form of the approach to the main level of pitch, intensity, or timbre in music and speech. There are four forms : the level, the rising, the falling attack, and the portamento. In the legato and related styles the portamento prevails as a continuous glide from one note to the next. The rising glide is the most frequent in free attack. The falling glide occurs in downward passage in the scale. All gliding attacks in good music including the portamento carry the vibrato (q.v.). The level attack generally makes the tone disagreeably sharp-edged or stiff. The gliding attack is a form of artistic license which adds much to the mellowness of the tone. The glide may vary in extent (q.v.) and rate of change in pitch, intensity, and timbre. It may be several semi-tones and many decibels in extent and may occupy a considerable portion of the total duration of the tone. Many singers can be identified by their prevailing tendencies in these respects. Attack is usually thought of as pertaining to pitch, but the concept is equally applicable to intensity and timbre. The same applies in principle to many instruments. See *Iowa Studies in Psych. of Music*, Vols. I and IV.—C.E.S.

attendant keys. *Mus.* (1) Of a major key:

the major keys with a tonic a perfect 5th higher and a perfect 5th lower ; and the three relative minors. (2) Of a minor key: the minor keys with a tonic a perfect 5th higher and a perfect 5th lower ; and the three relative majors. —F.M.G.

Attic base. The most common of all classic column bases. An upper and lower torus having fillets attached which are separated by a scotia. See base. —O.M.S.

attribute. Conventional symbol of identity. Such as Indra's *vajra* (q.v.).

aubade (Fr.). An early morning (dawn) open-air serenade or concert; a brief instrumental work of lyrical character.

Aubusson. A rug weave originating in France, seldom used as a floor covering and woven on either a high or low warp loom. All design lines which are parallel to the warp threads form a slit in the rug and must be sewn up later. —B.E.J.

audiles. See audiometer.

audiometer, audiometry. An instrument used in the measurement of keenness of hearing.

Musicians, like people in general, vary in their sensitiveness to sound. A sound that is audible to one may not be audible to another. It follows that this will affect not only their hearing of music but also their performance and direction of music. However, with progressive loss of hearing comes the power to make habitual allowance for the defect.

Persons who have fine auditory acuity live in a different world of experience and behavior from those who are dull in hearing largely because they tend to become **audiles**, i.e., to live in a tonal world, while others tend to become visualisers, i.e., to live in a visually constructed world. See C. C. Bunch, *Clinical Audiometry*, 1943, p. 186. —C.E.S.

auditory form. See PSYCHOLOGY OF ART.

augmentation. *Mus.* Doubling or increasing the time-value of the notes of a theme.

aural newsreel. See RADIO DRAMA.

aureole (or glory) and mandorla. In opposition to the nimbus (q.v.) or halo the aureole or glory is a splendor of light, surrounding not only the head, but the whole figure. It makes its first appearance in Greek painting, about the same time as the round nimbus.

Like the latter it is originally enriched by rays on the periphery. It is probable that the Christian aureole, like the Christian halo, is derived from its classical predecessors; as in the halo, however, the rays on the periphery were omitted during the early Christian and medieval periods; this secondary influence of the Roman *clipeus* (q.v.) which has been suggested with regard to the circular nimbus, is even more evident in the case of the aureole (cf. Elderkin). In spite of these undeniable relations of the Christian aureole to classical antiquity, it should be observed that there were powerful biblical motives for the use of the aureole that were lacking in the case of the mere halo: I am referring for instance to the Transfiguration of Christ in which His body was surrounded by light and to other kindred events from the Old and New Testaments. As to the aureoles of various shapes that occur in Hindu and Buddhist art, they are of too late a date to make it very probable that they influenced the classical or the Christian aureole (see nimbus).

The aureole is a symbol that occurs much less frequently than the nimbus. The first Christian examples are to be found in some of the mosaics of the nave of *S. Maria Maggiore* in Rome, illustrating the Old Testament. In early Christian art the aureole is also found around representations of the Lamb, the Phoenix and the Cross, and at least from the 5th cent. onward around the figure of Christ, later sometimes also around that of the Blessed Virgin. While the halo became the ordinary attribute of Christ and the saints, the aureole, before modern times, was reserved for a restricted number of subjects, particularly for Christ in the Transfiguration, the Descent to the *Limbo,* the Ascension, the *Maiestas Domini* and the Last Judgement. The shape of the aureole is dependent upon that of the human body; therefore it is often elliptical, but can be circular, esp. in the case of an enthroned figure. The oval-shaped aureole is also called by the Italian term *mandorla,* because of its almond-like form. In medieval art the aureole or mandorla is not infrequently combined with the globes of heaven and earth above which Christ is enthroned; this arrangement lead to complicated geometrical figures. The aureoles of that period look often more like an adorned shield than like a zone of light. In post-medieval art the aureole is comparatively rare. See W. W. S. Cook, The Iconography of the Globe Mandorla, *The Art Bulletin* 6 (1924) 38 ff.; G. W. Elderkin, Shield and Mandorla, *American*

Journal of Archaeology 42 (1938) 227 ff.; for the rest, see article nimbus.   —G.B.L.

aureolin. A pigment of yellow color made from cobalt goes by this name. See cobalt pigments.

Australian Aboriginal Art. The art of the aborigines of Australia is limited by the cultural level of the people themselves. Wandering from place to place, yet always within the bounds of their own hunting grounds, these early Australian blacks expended most of their artistic efforts on their bodies and transportable goods.

They did, however, like most stone-age hunting hordes, leave behind them outline drawings of fish, reptiles, birds, animals, weapons and human figures. These were carved or painted upon rock surfaces and are to be found in many parts of the continent. The art of rock carving, which is now extinct, was commonly practised on flat rocky sites. The examples of mural painting, being more ephemeral than the carvings, are placed under the protection of overhanging ledges or on the walls of caves. Unlike most primitive art, these illustrations are neither grotesque nor exaggerated and are executed with surprising restraint. Silhouette stenciling of hands is a common feature of cave painting, esp. in New South Wales where stencils of feet and weapons frequently appear. Sometimes the silhouette is filled in with a second color. In all painting in Australia there is no blending or shading of hues.

In spite of a low cultural development, the totemic lore and ceremonial rituals of these people appear very complex and depend to a great extent for their visual expression upon a symbolic type of art. Since much emphasis is placed upon the initiation of the youths, and as only the men take part in the sacred ceremonies, the women of the tribe have little understanding of the esoteric nature of the art forms.

The traditional and symbolic designs are made up of geometric and biomorphic elements which are based originally on nature forms. For example, a wavering line usually signifies a snake, while cross-hatching may symbolize water. Concentric circles, diamonds, lozenges, and triangles are basic forms. Oval shapes, serpentine zigzags, and dotted lines appear in great variation, while the use of herring-bone and chevron patterns are typical of certain regions.

In all these elements it may be noted that the principal characteristic is repetition. Lines, angles, and arcs are paralleled in a series. One shape is fitted within another. Even the backgrounds may be little more than a field of white dots.

Most sacred designs are closely associated with corresponding sóngs and chants, esp. those symbols which are found on the *Tjurunga* and *churinga* (sacred wooden or stone forms which are decorated with totemic motifs). In fact many of these designs are made to the accompaniment of particular songs which are also sung when the object decorated by the symbol is displayed. This close association of music with design most likely accounts for much of the repetitive nature of the visual form where the beat of the song is reflected in the dotted backgrounds and the paralleling of lines.

Besides the *Tjurunga* and *Churinga* clubs, spears, spear-throwers, boomerangs, shields, and bull-roarers are all decorated with symbolic designs usually of an abstract character. These are usually applied by incising or fluting the surfaces, the various geometric shapes being adapted to the particular areas to be ornamented. In the case of larger surfaces, such as found on shields, it is a common practice to use paint and even feather-down which is stuck on with blood. Often two or more techniques are combined. For example, the flutings and incisions are often filled with color in order to bring out the pattern. These pigments are the same as those used in mural painting and are common to most Australian art. The red and yellow are made from the ochres; white is produced from pipe clay and the black is made from charcoal. The pigments are mixed with grease and at times even with water. They are applied with the finger or with the aid of crude brushes.

Some mention must be made of the ceremonial paraphernalia made of feathers. While white feather-down is applied along each side of red or black lines traced onto the body, sacred feather banners are made up for each ceremonial ritual. While they are often carried as sacred banners in the totemic and historical ceremonies of northern and central Australia, they are also stuck in the ground and at times even worn as eleborate headdresses. They are known as *nurtunja* and *waninga* and represent the totem of the clan.

Earth drawings are also used for religious ceremonies, esp. in Central Australia. These are made on a circular area often six feet in diameter. After the ground has been suitably smoothed and dampened, the totemic designs of concentric circles and scrolls in a field of white dots are carefully painted in with the traditional colors. A new drawing is used for each day of a religious festival.

Symbolic designs similar to those used on weapons are also deeply engraved on tree trunks in the New South Wales and Queensland areas. These are used for religious ceremonies and are believed to have some mythological significance.

For the scholar of art the bark drawings from western Arnhem Land and the decoration of the baobab nuts in the Kimberly District are of particular interest as they show the decorative use of nature forms. The former are painted on the bark sheets forming the walls of huts and have some religious implication. Fish and kangeroos are commonly depicted in profile. The unusual aspect of this type of art is the portrayal of the internal structure of the creature which gives the drawing somewhat the appearance of an X-ray plate. The skeleton, the spinal column, and the alimentary canal are usually most conspicuous. Such treatment of animal forms is rare even in primitive art.

The painting and incising of baobab nuts show the skill with which the Australian artist can use animal motifs for allover decoration. Representations of emus, turtles, plants, and flowers are common, the outlines often being filled in with dots.

Twine baskets, skin rugs and mantles, bark belts and shell ornaments are all decorated with the customary designs adapted to localized traditions. The various articles themselves are often typical of particular regions. Whether these abstract and semi-abstract designs have symbolic and religious interpretation when applied to such mundane objects is still an unsolved problem which is fortunately of little consequence to the scholar of art.

There is much to be learned from a perusal of the wealth of colorful designs which appear in Australian art. The graceful curves and the interesting silhouettes of weapons and many of the totemic symbols offer much source material for the designer of to-day. Good color plates and lucid explanations are to be found in museum publications and especially in the Memoirs of the American Philosophical Society, Volume V, 1936, and Volume IX, 1937. See *A Preliminary Consideration of Aboriginal Australian Decorative Art*, 1937 and *Aboriginal Australian and Tasmanian Rock Carvings and Paintings*, 1936, Daniel Sutherland Davidson; *Australian Aboriginal Art*, Barrett and Kenyon, 1929; *Australian Aboriginal Decorative Art*, F. D. Mc-

Carthy, 1938; *Primitive Hunters of Australia,* Wilfred D. Hambly, 1936; *Studies in Australian Totemism,* A. P. Elkin, 1934 —C.B.S.

Australian Contemporary Art, like the contemporary art of many other countries, shows a variety of tendencies and directions which range from academic naturalism to modernism. However, on the whole the conservative group, i.e. Australian impressionism, is dominant and the value of modern tendencies in art was the object of lively controversies as late as 1940.

The year 1885 may be given as the beginning of the Australian school of painting which means primarily an art that depicts truthfully the peculiar characteristics of Australian landscape—a task which is often considered to be one of the most important for the Australian artist to undertake. Tom Roberts (1856—1931), returning from Europe in 1885, brought with him some landscapes painted in the impressionistic style which greatly influenced such painters as Frederick McCubbin (1855—1917), Charles Conder (1868—1909), Sir John Longstaff (1862—1941), Sir Arthur Streeton (b. 1867) and others. Under the influence of impressionism and "plein air" painting, Australian artists broke away from the academic studio painting; they were brought in contact with their own landscape and they were made aware of the subtle color schemes in their native surroundings. However, Australian impressionism maintained a great degree of careful draughtsmanship which has given it a peculiar character of its own. This new type of painting was first presented to the public at an exhibit in 1889 in Melbourne and was greeted with sharp adverse criticism. Such opposition did not, of course, prevent the growth of Australian impressionism which, as a result of the efforts of the artists just mentioned and such men as Julian Ashton, Max Meldrum (see Meldrum, school of) and others, rose to the dominant position it still holds.

Typical of this kind of impressionism are Conder's *Departure of the S. S. Orient,* 1888; McCubbin's *On the Wallaby Track,* 1890; Streeton's *Golden Summer,* 1889; *Still Glides the Stream,* 1890; *Road to Corryong,* or his more recent painting *Passing Showers,* 1937. Tom Roberts painted a series of large canvases depicting scenes from the life in the Australian bush, e.g. *The Breakaway, The Golden Fleece, Shearing the Rams,* 1890, *A Mountain Muster* and *Bailed Up.* The last picture was painted with great care as to

correct details from a model (i.e. a reenacted scene); it was started in 1898 and completed in 1928 (almost all the background being repainted) when it was acclaimed by Lionel Lindsay as part of Australian history and "completely removed from the category of academic story" (from the foreword to the catalogue of the exhibit at the Macquarie Galleries, Sidney).

The painter Hans Heysen (b. 1877) pointed out that the work of Roberts and Streeton made him and his friends realize that the atmosphere and color values of their landscape were quite different from the relatively low tones favoured in the English paintings of the time. In a great number of water colors and oils Heysen has embodied the results of this experience as for instance in his water colors from the Arkaba country (1927) in which he has depicted faithfully the subtle color gradations, the light effects as well as the structure of the Australian landscape.

Elioth Gruner (1882—1939) represents in a sense an intermediary stage in the development of Australian art. In his earlier works *Morning Light* or *The Valley of the Tweed* he, like J. J. Hilder (e. g. *At Close of Day*), shows sentimental and lyric qualities which appealed to the public and which helped to widen the popular interest in the Australian impressionism begun by Streeton, Roberts, et al. In this earlier phase the study of colour gradations and tonal values are dominant over structural form. The later phase of Gruner's work, as a result of his acquaintance with G. W. Lambert (returned from Europe) and his own stay in Europe, shows a change towards greater emphasis on form and design and greater clarity and simplicity of colours, e. g. *Devonshire Landscape,* 1925; *The Little Farm,* 1926.

The development of Elioth Gruner illustrates the changes taking place in Australian art and the transition from impressionism to modern art. When using the term "modern" one should remember its relative character; thus, in Australia, the term is applied to Rupert Bunny, whose work has been likened to that of Bonnard and Vuillard (e. g. *Olive Trees, Le Lavandou; Self-Portrait,* National Gallery, Melbourne), as well as to abstractionism and surrealism. Different and divergent as the work of the various moderns may appear they have certain aims in common—analysis and emphasis of the formal values of artistic composition. The intense interest in and the scrupulous observation of peculiar

Australian light and color effects had led to a neglect of the formal values of pictorial composition. Under the influence of Cézanne, van Gogh and Gauguin the moderns realized the necessity of a reconsideration and re-evaluation of the traditional principles and values of Australian "plein art" impressionism.

According to Roland Wakelin (*Art in Australia*, December 1928), the art of van Gogh, Gauguin and Cézanne became known in Australia ca. 1913. Color reproductions and the reports of Miss Nora Simpson, returning from England at about this time, inspired Wakelin and Roi de Mestre, who were studying at the Royal Art Society, Sidney, to experiment with intense and bright colors and draw in a cubistic manner. Their attempts met, of course, with opposition but A. Dattilo-Rubbo defended them as well as his pupils (Miss Simpson and Miss Grace Cossington Smith) and some of their works were accepted at the annual exhibitions of the Royal Art Society in 1916-18—without enjoying much popularity with either critics or public.

The period after the first world war saw a gradual growth of the modern tendencies among Australian artists—some of whom had come in contact with modernism in Europe during the war—and in November 1926 a number of those interested in modern art exhibited for the first time as a group at the Grosvenor Galleries, Sidney. Among the members of this group were Elioth Gruner (cf. above), G. W. Lambert, Kenneth Macqueen, Margaret Preston, Thea Proctor, Vida Lahey, John D. Moore, Roland Wakelin, Roi de Mestre and they were joined in the following year by Adelaide Perry, Grace Cossington Smith, Aletta Lewis, Mildred Lovett and Joseph Connor. In connection with the rise of Modernism in Melbourne (beginning ca. 1925) the names of William Frater, Arnold Shore, George Bell, Isabel Hunter Tweddle, Adrian Lawlor and Eric Thake should be mentioned.

George W. Lambert (1873—1930) was a most versatile artist, equally accomplished in painting as well as sculpture, e. g. the *Henry Lawson Statue, Memorial for Roman Catholic Soldiers and Sailors, St. Mary's Basilica,* Sidney, (assisted by Arthur Murch). Lambert exerted a great influence after his return from Europe in 1921; his "modernism", however, is actually an insistence upon a return to values of the earlier traditions of pictorial composition in the direction of classicistic form, e.g. *Important People,* 1921; his

Weighing the Fleece, 1921, and *The Squatter's Daughter* have often been referred to as examples for the renewed emphasis upon solid and constructive form.

In such paintings as *The Red House* or *Bay Road* of Roland Wakelin (b. 1887) the influence of Cézanne is discernible in the somewhat cubistic design of the picture. However, there is an emphasis on strong colours and in his later work (e.g. *St. James, Romantic Landscape,* 1937) colour is the carrier of the simplified design. Kenneth Macqueen (b. 1897), who manages his own farm in Queensland, combines in such water colors as *The Green Hill,* 1929; *Evans's Farm,* 1929, decorative design with authenticity of observation, while in his later work (e.g. *Cabbage Gums and Cypress Pines*) there is a freer handling of the natural forms and greater strength and movement of composition.

Margaret Preston (b. 1883) in *The Indigenous Art of Australia* (*Art in Australia,* March 1925) was the first artist to suggest the application of aboriginal art to modern design, and to advocate taking the art of aborigines as a basis for "an art for Australia from Australians" (*Art in Australia,* November 1940). In a great number of still lifes she has employed local forms and colors and in such later works as *Coral and Banksia,* 1939, *Aboriginal Still Life,* 1940, she shows well balanced strong colors and great vigor and firmness of design. In the work of Grace Cossington Smith strength and clarity of design are combined with a treatment of color that is reminiscent of van Gogh, e.g. *The Bridge Curve, Things on an Iron Tray on the Floor.*

George Bell (b. 1878) who, together with Arnold Shore (b. 1897), established a modern art school at Melbourne considers "abstractions" necessary for formal analyses and exercises. The results of these analyses he incorporates in paintings composed of wide planes in simplified design (e.g. *Lulworth Cove*). In such compositions as *Metamorphosis* Arnold Shore accentuates color strongly and in a manner reminiscent of van Gogh.

While some of the Australian artists had thus established contact with European modernism, the general public did not see a comprehensive exhibit of modern art until 1939. As a result of the efforts of Sir Keith Murdoch, the collector, and Basil Burdett, art critic for the *Melbourne Herald,* the *Herald* organized a travelling exhibit which comprised works of Cézanne, van Gogh,

Gaughin, Seurat, Picasso, Derain, Utrillo, Braque, Modigliani, Vlaminck, Bonnard, Steer, Tonks, John, Nash, Maillol, Epstein and others. The public in general did not respond very enthusiastically to this exhibit nor did the representatives of the conservatives among the artists and gallery directors, if the following statement by James S. MacDonald, Director of the National Gallery of Victoria, can be taken as an example. Mr. MacDonald wrote in 1940: "The art that Australian modernists profess is imported and is foreign to this relatively happiest of countries. The importers body-snatched the corpse abroad, smuggled it in, warmed it up. For it is dead, even if it has not yet lain down. European insecurity begat this yelling, shocking art . . . The distraction this leprous art furnished was pounced upon by overseas picture dealers and newspaper writers . . . They saw in it, respectively, profit and notoriety, . . . " (quoted from C. H. Grattan, *Introducing Australia*, 1942).

However, such adverse criticism in high quarters should not be interpreted to mean that the Australian artists of today are completely conservative and intend to remain so. In addition to those painters mentioned above, there is a very vigorous group of artists who are willing to take the risk of experiment and to face adverse criticism. They find support in the periodical, *Art in Australia,* (founded 1916 by Sidney Ure Smith) which, while not preferring uncritically everything modern, points out the necessity for judging modern art on its own grounds and makes a plea for the official recognition of an art which truly reflects contemporary attitudes. Thus in June-July-August 1941 *Art in Australia* editorializes, "Contemporary art means the true art of today . . . 1941 cannot be interpreted in the language of 1870 . . . Unfortunately, we possess too many painters, young and old, producing pale echoes of the Victorian era, and they are encouraged !"

Among the moderns, of whom only a few can be presented here, the following artists should be mentioned. Peter Purves Smith (b. 1913) develops his pictures in terms of simplified, subtly coloured planes without suppressing the expression of human qualities (e.g. *The Promenade,* 1938, *The Diplomats,* 1939). George Russel Drysdale (b. 1912), using colour with sensitivity, in such compositions as *Sunday Evening* and *Feeding the Dogs* sets the verticals of his elongated figures and trees against the horizontals of a wide landscape which seems pervaded by

a gentle melancholy. William Dobell (b. 1899) in a fresh approach to portrait painting subordinates accurate representation of his models to an analysis of expressive characteristics of their personality, e.g. *Squadron Leader G. U. 'Scotty' Allan, Portrait of a Strapper, The Student.*

The forms of Eric Wilson's (b. 1911) compositions seem to grow out of the swirling movement of colors, e.g. *In the Train,* 1924; *Mother and Son,* while his *Theme for Mural* and *Kitchen Theme* show the influence of Picasso. William Constable (b. 1906) in his stage designs has broken away from the traditional and conservative stage settings and works with strong color and bold, imaginative shapes (e.g. *Design for an Aboriginal Ballet,* No. 1 and No. 2). Elaine Haxton's work shows the influence of her stay in Europe and in the United States, as for example, her gouache *Early Colonial Architecture,* 1940, which, in the handling of color and space has something of the sophisticated effects of Raoul Dufy.

One of the spokesman of surrealism in Australia, Adrian Lawlor, author and painter, in *Banner of Blood, Symphonic Poem,* etc., gives expression to imaginative insight, accentuating emotional qualities rather than formal values. Somewhat in the manner of Dali, Eric Thake (b. 1904) in *Archaeopteryx* places realistically painted objects in fantastic juxtaposition. James Gleeson, Gordon Andrews, Albert Tucker, Max Ebert present the symbolic imagery of surrealism, while Geoffrey Collings and Alistair Morrison create abstractions emphasizing formal values.

In the field of sculpture the situation is similar to that in painting; the conservative and academic element is dominant and is best represented by such works of Sir Bertram MacKennal (1863-1931) as *Circe* (National Gallery, Melbourne), *The Earth and the Elements, Diana Wounded* (both in the Tate Gallery), and by a great number of memorials in Australia, England and India. C. W. Gilbert (1866-1925) and Harold Parker (b. 1873) are other representatives of an academic naturalism which, in the case of Gilbert shows some influence of Rodin.

Rayner Hoff (1894-1937), who was the first instructor at the first school of sculpture in Sidney (established 1924), departed from the traditional directions and shows in his figures for the *Anzac Memorial,* Sidney, a great restraint and a concentration upon the essential forms which is well suited to the theme represented. Ola Cohn's work is characterized by an accentuation of plastic values to which the shape of the natural objects depicted is subordinated (e.g. *Penguin*).

Among the Black and White artists David Low (New Zealand, b. 1892), since 1920 in London, is probably most widely known through his political satires which are characterized by an economy of line, a quality which is also cultivated by C. E. Finey (New Zealand, b. 1895) who contributes to various Sidney newspapers. There is a certain literary sophistication in the work of Will Dyson (b. 1881, in London since 1930) and his wit is rather subtle, e.g. his etchings satirizing psychoanalysis. Lionel Lindsay (b. 1874) who, through his contributions to *Art in Australia* has helped to make Australian artists known in their country, follows in his many etchings, drawings and water colours the criticism which he applies to others. ". . . The idiots who listen to modernistic critics," says Lionel Lindsay, "cannot see that . . . the best painting . . . is representational. Cezanne owes much of his fame . . . to his faults of drawing, . ." (*Art in Australia*, 1928). There are none of the "faults" of Cezanne in Lionel Lindsay's work which follows the conservative line of Australian impressionism. So does the work of his younger brother Norman Lindsay (b. 1879) whose etchings are filled with a great number of carefully executed details (e.g. *The Garden of Happiness, Enter the Magicians, Dionysus*).

Among the moderns a sensitive note is struck by Donald Friend in his delicately executed wash drawings. Francis Lymburner stresses the importance of drawing as a medium in which sculptor and painter may meet. James Gleeson presents his poetry in the fantastic forms of a surrealistic design. See William Moore, *The Story of Australian Art*, 2 vols., 1934; *Art of Australia* 1788-1941, compiled and edited by Sidney Ure Smith, O.B.E., 1941; *Art in Australia*, A Quarterly Magazine (founded 1916). —H.H.

AUSTRIAN ART. Already in prehistoric times important works of art were produced on Austrian soil, e.g. the so-called *Venus of Willendorf*. Numerous discoveries in settlements and burial places in Lower and Upper Austria furnish ample evidence of artistic activity. Particularly important are the discoveries relating to the Iron Age (from the 8th to the 5th cent. B.C.) known as the *Hallstatt* period after the town near which excavations were made. From the 1st to the 5th cent. A.D. the areas along the Danube, Upper and Lower Austria, and on the eastern fringe of the Alps,

Carinthia and Styria, were colonized by the Romans, who founded the larger settlements of Carnuntum, Loriacum, Virunum, Vindobona (Vienna). Roman mosaics, idols, notably of Mithras, sculptures like the *Athlete of the Helenenberg*, have been found in many places. The transition from the provincial Roman style to the style of the migrations can be best studied in ornaments and jewelry. The remains of barbarian cemeteries illustrate the art of the age of the migrations from the 4th to the 7th cent. A.D.

Latin culture was of decisive importance for further artistic development in Austria. Christianity was introduced at an early date. In the 8th cent. the first great monasteries and bishoprics were founded. Austrian medieval culture was chiefly ecclesiastical with its main strongholds in the numerous abbeys and monasteries, and spread from ecclesiastical centers, notably Salzburg. The Pre-Carolingian, the Carolingian, and the Ottonian periods, from the 8th to the 10th cent., are represented in Austria by remarkable works of art: e.g. the Tassilo chalice in Kremsmünster; the murals in Mals and Naturns in South-Tyrol; the ivories from St. Paul and Seitenstetten. Byzantine works of the minor arts were imported.

The Romanesque period in Austria covers the 11th, 12th, and most of the 13th cent. According to the traditional character of the Austrian people, it lasted longer here than in France and Germany. From the Romanesque period onward more numerous works of art have been preserved. Their chief importance lies in the field of architecture and painting (frescoes and illuminated books). Outstanding works are the monastic basilicas of Gurk, Millstatt, and St. Paul, all in Carinthia; Seckau in Styria; Heiligenkreuz, Klosterneuburg, and Lilienfeld, all in Lower Austria; Nonnberg and St. Peter in the city of Salzburg; the Cathedral of St. Stephen's in Vienna (West façade) and the old "Dom" of Salzburg (now replaced by the Renaissance structure). In these works are blended Lombardian and German influences. Plastic decoration concentrates on the portals, e.g. the Riesentor of St. Stephen's. Smaller buildings such as parish churches (Schöngrabern in Lower Austria) and round chapels (so-called "Karners") are often distinguished through richness of tectonic and plastic decor. The walls of the Romanesque interiors offered ample space for fresco painters to display their works. The West-Gallery of the cathedral of Gurk contains the most important and best preserved Romanesque murals of central Europe. Other examples are: Nonnberg, Pürgg in Styria, Brixen (now Bressanone) and Hoch-Eppan in South Tyrol. A remarkable school of book-illumination developed in Salzburg. The Abbey Klosterneuburg commissioned a multi-panelled altarpiece (completed 1181) from the Master Nicholas of Verdun, which remains the greatest work of Romanesque goldsmith art in the western world.

The Gothic style filtered through in the late 13th cent. but only gradually. While Romanesque art is mainly connected with the Benedictine order, the Cistercian and Dominican monks had an important share in spreading Gothic art as evident in the early examples: Heiligenkreuz; Friesach in Carinthia.

The flowering of Gothic art comes in the 14th cent., and extends through the 15th cent. Important schools of sculpture and painting developed. The court and the nobility played an increasing part as patrons of the arts. In the 14th cent. Vienna was a meeting place of great architects, sculptors, painters, glass painters, and goldsmiths. The Romanesque cathedral of St. Stephen's, due to the munificence of King Premyzl Ottokar of Bohemia, received a Gothic choir and naves under the Habsburg Dukes, Albert and Rudolph the Founder (*der Stifter*). The latter competed with the court of his father-in-law, Charles IV. in Prague, in making his residence a center of art and culture.

The period of High-Gothic extends in Austria throughout the 14th cent. The main examples in architecture aside from St. Stephen's are the Maria Stiegen church, the Minoritenkirche (Church of the Fratres Minores), and the Augustiner-Kirche, all in Vienna; the cloisters in Klosterneuburg, the monasteries of Zwettl and Neuberg. As in architecture, also in sculpture French influence prevailed at the beginning of the century. Works of classical beauty arose such as the virgins of Klosterneuburg and Wiener Neustadt by a sculptor trained in France, the *Servant's Virgin* in St. Stephen's. Later in the century, a specific Austrian variety of the Gothic style developed, largely inspired from Bohemia. The workshop of the master masons of St. Stephen's was connected with those of Prague and Ratisbon. Austria had a predilection for the spacious type of the so-called Hall-Church, characterized by the equal height of the naves. Gothic transcendentalism created in St. Stephen's tower one of the most fascinating works. The same feeling distinguishes the portrait sculptures of the Dukes' which adorn it, and the windows of the contemporary glass painters. A remarkable school of panel painting developed in Vienna after the beginning of the 14th cent. as manifest in the wings of the Verdun Altar. In the 15th cent., the century of Late Gothic, panel painting, wood-carving, and the graphic arts increased in importance. Leading schools of painting were those of Lower Austria, mainly Vienna, and Styria. Glow of color and highest pictorial refinement prove the affinity of Austrian panel painting of the early 15th cent. with the schools of Paris and Burgundy. With the decline of Bohemian art, native Austrian art rose in importance. The rising era of naturalism brought forward outstanding artistic personalities like the anonymous Master of the votive panel of St. Lambrecht and of the crucifixion in the Museum of Linz, the Master of the Carrying of the Cross from the Worcester Collection (now in the Institute of Fine Arts, Chicago), the Master of the Albrechtsaltar, the Master of Schloss Lichtenstein, Konrad Laib, and the sculptor Jakob Kaschauer. With artists like the Master of St. Wolfgang and the Master of the Mount Calvary, Austria contributed to the history of early engraving. In the 2nd half of the 15th cent., monumental altarpieces fitted with movable wings, consisting of wood-carvings and painted panels, became a specific artistic creation of the Austrian mountain and Danube countries. Tyrol, at that time, had the leadership. Michael Pacher, the greatest painter of the German speaking nations in the 2nd half of the 15th cent., was also a great sculptor. He created the altarpieces of Gries and Brixen in South Tyrol, and as the most famous, the St. Wolfgang Altar (1471-1481). Great painters like the Frueaufs in Salzburg contributed to altarpieces of this kind. Other important altars are: Kefermarkter Altar (Upper Austria), Schottenaltar (Vienna), of which only the paintings are preserved. Local communities gained increasing importance as patrons in this development. Many old Austrian cities received their characteristic features in this period, such as Steyr, Hall, Innsbruck. Among outstanding late-Gothic architects may be cited: Michael Knab and Hans Buchsbaum, the builders of the towers of St. Stephen's, Anton Pilgram, the creator of the pulpit and the organ gallery in St. Stephen's. Among the outstanding sculptors, foreign and native, were: Nicolaus von Leyden (Tombs of Emperor Friedrich III. and Eleonora of Portugal), and Lorenz Luchsperger.

The beginning of the 16th cent. brought an overlapping of Late Gothic and Renaissance. Signs of a new artistic period appear after

1500. Renaissance forms were introduced from Italy, but developed in the Late Gothic spirit. The distinction between Early and High-Renaissance, valid for Italy, is not applicable to Austrian art of the period.

During the first half of the 16th cent. the art produced for the court and for wealthy citizens takes precedence over ecclesiastical art. The reign of Maximilian I. (1493-1513) was an era of special splendor. It was distinguished by a great school of painting, centering in the Danube valley, one of whose achievements was to create an independent art of landscape painting and drawing. The **Danube School** (so-called because its main works originated chiefly between Passau and Vienna) was formed in Austria. The Austrians Rueland Frueauf the Younger, Marx Reichlich, Jörg Kölderer, Wolf Huber participated just as did the South Germans Lucas Cranach, Jörg Breu, Albrecht and Erhard Altdorfer. The main works of this school were painted for Austrian patrons and are still preserved in Austria (e.g. Altdorfer's altar at St. Florian, 1518). The Austrian spirit and the poetical charm of Austria's scenery largely shaped the character of the Danube School. The most prominent monument of Renaissance sculpture in Austria is the tomb of Maximilian I. in the Hofkirche at Innsbruck, mainly a work of Tyrolian artists in which also the German sculptors Veit Stoss and Peter Vischer participated.

The Late Renaissance covers the 2nd half of the 16th cent. and continues during the first decades of the 17th cent. It brought a complete victory of Italian forms. Austria as a Catholic country was open to the influence of the South in the period of the Counter-Reformation. Italian artists received great commissions (e.g. "Dom" of Salzburg). The international culture of court and aristocracy during the reign of Emperor Rudolph II (1576-1612) patronized Italian and Netherlandish artists to an equal extent.

Another great flowering period of Austrian art is the Baroque. Its roots are international, and Italian artists working in Austria had an important share in it (e.g. Burnacini, Carlone, Allio, Pozzo). We distinguish the periods of the Early Baroque (1st half of the 17th cent.), High Baroque (about 1650-1720), and the Late Baroque which in Austria goes over into the period of the Rococo, coinciding with the reign of the Empress Maria Theresa (1740-1780). Out of the international premises grew a genuine and national Austrian baroque art. Its climax was at the beginning of the 18th cent. marked by the activities of a group of great

architects. Vienna, flourishing after the victorious repulse of the Turks (1683), was the leading center of this activity. The era of the greatest Baroque splendor was during the reigns of Joseph I. (1705-1711), and Charles VI. (1711-1740). Baroque art answered not only the demands of the court and of the aristocracy for a magnificent representation but also involved a revival of religious art. Many medieval abbeys were rebuilt on a grand scale: Klosterneuburg, Melk, Göttweig, Kremsmünster, St. Florian, Wilhering, Wilten. The most outstanding architects were: Johann Bernhard Fischer von Erlach, 1656-1723 (main works: Kollegienkirche, Salzburg; Karlskirche, Vienna; Castle Frain, Moravia; projects for Schönbrunn and the Hofburg; Imperial Library, Winter Palace of Prince Eugene, Palais Trautson, all in Vienna); Joseph Emanuel Fischer von Erlach, 1693-1742 (Hofburg Reichskanzlei); Johann Lucas von Hildebrand, 1668-1745 (main works: Belvedere, Palais Schwarzenberg, Palais Kinsky, Peterskirche, all in Vienna; Monastery Goettweig); Jakob Prandtauer, 1660-1726 (main works: Monasteries Melk, Herzogenburg, Dürnstein, with the assistance of Joseph Mungenast); Matthias Steinl, 1644-1727, who designed the famous towers of Dürnstein and Zwettl.

The leading sculptors of the Baroque were: Georg Raphael Donner, 1693-1741 (Fountain on the Neuer Markt in Vienna), Balthasar Permoser, 1651-1732, and J. T. Stammel who continued the Late Gothic practice of wood-carving (*Allegories of the Four Last Things* in Admont). The works of the architects were embellished by the spirited frescoes of Johann Michael Rottmayr, Daniel Gran, and Paul Troger.

In the era of Maria Theresa, architecture was kept on a modest scale while painting reached an unsurpassed climax in the art of Franz Anton Maulbertsch (1724-1796). The pious mood of the contemporary Austrian ecclesiastic music (Haydn, Mozart) found a pictorial counter-part in the works of Maulbertsch and Martin Johann Schmidt (known as Kremserschmidt).

The era of neo-classicism during the reign of Francis I. gained greater importance through the creations of Beethoven and Schubert than through the works of its painters and sculptors although distinguished artists like Friedrich Heinrich Füger and Franz Anton Zauner were active.

The bourgeois era of the "Vormärz", between the Congress of Vienna, 1814, and the Revolution of March 1848, developed on one hand a religious and poetical romanticism in the works of Moritz von Schwind, Joseph Führich, and Scheffer von Leonhardshoff, and on the other hand a cultured and intimate pictorial naturalism in the works of Joseph Danhauser, Peter Fendi, Carl Schindler, Friedrich von Amerling, and Rudolf Alt. Georg Ferdinand Waldmüller (1793-1865) developed in his landscape paintings a vision of nature whose grandeur is paralleled only by the simplicity and straightforwardness of his portraits.

Historical styles in architecture flourished during the era of Francis Joseph I. The city of Vienna received its 19th cent. features (Ringstrasse with Opera House by Van der Nuell and Siccardsburg; Parliament; City Hall; Neue Hofburg). Hans Makart and Hans Canon revived a decorative baroque style in painting; August von Pettenkofen developed an Austrian impressionism, while Anton Romako foreshadowed expressionism.

Of greater creative importance became the following decades of the 20th cent. when Austrian art took the lead in the development of modern architecture (Otto Wagner, Adolf Loos) and progressive art of painting (Gustav Klimt, Egon Schiele, Oskar Kokoschka, Herbert Boeckl). See Otto Benesch, *Österreichische Handzeichnungen des XV. und XVI. Jahrhunderts.* Die Meisterzeichnung V, Freiburg, 1936; Georg Dehio, *Handbuch der Deutschen Kunstdenkmäler,* Österreich, vols. I, II, 1933, 1935; Josef Garber, *Die romanischen Wandgemälde Tirols,* Vienna, 1928; Karl Garzarolli-Thurnlackh, *Die barocke Handzeichnung in Österreich,* Vienna; Karl Ginhart, *Die Kunstdenkmäler Kärntens,* Klagenfurt and ed., *Die Bildende Kunst Österreichs,* vols. I-IV, 1936; *Österreichische Kunstbücher,* vols. I ff., Vienna, 1920 ff., special series, *Die Kunst in Tirol; Österreichische Kunsttopographie,* vols. I ff., Vienna, 1907 ff.; Otto Pächt, *Österreichische Tafelmalerei der Gotik,* Augsburg, 1929; Wilhelm Suida, *Österreichische Kunstschätze,* Jahrgang I-III, 1912-14; Hans Tietze, *Wien,* Berühmte Kunststätten 67, Leipzig, 1918; Joseph Weingartner, *Die Kunstdenkmäler Südtirols,* 4 vols.; F. Wickhoff, *Beschreibendes Verzeichnis der illuminierten Handschriften in Österreich,* Leipzig, 1905 ff.   —O.B.

authentication. See FORGERIES IN PAINTINGS.

authentic echoi. See EASTERN CHANTS.

authentic modes. See modes, ecclesiastical; MEDIEVAL MUSIC; idiom A (2).

author's alterations. *Book.* Type set or reset after original text has been composed.

auto-harp. See mechanical instruments.

automatic harpsichord. See mechanical instruments.

automatism in photography. See PHOTOGRAPHY.

auxiliary notes. *Mus.* Notes which are not essential to the harmony or melody; grace notes.

auxochromes. See COLOR.

Awata yaki (Jap.). A pottery ware made at Awata, Kyoto.

axis. See PERSPECTIVE.

Axminster. A rug carpet originally known as Moquette; an invention of Halcyon Skinner in 1876. Originated in Axminster, Devonshire, England, the seat of the imitation Oriental carpets known as Axminsters. It is a carpet with a chain of cotton or jute and a woolen or worsted filling; a heavy pile.   —G.W.R.

Axminster loom. Three fundamental features in the construction of an Axminster loom are: (1) the employment of yarn spools in the production of a figured pile surface; (2) the insertion into the carpet structure of tufts of pile yarn in one of two forms: (a) by cutting the yarn from the spools after being placed and secured in the carpet, and (b) by cutting the yarns from the spools into tufts-pieces and then inserting such tufts into the carpet; (3) the passing of the shots of weft into the sheds in the warps by means of a needle carrier.
—B.E.J.

Axminster, machine made. First known as Moquette and later as Royal Axminster. Developed in the U.S.A. and involves the use of highly intricate machinery which does the work of human fingers by looping each individual tuft of wool into the body of the fabric. Two distinct types, narrow width and seamless. The loom is equipped with a series of spools on which the pile has been wound. Each spool wound with different colored yarns represents a row of tufts in the rug. The spools are hand set according to the designers' pattern and are mounted in a long, endless chain which brings each spool off the chain and causes it to insert the yarn ends through the warp. A comb underneath the fabric loops the yarn around the filler or cross thread and the knives like giant scissors cut the rows of tufts,

The spool is put back on the chain, the next spool is put into position and the process is repeated.

Two things are outstanding about Axminster: It has unlimited color possibilities beyond any other woven floor covering, and the weave is produced in a greater yardage than any other in America. Axminster is woven today up to 18 feet wide, seamless. An Axminster is easily distinguished from any other weave because the fabric can be rolled lengthwise but is the only weave which cannot be rolled crosswise. This is due to the stiff jute construction. Axminster bears the closest resemblance to a hand-knotted carpet in its structure. This is owing to the fact that both are tufted, but in the Axminster the tufts of wool are inserted mechanically in rows and bound down in the weft but are not knotted. Each tuft shows on the surface and forms part of the design. None of the tuft yarn is buried in the back of the fabric, as it is in the Wilton weave, other than that which is required for attachment to the weft. The preparation of the yarns for weaving Axminster is a long process and takes weeks, while the actual time of weaving requires about one-tenth of the entire time of manufacturing.   —B.E.J.

Ayyubid art. See ISLAMIC ART.

Aztec. The term sometimes applied to the inhabitants of Tenochtitlan, the ancient Mexico City, but better used for the culture of the independent groups inhabiting central Mexico from 1300 to the Spanish Conquest in 1519-21. Theirs was a strong theological art based on a religion strongly stressing a cult of human sacrifice.   —G.C.V.

azure. *Her.* Blue.

azure dragon. See SYMBOLISM IN FAR EASTERN ART.

azurite. Common among the blue pigments of the Middle Ages and the Renaissance, this is now available only as a pure mineral. It is a basic copper carbonate and occurs in many parts of the world in secondary copper ore deposits. There it is often associated with malachite, the green basic carbonate of copper. The blue stone was ground and purified but retained something of its crystalline character. Because of the extensive labor in its preparation, azurite went out of use when artificially prepared blues came in to take its place.
                                    —G.L.S.

B

Babylonian art. See MESOPOTAMIAN ART.

Bacchanals. The Greek vegetation-god, Dionysus (Bacchus), was attended by ecstatic dancing women called Bacchanals (Bacchantes), whose worship was a favorite subject of many Greek vase-painters and sculptors. The best description of their rites is given in the choral odes of Euripides' *Bacchae*. Scopas, one of the leading sculptors of the 4th cent. B.C. made a famous statue of a Bacchanal, which may be reconstructed from a statuette now in Dresden, picturing a woman clad in a short Doric peplos, with her head thrown back, hair windswept, and hands brandishing a goat which she has killed in her frenzied revels. In neo-Attic reliefs and on Arretine pottery the subject was a popular one, giving artists the opportunity to represent groups of lovely dancers swinging along in joyous abandon. Titian and Tintoretto used the theme in their paintings of Dionysus discovering the deserted Ariadne on the island of Naxos. —W.R.A.

Bacchus. See Dionysus.

bachiru (Jap.). Ivory, tinted with a surface color, and incised to show the design in the original light tone.

backbone. *Book.* The same as spine, the back of a bound book.

backdrop. See STAGESETTING.

backed. See EDITION BINDING.

background. See STAGESETTING.

background music. Industrial music which is soft and sweet enough to be pleasant but non-distracting to workers at tasks requiring considerable concentration. —W.A.K.

backing. *Book.* A hammering process by which the sections are bent over at the back, so as to form grooves into which the boards forming the two sides fit.

Backstein Gotik. See brick Gothic; GERMAN ART.

badacco. See baldachin.

Baga, art of the. See AFRICAN NEGRO ART.

Bagafore art. See AFRICAN NEGRO ART.

bagatelle. A trifle. A musical sketch or short piece in a light style.

Baghdad cloth. See baldachin.

Baghdad wool. A dark carpet wool from Mesopotamia.

bagpipe. See MUSICAL INSTRUMENTS.

Bakelite. A synthetic substance combined by L. H. Baekeland, a native of Belgium and since 1889 a distinguished inventor and scientist in the United States. This new plastic, named after its inventor, is described as "a chemical synthesis from phenol and formaldehyde, replacing hard rubber and amber for uses in electricity and industrial arts where former plastics are unsuited." Baekeland started the commercial development of the substance in 1907. Like other plastics, bakelite has insulation properties, is not subject to corrosion and chemical action, is malleable, has great strength and hardness, can be easily treated for color and finish, and maintains a high degree of uniformity. It has been found an invaluable substitute for shellac, being electrically and thermally resistant, and is used for all electrical equipment which requires insulation or non-conduction. In the accessories of everyday life phonograph records, buttons, billiard balls, pipestems, and umbrella handles of bakelite are in common use.   —W.S.R.

baking. See CERAMICS I.

balalaika. A kind of guitar, usually triangular with a long neck and two or three strings. Common in Russia.

balance. (1) Originally, as applied to art, a rather broad and vague term denoting "a general harmony between the parts" (*Oxford Dictionary*), *repose,* or the special combination and arrangement of the parts of a work which was believed to be responsible for the impression of repose. Many of the specific meanings which the word acquired as the analysis of these arrangements progressed would have been discussed, if they had come up for discussion at all, under the topics of *contrast* and *proportion.* Its first specific application seems to have been to symmetrical figures. Fundamentally, the word *balance* suggests a gravitational equilibrium, and accordingly seems ideally applicable to any figure that is symmetrical with respect to its vertical axis. More remotely, it suggests a pair of opposites that complement each other so perfectly that the whole which they form seems complete and well-rounded; such pairs may be as arbitrary as straight lines and curves, verticals and horizontals, cold colors and warm colors, slow passages in music and rapid ones, or Shakespeare's clowns and tragic kings and still be recognized as constituting a balance, yet the ideal example is again the opposite halves of a symmetrical figure. But when this particular balance is analyzed it becomes obvious that it depends less on any innate difference between the two units involved than on their arrangement in space—and the whole field of equalities achieved primarily by means of arrangements in space is gradually recognized as the distinctive province of balance. Other names serve equally well for a mere opposition of qualities, or for qualities as general as harmony and repose, but here balance has few rivals. The word may of course be applied to a distribution in time, as in speaking of a song or a sentence that is built of balanced phrases, but distribution in space can be estimated so much more exactly and so many more equalities can be created within a given composition that it permits the creation of richer and subtler effects. The first decisive advance in our understanding of the subject was the realization that symmetry was not indispensable, since a satisfactory balance could be created with unequal and dissimilar units placed at unequal distances from the center of a composition. Progress was hampered, however, by two erroneous assumptions. The first was that symmetry and this balance of unequals were merely variant forms of a single phenomenon, which could be differentiated sufficiently as "formal" balance on the one hand and "asymmetric", "informal", "disguised", "subtle", or "occult" balance on the other. The second assumption was that, like balance in practical life, it was in all its forms essentially a gravitational phenomenon. A composition in which a large object near the center was balanced by a small one near the edge in the opposite half so inevitably suggested a seesaw, in which a large child sitting near the middle could be balanced by a small one at the end of the board that it was taken for granted that balance in a picture was an affair of the same sort. Writers spoke of the unequal "weights" of the balanced units and greatly overemphasized the slight discomfort of feeling that the "heavy" side of a composition that is not balanced is on the point of tipping downward. It was widely denied that there could be any other balance than balance across a vertical axis. Gradually, however, intimations of another ingredient in balance began to seep into the literature. Ethel Puffer wrote of the sort of excursions the eye preferred to make from the geometric center of a composition; other aestheticians spoke, more simply, of the different attractions which the units of a composition possessed for the eye of an observer and of the necessity for so distributing them that they will seem to balance each other; a few even recognized that a balance of this sort might be created across a diagonal axis, or possibly a horizontal one, as well as across a vertical one. Yet no one took the trouble to differentiate this newly discovered type of balance from the old; in nearly every discussion of the subject they were treated as, at most, alternative explanations of a single phenomenon, and remained intermingled as if in the strange confusion of a dream. Writers frequently began a paragraph in terms of one and ended it in terms of the other, without seeming to be fully conscious of the transition. It was not clearly realized that the attraction for the eye of any detail in a composition was equally effective in every direction, instead of merely across the center or across any axis whatsoever, and accordingly could be balanced in any direction; or that the frame, or other boundary, also created a set of attractions which must also be balanced; or that only a continuous network of balanced units covering the whole area within the frame could satisfy all these requirements, and that formal balance across an axis must be attributed to other factors. Neither was it understood that even a perfectly symmetrical figure at the exact center of a picture, no matter how irreproachable its gravitational balance, might still be too small to create a satisfactory balance with the frame, or that a symmetrical figure contained two factors which differentiated it sharply from every irregular form of balance —the repetition of the *shape* of each half by the other and the purely visual equality between the distances of every pair of corresponding points from the axis of symmetry. DeWitt Parker recognized that the new non-axial balance between visual attractions was something so different from balance in the old sense of the word that it needed a different name and suggested calling it *rhythm;* more recently, *equilibrium* (q.v.) has been suggested for the same purpose, but the problem still requires a great deal of analysis and experiment.

(2) In *architecture* the word balance, in addition to its usual meanings in the two dimensional arts, may refer to a balance of actual forces, such as the resistance of a column to the weight which it supports or the opposite thrusts of the two sides of an arch. In *dancing, to balance* is to take a few steps in one direction and then repeat them in the opposite direction, or it may refer to a pair, or a line, of dancers who approach each other and then withdraw. A *balancing position* is one in which a dancer stands on one leg with the other raised in a position that leaves him wholly free to choose his next step. The word is seldom used in connection with *sculpture,* either in the literature of the art or in the language of the studios.

(3) The adjective *balanced* is sometimes employed, like *harmonious, pleasing,* and similar words, as a casual term of praise for a work of art, with little or no intention of attributing to it any specific quality. —C.T.

(4) In *literary criticism* to indicate that in a work a proper respect is paid to all of the elements used. A work is balanced when each of its aspects receives due attention; it is unbalanced when some parts of the work are given a false emphasis. This distortion of balance may occur with reference to the subjects presented; or it may involve a sacrifice of form to meaning, of meaning to form, or of some of the values within these. —I.J.

baldachin, baldaquin, baldacchino (It., *Baldacco,* for the city of Baghdad, which was the center for the manufacture of a rich fabric of embroidered silk originally woven with a warp of gold thread; this fabric, *Baldacco* or Baghdad cloth, was preferred for the making of ceremonial canopies, the name of the cloth becoming associated with the canopy itself).

(1) A canopy of either permanent or temporary nature, stationary or portable.

(2a) A portable covering of decorative nature carried in ceremonial processions to protect and dignify distinguished individuals, treasured or sacred objects. The baldachin generally is supported by at least four poles carried by porters. It should not be confused with the ceremonial umbrella of the Orient; for example, see "Procession of *Corpus Domini*" by Gentile Bellini, Academy, Venice.

(2b) *Arch.* A stationary canopy of cloth over a dais or similar seat of a dignitary. The term sometimes is used in designating the canopy and curtains of a bed.

(2c) *Arch.* A fixed canopy, including its supports, of durable materials such as stone, marble, wood, or metal, built to shelter an altar (usually an isolated high altar) or sacred vessel. Baldachins of this nature are sometimes called tabernacles—example, Tabernacle of Or San Michele, Florence, by Andrea di Cione (Orcagna)—or ciboria—examples, S. M. in Trastevere, Rome, and Sant' Ambrogio, Milan. Many baldachins are elaborate in size and in use of materials, combining the art of sculptor, metalworker, and lapidarist; for example, that of the Cathedral of S. M. de los Angeles, Puebla, Mexico, and that of San Pietro in Vaticano, Rome, by G. L. Bernini, which measures approximately 95 ft. from the floor to the top of the finial cross. —J.C.

ballabile, ballabili (It. *ballare,* to dance). An evolution of a group or groups of dancers as climax to a scene, act or whole ballet as finale, when the entire company is merged into a collective moving mass, frequently executing a single repeated series of movements in unison immediately preceding a final held tableau. —L.K.

ballad. See song.

ballad dances. See chorovody.

ballad opera. An opera made up chiefly of folk songs, ballads, etc.

ballade. See MEDIEVAL MUSIC.

ballata. See MEDIEVAL MUSIC.

ball clay. *Cer.* A clay with plasticity and binding power. See CERAMICS I.

ballet (It. *ballare,* to dance). The *ballate* were Tuscan dance-songs of the 13th and 14th cents. These *canzone a ballo* received the diminutive *balleti,* from which we derive "ballad" as well as "ballet". A ballet is a theatrical representation achieved by means and in terms of dancing. It has been recent practice to term any danced action as ballet. Strictly speaking, a ballet is a particular kind of lyric or non-realistic spectacle, making use of a vocabulary of dance movement, based on Italian social dancing of the Renaissance and later amplified and theatricalized from inter-European sources, until in the late seventeenth century it was codified in the French Academy. The terminology is traditionally French, and terms once applying to social dance forms now specifically refer to a stage idiom.   —L.K.

balletto. (1) A ballet. (2) Name for an allegretto in 4/4 time (Bach).

balletomane (Fr., a ballet maniac or enthusiast). The ballet boasts an attendant body of devoted amateurs, like the *aficionado* of bull-fighting, the fan of baseball or boxing. These dispute the technical or personal qualifications of individual dancers, the merits of choreography and its specific performance.   —L.K.

ball flower. A carved ornament common in decorated Gothic architecture in the form of a circular flower having a ball at the center.

ball mill. *Cer.* Mill with porcelain lining, using hard pebbles for grinding. See CERAMICS I.

ballon (Fr., balloon). The quality of spring, bounce or lightness in a dancer. *La danse ballonné* is a type of movement based on leaps and broad movement, covering considerable air and floor space.   —L.K.

balloon framing (jocularly so-called because the buildings "go up so fast"). A simplified and practical western American type of framing for wooden buildings, mostly residences and stores of moderate size. The old *braced frame,* based on medieval traditions, was built up stage by stage, with elaborate mortise and tenon connections. This newer type was made possible in the 1830's by cheap nails for connections, and abundant saw-mill lumber (especially 2 x 4 or 6 inch studs in two-story lengths, 2 x 8 inch joists, and 1-inch sheathing boards). The exterior walls of a typical balloon frame are cellular, composed of vertical 2 x 4 inch studs which are set (about 16 inches center to center) upon a 4 x 6 inch *sill,* carry a notched-in *ledger board* at half-height to sustain the 2nd floor joists, and are capped by a 4 x 4 inch *plate* sustaining the rafters of the roof. Sill, plate, and corner studs (which must be stronger) are usually built up of 2-inch lumber. Interior walls are of 2 x 3 inch or 2 x 4 inch studs. Bridged openings receive door and window frames. The exterior sheathing, often applied diagonally, gives stiffness. This framing scheme, resulting in a notable economy of time, skilled labor, and materials, greatly facilitated the feverish growth of the western boom towns. The later *combination frame* incorporates bracing and other features of the braced frame; it is a further improvement, and is now in general use.

The earliest balloon frame building of note was the one-story shed-like St. Mary's, first church for Roman Catholics in Chicago (1833). Its builder was Augustine Deodat Taylor, from Hartford, Connecticut. Local tradition in Chicago ascribes the invention to the civil engineer and lumber dealer, George Washington Snow, from Keene, Vermont. Perhaps he worked out the typical 2-story scheme and/or as supplier, effectively spread knowledge of it. See Walker Field—A Re-examination of the Invention of the Balloon Frame, *Journal of the American Society of Architectural Historians,* vol. II, No. 4 (Oct. 1942), p. 3, and Voss and Henry, *Architectural Construction,* II, book I (New York, Wiley, 1926).   —K.J.C.

balsam. A few of the varnish materials used by painters come under this name. Copaiba balsam—frequently an ingredient in varnish mixtures—Canada balsam, Venice turpentine, and Strasbourg turpentine are others. In general, a balsam is the resinous exudate from coniferous trees. From it, by distillation, the volatile oils like turpentine are derived and the residue, after distillation, is some kind of crude resin.   —G.L.S.

Baluba art. See AFRICAN NEGRO ART.

baluster shape. Like the small pillar of a balustrade; swelling in the center or toward the base. A term applicable to many examples of Oriental ceramics.   —J.A.M.

balustrade. A handrail, usually resting on a series of small pillars (balusters).

bambino (It.). Representation of the infant Christ.

bambocciade (It.). A painting representing a grotesque scene from common or rustic life.

bamboo. See SYMBOLISM IN FAR EASTERN ART.

bamboo painting. See CHINESE ARTS.

banana oil. See amyl acetate.

band. *Mus.* (1). In the U.S.A., a group of ensemble performers upon wind and percussion instruments, as distinguished from an orchestra. *Military band* is such a band used by a regiment for marching or for concert purposes. *Brass band* is composed entirely of brass and percussion instruments; used for outdoor performance. (2) Hist., referred also to an orchestra or a chorus.   —M.E.

banded. Term applied to masonry in which there are definite bands or courses of stones. More clearly described as random coursed or alternating coursed masonry.   —J.M.M.

banderole, banderol. *Arch.* Frequent during the Renaissance. A sculptured band, often bearing an inscription.

banisters. See balustrade.

banjo. See MUSICAL INSTRUMENTS; AMERICAN NEGRO MUSIC.

Bänkelsänger (Ger., bench singer). Wandering minstrel who recounts romantic tales of adventure or history.

Banko jaki (Jap.). Pottery made in Ise province.

Banmana art. See AFRICAN NEGRO ART.

banquette (Fr. dim. of *banc,* bench). (1) Any bank, ledge, etc. (2) In southwestern archaeology: The term sometimes applied to the raised mass or ledge that is better known as the bench.   —J.M.M.

Baoulé art. See AFRICAN NEGRO ART.

bar (or **bar line**). *Mus.* (1) A line drawn vertically across the staff, measuring the music metrically according to the time signature. (2) Illogically used for *measure.* See also HERALDRY; ACOUSTICS.

barbican. See castle.

Barbizon school. See FRENCH ART.

barcarole, barcarolle. (1) A boatman's song. (2) Any piece in imitation of the songs of Venetian gondoliers.

barbotine. *Cer.* A slip or clay paste used in relief decoration of coarse pottery.

baren (Jap.). A circular pad made of a braided mat covered with a bamboo sheath used to transfer the image by pressure and circular motion from block to paper in producing Japanese wood-block prints.   —J.A.M.

barium yellow. This pale green pigment, known also as lemon yellow, is an artificial precipitate from neutral potassium chromate and barium chloride. As a pigment it is rather weak in color and rather translucent but has the advantage of being among the most stable of yellow coloring materials. It was developed during the first half of the 19th cent.
                —G.L.S.

barking vibrato. See VIBRATO.

baroque. From the Portuguese word "Barroco", meaning an irregularly shaped pearl. The term was used until the second part of the 19th cent. for "peculiar" and "overornate". It took a generation opposed to the classicist and rationalist theories of the first part of the 19th cent. and a matured notion of the genesis of styles before an understanding of the indigenous qualities of the post-Renaissance style called Baroque could be developed. This process of a transformation of a word of ridicule into one of a historically descriptive kind can be compared with the similar process the word "Gothic" underwent. We owe the elucidation of this style to Cornelius Gurlitt, Mâle, Woelfflin, Ricci, Dvořák, Sedlmayer, Weisbach and others. The term is used today for the art style of the period from about 1600 to 1720. If the *Rococo* which is really the last phase of the Baroque is included, the Baroque lasts until about 1760.

As far as form is concerned, Baroque in the Mediterranean countries appears as the organic outgrowth of the preceding Renaissance style. We call this development "organic" because it evolves features which can be likened to the "Baroque" elements in Hellenistic and late Roman art and which indicate that there exists a universal and natural tendency in the maturing of classical art styles to widen the scope of their expressive means and to enhance their language, until by mere evolution they have grown into a style in many ways opposed and contrary to their original concepts. It is therefore in our opinion not necessary to link the Baroque primarily to new spiritual concepts of the 16th cent. such as the Counter-Reformation (q.v.) but to see its basic stimulus in the maturing of pictorial and plastic problems in the later works of the High Renaissance masters such as Raphael, Michelangelo, Titian, Correggio, Sebastiano del Piombo, etc. In their work the constituents of the coming Baroque appear as an outgrowth of purely aesthetic concepts such as the meaning of art as an illusion of natural and psychic reality which bears in itself a tendency toward the "illusionistic" style of the Baroque.

Architecture. The architectural archetypes such as cruciform churches, centralized churches, temple façades, etc., remain basically the same as in the Renaissance and so do the ornamental parts such as columns, pilasters, cartouches, etc., yet they are all used for an intensification of the optical and sensorial effects. Proportions grow in height or become heavier. The architectural parts are increasingly deprived of their independence and become subordinated to a major theme. Consequently, ground plans present a rich variation and complication of the basic traditional forms Inner and outer walls undulate in curves just as figures move flame-like in a "figura serpentinata" (Michelangelo's term). In becoming the instrument of the Jesuit Counter-Reformation (i.e. Gesù in Rome by Vignola, 1568), the liturgical elements of the Catholic service are translated into dynamic visual symbols and the humanist restraint gives way to a fighting spirit which persuades, entices and seduces the devout. The exterior is conceived not only in context with its setting (previous centuries did this too) but in relation to its perspectivic appearance and its picturesque effects (Rome, St. Peter; St. Agnese in Piazza Navona). Façades are pulled together, buildings duplicated or multiplied in order to create the total effect (Rome, S. Carlo alle quattro fontane). Cupola and bell towers are merged closer with the body of the church and vitalize the contour of the building. Transitions from one part to another are organic and lend the impression of plastically moulded bodies. Ornamentation abounds, yet, in contrast to the late Renaissance, is not applied to a plane surface, but develops in form of plastic elements which emanate from the structural parts as an overflow of their dynamic energies.

In the interior all parts are used for the creation of one total effect. The longitudinal direction of the nave is received by the centralized and cupola-crowned transept. The old basilica scheme with side chapels all along the side naves has regained its old position. Monochrome treatment of the wall and its decorative elements changes to polychrome treatment. Surprising light effects, often from invisible sources of illumination, enrich the appearance and the mood of the interior. Marble columns and marble incrustation of the walls, stucco ornamentation and gilded wood carving on altars, confession chairs, etc. are treated in unison with sculpture and wall painting and tend toward the creation of one homogeneous picture to the eye of the observer. This means that the final effect is one of picturesque illusion rather than of intellectual demonstration as we find it in the previous Renaissance architecture.

The idea of the *Gesamtkunstwerk* (see universal artwork) shapes not only churches but also draws garden and palace together into one total effect (Versailles) and creates for the first time monumental solutions in city Planning (Rome; St. Peter's Square; Piazza del Popolo; Paris: Tuilleries; Bath: Crescent). Palaces expand to the size of castles indicating the growing importance and wealth of aristocracy in the dynastic organization of Europe in the 17th and 18th cent. London, Vienna, Prague, Madrid furnish a wealth of examples. Palace and castle both renounce the last traces of defensive buildings and open their walls with rows of windows, interspaced with balconies, thus changing austerity of appearance to urbanity and elegance. The dwellings of the citizen class follow on a more modest scale the example of palatial architecture and abound in picturesque solutions of the treatment of façades and roofs. Bridges, staircases, fountains, monuments help to create a consciously planned setting or an instinctively blended organism as we find it in Rome and Prague at its best.

The Baroque style in architecture originated in Rome stimulated by Michelangelo's three-dimensional plastic treatment of architecture to be seen in the choir and the cupola of St. Peter's. Galeazzo Alessis' (1512-1572) Bolognese palaces and Andrea Palladio's (1508-1580) building activity in Vicenza and Venice also contribute toward the maturing of Baroque architecture. Borromini (1599-1667) and Bernini (1598-1680), created the pompous and magnificent language of the Roman Baroque which spread all over Europe yet in France and England was counteracted by a tendency for classicist solutions (Paris, Louvre, where Bernini lost the competition against the classicist Perrault in 1665). On the other hand, Spain welcomed the Roman Baroque in accordance with its native tendency for ornateness and transplanted it into its American Colonial empire, thus making the Baroque the true architectonic European style in the New World. The Catholic countries of Central Europe (Bavaria, Bohemia, Austria) transformed the Italian style into an idiom of their own which surpasses the Roman Baroque in creative ingenuity. Especially in its latest phase, the *Rococo,* Central Europe contributed the subtlest solutions in the field of ecclesiastic and secular architecture. From the treatment of entire city units as in Nancy or Potsdam to the operatic intimacy of royal amusement places (Munich, Residenztheater, ca. 1730), the Catholic world conceived here for the last time an expression for its concepts embodied in the celestial and the secular hierarchy. Church and Court found the perfect vehicle for the symbolization of power, glory, divine installation and stratified organization in the Baroque style.

Sculpture. Baroque sculpture, created in the period between 1600 and 1750, is characterized by dynamic motion of body and garment, by an opening and splitting of contour, by an undulating fluency of all forms, by a richly concave and convex treatment of surface which admits light and shadow as an active factor in the total effect. Subordination to a larger architectonic unit such as an altar, a wall or a monument often determines the shape and the color scheme of statuary. Excellency of technical skill is growing together with the neglect for the indigenous laws of material, as typical of any illusionistic style. Wood is treated like marble, marble transcends the laws of gravity and stands for draperies or painted canvas. The new tasks such as large monuments and fountains create an awareness of distant optical effects but also a neglect for the subtle treatment of details.

Italian Baroque sculpture, prepared by the classicist ornateness of Florentine mannerism (Cellini, 1500-1571), by the massive exaggerations of the Michelangelo imitators (Ammanati, 1511-1592) and the courtly elegance of the French-Spanish-Italian school (Giovanni da Bologna, really Jean Boulogne, 1528-1608), came into its own in the extensive work of Lorenzo Bernini, previously mentioned as an architect. A stream of vitality emanates from his portrait busts (Louis XIV, Constanza Buonarelli, Urban VIII), from the active incorporation of water power in his Roman fountains (Triton fountain, fountains in Piazza Navona) and from his monuments which range from the delicate (St. Theresa in St. Maria della Vittoria) to the gigantic (Cathedra Petri in St. Peter's). His influence has helped to transform the sculptural style of Europe. Allegorical womanhood and the army of winged celestial messengers bloomed with new health and gaiety while in the field of equestrian monuments and portrait busts Bernini's manner became universal for the remainder of the 17th cent.

Spanish sculpture excelled in the Baroque period through its genuine blend of sensualism and mysticism which it derived partially from the influence of Italian Renaissance sculpture. The cunning use of polychromatic treatment enhanced its "naturalness" to the expression of ecstatic suffering and transcendental languor. Painters such as Francisco Pacheco (1571-1654) lent their art to the creation of the life-like surface of Sevillian sculpture. Gregorio Hernandez (1576-1636) represents the School of Valladolid, while Sevilla excells in the work of Juan Martinez Montañes (1568-1649) and his son Alonso (d. 1668). His student, Pedro de Mena (1628-1688) carries the highly emotional style to be compared with El Greco's mystical interpretations to the end of the century.

In Germany and Austria, the Baroque sculpture takes up many of the formal and emotional elements which this art had produced in the days of the late Gothic. Nowhere else around 1500 had sculpture reached a point of development so close to the Baroque spirit than in the statuary of Bavaria and Austria (cf. Hans Leinberger). Giovanni da Bologna's style was introduced into Southern Germany through a number of Flemish and Dutch students of his (Hubert Gerhard, Adriaen de Vries, Pieter de Witte, called Candido) and fused in the next generation with the native late Gothic undercurrent. In Andreas Schlueter (1664-1714) from Hamburg, Germany gave to the Northern world its greatest Baroque sculptor. In the south, Balthasar Permoser (1651-1733) developed Bernini's style toward the exuberant mobility of the Rococo. It is in this latest phase of the Baroque, the Rococo (1720-1770), that the Catholic and dynastic world of Southern Germany and Austria produced a host of excellent sculptors and an unmistakable style of its own. The creation of porcelain sculpture by Johann Kaendler (1706-1775) may be mentioned as an example of the transfer of the highly plastic feeling of the Baroque into a new medium.

French sculpture remained throughout the 17th cent. more in the line of its classical-Renaissance taste and contributed, accordingly, little to the history of the Baroque proper. It is with François Girardon (1628-1715) and Pierre Legros (1666-1717) that Bernini's style enters French sculpture. While Coysevox (1640-1720) and Coustou (1658-1733) represent the style of Louis XIV's court, Pierre Puget (1622-1694) follows his independent genius in the direction of an exploring yet monumental naturalism. The first part of the 18th cent. unites classicism with Baroque sensualism in the erotic-mythological genre of Bouchardon (1698-1762) and Falconet (1716-1791) which had a widespread influence on 18th century sculpture.

Painting. Out of three main components Baroque painting developed: the chiaroscuro style of Leonardo, the coloristic sensualism of Titian, the plastic dynamism of Michelangelo. In Correggio (1494-1534), a step beyond Leonardo toward the Baroque is made while in Tintoretto (1518-1594) a fusion of Titian's style with Michelangelo's was aspired and thus a further advancement of Baroque elements is achieved. All Northern and Spanish masters of the same period partake directly or indirectly in the same process of the Italian evolution. This evolution is one toward dramatization of composition, color and content. The *dramatization of composition* replaces Renaissance symmetry by asymmetrical balance and the horizontal and vertical scheme by a curvilinear fluency of forms. As in architecture, space becomes activated by the exaggeration of body foreshortening, by dramatic light and shadow movement and finally, by making space itself the primary motive of a painting's composition and mood. The *dramatization of color* expresses itself by a change from cool to warm colors, by a tendency toward the blending and modelling of colors into hues instead of localized color application and by the introduction of black and earth colors as the sonorous undertones from which to develop contrasting brilliancy. Accordingly, we observe a tendency to proceed gradually from the dark into the light, a process just the reverse of all previous painting. The *dramatization of content* bespeaks itself in an intensified apparatus of gestures and facial expressions reflecting a wider perception of sensorial experiences. The scale from horror to ecstasy is explored in Mediterranean art while the North delves into the unfathomable nuances of sustained psychic life. The appeal to the onlooker becomes more and more direct and new means are constantly invented to break down the "aesthetic barrier" between onlooker and art work. New fields of subject matter are opened up such as historical painting, the erotic genre, the allegory, the still-life and, most important of all, landscape painting.

As to the practical application of painting, its scope also becomes widened: fresco painting extends from the walls to the ceilings which open the space into an allegorically and religiously animated heaven and into the field of stage prospectus, inviting the architectonic-picturesque imagination. Costume designs, pageants and festivals remain as in previous periods a welcome field for the artist.

All these characteristics of Baroque painting appear full fledged in the exponents of the Bolognese Baroque art: Agostino Caracci (1557-1602) and his brother Annibale (1560-1609), Domenichino (1581-1641), and Guercino (1591-1666). Guido Reni (1575-1642), Carlo Dolci (1616-1686) and Maratta (1625-1713) continue their style and sensualize it to its extreme. For more than a hundred years the pictures of these painters and their innumerable students and followers set the standards in the history of taste and accordingly are represented everywhere in the dynastic galleries of Europe. Equally important is Michelangelo da Caravaggio (1565-1609), whose stark realism exerted a profound influence on Italian, French and Dutch painting. The illusionistic fresco painting of Cortona (1596-1669) and Pozzo (1642-1709) caused the introduction of celestial panoramas with daring foreshortening and uproarious agitation in monumental architecture all over Europe. Closely related with it are the imaginative stage designs by Ferdinando (1657-1743) and Francesco Bibiena (1659-1739). Salvator Rosa (1615-1673) and Magnasco (1681-1747) excel in the new Baroque landscape art with an atmosphere of operatic Romanticism. In the 18th cent., Venice makes its great contribution in the immense production of the painter families Tiepolo (Giovanni Battista, 1696-1770) and Canaletto (Antonio C., 1697-1768), spreading their works in fresco and canvas over the continent while Piazzetta (1682-1754), Longhi (1702-1762) and Guardi (1712-1793) carry the local Venetian note to its last flowering.

While Italian painting of the 17th and 18th cents. represent the virtuosity and the sensualism of a super-mature and slowly declining civilization, Flemish and Dutch art of this period stand for the maturing of all artistic problems prepared in the previous two centuries and for the ripening of the Protestant burgher civilization of Holland. The course of the art is determined by two great names: Rubens (1577-1640), who stands for the healthy and abundant Flemish Catholic country evolv: g his style out of a blend of native realism and Italian plasticity. The other is

Rembrandt (1606-1669), exponent of Holland's Protestant humanism, blending the local tradition with the notions of the Caravaggio school. In contrast to the prevailingly religious type of Italian Baroque painting, these two masters are exponents of the general trend of their civilization toward secular motives, expressed particularly in portraiture and landscape. In addition to Rubens and Rembrandt, there are the great landscape painters Jakob van Ruysdael (1628/29-1682) and Hobbema (1638-1709), accompanied by a flock of respectable secondary painters. A new type depicting interiors of rooms and courtyards with homely scenes finds its master in Vermeer (1632-1675), Pietre de Hooch (1629- after 1677) and Terborch (1617-1681). All of them are equally excellent in the field of portraiture and are joined by the brilliant Frans Hals (1582-1666), who develops tonality painting and preciousness of color quality to an unheard of level. Another specialty is the peasant genre in which Adriaen van Ostade (1610-1685), Jan Steen (1626-1679), and the Flemish artist Adriaen Brouwer (1605/6-1638) continue the Breughel tradition. Never again has a small nation produced a correspondingly large number of painters and rarely has there been achieved a similarly "visual" civilization.

The Spanish also see their greatest period in Baroque painting. Realism and mysticism determine its character. Religious subject matter embodies both these currents. In the art of Greco (really Domenico Theotocopuli from Crete, 1541-1613), ecstatic mysticism achieves its most ingenious representation while realism determines the work of Velasquez (1599-1660). Ribera (1588-1653), Zurbaran (1598-1664) and Murillo (1618-1682) embrace the entire range from the one to the other. While Greco's palette produced all means of a spiritualized Venetian luminosity, the other masters teach to later centuries the use of passive earth colors such as black, brown and grey in their maximum strength. The peasant and beggar genre, portraiture and religious art with an emphasis on the sombre and cruel prevail throughout.

French Baroque painting contributes two painters of international importance: Poussin (1593-1666), the master of the mythological and Claude Lorrain (1600-1682), the landscape painter. Yet as in architecture, the Baroque elements in French painting are more strongly interwoven with classicist doctrines. The brothers Le Nain (Antoine, 1588-1648; Louis, 1593-1648; Mathieu, 1607-1677) may be considered as the closest to the Dutch and Spanish

realists of this period. In the Rococo period French painting exerted its most widespread influence over Europe, being blessed with such gracious masters as Watteau (1684-1721), Boucher (1703-1770) and Fragonard (1732-1806). The vital substance of the Baroque era now begins to dissolve in the playful sophistication of a late aristocratic society.

At the same time in the late epoch of the history of the Baroque style, England produces its able and elegant society painter Gainsborough (1727-1788) and its deft satirist Hogarth (1697-1764), both of whom already reach out into a new era.

Germany in the 17th cent., perhaps under the influence of the 30 Years War, produced very few artists of more than local importance. Only Elsheimer (1578-1610), admired by Rembrandt, contributes his delicate romanticism to the field of landscape painting. The Catholic South, under the guidance of the Italian frescoists brought forth a large number of capable but superficial fresco masters active within the extensive building program of palatial and ecclesiastic architecture.

As a special field of artistic expression in this era we must consider the creation of the architectonic *Baroque garden* with its "parterres" of flowers, its symmetrically designed alleys with grand perspectivic effects and its dramatic use of cascades, fountains and canals. As a forerunner, the garden of the Villa d'Este in Tivoli (since 1549 by Pirro Ligorio) and as the mature solution Le Notre's (1613-1700) garden of Versailles (since 1661) set an international pattern for the Baroque garden. It subordinated nature under man's architectonic will and aimed for a total effect of wide distances presented in systematized spatial arrangements. In many ways, the Baroque garden appears as the most outspoken symbol of the entire epoch: dynastic will for space conquest, the tendency of the era for illusionistic deception, the strong sense for architectural and plastic form and life, the tendency for organized social life even in the out of doors, all these elements seem embodied in the Baroque garden. See THE SOUTH: Emile Mâle, *L'Art religieux après le concile de Trente,* Paris, 1923; Werner Weisbach, *Der Barock als Kunst der Gegenreformation,* Berlin, 1921, 2nd ed., 1924; Benedetto Croce, *Storia del' età barocca in Italia.* 1929; Julius Schlosser, *Die Kunstlitteratur,* Books 7 and 9, Vienna; 1924; Lionello Venturi, *History of Art Criticism,* chap. No. 5, New York, 1936; Heinrich Woelfflin, *Renaissance und Barock,* 4th ed., Munch, 1926; Werner Weisbach, *Die Kunst des Barock in Italien, Deutschland und Spanien,* Berlin, 1924, 2nd ed., 1929; Sacheverell Sitwell, *Southern Baroque Art,* New York, 1924; T. H. Fokker, *Roman Baroque Art,* London, 1938; Alois Riegl, *Die Entstehung der Barockkunst in Rom,* Vienna, 1st ed., 1907, 3rd ed., 1923; A. K. McComb, *The Baroque Painters of Italy,* Cambridge, 1934; N. Pevsner and O. Grautoff, *Barockmalerei in den romanischen Laendern,* Potsdam, 1928; Karl Justi, *Velasquez and His Time,* London, 193-; A. E. Brinckmann, *Die Baukunst des 17.und 18. Jahrhunderts in den romanischen Ländern,* Potsdam, 1916: M. S. Briggs, *Baroque Architecture,* London, 1914; Conrado Ricci, *Baroque Architecture and Sculpture in Italy,* New York, 1912; A. E. Brinckmann, *Barockskulptur,* Potsdam, 1919. THE NORTH: Willi Drost, *Barockmalerei in den germanischen Läundern,* Potsdam, 1926; Max Osborn, *Die Kunst des Rokoko,* Berlin, 1926; Max Rooses, *Art in Flanders,* New York, 1914; Wilhelm R. Valentiner, *Art of the Low Countries,* New York, 1914; Max J. Friedlaender, *Die niederländischen Maler des 17. Jahrhunderts,* Berlin, 1926; C. H. C. Baker, *Dutch Painting of the 17th Century,* 1926; S. Sitwell, *German baroque art,* New York, 1928; W. Pinder, *Deutscher Barock,* Ebenhausen, Langewiesche, 1914; A. E. Richardson, *Monumental Classic Architecture in Great Britain and Ireland,* 1914; Werner Weisbach, *Französiche Malerei des 17. Jahrhunderts,* Berlin, 1932; R. H. Wilenski, *French Painting.* New York, 1931; S. Rocheblave, *French Painting of the 18th Century;* Louis Hourtieq, *De Poussin à Watteau,* Paris, 1921.   —A.N.

baroque organ. See MUSICAL INSTRUMENTS.

barrel drum. See MUSICAL INSTRUMENTS.

barrel organ. See mechanical instruments.

barrel shape. Like a barrel, its height greater than its breadth, bulbous in the center and tapering equally toward each end.

barrel vault. A vault which, in section, is semicircular.

barrow. A tumulus.

baryta water. See fresco secco.

base (Fr. *base,* L. *basis,* Gr. *basis,* a step, base or pedestal). In architecture the lowermost member of a column, consisting of a plinth and mouldings between the shaft and the pavement or between the shaft of a column or pilaster and the pedestal on which it rests. In primitive Egyptian and Greek architecture the base was a raised slab of stone or cement whose function was to insulate the timber column resting upon it from ground moisture; when stone replaced wood for columns this simple base was retained, probably because its greater area gave increased stability. Each of the Greek orders, with the exception of the Doric in which the base was abandoned, developed a characteristic base in which the profiles varied by different proportions and combinations of torus and scotia mouldings and fillets. Common to all the Roman orders is an adapted Greek design known as the Attic base. In each of the Greek orders the base is round, and this practice was followed by the Romans, but frequently in Romanesque and Gothic work the roundness is modified by the addition of decorative spurs or *griffes* at the corners of the square dies to enrich the transition from round shaft to square plinth. Bases composed of elaborate mouldings appeared at an early date and are frequent in Assyrian and Persian architecture as well as in the classic styles. Base is also properly used to describe the plinth and mouldings which project at the bottom of the wall of a room or a church, and the lowermost course of masonry in a building; from Renaissance usage base is also used interchangeably with pedestal. (For profiles of the classic bases see ORDERS). Also see PERSPECTIVE.
                                                        —T.A.H.

base line. See PERSPECTIVE.

base of cones of rays. See PERSPECTIVE.

basic series. See twelve-tone technique.

basilica. *Rom. arch.* An oblong public building used for exchange or assembly, built with nave and aisles; an early Christian church building of similar form. See EARLY CHRISTIAN ARCHITECTURE.

Basket Makers. See Pueblo art.

bas-relief. A sculptural style whereby the design shows in low relief. See relief; relief sculpture.

bass. *Mus.* The tones below middle C.

basselice, basselisse. Low-warp.

basse-taille enamel. See ENAMELING ON METAL.

basset horn. See MUSICAL INSTRUMENTS.

basso fundamental. The fundamental bass or root of a chord.

bassoon. See MUSICAL INSTRUMENTS.

basso-relievo. See bas-relief; relief; relief sculpture.

bastard (script). See writing.

bat. See SYMBOLISM IN FAR EASTERN ART.

batik (Malay.). Fabrics decorated by the *batik* technique, which is a resist process. Parts, which are not to be dyed, are impregnated with wax. The fabric is then dipped in color and finally boiled to remove the wax. Repeated as many times as there are colors. See rogata-zome. —J.A.M.

batiste. Plain weave cotton or linen cloth.

bats. *Cer.* Shelving in decorating kiln; made of cast iron. See CERAMICS I.

battement. *Mus.* An old grace which in contrast to most other historic ornaments has no proper sign of its own. The battement consists of a shake starting on the auxiliary half-tone below the principal note. —F.D.

batter. Term applied to a wall that inclines inward from a vertical or plumb line.

battle dress. See COSTUME ART.

battle piece. Any work of art representing a battle.

Bauhaus. A German educational institution and research center for the training of architects, artists, industrial designers, etc. The Bauhaus was founded in 1919 by Walter Gropius in Weimar (as *Das Staatliche Bauhaus Weimar*), transferred to Dessau in 1925 and closed by the Hitler party in 1932.

The Bauhaus maintains that the separation of architecture, the so-called fine arts, applied arts, etc., from one another is a fundamental and dangerous error All these fields are different aspects of man's creative artistic ability, the ultimate goal of which should be "the composite but inseparable work of art, the great building" (Gropius). The Bauhaus therefore abolished the separations held to be artificial, and integrated the teaching and exploration of the various fields, taking building (*bauen*) as its basis, (hence the name *Bau* house). The teaching of the various aspects of art was supplemented by the study of related subjects (e.g. biology, sociology, accounting, etc.).

Since creative ability, according to the Bauhaus, is an integral part of life, an educational institution concerned with the development of such abilities must make the student aware of the forces which determine his age and hence his life (i.e. industry), and train the student so that his knowledge and abilities may best serve and express the true needs of his time. However, this program should not be understood as a complete subordination of architecture and the arts to the forces of industry and economics. While the Bauhaus is opposed to an "art for art's sake", it is equally opposed to the acceptance of industry as an aim in itself. In the integrated new culture which the Bauhaus envisages these two spheres influence each other mutually. The new conception of architecture and the arts ultimately implies a change in the social-cultural structure (and in many respects the products of the Bauhaus express a social ideal which is yet to be realized).

The integration of a harmoniously unified architecture and art into the contemporary culture has as a correlate, of course, the integration of the individual. This entails a general and a particular educational aim. The general aim would be: to make the student comprehend life as an integrated whole; the particular aim (concerning his professional training): to develop both the student's creative imagination and his technical proficiency. In order to achieve this aim the Bauhaus curriculum combined manual and intellectual training.

The manual training in the workshops was not intended to advocate a sentimental revival of handicraft, but was designed to serve as an introduction to industrial processes. The workshops of the Bauhaus were actually laboratories in which new designs for mass production were evolved. Since the advanced students also worked in factories which produced objects designed in the Bauhaus a close contact between the workshops and industrial production was maintained (while working in a factory the students studied all aspects of production, from actual work with the machines to price calculation).

The Bauhaus did not try to formulate a new "style" or a set of rules which could be handed down to the students. Its aim was rather to train students to understand new needs and to create objects which truly express and satisfy such needs.

As the result of its program and viewpoint the Bauhaus exerted a decisive influence on the formation of the modern style and became its center in Europe. It was but a logical extension of its basic ideas that the Bauhaus was international in character, accepting influences from all parts of the world, and in turn extending its influence beyond the boundaries of Germany. See GERMAN ART; functional architecture; also Walter Gropius, *Idee und Aufbau des Staatlichen Bauhauses Weimar*, 1923 and *The New Architecture and the Bauhaus*, 1937. —H.H.

Bautasteinar. See rune.

bay. *Arch.* (1) The principal compartment or division, as in a roof or ceiling, consisting of the space between rafters or beams. (2) The space between any two architectural features. —J.M.M.

Bayake art. See AFRICAN NEGRO ART.

bazaar. See ISLAMIC ART.

bead. A small molding having a rounded surface often carved with bead like forms alternating with another motif as in the Greek and Roman bead and reel. —O.M.S.

bead and reel ornament. Single or paired oblong beads or "olives" alternating with disks, all on a round convex molding.

beaker shape. Like a beaker. A cylindrical form narrowed in the center and flaring at both ends or flaring at the top only.—J.A.M.

beakhead. A Norman ornament having the form of a head with a beak.

beam. A long horizontal piece of wood, stone, or other material forming part of the frame of a building or other structure.

bearing. *Arch.* The part of a beam or other structural feature that rests upon a support.

beating up. Striking each warp thread into its appointed position.

beat. *Mus.* (1) Metric unit indicated by the time signature, e.g., ¾ time calls for three beats to the measure, the quarter note receiving one beat. (2) To express physically the unit divisions of the measure. (3) Acoustically, the throb heard when two tones of unsympathetic vibration numbers reach a point of coincidence. See ACOUSTICS. —M.E.

beauty. The quality of the "beautiful", ascribed to objects of aesthetic experience, is familiar to everybody. But the understanding of 'beauty' has proved to be exceedingly difficult. It is generally agreed that it is a value, primarily aesthetic insofar as it is enjoyed in its specific manifestations, and secondarily educational insofar as it is worth studying and also cultural insofar as it constitutes a vital phase of social progress. It is agreed also that beauty has a prominent subjective aspect, first, because aesthetic experience is always in a sense personal, and second, because persons contemplating a beautiful object are likely to contribute to it something of their own. But the objective aspect of beautiful objects has largely remained a puzzle or mystery. Some aestheticians are inclined to deny its very existence, while others assert that beauty is inherent in, or dependent on, the objects of aesthetic experience themselves; a few even maintain, following Plato, that beauty has a transcendent existence in which it coincides with the True and the Good. The puzzle is so profound that Kant came to regard it as an antinomy, or a contradiction that has to be nevertheless accepted.

It is possible, however, that the difficulty to comprehend 'beauty' is largely verbal. The term is, in fact, highly ambiguous in its use for three reasons: (1) Beauty is a matter of taste and opinion, and men disagree on what is beautiful and what is not; moreover, the experience is transient, and what is regarded as beautiful at one period of a person's life may not be so regarded at another. (2) Beauty, as an experience, throws little light on beauty, as a concept, with the result that persons who agree on what objects produce aesthetic experience may utterly disagree on its conceptual meaning. (3) Beauty applies to a vast field of aesthetic experience, including the beauty of nature and the beauty of art, though these two kinds of beauty have similar as well as dissimilar characteristics.

Among the characteristics which the beauty of nature and the beauty of art have in common are: (1) Beauty is ascribed in both cases, to external objects; e.g. when we admire flowers or paintings, we feel that it belongs to these objects rather than to our taste. (2) Beauty thus becomes an objective (or objectified) quality rather than a quality of our own experience. (3) The value of beauty, in both cases, can be enjoyed by more than one person, and thus differs from other values, such as those of physical pleasure or economic opportunity, which diminish when shared; in other words, an aesthetic experience is not directly affected by the number of participants.

Among the characteristics in which the beauty of nature and the beauty of **art differ** are: (1) Art is man-made, a product of man's creative ability, whereas nature on the whole is not; as a result, art embodies and expresses human feelings, desires and ideas to a much greater extent than nature. (2) Whereas the beauty of nature is necessarily pleasing, once it is experienced, art may take for its subject matter happiness or misery, the good or the evil, the sublime or the ugly, and thus cause pleasure or displeasure.

The latter distinctions make us conclude that the field of art, real and potential, is vaster than is usually supposed. Its subject matter may concern virtually everything in reality and social life, more or less modified by imagination, provided it is endowed, through an adequate use of artistic technique, with a message capable of arousing aesthetic feelings in those susceptible to it. Apart from certain purely psychological demands for a vicarious pleasure and satisfaction or fiction, the ultimate function of art appears to consist in freeing men from whatever self-imposed limitations they happen to possess; in refining and sharpening their sympathetic understanding of fellow-men; and in making the progress of mankind a matter of sensitive heart no less than that of thoughtful head and powerful muscle. See AESTHETICS; also Winn, R. B., The Beauty of Nature and Art, *Journal of Aesthetics and Art Criticism*, Spring, 1942; Dewey, John, *Art as Experience*, 1934; Gilbert, K. E., and Kuhn, H., *A History of Esthetics*, 1939; Parker, De W. H., *The Principles of Aesthetics*, 1920; Santayana, George, *Sense of Beauty*, 1896; Tolstoy, L. N., *What Is Art?* 1929.   —R.B.W.

Beauvais ware. See CERAMICS II.

bed. In masonry: (1) A layer of mortar in which stones or bricks are to be laid. (2) A horizontal course of a stone wall. (3) The lower horizontal surface on which the stone rests. See FURNITURE.   —J.M.M.

Bedford cord. A vertically ribbed cloth of great strength. First made in New Bedford, Mass., hence the name. A similar material in cotton which originated in France is called pique.   —G.W.R.

beeswax. Used now largely as a modelling and coating substance, this wax has been also

a painting medium. Among pictures in which it served that purpose, the so-called Fayum portraits—a group of mummy paintings—is probably the largest. Unwieldy, except perhaps in full tropical sunlight, it has the great advantage of stability. See also waxes.—G.L.S.

beige. Natural tan or ecru color; or undyed yarn or fabric.

bel canto (It.). Literally, beautiful song. The lyric style of singing as opposed to the declamatory or dramatic style.

bell. See MUSICAL INSTRUMENTS.

bell capital. See capital.

bell crater. See crater.

Belleek china. See CERAMICS II.

bell-shape. The form of a common hand-bell.

Bema. See synagogues.

bench. In southwestern archaeology: A mass of material, generally adobe or masonry, elevated above the floor of a chamber or given level; the top being more than twelve inches but not over three feet six inches above the floor or level; the top being at least twelve inches in width.   —J.M.M.

bench nook. In southwestern archaeology: Term applied to a recessed portion of the bench, as in a kiva.   —J.M.M.

bench singer. See Bankelsanger.

hend. See HERALDRY.

Ben Day process. *Etch.* Method of producing by machine a stippled, mottled, or shaded background on a line plate.

bend sinister. See HERALDRY.

benedictus. See Mass.

Bengal indigo. See indigo.

bengaline. A corded fabric, heavier than poplin, made of silk, silk and wool, or silk and cotton. Rayon may be substitute for silk.   —G.W.R.

Benham's discs. See COLOR.

beni (Jap.). A color designated as rose-red, used on early Japanese prints.

beni-e (Jap.). Early woodblock prints in which single coloring was added by hand to a black and white impression. The name was derived from *beni* (a rose-red pigment), which predominated.   —J.A.M.

Benin art. See AFRICAN NEGRO ART.

beni-zuri-e (Jap.). Woodblock prints in which red (*beni*) was prominent. The colors in *beni-zuri-e* were printed, whereas the earlier *beni-ɛ* (q.v.) were colored by hand.   —J.A.M.

benzoin. A dark gum or resin from trees native to Siam and Sumatra, benzoin is occasionally put into varnishes and lacquers to make them less brittle. It is mentioned in various manuscripts of mediaeval origin.
                                                    —G.L.S.

berceuse. A cradle song, lullaby.

Berlin blue. See Prussian blue.

Bes. *Egypt. Relig.* A god of many attributes but worshipped chiefly as a deity who warded off evil omens and witchcraft; god of pleasure.

bestiary. Medieval book on zoology reporting habits of animals, real and legendary and interpreting them as "symbols" of Christian verities, exceptionally of amorous pursuits (*bestiare d'amour*). Often illustrated and as such the source of motives in church decoration. Derived from the so-called "Physiologus" (q.v.).   —R.B.

Betatakin (Navaho, hillside house). An Anasazi cliff village built in a large cavern in the Laguna (or Segi) Canyon in north central Arizona. The houses and kivas, about 150 in number, are of stone and adobe or of adobe-covered poles. It is now part of the Navaho National Monument. See Pueblo art.   —H.G.

betterments. See CIVIC PLANNING.

bhadana, bandhana. Kerchief for the head or neck; originated in India, where *bandhu* or *bandh* referred to a cord or tie.   —G.W.R.

bhūmisparśa mudrā (Skr.). Mystic gesture symbolizing the right to call the earth to witness Buddha's power. Right hand extending downward over knee, palm inward, fingers extended, generally touching the lotus throne.
                                                    —J.A.M.

bibelot. *Book.* A small book, usually a curiosity.

Bicheroux process. See GLASS AND GLASS MAKING.

Bidri ware. See metalwork.

Biedermeier. A phase of German art (ca. 1830 - ca. 1860) following Romanticism. The name *Biedermeier* originally referred to a type of philistine—cheerful and honest, but limited in outlook. The term was invented by Eichrodt and Kuszmaul who, enjoying the unintentional humour of some poems of a village schoolmaster, published them (1855-1857) in the *Fliegende Blätter* (a humorous weekly) under the title, *Gesänge Biedermaiers* (Biedermaier's Songs, [the "ai" was later changed into "ei"]). The fictitious name then was applied generally to all sorts of philistine weaknesses and characteristics. Later *Biedermeier,* (losing its ironical connotations), was adopted as the name of the period, which is characterized, at least externally, by a dominance of sober orderliness and simple pleasures. The furniture and interior decorations clearly reflect this spirit which transformed the Empire style into a style of sober severity and simple usefulness.

In connection with the visual arts *Biedermeier* style is, in a sense, a reaction—although a mild one—to the later part of the Romantic period, replacing the historical, religious, and symbolic themes of that period by scenes from the every-day life of the "simple" peasant and of middle-class society. The forms of nature—plant, animal, human—are studied with loving care, and simplicity is depicted as a virtue found in nature and among those who are content with simple pleasures (e.g. the paintings of C. J. Milde, E. Engert, Karl Spitzweg). And yet this simplicity is artificial and sentimental; it is imported into nature. The peasants in G. F. Waldmüller's landscapes, for instance, are presented as neat and clean; in their picturesque costumes they move about in landscapes which are equally neat and clean. The drawings and paintings of Ludwig Richter and Moritz von Schwind have the appealing and sentimental qualities of folk-songs. Karl Spitzweg, J. P. Hasenclever, Th. Hosemann expose the weaknesses of their *Biedermeier* contemporaries with a gently ironic humour; the objects of their humour are mild eccentrics, e.g. slightly queer collectors of books or cacti who live contentedly within their own small circle oblivious to what happens in the outside world.

When the preoccupation with sentimental themes is abandoned, as in the numberless landscapes of Gensler, Blechen, Spitzweg, Rottmann, Pettenkofer, Lessing, Preller, Achenbach and many others, there result charming and intimate studies of parts of nature apparently done without an effort at composition or arrangement. Since, according to these artists, nature is best when not interfered with or spoiled by man, they avoided artistic composition trying to give nature as it really is. However, the scenes are carefully selected so as to reflect the sentiment which the artist wants to express—sunny clearings, pleasant and inviting valleys, gently rolling hills, etc. —the artistic composition is replaced by the picturesque motif.

The romantic historical narrative is continued in the paintings of Kaulbach, Rethel and Hildebrand. The meticulous care in the presentation of all objects and figures and the sentimental interest taken not only in the hero of the scene but also in minor figures (e.g. the paintings of Franz Krüger) tends to make the historical presentation anecdotal. In the art of Adolf Menzel this type of historical painting reaches its climax. Menzel, in whom the romantic interest in and love for nature finds expression in an almost fanatically realistic naturalism, combines great veracity in the historical details with the ability of binding together all the details into one unified composition while maintaining an air of the accidental.

The *Heimat Kunst* (regional art) of the turn of the century may be considered a late offspring of the *Biedermeier* art. Living in artist colonies (e.g. Worpswede, North Germany; Dachau, Bavaria; Willingshausen, Hessia) the *Heimat Künstler* paint peasants at work, peasants dancing, etc., in the *Biedermeier* manner with a technique which is strongly influenced by the impressionists. See GERMAN ART; FURNITURE; also Richard Hamann, *Die deutsche Malerei im 19. Jahrhundert*, 1914; Jos. Aug. Lux, *Von der Empire zur Biedermeierzeit*, 1906; Paul Ferdinand Schmidt, *Biedermeier Malerei*, 1923 (2nd ed.).　　　　　　　　　—H.H.

billet-molding. A Norman molding ornamented with short cylinders or prisms usually in a double row with regular spacing between the ends.　　　　　　　　　　　—O.M.S.

Bima (Heb.). See synagogues.

binder's stamp. *Book.* A design engraved in brass for stamping decorations and titles on covers.

binding medium. Any adhesive material put with pigment to hold it together in a film can be called by this name. It is sometimes confused with a diluent or solvent used to thin the adhesive, as water is used with gum arabic and glue or as turpentine is used with oil. These diluents are not painting mediums but serve only as temporary thinners There has been no standard classification of mediums as such, but practice has separated out oil, tempera—which frequently is extended to include all adhesives that are soluble in water at the time of application—and waxes.—G.L.S.

biotechnical elements of construction, the. See SCULPTURE.

bird sanctuary. A tract of land esp. reserved for the attraction and protection, under natural conditions, of wild birds. See CIVIC PLANNING.

Birüik art. See ESKIMO ART.

biscuit, bisque. Unglazed fired clay ware; the first firing or burning, converts dry, fragile clay into a hard, consolidated mass, generally used for clay products to be glazed (second firing). See CERAMICS I.

biscuit groups. See CERAMICS II.

biscuit kiln. *Cer.* For firing bisque. See CERAMICS I.

bistre. This, like asphaltum, is a tarry material and is derived from the soot of burned resinous wood. The color ranges from orange-yellow to brown-black, depending on the material and the method of manufacture. Unlike asphaltum, this can be readily used with water-soluble mediums. Though it has the drawback of being relatively unstable, it has been used largely for drawing since the 14th cent. It is still sold by artists' colormen.　　—G.L.S.

biting. *Etch.* Process of corroding or etching sections of a metal plate to form a design for intaglio printing. See line etching.

bitstone. *Cer.* Quartz rock grains for placing ware on bottom of glossed saggers. See CERAMICS I.

bitumen. See asphaltum.

biwa. See MUSICAL INSTRUMENTS.

Bizen yaki (Jap.). Pottery made in Bizen province.

blackface comedy and minstrelsy. See AMERICAN NEGRO THEATRE.

black-figured vases. During the first three-quarters of the sixth century B.C. the characteristic technique of Greek vase painters was black-figured, i.e., figures painted in black glaze silhouette on the terra-cotta background, with details of body and drapery incised in the glaze by a sharp metal tool. Sometimes the flesh of women was painted in white, and purple was used to vary the folds of the garments. Black-figured vases may conveniently be divided into two groups: (1) those made in Greek Asia Minor and the nearby islands, which show in their use of floral and heraldic designs a strong Oriental influence (see Ionian Vases); (2) those made in Greece proper, which emphasized human scenes, chiefly mythological. Of this second group the chief products were "Proto-Corinthian" (Sicyonian?), notable for their delicate shapes and polychrome designs; Corinthian, patterned after the Proto-Corinthian, but coarser in shape and decoration; Chalcidian, elegant and precise in form, with spirited scenes pictured on the sides; and Attic. It was in Attica that the black-figured style reached its highest point; previous shapes were refined and new ones invented; abstract decoration was confined to marking transitions, and emphasis was put on main friezes or panels, depicting with disciplined skill and vigorous energy scenes from heroic legend or everyday life. The first great example of Athenian black-figured ware is the so-called François vase, by the potter Ergotimos and the painter Klitias, dating about 560 B.C. Cups by the "Little Masters" have exquisite little figures in neat trim designs. Toward the end of the period came three great masters; Nikosthenes, who painted spirited scenes of revels on metallic-shaped amphorae; Amasis, more monumental in style; and Exekias, who designed his figures with unerring finesse and cut the details with great precision and delicacy. With them the possibilities of this technique were exhausted; in fact it is amazing, in view of the limitations of the technique, that they were able to produce such varied and intricate designs.   —W.R.A.

Blackfoot art. See Plains Indian art.

black tortoise. See SYMBOLISM IN FAR EASTERN ART.

blanc de Chine. French name for celebrated white porcelain made in China. See CERAMICS II.

Blaue Reiter, the (Ger. the Blue Rider). The "Blaue Reiter" was an editorial board which consisted of Franz Marc and Wassily Kandinsky and was set up in order to publish a magazine of the same name. Marc wrote on the 8th of September, 1911 to his friend, the painter August Macke, ". . . a magazine which will become the mouthpiece of all the new and sincere ideas of our day: painting, music, the stage, etc." By examples of old folk art they intended to demonstrate how deeply the modern art movement was rooted in the old one. A reconciliation between art and the people was the goal of the "Blaue Reiter", which was to be published at irregular intervals. On the 9th of November, 1911 the first copy was arranged, and was published in 1912. On the second of December, 1911, Franz Marc and Kandinsky left the "Neue Vereinigung", to which Jawlensky, Werefkin, Erbsloeh, and others belonged. These two artists then decided to enlarge the editorial organization to include art exhibitions. The first exhibition took place between the 18th of December, 1911 and the 1st of January, 1912, under the name the "Blaue Reiter" in the art salon of Thannhauser in Munich. From there the exhibition traveled to Cologne and to most of the larger cities of Germany. The "Blaue Reiter" is not, as is erroneously assumed, a society of artists, but the artists of the modern movement, German, Russian, French, etc., were invited to participate in these exhibitions. Only the first copy of the magazine appeared. All their efforts were interrupted by the outbreak of the world war and rendered useless by the death of Franz Marc in 1916. See Alois J. Schardt, *Franz Marc*, Berlin, 1936.   —A.J.S.

blazonry. See HERALDRY.

bled. *Book.* To bleed. To so print the page and trim the edges of a book that pictures and titles on covers run over the edge of the page.

blender. A large brush used by painters to soften and smooth coatings, usually of oil paint, the blender has a history that runs from some time at least as early as the 15th cent. until the present. Generally it is made of badger hair, is round in shape, fairly long, and flat at the end. This allows it to be tapped over the wet paint, as well as drawn over it with the usual brushing stroke.   —G.L.S.

bleu de roi. See CERAMICS II.

blighted district. See CIVIC PLANNING.

blind. *Book.* Blind-tooled. Without foil or color.

blind arcade. A range of arches attached to a wall without an opening.

block. (1) In masonry: Stone usually more than two inches thick; natural or dressed. (2) *Cer.* Plaster mold made from original model. See CERAMICS I.

blocked-out. See SCULPTURE.

blocking in. See design.

block print. See PRINTS AND PRINT PROCESSES.

blooming. The cloudy white film which appears on varnished surfaces. It is largely induced by moist atmosphere.

blossoming plum. See SYMBOLISM IN FAR EASTERN ART.

blottesque. Having blots or coarsely represented.

blue and white ware. Both over- and underglaze decoration in blue on a white ground.

blue bice. See blue verditer.

blue note. See AMERICAN NEGRO MUSIC.

Blue Rider, the. See Blaue Reiter, the.

Blue Rose group. See RUSSIAN ARTS.

blues. Melodies in dreamy, sentimental "blue" mood, of Negro origin. See AMERICAN NEGRO MUSIC; AMERICAN NEGRO LITERATURE.

blue verditer. Frequently called blue bice, this is an artificial basic copper carbonate, a blue pigment chemically similar to azurite. It probably was made at some time early in the Middle Ages and is still available, though rare.   —G.L.S.

blunger. *Cer.* Tank with revolving arms for mixing clay. See CERAMICS I.

boarding. See grain.

board of appeals. See CIVIC PLANNING.

board of survey. See CIVIC PLANNING.

bocasine (F.). A fabric similar to fine buckram.

Bodhisattva. See INDIAN ART.

bodhi tree. From *bodhi* (Skr.). The tree under which Buddha is said to have sat during the period of enlightenment. See INDIAN ART.

body. In pottery or metal, the main part of a receptacle.

body color. In painting, an opaque pigment as compared with a transparent finishing paint.

Boehm flute. See MUSICAL INSTRUMENTS.

Bohemia, art of. See CZECHOSLOVAKIA, ART OF.

bole. The inert or pigment material of the coating which is laid as a ground for gold leaf is usually called bole. The name is an ancient one and, in modern frame-making and gilding, is sometimes supplanted by the term, gold size. There is no fixed color. Traditionally, bole may be white, green, or one of many shades of dull red. The most common is the last, and the ordinary gold ground of the Middle Ages and the Renaissance was made of glue size with a brick-colored Armenian earth. Any bole must be somewhat amorphous and very finely divided, a clay rather than a purely crystalline material, which will provide a smooth and non-abrasive foundation for the leaf.   —G.L.S.

bolero. One of the classic Iberian dances of Spain, is a couple dance, in which the man and woman perform similar movements, the man with great vigor, the woman with more restraint. The intricate steps are characterized by high leaps and rapid turns in the air. The dance is divided into three parts, the second section being devoted to solos by each of the dancers. These solos give opportunity for individual improvisation within the traditional style of the dance. The dancers accompany themselves upon castanets with rapid rhythmic patterns in 3/4 meter.   —J.G.

Bologna, school of. The founders of the so-called eclectic school of Bologna are Lodovico, Agostino and Anniable Carracci, all born in Bologna between 1555 and 1560. They opened the Academy of Painting in Bologna in 1589. In contrast to the prevailing "Caravaggismo" (the realistic movement created by Michelangelo Merigi da Caravaggio), the Carracci followed the footsteps of Raphael and Correggio. The most famous work by the Carracci is the painting of the gallery of Cardinal Farnese's palace in Rome in 1600 by Anniable and Agostino.   —L.L.

bolt. *Book.* The fold of the paper in the outer edges of books; at one time found only at top and fore-edge but now also at the bottom edge or tail.

bombazine (Gr. *bombyx,* silk. Aristotle may have coined this term.). A light weight fabric of silk warp and worsted woof, chiefly used for mourning. Used as a mantilla material in South America.   —G.W.R.

bond. In masonry: The disposition or lapping of stones so that vertical joints may not fall over one another, but fall over or near the middle of the stone below.   —J.M.M.

bond clay. See ball clay.

bond-stone, bonder. In masonry: Stones whose longest horizontal direction is placed at right angles to the face of the wall. Bond-stones or bonders may be either "throughs" (extending through the entire thickness of the wall) or "headers" (extending only part way through the wall).   —J.M.M.

bone black. One of the many carbon black pigments which is made by charring animal bones in a closed vessel; it is said that so-called ivory black, used by artists today, is frequently made of charred bone.   —G.L.S.

bone china. *Cer.* Lower fired porcelain containing calcined bones. See CERAMICS I.

bones. See MUSICAL INSTRUMENTS.

book. See libretto.

bookbinding, early. See EARLY BOOK-BINDING AND FINE BINDING.

BOOK ILLUSTRATION is a graphic representation which explains, expands or embellishes the text of a book. It varies in its function from scientific documentation on the one hand to pure ornamentation on the other. Sympathetic pictorial interpretation, by artistic means, of a literary creation is considered by many as the ideal province of the illustrator. The artistic value of illustration is sometimes questioned by those who feel that the images arising spontaneously in a reader's mind are spoilt by different sets of images formulated and set down by an illustrator. This criticism, while justified in certain cases, is unfair in that it finds fault with the medium as such rather than with its improper use. Tactful and discreet interpretation of a text is an indispensable quality of good book illustration.

In its origin illustration is indistinguishable from the beginnings of writing. Pictographic writing is the seed from which both writing and illustration developed. It consisted of concrete images, graphically condensed into linear characters, arranged in definite sequences so as to convey messages, record events and to serve various other purposes. Illustration proper can be said to exist as soon as the same message is recorded twice on the same document, once in characters conveying words and again by images of mainly pictorial value. Just when this was first done is impossible to say, but both the early Mesopotamian culture and ancient Egypt have yielded examples of such early illustration.

Book illustration in classical Greece and Rome has left few traces. Documentary illustration of scientific, medical and botanical texts on scrolls was widely practiced, also the author's portrait, earliest form of the frontispiece (q.v.) was very popular. Of the illustration of literary texts we know little, but there is reason to believe that Homer, Virgil and certain books of the Old Testament were the subject of elaborate picture scrolls in which the text had shrunk to a few lines of caption for each picture.

Early Christianity and the introduction of the codex greatly stimulated book illustration, which in turn became a most important mouthpiece for the Church and one of its skillfully developed teaching devices. The illumination of mediaeval manuscripts is the graphic representation of the sacred Bible texts, the pictorial explanation of the doctrines of the church and, particularly in the later mediaeval centuries, an exposition of the life of the Virgin Mary and the life and passion of Christ. It is impossible to do justice in this article to the beauty, the wealth and variety of mediaeval schools of illumination. They have become the subject of intensive study and of a highly specialized literature.

Secular elements were slow to make themselves felt in mediaeval illumination and they appear at first as part of and connected with ecclesiastical texts and pictures. Apart from certain classical illustrations, inherited from ancient Rome and copied throughout the Middle Ages, no separate secular cycles of illumination appeared until the beginning of the Renaissance.

The invention of printing did not immediately revolutionize illustration. Picture printing first served as a mechanical duplicating device of established holy compositions, such as the early broadsides of various saints and other familiar Christian images. The block books of the 15th cent. too are to a large extent a multiplication of certain popular manuscripts. It cannot be denied, though, that the block book greatly contributed to the distribution of printed images among the people of Europe and to the development of the woodcut as a story telling device. From remote Asiatic sources and from its primitive European beginnings in the late 14th cent. the woodcut witnessed a century and a half of truly amazing development and refinements. It received early vitality at the hands of anonymous Dutch, German, French and Italian artists. Later on, such masters as Albrecht Dürer, Hans Holbein the Younger, Geofroy Tory and other artists of the first rank favored this technique. In the course of the 16th cent. the woodcut (q.v.) was superseded by the more refined, more sophisticated art of copper engraving and etching. These methods, enriched by specialized technical developments such as mezzotint and aquatint etching, stipple engraving and steel engraving (q.v.), reigned supreme from the 16th to the early 19th cent. Book illustration after 1500 showed itself completely emancipated from its mediaeval religious heritage. Holbein's *Dance of Death,* ostensibly an admonition to prepare for the world hereafter, introduced satire and social criticism. Emblem books, popular throughout the 16th and the 17th cent., expounded the wisdom and teaching of the ancient classics rather than of Christian theologians. Callot, Hogarth, Goya, Rowlandson and Daumier successively added portrayal of human folly in its many forms, of the horrors of war, of moral depravity and they developed satire to the point of caricature. They also laid the foundations for the modern political cartoon.

Book illustration proper was greatly benefited by Thomas Bewick's development of wood engraving around 1800, which restored much of the original directness, availability and ease of reproduction to the picture on the printed page. An undesirable element in the 19th cent. development of wood engraving was the increasing separation between artist and engraver. Lithography, arising about simultaneously, counteracted this tendency and supplied a new, very direct means of duplicating the artist's original drawing. Equally popular in 19th cent. Europe and America lithography has remained one of the favored mediums of illustrators concerned with faithful reproduction. This process, in its original form as well as in photomechanical adaptation,

has also contributed materially to the development of color printing.

The invention of photography has greatly affected book illustration. It has proved valuable in a double role as provider of pictures and as a reproducing agent. Photomechanical processes have made possible the inexpensive multiplication of a great variety of art work in line and halftone, in black and white and in color. For reasons of costliness the choicest of these methods have hardly been used for regular book illustration. Emphasis has been on quantity, speed and low production cost. This is one of several reasons why the oldtime processes of picture printing are being revived by many artists in many lands. Woodcut and wood engraving, linoleum cut and lithography are the chief beneficiaries of the current movement. See *Illuminated Manuscripts,* J. A. Herbert, London, 1912; *The Illustrated Book,* Frank Weitenkampf, Cambridge, 1938; *Modern Illustration Processes,* Charles W. Gamble, London, 1938. —H.L.H.

book of emblems. See emblem.

book of hours. The name given to illuminated prayer books during the Middle Ages for persons of high rank. The term is a translation of the French *belles heures* or *riches heures.* The most famous manuscript of this kind is the one called *Les très riches heures de Jean de France, Duc de Berry,* now in the Musée Condé, Chantilly, France. The scenes represented in this work were painted by the brothers Limbourg and are considered the peak of miniature painting of the Middle Ages. —L.L.

bookpile. See ex libris.

bookplate. See ex libris.

book sizes. In early book publishing, book sizes were known by the number of folds that made a signature. For example, folio meant a sheet folded once to form two sheets or four pages. The following sizes, although rapidly becoming obsolete, are occasionally used on book lists. They are only approximations, but will serve as a guide for determining the size of a book listed in that manner.

4 x 6½	18 mo (Octodecimo)
4½ x 6¾	16 mo (Sextodecimo)
5 x 7½	12 mo (Duodecimo)
5⅜ x 8	8 vo (Crown)
6 x 9	8 vo (Octavo)
6¼ x 10	8 vo (Royal)
9 x 12	4 vo (Quarto)
12 x 15	Folio —H.E.S.

border (of a rug). The part surrounding the center, or field, is technically known as the border.

bordure. See HERALDRY.

bore. See ACOUSTICS.

bosses. *Book.* Protecting pieces of metal on the cover, usually incorporated in the design, as knobs or studs.

bot (Siam.). Buddhist sanctuary for priests only.

botany. Used in the worsted yarn manufacture to designate yarns made from the soft, medium length varieties of Australian and South African merino wools. It is also used to signify all fine Australian wool, particularly in Great Britain; also fine worsted fabrics. —G.W.R.

bo tree. From Singhalese *"bo"* which comes from *bodhi* (Skr.) (q.v.) meaning enlightenment. Generally called pipal tree.

bottega (It. shop, working place; particularly the artists' workshop before the abolition of the guilds or *companie* in the late 18th and early 19th cents.). Like the workshop of other craftsmen incorporated in the guilds the *bottega* was a coöperative enterprise founded upon the patriarchal basis of intimate common living and of the master's responsibility for the bodily welfare of his associates. In many cases the *bottega* was a family enterprise inherited by successive generations. All artistic work was done under the agreement that the master was to be assisted in his exertions by his associates, helpers and apprentices who in turn would profit by his artistic example. The institution of the *bottega* provided for the early and thorough education of the novice in his future craft; apprentices were engaged when between 12 and 14 years old and learned the secrets of artistic technique in many years of first menial and later more responsible occupations. When risen to the rank of assistant they would be entrusted with the execution of designs by their master who would sometimes reserve for himself the finishing touches to bring the work up to his acknowledged and expected standards. Considering the extent of such collaboration by assistants it seems inappropriate to apply too rigorously to all works of art of the past the modern concept of authenticity—execution by the master; even an artist's signature may be a trade mark rather than a personal sign and may as such be placed upon the work of an associate as a stamp of approval. —R.B.

bottle shape. Like a bottle; cylindrical body, flat base and slender neck.

bouclé (F. lock). Irregularly twisted yarn. Frize, frotte, ondule, are all collectively called bouclé yarns. Curled or loop effects in cloths made with yarns of that description. —G.W.R.

boulevard. See CIVIC PLANNING.

bourrée, boutrade. The bourrée, classified today as a pre-classic form, was first danced by the mountain peasants of central France. They had several bourrées; a flirtatious couple dance, a large group dance similar in formation to English and American long dances, and a work bourrée danced to crush grapes in the vineyards. The basic movements were skipping, cut-steps, and stamps in 4/4 meter with a characteristic quarter-note upbeat and a stamped accent on the third beat of each bar. People accompanied each other by singing, shouting, and beating with their hands. In the sixteenth century, the French court adopted the bourrée for a short time, but its lusty nature evidently did not lend itself to refinement. The dance soon disappeared from court ballrooms. Many bourrée steps were carried over into the ballet, however, and composers of the period often included a bourrée in their instrumental suites. —J.G.

bow. *Mus.* A concave stick (formerly convex) controlling the length and tension of the attached hairs which are drawn across the strings of the stringed instruments to produce musical tones; the larger the instrument, the shorter the bow. —M.E.

bowl. Concave receptacle, small in size.

box set. See STAGESETTING.

braided rug (rag rug). Made from three narrow strips of cloth and braided together. The braided strips are then sewn together. The rug may be oval, circular or rectangular in shape. —B.E.J.

brain wave. The record of the action current (q.v.) generated by nerve impulses in the brain regarded as a measure of the nerve impulse under various conditions of mental and physical activity.

"The subject to be experimented upon in the laboratory is put into a room where he rests comfortably on a couch. Two or more electrodes are attached to different parts of the surface of his head, and elaborate electrical registering apparatus records on moving picture film the presence of nerve impulses by means of the accompanying electrical deflection. It seems fantastic to see these pictures of the nerve impulse revealing its rate and variation with location, complexity, intensity and duration of the processes. We can not only see action-current-waves but can convert them into sound which we can hear. This harnessing of brain waves is in electrophysiology for nerve impulse quite analogous to the harnessing of radio waves for the conduction and generation of musical sounds.

"The fundamental thing revealed is that the brain, like our electric lighting circuit, acts through alternating currents. Thus from the very beginning the principle of alternating current was adopted for our nervous systems because it is economical. That is an astounding fact.

"There are certain basic rays—such as the alpha ray which beats at about ten per second—and a series of other rays of higher frequency designated by Greek letters. The same principles that register the brain wave can also be used in tracing the course of the nerve impulse from the sense organ through various intricate centers to the brain or from the brain through various centers to the muscle. We now therefore, have, the means of discovering the origin and course of the nerve impulse, whether it be incoming or outgoing. We may look upon the brain as a central station at which incoming and outgoing impulses are distributed through various centers in the spinal cord and other parts of the nervous system.

"To give one illustration of the application of this to music, one of the problems in the study of the vibrato is to determine what elements of the nervous system control the pulsations of the vocal cords in the vibrato cycle affecting pitch, loudness and time. Pursuit of this problem is a fascinating one because it leads to the discovery of fundamental biological principles almost infinitely complex and yet frequently measurable and explainable. Here the musicologist is in a situation analogous to that of the astronomer, who with telescope and spectroscope, intricate mathematical theories and untiring observation, reveals law and order in the system as a whole, although he can observe only one infinitesimally small part of it at a time." C. E. Seashore, *Pioneering in Psychology,* University of Iowa Press, 1942.

branle of Brittany. See passepied.

branle of Poitou. See courante.

Brazil, The Colonial Architecture of. Throughout the colonial period (1500—1821) Brazilian architecture following the style of the mother country, Portugal, remained distinct from that of Spanish America and, on the whole, less original. The earliest buildings, around Baía, the old capital, and in the region of Recife, were of mud and wattle thatched with *pindoba* palm. The next stage, of wood and rubble (*pau a pique*), closely resembled the half timber architecture of northern Europe. It is found in the 17th cent. Pernambucan landscapes of Frans Post and in existing 18th cent. houses at Ouro Preto. Otherwise the Portuguese custom of covering the walls with painted plaster, except for angle pilasters, frames and cornices of cut stone, was universal. Roofing of tile was general, as in Spanish America, but after the Portuguese style, roofs were higher pitched, and terminated at the lower angles with projecting tiles in Oriental pagoda style (*bicos*). In the 18th cent. window sashes were employed, especially in the south, after a Portuguese custom derived from England, with panes in a variety of shapes.

As opposed to Spanish America (Mexico, Antilles, Peru and Bolivia) there were almost no reflections of the Manoeline Gothic or Plateresque styles because formal building in Brazil came only after those styles had ceased to be used in Portugal. The Jesuits, the first great builders, brought the severe Counter-Reformation style to the litoral, where it remained in vogue until the early 18th cent. The Franciscans in their convents of the Northeast introduced simple two-story Doric cloisters derived from the Florentine Renaissance. During the Dutch occupation of the north (1624—1654) some reflections of the Netherlands Baroque occurred, especially in Recife. In the 17th cent. country churches, convents and private chapels were often given entrance porches (*alpendres*) roofed in tile and supported on stubby Doric columns. Plantation houses were frequently surrounded by these porches. The 17th cent. church facade arrangement of a circular window over the door, flanked by two rectangular windows was expanded in the 18th cent. to systems of three and five doors surrounded by a corresponding number of windows. Twin lateral towers were, as in Spanish America a common feature of church facades, those of Minas Gerais being often round or oval in form. There was almost no elaborate use of baroque sculpture on these facades, as in the Churrigueresque buildings of Spanish America. But in the 18th cent. the Portuguese Rococo made itself felt in the graceful, curving lines of lightly sculptured doors and windows. In Minas Gerais, where the gold broom of the mid-18th cent. provided funds for ambitious building, much richer soapstone carving by Antonio Francisco Lisboa (*Aleijadinho*) and his school animated the facades. Toward the close of the century Custodio de Faria brought the incipient neo-classic style to Rio de Janeiro, the capital after 1762. At the same time neo-Palladian Italianate elements appeared in the church architecture of the extremes of the country, at Belem and in the Jesuit missions of the Sete Povos of Rio Grande do Sul, where architects like Giovanni Battista Primoli came from Argentina and Paraguay to work.

In the plans and roofing of Brazilian churches further contrasts with Spanish American methods are found. With the exception of a few buildings in Minas Gerais, simple rectangular plans prevailed. Round apses were avoided. Lateral corridors giving on to the nave often lead to a series of sacristy apartments behind the apse, although in country churches the sacristy is an outside excrescence. Projecting chapels almost never occur. True vaulting and cupolas, common in Spanish American building, were avoided in Brazil as they were in Portugal. Roofs were steep, while inside wood ceilings imitated shallow barrel vaults. In this way problems of engineering were avoided.

The decoration of church interiors was equally simple. Except in a few city churches of Baía and Rio de Janeiro, all-over Baroque polychrome wood carving gave way to isolated altars set against plain white washed walls. High altars were smaller and less complicated than the corresponding sculptured retables of Spanish America. Their centers were occupied by elaborate stage pyramids surmounted by the statue of a saint (*tronos*). This is a dramatic Portuguese feature usually covered by a curtain but on solemn occasions illuminated by ascending tiers of lighted candles. Chancels, corridors and sometimes the naves were ornamented with dadoes of the blue and white scenic Portuguese tiles. Jacarandá rosewood, handsome mahoganies, walnut and tropical woods were used for altar rails and sacristy and chancel furniture, handsomely carved in the Portuguese versions of Queen Anne, Chippendale, Louis XV, and Empire styles. Painted murals and altarpieces were fewer and less distinguished than in the churches of Spanish America.

The secular architecture of colonial Brazil followed Portuguese country models. Moorish or *mudéjar* influences, so important in Spanish America were scarcely felt; hence the inner patio, *artesonado* ceilings, and plaster arabesque were little used. Town houses were simple one and two story affairs, with window and door frames like the churches unceiled roofs, informal interior trim—very different from the lofty elaborate Spanish American palaces. In Baía and Recife some much higher houses were built, often with handsome sculptured doors and with kitchens on the topmost floor. In old towns of the Northeast some roofed wooden balconies are still found. Heavily latticed, these were a feature of colonial towns. In the streets, graceful, rococo wall fountains, often composed of dolphin motives, like those of church sacristies, were another Portuguese importation.

Public buildings, of which few have survived, imitated the Portuguese house forms. City halls in the Baía region had the façade, arcades, and central towers of the Spanish American *cabildos*. More frequently they were designed in the Iberian imitation of a Louis-XV *hôtel*. The prime example is the penitentiary (now museum) of Ouro Preto, begun by the governor Luís da Cunha Menezes in the 1780's.

Brazilian colonial building, like that of Portugal in relation to Spain, was, as compared with that of Spanish America, less imposing, less decorated, less varied, less structurally complicated, less influenced by Moorish construction and decoration. Its character is rural, rather than urban. Its distinction is its very simplicity, the justness of its proportions, and the delicacy of its limited decoration. See LATIN AMERICAN ART; also *Brazil builds,* New York, Museum of Modern Art, 1943; Cerqueira Falcão, (*Edgard de.*) *Reliquias da Bahia,* Sao Paulo, 1940; *Revista do Serviço do patrimonio histórico e artístico nacional,* Rio de Janeiro, v. 1-5, 1937-41; Smith, Robert C., The colonial architecture of Minas Gerais in Brazil, *Art Bulletin,* v. 21, 1939. p. 110-159.			—R.C.S.

breadth. An art object so characterized has its details massed in such manner as to give the effect of large size with unity.

breve (It.). *Mus.* Literally, short. Formerly the shortest note, now the longest note in music notation. Twice the length of the whole note (semibreve). **alla breve.** A doubling of the tempo, using the minim (half note) as the unit of beat instead of the crotchet (quarter note); i.e., 2/2 meter instead of 4/4. Also, sometimes indicates 4/2 meter. See neumes; NOTATION. —M.E.

breviary. See MEDIEVAL MUSIC.

brick Gothic. See GERMAN ART.

bridal. See COSTUME ART.

bridge. See RADIO DRAMA.

bridge. Bridges, constructed for carrying roadways or railroads across rivers and valleys, have always been and still are not a mere technical but an architectural task as well. Only the 19th cent., induced by the prevailing use of the new building materials iron, steel, concrete, left this problem entirely to the engineers. Bridgebuilding has to be done not more and not less functionally than the solution of any other architectural problem. There is only one phenomenon by which the bridge is distinguished from other works of architecture: it does not create and shape space but spans and cuts it.

The most primitive form is the post-and-lintel type of construction, a timber or stone beam, supported at both ends. Later, but still in prehistorical times we find the cantilever bridge of timber beams or stone blocks protruding from both sides. In Mesopotamia, the brick vaulted arch is already used around 3800 B. C. Building vaulted bridges in real stone was an essential part of Roman civilization. The Roman type of the barrel vaulted bridge characterized by the semi-circular arch and the perforation of the piers ruled European bridge architecture through almost 1000 years. Ancient writers like Julius Caesar (100-44 B.C.) and architects like Vitruvius (1st cent. B.C.) give so exact architectural details that we are enabled to reconstruct these bridges. Numerous examples are still preserved everywhere in Italy, France, Spain, Germany and the Balkans.

Mediaeval bridges do not show any principally new solutions. They are composed by arches of different diameters, later even by stilted arches. Fortifications, esp. watch-

towers, began to enrich the outline (e.g. bridges in Prag, Regensburg, Würzburg, Avignon, Montauban, Toledo, Carcassonne, Florence, Verona, all of them between 1100 and 1300). Some bridges are covered, framed by rows of houses (Old London Bridge, originally built 1176-1209, houses on both sides around 1300). Switzerland, Germany, and Austria excelled in wooden covered bridges.

The Renaissance bridge revived again the ancient principles of bridgebuilding. The artistic and technical theory is mainly developed in the treatise by Andrea Palladio (1508—1580), based on Vitruvius' *De Architectura Libri Decem* (Ten Books on Architecture). Some of the most wonderful Renaissance bridges, like those in Florence (Ponte S. Trinità, in 1567 by Bartolomeo Ammanati, 1511—1592) show already flat barrel vaults instead of the Roman semi-circular type.

The bridges of the 18th cent. in France stimulated mainly by the work of Jean Rodolphe Perronet (1708—1794) bridges of Orleans, Nantes, Neuilly, Paris, Pont de la Concorde, all of them between 1750 and 1790 connected technical progress with beautiful architectural forms. The arches became much flatter, the spans much wider than before. Perronet's works set the example for the architecture of stone bridges till today. The 18th cent. furthermore invented complicated systems of wooden constructions executed mainly in Switzerland, Germany and Scandinavia till about 1820, in the United States till about 1880. The famous covered bridges of Vermont, New Hampshire and other American States represented a special branch of this technique.

The 19th cent. stimulated bridgebuilding by two facts: the introduction of a new material, iron—later on steel—and by the invention of the railroad. Simultaneously with this technical progress the artistic interest receded. Only at the beginning of the 20th cent. people became interested again in the architectural aspects of the problem.

The first iron arch bridge was built 1776 in Coalebrookdale, England, with a span of about 100 feet. Five types of iron and steel bridges exist: the beam bridge, the arch bridge, the suspension bridge, the cantilever bridge, and the combined system, distinguished from each other by the different distribution of compression and tension in the individual elements of construction. Examples in Europe: Westminster Bridge, London (1854—1865), Garabit Valley (1885, span over 500 feet), Firth-of-Fourth Bridge (1890), Pont Alexander III, Paris (1899); in the United States: Eads Bridge, St. Louis, Miss. (1868–1874), Brooklyn Bridge by John A. Roebling, New York, N. Y. (1867—1883). The great steel bridges of the 20th cent. increase the span by improved construction, but more important is the re-gained interest in their architectural appearance. The suspension type is preferred. Examples: George Washington Bridge, New York, N. Y., (1927—1931), Waldo Hancock Bridge, Bucksport, Maine, (1931), Golden Gate Bridge, San Francisco, Calif., (1937), Oakland Bay Bridge, San Francisco, Calif., (1933—1937), Whitestone Bridge, New York, N. Y., (1937—1939).

Bridgebuilding received a new stimulus from the introduction of concrete and reinforced concrete, more in use in Europe than in the U.S.A. These materials combine the static advantages of steel and concrete.

The characteristic aesthetic element of the bridge is the emphasis of the outline. In any kind of material the bridge can become a work of architectural art only by the cooperation of the calculating engineer with the creative artist. See J. Furtenbach, *Architectura-civilis*, 1627; A. Martinelli, *Descrittione di diversi Ponti, etc.*, Rome, 1676: A Palladio, *The Architecture*, vol. III, 1730; J. J. Schübler, *Nützliche Anweisung zur Unentbehrlichen Zimmermannskunst*, 1731—36; C.Chr. Schramm, *Historischer Schauplatz, in welchem die merkwürdigsten Brücken aus allen vier Teilen der Welt*, 1735; C. Walter, *Theoretisch-praktische Anweisung, wie allerley Arten von Brucken, sowohl von Holz als von Steinen . . anzulegen sind*, 1765; J. R. Perronet, *Description des Projets et de la construction des Ponts*, 1788; M. Gauthey, *Traité de la construction des Ponts*, 1890—13; American Institute of Steel Construction, *Prize Bridges, 1928—1938*; Black. A., *The Story of Bridges*, 1934; Brangwyn and Sparrow, *A Book of Bridges*, 1914; Kirby and Laurson, *The Early Years of Modern Civil Engineering*, 1932; Parson, William Barclay, *Engineers and Engineering in the Renaissance*, 1939; Steinman, David B., and Watson, Sara Ruth, *Bridges and Their Builders*, 1941; Schuyler, Hamilton, *The Roeblings*, 1931; Thomas, William Norman, *The Development of Bridges*, 1920; Tyrell, Henry Grattan, *History of Bridge Engineering*, 1911; Watson, Wilbur J., *Bridge Architecture*, 1926; Watson, Wilbur J., *A Decade of Bridges*, 1937; Whitney, Charles S., *Bridges, a Study in Their Art, Science, and Evolution*, 1929; Zucker, Paul, *American Bridges and Dams*, 1941.   —P.Z.

brightness. See COLOR.

briiliance. Is a sensation attribute of color, the same as brightness. See COLOR.

brindisi. Drinking song.

broadcasting of music, the. The broadcasting of music belongs only to the most recent history of wireless communication. Early attempts to transmit and receive electrical impulses through the air produced signals which took the form of a visible spark or an audible buzz. The latter signals grouped as longs and shorts according to a code could be used to transmit messages. The classic experiments which established the possibility of wireless communication were made by Guglielmo Marconi in the closing years of the 19th cent.

The spark transmitters used for communication in code were intermittent in character and incapable of generating a sustained carrier wave which was necessary for the transmission of music and speech. It was Duddell, an English investigator, who in 1900 discovered that an electric arc could be used as a source of high frequency energy. By combining Duddell's singing arc with a microphone in a transmitting circuit, the Danish engineer, Vladimir Poulsen, produced the wireless telephone and by 1903 had demonstrated the possibility of transmitting speech over considerable distances. In 1908-09 engineers of the German Telefunken Company attempted to transmit speech and music by this method between Sandy Hook and Bedloes' Island, New York harbor, a distance of approximately eighteen miles. The music consisted of a record of Verdi's *Anvil Chorus* played by a cylinder phonograph of ancient design. The arc, however, was fluctuating, unreliable, and difficult to adjust.

It was the invention of the three element tube by Dr. Lee De Forest which provided a more reliable medium. This invention which was the Fleming valve modified by the interposition of a grid between the glowing filament and the cylinder, marked the end of the period of tentative experiment and the beginning of practical broadcasting. The development of the wireless telephone was enormously stimulated by the demands made by World War I when it was esp. valuable as a means by which observation planes might communicate with the ground forces.

Progress during the post-war period was

fumbling. A wireless link used by the telephone company to connect Catalina Island with the mainland had to be abandoned because of the lack of privacy, since conversations so transmitted could be picked up by any operator who tuned in. Much experimental broadcasting was done and the amount of amateur interest was enormous. A broadcast by Dr. Lee De Forest of the voice of Eugenia Farrar in 1907 was picked up by chance by an operator at the Brooklyn Navy Yard and excited incredulity. Programs of especial interest like those transmitted by Station 8XK operated by Frank Conrad, a Westinghouse engineer, attracted a considerable audience of radio amateurs.

It was largely with the idea of promoting the sale of radio sets that manufacturers of electrical equipment commenced broadcasting on a regular schedule. The first broadcast by a commercial station was the report of the Harding election returns broadcast by the Westinghouse Station KDKA from East Pittsburgh. Music emanating from this station consisted not only of phonograph records, but of actual musical performances by the Westinghouse band, an employee organization. Later the KDKA Little Symphony was organized. Early broadcasts originated in a tent pitched on the roof of a factory building. The erection of a tent indoors in the attempt to obtain similar favorable acoustical conditions led to the burlap draped studio which, in turn, has been largely replaced by acoustically treated wall surfaces by which the resonance of a studio can be controlled. Other important pioneer stations were WJZ broadcasting from Newark and WDY broadcasting from Aldene, New York, as well as WGY in Schenectady.

The advantage of remote pick-up soon became obvious since performers otherwise had to be induced (in the case of the New York stations) to make the trip from New York to New Jersey. Accordingly, we find WGY utilizing telegraph wires as a connection with New York and thus employing programs originating with WJZ. Similarly the American Telephone and Telegraph Station WBNY (later WEAF) utilized a studio in the old Waldorf Astoria Hotel. The development of large commercial stations was recognized by the Department of Commerce which attempted to resolve the growing problem of interference by establishing a group of Class B stations chosen on the basis of power, fidelity, and superior program content and assigning to them a new broadcasting fre-

quency, the 400 metre band. The other stations continued as hitherto on the 360 metre band. Congress tardily provided a regulatory body by authorizing the creation of the Federal Radio Commission, appointed by President Coolidge in 1927.

As early as 1916 David Sarnoff, then in the commercial department of the American Marconi Company, sent a memorandum to the general manager of that firm which anticipated in a striking fashion the salient features of subsequent American broadcasting. "I have in mind a plan of development which would make radio a household utility in the same sense as the piano or phonograph. The idea is to bring music into the home by wireless . . . The main revenue to be derived will be from the sale of the radio music boxes which, if manufactured in lots of 100,000 or so could yield a handsome profit . . . The Company would have to undertake to make the arrangements, I am sure, for music recitals, lectures, etc. . . . Aside from the profit to be derived from this proposition, the possibilities for advertising for the company are tremendous; for its name would ultimately be brought into the household and wireless would receive national and universal attention."

After a period of hesitation the sponsored program appeared in 1924, a fact which was to give a distinctive direction to American broadcasting. The makers of radio equipment who broadcast to secure a market for their products were gradually replaced by organizations which sold broadcasting time to commercial firms who sponsored programs in the hope of making their product known and thus increasing their sales. With this came the "commercial," the announcement praising the sponsor's product, but at the same time the plan offered a practical way of financing the mounting costs of broadcasting. Early performers had been lured to the microphone by curiosity and the promise of publicity. Once this initial stage was past, performers demanded a more substantial financial return. Fees rapidly increased as radio developed stars with a mass appeal.

The first commercial program was a ten minute real estate promotion talk sponsored by the Queensborough Corporation which was promoting the development of Jackson Heights, Long Island. Finding that speeches were a very dubious means of building good will, sponsors early turned to music. The Browning King Orchestra sponsored by a New York clothing firm of that name was first in this field. The Lucky Strike Company sponsored another pioneer musical program. Both of these programs appeared over WEAF.

The effective broadcasting range of an individual station was limited. Sponsors with a product of national appeal began to demand a wider coverage. Stations remote from the great metropolitan reservoirs of talent could also benefit by receiving the programs of key stations in metropolitan areas. Gradually the networks evolved. A pioneer step was the connection of Station KDKA with the Calvary Episcopal Church of Pittsburgh by telephone line. When Station WEAF was acquired by the National Broadcasting Corporation, its network connections had grown to the extent of 3600 miles of esp. designed telephone lines.

The Victor program, broadcast on New Year's Eve, 1925, was the first to utilize a national hook-up. This was preceded by a transitional stage in which there were two great broadcasting areas, the far west and the east, the Rocky Mountains serving as the dividing line.

Once continental America was linked from coast to coast by radio networks, intercontinental communication was the next step. As early as 1926 Station WJZ received and rebroadcast programs originating in Europe. By 1930 the feasibility of such programs was manifest, and at the present time news round-ups from the far corners of the globe are a usual feature of news coverage although frequently still subject to fading and excessive background noise. The distortion so often apparent in such broadcasts makes rebroadcasts of European musical programs of doubtful value at the present stage of development.

The important influence exerted by the three element tube on the phonograph and the talking film will be dealt with elsewhere. Two developments which promise to affect the future of radio should be mentioned here: broadcasting by frequency modulation and television. Stations employing frequency modulation have already entered the broadcasting field and some home radio sets are designed to receive broadcasts through this, as well as the usual channels. Since frequency modulation is not affected by static, it is an innovation of the greatest importance to musical broadcasts where unimpaired quality and freedom from background noise have always been of paramount importance.

Television, which was demonstrated in an impressive fashion at the New York World's Fair (The World of Tomorrow), excited much public interest. It is still in an experimental stage although a certain amount of broadcasting to a limited television audience has already been done. Its development was hindered rather than fostered by the advent of World War II since its operations do not lend themselves to military requirements as did radio broadcasting. Difficulties observable at present are the limited range of telecasts and the great expense involved in producing programs which include memorized texts (as in a stage play) without the possibility of a long run which is offered by a successful stage hit (see RADIO; DRAMA). Probably the transmission of films will play a role in telecasting comparable to that of the phonograph record in radio broadcasting.

—C.W.H.

broadloom. Carpets woven in widths 54 inches or wider, as distinguished from "narrow loom" widths of 27 inches and 26 inches. Broadloom carpet is produced as wide as 18 feet. —B.E.J.

broadsheet. A graphic print. A sheet of paper of more or less standard size, printed on one side only.

brocade (L. *broccus,* stitching). Originally heavy silk with elaborate pattern in silver and gold threads. Name now applied to many materials which resemble historic brocades. Brocade has embossed appearance and is of Jacquard weave. See also nishiki. —G.W.R.

brocade fabrics. Usually made of brocade light and medium weight silk; linen or cotton or rayon fabric of simple structure embellished with Jacquard figuring which may be developed by displaying either warp threads or picks of weft only, or both series of threads, more or less freely upon a ground texture usually consisting either of the plain calico or "tabby" weave or other simple and neutral weave, such as the smaller twill, satin and matt or dice weaves, according to the particular effect desired in the fabric. —G.W.R.

brocatelle. Name comes from *brocatel* and *brocatta,* referring to ancient patterned fabrics combined of wool and silk or cotton and wool. A rich silk fabric with a linen back that resembles a damask in weave, but a brocade in effect. The design stands out in relief from the background. No gold or silver is used in brocatelles. The fabric shows usually one color or two colors. —G.W.R.

broché (F. *brocher,* to stitch). Jacquard woven, it is known as swivel-broché. The threads are not carried across the whole width of the cloth. In hand woven brochés the pattern filling threads are floated from selvage to selvage.   —G.W.R.

brochure. *Book.* A small printed work. Also used to denote a "de luxe" or elaborately produced booklet.

broken. *Book.* A book is "broken" when the back (sewing, glueing, etc.) cracks inside from top to bottom, or head to tail. Paper is "broken" when it has been folded over.

broken consort. See chamber music.

broken ink landscape. See CHINESE ARTS.

broken pediment. A pediment often used in baroque architecture and in which one or both of the cornices are not continuous.

broken range. Term applied to masonry in which horizontal courses are continuous for short distances only (up to eight feet).

broken twills. Twill weaves in which the characteristic twill line is arranged to run part way of the repeat in the weave from left to right, and part way from right to left.

bronze mirror. In the Orient the early mirror was of bronze, polished to produce a first class reflecting surface on the obverse, and decorated in low relief on the reverse.—J.A.M.

brooch. See JEWELRY.

brotherhood of St. Luke. See POLISH ART.

Brown Decades. See POST-REVOLUTIONARY ARCHITECTURE AND DECORATIVE ARTS IN THE U.S.A.

Bruges school. A school of art that developed in 14th and 15th cent. Bruges out of the mediaeval tradition. This tradition is manifest in the work of the artists who worked in Bruges such as Hubert and Jan Van Eyck, Peter Christus, Hans Memlinc and Gheeraert David. Their work is often referred to as Flemish primitive art.   —R.L.W.

Brukskunst movement. See SCANDINAVIAN ART.

brush. The chief tools of the painter, brushes have changed little in their essential character through the entire history of this art. With the exception of a special type used in ancient Egypt, a reed macerated at one end to separate the fibres, brushes have generally been of animal hair tied into a tuft and set into a handle. A few of the larger brushes in earlier practice were tied around the handle. Quills were developed as a means of holding the tuft, allowing the tied hair to fit at one end of the cut quill and the handle in the other. Metal ferrules have taken the place of quills during the last century, though the traditional holder is still commonly made and sold. Modern painters' brushes are in two general types: bristle or coarse hair, usually that of the pig; and fine hair, sable or so-called 'camel' hair. Sable brushes are made of hair from the tails of the Asiatic mink, the kolinsky, native to a district of northeastern Russia. The color is reddish yellow. This is generally considered to be the finest of the hair brushes. 'Camel hair' comes actually from a squirrel and the best of these is found also in Russia or Siberia. The color may be red, gray, or black.   —G.L.S.

Brussels carpets. Woven by the Jacquard process and so far as basic construction goes are exactly the same as the Wilton carpets (q.v.). The only difference is that the wires have no blades on the ends so that when withdrawn the yarn is left in loops instead of being a cut pile.   —B.E.J.

buckling. Blisters in paint film. This condition usually applies to the ground as well.

buckram. *Book.* A very durable cotton or linen book cloth of a coarse, open weave and stiffened with size.

bucranium (L. *bucranium* fr. Gr. *boukranion,* ox head). An ox skull used as decoration in Roman architecture, particularly on altars and temple friezes, usually with a garland or fillet hung between each two bucrania.   —L.T.S.

Buddha's hand. The citron fruit with its fleshy, fingerlike parts; it often appears as a motive in Oriental art. See SYMBOLISM IN FAR EASTERN ART.

Buen Retiro pottery. See SPAIN, ART OF.

bugaku (Jap.). A classic court dance, now rare, in which large masks were worn. See JAPANESE ART.

Bühnenweihfestspiel (Ger.). The epithet Wagner bestowed on his last musical drama, *Parsifal* ("stage consecration play").

building line. See CIVIC PLANNING.

building regulation. See CIVIC PLANNING.

buisino. See MUSICAL INSTRUMENTS.

buke-zukuri. See JAPANESE ART.

bulb bowl. A circular shallow bowl, generally with three short legs; used in China as a container in which to grow flowering bulbs.

bulbous. A bi-symmetrical convex contour; swelled like a bulb.

Bulgaria, art of. When we pass over the remains of Thracian, Greek, and Roman art found on the territory of Bulgaria, the old Bulgarian art really commences with the foundation of the first Bulgarian Empire with its capitol at Pliska-Aboba in the northeast section of the country. Here from pagan times was a great palace with the foundations and lower parts of the columns constructed of large blocks of stone, many of which were obviously brought from the Roman ruins of Nikopolis. They show a strong similarity with various Asiatic arts, esp. that of the Sassanids, and this similarity is even more marked in the case of the monument of the mounted Bulgarian king of the 9th cent. carved on a rock at Madara. This is really a unique monument in Europe and the Balkans.

After the introduction of Christianity, a basilica of an Oriental type was built near Pliska, but the capital of the Bulgarian Empire was transferred to the now destroyed capital of Preslav and it is here that the Byzantine influences begin to appear. Tsar Boris also established churches in various parts of his domains including Ohrid; it is very likely that the oldest parts of the basilica of St. Sophia at Ohrid belong to this period. It is a vaulted basilica with pillars, with three naves and three aisles.

The greatest center of middle Bulgarian art is the city of Tirnovo, the capital of the second Empire, which is constructed largely of bricks and colored stones often arranged in layers. Most of the old churches are domed and adorned with frescos of a special style.

Near by in the village of Arbanassi are the best preserved private houses of the Middle Ages. They are plain with extremely thick walls, in some of which are passageways and hiding places. The main floor is essentially a store house without windows and the dwelling quarters are on the second floor with small windows.

Another common type of architecture are two-storied churches, in which the church below served as a mausoleum and the church above—but unconnected—was undoubtedly a chapel for the family. Such was the Church of Boyana near Sofia.

The Middle Ages saw extensive building of churches and monasteries such as the Monastery of the Transfiguration at Tirnovo and of St. John at Rilo. In all of these, and esp. on the iconostases, are exquisite examples of wood carving which often show the same type of oriental influences that have always been connected with Bulgarian art. There also remain examples of silver work which seem to come from a national school.

With the Turkish conquest, major works of art become fewer and fewer and Turkish influences appear, although there are relatively few important mosques in the country such as the Tombul Djamia of the Vizier Sherif in Shumen built in 1649. Most of the old private houses were of stone with wooden projecting balconies and approximate an oriental style.

Modern art, properly so called, begins with the rise of the movement for independence in the 19th cent. and the modern cities such as Sofia are being steadily reconstructed in a more modernistic style. Yet such monuments as the Church of St. Alexander Nevsky in Sofia, built by Russian architects after the liberation, are in a typical Russian style, much more ornate than are the more sober Bulgarian churches and buildings which rely for their beauty on interior decoration.

Modern painting has developed first under the influence of St. Petersburg and then of Vienna, but later the dominant influence was that of France. In its early stages, the modern art followed the same path as did the literature. The early artists were interested in depicting the village life, the local customs and traditions and had a narrow range of interests. They were succeeded by foreign trained workers, such as Andrei Nikolov in sculpture, the outstanding Bulgarian artist. Ivan Lazarov represents the modern stage of the more purely national art.

In painting too Ivan Murkvichka and Anton Mitov were the teachers in the first phase of work but since that time Bulgarian painting has branched out into all fields. Thus Boris Denev and Nikola Tanev are the leaders in landscape painting and views of village life with Nikola Petrov and Constantine Shterkelov among the still younger men. In decorative and imaginative art Nikolai Rainov is among the leaders. Special attention must be paid to the caricaturists Alexander Bozhinov and his younger contemporary Ilya Beshkov.

Also Vladimir Dimitrov Maistor with his simplified and symbolic figures and Boris Georgiev with his mystic symbolism are somewhat outside of the usual path of Bulgarian art.

In general, the fine arts of modern Bulgaria represent that same tendency which is so marked in the literature. There is an extreme emphasis on history and a preoccupation with the passing aspects of village life which has prevented the proper adjustment of the Bulgarian people to the world around them and has created feelings which the chauvinists and intriguers have led away easily from the normal democratic instincts of the Bulgarian people. The very healthiness and local patriotism of Bulgarian democracy have been counterbalanced with a narrowness which has involved the people in three disastrous wars within thirty years and the future of the national art depends upon the securing of a psychological balance and tolerance which has hitherto been lacking. See Bogdan Filow, *L'Ancien Art Bulgare,* Paris, 1922; R. H. Markham, *Meet Bulgaria,* Sofia, 1931.—C.A.M.

bulk. *Book.* The thickness of the book before binding.

bulk zoning. See CIVIC PLANNING.

bull-roarer. A sound-producing ceremonial instrument used in some parts of Oceania and consisting of a tube or slat that is whirled from the end of a string. See OCEANIA, THE ARTS OF.

bung. *Cer.* Tier of saggers (q.v.) or ware. See CERAMICS I.

bunjin-ga (Jap.). A modern school of painting in Chinese style.

bureau. See FURNITURE.

Burgundian school. See FRENCH ART.

burial robe. See COSTUME ART.

burin. See PRINTS AND PRINT PROCESSES.

burlesque. A form of variety theatrical entertainment in the U. S. comprising as its chief attraction scantily costumed dancing girls, some of whom "strip tease" or remove their garments during a bubble or feather dance. Sometimes the entertainment is a musical comedy; at other times it is a variety show of the vaudeville type. The humor is coarse

and frequently bawdy. Beginning about 1870, burlesque had its greatest popularity in the first quarter of the 20th cent.   —H.R.W.

Burma, art of. See SOUTHEASTERN ASIATIC ART.

burning. *Cer.* The firing of clay products in a kiln in temperatures from degrees Fahrenheit 1700 to 2100.

burnisher. (1) Gold leaf is commonly rubbed or polished after it is laid with some kind of a hard stone known as a burnisher. The most common stone for this purpose now is agate, but haematite is frequently mentioned in treatises of the Middle Ages and the Renaissance. During those periods, also, teeth of animals were made into burnishers as were fine stones such as sapphires, emeralds and rubies. (2) *Etch.* A smooth, highly polished, round piece of steel for reducing shadings that are too dark and for removing scratches. See PRINTS AND PRINT PROCESSES. (3) See GLASS AND GLASS-MAKING.

burnishing. See PRINTS AND PRINT PROCESSES.

burnt sienna. See iron pigments.

burnt umber. See umber; iron pigments.

burr. In an engraving or dry point, the rough or torn edge of the lines made on the metal plates by the graver or point; also the softened lines they produce in the prints if they are allowed to remain on the plate instead of being removed with a scraper. The burr is generally allowed to remain on dry points, while engravings are usually scraped so that their lines are sharp and clean. See drypoint (an intaglio process); see PRINTS AND PRINT PROCESSES.   —R.M.

bush dwellings. See DOMESTIC ARCHITECTURE.

Bushongo art. See AFRICAN NEGRO ART.

busine. See MUSICAL INSTRUMENTS.

busshi (Jap.). A carver of Buddhist images.

butsu-e (Jap.). Buddhist paintings.

butterfly. See SYMBOLISM IN FAR EASTERN ART.

buttress (Old Fr. *bouter,* to bear against). A mass of material, usually masonry, built against a wall to support or strengthen it.   —J.M.M.

byobu (Jap.). A folding screen, generally of six panels on which the best masters lavished their artistic skill.   —J.A.M.

bypass. See CIVIC PLANNING.

BYZANTINE ARCHITECTURE (4th cent. to the present). Constantine, a ruler who understood the times in which he lived, established the capital of the Roman Empire at Byzantium (324) and thereby gave shape and direction to the Eastern, Greek-speaking half of Christendom. Byzantine architecture dates from this foundation, being in succession to Roman, Hellenistic, Syrian, Sassanian-Persian, and all of the ancient styles of the Near East. In its development it constitutes a synthesis of principles and purposes inherent in all of these applied for the expression of its own inner spirit. This synthesis was essentially that of Greek and oriental elements and was fully attained in the reign of Justinian (527-565).

The formulating period is marked by experiment, creative imagination and bold engineering. It includes churches built by Constantine on the characteristic basilica plan in Constantinople and Palestine (Bethlehem), shrines such as the Holy Sepulchre at Jerusalem, the structures at Ravenna, examples at Salonika (St. George, S. Sophia, St. Demetrius) and in Constantinople St. John the Baptist of the Studion, the first S. Irene, SS. Sergius and Bacchus and Hagia Sophia. The basilica style, without cupola, was given vigorous independent handling in Asia Minor and esp. in the stone buildings of Syria, distinguished for admirable masonry, coloristic decoration and structural elements such as stone vaults, stone roofs, towers, etc. (The traditional basilica type of structure may not be considered further. Suffice it to say that it continued in the East for centuries and there is scarcely a location explored by excavators that does not reveal an example. The Syrian style, investigated thoroughly by H. C. Butler, possesses independent characteristics and merits special analysis beyond the scope of this article. Syria is also rich in the remains of civic buildings, houses, palaces, inns, shops, etc., all of which, as elsewhere in the Byzantine area, must be excluded from further mention.)

The first period closes with the dispute about images (Iconoclastic edict of Leo III, 726, to 843), and introduced the second great period known as Mid-Byzantine (11th cent. to capture of Constantinople by the crusading knights

in 1204, and later). It is characterized by the prevalence of the Greek-cross plan, esp. marked on the exterior by the cross arms, elevated drum and dome (often of small diameter), smaller domes on corners and elsewhere, and special attention to exterior decoration. This is the standard church of the Greek rite to the present day and is found everywhere, notably in Constantinople, Greece and the Balkan states. The style in Armenia represents an independent school, and Russia developed its own interpretation. Thus, while the Byzantine principle was standard it allowed flexible handling as national and racial instincts suggested. The last period, from the recovery of Constantinople by the Byzantines in 1261 (and marked by the loss of the city to the Ottoman Turks in 1453), on down to the present exhibits such variations, at times marked by loose and ostentatious usages, and on other occasions by traditional conservatism.

The general formula for Byzantine architecture may be stated thus: an organization of subordinate masses receiving the thrust which originates in the apex of the cupola which crowns the vertical axis. The two elements emphasized in this formula are (1) the dominating cupola, and (2) the subordinate masses on which it is lodged and their organization, all of which are functional architecturally and expressively.

Thrust is active within the mass of the whole. The buttress system is within. There is very little exterior buttressing, such as the tower-like piers which span the north and south aisles of Hagia Sophia. Structure is essentially self-buttressing. It creates an equilibrium of balanced masses, and being functional in all of its parts, it is accordingly, organic. The opposition of forces affords a sense of life, indeed of drama, being in this respect quite different in principle from the horizontal repose of Greek style (which is also organic but in a different way).

The typical Byzantine structure is of central type, with great variety in ground plan: (1) circle, polygon, square for simple structures such as baptisteries, tombs and memorials of martyrs and (2) radiating extension of the above; surrounding aisle for circle and polygon, cross with equal arms, projecting exedras and other masses; (3) approximations to rectangle and square, including within its lines all subordinate masses, with the exception of eastern apse. This is the standard plan, generally accepted through the centuries to the present day. This approximation was worked out by experiment during the 6th cent. (S. Vitale at Ravenna, S. George at Ezra, cathedral at Bosra, SS. Sergius and Bacchus at Constantinople) and attained an unrivalled climax in Hagia Sophia. It resolved the conflict between the vertical axis and the liturgical, which is longitudinal. Decorum in public worship is violated when the service is performed at the center of the building, and it requires the perspective of a nave to focus respectful attention on the altar. Byzantine structure placed the altar in the projecting apse (as in the basilica), contrived three aisles as in the basilica (but by novel means), and at the same time crowned the structure with a dome or cupola, effective both within and without. By such means the Byzantine builders accomplished their two objectives, length and height, and with no conflict, since the effect is that of harmony.

A comparison of Hagia Sophia with St. Peter's, the principal cathedral churches of the East and West areas of Christendom resp., is revealing: the dome of Hagia Sophia is the logical climax of the building, and the thrust descending from its apex is distributed justly through all of the masses of the substructure. Unity in composition is manifest thereby, but is unobtrusive; it appears to be in the very nature of things and affords no other suggestion. The dome is visible from all directions as one approaches the structure, and requires no vantage point, near or far, for effective view. On the other hand, the soaring dome of St. Peter's rises on the west portion of the cathedral only and its thrust has no relation with the bays and narthex of the eastern section (as composed by Maderna in alteration of the plans of Michelangelo and Bramante). St. Peter's dome is superbly effective from the west, and from distant points all over the Roman campagna. It dominates the entire city of Rome (or used to), but as one advances to the portals through the famous piazza, less and less of the dome is visible until it vanishes entirely. The whole is rather like a locomotive with a smokestack. Likewise, upon entering St. Peter's the visitor would scarcely suspect that the great barrel vaults support a dome. It is only as he nears the crossing and looks up that he receives the effect. But upon entering Hagia Sophia the entire interior bursts upon him instantly, in complete coordination. Therefore, Hagia Sophia is the historic example in all architecture of the successful integration within a large interior of longitudinal and vertical axes. Hagia Sophia stands alone, but almost all

Byzantine churches, even the most humble, share its principles, and reveal in the logical ordering of masses, solution of thrust and **organic unity**, the innate working of the Greek mind—granted the acceptance of the cupola from the eastern sections of the church. The Byzantine synthesis then, represents Greek and oriental elements in successful adjustment.

The cupola and the building of central type are regarded as Eastern in origin, various localities and periods receiving the credit and for sundry reasons (reed huts of Mesopotamia as prototype, brick as material in Assyria and Persia, technical resources in stone masonry in Syria and Armenia, etc., and the great dome of heaven over all). Considerable use of the principle had been made of it in Hellenistic and Roman architecture for tombs, shrines and memorials, but rarely for practical employment of space, with exception of the Pantheon. Christians had used it for the same purposes, and found it admirable for baptisteries and martyr shrines, and also to mark sacred places, such as the Holy Sepulchre and the place of the Ascension. The suggestion is that of emphasis, the celebration of an object of great importance,—sarcophagus, statue, baptismal font, consecrated spot. The new idea was to use it in churches for the audience hall but not for the altar which was placed in the projecting apse. What then, was on the axis of the domed church? Nothing tangible, only an idea; that of the validity of Christian doctrine as an entity, or of one dogma in particular.

Byzantine architecture is accordingly theological, with full intellectual implication of the term, and this is its distinction amid the historic Christian styles. The Eastern Church has been everlastingly interested in theology. It applied Greek philosophic usages to the organization of Christian belief, wrote the creeds and formulated the dogma. It is not without significance that it was host to the great ecumenical councils, that it weathered the bitter theological dispute about images, that it applied to itself the term orthodox, that it gave to its churches the titles of Divine Wisdom and Peace. Its architecture is fully responsive to this innate characteristic of its people and is amply revealing. Within the Byzantine structure one is assured of the logical coordination of Christian belief, its perfection and the unity of its doctrine. Again comparison with St. Peter's is instructive. The dome of St. Peter's expresses the idea of rule of competent ecclesiastical authority. It is truly Roman in its impressive suggestion of organization and administration of government. The dome of Hagia Sophia expresses the invariable authority of Christian doctrine.

Theology is the statement and exploration of abstract concepts. Likewise, Byzantine architecture is abstract, preeminently so amid the world's styles. Its distinction lies in this, that it contrives abstraction by architectural means, chiefly by its composition of space. Space in Roman architecture, in large examples, is handled almost as material, as if air were the invisible building material of which, together with the visible material a great building is constructed. But space in Byzantine architecture is an abstraction, the equivalent of the intellectual universe which the building connotes. Not that space is indefinite, unmarked by scale and uncertain in reliance upon structure. It is rather, that one scarcely notices such things in his preoccupation with the totality of space.

But the means by which space is made abstract are not mysterious. They are clear and obvious in their frank expression: a flat and richly colorful decorative system of marble veneering and mosaics or frescoes which masks walls and supports, draws attention away from elements of construction and seemingly denies the latter; together with a novel system of illumination precisely effective for the decorative scheme, such as the necklace of windows under the dome of Hagia Sophia, and a continuous flow of curves and spherical surfaces, leading upward to the hemisphere of the dome overhead. The icon screen too, has its part in constituting the abstraction. The liturgical celebration is largely behind the screen, so that the divine office itself is abstracted, not presented in detail for observation. The musical service can be and frequently is superb beyond words, as the interior is filled with sound, soaring upward to the dome. Space is then nothing other than music. Byzantine music (q.v.) known best through the masses of the great Russian composers, requires its characteristic architecture for complete satisfaction. The composers understood their architecture thoroughly and, as in music the master creates the substance of his composition on the statement of a theme, so in this architecture the theme is the curve. Byzantine architecture is a symphony of curves.

We turn now to some consideration of principles of construction, the anatomy of architecture, which made all this possible. The characteristic elements of the style—mass, arch, barrel vault, interesting groined vault and dome—were all at hand for Byzantine builders,

whatever the specific origins of these usages may have been. Whatever the materials— brick, stone or rubble, according to local supply—the outside walls are of thick, sturdy masonry, varying in height according to the effect desired in the several portions of the subordinate masses, and broken by openings, round-headed (and occasionally horseshoe-arched), and windows and doors. The lines are straight, interrupted by projecting apses at the east end and at times by exedras and transept arms of varied plan (Holy Apostles at Constantinople and the foliate style of Armenia). All of these masses, sometimes interestingly irregular in profile, are organized about the center and form a substantial base competent to receive the thrust from the dome.

The space within is directed into nave and aisles, as in the basilica plan, or into hall and rooms in the Greek cross and other plans, but in all cases with ready access to the center and to the sanctuary in the apse. The Greek cross plan, which became standard in the Mid-Byzantine period, is essentially that of the basilica within. Its cross effect is more clearly defined without. Massive piers and subordinate arch systems on columns are the supports, sustaining barrel vaults, half-domes, spherical pendentives and domes. All of these structural principles were resolved by the 6th cent. (period of Justinian) and reveal the progressive solution of the problem of lodging a dome on a square base, marked by four mighty piers. Various experiments in this century were verified in Hagia Sophia. In St. George at Ezra in Syria, length of space was achieved by exedras built in the four corners of the central structure and by a vaulted bay interposed before the apse. In San Vitale at Ravenna open exedras about the cluster of piers granted space to the surrounding polygonal aisle and supported both gallery and cupola. In SS. Sergius and Bacchus at Constantinople the features of both were combined, whereupon they were extended dramatically by the interposed crowning hemicycles of half-domes and fully exposed pendentives in Hagia Sophia. From there to the present, Byzantine architecture has given these elements of construction rich and varied expression, and has been content.

Constructing a dome on a square is the familiar Byzantine achievement, and has been given technical analysis in reference books. One method had been to reduce the square to a polygon at the desired height by throwing horizontal courses across the corners of the square, and continuing the process until a circle was approached on which the dome might be raised. This is a corbel system, and indeed the dome itself will be a corbelled one, ovoid in profile, and exerting vertical rather than lateral thrust by the nature of its construction of successive horizontal overlapping courses of rings of masonry and requiring height for safety as a consequence of the large number of rings of decreasing diameter.

A second method was that of squinches, arches of one sort or another spanning the corners of the square and affording a platform on which the circle base of the dome might be placed.

The third method was that of pendentives, i.e., spherical triangles. At first a dome with diameter equal to the diagonal of the square was conceived extending over and beyond the four piers of the square and supported on the piers, but with segments sliced off vertically over the sides of the square with resulting arches exposed, and leaving a flat dome above. This low dome and its pendentives are all a unit created out of the original true dome. It is the system employed in the tomb of Galla Placidia at Ravenna.

Hagia Sophia, however, presents us with dome on pendentives, the standard method ever since. The point to note is that here we have to do with two domes, the one (with diameter equal to the diagonal of the square) out of which the pendentives are formed by the vertical excisions and thereby affording the circular base for the second or true dome, the diameter of which is equal to the side of the square. The pendentives are all that are left of the larger dome, but being adequately buttressed by their substructures and supporting masses they are entirely competent to carry the thrust of the overhanging dome; a lateral thrust since the construction is by ribs (sometimes without centering, as in Persia today). Outside, the pendentives are covered by the four corners of the square, like a box. Presently a drum was interposed under the dome and over the box, and this became a feature of Mid-Byzantine and later periods, with varied provincial handling; esp. in the Balkan states and in Greece where on the exterior the drum is adorned with arched windows and arcades and the dome, usually small, snuggles down into the spandrels of the arches giving the pattern of the segments of a melon.

Domes presently began to increase in number, placed over selected masses; as on a second bay in the nave (St. Irene, Con-

stantinople), over the narthex or additional aisles, over the four corners of the subordinate structure in the Greek-cross plan (Church of the Chora, Constantinople), and most effectively in the plan of cross with equal arms (Holy Apostles at Constantinople, St. Mark's at Venice, St. Front at Périgueux). In the Russian version of Byzantine architecture domes really did multiply.

Thrust likewise imposed new burdens on columns, such as they had never been required to carry before, and made the **Byzantine order** distinctive. The shafts were monoliths when possible, and of colorfully veined marble, but the popular Corinthian capital could not safely support the lofty weight now placed upon it. The result was the secondary capital or impost block, trapezoidal in profile, which first received the weight and directed it to the axis of the lower capital and shaft. The flowing leaves of the Corinthian capital were out of harmony with such pressure and accordingly they were folded close to the core (windblown acanthus), the tendency being to simplify the planes of the block and adorn them with the characteristic flat pattern designs of the current sculpture (basket capitals, melons, lozenges, etc.) consistent with the system of wall decoration with curious optic effects. Indeed it is scarcely possible to overemphasize the Byzantine scheme of interior decoration. It is a style which is entirely architectural, inseparably associated with wall and surface areas. Being abstract in content and technique it is a major element in the Byzantine synthesis. In many examples it presents a color range that is at once harmonious in basic atmospheric value of gold and purple, with a glory all its own, orientally subtle in intricate pattern, rhythm and color, optic in effect and with a strange suggestion of life remote and pertinent to itself. Yet it is under Greek control and displays refined and sophisticated taste.

Following the earliest Christian practice such decoration is confined to interiors, with which the exteriors, at least in the first period, are in striking contrast and yet contributing to the dramatic unity of the whole. Plain and unadorned outside walls, sometimes of rude materials, strike the eye and at one time were disparaged. We have been instructed, however, by the organized cubic volumes of our modern functional architecture, and are in a position to reappraise the exterior effects of Byzantine masses, whether formally organized or composed of coherent irregularities which, of course, are the more subtle. Perspective silhouettes are now the subject of frank admiration, together with their bold geometry. If one imagines triangular planes imposed over the sloping four sides of Hagia Sophia and converging on the axis the structure is realized as a hollow pyramid, sensational with its silhouette of curves.

Structure, of great boldness and coherence, is then, the primary exterior decorative principle. It is self-decorative, as was Greek architecture, but with different means. In the Mid-Byzantine period and later, exteriors were given a decorative treatment which is quite distinctive. Attention is given to materials. Fine stone masonry is a feature in Armenia and also at Athens, together with occasional sculpture designed in one plane. Courses of stone or marble in two colors are found, or bands of brick alternating with stone. Brick is laid in geometric patterns, zigzag, chevron, guilloche, etc., in continuous bands, as under the edge of a roof, over bases, and over apses. Doors and windows are recessed in the thick walls and members are enriched with geometric treatment. Blind arcades are engaged to the wall, and at times windows are grouped in twin lights or triple arcades, as are doors. In the use of arches the impost capital on slender shaft supports the segment of a pier under the spandrel, delaying the turn of the arch, with consequent impression of lightness. These and other decorations are found in Constantinople (St. Theodore), Salonika (Holy Apostles), and in Serbia and other Balkan areas. They belong mostly to churches of the Greek cross plan, which as a group are now highly regarded. They are preferred by some to the earlier style, because they express the Byzantine formula with full richness, leading the eye from lower masses with their domes and other shapes, to the visible arms of the cross, surmounted by its drum and dome.

Byzantine architecture took special form in the provinces, as in Coptic Egypt, and in Russia where it had independent development. It was taken over by the Moslems who had no architecture of their own, and who promptly rejoiced in its domes even if they comprehended little the subordinate masses. Furthermore, the style had powerful influence at times on the Western church. It is well known in Italy; Ravenna, Sicily, Venice and its suburbs, Milan and even Rome (St. Theodore). From San Vitale at Ravenna it was taken to Aachen by Charlemagne, with modifications; and its use in Spain and western France during the Romanesque period and before

receives due notice (Oviedo, Périgueux, Angoulême, etc.). The style is alive today, not only in churches of the Greek rite, but in pretentious modern examples, such as Westminster cathedral in London, and in America where it has been appropriated by Jewish congregations for their more successful buildings. The principal modern modification is not in outward effect, but in means of construction. Steel frame can solve the problem of any dome.

Byzantine continues then, as one of the world's great styles in architecture, with a notable history of some 1500 years. It is both Eastern and Western, but is Greek in its essential being, and in its abstract quality. See N. L. Bréhier, *L'art byzantin*, 1924; H. C. Botler, *Architecture in Syria*, Princeton Expedition, 1899 and later; O. M. Dalton, *East Christian Art*, 1925; C. Diehl, *Manuel d'art byzantin*, 2 vols., 1925; J. A. Hamilton, *Byzantine Architecture and Decoration*, 1934; T. G. Jackson, *Byzantine and Romanesque Architecture*, vol. I, 1920; G. Millet, *L'art byzantin* in Michel's *Histoire de l'art*, 1905; Pierce and Tyler, *L'art byzantin*, 1932 and later; A. K. Porter, *Mediaeval Architecture*, 2 vols., 1912; G. T. Rivoira, *Lombardic Architecture*, 1933 and *Roman Architecture*, 1925; J. Strzygowski, *Origin of Christian Church Art*, 1923, *Kleinasien*, 1903, *Altai-Iran*, 1917 and *Die Baukunst der Armenier und Europa*, 2 vols., 1918; E. H. Swift, Hagia Sophia, 1940; O. Wulff, *Altchristliche und Byzantische Kunst*, 2 vols., 1924.   —C.D.L.

BYZANTINE ART (6th cent. to the present). The term Byzantine refers to the art originating at or associated with Constantinople, the site of the ancient Greek settlement of Byzantium. The title which is therefore technical is convenient and is universally agreed to. It covers the art of the East Christian world, that is, of the Greek speaking section of Christendom with its affiliations. There is, however, considerable difference of opinion on the matter of when the title should first be used. Some begin with Constantine (324-337), founder of Constantinople and noted as a builder and decorator of churches; others with Justinian (527-565) also a famed church builder and art patron. Still others hold rigid views and prefer to reserve the title to the recovery of art after the Iconoclastic Controversy (8th and 9th cents.), and restrict the term to the style specifically organized at Constantinople and trace developments from the influence of the capital. In such case the period before the 9th cent. is variously called

Asiatic (Morey) or First Golden Age (Diehl) or Proto-Byzantine. This sketch will begin with the 6th cent. since essential elements in the style are present in the age of Justinian.

Byzantine is an art of great distinction, power and tenacity. Like Egyptian, it is an art of formulas, and like Egyptian formulas are used for calculated purposes, not academically. It therefore attains great monumentality and is perhaps the greatest abstract art that men have ever created. Its consistent purpose is to present in visual terms an order of experience with a range of ideas pertaining thereto, heavenly, saintly or secular, which is utterly remote from actual circumstance and accordingly abstracted for such satisfactions as men may obtain from contemplating it. The satisfaction is immense for the art responded fully to the desires of its times and of its people. It is social in this respect and has a history unmatched in Christendom. Materials of utmost richness are employed for such purpose. The media then are mosaics, frescoes of high color, miniature and panel paintings (icons), ivories, enamels, jewels, textiles and objects of use. There is very little sculpture in marble, especially after the dispute about images. There is such an abundance of created objects that only selected references can be made in the following account.

Byzantine art combines Greek and oriental ingredients in style, technique and thought processes. The oriental contribution consisted in rich color harmonies particular to the Near East, organization by rhythmic accent and the sense of movement occasioned thereby, flat design with occasional vertical perspective, and in general the decorative principle. The East also contributed its characteristic mode of regarding both sensory and non-sensory phenomena as remote vision partaking of the nature of mystery and not subject to analysis but rather as the object of contemplation. Here the Greek mind made contact and under Christianity resolved the generality of supernal mystery into a series of concepts which invite the utmost effort in intellectual analysis. The Church had organized its dogma after some centuries of precise thinking and society had organized its institutions. Such was the material presented to the artists. Their task was to constitute these concepts in visual form, create in the visual arts equivalents of abstract dogmas (and also functions of the "apostolic" emperor), and display them both for contemplation and for intellectual stimulation, and in so doing afford pleasure to the eye and enrichment to the soul. Thus purposes implicit in Greek art, dissipated in the Hellenistic period, are recovered in their purity and under the inspiration of Christian faith, which supplied in its doctrine ideal concepts unknown to the ancient Greeks, attain a climax in Byzantine style of the 10th to 12th cents. Byzantine is thus the consummation of Greek art.

It is evident that in Byzantine we have to do with applied art. Technique is consciously applied for determined purposes, the creation of abstract concepts. It is therefore very intellectual both in the nature of the reflective thinking which supplied the requirement and in the technical processes by which the purposes were realized. The style is accordingly non-realistic, in environment, in figure and in episode. Environment is non-spatial, in one plane of no depth, with no recognition of perspective (save the vertical) and no atmosphere. It is all color, preferably gold, with obvious suggestion of the light of heaven. There are of course no cast shadows. Even the rich color of ivory is agreeable with such interpretation of environment. The figure is effectively distorted in characteristic ways. It tends towards the flat, although in the great period Greek sense of form is recovered with dignity and clarity. But ordinarily one sees gorgeous costume above which are outlined heads with strange staring eyes, and to which curiously distorted hands and feet are attached. Construction is by line and color within contours, and costumes at times become web, the patterns of which refer to the rhythmic folds of classic drapery and maintain a reminiscence of chiaroscuro. This formal denial of organic relation of costume to figure is strangely effective. In appropriate instances the pose is frontal, in immobile isolation, with powerful suggestion of monumentality.

In episode distortion becomes a virtue of high order. In some instances it is calculated with refined subtlety. Such distortion is expressive for its purpose, since it declares the significance of scene rather than the portrayal of it. Mutual relations are registered in one plane, and poses and gestures are formal. Movement is that of stately rhythm and takes place in the eye of the observer. Accessories are merely indicated, such as summary architectural data or foliage to suggest locality, though they hold equitable place in the pattern being in no wise subordinated.

From this account of characteristics of the style it appears then that whether we see episodes in the life of Christ or other narrative from the Scripture, great visions from the Apocalypse or from the ecstasies of the prophets of Israel, events in the lives of the apostles, saints and martyrs, the ceremonial dignity of the "sacred" *basileus,* nobles of his court or high ecclesiastics, in all cases we have the display of spectacle, rich in color and in materials, signifying a very special sort of experience, sensationally different from that of daily circumstances, remote, isolated and abstract. The style is indeed non-realistic unless we say that it makes vision real. Certainly it does all that art can do to intimate the realities of the heavenly world and indeed the essence of Christian experience of life in this world. The persons of the Trinity, angels, the Madonna, apostles and saints condescend by the aid of art to display their heavenly felicity and their abstract significance.

A few examples will serve to illustrate the above interpretation. The procession of martyrs holding crowns in their hands, is created in mosaic on the nave walls of *S. Apollinare Nuovo* at Ravenna (6th cent.). It is gorgeous in color, unnaturalistic in figure and is nonpictorial, but it is superb rhythmic decoration. It is not a picture of a procession, such as is afforded by the technique of illusionism in the documentary records of the triumphal parade in the Arch of Titus or the procession of dignitaries of the Altar of Peace at Rome. The parade of the martyrs is abstracted, and the sense of significance remains. In this respect it is like the procession of the Parthenon frieze, although the principles in design and organization are different.

The ivory panel of Christ bestowing crowns on the imperial couple, Romanos and Eudoxia (11th cent. Paris, *Bibl. Nat.*), constructed with complete mastery in technique is an assured abstraction of the concept of divine authority in imperial government. The panel of the Madonna and Child (11th cent., Utrecht), superbly wrought in ivory, declares the doctrine of the Incarnation. Nowhere is there a more impressive picture of the crucifixion than the mosaic at Daphni (11th cent.). The figure is realized with simple grace against no background save that of color. The mother and St. John are in formal balance. There is no environment or indication of time and place. From such categories the passion is abstracted, wherefore the divine sacrifice is made eternal and the Christian doctrine of redemption is offered to men for their contemplation. The effect is overwhelming. But it should be observed that Byzantine mosaics must be seen at first hand, as indeed frescoes

and all mural decorations. No reproductions in color can possibly give the effect. Byzantine mosaics are an authentic instance of the necessity of "exposing" the observer to the original material. Likewise it must be remembered that mosaics are associated with architecture, and their truly Byzantine function in this respect is illuminating. They mask walls, whether domes, semi-domes, pendentives or other areas, and practically deny the nature of the wall as well as of all structural supports. They make even architecture abstract, and leave nothing but experience, a rare experience indeed, especially when one includes music and the liturgical celebration.

The history of Byzantine art may be sketched as follows: The style was constituted upon the basis of experiments in East Christian art which attained a synthesis in the 6th cent. Chief examples are at Ravenna, seat of Byzantine government in Italy (*S. Vitale, S. Apollinare Nuovo*) and at Rome (*SS. Cosmas and Damian*). Mosaic is not an effective medium for chiaroscuro, and when such realistic effort was renounced in favor of flat plane and rhythmic accent, as well as rich and subtle color, a truly monumental style resulted. The oriental ingredient consisted in this decorative principle, whereas the Greek was that of figure and the underlying reason. Miniature painting is represented by the *Gospel of Sinope* and the *Gospels of Rossano,* in which the earlier struggles persist. Miniature is an intimate medium, inviting innovation and experiment, and the tendency in these paintings to reduce the planes to conform to non-spatial flatness results in obvious stringency.

The first period terminated in the Iconoclastic Dispute about art inaugurated by the Emperor Leo III in 726, and preceded by the rise of Islam with its non-representational art and the Arab conquests which removed Egypt and North Africa, Palestine and Syria from the Christian world. There were appropriate consequences: a loss of oriental influence, including Persian; heretical churches on the borders of the Empire no longer made demands; Constantinople was the acknowledged center and its influence extended more powerfully into Greece and the Balkan states, and also into Russia (the conversion of Russia was the sole important missionary exploit of the Greek Church and in this art was very influential); the orthodox theology and indeed the civilization of the area was reassessed and confirmed, and the culture was now overwhelmingly Greek. An especially significant phenomenon was the flight of Christians from

Alexandria, to Constantinople, to Sicily and to Italy, bringing Alexandrian style with them.

Recovery from all this resulted in the Mid-Byzantine style (with which some first recognize the art), or the true Golden Age, as others characterize it. It is essentially a meeting of the Alexandrian style with earlier Byzantine, with oriental elements restrained and Greek enhanced. New attention is given the figure which attains great nobility, and in miniature painting, such as the Paris Psalter, there is poetic realization of landscape. The 10th, 11th and 12th cents., are the great period. The decorative principles and the color sense and the organization of color accents into webbing are of oriental source, the figure, constructed at times with distinguished clarity and always with significance, is Greek, as is the trace of chiaroscuro and a certain freedom in modelling. The best examples in mosaic are at Daphni. The mosaics in Sicily are very well known. Some of the mosaics of St. Mark's at Venice belong here, as also Torcello. In recent years mosaics of *Hagia Sophia* at Constantinople have been uncovered. This is the supreme period for Byzantine ivories, for the best in miniature painting, and indeed for all media.

The purity of the style could not be maintained. The rhythm became mechanical, the iconography became static with the academic organization of formulas, and creative energy turned to drama, to excessive distortion and to sundry eccentricities. This period covers the 13th and 14th cents., and later. Examples are in sundry Balkan states and in Crete (whence came El Greco), with extended influence in Russia, where native vigor made it a truly Russian art. Here may be cited mosaics at Kahrie-Djami, Constantinople, noted for color, paintings at Mistra, Mount Athos, and in monasteries in Serbia and other Balkan states, which, however, are largely in fresco. This is an era rich in panel paintings (icons), and of course the illustration of books continues.

In Italy the style is known as Italian-Byzantine, and is basic in the school of Siena, modified by the grace of Duccio, until connection is made with Gothic. In Florence it is sharply renounced by Giotto. It continues to the present as the official art of the Greek Church and its national subdivisions and very effective examples of recent date are in the memorial chapel of the late king of Jugo-Slavia.

Byzantine style is thoroughly sophisticated, and is the reasonable expression of a learned culture which rejoices in intellectual exercise, and is content therewith. It reveals why the Greek section of Christendom remained static, untroubled by reformation movements and the progressive energies of the West. It required no recovery of antiquity since it possessed the true Greek heritage and took it for granted.

The perplexity of the barbarians of the West in their contact with and attempted use of Byzantine style is clarifying in this respect. Barbarism had destroyed the technique of Alexandrian illusionism in the West, together with all examples. Yet illusionism, the art of a practiced technique, gives pictures of visible reality, which the barbarian can see and understand but cannot create. Byzantine style is flat and in this respect is akin to the flat, linear, non-realistic usage of barbarians. The barbarians then could follow the formulas of Byzantine style but could not possibly understand the intellectual processes responsible for them. They were in a dilemma. What they could do they could not understand, and what they could understand they could not do. This is one reason why the art of mediaeval Europe is fascinating as well as bewildering. See O. M. Dalton, *Byzantine Art and Archaelogy,* 1911; C. R. Morey, *Medieval Art,* 1942; D. T. Rice, *Byzantine Art,* 1935; E. W. Anthony, *History of Mosaics,* 1935; C. Diehl, *Manuel d'Art Byzantin,* 2 v., 1925 and *La Peinture Byzantin,* 1933.   —C.D.L.

Byzantine chant. See MEDIEVAL MUSIC; eastern chants.

Byzantine music is the music of a semi-oriental people, for the Eastern Roman Empire was for centuries the meeting-ground of the East and the West. It was a very ancient musical heritage antedating the Christian era.

Many of the pagan ecclesiastical customs were not renounced when the Greek world gave up the worship of its ancient gods for the new faith. Music held one of the highest places in the educational system of the ancients, and the early Christians (Byzantines) conserved and saved that music in their religious worship. The pagan rhythmical, so-called Greek music, was introduced in the churches by the first Apostolic Fathers. The ecclesiastical hymnographers of the first centuries of the Christian era based their art upon the same intricate rhythmic patterns. Greek and occidental historians accept the technical arrangements of the ancient Greek music as the basis of the early Christian ecclesiastical modes.

Byzantine music is modal, divided into four authentic and four plagal; it is homophonic and employs both quarter tone and third of a tone. There are three general classifications: (1) *papathika,* which is florid and highly embellished; (2) *stihirarika,* our equivalent of which is andante and maestoso; (3) *ermologika,* our allegro and allegro vivace. It has its own notation (see NOTATION), originally stenographic—one sign expressed an entire melodic pattern. Today the notation is comprised of ten neumes, these neumes are used either simply or in combination to form a new note. Byzantine music, the inheritor of ancient Greek music, is the official liturgical music of the Eastern Orthodox Church throughout the world.   —C.V.

C

Cabiri (Gr. Kabeiroi). Early Greek nature deities (two male and two female) worshipped especially on the islands of Samothrace and Lemnos and in Thebes in Boeotia with mysterious rites, second only to the Eleusinian mysteries in popularity in Roman times.
—L.T.S.

cabochon (F.). An unfaceted cutting for gems, used almost universally in Oriental jewelry.

cabriole. A double-curved furniture leg, used widely from the late 17th cent. on. See FURNITURE.

caccia (chace). See MEDIEVAL MUSIC.

cachucha. A Spanish national dance of the Iberian group, recorded as being a species of sequidilla in triple time. Unlike most of the sequidilla type, it has virtually disappeared from popular performance, many of the steps having been incorporated into newer dances, variously named. The cachucha is remembered especially in connection with Fanny Elssler, the great 19th cent. ballerina who used many cachucha steps in one of her most famous dances. See sequidilla.
—J.G.

cacaphony. *Mus.* Extreme discord.

cadence. Arrangement of musical elements made in order to emphasize the termination of a phrase. If an idiom (q.v.) is used over a sufficient length of time, certain types of cadence formulae become standardized, e.g.: in modality, typical approaches of one or more voices to the final (raised leading tones, sets of suspensions and alternating tones, etc.); in tonality, typical chord progressions, classified according to their faculty of creating finality, such as authentic c. (dominant-tonic), plagal c. (subdominant-tonic), half-cadence (ending on the dominant), deceptive c. (substitution of another chord for the tonic in the authentic c.), etc. (see idiom). Cadential effects are enhanced by suitable metrical arrangements.
—E.K.

cadenza (It.). *Mus.* Literally, cadence. (1) A fantasia for display of virtuosity, played by the soloist just before the cadence of the first or last movements of a concerto, or an elaborate melismatic passage sung just before the cadence of an aria; in the nature of an extemporization though usually composed; based largely upon themes previously used. (2) In shorter compositions, short brilliant solo passages of unmeasured rhythm.

cadmium pigments. These comprise a range of colors from deep red to pale yellow. All are in some way sulphides of the element, cadmium. Differences are partly from addition of other elements and partly from conditions of manufacture. Commonly, these pigments are made by precipitating solutions of a soluble cadmium. Cadmium red contains some selenium. There is a group of colors known as the cadmium lithopones in which the pure cadmium is adulterated with barium sulphate precipitated with it. These have a slightly lower tinting strength but are otherwise not impared. All cadmium colors are of recent origin so far as their general commercial distribution is concerned. They are said to have been shown in the 1851 exhibition in London. Early in the manufacture of cadmium yellow some excess of free sulphur made it incompatible with many other pigments. That is corrected in modern production of this and the other cadmium colors. They change slightly when strongly heated but are, in normal temperatures, stable and fast to light.
—G.L.S.

Caeretan hydriae. See Ionian vases.

Cahokia Mound. A huge mound near the center of an area, near East St. Louis, containing 85 mounds. It is a truncated pyramid with a terrace, rectangular in plan, measuring c. 700 x 1000 ft., 100 ft. high and covering 16 acres. It is the type of mound that served as a base for a ceremonial building. It is also called the Monks' Mound, from a Trappist monastery built in 1809 at its base. The area now constitutes the Cahokia Mounds State Park. See Eastern North American Aboriginal Art. —H.G.

cairn (Gael.) Rounded heap of stones as a monument to the dead.

caitya (Skr.). Buddhist sanctuary. Particularly a chapel hall, as the caitya halls of Ajanta. See INDIAN ART.

cakra (Skr.). See Wheel of the Law.

calcography. Drawing with chalks or pastels.

.calefactory. See monastic architecture.

calico. Named from Callicut, a great trading center of India. Plain weave, it is one of the earliest cotton fabrics. Ancient Indian calico was printed with wood blocks. Calico is sometimes plain color or printed in colors. Printing of cotton calico started in London in 1676. First calico made in the U. S. A. in 1790, by power machine in 1826. A general term for calico up to the end of the 17th cent. —G.W.R.

California Indian art. The diverse topography of California tended to break the tribes into small units, while the climate and the ready availability of food made living easy. Conditions of life were in sharp contrast with the harsher ones of the broader and more unified areas of the Southwest. There were numerous small independent tribes, in general hunters and fishermen, and gatherers of the abundant acorns, nuts and seeds. Though sedentary they were not agriculturalists. Except for their elaborate ceremonials and for some stone jars and small stone carvings of sea creatures showing exceptionally fine feeling for simplified sculptural form which were made by the Gabrielino and Chumash tribes of the southwestern part of the state, the chief art expression was utilitarian: containers for storage, cooking and serving, transporting, berry and nut gathering. It was an art practiced by the women alone, who attained an unsurpassed level of form and

technique in astonishing variety. Materials were abundant: roots, stems, bark, grasses and rushes. Both coiling and twining techniques were used. Styles vary with the different tribes. The more important wares were produced in the central and northern part of the area. In the former, north of San Francisco Bay lived the Pomo, the virtuosos of the craft. The even texture of their baskets exhibits an amazing technical facility in both coiling and twining. In shape they are frequently flattened bowls; in size they vary greatly, from a few inches to several feet in diameter. Their designs, black or brown on tan, tend to triangular or rectangular motifs in diagonal or horizontal arrangement. An unusual feature is the frequent application of many colored feather ornaments. In the north the Yurok, Karok and Hupa produce finely twined baskets in red or black on white, or white on brown. Among the decorative motifs used, triangle and zig-zag predominate, frequently arranged with a diagonal movement. See F. H. Douglas, *The Main Divisions of California Indian Basketry,* Denver Art Museum Leaflets 83-84, 1937; A. L. Kroeber, *Handbook of the Indians of California,* 1925; O. T. Mason, *Aboriginal American Basketry,* 1902. —H.G.

calligraphic styles, the five Chinese. See CHINESE ARTS.

calligraphic. (F. *calligraphie;* 1. *calligraphia;* adaptation of Gr. *kalligraphía,* substantive of quality from *kalligráph-os, kállos* beauty — *gráphos* writing, writer, written. 1613 R. Cawdrey. *A table alphabeticall of English wordes.* ed. 3. *Calligraphie,* faire writing.) Beautiful writing as a product, also elegant penmanship as an art or profession.

Calligraphy is distinguished from writing only by its fine quality, hence in general the term may be applied to writing (q.v.) which shows excellence in design and execution in any of the three categories and of any period. In a more restricted use, the term is frequently employed to refer to the art and product of professional writing masters in Europe and America from the 16th to the 19th cents. Specimens of their work appear in the copy-books produced as models for students of handwriting. The earliest of these manuals, that of Ludovico degli Arrighi, also known as Vicentino, which appeared at Rome in 1522, gave a specimen of a semi-formal script, the chancery hand, with instructions for learning to write it. The later 16th cent. writing-books showed specimens of a similar script, sometimes with additional examples of the contemporary formal and cursive hands, both gothic and roman. In this century, however, the emphasis was on the semi-formal scripts for diplomatic and legal purposes. In the 17th and 18th cent., with the increase of commerce in France, Holland, and England, the cursive gothic hands gradually disappeared and the writing manuals show model scripts for business purposes, based on roman forms and much more cursive in character than their predecessors. In these hands open loops gradually replaced the former ascenders with serifs, until in the 19th cent. the usual hand of the copy-books had become the form popularly called "script", of which the typical, although scarcely calligraphic, example in America is the Spencerian hand. Most writing masters from the 17th to the 19th cent. included in their books specimens of ornament and drawings of animals, birds, etc. composed of pen-strokes and done by **command of hand,** i.e., with the pen lines written directly and freely without preliminary drawing. In the 20th cent. there has been a revival of calligraphy in the field of formal and semi-formal writing. The movement began in England with the teaching of Edward Johnston and was continued in Germany by Rudolf Koch and others. See WRITING and LETTERING; CHINESE ARTS; also A. Fairbank, *A Handwriting Manual,* 1932; P. Jessen; *Meister der Schreibkunst,* 1923; E. Johnston; *Writing and Illuminating, and Lettering,* 1906; S. Morison, *The development of handwriting,* in A. Heal, *The English Writing Masters and Their Copy-books,* 1931; R. Nash, *Some Early American Writing Books and Masters,* 1943.   —E.F.D.

calliope. A mechanical organ with keyboard by which tones are produced from a series of steam whistles; used in carnivals and on river boats.

calyn crater. See crater.

camaieu. Painting in monochrome.

camaak. A heavy silk fabric.

cámara (Skr.). See fly-whisk.

camarin. Domed chapel of the central type in Mexican pilgrimages churches (also Guatemala) usually immediately behind the apse and communicating with it by a window-like opening in which the cult image stands. Often also the repository of the jewelled wardrobe of the cult virgin.   —J.McA.

Cambodia art. See INDIAN ART; SOUTH-EASTERN ASIATIC ART.

cambric. Named after the French town, Cambrai, where it was first made. A fine cloth, originally linen, now usually cotton; a plain weave.   —G.W.R.

camelaucum. See tiara, papal.

camel hair. See brush.

cameo. See JEWELRY.

cameo-glass. Two pieces of colored glass fused together, the outer glass area being carved in outline and detail, thus showing in relief against the other.   —J.A.M.

camera lucida. A comparatively modern development of the camera obscura, this is a prism set in such a way as to deflect the image of an object and throw it on to a paper where it can be traced. It is listed by artists' colormen as early as 1848 and probably was in use somewhat before that.   —G.L.S.

camera obscura. The reflection of an object on to a surface where it can be traced or drawn is effected by this apparatus, as it is with a camera lucida. A camera obscura is larger and does not depend on a prism. It can operate with a mirror and some kind of a double convex lens. It is said to have been invented in 1540.   —G.L.S.

Cameroon art. See AFRICAN NEGRO ART.

camlet. A type of plush.

camp (Fr. *camp,* early 16th cent.; L. *campus,* field; Middle English used only *champ*). The place in open country where a body of troops is temporarily lodged in tents or make-shift structures, with or without entrenchments. In modern usage the term is also applied to a permanent station for the training of troops in the methods and duties of the field campaign, and includes all the buildings, tents, and equipment pertaining thereto. A secondary modern meaning is an informal house or lodge or assemblage of accommodations for the occasional use of hunters and fishermen. The term is also applied to certain of the ancient earthen fortifications of which traces remain in Britain.   —T.A.H.

Campā. See SOUTHEASTERN ASIATIC ART.

campana, campanetta. A bell.

campanile (It.). Bell tower, frequently free-standing.

campo aperto. See MEDIEVAL MUSIC.

campo santo (It.). Cemetery near a cathedral.

CANADA, ARCHITECTURE OF. The French Colonial architecture of Quebec is based on the 17th cent. building traditions of northern France. The first houses were of wood, framed and boarded. Such were the *habitations* built as trading-posts by the early explorers (Des Monts' habitation, Port Royal, 1605; Champlain's habitation, Quebec, 1608). But stone was abundant and though wood never went out of use, by about 1675 stone was in general use. Climate and living conditions modified the original tradition and produced a true Canadian architecture, simple but of great charm. In the woodcarving of the churches indeed it rises to high distinction.

The earliest houses now remaining (Batiscan presbytery 1696, Ferme St. Gabriel 1698) have sturdy stone walls and heavy shingled roofs with a slight bellcast. The plan is rectangular and compact; the roofs are large, often twice the height of the walls, and are gabled or hipped in the French *pavillon* form. (Villeneuve House, 1684, Baie St. Paul Manor, 1718.)

A distinctive type, with stone gable parapets surmounted by double chimneys, is common in and near Montreal. This is derived from the town house in which the parapets served as fire partitions. (Chateau de Ramezay, 1704.)

The curved bellcast, wide-spreading eaves and verandah gallery of the Quebec cottage seem to have been introduced about the end of the 18th cent. They apparently came from the French settlements of the Mississippi valley, which had learnt them from the Spanish settlements of the Gulf.

Skilled craftsmen were amongst the earliest colonists; in a procession held in 1648 twelve trades were represented. In addition, about 1668, an *École des Arts et Métiers* was founded in the Seminary. Here not only the trades were taught but also the arts of architecture, painting, sculpture and gilding.

The panelling in the refectory of the Hôpital Général (1674) and the fine stair-case in the Ursuline Monastery in Quebec (1686) show the skill of these craftsmen. They trained apprentices who carried on the tradition. The panelling of the Fargues House (1781), of the Briand chapel in the Seminary (1785) or of the Community Room in the Ursuline Monastery in Quebec, show a continuous tradition of fine design and workmanship.

The earliest existing churches date from about 1730. They are oblong halls terminating in a square or semicircular sanctuary. The roofs are steep, often covered by "tin tiles" which weather to a fine bronze colour. Over the west gable is an octagonal belfry surmounted by a slender flèche.

The sanctuary is fully decorated with woodcarving. Usually it has an architectural framing of Corinthian pilasters enclosing panels of trophies, fruit and flower garlands, niches and statues. The general style is that of Louis XIV or Louis XV but with the freedom natural in a colonial style. Such work was done in French Canada as late as the middle of the 19th cent.

In 1690 Jacques le Blond de Latour, an architect, sculptor and painter of Bordeaux, was teaching sculpture in the Seminary, and in Montreal Charles Chaboillez and Paul Jourdain dit Labrosse, French woodcarvers, were working in 1701. From them descend the great woodcarvers of the 18th and early 19th cents., the Sieurs Vasseur, Pierre Emond, the Baillargé family, Louis Quevillon and his associates and many others whose work is to be found throughout the province.

The leading woodsculptors were men of social standing, trained artists and skilled craftsmen. In their work the Grand Manner came to Canada; it is possibly the greatest achievement of traditional art in North America.

The old architecture of the Maritime Provinces is mainly New England Georgian, delicate in detail and proportion, showing clearly its derivation from the school of Robert Adam. Mount Uniacke, near Halifax is a high columned "Colonial" mansion, Acacia Grove in the Cornwallis Valley, is a fine square brick house, Matlock has a good ionic portico of the Greek revival. In Halifax the Governor's House and the Legislative Building by John Merrick, show an English flavour and remind us that men trained in English offices came to Canada in the early 19th cent., many of them attached to the military or naval services. The fortifications of Ile aux Noix or of Fort Henry at Kingston show that the Royal Engineers of that day were competent architects as well as military engineers.

Many of the smaller towns in Southern Ontario retain good houses of the late 18th and early 19th cents. The church of St. Andrew at Niagara, built about 1831, is particularly fine and we should mention the Town Hall at Kingston, a classic work of almost brutal strength.

The delicate art of the early 19th cent. could not withstand the rapid expansion of the 50's. The old traditions died and the need for architects was supplied from external sources. It is only of recent years that Canada has begun to train her own architects and for the greater part of the 19th and the early 20th cent. Canadian buildings are English, American or French rather than Canadian.

To take a few instances, the Canadian Pacific offices in Montreal are of Richardsonian Romanesque, the big railway hotels, in the style of François Premier, are named *chateaux* in compliment to our French Canadians, that at Quebec has even been taken for an ancient relic of the French Regime. Many Canadian architects received their training in the U.S.A. and returned to bring to Canada the American version of the *Beaux Arts;* others, trained in England, gave Canada fine buildings in the manner of Pugin, Cockerell, or Norman Shaw. Canada has many fine and dignified buildings, is thoroughly cosmopolitan, but has hardly got a Canadian architecture.

The East has her old traditions, the West her new aspirations. Time alone can unify Canadian arts and give us some day a true Canadian architecture.   —R.T.

CANADA, ART OF. (1) *Aboriginal Art.* The development of art among the native tribes of Canada was handicapped by the hardships of a semi-nomadic existence in a rigorous northern climate. Prehistoric artifacts of artistic significance are few and fragmentary, and it is difficult to determine exactly how far the Indians had progressed artistically before the coming of the white men. Due rather to unfavourable circumstances than to lack of ability, their work appears to have been restricted to decorative crafts and small carvings. Among the crafts known to have been practiced by them in prehistoric times are the making of pottery with incised decorations by the tribes of the St. Lawrence basin, the carving and engraving

of walrus ivory by the Eskimos, and the carving of rattles, masks, and other small objects in wood by the Indians of the Pacific Coast.

Most of the existing art of the Canadian Indians dates from the centuries following the discovery of the continent by white men and was directly or indirectly an outgrowth of white influence. Contact with Europeans gave the Indians hard metal tools, new sources of wealth resulting from the fur trade, and in some cases a European demand for their artistic products. These circumstances stimulated the latent artistic powers of the natives and resulted in a widespread flowering of Indian art. The Algonquin tribes of the eastern and central areas, for instance, developed an elaborate art of embroidery both in porcupine quills and glass beads. This art, skillful in craftsmanship and often charming in design, has been shown by Dr. Marius Barbeau to have been influenced by, and perhaps established as a result of, contact between the Indians and the trained European embroiderers of early French Canada.

Only on the Pacific Coast did the Indians of Canada press beyond decorative crafts to achieve art on a monumental scale. Here a milder climate and a more abundant food supply—the latter encouraging a relatively settled existence — occurred in conjunction with stimulating sources of raw material such as giant cedar forests and a deposit of black argillite, an attractive easily carved stone. Even with these advantages, West Coast Indian art reached maturity only after the Indians had received metal tools and surplus wealth from white traders. When all these circumstances finally converged, an incipient genius for carving suddenly blossomed into sculpture that constitutes one of the highest achievements of aboriginal art in Canada.

This sculpture first appeared about 1820 in the form of small **argillite carvings** of animate and inanimate forms. Although produced by the Indians for sale to the whites, many of these carvings are impressive both in sculptural design and vitality of expression. Outstanding among their makers were several members of the Edensaw family of Massett, Queen Charlotte Islands.

A decade after the first argillite carvings, that is to say about 1830, the carving of immense cedar logs into **totem poles** began its spectacular development. These totem poles, an outgrowth of the smaller frontal poles used at the entrances to plank houses, served a double function. They were monuments commemorating deceased nobles and also heraldic symbols of family pride and succession akin to European coats of arms. At their best they are imposing sculpture— monumental in size, rhythmic in design, awe-inspiring in imaginative conception.

West Coast sculpture was as short-lived as it was significant. By 1890 it had fallen into decline, crushed by the impact of the same white civilization that had stimulated its development.

Worthy to stand with West Coast sculpture at the summit of Canadian Indian art are the splendidly decorative **Chilkat blankets** woven of mountain goat's hair and cedar bark. These blankets originated on the Queen Charlotte Islands, but reached perfection in the hands of the Chilkat tribe on the mainland. Their unique patterns are based on the principle of dismembering natural forms, stylizing their component parts, and recombining them symmetrically in abstract relationship to each other; a type of design which in some respects anticipates 20th cent. European cubism.

See *Northwest Coast Indian art* elsewhere in this volume; also F. Boas, *Decorative Art of the Indians of the North Pacific Coast,* 1897; the chapter on art in D. Jenness, *The Indians of Canada,* 1932; and the following bulletins of the National Museum of Canada; H. I. Smith, *An Album of Prehistoric Canadian Art,* 1923; M. Barbeau, *Totem Poles of the Gitksan, Upper Skeena River, B. C.,* 1929.

(2) *French Colonial Period.* In the light of the foregoing paragraphs, the reader will not be surprised to learn that the first French Canadian art dates from two centuries earlier than the mature West Coast Indian art discussed above. Beginning with settlements at Port Royal, Nova Scotia, in 1605 and Quebec in 1608, French colonization spread through two chief areas: Acadia on the Atlantic Coast and New France along the St. Lawrence River. The material culture of the former area was virtually annihilated when the Acadians were expelled by the English in 1755. As a result, surviving examples of French Colonial art come almost exclusively from New France, now the Province of Quebec.

Like medieval Europe, the French Colonial period devoted its major energies to decorative arts rather than to painting, uniting a variety of crafts in the service of the Catholic church. Its governing purpose was to provide a resplendent setting for religious ceremonies; a setting to which the embroiderer or "tapestry maker," the wood carver and gilder,

and the worker in precious metals all contributed. Domestic arts and crafts were also practised, but it was religious art which particularly characterized the period.

The active history of French Canadian art may be said to date from the founding of the Ursuline convent in Quebec in 1639. Several of the nuns of this order were zealous practitioners and teachers of embroidery. Altar frontals, chasubles, and other church vestments engaged the chief energies of these devoted seamstresses. Gold and silver thread, combined with colored silks and sometimes enriched with semi-precious stones, gave their work a truly medieval magnificence. Among the leaders of the craft were Mother Marie de L'Incarnation (active 1633-71), the saintly Jeanne le Ber (active 1686-1714), and Mother Sainte-Helene (active 1714-59).

Interesting interaction of French and Indian traditions is shown by the fact that for reasons of economy the nuns sometimes embroidered with porcupine quills and dyed moose-hair secured from the Indians. Conversely, the rhythmic arabesques of the French floral patterns are believed to have inspired most of the decorative designs found in Indian embroidery.

About 1675 Msgr. de Laval, first bishop of Quebec, founded the first art school to be established in the New World: the *Ecole des Arts et Metiers* at Cap Tourmente, about thirty miles below Quebec on the St. Lawrence. The master craftsmen imported from France to serve as teachers at this school exerted a strong influence on the subsequent development of French Canadian art.

One outcome of Laval's initiative was a long line of French Canadian wood carvers and sculptors dedicated to the service of the church. Beginning with le Blond de Latour one of the original group of craftsmen who immigrated to Cap Tourmente, this line was still active two and a half centuries later in the person of Louis Jobin, who died as recently as 1928. These and several scores of intervening masters gave solicitous care to the decoration of altars, reredos, tabernacles, and other church fittings. Wooden statues of the Madonna and various saints also took shape under their chisels, to be finished with the brushes of the painter and gilder. The work is sometimes elegant, sometimes florid. Occasionally the sculpture is touched with real depths of expression, as in the fragments of a reredos at Les Eboulements.

As may be expected, Quebec silversmiths devoted their best efforts to the production of chalices, monstrances, and other church silver. Outstanding among the masters of this craft were Paul Lambert (1691-1749), Francois Ranvoyzé (1739-1819), and Laurent Amiot (1764-1839). Elaborately embossed ornamentation and fine simplicity of line can both be found in their work, the best of which compares favorably with American colonial silver and with contemporary silver from the Old World.

Students of period design can recognize in all the products of these several arts gradual changes of style following at a distance the influence of successive periods in Europe. The earlier work shows the influence of the contemporary French school of the period of Henri IV. This eventually gives way to more florid forms indicating Baroque influence, the latter in turn to be succeeded by Neo-Classic.

Important collections of early French Canadian art can be seen in Quebec City at the Ursuline Convent, the Hôtel-Dieu, and the Hôpital-Général; in Montreal, at the Hôtel-Dieu, the Museum of the Church of Notre-Dame, and the Congrégation of Notre-Dame. The Indian missions at Indian Lorette and Caughnawaga also possess outstanding collections.

See M. Barbeau, *Quebec, Where Ancient France Lingers,* 1936; *Maitres Artisans de Chez Nous,* 1942; *Saintes Artisanes,* 1943; R. Traquair, *The Old Silver of Quebec,* 1940; R. Traquair and others, *McGill University Publications, Art and Architecture,* Series XIII, Nos. 1-37; G. Morisset, *Coup d'Oeil sur les Arts en Nouvelle France,* 1941.

(2) *From the British Conquest to the Present Day.* The conquest of Canada by the British in 1759 coincided approximately with the transition between two fundamentally different cultural epochs. As already noted the traditions of New France, like those of 17th cent. New England were essentially mediaeval in character. After the Conquest the main currents of Canadian culture shifted their direction. The influence of the Renaissance and the Industrial Revolution replaced that of the Middle Ages. The unity of the arts which had resulted from a controlling framework of religious architecture disintegrated; hand crafts retreated before machine production to maintain a precarious existence in rural areas, and easel painting, the art of individualism, emerged as the dominant form of artistic expression. For the next century and a half the history of creative develop-ment in Canada was largely a history of painters and painting.

The early stages of this trend are to be seen, between 1770 and 1840, in the work of the so-called "topographers": English military officers and civil administrators who sketched Canadian landscapes either in connection with their official surveys or as a diversion for their leisure hours. Their work is usually classed as Canadiana and can be seen in public archives, both national and provincial, as well as in the imposing Coverdale Collection of the Manoir Richelieu at Murray Bay, Quebec. Done for the most part in drawing or water color, the work of the topographers was sometimes given wider circulation through the medium of engraving or lithography. Currier and Ives, as well as other publishers, drew upon it for Canadian subjects. As representatives of the school we may mention Lt.-Col. J. P. Cockburn (1779-1847) and W. H. Bartlett (1809-1854). Bartlett's *Canadian Scenery* (1842) ranks among the best productions of the period.

The topographical beginnings of painting in Canada merged almost imperceptibly into the work of the country's first professional painters: Paul Kane (1810-71) and Cornelius Krieghoff (1812-72). Kane was Canada's chief pictorial chronicler of the Indians. As recorded in his book, *The Wanderings of an Artist,* he made an epic journey across Canada to record the Indian scene in the then unsettled west. Inspired in manner by English historical painting of the 18th cent., Kane's work is dignified if somewhat constrained in effect, and constitutes a valuable record of the aboriginal life that was soon to be undermined by the advance of white civilization. The bulk of it is now at the Royal Ontario Museum in Toronto.

Krieghoff, though contemporary with Kane, differed from him in style, temperament, and subject. An adventurous young German who had gone to seek his fortune in the U.S.A., he fell in love with a French Canadian girl in New York, followed her to Canada, and became the jovial interpreter of French Canadian pioneer life. His most characteristic works show us the *habitants* bringing supplies to their frontier homes, stopping their sleighs to gossip with each other along frozen roads, or merrymaking at their parties. In style, these attractive pictures are reminiscent of 17th cent. Dutch traditions.

Though active at the middle of the 19th cent., both Kane and Krieghoff are essentially colonial. The Canada of their day was still a frontier country and the style in which they represented it was imported, more or less naively, from Europe. During the century which followed, successive European movements continued to influence painting in Canada as in other parts of the New World, but there was increasing effort on the part of artists to synchronize these influences with their own emerging sense of Canadian cultural and political identity. There was also increasing consciousness of the picture as an aesthetic creation.

Of the generation following Kane and Krieghoff, the two artists who probably deserve first attention are Homer Watson (1855-1936) and Horatio Walker (1858-1938). In their best work, both bring to Canadian painting a new power of simplification and emphasis; a new concern with pictorial construction. Watson applied these gifts to the study of sylvan landscape in Ontario, Walker to the elemental existence of the rural toiler on the Isle of Orleans, near Quebec. The landscapes of Franklin Brownell (1857—) rank highly in the judgment of Canadian collectors. William Brymner (1855-1925), for many years director of the Art School of the Montreal Art Association, is venerated for his constructive influence on his students, many of whom became leading artists of the succeeding generation.

Impressionism injected its powerful influence into Canadian painting through the work of Maurice Cullen (1866-1934) and M.-A. de F. Suzor-Coté (1869-1937), both of whom recognized a natural affinity between the Impressionistic technique and the varied lights and colors of Canadian snowscape. Ernest Lawson (1873-1939), perhaps the most brilliant of all North American Impressionists, was born in Canada and spent his boyhood there, but carried on most of his creative activity in the U.S.A. and is usually classed as an American artist.

Nationalism and internationalism interplay so precariously in the modern world that no nation has yet found a permanent balance between them. As a result contemporary art, in Canada as elsewhere, alternates between national and international tendencies. Typical of the latter in recent Canadian painting is the work of James Wilson Morrice (1865-1924). Morrice found so little encouragement for his Impressionistic and Post-Impressionistic art in Canada that he spent much of his life abroad. French, North African, and West Indian scenes occur more frequently in his pictures than do Canadian subjects. His work was respected in France and is now regarded by Canadian critics as among the most sensitive and original painting yet produced by one of Canadian birth. Another Canadian artist to work and win recognition abroad, first in France and later in the U.S.A., is the contemporary painter, Lillian Freiman. Her studies of humanity combine striking psychological insight with rare powers of graphic expressino.

Conscious nationalism in Canadian painting crystalized in the work of Tom Thomson and the **Group of Seven** during the years which preceded and followed World War I. A number of young artists developed a common enthusiasm for the wilder aspects of Canadian scenery, sensing in rugged northern landscapes a theme for distinctively Canadian art.

Tom Thomson (1877-1917), one of the major artists of the group, lost his life by drowning in a northern lake while the movement was still young. In 1919, his leading survivors organized themselves into the **Group of Seven** for the purpose of exhibiting and crusading together in the interests of progressive Canadian art. The artists belonging to this group were A. Y. Jackson (1882—), Lawren Harris (1885—), Arthur Lismer (1885—), J. E. H. MacDonald (1873-1932), F. H. Varley (1881—), Franklin Carmichael (1890—), and F. H. Johnston (1888—). Johnston subsequently withdrew, but the group was later joined by A. J. Casson (1898—), Edwin Holgate (1892—) and Le Moine FitzGerald (1890—).

Beginning in Ontario and Quebec, the leaders of this movement eventually covered every aspect of the Canadian wilds from the Atlantic to the Pacific and as far north as the arctic wastes of Ellesmere Island within a few hundred miles of the North Pole. Searching for a style appropriate to their subjects, some of these artists at one time emphasized surface pattern at the expense of depth, but their best work rises above this limitation to achieve dynamic and genuinely Canadian landscape painting. The Group of Seven continued its identity until 1933, when it changed its name to the **Canadian Group of Painters** and expanded its membership to include a score of the progressive younger artists of Canada.

Related to the Group of Seven in spirit and period are Clarence Gagnon (1880-1941), painter of Laurentian village scenes, and Emily Carr (1871—), interpreter of West

Coast forests and Indian villages. Of the same generation, but aloof from the Group as from all other movements, is David Milne (1884—), an artist with truly individual vision. His unique experiments reveal new and unsuspected possibilities in old mediums and are a delight to the cultivated observer.

So powerful was the influence of the Group of Seven that it dominated many of the younger painters of the succeeding decades. It is difficult as yet to say which of its many followers will make distinctive contributions of their own. The younger contemporaries who remained apart from the Group influence, or who early assimilated it with other influences, appear at present to be making the more important contributions.

Creative leaders in Montreal include Louis Muhlstock (1904—), one of Canada's outstanding draughtsmen as well as a prolific painter; Fritz Brandtner (1896—), a vigorous offshoot of German Expressionism; and Goodridge Roberts (1904—) whose monumental landscapes are subdued dramas of visual mood. Of the French Canadian painters in Montreal, two at least must receive special mention. They are Alfred Pellan (1906—) known in Paris and New York as well as at home for his exhuberent modernism, and Paul-Emils Borduas (1905—). Montreal is also distinguished by an unusual number of notable women painters. These comprise Mabel Lockerby (1887—), Ethel Seath (1879—), Anne Savage (1897—), Sarah Robertson (1891—), Prudence Heward (1896—), Lillias T. Newton (1896—) and Marian Scott (1906—). Mrs. Scott's mural in the Medical School of McGill University involves pioneer work in the artistic embodiment of scientific knowledge.

Among the contemporary artists living in Toronto may be mentioned Carl Schaefer (1903—), water color painter of rural Ontario; the sensitive pictorial composer, Paraskeva Clark (1899—); Thoreau MacDonald (1901—), typographer, graphic artist, and intimate interpreter of wild life; and Bertram Brooker (1888—), whose varied work includes interpretative illustrations, for the most part unpublished, of several literary classics. Henri Masson (1907—) of Ottawa, and Jack Humphrey (1901—) of St. John, N. B., both deal with varied themes but are particularly well known for their studies of the older sections of their respective cities.

Most of the painters listed above are of the experimental or progressive type. Others in considerable numbers, both progressive and conservative, are now active in Canada. They cannot be mentioned individually in the present summary, but their names are to be found in the membership roles of the leading Canadian artists' societies: the Royal Canadian Academy of Art, the Canadian Group of Painters, the Ontario Society of Artists, the Canadian Society of Graphic Art, the Canadian Society of Painter-Etchers and Engravers, and the Canadian Society of Painters in Water Color.

Sculpture, so active an art during the French colonial era, was slow to find a place in the subsequent development of Canadian culture. During the century which followed the English conquest, Quebec clung to its sculptural traditions but their force was slowly diminishing and nothing had appeared in other parts of Canada to replace them except the short-lived activity of the West Coast Indians. Then, during the latter part of the 19th cent., two French Canadian sculptors emerged to provide a link between the original French traditions and the growth of a modern interest in plastic art. They were Philippe Hebert (1850-1917), who provided sculpture for many public buildings and the painter Suzor-Coté, who modeled small *habitant* groups for casting in bronze.

The 20th cent. has seen a growth both in the number of Canadian sculptors and in their power of plastic conception. Walter Allward (1876—) has created impressive monuments, approaching sublimity in the vast Vimy Ridge Memorial in France. The work of Emanuel Hahn (1881—) reveals a solid mastery of plastic essentials, and that of his wife and former pupil, Elizabeth Wyn Wood (1903—), embodies some of the most original feeling for sculptural form yet found in Canada. The joint studio of Frances Loring (1887—) and Florence Wyle (1881—) is highly regarded, and there is creative promise in the work of several younger sculptors. A Sculptors' Society of Canada was founded in 1932.

As this summary is written (1944), twentieth century trends from many parts of the world are interplaying with Canada's native talents and traditions. Real artistic energies undoubtedly stand ready to serve Canadian life, but in this country as in most other parts of the world, recent political and social conditions have allowed them only grudging encouragement. What the future holds for them will depend to a considerable extent upon the social and economic developments of the post-war world.

Promising trends are discernable in several directions. The National Gallery of Canada, an institution supported by the federal government, encourages the development of native talent by purchasing and exhibiting native work, and by sponsoring travelling exhibitions, lectures, and other activities throughout the country. The Art Gallery of Toronto, the Art Association of Montreal, and a slowly growing list of other art museums, are also making valuable contributions. The dying or sadly commercialized folk arts are being restored to a healthier condition as a result of direction given by certain provincial governments, notably those of Quebec and Nova Scotia. The almost extinct Indian art is being assisted by the Society for the Furtherance of British Columbian Indian Arts and Crafts. A renewal of fine professional craftsmanship can be seen in various quarters, as for instance in the work of a number of contemporary Canadian potters. Canadian painters are being used to create official war records during World War II, as they were during World War I. Taken as a whole, the aspirations of Canadian cultural leaders are toward the increasing use of art in ways that will enrich, and be enriched by, the hoped-for "century of the common man."

See G. C. McInnis, *A Short History of Canadian Art,* 1939, which includes a general bibliography; F. B. Houser, *A Canadian Art Movement* (Group of Seven), 1926; A. H. Robson, *Canadian Landscape Painters,* 1932. D. W. Buchanan, *James Wilson Morrice,* 1936, and *The Story of Canadian Art* in the Canadian Geographical Journal, Dec. 1938.
—W.A.

Canada balsam. See oleoresin.

Canadian Group of Painters, the. See CANADA, ART OF.

Canal Builders, the. See Hohakam art.

canary vibrato. See VIBRATO.

cancella. See EARLY CHRISTIAN ARCHITECTURE.

cancrizans. See canon.

candae. See tiara, papal.

candelilla wax. See wax.

candi (Malay). Word of temple, as, Candi Sewu of Java.

canephoros (Gr.). A basket-bearer, basket usually being carried on the head and containing religious objects.

canon. A polyphonic composition in which one of its constituent melodic lines is repeated by imitation in its entirety by at least one of the other melodic lines. One or more parts presenting free counterpoints to the canon may be added.

double canon. Canonic imitation applied to a pair of simultaneously presented melodic lines.

canon by inversion. Canonic imitation using the inversion of the original melodic line.

crab canon (also **cancrizans,** from L. **cancer,** crab; **canon by retrogression**). A composition in which the counterpoint accompanying a melodic line is that same melodic line read backwards from its last to its first tone.

mirror canon. A canon which from a given point repeats itself backwards. The term is used figuratively, because the second half of a mirror canon may be thought of as being a reflection of the first half in a mirror placed vertically at the turning point. The term is sometimes applied also to a canon by inversion, interpreting the imitating part as a reflection of the original part in a mirror placed horizontally between the two parts. This usage, however, is misleading and should be avoided.

riddle canon. A canon in which the place of the entrance of the imitating part—or parts—is not indicated by the composer and has to be plotted by the performer. In elaborate cases of riddle canon the imitating part may enter at several different places and intervals.

endless canon. A canon leading into its own beginning so that it may be repeated without break.   —E.K.

canonical hours. See hours, canonical.

canon, sculptural. Although canons of anatomical proportions are implicit in earlier Greek statues, notably the "Apollo" figures of the sixth century B.C., Polyclitus of Argos (fl. 450-420 B.C.) was the first to make an exact study of the proportions of the human body and formulate, what he considered to be ideal relationships, in a treatise called "The Canon". Vitruvius attempted to reconstruct these ratios as follows: the palm

is the unit, the foot is three palms, lower leg six, thigh six, navel to ear six; the foot is one-sixth the total height, the face one-tenth, the head one-seventh. This was approved by Galen as medically sound. It is apparent, however, from a study of the extant copies of Polyclitus' statues, that Vitruvius' analysis was too mechanical, and that the formula was more dynamic, based on geometric rather than arithmetical proportions; but the statues indicate that Polyclitus favored a stalwart, muscular type. In the following century Lysippus of Sicyon modified this canon, substituting for the squarely-built figures of Polyclitus a more rangy type, with slimmer body, longer legs, and smaller head.
—W.R.A.

canopy. A projection or covering over windows, doors, niches, etc.

canso. See MEDIEVAL MUSIC.

cantata. (1) Originally, something sung, in contrast to something played (sonata). (2) Later, a composition for solo and chorus; a short oratorio (q.v.).

canticle, canticum. *Mus.* Church-service psalm or hymn.

cantiga. See MEDIEVAL MUSIC.

cantilena. A melody, air.

cantilever. A beam or other structural member projecting from a wall or column and supported only at one end.

cantillation. A chanting or half-singing recitation of biblical and liturgical texts practised by Hebrews and Christians. See JEWISH MUSIC.

canting. See ex libris.

canting arms. See HERALDRY.

canto formo. See cantus firmus.

canton. See HERALDRY.

Canton crepe. A fabric heavier than crepe de chine; may combine silk and rayon yarns.

cantor. See JEWISH MUSIC.

cants dels Romeus. See MEDIEVAL MUSIC.

cantus firmus. (1) A plain song (see Ambrosian and Gregorian chant). (2) A theme chosen for counterpoint which remains the same, i.e., "firm," while the other voices or

parts always change. See MEDIEVAL MUSIC.

cantus planus. See MEDIEVAL MUSIC.

canvas. The common support for painting since the 16th cent., this fabric has been used in this way since ancient times. The word, canvas, is now applied to any sort of fabric support that is made up primarily for use with oil paint. Linen with a thin ground was painted in tempera as early as the 12th dynasty in Egypt and probably much earlier. The practice continued steadily during classical times and through the Renaissance. Change to oil painting and to large-scale work has widened the use of it. For the most part, artists' canvas has been made up of a linen with plain cloth weave, though twill has been seen frequently in works from the 16th cent. on. Students' canvases are often made of cotton and a very recent development has been a prepared canvas of glass cloth. As made ready for the market, artists' canvas is prepared with a ground of complicated construction, the upper coatings including oil with white or colored pigments and inert materials.   —G.L.S.

canvas board. See academy board.

Canyon de Chelly (probably a Spanish and English corruption of the Navaho *Tsegi,* "down among the rocks"). A canyon in northeastern Arizona, with two tributaries, Canyon del Muerto (Sp. Canyon of Death, because of a massacre of Navaho in 1805) and Monument Canyon, which contain many cliff dwellings of the Anasazi. Important are White House (1066 to 1229 A.D. by tree ring dating), with about 50 rooms; Antelope House (of early Navaho time), so named because of pictographs of antelope on the cliff walls; and Mummy Cave (348-1284 A.D., tree ring dating), with about 65 rooms. The two latter are in Canyon del Muerto. The site, which has been occupied by the Navaho for probably several hundred years and figures prominently in Navaho mythology, is now the Canyon de Chelly National Monument.   —H.G.

canzone. (1) A folk song. (2) A part song. (3) An instrumental composition in two or three parts, with passages in imitation; somewhat like a madrigal.   —F.M.G.

capital. The top member of a column, effecting the transition from the circular column to the horizontal architrave course. In **Egypt**

the chief decorative shapes used were the conventionalized lotus flower or bud-cluster and the papyrus flower or bud-cluster. On **Persian** capitals a picturesque but structurally weak design of the fore parts of two bulls placed back to back above volutes was used. **Minoan** capitals had a cushion shape under a narrow crowning block. The **Greeks** evolved the three capitals which have since been used most widely in western architecture: the Doric, Ionic, and Corinthian. The **Doric** consists of a square crowning block (abacus), and a cushion (echinus), in its early form puffy, but by the 5th cent. B.C. subtly curving down into the necking that joins it to the column proper; in **Roman** times the echinus contour was reduced to an unimaginative diagonal. The **Ionic** capital consists of an abacus, a double scholl (volute), and an echinus elaborately decorated with ornamentation (bead-and-reel, egg-and-dart, guilloche); the gracefully swinging volutes make it highly ornamental, but it lacks the structural power of the Doric. The **Corinthian** is still more elaborate and less organic in character, consisting of a bell-shaped core from which long volutes arise to support the corners and shortened ones merge into a profusion of acanthus leaves in `two florid rows, producing a sumptuous effect which was greatly enjoyed by Roman architects. **Byzantine** architects used a form derived from the Corinthian, but flattened it and made it a more compact type of surface decoration; in addition to the acanthus they represented basket weaving, melon ridges, and interlacing circle between the abacus and the arch above. Sometimes they added an impost block, similar to the capital in shape. **Romanesque** capitals are also Corinthian in shape, but show a great variety of flatly carved decorative motifs: birds, animals, human figures, and robust foliate designs. In contrast, **Gothic** capitals are more deeply cut, with fantastic foliage, animals, and figures, emerging in picturesque decoration which calls attention to itself rather than contributes to the structural function of the capital.   —W.R.A.

Capo di Monte ware. See CERAMICS II.

cap of maintenance. See HERALDRY.

capriccio. A whimsical musical work of irregular form.

Capsian art. See PREHISTORIC ART.

caput mortuum. See Indian red.

caquetoire, caqueteuse. High-backed lightweight chair with curved arms, originating in 16th cent. France.

caravanserai (Ar.). An open or vaulted court with one or two stories of small rooms surrounding it. See ISLAMIC ART.

carbonated glass. See GLASS AND GLASS-MAKING.

carbon ink. See ink.

carcer (L.). Prison; starting stall in a Roman circus. See circus.

caricature. A drawing or description of a person in which the artist selects and emphasizes unusual characteristics to the point of grotesqueness with the intent of ridicule or burlesque. A process of characterization which over-emphasizes the individuality of a person.

This form of satire can be found in the frescos of the Romans at Pompeii and Herculaneum. In the Middle Ages caricature was manifest in the gargoyles, the characters of Reynard the Fox, the Devil and Death. In the 16th cent. Hans Holbein in his designs of the Danse Macabre drew a set of satirical moralities which caricatured the mysticism of the medieval period. Caricature as an art form was born with the Renaissance in the Netherlands with a multiplicity of prints by such men as Jerome Bosch and Pieter Breughel which were satirically intended. Jacques Callot, Hogarth and Goya drew telling caricatures. In the 18th and 19th cents. caricature developed in the works of Swift, Fielding, Rowlandson, Daumier and the English magazine *Punch*. In the United States Thomas Nast in *Harpers Weekly* created a vogue for caricature. The American school was strongly national as is shown in the works of A. B. Frost. This vogue for caricature has continued to the present time in the newspaper cartoons and the cinema cartoon comics.   —R.L.W.

carillon. A set of bells struck by hammers.

carmen. *Mus.* In early songs, the upper voice-part, above tenor.

carmine lake. See cochineal.

carnation. Flesh tints in a painting. *Rare.*

carnauba wax. This is a hard wax derived from the Brazilian palm where it occurs as a deposit on the leaves. It is yellowish in color and is distinguished by its hardness and high melting point. It is a frequent component in wax mixtures where a high gloss is wanted.   —G.L.S.

carol. Festal songs used esp. at Christmas and Easter.

Carolingian architecture. Within the nucleus of the Carolingian Empire (Northeastern France, Belgium, Rhineland, Switzerland) and in Rome, Carolingian architecture supersedes an early medieval "orientalizing" architecture from 770 on. Based on the political philosophy of Charlemagne, Constantinian Roman Christian building types are revived St. Denis, 775; Fulda, 790-819; Rome, S. Prassede, 817-824 and S. Marco, 827-844). Fused with surviving early mediaeval patterns they lead to new types: basilicas with "westworks," crossing towers and deep choirs (Centula, St. Riquier, 790 and Corvey, 822-875), or central buildings surrounded by aisles and galleries (Aix-la-Chapelle, 795), characterized by rich exterior group formations, monumental size, blank exterior, and lavishly painted and stuccoed interior. See GERMAN ART; also Gall, *Karolingische und Ottonische Kirchen,* 1930; Krautheimer, The Carolingian Revival of Early Christian Architecture, *The Art Bulletin,* 1942; Lehmann, *Der frühe deutsche Kirchenbau,* 1938.
—R.K.

Carolingian art. The Carolingian epoch in art is named for Charlemagne and his successors. It began about 800 and ended around the middle of the 10th cent., overlapping the Ottonian epoch. Its importance lies in the fact that during that time the late antique forms were transplanted into the north and were merged with the native northern tradition of art. In this way the Carolingian epoch became the basis for the entire postantique development of European art.

In architecture the stone building was taken from the south together with certain ground plans, two of which were of foremost importance, the centralized and oblong plans. The most important building of the centralized plan is still standing, the palace-chapel of Charlemagne (805), at present a part of the Cathedral at Aix-la-Chapelle. Another Carolingian building still standing is the church of St. Michael at Fulda (820). The second ground plan, the oblong plan of the basilica, was changed in the North in a very characteristic way. The Carolingian buildings of this type which are still preserved are St.

Peter in Mustail, Graubuenten (Tyrol), the Einhard basilica in Steinbach (Odenwals), and some parts of the present churches of Niederzell and Oberzell in Reichnau. Other Carolingian buildings of the oblong type are the West Gothic Royal Hall, now Santa Maria de Naranco (848), and some parts of the church in the Cloister of Corvay on the Weser. See also the preserved ground plan of the Carolingian basilica, which is a part of the entire ground plan of the Cloister of St. Gallen, built in the year 820. One very important example of Carolingian architecture is the entrance hall of the now destroyed cloister in Lorsch (774).

We know from documents that there were important murals from this epoch, but none of them are preserved. But there are a great number of illustrated manuscripts still in existence. One famous school of miniature painting was the **school of Godescalc,** so named after the writer Godescalc who, between 781 and 783, wrote an Evangeliar (now in Paris) for Charlemagne and his wife Hildegard. Another was the **school of the Ada Group,** named after the Abbess Ada of Mainz who, in about 800, ordered an Evangeliar (now in the city library in Trier). This latter school was localized in the country of the Lower Rhine. Among others of note were the **Palace school of Charlemagne** in which the famous Reichs-Evangeliar was written, the **school of Reims** where the Ebo Evangeliar and the Utrecht Psalter were written, the **school of Metz** (Drago Sacramentar, related to the school of Reims), the **school of Corbie** (Codex Aureus by the two brothers Beringar and Liuthard, written at the order of Charles the Bald in 879), the **school of Tours** (Evangeliar of Charles the Bald under the Abbot Vivian, 844-858), and the **school of St. Gallen** (Psalterium Aureum of St. Gallen).

In sculpture the ivory carvings of this period have become very famous. The different schools of sculpture and their various peculiarities parallel somewhat the different schools of miniature painting. Especially important and well known is the **Liuthard Group,** related in style to the school of Reims.

Starting about 900 virtuosity and baroque tendencies became predominate in painting and sculpture, characterizing the late Carolingian style which overlapped the Ottonian epoch in the last quarter of the 10th cent., and which was signalized by a great confusion of style.

Examples of Carolingian applied art, in so far as they are not identified with miniature painting and ivory carving, are the precious reliquaries like the Bursa of St. Stephen, the Reliquary of Enger, or the chalice of the last Duke of Bavaria, Tassilo. See GERMAN ART; also A. Michel, *Histoire de l'Art,* 1905; E. H. Zimmermann, *Vorkarolingische Miniaturen,* 1916; Wilhelm Koehler, *Die Karolingischen Miniaturen,* 1930; Amédée Boinet, *La Miniature Carolingienne, ses origines, son dévelopement,* 1913; *Schools of Illumination,* Reproductions from manuscripts in the British Museum, 6 vol. 1914-15 — 30; Albert Boeckler, *Abendlaendische Miniaturen bis zum Ausgang der Romanischen Zeit,* 1930; F. H. Stanford Robinson, *Celtic Illuminative Art in the Gospel Books of Durrow,* 1908; Alois J. Schardt, *Das Initial,* 1938; A. Goldschmidt, *Die Elfenbeinskulpturen aus der Zeit der Karolingischen und Saechsischen Kaiser,* 1914; G. Dehio und G. v. Bezold, *Die kirchliche Baukunst des Abendlandes,* 1892; C. Eulart, Manual d' Archeologie Francaise, *Architecture,* Paris, 1902, ff.; G. Dehio, *Geschichte der Deutschen Kunst I.,* 1919; Max Hauttmann, *Die Kunst des fruehen Mittelalters,* 1937.   —A.J.S.

Carolingian Renaissance. See GERMAN ART.

carp. See SYMBOLISM IN FAR EASTERN ART.

carpet (Lat., *carpere,* to pluck; this may refer to plucking wool from the sheep in order to make the carpet or it may have reference to the fabric as something which could be plucked, as the tufts or wool which form its surface.). A carpet is a textile floor covering, with heavy woven foundation, fortified with extra threads forming a pile. Tapestries and carpets in the early days were synonymous with the rugs of today. The general meaning for carpet today is a floor covering which is firmly fastened to the floor and covers the entire floorspace of the room. It can be either of a pile or regular construction. Early pile and tapestry weaving bears a definite relation to that of the pile and woven rugs and carpet production of today. The main types of carpets on the market are oriental, European, hand tufted Axminsters, machine made Axminsters, velvet, Wilton, tapestry, Brussels and chenille. Ingrain is rapidly disappearing due to its poor weaving quality and inferior appearance.   —B.E.J.

carpet structures. (1) *Eastern or hand tufted type*: woven in the highwarp loom, and now made in Donegal, some parts of England and Scotland, and on the Continent, as well as in Persia, Turkey, India, China, Japan, etc. (2) *Felt carpeting*: may be eastern and hand-made; western and machine-made; or woven felts, in which the operations of the loom determine the decorative features and the structure of the carpet, and felting or fulling produces compactness and strength of carpet surface. (3) *Compound plain woven structures*: may be Kidderminster, Scotch, and ingrain productions; or unions, comprising several types of manufacture, all of which are, however, made in a lower quality of warp, e.g. cotton or jute, than weft yarn, the latter consisting of wool, wool substitutes, and other animal fibres, and also of jute. (4) *Pile carpets*: may be loop pile, e.g. Brussels and tapestry; cut or velvet pile, e.g. Wilton and Axminster, with the pile of the carpet formed in weaving by the insertion of wires into the sheddings of the pile-yarn warp; "chenille" Axminster in which the pile is developed by using a "chenille" or "fur" yarn, i.e., a specially woven yarn composed of warp and weft threads, with the latter classified in the order of the coloring of the design in the carpet, and with the shots of weft in each chenille strand cut to give the pile effect (chenille rugs are producible with the pile characteristic on one or both sides, the latter being classed as double-pile or "reversibles.") ; royal or machine-wefted Axminster in which the pile is the result of inserting the pile yarns in lengths into prescribed warp sheds in the weaving of the carpet, such yarn being arranged on spools in the order of the color units in the transverse lines of the figuring (Each spool, with its full complement of pile yarn, is equivalent to the formation of a particular row of pile effect in the design. The yarns delivered through tubes or guides from the spools, after being inserted into the carpet ground work, are automatically cut to give an even length of nap.) ; or compound types of rugs in which the pile is "cut" and "loop" in the center and back respectively; or formed of ordinary yarn, mohair or lustrous worsted in one section of the rug, and in curled, crimped or frisé yarns in the border section. (5) *Inferior varieties of carpeting*: are of jute manufactures and union manufactures.   —B.E.J.

Carrara marble. A marble quarried in Luna, Italy, popular since the time of Caesar for sculpture, since it has been readily available at cheap cost. Due to its texture of very small crystals, it lacks luminous quality, and its dull white color is not suitable for expressing delicate modulations or sensuous values.   —W.R.A.

cartoccio. See scrollwork.

cartoon (F. *carton*, from It. *cartone*, pasteboard, from *carta*, paper; L. *charta*). (1) A full scale drawing on paper to be used as a model for easel paintings, mural paintings, mosaics, stained glass, tapestries, etc. The cartoon may be copied, or may be transferred to canvas or plaster by tracing or pouncing, and transferred to tapestry by cutting out figures and details and placing them behind the wool. The cartoon is usually carefully executed in line and value and, when employed, represents the major share of both invention and labor in the execution of a fresco or an oil painting. The practice of preparing accurate cartoons in chiaroscuro was general in the Renaissance, e.g. Mantegna's nine cartoons for the *Triumph of Caesar*, Raphael's cartoons for the Vatican tapestries, and the cartoons of Leonardo and Michelangelo for the *Palazzo Vecchio* frescoes. (2) The term 'cartoon' is also used to designate drawings for reproduction in newspapers and magazines, usually humorous as in the case of political satires or caricatures, or comic strips. Among journalistic sketches of this sort the caricature is the highest type; while with increasing frequency in America the term 'cartoon' connotes ideographic sketches of the comic strip type as contrasted with interpretive and individualized caricatures. See design.—L.D.L.

cartouche. An irregular, fantastic, scroll-like ornament, on which armorial symbols or bearings are frequently carved; used in baroque architecture.

caryatid. A draped female figure serving as an architectural column, so called after the dancing women of the town of Caryae. The earliest examples in Greece are found at Delphi, where two figures in gay Ionic costumes support the entablature of the porch of the Cnidian Treasury (about 550 B.C.). Similar ones were used in the Siphnian Treasury at Delphi a quarter of a century later. The most famous Caryatids are the six on the south porch of the Erechtheum at Athens;

these stalwart figures, subtly varied in pose and in the folds of drapery, which fall to their feet (suggesting the fluting of a column), with thick masses of hair behind the neck to strengthen that weaker element, seem to bear the weight of the entablature with serene dignity. Three caryatids, set back to back, served to support the tripod on top of an acanthus column at Delphi. The device was used infrequently in later times; but in general it has been agreed that the use of the female figure for such a purpose is structurally unfortunate.   —W.R.A.

casa (Sp.). House, dwelling, edifice, or other structure.

case. (1) *Cer.* Plaster mold made from block for making working molds. See CERAMICS I. (2) *Book.* The cover of a book apart from the book itself.

cased. *Arch.* Covered with other materials, generally of a better quality. See edition binding.

casein. Used largely as an adhesive for joining the wood of painters' panels or for similar purposes in building supports, casein has also served to a limited extent as a painting medium. It is prepared by heating skimmed milk with the addition of hydrochloric acid. This throws the curd of the milk out of suspension and, when dry, that forms a white powder. It can be dissolved in water if an alkali is added but, after the film of the adhesive has set, it is no longer water-soluble.   —G.L.S.

case-work or **casing.** *Book.* Inserting a book sewn, stitched, or pasted, into its case.

casing in. See edition binding.

cassapanca (It.). A chest converted into a settee by adding arms and a back. See FURNITURE.

cassone (It.). A large chest.

castanets. See MUSICAL INSTRUMENTS.

casting. Process of forming ware with slip in molds. See CERAMICS I; also METALWORK.

castle (OE. *castel*, fm. OF., fm. L. *castellum*, fortress, dim. of *castrum*, fortified place; mod. F., *château* or *château-fort*; It. & Sp. *castello*; G., *Schloss*, *Burg* or *Festung*). A large building or set of buildings fortified for defense, a fortress, citadel or stronghold, especially of a prince or nobleman; retained as a name for large mansions which formerly would have been feudal castles, especially if built on or near the site of actual castles; similarly in Fr. and G. **chateau** and **Schloss** have been retained to describe private country houses of noble dimension and tenure despite the total absence of fortification. The castle proper, built always to take advantage of naturally defensible terrain, and not infrequently with an eye to offensive strategy as well, consisted at its point of highest development of several distinct but well-articulated parts. At the outermost limits was a high curtain wall, battlemented, often protected by bastions and towers at the corners; in many cases outside this wall was a moat (in German such a castle is distinguished as a *Wasserburg*) crossed only by a strongly fortified drawbridge. Access to the castle was gained through a gate protected by flanking towers or contained within its own miniature fortress, the **barbican.** The gate opened into a ward or base court devoted to soldiers' quarters, stables and other offices connected with the needs of the armed retainers and servants. A second range of walls guarded the inner court where were the great hall, kitchens, chapel, and private apartments of the lord and his family. These were frequently contained within the **keep,** a massive structure at the heart of the castle which was capable of being maintained and defended when all the outer works had been taken by the attacker. In some cases there were as many as three sets of walls, and auxiliary fortifications to protect access to water supply or a river crossing. The arrangement and extent of defensive elements and the relation of domestic to military features varied in particular instances according to a number of factors; but until the castle, hitherto impregnable to nearly every form of attack but treason or starvation, ceased through the rapid development of the cannon in the 15th cent. to be any longer defensible, military considerations were paramount in its design. After this time its two major functions were separated; domestic requirements gradually became the more important and the castle merges into the history of the house in the one direction, or into pure military architecture in the other. The castle first began to acquire its feudal form and significance in the second half of the 10th cent., and received its first important

development in Normandy; during the dark ages local chieftains appear to have lived in the patched remains of Roman villas, but as the predatory instinct once again rose to the surface as a dominant factor in European life and fortification became a necessary condition of existence, the lords put palisades around their houses and farm buildings, then for greater security rebuilt the house on top of a mound (Fr. *motte*) surrounded with both a palisade and a moat. By the 11th cent., these crude timber castles which were constantly burning down either through carelessness or arson were gradually replaced with stone buildings, walled and moated, but still consisting, so far as domestic arrangements were concerned of little more than a great hall with an open hearth in the center, a type derived from the north countries, though Romanesque structural methods were used to vault the halls and provide support for the massive stone walls. In the period immediately following the Conquest the Normans invented two new types of castle; the citadel which took advantage of natural rock strongholds, as at Ludlow; and the massive high rectangular or square keep, of which the Tower of London and Rochester, Hedingham and Colchester Castles are the outstanding examples. The Crusades now provided unequalled opportunity for the laboratory study of castle-building; the art was revolutionized through the practical experience thus acquired by the Crusaders and through the lessons they learned from the advanced skill of Byzantine, Mohammedan and Saracen engineers and military architects. Such superb examples as Krak des Chevaliers, Margab and Kalat Sahyum in the Near East, Châteaux Gaillard, Loches and Chinon in France, Alnwick and Berkeley Castles in England bear eloquent testimony to the principles learned in this hard school: there must be concentric lines of defenses, equally strong, one within the other; walls must be protected by flanking towers, and round surfaces should be used where battering rams and scaling machines could be brought up against them; and that each part must be planned in relation to the mutual defense of all the parts. During the Gothic period fewer discoveries of defensive utility were made but there is a constant refinement of the domestic portions of the castle; the great strength of the outer works made possible generous window openings in the residential apartments at the protected core; the invention of the chimney and the hooded fireplace and the development of adequate sanitary systems (which did not carry over into the Renaissance) greatly increased personal comfort; and the taste for luxury which Crusaders and noble pilgrims acquired in Byzantium and Mohammedan lands bore rich fruit in the interior decoration of the castle. During the 14th and 15th cents., the most interesting phases of castle development are those having to do with these domestic improvements, and this is the case in even such brilliant examples of the military architect's genius as Pierrefonds and the Palais des Papes at Avignon; after the Crusades strictly military considerations and improvements in technique are found principally in those castles whose primary function was military rather than defensive, such as Carnarvon and Conway in Wales, Cocca and Turrégano in Spain. The last castle to be built as such in England was Longford (1578—1581) and this was an anachronism; many of the superficial features had lingered into early Renaissance country houses, but the castle as house was doomed as soon as the use of the cannon was mastered. The castles of the late 18th and 19th cents. were of course purely romantic in inspiration, though it cannot be denied that some are extremely effective pieces of rural decoration, and at least one reconstruction of this period, Windsor, is infinitely more convincing to the modern eye as a feudal masterpiece than would have been the building which Wyattville was commanded to transform.   —T.A.H.

cast stone. Cast concrete resembling stone.

catacombs. Any subterranean cemetery provided that it be of sufficient size to house more than the bodies of one family or clan and that its sepulcral chambers be interconnected. Dispersion of this type of burial over the regions adjoining the Mediterranean seems due to the adherence by exiled Jewish communities to the accustomed Palestinian methods of burying the dead. The Christians, who were at first no more than a Jewish sect, were naturally disposed to follow such prototypes and thus were lead to establish catacombs for many of their communities in Egypt, North Africa and Italy. By far the most extended as well as historically the most important of these were the catacombs of Rome. They alone had a history beyond early Christian times; they became centers of the cult of martyrs and in the 8th and 9th cents. the main source of supply for relics required for the establishment of altars in a rapidly expanding Christianity. After having fallen into neglect during the Middle Ages the Roman catacombs were rediscovered in 1578. See EARLY CRISTIAN ART.   —R.B.

catch. Originally, simply a round for three or more voices (unaccompanied) written out in length as one continuous melody. The catch was for each succeeding player to take up his part in time; this is evident not only from the manner in which it was written but also from the simple and innocent character of the words. But in course of time a new element was introduced into catches; words selected were so constructed that it was possible by mispronunciation or interweaving of words and phrases to produce the most hilarious and comical phrases. The singing of catches became an art, and was accompanied by gestures; the skill with which they were sung has become a tradition.   —F.M.G.

catharsis. The term occurs in Aristotle's famous definition of tragedy: "A tragedy, then, is the imitation of an action . . . with incidents arousing pity and fear, wherewith to accomplish its catharsis of such emotions." (1449 b28 translation Bywater). An elaboration of this statement by Aristotle is lacking. But there are a few passages in other Aristotelian writings that may be helpful in clarifying the obscure sentence. Cf. *Problems* 864a34; *Politics* VIII, 7; *Rhetorics* II, 5, 8; *Nic. Ethics* 128b11, 15; 136a8; 115a9; 107-a33; etc.

There is not a term in the catharsis clause that has not been the object of millenia of controversy.

(i) *eleos kai phobos,* pity and fear. *Eleos* has little to do with the melting, sympathetic Christian pity (misericordia) that the 18th cent., particularly Mendelssohn, saw in it; but seems to be closer to a strong gush of compassion. *Phobos* means really fear and not terror, as Lessing insisted against Dacier and Curtius. It is "a pain or disturbance arising from a mental presentation of impending evil, destructive or painful." (1382a24). Tragedy is to arouse both compassion and fear.— Corneille preferred to read: either pity or fear; and he added admiration as a third tragical emotion.—Mendelssohn reduced tragic terror to pity, pity being defined by him as a mixed sensation that is composed of love to an object and the displeasure (Unlust) caused by this object's bad luck. Terror is nothing but a pity that surprises us. Confusing fear *for* somebody and fear *with* somebody, he believed that tragic fear, too, springs from pity. Hence, he concluded that phobos has no place side by side with pity in the definition of tragedy. Following Corneille he suggested that it should be replaced by admiration.—Lessing held that the stimulation of pity alone is tragedy's function. However, led on by Aristotle's, "All things that we fear in our own case, the same arouse pity when they happen to others", he seemed to be inclined to explain tragic pity as reflective result of fear for ourselves. He objected to admiration as a tragic effect: it is too cold and moral a feeling. He tried in vain to reconcile Mendelssohn's and his own psychological concept of pity and fear, that reduced the one to the other and vice versa, with Aristotle's definition of tragedy, by claiming catharsis of fear to be of equal importance with catharsis of pity.—The simplest explanation, remaining close to observable phenomena, seems to be that, as a tragedy is the imitation of an action and as every "now" of an action is in between something that has happened and something that is going to happen, pity is the emotion evoked by what has happened, fear by what is going to happen "From mine eye too a swelling tear did start. No greater may the present evil grow!" (Euripides, *Medea,* transl. W. C. Lawton). A good tragedy fills the spectator with both pity and fear at the same moment. Neither can exist without the other, just as no action,—although it has a beginning and an end, (1450b26)—is without a past and a future. Quite naturally, fear will prevail during the first part and pity at the end.

(ii) " . . . *Its* catharsis . . . " "its" because, according to *Pol.* 8. 7, there are various other things that have a cathartic effect proper to their own nature. Music, for instance, has "its" cathartic effect on religious enthusiasm.

(iii) " . . . *of* such emotions . . . " Some arbitrarily interpret that to mean catharsis *of* the soul *from* such emotions; others, correctly, as catharsis of the emotions themselves.

(iv) " . . . of *such* emotions . . . " *toioutoon* has sometimes been changed into *toutoon,* thus limiting the catharsis to pity and fear. But most modern commentators prefer *toioutoon,* explaining that through the arousing of pity and fear, these *and* similar *pathoi* are purged and purified.

(v) "catharsis". There is a medical, a psychological, and an ethical aspect to the cathartic effect of tragedy; and it seems quite unwarranted to emphasize the one at the expense of the other. This, however, is exactly what has happened. The ethical interpretation, dominant in the 17th and 18th cents. (Corneille, Batteaux, Dacier, Heinsius, Crusius, Nikolai, Mendelssohn, Lessing) has been followed by a psychological (pathological) one in Bernays and Bywater, and a medical one in Margoliuth. It would be quite Aristotelian to describe one and the same process in medical terms as a medical event and in ethical terms as an ethical event.

(a) In medical terms, following Margoliuth, catharsis means the homoeopathic cure in the case of excessive cold in the black bile. Tragedy inspires fear, fear expresses itself in trembling, trembling, in turn, is a sign of cold. Thus homoeopathically, by excessive cold being introduced into the organism from the outside, the excessive internal cold of the black bile is equalized, and a proper balance restored between heat and cold. The cathartic effect of tragedy is this homeopathic restoring of equilibrium between heat and cold in the black bile.

To interpret catharsis in purely medical terms reduces tragedy to the status of a drug. The effect of tragedy, to be sure, has a physical aspect to be explained in medical terms. (It would seem, however, that Margoliuth is deliberately ignoring the definition of catharsis given in 864a34 and is misunderstanding 466a30.) But catharsis has above all an emotional aspect that has to be explained in appropriate terms, though with the aid of the medical analogy implicit in the term catharsis.

(b) The pathological interpretation of catharsis will differ according to whether one chooses as guide *Politics* 1342a or the definition of catharsis as given in *Problems* 864a34. In the first case (*Politics* 1342a), Aristotle would have meant by tragic catharsis the soul's liberation of an excess of fear and pity. Persons inclined to fall into religious frenzy are restored as though they had found healing and purgation, after having been excited by appropriate melodies to mystic frenzy. Similarly, the tragic catharsis would consist in exciting aesthetically pity and fear to a high pitch and thus restoring to the soul a healthful balance of these emotions.

This, however, seems to be more a purging of the soul from these emotions than a purging of the emotions themselves as demanded by the text of the *Poetics.* The medical definition of catharsis as given in *Problems* 864a34 will be more helpful in this respect.

To cleanse, medically speaking, is the function of certain substances, so-called drugs, that cannot be absorbed by the body (1) because of their excessive heat or cold; (2) because of their quantity. Dissolved in the stomach, but overpowering the intestinal tract, they rush through the body carrying with them various obstacles. (cf. 864a31). What is cleansed? Directly, the organs through which the drug passes; indirectly, the organs connected with these; and finally, the whole body. The cleansing substance is the drug which, though dissolved in the stomach, proves "overpowering" and therefore unabsorbable in the intestines. The body is cleansed of material obstructing the drug in its rush toward elimination from the body i.e., waste products that the body has been slow in eliminating. The fast-moving drives before it that which is sluggish.—This is the essence of catharsis.

How does this medical description of catharsis resemble the emotional effect of tragedy? The analogy is obvious enough. The fearful and pitiful overwhelm us through their quantity, bringing pity and fear and, through them, the whole soul into rapid motion. Thus they cleanse pity and fear, the emotions connected with them, and indirectly the whole soul of the sluggishness that in everyday life prevent pity and fear from being felt. Considerations of profit, interest, selfishness, etc. that leave us relatively unmoved and cold when witnessing a fearful and pitiful event in real life, are washed away on the waves of pity and fear, aroused by tragedy.

This interpretation, capable of being supplemented on the physiological side (as Margoliuth attempted to do), might well be called phenomenological in the popular sense of the term, since it remains close to the psychological and existential phenomena, observable in an aesthetic situation.

(c) A onesidedly moralistic interpretation of catharsis - - purification instead of purging—sees the effect of tragedy in the "moralische Verbesserung der Leidenschaften" (moral improvement of the passions—Lessing, *Hamburgische Dramaturgie*). Taking his orientation from the theory of the means in the *Nic. Ethics,* Lessing has too much or too little pity and fear disposed of by the tragic effect and the soul become virtuous by now finding itself situated in the middle between the extremes.

(d) A fourth trend of interpretation, metaphysical in scope, issues from German transcendentalism. From the aesthetically extraneous perspective of a deep, but doubtful philosophy of history, catharsis is given an important function in the history of the spirit. According to the scheme of this history, the Greek tragedy is a desperate attempt at overcoming the cosmic loneliness of Greek consciousness; and catharsis replaces the older dionysic unification with the All-One of nature, raising man from the limitations of self-feeling to sympathy with all being in its suffering. (Cf. Fritz Kaufmann, *Die Philosophie des Grafen York von Wartenberg*). From Herder through Schelling and Schopenhauer to Nietzche, this trend of interpretation indicates more about the standpoint of the interpreter than about Aristotle's own intentions which seem to be limited to an artistic analysis *within* the aesthetic situation.

—W.C.

cathedra. See EARLY CHRISTIAN ART.

cathedral. A church containing the cathedra, or official chair of a bishop.

Caucasus rugs. Inspired by Persia and Turkey. Wrap and weft of wool. Ghiordes knot always used. No predominance of red in designs. Rectilinear panel fringed with latchhoops and ground filled with detached devices such as octagons, stars and animals. —B.E.J.

cauri (Skr.). See fly-whisk.

causeuse (Fr.). A type of sofa for two.

cauterium. Among the few tools mentioned in the history of ancient painting is the cauterium, a spatula of metal with a rounded end. It was evidently used largely with melted wax and may have been responsible for some of the conformation in that group of mummy paintings known as Fayum portraits. —G.L.S.

cavatina. (1) A short song of lyric character. (2) In opera, a vocal air shorter and simpler than an aria, and in one division, i.e., not in ternary form *a-b-a.* —F.M.G.

cave art. See PREHISTORIC ART; INDIAN ART; AUSTRALIAN ABORIGINAL ART.

cave dwelling. See DOMESTIC ARCHITECTURE.

cavo reed. See ACOUSTICS.

cavetto. An Egyptian and classical moulding consisting of a single concave curve of approximately a quarter circle or ellipse cut back below a fascia; when ornamented in Greek architecture carries a Doric leaf pattern. —L.T.S

cavo-relievo. Hollow relief (q.v.). See relief sculpture.

C clef. See NOTATION.

ceiling. The upper side or overhead covering of a room or chamber. See INTERIOR ARCHITECTURE AND DECORATION.

celadon ware. A light-green glazed ware. The name is of French derivation originally implying the color of the coat worn by an actor of the 18th cent. who played the part of Celadon. See seiji; lung chùan yao. —J.A.M.

celesta. See MUSICAL INSTRUMENTS.

cella. Main chamber of classical temple wherein stood the cult statue. See HELLENIC ART.

cello. Abbrev. for violoncello, for which see MUSICAL INSTRUMENTS.

cellophane. A synthetic material compounded from cellulose as is rayon. It is poured out into flat sheets resulting in a transparent material of the thickness of paper. Cut into narrow strips it can be woven in combination with other fibres into a sheer fabric. —G.W.R.

celluloid. Rarely but occasionally used as a film material or varnish, celluloid is associated with the various cellulose products that have come into the paint trades during relatively recent times. It is cellulose nitrate plasticized with camphor. —G.L.S.

cellulose products. Chief among these are cellulose nitrate and cellulose acetate. Both are clear film materials, soluble in a number of organic solvents but not affected by water or turpentine. They have been used slightly as mediums for painting, but are generally classed with varnishes or surface film materials. Cellulose nitrate, known also as gun cotton or pyroxylin, has about 100 years of history. It is faintly yellow and has the disadvantage of being highly flammable. It is not stable to light for long periods and is particularly deteriorated by strong sunlight. Cellulose acetate is more stable but requires a large amount of solvent to convert it into a brushable fluid. —G.L.S.

celt. Implement in the form of an axe-head. in oriental art, sacrificial and symbolical forms, generally of bronze, stone or jade. —J.A.M.

Celtic art. The style of Celtic art as it is manifested in decorative designs and ornaments on swords, spear-heads, fibulae, bracelets, etc., originated probably in the Middle Rhine area under the influence of Mediterranean cultures and reached its climax on the European continent ca. 1st cent. B.C. during the last phase of the La Tène culture; hence the style is sometimes referred to as La Tène style. (La Tène is the site where the best known objects of this style were found.) The Celtic ornaments are primarily of a linear geometric design—developed into intricate patterns in the late phases—in which S-curves, spiral S-turns and the so-called trumpet forms occur frequently. The Celts of the West were renowned for their refined and intricate work in enamel, and they frequently employed red coral for the decoration of such bronze objects as fibulae, shields, brooches, etc.

The Celts were Romanized in the West of Europe ca. 25 B.C., and were Germanized or displaced by Teutonic tribes in the regions East of the Rhine at approximately the same time. The Celtic culture, however, remained dominant in England until the invasion of the Anglo-Saxons and in Ireland well into the Middle Ages. In the latter region the so-called La Tène style is sometimes referred to as late Celtic which is not very meaningful in view of the fact that Celtic culture in some places endured almost unchanged until a relatively late date, as noted above.

The 6th cent. saw the beginning of a revival of the Celtic style in Ireland. Some authors ascribe the flourishing of early Christian art in the following centuries in Ireland to this revival, which exhibited an admixture of foreign style elements, e.g. the animal style which is of Teutonic origin. In the 7th and 8th cent. the so-called La Tène (late Celtic) style is displaced by the interlaced style which, however, contains elements of the earlier stylistic phase (e.g. the *Book of Durrow*). See *Trésors Archéologiques de l'Armorique Occidental*, 1886; George Coffey, *Royal Irish Academy Collection*, 1910; *Christian Art in Ancient Ireland*, vol. I, 1932, Adolf Mahr, ed., vol. II, 1941, Joseph Raftery, ed. —H.H.

cembalo. A harpsichord (q.v.).

cement. In the arts this word is commonly used as a synonym of adhesive and means any kind of film material which will join parts of objects together. It may be referred to, also, as a support for wall painting and in that case Portland cement or concrete is meant.   —G.L.S.

cendal (L. *sendal*). Called sarcenet since the 15th cent. A thin taffeta used for banners for royal or ecclesiastical processions. —G.W.R.

censer. Generally, in oriental art, an incense burner with three legs and two perforated covers.

centaurs. These combative and amorous horsemen, who, according to the fertile Greek imagination, inhabited the mountains of Thessaly and Arcadia, were a favorite subject of Greek artists, as early as the 8th cent. B.C., both because of their picturesque exploits and because of their interesting combination of human and equine forms. In early art they were regarded as human beings in front, with the body and hind legs of a horse, but by the 6th cent. they were represented as men only to the waist. Their battles with the Lapiths were the subject of the west pediment at Olympia and many of the Parthenon metopes, and they were pictured often by Greek vase painters. In later painting, Botticelli's Pallas and a Centaur is the best known example. The subject continued to interest sculptors. Medieval imagiers, following the patterns established by the Bestiaries, carved on cathedral doorways and in cloisters squat little centaurs to personify the forces of evil that attack the righteous. Michelangelo, Bologna, Canova, Thorwaldsen, Barye, Degas, Manship and Bourdelle are among the great sculptors who made use of this theme. Bourdelle found it especially fascinating; he left several sketchbooks full of drawings and watercolors of Centaurs, and considered his Dying Centaur his finest sculptural achievement.   —W.R.A.

centering. A timber substructure supporting an arch in construction which is removed when the keystone is put in place making the arch self-supporting.

center of picture, of the vanishing line, of view, of vision. See PERSPECTIVE.

centipede. See SYMBOLISM IN FAR EASTERN ART.

Central American aboriginal art. See ABORIGINAL AMERICAN ART.

CENTRAL ASIAN ART (TURKESTAN). By the art of Central Asia is meant the architecture, sculpture, and painting that flourished in the Buddhist kingdoms extending along the highways of caravan and pilgrim that stretched from northwestern China to Afghanistan. The routes on which these capitals of religion and commerce were situated skirted the north and south of the great Taklamakan desert. The date of this Sino-Indian art is roughly from the 3rd to the 10th cents. A.D. In it are found those same elements that made up the international population of the silk-roads—Indian, Iranian, Classic, and Chinese. British, French, German, Japanese, and Russian expeditions have all been active in the archeological exploration of these regions since the beginning of the 20th cent. The most notable finds were made by Sir Aurel Stein and a number of German expeditions under Albert von Le Coq.

Since we know that as early as the 2nd cent. A.D. Syrian traders were exploring the commercial possibilities of Turkestan, it is not at all surprising that the 3rd cent. cycle of paintings from Mirān in southeastern Turkestan should reveal the same stylistic extension of Roman provincial forms as the art of Gandhāra in northwestern India. The wall-paintings of the circular cells, excavated by Sir Aurel Stein, consisted of a frieze of *Jātaka* scenes that are to all intents and purposes the pictorial equivalents of the Roman reliefs of Gandhāra. A high dado below this had representations of erotes bearing a garland, in the swags of which were busts of winged divinities, and what have been identified as personifications of the heavenly bodies. This is a familiar device on the sarcophagi of Late Roman and Early Christian art. The heads of the angels and planetary deities are abstract masks recalling the portraits of Palmyra and the Fayum. The lime-plaster sculpture found at Mirān and at the Rawak vihāra near Khotān again reveals techniques of Late Antique origin, such as the reduction of the drapery folds to a system of striated ridges; occasional heads betray something of the same realism and pathos that distinguishes the Greco-Buddhist sculpture from Hadda in Afghanistan.

The 5th, 6th, and 7th cents. A.D. saw the florescence of a number of styles, semi-Indian, semi-Iranian in character. This may be illustrated principally by the wall-paintings decorating the temples of the Thousand Buddha caves at Kyzil (Kuchā) on the northern silk-road. The people of the Kuchā oasis were of the Tocharian race, and are believed to be the descendants of the Scythian tribe of the Yüe-chih who began a westward migration from China in the 2nd cent. B.C. Their language belonged to the Indo-European group, and their costumes, as seen in the wall-paintings, seem almost medieval' European in style. A large collection of these wall-paintings is installed in the Museum für Völkerkunde in Berlin. Their subject matter confirms the testimony of the Chinese pilgrims, such as Hsüan Tsang, that the Buddhists of Turkestan were almost all followers of the Small Vehicle (Hinayāna), in which only the person of the founder, Śākyamuni Buddha, and the events in His earthly mission were presented for worship in art.

The earliest of the styles dating from ca. 500 A.D. may best be studied in the decorations of the Peacock Cave at Kyzil. An inscription in the Cave of the Painter gives a date of the early 6th cent. This is essentially a provincial Indian manner of painting. The svelte and languorous forms emanate the same sensuous warmth and grace that we find in the more truly Indian wall-paintings at Bāmiyān in Afghanistan. The heavy plastic shading, characteristic of Indian painting, is largely absent in this technique, and the color scheme, limited to dark reds and browns and malachite green, lacks the richness and tonal range of the famous Indian murals at Ajantā.

The second Central Asian style, defined by the German scholars as Indo-Iranian, has been dated 600 to 650 A.D. The wall-paintings in the Cave of the Red Dome contain inscribed portraits of three kings of Kuchā who are known to have reigned in the late 6th and early 7th cents. A.D. The best illustrations of this manner are the decorations of the Maya Cave at Kyzil. This phase of Turkestan painting is distinguished by its strident brilliance of coloring: green, orange, and lapis lazuli blue are the dominating hues in this completely non-realistic palette. Strangely inarticulated figures have their faces and bodies outlined with thick bands of orange shadow that confers a certain plasticity on these mannikin-like forms without, in any sense, recording actual effects of illumination. Whereas this technique is presumably Indian in origin, the round placid faces, the types of headdresses and jewels are reflections of the art of Iran in the Sassanian period. An abstract flatness characterizes the treatment of the costumes, in which the pattern of the stuff is represented without consideration for

either the foreshortening of the folds or the form of the body beneath. This strange combination of plastic and patternized elements reminds us of the hieratic forms of Byzantine art of the first Golden Age, in which the heads, set on flat bodies, retain something of the solid and realistic qualities of Roman art. What may be either a later development or a contemporary variant of this Indo-Iranian style may be seen in certain figures in which the thickened outlines have been replaced by contour lines of an even thickness and wiry, iron-hard quality. It is worthy of note that paintings in this Central Asian technique are to be found in the Buddhist cave-temples at Tun Huang in westermost China. In some of the *Jātaka* scenes painted at Kyzil the wall is divided into many interlocking chevron-shapes. Each one of these conventionalized mountain peaks frames an isolated figure or episode. This abstraction of what is essentially a landscape background into multiple space-cells may be seen in a further state of development in the earliest Buddhist wall-paintings at Tun Huang. The site of Kyzil has also yielded a large collection of highly polychromatic sculpture, which in style seems to be related to the Greco-Buddhist art of Gandhāra. The perpetuation of this Romanized Indian manner until such a late date is probably to be explained by the use of moulds, numbers of which have been found at this site.

The architecture of the cave-temples at Kyzil is very simple, and is not to be compared with the scale and grandeur of the grotto-temples of India, although probably the idea of hollowing sanctuaries from the rocks goes back to an Indian origin. The most common type of temple is either square or rectangular in form, usually with a small stûpa in the center of the chamber. In a slightly more elaborate type a porch or vestibule precedes the sanctuary, an arrangement that can also be found in the cave-temples at Bāmiyān. Occasionally, the shrine is in the form of a single long narrow chamber with a barrel vault cut out of the rock. The so-called lantern roof is also found in occasional examples at Kyzil.

The sculpture and painting of the famous Buddhist cave-temples at Bāmiyān, dated from the 4th to the 6th cents. A.D., must in a sense be regarded as Central Asian in character. Since all of the styles represented in the paintings at Kyzil may be found at this Afghan site, it seems possible that all these various styles originated at Bāmiyān. The two colossal Buddha statues, 120′ and 175′ in height, are magnifications of images in the Gandhāra style. The paintings in the niche of the larger image are partly in the first, partly in the second Kyzil style. A Bodhisattva in Group E at Bāmiyān, painted almost entirely in lapis lazuli blue, corresponds to the more linear phase of the Indo-Iranian style.

The paintings from the 8th to the 10th cent., recovered from the Turfān oasis in northeastern Turkestan, are almost completely Chinese in style. During these centuries this territory was under the rule of the Uighurs, a strong Turkish tribe, whose civilization was largely Western in character. It is evident from both the types and costumes represented in the paintings of Turfān that this Turkish culture with many elements of Western and Persian origin was greatly influenced by its contacts with the Chinese. The great series of wall-paintings from the monastery of Bezäklik, now divided between the Museum for Central Asian Antiquities in New Delhi and the Museum für Völkerkunde in Berlin, bear inscriptions in Chinese and Brahmi. The principal panels consist of enormous, almost identical compositions representing the Buddha Śākyamuni in various earlier incarnations, greeting the Buddhas of these past eras. The figures themselves show exactly the same synthesis of Indian and Chinese elements that distinguishes the mature art of the T'ang period in China. Both Chinese and Indian types are represented; the draperies of the Buddhas are drawn in a linear version of the Gandhāra formula; the architectural details and. the floral patterns of the frames are completely Chinese. The heads of the Buddhas, in their suggestion of the spheroidal mass of the head, in a completely linear technique, conform to Chinese Buddhist painting of the 8th and 9th cents. A.D.

Among the archeological finds in the Turfān region were numerous illuminated manuscripts dedicated to the Manichaean faith, a syncretic religion of Persian origin that had found favor with the Uighur chiefs. The style of these brilliantly colored book-illustrations has many reminiscences of Late Antique and Near Eastern art forms. It probably represents a perpetuation of a Sassanian Persian style of painting kept alive by the Manichaean tradition.

The Buddhist art of Central Asia comes to an end with the eastward advance of Mohammedanism. As early as the 8th cent., the monasteries of Kyzil were devastated by the

Islamic ruler of Kashgar, and by the 10th cent. A.D. only the easternmost reaches of Turkestan had escaped the rising tide of Mohammedan conquest. The Uighur civilization in this region was finally overwhelmed by the Mongol invasion of Chinghiz Khan in the 12th cent. See Grünwedel, A., *Alt-Kutscha*, 1920; Le Coq, Albert von, *Chotscho*, 1913; *Die Buddhistische Spätantike in Mittelasien*, 1922-33, *Bilderatlas zur Kunst und Kulturgeschichte Mittel-Asiens*, 1925, *Auf Hellas Spuren*, 1926 and *Buried Treasures of Chinese Turkestan*, 1928; Pelliot, P., *Mission an Asie Centrale*, Comptes-rendus de *l'Acad. d'Inser. et Belles-Lettres*, 1910; Stein, Sir Aurel, *Ancient Khotan*, 1907, *Sand-buried Ruins - of Khotan*, 1907, *Explorations in Central-Asia*, 1906-08, "Geographical Journal" for July and September, 1909, *Ruins of Desert Cathay*, 1912, *Serindia*, 1921, *Innermost Asia*, 1929 and *On Ancient Central Asian Tracks*, 1933; Waldschmidt, E., *Gandhāra, Kutscha, Turfan*, 1925.   —B.R.

centralization, centralizing. See CIVIC PLANNING.

central visual ray. See PERSPECTIVE.

centrolinead. See PERSPECTIVE.

ceramic sculpture. See CERAMICS I.

CERAMICS I: materials, processes, techniques. The art of ceramics had its beginning almost with the beginning of man. No other art traces the story of mankind on this earth so clearly as ceramics. The tides of time have washed away many races, but evidences of their existence has been left in the fragments of the humble art of the potter.

There are two reasons why this is true. The material, clay, is found in abundance in practically all parts of the world and since it is so plentiful it has no intrinsic value. The more important reason is that although seemingly fragile it has great resistance to atmospheric influences and is considered the least perishable of all things of all ages.

Ceramics or keramics (Gr. *keramikos*, potter's clay, Fr. *ceramique*, G. *keramik*) is a broad term given to all baked or fired clay articles. In Greek mythology *Keramos*, son of Ariadne and Bacchus was the patron god of the potters. The art is so ancient that its origin is unknown., but it is interesting that in every civilization of which we have any record of their religious beliefs, all give credit. for its beginning to the Gods. Aside from being a wonderful gift to mankind, many things seemed to happen, especially during firing, such as cracking and warping which primitive man could not understand. It was only natural to place the responsibility for good or bad pottery on the supernatural and as a result many interesting rituals and customs were observed in its making. Ceramics have told us of man's daily life, death and burial, his migrations, trade and conquests. It has been an essential part of his very existence.

As to its discovery, it is rather easy to imagine how, as prehistoric man walked through the rain-soaked mud, he noticed his footprints and how these impressions became hardened by the wind and sun. The earth over which he had built a fire was even harder and had changed in color. Just when he intentionally used these discoveries for making pottery is unknown, but it is generally believed that it may have been invented in many parts of the world. It is not as easy as it sounds and to the experienced potter it is much more than squeezing a piece of clay into shape and firing it. It is a long, tedious process which must have developed very slowly.

Material. The basic material in ceramics is clay. Natural clays are found everywhere and are usually fine grained, more or less coherent and become soft and plastic when wet. In early times the quality and character of the ware was largely dependent on local soil. This is no longer true as clays are now shipped from all parts of the world and combined to give the ideal mix (body) for the particular type of ware desired. The advantages as well as the limitations of the various kinds and colors gave inspiration to the potters and distinct styles soon developed. The economic value of clay depends on either the presence or absence of impurities. Some of these are organic humus, fossils of plants, animals and shells, carbonate and sulphide of lime, sand or oxide of iron. For instance, when iron is found in the ferrous state the clay may be blueish, greenish or grey and when in the ferric state is red, brown or yellow. Corinth was noted for its beautiful white clay while Attica was equally famous for its rich red.

There are many types of clays each having particularly desirable features: For instance, ball clay, also known as bond, pipe, fat or plastic clays, useful because of its bonding power; brick or tile clay which usually contains sand which prevents too great shrink-age; fire clay which is refractory to heat. There are many good American clays of practically every wanted characteristic.

Classifications. Ceramics may be roughly divided into two classifications, pottery and porcelain. Each of these may be again divided into two types, hard and soft. The differences are attributed to a few minor ingredients, preparation and the degree of heat to which they have been subjected. The results are their relative hardness of surface and their power in resisting the action of fire. Other terms may be used such as vitreous or non-vitreous, translucent or opaque.

With possible exception, pure clays exist in theory only. The ingredients in a typical pottery body are silica 60, alumina 30, iron 7, lime 2, as compared to porcelain, silica 66, alumina 30, potash 3½ and a small amount of lime and magnesia. The materials and amounts are similar, but with the proper preparation and firing the results are quite different.

There are many types of clay products other than art wares. A few of them are building materials—brick, wall, insulation and sewer tile, etc.; refractories—furnace and stove linings, grates, etc.; general ware—table, cooking, refrigerator, etc.; sanitary ware—bathtubs, lavatories, fountains, etc.; electric insulators and countless others. There is a best material and procedure of handling each. They may be made of terra-cotta, earthenware, stoneware, yellow ware, white granite or ironstone, semi-porcelain or one of the several types of porcelain. There are other terms such as crockery, pottery and· china—many of them misleading. For instance, Webster says under "CHINA—porcelain ware, originally brought from the Far East, loosely crockery." Then under "CROCKERY—earthenware." To most potters these are entirely different types. The word pottery (L. *Potum,* drinking vessel; Fr. *Poterie*) refers to all objects made of clay including porcelain. For the sake of understanding each other we will use the word pottery in reference to **earthenwares** which are first, non-vitreous, porous, absorbent, opaque (unless extremely thin), glazed or unglazed and also to hard earthenwares which are vitreous such as stoneware (G. *Steingut,* Gr. *grés or* Chin. *boccaro*). On the other hand we will use the word porcelain only in reference to translucent, vitreous ware (which means glass-like), having a sharp glassy structure and angular fracture, **non-**absorbent and impermeable.

Porcelain. The word porcelain was from the Latin and was in use in Europe before the substance as we know it was even known. The Italians used the word *Porcellana* for the cowrie shell. Marco Polo, after his visit to China in 1280 used it to describe the strange substance he had seen there. It was used to describe not only the material of Chinese porcelain, but also other things which in contrast to ordinary pottery had a porcelain quality of being transparent.

Some of the many varieties of porcelain are hard, soft, natural, artificial, chemical, electric, high tension, phosphate and dull. The main ingredient is kaolin, which is made up of silica and alumina, formed by the decomposition of granite rock. It gets its name from the mountain in China, *Kao-Ling* near the pottery center of *Ching-Te-Cheng*. It was first made by the Chinese about 206 B.C. At high temperatures the non-fusible silicate of alumina unites with the fusible bisilicate felspar (*Chin. pe-tun-tse*), to form the main ingredients. Natural hard porcelain is of dazzling whiteness, so hard that steel will not scratch it, impermeable to liquids and unaffected by acids. **Artificial soft porcelain** (Fr. *pate tendre,* such as old Sevres) in which glass or frit is used as a flux is never so white or hard. **Bone china,** made from calcined bones, phosphate of lime, is somewhere between these two in hardness, impermeability and whiteness. **Electrical or high tension porcelain** is porcelain in name only. The first true porcelain was discovered and made in Europe in 1709 by John Frederick Böttger in Dresden.

Preparation of Clays. Primitive man found that by searching for the more pure primary clays along the river beds or in the crevices in caves, his pottery was better. He had only to remove the coarse stones and other rough foreign materials, add water and knead the clay until it was uniformly soft and pliable. It is still prepared in much the same way today for handmade pottery. This process is known as **wedging.** A vast improvement in pottery was made when man learned to wash the clays of levigation, settling or straining making a more smooth, compact piece.

The preparation of clays for mass production of pottery is not basically different. The usual procedure is to weigh the mined, washed, dried clays to the desired proportions. They are then ground and mixed with water in a **blunger,** which is a huge tank with revolving arms for disintegrating and mixing the clay with water. The clay is now about the consistency of cream and is called **slip.** The slip is then strained through silk lawns to remove impurities and if a white body is desired, large magnets are used to remove the metallic iron. It is now ready to be used for one process known as casting. If it is needed in a more firm plastic state the excess water may be driven off by heat in a **slip kiln.** Another method is to put the slip through a **filter press.** By this method the slip is pumped into the center of a series of flat circular canvas bags which catch the clay allowing the water to seep out. The press is then tightened to squeeze out additional water and the clay is removed in the form of large pancakes. Clay is usually stored to age in this state. By proper moisture control bacterial growth is encouraged to accelerate colloidal degeneration which makes the clay tough and more easily worked. After it has aged it is put through a **pug mill** which wedges the clay by grinding and mixing until it is a uniformly homogenous mass, ready for use.

Forming of Pottery. In the beginning man's tools were his hands and fingers, sticks and stones. His first crude pots were squeezed into shape or a ball of clay was rolled and the center scooped out. Some may have been pounded over a smooth round stone and allowed to harden enough so that it would hold its shape when removed. Tiles were also made in this way, the clay being pounded out on smooth flat stones to the desired thickness. Another method was to roll out strips of clay and then by placing one coil upon another, working them together with his fingers, a hollow pot was formed. This same method is still used today and is known as **building.**

The most important change came about in the development of the **potter's wheel.** At first it was probably a simple flat stone disc, turned by hand. It was later mounted on a vertical shaft. By placing a lump of soft clay on the disc and turning, the clay was allowed to pass between the palm and the fingers forming a hollow round pot. Pictures of this type wheel are seen in the paintings on the walls of Egyptian tombs.

By extending the shaft and adding another disc at the bottom it was possible for the potter to turn the wheel with his feet, leaving both hands free to form the pottery. By pressing against the soft lump of clay, as the wheel revolved, a smooth round ball was formed. Then by pushing the thumbs down into the center of the ball and pulling outward and upward against the hands the even-walled round pot was formed. Some of the more complicated Greek and Chinese shapes were obviously thrown in several pieces and joined together while still damp. This same method, known as **throwing**, is still in use today.

There are many variations of the foot powered wheel. They may be pedal driven or others have a large weighted wheel at the bottom of the shaft. By pressing the foot downward and kicking forward the heavy wheel will run for some time. They are known as **kick wheels.**

Sometime later the power was supplied by a helper and more recently they were motorized. The modern equivalent for mass production is the **jigger** or **jolly.** This machine makes it possible to turn out large quantities of pieces which are alike. The **jigger head** is a metal shaped bowl into which a plaster of paris mold is placed. This mold has an impression of one side and as deep as the thickness of the piece of ware to be made. One of the **jiggerman's helpers**, the **batter-out**, selects a piece of clay and flattens it in the shape of a thick pancake and slaps it onto the mold. The **jigger arm,** which is suspended over the mold, has a scraping tool cut in the profile of the opposite side of the piece to be made. This tool is pulled down until it comes in contact with the clay, the amount of which is allowed to pass between the revolving mold and the profile is the piece of ware. It is allowed to dry on the mold, which may be used again when the piece has been removed. The latest development is an automatic jigger, which mechanically turns out several thousand pieces a day.

Pottery may also be made in a **press.** The leather hard clay is pressed between oil-lubricated revolving steel dies. Inasmuch as the clay contains little water the piece may be handled as soon as it is formed. These methods have definite limitations, handles, spouts and ornaments must be added. More complicated shapes with these projections are more easily made in molds.

Plaster of paris is used to make **molds** for pottery because it has the quality of absorbing water from the clay. After the original piece has been modeled a **block mold** is made and a mold made of this is called the **case,** from which the working molds are made.

The older method was to press or **pug** the clay into the molds by hand, allowing it to harden before removing. If a complicated piece was to be made, it was necessary to make it in several pieces and stick them together while they were still damp. The newer method is known as **casting** or **moulding.** The clay is thinned to about the consistency of cream, called **slip,** and is poured into the mold. The plaster absorbs the water from the slip causing a hard shell of clay to form. The longer this slip is allowed to remain the thicker the wall of the piece becomes. The surplus slip is then poured out and after a short drying period the mold may be opened and the complete piece, including handles, ornaments, etc. may be removed. This method is used almost exclusively today for the reproduction of art wares.

After the forming by any method a certain amount of finishing must be done. Built pieces may be scraped, thrown pieces turned, or those made in molds may have the seams removed by cutting, scraping or sponging. All ware formed but unfired is called green.

Many of the methods are the same in the preparation and forming of porcelain, although it is not usual to shape it by hand. A combination of pressing, throwing and jiggering is common, but perhaps most porcelain is made by casting. Porcelain slip is sometimes called **pulp.**

Firing. Perhaps the most vital change in ceramics comes about in the firing. In early times and in some places even today, pottery and bricks were sun baked. When man first intentionally fired clay is not known. Perhaps quite by accident, clay-lined grass baskets may have burned, destroying all but the clay lining, which was now hard and permanent. At first a fire was built over and around the pieces, but this had its disadvantages in uneven firing, causing warping and smoke discoloration. The most simple type oven or **kiln** has not changed very much from the kind used by the Egyptians and Greeks and they are still in common use in the Far East. Mass production methods required greater capacity and evenness or control of fire and larger kilns were developed. These were all **periodic kilns,** requiring the stacking of the ware, firing and then a cooling period before the kiln could be emptied. There were variations in direction of fire, such as updraft or down-draft, etc. The **muffled kiln** allowed the fire to pass through flues, heating the interior through the inner walls. The newer types are **continuous, tunnel kilns.** The time wasted in heating and cooling of periodic kilns has been overcome by placing the ware on cars which enter one end of the tunnel, travel slowly toward the firing zone which is somewhere near the middle. This gives the ware a chance to heat gradually until it reaches its highest temperature and then pass on slowly cooling, until it emerges at the other end. The firing zone in this kiln is continuously hot.

The newest type is a **merry-go-round or circular kiln.** The principle is the same as the tunnel, except that the cars travel on a circular track. One section being open allows for loading or unloading without stopping or removing the cars. Whether the kilns are for biscuit, gloss or decorating determines the size and control of fire. Fuels which might be used are wood, coal, oil, gas or electricity. The firing time may vary from a few hours to several days. In early times temperature was probably judged by the length of time the fire was kept going. **Optical pyrometry** which is the using of an experienced eye as a judge to determine the temperature by the color of the flame or the color of the objects in the flame was used before the development of **pyrometric Seger cones.** These are small cones made of various types of clays, carefully controlled to melt at certain heats. They were placed in various parts of the kiln to be visible from the outside and arranged in groups to melt in sequence. They range from cone 022 (1094° Fahr.) to cone 36 (3362° Fahr.). Most modern kilns are equipped with pyrometers, but cones are still used as a check for variation of heats in different parts of the kilns.

Saggers are refractory clay boxes in which the ware is placed to protect it from the direct contact with the flame. They also facilitate the stacking and are made in many shapes and sizes to accommodate the ware and allow circulation of heat between the bungs. Strips of moist clay, **wads,** are laid on the rim of the saggers to make a bed for the superimposed saggers and seal any openings between them. Fine sand is used as a cushion in the bottom of biscuit saggers. **Glost saggers,** used for firing glazed ware, have vertical rows of triangular shaped holes punched part way through the inner side walls into which pottery pins are inserted. These pins support and separate the pieces to prevent them from sticking together while the glaze is being fired. Ware placed on the bottom of the sagger rests on **bitstone.** Ware which has been fired once is known as **bisque** or biscuit; when glaze is applied and fired it is known as **glost ware.**

Glazes. The study of glazes is one of the most fascinating and unlimited phases of ceramics. Although they are of infinite variety, all of them are actually layers of molten glass fused to the surface of clay by firing. This coating of glass seals the surfaces of porous clay, making it smooth, shiny, hard and water tight. Potters have always been jealous and secretive about their glaze formulas and many of them have been handed down from father to son through many generations. Each age has contributed some new development or use.

As with most other phases of ceramics, the origin of glazes is not known. Whether it originated in Egypt, Assyria or the East is hard to say. The oldest known fragment is one bearing the name, in violet glaze, of King Mena about 3,000 B.C. However, the complicated technique suggests a much earlier period of development. The finest and most complete use of glazes and colors came in Egypt in the 18th dynasty.

There are several distinct types of glazes, each being best suited to a particular body. Preferably, body and glaze should have a similar coefficient of expansion. The first and oldest type is the **alkaline glaze.** It is made by the fusing of quarts sand (silicic acid) with an alkali, potash or soda. It was used by the Egyptian, Persian and Syrian potters and its use was carried on for thousands of years in spite of its shortcomings. Its use spread very little because it will not adhere to ordinary potter's clay. It must be used on a body which has something in common with it, i.e., a clay which is made up largely of silicious sand. This particular type of clay is very difficult to work unless mixed with a more plastic clay. Not every district had both kinds and as a result its use was continued only in certain places, while unglazed ware was made generally. It is a clear transparent glaze and may be stained with oxides of metals.

The next and most important type is **lead glaze.** This plumberiferous glaze is made by the addition of oxide of lead and will adhere to almost every type body. For this reason it is most widely used. It is as transparent as glass and may also be stained with various oxides. By the addition of tin oxide a **tin glaze,** a stanniferous, opaque glaze is formed. It hides the clay with its opacity and made the use of white slips to cover colored bodies unnecessary. This opaque enamel completely changed the whole character of many types of pottery and new styles resulted. It was used on Assyrian and Babylonian pottery and they also used it on their monumental architectural, and sculptured tiles. It may also be stained with oxides of metals and its use spread all over Egypt. We see it on the Hispano-Moresque wares, Italian maiolicas, Persian tiles and the Dutch delft ware, etc. In France it is known as faience (fayence or fayance), serving as an enamel base for painted decoration. Rouen became the center of a thriving faience industry in 1644.

Feldspathic glaze is used on hard porcelains. (Felspath, feldspar, felspar), is an essential part of nearly all crystalline rock containing silica, alumina and potash. It fuses with the body making one hard mass.

Another type is salt glaze. It is used on stoneware. When the temperature has reached its highest peak in firing the clay, common salt is thrown into openings made especially for that purpose in the kiln. The salt vaporizes and the soda in it combines with the silica on the surface of the ware to form a covering of soda glass.

Decoration. Although there are limitless varieties of shapes and forms possible in ceramics, the potter almost from the beginning has taken delight in adding some sort of decoration to his wares. At first these decorations were merely impressions made by his fingers or scratches made with sticks. Sometimes the surface was carved or incised or modeled in relief. Another method as seen in the Byzantine pottery and also in the later stoneware was to make wooden stamps and press them into the surface of the ware. At times these impressions were filled with various colored clays. Ornaments of all types were pressed in separate molds and attached while the clay was still damp.

Colored clays were found in a wide range of shades from white to grey, buff, cream, yellow, red, brown to black. They all have a characteristic dull, earthy appearance which makes them blend beautifully together. These colored clays could be thinned down and painted on, one over the other to form striking patterns. Another method of application was to squeeze the slip through the fingers and work the details after it was applied (barbotine). Some of the earliest Chinese pottery, about 3,000 B.C., was painted in red, black, purple and white clays over a buff or red body. This use of colored slips or engobe (Fr.), may be seen in a great deal of pottery today, having been applied by brush, spraying or dipping.

By combining the use of engobe with the earlier method of incising, a new style was developed known as sgraffito (It.). The red body was covered with a coating of white slip and the decoration was then cut or scratched away, allowing the red body to show through. The ware was then fired and left either in the bisque or was covered with a transparent clear or colored lead glaze. The best sgraffito was probably made in Bologna, Italy. One type of glazed sgraffito ware is known as mezza-maiolica, or half maiolica. The already fired red earthenware was dipped in white slip and the decoration was then scratched away. An easily fused metallic stain was daubed on, covered with lead glaze and then refired. These methods are still used today for fine decorative wares. The former Cowan Pottery in Cleveland, Ohio used a similar method and it was known as dry-point.

Colors. Because colors used in making pottery must stand relatively high temperatures in firing, oxides of metals are used. Some of the primitive tribes used stains made from boiled bark and plants to color their pottery. The acid in unripe cocoanut husk formed a black color when strips of the husk were placed over the pots but not fired. Various types of fuels for firing also gave black coatings which have been widely used. None of these methods of coloring are so permanent as metals. Native earths containing cobalt, iron, manganese and copper were found and used.

The height to which this simple process of painting metallic oxides directly on clay advanced is best seen in the Greek vases. These pieces were formed, given a light fire and then polished until very smooth. The black figures, probably iron oxide and manganese, were painted on the small details were scratched out and then refired, giving the surface a beautiful dull sheen. The red figures on a black background were done in the same way, except the background was painted, leaving the red of the body show through.

On a light colored body or on a light slip, copper gives blue, but combined with a little iron, green. Cobalt, gives blue; with manganese, violet; titanium, yellow; iron, brown. When used as underglaze colors these oxides are applied directly to the bisque, and are glazed and refired. The big advantage in using underglaze colors is that they are more resistant to wear because they are protected by the glaze. The high fire necessary to fuse some glazes limits the range to fewer colors and darker shades. These colors may be brushed, sprayed or applied by print.

Underglaze prints are made from copper plates, the process is similar to that used in making etchings. They are also made from steel engravings or lithographic stones. They are printed with underglaze color on thin tissue. The print is placed face downward and rubbed until the color adheres to the ware. It is usually necessary to harden on (light fire to burn out the oils used as a medium, to prevent glaze from crawling, pitting or bubbling) a color before the glaze is applied over the print and then refired. Here again the range of colors is limited. Aside from art wares it is widely used for hotel and other commercial ware.

Colors play an important part in glazes. To the layman who is not interested in glaze structure, color is the all important thing. We think of the Egyptians for their rich blues and green glazes, the Persians for their deep blues, the glorious rich blood reds (sang-de-boeuf) of the Hiang-hsi period, or the misty blue and green celadons, the delicate peach-bloom and plum colors of the Chinese, or the dark brown of English Rockingham. We think of Della Robbia for his thick white, blue and yellow enamels. Many of these colors have been made from the same oxides of metals; the clay, application, type of glaze and conditions in firing account for the differences.

Most wares are glazed all over, inside and out, but this is not always necessary. The Chinese as well as others, very often glazed only parts of their pieces, getting a striking contrast between the high shine of the glaze and the dull rough appearance of the bisque clay. This method is often used in American and other modern ceramic sculpture and pottery. It is also possible to apply glazes in patterns; this was popular with the Viennese.

Another interesting use of color and glaze to form decoration is found in the *Chinese crackle*. At first the method was the relatively unreliable one of plunging the hot piece of pottery into cold water causing the glaze to craze. These crazed marks were often accented by rubbing color into them. If metallic colors were used they could be refired and by allowing normal cooling the surface would be tight, leaving the pattern of the old craze underneath. Later, by the addition of a certain kind of stone (probably pegmatite) which was mixed with the glaze there resulted a disturbance of the relationship of body and glaze and a crackle was assured. The size and location of the crackles were controlled by the number of layers of this glaze used.

The interesting feathering of glazes and the crystalline formations, although at first accidental, were later controlled to produce another series of stunning effects.

When tin enamels were developed a distinct decorative style known as **maiolica** (majolica) was produced. It gets its name from Majorca, the largest of the Balearic Islands with which Italy carried on commerce as early as the 12th cent. Actually it was used to describe the wares imported from Spain in Majorcan trading ships. In Seville and Toledo, enameled tiles were produced, some were cut to form geometric patterns and others had the tin enamel separated to form the design. The enamel was kept apart by painting the spaces between with manganese and greasy medium (de cuerda seca). Tiles were later made with raised dividing lines molded in (de cuenca).

The Italian maiolicas are of earthenware bodies covered with an opaque tin enamel which served as a base for painting. The oxide colors mix somewhat with the glaze during firing, causing the pattern to be not under the glaze or over the glaze but actually in the glaze. In order to make this effect even more prominent a thin transparent glaze was often sprayed over the top and refired to thoroughly cover it.

As we have already seen, the high temperature necessary to develop most glazes limited the range of color. It was later found that these colors could be put on top of the body—overglaze. After the application of overglaze color the ware is again fired, but at a point much lower than it took to melt the glazes originally, but enough to open the surface so that the fluxed colors can attach themselves. These colors are less stable because they do not have the glaze as a protective covering.

One of the first types, probably discovered in the East, but famous on the Hispano-Moresque ware was the **lustre**. These differ from other metallic pigments in that they have an iridescent, reflecting surface. They are made from compounds of sulphur and copper, silver and iron. They may be applied by brush to the surface of fired opaque or transparent glaze and refired in a muffled kiln and become fixed to the surface. Lustres were used throughout Europe, especially by the Italians and the English. Imports to this country were in demand during the 18th and 19th cents. Some is still being made, although the use of gold and platinum has become much more popular. Golds are of two types, coin and bright. Coin gold is made by carefully grinding pure gold, quicksilver and flux. When fired and burnished with sand it has a dull, rich sheen. Bright gold is brilliant when fired without burnishing. Gold is also used for many overglaze colors such as reds and pinks as well as the base for fine ox blood glazes. Golds are applied in liquid form, the banding and ornamentation of handles is done with a brush by gilders and liners. It may also be applied with a rubber stamp for small filigree or intricate patterns.

Overglaze colors are brilliant, bright and limitless, but they are never so rich because they appear more thin and on the surface. Bands and lines are applied by brush while the piece is revolving on a liner's wheel. The air brush is also widely used for covering larger areas, masks made of rubber or metal being used to control the color areas.

Although at one time there was a great craze for hand painted china there is very little made today. It is a slow and expensive process and in order to make ware with the intricate floral patterns at popular prices a process known as decalcomania was developed. By the use of lithographic stones the patterns are printed on a special paper. The decal is applied face downward on the piece of fired glazed ware, which has been sized with varnish. A stiff brush is used to rub the color onto the size and the paper is then washed off. During the firing the varnish and oils used in printing are burned away and the colors are fused into the surface of the glaze. New methods of decal printing have recently been developed which give a greater smoothness and a more faithful reproduction of the artist's original drawing.

Ceramic Sculpture. The making of sculpture in fire clay has followed closely the developments in the making of pottery. The methods are much the same, so far as the preparation of clays and glazes. The method of forming depends a great deal upon the type of clay used and the size of the piece to be modeled.

For the making of unique pieces it is possible to model directly in fire clay. It is necessary to use a good plastic clay and knead it with the hands until it is of an even, firm consistency. There are several methods of modeling and they differ from regular sculpture in that no armature is used. Due to the fact that considerable shrinkage takes place in both drying and firing, the armature would prevent this action causing the piece to crack or break apart. It is advisable to

have a hollow, even-walled piece to prevent uneven shrinkage. These handicaps are overcome by modeling in the following ways.

The most simple method is to build the piece of sculpture solid and hollow it out later. It is best to build up with small enough pieces of clay to insure all air being squeezed out, so that no air pockets remain within the mass. During firing these would expand and cause the piece to explode or crack. The piece must be kept damp to assure adhesion of the added clay and again prevent uneven shrinkage. After the sculpture is completed, with perhaps the exception of the fine detail, it should be allowed to stand and harden only enough so that it can be handled without distorting the forms. If it is a broad based piece it may be hollowed out through the bottom. If it is rather complicated it may be necessary to cut it apart, hollow out each section and then reassemble them. These joints must be thoroughly worked together and the surface remodeled.

Ceramic sculpture may also be modeled by the coil method, the same as that used in building hollow pottery. It is imperative that the piece be thoroughly conceived, because it is modeled complete from the base up, the clay being allowed to harden enough to support the succeeding layers. A hole must be left somewhere in the piece to allow the air to escape during firing. It is possible to build clay supports on the outside of the piece to prevent the damp clay from sagging. This clay will shrink with the piece and may be removed after the piece is dry or has been fired.

Some decorative sculpture may be thrown on the wheel. In this case sections are thrown and then put together while still damp. Additional modeling of the surface forms may be done after it is assembled.

For larger architectural sculpture a rough terra-cotta clay may be used. The grog (fired clay which has been ground) which is added to fresh unfired clay gives an interesting coarse texture and reduces shrinkage and eliminates much of the strain and decreases the possibility of cracking.

It is of course possible to model with regular modeling clay with an armature and then make a plaster mold to form the final piece. Fire clay may be pugged or pressed into the mold, the piece being removed when it is hard enough to prevent distortion in handling. If the sculpture is complicated it may be made in several parts and then joined while they are still damp. Additional small detail may be added to the surface.

The method most widely used for reproduction of sculpture in quantities, is casting. In this case slip is used, being poured into the mold and allowed to remain until the desired thickness of wall is formed. The surplus slip is removed and after the piece is hard enough to handle it may be removed from the mold. Because of the difficulty in handling porcelain clay this method is used almost exclusively.

A great deal of ceramic sculpture is left in the bisque, especially when the clay used is interesting in color or texture. Additional interest may be given the bisque by the use of colored slips or stains. Sometimes partial areas are glazed and the contrast of the dull bisque and shiny glaze is very effective. The complete range of glazes used on pottery, from the thin transparent lead or salt to the heavy opaque tin enamels, mat or shiny may be used. If the heavy glazes are used it is necessary to overmodel the detail so that it will not be lost.

The firing of ceramic sculpture is the same as pottery, although, due to the uneven forms a longer drying and heating period is recommended.

Ceramics, although still a craft, has grown to a great industry. Most potters are born into the trade and the knowledge and understanding has been handed down from generation to generation. There is something about it that seems to fascinate and hold you to it; it may be the soft plastic feel or the smell of moist clay, or perhaps the glowing highlights of brilliant colored glazes or the dull earthy tones of bisque. As an industry it is often considered to be the most backward, perhaps because it is so old. Even with mechanical equipment in modern plants a piece of pottery may pass through as many as forty potters' hands. To the studio potter it is a constant challenge, full of disappointments and pleasant surprises.

America need no longer consider its commercial ceramics inferior to any produced in the world and in the field of art, pottery and ceramic sculpture is gaining world wide recognition. See *Pottery and Porcelain, Vol. 1,* Emil Hannover, 1925; *Pottery and Porcelain, Vol. 2,* Emil Hannover, 1925; *The Ceramic Art,* J. J. Young, 1878; *Chinese Ceramic Glazes,* A. L. Hetherington, 1937; *Ceramic Dictionary,* C. Merts Franzheim, 1924.   —V.S.

CERAMICS II: history of pottery and porcelain. The word ceramics, as a general term, is internationally used to define the study of the potter's art. The term pottery, then, broadly covers the entire field of clay products from bricks to porcelain or ceramic sculpture that takes its place with the fine arts.

The story of pottery goes back to the farthest reaches of prehistoric times, to a date unknown. Perhaps between the years of 10,000 to 2,000 B.C. Neolithic man was the pioneer potter of the world. From a study of primitive vessels made in many countries, it is apparent that in the very dawn of civilization the first objects of clay were constructed to contain food and drink. We know that at 6500 B.C. or even earlier the Sumerians in their stoneless valleys of the Euphrates used sun-baked clay for building bricks, for pots, for pottery images that were perhaps the most remote ancestors of the ceramic sculpture of today; and for clay tablets upon which they wrote.

Egyptian Pottery. The story of Egyptian pottery goes back to prehistoric, sun-baked bricks made from Nile mud by enslaved Hebrews who were taken captive in war, and forced to build the fortresses of Rameses; while at the same period in Assyria and Babylon primitive pottery was being made. But altho the potter and his art are frequently mentioned in the Scriptures, very few specimens of Hebrew pottery have been discovered, and the Mosaic law forbids the making of "graven images".

EARLY EGYPT AND THE OLD KINGDOM, 4500-2475 B.C. Bottles and vases of clay, contemporary with the Pyramids, were made with the potter's wheel (invented when or where we know not), as well as with other tools such as the lathe and moulds for stamping, and glazing was understood and practised. MIDDLE KINGDOM AND EMPIRE, 2160-1090 B.C. This period of wealth and magnificence included the craftsman's development of the brilliant blue glaze used for tiles and bowls, and skilfully baked in ovens constructed long before any devices for the regulation of the heat had been invented.

The art of Egypt, it must be remembered, including its pottery, was designed for use as well as for beauty; it served in the tombs as a protection for the souls of the dead; and it was employed by the Pharaohs to dazzle the common folk and to bolster their own power and importance.

Greek Pottery. The most remarkable craft of all antiquity was the Greek pottery, the development of which has now been traced from the Neolithic age, with Neolithic finds at Cnossus on the Island of Crete as ancient as any that have ever been unearthed. But in the early or archaic period, Greek pottery was derived from the Egyptian, whose wares were brought to Greece by Phoenician merchants.

Despite the Egyptians' earlier knowledge of it, invention of the potter's wheel was claimed both by the city of Marathon and by one Talos, the pupil of Daedalus, who, say the ancient records, "being cleverer than his master, invented the potter's wheel."

GREEK VASES AND VASE PAINTING, 2500-400 B.C. The story of Greek pottery is primarily the story of the unsurpassed Athenian vase. Marryatt tells us that a part of Athens was called *"Keramicus"*, from being inhabited by potters, and that their masterpieces were not only publicly exhibited, but were often filled with oil from the sacred olive tree in the Acropolis, and given as prizes to the victors in the Olympian games.

The vases of the early archaic period, from 2500 to 600 B.C. reveal animal and plant designs; the **black figured vases**, with designs illustrating legendary and mythological themes, date from about 600 to 500 B.C. while "the perfection of vase painting was between 480 and 450 B.C.", when the **red-figured vases** were produced. After the fall of Athens in 404 B.C. came the decadence.

Roman-Arretine Pottery, 2000 B.C.-5000 A.D. Following the decline of Greek pottery, a new kind of pottery was made at Arezzo, with these **Arretine vases,** as they were called, resembling the later Greek works on a smaller scale, and afterwards produced thruout the Roman world. The resemblance to Greek vases is explained by the fact that in the Punic Wars many Greek potters were taken prisoner, and, as a reward for their skills, were freed and honored by the Romans. Excavations in Britain have brought to light many examples of the best types of Roman pottery. About 100 B.C. stamps with the potter's name first appeared, usually with the name of the slave (who had probably made the vase) found beside that of his master.

Etruscan or Greco-Roman Pottery. Approximately from 1100 B.C. to the 3rd cent. B.C. pottery in imitation of the Greek products was developed in Etruria, Sicily, which also imported quantities of vases directly from Greece. Formerly called Etruscan, this ware is now called Greco-Roman, as it consisted

for the most part of red and black vases made by Romans after the Greek pattern.

Persian Pottery. From 641 A.D. **Rhages** pottery, made in Rhages, a city that had risen to importance prior to its destruction in the 13th cent., was remarkable for its iridescent blue and green glazes. These glazes were also used in Syria and thruout the Byzantine Empire and were the forerunners of all the glazed pottery of Europe that was to follow.

The great Persian period was from the 10th to the 16th cent. From the 13th cent., these unexcelled artist-potters produced "Persian porcelain"—translucent, entirely different in quality from the Chinese porcelain—and lustre ware vases and plates, at once superb in form and design, and glowing in rich color. Their decorative tiles were used in Moslem mosques and other buildings. The earliest dated specimen of Persian lustre is of the year 1216 A.D., and after the 16th cent. Persian products deteriorated.

Hispano-Moresque Pottery. From the 8th to the 17th cent., lustreware, undoubtedly derived from Persia, was first brought by Saracen invaders into Spain. The Moors, whose conquests covered Spain, Sicily and North Africa, introduced glazed tiles into Spain about 711 A.D. and the term Hispano-Moresque means "Moorish influence upon the art of Spain." Famous examples of their work, with its metallic iridescence, are to be found in the Alhambra. In the East, tin had been as costly as gold; but it was in Spain, where tin was found in abundance, that the distinctive tin-enameled Hispano-Moresque wares with their extraordinary beauty of lustre were produced. This ware was made at Malaga, in the Moorish kingdom of Granada; at Valencia; and on the island of Majorca.

Chinese Pottery and Porcelain. "The Chinese were the greatest race of potters the world has ever seen." The name "chinaware" comes originally from porcelain made in China, which so surpassed all other types of pottery that the term has been used to denote any and all other types of porcelain wares.

Dr. Johnson's definition of porcelain, given in his dictionary of 1818, and apparently omitted thereafter from all subsequent dictionaries, is interesting because it gives factual evidence that certain superstitions anent the Chinese porcelains were firmly believed. "Porcelain," he wrote, "—*Porcelaine*—French—said to be derived from *pom cent années;* because it was believed by Europeans that the materials of porcelain were matured under ground one hundred years."

In their skillful guarding of the secret of porcelain making, the Chinese were wont to spin "tall tales"; and even Bacon wrote: "Porcelain is a kind of plaster buried in the earth and by length of time congealed and glazed into that fine substance." Another fable is that "porcelain was made of egg-shells and sea-shells, beaten small and buried in the earth for a hundred years."

The most recent excavations in the province of Honan have proved beyond doubt that pre-dynastic pottery must have been made as early as 3000 B.C. This pottery, not unlike Neolithic pots found in other parts of the world, consisted for the most part of funerary vessels and articles for everyday use.

PORCELAIN. Altho certain early records state that porcelain was invented at Siu-ping at about 185 B.C., the exact date of the first making of porcelain in China is actually unknown.

Han Dynasty, 206 B.C.-220 A.D. The pottery of the Han dynasty, mostly found in tombs, was primitive—part of it unglazed, with stamped or incised decoration. Much of it was glazed, however, and it is believed that glaze was used for the first time during this period: possibly a lead glass brought from the Roman Empire, with which China is known to have been in touch during the Han dynasty.

T'ang Dynasty, 618-906 A.D. Recent excavations due to the building of railways in China by European engineering companies have added to our knowledge of the pottery of this great period of China's expansion and power. Again it is objects found in tombs that show us the progress that had been made since the Han dynasty. There are innumerable figurines, with vases and bowls of "porcellaneous stoneware" or a semi-porcelain in many instances revealing unmistakable Greek and Persian influences. And the first appearance of the pale green, known as celadon, has led to the belief that real porcelain was made for the first time in China during this dynasty.

Sung Dynasty, 960-1279 A.D. This era corresponded to the Middle Ages of Europe. The best of the Sung porcelains, now exceedingly rare, and declared to be stoneware rather than "true porcelain", were made in the province of Honan, and also discovered there thru comparatively recent excavations. It was during this dynasty that the pottery of China became known outside of its boundaries and it is recorded that about 1171

A.D. "Saladin sent a present of forty pieces to the Sultan of Damascus". This was followed by the beginning of China's export trade.

Ming Dynasty, 1368-1644 A.D. The Golden Age of ceramic art in China. During this period porcelain was decorated with colors fired over the glaze for the first time and the use of as many as five colors on one piece was first achieved by these amazing artist craftsmen.

The city of Ching-Te-Chen was famous for its imperial porcelain factory established about 1506 A.D. by Hung Wu, founder of this dynasty. Here was made for the first time the celebrated white porcelain, called by the French *blanc de Chine,* and considered "the outstanding contribution of the Chinese to ceramic art"; and from this town and district thereafter came the finest ceramic products of China. The use of this white china was reserved by the Chinese for religious ritual and, as tableware, for mourning periods in their own homes.

From this era have come the unsurpassed cobalt blues, the gorgeous oxblood reds *sang de boeuf,* the green *famille verte,* the extraordinary "eggshell" fabrique and the perforated or openwork wares of many kinds, including the so-called "grain of rice" porcelain— all fired in the highest kiln temperatures ever known.

K'ang-Hsi Dynasty, 1661-1722. This is also an important ceramic period, "from a decorative point of view the best period in Chinese history", with glazes begun in the Ming dynasty perfected; the introduction of designs etched and embossed, the imitation of jade and marble and metals in unusual glazes. From this dynasty came the blue and white porcelain familiarly known as "Old Nankin". But altho the Ching-Te-Chin factory was *near* Nanking, the city of Nanking itself boasted no potteries. So the name "Nankin" probably came from the *port* from which this blue ware was shipped to Europe; and it is a fact that "from 3000 to 8000 pounds have been paid for black ground Chinese porcelain of the K'ang-Hsi dynasty—the Chinese wares commanding high prices owing to difficulties of importation." Even as in Athens for the Olympic games, porcelain vases were presented as prizes and rewards for valiant deeds, and the best artists were highly honored.

During the Ming dynasty, the demand for Chinese porcelain had arisen in Europe—the first exports carried by Portuguese ships, the later ones by Dutch ships—leading to the tremendous efforts on the part of potters thruout the various European countries to reproduce this mysterious and beautiful fabrique: one of China's major contributions to world civilization.

European Porcelains. ITALY claims the first production of porcelain in Europe. From the fall of the Roman Empire, pottery making seems to have become almost a lost art until the 12th and 13th cents. when, after the conquest of Majorca by the Pisans in 1115 A.D. and the capture of many Moorish potters, work strongly influenced by the Hispano-Moresque wares was produced. It was 1420, however, before the first enamelled faience appeared with its tin glazes characteristic of Italian majolica. The word *majolica* is said to derive from the island of Majorca, originally called "Majorica" while *faience* is a French adaptation from the name of the town Faenza, the center for this particular craft. The superb 15th cent. majolica, produced at Faenza, the famous blue and yellow ware, is especially prized by collectors But after the advent of "true porcelain", with its superior fabrique, the production of majolica began to decline.

The sgraffito (Italian) process, a method of decorating by incised lines thru the slip coating to the red clay beneath, came out of medieval Italy, where, according to Picolpasso's ancient volume, *The Three Books of the Potter's Art*, the kiln at Castel Durante was closed with special ritual. "For," said he, "before fire is brought, care must be taken to observe the state of the moon. If the firing happens to take place at the waning of the moon, the fire lacks brightness in the same manner as the moon its brilliance."

LUCCA DELLA ROBBIA. Born in 1400, Lucca della Robbia of Florence, a pupil of Ghiberti. became perhaps the most distinguished forerunner of the ceramic sculptors who were to come afterwards. For with many orders to fill, and with the Dukes of Tuscany among his patrons, he turned to the more rapidly produced terra cotta figures, and evolved the beautiful white tin-enamel and other polychrome glazes that have long been associated with his bas-reliefs and sculptured Madonnas.

Venice claimed to be first in the production of porcelain—not only in Italy, but in Europe; but it is in Florence, under the patronage of the Medici, that at about 1580 the first "porcelain in imitation of china" was produced.

CAPO DI MONTE. This famous ware was made in a pottery established near Naples in 1736 by Charles the Third, whose consort, Queen Amelia of Saxony, is said to have brought the secret of porcelain making from Meissen; she was an enthusiastic patron of the Capo di Monte potters. And the King, it is recorded, amused himself by working in clay.

FRANCE. The enamelled wares of Italy passed into France about 1553, when the marriage of Catherine de Medici to Henry II took place, and Italian potters followed in her wake. There were potteries at Beauvais, Rouen and elsewhere; but it was at Saintes that Palissey, greatest of early French potters, evolved his fine enamel. After desperate struggles, he achieved success and the patronage of the King, which, however, did not prevent his dying in prison during the religious persecutions.

In 1696 porcelain of good quality was made at St. Cloud, "the invention protected by royal patent"; but later research now gives credence to the claim of Rouen's pottery manufactory that in 1673 the *first* porcelain of France was made there.

SEVRES. Stemming from the manufacture of porcelain at Vincennes, in 1756 the celebrated porcelain works at Sevres was built upon land owned by the Marquise de Pompadour, who was interested commercially in this project, and became the "Royal Porcelain Works" when Louis XV purchased the buildings and equipment four years later. Marie Antoinette brought knowledge of the Vienna potteries (supported by the Austrian court) to France when she arrived as a bride, and she gave many orders to the Sevres factory during her reign. The story goes that the kaolin needed for the manufacture of porcelain was accidentally discovered by a peasant woman near Limoges, who tried to use the white earth of the region as soap.

Famous colors of the Sevres fabrique are the yellow *jaune de jonquil* (the oldest one); the blues, *bleu de roi,* and the darker *gros bleu,* and the *rose Pompadour,* the latter often incorrectly referred to as *rose du Barry.*

Production at Sevres was abruptly interrupted by the French Revolution, but was resumed as a national project under Napoleon, who, "for the glory of France" decreed that this important industry should continue as a national factory.

The first exhibit of art treasures "free to the public" ever held anywhere in the world was opened at the Louvre after the Revolution, and consisted of loot stolen from the various palaces by the victorious Republicans. As large quantities of Sevres ware belonging to the court had been demolished or stolen, there was much demand under Napoleon for chinaware to replace the services that had been plundered. Thus began the era of monumental vases commemorating the victories of Napoleon, and the classical Empire designs.

Specialties of Sevres were the famous **biscuit groups**—portrait busts and figures, the work of Clodion, Pigalle and other noted sculptors; and the *pâte sur pâte* process—(successive layers of white and colored slip applied to a dark ground—an impasto decoration): The latter achieved by Louis Marc Solon from about 1762 and carried on under Taxile Doat, noted decorator and ceramist, from 1879 to 1905. Between 1880 and 1882, the great sculptor, Rodin, then a youth, was employed by Sevres.

Latest word, at this writing, of the world famous National Porcelain Manufactory at Sevres is the tragic report that it was bombed and wrecked in an R.A.F. raid in March, 1942. "According to a news dispatch, the pottery, in the district of Sevres, was close to a rifle bullet loading factory."

LIMOGES. The Limoges porcelain works was established in 1773, and afterwards annexed as a branch of the Sevres manufactory and discontinued in 1788: The modern Limoges (until World War II) a sort of French Staffordshire, with a number of porcelain factories that make the well-known Limoges tableware.

HAVILAND china was named for David Haviland of New York, an American who in 1840 established a pottery at Limoges (also producing prior to World War I).

GERMANY: MEISSEN. The first "true porcelain" made in Europe was produced at Meissen by John Böttger, a chemist accused of alchemy, who had fled from Berlin, and who, under the patronage of Augustus the Strong, King-Elector of Saxony—dubbed "King of China Maniacs"—founded the world renowned factory in 1709. This ware was called **Dresden porcelain**, as the Saxon court was nearby in Dresden. It is said that Böttger's factory was like a fortress, with his porcelain making secrets jealously guarded. In 1745, during the Seven Years' War, the Prussians under Frederick the Great attacked Dresden, looted the factory of its moulds and equipment and seized many of the workmen. This brought to a close the most distinguished period of Meissen production, for after this the Sevres porcelain factory became the most famous

in Europe. Thus the later Meissen ware has consisted largely of pieces that were imitations of the French products that were in such demand.

VIENNA. The Vienna factory was founded in 1720 by a runaway foreman of the Meissen works. In 1744 the factory was bought by the Empress Maria Theresa, and, first stimulated by her patronage, the production of wares of the Meissen type that were notable for their brilliant colors and technical excellence continued until the close of the factory in 1864. The pre-World War II *Wiener Keramik,* in collaboration with the *Wiener Werkstätte* in 1907 had become well-known for its contribution to modern industrial ceramic art and for its ceramic sculpture.

DELFT. Dutch factories were in production in 1650, six years after the close of the Ming dynasty in China. At one time Holland "was the only European power to whom the Japanese allowed an entrance into their ports" —resulting in Japanese and Chinese imports that could be copied: hence the Oriental character of this well-known blue and white ware —(also in continuous production prior to World War II).

DENMARK: COPENHAGEN. In 1772 Meissen potters began the production of porcelain in Copenhagen, where, in 1779, the factory became the Royal Porcelain Works under the patronage of King Christian VII and has continued to the present day (prior to the Nazi occupation). The modern factory of Bing and Gröndahl, established in Copenhagen in 1853, has combined superlative craftsmanship with original and outstanding work, executing the brilliant sculptures of Paul Gauguin, Kai Nielsen and others—and, in consequence, attracting wide attention in international expositions.

ENGLAND. Chinese porcelain had been imported to England as early as 1506, and gifts to Queen Elizabeth of "white and green porselyn" are recorded in 1587. In 1671 John Dwight of Fulham produced a "porcellaneous stoneware" which he called porcelain and which was somewhat similar to the Meissen products. In 1755 Richard Chaffers of Liverpool discovered "soap-rock" in Cornwall, and achieved a fabrique resembling the eagerly-sought Chinese ware. His first successful piece, it is told, was presented as a gift to his famous rival, Josiah Wedgwood.

Porcelain factories, with their products unmistakably related to those of France, were being established at Chelsea (where figures were derived from Boucher's paintings) and at Bow (known as "New Canton") in 1744; at Derby and at Worcester in 1751; while in the same year, "The case of the Undertaker of the Chelsea Porcelain protested imports from Dresden that were so detrimental to English manufacture".

It was 1768, however, before "hard porcelain" from native materials was first made in England by William Cookworthy, a Plymouth chemist, who also used the clay or "soap-rock" obtained from Cornwall. This factory, the forerunner of the celebrated potteries that came after, removed to Bristol in 1770, where it was carried on by Richard Champion until 1781, and afterwards absorbed by a group of Staffordshire potters.

With due respect to William Cookworthy, in the dispute as to who should be first, Thomas Frye of the Bow Manufactory contrived to have himself commemorated on his epitaph as "The Inventor and First Manufacturer of Porcelain in England"!

JOSIAH WEDGWOOD (1730-95) of Staffordshire was not only the greatest potter England has produced, but one of the greatest of all time. Born in 1730, the descendant of a century of pottery makers, he established his workshop at Burslem in 1759, when Queen Charlotte became his patron. Here, according to his epitaph, "Wedgwood converted a rude, inconsiderable manufactory into an elegant art and an important part of national commerce"; and his early experiments led to the beautiful jasper ware—stoneware with white classic designs in relief upon a blue ground: His masterpiece in this ware generally conceded to be his reproduction of the great *Barberini* or *Portland Vase,* the original of which was obtained from the Duchess of Portland's collection. (Two numbered copies are in the British Museum and Victoria and Albert Museum in London.) In fact, it was his love of classical designs that led him to name his pottery for *"Etruria";* and it is known that he imported Italian designers and sculptors to make copies of bas-reliefs in Rome.

It was after he had executed his famous service of 1300 pieces for Empress Catherine of Russia, which was exhibited in London in April, 1774 prior to its shipment, that Wedgwood became the most renowned potter in Europe. So influential was he that, exasperated by slow transportation for his mounting volume of orders, he was instrumental in obtaining better roads, and, of even more value, the development of canals thruout England.

So far as is known, a number of the original moulds are still in use in the Wedgwood Pottery in Stoke-on-Trent, England. For it will be remembered that "the Potteries" in the district of the "Five Towns" (including Burslem) were united in 1910 to form the city of Stoke-on-Trent.

Other notable figures in the story of English pottery include Josiah Spode, who began work in 1756 and Dr. Wall, who founded one of the most important of the English factories at Worcester.

LOWESTOFT. The Lowestoft factory, begun in 1756, produced ware the oriental designs of which stemmed from Chinese imports brought to Britain by Dutch traders. It is also known that a considerable quantity of so-called "Lowestoft" consisted of pieces made in China and afterwards decorated in England. The genuine Lowestoft did not possess the hard fabrique of the Chinese.

RUSSIA. The porcelain works established in 1744 under imperial patronage at St. Petersburg, now Leningrad, continues today as the State Porcelain Works. The following, direct from Soviet Russia, is interesting in its bearing upon the postwar future: "True Soviet art has been based on a highly developed industrial technique. This new movement in art known as 'constructivism' reflects the ideology and outlook of the technical workers and keeps production and industry constantly in view. Some of the artists identified with this trend, who are also productive workers in the pottery, glass and textile industries, have created beautiful examples of the applied arts, as, for instance, the wares of the State Porcelain Works at Leningrad. These artists will play an important part in remoulding living conditions among the masses and in creating characteristic Soviet styles not only in pottery and chinaware, but in other articles of daily use. Underlying all these efforts is the principle of every revolutionary artist—'Art for the toilers!'"

American Ceramics: The U.S.A. That the Americas also have an interesting pre-historic past, with aboriginal pottery of unknown date found in various sections of both North and South America is a fact vouched for by innumerable collections in museums of art and archaeology. Of special interest are the mound-builders' pots and the striking Indian pottery, the latter being reproduced today by the same primitive methods in pueblos of the Southwest.

It is known that as far back as 1612 "tylemakers" were at work in Virginia, where pottery of various crude types was made; and that in 1685 the first white ware manufactured in the Colonies was produced at Burlington, New Jersey — this ware referred to in records of the Bodleian Library at Oxford as "white and chiney ware", made in a pottery "with all necessary implements and diverse workmen", financed by one Dr. Daniel Coxe of London.

In 1735 John Remmey, a German, built a stoneware factory in New York, which was carried on by his descendants until 1895; and by 1750 over a hundred potteries of German origin were functioning in Pennsylvania. The earliest dated example of the Pennsylvania German slip decorated ware, popularly known as "Pennsylvania Dutch", is a carved white dish of the year 1762.

Back in 1745 we hear of William Cookworthy, England's first maker of porcelain "from native materials", importing the much-sought necessary kaolin, which he describes as "china earth", from Virginia, where several potteries were being carried on.

The Jugtown Pottery, still in existence in North Carolina, is said to date from 1750, when its first potter arrived from Staffordshire. In 1765 and 1766 certain "china clays", discovered by Indians in the Great Smokies, and dubbed by them *Unakah* (meaning "white") were shipped from South Carolina to the Worcester and Bristol china works in England. And it was an unsuccessful South Carolina pottery which, operated by a Staffordshire potter named Bartlem in 1766, caused Josiah Wedgwood undue alarm. For, wrote the famous English potter, who incidentally was himself importing "china earth" from the Carolinas and from Florida: "This trade to our Colonies we are apprehensive of losing in a few years, as they have set on foot some Pottworks there already, and have at this time an agent amongst us hiring a number of our hands for establishing new Pottworks in South Carolina."

It was actually 1769, however, before the manufacture of fine white china was undertaken in the U.S.A. The announcement as given out by Gousse Bonnin, who had been trained at Bow, England, quaintly stated: "Notwithstanding the various difficulties and disadvantages which usually attend the introduction of any important manufacture into a new country, the proprietors of the china works now erecting in Southwark have the pleasure to acquaint the public, they have proved to a certainty that the clays of America are productive of as good Porcelain

as any heretofore manufactured at the famous factory in Bow, near London." It is recorded in the History of Independence Hall that in 1771 this factory petitioned the Assembly for financial assistance. "For," said the proprietors, in part, "We, at our sole Risque and expense introduced into this Province a Manufacture of Porcelain or China Earthenware, a commodity, which by beauty and excellence, hath found its way into every refined Part of the Globe — — — America, in this general Struggle, hath hitherto been unthought of — and it is our peculiar Happiness to have been primarily instrumental in bringing her forward; but how far she shall proceed, in a great Measure, depends on the influence of your generous Support." The "generous Support" was evidently not forthcoming, and this abortive attempt at fine porcelain making came to a sad end in about two years.

Even as in Europe, other unsuccessful efforts to produce porcelain were made by divers potters thruout the country. But it was 1825 before William Ellis Tucker, the son of the proprietor of a small china shop in Philadelphia, discovered kaolin in Chester County, Pennsylvania, and first achieved "true porcelain" in these United States. His success was remarkable for, utterly unaided by the previous experience of others in the field, "he succeeded in a few years in perfecting from new and untried materials a porcelain equal in all respects to the best which England had produced after eighty years of continual experiment": the materials being taken from our soil "in great abundance and purity.'

Tucker's appeal to Congress for financial aid is also recorded in old Philadelphia archives, together with an interesting—and interested—letter from Andrew Jackson, who assured the applicant that "it would give him much pleasure to promote the objects he had in view, so far as they were within his constitutional sphere." Two months before Tucker's death in 1832, this ambitious potter had made another futile appeal to Congress for the passage of a tariff bill which would protect him from foreign competition, and Henry Clay had replied: "Such is the state of parties here, the friends of protection combating against the Treasury bill, sustained by the whole weight of the Administration, that it is extremely difficult to anticipate results or any part of the Tariff."

The firm continued under the name of Tucker and Hulme (later Tucker and Hemphill), for the most part turning out decorated copies of Sevres pieces for wealthy families in Pennsylvania and New Jersey, and finally came to an end in 1838. Thereafter, Thomas Tucker, William's younger brother, resigning himself to the craze for European wares, turned from the making of porcelain to the more lucrative pursuit of importing it from foreign shores. A few excellent specimens of this now rare "first American porcelain", for which only over-glaze colors were used, are to be found in the Barber Collection in the Philadelphia Museum of Art.

Early American potteries included the one at Bennington, Vermont, begun by the firm of Norton and Fenton in 1793, which was famous for its **Rockingham ware**, a yellow fabrique glazed with dark brown, and named for the Marquis of Rockingham, upon whose estate a similar ware had been originated at the Swinton Works in England. This American ware had a special showing at the first world exposition at the Crystal Palace in London in 1851, displaying objects that ranged from the favorite "Rockingham Lion" to pitcher-basin sets and cuspidors in infinite variety. The Bennington factory also specialized in **Parian ware**, the name derived from ivory white marble found on the island of Paros, Greece, and was carried on for more than a century.

1839 witnessed the founding of the pottery industry in East Liverpool, Ohio, a district which was to become one of the great ceramic industry centers of the United States; while in 1842 William Bromley of Stoke-on-Trent, England, opened a pottery in Cincinnati, Ohio; and about ten years later, the potteries in Trenton, New Jersey, presently known as "the Staffordshire of America", had their beginning.

Mention should also be made of that early American ancestor of the ceramic sculptors that are now legion: no less a personage than John Rogers of New York, whose terra cotta **"Rogers Groups"** were deservedly all the rage in the sixties and seventies as perfect examples of concentration upon the prevailing mid-Victorian "American Scene". And now it can be told that well-known sculptors, including men of the calibre of Daniel Chester French, were actually employed to model some of the figures.

Despite the impetus given to American ceramics by the Centennial Exposition in Philadelphia in 1876, when, in competition with the products of all the countries of Europe, it was apparent that "America had been left behind in the race"; and despite the increased production of fine wares in

the United States that followed such a rude awakening, it was not until 1918 that, under President Wilson, the White House for the first time purchased an American-made table service for the presidential table!

It was in the Lenox potteries, founded by Walter Scott Lenox, that the thin **Belleek china**, with its lustred, iridescent glaze, named for the famous product of the Belleek Porcelain Works in Ireland, was first made. Altho admittedly as perfect a fabrique as any found abroad, during the eighties and the "gay nineties" "this ware could not find a market, unless stamped with a foreign or misleading name!" Indeed so persistent was the senseless worship of imports thruout the country that perforce only the inexpensive domestic wares were readily marketable.

A direct outcome of the Centennial of 1876 was the founding of the well-known Rookwood Pottery in Cincinnati in 1880, at the instigation of Mrs. Maria Longworth Nichols. It was also in Cincinnati during this same period that a group of women, under the leadership of Miss M. Louise McLaughlin, undertook underglaze painting for the first time in the United States, and also experimented with considerable success in making single-fired porcelain.

The state of Ohio has always played a leading part in the history of American potting; for it was in 1894 (two years after the founding of the New York Ceramic Society) that Edward Orton, Jr. succeeded in the establishment of the "first ceramic school for the scientific study of ceramic engineering" at Ohio State University in Columbus —a school ably carried on today by the outstanding ceramist, Arthur F. Baggs, and his associates. Orton is also honored as the founder of the American Ceramic Society, "organized to promote the art, science and technology of ceramics", likewise with its headquarters in the city of Columbus. Furthermore, it is the great Cleveland Museum of Art which, under the directorship of William M. Milliken, has done so much to further the cause of ceramics and of the decorative arts in America.

The widely-known Cowan Pottery, specializing in ceramic sculpture and artistic wares, was operated in Rocky River, Ohio from 1913 to 1931 by R. Guy Cowan, who, with many personal awards and honors to his credit, was also for several years head of the Ceramic Department of the Cleveland School of Art. It was, in fact, under his leadership that the American school of ceramic sculpture received its first real impetus and inspiration. As Guy Cowan has written: "Ceramic sculpture offers infinite possibilities in color, texture and character of material, with permanence above all other materials."

ADELAIDE ALSOP ROBINEAU (1865-1929), internationally-known ceramist, was the first in this country to make porcelains fired at the high temperatures maintained by the famous Chinese potters (at 2400° F.). Moreover, altho she had begun work as a china painter, in an era abounding in bric-a-brac of the most atrocious "arty" period in history, her designs and vase shapes included many specimens of such classic beauty that they rank with the greatest ceramic achievements of all time.

Adelaide Alsop Robineau had studied painting for a few weeks in a summer class taught by William M. Chase, and had exhibited water colors and miniatures at the National Academy of Design. Two weeks at the New York State College of Ceramics at Alfred University, however, to familiarize herself with the elementary processes of work in clay, comprised her only formal instruction in pottery-making; this under Dr. Charles Fergus Binns, the noted craftsman, writer and teacher, whose father had been Director of the Royal Worcester Porcelain Works in England.

But the real inspiration for her porcelain came from books. After her marriage to Samuel E. Robineau in 1899, Mrs. Robineau and her husband together undertook the publication of a magazine on china decoration, which was increasingly popular, with imports of white undecorated ware continually arriving in huge quantities from Limoges, France. Thus the *Keramic Studio* (now the magazine *Design*) was begun. From Taxile Doat at the Sevres Porcelain works there came a series of articles on the making of art porcelain fired at high temperatures (afterwards published in book form under the title of *Grand Feu Ceramics*—high fire ceramics), which were translated from the French by Mr. Robineau and printed in the new magazine. Thereupon Adelaide Robineau decided that she would make high fire porcelain, which, as Charles F. Binns has written, "involves the pursuit of the most intricate and hazardous enterprise in the field of creative activity: her success the more remarkable for to this complex task Mrs. Robineau brought no special technical equipment—her resources were a high ideal, an extremely delicate touch, indomitable perseverance a n d unlimited patience."

Adelaide Robineau began her pottery making in 1903, with the skilled assistance of her husband in the firing of a kiln which he had constructed for her. But in a studio workshop on a hill-top in Syracuse she was destined to produce masterpieces of craftsmanship that are collector's items today. Mrs. Robineau did not care for the *pâte sur pâte* process used by Taxile Doat of Sevres, with whom she was associated for a short time in an ill-starred porcelain-making venture in St. Louis, and, instead, used almost exclusively a difficult process of excised carving, in which, with a single sharp pointed tool, the background was cut away, and the design made to stand out in relief. Exceptional, besides her delicate carving, were her *flambé* glazes, by means of which she obtained *sang de boeuf*, the pure oxblood red of the Chinese and her craquelled and crystalline glazes. She inaugurated, and for the last ten years of her life was in charge of, the ceramic department of the College of Fine Arts at Syracuse University where she received the degree of Master of Ceramic Arts; and at the time of her death in 1929, at the height of her career and fame, she was preparing for a scheduled exhibition in London.

In 1911 a group of fifty-five Robineau porcelains was sent to the International Exposition at Turin, Italy, where the exhibit was awarded the Grand Prize, "the highest possible award". In 1912 her work was exhibited at the *Musée des Arts Décoratifs* and at the spring *Salon* in Paris, this leading to her election to membership in the *Society Internationale des Beaux Arts*. Besides other prizes and awards, her porcelains received the Grand Prize at the Panama-Pacific Exposition in 1915.

Her work is included in the permanent collections of the Metropolitan Museum, the Philadelphia Museum, the Detroit Art Institute, the Newark Museum, the Cranbrook Museum, the Newcomb College Museum and the Syracuse Museum, as well as in many private collections, including that of the late Taxile Doat of Sevres. After her death, a memorial exhibition of her work was organized by the Metropolitan Museum of Art, and afterwards circulated to other museums.

Said Royal Cortissoz, writing in the New York Herald Tribune about the International Exhibition of Ceramics at the Metropolitan Museum in 1928: "The potters of the United States hold their own as regards vitality and range, with one virtuoso at the head producing some extraordinary work. This leader is Mrs. Adelaide Alsop Robineau of Syracuse — — Here are taste and technique magnificently fused. — — With a potter like Mrs. Robineau to the fore, it would seem as if almost anything were possible in the ceramic art of the country."

And from Taxile Doat in Sevres in 1929: "The Decorative Arts of the United States of America has suffered an immense loss with the death of Adelaide Robineau—its most remarkable and gifted leader."

THE NATIONAL CERAMIC EXHIBITION. "*American pottery and ceramic sculpture seem to me to be abreast of, if not superior to, anything that was being produced in Europe before the war.*" (Gisela Richter, Curator of Roman and Greek Art, Metropolitan Museum of Art, New York, February, 1943.) Syracuse had long been known as a "pottery city". At about 1845 William H. Farrar, formerly associated with the United States Pottery at Bennington, Vermont, was making "Rockingham and Yellow Ware Pottery" in the town of Geddes, New York, now incorporated as part of the city of Syracuse: This upon the same site today occupied by the well-known Onondaga Pottery, which was founded in 1857 by James Pass of Burslem, England.

With this background, and, in particular, on account of its large collection of porcelains by Adelaide Alsop Robineau, who had lived and worked in Syracuse, the Syracuse Museum of Fine Arts in 1932 founded in her honor the National Ceramic Exhibition, first known as the "Robineau Memorial": A non-commercial exhibition dedicated to the promotion of American ceramic art. And, besides pottery and ceramic sculpture, under a broad interpretation of the term "ceramic art", enamels on metal have been included. Ceramists from a mere eleven states responded to the invitation to participate in the first Ceramic National. Each year, however, the exhibition increased in scope and in importance until, in 1940, over one thousand entries had poured in from twenty-eight states, from Honolulu and from Canada; entries ranging all the way from decorative Indian jars from the pueblos of Santa Fe, or from the output of ambitious "unknowns" working in out-of-the-way mountain studios to major ceramic works of heroic size by many of America's leading sculptors. But owing to the high standards maintained year after year by distinguished jurors, quality kept pace with quantity: with all works judged "on the basis of decorative, creative and technical qualities".

An essential feature of this exhibition has been its annual circuit, following the initial Syracuse showing, which has carried the ceramics to well-known museums and galleries thruout the United States and Canada, with the exhibition in such demand that there has always been a waiting list for bookings. Organized as an "open show", to which any ceramically-minded American might submit his work, this annual exhibition resulted in the discovery of new talent every year, with new names inevitably appearing from territory thru which the ceramics had been circuited during the previous season. Furthermore, prior to the last decade, ceramic sculpture, formerly classed under "crafts", was not admitted to national sculpture exhibitions; while today sculpture in a ceramic medium will be found on an equality with bronze and marble in every important sculpture show in the country.

In 1936 the Ceramic National received an invitation from the *Kunstindustrie (Art and Industry) Museum* in Copenhagen, Denmark: an invitation conveyed thru Ruth Bryan Owen, American Minister to Denmark. Thus it came about that in 1937 the first all-American exhibition of Contemporary Ceramics ever invited abroad by a foreign museum was circulated thruout Scandinavia, with bookings, after Copenhagen, at the *Röhsska Museum* in Gothenburg, Sweden, at the Swedish National Museum in Stockholm, and at the *Konsthall* in Helsinfors, Finland (the latter booking arranged with the cooperation of Miss Maija Grotell, Finnish-American ceramist)—ending with a special showing, also by invitation, at the Hanley Museum in Josiah Wedgwood's own town, Stoke-on-Trent, England! This entire ceramic venture was financed by the Rockefeller Foundation, and the exhibition, the work exclusively of living artists, was shown, upon its return from a veritable triumphant tour, at the Whitney Museum of American Art in New York City. Said Richard F. Bach of the Metropolitan Museum of Art, Chairman of the Jury, in the Foreword of the foreign catalog: "These national exhibitions have rendered signal service in consolidating American interest in ceramics, for they have furnished a concentration point for ability and effort in this field, thus providing a 'proving ground' where criteria of quality may be established."

International recognition came again in 1939, when the Seventh Ceramic National was invited by Dorothy Liebes, Director of the Decorative Arts Section of the Golden Gate Exposition, to represent ceramic art of the United States at the San Francisco Fair. California, incidentally, has been second only to Ohio in its substantial representation in the Ceramic annuals, with Dr. Glen Lukens of the University of Southern California in the lead as craftsman and influential teacher, and with strong regional backing on the part of Reginald H. Poland, Director of the San Diego Gallery of Art, who has declared: "A National show such as this is interesting as an Index of American Civilization; in any case, a century hence it will be so considered."

The tenth anniversary of the Ceramic National was celebrated in the autumn of 1941 by an extensive exposition of Contemporary Ceramics of the Western Hemisphere, sponsored jointly by the Syracuse Museum and the International Business Machines Corporation: this exposition, the first of its kind, and the most extensive "all-American show" ever held, made possible thru the generosity and interest of Thomas J. Watson, Honorary Chairman of the National Ceramic Advisory Council. The Western Hemisphere show included work from eighteen countries, with Canadian pottery, assembled by the Canadian Potters' Guild, and South American pottery purchased especially for the exposition. The 1942 and 1943 Ceramic National annuals have been postponed on account of transportation conditions and other war-time difficulties.

Even before World War II, there was nothing in Europe that compared with the American ceramist's creative originality and the great variety evinced by a nation of individualists. For European potters, concentrating upon craftsmanship, had followed the same designs for years—sometimes for centuries—and, for the most part, were averse to innovations in forms or in technique. With contemporary European ceramics out of the picture, therefore, the American ceramist faces an increasingly important future. See *Three Books of the Potter's Art,* Piccolpasso, trans. by Bernard Rackham, 1934; *Pottery and Porcelain of the United States,* Edwin Atlee Barber, 1893; *The Story of the Potter,* Charles F. Binns, 1898; *The Craft of Athenian Pottery,* Gisela Richter, 1923; *Pottery and Porcelain,* Frederick Litchfield, 1925; *American Potters and Pottery,* John Ramsay, 1939; *Pottery: Its Craftsmanship and its Appreciation,* Edmund de Forest Curtis, 1940; *Pottery of the United States,* Helen E. Stiles, 1941; *United States Pottery, Encyclopedia Britannica,* Myrtle M. French.   —A.W.O.

Ceres. See Demeter.

ceresin wax. Among the various waxes used for surface coatings on paintings, sculpture, and other objects of art, ceresin has had an occasional place. It is harder than paraffin and more white in its tone. It melts at a point above 65° C. and has a rather smooth and unctuous consistency. It is a mineral wax and a derivative of ozokerite.   —G.L.S.

cerography. A method of painting which uses wax as a binder. The wax is heated with hot irons to make the colors fluid and to fix them.

certificate of authenticity. See FORGERIES IN PAINTING.

cerulean blue. As a bright, faintly greenish blue pigment, this synthetically prepared material has been available to painters since about 1860, though the process of making it was known before that. It is made by precipitating together cobaltous chloride and potassium stannate, the result being a combination of the salts of the metals, cobalt and tin. It is a fine-grained, stable, and inert pigment.
—G.L.S.

cestrum. Like the cauterium, the cestrum was an ancient tool of the painter and probably of other workers in the arts. It is mentioned by Pliny (XXXV, 149) and from its description appears to have been a pointed instrument used with wax.   —G.L.S.

Ceylon, art of. See INDIAN ART.

Chabad Chassidim. See JEWISH MUSIC.

Chaco Canyon. A canyon in northwestern New Mexico, about 10 miles long and 1 mile wide, in which were concentrated some of the most imposing open villages of the Great Pueblo Age. More than 15 major sites and a great many minor ones have been located. Pueblo Bonito (Beautiful Village) was one of the largest, with nearly 1000 rooms arranged on a roughly semicircular plan, and apparently one of the wealthiest, judging from its size, the large number of its kivas, and the rich turquoise ornaments and pottery found there. Chetro Ketl (Rain Village) nearby was roughly E-shape. The origin, history and fate of the inhabitants of the valley are unknown. Dates have been determined by tree ring dating. The site is now the Chaco Canyon National Monument. See Pueblo art.
—H.G.

chaconne. An ancient Spanish dance of possible Moorish origin, the *chaconne* or *cicona* is included among the *pre-classic* dance forms by virtue of its great contribution to classic music. Little is known about the original dance except that it was solemn in mood and performed in slow 3/4 meter, usually as a solo. It eventually appeared in 18th cent. society and French court as the final dance of a ball. This court form was carried over, with many variations, into musical composition. The chaconne, as danced by the nobility, consisted of one basic figure danced by the entire group in alternation with changing figures by various couples or smaller groups. In music, this pattern was developed into the *rondo, theme and variations,* and *air on a ground bass.* The latter musical form is also thought to have stemmed from another dance similar to the chaconne — the *passacaglia.* Whether the above arrangement characterized the ancient *cicona,* or was introduced by the French, is not clear. See passacaglia. —J.G.

chain lines. See wire-marks.

chaire (Jap.). A tea-caddy especially made for the powdered tea used in *cha-no-yu* (q.v.).

chaitya (Skr.). See caitya.

chakin (Jap.). An oblong piece of white linen used for wiping the tea-bowl during *cha-no-yu* (q.v.).

Chalcidian ware. See Ionian vases.

chalk. Common now as an ingredient in the grounds for paintings, this had a wide use, particularly in northern Europe, when panel paintings coated with white gesso were general. It is still a regular ingredient in certain oil grounds where it is mixed with white lead, linseed oil, and other materials.—G.L.S.

chalumeau. See MUSICAL INSTRUMENTS.

chamber. A space inclosed by walls and ceiling; a room.

chamber music. May be defined as music of an intimate character scored for solo instruments (one instrument to each part). Its proper place is in the salon in contrast to the symphony orchestra in the large concert auditorium or the opera company in a spacious theatre. Thus its identity depends on an intimate scale of performance. The forms employed were those usual at each period.

Chamber music emerges in a somewhat shadowy fashion from the other instrumental genres of the 15th and 16th cents. The two great climax periods coincide roughly with the lives of Bach and Handel and with the period of Haydn, Mozart, and Beethoven. The atmosphere of the Romantic period was less favorable to the development of chamber music than to the production of works for solo piano and for symphony orchestra. The rise of great permanent concert orchestras with the accompanying delight in color possibilities, the decline of the race of wealthy and cultured patrons of chamber music, the rise of the heaven-storming individualists (the virtuoso pianist and the professional conductor), all contributed to focus the attention of composer and public elsewhere. That significant and charming chamber music works were nevertheless composed during the Romantic period, and since that time, is true indeed. It is, however, significant that among the most successful composers of chamber music during the Romantic period and later were those who had the closest sympathy for classic music. Brahms is perhaps the best example.

The growth of a wider public for chamber music which is no longer limited to a privileged and cultured circle is a cheering development. This new audience is small when compared to the audiences for the symphony concert or the opera, but its existence suggests further possibilities for a form of musical art which has always been the delight of composers. To this result the broadcasts of chamber music, which still remain too infrequent, have contributed much.

Early chamber music developed in the courts of Europe, in the palaces and manor houses of cultured noblemen. It was performed by professional musicians attached to the court circle or belonging to the retinue of an individual patron. These performers were joined on less formal occasions by music-loving amateurs. During the 17th cent. amateur performances on the viols were an important part of English domestic music. University circles in Germany formed performing groups which were often headed by famous musicians.

Renaissance taste favored music performed on families of instruments the sizes of which corresponded in a rough fashion to the compass of the various voices. Thus the *Canzoni* of Florenzio Maschera (Brescia, 1584) though it contains instrumental forms, both dance-tunes and movements in imitation, nevertheless is written in a thoroughly vocal style. The English term for such a group is **consort.** Even at this time, however, stringed instruments (lutes and viols) were preferred for domestic music. The rarer case where unlike instruments played together was the **broken consort.** A fine early example of music for broken consort is the Morley *Consort Lessons* of 1599 which is scored for treble viol, recorder, and bass viol supported by a group of plucked instruments (lute, pandora, and cittern).

Music played during the 16th and 17th cents. may be divided into dance-airs which were gradually grouped in a contrasting series, the suite. On the other hand, an important group of forms was based on a polyphonic ideal and consisted in an adaptation of the basic principles of the vocal motet. Such forms were the ricercare, the canzona, and (esp. in England) the fancy or fantasia.

Much instrumental chamber music of early date was scored for five or six parts, as were many madrigals of the same period. The typical group for the period of Bach and Handel, however, was a trio consisting of two instruments of soprano compass (violins, oboes, or flutes) with a bass instrument (viola da gamba, cello, or bassoon). Furnishing a discreet harmonic background was a keyboard instrument or a lute. The melodic instruments were thus free to elaborate their melodic designs, relatively unhampered by the necessity of forming sonorous chords since the accompanying instruments could be depended on to fill in and unify the ensemble. This ideal which is completely foreign to modern conceptions of chamber style was dominant up to the classic period and even left perceptible traces on the music of that period. The **trio sonata** might be a **chamber sonata** (*sonata da camera*) in which case the music consisted of a series of contrasting dances; or it might be a **church sonata** (*sonata da chiesa*) in which case the principle of alternating lyric and animated movements was followed, with music more abstract and contrapuntal in style. In this connection the name of Arcangelo Corelli must be added to those of Bach and Handel. His first four works consist of trio sonatas which are models of elegance and perfection of style.

Chamber music of the classic period, the period of Haydn, Mozart, and Beethoven, was characterized by the dominance of a single form, the sonata form, and by two chief mediums, unaccompanied strings and stringed instruments with piano. To these must be added chamber music for wood-wind instruments, relatively important at the time of Mozart but diminishing in importance towards the present.

The chief medium for stringed istruments, indeed the most important chamber music combination, is the **string quartet:** two violins, viola, and cello. Subtract one violin, and a **string trio** remains. Add a second viola or cello, and the group is a **string quintet.** Larger ensembles are less frequent. The double quartets of Spohr are no longer played, but the Mendelssohn *Octet* remains a brilliant treatment of a most attractive combination.

The piano does not associate on equal terms with the stringed instruments. They constitute, rather, two opposing groups, the piano balancing and in more recent works often more than balancing the combined forces of the strings. The usual groupings are **piano trio:** piano, violin, and cello; **piano quartet:** piano, violin, viola, and cello; and **piano quintet:** piano with string quartet. The piano in these combinations is not merely a background instrument as in the preceding period but is an integral part of the musical texture, stating themes and developing accessory designs as well as accompanying the stringed instruments. Modern composers for the most part still compose for these combinations.

Romantic and modern chamber music is hardly distinguished by novelty of medium or form so much as by a new spirit. One may instance the Stravinsky *Octet for Wind Instruments* as novel in instrumentation or the *Varèse Octandre* as free from the influence of sonata form. In general, however, composers have remained faithful to the conventional combinations of instruments and, while treating the sonata form with freedom, have accepted its broad outline. It has, however, been difficult to keep a just balance of style at a time which is accustomed to the broad sonorities and kaleidoscopic color of the modern symphony orchestra. The limited color possibilities of the stringed instruments have been exploited in the most minute fashion. Orchestral traits like the bow tremolo have appeared and have not always been handled with suitable restraint. Such a blurring of stylistic lines is perhaps inevitable at a time which is orchestra-dominated.

At the same time professional chamber music has almost completely lost its domestic character and has become concert music for the small hall. Only enthusiastic amateur groups pursue the art of chamber music in what is perhaps the most ideal fashion. Thus a void appears separating modern chamber music, subtly colored, technically exacting, and molded to the requirements of concert performers, and the musical needs of the amateur quartet party. Such groups in view of their technical limitations and the lack of time available for rehearsal are likely to find that the best point of compromise may be found in a Haydn quartet or in a quartet from the *Opus 18* of Beethoven.

Meanwhile a mass audience for chamber music is perhaps in the making as a result of chamber music broadcasts. Here is the possibility of listening in informal surroundings to music small in scale, appealing to, rather than overwhelming, our musical sensibilities, yet music which can be transmitted to thousands of listeners without fading out in the depths of some huge auditorium and without losing its essential character.

In closing one should point out that certain vocal forms may properly be regarded as chamber music, not only the madrigal of the 16th and early 17th cents., but the later chamber duet for two voices with an instrumental bass part. Classic examples in the latter form have been left by Agostino Steffani, Carlo Maria Clari, and Handel. The interest in opera and in the large chorus have tended to remove vocal music from the sphere of chamber music. Nevertheless, such recent works as Hindemith's *Eight canons for two voices with instruments* (Op. 45, No. 2) represent an attempt to return to the chamber music ideal. —C.W.H.

champlevé enamel. A particular technique in enamel work generally applied to a copper background. In enamels of this kind the background not occupied by the design is hollowed out and the empty spaces are then filled with the vitreous paste; a mode of procedure entirely different to cloisonné enamel (q.v.). Champlevé enamel was employed in many outstanding goldsmiths' works of German origin during the Middle Ages. It is believed that it spread from there to France in the 12th cent., when Abbot Suger of St. Denis invited Lotharingian enamellers to his monastery to complete works of this kind. Later it was highly developed in the work shops of Limoges from where it spread all over Europe. In the beginning, champlevé enamel served solely ecclesiastical purposes and was applied to crosses, portable altars, chalices etc. Still later it was used as decoration on mundane objects such as hat ornaments, clasps, coats of arms. See ENAMELLING ON METAL. —L.L.

chancel. That part of a church east of the nave, including the choir and sanctuary, and reserved for the clergy.

chancery (script). See writing.

chang (Ch.). Ritualistic jade sometimes called a "half-tablet"; it is in the form of half a *kuei* (q.v.), if divided vertically.

changeable flats. See STAGESETTING.

cha-no-yu (Jap.). The serving of powdered tea in a formal, ceremonial-like manner. The utensils used are as follows:

chaire	*hibachi*
chakin	*hibashi*
chasen	*hishaku*
chashaku	*kama*
chawan	*kamashiki*
fukusa	*kan*
furo	*kōbako*
futa-oki	*koboshi*
habōki	*kōg*
haisaji	*ō*
	mizusashi

See JAPANESE ART; also *The Book of Tea,* Kakuzo Okakura, 1906; *Chanoyu, The Japanese Tea Ceremony,* A. L. Sadler, 1933; *Chanoyu, Tea Cult of Japan,* Yasunosuke Fukukita, 1932; *A Glimpse of Japanese Art* (chapter, Cha-no-yu as a Cultural Institution), Jiro Harada. —J.A.M.

chanson, chanson balladée, chanson de geste, chansonnier. See MEDIEVAL MUSIC.

chant, unrhythmical and rhythmical. See JEWISH MUSIC.

chapbook. *Book.* A small book in a paper binding sold by hawkers in the 17th and 18th cents., usually containing tales, bawdy ballads, lives of criminals, tracts, etc. —H.E.S.

chapter house. See monastic architecture.

character dance. Dances of *characterization* are those whose movements take on the qualities of another character. The creative imagination appropriates the experiences of another and enters into a point of view different from his own. The dancer "others" himself. He designs his movements to portray another's actions and feelings. Animals as well as people suggest a wealth of subject matter for characterization. See H'Doubler, M. N., *Dance, A Creative Art Experience,* 1940. —M.N.H.'D.

characteristic note, tone. See leading tone s.v. scale.

charcoal. The carbon made from roasting pieces of wood in a closed vessel has been a drawing and coloring material from prehistoric times. As thin sticks, made from close-grained wood like willow or beech, it is a regular drawing instrument. Pulverized, charcoal provides a common black pigment.
—G.L.S.

chardonnet silk. Named after its inventor, Count Hilaire de Chardonnet, a Frenchman, who first invented the nitrocellulose process in 1884. Syn. for nitrocellulose rayon. Now obs. in the U. S. —G.W.R.

charges. See HERALDRY.

charter (script). See writing.

chaseki (Jap.). See chashitsu; JAPANESE ART.

chasen (Jap.). A whisk of split bamboo used to whip each serving of powdered tea in the tea-bowl during *cha-no-yu* (q.v.). See JAPANESE ART.

chashaku (Jap.). A bamboo or ivory spoon used to transfer powdered tea from the caddy to the tea-bowl during *cha-no-yu* (q.v.).

chasse. See reliquary.

Chassidim. See JEWISH MUSIC.

châssis. *Painting.* A frame on which canvas may be stretched. *Sculp.* Modeling stand with revolving top on which wax model or armature (q.v.) may be placed.

chatta. See stupa.

chatty (Hind.). An earthen pot for holding liquids.

chawan (Jap.). The tea-bowl, invariably of pottery, used in *cha-no-yu* (q.v.).

chazan. See JEWISH MUSIC.

checkerboard. A decorative pattern which divides a surface into equal squares treated alternately in different ways, as with different colors or inset patterns or with high and low relief.

chef-d'oeuvre (Fr.). A masterpiece.

Chellean art. See PREHISTORIC ART.

Chelsea ware. See CERAMICS II.

chemical porcelain. Highly fired, resists rapid temperature change and reaction of chemicals. See CERAMICS I.

cheng. (Ch.). Banner paintings.

chenille (Fr. caterpillar). It is so named because its surface is composed of rows of fuzzy, V-shaped cord or fur, cut in strips from a blanket woven on the weft loom. These strips are attached, by means of strong linen or cotton catcher threads, to the coarse wool backing of the rug as it is being woven on the second or chenille loom. Chenille is woven up to thirty feet wide without a seam on a power loom. —B.E.J.

chenille Axminster. See carpet structures.

chest. See FURNITURE.

chevet (Fr.). Apsidal end of a church; esp. the entire east end of a church including the semicircular or polygonal vault over the end of the choir, the ambulatory, and the absidioles.

chevron. See HERALDRY.

chi (Ch.). Chinese word for lacquer ware. See SYMBOLISM IN FAR EASTERN ART.

ch'i (Ch.). Ritualistic jade axe. See also CHINESE ARTS s.v. calligraphy.

chia (Ch.). A sacrificial bronze vessel, three or four-legged, with handle at side, and two stanchions on top of lip as ornamented guides for cover. —J.A.M.

chiaroscuro. Meaning light and dark, a sister word to pianoforte, meaning soft and loud; was a term having to do with woodcuts. The finished picture displays a pleasant tone of contrasting lights and shades. Since the days of Leonardo da Vinci the term refers to the way the painter handles those atmospheric effects which permit him to create the illusion that his subjects are on all sides surrounded by space, letting them stand "free." See COLOR; PERSPECTIVE; PRINTS AND PRINT PROCESSES.

Chicago school. See functional architecture.

Chichimeca. Generic name given to the wild tribes which entered the Valley of Mexico around the 11th century. In this period there were a number of independent tribal groups which later took over the traits of Aztec civilization. —G.C.V.

chidori (Jap.). Small birds (plover). Often associated with waves, a common wave and bird pattern.

chief. See HERALDRY.

Chien yao (Ch.). Chinese pottery ware of the *Sung* dynasty. Thick glaze, iridescent purplish, bluish black or brown.

chiffon (1) Descriptive term indicating light weight and soft finish, as chiffon velvet or chiffon taffeta. (2) Light weight silk hose, 2-4 thread yarns. (3) Gauzelike silk fabric with soft or sometimes stiff finish. Warp and filling of hard twist singles.   —G.W.R.

chigaidana (Jap.). Shelves and sometimes cupboards, adjacent to the *tokonoma* (or place of honor) on which *objets d'art* are shown.   —J.A.M.

Chigi vase. See HELLENIC ART.

chih (Ch.). Sacrificial bronze vessel. Vaselike jar with cover and a base, for sacrificial wine; also the Chinese word for paper.

chih hua (Ch.). A style of Chinese pictorial painting made by dipping the finger or fingernail into color and producing a picture without the aid of a brush.   —J.A.M.

CHILDREN'S ART. *General.* Children's art can be defined as a visual means of expressing their mental attitudes. The mode of expression as well as the subject through which children express their approach to and position in the world is characteristic and unique. Once the mental attitude of childhood is outgrown and is changing into that of adulthood, whether at the age of nine or seventeen, art also is no more that of a child.

Since children's art is a means of expressing—visually—experiences, problems or simply observations, its development can be compared to language. Children's art, esp. children's drawings, fulfill a dual role. (a) They are a means of communication. Since the smaller child can draw more swiftly than he can write and has a picture vocabulary which is larger and more vivid than his abstract word vocabulary, he is in a better position to express himself through pictures than words, a situation which holds true for the average child until he is seven to nine years old. (b) Children's art provides them with an emotional outlet and an aesthetic satisfaction. Emotions find various ways of expression through lines, peculiar proportions or color, all of them carrying a symbolic meaning The

act of drawing or any other way of picturing is in itself a means of indirectly re-living, e-enacting or simply completing experiences o which otherwise the child could not react fully. Thus, at the ages eight to eleven children who ordinarily would not sit still for ny length of time, but would seek satisfaction in long periods of violent play exercises, substitute these purely physical activities by representing them in pictures. They experience these activities indirectly and derive in most cases an even greater satisfaction, since in their own representation they can be as successful as they wish to be and since, in the depicted play drama, unlike to real life, they are in a position to assign diverse parts to the people whose participation they desire.

History. Ever since children's art has attracted attention to the point of being studied methodically, i.e., since the eighties of the last century, it has been interpreted very differently. Its aesthetic qualities went first unnoticed because unrecognized. Attention was directed to the symbolism of its mode of expression and interpretation of it was undertaken in the light of children's personal growth and enrichment of observations.

Later an interpretation of child development in terms of their mode of representation was undertaken and children's drawings were studied on a larger scale in order to generalize and to find in their art generally applicable laws.

Still later, during the first years of the 20th cent., children's drawings were used as a proof for the assumption that each individual, in a more or less accurate way re-enacts the development of mankind from the primitive cave dweller to the renaissance uperman. This interpretation of child art was based on the similarity, and in some cases dentity of drawings of small children and primitive tribes as well as the similarity of drawings of all children throughout the world regardless of the nationality or kind of culture they came from.

After World War I children's art served as a simplified example of explaining art theory problems and as a special phase of expressionism. In fact, the attention paid quite generally to child art since the early twenties is largely due to the expressionist rt movement. At present, predominantly in the U. S. A., research in children's art serves the purpose of establishing and clarifying the facts and factors connected with it and their relation to child development. Hence, investigations have become less general and philo sophical and more specific and fact finding, thus more adaptable to educational objectives.

Developmental Stages in Children's Art. The function of and the qualities inherent in child art are extremely complex. It is not possible to separate and single out characteristics without distorting the pattern of their occurrence and interrelation. Although it is necessary to separate characteristics such as color, line or proportion in a drawing in order to acquire a more complete knowledge and to analyze in turn the qualities contained in each characteristic, one must keep in mind that there exists a functional relationship without which the analysis and interpretation of separate items is invalid. Children's art is a phase of their general development.

(a) *Subjects represented in Children's Art.* Younger children—4/5 to 9/10 years old—choose episodes of their own lives, activities in which they take part, such as outdoor plays, gardening, cooking, a party or picnic; places they see and can observe closely, such as their own house and garden, the park, the streets or the place where they spent their vacation; objects in which they are particularly interested, such as airplanes or automobiles. The content of their pictures is often characterized by changing some part of the reality they depict and fashioning it to suit their wishful thinking or express their admiration. The objects drawn in the pictures are various. People, i.e., men and women make up the largest percentage. This preference decreases as they grow older but comes back later, at the age of thirteen or so; i.e., during the transitional stage to adult observation and criticism. At this time their art takes the form of stereotypes of "pretty" girls and "strong" men. Animals, houses, trees and flowers, furniture pieces, eating utensils, toys and wagons are other objects of the young children's picture world.

(b) *Mode of representation.* It changes in both their drawings and their modeling according to age level. One can distinguish five developmental stages. The change from one to the next is gradual. Few drawings are entirely representative of one single stage, nor does all the art work of a given child have the characteristics of one phase only. The developmental phases of child art are irreversible. Though children will experience all or some of the stages, they do not go through a later one without having gone through the earlier ones, even if a given developmental stage sometimes lasts such a

short time — as happens occasionally with artists — as to be non-apparent.

1. The first stage, the scribble stage, is characteristic of children between three and six. During it objects or ideas are expressed by means of scribbling which, though meaningless to others, has a significance to the scribbling child and can be revealed by him during the making of the scribble picture.

2. The second stage, the schematic stage, is characterized by a pictorial representation in which use is made of simplified symbols, the shapes and contours of which bear a rough, diagrammatic resemblance to the real objects. Thus, each part of an object is outlined in the shape of rounds, ovals, near-squares, dots and straight lines and each part is finished before being joined to the next until all parts are assembled. The process of assembling is additive. Parts or details are often more important than the whole. One could say that the whole consists only of those parts that are essential at a given moment and hence the whole changes according to the changing importance of parts. Thus a human figure may be represented with one arm only, though with a multitude of details related to this one arm, while the other arm is omitted, because in the picture situation no function is assigned to the other arm. Another characteristic of the schema is the omission of a single point of vantage from which the picture is seen as is customary in all occidental pictorial representation. In the child's schematic picture, the point of vantage changes so that some objects are depicted as if seen simultaneously from all or several sides, from the top or from underneath. Each schematic picture object is worked out step by step. Though schemata differ somewhat among children, the schematic child's drawings have enough characteristics in common to give them the appearance of a style of their own and to set them apart from other schematic art forms.

3. The third developmental stage, the mixed or intermediate stage, is reached when children's schemata become intermixed with the characteristics of the fourth developmental stage: art true-to-appearance. Some objects will be partly schematic and partly true-to-appearance. Picture compositions may contain wholly schematic objects and also objects which are definitely true-to-appearance.

4. For the fourth developmental stage, representation true-to-appearance, it is characteristic that an attempt is made to represent

objects as they appear to an observer from a single point of vantage. Since depth is as yet not represented, the objects give an impression of flatness. Contrary to the schematic pictures, hidden parts of objects or whole objects are not represented because they cannot be seen.

5. The fifth stage, that of representation in space, is reached when depth, perspective or modeling in the round is added to the flatness of the contours used in true-to-appearance representation. One can distinguish between linear representation—convergence of lines, retaining of the verticals, eye-line; modeling of objects by means of shading and foreshortening; and color perspective, i.e., change of color to indicate distance such as faded colors in the background in contrast to the brilliancy of the foreground colors.

The developmental stages following the schematic stage are transitional stages to adult visual representation. The only stage truly representative of childhood is the schematic stage.

The primitive schema is interesting mainly for its psychological and developmental implications. It often represents nothing more than the human head from which hang down directly the legs, omitting the body entirely. In the course of perfecting the schema all parts of the human figure are included. First it is represented frontwise: the head as a near-round in which the eyes are dots or filled-in circles placed under and close to the top outlines of the head, the nose is a perpendicular single or double line in between and the mouth is a couple of horizontal lines with cross lines for teeth; the body as a near-oval with a row of buttons or a neckline or waistline to indicate a suit or dress; the legs as outlines of tubes hanging down from the oval body to which shorter tubes are fastened at a right angle, giving the impression of a pair of hockey sticks; arms resemble the legs and hang from the upper sides of the body ending in a leaflike hand. The frontview is gradually changed into a side view and both views are used in schematic pictures. However, the eye in the fully developed profile view remains frontwise, thus giving the head an appearance similar to certain Egyptian drawings; the outlines of the body, legs and arms remain the same, but are given a direction to either left or right. Both front and profile views are represented in rigid standing positions. Sitting or bending figures are exceptional. Sex is differentiated by given attributes.

The schematic animal, a horizontally laid out human schema, is usually represented in profile. In the course of developing the animal schema, particular attributes of mammal, bird or fish are worked out and at the height of the schema individual differences permit a differentiation of individual kinds such as the long flat bill of the duck as compared to the short pointed beak of the chicken.

In tree schemata a substantial double line is drawn for the trunk, representing a vertical axis, from which straight horizontal lines spread as branches from which in turn, again vertically and horizontally, shorter lines spread out, the twigs. From the latter hang leaves, blossoms and fruit, individually outlined, identical in shape, so arranged as not to interfere with each other. Besides this schema there is the near-circular shape, such as for the maple tree, the flame-shaped outline, such as for the poplar and the triangular schema, such as for the spruce tree. There are three distinct flower schemata with appropriate variations: the button type, a round with a dot in the center; the composite or daisy type, a circle of narrow cones or loops; and the tulip type, a drooping or upwardly directed bell shape. Single or double lines, slightly curved, represent the stem to which is added a narrow-shaped leaf-outline on one or both sides of it.

The house, a favorite of the child's picture world is shown with one to three or even four sides, unfolded side by side. A triangular roof is fitted exactly to the top. Windows are set in, shaped as small rectangles and at irregular distances. The door is always represented with a handle or knob. The chimney, out of which curls a black cloud of scribbled smoke is set perpendicular unto one side of the roof.

Characteristic of child drawing, and thus differing from populistic painting, is the lack of proportion among parts of a given object and among several objects. Thus the head of the human figure is very large as compared to the rest of the body; leaves of trees or fruit are gigantic in size as compared to the whole tree; flowers may have the size of the house along which they grow and people going to church may be as tall as the church itself. It has been shown experimentally that the child's estimate of proportion of real objects is as correct as that of adults. Since drawing fulfills the purpose of expressing a thought or describing an experience, the importance of certain parts of the experience is underlined by an exaggeration of size. Also, if an object has a number of important details, these details must be crowded in and, logically, the object becomes disproportioned. Furthermore, exaggeration of size symbolizes an action or the wish to attain a goal which is out of reach. Thus, one arm may have twice the size of the other, in order to indicate the necessity to reach or pull an object—and to represent strength. Conversely, uninteresting parts or details are shrunk or omitted.

Movement of objects in the schematic picture is not shown by bending of joints. It is achieved by zigzagging or curly lines and translates the child's experience of muscular sensations, not the appearance of movement to an onlooker. The shape of the object remains static, the lines have movement.

Another important characteristic of the child's schema is his desire to represent all that which is connected with his experience, whether simultaneously visible or not. Hence the transparency of certain objects such as a house or people's clothing or the picturing of objects hidden by a wall or fence.

(c) *Organization and Orientation.* The organization and orientation of pictures is also closely linked to general child development. The pre-school child scatters the objects of his representation over the paper. He does not distinguish between up and down, right or left and turns his paper during the process of drawing so that some parts seem upside down in comparison to others. Also, during this developmental phase, there are gaps between picture elements which are supplemented by oral narrative. As orientation proceeds, dislocation within a unit disappears and, in time, units are properly related to each other. Simultaneously, the graphic organization of the picture progresses toward an all-graphic unified composition. The desire of expressing some definite experience through the content is satisfied by either breaking up the representation into a series or by a repeated representation of some individuals or objects within the same picture in order to indicate various activities or situations. Whereas in the early stage of schematic organization few and single objects were placed far enough apart that they would not interfere with one another, the fully developed schematic organization represents crowds or masses of objects. To do so, single schemata are repeated identically in a multiple arrangement, a conclusion arrived at through reasoning, e.g., that a forest consists of very many trees and hence in order to represent a forest, rows upon rows of identical trees must be pictured.

In a schematic picture spatial arrangements are not interpreted through perspective of some kind but through organization. Though perspective is recognized and correctly interpreted in photographs or in perspective paintings, the child's way of expressing distance or depth is closer to oriental than occidental interpretation of space. In the average schematic picture figures or objects are arranged on a standline representing the ground—the earth—which includes objects in front and objects farther back. Above them is left an empty space—the air. Toward the top of the page a strip of blue indicates the sky and a yellow disk the sun. In order to express more intricate spatial arrangements the schematic child places several bands or standlines on top of each other and thus indicates by the bottom standline nearness, and by the top line farness. There are no differentiations of size. Another means of spatial arrangement is the maplike bird's-eye view of a given space, dotted with schemata of the objects involved.

Schematic drawings and modelings are made from memory. Even when supposed to draw from a model, children will look at it for the purpose of finding out what they are supposed to draw; they will observe details; and then they will start to draw by memory the object represented by the model but not the particular model in front of them. Memory is by no means purely pictorial. It is sense-mixed, i.e., a combination of remembered sensations of touch, hearing, taste or of a kinesthetic nature—all of which is interspersed by abstract concepts. The child necessarily evolves a memory stereotype which represents an abstraction. This abstraction, a symbol, is the schema and is being developed during a number of repetitions until it becomes as automatic as handwriting.

Painting and Color Use. Schematic child art uses color liberally. (1) Color is used during the scribble stage and in the primitive schema for manipulative purposes, i.e., to learn about color and for the pleasure of using it whether or not the color fits the pictured object. (2) It is characteristic of the schema that the color must be "true", i.e., that it must match the actual color of the object. If the local color of a tree trunk is brown and that of grass light green and that of the sky blue, then the colors applied in the picture must match accordingly. Even so, a large number of objects are observed for their shape and are of a nondescript color, in which cases color is either avoided or applied arbitrarily. The concept of "true" color is the reason for coloring distant hills in a bright color, thus matching the color the trees on the hill are known to have. Further development of the color schema leads to a modification of colors, i.e., to a variety of shades of a given color in order to match more closely the actual color of the object. Color remains independent of light effects or transparency all through the schematic stage, hence color as the most important mode of expression of the painter, e.g. impressionist painters, is foreign to child art. Its use may be likened to illumination in the Middle Ages. Though it is essential, it is subordinated to shape. (3) Color is used as a medium for emotional expression. In order to underline the importance of an object or of one of its parts a particular color is applied; or in order to symbolize taste, smell or sound certain "unreal" colors are used or one color is used exclusively. Peculiar coloring in some children's pictures may be indications of maladjustment, similar to the peculiar coloring used by certain types of insanes.

Technique and Media. (a) GENERAL. Left to themselves, children try a variety of media. The technique which they use is principally the same and is prescribed and limited by the nature of the schematic drawing as well as by the mental process which leads to its execution. Since all objects or portions of objects are outlined and set off against their surroundings, all drawings are ultimately line drawings, colored within their outline. Hence the treatment of all media is subordinated, to a greater or lesser extent, to this key-technique. When schematic children apply color with large paint brushes they strive even then to make an outline first, after which they fill in the area. Thus any medium which calls for a technique which abolishes contour and defined areas is contrary to the nature of the child's schematic art and is more of an obstacle than an inducement to its development.

(b) DRAWING. Children's drawing is based on a line technique, whether coarse or fine, whether of single objects or of whole picture organizations. The technique is an outcome of the child's process of thought and visualization; it therefore crystallizes a mental attitude and consequently is fundamental.

(c) MODELING. The technique of children's modeling during the schematic stage corresponds to and parallels their drawing technique. Though far less data are available than for drawing, it seems evident that first attempts at modeling follow the flat contour schemata of their drawings. Figures and ob-

jects give the appearance of a flattened slab, to which details such as eyes, nose or mouth are added either as kneaded rolls or balls of clay or are indented with the fingers, thus outlining a depression. Another procedure in modeling is that of rolling balls and cylinders in order to shape the head, body, arms and legs. In both methods the additive process is followed, parallel to the process of drawing schemata in that parts are made indepently and then joined together. Similar to his drawings, the child represents the parts he knows as if taking a walk—mentally—around his object. Eventually he thus achieves an all-around modeled piece with details indicated in flat lines, very similar to gingerbread men.

(d) PAPER CUTTING. Children are successful silhouettists at an early age. The scissors take the place of pencil or crayon in tracing contours. Through folding, a number of identical, symmetrical objects can be produced. The objects which the child wishes to represent can be cut out in parts and in various colors. Then, following the additive process of the schema they can be glued on a sheet of paper in order to form a suitable picture arrangement. It is also an ideal medium to represent space schematically, since children can "put on" the dress on the figure they are picturing or stick the house in front of the mountain and the flowers in front of the house, thus satisfying their feeling for reality and finding an expression for nearness and farness. Younger children use papercuts as a prop for dramatization: paper figures can be moved and bent; they also can be finished in the back as well as in front regarding hair, dress and ornamentation, thus giving the illusion of completeness. Papercut pieces of this kind take the place of modelings; they do not collapse and they can be evolved like any other schematic representation. The facility with which very young children make papercuts and their successfulness has been explained by some art theorists (Germany) in the following way: that it may be caused by an unusually strong response of the subject to two-dimensional, i.e., flat shapes; that a large number of individual, isolated and rigid — unchangeable — impressions are accumulated which tend to strengthen distinct and detailed contours, a phenomenon markedly present in eidetic individuals. The fact that facility of cutting contours, i.e., of making silhouettes, exists in very young children who otherwise are still in the developmental phase of the primitive schema can be interpreted as supporting the claim that the majority of children are eidetics who sooner or later, lose this quality.

(e) FINGERPAINTING. This is a medium especially fitted to the child's procedure of representation. The paints are tempera pigments to which starch is added as a binder. Opaque colors of this type can be superimposed on each other. The fingertips are used to apply the paint to wet paper. The technique is adapted to children's preference to work with their fingers directly. One of the main advantages of this medium is its therapeutic value. Also it has the advantage of making changing illustrations before a children's audience. Aesthetically, favor the child's inclination toward symmetry since both hands can be used simultaneously and in rhythmical movement. It permits painting of foreground over background so that the child can indulge in representing apparently hidden parts completely and subsequently cover them again. The handling of the paints, their mixture on the paper itself gives the illusion of modeling. The effects are often startling and create the illusion of expressionism.

(f) FASHIONING OF OBJECTS AND THEIR DECORATION. Very young children like to fashion objects. However, they have not yet attained the skill necessary to achieve results which would satisfy them. Similar to the scribble stage or the primitive schema, the fashioning of an object serves the purpose of creating something basically necessary for other activities. Later, children are more intent on decorating objects and fashion them for this purpose alone.

Aesthetics of Children's Art. (a) CHILDREN'S CONCEPT OF THE BEAUTIFUL is related to and dependent on their interests and activities, therefore on their participation, actually or mentally and on their sphere of interest. It changes according to age level and maturity. For younger children beauty is not static but associated with action or movement. Parades, bands, stage performances or dancing are beautiful. So are a number of things which can be enjoyed sensuously. An object is not beautiful because of its visual aspect alone. This is just a part of its beauty and not the most important. The enjoyment through other senses of sound, smell, touch or through kinesthesis are just as important or more so. The beauty of nature, too, is less a matter of visual enjoyment of scenery and its details, than of a background for real or imaginary activities, comparable to a stagesetting. Formal aspects, picturelike qualities of nature are not appreciated. Beauty of

people or animals cannot be separated from moral concepts. What is good is beautiful and what is beautiful must be good. Besides these two distinct elements—participation and moral values—enjoyment of beauty is limited by the child's comprehension of units. He understands simple units such as a flower or a bird, and gradually progresses to more complex units and their appreciation.

The aesthetic element as a form element is grasped when sustained by a particularly interesting content and even so seldom in an articulate way. In other words, aesthetic factors enhance already interesting contents and are noticed only in this context.

(b) AESTHETIC ELEMENTS IN THE CHILD'S CREATIVE WORK. Since the child's painting, modeling or building are play activities, he acts through his pictures or similar creations and the activity aspect dominates aesthetic considerations. The early, purely sensuous enjoyment of handling colors or manipulating clay is subordinated later on to the content. Childhood is over when the effect of the child's creations on others or on himself is more important than the activity of producing them. The aesthetic factors of the schematic child's picture are mainly the following. (1) *Symmetry*, partly due to commencing a picture by drawing the main object in the center and distributing further objects around it; partly due to a sense of balance which may have its root in the symmetry of the body and symmetrical movements. (2) *Repetitional design elements* caused by the nature of schematic symbols. Since people, animals, trees, flowers, houses and other objects are represented by schemata which are repeated identically or near-identically the effect is patternlike. The same element of repetitiousness is observed in the application of colors, again due to the fact that colors are applied according to their local trueness, therefore are coupled with like schemata and thus enhance the pattern effect. (3) *Brilliancy and color contrast.* They originate in the tendency to match the actual local color of objects e.g. blue of sky or water, green of grass or trees, with the colors applied in the picture and in the disregard of hues and tints as being unreal. Here must be mentioned certain "odd" colorings expressive of moods or sensations which bear a resemblance to certain characteristics of expressionism and have been interpreted as such. However, only a small number of schematic drawings of this kind gain aesthetically by these characteristics because of the haphazard way of application and therefore the failure of achieving a thematic unity. Older children, beyond the purely schematic stage are more successful aesthetically in expressing themselves in such manner. (4) *Compositional band arrangement.* It lends a formal effect. (5) *Decorativeness.* Although children do not strive to make decorative drawings they decorate the objects in their drawings, often very richly. Their intention is to represent a rich garment, or a house with elaborate windowframes. In decorating objects a similar attitude can be observed. The object's shape, proportion or curvature is of little importance. The main issue is the surface decoration. Decorations of any kind whether within a picture or on an actual object have usually some kind of narrative content. Few decorations are geometrical or abstract. They often represent a story within the story or a series of attributes related to the story. Thus it is not unusual to find that a child's schematic painting resembles a frieze in its arrangement and that the depicted objects are decorated in turn with figured bands or rows which in themselves constitute miniature friezes. The rigidity of objects and the resulting unreality contribute to the decorative effect.

(c) CHILDREN'S APPRECIATION OF VISUAL ART OBJECTS is less important and significant than their appreciation of other arts, esp. those involving any kind of activity. Only at the close of childhood does it rank first with children's interest in arts. The following facts can be stated as results from various investigations. (1) Children's picture—art—preferences vary according to age level and sex. (2) Their primary interest is the content of pictures or sculptures, even of patterns. (3) The interest of younger children centers on specific objects in the representation which seem to them the bearers of a real or imagined activity. They interpret the situation as actually existing and contemplate a picture as if looking on through a window. (4) Older children's interest in the content is less obvious and their associations are less crude. Their response is of a more emotional nature and tends to concentrate on character and morality. (5) Color interest ranges next to the interest in content and is therefore not primary. Color is interpreted emotionally, hence interpretations vary according to age level. Comparable to their own use of brilliant clear colors, younger children are partial to such colors in their art appreciation, while older children who are in the transitional stage are attracted by fewer assorted colors or by monochromes,

similar to the use of color in their own paintings. (6) Younger children are indifferent to techniques and skill, older children notice them, esp. if the medium used in the art object is familiar to some one they have tried in their own art activity. (7) In terms of style and art period children prefer naturalism or realism — photographic likeness — to expressionism or decorative primitivism, or the non-perspective of oriental art.

Generally speaking, children's aesthetic response in art appreciation is indirect and usually unconscious; this is in contrast to their direct response to the non-aesthetic elements of an art object. Therefore if the development of an aesthetic response seems desirable, aesthetic values must be represented by a content interesting to the age level in question.

Children's Artistic Ability. (a) TYPES OF ABILITY. Artistic ability is the ability of producing art objects or of understanding art that transcends that of the average child. One can discriminate between several types of ability. These may show separately or simultaneously. Artistic ability can be observed in varying degrees. One cannot state at exactly which point it has ceased to be average; it is more correct to conceive artistic ability quantitatively as a continuous quality scale on which some individuals rank very highly, others very close to average. Artistic ability correlates positively with higher intelligence. Among the types or kinds of ability one can observe are the ability of remembering and representing characteristics of an object at any time, an ability basic for the creative process in the visual arts; imaginative ability, i.e., the ability of the child to use visual concepts for representing his own phantasies, selecting certain elements and ignoring others; ability to draw from nature or model, i.e., the child's facility for a faithful reproduction of what he sees coupled with a limited amount of interpretation — an ability that appears during the transitional stage from schema to true-to-appearance; ability to copy exactly a given original, an ability which is usually found isolated from other artistic abilities and which is mostly observed in individuals with poor intelligence.

Children with artistic ability seldom represent one clearcut type of giftedness. Usually all types are present to a certain extent with one type predominating.

At the schematic stage the work of children of distinct ability resembles in some ways that of early European masters preceding the era of perspective interpretation of nature and full modeling—13th cent. It also has a certain relationship to modern expressionistic art, perhaps due to the fact that gifted children have the ability to express with intensity an idea or experience. The gifted child's art products are the ones in which one can see resemblances to other art forms. Thus, some similarity can be noticed between the gifted child's schema and the symbolism of the art of primitive tribes; its decorativeness and non-perspective representation and certain types of oriental art; its sharpness of outline and stiffness of pose and populistic art.

There exist theories which try to explain the development of and excellence in a specific medium, such as modeling *vs.* drawing. It has been traced to a constitutional difference of response to the three-dimensional or to flat optical impressions. The type excelling in modeling has been called haptic and is characterized by a dominance of kinesthetic and empathic sensations. The type gifted for contours is represented by the silhouettist who retains contours automatically but whose mental image disintegrates when he is faced with the problem of representing the various parts outlined within the silhouetted shape. Ordinarily both types exist in the same individual. The gifted child can resolve the contradictory elements of both types in one medium.

(b) CHARACTERISTICS OF ARTISTIC ABILITY IN CHILDREN'S PRODUCTIVE WORK. Gifted children treat of a greater variety of subjects. They share this quality with non-gifted highly intellectual children of the primitive schematic phase and even up to the height of the schema. However, the non-gifted children of high intellect abandon visual means of expression very early in favor of some other means of expression, e.g. verbal. In choosing his subject the artistically outstanding child selects and develops themes which are essentially favorable to visual representation. There is no way of finding out experimentally why it happens, but one can assume that his selective procedure is his ability to separate the visual from the a-visual elements of his experiences. This power of selection is perhaps unconscious at first, but it is definitely conscious in the older child. The gifted child's range of schemata, i.e., his graphic vocabulary, is wider than that of the average child. His ability to remember visual characteristics enables him to represent objects with facility, to elaborate on them and to enrich them.

It has been observed at an early stage of study that gifted children reach each developmental stage earlier than average children; in fact, for a long time this has been considered the only reliable characteristic of special ability. While it is true that accelerated development is an important characteristic and while the question has been raised as to whether great artists ever pass through the schematic stage, it is also true that one cannot rely on this characteristic alone, since many children with a very accelerated development arrive at perspective representation but without any other symptoms of special artistic ability; hence the early attainment of the last developmental stage can be considered as precocity, but not as artistic ability. The speed of representational development of gifted children varies greatly. Some reach the height of schematic drawing at a time when the average child is still in his scribble stage, others can represent perspective and foreshortening at the age of eight. The acceleration in development may be interpreted by the gifted child's predominance of the visual. This predominance leads to a wider graphic vocabulary, to selection of visual characteristics and probably to discrimination of an aesthetic nature which in turn is responsible for the development of the outstanding aesthetic characteristics which accompany accelerated development where one encounters artistic ability.

A large number of children whose art work seems highly promising do not fulfill the promise when they outgrow the schematic stage. They regress in their aesthetic qualities and lose interest in their visual means of expression. Generally speaking, gifted children differ from average children who did outstandingly good art work during the schematic phase and failed to carry over into adolescence in that the gifted are able to re-acquire aesthetic qualities and to apply them consciously to an adult way of representation. The process may be likened to some kinds of modern primitivism or expressionism where the artist consciously develops this style of expression because he believes in it and not because he cannot learn any other technique. One of the characteristics carried over by gifted children is the ability to express movement. It is not only the result of an especially vivid memory. Other children, not especially gifted in the visual arts remember vividly too. But while their memories are a combination of sense impressions and abstractions—a mixture which does not lend itself to clearcut visual expression—gifted children achieve a more complete integration of visual characteristics which, in the case of movement, leads to retainment of essential characteristics though they may be exaggerated or distorted.

The gifted child has a greater desire and greater ability to learn. He is open to suggestions and eager to follow direct instruction; he will observe closely artists' work or his surroundings; he will not get discouraged and will try again and again. Contrary to the average child who eliminates objects from his representation because of gaps in his visual knowledge and who thus lowers his standard of production, the gifted child will strive to fill these gaps in order to keep or raise his artistic standard.

Picture organization, i.e., the grouping of a number of objects, is more highly developed in gifted children who carry over this ability to the next developmental stage; this is in contrast to average children who at that time avoid grouping of any kind.

Artistic ability can be noticed in the handling of a new medium. Most young children are eager to try a new medium. Older children are disinclined to do so unless encouraged or helped. Gifted children do not need special encouragement. Contrary to the average child who tries to adapt a new medium to a previously used familiar technique, the gifted child foregoes an acquired skill that is unsuitable for a new medium and tries to work out a new technique which will suit the new medium.

(c) ARTISTIC ABILITY AND ART APPRECIATION. The gifted child, like the average child (cf. Aesthetics of Children's Art above), is strongly influenced by the content of a work of art; i.e., he is guided by his own general interests. But, contrary to the average child, his range of interesting art objects is wider, and far less personal. Gifted children show interest in design and technique. They are not satisfied to admire the illusion that has been created through the work of art or with identifying themselves with the pictured situation as do average children. They undertake a kind of analysis for the purpose of understanding the means by which the artist creates the illusion or produces his effects. They endeavor to assimilate their findings for their own creative work. See Barnes, Earl, *The Prettiest Thing, Stud. in Educ.*, 1902, II, 5; Britsch, Gustav, *Theorie der bildenden Kunst*, 1926; Kerschensteiner, Georg, *Die Entwicklung der zeichnerischen Begabung*, 1905; Kik, C. Die uebernormale Zeichenbegabung bei Kindern, *Zs.f.ang.Psych.*, 1908, II, 92-149; Lamprecht, Karl, Les Dessins des Enfants comme Source Historique, *Bull. de l'Acad. Roy. Belgique*,

1906, 9/10, 457-469; Lascaris, P. A., *L'Education Esthetique de l'Enfant*, 1928; Maitland, Louise, What Children draw to please themselves, *Inland Educ.* Sept., 1895; Munro, Thomas and Lark-Horovitz, Betty. Children's Art Abilities. *J. Exp. Educ.*, Dec., 1942: Wulff, O., Kernfragen der Kinderkunst und der allgemeinen Kunstunterrichts der Schule. *Zs.f.Aesth. allg. Kunstw.*, XXVI, 1932, I, 46-85 and Die Kunst des Kindes, 1927.

—B.L-H.

ch'i-lin (Ch.). A fabulous animal, suggesting the unicorn, which appears frequently in Chinese and Japanese art (*kirin,* Jap.) as a symbol of good government, or a wise statesman, or scholar. See K. M. Ball, *Decorative Motives of Oriental Art*, 1927. See SYMBOLISM IN FAR EASTERN ART.

—J.A.M.

Chilkat art. See Northwest Coast Indian art; CANADA, ART OF.

chill. Bloom, or clouded appearance, occurring as a defect in a picture.

chimera, chimaera. A representation of a monster with parts from various animals.

chimney. A flue for the smoke or gases from a fire.

chimney-pot. A pipe, pot, or other hollowed member on the top of a chimney, to improve the draft.

ch'in. See MUSICAL INSTRUMENTS.

china. Originally ware from China, usually vitrified. Also general term for dinnerware. See CERAMICS I.

China, arts of. See CHINESE ARTS.

China clay. Although the greatest use of this in the arts has been for the purpose of forming objects which were fired into pottery and porcelain, China clay, called also pipe clay, kaolin, and white bole, has been much used by painters and sculptors as an inert material in coatings and grounds. It was a frequent wash over clay walls in the painting of the Far East.

—C.L.S.

china porcelain. A term loosely applied to certain commercial types of ceramics.

China art. See CHINESE ARTS.

chinaware. See CERAMICS II.

chinchilla. A thick, heavy woolen cloth for women's and children's coats, with a long napped surface rolled into little tufts, in imitation of chinchilla fur.   —G.W.R.

Chinese architecture. See CHINESE ARTS.

CHINESE ARTS. *Painting.* The Chinese people always speak of painting and calligraphy together. They do so first because the two arts use the same materials (brush, ink, and silk or paper), are practiced by the same artists, and employ the same technique; and secondly because they follow the same aesthetic principles and require the same mental discipline, as we shall see. Very often the Chinese regard calligraphy as even a higher art than painting, because they consider it purer as a fine art and more spontaneous in production. It embodies the fundamental principles on which the art of painting is based.

(a) CALLIGRAPHY. Calligraphy to the Chinese is not merely good penmanship or an art of manuscript making. It is a fine art in the full sense of the word Fundamentally it is an art of the stroke or the line executed by the use of the brush (*pi*). Both the strokes and their composition are important. They must be organized according to the general principles of balance and dynamic posture. Each stroke is an end in itself, not merely a line to delineate a form, but a drama, a symphony, a dance with its own beginning and end, anticipation and suspense, delicacy and strength, contrast and harmony. The five calligraphic styles—the bronze or seal, the clerical, the formal or modal, the informal or "walking,' and the cursive or "dancing"—are distinguished not only by their characteristics in composition and general appearance, but also by the peculiarities of their strokes. Individual calligraphers, schools of calligraphy, and even types of calligraphic beauty are so distinguished.

Strokes are carefully analyzed. Traditionally they are classified into the slanting spot, the bridling horizontal stroke, the striving vertical stroke, the springing up-stroke, the whipping left-above-stroke, the skimming left-below-stroke, the pecking right-above-stroke, and the tearing right-below-stroke, all of which are represented in the character *yung*. Each of these strokes is further analyzed into many forms and tendencies, each with its own characteristic force and dynamic expression. It is this drama of force that makes Chinese calligraphy such an interesting art. Famous calligraphers speak of the "nine forces" of calligraphy, the "seven battle arrays of the

brush," and "the battle array of writing." As one writer describes it, "Writing is like breaking ice in a crystal jar, light as floating gossamer, or a cloud drifting across a clear sky, violent as an attack of wild beasts, or raging flames sweeping the prairie." The dynamic qualities of each stroke and the organic whole of a character must be such as to realize the "four essentials" of beauty in calligraphy: i.e., *shen* or a style full of spirit, energy, and vivacity; *ch'i* or the strength of the brush stroke; *yun*, rhythm or balance; and *wei* or aesthetic quality and interest and taste. In short, the ideal of calligraphy is rhythmic vitality and life movement.

(b) RHYTHMIC VITALITY. This is precisely what Chinese painting is driving at. The whole art develops on this very principle of "rhythmic vitality and life movement." This is *ch'i yun sheng tung*, the first canon of Chinese painting. The four words may be taken separately as *ch'i* or force, spirit, breath, soul; *yun* or resonance, rhythm, charm, feeling, reverberation; *sheng* or life, the will to live; and *tung* or movement. They may be taken in pairs as *ch'i yun* or spiritual resonance and *sheng tung* or life movement. They are, however, usually taken as one phrase, and often abbreviated to merely *ch'i*, which is fairly well rendered in English as "rhythmic vitality," "operation of the spirit of life movement," "spiritual rhythm expressed in the movement of life," or "the life-movement of the spirit through the rhythm of things." Hsieh Ho of the 5th cent. who formulated the canon neither defined nor explained the phrase, but from his comments on painting which were made on the basis of this canon, there can be no doubt that it denotes a style which expresses the spiritual essence and rhythmic vitality of things. He used such expressions as "the nature of things," "the principle according to which things are," "strong power," "style and charm," "the soul and mystery of things," "spirit," "life force," etc.

In the narrow sense of the phrase, it means rhythm. But in its broader sense, it denotes something more than mere musical quality. It is the creative force, the vitality of all life, the cosmic soul. For a painter to express the *ch'i* of a tree, for example, he must express the tree-nature, its structure, its peacefulness, gracefulness, and above all, the rhythmic vital force which gives it spirit and form. This *ch'i* may be expressed in various ways. As T'ang Chi-ch'i said, "There are different kinds of rhythmic vitality. There is the rhythmic vitality of the stroke. There is the rhythmic vitality of ink. And there is the rhythmic vitality of color. All of these are rhythmic vitality. Furthermore, there is the rhythmic vitality of movement. There is the rhythmic vitality of force. There is the rhythmic vitality of creative power."

(c) CONCEPTION AND BRUSH-STROKE. The fundamental factors of this creative process are two, namely, the conception and the brush-stroke. Of these two, the conception is more important, for according to the general belief of Chinese artists, "The conception precedes the stroke." This saying and also the dictum that "Painting proceeds from the mind" are the basic assumptions of the Chinese graphic art. To be able to express the rhythmic vitality of the object, the artist must first of all know the inner essence of the object and know it so well that he possesses it in his mind. This means a resolute hold on the reality and beauty of things, which can be achieved only after a long period of mental discipline so that there can be coherence and concentration of the artist's mind in relation with the object. The artist must "hold the universe in his hand," so to speak. It is only with this intimacy with the object that the artist can express freely and spontaneously its rhythmic vitality. Consequently, the artist must first of all have the proper conception of the nature of the object, the style, the expression the composition, and the mood before he takes up the brush. The execution of the stroke is an outcome of his conception. It is a translation of the conception on silk or paper. This translation must be accomplished spontaneously, sincerely, and surely, for there can be no "working over" once a stroke is drawn. The nature of Chinese ink and paper and silk prevents erasure or correction.

The stroke in painting follows the same principles as in calligraphy. The main thing is the controlling rhythm of the brush. With perfect control, a stroke may be simple, light, and delicate or varied, heavy, and powerful. It may proceed as a graceful curve or end in a sudden stop. It may progress as a swift and vigorous line or develop as a gentle and wavering stroke. Chinese painters demand "eight essential qualities" in a stroke, namely, simplicity, strength, freshness, elegance, penetrative expressiveness, roundness and smoothness, solidity and stability, and ever-changing liveliness. A stroke should have "sinews, muscles, bones, and energy," that is, precision, fulness, stability, and force. It must possess the "six fundamental characteristics," namely, fulness of spirit, clearness and lightness, rugged ma-

turity, strength, liveliness, and richness. It must avoid the "four defects" of stiffness, dryness, vulgarity, and weakness. It must be free from the "three shortcomings" of flatness, ugliness, and frigidity. It may require a lifetime to perfect. It determines to a great extent the merit of a painter. It distinguishes one school from another. Painters and schools differ in their types of strokes. But they all agree that the primary purpose of the stroke is to express rhythmic vitality. As in calligraphy, the stroke in painting has a drama of its own. But in addition, it expresses the inner essence of the object portrayed and also the conception of the artist.

(d) PAINTING AND POETRY. The formation of the conception and its expression in strokes are primarily intended to evoke a poetic mood, a mood which creates a sense of peace, gives a feeling of release from the vulgarity of city life, and provides a moment of brooding over life. This function of Chinese painting must be fully appreciated before one can understand why in Chinese painting landscape ranks highest, why the painting of the "four gentlemen" (plum, orchid, chrysanthemum, bamboo) form a special branch, and why inscription occupies an unusually important place. To the Chinese, Nature, especially in landscape and the "four gentlemen," is an inexhaustible fountain of poetic inspiration, and a poetic inscription can enhance the poetic mood of a picture. For this reason, Chinese poetry, which draws its chief inspiration from Nature, and Chinese painting always go hand in hand. One is not complete without the other. For this reason, most Chinese painters are poets at the same time.

A poetic mood can be expressed in just a few bamboo leaves or in a bare outline of a mountain range. Since a picture is not an end in itself, but a means to create a poetic mood, it must be beautiful enough to arouse the poetic consciousness instantly. This calls for economy of material and directness of expression. The painter includes only what is absolutely essential in his picture, expresses it in the simplest manner, and leaves a great deal of room for the free exercise of the imagination. The mood so created must continue to change and develop. In this sense, a Chinese painting is never a finished product. It grows with the beholder who places himself in the position of the artist, shares his conception, and carries on his process of re-creation.

To create a varying mood in the most effective manner, the Chinese have developed a form of painting as interesting as it is unique.

This is the **long scroll.** It is a horizontal painting many feet long, to be unrolled slowly and gradually, exposing only one small portion at a time. Each exposed portion is a good picture, good enough to express a full measure of rhythmic vitality and to provide a desired mood. As the scroll is unrolled, one goes from one scene to another, very much like following a symphony, watching a drama, or going through a journey. The rhythm here is three-dimensional, that of the two-dimensional rhythm of ordinary painting and the temporal rhythm of music. The mood changes and develops at every turn.

(e) COLOR AND PERSPECTIVE. The foregoing discussion should be sufficient to show that Chinese painting is allied with poetry (and music) rather than architecture and sculpture. Since the chief objects are the expression of rhythmic vitality and the creation of a poetic mood, it is obvious that color and perspective in the physical sense do not occupy as important a place in Chinese painting as they do in Western painting. To be sure, many Chinese painters paint with colors. But the ideal form of painting, to the Chinese way of thinking, is monochrome, on the assumption that Nature in her essence transcends colors. Chinese monochrome is not monotonous black and white drawing, but a painting in ink which has enormous range of effect and is capable of a great variety of shading and infinite tonal orchestration. To Chinese painters, the different shades of ink are sufficient to produce the effects of color. They resort to ink rather than color for tones and modulation. They say that ink has the "six colors" of black, white, dryness, richness, thickness, and thinness. As to light, shadow, and relief, Chinese painters pay little attention to them, if any, for they are not interested in the physical aspects of things.

In this idealistic type of aesthetics, physical perspective naturally assumes little importance. It is not that Chinese painters have not tried it. Ku K'ai-chih, one of the earliest painters, shows a highly developed sense of physical perspective. Chan Tzu-ch'ien of the 6th cent. is said to have experimented with perspective on murals. A century before that, a theory of geometric perspective was already well established and clearly formulated by Tsung Ping. He said that "if I spread the silk and hold it against an actual scene, the K'un-lan mountain can be included in one square inch. A vertical stroke of three inches on the silk is equal to a height of ten thousand feet, and a horizontal stroke of several feet is sufficient to represent several hundred miles." As a matter of fact, throughout the history of Chinese painting, the confusion of distances has always been regarded as a major blunder.

But Chinese painters have no desire for objective accuracy or factual description. Nor are they interested in mathematical exactness. Geometric perspective is based on a fixed point. This has no appeal to Chinese painters. They want the vision to move on continuously. To them the cardinal principle of perspective is that "the shape of a mountain changes with every step one takes." "A mountain viewed at close range," said Kuo Hsi, "has one appearance; a mountain viewed at a distance of several miles has another. When viewed from a distance of scores of miles, it has still another. The further the distance, the more different the appearance. This is called 'the shape of a mountain changes with every step one takes.'" A landscape painting must show all these changes.

Out of this conception of perspective grows the fundamental law of Chinese landscape composition, the **"law of three sections."** The appearance of the ground as the first level, trees as the second, and mountains as the third, represents the maximum concession of Chinese painters towards conformity with physical Nature. They place things nearby in the foreground and those further away in the background so that distance is conveyed by the movement of the eye from the bottom to the top of the scroll. But, significantly, there is lacking any center of gravity, any focus, or any vanishing point. Chinese artists refuse to arrest reality at a single instant of time or localize it at a single point of space. They want to grasp Nature in her essence, above the realm of space and time, through spiritual intimation and intuitive understanding instead of superficial imitation. In other words, they want to see Nature with an inner eye, with the perspective of the mind. Such perspective goes over and beyond geometric restriction. It is not sufficient to label this perspective as aerial, multiple, or even progressive, for these may still mean the point perspective. The Chinese perspective is that of the poetic mind, the inner vision, a sort of dream perspective if you like. Only with this type of perspective can Chinese painters express Nature as a whole without chopping her into pieces, and reveal her in her essence without distorting her physical appearance.

In such a scheme of perspective, space becomes extremely significant. It not only gives room for the free exercise of the imagination, but also provides an atmosphere of freedom and movement and gives a picture the sense of a satisfying whole. Very often in looking at a Chinese painting, one's eyes travel slowly until they come to some empty space. There they come to rest and there the mind broods over Nature and life. Gradually and unconsciously observation passes over to contemplation. As a result, one's experience is enriched and one's soul ennobled. Thus space is not a negative quality, but something alive, dynamic, constructive. As in calligraphy, it forms an integral part of the whole. As a matter of fact, for its structural and poetic qualities, space in painting draws inspiration from calligraphy. Orchid and bamboo paintings are closest to calligraphy, and it is not a coincidence that space is of special importance in these paintings. Space to these paintings is like air and breeze to the sweet fragrance of the orchid and the graceful bending of the bamboo.

(f) CHIN AND THE SOUTHERN AND NORTHERN DYNASTIES: BUDDHIST PAINTING, SIX CANONS, KU K'AI-CHIH. Chinese painting can be traced to prehistoric times when pottery was decorated with colored figures. From the dawn of recorded history, utensils, garments, banners, maps, and walls were painted with figures and designs. In the earlier part of the Han dynasty (206 B.C.-220 A.D.) murals with portraits of heroes were particularly common; both oil painting and water-color were practiced; and Mao Yen-shou in the reign of Yuan-ti (48-33 B.C.), the first known painter in Chinese history, distinguished himself as an outstanding portraitist. As we shall see in the section on Chinese stone carving, painting had reached a fairly advanced stage by his time. Early in the 3d cent., paper began to supplement silk as a medium.

It was during the Chin dynasty (265-420 A.D.) that Chinese painting was firmly established. This was a period of moral and intellectual revolution. The Confucian formalistic ethics of Han were breaking down. The imagination and the emotions were given free expression in poetry. The romantic, naturalistic philosophy of abandonment of Lao Tzu and Chuang Tzu captivated the literati and won many Confucianists over to Taoism. Buddhism was in ascendency. There was a new atmosphere and a new horizon, full of free spirit and fresh air. It was no wonder, therefore, that all the main branches of Chinese painting—Buddhist painting, landscape (or "mountain and water" as the Chinese call

it), flower and bird painting, genre painting ("people and things")—and the basic theories of art all emerged at this time. Furthermore, the substitution at the same time of ink for oil-paint and the brush for the reed provided artists with freer mediums of expression.

The originality of the Chin period can be seen from the works of many of its artists, especially Ts'ao Pu-hsing of the 3d cent. He was an eminent painter of dragons, the common symbol of cosmic vitality. He was the first one to experiment with painting on paper. And, most important of all, he was the founder of Buddhist painting in China. He imitated some Buddhist figures brought to China by Central Asiatic monks and inaugurated the vigorous movement of Buddhist art that was to last for many centuries. This movement gained momentum as the number of Buddhist temples increased and as more and more Indian and Central Asiatic Buddhist paintings were introduced. For some five centuries it dominated Chinese art and hardly any Chinese painter during this time escaped its influence.

The crowning art of China, landscape, advanced at this time from a secondary position as background to portraits to a position of equal importance. With the removal of the Chin capital to Chinyeh (present Nanking), the center of Chinese civilization shifted to the South. Here the Chinese from the North were overwhelmed by the abundance and charm of Nature. Artists were attracted to natural scenery and began to attach importance to landscape. This tendency was already noticeable in Ku K'ai-chih (392-467) who may therefore be considered the forerunner of Chinese landscape. In the beginning of the Southern and Northern Dynasties (420-589), the aesthetic foundation of landscape was laid by Tsung Ping (375-443) and Wang Wei (415-443). The former, as we have seen, had a clear conception of perspective. To him, "landscapes exist in material substance and soar into the realm of the spirit." "Through their shapes, they make the Way of Nature fascinating." He would therefore paint merely to "refresh his spirit." Wang Wei said that "the ancients painted not only to record sites and mark boundaries" but to express their feelings. "In painting," he declared, "what conforms to the object will produce harmony, but it is the mind that reveals the spirit and its life-movements." He believed that the painter should "depict the vast universe in one single stroke,"

With this type of aesthetic interest predominating, the time was ripe for the formulation of basic principles not only for landscape but for painting in general. This was accomplished by Hsieh Ho (c. 500). He laid down the Six Canons of art. The first and the most important Canon, "rhythmic vitality and life-movement," has been discussed. The rest are: "the structural use of the brush," "conformity with the object," "the application of colors according to their characteristics," "composition," and "transmission of style by copying and drawing". These Canons have been the guiding stars of Chinese painting from the fifth century to the present day.

While principles were being formulated by the aestheticians, the technique of painting was being refined by the Three Masters, Ku K'ai-chih, Lu T'an-wei (5th cent.), and Chang Seng-yu (479-502). Ku was one of the greatest painters in Chinese history. He was the first to practice outline drawing without color, shading, or wash. He was a great master of the "iron wire stroke," that is, the long, even, and flowing line drawn by a vertical brush. According to the *Hua Chi*, "In painting beautiful figures, Chang gives us the flesh, Lu gives us the bones, but Ku gives us the spirit." Copies of Ku's paintings in the British Museum and Freer Gallery show that his style has delicacy, lightness, refinement, and the rhythmic vitality of the brush-stroke. There is supreme elegance of form and poetry of attitude. His figures have graceful gestures, gentle manners, humane dignity, ivory faces with refined and subtle charm, and long, floating garments. In the words of the arch-critic Chang Yen-yuan, "His conception preceded the stroke . . . and therefore he achieved a perfect expression of spirit and rhythmic vitality." Lu T'an-wei was a master in all types of painting, especially Buddhist figures and dragons. His chief distinction, however, lies in his creation of the "one stroke painting" to which he applied the style of Wang Hsien-chih who wrote characters in one continuous stroke. Chang Seng-yu, besides being an expert painter of Buddhist figures and dragons, introduced the Indian technique of carved relief into Chinese painting, invented "painting without bones," that is, painting without preliminary outlines, and applied green and blue and red colors to his landscape, thus anticipating the "green and blue" painting of later periods.

None of the innovations of Lu and Chang, however, attracted much following. In the two centuries after them, Chinese artists chiefly confined their interest to Buddhist painting, and, to a lesser degree, to landscape, with Ku K'ai-chih's stroke-manner as the standard style. Both Buddhist painting and landscape continued to develop slowly through the Sui dynasty (581-618), with Buddhist painting predominating. The two outstanding artists of this era were Chan Tzu-ch'ien and Tung Po-jen. The former is generally considered to have laid the foundation of painting in the following T'ang dynasty.

(g) T'ANG: WU TAO-TZU, SOUTHERN AND NORTHERN SCHOOLS OF LANDSCAPE, PAINTING AND POETRY, PAINTING OF THE LITERATI, BUDDHIST PAINTING. The T'ang dynasty (618-907) gave China her greatest painters, notably Yen Li-te and his brother Li-pen (d. 673), Wu Tao-tzu, and Wang Wei (Mo Ch'i). The Yen brothers were exquisite in all styles, especially in Buddhist and Taoist figures. Wu Tao-tzu was epoch-making. And Li Ssu-hsun and Wang Wei founded the two rival schools of landscape. Few, if any, of their original paintings have been preserved. But from early copies of their works their styles can be clearly discerned.

The world is unanimous in calling Wu Tao-tzu (d. 792) the greatest of Chinese painters. To the Chinese he is "the sage of painting." In him, landscape declared complete independence from portraiture and started its way to pre-eminence as the greatest art of China. He was "perfect" in technique. In the words of Chang Yen-yuan, "In Wu's style we have the complete realization of the idea that the conception precedes the brush. . . . All the Six Canons are perfectly realized. In him, the stroke, especially the "orchid leaf line" which curls and changes in the middle to produce hues and enhance rhythm, achieved excellence. It is graceful, interesting, vehement, lively, vibrating, like "a ribbon flowing and dancing in the wind." It is no longer the delicate and fine stroke of his precedessors whom he at first followed, but "dynamic as the sudden wind and rain and forceful as lightning and thunder." Su Tung-po the poet-painter said that Wu was the only person in Chinese history "able to express new conceptions in ordinary patterns and to reveal essential truth in an unrestrained manner." As such he was the envy of all later Chinese painters. There is no doubt that Wu Tao-tzu drew his chief inspiration from calligraphy, and it was not a mere coincidence that his pupil Chang Hsu created the extremely swift, cursive, "entwining rope" style in calligraphy. Wu's style also reflects a certain Buddhist influence. He was equally a master of Buddhist and Taoist figures. It must be born in mind that throughout the Sui and T'ang dynasties, religious figures were the central interest of Chinese painters, although landscape began to offer strong competition.

Wang Wei (699-759) and Li Ssu-hsun (651-716) are traditionally called the founders of the Southern and Northern Schools of landscape, respectively. What they actually did, however, was to crystalize two divergent tendencies that had been asserting themselves for some time. The Southern School is characterized by the romantic and Taoistic spirit of the South, poetic suggestion, pliant lines, free and fast strokes, soft shades, subtle colors, imaginative quality, emotional expression, and a romantic, dreamy, and melancholic mood. There is in this school a keen sense for the spiritual and the most essential, a free intuitive mode of creation, a feeling of wonder and fancy, and the atmosphere of fresh air. The Northern School, on the other hand, is distinguished by the use of greens, blues, gold outlines, vigorous and rugged strokes, a formalistic and intellectual approach, vehement and bold execution, care for details, and a sense of stability and dignity. The landscape of the Southern School is often called "thin ink landscape," whereas that of the Northern School "landscape in greens and blues." The style of the former is often compared to delicate and graceful trees by the side of a lake, that of the latter to lofty and steep mountains. The Southern School uses the "rain-drop" stroke, that is, shading by the small, pointed, oval strokes, whereas the Northern School uses the "small axe" stroke, that is, shading by small strokes resembling axe splits. Actually, painters of one school also use the stroke of the other. The two schools did not develop in different geographical regions as their names may imply. They merely represent two different approaches to landscape, evidently inspired by and corresponding to the Southern and Northern Schools of Zen Buddhism. Famous followers of the Southern School were Ching Hao and Kuan T'ung of the Five Dynasties; Tung Yuan, Chu Jan, Li Ch'eng, Fan K'uan, Kuo Chung-shu, Li Lung-mien, Mi Fei, and Mi Yu-jen of Sung; the Four Masters of Yuan; and Wen Ching-ming and Shen Chou of Ming. Famous followers of the Northern School were Chao Kan, Chao Po-chu, Chao Po-hsiu, Ma Yuan, Hsia Kuei, Li T'ang, and Liu Sung-nien, all of Sung. Historians have classified practically all Chinese painters in the last ten centuries in one school or the other. Few painters, however, follow the style of one school exclusively.

To some extent the styles of the two schools reflect the environment and personality of their two reputed founders. Li Ssu-hsun was a member of the imperial family, served as a general, and enjoyed a life of aristocracy and nobility. Wang Wei, on the contrary, was a poet who loved streams and rocks and music and books, a hermit in his last years and one who shared the Buddhist and Taoist dislike of the vulgar life of the troubled world. He was an idealist who cared for the inner nature of things, not hesitating to paint flowers of different seasons in the same painting. He was as great a poet as he was a painter. It is often said that "there is poetry in his painting and there is painting in his poems." In him the mutual penetration of poetry and painting became complete. Beginning with him, monochrome was regarded as the best form for the expression of poetic sentiments. Beginning with him, too, the "broken ink" landscape became the ideal of Chinese landscape painters. Instead of traditional outlined painting filled in with colors, in this original style of Wang We, the configuration is effected by shading ("wrinkling") with woolly, light-colored ink-strokes. The soft and changing tones of this ink-painting render an atmospheric perspective both effective and charming. There is something fluid and ethereal about the style. This intuitive approach and free rendering definitely reflects the influence of Zen Buddhism which advocated "sudden enlightenment" and "direct intuition of Buddha-nature." Such a tendency suited the taste of the literati extremely well, and this poetic and subjective type of painting became known as "the painting of the literati." It has become the strongest tradition in Chinese painting, exerting no less influence today than it did a thousand years ago.

In addition to these new conceptions and new tendencies, the T'ang dynasty is important in the annals of Chinese painting in several other respects. First of all, the earliest paintings on silk or paper still existent belong to this period. Secondly, flower and bird painting developed in this era as one of the basic types, thanks to Pien Luan who brought the art to the level of excellence. Thirdly, specialization in painting began in this period. Many artists devoted their whole lives to perfect just one subject, be it the horse, dragon, tiger, water buffalo, a fruit, a bird, an insect, pine tree, bamboo, plum, water, fire, or clouds. The horse was particularly favored, undoubtedly because of the beauty of foreign horses newly imported from China's western neighbors. Both Tsao Pa and his pupil Han Kan (c. 700) excelled in this subject. In the fourth place, genre painting, especially that of beautiful women and their life in the court, the garden, or the home, a type of painting in which Chou Fang (c. 780) was outstanding, created a new conception of feminine beauty. Finally, Buddhist painting no longer imitated Indian models but became entirely Chinese in conception and manner. This is in sharp contrast to the Buddhist frescoes which remained partly foreign, were works of artisans, and were provincial in outlook. The most celebrated pieces are those discovered in the Tunhuang caves in 1907 and now mostly in the British Museum. They are admired by Westerners for their perfect combination of Chinese artistic conception and Indian imagery and formula, their tender and majestic figures, their graceful and gentle drapery, their profoundly religious feeling, their serene composition, and their harmony of colors. Because their lines lack the calligraphic quality, however, they are not highly regarded by the Chinese.

(h) SUNG: THREE MASTERS OF LANDSCAPE, MI FEI, LI LUNG-MIEN, ACADEMY, FLOWERS AND BIRDS, "PLAYING WITH INK." In the Five Dynasties (907-960) that followed T'ang, the Southern School, especially its "painting of the literati," became dominant. Bamboo painting, the most characteristic form of this type of painting, began at this time. Flower and bird painting reached new heights in Hsu Hsi and Huang Ch'uan, who became the standards of later generations.

Hsu Hsi used mere drops of ink to form his leaves, branches, and flower buds and then slightly spread colors on them. In this way he achieved an antique and distinctive effect. He is usually regarded as the representative of the Southern School in flowers and birds. Huang Ch'uan, on the other hand, first drew outlines and then applied brilliant and rich colors. In this way he achieved richness, charm, and a high degree of singular lightness and pervasiveness. He is usually regarded as the representative of the Northern School. The two exerted tremendous influence over flower and bird painters of subsequent dynasties, notably Chao Ch'ang and Emperor Hui-tsung of Sung, Ch'ien Hsuan and Wang Yuan of Yuan, Pien Wen-chin, Lu Chi, Lin Liang, and Chou Chih-mien of Ming, and

Yun Shou-p'ing and Chiang T'ing-hsi of Ch'ing.

Landscape in the Five Dynasties was predominantly Southern in spirit. There was no longer the delicacy of Chin or the peace and plainness of T'ang. Instead, it breathed an air of magnificence and power. With economy of strokes and loftiness of conception, both Ching Hao and Kuan T'ung, the two stars of the epoch, effected a strange vastness and overwhelming grandeur. As Hsu Hsi and Huang Ch'uan prepared for the "grand perfection" of flower and bird painting in the Sung dynasty, so they paved the way for the "grand perfection" of landscape in that dynasty.

The Sung period (960-1279) compares favorably with and in some respects surpasses T'ang in the field of painting. There was a greater host of masters than in any other period. The collection and study of paintings, enthusiastically encouraged by such artist-emperors as Hui-tsung (1083-1135), have never been equaled in Chinese history. Academies of painting were liberally supported by the government, and painting became a required subject both in the schools and in the competitive civil service examination. For three long centuries, the art of painting enjoyed unusual prosperity.

Under the influence of Zen Buddhism and the Confucian philosophy of *li* or Reason, that is, the inner principle of things, Sung aestheticians emphasized spiritual essence to the complete rejection of physical verisimilitude. The spirit of the Southern School dominated the age, in landscape, in flower and bird painting, and, especially, in "playing with ink." In all these arts, poetry was the end and calligraphy the means. Poetic inscription assumed more importance. Painting was exclusively the art of the literati.

Landscape reached the point of excellence at the beginning of the dynasty. Forms and styles were "completed" by the Three Great Masters, Tung Yuan (c. 903), Li Ch'eng (c. 970), and Fan K'uan (c. 977). They were all influenced by Wang Wei the poet-painter. Tung Yuan followed Wang Wei in his ink-painting, but resembled Li Ssu-hsun in the application of colors. He loved to paint the distant hills and changing clouds of the South in their natural simplicity, was exceedingly good in painting trees, woods, bridges, rivers, fishermen, and islands, all instinct with a sense of rural life and beauty. Li Ch'eng's ink-painting, coming from his free and sensitive brush, is precise, economical, subtle, especially effective in scenes of distant winter groves.

He could "sweep a thousand miles in the space of one foot and create ten thousand charms beyond mountain peaks." He combines ink-painting with greens and blues in perfectly harmonious blending. Fan K'uan is famous for his snow scenes, dense groves on mountain tops, and huge rocks by the water's edge. His strokes are strong and rugged, his "rain-drop" shading unique. He said, "It is better to learn from things than from people, and it is better to learn from one's own heart than from things."

These Three Masters held complete sway over the artists of their own period and the period immediately following. Hsu Tao-ning, Yen Wen-kuei (967-1044), Kuo Hsi (c. 1085), etc. followed Li Ch'eng, while Chu Jan (c. 930), who is sometimes called the fourth master of the period, and his pupils followed Tung Yuan. An outstanding painter of the time independent of them was Kuo Chung-hsi (c. 985), an expert in "measured painting," that is, architecture in landscape.

The influence of the Three Masters produced a great change in landscape about a century later. This change took place in Mi Fei (1051-1107) and his son Yu-jen (1085-1165), indisputably the greatest painters of Sung. With them Chinese painting entered upon a new epoch. Like Wang Wei, they are subjective, poetic, suggestive, imaginative. But unlike Wang Wei, they painted almost exclusively in monochrome and worked with tones rather than strokes. They painted in their novel "spilled ink" style, that is, piling wash upon wash as though working in oil. With heavy and broad touches they produced forcible silhouettes, vast mountain ranges, strange wooden peaks rising above rain and mist. They are especially admired for their "clouds and mist" and their ethereal atmosphere Mi Fei developed an original style of using clouds and mist to cover partially the trees. His son's landscape pictures seem to be composed of dots and dashes for the clouds and mist, made in a slipshod and hurried manner, and yet true to life. Both father and son possessed an intimacy with Nature and a conception of the universe in its inner essence never approached by other artists. Their mist, rain, and clouds are force, movement, and rhythmic vitality pure and simple. Their clouds and mist "flow across the scroll."

Another great painter of the time was Li Kung-lin, better known as Li Lung-mien (b. 1049). He was accomplished in all fields. His lines, particularly the curves, are delicate, flexible, fluid, rhythmic, harmonious. "com-parable to wandering clouds and running streams." He achieved consonant blending and perfect balance of different traditions. "He was better than Han Kan in painting horses, surpassed Wu Tao-tzu in Buddhist figures, equaled Li Ssu-hsun in landscape, and matched Wang Wei in his manner of ink and strokes." He is generally praised as the one painter since Wu Tao-tzu to have realized all the Six Canons of art, a "grand synthesis" of all masters. He was the greatest painter of religious figures of the Sung dynasty, especially the *lohan* or the Buddhist saint. He painted in black and white, setting a new style in figure painting. After his time Buddhist painting degenerated into an art of purely technical skill, partly because there was no new religious impulse and partly because Zen Buddhism deprecated art in favor of meditation and intuition.

After the Sung capital was moved to Nanking in 1127, the Southern School suffered a temporary setback. Practically all outstanding painters of the time were members of the Imperial Academy. They often painted more worldly scenes in a more realistic manner to please the emperors. Consequently the style of the Northern School became the vogue, complete with its delicacy, refinement, attention to details, and love of brilliant colors. This fact, of course, did not prevent its painters from being great or creative. Li T'ang (1049-1130), for example, distinguished himself for painting huge rocks with the "big axe splitting" stroke, thus altering the traditional stroke-manner of the Northern School. For the "vertical brush" which Li Ssu-hsun and other earlier leaders of the Northern School employed, he substituted the "slant brush," thus making a radical change which sharply differentiated the Northern School and the Southern School which continued to use the "vertical brush." He also could create an impression of roaring waves without the traditional "fish scale" line. He was superb in painting water buffaloes. Other great academicians were Chao Po-chu and his brother Po-hsiu (c. 1130) and Liu Sung-nien (1073-1157).

Before long, however, the Southern School reasserted itself, even within the Academy. Ma Yuan (c. 1195) and Hsia Kuei (c. 1208), both academicians, produced another change in landscape by synthesizing the style of Li T'ang and the ink-painting of the Southern School Their works show greatness of conception and broadness of stroke. They achieved strange effects by daring simplicity. Their plants seem to be alive and mountains seem to rear themselves with fierce energy. Their "heavy ink" or dense, black ink applied with the brush fairly dry, which was an innovation, has the fascinating effect of strength and antiquity mixed with fluidness. Equally splendid are their "axe split" strokes. They have been rightly called the school of "strong and antique ink-painting." They clearly betray the influence of the Three Masters and Mi Fei. In their expansive mood and rough manner, they erred in over-simplicity and abruptness. Their style was transmitted through Tai Wen-chin of Ming and later artists.

In flower and bird painting, the style of Huang Ch'uan was continued by his son Chu-ts'ai (b. 933) and that of Hsi Hsi by his grandson Ch'ung-ssu. Because of his aristocratic life in the Academy, Huang Chu-ts'ai not only perpetuated the richness, splendor, and elegance characteristic of his father but added to them sweetness and charm. He became the model of flower and bird painting in the Academy. His authority was not challenged until Ts'ui Pai (c. 1070) who modified the Huang Ch'uan tradition by substituting freedom for refinement and by introducing new forms. Hsu Ch'ung-ssu, Huang's rival outside the Academy, painted without outline but with rich colors. Beginning with him the Hsu Hsi school developed into two branches, one of ink-painting with subtle colors and one with rich colors but without "bones" or outlines.

At about this time a new tendency in the treatment of plant life commenced. This is called "playing with ink." Its subjects include groves, rocks, simple landscape, and plants. But the plum, the orchid, the chrysanthemum, and the bamboo are most favored. They are called the "four gentlemen," obviously because of their gentlemanly qualities. Artists painted them in the manner of the literary man to express their care-free feelings. Without the slightest attention to detail, convention, or factual accuracy, they painted like a child, spontaneously, freely, intuitively. They merely "played with ink" to suit their own tastes, to reveal their thoughts, and to express their feelings. They spoke of "writing" bamboo or plum, instead of "painting." Overcome by Zen Buddhism and the philosophy of li (inner principle of things), they "forgot both spirit and matter," but maintained an attitude of "seriousness" towards things, that is, an attitude of intimacy and identification with things. They religiously obeyed the principle that conception precedes the brush. They wanted rhythmic vitality, subtlety, simplicity, purity,

and spirituality. The result is a highly idealistic art, lofty in conception, simple in form, light in spirit, deep in poetic feeling, and calm but strong in rhythmic vitality. There is no artificiality, formality, or heaviness, but a child's delight coupled with a literary man's sense of nobility, refinement, and serenity. Almost all Sung painters "played with ink." Some devoted their whole lives to trying to master the art of painting bamboo. The two leading bamboo painters were Wen T'ung (1018-1079) and Su Tung-po (1036-1101). The former was the greatest master of bamboo in ink, while the latter was absolutely unconventional in handling his subject. Su Tung-po, himself a poet of the first order, said in a poem that "If in judging a painting you seek natural resemblance, you have the vision of a child." He therefore did not hesitate to paint bamboo in red or without joints. In him and in his circle, the painting of the literati reached its peak.

(i) YUAN: "CONCEPTION," FOUR GREAT MASTERS, INSCRIPTION. The literary tradition persisted throughout the Yuan dynasty (1280-1368). But instead of emphasizing the fa (technique) of T'ang or the li (inner principle) of Sung, Yuan artists concentrated on i (conception). The majority of artists "played with ink," were unusually fond of painting orchid and bamboo, liked to paint figures in outlines without color or shading, and put the poetic conception ahead of everything else. There was no longer the nobility, dignity, and spirituality that characterized the painting of Sung. These were replaced by melancholy, eccentricity, and purely subjective construction.

This is not to say that the Yuan dynasty had no great painters. Both Ch'ien Hsuan (1239-1302) and Chao Meng-fu (1254-1322) and later the Four Great Masters compare favorably with the masters of T'ang and Sung. Ch'ien and Chao continue the style of Li Lung-mien and retain the temper of the Sung painters. The former is good in figures, landscape, and flowers and birds. He combines strength and loftiness with tenderness. The latter is celebrated for all types of painting. His horses have excellent poses and a high degree of feeling and movement. His landscape shows perfect blending, lofty conception, masterly organization, and a sense of unity. The lines of his flowers and birds are simple, vibrant, and flexible. He applied the technique of carving and calligraphy to painting bamboo. As generally agreed, "he has all the delicacy of the T'ang artists without their weakness and all the strength of the Sung artists without their coarseness."

The Four Great Masters of Yuan were Huang Kung-meng (1268-1354), Wang Meng (d. 1385), Ni Tsan (1301-1374), and Wu Chen (1280-1354). They carried on the tradition of the Southern School following particularly Tung Yuan and Chu Jan. Their chief concern was poetic conception and rhythmic vitality. Their numerous mountain ranges and thick groves never cease to be interesting. Their strokes are extremely strong. They all used the "dried brush," that is, the technique in which the ink is used sparingly, with little moisture in the brush. In this they set a new style. Huang Kung-meng mostly painted in light red in which he combined strength and richness, and sometimes in simple ink and water in which he achieved telling effect with very little shading or "wrinkling." His pictures of hills and dales have ever-changing aspects and manifold beauty. Wang Meng who preferred to paint on paper rather than on silk, followed his grandfather Chao Meng-fu chiefly but applied the technique of shading-wrinkling of different schools, and therefore had richness and variety in his art. He led a roaming life and had nothing professional about him. As a matter of fact, most Chinese painters have been amateurs, but Wang was the most amateurish of all. Ni Tsan was the greatest master of the "dried brush," was "economical of ink as if it were gold," liked suggestion and simplicity, and was reticent and delicate in manner, placid and natural in style. He did not put human figures in his landscapes, and seldom used color. Like Wang, he lived a roaming life and was entirely free from the vulgarity of city life and the worldliness of the professionals. Wu Chen was expert in flowers in ink, figures, and landscape. His strokes are spirited and strong. Thus all the Four Masters were faithful to the Southern School tradition and yet each was unique in his own way.

Beginning with the Four Masters, inscriptions on paintings played a role of real importance. Poetic inscriptions were placed in prominent parts of the painting to re-enforce it in evoking a poetic mood. The unity of poetry and painting was thus strengthened. Calligraphy, too, was completely identified with painting. "Playing with ink" became "writing" *per se*. Different parts of bamboo, for example, were to be "written" in the styles of various written scripts.

(j) MING: FIGURES AND LIFE, LANDSCAPES. The care-free spirit of Chinese art rapidly de-clined in the Ming dynasty (1368-1644). Because of the dogmatic temper of rulers and the general concern for external matters of the time, artists lost their self-confidence. They were not at home with either the *hsing* (appearance), the *li* (inner principle), or the *i* (conception). They became formalistic, academic. They loved brilliant colors, over-laden composition, fine but laborous and meticulous lines, ornament, and nicety. They were increasingly interested in life and figures. They were more imitative than creative. The sixth canon, transmission of style by copying and drawing, meant to them not so much knowing great masters intimately in order to improve one's own style as meaningless imitation.

In spite of this enthusiasm for imitation, however, the Ming dynasty is not devoid of creative genius. It is found in both figure painting and landscape. Many artists painted Taoist and Buddhist figures, but as the religious impulse of the age was low, accomplishment in this field was negligible. Portraiture was more successful. The most remarkable achievement in figure painting, however, lies in the painting of feminine life and its surroundings. While the Ming painters of figures followed closely the technique of T'ang and Sung, they had a refinement, richness, and beauty of their own. The charming faces, elegant gestures, and supple gait of their figures are still an inexhaustible fountain of pleasure. Almost all Ming painters were productive in its line, but Ch'ou Ying (c. 1530) was the greatest of them all. It should be added that like painters in other periods, they were interested in atmosphere, expression, and psychological feeling, but not in physiological features. The human figure has never had much importance in Chinese painting, and the nude none at all.

The backbone of art in the Ming period, as in other periods, was landscape. Landscape painters far exceeded those of Sung and Yuan in number. They shunned the liberality and expansiveness of Yuan and as a reaction took special delight in minute details, in studied brush work, and in queer cliffs and odd rocks. There were many schools, each emphasizing or synthesizing certain preceding styles, but they fell under three major groups.

The first group is the Chekiang School. Painters in this group, all from Chekiang, hardly used color, imitated Ma Yuan and Hsia Kuei of Sung, but replaced their depth and quietness with a livelier tone. They became the stronghold of the Academy Tai Wen-chin (c. 1430), leader of the group, was expert in all types of painting and masterly in broad and free strokes. He distinguished himself in using in his figures the "iron wire" or the even, hard, and still line and also Wu Tao-tzu's famous "orchid leaf" line.

The second group was the Academy School led by T'ang Yin (1470-1523) and Ch'ou Ying. Members of this group tended more to the Northern School tradition than that of the Southern School, although in their technique they followed the Chao brothers Liu Sung-nien, and Li T'ang. They worked with greens and blues and gold outlines, had a strong taste for buildings and "measured painting," were fine in drawing and skilful in details, had richness, softness, and grace. There is prettiness, charm, elegance, and delicacy in them. The pictures of T'ang Yin have a suppressed kind of strength in them, giving a weird effect. Ch'ou Ying's paintings have classic elegance.

The most influential group was the third school which flourished outside of the Academy from the beginning of the sixteenth century and made a strong impression on the following generations. This is the Wu School, so named because its members all came from Wu and its neighborhood in Eastern China. The Wu painters rejected Ma Yuan and Hsia Kuei as "insane," and wanted to combine strength and broadness with elegance and tenderness. Their leaders Shen Chou (1427-1509) and Wen Cheng-ming (1470-1559) more than accomplished this aim. Shen Chou painted big branches and enormous leaves with just a few broad and powerful strokes. In landscape he was particularly skilful in monochrome. Never careless in his drawing he was powerful and fluid. Wen Cheng-ming closely followed Chao Meng-fu and Tung Yuan, approached them in rhythmic vitality, spirit, and charm, and probably surpassed them in ease and calmness. His lines are careful and delicate, his colors charming and elegant. The greatest master of the school, however, was Tung Ch'i-ch'ang (1555-1636) who combined the styles of Ching Hao and Huan T'ung of the Five Dynasties, Tung Yuan and Chu Jan of Sung, and the Four Masters of Yuan. His feeling is that of the learned man and his conception that of a noble soul. Out of him grew many schools of painting. He is the chief justification for the common contention that the landscape painting of Ming synthesizes the best elements of the past and sets the pattern for the future.

Both in flower and bird painting and in "playing with ink," Ming talents made a fairly good showing. Painters of flowers and birds generally followed Hsu-hsi and Huang Ch'uan. Painters "playing with ink" emphasized conception. They were particularly at home with bamboo and plum in monochrome. Although Ming art definitely lacks creativeness and high inspiration, it nevertheless has neatness of conception, clear definition of form, sobriety of composition, just sentiment for decorative effect, suppleness of stroke, harmonious coloring, and a fine taste in general.

(k) CH'ING: LANDSCAPE, FIGURE PAINTING, FLOWER AND BIRD PAINTING, WESTERN INFLUENCE. The Ch'ing dynasty (1644-1911) continued the major traditions of Ming. The whole period was dominated by the style of the Southern School transmitted through the Wu School. There were imperial encouragement, extensive collections, comprehensive study of previous works, and a great number of artists, probably totaling six or seven thousand.

In landscape the outstanding names of the period are the four Wangs, namely, Wang Shih-min (1592-1680), Wang Chien (1598-1677), Wang Hui (1632-1720), and Wang Yuan-ch'i (1642-1715). These four, Yun Shou-p'ing (1633-1690), and Wu Li (1632-1718) are called the Six Masters of early Ch'ing. Wang Shih-min, leading figure of the group, modeled after Tung Ch'i-ch'ang. There is a natural ease and a mastery of technique in his employment of dots and dashes which are very striking. Wang Chien, also following Tung, was accomplished both in ink-painting and in watercolor drawing. He often painted in greens and blues but avoided details and thereby synthesized the Southern and Northern styles. He is full of expression. He has an austere and antique beauty. His colors are so chosen as to give an atmosphere of culture and repose. Wang Hui has spirituality in content and life-movement in form, is good both in delicacy and in simplicity. He also synthesized the two schools. Wang Yun-ch'i's strokes are like carving on bronze. He has richness, mellowness, depth, and volume. Yun Shou-p'ing was outstanding in landscape but his real greatness lies in the field of flowers and birds. Wu Li believed in imitation and careful strokes. Being a Roman Catholic, he was influenced by Western painting. These Six Masters gave rise to many schools. Practically no subsequent landscape painter was free from their influence.

Figure painting in the Ch'ing dynasty was almost entirely secular. Hardly more than one artist in a hundred was interested in Buddhist and Taoist figures. In drawings of secular life, however, there were no less than five different schools. These include, first of all, that which followed Ch'ou Ying and paid chief attention to elegance; secondly, that which emphasized the classical style with its simplicity and greatness; thirdly, that which stressed lightness and outline drawing; fourthly, that which expressed its conception in ink-painting; and finally, that which was influenced by Western art. Chen Hung-shou (1599-1652) was an early master of all types of figures. Yu Chih-ting (b. 1647) was the outstanding painter of the entire period. Chin Nung (1687-1764) was the greatest master in religious figures. Giuseppe Castiglione the Italian Jesuit (Lang Shih-ning, 18th century) painted with Chinese material in the Chinese style in general but brought in a great deal of Western relief, perspective, and touch, giving the impression of a combination of Chinese painting and Western oil. He attracted few followers.

The most note-worthy accomplishment of the Ch'ing dynasty lies not so much in landscape or figure painting as in flower and bird painting. The glory that was Yuan and Ming was transmitted through Chu Na (Pa Ta Shan Jen, c. 1644) and his contemporary Shih T'ao (Tao Chi). Chu Na was free from conventional concepts and technique. There is in his few, simple, and powerful strokes much loftiness and nothing vulgar. Shih T'ao was the pre-eminent painter of flowers and birds of his time. His work is as eccentric as his person. By far the most celebrated master was Yun Shou-p'ing (Nan-t'ien) who is regarded as the greatest flower and bird painter in the Ch'ing dynasty, if not in Chinese history. Based on the Southern tradition of Hsu Ch'ung-ssu, he has lightness and neatness, as well as greatness, splendor, and dignity He painted without even the faintest outline, bringing the "boneless" style to a climax. He and his contemporary Chiang T'ing-hsi (1669-1732) set the standards for later generations. There were many followers, forming different schools. Of these followers, perhaps the most distinguished was Chin Nung (Tung-hsin) whose skill in calligraphy and seal carving gave his lines a peculiarly calligraphic and "bronze and stone carving" quality. He excelled in plums, bamboos, and horses. His coloring is unique. Hua Yen (Shin Lo Shan Jen, b. 1684) exercised the greatest influence over flower and bird painting in the latter half of the Ch'ing dynasty. His works are remarkably alive, permeated with a spirit of imaginative beauty. Chao Chih-ch'ien (1829-1884) combined the best of Chu Na Shih T'ao, and Hua Yen. Full of richness, majesty, and vitality, his works are also dignified, refined, and always full of interest. Wu Chunch'ing (1844-1927),the greatest painter in the last century was unrestrained, care-free, informal, lavish. In his unconventional spirit and expansive mood, there is freshness, novelty, vibration, expressiveness, power, maturity, and ruggedness attained by economical but strong and vehement strokes. He was a celebrated calligrapher of ancient scripts His strokes have the appearance of odd rocks and old vines characteristic of those ancient scripts.

(1) THE FUTURE. With the establishment of the Republic in 1912, China looks to the West for the solution of her problems. Painters likewise look to the West for new inspiration. Outstanding Westernists like Hsu Pei-hung, Liu Hai-su, Ch'en Shu-jen, and Kao Chien-fu, whether learning from the West directly or by way of Japan, created new styles. They emphasize light and shade and power of expression. They paint new subjects, especially those in daily life. They want to liberate Chinese art from the chain of old conventions and traditions. Their challenge has been strong and their influence extensive. Nevertheless, Chinese painters in general still devote their chief attention to landscape and flowers and birds, still rely on balance as the basic principle of composition, still center their technique around the stroke, still remain faithful to the major traditions of the Southern School. They have refused to give up their peculiar perspective in favor of the point perspective, or to allow light and shade much importance, or to divorce Chinese painting from calligraphy and poetry. The most renowned Chinese painter of the day, Ch'i Pai-shih, who is most celebrated for his "insects and grass" and flowers and birds, is not a Westernist. It may well be that future Chinese painters will paint a much greater variety of subjects. It may well be that they will use color as a medium of expression instead of decoration as it has been in Chinese art. It may well be that Chinese painters will be more creative and individualistic as Western painters are. In these three respects Chinese painting will likely learn from the West. But unless the Chinese people radically change their attitude towards calligraphy, poetry, and life in general, the basic philosophy and the basic technique of Chinese painting will remain essentially Chinese.

Stone Carving. To the Chinese, stone carving (*shih k'o*) is essentially calligraphy and painting executed on stone. Unlike Western sculpture, it is not primarily carving of figures in the round. As a matter of fact, in Chinese stone carving as in Chinese painting, the human body has little significance. The chief interest of stone carving lies in the line.

(a) STONE MONUMENTS. The art of carving goes back to times immemorial. In the Shang period (1765-1122 B.C.) carving on jade and bronze had already become a mature art. Whether stone carving rivaled carving on jade and bronze at the time, history does not tell. From literary records we know that at the end of the fifth century B.C., there were over 10,000 incised inscriptions on rock *in situ* commemorating the virtues and accomplishments of great men. All of these inscriptions have disappeared. The earliest stone monuments still extant are the well-known stone drums. They are ten in number, each three feet high. They were discovered in Shensi in the 7th century, moved to the Confucian Temple in Peiping in 1307, and transferred to Nanking in 1933. There are odes inscribed on them probably during the reign of King Hsuan (827-782 B.C.) to commemorate his expeditions. It is possible, however, that they belong to the Ch'in period (249-206 B.C.) as Prof. Ma Heng contended in 1923. At any rate the Ch'in period was an epoch in which engraving on stone tablets was commonly practiced. A number of these tablets have come down to us. They are very highly treasured by the Chinese literati for the excellent writing engraved on them. Their rubbings have served as models of calligraphy for many centuries.

In the Han dynasty (206 B.C.-220 A.D.) stone carving reached a very advanced stage. In addition to inscribing on precipices, there was the inscribed memorial pillars which was not known before. Some of these pillars are still standing, the oldest one dating back to 105 B.C. Their forms are dignified and majestic, their carving refined and strong, and, above all, their pictures and writing are among the best in Chinese history.

There was also the stone tablet. It was not new in the Han dynasty; it can be traced to the eighth century B.C. or even earlier when it was used as a sundial, as a memorial of thanksgiving placed in front of a temple, or as a post at the side of grave pits to facilitate the lowering of heavy coffins. But it was in the Han era that it assumed unusual importance in art. Its purpose was still utili-tarian, for use in lowering coffins. Long poles were inserted in the circular bores near the top of the tablet and the coffin was lowered with ropes suspended from the poles. But its writing and pictures are masterpieces of art. Rubbings of these masterpieces are today, as they have been for many centuries, models of Chinese calligraphers and stone carvers

A tablet was either circular or in the shape of *kuei,* that is, circular at the top and square at the bottom. The circular type has entirely disappeared. The other, however, has been preserved. The oldest tablet of this latter type is dated 25 B.C. As a rule, characters are engraved in the center to commemorate the deceased, and dragons and tigers are carved on both sides with a couple of mythological birds on top and tortoises at bottom. From the standpoint of art, the characters are the most important. It is they that rank the Han tablet as a supreme achievement in Chinese art.

As calligraphy is the triumph of the Han engraved tablet, so is painting the crowning success of the Han carved murals. The carving of figures on palace and temple walls started in the Chou period, but the most famous works existent today belong to the Han dynasty. In the Hsiao T'ang Shan Temple in Shantung province, a temple built in the latter part of the Earlier Han period (206 B.C.-24 A.D.), there are carvings on ten stone walls depicting historical, military, theatrical, and mythological scenes. As stone records of ancient civilization, they are the most ancient and as such are important enough. But they are even more important as works of art. Their clearness of conception, mastery of composition, excellence of execution, and gracefulness of expression have never been surpassed.

In the Wu Liang Temple, also of the Han period (147 A.D.) and also in Shantung, there are carvings on stones 4 ft. by 2 or 3 ft., in four stone chambers. Pictures are in bas-relief, arranged in two or three horizontal stories which possibly represent upper and lower floors but probably describe different scenes without any temporal or architectural relationship. There are scenes about ancient rulers, sages, heroes, filial sons and loyal ministers, military expeditions, funeral processions, the presentation of tribute, etc. Figures are extremely lively and individualistic. The narration of tales is clear. The composition of groups is pleasing.

Neither the Hsiao T'ang Shan nor the Wu Liang Temple carving shows much plastic quality. This is so because the Chinese regarded stone carving as essentially calligraphy and painting translated on stone. The main requirements were that the beauty of calligraphy and painting be successfully reproduced in carving and that the stone be of good quality, so good that it could be used as an ink slab. The Chinese value Han dynasty stone carving more highly than Han dynasty bronze vessels and mirrors which exhibit excellent workmanship but contain little painting or calligraphy of the first order.

(b) ANIMAL FIGURES. The preoccupation with calligraphy and painting in stone carving, however, did not prevent the Chinese from producing some amazingly artistic stone figures. These were made as early as the Shang dynasty, as recent excavations reveal. In the Eastern Chou period (770-481 B.C.), the Chinese began to bury clay, stone, or metal figures in tombs. The practice became extensive in the Han dynasty. Among these figures, Chou stone animals and Han terracotta are exceptionally beautiful. The Chou style continued the monumental qualities of Shang dynasty bronze, retaining its pleasing proportion, keen sense of modeling, and massiveness. In addition, there is a new sense of energy, for animals, whether standing by themselves or grouped together, show extreme liveliness and tremendous vigor. Very often they are conventionalized in geometrical patterns, but even in geometrical regularity and in symbolic abstraction, they are alive and dynamic.

The Han style is especially good in its plastic sense. On top of this there is more pronounced rhythm and linear movement, and more dramatic expression of energy than in previous works. Group compositions are in general excellent, full of organic unity without sacrificing the freedom of movement of individual animals. Fighting animals represent the Han style at its best. Their forms, vitality, tension, and dramatic postures are unparalleled elsewhere.

This outburst of energy and the variety of forms in the Han figures were definitely due to a new source of inspiration. China was in contact with India and Persia and her art was therefore influenced to some extent by the art of those countries. The Bactrian types embodied in Hellenistic art came into China through northern India. As a result the Chinese developed a definite type of horse with exceptional nobility and energy. The Persian influence resulted in the winged lions of Liang (502-557 A.D.), which show tense energy and a wonderful sense of line. Later in the T'ang

dynasty (618-907) when contact with Central Asia became more intimate, Central Asiatic horses and camels became objects of admiration by the Chinese and favorite themes of Chinese animal sculpture.

In the Northern and Southern Dynasties (420-589 A.D.), however, the Chinese spirit reasserted itself. Bodies of animals were prolonged and curves were exaggerated, indicating a return to the linear beauty of Chinese calligraphy and painting. This linear beauty was achieved without sacrificing the monumental characters of the figures, for they continued to be of enormous size, sometimes 12 ft long. Unfortunately it was this interest in size that developed many centuries later, in the Ming dynasty (1368-1644). Animal figures became massive. The trend was towards realism; the appreciation of linear beauty was slight.

(c) TOMB FIGURES. Tomb figures are of two types, huge figures erected outside tombs as guards and statuettes buried to serve the dead. Huge figures are of stone and are monumental and majestic in posture, but lacking in vitality. Small figures, on the other hand, are of pottery, and are full of vivacity and life. This is especially true of T'ang dynasty pottery figures which are considered the best of the kind. They are executed with feeling and with great care for details. They may represent warriors, servants, actors, magicians, musicians, and many others whose service may be needed by the deceased. Each figure has its own individuality and its own humor, be it a Persian magician, an Indian juggler, an Arabian horseman, a Central Asiatic camel driver, or a Chinese dancer. They are informal, intimate, and extremely characteristic. They are in an endless variety of posture, indicating a highly developed technique of modeling. Instead of being realistic human figures, however, they imitate the figures in T'ang dynasty painting, with long supple bodies, flowing draperies, and wide sleeves. The expression of linear rhythm is exceedingly effective. This is especially true of the dancing figures which are T'ang terracotta at its best. Aside from the fact that they are beautiful, they exhibit an infinite variety of posture and movement.

(c) BUDDHIST SCULPTURE. While tomb statuettes are human, lively, and personal, Buddhist statues are impersonal, calm, and wanting in individuality. They lack variety of posture or modeling effect, because they are usually in the frontal position. Buddhists believe that a Buddha or a bodhisattva (future Buddha) is a universal being devoid of specific characteristics. They have no desire, therefore, to represent a deity as male or female, or with any other individual characterization. Furthermore, they use images primarily for the purposes of worship and meditation, and consider the frontal position, together with the calm posture and merciful appearance of the statue, as most conducive to their religious experience. For these reasons they have almost totally ignored emotional expressions, organic features, and plastic treatment.

Buddhist sculpture must have begun in China as soon as Buddhism was introduced. In the Han dynasty, there were Buddhist images made of bronze, silver, gold, jade, sandal wood, ivory, and dried lacquer. There were large Buddha figures 20 ft. high. Also there were groups of 1,000 Buddha statuettes. In the fifth, sixth, and seventh centuries, Buddhist sculpture entered into a most glorious period. Many masterpieces were produced, notably in the Yunkang and Lungmen Caves.

The Yunkang Caves are situated in Tat'ung, Shansi province. The original work consists of five grottoes, which were started in 452 A.D. or later, and completed in 467. There are later additions, making a total of some twenty grottoes. Figures of Buddha and bodhisattvas are carved on the sides of caves in round form and tremendous size. Some of them are as high as 70 ft. The sculpturing of such large figures was undoubtedly facilitated by the regular shape of the caves.

It is certain that the sculpture of Yunkang is a result of the fusion of Chinese and foreign cultures. In the fifth century A.D., China was in constant contact with India and Central Asia. Stone carving in the round almost entirely eclipsed flat surface carving at this time. This fact might be explained as a gradual development of Chinese idol making before the arrival of Buddhism or as a sudden revival of Shang dynasty modeling in stone. But there is no doubt that the new movement drew its main inspiration from India and Central Asia. Chinese motifs are conspicuously absent in Yunkang. Evidence of Han art is found only in minor figures and in the treatment of draperies. The prominent nose and the thick lips make the Yunkang figures distinctly un-Chinese. In large figures, the style of the drapery is characteristically Indian. But we cannot conclude from this meager evidence that Yunkang sculpture is completely or even predominantly Indian. The nimbuses of the figures are pointed at the top, and hence different from the Indian style. There are also figures and hand signs not

known to India at the time. Besides, there are unmistakable marks of Central Asiatic influence. A number of floral ornaments are definitely Iranian in origin. Hellenistic motifs are present in many figures. Undoubtedly both Indian and Central Asiatic influences were at work. Authentic records show that Indian and Central Asiatic artists arrived in China at that time. The work at Yunkang may have been produced by these foreign artists. Or it may have been the creation of Chinese artists who either consulted these foreign artists or worked entirely on the authority of Buddhist texts. The scarcity of inscriptions in these caves leaves us very little literary record to support either conclusion. At any rate, one point is sure: along with the obvious elements of Indian and Central Asiatic influence, there is the unmistakable presence of the Chinese spirit. This spirit is expressed first in the energy and tension of the figures characteristic of the preceding Han dynasty. It is also expressed in the rhythmic lines and elongated forms that are definitely Chinese in feeling and style. Furthermore, there is pleasing harmony of decoration and sculpturing, a harmony which could hardly have been achieved without the graphic and plastic arts of Han as foundation.

When the Wei capital was moved to Loyang in present Honan province in 494 A.D., the center of Chinese sculpture shifted from Yunkang to Lungmen in the same province. Here the figures are smaller, due chiefly to the irregular contour of the caves. There are many styles not found in India, and many Indian styles not found here. While the most important pieces are products of Wei (386-535 A.D.) and the earliest sculptured image dates back to 483, the majority of the figures belong to T'ang and some to Sung (960-1279). In general, the works exhibit a finer technique than those in Yunkang, are executed in better material and freer spirit. In both Yunkang and Lungmen, fifth century sculpture is dominated by foreign models. At that time the approach to Buddhist art was abstract. Wei artists were intensely interested in the spiritual meaning of Buddhism, so that Buddha and bodhisattvas are represented as aloof and somewhat ascetic. In the later works in Lungmen, however, there is increasing softness and mellowness. The body becomes more slender and the neck lengthened. Drapery appears more graceful and flowing. There is more sheer delight in the display of rhythm and refinement. This is also true of Sui (581-618) sculpture, although it still retains the abstract quality of Wei to some degree. In T'ang sculpture, there is definite relaxation of energy. The spirit of artists became freer. Buddha figures became more human, more individual, more intimate, and more informal, so much so that there was the complaint that the Buddha was made to appear like court ladies. This change of style was due, first of all, to the gradual disappearance of Indian and Central Asiatic influence; secondly, to the revival of the humanistic spirit in the T'ang period; and thirdly, to the influence of painting. This last influence was destined to play a greater and greater role in Chinese sculpture. Under the influence of T'ang painting, sculpture became more pictorial, with the flowing line ascending in importance. Softer material like wood, clay, and dried lacquer came into vogue, and the chief interest of sculptors lay in subtlety, sophistication, charm, and rhythmic qualities. Color was used, partly due to the influence of painting and partly due to the weakening of the Buddhist impulse so that spiritual meaning was sacrificed in favor of superficial and easy decoration. By the Sung dynasty, interest in sculpture itself began to subside, owing, on the one hand, to the dominant position of painting and calligraphy over other arts, and, on the other, to the increasing popularity of Zen Buddhism which subordinated idol worship to the direct intuition of truth. Henceforth Buddhist sculptors were chiefly interested in making small figures of Kuan-yin, patriarchs, and *lohans* (saints). During the Yuan period (1280-1368) when Lamaism became the state religion, there was a revival of large-size figure sculpturing. The four Heavenly Kings on the gates of Chu Yung Pass are masterpieces of that period. In the Ming dynasty (1368-1644) many monumental figures were made in stone. The twelve stone human figures and the twenty-four animal figures, some measuring 12 ft. high, in front of the Ming Tombs are admirable for their magnificence and dignity. In the Ch'ing dynasty (1644-1911) there were also some remarkable achievements. The 70 ft. wooden Buddha of the Lama Temple in Peiping is an excellent example. So is the exquisite carving around the octagonal base of the White Pagoda Temple in Peiping. Nevertheless, from the Sung dynasty on, Buddhist sculpture was definitely overcome by painting. Chinese artists did maintain an interest in stone. The interest lay, however, not in sculpturing in the round, but in the engraving of calligraphy.

(d) ENGRAVING ON STONE. As has been pointed out, engraving on stone goes back to ancient times and reached a high level in the Han dynasty. To the marvellous accomplishments of Han, Buddhists of the fifth century added some remarkable tablets with calligraphy. The twenty inscriptions in the Lungmen Caves are among the most beautiful tablets ever produced in China. Rubbings of these tablets have been a constant source of inspiration to Chinese calligraphers. In the sixth century, not only inscriptions, but also Buddha figures were engraved on tablets.

However, the golden age of carving on tablets was not reached until the T'ang dynasty which gave China her most celebrated pieces of stone carving. These include many famous tablets which serve as excellent models of calligraphy. Of particular merit, however, is the portrait of Confucius painted by China's greatest painter Wu Tao-tzu and engraved on a tablet now standing in the Confucian Temple at Ch'ufu, the native place of Confucius. The Chinese attach special importance to this tablet because it most effectively expresses the personality of the sage who, according to his pupils, was "gentle but dignified, austere but not harsh, polite but completely at ease."

Equally admired are the six horses of Emperor Tai-tsung engraved on a stone 5 by 3 ft. The liveliness and the beautiful physique of the steeds are portrayed with perfect rhythmic vitality. The exquisite lines and elegant strokes compare favorably with the best in painting and calligraphy.

After the T'ang dynasty, Chinese carving developed along the lines of industrial arts and architectural decoration. Many beautiful objects of jade, lacquer, crystal, wood, ivory, etc. were produced. These, however, were works of artisans. Artists were not interested in these. Because of their primary interest in calligraphy, they developed a taste for a type of carving which is based on calligraphy. This is seal carving.

Seal carving may be traced to very ancient times. It was popular in the Han period when seals were carved of iron, jade, stone, and other materials. Its purpose was utilitarian and remained so in subsequent dynasties. Although pre-eminent artists of Sung like Mi Fei reproduced excellent calligraphy on seals, it was not until the Yuan dynasty (1280-1368) that purely aesthetic interest in them developed. In that period, painters like Ch'ien Hsuan and Chao Meng-fu successfully translated calligraphy onto seals. Later, artists like Wen Ching-ming and T'ang Yin of Ming, and Teng Shih-ju (1743-1805), Pao Shih-ch'en (1775-1855), and Chao Chih-ch'ien (1829-1884) of Ch'ing were as expert in seal carving as they were in calligraphy and painting. Different schools arose, with differing emphasis on the straight line or the curved line, the delicate stroke or the rugged stroke, and on the different styles in which the scalpel is handled. There are thirteen styles of cutting, such as perpendicular cutting, reverse cutting, double cutting, abrupt cutting, "flying cutting," etc. There are also different styles of strokes such as "hanging needle," "willow leaves," "iron wire," etc., comparable to styles in calligraphy. All styles require that "the scalpel must be handled exactly as the brush should be handled," so that the beauty of calligraphy may be re-created in carving. Both bas-relief and incision are popular. As in painting, there are the "Six Canons" of seal carving, namely, rhythmic vitality and life movement, the vigorous and classical way of incision, well-balanced composition of individual characters and of groups of characters, authentic etymological basis of scripts, the handling of the scalpel in the manner of the brush, and the absence of the vulgarity of artisans. To a great extent these canons are but a different version of the Six Canons of painting. The main object is to achieve a harmony of fullness and strength, delicacy and power, heaviness and lightness of stroke, the classical (i.e., Han dynasty) style and individual taste, as well as the strange and the commonplace. In short, seal cutting is calligraphy transferred to stone. This is why it is called "the art of the iron brush."

Seals are made of jade, bronze, gold, silver, lead, precious stone, amber, crystal, horn, ivory, porcelain, incense, seeds, and even bamboo roots and melon stalks. They may consist of a name, a proverb, or a poetic quotation. Their ideal use is to inscribe or decorate a work of painting or calligraphy.

Architecture. Chinese architecture reached maturity much later than sculpture or painting. From vague literary records and a few bas-reliefs, we know that ancient structures were simple and crude. The Ming T'ang or the Hall of Brightness of the Earlier Chou dynasty (1122?-770 B.C.), the supreme achievement of architecture of that period, had multiple units and many murals, but was still quite primitive. In the following centuries there were magnificent buildings. The palaces of Ch'in, built in 212 B.C. with the labor of 700,000 men, had a compound two miles in

extension. The terrace of their main hall was of such dimensions that 10,000 persons could be assembled in it and banners 50 ft. high could be unfurled below. A palace of Han (206 B.C.-220 A.D.) was surrounded by a wall nine miles long and contained a main hall 500 ft wide. Its walls, railings, pillars, and beams were freely painted, elaborately carved, and richly inlaid with jade and gold. The palaces of Sui (581-618) were even more gorgeous. They required the labor of 2,000,000 people to complete. Their park measured 60 miles in perimeter and included an artificial lake with hand-made hills more than 100 ft. high. The main building, called Mi Lou (Labyrinth), had "1,000 gates and 10,000 doors," and was such a maze that it was "impossible to find one's way out even after a whole day's struggle." Forty "Detached Palaces" were scattered over the country. In the T'ang (618-907) and Sung (960-1279) periods, architectural styles were well advanced as may be seen in temples, pagodas, and palaces, referred to in literary records, represented in paintings, and preserved at the present day in the ancient Horyuji Temple (607 A.D.) in Japan.

Not until the Ming dynasty (1368-1644), however, did Chinese architecture reach its maturity. All types were fully developed, as can be seen from famous remains of this period, notably the Altar of Heaven, the ancestral temple of the Ming Tombs the Five Pagoda Temple, the Taoist temple Ta Kao Hsuan Tien, and the imperial palaces, all in or near Peiping. The main features and the different types of Chinese architecture were all perfected during the Ming era.

(a) OUTSTANDING FEATURES. Chinese buildings, as a rule, face south. This convention can be traced to the ancient Hall of Brightness. Research by Wang Chung (1744-1794) and Wang Kuo-wei (1877-1927) revealed that the Hall faced south, consisted of four buildings of five rooms each, and was surrounded by a square courtyard. The buildings were arranged in a central axis forming a Greek cross, and were used to house the emperor, to hold courts, and to conduct state worship, education, feasts, etc. The central space was covered with a round concave roof and was used as an audience hall. Many features of traditional architecture originated from this arrangement. It certainly accounts for the fact that all formal buildings in China are symmetrical, built on an axis, and generally broad and low.

The basic material of Chinese architecture is wood. In ancient times buildings were constructed with wood or bamboo patched with earth, or, in elaborate buildings, with pulverized shell. Only terraces were of mud and stone. It is true that in the Han period stone construction was used to some extent and many centuries later, in the Yuan and Ming dynasties, under the influence of Western Asiatic architecture, stone was used in terraces, railings, balustrades, gates, walls and in imported features like artificial fountains, secret chambers, stone pavilions, and bathing pools. But the main material of architecture throughout the ages has been wood.

Tiles have been employed for roofs from very early days. At present they are both glazed and unglazed, and are used in large buildings, while in some small houses the roof is thatched instead. But the most important members of a structure are the pillar, the beam, and the cornice on which the building depends for support, and these are of wood. This material is well suited to a style of structure that is broad and low. Its chief defect is that it does not last long. This, of course, is responsible for the regrettable fact that no Chinese building earlier than the eleventh century and few before the Ming dynasty have survived.

Perhaps the most striking feature of Chinese architecture is the roof. It has two concave converging hips culminating in a massive horizontal ridge and gracefully curving, gently projecting eaves supported by intricately carved or ornamented brackets. The roof is often glazed and colored. Its origin is lost in mystery, but from the bas-reliefs and clay models of the second century B.C., we learn that the sweeping roof was already in vogue at that time, although the curve was not pronounced until the T'ang period. The curved roof is intended not only to accentuate its own gracefulness, but also to harmonize the structure with the surrounding landscape. It contributes a great deal to the feeling of calmness, contentment, peace, gracefulness, and gentleness so distinctive of Chinese architecture.

Attempts have been made to explain the upturned roof by associating it with the tent, by describing it as an imitation of the contour of a tree or the flight of a sparrow, by tracing it to the bending of bamboo in ancient buildings, by ascribing it to the influence of Chinese calligraphy which takes special delight in the curve, by interpreting it as a way to permit generous reception of sunlight, or by simply considering it as a matter of necessity to re-enforce the trusses in order to lighten the pressure of the tiles. The tent theory is definitely untenable because the Chinese people have had no experience of tent life, and the calligraphy theory is an anachronism. Other explanations may have some measure of truth. The ultimate explanation, however lies in the Chinese love of the roof's rhythm and linear beauty. It also eliminates the feeling of mass and weight so offensive to Chinese taste. Herein one may find the explanation why neither the dome nor the arch has been used since the Han dynasty.

Roofs are either continuous from the ridge to the eaves or gable-ended on both sides of the building. In pre-T'ang structures and in North China today, they are highly restrained, but in South China and in informal pavilions throughout the country, they may be so sweeping as to resemble horns. Double and triple roofs are quite common. The center of the roof ridge is often crowned with a golden knob or fire pearl, while the two ends are profusely decorated with dragon designs. At the edge of the eaves there are often human and animal figures from six to 16 inches high. Their origin, their purpose, and sometimes even their iconography are uncertain, although they are generally believed to serve as guardians against evil spirits. The finial of the roof was usually a metal phoenix in the Han and T'ang periods and a Buddhist gold vase in Yuan, but is today generally a dragon or phoenix in porcelain or clay.

As to walls, they are often movable partitions and are secondary in importance. They are intended to fill in the space after the frame of the building is completed. The ceiling too, is secondary, and is usually omitted or false when present. Columns and beams, or the other hand, are primary structural elements. Columns are generally of *persea nanmu*, seldom of stone. Their usually huge size and their position are determined chiefly by artistic requirements. They are widely separated, do not support the entablature, seldom have capitals, but as a rule have brackets below the beams by which they are tied. Beams, columns, and in most cases trusses are exposed, for in the Chinese way of thinking, lines have a beauty of their own. They are often elaborately painted, gilded, or carved with conventionalized flower and scroll designs, historical scenes, or poetic representations in brilliant colors, especially gold, vermillion, and azure, with black and white as subordinates. The favorite design for decorating columns is the dragon. That for the ceiling is the octagonal or round flower design, evidently a conventionalization of the Han dynasty square design of the water-lily painted in full bloom with its petals facing downward. In the walls, lattice-work plays a major role. This practice of rich decoration goes back to ancient times when murals beautified the Hall of Brightness and paper drawings covered pillars. In the Han period, even the earth floor was painted, until colored bricks were sufficiently developed towards the end of the dynasty. Aside from their artistic value, painting and gilding also helped to preserve the material.

The surrounding wall is another conspicuous feature of Chinese architecture, for no Chinese architectural unit, whether a palace or a temple, a city or a mansion, a park or a garden, can be considered complete without it. It dates back to the tenth century B.C. or even earlier. It was then, as it still is today, chiefly a matter of necessity—for protection. Nevertheless, it serves to give a structure an outline and unity. City walls, many of which are Ming remains, are high and thick and are generally of bricks. The Peiping city walls are about 60 ft. high, 40 ft. thick at the bottom and 20 ft. at the top, and consist of bricks 2 ft. by 6 in. and about 5 in. in thickness. Many city walls have bastions at regular intervals and watch towers at every corner, and often a moat all around. These walls are simple, symmetrical, majestic, and impressive. Walls surrounding buildings are usually painted or plastered, often in bright red, crowned with a roof of green glazed tiles, and richly decorated below the roof. In the case of an informal structure like the garden, the wall winds and zigzags, has irregular roofs and fancy doors, thus creating a sense of gentle rhythm. It is usually plastered in grey to serve as background for shadows of bamboo or some other shapely plant thrown upon it by moonlight. In such cases, the wall exists primarily for its aesthetic effect.

(b) PALACE STYLE. The foregoing features are common to practically all types of Chinese buildings, the palace, the temple, the dwelling house, the terrace, the pagoda, the pavilion, and the memorial arch. Especially, however, are they true of the first three types, which are often grouped together and called the "palace style." In structure and arrangement, the three do not vary radically from one another. They all follow the general pattern set by the Hall of Brightness. They consist of one or more buildings in a central axis, often with subsidiary buildings on both sides and in the back. Each building is usually one but sometimes two or three stories high, has from one to three halls connected with other parts of the structure by open courts and side corridors. To the back of the halls are living quarters. Additions are not built on top of the original structures but at the sides or in the back. Thus the symmetrical arrangement is preserved and expansion can be achieved without sacrificing unity. As a rule, the whole compound is enclosed by a wall, with the main gate in the south leading to an open court and the main entrance. This arrangement gives the impression of orderliness and peace, while the surrounding wall creates a sense of serenity and contentment.

In front of the entrance of the main building is a screen the use of which dates back to the Chou dynasty (1122?-249 B.C.). Originally it might have been erected to keep evil spirits from entering. Today, however, it is definitely for privacy and for weather protection, as the main door generally remains open during the day. Larger buildings are often accompanied by semi-artificial lakes or landscape gardens. The open courts themselves are in many cases gems of landscape architecture. These informal units help to minimize the simplicity and monotony of the general plan.

The foregoing description of the characteristic lay-out of Chinese architecture applies to both secular and religious buildings. From the days of the Hall of Brightness, religious and secular life in China has been a unity. Hence no distinction of the two types is necessary. The palace, the ancestral hall, the Buddhist temple, the Taoist temple, and the elaborate dwelling house have the same general appearance, differing chiefly in interior arrangement and in symbolism.

(c) T'ING. While buildings in the palace style are treated formally, the t'ing or the pavilion is treated informally. It is always an integral part of a landscape which is irregular in pattern. It may crown a hill of artistic outline, decorate a lake of interesting shape, or accompany a tree of strange contour. In it, all major features of Chinese architecture are present. The wall is often omitted, thus enhancing the importance of pillars, and the curved roof is often emphasized, thus accentuating the flow of linear rhythm. In or by the pavilion there are always artificial rockeries of picturesque pattern and strange charm.

(d) T'AI. The pavilion evolved out of the t'ai or tower, which is an ancient type going back to 2,000 B.C. or earlier. Originally the *t'ai* was merely an earth mound or a stone terrace, used for worship, meteorological observation, military review, festivals, and enjoying animal or human entertainments. In the period of the Contending States (480-249 B.C.), some *t'ais* had nine flights of terraces, showing the advanced stage of the development of this particular type. Eventually it gave rise to the secular pavilion on the one hand and the religious altar and pagoda on the other.

Of all altars in China, the most famous is of course the Altar of Heaven outside Peiping. It is a raised platform of three circular terraces with elaborately carved railings and balustrades. Measurements are based on odd numbers, especially the number 9 which is symbolic of infinity. In the middle of a cypress grove and accompanied by the charming circular, three-roofed Temple of Heaven with sweeping eaves and a golden top, the Altar never fails to create an impression of serenity and to arouse a sense of awe.

(e) T'A. While the altar has remained essentially a religious structure, the paogda has been to some extent secularized. When the Buddhist *stupa* was introduced into China from India about the beginning of the Christian era, it combined with the Chinese *t'ai* and formed the *t'a* or pagoda. For Buddhists it serves to house some relic of the Buddha. A pagoda dedicated to a *lohan* (saint) has four stories; to a bodhisattva (future Buddha), seven stories; and to a Buddha, at least eight and usually thirteen stories. On top of the pagoda is a chain of nine wheels or discs, pointing towards the Abode of Bliss, Nirvana.

The pagoda is no longer confined to Buddhism. It is used in Chinese geomancy which claims that a pagoda can control cosmic forces. It is also used in courts and in gardens purely as ornament to landscape. Today there are hundreds of thousands of pagodas throughout China, the earliest one dating back to c. 523 A.D. They involve more variety and change than any other type of Chinese architecture. Many kinds of material are used— wood, stone, marble, bricks, and even "jade." The shape of the pagoda varies from a cone to an octagon. Its roof may be radically sweeping or rigidly restrained. Its colors may be rich and varied or merely grey. Its height ranges from several feet to 360. Most in favor is the narrow and tall pagoda with many roofs of colored glazed tiles and projecting eaves. Because of its linear beauty, it has been compared to a stroke in calligraphy.

(f) P'AI LOU. The *p'ai lou* or the memorial arch forms a class by itself. It is built of wood or stone, consisting of two or four posts covered by single, double, or triple curving saddle-roofs. The posts and brackets under the roofs are as a rule richly decorated. In the center of the facade there is a tablet or *p'ai* commemorating some person's meritorious deed. Whether it grew out of the ancient simple gateway or originated from the Indian *toran* (from which the Japanese *torii* may have sprung), is still an open question. Like the pavilion and the pagoda, it has the main characteristics of Chinese architecture.

(g) CONCLUSION. In going through the various types of Chinese architecture, one cannot help noticing the fact that aside from the pagoda, Chinese architecture has not been influenced by foreign styles as Chinese sculpture has. It has not been modified by Buddhism, Mohammedanism, or Christianity to any appreciable degree. On the contrary, the Mohammedan mosque has adopted the Chinese style in its exterior, and the Chinese Buddhist pagoda is now a far cry from the Indian prototype. This failure to benefit from foreign styles is due possibly to the conservatism in Chinese architecture, but probably to the lack of interest in architecture as such on the part of Chinese creative artists. Throughout the ages, the art of building has been left to artisans. There is no great name nor great treatise associated with this form of art. The famous *Ying-tsao Fa-shih* (Patterns of Architecture, 1103 A.D.) by Li Ming-chung, the *Ch'iao-to T'ien-kung* (The Skillful Art of Building, 1631) by Chi Ch'eng, and the *Kung-ch'eng Tso-fa Tse-li* (Regulations for Building Construction) of the Ch'ing dynasty (1644-1911) are records of details rather than aesthetic deliberations on architecture. There has been a notable lack of leadership in the art. Furthermore, the belief in geomancy and the regimentation by the government through-out the centuries have undoubtedly discouraged experiment. For these reasons, Chinese architecture has not developed to the same high level as Chinese painting and sculpture. This does not mean, however, that there has been no progress in Chinese architecture or that there has been no new development since the Sung dynasty, as some writers believe. During the Yuan period, both the coir thatched roof and the flat roof were tried. Ming architecture was much more complicated than that of earlier periods, and there was in it a sense of refinement and delicacy not found in earlier works. Carving and lacquer works in Ming dynasty structures are the finest ever produced in China. In the Ch'ing dynasty the art of the glazed tile reached new heights. It was its golden age. There was a great variety of colors and shapes, and different kinds of clay were used. The Jehol Palace, the Yuan Ming Yuan, and the Summer Palace of the Ch'ing dynasty are constructions of supreme beauty.

There is no doubt that as more talent is directed to architecture, the art will soon enter into a new epoch. As a matter of fact, this new epoch is already at hand, for there has been an architectural renaissance in the last thirty years. In these recent decades, most governmental buildings, civic centers, memorial halls, libraries, museums, etc. have been built in the "palace style," complete with its sweeping roofs, glazed tiles in imperial yellow, lattice work, decorated beams and painted pillars, marble terraces and railings, movable partitions, and imposing gateways. Wood, however, has been replaced by steel and concrete, and modern lighting, heating, and ventilating systems have been introduced with ease. This does not mean that Chinese architecture will be replaced by Western architecture. In places where functional architecture is indispensable, China will readily bow to the West. But in places where edifices are to be monuments of art, China will, as she has in the last three decades, cling to the "palace style." Fortunately, Western scientific innovations can be incorporated into this style without sacrificing its main features. In no other case is the marriage of Western science and Chinese art so happy. If modern Chinese architecture can be taken as a pattern for the future development of other Chinese arts, there will be no conflict between Chinese and Western art in general but a synthesis of the two. This synthesis may take place not only in China alone. The West may take an interest in the curved roof, etc. as it has taken an interest in movable partitions. See GENERAL: *The Romance of Chinese Art;* Laurence Binyon, *The Spirit of Man in Asian Art;* S. W. Bushell, *Chinese Art;* John Ferguson, *Survey of Chinese Art.* PAINTING: Laurence Binyon, *The Flight of the Dragon;* L. Binyon, *Painting in the Far East;* Chiang Yee, *The Chinese Eye;* O. Siren, *A History of Early Chinese Painting;* Oswald Siren, *A History of Later Chinese Painting;* Arthur Waley, *An Introduction to the Study of Chinese Painting.* ARCHITECTURE: Oswald Siren, *History of Early Chinese Art,* Vol. IV; D. G. Mirams, *A Brief History of Chinese Architecture.*

SCULPTURE: L. Ashton, *An Introduction to the Study of Chinese Sculpture;* Oswald Siren, *A History of Early Chinese Art,* Vol. III; *Chinese Sculpture from the Fifth to the Fourteenth Century.* —W.T.C.

Chinese blue. See Prussian blue.

Chinese fiddle. See MUSICAL INSTRUMENTS.

Chinese ink. The traditional material of this name is made from a carbon black pigment, usually lamp black, combined with glue as a medium. In the Far East, this is regularly molded into sticks and the preparation of them has been given a great deal of care and attention. In use, the stick is rubbed with water on a stone slab, dissolving the glue and carrying the black pigment in suspension. An ink similar to this was the regular drawing and writing material in the West through the Middle Ages and the Renaissance.—G.L.S.

Chinese pottery and porcelain. See CERAMICS II.

Chinese insert wax. See wax.

Chinese theatre. See THEATRE.

Chinese white. See zinc white.

Chinese wood oil. See tung oil.

chine silk. Word did not originate in China. Has colored warp or filling threads woven to produce a pattern. Printing, tie dyeing and spot dyeing are used. —G.W.R.

Ch'ing art. See CHINESE ARTS.

chink. *n.* A long narrow cleft, a crack, or crevice. *v.* To fill, as a chink.

chinkinbori (Jap.). A lacquer technique. Shallow engraving traced with gold. A technique derived from the Chinese.

chinoiserie. TERMINOLOGY: *"chinoiserie', "à la chinois", "la chinage"* were terms used in the 18th cent. in France and other countries to cover not merely the products of the European craftsman influenced or inspired by the art of China, Japan and the Indies but generally the original art of these countries as well as the European imitations. In more modern usage the term chinoiserie has come to mean European art influenced or inspired by East Asiatic art only. The English lexicons of the 17th and 18th cents. do not mention an equivalent for chinoiserie; the term "china" for any kind of porcelain was first used in 1653. However, for the decorating of chintzes, furniture and especially lacquerwork the term "japanning" was used instead of chinoiserie. Similarly in the Dutch language, where the term "japon" for female dress and "kamerjapon" for informal apparel worn at home still testify to the 18th cent. fashion of printed cotton dresses with East Asiatic decor. In German the terms "sinesisch" and "indianisch" were used pretty much as synonyms for all East Asiatic art; for originals as well as for the European imitations. The Italians of the 18th cent. borrowed either the term "chinoserie" or used the expression "a la cinese" and in more modern times "influenza cinese".

History and Contiguity. The basis for the cultural and artistic relations between the Far East and Europe was trade; more specifically, silk trade along the old silk roads of which we have documentary and actual evidence (cf. Chinese damask of the Han period [202 B. C.—221 A. D.] found in Palmyra, Syria; excavations of Sir Aurel Stein in Central Asia). After the collapse of the Roman Empire and Hellenistic civilization it was the Islamic people who since the 7th cent. controlled the silk trade between the Far East and Europe. Chinese silk brocades of the 13th and 14th cents., some of them for the export to Islamic countries, have been found in the church treasures of western, central and northern Europe; their motifs of dragons, phoenix-like birds and lotus flowers were widely copied in Italy (Lucca and Venice) and amalgamated easily with the related motifs and the related dynamic style of the European Gothic. With the discovery of the direct sea route to East India (1498) a direct trade contact between the Far East and the West was again established which climaxed in the foundation of the East India Companies; English (1600), Dutch (1602) and French (1664). Especially the latter, the "Compagnie des Indies," was instrumental in flooding the European market with Far Eastern textiles, porcelain and lacquerwork. The second half of the 17th cent. and the first three quarters of the 18th mark the tidal wave of the chinoiserie. Before that time examples of Chinese and Japanese art had reached Europe as presents of legations sent from the Far East and as souvenirs of individual travelers (Marco Polo, 13th cent.). Knowledge of Chinese architecture, gardening, costumes and crafts was further disseminated through the engraved illustra-

tions of the travel books of the Jesuits (cf. Athanasius Kirchner, 1667; I. B. du Halde, 1736).

In order to cut down on costs and, to arrive at a compromise between Far Eastern and European taste, workshops were established in Asia where natives decorated porcelain, textiles and lacquer after European designs and engravings (cf. the so-called "Jesuit Porcelain" with Chinese decor after European engravings; the "ateliers" established by the Compagnie des Indies in Pondicherry since 1680 for the decoration of Indian "chints").

Of greatest importance for the development of the European arts were the attempts of the European artists to emulate directly the Far Eastern art in gardening and landscape architecture, furniture and interior design, lacquer, ceramics, textiles, wallpaper and metalwork.

Gardening and landscape architecture. The outstanding books which inspired European gardening were: Father Attiret, *Account of the Emperor of China's Gardens near Peking,* trans. from the French, 1752; and Sir William Chambers, *Dissertation on Oriental Gardening,* 1772. The examples of still standing pavilions and "pagodas", and every building with a curved, overhanging roof was called so—in European parks and gardens are too numerous to be fully recorded. Best known examples are: Kew Gardens near London built by Chambers; Englischer Garten, Munich; Chinesischer Pavilion in the park of Sanssouci, Potsdam, designed by Frederick the Great and Buering; the "jardin Anglo-Chinois" near Petit Trianon, laid out by the English gardener, Richard, for Marie Antoinette; the pagoda in the park of the Duke de Choiseul and in Het Loo in Holland. The garden of the type "Anglo-Chinois" with its natural, irregular layout, bridges, cascades and pavilions represents an important element in European 18th cent. romanticism.

Furniture and Interior Design. The interest in eastern motifs was very strong in England where they appear in conjunction with those of the Gothic (Horace Walpole's Strawberry Hill leased in 1747) to blend also with those of the French rococo style. Of broadest influence was Thomas Chippendale's *The Gentleman and Cabinet Maker's Director* (first edition, 1754) which in many designs shows the synchronization and fusion of the 18th cent "Gothic Survival," the French rococo and th Chinese.

Lacquer. First original coromandel lacquers, whole folding screens and other smaller objects were directly imported from China and Japan through Indian ports (e.g., Frederick the Great presented a whole room of coromandel lacquer to his sister in Bayreuth). Later lacquerwork was produced in England, where "Japanning" was done by craftsmen and fashionable dilettantes and where the term soon became a synonym for veneering and polishing; in Germany (Stobwasser in Braunschweig); in Italy (Venice); and in France, where the great "ébénists" decorated such pieces as writing desks, commodes etc. in imitation of East Asiatic lacquer. The *sedan-chair* which following a Chinese custom became fashionable in European high society gave further ample opportunity for lacquer decoration in the Chinese style.

Ceramics. Earliest attempts to imitate the effect of blue-white Chinese porcelain were made in the so-called "Medici Porcelain" during the Renaissance. These imitations were, however, merely a kind of stone-ware. Rare original pieces of Chinese porcelain were occasionally mounted in silver and gold by European craftsmen since the 15th cent. During the 17th cent. Chinese motifs were more or less faithfully copied on European "fayence"; Delft-ware, for instance. The collectors of the 17th cent. did not yet discriminate in the inventories between original Chinese porcelain and the European imitations in stone ware. This explains the high figure of so-called Chinese pieces in possession of Augustus the Strong of Saxony and Poland; a collection said to have numbered no less than 60,000 pieces and used for the decoration of the "Japanese Palace" in Dresden (built by Poeppelmann).

Boettger's discovery of porcelain in 1709, which was before that date a carefully guarded Chinese secret—was in the next 50 years followed by the founding of numerous porcelain manufacturers, patronized and often run by the European potentates, large and small, worldly and ecclesiastic. Mention can be given only to the most important: in Germany —Meissen, (Dresden) Nymphenburg, Hoechst, Berlin; in Austria—Vienna; in France— Sèvres; in England—Bow, Chelsea, Derby and Worcester; in Italy—Venice and Capo-di-Monte at Naples; in Russia—St. Petersburg. The decoration followed either Chinese originals or were free inventions in a pseudo-Chinese style.

Glass. Chinoiserie motifs are very frequent in Bohemian and Silesian glass of the 18th

cent., cut as well as decorated with gold and enamel.

Textiles. (a) *Silk Weavings.* A few silk weavings of Spanish colonial make with the Hapsburg double eagle, but of East Asiatic design, dating from the 16/17th cents. are known. The next group is that of "Bizarre Chinese" patterns found on Italian (Venice), French (Lyon) and Polish (Sluck) silk and gold brocades of the first part of the 18th cent. The bulk of silk weavings with chinoiserie are of an "illustrative", pictorial character, portraying "pagodas", dragon boats, Chinamen with pigtail, and bells, etc., mostly woven in Lyon during the second part of the 18th cent. (chief designers: Pillement and De La Salle).

(b) *Tapestries.* Chinoiserie motifs at the beginning are often mixed with Renaissance grotesque; for instance, in the designs by Bérain found in the products of Beauvais ca. 1700. This factory and Aubusson favored throughout the 18th cent. the chinoiserie. In English tapestries might be found "indo-Chinese" grotesques after coromandel lacquer (Design: John Vanderbanc).

(c) *Laces.* Chinoiserie motifs are very frequent in the laces of all countries since the second part of the 17th cent.

(d) *Chints.* (Chintzes). The Indian name for printed cotton weavings or calico, first imported from India, later (last quarter of 17th cent.) copied in the European countries, esp. England. In spite of rigid laws limiting or forbidding the importation and fabrication of chintzes, and even the wearing of such stuff in England as well as in France, the "Indienne" factories prospered, supplying not only material for clothing but also for the covering of walls and furniture. Most important among them was the Indienne factory of C. P. Oberkampf in Jouis en Josas near Versailles (founded 1760), who sent not only agents to the East to collect original motifs but also employed the best French designers of chinoiserie.

Wallpaper. In England the combination of chintzes and wallpaper being done in the same factory was common. The oldest document of the wallpaper industry in England figures in a patent given by Charles I in 1643 to Jerome Lanyer of London to fabricate "Londo-Indiana". Since then East Asiatic motifs have been preferred for the decoration of wallpaper.

Metalwork. Chinoiserie motifs are common in the design of metalwork during the 18th cent., esp. on wrought ironwork for elaborate gates and fences.

Ornament print. The chinoiserie motifs used in the different crafts during the 17/18 cents. were chiefly furnished by the so-called "ornament print" (Ornamentstich) in which the artists of France lead Europe. We mention here: Bérain, Gillot, Andran, Watteau, Boucher, Huquier, Peyrotte, Bellay, the elder Huet and especially I. Pillement (1709-1808) whose designs were used for textiles.

References to China and the chinoiserie in European literature during the 17th and 18th cents., either enthusiastically approving or satirizing, are numerous. See Voltaire (*Essai sur les moeurs; Orphelin de la Chine*) ; Defoe, Horace Walpole, Pope, Lamb, Goethe, Gozzi (*Re Turandote* transl. by Schiller). The influence of Confucius' moral philosophy and his stress on agriculture as the foundation of the state left its imprint on philosophic thought and economic theory (physiocrats in France.) See Allen, B. Sprague, *Tides in English Taste,* 1937. 2 vol., esp. chapters X-XIII; Belevitch-Stankevitch, H. *Le gout chinois en France au temps de Louis XIV,* 1910; Cordier, Henri, *La Chine en France au 18. siècle,* 1910; Graul, Richard, *Ostasiatische Kunst und ihr Einfluss auf Europa* 1906; Guèrin, M. J., *La Chinoiserie en Europe au 18. siècle, Exposition au Musée des Arts Decoratifs,* 1911; Laske, F., *Der Ostasiatische Einfluss auf die Baukunst des Abendlandes,* 1909 ; Reichwein, Adolf, *China und Europa, Geistige und Kuenstlerische Beziehungen im 18. Jahrhundert,* 1923; Scheyer, Efnst, *Chinoiserien in den Seidengeweben des 17. und 18. Jahrhunderts,* 1928. See FURNITURE.   —E.S.

chintz (Hind. *chint;* Skt. *chitra,* spotted or variegated). Includes chittes, painted calicoes, pintadoes, toiles peintes, perses, and indiennes. A cotton printed with all over patterns; sometimes glazed or calendered. See chinoiserie.   —G.W.R.

Chios, school of. One of the most productive and influential schools of sculpture during the 6th cent. B. C. was located on the island of Chios. It may have been a representative of this school who made the Nike of Delos, and it is likely that the kore type was invented there and exported to Athens, where it became so popular during the time of the tyrants. Pliny records the names of four generations of Chiot sculptors, beginning with Melas and ending with the sons of Achermos, who were considered the most famous

masters of their time. Characteristic of the Chiot faces are the oval contours, thin eyes, and engaging smiles. In metal work the sculptors of Chios were also outstanding; Glaukos of Chios is credited with having invented the soldering of iron about 600 B. C., and was famous for his relief designs in metal.   —W.R.A.

chipap. See sipapu.

Chippendale. See FURNITURE.

chiriji (Jap.). Plain black lacquer sprinkled with gold dust.

chiton. The universal Greek garment, worn by both men and women. There were two types: the Doric and Ionic, with slight differences in style for men and women. The Doric was an oblong woolen cloth wrapped around the body and sewn or left open on one side, sleeveless, and fastened at the shoulders with buckles or pins, with a belt over which the garment was pulled out. The woman's garment sometimes had an overfold (peplos). The Ionic chiton was longer and fuller, made usually of cotton or soft linen; it had sleeves fastened at intervals by brooches or pins, and was more richly decorated. Chitons were worn in a variety of colors and were ornamented with patterned borders. They were distinguished by their simplicity of material and design; they gave the maximum freedom of movement, and were effective in following rather than impeding the contours of the body. Hence they were of the utmost value to artists, both sculptors and vase painters, who used them to reveal and accentuate the dignity of bodies in repose, the rhythm of ones in motion. Greek sculptors were skillful in representing the delicate variations in fold patterns, without monotony or harshness. In comparison, the Roman treatment was usually mechanical and unimaginative.   —W.R.A.

ch'i yun sheng tung. See CHINESE ARTS.

Chod art. See CZECHOSLOVAKIA, ART OF.

choir. *Arch.* That part of a church accommodating the singers; more generally, the arm of the cross between the transepts and the apse.

choragic monument. *Gr. arch.* A small commemorative shrine built by a successful choragus (chorus leader).

choral notation. See NOTATION.

chord. Simultaneous sounding of several (usually more than two) different tones; harmony (q.v.). Chords have different degrees of tension as a result of the different degrees of tension which their constituent intervals have (see consonance; tension). Apart from these factors, the degree of tension in chords is conditioned by the location of the constituent intervals in relation to each other and by the context in which chords appear by virtue of their placement in the design, of voice leading, metrical situation, dynamics, etc. The term *chord* is sometimes reserved for chords built according to a particular principle; e.g., in intervals of thirds, of fourths, etc.   —E.K.

choreography (Gr. *choreos-graphos,* dance-plan). At the time of its first use (ca. 1700), spelled choregraphy, it indicated the written pattern of dance steps, the notation of composed dances. It has come to mean, through the 18th and 19th cents., the actual composition, creation or design of dance movements comprising the structure of a ballet, irrespective of its ultimate graphic notation. See design; NOTATION.   —L.K.

chorovody. The chorovody, or ballad-dances, form the most ancient group of Russian national dances. The dances of this class are closely interrelated and distinct from the other three fundamental groups, the trepak, kasatchy, and kamarienskaya. The chorovody are round dances, in which the dancers accompany themselves by singing ballads. A group of men and women move in a circle surrounding a solo dancer, usually a girl. The nature of the movement varies according to the content of the song, and may be definitely pantomimic or merely follow the general mood of the ballad. In either case, the motion approaches art dance in its expressive range and high technical level.   —J.G.

chou (Ch.) Round wooden rod around which a mounted painting is rolled.

chou shou (Ch.) Ornamental ends of the rod around which a mounted painting is rolled.

Christ and St. John. Devotional image (q.v.) which represents Jesus' favorite disciple trustfully leaning his head against the body of the Lord who is seated beside him. The theme is an embodiment of the desire in contemporary mysticism to be enveloped in the protection of Christ as St. John was, or even to be

in the latter's place. The subject is known only in the 14th cent. and in that region around the lake of Konstanz which was then the center of all mystical endeavor in central Europe. Its artistic formulation was brought about by the isolation of the central group from representations of the Last Supper.
—R.B.

chroma. See COLOR.

chromatic. *Mus.* See idiom, B (4) and C.

chromatic color. See COLOR.

chromatic notation. See NOTATION.

chromaticism. See scales and modes.

chromaticity. See COLOR.

chrome pigments. The most common of these and the most important commercially is chrome yellow, a lead chromate, synthetically formed by precipitation. The tint can vary from a pale greenish hue to orange. In character the pigment is crystalline and is not entirely permanent to light. It began to be manufactured and used in the early years of the 19th cent. Chrome green is a mixture of this yellow pigment with Prussian blue. Chrome red, also a lead product, a basic lead chromate, is made by boiling a solution of potassium dichromate with white lead and a small amount of caustic soda. It is only moderately stable, being readily affected by sulphur gases, and has had little use as an artist's pigment.   —G.L.S.

chromo. A chromolithograph.

chrysanthemum. See SYMBOLISM IN FAR EASTERN ART.

chrysanthine notation. See eastern chants.

chryselephantine. Several of the great cult statues in Greek temples of the 5th cent. B. C. were chryselephantine, i.e., made of ivory and gold. Notable among them were the Asklepios by Calamis, the Dionysus by Alcamenes and the Zeus at Olympia and Athena in the Parthenon at Athens by Phidias. The technique was probably imported from the Orient. In the Tomb of Tutankhamen in Egypt there are statuettes in which the flesh is ivory and the drapery and hair gold, and similar examples have been found in Mesopotamia and Crete. But Greeks made their cult statues on a tremendous scale. Phidias' standing figure of Athena was forty feet high, constructed on a framework of well-seasoned wood, the drapery made of plates of gold riveted to-gether, the flesh parts of ivory. His seated Zeus was nearly as high. Accessories of both figures were profusely decorated in relief. Ac-cording to Quintilian, the impression of beauty which the Zeus gave seemed to add some-thing to the revelation of religion, and Epicte-tus advised his disciples to see it before they died. Lacking adequate evidence for visual-izing how these statues actually looked, we can at least surmise that the materials of which they were made, as well as the majestic forms, seen in the dim light within the cella of the temples, inspired awe and adoration in the worshippers.   —W.R.A.

chüan (Ch.). The word for silk, the common medium for painting.

chuan chou (Ch.). A term applied to a stand-ard style of mounting for paintings, when they are rolled on a round stick which is incorporated into the mounting at the bot-tom of the picture.   —J.A.M.

chūban (Jap.). A term designating a wood-block print of medium size, vertical.

chüeh (Ch.). Sacrificial bronze vessel, three-legged, and with two extended lips for pour-ing.

ch'ui-ying wen (Ch.). Earthworm marks. A pattern sometimes seen in the glazed surfaces of pottery which simulate the tracks of an earthworm.

chung (Ch.). A clapperless bell with orna-mental hanging device; a sacrificial bronze form.

chün yao (Ch.). Chinese pottery ware of the Sung dynasty. Heavy with thick opalescence glaze.

Chumash art. See California Indian art.

churinga. See AUSTRALIAN ABORIGI-NAL ART.

churrigueresque (Mex.). An organized de-corative system with its own columnar order (see estipite), decorative vocabulary (see fal-doncito) and compositional syntax; employed particularly for *retablos,* facades, doorways, etc. in the Valley of Mexico ca. 1740-ca. 1780. Inaugurated by the Sevillian Gerónimo Balbás in the *Altár de los Reyes* of the Cathedral of Mexico, 1718-1736. See MEXICAN ARCHI-TECTURE (Native); SPANISH ARCHI-TECTURE IN THE NEW WORLD.
                        —J.McA.

cibobe. See sipapu.

ciborium (pl. ciboria, Med. Lat.). (1) A drinking cup, generally covered, from the Greek *kibōrion,* meaning cup-shaped seed pod of the Egyptian water lily (lotus); (2) a drinking cup made from or resembling this seed pod.

(3) *Art and Eccl.* (a) Any receptacle de-signed to hold the consecrated bread or wafers for the Eucharistic feast of the Christian Church, especially one shaped like a cup or chalice with a dome-shaped cover. (b) Any receptacle designed to form a de-pository for the vessels of the Eucharistic feast or other objects of sacred nature. Ciboria of this nature vary greatly in design, size, and materials used, ranging from elabo-rate designs in precious metals or marbles to small cupboards of simple workmanship and decoration set into a wall. Example, ciborium by Mino da Fiesole in Church of San Domen-cio, Siena. (c) *Early.* A fixed canopy of durable material, together with its supports, from which was suspended the receptacle containing the consecrated wafer of the Eucharist.

The name was soon transferred from the canopy to the receptacle itself, the canopy in the Western Church being called a bal-dachin (q.v.) or tabernacle. Much irregu-larity still persists, and the terms are often used as synonyms though incorrectly so. The use of the term ciborium has been further influenced by its early though mistaken con-nection with *cibus,* food. See EARLY CHRISTIAN ARCHITECTURE.   —J.C.

cicada design. A spear-pointlike motive, re-sembling a conventionalized cicada (insect of the cicadidae family).

cicerone (It.). A sight-seeing guide.

cicona. See chaconne.

cinnabar. As the natural red sulphide of mercury, this is closely related to the arti-ficially made pigment, vermilion. Cinnabar is an ore, somewhat duller in hue than the synthetic product. It was evidently known to ancient artists but may have been con-fused with the artificially made red lead. Pliny speaks of cinnabar as minium and the latter name became associated ultimately with the lead pigment.   —G.L.S.

cinnabar lacquer. See tsuishu.

cinquecento. Italian for five hundred, also abbreviation for *mil cinque cento* (1500). Therefore used in Italian chronology to designate the years whose numbers begin with 1500, that is the 16th cent., although this disregards the fact that the years 1500 and 1600 are the final years of the 14th and 15th cents. respectively.

In the arts the term cinquecento refers to the Italian styles of the High and Late Renaissance during the 16th cent. A. D. The term, however, designates a style quality rather than a time division, being particularly descriptive of the classic formalism of the first half of the 16th cent. and less appropriately applied to the latter half of the century when baroque (q.v.) elaboration, affection and stylization are clearly seen. This gives authority for including in the cinquecento artists such as Bramante and Leonardo da Vinci, though most of their work was done in the 15th cent.

The century is marked by the climax of the Renaissance in Rome, the decline of Florence as the leading center of activity and the rapid rise of Venice as the outstanding school of painting.

Individualism is a strong factor, particularly at the beginning of the century but there is a pronounced trend toward a more general style in which local schools are less easily discernible.

Architecture. The period begins with the maturity of the Italian Renaissance shown by the Roman work of Bramante (Donato Lazzari, 1444-1514), Baldassare Peruzzi (1480-1536) and Antonio San Gallo, the younger (1485-1546), and is marked by the complete understanding of classic form, both in mass and detail, as applied to 16th cent. requirements. Examples: *Cloister of Santa Maria della Pace* (finished 1504), *The Tempietto* (in courtyard of San Pietro in Montorio) (1502-1510), both by Bramante, *Palazzo Massimi* (1529) by Peruzzi and the *Palazzo Farnese* by San Gallo the younger (first two floors, 1517). In Venice and North Italy, designs show greater elaboration of surface treatment and materials. Examples: *Liberia Vecchia* (1536) by Jacopo Sansovino (Tatti), *Palazzo Grimini* (1549) by Michele Sanmicheli. A break with conservatism is seen in the brilliant designs of Michelangelo. Made chief architect of St. Peter's in 1546, his daring genius produced its choir, transepts and dome (model only), setting the style and scale of the finished building. His freedom in the use of established forms was both

the symptom and the cause of the desire for innovation, which in its unorthodox use of structural motifs anticipates the dynamic and theatrical designs of the succeeding century. This trend was slowed by the restraint of Vignola (1507-1572) and Palladio (1518-1580) ; however, both men present a fine balance between Classic adaption and Baroque invention. Examples: *Il Gesu, Rome* (1568) (facade by della Porta, interior decoration 17th cent), *Villa Farnese at Caprarola* (ca. 1547), both by Vignola; *Villa Capra (Rotunda), Vicenza*, the *"Basilica"* (1549), *Vicenza, Il Redentore, Venice* (1576) by Palladio. The period closes with the completion of the dome of St. Peter's by Giacomo della Porta and D. Fontana in 1588 and the early work of Maderna and Rainaldi.

The century sees the full development of the Renaissance dome (that is, a domical vault resting upon a high cylindrical drum, supported by arches and pendentives, usually four in number and arranged upon a square plan), the use of the colossal order (a column or pilaster, extending through two or more stories) and an increasing emphasis upon group and site planning in which symmetrical balance is sought.

Painting. Cinquecento painting begins with the development of a formal, monumental design, which has been styled "the grand manner" and which seems to be an outgrowth of Florentine science combined with Umbrian space-composition. It is exemplified by the painting of Raphael (1483-1520) (*Stanza della Segnatura, Madonna di san Sisto*). Light and shade (chiaroscuro) as an aid to tonal qualities or dramatic effect rather than to the definition of form or atmospheric depth is emphasized by Leonardo (1452-1519) (*Cenacolo, Mona Lisa*) and Correggio (1489-1534) (*Holy Night, Jupiter and Io*). Paradoxically, with this increase of formal and monumental elements in design, the human figure becomes less impersonal and far more a denizen of this world. Parallels could be drawn with Greek art of the 4th cent. B.C. Mural decorations tend to transcend the limits defined by architecture. The sciences necessary to naturalistic representation are thoroughly understood and are used to create the illusion of a desired reality. (*"To create three dimensions where there are but two."* Leonardo da Vinci.) This characteristic anticipated in different manners by Mantegna, Perugino and Pinturicchio is seen in developed form in Raphael's Stanze (Vatican), the *Sistine Chapel ceiling (Vatican)* by Michelangelo and the *dome of the Cathedral of Parma* by Correggio.

The most homogeneous school of painting is that of Venice. Due to preoccupation with form the central Italian schools, particularly Florence, did not take full advantage of tonal color, a quality peculiar to painting. Venice, with its eastern (Byzantine) heritage, made color a primary consideration. This accounts in a large measure for its preeminence in painting. Venetian characteristics, range, and merit of the cinquecento can be summed up in the life and work of Titian (Tiziano Vecelli, ca. 1477-1576). But three other painters equal or surpass him in certain limited phases; Giorgione (ca. 1478-1510) in subjectivism; Tintoretto (Jacobo Robusti 1518-1594) in emotional intensity and Veronese (Paolo Caliari, 1528-1588) in monumental decoration.

Sculpture. The century is so dominated by the work of Michelangelo Buonarroti (1475-1564) of Florence that all other efforts seem minor. This can be said in spite of the fact that his greater projects (*Tomb of Julius II, Rome* and the *Tombs of the Medici, Florence*) were never completed. His pronounced individualism, while conducive of a desire for massiveness on the part of imitators, is less typical of the century than the mannered elegance and stylizations of Jacopo Sansovino (1488-1570), *Bacchus;* Benvenuto Cellini (1500-1571), *Perseus* (Loggia di Lanyi, *Florence*) ; and Giovanni da Bologna (ca. 1524-1608), *Flying Mercury, Florence* and *Neptune Fountain, Bologna.*

In the cinquecento, scientific realism gives way to style and surface finish. The same general considerations that apply to both architecture and painting are equally applicable in the development of sculpture. See *Civilization of the Renaissance in Italy,* Jacob Burckhardt, 1909; *Renaissance in Italy,* J. A. Symonds, 1907-10; *History of Italian Painting,* F. J. Mather, Jr., 1923; *Handbook of Italian Renaissance Painting,* Lawrence Schmeckebier, 1938; *History of Sculpture,* Chase and Post, 1924; B. Berenson, *Central Italian Painters of the Renaissance,* 1907; *North Italian Painters of the Renaissance,* 1908; *Florentine Painters of the Renaissance,* 1907; *Venetian Painters of the Renaissance,* 1907; *Italian Renaissance Architecture,* W. J. Anderson, 1909; *Italian Renaissance Architecture,* Georges Gromort, 1922; *Gardens of Italy,* Bolton and Phillips, 1919; *Italian Gardens of the Renaissance,* J. C. Sheperd and G. A. Jellicoe, 1925.   —J.C.

cinquefoil. A form much used in Gothic tracery consisting of five arcs or foils separated by cusps.

circulating exhibition. See exhibition.

circus (L., from Gk. *kipos,* circle). (1) *Rom. antiq.* A structure composed of an oblong or elliptical area enclosed within rising tiers of seats for the exhibition of public spectacles of a sporting nature, particularly chariot and horse races; before the building of the Colosseum and other amphitheatres the circus also provided the setting for various military games and mimic battles, field sports, combats of animals and of animals with men. From this circumstance is derived the modern meaning of circus: a company of performers and animals, and the performances given by them. The circus existed from a very early period in Rome; at first simply an open space for such activities, seats for the spectators were introduced in the time of the kings; these were of timber and were frequently destroyed by fire. It was not until the 1st cent. A.D. that the circuses, by now primarily hippodromes, were built of stone or brick and took a definite architectonic form, though there was a Greek prototype in the *stadion* for the running of footraces Of the various circuses erected by the emperors within the city of Rome few traces remain, save that the shape of the Circus Agonalis of Domitian is preserved in the Piazza Navona. The most complete surviving example is the Circus of Maventius (311 A.D.) on the Via Appia, about two miles outside the city. This arena is 530 yds. in length, 86 in breadth. At the end nearest the Appian Way was a colonnade pierced with a monumental gateway over which was the loge of the exhibitor (*editor*) ; on either side were six *carceres* or barriers from which the chariots started. The ten rows of seats for the spectators, with accommodation for 18,000 run the full length of both sides of the arena and around the half circle at the far end, where there is a second triumphal gateway for the exit of the victors. Special boxes were provided for the emperor and for the judges. The arena is divided for about two-thirds of its length by a low wall embellished with statues and obelisks, the *spina,* and at either end of this barrier rise pedestals (*metae*) capped with three cones, goals around which the charioteers had to drive seven times to complete the hazardous three-mile course. The *spina* is placed at a slight angle to leave the entrance to the course from the *carceres* wider than the exit; the collenade containing the *carceres* was curved to place each chariot equidistant from the throat of the course on starting. The lowest tier of seats is raised and there is no protective moat separating arena from seats as there was in the later amphitheatres. The vaulted space below the seats formed a promenade in case of rain. Circuses were erected in various cities throughout the empire, of which traces remain at Orange, Tarragona, Anagnia and Istambul; there were timber circuses at Paris and Soissons. The magnificent baroque circus ('*Sferistereo*') at Macerata (by Alcandri) was designed for the game called *pallone*. (2) An enclosed building with a permanent circular or elliptic arena surrounded by tiers of seats for equestrian, acrobatic and other performances, and acts by trained animals, common in the 19th cent., and still represented in Paris by the Cirque Médrano and the Cirque d' Hiver; the earliest of these modern circus buildings was erected in Blackfriars-Rd., London, about 1780. (3) A circular range of houses or buildings surrounding a public thoroughfare at the junction of several streets; the thoroughfare is hence often entitled by this name, as, Oxford Circus (1771), Piccadilly Circus, and others in London and Bath. —T.A.H.

cire-perdue, cire perdue (Fr.). A process of casting bronze statues, etc. in which the original figure is modeled in wax over a core, and wax flows out of the space between the core and the mould when heated by the hot metal which runs into its place. See METAL-WORK.

cisele (Fr. *ciseler*, to carve). Velvet showing a pattern of cut and uncut loops.

citadel (from Fr. *citadelle*, 1586, from It. *cittadella*, dim. of *citta or cittade*, from Lat. *civitatem*: literally, "little city"). The highest and most impregnable and commanding part of a fortified town, its walls containing the permanent buildings of the garrison; hence a citadel is a fortress rather than a castle, though sometimes used as a synonym for a fortress-castle. The term has been in use since the Middle Ages; by extension it is incorrectly applied to ancient strongholds, including the Gr. *akropolis* and the Lat. *arx*. In medieval times the citadel served as much to dominate as to protect its dependent town. Notable examples: Carcassonne, Aleppo, Cairo, the Alhambra, Badajoz, Burgos and Ludlow. —T.A.H.

citadel-acropolis. See acropolis.

cittern. See MUSICAL INSTRUMENTS.

city hall, town hall. The municipal building of a city or town containing the offices of the principal officials.

city park. See CIVIC PLANNING.

city planning. See CIVIC PLANNING.

civic architecture. The architecture of structures that house activities pertaining to common society, or perform public services. Capital buildings, city halls, law courts, and museums are typical examples.

civic art. See CIVIC PLANNING.

civic center. See CIVIC PLANNING.

civic design. See CIVIC PLANNING.

CIVIC PLANNING (incl. *TOWN PLANNING, CITY PLANNING, and REGIONAL PLANNING*). The art and science of designing for varied human uses large outdoor spaces is commonly known by the term "planning" preceded by a noun indicating the kind of area involved, as **site p.** or **subdivision p.** in the case of a district (usually residential) smaller than a municipality, **village p., parish p., town p.** or **city p.** if a whole municipality is involved, **regional p.** if a larger territory including several municipalities having problems in common but usually not coextensive with county or state political boundaries, is included, and **county p., state p.** or **national p.** if one of these entities is the subject of consideration. **Continental p.** and **world p.** have not been attempted up to the time of this writing—although there has been some international regional planning—but these will probably be a development of the future as a by-product of increasing international organization.

Because of the present active growth of concepts in this field no single term for the subject at large has thus far received general acceptance. In past usage the English-speaking world has not been unanimous. In the U.S.A. **city p.** has predominated, **town p.** being applied only to relatively small communities, while in Britain it has been customary to use **town p.** more broadly in reference to large as well as small municipalities. In both countries **regional p.** has been a comparatively new term and used by most writers in the restricted sense given above rather than generically. **Land p.** has been used for inclusive purposes by some writers, but is not wholly satisfactory because it seems to imply the exclusion of bodies of water from consideration. **Civic art** has been used mainly with special emphasis on the architectural, landscape architectural and sculptural adornment of the community. **Civic design** is considered by many to be satisfactory as a generic term. **Civic planning** has been chosen as the heading of this article not because of any intrinsic superiority to the preceding term but because its resemblance to the traditional but inadequate **city p.** makes it more useful for reference needs.

Some of the boundaries of this field are well defined; others, where expansion is in active progress, are more vague. *Architecture* (q.v.) *landscape architecture* (q.v.) and *civil engineering* are commonly used in connection with planning enterprises, and in point of size or expense some projects of these three types exceed some of the fourth; but generally the contrast between the specialized character of the former and the more varied nature of the latter provides a ready means of distinction. On the other hand, while in the past **civic p.** has usually been concerned particularly with physical resources and arrangements there is now a marked tendenecy toward increasing attention to the relations between material and social conditions, having as a result the fading of sharp outlines separating planning from the social sciences.

The general purpose of civic planning may be broadly described as "the efficient adaptation of man's general environment to his needs". Practically all human acts are attempts at adaptation to needs, but most of them are concerned with the immediate rather than the general environment and are more or less impulsive in character—often far from well-considered and efficient. There has been considerable planning, but much of it has been ill-informed and short-sighted. For example, any decision as to the placing of a building may be said to be an instance of planning, and may serve the immediate purposes of the owner of the land, but if that site happens to be, because of special circumstances, the only suitable location for a highway, and consequently the building is later torn down, the placing of it there was short-sighted, wasteful, inefficient planning. When such mistakes occur in large numbers, as they are likely to in all communities where most of the planning is done only by private individuals, each in his own behalf, the expense

becomes enormous. Few private citizens have enough information—and many have not enough altruism—to enable them to plan in the public interest. Therefore effective civic planning is usually done by specialists whose training, experience and careful study of the facts in each case enable them to use wise, impersonal judgment.

RESOURCES PLANNING. The most fundamental of all planning is that dealing with the major resources of mankind in earth, water, minerals, living matter, sunshine and air. Its problems are extremely complex, involving interrelationships among geology, geography, biology, and sociology in their broadest aspects.

Some geological conditions are within man's control in spite of their tremendous magnitude. Minerals are very important to his welfare in this machine age, and, once exhausted, they cannot be replaced. If he continues to use the limited available supply wastefully, the future consequences will be most serious. Reckless commercial practices are now depleting his heritage at a rapid rate. In many cases mines are so managed that future access to relatively poorer veins of metal or coal is permanently cut off for the sake of speedy exploitation of richer veins. Oil wells are drilled too near together because of rivalries between adjacent land owners, and the natural gas accompanying the oil, which in the public interest should be utilized at the same time, is often wantonly burned in order to make quicker profits from the oil. The speed of the process will cause much of the potential oil supply to become inaccessible in the future because of the premature release of gas pressure. Of course the insatiable demands of a war enormously aggravate these evils.

The facts of biology and of the interrelations between biology, geology, and meteorology are also of great importance to man. This is especially true of those involved in the **hydrologic cycle**—the perpetual circulation of water between earth and sky. If the earth is well clothed with vegetation a large part of the rainfall is absorbed usefully by the roots of the plants and then transpired slowly back to the atmosphere; or any of it which escapes this, is at least delayed in its journey to stream and sea so that no harmful erosion results; while if ground is bare, the water runs quickly down any slopes, forming ever-growing barren gullies, washing away precious top-soil which is sometimes deposited as troublesome silt in rivers and harbors, lowering the level of ground water, with con sequent drying up of supplies of water for drinking and other human uses, and often causing disastrous floods. Other sources of waste are the leaching or dissolving of valuable chemicals from bare topsoil, and the depletion of soils from excessive specialization on one crop.

Many individual owners need considerable guidance in the allocation of land to various uses. Areas of which people are trying to make a more intensive economic use than is warranted by the conditions, as, for instance, ground used for tillage which is too barren for good crops and so should be devoted to pasture or forest, are called **marginal** or **sub-marginal districts.**

The steepness of slopes, together with the amount of rainfall and the fertility or rockiness of the soil, should largely determine whether a given area can best be used for wood, grass, or tilled crops. If rainfall is scanty, even level areas should be left in sod, or serious wind erosion ("dust-bowl" conditions) will ensue. Sometimes a series of unusually wet years, coupled perhaps with unusual demand for agricultural products, has encouraged owners to plow land which later proves to be too dry for the purpose—even if **terracing**, or **contour plowing** (making furrows curve in level sweeps around hills instead of straight up and down hill which encourages **erosion**) is practiced—with immense loss as a result. **Over-grazing**—permitting excessive numbers of animals, especially the close-cropping sheep, to feed on pasture areas—has almost equal effects.

Forestry has its special problems arising from the slowness of trees in maturing, which tempts owners to sacrifice long-term advantage for the sake of immediate profit. The best practice is to cut trees only as they reach full size, leaving young ones to develop later, eliminating excessive underbrush and trash and, where needed, planting seedlings of preferred species. Such policies have long prevailed in Europe, but in North America a tradition of **clear-cutting** has been inherited from pioneer days when the virgin forest was considered by many as merely an impediment to the settlement of the country, and large wooded tracts have been denuded of all sizes of trees at a time, the debris being carelessly left making tinder for forest fires. These have destroyed any saplings which have sprung up and often the best parts of the soil itself, exposing great barren areas to erosion. The new growth which manages to survive is always inferior to the original wood. Com-

munities which depend mainly upon the forest for employment of their inhabitants often become decadent or utterly abandoned "ghost towns" after the wood is cut.

Some owners voluntarily use good forestry methods but there is need for much education and some measure of public control over privately owned tracts, together with large additional purchases of land for public forests. Intelligent policy is especially urgent for woodlands on slopes draining into water supply reservoirs and into rivers which are important for water-power, irrigation, or navigation.

The control of floods caused by past mistakes in forestry calls for expert planning, as it involves intricate problems in the interrelationships of many natural and social factors. The most obvious remedy, the building of levees, is inadequate, and the most fundamental cure, the replacement of forests in the drainage basins upstream, is slow. The building of dams and the providing of reservoirs is expensive and often complicated by such problems as the removal of whole towns from the reservoir areas, but the benefits from the resulting flood control, navigation, irrigation, power, water supply, and recreation facilities usually make ample compensation. Swampy areas have sometimes been drained for the purpose of providing new agricultural land, or for mosquito control, and subsequently it has been discovered that they were more valuable for water storage purposes. Any radical change in natural conditions requires careful study from many standpoints to avoid such errors.

The discharge of untreated sewage and other waste matter into rivers and sea is a serious problem. A small amount of pollution in water is purified by oxidation but in too many cases the quantity is so great as to kill fish and other wild life and gravely to menace human health.

INDUSTRIAL AND BUSINESS PLANNING. Few of the materials taken from the earth are usable immediately in their raw condition. Good planning demands that any necessary processing be done with a minimum of effort. Manufacturing requires the combination of (1) at least one kind of material —usually several—, (2) labor, (3) power, and (4) shipping facilities. The less transportation is involved in bringing these elements together the greater the efficiency; so the problem of locating a given industry involves calculations of the comparative difficulties of procuring the different elements, together with such considerations as the availability and cost of necessary land or floor space, opportunity for disposal of waste material, and adequacy of water supply.

Since many industries have similar requirements, they often find it advantageous to be grouped in districts where suitable facilities may be had. An opportunity for spur tracks, for instance, might attract a number of factories all of which have a similar need for shipment of their materials by rail. The more advantages in common there are the more this tendency toward segregation is accentuated. Manufacturers of related products find it mutually helpful to be in proximity.

This tendency often produces whole cities in which one kind of industry is so predominant that if business conditions in that specialty become depressed the community is much more seriously affected than if it were more diversified in its activities. Therefore extremes of specialization are not altogether advantageous.

Many manufacturing plants are very ugly in appearance, produce disagreeable smoke, smells, or noises, pollute streams with their discarded products, or poison the air with fumes which kill all vegetation in the vicinity. These evils may be unavoidable in some cases but many could be remedied with little expense, sometimes with financial advantage, as when chemical research shows how valuable by-products can be obtained from wastes. Industries necessarily obnoxious should not only be located at a distance from residential areas but also should be toward the leeward with reference to prevailing winds. The most efficiently managed factories are usually also the most attractive. The effect of pleasant conditions upon employees and prospective customers is becoming increasingly recognized by enlightened manufacturers as being of pecuniary as well as humanitarian value.

Much of what has just been said applies also to business, whose function is mainly the distribution of the products of industry. The advantages of segregation are obvious here too, facilitating comparison of prices and interchange of related goods and services. Usually there is a sharp separation between wholesale and retail activities, the former being advantageously associated with manufacturing, shipping and storage facilities, while the latter are commonly either grouped in large central shopping areas, with considerable segregation of similar goods and services, or dispersed among residential districts as small neighborhood centers of mixed types,

or else placed beside heavily travelled highways in order to cater to motorists.

Offices for commercial administration, finance and miscellaneous other purposes are advantageously segregated also, sometimes near the wholesale business centers. Banks designed for the use of the general public usually are distributed like retail stores.

Public buildings serving essentially commercial functions, like a general post office or a custom house, should be in the commercial center of the city, and their efficiency should not be sacrificed for the sake of architectural ostentation. They, like all other structures, should be so designed as to function with a minimum of human effort, yet made as attractive as effective use permits. Beauty achieved at the expense of convenience awakens more annoyance than appreciation and so fails in its purpose.

Commercial premises are more likely to be aesthetically pleasing than manufacturing plants, partly because in most cases they have no stacks, condensers, and other such forms exposed to view and less waste material to be disposed of, and partly because they are to a greater extent in direct contact with their customers whose good impressions are of business value. But everything possible should be done to make both kinds of places more pleasant to the people who spend there so many hours of life.

HOUSING. Tastes differ greatly as to the amount and kind of residential space desired by different individuals, preferences ranging all the way from the solitude of the pioneer to the congestion of the apartment dweller. Most people however would probably agree fairly well upon a list of the characteristics of an ideal home, in spite of variation in their estimates of the comparative importance of the different items.

Such a list might include the following: (1) Healthfulness, with cleanliness, and abundant air, sunshine, beauty, and if possible some contact with nature. (2) Privacy, opportunity for restful sleep and a peaceful environment. (3) Easy access to educational, social, and creative opportunities. (4) Easy access to place of employment. (5) Convenience in use; ease and economy in maintenance. (6) Security of posession, at reasonable expenditure. (7) Protection against fire, disease and other dangers.

It is only too seldom that a home is to be found combining in large measure all these advantages. The city may furnish the first two only at high cost. A rural or suburban site is likely to provide them inexpensively but may lack accessibility to work and society except at cost of tedious travel. Often there is a shortage of acceptable, moderately-priced housing accommodations of all types.

The poor are, of course, most seriously affected by this problem, often being forced to live in tenements which are over-crowded, delapidated fire-traps, lacking adequate plumbing, lighting, heating and ventilation and altogether unsanitary. Disease, vice and crime are especially rife in slum districts.

One line of attack upon these evils has been through **building regulations** passed by some legislative body requiring certain minimum standards of construction and sanitation. However, generally such rules can be applied only to a limited extent or not at all to structures already built at the time of adoption, hence many of the oldest and worst specimens of bad housing have escaped. It has been difficult to secure enactment and enforcement of adequate laws in the face of opposition on the part of landowners and others who profit by the continuance of the bad conditions.

Zoning ordinances (which will be described in more detail later) regulating uses and heights of buildings and the preservation of minimum surrounding open spaces, thus protecting the occupants' supply of light and air, also are only applicable to new structures in most localities, and often even then have not been stringent enough to accomplish much good to the slum dwellers.

A more effective remedy has been the formation of public or semi public corporations which buy large tracts of land in slum districts, tear down or rebuild the miserable tenements and replace them with substantial, sanitary, pleasant dwellings having landscaped yards, playgrounds and nurseries for children and other attractive features or **amenities** with rents at considerably below commercial rates, often at less than cost.

Since these spacious developments usually accommodate fewer people than the congested arrangements they displace, this process, instead of relieving a shortage of housing, is likely to accentuate it. Many of the people removed from the old buildings tend to gravitate into some other slum, making it more crowded than before. Also there must be constant vigilance to prevent favoritism in the selection of families for subsidized dwellings, since people who are not genuinely needy often try to occupy them. Notwithstanding these drawbacks, most students of the subject agree that such **slum clearance** projects,

although not a complete solution of the housing problem, are of much social value, since they do definitely get rid of many filthy old hulks which otherwise would disgrace the community many years, always finding some tenants wretched enough to seek their dubious shelter. If the worst slums are eliminated, even though some of their inhabitants do move to others, some progress has been made. Clearly, however, this policy needs to be supplemented with other measures, providing both desirable houses and means for using them.

One of these measures is the **decentralization** of industries—dispersing them among many small communities rather than **centralizing** them in the large cities. This enables people to live within short distances of their work in districts where the comparatively low value of land makes cheaper rents possible, crowded dwellings less likely and often permits the supplementing of family income through home gardening, either in individual back yards or in **allotments**—strips within community gardens. Yet in too many cases squalid conditions exist, especially near factories and mines, even in the country. Some industrialists have provided for their employees row upon row of poorly built, ugly tenements, all alike. Some have used their dual function of employer and landlord as a means of exploiting the workers. On the other hand, some have built well-designed villages with attractive architecture and landscaping, including home gardens and good economic conditions. Similar developments of various sizes and types, some large enough to be called **garden cities**, have been built by philanthropists, philanthropic foundations or corporations, cooperative societies or governmental agencies.

A fundamental cause of the housing problem is the high cost of building construction in comparison with the income of the people. Anything diminishing the former factor, such as prefabrication processes putting housebuilding increasingly on a mass-production basis, helps reduce the difficulties. Also new developments in cheap, rapid transportation tend to improve the situation by promoting the commuting of workers, thus giving them easier access to inexpensive home sites, and also encouraging individual home ownership which is by many considered desirable if financial and other circumstances permit.

However it seems unlikely that reduction of land and building costs will be enough to win the battle against bad housing unless an attack is also made from the other side—the raising of popular income. It is doubtful if anything less than a great economic reform providing a substantial improvement in the distribution of wealth, together with an increase in the efficiency of education, stimulating people to use their available time and money more wisely, will suffice to actually eliminate wide-spread poverty and slums.

PUBLIC LANDS AND BUILDINGS. Even with excellent housing conditions there would not be sufficient space around urban and suburban dwellings to serve all the requirements of the inhabitants.

There is need for playgrounds, adapted in location, type and equipment to the various kinds of users. In large centers of population there is demand for athletic fields with elaborate provisions for seating and transporting great throngs of spectators.

Distinct from these arrangements connected with active play it is necessary to provide opportunities for quieter forms of outdoor enjoyment. **City parks** ranging in size from tiny plots at odd corners of streets to others occupying several blocks, usually more or less formal in design, make refreshing oases of green amidst the masonry. So-called **country parks** may be well within the congested part of a city yet perhaps be large enough for broad, informal landscape treatment, with public golf links, zoos, botanic gardens, and other spacious arrangements. It is particularly desirable that generous portions of the shores of rivers, lakes or the sea be kept open and developed for public use. Farther out from the population center may be still larger **reservations** (q.v.), **public forests** and **wild life sanctuaries** where natural conditions are encouraged, with few man-made features except roads, bridges, bridle paths, foot-trails, picnic facilities and shelters. Some very large reservations have cabins which are rented for brief periods to campers at nominal charge. It is desirable that as many as possible of the parks of a community be connected by **parkways** or **boulevards**—elongated parks enclosing highways usually limited in use to pleasure vehicles, the former usually informal in design, the latter formal—the whole comprising a **park system** in which one may walk or ride for long distances with beauty on every side. Planners aim to have some ramification of such a system within short walking distance of every city home.

Many of them also advocate that where possible a broad **green belt** of land surrounding each municipality be reserved for **park**, **forest** or agricultural use, through public purchase, zoning or other means, to provide spaces for the enjoyment of nature, for community gardens, and to keep the town from spreading shapelessly over the countryside, losing its identity and community spirit by merging with neighboring centers, and growing too large for the citizens to keep in close touch with their local government.

Often park functions can be combined to advantage with other uses. The parkways and boulevards just mentioned often provide important and pleasant traffic routes approaching or passing through a city. Cemeteries, especially if their monuments are not too obtrusive, the grounds around hospitals, colleges, and other large institutions, and those protecting drinking-water reservoirs, furnish agreeable landscapes for the enjoyment of passers-by and therefore blend well into a park system even though in some cases the public may not be permitted unrestricted entry.

However, care should be taken not to make incompatible combinations. A playground, for instance, may be adjacent to a park, provided there is considerable foliage or other insulation between them, but if the two are not well separated the noisy activity of the former will rob the latter of much of its value as a place of more quiet enjoyment. A park is often in danger of encroachment or even annihilation due to misguided civic leaders who look jealously upon its open spaces as sites immediately available without cost for public playgrounds, buildings, or other developments.

Frequently land least useful for other purposes because of irregular, rocky or swampy topography, and therefore comparatively inexpensive, is admirably suited for parks. There is great advantage in buying large tracts of such land as early as possible, before it is really required for use, and holding it for gradual refinement as need for it develops. The loss to the community in taxes by this policy is negligible in comparison with the savings effected in the cost of the land and the gain from the increase in valuation of neighboring properties.

It is desirable in purchasing land for park purposes to secure if possible complete topographical units, such as both sides of a valley or all the shores of a lake, in order that incongruous private developments may not spoil the landscape effect. Also it is best when feasible to have the territory terminate at public roads rather than private rear yards, for the same reason.

The placement of public buildings depends considerably upon their functions. Some, such as civic administration buildings, require a central location; others, like hospitals or pumping stations, may well be on the outskirts of a city. If their uses are compatible it is often desirable that they be grouped in **civic centers** where their combined architectural effect if well designed and with good landscaping around them may be impressive and an inspiration to the community. Some buildings may well be associated for reasons of convenience as well as aesthetics, as schools with libraries. Others should be separated, as police or fire stations from educational or recreational centers. Here, also, misguided efforts to economize sometimes lead to the crowding of a new building onto the grounds of an older structure, with unfortunate results. Consideration for the possibility of future expansion, as well as of the present appearance, demands ample open space around most public buildings.

Squares or **plazas,** important and enlarged street intersections, often closely related to civic centers, have been important throughout the history of civilization as focal points of community life, where marketing and all kinds of political and social gatherings have taken place. In many towns and cities much effort has been expended on their adornment with fountains, sculpture, arcades, and other decoration. In some old villages, a well or fountain in the market-place is still the principal water supply for the local population. In some other parts of the world it is customary to have a grassy, partially tree-shaded **village green** or **common** nearby, serving as a park, playground and site for local festivities and meetings, faced by churches and other public or commercial buildings.

Many old-world squares, dating from medieval times, when even main streets were usually irregular and very narrow, give an effect of practically complete enclosure and intimate unity. The beholder's eye is attracted by the picturesque facades of the surrounding ancient buildings and is not tempted to rove outside. In contrast to this, squares formed by intersections of modern wide streets impress with their spaciousness and distant views. Much as we may regret the loss of the charming older art-form, it appears inevitable under present conditions and the best available policy would seem to be to take as much aesthetic advantage as possible of the **closed vista,** or view terminating at a center of interest such as an impressive building.

Another modern problem arises from the increasingly urgent need for parking spaces for vehicles. There is strong temptation to use squares excessively for this need. A better plan is to provide if possible other near-by areas expressly for the purpose—**off-street parking.** Sometimes neighboring streets not needed for very active use are designated especially for parking.

STREETS. Clearly it is necessary that adequate provision be made for the movements of people and goods between the different parts of a city or region—especially between squares and other focal points. The natural pattern for the main streets of a town to take is in general likely to resemble somewhat that of a spider's web, with some streets radiating from the center and others circumferential. Large cities have several centers. A free adaptation of this spontaneous type of layout to the local situation is more likely to be convenient and economical than any rigid artificial design, rectangular or otherwise. The great increase in motor-driven vehicles and consequent traffic congestion has made it more important than ever that **arterial,** or **trunk** main connecting **highways** or **thoroughfares** be as direct and level as is feasible, and much wider than most of the principal roads of earlier days.

Augmented speed has brought added dangers of collision. These are lessened if the number of intersecting streets is reduced to a minimum, if acute angles in the intersections are avoided, if pedestrians are required to keep in special footways, and if vehicles having different directions and speeds are sorted into different traffic lanes or designated pathways, preferably separated by substantial curbs and **islands** (spaces in a street made slightly higher than the roadway to prevent their use by vehicles), or in some cases by wider strips of landscaped space, the shrubbery of which not only is pleasing in appearance but also serves to shield motorists' eyes from the glare of approaching head-lights. At a junction of several busy streets a **traffic circle** is often made, consisting of a large central island, usually landscaped, about which traffic rotates, all in the same direction. Where two especially important highways cross it is sometimes worth the expense to either raise one above the other, making an **overpass,** or lower one beneath the other, forming an **underpass;** in both cases traffic making a right or left turn is accommodated by a system of curving ramps so designed that no car meets another going in the opposite direction.

The resemblance of the typical plan of these ramps to the shape of a four-leaved clover has led to the name **clover-leaf** being applied to both of these types of intersection. In especially congested parts of some large cities highways are superposed, forming **high level** or **double deck roads** or **streets**, but the expense of such structures is enormous.

As a main highway extends out from a city, too often it becomes a center of **ribbon development**, lined on both sides by disagreeable urban-type buildings and also excessive quantities of outdoor advertising and commercial establishments intended for the attraction of motorists. In order to escape from this, from the tedium of following behind slow-moving, noisy commercial vehicles, and from the delays and dangers of collision at numerous intersections, most drivers of private passenger vehicles prefer to approach or leave the city by way of a beautifully landscaped parkway where these unpleasant features are prohibited. Thus many parkways originally intended for the enjoyment of leisurely strollers and riders have since become busy thoroughfares, providing attractive entrances to the city, but not without some sacrifice.

Abutters—owners of property *abutting* or bordering—on an ordinary street have the right to build driveway connections at practically any point they choose along their boundaries. In some localities they are allowed even to connect side roads to the main street with little or no control from public authorities. Since the many intersections resulting are a troublesome menace to commercial as well as passenger long-distance traffic, and since the former is not permitted to avoid the difficulty by using parkways, a demand has arisen for **freeways, express,** or **limited access highways,** fenced off from adjacent land except at occasional well-controlled junctions, on which either passenger or freight vehicles can go at high speeds with comparative safety.

Modern trunk highways usually **by-pass** or avoid all the smaller towns near their routes, being connected with them only by well-marked side roads, hence have sometimes been called **townless highways.** This prevents the dangers and interruptions which come from mixing high-speed long-distance traffic with local, permits the liberal use of low-cost land for the broad highway, and saves the peaceful country villages from complete spoiling of their charm.

Increasing attention is being paid in many localities to preserving and improving roadside beauty. The islands and other odd pieces of land incidental to designing for modern traffic conditions give many new opportunities for landscape architecture.

Secondary or **sub-arterial streets** usually lack the extreme width and elaborate separation of lanes characteristic of main arteries, but should be at least wide enough to allow an easy flow of movement in both directions when both curbs are fully occupied with parked vehicles. Their chief function is to gather the traffic of local streets and pour it into the main highways at well-organized junctions.

Under present conditions the crossing of a busy thoroughfare is a formidable undertaking. To minimize the number of such crossings, it is well to plan the areas bounded by main or secondary streets, when largely residential, as somewhat independent **neighborhood units,** each with its local school, playground, park, branch library, retail stores and other community equipment, the shops usually on or near the bounding streets, the school and playground centrally located—off the main streets to lessen danger to children from traffic. A unit should be large enough to require its own elementary school, but small enough to enable all the children to walk to the building—which often may serve also as a local community health, educational and recreational center for adults as well as young people.

In a well-planned residential neighborhood the local streets are quite different from main or secondary streets in many respects. They are varied and economical in layout and width, each especially designed to fit the needs of its section so that a maximum of communication service can be obtained with a minimum of street area. A moderate amount of irregularity is advantageous since it not only gives opportunity for especially interesting aesthetic effects but also tends to deter the entrance of through traffic thus shielding the neighborhood from much bustle and danger. A U-shaped street or a **cul-de-sac** (pl. culs-de-sac) or **dead-end street** connecting with another street at only one end, is often an economical means of providing access to irregular pieces of land. These are highly esteemed by many people as residential sites because they have so little traffic. The latter should be short to avoid undue inconvenience and fire hazard, and should be wide enough at the far end to permit easy turning of vehicles.

Streets should avoid climbing or cutting through steep hills directly but instead should wind around them, avoiding dangerous grades and providing attractive building sites and easy connections with private driveways. They should not be so far apart that excessively deep building lots are produced, since these may later, if the land increases considerably in value, lead to the construction of rear dwellings and development of bad housing conditions. Where feasible, streets should not run due east-west or north-south since those **orientations** give poor exposures to sunshine in many of the rooms of the houses.

Overhead electric wires along streets should be eliminated so far as possible by running them either under the surface of the street or else overhead along rear lot lines. Good shade trees add greatly to the attractiveness of a street, but modern waterproof pavements make it difficult for them to grow on curb-lines, so a common practice now is to plant them on private lawns near the street, by arrangement with the owners.

RAIL, WATER AND AIR TRANSPORTATION. Congestion often makes street travel slow. Cars moving on rails and separated from other traffic can make much faster progress. The form of separation ranges in cost from (1) the surface reservation, which is very inexpensive but rarely feasible under city condition; through (2) the **elevated** structure, ordinarily over a street, which is usually noisy and unsightly; (3) the **open cut**, where the railroad is below the level of its surroundings, relatively silent and inconspicuous, but requiring expensive excavation and monopolizing its space; and (4) the **subway, tube** or **underground,** so expensive that only large cities can afford it, (5) to the **tunnel** under a river, harbor, or hill which is the most costly of all such undertakings.

These **rapid-transit** lines need to be coordinated with all other passenger-transportation facilities in the city—particularly with airports, railroad stations and steamship piers. Any such point should be considered an entrance gate to the community, and so designed that strangers will receive a hospitable first impression.

Planning future provisions for air travel is especially difficult because requirements are subject to so much change on account of the progress of invention. However it is surely wise to provide ample landing areas, since if they later prove to be larger than necessary the surplus space can easily be used in other ways, and to choose locations of convenient relationship to other modes of transport, avoiding if possible places frequently shrouded in fog or smoke.

Railroad stations for freight or express should be separated from passenger stations but closely related to industrial and warehouse facilities, and provide means for efficient transfer of goods from one mode of transportation to another with minimum handling. Some large cities have been troubled by an excessive number of terminals belonging to rival railways; great improvement has come from combining these.

The necessity of avoiding steep inclinations and sharp curves in railroad design has caused many difficulties when new lines have passed through an established town, streets being intersected abruptly, necessitating in each case either a dead-end often coming at an awkward location, a **grade** or **level crossing** causing many accidents, or a bridge which is expensive. The smoke, dirt, noise and ugliness often produced by railroads are also troublesome. Electrification, which eliminates some of these evils, has been slow of development of its expense.

THE MAKING AND EXECUTING OF PLANS. The processes of making and executing civic plans consist essentially of four types of activity: (1) gathering of facts; (2) formulating of plans; (3) legislative adoption; and (4) construction and enforcement.

The first and second of these usually have been done under the direction of a **planning board, planning authority** or **planning commission** composed of representative citizens serving without pay, appointed by the executive of the governmental unit involved or elected by popular vote. Such boards should be small, of unquestionable disinterested honesty and ability, with fairly long, overlapping terms of office to insure continuity of policy. They usually have needed to employ part-time one or more specialists to advise them and attend to technical details.

The collection of adequate data as to the past, current, and probable future physical, economic and social geography of the area is most necessary before a plan can be prepared. Such information needs to be kept up-to-date by frequent supplementary surveys.

The designing process should be accompanied by public hearings and numerous conferences with civic leaders for the sake of both the fruitful suggestions often obtained and the need for a wide spreading of information as a necessary condition of the popular support upon which a plan so largely depends for its success.

In some localities school children have aided, under careful supervision, in gathering information in preliminary surveys. This not only has saved expense but has also given the young future voters civic education of great value. The formation of an "advisory council" of perhaps 100 leading citizens of the area to form a connecting body between the planning board and the general population has proved helpful in many places. Chambers of commerce, women's clubs and other community organizations have often assisted or even initiated planning movements.

In a democracy, plans ordinarily must receive some kind of legislative approval before they become effective. This may be piece-meal in form—even though the plan itself may be **comprehensive,** or take into consideration all important planning problems of the district— as when money for construction according to different parts of a plan is appropriated from time to time as need for each project arises; or in some places there may be formal adoption of a **master plan** as a whole, under a law which requires future conformity to the plan except in specified circumstances. In any case there is ample provision for amendments. All civic plans must be revised from time to time as conditions change.

Detailed legal provisions for putting civic plans into effect vary considerably in different countries and states but there are certain fundamental principles in common. One of the central problems in planning law is the reconciliation of the sometimes conflicting interests and rights of the community and the individual. One basic assumption, known as the **police power,** is that a government has the right and duty to make and enforce any regulation necessary to protect the health, safety, and general welfare of the public, without making compensation to any individual injured thereby. Another, called the **right of eminent domain,** is that the government and certain public service corporations, such as railroad companies, have the right to force individuals to sell property which is demonstrated to the satisfaction of a court to be needed for public benefit, at a price considered by the court to be fair, after a disinterested expert appraisal.

One troublesome issue is the extent to which legal recognition can justly be extended to aesthetic considerations. It is possible to demonstrate that, for instance, the building of an extremely ugly structure depresses the value of surrounding property, but the lack of agreement among alleged authorities on aesthetics as to what constitutes ugliness has made legislators and jurists reluctant to consider the problem. In some countries **architectural control,** the requirement that designs of buildings be approved by an official board of architects before construction is permitted, has long been in use; in others this would be considered an invasion of personal liberty. Some governments which have not adopted such control of private buildings do go so far as to require approval by an **art commission,** composed of recognized connoisseurs, of any design for a public building or monument before it is accepted.

Another approach to this problem is by way of **restrictions** written into real estate deeds which, being contracts, can include almost any provisions upon which the two parties agree. Common types prohibit certain uses of the property likely to be considered objectionable by neighbors, prescribe certain minimum open spaces around buildings, and require that the latter must have at least a certain minimum cost. Thus indirectly, by utilizing obviously measurable characteristics, a slight degree of aesthetic protection can be obtained from the law. But since the enforcement of private contracts depends upon private litigation many offenses go unchallenged.

However some sins against beauty are also demonstrable sins against public health, safety and general welfare; and, as we have seen, the government itself has the obligation under the police power to prohibit them and to enforce its edicts effectively.

Among these edicts are **zoning ordinances,** or **zoning by-laws,** which are based on the theory that different types of districts or **zones** should in the public interest have different regulations as to uses of property and spaces around buildings. For example, a city might classify its territory into the following **use zones,** and prohibit in each the building of any new structures which do not conform in use to the types permitted in that district: (1) "Single residence" zone, for houses containing one family (or cooking unit) only. (2) "General residence" permitting the above uses plus two-family houses. (3) "Apartment" permitting the above uses plus multi-family dwellings. (4) "Business" or "Shopping", permitting the above uses plus retail stores, offices, public garages, etc. (5) "Light industry", permitting the above uses plus wholesale ware-houses, etc. and factories which do not cause special danger to the public, or obnoxious smells or sounds. (6) "Heavy industry", permitting any use. There are many variations in different localties. Small towns usually adopt a simpler scheme, perhaps with only three types, residence, business and industry. In most localities non-conforming uses, or buildings of a type not permitted in a zone in which they were built before the zone was established, have been allowed to be maintained but not enlarged. An incidental or accessory use is one which although different from the principal uses of the zone is inconspicuous, not detrimental to them, and commonly associated with them, as for instance a physician's office in a residential district.

Bulk zoning regulates spaces around buildings, prescribing minimum sizes for yards or courts or a maximum percentage of lot coverage, and maximum heights. The latter through insistence upon a certain ratio between height and horizontal set-back (q.v.), also sometimes called envelope restriction, in order to let in sunlight around sky-scrapers, has had important influence upon the architectural effect of many large cities. Bulk zoning also provides a means, too often neglected, especially in the United States, whereby a proper adjustment of traffic volume to available capacity of streets and rapid transit lines can be maintained. The combination of use zoning and bulk zoning is called comprehensive zoning. An interim zoning by-law or ordinance is one adopted hastily for temporary protection during the preparation of a permanent one. Strictly speaking, however, no zoning scheme is ever permanent. It is expected that all regulations and plans will require occasional amendment as new conditions develop.

The enforcement of zoning is the duty of the local official who inspects building construction. There is always need for variances or exceptions to be made in some individual cases with unusual circumstances where a literal enforcement of regulations would be impossible or cause undue hardship. These cases are decided by a board of appeals—a small group of local officials—after a public hearing of which neighboring property-owners are especially notified. One serious problem is the tendency of many boards of appeal to grant variances when they are not actually necessary, thus robbing the community of much of the protection which zoning can provide. Another abuse is known as spot zoning, the making of small zones of inappropri-

ate type for the advantage of particularly favored property owners. These, like other civic evils, can be prevented by informed and alert citizenship.

When a zoning plan is being designed there is usually agitation from over-optimistic land owners to make business and industrial areas far in excess of the probable needs of the community. If the planning board yields to this pressure the land in question loses much of its value for residential purposes, and since only a small proportion of it ever is actually sold for the other uses, a frequent result is the creation of a blighted district—a term applied to any tract where values are depressed so low that it becomes a liability instead of an asset to the community.

Wise zoning tends to prevent blighted districts by forbidding the building of structures which are incongruous in use or bulk, thus stabilizing and protecting real estate values, adding the weight of public authority to the natural tendency toward that segregation which, as we have seen, is usually so advantageous to all concerned.

The minimum widths of front yards or setbacks prescribed by bulk zoning sometimes may have the incidental effect of preventing building upon space which later may be used for widening the street. The procedure particularly designed for this purpose, however, is the establishment of a building line, under the right of eminent domain instead of the police power. The owner can claim compensation, but since he still enjoys the use of his land it is usually nominal.

An important problem connected with executing plans for streets is the control of platting. When an owner of a large piece of land desires to cut it up into building lots, forming a subdivision or residential estate, he is required in a well-organized community to first submit his plan or plat to the planning board, or in some localities to a small group of officials known as a board of survey, for approval before he may proceed with the work. In the latter case the board of survey should have some members in common with the planning board or at the very least the two boards should keep in close touch, in order that all new streets shall be laid out so as to be consistent with the community plan.

No plan is complete unless it includes a consideration of how the work shall be paid for. A comprehensive plan should contain a tentative schedule of execution providing for priority of the most urgent projects, and distributing the program over a term of years so that the community will not have too heavy a burden of work or expense at any one time. Also it is wise to have a **shelf** or collection of detailed construction plans held in reserve against future periods of business depression when the execution of public works will help to relieve unemployment.

A widely accepted general principle for financing public works is that the burden of expense should be distributed among the citizens in proportions to their ability to pay and to the benefit they derive from the improvement.

Benefit may be apportioned with reference to time by considering how long the effect of the work will last. Regular annual maintenance expenses should obviously be paid for from current taxes; it is argued by some, however, that bonds may justly be issued to pay for major permanent improvements so that future citizens will share the expense, since they will share the benefits. On the other hand, interest charges on bonds often add so much to the total cost of a project that many governments have concluded that a "pay-as-you-go" policy, applied to all but the largest enterprises, is best in the long run.

Benefits may also be apportioned with regard to space, by laying special assessments called **betterments** upon land owners whose properties are especially increased in value by a local improvement, such as the abutters on a newly-paved dead-end street.

Sometimes parcels of land forfeited by their owners for non-payment of taxes are suitable for civic purposes, and the municipality may wisely keep instead of selling them. Some governments have been able to secure large parks or other improvements with comparatively little expense to the public, by means of **excess condemnation**—purchasing or taking by eminent domain not only the land needed for the project itself but also considerable additional land in the vicinity which is later sold at a substantial profit due to the increase in value caused by the improvement. Furthermore, the possession of a liberal margin of extra land has facilitated the planning of good connections blending the new development into its environment.

This is a practical illustration of the measurable worth of civic planning; but much more important are the innumerable other values which, since they are in terms of human happiness and well-being, are beyond measurement.

HISTORY. It is difficult to say when civic planning began. Man has probably always been gregarious, and the first groupings of huts into approximate rows or rings for convenience or defense might justly be considered such a beginning.

In practically all ancient towns security was a prime consideration, so they were characteristically small, compact and enclosed in walls, through gates in which, comparatively broad, sometimes splendid, processional ways led to a central market-place used for all sorts of public gatherings and surrounded by many of the principal buildings of the community. Other important structures were sometimes grouped on a hill to form a citadel or "acropolis". The populace usually lived in crowded hovels reached by narrow, crooked alleys and courts. Some of these very early cities show regularity of street patterns. In India remains have been found of highly developed cities which were flourishing at least 5,000 years ago, built in rectangular blocks. Kahun in Egypt was laid out in straight lines between 3,000 and 2,500 B.C. to house workers for the construction of a pyramid. Other Egyptian examples of formal planning were at Thebes, Memphis and Tell-el-Amarna.

Babylon, Assur, Ninevah, Jerusalem and Palmyra were representatives of ancient splendor, the first noted especially for its terraced or "hanging" gardens, the last for its magnificent colonnaded avenue. Neither Athens nor Rome were highly organized in general structure but the Acropolis of the former and the forums of the latter were among the world's finest civic centers.

The first city planner of whom we know was Hippodamus of Miletus, 480 B.C., who had considerable influence, particularly in the building of Piraeus, Rhodes, and probably Selinus and Priene.

Although early Roman cities were often irregular in pattern, those of later periods show the influence of the military camp in their conventional rectangular layouts. A similar relationship occurred in China.

In the Middle Ages, although there were some towns called "bastides" planned on rectangular lines expressly to house workers on monastery lands, most communities were very irregular in pattern within elaborate fortifications. Often they had so much picturesque charm that some modern writers, notably Camille Sitte, have attempted to revive the style for their own time, with limited direct success but with some indirect influence upon the development of the planned irregularity of the neighborhood unit.

The Renaissance, with its enthusiasm for the classical, brought a return to the emphasis on symmetry and the monumental. First in Italy, under the encouragement of various popes, then in France, especially under the patronage of Louis XIV and the influence of his architect, Le Nôtre, designer of Versailles, streets were widened and straightened and new ones cut through, often radiating from, and so affording vistas of, imposing buildings, which were fronted by spacious plazas with fountains and other embellishments. In Germany, Karlsruhe and Mannheim, and in Great Britain, Edinburgh and Bath were examples of this formal style as were also Sir Christopher Wren's unfortunately ignored plan for the rebuilding of London after the great fire of 1666, L'Enfant's plan for Washington, and later the development of the great boulevards, parks and plazas of Paris by Haussman under Napoleon III.

The 19th cent., with its unprecedented advances in science, invention, industry and transportation, was a period of fundamental civic changes. There was a marked increase of world population. Many of the people, lured by employment in the new factories even at very low wages, flocked to the cities, causing great expansion and the development of additional slums and other social distresses; others made use of improved travel facilities to emigrate to frontier territories or colonies.

In the United States the need for rapid subdivision of the vast western lands caused the adoption of a wholesale mode of surveying based on latitude and longitude which in turn led to the unfortunate imposition of a rigid, expensive and inconvenient rectangular street pattern, in the worst possible orientation, upon most of the country.

European cities tore down their out-grown and obsolete fortifications, and in some instances, notably Vienna, made good use of the space for circumferential streets and parks. Most old-world parks and playgrounds have been obtained from former royal pleasure grounds. Americans, with no such inheritance, have been stimulated into greater—although still inadequate—activity in purchasing recreation spaces.

Toward the end of the century the invention of steel framing and the elevator made possible the development in the United States of the skyscraper, a great architectural achievement, impressive when surrounded with sufficient space, but producing intolerable traffic congestion when closely grouped in quantity. Subsequent efforts to relieve the pressure by widening old streets or cutting through new ones and providing rapid transit lines have failed because owners profiting from the increase in land values due to the congestion have successfully resisted the enactment of adequate restrictions, and the building of new skyscrapers has outstripped the provision of new means of circulation.

Much of the demand for rapid transit has come from commuters living in **dormitory suburbs** who seek to combine the advantages of town and country life at the expense of a long ride to and from their daily work. Most large cities also have **satellite** industrial towns in their vicinity, arising from the desire of manufacturers to locate on cheap, abundant land but near a large supply of labor and good transportation facilities. (Some writers use the word *satellite* as a synonym of suburb.)

The publication in 1898 of a book, *Tomorrow,* by Ebenezer Howard, marked a milestone in civic planning progress. He proposed the purchase of large rural tracts by limited-dividend companies serving the public interest and the designing of them according to the best known principles of civic planning as attractive self-sustaining communities with provisions for well-balanced development of industries, local business and spacious, healthful housing, including ample open areas for recreation and a surrounding agricultural belt. His ideas have been embodied successfully in the garden cities of Letchworth and Welwyn, near London, and have had wide influence elsewhere.

The advent of the automobile early in the twentieth century brought along with its numerous social and economic benefits enormously increased congestion to already inadequate city streets, and spread the trouble into outlying towns and intervening country roads. The first remedy to be tried was the widening of existing ways, and many a beautiful tree-shaded village center was ruined before the concept of the "by-pass" came to the rescue. "Ribbon developments" wove cities and their suburbs and satellites together into great, indistinguishable, monotonously unattractive masses, unrelieved by open landscape.

The urgency of traffic problems greatly stimulated civic planning movements, which, however, had begun earlier—the decade between 1865 and 1875 having been particularly notable for the passage of European laws controlling town extensions and public health, the Chicago World's Fair of 1893 having stimulated the development of many civic centers in the U.S.A., and modern zoning having begun in Germany in 1894. The year 1909 was an important one on both sides of the Atlantic: it marked the passage of the "British Housing, Town Planning, etc., Act", which, with subsequent amendments, has been the legal basis of recent official planning in that country; and in the United States it saw the first meeting of the National Conference on City Planning, the appointment of a Plan Commission in Chicago, a report on Public Improvements for the Metropolitan District of Boston, foreshadowing the later development of regional planning, the beginning of university instruction in planning, at Harvard, and the first thorough-going zoning of an entire American city at Los Angeles. The time was ripe for unprecedented activity.

The approval by the courts of the Los Angeles zoning encouraged other municipalities to follow suit, and soon a wave of enthusiasm for zoning swept over the United States. By 1929, 754 communities of various sizes had been zoned, and 650 had official planning boards. There was also considerable highway planning. Superhighways—extra wide arterial roads—with separated traffic lanes and clover-leaf intersections were extensively constructed. Much interest was aroused by the designing in 1929 of Radburn, New Jersey, a new suburb of New York with a novel layout featuring cul-de-sac streets, footpaths and abundant open spaces, so arranged as to effect a virtually complete separation of pedestrian and motor traffic. This experiment has had much influence upon subsequent planning thought.

In England, although some new broad highways have been built, the majority of the roads are much narrower than in the U.S.A. The process of planning has been so rigorously controlled by elaborate laws that local initiative has been hampered, in the opinion of some critics. However, Britain has been a leader in the building of new housing villages, excellent in their sanitation and spaciousness.

In continental Europe and Latin America there has been continued emphasis upon monumental effects with grand avenues and plazas. In several countries the laws permit a considerable degree of architectural control, which has greatly promoted civic attractiveness. Many European ports have surpassed those of the U.S.A. in combining beauty with efficient utility in the designing of their water-fronts,

although the coördination of docks with railroads has not been so successful in most of the countries. An exception is Germany, where there has been excellent comprehensive planning, including zoning and industrial housing. Sweden, Holland, Czechoslovakia and Russia have also taken considerable progressive action in this field.

Among the cities on other parts of the earth for which more or less complete plans have been made are: Adelaide, Alexandria, Calcutta, Canton, Jerusalem, Johannesburg, Khartoum, Manila, Nanking, Greater Shanghai, Singapore, Tientsin, Tokyo, and Ottawa. Canberra, Australia, and New Delhi, India, have been planned from their beginnings, like Washington. This bare list indicates how the municipal planning impulse has spread thoughout the civilized world.

The history of the neighborhood unit goes back at least as far as about 793 A.D., in Kyoto, Japan, but its modern form was first given prominent notice in the "Regional Plan of New York and its Environs", published in 1929.

This ten-volume report was admirably representative of the metropolitan type of regional planning, comprehensively dealing as it did with the planning problems common to New York City and its surroundings, a territory lying in three states, extending to a radius of 40 to 50 miles and including 494 municipalities. The advantages of a large city and its satellites considering together their water, sewer, park and other problems were first officially recognized in the United States in 1890, when in Boston were established boards which later were merged as the "Metropolitan District Commission". Other cities which have done metropolitan planning include Chicago, Cleveland, Los Angeles, Philadelphia, Santa Barbara, and Washington. There also has been considerable of it in France, Germany, Great Britain, Italy and Sweden.

Another type of regional planning has developed in England, having the special purpose of preserving the character of areas especially notable for historical or scenic interest.

A third and more common type is concerned with the general economic and social development of a natural geographic unit, frequently a drainage basin containing a large river with its tributaries. In Germany there have been several enterprises of this sort, the one for the Ruhr district, including at least 1,470 square miles and 268 municipalities, being especially important.

By far the largest undertaking of this kind which has been done up to the time of writing is the Tennessee Valley project, including about 40,000 square miles of territory, comprising parts of seven states, and having among its purposes the development of navigation, flood control, electric power generation, reforestation, the proper use of submarginal lands and the "economic and social well-being" of the inhabitants. The work has been planned and executed under the supervision of three directors heading the "Tennessee Valley Authority", a corporation established by Congress.

The achievement of these ends is a most intricate problem, involving the stoppage of erosion by scientific agriculture and forestry; the building of great dams and power plants; the resettlement of the people who have been living in the reservoir areas above the dams, as well as others from sub-marginal farms, assisting them to move into well-planned new communities; sanitation, including the prevention of malaria through mosquito-control; the planning for new transportation, industrial, business, educational, recreational and social facilities; and numerous other factors. In short, such a project embraces practically the whole range of civic planning and of the relationships of human beings with each other and with nature.

The contemplation of such a stupendous task gives one pause. Yet when one reflects that man has succeeded before with many other difficult assignments, that he has the benefit of much experience with previous planning, and of a rich fund of scientific research, one feels reassured, and confident that not only will he accomplish this with a reasonable measure of success, but will boldly move on to still vaster undertakings—national, then continental, and ultimately world-wide, in their scope. Thus may planning—not dictatorial but always under democratic control—adjust man's environment to his needs and help him to achieve enduring peace, happiness and progress. See Adams, T., *Outline of Town and City Planning*, 1935; Adams, T., Thompson, F. L., Fry, E. M. and Adams, J. W. R., *Recent Advances in Town Planning*, 1932; Bauer, C., *Modern Housing*, 1934; Chase, S., *Rich Land, Poor Land; a Study of Waste in the Natural Resources of America*, 1936; Lewis, N. P. and Lewis, H. M., *The Planning of the Modern City*, 1923; Lohman, K. B., *Principles of City Planning*, 1931; MacKaye, B., *The New Exploration*, 1928; Mumford, L., *The Culture of Cities*, 1938; Sert, J. L. and the Congrès Internationaux d'Architecture Moderne, *Can Our Cities Survive? An A B C of Urban Problems, Their Analysis, Their Solution*, 1942. *American Planning and Civic Annual*, periodically published by the American Planning and Civic Association, Washington, D. C. —T.I.C.

clair-de-lune (F.). A color term applied to the glaze of Chinese pottery which simulates the light of the moon; a light blue.

clair-obscure. See chiaroscuro.

clarinet, clarionet. See MUSICAL INSTRUMENTS.

clarity. In criticism, the elemental meaning of this term is the simple one of transparency. Clarity indicates that a work yields its significance quickly and easily; it does not obtrude itself, as a work of art, between its meaning for appreciation and the person who would appreciate it. —I. J.

classical style. Although the art of classical Greece was actually extremely varied, including work which may be characterized as romantic, impressionistic, and realistic (see Hellenic Art and Hellenistic Art), certain of its most characteristic qualities, generally accepted since as "classical", have influenced strongly the art of Europe in various later periods. Broadly speaking, these qualities are: (1) the representation of the healthy human form at its best, without distortion or abstraction, tending toward the heroic but engaged in normal human activity; (2) a strict sense of formal design, monumental and typical rather than trivial and individual, appealing to the logical demands of the mind more than to merely sensuous delight or romantic moods. Copies or adaptations of such Greek art have been made in many later periods and places, but, capturing the external form, they have usually failed to incorporate the conviction and radiance of the originals. Genuine classical art, although it subordinated detail to contour and mass, did not suppress it, but infused into the powerful forms the subtlety and glow of resilient life. The adaptations have often only a superficial resemblance, with the negative virtue of restraint rather than the positive one of vitality. Roman artists thus failed to make their multitude of copies live. Among later sculptors, the craftsmen in Gandhara, India, fashioned adaptations of classical facial types and draperies, curbing their own native rhythmic exuberance. The influence of classical sculpture also appears in Provençal Roman-

esque statues, in which the earth-bound dignity
was inspired by Roman figures. In the Renaissance, Donatello realized in his less individualistic and dramatic work a classical dignity of form, and in France, Goujon was instructed by the more gracious classical reliefs.
Under the influence of the Beaux-Arts and
the French Academy in Rome, France became
devoted to the classical ideal, and the sculpture by such men as Girardon and Coysevox,
and paintings by Poussin, Lorraine and David,
dealt with classical subjects in classical types
of composition. The development of archaeological research in the 9th cent. led to great
enthusiasm for Greek and Roman art, which
was reflected in sculpture of the neo-classic
school, led by Canova, Thorwaldsen and Dannecker, who filled museums and homes with
coldly formal mythological figures. In modern
times a closer understanding of the best
Greek work has been achieved, and sculptors
like Manship, Jennewein and Cecere in
America, Bourdelle and Maillol in France,
and Milles in Sweden, have reinterpreted
classical themes and techniques with vigor and
originality, being genuinely guided rather than
confined by the classical tradition. —W.R.A.

classic ballet. A style of the academic theatrical dance employing pure movements of
the traditional school, apart from character
(theatricalized folk) dancing, or associative
or mimetic gesture. The impression of the
body in movement or repose is essentially
linear, with the line of the silhouette, clean,
sustained and noble, brilliant but measured,
deliberate but never dead.   —L.K.

classicism. A style incorporating the characteristics of classical Greek or Roman art by
a process of intellectual and aesthetic amalgamation. Many civilizations throughout history,
from India to Scandinavia, have taken over
elements of Mediterranean art, especially when
in search of a rational, harmonious and human
centered expression of their own cultural
values. The term, then, in distinction to the
genuine "classical", includes an element of the
derivative—yet, although derivative, it appears
with the claim of the absolute and timeless
validity of classical art.

We thus may speak of an Alexandrian
classicism, an Augustan classicism, a Renaissance classicism, a Palladian classicism, etc.,
thereby describing an art in which the national and time components are submerged
in the pattern of Greek (or Greco-Roman)
art. From this derives also, the peculiar

quality of classicism whereby its formal timeless characteristics often differ from the time-
bound meaning to be expressed such as, for
instance, a modern stock exchange in the
shape of a temple or Pauline Bonaparte as
a reclining Venus.

It must remain to some extent unexplained
why Greek art could exert such a recurrent
and stimulating but also often sterilizing influence on other civilizations. Besides the
highly rational organization of classical art
resulting in clarity of proportions, rhythmical
composition and visual application of geometrical and biological laws, Greek art had
been the first comprehensive expression of a
civilization of the white people handed down
in visible signs to later generations. All these
characteristics have bestowed upon it the
qualities of the exemplary, the normative and
the ideal.

Besides this general usage of the term
"classicism" there is the specific and more frequent one applying the term to the neoclassical
revival of the second part of the 18th and the
first quarter of the 19th cents. This revival
also is known under the name of "neo classicism"' (early part of it in America: "colonial
style"), while certain periods of it in the
history of furniture are called sometimes
"Louis Seize style" (up to 1790), "Directoire"
(ca. 1800), and "Empire" (ca. 1810).

Since the early Renaissance (ca. 1400),
classical aesthetics have increasingly taken
possession of Europe; yet all efforts toward
a pure application of classical forms and principles have been counteracted to some extent
by the dynamics of national and time-determined self-expression as a result of which
finally, the "Baroque Style" emerges. The
energies of this style had spent themselves by
the middle of the 18th cent. The fact that it
had become a means of propaganda for church
and dynasty made it also suspicious in the
eyes of the rising middle class brightened by
the light of "Reason".

The excavations at Herculaneum (1738) and
Pompeii (1748) provided the theorists, archeologists and academicians with the longed-for
samples of classical forms. The appearance of
J. F. Winckelmann's *History of the Art of
the Ancients* (1764) furnished the literary-
inclined world with the necessary foundations.

Thus by the middle of the 18th cent. the
baroque style divided into its two original
components—the classical and the Gothic. The
latter created the strange Neo-Gothic revival,
the former, classicism.

Its stylistic characteristics are those of Greco-Roman art but presented with the sophisticated asceticism of a refined society which yearned for lost simplicity. White, gold, soft blues, greens and yellows expressed the delicate sensualism of the era in an architecture and painting still connected by many ties to the previous rococo. Under Napoleon I the early Hellenic type of classicism changed to the more pompous Roman style known as "Empire". The forms became heavier, and accordingly, the color preferred was a deep red contrasted with gold. The imperial era wished to suggest a revival of the Augustan era.

After Napoleon's downfall, classicism became more and more an archeologically correct costume disguising the utilitarian purposes of modern city life until by the middle of the 19th cent. it had given way to the more ornate pseudo-Gothic, Renaissance and Baroque which the uncreative era of style imitations had brought about. Nowhere has classicism shown itself more conservatively preserved than in the U.S.A. with its classicist capital, Washington.

ARCHITECTURE. The conflict between the baroque and the neo-classical current appeared first in *France* at the competition for the facade of St. Sulpice in Paris (finished 1745). Meissonier's elegant Rococo solution, was defeated by the classical design of the Italian Jean Nicolas Servandino (1695-1766). Jaques Germain Soufflot's (1713-1780) *St. Genevieve* (1755-1790), better known as "Pantheon", was the era's first church built in the Roman design as a centralized, thermae-like building. Angle-Jacques Gabriel (1698-1782), the architect of the Place de la Concorde and Barthélemy Vignon (1762-1828), the architect of the "Madeleine", combined the baroque genius for large-scale planning with the sobriety and the archeological spirit of the new era.

Pierre Francois Fontaine (1762-1853) and Charles Percier (1764-1838), the court architects and decorators of Napoleon, exerted by the publication of their designs (1811) an international influence in spreading the "Empire" style. As a lesser-known but highly typical expression, the "architecture of reason" of Claude Nicolas Ledoux (1736-1806) may be mentioned in which architecture is reduced to the basic geometrical shapes of the universe.

In England the Palladianism of the previous era turned to Vitruvian purification by the publication of Stuart and Revett's *Antiquities*

of *Athens* (1761-62). Robert Adam (1728-1792) belongs among the most influential and refined architects of the period creating private homes (Sion House, 1761); city blocks and squares (the Adelphi, Fitzroy's, London); and public buildings (University of Edinburgh, 1788, only in parts); in which every detail of the interior and exterior is harmoniously designed.

James Craig (✠ 1795) designed a new *Edinburgh,* one of the few neo-classically laid out cities of Europe, while John Wood (✠ 1782) continued the noble style of his father, John the Elder (1754) in Bath. Equally important as a city planner is John Nash (1752-1835), the architect of Regent Street.

Sir John Soane's (1752-1837) Bank of England (since 1788) bespeaks still the Greco-Roman earlier manner, while Sir Robert Smirke's (1781-1867) British Museum (finished 1855) and Harvey L. Elmes (1813-1847) St. George's Hall in Liverpool (since 1838) represent the drier but archeologically more precise later phase of classicism.

In *Germany,* the new epoch excels in the "Prussian Classicism" of Friedrich Gilly (1772-1800) and his student, Karl Friedrich Schinkel (1781-1841), the architect of the Old Museum (1822-28) and the Schauspielhaus (1818-21) in Berlin.

Leo von Klenze (1784-1864), the architect of Ludwig I of Bavaria, transferred the Hellenic puritanism of the Gilly School to the South of Germany and to Russia (St. Petersburg, Eremitage—1840-52).

In *Italy,* the theatrical Roman, still half-baroque classicism of Giovanni Battista Piranesi (1720-1778) aroused a romantic longing among the architects of Europe to study the classical ruins.

Giuseppe Piermarini (1734-1808), the architect of the Scala (1776-78), Pietro Bianchi (1787-1849), the creator of San Francesco di Paola in Naples (finished 1831) and Pietro de Nobile (1774-1854) later city architect of Vienna, exemplify the new style in its different phases.

Scandinavia, Russia and Poland reveal in their cities and palaces, the great and lasting influence which the neo-classical style has had in the civilization of the late 18th and early 19th cents., continuing the large scale city planning of the previous baroque era on a more sober and conservative scale.

The first monumental architectural style of the U.S.A. is neo-classical. The so-called colonial style of the southern mansions as well as the architecture of New England, and the Hellenism of Washington, all express the Attic, Roman, and French-steeped traditions of the new democracy. Thomas Jefferson (1743-1826) himself presents the unity of the new aesthetic and political ideals in his plans for Monticello (1771), the Richmond state capitol (1785), and the University of Virginia (1817).

Charles Bulfinch (1763-1844), Benjamin Latrobe (1764-1820), and Thomas Walter (1804-1887), have systematized and spread the neo-classical style all the way from Boston to Washington. Theirs was the last sound architecture of America in the 19th cent. SCULPTURE. Theoretically, sculpture should have been the foremost expression of the classicist era since it is in the plastic field that Greco-Roman art has found its utmost expression. Rational art sensually experienced should have recognized in the human figure the noblest symbol of the universe. But practically the vitality of the fine arts in this epoch was too low, the experience of a humanism in the nude too remote to bring forth the expected sculpture. The two leading artists came from the southern and the northern ends of Europe; yet both spoke a very similar artistic language.

The Italian Antonio Canova (1757-1822) represents the realistic, often sweet and sensuous style of the first part of the classicist current with great skill and an equal mastering of the monumental (tomb for Clemens XIII—Rome, 1792; tomb of Maria Christina —Vienna, 1805) and the intimate (Amor and Psyche—c. 1795; Hebe—1814).

The Dane, Berthel Thorvaldsen (1770-1844) exemplifies perhaps best the Winckelmann ideal of "Noble simplicity and tranquil grandeur". Trained in Rome, he tried to reconquer the pure Greek style of Praxiteles. The classicist theory of the all-important contour (see PAINTING below) and the ever-present consciousness of his great examples prevented him, however, from achieving a vital plasticity. His Jason (1801), his bas-reliefs of Alexander's pageant (1811), his Christ (c. 1821) seem typical.

Other sculptors of significance are the English John Flaxman (1755-1826) (tomb of Nelson, St. Paul, London); the Frenchman Edmond Bouchardon (1698-1762) (Amor with the Club, Statue of Louis XV); and Jean Antoine Houdon (1741-1828)—only partially a classicist (countless portrait busts, Diana, 1780); and the German Johann Gotfried Schadow (1764-1850) (crown princess Luise and sister, 1797).

In general one can say that in subject matter, the erotical-allegorical type of the rococo has given way to a purer mythological genre, that religious sculpture nearly vanishes, and that portrait sculpture is stylized according to the ideals of Greco-Roman portraiture. Peaceful statecraft supersedes the vain-glory of war.

PAINTING. A revolution in painting took place at the same time under the leadership of theoretical writers such as Anton Rafael Mengs (1728-1779) and J. F. Winckelmann. The hostility of the theorists against the sensuous quality of color combined itself with a new emphasis on design as the solid foundation of the arts. This theory became further strengthened by Flaxman's and others' publications of Greek vase paintings in pure contour style which created the idea of Greek art being one of pure linearism. This tendency toward linear expression found universal acceptance.

Ingres states: "Even the smoke must be expressed by lines." The linearism of the classicist style appears as a part of a general reduction of the pictorial means in order to come closer to the believed clarity and serenity of ancient art.

As to subject matter, the heroique and the virtuous historical genre, such as Diderot (1713-1784) praised in his "Salon" reviews, became the favorite of the day.

The Parnassus (1761—Villa Albani, Rome) by Winckelmann's friend A. R. Mengs, was the first fresco in the new style. It exerted profound influence on the transitional masters such as Jean Baptiste Greuze (1725-1805) and Angelica Kauffmann (1741-1807). The new concepts of purified form and ideal subject matter concluded a treaty with the concepts of the French Revolution in the person of Jacques Louis David (1748-1825). This fact partially explains the enormous success of pictures such as his "Oath of the Horatii" (1784).

Yet, Republican Virtue became Imperial Grandeur in the "Coronation of Napoleon" (1805) and David, the sans culotte, became the court painter of the emperor. Besides his many historical paintings, David excelled as a realistic portraitist (Madame Recamier, 1800) and as the powerful leader of the best attended painting studio of Paris. His ideals were continued and translated from the Roman into a more refined Grecian sensualism by his student, Jean A. Dominique Ingres (1780-1867). He is the greatest portraitist of the era, its subtlest draftsman and the most uncompromising adherent to classicist theorems. As such, his influence prevailed throughout the 19th cent. with the masters of the neo-classical style.

Thomas Couture (1815-1879), Theodore Chasseriau (1819-1856) and Puvis de Chavannes (1824-1898) expressed the classicist doctrines in paintings and murals. Yet they fought an increasingly difficult battle against the naturalistic tendencies of the 19th cent.

In the other countries the classicist period has not produced great painters; which bespeaks perhaps, a certain exhaustion in the creative impulse of the visual arts. Sir Josuah Reynold's (1723-1792) eclecticism adhered only in parts to the rigid purity of classicism, while the American-born president of the Academy, Sir Benjamin West (1738-1820) raised American and English historical painting to classicist standards. Exclusively as draughtsmen, the sculptor Flaxman and William Blake (1757-1827), the illustrator of his own poetical writings, conformed clearly and purely to the ideals of their era.

In Germany, the religious art of the so-called "Nazarenes" under the leadership of Peter Cornelius (1783-1867) and Friedrich Overbeck (1789-1869), represented a blend of Romantic ideas with classicist form. Their academic teachings have exerted a widespread influence in Central Europe, especially in the field of fresco painting. Anselm Feuerbach (1829-1889), a student of Couture and Hans von Marées (1837-1887), seeker for greatness of concept and form interpreted the classical ideal for their naturalistic contemporaries. They remained tragically isolated.

The 20th cent. has seen new inroads of classicism. Pablo Picasso's (born 1881) linearism of the 1920's and at present, the so-called Neo-Romantic movement contain elements of Flaxman's and Ingres' art. It is the abstract in form and the abstracted in subject matter which are sought for in present day classicism. See Lionello Venturi, *History of art criticism*, 1936; H. J. C. Grierson, *Classical and romantic*, 1923; Hans Rose, *Klassik als Kuenstlerische Denkform des Abendlandes*, 1938; Gustav Pauli, *Die Kunst des Klassizismus und der Romantik*, 1929; L. Hautecoeur, *Rome et la renaissance de L'antiquité*, 1912; Siegfried Giedion, *Spaetbarocker und romantischer Klassizismus*, 1922; Fr. Benoit, *L'art francais pendant la revolution et l'empire*, 1897; Seymour de Ricci, *The style Louis XVI*, 1913; S. Rocheblave, *L'age classique de l'art francais*, 1931-2; A. E. Richardson, *Georgian England, Monumental classic archi-*

tecture in England, 1914; Carl Justi, *Winckelmann und seine Zeitgenossen*, 3 vol., 1898, 3rd ed., 1923; Franz Landsberger, *Die Kunst der Goethezeit*, 1931; F. Antal, Notes on Classicism and Romanticism, *Burlington Magazine*, April, 1935; June, 1936; Sept. 1940; Fiske Kimball, *American architecture*, 1928.

—A.N.

classic revival period, in American art. See POST - REVOLUTIONARY ARCHITECTURE AND DECORATIVE ARTS IN THE U.S.A.

classification of the arts. All arts fall into seven overlapping groups:
1. *Useful arts,* serving purposes outside themselves.
2. *Fine arts,* distinguished by self-sufficient expressive power.
3. *Lesser arts,* such as, furniture, rugs, printing, jewelry, masks.
4. *Decorative arts.*
5. *Social, civil, and religious arts*: graces, manners, ceremonies, rituals, and community plans which enrich human intercourse.
6. *Sportive arts,* pursued for pastime and amusement.
7. *Cosmic art,* not man-made, natural forms viewed as divine expressions.

The **fine arts** have been organized according to many principles, notably the following:
1. The senses: Hegel, Volkelt, Külpe, Delacroix . .
2. Kinds of imagination (visual, auditory, fanciful) condition formative, tonal, mobile arts: Vischer.
3. Medium: Bosanquet, Meumann: shaping, speaking, musical, mobile arts; T. M. Greene: representational arts (sculpture, painting), abstract (architecture, dance, music), symbolic (literature).
4. Degree of ideality: Schelling, Hegel: in symbolic art phenomenon preponderates over idea (typically, Egyptian architecture); idea and matter attain equilibrium in classical art (Greek sculpture); idea dominates in romantic art (painting, music, poetry).
5. Organic activity: Santayana, Dewey: automatic and shaping arts: expression through the human organism or through external materials.

(Adler's system below includes six other principles.)

The two following schemes perhaps succeed best in displaying the range, interrelations, and differences of the fine arts.

Adler, developing suggestions of Urries, constructs a cycle-system of the arts which integrates eight principles of division:

1. The use of external tools distinguishes mediate arts (architecture, sculpture, painting) from immediate arts (mimicry, music, poetry) which are expressed in the natural materials of man's organism and speech. Five other vertical perspectives qualify these contrasting groups respectively:
2. Formative versus musical.
3. Spatial versus temporal.
4. Static versus dynamic: rest versus motion.
5. Visual versus auditory (music, poetry), visual-auditory (drama, opera), and visual-rhythmic (dance).
6. Apollonian versus Dionysian.

By introducing fitting intermediate stages between neighboring pairs, Adler organized the six primary arts (in italics) into two cycles of kinship:

a. *Architecture,* monuments and architectural sculpture, *sculpture,* relief*, graphic arts, *painting,* murals and polychrome facades*, architecture. (*Means transition between two and three dimensions).

b. Dance, *mimicry,* drama, epic poetry, *poetry,* lyric poetry, vocal music, *music,* opera, dance.

Further, two horizontal perspectives intersect Adler's circles according to:

7. Theme of construction: body (sculpture, mimicry, drama); soul (architecture, music); world (body and soul; painting, dance, poetry).
8. Mode of expression: concrete-objective-imitative (sculpture, mimicry, painting, poetry); abstract-subjective-concrete (architecture, music).

Külpe divided the arts into three groups by senses (brackets enclose suggested supplements):

I. Optic arts:
   A. Surface arts:
      1. Uncolored or monochrome: Drawing [Graphic Arts, Photography];
      2. Polychrome: Painting, Tapestry [Stained Glass, Mosaic];
      [3. With motion: kinematic arts: Silent Cinema, Lumia, q.v.]
   B. Solid [or three-dimensional] arts:
      1. Semi-solid: Relief and Intaglio;
      2. Completely solid: Sculpture, [Ceramic Arts];
      [3. With motion; Pantomime, Eurhythmics, Fireworks].
   C. Aggregate arts: surface and plastic' effects:
      1. Tectonic Arts;
      2. Architecture, [Monuments, Landscape Design, Interior Decoration, Flower Art].
II. Acoustic arts:
   A. Of tones: Music;
   B. Of words: Poetry, [all Literature, Speech Arts];
   C. Aggregate arts: of tones and words: Song, Melodrama (recitation with music).
III. Optic-acoustic arts [often with costumes and architectural settings]:
   A. Of gestures and tones: Choreographic Art (dance with music), [with words: Talking Cinema];
   B. Of gestures, words, scenery: Drama, [Puppetry],
   C. Of gestures, words, tones, scenery: [Pageants], Opera.

See Leo Adler, *Zeitschrift für Aesthetik,* XVI, 1922, p. 258-61; B. Bosanquet, *A History of Aesthetics,* 1892; Oswald Külpe, Univ. of Toronto, *Psych. Series, II,* 1907, p. 1-21; E. Meumann, *System der Aesthetik,* 1919.
—R.F.P.

Claude Lorraine glass. A small reflecting surface for use principally in landscape sketching, this probably was a common implement of the painter's studio during the 17th and 18th cents. It was not a silvered mirror but a piece of black convex glass in which the weak reflection reduced the large scene to a small area and eliminated much of the fine detail.   —G.L.S.

clausula. See MEDIEVAL MUSIC.

clavichord. See MUSICAL INSTRUMENTS.

clavilux. A light projection instrument with attached playing console invented by Thomas Wilfred, president of the Art Institute of Light, for the performance of silent visual compositions in lumia (q.v.). The instrument consists of a varying number of projection units, arranged before a flat white screen and controlled from a keyboard with sliding keys. Each manual of keys contains three sets for form, motion and color. A special notation system of numbers on vertical staffs permits the exact repetition of a composition. Registers, not unlike those on a pipe organ console, permit the coupling of one or more projection units to any of the manuals.

The projection units have different functions and at least four are needed but any number may be added. The large permanent clavilux installed in the Art Institute of Light recital hall in New York City contains 32 individual units. In general a unit consists of a lamp house, a form section, a motion section, a color section and a final objective lens. The light passes from an incandescent lamp in the lamp house through condensing lenses and cooling cells into the form section. Here the formless white beam is shaped into one or more forms, motion is added in the motion section, color in the color section and the result projected on the screen through the objective lens—all modifications of the initial beam of light being under the control of the player at the keyboard. By the use of two or more units it is possible to create a visual counterpoint of independent form, motion and color sequences. See COLOR; LIGHT.

—T.W.

clay. Now largely the working material of sculptors, this material, varying widely in its composition, has had many uses in the arts. It is the substance of pottery and terra-cotta and, when colored by iron oxide and other minerals, has furnished pigments for painters. Under the name can be put any plastic earth consisting largely of hydrous aluminum silicate. Attributes of clay are its smoothness, its fine texture, and its rather unctuous quality when mixed with water. See CERAMICS I.

—G.L.S.

Clazomene ware. See Ionian vases.

clean. Used in literary criticism to indicate that a work contains only the features that are necessary to it for the performance of its artistic functions, with no additional parts or material that are added on gratuitously as simple decoration. —I.J.

cleaning of paintings. See RESTORATION OF PAINTINGS.

clear-cutting. See CIVIC PLANNING.

clef (L. *clavis*). A musical symbol that determines the pitch and note. At the present time three clefs are in use the G, or treble, the F, or bass, and the C clef. The earliest of these, the C clef, first came into use as marking the single line first placed in relation to the *neumes* (q.v.) as an indication of relative pitch. The F clef came into use shortly afterwards and the G clef had to wait until the 15th-16th cents. before it became part of the staff. The C line of the early staff was generally yellow or green while the F and G lines were red. This early G clef (gamma)

now obsolete, was below middle C, for G was the lowest note of the musical system in vogue at the time. Hence the term "gamut" for g was called **ut** (gamma ut).

The C and F clefs commonly were used in Gregorian Chant, the F clef being used in connection with the Second Mode and sometimes the Fourth Mode. The fact that the half-tone was directly below these clefs was a distinct aid to the singer. These clefs were movable and were placed on various lines of the staff which lessened or obviated the use of leger lines. Gradually, the clefs took fixed positions for specific voices and instruments. The C clef on the first line (lowest) was used for the soprano voice or "fiddle"; placed on the third line from the bottom it was known as the alto clef or viola clef; in turn the fourth line C clef became the tenor clef or cello clef.

The present day clefs bear little resemblance to their original forms and the intermediate steps in their evolution show interesting features. The C clef for instance was turned around to prevent a conflict with a similar symbol, a time signature. The thickening of the top and bottom and a lightening of the side stroke approaches the present day symbol. The present G clef or treble clef (on the second line) was not introduced until the 15th-16th cent. In this instance the association of G with "sol" gave rise to Gs as the symbol. This may be seen in Playford's "Dancing Master". The F clef (on the fourth line) commonly known today as bass clef went through a more drastic series, the original showing little resemblance to the original. An intermediate period shows some resemblance to the C clef.

Sometimes in the course of a composition the clefs may be changed or placed on another line. The latter is often the case in some of the melismatic Gregorian Chant Graduals. In modern compositions the alto clef used by the viola changes to the treble clef to avoid leger lines; the F clef used for the cello part may change to the tenor clef for the same reason. In regards to the tenor voice of a vocal composition present practice uses the notes as written in treble clef to sound an octave lower. Some publishers use a C clef on the third space to denote the tenor voice. —J.V.H.

clerestory, clearstory. That part of a church roof which rises clear of the roofs over the aisle and ambulatory and which is pierced with windows to illuminate the interior.

cliché. A stereotype plate or similar reproduction.

cliff dwellings. In the American Southwest: A term applied to designate the houses in the cliffs of the arid region, the former occupants of which belonged, at least in the main, to the group of tribes now known as the Pueblos. Two general classes of cliff-dwellings are recognized, (1) the cliffhouse proper, constructed of masonry, and (2) the cavate house, excavated in the cliffs.   —J.M.M.

climacus. See Mass.

climax. *Mus.* Approach to a point of emphasis, sometimes the point itself. A phrase accent being a point of emphasis, each phrase contains a climax, if one of very small dimensions. Complex climaxes are the result of carefully planning the relations of consecutive phrase accents. The climax plan of a composition is an important factor in regard to the articulation of the form.   —E.K.

clipeus (L. *clipeus*). Large, round shield of the Greeks and Romans; specifically, the round bronze shield of the Roman soldiers distinguished from their oval hide-covered wooden shield.   —L.T.S.

clivis. See neumes.

cloison. A term used in connection with cloisonné enamel (q.v.). It designates an interstice formed by the minute strips of gold which are attached to the metal background of an enamel work. These cloisons are then filled with liquid enamel paint, before the plaque is put in the fire.   —L.L.

cloissoné enamel. A particular technique in enamel work. It consisted in applying the design by attaching minute fences of gold to the metal plaque which formed the background and was generally of gold. The interstices or cloisons (q.v.) were then filled with vitreous pastes of various colors. This technique is the one used in enamels of Byzantine origin and differs from the so-called champlevé enamel (q.v.). See ENAMELLING ON METAL.   —L.L.

cloister. See monastic architecture.

closed vista. See CIVIC PLANNING.

cloth (1) *Book.* All woven cover materials including vellum, buckram, and linen, etc. This modern form of cloth binding was introduced early in the 19th cent., but cloth bindings have been in use for centuries. (2) *Theatre.* The painted cloth drops in a theatre. (3) See TAPESTRY.

clothes. See COSTUME ART; DRESS, EUROPEAN.

cloth of gold (Fr. *drap d'or*). Plain weave of gold thread. It is usually a silk or linen thread entwined with narrow strips of animal membrane which has been coated with gold leaf. The Romans used cloth of gold (Pliny). It was imported to Europe by Crusaders.   —G.W.R.

cloth of Tarsus. "Cloth of Tars couched with perles". *Chaucer.* Tarsus in south eastern Asia Minor specialized in this fabric. It was a fine silk usually dyed purple.   —G.W.R.

cloud band. A ribbonlike motive of conventionalized cloud forms.

clouds and mist landscapes. See CHINESE ARTS.

clover-leaf. See CIVIC PLANNING.

Cluniac architecture. Understood as the Romanesque churches and conventual structures of an international system of priories and monasteries ruled from the reforming mother house at Cluny (Saône-et Loire, France), founded in 910 and suppressed in 1790. The sober earlier works and the monastery plans have a considerable uniformity. Great advances in building technique, scale, and sculptured decoration were made by the French Cluniacs in the 11th cent. without producing a stereotyped inter-regional style. The third church at Cluny (1088-1130 and later) was the largest, boldest, and most highly evolved Romanesque building, but it failed to be an influential building because Gothic architecture was invented before it was finished. See Oursel, C., *L'Art roman de Bourgogne,* 1982; Evans, J., *Romanesque Architecture of the Order of Cluny,* 1938.   —K.J.C.

coat-of-arms. See HERALDRY.

cobalt pigments. Among the important additions to the artist's palette in the early years of the 19th cent. was cobalt blue, discovered by Thénard in 1802. It is a combination of the metals, cobalt and aluminum, is moderately fine in grain, bright in color, and very stable. Earlier blues were derived from cobalt, notably that which appeared in ceramic glazes, and a pigment of the late Renaissance known as smalt. These, however, did not carry the same name. A green made also from the mineral, cobalt, combined in this case with zinc, is as stable as the blue, but has less strength as a color. Cobalt violet is an anhydrous cobalt phosphate or arsenate, or may be a mixture of the two. Its hue is reddish violet, it is weak in tinting strength, and rather transparent. Like the other cobalt pigments, it is stable and unaffected by most chemical reagents. Cobalt yellow, often called aureolin, is a chemical compound of cobalt with potassium. It has fairly good strength as a color and moderate hiding power. In date it is somewhat later than the other cobalt pigments, for it appeared on the market in 1861. —G.L.S.

cobblestone. A rounded water-worn stone, as for paving.

cochineal. One of the many pigments made from dyes, this, called also *carmine lake* and *crimson lake,* is made from the dried bodies of an insect which lives on cactus plants in Mexico and Central and South America. The dye is extracted and precipitated to form a pigment. On different bases it produces tints from scarlet to purple. It is not stable to light, though its fugitive character is less evident when it is used with an oil medium. —G.L.S.

coda (It. tail). An additional termination to a musical composition, ranging from a few chords to an elaborate part.

codex. *Book.* A MS. volume. In the olden times, waxed tables fastened together. Pl., *codices.*

coelanaglyphic. *Sculp.* Indicating hollow relief.

coffer. A sunk panel in a vault, dome, or ceiling. See FURNITURE.

coherence. As a critical standard, this indicates a high degree of integration between the various aspects and elements of a work. A coherent work is one in which all of the parts reflect meaning upon one another, and in which there is, consequently, an easy transition across the work through all its dimensions. —I.J.

coign. See quoin.

coil method. See terra cotta sculpture, direct method.

coin. See quoin.

colascione. See MUSICAL INSTRUMENTS.

colcothar. See Indian red.

collage (Fr. *collage,* a pasting, something pasted). A term now generally accepted as the designation of certain pictures or other visual arrangements, sometimes Dadaist, but usually Surrealist. These are made, in part or entirely, of pasted pieces of paper, newspaper, wallpaper, chromos, illustrations, photographs, and other textured or figured material, which are assembled in a manner totally incongruous with ordinary phenomenal experience.

Sometimes arrangements are made of fragments of such materials, plus somehow related, drawn, painted, or three-dimensional passages; sometimes painted or drawn passages are added to, or incorporated into photographs, illustrations, and the like; sometimes whole cut-out images are inserted into the midst of already existing pictorial compositions; sometimes (according to Aragon) "the photography, pure and simple, of an arrangement of objects made incomprehensible by photography". A further variety is the **titre poème** (lit. **title-poem**) or cut-out poem, in which patches of writing or lettering are pasted into image-arrangements such as those described above.

It is held that the forcefulness of collage as a mode of expression derives from the novel, often bizarre and altogether unexpected, juxtapositions of the previously unrelated images, fragments of images, and stuffs, and through the psychological impact of the associations and fantasies which they evoke. (". . . we would come by chance, or as it seemed by chance, on [for example] the pages of a catalogue containing plates for anatomical or physical demonstration and found that these provided contiguously figurative elements so mutually distant that the very absurdity of their collection produced in us a hallucinating succession of contradictory images, superimposed one upon another with the persistence and rapidity proper to amorous recollections. These images themselves brought forth a new plane in order to meet in a new unknown [the plane of non-suitability]." M. Ernst).

By the Surrealists, who began making them ca. 1920, collages are considered (1) as a means of release of the fantasies of the subconscious, without dulling or inhibiting the process through the technical and mechanical restraints necessarily imposed by the more traditional methods of painting and sculpture; (2) as transforming the commonplace, the insignificant, and even the contemptible, without altering their appearance, through juxtaposition with other images and materials, a process somewhat akin to metaphor; (3) as eradicating personal taste, style, and technical virtuosity, which were considered to be self-advertising, thus inevitably diluting the stimulation-potentialities of the image by obtrusive indications of facture and the personality of the maker; (4) as providing a means of objectifying their fantasies and visions to persons untrained in the traditional artistic skills; (5) as another repudiation of the traditional artistic aims and conventions, which were considered to be moribund.

Collage is differentiated from **papier collé** (pasted paper) in that the latter employs various materials and stuffs primarily for their plastic or formal values as texture or pattern, whereas the materials of collage are used primarily for their representative, indicative, and associative values. Papiers collés employ snippets of newspaper, stamps, marbleized papers, street-car tickets, sand, feathers, wire, and the like. As a form of sophisticated artistic expression, papiers collés appear around 1910-1911, in the cubist works of Picasso and Braque. This development was due, in part, to formal preoccupations, the need for pictorial elements meaningless but recognizable, and impatience with conventional artistic materials.

During World War I and later, the Dadaists employed the various cut-out and pasting techniques as the vehicles of their cynicism and mockery of contemporary pretensions, in society generally, and in art; there was no deliberate attempt to prod the subconscious of the observer. Positively, Dadaist activities in the pasting techniques must be seen as another useful extension of the resources for artistic expression, whatever other values they may be found to have.

The terms collage and **montage** are sometimes used interchangeably. Montage, however, is used more often in connection with (1) arrangements made entirely of sections of photographs fitted together (the term **photomontage** is sometimes used), and (2) in connection with the techniques of the motion picture (q.v.). Whereas the ensembles of papier collé are devoid of narrational intent, and those of collage are generally of devious symbolism and suggestiveness, those of mon-

tage are commonly of the nature of fairly direct pictographic expression.

The various techniques described have had great influence in various fields of artistic work: advertising art, illustration, packaging, store-window display, photography, typography, stage decoration, and many others have been profoundly affected. See L. Aragon, *La Peinture Au Défi*, 1930; M. Ernst, "Au-Dela De La Peinture", *Cahiers D'Art*, no. 6-7, 1936; G. Hugnet, "Dada and Surrealism", *Bulletin of the Museum of Modern Art*, vol. 4, no. 2-3, 1936.   —M.S.F.

coll'arco. See pizzicato.

collate. *Book.* To collate is to compare. In ordinary binding it is sufficient to check the book by the signatures or pages; when there are insertions such as maps these must be collated with the instructions. In old books of value it is necessary to do more than this, to ascertain not only that the whole of the book is present, but that all that is present belongs to the book. See edition bindings.
                                                    —H.E.S.

collecting paintings. See FORGERIES IN PAINTINGS.

collector's mark. A stamp marked or impressed on the margin of a print by the owner. The mark of a well-known connoisseur denotes that the print has, in his judgment, excellent qualities.   —R.L.W.

colofonia. See colophony.

Cologne, school of. Although Cologne has been a famous center of art since the beginning of the Middle Ages we understand by the name "School of Cologne", the schools of painting of the 14th, 15th, and 16th cents. Shortly before the middle of the 14th cent. the paintings in the choir of the cathedral were created. In 1370 a series of frescoes was commissioned for the Great Hall of the Rathaus. Some fragments of frescoes, originally in the Hansasaal of the Rathaus, now in the Wallraf-Richartz Museum, are considered to have belonged to this work. Judging from these fragments, the work is among the most important paintings of the 14th cent. Another highly significant work of the late 14th cent. is an altarpiece commissioned by the nuns of St. Clara now standing behind the High-Altar of the Cathedral. Some of these paintings bear the marks of a really original and important master. Toward the end of the 14th cent. were created such famous works as the *Madonna mit der Wickentblüte* and *Christ on the Cross, before the Madonna and eight Saints,* both in the Cologne Museum, *St. Veronica holding the Sudarium* in the Munich Pinacothek. Some historians tried to credit all these paintings to a personality, called "Master Wilhelm". In the Limburg Chronical of 1380 an artist by this name is mentioned "as the best painter in the German lands". There have been several masters called Wilhelm in the 14th cent. One of them "Wilhelm von Horle" settled at Cologne in 1358, and died before 1378. But the entire question of the authorship of these frescoes in the Rathaus and the St. Clara altarpiece is not yet and may never be settled. In any case the paintings of the Hansasaal, the St. Claren altarpiece and those around the Madonna with the vetch blossom belong to very different artists. The latter works and a number of paintings more or less closely allied to them are ascribed to Master Hermann Wynrich von Wesel, born before 1360. Probably a pupil of Wilhelm von Horle, he attained to great wealth and distinction, and died in 1414. The character of these paintings is indicated by softness, loveliness, enamellike lucidity of color and a lyrical manner of narration. This line of works is concluded with the Little Garden of Paradise, now in Frankfurt, painted in the early 15th cent.

It is remarkable that Cologne was not in sympathy with the revolutionary movement of paintings in the manner of Multscher and Konrad Witz. Stephan Lochner, the main painter of the 15th cent., although conversant with the progressive development of his time, brought about a kind of counter movement to the naturalism of the 15th cent. Lochner himself came from the region of Lake Constance in 1430 to Cologne and died there in 1451. His main work is the *Altar of the Magi,* painted for the chapel of the magistrates, which now stands in the Cathedral. Dürer, on his voyage to the Netherlands, saw this work and was filled with admiration. Another important work of Lochner is the altar piece representing the last judgment, painted for the St. Laurentius Church. The individual pictures are now in the Museum of Cologne, Frankfort and Munich. Other well-known paintings are the *Madonna of the Rose Arbor* in the Wallraf-Richarts Museum, the *Presentation of Christ in the Temple* in the Hessisches Landes-Museum at Darmstadt, and the *Madonna with the Violet* in the Dom Museum at Cologne. The most important follower of Lochner was the "Master of the Life

of Mary". He was closely related to the painters of the Netherlands, especially Dirck Bouts. He was the leading master during the second half of the 15th cent. He takes his name from a series of panels, representing the life of Mary, seven of which are in the Munich Gallery, and the eighth in the London National Gallery. A pupil of his was the "Master of the Lyversberg Passion". This name is derived from eight panels representing the passion of Christ formerly in the possession of the magistrate Lyversberg, and now in the Museum of Cologne. Another Master, belonging to the second half of the 15th cent. is the "Master of the Legend of St. George" ca. 1450-65, whose name is taken from the history of St. George, painted by him. There is also the "Master of the Glorification of Mary" (Meister der Verherrlichung Mariae). He is influenced by Lochner and painters of the Netherlands. His name is derived from the "Madonna in Glory" in the Museum at Cologne. Influenced by the Master of the Life of Mary and the Master of the Glorification is the "Master of the Holy Kinship" (Meister der heiligen Sippe) who worked from about 1480 till after 1510. His name is derived from the painting of the Holy Kinship with Saints and Donors in the Cologne Museum. Excelling by his mastery of technique was the "Master of St. Bartholomew". He drew this name from the representation of St. Bartholomeus and other Saints in the Pinakothek at Munich. He is also called the "Master of the St. Thomas Altarpiece", a triptych representing the incredulity of St. Thomas (1499-1501) at the Cologne Museum. The "Master of St. Severin" lived at about the same time. His name is derived from paintings in St. Severin at Cologne. Other paintings by him are: the *St. Andrew Triptych* for the confraternity of the Rosary, the *Adoration of the Magi* (ca. 1513), and *Christ before Pilate* in the Cologne Museum. He further designed the paintings for the stained glass windows of the north side of the Cathedral (before 1508). The "Master of the Legend of St. Ursula", who painted series of eighteen pictures representing the Legend of St. Ursula for the church of St. Severin, is to be distinguished from the Master of St. Severin although closely related to him in style. Bartholomeus Bruyn and his students brought the School of Cologne to an end. He was born in 1493 at Wesel and died in 1555 at Cologne. He worked for the chapter at Essen and was commissioned to paint the high altarpiece of the collegiate church St. Victor at Xanten in 1529. But he is best known for his many portraits. He brought about the transition of the School of Cologne to the Italian manner of Renaissance painting. See J. J. Merls, *Köln. Künstler*, 2 Aufl. Herausgegeben von Ed. Firmenich - Richartz, 1895; Firmenich-Richartz, *Bartholomaeus Bruyn und seine Schule*, 1891; K. Aldenhoven, *Geschichte der Kölner Malerschule*, 1902; Mela Escherich; *Die Schule von Köln*, 1907; Hubert Schradt, *Stephan Lochner*, 1923; Heribert Reiners, *Die Kölner Malerschule*, 1925; Otto H. Foerster, *Stephan Lochner*, 1938. —A.J.S.

Colonial brass. See ENAMELLING ON METAL.

colonnade. A range of columns.

colonnette. A tiny, small column.

colophane. See colophony.

colophonium. See colophony.

colophony. Known commonly as rosin, colophony has little use as a resin ingredient in painters' varnishes. It forms a brittle film, easily discolored by exposure or by dampness, and easily scarred by friction. Mixed with oils, its mechanical qualities are improved. It is now most used as an ingredient in wax-resin mixtures for impregnating wood and for the relining of old paintings on canvas. —G.L.S.

COLOR is the general name for the nonspatial component of the sensation arising from the activity of the retina of the eye and its associated nerve systems.[1] Color may be further classified as **chromatic** or **achromatic** depending upon whether it does or does not exhibit hue. Hue is that attribute of certain colors which enables them to be classified as reddish, greenish, bluish, yellowish or purplish.

THE PHYSICAL BASIS FOR COLOR. The physical basis for color is light. Light has been recognized as a part of the great electromagnetic field, the visible radiations being of such magnitude that they must be measured in fractions of a micron (one thousandth of a millimeter), and falling within the range of approximately 380 to 740 millimicrons. Thus they form only a very small part of the total known electromagnetic emanations which range from the long radio waves through the thermally active infrared rays, through the visible light rays and the shorter

actinically active ultraviolet and x-rays to the radium rays and finally to the shortest cosmic rays.

Chromatic color is seen when the total light rays are selectively separated. The separated bands of light begin at the red rays (wave length approximately 740 millimicrons) and go through orange (600 millimicrons), green (520 millimicrons), blue (460 millimicrons), to violet (380 millimicrons). The names here assigned to the respective **chromatic color bands** are those traditionally used for the **rainbow hues**. In the selective separation of visible light rays into chromatic color bands, a complete separation is practically impossible and thus a pure chromatic color sensation is rare.

The process of breaking up light into chromatic color can be accomplished by one of two major methods, **refraction** and **diffraction**. The resultant series of chromatic color bands is called a **spectrum**. A spectrum obtained by refraction is known as a **prismatic spectrum**, ane one obtained by diffraction is a **diffraction grating spectrum**. The latter is the more pure and constant spectrum. A prism bends light rays according to their respective lengths, the shortest being bent the most. The grating which is composed of minute interstices, operates on the principle of intercepting conflicting circular wave fronts of light by a white screen. **Monochromatic light** will appear wherever the crest of two commensurable rays have crossed and been projected onto the screen. The spectra will appear on either side of a white center with the shortest rays appearing closest to the center.

Another method of breaking light into chromatic color is by the **polarization of light**. This is utilized for the chemical identification of substances which emit characteristic chromatic color bands. Certain substances have been found to possess the power of forcing a light ray, which ordinarily would travel in one direction but would vibrate in many different planes, to vibrate in one plane. This process is known as polarizing light. If such a polarizing substance (e.g., quartz) is placed between two prisms, the rotation of the substance will separate white light into a temporal sequence of monochromatic bands.

It will be important for the colorist to recognize that not all visible radiations and consequently not all color come from the sun. There are **incandescent rays** from hot bodies such as the sun or incandescent filaments and there are **luminescent rays** from cold bodies such as fire-flies or fluorescent tubes. Luminescent bodies are more efficient sources of light than are incandescent bodies. One type of luminescence is **photolumines-cence** which is light due to the secondary action of short wave radiations acting upon fluorescent or phosphorescent materials. Until recently most practical artificial light sources were incandescent bodies. But in the future we can expect practical development in lumin-escent and particularly in fluorescent lighting. For various reasons, the chief of which relate to the distribution of spectral colors in the illuminants, luminescent lighting will greatly affect color work. It will be necessary to study as soon as possible how colors of in-candescent and of luminescent light sources can be correlated.

An art of mobile colored light has been brought to a high degree of perfection by Thomas Wilfred who has invented the clavi-lux (q.v.) or color organ. Colored lights correlated with spatial patterns can be thrown upon the screen with this instrument.

THE CHEMICAL BASIS FOR COLOR. When light is diffused through space some of it reaches our eyes and causes the visual sensation. Most of it, however, is absorbed by opaque bodies and thus loses interest for the colorist. Some substances are not entirely absorptive towards color but are either selec-tively or entirely reflective or transmissive towards it. Such a substance is known as a **colorant,** the chief of which are the pigments and dyes. Pigments are colorants that are insoluble in water whereas dyes are soluble. When mixed with a carrier the colorants be-come the paints, lacquers, varnishes, dyes and inks of commerce. The process of producing chromatic color in colorants is known as selective reflection for opaque colorants, selec-tive transmission for transparent colorants or selective absorption as it would apply to both.

Chromatic color as seen by reflection or transmission has been altered qualitatively. The attribute of color especially affected is its saturation. Saturation is the second of the psychical or sensation attributes of chromatic color to be herein defined. Hue was the first. **Saturation** is that attribute of chromatic color which determines its degree of difference from an achromatic color of the same bright-ness. **Brightness,** the third and last psychical attribute, is that characteristic of any color which permits it to be classified as equivalent to some member of a series of achromatic colors.[1] With respect to the saturation of a color we find that transmitted and reflected colors are not usually as saturated as colors emitted directly from a light source. This is because they are not so spectrally pure.

The inherent chemical structure of a colorant is what affects its ability to reflect or trans-mit chromatic color. But other physical fac-tors will affect its appearance. It will appear more saturated when its placement makes multiple reflection possible. Likewise different hue and saturation effects (**dichroism**) may be caused by the same dye at relative depths of solution. The **refractive index** of the color-ant in relation to the refractive index of its carrier affects its appearance. The greater the difference in the indices of refraction the greater amount of light is reflected. But as any carrier is more dense than the air through which the light has been traveling, a coating of oil or varnish over a pigment will cause it to reflect less light although the light may be more spectrally pure. Pigments are classi-fied as relatively transparent or opaque de-pending upon whether the indices of refrac-tion of pigment and carrier are respectively similar or divergent. In the use of trans-parent paints the color of the under surface (**undertone**) and the depth of the color sur-face (**overtone**) are of importance. This is not true in using opaque paints.

Today the chemistry of the colorants is a very important and interesting branch of commercial chemistry. Until the 19th cent. most colorants were derived from nature. For instance an animal pigment was taken from the cochineal insect, a vegetable pigment from the indigo plant, a mineral or earth pigment from umber. The range was limited and few new colorants were added through the centuries. In 1856 Perkin in England pro-duced the first organic dye and since then color chemistry has progressed rapidly. Every colorist should be enough of a technologist to understand the limitations and possibilities of his media and so a basic knowledge of the theory underlying color chemistry is im-portant. The Research Laboratories of the International Printing Ink Corporation have published an excellent monograph on this subject.[2]

The real reason for the selectivity of a colorant to light is a matter of scientific con-jecture. Colorants may owe this selectivity to one or more of their components (e.g., chromium whose compounds are always chro-matically colored) or to their molecular struc-ture (e.g., alizarine, $C_{14}H_8O_4$). Most of the latter class of colorants are complicated or-ganic compounds and their molecules are built around carbon in ring formations. **Chromophore** or color-bearing groups usually containing nitrogen, oxygen, hydrogen or sulphur are linked to these carbon rings and the whole is rendered stable by hydroxyl groups known as **auxochromes** or **color-fixers.** The process of establishing new colorants and duplicating old ones requires infinite research and laboratory exactness.

From the craftsman's point of view colorants are quite naturally thought of in pairs which are known as complementary. **Complementary colorants** are two which when combined in the right proportion will produce an achromatic color. Such complementation is due to the very simple fact that if colorant A subtracts all but a limited band of chromatic rays and if colorant B subtracts that limited band, then the result is the absence of chromatic color due to a uniform absorption throughout the spectrum. This same principle operates when any two or more colorants are mixed. The resulting color will be that of the rays to which none of the colorants are absorptive. This process has been termed **subtractive color mixture** because each colorant subtracts from the total reflected or transmitted rays. The end product of subtractive color mixture would theoretically be black. The mixture of colored lights is known as **additive color mixing** because each chromatic light adds to the total light rays and the end product is white light. **Complementary lights** are two which when combined in the right proportion will produce a white light.

When the number of available natural colorants was limited, their interactions could be easily and pragmatically learned. Venetian red and emerald green, for instance, were well recognized pigment complements. Complementation then could be neatly diagramed. Today with the infinitely greater range of colorants it is not so easy to predict colorant complementation or the results of colorant mixing. It is possible that chemical combinations may occur and that the new product may not have the selectivity represented by the subtracted selectivity of its components. It is likewise possible that a colorant may exhibit a hue which does not belong to the spectral rays which it reflects. For instance an aqueous solution of neodymium ammonium nitrate looks yellow but transmits only red and green rays. These combine by additive mixture to form a yellow sensation which Luckiesh[3] rightly calls a subjective yellow. Or it is likewise possible that two colorants may have the same hue and have different spectral distribution curves (q.v. color interrelations). The difficulty which colorists are now experiencing in predicting the results of colorant mixtures has its rosy side which we will discuss under color interrelations.

Complementation of chromatic light and colorants has application in **color photography.** Emulsions which correspond to the yellow, red purple (magenta) and blue green pigments are superimposed in order upon a sensitized film which controls purple blue, green and red light respectively. In effect the picture is taken in three lights which are complementary to the emulsions and the image appears in the same colors as the emulsions. By further example of complementation when projected by a white light onto the screen it appears in its original colors.

THE PHYSIOLOGICAL BASIS FOR COLOR. The human eye has two distinct functions, transmitting the sensation of light and transmitting the sensation of form. The transmission of light is allied with the transmission of chromatic color. All visual sensation is dependent upon the functioning of the light transmitting mechanism. But light may be transmitted without the transmission of chromatic color or the transmission of form. These several sensations require specialized mechanisms in the eye. Thus it is not idle talk to separate form and color, or to separate chromatic from achromatic color. Many animals have eyes which limit their visual sensations to one or another of these.

This article is not concerned with the reactive media of the eye insofar as they effect point to point vision. It is discussing the **photoreceptors of the eye.** These are minute cells, some shaped like nine-pins and called **cones,** and some shaped like elongated cones and called **rods,** which are found in the second layer of the innermost coating of the eyeball, the retina. The retina, with its backing of pigmented epithelium is really an expansion of the fibers of the optic nerve and it lines all but the extreme front of the posterior chamber of the eye. The 30,000,000 rods, and the 7,000,000 cones are not uniformly distributed over the retina. Near the posterior end of the axis of the eyeball is the region called the **fovea centralis** where direct vision is centered. This contains only cones. Near the periphery of the retina there are only rods and the proportion of each type of cell varies in ratio to its proximity to each area. Each cone is connected to a single nerve fiber whereas several rods may share one nerve fiber, all of which send their impulses via the optic nerve to the brain.

Electromagnetic waves reach the eye but those below 380 and above 740 millimicrons are absorbed by the media of the eye through which they must pass before reaching the retina. A small proportion of light rays are likewise absorbed by these media, which consist of the **cornea** (a frontal continuation of the outer sclerotic coating), the **iris** (a frontal continuation of the second or vascular coating) and the lens and humors of the eye. The absorbed infrared and ultraviolet rays may in cases of extreme intensity prove very injurious to the several parts of the eye.[4]

The difference in the distribution of the rods and cones on the retina indicates a difference in function between the two. It is believed, on the evidence of their greater receptivity to images seen in dim light, that the rods (containing a reddish substance, the **visual purple,** which bleaches on exposure to light) are only capable of transmitting sensations of achromatic color and of functioning at a low illumination. The cones are believed to transmit chromatic color sensations and to function for distinct vision. The fact that chromatic color sensing is unequally distributed over the retina and that its distribution bears some relation to the distribution of the cones, has aided this theory. By means of an apparatus called a **perimeter** it is possible to determine the zones or distances from the eye at which various color sensations are perceived. The extremities of the visual field are sensitive only to the achromatic sensations; except for these margins the entire field is susceptible to blue and yellow and only the *fovea centralis* to red and green. This selective sensitivity of the visual field is likewise linked conjecturally with **color blindness,** of which the most common form is the so-called **red-green color blindness.** In this form both red and green appear a yellowish grey to the observer. Red-green color blindness occurs much more frequently in males and is testimony to the fact that in genetics color vision is a sex linked characteristic. The second type of color blindness, known as **monochromatic blindness,** in which there is complete absence of monochromatic color sensation generally occurs when there is complete destruction of the *fovea centralis* and so it is probably an accompaniment of loss of cone function.

Theories of color vision are in a conjectural state. The **Young-Helmholtz**[5] (Thomas Young, 1773-1829; Hermann von Helmholtz, 1821-1894, physicist) theory is perhaps best known. It assumes that different cones have nerve fibers giving rise to qualitatively different sensations based on the physical primacy of red, green and blue. (Primary chromatic colors whether in lights or colorants are those from which all other colors can supposedly be made.) There is no anatomical evidence that these sets of nerves are present or that nerve fibers can transmit qualitatively different impulses. The theory correlates with the facts of additive light mixtures and it agrees with the data expressed in the **Koenig sensation curves** where the various light rays were charted according to the sensations which they stimulated and where the sensations fell into three distinct groups, red, green and blue.

The **Hering**[6] (Ewald Hering, 1834-1918, physiologist) theory of color vision assumes six fundamental coupled sensations, black and white, blue and yellow, green and red. There is imagined in the retina three distinct substances each capable of anabolic or katabolic reactions under the influence of radiant energy. The anabolism of each of these substances creates the first of each of these paired sensations, the katabolism the second. This theory accords well with the fact of zoned retinal sensitivity and with the fact that black and white are distinct sensations.

The **Ladd-Franklin**[7] (Christine Ladd-Franklin, 1847-1930, psychologist) theory supposes that a photochemical substance exists in the rods. Upon dissociation it causes the grey sensation. In the cones the grey molecules undergo two stages of further dissociation. The grey molecules contain two groupings. The dissociation of one of these causes a yellow sensation, of the other a blue. In the second stage of dissociation the yellow grouping is divided into two new groupings, the dissociation of one giving rise to the red sensation and of the other the green. It is thought that the degree of dissociation is due to the wave length of light impinging upon the photochemical substance.

There are other theories of color vision, notably the so-called **Duplicity theory** which is associated with the name Von Kries (Johannes von Kries, 1853-1928, physiologist). It attempts to separate chromatic from achromatic color vision on the anatomical evidence of the rods and cones.

In completing the discussion of the physiological basis for color vision we must consider the eye as a refractive instrument containing a lens and other refractive media whereby point by point vision is made possible.

For this purpose the chief fault of the eye for chromatic vision is its lack of achromatism. All the rays of a continuous spectrum cannot be focused on the retina at the same time. If the long rays are focused on the retina the short rays will be focused in front of the retina and vice versa. The mixture of the two rays not distinctly focused will cause the image to have a violet fringe known as the **dispersion circle**. The achromatic lens is made by combining a convergent lens made of crown glass (more convergent for blue) with a divergent lens of flint glass (more divergent for blue).

THE PSYCHOLOGICAL BASIS FOR COLOR. The psychological aspects of color can be discussed under two headings. The first is concerned with receiving chromatic color sensations which have not emanated from corresponding spectral rays. One of these subjective sensations has already been discussed in the discussion of additive mixtures. Another example of subjective color sensation is when the chromatic color can be perceived when gentle pressure is applied to the closed lid over the eyeball or when a controlled current of electricity travels from the forehead to the hand of a patient who is seated in a dark room. The reason for this phenomenon lies in the excitation of the retinal nerves by pressure or by electricity. **Subjective color** can likewise be obtained by rotating achromatic discs (Benham's discs). This is due to an abnormal state produced on the retina by the alternate exposure to light and darkness.

After-images and **contrasts** are the principal ways of seeing subjective color. After-images refer to the experience of a color sensation after a color stimulus has been withdrawn. After-images are of two sorts, positive and negative. The former are the same color as the stimulus and are seen when the eyes are closed after looking for some time at an intense stimulus. The latter are complementary to the color of the stimulus and are usually seen when the eyes are directed toward a neutral tone after looking for some time at an intense stimulus. The reason advanced for positive after-images is the persistence of the chemical process in the retina after the stimulus has been withdrawn. The process of retinal fatigue is usually given as the reason for negative after-images.

Contrasts are closely allied to negative after-images. The only difference lies in the fact that negative after-images are projected upon an achromatic surface whereas contrasts are projected upon other chromatic surfaces thereby altering them in kind, e.g., in hue, brightness or saturation. Contrasts are subjective color phenomena whereby color sensations are being changed not by direct alteration but by controlling the color which lies adjacent. M. Chevreul,[8] one of the most famous and earliest of the theorists on color combinations, studied the subject of color contrast thoroughly and although his deductions were not proven by experiments of modern scientific exactness, nevertheless his perceptions were keen, his methodology was objective and his general laws of contrast stand the test of time. The fundamental **law of contrast** states that whenever the eye sees two contiguous colors at the same time they will appear as dissimilar as possible. In hue contrast adjacent hues (similar wave lengths) are pushed apart in hue and weakened in saturation, whereas dissimilar hues are pushed apart and strengthened and complementary hues are unaltered in hue but strengthened in saturation. Rood[9] illustrates this diagramatically. The reason for this is that each color is affected as though the after-image of the contiguous color were projected upon it. By contrast strong saturation seems stronger and weak saturation weaker in contiguity. Brightness contrast leads to the phenomenon called **induction** whereby in a graded series of grey papers the edge of a lighter strip that is adjacent to a darker one will appear lighter than the other edge of the lighter grey strip.

For the best demonstration of contrast two colors should be alike in the two attributes which are not expected to exhibit contrast. Likewise the spacing of colors is an important factor in color contrast. Hues which possess similar wave lengths operate according to the law of contrast if they are spatially isolated (e.g., spaced relatively far apart). If, however, they are spaced in narrow striped sequence, they strengthen each other because of the additive mixture of their reflected light rays. The same holds true for dissimilar hues which act according to the law of contrast when widely spaced in color areas and which exhibit the opposite effect and appear neutralized when the rays are diffused from a narrow striped sequence.

Another observable fact with relation to subjective color is in a sense the reverse of the phenomena of which we have just been speaking. **Color constancy** is the phenomenon whereby colors when placed in various illuminations seem to preserve their identity and to remain unaltered. This is a subjective color phenomenon in the sense that the color which the mind registers is not the color which the objective photographic plate registers. To date Katz[10] has done the chief experimentation in this field and has worked only with achromatic color. The basic experiment in color constancy is important and is as follows: Forty-eight squares of the achromatic color series were arranged upon a sheet of grey cardboard and were placed in such illumination as one would find at noon in the summer under a slightly clouded sky. This type of illumination is known for experimental purposes as **normal illumination.** The observers characterized each of the colors in a definite way in language, e.g., white, black. The experiment was then repeated at one-fifth the illumination and to the observers there was apparently no change in the colors. Thus by absolute standards of judgment color constancy within the limits of a one to five ratio in change of illumination seemed to be a fact.

When the comparative method was used, when two identical series of achromatic papers were viewed simultaneously at different levels of illumination, the illumination appeared to alter the color slightly although not in a comparative ratio. When the observer matched a "greatest whiteness" paper five metres away with one of a similar series of achromatic papers held in his hand, it was found that by photometric measurement the paper selected was reflecting approximately twenty times as much light as the more distant paper. The two papers were judged equally white but a difference was noticed between the two papers and Katz calls this difference one of **pronouncedness.** This Katz calls the fourth dimension, or more correctly, the fourth attribute of color. The colors near white vary as white in exhibiting pronouncedness. In other words the dimmer the illumination the less their pronouncedness. With the greys a region is reached where it is difficult to tell whether the more highly illumined or the less highly illumined show the greater pronouncedness. And for the blacks and the colors near black, the less the illumination the greater the pronouncedness.

These experiments in color constancy have led to two definitions. **Apparent color** is the immediately perceived color as seen at any time in any illumination. **Genuine color** is the color as seen only under the conditions of illumination described as normal. The colors which maintain their qualitative character most stably are the whites and the colors near white. The darker colors become the greater the differences that illumination will make between their apparent and their genuine colors.

Rood is one of the few observers who comments upon changes brought about in chromatic color by differences in illumination. He observes that a bright illumination causes all chromatic colors to appear more yellow and a dark illumination causes them to appear more blue. He explains this on the basis of the Young-Helmholtz theory of color vision. Mr. H. Barret Carpenter,[11] a worthy disciple of Rood, illustrates this law in his illustrations of objects as they show what he has termed "the natural order of colors."

There is yet another effect which changes in illumination bring to a color, known by the name of its discoverer as the **Purkinje effect.** At lowered illuminations the maximum of the luminosity curve has shifted toward the shorter wave lengths. At normal illumination the maximum of the luminosity curve is at about 550 millimicrons (a warm yellow). **Luminance** or the psycho-physical quality of appearing to reflect light, does not correlate directly with brightness but is the result of the product of brightness and hue. The reds and the violets are hues of low luminance. But according to the Purkinje effect if two hues of short and long wave length respectively are produced so as to have equal luminance at normal illumination, then as the illumination drops the hue of short wave length would appear to have more luminance. Thus the maximum of the luminosity curve would shift to the green yellows at lower illumination.

The psychologist has likewise defined the **modes of appearance of color.** In so doing he has left the field of subjective color and is discussing the second large heading, namely **objective color,** color emanating from spectral rays, as the mind perceives it. The most important modes are those of surface colors, film colors and volume colors. **Surface colors** are those which appear to have a surface in which the color lies. **Film colors** lie in a plane which is extended in space and which does not in the same sense possess a surface. A film color always has a frontal parallel character whereas the orientation of a surface color is always that of the surface upon which it lies. Surface and film colors may be further qualified with respect to their appearance of being seen through transparency. **Transparent film colors** are film colors as viewed through a piece of colored gelatin. This is different from the first or space-delimiting film color which is as though it were extended through space in the form of a bi-dimensional plane for which it functions as a rear boundary. **Transparent surface colors** are transparent colors which are obtained through the medium of opaque objects. For instance, if one eye is fixed on a point and a colored opaque cardboard is introduced at about half the distance before the other eye, the fixated object will give the impression of being seen through the color of the opaque object. Thus transparent surface colors present a texture derived from the opaque objects whereas transparent film colors do not present any texture. **Volume colors** fill three dimensional space and, like the color of a fog which is apperceived only as long as objects can be seen through it, they should be transparent. Volume colors can be seen in colored glass and colored transparent liquid.

There are other modes of appearance of colors which are less fundamental than the above. **Mirrored colors** are seen when the surface of an object is smooth and the light reflected from it is of such a nature that we can recognize images by it. When the surface is not in itself colored then the mode of appearance of the color of the image is that which was presented by the original object. Thus we seem to see mirrored objects behind rather than through the mirrored surface. But when the color of the mirroring surface is visible, the reflected object is seen behind that surface but through the color of that surface.

Luster is another color mode which a color assumes when the surface of an object is smooth but the reflected light is of such a nature that we cannot recognize images by it. Luster can take on different appearances such as the luster of silk or of metals. This does no mean that this type of luster is restricted to the kind of material which has given it its name but that it is most commonly seen as associated with this material. Luster has certain characteristics. It appears only on an object; it exceeds the color of the object in brightness; it partially destroys the surface structure of the object and it is apprehended as being distinct from the color of the object and as lying in front of the object. **Glitter, irridescence** and **opalescence** are terms used to refer to the luster of specific kinds of objects which are moved about. The research laboratories of the International Printing Ink Corporation have used the term luster, as though it were synonymous to the effect of bronze as dup-

licated by certain inks and they do not mean luster light. Katz describes various kinds of luster in detail and Birren 12/ illustrates Katz's types with colorants.

Luminosity is a color mode which has been variously described. To Katz and the psychologists it is the mode of appearance which is obtained when film colors are of greater brightness than their surroundings and when there is no definite defined figure. **Glow** is the same mode of appearance when there is definite defined figure. According to the Optical Society definition luminosity is a substitute for the older term, **visibility**, or the luminous efficiency of radiant energy. It is a correlative of light when one wishes to call attention to this particular attribute of light. The psychological and psychophysical definitions both contain the idea that luminosity describes emitted rather than reflected light and is thus the appearance of illumination.

Another field of psychological observation in objective color work is concerned with the effects that colors have upon the observer. It relates objective color to subjective effects. It is apparent, for instance, that certain hues seem to advance and to make objects seem nearer while other hues recede and make objects seem farther away. Likewise the hues of long wave lengths seem warmer than the hues of short wave lengths. The first phenomenon is probably related to the lack of achromatism of the eye and the second is probably due to the association with the colors of fire. Actually the hue exhibited by intense heat is white and blue rather than red. The fact that white reflects light and black absorbs it affects the actual warmth of these tones.

Again the psychologist is concerned with the effect that colors have upon the moods of the observer and he is interested in the color preferences of the observer. Much investigation along this line has been carried out by commercial interests and much valuable material of a pragmatic nature has been discovered. The material which the pure science of psychology has collected has not yet been of sufficient scope to formulate into general laws. Excellent bibliographies of this material are available[13] and the reader is referred to them for added study in this field. In addition to these two legitimate types of sources on this subject much material has been published which smacks of quackery. It is a ripe field for this sort of thing for there is the suggestion of occult powers in anything which is mysterious and is connected with man's emotions.

Humanity is apt to endow the things which it does not understand with many powers. Thus tertiary qualities or human and superhuman qualities have been projected by man into colors. From this it is only one step farther to accept the color as the symbol for this quality. Red, for instance, was the symbol of health, power and anger. Green symbolizes hope, immortality and victory. Then the color symbol became associated with the god who symbolized this quality. White was the symbol of Jupiter. This close association of color with the religions of primitive peoples retarded scientific investigation of its nature until the time of the rationalizing Greeks. The important hypotheses which they set forth lacked experimental proof and were forgotten for many centuries but they held the kernel of the scientific truths about color which have been discovered from the 16th cent. to date. In our day color symbolism has lost much of its meaning but powerful vestigial evidences remain in marriage and mourning colors, ecclesiastical and academic colors and even in sporting colors.

INTERRELATIONS IN COLOR WORK. Much of the difficulty in color work has been caused by the fact that the interrelations between its various aspects were not understood and defined. The fields which must be correlated are: color as radiant energy (the physical field) ; color as sensation (the psychical field) ; and color as the sensation of light (the psycho-physical field). In addition, colorant chemistry is part of the picture.

A word of explanation will show the reason for the fundamental three-fold division. Color is a form of radiant energy. Its rays can be measured in length and in the amount of energy emitted. A quantitative expression for the radiant energy at each wave length can be plotted on a graph in which the abscissus is the wave length and the ordinate is the energy radiated. Such a curve is called an **energy emittance curve, an energy transmission curve or a radiometric curve**. It is the basic data, the physical measurement data on which rest all photometry and all colorimetry.

This radiant energy would be a reality and a potentiality in our universe even if man were not equipped with eyes. But because he has a visual apparatus, a limited band of radiant energy possesses for him the quality of luminance or it becomes luminous energy

(light). Now he wants to know not the absolute amount of energy of the electro-magnetic rays but the amount of energy at each wave length relative to some standard source of luminous energy. He wants to know a physical measurement but he wants to relate it to a light sensation with which he is familiar, which comes within his experience. Thus we have a psycho-physical aspect to color. Such a psycho-physical measurement is found in the spectral distribution curve in which the abscissus is the wave length and the ordinate is relative to the energy of a specified wave length of a known illuminant. As light is likewise seen by transmission and by reflectance we have spectral transmission curves in which the wave length is plotted against the percentage of the incident ray which is transmitted and spectral reflectance curves in which the wave length is plotted against the percentage reflectance with respect to a standard white substance like magnesuim oxide which has a reflectance of approximately 98% throughout the spectrum.

We have already seen that the visual judgment of color depends upon many factors. But after all it is this visual judgment of color which is the final concern of the artist and the colorist for upon it will rest all subjective effects. This is the sensation aspect of color work. In so far as the visual judgment of a colorant is affected by a luminant the result can be determined by multiplying the energy emittance curve of the illuminant by the spectral reflectance curve of the colorant. The result is the energy distribution curve for that colorant under that illuminant.

Mention has been made of primaries and complementaries in lights and pigments. The psychological primaries are called red, yellow, green and blue as well as the achromatic black and white. The reason given for their primalcy is that they are unique sensations and that all other pure color sensations resemble one or another of these. In complementing sensations, yellow is coupled with blue and red with green. They are called complementaries because under proper viewing conditions they are the only sensations which will not alter each other except to give the utmost sensation of brilliance. Luckiesh has described an apparatus for viewing light complementaries. After-images are an index to sensation complementaries. Colorant complementaries can be discovered by colorant mixture and if the results are at present often indeterminate, that very fact is instant of the many new colorants which are continually being developed. Consequently it may soon be possible to produce a diagramatic system of material colored standards where the various kinds of complementaries exhibit the same hues. Theoretically this should be true.

The Optical Society of America under the auspices of the Inter-Society Color Council has been working for some time in an attempt to define and correlate interrelated terms used in color work.[1] Their latest recommendations are as follows: In considering achromatic color, radiant energy in the objective physical field correlates with luminous energy (light) in the psycho-physical field, and with color in the subjective psychical field. Calling these fields A, B and C respectively, radiance emittance in A is described by the radiant energy transmission curve (radiometric curve); luminous emittance in B is described by the spectral distribution curve and achromatic color in C is described by its sensation attribute. The corresponding attributes are radiance in A, luminance in B and brightness in C. For chromatic color we again speak of radiant energy in A, visual energy in B and chromatic as well as achromatic color in C. The attributes are the spectral composition plus the radiance in A, either the tristimulus values (q.v. color determination) or the dominant wave length, colorimetric purity and intensity in terms of reflectance, transmissance or luminance in B, and hue, saturation and brightness or brilliance in C. Relative brightness may be expressed as value or lightness. Chromaticity is a combination of hue and saturation.

In naming the sensation attributes not all colorists are in agreement. The Munsell nomenclature uses chroma for saturation and value for brightness. Prang charts use intensity for saturation. Birren uses tone as synonymous with an unsaturated color. Tone should more properly be reserved for the designation of any color considered with respect to its attributes but indefinite as to the characterization of its attributes. Tint and shade may be defined respectively as any color tone which has more or less brilliance than it would have in its spectral hue.

COLOR IDENTIFICATION. Color identification is dependent upon measurement and systematic specification. It utilizes certain instruments for measuring and translates the measurements into specifications with reference to the fields of color work.

Spectroradiometry is basic to all absolute photometry and colorimetry and all other types of measures can be obtained from the spectroradiometric curve. However spectroradiometry is still a difficult process with the available instruments.[14]

When spectroradiometry is abandoned for comparative measurement, the first essential is a standard set of viewing conditions. These were furnished in 1931 by the International Commission on Illumination and consist of specifications for a standard white light and for characteristics of the eye of the standard observer. There are two types of instruments which give comparative spectral energy distribution data, the spectrophotometers and certain of the visual colorimeters. The **spectrophotometers** are instruments so arranged that the intensity of rays of the same wave length in a known and unknown spectrum can be quantitatively and photometrically compared. The results may be given in terms of the already defined spectral distribution curve (comparative luminance at each wave length) or they may be translated into the simpler psycho-physical specifications known as tristimulus values.

To understand the tristimulus values which was the type of color determination standardized by the I. C. I. in 1931, we must go back to the Young-Helmholtz theory of color vision and assume the existence of the three sets of nerves particularly sensitive to red, green and blue overlapping bands of the spectrum. The I. C. I. then charted and standardized the sensitivity curves of these nerves (q.v. the Koenig sensation curves). These curves are plotted on a diagram where the abscissus is the wave length and the ordinate is the relative sensation produced at that wave length by a primary light source. The I. C. I. spectral sensitivity curves are based on color mixture data and although the presence of these nerves has not been confirmed, the spectral sensitivity curves are adequate as an aid for color mixture determination.

Tristimulus values are the values which indicate the degree to which the red, green and blue nerves are stimulated by a color with respect to the degree (100%) in which they are stimulated by a pure white material. They are strictly sensation values in that they represent a formula which if duplicated should provide the same sensation. They are related to definite physical measurements so they are psycho-physical values. They are obtained by multiplying the energy distribution curve of the standard white light by the spectral reflectance curve of the given material (obtained by the radiometer or spectrophotometer to get the energy distribution curve of that material which in turn must be multiplied by the three primary light sensitivity curves. In tristimulus symbols, X is the value for the red primary. Y is the green primary and the photometric quality and Z is the blue primary. There are other tristimulus systems besides the I. C. I. system and work is in progress to coordinate the various tristimulus systems.[15]

Another system of psycho-physical identification and specification of color is the **monochromatic plus white system**. These specifications may be obtained from the tristimulus specifications or they may be found on a visual colorimeter. This system is based on the matching of the unknown against a monochromatic light whose wave length can be varied throughout the visible spectrum and a source of white light. Every color except purple can be so matched and purple can be specified in terms of its complementary green. The monochromatic method gives a specification in terms of dominant wave length and colorimetric purity. The dominant wave length of a light is the wave length of the monochromatic light which must be added to the white light in order to match the unknown or, in the case of purple, it is the wave length of the monochromatic light which must be added to the unknown in order to match the white light. The ratio of the amount of monochromatic light to the amount of white light represents the **colorimetric purity**. Thus spectral colors have a purity of 100% and achromatic colors 0%. The brightness factor, if used, must be obtained directly from the Y tristimulus value. For instance, if the Y value is 17, then the brightness factor is 17%. This method of designation is often used not because of simplicity of execution but because it provides measurements in terms which are more easily visualized in relation to the sensation attributes of color. The dominant wave length correlates with a diagramatic hue angle and the purity factor correlates with a saturation radius whereas the luminous intensity (brightness) factor can be related to a polar axis. It can be seen that neither the tristimulus values nor the monochromatic plus white values give positive physical color identification. Consequently they might provide two colors with the same specifications which would not have the same physical measurements and so would appear different under different viewing conditions.

There are **visual colorimeters** which by utilizing mixtures of the three primary lights can give measurements yielding the tristimulus values directly. These are still farther removed from relation with the spectral distribution curves and so possess the limitations of purely sensation measurement.

Color temperature meters can measure color positively and visually but are of limited application for the color must fall exactly on the Planckian locus in order to be located by one point. The Planckian locus is the locus or energy radiation curve of an ideal theoretical body which emits more energy at each wave length than any other body at the same temperature.

COLOR SYSTEMS AND BASIC DIAGRAMS. In speaking of color identification mention was made of systems of color identification. In the following paragraphs we are concerned primarily with color systems. A **color system** is one providing a specified match for any color to be specified in terms of lights or of colorants.

Inasmuch as systems involving light specifications cannot easily be illustrated they are expressed in graphs or diagrams. The tristimulus specifications resulted in the **triangular diagram**. Clerk Maxwell was the first to describe such a triangle. He obtained his tristimulus values in an elementary manner by rapidly rotating chromatic discs known as Maxwell discs. On the Maxwell isosceles triangle the primaries are at the angles and a color is plotted by erecting three perpendiculars to the sides which are proportional to the tristimulus coordinates.

The monochromatic plus white specifications lead more naturally to the diagram of the **color solid**. As already mentioned, the dominant wave length specification can be expressed by an angle and the colorimetric purity by a radius. Brightness can be graphically described in either the triangular or the solid diagram by relating the chromaticity plane to an achromatic pole. Brightness in the triangular diagram is usually expressed directly from the green (Y) specification.

Systems of material standards (colorants) are more comprehensible and more usable for the average colorist. Some such systems utilize transparent media as standards. Among these are the **Lovibund glasses** consisting of three sets of primarily colored glasses from which by the subtractive method of mixing any color can be matched, and the Arny solutions whose concentrations are adjusted to produce the color match.

Other systems of material standards utilize pigmented or dyed surfaces. With these there can be no automatic and inherent system of designation unless the standards have been coordinated with the tristimulus or monochromatic plus white specifications. Usually the systematic aspect to the color specification is somewhat arbitrary although related to the method of measuring the standard surfaces.

Some so-called color systems of pigmented or dyed surfaces fail in two basic requirements of a system. Their pigmented surfaces are not carefully standardized and highly permanent and the number of these standard surfaces is not large enough to represent the considerable number of possible surface colors. One color diagram which could scarcely be called the basis for a material standards color system is the six and twelve hue **color circle of Chevreul.** Yet it is important because it is preserved today in the standard papers and colorants published by the Prang Company and by other companies. The names given to the six hues, red, orange, yellow, green, blue and violet are probably the most popularly used color names today. Using Prang colorants, the spacing of the hues on the diagramatic circle provides a quick clue to colorant complementation.

The **color system of Wilhelm Ostwald**[16] (1853-1932, physio-chemist) is of importance. Ostwald's work is based on the Hering color vision theory and his diagram follows the color rhomboid concept of the psychologist, E. B. Titchener. Ostwald arranged twenty-four hues around the equator of his solid so as to place the psychological complementaries opposite each other. He likewise claimed that these were optical (light) complements. His hue circuit exhibits an interesting correlation of these two sets of complementaries. The equator circumference hues possess the greatest spectral reflectance. Above the equator the hues are progressively mixed with white and below with black pigment. Every color is specified and located on the solid by a number (hue) and two letters (percent white and black respectively). By subtraction from 100% the percent pure color is derived. Thus the specification of a hue should not only locate it on the solid but should approximately indicate its pigment composition.

The Ostwald system is of such importance as to have elicited spectrophotometric measurement of its standards by various investigators and to have called forth studies on its correlation with various tristimulus systems.

Ostwald[17] himself originally published one hundred sixty-eight material standards and the English translation[16] of his work has given a more regular set of the same standards.

The **Munsell**[18] **system** (Albert Munsell, 1858-1918, artist) presents the most complete index of material standards to date. Mr. Munsell's original plan for this system was that it should conform to a purely psychological requirement and, at the same time, that the assignment of the notations should be based upon a reproducible system of psycho-physical measurement. There are many who believe that despite the difficulties inherent in perfecting such a system, the Munsell system comes closest to its attainment. It is used as the basis for standardized color work by the National Bureau of Standards and by many commercial enterprises. It is the object of continual critical study and revision by the Optical Society of America in conjunction with the Inter-Society Color Council.[19]

The Munsell system bases its diagram on the idea of an approximate sphere. The hues at maximum spectral reflectance are placed on the surface (or out from the surface) of the solid at their spectral brightness levels. Ten hues (five principal) were chosen (to coordinate with the decimal system) which would at equal saturation and brightness spin to a neutral grey. The placement of the hues is in accordance with optical (light) complementation.

A Munsell color is designated by a hue name (an objective rather than an associational terminology was used, e.g., yellow red rather than orange), a number which closely parallels the square root of its luminous reflectance (value) and a number which is proportional to its colorimetric purity (chroma).

A psychological color diagram (not a system) is the circuit of material standards which Mr. Birren calls the **Rational Color Circle.** It consists of thirteen hues which he claims have uniform psychological sensation steps between each other. The complementation thus bears no relation to light or pigment complementation. His nomenclature, which closely follows Ostwald's, uses associational terms, e.g., ice-blue, leaf-green.

There are several other arbitrary systems of material color standards which should be mentioned because they continue to serve a useful although somewhat limited purpose. Color dictionaries give us popularized color names in terms of material standards. The determination of the Munsell notations for all color samples in the Maerz and Paul Dictionary of Color[20] has been begun by the Inter-Society Color Council. The Textile Color Card Association publishes seasonal cards for its members.[21] It is the accepted authority for color names in the textile and allied industries. The Ridgeway Dictionary[22] was prepared in 1912 for the identification of colors in natural science. Today commercial color interest have coded color terminologies of their own which are usually coordinated basically with the Munsell system.

A method of designating colors which possesses qualities of both a color dictionary and of a color system is the ISCC-NBS method. It is the joint product of the Inter-Society Color Council and the National Bureau of Standards. The designations of about eight hundred colors are non-numerical but are systematic. The boundaries between color group names have been adjusted so as to accord as closely as possible with common usage and have been expressed in terms of the Munsell color system.

COLOR COMBINATIONS AND COLOR FORM. All this preliminary discussion from the artist's point of view would be useless if it gave him no clue to color combining and to color form. One difficulty in arriving at any theory of color combining is due to the many variables, both physical and psychological, which the subject presents. Absolute objective standards in the stimulus, as well as controlled conditions of viewing and objective standards of judgment are difficult to obtain. Conceptual principles, however, can and have been set down which are in the nature of prescriptions to be followed in ord r to gain certain kinds of results. Leonardo da Vinci examined some of these. Chevreul formulated the first systematic attempt to cover the subject of color combining. From his laws of contrast and harmony has stemmed the conception of monochromatic, analogous, complementary and triadic color schemes which are to be found in most modern textbooks.[23] Chevreul suggested the operation of his laws in terms of the three sensation attributes of color whereas many texts limit their discussion to hue. However the conception of balanced colors[24] whereby areas, brightness and saturation are so related that with given hue combinations an optical complementation by disc mixture results, is probably derived from Chevreul's laws and from the facts of the Maxwell disc mixtures. Ostwald based his color harmonies on the Ostwald color rhomboid. Birren's work is based on Ostwald's. The basic conception is

that harmonious colors have some underlying compositional factor which renders them allied. In the Ostwald harmonies this is the pigment factor, such as per cent black or white.

Carpenter has done work which illustrates the use of values (relative brightness) in handling analogous hues. The eye is more accustomed to the spectral order of values but in reversing this order more arresting effects may be produced.

Graves[25] has indicated nine paths through the Munsell solid which he calls color scales. A color scale would be a series of graded colors which would progress systematically by continuous variation with respect to one or two attributes of the component color. Graves, in scale 9, has a series wherein no attribute of the graded series is held constant but the progression is by systematic differences in all three attributes.

Birren uses the term, dimension, to describe the direction in which the eye is attracted along such progressive paths. Notan usually refers to such a progression in a value scale which is introduced for the sake of design, as in Japanese art, rather than for the sake of representational modeling. Chiaroscuro refers to the use of value progressions for representational modeling as was customary in Renaissance painting. In speaking of dimension Birren introduces the idea that to follow along the path of a scale produces a smoother effect than to jump backwards and forwards. Graves likewise mentions the concept of color chords and illustrates a limited number of such. A chord might in a broad sense be thought of as a progression on a color path or scale which has larger color intervals and where these intervals may have other proportions than are found in the repetitive spacing of a scale.

All of these concepts have made important contributions to the study of color harmony and color form. Color harmony is really a psychical phenomenon meaning a group of colors which seem pleasant when viewed together. Science is searching for the psychophysical basis, if any, for this phenomenon. Visual aesthetic form involves the selection and arrangement of the components of the visual arts (color, the appearance of texture, and the spatial component) into an orderly arrangement or composition. Thus it is easily seen that at present the basis for judging form can be more objective than the basis for judging harmony. Design is described by Dr. Thomas Munro[26] as one of the modes of composition in a total form wherein the details are organized so as to emphasize orderly arrangement (repetition, variation and contrast) among component traits. A component trait is a trait of a component with respect to which it can be compared with other traits which are like it in kind; e.g., in Munsell nomenclature the color red is a trait of hue, 8 is a trait of value. **Color form** is the design aspect of color so composed as to mesh with the design aspect of the other visual components in the total aesthetic form. Few colorists have considered the problem of **color design form.** Once again we refer to the conception of balanced colors as making a contribution to this subject because the concept of balanced colors relates colors to areas. Graves has made a contribution in relating his color chords to areas.

Although it is very doubtful and probably not especially desirable that many artists should synthesize color form by rote, nevertheless a background knowledge of how this can be done, such a knowledge as comprises a knowledge of the various bases for color and of the concepts of color harmony and of its integration into aesthetic form, should be helpful to every colorist. This is particularly true for such visual arts in which the design organization is of relatively great importance, namely the decorative arts, the theater arts, interior design and architecture. Colors take their places in color form in accordance with the way in which the color traits are organized and with the way in which the organization integrates with the organization of the traits in the textural and spatial components. This statement is broad enough to bear no exception and particular enough to indicate a definite line of reasoning. Armed with color knowledge and this basic concept we will still have color geniuses and colorists who do mediocre work.

1. Jones, L. A., "Colorimetry: Preliminary Draft of a Report on Nomenclature and Definitions," *Journal of the Optical Society of America,* XXVII (1937), p. 207.
2. International Printing Ink Corporation, 1935, Monograph No. 1—Color Chemistry; No. 2—Color as Light; No. 3—Color in Use.
3. Luckiesh, Mathew, *Color and its Application,* 1921.
4. Hardy, LeGrand H., *The Bases of Color Vision,* paper presented before the Thirty-Fourth Annual Convention of the Illuminating Engineering Society, September 9-12, 1940.
5. Helmholtz, Hermann von, *Handbuch der Physiologischen Optik,* translated by James Southcall, The Optical Society of America, 1924, 3 vols., 1896.
6. Hering, Ewald, *Lehre vom Lichtsinne,* 1878.
7. Ladd-Franklin, Christine, *Colour and Colour Theories,* VTBT.
8. Chevreul, M. E., *The Principles of Harmony and Contrast of Colours,* translated by Charles Martel, 1890.
9. Rood, Ogden Nicholas, *Students' Textbook of Color,* 1908.
10. Katz, David, *The World of Colour,* 1935.
11. Carpenter, H. Barret, *Colour,* 1932.
12. Birren, Faber, *Monument to Color,* 1938.
13. Chandler, Albert R. and Barnhart, Edward N., *A Bibliography of Psychological and Experimental Aesthetics,* 1864-1937, 1938.
14. Moon, Parry, *Color Determination,* paper presented before the Thirty-Fourth Annual Convention of the Illuminating Engineering Society, September 9-12, 1940.
15. Judd, Deane B., *Color Systems and Their Inter-Relation,* paper presented before the Thirty-Fourth Annual Convention of the Illuminating Engineering Society, September 9-12, 1940.
16. Ostwald, Wilhelm, *Colour Science,* authorized translation by S. Scott Taylor, 3 vols., 1931-35.
17. ——————, *Der Farbenatlas,* 1921.
18. Cleland, T. M., *A Practical Description of the Munsell Color System,* 1937.
19. *Journal of the Optical Society of America,* XXX (1940), pp. 573-645.
20. Maerz, A. and Paul M. Rea, *A Dictionary of Color,* 1930.
21. Textile Color Card Association, *Standard Ninth Edition Color Card,* 1942.
22. Ridgway, Robert, *Color Standards and Color Nomenclature,* 1912.
23. Burris-Meyer, Elizabeth, *Color and Design in the Decorative Arts,* 1937.
24. Munsell, Albert H., *Color Balance,* 1913.
25. Graves, Maitland, *The Art of Color and Design,* 1941.
26. Munro, Thomas, *Aesthetic Form: The Analysis of Form in the Arts,* 2 vols.

—V.K.B.

colorants. See COLOR.

color attribute. See COLOR.

coloratura. *n.* Ornaments and ornamental passages in vocal music.

color balance. See COLOR.

color blindness. See COLOR.

color chords. See COLOR.

color circle. See color wheel.

color constancy. See COLOR.

color contrast. See COLOR.

color design is one of the ways of organizing color in a total aesthetic form wherein details are organized so as to emphasize orderly arrangement (repetition, variation and contrast) among color traits. See COLOR.

—V.K.B.

color glow is color luminosity when there is a definite defined figure. See COLOR. —V.K.B.

color harmony. See COLOR.

colorimeter. See COLOR.

color in architecture. Color has been used as a conscious element in the design of buildings for various purposes and with varying degrees of skill by nearly all civilizations. It is inseparable as a negative element in construction of any sort, for no building material is devoid of color, whether or not employed with recognition of this characteristic. As an optical phenomenon—a property of the reflection, diffraction, diffusion or absorption of light, its transmission and our sensory perception of it —color is not a strictly structural element in architecture, nor is material color generally so conceived by architects. It is therefore exceptional in the history of architecture to find color considered and used as a major, primary factor in design, save as a function of light and shade; the customary practice has always been to apply color as a decorative adjunct, to treat it as an accessory material related only distantly and vaguely to fundamental design. Material color is of architectural utility in any form in which it may be applied or attached to the surfaces of a building or may inhere in the structural materials themselves, as, stone, wood, and compositions in which pigments may be mixed. The most widely used materials and composites of aesthetic value for their qualities of color are: glazed tile, first employed in the early Mesopotamian cultures, later an important decorative element in Gothic and Dutch Renaissance buildings; sheets or thin slabs of stone, as, marble, porphyry, malachite, lapis lazuli, extensively used in the more luxurious Roman and Renaissance architecture in flat areas or composed patterns for inner and outer walls and floors or as translucent panels; strips or slabs of wood chosen for color and grain for use in floors, ceilings and wall panelling, first extensively developed in the Gothic age, constantly refined in subsequent periods (marquetry, etc.), and restimulated in the 20th cent. by the invention of methods for producing large sheets of malleable, veneered plyboard; wood is further susceptible to painting and carving to increase its tonal values; brick, the color values of which are notably increased by age, the chemical effects of weathering, and the modifications produced by the lichenous growths for which it is frequently host; glass and stone mosaic, employed notably in Roman and Byzantine buildings; sheets of glass and mirror, whether colored or plain; and pigments in various forms; as paint or tint applied flat to wall surfaces or mixed in plaster and concrete; enamel, applied flat to wall surfaces; burned, as accidental or deliberately introduced earth colors into floor and roofing tiles, a method in universal use from very early times in oriental as well as western architecture; as lacquer,

conspicuously used in Chinese and Japanese architecture; as polychrome, a decorative expedient developed notably in classic Greece and in Gothic architecture, where it is usually applied directly on stone or wood; and as fresco, for the decoration of interior and exterior plaster walls and ceilings, practised throughout Europe and Asia from Egyptian times to the present. Modern experiment has developed a new source of color with vast architectural implications, light itself, produced by artificial means, which is suceptible of infinite changes, combinations and permutations. The fundamental importance of color in architecture is both psychological and technological; it has always been used to increase the comfort and aesthetic pleasure which buildings can provide; it is now also an important factor in increasing the utility of buildings through correcting the quantities and qualities of available light, whether natural or artificial. The major uses of color in architecture are: to induce the feeling of warmth or coolness; to decorate otherwise barren spaces; to modify apparent size, either through the progressive and recessive qualities of color itself or through illusory decorative treatment; to indicate function, particularly where certain colors are associated with a ritual significance; to create or simulate an atmosphere of luxury; to heighten emphasis and drama; to provide a subtle counterpoint to the bolder rhythms of architectonic forms; to produce harmony in the spatial relations of buildings with each other and with their landscape settings; and to provide the most efficient and restful reflective or absorptive surfaces in places requiring extended visual effort.

—T.A.H.

color and decolorizing agents in glass-making. See GLASS AND GLASS MAKING.

color intensity. See COLOR.

colorism, in sculpture. See EARLY CHRISTIAN ART.

colorist. One who is interested in some or all of the manifold aspects of color.

color mill. See grinding slab.

color music. See lumia; clavilux.

color organ. See clavilux.

color photography. See PHOTOGRAPHY; COLOR.

color print. See PRINTS AND PRINT PROCESSES.

color pronouncedness. See COLOR.

color purity. See COLOR.

color scales. See COLOR.

color scheme. Essential colors to be used in an artistic production and regarded as basic to the systematic conception of the art work.

color sensation. See COLOR.

color symbolism. See COLOR.

color symbols. See HERALDRY.

color systems. See COLOR.

color teaching. Instruction in the field of color as an aspect of art expression, such as the functional, creative, and appreciative aspects of color; may include theory and practice through drawing, painting, and designing in color and the application of color to work in other fields; sometimes organized as a separate course of study, including such concepts as *fundamental colors, chief color characteristics, color properties, color families, color harmony,* and *functional applications of color.* Whitford and Winslow in *Dictionary of Education.*

color temperature. See COLOR.

color traits. See COLOR.

color wheel. A popular name given for a circular color diagram or arrangement of standardized colored surfaces which places the most saturated material standards in a circuit so that the hues of shortest wave lengths and the purples join onto the hues of the longest wave lengths.   —V.K.B.

color value. See COLOR.

columbarium (L. *columbarium,* dovecote). A Roman subterranean burial chamber provided with superimposed rows of small semicircular shaped niches for the urns containing the ashes of the dead; for mass burial, slaves, freedmen, burial clubs, etc.   —L.T.S.

column (L. *columna,* a post). A vertical support, generally consisting of base, circular or polygonal shaft, and capital.

column, columnists. A signed article appearing under a byline regularly in the same position in a newspaper or magazine in the U.S.A. has been called a column and its author a columnist or colyumnist. These writers have been given almost free rein to comment upon affairs in general or upon topics of specialized interests. Some columns are primarily humorous and satirical with an almost equal mixture of verse and prose; other columns relate to literature, art, music, sports, etiquette, business, and so on through the full range of human activity.   —H.R.W.

comacine masters. See Lombard architecture.

comb. *Book.* A comb-like tool with teeth used for marbling edges, end papers, etc.

comb dovetailing. See TAPESTRY.

combination tone. See ACOUSTICS.

comic element in music, the. The most rudimentary variety of musical humor may be compared to such primitive practical jokes as those involving an unexpected ducking, sitting on a tack, and the like. The essence of these performances is a sudden and disconcerting physical shock. Such is the unexpected forte chord which interrupts the gentle course of the slow movement of Haydn's *Surprise Symphony* and furnishes the reason for the title.

Even in this example we can see the germ of the next type of which the essential characteristic is incongruity. In Saint-Saëns' *Carnival des Animaux,* for example, the elephant is depicted by the double bass which plays the melody of the Berlioz *Dance of the Sylphs* from the *Damnation of Faust.* Admittedly this passage is funnier if the listener knows the title of the tune quoted, but the unsuitability of the hollow and ungainly tone of the bass to this dainty waltz theme is clearly the core of the jest. In a less obvious manner, the ironic treatment of traditional dance forms was a favorite game with composers in the 1920's and one which may be exemplified by such pieces as the Polka from the Shostakovich Ballet *The Golden Age.* Here the humor lies in the dissonant and irrelevant harmonies applied to the familiar rhythms of a dance form which has become banal by repetition. It is the art of caricature applied to music, the distortion of a familiar profile. This factor of musical exaggeration may also be detected in music of earlier periods. We find it in the baroque fiorituri of the tenor who takes the role of the cantor in the *Hebrew School* of J. C. Seyfert. This is perhaps a vicious anti-Semitic jest in music, but it is pertinent to our topic because it pushes a real characteristic of certain songs of the Synagogue, a florid and highly ornamented melodic line, to the point of caricature. The same quality reappears in the delightful aria from the *Marriage of Figaro* by Mozart in which Figaro demonstrates the life of a soldier to little Cherubino who promises to be a most unwilling recruit. This is set to martial music which is amusingly at variance with the stage picture.

Operatic music, from the earlier music in buffa style to more recent examples, owes its effect more to the dramatic situation, to tricks of delivery, to stage business than to musical humor of a specific kind. Composers in this style, however, learned to employ a bubbling, vivacious, and voluble style which is indeed the musical counterpart of verbal wit and which finds a classic expression in Figaro's air *Largo al factotum* from Rossini's *Barber of Seville*. This characteristic of volubility finds a characteristic expression in the patter song. A most amusing early example is the duet of the two lawyers from Lully's music to Molière's *Monsieur de Pourceaugnac*. The pompous lawyer drones out a solemn succession of syllables in the bass while at the same time the voluble lawyer, the tenor, with breathless haste quotes every known legal authority. Devotees of the Gilbert and Sullivan operettas will recall other felicitous examples of the patter song besides the well known, "I am the very model of a modern major general."

Humor was not a salient characteristic of Wagner's genius. Where we do find it, as in the character of Beckmesser in the Mastersingers, it is marred by the almost sadistic completeness of the retribution which Wagner visits on the poor man. The treatment of the character throughout is in the vein of caricature. A charming and truly humorous effect occurs in the pantomine, in Act III, when Beckmesser enters Sachs's study. The orchestra quotes ruefully the melody of Beckmesser's unlucky serenade of the previous night and also the theme of the beating which the had suffered at the hands of the indignant David. Here we find a humorous use of the Wagnerian "leading motive."

Elsewhere in musical literature quotations frequently have the character of a riddle, the answer to which lies in the associations aroused by the title or the text of the tune. Sometimes the humor of quotation is musical as when Debussy quotes the opening bars of the Prelude to Tristan and Isolde in his *Golliwog's Cakewalk,* maliciously transforming the melancholy passion of the original into the sentimental idiom of the popular song. Sometimes the humor lies in factors associated with the music rather than in a purely musical effect. Thus Schumann's pointed reference to the Marseillaise in his *Faschingschwank aus Wien* is a joke at the expense of the censors who, though the performance of the tune was forbidden in Vienna, were unable to detect Schumann's rather obvious allusion to it. In the banqueting scene in Mozart's *Don Giovanni* the wind band on the stage quotes an air from Mozart's own *Marriage of Figaro.* Leporello comments tartly, "There's a tune I have heard only too often." Here we smile to hear Mozart disparage Mozart and at the same time neatly draw the attention of the audience to the enormous popularity which the *Marriage of Figaro* had enjoyed. In both of these cases the key to the jest lies in the associations of the tunes rather than in the music itself.   —C.W.H.

comic opera. See opera.

comic skit. See RADIO DRAMA.

command of hand. See calligraphy.

commedia dell' arte. See THEATRE.

commercial art. Art subordinated and adapted to the uses of commerce, e.g. advertising layout, package design, bookjackets, decorative designs for wall papers and textiles, and magazine and calendar illustration. In the broadest sense includes interior design, industrial design (q.v.), and painting or sculpture executed primarily to meet the demands of a popular market.   —L.D.L.

common charges. See HERALDRY.

communion. See MEDIEVAL MUSIC; Mass; Psalmody.

comparative aesthetics. See AESTHETIC INQUIRY, CURRENT TYPES OF.

comparative musicology. See MUSICOLOGY.

compartment ceiling. A ceiling divided into panels, sometimes deeply sunk or coffered and generally surrounded by mouldings.

compass. The drafting tool, compass or pair of compasses, has a long history and a regular utility in the studio of the painter and of other workers in the arts. In its simplest form, it was probably known from the earliest classical times. Similar to the compass is the proportional divider, used for laying off relative measures in scale. Sketches of this instrument are found among the notes of Leonardo da Vinci.   —G.L.S

complementary colors. See COLOR.

complementary color scheme. See COLOR.

component. An element in a work of art, or in aesthetic form; one of the factors which, when interrelated, produce an artistic composition; one of the ingredients or means which the artist uses—not a physical means such as paint or marble, but a type of psychological experience which he aims to convey or arouse. Linear shape, color, and other attributes of visual perception are components in painting and other visual arts. Some components are simple or *elementary,* such as pitch and timbre in music; others complex or *developed,* such as melody, harmony, and counterpoint. —T.M.

composite order. An order developed by the Romans based on the Greek Corinthian. The principal variation was the adaptation of the large volutes of the Ionic order to the capital of the column.   —O.M.S.

composition (L. *componere,* to put together). (1) The putting together and organizing of components in a work of art; or a product of such organization. There are four principal modes of composition: *utilitarian, representative, expository,* and *decorative* or *thematic.* (qq.v.). Four different types of factor in art result from these modes of composiiton; they may coexist (in varying proportion) within the same work of art.   —T.M.
(2) To *compose* a dance is to give a movement form, as significant design, to what the mind has created. Composition is the way in which inner experience is brought into existence by technique, not only as skillfully executed movements, but also as an artful relating to these movements so that their organization results in a dance symbolizing unity between content and the form of its expression. See design.   —M.N.H'D.

compound fabrics. See weaving.

compound interval. See interval.

compound pier. A pier consisting of a masonry core to which are applied or on which are clustered colonnettes, pilasters, etc., these applied members serving as supports for the arches and ribs of a vault.

compound plain woven carpet. See carpet structures.

comprehensive plan, zoning. See CIVIC PLANNING.

concave relief. See relief sculpture; negative carving.

concentric. Having the same center but not necessarily the same radii.

concentus. See accentus, concentus.

concertante. A display piece for two or more solo voices or instruments, with accompaniment.

concertina. See MUSICAL INSTRUMENTS.

concertino. (1) A small concerto. (2) The principal player.

concerto. A composition in sonata form for a solo instrument with orchestral accompaniment.

concert overture. See overture.

conch shell. See SYMBOLISM IN FAR EASTERN ART; MUSICAL INSTRUMENTS.

concord. *Mus.* Same as consonance (q.v.).

concourse. A large space usually enclosed which accommodates a large number of people, such as in a railroad station.

concrete. An artificial stone the usual ingredients of which are cement, sand and broken stone or other aggregate. When the ingredients are mixed with sufficient water the plastic mass may be poured into forms. The setting of the cement causes the mass to become hard.   —O.M.S.

conductus. See MEDIEVAL MUSIC.

cone. Stack or funnel of kiln. See CERAMICS I.

cone of vision. See PERSPECTIVE.

cones. Clay pyrometric measures of heat, established by Seger. See CERAMICS I; also COLOR for reference to cones of the eye.

confessio (L.). *Eccl. Arch.* The crypt or shrine, or the part of the altar, or occasionally a large subterranean chapel in which the relics are placed.

congo art. See AFRICAN NEGRO ART.

conical mound. See Eastern North American Aboriginal Art.

conical projection. See PERSPECTIVE.

conjugate vanishing points. See PERSPEC-TIVE.

connoisseur (F. *connaisseur*, formerly *connoisseur*, fr. OF. *conoisseor*, fr. *conoistre*, to know, fr. L. *cognoscere*, to become acquainted with). In art, one who has a trained and discriminating judgment of what is rare or choice, developed by the combination of historical knowledge of the art in question, practical understanding of its technical characteristics, and critical acumen in esthetic judgment. Connoisseurship may be described as the ideal goal of the historian of any art. See history of art. —L.D.L.

consignatorium. See EARLY CHRISTIAN ARCHITECTURE.

console. *Arch.* A projection or bracket for supporting a weight, usually formed of volutes or scrolls in an S-shape; a corbel.

consonance, dissonance. Antithetical terms designating the relatively small (consonance), or relatively high (dissonance) amount of tension which an interval between two simultaneously sounding tones has by virtue of the number of acoustical beats due to its vibration ratio. Since the octave is the only beatless interval, any boundary line between consonance and dissonance is arbitrary. Hence the principles according to which consonance and dissonance are treated in composition are a product of aesthetic consideration resulting from the assumptions of the idiom chosen. For practical purposes of contemporary composition, the intervals available in our tone system rank approximately as follows (from low to high tension degrees):

Perfect Fifth (Twelfth)
Major, minor Thirds (Tenths)
Major, minor Sixths
Perfect Fourth (Eleventh)
Diminished Fifth
Minor Seventh
Major Seventh
Major Second (Ninth)
Minor Second (Ninth)

In the equal temperament (q.v.) several intervals (e.g.: minor third and augmented second; diminished fifth and augmented fourth; minor seventh and augmented sixth, etc.) are acoustically equivalent. In the tonal idiom the equivalent intervals are distinguished in notation according to the harmonic functions which they represent in the particular context (see idiom, B.) In the atonal idiom (see idiom, C.) the notation is less relevant; the choice between different possibilities of notation depends on considerations of voice leading and of which version appears more convenient to the reader, viz. performer of the music. —E.K.

consonant interval. See interval.

consort. See chamber music.

constancy. See PSYCHOLOGY OF DRAWING AND PAINTING.

constants. See FRENCH ART.

construction. (art ed.) Work in the crafts, or industrial arts, where constructive activities are carried on; the translation of an idea into art form through building with materials such as wood, stone, metal, or clay; used in connection with grade project work of various kinds such as paper construction, sand table, model villages, etc. Whitford and Winslow in *Dictionary of Education*.

constructivism. Russian-French geometric-abstract movement in painting and sculpture founded by Naum Gabo and Antoine Pevsner in 1920 and flourishing during the 1920's. The movement included such artists as Moholy-Nagy, Lissitzky, Tatlin and Rodchenko. —L.D.L.

constructivism ceramics. See CERAMICS II.

contemporary dance. See modern dance.

continental planning. See CIVIC PLANNING.

continuous kiln. *Cer.* Kiln in which firing zone is continuously hot. See CERAMICS I.

contour. (F. *contour*, circuit, outline). The outline of a figure or body; the line that bounds.

contour line. In surveying: (1) A line joining points of equal elevation on a surface. (2) A line or level carried along the surface of a country or district at a uniform height above sea-level. —J.M.M.

contour plowing. See CIVIC PLANNING.

contra bassoon. See MUSICAL INSTRUMENTS.

contrapposto (It.) Opposition of contrasted masses.

contrast. Diversity of adjacent parts, as in color, tone, or emotion.

conventional. Following conventions in respect of design, technique, or conception; formalized; conventionalized.

conversation piece. A kind of genre painting in which a group of figures is represented.

cool colors. See COLOR.

copaiba balsam. See oleoresin.

Copenhagen ware. See CERAMICS II.

copies, imitations of contemporary paintings. See FORGERIES IN PAINTING.

coping. The highest and covering course of masonry on a wall. The coping should be waterproof to preserve the interior of the wall from dampness, which in frosty weather might burst.   —J.M.M.

copla (Sp.). See seguidilla.

copper point. Like the silver point, this was evidently much used as a drawing instrument in Western art and required, as did the other metal points, an abrasive ground in order to give it an effective line.   —G.L.S.

Coptic architecture. The architecture of the Copts, principal Christian sect among the native Egyptians.

coral. See SYMBOLISM IN FAR EASTERN ART.

corbel (F. *corbel,* a raven, hence a beak-like projection). A block, as of stone or wood, projecting from a wall to support or help support a projecting feature.   —J.M.M.

corbel table. A course of masonry projecting from a wall and supported by corbels which are often connected by arches.

Corbie, school of. See Carolingian art.

corda (It. string; Fr. *corde*). In piano scores, **una corde** is the direction to employ the soft pedal. **Due corde** (two strings) shifts the pedal only half way. **Tutte le corde** (all the strings) releases the performer from the use of the pedal. In violin playing, *due corde* calls for doubling of a note, which is performed on two strings simultaneously. **4me corde** means the G string; **3me corde**, the D string.   —F.D.

corduroy (F. *corde du roi*). A cotton velvet corded or ribbed.

core. (1) The heart or innermost part of a thing. (2) In masonry: That part of the wall between opposite facing stones.

Corinthian style. The architectural style in which the Corinthian version of the Greek Ionic order is used; i.e., the Corinthian capital with two superimposed rows of acanthus leaves and tendrils ending in volutes at the top of the four corners is substituted for the Ionic volute capital; in Roman times, modillions are added to the soffit of the cornice and the ornament of all members of the order is greatly enriched.   —L.T.S.

Corinthian vases. During the 7th and 6th cents. B.C., Corinth was a leading commercial center of the Mediterranean world. Among her chief industries was the fabrication and export of pottery. Her early vases show marked oriental influence, with carpet-like friezes of birds, animals, fish and flowers, and heraldic elements, including winged lions, sphinxes and griffins. In the 6th cent. these decorative elements were subordinated to mythological and genre scenes, including episodes from the potters' shops, mines and ships. Corinthian vases, robust in shape and vigorous in drawing, often show a lively feeling for color, with a cream background and figures in dark silhouette, varied by red, white and purple details. The quality of both clay and craftsmanship was not sufficient to meet the challenge which came from Athens in the late 6th cent., and Corinthian ware rapidly lost its vogue.   —W.R.A.

corners. *Book.* The corners of books. Leather, vellum, etc., used to cover the corners in half and three-quarter bindings. Metal corners for the outside and slips of metal driven into the board to strengthen the corners.   —H.E.S.

cornet. See MUSICAL INSTRUMENTS.

cornetto curvo, diritto, mutto. See MUSICAL INSTRUMENTS.

cornfield hollers. See AMERICAN NEGRO LITERATURE.

cornice (F. *corniche*). The course or courses of masonry at or near the top of a structure. The cornice often acts as a crowning feature and usually projects somewhat.   —J.M.M.

cornu. See MUSICAL INSTRUMENTS.

coromandel screen. Coromandel is an uncommon term used for a certain type of large inlaid screen made, in China, of calamander wood; thought perhaps to have come from the Coromandel Coast in India.   —J.A.M.

corona. See tiara, papal.

corps de ballet (F. body or collective group; a company). A body of subordinate dancers, used as a visual choral background, against which soloists are framed, projected and contrasted.   —L.K.

correct drawing. A term used by artist to denote specific information in terms of freehand drawing. See drawing.

corrente. See courante.

corridor. A gallery or passage of a building, usually having various rooms opening upon it.

Cosmati or **Cosmato work.** The Cosmati were families of marble workers, sculptors and mosaicists who flourished in and around Rome from the late 12th to the early 14th cent. The names Cosmas or Cosmatus appear in several of these families. Thus, for instance, in 1210 Jacobus with his son Cosmas are mentioned by name in an inscription on the architrave of their chief work, the portico of the Cathedral of Cività Castellana near Rome. The Cosmati are typical representatives of Roman decorative art of that period which, starting from the production of church furniture and decoration in marble, gradually turned to more ambitious tasks, such as making sepulchral statues and perhaps also figured mosaics. Their name therefore is often used to designate Roman artistic activity of the time, esp. that of the 13th cent. In this sense, however, it is more exact to speak of **Marmorarii Romani** which is a medieval term. Several families of Marmorarii Romani, besides those of the Cosmati, are known. Most noteworthy are the Vassalletti, their principal work is the magnificent Cloisters of *S. Giovanni in Laterano* from ca. 1230-40. Most of the interior decoration and furniture of the early Christian and early medieval churches of Rome, with the exception of wall-mosaics, having perished, it is difficult to say how much the art of the Marmorarii of the 12th cent. owed to that of their predecessors. There is no doubt that in the general reawakening of Roman city-life in the period after the victory of the Gregorian Church reform, i.e., from ca. 1100 onward, Rome and the neighbouring regions experienced an artistic revival which manifested itself first in the equipment of older churches with pavements, chancels, ambons, altars, ci-

boria, cathedras, Easter-candles, sepulchres, porticos, facades and cloisters of a refined and elegant character; some of these works are unsurpassed examples of decorative art. That the artists took pride in their works is evident from the inscriptions with their names which are rarely lacking.

The chief characteristic of the new Opus Romanum is the combination of architectonic elements of classical and early Christian origin —i.e., columns, architraves, arches, gables, sarcophagi, etc., all made of marble—with a geometric ornamentation that makes use of mosaic technique. In the pavements it is the ancient **Opus Sectile** of variegated marbles that is used. The term **Opus Alexandrinum** for these pavements is misleading; the ancient Roman *Opus Alexandrinum* was a not clearly defined type of stone-mosaic, mentioned in *Histor. August. Alexander Severus, 25, 7,* as having been invented under that emperor, but perhaps rather originating from Alexandria. The patterns used in the Cosmati pavements seem to have been unknown to the Roman mosaicists of earlier centuries. They were evidently taken over from Byzantium (cf., e.g., the pavement from Hosios Lucas in Phocis illustrated in O. M. Dalton, *Byzantine Art and Archaeology,* 911, fig. 251), perhaps by way of Monte Cassino (for this whole complex problem see A. L. Frothingham, Jr., *American Journal of Archeology;* E. Scaccia-Scarafoni, in: *Bolletino d'Arte,* Series 3, vol. 30, 1936). The most important characteristics of the geometrical Cosmati ornamentation are circles, usually of porphyry or serpentine, and around them endless bands of marble. Especially in the decoration of church furniture we find an enrichment of the *Opus Sectile* by glass-paste mosaic of the same technical character as that used in the early Christian and Byzantine representational wall mosaics; interspersed with the ornament of marble and coloured stones there is a kaleidoscopic arrangement of small glass-paste cubes. Related to the Roman Cosmati decoration is that of southern Italian and Sicilian church furniture of the Norman and Hohenstaufen periods; yet in it we meet also strong evidence of Islamic ornament, including floral and animal motives.

In the 13th cent. the fame of the *Marmorarii Romani* spread far through Europe. In 1268 the pavement of the choir of Westminster Abbey, and probably before 1269 (see *Flores Historiarum,* ed. H. R. Luard, 3, 1890, 18 f.) the shrine of Edward the Confessor there were decorated in Cosmati work. It is probable that Petrus Civis Romanus whose name occured in the shrine, was identical with Petrus Oderisii, the author of the sepulchre' of Pope Clement IV in Viterbo (see below); Odericus, whose name once appeared in the Westminster pavement, was probably the father. Other parts of the pavement and several other tombs in Westminster Abbey are likewise made in the Roman style, some perhaps by English pupils of the Roman artists.

From the latter part of the 12th cent onwards the Marmorarii Romani ventured upon the decoration of their works by sculpture. In this they were never very original, but assimilated influences from southern Italy and Tuscany. Among their earliest works in sculpture are the reliefs of the Easter-candle in *S. Paolo fuori le mura* by Nicolaus de Angelo and Petrus Vassallettus. Probably after his return from England Petrus Oderisii made the first Roman sepulchre with a canopy and a recumbent statue of the deceased; it is the aforementioned tomb of Pope Clement IV in Viterbo which was begun between 1268 and 1271 (today located in the Church of S. Francesco). The artist's name is preserved by the 17th cent. *Acta Sanctorum* of the Bollandists (Propylaeum Maii, p. 55). The statue of the Pope is strangely alive and presupposes the influence of French and English Gothic sculpture. It is chiefly for this reason that it seems advisable to identify Petrus Oderisii with the Petrus Civis Romanus who made the shrine of Edward the Confessor in Westminster Abbey (cf. H. Keller, in: *Jahrbuch der Preussischen Kunstsammlungen* 56 [1935] 205 ff.). Later Cosmati tombs like that of Pope Hadrian V in S. Francesco of Viterbo and other sculptural works are influenced by Arnolfo di Cambio and perhaps also by the art of the Pisani. Some of the 13th cent. sepulchres of the *Marmorarii Romani* have representational mosaics on the wall under the canopy. It is possible that these are the work of the same masters who made the tombs. Similarly, the modest mosaics over a portal of the Cathedral of Città Castellana and over the door of S. Tommaso in Formis in Rome may have been made by the Cosmati who did the portals themselves. See Pinzi, *Storia della Città di Viterbo,* 1887-89; Cristofori, *Le Tombe dei Papi in Viterbo,* 1887; A. L. Frotingham, Jr., in: *The American Journal of Archeology* 7, 1891, 38 ff.; also ibidem: 10, 1895, 152 ff.; G. Clausse, *Les marbriers romains,* 1897; G. Giovannoni, *Archivio della R. Società Romana di Storia Patria,* 1904, *L'Arte,* 1908, and *Enciclopedia Italiana* 11, 1931, 576 ff.; G. Swarzenski in Thieme-

Becker, *Allgemeines Lexikon der bildenden Künste,* 7, 1912, 505 ff.; P. Toesca, *Storia dell Arte Italiana,* 1, 1927, 583 ff. and 826 ff.; G. A. Sartorio, *I Marmorari Romani nella chiesa di Westminster Abbey,* 1896; W. R. Lethaby, *Westminster Abbey and the King's Craftsmen,* 1906 and *Westminster Abbey Re-Examined,* 1925.   —G.B.L.

costumbrista literature. See HISPANIC AMERICAN LITERATURE.

COSTUME ART. The purpose of these brief paragraphs is merely to indicate the scope of costume as human dress, worn for protection from the elements and from injury, or for propitiation and attraction. The subject is inevitably bound up with ethnology, pre-history and the history of all civilizations. The intention here is to suggest the allied fields where material can be found, and facilitate research depending on the angle or interest of the reader.

Among the first impulses of man has been the need to cover himself and to adorn himself. His creative instinct has led him to invent tools and techniques to accomplish this, using whatever materials he found at hand. Among his earliest inventions were the pin, the needle and the loom. Among the earliest materials used were skins, plant and animal fibers.

For the purpose of this article, the term *costume* includes every type of covering of the human form, no matter what the medium; elsewhere differentiation is made between clothing and costume, the latter implying characteristics or style.

Pre-history has left records of the bone pin, the eyed needle, and woven fibres; examples of the last are found in fragments remaining from the Hopewell culture (q.v.).

The first garments were skins of wild beasts wrapped around the body or limbs with thongs, later cut and sewed with thongs or fibres. Fibres and barks of trees pounded into cloth and, after the invention of the loom, strips of woven fibres were wrapped around the body.

These and other early techniques have survived among primitive peoples in various parts of the world. Invention and skill in using material at hand—shells, seeds, bone, grasses and numbers of other fibres besides skins of animals and fish, wool, hair, quills, feathers, minerals and metals, have been limited only by the imagination and craft of the artisan and instinct to create for adornment as well as need for protection. Examples of these skills can be found in ethnological departments of museums as well as in the jungles, icebound regions, seacoasts, mountains and other parts of the world where non-industrial cultures still exist.

Objects that are included in costume and costume accessories are tunics, shirts, cloaks, trousers, skirts or any garment to cover the body, foot coverings, headdresses, masks, earlaps, mittens and gloves, shawls, kerchiefs, girdles, garters, jewelry, pouches, bags, fans, parasols and any other object worn to adorn or protect, as well as skin painting, tattooing and "make-up" of all kinds.

In some instances costume has been conceived to enhance the human form, in others to conceal it. A theory exists that costume developed from man's instinct of modesty; another, that it grew entirely from climatic conditions—that in warm climates the skirt was used, and in cold, the trouser. These and other theories are difficult to prove because of obvious exceptions and the lack of exact data.

Early civilizations developed costume to a high art, according to what remains to us of objects unearthed or recorded on stone, pottery or painted documents. In Ur of the Chaldees, fringed and decorated garments are clearly indicated on stelae, and intricately fashioned jewels have been found intact in grave mounds. The Egyptians' skill in finely woven cotton and linen robes has been preserved in papyri, in wall paintings, sculpture and in mummy wrappings, along with necklaces, bracelets, hair ornaments and other adornments. Pre-Columbian robes, caps, headbands, and jewelry have been taken from sites in Peru and other Latin American countries. Source material for the study of costume of early civilizations can also be found on the stone, metal or painted records of Mesopotamia, Persepolis, Ajunta Caves, Chichén-Itzá, Luristan and in growing collections of the arts of peoples long buried and recovered by archaeological research and excavation, and are available for study in museums throughout the world. Sculpture, pottery, textiles, paintings, manuscripts are the handbooks that provide authentic information regarding the methods and styles of dress prevalent during past eras, and can be considered by the student of costume as the Godey Books of those times.

Notwithstanding this wealth of material, it is difficult to reconstruct a complete visual picture from description or two dimensional sketches or cuts. To understand the shapes and lines it is advisable wherever possible to investigate a garment at first hand. Such an investigation may prove not only inspirational to creative design but may help to determine the derivation of certain characteristics of garments; i.e., the slit in the modern man's coat which seems to carry down from the days when swords were worn. The cut of a traditional Palestinian robe, with its long pointed sleeve, may suggest the lines of a medieval dress for which it may have been the model in Crusader days. A well tailored Persian coat from the court of Shah Abas may have carried suggestions for European men's dress.

It seems to be a rule in most countries that social status or wealth is indicated by richness of material, color and elaborateness of decoration. Royalty wherever found wears not only a crown but other insignia of rank or position. Regal purple or imperial yellow furnish familiar examples, while green in the turban of a Mohammedan shows that he is descended from the Prophet or has made the pilgrimage to Mecca.

The **headcovering**, hair arrangement, or other typical ornament, often tell whether a woman is married or unmarried. In Japan, a different haircomb was used for each stage of a girl's development; these styles were also reflected in the design and brightness of color of the kimono. In Jugo-Slavia, studies have been made which show that certain embroidered patterns indicate if a widow, how many children she has, and even if she is open to remarriage.

Clothes are a fertile field for the study of symbolism and even calligraphy. They are among the first objects on which traditional designs are recorded, woven, stitched or painted. Basic nature symbols such as the sun wheel, the tree of life, are found in cultures as far apart as the American Indian, Mesapotamian, Ancient Greek. Beautiful script has been woven into garments by the Copts of Egypt and the Persians.

Special costume has been created by every people for their rituals. To propitiate their deity the finest craftsmanship is lavished on the garments worn for worship in all epochs. High priests, medicine men, holy Lamas of Thibet, punkis of Burma, Shamans of Central Asia, the Ethiopian prelates, whirling dervishes, wear some distinctive apparel or ceremonial garments. The habits of religious orders and sects—Christian, Buddhist, Mohammedan, Hebrew—form a detailed study in themselves, as do the vestments worn to celebrate masses, feasts, pilgrimages, and other religious observances. Symbolism enters into the methods of tying knots, bows, turbans and countless other arrangements of garments. The **tablitas** (high wooden headdresses) and masks worn in Pueblo Indian dances are no less creations of art than the magnificent brocaded church vestments.

Bridals, which are basically rituals of fertility, have always been distinguished by the care and workmanship expended on the robes and ornaments, and the modern bridal dress is no exception.

Burial robes and colors associated with mourning vary from the Biblical sackcloth and the white shroud to the rich trappings with which early Eastern people surrounded their dead on the journey to the after life.

The islanders of the Pacific spared no pains or fantasy on their elaborate headdresses, masks and ornaments, or in celebrating their rituals, as the magnificent collections in museums here and abroad testify.

The abstract art of African ritual **masks** has long been disclosed to us, while Guatemala, Mexico and other countries still furnish fertile fields for study of this form of folk expression still in use. Animals and birds are often models for masks, abstracted to suggest particular characteristics. Natural phenomena such as sun rays, thunderbolts, rain, are freely represented.

In Central Europe, in Russia, indeed in all countries where traditional costume is still in use, feast days are made particularly gorgeous by the addition of brilliantly embroidered shawls, scarfs, petticoats, shirts, jewels, footwear and headgear. Flowered ribbons, gay kerchiefs, feathered and beaded trimmings are often added to honor a seasonal celebration or saint's day ceremony.

It is hard to differentiate between **ritual** and **theatrical costume** because the theatre has had its roots in ritual and in many parts of the world is still a religious ceremonial.

In Mohammedan countries formal theatre has never developed but in such pageantry as the Passion Play of Kerbela, and in pilgrimages like Nebbi Mussah in Palestine, the usual handsome **abas** (coats) and turbans give suitable theatrical effect to the ecstatic sword dances and other devout practices.

In the Japanese No (ritual dramas) the handsomely woven and designed kimonos and carved wooden masks, the latter often signed sculptured works, are handed down like the acting convention itself. Gold tissue and heavy silk, tassels and cords whose red earth colors must not be confused when tied with the white heavenly section, are as rigidly prescribed as the gestures, language and vocalization.

In Indonesia costume for performance challenges the intricate technique and skill of the actors or dancers as they are called. The sarong is elaborate in design and trains, demanding art to manipulate gracefully. In Bali the torso is tightly bound with many yards of brocaded sash while a velvet jacket ornamented with perforated leather shoulder pieces is used in Java.

The Chinese theatre has developed a convention of its own; each class of characters is designated by a typical costume and make-up, such as the pheasant feather headdress of the military man and the long waistcoat over tight jacket and sash of the servant. "Make-ups" as elaborate as masks from which they were probably derived, are an essential part of the Chinese stage.

The theatrical clothes of Europe are familiar. Those worn in the mysteries and miracles were probably church and lay robes of the period, and are undoubtedly recorded on portals and other Medieval sculpture. Secular plays, the Comedia del Arte, and the masques, developed their own styles so vividly portrayed by Callot, Watteau and others.

As is well known the Shakespearean theatre used only the dress of the day. Painting and other documents reveal that in the later centuries there appeared elaborate costumes for ballets, operas and spectacles of all kinds that flourished under the Louis and the Charles, and in the luxurious courts of Italy, Vienna and Spain.

In more recent times costume for the stage reproduced the fashion of the day and of the specific characters represented. In the first quarter of the 20th cent. a new angle on theatre costume appeared. Designers conceived dress as part of the decorative ensemble, and strove to clothe each character to add atmosphere and express its psychological relation to the play in color, in line; to take costume out of the photographic state it had reached in the 19th cent. and again endow it with a certain theatrical convention. Developed lighting systems and other stage mechanics permitted treatments and handling of materials from a new and perhaps more imaginative perspective. In this day theatrical costume has sometimes become the inspiration for fashion.

Battle dress has in certain epochs called forth the greatest art and craftsmanship, not only in the finely wrought arms and chain mail of the Crusaders, but in the greaves, helmets, breastplates of the warriors of all ages and countries, and the warbonnets and trappings of tribesmen of all continents. To protect the body or limbs, to strike terror in or impress the enemy, to propitiate the gods of war or fellow countrymen, these battle costumes often have been wrought with the care and skill of the goldsmiths and were as highly prized as jewels. Modern warfare has transformed battle dress from display to concealment; the paratrooper's uniform has been devised to meet this need.

Occupational costumes seem to have developed as communities have become more and more complex. Shepherds, artisans, tillers of the soil have usually required certain types of garments as part of their work. In the Hungarian mountains a sheepskin coat is as necessary as a grass raincoat to a Mexican peon, or the waterproofed protective garments of fishermen on open seas.

As urban communities grew and occupations became differentiated in European countries, the butcher, the baker, and the candlestick maker each adopted his own style of dress, just as certain recognized professions—doctors, judges, civil officials, even jesters—had previously done.

Today occupational costumes are so numerous and functional as to seem commonplace, and generally are worn only during hours of work.

Footwear has called forth variations from the delicate classic sandals of infinite design to bark wrappings worn on the Russian Steppes; from the knitted sock to the slipper, the boot, the patten in all their ramifications.

Fastenings for these and other apparel have included lacings, thongs, straps, buckles and buttons, antedating the zipper which came into practical use in the 1920's.

Headdresses have been even more diverse as many peoples who never protected their feet, conceived plumage for the head to vie with Nature's efforts for the birds. Also like the birds, the males have usually carried this method of attraction even further than the females. Brilliantly hued feather pre-Columbian headdresses as well as robes, the delicate kingfisher and pearl crowns of Imperial Chinese, the ostrich plumed felt hats of swashbuckling cavaliers, the fabulous turbans of Turkish potentates, are merely a few examples of how man has taken a cue from nature. The haircomb both in itself and combined with stuffs and superimposed ornaments, is an intricate but intrinsic feature of headdress.

Jewelry, fans, bags, kerchiefs, parasols, gloves, veils, or what we term accessories, could each fill its own chapter (see JEWELRY).

Metal antecedents of the safety pin, fibulae of the Celts, nose-rings of the savages and the modern jeweled clip run the gamut of time and place. Unknown Cellinis have spent their art on delicately wrought breastplates, girdles, hair ornaments and rings for church and state; amulets have played important roles in life and death, in history and in legend.

The **veil** has had connotations with the most feminine qualities, both secular and religious. In only a rare instance, such as the Tuareg tribe, has it been associated with men. The fan is more than an implement to circulate air. It has symbolized rank, profession, joy, sorrow.

The parasol has not only functioned as a sunshade but has served in ritual. The glove, the bag, the kerchief have each evolved in form, design and purpose according to the fantasy and need of the generation or of geography.

Underwear, corsets, hoops, farthingales, bustles, have taken on as many changes as outer apparel and indeed have been devised to meet the requirements of a desired silhouette just as the style of a building is determined by its foundations. The nightcap and gown, the dressing gown, the pantelette and petticoat have appeared and disappeared according to the taste of an epoch.

Sportswear is fairly modern, although the falconer's glove and the hunting jerkin must have had their parallels in pre-Christian centuries. The Persian polo players and Parthian and other hunters seem to have worn their customary attire. The 18th cent. man's hunting clothes have come down to us in the traditional "pink coat", and peaked "jockey cap". Ladies' voluminous riding habits became more trim and practical with each generation until the side saddle and pommel went out of general use, and close fitting breeches became customary with the growing freedom of women. Fencing, badminton, tennis, golf, bathing, skating, ski-ing, camping, bicycling, motor driving and other sports developed special clothing in accordance with the basic styles of each generation, and their players' need for protection and ease of movement. Cricket, football, baseball and track suits are a late and strictly western innovation.

Make-up, the modern vanity case and lipstick have their antecedents in early times. Egyptian ladies and women of many remote civilizations knew and used kohl to attract attention to the eyes, which were often the only features visible to others than their immediate families. Henna preceded present day nail lacquers, and was not restricted to fingers, but also dyed the heels, soles and palms. Oils, unguents and perfumes were almost universally used in the East and eventually found their way to Europe. Elaborate make-up kits have survived many centuries.

But not only among highly cultured peoples has make-up been used to attract. A stippled face is part of the costume of the sturdy Tibetan women who enjoy the responsibilities and privileges of a polyandric state, and war paint is a familiar method used by tribesmen to terrify their enemies. Modern camouflage is a reverse, though related, use of this technique.

Tattooing, in some regions considered as adornment, is often a ritual. Boys at puberty are initiated into certain tribes by this painful operation. Tattooing as decoration of the person still seems to have an appeal for sailors, circus performers and other "he-men".

The costume art of one civilization has greatly influenced that of others. Since the 18th cent. France has been considered the fountain-head for the dress of Europeans and Americans in urban communities. Only in the last generations have men's clothes taken their cut from England. It is not alone in modern times that styles have been borrowed. Greece, the France of the Classic World, spread its design far and wide over Asia Minor, the Black Sea and all lands touching the Mediterranean, while the aesthetics of Iran reached far into Turkestan, as can be noted in the excavations of the caves at Turfan.

The Crusaders may have brought back from the east the wimple, the tall headdress and veil which took on many forms during the medieval period.

The Indians of Latin America stitched and wove into their garments designs brought by their Spanish conquerors. In Panama even the full belaced and beruffled skirt combine the traditions of Spanish women with the fantasy of native ornament.

In the Balkan countries reminiscences of Turkish domination are apparent in richly embroidered shirts, jackets, tunics, aprons, and veils. Metal threads, sequins and coins prized by Eastern peoples are profusely used to emphasize patterns or fringe the edges of caps, sashes, etc., and in many instances the full Turkish trouser, short sleeveless jacket,

diaphanous veil and upturned scimitar-shaped slipper were retained.

The Visigoths seem to have registered their descent on Spain in the cross-stitched and smocked linen shirts and heavily woven mantles bordered with strong geometric designs and crowned with hoods terminating in almost architectural patterns which as late as 1930 were still worn in the province of Zamora, and are probably still worn today.

Like language, many of these designs became traditional in the land of their adoption, and origins have become clouded in usage and in legend.

Design in modern costume or fashion has taken on a personal character, as well as expressing the psychology and life of a generation or an epoch. Names such as Worth, Poiret, Redfern, are inevitably connected with the dress of the 1890's, and first quarter of the 20th cent. The next decades saw other French designers emerge and at the present writing (1943) American designers' personal interpretations are being recognized as distinctly as a canvas bears the signature of the painter.

Since the introduction of the sewing machine and mass production, the art of costume has become paradoxically simpler and yet more complex, and is inevitably bound up with problems of industry. The motion picture too, has had a widespread influence in democratizing clothes and wiping out class distinctions. The farmer's wife wishes now to be dressed in the latest style worn by a favorite Hollywood star. She can shop through a mail order catalogue and acquire the newest model by a creative artist, or she herself can cut it from an easily available pattern, using perhaps a gay print which now replaces the unbleached flour sack.

Reversely, the blue jean formerly identified with the cowshed and the mine has swept to the four corners of the world and earned its place as a costume practical for most out-of-door work, play and factory labor.

All wars have dictated radical changes in costume, notably the French Revolution which brought a new social order and therefore a leveling of classes reflected in simplified and more universal styles of dress: man discarded frills and furbelows, adopted the trouser; woman sheathed the body instead of encasing it in countless rigid stuffs and grotesqueries prevalent in the 17th and 18th cents.

World War II has also precipitated upheavals and readjustments in those arts and industries related to fashion. Since World War II, designers in America and England are turning inward for their creative inspiration and also directly to the same historical and traditional sources that French designers formerly sought.

The limitations imposed by the U. S. War Prod. Board to conserve materials vital to the war effort, present a challenge to the ingenuity of designers which artists and craftsmen in costume have always faced in some form. As a result of experimentation required by war needs, a rebirth of creative design can be anticipated. New combinations of the natural and synthetic fibres, dyes, and media may be released after the war that may lead to a flowering of style to which easier intercommunication and understanding may be contributing factors.

The above paragraphs may emphasize the fact that costume is deeply enmeshed with other arts and sciences. In portraiture and in decorative painting artists have been as concerned with the textures and lines of the clothes as with the features. Sculptors, too, have often faithfully reproduced the wearing apparel of their day on pediments, stairways, capitals, busts and tombs. Art historians and archeologists turn to costume to identify the date of a particular work and to trace its origin. The crown of a King portrayed on coin or seal may give the sought-for evidence. The novelist, the journalist, the dramatist, turn to costume to verify atmosphere and history. The chemist also turns to costume to analyze and compare dyes, and the ethnologist finds much data in tracing customs and intermingling of cultures.

Functionally and decoratively, in every climate, arctic or subtropical, under all conditions and evolutions, in primitive states and in highly developed communities, man's ingenuity to protect and adorn himself has met every test. In no art has his genius for proportion and design shown itself more fertile.

Modern industry may provide ease and speed in meeting the need for clothes, but may add little to the level of beauty that has already been embodied in the garments of bygone eras and far flung civilizations. However, inspiration can be derived from a study of the past that may stimulate the creation of new skills, new designs, new avenues, to carry forward the art of costume into a world of the future and a way of life still unveiled. See JEWELRY; also *Costume Index*, ed. by Isabel Monro and Dorothy E. Cook, 1937; *Bibliography of Costume*, Hilaire and Meyer Hiler; *Accessories of Dress*, Katherine Lester & Bess Oerke, 1940; *Anat-*

omy of Abuses, Philip Stubbs; *A Cyclopaedia of Costume or Dictionary of Dress*, James Robinson Planché, 1876-1879; *Calico Painting and Printing in the East Indies in the 17th and 18th Centuries*, G. P. Baker, 1921; *Ciba Review*, published by the Society of Chemical Industry in Basle, Switzerland; *Decorative Motives of Oriental Art*, Katherine M. Ball, 1927; *Die Volkstrachten der Innerschweiz*, Julie Heierli, 1922; *English Women's Clothing in the Nineteenth Century*, C. Willett Cunnington, 1937; *Galeries des Modes et Costumes Français*, Ed. by Paul Cornu, 1910; *The Gay Nineties*, R. V. Cutler, 1927; *The Heritage of Cotton*, M. D. C. Crawford, 1924; *Historic Hungarian Costumes*, Joseph Hollrigl, 1939; *Hungarian Pageant*, Alexander F. Karolyi, 1937; *Glossary of Terms in Articles of British Dress and Armor*, Williams, 1851; *Journal des Tailleurs*, Plates, no author 1830-1840, 11 Volumes; *King of Fashion, The Autobiography of Paul Poiret*, trans, by Stephen Haden Guest, 1931; *Die Kunst des Islam*, Heinrich Gluck and Ernst Diez; *Die Kunst Indiens, Chinas und Japans*, Otto Fischer; *Kunstgeschichte der Seidenweberei*, Otto von Falke; *Late Antique—Coptic and Islamic Textiles of Egypt*, E. Weyhe; *Hungarian Dances*, Karoly Viski, 1937; *La España Incognita*, Kurt Hielscher, 1921; *The Language of Fashion*, Mary Brooks Picken, 1939; *Le Costume*, Jacque Ruppert, 1931; *Le Corset*, F. Libron and H. Clouzet, 1933; *Magyar Nep Muveszete, A Malonyay Dezso*, Franklin Tarsulat, 1909; *Ornament in Applied Art*, E. Weyhe, 1924; *Painted and Printed Fabrics; the History of the Manufactory at Jouy and other Ateliers in France*, Henri Clouzot, 1760-1815; *Recueil de Planches sur les Sciences, les Rartes, Denis Diderot*, 1762-1776, 11 Volumes, another added; *Spain*, Baron Ch. Davillire, 1876; *Studies of the Psychology of Sex*, Havelock Ellis; *Templedanser*, Tyra Kleen, 1931; *The Ways of Fashion*, M. D. C. Crawford, 1941; *Women's Wear Daily*, April 8, 1942 and May 25, 1943.   —I.L.

costume jewelry. See JEWELRY.

cotton. According to records unearthed in the ruins of the city of Mohenjo-dara in the Indus Valley of India, cotton cultivation and manufacture were pursued there as early as 3000 B. C. Definite information is to be found in the law books of Manu, 800-700 B.C. which show that cotton cultivation and conversion had long been established in India. The ancient costumes of India were draped and uncut. This single piece is called a **sari** and is usually decorated on the edges and at both ends. The **sari** forms a whole costume when draped by the Indian women.

Indo-Greek statuary of the 1st and 2nd cents. A.D. and the images of Buddha so evidently inspired by the Athenian statues, show an individual rendering of drapery. It is evident that the artist was familiar with the gossamer (cotton) muslins of India for which Dacca was once famous.

The lightness of **Dacca muslin** is made possible because of the long fine cotton yarn grown in the Indus Valley. In the 17th cent. we find a record of fabrics 15 yards long and one yard wide, of such incredible lightness as to weigh only 60 grains to the square yard—or 73 yards to the pound. (The lightest fabric made by a Swiss hand loom averages 16½ or 17 yeards to the pound.) This finest of cotton was sometimes called *mul mulkhas*— evening dew. These muslins were as precious as some of the finer rugs of Persia, being reserved for royal usage as gifts to friendly courts and for religious purposes. It is safe to say that the muslins of Dacca were the most delicate cotton fabrics ever fashioned in a loom. The spinning wheel was never used to spin these yarns (for the method of spinning see *The Heritage of Cotton*, D.M.C. Crawford, page 68.)

Few actual specimens of cotton from India date before the 16th cent. A great collection of Indian cottons in the Brooklyn Museum are early 17 cent. pieces from the ruined city of Amber. These are wall hangings representing English ambassadors in the costume of James First of England. One represents the sacred cotton plant of India which has large purple blossoms.

It was not until 400-300 B. C. that knowledge of cotton reached Europe through the writings of Herodotus and the chroniclers of the campaigns of Alexander the Great. Greek writers called cotton "tree wool."

In the records of the Byzantine Emperor Justinian appear the two words carbassa (meaning cotton yarn) and carbasum (meaning cotton fabrics), adaptations of the Sanskrit word for cotton, *karpasi*.

By 70 B.C. the Romans were reported to be using cotton, presumably imported from India over the Arabian trade routes, in tents, awnings and canopies. In 70 A.D. Pliny reported cotton cultivation and manufacture fairly extensive in upper Egypt.

Cotton growing and manufacture, however, did not gain a firm foothold on the continent of Europe until 912-916 A.D. when it became established in Spain under the Moors and in Sicily while that island was under Arab rule. Its European penetration was confined for the most part to those two countries until the Crusades brought to the attention of the north and west of Europe the Levantine cottons. For a time cotton growing and manufacture flourished in the Crusader states in Asia Minor and a lively trade between these states and the Italian city states developed.

Cotton appears to have made its appearance in England in the latter part of the 12th cent. when it was used as candle wicks, embroidery yarns and for mixture with flax and wool in the heavy cheaper fabrics of the poorer classes. It also became known about the same time in France and Flanders, but these countries failed to acquire the skill in its conversion, required to compete with the fabrics made in Asia until many years later.

The growth of cotton manufacture of Europe, however, was far from impressive by modern standards until late in the 18th cent. when Manchester and Bolton began to acquire fame for their cotton and linen manufactories. It was in that period that Arkwright invented the spinning frame. Crompton invented the spinning mule, and Cartwright invented the power loom and the machine age really got underway. In 1793 Eli Whitney invented the cotton gin. The effect of this was instantaneous and combined with the inventions of the Lancashire spinners and weavers gave the English speaking world a dominance in cotton growing and manufacture that went almost unchallenged for 150 years.

When Columbus landed in the Bahamas in 1492, he found the natives wearing cotton garments and it was partly this that led him to conclude that he had reached the Indies. Researches in recent years have disclosed that cotton cultivation had been known in the New World for many centuries prior to its discovery and there are fairly sound reasons for the belief that it was in use in pre-Inca times in Peru or as early as 200 B.C.

More than a thousand major uses for cotton are known and it is estimated 99 per cent of the world population uses cotton in one form or another. In addition to supplying innumerable articles of clothing and home furnishings such as sheets, blankets, mattresses, towels, wash cloths, draperies, upholstery, slip covers and rugs, cotton also is used in large quantities for bandage. As a base for explosives, it is essential in war, mining, road building and agriculture. There is in the course of development the use of cotton in pre-fabricated low-cost houses.   —G.W.R.

cotton weave. See weaving.

coulé. *Mus.* A slow appoggiatura (q.v.).

coulisse. See STAGESETTING.

count. Number of warp and filling threads per inch. Also diameter of yarn, largely worsted.

counterpoint. Set of principles concerning the intervals formed by two or more simultaneously presented melodic lines at any given point, to be obeyed in order to make the simultaneous presentation of such lines aesthetically meaningful in terms of the idiom chosen for the composition under consideration (see polyphony). *Educationally*: The discipline setting forth the principles of counterpoint. *Double counterpoint.* Set of rules to be obeyed in order to allow that a melodic line originally written as a lower, or upper, part in relation to another line be transposed by a given interval whereby it becomes an upper, resp. lower, part in relation to the other line, without violating the contrapuntal principles in validity; concretely speaking, the intervals between the original parts must be considered with respect to what becomes of them after the transposition of the movable part. The interval by which the movable part is transposed in order to change its relation to the stationary part specifies the kind of double counterpoint (e.g., double counterpoint of the octave, of the tenth, etc.).   —E.K.

Counter-reformation. The reaction of the Catholic Church to and its reorganization in the face of the Protestant Reformation; a movement which arose in the second quarter of the 16th cent., gained its greatest intensity in the second half and its greatest outer momentum in the 17th cent. Its central manifestation was the council of Trent which formulated it dogma.

In the 16th cent. the attitude of the Counter-Reformation towards art was mainly one of encouragement, but restraint; encouragement, since the value of art had to be upheld against iconoclastic trends in Protestantism; restraint, since the new orthodoxy, set as it was against the worldliness of the Renaissance, found it impossible to tolerate anything heretic, superfluous, indecent or Pagan. Hence the frequent interference of the ecclesiastic authorities in matters artistic. The positive

contributions of the Counter-Reformation to art were slower in coming and arrived at full fruition only during the baroque (q.v.). Apart from liturgical and iconographic innovations they were mostly connected with the new conception of art as a means of propaganda, to be used at best advantage in the effort to hold wavering souls, to reconquer lost and to gain new human territory. Art played its part in that program by virtue of its sensuous appeal to emotion; for no matter what their integrity of purpose, it was believed by leading personalities of the age (the Jesuits!) that the church could save great numbers of human souls only if she came to terms with empirical conditions of collective and individual psychology. Consequently, art came to be used as a means of impressing the community by the exploitation of extreme emotional situations: death, mystical ecstasy and the torture of martyrdom. Instead of educating the beholder as the art of the Middle Ages had done, the art of the Counter-Reformation meant to surprise, fascinate, elate or terrify him. By thus playing upon his sensibilities it discovered new powerful effects, but it lost much of the integrity and reticence of an earlier day.   —R.B.

country dance. This name designates a particular type of English national dance. The origin of the country dance has been hotly disputed, some authorities arguing that the name and the formations used prove descend from the contre-danses of Europe, introduced to England by the Normans. Others insist that dances of this type existed in England long before the Norman Conquest. This latter view is more generally accepted at present. The country dances were usually danced by couples in two lines facing each other and progressed through many figures, returning often to the original formation. The basic step was a light, springing run, performed with easy elegance. Accompaniment was by bagpipe, fiddle, or pipe and tabor in 2/4, 4/4, or 6/8 meter. See American folk forms, in music.   —J.G.

country park. See CIVIC PLANNING.

country planning. See CIVIC PLANNING.

country singing. See American folk forms, in music.

counts of yarn. Yarns are graded by the number of rubs, cuts, hanks, or yards required to make one pound.   —G.W.R.

county planning. See CIVIC PLANNING.

courante. As background for its existence at 16th and 17th cent. European court festivities, the courante had an ancient life among the people in both Italy and France. Both nations claim the dance, but apparently the similar forms had parallel origins—not an unusual or unnatural occurrence for a dance based on so fundamental an activity as runnnig. In both the Italian **corrente** and the French **courante**, or **branle of poitou**, as it was originally called, the dancers used a springing run characterized by a bouncing action of the knees. The figures made short advances and retreats with sudden changes of direction. The fast ¾ beat was subdivided into eighths in an accompaniment that followed the running movement. The branle of poitou, slower than the corrente, was the form adopted by the French court and traditionally incorporated a flirtation pantomine. The second movement of German musical suites took its name and form from this dance, with the result that the courante is classified as a pre-classic dance. —J.G.

course. In masonry: Arrow of stones of the same height, generally placed on a level bed.

coursed or range work. Term applied to masonry in which stone is laid with continuous horizontal joints.

coursing joint. In masonry: The joint between two courses of stone.

court. An open area within or surrounded by a building with its wings.

cove. *Arch.* A concave molding; a member, as a ceiling, whose section is a concave curve. *v. t. & i.* To arch over.

covers bound in. *Book.* The original covers bound in rebinding.

crab canon. See canon.

cracker box philosopher. See American folk forms, in literature.

crackle. Minute cracks often seen in the glaze of Oriental pottery. See also FORGERIES IN PAINTINGS.

cracoviac. A national dance of Poland, taking its name from the city of Cracow. It is a round dance performed by couples in a large circle. Partners dance close together in a position similar to that of modern social dance. The figures consist of a leaping waltz-balance in place, alternating with a polka step or vigorous waltz-galop moving around the

circle. Since it is in 2/4 meter, the dance seems more closely related to the polka than to the waltz. Sometimes all the steps are done with exaggerated springs into the air, stamping, and rapid whirling. —J.G.

Cracow renaissance. See POLISH ART.

Cracow workshops. See POLISH ART.

cradle. During the 19th cent. a common reparative appliance for wooden panel paintings was a system of strips attached to the reverse, known as a cradle. The purpose of this was to hold the panel without warping and, when well made, the cradle contained loose or sliding members which ran at right angles to the grain of the wood. These were held in by slots in longitudinal members that were joined to the panel proper. In practice, the effectiveness of the cradle has been open to much question, and it is less used now than formerly. See RESTORATION OF PAINTINGS. —G.L.S.

craft (As *craft*s strength, skill, cunning). In art, (1) skill, dexterity, or aptitude of manual or technical character in contrast to esthetic aptitude. (2) Those engaged in art or a branch of art taken collectively, e.g. a craft or guild of stonemasons, painters, goldsmiths, etc. (3) A handcraft, or work of art accomplished by the skill or cunning of the hand of a trained individual using simple tools, contrasting with the industrial art of mass production by machine, on the one hand, and with the fine arts of drawing, oil, fresco, water color, and tempera painting, design, sculpture, etching, and lithography, on the other. Typical crafts or handcrafts include wood-block printing, leather work, metal work and jewelry, bookbinding, weaving, ceramics, and other varieties of applied design in which each object is a unique product. —L.D.L.

crane. See SYMBOLISM IN FAR EASTERN ART.

craquelé (Fr.). See crackle.

craqueluré (Fr.). Cracking, as of varnish, color, or enamel, on a work of plastic art.

crater. A bowl used by the Greeks for mixing wine and water, with a large body, wide mouth, and handles on either side. Craters of gold and silver were mentioned in the Homeric poems. Among the most beautiful pottery shapes are the massive Corinthian craters with column handles enclosing the neck, the so-called Francois vase, an Athenian crater dating about 560 B.C., decorated with neat bands of silhouettes in black glaze representing scenes from mythology, the finely proportioned Chalcidian craters with slim curved handles, calyx craters made in Athens in the middle of the 5th cent. B.C., shaped like the opening calyx of a flower, and a very graceful elongated Athenian type with slim body, narrow neck, and long handles. In the 4th cent. B.C., two more florid and less attractive shapes became popular in Italiot Greece, the volute-crater in Apulia and the bell-crater in Leucania. The volute-crater was distinguished by an egg-shaped body, broad neck, and large volute handles rising high above the lip; ornate paintings on the sides represented sentimental scenes with technical skill but little sense of design. Bell-craters were so named because their shape was that of an inverted bell.   —W.R.A.

crawling. Running or creeping of glaze leaving parts unglazed. See CERAMICS I.

crayon. Any small stick made for drawing can be called by this name. It usually designates a combination of pigments or dyes in a wax medium, formed into a thin cylindrical shape. A few crayons contain water-soluble dyes. A kind of crayon has been made by cooking charcoal in linseed oil. As tools for the draftsman, they are said to have come into use in the 16th cent. and are found in drawings of that time and later.   —G.L.S.

crazing. Glaze fractures caused by greater contraction of glaze than body. See CERAMICS I; crackle.

creative dance is any dance experience in which the mind of the dancer is permitted to organize and endow its material with a specific structure and individuality that is its own. With the imagination it combines impressions creating new images out of past experience; with the will and energy the new images are executed and given an observable form.   —M.N.H'D.

creative experience. (art ed.). (1) That phase of the art experience characterized by actual application of art techniques and the making of original art products, rather than by examining, studying, and appreciating works of art; (2) that phase of the art experience characterized by the production of original art forms, rather than copied or imitated forms. Whitford and Winslow in *Dictionary of Education.*

credence. See FURNITURE.

credo. See Mass.

creeper. See crocket.

crenelated. Furnished with battlements.

crepe. Fabric containing hard twisted yarns and forming a pebbly surface character. A crinkled fabric. Produced in various ways.

crescendo. Increase in tone volume, gradual transition of musical dynamics; opposite **decrescendo.** Both have been employed for centuries as a generally accepted device in vocal and also in instrumental rendition. However, in orchestral performance, the crescendo-decrescendo technique took on special significance with the 18th cent. Mannheim school. See NOTATION.   —F.D.

crest. See HERALDY.

Cretan-Minoan. During the period from the middle of the 4th millenium B.C. to about 1200 B.C., the island of Crete developed a highly original and productive artistic culture. Archeological excavations begun by Sir Arthur Evans in 1900 have revealed that this civilization, the dominant commercial power of the eastern Mediterranean, was devoted to gay and luxurious living in which the artist played an important part. The architecture of the palace of the Minoan dynasty at Knossus was intricate in design, with scores of rooms, including a reception hall, royal apartments, chapels, a theatre and store-rooms, built in several stories about a central court. The broad stairways enclosed light-wells, and the system of plumbing was elaborate and effective. The palaces in Crete were liberally decorated with fresco paintings in bold color, including lively scenes of boys and girls in acrobatic games, gathering flowers, or serving at religious rites, and of animals, fish, and floral scenes, done in a wide gamut of clear color (red, blue, green, yellow, black, white and gold); the painting shows astonishingly accurate observation of nature, verve, and feeling for flowing rhythm. The products of the vase-makers were likewise outstanding (see Aegean vases). The sculpture produced by Cretan artists was decorative rather than monumental, but of exquisite quality. Figurines of glazed terra-cotta, ivory, and ivory and gold, especially the elaborately decorated figures of snake-goddesses, show admirable craftsmanship; and the reliefs carved on steatite vases have a vivacity and naturalistic charm similar to the fresco paintings. In metal work there was also superb artistry, with lovely floral patterns bordering bronze basins, hunting scenes skillfully worked in repoussé on cups of gold, and bronze dagger blades decorated with damascened scenes of lion hunts in gold and silver. The work of these artists was widely exported throughout the eastern Mediterranean, and exercised great influence on the island and mainland cities of Greece. The brutal invasion of Crete by Dorians about 1200 B.C. marked the end of this culture.   —W.R.A.

cretonne. Named for Norman village of Creton. May have a ribbed weave. Printed pattern not visible on reverse side owing to density of material. Drapery fabric.

crevé. *Etch.* A condition where the acid has widened and broken down the areas between lines, so that they print a gray and faint impression.   —K.K.

crewel. North England dialectic word, meaning twisted wool.

cribb. *In construction*: (1) To line (the walls of a pit or shaft) with poles, timber, or planking. (2) A frame of poles or timber, as to retain a bank of earth.   —J.M.M.

crimson lake. See cochineal.

crochet rugs. Made similar to a knitted rug using the crochet stitch and strips of cut cloth instead of yarn.   —B.E.J.

crockery. General term for common earthenware. See CERAMICS II.

crocket. An ornament, usually in the form of curved foliage, found on the sloping edge of a flying buttress, gable, pinnacle, etc. of a Gothic building.

croma. See NOTATION.

Cro-Magnon art. See PREHISTORIC ART.

cromlech. A dolmen; a stone circle.

chromophores. See COLOR.

cromorne. See MUSICAL INSTRUMENTS.

cross. See HERALDRY.

crossing. In a church of cruciform plan (q.v.), the space at the intersection of the nave and transepts.

cross ribs. See Gothic.

Cross River art. See AFRICAN NEGRO ART.

crotchet. See NOTATION.

Crow art. See Plains Indian art.

crown. The keystone or highest point in an arch or vault. See also book sizes.

cruciform plan. The plan of a building in the form of a cross.

crux ansata (L.). The ankh (q.v.); the cross of life.

crwth. See MUSICAL INSTRUMENTS.

crying vibrato. See VIBRATO.

crypt (Gr. *kryptos,* hidden). A secret recess or vault; generally partly or entirely under a structure.

crystal glass. See GLASS and GLASS MAKING.

cubism. An important movement in modern French painting and to a lesser extent in sculpture, begun by Picasso and Braque in 1907 and gradually expanding in the 1910's to acquire the scope of a significant international movement. It is semi-abstract and comparatively geometric (whence the name), and is spoken of as analytical or synthetic and two-dimensional or three-dimensional.

The movement was founded under the influence of African negro sculpture and Cezanne, and the founders were especially influenced by a statement of Cezanne in a letter to Emile Bernard, published in 1907, in which he said, "You must see in nature the cylinder, the sphere, and the cone". This led Bragne and Picasso to reduce natural forms to their fundamental geometric shapes, which, designated as analytical cubism, represents the first phase of the movement lasting until 1913. Picasso's *Young Ladies of Avignon* of 1907 is often called the first cubist picture and his *Head* of 1909 the first cubist sculpture.

At first merely geometric facets of natural forms were stressed, and the third-dimension was retained. This was followed by the development of "simultaneity"—the simultaneous presentation of different views of an object in the same picture. At the same time color was gradually eliminated and the pictures became monochromatic and more two-dimensional in design, eliminating movement or modelling in depth. The second phase of cubism, synthetic, developed in 1913 with the use of the "collage", in which pieces of paper and other materials were pasted on the surface of the canvas and became part of the painting. This led to the principle of constructing the cubist pictorial object synthetically, rather than abstracting a picture analytically from the model. The resultant compositions were increasingly two-dimensional and decorative, and in general were more colorful and less ascetic than analytical cubist paintings. This style was continued by Picasso until 1925, when he began to introduce psychic meanings and surrealist elements into his cubist work, and by Bracque in a purer and less psychic form until the 1930's.

In addition to the work of Picasso and Braque cubism includes the painting of Gleizes, Metzinger, Leger, Delaunay, Picabia, Gris, Marcoussis, Villon, la Fresnaye, Marcel Duchamp, Ozenfant and Jeanneret.

In sculpture, which is less well adapted to austere cubism than painting, there are fewer significant artists and few examples after 1925. As in painting the line of demarcation is tenuous between semi-abstract cubist forms and near- or pure-abstract forms. Sculptors who may be termed cubist, however, include Picasso (beginning 1909), Archipenko (as early as 1910), Boccioni (as early as 1911—futurist), Laurens (beginning 1912), Duchamp-Villon (from 1912), Lipchitz (from 1914), Belling (frequently), Brancusi (more often near-abstractionist). See abstraction, constructivism, FRENCH ART. See Alfred H. Barr, Jr., *Cubism and Abstract Art*, 1936.

—L.D.L.

cul-de-sac. See CIVIC PLANNING.

cullet. See GLASS AND GLASS MAKING.

culture. A culture is a social heritage. A culture comprises inherited artifacts, instruments, technical processes, ideas, habits, evaluations, language, and the liturgical paraphernalia of religion. Thus a culture will consist of material and psychological components. These components are made to interact with more or less intelligence by those born into the social organization or culture which those components constitute. As a consequence of this interplay of the material and psychological components, a culture develops the idiosyncrasies by which it is differentiated from other cultures. —R.W.C.

cuneiform. Wedge-shaped; applied esp. to characters of inscriptions of ancient Babylonia, Persia, Assyria, etc.

cupola. A roof or ceiling of rounded form; also loosely applied to any small structure built on top of a roof or building.

Cupid. See Aphrodite.

cupped mouthpiece. See ACOUSTICS; MUSICAL INSTRUMENTS.

cuprammonium rayon. Filaments composed of a regenerated cellulose which has been coagulated or solidified from a solution of cellulose in ammoniacal copper oxide.

cursive scripts. See writing.

curtal. See MUSICAL INSTRUMENTS.

curve of Praxiteles. The Athenian sculptor Praxiteles (fl. 370-330 B.C.), famous for his sensuous representation of lovely human bodies in moments of repose, secured this effect by placing the figure in a relaxed standing position, with the weight on the forward right foot, the left foot swung lightly back, the left arm extended to the side, often resting on a tree or an ornamental vase, the right hip curved out, and the head turned to the right, so that the entire body assumed the position of an inverted S-curve. —W.R.A.

curvilinear perspective. See PERSPECTIVE.

cusped arch. An arch embellished by pointed triangular shapes formed by meeting curves and projecting from the intrados of the arch.

cut-pile. Having a pile or nap composed of fibers or threads standing erect, produced by cutting or shearing the surface so as to cut the loops of the thread. (Velvets, corduroys).

cutting (or editing, montage). Generally considered the most important creative act in the making of a film, and the unique aesthetic attribute of the motion picture medium. Physically, cutting is the instantaneous transference from one pictorial image to another; aesthetically, it is the joining of images with a view to the emotional and intellectual overtones of each, so that two or more images in conjunction convey more than the sum of the visible content of each.

Through the cut, the director of a film is enabled to break down an action into its component visual elements, and thus to show on the screen only those parts of the action which advance the narrative or develop the theme (analytical montage) ; he is able also to destroy real time and real space and create **film time** and **film space** by showing two sets of events widely separated in time and space but shown alternately on the screen so that they appear to occur simultaneously (parallel action) or so that they build a new concept by presenting some comparison or contrast (contrastive cutting). The director may also create appropriate sensations in the spectator by cutting his film **"fast"** (a succession of short shots) or **"slow"** (a series of shots of long duration). The rate of cutting, and the "cutting tone" thereby produced, vary throughout the film according to the requirements of mood and action.

Alternatives to the cut are the **dissolve**, the **fade**, and the **wipe**. In the dissolve, a second shot appears on the screen seemingly under the first, and becomes increasingly distinct; the first shot then becomes decreasingly distinct and disappears. In a fade, an image gradually appears on, or disappears from, a dark screen. In a wipe, the screen image seemingly is peeled off, revealing another image beneath it. Dissolves, fades, and wipes are usually employed to mark the beginning or the close of a sequence. The cut may be used for the same purpose.   —I.B.

cutting plane. See PERSPECTIVE.

Cycladic architecture. See Aegean architecture.

cyclorama (cyclos, circle, and *horama*, sight). A photographic or light projection or a painted view, extended circularly so that the spectator is surrounded by it and so gets the illusion of seeing it as if he were out-of-doors. In the theatre the cyclorama curtain is the circular curtain upon which such views are projected. See MODERN STAGESETTING.
—V.K.B.

cylinder seal. In ancient Mesopotamia, a cylinder of stone, ivory, or clay inscribed all around with a design or inscription for sealing. See MESOPOTAMIAN ART.

cylix. A wide-bowled Greek drinking cup, one of the most popular shapes from Mycenaean times through the greatest period of Athenian vase-painting. Corinthian 6th cent. B.C., cylixes were heavy of body, with low stems, shallow bowls and stubby handles, and decorative patterns painted over a large part of the surface. Athenian black-figured cylixes, at first squat with thick stems, soon became more graceful, with more generous bowls,

high stems, and decoration confined to a band along the outside, and on the inner rim and bottom of the bowl. The finest cylixes were the product of such masters of the red-figured style as Euphronius and Brygus, who painted animated friezes of mythology and everyday scenes around the outside, and mastered the problem of filling the circle in the center with well-composed figures. Favorite themes of the painters were dancing and drinking scenes.
—W.R.A.

cyma recta (Gr. *kyma*, wave). A classical moulding consisting of a double curve below a fascia, made by swinging a reverse curve at the non-projecting end of a cavetto, i.e., the projecting part of the double curve is concave; when ornamented carries a lotus and palmette pattern.   —L.T.S.

cyma reversa (Gr. *kyma*, wave). A classical moulding consisting of a double curve made by turning a reverse curve at the non-projecting end of an ovolo, i.e., with its projecting curve convex; often ornamented with the Lesbian leaf pattern.   —L.T.S.

cymbals. See MUSICAL INSTRUMENTS.

cypress. See SYMBOLISM IN FAR EASTERN ART.

czardas. This ancient Hungarian national dance in 2/4 meter employs infinite variety of movement, figures, and tempi. It is danced by one or more couples, and is divided into two parts, the first very slow, and the second rapidly increasing in speed. In the first section, movements from side to side establish a horizontal feeling, while the jumps, leaps, and hops of the second emphasizes verticality. Great freedom is allowed in the improvisation of steps and formations. Thus the range of possible movement is great, including turning, cut-steps, deep knee-bends, twisting the hips, stepping sideward and clicking the heels, etc.   —J.G.

CZECHOSLOVAKIA, ART OF. *Folk art* gives a most faithful record of a people's peculiarities and endowments. The peasant art of Czechoslovakia is interesting for it reflects not only the temperament of the people, but the various influences to which they have been subjected, even to the very nature of their land. The western part of the country, Bohemia, which is inhabited by the Czechs, was subjected to the culture of Western Europe, more particularly the Germanic peoples, while Slovakia in the east was long under the influence of the Magyars and Roumanians. The differences nowhere are sudden but show a gradual transition between the four regions; Bohemia, Moravia, Slovakia and Ruthenia. Bohemia, always the most progressive of these territories, has lost her folk art with only one exception. The Chods, living in the Sudeten area, still retain their old customs and costumes. Domazlice and Klencin are the two towns richest in the Chod culture. Moravia's art more nearly resembles the old Czech art but is better preserved with most of its villages still holding to the old traditions. The Slovaks of the eastern region are an agricultural people whose villages are too remote to be affected by outside influence. The old Czechslovakia proverb, "Over every hill you find another costume", proves true, for hardly two villages show the same style. The fourth and most easterly region, Ruthenia, is still quite primitive showing a very definite Russian influence.

There is a natural tendency toward decoration and brilliant color. It is interesting to observe the harmony of art with the environmental conditions. For example, in the richer spa villages the art takes on a more elaborate form. The amount of embroidery on the costume seems to be in proportion to the wealth of the family. The use of gold and silver thread is quite popular, as is brilliant colored silk floss. In the poor mountain districts, where the women work in the fields, there is less time for handiwork and the costumes are noticeably plainer, though no less beautiful. The majority are executed in red cotton on a heavy linen crash.

The greatest difference between the costumes of the more prosperous Czechs and the other sections of Czechoslovakia was their use of manufactured materials. Luxurious colored silk brocades were used for the skirts and aprons, with bodices of velvet. Scarves were of patterned silk or wool with long fringe. What embroidery there was, was subtle in color—the most usual was white on white—or one color, such as blue, embroidered on a white ground. This handiwork was limited to sleeve edgings and caps, and was usually combined with lace. Compared to the Czech, the work of the three other groups are more similar and offer us a better study in the needlework craft. It is not unusual to find as many as twenty different stitches in a single piece. The motifs done on heavy homespun are intricate conventionalizations of flowers, leaves, and birds with an occasional use of hearts, stars, or some geometric shape.

Particularly worthy of note is the exquisitely fine, yellow embroidery on the sleeves and caps of Piestány, the beautiful white plaited blouses of Uhersky Ostroh, and the gay aprons of Kyjov. In some of the villages, like Detva and Svatoboric, the men's costumes are very elaborate; wide embroidered sleeves of extraordinary length, extremely short vests, and long streamers of flowered ribbons hang from neck to knees. These are the main characteristics of the strangely proportioned masculine attire of Svatoboric.

The dwellings of Bohemian villages are of stone or painted stucco. The roof line shows a very definite influence of the Baroque style; in fact this derivation is sometimes termed **village baroque**. Slovakian mountain villages are of whitewashed log houses with dark brown gables interestingly carved and all out of proportion in size to the house. Lumber is plentiful in the mountains, hence the log house instead of stucco. In the environs of Bratislava is the village of Modra (blue), so named because the houses are all painted blue. Aside from the color of the houses, Modra represents a good example of the towns in this region. Unlike the jig-saw arrangement of the villages elsewhere in the republic, Modra and its neighboring towns have an orderly pattern. The houses are lined along the straight streets. Each married son builds his home as an addition to the back of his father's house. The result is a long narrow building at right angles to the street. The interiors are particularly gay, with every conceivable wall space covered with free-hand paintings of bright colored flowers and decorative ceramic plates. From the beamed ceilings hang ceramic jugs, and lining the walls is a long, continuous bench gaily decorated too. In one corner of the parlor usually stands a bed piled high to the ceiling with pillows and featherbeds, all covered with richly embroidered cases. The painting of these interiors is done by the women who get help in the lay-out and design from the village **pisarka** (the woman whose profession it is to plan the designs for her village).

Nowhere are the houses so interesting or beautiful as those in Cicmany, one of the most remote villages in Slovakia. Here can be found some of the greatest treasures of antiquity. The thatched-roof houses are made of logs fitted together with clay. The clay is painted with geometric designs as are the corners of the house and areas surrounding the windows. The unusual feature of the interior is the open fireplace where the cooking is done, the smoke from which spreads through the room leaving the walls and ceiling sooty, and shining like pitch.

Other architectural interests are the strange wooden churches of Ruthenia with their obvious influence of the Byzantine, shown particularly in the onion-shaped domes. Throughout the entire country the little shrines, situated in the midst of fields, at the roadside, or crossroads, show an interesting development in peasant architecture, as do the carved and painted crosses in the country cemeteries.

Ceramics are an important peasant art. The Czech ceramics were influenced by the Italian Renaissance. The technique of the majolica ware was brought to Bohemia by Italian craftsmen who were invited by the nobles to teach the Czechs this craft. Ceramics in Moravia and Slovakia, on the whole, were not affected by outside influence. Some of the loveliest pieces are the **Haban ceramics.** The Habans were a group of Anabaptists who settled in Slovakia around 1546. The popular **Modra ware** is made in the village of Modra; it is well known, for these old designs are to-day manufactured on a large scale. In the Chod district of Bohemia the heavy sombre-colored pottery is still made in the most primitive of methods.

Architecture. Czechoslovakia, particularly Bohemia, with its capital, Prague, possesses many interesting buildings which display the whole evolution of European architecture, modified by the Czechoslovakian influence.

The churches are the prevalent architecture of the early styles. Toward the end of the 9th cent., the Macedonian apostles who Christianized the nation, brought with them the influence of the Byzantine. The rotunda buildings, which were developed in this period, were confined to the vicinity of Bohemia and Moravia—not extending farther westward. For the most part, these structures have burned or have been rebuilt.

The simple rotund building developed in the Romanesque period to a larger structure with a semi-circular apse, a nave and two aisles. St. George's Church, 1142, in the Prague Castle, is one of the best examples of this basilica type.

Around the end of the 12th cent., the Gothic culture, originating in France, brought impulses to Moravia, and the Cathedral of Trebíc, 1233, is a unique example of a traditional style. Later the Gothic style extended into Bohemia, quickly replacing the Romanesque without any transitional period. Gothic art flourished particularly under the reign of Karel IV, who had been educated in France and was greatly impressed by the elevating quality of the Gothic cathedrals. Karel laid the plans for the St. Vitus Cathedral situated high on the Hradcany, the most impressive of Prague's churches, whose spires tower high over this "Hundred Spired" City. Mathias of Arras, a Frenchman, began work on the Cathedral in 1344, and was then succeeded by the Czech, Petr Parlér, under whose guidance Czech architecture attained a world standard.

The towers of the Charles Bridge (Karluv Most), the Old Town Hall Chapel (Staromestska Radnice), the Tyn Church, the Powder Tower (Prasná Brána), and the well-known Karlstein Castle (Karluw Tyn), are all examples of the so-called **Vladislav Gothic style** which prevailed in Bohemia between 1475 and 1508, a Gothic style peculiar to this country, square towered and less elaborate than the French Gothic.

The 16th cent. marks the advent of the Renaissance into Bohemia, though the early Renaissance, like the late Gothic style, had a character all its own, which gives evidence of the independent spirit that so typifies Czechoslovakian art. Later there was a marked influence of the Italian Renaissance brought into the country by noted Italian architects who were working in the court of Ferdinand the First. The Spanish Hall in the Hradcany, Belvedere and Schwarzenberg Palaces, are examples of this style in Prague.

Throughout the baroque period there was an intense activity of building. Many features of Italian baroque classicism were imported by Italian architects from northern Italy, so many that Rodin, the famous French sculptor, called Prague the "Rome of the North".

Around the middle of the 17th cent., the Jesuits began their influence throughout the country, trying to recatholicize the population. They built elaborate churches and convents, which today are the best of the baroque architecture in Bohemia.

K. I. Dientzenhofer, the greatest architect since Parlér, was a master at baroque exaggeration. He overcame outside influence and brought the level of Czech architecture to the European standard. The most outstanding structures of this period are St. Nicholas Church (Svaty Mikuláse) and Waldstein Palace. From an architectural point of view Prague ranks among the foremost cities in Europe.

The 20th cent. is represented in this country by factories, administration buildings, chateaux and sanitariums, done in the extreme modern style. In the spa villages throughout the republic, the contrast between the modern sanitariums and the primitive homes of the peasants offer an interesting comparison.

Sculpture, around the earliest centuries, (11th and 12th), was not a separate art but was always found in conjunction with architecture. The earliest examples are carved in wood and it was not until the monks of the Sazava Monastery fostered this art (about the 11th cent.) that there is any record of modeled sculpture.

The Romanesque period is represented by the reliefs and decorations on the churches of this period. St. George's Church in Prague, the 12th cent. plastics in the church in Spis, Slovakia, and the portals of the Trebic Cathedral in Moravia (which is one of the most important Romanesque structures north of the Alps), are typical examples of Czechoslovakian Romanesque.

An exceptional development in sculpture was shown during the Gothic period, reflecting a great deal of the culture of Western Europe. At first the portals, capitals, and tympanums were mostly decorated with plant motifs; the use of figure compositions was rare until later. Czech Gothic sculpture reached its apogee under Petr Parlér, the architect, who was also a master in stone. Some of Parlér's works are the statue of St. Vaclav and the tombstones of the Czech kings, both in St. Vitus Cathedral; also the triforium of the church, which has a row of marble busts, portraits of the kings, queens and others who patronized or assisted in the construction of the cathedral.

Local sculptors in Moravia attained a high level and left magnificent examples of their work in the cities of Brno and Olomonc. The real period of creative work began in Slovakia around the 15th cent. with the late Gothic. The cathedrals in Kosice and Presov are rich in this style.

Czech Renaissance sculpture is characterized by its fine decorative craftsmanship. Some beautiful work is found in stucco ceilings, carved wood furniture, and decorative metal work. Unfortunately, a great deal from this period was destroyed or carried away during the Thirty Years' War. One of the few remaining pieces of plastic Renaissance sculpture is the "Singing Fountain" in the garden of the Prague Castle.

The baroque sculpture in Czechoslovakia at first developed under the influence of Renaissance craftsmen, but by the middle of the 17th cent., the pure baroque impulse was brought to this country from Bavaria, Austria, and Italy. The Charles Bridge (Karluv Most) is a regular museum of baroque sculpture. It is the only bridge of its kind in the whole of Europe and it consists of sixteen arches, the pillars of which are decorated with statues of the Saints. A statue of St. John Nepomucene (Sv. Jan Nepomuck) stands on the spot where it is alleged he was thrown off the bridge into the Vltava, in 1383. The bridge sculpture is the work of two important Bohemian sculptors, Mathias Braun and Ferdinand Maximillian Brokov. In the St. Vitus Cathedral is the tomb of St. John Nepomucene, an impressive piece done completely in silver and ornately decorated with figures. It is the work of J. E. Fischler, made around 1736.

Among the 19th cent. sculptors, Josef Vaclav Myslbeck rises considerably above the local standard. His monument of St. Vaclav stands at the upper end of the main square in Prague (Vaclavské Námesti), an inspiring sight of high artistic merit. The monument of Jan Hus, which stands in the Old Town Square, is also an excellent piece of work, done by Ladislav Saloun.

Painting. Unfortunately, little remains of early Czech painting. The few examples preserved are restricted mostly to paintings of religious scenes done on cloth or wood.

In the Romanesque period, fresco painting in the churches developed sooner than sculpture, dating from the second half of the 12th cent. St. George's Church in Prague, St. Catherine's (Sv. Kateriny) in Znojmo, Moravia, and the Cathedral of Sivetice in Slovakia, show outstanding Romanesque murals. The miniature paintings in the illuminated books surpass all other similar works of Central Europe at this period.

Karlstein Castle possesses a wealth of Gothic murals, most of which are done by unknown artists; the only known name being Theodoricus who executed a strong influence over the art of his time.

Toward the end of the 14th cent. the artist called "Master od Trebon" was the outstanding painter of Central Europe, and the equal to any in the west of Europe. He developed the light and shade technique hitherto unknown in this section of the country.

The Hussite Wars wrought great destruction to art in the 15th cent., after which Prague and Kutna Horá emerged as the two centers for late Gothic realism. The high altar of the Cathedral in Kosice, Slovakia, is made of painted panels, the richest of this type created in the whole republic.

Sgrafitto painting was introduced by the Italians during the Renaissance period, and not only the interiors but also the exteriors of public buildings were decorated in this manner, such as the Minuta House in Prague, and Schwarzenberg Palace.

The great building activity, following the lull of artistic endeavor caused by the Thirty Years' War, brought considerable development in decorative mural paintings. The work of Karel Skréa, Petr Brandl, and Václav Reiner can be found in the Prague National Gallery, representing the Baroque period. The subject matter of these paintings were partly religious and partly historical or allegorical battle scenes.

Painting emancipates itself from foreign influence in the 19th cent. The pioneer in this was Josef Mánes (1821-71) who made a study of native types and created an interest in the folk-lore of his people. Mikulás Ales (1852-1913), with his excellent illustrations of folks songs, was very popular, and through his sketches educated the people in the customs and costumes of the peasants. Joza Uprka, from Moravia, also found expression in the brilliance and beauty of the Slovak costumes.

The modern movement has quite a foothold in Czechoslovakia and while it is too new to make any judgment as to its quality, there is a great national interest and acceptance of it. Some of the artists who have led in this movement are Emil Filla, O. Kubista, Oskar Kokaschka, Vlastimil Rada, Frantisek Tichy, and Jan Zrzavy. See *Primitive and Peasant Art*, ed. Felix Payant; *Peasant Art in Austria and Hungary*, ed. Charles Holme; "The Arts of Czechoslovakia", *Art and Archaeology*, vol. XI, 5.   —V.N.

D

dabber. A pad used by engravers, etchers, etc., to apply ink, color, etc., evenly.

da capo aria. See opera.

Dacca muslin. See cotton.

Dadaism (F. hobby horse, cock-horse). A movement in painting, sculpture, and literature which began officially in Zurich in 1916, when the word *Dada* was discovered by chance in a dictionary and seemed to epitomize the aims of a group of artists and authors from various countries who were working in Zurich at the time. Their philosophy involved a complete nihilism, satirical disillusionment and violent protest, disgust with and ridicule of civilization, iconoclastic destruction and programmatic disorder, systematic demoralization, and a glorification of the irrational or anti-rational, and anti-aesthetic, and the amoral. In part at least, the movement may be said to be a product of World War I disillusionment, which aroused in the Dadaists a vicious disgust with all aspects of the civilization which produced such a senseless holocaust. Disguised by a thin veil of humor, Dadaism was in reality a cynical and diabolical rebellion against all social conventions and their accompanying inhibitions, and represented the cultural counterpart of political anarchy. Its chief accomplishment was not so much the merit of work produced, as in preparing the way for the more mature form of fantastic art which succeeded it under the name of surrealism.

The method of the exponents of the movement was to produce earnest and serious, essentially tragic nonsense with uncensored spontaneity, allowing forms to arise uninhibited from the subconscious, aided by automatic, semi-automatic, or hypnotic techniques of drawing or writing. Their products were fantastic, frequently symbolic, irreverent, ironic, amorphic or mechano-morphic concoctions, often typed in one or another weird category, e.g. rubbish constructions, fatagagas, *"merz"* pictures, ready-made objects, exquisite corpses, collages, rayographs (qq.v.). Examples of titles of specific pictures are *Catch as Catch Can; Amorous Procession; Infant Carburetor; Wet Paint; Object of Destruction; Self-constructed Little Machine; Here Everything is Floating; The Little Tear Gland that Says Tic Tac; The Gramineous Bicycle Garnished with Bells; the Pilfered Greybeards and the Echinoderms Bending the Spine to Look for Caresses.*

Dadaism was anticipated between 1910 and 1916 by proto-Dada works of de Chirico, Kandinsky, Duchamp, Picasso, Braque, Boccioni, Picabia, Archipenko and Klee of whom only Picabia was ever an official Dadaist. It lasted in Germany until 1920 and in France until 1922. The chief exponents of the movement, of whom many were both artists and writers, include Tristan Tzara, Hans Arp, Marcel Janco, Huelsenbeck, Hugo Ball, Francis Picabia, Man Ray, André Breton, Philippe Soupault, Guillaume Apollinaire, Louis Aragon, Max Ernst, Christian Schad, Kurt Schwitters, J. T. Baargeld. Members of the group held numerous exhibitions, published proclamations and manifestoes from time to time, published several short-lived periodicals of poetry and criticism, e.g. *Cabaret Voltaire, Sic, "391", Dada, Club Dada, Cannibale, Die Schammade,* staged dances, plays, public readings of poetry, *soirées,* festivals, opened a Dada nightclub in Berlin, and founded a newspaper in Cologne.

Dadaism differed from surrealism (q.v.), of which it was a direct antecedent, in emphasizing irrational and uncontrolled techniques of art production. It was the rebellious, anti-rational art of the unconscious, whereas surrealism is non-rebellious, super-rational, and a conscious, often deliberately Freudian presentation of dream or dream-like images, which fuse the real and the unreal into a super-reality. Many of the original Dadaists became surrealists after 1924. See FRENCH ART; also Alfred H. Barr, Jr., *Fantastic Art Dada Surrealism*, 1936.   —L.D.L.

dado. A plain flat, horizontal, and often decorated surface or band at the base of a wall.

Daedalic style. See HELLENIC ART.

dagaba (Singhalese). See dagoba.

dagoba (Singhalese). A monumental reliquary. See stupa; INDIAN ART.

dai (Jap.). A pedestal or stand. See also daiza.

dai-bou (Jap.). See key-block.

dai-sho (Jap.). Term used for companion swords worn by the samurai, or military class of feudal times. **Dai** (long sword, *katana*, q.v.) ; **sho** (short sword, *wakizashi*, q.v.).

daiza (Jap). The pedestal upon which a sculptured figure rests.

damascene technique. The application of metallic designs to iron or steel as seen on Damascus blades.

Damascus ware. See ISLAMIC ART.

damask. Named for the city of Damascus. Brought to Europe by Crusaders. Silk was material of the 12th cent. damasks which were woven on hand looms. Linen and cotton damasks are woven on Jacquard looms (q.v.) today. Wool, silk, cotton and rayon in combination are used in modern damasks. Damask fabrics in general are characterized either by warp or satin figuring upon a weft ground or vice versa. A twill weave may be employed for the figure and a satin weave for the ground. This fabric is reversible and sometimes equally interesting on both sides. Table linen is usually damask pattern.   —G.W.R.

dammar. A favorite among the resins used for varnish making, this is a product of a family of trees that grow in the Malay states and in the East Indies. It is pale in color, has a good lustre, and adheres well. It has the peculiar characteristic of being entirely soluble in hydrocarbons such as toluene and benzene

and in petroleum spirits. It dissolves, also, in alcohols and in turpentine. See RESTORATION OF PAINTINGS.   —G.L.S.

Dan art. See AFRICAN NEGRO ART.

DANCE. Every age has had its dance, and the fact that dance has not perished is evidence of its value to mankind. The fact that there has always been dance compels it to be accepted as an old and deeply rooted human activity whose foundations reside in the nature of man himself. The universal interest in dance rests upon the fact that it carries on and systematizes an activity that is operative in everyone's experience: it is co-existent with life.

Like the history of all the arts, the history of dance has followed those changes in attitude and feeling, and those fluctuations in man's concept of art which have given to every period its distinctive qualities.

As man lives longer and gains more experience and a better understanding of his world, his ability to adjust himself and survive depends more and more upon his mental powers rather than upon physical prowess alone. Along with the evolving intellectual life our aesthetic and emotional natures have developed, and with this complex scheme of development our sense of values and our tastes have grown. Therefore dance, as an art form, is a medium that has always reflected man's mental evolution. His artistic evaluations are reaching higher and higher, and in the process his aesthetic needs are preferring abstraction as suggestion, rather than realism as detailed description and copy. But the same life forces will actuate the dances of today as in the past. Man feels as deeply now as then. Feeling is constant. Only form is variable. What has happened is that racial and folk tendencies have gradually developed into more spiritual ideals, which have become the motives for expression. Experience tends to universalize the individual to the extent that concrete emotions and concrete dramatic situations take on more abstract form in the art expression of them.

Thus during the march of the ages man's expressive movements have become modified by his growing realization of the effect of his own actions, until at last these actions have been consciously and intentionally used as expressive tools. It was when thus modified that expressive movement became art dance — a form consciously pursued for its art values.

The desire and need for communication as well as for expression have led man to the discovery of aesthetic means. From this search for a means have evolved the knowledge, science, and technique of dance. At the same time this search has led to a refining of the basic impulses, causing various civilizations to elaborate and standardize forms of emotional expression.

The technique of dance is profiting from increased knowledge of motion and rhythm as applied to the movements of man. Physiological and psychological research have revealed to us the nature of the kinesthetic sense, the kinesthetic basis of rhythmic perception, and the relation existing between feeling and its motor expression—revelations which have made possible a new technical training. Also, the present scientific attitude has encouraged a habit of mind that is reflected with great benefit in our dance forms. It has made for clarity, simplicity, and directness. Its honesty of thinking leads to genuineness of feeling, which leaves little place for superficiality. Although the less forceful rhythms of 19th cent. romanticism have been replaced by the more vigorous, pulsating, and varied rhythms of our less leisurely age, that does not mean that the romantic spirit and sentiment are lost to us of today. Their mode of expression has merely changed to the modern idiom—meaning the discarding of unnecessary embellishments in the effort to attain a direct and frank simplicity of movement. Only such a dance form could be the correlate of the wide-ranging, complex, intellectual, and cosmopolitan character of our age. Its direction as a fine art is toward universal symbolism, much broader in its scope and meaning than any racial art or the art of any one age.

Today we are not concerned with traditional values as answers to problems that no longer exist. We make use of the same primitive elements with which our ancestors began, but with a difference: once a reflex outlet for strong emotional pressure, dance has become deliberate creation in which the intellect and will dominate the automatic and emotional impulses. There is a gain in consciousness, but no change in the essential working of biological and aesthetic processes. There is merely a refining of their functioning. We no longer expect dance to be the expression only of the more lofty and poetic feelings, but accept it as the expression of all that the heart can feel—its pangs, ecstasies, passions, moods, and aspirations. Its manner may include the satiric, the lofty, the simple, and the extravagantly strange. Dance will continue to grow despite confusion concerning its meaning and the various forms of its utterance.

The pleasure of obeying the impulse to move and to express in ordered movement our responses to the forces of our nature and of our environment remains the same in every time and place. The differences between the dances of the past and those of the present are but differences in outer form: in period, location, temperament, education, and taste, which together determine the cultural values of any age. Basically concerned with the primary issues of life, dance has been inseparably connected with the expression of the cultural development of every period, and in turn has exerted its influence on the social patterns of the past.   —M.N.H'D.

dance, a. As an art form, a dance, or a dance composition is a designed entity. It is an embodiment of emotional experience in expressive movements, upon which the principles of composition are consciously imposed by the personality which was the subject of the experience. It is an artistic image motorly conceived.

Subjectively, a dance is an ideal toward which the imaginative mind reaches and in which satisfaction is experienced in the attainment of the ideal; *objectively* a dance is a reality so formed that it becomes a movement symbol expressing and communicating this ideal.

A definition sufficiently broad to include the less highly developed forms, such as tap, folk, group and ballroom dancing, might be stated as follows: A dance is the rhythmic motor expression of feeling states aesthetically valued, whose movement symbols are consciously designed for the pleasure of re-experiencing, expressing, communicating, executing, and of creating form.   —M.N.H'D.

dance as art. The idealistic expression of man's emotional nature transformed by thought and consciously given movement form. Its significance does not change—only its forms have changed revealing changes in man himself, in his times, and in his beliefs, desires and growing sense of artistic values.

—M.N.H'D.

dance drama. A dance that has for its content some definite situation or story. The theme may be simple enough for a dance of a single interest, or sufficiently complex to take on the proportions of a dramatic plot. In either case, the dance movements depend upon a text containing some realistic human interest that kindles the imagination and arouses the emotions. And since the emotions are to be reached through ideas, the movement will be somewhat restricted by the necessity of following rather definite reaction patterns. Such dances are descriptive or narrative in character. (H'Doubler, M. N., *Dance, A Creative Art Experience,* F. S. Crofts & Co., 1940.)

dance music. The simplest accompaniment to the dance was produced by the movements of the dancers themselves, by the stamping of feet and the clapping of hands. These sounds were stressed and amplified by instruments of percussion In contrast to much vocal music which was based on the rhythms of speech, dance music was organized by the natural and periodic body movements of man. Its motor character was intensified by the noises which accompanied it. A pronounced motor impulse would seem to be almost lacking in certain Eastern dances which depend entirely on expressive and significant gestures for their effect.

When song accompanied the dance, it ceased to be recitation. The words frequently declined in significance, and nonsense syllables became more frequent as the rhythmic element assumed greater importance. As the beat of moving feet dictated the metric structure of dance music, so the figures of the more highly organized dances outlined the form of dance melodies. As steps forward are balanced by steps to the rear, so phrases in the melody must correspond in symmetry.

Once the musician had constructed his dance tune, the desire for variety led him to alter the too frequent repetitions of the melody by improvisation. Such practices ultimately passed into musical composition in the form of divisions over a bass such as *La Folia,* in the passacaglia, in sets of variations on folk-dance themes. Sequences of different dances which pleased both the dancers and the musicians permitted the latter to follow a stately pavane by a lively galliard, a *Tanz* by its *Nachtanz,* often by merely altering the metric basis of the melody. This development led to the classic suite with its varied sequence of dances, allemande, courante, sarabande and gigue (qq.v.).

There was always a natural tendency for the musician to treat dance music from a musical rather than a dance point of view. Thus we find Elizabethan variations on simple dance airs which rise to such a degree of complexity as to completely rob the tune of its energetic rhythmic character. Dancers ceased to move to the music of the pavane, the allemande, the minuet. Musicians have clung to these forms long after they have been forgotten by the dancers. Thus music has been enriched by many compositions which were not intended for dancing though they preserve dance characteristics to a greater or lesser degree. Even where music's connection with the dance is not shown by the title, characteristic melodic traits, or rhythmic pattern, it is still the dance which first employed those basic and powerful pulsations which animate and underlie all modern instrumental music. It was this great fructifying influence of the dance that Wagner had in mind when he spoke of Beethoven's Seventh Symphony as the "apotheosis of the dance." —C.W.H.

dance of death. A cultural folk drama in the allegorical pageants of the Middle Ages—developed from the death complex so prevalent at this time. Medieval man lived in constant dread and contemplation of death in the midst of daily exposure to the ravages of war, famine, and plague. There was no conception of the consolation of death. They only knew its horrors and expressed their feelings in the concrete embodiment of death in its most gruesome aspects. Death was personified as a skeleton to convey terrifying ideas about death's punishment for sin. The *dance of death* motive was a very popular theme of the writing and art of this period. Its basic theme—the leveling process that makes all men equal—has continued through the Renaissance to our times, each age expressing it according to its own philosophy. (H'Doubler, M. N., *Dance, A Creative Art Experience,* F. S. Crofts & Co., 1940.)

Danish art. See SCANDINAVIAN ART.

Danish porcelain. See CERAMICS II.

Dante chair. See FURNITURE.

Danube school. See AUSTRIAN ART.

dark raw umber. See iron pigments.

Daseian notation. See MEDIEVAL MUSIC.

daub. *n.* A sticky application, **as of mud or** plaster. *v.* To smear or coat with something sticky; to plaster. (**Wattle-and-daub construction:** A wattle, or frame of poles and twigs platted together and covered or daubed, **as** with mud or plaster). —J.M.M.

dead-end street. See CIVIC PLANNING.

decalcomania. *Cer.* Process of transferring decorations to ware See Ceramics I.

decandenza. See FURNITURE.

decentralization; decentralizing, etc. See CIVIC PLANNING.

de cuenca. See CERAMICS I.

de cuerda seca. See CERAMICS I.

deckle. *Book.* The unfinished edge of paper. In handmade paper this was the natural result of the frame in which the paper was made.

declamation. The correct enunciation of the words in recitative and dramatic music.

decoration, decorative. (L. *decus,* ornament). A mode of **composition** (q.v.) in art, in which details are arranged in such a way as to please, or with the intention of pleasing, the beholder through direct perceptual experience; especially through the nature and arrangement of sensory qualities such as lines, colors, rhythms, etc. The term is applied chiefly in the visual arts, but is sometimes extended to music and literature. It is sometimes identified with "aesthetic quality", in a narrow sense, as contrasted with representation, utility, meaning, content, etc. Decoration can be very simple, as in a plain color-area or the tone of a bell, or can be developed thematically (see theme) into complex pattern and design. It can be merged with other factors in aesthetic form, such as utility and representation, or can be applied separately as superficial ornament.
—T.M.

decorative art. All phases of art utilized as a means of ornamentation, enrichment, or decoration; sometimes called **applied art**; (for example, a fire screen may be decorated with ornament for artistic effects rather than as a structural necessity; a mural painting for the enrichment of a wall space in a building is a product of the decorative arts; many results of the handcrafts and industrial arts may be classed as decorative art products.) Whitford and Winslow in *Dictionary of Education.*

decrescendo. See crescendo.

Deësis. See RELIGIOUS PAINTING IN RUSSIA.

deflector. (1) A device to cause deflection. (2) In southwestern archaeology: The term applied to the raised stone, mass of poles and mud, or mass of masonry, located between the fire pit and the "ventilator". Known also by the terms "altar" and "fire screen". (Some archeologists believe the "ventilator" served to conduct air into the chamber and that the "screen" or "deflector" was constructed or placed to prevent the incoming current of air from blowing directly onto the fire. Others are of the belief that the so-called "ventilator" was thought to be the entrance and exit of the spirit beings and that the so-called "deflector" was an "altar").—J.M.M.

"degenerate" art (Ger. *Entartete Kunst*). A term used by the Hitler party to condemn modern art. According to Hitler and his followers, modern art is the expression of "political and cultural anarchy" and "art-bolshevism" and hence must be ruthlessly suppressed. In July 1937 an exhibit of modern art (for adults only) was opened in Munich (later travelling all over Germany) under the name of *Entartete Kunst*. This exhibit was supposed to reveal the decadence of modernism and thus to serve as a warning example. The works of the following artists, among others, were contained in the exhibition: Otto Dix, Emil Nolde, Franz Marc, Paul Klee, Marc Chagall, Oskar Kokoschka, Karl Hofer, Vasily Kandinsky, Max Beckmann, George Grosz, Lyonel Feininger, Lovis Corinth and Paula Modersohn-Becker.

In the same spirit of destruction, German museums and galleries were "purified" i.e. all modern paintings were removed and many of them sold outside of Germany e.g. works of van Gogh, Gauguin, Picasso, Derain, Barlach, Modigliani, Lehmbruck as well as works of the artists mentioned above. See GERMAN ART. —H.H.

de gustibus non est disputandum. See TASTE.

Delft ware. See CERAMICS II.

deliberate forgeries in painting. See FORGERIES IN PAINTING.

Delphi. Shrine of Apollo in central Greece, famous throughout the ancient world for its oracle, the Pythian games, and the buildings and sculpture dedicated to the god. It was excavated by French archeologists in the last decade of the 19th cent. Among the most important buildings were the Temple of

Apollo, the Siphnian Treasury (the first building to be decorated with two types of relief sculpture, one in low lateral relief, the other in three-dimensional mass), the Athenian Treasury, the Lesche of the Cnidians, with its famous murals of Hades and the Sack of Troy by Polygnotus, a graceful circular temple, the theatre and the stadium. Among the independent sculpture found are an archaic sphinx and kouroi, a 5th cent. bronze Charioteer, a figure of the athlete Agias (possibly a copy of an original by Lysippus), and three dancing maidens in the Praxitelean tradition, placed back to back on a high acanthus column. See T. Homolle et al, *Les Fouilles de Delphes.*
—W.R.A.

Demeter (L. Ceres). Greek goddess of the earth and harvest, symbolized by ears of grain, a basket of plenty, a pig, poppies. In mythology she is chiefly known for her sorrowing quest after her daughter, **Persephone (Proserpina)** was abducted by Pluto; the story personifies the death of vegetation. The most famous statue of her in ancient times was the 4th cent B.C., Demeter of Cnidus, a seated figure of the classical "mater dolorosa". In later sculpture she was pictured by Permoser, Dannecker, Jannewein, Fry and Storrs. In Bernini's *Rape of Persephone* the daughter of Demeter struggles with a very determined Pluto. —W.R.A.

demi relief. See relief sculpture.

demi-semi-quaver. See NOTATION.

dendrochronology. A method of dating ruins in the Southwest, originated by Dr. A. E. Douglass. It is based on the theory that trees each year add a ring of growth whose thickness is dependent upon the rainfall. Thus the trees of the same species and same locality will form a definite pattern. By matching and overlapping the ring patterns of the outer side of the older and the inner side of the younger trees, Dr. Douglass gradually worked backward in time and charted these patterns into a master ring calendar for certain areas of the Southwest, extending as far back as 11 A.D. By means of this calendar any beam of the same species and locality can be dated. See A. E. Douglass, *Dating Pueblo Bonito and Other Ruins in the Southwest,* National Geographic Soc., Pueblo Bonito Series 1 (1935); "The Secret of the Southwest Solved by Talkative Tree rings", *National Georgraphic Magazine* (Dec., 1929).—H.G.

dengaku (Jap.). A classic dance, now rare.

denim (F. *serges de Nimes*). A heavy coarse cotton twill weave. The warp is blue or brown with a white weft; washable.

dentils. A series of small, rectangular blocks projecting like teeth, as under Ionic and Corinthian cornices.

Der Blaue Reiter. See expression.

descort. See MEDIEVAL MUSIC.

design. (It. *designare,* which Hoare's *Italian Dictionary* derives from L. *de, signum,* to show by marks). (1) Fundamentally, the word seems to imply some application of drawing to the production of art, but it has spread over a wide range of derivative meanings. It can be applied not only to sketches but to far more complete works, which may have been produced by techniques as distantly related to drawing as painting and carving in wood. It may even be transferred, by analogy, to still more remote arts, as in speaking of the design of a symphony or of Dante's *Divine Comedy;* but there is probably a tendency to restrict it to work with a framework so simple and so definite that it could almost be outlined with a pencil. In modern usage the word refers oftener to some such framework than to a completed work—occasionally, as in the cases just cited, to the framework which an experienced observer can detect in the finished product but usually to the one that the artist himself uses as a sort of scaffolding to aid his work. It may exist only in his mind but, in the arts of space at least, he is more likely to make some record of it and it is this record that the word most commonly denotes. Ideally, it will be a graphic, shorthand solution of the intricate problem in relationships which the contemplated work presents—relationships between those aspects of his medium that he can modify and those that he cannot, such as its heaviness and solidity; relationships with the tools and processes by which this medium must be worked, and to the various uses to which the finished object will be put; relationships to the memories and character and desires of the special public for which it is intended; and finally the relationships between the flexible elements of the design itself—line, shape, color, mass, and light—which will give the work its distinctive aesthetic quality. A good design may be defined as one that allots to each of these relationships a weight proper to the task in hand and combines them all agreeably and as efficiently as possible. If the problems to be solved are more practical than aesthetic, as in designing a house, the solution is often called a **plan**; when the relationships involved are mainly internal, a **pattern**; and when, as in representative painting, the basic problem is the distribution over the canvas of the objects to be depicted we usually refer to the process of designing as **composition.** Certain arts, of course, have their individual traditions in the matter of terminology, which cannot be attributed to any universal customs. A three-dimensional sketch in clay for a piece of sculpture is called a **model**; a design for a tapestry is a **cartoon**; and we speak of the **choreography** of a dance. In the vocabulary of dancing **design** usually refers to costumes and stage-sets. Pepper has tried to differentiate design from **pattern** by defining the former as that aspect of a work which has been dictated by the laws of *interest* and the latter as the aspect which has been dictated by the laws of *attention*, but as yet this distinction has not been widely adopted. The earliest stage in the evolution of a design is sometimes called laying in or blocking in. For Ralph M. Pearson the design in such arts as painting is never finished until the work itself is; he uses the word as if it were essentially a synonym for form. There can be no question, however, that in most of the handicrafts design has to be sharply contrasted with treatment, or execution. And in modern machine production this contrast is intensified, because so many details that could formerly be left to the discretion of the workman must now be carefully prescribed in advance. It should be noted, too, that the mass-production that has come in with the machine has raised to a new importance the economic factors that influence design, such as cost of production, possible selling price, and the necessity of competing with a great number and variety of other machine-made products.

The tangible form which a design assumes varies considerably from one art to another, and so does its relation to the finished work. A design for a decoration to be applied to a piece of pottery may be sketched on paper but it will have to be translated by the artist into a form that will fit a curved surface. A design for a building will be a set of highly abstract cross-sections, sprinkled with numbers and arbitrary symbols, and supplemented with various elevations, perspective views, and written specifications, all of which will have to be interpreted with great skill and knowledge by a succession of contractors, subcon-tractors, and workmen. A design to be woven into a bolt of cloth may begin with a single colored sketch on paper, but it will have to be expanded by a draftsman into a technically complete repeat pattern and then translated—under the influence of the machine—into a set of perforated cards whose resemblance to the finished product will be very remote. A design for a painting, on the other hand, may be sketched very quickly on the canvas with charcoal, and modified endlessly as the picture evolves. When the artist is to be craftsman as well as designer he can limit his design to the scantiest network of lines and colors in which he can fix the special combination of relationships which he deems indispensable to his solution of the problem in hand.

As the proper management of the internal relationships in a design is an exceedingly complex and difficult business a number of formulas have been worked out to help the artist plan his efforts and check his results. They are commonly referred to as the **principles of design**, and they might be described as those subordinate types of organization which stand out most clearly within the organization of the whole work. It is rare to find any two lists of these principles that agree, but harmony, rhythm, repetition, symmetry, balance, proportion, dominance, subordination and variety may be cited as typical of the group. Like the major elements of verse structure—length of lines, number of lines, accents, and rhyme patterns—they may be combined in a great variety of ways, but it should be noted that they are far more likely to merge and to lose their individuality than are their counterparts in the field of verse. It is safer to think of them as rules-of-thumb for achieving some other end than as ultimate values in themselves. The term **elements of design** is more likely to be applied in the spatial arts to such tangible units or ingredients as walls, doors, windows, and roof in architecture, or color, light, and line in painting. The **motif** of a design is, roughly, the equivalent of a theme in music. It may be borrowed from nature—from the shape of an insect or the color pattern of a flower—or it may be a simple combination of lines and colors invented for the purpose, or merely some rhythmic pattern of spots and spaces. It might be described as a design for a design. See also decoration, dynamic symmetry, and the individual arts. Detailed analyses of various problems in design may be found in Harriet and Vetta Goldstein, *Art in Everyday*

Life; Lewis F. Day, *Pattern Design;* Walter D. Teague, *Design This Day.* —C.T.

(2) *Mus.* Artistic intention embodied in a composition; structural plan of a composition; characteristic outline, or contour, of a composition or of a particular aspect thereof (e.g., melodic design, motive design, contrapuntal design, etc.). —E.K.

design experience. (art ed.) (1) Practice in planning structural forms, such as in the relationships of space and mass in painting or architecture; (2) practice in creating unified expression in any medium of art; (3) practice in creating surface decoration; (4) the second stage in the development of a unit of teaching in art, the preceding stage being orientation. See design. Whitford and Winslow in *Dictionary of Education.*

desornamentado style. See FURNITURE.

de Stijl (Dutch, the style). A geometric-abstract movement in the visual arts and architecture, characterized by rectangles and primary colors, founded in Holland in 1917 by Theo Van Doesburg, and lasting until about 1931. The leading painters were Piet Mondrain and Doesburg, leading sculptor Vantongerloo, and leading architects J. J. P. Oud and Rietveld. The movement had a strong influence on industrial and commercial arts. —L.D.L.

deus ex machina (L. *deus ex machina,* god from the machine). In Greek tragedy, the device of introducing a deity at the end of a play to resolve the situation; from the term applied to the mechanical device in the theatre by which the actor impersonating the deity appears from above the level of the other actors. —L.T.S.

Deutscher Werkbund, (D.W.B.) A German association (founded 1907) of artists, architects, industrial designers, manufacturers, and writers which, by means of publications, meetings and exhibitions worked towards an integration of the various groups and directions of the moderns. Recognizing the importance of machines in all the various fields of modern industrialized society, the *Werkbund* emphasized the fact that high quality (*Qualität*) is not restricted to handicraft, but is compatible with standardized machine production. The efforts of the *Deutscher Werkbund* contributed greatly to the formation of the modern style and it was this organization which made the public familiar with it (e.g. the *Werkbund* exhibit at Cologne, 1914).

The example of the German association inspired the founding of a *Werkbund* in Austria (1910) and in Switzerland (1913), the reorganization of the Swedish *Slöjdsförening* (1910-1917), and the founding of the English "Design and Industries Association", D.I.A., (1915).

The names of Herrmann Muthesius and Alfred Lichtwark are of importance for the development of the German *Werkbund.* Muthesius, who was instrumental in bringing about the organization of the *Werkbund,* was a member of the German embassy in London from 1896 to 1903 and was strongly influenced by English ideas. Alfred Lichtwar (director of the Hamburg *Kunsthalle*), who greatly admired English architecture, must be mentioned here not only in connection with the *Werkbund,* but also because he exerted a very great influence upon the reformation and spreading of art education in Germany. Thanks to the efforts of Muthesius and Lichtwark modern architects and artists were appointed to head art academies and art schools (e.g. Peter Behrens, Düsseldorf; Pölzig, Breslau; Bruno Paul, Berlin; Henry van de Velde [a Belgian], Weimar). This policy was continued and expanded under the German Republic and during the period 1918-1933 many of the outstanding modern artists were teaching in art academies or similar institutions (e.g. Hofer, Kolbe, de Fiori in Berlin; Baumeister, Beckmann in Frankfort; Campendonk in Crefeld; Paul Klee at the *Bauhaus* and in Düsseldorf; Otto Dix, Kokoschka in Dresden; Otto Müller, Molzahn, Kanoldt in Breslau; Rohlfs in Hagen; Schrimpf in Munich; Schlemmer at the *Bauhaus* and in Breslau). One of the most important appointments was that of Walter Gropius to the Weimar art schools (1919) which he reorganized and amalgamated into one institution—*Das Staatliche Bauhaus Weimar* (q.v. Bauhaus). See also GERMAN ART. See H. Muthesius, *Die Werkbundarbeit der Zukunft,* 1914 and *Der Werkbundgedanke in den germanischen Ländern, Österreich-Ungarn, Schweiz, Holland, Dänemark, Schweden, Norwegen,* 1914; N. Pevsner, *Pioneers of the Modern Movement from William Morris to Walter Gropius,* 1936; W. Riezler, *Die Kulturarbeit des deutschen Werkbundes,* 1916; H. Waentig, *Wirtschaft und Kunst,* 1909. The official publication of the *Werkbund* is the periodical *Die Form,* vol. 1, 1925. —H.H.

deva (Skt.). A divine being.

devaloka (Skt.). See stupa.

devarāja (Skt.). See INDIAN ART. See SOUTHEASTERN ASIATIC ART.

development. *Mus.* See sonata.

devotional image. Any religious painting or sculpture made for purposes not of the cult but of private worship, no matter whether or not such purpose entails a modification of formal and representational character. In the case of Western medieval art devotional images, usually assumed the course of either the vivification of images of the cult or of the isolation and intensification of emotional traits found in historical narratives. By either process a humanization of the image was attained which made it easier for the individual worshipper to enter into an emotional relation with its subject. In their turn many emotional images are descriptive of visionary experiences which had been achieved through a sympathetic concentration upon isolated aspects of sacred history. See pieta; Christ and St. John; man of sorrow. —R.B.

devotional ring. See JEWELRY.

dexter side. See HERALDRY.

dextrin. This adhesive has an accessory use in the arts much like that of paste. Like paste, also, it is derived from starch, though when finally prepared it is a mixture of soluble starch with true dextrin and sugar. It has strong adhesive properties. —G.L.S.

dhāranī (Skr.). See stupa.

dharmacakra mudrā (Skr.). A mystic gesture symbolizing the wheel of the law or the gesture of preaching. Both hands against the breast. Left-hand palm inward, fingers bent. Right hand palm outward, fingers bent, certain fingers touching. —J.A.M.

dhoti (Skr.). Indian garment of muslin. A long loincloth draped so as to produce the effect of short trousers.

dhyāna mudrā (Skr.). A mystic gesture symbolizing profound meditation. Usually, hands in lap, three fingers extended, right overlapping left, index finger bent and touching thumbs. Sometimes, all fingers extended only thumbs touching. —J.A.M.

diabolus in musica. See tritone.

diadema. See tiara, papal.

Diadoumenos (Gr. from *dia + deo,* to bind, to fasten). Name given to a statue by Poly-

kleitos listed by Pliny in his Natural History XXXIV, 55. The work represents a youth binding his hair with a fillet. There exist several replicas, the best of which is owned by the National Museum of Athens. The lost original is generally dated at about 430 B.C. For illustration see Gisela Richter : *The Sculpture and the Sculptors of the Greeks,* 1929, Figs. 650-652. —L.L.

diagrammatic diagram. See drawing.

diagrammatic drawing. A form of drawing practiced by scientists or those whose intention is merely to inform the observer.

Diaguite culture. See PREHISTORIC ART.

Diana. See Artemis.

diaper. In the 15th cent. *linge d' Ypres.* A fine cloth with small geometrical pattern. Originally a silk fabric from the Orient, usually white, used for ecclesiastical vestments. Now linen or cotton with simple woven allover pattern. —G.W.R.

diaper pattern. Generally, an allover repeat design of floral or geometric motives.

diaphony (**organum**). See MEDIEVAL MUSIC.

diaphragm walls. Walls, the primary purpose of which is to give rigidity to construction.

Diasmetic notation. See NOTATION.

diatonic. (1) One of the three ancient Greek musical genera : diatonic, chromatic, enharmonic. (2) Any chord, interval, note, or progression confined to the tones of *one* major (or minor) key or scale. See scales and modes.

dichroism. See COLOR.

Die Brücke. See expressionism.

Dienst (pl. *Dienste,* Ger.). The term refers to the long thin shafts—circular, semicircular, etc. in shape—which, primarily in German Gothic architecture, are arranged around a column and which serve the purpose of supporting and strengthening the column in bearing the thrust of the vaulting. The *Dienste* usually have base and capital. In late Gothic the capital is omitted and the *Dienste* join directly with the ribs of the vaulting. A pier with *Diensten* can best be compared with a clustered pier. —H.H.

Die Scholle. The name of a group of Munich artists who (beginning ca. 1899) exhibited together and were prominent in the first decade of the 20th cent. Their work is characterised by an emphasis upon clear, strong colours and large, simplified shapes which are used to depict allegorical or idealized figures and scenes (e.g. Fritz Erler's decorative paintings in the *Kurhaus* in Wiesbaden). The best known members of the *Scholle* were the brothers Erler, Georgi, Münzer and Putz.
—H.H.

Dies irae. See sequence.

diffraction colors are the colors of the spectrum as obtained by a diffraction grating.

digital. A key on the keyboard of an organ, pianoforte, harpsichord.

diluent. In paint technology a distinction is usually made between a fluid which will dissolve a film material such as oil or resin and one which will dilute another fluid already formed through such solution. The latter, called a diluent, can be described only in relation to certain specific materials. Petroleum naphtha, for example, is a solvent for dammar resin; i.e., it can disperse all of that solid and hold it as suspended matter, but it is only a diluent for mastic resin. —G.L.S.

dime novel. A generic name for inexpensive tales of adventure, combat, or mystery first published by Erastus F. Beadle in the U. S. in 1860 and immensely popular until 1915. Sneered at by literary critics and reprobated by moralists, these brief historical tales of the Liberty Boys in the American Revolution, of Indian warfare under such leaders as Buffalo Bill (William F. Cody), of romantic love carried on under frontier handicaps were composed by writers of at least second-rate ability in conformity to a strict moral code. Nick Carter, master detective, became a universal hero; Frederick van Renssalaer Dey, the author, said of his 1,000 tales, "I never in my life wrote a 'Nick Carter' that I would be ashamed to read to a Bible class." William Patten under the pseudonym, "Burt L. Standish," created the most popular athletic hero, a possessor of all the manly virtues, Frank Merriwell. The tales ran from 15,000 to 75,000 words, were printed on cheap pulp paper with a colored poster on the cover, were sold from 5 to 25 cents a copy, and usually were issued in a series once a week. In recent years they have been replaced by the pulp magazines (q.v.). Edmund Lester Pearson, *Dime Novels,* 1929. —H.R.W.

diminished. *Mus.* **Diminished interval:** A minor interval contracted by a chromatic semitone. **Diminished chord:** A chord, the highest and lowest tones of which form a diminished interval. **Chord of the diminished seventh:** A chord consisting of three minor thirds.

diminuation *Mus.* The repetition of a theme in notes of smaller time-value.

diminuendo. See NOTATION.

diminutives. See HERALDRY.

dinanderie. Decorative objects of brass, copper or bronze used for ecclesiastic and domestic purposes, such as those made in the 13th and 14th cents. at Dinand (now Dinant), Belgium. See METALWORK. —R.L.W.

Dionysian. See Apollonian and Dionysian.

Dionysus (L. Bacchus). A Greek fertility god, symbolized chiefly by wine and worshipped with ecstatic dances by his devotees, the Bacchantes, Maenads and Thyiades. His chief attributes were the wine cup, the thyrsus (a staff ending in a pine cone), and the grapevine and cluster. On a great number of vases, especially 5th cent. B.C., Athenian drinking cups, he was pictured with his accompanying Satyrs, Silens, and dancing girls, especially by the Brygus painter. In classical sculpture he was represented as a child being carried by Silenus or Hermes (as in Praxiteles' famous group at Olympia), as a bearded god somewhat resembling Zeus, or as a blithe youthful divinity. In later painting he was pictured by Leonardo, Titian and Tintoretto; and in sculpture by Michelangelo, Sansovino, Tacca, Begas, Carl-Nielson and Paul Manship.
—W.R.A.

diorama. See STAGESETTING.

diota (Gr. *diotos* fr. *di-,* twice +*otos,* ear). In Greek, any vase with two handles, but usually an amphora (q.v.).

diploïdion (Gr. *diploidion* fr. *diploös,* twofold). Greek term for a woman's chiton with a double fold above the waist, in which the outer piece hangs loose.

dipping. *Cer.* Application of glaze by emersion. See CERAMICS I.

dipteros. See HELLENIC ART.

diptych. Two panels, generally designed as a

single composition. Used generally in connection with Japanese prints. *Book.* A folding writing tablet; a double codex, folding. See EARLY BOOKBINDING AND FINE BINDING.

Dipylon pottery. Athenian geometric vases, made in the 9th and 8th cents. B.C., are called Dipylon ware because they were found in the cemetery near the Dipylon Gate. They represent the finest examples of the Greek geometric style, which was brought to the Mediterranean by the northern invaders during the heroic age. These superb amphorae, over six feet high, were doubtless used as tributes at tombs. They are decorated with horizontal bands of geometric patterns (meander, zigzag, lozenge) and friezes of human and animal figures, likewise schematized in design, the men with triangular torso and angular silhouette. The drawings, in black on the terracotta background, represent for the most part battle scenes and funeral rites.   —W.R.A.

directed activity. (art ed.) Experience with information and materials of art that is guided or controlled or supervised by the teacher. Whitford and Winslow in *Dictionary of Education.*

directing line. See PERSPECTIVE.

direction (in dance). See movement.

Directoire style. See FURNITURE.

director. *Motion pictures.* Theoretically the actual "author" of the film, supervising every process of production from the writing of the script to the final editing; more frequently in practice, the director's work is confined to the supervision of the actors and the placing of the camera.   —I.B.

direct painting, school of. See POST-REVOLUTIONARY PAINTING AND SCULPTURE IN THE U.S.A.

direct projection method. See PERSPECTIVE.

discant (discantus). See MEDIEVAL MUSIC.

Discobolos (Gr. from *diskos+ballo*). The disc thrower. A famous statue by the Greek sculptor Myron of Eleutherai representing an athlete about to throw a quoit. The original is lost but the statue is preserved in several Roman copies. It is known for the new transitory movement of the body. The original probably dated from about 450 B.C. For illustration see Gisela M. A. Richter, *The Sculpture and Sculptors of the Greeks,* 1929, Figs. 578-582, and 583 on page 156.   —L.L.

disguised balance. See balance.

dispersion circle. See COLOR.

dissolve, the. See cutting.

dissonance. See consonance, dissonance.

dissonant interval. See interval.

distance (in dance). See movement.

distance of the picture. See PERSPECTIVE.

distance point. See PERSPECTIVE.

distemper. A method of painting which uses an egg emulsion as a binding medium. The emulsion is made with egg-yolk, size or the white of an egg. Pure distemper as distinguished from tempera makes use of size only.   —R.L.W.

distorted seeing. See PHOTOGRAPHY.

distortion (in dance). Hyperbole of movement, used as overstatement or understatement. Dance, like all the arts, distorts or exaggerates its medium that there may be a heightening of forces as a more effective stimulus, thus adding to its powers of expression and communication. To employ distortion artistically the dancer must first achieve an understanding and mastery of the normal. He is then free to deviate from it according to the demands of content and his artistic integrity. Artistically used distortion does not seem ugly or unnatural, for it is necessary to heighten expression of content. H'Doubler, M. N., *Dance, A Creative Art Experience,* F. S. Crofts & Co., 1940.

distribution. *Arch.* Arrangement of the parts, esp. in the interior.

divergent pattern. Definite motives receding from each other and moving from a common center.

divertissement (F. *divertir,* to amuse). *Mus.* (1) A light composition intended for amusement. (2) A medley of well-known melodies. (3) An entr'acte in an opera, i.e., a piece to be played between the acts. (4) In ballet, a single number, or suite of numbers aimed to display dancers, individually or in groups, through short dances, unconnected by dramatic scheme, although sometime set in the pretext of a feast or wedding. In the classic repertory, they are placed as interludes in character situations (gypsies, peasants, children, etc.), or as steps preceding a grand finale or apotheosis.   —L.K.

divisi. A direction for string instruments to play two different parts from the same staff, instead of double stopping.

divisionism. See impressionism.

doctrine of emotions. See MAIN TRENDS IN MUSICAL PERFORMANCE.

dog tooth. A type of ornament common in 13th cent. English Gothic consisting of radiating leaves suggestive of a dog's tooth.

doki (Jap.). Unglazed earthenware.

dolmen. A monument of megaliths suggesting a chamber.

dome. A large-scale cupola (q.v.); a polygonal or hemispherical vault.

domestic. Belonging to the house or household; concerning or relating to the house or family.

domestic architecture. Architecture pertaining to or concerned with the shelter and habitation of the human family group. The word domestic derives from "domus", Latin, for house.

As architecture has been primarily considered the art of designing public buildings serving religious or secular purposes, before the last century only the representational residences of wealthy families, of princes and church dignitaries were benefitted by the trained attention of especially commissioned designers, and then embodied many style characteristics of public or communal structures. Domestic architecture *per se* developed impersonally, and in its anonymity compares with folklore; a popular art production without specifically recorded authorship.

Domestic architecture has its beginning in the primitive furnishing of primeval natural abodes, such as birds' nest-like **bush shelters** and caves. It may be assumed with Violet le Duc and Gottfried Semper that original shelter construction consisted of roofs only, suspended by and affixed to a group of closely standing trees. Such roofs may have consisted of interlaced foliage-carrying branches, a thatching of large leafs of palm treets, aralias and other tropical or sub-tropical plants, or interwoven reeds piled up in several strata. Also the hides of killed game, we can assume, may have served as roofing material. The quickly deteriorable properties of all those items naturally accounts for it that no vestige of such early human dwellings are preserved, but certain similarities may be supposed with the primitive home making of natives in the Australian bush, the tropical woodlands near the upper valleys of African and South American rivers.

Contrasting with the openness of bush dwellings, caves with unmistakable traces of human shelter usage have been found in the moderate zones of the globe, especially in North America, Europe and Africa. The characteristic property of **cave dwellings** is the ease with which their often small outside access can be defended against aggression and weather attack, and the darkness and chill that called for the supplementation of fires built to furnish a minimum amount of light and heat. Only by this supplement the cave shelters were transformed into habitation. The tradition of a controlled room climate was initiated and produced a train of mental and domestic group activities, specifically conditioned by absence of violent air movement and by minimized change of moisture content and temperature.

Natural caves not found in abundance, were substituted for by walled windowless structures in rock, dobe or dirt and even of ice and snow (igloos of arctic tribes). The often clustered structures of neolithic pueblos continuously built and restored by settled native population in New Mexico and in remote arid zones of North Africa and Arabia, serve as examples of this early domestic architecture.

The bush dwelling on the one hand gave rise to the whole category of tectonically framed structures, from the nomadically portable tent of the grasslands with their scarcity of usable tree material, to the lake and lagoon dwellings, perched over the surface of inland- and sea-water in the European Alps or near the shores of Venezuela.

The dobe and natural stone dwelling on the other hand, induced to the techniques of brick making, brick baking, stone cutting and of joining the structural wall elements in stereotomic masonry. Arching of access- and light-openings and vaulting of ceiling spans were further consequences of these techniques and from domestic architecture, and were later adopted by public and communal building design.

Instances of a combination of the tectonic and stereotomic routines of early domestic architecture are found in the use of lintels over exterior openings, of wooden roofs and ceilings born by masonry walls, and in the reed reinforced dirt walls of certain central African tribes.

Due to powerful infantile conditioning of inhabitants, domestic architecture is everywhere until recently characterized by pronounced conservatism and traditional repetition. The solid enclosure of the cave and cavelike dwellings remains for many generations in psychological dominance in all civilizations developing in the temperate and colder zones of the globe. Nervous adaptation to a certain type of sheltered interior and of external appearances expressing it, persist in spite of many technical changes, and even resisting the normal technical evolution.

The **family dwelling**, individually protective and defensible, although unknown in certain collective societies of primitivity, has remained a dominant, if often subconscious ideal in the occidental civilizations, and in the post-Victorian era has tended to an over-individualistic expression. A counter weight to this trend was furnished by the spread of multi-family, cellular apartment buildings in metropolitan areas, which however were devoid of elements expressive of domestic architecture. Modern large scale housing projects, (see housing) and long incipient prefabrication of standard dwellings for the masses of civilized populations, are more recently handled by expert designers, and mark the full fledged entry of industrialization into domestic architecture. Both traditional repetition and individualistic extravagance seem gradually to withdraw and dissolve under the pressure of this newly evolving era in domestic dwelling design.
—R.J.N.

domestic art. See household art.

domicile. A settled place of abode; home, house, or dwelling.

dominant. The 5th note of a major or minor scale. See idiom B(1).

dominant key. A key the tonic of which is either a 5th higher or a 4th lower than that of the principle key. See key.

dominant seventh. The dominant triad with a minor 7th added

dominant wave length. See COLOR.

donsu (Jap.). Figured damask.

dorje (Tibet.). See vajra.

Dorian art. See HELLENIC ART.

Dorian mode. See scales and modes; idiom A(2).

Doric cyma. Term applied to the hawksbeak (q.v.), the regular moulding of the Doric order.

Doric frieze. In classical architecture, the middle member of the entablature, over the epistyle or architrave; in the Doric order an alternation of triglyphs and metopes, two of each to each intercolumniation in Greek architecture, more later.   —L.T.S.

Doric leaf. In Greek architecture, a decorative pattern consisting of a row of contiguous units of broad almost square shape with bottom corners rounded, each with a narrow tongue down the center stopping short of the bottom, and with a narrow border around the sides and the bottom; the regular ornament for the hawksbeak, the chief Doric moulding, also used on the cavetto.   —L.T.S.

dormitory suburb. See CIVIC PLANNING.

Doryphoros. The most famous statue of a Doryphoros (Spearbearer) was made by the 5th cent. B.C. Greek sculptor, Polyclitus; its stalwart form embodies his ideal proportions for the male body (see canon). There are several marble copies of this bronze figure, the best of which is now in the Naples Museum.   —W.R.A.

dosa (Jap.). A painter's sizing made of glue and alum.

dotaku (Jap.). An ancient bell-shaped metal form, the use of which is now unknown. See JAPANESE ART.

double. See RADIO DRAMA.

doublé. *Mus.* French term for turn.

double action harp. See MUSICAL INSTRUMENTS.

double axe. In Minoan Crete, a sacred religious symbol, made of gold or bronze, and represented on pottery, etc.; an axe with a double head of which the deeply concave sides connect the two convex blades which end in points at both ends.   —L.T.S

double bar. *Mus.* The two vertical lines used at the end of a piece, or at the end of some important division of it.

double canon. See canon.

double counterpoint. See counterpoint

double-deck street, highway, etc. See CIVIC PLANNING.

double fugue. See fugue.

double image. Any image that allows simultaneously of two irreconcilable interpretations. Examples : a cloud appearing also as a human face or a mountain appearing as a recumbent lion. Such simultaneity is proper to primitive strata of the mind and therefore manifests itself most persistently in dreams, in the mentality of children and of the insane. In art it is used as an element of playful surprise as well as of the weird and preternatural; for the funny and the uncanny dwell close to each other. A frequent device in primitive and surrealistic art. —R.B.

dovetailing. See TAPESTRY.

doxology. Hymn or psalm in praise of God (Blessed Trinity). The *Gloria in excelsis* in the Ordinary of the Mass is known as the "greater doxology" in contrast to the *Gloria Patri* or "lesser doxology" which concludes the psalms. —V.A.

drafting. See drawing.

dragon. A mythical animal with head of a camel, horns of a deer, ears of an ox, eyes of a hare, heavy eyebrows, beard, bristles, tusks, the body of a serpent with scales of a fish, dorsal spine, serpentine tail, four legs with feet that combine the paws of a tiger and talons of a hawk. In Chinese art, the Taoist symbol of cosmic vitality. See SYMBOLISM IN FAR EASTERN ART. —J.A.M.

dragon's blood. This material is a resin strongly colored purplish red. In the arts this color has probably been its chief claim to use, for it has served as a stain in varnishes. The pure color can be extracted and no doubt has been employed slightly as a precipitated dye or lake pigment. It was definitely known as such to the painters of manuscript illuminations but is no longer listed among artists' colors. —G.L.S.

dramatic lyric poetry. See POETRY.

dramatic oratorio. See ORATORIO.

dramatic poetry. See POETRY.

drawing. The art of representing or delineating an idea, emotion or object by the use of line, tone, or color. A mode of expression making use of symbols or literary ideas. In a strict sense drawing is the most direct means of expressing the beauty of form. **Pure drawing** realizes the abstract character of drawing. It implies that certain ideas about form cannot be expressed by words.

Drawings are usually made with outlines or tones. The purpose of drawing is to express the gesture of the object drawn. The **gesture** is that quality in the object which stimulates the artist to draw. The commonly accepted interpretation of the purpose of drawing is **pictorial representation.** Thus pictorial representation and drawing are often used synonymously. This comparison implies that the aim of drawing is a literal interpretation of the object seen. However, this idea of drawing is not universally accepted. The Oriental conception, for example, implies that drawing is a medium through which the inner-self finds expression. Drawing and writing are synonymous to the Oriental since both allow the individual to express his idea. This point of view was also shared by the Greeks and has its devotees among the artists of the modern school. The Oriental artist develops his idea completely before beginning to draw. The academic school of art is opposed to this conception of drawing. The academician considers good drawing to be an exact representation of the things seen. In this style the artist develops his idea by drawing. This is referred to as **sketching.**

Drawing is similar to composition (q.v.) in that each line or indication of dimension must compose itself in the realization of form.

There are two types of drawing. The first is that which is used by the creative artist to define his ideas. The second type is variously called **mechanical drawing, drafting, engineering drawing** or **precision drawing.** The process is mechanically controlled and imports specific information to the reader. It is made with the use of mechanical devices such as rulers, squares, and compasses. It is called drafting. The mechanical draftsman often sketches without the use of instruments. This is referred to as technical sketching.

The desire for precision in drawing accounts for the term **correct drawing** which is used by artists to denote specific information conveyed through **free-hand drawing.**

Another similar type of drawing is **diagrammatic drawing** such as that practiced by the scientist where the intention is to inform the observer. Although the drawing is freely done it is not intended to be expressive, a minimum of precision being necessary to convey the specific information desired.   —R.L.W.

drawing, architectural. The representation of architectural forms by means of lines.

drawing, memory. Representing an image on a surface through recall, from memory. Whitford and Winslow in *Dictionary of Education.*

drawing, perspective. Representation, on a two-dimensional surface, of two or three-dimensional objects surrounded by space so that they appear in the picture as they do to the eye. (Perspective drawing may be divided into linear and serial types each based upon special principles of representation. Linear representation may be divided into *parallel* or *one-point, angular* or *two-point,* and *oblique* or *three-point* perspective. The terms *curvilinear* and *rectilinear* are also applied to types of perspective drawing.) Whitford and Winslow in *Dictionary of Education.*

Dresden porcelain. See CERAMICS II.

dressed. *In masonry:* The term applied to stone which has been tooled or rubbed to a fairly smooth or even surface.

DRESS, EUROPEAN. INTRODUCTION. The study of man's dress is the study of mankind. Throughout the long and diversified record of human achievement, clothing has kept pace with man's development, leaving in each age a historical and philosophical record.

Over 8000 books have been written about clothing. Too few however have dealt with the subject from a purely scientific or philosophical aspect. The following remarks afford an outline approach to a philosophy of European dress.

Since clothing and adornment concern all peoples of the world, it is little wonder that there are so many different theories expounded concerning its origin. Most writers have their own pet theories. One or more of the following principles are frequently advanced:

1. Protection
   (a) From the elements
   (b) From physical enemies
2. Religious
3. Sex attraction
4. Economic
5. Modesty
6. Aesthetic
7. Social
8. Political

Assuming that adornment preceded clothing, what instinct in man prompted him to decorate his anatomical structure? Was it universal dissatisfaction with his naked form? Or was the cause more deeply rooted?

While each theory in itself invites a interesting argument, it is unsound to assume that any single isolated factor has directly influenced man either to adorn or clothe his body. The aforementioned factors are all so closely interrelated, each having a bearing in one way or another on the evolution of human dress, that exact differentiation is almost impossible.

No matter how time or geography have separated them, all the peoples of the world (past and present) are conditioned by their environment or mental attitude, and have been impelled by similar needs and desires which have led to the adoption of clothing.

Man's inventiveness throughout the ages has conquered condition. As a need arises, whether for bodily protection or spiritual expression, man's inherent skill surmounts the obstacle. He makes for himself tools with which to produce the necessities and comforts of life.

TYPES OF CLOTHING. Climate and occupational pursuits are determining factors as to the type of clothing used.

If intense cold forced man to kill the animal from which he removed the outer covering of fur in order to make a covering for himself, here is the beginning of one type of clothing—protection against the elements.

But does this theory stop here? What happened to man when he first put on this covering of fur? Was warmth all he sought? Or found? Was it reason that made man understand for the first time that the animal he hunted for food was also serving as protection against the elements? Was he awed at the first sight of himself when he donned the skin of the animal, or did he feel a strange magical power rising within? Did he assume some of the animal's attributes with its hide? Or did the animal serving his physical needs suddenly become a sacred being, one to be worshiped? Here are two intermingling influences, the protective and the religious, in man's first garment.

In tropical climates, uninfluenced by the need for warmth, primitive man resorted to body painting and then tattooing. Some of the theories given for undergoing this painful process are permanent identity with the guardian spirit or totem, initiation, courtship and marriage rites. This is a beginning of decorative ornamentation that may be compared to textile or embroidery design.

Man also early discovered that parts of his anatomical structure lent themselves naturally to suspending ornaments. The girdle, necklace, anklet, bracelet, headband, earrings, fitted easily into the hollow structures of the body, which supported the infinite variety of decorative ornament of man's ingenious art invention. The girdle and necklace are regarded by some authorities as the objects from which the skirt, trouser and poncho (later tunic or shirt) developed.

SUPERSTITION. Many of the art inventions of primitive man are the direct ancestors of some of the forms of decoration, particularly jewelry, used by people today. This is most certainly true of charm jewelry. When ancient man strung together the teeth and claws of the animals he hunted, or made himself other forms of "protective ornament", he did so not merely to satisfy his aesthetic sense, or boast his prowess, but also because he was afraid. He wore these because he feared things he did not understand—darkness, spirits, elemental forces—and he derived confidence and protection from the symbols of other strong creatures, later gods. Thus, through superstition, evolved the good-luck token and other forms of jewelry worn all over the world.

From these crude beginnings may be gathered how primitive man set a culture pattern to which each age has contributed.

As civilization advanced and the mental outlook and the physical demands changed, clothing changed. The more activity there was in a given period, the greater the changes in clothing.

BEGINNINGS OF COSTUME IN EUROPE. This, then, advances clothing to the point where it is no longer merely protective or purely adornment, and takes on the form of costume, which implies definite characteristics of an era.

In the panorama of world civilizations, each era and each country brought costumes characteristic of the time and place, running the gamut of man's imagination, and expressing in each age his weakness and power, success and failure, wisdom and folly, simplicity and grandeur, and last but not least, his wealth In peace or war man reaches out in search of beauty, in search of change, seeking to satisfy his soul and reflecting it in his physical appearance.

Time and again, clothes for men and women were practically identical, differing mainly in the manner in which they were worn. For great periods of time in agricultural areas there was little change of style; when it did come it was to man's costume more frequently than to woman's. This remained historically true until the 19th cent., when male garments became semi-static and women's changed radically over short periods. This may have been a direct result of the passing of predominantly rural life, the rise of the factory and its influence on life and the products used.

THE RECTANGLE, THE CIRCLE, AND THE CUT TO FIT. Technically, from the point of view of cut, most garments are constructed on the rectangle, the circle, and the cut to fit.

With the rectangle, the draped costume which adhered to the human form was as full across the body of the garment as at the bottom, and depended on the wearer for its gracefulness. In ancient Egypt, Assyria, Greece and Rome the draped costume was worn, based more or less on the rectangle. Starting with the Egyptian loin cloth, costumes underwent various changes and additions, in tunic, sleeves and mantle. Even when the loin cloth or wrap around skirt of the Egyptians changed to the tunic form, it was still constructed on the rectangle and in later developments, smaller rectangles were attached at one or either side of the armscye to form the sleeves.

The circle, or parts thereof, enables fullness to begin at any given point, and extend to the desired length, culminating in graceful folds. In ancient times the circle was first employed in the Roman toga, which later became elliptical in shape, and in varying degrees the circle has continued right through the centuries as the basic cut of the collar, mantle or cape.

The cut to fit produces a garment shaped to fit a given human figure, and may also employ either the circle or the rectangle or combinations of both. The earliest known representations of the cut to fit are probably in the women's costumes as pictured in the early Minoan art. The garment fits the figure closely, with very small waist, from shoulder to hip, which can only be achieved by skillful tailoring.

WARFARE AND FOREIGN INFLUENCES. Factors that have particularly affected the evolution and change in costume in any era are warfare and foreign influences—political and social principles.

The Romans and the Gauls were in constant conflict. Unaccustomed to the bitter northern climate of the barbarians, the Romans were led to adopt the warmer close-fitting trousers of the Gauls, which they wore under their tunics. The Gallo Romans gradually began to adopt each other's costumes.

With the fall of Rome, oriental influence centered around Byzantium and was reflected in the tunics so heavily weighted with embroidery and richly studded with stones that the rigidity of the fabric prevented it falling into folds.

War followed war, and the next great influence came from the Crusades. These two hundred years of martial pilgrimages took hundreds of thousands of men and women from Europe to the Near East, introducing them to strange new surroundings, clothing, materials and customs. The returning Crusaders brought back to Western Europe clothes totally different from their own, particularly the trouser and coat worn by Asiatic peoples. Magnificent fabrics and a wealth of jewels and metal work of the finest craftsmanship were incorporated into the garments, it was their pride to exhibit to those who stayed at home.

The foreign materials were adapted and embellished by the nobility and the wealthy clergy, and soon were emulated by the increasingly rich middle class and even the poor. Extravagance reached such heights that it became necessary to pass sumptuary laws, intended partly to curb the use of precious metals and jewels and the conversion of wealth into dress, but also partly to preserve class distinctions by limiting rich things to the nobility. As the classes continued to vie with each other or circumvent the existing laws, new restrictions were drawn up throughout Europe, limiting the use of fabrics and trimmings. When even these laws failed in their purpose, others were passed not only prohibiting the use of certain articles of dress, but even forbidding their manufacture.

THE CHURCH AND CHIVALRY. Of all the influences of the 1000 years. succeeding the fall of Rome, none was greater or more all-enveloping than the Church. It regulated the life of all Western Europeans from the cradle to the grave, and even more importantly, after. Eventual salvation, was expressed in Christianity, was to be obtained only by adherence to the Church's rules, and the greater this adherence, the sooner and greater the reward. Men and women turned to the Church, and the age of monasticism reached its height.

Even those not vowed to celibacy emulated or actually strove to achieve saintly existences; a natural expression of this came in clothing.

The flowing robes of monks and nuns were the models for the lay public. From the saints, and particularly the Virgin, women adopted the veil.

The elevation of the Virgin, as the intercessor for sinners, made a profound change in the status of women. The raising of one woman to such a position, the pattern thus set for other women, led to the elevation of womankind to a new position of respect and idealization, the core of the Age of Chivalry.

The relation of the sexes completely altered. Woman was raised to a pedestal, and emerged from the cloistered wife to a position of worldly understanding. Through the next four hundred years, there came an awareness of her womanly charms and although she retained the articles of costume, the robes, the veils, she expressed herself with new freedom in such ways as the low decolletage, and flirtatious arrangements of her draperies.

A prime factor in the evolution of men's clothing during the latter part of these 400 years preceding the Reformation was the development of armor from chain mail to moulded plates. The early link armor had hung loose over the tunics; the fitted plates required padded undergarments. Piece by piece solid metal replaced the yielding chain mail, and little by little men's garments became fitted to the body, heavily padded at the shoulders, thus minimizing the size of the waist. In the end armor completely encased the body, giving it a statuesque figure.

To preserve this heroic figure without armor, garments were stiffened or padded, stitched, puffed, or slashed, while trousers fitted close as tights, or added padding or quilting to make trunks. For the first time a sharp differentiation appeared between the costumes of men and women, and between clothing of Europe and Asia.

THE REFORMATION. With the opening of the 16th cent. there occurs such a sharp change in European costume trends that it is wise to suggest the probable thought shift which brought it about. After a thousand years of protective guardianship by the Church, with the Reformation man began to think for himself, untrammeled by spiritual restrictions. This freedom of thought found expression in increased activity in every direction, exploration, discovery, manufacture, new materials, new uses, and from them all, new costumes.

This same period saw the decline of armor; during the 16th cent. man still preserved the padded and corseted effect in his clothing, now emulated by women to such an extent that it is often difficult at first sight to identify the sex of a waist-length portrait. Gradually, during the early 17th cent. men turned to easier dress, but women retained the corset and hoop to a greater or lesser extent for three more centuries.

Was it social unrest that led both men and women to distort their bodies with artificial restrictions, or was "all the world a stage" and they the players, to exhibit their wealth on their persons?

Queen Elizabeth set the criterion for a whole era, an important emergence of woman as an acknowledged ruling force. She surrounded herself with a male court; she also surrounded herself anatomically with a farthingale, a barrel-shaped frame of Spanish influence, in which she resembled a dressing table in motion. Further, she laced her body flatly into a narrow corset; adorned herself with huge ruff, or upstanding collar; padded roll at the armscye, and stomacher copied from the men. Was this a form of subjugation of the more plentiful physical charms of her ladies until, as she grew older, by sheer wealth of dress she could surpass them to the eye as she did in mind and in rank?

From the age of Elizabeth to the 18th cent., individualism and the expression of personality emerged in full flower. The spirit of "newness" brought with it a new silhouette sequence, each distinctive in form and cut. No longer desirous of accepting anything medieval, woman threw off her trailing robes and concealing veils, and encased her body in a steel corset and iron or whalebone hoop. Over these were laid the rich and elegant fabrics of the Renaissance, and there emerged woman, a funnel-shaped silhouette. The emphasis in woman's dress was from waist to floor, in man's from shoulder to waist.

Although from the 17th cent. on men and women differed in the styles of their garments, nevertheless a certain other resemblance remained paramount until the French Revolution—a tendency toward elegance, lace, ribbons, and the use of other decorations, which increased in richness and profusion in both sexes to a point of effeminate softness, often reflected in the morality of social life. The development of the industries which produced

these elegancies grew with leaps and bounds, and was encouraged by the increased application of the product.

THE FRENCH REVOLUTION. If one retraces step by step the historical events of each period, one discerns that each great social change is preceded by a period in which there seems to be some spiritual recognition of the end of an era, a final flowering, a last ebullience, which expends itself in the refinement of luxuriousness, brilliant colors, fantastic exaggeration, but little real invention, the going-to-seed of the plants of culture before the new sowing.

Such a period existed in the quarter-century preceding the French Revolution. There were three classes, the nobility, the bourgeoisie who aped the nobility, and the common people who mattered not at all, barely covering their nakedness with homespun. Costume reached heights of exaggeration in silhouette and embellishment as false and superimposed as the society itself was superimposed on the restless masses of the people.

The Industrial Revolution had begun its upset of thousand, even three thousand year old traditions of living: machinery and the men to run it were shifting the populace, ruining old industries, creating new. The nobility and the bourgeoise strove to retain their old privileges, and secure advantages from new wealths. The pace of living became more and more artificial, more hectic; fashion followed the will-o-the-wisp of errant whim; living and thinking were chaotic and momentary, "après nous le déluge".

When it came, "le déluge" was so strong, so all-embracing that it changed all society, all customs and all costume with startling abruptness. Almost overnight, costume broke free of the corset, hoop and wig, and long trousers for men made their first modern appearance.

The influence of foreign wars and conquests reflected in the Greek renaissance, in Egyptian and Roman classic décors. Simplicity was the rule, admiration of the human form the base of male and female dress. For about thirty years the active spirit of a world at war kept fashion simplified.

THE NINETEENTH CENTURY. Increasing facilities for travel and communication, commerce, growth of manufacture, the invention of the sewing machine, a desire for knowledge and the availability of fashion magazines, all opened up new horizons for women of the 19th century. Heretofore man had played the dominant role, and was also the arbiter of fashion. From now on a gradual standardization of man's dress develops, while that of woman changes more rapidly.

What brought about this radical. change of dress? Was it the influence of two reigning personalities, Empress Eugenie and Queen Victoria? Or in asserting her new increasing spiritual freedom, was woman still clinging to man? Was she subconsciously accentuating her moulded torso from the waist down, encasing it again in a frame as women had done in the days of the Reformation when first freed of the shackles of medievalism? Was she wearing crinolines, hoops, bustles or pads as a means of distortion in order to attract attention—or was the exaggeration merely a madness of fashion?

The second half of the 19th cent. saw woman entering the economic world. With this new freedom, the distortion of the feminine form gradually disappeared and emancipated woman went forth untrammeled to take her place in the world.

MODERN COSTUME. Fashion in history has had phases of beauty, genius and madness. It has set the tempo of life of each period. It has had spurts of grandeur and simplicity. It has been affected throughout thousands of years by recurring cycles of world events, each manifesting itself in the pattern of life. Perhaps a realization of causes and their effects on costume may be found in the U.S.A. in the present World War II.

American costume begins with the 18th cent. Prior to that the Old World settlers in the New World continued to wear the clothes of the mother country. When their garments wore out they sent back for more, adapting them to their new mode of life. By the 18th cent. the colonists were established in their new homes and acclimated to the life in the New World—a leisure class had appeared to take an active interest in dress.

Costumes of the fashionable gentry were imported from France—Paris being the world center of luxury, leisure, fashion and taste. This leadership began during the reign of Louis XIV and was supported and favorably encouraged by the French Government, and in the past century by the American Fashion Press. It maintained its leadership until the fall of France in June, 1940.

Deprived of Paris leadership, American fashion began emerging on its own and is now beginning to be recognized, heralded and headlined along with other world events in the American newspapers of today. Historically, American Fashion begins with World War II.

CONCLUSION. Thus from man's garments which began as adornment or clothing, costume has evolved. This in turn has developed into one of America's major industries, known today as "Fashion".

Man's dress began with the dawn of civilization. It was invented by man because he needed it. It has survived because man still needs it. It will continue to survive as long as man has ideas and an opportunity to fulfill these ideas.

Man himself has been faced by physical, spiritual, social and geographical obstacles, which he has conquered by means of inherent creative ability. This conquest is written in man's dress throughout history and is expressed by the means and manner in which he invents and adapts materials beneath his hand.

He is standing in the dawn of a new age, an age of Synthetic creative invention. He is discovering the bowels of the Earth; he is discovering the might of the elemental forces. He is discovering a New World in which he will live—but before he can begin to live in this New World, he must first discover himself and his relationship to the new society in which he will live. Through this relationship will emerge the silhouette of the future. See JEWELRY; also *Ancient Egyptian, Assyrian and Persian Costume,* Mary G. Houston and Florence S. Hornblower, 1920; *The Conquest of Culture,* M. D. C. Crawford, 1938; *Customs of Mankind,* Lillian Eichler, 1924; *Costume and Conduct,* John Martin Vincent, 1935; *Descriptive Sociology,* II. Spencer, Vol. 1, London, 1876; *From Nudity to Raiment,* Hilaire Hiler, 1930; *History of Civilization,* J. Lippert, Stuttgart, 1887; *The History of Mankind,* F. Ratzel, New York, 1896; *The History of Human Marriage,* E. Westermarck; *Modes and Manners,* Max von Boehm —trans. by Joan Joshua—Vols. 1, 2, 3; *Modes and Manners of the 19th Century,* trans. by M. Edwardes, with an intro. by Grace Rhys, 1909; *Philosophy in Clothing,* M. D. C. Crawford, 1940; *Sartor Resartus,* Thomas Carlyle, London, 1838; *Studies in the Psychology of Sex,* Havelock Ellis, Philadelphia, 1923; *Women's Wear Daily,* Jan. 20, 1942; Feb. 17, 1942; April 8, 1942.   —P.W.

dressoir. See FURNITURE.

dried brush technique. See CHINESE ARTS.

drive. *Mus.* Devices of composition used to create the impression that a composition, or a section thereof, is moving with determination to certain goals; continuity; particularly applied in climaxes, by accumulating small rhythmic values, increasing speed, harmonic tension, dynamic volume, etc. —E.K.

drolery. The playful use in Gothic art of freely invented scenes or figures to give attraction to the functionally empty parts of architecture, furniture or books. Like other manifestations of medieval "humor" drolery is usually satyric or paradoxical and often borders upon the uncanny and demoniac. It takes the form of (1) scenes composed mainly of bizarre imaginary creatures, (2) animal fables, (3) the reversal of the cast of parts in real life (animal hunting the hunter), (4) jocular description of every day activities. —R.B.

drop folio. *Book.* The number at the bottom of the page of folio identification.

drum. *Arch.* One of the circular or near circular sections that go to make up a column: a circular or polygonal wall carrying a dome or cupola. See also MUSICAL INSTRUMENTS.

drumprinting. A printing process for worsted and woolen yarns in the manufacture of velvet carpets. See velvet.

dry. *Cer.* Insufficient glaze. See CERAMICS I.

drying oils. All the oils used in painting come under this head. Among them are linseed oil, walnut oil, and poppy-seed oil. More recently, though with little invasion of the field of artists' materials, different oils have come on the commercial market—tung oil, soya bean oil, sunflower oil, hempseed oil, and others. These oils have the property of forming, when exposed to the air in thin layers, solid elastic films. The process of drying or setting is largely chemical and can be briefly described as an absorption of oxygen into the complex oil molecule. Various physical changes accompany this: an increase of weight and a slow thickening. The process is a long one, continuing in some instances for a period of many years. Certain optical changes occur with it, often a slight yellowing, particularly if the oil is not exposed to normal light, and a slight increase of transparency. Linseed oil in the final dried film goes by the name, linoxyn. Over a long period it loses some of its elasticity, becoming brittle and subject to the action of moisture. The history of drying oils in the practice of painting has been open

to much dispute. The generally accepted belief of the last two or three centuries has been that the Flemish painters, the brothers Van Eyck, were responsible for its introduction. More recent study, however, has shown that at least in the crafts and certainly in medicine, the drying oils were familiar to the ancient writers, and descriptions of the preparation of an oil varnish—a combination of resin and drying oil—are found as early as the 8th cent. By the 12th cent. such records are numerous and by that time drying oils are mentioned as painting mediums. —G.L.S.

drypoint. *Etch.* A print made by the passage of a sharp point over a copper plate, raising a burr which holds the ink. This burr, which yields a rich velvety dark in printing, gives drypoint its distinctive character and charm. No acid is used; hence the term, drypoint. See PRINTS AND PRINT PROCESSES. —K.K.

drypoint (an intaglio process). *Etch.* Drypoint is a process which does not depend upon an auxiliary in the form of an acid to do the actual spadework. It is nearer engraving than etching.

Drypoint is one of the simplest of the intaglio processes to practice. All that one requires is a bare plate, a point (usually steel), a scraper, an oil stone, a burnisher, and some ink mixed with vasoline to show the progress of the work.

The peculiar beauty of this medium is dependent upon its power of yielding a wonderful velvety richness in the proof. This is due, not to the groove which is cut below the surface, but to the **burr**, or **ridge**, thrown up by the passage of the tool. It is the burr that catches and holds the ink on the surface of the plate during the action of wiping with rag or hand. If the burr is removed with the scraper or becomes worn off in the printing, the line below holds comparatively little ink, and the distinctive quality of the medium disappears. Usually the burr is retained in the heavy passage and removed in the delicate ones. Drypoint has a tremendous range in strength of line, far exceeding anything produced by etching.

The drypoint is extremely fragile, the usual edition being about thirty. If the plate is faced with chromium steel a great number of proofs can be pulled without injuring the delicate burr or any noticeable change showing in the proof. —K.K.

dulce-melos. See MUSICAL INSTRUMENTS.

dulcimer. See MUSICAL INSTRUMENTS.

dummy. *Book.* A book made up of blank sheets, or with title and contents only as sample for size and appearance; generally used in estimate of size, cost, etc.

Duncan Phyfe, 1768-1854, was a native of Loch Fannich, Scotland. Reaching America with his family at sixteen, he was apprenticed to a cabinet-maker at Albany, New York. By 1792 he was established in New York with his own joiner's establishment, marrying shortly afterwards and changing the spelling of his name from Fife. With growing success he established his shop on Partition (now Fulton) Street. During his long and prosperous career he enlarged his shops, added warehouses, employed many workmen, and associated with him in firm membership two of his sons.

As a furniture designer he outranks other American craftsmen of the time, revealing both manual dexterity and artistic taste. Combining Sheraton, Adam, and Hepplewhite grace with the ornateness of French Directoire, he achieved in his earlier work an original synthesis which rooted the European tradition in American soil. As time went on his restraint relaxed and with his **American Empire** he allowed the heavier forms popular at the time to control his style. His finest pieces in the 18th cent. English mode were made by 1814; in a graceful Anglo-French manner by 1825.

His pieces include principally chairs, sofas, and tables. Characteristic motives are lyre forms for chair backs and table supports, parallel rows of beads, acanthus leaves and outward curves on supporting members, and drapery swags. Good proportions are patent in all his best work. His preferred wood was mahogany, usually solid, but veneered on occasion. He also used satinwood, rosewood, even maple, and before his retirement was following the fashion in the employment of black walnut. Choice pieces by the master or his workmen are representative of the best of American furniture in the first half of the 19th cent. See FURNITURE; see C. O. Cornelius, *Furniture Masterpieces of Duncan Phyfe,* 1922; N. V. McClelland, *Duncan Phyfe and the English Regency, 1795-1830,* 1939. —W.S.R.

duocento school. See Florentine school.

duodecimo. See book sizes.

duodecimole. *Mus.* Same as duodecuplet. See scales and modes.

duodecuple scale. See scales and modes.

duplex longa. See NOTATION.

Dura-Europos. City of the Euphrates, in ruins since 265 A.D. Excavations by American and French expeditions (since 1932) discovered, in addition to monuments of Parthian, Hellenistic and early Christian art, the remnants of a synagogue with well-preserved frescoes. These represent stories of the Old Testament and are the only known examples of wall paintings in an antique synagogue. The frescoes painted between 245 and 256 A.D., are significant for their iconography and their stylistic relations. There are, however, wall paintings in the Jewish catacombs: Palmyra (2nd cent. A.D.), Rome (3rd-4th cent. A.D.). See M. Rostovzeff, *The excavations at Dura-Europos,* 1936 and *Dura-Europos and its art,* 1938; M. Aubert, Le peintre de la synagogue de Doura, *Gazette des Beaux-Arts,* 1938; R. du Mesnil du Buisson, *Les peintures de la synagogue de Doura-Europos,* 1939; Elizabeth Hill, *Roman elements in the settings of the synagogue frescoes at Dura, Marsyas,* 1941. —H.Gu.

duration. *Mus.* See NOTATION.

durchkomponieren (Ger.). See thoroughcompose.

Düsseldorf, school of. The term refers to a type of painting (fl. ca. 1830-50) that was closely associated with the Düsseldorf academy of art—one of the centers of *Biedermeier* art (q.v.) The Düsseldorf academy, founded in 1767, was closed in 1805 and reopened by the Prussian government in 1819. Peter von Cornelius was its first outstanding director (1821); he was followed in 1826 by Wilhelm von Schadow with whom the rise of the Düsseldorf school begins.

The style of the Düsseldorf school could be described as a compromise between the heroic-romantic tendencies of the late phase of German Romanticism, especially of the **Nazarenes** (q.v., also GERMAN ART), and the genre painting of Biedermeier art. In the historical paintings, the result of this compromise could be characterized as heroic genre. In landscape painting the landscape is often loaded with "inner meaning", conveyed by means of objects and figures saturated with sentimental associations.

Cornelius and Schadow were both Nazarenes, but Schadow, being an outstanding teacher, did not force his pupils to follow his interests exclusively—thus landscape and genre painting developed somewhat against his intentions. Schadow had carefully worked out a curriculum which, beginning with drawing from plaster casts, proceeded to the study of drapery and the copying of works of great painters. After this, came the study of composition, which began with a drawing of the central idea of the painting to be followed by careful studies of the details from a living model. This procedure—sometimes referred to as Düsseldorf "realism"—was supposed to allow "nature" to serve as a corrective and control during the final working out of the painting. Schadow's method, which was greatly acclaimed, produced in a short time a number of successful painters whose work showed the stamp of the "school", thus spreading its fame. Many of the Düsseldorf pupils were appointed to teach in other academies or at Düsseldorf itself.

Typical of the historical genre are Lessing, Hildebrandt and Bendemann; A. Achenbach represents best the Düsseldorf landscape painting, while Schrödter and Hasenclever are characteristic of the humorous genre. Alfred Rethel, a student of the Düsseldorf academy, is perhaps the only painter who, in his historical paintings, continues the heroic-monumental tradition of the Nazarenes rather than following the trend of the Düsseldorf historical genre painting.

Some of the Düsseldorf painters were strongly influenced by English artists, especially by William Collins and David Wilkie, e.g. Rudolf Jordan, Henry Ritter (born in Canada), Adolf Tidemand (born in Norway).

The Düsseldorf school has exerted some influence upon painting in the United States—its influence can be seen, for example, in the works of Emanuel Leutze, Worthington Whittredge, Albert Bierstadt, Eastman Johnson and others. See Wilhelm von Schadow, *Der moderne Vasari*, 1854; Wiegmann, *Die Künstlerakademie zu Düsseldorf*, 1856; Fr. Schaarschmidt, *Zur Geschichte der Düsseldorfer Kunst*, 1902; K. Koetschau, *Rheinische Malerei in der Biedermeierzeit*, 1926. —H.H.

dust cover. *Book.* The paper cover on a publisher's binding; the same as jacket.

Dutch art. See NETHERLANDISH ART.

Dutch glass. See GLASS AND GLASSMAKING.

Dutch metal. *Book.* In leaf and powder. An imitation of gold for gilding. It has not the depth of color of gold and "goes off."

Dutch porcelain. See CERAMICS II.

Dutch Renaissance. See RENAISSANCE.

dux. See fugue; counterpoint.

dvarāja. God-king. The king or the symbol of the king who rules by divine right as the god's representative.

dye. A coloring matter, to be called a dye as distinct from a pigment, is one which can be used in solution as a stain. The pigment is relatively granular, the color being contained in fixed or definite particles which are suspended in a medium. Dyes are generally organic, chemical compounds, and in the arts until comparatively modern times they were of natural origin; e.g., madder and indigo. The development of coal-tar as a source of dyestuffs has brought into the market an innumerable series of high tinting strength. The greatest use of dyes has been for the coloring of fabrics, but a few have been precipitated on a mineral base and used in that form as painters' pigments. See COLOR.
—G.L.S.

dyeing (AS. *deag,* color or tint). For modern usage all dyes are synthetic. Synthetic dyes were discovered in England by Sir Henry Perkins, developed in Germany, later in the U.S.A. Previous to the 20th cent., animal, vegetable and mineral substances were used directly, or mordanted on material.—G.W.R.

dynamic. The adjective dynamic comes from the Greek word *dynamikos* and means "powerful." Originally it was applied only to physical forces. In philosophy it means the reduction of all existence to a reciprocal relation of moving forces. Since the philosopher Leibniz, this external interchanging play of forces was thought to be related to an analogous procedure in the spiritual being within us. Since the World War this word has been increasingly applied to art, culture, and history. To Spengler, in his *Decline of the West,* dynamic is the essential attribute of the *Faust*ian man, Müller-Freienfels, in his book, *Persönlichkeit und Weltanschauung,* 1919, contrasts the dynamic type of man who looks at the world as being in eternal motion, with the static type. See also Troeltsch in *Die Dynamik der Geschichte nach der Geschichtsphilosophie des Positivismus,* 1919.

In art the word dynamic means the characterizing attribute of those artists who believe that all things are an indefinite interchange of forces influencing each other and who express this belief in their art. The word can also be applied to the works themselves. Generally speaking, one may say that the northern people have a dynamic point of view; therefore their works especially should be called dynamic. One can compare Germanic applied art of the time of the migrations (beginning in 375 A.D.) with their southern originals which served them as patterns and which show a static character. Or one may compare images of the evangelists and Biblical scenes of a static nature originating in the South with those of the Carolingian epoch which are based upon the southern pattern, as can be proved. The result of this transition was a wholly dynamic art.

Besides this general difference between different peoples, each art shows dynamic tendencies toward the end of its development.
—A.J.S.

dynamic sculptures. See SCULPTURE.

dynamics. *Mus.* The scientific explanation of the relative force, intensity or loudness of musical notes. The five main dynamic degrees are: pianissimo, piano, mezzo, forte, fortissimo.

E

Ea. Babylonian god of water, of the arts and sciences, etc.

EARLY AMERICAN ART. When we speak of "early American art" we are commonly referring to the artistic output of the New England colonies before the Revolution, particularly in the field of the so-called plastic arts, architecture, sculpture, and painting.

It is customary in such a discussion to ignore the Amerindians as belonging to an earlier and more primitive culture, requiring special treatment under a separate heading. This is especially reasonable since native forms of art, limited as they were almost exclusively to the Pacific Southwest, exercised no perceptible influence on the artistic development of the early settlers.

Excluded with less reason, perhaps, from a discussion of early American art is what has come to be treated separately as Spanish-American or Latin-American art (q.v.). This again, however, though in a different sense, belongs to a separate culture, which has exercised little or no influence on the artistic development of North America. For the purposes of this discussion, therefore, we shall be concerned only with the narrow strip of land along the Atlantic coast whose history for us begins with the first settlement at Jamestown, Virginia, in 1607.

The civilization of the Atlantic coast of North America had to be built up from the crudest beginnings, and its earliest contributions to art were of necessity also crude. The early English, Dutch, French and Swedish settlers lived a very primitive sort of life, and produced nothing at first which could properly be termed art. Certainly their early dwellings could not be dignified by the name of architecture, even when they abandoned temporary shelters for more permanent structures. By the middle of the 17th cent., however, they were building steep-roofed, gabled houses with overhanging second stories reminiscent of medieval England, and filling them with furnishings and utensils brought from the Old World. Primitive as these still were, they were characterized by good taste generally and had many charming qualities besides.

While the Spaniards were introducing to this continent the mature and often overripe art of the last flowering of the Renaissance in Europe with the object of proclaiming the grandeur and power of Spain, the settlers of the New England colonies were making their own way with little or no cultural or economic aid from abroad. Besides, the early Puritans had no use for art in any form, their emotions finding their only legitimate outlet in religious fervor. Any attempt to please the eye was regarded as a diversion from the main purpose of serving God. But, although it was deliberately excluded from their way of life, innate artistic instincts could not be permanently inhibited, and by degrees, helped by the influx of more liberal elements, a civilization developed in which art increasingly played a part.

Early 17th cent. architecture in the New England colonies was primarily the work of builders and craftsmen who rebuilt from memory on American soil the structures they had known in the Old World. These were substantial and livable in character, as were the houses of medieval England which served as their models. They were similarly well proportioned structures, solid, massive, largely of wood, well adapted to the climate and to existing social conditions. Many of these 17th cent. houses are extremely pleasing to the eye, having not only the charm of simplicity but good proportions and adaptability to use, all attributes of good architecture. While the aesthetic motive did not enter deliberately into their calculations, their builders built as well as they knew how, and among them were men of sound artistic judgment.

Although the British influence predominated, other nationalities left their mark architecturally in certain localities. The French in 1608 established themselves in Canada, at Quebec, and a century later (in 1718) at New Orleans, where they developed a cavalier civilization based upon social and economic conditions much more affluent than prevailed in the New England states. The Dutch, settlers of New Amsterdam, have also left an architectural heritage which is still in evidence in the New York of today. They followed the architectural patterns of their homeland in tall, narrow brick buildings not entirely suited to their New World environment. The Swedes, who in the middle of the century had a foothold temporarily at the mouth of the Delaware, never got farther than building what were probably the earliest log houses, largely defense structures, which were also patterned after the buildings they had known at home. The Germans likewise in Pennsylvania erected structures which reflected their nostalgic longings for the mode of life they had left behind them in the Old World.

18th cent. architecture in America reflects a greatly advanced standard of living, and the amply proportioned houses of that period were consciously designed with a view to pleasing the eye. These buildings are strikingly different from the unpretentious structures of the 17th cent., although they still reflect British architectural influences and ideals, being classified as **William and Mary, Queen Anne,** and **Georgian,** after the British monarchs whose reigns fall in this period. Many fine 18th cent. houses may still be found today in the Atlantic coast states which are models of good taste in both exterior and interior design. The Colonial Wing of the Metropolitan Museum in New York contains a series of representative interiors of this period.

The most striking example of the beauty of 18th cent. architecture may be seen in the recent reconstruction of Williamsburg, the colonial capital of Virginia, founded in 1690. Restored to its original form, it serves as a great outdoor museum of colonial architecture and civic design. As a monument to the good taste of colonial America, it should inspire future generations to solve their own problems with similar regard for the importance of art in the life of the community.

If the art of sculpture flourished in the colonies it has left no trace, and there is little evidence that sculptors found employment unless it was in the decorative ornamentation of buildings or perhaps in those naive manifestations spoken of as folk art. The figureheads of ships may possibly be regarded as samples of the sculptor's art, but apparently no public monuments were erected in the colonies before the Revolution.

The economic and social conditions which retarded the development of painting were even more effective in delaying the appearance of sculpture as an independent art. The early colonists brought no sculptures with them. Moreover, since sculpture is so largely concerned with the human body, the association of flesh with the devil was sufficient for the Puritans to bar sculpture from their lives.

In the 18th cent. what little there was of sculpture was largely the work of foreign artists. A notable exception was Patience Wright, whose portraits in wax became fashionable during the middle of the century. Occasionally plaster casts of classical statuary were imported from Europe, but largely for the private enjoyment of the well-to-do. The figureheads of William Rush, 1756-1833, were famous in their day, but none of these has survived. Rush was one of the company of those who in 1794 advocated the establishment of an art school in Philadelphia, which project, however, was not realized until 1805, when in Independence Hall seventy-one public-spirited citizens gathered to organize the Pennsylvania Academy of the Fine Arts, historically the oldest art school in the United States.

The number of paintings produced in the colonies is more impressive. Portrait painting did quite a flourishing business in the 17th and 18th cents., but can hardly lay claim to artistic distinction. Worthy of mention, however, are the so-called "primitives," who are highly regarded by those who react favorably to the naive qualities of these unskilled workers. Many of these early portraits bear no signature, but we have today an imposing list of names of persons who painted portraits as a means of gaining their livelihood. Practically all came from abroad, but few of them had ever studied drawing or painting as a preparation for their chosen profession. They were in their day spoken of as **limners,** a term derived from the medieval illuminer or illuminator of manuscripts.

Because of their unique methods no more interesting group of workers is to be found in the annals of American art, and their work is widely collected today both for its historic interest and for its quaint character. Many museums have also included the work of limners in their collections of early Americana because of the important role played by them in the history of American art.

While the early colonists brought few pictures to the New World, they brought with them a tradition of fondness for family portraits. In the 17th cent. relatively few of such portraits seem to have been painted, but in the 18th cent. the limner plied a lucrative trade. While the Puritan fought shy of the emotional upsets which contact with art might bring, he was not above the vanity of employing some itinerant portrait painter to record both his own likeness and those of members of his family, and a good many of these portraits have come down to us from colonial days. The work of the rank and file of these early limners is undoubtedly crude, without any structural solidity or plastic expression. The color is a brown monochrome and the technique is lacking in spontaneity and life. Considering the methods employed, however, this was inevitable. The winter months were spent at home in their studios in the preparation of numerous stock portraits in which everything was completed but the face. In the summer they went on the road, calling upon prospective patrons and visiting plantations and estates, where they were usually sure of finding a welcome. A single sitting commonly sufficed to complete a portrait, and the price was accordingly modest. They worked rapidly, and often earned a good income. They did not hesitate to advertise in the manner of the modern purveyor of medical panaceas, and they took every advantage of the opportunities offered by the New World.

The honor of being the first painter in the colonies goes to Capt. Thomas Smith who did a self-portrait in 1690 and a portrait of Major Thomas Savage inscribed 1679. William Dunlap, himself a painter of moderate ability but a faithful chronicler of the limners, many of whom he knew personally, in 1834 published his two volumes entitled *A History of the Rise and Progress of the Arts of Design in the United States.* In this work he accounts for the interesting company of those who constitute our Primitives—although it must be understood that their performance is not comparable to that of the Italian Primitives, who were craftsmen and artists of a high order. Mr. Dunlap's voluminous two volumes have recently been condensed and revised to include more recent discoveries, and this work will doubtless continue to be the most important source of information in regard to our earliest painters.

As in the case of architecture, painting gradually improved, and the work of the portrait painters who immediately followed the limners occasionally approached professionalism in quality. Robert Feke (1705-?), Matthew Pratt (1734-1805), John Smibert (1688-1751), John Greenwood (1727-1792), John Wollaston, ygr. (1672-?), John Hesselius (1726-1778), Joseph Blackburn (?), and Charles Willson Peale (1741-1827) show qualities in their work which entitle them to a higher rating than that accorded the limners, and thus prepare the way for the emergence of a group who may be called our first professional artists.

In the 18th cent. a number of really outstanding artists emerged, all American born, whose work belongs only partly to the period under discussion, since their lives and careers carry over into the post-Revolutionary era. These were John Singleton Copley (1737-1815), Benjamin West (1738-1820) and Gilbert Stuart (1755-1828). Copley, a Bostonian before his departure for Europe in 1774, had prospered at home as a portrait painter, and his numerous portraits of colonial dignitaries, divines, merchants, and their womenfolk are by far the best pre-Revolutionary portraits produced in America. When he settled in London, he came under the influence of the British masters Reynolds and Gainsborough, but while his later portraits are marked by greater refinement of form and color, they lack the sturdiness and objective power of his work done in the colonies. Copley also painted numerous historical canvases, among them *The Death of Lord Chatham,* which helped to establish his reputation in England.

Copley's methods were slow, and he required many sittings. His work, as a consequence, lacks spontaneity, although his compositions are occasionally lively and his color gay, particularly in the accessories.

Whereas Copley was a solitary figure and avoided public life, Benjamin West, on the other hand, became a noted public figure in England. Born in Springfield, Pennsylvania in 1737, he left the colonies when in his early thirties, after having impressed his friends at home by his talent and his ingratiating and likable personality, which was to play no small part in his rise to the position of court painter of George III, and to the presidency of the Royal Academy, which he had been instrumental in founding. In spite of his worldly successes, however, West's work is not highly regarded today. His preoccupation with moral values stood in the way of his producing really great painting. His vast canvases devoted to religious and historical themes seem empty, dry and uninspired. Sometimes in portraiture he succeeded better, but he never displays the robust quality of Copley nor the latter's power of characterization. West's school in London, howeper, was famous in its day and was the goal of all American artists who went to Europe for study. His generosity, his kindliness, his affability, cannot be denied, and it is to be regretted that his performance as a painter is so often remembered only to be held up to scorn.

Gilbert Stuart is today justly called our old master, his work being still highly esteemed for its fine qualities. His career as well as his personality and traits of character, were very different from West's. West was a conformist, Stuart an individualist. As compared with both Copley and West, Stuart was highly temperamental, with a colorful, often irascible nature and noted for his caustic wit. Irresponsible in his business relations, he was nevertheless a very gifted painter of portraits, conspicuous for their spontaneity and insight into human character. His work is limited to portraits, but within this limited range he produced masterpieces. His portrait of George Washington, the so-called Athenaeum Portrait, hangs in the Boston Museum of Fine Arts and has become the accepted official likeness of Washington.

Copley, West and Stuart represent together the culmination of colonial achievement in American art. The 19th cent., into which their careers entered, artistically fell into a decline before it rose again to significant and high attainments. See Fiske Kimball, *Colonial Architecture;* Suzanne La Follette, *Art in America;* Eugen Neuhaus, *The History and Ideals of American Art.* —E.N.

EARLY BOOKBINDING AND FINE BINDING. The desire to decorate the articles that he made is reflected in man's early attempts to devise for his writings a covering that would not only embellish them but also protect them. The form of early binding varies with the method used in making the primitive "book." The Babylonians (800 B.C.), who incised their cuneiform characters on clay tablets, covered the baked tablet with a second layer of thin clay on which was inscribed the title. To read the tablet it was necessary to break off this outer covering. The Egyptian papyrus "books" were first enclosed in wooden cases and then later folded in accordion folds not unlike oriental books today. In the ruins of Pompeii were found **diptychs** or two leaves of wood hinged together with leather thongs. The two inner surfaces were hollowed out to contain a layer of wax on which the writings could be scratched with a stylus. In the 5th cent. folded manuscript sheets of parchment or vellum were assembled and sewed together to form the forerunner of the modern book. Thin wooden panels were soon applied to protect the sheets and were fastened together with leather thongs, laced through holes bored in the back edge of the boards. A leather covering for the thongs was then introduced, which was finally extended to cover the whole area of the boards completing the essentials of modern bookbinding.

The application of decoration by blind tooling on leather bindings became common practice in the 6th cent., although other materials including gold, silver, and precious stones were used in binding and decorating the more expensive books. In the 15th cent. the art of gold tooling was introduced into Europe from the East and toward the end of the century, due to the advancement in papermaking technique, pasteboard began to replace the wooden board sides.

With the invention of movable type in the 15th cent., book publishing expanded rapidly and with it the art of binding flourished. The influence of the Renaissance binders, such as Jean Grolier with his interlacing of geometrical designs supplemented by floral motifs, is still imitated today by designers for the more ornate trade bindings.

The art of fine binding declined in the 19th cent. until T. S. Cobden-Sanderson, a disciple of William Morris, revived it in England. Partly due to the Cobden-Sanderson interest in the work of the outstanding Renaissance masters, binding today falls into three types: **fine binding,** usually done with hand tanned leathers decorated by blind or gold stamping by hand, **rebinding** or **repair binding,** and **trade binding,** produced by machinery with cheaper materials including cloth, cheap leather, and imitation leather, and decorated with plates which produce the design in one stamping operation. Leather and gold stamping alone, however, do not produce a fine binding, and in spite of cost limitations frequently trade binding, due to proper exercise of taste achieves a high degree of artistic success with less costly materials.

The fine binder today is that rare combination of artist and craftsman. He must be an accomplished designer in his medium and have attained the highest degree of skill in the use of his materials. Working entirely by hand he is able to use not only the best practices of the past but take advantage of the more uniform materials of today. His book is hand sewn, usually to cords which are fastened to the boards, and every effort is exercised to produce a flexible back that opens easily, lies flat, closes easily, and remains closed yet is firm and durable. The edges of the pages are usually gilded except when deckle edge paper is used, and then only the top edge receives this treatment. Head bands to support the top and bottom of the spine are applied either to the backbone or to the spine itself. The boards are covered with one of the best grade, hand tanned leathers, usually calf, goat, or pigskin. These operations are known as **forwarding**.

The final step, called **finishing**, includes the decorating of the cover. A suitable design is developed by pencil on paper and duplicated in ink by small stamping tools which may be prepared especially to produce this particular design. These tools (usually one motif to a tool) are made by cutting the motif on the end of a brass rod and inserting it in a long wooden handle. The leather cover is moistened and the design is transferred lightly to the leather by individual impressions of the tools. The gold size is applied to the leather and the gold leaf is laid on and a final and heavier impression of the design is made with the tools, which are heated to cause the gold to adhere to the leather. Occasionally colored leathers are inlaid into the cover to help produce a more ornate result. The edges and inside margins of the cover are frequently stamped with delicate border designs. A fine binder will spend days, weeks, and even months designing and producing a single book, which obviously limits the market to wealthy collectors and patrons. Possibly due to a greater appreciation and encouragement for the production of fine editions of books, this type of binding has found more favor in Europe than in the U.S.A. —H E.S.

EARLY CHRISTIAN ARCHITECTURE.

The small communities of the first two centuries held their meetings in any good-sized private room that was temporarily available (*Actus Apostol.* XX, 7-12). From the 3d cent. on they purchased houses in their own right and transformed them into permanent "community houses" (*domus ecclesiae, tituli, dominica*) containing a meeting hall for the Service, a baptistery, a **consignatorium** (for the confirmation), a vestry, rooms for board meetings and quarters for the clergy (Dura-Europos, "church" ca. 231 A.D.; Rome, building underneath SS. Giovanni e Paolo). The catacombs outside the city with their intricate galleries and small tomb chambers were never used for regular Services. Only occasionally were memorial Services held in chapels of trefoil, round or cross shape above or within these subterranean cemeteries (Rome, S. Sotere and *Capella graeca,* both Catacomb of Calixtus).

Independent church buildings may have first originated in the period of peace between 260 and 300: rectangular barn-like structures with or without interior supports, transversally divided for clergy and congregation and accompanied by baptisteries, *consignatoria* and rooms where the uninitiated *catechumen* could attend part of the Service (Rome, S. Crisogono I; Aquileia I, before 320). Their patterns are based on those of Roman public buildings such as the *curiae,* and possibly also on factory sheds. After the recognition of Christianity in 313 the early Christian **basilica** gradually evolved as the dominant church type. Its plan represents a variant of Roman secular *basilicae* (meaning "hall"), public meeting places near the town *fora,* consisting of a nave flanked or surrounded by lower aisles and of the more sacred *tribunal* where justice was administered under the image of the Emperor's divine majesty. Term and pattern are shared by "secular" and "ecclesiastical" basilicas with slight variations to accommodate the changed functions of the Christian buildings. Constantine's foundation (313-337) (Rome, Old St. Peter's, Church of the Lateran; Jerusalem, Holy Sepulchre; Bethlehem, Nativity) show the long nave, the four longitudinal aisles, all with open timber roofs, and the clerestory with numerous wide windows. Colonnades between nave and aisle carry an architrave or arches. In Jerusalem the aisles were surmounted by galleries as in some secular basilicas. This "congregation hall" was preceded by a colonnaded courtyard the *forum*-like *atrium* (from Greek *aithrio* not from *atrium* of Roman house), and terminated by a **memoria** over the venerated spot (St. Peter's tomb; Grotto of the Nativity) where the altar rose. This memoria is octagonal or circular in Palestine; in Rome is a long "continuous" transept, transverse structure between the nave and the *tribuna* like semicircular apse. The simple meeting halls of the pre-Constantinian period are superseded by the splendid audience halls of the King of Heaven (best preserved example of Constantinian type: Rome, St. Paul's 385-ca. 450, though restored 1825-1930).

During the 4th and 5th cents., basilicas intended for the regular Services superseded these Constantinian types inside the cities: the nave with only two aisles is terminated, usually at the east end, by a simple semicircular vaulted apse with a priest bench (**synthronos**) along its wall and the bishop's **cathedra** at the apex. The altar, surmounted by a canopy (**ciborium**) stands in front of the apse at the end of the chancel which protrudes into the nave, surrounded by precious marble screens (**cancelli**) and flanked by two pulpits (**ambones**). The transept is very rare. Apse and nave are decorated with murals or mosaics, curtains hang between the precious columns; marble incrustations cover the lower parts of the brick walls, a reddish golden light flows through the opaque glass or mica panes of the wide windows (Rome, S. Maria Maggiore, S. Sabina both ca. 430). This Roman type differs from that of other regions: the small but extremely massive stone churches of Syria with two-tower facades and with sacristies (**pastophories**) flanking the apse, emphasize the rich formation of the exterior rather than the interior (Qalb-Luzeh, late 5th cent.); similar, though more crude, are the tiny barrel-vaulted churches of Anatolia, Binbirkilisse). Timber-roofed basilicas often with galleries above the aisles and externally polygonal apses (Constantinople, St. John of the Studios, 463; Salonica, H. Paraskevi), sometimes with "tripartite" (Corinth, basilica, ca. 400; also Rome, S. Pietro in Vincoli, 420-50) or with three-aisled cross transepts (Menas city, basilica of Arcadius, 5th cent.), particularly emphasizing the wealth of interior decoration, prevail in the coastlands of the Eastern Mediterranean. The churches of North Africa and Spain are large sized with simple contrasts of horizontal and vertical planes, usually with three but sometimes with five, seven or nine aisles (Carthage, basilica Damous-el-Karita, ca. 400; Tipasa, Great basilica, ca. 400; Kh. Guidra first half 5th cent.; Tebessa, 5th cent. [?]), occasionally with vaulted aisles (Le Kef, Dar-el-Kous) and sometimes with double apses (Uppenna I, 4th cent; Vega del Mar). Along with these basilicas, octagonal and round domed baptisteries with deep founts (**piscina**) in their centers replace the plain annexed pre-Constantinian

baptismal rooms (Ravenna, Baptistery of the Orthodoxs, ca. 450). Memorias are erected over tombs or other venerated spots. They are circular or octagonal, related to Roman **mausolea** (Rome, S. Costanza) with or without galleries over the surrounding ambulatory and frequently with wooden domes (Jerusalem, Rotunda of the H. Sepulchre) or with open roofs (Jerusalem, Church of the Ascension). Others are large cross shaped structures with four either single naved or three-aisled wings of equal length (Antioch-Kaoussié, ca. 380; Kalât Simân, ca 450) or quadrifoil buildings with ambulatories and galleries and wooden domes (Milan, S. Lorenzo, late 4th cent.; Antioch-Seleucia, Martyrion, 5th cent.; Bosra, cathedral 526). Vaulting seems limited to smaller *mausolea* and baptisteries (Ravenna, so-called Mausoleum of Galla Placidia, ca. 450).

These different *memoriae* types form the basis on which Byzantine architecture develops from the early 5th century on It replaced early Christian architecture throughout the Mediterranean countries. Roman early Christian architecture is revived only within Carolingian architecture of the 9th cent. See Butler, *Early churches in Syria*, 1929; Crowfoot, *Early churches in Palestine*, 1940; Frothingham, *Monuments of Christian Rome*, 1925; Gsell, *Monuments antiques en Algérie*, 1901; Krautheimer, "Beginnings of Christian architecture", *Review of Religion*, 1939; Van Millingen, *Byzantine churches in Constantinople*, 1912. —R.K.

EARLY CHRISTIAN ART. It was the fortune of Christian art to originate and develop during a period (first five or six centuries of our era) when all of the arts, save architecture, were in a progressive decline, the causes being implicit in the times. The arts of Christian society accordingly shared in this regression, with occasional startling exceptions, until finally they emerged in Byzantine style and the arts of medieval Europe.

The earliest Christians had no interest in art, and naturally none in art theory. They were merely indifferent, with no particular feeling one way or another. Certainly, with the exception of sundry doctrinal puritans, they were not antagonistic. Surrounded as they were with the accumulated material of centuries they accepted it naturally and casually, until in the 4th cent. they began to apply the arts for impressive purposes, and especially for instruction.

The interest in early Christian art centers, first, in the subject matter supplied by Christianity itself, affording general unity and responsiveness to contemporary successive and also to provincial emphasis; and second, in the struggle with the technique of existing styles in giving expression to this body of Christian truth.

The two main sequences from late Hellenistic art dominated the entire era, Eastern (Neo-Attic) and Western (Alexandrian) under Greek and Latin modes of thought, with strong impulse from the peoples of Western Asia. These styles were modified by reacting forces until the Alexandrian style ended in complete ruin, and the Eastern resolved into the abstractions of Byzantine art. It will be convenient to treat of the Alexandrian sequence first.

I. *Alexandrian sequence.* Christian art began with the popular substitution of Scriptural subject matter for pagan mythology in the visual arts. The earliest existing examples and the most significant are the fresco wall decorations in the catacombs of Rome painted during the first 400 years. (The dates are afforded by archeological criteria.) They constitute a direct attack on the so-called Alexandrian style, as practiced in Italy, from which they are derived and accordingly are of primary importance. The attack was on the matter of environment in space composition, the outstanding characteristic of Alexandrian illusionism. The modification was due to accident, to incompetence and to the reaction of Eastern styles.

The first cause for the modification was that of accident, arising from conditions of place and workmanship. The **catacombs** of Rome consist of a vast mileage of underground passageways and small rooms, excavated by Christians for the burial of the dead, and for no other purpose. Following contemporary practice in the decoration of tombs they began, even in the 1st cent., to adorn the wall and ceiling surfaces with fresco paintings and stucco patterns, as inclination and resources suggested. It all followed the mode of house decoration, amply illustrated at Pompeii. The areas were organized by line into panels of various geometric shapes, but not by architectural members, since none were required in the catacombs where the granular tufa was itself the structural member. Garlands and festoons of vines and flowers were painted liberally as accompanying adornments, together with birds and pastoral animals, making

it clear that decoration was the primary intention.

The panels, as at Pompeii, invited subject painting and at once the Roman Christians turned to the Scripture, retaining a select few subjects from mythological sources, such as *puttos* and Orpheus with his beasts, but none of subjects which actively portray pagan episodes. (See H. Le Clercq, *Manuel d' Archéologie Chrétienne,* I, pp. 126-182). In so doing they were confronted with the double task of selection and composition.

The selection consisted of vital episodes from the Scripture stressing the saving intervention of Divine Providence in behalf of men and women of faith. From the Old Testament are featured Noah, Abraham, Moses, Jonah, Daniel, the Three Youths in the Furnace, and Susanna. The New Testament series is confined to the life of Christ in the Gospels; the nativity, baptism, the Good Shepherd, the Samaritan woman, miracles of healing such as the paralytic, the raising of Lazarus, and episodes interpreting the Eucharist such as the Multiplication of Loaves and Fishes and the Wine Miracle at Cana. The Passion history is entirely omitted, and in fact does not appear before the 5th cent. carvings. It is to be noted that all of these themes ignore death. They adorn tombs, but emphasize life which is regarded as a continuity. They stress faith, hope and the essence of Christian experience and are singularly cheerful.

The problem began in composition, and while at first there was some slight attempt to constitute the scene, as Nebuchadnezzar's palace as background in the theme of Daniel among the Lions (early 2nd cent., Greek Chapel in the catacomb of Priscilla. J. Wilpert, *Fractio Panis,* Pl. IX), this ambition was renounced almost from the start and a mode developed which is characteristic, though many times compromised with pictorial effort. It was based on the fact that everybody knew the stories and so there was no need to depict them, and proceeded as follows: (1) the theme was analysed, (2) the essential ingredients were isolated and all other data eliminated and (3) those data selected were then organized into a composition of great simplicity in traditional design. Mutual relation of figures was indicated and some suggestion of place, but real space (and above all distance) was ignored.

An extreme example is one of Abraham's sacrifice of Isaac in a sacrament chapel of the catacomb of Calixtus in the 2nd cent. It consists of Abraham with arms raised in prayer, Isaac on one side and the substituted ram on the other, an altar balancing a bundle of faggots, and a tree without leaves suggests a rugged landscape scene. These elements are formally displayed and graduated in size with Abraham on the axis as if they might fill a low triangle such as the pediment of a temple. (Wilpert, *Pitture delle Catacmobe Romane,* pl. 41).

It must be added that while accessories of environment are eliminated the painter was as realistic and vigorous as possible with what was portrayed. Figures are solidly constructed, and indeed with emphasis. The net result of this stenographic brevity in constituting a theme, and its consequent non-pictorial character, was to concentrate on its meaning and to invite the observer to reflect upon it and to extend his spiritual experience as far as he might care to. This is *symbolism*, the dominant characteristic of Christian art of the first four centuries, almost unknown in the arts of paganism since they had little to symbolize.

The function of a symbol is to stimulate imagination and to set free ideas, and its force is enhanced by emphatic concentration on its essential nature with exclusion of all else. And this came about by the accident that these paintings were executed underground, by artificial light and hastily, by artisans of medium ability for the most part (we can imagine what their work in house decoration must have been like), and it should not be forgotten that their efforts were for patrons who did not see them every day, but only at intervals when they had occasion to visit the catacombs; and finally, that these humble efforts made no pretense of being works of art. Furthermore, they became worse as time went on and no attempts on the part of 4th cent. painters to add lively touches or to bring back environment did any good. Many are incredibly bad. The later technique is especially bad. But they do constitute a cycle and inform us quite well of the fortunes of the art of painting in the last years of the Empire in the Latin areas.

The elimination of environment was accidental at first, and then consciously maintained when its symbolic effectiveness was recognized, and this was a decided modification of Alexandrian style. The painters eliminated distance, perspective, light and shade, cast shadows, atmosphere, though they retained tri-dimensional rendering of data and plausible mutual relationships on a restricted plane. Construction was by color, rather than by line, and in a spotted sort of impressionism, with occasional instances of decided merit. The earliest are the best, esp. in the creative period of the 2nd cent.

Greek principles in design were maintained with tenacity as formulas, and prevailed over historical data. For example, in the Epiphany when the Madonna and Child are at the end of a rectangular composition there are always three Magi, but when she is on the axis she is flanked by one or two on either side, as required by formal balance.

Changes in emphasis in symbolic thinking may be traced in the 3rd cent., responding to the forebodings of that era. The sense of evil in a declining civilization caused Christians to reflect upon sin and its origin in human nature and to introduce the primary anthropological symbol of Adam and Eve. Job also made his appearance as an example of misery, albeit enlivened by the figure of his wife handing him a cake on the end of a stick. (In this connection it may be pointed out that never, from earliest examples such as Jonah and Daniel of the 2nd cent., did Christians show any hesitation in depicting the nude figure.) In the 4th cent. there is definitely general confusion. The catacomb cycle ends with the capture of Rome by Alaric in 410, though the tombs of the martyrs received decoration until the 9th cent., when the catacombs were forgotten amid the troubles of the times.

Because of their sketchy character and general incompetence catacomb frescoes are given serious attention only by specialists. They are largely ignored in general works on the history of art, and such writings frequently indulge in misinformation. The most authoritative work (C. R. Morey, *Early Christian Art,* 1942, pp. 77, 102), states that, like the contemporary paintings at Dura, the Roman catacomb paintings did not have sequence in later styles. This is understandable since Rome now entered upon a period of disorder and chaos lasting for centuries and had little occasion to indulge in symbolic thinking, especially since the Eastern style now introduced presented work of genuine ability. Catacomb painting, however, did isolate experience and emphasize its significance and thus in a measure made it abstract. Accordingly, in this cycle we find one of the sources of Byzantine style.

Other examples are located in the catacombs of Alexandria, Naples and Sicily, with local variations, but the later fortunes of the Alexandrian manner in painting are revealed in the arts of mosaic and miniature.

Mosaic decorations in churches are a public art, and indicate the desire of the Church to apply the arts for its purposes. The change accordingly is from symbolism, which invites intimate personal exploration of ideas to a didactic program which is essentially public. Together with the decline of letters the Western Church in the 4th cent. was confronted with the problem of instructing the new converts in the Scripture narrative. The pictorial style of Alexandria was suitable for this, and the mosaic decorators attempted to transfer miniature illustrations of the sacred text, originating in Alexandria itself several centuries earlier, to the wall surfaces of churches in the medium of mosaic, continuing a practice of copying Hellenistic masterpieces. such as the Battle of Alexander mosaic at Naples.

The noted example is the series of mosaic pictures in the basilica of Santa Maria Maggiore at Rome of late 4th cent. and later. In these illustrations the struggle with illusionism, created originally by the brush, in the permanent medium of mosaic is very revealing in the essential nature of tridimensional atmospheric painting. A primary cubism is attained, as in the distinguished head of Simeon, literally created out of cubes, and impressive both structurally and in chiaroscuro. (Richter and Taylor, *The Golden Age of Classic Christian Art,* p. 37 in color).

Among other examples the 5th cent. mosaics of the tomb of Galla Placidia at Ravenna, esp. the lyric presentation of the Good Shepherd, may be cited.

Miniature painting is represented in the well known Joshua Roll of the Vatican, the pictures of which are dated in the 7th or 8th cent., but derive from illustrations created in the 2nd. Another famed example is the Vienna Genesis of 5th or 6th cent., the pictures having been copied from a roll illustrated centuries earlier at Alexandria or some eastern center. In these miniatures environment, including light and shade and cast shadows, is depicted with such skill as the artist could contrive, though with obvious strictures. The narrative purpose is emphasized fully, since the intention is to illustrate the episode and thereby edify the spectator. Through them the Alexandrian impressionism lingers on, strongly fortified in the 7th cent. in Santa Maria Antiqua in Rome by painters from Alexandria who fled from the Arab conquest of Egypt.

The Alexandrian manner is also continued in a languishing way in the sculptured relief decorations of some of the 4th cent. **sarcophagi.** These carvings constitute the last phase of the decline of Roman-Hellenistic sculpture. They are chiefly of the frieze type, some being in two ranges, and are quite lacking in decorative unity, though a few, such as those featuring the Jonah episode, continue an effect of overall pattern. The subject matter is mostly of the concise themes of the catacomb frescoes, with sundry additions, and continues the symbolic purpose in a rather mechanical manner. Content is the only interest since realization of form is at a minimum, and illusionism has vanished.

There is, however, genuine merit in ivory **carvings,** of such as stem from Alexandria, a metropolis for the export of ivory. There is considerable dispute regarding the source of consular diptychs, and they may be assigned to other style centers, but the masterly carving of the ivory of the Angel descending the stairs and of the superb chair of Maximian at Ravenna (6th cent.) continue the heritage of impressionism with distinction. The 5th cent. panels of the wooden doors of Santa Sabina at Rome likewise display traces of Alexandrian influence, intermingled with the technique contributed by the Eastern area.

II. *East Christian art* presents negligible existing examples before the 4th cent., earlier material having been destroyed during the centuries of violence which have plagued the lands of the Near East; or at best this material awaits discovery. Its sources are inferred from developments of late Hellenistic style, such as Neo-Attic sculpture, Asiatic sarcophagi and the mosaics uncovered at Antioch (together with the paintings at Dura), Persian and other styles of western Asia.

It is difficult to agree upon a single title to cover the entire field since it includes the output of scattered centers; Antioch, Jerusalem, Ephesus, Constantinople, Coptic Egypt, Cappadocia, Syria, and in the west, Ravenna, Milan, North Italy and Gaul and even Rome. East Christian is as good a title as any, though the term Greek-Asiatic has much to commend it because it signifies the meeting of Greek ideas with those of the peoples of western Asia. All of this implies a meeting, clash and reaction of the purposes of divergent racial stocks until a synthesis is attained in the 6th cent. and the first Byzantine style results. The varied expression of such a wide area is bewildering, affording considerable difference of opinion among specialists. The confusion is all the greater since objects were transported everywhere and made impression on local styles with consequence of further mixture. This is especially true in Italy and Gaul where contact with the lingering Alexandrian manner led to adjustments and compromises. To the person unacquainted with the material it looks much alike, appears to be incompetent in workmanship, and essentially strange.

The confusion may be resolved somewhat when we reflect upon a few essentials: (1) the content is Christian, (2) the figure is in the continuation of the Hellenistic and therefore maintains a classic reminiscence, (3) the decorative element, including design, is oriental.

In an attempt to simplify the confusion the following general sketch of causes and characteristics is offered. The free imaginative symbolism of the rather simple-minded Christians of the West did not appeal greatly to their brothers in the Eastern area. Here Greek methods of thinking prevailed. The verities of Christian faith were subjected to a turmoil of reflective thinking: definitions, subtle distinctions, analyses, interpretations, coherent organizations, resulting in creeds and systematic theology by reference to which orthodoxy was established and heresy confuted, though heresy was strong enough to organize several national churches on the fringes of the Empire. Greek philosophy, worn out by its scholastic struggles, now entered upon an era of new vigor and usefulness as Christian theology. Its own lingering pagan refreshment as neo-Platonism and neo-Pythagoreanism was sterile.

The intellectual interpretation of Christianity, nothwithstanding the clash of passions, tended to be impersonal and to remove men from the objects of devotion; a sort of optic point of view mentally, entirely consistent with the contemporary rule of this practice in the arts.

In curious harmony with the above was the impact of the traditional thought processes of the oriental ingredient, emerging from ancient Mesopotamia and desert lands, which had powerful effect. It was essentially non-intellectual in the grand manner, eschewing definitions and analyses, and relied rather upon contemplation without interpretation, and did so with awe and wonder; hence the oriental mysticism which dazzles the western mind. Bits of experience are thoroughly described but without investigation of causes. They are indeed in continuity, but without the flow of cause and effect in a linear sequence; the whole affording a pattern which may be as intricate as an oriental rug. The observer again is removed from the object but is amply rewarded by the rich color and rhythmic pattern unfolded before him. Such pattern is non-representational in its treatment of phenomena, and imposes the question of environment. On this East Christian art held definite views and made a contribution of utmost importance, constituting a strain of unity in the style.

The Greek and oriental processes converged in Christianity upon experience which certainly cannot be described but only inferred and contemplated; viz., that of the heavenly world. The divine majesty and glory, the felicity of the saints and martyrs and the entire heavenly host suggest an environment remote from earthly experience, but capable of intimation by art relying upon word-paintings in the Apocalyptic visions. The fruition of this is in Byzantine art, but the beginnings are in this period. This scene is properly two-dimensional, as befits vision, and invites rich display of color. With this the saintly experience in this world is in harmony. It is special, set-apart and precious, so far removed from the ordinary that it scarcely serves as an example to people in daily life, though men may contemplate it.

The academic phase of Hellenistic scripture had given concentrated attention to the single figure in the manner of the masters. Presently such important figures were further isolated on sarcophagi of western Asia by architectural framing (columnar and arcaded), and maintained on one plane. That is, they were non-pictorial, and the environment was limited by architecture, and with no depth.

This is the optic point of view, according to which the spectator realizes material by the eye, rather than by suggestion of touch, and therefore from a distance favorable for observation. He is manifestly apart from the objects portrayed which are physically and mentally isolated. It is an oriental process of constituting phenomena which made contact with Hellenistic art in the style known as Neo-Attic. Here the oriental mind made its primary contribution (Persia, Mesopotamia). It was that of color as the equivalent of environment and as a symbol of its quality. The technique in sculpture known as **colorism**, undercutting and perforations with the drill to a common depth, applied to architectural members afforded an effect of vibrating colored air when viewed from a distance. (The atmospheric enrichment of colorism is quite different from the chiaroscuro of Alexandrian illusionism which affects the realism of actual experience.) In coloristic technique embellishing details were sharpened, made intricate and flattened so that they suggested the pattern of textiles.

The tendency then, was towards one colorful plane, of no determined depth, in which well-rounded figures were placed. The effect was non-naturalistic, and a generalized formal experience was suggested; an experience to be observed but not one in which the observer might participate. It was in the nature of spectacle, and reflected the desire of men to reflect upon aspects of Christian truth. (Cf. *Christ and Two Apostles,* fragment of the 4th cent. sarcophagus in Berlin. This is the style of the best sarcophagi of the 4th cent., as was promptly recognized by people of taste at Rome and other western centers. Such objects are infinitely superior to the examples of the local Latin manner then being carved.)

The method was increasingly linear (q.v.), and primitive conventions returned: broad aspect of figure, frontality together with disjunctive and awkward pose. The projection was often inverted; another oriental contribution. Distortions are occasioned, however, by uncertainty as well as by incompetence, until finally the style appears to have made up its mind and created the Byzantine synthesis.

These processes are illustrated in small objects of descriptive content, ivories (consular diptychs, panels, boxes, covers, etc.), oil bottles and cases for relics carried home by pilgrims returning from Palestine, accessories of one sort or another. Description, while complete, is at times disjunctive in organization, with the several data treated in intense isolation and without logical sequence, each part being portrayed separately, but contributing to the pattern of the whole. The descriptive content varies in geographical areas, and the details of iconography invite endless archeological investigation, in such matters as the presentment of the person of Christ, the introduction of the angel to lead the magi in the Epiphany (Coptic), the standing Mary in the Annunciation (Syrian), the architecture of the Holy Sepulchre (Palestine and Gaul gave authentic record), the author Evangelists seated as philosophers (Ephesus), and so on.

The colorism in marble was fortified in painting by frank acceptance of oriental usage, the examples being chiefly in mosaics (Ravenna Baptesteries, e.g.) and a few min-

iatures (*Rossano Gospels, Gospel Book of Rabula*). Anticipated by the 1st cent. cult paintings of Dura, opulent figures appear in colors restrained by contours against a ground of one tone, such as purple and finally gold, —the obvious atmosphere of heaven. Presently the figures became flat, with slight suggestion of modeling and consequent loss of form and organic relation of costume to figure. Finally, all that we have is colorful costume, equipped with head, hands and feet. Such figures are represented in an unrealistic setting which is non-spatial, since it has no depth, or which is vertical in projection.

The use of the figure is implicit in both Greek and Christian art, but not in oriental. The oriental contribution then, consists in providing a significant, non-realistic environment, which it does largely by means of color, and also by its rhythmic decorative principle. Unity in composition is achieved by rhythm in the best examples. Greek principles, such as axis and balance continue, however, as in the sarcophagi of Ravenna. The period of 4th to 6th cents. presents only the beginning of such organization, and is of considerable importance in the struggle with style. It is marked by incompetence in the attempt to use the inheritance of age-old technique, Hellenistic and oriental, and by the refreshing experiments in original creation. It was progressive, not decadent as was the fearful decline of illusionism in the West, and accordingly was patronized by influential persons everywhere, Western as well as Eastern. Notable examples exist at Ravenna and Rome. Coptic Egypt presents it in such a summary fashion that it is well nigh an epitome and is highly regarded by modern critics. In any case, the unreal environment created was precisely required for the abstract concepts in which the Greek church delighted.

(There can be no discussion of East Christian art without reference to the insistent oriental theories of the Austrian scholar, J. Strzygowski. The prolific writings of this expert have now been assessed and there is general agreement on the essential merit of his contribution, viz., the forceful presentation of the oriental ingredient of nonrepresentational art with characteristic decorative principles.) See C. R. Morey, *Early Christian Art,* 1942; *Christian Art,* 1935; *Mosaics of Antioch,* 1938, and "Sources of Medieval Style", *Art Bulletin,* Vol. VII, 1924; J. Wilpert, *Pitture Delle Catacombe Romane,* 2 vols., 1903, also in German; O. M. Dalton, *East Christian Art,* 1925; O. Wulff, *Altchristliche u. Byzantinische Kunst,* 2 vols. 1914; H. Le-Clercq, *Manuel D'Archéologie Chrétienne,* 2 vols. 1907; J. Strzygowski, *Orient oder Rom?* 1901, and numerous works following; Cabrol, *Dictionnaire d'Archéologie Chrétienne et de Liturgie,* 1907; E. Baldwin Smith, *Early Christian Iconography,* 1918.　　—C.D.L.

early classical style. See HELLENIC ART.

early romanesque art. See GERMAN ART.

ear-mark notation. See JEWISH MUSIC.

earth color. Any colored mineral used as a pigment.

earthenware. Term for porous body, white ware with lead glaze. See CERAMICS I.

earth reds. See iron pigments.

earth yellows. See iron pigments.

easel. Any frame built to hold a painting, ordinarily during the time when it is being made, can be called an easel. The most frequently seen type in the representations of painters' studios during the late Renaissance in Europe is a three-legged piece of furniture on which the painting is held by the two forward legs, with the third standing out as a brace. More complex designs have been developed, particularly the studio easel with screw adjustments both for height and for the angle of the painting. Sketching easels made to fold up into a compact bundle are manufactured for landscape painters, and various types of small easels and table easels are available. The history of this piece of studio furniture goes back into remote antiquity, having been shown in a tomb relief of the Old Kingdom in Egypt. Mention is made of it in connection with legendary records about the Greek artist, Apelles, and many types are found in studio scenes from the Middle Ages on.　　—G.L.S.

east Christian art. See EARLY CHRISTIAN ART.

eastern carpet. See carpet structures.

eastern chants. The investigation of Eastern Church music is still in its initial stages. There is no great body of eastern chant (Armenian, Byzantine, Coptic, Ethiopian, Russian and Syrian) which remotely compares with the vast collection of Gregorian Chant. Although some pioneer work has been done in the various eastern chants, the Byzantine chant has received, and appropriately so, of late the most attention. To the student of music history the most vital question is the interrelationship and reciprocal influences of the chants of the east and those of the west— a question which for the most part remains unanswered.

It was not until the 12th cent. that the so-called **hagiopolitan** or **round** notation indicating precise intervals was invented. MSS. dating from the 8th and 9th cent. in the Ecphonetic notation based on grammatical accents are undecipherable. Nevertheless, it is possible that some of the extant Byzantine chants belong to the period of Romanos (fl. 491-518) and Sergios (fl. 610-41), the Golden age of Byzantine Hymnody. The hymns (**kontakia**) of this period were written by men who were both poets and musicians. The later hymnologists, among them St. Andrew of Crete (d. 730) and St. John of Damascus (d. 754), set the hymns (**kanon**) to pre-existing melodies. The Ecphonetic MSS. although undecipherable give in some instances chants with melodic contours similar to those of later MSS. in the round notation.

It is generally agreed that the rhythm of Byzantine chant was free, the melodies following the stress accents of the words. The system of 8 **echoi,** said to have been perfected by St. John of Damascus, who gave Byzantine musical theory a definite form, bears a superficial resemblance to the 8 modes of the west (See modes, ecclesiastical), but the cadential formulas are different. The 4 **authentic echoi** in ascending order on a, b, c, d. The 4 **plagal echoi** lie a 5th below. The classification of authentic and plagal is theoretical. The initial or final note of a melody is not always the regular final of the **echos,** but is determined by a special form of signature.

The system of modern or **Chrysanthine** notation codified by Chrysanthus, an Archimandrite, in the early 19th cent. and used in the Greek Church today should not be confused with the medieval Byzantine system.

The publication of the *Monumenta Musicae Byzantinae* comprising facsimiles, transcriptions, and critical studies of music of the ancient Byzantine Church is in progress under the editorship of C. Hoeg, H.J.W. Tillyard and E. Wellesz, the foremost authorities in the field.

See Chap. 3 in G. Reese, *Music in the Middle Ages,* 1940 and article on *Eastern Church Music,* in Grove's *Dictionary of Music and Musicians,* Sup. Vol. 1940.　　—V.A.

Eastern North American aboriginal art. Geographically the Eastern North American area includes that part of the continent from the Great Plains to the Atlantic and Gulf coasts. Unlike the situation in the Southwest, no coherent pattern showing interrelationships of cultures has been worked out for this area. The total picture is complex and confusing despite the large amount of excavation and the abundance of artifacts with rich aesthetic content. Names have been applied to important cultures, but they lack precise definition and no chronology has been established except tentatively in some locations.

This is a great woodland area whose earliest inhabitants were hunters and fisherman who fashioned polished stone tools with technical virtuosity and with a fine feeling for form. The introduction of corn precluded a more sedentary life which would make possible the introduction of pottery. From this basis centers of high culture gradually evolved, notably in the Ohio and Mississippi drainage and in the Southeast. Centering in Ohio were the Hopewell culture (q.v.) and the neighboring Adena (q.v.). Their most spectacular manifestations are the great mounds and earthworks (see Mound Builders) and their contents. The mounds, ranging from 4 to 70 ft. in height and enclosed with earth walls, are of several classes: the **conical mounds** for burial, in which numerous notable works of art have been found; the **platform mounds**, which were foundations for temples or domiciles, more frequent in the south; and low **effigy mounds,** made in the shape of a snake, bird or animal, such as the Great Serpent Mound (q.v.), and restricted to the northern Mississippi and Ohio valleys. Probably all the mounds had also some social or religious function. The earthworks, which are low enclosing embankments found chiefly in the Ohio basin, appear to have had a defensive, sacred, or social function.

Distinguished works of art, found chiefly in the burial mounds and apparently ceremonial rather than for daily use, comprise a large number of miniature **stone pipes,** copper and mica ornaments, intricately woven textiles, necklaces and ornaments of fresh-water pearls. The stone pipes were carved with flint tools; they represent bird, animal and human figures depicted naturalistically and with great vitality. Copper, obtained from the Lake Superior deposits, was hammered into thin sheets and by cutting, engraving or repoussé fashioned into headdresses, standards, bracelets, buttons, and various ornaments. The designs consisted of geometric motifs, which were handled with rare ability; human, bird and animal figures highly conventionalized; and dances in elaborate costumes, very much like similar figures found in the art of Middle America. Ornaments of varied designs were cut from thin sheets of mica obtained from Virginia and North Carolina—evidence of the wide trading of the Hopewell peoples.

In the Mississippi Valley arose another culture, sometimes called Middle Mississippi, centering between the Arkansas and Missouri Rivers and extending north, south and east. Lower Mississippi is a term sometimes applied to the southern reaches, but both terms are controversial. In this area the mounds, which are largely of the platform type, probably by influence from Middle America, served as bases for temples or chieftains' dwellings. Stone pipes again are characteristic but are large in size and, like the stone bowls with effigy attachments, represent animal, bird and human figures in a style that tends to a conventionalization required by ritual and stresses mass inherent in sculptural form. Yet surprisingly naturalistic figures have been found in clay effigy vessels discovered at Spiro Mound in Oklahoma and at Moundville, Alabama. Shell gorgets found widely in the southeastern area and engraved or cut into openwork patterns offer, both in their figures and their designs, additional evidence of contact with Middle America. The obvious influence of Middle American art in the southeastern area is a puzzling problem, for no actual Middle American artifacts have been found within the area. Pottery was abundant and various in style. Outstanding are the black bottles of the Caddoan tribe, which show spiralling designs incised either before or after firing. Frequently the incised lines were filled with color, or a polychrome decoration was obtained by the use of the lost-color technique. Though wood probably was used widely, only a few objects have survived.

A rare find of painted wood artifacts was made at Key Marco, Florida, where were discovered, miraculously preserved in muck, a large number of spear-throwers, human, bird and alligator figures, and ceremonial objects of all kinds, particularly the ceremonial masks in human and animal form which in their lively naturalism reach a high point of woodcarving among the native American peoples.

What became of these aboriginal cultures is uncertain. Some of them had disappeared or were decadent at the time of the coming of the Europeans; others can be traced to the ancestors of the historic Indians in this area. See F. H. Cushing, *Exploration of Ancient Key Dwellers' Remains on the Coast of Florida,* American Philosophical Society, Proceedings, 1896; F. H. Douglas, *Copper and the Indian,* Denver Art Museum Leaflets Nos. 75-76, 1936; Diamond Jenness, *The Indians of Canada,* 1934; Museum of Modern Art, *Indian Art of the United States,* 1941; Philip Phillips, *Middle American Influences on the Archaeology of the Southeastern United States,* in *The Maya and Their Neighbors,* George C. Vaillant et al., ed., 1940; H. C. Shetrone, *The Mound Builders,* 1930; George C. Vaillant, *Indian Arts in North America,* 1939; Clark Weissler, *The American Indian,* 1938.　　　　　　　　—H.G.

Easter oratorio. See oratorio.

eave. The projecting edge of a roof.

Eburnant group. See Ottonian art.

ecclesiastical modes. See scales and modes.

echinus (Gr. sea urchin). A convex molding on a capital, supporting the abacus.

echo. See ACOUSTICS.

échoppe. A needle used by the earliest etchers, the point of which is cut at a bevel, enabling them to make a line that swells and tapers, imitating the engraving process.　　　—K.K.

echos, echoi. See eastern chants.

eclecticism. The word comes from the Greek *eklegein,* which means to pick out, to choose, to gather. It is applied to the manner of those artists who compose their works by using the peculiarities of style of different artists or epochs without possessing the ability to concentrate these divers peculiarities in an organic unity. Working in a single style of a certain epoch, like in the Greek, Romanesque, Gothic, etc. style, may be called eclecticism also. The term stands in opposition to that artistic expression which arises within the nature of the artist himself and which results in a work of proper and organic quality.

Usually eclecticism comes into notice at the beginning and end of a whole era as well as singular epochs. Young peoples meeting old cultures superior to their own are pressed by this superiority to work in an eclectic manner until they have succeeded in digesting these influences and developing their own proper style upon a higher level. Correspond-

ing to this primitive eclecticism is the rational eclecticism at the end of a cultural development. The latter is caused by decreasing artistic substance and an increasingly critical and reflective view of the world. We notice primitive eclecticism, e.g., among the works of early Egyptian, early Greek, or early mediaeval art. Typical rational eclecticism may be noticed at the end of the Renaissance in the middle of the 16th cent. Eclecticism laid the foundation of the first European academy of art founded by the brothers Caracci. This academy originated from the opposition to Michel Angelo's late works which showed baroque tendencies. Many artists decided not to follow these baroque tendencies but to cling to that which the outstanding Renaissance artists had achieved. They tried to combine the charm of Raphael, the grandeur of Michel Angelo, and the light of Corregio. The result of this eclecticism was a set style. In the same way the classicism of the 18th cent. and its various renewals during the 19th and 20th cents. show eclectic tendencies. Together with the increasing discoveries of remote epochs of art and the critical and reflective view of art in recent times eclecticism has increased too. Sometimes, eclecticism becomes mannerism, as when the adopted elements of a foreign style are overstressed and applied in the way of formalism.　　　—A.J.S.

Ecole des beaux-arts (Fr.). A well-known endowed school of the fine arts in Paris, founded in 1648.

ecorché (Fr.). Anatomical manikin or figure showing the muscles.

écossaise. A spirited dance of Scotch origin in 2/4 time which was originally accompanied by the bagpipes.

ecphonetic notation. See eastern chants.

ectype. A copy of an artist's original.

edition. See PRINTS AND PRINT PROCESSES.

edition binding. A trade binding design produced in quantity is usually called *edition binding* to distinguish it from the less common *fine binding* which often consists of a special design for a single volume. The production of quantity (often with quality) binding relies to a large extent upon machinery that does more rapidly and cheaply the various operations of hand binding.

The first step in edition binding after the printed sheets are folded into signatures or sections is to **gather** or collect the book together in the order of binding. In most cases this operation can be accomplished by a belt that travels past hoppers which contain a quantity of the proper signatures and at the proper intervals drop a signature on the growing pile. At the end of the belt an operator occasionally checks or **collates** the order of placement to prevent misplaced signatures. In spite of this careful check books are bound and sold with either misplaced or even missing pages.

After gathering, or sometimes after sewing, an **end sheet** or folded piece of strong paper is pasted to the top and bottom signature. There are several types of book sewing machines. The most common method is to sew each signature and then connect it to the adjoining one with a loop of thread. For large catalogues and other books requiring unusual strength, machines are available that sew the signatures to tapes in a manner somewhat similar to hand sewing to tapes After sewing, a thin coating of flexible glue is applied to the back of the book and allowed to dry. The book is then **rounded** and **backed** or **smashed.** These operations form the back and give a concave curve to the foredge. Thin books are usually flat backed or **unrounded,** and instead of the almost unsupported cloth back of the rounded book, the flat backed type uses a flat stiff cardboard strip in the back of the case. After backing, the book receives another coating of glue plus a strip of thin cloth that extends over the sides onto the end sheet. This cloth hinge and the end sheet, when pasted to the case, will be all that holds the book and the case together. A piece of paper the width of the backbone is frequently applied on top of the cloth.

Most trade books are stained on at least the top edge or on all three edges and a few books are gilded. Finally, head bands are applied to the top and bottom of the backbone on the better editions. The book is now ready to be **cased.**

The making of the case and the **casing in** operation follow hand binding practices except that almost all operations are mechanical. The design is applied either by hot stamping with foil, real or imitation gold, aluminum, etc., or printed, blind stamped, embossed, or, in some cases, printed on the binding materials before the case is made. After casing in the finished book is placed by hand between brass-bound boards for drying and is ready for wrapping.   —H.E.S.

editor, exhibitor. See circus.

educational dance is a process, not an end in itself. Fundamentally, educational and art dance are the same. The dance of the professional artist is but a continuation of this basic educational dance—his art maturing as he the individual matures.

The concern of educational dance is the development of expression through the study of dance and not with the development of professional dancers. Its aim is the integration of personality by means of participation in dance as a creative art experience—affording students the opportunity to know dance as a special way of experiencing aesthetic values discovered in reality (see creative dance). Its approach is the study of dance as a whole and the use of creative motor experience as the basis of instruction, instead of centering dance interest in professional performance. Since art demands the unity of all aspects of our complex nature—emotional, intellectual, spiritual, and physical—dance, as a creative art experience, is especially adapted to educational ideals. In art the drives are emotional. When they are subjected to the restraint and directions of the intellect and executed by the physical, there results a fusion of all our energies with the focal point centered in the personality. For dance to realize these educational possibilities it must be emotional, intellectual, and spiritual, as well as physical. Its instruction necessitates a background of study in the fields of science, philosophy, and art and their related fields. Although such an approach to the study of dance does not insist on professional perfection, it does, nevertheless, insist on high standards, thus building for the development of an artistic foundation upon which the talented may build a superstructure according to his capacities to ascend.

Educational dance should be the basic foundation for dance as an art It is the beginning of art understanding with movement as the expressive medium.   —M.N.H'D.

educational drama. See RADIO DRAMA.

educational exhibition. See exhibition.

Edwardian. See GREAT BRITAIN, ARCHITECTURE OF.

effacé (F. *effacer,* to shade or diminish in plane). A term in classic ballet vocabulary generally applied to head and shoulders when they are set at certain angles to suggest greater plasticity, or to emphasize mass in space. —L.K.

effigy. Sculptured likeness, as on sepulchral monument.

egg-and-dart ornament. This design, used chiefly as a moulding in Greek and Roman buildings and their adaptations in Renaissance and modern times, originated probably in a leaf pattern, the "egg" sometimes showing a central spine and the "dart" derived from a lancelot leaf. No moulding has been more universally popular to indicate the division of architectural elements and to effect the transition from one to another gracefully, e.g., between wall and ceiling, between courses, and in ceiling coffers. Its vigorously conceived and sharply cut curved projections suggest the functional relationships of the building and enrich the surface. The most refined form of this motif appears on the Erechtheum in Athens. —W.R.A.

egg-shell porcelain. Porcelain so thin that it is often referred to as egg-shell porcelain.

egg tempera. In the regular panel painting of Europe before oil came into general use, the medium was yolk of an egg. The pigments were ground in water and to them was added enough of the yolk to serve as a binding medium. White of egg or glair mixed with various ingredients, principally water-soluble gums, or used without such additions, may have been a frequent vehicle of panel paintings and was the common tempera for manuscript illumination. Glair contains the adhesive substance, albumen. The egg yolk is an oily emulsion in which there is some albumen also. Being oily, it is relatively impervious to water when it is thoroughly dry, and the survival of large numbers of panel paintings from the late Middle Ages in Europe gives testimony of its favorable qualities as a painting medium. —G.L.S.

e-gorai ware (Jap.). Korean pottery of the *Korai* dynasty with surface under the glaze painted with floral motives. —J.A.M.

EGYPTIAN ART. Generally this term is understood to define the arts of ancient Egypt from prehistoric times until the conquest by Augustus in 32 B.C. It is sometimes limited to Dynastic Egypt, which is brought to a close with the conquest of Alexander in 332 B.C., and sometimes extended to include the art of the Roman period together with its later manifestations under the Copts (Egyptian Christians) until the Moslem conquest in the 7th century A.D.

Ancient Egypt proper included the entire Nile Valley and Delta from the Mediterranean Sea on the north to the First Cataract on the south, though this southern boundary during the new Empire was extended far into Upper Nubia and even to the Sudan; while Lower Nubia, the region immediately south of the First Cataract, was usually considered a part of the kingdom, being populated almost exclusively by pure Egyptians from the earliest times. Furthermore, Egypt generally claimed the deserts on the east to the shores of the Red Sea, including the Sinaï peninsula and the land directly north to the shores of the Mediterranean; and to the west the adjacent portions of the Libyan desert with their oases, including the fertile Fayoum district.

The ancient art of this region perhaps more than any other has a peculiarly unique character, which is established by a remarkable consistency of style. This was noted by Plato and has been reaffirmed ever since; yet Egyptian art did change, was acted upon by outside influences, though never to the extent nor with the rapidity that marks later Western styles, so that these changes are far less easily discernible. Moreover, none was strong enough to break the major conventions of this style, which had reached formalistic stability and mechanical precision at an extremely early date.

No survey of Egyptian art, however cursory, can be made without a brief review of the unique land, its government, and its religion, which controlled the nature of the arts even more completely than did Christianity during the Middle Ages in Europe, and for a greater period of time. Only slightly less important is some consideration of this time element involved.

The native name of Egypt was *Kemi* or *Kemet*, meaning "the black land," from the darkness of the alluvial soil of the Nile Valley. The modern name, Egypt, is derived from the Greek *Aigyptos* (origin obscure), which occurs in the *Odyssey* of Homer, where it is used as the name of the Nile River as well as the country, and with good reason, for the story of Egypt is the story of the Nile River (Egypt. *Hapi* or *Hapis*), which, in cutting its way northward through the eastern Sahara desert, makes fertile the narrow strips of land on either bank. The Nile valley, never more than ten miles wide and at many places less than two, is below the general level of the desert and is bounded on either side by cliffs and hills rising in some cases as high as 1800 feet above the valley floor. These cliffs and hills, composed largely of limestone and granite, are sources of a plentiful supply of durable building stone. About 100 miles south of the Mediterranean the bounding hills spread to the northwest and northeast, and between them lies the Delta, which, except for the section immediately adjacent to the sea, is the most fertile region of Egypt. The Delta, about 150 miles wide at its base, is a broad alluvial plain which rises so gently from sea level that its southern extremity has an altitude of scarcely 30 feet. Except for this coastal section Egypt lies in an almost rainless area. What rain does fall comes in occasional storms, generally in the winter months, but so infrequently that no regular rainy season can be plotted. The Nile therefore becomes the sole dependable water supply as well as the means of soil revitalization by its annual inundation. Moreover, it is the one great artery of commerce within the empire. It is not surprising then that the Nile was one of the deities in the Egyptian pantheon, but there is no evidence that it ever was accorded the veneration given by the Brahman to the Ganges, nor does the regularity of its yearly rise and fall, together with the continuous procession of cloudless days and the isolation, both actual and felt, of the valley seem to have exerted on the Egyptian and his art the profound environmental influence claimed by so many writers.

However, the fact that the ancient Egyptian found himself in an environment which emphasized the ephemeral nature of living things and in which only the gods and the dead were one with an unchanging nature accounts for his loathing of the idea of death, his attempt to identify himself with this changelessness by persuading himself that he did not die but continued to live, in some strange manner sustained by the preservation of his body, surrounded by models and painted representations of his ordinary life on earth. The tomb then was to deny rather than affirm the existence of death. The arid climate, which preserved rather than destroyed, heightened his belief, but it is well to bear in mind that this holds true for the Nile Valley only and not for the moist sea coast or the well-watered Delta, which destroyed as completely as the Valley preserved.

Ancient Egypt was divided into two regions, Lower Egypt, consisting of the Delta with its adjacent lands reaching south slightly beyond Memphis, and Upper Egypt, which was the remainder of the Nile Valley. These two regions represented the kingdoms which existed independently before Menes, the legendary founder of the 1st Dynasty, united them under one rule. From the time of the earliest dynasties, however, Upper Egypt took precedence over Lower Egypt in matters of government and religion. Beliefs that developed in the former would find acceptance in the latter. During Roman times Lower and Upper Egypt were separated by a third division called Middle Egypt, extending from the apex of the Delta southward approximately to the town of Asyut (modern Assiut).

The government of Egypt was monarchical. The king was the head of a hierarchy of princes and great landowners, who administered the affairs of a series of districts called nomes. At various times almost feudal conditions prevailed. Local rulers set up establishments which rivaled the royal court and were kept in order only by the use of severe measures on the part of the monarch. During the New Empire the king had all powers centralized in him but administered the land by means of an extensive bureaucracy headed by a vizier responsible only to the king. Sometimes two viziers, one for Upper and one for Lower Egypt, were employed, but in this case the vizier for Upper Egypt had precedence. The king or Pharaoh (Heb., from Egypt. Per'o, the old term for "royal palace" or "great house," which became the personal title of the monarch in popular language) was considered divine, one of his titles being "the Good God," and was the mediator between the gods and men. This divinity led the country to be unduly dominated by the priesthood, whose power increased as the power of the Pharaoh increased. Eventually a reigning Pharaoh was supplanted by the priests of Amon, who founded a dynasty of their own.

The priesthood, largely hereditary though not necessarily so, administered a state religion which was a collection of the ancient tribal cults, beliefs, and concepts, combined into some semblance of a whole, and as such imposed upon the people. By the time of the earliest dynasties it had secured the stereotyped form which characterized it as long at it endured. It included a vast pantheon of gods, some of them local, some of them general or cosmic deities, but the beliefs and rituals are so confused and self-contradictory that any clear explanation of them is impossible. Interpretations are as many and varied as there are writers interested in the subject, but it is clear that the Egyptian religion developed no spiritual concept or philosophy comparable to those developed in Asia. This pantheism was seriously challenged only once, under the reign of Amenhotep IV (Akh-en-aten or Ikhnaton), who introduced a religion of purest monotheism, the diety being the personification of the sun's disk under the name of Aten. The new religion scarcely survived the death of Akh-en-aten, and less than sixty years after its inception it had disappeared as completely as if it had never existed. Except for this unique circumstance, and possibly the late period under the Saites, according to H. R. Hall, the Egyptian's mental condition in religious matters was little above that of the Negroes of the Gold Coast.

Out of this mumbo-jumbo which passed as his religions the one clear fact emerged that the Egyptian resented death as he resented change. Perhaps here we can see the environmental influence of land and river. All evidence tells us that he enjoyed life and that he wished to project this enjoyable existence beyond his death. In order to do this all phases of his mortal life must be preserved in some manner: first his body in order that his soul might live—if not his body then a reasonable facsimile; next the persons and things that served him in life; and finally the actual scenes of his home, occupations, and diversions. All these guaranteed the perpetuity of this posthumous existence so long as they were preserved. Consequently all of these things must be embodied in the most durable materials in forms least likely to perish. During life the Egyptian was content with objects and materials of a relatively temporary nature. Even the Pharaohs lived in houses with walls of sun-dried brick and pressed mud roofs supported by wooden columns. Commercial buildings also were built for one generation to be replaced by the next. If metal was employed, it was for its ductility, color, and utility rather than for permanence. However, for the houses of the unchanging gods or the dead the most durable materials were sought and put into forms which had or suggested the greatest stability.

The art forms thus created were not marked by a disinterested search for beauty but rather by their utility. As the facts and objects represented were supposed to have the power of insuring existence after death, their immediate recognition rather than their aesthetic quality was of the greatest importance. In consequence, attention was paid only to those aspects of the object which most distinguish it from its surroundings and afford the clearest comprehension of it.

This purely conceptual idea of the visible world, which developed from as well as satisfied the necessities imposed by religion, habit, and economy, produced an art of pure illustration, which from the earliest time reduced all forms to a series of easily recognizable symbols and conventions executed in almost faultless craftsmanship. That Egyptian art was mainly literature in another form may be seen in the fact that neither sculptural relief nor painting ever lost the character of picture-writing completely; on the other hand, the Egyptian never abandoned the hieroglyphic for the alphabetic script, refusing to give up all reference to visual aspects even in his writing. Such an art of illustration and literary reference is necessarily an art of realism, but with Egypt this realism is descriptive and superficial, and, except in rare but noteworthy instances, is subservient to mannerism and style. Portraiture, which, because of the belief regarding life after death, was greatly developed, sacrificed vital realism to convention, advanced by the desire for forms of greatest durability. The close-knit, compact figures in the round present masses least likely to be damaged, just as the characteristic sunk-relief (see relief) protects surfaces from casual damage and affords as well the greatest legibility. Both of these types of sculpture undoubtedly owe part of their character to economy, being far less expensive in both time and money.

Furthermore, Egyptian art is noted for its anonymity. Few artists or craftsmen are known, though when known seem to have been individuals of exceptional ability. This anonymity must have been intended as inscriptions abound in names of kings, priests, and viziers.

All of the above factors combine to produce the singular uniformity of character to be found in Egyptian art.

Historical records, while plentiful, are fragmentary and present no strict chronology. Moreover, in spite of the great quantity of monuments, the information derived generally deals with works and expeditions of certain kings and gives little clue to the main lines of history. The most complete knowledge of Egyptian civilization is to be obtained from the biographical inscriptions and countless local scenes which are depicted on the walls of tombs and temples. Early in the 3rd cent. B.C. Manetho, an Egyptian priest, classified the kings of Egypt into a series of dynasties.

His work, preserved by early Christian historians, is full of errors and defects but still provides the accepted scheme of classification. These dynasties have been grouped into longer periods, usually named for the city or province which was the leading center of the time. These groups of classification vary in name and detail, depending upon the opinion and methods adopted by the particular authority, but mainly agree on the principal periods. No such agreement is seen when more precise dating is attempted. The records, methods, and theories by which widely varying dates have been advanced are too complex to be discussed here; it is sufficient to mention that the various dates set for the beginning of the 1st Dynasty vary as much as 2200 years. The following list of dynastic groups with approximate dates in round figures, representing a composite of the greater part of contemporary opinion, should serve for practical purposes. Where opinion approaches unanimity regarding the commencement of a particular dynasty, it is mentioned specially.

Pre-dynastic Period until 3200 B.C. Ancient Empire or Kingdom (Thinite and Memphite), Dynasties 1 to 10, 3200-2200. Middle Empire or Kingdom (Theban), Dynasties 11 to 14, 2200-1800; 12th Dynasty, 2000. Invasion of Shepherd Kings (Hyksos), Dynasties 15 and 16, 1800-1600. NewEmpire (Theban), Dynasties 17 to 20, 1600-1000; 18th Dynasty, 1580. Delta Dynasties (Saite), Dynasties 21 to 30, 1000-332; divided into two unequal periods by the Persian conquest of 525: 1st period, 21st to 26th Dynasties; 2d period, 27th to 30th Dynasties. (Many authorities introduce a 31st Dynasty representing the Persian occupation just preceding the conquest of Alexander.) Ptolemaic Period or Dynasty, 332-30.

Egyptian art then extends over a period whose length, by the most conservative estimate, is nearly two-thirds of man's recorded history. This fact alone gives increased importance to its various phases.

PRE-DYNASTIC PERIOD: With the usual early records of pottery and flint weapons we find a funerary art of painted pottery figures of women, either standing or seated, with arms raised in an attitude of mourning or supplication. The figures show little realistic representation, and their painted decoration seems to simulate tattooing. Ivory tusks with tips carved into heads of men with long beard are found. Combs and other useful articles carved with figures of animals come slightly later. Later pottery shows pictures of men and women (more prevalent) and animals

done in solid colors. The typical Egyptian blue glaze "faience" had also been invented.

The people who were to form the "Dynastic Egyptians" seem to have moved up the Nile from the north, and as their conquest progressed the level of the art was raised. Stone vase-making improved, and gold appeared as ornament. Stone sculpture appeared in rather rude flat relief on limestone grave monuments. Slate palettes, both painted and carved, developed in size. The carvings are characterized by processions of domestic animals usually arranged in horizontal rows, affording a strange parallel with the early art of the Mesopotamian Valley.

OLD EMPIRE: At the beginning of the Dynastic period there was a sudden and sharp development of all art forms. The 1st Dynasty, which together with the long and colorless 2d makes up the Archaic or Thinite period, is marked by conceptual power, strength of design, and technical skill. Though the conventions which mark Egyptian art are evident in relief and painting, fragments of stone sculpture in the round show greater freedom, while many of the small ivory figures are of extreme sensitivity and vitality.

In the reign of Zoser (Zosorthros), the 2d king of the 3rd Dynasty, a tremendous advance in architecture was made, which can be laid with great probability to his minister Imhotep (Yemhotep), who, later deified in his own name, is one of the few great figures to emerge from the anonymity (see above) of Egyptian art. Imhotep, the Imonthes of the Greeks, seems to have been the Egyptian Asklepios. Not only a scientist and physician, he was also an architect. It was under Zoser, according to Manetho, that the first stone house was built (probably a reference to the Stepped Pyramid at Sakkara); also the first funerary temple, which shows most of the characteristics of the developed Egyptian style —paneled limestone walls, rows of lotus-reed columns and other columns resembling the single papyrus stalk, and capitals shaped like its sample bell-like flower. The stepped pyramid, as well as subsequent pyramids, was a special form of the typical tomb of the nobility called a mastaba, from the native word meaning "bench," to which the tomb structure has a slight resemblance. Zoser's reign gave an impulse to architecture which resulted in the building of the Pyramids, the Great Pyramid of Khufu (Gr. Cheops), the 2d Pyramid of Khaf-Re (Gk. Chephren), and the 3d Pyramid of Menkaw-Re (Gk. Mycerinus) at Gizeh. The tremendous size of these structures together with the numerous smaller pyramids in their vicinity give the name Pyramid Age to the time, but it is to be noted that the pyramid form was used in many subsequent ages though not in the same magnitude or purity of construction. The pyramids, oriented with their faces toward the cardinal points of the compass, were built of large blocks of masonry (for Great Pyramid 4' x 6' x 20" approx.), which were then faced with carefully tooled stones so that when finished the sides were smooth. The nature of facing stone varied, limestone and granite being used. The stone masonry of the entire period is remarkable for its precision and finish. The famous Sphinx (Egypt. Harmachis) resulted from a fortuitous use of an outcropping of limestone in an old quarry. Its form at smaller size is common in Egyptian art.

Stone buildings were of post and lintel (trabeated) construction. The corbeled arch was used in some cases to span internal openings and to relieve lintels of excessive weight (see Great Pyramid, above), but the true arch and vault were used only in trenches or below ground, where there was adequate abutment. Tomb paintings and similar records show that some buildings employed the arch and vault and were sometimes capped by a form resembling a dome, but these types of construction seem to have been reserved for the more temporary buildings built of brick with pressed mud roofs.

During the first four dynasties we continue to see strong indications of earlier Mesopotamian influence. The paneled style of brick walls, the first stepped pyramids similar to the Babylonian Ziggurat, the character of early representation of animals, the use of the seal cylinder, which soon disappeared in Egypt though retained in Mesopotamia, and finally the knowledge and use of the true arch in the relatively temporary buildings of brick—all point to direct influence or to elements received by each culture from a common source. These indications increase in importance in view of recent discoveries in the lower Euphrates valley, which point to a greater antiquity for the early cultures of Mesopotamia. (See MESOPOTAMIAN ART.)

Both painting and sculpture now embodied the fully developed conventions which characterize Egyptian art through its long history. Neither form ever lost its association with picture writing, so that even in the periods of greatest realism colors were applied in flat tones practically devoid of shading, and no attempt was made to solve the pictorial problems of atmospheric depth or linear perspective. This resulted in an art in which beauty of line, silhouette, and color pattern predominated. Painting, except within tomb chambers, was employed least because of the relative impermanence of distemper, fresco not being used. In all periods, but particularly in the earlier dynasties, male figures in painting or painted sculpture are colored a red brown, while female figures are a light buff or tan. In both relief and painting the human figure shows the head in profile, eye in front view (a few exceptions show an attempt at profile; example, wood panels of Hesi or Hesi-ra, Cairo). Shoulders are in front view, but waist and hips again in side view, producing the peculiar "hourglass" type. Again, the legs are in side view, one advanced before the other, but with both feet flatly upon the ground line. A sense of action is produced by the quality of line rather than by naturalistic portrayal.

Sculpture in the round is marked by greater realism, enforced by its three dimensional nature, and the desire for a portrait image. (See above.) There was strong descriptive portraiture; however, it was confined to the head and face, characteristics of the body being indicated in a most general manner with no attention paid to accuracy of anatomical detail. While the figures show great variety, each follows certain rigid conventions. Seated figures have legs and feet close together. Standing figures (sometimes attached to a background slab of stone) present the same rigidity regarding the vertical axis. The weight is carried on both feet, but one leg, the left, is extended to the front. The arms are usually tight to the sides or one is extended forward, usually the left. The planes of front, back, and sides are strongly developed, giving the figures their characteristic squareness. The failure to bend or twist the figure about the vertical axis, which produces a distinct "front facade" in the figure, has been termed the Egyptian law of frontality. (Observed also in Babylonia, Assyria, and archaic Greece.) Practically all statues and reliefs were treated with color, conventionally applied. Most of this has disappeared. Outstanding examples— Sculpture: Sheik-el-Beled (Mayor of the Village) in wood, painted, Cairo; the large Khaf-Re in diorite, Cairo; the Seated Scribe of the Louvre, in limestone, colored; Pepi I, in beaten copper, Cairo. Painting: Geese of Medum, Cairo.

MIDDLE EMPIRES: While the political and art center was at Thebes in Upper Egypt, what little change there was in art forms is seen in the tendency toward greater stylization and formality. The 12th Dynasty is noted for the craftsmanship of its ivory carvings, scarabs, and various forms of glazed pottery (faience). In architecture, rock-cut tombs replaced the mastabas of Lower Egypt. Examples at Beni-Hassan.

HYKSOS: During this period the decline already noted was accelerated. About this time the rectangular burial chest was replaced by a coffin made of inferior native wood fashioned with a human head and roughly shaped to the body, which came to be the rule from that time on. The industry for the manufacture and decoration of mummy cases must have been prodigious.

NEW EMPIRE: This age saw an upturn in art quality, particularly in the 18th Dynasty. Except for the pyramids the architectural remains of the earlier dynasties are fragmentary, partly because of the rebuilding of temple structures at later dates. With the 18th Dynasty, however, this character changed; temples and tombs are more or less complete.

The temple now took its final form, which was maintained until the Roman era. It is symmetrically arranged about a major axis and is approached by a long avenue, usually flanked by recumbent lions or sphinxes (human-headed lions). The avenue terminates at a great gate structure or pylon, generally preceded by a pair of obelisks, and against which are fastened great poles from which banners were hung. A central gate through the pylon provides entrance to the forecourt, a rectangular enclosure bounded on its lateral sides by high walls, against which stand covered colonnades. Usually these colonnades are continuous on at least three sides of the court, forming an interior peristylar treatment adopted with minor variations by both Greeks and Romans. On the far side of the forecourt from the pylon lies the largest covered room of the ensemble: the hypostyle hall, so called by reason of the numerous columns needed to support the roof. Behind this in regular progression upon the main axis lie one or more antechambers, and finally the sanctuary containing the cult statue. Surrounding the sanctuary are numerous small rooms for the use of the priesthood, which are made part of the temple unit by an enclosing wall. The main rooms excepting the sanctuary, which varies, lie with their longer dimensions at right angles to the major axis; therefore their chief entrances are on the longer sides (also customary in Mesopotamia). The ceilings become lower as the sanctuary is approached, a condition which, together with the gradual shutting off of natural light, produces an effect well suited to a ritualistic cult. Walls both of the pylon and the inner rooms of the temple are profusely decorated with colored reliefs. Many temples multiplied the architectural features and added others, which gave variety to the more simple form, but the deviation from the axial scheme is made only in the most exceptional cases and is due mainly to topographical expediency. Two features, the entrance pylon and the hypostyle hall, evidences of which rarely occurred in earlier periods, were in common use; while the clerestory, i.e., the raising of the walls of the central section of a hall above the height of the roofs of the side portions in order to secure light by vertical openings in these upper walls,—which was used in a modest form in the Old Empire, reached full development in the New Empire. The classic example is the Hypostyle Hall of the Temple of Amon at Karnak (19th Dynasty), containing 134 columns within a space of 170' x 329'. The twelve columns of the central avenue are 70' high approximately. The large clerestory openings were filled with pierced stone trellises, ample fragments of which remain. The architecture, however, was clumsy, and the craftsmanship less skillful than in the earlier periods.

Rock-cut tombs and tomb temples reached their greatest size and magnificence, evidenced early in the 18th Dynasty by the tomb temple of Queen Hat-shepsut, constructed for her by the architect Sen-mut at Deir el Bahri, and in the 19th Dynasty by the Great Speos and Little Speos of Rameses II at Abu-Simbel.

In the 18th Dynasty painting confined itself largely to recording scenes from everyday events, and the delicate colored reliefs showing Queen Hat-shepsut's expedition to the land of Punt (Somaliland), as well as the reception of the ambassadors from Crete, are important as well as beautiful historical documents. Later in the 19th and 20th Dynasties painting became far more profuse and elaborate, sacrificing quality for magnificence. The general trend in sculpture and painting was toward greater stylization, formalization, and conventionality. The one exception was in the brief period of Akh-en-aten's religious revolt. At this time the shackles of conformity seemed lifted from the artist, and an art of brilliant and vital realism developed. Thutmosis, who evidently served Akh-en-aten as court artist, is one of the few sculptors who emerge from existing records as definite personalities. Sensitive portraits of the king, identified as his with reasonable certainty, show a depth of feeling entirely missing in the subsequent periods. A further example of this period is seen in the justly famed portrait of Akh-enaten's queen, Nofretete (Berlin), done in limestone, painted, with eyes of inlaid rock crystal. However, the highly stylized reliefs and statues of Seti I (Temple of Seti I, Abydos), and of Rameses II show an art of finished technique, whose grace and subtlety of line represents an attainment unequaled in its peculiar field. Toward the close of the New Empire sensitivity of feeling gave way to an almost vulgar display in which the lavish use of gold and color fails to compensate for the poverty of ideas.

SAITE PERIOD: Nothing noteworthy disturbed the relative mediocrity of the art forms until the 20th and 26th Dynasties. At this time there seemed to develop a conscious attempt to imitate and revive the art character of the Old Empire. Portrait statues were designed in the dress of the 4th and 5th Dynasties. Sometimes the imitation is so perfect that it is difficult to date the statue if its inscription is missing. Portraiture in sculpture reached a new high of technical excellence as well as literal fidelity to the model and may be compared to Flemish portraiture of the early 15th cent. A.D. However, this revival had little vitality, and its archaistic forms soon succumbed to the influence of Greece and Rome.

PTOLEMAIC PERIODS: Imitation of the Old Empire was replaced by imitation of the New Empire, from which the worst elements were retained and the virtues discarded. Added to this were mannerisms and motifs taken from the fully developed style of Greece and Rome. Several temples were built which have distinction if not brilliance, among them being the great temple at Edfu, the Hathor temple at Denderah, and the Isis temple with its accompanying buildings at Elephantine. These, though presenting variations in the design of details, emphasize the unchanging nature of Egyptian architectural forms.

MATERIALS AND TECHNIQUES: In the long period from its beginnings till its final extinction under the Romans Egyptian art shows a consistency in the use of materials as well as art forms. Good limestone and granite were plentiful, but so was the thick mud of the Delta and river valley, which was used for sun-dried brick. Wood was scarce, and from earliest times the finest timbers were imported from Syria. Other importations were the dense stones used for sculpture, such as diorite, basalt, and obsidian. Alabaster was plentiful and because of its softness was used ex-

tensively from earliest times. Ivory was used extensively and readily imported *via* the Eastern trade routes as well as from Nubia and the Sudan. Gold came largely from Nubia, and as early as the 1st Dynasty expert craftsmanship was shown in the fashioning of gold jewelry. Gold wire, however, was hammered. There is no evidence of drawn gold wire in ancient times. Silver, known as white gold, was considered almost equal in value with the yellow metal, owing to the necessity of importation and the resultant scarcity. The use of copper, both hammered and cast, though early casting was of solid metal in an open mold, is seen in Pre-dynastic times. The casting of figures by the "lost wax" process seems known as early as the building of the Pyramids. However, the large portrait statue of Pepi I of the 6th Dynasty seems to have been completely hammered out. The use of bronze, while not as early as copper, was thoroughly understood and developed at the time of the 12th Dynasty.

Glazed pottery was known from prehistoric times and by dynastic times the skill to glaze large surfaces was perfected. In early times the favorite colors were blue and blue-green. In the New Empire and later great varieties of colors were used. While the use of glaze was very early, glassware itself did not appear until the New Empire (*ca.* 18th Dynasty). Blown glass objects did not appear until late Ptolemaic times, the blow pipe seeming to be an invention of the early 1st cent. B.C. In all of the minor and decorative arts the artist was allowed greater freedom from the rigid conventions applying to architecture and the more monumental sculpture and painting.

The art of Egypt was strong as long as its gods were strong. Religious utility was always its motivating force. When that religion died because it could offer nothing to the concepts of the Christian era, the art died with it. The art forms themselves seemed only provincial and childish to the citizens of the Roman world. A few religious motives were taken by Coptic art; the old symbol of life, sometimes known as the Key of the Nile, became the Christian cross; the peristylar court, the clerestory window, and the leafed capital are reflected in different forms in Greek, Roman, and subsequent architectural styles. Beyond this Egypt offers only an abstract beauty of forms and surfaces which will last just as long as the materials from which they are fashioned shall last. See Jean Capart, *Egyptian Art*, 1923; Roger Fry, *Last Lectures*, 1939; H. R. Hall, "Egypt" (in part),

Encyclopaedia Britannica, 14th ed.; Gaspar Maspero, *Art in Egypt,* 1930; W. M. Flinders Petrie, "Egypt" (in part), *Encyclopaedia Britannica,* 11th ed.; George Steindorff, *Egypt,* 1943; H. E. Winlock, *Excavations at Deir-el-Bahri,* 1942.   —J.C.

Egyptian blue. The bright, rather pale blue color found in wall paintings of Egypt and of other parts of the Mediterranean basin through classical times is Egyptian blue. It is closely related to the blue glaze of Egyptian pottery making. It is artificially made and is inorganic, and, although the ancient method of manufacture is not known, it has been synthesized in modern times by heating a mixture containing silica, a copper compound, calcium carbonate, and the natural sodium sesquicarbonate. Recently such a pigment has been produced for the market under the name, Pompeian blue.   —G.L.S.

Egyptian fabrics. Earliest variety of pile structures on record. Pile was obtained by drawing selected shots of weft, at intervals in the width of the fabric, into loops or tufts. These looped yarns varied in length and frequency.   —B.E.J.

Egyptian pottery. See CERAMICS II.

Egyptian theatre. See THEATRE.

e-hon (Jap.). Literally, picture book.

eidotropic tendency. See PSYCHOLOGY OF DRAWING AND PAINTING.

eight. See SYMBOLISM IN FAR EASTERN ART.

Einfühlung (Ger.). See empathy.

Eirene (Gr. *Eirene*). In Greek mythology the goddess of peace.

ekkyklema (Gr.). See STAGESETTING.

e-kotoba (Jap.). A scroll painting which includes both painting and text.

electric action (of an organ). See electrical instruments.

electrical instruments (musical). Electricity has been one of the great transforming agents of the present century. It has not failed to affect the development of the musical art. It has served as an auxiliary, a substitute for a mechanical means as in the **electric action** of the modern organ. Here the finger merely makes an electrical contact, thus actuating an electro-magnetic apparatus which does the actual work of admitting a stream of air to the organ pipes. It has, through the agency of the **thermionic valve** or **three-element tube,** functioned in the most varied fashion. This tube not only has a fundamental function in radio broadcasting (q.v.) but has transformed the phonograph (q.v.) into an instrument of high fidelity. Moreover in its function as an amplifying agent it has served to fundamentally alter existing instruments and is employed to produce sound in ways which are new to music.

In the **electric guitar,** for example, the instrument is played in the usual fashion. The sound is received, however, by an electromagnetic pick-up and can be amplified to an almost unlimited extent by an amplifying stage and a loud speaker which are connected in the circuit. An apparatus similar in general principle has substituted electrical amplification for the mechanical amplification of the piano sound-board. The pioneer instrument of this kind was the **Neo-Bechstein piano.** Here the strings are thin, single, and are struck lightly by small wooden hammers in contrast to the grand piano with its thick strings grouped in twos or threes, save in the lowest register, and under tremendous tension so as to obtain the greatest sonority by mechanical means. The sound of the struck strings in the Neo-Bechstein piano, however, is picked up by a series of microphones, amplified, and passed through a cabinet containing a loud speaker.

The **Everett Orgatron** also uses a familiar sound source, in this case vibrating metal reeds of the harmonium type. The vibrations are received electro-statically by "tone-screws" placed opposite the ends of the reeds. These vibrations are amplified and made audible by a loud speaker in the usual manner. This instrument has the external appearance of a pipe organ with two manuals, pedal board, swell pedals, and tilting tablets to control tone quality and volume.

It has also been found possible to produce musical sound by using a purely mechanical means to produce periodic electrical impulses. These impulses may in turn be converted into audible sound. This was demonstrated by Thomas Cahill who, in the first part of the 20th cent., produced periodic electrical vibrations by wheels with regularly spaced teeth which were rotated in an electro-magnetic field. Among several instruments developed or similar lines the one which is the most familiar to American readers is the **Hammond organ** developed by Laurens Hammond of Chicago. Here, however, a revolving "tone-wheel" or disc replaces the toothed wheel of the apparatus described above. The controls of the Hammond organ are in general those of the pipe organ, save that a means of controlling the harmonics present and their relative intensies is provided in the form of adjustable draw-bars above the upper manual. This provides a novel means of controlling tone color.

Still more novel are instruments utilizing the light sensitive selenium cell to provide periodic electrical impulses. In the **Superpiano** of Spielman (1927) a series of electric light bulbs are placed behind revolving discs which are pierced with a series of holes. Thus an intermittent ray of light falls on the selenium cell which has the power of converting light into electrical impulses. These in turn are converted into audible sound vibrations. Though the instruments based on this principle have as yet played no considerable role in the concert hall, the use of an apparatus similar in principle in reproducing the sound track of moving picture films gives clear evidence of the practicability of the method.

Finally, a group of instruments produce sound by purely electrical means. If two electrical circuits each containing a thermionic valve are so arranged that the frequency of one of them can be varied by the use of a variable condenser, an audible beat-tone equal in pitch to the difference between the frequencies of the two circuits is heard. In the **Theremin** (named after its inventor, Prof. Theremin of Leningrad) the right hand of the operator, which is moved nearer or farther from a rod connected with one of the valves, serves as a variable condenser. The differential tone is higher in pitch when the hand is close to the rod, lower in pitch as it moves away. Improvements on the apparatus have taken the form of a switch operated by the left hand to eliminate the glissando effects produced as the right hand moves from one position to the other and of guides of various kinds to enable the performer to locate the various pitch positions more simply. Other workers have constructed keyboard instruments utilizing similarly produced beat tones. In these cases, however, the second circuit is no longer variable but is set at a point which will produce vibrations of the desired frequency. The **Klaviatur-Sphaerophon** of Jorg. Mager (1928) contained three series of such units, each series controlled by its own keyboard. Thus the

instrument was no longer restricted to melodic music but could play music in three parts.

Obviously, the field of electrical instruments is still so new that any study written at the present time can do little more than point out some of the broad areas which have been explored and some of the broad principles which are involved. The changes which may be effected in the future by electrical instruments may well be revolutionary in their results and might conceivably replace the conventional types of musical instruments with novel forms presenting possibilities which can be foreseen only dimly at present.

—C.W.H.

electrical porcelain. Hard porcelain for insulators; one fire body and glaze. See CERAMICS I.

electric guitar. See MUSICAL INSTRUMENTS; electrical instruments.

electric oscillation. See ACOUSTICS.

electrum. An alloy of gold and silver, natural pale-yellow in color.

elements of design. See design.

elemi. Known commercially as gum elemi, this is a sticky, resinous material, usually viscous like a balsam, which comes from a variety of trees common to the Philippine Islands, South America, Africa, and the East and West Indies. Its principal use in the arts is as an addition to varnishes, though it has been included in wax combinations for the relining of pictures. —G.L.S.

Eleusinian. Pertaining to Eleusis in Attica, Greece, the principal seat of the worship of Demeter and Persephone in Greece and the site of the shrine at which initiation into the Eleusinian Mysteries took place. —L.T.S.

elevation. The vertical arrangement, in an architectural design, of its elements.

Elizabethan architecture. During the reign of Queen Elizabeth, from 1558 to 1603, English architecture passed from the medieval through a phase corresponding to the high Renaissance in Italy into the baroque. Henry the VIII had broken the medieval church, and the new buildings, such as Longleat, Montacute House, and Wollaton, were expansive secular palaces, in keeping with the prosperity and relative security of the reign. Italy early contributed classical logic of planning and the ancient orders, but the latter were so superficially applied that they quickly gave way before the close of the 16th cent. to a new veneer in the baroque style.   —P.C.B.

Elysian fields (Gr. *Elysion pedion,* E. field). In Greek mythology, the abode of the blessed dead who had been righteous in life; believed to have perpetual springtime, flowers, happiness; in early Greek writers located in the western ocean or at western edge of the world, later in the underworld.   —L.T.S.

émail (Fr.). Enamel.

e-maki (Jap.). A scroll painting, usually with text included.

e-makimono (Jap.). *The makimono* is a rolled horizontal scroll; *e-makimono* is a rolled horizontal picture scroll.

emblazon. See HERALDRY.

emblem. An allegorical or symbolic device designed pictorially to convey an abstract meaning. As this definition implies, emblems do not constitute a logical or semantic category but merely a historically determined group. The vogue of emblems arose during the Renaissance in consequence of the then prevalent preoccupation with hieroglyphics (q.v.). As their popularity grew, the demand for variety resulted in the invention of more and more abstruse pictorial devices so that it became profitable to publish explanatory manuals, so called **books of emblems**. Since emblems often were metaphors or epigrams transposed into the visual medium, these books influenced the language of poets as well as that of sculptors and painters.   —R.B.

embossed. *Book.* Leather or other material with a raised design worked by hand or plates.

embouchure. That part of a musical instrument applied to the mouth.

embroidered rugs. Used in Germany as early as the 15th cent. Early American embroidered rugs were produced during early 19th cent. Only a few in existence.

emerald green. Occasionally confused with viridian or verte emeraude, emerald green is a distinct pigment, a copper aceto-arsenite. It is bright in color and rather bluish green. It was first made at Schweinfurt, Germany, in 1814 and has sometimes been known as Schweinfurt green. Another name is Paris green. It is identical with the insecticide which also carries that name. Although fairly permanent in an oil or varnish medium, it can be blackened by sulphurous air or sulphurous pigments, and it is poisonous and dangerous to handle.   —G.L.S.

eminent domain, right of. See CIVIC PLANNING.

Emmaus. According to *Luke* 24, 13, a village "which was from Jerusalem about threescore furlongs". After his resurrection, Christ went there with two of his followers who did not know him. When Christ sat down at table with them at Emmaus and broke the bread, they recognized him by the sacred action and by the wonder of the subsequent disappearance of Jesus. The subject has often been treated in art. Best known, perhaps, are the various versions by Rembrandt. He was greatly attracted by the Emmaus scene and has treated it in several etchings and paintings.
                              —L.L.

emotional buoyancy. A general name for the quality which enables a work of art to hold the attention and interest of an observer while its subtler and less insistent qualities produce an effect on him which they could not produce without some such aid. In music this buoyancy is supplied by the volume, the purity, and the essential continuity of the sound; in architecture, by the size, the height, and the obvious weight of the building—or occasionally by some less universal quality, such as the richness or rareness of the material. There are few arts that can dispense with this quality entirely. See Carl Thurston, *The Structure of Art.*   —C.T.

empaistic, empaestic. Inlaid, embossed, or stamped

empathy. A word, artificially composed of Greek elements (*em-pathein*) to serve as an equivalent for the German **Einfühlung**, which literally means "feeling-into". It denotes the subconscious act of projection by which we attribute to an object our own kinesthetic sensations, motor impulses, moods, emotions, attitudes, and thoughts, perceiving these mental features as if they belonged to the object and formed what has been called its "tertiary qualities." The hill is experienced as 'rising', a spire as 'pointing to heaven', a spring day as 'smiling'. The phenomenon was described as the "animation of the inanimate" by Aristotle (*Rhetoric* 1411 b 32), and as "pathetic fallacy" by John Ruskin (*Modern Painters* Part III, Sec. II, Ch. 3, §31). But only after the term **Einfühlung** was ushered into the aesthetic discussions by Robert Vischer (*Das* *optische Formgefühl,* 1873), attempts have been made to find in empathy the clue for an interpretation of aesthetic enjoyment. The chief representatives of modern empathy aesthetics are Theodor Lipps, Johannes Volkelt, Karl Groos, Victor Basch, and Vernon Lee. See Earl of Listowel, *A Critical History of Modern Aesthetics,* 1933, pp. 51-82; K. E. Gilbert and H. Kuhn, *A History of Esthetics,* 1939, pp. 537-540.   —H.K.

Emperor. See ORIENTAL MUSIC.

Empire style. A term applied to the neoclassic mode which prevailed in France during the ascendancy of Napoleon Bonaparte, from about 1796 to 1815. A natural outgrowth of the stricter classicism of the late 18th cent. which was promoted by scientific archeology, it was particularly congenial to Napoleon's dreams of Roman grandeur. After 1798, sphinxes and other Egyptian motifs were added to the Roman repertory to celebrate the Egyptian campaign. The furniture in the style tended to a combination of rectangular massiveness and swelling curves, and was embellished both with heavy textiles, often exhibiting the "N" of Napoleon or the symbolic bees, and with much bronze appliqué. In America the style is associated with the relatively simpler furniture named after **Duncan Phyfe.** Probably the most noted architectural representatives of the style are the Arc de Triomphe de l'Etoile and the Temple of Glory (now the Church of the Madeleine), begun by Napoleon in 1806 and 1807, resp.
                                              —P.C.D.

emulsions. Among the painting mediums is a group in which drops of one kind of liquid are suspended in another liquid with which the former would not form a stable mixture. Perhaps the most common emulsion in the history of painting is the yolk of egg where a natural emulsifying agent keeps the two types, the egg-oil and the watery, albuminous mixture, in a stable suspension. Other emulsions can be made by mixtures of gums or glues with oils and varnishes, with the addition of a suitable emulsifying agent. Oil added to the egg yolk is still another. There has been some argument in favor of the theory that emulsions explain much of the character of late Renaissance oil painting and that they were important in the development of the handling of oil paint through the 17th and 18th cents. No very great amount of evidence has been brought together to support these arguments, but specific evidence about

painting mediums during this period is still very slight.   —G.L.S.

enamel. Fine glaze, opaque. See CERAMICS I.

ENAMELLING ON METAL. The process of enamelling consists of applying a thin coat of glass to certain metals, raising them both to a red hot heat, thereby melting the glass, and fusing it to the metal.

This type of enamelling should rightfully be termed **vitreous enamelling** to differentiate it from enamelled furniture, or automobiles which is accomplished by applying a resinous substance to a metal surface, and hardening it by baking in an oven at slightly above the boiling point.

There is some vagueness connected with the origin of the word "enamel", although the French word *esmail* leads us to believe it is connected with our word "smelt", and the German word *schmeltzen,* from which we also derive the word "smalt".

The vitreous glaze will adhere to some metals such as gold, silver, copper, and fine bronze (copper with a small admixture of tin), but will not adhere to nickel, zinc, or brass, which is a mixture of copper and zinc. A metal known as **colonial brass,** which is either 90 or 95 percent copper can be successfully enamelled if only one firing is required. However, on subsequent firings the alloy always causes trouble, and gives a streaked, or blistered effect. For the most beautiful transparencies it is advisable to use pure gold, fine silver, or pure copper.

Enamel is composed of silicates of various materials forming a colorless transparent glass called **fondant** in French, and **flux** in English. To this flux color is added by means of introducing small quantities of metallic oxides. An opaque white is made by melting the flux with oxide of tin, a yellow is obtained by the use of oxide of iron, or uranium. Manganese gives violet, and gold oxide produces our most beautiful reds. Cobalt will give an ultramarine blue, chromium a certain shade of green, and iridium a steel gray, or black.

The historical importance of the art of enamelling cannot be ignored. Its antiquity is assured, although confusion as to the authenticity of Egyptians, Babylonians, and Assyrians using enamels is still extant. The close resemblance to enamels in these cases is said to be pieces of inlaid glass, or colored stone.

There is no doubt that the work of the Celts, and the Saxons on the British Isles in the year 240 A.D., and continuing from the 6th to the 9th cents., was truly enamelling as we understand it today. They were said to have poured colored glass into molds to decorate their horse-trappings, shields, and armor-plate of fine gold and bronze. Originating in Persia was another type of enamelling called cloissonne and as that from the British Isles travelled eastward, the Persian type travelled westward, and met in Byzantium, where from the 9th to 11th cent. flourished the greatest enamelling era in the world's history. It was the strong religious feeling, and the desire for beautification that found in enamels the perfect vehicle for expression.

From Byzantium enamelling found its way to Europe, and followed the spread of Christianity. We find superb examples which were produced in Saxony, Brunswick, and along the valleys of the Meuse and the Rhine. By the second half of the 12th cent., France had acquired enamellers from Germaney. It was then passed on from the French to the Italian craftsmen during the 13th and 14th cents. and on into the Renaissance. We find the cities of Lorraine and Limoges the most important centers of enamelling in the 15th and 16th cents. Four top-ranking personalities from this great period stand out. First there was Nardon, or Leonard Penicaud apparently the eldest of the family, then Jean Penicaud, probably a brother, but often spoken of as Penicaud II, Leonard Limousin, and Pierre Raymond who were equally important during this time, produced quantities of fine pieces. A decided decline came about through the unwise dictatorial powers which Louis XIV exercised over the artisans of his time. The atmosphere surrounding the court was not conducive to the higher forms of art, and we find less opportunity given for creative work. Copies of paintings by Watteau, and Fragonard of superficial court life were adapted to snuff-boxes, and watch-cases. These made chiefly in Battersea, and Bow in England, showed skill in craftsmanship, and delicacy in drawing, but could hardly be considered as much more than pretty art.

The Japanese enamels are almost entirely done in the cloissonne method, and while superbly executed, are sometimes monotonous in their use of pale opaque colors. The more glaring work of the Chinese usually done in brilliant reds, blues, greens, and yellows on a white ground, is inferior to the Japanese enamels in many cases.

After an almost total lapse of interest in handicraft during the 19th cent., enamelling has emerged as one of the important forms of decoration, made possible with many new discoveries in chemistry, and mechanical inventions. A renewed interest in creating more beautiful utilitarian objects has inspired a handful of craftsmen throughout this country to keep alive the great traditions of enamelling as a fine art expression. Paralleling this effort, we also find enamelling being commercially produced for a variety of purposes, including bath tubs, kitchen sinks, automobile name plates, gasoline stations, and imitation shingles.

The process of enamelling is within reach of anyone with a sense of craftsmanship, and artistic ability. The tools for applying the enamel consist of a small spatular, a scriber or awl, and a spreader, which is made by bending a wire at 60 degrees and inserting it into a wooden handle. In general, the process can be divided into three parts; cleaning and preparing the metal to be worked upon; applying the enamel; and firing. The cleaning consists of three simple operations, which if followed carefully will assure success.

Careless preparation is the common cause of inferior work. First, the metal is cleaned in acid. In the case of copper, which is generally used, a solution of one part chemically pure nitric acid to one part water or two parts commercial nitric acid to one part water make up the acid bath. Secondly, the copper is rubbed briskly with fine steel wool. Thirdly, an application of saliva, being a weak alkaline solution, guarantees a perfectly neutralized surface upon which to work.

After scratching the design with the **scriber,** a small amount of enamel is taken from the jar with the **spatular,** and worked into place with the scriber while still moist, and then carefully leveled off with the **spreader.** The entire surface must be covered before firing, and care should be taken in juxtaposing the colors. It is necessary to keep the whole design continually wet. This can be accomplished by the use of a small atomizer. A weak solution of gum tragacanth is now sprayed on the design to help hold the particles in place. It is customary to use enamel ground to 60 or 80 mesh, but for detail work it may be ground to 200 mesh, and applied in the form of a paste, using oil of sassafras as the vehicle. When the piece is thoroughly dry, it is placed in a muffled electric kiln, and raised to 1400 deg. F., or 1800 deg. F., according to the average melting point of various hard and soft enamels which have been used in the design. A concave tray or bowl, may be fired on the concave side only, but if a convex plaque is to be made, it is advisable to counter-enamel the copper, to counteract the coefficient of expansion in the metal and the enamel as it cools.

When working on copper, more brilliant effects can be obtained with the transparent colors, by firing silver, or gold foil (No. 4, non-adhesive) onto a layer of enamel, and then proceeding as if working on the more precious metal. The cold colors are more suc-cessful over silver, and the warm colors over gold. Opaque colors can be used over any of the above mentioned metals.

For a fine finish, the work should be stoned with a carborundum stick under constantly flowing water, then refired.

The type of enamelling just described is called **painted enamel**. The colors are merely fused to the copper, and allowed to flow to-gether. In the type called **cloissonne**, thin wires are used to separate each color. This is the most ancient process, and a term which is greatly misused. The word comes from *clois-sons* meaning cells, into which the colors are placed. In the **champleve** type, the area which receives the enamel is either etched, or carved away, enabling the metal to show in places. There is a type of enamelling called **plique-a-jour**. It is a translucent enamel without a background which is accomplished by cutting away small areas from the metal and holding the enamel in place by capillary attraction, and then firing on a sheet of mica. After the mica is removed, the effect of small stained glass windows is achieved. **Basse-taille** enamel-ling is really a low relief, upon which trans-parent enamel is fused. **Grisaille** is an effect of light and shade produced in painted enamels, whereby a background is covered with opaque white, and modulated to produce the desired gradations.

The possibilities in the medium of enamel-ling are endless. Not only is there the varia-tion of coloring caused by different heats, but the combinations of enamels on various metals, and the effects of superimposition of the trans-parent colors and refinement of detail make enamelling an art which warrants the time and study of the artist, and repays in gratify-ing dividends. See H. H. Cunynghame, *Art-Enamelling on Metals;* K. Gibson, *The Gold-smith of Florence;* A. Rose and A. Cirino, *Jewelry Making and Design.*   **—K.F.B.**

encarpus. *Arch.* A festoon, flower, etc. orna-ment on a frieze or capital.

encaustic painting. An ancient method of easel and mural painting which employs pigments mixed with refined beeswax, with or without modifying ingredients (e.g., oils or resins). The paints are applied and manipulated with the aid of heat but the term, which implies a strong burning in of the colors does not apply literally to any of the accepted versions of the process in which the molten wax colors are manipulated over the surface with a brush and **cestrum** (one of an assortment of spatulate metal instruments or **cauteria**). En-caustic was apparently a major, if not the principal painting method employed during the entire classical period. No Hellenic Greek specimens or technical accounts of the process exist, but there are many literary allusions to it. The method was described in some detail by Pliny the elder, and referred to by Theophrastus and Dioscorides. Best known surviving examples are the Fayoum mummy portraits; these are described by some as Greek, others cite evidence to show that en-caustic may have originated in Egypt. A notable find in 1845 of a complete encaustic painter's equipment in a tomb at St. Médard-des-Prés established or confirmed the details of several of the materials and instruments used. Encaustic became obsolete during the 9th cent. Although the medium is extremely permanent and has desirable textural and op-tical qualities, its manipulation is rather diffi-cult to control. 19th and 20th cent. revivals have been sporadic and isolated. See mural painting; also *Beiträge zur Entwicklungsge-schichte der Maltechnik,* Ernst Berger, 1904; *Greek and Roman Methods of Painting,* A. P. Laurie, 1910; *Ancient Egyptian Materials and Industries,* A. Lucas, 1934; *La Reconstitution du Procédé à l'Encaustique,* Hans Schmid, 1933.   **—R.M.**

enchainement (F. *enchainer,* to link). A link-ing or combination of steps and movements, which collectively form the phrases of a com-plete dance. Also, an academic term for a short class-room exercise.   **—L.K.**

end blown flute. See MUSICAL INSTRU-MENTS.

endless canon. See canon.

endless knot. See SYMBOLISM IN FAR EASTERN ART.

endpapers. *Book.* The paper pasted to the inside of the boards and also the first loose leaf.

end sheet. See edition binding.

energy distribution curve. See COLOR.

energy transmission curve. See COLOR.

engaged column. A member belonging to and projecting from a wall, with the appearance of a column but not free-standing; an applied column.

engineer. See RADIO DRAMA.

engineering, aesthetics of. Considering engineering constructions as tasks of architecture and therefore as phenomena of art is not a discovery of modern times. Roman aqueducts, mediaeval fortifications, and Renaissance bridges are exactly as much solutions of specific technical problems as modern factories and railway stations. The only distinguishing fact is the use of new materials of engineering, iron, steel, and reinforced concrete. These new materials began to find their artistic expression beyond the mere fulfillment of technical needs at the beginning of the 20th cent. Some pioneer work in this direction was done already in the 19th cent.: Paxton's Crystal Palace at the World Exhibition, London, 1851; the Engineering Hall at the World Exhibition, Paris, 1884; the Eiffel Tower, Paris, 1889; many iron and steel bridges throughout Europe; the Brooklyn Bridge in New York, N. Y., 1883, etc.

Today, the borderline between technical construction and architectural creation is hard to fix, even in mere technical constructions like silos, hangars, bridges, and plants. Cooperation of engineer and architect is' becoming usual. The same is true for the shaping of non-architectural utensils and machines, like locomotives, cars, etc. Objects of daily use like lighting fixtures, kitchen units, telephones, refrigerators, etc., originally mere problems of engineering and fabricating calculation, become subjects of artistic consideration as tasks for the industrial designer. See traffic, aesthetics of; functional architecture. See also Lewis Mumford, *Sticks and Stones,* 1924; Henry Russel Hitchcock, Jr., *Modern Architecture, Romanticism and Reintegration,* 1929; Museum of Modern Art, *Machine Art,* 1934; Talbot Hamlin, *Architecture through the Ages,* 1940; N. Pevsner, *The Pioneers of the Modern Movement, from William*

Morris to Walter Gropius, 1936; Sigfried Giedion, *Space, Time and Architecture,* 1941; Paul Zucker, *American Bridges and Dams,* 1941; David B. Steinman, *Bridges and Their Builders,* 1941; L. Moholy-Nagy, *The New Vision,* 1938.   —P.Z.

engineering drawing. See drawing.

England, architecture of. See GREAT BRITAIN, ARCHITECTURE OF.

ENGLISH ART. The beginnings of English art reach back to Anglo-Saxon times. A crude country slowly developing under the civilizing influence of the medieval church, the English were largely dependent on the Continent for both art and decoration. The Venerable Bede's account of the building of the monastery and church of St. Peter near the mouth of the river Wear in Northumberland, may be taken as typical of the methods of the times. Biscop, called Benedict, in 674 began the building by importing masons from Gaul to build a church in the "Roman style"; he also brought over glaziers to make and decorate the windows. Finally, on one of his numerous visits to Rome, he purchased pictures of the Virgin and the Twelve Apostles not only for the adornment of his church but also for the edification of all who could not read. The Danish invasion destroyed Biscop's work to such an extent that only the foundations of his church remain.

English artists doubtless learned from Continental artists; and during the period of the building of the great churches and cathedrals the work of natives and foreigners is inextricably mixed. Of the English who are known by name the most prominent was William of Winchester and later of Westminster. His greatest work was the Painted Chamber at Westminster (1230, *temp.* Henry III), which stood south of Westminster Hall and was destroyed by fire in 1834 together with the Houses of Parliament. That there was much pictorial decoration in the English churches is evidenced by the remains that are scattered over the country, remains which have usually suffered severely in the passage of time or at the hands of later improvers.

With the foundation and development of the monasteries came also the production of manuscripts. The rule of the orders was brought from the Continent and similarly the methods of making and illuminating manuscripts. Matthew Paris of St. Albans (c. 1195-1259) was not only a notable author and illustrator (see his *Historia Major*) but he was also the director of other works written or copied and illuminated by monks working under his direction. After the Conquest as the monasteries rose to the fullness of their life and power, the making of beautiful books flourished. Not all of the work was original, for much of it was based on older pictures and designs which were well known; but every so often there arose artists of great skill and originality whose names are buried in the anonymity of their lives. The works which have survived show much of the outpouring of books in mediaeval England: Psalters (e.g., *Queen Mary's Psalter,* the *Tickhill Psalter,* and that which belonged to John, Duke of Bedford), Horae (e.g., the *Taymouth,* the *Carew-Poyntz*), Missals (e.g., *Sherbourne*), Gospels (e.g., one at Pembroke College, Oxford), and innumerable Bestiaries, Chronicles, and Romances. Once again, however, it is necessary to keep in mind the fact that many manuscripts made on the Continent found their way to England and cannot, because of what one may call an international style of writing and illumination, be divided from the native product. But there is sufficient authentic English work, as in the *Psalter and Hours* of John, Duke of Bedford, to justify the statement that at times that work rose to a level equal to the best produced on the Continent.

Upon the conclusion of the Wars of the Roses and under the well established government of Henry VII (1485-1509) came a demand for portraits and secular decoration. Religious painting and church decoration, which languished under this reign, came to an abrupt end in the days of Henry VIII (1509-47). In the matter of portraiture the threads are again mixed, the most notable work being that of foreigners together with some successful portraits by minor English artists. Hans Holbein the Younger (1497-1543), a German, was in England from 1526 to 1528 and again from 1537 until his death. His portraits of the court of Henry VIII are notable both for their style and for their portrayal of character. He was followed by Antonio Mor (c. 1512-75), a Dutchman, who made the great portrait of Queen Mary in 1554. Of the native Englishmen of the time of Elizabeth, Nicholas Hilliard (1537-1619), goldsmith and miniaturist, stands very high because of the radiance of his portraits in color, line, and pattern. The success of Hilliard gave rise to a large school of English miniaturists of varying abilities (e.g., Isaac Oliver, John Hoskins, Alexander and Samuel Cooper). The stabil-

ity of life in England under the firm government of the Tudors together with the development of a definite court society, gave opportunity for these artists to follow their calling. The Tudors did not, however, show any great inclination to foster the arts and such patronage as they bestowed was incidental and haphazard.

Under James I (1603-25) and Charles I (1625-49) the foreigners are still the prominent painters. Marc Gheeraedts the Younger (1561-1635), a Fleming, was more English than any of these, for he lived in England from the age of seven; his portraits of women and children (e.g., *Prince Henry; The Countess of Pembroke*) are notable for their gentle manner and detailed charm. Daniel Mytens (c. 1590-1642), a Dutchman, was in England from 1614 to 1634 (e.g., *Duke of Hamilton*); Cornelius Johnson c. 1593(-1664), the son of a Fleming, was born in England and appears from his work to have been a pupil of Gheeraedts (e.g., *Lady Waterpark*); after the beginning of the Parliamentary Wars he removed to Holland. Of all the foreigners in England at this time Anthony Van Dyck (1599-1641) was the most prominent. He was in England in 1620-21 and in 1629; in 1632 Charles made him court painter, a position which he held until his death. Van Dyck is of importance not only for the portraits which he painted (e.g., *Archbishop Laud, Lord Philip Wharton, Charles I, Sir Kenelm Digby*) but also for his influence upon English painters in setting a pattern for portrait painting. William Dobson (1610-1646) was probably his most successful pupil. It is interesting to note that the Van Dyck influence, which was Cavalier, continued through the Commonwealth period, as is instanced by Robert Walker's (c. 1600-c. 1660) *Oliver Cromwell and his Squire,* which is wholly in the Van Dyck tradition.

Lely (Peter van der Faes, 1618-80), a Dutchman, who lived in England from 1641 until his death, constitutes the link between the pre-Commonwealth period of Van Dyck and the Restoration; fitting himself to the political situation of the moment, he was always fashionable: his Puritans are dour; his Restoration *Beauties* are sensual. His successor was Godfrey Kneller (1646-1723), a German, who first followed Lely's style but later developed a more free expression of his own. Both of these men reflect the low spiritual level of the Restoration period. Like Lely, Kneller was adaptable and so adjusted himself to the situation after the Revolution of 1688 that William knighted him. Of equal importance with his pictures is the fact that in London he founded and directed the first academy for teaching painting. Henceforth the English were to develop their own painters and the reign of the foreigners was over.

With the accession of Queen Anne (1702) began the so-called **Age of Manners** supported by a sophisticated, albeit a rather sceptical, society. The accumulation of wealth under the Whig rule, the building of great houses on estates, and the settled government of the nation, all made possible the patronage of art by the upper classes. As the great fire of London gave Sir Christopher Wren his opportunity to build churches, so the new St. Paul's provided Sir James Thornhill (1676-1734) with a dome to be decorated. It is noteworthy that an Englishman was chosen for this work, an Englishman whose first art education was under Thomas Highmore, a minor artist. Moreover, by virtue of his local reputation Thornhill continued the painting academy begun by Kneller.

William Hogarth (1697-1764), wholly English trained, became the great champion of the English artist in his own country and his efforts were not without success. Because of his method of publishing engraved reproductions, his series of story-telling pictures (*Harlot's Progress, Rake's Progress, Marriage à la Mode, Industry and Idleness*), satirical and moralizing at once, were more widely known than the work of any other artist of his day. His efforts to show ability in great mural paintings were unfortunate and only a few of his portraits are worthy of notice. But he strove valiantly to show that the English could do what the foreigners did, and although his skill was not equal to his patriotism, he gave much encouragement to English artists and patrons.

The latter half of the 18th cent. saw the happy co-existence of a continually expanding upper class able and willing to patronize the arts and a number of artists, particularly portraitists, of genuine worth. Sir Joshua Reynolds (1723-1792), trained at home and abroad, after 1752 speedily became the foremost painter of his day. For a time to be painted by Reynolds was a social requirement. When one considers the large output of his studio, for in his great days he employed assistants, one is amazed at the great number of excellent portraits (e.g., *Captain John Hamilton, Nelly O'Brien, Duchess of Hamilton, Admiral Keppel, Sarah Siddons as the Tragic Muse*). Reynolds knew his genera-

tion thoroughly and painted it with just the right mixture of classicism and sentimentality.

Reynolds' influence was greater than his painting; for in 1768 with others he founded, under the patronage of George III, the Royal Academy of Arts. He was its first President and was reëlected annually for twenty-four years. For better or for worse the Royal Academy, with its schools and its annual exhibition, is a factor henceforth to be reckoned with in the history of English painting. In its schools, at least until the end of the 19th cent., nearly all English artists studied and to its exhibitions most of them submitted pictures. Like similar organizations the Royal Academy has developed and taught standards and tradition. Slower to change than the individual, it has at times been behind current thought and has therefore been accused of hampering development; nevertheless, the Royal Academy has given standard and focal point to English art which particularly fits the genius of that nation

Contemporary with Reynolds and by many ranked as his equal was Thomas Gainsborough (1727-88). Wholly English trained, he became in 1759 a popular society painter at Bath, and in 1774 carried his reputation to London where he became the rival of Reynolds, with whom he had a part in the founding of the Royal Academy. His portraits are notable for their delineation of character (e.g., *Mr. Nugent, Karl Abel, The Blue Boy, Mrs. Graham, Perdita Robinson, Captain Wade*). From the point of view of popularity Sir Thomas Lawrence (1769-1830) was Reynold's successor. In demand by 1787, elected A.R.A. in 1791, appointed Court Painter in 1792, and elected R.A. in 1794, this son of a Bristol innkeeper rose to the top with astonishing swiftness. Later times have somewhat lowered this high estimation of his work, for his women have a tendency to be too sweet and his men too theatrically ideal; nevertheless, his portraits have quality and must be accorded a better rating than many others (e.g., *Sir Philip Sansom*, the *Calmady Children, Caroline Upton, Pinkie, George, Duke of Grafton*). Three other society artists of the period must be mentioned: George Romney (1734-1802), who painted some fifty pictures of Lady Hamilton until she became a kind of stock character for him; Benjamin West (1738-1820), American born, who lived in England after 1763 and eventually became President of the Royal Academy; and John Singleton Copley (1737-1815), also American born, who took up residence in London in 1775 and became famous not only for his portraits but also for his rhetorical historical paintings (e.g., *Death of Chatham*). Of Reynolds' students James Northcote (1746-1831) and Thomas Beach (1738-1806) were the most successful.

The 18th cent. in England was much concerned with gardens and the picturesque. In the early decades of the century the formal classical garden with its axis and balance, with its mount and artificial ruined Roman arch, was very popular; later came the so-called natural garden and landscape which by means of a vista maintained an axis but kept the other parts in imbalance. Because this interest in nature pertained to small cultivated and controlled areas, patronage for landscape painting was almost nonexistent. The life of Richard Wilson (1714-82), a landscape painter of no mean ability, is an eloquent example of the difficulties of an artist in this field: in his latter days he was saved from poverty by his appointment as Librarian of the Royal Academy. But in spite of lack of patronage landscape painting, particularly in water color, made progress. Samuel Scott (1710-72), Paul Sandby (1725-1809), and John Robert Cozens (1752-97) were all successful painters of landscape in water color; and their group is fittingly brought to a conclusion by the greatest of them all, Thomas Girtin (1775-1802).

It is often said that Joseph Mallord William Turner (1775-1851) made his way rapidly in the Royal Academy (A.R.A., 1799; R.A., 1802) because there was so little competition in the field of landscape painting, but one hopes rather that the members of the Academy thus early recognized the genius and ability of the man who was to become one of the greatest painters in England. In water color and in oil he had equal facility. Of the quality of his work one must note his skill in giving impressions without attention to minute detail Ruskin fought hard to demonstrate that everywhere Turner was true to nature, a demonstration which today seems somewhat needless. The greatness of Turner lies in his scope, his grasp of the essence of things. His mountains at times loom large and are overpowering, but such was their emotional effect and Turner has produced it; his skies are luminous beyond any that had ever been seen before and the play of color in them was a revelation to the studio artist. His life-long, one-sided combat with Claude Lorrain (1600-82) damaged some of his work, for his paintings on classical subjects have not the life of his other work, Ruskin notwithstanding)

That later the French Impressionists should look upon Turner as their founder and forerunner is wholly understandable, for to Turner form and effect were always greater than detail. Of his pictures the following represent different types of his work: *Coniston Falls; Garden of the Hesperides; Sun Rising Through Mist; Death of Nelson; Crossing the Brook; The Slave Ship; The Fighting Téméraire; Venice; Snow Storm; Rain, Steam, and Speed; Norham Castle*. With Turner landscape painting came into popularity in England, a popularity which it has never lost.

Contemporary with Turner was John Constable (1776-1836), as honest a painter as England ever saw. Whereas Turner frequently rearranged nature to suit his effect, Constable selected but never changed the relationship of objects as he found them. Not being gifted with the rapid and unerring skill of Turner, Constable had to work hard to achieve his purpose; and like Turner he was interested in the portrayal of light and its effect. The following pictures are representative of his work: *The Cottage in the Cornfield; Dedham Mill; The Hay-Wain; Salisbury Cathedral from the Bishop's Palace; Stonehenge*. Other landscapists of the time can only be mentioned: Copley Fielding (1787-1855); W. H. Hunt (1790-1864); David Cox (1783-1859); and John Sell Cotman (1782-1842).

Alone and unheralded stands William Blake (1757-1827) whose scope was that of the universe. By virtue of his religious beliefs he moved in his mind from heaven to earth, to hell and chaotic void, peopling them with characters whose actions and fates are frequently hard to follow and difficult of interpretation. The lyricism of his poetry is marred by defects and yet the lyric quality surmounts the faults; and in his pictures his distortions of the human figure are forgotten in the sweep and grace of the movement which they portray. The colored engraving was his chief medium, for his early training was in engraving; and throughout his work the engraver's precision of line is everywhere evident. Endowed with an imagination far beyond that of the average man, he frequently leaves those who look at his work far behind and rather breathless as they perceive the scope of his beauty. The following represent different aspects of his work: *Pity; Glad Day; The Four and Twenty Elders;* illustrations for Milton's *Paradise Lost, The Book of Job,* Bunyan's *The Pilgrim's Progress; Songs of Innocence* and *Songs of Experience; Jerusalem*.

During the Victorian era the Royal Academy was easily the dominating force in the field of art. Literary painting, i.e., paintings based upon passages or characters in books, flourished (e.g., E. M. Ward's *Doctor Johnson at Lord Chesterfield's House;* C. R. Leslie's *My Uncle Toby and the Widow Wadman;* Frederick, Lord Leighton's *Romeo and Juliet*). The competition for the decoration of the new Houses of Parliament gave added impetus to historical painting. Portrait painting, largely in the tradition of Reynolds, constituted a steady and assured income for all artists.

Perhaps the popularity of the genre picture is something of a key to the Victorian point of view. At this time the number of purchasers of works of art was the largest that had ever existed in England. It was made up not only of the upper classes but also of many who through the prosperous days of the Empire had made money and were willing to spend it. The people of the second category were filled with memories of their earlier and less affluent days and from their vantage ground of comfortable financial security looked back sentimentally on their childhood and youth. Supported by these persons genre painting was much in demand. The Scot Sir David Wilkie (1785-1841), though not the first to do this type of work in England, made genre painting popular (e.g., *The Blind Fiddler; The Penny Wedding*). After him came such men as William Mulready (1786-1863) (e.g., *Crossing the Ford*); William Collins (1788-1847); and William P. Frith (1819-1909) whose *Derby Day* in its size and in the multiplicity of its characters is almost the climax of this type. Even Turner tried his hand in *The Blacksmith Shop* but fortunately was satisfied with this one demonstration of his ability. At the close of the Victorian era with the dying of sentimentality as a dominant force, the vogue for genre painting fell away.

Against all of this kind of painting and the domination of tradition in the Royal Academy rose the **pre-Raphaelite Brotherhood.** In 1848 three young painters, Dante Gabriel Rossetti (1828-82), William Holman Hunt (1827-1910), and John Everett Millais (1829-96), in an effort to get back to truth and reality as they understood them, thought they saw in the work of the artists who preceded Raphael the validity they sought. A noble subject, truthfulness to nature, and extraordinary attention to detail were their cardinal Tenets. Because they were young and had not yet mastered their craft, their early work was stiff and awkward; but it did not deserve the torrent of abuse which was heaped upon it (even Charles Dickens, who knew nothing about art, attacked it) until Ruskin stepped in and quieted the storm. The Brotherhood lasted only from 1848 to 1851. Rossetti, who had never been a very faithful member, went off to painting women in beautiful clothes and colorful backgrounds. Millais fell away to follow the popular patterns of the day which brought him finally a knighthood and the presidency of the Royal Academy. Holman Hunt remained true to his principles and won gradual recognition, as evidenced by the Order of Merit which he received in his old age. The following pictures are representative: Rossetti, *Ecce Ancilla Domini* (P.R.B.); *Beata Beatrix; Monna Vanna; Veronica Veronese*: Millais, *Christ in the House of his Parents* (P.R.B.); *The Order of Release; My First Sermon; The Yeoman of the Guard*: Holman Hunt, *The Light of the World; The Scapegoat; Triumph of the Innocents; May Morning on Magdalen Tower.* Ford Madox Brown (1821-93), although he was not a member of the Brotherhood, was sympathetic (e.g., *Christ Washing St. Peter's Feet; The Last of England*); and Sir Edward Burne-Jones (1833-98) was the Brotherhood's most prominent follower (e.g., *King Cophetua and the Beggar Maid; The Golden Stairs*).

Whatever eventual effect the pre-Raphaelite movement might have had on English art was broken off by the influence of French Impressionism, which was carried to England and championed by the American born, irascible, James McNeill Whistler (1834-1903). Whistler's emphasis on design as opposed to the story-telling picture of his contemporaries, was sufficiently revolutionary to keep him the storm center of British art throughout his life, a position which because of his personality he must have thoroughly enjoyed. In painting, etching, and lithography he did notable work. In his *Portrait of his Mother* and *Carlyle* he achieved a simplicity and effectiveness of character portrayal which not only transcended but also was in complete harmony with his design. The influence of his study of Japanese art is nowhere better shown than in his paintings and etchings of the Thames (e.g., *Nocturne in Blue and Silver* and *Old Battersea Bridge*). Significant of the new forces which were abroad in the land was the founding of the International Art Society of which Whistler was the first president.

The pre-Raphaelite Brotherhood experienced the life of Jonah's gourd; Whistler, by virtue of his personality, was pretty much a lone wolf; but the reaction against the domination through tradition by the Royal Academy was bound to come. In 1885 the **New English Art Club** was founded to give opportunity for those who found inspiration and validity in Impressionism. It was, however, more than a *Salon des Refusés*, for it had organization and flexibility of point of view, factors which have kept it alive to this day. That it eventually influenced the Royal Academy can be seen in the number of its members who later became Academicians. Of these two at least should be noted: George Clausen (1852—) and John Singer Sargent (1856-1925). In landscape Clausen, under the influence of Bastien Lepage, Millet, and Monet, interpreted the English scene with new design and luminosity (*e.g., Building the Rick* and *The Road: Winter Morning*) and was one of the leaders in revitalizing English landscape painting. Sargent, after his training in France, became a popular painter of portraits in London and in the United States. His work was uneven in that at times his facility ran away with him but often his portrayal of faces showed not only likeness but also penetration of character (*e.g., Asher Wertheimer* and *The Misses Vickers*). Some of his superficiality may be, probably unconsciously, an interpretation of the character of the generation whom he was painting.

The record of English art of the last thirty years is that of other countries; post-impressionism, cubism, and all of the other movements were and are reflected in the work of British artists, and to mention names in this short account would merely give undue prominence to some who are no more worthy than their fellows. These decades are very much alive. The Royal Academy is still the great fortress of British respectability in art but its influence has been greatly diminished. It no longer conducts the only art school; there are many very good ones. Its exhibitions are always attended and carefully criticized; but there are many other exhibitions which are also patronized and studied. English art today is vigorous and many English artists are doing competent work. The days of dependence on foreign artists is long since past and in its place has developed an English art which is in its way an interpretation of the nation. See Baker, C. H. C. and James, M. R. *British Painting*, 1933; Baker, C. H. C. and Constable, W. G., *English Painting, 16th and 17th Centuries*, 1930; Baker, C. H. C., *Lely and the Stuart Portrait Painters*, 1912· Binyon,

L., *English Water-Colours*, 1933; Borenius, T. and Tristram, E. W., *English Mediaeval Painting*, 1927; Finsberg, A. J., *English Water-Colour Painters*, 1906; Fry, R. and others, *Georgian Art, 1760-1820*, 1929; Fry, R., *Reflections on British Painting*, 1940; Hunt, W. Holman, *Pre-Raphaelitism and the Pre-Raphaelite Brotherhood*, 1912; Johnson, Charles, *English Painting from the Seventh Century to the Present Day*, 1932; Long, Basil, *A History of British Miniatures*, 1929; Millar, E. G., *English Illuminated Manuscripts:* Vol. I, *Tenth to Thirteenth Centuries:* Vol. II, *Fourteenth and Fifteenth Centuries*, 1926-28; Reynolds, Sir Joshua, *Discourses*, 1924; Saunders, O. E., *English Art in the Middle Ages*, 1932; Walpole, Horace, *Anecdotes of Painting in England*, 1871; Whitley, W. T., *Art in England, 1800-37*, 2 vols., 1928-30; Wilenski, R. H., *English Painting*, 1940.

—F.F.

English glass. See GLASS AND GLASS-MAKING.

English guitar. See MUSICAL INSTRUMENTS; mechanical instruments.

English horn. See MUSICAL INSTRUMENTS.

English porcelain. See CERAMICS II.

English red. See iron pigments.

English Renaissance. See RENAISSANCE.

engobe. *Cer.* Coating of slip, usually different in color from body. See CERAMICS I.

engraving. This is the process of incising lines on a plate with a graver or burin to produce intaglio prints that have a precise angular beauty. As it is easier to make straight cuts with the burin than curved ones, many parallel straight lines and cross hatchings are characteristics of this process. When the design is composed predominantly of little dots and short lines it is called **stipple engraving.** See PRINTS AND PRINT PROCESSES.

—K.K.

enharmony. The fact that in the equal temperament (q.v.) three different notations can be used to designate the same tone (e.g.: c double sharp, d, e double flat; d double sharp, e, f flat, etc.)

—E.K.

enharmonic interval. See interval.

entablature. The superstructure which lies horizontally upon architectural columns or piers; generally of several units.

entasis (Gr.). A slight convex curve sometimes given to a column to counteract the appearance of weakness. Seen on the columns of 7th cent. Japanese architecture. —J.A.M.

entelechy. See form.

entr' acte. See divertissement.

entrée (F. *entrer,* to enter or come in). The arrival by groups or individuals of dancers onto the stage, especially in a divertissement (q.v.). —L.K.

entwining rope style. See CHINESE ARTS.

envelope restriction. See CIVIC PLANNING.

épi. *Arch.* A covering for the peak of a sharp-pointed roof.

epigraphy. See writing.

epiphany. See EARLY CHRISTIAN ART.

episode. *Mus.* A digression or incidental passage. See fugue.

episodic. Lack of organization with specific reference to plot or story. Here, the term indicates that the various incidents have insufficient internal unity and cohesion; they do not flow into and follow from one another, but are merely a series of unconnected events. There is a lack of logical pattern, and the successive parts of the plot do not seem to demand or influence one another. Hence, though much may happen, nothing develops. —I.J.

equal temperament. See ACOUSTICS; interval.

equilibrium. A term suggested as an aid in differentiating a balance between *attention-values* from other types of balance (q.v.) found in art. (See Carl Thurston, *The Structure of Art.*) This particular form of balance has grown so indispensable to certain arts that it is important to understand its distinctive structure. A long series of experiments in the laboratory will be needed before this structure can be understood completely but its major outlines seem fairly clear. The forces to be balanced are the attractions which the various units in a composition have for the eye. The attraction which a given unit exercises at any point in the composition will diminish with the distance from that unit but will not be modified by the direction (except in a few special cases which need not be considered here). The sum of the attractions to any unit may accordingly be regarded as constituting a *field,* roughly comparable to the gravitational field surrounding the earth, and any balance that may be created between the attractions exercised by any two units may be most clearly understood by regarding it as a balance between their two fields. It may be assumed, in general, that no balance will be perceived if either (1) the two units are so far apart that a zone exists between them in which their attraction has become so weak that an observer is not conscious of any rivalry between them or (2) they are so close together that the weaker one can no longer compete with the stronger. The possibility of a balance depends on the existence of a point or a zone, at which the attraction of each is felt to be equally strong. But when a pattern or composition contains many units the problem of the artist is not so much the creation of a series of individual balances between them as the merging of all their fields, including those generated by the border or frame if present, into a single field which will appear to be in an agreeable equilibrium. If he is depicting more of the third dimension than is inherent in his medium, as in painting, this imaginary space must also, if possible, be included in the same field. The individual forces involved are extremely slight but as their total value increases, roughly, with the square of the number of units in a composition this total becomes impressive in an art as complex as painting. But what makes it an indispensable ingredient in this art is the infinite flexibility which belongs to it by virtue of its independence of all axes and of the ease with which it can be readjusted by either moving its units, modifying their attractive power, or adding new units, of any desired intensity, wherever they may be needed. It is the only system of space relationships capable of functioning satisfactorily as a complete solvent for all the other ingredients in a highly complex art. It constitutes, to be concrete, the major part of the difference between a Vermeer and a Gerard Dou or a Meissonier. It seems to belong to at least the same aesthetic genus as beauty (q.v.): both create an illusion of simplicity yet are so complex and so elusive that they produce their effects without betraying the secret of how it is done. —C.T.

equipoised sculpture. See SCULPTURE.

Erato (Gr. *Erato* fr. *erasthai,* to love). In Greek mythology, the Muse of lyric, love poetry; represented crowned with roses and myrtle and holding a lyre.

Erechtheum. Greek Ionic temple on the Acropolis at Athens. Built 410-409 B.C. to enshrine an ancient and venerated wooden statue of Athene supposed to have fallen from heaven. The design is attributed to Mnesicles, architect of the Propyleia. The temple is built of Pentelic marble with friezes of black Eleusinean marble. It is on three levels, with two Ionic porticos of different scale, both of unrivalled beauty. On the north side is found the exquisite Porch of the Caryatidae.

—L.H.

Eresh-Kigal. Sumerian goddess of the underworld.

ermine. See HERALDRY.

Eros. See Aphrodite.

erotic. *n.* An amorous composition or poem. See also ex libris.

eschequier. See MUSICAL INSTRUMENTS.

escritoire. A secretary desk. See FURNITURE.

escutcheon. See HERALDRY.

ESKIMO ART. By most authorities the Eskimo are thought to have been late comers, probably the last of the Mongoloids to enter North America from Asia. Several thousand years ago they reached Alaska and spread eastward across the treeless tundras that fringe the 6000-mile coastline of the continent from Bering Sea to Greenland. A few turned inland to the forested land up the river valleys and to southwestern Alaska, where, and only where, contact with the Indians was possible. Otherwise they have been a self-contained people and present a relatively homogenous culture pattern evolved by an ingenious people in an inhospitable land. They were hunters and fishers, partly nomadic and partly sedentary, in search of the animals on land and primarily on sea that could furnish them food, fuel, materials for clothing, hunting and fishing equipment, and other artifacts for daily living. In winter many lived in snow houses out on the ice, hunting seal, walrus and whale; in summer they camped in skin tents on the land, seeking land game and fishing in dugouts and kayaks.

A series of epochs has been tentatively established to show the evolution of Eskimo culture. The oldest stage, probably the climax, appears in the **Old Bering Sea culture** found on St. Lawrence and Diomede Islands. It was probably already highly developed in the early Christian centuries. Houses were built of stone, timber and whale bone. Seal, walrus and whale furnished flesh and blubber for food and fuel, skins and membranes for clothing and covering of kayaks, bone and ivory for various artifacts, the shaping and embellishing of which constitute the chief art expression. Besides stone for chipping implements, walrus ivory furnished excellent material for the exploitation of the chief characteristic of their style, linear decoration. Harpoon points, spear heads, skin scrapers and handles of various utilitarian objects were polished to a smooth surface and then engraved with circles or ellipses swung lightly but firmly around a central dot. This linear design produces movement that accents the planes of the object and at the same time an exceptionally delicate surface decoration. The designs are either purely geometric or abstractly representational, depicting the head of a fish or animal where the controlling dot is the eye.

From this Old Bering Sea culture evolved the **Punuk,** whose artifacts are similar. The carving, however, lacks the sensitive delicacy of the former, tends toward the straight line and is cut deeper, probably because of the introduction of iron somewhat before 1000 A.D. Punuk is the transitional stage to modern Eskimo.

In the vicinity of Point Barrow centered the Birnik phase, important chiefly in that it formed the basis of the **Thule** culture which extended eastward from Alaska through Greenland and was based upon seal, walrus and whale hunting. It had much in common with the Old Bering Sea epoch whence it appears to have originated. Its art expression, though similar in kind, is less sophisticated. The Thule culture flourished about a thousand years ago and gave rise to the historic Eskimo in this area.

The Eskimo have adapted themselves most ingeniously to the rigorous climate and limited resources of the far North. They remained isolated from both the Indians and the white men until late in the 19th cent., with the exception of those groups that moved into southwestern Alaska, where they made contact with the Northwest Coast Indians. Here they found an abundant new material, wood, and also metal tools; and from it, with the addition of paint, fur and feathers, produced astonishingly imaginative masks, lively in character, some apparently for pure amusement, but many for a magical purpose, to insure success in the hunt or to appease terrifying evil spirits. Carving from walrus ivory continued on harpoons, throw-sticks, and fishing equipment; but to this utilitarian art was added the engraving and carving of human and animal figures with no particular function. These small carvings are quite abstract in their highly generalized form yet realistic in their characterization.

The Eskimo are skillful in making clothing that is not only suitable to an intensely cold, damp climate but particularly pleasing because of the combinations of furs differing in color and texture, or because of the deftly patterned borders of raincoats made from animal membranes. See Kaj Birket-Smith, *The Eskimos*, 1936; Henry B. Collins, Jr., *Outline of Eskimo Prehistory*, in *Essays in Historical Anthropology of North America*, Smithsonian Miscellaneous Collections, 1940; *Prehistoric Art of the Alaskan Eskimo*, Smithsonian Miscellaneous Collections, 1929; J. A. Mason, *Eskimo Pictorial Art*, University of Pennsylvania, Museum Journal, 1927.   —H.G.

estampie. See MEDIEVAL MUSIC.

estipite. Shaft in the form of an inverted obelisk or herm base which constitutes the main element in the compound shaft of the Mexican churriqueresque order. It is regularly surmounted by a square block with round medallions and a Corinthianesque foliate capital.   —J.Mc.

Estonia, art of. Estonian art well reflects the history of the country and the long periods of foreign domination. The original Estonians, a Finnic speaking race, were conquered by the Danes in the 13th cent. and King Waldemar of Denmark erected the castle of Tallinn. The country finally passed under the control of the Knights of the Sword and later the Teutonic Knights until its union with Sweden in 1561. Then in 1710 Russia, which had repeatedly invaded the country, captured it and held it until the Soviet Revolution. During the confusion of World War I, the Estonians recovered their independence and were recognized by the other nations.

There are a few remains of the Stone Age and of the Iron Age but the bulk of the peasant art dates from the 18th cent Like the other nations of Eastern Europe, wood was the most favorite medium for decoration with floral motifs in the north and geometric in the south. Woolen and linen weavings show the same type of design. Metal work is relatively rare, although there are considerable numbers of silver articles.

The medieval architecture, esp. in Tallinn, consists of churches and castles in Baltic Gothic. Among these may be mentioned the Bishop's Church (ca. 1223), the Gothic City Hall of the 14th cent. and the towers of the various ramparts as the Fat Margaret, the Kik in de Kök and many others. Nearby in Pirita is the Church of St. Brigitta which was destroyed by the Russians in 1577 and has since been excavated and restored.

There are a few Renaissance buildings as the House of the Black Heads in Tallinn and in the 17th cent. there were many baroque monuments, esp. in Narva. Later, under Russian influence there was an extensive development of the classical tradition so favored by Peter the Great and his successors. We may mention many of the buildings in Tartu and the Kadriorg or palace of Peter near Tallinn.

During the 19th cent., the modern buildings show the conventional European influences and since the liberation of the country there has been a definite influence of some of the Finnish architects.

In the field of painting, there exist some religious frescos from the medieval period but there is little of value until the 19th cent. when K. A. Senff (1770-1838), a German, became professor of art at the University of Tartu. Yet, during the century the influence of the Imperial Russian Academy of Arts was very prominent and J. Köler (1826-1899) was the first Estonian to be elected to membership in it. He was a portraitist and landscape painter influenced, to a certain degree, by French realism. Later through the influence of Hoffmann (1851-1912) and K. F. E. von Gerhardt (1838-1925) the Düsseldorf Academy exerted considerable influence upon the younger painters. Konrad Mägi (1878-1925) introduced French post-impressionistic traditions; since his time practically all schools of painting have made their appearance.

Since the independence of the country, the Pallas School of Arts at Tartu has been the chief influence in the country. There has been a return to realism among some of the most prominent artists as A. Johani (b. 1906) but this has not excluded the development of artists who have been influenced by German expressionism, French monumental art, cubism and abstract geometric art.

Sculpture has been less developed but August Weizenberg (1837-1921) was trained in the Imperial Russian Academy and such men as Jaan Koort (b. 1883), the greatest of Estonian sculptors, has been influenced by Egyptian and various primitive techniques.

The sober realism of the Estonian character has left its effect upon the art of the country; and since the period of liberation this has been taking the foremost place in the artistic production. Yet this has not meant the elimination of foreign influences but rather the welding of them into the formation of a national style which is still not in final shape. See *Estonia: Population, Cultural and Economic Life,* ed., Albert Pullerits, Tallinn, 1938.

—C.A.M.

estufa (Sp. stove). (1) Term applied to the chamber used as a "sweat house" by various Indians. (2) Term sometimes applied to the chamber that is better known as the "kiva" in southwestern archeology. —J.M.M.

étagère (F.). An open-shelved cabinet.

etched glass. See GLASS AND GLASS MAKING.

etching (from the Dutch, *etzen,* to eat). Denotes an eating away process, using acid for this purpose. In print making, includes not only bitten plates but also proofs from these plates. The term, used in a general way, covers the following intaglio processes: line etching, aquatint soft ground, pen process aquatint, stylotint (q.v.), and other types of bitten graphic work. See PRINTS AND PRINT PROCESSES. —K.K.

etching line. This is what is usually meant by the term, etching, used in a restricted sense. Line etchings are entirely made up of lines, some bitten deep, some very delicate, sometimes single lines, sometimes cross hatched many times. The paper and ink molded in the tiny etched channels of the plate gives a rich raised line. The delicate film of ink on the surface of the plate, controlled by the printer, can focus light on an appropriate section of the plate, giving a sustaining tone to the darker passages. It is the most widely used and renowned of the intaglio printing processes, used by the world's most famous artists. See PRINTS AND PRINT PROCESSES. —K.K.

etching needle. Steel point used for making the drawing on a grounded plate for a line etching.

etching paper. Specially made paper, soft, and with a minimum of sizing, for printing etchings.

etching press. Printing press for pulling proofs or impressions on paper from intaglio designs on metal plates.

etching, soft ground (*vernis mou*). A type of etching that has a soft broken line resembling a pencil or crayon line. It does not have the decisive quality or control that characterizes line etching, but it does have a pleasing line well suited for masses, textures and use in conjunction with aquatint. See PRINTS AND PRINT PROCESSES. —K.K.

etchuseto yaki (Jap.). Pottery made in Etchu province.

Etruria ware. See CERAMICS II.

ETRUSCAN ART. Etruscan civilization (ca. 700-100 B.C.) centered in Tuscany on the west coast of Italy. The Etruscans, seafaring invaders from the eastern Mediterranean, were for three centuries the leading political power of Italy (8th-6th cent. B.C.). Later (400-100 B.C.) they succumbed to the attacks of the Gauls and the Romans. Early Etruscan architecture is represented by tombs, some rock-cut and others built of masonry (Regolini-Galassi, Caere; Pietrera, Vetulonia; Populonia). The accent is on the masses of the walls; narrow and intimate spaces are hollowed into the big mounds. The decorative vocabulary of the minor arts combines central European (Hallstatt) and orientalizing traits. Adorned with images of oriental gods and monsters in exquisite granulation, the superb Etruscan jewelry derives its effects from a rhythmic alternation of light and shade on the gleaming metal.

Greek influence becomes paramount in the later 7th cent. B.C. and henceforth dominates all forms of Etruscan art. The Etruscan temples derive their tripartite cella from a Mediterranean prototype. Their division into a roofed porch and a broad cella results from exigencies of the Etruscan cult. Their use of columns and architectural decoration is based on archaic Greek models. The best examples of wooden temples revetted with polychrome terra cottas date from the archaic period (600-450 B.C.). This period abounds in large terra cotta images and in funeral statues and funeral reliefs in native sandstone (Veii, Caere, Met. Mus., N. Y.) (Chiusi, Tarquinia, Fiesole). The reliefs depict battle scenes, funeral games, banquets, and religious ceremonies; similar subjects are shown in the vivid paintings of the tombs.

Etruscan work lack the disciplined order, the logic, the tectonic poise of their Greek models. They exhibit broad, voluminous forms covered with flat colors and express an unbridled, animalistic spirit.

The classical art of Greece (5th and 4th cent. B.C.) was imitated by the Etruscans with indifferent results. In architecture some of the decorative motifs change following their Greek models and sculptured groups are introduced into the pediments (Orvieto). In sculpture, the mechanics of anatomy are gradually grasped with no perception of their organic unity. And the exuberance of Etruscan archaism is replaced by vacuous passivity (terra cotta head, Chiusi; bronze statue of Mars from Todi).

The revival of Etruscan art in the 2nd and 3rd cent. B.C. forms part of the rise of provincial Hellenism in Italy, an art often lax and barbarized but vigorous and rich in experiments. In architecture, arcuated forms developed by the Greeks stimulate the Etruscans to new achievements in arched and vaulted structures (barrel-vaulted tombs and cisterns in Chiusi, city gates of Volterra and Perugia). In sculpture, the dynamic style of the Hellenistic school of Pergamon is reflected in the excited, loosely modelled reliefs of Etruscan urns and, on a larger scale, in the terra cotta sculptures of temple pediments (Civit'Alba, Telamon, Vetulonia). Hellenistic interest in the individual is echoed in Tuscany by a series of magnificent portraits. Some are pensive and introspective (bronze boy, Florence); some are overladen with realistic detail to the point of caricature. Others portray an aggressive spirit with a few incisive traits. But all of these portraits are concerned with the emotional rather than the intellectual or spiritual aspect of man. In painting, Greek Hellenistic prototypes of sculptural forms and richly graded palette are reduced to flat outline drawings with strong contours and a few expressive accents. (Tomb of Typhon, Tomb of Cardinal, Tarquinia). The last Etruscan monuments (after 100 B.C.), represented by small Etruscan urns in Perugia, can scarcely be distinguished from the poorer products of the art of the Roman Republic.

The Etruscans have not contributed any new significant visual forms to the history of art and too little is known about the function of art within the framework of Etruscan culture to give a true historic interpretation.

Yet in the best Etruscan painting and sculpture, technical competence combines with a rich decorative pattern, strong colors and voluminous masses to express convincingly a passionate vitality which strongly appeals to many modern critics. See G. M. A. Richter, *Handb. Etruscan Coll., Met. Mus., N. Y.,* 1940; E. G. Giglioli, *L'arte etrusca,* 1935; P. Ducati, *Storia dell'arte etrusca,* 2 vols., 1928; *Etruscan Sculpture* (Phaidon), 1940.
                                                    —G.M.A.H.

Etruscan pottery. See CERAMICS II.

etude. *Mus.* A lesson designed to afford practice in some special difficulty; occasionally used as name for artistic compositions (Chopin).

euouae. A formula or abbreviation found in chant books for the last two words, *saeculorum amen* of the *Gloria Patri* or lesser doxology. The abbreviation is made up of the last six vowels.   —V.A.

euphony. An agreeable combination of sounds or tones.

Evangeliar (L., *evangeliarium*). It contains the four Gospels in unabridged form. At the beginning of the medieval Evangeliars there was usually the introductory letter which St. Jerome, the translator and redactor of the Vulgata, wrote to Pope Damasus who had ordered the translation. The Evangeliars have become of great artistic importance because of the habit of ornamenting letters and illustrating the texts. They contain the oldest extant examples of Teutonic culture in the form of painting. Famous Evangeliars include the following: SCHOOL OF IRELAND: *The Book of Kells,* beginning of the 8th cent., Trinity College Library, Dublin; *Evangeliar from Lindisfarne,* beginning of the 8th cent., London British Museum; *Evangeliar from the St. Gallen Monastary,* library No. 51, about 750 to 780. SCHOOL OF ENGLAND: *Cuthbert Evangeliar,* 770 to 780, Vienna, Hofbibliothek; *Evangeliar of the School of Canterbury,* about 785, London British Museum; *Evangeliar of Cambridge,* beginning of 11th cent. FRANKISH SCHOOL: *Godescalc Evangeliar,* about 800, Paris and London; *Evangeliar Grandval,* School of Tours, 834 to 843; *Evangeliar of Charles the Bald,* Franko-Saxon, after 865; *Codex Aureus of St. Emmeram,* School of Corby, 870. GERMAN SCHOOLS: *Evangeliar of Otto III,* School of Reichenau, about 1000, now in Munich; *Evangeliar of the Abbess Uta of Niedermuenster,* School of Regensburg, 1002-

1025; *Bernward Evangeliar,* School of Hildesheim, 993-1022; *The Golden Evangeliar of Henry III,* School of Echternach, 1045, now in the Escorial. See literature under miniature and initial.   —A.J.S.

Evangelistary, the. Contains the Gospel texts of the *Missale Romanum.* These texts are distributed through the whole of the Church year in accordance with that which is read each Sunday. They are artistically important because of their ornamented letters and illustrations. Famous old Evangelistaries are among others: Evangelistary in Oxford, Bodleian Library, north east Frankish, about 800; Evangelistary at Leipzig, Stadtbibliothek, School of Reichenau, group of Eburnant, third quarter of the 10th cent.; *Gero Codex* (Evangelistary) Darmstadt, Hessische Landesbibliothek, Cod. 1948, School of Reichenau, Eburnant-group, third quarter of the 10th cent. See literature under miniature and initial —A.J.S.

Everett Orgatron. See electrical instruments.

ewer. A wide-mouthed pitcher or jug with extended lip for pouring liquids.

exact seeing. See PHOTOGRAPHY.

excess condemnation. See CIVIC PLANNING.

execution. See design.

exedra (Gr. *exedra* fr. *ex,* out+*hedra,* seat). An open recess, semi-circular or rectangular, provided with a bench around the wall, opening off the colonnade in Greek gymnasia or private houses, or free standing in sanctuaries; for conversation.   —L.T.S.

exhibition. In museum terminology the word "exhibition" means a temporary display of art objects based on a central theme. Many museums arrange a varied program of exhibitions which change every month. In a broader sense "exhibition" is used to refer to the display of objects in an art museum's permanent collection. Art exhibitions are also held in schools, colleges, galleries of art dealers, clubs, theatres, stores, and other public institutions.

Not only is the temporary exhibit important for enjoyment and educational value, but it also serves to lead visitors elsewhere in the museum and into other museum activities. The importance of temporary exhibitions has been recognized by museums in recent years as a means for stimulating and maintaining interest in the museum and for keeping it a living institution. Often the temporary exhibition is used as the focus for lectures, seminars, movies, and as an integral part of the museum's educational program.

Loan exhibitions consist of objects borrowed from private and public collections and from art dealers. These are often supplemented by objects from the museum's own collection which are adapted to the idea of the exhibition. **Circulating exhibitions** are assembled or constructed by an institution and rented or lent to museums and schools. The materials of circulating exhibitions are sometimes mounted on panels to facilitate transportation. These are often **educational exhibitions,** which include both original works of art and explanatory material: photographs, diagrams, and models. The **permanent collection** of a museum includes all the works of art it owns. In displaying its objects according to periods and countries, a museum often makes them into organized exhibitions.

Although the subjects of exhibitions are infinite, specific types of subject matter can be listed. The most common subjects are the art of a single country, period, or type of art (painting, sculpture, architecture, prints, furniture, etc.). The "one man show" of the work of a single artist, living or dead, is a common theme. Other subjects include types of subject matter (portraits, landscapes, the Christmas story, fashion in art, etc.). After the idea of an exhibition has been developed, a good title is important, just as for a play or book.

The arranging of exhibitions is an art in itself. Even the simplest exhibit of paintings in a single room requires care and thought in its display. A symmetrically balanced arrangement is usually made in a case of this kind. Large pictures are located in the centers of walls, as centers of interest and balance, with smaller pictures of equal size on either side. On each side of the central group an alternation of picture sizes and shapes is then made. Two small pictures may be double hung to form a group equivalent to a large picture. Sometimes pictures must be balanced with respect to the direction of their internal lines. In this connection, paintings in the corners of rooms should never face the corner (e.g., a profile portrait facing a corner). In general, pictures are hung at eye level with equal distances between them. The aim, of course, is to make as interesting a wall as possible, for a wall arrangement can easily be monotonous.

In contrast to exhibitions with balanced arrangement are exhibits which are intended to be started at the beginning and read through to the end. By their nature exhibitions of this kind are educational. The primary consideration in the arrangement of such an exhibition is to induce the observer to follow the material in logical sequence. This requires not only signs and arrows to point out the starting place and continuity, but also an arrangement of objects so that one will lead to another. In the informal sequence type of exhibition, there is usually more grouping of objects than in the formal balanced type. Often objects are arranged on the diagonal and in unsymmetrical balance. Sometimes a unifying horizontal background is used in the form of a band of colored paper, cloth, or wood extending around the room on which the objects are arranged. To make the observer look at objects in the proper sequence, many museums form corridors by erecting partitions. Corridors and an informal arrangement are also used in exhibitions which do not have a strict sequence or educational aim. The arrangement of an exhibition develops as the logical result of the material.

An important principle in exhibition arrangement is clarity, both in layout and in labeling, so that unanswered questions do not distract the observer. In some cases explanation is not included in labels or signs but in a catalogue or gallery book. The arrangers of exhibitions have learned much from advertising art, the theatre, and store window display. Among the properties used are different types of pedestals, backgrounds, shelves, moving diagrams, wall movies, and spotlights.

In planning an exhibition every aspect is important from beginning to end, from the original idea to the publicity, opening reception, and museum program based on the exhibition. Although to the observer the finished exhibition should have the appearance of being an almost effortless undertaking, it is the work and thought which have gone into every phase that make it a success.

—D.T.

exile melodies. See JEWISH MUSIC.

ex libris. The international term for **bookplate,** a decorative name label placed (usually) on the inside cover of a book to indicate ownership. Its history parallels closely the history of printing, the earliest known plate dating back to 1450. Albrecht Dürer engraved a number in the early 1500's as did Altdorfer,

Cranach and other artists contemporary with him. The earliest dated English plate yet found is of 1520. These early plates were nearly all armorial, many of them with the coat of arms only, as everyone could read the armorial bearings even if unable to read the name. The first plate printed in America was the typographical label of Steven Day, dated 1642.

All art museums and most libraries have collections of bookplates mounted and classified. Classification according to style is important in the description of plates, as "plain armorial", "Jacobean", "Chippendale", "ribbon and wreath", "urn" (which had a vogue after the publication of Gray's *Elegy*), "pictorial", "armorial-pictorial", "bookpile", "portrait", "canting", "erotic", "humorous", "juvenile", "typographic". Plates are distinguished again according to the method of reproduction. The earlier plates were all engraved on copper and this is still considered to be the finest and most formal method, but unfortunately there are very few artist-engravers now living. Etching on copper is a popular medium, particularly for pictorial plates and some of the great contemporary etchers have made beautiful bookplates. Wood engraving is a fine medium for creative expression and the many striking plates by Rockwell Kent are the best modern wood-block examples. Lithography and photogravure are both used successfully in the reproduction of bookplates, but the half-tone process is ineffective. In point of numbers more plates are made as zinc etchings from pen drawings than are produced by all other methods combined. The cheapness of the process makes it popular rather than exclusive and the success of the plate all depends upon the artistry of the original drawing.

Collectors classify plates under different subject heads and specialize in their collecting under one or more divisions. Some collect only Early American, others famous personages, others Masonic or medical or angling or dramatic plates. Some collect authors, others music markers. Many collect only the work gardens, ships, skulls, canting plates, juveniles, of one or two noted artists such as Sherborn, Eve, Spencely, E. D. French, Sidney Smith or Macdonald.

A bookplate is first of all a name plate to denote ownership and prevent loss. It is a design with the owner's name and, to make it individual, some pictorial indication of his profession or hobby or ambition or favorite recreation, but ideally it should be more than

this, it should be a composition to be enjoyed for the intellectual pleasure it gives from its organized pattern of form and line, a design whose elements are the name and individual symbolism of the owner but which are used as means to the end of creating a complete and satisfying piece of art. A bookplate is a little thing, two inches by three, more or less, but it *can* be a distinct work of art. It is like a sonnet in literature, complete and self-contained. A long list of the world's great artists who have made bookplates could be compiled, from Dürer, Holbein, Hogarth, Bartalozzi, Millais, Abbey, down to Brangwyn, Cameron, Heintzelman and Kent of the present day, all of the plates containing that indefinable quality that makes true art. It must be admitted, however, that the majority of bookplates now in use do not reach that height, and it might be said incidentally that most amateur designs fail because of poor lettering. See Allen, *American Bookplates;* Fowler, *Bookplates for Beginners;* Doane, *About Collecting Bookplates;* Ward, *Some American College Bookplates;* Fuller, *A Bibliography of Bookplate Literature.*
—T.E.F.

experience of beauty. See PSYCHOLOGY OF ART.

experimental aesthetics. See AESTHETIC INQUIRY, CURRENT TYPES OF.

experimental productions. See RADIO DRAMA.

EXPERIMENTAL PSYCHOLOGY OF MUSIC. Viewed comprehensively, the experimental psychology of music is based on pure psychology, general aesthetics, physics, particularly acoustics, anthropology, ethnology, genetics, and in the case of vocal music, phonetics and linguistics. Pure psychology and aesthetics present the general problems and hypotheses, while the other sciences furnish methods of research, apparatus and techniques, and an adequate variety of material in space and time.

The beginnings of such an experimental science appear in the work of the Pythagoreans on the relation between musical tones and the length and tension of vibrating strings, and in empirical observations on the influence of different musical modes on the individual and society recorded by Plato and other Greek authors; but the experimental approach remained undeveloped through the decline and eclipse of science during the later classical and medieval periods.

Beginning with the Renaissance, the rapid development of experimental physics, physiology and anatomy, including many researches on acoustics and studies of the auditory apparatus, prepared the way for the first comprehensive treatment of the conditions and laws of musical sensitivity presented by Helmholz in his classic on musical sensations (*Tonempfindungen,* 1863). In this work, mathematical analyses of sound waves, physical attributes of sound, sensory properties of tones and tone complexes, and a detailed account of the structures and functions of the ear are brought into fruitful contact and given a systematic interpretation.

The contribution of Helmholz may be appreciated when it is realized that "every phase of vocal or instrumental music, artistic or inartistic, every emotional touch as actually expressed and conveyed by the musician can be represented in the four attributes of the sound wave; namely, the frequency, the amplitude, the duration and the wave form." (Seashore). In short, all music is a matter of sound waves, which may be photographed and of sensory receptors and effectors which may be studied in detail.

Helmholz confined his attention to musical sensations, formulating theories of tonal fusion and consonance based on an experimental study of "beats." Rival theories of consonance and dissonance, also based on experiment, were presented by Stumpf, Lipps and Külpe, and fruitful experimental studies of melody and harmony have also grown out of Helmholz's work.

Other psychologists applied the experimental method to musical ideation and affective processes. The result is a general agreement that **musical imagery** is never specific and that musical synaesthesias are variable products of individual experience.

On the other hand, emotional responses to music appear to be well established. Bingham has shown the presence of constant **mood effects** in response to specific musical patterns and the traditional correlation of gay and melancholy responses with major and minor modes, receives considerable support. The modification of physiological functions and bodily reflexes involved in emotion, and even in the absence of an affective state, is marked. As to motor and physiological responses there appears to be general agreement that music increases metabolism in man and higher animals, increases or decreases energy according to type of music, accelerates rate and decreases regularity of respiration, produces marked but fluctuating effects on blood circulation, is reflected in the psychogalvanic reflex, and reduces sensory thresholds in several sensory modes.

Types of musical experience as a whole have also been studied experimentally, and several useful classifications of musical listeners have been presented. Among these are Gurney's indefinite and definite listeners, Ortman's genetic classification into sensorial, perceptual and imaginal types, and Myers' division of musical auditors into intra-subjective, associative, objective and character types according to their tendency to regard music as an end in itself, or on the other hand, to read into it experiences of a personal or subjective nature.

The existence of different types of listener points to differing degrees of musical receptivity and capacity for production, and suggests that aesthetic response to music as such is a definite function which Schoen terms "form-mindedness." This must be defined in terms of acquired and inherited sensitivity to the principal aspects of musical form, viz: pitch, intensity, duration, timbre, consonance and rhythm,—all available for experimental study.

Recognition of this inaugurated the third phase in the development of an experimental psychology of music,—viz: an applied psychology, seeking the definite limits of heredity and acquisition, the order and sequence of musical development as revealed by comparative ethnology and child psychology, and reliable tests of musical aptitude as a whole and musical abilities in detail. The **applied psychology of music** is likewise concerned with tests, measures, and relevant methods of investigating musical performance, production or creation.

Professor Seashore of Iowa may be regarded as the great pioneer and principal founder of an applied psychology of music on an experimental basis. Several unstandardized and four standardized tests for musical capacities exist. Of the standardized tests by Seashore, Schoen, Kwalwasser-Dykerma and Ortmann, those of Seashore are best known and the most widely used. Seashore presents tests of pitch intensity, time memory, consonance, and rhythm.

Seashore and his pupils have also evolved exact experimental techniques and apparatus for recording the finer unconscious variations in the vocal performances of singers. This work, as it involves similar equipment and techniques, establishes connection with the psychology of phonetics and speech. Seashore's

studies of the vibrato (q.v.) mark a fruitful extension of the experimental psychology of music.

Experimental studies of the development of musical sensitivity in young children and primitives suggest that both are comparatively indifferent to consonance and dissonance, but civilized children develop the tastes of adults at the age of twelve or thirteen, while primitives remain retarded in this direction. In this connection the comparative phonographic researches of Von Hornbostel, and of members of the Bureau of American Ethnology have supplied invaluable data. Attempts to study the inheritance of musical ability by statistical studies of families of musicians, and intensive tests of musical prodigies have yielded no definite conclusions respecting the inheritance of musical talent as a whole, but suggest that certain specific capacities may be inherited.

On the whole the experimental psychology of music has resulted in a solid contribution, useful to the theorist, teacher, musical performers, and composers, as well as to all concerned with what we might call the economic utilization of the musical resources of society. See Schoen, *The Psychology of Music,* 1940, (best single reference); Helmholtz, *Tonempfindungen,* 1863, Eng. trans., *Sensations of Tone,* 1912; Stumpf, *Tonpsychologie,* 1883; Seashore, *The Psychology of Musical Talent,* 1919 and The University of Iowa Studies in the Psychology of Music, 1932-1937; Diserens, *The Influence of Music on Behavior,* 1926; Schoen, *The Effects of Music,* 1927; Diserens and Fine, *A Psychology of Music,* 1939.   —C.M.D.

exposition. *Mus.* (1) The first section of a fugue. (2) The section before the double bar in a sonata's (q.v.) first movement. See fugue.

exposition, expository composition (L. *expositio*). A mode of composition (q.v.) in art, in which details are arranged in such a way as to set forth, explain or suggest general relationships, as of casual or logical connection, abstract meanings, pervasive qualities, common or underlying principles. It is most fully and clearly developed in scientific and literary discourse, as in the essay; but occurs also as a factor in other arts. Religious painting and sculpture often contain a strongly expository factor, in the setting forth of doctrines about the nature of divinity, the universe, morality, etc., often suggested in a vague or cryptic way through mystic symbols. Exposition may coexist with decoration, representation, and utility as a factor in the total form of a work of art.   —T.M.

express highway. See CIVIC PLANNING.

expression. A process through which something hidden and diffused is concentrated and brought out into the light (for instance the squeezing out of the juice from the fruit). The twofold movement from diffusion to concentration, and from inside to outside is retained in the aesthetic employment of the term. There is also retained, to a certain extent at least, the idea that the juice squeezed out is the essential part of the fruit—*sugo*, juice, is in Italian also the colloquial term for essence—whereas the remainder, such as seed, shell, etc., can be disposed of.

In art the term expression used to be employed exclusively for a relation taking place in the subject matter itself, the relation between the visible or audible movements of a body and the state of mind of the owner of the body. A painting, for instance, was said to be expressive if the movements and physiognomies of the persons represented left no doubt as to the state of mind of these persons. A state of mind, diffuse by nature and hidden to our eyes, is concentrated and made visible in the movements of the face and body (gestures). Thus the essence, the "idea" of that state of mind gains visibility, while the accidental is left out. In this objective sense of the term Raphael was thought by the classicists to be the greatest, i.e., the most expressive of all artists.

Today such a judgment would seem almost incomprehensible. Many call Raphael expressionless because instead of acquainting us with the passions of his soul he projects by some magic other people's emotions into the realm of beautiful gestures. Our subjectivistic age prefers the direct expression of the artist's interesting soul. With increasing emphasis on the subjective side of art, expression has been losing more and more the function of concentrating the diffused and separating the essential from the accidental. To express is still to bring to light what is hidden; but in the heyday of expressionism, anything in the artist's soul was considered worthy of being expressed, and artistic productivity had come to mean obedience of pen and brush to chance associations in the artist's mind, chance associations which are his private affair and quite incomprehensible to anybody else.

Between objectivism and extreme subjectivism stands Croce's famous theory of art as intuition. To be sure, it is the artist's state of mind that is being expressed. Yet it is being expressed not directly, explosively, catastrophically, but indirectly, through an image, in which the artist's state of mind finds fulfillment and satisfaction. The union of the state of mind with this image Croce calls the aesthetic synthesis *a priori*. The image, repleted with the artist's soul, is, in turn, being translated into the terms of the artistic medium. This translation is the function of the artistic technique. The decisive artistic stage is, then, what might be called the conception of the artistic idea, the moment when a state of mind seems to find its full expression in a sequence of sounds, called melody, or a combination of colors and shapes. The elaboration of this initial conception, of the melodies into a symphony, of the pattern of colors and shapes into a painting, would be a matter of mere technique, and artistically much less relevant.

Dewey, however, recognizes the intrinsically artistic function of what to Croce is the mere translation of the original conception into terms of the artistic medium. The resistance offered by the medium causes the artist's emotion to reflect upon itself and thus raises expression from a mere outcry to a poem. On the other hand, Dewey identifies the act of expression and the expressive object. To him every experience is aesthetic which is consummate—as if an object were a work of art because our experience of it (both creative and recreative) is consummate.

When the expression aesthetics was at its height, understanding of the term expression was at its lowest. It contained various ingredients that remained undistinguished. There is, first, the formal concept of expression according to which anything present to our senses may signify something absent to them. Behind this formal concept of expression are hidden three relations which are hopelessly confused by indiscriminately calling them all "expression". We may call them discharge, expression proper, and sedimentation. All three view expression from the perspective of the expressing agent, whereas the formal concept of expression is drawn from the perspective of the onlooker. **Discharge** may be defined as a direct expression, translating an emotion into motion, with no intervening judgment of taste, morale, reason. **Expression proper is** the deliberate objectification of a state of mind in an image—this is Croce's aesthetic synthesis *a priori.* Sedimentation, perhaps the most enigmatic of these processes, is the way in which unconscious evaluations that make up much of the artist's individual, racial, social, cultural character, become unintentionally perceptible in the work of art.

The metaphysical phase of the problem of expression is part of the traditional mind-body problem—an observation that cannot here be elaborated. For the historical relativism implied by the expression aesthetics see style.

—W.C.

expression in dance refers to the quality of its movements being indicative of feeling, mood, or character. Vividness of expression depends upon the strength of emotional tone which in turn depends upon the clarity and strength of the image (the mental state) to be expressed. The wealth of image recall is dependent upon the richness of imaginal materials of the mind and not upon the will to be "expressive". When the final image is clearly and vividly sensed, it demands release. It expels itself from the mind over the motor paths and finds expression in movement. If the emphasis is on the dancer's personal way of experiencing and reacting to the mental state seeking expression, the dance tends toward "self-expression." But if the emphasis is on the interpretation of content in relation to other selves, the dance becomes less personal and more universal. A dance, of course, must be an individual thing, but not a personal thing. A dancer must have the capacity of expressing and arousing human emotions without appearing to share them personally. His audience should feel with him—not for him.   —M.N.H.'D.

expressionism. One of several currents of post-impressionistic art, but also the whole post-impressionistic period itself, including abstactionism, cubism, etc.

The common denominator of all post-impressionistic art is negative: Expressionism is non-imitative. What, then, is being painted? The various answers to this question indicate the several trends of post-impressionism.

I. Subjective Expressionism. (a) The artist paints his emotions, or rather his emotions do the painting. Hand and brush form the immediate, automatic outlet for his moods and feelings. (The early Kandinsky; many minor German and Russian artists.) (b) He paints his associations or arbitrary symbols of such (Klee, Kandinsky, some of Marin). The resemblance of this art to the creations of schizophrenics has often been observed (cf.

Oskar Pfister, *Expressionism in Art,* London, 1922). (c) He paints his representational images. (Matisse, Picasso, some of Marc).

II. Objective Expressionism. The artist paints the expressive character of the object. Instead of painting a tree, he paints its convulsiveness or its strength. Sincerity becomes the main aesthetic category. (Rouault, Nolde, Hofer, Beckmann, Kokoschka. In sculpture: Barlach, Zadkine, Epstein, Lehmbruck).

III. Abstractionism (q.v. abstraction). (a) The artist paints wholly abstract compositions of colors and forms (Picasso, Braque, Kandinsky. In sculpture: Archipenko). (b) Decorative patterns, mostly planear. (Matisse: ". . . expression for me . . . is in the whole disposition of my picture" Walden: "Painting is the art of the plane" (c) The stereometric or geometric essence of some object, varying this motif according to aesthetic laws. This is Cubism (Picasso, Bracque, Feininger. In sculpture: Brancusi, Archipenko, Zadkine.)

IV. Magic Realism and Surrealism, usually classed with the post-expressionistic movements (q.v. surrealism).

These currents are derived from the four great masters who were the first to move beyond impressionism, viz., Cézanne (1839-1906), Odillon Rédon (1842-1916), Gauguin (1848-1903) and Vincent van Gogh (1853-1890). (Seurat also is nowadays counted among the direct progenitors of post-impressionism). The decorative tendencies of post-impressionism originate with Gauguin, whose planear decorativeness is plastic without being spatial; the cubistic ones with Cézanne who builds his cuboid forms and spaces out of densely interlocking color planes. The objective expressionists see their great precursor in van Gogh, who changed the things painted more and more into symbols of expressiveness; the magic realists and surrealists in Rédon. These trends now join forces, now remain separate and distinct.

The meaning of expressionism has been conceived differently by French and German artists and art-writers. To the Germans, expressionism meant above all a revolution from the 'superficial', 'technical' art of impressionism to a style directly expressive of the artist's soul in all its hidden depth and with as little interference as possible from formal and compositional elements. Here we have a revolution against Renaissance this—worldliness with its culmination in impressionism (Hermann Bahr, Paul Fechter).

In France, however, according to the particular genius of this nation, the formal and

340

truly artistic problems have dominated the scene. The emotional eruption was left to the Eastern barbarians. While there are no intermediaries between German, impressionism and German expressionism, a definite artistic continuity can be pointed out in the development from French impressionism to French expressionism (for example Monet's murals in the Musée du Jeu de Psaume anticipate Matisse's planear decorative patterns), where in spite of all savagerie (Les Fauves) good taste, elegance and workmanship prevail.

Herwarth Walden was one of the very few German expressionists who, like the French Appolinaire and Gleizes, laid less emphasis on soul and metaphysics than on the formal structure of the work of art. The "painting is an organism the parts of which are composed by colored forms", the idea being that what music does with sounds, painting should do with colors and forms, in abstraction both from subject matter and from the artist's soul.

Post-impressionism's real contribution to the history of art lies in its emphasis on pure form and structural integrity—an assertion corroborated by the fact that cubism alone of all the post-impressionistic movements has been able to express itself in the medium of architecture, there creating a new and truly great style (Le Corbusier, Gropius and das Bauhaus, Lescaze, Neutra, some buildings of Frank Lloyd Wright, etc.). See FRENCH ART.　　　　　　　　　　　　—W.C.

Expressionismus (Ger). The collective name usually given to the various movements of modern German art (with the exception of *Neue Sachlichkeit*, q.v. new objectivism). For the development of German expressionism two dates are of importance: 1903—the founding of the first modern artists' group, *Die Brücke*, (The Bridge) at Dresden by E. Heckel, Max Pechstein, Emil Nolde, E. L. Kirchner, K. Schmidt-Rottluff, and 1911—the organization of the artists' group, *Der Blaue Reiter*, (The Blue Horseman) at Munich by Paul Klee, Franz Marc and Vasily Kandinsky, later joined by Jawlensky and M. Chagall. ("The Blue Horseman" grew out of the *Neue Künstlervereinigung München* of which Kandinsky was one of the leaders.)

In its beginning German expressionism was greatly influenced by the art of Gauguin, van Gogh, and Edvard Munch, and by the French moderns. The difference between the German modernists and their French contemporaries might be seen in the greater individual variety and the greater radicalism in the deformation and distortion of natural forms by the German artists. The expressionists however, do not aim for purely aesthetic-artistic creations: the accent lies (according to their declared aims) on the "expression of the innermost soul", the "thing as such", etc.

Emil Nolde's interpretations of biblical scenes, Schmidt-Rottluff's figures and portraits, Max Pechstein's South-Sea idols (and one might add the names of Macke, Nauen, Kirchner, Heckel, Otto Müller) are violent distortions of forms found in nature, painted in bright, strong and often sharply contrasting colours. These pictures owe their strength and violence to a great extent to the fact that the natural shapes and forms are not sacrificed altogether to the artistic effect but that there remains just enough recognizable similarity to make the change appear as a radical if not brutal deformation. More concerned with artistic form, but justifying it by means of metaphysical considerations, are the pictures of Franz Marc, who in his letters explains that he turned to painting animals because he found them purer than men, who were ugly, and that he tries to make nature transparent for the clear line of "pure expression". The Austrian Kokoschka's early pictures show similarities to the above mentioned group (e.g. *Woman with Parrot*, 1915); in his later paintings his colors have become lighter and there is less distortion in his paintings (e.g. *Port of Dover*, 1926). Lyonel Feininger (American born) transforms natural forms, especially buildings and streets, into crystal-like shapes which are arranged with geometrical precision into quite unreal perspectives.

Willy Baumeister and Oskar Schlemmer construct their compositions of figures and objects in a manner reminiscent of F. Léger. While Baumeister builds up his forms with clear contours, often using color as a modeling shadow, Schlemmer uses color for the construction of the figures, gaining three dimensional effects through shading and color transitions. J. Molzahn paints bent and curved geometrical shapes (e.g. *Flowering Chalice*, 1920), in rich and glowing colors. Campendonk's treatment of colors is similar to that of Molzahn, but his treatment of the shapes of men, animals or plants shows the influence of Marc Chagall (e.g. *The White Tree*, 1925).

The most consistent of the expressionists are Vasily Kandinsky and Paul Klee. Kandinsky, a Russian (born 1861, living in Germany 1897-1914 and 1922-1933), who must be mentioned here because through his painting, writing and teaching (he belonged to the staff of the *Bauhaus*) he has exerted great influence upon German expressionism. Kandinsky gives up completely any similarity to shapes and forms of nature. Naming his paintings *Composition 8* (1923), *Light Blue* (1929), etc., Kandinsky presents what he calls "the inner value or melody of objects"; this he believes is achieved by painting the "abstract in the form" and by using a color harmony which is based upon the principle of "inner necessity," i.e. the principle of the "best contact with the human soul." In a great number of vigorous and phantastic line-color-shape compositions, Kandinsky demonstrates his principle that "the artist is not only justified in using forms as it is necessary for his purpose, but that it is his duty to do so,"—he considers this an obligation to his artistic honesty (*Über das Geistige in der Kunst*, Munich, 1912).

Paul Klee (born in Switzerland 1879, in Germany 1898-1933) has described some of his paintings as "a line taking a walk," and he begins his *Pädagogisches Skizzenbuch*—the original basis for a part of the theoretical instruction at the *Staatliche Bauhaus* at Weimar—(Munich, 1925, 2nd ed.), with definitions of various types of lines, e.g. "An active line which freely wanders along, taking a walk for its own sake without any aim," etc. The ascribing of active forces and expressive energies to the elements of composition is not only characteristic for the theory of expressionism, but it seems also to describe well the peculiar quality of Paul Klee's art. With thin nervous lines and with subtly shaded subdued colors Paul Klee creates exquisitely fantastic landscapes or delicate, weird and whimsical constructions (e.g. *The Twittering Machine,* 1922) which anticipate surrealism. Surrealism did not exert a very great influence in Germany, though Grosz as well as Klee are sometimes claimed for this movement which is mainly connected with the names of Kurt Schwitters and Max Ernst.

Expressionism slowly lost its dominating position about 1920 giving way to the movement of the *Neue Sachlichkeit* (q.v. new objectivism). See GERMAN ART. See also H. Bahr, *Expressionism,* 1925 (translated by R. T. Gribble); P. Fechter, *Der Expressionismus,* 1914; V. Kandinsky, *The Art of Spiritual Harmony,* 1914, (translated by M. T. H. Sadler); *Modern German Painting and Sculpture,* Museum of Modern Art, New York, 1931.   —H.H.

expressionistic criticism. See ART CRITICISM.

exquisite corpses. See Dadaism.

extensity. As a criterion of literary value, this term refers primarily to the range of subject-matter covered in a work. It is used almost exclusively by those critics who attach high importance to the content and meaning of a work of art: and for them it measures the greatness of a work, in accord with the light this throws on matters of human interest.   —I.J.

extent of pitch. See vibrato.

exterior kiva corner. As applied in southwestern archeology: The roughly triangular spaces resulting from the construction of a circular kiva within a rectangular walled area or room. These spaces are believed to have been waste spaces and to have been intentionally filled.   —J.M.M.

extra cloth. *Book.* Cloth binding, heavily colored, concealing the weaving of the cloth.

extrados. *Arch.* The exterior curve of an arch or vault.

eye. See PERSPECTIVE.

ezo (Jap.). A portrait painting.

F

f. See NOTATION.

fabliau. A versified tale or romance popular among the trouvères of the 12th and 13th cents.

fabric. Cloth made of threads either woven, knitted or knotted or felted together.

fabrikoid. *Book.* An imitation leather.

faburden. See fauxbourdon.

façade (Fr.-L. *facies,* face). The front elevation or chief face of a structure.

facial angle. Angle formed by the crossing of the axis of the face with the axis of the skull.

factura. See RUSSIAN ARTS.

facture. Act or manner of producing an art work.

faïence (F.). A very friable pottery. Also enamel base for painted decoration. See CERAMICS I, II.

faille. Soft, flat ribbed silk fabric Ribs are wider and flatter than grosgrain. Wears well, if not too loose in weave or heavily weighted. May be rayon and cotton.

faldoncito. Pendant scalloped lambrequin-like ornamental motif in Mexican churrigueresque (q.v.).

fall-front desk. See FURNITURE.

false biting (foul biting, English usage). *Etch.* A tone bitten on a plate due to a defective ground.

false door Simulated openings in the inner and outerwalls of a mastaba, for the passage of the *ka* or spirit.

false tones. See NOTATION.

famille jaune (F.). A term often applied to Chinese porcelain when a polychromed floral pattern has yellow as a dominant color.

famille noire (F.). A term often applied to Chinese porcelain when a polychrome floral pattern has black as a dominant color.

famille rose (F.). A term often applied to Chinese porcelain when a polychromed floral pattern has the rose as a dominant motive, or rose-color as a dominant tone.

famille verte (F.). A term often applied to Chinese porcelain when a polychrome floral pattern has green as a dominant tone.

family dwelling. See domestic architecture.

family tradition and paintings. See FORGERIES IN PAINTING.

fan. See Sensu and uchiwa (Jap.).

Fancy, Fantasia. Was one of the early instrumental forms which developed from the vocal motet. It reached its highest development in England during the period 1550-1660 and was most appropriately performed on an ensemble of viols though many Fantasias for keyboard instruments are found in collections of the period. Though contemporary theorists prescribe no very exact bounds for the form, most examples consist of a number of fugal sections often contrasted with intervening passages in a chordal and homophonic style. Later examples by such composers as William Lawes and John Jenkins are decidedly instrumental in style. In some cases the Fancy was followed by one or more dances or served as a serious introductory movement to a suite.

The list given by Thomas Mace in his *Musick's Monument* mentions many of the best known composers of Fancies. "The Authors of such like Compositions have been divers Famous English Men, and Italians; some of which, for Their very Great Eminency and Worth in that Particular Faculty, I will here name, viz. Mr. Alfonso Ferabosco, Mr. John Ward, Mr. Lupo, Mr. White, Mr. Richard Deering, Mr William Lawes, Mr. Christopher Simpson, Mr. Coperario, and one Monteverde, a Famous Italian Author . . ." No Fancies by Monteverdi have been found.

Designed as they were for domestic chamber music, the Fancies vanished with the consort of viols in the change in English taste brought about at the time of the Restoration. Modern interest in the form is almost entirely due to the pioneer efforts of Arnold Dolmetsch and his associates. The late Fantasias of Matthew Lock should be mentioned as well as the very beautiful examples by Purcell.

The term Fantasia is also employed for a keyboard composition usually improvisatory in style and governed by no fixed formal characteristics. With Bach such a movement may serve as a prelude to a fugue (*Chromatic Fantasy and Fugue*) or as an introductory movement to a suite. The fine Mozart *Fantasia in C minor* leads into a complete sonata in the same key. The independent work in D minor has a looser and less unified character. Beethoven who uses the term infrequently twice employs it as if he were explaining that the sonatas in question were treated with unusual freedom. The more familiar example is the so-called "Moonlight Sonata" (*Op. 27, No. 2*) which is marked "Quasi una Fantasia". More recent composers have not favored the form though Schumann has left an important example in his Opus 17.
—C.W.H.

fandango. Has been one of the most popular of the classic Iberian Spanish dances. It is danced by men and women facing each other in lines, and playing their own accompaniment upon castanets. The general form and style are closely related to those of the sequidilla, from which it is said to have originally developed. See sequidilla. —J.G.

fang (Ch.). A Chinese word applied to a painting which has been created in the style of another.

fan tracery. Decorative tracery on **fan vaulting**; vaulting in which the ribs diverge like the rays of a fan.

far eastern art, symbolism in. See SYMBOLISM IN FAR EASTERN ART.

farandole. A French national dance traditional in Provence, is one of the most spontaneous of all folk-dances. A leader guides the dancers through the streets in a long line lin'ed by holding hands, ribbons, or handkerchiefs. The procession, continually growing longer, weaves back and forth or winds and unwinds according to the fancy of the leader, who is accompanied by musicians playing flutes and tambourins. The music is in strongly accented 6/8 meter, stimulating the brisk walk or skip of the dance. The farandole is performed on feast days as the prelude to an evening of dancing, leading the crowd to a central gathering place. —J.G.

fat clay. See ball clay.

Fatamid art. See ISLAMIC ART.

Fat-shan Chün yao (Ch.). Place name—imitation of Chün yao (q.v.).

fauces (L.). Passage from the door of a house to the atrium.

Fauves. See FRENCH ART; post-impressionism.

fauxbourdon (mid. Eng. *faburden*, It. *falso bordone*). A form of rudimentary harmony or discant using progressions of chords in the 6th, i.e. 1st inversion chords, beginning and ending in chords of the fundamental position. There are two varieties, the older "English discant" style in which the lowest voice is the *cantus firmus*, and the continental style in which the *cantus firmus*, though written in the lowest part is performed an octave higher, hence false base.

The testimony of theorists and available MSS., indicates an English origin. The expansion of harmonic resources during the 14th and 15th cents, in which the role of the 3rd and 6th is in evidence points to the marked influence of fauxbourdon. See M. Bukofzer, *Geschichte des Englischen Diskants und des Fauxbourdons*, 1936. —V.A.

F clef. See NOTATION.

federal architecture. The architecture that houses the activities of the sovereign government in a federation of states such as The United States of America, as distinct from the architecture of the subdivisions. The Capitol and Supreme Court buildings in Washington, D. C. and Post Office and Federal

Reserve Bank buildings throughout the nation are examples.   —O.M.S.

felt. A material made of matted fibres of wool, fulled or wrought by rolling and pressure with "lees" or size, without spinning or weaving. Today a fine felt is sometimes a woven material with a felted surface. Man probably produced true felt before he developed fabrics.   —G.W.R.

felt carpet. See carpet structures.

felted rugs, primitive. Preceding discovery and practice of manual crafts of carding, spinning and weaving, skins of animals were used as clothing and mats or rugs on which to recline. These applications perhaps suggested feasibility of working fibre, hair, or fur into a matted or felted texture. Felt rugs originally were an eastern production produced from primitive times in various parts of Asia.   —B.E.J.

felting matting. One of the earliest varieties of carpeting. A type of cloth producible independently of the operations of spinning and weaving. Yarn is not used. Produced by the opening and separating of the filaments of wool followed by reblending into compact adhesive layers of uniform thickness and density.   —B.E.J.

felt pattern. Obtained in two ways: (1) Block printing on felt surfaces; (2) by felting color ingredients consisting of portions of selected dyed wool into the nŭmŭds in the operation of fulling.   —B.E.J.

felts Persian. Designated as *numuds* or *nammads*. A *nŭmŭd* is not a solid colored felt like that made by machinery but a decorative floor covering diversified in colors and patterns.   —B.E.J.

fenestration. The arrangement and disposition of the window and door openings of a building with regard to proportion and detail.

fenestella (It.). A small windowlike opening in the front of an altar, so the relics within can be seen.

fêng-huang (Ch.). Bird of good omen. A long-tailed pheasant-type of bird, commonly called the phoenix. Scientifically known as Rheinart's ocellated argus. See SYMBOLISM IN FAR EASTERN ART; also Phoenix in Fact and Fancy, Alan Priest, *Bull. Metropolitan Museum of Art*, Oct. 1942, p. 97-101.

fên su jên wu (Ch.). Genre painting.

fen-ts'ai (Ch.). Enamel colors.

feretory. A highly decorated, often movable, bier or shrine for the relics of a saint; the chapel inside which this was kept.

ferroconcrete. Reinforced concrete.

ferronnerie (F. hand wrought iron work). Lustrous velvets of the 15th and 16th cents. having slender tracery designs resembling wrought iron work.

fertility cult. See PRIMITIVE ART.

fesse. See HERALDRY.

fetish. See PRIMITIVE ART.

ff. See NOTATION.

fibers, textile. Slender filaments or strands that cling together, enabling them to be spun into yarns of appreciable strength and sufficiently pliable to be woven into fabrics. Textile fibers include cotton, flex, jute, and other fibers of vegetable origin, silk, wool and various hairs of animal, rayon, and allied synthetic or artificial fibers, asbestos and glass.   —G.W.R.

fiberglass. See GLASS AND GLASSMAKING.

fiddle. See MUSICAL INSTRUMENTS.

field. See HERALDRY.

field, of a rug. The central or main part.

field of view. See PERSPECTIVE.

fife. See MUSICAL INSTRUMENTS.

figuration. *Mus.* (1) The development of florid counterpoint by the introduction of figures, runs, etc. (2) Embellishing a theme by adding to or by ornamenting the melody with grace notes, runs, florid passages. (3) The working-out of a figured bass.

figured bass. *Mus.* A bass with chords indicated by figures.

Fikellura ware. See Ionian vases.

filler panel. See FURNITURE.

fillet. *Book.* (1) The tool—a wheel fixed on an axle—with which lines are made on book covers. (2) The ornamental line, often of gold, made on a book cover, usually at the top and bottom of the back. (3) That part of a cover design which completes the design after outline portions are made. *Arch.* A narrow flat member; esp., a flat molding separating other modlings; also, the space between two flutings in a shaft.

filling. The woof of a woven fabric. Also called filler, tram.

filling motifs. Various ornaments used to fill the space between figures in Greek pottery of the 8th to 6th cent. B.C., e.g., spirals, rosette, circles, rhombus, meander, swastika, etc.

film color. See COLOR.

final, finalis of a mode. *Mus.* The note on which a melody must end in any of the church modes, answering to our tonic or key note. See scales and modes; idiom A (2).

finale. *Mus.* The last "number" of an opera act; the last movement of a symphony.

fine art. See classification of the arts; art.

fine arts, academy of. A school or institute of learning where courses of instruction are given in drawing, painting, sculpture, design, architecture, and other visual or space arts. (First academy of art in Europe was founded by a group of Venetian painters in 1346.) Whitford and Winslow in *Dictionary of Education.*

fine binding, bookbinding. See EARLY BOOKBINDING AND FINE BINDING.

fingerpainting. See CHILDREN'S ART; chih hua.

finial. The decorative foliate ornament forming the upper extremity of a Gothic gable, pinnacle, buttress, etc.

finishing. *Book.* The last stage of binding, including the gilding, tooling, etc., in hand work. The "finisher" is the one doing the work. See EARLY BOOKBINDING AND FINE BINDING.

fioritura, fioriture (It.). *Mus.* Embellishment (s) interwoven into a melody.

fireback. The rear wall of a fireplace

fire-gilt process. Amalgam of gold and mercury washed onto a metal base, heated to drive off the mercury, then burnished.

fire pit. A pit or cavity, generally sunk entirely below the floor or given level, in which a fire is built; a fireplace.

fireplace. A recess, structure, pit, or place in which or on which a fire is built. See INTERIOR ARCHITECTURE AND DECORATION.

firing. Process of heating or burning of all ceramics. See CERAMICS I.

First Federal (National) Period. See POST-REVOLUTIONARY ARCHITECTURE AND DECORATIVE ARTS IN THE U.S.A.

fishroe pattern. Often a punched pattern representing a mass of fresh fish roe.

fivecolor ware. Chinese porcelain on which the colors, red, yellow, green, blue, and violet, are used.

five Dynasties art. See CHINESE ARTS.

five poisons. See SYMBOLISM IN FAR EASTERN ART.

fixative. A liquid used by artists to bind the loose particles of charcoal, pastel or crayon pictures and prevent them from rubbing off. It acts only in a weak, surface manner; for this purpose it is neither necessary nor desirable to produce an impervious film as do the varnishes which are applied to oil and tempera paintings.   —R.M.

fixed do. See movable do.

flageolet. See MUSICAL INSTRUMENTS; ACOUSTICS.

flagon. A velles with handle, spout and lid, with bulging body, contracted neck, flaring lip and stable foot.

flagstone. A broad, flat stone suitable for foot-pavements.

flake white. See white lead.

flambé (F.). A term applied to Chinese porcelain when glaze is splashed or irregularly applied.

flamboyant. See Gothic.

flame ornament. See Gothic.

flamenco dances. See tango.

flanning. The internal splay of a window or door opening.

flashback. See RADIO DRAMA.

flashed. *Cer.* Irregular discoloration caused by direct contact with flame. See CERAMICS I.

flat. *Mus.* The sign *b* which when placed in the signature or after a note, lowers the pitch of the note involved by a semi-tone.

flattening (or stretching). Intaglio prints are usually printed on damp paper, which necessitates drying the proofs between sets of blotters under pressure to prevent the proofs from wrinkling.

flautando. Producing a flute-like tone on the violin.

flax (AS. *fleax*). The soft, silky fiber, 2′ to 3′ long, comes from the inside of the bark of the flax plant. There are more than one hundred species of this plant, from the fiber of which can be made the sheerest linen, the most exquisite lace or the heavist ropes.
—G.W.R.

flèche. A spire, esp. a long tapering one above the crossing of the nave and transepts of a church or cathedral.

fleece. Comes from the back of the sheep and is held together by the intertwining of the fibres.

FLEMISH ART. The art of all the provinces which now make up the kingdom of Belgium is called Flemish art. The Dutch contributed greatly to the development of this art long before their cities supported artists. Although some good sculpture and architecture was created, Flemish art generally refers to the style of painting developed in Flanders from the 14th to the 17th cent.

The general aesthetic quality which distinguishes the Flemish school is a sharply focused realism manifest in all phases of its development. The Flemish artists' uncritical literalness expressed itself through a passion for accuracy and precision of outline. Their love for craftsmanship led them to develop and gain complete control over an oil painting medium at an early period. A delight in the commonplace and a lack of generalizing spirit caused them to imitate familiar things with a keen observation, brilliance and solidity of technique. Their love of life stimulated their sense of color and pageantry. A taste for satire and symbolism suited to the conventions of the time imbued their work with a vivid realism.

This early manifestation of realism in the Flemish school was a result of a long tradition of miniature painting extending from Romanesque times through the Gothic period into the Renaissance. This art, coupled with a long tradition of craftsmanship developed in the tapestry industries, favored the development of art in the Low Countries.

Sculpture and architecture in Flanders followed the Romanesque and Gothic traditions. Gothic art continued in Flanders long after it had waned in Italy. The abstract design of the Gothic period fused with the realistic tendency of medieval Flanders to form a new style of art essentially different from any development in Italy. The southern artist was interested in arrangement of form and color for representation while the Flemish artist was interested in a literal presentation of significant activities. The Italians therefore, used color for its plastic effect while the Flemish artist used it for its effect of pageantry.

Primitive Flemish art, which is only primitive chronologically, emphasized the flat, decorative quality of Gothic design and used paint primarily as a vehicle for drawing. The flowering of Flemish art came in the 14th and 15ht cents. in Bruges and in the 17th cent. in Antwerp. The great period in the 15th cent. begins in Bruges with the work of the brothers Hubert and Jan Van Eyck who developed and perfected the oil painting technique of the early Flemish painters. The Van Eycks painted religious pictures and portraits of such accuracy as to mark the beginning of realistic art in Europe. They pursued realism tenaciously until the resemblance was complete and the external characteristics were copied down to the last hair or wrinkle. They attempted to capture moral resemblance by copying the appearance of things. Their contribution to the craft of painting is exemplified by the marvelous state of preservation of their paintings.

In the second half of the 15th cent. Peter Christus worked at Bruges and began painting episodes from ·real life such as his *Legend of Ste. Godeberte*.

A popular school of painting developed in Tournai which was conventionally religious and influenced the schools of Ghent, Haarlem and Louvain. The leaders of the school at Tournai were Robert Campin and Roger Van der Weyden who were contemporaries of the Van Eycks. Campin's work is closely related to the school of sculpture which was flourishing at Tournai. Roger Van der Weyden introduced a new note into Flemish art with his painstaking portraits. His work refined and enlarged on the art of the Van Eycks.

Dierick Bouts came to Flanders from Holland and his work resembles that of Roger Van der Weyden. He painted important historical pictures such as *The Injustice of the Emperor Ohio*.

Hugo Van der Gos, who worked a generation after Peter Christus, led the Flemish school into a broader path of realism which survived for several generations.

During the second half of the 15th cent. Flemish painting entered a new stage of freedom with the religious paintings of Hans Memlinc. He settled in Bruges and painted many religious pictures and small portraits. They are fused with a hazy, pervading light and handled more broadly than those of his predecessors. He acquired the plastic quality of the Italian style while retaining the microscopic fidelity of the Flemish style.

The last great painter of the Bruges school is Gheerardt David who came from Oudewater. He maintained the Bruges tradition while introducing a Dutch note of serious calm in his work. Although the Primitive tradition did not end with the Bruges school, its greatest exponents painted there.

At the beginning of the 16th cent. Antwerp succeeded Bruges as the center of Flemish art. With this shift architecture, sculpture and painting began to be modified by the Italian Renaissance influence. The first great artist of this school was Quentin Massys. His work was still in the Primitive tradition but he introduced a new note in his understanding of the artistic merit in the trivial and vulgar reality of everyday life. His work also shows the increasing influence of Italian art. Two other members of this school, Joachim Patinir and Hendrik Bles, made their reputation as landscape painters. Before it died out the Primitive school produced two more great Holland realists in Jerome Bosch and Pieter Breughel. Bosch did not confine himself to imitation but invented wild and grotesque fiction. His biblical paintings were very popular in Catholic Spain where he was considered a great moralist. Pieter Breughel was a painter of his time and for his people and his work portrays wit and homely moralizing. He painted many scriptural subjects, genre scenes and made numerous drawings and engravings to illustrate proverbs. He developed the art of landscape painting to a new height.

From this period on the Italian influence became more pronounced. At first it destroyed the Flemish tradition but gradually the two styles merged. This process took place during the greater part of the 16th cent. By the beginning of the 17th cent. the real principles of Italian art had been absorbed. Among these Italianizers were Jan Gossart (Mabuse), Van Orley, Lancelot Blondeel, Jan Massys and Frans Floris. So great was the Italian influence that many of the artists called themselves "Romanists."

Portrait painting, an integral part of the Flemish tradition, became popular in the middle of the 16th cent. and is well exemplified in the work of Antonio Moro.

During the last half of the 16th cent. the artists divested themselves of both the Italian and early Flemish influence to develop a clever style of historical painting. At the beginning of the 17th cent. a taste for more naturalistic art developed and copper-plate engraving became popular in Antwerp.

The beginning of the 18th cent. ushered in a type of renaissance church building sponsored by the Jesuits and known as the "Jesuit" style. In the early 17th cent. Peter Paul Rubens, an artist, scholar, courtier and diplomat, brought about a resurgence of the Flemish style. In his workshop was developed an art style that greatly influenced painters and sculptors of the period. His work combines the best qualities of the Italian and early Flemish styles into a new synthesis that was to influence the direction of future painters. He painted allegorical, historical and mythological subjects, portraits, landscapes, still-life, and biblical scenes. Among his distinguished pupils and followers were Anthony Van Dyck who was noted for his portraits, Gerard Seghers and Frans Snyders, the last of whom was famous for his still-life and animal pictures. These artists and many other collaborated with Rubens in the execution of a large volume of pictures. Jacob Jordaens, Sustermans and many other painters followed in Ruben's style.

The native bourgeois and genre tradition was continued by Adriawn Brower and the Teniers family. After 1700 painting continued in Flanders on a mediocre scale compared with former times.

Belgian art flourished in the 19th cent. and the sculptures of Constantin Meunier attracted considerable attention. Painting followed the academic dictates of the French school and centered in Brussels.   —R.L.W.

Flemish primitives. That group of painters of the 14th and 15th cents. whose work still retained the naiveté and rigidity of style characteristic of the medieval ages. Primitive does no refer to a lack of facility or ineptness, but more specifically indicates a quality of design peculiar to all art forms in their early stages. The Flemish primitives include Hubert and Jan Van Eyck, Peter Christus, Dierick Bouts, Hugo van der Gos, Hans Memlinc, Gheerardt David, Roger Van der Weyden, Robert Campin, Jerome Bosch and Pieter Breughel.   —R.L.W.

Flemish renaissance. See RENAISSANCE.

Flemish style (in furniture). See FURNITURE.

flesh color. The average color of a Caucasian's skin; low saturation of red-yellow and high in brilliance.

flexible. *Book.* Flexible sewing or binding generally means sewing right around the cords or tapes, or raised bands with the leather, or other back material glued to the back of the book itself so that the back of the cover bends with the book when it is opened. More properly this is a "tight back" (q.v.).   —H.E.S.

flint glass. See GLASS AND GLASS-MAKING.

floating material. See American folk forms, in literature.

floats. Warp or weft threads that are carried loose over the surface or back of the cloth.

Florentine school. The term Florentine school in its general sense defines the successive groups of artists (architects, painters, sculptors, and workers in the allied arts) who were citizens of or closely associated with the city of Florence (Firenze), Italy, from the last quarter of the 13th cent. until the close of the 16th cent., and who were united by common humanistic aims expressed by a variety of viewpoints and technical methods. The school is generally considered as the leading one of the Italian Renaissance (1400-1550 A.D.) due to the completeness with which it demonstrates the humanistic viewpoint of that time.

More precisely, the term refers to the painters of that city, over the same time periods, though many of these were equally proficient in sculpture and architecture. The school in reality is a group or series of strong personalities presenting individual points of view, specialized interests, and technical methods, yet united by a common humanism which is shown by a continuous and outstanding concern for form as the chief means of expression, with the accompanying interest in the pictorial analysis of observed phenomena and the investigation of all techniques necessary to representative painting. The resultant natural tendency toward an art of complete realism is modified by a common regard for classic impersonality and nobility of form.

The Florentine school of painting is divided chronologically into the schools of the 13th (duocento), 14th (trecento), 15th (quattrocento), and 16th (cinquecento) cents. The schools of the 13th and 14th cent. (Gothic) are generally grouped together as they are dominated by Cimabue (Cenni di Pepo), active during the last quarter of the 13th cent., and his greater follower, Giotto di Bondone (1266/76-1337). The remainder of the 14th cent. is given over largely to the emulation of Giotto by his followers.

The 15th cent. is marked by the complete supremacy of Florence as the leader of the Renaissance. The school at this time falls logically into three groups: first, the painters who continue largely in the Gothic tradition, represented by Fra Angelico (1387-1455); second, the progressive realists, led by Masaccio (1401-ca. 1428) and represented toward the close of the century by Andrea Verrocchio (1435-1488) and Leonardo da Vinci (1452-1519); third, the narrative group, which combined realism with documentary recording, represented by Fra Fillippo Lippi (ca. 1406-1469) and Domenico Ghirlandaio (1449-1494). It is also feasible to form a fourth group of extreme individualists working in the last quarter of the century, such as Sandro Botticelli (1444/45-1510) and Piero di Cosimo (1462-1521). There is no unified agreement as to the artists to be included in or excluded from the school. Some authorities list such men as Piero dei Franceschi (della Francesca) and Loca Signorelli because of their acceptance of Florentine aims. (Michelangelo is often classified as Roman due to his long residence in that city, though Giotto is always listed as Florentine in spite of many years in Assisi, Rome, and Padua.)

The 16th cent. is opened brilliantly by such men as Leonardo da Vinci, Michelangelo Buonarroti, and Andrea del Sarto (1486-1531), but with certain exceptions (Agnolo Bronzino) is marked by a rapid decline in quality and leadership. The last half of the century is barren when compared with the first thirty years.

The Florentine school of sculpture rivals that of Pisa in the 14th cent. and dominates Italy in the 15th cent. It contains such men as Andrea Pisano (14th cent.), Donato di Bardi (Donatello), known as the Father of the Renaissance, Lorenzo Ghiberti, Luca della Robbia, Andrea del Verrocchio, and Benedetto da Majano, all of the 15th cent., and Michelangelo and Benvenuto Cellini of the 16th cent. See ITALIAN ART; also Vasari, Giorgio, *Lives of the Painters,* ed. by E. H. and E. W. Blashfield and A. A. Hopkins, 4 vols., 1926; Van Marle, Raimond, *The Development of the Italian Schools of Painting,* 18 vols., 1929-37; Berenson, Bernhard, *Italian Painters of the Renaissance,* 1932 and *Florentine Painters of the Renaissance;* Offner, Richard, *A Critical and Historical Corpus of Florentine Painting,* 1930 ff.; Mather, Frank Jewett, *A History of Italian Painting,* 1923; Schmeckebier, Laurence, *A Handbook of Italian Renaissance Painting,* 1938.   —J.C.

florid. *Mus.* Embellished with runs, passages, etc.

flossa. An old Swedish technique for pile rugs similar to the Turkish or Ghiordes knot (q.v.) in oriental rugs.

flower and bird painting. See CHINESE ARTS.

FLOWER ARRANGEMENT. An art using as its medium cut flowers and branches, fungus, moss and so forth, arranged in unified compositions either in vases, or in garlands, wreaths, bouquets or other forms. The medium has unique aspects different from those of most other mediums used for creative expression, whether conceptual and representational, or purely decorative. The most conspicuous of these aspects is fragility, impermanence; flowers fade and arrangements disappear. This has not led to their being treated with less care or technical virtuosity than any other art medium, but it has, in Western countries, affected both the development of the art and man's attitude toward it. Without tangible objects to deal with, the art has, in a measure, been taken for granted. In the West, where only the decorative and symbolic potentialities of this art form have been exploited, the record of its achievements has, with rare exceptions, been incidental and accidental. This record is found in representational arts, paintings, mosaics, miniatures, sculptures, and tapestries, where flower arrangements are a part of the "taken for granted" decorative scene in which the main action of the picture takes place. (The exceptions are the still life flower paintings and prints of the 17th and 18th cents.) There is hardly a book in existence dealing with the arts of particular countries where flower arrangements are mentioned. The exceptions are notable and prove the point. Howard Carter, in his second volume on the *Tomb of Tut-Ankh-Amen,* because he discovered actual flower chaplets and necklaces, gives several paragraphs to a description of their elaborate technique; and Mr. H. E. Winlock, in the presence of a gold dish from Egypt definitely proven to have been made for flowers and for no other purpose, writes a complete and illustrated article on one type of Egyptian flower arrangement. (*Metropolitan Museum Studies,* vol. V, 1934-36, p. 151.) In Japan the story is quite a different one. Here, as in China to a more limited extent, the conceptual possibilities of this art form have been developed, with the result that meaning in flower compositions has caught the human imagination and has given a basis for discussion, comment, judgment and evaluation. The art has had in Japan as much recognition as any other and has furthermore a long recorded history as well as its own aesthetics. (Both countries have a highly developed flower symbolism, and flowers or branches grouped together to convey a symbolic message are used for special occasions.) It is noteworthy that in the West the invention of photography, esp. color photography, has given a kind of permanence to the art, and that with this a definite body of opinion and judgment, even the dawn of a few ideas, is appearing.

Another distinguishing characteristic of the medium is the strong symbolic and associational nature that flower shapes and colors have assumed in the minds of men. This is natural enough in view of the fact that flowers have played an omni-present role in our lives for centuries; as offerings in temples and churches, as gifts to honor the dead, and as adornments for the living on occasions of importance when seasons and anniversaries are being appropriately observed. This symbolic character of the very medium itself, as well as its predetermined form, is both its strength and its limitation as material for creative expression. Its strength is in that it develops its representational possibilities. The Chinese and Japanese can convey a specific meaning of good will in a flower composition through the proper selection and combination of different plants (the pine for constancy, the plum for wedded bliss, the magnolia for a woman's grace and charm, etc., etc.). This was done in a sentimental, literary way in the West in the Victorian **tussy mussy**. Its weakness is that symbolic meaning and associations of ideas are apt to cling to the material in whatever context it may be used. This is scarcely true of any other artistic medium. The potentialities of the medium for the expression of abstract decorative themes and all that these may be led to suggest or to impel one to *feel,* through empathy, are almost limitless. Line, color, mass, texture, shape, scale, with the opportunities for their thematic development are all there with the added factor of fragrance. It is these potentialities that have been developed in the West (until the moment of Japanese influence) to the exclusion of all others, except the literary symbolic combinations of religious and heraldic content. Through the centuries flowers have been formed into thematic schemes of color, line and mass which reflected the prevailing decorative taste of the period. Baroque arrangements were large in scale, with heavy masses, strong, and dark in color, composed along a swirling S curve. (There is probably a certain amount of suggested matter here: *abundance* in the heavy masses; *confidence* in the sweeping, bold curve.) The abstract phase of modern art has had its counterpart in flowers; material such as cacti, succulents and other exotic forms, were skillfully chosen to contribute through shape and other characteristics to clear-cut, precise, machine-like compositions, and were manipulated into severe repetitions of line and shape that suggested the staccato beat of the piston. It was interesting to observe how much variety there was in the enormous amount of rare and exotic flower material that suddenly became available when this taste was in the wind.

Further decorative possibilities of the medium, necessitating the development of the highest degree of technical ingenuity and skill, have been developed in countries as far apart in time and space as Siam, Bali and Ancient Egypt. In Siam, flowers are taken to pieces down to their very stamens and recreated into new and different flower forms. The ancient Egyptians also made new forms out of the parts of flowers. Because of their taste for stiff, formal, tightly and symmetrically balanced designs, with borders of repeated units, their flowers were organized in the same way. They carried long **thyrsi** in funeral processions and short, stiff, fan-shaped bouquets in everyday life. These were miracles of patient and skillful craftsmanship. At the top there were three heads of either the lotus or the papyrus blossom, symmetrically arranged and held in place by a band made up of rows of petals and tiny buds or berries; along the length of the stick, which was the foundation of the arrangement, spaced at regular intervals and held in place by the same kind of flower band as was used at the top were groups of large flower heads. A pretty woven handle of reeds finished it off. Chaplets and necklaces of real flowers, buds, petals and berries were designed and executed with a skill to rival that of any jeweller. The resulting artificial effect would not accord with our ideas of how flowers should look. In Bali the towers, or **kbogans,** composed of tier upon tier of fruit, flowers and leaves, with a waving mass of flowers on top are much like Egyptian compositions, in which contrasting shapes, sizes and colors create the decorative interest. These examples of the decorative possibilities of the medium, while they do not cover the historic field, give some idea of the range of experiment that has been made.

When we turn to the representational aspects of flower material, distinct from symbolism, we must turn to the East to see what has been realized. *Direct representation* is obviously easy enough, and both the Chinese and Japanese have over centuries made flower arrangements, in flat containers, that imitate not only growing trees and plants but broad landscape effects with foreground, middle ground and distance, the shapes of mountains and contrasting valleys, as well as more restricted scenes, a curving shore line or the corner of a garden. To accomplish these effects, they use various rocks of interesting shape and texture as well as weathered wood, mosses, fungus and other accessories. (It may be added that one of the rules in Japanese flower arrangement is that all flower material used shall be so placed in the vase that it looks as though it were still growing, not like a cut flower stuck in a vase.) This style of landscape composition is called by the Japanese *moribana style* (*moribana* means piled-up flowers). But more than direct representation is possible with this material. Certain suggested meanings are inherent in the medium itself. Flowers and branches are out of Nature and can be used to express man's enjoyment of Her, his reactions to Her, even to suggest the moods that She induces in him, and certain comments he might make upon his place in Her scheme of things. Such experiences as vastness, bleakness, coldness, windiness, and the character of the seasons can be suggested. The Japanese style of flower arrangement called **rikkwa** (meaning "standing-up plant-cuttings") which was evolved by a flower artist in the 11th cent. to convey his impressions of natural scenery is more abstract, formal and suggestive than the moribana style. Rikkwa and all Japanese styles have a romantic tendency. To make the medium adequate to express their meanings the Japanese early developed precise techniques and equipment. They have various holders, metal, forked sticks, and other devices to keep the flowers firmly in place; containers, in many different shapes, are made specifically for flower arrangement, of bronze, pottery, basketwork, bamboo and other woods. Techniques and personal modes of composition were taught by masters of the art, who thus founded schools which have maintained the tradition of the founder to the present day. New schools have appeared when artists have presented sufficiently original ideas to mark a real departure from tradition. Today the tendency is away from representation and toward the decorative.

With the large amount of written tradition and theory that exists in Japan, it was easy enough when we in this country became interested in their flower arrangement to present us with a clear account of its aims and values. There are now many excellent books in English on the subject. Flower arrangement in this country gained enormously when the influence from Japan was felt. While we were learning in the 1920's, chiefly through the offices of John Taylor Arms, to consciously apply the principles of good design to meaningless Victorian bunches and shapeless masses of flowers there comes a time when one gets tired of exercises and wants to play a real piece of music. The Japanese consciousness of the expressive possibilities of flowers was as stimulating to us as a breath of fresh air.

There are few names of artists to record in this field of art in the West, while Japan has many. It is mentioned that Charles LeBrun made flower compositions for the gardens and galleries of Louis XIV. It seems safe to assume that the art was often practised by women, as it is today in Bali, Siam and in this country, and that, in the past as now, when men went into the field they did so because it was a lucrative trade where they could turn out wreaths and bouquets, cor-

sages or other marketable flower pieces. The French artists Odilon Redon and Henri Rousseau show a remarkable feeling for the medium in their paintings. In Japan it has been men rather than women, artists rather than artisans, who have distinguished themselves in the field. In the past few years we in the West have a real artist in Constance Spry, an English woman, and because her work has been preserved in photographs it is possible to evaluate it. She has daring originality and has mastered the real technical problem of getting her material to hand (which means, in this art form, that she is a real horticulturalist, not only growing exotic plants in her own greenhouses, but being also familiar with sources outside of her own territory. This is not so necessary an asset in Japan where, due to the popularity of the art, there is a wide range of material on the open market.). She has invented some very useful containers, and has adapted others from various sources. She is a master of monochromatic color arrangements of modified baroque and rococo form. While she has little interest in the expressive possibilities of the medium beyond suggestions of opulence, etc., she can arrange a group of smooth white flowers in a niche so that they have as much presence as a fine piece of sculpture, and her masses of roses in color and texture are as sensuously appealing as Renoir's paintings. No discussion of flower arrangement as an art could fail to mention her as both improvisor and artist.

In closing it may be said that as one weighs the achievements and possibilities of this art medium, one is reminded more often of music than of any other art form. The possible parallels are the following. Both arts have common abstract tendencies and yet in the hands of artists can approach suggestive regions of expression. Comparisons can be made between Debussy's music, the *Waves,* for instance, and certain Japanese compositions, esp. rikkwa. Furthermore, improvisation and virtuosity in performance are qualities that they both have in common. We are all familiar with musical variations on a theme. In Indian music, such variations are the spontaneous expression of a singer or the master of an instrument before his audience. Japanese flower arrangement has, in its tradition, flower artists who were masters of improvisation. They tell of competitions held long ago, where the artist, presented with flowers and vase, who could create an artistic achievement with technical brilliance, as well as wit and ingenuity, won the prize.

While such comparisons may seem tenuous they throw into relief certain illusive qualities of this art form. See John T. Arms, *Design in Flower Arrangement;* F. F. Rockwell and E. C. Grayson, *Flower Arrangement in Color;* Alfred Koehn, *The Way of Japanese Flower Arrangement;* Oshigawa and Gorham, *Manual of Flower Arrangement;* Mary Averill, *The Flower Art of Japan;* Constance Spry, *Flowers in House and Garden.*   —M.F.M.

flowers of the four seasons. See SYMBOLISM IN FAR EASTERN ART.

flue. A channel or passage for smoke, air, or gases of combustion; a chimney.

fluff mats. Made by cutting cloth into small strips about ½ in. to ¾ in. wide by 2 in. to 2½ in. long and crocheting these into the mat. Coarse yarn used for crocheting and the pieces of cloth were caught at their middles into the stiches leaving both ends on top of the crocheted web. This produced a mat covered with a pile formed by cut ends.—B.E.J.

fluorescence. Some objects when seen under ultra-violet light reflect a characteristic glow or fluorescence This property is useful in detecting repairs on paintings and objects.

fluorescent bodies. See COLOR.

flute, flute d'amour. See MUSICAL INSTRUMENTS.

flutes. Grooves of curved section, used to decorate columns in classical architecture where they were cut vertically along the shaft.

flux. *Cer.* Material which melts to form binding agent when cooled. See CERAMICS I; ENAMELLING ON METAL.

flying buttress. A masonry structural member usually arched which carries the thrust of a ceiling vault or roof to a detached pier. See Gothic.

fly-leaf. *Book.* A blank leaf at the beginning and end of a book, usually in addition to the loose leaf of the end paper and next to it.

fly-whisk. Often depicted in East Asiatic art in the hands of deities, bonzes or sages. Generally of white yak- or horse-tail hairs fixed in a short handle. Symbolic significance, "to clear away the dust of this world." See Cāmara; canrī; hossu.   —J.A.M.

focus, in dance. See movement.

foil. A leaflike space or arc between the cusps in Gothic tracery. **Trefoil** indicates three such arcs in the ornamental unit.

folding chair. See FURNITURE.

folia. *Mus.* A slow tempo. Spanish dance in 3/4 time

folio. *Book.* A book size (q.v.). Also a sheet of paper folded once to make four pages.

folk art. Basically, folk art is an aspect of folklore which characterizes the change of a group from a primitive to a rural or cultured status. It is a part of the pattern of the folkways of the group, the mores of which may dominate, while the arts liberate, in a complex of traditions, festivals, songs, and ornament. Leaving the point of view of sociologist and psychologist, the student must next distinguish folk art from or mediate it with, other forms of art. It is comparable to primitive art only if survival elements predominate; it is peasant art only if unsophisticated and strongly traditional elements are patent; it is popular art only if at the chronological level under consideration widespread employment of the forms is clear; it is regional, provincial, colonial, immigrant, or frontier, dependent upon the geographical, political, or environmental setting of its expression. Folk art is never aristocratic, dictated by fashion, or fostered by a patron It is rather the expression of the people, traditionally, naively, economically.

The mixed influence of folk art on other art forms or *vice versa* are also worthy of note. A folk art may influence in its later phases art forms on levels far different from the one of its origin. One thinks of Japanese prints and Manet, or of African negro sculpture and Picasso. The influence may, again, come from an art form of a sophisticated mode and help define the appearance of a popular form. One recalls della Robbia's glazed terra-cottas, the printed page which long echoed illuminated manuscripts, and the color reproductions of our own day. The influence may, again, be horizontal, rather than vertical, as when the textiles of a museum collection are reproduced on electrically-run looms.

Folk art, then, is an essentially naive, nonacademic, frequently untrained type of art. It is founded on traditional techniques; it concentrates on things rather than on ideas; its craftsmen know the satisfaction of recreation rather than that of creation Everyday objects of dress, utensils furniture, or portraiture are its major concern. It is a minor art in a world where nature is the producer of the major. See T. Munro and P. Guillaume, *Primitive Negro Sculpture*, 1926; *American Folk Art*, 1932 and *Masters of Popular Painting*, 1938, Mus. of Modern Art; F. H. Haire, *The Folk Costume Book*, 1926; C. H. Holme, editor, *Peasant Art in Sweden*, 1910, *Peasant Art in Austria and Hungary*, 1910, *Peasant Art in Russia*, 1912, *Peasant Art in Italy*, 1913; D. Baud-Bovy, *Peasant Art in Switzerland*, 1924.   —W.S.R.

folk dance. Literally means the dance of people and in that sense is synonymous with all "dance". The distinction habitually drawn between folk and art dance may be false unless it is made with an understanding of the fundamental inter-dependence of the two. The difference between them is in fact more a difference between two growth stages of one human activity, comparable to the difference between a plant and its seed.

Folk dance is the growth stage which stands midway between dance as a partly instinctive and reflex reaction to environment and dance as a form consciously pursued for its own art value. The partly instinctive activity became more deliberate in folk dance, and, though its basic purpose remained the expression of human feeling, it acquired other associated purposes. The people of individual nations danced also for the joy of communal activity, for the expression and heightening of their common emotion, and for the sense of unity such group expression gave them.

The form and content of such dances varied within limits according to the national or racial differences between groups. These limits were narrow, however, as is repeatedly shown by the universality of certain patterns and movements among dances of all nations, and stand as proof of the constancy of all basic human reactions to living.

Folk dance has been and is the nutritive source which provides art dance with its elemental material, however the expression of that material may be developed for more powerful communication.   —J.G.

Folkemuseum. See SCANDINAVIAN ART.

folk-radio. See radio and music.

folk song. A simple song in ballad-form tinged by the musical peculiarities of a nation. See song.

folk song, Jewish. See JEWISH MUSIC.

folly (from ME and OF *folie*, foolish, mad), in architecture, an extravaganza, a monument without functional intention or significance; a concrete expression of the builder's private and cabalistic theology, an embodiment of his wit or spite, a mirror to his vanity; a house abandoned uncompleted because its scale exceeded its owner's purse; any building which completely lacks utility or meaning in the eyes of the neighbors. The folly is particularly associated with 18th cent. England, a time and place when indulgence in this aberration of the art of building attained the proportions of an epidemic and its survivors stand as minor, characteristic expressions of an age. Yet the folly knows neither style nor period nor nationality, and seldom speaks to reason. Conspicuous examples litter the centuries, from the Tower of Babel to the Maginot Line, but the hair dividing what is folly from what is not is difficult to define. Whether or not a particular object be a true folly depends upon the sensibilities of the beholder. Some are held to be so by common consent, others are arguable. The *folies de grandeur* committed on the orders of certain Caesars, contemporary as well as Roman, do not fall within this classification, nor do most of the wilder flights of baroque imagination in civil architecture; the palace and gardens of the Prince of Palagonia, La Bagaria in Sicily, provide a notable exception, as does the earlier Palazzo Cattaio, near Monselice, built from strictly literary specifications; Marco Polo's description of the Imperial Palace in Peking. Architectural expressions of a social as opposed to an individual psychosis in which the mental unbalance is clearly mirrored in the architecture itself as in the unfinished Cathedral of the Sagrada Familia by Gaudi in Barcelona, are genuine follies; but it is unfair to classify monuments to unfulfilled ideals, as the Palace of the League of Nations in Geneva, by this title. The earliest authentic follies in England were both built in Northamptonshire by the recusant Sir Thomas Tresham who designed Rushton Lodge (1595) and the unfinished house called Lyveden New Building to symbolize his private views on the Passion; subsequent follies of a religious nature include the Georgian church built by "Hellfire" Sir Francis Dashwood on the crest of a steep hill at West Wycombe in the cynical hope that no parishioners would ever ascend to it; the group of cottages embellished with a false-front Norman church tower of only three sides at Tattingstone, Suffolk (1790) to improve the Squire's view; and Jezreel's Temple, near Rochester, projected and partially built by James White in 1885 in preparation for the end of the world. The most conspicuous follies took the form of isolated towers, many of them subsequently destroyed by lightning. Freston Tower, Suffolk (c. 1595) and Eyre's Folly, Wilts., (Jacobean), are early surviving examples; of the 18th cent., Sir William Chambers' delightful Chinese pagoda in Kew Garden, Stratton's Folly at Little Berkhamsted (1789), the Sugarloaf Folly above Dallington, Sussex, hastily erected by "Mad Jack" Fuller to win a rash bet that Dallington Church spire was visible from his drawing room, and William Beckford's Lansdowne Tower at Bath are notable. The latest and loftiest is Wainhouse Folly, Halifax, reared to a height of 282 feet between 1871 and 1874. Nearly every 18th cent. country house boasted its Temple, Artificial Ruin, Triumphal Arch, Pyramid, Tower, Gazebos, Grottoes, or Ornamental Mausoleum; some parks were ornamented with all these species, as at Stowe, which afforded a tasteful collection of follies without equal in the kingdom. The most modest follies were grottoes, stemming from memories of baroque gardens in Italy and France: Evelyn and Sir William Temple had the earliest, Pope popularized them with his celebrated (and utilitarian) one at Twickenham; the Duchess of Richmond and her daughters built a famous one with their own hands (1740), adorned with shells in striking anticipation of the Adam manner, at Goodwood House; Payne Knight's Cold Bath at Downton Castle was admired by tourists; and none exceeded in luxury Beckford's Grotto at Fonthill, inhabited by a hired hermit. In the next century the grotto follies attained their apotheosis at Liverpool, where Joseph Williamson built himself a huge underground establishment (c. 1820, ostensibly as a private work-relief project), and at Welbeck Abbey where the 5th Duke of Portland excavated a still more vast subterranean palace (without excuses). The most magnificent Triumphal Arch, popularly known as "The Gates of Jerusalem", was erected at Shugborough Park in 1763 from designs of James Stuart, ostensibly as a memorial to Admiral Anson. The Pyramids were generally intended for tombs, though sometimes merely as epigrammatic incidents in a landscape; outstanding are that of John Knill above St. Ives in Cornwall (for himself) and the two built by Jack Fuller, one of them at Brightling for himself, the other on Farley Mount, Hants, for a favorite horse. Francis

Dashwood's mausoleum at West Wycombe and the unfinished colosseum overhanging Oban Harbour are other notable sepulchral follies. The most curious coincidence of imitation Roman *tempietto* and sham Gothic ruin is still to be seen in the grounds of Colchester Castle, an absurdity undoubtedly considered an excellent evidence of *gusto* and *ton* when fresh, but surely superflous next to a genuine and large Norman castle which stands on the floor of a genuine Roman temple? The most engaging of 18th cent. follies are the occasional **picturesque villages** designed and built not merely to house retainers but primarily to improve the view. Two of them, those at Milton Abbey, Dorset, and at Southill, Beds, designed respectively by James Wyatt and Henry Holland, replaced existing but uncomely and unfavorably situated villages. Two others were entirely new, the delightful hamlet at Blaise Castle in Somerset, designed for the Harfords by John Nash, and the coal-miners village on the Ellis estate, Debdale Hall, Notts; the latter, successfully combining the owner's aesthetic and philanthropic impulses, stands as the earliest industrial model village in England. Fortunately none of these had the political consequences of the most celebrated village folly, Maria Antoinette's *hameau* at Versailles. The most elaborate follies were houses meant to be lived in. Between Walpole's Strawberry Hill and P. F. Robinson's Swiss Cottage (1829-32) lie several generations of English country houses which range from the eccentric to sheer folly. The neighborhood of Bath is rich in them; the most characteristic is Midford Castle, built in the shape of a club to commemorae a killing at cards. But none can match the three most spectacular examples: William Beckford's Fonthill Abbey, Wilts, by James Wyatt, 1796-1807) which was destroyed only a few years after its completion when the colossal central tower collapsed in a storm; Ashridge, Bucks (also by Wyatt, 1807-13); and Brighton Pavilion, built by John Nash as an extravagant whimsy for George IV.

—T.A.H.

Folsom culture. An early American culture apparently of the last glacial epoch, at least 10,000 yrs. ago, evidence of which was found near Folsom (hence the name) in northeastern New Mexico in 1925, through the discovery of chipped stone artifacts with the remains of extinct species of animals. Knives, blades, darts, gravers and other tools of refined shape and skilled workmanship reveal a hunter people of whom no skeletal remains have as yet been found. Similar finds in other sites show a

wide distribution of the culture over the Great Plains area. The relation of this culture to that of the Anasazi is unknown, and a gap of some 8,000 years between the two is still to be filled. See PREHISTORIC ART; also Frank H. H. Roberts, Jr., *Developments in the Problem of the North American Paleo-Indian,* Essays in Historical Anthropology, Smithsonian Miscellaneous Collections, 1940.
—H.G.

fondant. See ENAMELLING ON METAL.

font. *Book.* A set of letters, numbers, etc. But also used in another sense, as representing style of letters, as for instance when a letter of a different size or style appears in a line of print, or a word, it is said to be of wrong font. —H.E.S.

Fontainebleu, school of. Barbizon school. See FRENCH ART.

foot. *Cer.* The bottom part of the base of a vessel.

footings. The spreading courses at the base or foundation of a wall. When a layer of different material is used, it is called the "footing".
force, in dance. See movement.

foredge painting. *Book.* Pictures found, usually in old books, painted on the fore-edge of books.

foreground. That part of a scene in a painting, bas-relief, mosaic picture, etc., which is nearest to, and in front of, the spectator.

foreshorten, foreshortening. See PERSPECTIVE; PSYCHOLOGY OF DRAWING AND PAINTING.

FORGERIES IN PAINTINGS. The theory that the rise of the faker and forger of art objects coincided with the beginnings of private collecting is advanced by Riccardo Nobili in his entertaining book, *The Gentle Art of Faking.* He points out that the arts in Greece were practiced for the benefit of the state and that personal ownership of art objects was not the fashion. Architects, sculptors and painters lavished their talents in building and embellishing temples, theatres and public places where citizens came to worship, find recreation and enjoy the current productions of a living art. Doubtless much the same condition had obtained in Egypt where the artist and artisan were intimately associated in the creation of monuments of religious nature, their

creations being considered as current commodities rather than objects of virtue.

It was in Rome of the Empire, rendered fabulously wealthy through conquest and plunder, that the **private collector** emerged. When the Temple of Concord in the Roman Forum was erected in the reign of Tiberius, it housed art treasures looted in conquered lands. Agrippa, Caesar, Mark Antony and Sulla assembled vast collections and Verres plundered Sicily while serving there as proconsul. It was inevitable that the lesser fry and even the soldiers should return with objects which they little understood and which quickly found their way into the hands of dealers. There existed in Imperial Rome, as in America today, a complex art world with its dealers and auction rooms, its collections and its forgers.

The revival of interest in classical culture and art which fostered the renascence of the arts in Italy awakened the collector's instinct anew. The princely collections of the Medici, the Dukes of Urbino, the Gonzagas, of Isabella d'Este, the Dukes of Milan and a host of others have not been surpassed even in our days of fabulous fortunes. It is known that Donatello, Ghiberti and others were greatly influenced by antique sculpture and that extraordinary skill in repairing and imitating these works was rapidly acquired in Italy. Imitation of paintings was somewhat retarded because few if any antique works had survived and the churchly Gothic art was not likely to be sought after by the collectors of the Renaissance. By Vasari's day, however, the deliberate creation of false works was practiced and the skill and cunning of the Italian hand has been proverbial ever since.

Through the 17th, 18th and 19th cents. the collector's mania continued to spread and with it the traffic in works of doubtful character. This traffic has flourished in periods of unusual national prosperity with its crop of new fortunes engendering a class of collectors possessed of enthusiasm and, at times, little taste or knowledge. It is interesting to note that whenever artists have been employed directly as they were during the 15th cent. in Flanders that little if any evidence of faking within the epoch exists. It is only when these works, with the passing of time, become objects of commerce that dishonest falsifications begin to appear in numbers. This seems to be borne out by the fact that today works by such masters as Picasso and Matisse are collected for high prices by the comparative few and already have been the subjects of criminal imitation. Daumier and van Gogh died in obscurity and poverty, their works appreciated by a handful of friends, yet today, the collector of their works must beware. For the explanation of this phenomenon we must look into a number of places.

Fashionable collecting has always invited the production of forgeries. Of late years we have witnessed in this country an enlightened interest in works by the three pillars of modern American painting, Homer, Ryder and Eakins Crass imitations of these, fully signed, have already flooded the market. Earlier in this century pictures by Corot and Millet were in much favor and many worthless imitations entered collections in this country, the grandson of Millet being guilty of fraudulent imitations of this artist's works. Not long ago, in Germany, a sizeable group of forgeries, some quite clever, were sold widely as the work of Vincent van Gogh. Renoir and Cézanne have been exploited and a picture said to be by Modigliani must be carefully traced and studied before it is purchased. These painters and others in their circle are being collected and are fetching large prices today, hence their imitation is a profitable occupation. There was a time when the works of Monticelli were first-string collectors' items and imitations of them were numerous. Today neither originals nor imitations have many buyers. The forger, the unscrupulous dealer and their numerous accomplices, obviously function to supply the current demand or fashion.

Picture dealers have been held in much suspicion, so much so that many have come to consider them dishonest as a class. This is far from being the case—indeed, it is the exception. Reference is made, of course, to the numerous houses with established reputations and long experience with fine pictures. It is true that even with these mistakes may be made, sometimes serious ones. Generally, however, the errors concern faulty attributions, seldom involve the purchase of a completely worthless imitation. These dealers treasure their good name as their greatest asset. Many of them are intelligent and well informed and a few are among the most accomplished connoisseurs of our day. The collector who pays most dearly at the hands of a dealer is the bargain hunter with more trust in his judgment and keen eye than knowledge and good sense. There is a class of dealers specifically in business for this kind of amateur and curiously enough both parties to the bargain are usually well satisfied. There is nothing more repugnant to such a collector than hearing the truth concerning his mistake. Thus fraudulent works may remain in private possession for years and the thieving dealer continues, unexposed, in successful practice.

Certificates of authenticity given by over-sanguine scholars frequently figure in advancing the price of pictures of average importance. The practice of writing certificates indulged in by some European museum directors and curators is frowned on by the ethical code of American museum men. In all such cases the buyer must weigh carefully what is *actually* said in the certificate. The clever use of language can frequently hide the truth concerning a work which a certificate is supposedly supporting. It is also important to know whether the writer of such a document is a competent and recognized scholar in his field. Knowledge in the field of paintings has advanced so in recent years that one would do well to secure the specialist's opinion. To all those buying names rather than works of art, however, there is no sure guarantee that certificates will infallibly produce a fine work of art.

Provenance or pedigree consisting of bills or receipts given by the artist, published descriptions in documents or journals of the epoch, engravings of works made during or shortly after the artist's lifetime, may usually be accepted if they actually refer to the picture in question. Likewise pictures which have figured in a long succession of well known collections or have appeared in important exhibitions may be credited. Here again the utmost care must be taken to assure the common identity of the works so known with those being studied.

Family tradition is rarely dependable unless it is supported by documents. Word of mouth statements passing from generation to generation are generally suspect. So frequently an indifferent copy of an original by Gilbert Stuart made, let us assume, in 1850, becomes by 1900 one of his own. In such cases only knowledge of the artist's painting habits, his canvas and color, should determine one's opinion. Many such inaccurate statements are made quite honestly by owners but some are deliberately fabricated to deceive the inexperienced. Worthless portraits supposedly by good early American painters have been planted in apparently respectable families and sold for important sums. Many times these pictures change hands so frequently before being "placed" that the fraud is well nigh impossible to trace. It must be borne in mind also that we have no laws in this country designed to punish such frauds.

Deliberate forgeries may be classified as imitations of an artist's work made with the intent to deceive. They must be distinguished from imitations made honestly by a master's pupils, by copyists or mannerist imitators. The van Gogh imitations referred to earlier were deliberate and criminal forgeries. Such forgeries are usually signed with a carefully faked signature. They attempt to reproduce the artist's style, his drawing, his color and his materials. The most clever ones are made on an old foundation so that the fine crackle of age will be found upon close examination. They are at times made up of motifs taken from several sources within the master's production put together skillfully to appear as plausible originals. Their detection will also depend upon a study of the art forms themselves. Imitators intent upon reproducing the "style sensation" of a picture will rarely understand the basic forms, and mistakes in construction will stand out to proclaim the forger. Early works imitated on old grounds can be detected by use of **photomacrographs** of 2½ x to 3 x. With this magnification the fresh paint film can usually be seen extending over unbroken pigment as well as between the old separations. Such superimposed paint is necessarily more recent than the foundation. True **crackle** in old painted surfaces causes a definite interruption, the cracks extending through to the support. Less accomplished forgers will attempt to create the appearance of age artificially. The fine crackle can be produced by varnishing a paint film before it is completely dry or by exposing it to heat. In such cases the crackle will affect only varnish and paint film. Still clumsier forgers have attempted to paint the fine crackle over a freshly painted imitation. Only close inspection with a glass is required to detect this common practice.

Old copies and **imitations** frequently figure as forgeries years after they have been honestly produced. Students in all epochs have endeavored to emulate their masters to the minutest detail. Copies and imitations so created have at times been modified, signed and given faked pedigrees or declared newly discovered works. In many ways they form the most plausible class of forgeries because they have the authentic appearance and their materials are of the epoch. In such cases stylistic comparisons of line, form, colour and technique will aid in detecting which is a copy or imitation and which the original. Knowl-

edge of the artist's style is essential but technical aids in the form of photomacrographs, radiographs and infra-red ray photographs will be found useful in checking and amplifying one's visual examination. The procedure is to assemble a group of such documents from unquestioned works by the master under study. By comparing these with similar material taken from the questioned work style differences will emerge and plausible conclusions can be reached.

Modern copies and **imitations of old masters** offer less serious problems. The professional museum copyist has never been a familiar figure in our museums. Such pictures, mostly produced abroad, find their way to auction rooms and smaller antique shops where they are bought for decorative purposes although, at times, an unlucky purchaser mistakes them for originals. These works can be recognized by examining their materials, canvas or panel and their manner of execution.

Copies and **imitations of contemporary work** are more difficult to detect because many of these are made to deceive and some are quite clever. Fortunately one encounters such pictures seldom although the danger is ever present. The best counsel to the collector is to secure competent advice and to remember that good pictures by celebrated artists have their price. He should beware of "recently discovered" and "unknown" paintings found in out of the way places. Such works, offered at small prices are seldom genuine.

Signatures on pictures are not positive proof of authenticity. Indeed a large percentage of artists in the past failed to sign or identify their pictures in any way. Genuine signatures are usually an integral part of the paint film. When added over old painted surfaces, the writing will interrupt and fill the fine cracks characteristic of old paint films. Such signatures, apparently lying upon the surface are suspect. The validity of the signature can be accepted only when the style of the picture is clearly that of the artist. Dictionaries listing names of painters and giving various known forms of their signatures are useful in checking one's conclusions but they do not furnish final evidence, because, obviously, forgers have access to them as well.

Modified fragments constitute a well known class of pictures masquerading as completed originals. This is a large and deceptive group of forgeries because at least a portion of such works is original. Incomplete works, sketches and partially damaged pictures are often completed or modified to increase their desirability and value. Unscrupulous dealers and clever restorers are at fault here. This practice was widely used in the last century and many a *pasticcio* of this kind has remained undiscovered in private and public collections. The experienced eye will be able to detect such modifications by the presence of *pentimenti* which do not function with the drawing, brush work or composition of the picture but he may not be able to positively state the extent of the changes. The x-ray is the most useful means of detecting such additions. At times infra-red and ultra-violet ray photography will aid but these results are not always clear cut.

Modifications by the artist must be recognized as distinct from the subsequent changes of restorers. These are legitimate and their treatment in restoration constitutes a special problem. They do not affect the value of a painting and often furnish instructive clues to the artist's methods.

Repainted "wrecks" are old pictures which have survived in a state of delapidation and have, by clever restoration, been reborn. Many times the extent of original paint film is less than 10%. This fairly large class of forgeries are worthless except as study pieces. Here again, the x-ray and the infra-red ray photograph will furnish positive evidence of condition. Because varnishes have a fluorescence of their own, the ultra-violet ray lamp is less useful.

Reproductions, photographs, prints and **drawings** have also been used as foundations for forgeries. As a class, they are not especially clever nor are they too difficult to recognize. The paper support of coloured reproductions is removed so that the printed surface alone remains. This is then mounted on canvas and care taken that the weave of the fabric shows through on the face of the print. Varnishing and artificial ageing finish the product. Much the same process is followed with prints and drawings although these must be colored with glazes before being varnished. When such works are encountered they will arouse suspicion by their flat, papery appearance lacking the slight relief and varied surface texture of an oil painting. Examination of the edges of the picture will provide further proof. A warning should be noted lest all oil sketches on paper be suspected. Artists of past times and of our day have utilized paper supports, despite their flimsy and temporary nature, to produce sketches and informal experiments.

Interpretation of technical photographs correctly is of utmost importance in study of style and hence in deciding between the master's work and that of the copyist. Radiographs record the substructure of a painting produced with pigments dense enough to impede the passage of x-rays. The denser the pigment the greater the clarity of the shadow cast. Since white and many light pigments contain lead, a material impervious to x-ray, it follows that their shadows in pictures will be recorded with greater clarity than dark areas in which lead pigments are absent or exist in smaller proportions. The shadowgraph will, therefore, give only an approximation of the visible surface conditions. This approximation will approach the truth in heads and hands where a larger portion of white is used. Such areas furnish valuable clues on technique and work habits which are personal with each artist. The modern copyist will reproduce only the surface characteristics of a painting, not the master's own personal habits of work. These are more likely to be known to pupils of an artist and their copies or imitations are therefore more convincing. This is the case with works of painters in Rembrandt's circle, many of which are or used to be attributed to the master. A sufficiently large group of radiographs by a given artist will establish a performance pattern which is apt to be conclusive and shadowgraphs which do not belong in the pattern cannot be accepted as his work. All technical photographs are only aids in enlarging one's observation and recording it for future comparison. The popular belief that these do away with the need for connoisseurship is, of course, erroneous. To be useful such photographs must be compared with one another and with the work of art so that a logical chain of reasoning can be evolved. See *Trucs et Truquers*, Paris, 1907 and *Le Truquage*, Paul Eudel, Paris, 1908; *Mouseion*, Paris, 1920, vols. 17-18, pp. 132-136; *The Gentle Art of Faking*, Riccardo Nobili, London, 1922; *Three Essays in Method*, B. Berenson, Oxford, 1927; *The Scientific Examination of Paintings*, A. Martin de Wild, London, 1929; *Echt und Unecht*, Max J. Friedländer, Berlin, 1929; *The Analyist*, London, 1934, vol. 59, pp. 657-664; *Metropolitan Museum Studies*, vol. 5, 1934-1936, pp. 1-19; *Technical Studies*, vol. 6, Oct. 1937, pp. 75-105; *Art Critics from a Laboratory*, Alan Burroughs, Boston, 1938; *Journal of the Walters Art Gallery*, Balt., Md., 1940, pp. 9-41; *Burlington Mag.*, London, vol. 78, 1941, pp. 143-151; for mag. articles vide *Art Index* 1929 to date.

—H.M.

forlana, furlana. A lively Italian dance in 6/8 or 6/4 time.

form (L. *forma*). In general, mode of arrangement; structure; order; organization. (1) In comparative aesthetics, and in regard to any art: (a) Mode of arranging or co-ordinating the factors in a work of art. As distinct from the physical form of the object, its **aesthetic form** is that arrangement of details and meanings which can be either directly sensed and verified by other observers, or demonstrably assigned to it on the basis of established cultural usage. For example, the form of a poem includes patterns of word-sounds and also established meanings of words. (b) A particular type of such arrangement; especially, a recognized, conventional type such as the sonnet or sonata. (2) In visual arts: shape, especially solid shape; as in the statement that line, form, color are elements in art. (To avoid confusion with sense (1) a, the term **shape**—linear, surface, or solid shape—is preferable).   —T.M.

(3) For dance to exist as an *art form,* movement must be associated with imaginative content and mental discipline. This necessity presents two phases belonging to its art form. One of the unseen, **inner dance,** which is the organization of the mental attributes into content; the other is the outer **observed dance,** which is the result of the organization and execution of the motor elements. When the fusion of inner subjective experience and outer objective motor experience is attained, form in dance is achieved in its fullest meaning as *art form.* The observable form as art form is, therefore, biologic and organic, for it is an extension of inner conditions into their expressive form. In the last analysis the term "form", in all its implications, means the organization of constituent elements into a defining characteristic appearance by which it is known.   —M.N.H'D.

form: a philosophical analysis. During the two millennia of European thinking about art this term has acquired so many meanings, and such confusing ones, that order will have to be brought out of chaos by applying some scheme of classification.

A. *Form as an ontological category.* (1) **Platonic form.** The form of a particular work of art is the idea, the essence, the prototype which is made perceptible in the work of art. (a) It is perceptible in what the work of art is *about.* The prototype of a chair is made visible in the painting of this or that chair.

What is usually called content (or matter) thus becomes the locus for the idea, the form. This is roughly the standpoint of the **aesthetics of content.** (b) The idea of form that becomes perceptible is not this or that idea, but the idea of the beautiful in general. Its locus is not the content but the composition of the work of art, the law of order ruling over the parts that compose it. (c) There is no reason why these two formalisms of form and content should not be joined and the work of art defined as the beautiful representation of a prototype, beautiful here meaning a representation in terms of the Platonic idea of beauty. (2) **Aristotelian** and **pseudo-Aristotelian form:** Form as entelechy of matter. (a) Form and matter do not exist separately; they exist only as formed matter or mattered form. According as one understands by matter in art the artistic medium (colors, sounds, words, etc.) or the subject matter, form means the entelechy of the medium, or the entelechy of the subject matter, or both.

This corresponds to T. M. Greene's distinction (made in an un-Aristotelian context) between aesthetic and artistic form. **Aesthetic form** lies in what Prall calls the aesthetic surface and is the relationship established by the artist between the ultimate sensuous data that constitute the artist's medium. **Artistic form,** on the other hand, is this aesthetic form, now not taken as an end in itself, "but also, and essentially (as) a means, in fact the only means, whereby the artist can express himself and communicate his ideas to others." According to Greene, artistic form, as "means to the end of significant expression" "is the *peculiar* locus of its (the work of art) artistic quality."

Returning now to form as entelechy, form in art is somehow in between the useful form that is imposed by man upon indifferent material—as for instance in the case of human tools—and the biological form that develops from inside the matter itself. With respect to these teleological relationships see Kant's *Critique of Judgment.* (Cf. also Dewey, *Art as Experience,* p. 116.) (b) By a process of crass substantialization, form and matter become substances themselves, subsisting independent of each other like soul and body, and brought together by fate or force to constitute another more complex substance This view can easily be adopted by Platonists. What was the form, before it was joined to matter? An idea, or perhaps better, the vision of an idea. This vision, however, is a vision in colors, or in sounds; it is itself a hylomorphic thing.

The accent can now be shifted upon this vision and the translation of the vision into real matter becomes the task, artistically rather irrelevant, of what Croce would call mere technique.

B. *Form as instrument of aesthetic analysis.* Form and matter are mere instruments of analysis. The scalpel and retractor with which we dissect human bodies are not themselves parts of the body. Similarly our concepts of form, matter, etc. are merely operational devices; they are no real parts (nor even moments) of the work of art. The same thing viewed in one perspective is form, viewed from another point, matter—just as one and the same nervous process is, for the biologist, a chemical process, for the psychologist, a psychological process

We cannot discuss this view. It is suspicious, however, that even where form and matter are regarded as mere concepts of analysis, they tend to take on again a definitely ontological meaning. Cf. T. M. Greene, *The Arts and the Art of Criticism,* pp. 123, 126, for whom form, matter, etc., are categories of analysis.

C. *Form as a principle of classification.* Works of art are grouped according to similarities. The characteristics wherein they are similar are abstracted from the rest and lead to the establishment of classes. The interest guiding these abstractions may be either systematic or historic. The systematic abstractions lead to such formal concepts as epic, novel, drama, comedy, etc. The characteristics which were basic in making up these groups are easily turned into normative concepts. Every good epic for example, must be written in the form of alexandrines, these alexandrines themselves must have a certain form, etc. It is in this sense that academicians are called formalists.

The historic interest leads to classifying works of art according to stylistic characteristics (see style). The form of a work of art here consists of all those characteristics that show the work or art to be of a certain period, of a certain country, of a certain painter, etc. (Cf. Woelfflin, Panofsky.)

The systematic forms are supposed to be "right" at all times and in all places. The beauty of which they are the *conditio sine qua non* is thought eternal. The historic forms, on the other hand, are relative to place, time, and race. They are called beautiful only as they give expression to the unique spirit that created them. —W.C.

formal balance. See balance.

formal poetry. See POETRY.

formalism. Indicates the use of those transcendent forms by which all form is achieved; i.e., the translating of any subject matter into a thing which may be perceived by the senses.

Besides this transcendental meaning there is the meaning in art of form which is sensually perceivable but which has become divorced from its content and which has no longer any relation to it. Form itself is important only because of its relation to the subject which is to be formed and to which it stands in a certain organic kinsship. But if one dissolves this relationship with the content or annuls the organic partnership, then form without content is the result, and that is the exact meaning of formalism. In some degree formalism may be compared with governmental inefficiency in which governmental functions are no longer related to the things which they govern, and the relation between them has become only a formal function, not an organic one.

In art this kind of formalism is used by persons of critical mentality, who know that a certain content is the basis of each form, and who have in addition an imitative ability which makes use of this knowledge to imitate forms, to make the spectator believe that the content is really expressed by the form. Therefore formalism always means the illusion of something which is not really there. This deception can be achieved either unconsciously by those with a lack of spiritual substance and an abundance of ability for formal expression or consciously with the intention of creating effects by means of forms behind which there is an insufficient fund of substance. This deception of value by means of empty forms, or form husks, is only possible when the spectator has an inexact or superficial feeling for form. In reality, empty form never can be the same as form filled with substance, because between substance and form there exists a relation which cannot be broken, so that neither can be mistaken by the keen observer.

Formalism plays a great part in epochs that terminate a cultural period in which the substance of feeling is at a low ebb and the emphasis on form over-developed. —A.J.S.

formal script. See writing.

formant, formant regions. *Mus.* A dominant group or groups of adjacent partials in a tone spectrum which gives character to a rich tone. A sound may have one or more formants. It is largely in terms of the number, location, and relative dominance of the formants that we distinguish a voice, an instrument, a vowel, or any other sound from another.

The characteristic of a tone, such as an *o*, an *a*, or an *e*, is revealed by the number and location of the formant regions usually from one to three in a rich tone. Thus there are characteristic formant regions, for each vowel in music or speech for each solo instrument so that one can distinguish at a glance a clarinet tone, a flute tone, a violin tone, or the tone of a bassoon in part by this. A pure tone has only one partial, a fundamental. A rich tone may or may not have a formant or a formance.   —C.E.S.

format. *Book.* In French, size only; but also size, shape, style, etc., in English.

forming of pottery. See CERAMICS I.

form, in music. (1) Opposite to extra-musical content or subject matter. (2) Sum total of relationships among consecutive elements of a composition insofar as such relationships are relevant factors constituting the coherence of the composition. The elements in question may be simple (motifs, phrases, themes), or complex (sections, movements). The relationships in question may be identity (literal repetition), similarity (variation, allusion), or heterogeneity (contrast).

Set forms (sonata, rondo, etc.) are generated when certain types of relationships are applied to certain types of elements by numerous composers in a typical way over a considerable length of time.   —E.K.

formism, formists. See POLISH ART.

fortifications. Any works constructed for the purpose of military defense. Early fortifications consisted primarily of a parapet and a ditch.

forum. See ROMAN ART.

forwarding. *Book.* The stage of a work on a book between sewing and tooling, etc., including rounding, backing, putting in boards, etc. See EARLY BOOKBINDING AND FINE BINDING.

foundation. A structure upon which something is erected, as a building below the surface of the ground, or the portion that constitutes a base; sometimes, a platform, on which the upper portions rest.   —J.M.M.

foundation weaves. See weaving.

founding. The art of melting and casting.

found object. See object.

found object assisted, interpreted. See object.

fountain. A natural or artificially produced jet of water. Architecturally, the structure or basin, often embellished, through which the water flows.

four attributes of the scholar. See SYMBOLISM IN FAR EASTERN ART.

four gentlemen, the. See CHINESE ART.

four leaf motif. Also called quatrefoil; a decorative ornament having four lobes or foils with either pointed or rounded ends; the pointed form common on Greek pottery, sometimes hatched.

fovea centralis. See COLOR.

foxed. *Book.* Discolored; spotted. The term is generally used to describe the yellow spots left in paper by damp.

fractional concept. A perspective or conception involving visual description of an object as a combination of different parts rather than as an organic unity; found in early or primitive art forms.

frame. In the sense most commonly applicable to art, the word frame is primarily used for a construction of wood, metal or other material forming an enclosure or border around a work of art, such as a painting, relief or stretched tapestry, etc., to provide a neat or ornamental finish around the work, to isolate it from its surroundings or to harmonize it with them, and serving as well as a protection and often as the means of attaching the work in its appointed place.

In one aspect of its use the frame is a device for setting successfully a painted or sculptured picture or ornamentation into its architecturally appointed place. In this sense the use of moldings to set off elements of a building has relation with frames. Related also are borders such as occur in wall paintings in Pompeii and Herculaneum, in mosaics as there and at Antioch, and later in mediaeval Italian churches, as at Ravenna and Rome, around decorative medallions as in Coptic textiles, in decorative bands around a page of manuscript or in connection with miniatures in manuscripts of the Middle Ages, or in mounts for ivory carvings and enamels as in medieval reliquaries and book-bindings.

In modern usage a frame usually is thought of as a constructed device for holding in place, protecting, and presenting appropriately for inspection a painting, a mirror or the like, and it may or may not have architectural relation with the spot where it serves. The tendency has been toward less and less architectural relation with the environment, as, during the development of European art, the painting has become increasingly an independent, studio product unrelated to its probable setting, and important in its own right apart from any decorative or other purpose it may serve. Naturally, frames have reflected dominant styles of decoration of the period in which they were made.

The earliest use of the frame in a way approximating modern usage is contemporaneous with early painting in Europe. The structures holding in place the multiple painted panels of saints and sacred history used in churches and chapels in the medieval period, and, as the Gothic period progressed, repeating as ornament some of the crockets and finials used in architecture, are the earliest, and authentic examples are rare. They still are close to architecture, have usually been designed, like the paintings they enclose, for a specific space. The reredos (q.v.) of chapels and churches, set with painted panels, used in medieval times and finding elaborate and complex expression in Spain and Latin American countries into the 18th cent. are more complex, but thoroughly architectural developments of the frame.

The Renaissance used the frame and developed it in accord with modern practice, apart from any architectural connection, from the 16th cent. It took on size, weight and baroque decorative elaboration in the 17th cent., became more delicate and detailed in common with each change of style and taste in the 18th cent., reflected classic influences and used classic motifs at the beginning of the 19th cent.

Until the 18th cent., though the frames were often of other materials—for example ivory, silver, ebony, tortoise-shell, etc.—the principal material employed was wood, carved, and then usually gilded. The finest craftsmen (e.g. Grinling Gibbons in England) frequently turned their hand to carving frames and examples exist which are as fine in their expression of the time as the works they enclose.

In the 18th cent., in the effort to meet the demand for cheaper frames than the hand-carved type, a composition, which could be molded to imitate carving and then gilded to resemble the solid wood frame, was perfected. From that time on only rarely have competent wood carvers worked on frames. The composition type frames, still produced, flourished in abundance, and in great size and weight as in brilliance of gliding, through the 19th cent.; and the heavy gold frame, sometimes somewhat eclipsing the work of art it enclosed, was a characteristic interior decoration of the Victorian home. For the most part these frames reproduce 18th cent. designs, and have been widely responsible for the persistence of this style of decoration. In the late 19th cent. Seurat experimented with frames painted in harmony with his pictures, and many contemporary artists design, and sometimes also make, their own frames. The classic paintings of modern art, impressionists, Cezanne, etc. are most frequently sold by the dealers in old 18th cent. frames, preferably of carved wood, but sometimes of composition, from which the gilding or a great part of it has been removed with caustic, and which, as a result, are of an unassuming neutral color and texture flattering to the vividly colored works they enclose. Today, some artists use old frames similarly treated, or refinished to their taste, design their own frames, or even entirely omit frames. The frame has, however, a functional purpose in protecting the painting in handling and providing a convenient and solid material by which it may be attached to the wall. A few designers have made frames of modern materials used in modern ways for a decorative purpose, but generally speaking, the functional aspect of the frame prevails and even commercial framers offer honest milled moldings of varied and fairly simple profile for the public choice. Contemporary paintings, which are often painted as much for exhibition in galleries as with their possible eventual place in a home in mind, have special need of frames for protection in shipping, handling and hanging. From this point of view, simple frames, harmonious, but not too distracting or insistent in color or tone, without composition protuberances likely to be knocked off, and placing the principal emphasis on the work enclosed, are the most satisfactory. Such simple frames perform their functional purpose, and, at the same time, their aesthetic duty of isolating the painting from its background, of setting it off from competing and disturbing details, and of directing attention discretely to it.   —G.L.M.M.

frame of reference See AESTHETICS, RECENT TRENDS IN (1).

frames. A technical term referring to the Brussel loom—the number of worsted pile threads which pass through each dent of the reed.

framework chair. See FURNITURE.

francaise. A French dance in triple time.

freehand drawing. See drawing.

freehand perspective See PERSPECTIVE.

free-standing. Term used to characterize a carved figure or column which is not attached to or part of a background or wall.

free-stone. Stone which may be easily cut or shaped into blocks and worked with a chisel; so called from having no grain; it may therefore be cut in any direction.

free verse (vogue in U.S.). Poetry without a fixed metrical accent was introduced into the U.S. by McPherson's Ossian, whose Celtic cadences were imitated extensively after 1783. Whitman's poetry gave impetus to the movement for unshackling verse from traditional metrical patterns. Thoreau, Margaret Fuller, Emily Dickinson, Stephen Crane, and others deviated from classical formulae but it was not until the new poetry movement of 1912 that organized resistance to tradition succeeded in enfranchizing non-metrical verse. Ezra Pound and Amy Lowell, the proponents of imagism (q.v.), as well as the magazine *Poetry*, defended the new form. Much experimentation in the following thirty years led to a discovery of undreamed richness in the musical use of language. No poet remained unaffected by free verse, although a tendency appeared by 1940 to return to formal patterns and to achieve these new effects within prescribed limits. See L. Untermeyer, *Modern American Poetry*, 6th ed., 1941; Amy Lowell, *Tendencies in Modern Am. Poetry*, 1917.   —H.R.W.

freeway. See CIVIC PLANNING.

FRENCH ART. There was no single center of art in France during the Hundred Years War (1339-1453) and consequently no school that inclusively represents the French temperament in art. In the early 15th cent. Charles VI (1380-1422) was banished from Paris to that part of France that is bounded by Touraine and Champagne. Moulins, Tours and Orléans all played their parts in art production but it was at Bourges that Charles VI and Charles VII (1422-1461) patronized those artists that went to make up the **school of the Loire,** or as it is sometimes called **Touraine.**

The Burgundians, who had allied themselves to the English, were the sovereigns of both Flanders and Burgundy and at Dijon encouraged the art genius principally of Flanders and Holland. In the south (Provence and Languedoc) the Popes, during the "Babylonian Captivity" at Avignon, in need of religious decorations, were naturally more predisposed to the Italian temperament and employed many Italian artists preponderantly of the Siennese school. Although the captivity ended in 1377 Avignon and Aix continued their tradition as great centers of art. It was only toward the end of the reign of Louis XI (1461-1483) that France was once more united and French art began to harmonize its scattered influences. The Franco-Flemish school gave to French art its precision, force and dynamism, its preoccupation with realism, its color and its sense of linear form. From Avignon and Aix the spirit of Italian classicism manifested itself in the close-knit composition of Giotto and the three-dimensional qualities of Massacio. The generalized idealism of humanism unloosed in French art the tension of Flemish angularities and heavily detailed masses. The regal court of central France south of the Loire, deprived of imported foreign artists for so long a time, retained the Gothic feeling of 'infinity' and an inchoate naturalism that finally became one of the leading elements in the international style of all Europe. In Provence (Avignon) Froment of Avignon, Jean Perréal and even Jean Fouguet (1415-1485) emulate certain Italian qualities: Froment, a linear delicacy, Perréal, a bi-symmetrical decorative element, and Fouquet a close-knit order not to be found in former miniature painting. But these three men, over and beyond their northern and southern influences, began to express the French spirit of elegance, taste and particularly that balance of northern, formal precision and southern formal idealism. While the Franco-Flemish art of the north was producing masterpieces by the Van Eycks, Van der Weyden, Bouts, Memling and Massys, Jerome Bosch, Van der Goes and a number of anonymous workers, and while Avignon and Ville Neuve had epitomized their great work in the justly celebrated Avignon Pietà, the school of Touraine was still laboring under the handicap of isolation from the dynamic art trends about it.

Image makers **(Imagiers)** were turning out sacred statues in ivory, stone and wood, and the book illuminators inspired by Pol de Limbourg and his followers were still working, to some extent, in the spirit of Medievalism. Following the abortive Italian ventures of Charles VIII, Louis XII and Francis I, Italian art became the ideal of the French ruling class, and under Francis I a number of Italian artists were invited to France, among whom were da Vinci, del Sarto and Cellini. Later (ca. 1530) Rosso the Florentine and Primaticcio were engaged to make the decorations of the King's palaces. Their French admirers founded the **school of Fontainebleau,** which is generally regarded as Italianate, but it was in this school that French genius finally asserted itself.

Italian elements can be distilled from most of these anonymous painters, but these elements are no more than tools with which the French temperament carves its own likeness.

In the 16th cent. the sculptor Michel Colombe (d. 1512) was still unemancipated from Gothic conceptions; Germain Pilon and Barthelèmy Prieur, chose Italian guise and Jean Goujon, one of the glories of all French sculpture, used certain Italian details and even the Michel angelesque "hole and bump" postures, although very French in flavor and conception.

Throughout the French progressus there is apparent a facile solving of the most weighty problems presented to the painter or sculptor. The French artist, seems never to labor over his work; there is a smiling and almost off-hand acceptance of life. With the Flemish or Italian artist life as expressed in their art is a serious business; in the north we find problems that become burdens and one feels that he is imprisoned by the mere handling of his brush. In the south, idealism of form, never obscures the pathos, the histrionic drama, the struggle, maternity and martyrdom he depicts, and even in classical legend there is serious concentration on the figures of the myth that his color and composition mastery only served to intensify.

The final establishment and unification of French traits in art of the 16th cent. prefigured the strong French state of Louis XIII (1610-1643). In spite of the fact that French taste in the first part of the 17th cent. was for Italian eclecticism even the French artists who lived and worked in Italy could not divest themselves of their racial traits. Jean Cousin, called by some the founder of the French school and by others a degraded imitator of Italian decadence, was in his lesser sphere as French as Poussin or Claude. Jacques Callot (1593-1635) a caricaturist and depictor of beggars and soldiers inaugurated a type of art in France that was the foundation on which Daumier, Guys, Gavarni and even Toulouse de Lautrec and Foraine built. The brothers Le Nain, using the contrasted and heavy light-and-shade method of Caravaggio, (the artist of the Counter-Reformation) depicted the genre subjects of the downtrodden peasant and the earth's humble. These artists mark the first ripple of the French revolution still a century and a half in the future and are the prophets, sired by the religious wars of Henry III and the waning power of the nobility, of the coming ascendancy of the Commune. In 1648 this tendency was thwarted by another authoritarian movement. Mazarin and Colbert founded the French Academy, an institution based on the intellectual concepts extractable from the Italian painting of the High Renaissance. Needless to say, the effort at making geniuses by means of laws was abortive, and although under Louis XIV there are a plethora of well-known names, there are few indeed that add substantially to the glories of French art.

Le Brun became professor in the Academy in 1648 and its director in 1683. A veritable czar of aesthetics, he based all instruction on the suggestions of his friend Poussin, after having submitted them to a sort of Cartesian tribunal. The geometrical and mechanist approach was the desiderata of this strongly intellectual and purposeful professor, and the belief is held that he suborned all the talents of his time. As a matter of fact, such an authority was sorely needed by the artists, who, in being liberated in too quick succession from mediaevalism, the authority of the Church, the guild system, feudalism and Italian art would have lost themselves in the by-ways of idiosyncrasy before their wings were strong enough really to fly. As a foundation for art creation the Richelieu-Mazarin-Colbert-Le Brun Academy was worthless but from the bureaucratic standpoint of raising insignificant men to the level of craft capability and setting a technical goal as an ideal, it was salutory. The fact that it had no place for originality or genius only proves that all institutionalism must be considered as a breeding place of mediocrity; genius pays it no subservient respect, it simply ignores its existence.

In Le Brun's own work we see a strong man of exceptionally expressive talent, working in the service of his monarch, using a style wherein exact proportions and voluntary arrangement form a minutely measured-out appearance. His drawing was meticulously sincere in what he erroneously imagined was the Grand Style of the Italians, and his composition was a feeble approach (insensitively based on the mistakes of Poussin) to the Italian High Renaissance conception. His contemporary and follower was Le Sueur, a more Italianized imitator and a lesser man intellectually, though just as artistic a one. Hyacinthe Rigaud added a factitious pomposity in his portraits and shows all the numerous faults that can accrue when inferior artists take themselves and their ideas too seriously. With Largillierè we have a tendency toward a greater freedom in drawing and while still enslaved to the superficies of monarchial taste, he nevertheless has a grace and a litheness that marks him of the French tradition of Greuze, Watteau, Ingres and Renoir. The two great painters of the day are Poussin (1594-1665) and Claude Lorrain (1600-1682). Poussin was a highly cultured man who spent the greater part of his life in Italy for the purpose of study and inspiration. He never quite sounded the depths of Italian art in spite of the recipe books of the Italian guilds, the *Poetics* of Aristotle or of Bacon's *Essays on Learning*. His composition is elementary, generally little more than balance; his color is unattractive but his drawing is highly correct and even sensitive. The landscapes in which he places his figures, have, relatively speaking, an organic relationship to these figures and while the emulation of Le Brun's work is the usual achievement of the best French academicians, the art of Poussin is their unattained ideal. Lorrain is a painter through his wonder at and love of light. Landscape is his forte, and even today his pictures, while less actual than those of the impressionists seem more lastingly luminous. Such a treatment of nature as a theatre in which all the rôles are played by light, link Lorrain to such masters as Rembrandt, Watteau, Turner, Monet, Vermeer and Cuyp.

In the sculpture of the 17th cent. we find, besides a vast number of magnificent portraits, several men of genius. Perhaps Puget and Girardon are its greatest examplars. Pierre Puget was passionately enslaved by the tortured soul of Michael Angelo and sought to express in large masses, that movement and tension that the Florentine master employed to exteriorize and formulate his inner psychic struggle. There is force here and the drama of the lonely man who shuns the too easy answering of life's questions and yet at the same time the facility and the verve that brand him French. Girardon both as a portraitist and the sculptor of the bas-reliefs of Versailles shows his mastery of form, grace, and material. His handling of the nude foreshadows both Ingres and Renoir in its drawing and is as French as Mignard and Fragonard.

Coysevox and his pupils the Coustous, are more naturalistic in a diluted classical and decorative sense, but energetically worked to found the academic ideal. This ideal looked upon Bernini as a great man and its pre-occupation with the baroque was leading it to the *cul de sac* of insignificant clock ornamentation so prevalent in the French salons of the 20th cent.

In spite of monarchial authoritarianism, Colbert and the French academy, the 18th cent. was Jansenist and masculine. The first great artist of this revolutionary era was Antoine Watteau (d. 1721) who turned to Rubens for his inspiration and tools. One might say his art was the French visage reflected in a baroque Flemish mirror. On him devolved the pleasure of depicting the lighter moments of the court circles, in glowing colors, flowing lines of movement and bathed in an all-encompassing light only equalled by Lorrain. This subject matter was an escape from the vacillating political economy of Louis XV and a summation of ideal condition in contrast to the poverty and oppression of the French people. Watteau all unconsciously, with Boucher and Fragonard, Lancret and Peter was a propagandist for the Revolution. Here was too much pleasure and beauty that belonged to one class while all others were engaged in a life and death struggle both at home and on the battle front. Voltaire, Montesquieu, Rousseau and D'Alembert opposed everything for which the Court stood while Watteau distilled, through sheer delight, all the Elysian happiness that he felt could be man's inheritance. His philosophy was as limited as that of the Trouvères of an earlier day or of his opposing contemporaries, but his art is a magnificent expression of the stable qualities, fundamentally unaltered by transient upheavals, of the French temperament. Here began the modern expression of a romanticism whose earlier expression in the school of Fontainebleau took the classical myth as its theme.

J. B. Chardin, the other great artist of the 18th cent., also looked north for inspiration. His point of view was diametrically opposed to that of Watteau. Interested in genre like the Dutch he painted the homely things of the middle class domicile; single figures, interiors and particularly still-lives. A realist, so-called, he was an artist dedicated to formal values which included chiaroscuro, texture and the minute study of light effects. From this standpoint and on this limited ground he was as expert as Rembrandt. It is unfortunate that the late 19th cent. student, instructed by the official schools, should so miserably have misunderstood Chardin's work as to have made of him an authority for the *trompe l'oeil*.

Rousseau's influence on Diderot made him inveigh against the voluptous implications of Watteau and threw him into a trap of moral issues where he found Jean-Baptiste Greuze. This artist was the great 'story-teller' par excellence, a calculating and opportunistic soul whose mask was a didactic uprightness and sympathy with the people, but whose real message was a weakening sensualism far beyond that of a frankly licentious Boucher. Greuze banalized Chardin in much the same way that the 'jazz style' decoratively popularized cubism, but unlike the interior decorators of our day Greuze, as a painter, is by no means insignificant. It took a world shattering revolution to divorce him from the mawkish esteem of the public.

Thus during the 18th cent. there appeared four tendencies in the art of France. Watteau represents the nostalgia of idealism with textural, atmospheric and voluptuous beauty as its supports. Chardin is the formalist, the actualist, whose significance in the new outlook resides in his ability to make art of the materials that have no specific claim to beauty per se. The third approach is by way of playing to the bourgeoisie and the proletariat. Its methods are unimportant, its subject matter is everything. It has a literary basis that elevates itself sporadically in the progressus of all the arts, not only in France but universally. The fourth tendency is that represented by Jacques Louis David. His was a revolt against the other three; an art concocted for the soldier of Napoleon as well as for the fanatics of the Reign of Terror. A cold and aloof draughtsmanship, (it is difficult to conceive of his work as painting) he had a correctness unequalled even by Le Brun. He was dessicated by political theory and the too-long observations of Greco-Roman sculptural copies. He stems from the archeological enthusiasm of Winckelmann rather than from the vivid and viable paintings of the Renaissance and his work became the final rallying point for the now dominantly vocal distrust of the revolutionaries for all that had gone before them.

Sculpture of the early 18th cent. retained the correctness and dignity of Louis XIV and followed the traditional convention of the Coustous. Le Moyne and Falconet are representative of this serious academic effort, but two other artists arose to eclipse them. Pigalle was a vigorous artist with a great understanding of the antique which he applied to portraiture in a striking and epic manner; Houdon, better known in this country, was less classicist than realist. His handling of the human form is sure and penetrating and yet he instills a grace and order that could only come from sounding the depths of Hellenistic principles. Clodion (1738-1814) or Claude Michel was the boudoir sculptor par excellence. Using terra cotta for greater freedom in modeling he produced a multiplicity of statuettes which, while bordering on the licentious, are replete with excellent observation of realistic form. One might say he translated Boucher into formal naturalism and not be far from exact.

David became a political figure; was selected by the Revolutionary Assembly as the official painter of the Commune, was later popularized by his Napoleonic illustrations and after the return of the monarchy was exiled. Raphael Mengs in Rome and Vien in France were instrumental in David's development but to him is usually given the credit as the founder of the **Neo-Classical school.**

Jean Auguste Dominique Ingres after eighteen years returned to France from Italy in 1824 and became associated with the Neo-Classicists. One may be sure that his leadership of this school was more in the way of a protest against Delacroix than a feeling of relationship with the spirit of David. Both he and David were inept at compositions in which more than one figure was painted; both painted magnificent portraits. But it is to Ingres that we must turn when great draughtsmanship is in question. No matter how flat and thinly decorative might be his actual painter's technique, his drawing sets him in the forefront of the greatest portraitists of occidental art. His line is tenuous, melodic and very sure and it is to the study of Ingres' drawings that we owe the draughtsmanship of such men as Degas, Renoir, Matisse and other lesser artists. He synthesizes his models by the abrogation of every nugatory protuberance and arrives at the essential form with never-failing and sensitive acumen. While using the material means of neo-classicism, Ingres was at heart a romantic, and it was perhaps, the consciousness of this, to him, shameful tendency, that made him so intolerant of his more straightforward contemporaries. Among these Girodet had most of Ingres' faults and few of his undoubted virtues. He, too, was a romantic in spirit inspired by literary imitations of antiquity. But it was the work of Baron Gros that inaugurated romanticism, one of whose dicta was the depiction of the topical. Prud'hon, a student of Correggio, extended Gros' technical means into the realms of closely-observed, logical chiaroscuro, which at times used a rich color ensemble for its effect. His subject matter, however, never escaped the classical.

Gericault takes up the subject matter of Gros and uses the three-dimensional lighting of Prud'hon and it is in his great picture *The Raft of the Medusa* that romanticism shows itself in full swing. The leader of the romantic school is undoubtedly Eugène Delacroix. Having studied the Venetians, Rubens and Gericault (from all of whom he absorbed qualities relative to his genius), he began to paint subjects that mark the high moments of many literatures. Byron, Shakespeare, Dante and the Bible, the Greek revolt against the Turks and the French Revolution,—all furnished him material for his brush. He made a study of color-spectra, observed the broken tints of Constable and Turner in England, and formulated theories that were instrumental in the later impressionistic experimentation. His drawing is much looser than that of any of his immediate forerunners and his painted figures have a plastic value that at times equalled those of Tintoretto.

Romanticism as a movement in French art is closely associated in art histories with technical methods. It has little meaning if restricted to subject matter, for most painters, today and yesterday, have been romantics by temperament. When David painted the *Oath of the Horatii*, the very gestures are romantic, and where the coldness of the conception and the theatricality of the background give one the feeling of rigid intellectualism, the picture's effect on the revolutionaries of the day

was to intensify their political hysteria. The painting of classical myths can be conceived only as romantic creations and even the archeological researches of Winckelmann as of Schliemann of a later day are the result of impelling and purposive fantasy. In the 19th cent. romanticism was synonymous with the desire for, and the feeling of freedom from any authoritarian group and it manifested itself as the emotionalism, realism, natural science, experimentation in the realms of fantasy and philosophy and finally the 'back to nature' impulse. Man was freed from Church, priest, noble, king, state and now from God. The artist successively in service to all these 'authorities'; having accepted their dicta as final and having found them a stultification to his spirit, now believed that if truths were to be known he must search them out pragmatically and personally. Empiricism was abandoned, the Industrial Revolution extended trade and the atheistic and democratic mask of science gave him a new and infinitely diversified public, a myriad new arts for his contemplation and use and a legal right to say his thoughts. Needless to say he indulged his preferences. He was exotic, socialistic, communistic, monarchial, democratic, anarchistic, maudlin, fantastic, literary. He was all that man has ever been, only now it could be expressed with impunity and romanticism was the cloak that covered all his dreams.

Man has long contemplated the face of nature and for at least 3500 years has painted it. Lorrain distilled as much mood and Watteau as much shade and light from landscape as did the painters of the Barbizon woods, but with these later nature-lovers landscape was treated realistically. The prearranged trees and hills of Poussin and the backgrounds of the painters of the High Renaissance gave place to the actualities of the French countryside. Diaz (1808-1876), Rousseau (1812-1867) and esp. Corot (1796-1875) are the great men of the group. While Rousseau was more of a formalist and actualist than were Diaz and the Corot of popular knowledge, Corot, in his Italian sojourn produced some of the most solid figure pieces and city-scapes of the entire French development. He was the forerunner in attitude of Monet and the Impressionists and his handling of streets and houses had a profound effect on the style of Cézanne. In his complete career we are witnesses to the 'back to nature', topical actuality, classicism and the 'mood painting' ideals of the day. With Courbet (1819-1877) who proclaimed himself realist, we see that side of romanticism that demands models, present day subject matter, the close attention to realistic lighting and a mind closely akin to that of the sociological Le Nains. He abhorred all mention of classical myths and even picture subjects in the literary sense and with unerring intuition based his effects on the technical approaches, of the Spanish and Dutch. Also sociological and at times more romantic than Courbet, was Honoré Daumier (1808-1875) an artist who began his career as a political cartoonist. By a great economy of means he achieved such solidity of volume that even today the French say he had "Michelangelo in his skin." A succinct and pitiless critic of the foibles, abuses and pretenses of his day, his very ardor of hate transliterated itself into a spark of intense life in his pictures. He opposes strong lights to strong shadows in the manner of Caravaggio and at times like Prud'hon or Millet but his drawing is rapid, nervous, loose and essentializes everything it delineates in a synthesis that may be due to an admiration for Ingres. He is the transition from Goya to Forain.

Impressionism was a close study of light and the effects of light in its rôle of presenting visually colored form to the eye. Sanctioned by the realism of the Barbizon painters the Impressionists worked on the theory that whatever is (in Nature's light effects) is right and throwing aside all ulterior motives of classicism, romanticism, literature and subject, they painted nature as they found it. To do so they were necessitated to start afresh with a new palette and a new approach. Turner and Constable had changed the color habits of Delacroix and these three men now were the guiding technical spirits of the new school. Finding that there are no large uniform color planes in nature (Ruskin had noted this fact) they broke their color into small variegated touches and thus achieved the scintillating and ephemeral effects of shifting light. They discovered that sunlight was yellow and that its complementary, shadow, was violet; that local color existed only in half tones and that the complementary of the light portion of the painted object invariably appeared, in some degree, in its shadow. Monet was the great technician of the movement, and Pissarro its high priest. There is not a technical nor formal development in art since their day that is not directly or indirectly affected by their works. In spite of its realism, Impressionism is probably the most romantic of all 19th and 20th cent. painting, for in it there is no room for political theory or prac-

tical intellectualization. For sheer nature-beauty and the portrait of every mood-provoking atmosphere of the outdoors, Impressionism can never be surpassed. It adds life and meaning to the colored photograph and naturalism to the Japanese print. It is the culmination of all the artists's researches into optical realism and brings topical pictorialism to a conclusive impasse. The greatest artist of this movement was Auguste Renoir (1841-1919) who in his middle and last period utilized the impressionistic means to the end of form and order.

Neo-Impressionism, founded by Georges Seurat (1859-1891) and Paul Signac was a rationalistic summation of the Impressionists quasi-intutive methods. These men strove to make an academic formula, a psychological pragmatism of all the observations that had preceded them and attempted to express these theories by an intellectualized ordination of separated color spots built on the writings of Chevreul, Helmholtz, Rude, Le Blanc and Delacroix. Seurat's art fortunately went beyond his verbal dicta and in his greatest work we find magnificent pattern, drawing based on the synthesis of Ingres, combined with an almost Persian handling of interstice.

It must be borne in mind that impressionism marked the beginning of the use of color in the modern sense and that in destroying the academic barriers of traditional chiaroscuro opened the door to all the uninhibited essays that followed them. Technically speaking, color became the first consideration of Gauguin, van Gogh, Matisse, Cézanne, Bonnard, Vuillard and a host of lesser painters.

Paul Gauguin (1848-1903) called for the abrogation of both the model and of tradition in his followers of the school of Pont Aven and Pouldu in Brittany. He was probably the most radical adherent of the 'back to nature' impetus, even exiling himself to the South Seas to make a stricter contact with the primitive. His work is the first great color decoration of modern times, flatly conceived but savantly varied as to lights and darks. His theories concerned themselves mostly with color and the necessity for its brilliance. He utilized as much contrast as is possible and applied it to a drawing that sometimes is naïve sometimes inept. He never worked over a first impression in his drawing thus saving, as he contended, the spontaneous freshness of vision. A decorator par excellence, he represents the highly romantic element of a romantic period of adventurous individuality.

Vincent van Gogh (1853-1890), although a Dutchman, is usually considered as belonging to the French progressus. He was a participant in the more or less chaotic élan of the Neo-Impressionists but changed their spots of color into long streaks of color. A victim of paresis and of the reformer's frenzy, his works gained in hysterical intensifications by his malady which eventually ended in suicidal mania. There is perhaps, no example in history of work brought to so febrile a focus, and this, for an age of lightning changes, theatricality, rapid and chaotic evaluations, combined with the tragic story of his life has posthumously made for him a repute that time will probably revise.

While Renoir was inspired by Rubens and the classical Italians in his mature life, Paul Cézanne (1839-1906) was a great admirer of Delacroix. He saw the impasse into which Impressionism was leading and realized the necessity for formal composition, the basis of art, to which Monet and his school paid scant attention. Profiting by the color theories of his day he employed them in the production of ordered three-dimensional objective extensions. To achieve this he disciplined himself to view nature as though he were a chromophotographic plate or a mirror, erasing from his receptivity all the significance of objects as such and viewing his field of observation as a series of contiguous and related colors. By this combination of knowledge and pure objectification he approached closely to Morey's Gothic 'infinitude' and the architectonic stability of the Romanesque church. He belonged to no school as such, but he has created at least three, besides having influenced the work of every serious student of modern art since 1906. His letters became text-books for artists before World War I and his approach to art, both the traditional and revolutionary sides carried incalculable weight in the works of the younger artists of the time. Criticism also, was renovated by his findings and aesthetics became the theme of all writings on art since 1914. Form and order were once more viewed as significant necessities, and technical means supplanted, in these writings, the consideration of literary or psychological theories.

In 19th cent. sculpture we see the same romantic individualism that is present in painting with the same type of left-overs, the classicists and the 18th cent, schools of academic and royal absolutism. Francois Rude (1784-1855) was perhaps the first dramatic sculptor of the 19th cent. and incorporates some traditionally symbolic elements in his romanticism. Puget, Houdon and the Roman arches play a part in Rude's work, but he has added an emotionalism that vitalizes the often academically insensitive forms. The tradition inaugurated by the unconsciously eclectic Rude was carried on by Carpeaux (1827-1875). Barye (1796-1875) was the Courbet and the Michelangelo of animal sculpture, and his works of realistic animal portraiture, every one so characteristic of the fundamental traits of his model, have not been surpassed.

In Rodin we discern a sculptor of varied and noble attainments, at times a poet, a psychologist, but invariably traditional. Jacopo della Quercia, Donatello, Michael Angelo, Ghibertti, Goujon, Girardon, Rude and Carpeaux, have all donated poses and forms to his mercurial talent. He has even gone to the Hellenistic Greeks, and some of his finest figures have been transliterations of these 3d cent. artists. Rodin represents the most facile and expert type of modeling and if his sense of order never equals the works of the greatest of his inspirations from former times, his emotionalism and fervor often outstrip them.

Specialization in science and industry were adumbrated a century earlier in painting. The 20th cent. gives us in its first fifteen years an extension of this tendency in the partitioning of the elements of the work of Cézanne. First we have Henri Matisse (b. 1869) and his Fauve following. Much of Matisse's art is due to the boredom he felt in making copies of classical art for the French Government. He sought and found a more exotic inspiration in Negro sculpture and, according to him, in Persian miniature. As a matter of fact there was much in his second period of both Lorenzetti and the school of Alexandria. Be this as it may, color was Matisse's forte, color used for its brilliant decorative effects and arranged in simple areas. His formal side was never developed and his drawing, when not academic was loosely nonchalant, charming, generally sensitive but never significant in either the classical or realistic sense. His finished works today are like richly illuminated tapestries, extremely harmonious, often rich in chromatic saturation but usually light and ephemeral in their effect upon us. A Persian miniature of the 16th cent. fleetingly seen, a magnificent bouquet of flowers, the faience mosaic work of an Islamic mosque, these superficially resemble the total effect of a number of

Matisse's works when viewed together. Gauguin gives us the impression of greater solidity and permanence just as he gave Matisse the sanction for his unnaturalistic translations of objectivity. Matisse in turn widened this sanction for the men of his day and we should recognize his work as that side of the French temperament that numbers such artists as Girandon, Boucher, Cousin and Hébert.

Cubism was sired in Paris in 1911 by Pablo Picasso (b. 1877), Braque (b. 1878) and Derain (b. 1876) and was a further sounding of the depths of formal values. Having loved the world, observed the world and enjoyed the world; having developed means to depict absolutely the world, little was left but the world's disintegration into its formal elements. Matisse extracted, as his specialty, the decoratively colored elements of nature and Cubism delved into that part of construction that lies behind the mensurable visual aspect. Picasso, having seen a collection of Negro sculpture in the studio of Matisse, grasped the elementary forms to carry out the suggestion of Cézanne that nature must be reduced to geometrical fundamentals. Color was discarded at first; black, burnt sienna and white giving the thermic and tonal desiderata. Nature in the minds of these artists became wholly subjective and objects as such reduced themselves to partial planes, cubes, spheres and cones. Behind this new experimentation a whole library of pseudo-psychology and pseudo-philosophy sprang up based upon the desire for justification rather than on observation. Its method was verbal logic which often belied the logic of human reaction and like all art movements in which theory plays an official rôle, the art achieved vastly outstripped the literary ultimates. The veritable background for Cubism and succeeding schools was the consciousness of individual freedom, the desire for publicity and a fatigue in the contemplation of hackneyed shapes. The world had grown smaller, universal histories of art had been written by archeological and research aestheticians, the Viennese psycho-analysts had turned public thought to psychology, the Industrial Revolution had regimented mechanically a large part of living, democratic ideals had greatly enhanced man's evaluation of his idiosyncrasies and fo cap these climaxes there was a great surge of talent in Paris that recognized the imperative necessity of feral competition. Beyond all this the cyclic return to stable and permanent forms was at hand and the wholly inadequate composition of im-pressionism had to be corrected again. Cézanne was the bridge that led men from the chaos of modern unrest to the foundations of the great tradition. Over this bridge Cubism passed to assert once more the infinitely subtle mathematics of traditional skeletal structure. This search sums up the first years of Cubism as a student essay to recapture the anatomy of the High Renaissance. Thus, like science, cubism must flay the specimen in its search for the life principle, but that life principle did not reside in qualities, elements or forms, it lay and will always lie in the spirit of the artist who creates better than he thinks.

Two movements toward non-objectivity were the **Orphist** and **Synchromist** schools. Robert Delaunay founded the school of Orphism, later called **Simultaneism**, a lyrical color-expression that at first extended Impressionism into cubistic forms. Instead of acromatic tonalities Delaunay produced a prismatic effect by separately coloring the innumerable geometric planes of enormous pictures. Later in 1912, this prismatic effect largely disappeared while the color, applied in larger planes had greater effect. A year later the planes were interspersed with swirls and eddies of pure color. Synchromism, although founded by two American' painters, Morgan Russell (b. 1886) and S. Macdonald-Wright (b 1890) had its inception in 1913 and is included in the French progressus by the official *L'Amour de l'Art*. The theory underlying Synchromism was that color inherently extends itself into an emotional third dimension and that the Impressionists, in recognizing the two extremes of light and shadow (as yellow and violet) neglected to exploit all the intermediate tones as pure color. Russell's work was a translation of these tonal values into pure color while Macdonald-Wright attacked deep space with undiluted pigment.

During this period of intellectual research and art activity three older men had launched the school of the **Intimistes**. Bonnard (b. 1866), Vuillard (b. 1866) and K. X. Roussel were little moved by the more radical tendencies of their time, but had taken advantage of the impressionist concepts which they handled in individual fashion. The color of Vuillard and Bonnard is that of the richest textiles. It has the color that seems to come of the patina of age, besides representing in its most attractive and exquisite style the topical subject matter of the Latin Quarter and the French countryside. Due to louder voices, the Intimistes were for sometime considered as a slightly varied academic tendency, but are now belatedly being acclaimed for their sane and traditional drawing qualities that in the French spirit always include a modicum of stubborn revolt.

Expressionism, while not known as a French movement, nevertheless saw its first light in France. Vincent van Gogh well epitomizes the ideals of the Expressionists, which are simply those of direct emotional release devoid of the circumlocutions of any traditional traits. Rouault (b. 1871) is today the great artist of the school. His work is done mostly on prepared and toned paper and depicts dancers, clowns, models and numerous heads of Christ. His reputation is that of a profoundly religious painter, and his work is regarded with a sort of mystic veneration. Having been employed in a stain-glass window factory, where he was immersed in the contemplation of medieval, Byzantine and Gothic holy figures and the technique of their depiction in church windows, he uses black as heavy leading is used in the juncture of the glass segments, with the pure ultramarine, red lakes, purple and yellow of such decorations.

During and since World War I there have been no technical movements launched, whereas before 1914 every advance in French art history was a step in some way directed by new methods or in extending man's visual and emotional horizon by revaluations or new uses of old techniques.

Ozenfant's Purism and the German Dadaists (Hobbyists), ineradicably opposed schools, were both ideational as opposed to technical essays. Purism was based on the belief that art is greater than the artist; a sort of archeological architectonic nostalgia that longed for functional art as closely related to its day as classical art was related to classical times. The demand was for "Constants", viz. the depiction of objects of permanent functional value such as the egg and the water-pitcher, intimately part of the life of man and animal for countless generations. Purism was launched in 1918, having been known in its earlier aspect as the Style Mécanique, inaugurated by Marcel Duchamp and Francis Picabia in New York at 291 Fifth Avenue with the backing of Alfred Stieglitz in 1915.

Dadaism was a wholly anarchic idea that demanded the total eclipse of all aesthetic, formal or traditional concepts and the destruction of all social or political convention. The only reason for mentioning either Dadaism or the Style Mécanique (whose single famous practitioner is Fernand Léger) is that both had a vague relationship to Surréalisme. Wilenski divides Surréalisme into two parts: the first includes that branch which existed before World War I and Neo-Surréalisme which he places between the two world wars. The later branch pursued the spirit of wonder and incongruity, of mystery and shocking unrelatedness, of neurosis and the invitation to unreality as expressed by Giorgio de Chirico at its inception. The writers of the manifesto of the post-war movement adopted the name Surréalist, meaning 'beyond the natural', and base their ideals on the Freudian researches into the subconscious. De Chirico had painted Poesque pictures dictated by the lesser neuroses and had juxtaposed articles that ordinarily would appear together only in the dream state. The later men basing their anarchism on that of Dadaism wished to produce by means of a sort of automatism, directed by the subconscious, a complete therapy. To do this they subverted natural shapes and depicted palpable impossibilities. Thus they foresaw the final achievement of man ascendant over his own subliminal self; happier, freer and at last complete. Salvador Dali (b. 1903) is the latest and perhaps the last disciple of Néo-Surréalisme. He is a competent academic draughtsman with little color talent; a painter like Greuze, of anecdotic pictures, and a great showman. His technical means are as minute as Meissonier and his romanticism, unhealthy and tinged with cruelty recalls at times the great Bougereau.

The sculpture of the 20th cent. is as diversified in its personal expression as is its painting. Aristide Maillol comes immediately to mind as the rebel against the baroque and sometimes rococo modeling of the romantic Rodin. Maillol's figures, while superficially inspired by the genuinely classical are, none the less, abstract structures in which volumes are weighed against volumes in the same way in which Cubism balanced its abstractly conceived planes. The fact that Maillol clings closely to synthesized and over-robust human forms often gives one the impression of adipose bodies modeled from the outside. But the very fact that his volumes have this inflated appearance has been a factor in his reputation as a monumentalist.

Constantir Brancusi (b. 1879) reduces objectivity to a strictly personal synthesis always maintaining an elegance of taste, a perfection of craftsmanship and an acute sense of delicate equilibrium. Those artists influenced by his style have made of it a puerile architectural adjunct. The Martels in their Debussy monument in Paris are cases in point.

Antoine Bourdelle is a dynamic modeler of reliefs, an illustrator by temperament and a borrower from the antiquity of Greece, Assyria and Egypt. His work has the character of wood-carving and while much of it is well ordered its greatest claim to popular esteem is its violent movement and rugged drawing.

The sculpture of Matisse, Picasso and Renoir precisely follow their individual conceptions of form as seen in their painting. In Matisse, the dislocations and the amorphism of parts; in Picasso, a series of composed, disintegrated masks; in Renoir, the solid and classical conception of synthetic naturalism. See H. Buchthal, *The Miniatures of the Paris Psalter*, 1938; Charles Diehl, *La peinture Byzantine*, 1933; A. Gardner, *Medieval Sculpture in France*, 1931; E. Male, *L'Art religieux du XIII siècle en France*, 1923 and *L'Art religieux de la fin du Moyen-âge en France*, 1925; G. Graf Vitzthum, *Die Pariser Miniaturmalerei*, 1907; Osvald Siren, *Giotto and some of his Followers*, 1917; Ch. Sterling, *Les Primitifs Français*, 1939; Ch. de Tolnay, *Le Maître de Flémalle et les frères Van Eyck*, 1939; O. Cartelliere, *The Court of Burgundy*, 1926; E. Delacroix, *The Journals of Eugène Delacroix*, ed. and trans. by Walter Pach, 1937; Arthur Hoeber, *The Barbizon Painters*, 1915; W. H. Wright, *Modern Painting*, 1915; Louis Hourticq, *Art in France*, 1917; R. H. Wilenski, *Modern French Painters*, 1939; C. Terrasse, *French Painting in the XXth Century*, 1939; S. Cheney, *Story of Modern Art*, 1941; F. J. Mather, *Western European Painting of the Renaissance*, 1939.   —S.M-W.

French crepe. Flat crepe, originally made in France. Now, light weight flat rayon-crepe suitable for lingerie.

French glass. See GLASS AND GLASS-MAKING.

French horn. See MUSICAL INSTRUMENTS.

French joint. *Book.* A revived style affecting the hinge of the cover. The boards have a sufficient distance between their back edge and the "round" of the back of the book to allow thick material to be well pressed in and to work freely as a hinge.   —H.F.S.

French porcelain. See CERAMICS II.

French ultramarine blue. An important blue pigment was added to the artist's palette when, in 1814, a compound was produced analogous to the ancient ultramarine derived from lapis lazuli. The artificial pigment is the same in chemical composition but is far more intense in its color and much finer in its particle size. It may have a somewhat more purplish tinge than the natural ultramarine but is equally stable, being unaffected by light or by high temperatures or by alkalis. It is, however, readily decomposed in dilute acid. It is relatively inexpensive and, by 1830, was a regular article of trade.   —G.L.S.

fresco. The art of painting on a surface of plaster; also, a picture so painted. See mural painting.

fresco secco. A traditional mural painting method of ancient origin, specifically the process of painting with fresco pigments ground in a glue or casein solution on a finished, set, lime-plaster wall which has been made wet by saturating it with a limewash (lime water or baryta water). The term has also been applied to several variants of this process and has also been used generally, but not accurately to designate any painting which imitates or approximates the effects of true fresco by painting on a dry wall with pigments ground in an aqueous binding medium such as tempera. In various accounts of the true fresco technique the term in *seco* or *a seco* has been used by writers from the 14th cent. down to recent times to denote the use of such paints as finishing touches to a dried fresco painting. This is not a confusion of terms but merely the use of the Italian word in a more literal sense. Fresco secco paintings approximate the visual effects of true fresco rather well, but lack much of its brilliance, clarity, durability and manipulative qualities.   —R.M.

fret (Old Fr. *frettes*, grating). An ornament or decoration characterized by angular interlocked or interlacing lines. See meander motif.

frieze (It. *fregio*, ornament). (1) Any ornamental band or strip in a wall. (2) The middle division of the classic entablature.

frieze of buds. In Greek pottery, a decorative pattern consisting of a row of tall pointed buds of which alternate ones are connected by half circles, at the bottom by one swinging down from the center of the bottom, and at the top by one curving up from each side of the bud below the tip.   —L.T.S.

fringe. Exposed cut ends of warp threads of rugs and carpets. The process of knotting prevents the unravelling of the weft threads.

frit. *Cer.* Semifused compounds used for glaze base. See CERAMICS I.

frize (Fr. *friser*, to curl). Fabric used chiefly for upholstery; the better types are wool, mohair or heavy cotton.

frontality, law of. Primitive artists as a general rule represent their figures in such a manner that the parts are presented in their broadest and most familiar aspect. With sculpture in the round the most characteristic and familiar attitude selected by the sculptor has been the directly frontal one. The law of frontality dictates that the postures be such that a vertical plane through the nose and the navel will divide the statue symmetrically, except in the disposition of the arms and legs. In standing figures the left foot is often advanced and in seated figures the arms are not always similarly placed. This formula persisted in archaic Greek sculpture through most of the 6th cent. B.C. Egyptian sculpture was largely religious in character and the natural conservatism: caused these conventions to be retained long after the lack of technical skill imposed them upon the artist.   —O.M.S.

frontispiece. In its current meaning frontispiece designates an illustration facing the title page of a printed book. However, the frontispiece is older than the title page and is found in illuminated manuscripts previous to printing. In the form of author's portrait it dates back even to the book rolls of ancient Rome. At the beginning of mediaeval manuscripts or of important text divisions one frequently sees portraits of the four evangelists with their symbols, of the Church fathers, or of the founders of monastic orders. The secular element appears with the beginning of the Renaissance. Emperor or king, members of their families or court, other worldly potentates, burgomasters and magistrates are depicted as patrons of the book on its frontispiece. The scholar appears, alone as author, or with colleagues in disputation, or as teacher with students. The *magister cum discipulis* is particularly popular in early woodcut frontispieces. Title pages appeared a generation after the beginning of printing. They were either merged with the frontispiece into elaborately decorated and illustrated title pages, or printed on a separate page. In the 16th cent. the frontispiece retained its position opposite the beginning of the text and on the back of the title page. The 17th cent. saw experiments with elaborate new arrangements, sometimes involving a two-page frontispiece in addition to the title page. The current form emerged in the course of the 18th cent. The woodcut was replaced after the middle of the 16th cent. by copper engraving. Emblematic, symbolical and architectural frontispieces became fashionable, the latter particularly in England. Mezzotint etching, steel engraving, lithography, photography and various color printing methods were successively employed through the 18th, 19th and 20th cents.

In architecture frontispiece designates the decorated front of a building, particularly entrance or portal, and the pediment over a door. See "In search of the Frontispiece", Hellmut Lehmann-Haupt, *The Bulletin of the Garden Club of America,* May, 1940.
          —H.L-H.

front matter. *Book.* The same as preliminary matter. When these were printed apart from the body of the book it was a separate section.

frottage (Fr. *frottage,* a rubbing, the act of rubbing). A technique employed by some Surrealists, notably Max Ernst, which results in the transference of the superficial topography of an object or surface — like weathered wood or stone, sacking material, leaves, an unravelled spool of thread — to another surface. A piece of paper, for example, placed on a rough or irregular surface, is rubbed with pencil, paint, etc., and an approximate image of the peaks and valleys results; this image also is called a frottage.

The irregular and unpredictable patterns are sometimes found to be highly stimulating in their suggestiveness, as Leonardo found the markings on old walls to be. (". . . I was surprised by the sudden intensification of my visionary faculties and by the hallucinative quality of the contradictory images superimposing themselves on one another, with the persistence and rapidity of amorous souvenirs . . . the design thus obtained loses more and more the character of the interrogated material, and takes the aspect of second images, capable of unveiling the first reason of the obsession or to produce a symbol of this reason. This new image forms itself passing by a series of suggestions and transmutations which offer themselves spontaneously in the manner of the hypnagogical visions. Therefore the process of frottage rests only on the intensification of the irritability of the mental faculties by special technical means

It excludes all conscious mental conduct, reason, taste, morale." M. Ernst). Nevertheless, the producer of the frottage often "assists" the original impression made on the paper.

For further description of the motivations behind frottage, see collage, objects, and the bibliographies given there.   —M.S.F.

fu (Ch.). A sacrificial bronze vessel. Quadrangular, four low feet; troughlike for holding sacrificial food. The cover nearly identical with dish so that it can be used as a second receptacle. See SYMBOLISM IN FAR EASTERN ART.   —J.A.M.

fuchi (Jap.). An ornamental metal collar on the Japanese sword at the lower end of the handle, against which the swordguard makes contact.

fude (Jap.). Painting and writing brush.

fugue. Polyphonic composition, usually in the tonal idiom, based on the principle that a melodic phrase, or motif, (**subject**) presented by one part is imitated in the dominant region of the principal key by the second part (**answer**); if there are more than two parts they alternate in presenting subject and answer by their consecutive entrances. A fugue usually has several sections of the structure indicated above, called **expositions** which are connected by **episodes,** or **interludes,** developed from motivic material related to the subject. **Stretto** is an exposition in which imitations of the subject occur in time intervals shorter than the subject. **Double, triple** (etc.) **fugue.** Fugue with two, three, or more subjects which may appear simultaneously by virtue of their being written in double, triple (etc.) counterpoint.   —E.K.

Fujiwara art. See JAPANESE ART.

fukusa (Jap.). A nearly square, double piece of heavy silk on which the tea-bowl is ceremoniously passed during *cha-no-yu* (q.v.). See TAPESTRY.

full anthem. See anthem.

full-bound. *Book.* Generally used for leather bindings when the term denotes that the book is entirely covered with leather in one piece; more often used "full leather" or "full cloth," etc.

functional. See utilitarian.

functional architecture. This type of architecture is characterized by the tendency of expressing and showing through the shape of a building its function, its construction and its material as clearly as possible. That refers not only to the layout, to the façade, and to each individual part of a building, but also to the specific character of the used materials and techniques of construction. Although this tendency is esp. stressed in modern architecture, it is as a whole not an entirely new phenomenon.

Roman architecture with its aqueducts, theatres and public baths, medieval architecture with its fortresses and castles, the bridges of the Renaissance, and even the layout of classicistic Protestant churches, to mention only a few examples, prove that the idea of functionalism in architecture recurred again and again.

Actually each revival of ancient forms, from the early Renaissance to the classicism of the end of the 18th cent. did refer not only to the alleged "eternal beauty" of antique forms, but to their intrinsic "truth", too. The pioneers of the respective revivals always emphasized that the ancient forms expressed most clearly the struggle between weight and support, showed the most simple forms of elevation, and were in any way the most natural. Even if our conception of Greek architecture does not agree with these statements, the mere fact of mentioning these reasons as positive advantages proves that the inner tendencies of these periods approved functionalism in architecture.

Modern functionalism represented first a revolt against the use and the misuse of the borrowed forms of earlier periods by the eclectic architecture of the 19th cent. The paradox of a modern theatre in the form of ancient Greek temples, of railway stations which looked like Roman baths, etc., was felt and conquered. The real practical purpose of a building should become visible. Real architectural beauty could not originate if this first supposition of building was not fulfilled. Equally stucco should not appear as marble, sheet metal as bric-shingle, etc. A modern construction in steel should not be dressed as if built in stone, the materials themselves should become visible as such.

Thus the elements of building, material, construction, organization of the layout became more and more essential. As a reaction against the make-believe imitation and the borrowed splendor of earlier styles, those above mentioned factors were recognized as the essence of building. By emphasizing *only* these newly rediscovered factors, however, the architect voluntarily renounced—at least theoretically—the creative power of his spatial imagination. The engineering part, everything that could be calculated and computed, took the lead over the intrinsic imaginative shaping power.

Thus it was only natural that industrial architecture was the first realm in which the best works of new architecture were created.

In the U.S.A. the first pioneers were the members of the so-called **Chicago school** who based their buildings upon steel skeleton constructions, excelling among them Louis Sullivan (1856-1924). In some respects Frank Lloyd Wright (b. 1869) worked in the same way. In France it was Tony Garnier (b. 1869) and Auguste G. Perret (b. 1874); in the Netherlands, H. P. Berlage (1856-1934); in Germany, Peter Behrens (b. 1868); in Austria, Josef Hoffman (b. 1870) and Adolf Loos (1870-1933); in Finland, Eliel Saarinen (b. 1873). The whole movement gained impetus after the World War I. In Europe the leading architects of the new generation were in France: Le Corbusier (b. 1887), André Lurcat (b. 1894), Robert Mallet Stevens (b. 1886); in the Netherlands, J. J. P. Oud (b. 1890), Van der Vlugt (b. 1882), Wilhelm M. Dudok (b. 1884); in Germany, Walter Gropius (b. 1883) and his **Bauhaus Kreis**, Mies van der Rohe (b. 1886); in Scandinavia, **Alvar Aalto** (b. 1898). In England, an independent modern movement did not develop.

In the U.S.A., Frank Lloyd Wright continued working; besides him Albert Kahn 1869-1943), G. Howe, and William Lescaze (b. 1896), Richard J. Neutra (b. 1892), Raymond M. Hood (1881-1934) and many others. Fortunately these artists who theoretically relied entirely on the expression of function and material, were, nevertheless, creative artists in the original meaning of the word in so far as they went far beyond mere engineering construction.

Since the 1930's, the U.S.A. developed a new style which although entirely functional was saved from the exaggerated dogmatism and coolness which characterized creations of the pioneering period in the various countries abroad.

Although the time of overemphasis of mere functionalism is over, we have to be grateful to this period for clearing the field by abolishing entirely the imitative historical eclecticism of the 19th cent. See international architecture; streamlined; also Geoffrey Scott, *The*

Architecture of Humanism, 1924; Lewis Mumford, *Sticks and Stones,* 1924 and *The Culture of Cities,* 1938; Le Corbusier, *Towards a New Architecture,* 1927, *The City of To-Morrow,* 1929 and *La Ville Radieuse,* 1934; G. H. Edgell, *The American Architecture of Today,* 1928; Sheldon Cheney, *The New World Architecture,* 1930; Francisco Mujica, *History of the Skyscraper,* 1930; R. W. Sexton, *The Logic of Modern Architecture,* 1929; Henry Russell Hitchcock, *Modern Architecture,* 1929; Frank Lloyd Wright, *Modern Architecture,* 1931; Catherine Bauer, *Modern Housing,* 1934; C. G. Holme, *Industrial Architecture,* 1935; N. Pevsner, *The Pioneers of the Modern Movement, from William Morris to Walter Gropius,* 1936; Cahill, Holger, and Barr, A. H., eds., *Art in America in Modern Times* (chapter on Architecture by H. R. Hitchcock), 1934; Alberto Sartoris, *Gli Elementi dell'Architettura Funzionale,* 1937; Oliver Reagan, *American Architecture of the 20th Century,* 1929; Rexford Newcomb, *Outline of the History of Architecture* (Part IV), 1939; Walter Gropius, *The New Architecture and the Bauhaus,* 1935; Talbot Hamlin, *Architecture Through the Ages,* 1940; Sigfried Giedion, *Space, Time and Architecture,* 1941.   —P.Z.

functionalism. See POST-REVOLUTIONARY ARCHITECTURE AND DECORATIVE ARTS IN THE U.S.A.

fundame (Jap.). A lacquer technique. Powdered gold or silver laid on lacquer and polished flush with the lacquer surface; dull finish.

fundamental. See ACOUSTICS; scales and modes.

fungus. Used as a motive in oriental art to symbolize longevity; in China called *lingchih,* in Japan *kinoko.*

furiant. A rapid Bohemian dance of changing accents and rhythms.

FURNITURE. In its limited definition in America, means movable objects of utility, corresponding to the French *meubles* or the German *Möbel.*

Design in furniture is an ever-changing effort to reconcile utilitarian demands with current decorative expressions, technical skills and processes, shifting interest in new or revived materials, economic, social and political moves. The hybridization of basic types as well as the variation of decorative themes stems from this process of reconciling the background and the wishes of the user.

The critical elements of furniture design are function, material and technique.

Function divides categories of furniture by their uses. Furniture as we know it is conceived fundamentally for residential use, and may be divided into forms for (a) *rest or repose*—chairs, benches, stools, settees, sofas, couches, chaise lounges, beds, daybeds, divans, etc.; (b) *work forms*—tables, desks, stands; (c) *storage forms*—chests, cupboards, cabinets, armoires, bureaux, bookcases, wardrobes, boxes, etc.; (d) *decorative forms*—frames (for mirrors and pictures), brackets, consoles.

Materials comprise woods, metals, stone, textiles, glass, compositions or synthetics, ivory and other precious accessory materials.

Technique of furniture harmonizes the skill of designing and the skill of manufacturing. Manufacturing utilizes knowledge of materials, methods, tools and machines. Designing adds to this knowledge an understanding of the emotional factor of furniture, of its capacity to satisfy a human craving, an expression of the quest for something transcending sheer utility. Variably, the artist as designer stresses one factor or another according to his taste, and his client's. His repertoire includes: (a) outline or silhouette, largely dictated by consideration of function, ultimate background, materials available; (b) surface treatment. The latter offers choice of wood or material selected for color, texture, use; and decoration or ornamentation. In this there is a vast library of historical themes and methods of using them. Painting, staining, polychromy; relief, scratch and chip carving; veneering, inlaying, appliques, metal mounts, mouldings, are all means to the expression of decorative motives. Nature supplies animal and plant themes; mythology has amplified these into gargoyles, chimerae, imaginative creations; conventionalization has subdued the realistic forms and geometry has supplied a catalog of its own.

The use of historical or traditional ideas is more persistent in furniture design than in any other of the arts, and the present generation has seen this carried to its farthest extreme. In all the history of furniture no electicism has made such a virtue of itself, nor so enthusiastically resorted to more slavish copying, as it has in the U.S.A., in the first third of the 20th cent. It may well be that the very ease and abundance of life, the height of technical skills, the universality of some knowledge have encouraged this dilettantism, instead of fostering true design as it should be inspired by use, material, technique. This element of capriciousness has appeared before, always in eras of soft living; it may be the debutante stage in the nation's artistic lifetime.

For all practical purposes there is little value in examining the history of furniture preceding the modern world. This does not deny the artistic achievements of earlier civilizations, but it does isolate those achievements from the social-economic aspects of relatively modern times which produced new needs and new solutions in furniture. Egypt had furniture, and so did Greece and Rome, and medieval Europe blossomed in superb woodwork. But we must look to the Renaissance for the beginnings of recognizable forms, because it was in this era that life took on those outward forms, socially, politically, economically, that still form the framework of everyday life.

Egyptian remains testify to an original, highly developed furniture art, both secular and religious. The latter was highly ornate and richly wrought as befits objects dedicated to the gods, but domestic articles were of simple functional design. The evidence of actual remains as well as that pictured in documents — papyrii, wall paintings, burial models, etc.,—reveals a beautifully direct approach to design, with subordinated ornamental features of great beauty. Wood was not common, so it was used with discretion and taste, carved naturalistically in the manner of Egyptian sculpture, and supplemented with veneers and inlays of precious metals, faience, ivory, mother of pearl and painting in conventional and pictorial designs. Animal forms appear as legs and arms of chairs, tables, couches:—lions' paws for feet, duck bills, serpentine heads, etc., for arm rests. Folding chairs and beds were common. Boxes and cases for storage, for dressing and writing materials, sarcophagi of many types and degrees of splendor are among the exhumed tomb relics.

Other Near Eastern furniture arts—Assyrian, Persian, Phoenician, Judean, etc.—appear to have been derived largely from the Egyptian, lacking the vigor and originality of the latter. Our knowledge is conjectural, based on bas-relief decorations.

Greek sources indicate a lively development and understanding of furniture, although our judgment is derived from vase paintings and bas-reliefs, rather than from actual remains. Abstract forms of graceful lines are indicated;

the catalog comprises chairs, beds, and couches, tables and chests. Mediterranean woods—olive, cedar, oak and cypress were enhanced with bronze, gold and silver. Rich fabrics were used for cushions in profusion.

Rome borrowed and adapted freely, and produced finally the Greco-Roman style of which examples are found in the buried cities. The range of materials and decorative details was enlarged from Greek and Egyptian sources, and developed types of chests, armoires, tables, benches, stools, and chairs appeared.

The Middle Ages, until the triumph of the northern Gothic, left few relics of furniture art. Byzantine and Romanesque remains are few, and scarcely indicative of any substantial crafts. Barbaric and debased, they were ecclesiastical in function, ornately architectural in form and ornamentation.

The great centuries of the continental Gothic —13th, 14th, 15th—left a complete furniture art, vigorously original and almost exclusively ecclesiastical. Both its structural system and ornamental vocabulary are completely architectural, scaled-down representations of building forms and details. Since the function of this furniture was an integral detail of the function of the building, this technique of design is admirable and thoroughly sound. It produces a harmony of parts, a consecutiveness possible only in such single-minded compositions. There is, furthermore, no considerable difference between secular and religious types, since the church idiom was dominant in every artistic expression; the social organization demanded little else. The mass of the people had nothing. Nobles and clergy lived a semi-nomadic existence in fortress-like castles, requiring little furniture. Important throne-like seatings show origins in the developed panelling of the room as well as in the stately throne of Romanesque form. Lesser seatings were of folding types. The least were mere planks on legs.

Storage forms began to evolve in earnest in this era, growing out of the portable chest that could be packed upon a mule, up to the stately hutch form, the chest on trestles. The credence, hutch, settee, dressoir, are all offsprings of the coffer. In ornamentation it advanced rapidly from the Romanesque iron bound box to an architectural scale model, featuring arches and tracery of exquisite intricacy, as well as the more abstract linenfold drapery on one hand, or fairly naturalistic relief pictures on the other. However, the real significance of the developed chest form lies in the progress from the structure of rude box construction, mere joined planks, to the ultimate panel-in-a-frame construction. This appeared about 1300 and reflects the structural wisdom of the strong skeleton with the light filler panel, the system which is the secret and the innovation of Gothic construction.

Tables appeared late in the period. Earlier the table was a mere board on trestles, and this form crystallized as the permanent trestle table, or refectory, with infinite variations. Beds, in the transportable form, were mere rough frameworks upon which were draped the bedding—the canopy, the curtains, etc., which formed the medieval bed. With permanent abodes came decorative woodwork, but the bed as a monumental composition of textiles only began to decline in the late 17th cent.

The materials of Gothic furniture were invariably local, but predominantly oak. Walnut, beech, and pine appear in sections where these woods abound, as in southern France and the Alpine regions respectively. As significant as the development of joinery technique is the superb carving style which grew straight out of the tactile nature of the wood at hand, and the motives of familiar things. Seen through deeply religious eyes, all the common natural forms,—plants, animals, symbols—are the themes of conventionalized and naturalistic representation in carving and painting. Wood, stone, metal, textile, ivory, or whatever the medium, it is almost uniformly handled directly in good scale and with commendable regard for texture. In all media we find the themes of leaves, vines, flowers; grotesque human and animal representation; complex geometric outlines like cusped arches, trefoil and quatrefoil; the dramatic shadows of full moldings and strong ogee curves.

Strictly speaking, there was no decline of the Gothic style. It reached its zenith in a flamboyant flush, at the very height of which it found itself adding new, alien, irrelevant details. These, the product of an almost contradictory line of thought, were the first surges of the Renaissance, pushing north from Italy.

The growth and spread and subsequent phenomena of Renaissance furniture are analogous, diagramatically to the effects of a stone cast into a quiet pool. Concentric, expanding rings strike an irregular shore, at each point forming a different pattern, the whole effect similar. The Renaissance emanated from Italy, never truly Gothic. It spread geographically to those lands closest to Italian thought:

France of the Medici, Spain, the Spanish Netherlands, Tudor England. In each of the coalescing nationalities grew a social organization consistent with its political rise, and in each a distinguishable idiom of furniture design. The varying impact of similar forces upon more or less impressionable material, the time lag, the revaluation and the individuality of interpretations gave rise to styles. The styles of the last four centuries are today the repertoire of furniture design.

In Italy the Gothic was sheer affectation; Italian Gothic was a medley of Byzantine polychromy, the half-remembered classicism of the Romanesque, and a smattering of irrelevantly applied northern details. With the 14th cent. a conscious revival of interest in ancient learning brought a reawakening to Roman art and architecture; before long these themes began to appear in furniture designs. More, the revival produced a change in living habits which engendered new furniture forms.

The **chair,** a ceremonial object of remarkable uncomfortableness, struck root in every known form and became an object of common use. By 1600 the **framework chair** had descended from a stiff, high structure to a shape we recognize today; the wood seat became leather bands or had applied cushions, which presently appeared as the upholstered seat. The ponderous **folding chairs,** lightened and decorated, are identified as **Dante** and **Savonarola** chairs. Up from the rude three-legged stool came the **sgabelle,** ancestor of all light side chair forms.

The ubiquitous **chest,** a utilitarian necessity most often built for storage and readiness for transport, grew in size and splendor. Become overlarge for travel, it took new forms. Set up on high legs, the lid became hard to handle, so drawers appeared in the lower part, and the **chest of drawers** is born. Other solutions produced doors in the lower part, giving rise to the hutch and credenza types, and the concept of the high cabinet on legs.

On the other hand, the chest which is in its nomadic stage provided seating surface, and consequently a surface upon which a retainer might sleep, took on the aspect of the familiar bench when it appeared with high arms, later with a back, finally with cushions; hence the whole category of **long bench** (cassapanca), **settles,** settees, **sofas.** Still another branch was the desk group, the great Italian **fall-front desk** with its many compartments and drawers, parent of the Spanish **Vargueno,** the **bureaux,** the **escritoire** or **secretary.**

Bed types in Mediterranean countries have changed little since ancient times; the elevated platform on decorative legs, and the headboard for reclining are the only essentials, and only the superficial details and the padding have changed. This is contrary to a tremendous metamorphosis in the bed type which took place in northern countries.

The table form was projected into astonishing variations. Basically two forms, the oblong top on trestles or legs, and the round or equilateral shape on a central pedestal. The types were merged, crossed and combined into most of the shapes known today. Most distinctive is the highly carved slab base bearing a long narrow top, the so-called **refectory** shape, an echo of ancient Rome.

Italian furniture of the 15th and 16th cents. exhibits some general characteristics irrespective of locale. The *quattrocento* is everywhere a style of great purity and restraint. Scale is noble, but quite human. Ornament, sparingly used, is classical in theme, mostly carved; mythological symbols, foliage and scrolls in the ancient manner, architectural details like egg-and-dart, dentils and other molding enrichments. The wood is preeminently the local walnut. In the *cinquecento* the scale became bolder, the ornament less restrained. Bolder carving was supplemented by polychromy, decorative and representational painting, gesso, intarsia, gilding, metal mountings. The classic motifs were expanded, the whole vocabulary enlarged, and added were courtouches, strapwork, broken pediments and capricious recasting of every accepted classic detail.

Between the cinquecento and the climax of the bároque occurred devastating political changes which caused a backwash in Italian design. Formerly exclusively a product for export, furniture ideas from other lands came to Italy during the 17th cent. Marked in Italy as the **decandenza,** this period must be viewed from the perspective of other countries. Least dissimilar in Spain, a rising Italianized French court imported and exported ideas, while far off England put its own stamp on its imports, and created fresh decorative forms.

Furniture of medieval Spain shows first the conflict between Moor and Christian. Mohammedan elements persisted in the fine geometric detail and brilliant light and shade. Even Spanish Gothic uses dramatic blank areas as a foil for brilliant detail. This style, the **Mudéjar,** succumbed to Early Renaissance influence from Italy. The adapted style is the brilliant **plateresque,** its apex coincidental with the climax of Spanish world power, and so reflected in Spanish Colonial art around the globe. With relatively few essential improvements over the Italian, the rendition is highly individual, the craftsmanship inferior. Rich painting, extravagantly scaled detail, extensive use of metal mountings, repetitious turned elements, wide employment of leather are recognizable details. The **Vargueno**, high desk on stand, is the outstanding achievement.

The plateresque was followed by a brief period of reaction, a harsh, ascetic style sometimes called **desornamentado**, sometimes **herrera** after its designer, architect to Philip II. Inevitably arose the colorful **churrigueresque** style, a vivid imaginative outburst of Baroque splendor, not too distinguishable from the more violent Italian prototypes, strongly mixed with irrelevant borrowings from everywhere. Spanish furniture never again rose to the vigor of a complete individual style.

The Renaissance era in France is most significant. At first the Gothic forms were merely modified with Italian detail. Francois I brought the chateau form up to the great monuments of Blois and Chambord, and for the furnishings of the interiors he imported Italian workmen, their habits, ideas, materials. French furniture of the 16th cent. is magnificent, ornate, heavy. Great cabinets are elaborately carved with complex motives; there were inlays of stone, metal, rare woods. Tables and chairs acquired new importance. Beds were voluminous masses of drapery. Oak is extensively supplemented by walnut.

In the Netherlands influence was Spanish through the 16th cent. Cabinets, tables and chairs showed the same development as in France, but its opulence was in the more sober Spanish vein. A typically restrained, full richness persists in the Lowlands for several centuries, regardless of style, and features like spiral or twist turnings, arcaded galleries and chair backs, deep flutings and a sturdy constructional sense are known as **Flemish**, whether they occur in English or Continental work.

Germany as a whole showed a decided time lag in the acceptance of the Renaissance. In the south a clear Flemish-French infiltration took place, although the general mass and texture remained Gothic. The trading ports in the north likewise accepted decorative themes, but retained simplicity of outline, a low rectangular quality, and, in the carving, much lower relief in the Scandinavian tradition.

England of Henry VIII and Elizabeth gives the most complete picture of 16th cent. furniture evolution from the medieval. **Tudor** oak furniture retains its essentially Gothic style, probably the best developed truly Gothic furniture; but it begins to acknowledge Italian, French, Flemish influence in ornamental detail and in the enlarged catalog of shapes and uses. Structurally the designs are not subtle. Tables and chairs are extensively underbraced; members are unnecessarily heavy, the joinery elementary. Great bulbous or melon turnings dramatically exaggerate the legs of tables and bedposts. The latter were great structures often independent of the beds. Rather crude members were elaborated with spirited carvings, inspired by but certainly not in the Italian manner. In common with all 16th cent. furniture, Tudor-Elizabethan work evidences the enrichment of everyday life.

This development in England continued evenly under the Stuarts through the first half of the 17th cent. Better known as the **Jacobean** (q.v.) period, the reigns of James I and Charles I saw the evolution of a rich woodwork style, increasing comfort, the steady progress away from Gothic ideas, a free use of Flemish, Italian, French details, with no sacrifice of the distinctly English quality. The Puritan Revolution swept away the ornate grandeur, yet Cromwellian furniture is a simplified, lightened, severe variation of Jacobean forms and proportions. Knobbed or sausage turnings and scant carving were the only decorations on the low, rectangular shapes.

In France, Louis XIII continued the political development of the French nation, and permitted steady growth of its substantial furniture art. Two significant branchings should be noted in this period. First, the rise of the bourgeoisie, who, taking over the furniture mannerism of the period retained and developed its characteristics into a collateral set of styles referred to as **Provincial French**; second, the infiltration of the baroque from Italy, and its flowering into the grandiose **style of Louis XIV**. In a sense, the latter is the result of the former, for the Sun King could not permit his grandeur to be imitated by inferior classes, and was so constrained to evoke a new kingly style.

The 17th cent. everywhere expanded the modern spirit. Renaissance art attained its height in Italy, and exploded in the movement known as the **baroque**, which replaced classic restraint and poise with a quality of surprise, of drama. In the beginning baroque furniture merely amplified stately regularity giving way to freedom of outline and movement. The style of Louis XIV epitomizes this amplification, for here furniture attains its greatest splendor in monumental scale, formality, lavish ornamentation. The royal concern with **meubles de luxe** is seen in the state control of the Gobelins factory, which manufactured not only tapestries, but furniture of precious foreign woods, often overlaid with gold and silver, or inlaid with brass and bronze, ivory, tortoiseshell. The name of André Charles Boulle is associated with this excessively complex surface design, but no single name applies to the superbly chased bronze mounts which protected these fine surfaces, and which themselves became the chief ornamental medium during the succeeding century.

The baroque of Louis XIV is restrained and formal in outline, massive in scale; these qualities were the chief features borrowed by the English after the **Restoration**. The splendor of Charles II is an echo of France, translated into English. Veneering is a prime development, and there is a clear association between Boulle's work and the intricate pattern of Restoration inlaying. Scrolled legs and robust curves betray the baroque, whether in cabinets, chairs, or tables. Beds were prodigious compositions of textiles. Mirrors became common. The chair and its allied forms developed along lines which still persist. Walnut was the preeminent wood; joining technique is more knowing and more daring.

Chinese influence appears as an affected mannerism during the 17th cent. and in repeated waves enters subsequent styles everywhere as a phase. Chinoiserie appears in Louis XIV work as decorated panels, in textile motives, in simulated lacquer effects. Dutch traders brought screens, boxes, textiles, small objects; and even carried cabinets to China to be decorated. England had periodic crazes for Eastern motives and "Japanning" — a process of imitating oriental lacquer—covers much late 17th and 18th cent. work (see chinoiserie; Japonism).

The turn from the 17th to the 18th cents. in England is marked by the accession of Dutch influence in the eras of William and Mary and Queen Anne. The grandiose swagger of the French style of Charles II gave way to a smaller, intimate scale, lightness and comfort, at no loss of elegance. Walnut was chiefly used; veneering was less complicated. The **cabriole** leg developed into its best form, and appears without stretchers, as a distinguishing feature. There is an ever growing list of furniture articles, and its general character becomes similar to the furniture in use for the next two centuries. A

distinct Englishness appears, and remains.

A most significant transition took place in France in the first quarter of the 18th cent. The periods of the **Regence** and **Louis XV** are marked by the change from the rectangular to the curved line, the thinning-out of the stately baroque of **Louis XIV** into the feminine prettiness of the rococo. Symmetry and straight lines give way to unsymmetrical compositions curved in every plane. Capricious, fantastic ornament was based on natural forms—flowers, rocks and shells, animals, ribbons and scrolls. Probably the most decorative forms ever produced, Rococo furniture is smaller, more elegant, than **Louis Quatorze**; it employs all materials known before—precious woods, marquetry, marble and faience, bronze and gold, lacquering in the ornamental manner, and pictorial painting—in free designs, forsaking all balance and forcing the structural lines into curves. Chinoiserie cropped out incessantly. There were new types: writing tables, chaise longues etc., all contributing to the polite life and the feminine elegance of the time.

The **rococo** swept over all Europe, and persists in details without interruption up to the present day. Its local variations are most interesting. The great cities of Italy, now in decline, seized upon the style and exaggerated, cheapened it into highly theatrical excesses. In southern Germany the rococo completely ran away with taste, and a wedding-cake architecture was supplemented by an effusion of ornamental extravagance. It spread north and east; to north Germany and the Scandinavian countries, to Poland and Russia and Austria, everywhere being handled with as much or as little artistic discretion as local taste dictated.

The rococo did not overwhelm England. The years of the first Georges produced a rich furniture style, fostered by the spread of wealth and good living. While the period is often referred to as **Georgian** (q.v.), the term is chronological only. The Georges did not influence design as did the Louis, or as had earlier British monarchs. Instead the source of design is found in those effective individuals whose names stand for 18th cent. English furniture. Kent, Chambers, Vanbrugh, the Halfpennys, Manwaring, lead up to **Chippendale** (q.v.), in whom culminates a combination of eclecticism, craftsmanship and salesmanship. Chippendale borrowed freely, using a baroque basis for his essays in the French, rococo, Gothic and Chinese "taste" or whims of his clientele. He produced superb furniture in his own excellent shops, often working in collaboration with other designers, and acquired a most catholic range of taste which he embodied in his important publications. These books served as guides to cabinetmakers in England and her colonies, and so the whole manner of the middle 18th cent. is labelled Chippendale.

A revival of classicism features the fourth quarter of the 18th cent. Even before Louis XVI ascended the French throne in 1774 the sweetness of the rococo had begun to cloy and the reaction was violent and complete. The straight line returned, chaste, austere, refined, imitating classical antiquity. Scholarly archeology tinctures the whole thought of the period. In France it was the intellectual scenery of the Revolution, but it first contributed to the sophisticated, luxurious style known as **Louis Seize**. Graceful, delicate scale, classically conventional ornament, simple surfaces of paint or fine woods elegantly treated, are elements of this style. It was accepted gradually throughout Europe, appearing in local versions of remarkable individuality.

Classicism represented no such revolt in England as it had in France, because many British designers had never honored any other influence. Notably the Brothers **Adam** (see Adam style), architects who designed every detail for their buildings, were the masters of the "Antique"; their symmetry, square lines and classic ornamental details drove out the claw-and-ball baroque, the pseudo-Gothic and the limited rococo sponsored by Chippendale. **Hepplewhite** on the other hand took more license, and only later abandoned these influences, and then devoted himself to a more congenial classic touch. **Sheraton's** work is closely parallel to the Louis Seize at first, but later sacrifices to a confusion of semi-classic themes. Nevertheless Hepplewhite, Sheraton, Shearer and their contemporaries produced a body of furniture design unsurpassed in grace, simplicity, and technical excellence. Sheraton excelled particularly in designs embodying the extremes of mechanical ingenuity and of light, dignified elegance. The style favors tapered or simple turned legs, restrained ornament of classic nature, emphasis on the wood quality, which was prevailingly mahogany. Toward the end of the century satinwood and other exotic materials came into favor.

The French Revolution at first produced a modification of the Louis Seize style known as the **Directoire**, a simplified reflection of the grand manner. Napoleon superimposed his **Empire** style practically by edict. This is a conglomeration of themes from all antiquity —Egyptian, Greek and Roman,—heavily rendered. Its strained classicism dominated all Europe and produced collateral styles of dignity and directness. The **Biedermeier** (q.v.) in Austria and Germany and the Neo-classic of northern Italy rendered the restrained outlines in native woods, and even translated the imperial motives into the local fruits and vegetables. England was too rich to do the thing simply. The precious eclecticism of Thomas Hope inspired much of the style of the Regency and of Victoria's early years, and the descent of taste that marked the 19th cent. was well under way.

Furniture in America, like all colonial interpretations, adapted the patterns of the mother country to native materials, skills, specialized wants, plus the usual time lag. The settlers were rarely of noble origin, so their production can be assumed to follow the lines of provincial work, the aristocratic manner simplified or even misunderstood, and a generation late. Thus the New England colonists brought elements of mediaevalism which for two generations colored the architectural background. Dutch, German, Swedish, French and Spanish groups, developing their traditions on alien soils, produced designs of earnest purposeful quality, in their native idiom. In the 18th cent. life grew easier and aimed at deliberate style, leading to importation of ideas as well as materials. Thus the Philadelphia **Chippendale style** rendered by Savery and Gostelowe, its derivative in the work of Goddard and the Rhode Island school, and finally the **Sheraton-Directoire** inspired work of **Duncan Phyfe** (q.v.). Great masters these, but interpreters first. The **Colonial** (1600-1775) and **Federal** styles (1775-1840), the **Neo-Classic (American Empire,** (1810-1850), the **Neo-Gothic** and various other Neos were truly individual so far as material and execution went, but they always reflected the European scene.

The middle 19th cent. saw the furniture aesthetic bogged down everywhere. The machine confused everybody, chiefly the furniture maker who saw in it only a means to fake the virtuosity of hand craftsmanship. In the '70s arose a sporadic discussion of the state of design, which brought positive gestures from Eastlake, Pugin, William Morris and others, but unfortunately their efforts were toward the neutralization of the machine rather than toward manipulation. The Art Nouveau movement and its branchings of

Arts-and-Crafts, Jugendstil, Mission (q.q.v.), etc., failed to arouse any continuous interest, and for the greater part yielded to pure copying and the glorification of stylism and the antiques industry.

The so-called **Modern** movement caught the public eye about 1925. It had no single clear idea, and proclaimed a functionalism it did not practice, even in some of its most austere phases. At this stage it appears to have sounder motive force, through the exigencies of war, than it has had previously. Expediency and the discipline of strict necessity will probably stimulate sounder creative thinking than did the sheer intellectualism and artistic snobbery that preceded the war. Certainly the talk about "machine processes" is materializing, for we are now confronted with the beginnings of a wood technology which cannot but stimulate designing of a new order.

Woodworking machines have hitherto been chiefly tools, directed at one or another of the traditional processes of furniture making. The cutting of the log into boards, the seasoning and drying, the various steps of cutting, planing, turning, shaping, smoothing have all been handled mechanically, but *each as a separate process*. Finally the assembling, the joinery, is a hand operation, its quality entirely a product of painstaking craftsmanship. The wastefulness of each part is just about the same as it was in Egypt four thousand years ago.

The new approach springs from the changing nature of wood, wood as a *reconstructed natural material* rather than a raw material. If the nature and properties of wood can be changed, as now appears likely through the developments of new adhesives, new molding processes, and the plasticizing of wood, furniture will automatically be designed in a new idiom. This will not be the precious design of aesthetes, weighing the advantages of stylism; it will be laboratory, shop design, the design of the technologist, of the production line, for better or worse. And if it will be cheap, strong, truly functional, conserving of material and labor, no power of critical taste will be able to stop it. Only then will the Industrial Revolution have reached furniture See Bajot, E., *Encyclopedia Du Meuble*, 1900; Foley, Edwin, *The Book of Decorative Furniture, Its Form, Colour and History*, 1912; Hunter, George Leland, *Decorative Furniture*, 1923; Aronson, Joseph, *The Encyclopedia of Furniture*, 1938; Richter, G. M. A., *Ancient Furniture*, 1926; Hunter, George Leland, *Italian Furniture and Interiors*, 1918; Pedrini, A.,

L'Ambiente, il Mobilio e le Decorazioni del Rinascimento in Italia, Turin, 1925; Dreyfus, C., *Le Mobilier Francais, Paris*, Vol. I — Epoques de Louis 14th and 15th, Vol. 2 — Epoque de Louis 16th; Janneau, G., *Les Beaux Meubles Francais Anciens*, 5 vols., Paris; MacQuoid, P., *A History of English Furniture*, 4 vols., 1904-08; Brackett, O., *An Encyclopedia of English Furniture*, 1927; Cescinsky, H., *English Furniture from Gothic to Sheraton*, 1929; Baer, C. H., *Deutsche Wohnund Festräume aus 6 Jahrhunderten;* Lockwood, L. V., *Colonial Furniture in America*, 1902; Wells & Hooper, *Modern Cabinetwork, Furniture and Fitments*, 1909.   —J.A.

furo (Jap.) A portable charcoal brazier on which the water is heated for *cha-no-yu* (q.v.).

fusa. See NOTATION

fused art program. See art program, integrated (2).

fusma (Jap.). An opaque, movable roompartition upon which Japanese artists lavish their best pictorial efforts.

fusuma-e (Jap.). The painting applied to *fusuma* (q.v.), movable room partitions in Japanese homes and temples.

futa-oki (Jap.). A small pottery cylinder, a pedestal, on which the cover of the hot water kettle or the hot water dipper may be rested during *cha-no-yu* (q.v.).   —J.A.M.

futsujin (Jap). Fly whisk made of white hair fixed to a short handle, "to clear away the dust of this world."

futurism. An Italian doctrine in painting, sculpture, and literature, which flourished from 1911 to 1915, and which endeavored to portray the essence of movement without the thing that moves. The first manifesto of futurism was published by the leading critical and literary exponent of the movement, Marinetti, in 1909, but the first examples of painting and sculpture appeared in 1911. Carra, Russolo, Severini, Balla, and Boccioni were the leading futurist artists, the last being a sculptor as well as painter. Marinetti was the leading futurist writer, and was proportionately the most successful futurist, since the objectives of the movement were best adapted to literary expression.

In content, futurism stressed the dynamism and violence of our age and opposed a culture which looks to the past and smothers new art forms. It glorified the "dangerous life", war, blind patriotism, and the age of machinery. Politically it was fascist; ethically Nietzschean; philosophically Bergsonian.

In form, futurist painting was based on neo-impressionistic bright color, and cubist design. It endeavored to destroy the materiality of objects and to depict kinetic and dynamic effects by the principle of simultaneity (q.v.) borrowed from cubism. Painters endeavored to fuse objects with their surroundings to express the speed and character of movement, and at the same time they desired to retain decorative two-dimensional pattern. In sculpture Boccioni tried to do away with circumscribed natural form, to prolong the forms into space, to open them up, and to reveal the dynamics of their movement.

In spite of its short life futurism had some influence on the art of other countries, on French Cubists and Purists, English Vorticists 1913-14, Russian Constructivists 1913-22, and Franco-German Dadaists 1916-22.—L.D.L.

fylfot. The swastika.

G

gable. (1) The upper part of an end wall, above the level of the eaves, beneath the end of a ridge-roof that is not hipped or returned on itself; commonly triangular. (2) The entire end wall of a building. (2) Any gable-like member. —J.M.M.

gable roof. *Arch.* A ridge-roof terminating in a gable.

Gabrielino. See California Indian art.

Gabri ware. See ISLAMIC ART; PERSIAN ART.

gadroon. Notching or carving in a rounded molding; a fluting or reeding, often nearly oval, used in silverware, etc.

gaku (Jap.). A panel-painting. Mounted and enclosed in a wooden frame.

gakumen (Jap.). A framed picture.

gallant style. represents an attempt on the part of musicians to write music which should be pleasing, graceful, and easily comprehensible. It is the music of an ornamental aristocracy which, though it still demanded music of pomp and ceremony for official occasions, had learned to employ music in less serious hours as a language of compliment and of courtly discourse, pleasing without excess of passion, devoid of difficulties for the ear. It represents a stage of transition between the baroque music of Bach and Handel and the fully developed classic style of Haydn and Mozart, but looks forward to the elegance of the classic style rather than back to the grandeur and the musical science of Bach and Handel.

We may trace this general trend in polyphonic music in the work of composers who, against the opposition of such conservatives as Fux, wrote fugues in a lighter polyhonic style with much freedom in the treatment of dissonances and with such emphasis on the most important voice that the rest are reduced to accessory designs. The opposition of Fux though bitter (he wished to suppress the new "licentious" style by imperial edict) was in vain. Marpurg admits in his treatise on fugue that such composers as Telemann "long ago silenced the false opinion that the so-called gallant style did not permit a fusion with features derived from counterpoint."

More important to modern music lovers is the effect of the **lute style** of such great performers as Denis Gaultier on the early harpsichord composers of France: Chambonnières, d'Anglebert, the Couperins, Rameau. The accompaniments, arpeggiated in character, were no longer carried out in a fixed number of parts, but the texture was varied at will, governed by a nice feeling for purely instrumental sonorities. This style, often called the **rococo style**, was also characterized by a graceful use of chromatics and flowing melodic line and a charming, if sometimes excessive, use of melodic graces, turns, trills, and mordents of various kinds. The use of characteristic titles, frequently personal names, was so frequent among the lutenists that Baron can say in his treatise on the lute, "Seldom do we find a French piece which does not have the name of a gallant lady by which, if it pleases her, the piece is named." Though the style, understood in this sense, originated in France, it rapidly conquered Europe; so that we find in the treatise of Carl Philip Emmanuel Bach on keyboard performance and in the work by Johann Joachim Quantz on playing the flute perhaps the most careful and precise accounts of the genre. —C.W.H.

galliard. A *pre-classic* dance form of Italian folk origin which became popular in Continental and English courts during the 16th and 17th cents. The style and spirit of the dance are implicit in its name, which means literally *a gay and dashing person*. The galliard was danced in fast 3/4 meter. The accompaniment had a characteristic two-measure rhythmic pattern, in which the second beat of the second measure was omitted, giving emphasis to the jump climax of the Galliard step. Running, jumping, and kicking steps formed the basic dance, which was subject to three major variations. The earliest of these, the *tourdion,* was the most restrained, the *galliard proper* was livelier, and in the extremely vigorous *volté,* the men lifted their partners into the air at the climax of each phrase. As the galliard became the second dance in court balls, it was used by French composers as the second piece in the musical suites first written for court ball accompaniment.   —J.G.

Gallican chant. See MEDIEVAL MUSIC.

galop. A very spirited dance in 2/4 time.

gambang. A Javanese xylophone.

gamut. See solmization.

Gandhāra art. See INDIAN ART.

ganosis. A process of toning down the glare of marble in sculpture.

garba grha. See INDIAN ART.

garden rugs, Persian. Among most beautiful and important rugs. The Persians spread their garden rugs on the floor in winter to surround themselves with the garden.   —B.E.J.

garden city. See CIVIC PLANNING.

garland. In Roman decoration, a festoon of flowers, leaves, or fruit suspended at both ends and hanging in a curve, often from a bucranium, patera, etc.; also a rope of flowers, etc. running continuously as a border.—L.T.S.

gatch (Pers.). Stucco, used in architecture.

gather, a. See GLASS AND GLASS-MAKING.

gather, to. *Book.* In gathering the folded sections are placed in piles in their proper order. These are then "gathered" one by one to make complete books. See EDITION BINDINGS.

gaucho literature. See HISPANO AMERICAN LITERATURE.

gauze fabrics. See weaving.

gavotte. A member of the *pre-classic* group of dances, had its origin among the Gavots, peasants of a region in south eastern France. A merry and active couple dance in fast 4/4 meter, it began traditionally on the third beat of the measure. The basic movement consisted of small leaping steps. After its adoption by the 16th cent. French court, the gavotte underwent a formalizing and devitalizing process until it reached an extreme of artificiality. Composers of the instrumental suite based on court ball dance music used the gavotte for the fifth or sixth piece, between the *sarabande* and the *gigue.*   —J.G.

G clef. See NOTATION.

geisslerlieder. See MEDIEVAL MUSIC.

gekkin. See MUSICAL INSTRUMENTS.

general ware. See CERAMICS I.

genius. This word has been used so widely in so many contexts that it almost has lost its usefulness as a vehicle of precise expression. To salvage the term two steps are necessary; first, to strip it of its undesirable, confusing and scientifically erroneous connotations; second, to provide a clear statement of useful referents.

The term "genius" is not the sole property of any one discipline. Indeed, it is used as frequently by men-on-the-street as by the technical writers. Let us consider these usages. The man-on-the-street refers to his nephew as a genius if he makes his automobile function after it is apparently beyond amateur repair or performs a similarly surprising feat. In this context even slightly unusual accomplishment is evidence of genius.

In artistic usage, genius is used to connote unusual creative ability with the added emphasis upon inspired activity. The mystical assumption is often made that the genius has contained within him the art product, full grown, awaiting release through appropriate stimulation. Thus, it is assumed that, once inspired, the genius spews forth his creative offspring as a full grown product, while lesser artists must labor, revise, strive and strain to accomplish their purposes.

In many respects artistic usage converges on superstitious and semi-religious interpretations. The latter are inclined to personify the quality of genius even more than artistic usage. Thus, an individual is "possessed by a genius" which may, on whim or perhaps for mystical reasons, leave him. His products are really products of this spirit which is using his body as a medium.

None of these connotations can provide a satisfactory basis for acceptance of the word as a construct for science in general and art and psychology in particular. The man-in-the-street is too inclusive, the frequent artistic and superstitious usages are too vague, and too dependent upon mysterious non-existent entities.

Formal definitions of this term provided by the *Webster International Dictionary* and *Warren's Dictionary of Psychology* which are in essential agreement, provide a more satisfactory basis for usage. Webster's preferred definition is stated: "extraordinary mental superiority; esp. unusual power of invention or origination of any kind." Warren's statement is very similar: "very superior mental ability; esp. superior power of invention or origination of any kind or execution of some special form such as music, painting, or mathematics."

However, the slight differences in the choice of words do reflect rather definite differences in use of the term. Comparison of the two statements reveals that the difference in concept is relected in the comparison of the first statements to each definition. Webster uses the phrase "extraordinary mental superiority", while Warren says "very superior mental ability". "Extraordinary superiority" is opposed to "very superior". The former implies much more atypicality than the latter. This latter statement reflects a bias in interpretation which was emphasized by Terman's definition of genius in terms of his scale of intelligence viz. an I.Q. of 140 or greater. This is a statistical interpretation of genius which is at variance with artistic usage. In the latter context, there is a decided tendency to reserve the appellation to artists and artistic works that have withstood the test of time. On the other hand, the criterion of genius as implied by Warren and Terman is that the individual or his work be sufficiently above that of his contemporaries so that only one per cent of the total population could be said to equal or better it. Further, in Terman's usage genius is treated as an inherent quality of the individual apart from any demonstration of this quality in terms of socially significant behavior. Thus, large numbers of children in this country earn the title

of genius by virtue of an intelligence test performance, while artists and art critics find only a few in each generation who are worthy of the title in terms of achievements.

To gain full understanding of Terman's concept, consideration must be given to the heredity-environment question. The conception that the upper one per cent or any top per cent of individuals in performance on an intelligence test are worthy of the name genius implies that even though an extremely small proportion of them actually perform like geniuses, they are all endowed by nature to be geniuses. Those who do not earn the title by their achievements have been blocked by environmental handicaps. The opposed point of view places complete emphasis upon the individual's developmental history, and expresses doubt that all who have been rated as genius on the basis of accomplishments would necessarily score I.Q.'s of 140 or better on the Stanford-Binet scale. As a difference of opinion over the relative importance of hereditary and environmental influences, this controversy has little to offer in the direction of the better understanding of genius. It seems clear that the final criterion of genius will be accomplishment and that accomplishment cannot take place independently of either hereditary or environmental influences.

If this conclusion is acceptable, then genius can be defined as extraordinary superiority of accomplishment; esp. unusual power of invention or origination of any kind. This definition makes no assumptions with regard to the origin of the accomplishment nor the manner of procedure in the act of accomplishment. It does emphasize the exclusiveness of the quality and the characteristics of origination and innovation. Attempts to extend its meaning to include *specific* assumptions as to origin will go beyond the bounds of established fact. See Terman, L. M. et al, *Genetic Studies of Genius*, 1925; Warren, H. C., *Dictionary of Psychology*, 1934; *Webster's International Dictionary*, 2nd ed., 1934.
—E.S.B.

genre painting. In oriental art the term applies to subjects "of the passing world", or every day life, in opposition to the grand style or to religious subjects. See PAINTING.   —J.A.M.

genre tradition. A tradition of painting in the Flemish school that portrays the rustic life. It was an integral feature of Flemish art almost from the beginning. Such famous artists as Jerome Bosch, Pieter Breughel,

Adriaen Brower and many less noted painters worked in this tradition.   —R.L.W.

genuine color. See COLOR.

geometric design. A formal arrangement of the elements of art structure created by using shapes geometric in character.

geometric ornamentation. See HELLENIC ART.

geometric style. This type of decoration, based on geometric patterns, occurs in the early stages of many cultures. During the 9th and 8th cents. B.C., it dominated the art of the Mediterranean world, supplanting the naturalistic curvilinear designs of the Minoan culture. It was doubtless introduced by the conquering northern invaders. Characteristic are the abstract rectilinear patterns, such as the meander, lozenge, cross, triangle, rhombus and zigzag, and the geometric schematization of the human form. The patterns appear on gold and bronze ornaments and bronze statuettes, but are chiefly seen in pottery, where they often fill the surface of vases with their firm, exact linear decoration. On more ambitious vases there are bands representing scenes of fighting, funeral rites, and mythological events, but these also were designed in a highly formalized fashion, without any spatial sense or fluid movement, and the background was often filled with carpet-like abstract shapes. Centers of this artistic production were Athens, Boeotia, Eretria, Delos, Thera, Rhodes and Argos, but the technique was universally accepted throughout the Greek world. As colonization and increasing trade brought the Greeks into contact with the Orient, where the decorative elements were more varied and naturalistic, the limitations of the geometric style were revealed, and it speedily lost favor. Yet its austere influence remained, as an architectonic restraint which guided the design of later Greek artists. See HELLENIC ART.   —W.R.A.

georgette. Thin silk fabric, dull in texture, with crepe effect due to tightly twisted yarns in both warp and filling. Right and left hand twists alternate.

Georgian. A period in English history nominally associated with the supremacy of the House of Hanover under the first three Georges, from 1714 to 1820. Before its conclusion England had gained a mighty empire, survived the Napoleonic era, and embraced the Industrial Revolution. In architecture, the baroque tendencies of the 17th cent. succumbed to an academic purity which, despite incipient romanticism, became generally stricter as the century progressed and ended in a forthright classicism. The most significant names in the profession are, perhaps, James Gibbs (St. Martin-in-the-Fields in London) and John Wood (Prior Park and the Circus at Bath). But this was England's Golden Age of furniture and interior design, and even renowned are the names of Chippendale, Sheraton, Hepplewhite, and Robert Adam. See EARLY AMERICAN ART; FURNITURE.   —P.C.B.

GERMAN ART. A historical survey of German art as it is attempted in the following pages meets with a number of difficulties because it involves the separation of a cultural-historical phenomenon from the context from which it is in fact inseparable. The particular qualities and characteristics of German art become fully clear only if German art is presented in relation to the art of other European regions which greatly influenced it in many cases. The fact that German art is treated here as an independent subject is not intended to suggest that it is an independent phenomenon and that the art forms presented here are unique, springing from sources solely within Germany.

It has been argued that the native Germanic creative ability has never been understood and properly appreciated despite the fact that it produced original and valuable works and gave to German art those characteristics which differentiate it from the art of other European regions (W. Worringer, H. Read). The dominance of the canons of taste which grew out of Greek and Greco-Roman culture is held responsible by these writers for this fact. It is of course at the present time no longer necessary to demonstrate that the standards of Greek idealized naturalism are only one of a number of possible different standards and it will be readily admitted that different criteria are needed to judge fairly different types of art (e.g. the art of primitives, children's art, etc.). Furthermore, it will be admitted that these standards are of equal value. However, admitting all this— while it makes us more appreciative of a greater variety of art forms—does not change historical facts and it is an undeniable fact that the forms of Greek and Greco-Roman art as well as the standards of taste derived from them have played a most important role in the historical development of European art in general as well as of German art in particular.

There is little, if any, evidence that the early phases of Germanic art were markedly different from the primitive and archaic art forms produced in other regions or by other people. The art of the early phase consists mostly of intricate two-dimensional surface decoration which is primarily non-naturalistic. These art forms were originally brought to Germany from the Black Sea region during the period of the Great Migration. The early phases of this art of the Migration-period are common to the Southern as well as the Northern Germanic tribes. In the 8th cent., however, these art forms disappear in the South of Germany, but they are continued in Northern Germany and in Scandinavia until the 10th cent. If these ornaments are contrasted with classic Greek art, one might say that they contain strong and violent movement. However, it is not sufficient in this case to speak merely of dynamic movement as contrasted with the static restfulness of classic forms. It is necessary also to describe the peculiar quality of the movement in the Germanic ornaments because the element of movement is also contained in Hellenistic and baroque works of art. (It is necessary to make this distinction because it will be helpful in characterizing the German art of later periods). In Hellenistic and baroque art the movement seems to grow out of the organic functions of the object depicted while in the Germanic ornaments an abstract-decorative movement seems to be imposed upon whatever organic form or functions are depicted, distorting or obscuring these forms. Whether the forms of Germanic art had been developed to a point beyond which further progress was not possible or whether the advance of new influences suppressed and prevented such progress is a moot question with which we cannot be concerned here. Whatever the cause —as an independent dominant art these forms disappeared. They lived on to a certain extent in the so-called folk-art (e.g. decorations on utensils of daily use, etc.) but in the field of art the forms of Christianized Greco-Roman civilization became dominant, modified and changed by what must be assumed to be the tendencies of the earlier Germanic cultural tradition.

German art may be said to begin with the **Carolingian Renaissance** in the 9th cent. The efforts of Charles the Great to introduce into the Northern part of the newly established Holy Roman Empire the forms of Greco-Roman civilization are not without precedent. The policy of Charles the Great, however, was more deliberate and more consistent than that of others. For Germany, this policy meant that the forms of the, at that time, most sophisticated civilization were imposed upon a culture that in comparison was simple and primitive. The Carolingian Renaissance introduced into Germany not only art forms, but also themes and contents which were very alien to those who with admirable energy and sincerity strove to imitate and accept them. Due to this lack of understanding, the new forms were accepted and copied more or less indiscriminately. In the process of adaptation the sophisticated was simplified and often enough distorted and transformed into something much more crude. In the field of architecture a comparison of *S. Vitale,* Ravenna (ca. 500-550) with the *Munster* in Aachen (dedicated 805) will serve as a good illustration. In the visual arts the illustrations of the Gospel Books (e.g. the Gospel Book of Charles the Great, ca. 800), as well as ivory carvings (e.g. *Crucifixion,* ca. 870, bookcover, Munich *Staats Bibliothek*) are good examples. In summary one might say that in the Carolingian period a sophisticated painterly form of art was reduced to the levels of an archaic civilization.

From this mixture evolved slowly a tradition which determined decisively the historical development of German art for centuries to come. This tradition is basically non-classic, i.e. the accent lies upon the particular and personal rather than upon the general, upon the realistic and naturalistic rather than upon the idealized, upon the narrative and dramatic rather than the representational and harmonious.

There is no evidence in support of the claim that the German artistic tradition is racially conditioned in the sense that only the Germanic races (whatever that term may mean) were able and/or destined to create these particular art forms. As pointed out, they are the product of a combination of influences and circumstances; furthermore, it should be remembered that (if one wants to consider the racial background at all) the typical Romanesque and Gothic styles which differ markedly from German art were produced by people who were racially related to the Germans (Burgundians, Franconians, Normans). And lastly there is during the Middle Ages great similarity between the art of Germany and Southern France—a predominantly Celtic region.

In France a continuity of contact and familiarity with Greco-Roman civilization guaranteed a better understanding of and a greater freedom with its forms and hence permitted a development which is independent and yet closer to the principles of classic style than German art; thus France was able to develop the Romanesque and the Gothic style. However, before these two styles can be discussed a phase of German art must be mentioned which lies between the Carolingian and the Romanesque period, the so-called Ottonian period. As compared with Carolingian art, the **Ottonian art** appears simpler, clearer and more archaic; it has a simplicity which accentuates essentials and seems to result from a better understanding of the themes depicted and the forms used. The phase is retrogressive in the sense that the imitataon of the imported style is not continued and improved. On the contrary, there is a movement away from the original models towards an archaic simplicity more appropriate to the general cultural level. The effects of the Carolingian Renaissance and French influences, however, prevented the formation of a truly archaic style.

Whether Romanesque and Gothic are the styles which (in European art) naturally follow the archaic style is a question which need not be discussed here. In the historical sequence we observe a recrudescence of archaic tendencies which shows an affinity to French Romanesque. This relationship made Germany more receptive to French influences which determined her artistic development decisively. (Cluny is one of the centers from which these influences emanate). In many respects the Ottonian phase prepared the Romanesque style and it seems justifiable to designate this stage (as some authors do) as **Pre-Romanesque** or **Early-Romanesque.** This seems permissible esp. in the field of architecture where the distinction is less clear partly because many of the cathedrals were constructed during both periods, partly because the French influences go back to the 11th cent. For this reason the Pre-Romanesque and the Romanesque architectures can be treated together for the purposes of this survey. The difference between French and German Romanesque cathedrals concisely expressed, lies in the following factors: the German structures are in general longer and narrower cf. the ground plans of the abbey church of Paulinzella, 12th cent., and Paray-le-Monial, Notre Dame, late 11th—early 12th cent.), they are higher with a steeper roof

and they appear heavier and more somber; furthermore the arrangement of the towers is different. The cathedral of Speyer (begun ca. 1030, alterations ca. 1100 and after 1150) with its two transepts, its two central towers rising above the crossings and with its four flanking towers, placed at the end of the transepts, is a good example of German Romanesque. Many of the German Romanesque cathedrals can be considered as variations of this design (e.g. Worms, Mainz, Maria Laach, and others).

The tomb-relief of Archbishop Friedrich von Wettin (Magdeburg, Cathedral, ca. 1152) is perhaps one of the clearest examples of German Romanesque sculpture. A comparison of the Wettin-tomb with the tomb-relief of Rudolf von Schwaben (Merseburg, Cathedral, ca. 1080) illustrates very well the development from Ottonian (Pre-Romanesque) to Romanesque art. In the Ottonian relief, with its almost too carefully arranged symmetry and clarity of contour, the different parts of the figure are more or less equally emphasized and this lack of unification gives it an air of uncertainty which, despite its impersonal qualities, makes it appear reserved rather than monumental. By means of accentuating the essential form elements and through the subordination of the single parts to the almost cube-like simplicity of the figure, the Wettin-tomb achieves a monumentality which nevertheless contains a certain human quality entirely lacking in the Ottonian sculpture.

The cathedral of Magdeburg (begun 1209) presents the first attempt to introduce into Germany Gothic architectural principles and the Gothic portal with its statuary (see Gothic). The not very successful attempt met with great difficulties as shown by the four successive changes in the plan of construction. French ideas were more successfully assimilated at Strasbourg, Bamberg and Naumburg. An examination of the sculpture of these three cathedrals will show the characteristic traits of German Gothic which are most strongly expressed in Naumburg. (e.g. Strasbourg, figures of the Southern portal of the transept, ca. 1225 and the so-called *Pillar of the Angels,* ca. 1225; Bamberg, figures of the *Portal of the Princes,* ca. 1230-1240; Naumburg, the *Figures of the Donors,* ca. 1250-1260). If compared with French works of equal rank the sculptures of Strasbourg, Bamberg and Naumburg lack the idealizing grace and elegant formality of French Gothic. On the whole the German figures seem to be filled with a certain tense energy; they are stronger, more forceful and monumental than the French. Especially in Naumburg individual human qualities are presented with a strength that raises these works from the level of portraiture to that of lasting monumentality.

The different phases of Gothic art in Germany do not merely grow one out of the other, but result also from successive French influences. For the transmission of such influences three centers can be distinguished, Strasbourg, Marburg and Cologne. The earliest typical German Gothic cathedral was constructed in Marburg. With its two steeples, a system of buttresses and great, high windows and with a system of piers and arches the St. Elisabeth Church (1235-1285) shows important structural similarities to Reims, but the whole building appears more compact and severe. In the Marburg St. Elisabeth Church architectural principles are embodied which are more clearly worked out in the cathedrals of Wetzlar (ca. 1250-1350) and Paderborn (ca. 1235-1275). These cathedrals are examples of a type of construction which is known as *Hallenkirche*—i.e. a cathedral the nave and aisles of which are of equal height and which needs no flying buttresses since the thrust of the vault is carried directly by the aisles to the buttresses, with one great roof covering nave as well as aisles. Although the *Hallenkirche* is found frequently in Germany it is not a purely German invention; its antecedents can be traced to Southern France, as a comparison of the cathedral of Paderborn with the cathedral of Poitiers (1166 - ca. 1300) will show. Of the numerous examples of the *Hallenkirche* type the following might be mentioned: the cathedral of Münster (ca. 1225-1275) and the *Wiesenkirche* at Soest (Middle of the 14th cent.).

An interesting variety of Gothic architecture is the so-called *Backstein Gotik* (Brick Gothic) to be found mainly in Northeastern Germany (e.g. Lübeck, Rostock, Wismar, Danzig, Prenzlau, etc.). The cathedral of Cologne (begun 1248, completed in the 19th cent.), perhaps the most widely known, is actually the least characteristic of German Gothic, being a rather faithful copy of the cathedral of Amiens.

German art of the Renaissance (q.v.) presents a combination of European, esp. Italian, tendencies and the German artistic tradition, in which the latter, however, in most cases is dominant. In so far as such a complex phenomenon as the Renaissance can be reduced to simple formulas, three phases are distinguishable in the development of the Renaissance. The first phase, which is characterized by a naturalistic realism, (e.g. in Italy, Donatello; North of the Alps, Claus Sluter, Konrad Witz, et al.), means a breaking away from the elegant formalism of the Gothic style. In Germany, where the formalizing Gothic style had been accepted with reservations this first phase had a natural affinity with the native artistic tradition. The German works of this phase are considerably lacking in formal unity of composition, but they reveal a great interest in and a feeling for nature and the intimacy of human, personal experience which is of course carried into the presentation of religious themes. (e.g. Master-of-the-Life-of-Mary, Master Franke, Lukas Moser, Konrad Witz.)

In the second phase of the Renaissance which has been named Late Gothic or Neo-Gothic (beginning ca. 1450), there is a revival of the idealizing, formalizing tendencies of the Gothic. This retrogression—not restricted to the North of Europe, e.g. Botticelli, Lorenzo di Credi, Verrochio—is in Germany best represented by the sculptors Pacher, Veit Stosz and Tilman Riemenschneider. The large altars carved in wood of Pacher (*Coronation of St. Mary*, St. Wolfgang, 1479-81), Veit Stosz (*Ascension of St. Mary*, Cracow, 1477-89) and Tilman Riemenschneider (*Ascension of St. Mary*, Creglingen) are the climax of the Neo-Gothic of the 15th cent. In the Mannerism (q.v.) of the 16th cent. Neo-Gothic principles are carried to the extreme in the over-elaborate, swirling, and twisted sculptures of Master H. L. (*Coronation of St. Mary*, 1526, Breisach, cathedral), Claus Berg (*Apostles*, ca. 1532-35, Güstrow, cathedral) Hans Leinberger, and others.

In Italy the Neo-Gothic phase was followed by a turning towards classic form. In Germany the development moved in a different direction; the Neo-Gothic style was abandoned, but it was followed in the majority of cases by a modification of the naturalism of the earlier phase (of the Renaissance) and the break with the medieval tradition in favor of classic concepts was not as clear as it was in Italy. Painters like Albrecht Altdorfer, Lucas Cranach the Elder, Hans Baldung Grien, Hirschvogel, Lautensack, and others follow the tradition of Konrad Witz or Master Franke — a naive naturalism which shows lyrical qualities in landscapes and which tends to become sentimental in religious paintings.

The artistic development of Albrecht Dürer as he himself, according to Melanchton once described it, is also a reflection of the progress of the Renaissance. From a naturalistic realism with great interest in the accidental, bizarre and narrative he advances to simplicity and clarity which he describes as depicted the "original face" (*ursprüngliches Antlitz*) of Nature. Dürer's early graphic work shows effects of the Gothic tradition (e.g. the woodcuts of the *Apocalypse,* before 1498)—intensity of movement and intricacy of design which later give way to greater clarity and simplicity (e.g. the woodcuts of the *Great Passion,* 1510). However, Dürer never loses the intimate and intensely human qualities which can be brought out esp. well in woodcuts, engravings, etc. because these are addressed to a single observer rather than to a large gathering of people (as an altar painting is) His paintings show more strongly the influence of the ideas of the Italian Renaissance (e.g. *St. Mary with the Finch,* 1506 or the *Selfportrait* of 1498). In the *Four Apostles* (1526) Dürer achieves a complete unity of form and content as well as the simplicity and clarity which he called the essence of Nature. If compared with contemporary Italians of equal rank (e.g. Giovanni Bellini) his figures seem to have greater strength and there is an intense, almost aggressive sincerity in the expression of the figures and faces of the four men. The robes follow the movement of the body in bold and sweeping curves with folds which are sharply and clearly cut but nowhere counteracting the movement or breaking the unity of the composition

None of Dürer's contemporaries succeeds to this degree in combining clarity and unity of composition with intensity of expression. In comparison with Dürer, Hans Holbein the Younger appears cool and reserved and his series of woodcuts, the *Dance of Death* (published 1538) seems to lack the intensity of Dürer's graphic work. Matthias Grünewald (Mathis Gothart, called Nithart) in his paintings for the Isenheim Altar (ca. 1510) combines a monumental effect with naturalistic realism, and the grandeur of forms seems sometimes incongruous with the intimate and humanizing tendencies in the conception of the religious themes. In the *Crucifixion* (of the Isenheim Altar) the human suffering is depicted with an almost brutal realism which contrasts strongly with Gothic beautification, but which lacks entirely the dignity and noble simplicity of Dürer's art.

In architecture the ideas of classic Renaissance were even less assimilated than in the visual arts. This fact is important not merely in regard to the classifications of so-called Renaissance architecture, but also because it explains the different character of German art and architecture of the baroque and rococo period. When analyzing the character of movement in Germanic ornaments the exaggerated organic movement of Italian baroque was distinguished from the abstract-decorative movement imposed upon organic forms. As pointed out above, the Renaissance (in the first stage) means the overthrowing of the conventionalized formality of the Gothic which then in Italy was replaced by the discipline of classic form. In Germany the Renaissance movement was instrumental in overcoming the formal Gothic style (accepted with reservations anyway), but since the classic principles were not widely accepted the baroque art in Germany meant a dominance of the German tradition (i.e. dominance of abstract-decorative tendencies) modified through Italian influences. Besides this art developed within Germany there are works of art in a baroque style more or less directly brought from Italy (e.g. Andreas Schlüter's equestrian statue of the *Great Elector* in Berlin, 1698-1703).

In architecture the 16th and early 17th cent. is the period of the town halls, guild halls, and stately burgher houses. The town halls in Rothenburg, Bremen, the *Salzhaus* in Frankfort, the *Essighaus* in Bremen, the *Zeughaus* in Danzig, the *Rattenfangerhause* in Hameln, and many others in Nürnberg, Hildesheim, Halberstadt, Braunschweig, Münster, etc., are typical for this period. These buildings were monuments of the rising power of the German cities. With all their elaborate richness and enjoyment of detail they have a homelike quality but they lack the impressive dignity of Italian Renaissance architecture.

Around the turn of the century architecture becomes somewhat more simple and unified as a comparison of the *Otto-Heinrichs-Bau* (1556 - after 1560) with the *Friedrichs-Bau* (1601-1607) of the Castle of Heidelberg will show.

It is futile yet tempting to speculate what course the artistic development in Germany might have followed if it had not been interrupted by the Thirty Years War; whether for instance the cities might not have become centers of a culture similar to that of the Netherlands. The outcome of the Thirty Years War brought the rule of numberless absolute princes who were anxious to model their courts after that of Versailles. The palaces built as a result of such desire for imitation are variations of the castle at Versailles (e.g.

Solitude near Stuttgart, the Castle at Münster, *Sanssouci* near Potsdam, the palace of the archbishop at Würzburg, etc.).

The Royal Castle in Berlin (begun 1538, remodeled 1698-1706 by Andreas Schlüter), a Prussian version of an Italian palace, is a good example of German baroque. The somber façade of the heavy cube-like structure is somewhat enlivened by the vertical rhythm of the window arrangement. On the southern part two huge groups of columns are set into the building interrupting the facade yet adding to the forbidding heaviness of the whole building rather than enlivening it. The buildings of the Dresden *Zwinger* (1711-1722 by Matthäus Daniel Pöppelmann), arranged around a square, have an elegance and an elaborate richness of decorative ornaments diametrically opposed to the sobriety of the Berlin Castle. The *Zwinger* is typical for German rococo (see rococo), which has less clarity and unity than the French, but which shows instead a greater variety of and emphasis upon individual parts—resulting in a more friendly if sometimes somewhat heavier appearance. In church architecture there is, besides direct Italian baroque influences, a tendency to return to the type of the *Hallenkirche* of the Gothic. The *Wallfahrtskirche* in Vierzehnheiligen (J. B. Neumann, begun 1743) presents this kind of rococo architecture very clearly. The strict cross-shaped ground-plan of the Italian baroque churches (e.g. *Il Gesù*) has been transformed somewhat in the manner of the early German churches, thus creating a high and wide nave to which aisles as well as transept are subordinated. Any reminiscences of medieval gloom are removed through the lightness and richness of the rococo decorations.

The breaking away from the formalized conventions of the rococo during the **Sturm und Drang** (Storm and Stress) period (latter part of the 18th cent.) and the movement towards a new natural humanity meant in Germany that the native artistic tradition came more strongly to the fore. The majority of the German rococo painters were bourgeois, and they had transformed the art of the court of Versailles into something rather sober and simple (e.g. Daniel Chodowiecki's paintings are carefully recorded reports of garden parties of a most honorable society). In the paintings of Chodowiecki and his contemporaries (e.g. J. A. Herrlein, J. K. Seekatz, J. L. E. Morgenstern, et al. there is a certain conflict between the accentuation of the human figure in the composition, the

graceful curves of the design, the play of light and the simple pleasures and events which are depicted. Their art already contains elements of the new natural humanity proclaimed as the aim of Classicism and Romanticism. However, the new natural state to be achieved is an intellectual product, a sentimentalized fiction—all these natural men, the peasants or savages, are noble, sensible and sensitive. Nature and natural beings are invested with all the feelings of those who are seeking this better state, nature is approached sentimentally and as a consequence is itself sentimentalized. Classic antiquity is approached with the same attitude, to be classic is to be natural. It is a sentimentalized classicism, particularly in Germany, and we witness the strange contradiction that the art from which the very idea of form is derived is used in a romantically transformed fashion to protest against an art considered to be artificial because it is formal. The opposition between Classicism and Romanticism of the late 18th and the 19th cent. is actually no conflict at all. The classicism of Ph. Fr. Hetch, of A. J. Carstens or of G. Schadow is a romantically distorted version of classic antiquity—it is the same honorable sobriety of Chodowieck only in classic robes, narrative rather than representative, intimate rather than great, and nobler in the intention than in the execution. On the other hand the so-called Romanticists' manner of painting has many of the characteristics of Classicism. For instance in Gottfried Schick's *Portrait of the Daughters of Wilhelm von Humboldt* (1809) the forms are contained within a clear contour and the two children are placed in the center of the composition before a landscape which widens into indefinite distances. The romantic sentiment is depicted in the soulful look and expression of the faces and repeated more clearly in the landscape of the background. The same holds true for the paintings of Philipp Otto Runge. The contemplative gaze of the figures in *We Three* (1806; destroyed 1931 in the fire of the Munich *Glaspalast*) is not directed towards the observer but goes beyond him; it expresses the vague and indefinite longing for something which one feels rather than knows, a desire to be in harmony with the rhythm of the universe. There is a conflict between the clearly painted figures in the foreground and the romantically treated landscape. Caspar David Friedrich overcomes this conflict by abandoning the human figure as a primary and independent carrier of emotions His men are completely part of the landscape; they are subordinated to it. Together with trees shrubs, with ruins or with masts of boats the figures form a part of the foreground. By means of accentuating the foreground a framework is created through which the observer perceives the landscape; often he surmises rather than sees it beyond the framework and by emphasis on the foreground the landscape seems to become more vague, wide and indefinite (e.g. *Cliffs of Rügen* ca. 1820).

In Friedrich's *Stimmungs*-landscapes the feeling for nature and the new natural state of existence is expressed in and by means of the landscape itself; nature has become the carrier of the romantic sentiment. The feeling of longing and expectation which Runge and others narrated by means of the expressions in the faces and the attitudes of men are expressed by C. D. Friedrich through selecting moments and situations in nature which arouse expectation and in such a manner as to leave it to the observer's imagination to complete the scene. For instance in *Before Sunrise* (ca. 1811), *Sunrise near Neubrandenburg* (1820-1830, not completed), or *Morning in the Riesengebirge* (1811), the morning has not yet come—the rising mist, the first rays of the sun reflected on the hills or buildings, make us expect the arrival of the morning. By creating such a suspended state of emotion filled with expectation of that which the observer imagines will occur, C. D. Friedrich satisfies the criteria of the aestheticians of Romanticism who requested an art which taught them to "feel their feelings" (Wackenroder).

Neither Friedrich's contemporaries nor the painters of the later phase of Romanticism attempt to embody the elusive quality of the romantic sentiment in nature itself. The vagueness and the indefinite feeling of which Runge's men seem to dream, the emotions which Friedrich suggests and indicates in a pantheistically enlivened nature is in the later phase crystallized and directed towards a definite and historically located aim. A goal is set for the romantic longing—the Middle Ages, i.e. a sentimentalized Gothicism and with it a romanticized Catholicism (e.g. the brothers Schlegel, Wackenroder, Philipp Veit) as illustrated by the historizing and symbolizing narratives of Fr. Pforr, J. H. F. von Olivier, Schnorr von Carolsfeld, and others. While these painters present their stories as sentimental idyls, the **Nazarenes** (q.v.) (P. von Cornelius, Philipp Veit, Friedrich Overbeck) attempt to set forth their ideas in monumental

form. The result (e.g. the frescoes of the Casa Bartoldi) is a compromise between Renaissance forms and romantic religious sentiment inspired by medieval mysticism. The change of sentiment finds expression in a type of painting in which nothing is left indefinite. The landscape is clearly presented and limited by a distinctly drawn horizon of hills or houses and the religious or historical scenes are recorded with great care and accuracy. The romantic interest in and feeling for nature which in this later phase of Romanticism is somewhat hidden behind the historical religious and symbolic themes comes to the fore again (ca. 1830) in the art of the **Biedermeier** (q.v., also Düsseldorf, school of) expressing itself in careful studies of natural forms and in a preference of simple themes and people.

In the art of the last decades of the 19th cent. general ideas and idealized forms are emphasized instead of the natural and intimate qualities of Romanticism. However, the artists of this phase—Böcklin, Feuerbach, H. von Marées, Leibl, Thoma, et al.—do not overcome completely the sentimental naturalism and realism of the previous phases and their art contains a great deal of the motifs and themes as well as of the sentimental approach of the Romantic and *Biedermeier* art. However, their paintings contain also certain elements which seem to point towards the new art which follows and in this sense the art is transitional. In the selection of themes idealized and heroic figures of classic antiquity, Christian mythology or early history are preferred and instead of the anecdotal narrating of incidents the general and symbolic meaning of the figures and events is emphasized. The themes are painted in a style that aims to be monumental and representative. The unity of man and nature, so important to the Romantics, is dissolved and a type of composition is introduced in which the human figure stands out clearly from the background to which nature, i.e. landscape, etc., is relegated. The important factor as far as the development of the new art is concerned is that compositional principles are emphasized again. The forms of nature while they are subordinated to the theme of the composition are also subordinated to artistic principles of composition—by becoming decorative this art turns away from the *Biedermeier* imitations of nature.

German **Impressionism** is closely linked to the names of Max Liebermann, Max Slevogt, and Lovis Corinth. Liebermann's early work is related to the art of the previous phase inasmuch as he, like Leibl, paints peasants or workingmen unsentimentally and simply. Unlike Leibl, however, he does not stylize these figures nor does he build his composition around them. Somewhat like Menzel, Liebermann presents momentary action, the moving about of people of whom he seems to have become aware more or less accidentally. On the other hand Liebermann paints his people as well as the space in which they move quite differently. The people are observed with the same detached interest with which other objects are considered. Thus in overcoming the sentimentality of the 19th cent. Liebermann's paintings become at once more artistic and more realistic in the portrayal of workingmen. A comparison of Liebermann's earlier works (e.g. *Shoemakers,* 1881) with some of the later pictures (e.g. *Poloplayers,* (1903), will show that he became increasingly interested in the artistic problems of depicting movement and delicate and most subtle color gradations. Influenced by Degas, whom he considered the most gifted of modern painters, Liebermann develops a technique by means of which figures and objects alike seem to be dissolved in vibrating light and atmosphere. Max Slevogt, 21 years younger than Liebermann and since ca. 1900 working in Berlin with him, shows great similarity to Liebermann's impressionism. In clear, light and glowing colors with a vibrant atmosphere he paints portraits, scenes from race courses or from the theater, of which *D'Andrade as Don Juan* (1902) is a brilliant example. In his early pictures Lovis Corinth shows a delicacy of color and a lightness of tones equal to that of Liebermann or Slevogt, but in the course of his artistic development his painting becomes broader, heavier, and his colors less transparent (e.g. *Nude,* ca. 1895, formerly Bremen *Kunsthalle*). He is more radical in dissolving the human body or the forms of nature into masses of color; most intensive and revolutionary in this respect are his *Walchensee landscapes.*

Of a group of artists concerned with the proletarian milieu Käthe Kollwitz is the only one who formulates a sharp protest against social conditions which she considers wrong. Her etchings and drawings have the rousing quality of political pamphlets; her artistic ability prevents her from becoming sentimental.

Modern art in Germany is usually classified into two movements. *Expressionismus* (see expressionism) and *Neue Sachlichkeit* (see New Objectivity). The art of Gauguin, van Gogh and Edward Munch and of the French

moderns exerted great influence upon the development of German expressionism. The difference between the German modernists and their French contemporaries might be seen in the greater individual variety which results in the formation of a number of "schools" and groups within German expressionism. The expressionists are also more radical in the deformation and distortion of natural forms. However, the expressionists do not aim for purely aesthetic-artistic creations; the accent lies (according to their declared aims) on the "expression of the innermost soul," the "thing as such," etc.

Of modern German sculptors Wilhelm Lehmbruck achieves with thin and elongated figures an expression of graceful movement and clarity of contour (e.g. *Kneeling Woman,* 1911; *Ascending Youth,* 1913). Rudolf Belling is the only non-naturalist and truly experimental sculptor; he reduces figures to simple and sharply cut cubes by means of which the various axes of space are explored (e.g. *Triad,* 1919). In his metal portraits Belling achieves most startling effects by means of a combination of naturalistic elements with abstract construction (e.g. *Portrait of J. von Sternberg,* 1930). In comparison with Belling, Georg Kolbe and those who follow more or less his trend (G. Marks, de Fiori, Scheibe, E. Scharff) appear conservative. Kolbe's early work shows the influence of Rodin, from which he freed himself later. His figures have a quality of reserve and restraint even when movement or strong emotion are expressed (e.g. *Grief,* 1921; *Descending Woman,* 1927).

The strongest of modern sculptors and probably one of the greatest German artists is Ernst Barlach. Barlach's art has been described as Gothic (e.g. H. Read), presumably indicating a German quality in his sculpture. Such a description, however, is quite misleading since Barlach's work shows no similarity to the gentle and graceful figures of Reims or Strasbourg. Barlach's figures, usually shrouded in heavy cloaks, are reduced to simple geometrical shapes; the few folds of the garments are straight and clear-cut; they support and emphasize the expressive qualities of the figures without counteracting their organic forms or movements. The heavy vigor of Barlach's figures comes out most strongly in sculptures in which movement is depicted, as for instance in the *Avenger* (1923) in which every part of the figure contributes to and seems to be compressed into the forward rush. If one wants to discover peculiarly German characteristics in the vigorous expressiveness of Barlach's figures the observer must consider the fact that the formal values of his sculptures are not sacrificed to the expression and that Barlach, in fact, achieves often enough a complete unity of content and form seldom found in the non-classic German tradition. The geometric simplicity is probably explainable from his position within the development of 19th and 20th cent. art and should not be simply put down as a Gothic, Nordic or Germanic quality. Barlach is closer to the Dürer of the *Four Apostles* than to the intricacies of Veit Stosz, Pacher or other Gothic artists.

It would be a grievous omission to neglect the development of architecture and industrial design of the 19th and the 20th cent. in this survey. No new architectural style was created in the Romantic period. In Berlin Karl Friedrich Schinkel built the *Neue Wache* (1816-18), the *Schauspielhaus* (1818-21), the *Altes Museum* (1822-28) in an austere classicism after the architecture of early Italian Renaissance (among his designs imaginative Gothic constructions can be found, e.g. the projected mausoleum for Queen Louise of Prussia, ca. 1810). A similar cold and rather academic classicism was inaugurated by Leo von Klenze in Munich (e.g. the *Glyptothek* [1816-30], the *Propylaea* [1830-42]). The classicism of Schinkel and Klenze was the basis for the official architecture of the later 19th and the beginning 20th cent. The newly founded German Empire of 1871 adopted as its official style a bombastic mixture of classicism and baroque (known as *Neudeutsche Renaissance*) of which the *Reichstag* (1884-94, by Paul Wallot) and the Cathedral of Berlin (by Raschdorff) are characteristic examples.

While Germany thus was being covered with courthouses, postoffices, theatres, etc. in New German Renaissance style and with churches in a pseudo-Gothic style a new architecture developed that was first applied to buildings which were the expressions of the new needs of a changing social-cultural structure, such as department stores, factory buildings, railway stations, etc. (e.g. *Departmentstore Wertheim*, Berlin, 1896-1904, by Messel; power station of the A.E.G., Berlin, 1909, by Peter Behrens; *Fagus Boot-Last Factory*, Alfeld-on-der-Leine, 1911, by Walter Gropius and Adolf Meyer. This new movement in architecture and the applied arts known in its beginning as *Jugendstil* (q.v.) is the basis for modern architecture and industrial design. Artists, engineers, manufacturers, de-

signers, writers, etc., interested in furthering and integrating the efforts and experiments of the various groups among the moderns, founded in 1907 the *Deutscher Werkbund* (q.v.), an organization which exerted a great and far reaching influence upon the development of modern style.

One of the most important phenomena of modern Germany and the outstanding exponent of the new spirit in art and architecture was the *Bauhaus* (q.v.), an educational institution as well as a center for experiments and research which extended its influence far beyond the boundaries of Germany and played a decisive role in the formation of a new European style.

The beginning of the Hitler government is the end of German culture. In the visual arts and in architecture a gruesome mixture of a forced-academic classicism and a frightfully sentimental and stuffy *Biedermeier* is proclaimed as the official and only permissible style. Imitations of Klenze's classicism (e.g. the Munich party buildings), hundreds of square yards of canvas filled with marching elite guards, green forests, fertile fields, fertile peasant women, symbols of fertility, and enthroned above all Herr Hitler in shiny armor on horseback bearing the party flag, are the results of this government-regulated art. At the same time the works of Ernst Barlach, Franz Marc, Paul Klee and those of many others are condemned as "**degenerate art.**" One may or may not approve of modern German art—it is impossible to approve of the methods used to suppress it. A total lack of understanding of German cultural history is revealed by the establishment of the above described official style which is as futile as the methods of its enforcement are barbaric.

It is a tragic irony that at the moment when Germany for the first time in the history of art was taking a leading part in the creation of a European style the *Bauhaus* and all the achievements and hopes for which it stood were destroyed. See F. Adama van Scheltema, *Die altnordische Kunst,* 1923; G. Biermann, *Deutsches Barock und Rokoko,* 2 vols., 1914; G. G. Dehio, *Geschichte der deutschen Kunst,* 4 vols., 1930-34, 4th ed.; *German Art from the 15th to the 20th cent.,* Catalogue of the Exhibition of Paintings, Watercolours, and Drawings held under the Auspices of the Oberländer Trust and the Carl Schurz Memorial Foundation, 1936-1937; K. Gerstenberg, *Deutsche Sondergotik,* 1913; E. Heidrich, *Die altdeutsche Malerei,* 1920, 2nd ed.; F. Landsberger, *Impressionismus und Expres-*

sionismus, 1922, 6th ed.; *Modern German Painting and Sculpture,* Museum of Modern Art, New York; E. Panofsky, *Die deutsche Plastik des 11.-13. Jahrhunderts,* 2 vols., 1924 and *Albrecht Dürer,* 2 vols., 1943; G. Pauli, *Die Kunst des Klassizismus und der Romantik,* 1925; W. Pinder, *Die deutsche Plastik vom ausgehenden Mittelalter bis zum Ende der Renaissance,* 2 vols., 1924-1928; S. Sitwell, *German Baroque Art,* 1928. —H.H.

German glass. See GLASS AND GLASS-MAKING.

German porcelain. See CERAMICS II.

Gesamtkunstwerk (Ger.). See universal artwork.

gesso. A mixture of chalk and glue applied to a panel to furnish a painting surface. It takes a smooth polish and gives brilliance to pigment applied over it.

gestalt psychology and music. Ever since its origin by C. v. Ehrenfels, (1890) the theory of a gestalt—a configuration that has more qualities than the sum of the qualities of its parts—used music as one of its most convincing examples.

Obviously the sensation of a melody is much richer than, and entirely different from, the sum of tone sensations. Thus the melody served as the classical example of a gestalt in time. The main representatives of this theory, W. Köhler, M. Wertheimer, E. v. Hornbostel, G. W. Hartmann, K. Koffka, were gifted with special musical understanding; and such contemporary musicologists as E. Kurth, H. Reichenbach, F. M. Gatz, and H. Eames applied the results of this theory to musicology. Not only the melody but also rhythm, harmony, and form in music have to be evaluated as gestalt.

However not every musical performance enjoys the quality of gestalt. Oriental dinner music or the incessant radio are permanent background and not a figure distinguished from a background. In that respect they are comparable to colored wallpaper. But if on the wall there is a picture in a frame the design requires gestalt quality. The frame of a piece of music is the silence before and afterwards. Beethoven's request for a devoted silence before and during his playing was new to the Vienna aristocracy which used to regard music as social background.

We must regard musical form as a gestalt of higher order in that its components themselves have the quality of gestalt: the movements of a cyclic form, the parts of a song form, the themes, cadences, rhythmical patterns, etc.

The amount of gestalt quality is a direct measure for the perfection of a composition. Classical composers excel in integration as well as differentiation of the gestalt, although some stress its closeness, others its richness. Their eclectic followers developed, at most, one of these two qualities. Popular music of all times is esp. strong in closeness, and is therefore easily memorized.

Experimental investigations of music on the basis of this theory promise to furnish further valuable information about the psychology of music, the elements of listening, the logic of compositions, the act of performance, as well as the discovery of the best means for musical education. —H.R.

gesture (L *gestus,* a thing done, an act). (1) Visible action of the human body, preponderantly by use of head and arms, conveying a mimetic or associative idea. In ballet, gesture serves to relate purely danced portions of the action by visual statements of psychological reference, in dumb-show. By physical and literary association, love is indicated by hand on heart, grief by attention to the eyes, vengeance by menacing with the hands, etc. (2) That quality in an object which stimulates the artist to draw. See drawing.

Ghent school. An important 15th cent. school of miniature painting in Ghent including such famous families of miniaturists as the Binninks and the Horenbauts. The school also produced competent painters such as the vigorous realist Hugo van der Gos.—R.L.W.

Ghiordes knot. Sometimes called Turkish—used in the weaving of oriental pile rugs. Two loose ends project between adjacent warp threads and two warp threads are included between adjacent pile ends. See ISLAMIC ART. —B.E.J.

ghost writer. One who prepares literary or artistic material for another person for issuance or publication as his own. The vogue of the 'big name' in newspaper and magazine offices led editors to assign skilled reporters to prepare copy purporting to reflect the thoughts and experiences of a famous person. Although amanuenses and literary assistants had done work of this character since the beginning of writing, the practice of ghost writing became notorious in U. S. sports, politics, and industry after 1918. —H.R.W.

gift books (annuals). Well printed and ornately bound, these books contained a variety of prose and verse together with a series of engravings. Adapted from the almanac, these annuals served as Christmas presents and as symbols of elegant taste. The first was *Almanach des muses,* published in 1765 in Paris. The idea spread to Göttingen five years later, where was issued a *Musenalmanach,* and soon thereafter to England. In the U.S.A. there was a great vogue of annuals between 1825 and 1860. Generally the books were for ladies; the contents were sentimental, exotic, romantic, while the drawings were emotional and unrealistic. Painters, engravers, and authors often found outlets for their work, as well as a fair income, for contributions to these resplendent publications. Although famous names like Hawthorne's are represented, the artistic and literary importance of the annual is small; these books symbolize the garish middle class taste of their era. See Ralph Thompson. *American Annuals & Gift Books, 1825-1865,* 1936.   —H.R.W.

gift cloths. See TAPESTRY.

gigaku (Jap.). A classic dance, now rare, in which masks are worn. See JAPANESE ART.

gigue. (1) Old name for viol. (2) The *gigue* or *jig* is an ancient dance form native to nearly all European peoples. Since the French and other courts of the 16th and 17th cents. made it an elegant ballroom dance, the gigue is included in the list of *pre-classic* forms. After this transmutation, French composers used gigue music to close their instrumental suites, finding that the rapid eighth-notes grouped in threes and the rollicking gigue spirit gave a lively finish. In spite of its life among the courtiers, the dance retained much of its native vitality and survives today in folk-dance form. One 16th cent. authority described the court gigue as "resembling . . . the dances of savages." The rapid and vigorous footwork typical of the dance were apparently retained in an only slightly more refined manner. See Irish jig.   —J.G.

gillotage, gillotype. A type of mechanical photography for reproducing line drawings.

gilt. *Book.* The gilding on a book, including covers and edges.

gingerbread. See POST-REVOLUTIONARY ARCHITECTURE AND DECORATIVE ARTS IN THE U.S.A.

ginger jar. A popular name given to a bulbous jar with cover in which the Chinese store preserved ginger.

girder. A principal horizontal beam, or a compound structure acting as a beam, receiving vertical load and bearing vertically upon its supports.   —J.M.M.

girouette (Fr.). A weathercock.

glair. See egg tempera.

GLASS AND GLASSMAKING. Glass is an amorphous, brittle, hard substance which has passed from the liquid to the solid state continuously and with sufficient rapidity to prevent the forming of crystals in solution. It is usually transparent and colorless, but may be colored and also either translucent or opaque. It is produced by the melting or fusing together of acidic oxides such as silica, oxide of arsenic, boric acid, oxide of antimony and phosphoric oxide, or, more frequently, by the fusion of both acidic and basic oxides, the latter of which soda, magnesia, potash, lead oxide, lime, zinc oxide, barium oxide and alumina are the most common.

The three basic kinds of glass are **green glass,** glass of soda, and glass of lead. Green glass is glass in its natural color, neither colored nor colorless, used mainly for bottles and flasks. It is generally made from coarse, rough materials, less pure than those used for the other, finer kinds of glass. **Soda-lime glass,** sometimes called **alkaline,** is used today in windows and in certain types of bottles and other inexpensive vessels. It is of ancient origin and was made by the Egyptians with approximately the same formula as is used today. The first glassmakers in this country made soda glass to a great extent because lead oxide was not available and potash, easily obtained from wood ashes, could be used as the source of alkali. Now, however, **lead glass** has won preference, especially for delicate work. Lead glass is also known as **crystal,** or, more recently, as **flint glass.** It can be blown with great ease as compared to the older type of alkaline glass, but is more expensive. The addition of lead, a 17th cent. English discovery, makes the glass softer for cutting, and adds to the luster and clear, full ringing tone of the glass as well as to the quality of refraction.

Glass Composition. The composition chosen in making glass depends upon the cost of ingredients and manufacturing, and upon the properties desired in the glass:—the stability and durability, the rate at which it hardens, the ease of melting, and the service the finished piece must perform. The **batch**, or mixture from which the glass is to be made contains, first of all, the fundamental materials, (sand, soda ash, red lead, lime), together with **cullet** which is the waste glass left over from a previous melting. Sometimes between twenty and eighty per cent of the total batch is made up of cullet, for it assists in the melting of the materials and lowers the cost of the composition. The proportion to which the basic ingredients go to make up soda-lime glass is approximately: silica, 70 parts; soda, 14; lime, 13; and alumina, 3. In flint glass it is: silica, 54 parts; lead oxide, 32; potash, 12; lime, 1; and alumina, 1. To these basic materials and the cullet are added either a reducing agent, as carbon, or an oxidizing agent, such as sodium or potassium nitrate. This is to prevent the lead oxide, e.g., from melting into metallic lead instead of fusing with the other ingredients.

Coloring and Decolorizing Agents. Glassmaking ingredients are seldom found in a pure state. The impurities contained in each tend to taint the glass unless some decolorizing agents are used to neutralize them. The most successful of these are manganese and arsenic, but nickel oxide and selenium are also employed.

In some glass, color is a requisite, and is obtained by the addition of various metallic oxides, depending upon the color desired. The common coloring elements are iron oxide for amber, brown, and black; nickel oxide for brown and yellow; cobalt oxide for blue; chromium oxide for green and yellow; manganese oxide for purple; copper oxide for green and blue-green; and uranium oxide for orange and yellow. Combinations of various oxides produce secondary and other colors. What color is actually obtained depends on the quantity of oxide or oxides used, the composition and consistency of the glass mixture, the length of time the batch is heated, the temperature and the gases in the melting furnace.

The Process of Glassmaking. The raw materials are melted together in either a **pot furnace,** in which any number of from three to fifteen containers are set in a single furnace, or in a **tank furnace** where the tank serves as one main receptacle. The pots used in the pot furnace are made from fireclay and may each hold from fifty to about twenty-five hundred pounds. Before the ingredients are put into these pots they are heated for about a week at a temperature of over a thousand degrees Centigrade. The raw materials are then put in and heated for anywhere from twelve to thirty-six hours, or until they are melted together forming liquid glass or **metal.**

Bubbles have been forming on the surface of the melting glass during this process and must be removed. One good method used is thrusting water-soaked blocks of wood into the metal. As the steam generated by this wet wood rises it takes out the gas bubbles. The temperature of the metal is then gradually lowered until the glass has thickened slightly and has reached a workable consistency.

The method in the tank furnace is somewhat different in that it is a continual process twenty-four hours a day. During this time the raw materials are constantly fed into the furnace at one end and the metal drawn from it at the other.

From "Metal" into Glassware. Glass blowing is one commonly employed method for making articles from the molten glass. First a ring shaped piece of clay is floated in the top of the hot metal to keep a spot clear from the scum which forms when the metal boils. One of the workers in the factory dips an end of his blow-pipe into this clear spot and gets a **gather** or small amount of hot glass which adheres to the pipe. Then putting the other end of the pipe to his mouth, he blows, forcing the glass to increase in size like a soap bubble. During this time he has been rolling the pipe back and forth continuously on his work bench to keep the glass bulb as circular as possible. Then he swings the pipe through the air letting centrifugal force help stretch the glass further into shape, and passes the pipe on to another worker. He, in turn, gives the glass further shape, adds the handles, and so on. He has to reheat the glass to keep it in a workable state. He does this either by dipping the glass into the hot metal for another coating, being careful meanwhile that the whole glass ball does not slip off his pipe and back into the furnace, or else by putting the glass into a small reheating oven called the **glory hole.** When the glass is reheated he blows it a little more and then rolls it on the **marver,** or flat, oiled marble slab, so that the thickness of the glass ball is consistent throughout. From this hollow bulb of glass can be made bottles, Christmas tree ornaments, dinner glasses, and vessels of various sizes and shapes. In making a goblet, for instance, a small portion of hot glass is fastened to the bottom of the glass bulb and is pulled out forming a stem, the glass being rotated continuously during this process. To this stem is fastened a smaller bulb of glass, separated from its own blow-pipe. The small bulb, still hot, is pressed against a flat iron and rotated until it forms an almost flat disc. An iron rod, or **pontil**, is fastened to the bottom of this flat disc for handling the glass, as the large bulb is separated from its blow-pipe by breaking it very near the point the bulb joins the pipe. The glass is reheated and worked until the desired shape is obtained, after which the edge of the flat disc base and the lip of the round glass goblet are cut with scissors and fused. Occasionally the edge of a vessel is cut by scratching the glass with a diamond point and then using a series of small horizontal flames around the glass on the scratched line. A crack soon starts and follows the line around. The edges are then rounded off with a flame.

Another technique for making articles from the hot molten metal is that of **mold-blowing**. After the craftsman has obtained a gather of glass from the furnace and blown a slight glass bulb, he places the hot bulb into the bottom half of a cast iron, or in some cases a wood mold, hinges the top half of the mold down, and blows his blow-pipe until the hot glass has completely filled every corner and crease in the mold. After allowing the glass to cool and harden, the mold is opened and the glass taken out and finished. Sometimes, to prevent the glass from being scratched, a paste of some sort is spread on the interior surface of the mold before the glass is blown in it. This is called a **paste mold**.

A third process of working with glass is **glass pressing**. It is like mold-blowing in that molds are used, but unlike it in that the glass is not blown before it is put into the mold. A quantity of hot metal is put into the mold and an iron presser or plunger is trust down, forcing the hot glass into all parts of the mold. The glass pressing process is now used on a mass-production level, molds being rotated mechanically under the plungers.

Some glass is **rolled** out in flat sheets for plate glass, reinforced glass, and wire glass. The hot metal is poured from the furnace on to large, flat tables upon which has first been scattered a layer of sand to prevent the glass from adhering. On these tables are mounted rollers which run the full length of the table rolling the glass out into thin layers approximately one-half inch thick. Each roller is slightly rough to prevent the hot

glass from sticking to it. The next step, **annealing**, plays a big part in glassmaking. If a piece of glass is cooled too quickly it will, of course, crack or break into hundreds of pieces. And so the sheets of rolled glass are passed on through the annealing furnace where they are cooled gradually. When cool the plate glass is ground, using iron tools for grinding and sand and water as abrasive. After this the glass is placed on felt so as not to scratch the one side while the other is being polished with water and rouge. Another process is also used, the **Bicheroux process**, in which the glass is rolled between two smooth rollers. This cuts down on both the time and expense of grinding the glass.

More complicated than glass rolling is the process of **drawing glass** which is used mainly for making glass tubing, but also for making some plate glass. The metal is put into a shallow container and a blowpipe lowered into it. When some hot glass adheres to the pipe, it is steadily raised out of the container, the glass being constantly drawn up also. Tubes or cylinders can be made up to three feet in diameter and about thirty-six feet long. For plate glass these cylinders are split and flattened in a hot furnace.

Glass Decorating. Besides coloring the glass, decoration can be obtained through glass cutting and engraving, sand blasting, etching, and through the process of spun glass. Glass cutting is done in one of two ways,—either **intaglio** or **relief cutting**. The former is used most often and consists in the decoration being cut into the surface of the glass. Relief cutting, on the other hand, is more difficult, for the glass surface is cut away leaving the decoration projecting out. In cutting or engraving, the pattern is first traced on the glass with chalk or quick drying ink and is then roughly cut out by holding the vessel against a rotating disc of iron called the **wheel**. A constant stream of sand and water runs onto the wheel during this process, the sand doing the actual cutting under the pressure of the metal wheel, and the water washing away the sand and glass particles. After the areas of rough work are ground away, the glass vessel is finished up much more carefully on the smaller engraver's wheel, this time of copper instead of iron. The size of copper wheel used depends upon the fineness of detail desired; the wheels themselves vary from four inches in diameter down to about one-sixteenth of an inch. It is in this process that both artistic and technical skills are needed, for the engraver must know how to execute the design so that the finished product will be one of perfection The designs cut or engraved on glass must be such that they go with the glass medium. Light, airy, clear designs which follow the form of a circular transparent object are what is desired and not weighty, heavy decoration, nor that which should only be seen from one side on a flat surface. Only by having the high quality design to work with can the engraver turn out a masterpiece even though he has developed his technique very well. After the glass is both ground and cut it is polished with emery powder or with a small disc of metal or wood called a burnisher

Another technique for decorating glass is that of etching. The parts of the glass which are not to be eaten away by the acid are first covered with a mixture of asphalt, beeswax, resin and turpentine. Then the glass is put into an acid solution containing one part of hydrofluoric acid to four parts water. Different variations in the portions of acid used give different etched effects, such as dull, rough finishes, or semi-smooth ones.

With the use of the **sand blasting process,** a slightly irregular matt surface is obtained. A metal stencil of the design is made and placed against the glass. Sand is then forced through the stencil and against the **glass,** wearing down the glass surface where it is exposed through the stencil.

The most complicated technique for decorating glass, however, is that of using **spun glass.** A small quantity of colored glass is rolled out with an iron rod on the marver until it adheres to the sides of the rod, the whole of which is then dipped into transparent glass and cooled. The iron rod is now covered with a layer of colored glass and a layer of transparent glass over that. The iron is then removed and the hollow shell of glass heated and pulled out into a long, thin string about one tenth of an inch in diameter. Long threads made this way are then cut up into shorter pieces. A number of these threads are arranged around the inside of a clay vessel the shape of a drinking glass. Sometimes they are alternately all clear and colored threads; sometimes there are two or three colors alternating; sometimes there are three or four colored threads on one side and the same number directly opposite with clear threads in between, and so on. The way the threads are arranged, determines the pattern of the glass. The center of this clay vessel is next filled with clear glass which fuses the

threads all together This piece of glass is then removed from the jar, stretched out until it is thin as a fine thread, all the time being twisted to form a rope-like pattern. Occasionally a number of these twisted threads are, in turn, put inside a mold of some sort and a glass bulb blown inside them, fusing them together and making a decorative dish or vessel. There are many variations of this technique that are used in making ornamental glass.

The History of Glass. The exact origin of glass is not known. We cannot tell when or where it was first discovered, nor whether it was deliberate or accidental. Perhaps the Egyptians are responsible, for the earliest definitely dated glass vessels which have survived to this day came from Egyptian tombs of the 15th cent. B.C. They were merely a kind of opaque paste made into beads, charms, etc. Perhaps the Phoenicians first discovered how to make glass and brought their invention to Egypt. We are not sure. But the discovery that glass could be blown did not take place until the beginning of the Christian era. This event, which took place in the Phoenician city of Sidon, brought about a change in glass in every respect. It was now translucent and transparent instead of being opaque; it could be made into shapes and sizes never before possible, and could be made more quickly. Knowledge of the possibilities of glass spread rapidly up into Europe, and particularly into the Rhineland where places like Cologne and Treves produced high quality, artistic glassware between the 2nd and 4th cents. By this time almost all the major technical processes for making and decorating glass had been discovered and put into use. Greece seems to be one of the few countries in which glass was slow at getting started.

About the time of the 9th cent. glassmaking was well under progress in Mesopotamia and by the 11th cent. the Arabians were nearing a peak in their production of enamelled glass, a development which lasted until the 1300's.

Venetian Glass. About the middle of the 15th cent. we begin to find Venetian glass assuming some artistic form although it was not until the 16th cent. that it became the most perfect glass, both artistically and technically, of any glass produced in the world at this time. The light, airy, colorless forms and graceful shapes of this period made Venetian glass famous. In the 17th cent. the Baroque Movement had its influence and glass became highly ornamental and decoratively complicated. "Venetian Glass" became a well-known name but it is a mistake to think that all such glass came from Venice. Some of it was also produced in other Italian cities like Padua, Florence, Genoa, and Mantua. By the 18th cent., however, the cut glass of Silesia and Bohemia had outshadowed that of Venice. Italian glass, in fact, even now in the 20th cent., has never come up to the peak it established with Venetian Glass of the 1500's. Their contemporary products are technically good, but they still rely upon older glass for designs and shapes.

German Glass. The Rhineland was an important center for glass works between the 2nd and 4th cents. but glassmaking soon spread to other sections,—to Hesse, Bohemia, Bavaria and Silesia. In the 16th cent. the famous German green wine-glass, the **Römer**, was produced and in the latter part of the century opaque enamel painting on hollow-glass was developed. Then around 1600 in Prague a jewel-cutter to Emperor Rudolf II tried the process of jewel and gem cutting on glass and found that **glass cutting** could be successful. By about 1700 glass cutting had come into its own in Central Europe and the Silesian and Bohemian glass-cutters in particular were using the technique with great skill and perfection. Cut-glass survived through the periods and movements that followed,—through the baroque, the rococo, and so on until today when glass-cutting and engraving is one of the finest techniques we have for producing modern decorative glassware. Some of the best 20th cent. glass in Germany was turned out at the Arts and Crafts school of Zwiesel and, of course, at the Bauhaus at Dessau.

French Glass. Some small pieces of Nevers glass and a few pieces of enamelled glass of the 16th cent. are about all the good decorative glass France has produced until quite recently. Their main concern had been more practical glass like mirrors and window glass. The Paris Exposition in 1870, however, was a real impetus to artistic work in French glass. Three artists in particular, Brocard, E. Rousseau, and Gallé, began experimenting with glass coloring and decorating, and were the forerunners of the contemporary French artists like Marinot, Navarre, Daum, Marcel Goupy, Pissaro, Simonet and Dufresne who have produced some very fine glass for modern times. Marinot esp. has done unusual work with smooth, thick glass using air bubbles for ornamentation.

Dutch Glass. During the 16th and 17th cents. the glass factories in the Netherlands were influenced both by Venetian and German glass and during the 17th cent. the English-discovered lead glass was also put into use in the Netherlands. Dutch glassmakers developed a method of decoration by scratching the glass with the point of a diamond, and later by dotting the glass surface with the diamond point. Greenwood and Wolff became the experts at this decorative technique. In the very late 19th cent. the idea of functionalism began to take form,—the idea of making useful, yet beautiful household articles. The Dutch architect, Berlage, helped promote the idea when he designed a glass dinner set in 1900. Soon there developed the glassware of simplicity, of pure shapes beautiful in themselves. When engraving was used it too was kept simplified, lending a dignity to the glass. C. de Lorm added his contribution to Dutch glass by carefully considering the use of the glasses first and foremost in his designing, but not forgetting the aesthetic qualifications in so doing. Other Dutch glass-artists of importance are Copier and Lebeau, Lanooy and Gidding.

Scandinavian Glass. No history of glass would be complete without something about Scandinavian glassware, even though it was of no outstanding importance until comparatively recent times. A factory for making plain bottles and household glassware was established at Kosta, Sweden, in 1741, but it was not until 1898 when the **Orrefors** factory was established that Swedish glass began to draw attention from other parts of the world. The Orrefors glassworkers are now concerned mainly wiht *Vackrara Vardagsvara,* or 'More beautiful things for everyday use', artistically producing even the cheaper soda **glass** so that the average working man and his family can enjoy glass designed by the country's leading glass-artists. At the same time they do exceptional work in luxury glass as well. It is at Orrefors where the noted artists Edvard Hald and Simon Gate create their glass masterpieces. Mr. Hald is the director of Orrefors, but he still finds time to design. Both he and Mr. Gate realize that the engraver's tool is a circular wheel and base their designs upon circles and curves. For this reason they often use the human figure in their designing for it lends itself to circular design very readily. They are assisted in their work by young designers like Viktor Lindstrand, Nils Landberg, and Edvin Öhström, all of whom help Gate and

Hald prove that no higher quality glass is produced in the world today than that of Orrefors.

Sweden is not alone when it comes to modern glass, for Norway and Denmark, too, have their contributions to make. The most important glass factory in Denmark is the Holmegaard factory in South Zealand, which is managed by the architect-designer, Jacob E. Bang, while in Norway it is the Hadeland Works where the artist-craftsman Sverre Pettersen does both engraved and hand-chased work in glass and crystal of striking modern character.

English Glass. Just when in between the 1st and 7th cents. A.D. glass was introduced into Britain, we are not sure. It is believed to have been before the 4th cent., however, for fragments of glass-making furnaces of that time have been unearthed. At any rate we know that in the 10th cent. a type of stained or colored window was used in the churches and that in the 1500's Edward VI, and later Queen Elizabeth, employed Venetian glass-workers in their courts. English glass became most important about 1675 when the famous English flintglass was developed. This was followed by the introduction of glass cutting with diamonds which made highly decorative glass fashionable about this time, and particularly decoration on the stems of the glasses. A government tax levied in 1746 upon the weight of glass, rather than its value, furthered the making of elaborate cut-out work. Enamelled glassware came into much use until 1777 when the government began taxing that as well as the clear glass. For a while during the middle part of the 19th cent. the English people tired of elaborately decorated glass although by the latter part of the century they once more delighted in it. 20th cent. Britain is concerned with glass as a science. Sheffield University's Society of Glass Technology is now carrying on scientific research and experimentation as part of England's contribution to the realm of glass.

American Glass. The first glass made in America was in the spring of 1609 at Jamestown, but the attempt soon died out. Two more trials were made at starting glass manufacturing in America, another one at Jamestown in 1621 and one in Salem, Massachusetts in 1641, but neither of these were successful either. The first glass industry of any true success in America was on Manhattan Island. Here in the Dutch settlement glass was made from 1645 on until about 1767. And in the

meantime other plants were growing up in the new world. A Caspar Wistar, for example, started making bottles and window glass at South Jersey in 1739. After the death of Wistar in 1752 his son carried on with the plant and the work. Wistar glasses have become famous because of their broad bases and wide tops, and their decoration of floral designs in glass welded on to the surface of the vessels.

The next big name in American glass manufacturing is that of "Baron" Heinrich Stiegel, the czar of glassmaking from 1763 until the year he went bankrupt, 1774. His favorite color being blue, much of the work at his factory was produced in that hue. Part of the Stiegelware is thin, plain surfaced, light glass with a brilliant reflective quality, but some is quite ornamental,—either engraved, etched, gilted or enamel decorated.

The Boston and Sandwich Glass Company of Sandwich, Massachusetts, as the third important glass factory in America, was founded in 1825 by Deming Jarves. For the first few years the company turned out only blown glassware, but with the invention of the glasspressing machine in 1827, they changed their technique and pressed-glass soon became very popular. The discovery of petroleum called for lamp chimneys and Sandwich glass contributed its part, although the Boston and Sandwich Company has become more famous for the making of their strikingly colored glass in blues, greens, purples, and various color combinations.

The American glass produced during the period from about 1860 to 1890 was of poor design and craftsmanship. Shortly after 1890, however, the Libbey Glass Company of Toledo, Ohio, began making cut glass of very high quality and helped bring the glass industry back to its standard once more. Libbey did much for the glass industry, too, by his extensive glass exhibition at the Chicago Fair in the 1890's which drew wide attention. In his exhibit workers were shown making, cutting, and polishing glass. A spun glass dress for the Infanta Eulalie of Spain was also on display. A Libbey Plant worker, Michael Owens, in 1906 invented an automatic machine for blowing bottles and this, too, greatly furthered the production of glass in America. The Libbey Company now has developed into the Libbey-Owens-Ford Company. Together with the Pittsburgh Plate Glass Company they manufacture some of the most technically perfect and beautiful window and plate glass in the world. "Pyrex" is another name well known in America to-day, particularly to the housewives. Glass bearing the Pyrex trade-mark can withstand oven heat and the Pyrex "Flameware" can even be used for cooking over a direct flame without breaking. The Corning Glass Company is doing further research in heat—withstanding glass and other phases of modern glass and production. The Steuben Division of Corning is now even taking first-rate artists into industry and turning out beautiful engraved glassware. Sidney Waugh is their best known regular glass designer to date. Glass-making in America, now developed into a highly technical science, is once more employing trained designers to work along with the production staff in the factories with the aim that excellently designed glassware can be mass produced and enjoyed by all.

Modern Glass. Glass has come to be accepted as part of our everyday lives almost as much as the food we eat or the clothes we wear. Everyone comes in contact with glass, hundreds of times each day. Besides vases and dinnerware, glass has found its all important place in architecture, not only in windows, mirrors, and parts of furniture, but in construction and insulation as well. **Glass brick**, for example, is used for parts of walls, or even for whole walls. These hollow, translucent blocks are so constructed that they will not crack or break even when subjected to the change of temperature from the cold outdoors on the one side to the warm interior on the other.

The glass used for insulation is **fiber glass**, the threads of which are between ten or fifteen times finer than a human hair, and yet greater in tensile strength than steel. These fine threads made from ground up marbles, are used either massed together in a web or in sheet form or are rolled into nodules and blown into the walls of old buildings. Fiber glass is not only used as an insulator of heat and cold in buildings, of sound and electricity, but also for deadening vibrations. Some fiber glass is used as a plant mulcher and a great deal of it is twisted into threads and woven into shower curtains, draperies, upholstery, etc. The outstanding features of fiber glass are that it cannot be destroyed by fire, water, acid, (except hydrofluoric), or insects, and that it will not rot or decay. These qualities find for it numerous other uses as well as those mentioned.

The glass industry is now making worthy contributions in the war, particularly in producing glass to replace much needed metals.

One noteworthy example of this is **glass plumbing**. The glass pipes have been so perfected that they can stand rapid temperature changes and can be annealed and welded together for installation and repairing. Household utensils, too, are being made to withstand the heat of cooking and can replace metal pots and pans.

Other recent developments in glass include a *glass which absorbs infra red rays* and consequently serves as a shield to cut off the heat. This is being made use of mainly in hospitals as is the ultraviolet ray transmitting glass which helps kill germs. In addition there are the following types: **one-way glass**, which looks like a mirror in a lighted room but from an adjoining dark room appears as blue, transparent glass; **carbonated glass**, a honeycomb-like product, easily cut, sawed, or drilled, which is used chiefly for insulation, particularly in refrigerators; **tempered glass** which can be twisted or bent to about twenty degrees; **safety glass** which is shatterproof due to the layer of cellulose or plastic between the sheets of glass; and Polaroid which eliminates the glare of light.

The day of taking glass for granted is past; we are now beginning to realize its endless possibilities. Research and experimentation is going on constantly, progressively, scientifically to create new glasses and new uses for them. Artists are being called into the factories to design for mass-production manufacture. Architects are using glass as the key means for bringing interiors and exteriors together as one for more pleasant, healthful living. Manufacturers are packing their products in glass for greater sales appeal. In short, glass has arrived! See Glendinning, R. E., "American Craftsmanship in Glass", *Country Life Magazine,* Jan. 1941; Hildebrand, J. R., "Glass 'Goes To Town' ", *National Geographic Magazine,* Jan. 1943; Keyes, H. E., "Glass: Ancient and Antique", *Antiques Magazine,* Aug. 1937; Maas, Carl, "Glass Comes of Age", *Arts and Decoration Magazine,* Jan. 1939; McGrath, Raymond and Frost, A. C., *Glass in Architecture and Decoration,* 1937; McKearin, Geo. S. and Helen, *American Glass,* 1941; Norton, F. H., "The Scientific Identification of Glass", *Antiques Magazine,* Aug. 1937; Remlov, Arne, "Modern Norwegian Glass", *Studio Magazine,* Nov. 1938; Rogers, Frances and Beard, Alice, *5000 Years of Glass,* 1937; Tillotson, E. W., "Concerning Glass Composition", *Antiques Magazine,* Oct. 1940   —N.P.

glasses, musical. See MUSICAL INSTRUMENTS.

glass harmonica. See MUSICAL INSTRUMENTS.

glass painting. A type of comparatively modern painting in China which has the painting applied directly to a sheet of glass. The glass is backed and framed and a metal hooklike device is added at the top so that the painting may be hung. —J.A.M.

glass rolling. See GLASS AND GLASS-MAKING.

glaze. Literally, glass. Covering for clay bodies, ceramic wares. When subjected to fire, glazes melt into glassy coatings. Used for decoration and protection against moisture. Glazes are silicates. See CERAMICS I.

glee. A composition of three or more unaccompanied solo voices.

glissando. (1) A rapid slur, or portamento on stringed instruments. (2) A rapid scale-passage on the piano, slurred instead of striking each note separately.

glockenspiel. See MUSICAL INSTRUMENTS.

gloria. See Mass.

Gloria in Excelsis, Gloria Patri. See doxology.

Gloria Tibi Domine. Short doxology. "Glory be to Thee O Lord.'

gloriole. An aureole.

glory. In painting, a representation of the heaven opened.

glory hole. See GLASS AND GLASS-MAKING.

glove silk. Warp knit fabric originally used for gloves now for undergarments, dresses and gloves. May contain one or a combination of rayon yarns.

glue. Although commonly used as an adhesive for joining purposes, glue has been also a binding medium in paints. Through the Far East this is the traditional vehicle and is still the usual one in the tempera painting characteristic of the Orient. It is prepared from a wide variety of organic materials, bones, skins, and intestines of animals and fish. All of these supply gelatinous tissues from which a gelatin or glue is extracted by cooking with hot water. With the exception of fish glues, most of these dry to a hard gel that is dissolved first by soaking in cold water and then by heating until solution occurs. The finest gelatin or size is prepared from skins, often from parchment. This was a frequent medium in manuscript illumination. —G.L.S.

glutton motif. See PREHISTORIC ART.

glyphic art. The branch of art concerned principally with modeling plastic material and carving. Syn. *sculpture; modeling.*

gniezno. See POLISH ART.

Gobelin tapestry. See TAPESTRY.

Godescalo, school of. See Carolingian art.

gofun (Jap.). A white chalk wash often used as a ground by painters.

gohei (Jap.). Strips of cut paper attached to a straw rope and hung before Shinto temples.

Gojo yaki (Jap.). Pottery made in Yamashiro province.

Gold Coast art. See AFRICAN NEGRO ART.

Golden Fleece, The. See RUSSIAN ARTS.

golden section. That part of a line or figure in which the size of the smaller part is to the size of the greater part as the greater is to the whole.

gold point. Comparatively little used as a drawing instrument, there is some record to show that a wire or point of gold like that of silver, drawn over a slightly abrasive ground, has been employed in the arts. It is said to give a somewhat warmer tint than the line made by silver. —G.L.S.

gold size. See bole.

Golgotha. Calvary. (not cap.) A burial place. A place of torment or martyrdom.

goliard. See MEDIEVAL MUSIC.

gondola pattern. See JEWELRY.

gong. See MUSICAL INSTRUMENTS.

gongorism. See HISPANIC AMERICAN LITERATURE.

gorge. The concave portion of a molding or a groove.

Gorgoneion (Gr. *Gorgoneion* fr. *Gorgo* fr. *gorgos,* terrible). In Greek art, the face of the terrible, ugly Gorgon with exaggeratedly large features, wide open eyes, broad nose, and grinning mouth, and spiral curls; sometimes surrounded by curling snakes; has apotropaic significance.   —L.T.S.

Gothic. Literally, in the manner of the Goths, which means in the style of the Northern barbarians before the light of the Renaissance shone. This derogative use of the term *more Gothico* for the whole of medieval-Christian art was used by Vasari in his *Life of the Painters* (1550), who followed in it, to some extent, Ghiberti's interpretation of the three eras in art: Golden Age of classical art—decline since Constantine — Italian revival through Giotto. Yet it is Vasari who emphasizes first the devastating influence of the barbarian Goths on the continuity of classical art. This interpretation (esp. in *proemio delle vite,* 1550, ed. Karl Frey, vol. 1, Munich, 1911, p. 188) was accepted by the author's contemporaries throughout the Renaissance and remained a stock phrase as long as classical and baroque aesthetics prevailed. Pre-Romanticism in England and the Central European countries and Romanticism throughout Europe since the last quarter of the 18th cent. destroyed the pseudo-historical pattern of Renaissance aesthetics. The reinstallation of Gothic art begins with the emotional-sentimental interpretation of Horace Walpole, the exponent of the "Gothic novel" and the artificial ruin. In the later Romantic era, esp. since the practical and theoretical contributions in the field of restoration and analysis of mediaeval buildings by Viollet-le-Duc (1814-79) have been made, the scientific approach gradually replaces lyrical enthusiasm. This second epoch based on empirical knowledge owes much to Lasteyrie, Mâle, Vitry, Aubert, Focillon, Dehio, A. Goldschmidt, P. Frankl, M. Dvorak, Kingsley Porter, C. R. Morey and others.

The present understanding is that Gothic describes the style of mediaeval art flourishing from about 1150 to 1420 in Italy, and to 1500 in the North. It has its origin in architecture and is therefore primarily an architectural style; yet the term is used in a derivative sense also for sculpture and painting. (Here it basically differs from the term *Renaissance* which has its roots in painting and sculpture.)

The Gothic style originated in the 12th cent. in the church architecture of Normandy and Burgundy. It is the first architectural conception in history in which building with solid masses is transformed into one of void spaces over a skeleton framework. The elements of this type of structure are: rib vaulting, the pointed arch, and the flying buttress. These features represent constructional improvements and each of them used individually can be found in preceding Romanesque French buildings of the late 11th and early 12th cents. Yet it is the combination of the three devices which transforms the structural element into a new aesthetical unit. **Cross ribs,** due to their function as weight carriers and distributors, make the vault supporting pilasters and columns more independent from the thrust of the ceiling and allow them to stretch out accordingly in a vertical direction. Gaining thus in height, the distance from pillar to pillar can now be varied to conform with the needs of the groundplan. The space between the supporting carriers becomes bridged by *ogivale arches* which, because of their shape also diminish the direct thrust. Finally, the **flying buttresses** are supporting cantilevers on the outside of the church which carry the weight of the ceiling away from the inside walls to the outside walls and down to the ground.

It becomes the main tendency in the development of Gothic architecture to fuse these structural parts more and more together. The number of subdividing ribs, forming an ornamental net along the ceiling, increases, and conducts the weight of the ceiling to the ground. Where the downward flowing ribs meet the clerestory, they often burst forth in flowers and buds. The ribs continue along the capital crowned columns or pillars as bundles engaged to their surface and lead the eye from the ground to the vault with their energetic action upward. Thus the functional downward direction implies at the same time aesthetically an upward trend of the architectural design. The vault stretched over the ribs becomes in consequence thinner and higher. The nave grows in height to unprecedented proportions while the walls become more and more perforated by screens of stone-carved galleries and stained glass windows. Colored glass transforms light into an expression of supernatural mood and significance. The ingenious relation of thrust, counterthrust and support increasingly replaces the solid walls, basic to all previous architectonic styles. The string course of the nave leading the eye toward the choirs and ambulatories around the choir enhance the importance of the main altar. The ambulatories also increase the number of individual chapels and the possibilities for processions. Sub-divided rooms along the side naves multiply and honeycomb the church interior. A balcony for the organ and the choir and a rose window, both of which on the entrance wall, create an answering accent to the choir and the altar. Altogether the interior is unified—not only vertically, but horizontally. The cross arms grow shorter, thus fusing to some extent with the main nave while the choir continues in the direction of the nave. The cruciform basilica with eastward orientation prevails, but toward the end of the Gothic style, hall churches with naves of equal height appear frequently.

On the outside the flying buttresses developed into a system of semi-arches adorned with pinnacles, canopies, and statues. This lace-like perforation of the walls and the buttresses in combination with a large amount of statuary lends an impression of great richness and lightness to the exterior. The portals further hollow out the walls, decorating the voided spaces with column-bound statues and bas-reliefs, the latter mainly above the doors. Towers are merged with the body of the building and express the vertical tendencies of the design with aspiring keenness. The cross-shaped groundplan, the verticalism of the elevation and a unified program of statuary on portals, flying buttresses, water spouts and balconies, together with the central rose window and the stained glass windows, transform the achievement of engineering calculation into the polyphonous symbolical ensemble of the *Corpus Christi* in architectural form. It is, as far as its theological message is concerned, a sermon in stone of sin, repentance and final redemption. The celestial hierarchy represents and protects the Christian universe while the world of Satan with chimeras and grotesques appears as its demonic counterpart. Thus medieval Gothic art, considered in terms of its spiritual goal and practical purpose, is a transcendental-ecclesiastic art; and although it abounds in realistic discoveries they are subordinated to and influenced by the transworldly spirit of medieval religiousity

We speak of an **early Gothic** period (ca. 1150 in France, 1180 in England, 1230 in Germany, 1220 in Spain), a **High Gothic** period (1250-1400) and a **late Gothic** or *Style Flamboyante* (1400-1500). With some of its characteristic features, the Gothic style announces itself in the churches of St. Etienne and St. Trinité in Caen in Normandy (1080) and appears developed in St. Denis in Paris (1140). From there it spreads eastward to Chartres (1130), Notre Dame, Paris (1160), Reims (1180), Amiens (1220), Strassburg (1220), Freiburg (1230), Magdeburg (1230), Köln (1250), Regensburg (since 1275), Wien (14th cent.), Prag (since 1344). In the westward direction, we find the cathedrals of Canterbury (since 1174), Peterborough (ca. 1200), Ely, Lincoln (ca. 1200), Salisbury (1220), Westminster Abbey (1245), Exeter (14th cent.), York (14th cent.), Gloucester (1330) as examples of the early and High Gothic, often rebuilt on Norman (Romanesque) structures.

Generally, these English cathedrals present double transepts and no flying buttresses. A tendency for unstructural ornateness finds its expression in the so-called **lierne vaulting**, an elaborate design of ribs on the vault, beginning with Gloucester cathedral. In the 15th cent. the *perpendicular style* transforms masonry practically into an art of carving as we see it in Kings College, Cambridge (1440) or in the Chapel of Henry VIII in Westminster, London (1503-1520). Actually, wooden ceilings in which the direction of the ribs are inverted like stalactites, or open ceilings, frequently replace the stone vault.

In Italy, the Gothic always remained an alien element and the Latin feeling for a balance of horizontals and verticals never subsided. The cathedrals of Siena (1260), the Pisa Campo Santo (1278), the cathedrals of Orvieto (1285), Florence (1296) and Milan (since 1386) may stand as examples.

In Spain, dependence on French groundplans fused with the native tendency for ornate even abundant decoration. The combination of Gothic with Moresque elements resulted in the so-called *Mudejar* (q.v.) style, flourishing in the 14th cent. The cathedral of Burgos (since 1221) and Toledo (1227) present typical examples of the somber and sumptuous qualities of the **Spanish Gothic.**

In *secular architecture,* the Gothic style has expressed itself abundantly in the diversified functions of civic life and of knighthood. Castles rise from picturesque and strategically dominating points (Mont St. Michel, Marienburg), city halls accentuate the market squares with their richly decorated façades (Louvain, Brussels, London, Westminster Hall), hospitals (Ghent, Lübeck) and patrician dwellings

(Venice, Ca'D'Oro) express civic pride competing with aristocracy and monastic orders. Gothic towns in the North and South present the appearance of a unified city plan, the first since the days of antiquity (examples of prevailingly Gothic forms: Oxford, Ghent, Luebeck, Rothenburg, Siena, Bologna). Irregular arrangement of streets, squares and dwellings, manifoldness in the treatment of each new task, abundant wealth of decoration, lend to the Gothic town, with its secular architecture, the most picturesque quality.

SCULPTURE. Sculpture was ordinarily part of the architectural setting which it accompanied symbolically and aesthetically. Never before had there been produced in Europe such an abundance of figural and decorative works in stone, wood, metal and ivory, created by craftsmen organized in guilds. Polychromic treatment of the surface with color or with precious and semi-precious stones is preferred. In subject matter, prevailingly religious or allegorical, Gothic sculpture, in spite of its transcendental attitude, shows more and more the growing naturalism and individualism of the later medieval period. The great statuary programs of Chartres, Reims, and Strassburg may represent the beginning while the statuary of the Burgundian Chartreuse of Champmolle, executed by Claus Sluter (✠1406) and his workshop, must suffice to represent the increasing number of individually known masters of the later period. It is the garment draped over the undulating curve of the body which furnishes the expressive material for the sculptor. Its linear traces, its indentations and bulging convexities are treated by each generation, often under the influence of one outstanding masterpiece, in a different manner and allow (based on these evidences in most cases) precise dating and localization. The human body as such was not yet studied anatomically and the nude is avoided in general. And yet, the body is greatly important as the transmitter of generalized aspects of motion and tranquility reflected once over in the naturalistically rendered features of the statue. In its greatest works at the beginning of the Gothic era, a study of Antique statuary (Reims) enhances the "classical" characteristics. Yet from decade to decade, the distance from antiquity becomes greater and the blend of realistic details with an idealized and abstracted curvilinear style results in the unique Gothic expressiveness. The 15th cent. shows an ever growing amount of realism paralleling a similar tendency in Italian Renaissance sculpture of the same period. Sluter

(works in Dijon from 1390 to 1406), the Dutch Gothic master, and Quercia (1374-1438), the contemporary Italian sculptor, half Renaissance and half Gothic in his style, must be understood as exponents of one trend. The latest phase of Gothic sculpture from about 1480-1520, is characterized by mannerism, expressionism and sentimentalism, showing a rich production especially in Germany (Leinberger (active 1510-30). Notke (1440-1509), Riemenschneider (1460-1531) they all are indicative of the refinement and sometimes the decadence of the latest phase of the Gothic style.

While Gothic sculpture may be studied today in most of the American and European museums, it reveals its intrinsic beauty only if connected with its original architectonic setting. England and the Central European countries (better than France which, with some glorious exceptions, has suffered from the devastations of the French Revolution) can reveal in its churches, city halls, fountains, etc., the decorative and symbolic function of Gothic sculpture.

PAINTING. Mural painting and miniature illumination appear as the two poles of monumental and of intimate recording in our period. Between them a new type slowly rises: easel painting. It takes care of the increasing number of orders for altar panels, painted crucifixes, memorial images, etc. The technique applied is tempera with its opaque quality until the brothers Van Eyck (ca. 1370, Jan died 1441) at the beginning of the 15th cent. introduce the richer oil medium and with it a new luminosity and transparency. The subject matter as well as the purpose of Gothic painting is prevailingly religious. It teaches the Christian dogma from the walls of its cathedrals, it illustrates the story of Christ and his Saints in manuscripts and it visualizes it on altar panels. Yet also there is the beginning of profane illustration as we find it e.g. in the political admonitions of the Palazzo Publico in Siena, painted by Ambrogio Lorenzetti (1337-1339). There are manuscripts with calendar illustrations, medical treatises and since the 15th cent., moralizing interpretations of Antique authors (c.f. *Ovid moralisé*) which widen the circle of pictorial representations. However, nothing bespeaks more the spirit of rising individualism, so closely connected with the introduction of easel painting, than the appearance of portraits. In the French-Burgundian court atmosphere, we must look for its beginnings (portrait of Jean le Bon, 1350-64, Paris, Bibl. Nationale). With the Van Eycks in the North and the first Renaissance masters in the South (Masaccio, Uccello, Domenico Veneziano, Pisanello), portraiture becomes universal early in the 15th cent.

The characteristics of the new style, derived from Gothic statuary with its S-shaped curves and gentle individualism, appear first in French and English miniatures around 1200. Monastic scriptoria and transportable tapestries help to spread the new style. Gothic painting begins as a flat pattern design on abstract gold or ornamental background but takes on, at the end of the 13th cent., a vigorous trend toward three-dimensional space, naturalistic details and psychological individualization. All these elements appear combined and powerfully realized in the art of Giotto (ca. 1276-1337), whose works establish new standards for European art. From Siena, these characteristics, slightly modified and in a more lyrical manner, are transferred by Simone Martini (ca. 1283-1344) to Avignon, the residence of the popes in exile. From there the new style spreads eastward and westward, blending with the local Gothic idioms of France, Germany, England, etc. In the second part of the 14th cent. new impulses from the Northern Italian followers of Giotto bring about the flourishing of an influential Bohemian group, centered in Prague, then the crownland and residence of the German emperor. It is a truly "international style" which dominates Europe from the beginning of the 13th cent. However, painting does not acquire the dominating place in the field of medieval arts before the 15th cent., and this is the time when the international Gothic (which really is a French one, nationally modified) divides itself into its individual national components. The greatest impulse radiates now from the Burgundian-Flemish countries. Out of the germ of illustrative miniature painting, as fostered by the Dukes of Burgundy for their prayer books (*livres d'heure*), grows the new realistic landscape painting, the portraiture and the intimate devotional easel paintings of Hubert and Jan Van Eyck, the founders of the Flemish school, of Rogier van der Weyden [after 1400-1464], Hans Memling [ca. 1430/40-1494], Hugo van der Goes [died 1482].

From this time on the Central European countries follow the line of late Gothic naturalism and expressionism for another century, while Italian painting thrives under the sun of its classical-Mediterranean revival in the Renaissance. Around 1500, the Gothic comes to an end in the North greatly under the influence of Italian form and aesthetics. Albrecht Dürer (1471-1528) from Nürnberg, brings the classical message to the Cisalpine countries. At the same time, the mediaeval world seems to burst forth in one glorious mystical finale in the Isenheim altar (now Museum, Colmar) of Mathias Grünewald (died ca. 1530).

In the 16th cent. and even in the 17th cent., certain elements of Gothic church architecture survive in Germany, Belgium and England as a Post-Gothic resisting in the native tradition the ever increasing thrust of the Italianate Renaissance, Mannerism and Baroque. (The artificial revival of the middle of the 18th cent., originating in England, is discussed under Neo-Gothicism). See MEDIEVAL CIVILIZATION: Coulton, G. G., *Life in the Middle Ages*, New York, 1928/30, vol I-IV; Huizinga, J., *The Waning of the Middle Ages*, Berlin, London, 1937; Taylor, H. O., *The Medieval Mind*, 4th ed., New York, 1925, 2 v. GENERAL HISTORIES OF GOTHIC ART AND MEDIEVAL BOOKS ON TECHNIQUE: Cennini, Cennino, *The Book of the Art of Cennino Cennini*, ed. by Charles J. Herringham, 3rd ed., London, 1930; Hahnloser, Hans R., *Villard de Honnecourt*, Vienna, 1935; Clasen, H., *Die Gotische Baukunst*, Potsdam, 1930; Fletcher, Sir B. F., *History of Architecture on the Comparative Method*, 10th ed., London, 1938; Herbert, J. A., *Illuminated Manuscripts*, 2nd de., London, 1912; Karlinger, Hans, *Die Kunst der Gotik*, Berlin, 1927; Kimball, Fiske and George H. Edgell, *A History of Architecture*, New York, 1918; Mâle, Emil, *Art et artistes du moyen age*, Paris, 1927; Morey, Charles R., *Medieval Art*, New York, 1942; Worringer, Wilhelm, *Form Problems of the Gothic*, Tr. by H. Read, London, 1927. INDIVIDUAL COUNTRIES: Mâle, Emil, *L'art rèligieux du XIIe siécle en France*, Paris, 1922 and *Religious art in France, XIII century*, Paris, 1913; Dehio, Georg, *Geschichte der Deutschen Kunst*, Berlin, 1927, vol. II, pts. 1 and 2; Jackson, Sir T. G., *Gothic Architecture in France, England and Italy*, London, 1915, 2 v.; Street, G. E., *Some Account of Gothic Architecture in Spain*, 1914, 2 v.; Gardner, Arthur, *Medieval Sculpture in France*, 1931; Vitry, Paul, *Gothic Sculpture in France*, Florence, New York, n.d.; Pinder, W., *Deutsche Plastik*, Potsdam, 1924, 2 v.; Gardner, Arthur, *A Handbook of English Medieval Scultpure*, New York, 1935; Vitzhum, G. Graf and W. Volbach, *Die Malerei und Plastik des Mittelalters in Italien*, Potsdam, 1924; Lemoisne, P. A., *Gothic Painting in France*, Florence, 1931; Saunders, O. E.,

History of English Art in the Middle Ages,
London, 1932; Tristram, E. S. and T. Borenius, *English Medieval Painting,* Florence,
New York, 1926; Stange A., *Deutsche Malerei
der Gotik,* Berlin, 1934, 3 v.; Crowe, A. and
G. B. Cavalcaselle, *A History of Painting in
Italy,* ed. by L. Douglas, 2nd ed., London,
1923, vols. II and III; Van Marle, R., *The
Italian Schools of Painting,* The Hague, 1923,
vol. I-IX; Toesca, P., *Florentine Painting of
the Trecento,* Florence, 1929; Weigelt, C. H.,
Sienese Painting of the Trecento, Florence,
1930; Conway, Sir Martin, *The Van Eycks
and Their Followers,* London, 1921; Friedlaender, M. J., *Die altniederländische Malerei,*
Haag, 1934, vol. I-XIV; Post, Charles, *History of Spanish Painting,* Cambridge, 1930,
vol. 2-4.   —A.N.

Gothic notation. See NOTATION.

Gothic novel. See NOVEL.

gouache. A type of water color painting made
with opaque water colors. A pliable adhesive
is usually added to the binder to give the
surface a soft sheeny quality and to make
the paint dry more slowly.   —R.L.W.

gourd shape. A form often seen in oriental
art which simulates a true gourd.

Gouro art. See AFRICAN NEGRO ART.

grace. *Mus.* A vocal or instrumental ornament
not essential to the melody or harmony (grace
note).

gradation. A gradual passing from one tint or
shade to another. *Mus.* A diatonic succession
of chords.

grade crossing. See CIVIC PLANNING.

gradine. A toothed chisel.

gradual. See MEDIEVAL MUSIC; Mass.

gradual responsorium. See MEDIEVAL
MUSIC.

graffito. See sgraffito.

grain. *Book.* The arrangement or direction of
the fibres, etc. in paper, the warp in cloth, the
texture in leather. To dye in "grain" is to dye
deeply. Graining cloth or leather is done in a
variety of ways; by rolling between rollers
with an engraved grain on the one; by pressing between flatplates; or by hand with a
cork-covered board, sometimes termed **boarding.**   —H.E.S.

grain of rice porcelain. See CERAMICS II.

gramophone. See phonograph.

Granada ware. See CERAMICS II.

granary urn. In oriental art, a cylindrical covered earthenware receptacle with overhanging
cover somewhat resembling a granary.

grand adagio. See adagio (2).

grand opera. A tragic opera in which there is
no spoken dialogue (*opera seria*). See opera.

grand relief. See relief sculpture.

grant of arms. See HERALDRY.

granulated work. See JEWELRY.

grapes. Also called grapevine pattern; in
classical art, especially Greek pottery, a decorative pattern in which serrated edged vine
leaves and bunches of grapes are arranged on
either side of a straight or winding stem line,
the leaves usually set opposite each other regularly, the bunches of grapes more often irregularly dispersed.   —L.T.S.

graphic art. (1) (Newer usage) those expressions of art produced by printing from various
kinds of blocks, plates, or type, as etching,
drypoint, lithography, wood and linoleum block
printing, rotogravure, off-set, letter press, and
all other forms of printing (usually *book art*
is considered a part of *graphic art,* though
sometimes included under *commercial art*);
(2) (older usage) all forms of representation,
including drawing, painting, and, sometimes,
modeling; art forms based upon drawings,
painting, or engraving. Whitford and Winslow
in *Dictionary of Education.*

graphic vocabulary. A term coined by Walter
Sargent in 1916 to designate a method of
teaching drawing whereby a "vocabulary" of
simple forms is acquired by pupils as a basis
for graphic expression. Whitford and Winslow in *Dictionary of Education.*

graphite. A form of carbon, this mineral probably had little regular use in the arts until
crayons or pencils were made of it. Early it
was confused with lead, and the ordinary
graphite pencil still carries that name. It is
dull gray in color and has a greasy texture.
Though rather easily abraded, it is entirely
permanent and, because of its texture, can be
used on soft papers. It is widely distributed
as a natural mineral but has also been made
artificially since about 1891.   —G.L.S.

grass orchid. See SYMBOLISM IN FAR EASTERN ART.

graver. See PRINTS AND PRINT PROCESSES.

Great Benin art. See AFRICAN NEGRO ART.

GREAT BRITAIN, ARCHITECTURE OF. The English genius, which has expressed itself with such great force in law, in government, and in the written and spoken word, has often seemed to the purist deficient in that plastic sensibility which is the foundation of great architecture. Yet the British people can justly lay claim to a great and ingratiating architectural heritage. Many of its elements were born abroad, but they have been transformed by British conservatism into something so expressive of the English character as to warrant the merit of originality. The same conservatism has avoided extremes either of Mediterranean classicism or Teutonic exuberance; at the same time it has fostered a love of the old buildings which weaves them into the very fabric of English life and history. If traditionalism and reserve have somewhat dampened the ardor which has carried other races to the highest levels of logic, daring, or refinement, compensation may be found in the positive genius of the British people for the landscape art. In no other equal area can one find so many perfect marriages of building to exquisite setting. If the designers have been sometimes lacking in the strictly architectural sense, they have been incomparable masters of the ensemble.

The specific periods in English architectural history are treated fully in the special references; this cursory account may confine itself therefore to an emphasis of major trends. The condition of British architecture prior to and immediately following the Norman conquest of 1066 may be summarized respectively by the tower at Earl's Barton (early 11th cent.), a structure of massive impressiveness, and the cathedral built at Durham between 1096 and 1133. Upon its completion the latter was momentarily the most imposing Romanesque building in the world. Boasting Gothic proportions, it superseded even the enormous monastery at Cluny until it was in turn outmoded by the spread of international Gothic.

The Gothic buildings of England illustrate the transformation to which a movement as powerful as the French Gothic was subjected once it had crossed the Channel. In adopting it the English architects missed entirely the lessons in engineering, planning, and embellishment offered by the Gallic development, but they compensated for this by the perfection of the settings which they provided for their cathedrals. Except at Canterbury (after 1170), they were unable to obtain glazing which in any way rivalled the windows of Chartres or Paris, but in the crossing lantern, esp. the magnificent tower and spire at Salisbury (1220-c. 1258), they designed one of the most impressive motifs in all architecture.

The Gothic period also witnessed the foundation of the great universities at Oxford (13th cent.) and Cambridge (13th cent.), whose ideals and buildings have exerted such a widespread influence upon American academic institutions; the University of Chicago, Yale University, and Duke University are important examples.

The Renaissance, a highly mundane and modern period compared to the Middle Ages, saw an almost complete shift from ecclesiastical to secular building, and the Tudor era (16th cent.) is most prominently marked by the appearance of a large number of palaces, such as Hampton Court (1515-40), the Palace of Nonesuch (1537-50), Kirby Hall (1570-1640), Wollaton (1580-1588), Sydenham (16th cent.), and Haddon Hall (1567-1584). The best known designer of the day seems to have been John Thorpe (late 16th cent. and early 17th). At first glance his buildings reveal only a superficial appliqué of the Italian Renaissance motifs which Henry VIII had imported so eagerly, but their plans contain an orderly symmetry which was a more profound derivation from the classic spirit. Several plans are based upon an interesting H or E plan out of respect for Henry VIII or Elizabeth, and a more confident openness is also apparent. It was, indeed, due to the order, prosperity, and highly centralized government promoted by Elizabeth that the medieval fortress gave way to the house with open baywindows overlooking unprotected lawns and gardens.

England suffered through civil war and revolution during the 17th cent., and her architecture reveals her uncertainty. The closing decades of the century brought in rather unsightly motifs from Germany and the Netherlands. Blenheim Palace, built between 1705 and 1724, betrays the painful persistence of the continental baroque characteristics well into the 18th cent. Nevertheless, in the same century Inigo Jones (1575-1652) imported the graceful Palladian style from Italy, an event of far-reaching significance for both England and America; and Sir Christopher Wren (1632-1723) began his notable career.

Wren left an imposing monument in St. Paul's, London (1668-1710), and he embellished that city with a forest of church spires which testifies to his fecundity of invention; but his broadest conception remained only a plan. It was a layout for the city of London which Wren offered after the great fire of 1666, and which would have brought classic axes and focal points into London's haphazard medieval maze. Property interests thwarted its adoption, but it is possible that L'Enfant borrowed from Wren, as well as from Versailles, the plan for Washington, D. C. in 1792.

By contrast with the 17th cent., the 1700's in England were distinguished by architecture of a most satisfying character. Owing to Palladian influence, prosperity, social and other factors, designs of both exteriors and interiors exhibit a high degree of refinement and finesse which in turn had a pronounced effect upon the bulk of what we think of as colonial architecture of the region from Maine to South Carolina. Though there were fewer noted monumental architects, there arose a series of brilliant and renowned designers of furniture and interiors. Chippendale (1718-1779), Hepplewhite (a. 1786), Sheraton (c. 1751-1806), and the brothers Adam (c. 1728-c. 1792) being the most prominent. In awarding them a high place in the decorative arts, we recognize the English conception that architecture is an harmonious ensemble of furniture, interior, building, and grounds; and the old houses of Salem, Massachusetts, reflect the atmosphere of graceful living which this ideal has fostered.

The foremost position among British architects of the Georgian era rightly belongs to John Wood (1704-1754) and his son, whose designs at Bath, such as Prior Park (1734), Landsdowne Crescent (1794), Royal Crescent (1769), and the Serpentine (1727-54), are only now being fully recognized as landmarks in the history of town planning and as superb examples of the baroque integration of structure and space.

The end of the 18th cent. saw the irresistible rise of the Industrial Revolution, with England playing a prominent part. With it came prophecies of revolutions in economics, society, politics, and architecture, but the ensuing hundred years witnessed a denial of this change. Fearful of the machine in its midst and lacking the ability to create a style of its own, the new century clung desperately to the past through a series of revivals which culminated in outright eclecticism. The productions of this conservatism dominated the outward character of the era; but beneath this veneer the engineers—who make possible any architectural revolution—were laying the groundwork for the 20th cent.

England has the doubtful distinction of being in the vanguard of the revivalists. Neoclassicism became a certainty when Stuart (1713-1788), after a trip to Greece (1751-54), built a Greek temple at Hagley (1758). The remodelling of Kedleston (1761) gave impetus to the movement; and the erection of the Bank of London (1788-1833) gave it genuine authority. Sir John Soane (1753-1837) employed Roman, Greek motifs, and a modern-looking stripped-classic (in the Governor's Court) with freedom and true distinction. Smirke (1780-1867), in the British Museum (1825), employed Greek instead of Roman orders, but the change was merely a substitution. Meanwhile, Romanticism was developing, assisted by important factors. On the one hand romanticism has been a persistent strain in the British character, and during the medieval period it had created the great Gothic edifices which the British so deeply cherish. As early as 1720 Hawksmoor (1661-1736) had obliged All Soul's College at Oxford with a Gothic façade. This was understandable, but even in the 1750's of the Georgian reign Chippendale had to pause to do "Gothick" pieces for several clients, and Walpole built a large residence, the fantastic "Strawberry Hill" (1753-76), in the Gothic "manner," perhaps as a caprice. But serious attention was drawn to the movement when Beckford, a confirmed mediaevalist, employed Wyatt to build his enormous and costly house called "Fonthill Abbey" (1796-1814). When the weak central tower crumbled, Beckford had a ruin on his hands—and was perfectly delighted.

Romanticism scored a triumph when the Houses of Parliament (1838-60) were built, quite naturally, in the perpendicular Gothic around the nucleus of old Westminster Hall. It represented, in one sense, a union of the two competing revivals, for the plan was developed by Barry (1795-1860), a classicist, and the superstructure was designed by Pugin (1812-1812), an erratic but devoted and brilliant mediaevalist. Street's (1824-81) Law Courts (1868-84) paid the same respect to tradition, in this case the nucleus being the Old Temple; and mediaevalism prospered under the hands of Ruskin, Sir George Gilbert Scott, Bently, and others into the 20th cent., when the huge Cathedral at Liverpool was conceived in the Gothic style.

The second half of the 19th cent., however, was dominated by a frantic uncertainty which can only be called eclecticism. The ransacking of all styles of the past was an international disease which England merely shared. Its insincerity is illustrated by the notorious instance of Sir George Gilbert Scott (1811-1878), then an esteemed practitioner. When his Venetian Gothic design for a government administration building failed to please Lord Palmerston, Scott calmly used it for St. Pancras Railroad Station, and satisfied the Prime Minister with something more in the Renaissance "manner." Such were the typical copybook practices of the day.

Meantime, English engineers were quietly leading the world to a new architecture in the last places that the academic architects would have thought beauty could be born, in factories, bridges, and light-houses. These were the true progeny of the Industrial Revolution which England had fostered, and in them materials of the future—metal, glass, and concrete—were first used with logic and daring. As early as 1758 John Smeaton (1724-92) built one of the landmarks of modern architecture, the famous Eddystone Lighthouse near Plymouth. Its binding of cement allowed it to stand where its predecessors had been smashed, perhaps, also, because its lines were "functional" as the word is understood today. Smeaton's triumph pointed the way to Joseph Aspdin's perfection of Portland cement (1824); it was a material incomparably stronger than ancient Roman concrete, and without it a vast portion of modern architecture would be unthinkable.

The workers in metal also kept apace. The first country to boast of an extensive railway system needed new bridges. To this demand Abraham Darby applied metal when he built the first cast iron bridge over the Severn near Coalbrookdale (1775-79), and his success was only the first of many. The Sunderland Bridge (1793-96) covered an unprecedented 263 feet with a single arch. Only five years later (1801) Thomas Telford (1757-1834) submitted a perfectly practicable design for replacing the old London Bridge with a single-arch metal span of 600 feet. And in 1836 Brunel (1826-59) built the Clifton Suspension Bridge near Bristol, covering 702 feet with beautiful ease. These were notable achievements, and served to dramatize the new materials.

Likewise, important advances were made in the expanding factories of England, far beyond the world of "taste." The engineering problem was to free the interior from the tyranny of the masonry tradition: to lighten walls and enlarge windows, to provide through multi-storied structures a beehive of clearly-lighted and unimpeded space-blocks. In one of the most conclusive solutions in architectural history Boulton (1728-1809) and James Watt (1736-1819) solved the problem in a seven-story mill at Salford, Manchester (1801), the forefather of all metal-frame buildings. William Fairbairn's (1789-1874) English Refinery of 1845 improved upon this construction; but mill-designers up to the present day have really only refined upon Watt's stroke of genius.

Factory architecture came into its own in spectacular fashion in 1851 when Sir Joseph Paxton (1803-1865) adopted greenhouse construction on a gigantic scale for the Crystal Palace which housed the International Exposition at London. Its pre-fabricated metal frames encased 1851 running feet—one for each year of the Christian era—and occupied only 1/200th of the floor space. The interior was a procession of space-blocks flooded by a sea of light, protected from the weather by a hovering envelope of glass. This was a new concept of architecture. The world was enthralled and men of vision must have dreamed of unlimited possibilities. Henceforth, no exposition was complete without a similar attraction, and the Galerie des Machines and the Eiffel Tower at the Paris Exposition of 1889 were but breath-taking fulfillments of Paxton's prophecy.

The early achievements of the modern English engineers have, of course, been superseded; they were, nevertheless, great innovations. A further word should be said about a group of designers who, because they worked on a less impressive scale, have received less attention. These men avoided the morass of eclecticism which mired the whole world of academic architecture during the second half of the 19th cent. Outstanding was William Morris (1834-1896), who saw clearly by 1858 that mass-production was filling the world with design-less horrors. The industrial displays in the Crystal Palace—rugs, ceramics, textiles, furniture, etc.—were unbelievably bad. Unfortunately, Morris saw the ill as a moral one, and tried to promote through his **Arts and Crafts movement** a return to the medieval work bench. He produced some handsome designs which make the machine products of that day appear hideous, but they were a trickle beside a flood and could only be afforded by the well-to-do. Morris would not compromise with the Machine Age or make his designs available to it; yet his influence was not lost. The famous Red House, which Philip Webb (1831-1915) built for Morris and under his direction at Bexley Heath (1859), is so simple and tasteful as to be styleless and timeless. It was certainly unique in its day, and it is possible that it guided the busiest English architect of the time, R. Norman Shaw (1831-1912) in his well-known London houses. These, though hinting of Renaissance and Queen Anne precedents, possess the orderly simplicity for which Morris pleaded; and we must constantly remember the prevailing gaudiness of eclecticism to appreciate the assurance and restraint of Webb and Shaw.

At the end of the 19th cent. the British Isles produced one of the great pioneers of Modernism, the solitary Scotchman, Charles Rennie Mackintosh (1869-1928). He was a contemporary of Berlage (1856-1934), Otto Wagner (1841-1918), Frank Lloyd Wright (b. 1869), and Peter Behrens (b. 1868), and of their stature. His Art School in Glasgow (1898-99) is a landmark comparable to Berlage's Amsterdam Bourse (1898-1903), and his houses, esp. the one for Dr. Blackie at Helensborough (1902) pointed the way for many subsequent developments.

It was not, however, until the post-war period that Modernism enlisted the energies of a whole generation of young architects in conservative England. The movement was augmented significantly in 1932 when some of the foremost German modernists fled to England; and they were joined by other continentals, like the Russian Lubetkin. Lubetkin's Penguin Pond at the London Zoo (1933) dramatically popularized the movement, and captured the attention of the world. Such masters as Lescaze, Marcel Breuer, Walter Gropius, and Eric Mendelsohn brought with them the most advanced ideas of the continent; and the theories of Le Corbusier (b. 1887) were published (1927) and keenly appraised. Some of the newcomers formed partnerships with the younger men which must have been mutually instructive and beneficial; Mendelsohn and Chermayeff, Lescaze and Henning, Tecton and Lubetkin, Gropius and Fry were firms which commanded wide attention. At that moment in the early 1930's England was the world center of the International Style. But the production was by no means wholly foreign. Progressive young Englishmen began to earn reputations in impressive numbers. In a limited space only a few can be mentioned: Burnett, Tait, and Loring; Anthony Chitty; Wells Coates; Joseph Emberton; Cornell, Ward, and Lucas; L. A. Heaps; Slater and Moberly; Marshall Sisson; E. Owen Williams; Christopher Nicholson; Geoffry Allan Jellicoe; Samuel and Harding; Oliver Hill; and Valentine Harding.

This group is ready and eager to undertake the rebuilding of England after World War II is ended, and they are determined to reassure those who fear that a commission of elderly conservatives will reconstruct England along merely picturesque and half-modern lines. The Industrial Revolution may yet come to its artistic fruition in the country where it started.
—P.C.B.

Great Serpent Mound. An effigy mound in southern Ohio, built on a high ridge in the shape of an undulating serpent 1330 ft. long and 2-3½ ft. high. Its function was not burial but probably religious. See Eastern North American Aboriginal art.

great staff. See NOTATION.

Great Wheel. See INDIAN ART.

Greco-Buddhist art. See INDIAN ART.

Greco-Roman pottery. See CERAMICS II.

Greek art. See HELLENIC ART.

Greek-Asiatic art. See EARLY CHRISTIAN ART.

Greek music, ancient. With the music of the ancient Greeks the music historian finds the earliest musical system which can be studied in any great detail. Only very little actual music exists which can be identified as coming directly from the ancient Greeks.

Music played a large part in the social life of Greece. The performance of poetry with a musical accompaniment was a highly cultivated art. Music was important in religious rites, in the theater, and was even contested in the Olympic Games.

The Greek musical system grew out of the use of the chief musical instrument, the kithara or lyre, received its definite tuning through the mathematical and experimental discoveries of Pythagoras (582-507 B.C.), and eventually included the seven-tone modal scales which, judging from their geographical names —Dorian, Phrygian, Lydian, Mixolydian— had a much earlier origin than the complete system.

The Greeks themselves perceived qualities in music which they felt were inherent in the modal scale in which the music was cast. Plato and Aristotle discussed these qualities when they talked of the *ethos* of music. Music in the Dorian mode was conceived to be masterful, suited to military use. The Phrygian was slack, the Lydian soft and effeminate, the Mixolydian mournful and depressing.

For a more detailed discussion of Greek music see Finney, *A History of Music.* For a highly technical discussion and a detailed bibliography see Reese, *Music in the Middle Ages.*   —T.M.F.

Greek pottery. See CERAMICS II.

Greek rugs. Resemble the so-called Smyrna rug. Two kinds—the heavy rugs served for floor coverings in the winter, and the thinner used all the year round.   —B.E.J.

Greek theatre. See THEATRE.

green belt. See CIVIC PLANNING.

green earth. Under the names, **terre-verte** and **terra verde**, this was the most usual green pigment of the Middle Ages and the Renaissance. It was known long before that and has been found on wall paintings of classical times. It is a natural earth which owes its color to hydrous iron, magnesium, and aluminum potassium silicates. Shades of it range from grayish green to yellow green. It is very stable and, with thorough grinding, provides a smooth and workable pigment. Its tinting strength, however, is slight.   G.L.S.

green glass. See GLASS AND GLASS-MAKING.

green ware. Unfired finished ware. See CERAMICS I.

Gregorian chant. See MEDIEVAL MUSIC.

greige goods. Term designating rayon cloths just off the loom and in unfinished state.

grey (or **gray**). Yarns or fabrics in an undyed or unbleached state; also not scoured.

griffes. See base.

grill, grille. *Arch.* A grating or screen, as of wood or metal, often used in or covering window openings.

grinding slab. The stone on which paint is hand-ground goes by this name. Traditionally, the best was of porphyry or granite. In Re-

naissance painting it was of fair size, being more than a foot across, and the pigment was worked on it with another stone, small and fitted to the hand, known as a **muller.** It was probably developed from prehistoric means of grinding grain and examples of it in different forms are found from the earliest records of the painter's art. In modern practice ground glass has proved to be more convenient than stone. Hand grinding of colors is, however, comparatively rare, having been supplanted by the **color mill,** usually of rotating cylinders and operated by machinery.   —G.L.S.

grisaille (Fr.). (1) Decorative painting in gray monochrome. (2) A cotton and wool dress fabric with a fancy design. See also ENAMELLING ON METAL.

grit-stone. A course or fine-grained sandstone of various degrees of hardness. It is composed of small grains of sand united by a cementing material of an argillaceous, calcareous, or siliceous nature.   —J.M.M.

grog. Clay that has been burned and crushed. 30 to 40 parts grog (10 to 50 mesh) to 70 to 60 parts clay may be used in ceramic sculpture.

groin. The projecting solid angle formed by the meeting of two vaults, growing more obtuse at the top.

Grolier. *Book.* Ornament following the style used by Grolier in the 16th cent.

gros bleu. See CERAMICS II.

grosgrain. Firm, stiff, closely woven, corded fabric. Ribs vary from 50 to 70 per inch. Filling may be of cotton but usually silk or rayon.

grosse verdure. See TAPESTRY.

grotesque. As a decorative element means an ornament, painted or sculptured, which consists of fantastically shaped human beings, animals and fabulous beings, joined together by garlands, wreaths of flowers, fantastic architectural elements and other ornaments like arabesques (q.v.) and scroll-work (q.v.). The word comes from the Italian *grottesco,* an adjective formed from *grotta,* for in the excavated ancient Greek and Roman palaces this type of decoration has been especially found. These antique decorations became known after 1490 from which time on they were widely used in Italian decoration. But it was Raffael and his collaborators who really mark the starting point for the revival of this decora-

tive element in modern times. It has to be stressed that the grotesque did not develop in contrast with the arabesque but in close connection with it (cf. Giovanni Paolo Lomazzo, *Rime*. Milan, 1587). The usage of grotesques became favorite with painters and sculptors as well as with ornament engravers. The development, enrichment, variations, and spreading of this ornament were up to the individual artists who had no rule to follow except the symmetrical built up of grotesque design. From Italy, the grotesque went to Northern countries, too (esp. by means of ornament engravings), and the Netherlands were very industrious in developing an original form in mixing grotesque elements with their typical scrollwork. See Alois Riegl, *Stilfragen*, Berlin, 1893; Jacob Burckhardt, *The Civilization of the Renaissance in Italy*, Esslingen, 1912; English trans., London, 1937; Robert Hedicke, *Cornelis Floris und die Florisdekoration*, Berlin, 1913; Peter Jessen, *Der Ornamentstich*, Berlin, 1920; Rudolf Berliner, *Ornamentale Vorlageblätter*, Leipzig, 1926 and *Katalog der Berliner Ornamentstich-Sammlung*, Berlin, 1935; Fiske Kimball, "Sources and Evolution of the Arabesques of Berain," in *The Art Bulletin*, vol. XXII, No. 4, 1941.
　　　　　　　　　　　　　　　　　　—L.P-E.

grottesque. See arabesque.

grotto. See folly.

ground. (1) The ground of a painting is the preparation laid over the support, providing a smooth, even-textured, and even-toned surface for the design proper. The most widely applied of such grounds for many centuries was a mixture of either gypsum or chalk with glue, a substance known as gesso, put over the wooden panels that were painting supports during the Middle Ages and the Renaissance in Europe. Later, oil grounds containing similar inert materials, probably with a frequent addition of white lead, were used on canvas supports. Prepared commercially, these are still common. (2) *Etch.* An acid-resistant coating on a plate.　　　　　—G.L.S.

ground, aquatint. *Etch.* Finely powdered asphaltum or resin, used in making aquatints.

ground bass (It. *basso ostinato*). A short theme repeated over again in the bass with varied melodic and harmonic accompaniments.

ground, etching. Hard ground used for line etching, composed of asphaltum, beeswax and other ingredients.

ground harp. See MUSICAL INSTRUMENTS.

ground line. See PERSPECTIVE.

ground, liquid. Hard ground dissolved in chloroform, used in making line etchings.

ground plane. See PERSPECTIVE.

ground psaltery. See MUSICAL INSTRUMENTS.

ground, soft. Same as hard ground (see ground, hard) but with 50 per cent tallow added, used in making soft ground aquatints.

grout. A mixture of cement or lime and sand or gravel, poured when semiliquid between stones or bricks in a structure, as a wall.

guardant. See HERALDRY.

guard bands, of a rug. The border and field of a rug are generally flanked with narrow strips called guard bands.

Guidonian hand. See solmization.

Guidonian notation. See NOTATION.

guilloche. (1) *Book.* A design composed of two or more bands intertwining and a continuous series. (2) *Arch.* In ancient eastern and classical art, an ornamental pattern composed of two or more curved lines or bands intersecting and interlacing, leaving circular centres or eyes, sometimes filled with rosettes.

guitar. See MUSICAL INSTRUMENTS.

gules. *Her.* Red.

gum elemi. See elemi.

gunbad. A monumental tomb. See ISLAMIC ART.

Gupta art. See INDIAN ART.

guri (Jap.). A lacquer technique. Successive layers of various colored lacquers carved V-shape to show the striated colors as a pattern.
　　　　　　　　　　　　　　　　　　—J.A.M.

Gustavian style. See SCANDINAVIAN ART.

guttae (pl.). A series of droplike ornaments, as on the lower face of a mutule in a Doric entablature.

gutter. A channel or trough, generally along the eaves of a structure, to carry off rainwater.

gymel. (L. *gemellum*). Twin song. A form of organum or part-singing in 3rds, used in England in the early Middle Ages.

Gymnopaedia. An exhibition and festival held in honor of Apollo, Artemis, and Leto from about the 6th to the 10th of July at Sparta; included awards for accomplishments of boys, youths and men in dancing, gymnastics and music. Old bachelors were excluded.

gypsum. Best known now as **plaster of Paris,** some form of gypsum has been used for a substance to be molded or carved since ancient times. Pulverized, it has served as the common inert material of grounds, the gesso in panel paintings. As a natural deposit, a calcium sulphate dihydrate, gypsum is found widely over the earth's surface, though it occurs in many varieties. Most of that used in the arts is burned and, when it is again combined with water, sets rapidly to a firm plaster. It is the most common of casting materials. It is generally stable but is slightly soluble in water and is fairly soluble in dilute hydrochloric acid.　　　　　　　　　　　　—G.L.S.

gyron. See HERALDRY.

H

Haarlem school. A school of art centering in Haarlem whose chief characteristic was truthfully depicted garden backgrounds first introduced by Dierick Bouts. This school was a forerunner of painting-schools that were to flourish in Holland in the 17th cent.
—R.L.W.

habaki (Jap.). A metal stop fitting both sides of a Japanese sword-blade to keep the edge of the blade from coming in contact with the hilt. —J.A.M.

Haban ceramics. See CZECHOSLOVAKIA, ART OF.

habanera. A dance in 2/4 time popular in Havana; frequently syncopated and performed in a slow, voluptuous manner.

Habbé art. See AFRICAN NEGRO ART.

haboki (Jap.). A feather brush used to dust up the ashes of the fire brazier in connection with *cha-no-yu* (q.v.).

hematite. Although there is some literary reference to the use of this mineral, a hard, natural variety of anhydrous ferric oxide, as a pigment, probably its chief utility in the arts has been to supply a stone suitable for making burnishers for gold leaf. —G.L.S.

Haggadah. The report of the exodus of the Jews from Egypt, as told on the Passover Evening in the Jewish family. More frequently than any other Jewish text the Haggadah was written and illustrated during the Middle Ages and the Renaissance. See JEWISH ART.
—H.G.

hagiopolitan. See eastern chants.

Hagi yaki (Jap.). Pottery made in Nagato province.

hagoromo. See SYMBOLISM IN FAR EASTERN ART.

Haida art. See Northwest Coast Indian art.

hainsa (Skr.). The emblem of *Mon* Sovereignty, often seen in Siam adorning temple flag poles.

haircloth. A cloth combining cotton or linen warp with a weft of horse-hair.

haisaji (Jap.). A metal spoon for shaping the ashes around the charcoal fire. A utensil used in *cha-no-yu* (q.v.).

hakemei (Jap.). Lacquer technique in which brush marks are deliberately shown as a style of decoration.

hakudo (Jap.). "White bronze," composed of copper and nickel.

Hakuohô art. See JAPANESE ART.

half-binding. *Book.* A book with leather corners and leather back coming well over the side of the book is said to be half-bound. In three-quarter binding, the back leather covers more of the side, and the corners (q.v.) are larger. The term is obviously short for half-leather binding. The term is also used for any binding in which the covering of the spine and corners is different from the material covering the sides. Also used for the material itself. —H.E.S.

half circles. In Greek art, esp. pottery, half circles are used concentrically to make an ornamental pattern.

half distance point, half measuring point, half point of distance, half station point. See PERSPECTIVE.

418

half relief. See relief; relief sculpture.

half-timbered. *Arch.* Built of a timber frame, the spaces in between being filled in with masonry or with plastered laths.

Hallenkirche. See GERMAN ART.

Hallstatt art. See AUSTRIAN ART; PRE-HISTORIC ART.

Halmstadgruppen. See SCANDINAVIAN ART.

halo. Seen in oriental art as a nimbus (q.v.) back of the head and sometimes completely surrounding the figure. Said to be derived from the fact that the ancients were believed to have been able to see an aura emanating from the body of a holy person.   —J.A.M.

halveflossa. A Swedish technique which consists of a flat texture forming the background and the knots or tufts woven in to form the design. Both the loop knot and the cut knot are used.   —B.E.J.

hammer dressing. In masonry: Roughest description of dressing or tooling after scabbling.

Hammond organ. See MUSICAL INSTRUMENTS; electrical instruments.

han (Ch.). Flat jade ritual ornament in the shape of a cicada; placed on the tongue at time of burial.

Han art. See CHINESE ARTS.

hand. The texture or feel of a fabric, esp. of silk.

handcraft. Productive creative work done by hand, with the aid of simple tools and machines. (Note the new spelling, *handcraft,* now coming into general use by art educators and regarded as an improvement over *handicraft.*) Whitford and Winslow in *Dictionary of Education.*

hand tufted carpet. See carpet structures.

Han dynasty porcelain. See CERAMICS II.

haniwa (Jap.). Unique hollow pottery post-like forms representing human beings, animals and houses, which were apparently implanted around the exterior of ancient tumuli in Japan. Literary tradition explains them as humane substitutes for interment, alive, of wives, retainers, etc., in the tomb of the deceased. See JAPANESE ART.   —J.A.M.

hardening on. *Cer.* Low firing of underglaze decoration to remove oils before glazing. See CERAMICS I.

hare's fur glaze. Radiating glaze sometimes seen on Chinese pottery of the Sung dynasty, especially on Temmoku ware (q.v.).

harmika. See stupa; INDIAN ART.

harmonic. *Mus.* (1) An upper partial (see ACOUSTICS), frequently used in the pl. **harmonics.** (2) Relating to harmony.

harmonica. See MUSICAL INSTRUMENTS.

harmonic analysis. The analysis and measurement of the cross section of the structure of a tone in terms of the number of partials present, their distribution, the relative amount of energy in each, and their phase relationships.

This type of analysis has long been known in mathematics and physics but has not come into general use in music and psychology on account of the complicated nature of the measurement and, therefore, the general ignorance prevailing on the subject. Now, however, we have instruments which give us measures of precision and are great time-savers so that we can say that timbre is very satisfactorily harnessed for experimental work in the laboratory, and we can collect samples of sound waves in any form of music and submit them to exact measurement. The term harmonic analysis as here used with reference to the analysis of the cross section of a tone should be distinguished from the term harmonic analysis as it prevails in the treatment of musical harmony. In radio and in the recording of music, utilization of knowledge of the harmonic structure of sound plays a very important role.

There are three fundamental steps in the measurement: (1) the taking of an **oscillogram,** which is a large and detailed picture of the form of the sound wave; (2) the running of this wave form through an harmonic analyzer; and (3) the representation of the readings from the analyzer in a diagram called the **tone spectrum** (q.v.). The analyzer works like a very complicated calculating machine and delivers the results of the analysis of the wave form in terms of figures on dials, which show (a) which partials are present within a range of 40 or more, and (b) what per cent of energy of the whole tone comes from each of the partials. In physics we speak of the component elements of a rich tone **as partials,** calling the fundamental tone the first partial; whereas, in psychology and music, we speak of **overtones**, calling the second partial the first overtone and the first partial the fundamental. —C.E.S.

harmonic interval. See interval.

harmonic inversion. See inversion.

harmonic minor scale. See scales and modes.

harmonium. See · MUSICAL INSTRUMENTS.

harmonization in Jewish music. See JEWISH MUSIC.

harmony. (1) The representation of all opposed elements in a work of art in such a way as to become a pleasing unity. Since quite generally the task of art is to bring the distinct parts into a unified whole, or to demonstrate them as components of one unified law and thus to excite aesthetic satisfaction, harmony is the main requirement of every art.

But we must discriminate between this more general meaning and its more limited sense. The latter has been restricted to Greek art and to all art which is related to it, such as Hellenistic and Roman art, the Renaissance and classicism. The harmonic effect is realized in classic works of art because the different parts which are represented have become the parts of one idea or of an ideal whole. The resulting effect is that the whole may be seen immediately and easily, that the highest possible equilibrium is achieved, and that all lines are continuant and tending to return to their starting point. Only by showing these elements unmistakably clearly can there be harmony in the Greek and classic sense.

In order to achieve this harmonic pleasure certain rules and measures were set down in the so-called canons from the very beginning. On the basis of these canons the measurements and proportions of the human body were exactly fixed. One of the most famous and well known systems of proportion, of dividing the whole into pleasant parts, is the *Linea Aurea*. —A.J.S.

(2) *Mus.* Simultaneous sounding of several different tones; chord; system of relationships between chords to be applied in order to make successions of chords aesthetically meaningful in terms of the idiom chosen for the composition under consideration (see chord; idiom). Educationally: the discipline setting forth the principles of harmony. —E.K.

harp. See MUSICAL INSTRUMENTS.

harpsichord (Fr. *clavecin*, It. *arpsichordo*, *clavicembalo*). The precursor of the pianoforte. The strings were plucked by means of quills attached to "jacks". See MUSICAL INSTRUMENTS; mechanical instruments.

hashira-e (Jap.). *hashira*, pillar; *e*, painting; thus a pillar painting or a narrow panel to hang on a pillar. Generally applied to a long narrow form of Japanese print, ca. 28 in. x 5 in. —J.A.M.

hatchway, hatch. An opening in a deck, floor, or roof of a structure affording passage from one level to another.

haunch. Either of the parts of an arch at the sides of the crown between the crown and the springings.

Haviland china. See CERAMICS II.

hawksbeak. A Greek compound moulding based on a cavetto of which the fascia has become añ ovolo or a cyma reversa and the concave curve has been undercut and may or may not terminate in a short reverse curve at the bottom; when ornamented carries a Doric leaf pattern. —L.T.S.

hawthorn design. A pattern often seen on Chinese blue and white porcelain which is miscalled for the plum pattern.

head. (1) *Book.* The top of the book is described as the head. But a headpiece is ornament (in printing) at the top of the page commencing a chapter. (2) *Arch.* The lintel of an opening.

headband. *Book.* The silk or other band at the top and bottom of the back of a book. They are of two kinds, the one worked or made, the other simply stuck on, as it were. The former, besides being ornamental, is useful, but the latter is ornamental only. —H.E.S.

headdress. See COSTUME ART.

header. See bond-stone.

headers. In masonry: The name applied to stones, the lengths of which are 2/3 to 3/4 the thickness of the wall, laid transversely.

heading. In masonry: The vertical side of a stone perpendicular to the face.

heading joint. In masonry: The stratum of

mortar between the vertical surfaces of two adjacent stones.

hearth. *Arch.* The floor of a fireplace.

heat absorbing glass. See GLASS AND GLASS-MAKING.

heaume. Ancient spelling of helmet. See HERALDRY.

heavy ink technique. See CHINESE ARTS.

Hebrew theatre. See THEATRE.

heckelphon. See MUSICAL INSTRUMENTS.

Heian art. See JAPANESE ART.

heidatsu (Jap.). A style of decoration which makes use of thin sheet metal, especially gold or silver, cut into perforated patterns (which may also be engraved) and laid into lacquered surfaces. As the lacquer hardened the decoration became part of the surface itself.
—J.A.M.

heien (Jap.). A term indicating "level distance" in a painting; mountains depicted as seen across water.

height line. See PERSPECTIVE.

Heimatkunst. See Biedermeier.

Helladic architecture. See AEGEAN ARCHITECTURE.

HELLENIC ART developed in the Greek peninsula, on the islands of the Aegean, and on the shores of Asia Minor in the first millennium B.C. Greek colonists carried it to Southern Italy, Sicily, North Africa, Southern France and Spain as well as to the Balkans and the Crimea. In the 3rd and 4th cent. B.C. Alexander the Great and his successors extended the influence of Greek art to Syria, Egypt, Mesopotamia, Iran, and India. Hellenic art supplied the foundations for Roman and Byzantine art; as a normative expression of the humanistic idea it has remained a living force in the later development of European and American culture.

The history of Hellenic art may be divided into six major phases: Proto-Geometric, 1100-900 B.C.; Geometric, 900-700 B.C.; Orientalizing, 700-600 B.C.; Archaic, 600-500 B.C.; Classical, 500-300 B.C.; and Hellenistic, 300-100 B.C. The transition from Greek to Roman art occurs in the 1st cent. B.C. and 1st cent. A.D.

The origin of Hellenic art has long been a subject of controversy. When Mycenaean art was discovered, many scholars tended to emphasize the importance of Mycenaean elements for the formative stage of Hellenic art. Others regarded the Dorian invasion (ca. 1100) as a decisive event and the Dorians as the originators of the new Geometric art. Others yet observed that many Geometric styles developed in the Mediterranean area during the period of migrations (13th—9th cent. B.C.) and regarded the Greek Geometric style as one special type of this general Mediterranean style of the period.

Although the excavations in Athens (Kübler and Kraiker, *Kerameikos,* 1939; O. Broneer, *Hesperia,* 8, 1939, 416) illustrate the transition from late Mycenaean to the earliest Hellenic style, the birth of Greek art remains miraculous. Athens was never occupied by the Dorians; the Dorian invasion cannot, therefore, be directly responsible. Yet the change from the debased, de-naturalized late Mycenaean style to the crystalline system of the Proto-Geometric signifies a change of fundamental principles. Despite the modest character of the Proto-Geometric vases and the simplicity of decorative elements the Proto-Geometric style already partakes of that lucid logic that is a fundamental trait of Hellenic art. In contrast to the dynamic movement of the Minoan and Mycenaean ornament, the new style is dominated by tectonic order, by rhythmic spacing of decoratice elements, by close relation between the structural form of the vase and the horizontal zones of ornament.

Geometric. "Geometric" elements of decoration such as circles, parallel lines, triangles, meanders, and hour glasses are found in many arts. What distinguishes the Greek "Geometric" style is the completely abstract, mathematical character of the underlying compositional system and the perfection of draftsmanship characterized by the "tyranny of compass and ruler" (Payne). The Greek artists knew at all times how to concentrate upon a few clearly limited problems which they pursued with single-minded devotion until all possibilities of the approach were exhausted. They were really the first to recognize artistic problems and to conceive of art as a rational activity. Yet Greek art expresses the concept that art reflects an objective pre-established order of the universe. The Geometric period symbolizes this order by a static geometric system of abstract forms; the Orientalizing, by its sequences of monsters, animals, and plants; the Archaic through automatic angular movement expressed by human beings; the Classical through the organic flow of movement again expressed through human beings; and the Hellenistic through a vast variety of naturalistic rhythmic motions that pervade the entire realm of nature. Two-dimensional geometry is the most striking manifestation of early Hellenic art, but no less important is the feeling for three-dimensional structure displayed in the shapes of the Geometric vases. Dominating the entire Greek art is the absolute conviction that three-dimensional structure is the true essence of all things. In spite of their scientific inquiries into the nature of optics and their great knowledge of the phenomena of color and light, the Greeks never completely entrusted themselves to the optic vision. This remained the prerogative of the modern cycle of art (15th to 19th cent. W.M. Ivins, *On the Rationalization of Sight*, 1938).

Painted pottery is the leading art of the Geometric period. The shape of the vase and its painted surface are in complete harmony. The decorators seek to visualize the structure of the vase. As the vase is built up of added rings so is the ornament built up in uniform, horizontal zones. The two-handled jars (*amphorae*) and the huge mixing bowls (craters) were placed on tombs or in sacret precincts. In Athens ("Dipylon" vases), Corinth, Thera, and the Peloponnesus the vases are decorated with circles, parallel lines, triangles, and meanders drawn with wiry precision. In the Eastern islands, in Crete, and in Asia Minor connected circles, spirals, parallel lines prevail; the composition is looser, the draftsmanship broader. Animals and men are represented in the developed Geometric style. At first they are displayed in uniform rows that convey no definite meaning. Later, they are organized in simple compositions with recognizable types of subject matter such as battles on land and sea, chariot races, dances, and the solemn lament for the dead. The figures, mere black silhouettes, are composed of geometric forms and serve as a symbolic shorthand transcribing but not reflecting reality. In size and arrangement they are treated exactly like the geometric ornaments and do not break the rigid compositional divisions.

Geometric sculpture features small bronzes and terra cottas of birds, horses, and bulls (Delphi, Olympia) which are quite similar to the bronze figurines of the Early Eurasian Iron Age (Hallstatt). The few human figur-

ines, which include some groups (dance, Olympia), are loosely constructed and tentative, and only the best of the animal groups approach the tectonic clarity of vase decoration (mare and foal, Olympia; fawn, Boston; stag and dogs, Olympia). Cf. V. Mueller, *Antike Plastik in Griechenland*, 1929, W. Lamb, *Greek Bronzes*, 1929.

The architecture of the Geometric Age is as yet imperfectly known. House foundations show rather irregular plans (Crete, Eleusis, Thermos, Olympia, Samos). Temples are either long narrow halls or short, almost square rooms (*Dreros*). The central column or the central row of supports inside seems a survival from Minoan architecture. Terra cotta models of buildings from Argos and Perachora have columns placed in front of a small rectangular cella and a (prostyle) high pitched roof. (Payne, *Perachora*, 1940). Some knowledge of stone building survived from Mycenaean times but unbaked brick and wood are the important materials. Altogether these Geometric buildings must be visualized as rustic sheds and huts, perhaps decorated with painting or woodwork; they do not show the definite stylistic system of vase painting.

Orientalizing. The Greek feudal system underwent a transformation toward an urban, commercial culture. The adoption of the Phoenician alphabet led to literacy. The cosmogony, the science, and the law codes of the Near East began to exercise considerable influence upon Greek thought. Hesiod interpreted the universe in terms of Oriental hierarchies of gods and monsters. He opposed the feudal ideal of noble birth, physical strength and undaunted courage with a glorification of justice and equality as the divine foundations of human society. The lyrics of Alcman portray a rich new world in which real events enter the realm of mythological fancy. And as Greek mythology achieved a more grandiose and universal quality through the influence of Oriental cosmology, Greek art also gained a sense of powerful grandeur, when it was brought in contact with the colossal creations of the Near East and later of Egypt. The symbolic transcription of mythological reality was discarded in favor of representation. Vase-painting displays in large panels or friezes pictures of full-blooded monsters, animals, and occasionally mythological subjects (Cretan, Proto-Corinthian, Proto-Attic, Melian). The subordination of surface decoration to the structure of the vase is relaxed. The ornamental vocabulary changes from static geometric motifs to highly stylized, floral arabesques. The figures, though still two-dimensional and conceptual, show a physical reality which is expressed by bulky forms, ornamentalized details, and symbolic polychromy. The luxurious splendor of painting is restrained and systemized by the end of the period, in the miniaturistic battles and friezes of the Chigi Vase (Proto-Corinthian) or in the grand, sculpturesque chariot and lion of the Pyraeus Amphora (Proto-Attic). And the first examples of large-scale painting appear (metopes Thermos).

Sculpture was eminently suited to express the massive physical power that appeared to the artists as the fundamental feature of "reality". This explains the rise of monumental sculpture in stone. Draped figures, standing and seated (Prinia; Auxerre-Louvre; "Hera", Samos; Nikandre, Delos) are fashioned after Near Eastern types and the nude walking youths follow Egyptian models. The earliest reliefs depict the same rows of riders, monsters, and animals as the Orientalizing vases (Prinia, Vrocastro). In the marble youths from Attica (Dipylon head; Met. Mus., N. Y.; Sunion) there is a synthesis of Geometric order and Orientalizing mass. They represent a generalized human ideal, as opposed to the specific religious social concepts expressed by the sculpture of the Near East and Egypt. They surpass their Egyptian prototypes in tension of forms and energy of movement; and their Oriental models in systematic organization and correlation of forms. This formative, "Daedalic" style, is represented, with local variations, throughout Greece by large stone-images and small bronzes, ivories, and terra cottas. Cf. H. Payne, *Necrocorinthia*, 1932, R. Jenkins, *Daedalica*, 1936, P. Knoblauch, *Studien*, 1936, F. R. Grace, *AJA* 46, 1942, 341 ff.

The development of the Doric and the Ionic orders in architecture parallels the development of definite types in sculpture. The temples gain in substance and volume, and their proportions widen. There is an initial use of stone rather than wood, although a combination of wooden structure and terra cotta revetment remains popular far into the archaic period. During the early phase the buildings were probably burdened with floral and figurative motifs. Traces of this experimentation appear in the door-sills of the temple in Prinia, and in the discarded decorations from Thermos and Calydon. The brief use of the luxurious Aeolic palm-capitals derived from Syria (Megiddo) indicates the same tendency (Neandria). Order and restraint predominate by the end of 7th cent. The Doric order has developed its essential features (Tiryns; Heraeum, Olympia; Heraeum, Argos); the Ionic is soon to follow. A number of temples without porches, (Prinia; Gortyn; Demeter, Selinus) particularly in Crete, represent perhaps an older type.

Archaic. In contrast to the experimental and revolutionary character of the Orientalizing period, the archaic period (6th cent. B.C.) is a time of steady progress toward humanization and refinement. As the solemn grandeur of Solon's poetry is followed by the joyous refinement of Anacreon's so is the massive strength of early archaic sculpture replaced by a courtly refinement in the **Peisistratid era.** Archaic painting and sculpture is unsurpassed in beauty of the individual form, feeling for material and in its flawless craftsmanship. Sculpture emerges as the leading form of artistic expression in Greek culture. In the numerous statues of youths and maidens (esp. Acropolis, Athens; Argos; Delphi; Corinth (Tenea); Samos; Miletus) and in the architectural sculpture of friezes, metopes, and pediments (Korfu; Acropolis, Athens; Assus; Selinus; treasuries of the Syracusans, Siphnians, and Athenians in Delphi, of Megarrans in Olympia; of Artemisium, Ephesus) the parts of the human figure are transformed from a linear ornamentalism to a sculptural stylization. The growing superficial naturalism of details does not change the basic structure of the figures which is still abstract. The generalized expression of austerity prevalent in the early archaic period is differentiated into a number of typical expressions dictated by the conventions of an aristocratic ideal; they range from exaggerated friendliness (goddess, Berlin), lusty good nature (calf bearer, Athens), modest confidence (head Rayet, Copenhagen), to courtly politeness (many Korai, Acropolis; pedimental group from Eretria). The interest in physical beauty far outweighs any concern for emotion or intellect.

Archaic vase-painting is an illustrative art always conscious of its decorative function. Nearly all Greek mythology is represented, and gradually scenes of sports, dances, concerts, dinners, and even of business and trade rival the earlier subject matter. At first the painters tell their stories with epic uniformity; then, attending the birth of Greek drama, dramatic concentration becomes an important concern. Schools of vase painting flourish in Sparta, Corinth, Chalcis, and Ionia ("Caeretan" hydriae), but ultimately a brilliant series of draftsmen headed by Exekias wins the artistic leadership for the black-figure style of Athens (J.D. Beazley, *Attic Black-Figure,* 1929). The Attic red-figure technique (530 B.C.) alters that character of vase-decoration by introducing foreshortening which gives to the figures a space of their own. Clear compositions, beauty and economy of lines, and ornamentalization of details place the red-figure painters Epictetus, Euphronios, and Euthymides among the greatest outline draftsmen of all times.

Archaic architecture amplifies and elaborates the types created in the Orientalizing period. The heavy proportions of early archaic are gradually lightened; capitals and profiles are made more elastic and tense. The different kinds of ornament are brought into definite relation with the structural system. Color, which dominated the buildings with terra cotta revetments, is used to enliven the ornament in stone and marble buildings and to emphasize parts that are structurally important. The coherence of archaic temples reflects the growth of systematic rational inquiry into relations and proportions. Definite mathematical ratios as well as technical advice on problems of construction were probably included in the publications of the designs. The typical plan of the Greek temple now features an entrance porch (*pronaos*), the main chamber containing the image (*cella, naos*), and often a room in the rear (*opisthodomos*). This structure was surrounded by a colonnade (*peristasis*). A sloping roof covers the entire building. The cella is sometimes divided into nave and aisles by two inner colonnades. Notable Doric examples were found in Corfu, Thermos, Selinus ("C"), Sele (Hera), Paestum ("Basilica", "Ceres"), Athens (Old Athena), Cyrene (Apollo), Corinth (Apollo), Sunium, Assus, and Delphi. Huge Ionic temples were erected in Ephesus by Chersiphron and Metagenes and in Samos by Rhoicus; they include a double colonnade (*dipteros*). The subordination of ornament and sculptural adornment to the tectonic elements and the exacting finish of every part bestow a peculiar purity and strength upon these temples.

Classical. The foundations of the entire Greek culture undergo a change in the transition from the archaic to the Classical period. Human reason is regarded capable of finding *a priori* the nature of reality. Man and the universe are conceived in a divine order ruled by rational and lawful deities. Characterized by free will and rationality, the new human ideal is projected into the forms of traditional mythology where the gods and mythical heroes typify human attitudes in normal and ethical problems. The conflict of the tragic hero with the divine order is a problem of universal validity. The political recognition of the belief in man is reflected by the rise of democracy. The power of self-analysis is shown by the description of the war with Persia as a conflict of two different ways of life. Rational idealization thus constitutes the basis of Classical thought.

Greek drama and sculpture lead the way, while in philosophy, science, and painting the change is more gradual. Of the two leading arts drama develops a greater emotional insight, but sculpture makes an epochal advance in structure that remained unrivaled until the advent of modern abstract art. In archaic art the composition of statues was based on semi-abstract rhythms. The advance toward verisimilitude was limited to external appearances . In Classical art, the statue expresses an equilibrium of organic motions affecting every part of the body. Dynamic interrelation replaces static correlation. The relation of the statue to space undergoes a similar change. The archaic statue is like a rectangular pillar, and all the major forms are developed within the four planes. Although the four planes are still ideally retained in the classical statue and the mass of the body is roughly parallel to the frontal plane, the lower part and the head and shoulder are turned in rounded movements. The expression of unified movement has replaced the accentuation of the four different views.

The Classical period is the age of great artistic personalities. Unfortunately, the style of the greatest artists—Phidias, Polycleitus, Myron in the 5th cent., Scopas, Timotheos, Praxiteles, Bryaxis, and Lysippus—in the fourth—must be recognized from fragments, reflections, and Roman copies, while other masters, equally famous, remain phantoms. The marble statue of a boy by Critios, the magnificent Victory of Paeonius, possibly the Hermes of Praxiteles (doubtful, cf. *AJA* 1931) are among the few Classical sculptures whose authors are known. We owe our knowledge of Classical standards to anonymous but great originals; the bronze statue of bearded god from Cape Artemisium, easily the grandest of all Early Classical sculptures; the austere charioteer from Delphi; the poetic relief of the Ludovisi Throne; and for the later Classical sculpture the bronze boy from Marathon, the Demeter from Cnidus, the pensive head of Aphrodite (Boston), and a vigorous and brutal portrait of a boxer from Olympia. Yet we could not have traced the development of Classical art, had the architectural sculpture been lost. Aegina (480), Olympia (460), Parthenon, Athens (448-432), Hephaestium, Athens (440), Erechtheum, Athens (420-405), Nike Balustrade, Athens (405), the Nereid Monument, Xanthus (ca.400) and a number of unattached pedimental sculptures and acroteria (Niobids, Rome and Copenhagen) reveal to us the harmony of lofty spirit. The sculptures from Tegea (380), Epidaurus (360), and the Mausoleum of Halicarnassus display the increased laxity of form and complexity of movement that distinguish later Classical art. Numerous votive and sepulchral reliefs round out the picture.

Classical art is often praised for its naturalism or, conversely, for its idealism. Classical sculpture, although humanized, represents a general type. The statues are expressions of the universal order in human form; they are a perfect harmony of physical beauty, cosmic validity, and ethical greatness. Formally as well as psychologically, they express not the accidental appearance but the underlying principles of the organic universe moved by eternal laws. The High Classic age of Phidias insists upon the enduring states of existence; the Later Classic explores the contrasts of restful contemplation and emotional action.

Classical architecture is infused with a sense of organic growth and equilibrium; but its proportions are perfected by mathematical or geometric formulae. For the Doric order, the temple of Zeus in Olympia, built by Libon (456) is the first great Classical building. A complex of fine classic temples is concentrated on the Acropolis of Athens reconstructed under the leadership of Pericles (450-430). As their entrance, Mnesicles designed a festive two-winged gate, the Propylaea (437-432). Crowning the Acropolis is the most perfect Doric temple in the world, the Parthenon, built by Ictinus and decorated with sculpture after designs by Phidias; a work in which the smallest form vibrates with musical life. Compared to their archaic predecessors the Ionic temples of Athena Nike (425 ?) and Athena and Erechtheus are small, almost fragile expressions of a poetic grace which is enhanced by their pure, rhyth-

mic ornaments. Ictinus also designed the Mystery Hall (Telesterion) in Eleusis and a temple of unusual plan in Phigalia, while another great but anonymous architect designed the Hephaestium in Athens and a temple in Sunium (W.B. Dinsmoor, *Hesperia* suppl. T, 1941). The Doric and Ionic orders had symbolized organic life through abstract and semi-abstract forms. Later Classical architects portray organic growth more literally by means of the acanthus ornament and other forms adopted from actual plants. The popular Corinthian order (Choregic monument of Lysicrates, 334 B.C.) in which the capital consists of vegetable forms, is the last order of Classical architecture. The architects use its rich, natural forms in the interior (Athena, Tegea, by Scopas; Tholos, Epidaurus, by the Younger Polycleitus) reserving the traditional Doric for the façade. The Early Classical temples are unified by a consistent use of the Doric order. These later temples, however, separate the luxurious complex life of the interior structure from the restrained appearance of the exterior, a principle which applies equally to much fourth century sculpture. The end of Classical architecture coincides with the **Ionic Renaissance** championed by the architect Pytheos (Maussoleum of Halicarnassus, 350 and Temple of Athena, Priene, 334); he abandons the pursuit of complex refinement and aims to make his structures dominate their surroundings through colossal scale, largeness of detail, and accentuation of height.

The Early Classical period boasts a galaxy of draftsmen. Without the vase-paintings by Kleophrades Painter (Epictetus), by the "Berlin Painter", the "Pan Painter" by the "Pistoexenos Painter", by Brygos and Douris we could never appreciate the varied aspects of this period. Their complicated compositions and isolated figures of solitary grandeur rival the pediments of Olympia. The subjects range from the loftiest myth to the aftermath of a drinking bout. The best vase painters parallel and follow the lead of sculpture; others seek to emulate the advance of painting ("Niobid Painter") and are confronted with a dilemma: either deny the tectonic character of the vase altogether, introduce color, and make miniature painting on vases, or retain the red-figure technique, the decorative arrangement, and make imperfect imitations. The problem was never solved. The best High Classical draftsmen reject ambitious subject matter to draw quiet groups of two and three figures on vases with white ground, filling the outlines with a few flat colors (Achilles Painter). Thereafter vase-painting drifts into mediocrity.

Classical painting explores for the first time in Greek history problems connected with the optic illusion: foreshortening, perspective, local color, and light. Polygnotus (ca.480-440), "the painter of ethos", is extolled by literary sources as an exponent of universal, tragic conflicts, who unified his vast compositions by psychological rather than formal relations. Yet he also broke the architectural system of frieze-like zones, by adopting a symbolic high space in which the figures were grouped with reference to isolated landscape elements. Apollodorus (460-420), Zeuxis (430-390), and Parrhasios (430-?) are credited with the fundamental inventions in the use of local color, light, and three-dimensional construction of figures. Finally ,the proverbial Apelles (370-320) is thought to have developed a convincing and refined coloristic system for the rendering of textures. His flowing sensitive rhythm of composition harmonized those currents of restrained sentiment and emotion that unite gods and men in a self-sufficient world of their own. Although no work of these painters has survived, the transition from the symbolic, two-dimensional reality of archaic to a direct reflection of reality based on optic illusion can be surmised from literary evidence; reflections in vase painting and later Roman (Pompeian) copies help to complete this theoretical reconstruction. They prove beyond any doubt that the Greeks stopped short of a unified visual illusion. Thus individual figures and objects show correct foreshortening and are often grouped in approximate perspective but never according to a unified scientific perspective. Abstract light and shadow are used to model figures and objects. The coloristic scheme employed is highly differentiated but does not present a consistent application of local color. Objects and figures always retain a sculptural coherence and the color is never allowed to dissolve their outlines. The space is a limited, stage-like setting and there is no attempt to suggest or characterize atmospheric effects. The magnificent effect of the Theseus and the Minotaur, of Achilles and Briseis, of The Battle of Alexander is created by the rhythmic compositional arrangement, by free and easy movement of heroic bodies, and by the lofty psychological interpretation. In consummate rendering of texture and in emphatic expressive strength the painting of the fourth century forged ahead of the contemporary sculpture. Indeed, the sculptor Praxiteles relied upon the painter Nikias to give the finer animation to his statues. We can appreciate the richness and vitality of such painted sculpture in the magnificent "Alexander Sarcophagus" from Sidon.

Hellenistic. Geographical horizons expanded and scientific thought quickened in the age of Alexander, but Hellenism does not initiate a new cycle. It is a period of intellectual dispersion and specialization. The Classical concept of an orderly, rational universe is maintained. But the concrete character of the Classic universe that was due to the anthropomorphic character of its ethic religious concepts, is lost. The variety of types in architecture, and of subject matter in sculpture and painting is enormously increased; but this gain is nullified by the loss of intensity which the Classic period achieved by concentrating all its thought and emotions in a few clearly defined types. Art becomes secularized. Hellenistic religious ideals are too abstract to be embodied convincingly in human form, or to be confined residents of narrow temples. Civic architecture, portraiture, genre, and landscape painting are the leading artistic expressions of the new world. Scientific observation aids sculptors to master external appearances and to portray a variety of psychological effects. The individual with his evanescent moods, his immediate physical and emotional reality, dominates the stage. But in contrast to modern realism even the late Greeks were never satisfied with the representation of purely external appearance; like the "Characters" of Theophrastus Hellenistic sculptures always suggest a typical element or experience of the individual. The powerful portraits of Hellenistic Kings from Alexander to Mithridates share an element of superhuman vigor and dynamic power. The Demosthenes, outwardly realistic, stands for the struggle of body and spirit, the Girl of Anzio, for the self-oblivious piety of an adolescent, the Lacoon for heroism before death. The Classical world found its subject matter within itself; the subjects of the Hellenistic world are projected into monsters and barbarians (Pergamon Frieze and the "Large" and "Small" Gauls), or into the world of lower mythology to express very human experiences from the healthy sleep of a rugged peasant (Faun Barberini) to the sentimental petting of courtly lovers ("Invitation to dance", "Eros and Psyche"). Rather than humanize ethical laws Hellenistic art objectifies individual emotions. The abstract ideology of the new world is expressed in personifications and allegories, ("Tyche of Antioch", 300 B.C.) but rarely is the gap between the concept and its embodiment bridged so successfully as in the Victory from Samothrace (ca. 200 B.C.) who sails forth in a jubilant sweep.

Hellenistic painting must also be reconstructed from Roman copies. It was a suitable medium in which to represent the expanded concept of the universe. Space construction was deepened and unified, although the visual illusion was not complete. The representation of light was improved. And the new relation of man and nature was expressed in landscapes which subordinated man to nature (Odyssey, Rome; mosaics, Palermo). The representation of animals, of still life, and of peculiar ethnic types runs parallel to the specialized natural and geographic studies (Dove mosaic, Pergamon). Copies of the Finding of Telephus, of Medea and Her Children show the psychological individualization as it is applied to the mythological sphere; the mosaics of Dioscurides illustrate the bristling vivacity of genre.

The Classical architects had conceived each building as a separate organic unit; Hellenistic architects, accustomed to planning new cities and constructing vast residences, think in terms of architectural complexes (Cos, Pergamon, Antioch, Seleucia, Magnesia). The interest in magnitude overshadows the attention to detail in the temples of Cossutius (Zeus, Athens, 175 B.C.) and Hermogenes (Artemis, Magnesia, ca. 140 B.C.) or in the great Altar of Pergamon (180 B.C.). Their creative efforts are most clearly manifested in secular or semi-secular buildings such as public walks (colonnades in Priene, Pergamon, and Athens), market places, assembly halls (Miletus), libraries (Pergamon), palaces, and ultimately in villas and residential houses. Just as much of Hellenistic sculpture is conceived with reference to a definite architectural setting, so are many Hellenistic buildings planned with reference to other buildings, to architectural zones, and finally to landscape. The contact with the non-Greek architecture of Egypt, Syria, and Mesopotamia influenced the production of new types of buildings (sanctuaries of Egyptian and Oriental gods) and increased the ornamental vocabulary. Conversely, the Greek orders spread into Persia, Bactria, and India. The rhythmic coherence of ornament yields to

naturalistic verisimilitude; animal forms join the vegetable motifs. Often the ornaments are conceived as realistic replicas of the actual cult objects (bucrania, garlands, sacrificial implements). Within each building, the objective relation of the tectonic elements comes to mean less than their optic appearance.

It has been argued that Roman art is actually just another phase of the Hellenistic; assuredly the former would have been impossible without the latter. Yet, by the end of the 2d cent. B. C. the unity of Hellenistic art has broken down into a multitude of regional developments. A few migrating artists and workshops showed technical competence; but their products cannot conceal the lack of common aims and ideas; local arts of the Greek lands deteriorated rapidly. Rome restored the political and economic foundations of art and supplied the leading ideas for a fresh start.

Phoenix-like, Greek art continues to provide new inspirations for posterity, because it has encompassed so many eternally human interests, desires, emotions and ideas. In its statues and temples it had accomplished a balance of nature and ideal, of reason and belief, and of emotion and restraint. Greek art is a triumphant affirmation of faith in man as a spectator of the universe and as master of his fate. See J. D. Beazley and B. Ashmole, *Greek Sculpture and Painting*, 1932; L. Curtius, *Griech. Kunst*, 1938; H. Payne, *Necrocorinthia*, 1931 and *Greek Sculpture on the Acropolis*, 1936; E. Buschor, *Greek Vase Painting*, 1922 and *Griech. Vasen*, 1940; G. Richter, *Greek Sculptors and Sculpture*, 1930; Ch. Picard, *Manuel d'archeologie* I, 1935; M. Bunim, *Perspective Ancient and Medieval*, 1940; M. Swindler, *Ancient Painting*, 1929; A. W. Lawrence, *Class. Greek Sculpture*, 1929 and *Later Greek Sculpture*, 1927; D. S. Robertson, *Handbook of Greek and Roman Archit.*, 1929; W. J. Anderson, R. P. Spiers, W. B. Dinsmoor, *The Architecture of Ancient Greece*, 1927; T. B. L. Webster, *Greek Art and Literature*, 1939.

—G.M.A.H.

helm. See HERALDRY.

helmet. See HERALDRY.

hemi-demi-semi-quaver. See NOTATION.

Hepplewhite. See FURNITURE.

Heracles (L. Hercules). The leading pioneer hero of the Greeks, son of Zeus and the mortal Alcmena, who by sheer strength overcame many natural and human obstacles during his spectacular career, and eventually was received into Olympus as a demigod. He was usually represented wearing a lionskin and armed with a bow and club. His exploits were extensively treated by 6th and 5th cent. B. C., Greek vase painters, and appeared in architectural sculpture at Delphi (Athenian Treasury), Olympia (Temple of Zeus), Athens (Temple of Hephaestus), and in independent sculpture by Myron, Scopas, Lysippus, Glycon, etc. Pollaiuolo's painting of Hercules strangling Antaeus, the earth giant, gives a spirited representation of him. In post classical sculpture he has been pictured by Bologna, Bandinelli, Pollaiuolo, Canova, Thorvaldsen, Manship, and Bourdelle.   —W.R.A.

HERALDRY. The art of heraldry includes the designing and authenticating of armorial bearings or coats-of-arms and the preparation of their blazonry, their verbal description in correct heraldic language.

From the earliest times distinguishing emblems and symbolic devices have been worn by individuals and groups in battle, but the essential difference between such symbols and heraldry as now known is the basic hereditary feature of the latter. Present heraldry began in the 12th cent. at the time of the Third Crusade when international participation, combined with the advent of the cylindrical helmet covering the whole face, made identifying marks necessary for recognition in combat, so each knight painted an individual sign on his shield. Later the same device was embroidered on the surcoat worn for protection over his polished armor, from which the term **coat-of-arms** originated. The device was also engraved on the owner's seal used on official documents, whence the study of **sphragistics** (q.v.). These earliest arms, assumed at will by the bearers, were simple bands of color or a single emblem on the shield, often with no symbolic meaning. They were recognized as family property and sons would adopt the same design with a change of color or some added mark of cadency. New grants of arms and judgments of dispute were made by the Kings until 1464 when the Heralds' College was established for designing and granting armorial bearings, together with tracing and preserving genealogies, which it has done from that time to the present.

The emblems pictured on the shield as "charges" came from many sources. Besides those chosen without significance one group includes those which symbolize some valorous deed or momentous event in the life of the original owners, the story often forgotten by his descendants. Another large group is that of **canting arms** or **armes parlantes**, sometimes called **allusive arms**, which are puns of the rebus type on the owners' names. These are sometimes very evident, sometimes far-fetched, sometimes obscure.

After the Crusades many changed their coats-of-arms, replacing some charge of minor significance with a symbol indicating their participation in the Holy War. The most common charge of this type is some form of the cross, of which over 400 varieties have been listed and a score or more are in very general use, such as the cross anchory, cross botony, cross crosslet, cross crosslet fitchee, cross patée, cross moline, cross passion, cross raguly, cross voided. Other Crusade charges include Saracen heads, escallops, coultraps, scimitars and water bougets.

The term **coat-of-arms** can refer either to the shield only, or to the shield and crest, or to the assembly of shield, helmet, torse, mantling, crest and motto, with supporters when granted, all of which together is called the **achievement.** The most important item is **shield** or **escutcheon.** Its shape has nothing to do with the coat-of-arms and is not specified in the blazonry but is entirely a matter with the designer. From the position of the bearer of the shield the side on his right is called the **dexter side** and that on his left the **sinister side.** The arms of unmarried ladies are emblazoned on a lozenge shape and those of churchmen on a vesica.

The **helmet** or **helm,** anciently spelled *heaume,* has changed shape through the centuries from the cylindrical or stovepipe form supported by the head to the type with flanged base supported on the shoulders. The designer must stay in period and not put a 13th cent. helm on a 15th cent. shield. The royal helm is drawn affronté with visor up and the esquire's or gentleman's in profile, closed. To aid in fitting the crest many good designers turn it to a three-quarters position.

The **torse** or **wreath** is a ring of twisted cloth on top of the helmet, covering the joint between helm and crest. It is always drawn with six twists and of the first two colors of the shield. In certain cases a coronet or a **cap of maintenance** is specified in place of a wreath.

The **mantling** is an ornamental flourish issuing from under the torse, originating probably from the cloth worn over the helmet to keep the back of the knight's neck from getting sunburned. It again has nothing to do with the **grant of arms** but is purely the artist's fancy and may be elaborated or omitted at will. When emblazoned in color the first two colors of the shield are used.

The **crest** is a specified part of the arms. Starting originally as a device of molded leather or carved wood worn on top of the helmet to identify the bearer in battle it later became a more elaborate ceremonial headdress in pageants and tournaments. Still later when armor was no longer worn it became only a part of the design in so-called **paper heraldry** and many crests were designed that could not have been worn. The careless misuse of the word *crest* to mean coat-of-arms is quite inexcusable.

The **motto**, usually in Latin or Norman French and generally placed on a ribbon below the shield, is a word or short phrase expressing some lofty sentiment or quality of the owner, now and then boastful, sometimes canting, oftener dedicatory. The war cry or *cri de guerre* was an early form, even earlier than heraldry itself.

Supporters are animate figures placed one on each side of the shield. In general their use is restricted to the arms of royalty and those of state and municipal corporations.

The **tinctures** include three classes of coverings used on shields, the metals, the colors and the furs. The metals are gold and silver, in heraldic language **or** and **argent**. The usual colors are **gules** (red), **azure** (blue), **vert** (green), **purpure** (purple), and **sable** (black). The commonest furs are **ermine** with black tails on a white ground and **vair**, alternating blue and white shapes representing squirrel pelts.

When a charge is shown in its natural color, which may but need not be other than one of the heraldic colors, it is said to be *proper* and may be charged on any tincture.

Color symbols. When arms are drawn or engraved in black and white a universal standard system of line symbols is used to designate the colors. Red is indicated by vertical linings, blue by horizontal, green by diagonals from dexter chief to sinister base, purple from sinister chief to dexter base and sable by crossed vertical and horizontal. Gold is represented by dots and silver is left blank.

Charges. The surface of the shield is covered with one of the tinctures, upon which **field** is superposed one or more **charges** of another tincture. The first rule of heraldry is that a color must not be superposed on another color, nor a metal on a metal nor a fur on a fur. Thus a red lion could not be shown on a blue field but could be placed on a gold or silver or ermine field. Sable, however, while classed as a color, is not subject to this rule but may be charged either on a color or a metal. It is often used to represent iron objects.

The **ordinaries** are the oldest and most frequently used of all the charges. Originating no doubt from bands placed across the shield to strengthen it, they form most effective and legible distinguishing marks. They include the **chief**, a band covering the upper third of the shield; the **fesse**, a broad horizontal band across the middle point; the **pale**, a broad vertical band down the middle, the **bend**, a diagonal band from dexter chief to sinister base; the **bend sinister**, from sinister chief to dexter base (rarely used); the **cross**, a combination of fesse and pale; the **saltire** or St. Andrew's cross, a combination of bend and bend sinister; the **chevron**, formed of the lower part of the saltire; the **pall**, the **quarter** and the **gyron**.

Diminutives are narrower bands running in the same direction as the corresponding ordinaries. Thus the diminutive of the **pale** is a pallet, of the fess a **bar**, of the bend a bendlet, of the chevron a chevronel. (Since the bar is a horizontal stripe, and not used singly, there is no such thing as a "bar sinister", in spite of the persistent use of that term by fiction writers.)

The name **subordinaries** is given to a group of charges including the **canton**, a square about 1/5 the width of the shield in the dexter chief; the **inescutcheon**, a small shield in the middle of the large one; the **pile**, the **bordure**, and the **tressure**.

Parted coats. The shield may be divided in various ways giving two tinctures in the field. If divided vertically it is *party per pale*. Similarly it may be divided per fesse, per bend, per chevron, quarterly, saltirewise and gyronny.

Partition lines. Lines of division and edges of ordinaries may be straight or in one of several patterns, as wavy, indented, invecked, engrailed, etc.

Common charges. In addition to the ordinaries there are literally hundreds of devices known as common charges which are superposed either on the field or the ordinary, or both. They may be divided broadly into animate and inanimate classes, the former including animals, birds, fishes, human figures, monsters and parts of each. Single animals must always face the dexter side (except when affronté). Charges may have any tincture, but the rule against putting color to color or metal to metal must be remembered.

The lion is by far the most popular animal charge and the position **rampant** with one foot on the ground and three in the air the commonest pose. Other positions, *salient, passant, statant, sejant, couchant* and *dormant* are seen occasionally. Normally both body and head are in profile, if the head is turned to look directly at the reader he is said to be **guardant** and if looking behind, **regardant.**

The stag is another popular charge and it requires another set of words to describe his positions. If walking, with three feet on the ground he is not **passant** but **trippant** and if looking at the reader not *guardant* but **at gaze.** The boar, the bear, the bull, the horse and a score of other animals are found as charges. Heads of animals, erased, couped or cabossed are quite common. Of birds the eagle *displayed* is best known for its use in the arms of the United States and other countries. The martlet, a swallow with beak and legs cut off is a well-known charge. The dolphin is the commonest marine charge. Fabulous animals called *monsters,* as the griffin, the dragon, the wyvern and the cockatrice are not uncommon.

The inanimate classification covers everything in the vegetable kingdom, astronomical charges and hundreds of traditional artifacts. In the decadent period of the 17th-19th cents. it was made to include such objects as locomotives, steamships, bridges and buildings, now considered as very bad heraldry.

Blazonry. To blazon an achievement is to describe it accurately in words and a blazon is this verbal description. To **emblazon,** however, means to paint the arms in full color on paper or other surface. A designer who is asked to use a coat-of-arms in a design would much prefer to have the blazonry given him than a painting or drawing of the arms, which would be only another artist's rendering of it. The good designer knows that heraldry is like etiquette in that one must not make a mistake in it. He not only knows the vocabulary but will avoid any incongruities or anachronisms and should always produce a fine piece of design, sometimes even achieving a work of art.

In the layman's study of heraldry, aside from the appreciation of the beauty of a well-rendered achievement, the ability to read and write a blazon is the most important item. The language may seem stilted and the sentence arrangement peculiar but it is done in the interest of economy of words as well as accuracy. The standard order is to name first the field, then the ordinary, next the charges on the field and finally those on the ordinary. A tincture is named once and afterward referred to by position in the blazon, as "of the field" or "of the second". The descriptions of the crest and motto follow in that order.

It is a mistake to think that heraldry is a dead subject. A working knowledge of it is indispensable to the genealogist, the historian, the architect and the artist-designer. The present use of seals, crests and coats-of-arms by the various branches of the government, the armed forces, states, cities, colleges, guilds and clubs indicates the timeliness of its study by every educated person.

The United States Army has an Heraldic Section under the Quartermaster General, in which all insignia are designed and authorized. This department's rules agree entirely with those of the Herald's College.

One of the interesting applications of heraldry in design is found in British and American armorial bookplates (see ex libris) by master engravers such as C. W. Sherborn and G. W. Eve in England and E. D. French,, J. W. Spenceley and others in America. See Gwillim, *Display of Heraldry*; Whittemore, *Origin and Antiquity of Heraldry*; Fox-Davies, *The Art of Heraldry;* Hope, *Heraldry for Craftsmen and Designers;* Eve, *Heraldry as Art.* —T.E.F.

Herat rugs. See ISLAMIC ART.

Hercules. See Heracles.

Hermes (L. Mercury). The Greek god of fertility and commerce, messenger of the gods, usually represented as a handsome youth with winged helmet and sandals, carrying a herald's staff. On the Greek funerary vases he was often pictured escorting the souls of the dead to Hades. In later art he was the subject of paintings by Correggio and Rubens, and of sculpture by Bologna, Cellini, de Vries, Coysevox, Thorvandsen, Begas, Idrac and Bottiau. —W.R.A.

heroic realism. See RUSSIAN ARTS.

hero legends. See American Folk Forms, literature.

Herrera style. See FURNITURE.

herringbone. A decorative pattern in which lines are set diagonally; small parallel lines are set at 45 degree angle with the general direction of the row and at right angles with the lines (or members) of the adjoining rows. —L.T.S.

hexachordal system. See MEDIEVAL MUSIC; solmization.

hibachi (Jap.). Fire-box or brazier in which a charcoal fire is maintained. An appurtenance of *cha-no-yu* (q.v.).

hibashi (Jap.). Fire sticks of metal resembling a pair of chop-sticks, with which charcoal for the fire is handled during *cha-no-yu* (q.v.).

Hieroglyphics. The title of a book on Egyptian hieroglyphs supposedly by Horapollo Nilus (4th cent. A.D. ?), who interpreted them metaphorically and mystically without knowing their significance as a script. This book, together with other Roman writings, was the basis for revival of hieroglyphic studies in the Italian Renaissance. The humanists of the 15th and 16th cents. believed they were imitating the Egyptians when combining isolated images of their own invention so as to convey a secret meaning. Hieroglyphics in their hands became means for the visual representation of poetic epigrams and thereby acted as a stimulus for the development of emblems. —R.B.

high Gothic. See Gothic.

Highland fling. One of the most ancient Scotch national dances, the Highland fling has for centuries been closely interwoven with the life of the people. It traditionally expresses victory or joy. In form and technique, the dance is perhaps more precise and less subject to improvisation than any other folk-dance. The movement is confined to fast and intricate foot-work combined with clearly defined arm motions. The dance is traditionally a man's solo, accompanied by bagpipe music in 2/4 meter with an almost unvarying, irregular rhythm. —J.G.

high-level street. See CIVIC PLANNING.

high relief. See relief; relief sculpture.

hi h tension porcelain. See CERAMICS I.

high warp. Has its warp placed in a vertical position as a painting is hung.

high warp loom. An upright loom; probably the earliest type. The warp is in a vertical position in front of the weaver.

highway. See CIVIC PLANNING.

hilliers. *Cer.* Cap for sagger (q.v.), same material and shape. See CERAMICS I.

hill-jar. A certain form of Chinese Han pottery which has a cover cone-shaped, representing mountain scenery with peaks and valleys and oftentimes hunters and hunted animals. —J.A.M.

Himejitozan yaki (Jap.). Pottery made in Harima province.

Hindu art. See INDIAN ART.

Hindu theatre. See THEATRE.

Hinnokogi yaki (Jap.). Pottery made in Yamashiro province.

hinoki (Jap.). The Japanese cypress, used extensively as a medium for both architecture and sculpture.

hip. (1) The external angle in which adjacent roof-slopes meet each other. (2) A truncated roof or gable.

hippocampus. A fabulous monster with head and forequarters like a horse, tail like a dolphin.

hip-roof. (1) A roof rising directly from the wall-plate on all sides, and so having no gable. (2) A short portion of a roof over a truncated gable. —J.M.M.

Hirado yaki (Jap.). Pottery made in the province of Hizen.

hiramakie (Jap.). A lacquer technique. Design in low relief in one plane, produced by successive layers of pure lacquer.

hirame (Jap.). A term applied to lacquer-ware when gold-foil is cut in fragment-like forms, applied to the lacquer surface and, when dry, polished.

hishaku (Jap.). A dipper made of bamboo, used to transfer water from the boiling water-kettle to the tea-bowl. A utensil for *cha-no-yu* (q.v.).

HISPANIC AMERICAN LITERATURE.

Since none of the Pre-Hispanic native groups of the New World had yet discovered phonetic writing, Hispanic American literature, properly speaking, begins with the colonial period. The various "literary" pieces which undoubtedly existed prior to 1492 were handed down from generation to generation by word of mouth. Hence, in evaluating their merits, whether they be the cryptic Mayan folklore tales or the delicately melancholy verses attributed to the Texcocan King Netzahualcoyotl or the simple Andean lyrics of the kind recited by professional bards at court, in the street or in the market, it is well to bear in mind that most of this stock of poetic or oratorical lore has reached us in Spanish, a fact that makes it difficult to determine the extent to which the original thought and emotions have been faithfully preserved.

In a rapid survey of this sort no attempt at completeness can be made. Often a number of writers or even an entire genre with historical rather than intrinsic significance has been left out. In either case a general statement has been considered enough for the purpose of this discussion.

I. The Colonial Period (1492-1808). The first productions in the colonial period were descriptive or epic in character, fraught as they were with the din and clamor of the conquest. This literature takes the form of lengthy reports or still lengthier chronicles, in which the deeds of the conquistadores are mingled with meticulous descriptions of places and peoples. The vastness and novelty of the New World led writers to fix their attention almost exclusively on concrete things. There was little time or predisposition for poetry or a more complex genre such as the novel. These productions were penned by Spaniards who were government officials, soldiers or friars, all of them intent upon revealing to the Old World the wonders of the New. Such are Columbus's letters and memoranda, pervaded with a curious mixture of religious zeal, practical sense and unbridled imagination. Equally vehement are the writings of the "Apostle of the Indies", Friar Bartolomé de las Casas, the renowned author of *Brevísima relación* (1552) and *Historia General de las Indias.*

The conquest of Mexico elicited several long accounts from soldiers and historians. Among these are the five dispatches sent by Hernán Cortés to the Emperor Charles V between 1519 and 1526; the fascinating narrative by Bernal Díaz del Castillo, *Verdadera historia de la conquista de la Nueva España,* whose garrulous style contrasts sharply with the laudatory and methodical account by Francisco López de Gómara, *Conquista de México* (1552). In the first one of these the heroes are the soldiers and horses that came with Cortés; in the other, the conqueror himself, who overshadows all others.

Peru produced the first American chronicler in the Inca Garcilaso de la Vega, whose *Comentarios Reales* (Lisbon, 1609) is the most valuable single work for the study of the Inca period. Garcilaso recreates the imperial splendor of the proud Inca race from which he descended. The author's credulity and pathetic attachment to his subject do not detract from the intrinsic merits of this colorful and eloquent narrative. The conquest and settlement of Peru was one of the most dramatic clashes of two different races ever recorded. Atahualpa's tragic fate and the disintegration of his empire were followed by rivalries among the conquerors. Many accounts of the incidents of the conquest and the subsequent civil wars were written. Among them are the *Historia del descubrimiento y conquista de la provincia del Perú* by Augustín de Zárate and the lengthy chronicles by Pedro Cieza de León.

The wonders of the American world were no less fascinating than the conquest itself. It is then natural that a goodly number of observant men should have described the flora and fauna of the new lands. Foremost among them was Gonzalo Fernández de Oviedo, who included a most interesting discussion of American natural history in his *Historia general y natural de las Indias.*

In the deluge of historical writings there appeared the greatest epic poem in the Spanish language: Alonso de Ercilla's *La Araucana,* in three parts (1569, 1578 and 1589). *La Araucana,* written in octaves and under the influence of Ariosto, relates the bloody wars against the indomitable Araucanian Indians of southern Chile. Interspersed with admirable accounts of battles are various interpolated philosophical reflections and arresting scenes of Indian bravery and endurance. The same theme is again presented in Pedro de Oña's *Arauco domado* (1596). Here the attention is focused on the conqueror Don García Hurtado de Mendoza rather than on the Indian warriors, thus making amends for Ercilla's disregard for the Spanish nobleman. This poem, obviously inspired by *La Araucana,* lacks genuine epic inspiration and betrays the author's haste and laudatory purpose.

Two other epics were composed by men who lived in the New World: *La Cristiada* (1611) by Diego de Ojeda, and Bernardo de Balbuena's 5000 octave poem which appeared in 1624 under the title of *Bernardo o victoria de Roncesvalles*.

In the chronicles and poems mentioned there is an evident influence of Spanish literary tradition, which in turn had been nurtured in medieval and Renaissance canons. Throughout the colonial period, literary taste continued to be guided exclusively by the mother country. The most important single influence during the first half of the 17th cent. was that of Góngora, the master of literary preciosity in Spain. Unfortunately, **Gongorism** degenerated, especially in the colonies, into mere intellectual gymnastics. Generally speaking, we find none of the better aspects of Gongorism in the colonies. Banal artificiality contaminated even the better minds. An exception, however, was Sor Juana Inés de la Cruz of Mexico, the lyric poet par excellence in the colonial period. A precocious child, endowed with beauty, charm and intelligence, Sor Juana entered a convent at sixteen seeking "assurance of salvation". Her poetry, intensely human and sincere, betrays the vehemence of a profoundly feminine soul. Her defense of women makes her the first feminist in the American world.

Gongorism did not spare scholars such as the Mexican Carlos de Sigüenza y Góngora (1645-1700), better known as an erudite than as a man of letters, and the learned but erratic Pedro de Peralta Barnuevo of Peru (1663-1743), whom the Spanish critic Menéndez y Pelayo called "a monster of erudition".

In the second half of the 18th cent., new ideas from abroad had a profound effect on intellectual circles in the colonies. A new mentality now existed, the result of contact with foreign scientists, the acquaintance with European works from countries other than Spain and the change in ways of life and customs made possible by the surprising liberality of the Bourbon dynasty. Typical of this new mentality was Pablo de Olavide. A friend of the French encyclopedists, Olavide became the personification of colonial heterodoxy. The expulsion of the Jesuits in 1767, although very detrimental to the continuation of intellectual pursuits, also marks the beginning of a freer age, which was to witness the emergence of native writers and

scientists to challenge the principles and modes of life consecrated by centuries of Spanish rule. This new frame of mind is evidenced by Esteban de Terralla y Landa's poem *Lima por dentro y por fuera* (ca. 1792), a satire on prominent men and customs. Very satirical also is one Calixto Bustamante who wrote under the pen name of Concolorcorvo (the swarthy one). His festive spirit strikes a gay note in *El lazarillo de ciegos caminantes* (1773), the story of a long trip, containing keen observations on peoples and customs of the time.

As the 18th cent. draws to a close, symptoms of restlessness are apparent everywhere. The newspapers, social intercourse in the streets and cafes, the discussion of books surreptitiously brought in and the circulation of new ideas on government which had found expression in the American and French revolutions, all these contributed to the increase of the intellectual and social agitation which was to culminate in the wars of independence.

II. The Struggle for Independence (1808-1824). The early years of the 19th cent. were chaotic. Politics and warfare occupied the minds of men. The lengthy composition and the gongoristic poem had given way to the newspaper article on social, political and economic questions. The literary and artistic societies founded by men born in the colonies became plotting centers which attracted the best men of the time. Aside from scientific articles like those of Francisco José de Caldas of Colombia and a great abundance of patriotic poetry, this period was not productive of first rate literature. There do abound, of course, political manifestoes and proclamations, some of them written by the greatest men in Hispanic America. Many of them had studied in universities under the impelling force of late 18th cent. enlightenment. Among the outstanding political thinkers of that day is, of course, the Liberator Simón Bolívar. His celebrated *Letter from Jamaica* (1815) is a rare example of penetrating insight into the future of the newborn republics.

A representative prose writer of this period is José Joaquín Fernández de Lizardi (1774-1827), the author of the first Hispanic American novel: *El periquillo sarniento* (1816). In true picaresque fashion the hero of this didactic narrative passes from one adventure to another, thus affording the author an opportunity to point out the virtues and defects of contemporary Mexican society. Also a journalist, Fernández de Lizardi was a bold defender of the revolutionary cause. His contributions, published under the pseudonym of "The Mexican Thinker", helped notably to keep alive the spirit of revolt in his country.

With the rapid multiplication of periodicals and the appearance of a new reading public, there developed a taste for popular poetry. One of its manifestations is **gaucho poetry**, a sort of continuation in America of the Spanish popular ballad. Among the earliest cultivators is the Uruguayan Bartolomé Hidalgo, whose heroic verses (*Cielitos heroicos*) set a pattern that was to evolve into noteworthy literary works.

In 1824 Hispanic American independence was assured with the great victory at Ayacucho. With the return to a fair degree of normalcy literary life began anew.

III. The Romantic Age (1824-1888). FORERUNNERS. Romanticism reached different parts of Hispanic America at different times but some of its literary accessories are present in Mexico and Argentina in the period immediately following independence. Among the forerunners of Romanticism are two great poets: José Joaquín Olmedo of Ecuador (1790-1847) and José María Heredia of Cuba (1803-1839). Olmedo's best known work is the poem *La victoria de Junín: Canto a Bolívar* (1825), a resounding tribute to the Liberator. In it grandiloquence blends with imagination, sonority with vehemence. Heredia, better known than Olmedo, was a standard bearer of Cuban independence and the majestic singer of nature's moods. His odes *En una tempestad* (1822), *Al Niágara* (1824), *Al sol* (1830) and his mediative poem *En el Teocalli de Cholula* (1820) all have a ring of sincerity and genuine inspiration.

Contemporaneous with these pre-romantic exponents of Hispanic American spontaneity and poetic arrogance there rose a smaller group of "classicists". The greatest of them all was Andrés Bello (1781-1865), a scholar and a patriot born in Venezuela and later an adopted son of Chile. A poet and a grammarian, a philosopher and a jurist, Bello stands out as the personification of the self-restraint and method of a first rate humanist. His *Gramática castellana* and his literary investigations reveal the breadth of his preparation. His poetry, original and translated, bespeaks the sensitiveness of the scholar's heart. But like a mighty torrent Romanticism broke all dikes. This occurred after the epoch-making polemic between Bello and the brilliant and pugnacious Argentine exile and journmalist, Domingo Faustino Sarmiento (1811-1888).

Sarmiento, a schoolmaster and outspoken foe of the tyrant Rosas, had arrived in Chile to earn his living as a newspaper writer. He was tender in his affections and uncompromising in his hatred. Sarmiento became the champion of civilization. He waved aside with disdain everything that smacked of lifeless conservatism. His magnetic personality fired the South American intellectual world. He had the reformatory and progressive spirit of a convinced romanticist. His best known work is *Facundo, o la civilización y la barbarie* (1845). This is a pitiless condemnation of the tyrant Rosas and of his henchmen, symbols of barbarity, ignorance and oppression. Back in Argentina after the fall of Rosas (1852), Sarmiento was successively deputy, senator, minister, governor and eventually president of the republic.

PROMINENT ROMANTICISTS. By the middle of the 19th cent. romanticism had spread all over the Hispanic American world. In point of time in this sketch, first place belongs to the Argentinian poet Esteban Echeverría, author of *La cautiva* (1837). This poem is the dramatic story of a married couple and their son who had been captured by Pampa Indians. Its best asset is the description of Pampa scenes. Also a relentless enemy of Rosas, Echeverría compared in *El matadero* (a sort of novelette) the barbaric practices of the tyrant with the carnage of a slaughter house.

Other distinguished romanticists were the exemplary and exalted Colombian citizen, José Eusebio Caro, an intense reformer and thinker; Julio Arboleda, also a Colombian and a champion of liberty, whose verses, though not abundant, show deep sentiment and refinement; the unfortunate "Plácido", the Cuban mulatto of tragic memory; the Cuban Gertrudis Gómez de Avellaneda, whose verses tell of the disillusion and despair of a passionate soul; the somber Manuel Acuña who ended his own life at twenty, and Juan de Dios Peza, the Mexican, whose verses, full of devoted love, made him very popular at the time.

Romanticism held sway until the end of the century, long after it had died away in Europe. This is proved by the late appearance of productions like Juan Zorilla de San Martín's *Tabaré* (1888). In it the author proposed to delve into the ancestral soul of the Uruguayan native, the Charruan Indian. Like many other pieces of **Indianist literature**,

Tabaré is a sentimental conception of the Spanish American native.

Not a few romantic novels with Indianist themes show a marked influence of foreign authors: Chateaubriand, Scott, Fenimore Cooper. In them the Indian is endowed with a sensitiveness and refinement he did not have. A novel of this type is Juan León Mera's *Cumandá* (1871). On the whole only mediocre works are found in this Indianist genre.

The greatest of all the romantic novels is Jorge Isaacs's *María* (1867), a sweet and tender story that all generations have read. The delicacy of sentiments and idyllic beauty of this tragic romance have impressed millions of young readers. Also popular, although inferior to *María,* is José Marmol's *Amalia* (1851-1855), an absorbing love story with Rosas's tyranny as its background. A unique romantic variation in prose is the historical "tradition". Unequalled in this type of short story is Ricardo Palma of Perú. His *Tradiciones peruanas* have had many imitators but none that matched his wit and charm.

Love for the unspoiled simplicity of the country people led Argentinian romanticists to turn their eyes to the gaucho as Hidalgo and others had done before them. This **gaucho literature** was popular in form only. Its cultivators were men from the cities. Among them are Estanislao del Campo, author of *Fausto* (1866) which relates the impressions of a simple gaucho at a performance of Gounod's opera, and Hilario Ascasubi, whose *Santos Vega* (1872) recounts the life of a gaucho troubadour. But the most notable gaucho piece is José Hernández's *Martín Fierro* (1872 and 1879), a poem which has been called "the epic of the Argentine".

The influence of such Spanish **costumbrista writers** as Larra, Mesonero Romanos and others gave rise to cultivation of the short narrative of customs which later developed into the full length realistic novel. Again, in the latter genre, the influence is Spanish, through authors like Pereda and Pérez Galdós. An important figure in this field is Alberto Blest Gana, who describes Chilean manners in *Martín Rivas* (1862) and the foibles of his fellow countrymen living in Paris in his masterpiece, *Los trasplantados* (1904). In Mexico, Ignacio Manuel Altamirano, José López-Portillo and Rafael Delgado portray Mexican society of both the city and the country. It is in Colombia, however, that realism produces the greatest number of works. At least passing mention should be made of *Manuela* (1866) by Eugenio Díaz,

and *Pax* by Lorenzo Marroquín. The acknowledged master of Colombian realism is Tomás Carrasquilla who links one century to another. Among his works are *Salve Regina* (1903), *El padre Casafús* (1914) and his best work, *La marquesa de Yolombó* (1928), in which he has given us a study of social life in Antioquia.

In the latter part of the 19th cent. French naturalism won a few followers. This school still exists at the present time. Although scientific determinism was very much discussed in Hispanic America it did not produce truly great works. Among the better ones are *Sin rumbo* (1885) and *En la sangre* (1887) by Eugenio Cambaceres of Argentina; *Las honradas* (1917) and *Las impuras* (1919) by the Cuban Miguel de Carrión and the several novels of the Mexican Federico Gamboa, such as *Suprema ley* (1896), *Santa* (1903) and *La llaga* (1912). The vitality of the genre is attested by the late appearance of *Juan Criollo* (1927) by Carlos Loveira of Cuba ,a naturalist with all the makings of a great novelist. This work is a penetrating analysis of Cuban traits.

The tempo of cultural and political life in the latter part of the 19th cent. is best revealed by the essayists. Some of them, like Cecilio Acosta of Venezuela and Juan Montalvo of Ecuador were champions of liberty. Each in his own way resisted tyranny. Of the two, Montalvo is the greater man as a literary figure. His breadth of thought, mental loftiness and impeccable style make him inimitable. Most representative of his works is the collection entitled *Siete Tratados,* written about 1873. His indomitable spirit and contempt for mediocrity and narrow-mindedness led him to write the burning pages of *Mercurial eclesiástica* (1884) and *Catilinarias* (1894).

Peru also had a great essayist and leader in Manuel González Prada. The defeat of Peru in the War of the Pacific (1879-1883) aroused this author's civic ire. He organized the youth of Peru and proceeded to tear down the old order mercilessly. His *Páginas libres* (1894) and *Horas de lucha* (1908) mark the birth of a new national consciousness. His example was to be followed later by the Aprista group under the leadership of Víctor Raúl Haya de la Torre.

Less spectacular but just as much imbued with reformatory zeal, the Porto Rican Eugenio María de Hostos energized the American world with his exemplary life and inspired teaching. In Santo Domingo, Porte

Rico, Chile and other countries, Hostos preached the doctrine of orderly social conduct and enlightenment. His best work is *Moral social* (1888), a call to order and social morality in accordance with the laws of Nature.

IV. *Modernism* (*1888-1910*). The last quarter of the 19th cent. witnessed a profound literary reform, the most important ever to originate in Hispanic America. The rise of a liberal middle class, the prevalence of positivism in intellectual circles and the spread of realism and naturalism in literature gave rise to "Modernism". This was a personalistic and aristocratic counter-current in poetry which was none the less a symptom of the general awakening in all spheres of intellectual and social life. Modernism sought above all the creation of beauty, the untrammeled expression of personality and the rejuvenation of the Castilian language. Modernism was aesthetic in its import and cosmopolitan in its scope. It fused together Romanticism, Parnassianism and Symbolism, thus holding in one channel widely different literary currents which in Europe had been non-contemporaneous and even antagonistic. This unification can be seen in the poems of the precursors of the movement: musicality in José Asunción Silva, objectivity in Julián del Casal and a marked elegiac tone in Manuel Gutiérrez Nájera.

The publication of *Azul* (1888) by Rubén Darío, the greatest figure within Modernism, marks the year of definition and self-assertion. This volume was followed by the sumptuous *Prosas profanas* (1896), (the apogee of Modernism), and the more human *Cantos de vida y esperanza* published in 1905. The variety and exquisiteness of Darío's moods, his sincerity and devotion to art, made him the pivotal center of the new school, In later years his aristocratic aloofness gave way to a more universal note. He left his ivory tower and sang of the cares and sorrows of man. Darío's influence in the Spanish speaking world was tremendous. With him, Hispanic America is incorporated into world literature.

Modernism was as varied as were its cultivators: sonorous and epic with José Santos Chocano of Peru, philosophical with Guillermo Valencia of Colombia, spiritual and devout with Amado Nervo of Mexico, refined and self-assertive with Salvador Díaz Mirón, also of Mexico. Argentina contributed the versatile Leopoldo Lugones and Uruguay the neo-gongoristic Julio Herrera y Reissig. Final-

ly in 1911 Enrique González Martínez sounded the death knell of the school in his poem *Tuércele el cuello al cisne*.

Hispanic America also had one great modernist in prose, the Uruguayan thinker José Enrique Rodó, best known for his essay *Ariel* (1900). Written shortly after the Spanish-American war, this long discourse voiced a new credo of life and conduct which gave Hispanic America a sense of self-respect. The analysis of Hispanic traditions—in contrast with North American ideals and accomplishments—is not always sound, but Rodó's olympic attitude and impeccable style made *Ariel* one of the most widely read essays. *Los motivos de Proteo* and *El mirador de Próspero* are also indispensable for an understanding of this Emerson of South America.

V. *The Contemporary Period* (*1910-1943*). Post-Modernism preserved the worthwhile values of Modernism. It veered off, however, into various new directions, now striving for simplicity and deeper human content, now going back to nature and common every-day life. Some representative figures in this school are Manuel Magallanes Moure of Chile, Enrique Banchs, Fernández Moreno and Arturo Marasso of Argentina, Emilio Frugoni and Carlos Sabat Ercasty of Uruguay, Luis Carlos López and Miguel Angel Osorio of Colombia.

The most significant development within Post-Modernism is the appearance of several poetesses: Gabriela Mistral of Chile, sad and sweetly maternal; Alfonsina Storni, disillusioned and ironic; Delmira Augustini, passionate and fanciful, and María Eugenia Vaz Ferreira, a woman of intelligence and pride. The most captivating of them all is Juana de Ibarbourou, poet laureate of Hispanic America.

A still greater refinement was achieved in more recent years by such artists as José María Egurén of Peru, Emilio Oribe of Uruguay and Ramón López Velarde of Mexico, to mention only three of a much larger group. Among the latest poets the most significant are Pablo Neruda and Vicente Huidobro of Chile, Javier Villaurrutia of Mexico, the Ecuatorian Jorge Carrera Andrade, Carlos Pellicer of Mexico and César Vallejo of Peru. At least passing mention should be made here of Negro verse. Its most significant cultivators are Nicolás Guillén and Emilio Ballagas of Cuba and the Porto Rican Luis Palés Matos.

In the novel, Hispanic America has in recent years produced some truly outstanding works. The relation of man to the land he lives on is masterfully presented by Rómulo Galiegos in *Doña Bárbara* (1929). Before him, José Eustacio Rivera of Columbia had written the odyssey of man in conflict with the monstrous in nature. His novel, *La vorágine* (1924), is the best of the jungle novels. Other writers turned their eyes to the great convulsion of the Mexican revolution. Chief among them is Mariano Azuela. His novel *Los de abajo* (1916) is considered one of the best in the contemporary period. In Argentina the gaucho theme blossomed anew in Ricardo Güiraldes's *Don Segundo Sombra* (1926), which is a poetization of the pampa and the gaucho. The prosaic *peón,* a descendant of the independent gaucho of old, has been studied in the works of Justino Zavala Muniz of Uruguay and Benito Lynch of the Argentine. The re-discovery of the common man has brought the Indian and the Negro to the novel: the Mexican Indian in Gregorio López y Fuentes's *El indio* and Mauricio Magdaleno's *El resplandor;* the Andean Indian, in Jorge Icaza's *Huasipungo,* a pitiful story of the native of the Ecuatorian mountains. Among the most recent works of the latter type is Ciro Alegría's *El mundo es ancho y ajeno,* awarded first prize in the Latin American novel contest of 1941.

Among the writers of psychological novels none compares with Eduardo Barrios of Chile. His *Un perdido* and *El hermano asno* have justly made him famous. In Argentina, Manuel Gálvez has also studied various phases of city life in *El mal metafísico,* one of his best novels, and in *La maestra normal* and *Nacha Regules.* His last few novels are inferior, particularly those that followed his trilogy on the war with Paraguay.

Opposed to the novel of the ordinary man is the novel of "evasion", as the Peruvian critic Luis Alberto Sánchez has called it. Its themes are bygone days, the spell of foreign lands and the world of dreams.

In the short story not a few writers have achieved distinction. Among them are: Ventura García Calderón, a master in the recreation of legendary and mysterious Peru; Horacio Quiroga, tormented and bordering on insanity, the interpreter of the mysterious and of impending fatality; Mariano Latorre of Chile, a landscape painter; the lamented José de la Cuadra of Ecuador and the prolific Javier de Viana of Uruguay.

In contrast with the abundance of fictional literature is the scarcity of dramatic productions. In most countries the drama has appeared only sporadically. A notable exception is Argentina where the Teatro del Pueblo, ably directed by Leónidas Barletta, has kept alive the interest in native and foreign drama. The best known of the Hispanic American dramatists is Florencio Sánchez, the initiator of the modern theater in South America and a keen observer of rural life and native types. The dominant notes of his plays are accurate observation and a marked feeling of compassion.

In the ideological field, Hispanic America is becoming better known through its essayists. Aside from the older thinkers like José Vasconcelos, Francisco García Calderón, Alejandro Deustua, Enrique Molina, Alejandro Korn, Enrique José Varona, Carlos Vaz Ferreira and brilliant Alfonso Reyes there are several younger groups that have made themselves known. In Argentina there is the group gathered around the indefatigable Francisco Romero. Important too is the Aprista group of Peru, which inherited the combative spirit of Manuel González Prada. Still others are discovering the personality of their own country or that of their neighbors: Ezequiel Martínez Estrada of Argentina, Jorge Mañach of Cuba, Luis López de Mesa of Colombia, Mariano Picón Salas of Venezuela, to mention only a few.

The visits of noted European thinkers and more recently the arrival of European refugees have contributed to the creation of an even greater interest in various fields of intellectual endeavor. The present world conflict has also had profound repercussions. Hispanic America is now living its hour of decision. Its intellectual and artistic potentiality will be revealed in the years to come.

MINIMUM BIBLIOGRAPHY

See Barrera, Isaac J., *Literatura hispanoamericana,* Quito, 1934; Blanco-Fombona, Rufino, *Grandes escritores de América,* Madrid, 1917 and *El modernismo y los poetas modernistas,* Madrid, 1929; Coester, Alfred, *A Literary History of Spanish America,* New York, 2nd. ed., 1928; Donoso, Armando, *La otra América,* Madrid, 1925; García Calderón, Ventura, *Del romanticismo al modernismo,* Paris, 1910 and *Semblanzas de América,* Madrid, n. d.; Goldberg, Isaac, *Studies in Spanish American Literature,* New York, 1920; Hespelt, E. H., *et al.,* An *Outline History of Spanish American Literature,* New York, 1941; Menéndez y Pelayo, Marcelino, *Antología de poetas hispanoamericanos,* 4 vols., Madrid, 1893-1895; Moses, Bernard, *Spanish*

Colonial Literature in South America, New York, 1922; Onís, Federico de, *Antología de la poesía española e hispanoamericana,* Madrid, 1934; Sánchez, Luis Alberto, *Historia de la literatura americana,* 2nd. ed., Santiago, 1940 and *América: novela sin novelistas,* Lima, 1933; Santos González, C., *Poetas y críticos de América,* Paris, 1913; Torres-Ríoseco, A., *Novelistas contemporáneos de América,* Santiago, 1940, *Precursores del modernismo,* Madrid, 1925 and *The Epic of Latin American Literature,* New York, 1942. For the literature of individual countries see: *Bibliographies of Spanish-American Literature,* Cambridge, 1935, 3 vols., and Lewis Hanke, Miron Burgin (editors), *Handbook of Latin American Studies,* Cambridge, Harvard University Press, (1936-1942), 7 vols.
—E.N-S.

Hispano-Flemish style. See SPAIN, ART OF.

Hispano-Moresque pottery. See CERAMICS II.

historiated. Adorned with figures having significance, as flowers, animals, as disting. from scrolls, diapers, etc.

historical musicology. See MUSICOLOGY.

historical novel. See NOVEL, THE.

history of art. A subject of study in the general field of the "humanities", concerned with the graphic and plastic arts; primarily sculpture, architecture (including city planning), and painting in oil, tempera, fresco, water color, encaustic, ink, etc.; and secondarily the minor arts, crafts, applied arts, and industrial arts—including prints and drawings, manuscript illumination, mosaic, stained glass, ivory carving, wood carving, metal work and jewelry, ceramics, textiles, tapestries, printing, book binding, weaving, basketry and varied peasant crafts, ornament, lettering, furniture, interior decoration, costume design, advertising and industrial design, photography, and the cinema.

The study of the history of art involves, in the first place, the usual historical approach. Periods, styles, movements, schools, and individual artists and works of art are investigated in historical perspective; and the attempt is made to discover correct dates and chronology, proveniences, sources, interinfluences, authorship, authenticity, biographical data and relevant documentary facts, iconography, and cultural and social contexts. This research combines the scientific accuracy and objectivity of archeological investigations and the philosophical discipline of theoretical interpretation. In some periods the study of art provides the chief source of historical knowledge, and the contribution of this subject to general history is always important to the extent that it succeeds in its essential purpose, viz. to reveal and interpret the past through the visual records of its emotions, thoughts, ideals, and aspirations.

The modern art historian, however, is more than a cataloguer or statistician of historic fact, and more than an interpreter of historic meaning in an objective, scientific sense. Ideally art history today leads to connoisseurship (q.v.), which may be attained only with the development of critical sensitivity through discipline in aesthetic judgment. This involves analytical studies in the formal aspects of the visual arts, the language of expression, the analysis of content; and it requires a systematic investigation in the philosophy and psychology of art. The true art historian, as connoisseur, is thus professionally versed in that which is genuine, rare, and choice in the field of art, both in the past and in the present. He is capable of re-creating in verbal terms the true and unique meaning of individual works of visual art of any age, not only in terms of the historical and cultural context, but also in terms of the individual ideas, experiences and insights of the artist. And finally, the art historian, as connoisseur, is competent and obligated not only to interpret the aesthetic meaning, but also to appraise the aesthetic merit of works of art in terms of their broad philosophical or human significance.

Arising out of the simple archaeological studies of the 18th and 19th cents., the history of art has not always recognized the comprehensive obligations it now assumes. Modern art history is a complex study, in part scientific and objective, in part philosophical and normative, involving an attitude at once historical, analytical, interpretative, and judicial. Moreover, the zealous historian of the arts today understands the implicit needs of contemporary life and art, and, as the historian of political theory constantly is mindful of his contribution to contemporary practice, so the historian of the arts increasingly exercises his judicial function in a salutary and responsible endeavor to quicken and inform both the artist and the amateur of the arts. See ARCHAEOLOGY, AESTHETIC ASPECTS OF.   —L.D.L.

history of music. See music history, periods in.

hitsui (Jap.). Brush stroke.

Hizen yaki (Jap.). Pottery made in Hizen province.

ho (Ch.). Sacrificial bronze vessel. Three hollow legs, handle at side, spout and cover. Used for mixing sacrificial drinks. See SYMBOLISM IN FAR EASTERN ART.

Hobbyists, the. See FRENCH ART; Dadaism.

hocket (hoquetus). See MEDIEVAL MUSIC.

hogan (Navaho, house). A dwelling built of logs set upright like a tripod or laid horizontally in courses on a hexagonal plan, covered with poles, bark and a thick layer of earth. A smoke hole is left at the apex, and an opening is left for a door, usually on the eastern side. The hogan is used by the Navaho chiefly in winter for protection from the cold and for storage.   —H.G.

Hohenstaufen art. This period parallels almost entirely the reign of the German Hohenstaufen Dynasty (1138-1254). It is noted for its psychological tensions and artistic antagonisms. The proper trend of Hohenstaufen art suffered from a great deal of opposition which makes the whole picture difficult to review but which also makes it very interesting.

Generally speaking, one may say that the Hohenstaufen period was interested in human individuality, in centralization and in rationalization and, because of that, has been called the **proto-Renaissance** or the predecessor of the Renaissance.

There were three characterizing attributes in the architecture of this period: first, an inclination toward the circular plan, which means that all peripheral parts of the building are placed around a dome as center; secondly, an anti-Gothic handling of vault and wall, which means that the pressure of the vault was placed upon the wall from which had been taken those parts not immediately necessary for the support of the pressure; thirdly, a final effect which was picturesque and which was accomplished in an eclectic manner.

The Hohenstaufen architectural period begins with the two-storied building in Schwarzrheindorf near Bonn (begun in 1151). The

ground plan was a Greek cross. Examples of this period are the rebuilt cathedral in Speyer (second half of the 12th cent.), the eastern portions of the Church of the Apostles in Cologne (after 1192), the eastern portions of the Cathedral of Strassburg (after 1176), the Cathedral in Worms (end of the 12th to the beginning of the 13th cent.), the dome of St. Gereon (1219-1227), the choir of the Church of Our Lady in Gelnhausen (1230-1250), the Abbey of St. George in Limburg-Lahn (about 1235), the west choir of the Cathedral in Mainz, (beginning of the 13th cent. to 1239), the west portion of the Abbey of St. Patroclus in Soest (the end of the 12th cent. to 1220), the ruin of Heisterbach (1227), and the Kaiserpfalz in Gelnhausen (beginning of the 13th cent.).

Examples of the reactionary movement against the Hohenstaufen style are ,among others, St. Michael in Altenstadt near Schongau, (2d half of the 12th cent.), the eastern portion of the former abbey of the Benedictines in Murbach, in upper Alsace (about or shortly after the middle of the 12th cent.), the abbey of the Scottish monks of St. Jacob in Regensburg (about 1180), and the former Praemonstratenser Abbey in Jerichow (1144-1250).

In sculpture, special importance was given to the representation of the human figure. Two opposing conceptions are to be noticed. The followers of the one trend started from a metaphysical aspect as the predominant view of life, the others from a natural, human aspect. Both divisions were split into two, or even more, specialized groups. Among the representatives of the metaphysical viewpoint there was one strongly conservative group which clung to the old Salian ideals, and sometimes overdid the Salian attributes to the point of rigidity. Examples of this trend are: the limestone relief in the former abbey in Oberpleis (about 1151), the Imerward Crucifix in the Cathedral of Braunschweig (3d quarter of the 12th cent.), the statue of Mary and Child in Hoven near Euskirchen (about 1175), the tombstone of Plektrudis in the crypt of St. Maria im Kapitol in Cologne (last quarter of the 12th cent.), Mary and St. John at the Crucifixion from the Abbey Sonnenburg near Bruneck (about 1200), now in the Schnuetgen Museum, Cologne. The second of these metaphysical groups stressed the emotional movement of the soul, ranging from soft emotions to ecstacy. Examples of this group are: the stone relief of Daniel in the Lions' den in the

Cathedral of Worms (last quarter of the 12th cent.), the Madonna of Dom Ruppert from St. Laurentius, in the Luettich Museum of Archeology (last quarter of the 12th cent.), and the Mary of the Wessorbrunner choir chancel (about 1250), now in the Bayrisches National Museum, Munich.

Examples of the ecstatic group are: the Gero Crucifix in the Cathedral of Cologne (about 1180), and the Tympanon relief in the Cathedral of Trier (third quarter of the 12th cent.). The other trend in sculpture in which importance was put upon the more natural-human aspect was also divided into two different groups. One group emphasized the dependence of the human body upon certain natural laws which are the activating principle of bodily life. But these laws, and therefore the human body, are dependent upon the metaphysical aspect to which they are subject. This was a pre-Gothic conception. The other group, however, stressed the point that the human body is independent of the metaphysical, that it follows its own natural laws and therefore is self-sufficient. This latter group may be called Hohenstaufen in the proper meaning of the word. The reliefs of the choir chancel in the Church of Our Lady in Halberstadt may be considered as the point of origin of the two aspects.

Examples of the pre-Gothic group are: the figures of the Prophets and Apostles on the reliquary of the Magi in the treasury of the Cathedral of Cologne (1206-1230), the prophets and apostles on the porch of the Prince's Portal of the Cathedral of Bamberg (about 1220-1230), the reliefs on the choir chancel of Bamberg (1220-1230), and the reliefs on the reliquary of St. Elizabeth in Marburg (about 1236-1240).

Examples of the true Hohenstaufen style are: the statues on the gilt porch of the Cathedral of Freiburg in Saxony (about 1230), the Bamberg Equestrian and the statues of the Adam Porch in the Bamberg Cathedral, the statues of the so-called Sibyl and of Mary in Bamberg, the reliefs of the Passion on the choir chancel in Naumburg and the statues in the west choir of the Naumburg Cathedral (about 1250), and the reliefs and statues of the south portal of the Cathedral in Strassburg (1240-1250).

In the field of painting there were similar opposing trends. The Hohenstaufen style in its true objective endows the human figure with a self-sufficient, innate human dignity. This line begins with the murals in the lower church in Schwarz-Rheindorf (1151-1156), and is continued in the murals on the vaults of the chapter house of the former abbey of the Benedictines in Brauweiler near Cologne (about 1174). Striving toward the same goal are the enamel paintings on the casket of St. Heribert in Deutz and the enamel paintings by Nicolaus Virdunensis, in the Abbey of Neuerburg near Vienna, (1181), the paintings on the ceiling in St. Michael in Hildesheim (late 12th cent.), and the murals on the west choir in the Cathedral of Gurk (about 1220).

The combination of the natural bodily aspect with spiritual emotion is shown in the murals of the Baptistry of St. Gereon in Cologne (2d quarter of the 13th cent.), and in the murals on the choir of the Church of Our Lady in Gelnhausen (1240-1250). Those painted from a purely metaphysical point of view are: the miniatures of the Evangeliar from Gengenbach (about 1150), the illustrations in the "Scivias" tractate of Hildegard of Bingen (2d part of the 12th cent.), and murals of the choir of St. Maria zur Hoehe in Soest (about 1230), which belongs to a more visionary and ecstatic part of this metaphysical group. At the end of the Hohenstaufen epoch a strongly agitated and baroque style was developed, as can be shown in the illustrations of the Missale of Halberstadt (about 1250), which shows a Byzantine influence, in the illustrations in the Psalter of Baumont, (after 1250), and in the illustrations of the *Liet von der Maget* by Wernher von Tegernsee (after 1200).

GEN'L.: G. Dehio, *Geschichte der deutschen Kunst,* Berlin, 1914, new edition by Gall; W. Pinder, *Die Kunst der deutschen Kaiserzeit,* Leipzig, 1933; Max Hauttmann, *Die Kunst des frühen Mittelalters,* Berlin, 1937. ARCH.: G. Dehio and G. V. Bezold, *Die Kirchliche Baukunst des Abendlandes,* Stuttgart, 1892; Paul Frankl, *Die Baukunst des Mittelalters, Handbuch der Kunstwissenschaft,* Berlin, 1918. SCULPTURE: J. Baum, *Malerei und Plastik des Mittelalters, Handbuch der Kunstwissenschaft,* Berlin, 1930; H. Beenken, *Romanische Skulpturen in Deutschland,* Leipzig, 1924; E. Panofsky, *Deutsche Plastik des 11. bis 13. Jahrh.* PAINTING: Bernath, *Malerei des Mittelalters,* Leipzig, 1916; Paul Clemen, *Die romanische Monumentalmalerei in den Rheinlanden, Düsseldorf,* 1916; Josef Gerber, *Die romanischen Wandgemälde Tirols, Wien,* 1928; Georg Leidinger, *Meisterwerke der Buchmalerei,* München, 1920, ff.; Hans Swarzenski, *Vorgotische Miniaturen,* Koenigstein, 1927; Adolf

Goldschmidt, *Die deutsche Buchmalerei,* München, 1928. APPLIED ART: G. V. Falke and G. Swarzenski, *Das Kunstgewerbe im Mittelalter, part of Lehnert, Illustrierte Geschichte des Kungstgewerbes* I; Falke-Frauberger, *Deutsche Schmelzarbeiten des Mittelalters,* Frankfurt, 1904; Josef Braun, *Meisterwerke der deutschen Goldschmiedekunst vorgotischer Zeit,* München, 1922.   —A.J.S.

Hohokam art (Pima, ancient ones). The culture of the Hohokam, though contemporary with that of the Anasazi (q.v.), is less well known because less intensively investigated. They lived in the desert lands of southwestern Arizona, whither they may have migrated from the south, probably in the early centuries of the Christian era, with a culture pattern already established. The evolution of this culture in its new habitat seems fairly clear in its general outline. At first they built rectangular pit and surface houses, of the single unit type, with walls of brush, poles and mud, which were grouped into walled villages spread widely over the arid valleys. Agriculture was basic in their economy because of extensive, ingenious systems of irrigation. Hence they are sometimes called the Canal Builders. All through their history, pottery was one of the most important of the arts and was produced in great abundance. The most characteristic shape was a large jar with a low, broad shoulder, built up by coiling but finished by the paddle and anvil technique; that is, smoothing the coils by beating them with a paddle on the outside, against a stone held on the inside, instead of smoothing with a gourd tool, the usual method in Pueblo pottery making. Designs in red upon the buff surface consisted of vigorously drawn rectangles, containing hatchings, frets and zigzags apparently derived from textile design, varied with bold spirals. A less well known but unique ware consists of bowls with decorations of representational content, figures of men, birds and animals freely sketched in a style quite different from the abstract quality of Pueblo pottery decoration but akin to that of the Mimbres potters (q.v.).

This early stage was followed by a concentration of villages which may have prefaced an invasion of Pueblo peoples from the north, lasting from ca. 1300-1350 to ca. 1400-1450 A.D. Communal dwellings of adobe with many stories appeared alongside the one-story surface houses of the earlier type. Together they constituted a compound surrounded by a wall with no opening and entered by a ladder. Casa Grande, now in the Casa Grande National Monument, affords the best example. Cliff dwellings were also built.

The Hohokam were unique in the Southwest in their use of shell, probably obtained from the Gulf of California. From it they carved and engraved necklaces, rings, bracelets and pendants in the form of or decorated with lively figures of frogs, sheep, birds and humans, both for personal adornment and for burial purposes. These all show a sense of essential form and decorative value. Fragments reveal a skill in weaving fine cloth with intricate patterns closely related to ceramic ornament.

After about a century of invasion the northerners appear to have left. Their influence is still seen in the communal type of building which continued alongside the original type and in the appearance of a polychrome pottery, which, however, did not supplant the characteristic red on buff ware.

What became of the Hohokam is not known. The historic Pima and Papago tribes are believed by some to be their direct descendants. But that is a moot question. See Charles A. Amsden, *An Analysis of Hohokam Pottery Designs,* in Gila Pueblo *Medallion Papers,* No. 12 (Globe, Arizona, 1936); Harold S. Gladwin et al., *Excavations at Snaketown,* in *Medallion Papers,* Nos. 25-26 (Globe, Arizona, 1937); Frank H. H. Roberts, Jr., *A Survey of Southwestern Archeology,* in Smithsonian Institution Annual Report, 1935; George C. Vaillant, *Indian Arts in North America,* 1939.   —H.G.

hold (It. *fermata*). *Mus.* A note or a rest prolonged.

hollow relief. See relief sculpture.

homespun. (1) A loose but very strong and durable woolen, woven on hand looms. (2) A coarse and loosely woven material, made in imitation of actual home made cloth. Irregularity of mixed colored yarns is main characteristic, also rough finish.   —G.W.R.

homophony. Process of composition by which one melodic line is presented simultaneously with an accompaniment of chords, or the intervals formed by several simultaneously presented melodic lines acquire the character of chords subject to the principles of harmony, one of these lines usually standing out as a dominating element.   —E.K.

honzon (Jap.). Principal sculptured image in a Buddhist temple.

Hoo (Jap.). Bird of good omen. A long-tailed pheasant type of bird commonly called the phoenix. See "Phoenix in Fact and Fancy", by Alan Priest, *Bull. Metropolitan Museum of Art,* New York, Oct. 1942.

hooked rug (drawn in). Originated and practiced by prehistoric workers for clothing and later by poor people to give warmth to bed and covering for damp bare floors. A tufted rug made on a foundation of burlap or linen. The pile is made of long narrow strips of cloth or yarn which is pulled into the foundation by means of a hook, leaving an uncut loop on the surface of the foundation. The loops can be cut with rug shears after the drawing in process is complete. Many colors and patterns are possible.   —B.E.J.

hoop. See JEWELRY.

Hopewell culture. An aboriginal American culture centering in southern Ohio but widespread in the eastern United States. Its name derives from the owner of a site near Chillicothe, Ohio, where remains of it were first discovered and where some of its finest products have been found. See Eastern North American Aboriginal art.   —H.G.

Hopi art. The Hopi (the name a contraction of the Hopi *Ho-pi-tu,* peaceful people), formerly called Moki or Moqui, are an isolated tribe living in nine villages on three mesas which jut out like headlands from the Black Mesa toward the Painted Desert of north central Arizona; one valley village lies to the west and several modern towns have sprung up at the foot of the mesas. Best known are Walpi on First Mesa, and Oraibi on Third. The origin of the Hopi is not known with certainty. They differ racially from the other Pueblos, being of Shoshonean stock, except the inhabitants of Hano, a Tewa village on First Mesa, settled ca. 1700 A.D. At first they appear to have lived at the base of the mesas, choice sites because of springs; later, for protection against raiding nomads, they moved up on the mesas, where their stone and adobe houses and kivas are crowded along the ridges of the steep-walled headlands. Because of their inaccessibility the Hopi have retained their ancient cultural pattern more nearly intact than other tribes. They are expert farmers. Their fields of colored corn, beans and squash, and their orchards of peaches, a gift of the Spaniard, stretch many miles from the mesas. From prehistoric times they have been fine craftsmen and their wares have been in demand for trade along ancient routes. Their ceremonials are most elaborate and require for their preparation and celebration a large amount of time and activity, and are a determining factor in many of the crafts. These ceremonials involve drama, costume, song and dance, and their function is not amusement but a ritual, prayers for rain, for increase in crops and for the welfare of the tribe. The kachina (q.v.) cult involves a continuous ceremonial with masked dancers, lasting from January to July. The unmasked dances, such as the Snake and Flute, take place during the remaining six months. Kachina dolls, representations of the kachinas, are carved by the men from cottonwood, painted, and decorated with feathers and other embellishments in imitation of the costumes of the dancers. They are given to the children by the kachinas at the time of the dances or are hung up in the houses for ceremonial purposes.

Basketry is a craft of the women. Plaques and bowls for both household and ceremonial use, and, recently, deep baskets for trade, are made of local grasses, stems, yucca and twigs, and decorated with geometric motifs or human and animal figures highly conventionalized and adapted to the shape and weaving technique. Styles differ on the different mesas. Second Mesa produces a thick oil product; Oraibi and Third Mesa a fine type of wickerwork.

Pottery, also a woman's craft, was made in all the villages in prehistoric times, a black and white ware common to the Pueblo region. The contribution of the Hopi to the ceramic art of the Southwest was the development of a polychrome style which culminated in the Sikyatki ware (q.v.) of Pueblo IV period (see Pueblo Art). It was made on First Mesa, where the pottery craft was concentrated. The shapes consisted chiefly of large bowls with a broad flattened shoulder, an excellent surface for decoration, and shallow bowls with decorations on the interior. The decorative motifs, in red and brown on a yellow or orange base, consist of geometric shapes and highly conventionalized birds and animals. In shape, color, and the bold vigor of its decoration this ware is an outstanding ceramic product of the Southwest.

Weaving was a craft practiced by the men. Native cotton, before the coming of the Spaniards, and wool after the arrival of their sheep, furnished the materials for making blankets and garments for daily use, and ceremonial garments, kilts and sashes. The few colors used were those of the native wools and cotton, of natural dyes and imported indigo, until the advent, late in the 19th cent., of aniline dyes. The designs were and still are simple stripe patterns or borders with diamond, triangular and terraced motifs either woven in the fabric or added by brocading or embroidering with wool. See Ruth Bunzel, *The Pueblo Potter*, 1929; Mary-Russell F. Colton, *The Arts and Crafts of the Hopi Indians,* Museum of Northern Arizona *Museum Notes,* Vol. 11, No. 1, July, 1938; Denver Art Museum, Dept. of Indian Art, Bulletins: *The Hopi Indians,* Leaflet No. 13, 1930, *Hopi Indian Basketry,* Leaflet No. 17, 1931, *Hopi Indian Weaving,* Leaflet No. 18, 1931, *Hopi Indian Pottery,* Leaflet No. 47, May, 1932; Edward Kennard, *Hopi Kachinas,* 1938.   —H.G.

hora. A folk-dance of disputed nationality. Most authorities include it among the dances of Roumania, but in the recent revival of Palestinian folk arts, it has emerged as a dance of Hebrew origin. It seems possible that Jewish people living in Roumania introduced the hora to Roumanian folk-culture. The dance as performed by Jewish people today is similar in many ways to the Roumanian version, but different in that the Jewish hora has a chanting accompaniment which is sung in Hebrew by the dancers. The Jewish hora is a gay and vigorous dance in 2/4 meter, usually performed in a close circle which symbolizes the unity of the group. The Roumanian hora has a slow introduction, during which the men dance alone while the women gradually approach the circle. Both dances are characterized by a gradual increase in speed and range of movement.   —J.G.

Horai (Jap.). Buddhist land of eternal spring —paradise.

horizon, horizon line. See PERSPECTIVE.

horizontal. *Mus.* Term used figuratively to designate the succession of musical elements, particularly the progress of melodic lines.

horizontal line. See PERSPECTIVE.

horn. See MUSICAL INSTRUMENTS.

hornacina (literally, little oven). Niche in the corner of a Mexican 17th-18th cent. palace for the figure of the patron Virgin or

Saint of the family, often placed above the main cornice in a raised and specially ornamented section of the parapet.   —J.Mc.

horned lions. See SYMBOLISM IN FAR EASTERN ART.

horror vacui. See SYMBOLISM IN FAR EASTERN ART.

horse hair, artificial. A rayon product, made in imitation of the natural horse hair. It consists of single strands of any desired length, and in very heavy deniers, usually 300 to 450. It is made either round or flat. Its advantage over the natural horse hair is that it can be produced in optional lengths. Artificial horse hair behaves exactly the same as the viscose rayon yarn. Used for mats, ribbons, belts, millinery, braids, galloons and hats.
                                                         —G.W.R.

horseshoe arch. See ISLAMIC ART.

Hoshino yaki (Jap.). Pottery made in Chikugo province.

hoso-e (Jap.). A vertical style of print about 12 x 6 in. in size.

hossu (Jap.). See fly-whisk.

hourglass drum. See MUSICAL INSTRUMENTS.

hourglass motif. In classical art, an ornament consisting of two triangles set one on top of the other, point to point; usually this unit is repeated continuously in a row.
                                                         —L.T.S.

hours, canonical. The matins, lauds, prime, terce, sext, none, vespers and compline—portions of the day set aside by rule (canon) during which devotional services are prescribed such as singing of the psalms, hymns, etc. Of eastern origin, the canonical hours were adopted by monasteries and the Church itself in the early formative period.   —V.A.

house. Structure of moderate size to shelter the group life of one single family group. A more or less strict segregation of the family group within the tribe occurs in all primitive societies, although collectivism may prevail in many activities. Apart from the clustered dwelling structures found with cliff and mesa dwellers and in certain timber construction as in North America, the use and construction of compartments for individual matrimonial and family units seems to have been one of the earliest customs.

Nomadic populations speedily erected temporary structures as homes, or where their migration habitually took them through areas, poor in handy structural material of any kind, as the drylands of Arabia, or the grasslands of the North American Middlewest, prefabricated, collapsible, transportable dwellings in form of tents were substituted. Like with tepees, the ownership of the home and its furnishings, esp. its floor covering, was often fixed with the wife, not the husband. In case of polygamy, each wife frequently produced, owned and maintained the mat on which to receive the husband, as well as the tent or abode in which these simple furnishings of daily life were placed. Reed constructions and entire adobe villages were structurally processed and often maintained by women in ritualistically repeated activities. The introduction of heavy materials, such as timber and rock, supplanted female by male labor in house construction; but in spite of the individual house, collective construction of each house in the community by cooperative effort of the village has subsisted in many regions from Yucatan to Slovakia.

The early house frequently is not merely a dwelling place but a place of production as far as such production of a pre-industrial economy depends on and requires indoor and controlled climate. Up to the recent time of the North American pioneer, spinning, weaving of textiles, making of pottery, of candles, of crude wood furniture, sewing of clothes and above all the processing of food stuffs, baking, pickling, salting of meat, preserving of fruit and a hundred other productional activities took place, required space and found architectural expression of some sort in layout and design of the house. Animal husbandry, the care of domesticated animals segregated itself but slowly from its concept, and chickens, rabbits, goats, cows shared long with dogs and cats the right of the master's and owner's roof. This type of peasant dwelling with lean-to's, and consequently a plan of picturesque accumulation and roof configuration, sentimentally influences to this day the idea of home, while the derivative and diminutions of the landowner's mansion and the nobleman's castle furnish other historico-psychological components. Pronounced protectiveness against intrusion and against the discomfort of climate and weather, a minimum of openings, heavy walls for insulation, fireplaces and expressive chimneys are in many ancient traditions identified with the idea of comfortable home, and the house of the forefathers. Cottages reminiscent of English and French peasants' cottages, Swiss chalets, Mexican ranch houses, Cape Cod fishermen's huts have in painfully variegated rows invaded the suburban subdivision of yesterday's metropolis.

The unprecedented increase of population, the great density of settlement in even very decentralized and fully motorized sectors of civilized countries, further the irreversible industrialization of practically all commodity production now placed apart and outside of the home. All these facts profoundly change the destiny of house design and home comfort. It is anomalous to expect that the requirements of a greatly modified usage, the very much changed aspirations of a new generation, and finally, the new and so different industrially processed materials, tools, construction methods would permit the maintenance or revival of historical design pattern for the contemporary house or the house of the near future.   —R.J.N.

household art. (art ed.) A phase of art concerned with the selection, arrangement, furnishing, care, and maintenance of the home and of its immediate surroundings, often including a study of exterior and interior architecutre, landscape design, period styles of furniture and furnishings. Whitford and Winslow in *Dictionary of Education.*

housing. An expression and a concept relating social reform to conditions of shelter and habitation. Emphasis is hereby placed on needs of the masses of population.

Apart from a certain collectivism in the design or in the structural process in primitive villages (see domestic architecture; house) the housing of families, understood as a large scale socio-economic issue, has historically occurred in certain efforts of colonization, and similarly, in order to secure labor for a certain local manufacture (Fuggerei, 16th cent., Augsburgh, Germany), or to induce the migration of trained workers into a less civilized but not directly colonial region (Frederic II, settlements of skilled French weavers in Brandenburg, Germany, middle 18th cent.).

Housing as a remedy for consciously observed socio-economic deterioration, was first conceived in conjunction with other allied and general reform movements, such as those initiated by Robert Owen, Fourrier, Saint Simon; Marxism in its earlier stages did not pay programmatic attention to this particular phase of societal reconstruction. Up to the conclusion of World War I, remedial criticism of housing conditions, and of the consequential significance of slums, remained largely in the hands of middle class and moralistic reform societies; but problems of sanitation esp., caused at least preventive legislation by states and municipalities, to curb boundless deterioration of living standards and the manifold threat of blighted dwelling areas to the community as a whole.

The garden city movement based on ideas and exemplary action of Ebenezer Howard and Raymond Unwin, originated in England, produced model housing for medium, but not for low incomes. It spread to Germany, Switzerland, Belgium, Holland, and influenced plans of consumer cooperatives in the Scandinavian countries.

After World War I, housing of the workers and the lowest income groups was recognized by Continental governments as in line with other public utilities, and as an object of administrative responsibility. The municipalities of Vienna, Frankfort, A. M. Amsterdam, Rotterdam, Berlin, et. al., during the 20's of this century, prided themselves on having rehoused between 10 and 20 per cent of their respective populations in model housing projects. A scattered *avant guard* of the architectural profession in Europe, North and South Africa, West and East Asia, concentrated attention on housing as a vital ingredient of city and community planning. (C. I. A. M.—Congres Internationaux D'Architecture Moderne).

The American countries, esp. the U. S. A. and Mexico, followed this worldwide movement since the economic depression of the 30's and housing of newly migrated defense workers speeded this activity for a brief period until the current material shortage interrupted most construction during the exhaustive efforts of World War II. Housing is recognized as a peace work reserve of staggering magnitude, to combat post-war economic depression and unemployment. Its significance in improving and stabilizing society can hardly be overestimated.

In contrast to post-Victorian subdivisions, the most advanced recent housing projects excel in an *extension and continuity of communal areas, uninterrupted* by *rolling traffic,* safely enjoyed by children and endowed with *community buildings, day nurseries, kindergartens* and *recreational facilities* for all age levels. The tendency is to produce a rather self-contained *restful neighborhood, in which coherent social activities may develop,* and the amorphous vasts and wastes of yesterday's urban life are avoided. See CIVIC PLANNING; also Catherine Bauer, *Modern Housing* and *Citizen's Guide to Public Housing*; C. A. Perry, *Housing and the Machine Age*; Nat'l. Assoc. of Housing Officials, *Housing Yearbook 1937-42;* The Pacific Southwest Academy, *Los Angeles, Preface of a Master Plan*; Mabel L. Walker, *Urban Blight and Slums*; Edith E. Wood, *Recent Trends in American Housing*; P. W. A., *Urban Housing*; R. J. Thomas, *Housing for Defense*; Miles Colean, *Can America Build Houses?*; Annual of Amer. Acad. of Political and Social Science, *Current Developments in Housing*; R. J. Neutra, Peace Gains from War's Forced Changes, *The New Pencil Points,* November, 1943.   —R.J.N.

hsiang (Ch.). A portrait.

hsieh-chai. See SYMBOLISM IN FAR EASTERN ART.

hsieh-i (Ch.). Free sketch.

hsien (Ch.). Sacrificial bronze vessel. Three hollow bulbous legs as a lower section and a flaring jarlike form above, with two upright vertical handles on the lip. Thought to be a steamer or cooker for sacrificial food.   —J.A.M.

hsi pi (Ch.). Small *pi* (q.v.), used as an ornamental jade girdle pendant.

hu (Ch.). (1) . Sacrificial bronze vessel. A vaselike jar with contracted neck and a base. Sometimes with ring handles at the side. Used for holding wine at the time of sac— (2) Ritualistic jade in the shape of a tiger; symbol of the west.   —J.A.M.

hua (Ch.). A painting; or, to paint.

hua ch'i (Ch.). Literally, painted lacquerware, with pure lacquer as the painting medium.

hua chüan (Ch.). Silk, properly sized and prepared for painting.

hua hui (Ch.). Flowers and plants; one of the stipulated subjects in Chinese schools of painting.

huang (Ch.). Ritualistic jade symbol of the north, in the shape of a half-disc.

Huastec. The name describing the linguistic group living in northern Vera Cruz and southern Tamaulipas who spoke extreme

variations of one of the Maya languages. This term is also applied to the culture found in that region which is fairly homogeneous, although subject to the variations implicit in development over a long period of time.
—G.C.V.

Hudson River school. See POST-REVO-LUTIONARY PAINTING AND SCULP-TURE IN THE U. S. A.

hue. See COLOR.

humanism, the new. A philosophical and critical doctrine popular in the 1920's. Founded by Irving Babbitt and Paul Elmer More, this ethical interpretation of man's place in the universe gave precedence to human free will guided by intuition over theological or scientific determinism. Being the master of his own fate, man can direct his own pro-gress; he must avoid extremes and follow the Aristotelian middle path in conduct and in art. Rousseauistic romanticism and mate-rialistic naturalism became arch enemies to be destroyed, for the former cultivated un-fettered individualism and the latter permit-ted an intellectual attitude of irresponsibil-ity. Classical art and derivative principles were considered the upholders of established cultural values; emphasis was placed upon tradition to such an extent that critics con-sidered the doctrine untenably aristocratic in a democratic society, as well as anti-scien-tific in an age of science. See N. Foerster, ed., *Humanism and America*, 1930; C. H. Grattan, ed., *The Critique of Humanism*, 1931.   —H.R.W.

humanist aesthetics. See AESTHETICS, re-cent trends in (3).

humorous. See ex libris.

hundred antiques. See SYMBOLISM IN FAR EASTERN ART.

hunting rugs. 16th cent. Persian. The field usually showed wild animals portrayed in the position of being pursued, overtaken by and struggling with their hunters, interspersed with scrolls and floral forms. Were hung in palaces and highly prized.   —B.E.J.

hunting horn. See MUSICAL INSTRU-MENTS.

hupa. See California Indian art.

hurdy-gurdy. See MUSICAL INSTRU-MENTS; mechanical instruments.

husflid school. See SCANDINAVIAN ART.

hutch. See FURNITURE.

hydraulis. See MUSICAL INSTRU-MENTS.

hydria. A Greek water pitcher. In the 6th cent. B.C., these vases were characterized by broad-bellied, egg shapes, sometimes with two stubby handles but usually with a large one at the back and two smaller ones at the sides. By the beginning of the 5th cent. B.C., Athenian potters refined the shape, slimming the body, flattening the shoulder, and uniting the neck and body with a grace-ful curve, thus making the hydria among the most attractive of Greek vases.
—W.R.A.

hydrologic cycle. See CIVIC PLANNING.

hymn. According to St. Ambrose (c. 340-97) a hymn was a song in praise of God. Later hymns also honored the Virgin and Saints.

During his exile in Phrygia, Hilary of Poitiers (d. 366) became acquainted with Syrian hymnody. Upon his return to Gaul (c. 360) Hilary's attempt to introduce hymn singing failed because the Gauls apparently lacked artistic perception. Although Isadore of Seville (c. 570-636) refers to Hilary as the first Latin hymn-writer, to Ambrose goes the credit for introducing the hymn from the east into the services of the Western Church. Four hymn-texts with certainty can be as-cribed to the Saint: *Aeterne rerum Conditor*; *Deus Creator omnium*; *Iam surgit hora tertia*; and *Veni Redemptor gentium*. It is impossible to say if the melodies associated with these texts were also written by Am-brose. They may well have been set to pre-existing melodies. Each hymn consists of eight four-line stanzas in iambic dimiter, and each stanza is set syllabically to the same melody. This simple structure was ideal for congregational singing in the antiphonal man-ner. Metrical hymns written in this form in the following centuries were known as *hymni Ambrosiani*. The famous *Te Deum* known throughout the Middle Ages as the *Hymnus Ambrosianus* is not by Ambrose as was formerly supposed but probably by Niceta of Remesiana (c. 335-414).

St. Benedict (c. 480-543) gave hymnody order and method which characterized the Western ritual of later times. The Rule of St. Benedict prescribed the regular singing of Ambrosian hymns in the Offices for the

Canonical Hours (q. v.). Eventually hymns found their way into the Divine Service.

Among the hymn writers who followed Ambrose are Prudentius (348-c. 410), Sedulius (1st half 5th cent.), Gregory I (c. 540-604), and his friend Venantius Fortunatus (530-609). New meters were introduced from time to time but the Ambrosian model remained dominant. Also must be mentioned the Venerable Bede (c. 672-735) and Theodulph, Bishop of Orleans (d. 821) who wrote the celebrated hymn for Palm Sunday in hexameters and pentameters, *Gloria, laus,*

et honor tibi sit, Rex Christe Redemptor. As in the case of Ambrose, the authorship of the melodies is uncertain. Many of these melodies are to be found in the *Antiphonale,* the *Vesperale* and the *Liber Usualis.*

With the "invention" of the *Sequence* (q.v.) by Notker (d. 912) a new era came into Latin hymnody. See Julian, J., *A Dictionary of Hymnology,* 1925. —V.A.

hyomon (Jap.). See heidatsu.

hypo-mode. See idiom A (2).

I

i (Ch.). Sacrificial bronze vessel. Two-handled with flaring rim, to hold sacrificial food. Sometimes rectangular with cover. *I* is also a generic term for all ritual bronze vessels. —J.A.M.

I. C. I. standard observer, white light. See COLOR.

ichi-mai-e (Jap.). A single-sheet woodblock print in black and white.

iconoclasm. The rejection of and active enemity against the use of images in religious cults; an attitude which is the antithesis not so much of the aesthetic and sensuous as of the magic approach towards art. Its argumentation therefore, usually either draws attention to the magic practices connected with image worship (medieval iconoclasm) or it accepts the presupposition of such practices by identifying images with the divinities they portray and then proceeding to decry them as inimical to a spiritual God (Hebrew iconoclasm). Underlying the contest between *iconoclasts* and **iconophiles** (the friends of images) is the problem whether man should try to reach God directly by shunning all sensuous blandishments of the world or whether he should penetrate to him through images and symbols. The term iconoclasm came to prominence first on occasion of the iconoclastic struggle, which from 725-842 A.D. divided the Byzantine world into the hostile camps of friends and enemies of images. In present terminology it is frequently used to designate any movement against established idols, material or spiritual. —R.B.

iconoclasts, Byzantine. The struggle against religious images in the Eastern Roman Empire which began between 724 and 726 and found its final end in 843, when the Feast of Orthodoxy was instituted to commemorate the victory of the upholders of religious imagery, was one of the great religious, political and cultural crises of Byzantine history. The emperors who initiated and chiefly encouraged iconoclasm were Leo III (717-41) and his son Constantine V (741-75), and then, after the iconophile interval of Irene's reign (780-802) and the temporary rehabilitation of the holy images by the second council of Nicaea in 787, again Leo V (813-20), Michael II (820-29) and Theophilus (829-42). The reasons for the outbreak of iconoclasm in the Byzantine Empire should not be sought merely in puritan and even less in rationalistic tendencies. Byzantine iconoclasm was an outgrowth and indeed the climax of the caesaropapistic theory and praxis of the State, as represented by some of the most successful emperors. The example of Jewish and Mohammedan hostility against images seems to have played a not unimportant role. Early-Christian anti-idolatrous tendencies were to some extent revived, but they alone do not suffice for an explanation of the struggle, as the destruction of religious images was accompanied by a remarkable increase of secular imperial imagery. It seems that the iconoclastic emperors understood the old idea of priestly rulership in such a way that only their sacred empire was to be the material form of Christendom in the world. Accordingly, the supra-natural sphere should remain as abstract as possible, and Christ and His saints should not be expressed visibly in images.

The iconclasts succeeded in destroying most of the pre-iconoclastic Christian imagery in the central regions of the Byzantine Empire. During the reign of Irene and after the ultimate victory of orthodoxy the upholders of the images destroyed practically everything

of iconoclastic church art which had been ornamental and symbolical. As a lasting consequence of iconoclasm, sculpture in the round disappeared completely from Byzantine art, while reliefs were allowed. There was never an official prohibition of statues in particular, but the esp. close association of statuary art with pagan idolatry as well as the oriental artistic trend which transformed plastic forms into pictorial patterns, led to this result.
—G.B.L.

iconography. Art of representation by pictures or images; the description or study of portraiture or representation. See RELIGIOUS PAINTING IN RUSSIA; INDIAN ART.

iconophile. See iconoclasm.

iconostasis. See RELIGIOUS PAINTING IN RUSSIA.

ictus. See MEDIEVAL MUSIC.

idealism. Idealism grows out of the conception that all individual things, in so far as they belong to a certain genus, go back to an original, primeval image. This primeval image is the lasting essence through its changes of manifestation. It cannot be found in any individual form which can be perceived by the five senses. It is immaterial. For instance, behind all individual men who have been, who are, or who will be, there lies the idea of man. Imagine, perhaps all human forms photographed upon the same negative; all the qualities characterizing and distinguishing one single individual from another would become equalized and all qualities which men have in common would be emphasized. From the modern point of view, it could be called a "standardized" form, a standard necessarily arising from the manifold variety of individual figures. This idea, therefore, represents the primeval law, or the primeval image from which every separate figure is descended. In the same way that the idea of "mankind" exists, so the idea of "man", and of "woman" exists. There are as many ideas as there are general; e. g., the idea of animal, plant, tree, landscape, etc.

Since this primeval image is eternal and immutable, it must be calm and since this image realizes the primeval law, it must be self-sufficient. Consequently all powers contained in the image become equally, or even symetrically balanced. Since all opposed variations which characterize and distinguish the individuals are made equal, a primeval calm

arises from it and causes the entire disappearance of all such variations; this means that all lines must be continuant and must be retraceable to their starting point. Since these qualities are to be found most perfect in a circle and in forms similar to a circle, idealistic art will express itself mainly in these forms.

The artist devoted to idealistic art should demonstrate the qualities of primeval images in his works; he stands in opposition, let us say, to the artist who is near the individualized or characteristic art. The difficulties of idealistic art lie in the fact that the artist should keep away, on the one hand from the single living individual, and on the other hand from some inanimate pattern, and he should combine that which fills with life the single being with the immutable law. The creators of idealistic art were the Greeks. The climax of this art occurred in the 5th and 4th cents. B.C. In Hellenistic and Roman times idealistic art continued with certain deviations characterizing the changed situation. During the development of Roman art the ideal conception became gradually so very changed by oriental and Germanic influences that in the medieval times following, art took its origin from a quite different point of view than in the antique world. In the 2d half of the 12th and the 1st half of the 13th cents. a distinct inclination toward ideal conceptions is to be noticed in European art. This we call the epoch of the proto-Renaissance.

The renewal of idealism upon a broader basis began in Italy during the 15th cent. This movement, called the Renaissance, invaded the whole of Europe from the South. But, because the point of origin of the post-medieval period was motion rather than calmness, the Renaissance was entirely unable to create and continue idealism. As this element of movement gradually became more and more pressing, the original idealism was forced to change into an overstressed idealism, which we call the baroque. This transition began with Michel Angelo. There is a renewal of idealism in the 18th, 19th and 20th cents., the so-called Classicism. —A.J.S.

idée fixe (Fr.). *Mus.* Berlioz's term for a theme which constantly reappears.

ideographic notation. See NOTATION.

ideological art. See art for propaganda.

idiom. *Mus.* Fundamental organization of musical materials, brought into evidence through the common practice of numerous composers during a considerable length of time and forming the assumptions from which the principles of composition applied in the period under consideration can be derived. The organization of the material constituting an idiom is manifest in choices of preference concerning particularly the **vocabulary** (selection of tones to be used); the character of the basic elements (e.g. intervals in melodic progressions and between simultaneously sounding tones; chords; rhythmic and metrical principles); the type of textural relationships (e.g. monophonic, polyphonic, homophonic; qq.v.) between the elements; the distinction between consonances and dissonances (qq.v.); the treatment of dissonances, etc. (The term **idiom** is also used to designate individual features peculiar of a style (q.v.); e.g. certain melodic figures are idiomatic in the Palestrina style, certain harmonic progressions are idiomatic with Wagner, certain rhythmic phenomena are idiomatic in Spanish folk-music, etc.) In the music of the Western civilization three chief idioms can be distinguished: modality, tonality, atonality.

A. **Modality** is the oldest of the three idioms. Its main principles are: (1) The vocabulary of modality is the seven tones of the diatonic series which has within each octave segment five whole-tone and two half-tone steps. (2) For systematical purposes, tones appearing in prominent places (mainly at phrase endings) of modal music are considered **key-notes** of different modal scales which thus are distinguished by the different locations of the whole-tone and half-tone steps in relation to that key-note which is called the *finalis* (final) of the mode. Definition and nomenclature of the modes have varied considerably from antiquity throughout the Middle Ages. The names given to the modes are derived from the terminology evolved by the theorists of ancient Greece. The following classification, formulated in the Renaissance period, accounts for most cases of modal music (*finales* in brackets after the name of the mode): Ionian (C), Dorian (D), Phrygian (E), Lydian (F), Mixolydian (G), Aeolian (A). These are the authentic modes. There is an equal number of **plagal**, or **hypo-modes**, so designated because their names are formed by adding the prefix *hypo* to the name of the corresponding authentic mode. The plagal modes have the same *finales* as the corresponding authentic modes. Roughly speaking, a melody is ascribed to an **authentic mode** when its lowest tone is identical with the final of the mode and the range of the melody covers approximately one octave above the final. A melody is ascribed to a plagal mode when its range reaches approximately four tones below and five tones above the final (e.g. a melody with final C and the range G-g is called hypo-Ionian, etc.). Thus the modes are a system useful for the classification of melodies according to what segments of the diatonic series they characteristically cover. (3) Alterations of the tones of the modes (modifications through raising or lowering tones by half-tone steps) are used sparingly and conditionally. On the basis of the diatonic series C-D-E-F-G-A-B, the following alterations were admitted almost exclusively: C sharp, E flat, F sharp, G sharp, B flat (not their enharmonic equivalents; see enharmony). (4) Early modal music was monophonic (see monophony) (e.g. Gregorian chant). Later (particularly ecclesiastical) modal music was polyphonic (see polyphony). Because of the prevailing contrapuntal texture (see counterpoint) of this music, the intervals formed between the various voices were of paramount relevance, and increasing attention was paid to their different degrees of tension (see consonance), until definite and consistent distinction was made between consonances and dissonances, the use of the latter being restricted by detailed regulations as to preparation, resolution, metrical placement, etc. In the course of this evolution, the allegiance of a melody to a particular mode became determined rather by the more and more typified approaches to the final (see cadence) than by the range covered by that melody. A beginning of harmonic orientation became manifest particularly in the behavior of several voices participating in cadences, so that in the latest period of modality homophonic texture gained increasing significance. (5) In modality, cadences on other steps than the final of the mode can have one of the following forms: [a] in the approach to the cadence tone, only tones of the original mode are used; [b] a cadence formula typical of the mode of which the cadence tone is the final is used; [c] the cadence tone is treated as the final of the original (or some other) mode transposed to a pitch level different from that of the original mode (e.g., a phrase in the Ionian mode may have an intermediate cadence on A; in the case [a] the cadence tone A may be reached from G; in the case [b] it may be reached from G sharp which suggests a cadence formula typical of Aeolian; in the case [c] another voice may have C sharp (the major third of A, instead of the minor third, C, available in Ionian), which suggests that the tone A is considered the final of an Ionian mode beginning on A, in other words: that the phrase "modulates" to "Ionian in the key of A" (see key). The use of this modulatory principle was restricted to such processes which did not involve the introduction of other alterations than those listed under A.(3). (6) In ecclesiastical modal music, the relative metrical weight of melody tones is determined chiefly by rhythmic conditions (length; see rhythm) and location within the range of the melody (pitch). The various contrapuntal principles applied in different periods of modality presuppose an arrangement of the basic rhythmic units of the melodic lines in groups of two or three (double, or triple, time). This concept, however, does not imply a dynamic stress (see accent) on every first unit of such a group. Especially in ecclesiastical modal music, points of emphasis appear in the various voices at irregular time intervals. In secular modal music a tendency towards coincidence of the points of emphasis with the first units of the basic rhythmic groups is manifest.

B. **Tonality** is the idiom which superseded modality in the later part of the 16th cent. As far as the vocabulary was concerned, the transition from modality to tonality consisted mainly in that two of the Renaissance modes, Ionian and Aeolian, were used preferentially, later exclusively, under the name of major and minor modes. Intermediate cadences on other steps than the *finales* of these two modes were regularly treated according to the process described under A.(5)[c], so that each step of the two basic modes could be considered the final of a transposition of one of the basic modes. In the late 17th cent., especially under the assumption of the Equal Temperament (q.v.), this concept was made applicable to each of the twelve tones available within the range of an octave. On account of these evolutionary processes, tonality can be considered a specific case of modality. Since, however, the transition from modality to tonality implied essential changes of fundamental principles of composition, it is advisable to reserve the term modality for the idiom described under A. The principles of tonality, as compared to those of modality, are the following: (1) Tonal music is characterized by prevailingly harmonic orientation, even in cases of contrapuntal texture (e.g. J. S. Bach). Therefore the tones of the tonal scales have significance above all by virtue of the functions ascribed to the chords built in intervals of thirds upon the degrees of the major and minor scales (triads, seventh chords, etc.), the functions being a set of principles by which chord progressions are evaluated aesthetically mainly with respect to the position of the roots of the chords in the scale and to the intervals between the roots of consecutive chords. In order to classify the functions, the tones of the scales are given the following names (in ascending order): Tonic, Supertonic, Mediant, Subdominant, Dominant, Submediant, Leading Tone. (2) Each tone of the twelve tones available within the range of an octave can be made the reference point for identical sets of harmonic functions. In other words, each of the twelve tones is the key-note of a major and a minor scale. Thus the major and minor modes appear each in twelve different keys. The keys are given names after their keynotes (e.g.: C major, C minor, C sharp major, C sharp minor, etc.). (3) The concept of **modulation**, viz. transition from one key to another by interpreting elements common to both keys as having functions in the key to be left as well as in the key to be' introduced, is used without the restrictions attached to it in modality (see A. (5)) and became one of the most effective devices of articulation of form in tonal music (see articulation). (4) Tones not belonging to the scale of the basic key were used with increasing frequency, as tonality developed. Such tones are considered alterations of, or substitutions for, tones of the basic scales, and as such they affect the harmonic functions in various characteristic ways. The five tones available in each key for such purposes are called **chromatic tones.** More recently the term "chromatic" is used for any melodic progression in half-tone steps. (5) In the course of evolution, distinction between consonances and dissonances, from the outset overshadowed by the principle of harmonic functions, became gradually less relevant. (6) The basic groupings of rhythmic units, similar to those of modality (double, triple time, or composites of these like six-eighth, five-four, etc.), have metrical significance in that musical elements placed on the first units of such groups (bars) carry accents (see accent). Phrase accents by which articulation in spans larger than the basic rhythmic units is secured may, or may not, coincide with the accented rhythmic units. Symmetry (q.v.)—recurrence of metrical situations in regular time intervals—is characteristic of tonality. The evaluation of chord progressions laid down in the system of harmonic functions is brought into close reference to the rhythmic and metrical conditions of tonal music. (The term **tonality** is sometimes used to designate the existence of any kind of relationships between musical sounds, necessary to make their presentation aesthetically meaningful. In this sense, tonality is a synonym of **music.** If the term is so used, the three idioms discussed here appear as different forms of tonality. In this case it would be necessary to apply another term at least to the idiom described under B., in order to discuss the differences between the three idioms. Hence it seems advisable to use the terms tonality only in the sense outlined under B.)

C. **Atonality,** in a purely linguistic sense, is any idiom characterized by the absence of the properties of tonality, as outlined under B. (Thus, modality might be considered a case of atonality.) The term atonality is more specifically used to designate the idiom which evolved from the tonal idiom in the 20th cent. In the latest period of tonality, the increasingly frequent use of chromatic tones obscured the harmonic functions and the principles related to them to such an extent that they could not any longer be relied upon for the derivation of the principles of composition applied in a large portion of contemporary music. Although it is possible to identify any isolated musical element as belonging to one, or more, of the keys of tonality, many of the contexts in which elements were placed in the 20th cent. suggest the formation of a basic organization different from that of tonality. The main principles of atonality, as compared to those of the other idioms, may be outlined as follows: (1) The vocabulary of atonality is the twelve tones available within the range of an octave. They are used without reference to a normative selection, or selections of tones (modes) from that vocabulary. (2) Factors of reference (tones, chords, motifs, etc.) emerge through the relative emphases put on them in their particular contexts rather than from a generally binding system of relationships

(such as the harmonic functions of tonality, the cadence formulae of modality, etc.). Melodic, rhythmic, harmonic (in this order) correspondences between different parts of a structure are the principal factors in establishing unity of design and articulation of form. (3) Polyphonic orientation prevails in atonality. Therefore, and because of the absence of a harmonic reference system, the degrees of tension of intervals between the various voices are of a relevance similar to that which they had in modality. Consonant combinations, however, are used rather sparingly. (4) Increase and decrease of tension are also the criteria according to which chord progressions are mainly evaluated wherever atonal music has a more homophonic texture. Factors modifying and specifying the amount of tension which a chord has by virtue of its constituent intervals (see Chord) are location of those intervals in relation to each other, dynamic conditions, sound color (timbre), **voice leading** (character of the motion by which the different voices, especially the top and bottom voices, reach the chord), rhythmic and metrical situation. (5) Chords may be built on any of the twelve tones and be constituted by any kind and number of intervals. (6) Rhythmic and metrical conditions of atonal music, especially of the polyphonic type, resemble to a considerable extent those of modality, although the systematical accent (dynamic stress on the first unit of a basic rhythmic group; see Accent) still plays a more or less important part. Phrase accents are distributed prevailingly in irregular time intervals.   —E.K.

Idolino. A bronze statue in Florence, representing a graceful standing youth. It has many of the characteristics of Polyclitus' sculpture, especially the wavy pattern of the hair and the serene pose of the body and facial expression.   —W.R.A.

Iga yaki (Jap.). Pottery made in the province of Iga.

Igeta yaki (Jap.). Pottery made in Tanba province.

ihia (Jap.). Ancestral tablet. A small lacquered tablet on which the name of a deceased ancestor is inscribed. These ancestral tablets are hung in the family shrine.
                    —J.A.M.

ikake-ji (Jap.). A lacquer technique in which the entire ground is covered with gold.

ikat (Jav.). A type of weaving whereby, before being woven, yarn is dyed by the tie-dye method to synchronize with the pattern desired.   —J.A.M.

ikebana (Jap.). The art of flower arrangement. See *Japanese Flower Arrangement,* Mary Averill, 1928; *The Art of Flower Arrangement in Japan,* A. L. Sadler, 1933; *Japanese Flower Arrangement for Modern Homes,* Margaret Preininger, 1936; *The Art of Japanese Flower Arrangement,* Alfred Koahn, 1934.

illuminating. *Book.* Ornamentation in gold and colors, usually on vellum.

illumination. See BOOK ILLUSTRATION; PSYCHOLOGY OF ART.

illusionism. The effort in painting or sculpture to create as nearly as possible an illusion of visual reality. The painting or modelling of "substitute objects", i.e. objects so like their prototypes as to serve in the manner of substitutes for them. Naturalism (q.v.) and impressionism (q.v.) are forms of illusionism. Perspective, foreshortening, chiaroscuro for the sake of modelling form or defining transient effects of light striking a surface, representational line drawing, and microscopic and *trompe l'oeil* detail are all potentially aids to illusionism, which is more essentially an applied science than an art and can be taught by academic rules and demonstrations. Photographs and casts from the live model may be used by illusionistic painters and sculptors as crutches to aid in achieving their ends. In sculpture the material used is made to imitate real flesh or drapery; painting of the figure in natural colors may be employed; real hair or clothing may be added; a base may be omitted so that under ideal conditions the spectator may indeed be led to an erroneous perception and believe himself actually in the presence of the original imitated by the sculptor.

In practice few artists have coveted pure illusionism at any time in history, but in the late 19th cent. and in the Hellenistic period they came nearest to it. The term "illusionistic" is used comparatively, however, to describe West Christian art as opposed to East Christian, the Odyssey Landscapes as opposed to Greek art of the 5th and 4th centuries B.C., *quattrocento* (q.v.) Italian art as compared with medieval Byzantine or Gothic, Renaissance art in comparison with

contemporary, Western art in contrast to Oriental.   —L.D.L.

image sequence. See PHOTOGRAPHY.

imagination. The faculty of having images, i.e., sensuous mental concepts; or, in a less restricted sense, the faculty of building up any kind of mental concept; with an emphasis on the power of evoking these images or concepts in the absence of the real objects represented by them. As expressing the power of free evocation, unfettered by adherence to factuality, the word describes an important aspect of artistic creativeness. In modern aesthetic discussions, the term usually has for its background the idealistic philosophy of Kant and his followers, of F. W. J. Schelling, S. T. Coleridge, R. W. Emerson, and others. These thinkers viewed art as the product and manifestation of human creativity. "Imagination" (*Einbildungskraft*), adopted as a name for the faculty of artistic conception, was considered by them an effluence of the creative center of human personality. Coleridge defined imagination as "the living Power and Prime Agent of all human Perception" (*Biographia Literaria,* Ch. XIII), and also as the "soul" of poetic genius (*Ibid.,* Ch. XIV). He distinguished it as an animating and integrating power from "fancy", the "drapery" of genius, which "has no other counters to play with, but fixities and definites." Much in the same sense a later author, Bernard Bosanquet, asserted that imagination is not a separate faculty but "the mind at work" (*Three Lectures on Aesthetic,* 1915, p. 26).   —H.K.

imagism. A poetic movement which flourished in Eng. and U. S. from 1909 to 1917. T. E. Hulme's esthetic philosophy stirred Ezra Pound to unite a group hostile to romanticism and friendly to the innovations of modern French poets, to the recently translated Chinese and Japanese epigrammatic verse, and to Greek and Roman classical poetry. Chief members were Hilda Doolittle, Richard Aldington, and John Gould Fletcher. After editing *Des Imagistes* (1914), Pound withdrew, and Amy Lowell assumed active leadership by asking that the group subscribe for three years to a fixed program. Their credo, announced in *Some Imagist Poets* (1915), included the use of exact words from common speech in condensed and suggestive expression, the avoidance of clichés, the creation of new rhythms to express new moods, the free choice of subjects from modern life, and the presentation of concrete, firm, precise pictures or images (hence the name). They wrote chiefly in free verse (q.v.) forms. See Glenn Hughes, *Imagism and the Imagists,* 1931.   —H.R.W.

Imarki yaki (Jap.). Japanese pottery made in Hizen province.

imitation. *Mus.* Device of polyphonic composition by which a melodic phrase, or motif, presented in one part is repeated shortly afterwards in another part while the first part continues with a suitable counterpart. **Imitation by inversion** is imitative repetition of a given melody using its inversion (q.v.).
                                                    —E.K.

imitations of old masters. See FORGERIES IN PAINTING.

impasto. Used to describe the mixture of pigment and medium (oil or turpentine, or both) with which a picture is painted.

impost. The top member of a pillar, pier, wall, etc., upon which the weight of an arch rests.

impregnation method. See RESTORATION OF PAINTINGS.

impresa. Any pictorial emblem when used as the insignia of a person (or group of persons) provided that it refers through metaphorical implication either to the life story or to the aims, beliefs and convictions of that person. In absence of such metaphorical implication any impresa will degenerate into a mere mark of cognition or heraldic sign. Although often no more than a piece of fashionable pedantry the impresa was originally and primarily meant to be a tool for the training of the will designed to remind its "owner" by its ubiquity in his environment of his permanent ideals and aspirations.
                                                    —R.B.
impression. See PRINTS AND PRINT PROCESSES.

impressionism. A variety of naturalism (q.v.) which depicts objectively the world of ephemeral appearance. (1) The effort to present a general impression of an incident, a view, or an object, rather than to record it in detail, to paint or model what the eye sees at a glance, not what it knows to be there,—accomplished ordinarily with comparative rapidity and suggesting a sketch of the bare essentials. Ideally the doctrine requires an objective attitude with no personal com-

ment, no alteration or exaggeration of the record of instantaneous vision for the sake of design or personal self-expression, as in the case of expressionism (q.v.); but this ideal is seldom completely realized in practice either in painting and sculpture or in poetry and prose. Normally the attention of the artist is concentrated upon superficial appearances, as opposed to inner structure of forms or events, which distinguishes impressionism from abstraction (q.v.). The human meaning or underlying essence of forms or events is programmatically neglected by the impressionist, who therefore has nothing in common with realists, idealists, and romanticists (q.v.). Like all formal naturalists he restricts his interests to the world of vision, but some impressionists are also philosophical naturalists, i.e. naturalists in content as well as form.

Used in the broadest sense the term impressionist includes such artists as Frans Hals, late Velasquez, some Hogarths (e.g. the *Shrimp Girl*), the antique painter of the *Odyssey Landscapes,* Turner, some Constables, Whistler, Sargent, Liebermann, Sorolla, Rodin, et al., as well as the French artists of the late nineteenth century to whom the term applies in a special sense.

(2) Specifically impressionism implies the study of light reflecting on surfaces as exemplified in the work of Monet, Pissarro, Sisley, et al., in late 19th century French painting. These artists made a scientific study of light and color, and have sometimes been called "luminists" to distinguish them from impressionists in the broader meaning of the term. They used the "pointillist" or "divisionist" method of applying paint in small spots of pure color (i.e. color not previously mixed on the palette), and by this method succeeded in getting the bright tones of sunlight. They painted rapidly in the open rather than in the studio and, foresaking composition and design, form and inner structure, interpretation and subject interest, recorded short-hand impressions of light striking on the surfaces of the same objects at varying times of day and under varying atmospheric conditions. For the most part they painted landscapes.

They were first called impressionists after an exhibition held in Paris in 1874. Some of the other artists who exhibited with the impressionists at the various group shows of the 1870's, when impressionism was the latest movemen in art, were at most transient impressionists, or else were never consistent believers in the doctrine in the "luminist" sense just described, or were more interested in capturing fleeting movement than fugitive light effects. Such was the case with Cézanne, Degas, Renoir, and Gauguin. Other impressionists of the late 19th and early 20th century include Bazille, Guillaumin, the late Manet, Berthe Morisot, and such Americans as Mary Cassatt, Sargent, Childe Hassam, Twachtman, Weir and Friesecke.

(3) As applied to sculpture, impressionism refers to modelling of forms with bosses and hollows, which do not describe form with anatomical accuracy or reveal the essential structure of form, but which reflect light in such a way as to create the illusion of natural form; and it further refers to modelling which captures the sense of fleeting movement. Impressionism in sculpture developed later and was influenced by the movement in painting, and is more pictorial than plastic. Hence impressionist sculptors are exclusively modellers rather than carvers and their natural media are bronze and terra cotta. Rodin is the chief representative of impressionistic sculpture, but the sculpture of Degas and some of the modelled works of Carpeaux, Barye, Epstein, George Gray Barnard, and Gutzon Borglum, are also impressionistic.

(4) As applied to literature, impressionism is an endeavor uncritically to express the immediate, hyperesthetic, vibrant sensations produced by the external world. It involves an intensely nervous style of picturesque virtuosity and is little concerned with formal clarity. Its pictorialism shows the influence of impressionist painting of the day. In literature, more often than in painting, subjective attitudes creep into impressionism. The Goncourt brothers represent impressionistic literature in purest form. Later writers like Pierre Loti and the Symbolist poets use impressionistic methods, but in order to attain more subjective and expressionistic ends. In America impressionistic form is used by Ezra Pound, Carl Sandberg, Amy Lowell, Sherwood Anderson, and John Dos Passos, but without a consistent objectivity.

(5) Applied to music, impressionism is sometimes used to describe the work of such men as Debussy and Ravel, and is used in general, whatever the date, in referring to descriptive music based on pictorial subjects, but, as in literature, subjective qualities and formal order are stronger in impressionistic music than in analogous painting. —L.D.L.

impressionism and photography. See PHOTOGRAPHY.

impressionistic criticism. See art criticism.

impromptu. *Mus.* Extempore; an improvisation; a piece in the manner of a fantasia.

in (Jap.). See seal.

Inbe yaki (Jap.). Pottery made in Bizen province.

Inca art. See ABORIGINAL AMERICAN ART.

incandescent bodies. See COLOR.

incense burner. See koro.

inchoate. Lack of organization with specific reference to the treatment of the emotional aspects of a literary work. The word indicates that the emotional responses recorded in the work have been inadequately felt, reflected upon, and analyzed. Hence, the work does not tell with any accuracy or finesse what the emotional effect was: it can only say that it was strong or 'overwhelming'. The inchoate work of art is bad because it exhibits an inability to bring order and clarity into one's feelings. —I.J.

incidental use. See CIVIC PLANNING.

incised relief. See relief sculpture.

incubation. See PSYCHOLOGY OF ART.

independence, musical. See polyphony.

India, art of. See INDIAN ART.

India rugs. Introduced into India by the Mohammedans in the beginning of the 11th cent. The Emperor Akbar introduced Persian workmen about end of 16th cent. Followed Persian design at first. Two types of patterns: (1) Field divided into quatrefoils or ogee compartments each containing a naturalistic plant or floral forms. (2) Detached sprigs of flowers arranged in various ways. —B.E.J.

INDIAN ART. Art in India, since its beginnings, has been dedicated to the great religious systems of India: Brahmanism or Hinduism, Buddhism, Jainism, and the many indigenous nature cults that have always flourished in southwestern Asia. It has been an art concerned with the statement of the traditional principles embodied in these faiths and never with the self-conscious creation of beauty for its own sake. The monuments of the great periods of Indian art history are icons with the primary utilitarian function of presenting the divine prototype in material form for the express veneration of the worshipper. If they are beautiful or moving, it is because they have been effectively fashioned to fulfill this purpose and not because the craftsman deliberately set out to make something "artistic" with superficially pleasing surfaces. It was the final purpose of art in India to present to the believer all of the truths and certainties of his religion.

The Indus Valley Culture (*c. 3300- c. 2000 B.C.*). The earliest known examples of art in India are the material fragments of a great civilization that flourished in the Indus valley from 3300 to ca. 2000 B.C. Little is known of the people who built up the great commercial city of Mohenjo Daro, but it can be definitely established that this culture antedated the invasion of the Aryans in the 2nd millenium B.C. From the finding of objects of Indian manufacture in the ruins of Tell Asmar and other centers of early Babylonian culture it has been determined that commercial and artistic links related the civilizations of the Indus and the Two Rivers. It is for this reason ,that the name "Indo-Sumerian" has sometimes been used to describe the culture of Mohenjo Daro. The designation of "Indus Valley Culture" is, however, to be considered more appropriate for a period so predominantly Indian in character. The few fragments of sculpture found at Mohenjo Daro include a number of male heads and busts faintly suggestive of Mesopotamian forms in their conventions and heavy, static form which may perhaps be identified as priests of a Shamanistic cult. A small male torso, discovered at Harappa (Pañjāb), is completely Indian and, in certain respects, already prophesies the expression and technique typical of the historical periods of Indian art; it is distinguished by that miraculous realization of the very quality of flesh in stone that has always been one of the special achievements of the Indian craftsman. The surface of the skin is taut, as though undergoing the tension of an expanding inner force. It is this quality that is responsible for suggesting the roundness and fullness of the form. This is a technique of elimination in which all details of superficial imitation are avoided and only the essential articulation and form of the body are given. By far the most numerous class of objects

found at Mohenjo Daro are the small steatite seals or talismen with remarkably living carvings of such typically Indian animals as the zebu, the urus ox, and the elephant in addition to representations of divinities both Indian and Mesopotamian. The animals are represented from the conceptual point of view in that each element of the anatomy is shown from its most characteristic aspect; and the creatures appear marvellously imbued with life.

The Maurya Period (*322-185 B.C.*). With the final disaster that overwhelmed Mohenjo Daro it was as if a shroud had been drawn over Indian art history for more than a thousand years. No authenticated objects of art can be assigned to that epic period from 1500 to 400 B.C. which saw the compilation of the Vedic hymns and Brahmanas, the rise of Buddhism and Jainism, and the emergence of modern Hinduism. Indian art, indeed, seemingly only emerged from the darkness with the rise of the Maurya dynasty and the creation of a new tradition of monumental art, possibly under Western influence as a result of the invasion of Alexander the Great (327 B.C.). Now, for the first time, we find a new art, dedicated to the propagandizing of the religion of Buddha. The forms of this art are in all likelihood of Iranian and Greek derivation, but its symbolism is explicitly Indian. Generally associated with that great patron of Buddhism, the Emperor Aśoka (*272-232 B.C.*), are the tall columns or lats, many of them over fifty feet in height, which were erected at the sites sacred to the omission of Buddha both in India and in Nepal. The most famous and beautiful of these monuments is the pillar that once stood at Sārnāth, scene of the Buddha's first preaching. It was surmounted by a capital consisting of four lions upholding a gigantic wheel. Although it is possible that this memorial was raised as a solar symbol prior to the time of Aśoka, it came to be regarded as emblematic of the universal domination of the Buddha's Law, typified by the great Wheel or *dharmacakra*. The lions, which formed a throne for the wheel, are reminiscent of the style of Achaemenid Iran; the four smaller animals, carved on the plinth, might have been done by workmen imported from the Hellenistic regions with which the Mauryan emperors maintained diplomatic contacts. If the art of the Mauryan column is properly speaking a royal art wrought largely by foreign craftsmen, forms of a more popular and Indian character are represented by the many colossal statutes of *yaksas* and *yaksis* dating from this same period. These figures, as an example of which one may select the Parkham *yaksa* in the Muttra Museum, are the earliest examples of monumental figure sculpture in stone. They are characterized by an absolute frontality and an almost overwhelming weight and massiveness. It is almost certain that they represent the first attempt of sculptors long accustomed to working in wood or metal to translate the techniques of these media into stone. It must be remembered that these statues of nature spirits, like all later Indian icons, are not conceived as possible biological organisms based on an observation of human models, but rather as symbols of great simplicity and power in which only those features essential to expressing the protective and generative faculties of these beings is presented to the worshipper.

The Sunga and Early Āndhra Periods (c. 200-25 B.C.). If the sculptured figures decorating the Buddhist monuments of the Sunga and Early Āndhra periods, such as the *yaksis* on the Buddhist railing at Bharhut, seem to mark an improvement over the seemingly archaic conceptions of the Maurya craftsmen, this is not to be interpreted as a sudden turning to the observation of nature, but rather as the more direct and more effective realization of mental images and their projection into material form by craftsmen who were now completely conversant with the technique of stone carving. In this as in all other periods of Indian art the Indian artist was guided by a system of prescribed canons and proportions to which he accommodated the object of his making, the object with which he identified himself in yoga meditation. The sculpture of the Sunga period consists mainly of the reliefs decorating the Buddhist railings surrounding the stupa at Bhārhut and the enclosure of the sacred precinct at Bodh Gayā. Some of the *yaksi* figures reveal a poignantly direct sense of the full beauty of the human form, conceived not as an articulate or possible biological organism but as the totality of so many individually beautiful and mechanistically joined parts. Here for the first time we may see developing the iconography of the Buddha story. In this period of Indian art He who had passed into the realm of invisibility where neither gods nor men shall know Him was represented only by symbols, such as the Wheel and the **Bodhi Tree**, emblematic of the great events in His earthly mission. The carvings of this period are concerned with directness of communication; laws of normal vision and all such considerations as perspective and spatial arrangement are of little importance for the representation of these events of no time and no place which exist as eternal certainties in the heart and mind of the worshipper. Among these Buddhist primitives one may select as especially magnificent embodiments of the Indian ideal the decorations of the four gateways of the stupa at Sāñchī, erected in the Early Āndhra period (c. 72-25 B.C.). No more eloquent and expressive embodiment of the sensuality and desirability of the feminine form exist anywhere in the art of the world than the *yaksis* which swing like living vines from the *toranas* of the sacred enclosure. The parts of the body are simplified and emphasized with the clarity of poetic metaphor. Never is there the least suggestion of the imitation of the accidental or actual form of any human model, but rather the presentation of the essential or permanent structure beneath the surface appearance of things. The narrative panels at Sāñchi, very deeply carved so as to gain full advantage of the brilliant Indian sunlight, show us a number of consecutive incidents shuffled together without regard to chronological associations almost in the same way that these images are stored all together in the mind of the artist.

Something must be said about the **stupas** or relic mounds, of which the sculpture discussed above provided the principal decoration. These in their simplest form were hemispherical tumuli on a square or round base and surmounted by a superstructure consisting of a balcony-like member or *harmikā* and a mast supporting a number of parasols. It seems that originally such mounds were raised for royal sepulchral type was used to enshrine the relics of the Buddha and His saints. In addition to its function of enclosing the corporeal remains of the Tathāgata and as a symbol of His *Nirvāna*, the tumulus embodied in its architecture the Indian concept of the world. The base represented the earth; the hemispherical cupola, the enclosing dome of the sky; and the umbrellas, the various heavens or planes of reference that rise one above the other on the world axis above the finite realm of man. The dome of the stupa figuratively encloses the shape of the world mountain Meru, on the summit of which is set the heaven of the Thirty-three Gods, architecturally represented by the *harmikā*. This symbolism is thoroughly compatible with Buddhist doctrine in that the Buddha had come to be regarded as equivalent to the world itself; the stupa is that world; it is the architectural body of the Buddha miraculously animated by the quickening presence of the relics.

Also dating from the Sunga period are a number of rock cut sanctuaries or *caitya* halls, notably the shrines at Bhājā, Bedsa, and Kārli in the immediate vicinity of Bombay. These Buddhist cathedrals are basilican in form with a rounded apse usually containing a carved stupa as the principal object of worship. The body of the grotto temples is divided into nave and side aisles by rows of columns terminating in the ambulatory. It is believed that all of these elements including the rounded vault and the façade in the shape of the *pipal* leaf are imitations in stone of pre-existing free-standing temples of wood and thatch. The exact symbolism of these impressive cave-temples is not known, but it is believed that, like the stupa, they are reconstructions of the fabric of the cosmic house. The earliest rock cut shrine in India is the Lomas Rsi cave dating from Maurya times; the Bhājā temple has been dated about 200 B.C.; and the largest of these monuments at Kārlī was dedicated in 80 B.C.

Greco-Buddhist Art (1st-6th cents. A.D.). It seems strangely paradoxical that one of the schools of art most important for the whole future development of art in India and all Asia is not properly Indian at all but largely the creation of foreign craftsmen: this is the so-called Greco-Buddhist school of sculpture that flourished in Gandhāra (northwestern India and Afghanistan) from the 1st to the 6th cents. A.D. It has been assumed without really suffiicient evidence that the hypothetical existence of a school of Hellenistic art in Bactria was directly responsible for the development of the debased Classic style in Asia; however, from the date of the monuments and from their style it is apparent that Gandhāra sculpture is simply the easternmost florescence of Late Antique art (q.v.) and might indeed be regarded as a provincial Roman school created with the participation of artisans imported to these regions from Syria or some other province of the eastern Roman empire with which the sovereigns of Gandhāra are known to have maintained an intimate commercial relationship. The Gandhāra sculptures were largely the donations of that foreign dynasty of kings, the Kushanas, of Scythian stock, who were masters of all northwestern India and Afghanistan in the period under discussion. The Gandhāra sculptures are, of course, Indian in content in so far as their subject matter is entirely Buddhist, but their style is marked by that same abstraction of the humanistic Classical formula found in late Roman and Early Christian art. The principal contribution of the school to Asiatic art was its creation of the Buddha image. The Great Teacher is represented with the features of a Greek Apollo and in the pose and costume of a Greek philosopher. Only in the very last phases of its existence did the Gandhāra school produce sculpture of a marked esthetic character. The images in lime plaster that decorated the monasteries of Hadda in southern Afghanistan are marked by a sort of spiritualized realism that seems to prophesy the achievements of Gothic art in the 13th cent. Especially significant for their influence on Chinese Buddhist art are the two colossal Buddhas, 120 and 175 feet in height, that were hewn from the sandstone cliffs at Bāmiyān in the 5th and 6th cents. A.D.

Architecture in Gandhāra is represented chiefly by the ruins of monastic establishments in the environs of Taxila and Peshawar. The plan of these buildings is very simple, consisting of a number of courts with cells for the monks' habitation and niches for the images. The stupas of northwestern India and Afghanistan are more elaborate than the earlier types, and in their original state were clothed in a revetment of Buddhist statuary in lime plaster and stone.

The Kushan Period (c. 50-320 A.D.). Exactly contemporary with the hybrid productions of the Gandhāra school is the sculpture that once ornamented the sanctuaries of the southern capital of the Kushan kings at Muttra (Mathurā). Some scholars believe that the artists of the Kushan school and not the foreign workmen in Gandhāra were the first to represent the Buddha in an anthropomorphic shape. The Buddha statues from Muttra, some of which date from the reign of King Kanishka (128-160 A.D.), are thoroughly Indian in their form and expression. They have the heroic proportions of the *yaksas* of the Maurya period. The magic marks or *laksana* and other attributes calculated to express the superhuman proportions of the Buddha are all explicitly portrayed. The most famous of these is the statue dedicated by the monk Bala at Sārnāth in the third year of Kanishka. It is distinguished by that same remarkable suggestion of the warmth and softness of the flesh already described in works of earlier periods. The figure has none of the effeminate beauty of the Apollonian Buddhas of the Gandhara school but is conceived in completely Indian terms. No less Indian in their overblown voluptuousness are the extremely sensuous carvings of *yaksīs* that ornamented the enclosures of the stupas at Muttra. A unique type of sculpture at Muttra is to be found in the portraits of the Kushan monarchs. These absolutely rigid and frontal effigies of Kanishka and other princes of the dynasty have little that is Indian about them and seem more nearly related to the statues of the royal portraits of Parthia.

It seems likely that the famous Mahābodhi temple at Bodh Gayā, although considerably modified by restorations in the Pāla period (730-1197 A.D.) and an almost complete reconstruction in the 19th century, was built as early as the 2d cent. A.D. Its form is that of a towering truncated pyramid flanked by four lesser towers raised on a podium-like foundation storey. Originally, the exterior was decorated with multiple Buddha images set in niches. The most interesting architectural feature of this building was unfortunately eliminated during the restorations of the 19th cent. This consisted of structural pointed arches and vaults in the inner chamber. This was an architectural element so thoroughly un-Indian that we are forced to conclude that it was introduced either from Iran or from the eastern Roman empire.

The Later Āndhra Period (*150-300 A.D.*). The art of South India in these same centuries is represented by the luxuriant and exquisite limestone sculptures from the great stupa at Amarāvatī, dedicated under the patronage of the kings and queens of the Later Āndhra dynasty. The svelte and languorous beauty of the figures that crowd the reliefs of the Buddha legend are at once a continuation of the canons of perfection of the Kushan school and a prophecy of the culmination of the Indian esthetic ideal in the work of the Gupta period.

The Gupta Period: Painting (*320-600 A.D.*). The Gupta period is one of the great epochs in Indian civilization, an exquisite and talented civilization, marked at once by the unparalleled magnificence and dusty splendor of the imperial courts and a flowering of all the arts—painting, sculpture, literature, and music. The most perfect expression of the luxurious and sophisticated elegance of this Golden Age is to be found in the great cycle of wall-paintings that cover the walls of the rock cut Buddhist sanctuaries at Ajantā. These wall-paintings are not illustrations of that primitive Buddhism reflected in the art of the Gardhāra and Kushan periods, but are dedicated to that developed form of the religion, the Buddhism of the Great Vehicle or Mahāyāna. Predominant are the princely forms of the **Bodhisattvas,** at once saving deities and incarnations of the Buddha's virtues, who throng the pantheon of this now thoroughly mystical and esoteric faith. One of the great masterpieces of Indian art is the Bodhisattva of the Blue Lotus in the first of the twenty-six caves at Ajantā. The figure looms as a mystic vision of divine loveliness and compassion before the ecstatic eyes of the humans and animals that fill the giant composition. The figure is not modelled on any standards of beauty, but is composed in a canon of proportion and ideal shapes calculated the more effectively and appropriately to evoke the divine and superhuman nature of the Great Being. Just as the poet employs the metaphor to suggest the beauty of his subject, so the Indian artist employs shapes drawn from the animal and plant world to describe the final perfection of the godly anatomy; as is specifically indicated in the manuals of artistic practice, the eyes are in the shape of lotus petals; the tensile curve of the Indian bow describes the arched loveliness of the brows; leonine is the sinuous torso; the truly flower-like hands suggest the orderly beauty of the growth of lotus blossoms. Certainly, the languorous ease of gesture and pose in this as in all the Ajantā figures is based on that language of gesture that was so vital a part of the Indian dance and drama. The compositions of the Ajantā paintings are not clear and symmetrical, but are densely crowded arrangements of figures and setting in which there is a continuous stirring and movement from figure to figure and group to group that provides a kind of rhythmic internal unity. These paintings, although Buddhist in subject matter, seem to affirm an almost lyric devotion to the beauty and warmth of the world of the senses. They are marked by that dualism of spirituality and sensuality that in a sense is not a dualism at all, so united are these opposites here as in all Indian art.

The Gupta Period: Sculpture. The Buddha images of the Gupta period are the final realization of the Indian aesthetic ideal in the cult image. The humanistic Gandhāra Buddha, so inappropriate as an object of worship because of the distracting element of naturalism, has been replaced by an image completely Indian in conception. These images carved at Muttra in the 4th and 5th cents. A. D. are a combination of traits and techniques developing out of the Gandhāra and Kushan schools: the contribution of the Gandhāra style is the anthropomorphic conception of the Buddha, the technique of representing the drapery in string-like folds, and the carving of the face in simplified, sharply cut planes; the Kushan school has contributed the heroic proportions of the superman and the typically Indian technique of suggesting the warmth and softness of the flesh. In the sandstone images excavated at Sārnāth all reminiscences of Greco-Roman techniques have fallen away, and not even the slightest indication of folds interrupts the smooth, abstract surfaces of the bodies revealed in garments whose presence is shown only by the borders. These figures are composed in accordance with pre-conceived canons of mathematical proportion. The features and the body are built up in the same metaphorical language as the forms at Ajantā. A fixed vocabulary of gestures or *mudrās* (q.v.) determined the position of the hands. The statues have a crystalline harmony of abstraction, the final perfection of the religious diagram so often used in place of icons in the religious art of the East. Images like the famous Buddha in *dharmacakra mudrā* at Sārnāth are the last and fullest embodiment of the serenity and spiritual power of the Thathāgata manifested in material form. Another master work of this period is the torso of the Bodhisattva Avalokiteśvara from Sāñchī in the Indian Museum, London. The numerous steles from Sārnāth with reliefs of the Buddha show a translation into Indian terms of the iconography developed in the school of Gandhāra.

The Gupta Period: Architecture. In the Gupta period there emerges a type of temple which, in its essential elements, provides the arrangement of sanctuaries for all later periods. In such temples as No. 17 at Sāñchī and the 6th cent. shrines at Aihole a cella-like sanctuary or **garbha gṛha** is preceded by one or more pillared porches. The shrine proper is surmounted by a conical spire or

śikkhara. The final development of this type may be seen in the medieval temples of Orissa, consisting of a towering *śikkhara* and a number of terraced porch-pavilions or *mandapa.*

The Medieval Period: Sculpture. (The chronology of the Mediaeval period is generally given as 600-850 A.D. for Early Mediaeval, and 850-1200 A.D. for late Mediaeval: actually the date of the latter period may be extended to the 19th cent. to include such phenomena as Cola art and Rajput painting.) The art of the Mediaeval period is almost entirely Hindu in content. As early as the 6th cent. Buddhism, permeated by doctrines of a magic and secret nature, entered the period of its final decline that culminated in its extinction or re-absorption into Hinduism. The last school of Indian Buddhist art flourished under the Pāla and Sena dynasties which ruled in the Bengal valley from the 8th to the 12th cents. In style this sculpture is a rather dry and mannered continuation of Gupta techniques. The chief importance of this school is that it furnished the canons for all the later centuries of Buddhist art in Tibet and Nepal. At the same time that great Buddhist teachers were imported into Tibet from Nālandā and other Indian centers by Sron Tsan Gampo, artisans from these places found their way over the Himālayas as well. The earliest monument (8th cent. A.D.) heralding the revival of Hinduism is the great relief of the Descent of the Ganges at Māmallapuram. This was a dedication of the Pallava dynasty that had succeeded the Āndhras in eastern and southern India. This relief covers the face of an enormous boulder on the sea-shore south of Madras. In it are represented life-size figures of elephants, deer, monkeys, and all manner of creatures human and divine gathered to give thanks for the miraculous descent of the sacred stream from Heaven. The animal forms, although not direct copies from nature, reveal such a wonderful sense of the articulation and movements specific to each of these species that they seem almost to be endowed with an actual life of their own. This seeming naturalism reserved for the members of the animal kingdom is in direct contrast to the abstract canons in which the figures of the celestial beings are conceived. Although much more attenuated and even lighter than the figures of the Gupta period, the forms of the *devas* are really a prolongation of the proportions and standards of beauty of the Golden Age.

The figures are portrayed in such radically simplified planes that they both suggest the glyptic nature of their material and are magnificent embodiments of sculptural form.

The most notable single sculpture at the famous site of Ellura is the deep, grotto-like relief in the Kailāsanātha temple depicting Siva's subjugation of the demon Ravana. This composition, which is one of a number drawn from the legend of the *Rāmayana,* is so deeply carved that the figures appear in the full round in a box-like stage, and the most violent effects of light and shade are thereby achieved to enhance the dramatic emotion of the scene. The attitudes of the principal figures are all calculated to stress the fear and tension of this moment when Ravana threatens to uproot the sacred mountain. In their svelte attenuation and dynamic movement the forms are a continuation of the Pallava style of eastern India.

Stone sculpture in the Later Medieval period seems to represent a kind of drying-up and almost mechanical reproduction of the great style of the 8th cent. With few exceptions the images encrusting the later temples of eastern and southern India are only parts of a decorative symbolical scheme and hardly worthy of individual esthetic consideration.

The greatest artistic achievements of Hindu art in the Medieval period are in the South Indian metal images of Saivite gods and saints. Most notable among these are the many representations of Śiva as Lord of the Dance that embody in plastic form the flux and vibration of the god's endless destruction and re-creation of the universe. The statues of Śiva saints in their suggestion of an inner quality of vibrant and ecstatic adoration are almost symbols of devotion itself.

The Medieval Period: Architecture. Hindu architecture of the Medieval period is sometimes rather conveniently divided into the Northern and Southern styles, although probably no such geographical division is really tenable. Distinctive of the northern type is the so-called *Śikkhara,* represented principally by the temples at Bhuvaneśvar in Orissa. The *Śikkhara,* rather like a bee-hive in shape, is constructed in clearly defined courses of masonry, emphasized by lotiform quoins or *amalakas* which, since the temple is a cosmic diagram, typify a hierarchy of deities or powers in the Hindu pantheon. Sanctuaries in the shape of stepped pyramids covered with numerous *stūpikās* are sometimes believed to be especially characteristic of southern or Dravidian India.

To this category belong two of the seven small sanctuaries at Māmallapuram: these, the so-called Seven Pagodas, are not true architecture, but rather sculptural replicas of free standing structures in wood and thatch. Another example of this type is one of the greatest monuments of Indian art: the Kailāsanātha temple at Ellura. This vast Saivite sanctuary whose architectural shape represents the form of the sacred mountain, Mount Kailāsā, together with the many porches, free standing columns, and vast sculptural decoration was directly hewn from a great quarry of rock. It was carved under the Calukya dynasty (650-750 A.D.). The dominant shrine is in the shape of a terraced pyramid, dominated by a bulbous member or *stūpikā,* the shape of which is repeated in smaller scale on the tiers of this terraced stupa structure.

The Medieval Period: Painting. No account of medieval art in India would be complete without at least a mention of the schools of Rājput painting that flourished in Rājputāna, Bunkelkhand, and the Pañjāb Himālayas from the 16th to the 19th cent. The universal subject matter of these exquisite pictures is Hindu epic legends; most often repeated of *Krsna-lila* legends is the refrain of Krsna's love for Radha in all its passionate beauty. The themes are expressed in terms of a stylized and linear loveliness; the lyric grandeur of the compositions harks back to the wall-paintings of the classic period. The colors have the translucency of stained glass. Rājput painting is medieval in its idiom and totally different from the Mughal school's preoccupation with realistic effects and the happenings of the contemporary world.

Art in Ceylon. The island of Ceylon was converted to Buddhism by Mahinda, the missionary-son of the Emperor Aśoka, in the 3d cent. B.C. Unlike India, Ceylon has remained a stronghold of Buddhism ever since. The earliest center of Buddhist art was the capital at Anurādhapura where a number of the giant *dāgabas* or stupas and other dedications of the early Buddhist kings may still be seen in the jungle. The sculpture found at this site appears to be derived from the Later Āndhra style of eastern India. Most of these remains date from the 2d to the 5th cents. A.D. In the succeeding period of confusion the Tamil invasions from southern India forced the removal of the capital to Polonnarūva. This was the last important center of Singhalese culture in the 12th and 13th cents. The Buddhist art of Polonnarūva reveals the unchanged persistence of the forms of the early period. There have also been found at Polonnarūva copper images of Hindu deities which, although based on the canons of Medieval South Indian art, are superior in their refinement to their continental prototypes. Ceylon is not lacking in examples of the painter's art: the series of *apsaras* painted at Sīgirya in the 6th cent. A.D. are the vigorous local equivalent of the Gupta style. The very much ruined cycle of paintings at Polonnarūva is related to the painting of South India in the Medieval period.

It must not be supposed from the above that the art of Ceylon is completely without originality. The Buddha statues of Anurādhapura show a grandeur of conception that in its expression of the self-contained serenity of the master surpasses the Indian models.

Art in Indo-China. The introduction of the Indian art and religions into Indo-China and Siam follows a pattern somewhat similar to that presented by the art history of Ceylon. The earliest Buddhist and Hindu sculpture of the so-called pre-Khmer period (5th-7th cents. A.D.) reveals a more or less faithful transcription of Gupta prototypes, although a few masterpieces like the Hari Hara of the Phnom Penh Museum display a sculptural perfection surpassed in Asiatic art. What may be recognized as a definite Khmer formula manifests itself in the sculpture of the Classic period (8th-13th cents. A.D.), represented chiefly by the carvings decorating the temples of the capital at Angkor. There we see the developed Cambodian formula for the expression of the Buddha nature. The inner radiance of the deity is expressed largely through the eyes closed in reverie and the oft-repeated long slow smile of the lips. From the fact that the kings of Cambodia even in their lifetime were worshipped as earthly personnifications of the Buddha or one of the Hindu gods it is apparent that something like a recording of personal traits is frequently included in the abstract framework determining the representation of these cult statues of the god-king. The greatest monuments of Khmer architecture are the temples of Angkor Vat and the Bayon, built in the 12th and 13th cents. resp. The shrine of Angkor Vat represents the final development of Khmer architecture: in it the isolated towers which were the sanctuaries of earlier centuries are joined by galleries on several levels. Only the most primitive corbelled type of vault is employed in the Cambodian buildings and the stories are laid without mortar of any kind. Angkor Vat is at once the temple and the tomb of the *devaraja Suryavarman II* (1112-1152 A.D.), whose image in the guise of Śiva was enshrined in the topmost tower of the structure. Allegories of the king's earthly triumphs are contained in the reliefs from the Indian epics that cover the walls of the first gallery. The many smaller towers that echo the shape of the central spire are believed to have immortalized the great generals of the realm. The temple of the Bayon which stood in the center of Jayavarman VII's (1181-1201 A. D.) capital at Angkir Thom is another vastly complicated structure, dominated by multiple towers that have on each of their four sides carved faces of the Bodhisattva Lokeśvara. This is intended to indicate the spread of the royal power to all points of the compass. The statue of the god-king in this temple was a Buddha seated on a Nāga. The temple of the Bayon in conjunction with the walls and moat of the capital was a magic reconstruction in architecture of the world structure with Mount Meru at the center surrounded by ramparts of mountains and the great ocean encompassing all. The sculpture of the Bayon represents a softer and more subtle development from the sculpture of the Classic period, just as its architecture is the final and most complicated evolution from earlier and more simple types.

Art in Java. One of the great centers of Indian colonial art was the island of Java where, under the powerful dynasty of the Śailendras (ca. 750-860 A.D.), Mahāyāna Buddhism produced its noblest monument in the great sanctuary of Barabudur. This structure has the hemispherical profile of a giant stupa enclosing a stepped pyramid or *prāsāda.* The ancient symbolism of the sky-dome enclosing Mount Meru is easily recognizable in these two architectural elements; in fact, Barabudur is the most complicated illustration of the principle of *pratibimba* whereby the cosmos is magically reconstructed in architecture. The temple is more than this; it is a magic diagram or *maṇḍala* of the material and spiritual worlds comprehended within the mind of the Universal Buddha. The subjects of the reliefs of the successive galleries lead the pilgrim upward through the worlds of desire and form to the final contemplation of the world without form and action symbolized in the seventy-three stupa-enclosed statues of Vairocana Buddha. The allegory of the monument is brought to completion by the statues of the Buddhas of the Four Directions that fill the niches on the four façades of the building. The style of the reliefs of the galleries, as though confirming the hierarchy of their subject matter, progresses from a direct and naturalistic treatment of the subjects from the world of desire to a very abstract and spiritualized presentation of the realms of the mystic Buddhas that adorn the uppermost corridor. The Buddha statues are the final crystalline perfection of the technique and canons of proportions of the Gupta period. See Anand, M. R., *The Hindu View of Art*, 1933; Codrington, K. deB., *Ancient India*, 1926 and *Introduction to the Study of Medieval Indian Sculpture*, 1929; Cohn, W., *Indische Plastik*, 1921; Combaz, G., *L'Évolution du Stūpa en Asie*, 1933-37; and *L'Inde et l'Orient Classique*, 1937; Coomaraswamy, A. K., *Arts and Crafts of India and Ceylon*, 1913, *Introduction to Indian Art*, 1923, *Bibliographies of Indian Art*, 1925, *History of Indian and Indonesian Art*, 1927, *Visvakarma*, 1914, *Catalogue of the Indian Collections in the Museum of Fine Arts, Boston*, 5 vols., 1923-24, *Introduction to the Art of Eastern Asia*, The Open Court, 1932, *The Christian and Oriental or True Philosophy of Art*, 1939 and *The Dance of Siva*, 1918; Diez, E., *Die Kunst Indiens (Handbuch der Kunstwissenschaft)*, 1925; Fergusson, J., *History of Indian and Eastern Architecture*, 1876; Fischer, O., *Die Kunst Indiens, Chinas, und Japans*, Propylaean Kunstgeschichte, IV, 1928; Gangoly, O. C., *Indian Architecture*, Little Books on Asiatic Art, 1928 (?) and *Southern Indian Bronzes*, Little Books on Asiatic Art; Grousset, R., *Civilizations of the East*, vol. 2, *India*, 1931; Grünwedel, A., *Buddhist Art in India*, 1901; Hackin, J., *La Sculpture Indienne et Tibétaine au Musée Guimet*, 1931 and *Les Collections Bouddhiques*; Musée Guimet—Guide Catalogue, 1923; Havell, E. B., *Ancient and Medieval Architecture of India*, 1915, *Handbook of Indian Art*, 1920, *The Himalayas in Indian Art*, 1924, *Ideals of Indian Art*, 1924 and *Indian Sculpture and Painting*, 1908; Kramrisch, S., *A Survey of Painting in the Deccan*, 1939, *Grundzüge der Indischen Kunst*, 1924 and *Indian Sculpture*, 1933; Le Bon, G., *Les Monuments de l'Inde*, 1893; Mackay, E., *The Indus Civilization*, 1935; Ramaprasad Chanda, *Medieval Indian Sculpture*, 1936; Reuther, O., *Indische Paläste und Wohnhäuser*, 1924; Rowland, B., *Outline and Bibliographies of Oriental Art*, 1940 and Rowland, B., and Coomaraswanny, A. K., *The Wall-Paintings of India, Central Asia, and Ceylon*, 1938; Smith, V. A., *Fine Arts in India and Ceylon*, 2nd ed. revised by K. deB. Codrington, 1930; Strzygowski, J., and others, *The Influence of Indian Art*, Ind. Soc., 1925.   —B.R.

Indian lake. See lac.

Indian red. The name of this pigment originally indicated a natural iron oxide imported from India. It was slightly different from most other varieties of red earth in having a somewhat purple tinge. Now the name is used for any pigment that has such a color, even for one that is artificially made by calcining copperas. The words, **rouge**, as used in industry for a polishing material, **colcothar**, and **caput mortuum**, all stand for this same pigment.   —G.L.S.

Indian yellow. As an artist's pigment, this was always rather rare and is now practically out of use. It was formerly prepared in Bengal and was a dried extract from the urine of cows that had been fed on mango leaves. Its color is deep, translucent yellow-orange. For an organic pigment, it is fairly stable, even to light, is slightly soluble in water, and is decomposed by hydrochloric acid. A synthetic substitute is now often sold under the same name.   —G.L.S.

Indianist literature. See HISPANIC AMERICAN LITERATURE.

Indigo. Probably the oldest of the organic blue colors, indigo is strictly a dye. It is yielded by different plants of the *Indigofera*, and has been grown all over the world but particularly in India and China. Bengal indigo was considered one of the best grades and was widely used as a dye for fabrics. Unlike most of the organic colors used as a painter's pigment, this was not precipitated on a base but was ground to a fine powder as a dye and thus mixed with different mediums. Synthetic dyes have largely displaced it but it is still used to a limited extent as a water color. In an aqueous medium it is more satisfactory than in oil and is moderately stable when well bound and covered with a varnish film.   —G.L.S.

Indo-China, art of. See INDIAN ART.

Indo-Iranian art. See CENTRAL ASIAN ART.

Indo-Sumerian art. See INDIAN ART.

Indus valley art. See INDIAN ART.

industrial art. (1) Art of the machine in which manufacture and, usually, production is sought; (2) (as distinguished from *industrial arts*) art as applied to industry. Comp. w. *industrial arts*. Whitford and Winslow in *Dictionary of Education.*

industrial arts. (1) Broadly, an area of the school curriculum, or a field of study, concerned with the materials, processes, and products of modern industry; intended to familiarize pupils with the industrial elements of modern civilization vocations, and to provide opportunities to acquire skill in the use of tools and materials in the construction of useful objects; (2) more narrowly, a term used in preference to the older designation, *manual training*. Dist f. *industrial art.* Whitford and Winslow in *Dictionary of Education.*

industrial art school. A school that specializes in the training of students for employment as artists in the industries. (Such artists are often called *stylists* or *industrial designers*.) Whitford and Winslow in *Dictionary of Education.*

industrial design. Structural or three-dimensional design of objects for industrial mass production by machine tools, e.g. radios, clocks, light fixtures, electric irons, automobiles. Contrasts with two-dimensional design for commercial advertising or decoration, and with pictorial design in the fine arts of painting and sculpture.   —L.D.L.

industrial music. Music over plant communication systems to industrial workers; now provided by several hundred plants in the U. S. A. and most of those in the British Isles.   —W.A.K.

industrial music library. A collection of current and standard phonograph records used for broadcast over plant communication systems to industrial workers. One firm (RCA) supplies a factory with an initial library and then provides for a monthly exchange service so that the library may be kept up to date.   —W.A.K.

INDUSTRIAL MUSIC RESEARCH. Secretary of Labor James J. Davis stated in 1922 that "We have come to realize that there is a big field for music in the industrial and commercial world". Before the end of that

decade, music was being broadcast to some American workers over industrial sound systems. Consensus at that time, according to Clark (2), was that music played while employees worked had a beneficial effect on morale, fatigue, and earnings. Anecdotal evidence favorable to music has been so positive that relatively few serious attempts at controlled scientific evaluation of music's effects have been made. It is now realized that this is a vitally important research field for socio-industrial psychology.

Industrial music research is primarily concerned with the determination of the influence of recorded music as broadcast over factory communication systems upon workers' efficiency, aesthetic appreciation, attitudes, feelings of pleasantness and tiredness, and general morale. It is apparent of course, that this research also faces the task of evaluating the effect of myriad *kinds* of music upon the same important factors. Current opinion on operation of industrial sound systems holds that "hot swing" and certain other types of music are not good from the standpoint of factory production. There is no agreement as yet as to types of music most valuable at various periods in the work spell.

Quantitative reports of effect of music on industrial output are meager but consistent. The classical study to date is that reported by the British Industrial Health Research Board (17) in 1938; in this study Wyatt and Langdon found that over a period of 24 weeks during which twelve employees doing repetitive-type work experienced periods of no music and several kinds of music, daily production was increased 2.6 per cent by the application of music. Relative effectiveness of types on output (not conclusive because of small number of workers in experiment) are reported in the following order: one steps, fox-trots, waltzes, light classics. Their study of 350 other factory workers revealed that these employees feel that time drags worst during the first two hours of each half of the work-day, and that from 77 to 97 per cent of these same workers feel that they *can* think of other things while they work and that time passes more quickly when they *do* think of other things. The significance of this last sentence is considerable in the light of their further finding in an experiment with 19 employees in which those reporting boredoom did significantly less work than those not bored. Music's apparent favorable influence upon output is partly due to its ability to "take up the slack" in the mind of the worker which may be dulled by the constant concentration upon a repetitive task long since mastered.

In an experiment performed by Humes (5) at a Hygrade Sylvania tube factory, it was found that quality of work done by 88 female operators was significantly higher on the average (as indicated by scrappage data) during music than during no-music weeks. The last no-music week was interrupted by an employee petition demanding that the recorded music broadcasts be restored.

Less certain is the favorable effect of music on those less repetitive operations which require considerable continued mental concentration. Jensen (6) in a school experiment found that typing output was somewhat reduced by jazz and dirge music; of course he used perhaps the two worst types of music for stimulating output; it is possible that he might have obtained different and favorable results had he applied familiar sweet popular music or soft background music. As a matter of fact, the dirge music reduced speed but improved accuracy.

In a series of carefully controlled experiments, Hevner(4) has shown that for certain compositions, major modality, fast tempo, high pitch, flowing rhythm, and simple harmony tend to express happiness best. Unfortunately it is not yet known whether music with the best effect on worker output is the same kind of music which has best effects on the worker's morale and feelings of well-being, although there is strong indication that almost *any* pleasant kind of occasional music has more favorable effect on both production and morale than does no music.

Podolsky(11) has compiled facts which show that music tends in general to increase pulse rate, respiration, and metabolism, lower the threshold for sensory stimuli of different modes, and reduce the regularity of respiration. These conditions are certainly not characteristic of the organism when in a state of boredom.

In addition to the as yet meager scientific evidence, there is much published opinion to substantiate the partly experimentally confirmed thesis that music has several desirable influences in industry. Ramsay and Rawson (12) report from a 1939 British survey that 74.5 per cent of employers using music believe that it increases work efficiency. Wynford Reynolds(13), in charge of a British program, has declared of industrial music—"It is a tonic like a cup of tea, something to cheer the mind.

You will get increase output all right, but it will be spread over the work-spell as a whole. You will not necessarily get it while the music is actually being played." Reynolds advises use of not more than 2½ hours of music a day, in periods lasting from fifteen to twenty minutes.

According to the British Industrial Welfare Society(13), "On the whole the concensus . . . seems to be that music at work does much to relieve the monotony of repetitive work, and produces a stimulus to increased output, and in the opinion of the Industrial Welfare Society there is no doubt that this development is not merely a wartime one, but that music at work will remain a definite feature of industry." As just indicated the British are making extensive use of industrial music and a recent headline dated from Switzerland, "Arms Output Slows So Nazis Try Music," indicates that it is also being adopted on the continent. Use of industrial sound systems is rapidly spreading in America as is shown by the fact that representative factories throughout the nation have made installations and by the additional fact that the largest sound manufacturer, RCA Mfg. Co., Inc., has a separate service for such industrial sound systems.

There are many categories into which music may be divided, although Peters(10), summarizing a review of aesthetic studies, observes that "It is highly significant that these studies . . . should find only two types and that all experiments of both kinds should identify the two corresponding *sets* in terms suggestive of form and meaning." Convenient practical terms for categorizing music for industrial research purposes include cultural type, tempo, familiarity, instrumentation, vocalization, styling, seriousness, volume variability, and recording level.

There is much opinion but few experimental results on effects of types of music. Mr. Wynford Reynolds maintains that British experience indicates that slow waltzes, rhumbas, hot music, music that is too thickly scored, and vocals should be avoided; much American experience challenges this ban on vocals. A survey of British employers using music showed that two-thirds of those reporting want vocals occasionally and a majority prefer men vocalists; fourteen types of broadcast programs received this rank order: light orchestra without vocal, ballroom orchestra without vocal, brass band without vocal, swing orchestra or accordion without vocal, small novelty combination featuring xylophone, band with five vocals, light orchestra dance band without vocal, theatre organ, rhythmic records of light classical music, dance-time records, military band, salon orchestra, dance band, band playing folk songs and dances of another nation.

Thorpe(15) studied the type preferences of 475 college and high school students after they heard an orchestra play eight types and found that the top four fell into approximately this order: military march, semi-symphony, concert waltz, descriptive piece (*Whispering Flowers*); type preferences were not notably related with intelligence, college grade, or curriculum pursued. Fay and Middleton(3) played four types of classical and two types of popular music over a sound system to 54 college students and the students ranked the types from most to least pleasant in this order: light classical, old classical, romantic classical, swing, modern classical, and sweet; all were rated as more pleasant than unpleasant. Women rated all types of classical higher than did men. Freyman(13) reports that analysis of 190 replies received from 250 British workers indicates a demand for more modern popular tunes, music-hall songs, dance-time music and waltzes and less light classical, marches, and hot jazz. All of these 190 replied that they consider music a pleasant background to their work.

Humes(5) concluded from an experiment in a tube factory that quality of output is generally better under all fast music or all slow music than under programs arranged with pieces proceeding from most to least familiar.

After experiencing several months of music, Wyatt and Langdon's(17) British factory subjects gave all their votes to fox trots and waltzes and none to one-steps, marches, or light classical. One-steps, however, appeared to have the most favorable effect on output.

Since gratification of felt needs tends to raise morale, it may be expected that providing music for employees will help morale; in a survey by Kerr(7) of 132 applicants in one U. S. Employment Office, it was found that a significantly larger number would rather work on a floor with music than on one without music and that such attitude tends to be negatively correlated with age. These findings may imply that in a scarce labor market, an employer with music may have the advantages of more and younger applicants to select from. Humes in a tube factory and foremen in many other plants have found that when broadcast music ceases for a few days for any cause, employees frequently protest and request its resumption. The fact, as shown by Wiebe(16),

that frequent repetition of an unfamiliar song will tend to make it more popular tends to indicate that industrial music might be capable of raising average employee appreciation for semi-classical and classical music. In a study of 457 college students, Rigg(14) found that mere repetition increased appreciation and also found that almost any comment, even if unfavorable, increased appreciation. Fay and Middleton(3) conclude from one study that "For individuals who are sufficiently gifted . . . frequent exposure to the good may lead to a preference for the good." These studies strongly indicate that use of industrial sound systems should have considerable value in raising both employee's morale and level of appreciation for good music.

Tests to be used in measuring employees' preference for representative songs and types of music may be obtained from the Personnel Research Department of the RCA Mfg. Co., Inc., Indianapolis. For small scale experimental studies of program and music popularity, the Program Analyzer used by Peterman and Lazarsfeld(9) is a highly refined measuring instrument. This latter device makes it possible for a listener to record like or dislike for any part of a song or program by squeezing an appropriate button. A more useful instrument for general survey purposes is the *Attitudes Toward Music* scale developed by RCA Mfg. Co. to determine music type preferences of employees in order that plant broadcast programs will have optimum "fit" for the plant's personnel.

In an article on recent advances in human engineering, Kirkpatrick(8) observes that "The instinct with which the repetitive work of modern industry is said to come into conflict most seriously and most frequently is that of workmanship, or creativity. . . . He may experience . . . a pronounced feeling of boredom —an overwhelming tiredness that is not the result of actual physical fatigue, but an expression of monotony." Relief of this psychological fatigue is believed by many to be the greatest single value of music in industry. Theoretically the music may provide an element of creative expression which is absent from the work—or, as Cantril and Allport(1) point out, "Familiarity means progress toward mastery, and so long as the progress is *under way* the sense of enjoyment is retained. Perfect aesthetic mastery . . . is easily achieved in the case of popular music, at which time its appeal diminishes." REF. (1) Cantril, Hadley & Allport, G. W. *The Psychology of Radio,* 1935. (2) Clark, K. S. *Music in Industry,*

1929. (3) Fay, P. J. & Middleton, W. C. Relationships between musical talent and preferences for different types of music. *J. Educ. Psychol.*, 1941, Nov., 573-583. (4) Hevner, Kate. The affective value of pitch and tempo in music. *Amer. J. Psychol.*, 1937, *49*, 621-630. (5) Humes, J. F. The effects of occupational music on scrappage in the manufacture of radio tubes. *J. Appl. Psychol.*, 1941, *25*, 573-587. (6) Jensen, M. B. The influence of jazz and dirge music upon speed and accuracy of typing. *J. Educ. Psychol.*, 1931, *22*, 458-462. (7) Kerr, W. A. Attitude of job applicants toward industrial music. Unpublished manuscript. (8) Kirkpatrick, F. H. Human engineering advances. *Radio Age*, 1942, July, 10-12. (9) Peterman, J. N. The program analyzer. *J. Appl. Psychol.*, 1940, *24*, 728-741. (10) Peters, H. N. The experimental study of aesthetic judgments. *Psychol. Bull.*, 1942, *39*, 273-305. (11) Podolsky, Edward. *The Doctor Prescribes Music*, 1939. (12) Ramsay, J. & Rawson, R. E., et al. Rest-pauses and refreshments in industry. *Nat. Institute Industrial Psychol.*, Report No. 8, London, 1939. (13) Reports of British Library of Information, 1941-42. (14) Rigg, M. G. Favorable v. Unfavorable propaganda in music. *Psychol. Bull.*, 1941, *38*, 543. (15) Thorpe, L. P. The orchestral preferences of students. *J. Appl. Psychol.*, 1936, *20*, 778-784. (16) Wiebe, Gerhart. The effect of radio plugging on students' opinions of popular songs, *J. Appl. Psychol.*, 1940, *24*, 221-227. (17) Wyatt, S. & Langdon, J. N. *Fatigue and Boredom in Repetitive Type Work*. Med. Res. Council, Industr. Health Res. Bd., London, 1938.   —W.A.K.

inert. In paint technology those materials are called inerts which are used for body or bulk rather than for their tint. Generally they are white in the dry form. Chalk, gypsum, and China clay are typical examples; others such as aluminum silicate are used as extenders in the manufacture of paints.   —G.L.S.

inescutcheon. See HERALDRY.

informal balance. See balance.

infra-red ray photograph. Photograph made on plates or films especially sensitive to the long wave length in the infra-red end of the spectrum. A special filter is used on the camera.   —H.M.

infulae. See tiara, papal.

ingrain carpets. Known as Kidderminster or Scotch carpet, is a flat weave and is usually

made in a two-ply fabric with the aid of a "double cloth jacquard" machine. The term "two-ply" fabric in this case means two sets of weft yarns interchanged in such a way that while the pattern is alike on both sides the colors are reversed and can be used on either side.   —B.E.J.

initial. An initial is the large letter at the beginning of a text, section, or paragraph. The word comes from *litera initialis,* from which the noun *litera,* letter, has been dropped; the adjective has taken over the meaning of the whole phrase.

The Romans had already stressed the beginning letter, as can be proved by the oldest extant manuscripts of Vergil dating from the 4th cent. A.D. These initial letters were enlarged in about twice the size of the other letters. They were enlarged in order to call attention to the beginning of a new section. The oriental people began decorating this initial letter. But only the people of the Celtic-Germanic cultural family gave the greatest importance to it, esp. in the Bible where one single letter or a compound of some letters covered an entire page and were decorated in a greatly enriched and costly manner. The oldest of these big ornamented letters appear in the Irish Evangeliar, the so-called Book of Kells, now in the Trinity College Library at Dublin. The Anglo-Saxons and the Frankish Merovingians also cultivated this art. The initial letter was taken over by the schools of Carolingian culture, and became the vogue for many centuries. In recent times the custom of emphasizing initial letters has been revived to a certain extent. See Lamprecht, *Initial-ornamentik des 8. bis 13. Jahrhundert,* Leipzig, 1882; Von Kobell, *Kunstvolle Miniaturen und Initialen aus Handschriften des 4. bis 16. Jahrhunderts,* München, 1891; K. Loeffler, *Romanische Zierbuchstaben und ihre Vorlaeufer,* Stuttgart, 1917; Alois J. Schardt, *Das Initial,* Berlin, 1938; *Illuminated Manuscripts in the British Museum, Miniatures, Borders and Initials,* G. F. Warner, London, 1903; *Schools of Illumination,* Reproductions from manuscripts in the British Museum, 6 vs., London, 1914/15-30; *Beschreibendes Verzeichnis der illuminierten Handschriften in Oesterreich,* Neue Folge, herausgegeben von J. Schlosser und H. J. Hermann, Leipzig; *Miniaturen aus Handschriften der Kgl. Hof-und Staatsbibliothek in München,* herausgegeben von Dr. Georg Leidinger; Ph. Lauer, *Les enluminures Romanes des manuscripts de la Bibliotheque Nationale,* Paris, 1927; Albert Boeckler,

Abendländische Miniaturen bis zum Ausgang der Romanischen Zeit, Berlin, 1930. —A.J.S.

ink. The modern ink for writing is some kind of dye, the more traditional being the so-called iron gall ink. This is made from tannin or gallotannic acid derived from oak galls and combined with ferrous sulphate. The combination alone has no color but turns black when exposed to the air. These iron gall inks were probably taken up at some time in the early Middle Ages. In common use then and earlier was the carbon ink like that still prevalent in the Far East, made usually from finely ground lamp black with a weak medium of glue. The ink stick of China and Japan is of such composition and a similar mixture known to scribes and painters by the name, ink, was a common preparation in Europe during the Middle Ages and the Renaissance. —G.L.S.

ink-painting. See CHINESE ARTS.

inlaid. *Book.* An inlaid design in leather bindings in one having leather of another color or style inset into the leather cover.

inner dance. See form (3).

In Nomine. Was a composition based on a given melody sounded in long tones in one voice while the other parts interwove polyphonic and frequently imitative passages around it. The name of the form was derived from the text associated with the given melody which was most frequently employed (*Benedictus qui venit in nomine Domini*) though other subjects were also used. Even the **fantasia** on one note might fairly be included here, though the repetition of a single tone in one part undoubtedly reduces the concept of a given melody to its lowest possible terms. The form, though conservative in tendency and, in fact, an offshoot of the old Netherlands cantus firmus technique, was long practiced with interesting results by English composers. John Taverner appears to have been a pioneer in this form of composition. The roster of composers of In Nomines is a long one, and the form was much practiced during the latter part of the 16th cent. and the first decade of the following century. The works of Henry Purcell appearing after a long silence close the history of the form (c. 1680).

The delight of English composers in exhausting the possibilities of a single subject was not confined to the In Nomine. The *Miserere* was similarly employed as was an old folk theme, *The leaves be greene* or *browning.* Perhaps a unique record of a friendly contest in this kind of composition must have been contained in the *Medulla Musicke.* "Sucked out of the sappe of Two of the most famous Musitians that ever were in this Land, namely Master William Byrd . . . and Master Alfonso Ferabosco . . . either of whom having made 40tie severall waies . . . showing most rare and intricate skill in 2 partes in one upon the playne songe 'Miserere'". This volume has, however, been lost. Like the **fancy** (q.v.), the In Nomine was predominantly intended for performance on the viols though examples in the Mulliner Organ Book and elsewhere are for keyboard instruments. —C.W.H.

inro (Jap.). A small receptacle which was suspended by a cord from the belt and in which pellets were kept. Generally divided into five compartments synchronized one over the other. See also netsuke and ojime, standard accompaniments of the *inro;* also "Catalogue of Japanese Lacquer, Part II, *Inro*", Victoria and Albert Museum, London, Edward F. Strange, 1925. —J.A.M.

insert. *Book.* Usually applied to a circular or leaflet placed loose between the leaves of a book.

inside margins. *Book.* Of two kinds : (1) The narrow border of leather turned in over the board of the cover leaving the margin around three sides of the pasted down end paper. (2) The white at the back center of the opened book between the two print pages. Also known as the **gutter margin.** —H.E.S.

inso (Jap.). See mūdra.

inspiration. Inspiration is well defined by Webster as "A supernatural divine influence which qualifies men to receive and communicate divine truth." The word itself implies the inward breathing of an informing spirit. In this sense, "All that is true, by whomsoever it has been said, is from the Sanctus Spiritus" (St. Ambrose on I Cor. 12.3). The Synteresis as "conscience" is the principle equally of prudence and art (cf. Renz, O., *Die Synteresis nach dem Hl. Thomas von Aquin,* 1911, p. 172; St. Augustine, *Conf.* XI. 5 *ingenium,* whence our word "ingenious"). Thus Meister Eckhart rightly speaks of the artificer as "inspired by his art."

It is in this way that "inspiration" has always been understood. Thus Hesiod, "The Muses breathed into (*enépneusan*) me a divine voice, and bade me sing" (*Theogony,*

31); Homer, "The Genius breathed into (*en-épneuse*) my heart to weave" (*Odyssey,* XIX. 138); "It is the God himself that speaks . . . the makers are but his exponents" (Plato, *Ion,* 534, 535); "I do nothing of myself, but as my Father taught me, I speak" (John, VIII. 28) "I am one, who when Love (*amor,* the divine Eros, Apollo, Sanctus Spiritus) inspires me (*me spira*), attend, and go setting it forth in such wise as He dictates within me" (*Purgatorio,* XXIII. 53, 54, cf. *Paradiso* I. 19). The artist who can claim to have been inspired is one who does his work in accordance with "the pattern of all that he had by the spirit" (I. Cor. 28,12).

Inspiration pertains to the artificer's contemplative *actus primus* in which he "sees" or "hears", i.e. "imagines" the shape of the work to be done. The revealed scriptures of India are, accordingly, spoken of as "audition" (*śruti*); the sacrificers, when at a loss how to proceed with the construction of the Fire-altar are told to "reflect" (*cit*). Incidentally, the word "reflect" itself is significant of the essential of what is always an "imitation" (Platonic *mimetis,* Skr. *anukaraṇa*). There are many Indian stories of artists who ascend to inspect what Hebr. IX. 23 calls "the patterns of things in the heavens," and having taken note of them, copy their forms in the physical material here below; so that "it is in imitation of the divine works of art that any work of art is accomplished here" (*Aitareya Brāhmaṇa* VII. 27); "the crafts such as building and carpentry . . . take their principles from that realm and from the thinking there . . . such arts as are the offspring of intellect (*nous*) must be there" (Plotinus, *Enneads,* V. 9,11, 12).

The term "inspiration" has thus had always a precise meaning. The term is nowadays frequently misused by art critics who do not realize that the word "inspire" cannot be used in connection with effects produced on the artist by concrete objects external to himself. Thus we are told the female nude was Maillol's "exclusive inspiration" (*Parnassus,* May 1941); that the modern artist derives his inspiration from the very physical materials he works with" (Greenberg in the *Nation,* April 19, 1941); and that "the poet or artist may let the rain inspire him" (Rose, *Greek Mythology,* 2nd ed., 1933, p. 11). In all these cases the authors are using the word "inspire" when they mean "stimulate". The modern critic, if a rationalist, may deny the possibility of inspiration; but in this case he must never speak of an artist as having been "inspired"; for the word is excluded, by his own assumption, from his vocabulary.   —A.K.C.

instrumental anthem. See anthem.

instrumental vibrato. See vibrato.

instrumentation (orchestration). The practice of adapting music for a group of different instruments; to arrange for an orchestra.

instruments, musical. See MUSICAL INSTRUMENTS.

intaglio. See aquatint; engraving; GLASS AND GLASS-MAKING; PRINTS AND PRINT PROCESSES; relief sculpture.

intarsia. Decorative designs produced by inlaying wood in a background of wood; much practiced in Renaissance Italy.

integrated art program. See art program, integrated.

integration. (Art ed.). (1) Promoting unified personality by making art contribute its share to experience as a whole; (2) making art in the school contribute its share to the curriculum as a whole. See *art program, integrated.* Whitford and Winslow in *Dictionary of Education.*

intensified seeing. See PHOTOGRAPHY.

intensity. (1) This term is used in two quite different senses in literary criticism. In one of these it is synonymous with *passion,* and indicates that the work issues from a vivid partiality and conveys the strong and spontaneous convictions of the artist. In another sense, intensity is a criterion of the artist's perceptual and intellectual acumen. Here, it indicates that a work exhibits careful attention to detail, and is a subtle and refined exploration of its subject-matter. (2) *Mus.* See NOTATION.
  —I.J.

intensity and timbre pulsations. See vibrato.

intercolumniation. *Arch.* The space or method of spacing between columns.

interim zoning by-law, ordinance. See CIVIC PLANNING.

INTERIOR ARCHITECTURE AND DECORATION (INTERIOR DESIGN). Interior decoration, interior architecture, and interior design are not strictly synonymous, although they are commonly used to describe the process of deliberate planning of utilitarian and decorative elements within rooms. In its best sense, interior architecture or interior design cannot be dissociated in any way from the function of the architect, insofar as the ideally planned interior, reflecting the usability of the room and its relation to the other spaces, is the key to the plan of the whole structure. Interior decoration, on the other hand, more frequently sees a room as an arbitrary enclosure within a structure and imposes upon this room a plan of applied decoration and furnishing with no more reference to the structure than a stage setting bears to the shape of the theater.

The orthodox method of designing interiors is still preponderantly a matter of combining or blending articles of furniture of harmonizing style with background features—flooring, wall and window treatments, lighting and accessories, of sympathetic form, color, texture. In this method the utilitarian aspects of room and furnishings are largely taken for granted. Deviations from the ordinary procedure are canalized, more or less ingeniously, to fit the preconceived scheme. The output of furniture in recent years having been chiefly eclectically stylistic, most American interiors have inevitably assumed arbitrarily stylized pretensions, so far as mechanical innovations of lighting, heating and construction could be circumvented.

In ancient times the rooms that served the higher civilizations of the Mediterranean basin were of the simplest organization, as life was largely lived out of doors. In all likelihood, the rooms of Egyptian, Greek and Roman antiquity were small and built around central courtyards. There were probably no windows. In this elementary house organization interior design was, therefore, purely a matter of decoration, and that, most likely, surface effects only, aided by powerful colors. The quantity and nature of the furniture is conjectural, but it is reasonable to suppose that such articles were few in number and portable rather than fixed. In public buildings, inevitably religious, interior design was inspired entirely by ritual. The effects were monumental, consistent, imposing.

Buildings of the Middle Ages were essentially religious in motivation. The architecture of the structure was a completely integrated design; the whole shape, details and interior aspect emanated from a single impulse. Inside and out, Gothic building exhibits a concerted directness of planning and embellishment that is the architectural glory of the era. Insofar as this method met the conditions of usefulness, it produced superb functional designs.

Rich colors and gold leaf were applied to ceiling and wall area between structural members. Woodwork was richly carved.

Domestic life of the Middle Ages was an entirely different affair from present standards. The mass of people lived in hovels or huts of such elementary character as to be beyond the consideration of this subject. Above that propertied persons appear to have lived a somewhat nomadic existence with military expediency a prime factor. It follows that the rooms they inhabited in their fortified castles were furnished with articles of a portable nature and that the harsh aspect of the interiors was ameliorated by such decorative elements as tapestries (Arras), carpets and rugs. Tile and painted plaster walls and stone floors were the background; textiles were embroidered and woven into tapestry pattern and woodwork was extensively carved.

The shapes and uses of rooms were probably poorly defined. A great hall in a feudal castle might have been the quarters for the lord and his lady and her attendants and the entire retinue. Probably the cooking was the first domestic function to have a room to itself. The ladies slept in a space separated from the rest of the hall by hastily hung curtains, while the retainers arranged themselves for sleep on the floor, on benches, and on the coffers in which were carried the possessions of the household.

At a very early date the specialized room appeared. The great hall remained as the living space for the entire household, but sleeping spaces were probably detached into individual rooms before the 12th cent. Windows were not generally glazed until the 15th cent., so that before that time window opening was minimized, fitted with wooden shutters that admitted a trifle of light through holes filled with horn, mica, or waxed cloth. Open fires were built in braziers or on the floor until the development of the fireplace. When this feature appeared during the 13th cent. it became the decorative focus of the whole room, and inspired the symbolism of hearth and home.

The great halls were usually of monumental proportions. The ceilings made no effort to disguise their structural plan, revealing open beams or trusses which at an early date became the subject of decorative painting and carving. Flat beamed ceilings, exposing the beams, developed into coffered types. In the Mediterranean lands a dark polychromy was preferred, but everywhere extensive decoration was lavished on the ceiling. The floors were of stone, brick, or tile and in northern homes always covered with a thick loose mat of rushes, straw, or leaves. The Crusaders brought refinements from the East in the form of Oriental rugs and textiles.

Interior walls at first were of the structural stone, but before long the need for some insulating quality led to plastering and, very soon after, to decorative painting and frescos. About 1400 the use of tapestries from Arras in France became universal in colder countries. They were used as wall coverings, to enclose beds or to form partitions in large rooms, and to hang over windows and doors. Presently the practice grew of simulating tapestries with paint on the plaster walls.

The use of wood panelling for interior finish appeared about the 12th cent. In the great houses this was evidently a sheathing designed to insulate. It is also likely that forms of panelling derived from the filling-in with boards between structural wood members where the exterior shell was filled in with wattle. Various designs of panels grew naturally out of structural elements, since the wider panels had to be held rigid by regularly spaced heavier members. Early builders saw the decorative possibilities inherent in these panels, and repeated patterns in the larger areas became one of the staples of medieval wall design.

The staircase was another vital element which appeared early, also as a consequence of the division of the great hall into specialized rooms. Quite possibly the first rooms were built in the form of balconies for sleeping quarters, suggesting the multiple-story house. As the specialized character of these additional rooms developed, the stairway grew in importance and finally vied with the fireplace for focal interest in the great hall.

The actual development of the house form with its specialized rooms is a product of the Renaissance. The stabilization of living conditions promoted the growth of physical comfort, and the nobles and merchant classes were quick to embody the new luxury into their dwellings. Beginning in Italy in the 13th cent. a recognizable house form appears, both in luxurious city dwellings and in suburban villas. The central court motive survived, and Mediterranean houses are still basically planned to look inward rather than outward. In Italy and Spain the rooms present their most gracious aspect to the court or patio, with windows and balconies a feature of the design. The earlier Renaissance rooms, invariably large and high-ceilinged, were on a splendid scale. Walls were painted over plaster,

floors were stone, and the ceilings were of rich designs developed from the pattern of the beams, elaborated by paint and mouldings. The furnishings of these rooms were consistently rich and splendid, proceeding from simple restrained forms early in the period to very elaborate carved and inlaid efforts later. While there was a multiplicity of rooms, there was relatively little specialization and few rooms appear to have been used for one exclusive purpose.

The same years in France saw a very similar development in the nature and use of rooms, although Gothic details persisted. The uses of rooms were undefined although their number multiplied. Decoration was rampant, the whole criterion of a room being the amount of ornament applied to ceilings and walls. Furniture was sparsely used, and not usually related to the design of the room. Dominant cabinets such as dressoirs and armoires appeared early and had an architectural affinity with the room, but other furniture was quite unrelated.

Like the Italian, the French architects were primarily concerned with an interior that expressed sumptuous magnificence rather than any human living quality, and employed various motives and materials as embellishment more than for any conceivable comfort that might derive from their use.

The Alpine countries had a lesser aristocracy and a more important bourgeoisie, and their efforts at interior design were largely directed toward making their rooms a refuge from the severe winter climate. At an early date we find such rooms sheathed with wood of great decorative pretense, a very considerable effort toward the humanization of the room and its furnishings.

The English house development quickly succeeded the feudal castle. The 16th cent. witnessed the growth of half timber, brick and stone dwellings of advanced form. Gothic details survived although the architectural planning was new, and rooms for specialized purposes developed quickly. The great hall persisted throughout the Tudor period and even later, although it had long ceased to be the whole of the house. A multitude of rooms were added on a rambling plan without too much regard for the architectural symmetry that typified Continental work. The quality of informality is the key to the livable aspect of English domestic architecture, as opposed to the purer plan designs of France and Italy. It persisted in spite of the Renaissance accent on classical propriety. Rooms were often of odd shapes dictated by convenience rather than by exterior appearance.

The general aspect of early Tudor rooms was vigorously masculine, dignified and austere. Windows were as emphatically part of the composition as fireplaces, both important factors in a chill gray climate. In lesser buildings wall treatment appeared in the form of interior half-timbering, in which the structural skeleton was visible, the intervening spaces being filled with rough-textured plaster. The panels were occasionally carved with either the vestigial linen-fold panel or newly borrowed ornaments of the Renaissance. To a lesser extent panels were painted. Plaster work became significant, the method of moulding ornaments into ceilings or walls being known as **parge work**. Wood floors appeared in the upper stories. Furnishings and accessories were few. On the whole the 16th cent. English room reflected a boisterous, masculine social life, with small emphasis on comfort.

The 17th cent. generally saw the emergence of the room form as it subsequently developed. Manners and customs quickly reflected growing wealth and political stability. The feudal aspect of the room disappeared, except for those state chambers which bore a certain political significance and were first dedicated to the use of large numbers of people. The domestic quality of life reduced the size and scale of rooms to a few elementary features: the range of the human voice, the dimensions of the human frame, considerations of heating and ventilation, and the particularized activity for which the room was planned. This was accompanied by a general softening of textures, a toning of the chromatic scale, and the inclusion of articles of furniture or fitments planned to facilitate the activity within the room.

In Italy the suburban villa flourished under the influence of architects like Palladio and Vignola. Their houses, particularly those in the Veneto, were exquisite compositions of well-planned rooms behind a symmetrical facade, in which neither the design of the room nor the exterior was sacrificed one to the other. The rooms were superbly adapted to the climate and to the stately cultured Mediterranean scheme of living.

In France the great palaces carried the regal concept to extremes in the palatial scale that typified Louis XIII and Louis XIV. Colossal ostentatious rooms were calculated less to render human comfort than to bedazzle and astonish. The regal manner was stepped down in scale in lesser buildings, but never abandoned.

The more significant development followed the growth of the *petite bourgeoisie* who utilized some of the decorative inspiration but retained their sense of livability and creature comfort. The group of styles labeled French Provincial comprises an infinity of regional variations and reminiscences of court manners from Henry II to Louis XVI, but never loses sight of human scale and utility.

English domestic life, like the French, advanced by rapid stages during the 17th cent. The Cromwellian Revolution, discarding opulence and ostentation, advanced notions of simplicity and utility in room design which were not altogether lost in the subsequent return of extravagant living. The Restoration produced rooms strongly influenced by Italian and French contemporaries but later prompted by influences from the Netherlands which tended to simplify and render more comfortable the whole room as well as the individual articles of furniture. Paintings of the Flemish school (q.v.) depict interiors of dignity and comfort. Rooms were smaller, lower, better lighted and ventilated. Ceilings were plain, walls were most frequently of wood, and floors almost universally of wood made more comfortable with Oriental rugs. The architectural influence was strong and the simulation of structural members was a motive of the panelling. Wallpapers appeared, at first in imitation of the tapestries and embroideries. The bed, an outstanding feature of this era, was virtually a room within a room, a voluminous composition of draperies.

With the accession of the Dutch monarchs came a further tendency toward simplicity and delicacy. Reaction to the baroque extravagancies of the Restoration produced simple forms in furniture and rooms of intimate scale and unpretentious harmony. While panelling persisted, it was now more often painted white, and the use of wallpapers became virtually a rule. Rooms of the Queen Anne period show a reduced fireplace, improved window areas, built in features like niches and bookcases, and a superior quality of domestic functionalism that set the style for 18th cent. interiors not only in England but throughout Europe.

In France the baroque opulence of Louis XIV tended, in the period of the Regence, toward a reduction in scale and a softening of contour. A process of feminization set in; this was the counterpart of the simplification of English rooms, but untouched by the democratic germ.

The 18th cent. witnessed the evolution of the house form and its interiors up to the prototype of the traditional house as known today. The decline of a dominant aristocracy was met by the rise of the lower classes; and in between, the development of a great middle class whose social idiom established the living technique of the next two centuries. This was accompanied by a new consciousness of material comfort. Habits of eating and drinking, sleeping, work and entertainment were modified by a new worldliness. Food, books, woods, music and ideas became the elements of cultured design rather than merely royal prerogatives. 18th cent. rooms are notably smaller and more intimate. In England and France a rich baroque manner persisted in the earlier years of the century. The romantic influence reached its apogee at this time. The fondness for curved lines culminated in the rococo style. Architectural motives were abandoned. Rooms of Louis XV's reign have, in the best examples, wood panels with irregular carved forms and broken corners. In the lesser chateaux painting was resorted to for economy, the strong primary colors of earlier years being succeeded by pastel tones of rose, sage green, putty, mustard and straw tints. Decorative motives after Chinese and natural sources were freely rendered, and wallpaper displaced both. Mantels were now decorative gems, small and exquisitely carved in marble, and were emphasized with handsomely carved and painted overmantels with mirrors, called **trumeaux.** Textiles for draperies and upholstery were of fine scale and texture and patterned with scrolls, ribbons, flowers, etc. Printed curtains, the toiles-de-Jouy, had pictorial designs on light grounds. Exquisitely chased metal work formed lighting fixtures, fireplace accessories and hardware. Floors were of wood arranged in marquetry patterns or rectangular parquet and were covered with the remarkable rugs from the Aubusson and Savonnérie looms.

In England early Georgian rooms were rather more architectural, under the influence of Wren, Langley, Swan, Kent and others. This merged into the Chippendale period, and although Chippendale was primarily a furniture designer and manufacturer, he influenced the design of whole rooms to some extent. The great rooms of the period were freely architectural with sumptuous ornament. In the classic Italian manner, columns and fluted pilasters and entablatures with broken or scroll pediments were supplemented by sculptured figures of classic antiquity. Chippendale was influenced by the rococo fashion, but not to the exclusion of other sources. Indeed, the rococo never dominated English work, and Chinese lattice work as well as misunderstood Gothic details appear frequently.

The rococo was most enthusiastically received in the *Schlösser* of the German principalities where it exceeded even the French examples in capriciousness and fanciful extravagance. In Italy the rococo developed a special theatrical quality of moving fanciful lines, lightly rendered. Proportions were less suave than the French work, and ornament, charming in itself, was applied unsuitably and, on occasion, produced an effect of gaudiness and vulgarity. It was a superficial expedient style.

The extravagance of the rococo began to wane before the death of Louis XV, and the style of his successor, Louis XVI, is one of consistent classical austerity. Straight lines and right angles supersede the sinuous curves. The essential characteristics of the interior design continue to develop insofar as the rooms were smaller, less formal, specialized in purpose, charming in scale and detail. Bedroom, boudoir, library and dining room became distinct types. They were furnished with articles reflecting the intimate social life of the period—the chaise-longue, the bèrgere, small desks for note writing, tea-tables, gaming-tables, all symbolizing the current mode of living. Wall treatments of the Louis XVI period were less profusely ornamented whether on wood or plaster. Fabrics as well as wallpapers were applied to the walls. Both wood and plaster areas were painted in soft neutral colors. Naturalistic themes were replaced by elements of classic ornament. Marble mantels were of classic rectangular design, as were also doors and windows. Ceilings were usually plain, although some elaborate rooms were painted with sky and cloud effects.

In England classicism was a continuous line of development. The classic architectural style reached its height in the work of **Robert Adam**, who may be considered the first interior decorator. The brothers Adam were architects, but carried their architecture through every detail of the interior, summoning the talents of artists and designers in every field to execute the details of their broad concepts. Robert Adam designed rooms that share the classic attitudes of the Louis XVI style. Color schemes, as well as proportions, were excessively delicate. The fineness of Greek and Roman detail was offset by broad surfaces of delicate hues of pea green, blue, straw, lilac, gray and often white. An air of formality, of cold symmetry, pervaded the Adam work, and contemporary critics objected vociferously to the austere perfection which appeared to them as too contradictory to the comfortable opulence of the Chippendale era. The last half of the century saw fewer innovations resulting from the manner of living than in the ornamental aspects of room design; indeed, there was no substantial difference in the decorative or utilitarian aspect of the important rooms in great houses from the late 18th cent. to the early 20th. and it may be said that the palatial interior never surpassed the splendor attained in the 17th and 18th cents.

The 19th cent. is characterized by the decline of the aristocratic ideal and the ascendancy of the middle class. The new wealthy were satisfied to aspire to the artistic achievements of the aristocracy, a backward-looking process which resulted in confusion, vulgarity, a vast output of works of questionable taste. Fads and short-lived styles spotted the design history of the 19th century. The significance of this decline in taste lies in the corruption of the standards of basic organic design. The most fortunate leavening influence was the fact that so many houses were built by people of modest wealth, who were prevented by the stern dictates of economy from departing altogether from their sense of the substantial and useful.

Interior design in America exemplifies the rise from absolutely utilitarian design through its various stages of embellishment. Colonizations are not made by migrations of great wealth. According to their means the houses of the various parts of the new continent were more or less rudimentary. The New England colonists were yeomen of strain dedicated to austerity and with a background of rustic building. Their first houses were shelters pure and simple, and such artistic value as graced these dwellings was the result of unconsciously good purposefulness, mechanical skill and ingenuity, and directness in the appreciation of useful form and of the materials at hand. The great fireplace and the small windows testified to the primary requirement,—shelter from the stern climate. At least two generations passed in New England before the house took on an air of comfort and convenient living. The walls were finished with rectangular wood panels of upright boards; the ceilings were open timbers; the fireplace was a large part of one wall and usually spanned with a heavy beam ornamented with primitive carving. The floors were of broad boards with an occasional small Turkey carpet. The Virginia colonies of the same era, exemplified in the Williamsburgh restoration, were in the more highly decorative vein which the Cavaliers, with their greater wealth and their broader sense of beauty, were able to import. The Dutch settlements were chiefly homes in the burgher tradition, substantial merchant types, addicted only to the broader aspects of the Netherlands baroque influence. Swedish and German settlements were entirely of peasant character, the log cabin being the conspicuous contribution of the Swedish.

In the 18th cent. the rising merchant class began to import not only an occasional piece of furniture, but the books of the great designers, and local cabinetmakers reproduced the substance of these designs in their own manner and materials. Echoes of Chippendale appear in the work of Randolph, Savory and Gostelowe in Philadelphia, Townsend and Goddard in Newport, among others. Later, the Adam influence motivates Bulfinch and McIntire and, finally, Sheraton and the Directoire style reappear in the skillful reproductions of Duncan Phyfe. It might therefore be said that colonial arts are always of less value than their aristocratic progenitors except for the factors of simplification and adaptation which provide special interest. 18th cent. American rooms were, in their best aspects, faint echoes of the finer houses in England. Woodwork was chiefly painted white; all over panelling is rarer than dado panelling with plaster walls above, although architectural members, like pilasters and cornices, were abundant. Mantlepieces were of wood, distinctively carved, and floors of broad boards. The staircase was made an important feature of the central hall. Wallpapers were imported freely along with damasks and satins for draperies, and *toiles-de-Jouy* came with other French influences during that period after the Revolution in which British inspiration was patriotically discarded.

The early 19th cent. responded to Napoleon to the extent of patterning most of its work after his synthetic **Empire** style. Everywhere in Europe and America a stiff architectural conglomeration of motives from ancient Egypt, Greece and Rome was accepted. A classical imperial attitude prescribed strong colors, stern architectural and military motifs. The Biedermeier style (q.v.) in Germany and Austria is a provincial, graceful variation, and similar reduction of the imperial manner characterized the **American Empire.** Provincial styles in France were more casual about mixing *Empire* and *Directoire* designs with vestigial Louis XV and Louis XVI details.

Interior design and decoration in the 20th cent. advanced very slightly from the preceding hundred years. In England and the U. S. A. organic room form was given relatively little thought. It was regarded as a box in which certain activities were contained and, in its turn, contained in a larger box. The shape of the outer shell was too often the starting point and the various rooms were fitted into a preconceived mass of house. Unfortunately, this outer mass was designed less from a consideration of activities than from eclectic notions of silhouette and site requirements. The practice of interior decoration then attached each room as an entity, bestowing upon it such elements of historical design as suited the whim of the owner. This unwholesome practice prevailed in the more costly work even more than in the lesser, as the rich were able to buy antiques and were prompted to simulate backgrounds to harmonize with the antique furnishings. A spurious archeological scholarship became the stock-in-trade of the interior decorator, and decoration acquired a bad name through having become aesthetically sterile, eclectically correct. There were in all countries revolts to this slavish copying. Intellectual movements in the later 19th cent. endeavored to dissociate aesthetics from machine products to the extent of overvaluing the amateur. The culmination of this idea in the Arts-and-Crafts (q.v.), Mission and equivalent homemade movements produced a crude graceless manner of decoration. The **Mission style** in the U. S. A. manifested itself in badly lighted interiors of morose colorings. Furniture was heavy and sturdy by virtue of its primitive joinery and lack of subtlety and sheer weight. There was also an admixture of the *Art Nouveau* (q.v.) at the turn of the century which exaggerated natural motives, with generally unhappy results. The whole approach, while it had widespread effects on commercial design, failed to kindle any lasting interest.

Architectural thought after World War I developed a clear cleavage between the exponents of traditional revivalism and rebel schools seeking to re-appraise decorative and architectural impulses. The traditionalists were more correct archeologically and made better copies than ever before, thanks to superior research and documentation. The modernists on the other hand followed many avenues of thought in the 20's and 30's. One school worked along essentially traditional lines modifying only the decorative idiom. These produced rooms organically the same as they had been before, but often possessing qualities of decorative freedom and ingenuity. Much of the French and German work (which inspired like work in England and America) was reminiscent of the *Art Nouveau.* Fine materials were used. Restrained pastel color schemes and rich textures prevailed. Among these may be cited the work of Ruhlmann in France, Bruno Paul and Peter Behrens in Germany. There was another school that shrieked of dynamics and the Jazz Age, emulating cubistic patterns in harsh forms and strident color schemes. Neither of these schools gave much evidence of a sound philosophic revaluation of architectural design, and the rising school of deliberately functional analysts experienced some difficulty in making itself heard above the clamor of the three other mentioned disputants.

It nevertheless became clear, largely through the external pressure of world events, that humanity must, willingly or not, accept and learn the new living technique. Houses must accept mechanical and social innovations as a factor in design, not by a process of reconciliation. Rooms and houses are no longer composed of boxes. The new approach to houses begins with one or more functions and establishes their relationships in rooms.

The functions of architect and interior decorator in the new houses are not easily dissociated as the external form of the houses derives from the minutiae of the activities within. The room is the first consideration in the design of the house. Its shape and boundaries, lighting, color and furnishings determine its appearance. Heating systems are not limited to the range of a fireplace or stove, so that a large area may be heated and ventilated as readily as a small one. Features like sunlight and seasonal breezes may well become the deciding feature in the appearance of a room. Colors and textures are disposed according to their composition with light and shade, and in terms and shapes and proportions. These factors eliminate the four square wall concept. Symmetry has no purpose, visual or functional, but balance may be achieved without symmetry and the sacrifices it sometimes demands.

The interior decorator in the traditional sense must operate in direct conjunction and complete harmony with the architect, if he participates in this type of design at all. More practically, the architect must conceive the interior aspect of the house as well as the shell. There is no separate decorative approach. It is possible and practical that separate individuals can work harmoniously together for a clearly understood end in the same way that the great Gothic cathedrals were one blended thought inside and out. This will demand either that the architect function as interior designer or that the interior designer enlarge his scope to design the whole house. See Abercrombie, P., *The Book of the Modern House*, 1939; Aloi, R., *L'Arredamento Moderno* (Second Series), 1939; Aronson, Joseph, *The Book of Furniture & Decoration*, 1924; LeCorbusier, *Toward a New Architecture*, 1931; Dilke, Emilia, *French Furniture and Decoration in the 18th Century*, 1901; Eberlein and Hubbard, *Colonial Interiors, Federal and Greek Revival*, 3rd Series; Ford and Ford, *The Modern House in America*, 1940; Frankl, Paul T., *Space for Living*, 1938; Frohne, H. W., and Jackson, B. and A. F., *Color Schemes for the Home and Model Interiors*, 1919; Holme, H. M., *Colour in Interior Decoration*; Jourdain, Margaret, *English Decoration and Furniture of the Early Renaissance*, 1924 and *English Decoration and Furniture of the Later 18th Century*, 1922; Kimball, Fiske, *Domestic Architecture of the American Colonies and the Early Republic*, 1922; Lenygon, Francis, *Decoration and Furniture of English Mansions During the 17th and 18th Centuries*, 1909; Maas, Carl, *Common Sense in Home Decoration*, 1938; Mumford, Lewis, *Sticks and Stones*, 1924; Parsons, Frank Alvah, *Interior Decoration*, 1925; Retera, W., *Het Moderne Interieur*, 1937; Sale, Edith Tunis, *Colonial Interiors*, 1930; Storey, Walter Rendell, *Period Influence in Interior Decoration*, 1937; Todd, D., and Mortimer, R., *The New Interior Decoration;* Whiton, Sherrill, *Elements of Interior Decoration*, 1937.   —J.A.

interior decoration. See INTERIOR ARCHITECTURE AND DECORATION.

interior design. See INTERIOR ARCHITECTURE AND DECORATION.

interleaved. *Book.* A book is interleaved when blank leaves are inserted between the printed pages.

interlude. An instrumental passage connecting different periods or parts in instrumental or vocal music. See fugue.

intermezzo. (1) Interlude. (2) Entr'acte. (3) A short operetta.

international architecture. The development of modern architecture in the 20th cent., esp. in the years between 1920 and 1930, in Europe brought forth a trend which influenced the U. S. A. too, called "International Architecture." The borderline between "International Architecture" and "Functional Architecture" is not quite clearly drawn. For its definition, the history of architecture in the 20th cent. has to be scrutinized. The common trend was primarily characterized everywhere by the fight against the historical eclecticism which dressed each building independent of its practical function with the same repetitions of forms of earlier periods.

The reaction began in Austria, Germany, and the Netherlands. It later was carried on in France, Scandinavia, and Russia. Around 1920, two currents had clearly developed: The one based upon earlier works by Otto Wagner, Van de Velde, and Joseph Maria Olbrich was now, in this generation, represented in Austria by Joseph Hoffman and Koloman Moser; in Germany, by Hans Poelzig, Bruno Taut (Expressionism); in the Netherlands, by M. de Klerk, P. Kramer, C. I. Blaauw; in France, by Auguste Perret. These architects, although denying the eclecticism of the 19th cent., developed very soon a new kind of technical romanticism. Certain forms continuously repeated began quickly to stale.

The other group of architects, represented by J. J. P. Oud, W. M. Dudok in the Netherlands, Adolf Loos in Austria, Walter Gropius (Bauhaus) and Mies van der Rohe in Germany, Le Corbusier and André Lurcat in France, Lescaze and Neutra in the U. S. A., denied equally the historical eclecticism. However, their works and those of their followers emphasized the composition in individual loose plans instead of in solid compact masses, stressing more the specific qualities of the respective materials and construction methods. The artistic result of these tendencies was the opening of the façade by large porches and windows, cubic concentration of crystallized masses, emphasis on horizontal lines. It is this type of architectural planning which is generally called "International Architecture."

Practically, very soon national shades of this international movement became apparent. Although strongly functional planning produced a certain alikeness, the respective national traditions, preferences for certain materials and construction methods began soon creating variant external shapes. Thus today, modern architecture after having gone through its fighting and pioneering stage begins gradually to lose its dogmatic, cool strictness and to fit into the lines of the respective national traditions. In spite of this fact it should never be forgotten that the whole modern development in architecture is entirely based upon the fundamental and essential achievements of the generation working between 1920 and 1930 in Europe, and after 1930 in the U. S. A. See functional architecture; also Bruno Taut, *Modern Architecture,* 1929; Henry Russell Hitchcock, Jr., *Modern Architecture, Romanticism and Reintegration,* 1929; Le Corbusier, *Towards a New Architecture,* 1929, and *The City of To-Morrow,* 1929; Cahill, Holger, and Barr, A. H., eds., *Art in America in Modern Times* (chapter on Architecture by H. R. Hitchcock), 1934; N. Pevsner, *The Pioneers of the Modern Movement, from William Morris to Walter Gropius,* 1936; C. G. Holme, *Industrial Architecture,* 1935; Rexford Newcomb, *Outline of the History of Architecture,* 1939. (Part 4); Talbot Hamlin, *Architecture through the Ages,* 1940; H. Russell Hitchcock, *The International Style,* 1932; "International Architecture 1924-1934", Catalogue of the Centenary Exhibition. R. J. B. A.

—P.Z.

International pitch. See ACOUSTICS.

International style. See INTERNATIONAL ARCHITECTURE.

Interpretative dance. See natural dance.

Interval. The distance between two tones is called an interval. An interval is referred to as melodic if they are sounded successively and harmonic if sounded together. In naming the intervals the major scale is the usual standard. Intervals are reckoned from the lowest to the highest note and given a "number" name such as a second (c-d); third (*c*-d-*e*); fourth (*c*-d-e-*f*) etc. Should two voices sing the same pitch, the unison is called a prime. The "number" names is qualified by a "specific" name for which the terms perfect, major, minor, augmented and diminished are used. In the major scale the intervals formed by using the key-note as the lowest note are either perfect (prime, fourth, fifth, octave) or major (second, third, sixth, seventh). To calculate the specific name "whole" and "half-steps" are used to measure the interval, thus a major third is two whole-steps or four half-steps.

By the use of sharps, flats or double sharps and flats intervals may be decreased or increased. If a **major** interval is decreased by a half-step it becomes **minor,** (C-E reduce to C-Eflat). If a **perfect** or **major** interval is increased by a half-step it becomes augmented. (*Perfect* C-G; C-Gsharp, augmented: Major sixth C-A; C-Asharp, augmented). If a *perfect* or *minor* interval is decreased by a half-step it is diminished, (*Perfect* C-G; C-Gflat, diminished: *Minor* third C-Eflat; C-E double flat diminished). It will be noticed that on the present day piano the interval C-Gsharp and C-Aflat will sound the same whereas on string instruments the slight difference may be demonstrated. These intervals sounding the same but labeled with different staff names are called **enharmonic intervals.** In keeping with theoretical practice, however, the interval C-Gsharp is reckoned as a fifth (augmented) and C-Aflat as a sixth (minor).

Intervals beyond the range of the octave (compound) such as the ninth, tenth, etc., are ordinarily reduced an octave and spoken of as a second (ninth), third (tenth), etc. In harmony, however, it is common to refer to chords as chord of the 9th, 11th, and 13th with the 15th completing two octaves.

Harmonically, intervals are either **consonant** or **dissonant.** The perfect intervals and the major and minor thirds and sixths are classed as consonant while the seconds, sevenths and the augmented and diminished intervals are dissonant.

Intervals may be **inverted.** That is the lower note becomes the higher or vice versa. Under these circumstances the perfect intervals remain perfect; the augmented become minor; and the minor major. As regard the number name the seconds become sevenths; the thirds become sixths, etc. A common device is to subtract the original "number" from nine to find the new interval.

Acoustically, an interval is the ratio between the number of vibrations of the vibrating media, string, pipe, etc. In **just intonation** the vibrations bear a relationship shown in the following table:

Octave 2:1
Fifth 3:2
Fourth 4:3
Major Third 5:4
Minor Third 6:5
Major Sixth 5:3
Minor Sixth 8:5

In the tuning of keyboard instruments just intonation, mean-tone temperament and equal temperament have been used at different periods. The just intervals are in tune in one key; those in mean-tone permit modulation (q.v.) to several keys; and with equal temperament, the present system, modulation to all keys is possible. The ear is not capable of discerning moderate differences in vibration and the intervals in equal temperament are only slightly out of tune with their just intonation. The ear likewise is unable to resolve intervals that are octaves apart.

At times aesthetic qualities have been attached to certain intervals but this is a personal interpretation and what may appear to be associated with the individual interval may be lost when placed in harmonic surroundings. Certain intervals however have been associated with particular races of people.

Smaller intervals than the half-tone have been the subject of study and experiment. Instruments have been constructed on the principle of the quarter-tone idiom. It is interesting in this light to refer to a 17th cent. manual which refers to quarter-tones and remarks that they are impractical for vocal writing.   —J.V.H.

Intimistes. See FRENCH ART.

intonation. (1) The method of tone production of a voice or instrument. (2) Pitch. (3) Tone quality or timbre. (4) The opening notes of a Gregorian chant.

intrada. (1) The pompous introduction to early dramas and operas. (2) An instrumental overture to instrumental compositions.

intrados. The interior face of an arch or vault.

introit. See psalmody; Mass; MEDIEVAL MUSIC.

invention. *Mus.* A composition of fanciful or impromptu character (Bach).

inverse process. See PERSPECTIVE.

inversion. *Mus.* Device of composition by which a harmonic interval is transformed into its complementary interval within the range of an octave (**harmonic inversion**, e.g.: a minor sixth becomes a major third, a perfect fifth becomes a perfect fourth, etc.), or a melodic interval is transformed into an equivalent interval of opposite direction (**melodic inversion**, e.g.: an ascending major third becomes a descending major third, etc.; in the modal and tonal idioms melodic inversion is usually applied with the proviso that minor intervals stand for major, and vice versa, whenever literal inversion would interfere with the mode, or key, of the original melody). Sometimes the term inversion is applied to the transposition of melodic lines in double counterpoint (see counterpoint); this usage, however, is misleading and should be avoided.   —E.K.

inverted interval. See interval; inversion.

Ionian mode. See idiom A (2).

Ionian vases. During the 7th and 6th cents. B.C. there were many productive potteries on the coast of Asia Minor and the islands of the Aegean, which produced vases combining Greek and oriental motifs in an interesting way. Notable among them were those at Miletus, Ephesus, Colophon, Priene, Clazomene, Rhodes and Melos. Oriental influence, causing the breakup of the geometric tradition, first appeared in the Cyclades, where 7th cent. vases found in Delos, Melos and Thera show heraldic animals and birds beginning to supplant the earlier abstract patterns. The so-called **Melian amphorae** have rich decorative bands of birds and animals, some of them imaginative ones such as sphinxes and sickle winged horses, painted on a cream slip with geometric ornament still filling in the background. "**Rhodian**" **ware**, including a lovely series of robust pitchers, has similar friezes of birds and animals, but the color scheme is more brilliant, including crimson, maroon and black against the cream slip. The "Ionic eye" was often painted on them to ward off evil. During the 6th cent. the oriental tapestry effect was generally abandoned in favor of the organization of human figures in mythological scenes (often humorously interpreted) or everyday life: sport, battles, festivals; and plant decoration became conventionalized for borders. Among the most important vases of this period were gay and fantastic vases from **Clazomene,** with scenes of dancing and riotous Satyrs and a liberal use of foliate ornament; **Fikellura ware,** notable for its spirited scenes of dances and animals painted on squat-neck amphorae; a polychrome series found at Naucratis, in which the color scheme includes red, black, white, yellow, maroon and purple on a cream ground; ware found at Cyrene, picturing incisively scenes of everyday commercial activity; "**Caeretan**" **hydriae**, stout water jugs with white, black and dark red pictures representing mythological scenes, such as the exploits of Heracles; "**Pontic**" **ware**, with lovely plump lotus and palmette borders and mythological scenes which are frank caricatures, such as the Judgment of Paris vase; and a fine series called **Chalcidian**, elegant in shape, with energetic pictures crisply painted in black on the deep orange ground.   —W.R.A.

Ionic cyma. Term applied sometimes to the cyma recta (q.v.) or to the cyma reversa (q.v.), both of which mouldings are commonly used in Ionic order.

Ionic frieze. In classical architecture, the middle member of the entablature, over the epistyle or architrave; in the Ionic order left a plain band with a crowning moulding or decorated with a continuous band of figures or ornament in relief.   —L.T.S.

Ionic Renaissance. See HELLENIC ART.

Iranian art. See PERSIAN ART.

iris. See SYMBOLISM IN FAR EASTERN ART.

Iris green. A rare pigment with fine green color, this can be classed among painting materials now obsolete. It was used extensively for manuscript illumination during the 14th and 15th cents. It was an organic dyestuff made from the juice of the iris flower and the best color came from mixtures with alum.   —G.L.S.

Irish jig. The word "jig" designates a large group of Irish national dances, group and solo, each of which has its individual name and particular arrangement of the traditional content. Jigs are characterized by fast shuffling, tapping, jumping, and hopping steps in 6/8 or 9/8 meter. The solos are intricate and difficult, with great stress upon the complicated foot-work. The group jigs are simpler, and may be round, square, or long dances, sometimes differing from the reels only in meter, but usually employing the jig type of step. See Irish reel.   —J.G.

Irish reel. The reel is a type of Irish national dance in 2/4 meter. The name applies to a large group of dances, each having its individual title and arrangement of traditional steps and figures. There are reels for solo and for small or large groups of couples. The steps of all reels are gliding and rapid with little torso movement, but more intricate in the solo dances. The group reels are round, square, or long dances, elaborate in pattern, with weaving and turning figures, promenades, advancing and retiring of couples in turn, etc.   —J.G.

Iron gall ink. See ink.

iron pigments. The best known of these are the earth reds and yellows, and green earth or terre-verte. The red iron oxides found as natural deposits are haematite, Indian red, light red, Tuscan red, Venetian red, English red, and others. Synthetic iron oxides have been made and bear the trade names, Mars red and Mars yellow. The yellow iron pigments, also oxides, are somewhat more hydrous and go by the names, yellow ochre, raw sienna, and the dark raw umber which contains also a small amount of manganese. Burned to a dull red color, the two latter give burnt umber and burnt sienna. Green earth contains not only hydrous iron but magnesium and aluminum potassium silicates.   —G.L.S.

iron wire stroke, the. In Chinese painting, the long, even, and flowing line drawn by a vertical brush, mastered first by Ku K'ai-chih of the 5th cent.

ironwork. See METALWORK.

ishi yake (Jap.). Stoneware.

ishizuri (Jap.). An impression secured by taking a rubbing from a stone. Also used to define any print which is similar in style. See rubbing.   —J.A.M.

ISLAMIC ART. The categorical fine arts have all been practised in a characteristic manner by Islamic peoples. But Muslims did not conceive our distinction between fine and useful arts. The Encyclopedists who afford the best indices of the intellectual importance attached to the various human activities include painting among such crafts as weaving and metal-work; sculpture as such is rarely mentioned. Architectural design, in theory at least, was a part of geometry (*handasa*) and in practice often the work of master-masons. "Classic" Persian painting was in practice a subordinate part of book-making. Of all the visual arts calligraphy (*khatt*) alone appears to have been regarded as a fine art by Muslims(it is termed "a spiritual geometry," see also Koran LXVIII) and enthusiastically practised for its own sake by princes and statesmen. The Arabic alphabet in various scripts, generally in "contrapuntal" or "polar" combination with arabesque (*islimi*) ornament, became the most august decoration for architecture and other deliberately beautified artifacts.

Muslims, then, have never looked to artists (with the exception of poets and perhaps calligraphers) for special insights or meanings. They regarded the arts as we regard the decorative arts.

In spirit this art has been characterized as "polar". Tension between simple bulk and minute two-dimensional surface-elaboration, between curved and straight lines, has perhaps never been so extreme as in the "classic" manifestations of Islamic art (Persia 11th-16th cents., Syro-Egypt 12th-14th cents.). The mature color-systems exemplify the same polarity in hue (*ablaq* masonry; checkered, etc. revetments; equality of saturation giving a curious "pull" to juxtapositions of scarlet and blue, orange and green in Safavid paintings and textiles). The spirit was present at the beginning of Islam (Korans of the Abbasid period) and even in Sasanian Persia (*ivan* facade with its violent antithesis of air and solid, e.g. Ctesiphon).

Probably because Islam historically is to be regarded rather as a reaction in Eastern Christianity than as a new culture, and because the Arabs among whom the Faith arose did not practise the visual arts, earlier Islamic architecture, sculpture, and painting are best approached as final forms of the Byzantine-Sasanian style, alternative forms to those prevailing in the Christian lands which were not conquered by the Muslims.

In the 10th and 11th cents. a revival among the Iranian peoples opened a new phase. The transformation of the older Islamic style then accomplished was spread, in successive phases of development, by their conquerors, first by the Seljuq Turks, then by the Mongol Il-Khans, then by the Timurids. Lastly, by its own splendor in its period of conclusive fulfilment (16th cent.) it permeated afresh the Moghul and Ottoman courts.

There is thus a certain want of organic unity in the development of the Islamic fine arts which underlies the apparent consistency of the Islamic style.

Architecture. The essentials of the Muslim town are a mosque, a bazaar, and a public bath. In addition to palaces (for which the Central Asian conquerors of Persia contributed a special type: a garden with tents for habitation and kiosques, often of great grandeur, for ornament), castles (in which the Muslims developed Sasanian and Byzantine forms), bridges, and other great forms common to all highly developed architectures, certain characteristic Islamic forms were developed, including: (1) the **mosque** (*masjid* and, later *jami*) or normal place of worship (*sajd*: prostration), consisting of a court (*sahn*) surrounded ordinarily by roofed arcades (*rivaq*). Mosques are generally oriented towards Mecca (this direction is called the *qibla*), and in the sanctuary, or arcade on this side, are generally a niche, (*mihrab*) showing the qibla, a pulpit (*minbar*)and often a *maqsura* or fenced-off area in the arcade. From one to six minarets, tall towers for the call to prayer and for architectural ornament, were often built near mosques, or at their sides or corners. The mosque form may be regarded as the incorporation of certain features of early churches in plans modelled on that of the Prophet's house at Medina which served as the first center of worship. (2) the *madrasa* or *college,* originally a school of Sunnite theology, but used by the Seljuqs and their successors as schools for the administrative bureaucracy. At first of merely domestic architecture, they were later characterized by the use of a pre-Islamic cruciform plan, with four great *ivans* round a court. (3) the *monastery* (at first *ribat,* or military station for the Holy War against unbelievers; later *khanaqah* of Sufi mystics on the Persian model, and, in the Ottoman empire, *takya* or dervish hostel): architecurally *ribats* appear to have been fortified caravanserais with tall watch-towers; *khanaqahs* were in general cult-buildings of mosque or madrasa type with subsidiary courts surrounded by rows of cells. (4) the **monumental tomb** (*turbat, qubba, gunbad, pir,* or even *sayyid*) generally a square chamber with a domical roof. A distinctive Persian type common from the 11th to 14th cents. is a tall tower. Tombs are sometimes the most ambitious of all Islamic buildings (Sinjar at Merv, Taj Mahall, Bijapur dome) and are of importance since they were frequently placed at the corners of the qibla side of mosques or madrasas. (5) the **bazaar,** *suq,* or *qaysaria,* a street often vaulted or ceiled, with shops on both sides. Bazaars are often in the form of a cross, and seem to develop from the crossed streets of booths which have been for many centuries the Asiatic nomad markets. (6) the **caravanserai** or **khan**, an open or vaulted court with one or two stories of small rooms surrounding it.

The most characteristic formal specialities of Islamic building, are, in addition to the minaret and the *ivan* or open-ended vault, peculiar dome-profiles, squinches of great variety of filling, webbed armatures in pendentives, half-domes and vaults, "stalactites" (*mugharnas*), and carved plaster diapers.

The first great building of Islam is the Dome of the Rock at Jerusalem (691 A.D.), a wooden dome on a pillared and arcaded ambulatory, richly decorated in mosaic, essentially Byzantine. Similar mosaics decorate the Great Mosque of the **Umayyads** at Damascus (705-715), which has a great three-aisled prayer-hall crossed by a transept parallel to the *qibla* having a domed center. Other Umayyad monuments are Qusair 'Amra (712-715), a bath with erotic, astrological, and propagandist murals, and Mshatta (743-744), a palace in the desert, half the elaborately carved facade of which is in the Berlin SM.

With the fall of the Umayyads Iraq became the seat of empire, and a more Sasanian, a less Christian imperial or metropolitan style prevailed. The Round City of Baghdad, with palaces, barracks, and offices in its center, and its popular quarters disposed circumferentially within the triple defense system and the four gates, expresses the Caliphal determination that no *émeute* of the type to which they owed their own power should ever take place again in the capital. The Round City has totally disappeared, but has been reconstructed by Herzfeld and Creswell. Apart from the mosque of Qayrawan in the west (v. inf.) the middle 9th cent. ruins of the palaces and mosques of Samarra give our clearest picture of **Abbasid** architecture. It was extravagantly ostentatious in scale (the Bulkuwara palace is about 1250 m. a side), lavishly and rather coarsely decorated with carved plaster, mural painting of debased Sasanian-Hellenistic type, and precious materials. Its effect was probably largely dependent on hanging and rugs. Huge conical "minarets" with winding ramps up which donkeys could be ridden were for pleasure rather than for religious use. Ukhaydir and Raqqa are important Abbasid monuments.

Carved plaster remained a principal ornament of Islamic interiors up to the present day. The mosque of Ibn Tulun at Cairo (876-879), with plastered brick arcades, is the finest early Islamic building in Egypt.

The schismatic **Fatimid** caliphs appear to have favored the massive ashlar construction with delicately-cut surface ornament which was to set a style for the noblest West-Islamic buildings (Cairo: mosques of al-Azhar, 970-972, al-Hakim, 990-1003, al-Akmar, 1125, gates of Bab al-Futuh, Bab al-Nasr, Bab Zuwayla).

Little remains of **Ayyubid** work in Egypt. Citadels, mosques, madrasas, and hospitals (mostly on a modest scale) at Damascus and, more important, Aleppo, show the perfect mastery of Syrian stone-cutters over the now perfected Islamic arch, surface-arabesque, and stalactites (Jami' of Aleppo; Firdaw's mosque and madrasa, Aleppo, 1235).

Under the **Mamluk** successors to the Ayyubids Syro-Egyptian architecture reached its conclusive form. Increasing use of varicolored (*ablaq*) masonry, red and white or black and white marbles and limestone, interiors of stone marquetry (later imitated in paint), stripes, checkers, polygonal entrelacs, guilloches, a preference for lines of stability e.g. in the strongly horizontal organization of stalactite squinches, half-domes, and cornices and in the avoidance of strong diagonals, these features are what distinguish the Mamluk, one of the supreme expressions of the Islamic style, from contemporary Persian architecture. A very deeply stilted dome, and a characteristically Egyptian way of emphasizing cubical form by the suppression of corner-punctuation are the most significant formal peculiarities. The principal monuments are all in Cairo: madrasa of Baybars, 1262-3; madrasa of Sinjar al-Jawli, 1303-4; madrasa-tomb of Sunqur Sa'di, 1315, mosque of Muhammad Nasir, 1318; Almas mosque, 1329-30; madrasa-tomb of Sultan Hasan, 1356-62; Khanaqah of Barkuk, 1400-10; mosque of Sultan Mu'ayyad, 1414; madrasa-tomb, 1472-4, and city mosque 1475, of Qa'itbay; madrasa of al-Uzbek, 1487-1500; madrasa of Abu Bakr Ma'shar, 1497; madrasa of Qansawh al-Ghawri, 1503-4; the so-called "Tombs of the Caliphs", 15th and early 16th cents.

The Ottoman conquest introduced the **Ottoman** style (v. inf.).

In the east, mosques were at first **Sasanian** in construction even if raised over an Arab plan (Tarik Khana of Damghan, pier and barrel vault *rivaqs*). The decline of the Abbasid caliphate coincided with the revival of Iranian national culture, of which the most important architectural monument is the tomb of Isma'il the Samanid at Bukhara, c. 900, a dome on tripod squinches, with very elaborate bricklays and a vaulted gallery round the springing. The chief buildings of the pre-Seljuq period (towers of Gunbad-i-Qabus, 1006-7, Radkan West, Pir Alamdar at Damghan, 1026; *turbat* and minaret of Sangbast; minaret of the Tarik Khana; towers at Ghazni; Dawazdah Imam at Yazd, 1037) prove that forms (flanged towers, tall cylindrical minarets, squinch with oversailing quarter-domes), techniques (elaborate bonds, cut terra cotta), and decoration (fine-scale arabesque, plaited Kufic) of the Seljuq period existed, though severally, before the Seljuq conquest. Even glazed tile (*kashi*) inlay for brickwork occurs in the Jami minaret of Damghan.

Under and after the **Seljuqs** in the later 11th and 12th cents. these elements were combined in a series of masterpieces: Isfahan Jami', especially the North Dome, 1088, which is perhaps the most wonderfully constructed dome on the Earth's surface; mosques of Gulpaygan, 1104-17, and Qazvin; Ribat-i-Malik near Merv, with its wall of huge cylindrical pleatings; towers at Rayy 1139, Kunya Urgenj; the Haydaria of Qazvin; tower at Maragha, 1147; Gunbad-i-Alaviyyan at Hamadan; tombs of Jalal al-Din Husayn at Usgen, 1152, and of Sinjar at Merv 1157-60; Ardistan mosque, 1160; Jabal-i-Sang of Kirman; tomb of Mu'-mina Khatun at Nakhshivan, 1186-7; octagonal tower at Maragha of 1196-7. Interest in surface-enrichment by outset entrelacs, *kashi*, pleatings, etc., is marked in the latter of the foregoing.

The first **Jinghizids** built little; at the end of the 13th cent. grand architecture recommenced with the now ruined tomb of Ghazan near Tabriz (parts of revetment in the Berlin SM.). The mosque of 'Alishah at Tabriz, with a vault over 30m. wide, now fallen, the dome of Sultania, which had a "coronet" of eight minarets, shrines at Bistam and Natanz, all show the increased elaboration of colored ornament, esp. of *kashi* marquetry or "mosaic", with which the early 14th cent was preoccupied. Of this type of decoration the first "mature" or "late" example, with curvilinear arabesque in five colors, is the Baba Qasim shrine at Isfahan, 1340-1. Its development in the buildings of the Muzaffarids in Fars and Jibal brought it to an indescribable liquid brilliance (Jami' of Kirman, 1349; extensive rebuilding of the Jami' of Yazd; the former is the oldest complete example of an important mosque-plan with a huge portal on the main axis, opposite the *mihrab*, with a

domed vestibule leading into the *ivan*).

Under **Timur** and his successors Persian architecture of the Islamic period approached its final form: the differences between the great buildings of about 1400 and those of about 1700 are differences of detail. Now appears, at first in the Oxus region, that dome of bulbous profile on a high drum which has always fascinated the West. Early examples, generally "ribbed" or pleated; Hazrat Yassavi at Turkistan, 1394 or 1397; Gur-i-Mir at Samarqand, before 1404; Shah Zinda cemetery, Samarqand. The most important standing monument is the mosque of Gawhar Shad in the shrine of Imam Riza at Mashhad, 1405-1418, the finest colored exterior surviving, a court with four great ivans, two-story facades, and minarets flanking the sanctuary *ivan*. The whole visible surface is either *kashi* or a deliberate ground or foil to it in brick or plaster. Gawhar Shad's *musalla* at Herat, of which two minarets remain, appears to have been even more splendid. The chief architect and decorator of the early Timurid period was Qivam al-Din of Shiraz. Many Persian buildings were rebuilt or redecorated in the XV century. The most famous monuments are the Blue Mosque of Tabriz, 1437-67, and a madrasa at Khargird, 1444-5.

The **Safavids**, extensive builders, innovated little. Widening of the decorable surface by the elimination or chamfering of reveals was carried to the limit. After about 1600 five-color or seven-color figured tiles tended to replace the more expensive mosaic. Principal monuments are: Harun Vilayat at Isfahan, 1512; Shrine of Safi at Ardabil; the Ali Qapu palace, Royal Mosque, mosque of Lutfallah, and Qaysaria in the Maydan of Isfahan (early XVII century); Khwaja Rabi' at Mashhad, 1622; Court, dome, and embellishments at the Mashhad shrine; Qadamgah near Nishapur 1643; Madrasa-i-Madar-i-Shah at Isfahan, 1707-11.

Under the short-lived Zend dynasty at Shiraz were built several extreme examples of the bulbous dome, only a few decades after the building of the Isfahan madrasa dome of 1707-11, which is in contour the subtlest and best of all Islamic domes. In the Qajar and Pahlavi periods the increasing influence of Europe has affected the traditional forms. Various Teheran palaces (e.g. Gulistan, Baghi-Firdaws) show the style best.

ASIA MINOR, ETC. When the Seljuqs mastered Rum (Asia Minor), the old sculptural technique of that region was only gradually adapted to the expression of Islamic design. Early examples (e.g. Divrigi, 1229) show ornament apparently designed by illuminators executed in deeply-cut relief and three-dimensional arrangements; the effect is extraordinarily turbulent. Later examples (Chifta Manara, Sivas, 1271-2) though generally richer than Mamluk or Almohad masterpieces, conform to the Islamic norm for relation of bulk to surface. Principal monuments: at Konya, mosque of 'Ala al-Din, Kara Tai Madrasa, 1251-2, "Indian Minaret".

The extinction of the Byzantine empire left the Ottoman successors to the Seljuqs heirs to the Byzantine style, and they built great enclosed mosques with saucer-domes, and often with abutting half-domes, curiously like the grandest churches. Principal monuments: at Brusa, Ulu mosque 1421, Green Mosque, 1423; at Istanbul, mosques of Shahzada, 1548, Sulayman, 1557, Ahmad I, 1617, Nur-i-'Uthmania, 1755; at Adrianople, mosque of Salim II, 1574. Some details such as *ablaq* voussoirs derive from the Mamluk style, others such as tile revetment from Persia, others such as baroque cornices and mouldings from Europe; but at its best the Ottoman style is, though frigid, nobly monumental. Its great masters were Sinan and Agha. A peculiarly slender minaret with elongated conical head, and often with two or three stalactite-corbelled balconies, was much used (sometimes six to a mosque). To Western eyes the minarets of Istanbul are more masterfully grouped than any in Cairo, Persia, or India.

INDIA. In India under the Ghorid successors of the Ghaznevids, her first Muslim conquerors, was produced another variant of the characteristic architecture which Islam imposed upon stone-working countries. The mosque-facade and minaret of Qutb al-Din at Old Delhi (late 12th cent.) and the 'Ala Darwaza at the same site, 1310, are so much akin to Almohad work that a comparison is startling proof of the unity of an Islamic art-style over almost an entire quadrant of the Earth's 30th latitude. Under the medieval dynasties the style reverted somewhat to Indian character (Sahsaram, tomb of Shir Shah; Bijapur architecture, esp. tomb of Muhammad Adil Shah, early 17th cent., a huge dome with an inner diameter of c. 45 m., larger than the Pantheon or S. Sophia of Constantinople; Golconda architecture of the Qutbshah period). The **Moghul** emperors, whose ideas of culture were strongly colored by their Timurid ancestors and their Safavid contemporaries, imposed typical Islamic refinement on the architecture of the 16th and

17th cents.: tomb of Humayun at Delhi; tomb of Akbar; Taj Mahal, tomb of I 'timad al Dawla at Agra. These and the various palaces at Agra and Delhi are remarkable for rich interiors of marble inlaid with illuminators' flower- and arabesque-designs in variegated and semi-precious stones. Cusped arches, flat as well as vaulted roofs, pierced marble grills, corbels with massive drops, heavily-domed roof-pavilions on slender columns are characteristic of the **Moghul style**. Its normal material, apart from marble, was red sandstone.

WESTERN LANDS OF ISLAM. Though Ifriqia, Maghrib, and Andalusia have really their own artistic characters and traditions, their interaction in the Muslim period and their homogeneity vis-à-vis the Persian style suggest a general treatment. Algeria is essentially provincial.

In Ifriqia the conquerors founded Qayrawan, where about 800 the Aghlabids set up a dynastic culture in the **Abbasid** style. The Great Mosque of Qayrawan is the only great unruined monument of Abbasid architecture (836-875 and later). It has a hypostyle hall (main aisles in a T along axis and *qibla* wall; sixteen lateral nine-bay aisles) and an enormous court with narrow *rivaqs* (total area: c. 135x 80 m). On the axis opposite the *qibla* is a minaret of three square stories, and the axial aisle of the *qibla rivaq* is punctuated with domes before the *mihrab* and next the court. In the aisles, re-used classical and Byzantine columns and capitals support horseshoe arches, with an over-abacus, impost, and cornice mediating. On the arcades rest timber roofs; the axial aisle is pitched. The *mihrab* dome has conch-shaped squinches supporting, on an arcade of sixteen niches, a hemispherical fluted or melon dome. Other monuments; Zaytuna mosque of Tunis, 865; ruins of Sedrata; mosque and *ribat* of Susa.

The **horseshoe** (*manfukh* swollen) **arch**, either round, deformed, or pointed at the head, remained characteristic of West Islamic architecture. Qayrawan's influence is only less than that of the Great Mosque of Cordova (785-961 and later). Here, on the model of Damascus, the Spanish **Umayyads** employed Byzantine mosaicists, but this technique was little imitated, whereas reflections are to be seen everywhere of the "Villa Viciosa" and the sanctuary bay, one of the most fascinating structures ever built by man. At the culmination of the Italian baroque Guarini's San Lorenzo at Turin does little more than repeat this extraordinary form. Within and

beneath the main triple horseshoe arcade are
interlaced cusped half-arches in relief-carved
vari-colored ashlar. Above, cusped squinches
form an octagonal "drum" from the angles of
which spring eight interlaced arches, whose
crowns provide the narrowed base for a
fluted hemispherical "lantern". Other monuments: mosque of Bib Mardum ("Church of
Cristo de la Luz") at Toledo, ruins of Madin-
at al-Zahra. A post-Umayyad monument of
Saragossa, the al-Jafaria, shows the Umayyad style at its climax: the capricious intricacy of its interlaced arcades, though startlingly beautiful, appears never to have been
imitated.

The **Fatimids** continued (mosque at Monas-
tir) and the Sanhaja developed (Qal'a of the
Beni Hammad; Sfax) the Aghlabid style. Of
the dynasties which followed, the **Almoravids**
probably gave their present form to the Great
Mosque of Algiers, the Qarawin, Fez, and the
Great Mosque of Tlemcen, 1135, which has
a stalactite-dome lantern resting on sixteen
interlaced arches with pierced plaster panels
between them.

The **West-Islamic** style reached its fulfilment under the Almohads (1145-1269) of
Maghrib, who for the last time united the
whole in a single empire. Principal monuments: Qutubia of Marrakesh; Tinmal mosque; Hasan's mosque at Ribat; the Giralda
and Golden Tower of Seville. The majestic
Almohad gates of Ribat and Marrakesh are
among the noblest creations of Islamic art
(Bab al-Ruwa, Udaya Qasba, Bab Aganaw).
Western mosques in general have proportionally smaller courts than those of Eastern
Islam: in the enormous unfinished mosque of
Hasan at Ribat (183 x 139 m.) the three
courts occupy only about one-sixth of the
total area.

Of later West-Islamic monuments the most
famous is the Alhambra palace of the Nasrids
at Granada (mid 13th-mid 14th cents.), a
complex of chambers covered with carved
stucco and stalactite work built round two
courts, the Alberca water-court and the famous Court of the Lions. The latter has two
pavilions emerging from its narrower facades;
this scheme was several times copied in Bar-
bary (e.g. 17th cent. pavilions in the Qarawin of Fez).

After the collapse of Almohad power there
appears comparatively little architectural invention, the principal evolution being the extension of tile-marquetry. Principal monuments of the Maghrib: Great Mosque of
Taza, 13th-14th cents.; Sidi bil Hasan at

Tlemcen, 1296; Mansura minaret at Tlemcen,
1303-1336 or later; various Marinid madrasas
at Fez, especially al-'Attarin, 1323-5, and Abu
Inania, 1350-5; the Sa'dian Mausoleum at
Marrakesh (early 17th cent.), the Madrasa
al-Sharratin, Fez, 1670, the Mansur gate at
Meknes.

Algeria in the days of its wealth produced
a bastard architecture of Ottoman, European,
and African elements: 'Ali Bichnin mosque,
ca. 1622; Jami' al-Jadid, 1660; Kechawa mosque, 1794, now much altered.

Tunisia has continued to produce buildings
in which decadence is less evident. Taut ar-
cading of ancient type and sober proportion
distinguish such buildings as the exterior galleries of the Zaytuna; the tomb-mosques of
Yusuf Dey, 1610-1637, and Hamuda Bey,
1654. The strength of rooted native tradition
is shown, even more than in the houses of
wealthy modern Tunisians, in the grand modern "Mosque of Swords" at Qayrawan.

The most distinctive decorative features of
West-Islamic architecture are its arches,
horseshoe, cusped, and "slittered" (an elaborate
form with much vertical detail got by the
grouping of cusps and stalactites), and the
richness of its lozenge and trellis diapers.
The minarets, of which the different stories
are sometimes used for a display of virtuosity
in various vaulting, are of great structural
interest.

Painting. Earlier Islamic painting, ceremonial, magical, erotic, or astrological in content (fragmentary murals at Qusayr Amra,
Samarra, pornographic papyrus at Vienna
SB.) derives partly from Sasanian but largely
from Byzantine and late classical art. The
same heritage, considerably assimilated to
linear and two-dimensional Islamic style, appears in the earliest surviving illustrated manuscripts (Cairo Royal Lib. Kitab al-Baytara
of 1209; Mashhad shrine Khawass al-Ashjar
and Mufid al-Khass; Vienna SB. Galen;
Paris B.N. Hariri "Assemblies" of 1222-3, and
Bidpai fables of about the same date; Dioscurides "Materia Medica" (in translation)
of 1224 (dispersed: Boston M.F.A., N.Y.
Met. Mus., Freer Gall. Washington); Paris
B.N. "Schefer" Hariri of 1237 with pictures
by al-Wasiti). An evident old-Asiatic tendency to break down classical illusionist
painting procedures into representation by line
and local tone is still incomplete: drapery
is not yet pattern, although the folds become
progressively less realistic until they finally
become the so called *Schnörkelfalten* pattern
of whorls in Mamluk miniatures (Oxford

Bod. Lib. Bidpai of 1354; Paris Bidpai ar. 3467). The earlier Islamic style appears to die out with Mamluk painting. Ottoman painting was to begin as an imitation of a new style which had meanwhile grown up in Persia.

Persian miniature painting is in scale the most delicate and in color the most brilliant painting ever executed by man. Fairly fine post-Seljuq painting survives on *minai* ceramics (Bowl, Kelekian coll. N. Y.), and a rather decadent style of it in illustrated Shahnamas, with scenes on red and yellow backgrounds (Istanbul 1330 ms.; Leningrad 1332 ms.), and similar Bidpais. Towards 1300, however, the Mongol rulers and their wazirs had assembled Chinese, Persian, and Western painters near their courts in Azarbaijan (Morgan Library Bestiary of 1291 and later; Edinburgh Univ. Lib. Biruni of 1307-8; Edinburgh and Royal Asiatic Society Jami' al-Tawarikh of 1306-1314 are the chief monuments of this eclectic or encyclopedic period).

In the 2d quarter of the 14th cent. Ahmad Musa is said to have founded the "modern" style of painting. What may be his illustrations to Bidpai are remounted in an album in Istanbul (former Yildiz Lib. album); they are the oldest Persian paintings with great range of color, and are based on an exceptional analysis of contemporary Chinese method. The Shahnama was illustrated a generation later in the new style by a group of artists who produced the most powerfully dramatic of Persian paintings ("Demotte" Shahnama, dispersed; collections of its miniatures in the Louvre, Fogg Museum of Harvard, Boston M.F.A., Freer Gallery, etc. Finest individual painting, Rockefeller coll. N. Y.). A Khwaju ms. of 1396 (B.M.) illustrated in a very sophisticated style marks the complete emergence of the Persian manner: tall compositions in so-called vertical perspective, excessively slender and upright figures, crowded and delicate detail. This style, which had developed at the Jalairid court at Baghdad, was patronized by the **Timurid** princes and their Western neighbors (Gulbenkian and B.M. Miscellanies made for Iskandar of Shiraz, 1410-11; Teheran Bidpai; Berlin 1420 Miscellany for Baysunghur of Herat; Vienna SB. Khwaju of 1427; Teheran Shahnama of 1429-30; Istanbul Bidpai of 1430; Upsala Univ. Lib. Nizami of 1439; Roy. As. Soc. Shahnama for Muhammad Juki; Tabari of 1469, Chester Beatty coll., London).

About 1470 appeared Bihzad, justly the most famous of Persian painters; the silly epithet "Raphael of the East" has been applied to a man whose genius lay chiefly in a wholly original realism and a power to render the hurried, the vulgar, and the humorous in perfect two-dimensional beauty (Garett Zafarnama at Princeton Univ. Lib.; Cairo Sa'di of 1488-9; Teheran "Garden Scene"; paintings in B.M. Nizani Or. 6810). His most eminent follower was Qasim Ali (Oxford 'Alishir of 1485).

The Bukhara Shaybanids captured many Herat artists, and a Bukhara group of mss. includes the Kalebdjian Mihru Mushtari of 1523; the Vever Bustan of 1524; the Paris B.N. Makhzan al-Asrar s.p. 985, Alishir of 1553, and Bustan of 1555; and the Kevorkian Jami of 1565 N. Y.

Bihzad and others fled to Tabriz, served the first **Safavid** shahs and probably helped to train the great Safavid masters Mir Musavvir ("Fable of the Owls" in the B.M. Nizami for Tahmasp of 1539-43, drawing: "A King at an Encampment" in the Boston M.F.A.); Sultan Muhammad ("Sinjar and the Old Woman" and labelled miniatures in Tahmasp's Nizami, Leningrad National Lib. "Hunting Scene", Cartier coll. Hafiz, Paris); Mir Sayyid 'Ali (miniatures in Tahmasp's Nizami and in the Beatty coll.). Mirak, Mirza 'Ali, Muzaffar 'Ali, and Shah Muhammad were other meritorious artists of the period, and other rich Safavid mss, are the Met. Mus. N. Y. Nizami of 1524-5 and a Jami in the Kevorkian coll. N. Y. The best artists of the later 16th and the 17th cents., Shaykh Muhammad Shirazi, Muhammadi, Sadiqui, Aqa Riza, Riza 'Abbasi, Afdal Husayni, Mu'in Musavvir, Muhammad Qasim, Muhammad 'Ali, are known chiefly by isolated miniatures in the great collections (Bib. Nat. and Louvre at Paris, Boston M.F.A., Freer Gall., Beatty and Vever colls., albums in the Istanbul Libs Fogg Mus).

Persian painters after 1600 imitated European light-and-shade and landscape. Flower-paintings of extraordinary delicacy are the best 18th cent. work. Large oil-paintings (usually portraits, occasionally erotic) were made to fit the niches in palace walls by Mihr Ali and others from the late 18th cent. onwards (Leningrad Winter Palace; V. and A., London).

In Turkey Salim the Grim inaugurated the **Ottoman** school of painting by kidnapping all the Tabriz masters he could lay his hands on in 1514. Turkish painting is essentially provincial, and throughout the 16th cent. Persians continued to command high salaries at Istanbul (Shahquli, Walijan). "Physiognomy" mss. or series of portraits of the Ottoman Sultans are a characteristic specialty (Istanbul Univ. Lib.; Beatty coll.), and Turkish battle-painters are particularly fond of representing the effusion of blood. Ustad 'Uthman is perhaps the most famous Turkish painter. Another signs himself Amin ai-Khalafa (Boston M.F.A., Fogg Mus.). Most of the great Turkish mss. are in the various Istanbul libraries, and are unknown to the West, but the Paris B.N., the B.M., the Berlin Islamische Kstabtng., Boston M.F. A., Met. Mus. of N. Y. and Beatty coll. all have good examples of Turkish painting.

In India the Moghul "school" was somewhat similarily begun, Humayun hiring the Persians Mir Sayyid 'Ali and 'Abd al-Samad in the mid 16th cent. But a characteristic Indian palette of varied greens and glowing reds and oranges, and the fusion into a single style of old Indian formulae for scenery and figures, European shade and would-be perspective, and Persian delicacy of detail and linear grace produced a number of remarkable mss. and album-paintings. Most Moghul painters were of Indian blood (Daswanth, Basawan). They illustrated a copy of the Hamza Romance, probably the largest Islamic illuminated ms. (dispersed miniatures in the Vienna Indust. Mus., the V. and A., Boston M.F.A., Met. Mus. of N. Y., Fogg Mus.); the Razmnama, a Persian translation of the Mahabharata; lives of Babur and Akbar; the "Lights of Canopus" or modernized Bidpai, and the usual Persian poets and historians; but much of the finest work was isolated miniatures for albums: portraits, incidents of court life, curious or beautiful animals or flowers, wives and concubines of the sovereign, the sovereign visiting saints or sitting with his deceased ancestors, etc. The portraitist Abu'l-Hasan, the animal-painter Mansur, Gowardhan, Manohar, and others are represented by album paintings at Teheran, (Gulshan palace album), Berlin (Jahangir album), Boston M.F.A., V. and A., London, Beatty coll. etc. Under Awrangzib in the later 17th cent. the eclectic style gave way to local styles, fusing with traditional Hindu painting, and ceased to be in any real sense an Islamic art, although imitative work of considerable skill continued to be made in the great Muhammadan cities for two hundred years.

Calligraphy and Illumination. The Arabic alphabet, extant before Islam, was written in three distinct styles as early as the first Islamic century: a rounded cursive, a formal style with extremely elongated uprights, and varied formal styles of generally rectilinear character and elongated connectives, all nowadays mistermed "Kufic", Terminology is only provisional, since no acceptable identification of the various historic scripts has yet been made; though minutely, they are not consistently differentiable, and Oriental connoisseurs are not historiographic in our manner.

"Kufic", the imperial script of the Caliphate, was used for Korans up to c. 1000, and for inscriptions at intervals into the 15th cent. The most celebrated masters of the **Abbasid** period were Khoshnam of Basra and al-Mahdi of **Kufa.**

Probably to be associated with the Persian revival, and possibly regularized by the Abbasid wazir Ibn Muqla, is a dramatic script normal in 10th cent. Korans, found in a stone inscription on a tomb at Ghazni.

Naskhi, a rounded script of rather level ductus, was the characteristic writing of the Seljuq period. Masters: Muhammad ibn Khazin of Dinawar (d. 1124), Yaqut of Mosul, Abdallah Sairafi.

Under the Mongols a variety of far more violent scripts were used: *thuluth, muhaqqaq, ta'liq,* etc., not clearly differentiated. Chief monuments are the early 14th cent. Korans for Uljaytu at Cairo and Leipzig, and a late 14th cent. Koran for Bayazid I in S. Sophia with abstracted illuminations in Gulbenkian and Beatty collections. The most famous master was Yaqut al-Musta'simi (d. 1298). Thuluth in particular was continued in Rum under the Ottomans, Shaykh Hamdallah (late 15th cent.) being the most celebrated master (Koran in S. Sophia). The greatest later master was Hafiz 'Uthman in the late 17th cent. (Koran and album at S. Sophia; model-book at Nur-i-'Uthmania, Istanbul).

Nasta'liq, the most completely Persian of the forms, with a drooping ductus, strongly repetitive curvature, and an almost complete elimination of straight lines, evolves gradually in the late 14th and early 15th cent. Masters: Mir 'Ali Tabrizi its "inventor", the Timurid prince Baysunghur (inscriptions in the mosque of Gawhar Shad, Mashhad), Ja'far Tabrizi (Teheran Shahnama of 1430). Later masters, represented in most of the great collections of mss., are: Sultan 'Ali Mashhadi,

his son Sultan Muhammad Nur, Shah Mah-
mud Nishapuri, Mir 'Ali Harawi, the great
master of album-pieces (*mashq*) Mir 'Imad
al-Hasani, and his rival the designer of many
of the Isfahan building inscriptions, 'Ali
Riza 'Abbasi.

Shikasta (broken) is an almost illegible and
dissipated "decadent" script, found in albums
of the 17th and 18th cents.

Of the numerous fanciful scripts the most
important is **Tughra** in its monogrammatic
form as used by the Ottomans.

Calligraphy in the lands beyond Persian
influence shared little in the later glories.
In Egypt and Syria the **Mamluks** used curious
dilated scripts for monumental inscriptions,
and in the West "Maghribi" script kept until
the 18th cent. much of the appearance of the
early centuries of Islam.

Illuminations were at first largely in gold,
with tricks of brown, red, blue, and green
(Kufic Korans). From the Abbasid caliphate
at least, whole pages were devoted to illumination with little or no script. In the
Mongol period for the first time really bold
antithesis of color were used (Uljaytu
Korans). In the late 14th and early 15th
cents. delicate black or black-and-gold drawing in margins developed (Divan of Ahmad
Jalair, Freer Gall.; Iskandar Miscellanies in
the B.M. and Gulbenkian colls.), and the
richer pages and headings assumed a characteristic minute scale and blue-and-gold tonality.
Pinks, violets, orange, and blue-greens invaded the cool harmony in the 16th cent.,
and many 17th cent. illuminations are offen-
sively colored to Western eyes. An alternative
style of rich margin also came in with the
16th cent., in colored papers sprinkled or
elaborately figured with gold. Examples of
the illumination are the same manuscripts as
examples of the painting of the later period.

Sculpture. Of figure sculpture in the round
the remains are negligible; literary descriptions of gold, silver, or bronze trees, horsemen, birds, lions, etc. in Islamic palaces indicate that metal was always its chief vehicle. Only one large piece remains from
the whole medieval period: a bronze griffin
(probably from Fatimid Egypt, 11th cent.)
now in the Campo Santo of Pisa. Is is a
work of inflated rotundity, all minor modelling
suppressed in favor of energy curvature in
the silhouette. Textile-like diaper-patterns and
borders cover the purely decorative divisions
of the surface. Lion-shaped incense-burners
(Louvre; Met. Mus., N. Y.) and pumice-
holders (the finest is in the Brummer coll.

N. Y.), and other theriomorphic utensils
(Hermitage Mus. Leningrad, esp. a cow nursing a calf) prove that the style was universal
and long-continued in Islam. A few stone
sculptures such as the lions of the Alhambra,
the marble throne of the Gulistan Palace,
Teheran, and the "nymphs" of the Chil Sutun
Palace at Isfahan are far inferior in merit
to the metal works. Decorative surface-carv-
ing is at its best in the Fatimid, Seljuq, and
Mamluk periods.

Minor arts. Systematic description of the
minor arts of Islamic peoples is not here
feasible; nor is it desirable, since in many
regions and for long ages they remained folk-
arts, like the rugs of Turkestan, only specifically 'if at all affected by the true Islamic
style. Some minor arts are of great beauty:
Egyptian and Persian bookbindings; Egyptian
marble water-vessels; wooden doors, panels,
coffers, and furnishings, carved in medieval
Turkestan, Persia, and Egypt, or painted in
Safavid Persia and Ottoman Syria; the carved ivories (caskets, writing-cases, etc.) of
the Cordovan Caliphate (Louvre, V. and A.,
Hispanic Society of New York) and later
(Pamplona Cathedral, Burgos Mus., Arch.
Mus. of Madrid); the intarsia furniture and
bibelots produced in Syria and Egypt and,
with the additional ingredient of metal, in a
very characteristic form in 18th cent. Shiraz;
Syrian glass of the early Islamic period and
Persian glass of the 18th and 19th cents.;
Moghul jewelry and early Qajar enamel on
gold; Persian lacquered *papier-maché* and
wood (notably a Safavid box in the Berlin
SM. and the common pen-boxes with exquisite
floral decoration of the 18th cent.); astro-
labes in all periods; gold-inlaid steel weapons
and implements made in Persia, Turkey, and
Northwest India from the 16th to the 18th
cents.

Perhaps less beautiful, but important to
their users by the preciousness of their materials, are such objects as the Fatimid wheel-
cut rock-crystal vessels (ewer of Caliph al-
Aziz at St. Mark's, Venice; crystals in the
Ksthist, Mus. Vienna ,the Louvre, the Rijks-
mus., Amsterdam); the rare pieces of early
gold and silver (gold vessel of Bakhtiyar,
Freer gall. Washington; Alp Arslan tray at
Boston M.F.A.; 12th cent. gold wine-cup
in the B.M.); the Ortukid enamelled bowl in
the Landesmuseum of Innsbruck; the opulent
Persian, Turkish, and Indian gold services in
the Gulistan, Teheran; the Hermitage, Leningrad; the Moscow Museum; the Topqapi
Saray, Istanbul.

But there are two classes of artifacts profoundly expressive of the characteristic spirit of Islamic culture. The first may be subsumed under that group of arts which were, for limited periods only, sufficiently important to enlist the service of first-rate calligraphy, the recognized fine art: it includes seal-cutting, damascened metalwork from the 12th to the 15th cent., Syrian enamelled glass of the 13th and 14th cents., and ceramics in the Eastern Caliphate lands from the 10th to the 14th cents. The second class is the textiles and carpets of the whole Islamic period. Although it would seem that the capacity to weave expressive textiles arrives with the maturity of cultures, Islam supervened upon an already mature culture, in which architecture, the most significant of the arts, used textiles as an essential organ; and their importance was kept up by a general feature of Islamic sovereignty, the customary giving of robes of honor by way of reward, compliment, and investiture. The importance of carpets is connected both with that nomadic or open-air habit of life which even the city-dwelling Arabs, Persians, and Turks have never entirely lost and with the value of the carpet as an image, felt by the Persians with their peculiar world-view and inconceivable to us with ours.

The appreciation of Islamic seals lies entirely beyond the range of Western connoisseurship; the most renowned master was perhaps Ahmad Beg of Mekka (late 16th cent.).

Metalwork of the early Islamic period elaborates that of Sasanian Persian and the Christian East (post-Sasanian jugs and shallow cups, Hermitage, Leningrad; ewer from the treasure of Marwan II and similar bird-spout ewers, Arab Mus. Cairo and Hermitage, Leningrad). The dissolution of subordinate relief and approach to final Islamic form is seen in a bronze hawk (Berlin SM.) and a bronze stag (Nat. Mus. Munich). The final form as expressed in the Pisa griffin (v. sup. under "Sculpture") remained alive principally in Persia, where birds, animals, fishes, and fruits of gold-inlaid steel show little decadence even in the 18th cent Isfahan work.

Meanwhile, the inlaying of the metal surface with other metals, known to Sasanian smiths, had undergone a curiously rapid exploitation in "damascening", which appears practically complete in the earliest dated piece, the "Bobrinsky" caldron made at Herat in 1163 in the Hermitage, Leningrad. The bronze body of this vessel appears dissolved

in the fine-spun figural and calligraphic decoration of inlaid silver and copper plates. This ambiguity of aspect is characteristic of all the great damascened vessels (late 12th cent. candlestick, Gulistan, Teheran; ewer of 1232, B.M.; basin made in Mosul for Badr al-Din Lulu, 1233-59, S. Bibl., Munich; basin for Najm al-Din Ayyub of Syria, Arenberg coll. Brussels; "Baptistere de S. Louis", Louvre; canteen with Christian subjects, Freer Gall., Washington; candlesticks, braziers, ewers, basins, of the early Mamluk period in the Ar. Mus. Cairo, the Met. Mus. New York, the B.M. and V. and A., London, Louvre, Berlin SM., etc.).

The same magical ambiguity of appearance was recognized (as Hariri's 18th. Assembly indicates) and prized in glass-ware (a Muslim traveller at Aleppo states that "when a man has gone into the Glass Market there he can hardly make up his mind to go away"). Blown vessels of grayish or honey-colored glass were painted with powdered glass of red, green, blue, and opaque white and gilded. Refiring fixed and fused the decoration, which rendered the vessels almost equally pervious to and reflective of light. Bottles, tall cups, standing bowls, and lamps were the usual forms. Aleppo was the principal seat of manufacture, and the period of greatest perfection extended from the late XIII to the middle XIV century. The only large collections are in the Ar. Mus. Cairo and the Met. Mus., New York (other fine examples; Freer Gall. Washington, V. and A. London, Louvre, St. Stephen's at Vienna.)

POTTERY. To the taste for the marvelous and mysterious so clearly evinced in the finest metal- and glass-wares rather than to the vulgar or orthodox imitation of gold and silver by which it has been very often and very naively explained we must attribute the development of the most characteristic of Muslim ceramic wares: luster. It seems that luster wares were first extensively made in Abbasid Mesopotamia, along with cobalt-painted white wares, imitations of T'ang splashed wares, and other significant early types (for the very earliest Islamic wares have nothing Islamic about them except their often disputable dates). Yellow, green, and brown luster designs were painted on an opaque tin-enamel ground. The subtle variations of tone in the material are not fully exploited in the bold designs of most early Mesopotamian pieces (griffin plate and dish with nursing camel, Louvre; jar, Art Inst. of Chicago), nor in the Fatimid lusters of the succeeding period (Louvre; bowl with tree full of birds, Cote coll., Lyons), nor in the large dishes and fantastically moulded jars of Western Islam (Alhambra vase, Granada).

In Persia from the 12th to the 14th cents. luster was made at Rayy, at Nishapur, and probably elsewhere, the finest wares being manufactured at **Kashan**, especially in the early 13th cent.. Words cannot describe the intimate and dreamy enchantment of the best Kashan pieces (*mihrab* from the Maydan mosque of Kashan, Berlin SM.; Eumorfopoulos bowl of 1210 in the B.M.; Havemeyer plate, New York; Huntsman bowl in the Kelekian collection, V and A.; smaller pieces in the Boston M.F.A.). For *mihrabs*, which were frequently executed in this technique at this period, very strong blue inscriptions appear to establish the Revealed Word as an apparition floating before the impalpable luster surface. Later Kashan lusters show Mongol motifs and degenerate drawing. Rayy lusters, though very freely drawn, are essentially cruder. Ruby- and gold-toned luster was used again by Safavid potters.

Another ware sometimes graced with superb calligraphy is a creamy pottery with brown slip and tomato-red bole designs made in East Iran about the 10th cent. Only two large pieces are known (Kann plate, Louvre; Schroeder bowl, Boston M.F.A.; fragments in Berlin SM.; "provincial" variants from the Nishapur excavations in Met Mus. New York).

Although there is reason to believe that the great Kashan potters made both luster and other types of ware, the more perfunctory even where equally skilful execution of inscriptions upon some exceptional pieces of underglaze painted pottery (reticulated jug from Macy coll. Met. Mus. New York; tile with Shahnama scene, Boston M.F.A.) prove that less importance was attached to them; on the less elaborate pieces the "writing" is often an illiterate imitation of letter-forms. Three ceramic types have remained characteristic of Islamic lands to today: blue-glazed wares, sometimes moulded; blue-glazed wares with black **underglaze** painted designs; and clear-glazed wares with underglaze painting in blue, black, and occasionally other colors. Of the first type an exceptional masterpiece is a turquoise-glazed lion, over two feet high, in the Kevorkian coll. New York; noble jars in this color were made at Raqqa. Of the other two types the finest pieces appear to have been made at Kashan (examples

in all important colls.). A luxury ware of great gaiety is the *minai* overglaze painted pottery, with representations in Seljuq style of courts, picnics, horse-races, and incidents from romances. The most interesting piece is a huge plate with a picture of a siege, which even in its incomplete state has about seventy figures (Kelekian coll. New York). A similar ware with low relief and gilding is the most sumptuous of Persian ceramic types (bowl with lovers, Boston M.F.A.; horseman bowl, Met. Mus. New York; Edsel Ford coll., Detroit; harpy bowl, B.M.).

The so-called **Sultanabad and Sultania wares** of Mongol Persia, with animals, phoenixes, revellers, and cavaliers reserved against leafy thickets of Chinese foliation-motifs often in low relief, generally in grayish tonalities, are sometimes of great beauty ("Running Buck" bowl, Dumbarton Oaks [Georgetown], Washington).

Numerous other types of pottery express, though less eloquently, the singularly lyrical spirit of Persia in that age of fire and sword. The **Seljuq ceramics** of the immediately preceding period included a sgraffito ware with animal designs often of great strength, probably made chiefly in Western Iran (so-called "gabri" ware: examples in all important colls). The only original **Mamluk ware** is a coarse armorial style of pottery in similar technique.

But nearly all the eastern types enumerated were exported to and imitated in the East Mediterranean Islamic lands; the animal-drawing of some Mesopotamian underglaze-painted wares (associated with Raqqa) has **a** unique "heraldic" haughtiness of aspect. These Mediterranean lands preserved some late-classical formal qualities, and show a liking for flanged shapes (blue and gold albarello with spiral flange, Godman coll., Horsham, England).

In Persia the Timurids and their successors preferred imported Chinese pottery, so that although some 16th cent. Persian monochromes and lusters have a characteristic charm, most of the typical Safavid imitations and adaptations of Chinese models, and the late wares called Kubacha, Gombroon, etc. are of comparatively small artistic significance.

One more group of Islamic potteries ranks with the great types by its vitality and the importance which the quality of its calligraphy proves (blue-and-white inscribed bowl, B.M.): the **Ottoman wares** (formerly called "Damascus" or "Rhodian") believed to have been made principally at Isnik (Nicea), and at their finest in the middle and late 16th cent. Blue-and-white, or cobalt-blue, copper-green and either tomato-red bole or manganese violet are the normal colors. Tulips, hyacinths, carnations, pomegranates and the other typical elements of contemporary Ottoman decoration, as well as lateen-rigged ships used as a repeat-spray, are drawn on the bottles, jugs, bowls, plates, and tankards as well as the tile-revetments of Isnik pottery with irresistible boldness, and occasionally with a marked poetical feeling (broken plate in the Boston M.F.A.; jug with Dutch mounting of 1580, V. and A., London).

TEXTILES. The history of Muhammadan textiles does not exist and cannot be summarized. No agreement exists among authorities either as to the provenance of many of the more important monuments or as to what associations of pieces are permissible.

Important textile-producing regions were early conquered by the Muslim Arabs. At least two types of splendid weaving were prized: tapestries of wool and sometimes of silk upon linen, and figured silks. Egypt especially produced tapestries, often figured with Christian subjects, to adorn linen garments with rich stripes or medallions.

Figured silks were made in China during the Han period (B.C. 206- A.D. 220). Raw materials for silk-weaving were exported thence for Western manufacture, and appear to have been first and principally woven into figured textiles in East Mediterranean lands (Syria? Egypt?) from the 4th cent. Justinian (6th cent.) established seri-culture in the Empire and textile factories at his capital. His contemporary Khusraw I of Persia appears to have interrupted the passage-trade of silk through his empire and may have established factories for figured silks. It seems probable that China, Iran, and Byzantium all produced silks in a Sasanian style of pattern; these grandiose stuffs, with beasts or monsters, paired or single, in medallions, are often considered the most noble textiles ever woven (Peacock-tail-monster or Senmurv stuffs in the Mus. d. Arts Dec., Paris, and V. and A., London; similar silk in Cooper Union Mus., New York).

Continuation of this style was the principal factor in the first three Islamic centuries ("sudarium of St. Columba and St. Loup", Sens Cathedral; lion silk in the Vatican; excavated fragments from Tun Huang). One of the most gorgeous monuments of Abbasid luxury is a silk-and-gold embroidery with peacocks and other birds, beasts, and mon-

sters in roundels (Boston M.F.A.). But Islam itself contributed a characteristic variant of style: auspicious inscriptions, Koranic or Caliphal, often on bands alternating with bands, figured with birds, beasts, and flowers. The oldest textile which can with certainty be associated with Muslim ownership is a band-design silk with an embroidered inscription datable between 684 and 750 (V. and A. London). Such Egyptian pieces as a silk tapestry on linen with the name of al-Hakim (V. and A.) and an apparently Spanish piece (the "Veil of Hisham" at the R. Acad. Hist., Madrid) are comparable products of the Imperial Caliphal style.

Fine silk tapestries with Kufic and, later, round-hand inscriptions were woven in **Fatimid** and **Ayyubid Egypt** (Boston M.F.A.). The mantle of Roger II used as the Coronation robe of the Holy Roman Emperors is an embroidery in Fatimid style apparently made by Muslim workmen in Palermo in 1133 (Schatzkammer, Vienna). The finest "**Mamluk**" stuffs appear to have been imported from China; they attest the extraordinarily careful adaptation to Muslim tastes of Chinese manufacture for export in the Middle Ages ("Nasir" brocade with addorsed falcons, Marienkirche, Danzig; probably the silk from the tomb of Cangrande, Verona).

Curious stuffs (which have been associated with Sicily) were woven displaying bands of color woven in independently of the design. Sicilian stuffs were less esteemed than those of Spain, but satisfactory differentiation of the styles is not possible (silk with checker of entrelacs and addorsed griffins, V. and A. London; double-headed eagle silk, Kstgew. Mus. Berlin and Cooper Union, New York; 13th cent. mantle of Infante Don Felipe, Boston M.F.A. and Arch. Mus. Madrid).

It is notable that the Shahnama, written in Eastern Persia in about 1000 A.D., refers frequently to brocades: they are always "Chinese" or "Ruman" (Byzantine). A many-colored silk-and-cotton stuff called 'Attabi was woven at Baghdad, and perhaps striped silks were woven in Khuzistan. The famous "St. Josse" piece (Louvre) with confronted elephants, a border of camels, formalized ornamental stripes, and a Kufic inscription in the name of a 10th cent. Khurasan amir, may be an example of the silks known to have been produced in the Zarafshan valley of West Turkistan.

The silks in so-called **Seljuq** style, in a limited color-range, and often in two contrasted colors, are less spacious in design than the earlier Islamic textiles. They sometimes employ very small-scale ornamental patterns (silk with winged lions and birds, V. and A. London; "Tomb-cover" and blue-and-red silk with guilloche in roundels, Text. Mus. of D.C.; double-headed eagle silk, Dumbarton Oaks, Washington). It is not known where such pieces were made.

The **Mongol** and **Timurid** rulers of Persia appear to have used mainly imported Chinese silks. Under the early **Safavids** European and Turkish velvets and brocades appear to have shared the favor of the rich, until the Veneto-Turkish wars choked off the traffic. But about the middle of the century it seems certain that precious textiles were being produced in Persia itself; the principal centers were Kashan and Yazd, old weaving towns. Strongly contrasted color, often based on crimson-and-white opposition, and a close dependence of design upon contemporary miniature-painting and illumination mark the earlier brocades and velvets. Ghiyath is a name found upon many of the finest pieces of the period. (Ghiyath's Layla and Manun silk, Boston M.F.A.; "Iskandar and the Dragon" brocade coat, Mus. Moscow; velvet of similar design, Met. Mus. New York; yellow-ground cup-bearer silk, Met. New York, and V. and A. London; hunting velvet from the top of a tent, Boston M.F.A.) Under Shah Abbas I (1587-1629) the capital, Isfahan, became a chief center of all arts and crafts. Brocades and gilt velvets were woven, sometimes with figure-subjects (lovers, cup-bearers, hunters), and sometimes with flowers in a new and less formal style. The colors are different: although it is hazardous to speak of stuffs which may have once been far more vivid, it seems that oranges, pinks, yellow-greens, etc. may have been combined in harmonies of saturation to give a peculiar "glow" to the stuffs of this period (Dated silk of 1599-1600, Met. Mus. New York; velvet brocade in Riza Abbasi style, Art Inst. of Chicago and V. and A. London; velvet brocade with flowers, rocks, and butterflies, silver brocade with doves, ducks, and roses, carpet-design velvet formerly in the Saxon royal coll., all now in the Met. Mus. New York; pieces in the Benaki Mus. Athens; coat in green and gold on pink, and silver brocade with jasmines, carnations, lilies and sunflowers, both in V. and A. London; velvet with Madonna, Correr Mus., Venice). The spacing of the sprays in many of the loveliest of the less elaborate brocades, the prevalence of a rectangular type of spray, and some characteristic color-combinations suggest that these may have been woven to replace or to surpass Indian textiles.

In India Muhammadan weaving was either modification or continuation of ancient Indian techniques or, in the 17th cent., emulation of Persian methods such as silk velvet-weaving (rug-design velvet, Blumenthal coll. New York) or brocades, often exceptionally rich in gold thread.

In Turkey the old Ruman style was continued by the Seljuq conquerors ("Kaikobad" gold and silk stuff with confronted lions in roundels, Text. Mus. Lyons). In the 15th or early 16th cent. a definite **Ottoman** or Turkish style arose. Pieces of the earlier 16th cent. show already the characteristic ogival trellises and diapers and the normal hyacinths, tulips, and pomegranates of Turkish decoration (green-ground silk no. 1356. 1887, V. and A., London; gold brocade coat with undulating stems, Met. Mus. New York; stuffs in Boston M.F.A.). In one well-known type of velvets for hangings, with few colors and bold designs, there is a certain strength or energy of curvature which is unique (red-and-silver or red-and-gold stuffs generally with pomegranate design, in all great collections of textiles or of Islamic art).

CARPETS. Both pile and tapestry rugs were woven; but all rugs of the first artistic importance are pile rugs, except for the tapestry weaving of gold and silver threads in certain luxurious **Safavid** and related rugs. Three types of knot occur: a knot round a single warp-thread characteristic of the oldest Central Asian and of Spanish rugs, the **Ghiordes** or **Turkish knot** in which two ends of yarn emerge between two encircled warp-threads, and the **Sehna** or **Persian knot** in which the two ends emerge between and outside (to left or right) respectively of the warp threads. The number of dyes was limited in the classic period: for red, madder and *kirmiz;* for blue, indigo; for yellow, Persian berries and turmeric; for brown, catechu; for black, logwood with iron. Double-dipping supplied secondaries.

The earliest recovered pile-rugs are fragments from Lou-Lan, Tun-Huang, and Antinoe in Egypt; the latter show imitations of mosaic design. A few fragments of the **Fatimid** period with Kufic inscriptions (Mus. Ar., Cairo; Text. Mus. of D. C., Washington) and some archaic carpets from the mosques of Konia and Bayshahr (Mus. of Turk. and Isl. Art, Istanbul) with simple geometric and "debased Kufic" designs indicate the medieval style. This style was continued by the **Mamluks** and by the **Ottomans** in Egypt, under whom were produced the so-called "Damascus" rugs (silk rug, State Mus. Vienna; Met. Mus. New York).

A curious rug in the Berlin SM. displays a reduction to primitive knotting technique of a Chinese representation of the strife between the Dragon and the Phoenix; it is datable in the mid-15th cent. by its resemblance to a rug in a Sienese fresco of 1440-44. The so-called "Holbein" rugs such as that in the City Art Mus. of St. Louis, with geometrical designs in square fields or star and cross patterns, are sufficiently like representations in both Persian and Italian 15th cent. paintings to justify the belief that these were the typical rugs of Eastern Islam; they may have been woven both in Persia and in Anatolia, where the Persian art of the later Mongol period was admired. Or the Persian courts may have imported Anatolian rugs.

Late in the 15th cent. a new style of carpet first appears in Persian miniatures, adorned with curvilinear compartments, medallions, stars, and arabesques. The type has been called **Ushaq** after the great weaving town of that name, and its direct descendants (called **"Smyrna" rugs**) were woven in Anatolia as late as the 18th cent. The finest examples are in the V. and A., London; dated rugs which may be English copies (1584 and 1585) are in the possession of the Duke of Buccleuch.

Even if the analogy of the Ushaqs be held grounds for attributing the "Holbeins" to Anatolia, there is no doubt that in the early 16th cent. at latest the Persians began to weave what are considered the most wonderful rugs ever made. **Safavid rugs** are generally classified iconographically: as medallion carpets (with designs similar to illuminations and the more conventional bookbindings), as hunting carpets (with scenes of the chase), as animal carpets (similar to the last, but without human figures), as vase carpets (with exceptionally grandiose complex flowers spaced over a trellis of which some stems generally spring from vases), and as garden carpets (in which gardens are represented more or less in plan, with rectangular flower-beds, canals, pools, and trees). Many carpets combine two types. Shah Tahmasp himself designed carpets, and it is almost certain that his greatest painters and illuminators also did so. Several of the very finest are dated: two medallion carpets from the Ardabil shrine

(1539) by Maqsud of Kashan, V. and A. London, and Duveen coll., New York; hunting carpet (1542 or 1522) by Ghiyath al-Din of Jam, Poldi-Pezzoli Mus., Milan; floral carpet (1656) by Mu'min, son of Qutb al-Din of Mahun, Mus. Sarajevo; silk carpet with flowers and trees (1671) by Ni'mat Allah of Jawshaqan from the tomb of Shah 'Abbas II. Amongst the finest undated Safavid carpets are a medallion rug in the Mus. des Gobelins; an animal medallion rug in the Mus. des Arts Dec., Paris; the "Coronation Carpet" in the Mackay coll. New York; a compartment rug (Yerkes coll.), Met. Mus., New York; an animal rug in the Ottoman Mus. Istanbul; a vase carpet in the V. and A.; a fragmentary vase-carpet with immense flowers in the Berlin SM.; a white-ground vase-carpet at Vienna SM.; a vase-carpet (former Lichnowsky) in the Altman coll. New York; a garden carpet formerly in the Figdor coll. Vienna. **Silk rugs**, often enriched with gold and silver thread, apparently made for royal use and royal gifts (especially to foreign rulers), were made during the 16th and 17th cents. Only three large 16th cent. examples are known; the Imperial Hunting Rug in Vienna, the Maurice Rothschild hunting rug, Paris, and a rug in the royal coll. at Stockholm. In the 17th cent. Persian looms produced a new type in these precious materials, in the same rather "Indian" color harmonies as some contemporary brocades, and generally with a very *mouvementé* design with long acanthus-like leaves. These silk rugs (called *Polonaise*) may have been woven principally at Jawshaqan near Isfahan. What are often considered typical **"Herat" rugs** may be provincial or village versions of these designs in wool. Olearius (1637) reports Herat as a principal center of rug-manufacture.

The lands of the **Ottoman** sultans had long produced carpets, as we have seen (Armenian carpets were preferred even in Umayyad times). In the Caucasus and neighboring regions strongly geometrical forms give typical rugs an extremely archaic appearance. Reductions to this style of Safavid medallion and compartment rugs resulted in the so-called **Armenian Dragon-carpets**, made from the 16th to the 18th cents. (once thought to be far older). Fine examples are in the V. and A. and the Berlin SM.; a piece dated 1689 is in the G. H. Myers coll., Washington.

Other versions of **Safavid** rugs in the period of Safavid cultural prestige (16th-

17th cents.), probably made in Western Anatolia and Istanbul, incorporate the typical hyacinths, tulips, and carnations of contemporary Ottoman decoration. More distinctive are the **prayer-rugs**, with clear niche-shaped fields, often between columns and sometimes with the representation of a mosque-lamp. The field is generally red or green. Early examples are comparatively rare (Mus. des Arts Dec., Paris; Ballard coll. in the Met. Mus. New York), but the type was multiplied in the common 17th, 18th and 19th cent. prayer rugs of Ghiordes, of Kula (with more ornament in the field), of Ladik (with "arrowheads" below the niches), and of Bergama (miscalled "Transylvanian" or "Siebenbuerger", with compartment borders and often floral fields).

Indian carpets of a specifically Islamic character were probably not made before the introduction by Akbar in the later 16th cent. of weaving on the Persian model, and probably at first by Persian workmen, at Lahore, Fathpur, and Agra. A magnificent rug in the Met. Mus. of New York gives an idea of the early style: a certain profusion and intimacy wholly Indian seems to inform the assemblage of the elements of an animal rug of Persian type. A rug at the Boston M.F.A. (early 17th cent.) with Indian interior and hunting scenes, beasts, monsters, and landscape is closer to contemporary painting than any surviving Persian rug. Other famous Indian rugs are in the Vienna Industrial Mus. and in the possession of the Girdlers' Company, London the latter was made at Lahore before 1634). Certain Indian rugs have in their borders vertically arranged, botanically drawn flowers, characteristic of Moghul album-margins (Met. Mus. New York). As *tours de force*, though not as works of art, some Moghul carpets surpass their Persian models: a silk fragment in the Met. Mus. has 2552 knots to the square inch.

CHIEF COLLECTIONS OF ISLAMIC ART, all partially published in periodical or cataloque form:

Cairo. Musee Arabe, Royal Library (pub. G. Wiet et al.). *Baghdad.* Museum. *Istanbul.* Topqapu Seray; University and other Libraries. *Teheran.* Museum; Gulistan and other palaces. *Leningrad.* Hermitage Museum; Academy of Sciences; Inst. for Material Culture. *Paris.* Louvre (pub. G. Migeon et al.); Bibliothèque Nationale (pub. E. Blochet). *London.* British Museum, Victoria and Albert Museum, Chester Beatty coll. (pub. J.V.S. Wilkinson). *Berlin.* State Museums, Islamische Kunstabteilung, (pub. F. Sarre, E. Kühnel

et al.). *Boston.* Museum of Fine Arts (pub. A. K. Coomaraswamy). *New York.* Metropolitan Museum (pub. M. S. Dimand et al). *Washington.* Freer Gallery.

Other important American collections are the Walters gallery at Baltimore, the Buffalo Museum, the Fogg Museum of Art at Harvard University, the Detroit Institute of Arts, the Nelson Gallery at Kansas City, the Museum of Arts and Pennsylvania University Museum at Philadelphia, the Princeton University Library.

For extensive bibliographies see W. Bjoerkman and E. Kühnel, "Kritische Bibliographie: Islamische Kunst 1914-1927", in *Der Islam* XVII, 1928, pp. 133-248; *Ars Islamica*, I—, Ann Arbor, 1934 —; L. A. Mayer et al., *Annual Bibliography of Islamic Art and Archaeology*, pub. currently at Jerusalem. A useful short bibliography is in M. S. Dimand, *Muhammadan Decorative Arts*, N. Y. 1930.

GENERAL WORKS: *The Encyclopaedia of Islam*, ed M. T. Houtsma et al., London and leyden, 1913-1938; *A Survey of Persian Art*, ed. A. U. Pope, Oxford, 1938; E. Diez, *Die Kunst der Islamischen Völker*, Berlin, 1918; H. Glück and E. Diez, *Die Kunst des Islam*, Berlin, 1925; M. S. Dimand, op. cit.; R. Ettinghausen and E. Schroeder, *Iranian and Islamic Art*, University Prints, Newton Mass., 1941; E. Kühnel, *Islamische Kleinkunst*, Berlin, 1925; E. Kühnel, *Die Islamische Kunst*, in *Handbuch der Kunstgeschichte*, VI, pp. 373-548, Leipzig, 1929; E. Kühnel, *Maurische Kunst*, Berlin, 1924; G. Migeon, *Manuel d'Art Musulman: Arts plastiques et industriels*, Paris 1927; F. Sarre and F. R. Martin, *Die Ausstellung Meisterwerke Muhammadanischer Kunst*, Munich, 1912.

ARCHITECTURE AND DECORATIVE SCULPTURE: K. A. C. Creswell, *Early Muslim Architecture*, Oxford, 1929 and 1940; F. Sarre and E. Herzfeld, *Die Ausgrabungen von Samarra*, Berlin, 1923—; A. U. Pope, E. Schroeder, et al. in *A Survey of Persian Art*, vols. II, IV; C. Preusser, *Nordmesopotamische Baudenkmäler Altchristlicher und Islamischer Zeit*, Leipzig, 1911; A. Gabriel, *Monuments Turcs d'Anatolie*, Paris, 1931-4; M. S. Briggs, *Muhammadan Architecture in Egypt and Palestine*, Oxford, 1924; L. Hautecoeur and G. Wiet, *Les Mosquées du Caire*, Paris, 1932; C. Gurlitt, *Die Baukunst Constantinopels*, Berlin, 1912; G. Marcais, *Manuel d'Art Musulman, L'Architecture, Tunisie, Algérie, Maroc, Espagne, Sicile*, Paris, 1927; *Athar-é Iran*, I—, Paris, 1936—; *Iraq*, I—, London, 1934—; *Syria*, I—, Paris, 1920—; *Archaeological Sur-*

vey of India, Annual Reports, classified by districts.

PAINTING, CALLIGRAPHY, AND ILLUMINATION :
T. W. Arnold, *Painting in Islam,* Oxford, 1928; T. W. Arnold, *The Islamic Book,* Paris, 1929; L. Binyon, J. V. S. Wilkinson, and B. Gray, *Persian Miniature Painting,* Oxford, 1933 (best historical account); P. Brown, *Indian Painting under the Mughals,* Oxford, 1924; E. Kühnel, *Miniaturmalerei im Islamischen Orient,* Berlin, 1922; E. Kühnel et al. in *A Survey of Persian Art,* vols. III and V; G. Marteau and H. Vever, *Miniatures Persanes,* Paris, 1912; F. R. Martin, *The Miniature Painting and Painters of Persia, India, and Turkey,* London, 1912; B. Moritz (ed.), *Arabic Palaeography,* Leipzig, 1905; A. Sakisian, *La Miniature Persane,* Paris, 1929; E. Schroeder, *Persian Miniatures in the Fogg Museum of Art* (extensive revision of work of Kühnel and Binyon, Wilkinson, and Gray), Cambridge, Mass., 1942; P. W. Schulz, *Die Persisch-Islamische Miniaturmalerei,* Leipzig, 1914.   —Er.S.

isocephaly (Greek fm. *isos* + *kephale,* equal— head). A style of composition in the visual arts in which the acting persons are arranged iu such a way that they are of the same height; a manner of representation mainly pertaining to the Classical period of Greek art.   —L.L.

itajime (Jap.). The dyeing of fabrics by an unusual method, in which the fabric is clamped tightly between two thin boards with perforated designs; when the dye is applied it seeps in only through the perforations. Used in the *Suiko* Era, c.600 A.D. Ancient name, *Kyokechi.*   —J.A.M.

ITALIAN ART. Probably no country has played a greater role than Italy in the formation of the ideals of art in Western Europe and the highest expression of human endeavor in architecture, sculpture, and painting. The art of the Early Christian Church like all art, pagan or Christian alike, in the period of the disintegration of the Roman Empire is not, properly speaking, Italian at all, but belongs to the universal phenomenon of Late Antique art (q.v.). From the 6th to the 10th cents. there was an emergence of classical and oriental elements generally described as Byzantine art (q.v.). The monuments of Justinian in Ravenna and the later church of St. Mark's in Venice are eloquent proof of the extent of Byzantine influence in Italy.
The Romanesque Period. (10*th*-13*th cents.*

A. D.). ARCHITECTURE. The first truly Italian art of the Middle Ages makes its appearance in the Romanesque (q.v.) period, roughly from the 10th to the 13th centuries A.D. As might be expected in a period distinguished by the rise of the great free communes in northern Italy, art found its greatest expression in monuments of civic and religious pride. The churches of Lombardy are marked by their massive construction, and by their barbaric decoration recalling the ingenuity of Lombard jewelry. The building was entirely in the hands of the masonic guilds, the Magistri Comacini (q.v.), who were instrumental in spreading the Lombard style to the furthest reaches of the Pilgrimage roads in Spain. North Italian architects developed a form of the ribbed groin vault which is often regarded as the precursor of Gothic construction. The best example is in the famous church of Sant' Ambrogio in Milan. The architects at this period retained the traditional basilican form; as in later periods of Italian architecture the spaciousness of the interior is enhanced by the retention of the classical square bay. The principal decorative features were the corbel table and the use of open and engaged colonnades on the exterior.

The architecture of Tuscany was exemplified most nobly by the celebrated group at Pisa comprising the Baptistery, Cathedral, and the famous Leaning Tower. These buildings are in no sense marked by the structural solidity and logic of Lombard Romanesque. A wooden roof spans the aisled basilica interior. Exterior and interior of the cathedral are almost extravagantly decorated with varicolored marbles. The church, the Baptistery, and the tower are harmonized by an identical decorative scheme; continuous colonnades of slender pillars girdle the buildings in successive stories which increase the feeling of height and unite the group in a decorative whole. It has even been suggested that the Leaning Tower was a deliberate caprice of the architect Boscatus.

The Romanesque cathedrals of Sicily, notably the great shrine of Monreale, and Cefalú, reflect the tastes of the various races that contributed to Sicilian civilization of the 12th cent. Saracenic interlaces twine on towers of Norman inspiration. The interior of Monreale is ablaze with mosaics of Byzantine inspiration. In the wonderful interior of the Palatine chapel in Palermo Islamic vaults and arches are resplendent with the Greek mosaicist's art.

PAINTING. The Romanesque painting of Italy as exemplified principally by certain 11th cent. frescoes at Sant' Angelo in Formis shows a revivification of the Byzantine heritage that already foreshadows the tremendous moving power of Italian religious art in centuries yet to come. What can only be described as a Latin vigor, seen in the almost brutal heaviness of line and brilliance of color, makes these decorations rank among the greatest religious paintings of the time.

SCULPTURE. Italian sculpture of the 12th and 13th cents. is a part of that international style of art, with mixed borrowings from the classic, the Byzantine, and the barbarian traditions, which flourished all over Europe in the Romanesque period. Certain sculptors, such as the Lombards Guglielmus and Benedetto Antelami, are truly Italian in their crude attempts to reveal the beauty and sturdiness of the human form in a realistic manner quite apart from the patterns and formulae of their contemporaries.

The Gothic Period. (*13th-15th cents. A.D.*)
ARCHITECTURE. The Gothic period in Italy from the 13th to the 15th cents., marked by the greatest spiritual expression in the arts, is in many respects the prelude to the Renaissance. The Gothic architecture of central Italy has in reality very little to do with true Gothic construction. Churches like the Duomo at Florence retain the old basilican plan. The architects continue to show a marked predilection for the square bay, a feature which in itself mitigated against the attainment of those effects of loftiness so distinctive of the French cathedrals. Again, for climatic reasons, and even more because of the ineradicable classical heritage, the Italians were unwilling, and for structural reasons unable, to eliminate the walls of the building. Except for a few isolated instances where French masons were employed, the Italian Gothic churches can be recognized as such only by the employment of pointed arches which on no occasion were utilized to the same effect as in France. The exteriors, particularly the façades, were given extraordinary decorative treatment, mosaics and colored marbles contributing to the gorgeousness of the effect.

The domestic buildings of the period, as exemplified by the Palazzo Vecchio in Florence, are fortress-like structures distinguished by their heavy rustication and, in contrast to this massiveness, by that final symbol of civic pride, the slender campanile.

PAINTING. It was in the field of painting that the first true signs of Italian greatness became manifest in the 14th cent. In the works of the Sienese painters Duccio di Buoninsegna (active 1285-1311) and Simone Martini (active 1315-1344) we may note a gradual emancipation from the Byzantine tradition. Duccio's work, although based on Byzantine formulae, is marked by an effectiveness of dramatic presentation that is typically Italian. Simone, greatest of the mystic painters, is almost Oriental in his delineation of the supernal forms. The real giant of the period was the Florentine, Giotto di Bondone (1266-1336), sometimes called the father of modern painting. His study of Antique and Early Christian works of art combined in him to produce the first truly monumental painting since Classical times. His figures are imbued with an enormous solidity and gravity that give them the aspect of being hewn from granite. The very simplicity of his style contributes to Giotto's direct and masterly presentation of the Christian drama. Giotto's figures by their impersonality have the universal power of persons in Greek tragedy. They are a kind of super-humanity of Giotto's own imagining. Giotto was the first to immortalize the legend of St. Francis and to imbue the pictorial story of the Passion of Christ with a sober pathos that is the more moving for the simplicity of its eloquence. The Lorenzetti (d. 1348) of Siena combined Giotto's form with a dramatic intensity that is completely Gothic.

SCULPTURE. The sculptural equivalents of Giotto are the marble-workers of the Pisani family. Niccolò Pisano (ca. 1205?-1278?) received his training in the workshops of Capua where a school of classical sculpture was sponsored by Frederick II. His reliefs of the New Testament which decorate the pulpits of Siena and Pisa have the same massiveness of form and restrained drama found in Giotto's frescoes. Giovanni Pisano's (ca. 1250—ca. 1317) figures are tormented and wasted forms writhing in a frenzied movement that suggest that same imminent exhaustion found in the flamboyant art of northern Europe. We may see here, however, an emotional expressiveness through the violent contortions of the human form, contortions which in Northern art are merely affected posturings.

The Renaissance. (*15th and 16th cents. A.D.*) The Renaissance, as the name implies, is a period of awakening and, by popular definition, the rebirth of the classical spirit. This was no sudden sporadic flowering but the fruit of a long period of development. The Renaissance interest in man and the realities of this world can already be discerned in the art of the late Middle Ages. We may perhaps suppose that the mediaeval idea that all things in our ken are reflections of the beauty of God fostered a crude realism in art that needed only the scientific spirit of the Renaissance to bring it to perfection. Again, the 15th and 16th cents. only emphasized the attachment to the classical past that had never been entirely lost. Perhaps the most concise explanation of the phenomenon known as the Renaissance is that whereas in the Middle Ages God was the center of the cosmic Machine, in the Renaissance Man became a cosmos in himself, and all things in life and art alike were measured by the human rather than the divine standard. Man saw Beauty reflected in himself rather than in the ineffable Godhead. Indeed in the Italian art of the 15th and 16th cents. it is the beauty and dignity of humanity in that age and all other ages that is the keynote of creative endeavor. In this period as never before nature in all its manifestations was explored. Architecture became a work of human pride, its magnificence and taste intended to reflect the magnificence and taste of the human builder. The medieval cathedral was a symbol of God; the Renaissance palace a symbol of Man. In the 15th cent. Science brought to fulfillment and began the ruin of Western art. The beginning of self-conscious expression in the Renaissance was ultimately to lead to the emptiness and meaningless expression of modern art.

PAINTING OF THE RENAISSANCE. It would be difficult to nominate any one painter as the founder of Renaissance painting in Italy. We can only single out certain individual artists who were the first to apply the principles of the new scientific vision and scientific experimentation which replaced the certainty of religious belief and formulae of the Middle Ages. The first astonishing monument of Renaissance painting was the cycle of frescoes painted by Masaccio (1401-1428) in the Brancacci chapel of the Carmelite church in Florence. His figures retain the statuesque bulk of Giotto's forms, but for the first time they appear as living things in a defined space and atmosphere. No painter ever succeeded in imbuing his forms with the dignity of man more completely than Masaccio. In the great painting of the

Tribute Money the heroic group of Christ and the apostles is set off against a landscape suggestive of the Arno valley and composed for the first time according to the laws of atmospheric perspective. Masaccio was one of the first painters to represent the diminution of color-intensity in shadow and to abandon the mediaeval convention whereby in modelling colors were presented with their highest intensity in deepest shadow. Masaccio's contemporary, the beloved Fra Angelico (1387-1455), was essentially a mediaeval painter who did, however, make certain innovations in landscape and in the painting of figures and architecture in proper rather than symbolical scale. Uccello (1397-1457), whose dreams were inspired by the researches of the mathematician Manetti, seemed to paint largely for the sake of demonstrating his theories of scientific perspective. His battle-pieces are like strange fairy-lands with cubistic wooden figures and splendid details of military gear arranged in attitudes calculated to lead the eye into the depths of the panel. Another pioneer was Antonio Pollaiuolo (1433-1498) whose interest lay in the exploration of the structure of the human body. His representation of battling men and gods are more than anatomical *écorchés*: they are drawn with a real suggestion of struggle and action that communicates itself to the spectator. The painter who perhaps more than any other exemplifies the nostalgic longing of the Renaissance for the classical past and who best reflects the Platonic visions of the Medicean court was Sandro Botticelli (1447-1510). Botticelli's mythology is scientific insofar as it is based on the investigations of contemporary humanists, but it has a poetic and mystical quality that is strangely reminiscent of the medieval. Although thoroughly aware of the scientific innovations of the day, Botticelli was not interested in the exploration of the realm of Science. He developed a technique of line drawing that invests its figures with wraith-like insubstantiality and the movement of flowers stirring in the wind. The strange translucent pallor of his people, their very insubstantiality, suggest the longing of the neo-Platonic soul for the ineffable and eternal beauty of the Divine, a longing which Botticelli expressed in pagan and Christian allegories alike. Botticelli was in every way a Renaissance Christian personality moved alike by the Latin poetry of Politian and the fanatic Christian eloquence of Savonarola,

If one were to pick one individual representative of the Renaissance mind in all its facets, one would turn to Leonardo da Vinci (1452-1519). This great Florentine genius was primarily a scientist and inventor. His experiments in aeronautics and military engineering were among his many magnificent failures. In a way painting was simply part of that nature and universal science whose secrets he sought to plumb. Leonardo was interested in recording both the physical action and the psychological states of the human animal in much the same way as he studied the movement of water and the growth of plants. His famous *Last Supper* is a kind of tour de force attempting to register the reactions of the group of apostles to Christ's accusation of betrayal. They are real persons and at the same time personifications created from his sketches and memories of hundreds of real models. The *Mona Lisa* again is as much a portrait of an enigmatic introspective personality as a replica of a personage of flesh and blood. The scientist Leonardo brought many innovations to painting, notably the use of deep chiaroscuro to render most effectively the subtleties of facial expression and bodily form. As a draughtsman who was able to suggest the articulation and inner movement of the human fabric Leonardo has never been surpassed.

The last and greatest of the Renaissance giants was Michelangelo Buonarroti (1475-1564). Michelangelo considered himself primarily a sculptor. His schooling was in the studio of a conservative Florentine painter and in the classical collection of the Medici family. Michelangelo presents the curious phenomenon of a medieval Christian in a pagan world. The dynamic tormented movement of his giant forms is a reflection of the struggle and unhappiness of the man himself. The decoration of the ceiling of the Sistine Chapel is a vast allegory of the Fall and Redemption inspired by the pages of St. Jerome. The *Last Judgment* was a kind of giant poster intended to advertise to Michelangelo's lost and sinful generation that, as Dante stated, eventual redemption awaited even sinners through the cleansing torments of Limbo and Purgatory. Michelangelo has always been admired for the accuracy and power of his drawing of the human nude; like no other artist he was able to use the human form to express the greatest depths of suffering and the highest exaltation of the human soul. In the hands of his imitators the same bodies

became simply huge posturing mannequins devoid of meaning.

The 15th cent. painters of **Umbria** are renowned chiefly for the development of landscape and the suggestion of spatial effects. These features can be noted in the work of Perugino (ca. 1450-1523), whose work is distinguished also for its almost pietistic sentimentality. In earlier centuries Umbria had always been the home of saints and mystics. A much greater figure and entirely lacking in the popular sentimentality of Perugino was Piero della Francesca (ca. 1416-1492). His figures have the statuesque simplicity and grandeur of Egyptian sculpture. They are for this impersonality tremendously heroic, and move in landscapes austerely furnished and bathed in the cold blue Umbrian air. Piero was one of the first painters to suggest the presence of outdoor light as a factor in the picture enhancing form and color alike. Luca Signorelli (1441-1523) might well be described as the greatest of the Early Renaissance anatomists. His researches into the structure of the human frame enabled him to paint with tremendous conviction the armies of naked figures that move in the scenes of the last days of the world in his great eschatological drama painted in the San Brizio chapel at Orvieto. The work of Luca Signorelli is but one illustration of how the Renaissance artist, like the masters of that antiquity which they sought to recapture, used the nude human form as a vehicle for powerful emotional expression. His work illustrates, too, how Science, in this case the science of anatomy, was opening up new vistas to the artist. In the medieval period anatomy was a thing prescribed by formulae, designed to produce a divine protion. In the Renaissance it was based not on systems of *a priori* divine perfection, but on the knowledge gained in the dissection of cadavers.

The last great painter of Umbria was Raphael Sanzio (1483-1520), the pupil of Perugino. In the early years of his career Raphael showed himself no more than a simple improvisor on the sentimental themes of his teacher. His real greatness is to be measured by those works which he produced under Papal patronage in Rome. His masterpieces are the series of frescoes decorating the Stanza della Segnatura in the Vatican. The *School of Athens* and the *Disputà* are not only extremely profound and recondite symbols of pagan and Christian metaphysics, but masterpieces in the suggestion of tangible space and depth on a flat surface. Even the sentimental *Sistine Madonna* is extremely moving in the subtle suggestion of the Madonna's floating down toward the spectator out of the infinite sky that forms an aureole behind her.

A north Italian collector and passionate admirer of antiquity was Andrea Mantegna (1431-1506). He filled his religious panels with *membra disiecta* of Roman monuments, not so much as symbols of the decay of the pagan world, but because he loved the cold perfection of classical forms. Mantegna is notable also for his startling experiments with perspective and fore-shortening. He was one of the first artists to suggest that the space of the painting was a continuation of actual space.

If the humanism of Florence was one of the mind, the humanism of Venice was dedicated to the senses. Whereas painters like Botticelli recorded in classical allegory the intellectual triumphs of the Medici, the painters of Venice even in religious painting were concerned with recording the color and pageantry of this semi-Oriental capital on the Adriatic. The paintings of Gentile Bellini (1426-1507), although religious in subject matter, are most notable for his figuring in an almost anecdotal style the costumes and architectural appearance of the city in his time. Giovanni Bellini (1428-1516), the most famous member of the Bellini family, was the first to develop that splendor of color which is the special glory of the masters of the High Renaissance. He inaugurated the technique of painting in transparent oil glazes, a method practiced extensively by the Flemings and supposedly introduced to Venice by the south Italian master Antonello da Messina. Giovanni Bellini is able to impart an almost Flemish pathos to his painting of the *Dead Christ in the Tomb*. His many representations of the *Madonna and Child* fall just short of being likenesses of contemporary beauties. In the backgrounds of his pictures Giovanni Bellini paints some of the most distinguished landscapes of the Renaissance. The blue hills of the Trentino, the square and simple white houses on distant slopes are bathed in a really convincing impression of light and atmosphere. Giovanni Bellini's pupil was short-lived, but brilliant, Giorgione (1478-1510). His famous reclining *Venus* in the Dresden Gallery is the sensualist Venetian counterpart of the intellectual nudes of the Florentine painters. His representation of the nubile fullness and provocative softness of the

feminine form is the complete expression of Venetian humanism that sought perfection in physical form and not in a neo-Platonic dream of loveliness. The composition with the figure and a screen of trees, half concealing the background and leading the eye to an exploration of the distance, is one that was used over and over again by the famous Titian (1477-1576). This long-lived and exceedingly prolific master was like all the men of Venice totally lacking in those intellectual interests and qualities which dominated the lives and painting of the artists of Florence and Rome. Titian, like all the Venetians, was entirely a painter of the physical beauty of man and nature. He developed to its fullest extent the Venetian technique of painting in transparent glazes so that his figures and landscapes alike appear transfigured with a magnificent golden light. It must be pointed out that neither Titian nor for that matter any master of the period ever attempted to reproduce directly the actual effect of outdoor light. He simply suggested its brilliance and warmth by formulae developed in the studio. Titian's color was probably the most beautiful of any artist of the Italian Renaissance. His famous *Bacchus and Ariadne* is a superb color poem of the warmth of the Mediterranean sun, a Renaissance pagan's vision of beauty when the world was young. Titian's most famous pupil was Tintoretto (1518-1594) who was chiefly notable for his dramatic innovations in the composition and especially the lighting of religious scenes. His famous painting of the *Last Supper* in San Rocco is built on the dramatic diagonal of the table receding into the background. The multiple forms that throng this Venetian feasting scene are dramatically illuminated by the light emanating from the person of Christ. Tintoretto gains much of his dramatic effect by the violent juxtaposition of lights and darks in his paintings. The last of the Venetian Renaissance masters was Veronese (1528-1588), a painter of religious scenes that were criticized even in his time for their irreverent qualities. The *Wedding at Cana* is a Venetian feast laid in a Palladian hall, painted with great breadth and richness and totally lacking in spirituality.

Correggio, (1489-1534), the famous master of Parma, continued Mantegna's experiments in perspective and foreshortening in his decoration of the dome of the cathedral of Parma, a fresco that prophesies the elaborate representations of celestial space by the painters of the baroque period. He preferred human beauty of an exotic, alluring type. Correggio had his own technique of painting flesh in melting silver tones that makes both his religious and pagan subjects the most sensuous ever painted.

ARCHITECTURE OF THE RENAISSANCE. The architecture of the Renaissance was as much as painting a reflection of the material and spiritual attitude of the day. Building, perhaps even more than painting, was affected by the re-discovery of antiquity. The architects of the early 15th cent. were content with a timid application of classical detail to structures still essentially medieval. Only later did the architects turn to embodying the proportions and structure of antique prototypes into their buildings. This was an intelligent borrowing and not, as in the work of the neo-classic movement, a slavish reproduction of classical models. As Botticelli in his *Birth of Venus* was in a way competing with the lost original by Apelles, so the architect of the Renaissance sought to create a style based on the ancients but suited to modern usage and surpassing the work of the classical masters. Architects like Brunelleschi (1377-1446) were not only designers but great engineers. Brunelleschi's famous dome of the cathedral of Florence was essentially mediaeval in form but thoroughly Renaissance in the magnitude of the undertaking and the application of certain principles deprived from the structure of the Pantheon. The heavily rusticated facades of the Florentine palaces recall the exterior of the medieval Palazzo Vecchio; classical details appear in the windows of the famous Medici-Riccardi palace, its colonnaded courtyard with arches resting on Corinthian columns is a direct borrowing of a famous Roman device. Brunelleschi's Pazzi chapel is Rennaissance mainly in the application of pediments and Corinthian pilasters and columns. This rather illiterate use of classical detail is replaced by a much more scholarly, one might say humanist, approach in the buildings of Alberti (1404-1427). To the first-hand craftsman's knowledge which Brunelleschi had gained by studying the stones of Rome Alberti added a profound knowledge of the principles and aesthetics of Roman architecture. His façade for the church of San Francisco at Rimini is an improvisation on the theme of the Roman triumphal arch The same motif was enlarged to a gigantic scale at the church of Sant' Andrea at Mantua. The interior of this building uses the massive barrel vaults of the Roman bath.

The great epic of Italian architecture in the Renaissance was the rebuilding of the basilica of St. Peter's in Rome. From the time that the Early Christian Church was demolished by Pope Julius II practically every well-known Florentine and Roman architecture submitted plans for the magnificent edifice in the very center of the Christian world. Michelangelo, more than any other man, made his architectural personality felt in the present structure. According to his original plan the church was to be a Greek cross in form with four massive piers to support the lofty and magnificent dome. Although both the plan of the church and the great cupola itself were modified by architects of the baroque period, whatever is magnificent in the construction is due to Michelangelo's conception. The effect of spaciousness that would have been present had the Greek cross plan been retained was spoiled by the lengthening of the nave by the 17th cent. architect Maderna; this baroque nave also spoils the effect of the dome by partially concealing it from the east. The cupola is the final development in dome construction; the result, like Brunelleschi's Florentine dome, is in two shells and is raised on a lofty drum. Throughout the church the giant order is employed. So massive is the structure that, especially from its west end, it appears like a great granite plateau on which the dome has been raised. The one great criticism of the building is that no sense of scale is provided to judge its vast dimensions.

One of the architects who preceded Michelangelo in the work on St. Peter's was Donato Bramante (1444-1514) of Milan. Although his early work in that city is in the florid picturesque style of Lombardy, his buildings in Rome reveal a mature and distinctly classical style. The famous Tempietto consists of an almost archeological copy of the Temple of Vesta surmounted by a ribbed Rennaissance dome. The building is characteristic of that sobriety and dignity that distinguish all the buildings in the Eternal City in the High Renaissance. Michelangelo's famous group of buildings on the Capitoline Hill is perhaps most notable as the first example of assymetrical planning on a central axis. The lateral buildings of the group are aligned so as to direct attention to the central member and to provide a feeling of spacious expansiveness that was to reach its highest development in the baroque period. One of the most influential and classic of the Renaissance architects was the Venetian Palladio (1518-1580). He studied Vitruvius and the writings of Alberti. His style came to influence profoundly the buildings of Thomas Jefferson.

SCULPTURE OF THE RENAISSANCE. The history of Italian sculpture in the Renaissance in many ways parallels the developments seen in painting. Ghiberti (1378-1455), author of the famous *Doors of Paradise* of the Florentine Baptistery, was in many respects still a medieval artist. The suggestions of actual depth and atmospheric perspective in his reliefs of the *Creation* have their parallel in Masaccio's frescoes in the Brancacci chapel. The sturdy forms of Jacopo della Quercia (1371-1438) prophesy Michelangelo in his sensitive understanding of the beauty of articulation in the human form. The great sculptural genius of the Florentine Renaissance was Donatello (1386-1466) who in his youth had gone with Brunelleschi to study the antiquities of Rome. His famous bronze David was indeed the first free-standing nude figure to have been made since the Classical period. Donatello's greatness lies not only in the ease with which he was able to suggest the animal beauty and movement of human beings but in his ability to suggest the existence of thought and life behind the masks of his statues. Donatello seems to have been profoundly affected by the realism of Roman portraiture but his heads are more than a mere topographical recording of the physical envelope. They appear imbued with thought and in the true interpretation of the "speaking likeness" seem ready to become articulate. Donatello's many representations of the haggard John the Baptist are saved from being mere veristic recordings of emaciated anatomy by the extraordinary spirituality of the pathetic features. Donatello was a true Renaissance artist in his interest in showing an action not only physical but mental. An artist famed mostly for his many sentimental renderings of the Madonna and Child was Luca della Robbia (1400-1482). The glazed terra cotta medium he employed was developed to its highest point by this sculptor and his successors. His greatest monument is perhaps the *Singing Gallery* in Florence, beautiful in its recording of the healthy Tuscan childhood. One of Donatello's most powerful monuments was his equestrian statue of the Condottiere Gattamelata. Its conception was based in part at least on the antique equestrian group of Marcus Aurelius. It remained for Andrea Verrochio (1435-1488) to produce the greatest equestrian statue of the Renaissance, the memorial to Colleoni, which may well stand for the eternal per-

sonification of the cruelty and power of the professional warrior.

Italian sculpture of the High Renaissance finds its final perfection in the work of the universal genius Michelangelo. Sculpture was his favorite medium, and it was in marble that he achieved his greatest triumphs and failures. His inability to complete the vast sepulchre commissioned by Julius II was the great tragedy of his life, and yet the fragments of this uncompleted monument are among the greatest wrought by his chisel. The *Moses* may be taken as an example of that terrible and awe-inspiring power with which Michelangelo was able to invest his statues, partly by their giant scale and partly by Michelangelo's development of the principle of contraposto whereby the body is twisted on its axis, suggesting emphatically a kind of struggle physical as well as spiritual within the fabric of the stone being. The *Bound Slave* again reveals a relaxation, an exhaustion that is a kind of personification of the futility of existence. A great deal of obscure and probably unjustified symbolism has been read into Michelangelo's statues, especially the Herculean forms on the tombs of the Medici. It is certainly true, however, that these vast forms seem to reveal a weariness as though from an inner struggle that parallels the struggle between Christian and pagan in the soul of Michelangelo himself.

Mannerism. The early 16th cent. in Italy saw the florescence of a style generally defined as *mannerism* (q.v.), not necessarily because the artists worked in the manner of their predecessors but because their style was mannered in the sense of being eccentric and distinctly self-conscious. The figures of painters like Parmigianini and Pontormo are enormously attenuated and of a languid grace strangely out of keeping with the giant bodies with which they have been endowed. Fugitive shades of lavender, rose, and lemon-yellow lend a strangely cold and twilight atmosphere. It is almost as if the artist were catering to the strange exotic tastes of the exhausted generation in which he lived. The same fondness for attenuation and mannered grace may be seen in the sculpture of Benvenuto Cellini (1500-1571). In a sense it was a search for novelty through perversion in a world in which there was nothing left to say. The work of the mannerists shows the first self-conscious straining for effect through distortion of the normal proportions. In the field of portraiture men like Bronzino and Parmigianino were masters. Their over-elegant style was admirably suited for interpreting the over-sophisticated personalities who were a part of the decay of the Renaissance world.

The 17th and 18th Cents. Just as it is impossible to fix an exact date for the beginning of the Renaissance, in like manner would it be foolhardy to single out an exact year for the inauguration of the baroque epoch. Just as Giotto already anticipated many of the concepts of the Renaissance, so it could be said that men like Michelangelo had already developed many of the concepts of the 17th cent. style.

The definition baroque has always been one of disparagement, implying floridity and lack of refinement. Certainly the baroque art of Italy is not classic: it lacks restraint, but it is as powerful and emotionally exciting as any form ever devised by human artists. In the art of the 17th cent. there is a strangely fluid and effective blending of mediums: sculpture becomes pictorial; painting, plastic; and architecture frequently becomes painterly and trembles with movement. This was an art for effect and effect alone.

Baroque art in Italy is first and foremost an art dedicated to the propagandizing of the Roman Catholic Church; that is, the new and powerful Church that emerged with the founding of the Jesuit order. It is an art of ostentation intended to surprise and move the emotions. It was intended to re-enforce the appeals made to the heart by the sermons of the Jesuit fathers.

BAROQUE SCULPTURE. One of the greatest of the Italian baroque artists was Gian Lorenzo Bernini (1598-1680) whose architecture and sculpture are in every way characteristic of the tastes of the period. Bernini's sculpture, as illustrated by his group of *Apollo and Daphne,* is a far cry from the almost frontal concept of statuary in the Renaissance period. It is specifically meant to be seen from all sides. The figures are no longer enclosed within themselves but definitely suggest that they are part of space in general: their realism, with the imitation of texture in marble, prepared the way for the makers of mortuary sculpture in modern Genoa. Bernini's famous *Ecstasy of St. Theresa* is not only a representation of a mystic experience in concrete, it has been said even Freudian, terms, but a new and pictorial and sculptural form in which the stage and spatial setting of the group are a part of the ensemble.

BAROQUE ARCHITECTURE. Bernini's architecture, too, is filled with devices intended to suggest a vast scale and expansiveness in space. This is particularly notable in his famous colonnades of St. Peter's which reach out like giant calipers to embrace the ancient square by their inclination from the basilica's facade artificially enhancing the feeling of space and distance. The architecture of the baroque, like the architecture of a stage, is built for effect. The interior of churches like Vignola's (1507-1573) Gesú in Rome eliminated the aisles in order to enhance the almost overpowering sense of expanding spaciousness, to concentrate attention on the pulpit, and to accommodate the large audiences of the Jesuit sermons. Stucco clouds and marble angels on the cornices lead the eye to a vast ceiling-painting of *Christ in Glory,* creating the illusion that the infinite reaches of Heaven itself open directly from God's temple on earth. It is not surprising that a material age which required such material concepts for its spiritual nature should have demanded a new magnificence for the physical world as well. No better illustration of this could be found than in the great villas that surround Rome and Naples: the Villa d'Este at Tivoli with endless picturesqueness of garden vistas and Caserta where the nightingales sing. In contrast to the façades of the Renaissance churches which might be described as closed and plastic in the non-projection of any salient elements, the exteriors of the baroque shrines of Rome are deliberately startling and pictorial. A staccato effect of light and shade is achieved by constructing the façade in a number of planes projecting one beyond the other. The violent breaking of entablatures, the employment of curve and counter-curve, sometimes, as in the fantastic edifices of Borromini, almost produce an effect of actual rippling movement in architecture. The effects are deliberately bizarre in what is really a kind of ecclesiastic opera scenery, intended by its very novelty and richness to advertise the power and richness of the new Church.

BAROQUE PAINTING. Painting, no less than architecture and sculpture, was intended to startle and move by direct appeal to the heart and senses. New techniques of realism came into being in the effort to interpret the Bible story in completely human terms. Caravaggio (1569-1608) of Naples devised a technique of violent chiaroscuro whereby the figures, usually in a dark setting, are illuminated as though by a spotlight to lend a new and dramatic violence to the interpretation of the martyrdoms and Gospel incidents which he pictures. The Eclectics, principally the members of the Carracci family in Rome, founded an academy and attempted by a formula intended to combine the features of the best Renaissance artists to produce a final perfection in painting. This search for a kind of philosopher's stone in art shows the strange exhaustion of the creative tradition in the 17th cent. It marks too the beginning of academic art which attempts by setting up such *a priori* standards to produce an art which *ipso facto* will be good. Appeal through cheap sentimentality which had been latent even in Renaissance art was developed as never before by such saccharine masters as Guido Reni. This magazine-cover type of religious art was enormously popular and greatly encouraged by the Church whose needs it suited so admirably.

If the baroque painters lack the intellectual stature of the humanist masters of the 15th and 16th cents., they excelled as the tastes of their times demanded, in the development of various aspects of realism, notably the effects of endless celestial perspective achieved by the painters of ceilings in the churches of Rome and Naples. Landscape, which in the Renaissance had been only a kind of timid stage setting, emerges as a separate form of art. We may see this in the rather classical landscapes of the Carracci, in the wilder aspects of nature pictured by the romantic Salvator Rosa, and finally in the architectural vistas by the 18th cent. Venetians, Canaletto and Guardi.

The Neo-Classic Movement. (18th - 19th cents.) It must not be supposed that the classical spirit or the taste for classical things was in any sense lost in the extravagance of the high baroque. Even the architecture of Bernini is classical in his continual employment of the classical orders and in its extreme severity. Indeed the attachment to the classical past which had lived on in Italian history for a thousand years after the fall of Rome was to enjoy one final moment of supremacy in the latter half of the 18th cent. This was in the so-called neo-classic movement that had its origin in Italy with the discovery of the ruins of Pompeii and Herculaneum. The sculptor Canova (1757-1822) was only one of many artists all over the world who sought to embody the dictates of the German archeologist Winkelmann that perfection in art was to be found only in an imitation of the "noble simplicity" and "quiet grandeur" of the antique. This was the first regrettable instance in art history when artists sought inspiration neither in nature

nor in their own spirits but in the imitation of the art of the past.

Conclusion. From the close of the 18th cent., the artistic supremacy in Italy gradually vanished, perhaps because of the disorder and exhaustion during the 19th cent. Except for imitations of the prevailing Parisian fashions no further original art was produced. In the 20th cent., esp. in the last fifteen years, conditions have hardly favored the growth of the creative spirit. One may mention only Chirico with his symbolic nightmare visions of classical fragments as the last of a great tradition. See Anderson, W. J., and Stratton, A., *Architecture of the Renaissance in Italy,* 1927; Brown, A., and Rankin, W., *A Short History of Italian Painting,* 1914; Fokker, T. H., *Roman Baroque Art,* 1932; Maclagen, E., *Italian Sculpture of the Renaissance,* 1933; Mather, F. J., *A History of Italian Painting,* 1923; Porter, A. K., *Medieval Architecture,* 1912; Post, C. R., *A History of European and American Sculpture,* 1921; Ricci, C., *High and Late Renaissance Architecture,* 1923; Robb, D. M. and Garrison, J. J., *Art in the Western World,* 1942; Van Marle, R., *The Italian Schools of Painting,* 1923-1934; Wölfflin, H., *The Art of the Italian Renaissance,* 1913.   —B.R.

Italian notation. See NOTATION.

Italian porcelain. See CERAMICS II.

Italian style. A style of art essentially different from Flemish art in that the emphasis was on the plastic effect of form and color while Flemish art emphasized a literal presentation of reality. Its influence permeated all of Europe during and after the Renaissance.
                                           —R.L.W.

Italianizers. A group of Flemish artists of the 16th and 17th cents. who travelled in Italy and imitated the Italian style. This influence created a fusion of the two styles. Some of the Italianizers were Jan Gossaert (Mabuse), Van Orley, Michael van Coxcyen, Lambert Lombard, Pieter de Kempenaer, Jan Massys and Frans Floris. The painters and others who worked in Rome called themselves "**Romanists.**"   —R.L.W.

ithyphallic (Greek fm. *ithus* + *phallos*). A mode of representation in which male persons are shown in a state of sexual excitement. Frequent in the reproduction of Satyrs on Greek vases of the 5th cent. B.C.   —L.L.

itomaki (Jap.). The cord wrapping of the handle of a sword.

ivan. (Ar.) An open-ended vault. See ISLAMIC ART; PERSIAN ART.

ivory. Widely used as a material for carving and, to some extent, as a support for paintings, ivory has been a material familiar to artists from ancient times. Strictly, the word indicates the tusk of an elephant, but practically those of the walrus, the hippopotamus, and other animals, some of them even from prehistoric remains, have been used. In substance and structure this material is a tooth formed out of phosphates and similar substances lying in layers deposited by the growth process. Unlike bone, it can be worked as soon as it is cut.   —G.L.S.

ivory black. See bone black.

ivory carving. See EARLY CHRISTIAN ART.

Ivory Coast art. See AFRICAN NEGRO ART.

ivory tusks. See SYMBOLISM IN FAR EASTERN ART.

ivy. In classical art, especially Greek pottery, a decorative pattern in which heart shaped leaves are set on either side of the continuous stem line, either directly opposite each other or where the stem is slightly wavy, set to fill in the hollows.   —L.T.S.

Iwakurayama yaki (Jap.). Pottery made in Yamashiro province.

Izumo yaki (Jap.). Pottery made in Izumo province.

J

Jack of Diamonds group. See RUSSIAN ARTS.

jacket. *Book.* The wrapper of a book from the publishers. Usually printed and decorated but sometimes unprinted, and also a transparent wrapper showing the cover design on the book itself.

Jacobean. The Jacobean style, a term derived from Jacobus, the Latin name for James I, who ruled England from 1603 to 1625.

The Jacobean manner was actually born during the last years of Elizabeth, when the Italian classicism imported by Henry VIII gave way before the rising baroque; but it was a German and Flemish baroque, full of bizarre effects and heavy forms. Among interior designers the period is sometimes known as the **"Age of Oak"**; generally it is typified by the most popular of its contributions to the development of furniture, the ponderous refectory table with bulbous legs. See ex libris; FURNITURE.

—P.C.B.

Jacquard attachment. Mechanism on a loom which selects the proper color. Its operation is controlled by a perforated record which resembles very much the record that is used for a player piano. —B.E.J.

Jacquard loom. Invented about 1800 and is now used in the making of Brussels and Wilton carpets.

jade. A mineral, ranging from white to black, used extensively in oriental art. For terms, see the following: *chang, ch'i, han, hsi pi, hu, huang, kuei, kuei pi, ku-pi, lung, pi, spinach green, sui, susan chi, ts'ung, and ya chang.* See also *Jade*, Berthold Laufer, Field Museum of Natural History, 1912; *Early Chinese Jade*, Una Pope-Hennessy, 1923.

—J.A.M.

jamb. The side of a window or door opening.

jami. (Ar.). A mosque. See ISLAMIC ART.

JAPANESE ART. *Pre-Buddhist Art.* The early cultural history of Japan is rather obscure but the few surviving examples of Pre-Buddhist art are of interest chiefly because they exhibit certain qualities peculiar to native Japanese art existing before the succession of waves of influence from the outside and reappearing after each wave has been absorbed. These characteristics, expressed in the *haniwa*, archaic clay grave figures, and *dôtaku*, bronze bells covered with engraving, have been described with the words, *heimei, meikai,* and *meiro*, suggesting a liking for simplicity and directness, cheerful ingenuousness, unclouded by philosophy.

The native style of architecture, *tenchi-kongen-miyazukuri*, was a primitive wooden building consisting of two posts set in the ground supporting a ridge-pole to each end of which were fastened two rafters which sloped to the ground. To these rafters a number of beams were tied horizontally to support a thatch which served for walls as well as roof. Later this whole structure was elevated by introducing four walls and a floor. Four early types of Shinto architecture based on this simple form were, *Taisha, Otori, Sumi-yoshi,* and *Shimmei*.

Suiko Period (580-650). In the 6th cent. Buddhism pushed its way through China and Korea and came to Japan and the art so intimately connected with it came also. The first Buddhist sculpture was sent over by the King

504

of Paiche in Korea. Korean art was then following the style of Northern Wei and this style developed rapidly in Japan during the reign of Empress Suiko. It was a formal art, sharp and rigid.

A large number of temple builders, painters, sculptors, tile makers, and other artisans came from Korea. Buddhist temples were built on a grand scale and what·remains of these buildings eloquently speaks of the magnificence of the imported style.

Hakuohô Period (650-720). The Hakuoho was a transition period marking the gradual development of the intensely nationalistic art of the Tempyô. In the early part of the period there was increasing direct intercourse with China. Customs and manners, art and religion were industriously copied. Sculpture followed that of Sui and early T'ang in losing the Wei stiffness. It became more sensuous and three-dimensional, and toward the end of the period it began to develop independent characteristics, although the painting of this time remained faithful to its continental origin.

The court was established at Nara in 710 and the capital was laid out after the Chinese plan. The Imperial Palace buildings had roofs of green glazed tile and pillars painted red. The temples were painted with red oxide and the interior in full color, the peculiarity of the decoration of this period being the gradation of different shades of color, the result being known as *ungen*.

Tempyô Period (720-810). The art of this "blossom-time of Japanese civilization" reflects the virility and vitality of the times, a period of great political and religious ardor. The influence of China was still strong, for fixed canons of religious art came from there, but the native character predominated. There was a great output of sculpture. It was realistic and had a three-dimensional quality best expressed by the word *ryo* meaning "volume" but also suggesting solidity and an active rather than passive strength. They contain an inner force pressing outward, ready to overflow. The statues produced around the middle of the 8th cent. give an impression of animation and an open frankness which makes them pleasant as well as imposing. Toward the end of the period, however, they become heavy and the full curving flesh gets fat.

Beside the religious art realistic portrait statutes were made and grotesque masks used in *Gigaku*, a comic dance imported from the continent. These masks differed from Buddhist art in being wholly worldly and from the portrait statues in being unrealistic.

The materials used by the sculptors were, painted wood, lacquered wood, dry lacquer, hollow lacquer, paper mache, and some bronze and clay, and toward the end of the period woodcarving.

Jogan Period (810-980). This and the following period are often united and called **Heian**; it was another transitional time in which the vigorous Tempyo art declined and was replaced by the delicate and fragile Fujiwara. However there was a special influence of the time which had its effect on the art. This was the introduction of the religious sects of Shingon and Tendai. These esoteric sects, from one point of view may be called the sects of painting and sculpture. In Kobô Daishi's *List of Importations* it is said that "the inner meaning of the esoteric doctrine is different to put down in words but by the use of painting and sculpture it will be comprehended." The motivating spirit of these sects was an occultism that transcended realism and their painting and sculpture were consequently ideological and removed from realism. Certain characteristics were added that derived from southern India. Formalism set in; realism disappeared. In painting an expansive style of treatment was in favor, the figures drawn to such a size they fill the face of the picture and almost overflow its borders. A famous painter of the 9th cent. whose name still survives though none of his pictures do, is Kanaoka who founded the Kose school.

The esoteric sects also had a vital effect on religious architecture. Hitherto the temples had been built in cities and on level ground but now they came to be built on mountain tops, necessitating certain changes in the construction. The symmetrical arrangement was no longer possible and greater freedom was allowed in the design. A curve was given to both gable and roof.

Fujiwara Period (983-1170). This period is named after the Fujiwara family who intermarried with the Imperial clan and managed to monopolize all the high official positions of the government. The court was moved to Kyoto where amid wealthy and aristocratic circles, art and literature flourished. Elegance and refinement were carried to extremes and the art acquired a graceful and feminine beauty. It is sometimes called the period of decadent sentimentalism.

Chinese, heretofore the language of learning as Latin was once in Europe, gave way to the use of Japanese in literary expression and in the 10th cent. there were enough Japanese poems to be collected into a book. Poetry had long been a favorite form of expression. The poems were usually 17 or 31 syllables in length and arranged in a special way. They did not describe but suggested, the aim of the poet being to stimulate and then direct the imagination of the reader, trusting him to make the poem for himself. Sometimes they expressed a complete idea, other times a sigh of regret or an exclamation of joy.

Another form of literature popular at this time was the romantic novel, half historical, half legendary, idealistic tales of the heroes of medieval wars. The literature with few exceptions never reached the heights it did in the west, nor was there much of it. An interesting book, *Tale of Genji*, by Lady Murasaki gives a great many significant pictures of the manners and customs of the court life of this time.

The pictorial illustrations of these tales and verses was a very popular form of art. These were painted on scrolls which like the movies obtained their effect from a development of the subject corresponding to the flow of pictures. Paintings were also made on poem card size paper, *uta-e*, or poem-pictures. One of the esoteric sects used landscape screens in the religious ceremony and a technique of landscape painting developed, "piling up of mountains in many layers." The painting of this period was designated by the term *yamato* to indicate its essentially Japanese character.

The aristocrats built temples and mansions on an elaborate scale, developing a style known as *shinden-zukuri* which consisted of a number of rectangular buildings joined by long corridors, with a landscape garden on the south side containing a large pond with an island in it connected by bridges, one in front and the other in back, the front one enabling boats to pass under it. Such was also the plan adopted for palace architecture. The houses of the common people remained simple with thatched roofs.

Kamakura Period (*1170-1350*). Historically this was a period of reconstruction after the civil wars that ended the Fujiwara period. Minamoto no Yoritomo moved the government to Kamakura to preserve the Bakafu from the degenerating influence of the luxury of Kyôto, and his successors, the Hojo family, continued the tradition of soldierly simplicity for the rest of the period. The resulting spirit did not supersede the dreamy grandeur of Fujiwara all at once, but a new vigor and love of nature was injected.

Sculpture flourished under the genius of Unkei and his followers, it was full of strength and solidity and common sense, but later developed mannerisms and became overelaborate. Painting followed the same general lines though the influence of Sung is more clearly visible. *Bugaku*, a new operatic dance brought from China replaced the *Gigaku*. The masks were smaller and shallower than *Gigaku*.

The Zen sect of Buddhism brought to Japan from China spread among *samurai* and aristocrats and had a profound influence on all phases of Japanese life and art. This religion which combined soldierly virtues with a refined aestheticism promoted detachment from worldly desires and the cultivation of concentration, decision, and simplicity.

The Zen temples of Sung were reproduced in Japan and the style of these new buildings were called *kara-yo*, Chinese style, the older style which continued to exist from the previous period was named *wa-yo*, Japanese style; finally they merged into one and developed a mixed style. The *wa-yo* allowed great freedom in the planning of the temple and in the arrangement of the different buildings while the *kaya-yo* retained, as in the case of the Buddhistic architecture first introduced from China in the 7th cent., the symmetrical arrangement. It simplified the interior of the temple and at the same time added more decorative detail to the exterior, such as carving for the gable ends. A third style was the *tenjiku-yo*, or Indian style, which featured an elaborate system of bracketing.

The powerful war lords rivaled each other in building magnificent mansions for themselves thus giving stimulus to the development of painting, architecture, gardening, and the various branches of applied arts. *Bukezukuri* was the style developed for the *samurai* class. It was customary for the *buke* style to surround the house with a ditch and fence. Instead of having many separate buildings as in the *shinden,* the *buke* had many rooms under one roof, or groups of roofs joined together.

Ashikaga Period (*1350-1570*). The Ashikaga clan abandoned Kamakura and Kyôto again became the political center. The simple ways of the *samurai* were forgotten but the popularity of Zen increased. The religiophilosophic principles laid down by that religion for every form of art were assidiously cultivated. There arose a type of architecture based on the *shinden* and *buke,* called *shoin-zukuri.* This style introduced into the dwelling houses the *tokonoma* (an alcove for paintings and flowers), shelves on the wall for ornaments, sliding paper screens. The tea-ceremony, *Cha-no-yu,* developed into a fine art and a special form of architecture, *chaseki,* arose in connection with it. The *chaseki* was like a primitive hut in the middle of a forest. A tiny and simple room with no decoration other than a single painting or example of calligraphy, and a flower.

Also in regard to the tea-ceremony the art of the potter must be mentioned. In ceramics as in other branches of art the Chinese influence was great. Much of the porcelain of the kind usually exported, Imari, Satsuma, shows little of the refined taste of the Japanese found in the work of the potter. These artists allowed their personality and individuality to appear in their work. The bowls and jars made to be used in the tea-ceremony were not made for commercial purposes but to be loved and cherished for their beauty and the skill of the craftsman.

Another development of the aesthetic of this time was the *No* drama. These are religious or at least solemn and serious plays, inculcating Buddhist morals. They are played in skillfully carved masks suitable to the character portrayed and are chanted or intoned to a particular kind of musical accompaniment. Descriptive and explanatory passages being sung by some of the musicians. The dancers move through a series of stately posturings prescribed by tradition. The text is mainly in verse and filled with scholarly allusions which makes it difficult to understand. This was (and is) the theatre of the aristocrats, highly conventionalized and intellectual. They are short plays with only four or five characters and it is customary in one evening's performance to give five *No* and three short farces called *Kyogen* which ridicule everything.

A style of painting, a swift ink sketch in black and white line and wash, brought from China during Kamakura by Zen priests, *suibokugwa,* attained high development during this period. Nearly all of the early *suibokugwa* artists were Zen priests and the art kept its religious quality until about the end of the 15th cent. when the Chinese spirit left and then the paintings represented pure artistic enjoyment of the medium. The first of the great *suibokugwa* artists was Shûbun;

he founded a line of painters, Jasoku, Bunsei, Oguri, Sotan, Gei-ami, Sôami, Nôami, Keishôki, and other masters. These belong to what later became known as the Chinese School or *Kangwa.* A greater artist Sesshû, the "ink-splash painter" formed a more personal style. He represented his own feelings rather than the quality of the landscape. His followers were Sesson and Shôkei.

Buddhist painting and sculpture by this time had fallen by the wayside. It had become either stylized and over-elaborate, or stylized and crude. The *Yamato-e* painters now represented by the *Tosa School,* continued but the refinement is gone. Kano, a new school founded during this period by Kanô Motonobu, the first to study both *Kangwa* and *Yamato-e,* gave a Japanese flavor to Chinese-style painting.

Momoyama Period (1570-1630). This time saw the consolidation of the states and there was a general reaction from the severity of Ashikaga. Momoyama art was extraordinarily gorgeous and brilliant. Things were done on a grand and ostentatious scale barely saved from vulgarity by the vigor of the artists. The latter had by now turned their attention completely toward men and things connected with daily life. One of the great contributions of the period were the beautiful six-fold screens the Kano artists painted by the hundreds to decorate the new castles and palaces. They chose as subject matter, flowers, animals, trees, seasonal landscapes, using the gold ground as clouds or space in an integral part of the design. Screens with clothes for their subject are known as *tagasode-byoha,* "Whose clothes? screens."

An outstanding individual artist, Kôyetsu, a distinguished painter, incomparable calligrapher, designer in wood, metal, and lacquer, together with his friend and follower Sôtatsu, founded a school intimately Japanese. Their art was a fusion of Tosa and Kanô. They started with an abstract design of related or opposed forms and melted natural form and color into it.

Tokugawa Period (1630-1867). The Tokugawa dictatorship which lasted over two centuries and a half was distinguished by the orderliness of the feudal system and the elaborate organization of the government. The social structure was necessarily founded upon a rigid distinction between the rulers and the ruled and this distinction was preserved by force and only so could it be preserved especially when the accumulation of wealth by the merchant class began to threaten the order. When at this time foreign intercourse was forbidden Japan was forced into a period of national isolation. Under such stagnant conditions the people could only elaborate what they had inherited from the previous ages. The painters produced by the now academic Kanô and Tosa schools engaged only upon refinement of their traditions and their work became nothing more than tedious repetition. Mausoleums and edifices were built in the old style overlaid with elaborate decoration until they became a crowded medley of carvings and pictures.

The evolution of the common dwelling house was now completed. Based on *chaseki* and *shoin* the houses developed so that the landscape gardens became an indispensable part of the home. Of one or two stories, a grey tile or thatched roof, the house is divided into rooms by sliding screens. Light is admitted by paper-covered lattice movable so as to throw the rooms and the garden into one. The aim was to bring man closer to nature and the art of the gardens was to conceal beauty in such a way that it might be discovered individually. *Shibumi,* "an unassuming quality in which refinement underlies a common-place appearance, appreciable only by a cultivated taste", was in demand.

One outstanding exception to the rule of solid conservatism was Korin whose refinement on tradition resulted in a daring and original decorative art. He followed in the path of Kôyetsu and Sôtatsu and produced a gorgeousness tempered by refined taste. He was a master of every branch of the decorative arts. His brother, Kenzan was also a fine painter but even more distinguished as a potter.

Matabei, who lived at the end of the 16th cent. and through the first half of the 17th, founded a kind of genre painting called *ukiyo-e* ("Floating World"), paintings of ordinary life. He originated the manner followed by the artists who produced the color prints more appreciated in the West than in Japan. Moronobu, in the latter half of the 17th cent. was the first of this school to produce prints, although in black only. His followers carried the process further. At first the black prints were touched by hand with a red pigment called *tan*; these *tan-ye* as such prints were called soon gave place to prints with fuller color. Then black lacquer was used to reinforce the moderately full palette in the hand-colored prints, these are known as *urushi-ye*. This was the final form of the hand-colored print. Kiyonobu pro-

duced the first sheets made wholly by printing and this was the method followed by the rest of the printmakers. He was also the first to design portraits of actors which remained one of the staple themes along with portraits of fashionable beauties, esp. courtesans.

All through the early part of the 18th cent. prints were made of increasing complexity until at last Harunobu pushed the printing process back to its furthest limits. To mention only a few of the printmakers, Kôryusai, Kiyonaga, made prints of great dignity and beauty, Shunshô and Sharaku, noted for their portraits of actors, Utamaro, whose absorbing theme was woman, Hokusai and Hiroshige captured on their landscapes the various moods of nature, Kuniyoshi and Kunisada were outstanding masters of figure design. At the close of the 18th cent. the character and quality of the woodcuts declined, cheap pigments were used and an attempt was made to reproduce paintings.

In late Tôkugawa an interest in the decorative colored style of later Ming gave inspiration to a number of painters, Bunchô, Rikurikio, Taigadô, Buson, Kwanzan, and others. The naturalistic movement produced such masters as Goshun, Ikyo, Ganku, and the most eminent of this school, Mori Sosen, painter of monkeys, deer, and other animals which he studied in their native forests. Jakuchû painted gorgeous cocks, hens, and fishes, while Soga Shohaku, another contemporary pursued an independent line and tried to recapture some of the spirit of the 15th cent.

Meiji Period (1868-1912). The restoration of power to the Emperor in 1868 marked a new opening to every outside influence, largely to the neglect of national heritage. In the first two decades it seemed as if the national tradition, everything inherited, were to be wiped out, but soon a reaction set in and the cultural heritage was revived. Occidental manners in many phases of life and art had been adopted and an attempt was made to reconcile these with the Japanese culture but the result has not been a happy one. See *The Flight of the Dragon,* Laurence Binyon, 1911-35; *Painting in the Far East,* Laurence Binyon, 1913; *The Spirit of Japanese Art,* Yone Noguchi, 1915; *An Illustrated History of Japanese Art,* Minamoto; *The ABC of Japanese Art,* J. F. Blacker; *Epochs of Chinese and Japanese Art,* Ernest F. Fenollosa, 1913; *Art, Life, and Nature in Japan,* Masaharu Anesaki, 1933; *A Glimpse of Japa-*

nese Ideals, Jiro Harada, 1938; *The Art of Japan.* Louis V. Ledous, 1927. —Y.K., M.M.

Japanese prints. See PRINTS AND PRINT PROCESSES.

japanning. See FURNITURE.

Japonism. *Japonisme, Japonaiserie,* used by French writers of the second part of the 19th cent. to cover the whole complex of interest in the art of Japan. A society of Japanophiles established ca. 1900 in Paris called themselves *Japonisantes.* Today the use of the term Japonism has been limited to the influence of Japanese art, esp. that of the Japanese colour print upon the graphic arts, painting, crafts and interior design of Europe and America during the 2d part of the 19th cent. and the 1st decade of the 20th.

The *chinoiserie* of the 17th and 18th cents. (q.v.), terminated by neo-classicism survived only sporadically in the crafts of the Biedermeier style in Germany and Austria and fused in England with neo-Gothicism during the Victorian era. It was through the channels of the French "realistic" graphic arts that East Asiatic influence reasserted itself, but this time almost exclusively limited to Japanese art,—more specifically to that of the Japanese print of the Ukiyo-é school, a popular branch of Japanese painting during the Tokugawa period (1603-1867), in very low esteem, among the Japanese conoisseurs themselves.

Dates most frequently mentioned in connection with the history of Japonism are: 1856, 1862, 1867. In 1856 the French etcher, Félix Braquemond (1833-1917), "discovered" Hokusai's "Mangwa", used as packing material in a parcel of porcelain sent from Japan in the shop of his printer Delâtre. In the year 1862 the movement spread in Paris to circles of etchers, painters and collectors among them: the etchers Bracquemond and Legros; the painters Manet, Monet and Degas; the writers Edmond and Jules de Goncourt, Champfleury, Zola, Burty and Duret; the editor and collector Charpentier, the Count Cammondo, names all well known in the movements of French realism and impressionism. These Frenchmen were joined by the Belgian painter Alfred Stevens, the English painter James Tissot, and the American Whistler as habitués of the *"Porte Chinoise"* in the rue de Rivoli, a curio shop run by Mr. and Madame de Soye who had lived for a while in Japan. All of them, esp. the Goncourts and Whistler, were more or less collectors of East Asiatic art, chiefly Japanese.

In 1867, the year of the first Japanese department organized by the Japanese Government at the Parisian World Fair, came the foundation of *"La Société Japonaise du Jinglar"*—named after a French wine—a club of Japonophiles, who met in Sèvres in the house of Solon, the director of the porcelain manufactory of this place. Among others belonged Solon, Braquemond—who introduced Japanese decor to Sèvres porcelain—Zacharie Astruc, the manysided friend of Manet, the writer Burty, and the painter Fantin-La-Tour. Claims of having been the discoverers of the Japanese print were also put in by the brothers de Goncourt who in their "Journals" as early as 1866 became champions of Japanese art, which they collected on a large scale and which Edmond made popular through his books on *Outamaro, le peintre des maisons vertes* (1891) and *Hokusai* (1896).

The influence of the Japanese print was naturally felt first in the graphic arts, where it coincided with the revival of etching in France (*Société des Aquafortistes* founded in 1862). Braquemond, the key figure in this movement, advised both Manet and Degas in their attempts at etching; the not too numerous graphic work of these artists shows in the quality of line, in the flat treatment of areas, in the asymmetrical, casual arrangement of the composition and in the way in which foreground figures are "cut off" and only partly visible,—a marked Japanese influence. Yet there were in the arts of these men no obvious ethnological borrowings as, e.g. in the prints of Paul Rivière who like Whistler signed with a Japanese signet. Degas' American pupil Mary Cassat gave to a series of 10 coloured engravings one print of (1891) the title *Attempted Imitation of a Japanese Print.* Whistler's etchings are proof of the application of what he called "the Japanese theory of drawing", while in his early oils done between 1862 and 1864 Japanese setting and costumes occur; e.g., in his *La princesse du pays de la porcelaine.*

In England, tendencies towards Japonism allied themselves with the pre-Raphaelite movement—both brothers Rossetti were collectors of Japanese prints. Beardsley's sophisticated black and white art is an interesting fusion of pre-Raphaelitism, Greek vase painting, French rococo and very decisively, the Japanese print.

Book illustration and ornamentation, esp. in England, Germany, Austria, Belgium, and the Scandinavian countries, becomes one of the chief vehicles for the dissemination of Japanese motives and compositional principles. The illustrated art magazines such as the English *Studio* (founded 1893), the German *Pan* (1895), *Jugend* (1896), *Simplicissimus* (1897), *Deutsche Kunst und Dekoration* (1897), the Austrian *Ver Sacrum* (1898), the French *Art et Décoration* and *L'Art Décoratif* (1897), all of which were in the front line of the struggle for a new style independent from historical prototypes (known as *art nouveau* in Belgium, France and England, *Jugend Stil* in Germany, "style liberty" in Italy) testify to the great importance given to the Japanese print and crafts as an inspiration.

Of even more lasting influence and of greater social significance is the role played by the Japanese print in the evolution of the poster. Toulouse-Lautrec's lithographic coloured posters (the earliest from 1891-2, among them one for the cabaret, *Divan Japonais*), book jackets and music covers adjust Japanese decorative principles, colour scheme and line quality to Western taste and needs.

Most of the aforementioned artists, esp. Manet, Degas, Whistler, Toulouse-Lautrec, show Japanese influence also in their water colors and oils. Yet the influence of Japan upon the painting of the impressionists, such as Monet, Renoir, Pissarro and Sisley, although undeniable, has been exaggerated, since the two-dimensional space conception of East Asiatic art and the stress upon light and atmosphere in impressionist painting, creating there a strong three-dimensional effect, are mutually exclusive.

In the paintings of the post-impressionists, such as van Gogh and Gauguin, where tendencies toward two-dimensionality and line quality are most marked, the influence of the Japanese colourprint is most evident. It finds expression also in the numerous references to Japanese art in the writings of these men; in the letters of van Gogh to his brother Theo and to his friend the painter, Emil Bernard; in Gauguin's book *Avant et Après*. In the art and theory of Gauguin it is already part of his interest in primitive art. It is this "primitivism" which succeeded Japonism as "exotic" influence upon the arts of the West.

The very considerable influence of Japan on the crafts and interior design in Europe and America is an integral part of that movement for the revival of the handicrafts which we trace back to William Morris and for which no general name yet exists. It continued in the style referred to above as *art nouveau*, *Jugend Stil*, style liberty. It is of great significance that L. Liberty, the founder of the craft shops which bear his name in England and the continent, as well as S. Bing, whose shop "Art Nouveau" in the Rue de Provence in Paris (founded 1896) gave their names to the movement, both started as dealers of Japanese prints. In the early designs of the Belgian Henry van de Velde, the Germans and Austrians Behrens, Eckmann, Endell, Moser, Obrist, Pankok and Bruno Paul, motifs from Japanese prints have been applied. Most of these men were in the beginning of their careers more designers of ornament (for tapestries and wall papers, for instance) than architects. Therefore, the Japanese exterior architecture, and most of all the Japanese interior with its emphasis on empty space—"the domestication of infinity" —was not of the same interest to them as the decorative accessories, of ceramic, lacquerwork, iron sword guards, flower arrangement, etc. One of the first to value the qualities of the Japanese layout of house and garden in its dynamic freedom and natural adaptation to the surrounding landscape was Frank Lloyd Wright who, before he had an opportunity to travel and build in Japan (1915-22),—especially in his domestic architecture during the nineties and the first decade of this century—was pursuing similar aims. The U. S. A. had in Ernest Fenollosa (the American, Lafcadio Hearn), John La Farge (*An Artist's Letters from Japan,* 1886) and Henry Adams (*Letters from Japan,* 1886) men with fine understanding for the values of East Asiatic art who did not merely measure them with the yardstick of western aesthetics.

Among the crafts Japanese influence was most strongly felt in ceramics, glass and metalwork where the objects in the Japanese departments of the Parisian World Fairs of 1867 and 1878, and further, the enthusiasm of private collectors and museums had made numerous artists and laymen familiar with the skill and taste of the Eastern craftsman. Especially the coarser Japanese ware of the "raku" type with its thick and irregularly flowing glazes, ornamented as well as unornamented, inspired the Western potter.

Outstanding in French ceramics were Bigot, Chaplet, Damouse, Delaherche; in the U. S. A.: Mrs. A. Robineau in Syracuse (1865-

1929), Prof. Ch. F. Binns (1857-1934), in New York, Mrs. Mary Chase Stratton in her Pawabic Pottery, Detroit, all of whom appreciated and studied Japanese ceramics. In Denmark the porcelain of Royal Kopenhagen shows in its decor the marked influence of such Japanese artists as Korin.

Lalique (Paris) and Gallé (Nancy), the outstanding French craftsmen in glass, used Japanese decoration for their cut glass, although the technique of multi-coloured, deeply cut glass seems to have been inspired by the so-called Chinese "snuff bottles" of the later periods.

To this group of French craftsmen belong also the American, Charles L. Tiffany and his son Louis C. who in their designs for jewelry and other crafts employ the florid curvilinear character of Japanese decoration.

John La Farge in some of his stained glass windows, e.g., in the "Peacock Window" follows somewhat the example of Whistler's famous "Peacock Room" (Washington, Freer Coll.) done for the house of his patron Leyland on 49 Prince's Gate, London in 1867—one of the earliest although not too successful attempts to design a whole room with its furniture, pictures and decorative accessories in the East Asiatic—or better—pseudo-East Asiatic style.

The echo of the 19th cent. interest in Japan in European literature and music ranges from the serious to the burlesque, from Pierre Loti's *Madame Chrysanthème* (1887) which enthused van Gogh and furnished ideas for the libretto of Puccini's successful opera *Madame Butterfly* to Gilbert and Sullivan's *Mikado* (1885). See Bénédite, Léonce, Whistler, *Gazette des Beaux Arts,* 1905, vol. II and Braquemond, *Art et Decoration,* February 1905; Chesneau, Ernest, *Le Japon à Paris, Gazette des Beaux Arts,* 1878, vol. II; Goldwater, Robert J., *Primitivism in Modern Painting,* New York, 1938; Michalski, Ernst, Die Entwicklungsgeschichtliche Bedeutung des Jugendstils in *Repertorium für Kunstwissenschaften,* 1925, vol. 46; Pevsner, Nikolaus, *Pioneers of the Modern Movement; From William Morris to Walter Gropius,* London, 1936; Scheyer, Ernst, Eastasiatic Art and French Impressionism, *The Art Quarterly,* Detroit, Spring 1943; Schmalenbach, Fritz, *Jugendstil,* Würzburg, 1935. —E.S.

jar. Generally a pottery vessel, deep and broad-mouthed.

jaune de jonquil. See CERAMICS II.

Java, art of. See INDIAN ART.

Javanese theatre. See THEATRE.

jaw bone. See MUSICAL INSTRUMENTS.

jazz. A style of dance music, played by a smaller or larger ensemble, the band, which began in the U. S. A. at the time of World War I and has since spread over the whole world. This style is primarily one of *performance*. It referred originally to improvisatory circumscriptions, particularly rhythmical ones, of pre-given, generally rather simple compositions. These improvisations were done either by individual players or by the whole ensemble. In commercial practice, improvisation has more and more disappeared. It has been replaced by the jazz arrangement, by the sometimes very sophisticated adaptation of the basic tunes by specialists, either as stock arrangements for general use or as special arrangements for particular bands. The basic materials of these arrangements, however, are, with few exceptions, either older established hit tunes or the current ones of the day, "plugged" and exploited by a small group of publishers. Very often, these tunes as such have very little to do with jazz style proper. They may be treated in many different ways. An exception is only the so-called "rhythm numbers" which are from the very beginning conceived in terms of jazz performance.

The most obvious characteristic of jazz is the prevalence of the syncope which may be expanded in such a way that the syncopations form a kind of new symmetry or "pseudo-measures" among themselves. Even the simplest cake-walk rhythm may be interpreted in terms of pseudo-measures; i.e., $3/16 + 3/16 + 2/16$, within a $2/4$ measure. What distinguishes jazz, however, are not these syncopations as such,—which are the equivalent of the element of rhythmical improvisation—but rather their relation to the ground beats which throughout the piece are rigidly maintained in a machine-like manner against the syncopated improvisations. These ground beats are either actually marked (in the bass drum part and by *pizzicati* in the double bass part) or they are implicitly understood and observed. The idea of jazz as well as its understanding are bound up with the simultaneous appearance of something inexorably regular and of something that breaks away from this regularity—in a stumbling manner, as it were—only to ever come back to safe rhythmical ground again. One might say that jazz subjects the performer as well as the listener to an incessant test: how far his musical consciousness is capable of snapping with the fingers at the norm without ever abandoning it seriously. This double character is peculiar to jazz in all its elements. Even the sound which "vocalizes" the instruments, making the mechanical musical elements subjectively vibrate without ever breaking the command of these elements, manifests the same intention.

Historically, the jazz style was engendered partly by the folk music of American Negroes (spirituals and blues), partly by syncopated American ditties which can be traced back to the earlier part of the 19th cent. Since Winthrop Sargeant published his careful and learned book, *Jazz Hot and Hybrid,* the Negro origins of jazz are clarified and identified in all technical details. At the same time, however, this book repudiated the belief in the primitive spontaneity of present-day jazz.

With regard to the final establishment of the style, the introduction of step dance, defining the ground beats in terms of marching, must have been of the utmost importance. The organization of the jazz band is akin to that of the military band. The sentimental features of jazz expression are derived from *salon* music; its particular harmonic stimuli coming from musical impressionism. The idea of jazz in a somewhat broader sense, is most intimately related to that of the eccentric clown and the American slapstick and film comedy. All the latter aspects of jazz, however, have so far been much less stressed by musicology than the folk art aspects. Yet, as far as the basic structure of melody, harmony, and metrics is concerned, jazz stands absolutely on the level of traditional dance music which it has embellished but has not essentially changed. Its innovations belong mainly to the sphere of rhythmical and instrumental tricks. In particular, the instrumental techniques of the clarinet, trumpet, saxophone, trombone, and percussion instruments are indebted to jazz.

All the musical essentials of jazz could already be found in ragtime, before World War I. Ragtime, however, was primarily limited to the piano. The first jazz fad was brought about by the appearance of the first jazz bands. At that time also, the name "jazz" was introduced. Since then the basic idea and the rules of the game have settled. Hence, it is difficult to speak of a "history" of jazz in the proper sense.

The changes it undergoes are comparable rather to those which fashions in clothes undergo. They are engendered chiefly by the desire to stimulate consumption of what remains ever the same by constantly changing its mode of occurrence; each such change being rigorously stylized and made as obligatory as possible.

With the increasing technological and economic concentration of the popular music industry and the standardization of its products, the stylistic changes of jazz often terminate in mere manipulations for advertising purposes.

As far as there are any genuine developmental tendencies within jazz, they are bound up with this very tendency towards concentration and standardization, and with the desire to escape this tendency. The practices of the radio and recording industries have smoothed jazz more and more, have tamed its "shocking" features which never went very far anyway. Today, jazz practice tends towards two extremes. On the one hand, all its "corners" are being blunted, all its "rawness" is being sacrificed to a round, mellow, often over-sweetened sound. On the other hand, there is a trend to expand syncopation and rhythmical somersaults into a smart, virtuoso trick system that combines rhythmical sophistication and harmlessness. The advertising slogans "sweet" and "swing" refer to these two extremes. In practice, the difference is often much smaller than one would expect. Swing was first a countertendency against standardization and "smoothing" and originated with the best bands aiming at a bolder and more spontaneous style of performance. It was seized, however, at once by business.

Since Debussy the influence of jazz upon the art music of both continents has been considerable. It cannot be disputed that many "serious" composers tried to escape their isolation and get in touch with the public by experimenting with the highly successful and technically stimulating new kind of dance music. Even within autonomous production there is almost no composer who did not somehow react to the impulse of jazz. This is not only due to the so-called mood of the time and the supposed up-to-dateness of jazz but also to purely musical reasons. In serious music the emancipation from tonality and its intrinsic symmetries, and esp. the emancipation from the accent upon the down-beat, met the idea of jazz half-way. Mention may be made of Milhaud (*Le Boeuf sur le Toit*).

Hindemith (*Kammermusik* op. 24, No. 1; *Suite "'1922"*), Krenek (*Jonny spielt auf*), and Kurt Weill (whose *Dreigroschenoper* was played from the beginning in jazz arrangement). The most important results of the process between art music and jazz, however, are probably Stravinsky's *Ragtime* and *Piano Rag Music*; and above all, his *Histoire du Soldat*. In the latter, the whole technique of jazz, particularly that of percussion, is put into the service of a genuine intention of composing which reveals, as it were, the hidden meaning of jazz itself.   —T.W.A.

jên wu (Ch.). A style of painting which includes figures and objects of domestic environment.

Jesuit style. A style of church architecture developed by the Jesuit Order. It was the style of almost all of the churches of the 18th cent. Its main characteristic was an interior nave supported by two rows of superimposed columns, on either side a low aisle with flat ceiling, above which runs an open gallery; all features reminiscent of antique Roman architecture.   —R.L.W.

Jeu de Robin et Marion. See MEDIEVAL MUSIC.

Jeu parti. See MEDIEVAL MUSIC.

jewel point. *Etch.* A very useful tool, the diamond or ruby point of which can be used with extraordinary freedom in making drypoints.

JEWELRY, HISTORY OF. In current precise use, the term "jewel" is applied to a gem that is worn on the person. But the term originally referred to an article of adornment, and this usage will be adopted here.

From the beginning, jewelry seems to have been closely associated with costume. Indeed, the sociologist, Edward Westermarck, believes that ornament preceded clothing, even that clothes have developed from decoration in some instances.

The parts of the body destined to carry ornaments were those contracted or narrower portions above large bony or muscular structures—the forehead and temples, the neck and shoulders, the waist and hips, the ankles, the wrist, and the fingers. This kind of decoration has often been carried out for reasons of pleasure. It is as if the figure has been considered a kind of vase or bowl. It has been conceived as a whole and in terms of the relations between subdivided parts. Parts may be accentuated by means of a necklace, a tiara, a brooch or a ring. As a potter would run a band of color around the rim of a bowl, the jeweler would border the extremities of the human body.

It must not be supposed, however, that jewelry has been designed for hedonic purposes alone. Throughout history articles of this class have enjoyed a wide range of utility, from the **talisman** which rendered its wearer invulnerable, to the clasp which secured his cloak. Devotional rings and beads testify to the part which jewelry may take in religious ritual. Jewelry has been employed for many other interesting reasons, for sexual attraction, for "conspicuous leisure", to imitate or emulate.

Ancient Egypt. A rich range of jewelry has been disinterred from the archeological sites of Egypt. The types of ornament include crowns, necklaces, pectorals, bracelets, anklets, and rings. Many techniques are represented—chiselling, molding, inlay, filigree, cloisonné. This period supplies the earliest instance of **granulated work** in which small grains of gold are soldered on a flat surface. Gold was commonly set with precious and semi-precious stones such as lapislazuli and turquoise, with pastes and even glass.

The selection of motifs was apparently determined by religious considerations. Many anthropomorphic and zoomorphic forms of the deities appear in the jewelry, as well as certain abstract figures of religious signification.

It is sometimes difficult to distinguish between the representations of crown and coiffure in the early periods of Egyptian art. Certainly it seems that the **vulture headdress**, the most important ornamental head covering of the early period, included a fabrication of more than hair. In later times, however, the distinction becomes clear, as may be seen in the tall crown of *Nofretete*, in the bust at the Berlin Museum.

Elaborate wigs were more common than caps or crowns. The early hairpins which secured the coiffure were bodkins, of single shaft, fashioned in bronze or gold.

Large silver or gold **hoops**, some more than two inches in diameter, were worn through the pierced lobe of the ear. In some cases, a pendant was suspended from the hoop. During the Ptolemaic period, under Greek influence, the hoop was shaped into a convex crescent which often took on a granulated surface.

Lapis-lazuli, carnelian, amethyst, felspar, agate and pearl in the form of drops, diamonds, cylinders, and flat disks were used singly as **amulets**, or in series as strands, amounting in some instances to ten concentric bands. Both men and women wore deep **collars** of string beads. Good representations are to be found on the male in the famous *Hunting Scene* in the British Museum, and on *Nofretete* at Berlin. Sacred emblems, such as the scarab, utchat, uraeus, and lotus, were worked into the pattern of many **necklaces.**

A plate of approximately four inches at the base was, on occasion, worn as a **pendant** to a necklace. Usually gold, this carried symmetrical designs of representational and symbolic figures which were engraved, enamelled, or inlaid with colored stones. Good examples are the *Pectorals of Sesostris II and III* at the Cairo Museum; and the *Pectoral from the Necklace of Princess Sathathor-iunut* at the Metropolitan Museum, New York.

Both metal and beads formed bands for the arm and ankle. Some were simple band rings, others were serpentine. Gold and silver were ornamented with enamel or with stone inlay. **Bracelets** were worn on both forearm and upper arm, as may be seen in the relief of *Seti Making Offering to Osiris* in the Temple of Seti I at Abydos. The Leyden Museum collection includes a *Gold Anklet* one-and-a-half inches high by three inches in diameter, bearing the name of Thotmes III. While the less well-to-do classes wore **rings** of ivory and porcelain, the wealthy wore gold and rarely silver. Many metal rings were set with semi-precious stones. A red carnelian cut in the form of a scarab often formed the **signet ring** of the Pharaoh. Markings indicated the name of the owner, the ruling monarch, or were emblems of certain deities. Scarab, snake, snail, and knot patterns were popular. There are examples of settings which turned on pins. It was the fashion among women to wear many rings, two and three on a finger, and paintings on mummy cases testify that the thumb was not ignored. The use of the ring in the marriage service began in Egypt.

Babylonia and Assyria. The relief sculpture of this civilization indicates that both men and women wore necklaces, earrings, and bracelets. These were made of either gold or silver. In the Louvre Museum there are reliefs of *Gilgames, the Hero, A Winged Genie,* and *Worshippers* which illustrate the types of ornamentation employed by the people.

Earrings are usually long with pear-shaped drops or cones attached to a ring or a crescent. During later periods, crosses or groups of balls were favorite earring designs. Bracelets were worn on the upper arm as well as on the wrist, the upper arm bracelets usually being of the serpentine variety winding several times about the arm. Many of the bracelets clamped over the wrist and in some cases were ornamented with a rosette design. Necklaces were worn rather closely about the throat, some of them resembling "chokers". In the British Museum, a relief of *Ashurbanipal and His Queen at Dinner* depicts the royal family surrounded by attendants who are wearing closely fitting necklaces.

The British Museum and the University of Pennsylvania sponsored an expedition to the ancient city of Ur where many objects of ornamentation were found.

Aegean Civilization. Widespread excavation on the islands and along the shores of the Aegean Sea have revealed an extensive store of jewelry which was produced over a period of about 1900 years. The types of ornament include diadems, earrings, necklaces, bracelets, pendants, brooches and rings. Metal was worked in various ways, among them repoussé, twisted wire, and granulated work. The prevalence of motifs such as the sphinx, griffin, and bull's head point to a connection with religion.

Diadems reached an extreme of elaboration as in one example which, twenty-five inches in length, was covered with rosette ornaments in repoussé and further complicated by attachments of thirty-six large leaves of gold. **Fillets** with pendants of figures were worn on women's foreheads, the longest pendants falling on each side of the face. Certain other articles such as grasshoppers or tree crickets in gold repoussé suspended by chains likely were worn in the hair.

Gold butterflies, cuttlefish, rosettes and leaf designs were mounted on small **plaques** which in turn were perforated to allow attachment to clothing.

The Schliemann excavations at Hissarlik and the graves of Mycenae, the *Gold Treasure* at the Artemesion at Ephesus gave up a great variety of material including, as well as those already mentioned, cross and star motifs, meander patterns and concentric circles, spirals of twisted wire, and rosettes with fragments of stones in the center. Examples of jewelry excavated on the Island of Cyprus between 1872-1875, which include enamelled ware, now comprise the Cesnola Collection of the Metropolitan Museum.

Ancient Greece. The many types of Greek jewelry include diadems, hairpins, earrings, necklaces, fibulae, brooches, bracelets and rings. While geometric motifs prevail, there are numerous representations of animal and human figures, some of which stood for the gods of the Pantheon. Greece inherited certain techniques from previous cultures, and it is common to find specimens of filigree, enamel, and granulated work.

Intricate designs in ivory or metal surmounted **hairpins** with a single shaft. In some instances, the designs were geometric; in others, they formed representations of figures or insects, such as the cicada. The most pretentious pins were ornamented with enamels and jewels, and were sometimes tipped with gold.

Plato, it will be remembered, mentions golden **earrings** in his will. Men as well as women are known to have worn this type of jewelry. Winckelmann reported that many of the statues originally had ear pendants. For the most part, rings were worn symmetrically, one at each ear. Later, however, it was the fashion to wear only one earring. Some earrings were very simple, but others reached a remarkable degree of complexity. One of the latter from the Golden Age shows in fine detail *Nike Driving a Two-Horse Chariot.*. This is owned by the Museum of Fine Arts in Boston.

Colored beads and stones were not generally worn. On the other hand, the gold smith excelled in filigree work and in the arts of engraving and embossing. Many **necklaces** were made of plaited wire which terminated in pendants of enamel or chased gold. Others were formed by linking together various ornaments such as disks and balls. The characteristic Greek necklace, however, was a deep fringe made of fine chains and little vase-like drops. Rosette shapes in white, green and blue enamel were interspersed among the chains.

The use of **bracelets** seems to have been confined to women. Some statues show a simple bracelet encircling the upper arm. This is to be seen, for example, in the *Knidian Aphrodite* in the Vatican. Bracelets were made of gold, silver and bronze. Designs were either embossed or outlined by thin strands of gold wire in curvilinear arrangements. Gems were rarely used before the 3d cent. B.C. Cloisonné bracelets were fairly common.

The **finger ring** was introduced from Asia. Worn sparingly, in the early period it was restricted to the third finger of the left hand. Later on, it appeared on the index and little finger. During the Golden Age, rings were set with carnelian, jasper, and quartz with intaglio design. Others were set with sardonyx and chalcedony which lend themselves to cameo cutting.

Etruscan Civilization. While certain Etruscan designs bear a close resemblance to Greek motifs, others, in most cases later, are not so precise. Later pieces are relatively florid. Filigree and granulated work in gold attained such a degree of refinement that craftsmen of modern times were mystified and quite unable to imitate the process. In the last century, however, the method was restored to the common lore of jewelry by Castellani of Rome, who had discovered goldworkers in the Abruzzi to whom the technique had descended. Among popular Etruscan patterns were those known as the "**handbag**" and the "**gondola**" which were prevalent in types of jewelry with suspended parts such as necklaces and earrings. Gems were infrequently used, although pearls and even white glass have been found in a few examples. Cloisonné enamel is not unknown.

Ancient Rome. Rome carried on the Etruscan's love of gold ornaments for the person. As it was in the case of the other arts, Greek design was subsequently adapted to Italian taste. But where the Etruscans were spare in their use of gems, the Romans were lavish. Where the Etruscans decorated gold surfaces with complex patterns of filigree or granulation, the Romans preferred large plain surfaces. Greek design is fine and graceful; Roman design is magnificent and heavy.

Hairpins were made of gold, silver, or ivory and were seldom without some form of representational ornament. Dogs, bears, and military standards were frequently formed out of the superstructure of the pins, but more often the subjects had a quasi-religious significance and were drawn from the more amorous members of the Pantheon.

It has been said that the Greeks valued workmanship, whereas the Romans esteemed material. Certainly the costliness of an article seems to have inspired a respect which was mixed with other causes for admiration. For example, Seneca has said that some **earrings** were so expensive that their price was equal to the revenue of a large estate. A major cause of such prodigious cost was the extravagant use of precious stones. Emeralds, rubies, sapphires, garnets and pearls were common embellishments of the ear.

If only by virtue of size, **necklaces** were among the most expensive items. There were ropes of pearls and it was no rarity to see diamonds, amethysts, sapphires and opals linked in generous lengths about the neck. Settings for these stones have been adapted by modern jewelers, and their like is now widely familiar.

The **serpent bracelet** seems to have been the most popular, but many others were more massive and ran even more to display. Some of these opened and closed on hinges. Broad bands or links provide elaborate settings for precious stones of several colors.

The prodigality to be found in necklaces and bracelets also is to be found in **finger rings.** Here, too, precious stones were conspicuous. Diamond, pearl or amber complemented the rich settings, and in some cases sapphires and rubies were cut as seals. Other rings were decorated with religious or mythological subject matter. There were iron as well as gold rings. At one time iron rings were worn as signs of mourning by knights and patricians who otherwise by right wore gold. Men and women of the Empire were laden with rings, even to the point of placing them above the second joint of the finger. Thumb rings were popular. Finger bands made convenient emblems of political, social and domestic functions. The **"key"** ring was a characteristic Roman institution. It is supposed to have derived from the seal which signified the right of the mistress to seal the household stores. Later, the stores were more firmly secured by a lock, the key being a projection from the natural body of the distaff ring.

Byzantium. When Emperor Constantine established his court at Constantinople, the fashion center of the world moved from the classical world to the Near East. Based on three stylistic sources, the Greek, the Roman and the Eastern, Byzantine jewelry, like its costume, was composite in its design. Earrings, necklaces, rings, tiaras and bracelets illustrate the luxurious taste of the day. The famous mosaic, *Empress Theodora and Her Court,* in San Vitale, Ravenna, pictures a lavish display of ornamentation upon the figures of her lady attendants. Both men and women wore jewelry.

Four different shapes were used for earrings—the circle, the square, the triangle and the crescent. Sometimes these were engraved someties pierced, at still other times were decorated with cloisonné. **Earrings** were often four inches in length. Pearls were one of the favorite gems—either used in a strand or combined with gold and other precious stones. **Necklaces,** in some instances, assumed such large proportions that they resembled wide collars. These were encrusted with jewels *en cabachon,* inlaid with colored pastes, or were simply heavy plates of gold. Filigree tracery and granulations are to be found on the collar necklaces as well as on the single strand necklaces and others of less ambitious design. Glass and clay were employed in lieu of the more costly materials.

Middle Ages. With the decay of the Roman Empire and the removal of the court to Constantinople, Europe saw the rise of the barbarian tribes. Now preserved in the Museum of Bucharest is the remarkable *Gold Treasure of Petrossa* which was discovered in 1837 in the Transylvanian Alps. This find indicates the type of ornamentation produced by the Goths. Its style is a decadent form of the classical tradition with barbaric elements included. Its chief characteristics are: conventionalized animal forms (i.e., bird-shaped **fibulae**) ; pierced gold work and a free use of stones inlaid in cloisonné fashion or in a perforated gold plate. The *Petrossa Treasure* contains objects which are similar to those found from Siberia to Spain. The migrations of the Teutonic tribes no doubt accounts for the dispersement of these objects. The later and more refined forms of this type of decoration are to be found in the Merovingian style of the 5th cent.

Of an equally long but independent line of descent is the Celtic jewelry. Typical of this style of decoration is the hammered work with details in repoussé and the fillings-in of vitreous paste, coloured enamels, amber, and in the later examples rock crystal with a smooth rounded surface cut *en cabochon.* The more ancient examples of Celtic ornamentation accent curves, skilful uses of inlaid enamels, and the chased line. After the introduction of Christianity, other motifs were introduced, such as interlaced winding scrolls which led to the complexity of Irish illumination and metal work. Examples of 1st cent. gold work is the find discovered in the northwestern part of Ireland. One of the finest examples of Celtic art is the *Tara Brooch* in the Royal Irish Academy, Dublin. This was found near Drogheda and is made of white bronze, copper, tin, and silver, the lower half of the ring being broadened out into a much-ornamented lunette. Scrollwork of fine wire, translucent enamels, filigree gold work, colored glass, little human masks in red glass ornamenting the large bosses make up the design of the brooch.

The contents of the tomb of King Childeric (5th cent.) in the Bibliothèque Nationale, Paris, are typical examples of the jeweler's craft of the Merovingian period. A thin slab of garnet was set on a plate of gold and secured by shallow walls of gold which were soldered to the surface. Sometimes very decorative details of filigree work, beading and twisted gold wire were added. **Buckles, girdle ornaments**, earrings, bracelets, rings and fibulae were other objects similarly treated,—hammered in relief, or set with precious gems.

Although based on the motifs employed during the classical era, the jewelry up to the 10th cent. is impressive because of its barbaric splendor. The refinement of the jewelers of Greece was no longer in evidence; its place was superseded by a heaviness and a richness, reflections of barbaric taste. The Gallo-Romans, the Frankish, and the daughters of Charlemagne wore this type. The Anglo-Saxons, on the other hand, used **beads** in great quantity. All sorts of material were used for these: clay, stone, crystal, garnet, amber and amethyst. This vogue for beads gradually declined with the result that during the Middle Ages beads became *passé* with ornaments of gold taking their place in fashion's favor. In the 14th cent. chains began to appear and were liked so much that it became the fad to wear several at once.

Invading barbaric tribes used **T-shaped fibulae** a great deal. The Celts and the Anglo-Saxons found **annular** and **penannular brooches** very much suited to their taste. During the later Middle Ages, a round brooch with the pin placed behind was developed out of the circle and long pin of the Celtic period. Until the 13th cent. the stones were polished but uncut.

The **bracelet** and the **earring** suffered because of the medieval type of costume. Although in the 9th and 10th cents., gold and bronze were popular, the long flowing sleeves of later date did much to overcome the fashion for arm decoration. The earring, too, shared the same neglect, for, although the Merovingian period continued the Byzantine taste for these articles of adornment, they gradually went out of style because of the medieval custom of using veils to swathe the head.

From the 10th to the 13th cents., the **ring** was the chief article of medieval jewelry. The massiveness of these rings was the result of the combination of the Byzantine tradition with that of the barbaric. There were many different types of rings: the spiral ring of gold, the betrothal ring, the wedding ring, the gift ring, ecclesiastical rings to indicate authority and the union of the priesthood and the church, and many others. During the 15th cent., **charm rings** were worn to invoke miracles, such as to bring about the ability to converse with the birds, and the power to become invisible. **Talismanic pieces** were set in rings for protection of one kind and another. For example, a wolf's tooth would be protection against assault; a badger's tooth would eventually bring wealth. One of the most popular rings was the **devotional ring** which was made of gold, bronze, or ivory and which had ball-like projections around it for the saying of "Aves".

The Renaissance. Even today jewelry has not outgrown the influences which were first imposed by the Renaissance. But while there is a family resemblance between objects of the craft which were made four centuries apart, the differences mark interesting divergences of taste.

The Quattrocento lady, for example, affected a profuse if dainty display of jewels which at times became indistinguishable from the surface decorations of her costume. It was not uncommon to fasten myriads of tiny pearls to a sleeve or a bodice. On the other hand, a close set cluster of stones often served to accent some part of an ensemble. This occurs in many portraits of fashionable women, where a pendant of large pearls hangs isolated from a thin cord about the throat.

Women of Cinquecento, however, apparently scorned such preciosity. Their jewelry was rich and elaborate, but it was concentrated rather than diffuse and enriched by contrast with simple surroundings. A **brooch**, often the work of a master, would be the solitary decoration on a dress. A ring, a necklace, or a pin became, in the wearing as much as in the making, an epitome of the jeweler's art.

Later on, prodigality became once more the order of the day, and in turn a period of refinement set in. Yet throughout this flux, certain characteristics of the Renaissance prevailed.

The greatest artists of the time designed jewelry. Indeed, one of them, Benvenuto Cellini, was more celebrated for his creations in this craft than he was for his sculpture. Leonardo and Dürer were among those who designed articles of personal adornment. Their predecessors included Mantegna, Verrocchio and Ghirlandaio.

Elaborate **chains** and **collars** composed of massive links were regarded as emblems of wealth and distinction when worn by gentlemen of the High Renaissance. A superb example of this practice may be seen in Titian's portrait of *Pietro Aretino,* ✝the Frick Collection, New York. Women also wore chains about the neck, usually with jewelled settings and an expansive display of pearls. **Pendants** and **pendant brooches** were popular. *Isabel, Empress of Portugal,* is shown by Titian in the picture at the Prado wearing a large brooch which divides a heavy rope of matched pearls into two deep loops. Antique **cameos** also were esteemed by the quasi-scholarly society of the period. In the 17th cent., brooches were pinned like a badge to hats for men, whereas both men and women used them to keep lace collars in place. At the close of the century the brooch became unfashionable.

Toward the middle of the reign of Louis XIV, stones took precedence in importance over settings. A lapidary known as Jaquin of Paris invented a process for making **imitation pearls.** Blown glass beads were lined with powdered fish scales and filled with wax. During the Revolutionary period in France luxurious ornamentation was viewed with suspicion. A simple ribbon was substituted for the necklace; only later was the miniature or the locket added as a pendant to this.

Earrings added to the spectacle of Renaissance dress. For a time, they were an item *de rigueur* in the gentleman's costume. Charles I, Raleigh and Essex were exemplars of the mode. The pearl was the favorite gem for the ear until early in the 18th cent., when the brilliant-cut diamond replaced it. Bracelets were seldom seen until late in the 18th cent., shortened sleeves having become the vogue.

Rings were lavished on fingers and thumbs in the 16th cent.; and if there were still too many, the excess numbers were carried on a chain from the neck. Portraits of Holbein of *Jane Seymour, Anne of Cleves,* and others testify to the admiration of rings in those days. Among the several novel types of ring was the **"posy"**, with inscriptions such as "Let us love like turtle-doves".

Portraits by van Dyck and Sir Peter Lely illustrate the sudden lapse of popularity of the ring. Indeed, later on, even the custom of the wedding ring was given up, on the basis of its un-Christian origin. The execution of Charles I revived an earlier habit of wearing **"memorial rings"**. The **mourning ring** was in fashion for a while. It was usually black, massive in design, and often bore a portrait of the deceased with an appropriate inscription. Certain rings of this order contained a twist of the deceased's hair.

The Nineteenth Century. The Industrial Revolution converted the art of jewelry from a hand-made production and individual creation into a commercial industry and large-scale mass production. Instead of a bracelet being created as an independent work of art, it now very frequently became merely one of a set. During the 1840's, black onyx and jet with gold and pearls were used for sets of brooches, bracelets and earrings. At about this same time, necklaces were seldom seen. For a decade or two following, jewelry seems to have declined in public favor, but gradually it came back into style again. Coral and enamel brooches were a lady's delight to be worn with her Cashmere or Paisley shawl, lace collars, or fichus. Gold, silver, and glass as well as precious stones were likewise used for brooches. **Rings** were very popular in the early 19th cent. One of the most interesting styles in the history of the ring occurred during the Napoleonic era. After Napoleon's exile, his still faithful followers wore rings which had a stone set in a hinged lid. This lid opened and inside there was concealed the portrait of Napoleon. The ring, like other articles of jewelry, was not worn very much until 1865 when the signet ring became very popular. This fad was followed by a flair for cameo rings which produced a taste for intaglio rings, cut in black onyx, carnelian or "sard". In the 1870's long gold and enamel **earrings** with gold fringe enjoyed short-lived favor, for in the decade between 1880 and 1890 the popularity of the earring declined. But in 1900 the screw device was invented with the result that the earring came back into style again. While the earring was not being employed as an object of decoration in the 1880's, the **bracelet** was developed into a serpent design which twisted about the arm heavy circlets of gold ending in some favored animal's head. The late 19th cent. saw the manufacture of long bars of pressed gold used for brooches, the cost was modest because of machine production. **Lavalieres,** named after the famous

French beauty, Louise de la Valliere, were *haute mode*.

About 1880, a reaction to machine-made jewelry set in. A jeweler whose name was Massin created designs very unlike the necessarily more rigid patterns of a machine product. He used motifs inspired by natural flower forms and emphasized the craftsmanship of his design. Another artist René Lalique turned away from commercialism and relied upon the designs of past traditions. He used free double curves, opalescent harmonies of colouring and was influenced by the ancient jewelry of the Orient, Egypt, Chaldea, Greece and Italy. He ignored the hierarchy of gems, using a piece of flint if his design warranted it. He believed that no stone had any value beyond the characteristic expression he lent it as a means to his end.

The "arts and crafts" movement in England purged the jeweler's craft of its character of mere gem-mounting. Feeling the need for the creative hand of the artist to come into direct contact with his craft, many people, among them L. C. Tiffany of America, and Philippe Wolfers of Belgium, allied themselves to this movement because of the disastrous effect the machine had had on the art of the jeweler.

The Twentieth Century. Jewelry has become in this century a large modern industry with centers at Paris, Vienna, London and New York. Jewelry seems to fall into three classifications: that in which gems and stones form the principal portions with the metal merely used as the support; that in which the gold or silver or platinum work is an important element in the design with the gems subordinated to the metal; and that in which the gold or other metal is used alone. The designs are wrought out by hammering in repoussé, casting, engraving, chasing or by the addition of filigree.

Bracelets during this time have been in and out of fashion, depending upon the sleeve length. Wrist watches have developed into a kind of bracelet. Gold, silver, platinum, precious and semi-precious stones are used for bracelet design. Sometimes even compositions of one sort or another are called into use since the advent of so-called **"costume"** jewelry. Because of the fleeting fashions in dress and the rapidity with which change follows change in this century, the industry of "costume" jewelry, made of imitation stones and metals, and so forth, has been created. Necklaces, clips, pins, rings are products of this industry as well as products of the more expensive jewelers.

The 20th cent. has made three contributions to the field of ornamentation: "costume" jewelry; the introduction of platinum jewelry; and the revival of hand-wrought jewelry. Working at present in the tradition of the Renaissance craftsmen are many artists, among them some who have made their name in other fields of art. Salvador Dali, the painter, has used precious stones and metalwork in a fantastic way. Like Lalique, Alexander Calder, known chiefly for his mobile sculpture, shows less respect for precious material than for design. His most notable pieces are composed of twisted copper wire and hammered brass. See Alexander, Christine, *Jewelry, the Art of the Goldsmith in Classical Times,* 1928; Allen, J. R., *Celtic Art in Pagan and Christian Times,* 1908; Boehn, Max von, *Modes and Manners; Ornaments,* 1929; Buckhardt, Jacob, *The Civilization of the Renaissance in Italy,* 1890; Davenport, Cyril, *Jewelry,* 1908; Lester, Katherine, *Accessories of Dress,* 1940; Norris, Herbert, *Costume and Fashion,* 1925; Speltz, Alexander, *The Styles of Ornament,* 1910; California Palace of the Legion of Honor, *Vanity Fair Catalogue,* 1942; Woolley, C. L., *Ur of the Chaldees,* 1930.   —J.M.

JEWISH ART. This term can hardly be found before the 19th cent. when discussions were conducted concerning the essential Jewish contributions to civilization. Even those who think of Judaism as a nation, which has temporarily lost its political organization but never its national qualities, do not claim the existence of a Jewish art. The term, however frequently used, refers to art for Jews and Jewish religious purposes, or to artistic creations by Jews. There is no specific tendency toward form or content in the artistic creations of Jews or for Jews, but there is an intimate connection between their works and the art forms and tendencies of the peoples among which Jews have been living. There is no connection in the art works of Jews binding them through space and age to a Jewish art, nor to a complex group of distinct artistic patterns, nor is there evidence for a need toward artistic expression as a result of an artist's Jewish origin.

The reasons for the non-existence of a Jewish art are among others: the interpretation of the second commandment, leading to great reluctancy in accepting the possibilities of the fine arts. That attitude changes from rejection of the arts to indifference toward art, but never to an acceptance of the fine arts as a function of life. Though the Bible sees the artists like the prophets filled with the spirit of God (*Ex.* 31, 1ff., 35, 30-36, 1ff.), the rabbis and sages are not inclined to have the arts enter into the religious life of the Jews. A further reason for the nonexistence of a Jewish art (in the sense of Italian art, French art) are the political-social conditions under which Jews have been living. Lack of security and forced migrations, as well as exclusion from guilds and crafts made the development of technical knowledge and craftmanship impossible.

Because of these limitations the history of art of the Jews centers primarily in architectural tasks. After the canaanitic time with its Egyptian influences, tendencies of the Near East joined with those Egyptian trends in the Temple of Solomon (by 1000 B.C.). Political conquest by Babylonia and Assyria caused a strengthening of the West-Asiatic influence. The Temple of Herodes (1st cent.) was built in Hellenistic forms. The synagogues, developed first in Egypt around 250 B.C., are basilicas, often with two stories (q.v. synagogues). Jewish catacombs are found in Malta, Syracuse, Rome and North Africa.

In the minor arts influences can similarly be drafted. The art of glyptics shows the Phoenician sources, ceramic excavations represent Amorite and Phoenician influences. There are no remains of metalwork, but the Jews in Palestine seem to have known the technique of covering wooden carved forms with silver or gold plates (Golden Calf, doors of the Temple). Ivory-carving was used for the throne of Solomon. There is no example of sculpture in stone or clay. (For wall painting see Dura-Europos.)

In medieval and modern times the religious cult stimulated works in silver, gold, textiles and ceramics for domestic and synagogal use. The decorations for the Scroll, textiles for the Holy Shrine, lamps and spice boxes were decorated with Jewish symbols, among them the chandelier with seven arms, the signs of the Zodiac and others. Many of these works are certain to have been created by Jewish craftsmen and artists. Bookwriting and printing became a main chapter of Jewish artistic interest. The earliest manuscripts with Hebrew texts are Pentateuchs of the 10th cent., mostly from Egypt and Syria. The earliest known European ex-

amples were written in Spain around 1200. Many manuscripts were *Haggadahs* (q.v.), written in Italy, some in France and Germany. Other manuscripts with illustrations were the "Story of Esther" and prayer-books. The Italian Jews in the 17th and 18th cents. had richly illuminated marriage contracts. Though the artistic styles from Gothic to rococo are to be found in the miniatures, there is a tendency to perpetuate traditional forms and subject matters in the way of a folk art. See JEWISH MUSIC; also *Encyclopedia Judaica; Jewish Encyclopedia;* E. Cohn-Wiener, *Die Juedische Kunst,* 1929; K. Schwarz, *Die Juden in der Kunst,* 1936; *Schriften der Gesellschaft zur Erforschung Juedischer Kunstdenkmaeler.*   H.Gu.

Jewish hora, the. See hora.

JEWISH MUSIC. *Music in the Bible.* That music played an important part in the life of the Jewish people from the earliest days of its history is attested by the many musical references to instrumental music and song found in the Bible. The Song of the Sea (*Exodus* 15:1-20), which was sung to the accompaniment of a percussion instrument, as well as the account in the latter part of the Bible (*Chronicles* 2, Chap. 29:26-30) of the part which song and instrumental playing played in the observation of a Passover during the reign of King Hezekiah, point clearly to the place of music during Biblical times.

Everywhere and at all times was music to be found among the Jews in Biblical days. Children danced in the streets and young people played various percussion instruments and the **Kinnor** (small harp). Music at meals was quite common, but the use of dancing girls for entertainment was censured by the Prophets. Dancing, however, was common on religious occasions and celebrations. David danced before the Lord, and so did Jephtha. Much dancing took place at the celebration of the Ceremony of the Water Libation on the second night of the Feast of Tabernacles. The music which accompanied these dances was chiefly rhythmic. Melody played a secondary part. The instruments were played in unison and without harmony. Music was heard in private life at weddings and funerals as well as in public life, when a warrior returned victorious or when a king was crowned. We find (Samuel I, 18-6) that David danced before the Ark of the Covenant when he recaptured it from the Philistines. The music in the First and

Second Temples was performed by a choir of Levites and instrumental players. The following account of a temple service in the last century B.C.E. is given in the Mishna (Tammid V): After the priests on duty had recited a benediction, the Ten Commandments, the Shema (*Deut.* 6:4-9), the priestly benediction (*Num.* 6:22-26) and three other benedictions, they proceeded to the act of the offerings. After they were through with the arrangement of the sacrifices, one of them sounded the Magrepha which was the signal to enter the Temple in order to prostrate themselves, whereas for the Levites, that sound marked the beginning of their musical performance. Two priests took their stand at the altar immediately and started to blow the trumpets. After this performance they approached Ben Azra the cymbal player, and took their stand beside him, to the left and right. At the sign of a flag given by the superintendent, this Levite sounded his cymbal, and the Levites began to sing the Psalm of the Day. Whenever a section was finished they paused, the priests repeated their blowing of the trumpets and the people prostrated themselves.

The texts sung by the Levites were not only the Psalms, but also sections of the Pentateuch.

Music in the Psalms. Song occupied the more important part in religious worship, as compared to instrumental playing. In Psalm 137, the Israelites in Babylonian captivity are asked to sing the "Songs of Zion", for these songs had become well-known for their beauty. Many are the references in the Book of Psalms to the musical instruments and to the popular songs of the day. Psalm 150 gives us a good idea of the wind, percussion and string instruments used in Biblical days. The Book of Psalms has become the chief pillar of Christian Liturgy. Such terms as "Amen", "Hallelujah", "Hosannah" (Hoshia-na) have been taken over from the original Hebrew. St. Paul and Pliny the Younger acknowledged that Christian songs and hymns were taken from the Jews.

Cantillation. Poetry, lore and prayers were studied to song, for through song the word was more easily remembered and the meaning of the word became clearer. All study and reading of the Torah among Jews was commanded to be done "in sweet musical tones" for it is written that "whosoever intones Holy Scripture in the manner of secular song abuses the Torah" (B. Meg. 32A. San. 101A).

The music with which the Torah is intoned is called cantillation. These cantillation melodies, known as *Ta-amim* or *Neginoth,* existed long before their syntactical force was felt and were in the general musical style of the songs which the people sang in those days. The signs are to be found above and below the Hebrew word in the Bible and serve to remind the reader of a group of notes which each sign denotes. These signs are either conjunctive or disjunctive. Some are prepositive, others are post-positive. Most of the signs are to be found on the accented syllable of the word. In some cases, where there are two or more syllables, two or more signs may be found.

Only those books of the Bible which were read in public are provided with cantillation modes. They are Pentateuch, Prophets, Esther, Lamentations, Ruth, Ecclesiastes, Song of Songs, and in some communities, Job. Proverbs, Ezra, Nehemiah and Chronicles have no modes because they were not read in public. Eighteen accents are used for the twenty-one Books, and twelve for the Psalms, Proverbs and Job. Three systems of signs have come down traditionally, viz.: the Palestinian, Babylonian and Arabian. The Palestinian system of cantillation has been adopted by Western Jewry.

The cantillation modes and interpretation of the many tropes vary according to the need of the text and occasion. The tropes are interpreted differently for the reading of the Pentateuch and for the reading of the Prophets. A special interpretation of the tropes for the Pentateuch is employed on the New Year Day and Day of Atonement. Special modes are sometimes used for certain parts of the Bible, as for example "The Song of the Sea". These Biblical intonations were preserved in the memory of the people for many centuries.

Attempts were made, however, to preserve neum interpretations by such ancient nations as the Indians and the Greeks. These attempts constitute the first efforts at musical notation. This system of "ear-marks" consisted of lines and curves which the voice was to make.

A system of chironomy practiced in ancient Palestine and up to the 12th cent. in Bagdad and even to this day in Yemen, consisted of manual accents, whereby the rise and fall of the finger by an assistant shown to the reader, served to remind him of the trope associated with the word.

There were teachers at all times who taught musical accentuation and the art of chironomy. Private scrolls with musical accents came into existence gradually, but the first to furnish the Bible with a complete system of accents was Aaron Ben-Asher of Tiberias in the 10th cent. The Ben-Asher family, from the 7th cent., seemed to have been interested in musical accentuation. In public, however, the reading had to be done from an unpointed and unaccented parchment scroll.

Upon examination of the various ancient systems of cantillation one is led to believe that the pentatonic scale must have been the scale which was prevalent and which was used by the people in their daily music.

Tropes frequently serve to accentuate the meaning of the word and to define its fine shades of meaning. They frequently are aids to grammatical analysis. When intoned by a capable reader, the cantillation of the Bible gives us a fair idea of the spirit and manner of ancient recitation. These cantillation modes served as the foundations of the early church chants which later crystallized into the Gregorian chant of the 5th cent.

Prayer Modes. The cantillation modes influenced the formation of the prayer modes. Israel not only praised and adored his God, but he also cultivated supplication. The Psalter is not only a book of praise and song, but a good part of it is comprised of prayer and supplication.

As time went on new prayers were improvised by the precentors who led the religious services. Many of these prayers found their way into the prayer book which was finally written down in the 5th century. Around these prayers and laudations for every day, holiday and ceremony in the Jewish calendar year, a tremendous musical structure was built, during Biblical days and through 2000 years of exile. Distinctive traditional modes and melodies were evolved for every holiday, and for every service celebrating a holiday. Special melodies were evolved for such special prayers as "Kol Nidre", for the evening service of the Day of Atonement and for every similarly important prayer. The prayer modes are based on certain scales. Out of these scales motifs are extracted and upon these motifs the cantor or precentor improvises his prayer. Sometimes at a certain point the cantor may modulate to another mode, but he will almost always manage to return. While these modes and melodies seemingly stem from the pentatonic scale, we can best understand them when related to our scales of today.

1. Magen Avoth Mode: d-e-f-g-a-b♭-c-d.
2. Adonay Malach Mode: c-d-e-f-g-a-b♭-c.
3. Ahavah Rabbah Mode: e-f-g#-a-b-c-d$^{(\#)}$-e.
4. Slicha Mode: d-e-f-g-(a).
5. Viddvi Mode: c-d-e-f-g.

Unrhythmical and Rhythmical Chant. We still have a great deal of unrhythmical chant in Jewish liturgy but rhythmical poetry influenced Jewish liturgy through the development of Islamic poetry in the 6th cent. Beginning with this period a large number of paytan-chazannim (poet-cantors) arose. For the rhythm which came to this new religious poetry, specialized handling was necessary by those musically gifted. This gave rise to the professional chazan or cantor. It was common practice in those days (and even in our own) for any worshipper who knew the prayers and modes, to lead the religious service. In many cases in mediaeval times and in some cases today the offices of rabbi and cantor are combined. Among these paytan-chazannim were Jose ben Jose (ca. 500 C.E.), Yanai (ca. 100 C.E.), composer of Mahzor Yanai, and Eliezer Kalir (ca. 700 C.E.). These lived not only in Europe but also in Palestine.

Many of the traditional melodies known to the western synagogue are believed to have been composed between the 13th and the 15th cents. A number of these are attributed to Rabbi Maier of Rothenberg (Worms, 1215-1293). Some of these melodies may here and there show western influence, but one can always find in them the traces of the cantillation modes.

The Cantor. Persecution, which is usually followed by ignorance, eliminated the honorary precentors and made way for the professional cantor. The rise of the troubadours in France and the Minnesingers in Germany in the 16th cent. made the Jews, too, feel the need of one who would express for them their prayers and sentiments in a musical manner. Soon the cantor became a very important factor in the Jewish community. He officiated at all services, while the Rabbi preached only from time to time during the year. The cantor in the community expressed the joys and sorrows of the people and was with the members of his congregation from birth to death. This circumstance led in some cases to conceit among cantors and neglect of study and duties. They were frequently censured by the Rabbis for attempting to bring in foreign melodies into the synagogue. But the people always followed the cantor, for he was their only means of musical nourishment.

Young men with beautiful voices turned to this profession. Concert and operatic careers were out of the question for religious reasons. We have records of cantors who possessed great voices during the 18th and 19th centuries. In some cases cantors possessed creative talents and contributed compositions to the musical liturgy of the synagogue. Israel Lowy (1773-1832), Solomon Kashtan (1781-1829), Solomon Sulzer (1804-1890), friend of Schubert, Solomon Naumbourg (1815-1880), Hersch Weintraub (1811-1882), Osias Abrass (1880-1896), Abraham Baer (1834-1894), Pinchos Minkowsky (1859-1924), were some of the great cantors of the 19th cent. who helped to develop the music of the synagogue.

In our own time we have had a number of cantors with great voices. Among the most important are Josef Rosenblatt, Zavel Kwartin, Mordecai Herschman, Don Fuchs, David Roitman and Adolf Katchko.

There were also cantors with lesser voices but with strong creative ability, such as Yeruchum Hakaton (1798-1891), Nissi Belzer (1824-1906), Abraham Frachtenberg (1861-1929) and Baruch Schorr (1823-1904).

Zemiroth. The Sabbath has always been considered a day of "delight" among Jews. The singing of the 92nd Psalm, abounding in musical terminology, represents one of the many ceremonies which took place on that day in biblical times. Mourning on the Sabbath was prohibited even during the gloomy period of exile, and the singing of the Zemiroth—appropriate table songs at the Sabbath meal—was particularly encouraged. At a later date, the Cabalists propounded the belief that an additional "Sabbath Soul" may be induced to descend upon the Jew through the medium of song. The character of the community often influenced the types of melodies to be used for its "Zemiroth", most of which were composed since the 10th cent. onward. The Chassidim used highly rhythmic and joyous tunes, generally, while the Chabad Chassidim used prayerful and mystical ones. (*The Sabbath In Music.* A. W. Binder.)

Folk Song. There is no question as to the existence of secular songs during Biblical times. For a people in its own land and on its own soil creates, along with other values in civilization, its own folk lore. Ben Sirach (Chap. 30-40) praises song at a wine banquet, while he warns the people against association with female singers. Sages maintained that

songs of wine and lust cause destruction in the world, while Israel's sacred songs save it (Shir Hashirim, Rabah, 8-end). It was generally maintained that when one had a good voice, he was to honor God with it. If we are to accept the Psalm headings, like Al Yonath Elem Rechokim (Psalm 56), and Ayeleth Hashachar (Psalm 22) as referring to popular songs of the day, and that these Psalms are to be sung to their tunes, this should give us additional proof that folksong singing existed during Biblical days. It is also maintained that the Song of Songs was a series of secular folksongs, incorporated into the Bible when a sacred interpretation was given to them. This interpretation spoke of God as the lover and Israel as the beloved.

After the Destruction, the Jewish ear was forbidden to listen to instrumental music. The use of secular song was forbidden (Hoseah 9-1). But the love for Israel's land was constantly in his heart. This he expressed through prayer and song in the synagogue. He hoped and prayed for return to his land where he might again be a free nation among other nations. This sentiment expressed itself in various forms of poetry which was set to music. So the earliest folksongs of Israel dealt with Israel's longing and hope for return to his land led by the Prophet Elijah, who was considered the legendary guardian of Israel's land (Mal. 3:23-24).

We have no folksongs recorded until the 18th cent. Even when they did come into existence their texture was of a religious and ethical nature. They were songs dealing with the various holidays. In these songs customs and rules for the observation of holidays and festivals are given. The oldest of these published collections is Simchath Hanefash (E. Kirchan; Furth, 1727).

The ghetto walls which rose in the 16th cent. gave rise to the Jewish secular song. The first German text collection of folksongs was compiled by Eisik Walich (Worms 1595-1605). Many of these songs were a Judeazation of German folksongs. One also feels here the influence of the troubadours and minnesingers of the 16th cent.

The ghettos of eastern Europe huddled the Jews closely together in small areas where signs of nature were scarce, and so we find in the songs of the 18th and 19th cent. very few which deal with nature and the outdoors. They do, however, traverse the entire gamut of human emotions from the cradle to the grave. (Jüdische Folks Lieder—Kipnis.)

The texts of these songs are sometimes original and sometimes translations, with some variations, of the songs of the people among whom the Jews lived. When the subject is a religious one, as, for example, God, the Torah or Israel, we may be sure to find an original text.

The same may be true of the music, whereas with secular subjects we almost always find borrowed tunes. The contrary is true when a religious subject is used. And so the most original Yiddish folksongs are those where the text and the tune are of Jewish content. (*Die Schönsten Lieder der Ost Juden*: Kaufman: Leipzig, 1920.)

Music of the Chassidim. The Chassidic Sect, which was founded by Israel Bal-Shem Tov at the beginning of the 18th cent. (*Romance of Chassidism,* Minkin), contributed greatly towards Jewish folk-lore and song. Music became an integral part of the Chassidic program. The slogan of this new sect was "Serve the Lord with Joy", and music became the hand-maiden of this slogan.

The Chassidim developed two types of songs. The first was a meditative type which was utilized when the Chassid attempted to throw off his earthly garb and rise to heavenly heights, there to join his soul with that of his creator. The second was the dance type which was used for moods of high exaltation. Both were frequently sung without words at Chassidic gatherings. Many of these tunes (Nigunim) were joined to prayer texts when sung in the synagogue. Emphasis was, however, placed on the Nigun, the song without words. The Chassidic Rabbi, Shneor Zalman, of Ladi (1747-1813) believed that in a song without words the heart can express itself to the full, whereas in a song with words the song must cease when the words come to an end. Rabbi Nachman of Bratslaw (1772-1811), another great Chassidic Rabbi, told his Chassidim that "There are gates in Heaven which cannot be opened save through the power of song". Some of the Chassidic Rabbis were musically gifted and composed tunes which their Chassidim sang and which became associated with a particular Rabbi. Rabbi Levi Yitzchok of Berdichev (1740-1810) is the poet and composer of a number of folksongs which may be considered as genuine examples of the Yiddish folksong. Among them are "A Din Toireh Mit Gott", "Dudele", "Mayerke Mein Zuhn", "A Gesang Funm Berditchever Rebben".

Those who opposed this new Chassidic sect were called "Mithnagdim". They sang pseudo-Chassidic songs, in which they ridiculed the Chassidic Rabbi, his followers and the relationship of both. These must not be confused with the songs which the Chassidim themselves sang. Examples of Mithnagdic songs are: "Der Rebbe Hot Gevolt", "Der Filizof", and "Nissim V'nifloos". (*Chassidic Songs*: A. W. Binder.)

Palestinian Folk Song. The love for Palestine and the hope of returning to his homeland never died in the heart of the Jew, from the day when he was exiled and throughout the two thousand years of exile. This hope expresses itself in various forms of literature, poetry, prayer and music. It reached its climax during the Middle Ages with the Golden Age of poetry in Spain from the 10th to the 15th cents. This period brought forth the greatest of Jewish poets, Jehudah Halevy (ca. 1085-1145), in whose poetry Palestine was glorified. His longing to see the land (which, indeed, he did) is expressed in numerous poems (*Selected Poems,* Jehudah Halevy. Translated into English by Nina Solomon). This hope persisted and manifested itself through religious and secular poetry and reached its climax when an actual effort to resettle the land in 1881 was made by the Bilu settlers. Eliakum Zunser was one of the first to write of this return. His songs, "Shivas Tsion", "Die Soche" and "Die Blum" (*Songs of Eliakum Zunser,* New York), became very popular among the early Zionists. During this time, too, Naphtali Herz Imber (1856-1911) wrote his poem *Hatikvah* (The Hope), which became the Zionist Anthem in 1897. From that time on many folksongs of Palestine came into being. Many Yiddish folksongs were translated into Hebrew and many original poems were composed and set to music.

In most cases the music applied to these songs in the diaspora, as well as in Palestine, were borrowed from the countries in which the composer formerly lived. But there was the desire to create a Palestinian folksong, a desire not to be fulfilled until fifty years later.

The Balfour Declaration, issued in 1918, after the World War I, started emigration to Palestine, particularly from eastern Europe. During this period a great many folksongs were composed and sung, about every phase of Palestinian life. The people of Palestine, however, regretted the fact that these songs were not Palestinian in character, but borrowed for the most part. (*New Palestinian Songs*—Book I, A. W. Binder.)

In the early 30's of this century Palestine began to develop a new type of folksong and was singing more discriminately. Melodies began to be classified as "exile melodies" and "eastern melodies". The new favorite tunes were characterized as having a distinctive "eastern" flavor. Palestine at that time was singing a new song, composed not by the professional composer, but by the peasant folk. Upon analyzing the tunes of Zaira or Matithyahu Weiner, the most popular of Palestinian song-writers, and some of the new tunes created by others, we find that these new songs draw from three musical sources: (1) The Jewish liturgical song, (2) Yemenite songs, (3) The song of the Palestinian Arab.

The new Palestinian songs have musical figures which interpret Jewish folk-ways and Jewish characteristics. In these we find also expressed the longing of the Jew for his homeland, as well as the enthusiasm which he experiences in working toward its rehabilitation. (*New Palestinian Songs*, Book II, *Palestine in Song*, Book III, A. W. Binder.)

The most distinguishing features of the songs of this period are not as yet found in the melodies, but in the rhythms, tonalities and texts. Almost all contain rhythmic features which are buoyant, moving, enthusiastic and in some cases individual. These are indeed different as compared with the folksongs of the exile, which in most cases are sad, slow-moving, monotonous and imitative.

The songs of the latter part of the 30's represent a constant striving towards a purer style. Many of the songs show pentatonic characteristics, liturgical and cantillation elements.

Harmonization. The problem of the harmonization of the ancient and modern Jewish music has occupied the minds of all serious Jewish composers of the present decade. The western harmonic system of the 19th cent., when applied to the harmonization of Palestinian folksongs, does not reflect the spirit of this highly characteristic oriental music. And so composers, during the last decade, have been experimenting in many ways with new harmonic styles in the effort to bring out the true color of the Palestinian song.

Folksongs of Palestine reflect the many-sided musical experience in Palestine, as well as the activities of its inhabitants. There are national songs, watchman's songs, shepherd songs, hora (dance songs), love songs, songs praising various localities in Palestine, and worker's songs. The most characteristic and purest of these come from the Chalutzim in the rural localities. Among the best-known composers of modern Palestinian songs are M. Zaira, M. Weiner, Y. Ezrachi, N. Nardi, S. Fastalsky, N. Gurachow. (*Pioneer Songs of Palestine,* Book IV, A. W. Binder.)

Synagogue Music of the 19th and 20th Centuries. The impact of the tremendous development of Catholic and Protestant church music during the 17th and 18th cent. did not fail to make itself felt on the music of the synagogue. The musical performing structure of the synagogue at the beginning of the 19th cent. was composed of the cantor, a boy singer and an adult. This adult was a bass when the cantor was a tenor and vice versa. This combination sang in unison most of the time, hummed a chord during certain portions of the cantor's improvisations and improvised harmonizations during the rehearsals and at the service. Frequently the harmonization at the rehearsal was different from that which was heard at the service. This was done without musical notation, for musical education as such was prohibited, even as were the other sciences and arts among the Jews. Religious education alone was permissible. But musical reformers appeared during the latter part of the 18th cent. in the person of Israel Lowy (1783-1832), who began to bring ordered and rehearsed choir singing into the synagogue from musical notation. It was, however, left to Solomon Sulzer (1804-1890) to bring order into the music of the synagogue, when he assumed his position as cantor of the Kultus-Gemeinde Synagogue in Vienna in 1825. His influence was felt throughout all European synagogues, reform as well as orthodox. His compositions for the synagogue, which are embodied in his two volumes entitled *Shir Zion* gradually became the musical liturgy of the synagogue. His influence is felt even to this day.

Louis Lewandowski (1821-1894) in Berlin followed in the footsteps of Sulzer, as did also Solomon Naumbourg (1815-1880) in Paris, as well as a host of other composers of synagogue music who were both cantors and choir directors.

While these musical reforms did much toward bringing harmony out of chaos in synagogue music, they deserted for the most part, the musical traditions of the synagogue. This was in keeping with the spirit of the reform movement which swept over western Europe along with the period of emancipation in the first part of the 19th cent. These reformers wanted their music to sound Protestant-like, and the composers of synagogue music accomodated them. They endeavored to eliminate all oriental traces found in synagogue music. They eliminated the cantillation modes of the Pentateuch when it was read on the Sabbath, and the traditional melodies and modes of the synagogue liturgy, substituting for them the musical style of the Protestant church of that time.

While eastern European composers liked the newly ordered music, they felt that the music of Sulzer and Lewandowski was alien to the synagogue. So men like David Nowakowski of Odessa (1848-1931), Baruch Schorr of Lemberg, and Nissi Belzer of Belz, Russia, took these new forms and employed them while utilizing for the most part traditional musical material. This improvement came toward the end of the 19th cent.

The western harmonic structure was not always successful in serving as a harmonic background for these ancient oriental modes and melodies. Efforts, conscious and unconscious, were made now and then to reconcile melody and harmony. Some successful results were achieved in the works of Hirsch Weintraub (1811-1882) and Eleazer Gerowich (1844-1913). But it was David Nowakowski in Odessa who succeeded to the greatest extent toward this end. His two splendid published works "Neilah" and "Shire David" and many unpublished manuscripts are proofs of this fact.

Synagogue Music in America. In our own country the composers of synagogue music who came here during the middle of the 19th century were of meagre stature. The best which they achieved resulted only in a mediocre imitation of Sulzer and Lewandowski. Especially in the reform synagogue, where there was a new liturgy and no music to accompany it they were faced with a difficult situation. The first American composer of synagogue music for the reform synagogue to achieve some distinction was Edward Stark (1863-1918), cantor of Temple Emanuel of San Francisco. He was the first composer in this country to make an effort to preserve the musical tradition for the reform synagogue in America.

Gradually the synagogues began to feel the lack of Jewishness in their music. The third edition of the Union Hymnal (edited by A. W. Binder, 1931) makes use of many traditional melodies and modes. The reform synagogue gradually attracted musicians who were interested in preserving the Jewish musical tradition and so in the twenties and thirties of this century a large number of musical liturgies by such composers as Joseph Achron, Ernest Bloch, Frederick Jacobi, Isidore Freed, Lazare Saminsky, Jacob Weinberg and A. W. Binder and many others were published. These services combined tradition, musical technique and a striving towards a harmonic system in consonance with the musical material.

Jewish Art Music. The consciousness of the existence of a Jewish folksong and the development of the folksong in Palestine led many composers in Europe and America to apply themselves toward the arrangement and development of this material. Through the Jewish Folksong Society, organized in Petrograd in 1908, many folksongs were collected and arranged for concert performance. Many compositions in all forms were composed in which were utilized the various types of Jewish musical material collected. These compositions range from simple folksongs to chamber and symphonic works. Active in this group at that time were Julius Engel, Joseph Achron, Solomon Rosowsky, Moses Milner, Alexander Krein and others. A number of these pioneers in Jewish art music came to America after World War I. They brought with them their music and their ideas, which immediately influenced many of the younger Jewish composers in this country. The Zimroh Ensemble, headed by Simeon Bellison, clarinetist, was instrumental in performing much of the chamber music which was produced by the Jewish Folk Song Society. In 1931 Maillam, an organization for the support of music in Palestine, and for the performance of Jewish music in America, was organized by Solomon Rosowsky and later headed by Mirian Zunser. This organization functioned for eight years.

The Jewish Music Forum, was established in September 1940, with the purpose of enabling those interested in the history and development of Jewish music to gather and discuss their common problems. This organization has to date brought forth many interesting papers based on research in Jewish music. The organization sponsored a "Conference on the Status of Synagogue Music in America" in June 1941, at which the problems of synagogue music were discussed by professional Jewish musicians, composers and laymen.

At this time there are many Jewish musicians all over the world who are working toward the creation of a Jewish musical idiom. Many works in all forms, large and small, have been created, published and performed by major musical organizations throughout the world. See *Jewish Music*, A. Z. Idelsohn; *Jewish Liturgy*, A. Z. Idelsohn; *Music In the Old Testament*, C. H. Cornill; *History of Musical Instruments* and *The Rise of Music in the Ancient World*, Curt Sachs; *Music In Western Civilization*, P. H. Lang; *Medieval Hebrew Minstrelsy*, Lowe; *The Music of the Pentateuch*, S. Rosowsky; *Sabbath in Music*, A. W. Binder; *Quartel Harmony*, Joseph Yasser.   —A.W.B.

Jew's harp, Jew's trump. See MUSICAL INSTRUMENTS.

jig. See gigue.

jigger, jolly. *Cer.* Machine for making round or oval ware. See CERAMICS I.

jig-tunes. See AMERICAN NEGRO LITERATURE.

jiki (Jap.). Name for porcelain.

jiku (Jap.). Ornamental knobs at each end of the round stick on which Japanese paintings are mounted and rolled.

jimotsu (Jap.). Attributes (q.v.).

Jinghizid architecture. See ISLAMIC ART.

Pögan art. See JAPANESE ART.

joint. *Book.* The term is applied in several ways in bookbinding. (1) The complete hinge of the cover (see French joint). (2) Strips of various materials attached to the fold of end papers, and first and last sections, etc. (3) The groove only, as opposed to the whole of the hinge. (4) A mend.   —H.E.S.

joist. A horizontal member, as a timber, forming part of the structure of a floor or ceiling.

jolly, jigger. *Cer.* Machine for making round or oval ware. See CERAMICS I.

jongleur. See MEDIEVAL MUSIC.

jota. A national dance of Spain; one of the classic Iberian dances. In its present form, it is perhaps closer to its origin in peasant dance than are the others of its group. The movement is strong, rapid, and staccato in quality with a certain rustic stiffness and angularity. It is danced in four/four meter by a man and woman, giving rollicking, pantomimic suggestion of simple courtship. The rhythmic patterns of the dance and the castanet accompaniment form a fast, syncopated counterpoint to the melody, which is slower and paradoxically melancholy in mood.   —J.G.

jubilus. See MEDIEVAL MUSIC.

jug. A deep vessel with a narrow mouth and a handle.

Jugendstil. The name given to the style of a movement for a renewal of the applied arts and architecture in Germany in the last decade of the 19th cent. and the early 20th cent. The name is taken from the magazine *Jugend* (first published 1896 in Munich). The illustrations, decorative designs, etc. of this magazine—reminiscent of A. Beardsley, Edvard Munch—are typical for the *Jugendstil*. The corresponding style in England and France is known under the name of *Art Nouveau*, in Italy as *Stile Liberty*, the names being taken respectively from the shop *Art Nouveau* opened by the Hamburg art dealer S. Bing 1896 in Paris and from Liberty's of the Strand.

In its beginning this new movement was closely connected with the visual arts, as evidenced by the fact that many of the architects originally started as painters (e.g. Peter Behrens, R. Riemerschmid, Bruno Paul, Bernhard Pankok, Henry van de Velde [a Belgian who exerted great influence upon the German movement]). The interiors or exteriors designed in the early phase, such as August Endell's facade of the Elvira studio in Munich (1898), look somewhat like enlarged decorative drawings transferred into different material (cf. drawings or etchings by Klimt, Max Klinger).

The *Jugendstil*, which is greatly indebted to the work of William Morris and his followers in England, prepared the way for the modern style in architecture and industrial design. Those among the moderns who ridicule the *Jugendstil* for its elaborateness forget that it is due to the efforts of this movement that the artistic qualities of good workmanship and the aesthetic values of materials and of textures were rediscovered and recognized. The consideration of the use and function of materials is the first step towards an objectivism (*Sachlichkeit*), which solves problems of design in architecture and industrial production by reference primarily to the functions involved and the materials available and best suited to the functions. See GERMAN ART; art nouveau; also E. Michalski,

Die entwicklungsgeschichtliche Bedeutung des Jugendstils, Repertorium für Kunstwissenschaft, vol. 46, 1925; N. Pevsner, *Pioneers of the Modern Movement from William Morris to Walter Gropius,* 1936; F. Schmalenbach, *Jugendstil,* 1935.   —H.H.

Jugtown ware. See CERAMICS II.

jui (Ch.). A short curved wand or sceptre, the symbol of good wishes.

juke box. See mechanical instruments.

Jupiter. See Zeus.

just interval. See interval.

just intonation. See interval.

just scale. See ACOUSTICS.

jute. A glossy fiber growing between the bark and stalk of a large plant grown in India. It is shredded and spun into a very strong and durable yarn, sometimes used for backing to add strength and stiffness to floorcovering fabrics.   —B.E.J.

juvenile. See ex libris.

juvenile art. See CHILDREN'S ART.

ju yao (Ch.). Chinese pottery ware, heavy, with glaze like "the blue of the sky after rain". *Sung* dynasty.

K

kabe-e (Jap.). A mural. *Kabe*—wall; *e*—painting, wall-painting.

Kabuki drama. See THEATRE.

kachina, katcima. Supernatural beings, hundreds in number, whose cult is widespread among the Pueblos of the Southwest but strongest among the Hopi and Zuñi. Their home is in the San Francisco mountains, according to the Hopi, whence they come to visit the villages for six months to dance, sing, bring presents to the children and, primarily, to take to the gods the prayers of the people for rain and fertility. A long succession of ceremonies takes place during their presence in the villages. The term also applies to the masked dancers who impersonate the kachinas and to the dolls made to represent them.
—H.G.

kacho (Jap.). A painting composite including rock, tree, flower and bird.

kakemono (Jap.). Literally, "hanging thing". A painting, or example of calligraphy, mounted with brocade margins incorporating a round stick at the bottom on which the painting can be rolled up when not in use, and a small stick at the top by means of which the painting can be hung on the wall.   —J.A.M.

kakemono-e (Jap.). A long vertical woodblock print, about 28 by 10 inches; or a horizontal print of unusual size.

Kakiemon ware (Jap.). Porcelain made by the potter Kakiemon.

kakihan (Jap.). A hand-written seal mark; a monogramlike signature.

kalamaika. A lively Hungarian dance in 2/4 time.

kalamkar. The Persian name for those gay prints was *kalamakari*. A printed cotton cloth from India.

kama (Jap.). An iron kettle with a removable cover in which the water is boiled for *cha-no-yu* (q.v.).

Kamakura art. See JAPANESE ART.

Kamakura-bori (Jap.). Carved wood thickly lacquered in red or black. A lacquer style particularly favored in the city of *Kamakura*.

Kamares ware. See Aegean vases.

kamarienskaya. The kamarienskaya dances form one of the four fundamental classes of Russian national dances. They are the romantic group as contrasted to the chorovody, the trepak, and the kasatschy. The kamarienskaya are solos, the dances of the bride-to-be, in which she describes her romantic anticipation of wedded bliss. The dances are usually divided into two phases. The slow and flowing movement of the first changes in the second to a figure of increasing speed and excitement, ending in an abrupt climax symbolic of the meeting with the groom.   —J.G.

kamashiki (Jap.). A metal or pottery stand on which the hot water kettle may be placed when and if removed from the fire during *cha-no-yu* (q.v.).

kami (Jap.). Paper.

kamptulicon. An early floor covering material using India rubber to bind together particles of cork.

kan (Jap.). A pair of open metal rings by which the kettle may be removed from the fire, during *cha-no-yu* (q.v.).

kanagai (Jap.). See raden.

K'ang-Hsi dynasty porcelain. See CERA-MICS II.

Kanga school (Jap.). A style of painting which, as the Chinese word implies, was deliberately Chinese in manner.

kangwa. See JAPANESE ART.

Kano school (Jap.). School of painting after the style of Chinese painting. See JAPAN-ESE ART.

kanon. See Eastern chants.

kanshitsu (Jap.). A lacquer technique whereby cloth is saturated with lacquer and modeled over armatures to produce sculptural forms. In vogue in China and Japan in the 8th and 9th cent. Sometimes called "dried lacquer" work.   —J.A.M.

kaolin (Fr. fm. Ch.). A pure white clay (hydrous silicate of aluminum) used in the manufacture of porcelain. See China clay; CERAMICS I.

kapists. See POLISH ART.

kap kap. A type of ornament common in some parts of Oceania consisting of incised tortoise shell mounted on polished sea shell. See OCEANIA, THE ARTS OF.

karakul (fm. Kara Kul, lake in Pamir, literally black lake). A broad tail sheep of hardy breed. Brown wiry fur on adult sheep. New born lamb glossy black. The term is applied to fabrics made in imitation of this fur.
—G.W.R.

kara-ori (Jap.). Literally, "Chinese fabric", referring to the sumptuous imported brocades; any heavy, elaborate brocade.

karashishi (Jap.). The "Chinese lion" motive.

Karatsu yaki (Jap.). Pottery made in the province of Hizen.

kara-yo (Jap.). See JAPANESE ART.

Karminian. Another name given to the Khilim rug.

Karok. See California Indian art.

kasatsky. A group of Russian national dances, closely interrelated and distinguishable from the other three major groups, chorovody, trepak, and kamarienskaya, by their dramatic content and the fact that they are always performed by one couple only. These dances are devoted to a spirited portrayal of courtship. The man's role is more vigorous and technically difficult than the woman's, beginning quietly, but increasing in power and speed to a tremendous climax. Like most Russian folk-dances, the kasatsky stress and depend upon the technical ability and inspiration of individual dancers.   —J.G.

Kashan ware. See ISLAMIC ART; PERSIAN ART.

kashi. (Ar.). Glazed tile inlay used for brickwork. See ISLAMIC ART.

kashira (Jap.). An ornamental metal cap on the upper end of a Japanese sword handle.

kata-kiribori (Jap.). Incised chiseling, in which the lines imitate brush strokes.

katana (Jap.). Sword with a single cutting edge.

katcina (kachina) niche. In southwestern archeology: A niche, often found in ceremonial chambers, seemingly used during some ceremonies for the depositing of certain masks, etc. when not in use by the participants. Among the Hopi this niche is called the Katcina kihu or house of the Katcinas.
—J.M.M.

kbogan. See FLOWER ARRANGEMENT.

keep. See castle.

Keet Seel (Navaho, broken pottery). An Anasazi cliff village built in a cavern in the Laguna (or Segi) Canyon of north central Arizona. It contains more than 150 rooms and circular subterranean kivas. It is now a part of the Navaho National Monument. See Pueblo art.   —H.G.

kesa (Jap.). A priest's special outer robe in the form of a rectangle which is thrown over the shoulders and caught at the left shoulder with a single cord.   —J.A.M.

kettledrum. See MUSICAL INSTRUMENTS.

kettle-stitch. Book. In some hand-sewn books and some sewn by machine the stitch at the head and tail—or top and bottom—of each section joining it to those on either side. In other cases the needle holes nearest top and bottom.   —H.E.S.

key (Fr. *tonalite;* Ger. *Tonart;* It. *tonalitá*). *Mus.* A term denoting a series of tones or scale and harmonies that center on a specific note. The term also applies to the mechanism of various musical instruments. Although often used interchangeably with "scale" the substitution is not strictly correct. A scale consists of a melodic succession of tones whereas the "key" as reference to the tonal series and the chords connected with them. Tones foreign to the key, however, may be introduced without disturbing the tonal center. The key of a piece is indicated at the beginning of a composition by placing the proper signature of sharps or flats at the beginning. In classical compositions the last bass note is likewise the key-note.

Historically the major and minor keys of to-day are an outgrowth of the older modes. Through the use of Musica Ficta notes extraneous to the mode were gradually introduced and in time (17th cent.) the modern key feeling was established. There are twelve major and twelve minor scales. The key of the relative minor has the same signature (G and e minor) and that of the Tonic minor is built on the same key-note (C and c minor). Keys bear a close relation to each other and passing from one these tonalities to another is termed modulation. The common circle of fifths exemplifies the simplest of these modulatory relations. There are many other connecting links between these different tonalities which are revealed by a study of modulation. The tendency in many contemporary scores is to reject those commonly accepted by using two or more tonalities (polytonality) while others have used a scheme based on the twelve-tone scale which results in no tonality (atonality).

Although there were others who were vitally interested, Bach's *Well-Tempered Clavichord* is regarded as the turning point toward establishing the tempered scale rather than the mean-tone system formerly in use. The mean-tone tuning prevented the use of keys beyond three sharps or three flats as they would be out of tune. Modulation was, of course, restricted. In many of the compositions of the Bach and Handel period the signatures will be found to contain a flat or sharp less than in those of the present era. This is evidence of their connection with the modal era which was largely in disuse but which still influenced the composers. In modern scores based on the chromatic scale or twelve-tone system, signatures are very often omitted to simplify the reading for the performer and the sharps and flats added to the notes that require them. For a consideration of *key* in relation to the mechanics of an instrument such as the piano, organ, etc., reference may be made to these subjects. See idiom A(5), B(2), (3), (4), C. —J.V.H.

key-block. A wood-block (q.v.), on which are cut contour lines only. This block, when applied to a print, outlines all color areas with a black line. —J.A.M.

keyboard. *Mus.* Row of keys (pianoforte, organ).

key-note. See idiom A (2).

key novel. See NOVEL, THE.

key pattern. A fret pattern similar to the Greek fret but after the form of a typical oriental key to a lock.

key plate. *Etch.* Usually the blue or black plate in multiple plate color acquatint work. This plate carries most of the outlines and is used to offset onto the other plates. —K.K.

key ring. See JEWELRY.

keystone. The voussoir at the crown of an arch, regarded as binding the whole.

khan. (Ar.). An open or vaulted court with one or two stories of small rooms surrounding it. See ISLAMIC ART.

khanaqah. (Ar.). A cult-building (usually) of mosque type with subsidiary courts surrounded by rows of cells. See ISLAMIC ART.

khatt. (Ar.). Calligraphy. See ISLAMIC ART.

Khilim. Written also Ghileem, Kilim, is a flat stitched rug without a nap and woven without a shuttle by the nomads in Turkish Kurdistan and the surrounding country. This rug is alike on both sides. See TAPESTRY.
—B.E.J.

Khmer art. See INDIAN ART.

kickwheel. *Cer.* Foot-driven throwing wheel. See CERAMICS I.

Kidderminster. A place in the British Isles famous for carpet made without a nap.

kilims in Poland. See POLISH ART.

kiln. An oven or furnace for baking, burning, or drying, as for bricks, pottery, or limestone; may be heated by gas, oil, electricity, wood or coal.

kinesthesia. Consciousness of one's own muscular sensations in terms of the amount of effort and speed demanded in the performance of any act. It is motor observance. —M.N. H'D.

kinesthetic sense (muscle sense). The special sense employed in the perception of the sensations from active muscles, tendons, and joints. Just as the visual sense conveys sensations of sight to the brain, so does the kinesthetic sense, in combination with pressure sensations convey impressions of the body in activity and in states of equilibrium and rest. Upon them are based judgments of force, range, and duration of movement. Knowledge of the positions of the body and its parts in relation to one another and to space are also ascertained from kinesthetic sensations. And further—ideas concerning the form and solidarity of objects have a kinesthetic basis. The distinguishing characteristic of muscle sensations by which movements are known are time (duration) and stress (force) whose ratios determine the rhythmic structure of all muscular activity (see rhythm). Therefore, kinesthetic is fundamental to rhythmic perception. A keen and reliable kinesthetic perception is essential to all effective uses of the body and is an invaluable endowment to a dancer. —M.N. H'D.

kinetic sculpture. See SCULPTURE.

kingly pose. A formal pose, seen in East Indian art, whereby the right foot is raised to the seat level and the right arm rests on the raised knee. —J.A.M.

king's yellow. See orpiment.

kinji (Jap.). A lacquer technique. A plain gold ground.

Kinkazan yaki (Jap.). Pottery made in Mino province.

Kinnor (Heb.). A small harp. See JEWISH MUSIC.

kinoko (Jap.). The fungus (q.v.).

kira-e (Jap.). Woodblock prints with backgrounds of powdered mica.

kirikane (Jap.). (1) A painting technique. Gold-foil cut in hairline strips and applied to the painting, especially to represent the pat-

terns on fabrics. (2) Also a lacquer technique. Gold or silver-foil cut in small rectangular pieces and applied to lacquer to make an all-over pattern. —J.A.M.

kirin (Jap.). Fabulous deerlike animal with single horn, similar to the unicorn. See chi'i-lin.

Kissi, art of the. See AFRICAN NEGRO ART.

kithara. See MUSICAL INSTRUMENTS.

kiva (Hopi). In southwestern archaeology: A chamber especially constructed for ceremonial purposes. Two general types are recognized, (a) circular, and (b) rectangular. The circular group falls into two major divisions, the ordinary-sized chambers which are frequently termed clan kivas, and the super-ceremonial structures, or great kivas. It is thought by many southwestern archaeologists that the circular kivas, of the ordinary-sized group, represented a survival of an older original type of dwelling. The round form of kiva reached its greatest development in the nuclear portion of the Pueblo region, in the Great Period of prehistoric Pueblo construction. The rectangular form of kiva is believed to be of later origin in the Pueblo system of building. —J.M.M.

Kiyomizu-yaki. (Jap.). Pottery made in Kiyomdsu, in Kyoto.

kiyose-ho (Jap.). The technique of forming a statue from several sections of wood instead of carving it from a single piece.

Klaviatur-Sphaerophon. See electrical instruments.

knei (Ch.). A shape characteristic of some Chinese stone tablets; i.e., circular at the top and square at the bottom.

knitted rugs. Made by strips of material cut and sewn together endwise and wound into balls of string to be knitted into floor pieces.

knots. The yarn which forms the substance of a rug is tied around the warp threads, forming knots. The texture of the carpet depends upon the fineness of the knots. —B.E.J.

knots, single warp. The strands of yarn are wrapped all the way around a single thread of warp, crossed at the back and the ends brought to the front, one on either side. It is tied on alternate threads. As in other weaves, after each row of knots has been tied, one or more weft threads are put in. This knot technique produces smooth diagonal lines instead of perfectly even vertical lines. This knot appears in the early Spanish carpets and rarely in the Oriental rugs. See *European and American Carpets & Rugs*, C. B. Faraday. —B.E.J.

ko (Ch.). Generic term for arrowheads, knives, daggers, etc.

ko (Jap.). See *vajra*.

kobako (Jap.). A utensil for cha-no-yu (q.v.). See *kogo*.

koban (Jap.). A vertical woodblock print slightly smaller than a *chūban* (q.v.).

koboshi (Jap.). A receptacle for waste water, used in *cha-no-yu* (q.v.).

Kodo (Jap.). Lecture hall of a Buddhist temple.

koen (Jap.). A term used to denote "high distance" in a painting; mountains painted as though seen from below.

Koenig sensation curves. See COLOR.

kogai (Jap.). A pair of skewers, sometimes called hairpins, inserted in the scabbard of the "long" sword.

kogo (Jap.). A small box of lacquer or pottery in which are kept the pellets of incense used in *cha-no-yu* (q.v.).

kohai (Jap.) Japanese word for halo.

kojiri (Jap.). An ornamental cap fitted over the lower end of a sword scabbard.

koka-ryokugo (Jap.). A lacquer technique in which the object is first coated with layers of red and of green lacquer and then carved in a pattern of crimson flowers among green leaves. —J.A.M.

kokechi (Jap.). Japanese word for the technique of tie-dyeing.

kondo (Jap.). Gilt-bronze.

Kondo (Jap.). Literally, "golden hall", the hall of worship in a Buddhist temple.

kontakia. See eastern chants.

Korai ware (Jap.). Korean pottery ware of the *Korai* dynasty (918-1392).

koro (Jap.). Incense burner.

kose. See JAPANESE ART.

Kosobe yaki (Jap.). Pottery made in Settsu province.

koto. See MUSICAL INSTRUMENTS.

koto-buki (Jap.). The Japanese word for the Chinese character, *"shou"*, meaning long life and happiness. Often used as a decorative motive. —J.A.M.

ko yao (Ch.). Chinese pottery ware of the *Sung* dynasty.

kozuka (Jap.). Small knife, inserted in the side of the sword scabbard.

krakowiak. See cracoviac.

krater. See crater.

kremnitz white. See white lead.

k'ssu. See TAPESTRY.

ku (Ch.). Sacrificial bronze vessel, beaker-shaped, for holding sacrificial wine.

k'uan (Ch.). Signature or colophon of an artist.

kuang (Ch.). Sacrificial bronze vessel, sometimes three-legged, with handle at side and large open spout. When the cover is in place, the spout is covered and the vessel then appears like a quasi-animal form with curled tail (handle), long neck (spout), and horned head, which is a part of the cover. —J.A.M.

Kuangtung yao (Ch.). Chinese pottery ware of the *Sung* dynasty.

kuan yao (Ch.). Chinese pottery ware of the *Sung* dynasty.

kuei (Ch.). A ritualistic jade tablet, thin and rectangular with a pointed end, which is symbolic of the East and used as a symbol of authority. —J.A.M.

kuei (Ch.). Sacrificial bronze vessel, with two or four handles at side usually, and a base. Used to hold sacrificial food.

kuei pi (Ch.). A jade form which combines a disc (*pi*) with a tablet (*kuei*). It is said to be symbolic of the sun, moon and stars, and is used ritually. —J.A.M.

Kufic script. See ISLAMIC ART.

kulepa. See MUSICAL INSTRUMENTS.

kuljak. This Esthonian national dance, like others of that country, reflects more strongly than most folk-dances the primitive religious significance of dance. It is performed by men and women in circular formation around a fire. The dancers circle with joined hands, walk in promenade by twos, or dance singly with small angular movements. The dance is accompanied by harp music closely related in meter and tempo to the Hungarian czardas (q.v.).   —J.G.

Kulturkreis (Ger.). The social-cultural complex; a concept frequently employed in ethnographic approaches to the study of art.

kung pi (Ch.). A precise and meticulous method of painting in the academic style.

Kunst For Varer. See SCANDINAVIAN ART.

Kunstforeninger. See SCANDINAVIAN ART.

Kunstnärsforbundet. See SCANDINAVIAN ART.

ku-pi (Ch.). A *pi*, q.v., decorated jade with a grain or "millet" pattern.

kurikata (Jap.). Oval knob near the top of a scabbard with a channel opening in the side through which a cord passes (*sageo*, q.v.) to fasten the scabbard to the belt or to fasten the sword in the scabbard.   —J.A.M.

Kushan art. See INDIAN ART.

Kusuura yaki (Jap.). Pottery made in province of Buzen.

Kutani yaki (Jap.). Pottery made in the province of Kaga.

Kwakiutl art. See Northwest Coast Indian art.

kylix. See cylix.

kyogen. See JAPANESE ART.

kyokechi (Jap.). Ancient name for *itajime* (q.v.).

kyrie. See MEDIEVAL MUSIC; Mass.

L

Lac. A natural organic red dyestuff usually has been given this name, and it is also called "lac lake" and "Indian lake". It comes from the resinous secretion of the larvae of the *Coccus lacca* which lives on certain trees native to India and the Far East. This is similar to the secretion from which seed lac or shellac is obtained. It is similar, also, in composition and color to the carmine lakes from cochineal, but lac is slightly duller in tone and somewhat more stable. It seems to have been used more largely in the East than in Europe, but became moderately familiar to Western painters during the Middle Ages. —G.L.S.

lace. Hand made or *real lace* exists in two main classes: (1) needle point or point lace made by the needle; (2) Bobbin or pillow lace made with bobbins and pins on a pillow. Machine made lace sometimes imitates hand made lace—sometimes produces original designs producing the effect of hand made lace —or produces an entirely unique effect. It is always possible to detect the difference between real and machine made lace. Sometimes a fabric is made with a combination of machine work and hand made work.

Intricate cords, fringe and nets fashioned of fibers of flax, hemp, and wool are the forerunners of lace. The priests of Egypt sometimes cut holes in gazelle skins making a lace effect. Peruvian laces show diagonal serrated stripes with fretted key devices, chevrons, crosses, roundels, squares, lozenges and representations of the puma, the duck and the fish. These laces are made of acuna, wool and fibers of the maguey, a species of cactus plant. There are a few specimens of lace dating from the Byzantine Emperor Justinian. All pre-Renaissance lace consisted of drawn work, cut work, darned work and macrame. Some of the stitches used are called *punto avora, punto saracen* and *point mouree.*

Lace making flourished in the Grecian Archipelago and it is from these sources that lace was first introduced into Venice during the Byzantine period. About the year 1530 the Venetians abandoned all foundation material and relied on the needle to create the fabric. The first real lace was the fine Italian needlepoint lace we know as **punto in aria.** The design took on floral forms with curved lines.

Reticella was the earliest of needlepoint laces. It was a development of cut work and drawn work. Brides and picots were introduced at intervals. The late development of reticella show circles and curved, free flowing lines in the design. A pattern book of laces was printed in Venice in 1560 which tends to establish Italy's claim to have been the first European country to develop the making of true hand-made lace. Flanders has for years contested Italy's claim as the originator of the European industry.

At the same time lace-making was developing in Italy it was developing independently in Flanders by an entirely different process, employing pillow, bobbin, and pins. Flanders lace industries began to flourish at the end of the 16th cent. Mixed laces in both countries were of a later date, after each country had copied the work of the other.

Pillow bobbin and fringe lace all developed from plaited fringe work. The pattern is developed thru crossing, plaiting and braiding threads. The pillows used vary in shape and mechanism. The design drawn on parchment must not measure more than the circumference of the pillow. The lace maker tosses her bobbins about, braiding the threads which hang from the top of the pattern fastened on the pillow. As one pattern ends

535

another commences. Pins are used to fasten the threads in place on the pillow. The pins are removed as the pattern progresses.

From 1540 to 1590 lace showed geometric forms set within square or crossed and radiating line devices, in a very open fabric.' No brides or reseaux were used. From 1590 conventional floral and even human and animal forms and slender scrolls in a tape-like texture held together by brides appear. From 1620 to 1670 the development of long, continuous scroll patterns with reseaux and brides accompanied in the case of needle made laces with an elaboration of details (coordinated with massings of picots). From 1650 to 1700 the scroll patterns gave way to arrangements of detailed ornamental details. From 1700 to 1760 more important schemes or designs were made into which were introduced naturalistic rendering of garlands, flowers, birds, trophies, architectural ornament and human figures. From 1760 to 1800 small details lognets, sprays of flowers, single flowers, leaves, buds, sopts, were adopted, and sprinkled over meshed grounds, and the character of the texture was gauzy and filmy.

Different countries developed distinctive designs: *gros point* de Venice in Italy; *meclin* in Flanders; heavy *blonde* in Spain; *point d'Alencon* and *chantilly* in France; *Honiton* in England; *Carrick ma crosse* and *Irish crochet* lace in Ireland.   —G.W.R.

lacing. *Book.* When the cords or tapes—slips—are passed through the holes in the boards to attach them to the book.

lacing course. In masonry: The term applied to a horizontal band of stone placed in rubble or rough walls to form a longitudinal line.

lacquer. Numerous synthetic resins are grouped under the heading, lacquer, but in the arts the term still keeps its traditional meaning as the specific name for a natural resinous exudation from the tree, *Rhus Vernicifera* DC. This is most common in China and Japan but there are lacquers from Burma, Indo-China, and Formosa. The lacquer is extracted as a sap and seems to have been used directly as a coating material for various objects of fine workmanship. Precise methods of application have been largely kept as secrets, and possibly the poisonous nature of this sap has prevented it from gaining a wider use. Its affect is somewhat like that of ivy poisoning. As a film it has unusually stable characteristics. It hardens in the presence of

moisture, does not become brittle, and can be highly polished. When thoroughly dried, it is unaffected by acids, alkalis, or alcohol, or by heat up to about 160 degrees C.
                                        —G.L.S.

la ch'in. See MUSICAL INSTRUMENTS.

lacquer print (so-called). A broadsheet, classified as a print, but painted in parts to represent a lacquer medium.

lacquerware. A technique peculiar to the Orient, whereby the sap of the poisonous sumac tree is used as a painting medium in the fine arts. In the crafts it is used over a wooden base producing a surface of permanency and great beauty, with all the aspects of the painter's art.

The lacquerer is nearly equal in rank to the painters of the Orient. For further details see the following:

chi	*Kamakura-bori*	*sabiji*
chinkinbori	*kanagai*	*shikki*
chiriji	*kanshitsu*	*soku*
cinnabar	*kinji*	*suzuri-bako*
fundame	*kōka-ryokugō*	*takamakie*
guri	*maki-e*	*tiaoch'i*
hakemei	*makkinro*	*togidashi*
heidatsu	*mokume*	*togidashi-makie*
hyōmen	*Nagasaki ware*	*tsuikoku*
hiramakie	*nashiji*	*tsuishu*
hirame	*raden*	*urushi*
hua ch'i	*raten*	*urushi-e*
ikake-ji	*roiro*	*wakasanuri*
		zōgan-muri

See also *Catalogue of Chinese Lacquer,* Edward F. Strange, Victoria and Albert Museum, London, 1925; *Catalogue of Japanese Lacquer,* Edward F. Strange, Victoria and Albert Museum, London, Part I, 1924, Part II, 1925; *A Glimpse of Japanese Ideals* (chapter, Ancient Lacquer in Japan), Jiro Harada, 1937.   —J.A.M.

lad. See POLISH ART.

lai. See MEDIEVAL MUSIC.

laid lines. See wire-marks.

lake pigments. The coloring materials used by painters and made from dyestuffs are usually called lakes. Possibly the word came from association with lac, a natural red dye. The lakes are completely soluble and transparent and become usable as pigments when combined with a solution of a metal to form a precipitate with body, grain, and some amount of hiding power. —G.L.S.

laksana. See INDIAN ART.

La Libre Esthetique. See art nouveau.

lamé. A fabric shot through with metal threads or having a brocaded pattern in metal with silk or rayon.

lamp black. Among the various carbon blacks, this is probably the finest in texture. It is made from the condensed smoke of burning oil, tar, gas or resin. Such black pigment was known in ancient times and has had a continuous use since then.   —G.L.S.

lancet window. A high narrow window (without tracery) with a sharply pointed head.

ländler. A Styrian peasant dance in 3/4 time; a kind of waltz.

land planning. See CIVIC PLANNING.

LANDSCAPE ARCHITECTURE. Landscape architecture, of ancient lineage, had its rise when man first began to modify his intimate surroundings for more practical use and, shortly afterwards, for more pleasing arrangements. No doubt aesthetic considerations in the beginning were correlated with primitive religious concepts; but the relative precedence of personal desire for aesthetic appearance as against that of religious influence is not known, and the preponderance of one factor over the other can only be surmised by comparative study of the contemporary arts. The names of the earlier landscape architects have not been preserved, although the evidence of thir handiwork is well established by archeological research.

At first the ordered arrangement of ground about the habitations of man was purely an expression of individual taste: for the earlier adepts in development of ground for better use and enjoyment were part of the retinue of some individual whose land, because it was unplanned, had been found both inconvenient and unproductive. But as time went on, as in all of the fine arts, certain basic principles became the common knowledge of all employing the art.

Probably the highest development of the art of landscape architecture, in the sense of its most widespread contemporary use, was in Italy during the Renaissance. Many examples of this period exist today, but most people who visit them understand them only from the background of modern experience. The gardens are beautiful, and as such the power of their beauty obscures the fundamental fact that they were primarily useful to the builders. Since appreciation of their original utilitarian purpose has been largely lost, and because they are a source of visual pleasure to the visitor, the art which brought them into being is incorrectly judged to be concerned only with beauty. Equally unfortunate, it is also assumed to be concerned only with large properties because the Italian villas of the Renaissance were large.

In evaluating the place of the landscape architect in our present-day social structure, it is peculiarly pertinent to observe that when the outstanding works of landscape architecture were achieved in Italy, and somewhat similarly in France and England, it was the time when the individual of force, character, and position dominated society. Public service as we know it did not exist; there was only the most rudimentary concept of the State as separate from the powerful individual. This circumstance was precisely set forth by Louis XIV: "I am the State." The practitioner of any of the fine arts at that time could exist only by the pleasure and grace of powerful patrons.

With the decline of the power of monarch and nobility, and the rise in power of the people, the idea of public service as well as service to the public came into being; and at the same time the place of the architect, doctor, lawyer, and landscape architect as independent and free agents related to society became fixed. The earliest example of landscape architecture conceived as a public improvement, carried forward to completion as such, and financed from public funds, was Central Park in New York City. Earlier examples, such as the squares and greens of Colonial settlements were not founded on this philosophy, but were outgrowths of community necessity or grants made by the great land development companies for pasturage or other specific land uses other than that for park purposes as they are now used. The circles and plazas of the L'Enfant plan of Washington were in part military,—artillery emplacements for efficient quelling of rebellion. Today, landscape architecture is still one of the arts of civilization, assisting man in his effort to modify his surroundings for more efficient and orderly use, and to bring to these revised or corrected surroundings such pleasure as may be compatible with the situation. The landscape architect as an individual rendering service to the public is now as interested in small properties as in large ones. Wherever there is a problem of bringing ordered arrangement to a large tract or a small parcel of land, the landscape architect can make his contribution to its development, and in this he is a working member of society.

With the growth of the power of the people, supplanting the functions of the monarch, it is worthy of note that great current examples of landscape architecture in the democracies throughout the world have taken the form of national parks and national monuments, national forests, extensive metropolitan and city parks and parkways, landscape improvement of public highways, landscape development of subsidized low-rent housing, and other similar works which are for the benefit of the community as a whole. Modern landscape architecture serves democratic ends; for this reason work comparable with Versailles in intensive development has not been done in recent years. In breadth of conception and monetary value, however, several of the larger public works projects executed in this country exceed those of kings and nobles, and in respect to man-hours of work there is little doubt that some WPA projects exceed the undertakings of Louis XIV.

The work of the landscape architect, in the public field as well as in relatively smaller problems for the private individual, is first of all planning land areas for specific uses, and subsequent development is secondary to the primary allocation of land. In the preservation of natural conditions, construction and planting are minimized when they cannot be avoided. The landscape architect, whose training is based upon land use, is always conscious of the land; and for this reason it should be remembered that, while of itself a private residence project may be a relatively small undertaking, the training and experience brought to bear upon it by a competent landscape architect embrace consideration of certain aspects of town and regional planning, transportation and traffic, public service facilities, and zoning, and may well include problems of erosion control, soil conservation, reforestation, and water-shed preservation, in addition to the specific problems of the site, —all because the landscape architect is conscious of the fact that all the surface of the earth is continuous, and that land planning which fails to recognize this fact cannot be completely successful. Herein lies a fundamental difference between landscape architecture and civil engineering or architecture.

A concise statement of the several types of work with which the landscape architect may be concerned appears in the following statement prepared by the American Society of Landscape Architects:

(1) *GENERAL AND BROAD-SCALE PLANNING: General Considerations External to a Definitive Project.*
Selection of a site to conform to predetermined requirements, accompanied by a report upon its relation to the surrounding region and an estimate of the probable effect of the project upon the region.

Professional work would include: Reports on transportation and traffic; recommendations for new planning legislation or for amendment of existing planning legislation (including zoning); appraisal of recreational and social facilities; public service facilities in respect to their adequacy; financial structure of the region affected by the project; cooperation with local planning authorities; and coordination with local physical development programs and local social or economic activities.

(2) *LAND USE PROBLEMS AND GENERAL LAND DEVELOPMENT PROGRAM.*
Problems of a *regional significance*: Allocation of land for economic, recreational, social, or scientific purposes such as agriculture, industry, housing, erosion, erosion control, wildlife conservation, reforestation, parks, parkways, and park system of national, state, regional, or municipal character.

Professional work would include: Reconnaissance investigation, formation of programs, drafting of legislation, and coordination of the various levels of government, etc.

Problems of *land use upon a specified area*: Allocation of land within a limited area in conformity with the purpose, dedicated to some form of public use or benefit, such as recreation, reforestation, wildlife restoration, development of area to demonstrate one or more scientific concepts, and allocation or development of outlying land about a given project for purposes of "buffer" or protection.

Professional work would include: Determination of the various types of land uses in which an area should be divided; general locations of special improvements or alterations; recommendations as to extent, character, and specific use of improvements, accompanied by estimates, reports, outline specifications, and contractural conditions if necessary.

(3) *SITE PLANNING AND DEVELOPMENT.*

Location of buildings and other structures in relation to topography; drives and walks for vehicular and pedestrian circulation, with parking spaces; control of ground forms through grading; location of recreational areas, playgrounds, athletic fields, and their necessary facilities and equipment, lawns, and planting areas; drainage, irrigation, and their appurtenances; structures incidental to landscape development, such as swimming pools, wading pools, shelters, etc.; and general or specialized planting arrangements pertinent to the development. The work of the landscape architect in site planning also includes the planning of parks and other public properties, institutional properties, land subdivisions, housing projects, cemeteries, and private properties.

Professional work would include: Usual preliminary studies and reports and final working drawings, specifications, preliminary and final estimates, material schedules, contract documents, and supervision of construction. Landscape architecture draws upon the specialized fields of technical knowledge such as geology, agriculture, and particularly its handmaiden, horticulture, and upon architecture and engineering for incidental and necessary supplemental data, but primarily it is a field of its own with established and ever-accumulating basic principles necessary for the planning of land for human use and enjoyment.

The materials of landscape architecture are for the most part natural,—earth and water forms in their infinite variety, and living plants,—but include a limited number of processed materials. Both plants and processed materials must be either climatically adapted or weather-enduring. A completed project in landscape architecture is not finished when the designer ends his work; it must mature over a period of years, the number required depending upon the character of the development. In this, landscape architecture differs from all other arts, for its works—unlike those based on processed materials—do not begin their decline upon completion. There is a general misconception that the work of the landscape architect primarily deals with plants and horticultural problems. On the contrary, plants and planting are but the last step in the development of any project, and must always follow problems dealing with location of buildings, grading, drives, walks, etc. Of course, vegetation is an important element in landscape composition, but must be coordinated with other elements of design and construction to complete the final effect.

Inasmuch as the elements comprising landscape architecture are as variable as its terrain and its materials, it cannot be defined by unbreakable rules, and for this reason it is often defined to suit the particular limitations of its application. Most of these definitions overlook the fact that it is primarily concerned with three dimensions, and also, that substitute terms for landscape architecture (and the landscape architect) are specific limitations rather than a statement of general principles. There is no approved definition, but in lieu of an authorized version it may be stated that: Landscape architecture is the planning of land by allocation into ordered arrangements for various purposes and its subsequent development whereby economic, social, physical, and aesthetic values are simultaneously recognized and proportionally emphasizbed according to the requirements of the problem for the purpose of deriving maximum use and human enjoyment.

Landscape architects are found practicing their profession in private offices, and in many public offices at all levels of government,—some under titles which give no clue to their professional training. A large number of city or town planners are trained landscape architects, as also are many government officials in charge of broad-scale planning and in the fields of recreation and conservation. The landscape architect, whether in private practice or in public service, looks upon his work as a profession, and therefore is not concerned with speculative profit on labor or materials. His method of rendering service follows a rigid code of accepted practices, and is analogous to that of the medical or architectural professions. The official organization sponsoring landscape architecture in this country in which qualified professional landscape architects may become members is the American Society of Landscape Architects, founded in 1899.

In a current dictionary of fine arts the influence of the modern attitude should be particularly noted. Most landscape architects consider their profession to be fully in conformity with today's demands since their efforts are directed toward public welfare as well as for the service of the individual. However, those who are drawn to the current trend believe that modern landscape design must express itself and be inseparable from modern architecture in spirit, technique, and development, and that the design of gardens should change to reflect the contemporary spirit rather than to cling to precepts of the past, many of which are now archaic or sentimental. But landscape architecture is both conservative and radical simultaneously. In its larger works, where extensive units of water, vegetation, broad sweeps of land and sky are the elements of a composition, it is to a great extent at the mercy of its materials. To conserve and preserve the natural compositions or to reconstruct them for posterity in perpetuity is still a radical concept that is not fully appreciated. In areas of smaller extent a designer may impose his will and design according to style. Competency of design is judged in the final analysis as to economic values, and for this reason recent work strives for low operating costs; similarly, older work is revised to make it economically maintainable and as pleasurable as may be compatible with economic limitations. See CIVIC PLANNING.

Glossaries: Terms used in landscape architecture are drawn from the allied fields of architecture, engineering, construction, and from subdivisions of agriculture such as botany, forestry, horticulture, etc. The terms borrowed are defined in the references to these fields and practically all are in one of the unabridged dictionaries. A general or complete glossary of the terms applicable to landscape architecture has not been published. Specialized glossaries of limited application are:

Housing: "A Glossary of Landscape Terms", prepared by the Sub-committee on Landscape Work for the Central Housing Committee, Washington, D. C., 1942.

Horticulture: *The Complete Garden*, Taylor and Cooper, N. Y., 1923.

Botany: The botanical manuals contain glossaries for botanical subjects and works devoted to a specialized plant group contain abbreviated glossaries suitable for their purpose. —W.A.S.

language of art. A metaphorical phrase indicating the expressive quality of art, and implying that the elements of art, such as line, form, light and dark, color, and texture, when arranged according to aesthetic principles, produce a structure, pattern, or composition that may be interpreted or read as a language of expression. Whitford and Winslow in *Dictionary of Education*.

lapidary. A supplement to a bestiary (q.v.) describing the miraculous qualities of different species of stones. See JEWELRY.

lapis lazuli. One of the semi-precious stones, this has served as a material for carving and also as the mineral from which genuine or true ultramarine blue, the painter's pigment, is derived. That comes directly from pulverized lapis lazuli and is made somewhat more intense in color by a treatment which separates out the more highly colored particles from those which are colorless or have a contrasting color. —G.L.S.

lappet weaving. A process of decorating plain woven or gauze fabrics with embroidery-like motifs simultaneously with the weaving of the ground. The pattern is formed by an extra warp thread, heavier than the ground. See weaving. —G.W.R.

lat. See INDIAN ART.

LATE ANTIQUE ART. (NOTE: The present article on Late Antique art will be limited to a consideration of the last monuments of pagan art to be made in the Roman empire. Although Early Christian art, q.v.) in both its eastern and western manifestations is a part of Late Antique art, this development is omitted here for reasons of clarity and brevity.)

Introduction. By the Late Antique period is meant chiefly the twilight of the classical era, the final chapters of Roman imperial art, particularly in those most remote provincial centers within the artistic web that Rome spun over the world. Late Antique art, esp. in its regional manifestations, represents a phase of artistic expression interesting not only for its intrinsic aesthetic merit which, contrary to popular opinion, is sometimes considerable, but also for its revelation of a period of culture when the old classic humanistic values were locked in a death struggle with the dynamic and overwhelming forces of Oriental and barbarian art, a struggle that was to end with the victorious emergence of mighty and new spiritual forces that produced mediaeval art in the West and the great and truly ghostly beauty of developed Buddhist art in India and the Far East. Classic art, which held a mirror to catch the familiar friendly face of nature, was basically no more compatible with Oriental art and its endless yearnings after the other world than it was with the fantastic and dynamic imaginings of the barbarian soul in Gaul and Britain. In Late Antique art we have the spectacle of artists completely reshaping the material terms and techniques of classical art that were fundamentally unsuited to expressing the spiritual ideals of non-materialistic beliefs. Herein lie the reasons why classical art could not survive in a world whose thoughts were beyond Nature and the accidental beauty of the human form. And it is precisely as an exemplar of this universal process involving the death of classicism and the rebirth of spiritual expression in art that the production of the Late Antique period is of such particularly vital import.

The changes that took place in Late Roman art are sometimes attributed to a falling-off in technical ability co-incident with the gradual disappearance of schools and training centers for artists in the period of confusion that accompanied the disintegration of the Empire. Although this is partly true, it is also undeniable that many of the distortions and departures from the naturalistic norm of earlier centuries were deliberate and influenced to some degree by the ideals and techniques of Oriental art as represented by the artistic traditions of the peoples in the eastern Roman provinces.

There are a certain number of formal and symbolic tendencies distinctive of Late Antique works of art as a whole which, as is to be expected, may be seen developing in earlier monuments of Roman art. So, for example, the heraldic symmetry, notable in the strict balance of equal numbers of figures on the arch of Constantine of 315 A.D., may be discerned in works as early as the Ara Pacis of 9 A.D. The method of continuous narration in which successive episodes are presented within the confines of the same frame was of course developed in the spiral reliefs of the triumphal columns of Trajan (98-117 A.D.) and Marcus Aurelius (161-180 A.D.). So, too, the universal tendency to frontality may likewise be discovered in certain reliefs from the monuments of Trajan, such as the arch of Benevento. Again, the principle of hierarchic scaling has its beginnings in the column of Trajan in which the figure of the Emperor is enlarged to emphasize his importance. The Late Antique device of inverted perspective might be pointed out in monuments as early as the 2nd cent. A.D. The general disproportion in the scale of the figures and their setting, so pronounced in the reliefs of the Constantinian period, is already a fully developed formula in the purely symbolical architecture of the reliefs on the column of Trajan. The lack of proportion in the human body, marked by an expressive rather than a normal enlargement of the head, may be already seen in the 3rd cent. reliefs of the arch of Septimius Severus (193-211). In exactly the same way the total disintegration of a unified spatial conception may be seen again in the Trajanic reliefs in which the suggestion of spatial existence is symbolical rather than optical. At the same time the disappearance of the unity of time and place in Late Antique reliefs is to be noted in monuments of the 1st cent. A.D., in which actions taking place at different times are arbitrarily shuffled together in the same composition. The violent contrasts of light and dark, which completely displace the earlier illusionistic style of relief of such monuments as the arch of Titus (79 A.D.), make their appearance as early as the Hadrianic period (117-138 A.D.) and in the impressionistic treatment of certain heads in the column of Marcus Aurelius. The trend toward the colossal, typical of 4th cent. portraiture, had its beginnings in the statues of earlier emperors represented slightly larger than life-size. Again, the employment of symbolical attributes in Late Roman portraiture is simply an outgrowth of such earlier types like, for example, the Prima Porta statue of Augustus (27 B.C.-94 A.D.) representing the Emperor in military gear, emblematic of his power as *Pacificator Mundi*.

The gradual breaking down of the Hellenistic tradition was already under way in the far-flung provinces of the Empire as early as the 1st and 2nd cents. A. D. There the local Oriental or barbarian traditions hastened the disintegration of the humanistic classical ideal. It is customary to classify under the Late Antique period the art of Byzantium from the founding of the new Rome by Constantine until the emergence of truly Byzantine art under Justinian.

It seems that whatever creative impulse was left in the 3rd and 4th cents. flourished not so much in Rome the city, but along the axis of the Empire from Britain to the Parthian border: more and more strongly the forces that were to culminate in the medieval ideal came from the circumference of the Roman orbit; by 300 A.D. the creative power at the center had died. In these later centuries we should think in terms of Roman imperial art—the art of the Empire—rather than Roman art. This will account for the uniform character of all Roman provincial art and the sometimes baffling synthetic character of its later development.

The principal monuments of Late Antique art, such as the arch of Constantine in Rome and the later Imperial portraits, are conceived in a form language completely distinct from the standards of earlier centuries. Classic forms come to be disintegrated, and the conception is now in a linear, frontal style that seems almost like a return to the archaic. The figures in relief become isolated and take on an inhuman rigor. A luminous spiritual quality animates the mask-like faces with their enormous eyes. The drapery is reduced to a kind of mesh of ornamental striations. These are all devices intended to emphasize the spiritual rather than the material nature of humanity, the ghostly inner self rather than the outward physical body.

An analysis of a few monuments selected from the principal centers of artistic production in the 3rd to the 6th cents. A.D. will suffice to reveal the essential character of Late Antique art in general.

Rome. In Rome itself those sections of the arch of Constantine which were actually carved in the 4th cent. are typical of this last phase of classical art. In the reliefs of Constantine's triumph over Maxentius the figures arranged in bands with a strict adherence to the principle of isocephaly appear as isolated units in a poster-like flat pattern of light and shade. They are arranged in a completely frontal and hieratic fashion, and appear as symbolic rather than descriptive portrayals of the human form. There is no projection forward or back, and what movement there is is completely lateral. The principle of hierarchic scaling makes its appearance in the slight enlargement of the figure of the Emperor which is also somewhat raised above the crowd to signalize his eminence.

A style of portraiture of a spiritual effectiveness such as the world had never seen before is to be found in the likenesses of the emperor Constantine and his successors. We find a new and abstract system of construction in which all signs of physical life in the face are subordinated to the radiation of a ghostly presence. The sense of human strain already characteristic of certain earlier Roman portraits is transmuted into a kind of

ecstasy. The eyes begin to gaze upward out of the world with a blazing fervor; so—Constantine's chronicler Eusebius tell us—the Emperor was invariably portrayed in prayer with his gaze straining heavenward. The eyes become the chief unit in what is no longer a real physical personage but a soul aspiring towards its god. All the other features are no more than a decorative enframement of the spiritual power of the eyes. Here we have no ephemeral, momentary likeness, but that constant structure lying behind the incidentals of phenomenal appearance. The Late Antique period is marked by a re-appearance of the colossal statue, no longer for the representations of the Olympian god but for the specific designation of the Emperor as the more than mortal Cosmokrator and stupendous symbol of Empire.

ARCHITECTURE. The tendencies toward the dissolution of classical form, illustrated by the sculpture of the Late Antique period in Rome, are no less apparent in the architecture of the period. So, for example, the carving of the Corinthian capital, as seen especially in the buildings of Baalbek, Palmyra, and Palestine, could be taken as an index of the reduction of organic form and structure to a shimmering, immaterial pattern of staccato light and dark. In exactly the same way the façades of Late Antique buildings, notably the triumphal arches, become a sharply defined web of chiaroscuro in which all structural solidity is dissolved. One would have to consider, too, the culmination of the treatment of the orders in the arcades of Diocletian's palace at Spalato, in which the Roman arch is wedded directly to the Greek column. The arcade itself is a new spatial device peculiar to the Late Antique period. The palace complex itself is a symbol of the isolation and separate existence of the divine soverign. It is not surprising that following the new spiritualizing tendencies the dome, immemorial emblem of the sky in eastern architecture, comes more and more into prominence in the buildings of the Constantinian period that prophesy the triumph of domical construction in the symbolical architecture of Byzantium.

PAINTING. The painting of the Late Antique period is marked by exactly the same changes in the conception of form and space demonstrated by the sculpture of these centuries. This transformation, already discernible in Late Roman wall-paintings, may be admirably illustrated by the illuminations of the famous Vatican Vergil. All suggestion of material space has disappeared. The landscape is arranged in a series of zones or flat bands behind the prominent figures in the foreground. An exotic impressionism in color seems to parallel the treatment of sculpture as a design in chiaroscuro. Other features of Late Antique painting will be discussed at greater length in the section devoted to art in the Near East.

Byzantium. Constantinople, the new Rome founded by Constantine on the Golden Horn, was perhaps even more than the capital of the western Empire one of the last citadels of Hellenism. Some of the most famous statues of classical antiquity ornamented the squares and porticoes of the city until they were destroyed by the Venetians in 1204. The study of pagan Greek literature had never completely died out. It is for these reasons perhaps that so many monuments of the 4th and 5th cents. in Byzantium retain a distinctly Hellenic flavor. So, for example, the relief of a Nike from the Golden Gate, now in the Ottoman Museum, might at first be mistaken for a monument of the 5th cent. B.C. A closer inspection will reveal, however, that the body is hardly conceived as a physically articulated organism, and that the drapery, far from revealing either its own or the body's structure, is a reduction to a completely linear pattern of the Phidian scheme of drapery.

One of the most typical examples of Late Antique art in Constantinople is the base of the obelisk of Theodosius, erected in the Hippodrome in 405 A.D. Many of the techniques and concepts noted in the arch of Constantine are here brought to their final development. Figures are completely frontal in their rigid alignment. In a sort of combination of the principles of inverse perspective and hierarchic scaling, the figures performing below, in front of the royal box, are represented in a much smaller scale than the effigies of the Emperor and his courtiers. The only truly realistic figures are those of the kneeling Gothic barbarians. Extremely moving heads with their straining intensity of expression reveal a type of naturalism stressing pathos and suffering that is found in many examples of Roman provincial art in Europe.

Provincial art. It has been suggested that during the 3rd and 4th cents. A.D. the real centers of vitality in Roman art were in the provinces of the Empire where the gradual rise to dominance of Oriental and barbarian tendencies led to just those stylistic changes in Roman sculpture that have been noted in

such monuments as the arch of Constantine. The human element in the art of Rome provided an acceptable and often vigorous means of expression. The change from classicism in Roman provincial art to a kind of dynamic expressionism was a turning from a cold and exhausted idealistic art to an art expressive of religious and ethnic ideas. The progressive disintegration of the classic ideal in the provinces was quickened by the existence of religious and racial groups that conceived their deities in abstract rather than representational, symbolic rather than concrete, terms. The best of the provincial Roman sculpture—from Gaul, Germany, and Bulgaria, to name a few centers—represents a purposeful transformation of the classical style into very much the same abstract and expressionistic formulae that distinguish western religious art at its moment of greatest tension in the Romanesque period. The notable triumphs of ethnic portraiture, seen, for example, in the reliefs of the Neumagen grave monument, seem marked by that suggestion of an inner radiance and spiritual intensity that distinguishes the sculpture of the Gothic age.

The Near East. The art of the Roman province of Syria comprises the remains from Antioch on the Orontes, the garrison town of Dura Europos, as well as many examples of sarcophagi generally classified under the designation Sidamara, from the site where most of the important examples have been found. The monuments of Palmyra and Nabataea represent an even more Orientalized type of Hellenism.

The principal remains from Antioch consist mainly of the pavement mosaics that decorated the patrician villas of this famous capital. Many of these decorations may be classified as Late Antique in their revelation of the gradual breakdown of the illusionistic technique, seen in the Pompeiian figure-painting of the third and fourth styles. Both subtlety of modelling and suggestions of light and atmosphere have disappeared, and the figures are now harshly modelled by shading that is little more than a thickening of the outlines. The forms have a strangely rigid and hieratic quality; in the nudes the muscular structure is more of a pattern than a definition of anatomy.

The city of Dura Europos on the Euphrates was essentially a military post that changed hands on a number of occasions from the Romans to the Parthians. Its art presents just that intermarriage of occidental and oriental techniques that is so distinctive of all Late Antique art. The most notable example of painting at Dura was a long painted frieze in the temple of Bel. The priests of Bel, like frozen effigies fixing the spectator with their great hypnotic eyes, are isolated against the background essentially flat and without depth, as though by this elimination of all suggestion of actuality it was intended to project the principal figures—the priests as symbols of perpetual sacrifice—the more forcefully and with the minimum of distraction. In this work of the 1st cent. A.D. hierarchical rather than optical criteria are dominant. Attributes and ritual gestures have completely replaced action and drama. Among the other pictorial remains in Dura include the decorations of the synagogue arranged in hieratic zones on the walls of the sanctuary. These were presumably completed about 250 A.D. Hieratic frontality, disproportion of figures and architecture, the conception of the forms in flat linear terms are among the many elements specific to Late Antique art. Both paintings and sculptures dedicated to the cult of Mithra have been among the principal finds at Dura Europos. It seems reasonable to suppose that the diffusion of the cult of Mithra, the divine toreador, to every province of the Roman empire was one of the most potent factors in the interweaving, not only of the Oriental mystery religious, but also of Oriental concepts and forms in art, into the whole fabric of the Roman empire.

The principal examples of the Asiatic sarcophagi are now gathered together in the Ottoman Museum in Constantinople. Although there has been some dispute as to their origin, it is now generally conceded that the chief center for the manufacture of these sepulchres was Sidamara in Asia Minor. Their decoration generally consists of figures of gods and goddesses centered in the niches of an arcade that enframes the sarcophagus. The resultant isolation of the forms is one of the chief traits of Late Antique art. The so-called *homme-arcade* motif was to find its way into Early Christian in the West, and is frequently found as a decoration on the Buddhist monuments of Afghanistan and northwestern India. Although many of the figures on Sidamara coffins reproduce heroic classical types, the forms have a sharpness and hardness in modelling and are conceived more as effective silhouettes than as plastically conceived masses. Not only the figural sculpture but also the lace-like decorative patterns clearly suggest the *Tiefendunkel* that comes to be distinctive of 4th cent. sculpture in Rome.

The art of Palmyra consists mainly of the innumerable grave portraits carved from the 1st cent. A.D. until the destruction of the desert metropolis by Aurelian in 273 A.D. Here again is a method of direct formalized expression with the elimination of all suggestion of physical realism. The body is reduced to a linear pattern of lines and simple abstract surfaces of planes. Absolutely rigid frontality prevails in all these grave portraits, and the eyes are given an enormous ghostly prominence. The minute treatment of the drapery patterns and jewelry in many of the Palmyrene portraits is to be interpreted not as realism but as a symbolic attribute of the rank and wealth of the deceased. These sculptures from Palmyra and the highly similar grave monuments from Nabataea are the most striking examples of the dematerialization of solid sculptural forms with the express intention of emphasizing the spiritual rather than the material nature of humanity.

Egypt. The grave portraits from the Fayum in Egypt, dating from the 2nd cent. A.D. and later, although made as pictures of individuals, are definitely abstractions: they reveal a reduction of the illusionistic and seemingly real light and shade of Roman and Pompeiian painting to an abstract formula of flat planes and thick contours—a simplification that immediately detracts from the reality of the form. The eyes too come to be enormously enlarged as if the better to suggest the indwelling ghostly presence of the dead. One could rightly say that they are "soulful" because, like the Palmyrene grave reliefs, these are portraits of the *spirit* of the deceased rather than replicas of his physical self.

Although the discussion of Christian art is omitted from this article, it is to be noted that the art of the Coptic Church in Egypt during the first six centuries of the Christian era must be regarded as a phase of Late Antique art. Subjects and techniques of pagan and Egyptian mythology survive, but these, as well as the Christian subjects, are handled in a manner distinctive of this local school. It happens that textiles are the principal survivals of Coptic culture, and even the sculpture is reduced to a patternized formula dryly and deeply cut, that is distinctly suggestive of a flat black and white design in weaving.

The Orient. Continuing our investigation of Late Antique art in the East, we find that in many respects the art of Sasanian

Persia (226-632) presents the same mixture of classical and Oriental elements that is at the root of this whole world-wide manifestation. In this case the oriental elements are revivals of themes and techniques of the Achaemenid period; these are combined in rather haphazard fashion with Roman motifs and methods. Recent excavations at Shapur have revealed that Roman craftsmen were employed by the King of Kings, following his defeat of the Roman emperor Valerian in 260 A.D. The famous relief at Naqsh-i-Rustam, memorializing this victory, has the rigid symmetry and frozen, static quality of Achaemenid art, combined with such devices as over-lapping planes of relief and other details of Roman origin. The famous Victories or angels decorating the grotto of Khosrau II (590-628) at Taq-i-Bustan are the exact Sasanian counterparts of the Nike of the Golden Gate of Constantinople.

It was largely due to the intimate commercial relations between northwestern India and the Roman Orient that a local school of Late Antique art came into being in the province of Gandhāra in about the 2nd cent. A.D. Although a survival of Hellenistic culture in these regions during the centuries after the invasion of Alexander of Macedon may have had something to do with the origins of this school, both the types and techniques of Gandhāra sculpture are so closely related to Late Roman art and to the work at Palmyra there can be little doubt that the so-called Greco-Buddhist school of art is simply the easternmost extension of the Late Antique styles. (See INDIAN ART.)

Conclusion. It must not be supposed that the development seen in Late Antique art came to a sudden and abrupt end with the final collapse of the Roman empire. The tendencies initiated in the twilight of the Roman world really attain their final expression in the art of the Byzantine empire. It could even be said that certain aspects of Romanesque and Gothic sculpture are the final steps in what might be described as the spiritualization of Graeco-Roman art. In exactly similar fashion the local schools of Late Antique art in India and Iran exercised a powerful influence on the entire later development of religious art in Central Asia and the Far East. In many respects Late Antique art belongs to the culture of the Middle Ages. It could be said to represent the same metaphysical reinterpretation of classical form as the doctrines of Plotinus in relation to the thought of the Greek world.

See Chabot, J. B., *Choix d'Inscriptions de Palmyre,* 1922; Delbrueck, R., *Die Consulardiptychen,* 1929 and *Spätantike Kaiserporträts,* 1933; Duthuit, G., *La Sculpture Copte,* 1931; Ferri, S., *Arte Romana sul Danubio,* 1933 and *Arte Romana sul Reno,* 1931; Haseloff, A., *Pre-Romanesque Art in Italy,* 1930; Hinks, Roger, *Carolingian Art,* 1935; Ingholt, II., *Studier over Palmyrensk Skultur,* 1928; Morey, C. R., *The Sarcophagus of Claudia Antonia Sabina,* 1924; Peirce, H. and Tyler, R., *L'Art Byzantin,* I. 1932, II. 1934; Riegel, A., *Spätrömische Kunstindustrie,* 1927; Rostovtzeff, M., *Dura-Europos and its Art,* 1938; Sarre, F., *Die Kunst des Alten Persien,* 1922; Strong, E., *Roman Sculpture,* 1907.   —B.R.

La Tène art. See Celtic art.

lateral parts. See STAGESETTING.

LATIN AMERICAN ART. Twenty independent countries, from Mexico in the North to Chile and Argentina in the South, occupying more than half a hemisphere, extending from the temperate zone across the tropics to the temperate zone again, with great variety of climate and topography, and varying national and racial heritages and mixtures, necessarily present a diversified historical art development and considerable variety in contemporary art.

Historically this area of the Western Hemisphere formed the Portugese Colony which is now Brazil, and, at the greatest extension of the Spanish power, the 8 Spanish colonies known as Vice-royalties and Captaincies General, administratively distinct, and also distinct in cultural development and in character. These original divisions, based in part on the order of Conquest and in part on pre-Conquest native circles of influence, furnished the frame of development of art during Colonial times, and to an extent determine certain art tendencies even today.

All 20 countries use Spanish as their official language, with two exceptions: Brazil, where Portugese is spoken, and Haiti, French since 1697, where French is the established language.

Colonial period (16th to 19th cent.). The Spanish-speaking countries—all colonies of Spain before the 19th cent. wars for independence,—derived their principal influences in all the arts through and from Spain. Soon after the Conquest (Mexico, 1521; Peru, and Ecuador, 1534), plans for towns and buildings, and in some cases architects, painters and sculptors, arrived in the principal centers to fill the need for construction of settlements, administrative buildings, and the churches that were the first permanent structures after military conquest.

In the great early centers of the Spanish Colonial Empire, where Colonial art in all its forms developed and flourished most richly during three centuries (the Vice-royalties of Mexico, Peru and New Granada and the Captaincy General of Guatemala, corresponding approximately to what are today Mexico, Peru, Bolivia, Colombia, Ecuador and Central America) the Spaniards found well developed Indian civilizations. These were very different from Spain's European-Moorish Christian tradition, but they had achieved impressive tangible artistic expression. Their Indian creators had trained hands, skills in construction and decoration, that made them apt workmen in the imported style imposed by the Spanish conquerors.

The great numbers of buildings erected during the Colonial period reflected Spanish styles, with more or less local adaptation and detail. The earliest structures rose on the West Indian islands, first stronghold of the Spanish power, where, in Santa Domingo, Porto Rico and Cuba, fortresses, churches and fortified dwellings date from the early 16th cent. and are little more than direct importations of utilitarian forms. The original and vital Spanish American architecture, derived from Spain but with character of its own, and all the arts that accompanied it, took form slightly later in the continental colonies that coincided with the regions of high pre-Conquest civilization. (See Mexican Colonial Architecture; Spanish Architecture in the New World.)

Sources of buildings, and even more of decoration and other art work, were varied. Among the missionary builders of churches were men who knew a little of architecture, painting, and sculpture, when professionals were lacking, as they frequently were outside of the principal settlements. They planned the adornment of their churches inside and out. Spanish, Italian and Flemish art works were imported, and sometimes ornaments as well as buildings were fashioned after remembered Spanish originals. Illustrated books were fertile sources, and engravings of European architecture, painting and the other arts served as models and suggestion for paintings and sculpture and ornament as well as for architecture and detail in the New World in places and cases where the con-

nection with Spanish arts was not more direct. As always in Colonial societies great effort was made to establish in the new setting all that had been the customary adjuncts of civilized life at home, as quickly as it was possible to do so. Here it was not only a need of the settlers, but as well a device for subduing the Indians and establishing a pattern of life and of belief for them.

Side by side with the importation and imposition of Spanish patterns of living and of art styles, which in many instances absorbed some aboriginal elements or influences, or took on adaptations to new conditions, there continued intact native arts and crafts, notably those for every day use. They profited in some cases by improved techniques and added resources acquired from the Spaniards, but continued essentially unchanged otherwise, and apart, even as many habits of living did. Many of the arts and crafts existing today among the people in countries where large Indian populations persist undoubtedly exemplify such a history of continuous practice, side by side with those imported, just as details of local customs and living intermingle the influences that are so difficult to disentangle of the double inheritance of the aboriginal and of the superimposed Spanish civilizations.

By the end of the 16th cent. a considerable number of European artists were in Mexico and in the other older colonies. At the same time native artists and artist-craftsmen, of Spanish, of Indian and of mixed Spanish and Indian descent, but trained entirely in Spanish styles and traditions, began to appear, and from that time on took a dominant part in the development of Spanish Colonial art. Some few went to Europe for training and returned. Most learned from imported European art or from the immigrant European masters, working out in some cases a style reflecting faithfully their originals and sources, in others making a considerable departure to form a personal style or to conform to a local group style.

All the principal colonial capitals had by the late 16th or early 17th cent. groups of painters and sculptors of some interest. In Mexico, the diverse influences of the Renaissance were firmly established by 1600. A little later local centers with local styles were to develop, and native-born artists with distinctive personalities became numerous, not only in Mexico City, but in other cities throughout the Vice-royalty. In general, Mexico's colonial painting carried on faithfully the Renaissance tradition and reflected Spanish styles and tastes, with some time lag to be sure. Folk and popular and provincial artists did not conform, of course, but the main current of competent professional Mexican painting found culmination in a baroque decorative and monumental style of originality and considerable grandeur and power in the late 17th and early 18th cents.

In the other colonies, the same influences were active and much the same course of development occurred. In the 17th cent. each capital or cultural center had its Colonial master, thoroughly trained in European tradition, familiar with European styles of his time, working brilliantly in accord with them, but competent in his own right and making his own contribution, to stand as the Old Master of national art history.

The complete roster of those painters counted important in the four Colonies which contributed most to art development from the late 16th cent. to the 19th is too long, but the significant achievements can be summarized in a few recognized leaders of each place and time, of whom something is known. and to whom extant works of some importance are attributed, viz.: *for Mexico*: Baltasar de Echave Orio (Sp. c. 1548-Mex. c. 1620) ; Baltasar de Echave Ibia (c. 1583-c. 1650), son of preceding ; Baltasar de Echave Rioja (1632-1682), grandson of Echave Orio; Cristóbal de Villalpando (c. 1639-1714) ; Miguel Cabrera (1695-1768) ; Fray Miguel de Herrera (act. 1725-1752) ; José de Ibarra (1688-1756) ; José de Paez (c. 1715-after 1790) ; *for Guatemala*: Francisco (de) Villalpando (17th cent.) ; Antonio de Montúfar (17th cent.) ; Thomas de Merlo (late 17th cent.-1739) ; *for Columbia*: Gregorio Vásquez de Arce y Ceballos (1638-1711) ; *for Ecuador*: Miguel de Santigo (c. 1605-1673) ; Nicolas Javier de Goríbar (act. c. 1656-1688) ; *for Peru*: Francisco Bejarano (act. early 17th cent., Lima) ; Pedro de Saldaña (late 16th cent., Cuzco) ; Lorenzo Sánchez, Juan Osorio, Marcos Zapata and Juan Espinoza de lós Monteros (all active in the 17th cent., Cuzco).

Naturally, most painting, esp. of the earliest period, was religious in subject. A certain amount of portraiture was done from the beginning, and became relatively more important in the 18th and early 19th cent.

In some places and at some periods, the imported styles, were weakened by lack of direct contact, or diluted or modified by divergent personal interpretations, local influences, in part indigenous, or by local taste, to take on the character of a distinctive style, derived from the common tradition but changed profoundly. Cuzco is the clearest example. It developed its own recognizable series of styles, in part production of workshops or anonymous artists but with some leaders known by name. Quito, Lima, some of the provincial cities of Mexico in the 17th and 18th cents. had groups practicing distinctive styles with regional provincial characteristics of great interest.

In some cases it was a special product as well as a style which made a center famous. Most centers probably produced for local consumption, but in a few cases their specialties became famous and they exported. Thus Quito, which attained enough celebrity in painting to send works as far as Chile, developed in addition a specialty of fine polychrome religious sculpture. Spanish sculptors brought knowledge of the art to Quito, but the long line of gifted Colonial sculptors invented new types and refined the technique. Among many, Father Carlos of the 17th cent. and the Indian Caspicara of the 18th are perhaps the most important. Tradition has it that in the 18th cent. Quito exported its figures to every part of the Spanish-speaking world.

Guatemala likewise became famous for polychrome sculpture which was sought throughout Mexico and Central America. Among a number of sculptors famous in the 17th cent. and known by name and by attributed works Alonso de la Paz (1605-1676) is the recognized great master. Quirio Cataño, active in the last half of the 16th cent. was scarcely less celebrated, and Evaristo Zúáiga whose important work dates from the early 18th cent. carried on the tradition.

Polychrome sculpture, to adorn altars and decorate chapels and churches, was produced widely, and ranged in quality from the delicate perfection and richness of Quito and Guatemala to crude, late folk art figurines —still most frequently of saints,—but heartily popular and rudely provincial, produced at a distance from the sophisticated centers.

Sculpture in both stone and wood was highly developed in the Colonies of Mexico, New Granada, Guatemala and Peru. Stone sculpture had ample scope as decoration surrounding doorways and on the façades of churches, and ranged from the elaborate and rich detail of cathedrals and important churches in such leading centers as Mexico,

Puebla, Lima, Cuzco, Quito, La Paz to a few moldings or symbolic motifs for the simple chapels and churches of monastic establishments and of small cities and villages everywhere. Some was used on public buildings and on the more pretentious private dwellings as well, usually above doorways. Sometimes pulpit or font was carved stone, or a fountain or a free-standing cross in a churchyard had carved ornament. Spanish styles were influential, but very often in detail they were modified or enriched by local influences, sometimes clearly indigenous, or by personal fantasy, or perhaps improvisation taking the place of academic knowledge.

The richly ornamented altar, reredos, chapels, doors, choir loft, pulpit, choir stalls, and other furniture of church and sacristy, and the furnishings of public buildings and homes, offered opportunities for wood carvers. Usually these artist-craftsmen in wood, as in stone, were anonymous. Though the general quality of their work is fine, with abundance of skill and imagination and a sure sense of decoration, only by exception was it thought of as creative art in the same sense as paintings and the polychrome sculptures were. In the majority of cases the carvers were probably of Indian or part Indian descent. Skilled gilders and painters usually completed the work of the carvers, and in a few cases also gained such fame as to be known by name. In Peruvian, Bolivian, Ecuadorian and Colombia churches, the original rich interior decoration, including the carved and gilded altars, with their paintings and polychrome saints, are usually preserved. Mexican churches have in most cases lost their altars and chapels, and with them something of the richness characteristic of the best of the Latin-American decorative styles.

In Mexico, Ecuador and Peru the abundance of silver fostered fine work, in church ornaments and domestic ornaments and tableware of great weight and richness, baroque in style. Fine work in iron and bronze was done also, in window grills, door grills and studding, on locks and hinges and other hardware for house and furniture.

Art has no such long nor rich history in the other four Colonies (the Captaincy General of Cuba, the Captaincy General of Venezuela, the Vice-royalty of Buenos Aires, and the Captaincy General of Chile). These regions were remote from the great centers of Mexico and Peru, could not draw on established Indian civilizations with their ready prepared skills, and, in the case of Buenos Aires and Chile, settlement came later and material growth was slower.

Venezuela, notwithstanding its proximity to Columbia and the Caribbean, has little to show before the end of the seventeenth century, perhaps partly because of losses in the disastrous earthquake of 1641. In the eighteenth century, it had stone and wood carvers of competence who decorated churches and houses, and skilled cabinet-makers who turned out fine furniture and woodwork. There were painters and religious sculptors from the seventeenth century on, but they are not to be compared in number and achievement with those of the more active Colonial schools.

Cuba began immediately after the discovery of America its growth in architecture, but in painting nothing remains earlier than the work of José Nicolas de la Escalera (c. 1734 c.-1804), a painter of religious subjects in the accepted European style of the time.

Northern Argentina, in close contact with Upper Peru, shared its artistic development to an extent, and churches in Córdoba illustrate admirable achievement in stone carving and woodwork by the late 17th and early 18th cents., and in the old houses of Salta, fine 18th cent. metal work, wood carving and stone work are proof of the skill of the local artist-craftsmen. The Colonial churches of the region, founded by missionaries, recall their stately and rich prototypes in Peru, in some cases, but with less sophisticated style, and a sincerity and directness and, frequently, indigenous influences as well, that give them a special savor.

In Buenos Aires and elsewhere in Argentina, architecture, and in general the accompanying arts, date in their oldest examples from the late 18th cent. However, in addition to the late art development under Peruvian influence in the North, the Vice-royalty of Buenos Aires (which included, in addition to Bolivia and Argentina, what is now Uruguay) offered one native art development:— that fostered by the Jesuit missionaries in the 17th and first half of the 18th cent. among the Guarani Indians. This was in territory which today is divided between Argentina, Paraguay and Brazil. Now known only by ruins and a few pieces of sculpture which have found their way to museums, the Guarani towns of brick and adobe, and the churches of stone, roofed in wood, represented an individual development of great interest, dependent on the skill of the Indian converts under the able and energetic direction of the Jesuits. In addition to elaborate decoration on the façades of the churches, in which the detail appears almost always to be indigenous, religious figurines of saints in polychromed wood were produced for church decoration, for the local need, but also for export as far as Buenos Aires. Both carvers and decorative painters—trained Indian craftsmen,—are supposed to have worked in Buenos Aires and elsewhere when needed. The Guarani artists included painters of religious pictures, and engravers, but only scattered examples of their work are known, and it appears to have been decorative rather than strongly creative.

Architecture and art developed relatively late in Chile. A severe earthquake in 1647 destroyed earlier buildings and with them work of native craftsmen in altars and other church ornament. By the late 17th cent. much art had been imported from other centers in South America, some native sculptors had appeared, painters from Cuzco had made some contribution to the development of local painting, and the baroque style also was having its influence. In the 18th cent. a group of European craftsmen was imported by the Jesuits and gave considerable encouragement to art of all kinds.

Brazil stands apart from the remainder of Latin America, for its vigorous Colonial art derives, like its language, from Portugal, not Spain. In its territory no great Indian civilization existed and the flowering of its architecture—an original development of Portuguese baroque—took place in the 18th cent. (See Brazil, Colonial Architecture of.) Franz Post, one of the six Dutch artists imported by Prince Maurice of Nassau during the 30 years of Dutch occupation in the 17th cent., was the first to introduce Brazil's tropical landscape to European art. Neither he nor his companions left any trace on the art of Brazil, however. Church painting followed European styles, with something of the same exuberance of the architecture. The work that stands out in the Colonial period is the elaborate and sometimes somewhat bizarre sculpture of the celebrated and romantic cripple, called "Aleijadinho", who is associated principally with the statuary in Minas Geraes. His figures in both stone and wood never fail in power and expressiveness, and though their origins in Portuguese art are clear, they represent a personal and native development.

The Nineteenth Century in all Latin American countries was politically a period of unrest and revolution, marked by the continuous struggle, with greater or less difficulty, through battle and a varied series of political transitions, from the status of colonies of Spain or Portugal to independent republics. In the 18th cent. religious art had been less important; portraits, painted from the beginning of important personnages of the colonies, became increasingly numerous. In the 19th cent. portraits of the heroes of the revolution, and some historical academic painting—usually on a large scale—came into prominence. Except for portraits by self-taught artists, successful because of the intense desire for realism and expression, and the sincerity of the conscientious painters, European influences, largely French, but also Italian, were dominant. In the early years of the century foreign artists visited most of the countries, recorded charmingly their picturesque life, and sometimes stayed to become masters of drawing and painting. In 1828 an Academy of Arts was formed in Brazil and French teachers were installed. In most other countries, some comparable academic European direction was established by the middle of the century. Especially promising art students were sent to Europe for study, and invariably fell into academic styles. They returned, bringing the skills, but also the art ideas of Europe with them. There resulted everywhere, except among a few self-taught, naïve and dissident artists, whose work was relegated by their contemporaries to inferior rank if considered at all as art, a dominant, vigorous, transplanted European academism in both painting and sculpture, everywhere in Latin America.

For the most part, though these men did found the tradition of the craft of the arts in their respective countries, their work and their names have only historical interest. However, a few painters by their personal force either escaped occasionally from the academic stamp to produce some work of essential quality, or stood aside from the common tradition and yet made a direct contribution to art development, sometimes through rediscovery by artists of today. A few type examples are worth noting in this period: Franklin Rawson (1819-1871) for portraits, sensitive and occasionally naïvely decorative, and Prilidiano Pueyrredón (1823-1870) for portraits and genre scenes of quality and power, both of Argentina; Juan Manuel Blanes (1830-1901) for portraits, historical compositions of great size, and genre paintings of vigor, of Uruguay; Pancho Fierro (act. mid 19th cent.) lively recorder in watercolor and drawings of contemporary types and customs in a direct, personal, and somewhat naïve style, of Peru, whose work is greatly savored by the Peruvian *indigenistas* and has had some little influence on contemporary painting there.

Contemporary art. In the 20th cent. gifted students continued to go from their respective Latin American countries to Europe to complete their art training. Paris was the most popular center for study, though a good number went to Spain and Italy, and a few to Germany. Most traveled also in Italy, some in Spain and a few in Germany, to study the art of the museums. By far the majority, wherever they went, followed the traditional course of academic art, and that was what they took back to their own countries, what prevailed also in the academies of art,—usually national schools supported by their respective governments,—and what was approved by cultivated taste among the public at home. Some few were deeply stirred by the currents of futurism in Italy, of cubism and other new movements of the period from 1910 on, in France and in Germany. Some few, like Diego Rivera (1886-) of Mexico, Emilio Pettoruti (1892-) of Argentina, entered directly into current movements, assimilated them and contributed to European styles for a short period, but for most the new tendencies were a stirring to self-examination, an encouragement to venture from the deep-traced paths of tradition, and a stimulus to seek their own way. At second hand, the impulse toward freedom affected even those who developed at home, as well as those abroad who did not directly enter into any of the new European movements. This stimulus from Europe, and the lifeless state into which academic art had come in its imported forms, together account for new developments in the art of all countries during the 20's and 30's.

In general, it can be said that there is everywhere a tendency to develop art in increasing independence from Europe, and with a growing reference to national environment and sources. Sometimes it is a deliberate effort to discover the new and exotic, to derive from native sources, and, sometimes, to depend on content alone to create a new art. More often it is a sensitive exploration of the environment, which may . reflect its conditions and characteristics without any obvious recourse to subject matter. The results range all the way from Mexico's vigorous, original, independent school of painting, deeply rooted in the past and present of its people and country, to the gradual and subtle adaptation of international expression to the national scene in the contemporary art of such countries as Argentina and Chile.

Interestingly enough the two major tendencies exemplified respectively by Mexico and by Argentina, coincide to an extent with the presence or absence of the pre-Conquest Indian civilizations, so that it is no exaggeration to say that the pattern of the Indian past contributes to contemporary art just as it established the distribution of art development during the Colonial period.

Mexico's is the most brilliant example of a Latin American art development consciously turning to the sources of its own land and working out an independent movement. It has had numerous brilliant painters, and continues its development uninterrupted, and enriched by a vigorous evolution of styles in the work of successive generations of younger artists. (See MEXICAN PAINTING, CONTEMPORARY.) By virtue of its accomplishment it leads in this modern movement—that tendency to draw on indigenous material as subject and as source for contemporary art.

Developments similar to that of Mexico are to be seen elsewhere, but less powerful and less important. They appear logically enough as one of the accepted art expressions in most countries of strong Indian heritage, especially where the Indian past continues into the living present by virtue of large Indian or predominantly Indian populations. There is no doubt that the example of Mexico has had some influence both on the tendency in general, and on individual artists.

Peru is second only to Mexico in the development of its *indigenista* school of contemporary art. Its use of Indian subjects, as frequent though not exclusive material, gives it a superficial resemblance to Mexican painting, which disappears on closer examination. It draws its strength from simplified and rhythmic handling of themes of the country: Indian life, Indian villages, mountains, llamas, Colonial architecture, characteristic types and customs of the country. Its artists derive their patterns from the study of pre-Columbian Peruvian art, the Colonial period, and the Indian arts of today, with a tendency to stylize and abstract which results, in the work of some of the artists, in a type of expressionism, while others have developed a more purely decorative style. For the most part, there is avoidance of illustration, which is the danger of an art dependent on subject. No such impressive development has taken place as in Mexico; neither in the dominating personalities nor in the number of active artists can Peru match Mexico. There is, however, the authentic savor of a sincere, workmanlike tradition deriving its themes and its expression from the country and its people, and feeling its differences from European art as a reflection of the differences from European environment.

Among the Peruvians should be noted: José Sabogal (1888-), painter and teacher chief theorist and in many ways the leader of the group; Julia Codesido (1892-), sensitive colorist and increasingly expressionistic painter; Camilo Blas (1903-), working in bold color, often with humor, and with a tendency to stylize and to create linear patterns. A younger group continues exploring native themes and feeling, contributes personal styles of some interest, and promises to carry on development of a national art, freed from academic traditions, but sound in technique.

In other countries of Indian background and large contemporary Indian population there is also semblance of an *indigenista* movement in some form.

Bolivia has turned to indigenous material, and the most active contemporary tendency has been a decorative treatment of Indian types or typical scenery. For the most part, however, the indigenous interest has been illustrational—a discovery of picturesque and exotic subject matter by artists trained in Europe and essentially European in point of view. There has been no intimate understanding and no real penetration in art into the land and its people. The dominant style has remained true to its academic origins, and has in no sense,—but content,—developed anything new, original nor really modern. A few younger Bolivian artists, both painters and sculptors, give evidence of having more to offer. Not all of them exploit indigenous themes, though all have a profound sense of the life of the Indian people and the ancient past of Bolivia in pre-Columbian and Colonial times. It is in their work that contemporary development of value is to be expected. Among a number should be noted Marina Nuñez del Prado, sculptor of Indian types and dances, in increasingly abstract rhythmic style; Roberto Berdecio and Antonio Sotomayor, painters of Indian types and scenes, occasionally. None of these artists is now resident in Bolivia.

In Ecuador, there are a number of young, gifted, powerful artists imbued with Indian life as it is a part of the present and past of the country, and using their studies of it and of the country as an avenue of emotional expression. They identify themselves with this Indian life and paint from within it as a well understood and valued heritage. Eduardo Kingman and Oswaldo Guayasamin (Calero) are promising examples chosen from a number. Beside them are Ecuadorians of well formed European training and tradition, some few academic and illustrational, most modern and sensitive, but not associated with advance guard movements. They paint either material that has no obvious connection in subject or feeling with the country, or when they paint native themes do so ably and well, but as outsiders. In this group Pedro León and Sergio Guarderas are examples. Finally there are some resident Europeans who find in the native themes occasion for stylizations, expressionistic distortions or decorations. Olga Anhalzer-Fisch and Jan Schreuder are typical.

The other country of large Indian population today, Guatemala, has no great art development. Its most eminent painter, Carlos Merida (1893-), was originally associated with the Mexican movement, and at present tends toward abstraction, influenced in character, color and form certainly by his rich experience and feeling for Indian arts, but subtly, not obviously. Other painters in Guatemala, except for a minority who study Indian types in a purely illustrational if competent fashion, work entirely in an international modern style, sensitive and adequate and experimental, treating Indian and native themes incidentally.

Colombia, the remaining one of the regions coinciding with the great Colonial centers in which art and architecture flourished, and which before the Conquest had developed a high civilization, does not have a large Indian population today. It has artists of European training who use native subject matter as exotic illustration, a few younger artists, like Luis Albert Acuña, who know well the arts of the Indian past and from them have drawn stimulus for a personal style, and a large group of artists, for example, Ignacio Gomez Jaramillo, some of whom know Europe, especially Spain, who work in the Spanish and other European contemporary traditions with little regard for such native elements as persist still in their own environment. In comparison with the three foregoing countries these are scarcely perceptible in modern Colombia, for the Indian past is well overlaid with European culture. The rise of an *indigenista* feeling is hardly to be expected therefore, and would indeed seem artificial except as it prompts a personal, lyrical and decorative expression in individual artists.

This is even truer of the other Latin American countries, which had no great Indian civilizations, and in which the Indian populations have either disappeared completely as in Uruguay, or have made no direct contribution to the cultural development of the country. It is not surprising to find the international patterns of modern art strongly established in all of them. A few of the leading countries have art movements and artists to note, with marked tendencies toward individual development within the European tradition.

Cuba has always felt close to both Paris and New York and reflects clearly the activity of both centers. Some of the School of Paris styles flourish there side by side with less advanced and more individual styles, but all derived predominently from French 20th cent. painting. Names of interest are Mario Carreño, Antonio Gattorno, Amelia Pelaez, Jorge Arche, Cundo Bermúdez.

Chile, following an extensive program of training its most promising artists in Europe in the late 20's, has developed a contemporary school in which Impressionism is dominant, with noticeable interest in the post-Impressionists Cezanne, Renoir and Van Gogh occurring, and a very few artists reflecting the School of Paris, and exhibiting a touch of surrealism and abstraction. Sculpture, well developed, has been influenced to good effect by Bourelle and Maillol. Representative tendencies are exemplified by Jorge Caballero, Hector Banderas, José Perotti, Camilo Mori, Armando Lira, Laura Rodig, Raul Vargas, Lily Garafulic.

Argentina shows more clearly the influence of the School of Paris, in the work of individuals and in the variety of styles. A few have come under the influence of Italian and Spanish modern movements, but French influence is dominant. Notable among the mature artists, European trained, who began by close association with European styles, later to evolve highly personal expressions of their own, are Horacio Butler (1897-) and Emilio Pettoruti (1892-). Butler, early interested in French modern movements, turned to scenes of hsi own land, deeply felt, strongly modelled, in well composed rather personal color harmonies. Pettoruti, who was associated with Italian futurism, continued

a personal development of abstraction on his return to Argentina. Other names to note are Onofrio Pacenza, Lino Spilimbergo, Antonio Berni, Ernesto Scotti, Ramón Gómez Cornet, Alfredo Bigatti.

European influences are strong in Uruguay also. From the large group which reflects European styles in great variety, most interesting are perhaps the abstract painter J. Torres García and the original Pedro Figari (1861-1938) in his naïve, direct, clear-colored, sprightly memories of the Montevideo of his childhood.

Venezuela, like the other countries, sent its most promising artists to Europe for study. On their return these artists have carried on the traditions of contemporary Europe for the most part, though through Armando Lira, Chile's contemporary development has had some influence there, and a few of the younger artists have been interested in Mexico. Armando Reverón, Paris trained, but whose work has developed a highly personal style, is probably the outstanding personality among a large group of competent artists. Francisco Narvaez is an interesting sculptor.

In Brazil, too, the European modern art styles, and especially those of France, have had fertile influence. Despite a great development in functional modern architecture, which has made its own distinguished contribution to the movement, Rio de Janeiro inclines to be less progressive in the other arts than Sao Paulo, in which is centered the Salao de Maio and the whole focus of the more advanced art ferment of Brazil. European movements of the advance guard find adaptation and local exponents there in great variety. Candido Portinari is the only name as yet to be well known outside the country, but among others should be noted Lucy Citti Ferreira, Barbara Ruchti, Flavio de Carvalho, Manoel Martins.

The influence of European art is clear and has been dominant in these Latin American countries, and also in all those remaining which are not specifically mentioned here. This influence, however, has in most cases been a point of departure, and a fertile guide rather than a limitation. The artists of each country have worked freely within the congenial tradition, making their own personal contribution and adapting themselves and their work to their own environment. In general they have thought of themselves as belonging to an international movement, have thought of their respective countries as they resemble Europe. Only as a minor trend, and not in the deliberate manner of Mexicans and Peruvians, have they usually thought of the art of their country as a nationalist expression, or of its possible national styles. In the last years of the 30's, however, there had been less movement to Europe, and with the attainment of maturity and assurance by those who had studied there earlier, a tendency to feel more independent artistically, more assured and self-sufficient, within the art growth of their own country, began to appear. This trend may foreshadow a growth of national styles in a more conscious way, as national local styles already are perceptible in fact. To be entirely self-sufficient in these countries of European art tradition seems scarcely possible, since, except for Argentina, there are no large collections to exemplify the tradition. There is likely to be, however, as a result of the war, a deepening of the consciousness of differences from Europe. This feeling may foster the development of national feeling and adaptation of European styles to a more consciously national expression.

In nearly all countries, even where there is no indication of any tendency toward national expression or feeling in painting or sculpture, there have been established within the last decade or two schools of applied arts, or movements among artist-craftsmen, which have deliberately, and with varying success, turned to historical national sources for design,—in pottery, ornament, textiles, etc. It is interesting to note also, that in the less formal arts of prints and illustration, well developed but scarcely regarded as art on the same level as painting and sculpture, there is much exploration of native material, even to the point of some influence on style, in countries appearing in their painting as predominantly European in tradition.

Countries which have produced notable contemporary work in prints are Argentina, where monotypes, etchings, and engravings achieve technical excellence; Uruguay, which also shows preference for metal plate prints; Peru and Ecuador, in both of which bold, decorative woodcuts, often on indigenous themes, are outstanding; Brazil, where some of the finest work by Portinari and Santa Rosa is in lithography, produces work in the other print mediums as well; and Mexico, which has established an active group of print-makers in all mediums, but finds the autographic lithograph and the decorative wood cut especially sympathetic.

Mural painting. In accordance with church tradition, mural painting was introduced early in the Spanish New World. Again in the countries of Indian civilization, Mexico and Peru, it was not a foreign idea, as Mayas, Aztecs and Peruvian peoples all had painted walls. Many of the early churches and monasteries were decorated with wall paintings, usually tempera on plaster, in color or in grisaille, with saints or with ornamentation, perhaps copied from books. The important development of murals in Latin American countries has been contemporary, however. Mexico led with the revival of true fresco in the early 20's under the leadership of Diego Rivera and José Clemente Orozco and others. This revival stimulated similar work in all other American countries, first perhaps in the United States, where both Orozco and Rivera executed important commissions in fresco, trained assistants, and by the topical and symbolic subject-matter designed for the instruction and indoctrination of the masses, showed the way to a large following who worked in fresco and other mediums with a like purpose. Their example had some influence everywhere in Latin American countries. José Sabogal of Peru has worked in fresco, but has not had an opportunity to do a large wall in his own country; Alfredo Guido of Argentina has done some murals and instructs in mural design; Candido Portinari has painted numerous murals, in fresco and in other mediums, both in Brazil and in the United States; Ignacio Gomez Jaramillo of Colombia has done a few frescoes in Bogotá. However, the only artist who has executed any considerable number of murals, designed, like those of the Mexicans, to teach a lesson and illustrate a theme, instead of serving a decorative purpose only, is the Colombian Pedro Nel Gomez, who has painted for public buildings in Medellín numerous monumental frescoes illustrating social problems and historical subjects of national life.

Folk and Popular Arts. The native crafts of the Indian peoples, as well as adaptions to their understanding of imported crafts and arts, all used as a part of everyday living, are the basis of folk and popular arts in the countries of Indian inheritance and population. Weaving of great variety and quality, and pottery of diversified forms and uses,—from pots to toys,—illustrate well such arts in Mexico, Guatemala, Ecuador, Peru and Bolivia, all notable centers of such production. Individual towns or localities often have their specialties as, the pottery of Puebla, the lacquers of Michoacan, the textiles of the diverse villages of Guatemala or of Peru, the topos or shawl pins of Bolivian settlements. The wide range of Mexican popular arts and the variety of Guatemalan textiles are well known, for they have developed into an export and tourist trade as well as production for local use. The folk arts of the other countries are less known, for no tourist trade to speak of has developed. In Ecuador, baskets, textiles and carvings are the principal products. In Peru, besides weaving, elaborate knitting of dolls, caps and mittens is carried on, silver ornaments are made, wood carvings of llamas, and pottery depicting bulls are produced as toys. The most interesting craft is, however, undoubtedly the carving of gourds in lively scenes of musicians, markets and other episodes of everyday life, with great spirit and a sure sense of decoration.

In many countries of Indian culture, masks for dances given on religious festivals are an important craft. That is especially true of Mexico, Bolivia and Guatemala.

In the countries of European heritage some crafts, brought from Europe with the original settlers, or developments in response to special conditions, persist. Some forms of pottery and weaving in Chile and Argentina, the gaucho's silver studded belts and braided leather quirts in Argentina, are such examples, but they are rarer and less exotic than the crafts the Indian peoples preserve. In Brazil a certain amount of popular work is done by the Negroes in the Northern cities; —especially interesting are crudely but powerfully carved small figures that are probably fetishes much like those more aesthetically mature ones produced by their ancestors in Africa.

The ex-votos or miracle pictures produced in most countries on the occasion of cures, recoveries, or escape from accident or danger and put in churches as commemorative tablets,—naïve and childish often, but sincere and decorative work of some amateur or sign painter,—are among the most charming works of popular art. They are well known and valued in Mexican art, but they occurred everywhere, probably from very early times. Many were produced in the 19th cent. everywhere, and occasionally are still produced, just as the silver representation of legs or arms or hearts, ex-votos also, are still used everywhere as they have been for several hundred years.

The boldly carved and colored saints, often with homely attributes of daily and familiar life, and the processional images of provincial churches furnish other examples of folk arts.

In all countries, once the large cities are left behind, even including countries of European culture and good or comparatively good communications, like Argentina and Chile, individuals are still dependent on their own skills, and in more remote sections in less developed countries, like Bolivia and Peru and Ecuador, are largely self-dependent for all they use. The result is the making of many articles for their own use or for trade against other needed articles made by someone else. Usually these objects have some decoration or fineness of form that puts the best examples in the class of popular arts.

Few countries, at least as far as known, have the immense variety and richness of crafts that Mexico displays, but in the other Latin American countries there is undoubtedly much more to be discovered and explored in the field of traditional popular arts as well as of those of today, than has been as yet reported and described. See Academia Nac. de Bellas Artes, *Documentos de Arte Argentino,* 1940; Argentina Nat. Committee, *Fine Arts in Argentina,* 1939; Diaz, Victor Miguel, *Las Bellas Artes en Guatemala,* 1934; Goodwin, Philip L. (Mus. of Mod. Art cat.); *Brazil Builds,* 1943; Gómez Sicre, José, *Cuban Painting Today,* 1944; Inst. Nac. de Artes Plásticas, *300 Años de Arte en Cuba,* 1940; Kirstein, Lincoln (Mus. of Mod. Art cat.), *The Latin-American Collection of the Museum of Modern Art,* 1943; Morley, G. L. M., *Introduction to Contemporary Peruvian Painting,* 1942; Navarro, J. G., *Ten Lectures on Ecuadorian Art,* 1935; Nucete-Sardi, José, *Notas sobre la Pintura y la Escultura en Venezuela,* 1940; Pagano, José León, *El Arte de Los Argentinos;* Salao de Maio, *RASM,* 1939; Soc. de Acuarelistas y Grabadores (Argentina), *25 Aniversario,* 1939; Solá, Miguel, *Historia del Arte Hispano-Americano,* 1935; Toledo Mus. of Art, *Chilean Contemporary Art,* 1942; Velásquez Chavez, Agusín, *Tres Siglos de Pintura Colonial Mexicana,* 1993; Zalamea, Jorge, *Nueve Artistas Colombianos (contemporáneos),* 1941. (NOTE: Many of the general historical surveys are incomplete and often inaccurate for lack of sufficient sources and of basic research. Few general surveys of contemporary art exist. Very little in English has been published as yet and this mostly in periodicals and on single artists. For helpful references and illustrations, usually periodical, see *Art* in annual *Handbook of Latin American Studies*.)   —G.L.M.M.

Latin American Music. The music of South America is of Indian and Latin heritage. Analogous to the history of her countries, so in her music the Spanish and Portuguese elements are dominant, both interwoven into the features of an ageless native art. Yet, in addition to such a blend of musical idioms from the Old and New Worlds, there are other factors at work, ideological and technical, which are leaving a distinct imprint of modernism on contemporary music South of the Rio Grande. Thus modern Mexican scores, in spite of a certain affinity with the ancient forms and rhythms of the Indians, display a progressive attitude achieved from the study of the technically most advanced trends in European composition. Likewise, the truly representative works from Brazil, Argentina, Chile or Peru all show modern strides—from the advanced employment of the new electrogenic media of performance to that of the twelve-tone scheme.

Obviously, the geographical location of South America no longer involves artistic isolation. Today, radio and records flood music all over the vast continent with its wide prairies, thick jungles and high mountains. Formerly, it was but a small number of cosmopolitan musicians that had, in Latin America's big cities, real access to the new art from abroad. Now, with the turn of a switch the average South American may hear the music of Schoenberg, Shostakovitch, or of his progressive North American neighbors. It is clear that the contemporary style in Cuba, Guatemala, Colombia and the other Latin American countries could not remain unaltered with these revolutionary inventions of electrogenic rendition.

On the other hand, nationalization appears to be one of the outstanding trends in the music of many South American countries. Whatever its basis—nationalistic ideology or mere *l'art pour l'art* exploitation of the rich native folklore—there is a group of composers, esp. in Argentina and Brazil, who want to throw overboard any model imported from the old continent and want to retain as much as possible from their own tunes and forms.

Among the forms of specifically Latin American origin certain dance types are in the foreground. In fact, dances from South America are the very exportations which the rest of the world has eagerly accepted for more than one hundred years. Today, the Latin countries continue this tradition of vitalizing their own musical performances and those of the other continents with terpsichorean spirit. Several of the fiery and sentimental types, like the Brazilian Congo, the Cuban Habanera, the Argentine Tango, appear now in symphonic garb: their style has been transformed just as was the old Hispanic sarabande with its integration into the instrumental suite of the baroque.

Reviewing the composers from South America, the name of the Brazilian Antonio Carlos Gomes might be mentioned first—since his opera *Il Guarany* (using Amazon-Indian themes) had, as early as 1870, great international success and threw the spotlight on the musical production of his country. Today, the dominant position is held by Heitor Villa-Lobos, an extremely prolific musician of many activities and remarkable imagination. With the Brazilian Villa Lobos, the Mexican Carlos Chavez is today one of the best known Latin American musician. Dividing his activities between composing, conducting and teaching, he has placed organizations and men under his leadership in Mexico City into the *avant-garde* of interpretative progress. The Argentine composers José Maria Castro and Juan José Castro have gained reputation outside Buenos Aires. The latter is also musical director at the Teatro Colón, the most important South American opera house. In connection with Argentina the fact is noteworthy that Manuel de Falla, the greatest living Spanish composer, is now making his home there: this will doubtless cause further interaction between the musical idioms of the old and new Hispanic countries.   —F.D.

Latin American Literature. See HISPANIC AMERICAN LITERATURE.

lattice. A decorative pattern of lines crossing each other at regular intervals to make regular openings of square or diamond shape.

Latvia, art of. Latvia, the central one of the Baltic Republics, was inhabited in prehistoric times by Finnic and Baltic populations and the early remains show the various types of East Baltic prohistory. They were abundantly adorned with swastikas of various forms in red and green areas.

Many of the antique decorations from the Iron Age still continue as popular adornments and motifs and the folk art still maintains the purest native inspirations.

During the medieval period Christianity was introduced and most of the country fell under the control of the various archbishops and the Knights of the Sword. There were bloody battles between these groups but both represented Germanic influence and introduced into the country **Baltic Gothic** which is represented in Riga by such monuments as the Dome Church (originally started in Romanesque times early in the 13th cent.) and the St. Peter's Church with the highest wooden steeple in the world (commenced by 1416). Here belong also the House of the Black Heads started in 1330 but often remodelled.

Later during the Swedish and Polish occupations after the turning of the Teutonic Knights to Protestanism, the architecture shows the usual influences. With the coming of Russian domination in the time of Peter the Great, we begin to find the same types of architecture that were adopted in Russia. As a result, Riga represents the usual architectural features of the various centuries, with a great deal of restoration and reconstruction, while in the country districts there are also monuments of all periods.

In the field of painting, while there are some remains of medieval work, the various artists fell under Russian and German influences and it was not until the time of Adam Alksnis (1864-1897) that there begins a native Latvian school of painting. The artists of this group are particularly interested in landscapes and they show the same melancholy lyricism, patient labor and soundness of character that are found in the literature. V. Purvits (b. 1872) won international fame with his landscapes and J. Rozentals (1866-1916) also won fame in ment lines. French influence became very strong even before the restoration of national independence. Since that time the modern developments have maintained the Latvian spirit and followed the various trends of European and esp. French art.

The same is true also of sculpture in the person of B. Dzenis (born 1879) and Z. Zalkalus (born 1876), a student of Rodin. Among the leaders of the younger generation are Emils Melders, Marta Skulme, K. Zale and Arnolds Dzirkals. See Marcel Segreste, *La Lettonie*, 1930; Alfred Bilmanis, *Latvia in the Making*, 1928.   —C.A.M.

lauda spirituale. See MEDIEVAL MUSIC.

laughter vibrato. See vibrato.

laurel. In classical art, a decorative pattern with long thin pointed leaves arranged opposite each other on a stem; used in wreath form as an emblem of honor or crown of victory.   —L.T.S.

law of frontality. See frontality, law of.

law of three sections, the. See CHINESE ARTS.

lay figure. A mechanical figure jointed in such a way that it can be given a pose somewhat like that of a living human figure is often used as an artist's model, particularly as a support for drapery. It is like a manikin but the term, lay figure, has been applied usually to somewhat more realistic devices in which the mechanism and the joints were covered. It appears not to have been much used before the 19th cent.   —G.L.S.

laying in. See design.

lead glass. See GLASS AND GLASSMAKING.

leading note, leading tone. See idiom B(1).

leading seventh. See idiom B(1).

leaf and dart ornament. A classical molding enriched by alternating the leaf and dart forms.

leaf pattern. See Lesbian leaf.

lean-to. (1) A structure, usually comparatively small, having a single-pitched roof with its apex against another building, or against a wall. (2) Having rafters, as a roof, sloping only one way.   —J.M.M.

leather. The large use of leather in the crafts does not have a parallel in its use for objects of fine art, though it has served occasionally as a support for representational painting. Most of this seems to have disappeared and is only a matter of literary record.   —G.L.S.

lecythus. A Greek oil-flask, with long body, narrow neck and small mouth, used for bath, gymnasium, and funeral purposes. Early Corinthian lecythi had a short, thick neck and cup-shaped mouth. The most beautiful vases of this type were made in Athens from 550 to 300 B.C. Their shape was cylindrical, tapering gracefully to the base, with a slender handle attached to a long neck and rather flat shoulder. Vases used for memorials at graves were covered with a yellowish-white slip, on which there were paintings in brown glaze or dull matt picturing home life and poignant farewell and commemorative scenes. Often purple borders were added on the garments, and green, blue and yellow color was sometimes used. The designs are notable for their flat effect, simplicity of line, and modestly monumental compositions. —W.R.A.

ledge. A horizontal top set into or against a wall, resembling a narrow shelf, and being usually less than twelve inches in width.
            —J.M.M.

legato. *Mus.* Smooth, connected; opposite of staccato (q.v.).

legno, col. *Mus.* A direction in violin playing to strike the strings with the back of the bow.

lei (Ch.). Sacrificial bronze vessel. Vase-like form with wide mouth and small boss-like handles at side of neck.

leich. See MEDIEVAL MUSIC.

leitmotiv (Ger.). *Mus.* The leading theme or motive (motif) repeated throughout a work. See idée fixe; opera.

lei wen. See PREHISTORIC ART.

lekythos. See lecythus.

lemon yellow. The pigment which carries this name is perhaps better known as barium yellow. It has a slightly greenish tinge and is pale. Chemically, it is a barium chromate and its preparation was first described in 1809. It is moderately stable, being very little affected by light but decomposed by heat at high temperatures and soluble in dilute alkalis and in dilute mineral acids.
            —G.L.S.

leno fabrics. See weaving.

Lenox china. See CERAMICS II.

Lesbian wave. An ancient Greek pattern used in architectural and sculptural works, frequently in moldings and cornices; also called the Lesbian or water leaf, or Lesbian cyma. A decorative molding the pattern of which consists of a series of heart-shaped leaves with a deeply marked midrib. (For ill. see *Enc. Brit.,* 14th ed., Vol. 15, page 926, ill. A.)
            —L.L.

lettering (verbal noun, fm. *letter* verb, to affix an inscription upon anything, fm. *letter* noun, an alphabetic character, which represents one of elementary sounds of speech. (1712 Addison *Spectator* no. 463, p. 7, "I observed one particular weight lettered on both sides"). The action or process of putting letters upon anything by inscribing, painting, gilding, stamping, etc. Also, concretely, the letters so inscribed.

Lettering is the most formal method of making an inscription. Its formality, evident alike in the forms of the letters and in their arrangement, results from the purpose of the lettering and the method of its production. By intent, a piece of lettering is meant to have maximum legibility and, usually, more or less permanence. In its production, these ends are achieved by the use of a deliberate process, which includes two main operations: (1) the making of a preliminary plan in a temporary medium to determine the letter-forms and their arrangement; (2) the completion of the letter-forms in a more permanent technique. It is this dual process which differentiates lettering from the simple and direct method of writing. In ancient times, as is evident from certain surviving inscriptions in stone or metal, the preliminary design was usually made in formal writing on the stone or metal surface with a chisel-shaped brush and red pigment and afterward completed by incising with a chisel. This use of a free preliminary rendering with a formalizing secondary technique appears to have been the usual classical and medieval procedure for all kinds of lettering. In the late 14th and early 15th cents. a great formality was sometimes introduced into inscriptions by the use of letters drawn mechanically with draughting instruments and constructed geometrically to control their proportions. There exist three 15th cent. manuscripts with designs of the geometrical construction of letters and from the same period one printed book, the diagrams of a Roman capital alphabet issued by Damiano da Moile at Parma ca. 1477. In the early 16th cent. there were published a number of subsequent treatises on the subject, of which the most important are those of Luca Paccioli (Venice 1509), Sigismondo Fanti (Venice 1514), Albrecht Dürer (Nuremberg 1525), and Geoffroy Tory (Paris 1529). Since the 16th cent. the growing volume and influence of printing has caused lettering in most cases to be modelled on the designs of contemporary printing types (type design itself being by definition a kind of lettering), although throughout this period there have usually appeared a few examples derived directly from classical or Renaissance inscriptions. With the modern revival of calligraphy there has also been a return to the classical method of a preliminary design in formal writing to be completed later in some more permanent technique. See J. H. Benson and A. G. Carey, *The Elements of Lettering*, 1940; British Institute of Industrial Art, *The Art of Lettering*, the report of a special committee, 1931; H. Degering, *Lettering*, London, 1929 or German edition *Die Schrift*, Berlin, 1929; E. Johnson, *Writing and Illuminating, and Lettering*, 1906.   —E.F.D.

letter notation. See NOTATION.

level crossing. See CIVIC PLANNING.

li (Ch.). Reason, i.e., the inner principle of things.

li (Ch.). Sacrificial bronze vessel. Three hollow legs, two upright handles at lip, and tripartite body.

library binding. *Book.* At one time an edition de luxe bound in leather, but now used mostly for strong bindings for public and other library work. Usually bound in buckram cloth.   —H.E.S.

libretto (It. a little book, a plot). (1) In the ballet repertory, the libretto is the literary statement of the ideas performed in a given work by terms of dancing. The libretto may be of a logical nature, a plot for drama in dumb-show, or a merely atmospheric or suggestive pretext for a loosely linked suite of dances. (2) *Mus.* A book containing the words of an opera.   —L.K.

lied (Ger.). A song composition. See song; MEDIEVAL MUSIC.

lien. See SYMBOLISM IN FAR EASTERN ART.

lierne. A rib in Gothic vaulting which is not a ridge rib and does not spring from an impost. It is intermediate between the principal ribs or bosses. See Gothic.   —O.M.S.

ligature. See NOTATION.

LIGHT, CREATIVE USE OF. Because of the diversity of the uses of light, the word light has assumed a many-sided and somewhat ambiguous meaning. To the artist light is a medium for creative expression. It is

used as a physiological and psychological stimulant for inducing emotional and intellectual response. It is this aspect of light we are primarily concerned with, and its physical properties will be considered only in respect to their relationship to visual sensation.

However, in order to evaluate the use of light in the visual arts we must first understand the role light plays in our understanding of space, and the role space plays in human experience.

Everything in the outside world presents a possible threat to man's existence. Without complete knowledge of the position and arrangement of the object world in relationship to himself, man could not hope to survive. He must be able to measure distances and determine the size of objects and the speed of their movements. This necessity develops in him an acute consciousness of space.

The measurement of space is done through the medium of the sense organs. And while to some extent it involves such senses as touch, hearing, equilibrium, and so forth, it is primarily based on the sense of sight, which is the impact of light on the eye. Without light or capacity for perceiving and measuring, space would be almost negligible.

In this sense, space, and the light by which we know it, become one. And as the principal vehicle for space experience, light acquires the power to produce the same emotional response as space.

We have evidence throughout history of man's profound sense of dependency upon light. In early times it took the form of attributing omnipotent powers to light sources. There were cults of fire worshipers and sun worshipers. Even the words light and space, in the languages, suggest the important influence they had on man's habits and living conditions. The root of the word space is variously given as—power, to be successful, to be able to, to increase; and in contemporary language it invariably has connotations of comfort, security, and pleasure. The word light is variously defined as enlightenment, awareness, orientation; and the definition of the opposite of light, darkness, is equally significant—to obscure, to hide, gloomy, hopeless.

So in view of this it is only natural that man in his creative expression should attempt to imitate light in order to represent the world of space he lives in.

Light can be seen either directly, as in the case of the sun, fire, electric bulb, luminous gas, or indirectly, as a reflection. Objects are recognizable to the eye because of its ability to discern differences in brightness and hue; that is, differences in light, shade, and color. These differences are revealed by the characteristics of the light reflection, refraction and absorbtion.

In a sense, the world can be conceived as being composed of innumerable light modulating surfaces or substances. Man, desiring to express himself and communicate his experience to his fellow man, recognized and progressively controlled the light articulating properties of the materials in his reach. In time his experiments resulted in the arts of painting, sculpture, architecture, photography, motion picture and stage design. All these activities are directed toward the optical sense. In all of them the control and articulation of light in its interaction on materials is of dominant importance.

In painting and graphic arts the light reflecting and absorbing qualities of pigments are utilized. One objective is to create the illusion of a three-dimension object world on a two-dimension surface.

In sculpture, clay, stone, metal, and other materials were modelled in such a way that the action of light upon it would explain its spatial extension.

In architecture, space is achieved also by the light articulating qualities of the walls. Opacity, transparency, and surface qualities all contribute to the explanation of space.

In stage design, by controlling the interplay of artificial light on the mobile reflecting screens—the actors,—and on the static screens —the props,—kinetic spatial unity is achieved.

In photography, through the optical system of the camera, the reflected lights of the objects are collected and reproduced on a photo sensitive emulsion, creating an illusion of the spatial world.

In motion picture, as in photography, light coming from the object can be recorded on a photo sensitive emulsion, but unlike photography it can in addition reproduce space in motion.

The development of man's understanding and control of light can be best observed in the study of the history of painting. Primitive drawings and paintings are the first material we have showing man's conscious ability to interpret the outside world. They are mostly in flat silhouette, and although they reveal the immature state of primitive man's visual development, they show an important, if elementary, grasping of the significance of light. The ability to recognize and crystalize

the myriad light tones that are involved in the fixing of even a flat image on a flat plane was a great achievement toward the utilization and control of light.

We assume that at first man was able only to distinguish the light quality differences between objects and their background, and that familiarity with these tonal differences gradually developed into certain and immediate recognition. The light relationship between object and background became a familiar pattern of light sensation and in time man identified this light pattern as the object itself.

Not being able to control actual light sources, man used pigments as his first means to articulate and modify light. In these early representations man was entirely preoccupied with the objects of his surroundings. The bodies of animals, the shape of trees, the sun, and all the important objects of his environment, the friendly and the dangerous, had characteristic forms, and it was important to recognize them.

Of course, this does not mean that the early cave paintings are equivalent to primitive man's visual development, because his lack of experience with, and the actual lack of implements of expression (pigments, brushes) must be considered.

Cave painting, children's painting, and in fact the painting of all early cultures show this period of development. An object is represented in outline without regard for the relationship it bears to other objects or the internal relationship of its details. But as the visual perception develops further, the area of recognition becomes larger, and the interrelation of objects becomes evident as well as the more complex inner details of the objects themselves.

Visual development, the growth of sensibility to the subtleties of light differences, can be observed clearly in the paintings of the different culture periods. In this development, all culture showed a similar evolution. In the early stages of each culture, drawing and painting show one flat surface against another. As the culture advances, the paintings begin to show signs of modelling by use of light and shade. For example, the art of early Egypt, Mycenaen, Greek, Roman and Western civilizations, all represented the object world as flat and without depth dimension. Later Mycenaen, Greek and Pompeiian frescoes introduce in their respective cultures the conscious use of light and dark variation to show depth and consequently space.

In Western culture, the dawn of the Renaissance found painters such as Giotto, Cimabue, and Duccio painting with sculpturesque treatment, modelling the surface by the use of light and shade. Of this period Masaccio showed the clearest understanding of the newly conceived object representation. In his paintings, color and form became closer to their actual appearance in nature. Bright colors were softened by distance. Later, Michelangelo and Leonardo da Vinci, by constant studies of the effect of light on form, brought this naturalistic rendering of the object to an even higher level.

Leonardo da Vinci's contribution was especially noteworthy. He systematically recorded and collected existing information on light phenomena. He investigated the properties of light in much the same way that his scientific contemporaries dissected and listed parts of the body. Not only did his work show a clear understanding of light as an agent in determining form and of the importance of the control of light in chiaroscuro, but he prophetically sensed other important properties, some of which later painters used and some which we are only today beginning to use, such as light mobility, aerial perspective, certain actual physiological effects of color upon the eye, tone and color contract, and the spatial value of sharp and unsharp definition.

In rendering the apparent accidental conditions of reflections, Leonardo was the first to instill in his paintings the transitory elusiveness which is characteristic of nature. But he and his school were still engrossed with the task of naturalistic rendering of the object. The object remained as the complete and sole focal point of interest. The remainder of the painting was in most cases a passive background. In the time of the early Baroque, we find a maturing of the seeds planted by da Vinci. In this period Coreggio, Titian, Veronese, and Tintoretto begin to show an acute consciousness of the power of light. They were no longer content solely with imitating an object, but were much more interested in showing the interrelationship of forms. They sensed the fact that objects were completely dependent on light, and that their paintings were little worlds of light, which they indicated by the arrangement of the object. Tintoretto actually constructed a small box in which he placed small wax figures in order to experiment and study the effects and interrelation of light on forms.

More and more light, rather than the object, was being recognized as the active and important element in the painting. But it was not until later that light began to be used as an intrinsic element for bringing together compositions. (The words light and color will be used interchangeably in this article, color being a physical phenomena directly dependent upon light.) And eventually in Rembrandt we get the actual experience of light space. In his compositions the entire surface with frequently only two or three bright spots seems to quiver brilliantly with light. When we look at his paintings, we know that the light is not confined to the bright spots we see, but that the entire surface is charged with the passage of light, and that it is latent even in the darkest corners. The object has now definitely lost its rigid mooring, and isolated independence. It is afloat in a volume of light space, maintaining its position only in relationship with other forms.

After Rembrandt we find the painters giving much more attention to organizing of light and dark areas, than to the subject matter. The paintings of El Greco, Velasquez, Ribera, and Zurbaran are violently dramatic in light arrangement. El Greco experimented with light by using clay figures in a small box. There is now an unquestionable realization of the importance of light as the organizational element in the painting. Gone is the slavish fidelity to actual appearance of objects. Shapes and lines are distorted, detail is frequently omitted altogether, and in general the significance rather than the appearance of an object is sought for.

Prime attention is given to light relationship between objects, and the paintings acquire a spatial depth that is no longer solely dependent on artificial devices such as perspective and size relationship, but rather upon the skillful relating of the dark and light picture areas.

And still, light was not completely liberated from its bondage to form. For despite distortion and lack of detail there remained a definite structural shape in object representation, which does not disappear until the time of Turner and Constable. In their work, forms become almost dematerialized. This is especially true in the later landscapes of Turner where the forms become dissolved into translucent and luminous space.

This marked the highest pinnacle man had achieved in the conscious control of objective light representation. The almost complete dissolution of form was the keynote of freedom for the Impressionist painters. They realized that the sensation of space could be produced by stimulating the eye by light pulsations alone. This was in recognition of the fact that the experience of space is conditioned by the neuro-muscular structure of the eye.

However, in practice they were confronted by the same problem which centuries of painters before them had tried to solve. The problem was a fundamental one concerning the nature of the eye. When one color pigment is placed over another one, the light given off by the under pigment is subtracted by the color placed above it. This is true even if the colors are transparent. The result, of course, is a diminishing of brightness. Since the impressionists were concerned with faithfully reproducing the brilliancy and vividness of the outdoors, this presented a stumbling block. The difficulty was solved by placing the different colors side by side in close proximity to each other. The colors are then combined by the eye into a single additive mixture, the final result being the added brightness of all the colors.

In the past there had been many painters who had intuitively grasped the effects of these additive and subtractive mixtures. This accounted for the remarkable radiance and brilliancy in the paintings of Fra Angelico and Fillipino Lippi, and Botticelli, as well as the almost unearthly luminosity in the skin coloring of Rubens. But the theories of the impressionists differed from these painters in that they were directly influenced by the scientific discoveries of their time. The findings of Helmholtz and Chevreul were consciously exploited by painters like Monet, Signac, and Seurat. The discovery and development of photography also contributed greatly to the growing consciousness of the inherent power of light. In photography light was the active and dynamic element. It is most interesting that in the short period of one century, the evolution of photography arrived at a stage almost identical to that of painting. In photography the importance of light as a technical agent was obvious from the first, but its importance as a medium for giving visual space experience developed apace with the late stages of painting. The photogram in photography can be compared with the final results of cubist analysis in painting. It liberated photography from the limitations of realism and presented the opportunity to observe the action of light and shadow in its most refined and subtle interrelationships.

The future is sufficiently revealed to warrant certain predictions. Light itself is assuming its place as the medium for a new art. What has been dimly perceived through, out our cultural history and has been attempted in various forms such as in the stained glass windows and the experimentation in stage lighting is now a reality.

Three factors made possible the work in this new medium. First, scientific progress supplying new data concerning the physiological and psychological attributes of the eyes and vision; technological progress, the invention of electricity and new light sources, and the many devices for controlling these sources, switches, rheostats and so forth; and thirdly, environmental conditioning. For the technological advances had introduced new elements of visual stimulus into the every-day life of the people. The blinking electric bulb, the brilliancy and color range of the neon light, both used extensively by the advertiser, made people more receptive to experimentation with these daily phenomena.

All these developments opened the way for a new form of visual expression—the use of light as a primary medium in itself. In creative expression in the past, light has been the auxiliary medium for revealing the qualities of other media and materials, such as, color pigment, clay, glass, paper, pencil, pen and so forth. Now cognizant of the fact that light in itself contains the power of awakening strong emotional reaction, certain artists started to use it as a plastic medium.

In this progressive work, probably the first form is the motion picture. Here for the first time light is used, not as an agent, to make articulate a controlled two-dimensional screen (such as painting or the photograph), which in reality modifies the light which falls upon it, but conversely the light which falls upon this blank white screen is in itself the articulating factor. The screen no longer is used to modify the light. The projected image, with all of its inherent power to stimulate emotional reaction, is simply a controlled succession of light rays of various intensities illuminating the even white screen. The blank screen is now entirely dependent on the light for its meaning. The screen, then, is not limited to one characteristic image(as in the painting) but thousands or millions of images. All organization is now mobile light and shade relationship.

With these new elements available, the most subtle and refined manipulation and control of light became possible. Many contemporary artists contributed to this work. Probably the earliest who tackled the problem was the Russian composer, Scriabin, who in 1911 synchronized his composition of *Prometheus,* the poem of "fire," with a color light play.

Viking Eggeling's *Diagonal Symphony* (1919) was the first abstract film based entirely on the plastic treatment of light. Shortly afterwards, Hans Richter (*Prelude and Rhythm,* 1921) and Walter Ruttman (Opus I, II, III) made similar films. Moholy-Nagy's film *Black, White and Grey* appeared in 1930.

In 1922 Hershfield Mack wrote a color sonata. This sequence of color and form projected on a screen was in symphonic notation. This instrument was called a color organ.

Thomas Wilfred and Alexander Lazlo made further developments in the color organ. In the color organ of Lazlo, prisms, lens and colored filters are revolved in a complicated interplay, while all of the elements, the speed of the movements, light intensity, color mixture, etc., are played directly on a keyboard. There has been additional experimentation in the use of projected light directly in painting and also in sculpture but much of it is still in a formative stage.

It would be well to acknowledge here the indebtedness the entire movement has to Adolph Appia. As early as 1895, in his book *Music and The Stage Setting,* he clearly stated many of the basic principles of light which the foremost present-day exponents of the art recognize.

The word done in the exploitation of this medium has not been extensive but is of great significance, for it indicates an attempt to sensitize the vision so that it can respond to abstractions of form and color, with the same pleasure and awareness as the ear to music.

Eventually a heightened sensivity such as this cannot but have the most direct influence on all of our entire controllable environment. Much of this is, of course, unpredictable, but e. eg., the architect in planning a home may have to consider not only room and convenience areas as he does now, but light areas, in which the subtle reactions of the dweller to the fluctuations of light in various parts of the home would have to be considered and solved.

There are increasing evidences that people are becoming more and more aware of the possibilities of light as an expressive medium. In recent years the use of light in world fairs and similar large exhibitions, has long since departed from the simple task of illumination and has been used to create veritable three-dimensional color panoramas. Another use stemming from ancient times, but now developed to high degree, is the pyrotechnic or fireworks displays. The dramatic theatre has for a long time used light purely for evoking emotional effects and many experimental plays have been produced, containing no scenery but depending entirely on the manipulation of light and color to achieve mood and situation.

Difficult as it is to predict the future of the art of light, we can without knowing the exact direction and form it will take, prophesy for it a role of great importance.

It has captured the imagination of many creative artists. One of the artists L. Moholy-Nagy, who has worked extensively in the light medium, writes—

" . . . a future in which light displays of any desired quality and magnitude will suddenly blaze up, and multicolored floodlights with transparent sheaths of fire will project a constant flow of immaterial, evanescent images into space by the simple manipulation of switches, . . . "

As has been pointed out, the potentiality of light as a plastic medium has until now merely been suggested. In the future lies its maturing. See COLOR; lumia; clavilux.

—G.K., N.L.

light modulator. See PHOTOGRAPHY.

light records. See PHOTOGRAPHY.

light red. See iron pigments.

light tracks. See PHOTOGRAPHY.

lily. In classical art, a conventionalized ornament based on a lily form, having a petal ending in a spiral at each side of the central stamen lines.   —L.T.S.

lime. This is chiefly known in the arts as the principal ingredient of plaster and an important factor in the process known as fresco painting. Lime oxide is made by burning limestone, marble, or chalk to drive off carbon dioxide. This mixed with water becomes a lime hydrate or putty and, combined with suitable amounts of sand or other granular ingredients, forms the traditional lime plaster.

Pigments mixed with water and applied on this are held in place by changes in crystalline character as the lime becomes a hydroxide and later a carbonate.   —G.L.S.

limited access highway. See CIVIC PLANNING.

limners. See EARLY AMERICAN ART.

Limoges ware. See CERAMICS II.

limp. *Book.* Limp binding, limp boards,, limp covers, are all terms used to describe a book bound with covers that readily bend without cracking; and further described as limp leather, or limp cloth—seldom, if ever, applied to paper covers. The covers may be lined or not.   —H.E.S.

line engraving (an intaglio process). Line engraving is older than etching, having been used by armourers and jewelers before the 15th cent. It reached its height as a print process in the days of the artists Dürer and Schongauer.

In this process the metal is cut away with a burin, instead of using an acid to eat out a line as in an etching or instead of using a metal point to raise a burr as in a drypoint. It is much easier to make a straight line with the engraving tool than a curved one. These characteristics giving the engraving a stiff angular quality, although the lines have a clear regular perfection.

Sometimes the print is made by using dots of various sizes and depths instead of using lines. This is called **stipple engraving.**

Modern print makers have brought out most effectively the stiff angular beauty of this process. The great modern French engraver, Laboreaur, and the Czech, Bouda, have done this esp. well.   —K.K.

line etching (an intaglio process). Line etching is one of the most distinguished of the graphic processes. Etching was used by jewelers and armorers before the 15th cent. for decorative purposes. In the 16th cent. line etching was used as a short cut to engraving and became popular for its freedom and quickness. Among the first to use it was Albrecht Dürer (1471-1528), the great German wood and copper engraver.

Line etching is one of the intaglio processes. The design is carried by the deep indented parts of the plate instead of by the raised parts as in **relief printing.**

Copper, ground and polished to mirror brightness, is the ideal metal to use, though zinc and occasionally other metals are sometimes used. The plate is heated and an etching ground made of wax asphaltum and other ingredients is dabbed or rolled on the surface. The plate is held in a hand-vise and smoked with a taper. The ground acts as an acid resistant. The drawing is made on the grounded plate with a pointed steel stylus that breaks through the ground coating to the copper. When the plate with the drawing scratched through the ground is laid in an acid bath, the acid will attack and dissolve the copper wherever a stylus line has laid the copper bare. This is the process of biting the plate. The three most common acids used for biting are nitric, Dutch mordant, and iron chloride. Certain areas are exposed to the acid longer in order to make the line deeper and blacker while other areas are stopped after a short bite with a varnish called the **stopping out varnish.** The varnish and ground are removed after biting and the plate is ready for printing.

The entire plate is covered with the etching ink. The ink is wiped off the surface with tarlatan and the palm of the hand, leaving ink only in the lines. A delicate film of ink also remains on surface of the plate which helps to give etching its peculiar charm.

The etching press consists of two heavy iron rollers with a flat iron bed between. The inked plate is laid face up on the bed; dampened etching paper is laid on it, followed by a piece of blotting paper and a felt blanket. In passing through press, the rollers force the soft damp paper down into the lines, producing the characteristic plate mark, the smooth pressed surface and the raised lines of an etching. The damp proof is now flattened and dried between blotters and is ready for matting.   —K.K.

line of direction, of sight. See PERSPECTIVE.

linear. i.e. forms expressed prevailingly by lines. (The term has been introduced into our aesthetic vocabulary by Henrich Woelfflin. who uses it in his *Kunstgeschichtliche Grundbegriffe* (1915), [*Principles of Art History*, New York, 1932] in contrast to "painterly".)

It describes an artistic expression in which objects or ideas are rendered by circumferential lines. Yet the use of lines alone does not suffice to describe a painting or a drawing as linear. These lines must be made significant by the absence or at least the subordination of light and shadow under the linear forms. Accordingly, color too is of secondary importance in linear rendition. The term can be used in a derivative sense for sculpture.

Since there are no lines but only masses in nature, visual conception furnishes the human eye with an abstraction which offers the designer a means of simplified statements for visual facts or for the visualization of ideas. The strongest emphasis is given to the contour. Leon Battista Alberti in his second book on painting and Friedrich Schiller in his poem *Der Künstler* (The Artist) follow Pliny's (xxxv, 15) aesthetics when they ascribe the origin of design to the tracing of a line around the shadow cast by an object.

The relationship of lines to each other implies other aesthetic qualities: the clarity and evenness of statement calls for a decorative arrangement of lines. Linearism has consequently, a tendency toward the decorative which may be observed e.g. in the Greek vase painting of the 5th cent. (Sosias, Euphronios).

It must further be stressed that it. is the relative isolation of each line which makes a design linear, while the fusion of lines into groups tends toward a painterly effect. Evenness of muscular pressure applied to drawing creates a linear form, unevenness of pressure resulting in changing darkness and discontinuity of form which create a painterly line quality.

It is, therefore, a quality of mental control and an ability for abstraction from reality and from self-consciousness; it is a tendency toward objective statement which is found in artists who express themselves in a linear style.

The simplicity and clarity of lines appeal particularly to periods or individuals whose aesthetic ideals aim toward conciseness of statement. By its method of abbreviation the linear style is esp. capable of denoting not only visual facts but also ideas or abstract notions. In the latter case the linear design becomes an ideogram or a hieroglyph. We find linear expression favored in Egyptian art, in Greek art down to the 4th cent., in medieval painting, in early Renaissance art, in the art of the neo-classical era, in contemporary abstractions and modern classicism.

Summarizing we may say: the linear style implies a tendency toward rhythmical clarity, decorative balance, and objectivity, all of which are characteristic of *Seinsstilen* ("styles of being", a term used by Woelfflin) in contrast to *Werdensstilen* ("styles of becoming") which latter usually tend toward the painterly expression.

The theory of the linear style is to be found wherever artistic tendencies stress the before mentioned qualities. We have already spoken about Alberti as the early Renaissance exponent of linear aesthetics. With Leonardo da Vinci the problems of light and shadow become more strongly emphasized and from then on these problems counterbalance the emphasis on linear treatment. The full impact of the linear theory is to be found in the neo-classical era, esp. in the writings of Kant, Schiller, Goethe, etc. Hogarth's "beauty line" in his *Analysis of Beauty* (1753) stands at the beginning of English linearism theoretically as well as practically. The last important revival of the neo-classical linear theory is developed in the essay *Das Problem der Form in der Bildenden Kunst* (1893, 2nd ed. 1914) by the German sculptor Adolph von Hildebrandt. This essay has influenced Woelfflin's basic theory of the linear which was quoted in the beginning.   —A.N.

linear elements. See PAINTING.

linearism. See linear.

linear perspective. See PERSPECTIVE.

linen. (1) The principal use of this material has been as an accessory in the arts and probably its greatest use has been as a support of paintings. Since the late Egyptian dynasties when it served, along with thin panels of wood, as a material on which mummy portraits were executed, it has had this kind of utility. With the development of painting in the 16th cent. and, more particularly, in the 17th cent., linen became the principal painting support, and the name has become practically synonymous with canvas. It is made from the fibres of the flax plant and, like most of the textile fibres, is largely composed of cellulose. It can be formed into a firm thread capable of being bleached white and, when used as a textile, of taking a variety of colors by dyeing. (2) *Book.* A woven material made of lint or flax and loaded or filled.   —G.L.S.

linen weave. See weaving.

lingam. Phallic symbol of divine power of creation.

ling-chih (Ch.). The fungus (q.v.).

ling mai (Ch.). Literally, feathers and furs. A major school of painting in which birds and animals are the subjects.

lining. *Book.* Linen linings are strips of linen on the inner folds of a section sewn through with the section and pasted down. Lining papers are the same as end papers. Also applied to the process of lining the back with brown paper or leather before covering.
—H.E.S.

linoleum. From *linum,* the Latin word for flax (the plant which produces linseed oil) and *oleum* meaning oil, is a floor covering made from cork ground to the fineness of flour, color pigments and a linseed oil "cement" which holds the particles of cork and color pigments together. —B.E.J.

linoleum cut. See PRINTS AND PRINT PROCESSES.

linoxyn. Though rarely used in the technology of the arts, this term is common in general paint technology. It stands for the fully dried and hardened film of linseed oil.
—G.L.S.

linseed oil. Although other drying oils, that is, oils capable of hardening into a firm film through the addition of oxygen to the molecule which forms the oil fluid, have been used as painting mediums, the oil of linseed has undoubtedly been the principal one taken for this purpose. Such oil is expressed from the seed of the flax plants, and the better grade for artists' paint comes from cold pressing. Unbleached, this has a bright golden yellow color. It is refined by washing or by settling or by chemical methods. Bleaching is best done by exposure to sunlight. The oil of linseed contains mixed triglycerides of linolenic, linoleic, oleic, and stearic acids, together with small amounts of other acids. It has been usually supposed that the finest oil comes from India and is known as Calcutta oil. Its history is indefinite in the past of the painting art. It was known as early as the 8th cent. but had its greatest use as a medium beginning at some time in the early 15th cent. —G.L.S.

lintel (Med. Lat. *lintellus,* head piece for a door or window). The horizontal top member spanning an opening, as of a doorway or window. —J.M.M.

lion. See SYMBOLISM IN FAR EASTERN ART.

lip reed. See ACOUSTICS.

Litany. An ancient form of prayer in which the priest lead and the people responded.

LITERARY CRITICISM. Of all the branches of criticism, that of literature is at once the most understandable and the most confused, the easiest to practice and the least rewarding as a guide. The resolution of this seeming paradox resides in the nature of the material that is here subjected to criticism: works of literary art, as compared to works of the other arts, are both more obvious and more complex.

Due to the first of these qualities—the obviousness of literature—literary criticism is temptingly easy to practice and deceptively easy to understand. Where a large portion of the other arts is, strictly speaking, meaningless to many persons, poems and stories, essays and dramas, convey some kind and degree of meaning to almost everyone. Consequently, literature being by far the most familiar of the art forms, criticism of literature appears as a natural and simple exercise of judgment upon materials that are accessible to everyone.

Due to the second of these qualities—the complexity of literature—literary criticism is in fact an intricate and delicate enterprise, and one that is almost always accompanied by confusion. Works of literary art are complex in the sense that they contain a plurality of values and so have different meanings for different readers. Put differently, this is to say that literature is the most impure of the arts, because there is here the greatest intrusion of reference foreign to the artistic form, and the highest ambiguity of artistic meaning. This of course entails that works of literature lend themselves readily to various interpretations, with the result that the same objective work of art will serve as stimulus to several quite different subjective acts of appreciation. Since it is, fundamentally, the work-as-appreciated that is criticized, the effect of this ambiguity of value and meaning upon criticism is obvious. Literary criticism has suffered greatly from this fact: different critics have found in literature different value and have lent to literature different purposes—have subscribed to conflicting aesthetic doctrines—and have done this unconsciously. Then, they have insisted that the value they find is unique, and all others spurious. And criticism degenerates into debate. Hence, the first step in an intelligent consideration of literary criticism is the thorough recognition that literature is a locus of many values. And the prime task facing the philosophical analysis of criticism is a discussion of these values, and of the various schools that have developed from them.

The general function of criticism can be summed up as consisting in the *evaluation* and *interpretation* of works of art. The function of the critic is to act as a mediator between art and the public: it is the critic's proper business to advise the public as to what is good and what is bad in art; and then, further, to aid the public toward an accurate and sensitive appreciation of art. Of course, objection can and will be made that this is to endow the critic with the tasks and powers of the censor and the educator, and that these do not properly belong to the critic. This is to adopt a thoroughly dilettante attitude toward both art and criticism: an attitude that can be defended only on the contention that art is both trivial and insignificant, incapable and unworthy of being accurately evaluated and interpreted. If art is a serious enterprise, then it certainly has some public function. And if art has a public function—if art is a matter of individual and social import—then there is a place for the critic. This place is to distinguish good art from bad; to prevent bad art from being foisted on the public; and to aid this public toward the appreciation of good art.

Within the field established by this basic agreement, there occur the differences of opinion which give rise to the various schools of criticism. Granting that art is the product of a serious human activity, with a definite nature and function, there have existed legitimate disagreements as to what this nature and function are. The act of evaluation obviously demands a frame of reference: to judge the worth of an object, it is necessary to appeal to some criteria; and these criteria can themselves be established only on the basis of what the work of art intends to be and to do.

So literary criticism has its point of departure in some aesthetic doctrine of the nature and function of art, even though this theoretic background be unrecognized by the critic. Criticism, admittedly or not, estimates the beauty of works of literary art. So critics will differ basically in their estimates as they differ in their opinions as to what makes things beautiful. There are four general interpretations of art that have been of special historic significance; and there are four corresponding sets of artistic criteria, or frames-of-reference for the evaluation of art, that have largely constituted the arsenal of practical literary criticism.

(a) The *revelatory* aesthetic doctrine and critical dogmas. This school is based on the general position that *art is an imitation;* it holds that art reveals the essential truth about the antecedently real. Of course, there is wide disagreement as to the nature of the antecedent reality that art imitates: specific imitationist schools vary from subjective impressionism through "factual" realism to objective idealism. The core of the aesthetic doctrine is the thesis that art has a reference beyond itself. Critical schools based on this doctrine tend to evaluate art in terms of the subject-matter it imitates and the success achieved in exhibiting this subject.

(b) *Formalistic* aesthetic doctrine and critical dogmas, based on the general position that art is essentially a creation, or a "making". This theory interprets the work of art as being primarily the imposition of form upon matter; the artist takes the mere material of his craft, and he creates from this an object of formal beauty. The critical schools that evaluate art from this frame of reference emphasize values of structure and composition; the work of art is treated as an end in itself, and the artist is judged for his success in making an object that is beautiful in and for itself, with no values borrowed from without.

(c) Aesthetic theory of *expressionism* and derivative critical groups. The central tenet of this theory holds that art is an expression of the artist's emotions and sentiments, as evoked on a particular occasion. The work of art records these sentiments. There are again divergent schools which all accept the fundamental position of expressionism, with romanticism as perhaps the most famous. Expressionistic criticism is loose and inchoate, as its chief criteria must be those of *passion* and *sincerity,* both of which are difficult to apply and measure.

(d) *Moralistic* aesthetic doctrines and critical dogmas. This movement can be more readily identified to the modern reader through its most recent specialized form: the sociological interpretation and criticism of art. All such theories hold, primarily, that art is a medium for fashioning the beliefs, attitudes, and habits of people. That is, art is a formal structure that has a peculiar ability to influence those who behold it. Consequently, it is the function of art to instill into the populace a correct and healthy set of opinions. Special schools of moralistic theory and criticism differ according to the fundamental beliefs behind them, and so vary from catholic to communistic. All have in common the intention of judging art by the criterion of its propaganda value: to be good, art must carry the right moral or lesson, and it must indoctrinate its audience quickly and thoroughly.

Before discussing in more detail the actual critical methods and practices of these different schools, there are several remarks concerning them all simply as schools that need to be made.

In the first place, it is most important to emphasize that every one of these aesthetic doctrines has its just measure of truth. Art is in fact a locus of many values, a complex of several characters; and each one of these values or characters can be criticized and judged. Hence, each aesthetic thoery is a partial truth, and each method of criticism can but partially exhaust the possibilities of the art work that it seeks to evaluate.

The natural and expected result of this aesthetic fact is that critics, and critical schools, find it all but impossible to be consistent. A critical group bases itself on the correct recognition of one type of aesthetic value, and announces its determination to judge works of art as they exhibit this value. But then, in the act of aesthetic appreciation, a critic of this group becomes aware of another type of value in a work. This value is not, and cannot be, recognized by him as an official critic; but it is recognized, and can not be denied, by him as a person. So it inevitably influences his evaluation of the work; and he must broaden his critical frame of reference to include this value, or must distort his criticism so as to honor it without acknowledging it.

Finally, this emphasizes again the fact that it is the prime responsibility of a conscientious critic to remain always aware of the aesthetic principles upon which his practice is based, and to submit these principles—as well as their application—to periodic scrutiny. Criticism is a type of measurement; and as such, the measuring tool is prior to and of at least equal importance with the object measured. Hence, the critic must remember not only to search out the exact quality of the work before him, but also to search out the meaning and accuracy of the standards he applies to the evaluation of this work.

We can turn now to some consideration of the critical standards and techniques employed by each of these schools.

(a) *Criticism based on the content, or external reference, of the literary work.* Such criticism regards the work of art as essentially a report of something existing independently of the work. Obviously, then, there will be two fundamental criteria available to critics in their evaluation of any particular work. First, the work can be judged on the basis of the worth or value of that which it represents. Secondly, it can be judged as a more or less adequate report of this subject-matter.

When art is referred to as *great,* and is praised for its "nobility", "depth", or "importance", it is being evaluated on the first of these bases. Such criticism depends primarily upon the fact that art is significant, in the primitive sense of signifying, or pointing, beyond itself. Thus, the standard of greatness in art is one that measures the work of art in terms of the scope or dignity of its subject-matter. This reportorial aspect is probably the most obvious quality of art, and this element has always weighed heavily in criticism. The most naïve and spontaneous artistic judgments are our statements that a book has a "good story" or that a painting is a "fine likeness". And much of the most sophisticated criticsm consists only in a refinement and elaboration of such judgments.

Historically, criticism of this general character has been practiced under the guise of many specific schools, which differ so acutely and so loudly among themselves that their common nature is all but lost. These schools depend upon, and arise from, divergent interpretations of what is independently real and so the proper object of artistic exploitation. Generically, all such criticism evaluates and interprets art as a record of reality; specifically, the criticisms vary as the critics hold different opinions of the nature of the real. The most familiar critical schools of this type are the *idealists* and the *naturalists,* or *factual realists.* The idealists, of course, attach faith to a realm of perfected ideal essences, more or less akin to the Ideas of Plato and Schopenhauer. They hold that the function of art is to reveal this realm, and that the artist must first possess the vision to grasp these essences, and then the technical skill to exhibit them clearly to men. Such criticism has encouraged an intensive exploration of the realm of values, and has promoted much art of an inspirational nature. It has also, of course, fostered a good deal of dull and platitudinous art, and has sometimes had the unfortunate effect of submerging the art work in its subject matter.

Naturalistic, or realistic, criticism, depends upon the metaphysical hypothesis that only physical particulars are real. It says that literary art should give a factual report of the details of objects, events, and situations. Critics of this group demand of art a minute attention to physical data, abstention from generalities and abstractions, and a profound adherence to the laws of cause and effect. This criticism tends very strongly to deny any of the so-called higher interests and motivations of man, and usually reduces human behavior to the most primitive appetites: sex, wealth, power, pride, and jealousy. The effect on literature has been salutary in that it has torn away the false platitudes of idealism, and has encouraged a facing of the facts; it has been unhealthy in that it has blinded men to some real facts of human nature, and has reduced the perspectives that artists need.

Two other sufficiently familiar critical schools of this type are the *sur-realists* and the *impressionists*. The first insist on the falsity of all the phenomena of "ordinary" consciousness, and strive, through art, to achieve and reveal the "true" reality that lies above and beyond this conventionalized shadow. Impressionistic criticism emphasizes the Heraclitean doctrine of flux, sees all things as always changing, and finds the value of art in the recording of these ephemeral moments.

The first tendency of all of these specific schools of imitationist criticism is to evaluate works of art in terms of their content; and here, the standards used will vary between groups. But, in the second place, all such schools also evaluate works of art as a medium of expression or communication: i.e., works can differ as to the clarity and force with which they exhibit their subject, and so can be of different value in this respect. The criteria that are used in this phase of evaluation are common to the various schools, since they are meant to measure the same characteristic simply used to different ends: i.e., they judge the efficacy of the work in revealing clearly and convincingly some vista of the real.

(The most important of these criteria are: truth, clarity, intensity, range, extensity, organization, structure, meaning, coherence, compactness, unity, variety [q.q.v.].)

(b) *Criticism which centers around the purely formal or structural aspects of the work of art.* Such criticism, a development of the aesthetic doctrine that beauty is form imposed upon matter, regards the work of art as essentially a composition of material parts into a formal whole. Here, the artistic process is interpreted as the exercise of a technique which produces aesthetic value from material that is only potentially beautiful; it does this by molding the matter of its craft into a pattern or design that is inherently pleasing.

This type of criticism arises from the recognition that works of art are products of craftsmanship; that they are brought into being by operations performed upon materials and resulting in the creation of a design that will attract and hold attention. The directions then taken by formalistic criticism are, first, toward a study of the structural principles of an art form, and, second, toward an analysis of "acceptable" or "approved" types and styles.

The first path of inquiry is meant to terminate in the enunciation of the rules that must be satisfied if a work of art is to be successful. That is, the effort here is always and unavoidably to reduce art to a science: to achieve a position where the necessary and sufficient conditions of beauty can be determined and set forth for a certain art form. By far the most familiar case of this is the attempt at complete formalization made by the French tragedians; but any classicism is a case, more or less thorough, of this enterprise. The attempt is made to say, once and for all, "follow this path and success will crown your efforts, turn from it and you fail".

The second line of formalistic investigation has consisted, historically, of a steadily increasing discrimination within the various art forms. Literature, or a literary art, becomes poetry and prose; these in turn become tragedy, comedy, lyric, romance; these are broken down into yet more finely discriminated classes; and then, finally, the various styles in which these forms have been developed by different individual artists are dissected and evaluated.

Both the salutary and the malicious effects of formalistic criticism are theoretically obvious and historically familiar. Such criticism has performed services of great value in clarifying the structural elements of art, in analyzing the principles of design, in establishing certain rational and healthy artistic "standards" or "models", and in refining our awareness of the subtle features and differences of works of art. Like any other human enterprise, art demands continuity, and the critics of the various formalistic schools have done much to assure this. Such criticism tends to establish types or models; that is, it produces accepted forms of beauty and value. And in doing this, it promotes continuity, because it establishes ideals and techniques that will be passed on from one generation of artists to another.

Conversely, criticism of this type has an unavoidable tendency to discourage change, and so to inhibit the development of new art forms. The models and rules once established by a critical school come gradually to dominate the artistic endeavours they are supposed to guide, and so to thwart the production they are meant to further. The history of each school of formalistic criticism and art has been the same: birth in the discovery of a new art form; maturity through a constantly progressing exploration of the possibilities of this form, until all of its subtleties and refinements have been exploited; senescence in dull mediocrities and unintelligible preciosities. The same cycle can be traced in only to many historical cases.

Fortunately, the positive values of formal criticism outlast its weaknesses; and this simply because, though models and rules may be discarded, the advances in technique and in style that such criticism exposes are permanently at the disposal of all future artists. The refinements of style and the more acute consciousness of detail that such criticism brings may be abused and so fall into disrepute; but they remain, and can be properly employed by artists of a later and healthier movement.

In the course of literary history, and coincident with the development of literature as a fine art, there have arisen many different schools of formal criticism. They have shared a common interest in the form and structure of literary works: i.e., in the organizations that can be wrought with words, sounds, sentences, and meanings. Consequently, they have all criticized literary works from the point of view of craftsmanship and technique. They have instinctively held that literary worth is a function of skill in the arrangement of elements; and so they have praised those works which seemed to them to exhibit a successful use of design. They have differed with respect to the forms

that they have valued, which is to say that they have had divergent preferences and have explored in various directions.

Throughout these developments, there has been one criterion that constantly reappears in different guises: that of *unity in variety*. This principle has been so permanent because it merely is a statement of those objective conditions which will satisfy the most basic and persistent of our subjective aesthetic demands: that our attention shall be kept interested, but shall not be exhausted. In these terms, the demand for variety in artistic pattern is the demand for constantly new elements, or organizations, that will revive and stimulate aesthetic response. Conversely, the demand for unity is the demand for a pattern or structure that will bind these various elements together and facilitate our ready and easy grasp of them as a whole and as one.

Thus, the inevitable direction of all classicisms—of all schools of artistic structure—is toward a constant development of a particular form into all the richness of detail that this form can support before unity of pattern and purpose is lost. Schools of formal criticism all start off with a severe austerity: purity and simplicity of form are praised above all, and any tendency toward elaboration of structure is condemned as "decoration". This corresponds to the primitive epoch of artistic schools. The period of maturity and influence of such critical schools consists in the gradual exploration of all of the refinements and subtleties of which the particular form is capable. Here, the unity of form is covered with a vastly greater wealth of detail, and the form is treated as a skeleton to support the living richness of the artistic matter. Finally, such criticism degenerates into the inane praise of subtlety as an end in itself. Here, the detail of the work completely supersedes the structure, and the work ceases to be an intelligible vehicle of meaning.

(For the more specific criteria employed in formalistic criticism, see the following: harmony, proportion, balance, richness, purity, clean, coherence, clarity, strength, looseness.)

(c) *Impressionistic or romantic schools of criticism.* Expressionism is the most vocal and the least articulate of all aesthetic theories, and the same is true of the critical doctrines and writings that arise from this theory. This remark is *not* meant as a condemnation and utter rejection of expressionistic aesthetics and criticism: expressionism, in its insistence that art reflects the feelings and emotions of the artist, has hold of a real and valuable truth. But the remark *is* meant as an indication of the necessary limitations of expressionism as a basis for explanation and criticism: such a doctrine defines the work of art by referring it to the artist's sentiments and intentions; and since these are utterly private, discussion of the value of the work, by anyone other than the artist, becomes, at best, a dubious enterprise. In honesty, the most that a critic can here say is, first, that a work seems to him to reflect, or to be a fine expression of, a feeling that the artist has had; and, second, that this feeling is itself a healthy and interesting reaction to some certain aspect of the environment.

Of course, this second judgment is extraneous to the expressionistic doctrine; it judges the work by reference to an external world that it represents, even if indirectly. Hence, such evaluations are condemned by strict expressionists, and those who make them openly, as Tolstoy, have ridicule heaped upon them. In fact, however, such judgments always creep into expressionistic criticism, though surreptitiously. It is all but impossible to attend to a person's emotions and reactions purely as such: we spontaneously approve them as fitting and proper, or condemn them as irrelevant and indecent, to the situation which aroused them. The critics of expressionism have proved no exception to this human rule, and have passed such judgments. In so far as they do this, their criticism becomes of the first type discussed, where the work of art is regarded as a report; but their criticism of this type is usually quite shallow, as they have no coherent imitationist theory in terms of which to couch their judgments, and so their evaluations are purely personal and impressionistic.

When expressionistic criticism stays within its avowed province, it concerns itself only with the first type of judgment mentioned above. As J. E. Spingarn has put it, the critic only asks, "What has the poet tried to do, and how has he fulfilled his intention? What is he striving to express and how has he expressed it?" Hence, all expressionistic criticism is written in terms of three basic criteria: *passion, sincerity,* and *vividness*.

Passion is here used, perhaps unwittingly, almost in its primitive sense of subjection to and dependence upon that which is ex-

ternal to the self: it is used to measure violence of reaction. An artist works with passion, and exhibits it in his creations, when he is completely dominated by the environment, carried away beyond himself, and responding not with intelligence and will, but only with a powerful emotion. Hence, to say that a work of art is highly passionate, is to say that it is the record of an intense and violent reaction on the part of the artist. Passion is valued and praised because it indicates that the artist has *felt* strongly; and this in turn is supposed to guarantee that the artist has something new and different to say. The absence of passion—calmness or aloofness or tranquility—is deprecated on the ground that this means that the artist has not really felt anything, and that the work is merely a cold record of matter of fact.

The criterion of *sincerity* is used to indicate that the artist is reporting truly his reactions to his environment. The expressionistic attitude would seem to be that the artist has no obligation to seek a "true" or "correct" interpretation: he has only to state as vehemently as possible his own spontaneous response. The criterion of sincerity then means that the artist has reported what he "really" felt, and has not colored this by any effort to accommodate the opinions of others, or even his own previous attitudes. Sincerity is obviously a valuable trait in art; but it can equally obviously be abused, and made to excuse hasty and careless work, on the ground that this is "what I felt".

The two criteria hitherto discussed, those of *sincerity* and *passion*, refer to the relation between the artist and his work: i.e., they evaluate the work of art as being a more or less faithful and adequate manifestation of the artist's feelings and intentions. The third common standard of expressionism, that of *vividness,* refers primarily to the relation between the work and the audience: i.e. it seeks to evaluate the relative success of the work in conveying its content and meaning to the people who encounter it. A work is vivid to the extent that it promotes a quick and facile grasp of itself; and vividness is valued in art because it helps to clarify, to make external and public, to *express*, a content that was originally private and subjective.

In summation, it should be said that critics of the expressionistic school have on numerous occasions performed services of real value in fighting against a prevalent classicism, and in freeing art from a narrow set of rules. On the other hand, such critics have done art a disservice by sponsoring and even encouraging artists to scorn all rules and principles, to deny all responsibility to anything objective, whether the real world or the real audience, and so to recognize no standards but their own whims. In this respect, classical and expressionistic criticism are invaluable foils to one another, and periods of real artistic merit always exhibit a balance of these creative and critical tendencies.

(d) *Criticism based on the moral significance of the work of art.* Criticism of this type is of far less aesthetic or literary interest than the three types already discussed, since it has no interest in the work of art apart from the effect that this makes on the audience. Critics of this school are concerned primarily with the content of the work: its subject-matter and the manner in which this subject is presented. It is only secondarily, and to a much lesser degree, that they are interested in those formal aspects of the art work which make it an effective carrier of its message.

This kind of criticism is based upon the conspicuous fact that art does have what we would now call a propaganda value and function. It has been vehemently maintained that art is not intended to serve the purposes of propaganda—to mold the opinions of people —and should not be viewed or criticized from this point of view. But the fact remains that art *does* have a propaganda effect; and so long as it does this, people are going to be intensely interested in the message that art carries, and the direction in which it tends to influence opinions. Hence, moralistic criticism has been practiced as persistently as it has been deplored, and probably always will be.

The body of such criticism has been as various as the beliefs that men have held and the doctrines that they have defended. Historically, critics of the moralistic school have been of the greatest importance: they have determined artists to develop some themes and neglect others, and they have cultivated in the reading public the literary tastes which they regarded as "right" and "healthy". The chief value of such criticism has been to promote a close relation between literary work and significant contemporary issues. That is, such criticism simply espouses the common-sense recognition that art has a content, takes up a certain attitude toward this content, and so presents a definite argument.

The weaknesses of this type of criticism are obvious: it tends to judge the work of art only on the basis of its message, and so neglects the formal, expressive, and structural features of art. The critics of this general caste are of more interest to the historian of ideas than to the aesthetician, and the schools need little detailed consideration from the artist's frame of reference. They have contributed greatly to intellectual history; but they have contributed very little to criticism, because they have not been interested in criticism as a process and profession, but only as a means to an end.

In conclusion, it should be emphasized again that all criticism has its basis in the simple statement, "I like that". That is, criticism depends upon the antecedent discovery of value. Hence, in the first place, there will be as many legitimate schools of critics as there are types of value to be found in literature: values of form, of meaning, of emotional effect, and of moral influence. Again, the critic is mainly concerned to discover and promote the value that he has discovered; which means, that he analyzes art in order to improve its quality. And it is in pursuit of this quite simple and very understandable goal that there emerge all of the refinements and distinctions that we have already discussed.   —I.J.

litharge (Fr.). A form of lead monoxide, combined wtih various colors and used as painting media. See also mitsudaso.

lithography. See PRINTS AND PRINT PROCESSES.

lithophone. As a white pigment, this has had a very small use in the fine arts, though it is common in commercial paints. It is comparatively recent in origin, having been first produced and patented in England in about 1874. Commercially it is a co-precipitate of zinc and barium salts which produce a mixture of zinc sulphide and barium sulphate. This precipitate is commonly calcined before it is ground as a pigment. It is frequently used in connection with the cadmium sulphides as an extender and to a limited extent with other intensely colored pigments.   —G.L.S.

lithotint. See PRINTS AND PRINT PROCESSES.

Lithuanian art. Attempts to study the development of Lituanian art meet with tremendous difficulties in view of the political and cultural changes that have marked the history of the people. The Lithuanians were among the last peoples of the eastern Baltic area to be definitely Christianized and by that time they had already created a powerful state with important castles on the East Baltic pattern in Trakai and other centers. There is a rich peasant art and among the most striking examples of this are the ornate crucifixes scattered throughout the country and which contain motifs drawn from pagan times adapted to their present purpose in a truly national manner and spirit.

Later part of the royal family, e.g. the descendants of Gediminas, came into contact with the White Russians and became Orthodox. White Russian became then the official language of the state and later when the pagan Jagiello was baptized in the Roman Catholic Church and married Queen Jadviga of Poland in 1386, Polish influence and culture was extended into Jagiello's capital of Vilnius (Wilno, Vilna). The higher artistic genius of Lithuania flowered in this capital with its superb brick Gothic churches (e.g. St. Anne), and later its baroque and classical monuments. These are claimed by both the Poles and the Lithuanians in view of the complicated way in which the two elements were united in the Polish Republic. Later came the Russian period and for the greater part of the 19th cent. Lithuania felt sterner methods of repression than did any of her neighbors.

The modern Lithuanian art, therefore, based on a revival of the peasant traditions as they have been handed down, began only at the ending of the 19th cent. and has followed the trends of modern times. Among the outstanding artists were K. Cviurlionis (1875-1914), a distinguished painter and musician who had been educated in St. Petersburg and who became one of the first to attempt a new national art; Antanas Zemaitis a painter of poetic delicacy; and the sculptor Petras Rimsa.

The period of liberation as elsewhere released the Lithuanian talents and a large number of new artists appeared. Yet the fact that the traditional capital of old Lithuania, Vilnius, remained in the hands of Poland, served to prevent the closest possible contact with the monuments of the past claimed by the Lithuanians; the question of the capital occupied an excessive part of Lithuanian energy. A great deal of work was done in the modern-

izing of the temporary capital of Kaunas and in architecture there was being developed a modernistic type based on the local needs. Nevertheless the coming of World War II and the difficulties caused by the Soviet and then the German occupation of the country disrupted most of the definite programs of work and has thrown the burden of maintaining the traditions on the Lithuanian groups abroad, esp. in the U.S.A. See E. J. Harrison, *Lithuania Past and Present*, 1922; W. St. Vidunas, *La Lithuanie dans le passé et dans le présent*.

—C.A.M.

little magazine. The journal of a coterie for the expression and propagation of doctrines looking to the reform of art and society. In England *The Yellow Book* (1894-7) and *The Savoy* (1896) enunciated an art-for-art's-sake theory in opposition to the prevailing Victorian standards of taste and morality. The *Chapbook* (1894-8) of Chicago for a time expressed similar *fin de siecle* opinions. Not until *Poetry* (1912-) founded by Harriet Monroe in Chicago, *The Masses* (1911-7) edited by Max Eastman and Floyd Dell in New York, and *The Little Review* (1914-29) edited by Margaret Anderson and Jane Heap in Chicago, New York, and Paris arrived on the scene were there U. S. magazines effective in supporting experimentation and revolt. *The Masses,* which was discontinued in 1917 because its editors and some contributors were tried for treason and which continued as *The Liberator* (1918-24) edited by Robert Minor and as the monthly *New Masses* (1926-1934) edited first by Max Eastman and later by Michael Gold and then by Joseph Freeman, was the first of the little magazines in America to support social as well as literary experimentation. The weekly *New Masses* (1934-) is said to be controlled by the Communist Party of the U. S. Another early advance guard magazine was *Blast* (1914-5) edited by Ezra Pound and Wyndham Lewis in London. *The Seven Arts* (1916-7) edited by James Oppenheim, Waldo Frank, and others in New York was discontinued because its patron objected to the magazine's opposition to World War I. It published important essays by Waldo Frank, Randolph Bourne, etc., *S4N* (1919-25) edited by Norman Fitts in Northampton, Mass., and New Haven, Conn., and *The Freeman* (1920-4) edited by Frances Neilson and Alfred Jay Nock in New York, contributed to the revolt which was to characterize the 20's. The latter was revived as *The New Freeman* (1930-2) to compete with the *New Masses,* both of which were housed in offices at 112 E. 19th St., N. Y. C. The most august of the advance guard magazines was *The Dial* founded in New York as a monthly after an earlier career as a weekly in Chicago (1920-9) and edited first by Scofield Thayer (1920-5) and later by Marianne Moore (1925-9). There were other little magazines to swell the list: *Broom* (1921-4) edited by Harold Loeb, Alfred Kreymborg, Malcolm Crowley, and Slater Brown and published in Rome, Berlin, New York consecutively. *Contact* (1921) edited by Robert McAlmon and William Carlos Williams in Paris for five monthly issues and resumed in New York (1932) for four quarterly issues under the editorship of William Carlos Williams. Norman Macleod edited another number which was not issued by Martin Kamin, the magazine's publisher. The first little magazine to be published in the South was *The Double Dealer* (1921-6). It was edited by Julius Weis Friend and Basil Thompson in New Orleans. The next was *The Fugitive* (1922-5) edited by John Crowe Ransom, Donald Davidson, Allen Tate, and others in Nashville. Another important publication of the twenties was *Secession* (1922-4) edited by Gorham B. Munson, Kenneth Burke, and Matthew Josephson and published successively in Vienna, Berlin, Reutte (Tirol), and New York. The two most important little magazines edited by Americans in Europe were *This Quarter* (1925-6 under editorship of E. Walsh and Ethel Moorhead in Milan, Italy, and Cannes, France; 1929-34 under editorship of Edward Titus in Paris) and *Transition* (1927-36) edited by Eugene Jolas and published monthly in Paris (1927-8) and quarterly (1928-30). Discontinued in 1930. Resumed publication as a quarterly (1932-6) published by N. V. Servire in The Hague, Holland. Several issues in New York (1936). Discontinued. The magazine to continue from where *The Dial* left off was *The Hound & Horn* (1927-34) edited by Lincoln Kirstein primarily and published first in Cambridge, Mass., and later in New York. Ezra Pound contributes another magazine as the editor of *The Exile* (1927-8), which was published for four issues by Pascal Covici in Chicago. Surrealism was first given group expression in the U. S. A. by *Blues* (1929-33) edited by Charles Henri Ford first in Columbus, Miss., and later in New York. In competition with the Southern Agrarians (Allen Tate, John Crowe Ransom, etc.), Yvor Winters founded *The Gyroscope* (1929-

31) and published it from Palo Alto, Calif. The bi-lingual (French and English texts) *Tambour* (1929-32) was edited by Harold Salemson and published in Paris. The most important advance guard magazine of the 30's to be published in America was *Pagany* (1930-3) edited by Richard Johns, first in Boston and later in New York. One of the most important advance guard critical journals was *The Symposium* (1930-4) edited by James Burnham and Philip E. Wheelwright in New York. Social and literary revolt are combined with internationalism in *Front* (1930-2) which attempted to present "the complex literary countenance of a world generation". It was a tri-lingual publication with English, French, and German texts and was composed of Soviet Russian (editor: FOSP, Moscow), Asiatic (editor: Masaki Ikedo, Tokyo), Latin American (editor: Xavier Abril, Lima, Peru), American (editor: Norman Macleod, New York), and European (editor: Sonja Prins, Amsterdam) sections. The two most important editors were Sonja Prins, who organized the European and Soviet sections, and Norman Macleod, who organized the American, Latin American, and Asiatic sections. Published by N. V. Servire, The Hague, Holland. Discontinued in favor of *International Literature* (1928—   ) published in Moscow in separate Chinese, English, German, French, and Russian editions. Another tri-lingual advance guard review was *The Morada* (1930-32) published first in Albuquerque, N. M., and later in Cagnes, s/mer, France, by Norman Macleod and Donal McKenzie. The first little magazine (other than *New Masses*) to go Communist was *The Left* (1931-2) edited by George Redfield, Jay Du Von, and others in Davenport, Iowa. An International Note Book of the Arts was the sub-title of *The New Review* (1931-2) edited by Samuel Putnam in Paris. *The Partisan Review* (1935-   ) was first published as the official organ of the New York John Reed Club which belonged to the American section of the International Union of Revolutionary Writers and was edited by Alan Calmer, Jack Conroy, Ben Field, William Phillips, and Philip Rahv. The last two named in 1937 took the magazine with them when they broke with the leftist group above mentioned and continued its publication together with Clement Greenberg, Dwight Macdonald, and George L. K. Morris, who supported the magazine financially. *The Partisan Review* is now an independent left literary little magazine which neither supports World

War II nor opposes it. *The Southern Review* (1935-42) was edited by Cleanth Brooks, Robert Penn Warren, etc., and published at Baton Rouge, La. *Accent* (1940-) is a conservative little magazine published in Urbana, Ill. *View* (1940-) edited by Charles Henri Ford in New York and *VVV* (New York) reflect the influence of André Breton and French Surrealism, which has come to New York to escape annihilation at the hands of the Nazis. The American Surrealists maintain close communication with their colleagues in South American who are said to constitute one of the main literary developments south of the Panama Canal.
—N.M.

lituus. See MUSICAL INSTRUMENTS.

Liuthar group, the. See Carolingian art; See Ottonian art.

lizard. See SYMBOLISM IN FAR EASTERN ART.

loan exhibition. See exhibition.

local color. A form of fiction popularized in the U.S.A. by Bret Harte in 1868, although stories of this type had been written as early as 1834 by Harriet Beecher Stowe and A. B. Longstreet. Emphasis is placed upon unique geographic or atmospheric effects; upon odd, whimsical, or unique characters who speak in dialect; and upon local customs, dress, and superstitions. Harte's stories, set in the California Gold Rush of 1849, pictured against the red hills in dry or snowy weather a set of moral reprobates—gamblers, saloon keepers, and prostitutes—who revealed heroic, saintlike qualities in an emergency. By combining certain narrative techniques of Dickens, Irving, and Hawthorne, Harte gave surge as well as depth to his narratives; and by employing the comic devices of telltale (q.v.) humor, he interested a vast audience. Writers in other areas immediately saw the possibilities in their local material, so that by 1910 almost every region in the U. S. was pictured. The other most memorable writers with their localities are: Sarah O. Jewett, Maine; Mary E. W. Freeman, Mass.; Alice Brown, N. H.; Rose T. Cooke, Conn.; E. N. Westcott, Upper N. Y. State; Helen R. Martin and Elsie Singmaster, Penna. Deitsch; Margaret Deland, Western Penna.; T. N. Page, Va.; J. L. Allen, Ky.; Mary N. Murfree, Tenn.; C. W. Chestnutt, N. C.; J. C. Harris and H. S. Edwards, Ca.; Mary H. Catherwood, Ohio; E. F. Eggleston, Ind.;

Constance F. Woolson, Mich.; Hamlin Garland and Zona Gale, Wis.; Alice French, Ark.; G. W. Cable, Crace E. King, Ruth M. Stuart, and Kate Chopin, La.; T. A. Janvier and C. F. Lummis, N. M.; P. V. Mighels, Nev.; Mary H. Foote, Idaho; and Frank Norris, San Francisco's Chinatown. Under the impact of the realistic theories of fiction introduced from Europe, local color merged into the New Regionalism (q.v.) or became the sublimated basis for universal studies like those of Willa Cather and Sinclair Lewis. See H. R. Warfel and G. H. Orians, *Am. Local-Color Stories,* 1941.   —H.R.W.

locus. See PERSPECTIVE.

log. A bulky piece of timber cut down and cleared of branches; usually more than five inches in diameter.

lohan (Ch.). Buddhist saint.

Loire, school of. See FRENCH ART.

Lokeśvara. The form of Avalokiteśvara found in Cambodia, and elsewhere. He is the god of compassion and power.

lokweave. Type of carpeting particularly adaptable to practical use. This fabric requires no binding and due to the fact that it can be cut in any direction without raveling, it is excellent for use in odd-size rooms. Also as this fabric permits the joining of any number of pieces together through the application of a patented sealer on the back, no visible seams spoil the appearance of the completed installation. Therefore, any pattern or design can be executed in any desired color scheme. One of the other advantages of this type of carpeting is that if any damage is done to the rug, such as a bad stain or burn, etc. the damaged spot may be cut out and a new piece inserted and sealed into place, thus protecting the life of the carpet.   .—B.E.J.

Lombard architecture. The style of medieval building in the north-Italian region which took its name from an invading tribe of German barbarians, but developed its architecture on Roman traditions under strong Byzantine influence received through Ravenna. King Rotharis (636-52) set up a code of the Comacine masters (q.v.) which has been widely interpreted as the basis of masons' guilds centered at Como, though the word probably means co-workers on the scaffold (*macigno*). The simple early Lombard structures are built of brick or of small stones resembling bricks, with some vaulting, and decorations of pilaster strips and corbel tables. The Lombard style spread to Dalmatia, Southern France, Catalonia, and the Rhineland in the course of the 9th, 10th, and 11th cents. Outside Italy it was superseded by regional schools of Romanesque architecture after 1100. By that time notable structures in developed Lombard Romanesque were building. Square bays with rubble groin vaulting on ribs supported by grouped shafting were then in use, and it has been thought that influential Lombard churchmen going to Normandy and England were responsible for the appearance there of these features, which soon brought about the development of Gothic architecture. See Porter, A. K., *Lombard Architecture,* 1915-17: Puig i Cadafalch, *La géographie et les origines du premier Art roman,* 1935; Clapham, A. W., *Romanesque Architecture in Western Europe,* 1936. —K.J.C.

Lombard porch. A porch projecting from a church portal and supported by disengaged columns resting on bodies either of lions or of griffins. Introduced into Lombardy in the beginning of the 12th cent. —R.B.

long. See neumes.

longa. See NOTATION.

longa imperfecta. See NOTATION.

longa perfecta. See NOTATION.

long bench. See FURNITURE.

long room. See MESOPOTAMIAN ART.

long scroll. See CHINESE ARTS.

loom, hand weaving. A mechanical apparatus upon which the rug is woven, consisting of a heavy wooden framework over which the threads that are to be the foundation of the rug are stretched. —B.E.J.

looseness. As applied to literature, this term indicates a lack of internal connection between the various elements of the work. Looseness is the condition that holds when the passage from one part of the work to another is weak and unstable; it has the effect of isolating the various segments of the work, and so destroys artistic unity. —I.J.

Lopburi, school of. See SOUTHEASTERN ASIATIC ART.

lost wax method. See cire-perdue.

lotus. A conventionalized ornament based on a water lily of Egypt or Mesopotamia, a symmetrical unit either (1) in bud form, a long thin pointed bud, or (2) in blossom form, a petal curving out toward the top on each side of a central pointed member; widely used in ancient Egypt, Mesopotamia, and Greece. See SYMBOLISM IN FAR EASTERN ART. —L.T.S.

lotus and palmette. Also called lotus and palmette chain, or anthemion; a continuous classical ornament in which the units are alternately a lotus blossom and a palmette, and are connected at the bottom by a double curved or S-scroll; widely used on Greek pottery and in Greek and Roman architecture. —L.T.S.

lotus throne. Pedestal designed with lotus petals surrounding a lotus pod motive, on which, in pictorial and sculptural art, the Buddha is usually seated.

loud, loudness. See ACOUSTICS.

Louis Quatorze (XIV) style. See FURNITURE.

Louis Quinze (XV) style. See FURNITURE.

Louis Seize (XVI) style. See FURNITURE.

Louvain school. A school of 15th cent. Flemish artists at Louvain. It was here that Dierick Bouts developed his style of landscape which influenced the school of Cologne. —R.L.W.

low relief. See relief; relief sculpture.

low warp loom. A loom with the warp in a horizontal position. The worker leans over such a loom while weaving as if writing at a table.

Lowestoft ware. See CERAMICS II.

Loyal subjects. See ORIENTAL MUSIC.

Lucca della Robbia ware. See CERAMICS II.

Luhrs. See PREHISTORIC ART.

Lumia (also called mobile color, color music, the art of light). An eighth fine art form in which light is used as a direct and independent medium for aesthetic expression. The aesthetic treatment of mobile form and color in apparent space.

A lumia composition is a silent visual sequence performed on a white screen by means of a light projection instrument controlled from a console (see clavilux). A special notation system is used by composer and performer (lumianist.)

The basic factors of lumia have been set forth by Thomas Wilfred in the following frame of reference:

FORM
{ POSITION
  VOLUME
  OUTLINE
  CHARACTER
    (Texture,
    Opacity) }

MOTION
{ ORBIT
  TEMPO
  CYCLE
    (Recurrence)
  FIELD* }

COLOR
{ HUE
  CHROMA
  VALUE
  INTENSITY** }

The periodic change within any one or any combination of the twelve sub-factors constitutes RHYTHM.

*FIELD is that area of imaginary space visible to the spectator. A composition may either be completely contained within this area (single field)—or much of the sequence may, by inference, develop without and be visible only as orbit and field coincide (double field).

**In lumia it has been found expedient to add intensity to hue, chroma and value since a given combination of the three latter may remain relatively unchanged while being moved into a higher intensity dimension by means of added candlepower from the light source.

Lumia, being in its purest form a space-time, art, color is the only dispensable basic factor. Experimental programs of black and white compositions have been successfully played by Thomas Wilfred in the recital hall of the Art Institute of Light in New York City.

The lumia artist must first of all create a perfect illusion of depth. The flat white screen must become a window, opening on infinite space in which form, motion and color interweave. A composition may begin with a tiny sphere of pale blue in the far distance, approaching the spectator through rising clouds of green tendrils and opening up into a flaming climax of intense warm colors. This cycle may be repeated with variations until the composition ends with the sphere receding through the undulating curtains of green tendrils until it vanishes in the distance.

Lumia composition ranges from the purely abstract to the stark representational—from the majestic to the grotesque. Among the pioneer artist Thomas Wilfred's 132 compositions we find such titles as *Study in Rising Forms,* Op. 75; *Rhythm in Steel,* Op. 71; *Counterpoint in Space,* Op. 96; *Triangular Etude,* Op. 39 and *Chorus,* Op. 69.

Lumia has been used in conjunction with music and drama (see *Encyclopedia Britannica,* 14th Ed. Vol. 21, pp. 189-190), the dance and architecture (projected mobile murals, interior and exterior decoration with light).

The art form is still in its infancy and its instruments primitive but it opened up a new field of great importance in aesthetics. Lumia has also been applied with success in psychotherapy through a series of special arrangements built at the Art Institute of Light.

—T.W.

luminance. See COLOR.

luminescent bodies. See COLOR.

luminism. See impressionism.

luminosity. See COLOR.

luminous emittance. See COLOR.

luminous (visual) energy. See COLOR.

lunar cult. See PRIMITIVE ART.

lung (Ch.). Dragon. See SYMBOLISM IN FAR EASTERN ART.

lung (Ch.). Jade disc, or split disc, with circular perforation in center, and with dragon heads *en face;* symbol of fertile rain and therefore used ritually in prayers for rain.

—J.A.M.

Lung-ch'üan yao (Ch.). Chinese ceramic ware with either a porcelain or pottery base and the gray-green glaze popularly known in the occident as celadon (q.v.).

lung-mên. See SYMBOLISM IN FAR EASTERN ART.

Lungmen caves. See CHINESE ARTS.

lur. An ancient Scandinavian trumpet or horn. See MUSICAL INSTRUMENTS.

Luristan bronze . See PREHISTORIC ART.

lustre. Luster, an iridescent sheen or glass-like surface. See CERAMICS I; COLOR. See ISLAMIC ART.

lute. See MUSICAL INSTRUMENTS.

lute style. See gallant style.

lutschism (Ger.). See rayonism.

Lydian mode. See idiom A (2); scales and modes.

lyra, 1. da braccia, 1. da gamba, 1. viol, lyre. See MUSICAL INSTRUMENTS.

lyric oratorio. See ORATORIO.

lyric poetry. See POETRY.

M

machine art, exactly speaking, is distinguishable from handicraft, though it is clear that a sharp separation cannot be made. Perhaps the dividing line should be drawn where the motive power is or is not human, rather than where the degree of complication of the tool used suggests a mechanical emphasis as opposed to a human one. As commonly understood, however, the term, *machine art*, applies to the articles produced by mass production methods, a process developed since the Industrial Revolution. With this connotation the term separates articles mechanically produced, which make claims to artistic form, from those which do not.

Historically speaking, the interest in machine art followed that aroused by the arts and crafts movement (q.v.) in the late 19th cent., as a reaction to that movement's total condemnation of the machine when used to create art.

In the early stages of machine art various decorative formulas were followed, called now art nouveau, now Viennese Secession, art moderne, and latterly, streamlining—all attempting to use the machine, but denying its total validity. Later, technical problems as solved by engineers tended to dominate individuality in artistic creations which stressed utility and functionalism in design. Following the First World War, a reaction set in which emphasized the originality of the artist's creation. In the 20's and 30's a counter-reaction flourished, this time back to techniques derivative from new materials and processes and uses, as illustrated by tubular metal and plywood furniture. As the 1940's pass and a post-war world is envisaged, it appears that the machine may in time be humanized, and that the forms which man designs through its instrumentality will develop

their own range of aesthetic values. The machine will not be forced in that event to imitate handicrafts, but it will be so controlled that the product will express both the creating mind of the artist and the guiding hand of the operator, as well as the process, the material, and the purpose which the object will serve. That a machine aesthetic is gathering force and clarity has been indicated by the Machine Art Exhibition held at the Museum of Modern Art, New York City, in 1934, where Plato and St. Thomas Aquinas were summoned to endorse the beauty of machine forms, and where industrial units, household and office equipment, kitchenware, home furnishings, and accessories, scientific instruments and laboratory glass and porcelain were expertly displayed to reveal unsuspected beauty of geometry and rhythm, of technique and material, of intricacy and simplicity. Pertinent relationships have also been pointed out between the beauty of machine art and that of natural forms, between machine aesthetic and that of abstract art, and between machine art and the new awareness of time-space which tends to color our sociological thinking, as it encompasses housing, transportation, and regional planning.

In America the former leaders of the Bauhaus, Dessau, Germany, as well as Norman Bel Geddes, Walter Dorwin Teague, Harold van Doren, Alvar Aalto from Finland, and many of the most distinguished modern architects are leaders among designers of Machine Art, though there is hardly a craft which has not its forward-looking advocates who are helping to hasten the day when even the peculiar beauty of machine art will no longer be exploited, but when the human being, with his manual powers extended by the machine he has designed will produce objects, both those made

578

to order and those completed on a moving belt, of human significance. Lewis Mumford in *Technics and Civilization* has written a suggestive introduction to the understanding of such an environment.

From a world of mass production and objects composed of standardized units only a representative series of examples can be suggested here. Greenbelt towns, sponsored by the American government, great Federal engineering and regional developments such as the Tennessee Valley Project, the motor parkways of Westchester County, New York, the concrete bridges of Robert Maillart in Switzerland, the Johnson Wax Company office, Racine, Wisconsin, with mushroom supports and imaginative lighting created by Frank Lloyd Wright, make quite clear that the lesson of motor car, and steamboat, and airplane have been learned, as well as that of the Parthenon and of the human body and arrow-heads.

On a smaller scale such details as the metal doors of vaults at the Philadelphia Savings Fund Society Building by Howe and Lescaze, the standardized telephones of the Bell System, the basic equipment of the transcontinental flyers, the revolutionary uses of glass used to relate interiors to environments, and the transformation seen in the design of every article used in domestic furnishing and consumption from stove to lighting fixture to textile to easy chair are too numerous and too obvious to mention further. The machine is clearly being accepted and allowed to create its own type of beauty as the values of metal and wood and plastics are sought and found.

But more amazing, perhaps, than the novelty seen in new forms occasioned by new practices and needs, and the exploitation of new materials, is the revolution to be seen in the traditional art forms. Siqueiros paints with Duco-spray, photography is developing a mural phase, pre-cast concrete blocks are used for architectural decoration, machine-made glass is produced in bendable form for structural use and in mass production rivals the beauty of hand-made products, and premiated furniture designs, resulting from understanding raw materials, new techniques, and the human body, are turned over to mass production as soon as prizes are announced. Even the province of typography and book-making is being re-explored and type-faces expressive of modern ideas and new formats for a visual-minded and hurried reader are making cautious advances to the machine, while the late Grant Wood admittedly painted pictures with the demands of magazine reproduction in mind. Thus does a democracy move to the mastery of the machine.

For the theories of machine art forms, cf. J. L. Martin, etc., editors, *Circle*, 1937; *Machine Art*, Museum of Modern Art, New York, 1934; S. Giedion, *Time, Space, and Architecture*, 1941; L. Moholy-Nagy, *The New Vision*, 1938; L. Mumford, *Technics and Civilization*, 1934. For historical backgrounds, cf. E. A. Park, *New Backgrounds for a New Age*, 1927; L. F. Day, *Of William Morris and His Work*, 1899; N. Pevsner, *Pioneers of the Modern Movement*, 1936. For architecture and machine art, cf. F. L. Wright, *Modern Architecture*, 1931; W. Gropius, *The New Architecture*, 1935; Le Corbusier, *L'art decoratif d'aujourdhui*. For interiors, cf. P. T. Frankl, *Form and Reform*, 1930, and *New Dimensions*, 1928; J. Aronson, *Furniture and Decoration*, 1941. For types of machine art, cf. *Organic Design*, Museum of Modern Art, New York, 1941; S. and M. Cheney, *Art and the Machine*, 1936; N. Bel Geddes, *Magic Motorways*, 1940, and *Horizons*, 1932; H. Read, *Art and Industry*, 1934; C. R. Richards, *Art in Industry*, 1939; W. D. Teague, *Design This Day*, 1940; Harold van Doren, *Industrial Design*, 1940. Cf. also, K. Blossfeldt, *Art Forms in Nature*, and D. E. Mansberger and C. W. Pepper, *Plastics: Problems and Processes*, 1938.   —W.S.R.

madder. As one of the lake or dye pigments, the madder or madder lake was probably as well known as any of the red coloring materials used by painters since classical times. It is usually considered to be the *rubia* mentioned by Pliny, and specimens of it have been found on paintings of Egyptian and Greco-Roman times. It is a natural dye extracted from the root of the *Rubia Tinctorium*. Until recently this was cultivated exclusively in Europe and Asia Minor. Synthetic dyes such as alizarin have largely displaced it.   —G.L.S.

madras. A cotton fabric made with leno weave.

madrasa. See ISLAMIC ART.

madrigal (matricale). A vocal, unaccompanied composition, generally in imitative counterpoint in from 3 to 8 parts. The madrigal is closely allied to the motet. It differs from the glee in that it is sung by a chorus, while the glee is intended for solo voices. See MEDIEVAL MUSIC.

magatama (Jap.). A bead or pendant, shaped like a comma. Its significance is lost in antiquity.

Magdalenian art. See PREHISTORIC ART.

Magen Avoth mode. See JEWISH MUSIC.

magenta. The name given to a brilliant reddish purple color, this is also the name of a particular dye synthetically made and belonging to the triphenylmethane group. It was first prepared in the middle of the 19th cent. and, although a fugitive material, is used still as a water color.   —G.L.S.

magic realism. See new objectivity.

mahlstick. Held in the palette hand of the painter and used as a rest for his painting hand, especially in the execution of fine work, is the mahlstick. Evidence of its use goes back to the 16th cent. where it is seen in representations of painters' studios, particularly of St. Luke. It is a light rod of wood, ordinarily with a soft leather-covered ball at one end. This ball is made to rest against the painting, if necessary, or against a part of the easel. Commercially made mahlsticks are of hardwood or bamboo jointed to give them a total length of about four feet. The name, rest stick, is also applied to them.   —G.L.S.

maitre de ballet (Fr. ballet-master). In the original 17th cent. meaning, the ballet-master trained the company, was responsible for its schooling as well as its performance on the stage. Today, this work is divided into the teacher's, the rehearsalist's, and the choreographer's, while the choreographer is usually understood as *maitre de ballet*.   —L.K.

majolica, maiolica ware. Lustrous, colorful, opaque glazed pottery. See CERAMICS I, II; faïence ware.

major. See key.

major interval. See interval.

major mode. See scales and modes.

major scale. See NOTATION.

majuscule. Capital letter. See writing.

makara (Skr.). A crocodile-like mythical monster with fish tail; often used decoratively

in the sculpture of India and the Indonesian countries.

make-up. See COSTUME ART.

maki-e (Jap.). Lacquerware (q.v.), in relief.

makimono (Jap.). Literally "rolled thing". A painting mounted so as to be rolled or unrolled horizontally.

makkinro (Jap.). An ancient lacquer technique in which a design in coarse gold dust is laid on a ground of black lacquer, then covered with black lacquer and polished through.   —J.A.M.

malachite. Closely associated with the blue known as azurite, malachite is a similar mineral, a basic copper carbonate. It is green in color and has sometimes been given the name, mountain green. The mineral is prepared as a pigment by selection, grinding, and sieving. Formerly much used in Europe through the Middle Ages and the Renaissance, it is now no longer prepared by artists' colormen. It appears still with azurite as a pigment used in the Far East, and has evidently been in the palette of artists in that region since Han times.   —G.L.S.

Malaga ware. See CERAMICS II.

malagueña. A national Spanish couple dance in the sequidilla tradition belonging to the classic Iberian group. The dance is partly mimetic in character, using flirtation as its theme. The woman carries a fan and the man a cape, which he flourishes in movements suggestive of bull-fighting. The movement is fast with intricate, rapid footwork, punctuated by abrupt pauses. In form, the dance consists of three sections; the promenade, the pantomime, and the dance proper.   —J.G.

mallet of daikoku. See SYMBOLISM IN FAR EASTERN ART.

Mamluk art. See ISLAMIC ART.

manaia (Maori). The squat human figure, a recurrent and basic motif in Maori carving (q.v.).

mandala (Skr.). A temple painting showing a portion or all of a pantheon with mystic symbols often arranged geometrically. See INDIAN ART; stupa.

mandapa. See INDIAN ART.

mandara (Jap.). See mandala.

mandarin duck. See SYMBOLISM IN FAR EASTERN ART.

mandolin, mandoline. See MUSICAL INSTRUMENTS.

mandorla. See aureole and mandorla.

mandriale. See madrigal.

manfukh (Ar. swollen) arch. Horseshoe arch. See ISLAMIC ART.

mang. See SYMBOLISM IN FAR EASTERN ART.

manga (Jap.). Sketches, generally assembled in book form; cartoons.

manganese pigments. The blue and violet colors from the manganese metal are of quite modern origin. Manganese violet, a manganese ammonium phosphate, first appeared on the market in 1890. A synthetic pigment, this is inorganic and is quite permanent to light and heat. It is decomposed by strong acids or by alkalis. Its color is not extremely brilliant and its hiding power is weak. Manganese blue is still more recent in origin and is first mentioned in the patent literature in about 1935. It is somewhat more complex, being essentially a barium manganate fixed on a barium sulphate base. Chemically, it is inert and is not affected by heat or by strong acids or alkalis. Like the violet color, it is weak in tinting strength and in hiding power.
—G.L.S.

Manieren. *Mus.* German term for ornament. Philipp Emanuel Bach devotes in his famous treatise *Versuch über die wahre Art das Clavier zu spielen* nine chapters to Manieren, offering a detailed study of ornaments. He specifies the following types: I. Manieren in General; II. On Appogiature; III. On Shakes; IV. The Turn; V. Mordents; VI. The Anschlag; VII. The Schleifer; VIII. The Schneller; IX. On the Ornamentation of the Fermata.
—F.D.

manikin. Evidently older in the history of the art than the lay figure, the manikin is similar. As an adjustable model, it is made to imitate the human figure and is used particularly in the representation of costume and drapery. In it there is no attempt to conceal the mechanical articulation of joints and there is no attempt to imitate superficial forms. The commercially made manikins are usually of wood and the size ranges from about a foot in height to approximately life size.

Figures of this type were known as early as the 16th cent. in artists' studios and may have been part of the equipment of such rooms at earlier dates.
—G.L.S.

manila. *Book.* A paper and a card. Made from manila hemp in the best qualities, but imitated with other materials.

manji (Jap.). Swastika.

Mannerism as a universal phenomenon occurs whenever in any art the exhibition of formal dexterity is dominant at the expense of the rendition of expressive or representative content. Its appearance can accordingly be due to the exhaustion either of the creative impulse or of the ideas underlying creative activity.

As the name of a style, the word is applied to most European art between 1520, the end of the High Renaissance outside of Venice and 1600, the beginning of the baroque, its applicability being coextensive with that of the term "Late Renaissance". The style of Mannerism is a "manneristic phenomenon", since (1) it relies on ready-made formulae with disregard for their functional context; since (2) it lacks the naïveté of an art aware of tasks ahead; since (3) it puts a premium on ingenuity in the planning of involved compositions and of abstruse literary programs.

Mannerism is an anti-classical style in that it sets itself against the progressive rationality of the Renaissance. In some cases (Michelangelo, Pontormo) this is due to religious desires and may then involve a resumption of artistic forms of the Middle Ages, just as some phases of Mannerist theory of art have a mystical and medieval flavour (Lomazzo, Zuccari). Usually, however, the dissonances of Mannerism are no more than free variations upon motives of the High Renaissance, which remain the basis of the new art: witness the adherence even in the most anti-classical architecture to Vitruvius' orders of columns. Mannerism, then, presupposes classicism as any deviation or irregularity presupposes a rule. It indulges in deviations from the classical style, because it regards it as the embodiment not of a valid view of the world, but only of a set of prescriptions which the artist feels at liberty to accept or to reject.

Typical traits of the Mannerist style are (1) the general instability of composition, which in painting is often without any aesthetic center and in architecture sometimes gives the impression of the upper parts being overweight; (2) the denial or exaggerated assertion of space, which is either compressed into a narrow frontal zone with disregard for the real distance of the figures from the picture plain or lengthened into a bottomless chasm. In both cases the space composition is unstable, in the first also paradoxical. (3) The ambiguous interpretation or outright perversion of functional relationships. In architecture this leads to such paradoxes as the incorporation of columns into the walls which they are to support, or the treatment of brackets as if they were suspended (vestibule of Bibliotheca Laurentiana). In painting, the divorce of form and function is expressed by the emptiness of gestures which instead of arising from a situation, are merely superficially adapted to it. Frequently several conflicting interpretations of the same group of forms are simultaneously forced upon the spectator, who will be both attracted and repelled by such duplicity. Mannerism is therefore (4) the style of interlocking forms and of conflict without issue. Therein lies its essential futility.

Escape from this impasse was sought by means of the following devices: (1) the reversion from structural form to ornament. In architecture this implied in some cases the annihilation of all specially architectonic content (P. Ligoria). (2) The reversion from consciously elaborated form to the pathological forms of the "subconscious": witness the frequency of double images (q.v.) or the interpretation of ornamental details as threatening physiognomies and masks. (3) The reversion from artificial form of any kind to the crude unformed matter of inorganic nature. Witness the introduction of artificial grottos and the use of uncut rock in the midst of highly elaborate architecture (Giulio Romano). (4) The reversion from unresolved conflict to rigidity: witness the coldness of classicistic form and the absence of expressive content in the work of the latest Mannerists (Cavalier' d' Arpino.). Witness also the iciness of Mannerist portraiture (Bronzino) which instead of rendering living human beings renders only their masks.

The rise of a Mannerism in the 16th cent. is due to the interplay of two circumstances: (1) the incipient emancipation of art from medieval bondage as a result of the pride of artist in the achievements of the Renaissance; (2) the worthlessness of these achievements in the face of the new spiritual demands of the day (see counter reforma-

tion). As a result of this conflict the new formal mastery was deprived of its ideological justification and became pointless artistry. The ensuing spiritual confusion is expressed through images of unresolved contrast and often of oppression and anguish. See GERMAN ART.   —R.B.

In dancing, a mannerism is a personal idiosyncratic accretion or emphasis on the corpus of the academic traditional vocabulary presupposed by every technician, which is the individual contribution of every dancer.
                                                          —L.K.

man of sorrow. Late medieval devotional image (q.v.) representing Christ after his death, upright and suffering from the wounds inflicted during the Passion, frequently also exhibiting his injuries and thereby inviting the compassion of the beholder.   —R.B.

mansions. See STAGESETTING; THEATRE.

mantel. The work, or facing, over a fireplace in front of the chimney. See INTERIOR ARCHITECTURE AND DECORATION.

mantling. See HERALDRY.

Maori. A Polynesian people living in New Zealand. For Maori art see OCEANIA, ARTS OF; Maori carving.

Maori carving. Few primitive peoples have such an individual form of art expression as the Maoris of New Zealand. An isolated geographic position and relatively rigorous climatic conditions tended to force the development of a local art style which was quite distinctive from that of other south sea island groups.

A careful survey of a map of the southern Pacific will show that the land of the Maoris is indeed at the very edge of the inhabited world. In spite of this, a fleet of Polynesian outrigger and double canoes carrying colonists from Hawaii crossed a broad expanse of the Pacific and settled in New Zealand a hundred years or so before Columbus dared to leave the shores of Europe.

For over three hundred years these people remained unmolested, developing an individual culture pattern and adapting themselves to their new environment. Among other things, the Maoris discovered that the fine-grained totara wood offered excellent material for carving. From the greenstone (nephrite) which was found locally, they were able to fashion sharp cutting-tools which were as hard as common steel. With such materials at hand is it any wonder that the Maoris turned to wood carving as the means of preserving their traditional art forms? Being a rhythmic people with latent abilities they gradually attained a technical skill seldom reached by stone-age cultures.

Living in a country where practically no animals existed and where even the birds were relatively small and timorous the Maori carver lacked the fearsome models which so commonly inspired the primitive artist to create terrifying animistic forms. Instead the Maoris worked in a profuse decorative manner using few major motifs and filling background areas with abstract curvilinear patterns. Most of the carving was done in relief.

Of the larger motifs the most important were the squat human figure, the **manaia**, and the double spiral. These appeared most frequently and with the greatest variation both in treatment and size. Other large motifs such as the **marakihau**, the whale and the lizard were much more standardized and limited in their use.

Apart from the double spiral, the squat human figure motif seems to be basic in Maori carving. Unhampered by any desire for realism the trained **tohunga** adapted the human form to the rectangular plank which he carved. The head, being most important, was enlarged to fill the top part of the rectangle. The eyes, which were represented by disks of inlaid *paua* shell, were set under slanting brows. The nose was little more than a stylized "m" shaped unit. The mouth was greatly emphasized, with wide decorated lips and a tongue which protruded as a gesture of defiance. The body was greatly shortened and subordinated to the shoulder and hip joints which were usually expressed by large double spirals. The arms were little more than curving bands ending in three-fingered, claw-like hand designs. The feet were treated similarly to the hands being joined directly to the hip-spirals. Over most of the exposed surfaces were carved variations of notched, seed-like elements contained in parallel grooves.

While this squat human motif symbolized the story of the great ancestral heroes on the interior panels of the large community houses, at other times it seemed to serve as little more than decoration.

Another major motif which was just as important as the squat human figure and which indeed appears to be interchangeable with it was the sinuous grotesque form known as the *manaia*. This motif has a curving body surmounted by a bird-like head, which on closer inspection seems to be nothing more than the regular head-design split in half. This process of division is not uncommon in other Pacific arts, particularly those of the West-coast Canadian Indian. The body is an "s" curve which is grasped at the middle of the forward thrust by the large three-fingered hand motif.

A study of the taiaha, the canoe prow, the door lintel and particularly the exterior of the carved storehouse will show how both the squat human motif and the manaia design were variated and adapted to the shape of the area they had to fill. It will also be noted that in many places the figure disintegrated until the various members of the body became abstract units of decoration, complete in themselves.

The double spiral is not so easy to explain. Neither the Maori chiefs nor the scholars of Maori culture have reached any agreement upon its meaning. It appears most prominently on the canoe prows and on door lintels. Its very structure suggests that it does not originate from nature. This motif diminishes at times to small whorls of surface decoration.

Three creature motifs, the *marakihau*, the lizard and the whale all resulted from environmental factors. As each of these designs were reserved for the decoration of a particular place they did not tend to develop as to either complexity of form or use, and may be considered as of minor importance.

The *marakihau* symbolized a human ancestor who had assumed the form of a legendary sea-monster. In appearance it was similar to the squat human figure except that the feet were replaced by a fish tail, the tongue was long and tubular, and the head showed two horn-like appendages. This design usually appeared on one or two of the carved panels of the large community houses.

The lizard, which was the most naturalistic motif of Maori art, was copied directly from nature. As in other aboriginal cultures it symbolized death and was used in the decoration of coffins.

The whale motif was carved with a fairly naturalistic body and tail but with the head represented by two interlocking curves. This design symbolized a period of plenty and was most appropriately chosen to ornament the façade of the carved storehouse.

Unlike most primitive peoples the Maoris did not evolve different motifs or totem designs to signify the various tribes or clans. Instead, the same major motifs were used throughout the entire culture of the Maoris. The individuality of each district was displayed by the local treatment of these motifs and their particular arrangement. Thus, the placing and the emphasis of the spirals and squat human figure designs on a door lintel would intimate to the scholar where it was carved.

While it is true that the Maoris attempted to crystalize their history and mythology in their art, the very decorative and ornate profusion of the carving, plus an intense community pride suggests very strongly that there was still another underlying factor—the prestige element. Even though Maori carving is preponderately symbolic, nevertheless it is definitely used to express and increase the prestige of the community both in the eyes of the group and of their neighbors. See OCEANIA, ARTS OF; also *Maori Artistry*, W. Page Rowe, 1928; *Maori Carving*, Carter B. Storr, 1943; *The Maori As He Was*, Elsdon Best, 1934; *South Sea Folk*, Gilbert Archey, 1937.   —C.B.S.

maple. See SYMBOLISM IN FAR EASTERN ART.

maqsura (Ar.). A fenced-off area in the *rivaq* (roofed arcade) of a mosque. See ISLAMIC ART.

maraca. See MUSICAL INSTRUMENTS.

marae. A sacred enclosure or place of worship of the Polynesians. See OCEANIA, ARTS OF.

marakihau (Maori). Sea-monster motif in Maori carving (q.v.).

marbling. *Book.* The process of imitating marble on paper, etc. Edges so treated are marble-edges; and papers are marbled endpapers, and so on. The man doing the work is a **marbler.**   —H.E.S.

marginal (district). See CIVIC PLANNING.

margins. *Book.* The white borders around the type of a book page.

marimba. See MUSICAL INSTRUMENTS.

marine painting. A painting making use of seascapes or marine objects.

marmorarii Romani. See Cosmati work.

marquetry. Inlaid work, as in furniture.

Mars. See Ares.

Mars pigments. A range of colors from yellow to violet through orange and red have been made artificially by precipitating a mixture of a soluble iron salt and alum with an alkali like lime or potash. These are similar in a general way to the earth yellows and reds. They may be somewhat brighter in color and are rather more fine in grain than the natural products.   —G.L.S.

Maruyama school (Jap.). School of painting depicting subjects of nature in a realistic style.

marver. See GLASS AND GLASS-MAKING.

masjid. (Ar.). A Mosque. See ISLAMIC ART.

mask, masque. See THEATRE; OPERA; STAGESETTING; COSTUME ART.

Mass (L. *Missa*). The ritual in celebration of the Eucharist or Lord's Supper. The Mass falls into two divisions, the Ordinary and the Proper. The former consists of unchanging texts: the Kyrie, Gloria, Credo, Sanctus and Benedictus, and Agnus Dei. The texts of the Proper, principally the Introit, Gradual, Allelulia or Tract, Offertory and Communion, change according to the commemoration of the season or saint. Apart from the original plainsong settings, little music has been composed for the Proper of the Mass. The Ordinary, on the other hand, because of its fixity and range in religious expression, became in the hands of great 15th and 16th cent. schools the most significant art-form of the period. See Liber Usualis for plainsong melodies. See requiem mass; MEDIEVAL MUSIC; for mass (small letter). See PSYCHOLOGY OF DRAWING AND PAINTING; also for Mass see P. Wagner, *Geschichte der Messe*, 1913.   —V.A.

massicot. Derived from the mineral, lead, of which this is a monoxide, massicot has a clear yellow color. Traditionally, it is made by the gentle roasting of white lead at a temperature of about 300°C. Litharge is another name given it, although that may be used to designate a pigment more orange in color. The yellow lead monoxide, massicot, undoubtedly had a common use with painters during the Middle Ages and the Renaissance, and there is evidence to show that it was known from predynastic times in Egypt.

—G.L.S.

mastaba, mastabah. A type of tomb, oblong with sloping sides and connected with a mummy chamber in the rock beneath; characteristic of the tomb masonry of the Old Kingdom in Egypt. See EGYPTIAN ART.

masterpiece. A term which can be traced back to the medieval custom of requiring a craftsman who applied to his guild for the title of "master" to present a specific piece of work as evidence of his skill. The word was later applied to anything that seemed worthy of a master-craftman; but as the guilds disintegrated and the competition between skilled workmen grew freer and more intense a demand developed for more superlatives and the term *masterpiece* was reserved for the finest item in any given group, instead of being used merely to indicate the attainment of a certain level of excellence. Raphael's masterpiece was the *Sistine Madonna*; the architectural masterpiece of Rome was St. Peter's. The next phase in the evolution of the word consisted in changes in the comprehensiveness of the groups to which it was applied, or in the principle by which they were selected; we encounter lists of the masterpieces of painting, from Cimabue to the present day; of the masterpieces of genre, in painting, sculpture, etching, and other arts; or of the masterpieces of art, from the Parthenon and the Iliad to Hamlet and Beethoven's *Fifth Symphony*. But it is noticeable that this change was accompanied by a tendency to use the word in the plural and to preface it with the adjective *great*; it was beyond human power to select a single unquestioned masterpiece from such vast fields—and for some obscure reason users of the word have tended to avoid applications of it that were sure to lead to controversy. *Great* involves innumerable problems in absolute aesthetic value and arouses endless arguments, but *masterpiece* indicates only relative values, and limited comparisons, and it is employed chiefly to record widely accepted judgments. For still more obscure reasons the word is applied much oftener to the various arts of

space than to either music or poetry or the arts of the theater; it occurs most often, of course, in arts such as painting and sculpture in which there are no bars except lack of talent to the attainment of the highest possible level of artistic achievement. It must be recognized, however, that in all these fields the word has been losing caste in recent years. It is perhaps because its meaning has grown too flexible—we can say, for example, without arousing much argument, either that Vermeer left us no masterpiece or that he left few works that are not masterpieces—but it is more probably because our interest has turned from the superficial and rather fantastic problem of determining the precise rank of any given work within its group to the profounder and more realistic problem of analyzing its internal structure and realizing its individual potentialities, and because we are less intrigued by the notion of "permanent" values. We seldom find *masterpiece* in the index of any modern work on art and its appearances in the text are growing less frequent. When it does occur it is a little more likely to be used as a simple indication of value, or as a device for imparting color and rhetorical force to a sentence, than as a carefully considered superlative. It is still a permissible word, and even a respectable one, but under the pressure of the exacting modern standards for the study of art it is losing a little of its former glamour. —C.T.

master plan. See CIVIC PLANNING.

mastic. As a varnish-making resin, this is probably the most commonly used of all such materials at the present time. Mastic varnish is ordinarily prepared from the pure resin by selection and solution with a solvent like turpentine, with the addition of a small amount of drying oil or other plasticizer. The resin is derived from the tree, *Pistacia Lentiscus,* native of the Greek Archipelago but found, also, in other regions of the Mediterranean. The best known commercial source is the island of Chios. See RESTORATION OF PAINTINGS.

—G.L.S.

metabami (Pers.). Celadon (q.v.).

matelasse fabrics (Fr. *matelasser,* to cushion, to cover). An interesting modern fabric used for ladies' high priced dress materials. These are compound fabrics and have two distinct series of warp and filling threads. The face shows a modeled surface or pattern in quite high relief. The back shows the complicated nature of the weaving.

—G.W.R.

materialism. Materialism in art must be understood as the representation of that which is taken exclusively from external nature, as it is perceived by our senses. The only focal point of this art is material nature, which has for its main characteristic, the accidental. This type of materialism began in the early 15th cent. with the brothers Van Eyck, Konrad Witz, and Hans Multscher. In this art it is important that the world which is perceived by our five senses is understood as of the last and highest value, and from which there is no appeal. The last theoretical conclusions were drawn by the French Encyclopedists of the 18th cent. (see Diderot's works, esp. *La Système de la Nature*). Since for them nature has no purpose, no order, no value dependent upon purposes or order lying outside natural objects and nature is the only thing existing, no beauty of art is possible. For beauty is a value arising in the human mind and fixed by it. Furthermore, materialistic art can have no ideals and cannot consider the ideal as the goal for which it strives. Upon the basis of this materialism the only purpose of art can be the representation of nature in its entire and accidental appearance. An art thus unmistakably achieved must consequently be entirely indifferent to the human soul. The more it succeeds in eliminating all human value, the more precious it becomes.

A complete achievement of this materialistic program in art is not possible, because the main requirement of art is unity; and unity is achieved by ordering all single parts into a system of balance. The characteristics of unity and balance are qualities not lying within the material itself but arising from the activity of the human soul.

The more materialistic art grew away from the principles of the Middle Ages, the more all spiritual aims tending beyond the represented object vanished. Approaching nearest to the materialistic program were the so-called Naturalists of the 19th cent., such as Courbet and Leibl, the Impressionists such as Manet, Renoir, etc., and the Pointillists such as Signac. Only these artists seriously tried to put upon the canvas exclusively sensual perceptions and to indicate them as of the highest values in themselves. In connection with these works it is interesting to notice how the artist tried to evade the prob-

lem of "form", and to conceal unity and balance in order to give the appearance of accident and self-sufficiency.   —A.J.S.

mathematical aesthetics. See AESTHETICS, recent trends in (1).

mathematical objects. See object.

matte. Without shiny reflections.

maulstick. See mahlstick.

mauresque. See arabesque.

Mauryan art. See INDIAN ART.

mausoleum. See EARLY CHRISTIAN ARCHITECTURE.

maxima. See NOTATION.

Maxwell discs, triangle. See COLOR.

Maya art. The Maya were the greatest of ancient American peoples and their art was the finest of pre-Columbus American art. In fact, the three profound achievements of the Maya were art, architecture, and astronomy.

Although the astronomical data upon which is based the ultimate Maya calendar may have begun to be collected as early as the 7th cent. B.C., the Maya as an integrated, identifiable culture did not come into being until less than a hundred years before the birth of Christ. Suddenly, in the densely rain-forested plains of north-central Guatemala and neighboring British Honduras, the Maya were building splendid stone cities whose lofty truncated pyramids even today lift their ruined temple crowns as high as 280 feet in the air. Maya architecture was marked by the use of the corbelled arch. From their complex calendar the Maya carved dated inscriptions upon their towering monolithic stone monuments. Their writing-system was original, complete. Maya culture had flowered almost overnight. And with it, Maya art.

During the past hundred years Maya archeology has tended to emphasize the importance of the Petén area as the home of the so-called "Old Empire" of the Maya during the first five or six cents. A.D., and to bespeak the succeeding value of northern Yucatán as the site of the "New Empire", particularly between the 10th and 15th cents. A.D. The potential archeological value of the highland region of southern Guatemala has been neglected. Historically, this region promises to yield much; artistically, the prospect is more problematical. Unquestionably, Maya art reached its apex in the "Old Empire" cities, particularly in Quirigua, Piedras Negras, Palenque, and Copán. It had a strong resurgence some centuries later in Chichén Itzá, in Uxmal, and in several lesser cities of the Yucatecan area.

Like Maya architecture, the Maya calendar, and the Maya system of writing, Maya art was intensively religious. This was logical in a hemisphere where all cultures based most of their personal and national conduct upon religion: that is, upon the propitiation of the strenuous forces of nature surrounding them.

Maya art was mature from its identifiable beginnings. It simply grew more complex as the Maya culture grew older. But in the process it lost its earlier freshness and realism. Increasing emphasis was placed upon geometric design. There was a steady formalization of the nature-motifs, resulting finally in the most stylized ornamentation of stone, wood, and clay achieved by any people.

Living in an area of luxuriant tropical growth, the Maya in their art reflected their surroundings. They included profuse quantities of decorative detail. Like nature itself, the Maya abhorred a vacuum, and usually endeavored to fill all blank spaces with design. In the world about them there was no lack of motifs, either in foliage, animal life, or astronomical phenomena. Despite the urgency of pleasing the gods of fertility, however, there was in the art of this agricultural people a marked lack of phallic symbolism.

High among examples of Maya art are the stone sculptures in the round and semi-round at their great eastern city of Copán, in present-day Honduras (particularly a maize-goddess whose original is in the British Museum); the huge monolithic sandstone monuments at Quirigua, in Guatemala, with their complicated carved designs and hieroglyphic inscriptions; the carved and painted walls at Chichén Itzá, in Yucatán, México; a magnificent bas-relief on three walls of a nobleman's tomb at Comalcalco, in the Mexican state of Tabasco; jadeite figurines and plaques of exquisite workmanship, dredged from the great Sacred Cenote at Chichén Itzá; and painted ceramics from the Usumacíntla valley between Guatemala and México.

These, like all Maya art, were produced not by professional artists but by superb craftsmen. None of the ancient American nations supported an artist class. Their art was produced not as tours de force, not as the personalized expression of the artist, not on commission from some wealthy patron, but essentially as the conscious effort of the skilled artisan class to produce essentially utilitarian objects pleasing to the deities. In this, no people has been more successful. See ABORIGINAL AMERICAN ART.

—M.R.

mazurka. A national Polish couple dance usually performed by four or eight couples, in 3/4 or 3/8 time, the tempo being slower than the usual waltz. The basic step consists, in general, of leaping, sliding, and hopping combinations, with the greatest accent placed upon the second beat of the measure. When the dance was most popular, great freedom of invention was allowed, with the result that many mazurkas had a fresh, improvisational quality. —J.G.

meander motif. The meander (or fret) ornament, a simple, interlocking geometric pattern, was used in early Chinese art as a symbol of thunder and lightning; it is frequently found on Shang and Han bronzes. Among the Greeks it was employed to enliven architectural surfaces, especially on ceiling cornices and on the bases and capitals of columns, and as a border on vases. Several variations of the meander were devised, and sometimes a fret border was broken with insertions of squares or stars. —W.R.A.

meaning. As used in literary criticism, this term usually indicates the reference of the work of art beyond itself. The distinction involved here is that between the work of art as a formal and material structure, and what is conveyed by this structure. The concept of *meaning* thus depends upon the concept of *content* or *subject-matter*: the art work is regarded as referring to this content, and the meaning of the work is what it says about the content.

The term is also used, less often, to refer to the total effect produced by the work, without regard to the formal, material, or contextual elements of this effect. —I.J.

mean-tone temperament. See interval.

measure. *Mus.* A metrical unit of fixed length and accentuation, forming the smallest metrical subdivision of a period; presented by a group of notes or rests contained between two bars; sometimes called a **bar**.

measured music. See MEDIEVAL MUSIC.

measured painting. In Chinese painting, architectural in landscape. Kuo Chung-hsi (ca. 985) was an expert in this form of painting.

measuring point. See PERSPECTIVE.

mechanical arts. Productive activities of man which require mechanical labor and consequently cannot be listed among the liberal arts (q.v.). This division which was universally accepted during the Middle Ages and very largely even during the Renaissance and baroque periods, has its origin in social conditions of classical antiquity. For according to ancient Roman thought, while it was desirable that a citizen and free man give his attention to the philosophical and political interests embodied in the liberal arts, the pursuit of activities requiring physical labour (i.e., of the mechanical arts) was proper only for slaves. So great was the conservatism of medieval Europe that in spite of fundamentally altered social conditions this obsolete classification was retained. Medieval man was compelled consequently to list all that we now call the fine arts (q.v.) among the mechanical, since they require physical exertion; he could exempt them from this classification only in so far as they presupposed the liberal art of geometry. Therefore, architecture, e.g., was a liberal art as long as in the stage of geometrical planning, but a mechanical art when in the stage of actual construction. To raise the standing of the artistic profession to the level of liberal pursuits was an important purpose of Renaissance theory. See paragone. —R.B.

mechanical drawing. A mechanically controlled process of drawing which intends to import specific information to the reader. The same term applies to the terms, drafting, engineering drawing and precision drawing. See drawing. —R.L.W.

mechanical instruments (musical). In a sense all instruments which produce sound are machines. They differ, however, in the amount of mechanism intervening between the operator and the sound produced. Thus the vocal mechanism is part of the human body, responding in an intimate fashion to the mood of the singer. The keyboard instruments are much more remote, since a very complex machine intervenes between the will of the operator and the sound produced. We must distinguish the extent to which various musical instruments are mechanized. In the first or simplest stage a musical instrument produces sounds when manipulated by a performer. (For a discussion of this subject see the article entitled MUSICAL INSTRUMENTS.)

A second stage is reached when part of the operation, usually accomplished by the performer, is mechanically realized. Thus the **English guitar**, a stringed instrument which was played by a plectrum held in the fingers of the right hand, was in certain examples of late date automatically plucked. All the player did in such instances was to depress a key (like a small piano key) above the proper string to set the plucking mechanism into operation. In a sense the **harpsichord** and **piano** must be included here, since the ancestors of these instruments were sounded by plucking the strings with a plectrum or by striking them with small hammers. In another group of instruments the pitch of the sounds produced is controlled by operating a button or lever. A familiar though musically unimportant example of this group is the **auto-harp** where accompanying chords are automatically stopped by depressing a button.

Finally we reach a group of instruments which are completely or almost completely automatic, human intervention being essentially limited to setting the mechanism in operation and stopping it. Here we must include self-playing keyboard instruments, music boxes, and the like. This is the group which is usually designated by the term "mechanical instrument", and it is to this group that this article is chiefly devoted. The phonograph and radio (q.q.v.) are separately dealt with under the appropriate headings.

The tale of the *Golden Cockerel* of Pushkin with its magic bird which could forewarn of invasion, the mechanical nightingale of Andersen's fairy stories like many early tales of wonder reflect a deep desire to impose man's will on the most impalpable element as well as a naïve wonder which assumes that mechanisms which sing must be magic. Historical automatic instruments evolved at an early period and continued to follow a relatively uniform pattern through the period of Beethoven and (with diminished importance) to the present. The **automatic harpsichord** of the 16th cent. and the modern Swiss music box are closely related as far as the essentials of the action are concerned.

A series of pipes with their appropriate valves or a harpsichord mechanism were actuated by projecting studs on a revolving barrel. Père Engramelle in his very curious volume, *La Tonotechnie,* Paris, 1775, describes the manner of pricking the studs on the barrel with clarity. "Notation as I shall teach it, is nothing else than an easy system of calculating music, of measuring notes by figures, and of dividing the circumference of the cylinders in as many equal parts as may be necessary, in order to apply nails to them at precise and regular intervals, and to arrange them in such a fashion as to execute with taste and precision the pieces of music which one wishes to have played by these machines."

The invention of this mechanism dates back to the 16th cent. at least. Athanasius Kircher (*Musurgia,* 1650) describes a glockenspiel with a self-playing mechanism. Mersenne (*Harmonie universelle,* 1638) who was familiar with the device seems to consider it a German invention and refers to it as "of our time". Earlier than these descriptions, however, is an actual automatic instrument of the 16th cent. constructed by the Augsburg organ builder, Samuel Biderman. This, like the hurdy-gurdy, was operated by a crank, and the cylinder was pricked, producing six pieces of music. The wonder with which a modern listener might hear this echo of the music of so remote a period had already been felt by Père Engramelle who wrote a prophetic paragraph concerning the possibility of preserving the sound and the style of music by earlier composers, a possibility which we still have only partially realized with the phonograph, a much more perfect instrument at our disposal.

"We would still enjoy at present the execution of Lulli, of Marchand and of all the great men who have filled their contemporaries with astonishment if they had understood the system of pricking their best pieces, which transmitted by themselves to posterity on unalterable cylinders, would have preserved this form of expression of which we can only form an idea through history."

This wish to preserve the performances of famous performers was no doubt the force which inspired the unknown inventor who described "a Machine that shall write Extempore Voluntarys or other Musick as fast as any Master of Musick shall be able to play them upon an Organ Harpsichord &c." in an anonymous manuscript of the 18th cent. Each key was to have a stylus on its lower surface which would trace straight lines on a roll of paper revolving under them. The length of each traced line would indicate the duration of a note, and its position from left to right the pitch. The resulting record would resemble a player-piano roll, and, indeed, this unknown inventor would seem to have anticipated certain basic elements of the later player-piano.

The famous engineer Samuel de Caus in a book at once naïve and ingenious (English translation entitled *New and Rare Inventions of Water Works,* 1701) proposed various musical devices operated by water power. Thus, for example, a bird whistle might be operated by the air pressure produced by admitting water from an upper reservoir into a lower air-filled reservoir. He also describes **water-organs** in which both the barrel mechanism and the bellows are actuated by a water-wheel, the latter by a crank action so that one bellows is deflated while the other is inflated. Such toys, no doubt, were intended to add to the pleasure of formal gardens of the period.

One must note that the best of these early devices were by no means inflexible and terrifying mechanisms like the early player-piano, but were gentle in tone; and one must further note that the controlling cylinders were not laid out in a mechanical fashion, but were so calculated as to produce effects of rhythmic nuance. That great composers did not despise such machines is shown by Haydn's music for the tiny flute-like pipes of a mechanical clock, by Mozart's *Fantasia,* better known in the version for organ but originally for a mechanical instrument, and Beethoven's *Battle Symphony,* originally composed by Maëlzel's Panharmonicon.

This early art survived in such pretty toys as the **Swiss music box** in which the actuating pins plucked slender vibrating metal tongues of various lengths. The motive power was supplied by a clockwork motor. The principle also survived in the **hurdy-gurdy** which was operated by a crank and which contributed to the spice and variety of street noises. The **barrel organ** invaded even the parish churches of England as readers of Thomas Hardy's charming tale *Absentmindedness in a Parish Choir* will recall. We find as distinguished a figure as Edward F. Rimbault recommending a variant of this mechanism, concluding "we need scarcely point out the superiority of an accurate mechanism over the imperfect manipulation of an inferior performer".

The 19th and early 20th cents. marked the full development of new types of player mechanisms adapted to the piano. Earlier types were operated by two treadles which were alternately depressed. The barrel of earlier examples was replaced by a roll of paper perforated by dots and slots of various lengths. These openings permitted a pneumatic apparatus to actuate the appropriate key for a duration corresponding to the length of the slot in the roll.

Early examples were formidable indeed, and capable of boundless technique. In spite of an almost complete lack of nuance (the levers or other controls which supposedly provided expression were unable to alter the fundamental rigidity of the instrument) these instruments proved attractive not only to the general public but to certain composers such as Hindemith and Casella who wrote music for the instrument. A newspaper clipping of the early years of the 20th cent. pictures the vogue for these machines in an amusing fashion and at the same time points shrewdly to a real function of reproducing instruments. "A music festival is really hardly needed this year, with so many free concerts given to the public by the agents of automatic piano players. . . . Almost every week it is announced that some piano-making firm is to put a new kind of self-player on the market, and the purchaser, who finds it hard enough already to choose a piano, will be more and more embarrassed in selecting among the many playing attachments, of which the pianola was the pioneer. . . . It is precisely in supplying this general lack of opportunity for the frequent hearing of good music that the self player finds its field of utility."

Later developments resulted in such instruments as the Duo Art and the Ampico in which the rolls were the reproduction of a performance by a performing artist. The mechanism was actuated by an electric motor and a greater range of expression was striven for. Partly due to inherent defects but chiefly to the phenomenal development of radio and the electric phonograph these instruments have ceased to play an important role. The juke box, an electric phonograph with a record selector and a nickel-in-the-slot attachment, furnishes a loud and strident musical background in saloons, road houses, and other places of entertainments where the player-piano used to flourish. In another musical sphere the radio offers a far wider variety of musical fare than was possible on the earlier instrument. The mechanical age in music has been succeeded by an electrical age which is still revealing its possibilities.

—C.W.H.

medallion carpets. See ISLAMIC ART.

mediant. *Mus.* The third note of any major or minor scale, the "middle" note between tonic and dominant. See idiom B(1).

MEDIEVAL MUSIC: *The Monodic Ecclesiastical Phase.* The initial stages in the development of ecclesiastical music, more specifically the **plainsong,** or sung prayer of the Church, are intimately connected with the beginnings of Christianity. The term plainsong (L. *cantus planus;* Fr. *plainchant.*) meaning unaccompanied, unisonous, monodic, unmeasured melody, is a generic one, and includes the chants of the East (Armenian, Byzantine, Coptic, Ethiopian, Russian and Syrian) as well as those of the West (Ambrosian, Gallican, Gregorian, and Mozarabic). Since Christianity originated in the East, it follows that the sources of early Christian music are connected with those localities of the new religion in its inception—Jerusalem, Antioch, and Alexandria (see eastern chants).

The adoption of Hebraic forms of worship, e.g., the Alleluia, a direct outgrowth from the Hallel-psalms, and the Trisagion or Thrice Holy (the *Kedushah*), is an indication that Hebraic melodies were utilized by early Christians.

The spread of Christianity in the East brought the chant in contact with Greek musical theory and the Greek language, the liturgical language of the Church in both East and West up to the end of the 3rd century. The inclusion of the Kyrie into the Mass, the celebrated **Oxyrhynchus hymn** (q.v.) dating from the close of the 3rd cent. A.D., and the astounding similarity between the Greek hymn, Epitaph of Seikolos (variously dated from 2nd cent. B.C. to 1st cent. A.D.) and the Gregorian antiphon, Hosanna filio David —all of these constitute concrete evidence of the Greek influence.

The diverse Hellenic and Oriental elements were fused and crystallized by the Byzantine Church whose tendencies in the intellectual and religious spheres strongly affected the Roman Church of the West. Although the East continued to exert its influence with varying force on the West up to the middle of the 8th cent., it is at present impossible to determine the extent and the precise nature of that relationship. The first complete development of liturgical chant is to be found in the East, but it is the Western Chant which represents the earliest efflorescence of music known to us.

To the Hebraic, Greek, and Byzantine factors in the development of the Western Chant must be added another—the Latin language which dominates the rhythmic flow of the melodies. That Roman secular melodies found their way into the chants when Christianity was Latinized in the West, is probably, though not demonstrable.

Before giving an account of the Western Plainsong, it is well to consider the attitude of the Church toward music. The master-motive of the Christian Church was salvation. To this end the arts were pressed into service. As has been already intimated, the development of the liturgy is identified with the rise of the Chant. The function of melody, then, was to enhance and make more potent the meanings of the liturgical text. The notion of music as an end in itself was associated with evil and therefore, vehemently rejected. The memorable words of St. Augustine at the time of his conversion sum up the outlook of the middle ages thus: "Yet again, when I remember the tears I shed at the Psalmody of Thy Church, in the beginning of my recovered faith; and how at this time, I am moved, not with the singing, but with the things sung, when they are sung with a clear voice and modulation most suitable, I acknowledge the great use of this institution. Thus I fluctuate between peril of pleasure, and approved wholesomeness; inclined the rather (though not as pronouncing an irrevocable opinion) to approve of the usage of singing in the church; that so by the delight of the ears, the weaker minds may rise to the feeling of devotion. Yet when it befalls me to be more moved with the voice than the words sung, I confess to have sinned penally, and then had rather not hear music." (*Confessions* xxxiii, 50).

It has been properly maintained that the four great chants of the West—the **Ambrosian, Gallican, Gregorian** and **Mozarabic** represent four dialects of a common language. Tremendous interest centers around the plainsong of the west not only because of its intrinsic value—one of the greatest artistic manifestations of the middle ages—but also because the Chant later constitutes the basis for the new polyphonic art which emerges

about the 9th cent. and reaches its climax with the great 16th cent. polyphonic schools. The Gallican chant was superseded by the Gregorian when Charlemagne imposed the substitution of the Roman rite in 803 at the Council of Aachen. In Spain the Mozarabic Chant persisted for a time even after Alphonso VI (1085) against much opposition ordered the adoption of the Roman. There are little or no remains of the Gallican chant except for what was absorbed in the Gregorian. These include the *Improperia,* the *Crux fidelis,* and the hymn *Pange linga . . . certaminis,* all of which are part of the Good Friday service. Similarly, the Mozarabic chant did not survive except for 21 melodies, mostly from the Office of the Dead.

Named after St. Ambrose, Bishop of Milan (c. 340-97), the **Ambrosian chant** embraces all the music of the Milanese liturgy, a considerable amount of which was composed after the death of the saint. Although the Ambrosian Chant has survived, it has never been widely diffused, confining itself for the most part to Northern Italy. It was also used in the monastery of Monte Cassino up to the middle of the 11th cent. when it was replaced by the Gregorian chant. In spite of its antiquity, the earliest MS containing Ambrosian chant dates from the 12th cent.

Many Ambrosian melodies have found their way into the Gregorian collection. Indeed, the relationship of the Ambrosian to the Gregorian is reciprocal rather than one-sided. Comparative study of similar ornate chants reveals that the Ambrosian version tends to be more ornate than the Gregorian. On the other hand, the simple chants of the former are even simpler than those of the latter.

By far the largest and most important collection of ancient ecclesiastical music is that of the service of the Roman Church, or the **Gregorian Chant** (after Pope Gregory). This vast collection falls into two divisions, the music of the Mass (q.v.), contained in the Gradual, and the music of the Daily Hours of Divine Service in the **Antiphonary.** The texts for the first are available in the modern **Missal,** those for the second in the modern **Breviary.** The bulk of the music of the Proper of the Mass dates from the turn of the 7th cent. or earlier. The remainder was composed in the following centuries, some as recent as the 15th cent.

Of the role played in the development of the chant by Gregory's predecessors little is known. It appears that a papal school for singers existed in Rome at the time of

Pope Sylvester (314-36). Celestine I (422-32), Sixtus (432-40), Leo the Great (440-61), Gelasius (492-96), Symmachus (498-514), Hormisdas (514-23), John (523-26), and Boniface (530-32) are all said to have contributed to the liturgy and chant in some form or other. It is certain that the papacy at Rome furnished the impetus toward unity in the liturgy and chant. The climax in this direction came with the so-called Gregorian reform. According to a tradition based on the writing of John the Deacon (c. 872), Egbert, Bishop of York (732-66), and others, Gregory "arranged for the singers a most useful collection, the *Antiphonarius Cento*", made the liturgical chant equal to the liturgy itself as law of the Church, and imposed a uniform ritual and chant on all western congregations. The nature of Gregory's reform is disclosed in the meaning of the word *cento,* patch-work, hence compilation. With some additions made in the following centuries, this codification still constitutes the great body of Gregorian chant in use today.

The mission of St. Augustine in 596 to England at the behest of Gregory was but one important step in the propagation of the Roman chant in that country. In general, with the spread of the Church over Europe, the diffusion of the chant followed. On the continent the famous monasteries of Metz and St. Gall founded *Scholae Cantorum* based on the Roman model. By the 9th cent. the Roman chant was firmly established in Gaul through the medium of monasteries, cathedral and parochial schools. To be mentioned also are the monasteries of Reichenau, Fulda, and Cologne and Worms. In France the Abbey Würzburg and the schools in Mainz, Aachen, St. Martial in Limoges took a leading role in the dissemination of the chant. By the end of the 11th cent., Gregorian chant had established itself in Spain.

The concordance of the numerous MSS. preserved in these monasteries and schools from the 9th cent. on, demonstrates first the extraordinary zeal for unity in the chant and liturgy on the part of the Church, and 2nd that they must have been copies of an original collection stemming from the lost *Antiphonarius Cento* of Gregory I.

During the early centuries, the Chant was transmitted by oral tradition. *Neums* (q.v.) based on the grave, acute and circumflex accents (of probable Byzantine origin) indicating the rise and fall of a melodic line were used to recall known melodies. The shortcomings of such a method of notation were manifest to many medieval musicians. Numerous efforts were made to establish a system of precise notation. Among the systems of notation in vogue was the *daseian* notation (9th cent.) in which letters in various positions represented different pitches. That of Hermannus Contractus (1013-54) in which letters were used to indicate melodic intervals was somewhat similar in principle. The staff notation favored and perfected by Guido D'Arezzo (c. 995-1050), was really one among many in use at the time. Guido's interests were those of the practical teacher and musician. His method of **solmization** (q.v.) and adoption of the syllables ut, re, mi, fa, sol, la for the notes of the hexachord are unique achievements of far-reaching consequences.

Medieval music is based on a system of eight modes—4 authentic modes, and 4 derivative plagal modes. (See modes, ecclesiastical.) In modern chant books the mode is indicated by its appropriate number at the beginning of each composition. There is substantial evidence that the medieval modal system was in reality super-imposed on the Church melodies the basis of which is pentatonic. (See pentatonic scale.) The presence of the *quilisma* (a jagged note to be sung softly) occurring within the minor third adds weight to this view. The quilisma acts as a filling-in-tone, or non-essential tone which gives diatonic character to the fundamentally pentatonic structure of the ancient melodies. That numerous chants were revised in order to make them conform to the modal system is certain. Although theory and practice are sometimes at variance, for practical purposes it is best to treat the chants according to the modal system.

From the viewpoint of melodic structure plainsong falls into two styles: 1st the syllabic style in which for the most part each syllable of the text is set to one note, with an occasional syllable set to 2 or 3 notes, and 2nd the melismatic in which the syllables are set to 2 or more notes, and groups of notes. In general the capacity of the singers and the significance of the occasion determine the style.

The greater portion of Gregorian chant is either *responsorial* or *antiphonal*. (See psalmody.) The responses of a group to a soloist characterize responsorial chant. Representative of this category in the Mass are the **Gradual** (*Gradualresponsorium*) and **Alleluia,** in the **Office,** the **Respond,** (*Responsorium*). The alternate singing of two groups is the essential feature of antiphonal chant. This type is found in the Introit, Communion and in a certain sense the Offertory. More elaborate than the antiphonal chants of the Office, those of the Mass were performed by trained singers. Belonging to neither the responsorial nor the antiphonal is the **Tract** (*tractus*—straightway) in which the text is sung directly from one end to the other without alternation.

To the 9th cent. must be credited two of the most outstanding developments of medieval music, the *sequence* and the *trope* (q.q.v.). In the Alleluia it was customary since pre-Gregorian times to sing a long melismatic passage on the final syllable "a". This wordless melody was known as a *jubilus* or jubilation. Historians have attributed to Notker Balbulus (the stammerer), monk of St. Gall (d. 912) the mnemonic device of supplying these *longissimae melodiae* with words. The adaptation of words to a jubilus was called *sequentia cum prose*. (By the 12th cent. the terms prose and sequentia appear to have been used interchangeably.) In his *Liber hymnorium,* Notker states that he followed the example of the monks of Jumièges, who in turn probably obtained the idea from Byzantine sources. It appears therefore, that the sequence originated in northern France. Notker apparently was a writer of words to pre-existing melodies rather than a composer.

The trope which legend associates with Tuotilo, monk of St. Gall (d. 915) was an interpolation or addition in the chant. Of Byzantine origin this practice gradually penetrated the Ordinary of the Mass, and the Hour services. The interpolated melismatic melodies were later set to a text usually appropriate to the character of the feast according to the principle—one note, one syllable. Thus the sequence can be regarded as a trope appended to the Alleluia. Both tropes and sequences continued in vogue for several centuries. The former, never attained a place in the liturgy, while the latter after achieving a popularity which menaced the integrity of the liturgy were banned by the Church with the exception of 5.

There was little difference in musical style between the chants of the 9th cent. when new feasts were added and those of Gregorian times. As the need for new texts arose, the older melodies, or segments of them were utilized. The compositions of the 11th and 12th cents., on the other hand, no longer attained the simplicity, depth, and robustness

of the primitive melodies. Affectation and histrionics replaced sincerity and sobriety. The seeds of decadence were already in evidence during the 9th cent. when the new art of polyphony was first practiced in the Church. With the emergence of measured music during the 12th cent. came a misunderstanding of the Gregorian melismata. The rapid diffusion of the chant during the 9th, 10th, and 11th cents. is another cause which contributed to its decline. No sooner was the supervision of Rome relaxed in distant parts of Europe than the execution of the chant suffered. As the impetus in the cultivation of polyphony gained momentum, the interpretation of the chant became more and more uncertain.

After some centuries an abortive attempt to "reform" the chant resulted in the Medicean Gradual of 1614-15 in which the primitive melodies were abbreviated and shorn of their rich melismas beyond recognition, and interpreted according to the rules of measured music. Knowledge and interest in the Gregorian chant was so meagre in the years that followed, that no reaction against the crudities of the Medicean editions occurred until the 19th cent. The credit for the revival of Gregorian chant goes to the Benedictines (Solesmes) of the Congregation of France, especially Guéranger (1805-75) Pothier (1835-1923) and Mocquereau (1849-1930). "Where the MSS of different periods and different countries agree in their version of a melody, it may be affirmed that the true Gregorian text has been discovered." With this rule as guiding principle, an intense comparative study of hundreds of MSS from the 9th to the 14th cents. led to the restoration of the ancient Church melodies. In 1889 Mocquereau started the monumental *Paléographie Musicale* containing facsimiles of Ambrosian, Gallican, Gregorian and Mozarabic MSS., as well as studies on the history of the chant and its interpretation. The researches of the Benedictines received ecclesiastical sanction in the *Motu proprio* (Nov. 22, 1903) of Pius X, which provided for an *Editio Vaticana* (1905) containing the authoritative version of the Gregorian chant.

A theory of rhythmic interpretation has been developed by Mocquereau based on the equal duration of the square punctum and the virga. According to this theory note-groups of 2's and 3's freely mixed make up the rhythmic flow. The 1st note of each group bears an *ictus* which is sometimes indicated by a vertical line (|) or implied by the context according to well-defined rules. The ictus however, does not express any material emphasis being independent of the Latin tonic accent. "The ictus is more in the mind than in the voice" is a Solesmes slogan.

The vast labors of the Solesmes school have brought to light once more the ancient melodies, but while conceding the beauty of the Solesmes interpretations many scholars do not agree with their rhythmic principles. The so-called **Accentualists** (Pothier) who maintain that verbal accents should be stressed in rendering the chant, and the **Mensuralists** (Dechevrens, Jeannin) who insist that the note values of the medieval MSS. indicate longs and shorts (long twice duration of short) both find support for their contentions in medieval theory. Because the plainsong passed through various stages during its long course, it is doubtful if a general agreement on rhythmic interpretation will ever be reached. In any event, there is still much important work to be accomplished in this direction. The "Old Vatican Music" MSS. allegedly containing late copies of pre-Gregorian chant remain for the greater part a field for investigation.

The Monodic Secular Phase. That secular music has existed at all times requires no proof. In contrast to the survival of sacred music, no secular music of the early Middle Ages is now extant. There was no necessity for an oral tradition resembling that of the Church. MSS. of the 9th-11th cents. in staffless neume notation containing non-liturgical songs in Latin are undecipherable. Of the music of the **goliards**, wandering students and minor clerics—drinking songs, satirical songs, etc.,—nothing is known. With the exception of one melody, if it can be called such (*Audigier*, incorporated in the pastoral play by Adam de la Hale), nothing of the music of the *chansons de geste*, epic narratives on the exploits of Charlemagne, Roland, etc., remains.

It is quite different with the songs of the **troubadours** and **trouvères** whose sophisticated art coincided with the Age of Chivalry from the end of the 11th cent. to the end of the 13th. Over 250 melodies and 2600 poems by the troubadours are preserved in various MSS. The trouvères were more fortunate in the survival of their works—some 1200 melodies and about 4000 poems, in many cases more than one melody to the same poem. This outburst of monodic song must be considered in the light of the crusades, the stimulating contact with the east,

and the use of the vernacular languages. The new art brought with it a new theme—chivalric love, fealty, and service.

> *"À Dieu mon âme,*
> *Mon coeur aux dames,*
> *Ma vie a roi,*
> *L'honneur pour moi."*

In reflecting the varied thoughts and feelings pertaining to the mundane aspect of medieval life, troubadour and trouvère art for the first time in history emphasized the role of music as an end in itself.

The troubadours, amateur musician-poets of noble birth first practiced their art in the ancient province of Limousin, south of the Loire (Provence). Their language was the *langue d'oc*. The trouvères who imitated them came from the north of the Loire. Except for the use of the *langue d'oïl* there is no essential difference between the music of the trouvères and that of the troubadours. The cultural contact which paved the way for the art and ideas of the Provençal poets in northern France was effected during the second Crusade of 1147 when the nobility of the north and south was brought together. Practiced originally in the courts of Provence and the French court at the time of Louis VII, secular monodic art soon found its way into the feudal court of Burgundy, the Spanish courts of Aragon and Castile, as well as those of England and Italy.

According to all accounts, Guilhem IX, Duke of Aquitaine (1071-1127) was the first troubadour. Among the more famous were Marcabrun (c. 1120-95), one of the first to cultivate that obscure genre called *trobar clus* (closed poetry i.e. obscure) containing secret forms of verse accessible only to the initiated, Bertran de Born (d. 1215) who took part in the struggle between Henry II of England and his rebel sons, Peire Vidal (d. c. 1215) a rash scatterbrained individual known as "terror of husbands", Guiraut de Bornelh (d. c. 1220), *lo maestre dels trobadors,* and Folquet de Marseilles (d. 1231) who from being a troubadour ended his career as bishop of Toulouse. Also to be mentioned are Jauffre Rudel (1st half of 12th cent.), Raimon de Mirval (d. c. 1220) and Raimbaut de Vagueiras (d. 1207). Greatest of all troubadours was Bernard de Ventadour (d. 1195) who rose into prominence at the court of Eleanor of Aquitaine, grand-daughter of the first troubadour, and whose perfect specimens of love poetry are wedded to veritable melodic gems.

Included among the trouvères were Chré

tien de Troyes (12th cent.), Châtelaine de Coucy (fl. c. 1186-1203), Gace Brulé (d. c. 1220), Quesnes Béthune (1150-1224), and Blondel de Nesle (12th cent.) associated with Richard-Coeur de Lion (1157-99), himself a trouvère. Actual performance of the songs was in the hands of the wandering *jongleur*, a peculiar combination of executant musician and mountebank, who in return for wages placed his talents at the disposal of the troubadour (or trouvère). To the accompaniment (probably consisting of a simple prelude and postlude), of the harp, veille, guitar, lute or even a small portative organ, the jongleur performed his master's songs from castle to castle.

The relation between troubadour and jongleur was much like that of knight and squire. Occasionally the lowly jongleur wrote and composed, and thus raised his status as in the case of the troubadours Bernard de Ventadour and Gaucelm Faidit (d. c. 1216), and the trouvère, Colin Muset (c. 13th cent.). By the 13th cent., however, the distinction in social status between jongleur and trouvère appears to have no longer existed. During the 13th cent. supremacy in the art of song shifted to the *bourgeois* school of Arras, the most outstanding being the trouvère, Adam de la Hale (c. 1238-88), author of *Jeu de Robin et Marion*, the earliest French play with music.

The theory that the songs of the troubadours were originally imitations of Spanish models which in turn were based on Arabic forms must be dismissed. Despite its plausibility in view of the fact that the lute, a favorite of the troubadours, is of Oriental origin, the complete lack of Arabic MSS. renders this theory untenable. One must turn to the forms practiced by the Church—the litany, the rondeau, the sequence and the hymn—as the derivative elements of troubadour-trouvère lyrical poetry. The popularity of the sequences, tropes, and hymns naturally led secular artists to similar forms of expression. The themes of love and service, on the other hand, had their antecedents in medieval Latin poetry. They had but to await the Crusades for the full flowering.

As the following listing of poetic types will show, the subject matter included themes other than love and service. The *canso* or *chanson d'amour* treated love according to the "théorie de l'amour courtois", the *sirventes* of moral and political topics, the *pastourelle* of the love adventures of a knight with a shepherdess. The *alba* or *chanson d'aube* was

a song of warning in which the lovers were informed that the dawn was approaching. The *chanson de danse* (*estampie*) as the name suggests, combined song with dance. More complex were the *partimen* (*jeu parti*) and the *tenson*, debates between two interlocutors, sometimes on a moral or political subject, sometimes on a point of amorous casuistry. The *chanson de toile* supposedly sung by a woman at work treated of unhappy romance. To be mentioned also are the crusaders songs and the *planh*, a dirge on the death of a hero.

The most prevalent musical form may be described as A-A-B. This simple formula was capable of infinite variation. Indeed it was the rule that no two songs should be alike—the slightest dissimilarity satisfied this canon. The first strophe, A frequently ends with a half-close—*ouvert*, and the antistrophe A set to the same melody with a full-close —*clos*. The episode B set to a different melody may be short or long and is often subdivided.

Different from the above in form are the *rondeau* and the *descort* (*lai*). The former may be described by the following formula:

music: A-B-A-A-A-B-A-B

text: a-b-c-a-d-e-a-b

Lines a-c-d and lines b-e have the same meter and the same rhyme. In the *descort*, on the other hand, each verse possesses a different setting.

The ecclesiastical modal system is the basis of the melodies, but many of them border on those modes scrupulously avoided in church music—the major and the minor. In the various *chansonniers* of the 13th and 14th cents. which preserve the songs, the plainsong notation on staves is used. Since this type of notation indicates no time values, the interpretation of rhythm has caused considerable difficulty. The most widely accepted solution to this problem (formulated by Jean Beck and Pierre Aubry) is that the poetic meter of the text determines the rhythm of the melody. Through the application of the *rhythmic modes* (q.v.) the melodies acquire real meaning. Balanced phrases four measures in length (sometimes six), the prevalent feature of modern music are common.

The art of the troubadours was stifled by the Albigensian crusade (1209-29). This implacable war carried on by Innocent III against the Provençal nobility who constituted an anti-sacerdotal party in opposition to the Roman Church, resulted in the complete destruction of Provençal civilization

"Song should express joy, but sorrow oppresses me, and I have come into the world too late," mournfully wrote Guiraut Riquier (d. 1292) last of the troubadours. The decline of the trouvères was a gradual process, social changes and interest in the new art of polyphony both playing their inexorable roles.

'With Guillaume de Machaut (c. 1300-77) monodic song experienced a momentary resurgence in France. But the great days of the Age of Chivalry were over, and Machaut's songs were really an emulation of the past and not a reflection of contemporary mood. Machaut's monodic *lais* consist of 12 pairs of stanzas, each having a different metrical form and melody with the exception of the last which is the same as the first in meter and is set to the same melody. His *virelais* (*chansons balladées*) are based on a form frequently found not only in troubadour and trouvere songs but also in the non-liturgical songs of the 13th and 14th cents. In its simplest form the *virelai* (also equivalent in form to the Italian *ballata*) answers to the following formula: Music: A-B-B-A
Text: a-b-c-d.

The German counterpart of the troubadour and trouvère is the **Minnesinger** (Minnelove). Using the lyrical forms of the troubadours as their models and in some instances fitting German poems to Provençal melodies, the Minnesingers are by no means to be considered as slavish imitators. They are as thoroughly German in spirit as the courts of the Hohenstaufen, Thuringian, and Austrian nobility which they graced.

Outstanding among the Minnesingers, as a rule members of the lower nobility, were Friedrich von Hûsen (c. 1190), Walther von der Vogelweide (c. 1170-c. 1230), most famous of German medieval poets, his great contemporary, Wolfram von Eschenbach, Neidhart von Reuenthal (c. 1180-1250), and Ulrich von Lichtenstein (c. 1200-76). Of especial interest is Heinrich von Meissen (1250-1318), better known as Frauenlob (ladies' praiser), who is said to have established the first guild for singers at Mainz in 1311. The Minnesingers did not have jongleurs, they performed their own songs.

In their praise of love and gallantry, the Minnesingers assumed a chaster attitude than the troubadours and trouvères. Their poems were permeated with a feeling for nature and a religious mysticism totally foreign to the skeptical and volatile tone of their western confrères. The songs in honor of the

Virgin Mary are typical of a religiosity peculiarly German.

Practically identical are the poetic types: the **Lied** corresponds to the *canso*, the **Leich,** the *lai*, the **Tagelied,** the *alba*, etc. The **Spruch** usually didactic in character, dealt with social and political matters. The most frequently used form consists of a couplet and a conclusion i.e. two **Stollen** and the **Abgesang.** The two **Stollen** are metrically alike and set to the same melody. The *Abgesang* has its own melody, thus making an A-A-B. In some songs there is a repetition of the couplet melody following the *Abgesang*.

Based on the ecclesiastical modes, the melodies show the influence of Gregorian chant. Like the melodies of the troubadours and trouvères, those of the Minnesingers are interpreted rhythmically according to the meter of the verse. (See rhythmic modes.) In melodic invention and sheer beauty, the art of the Minnesinger as a whole compares less favorable with that of his western colleagues.

With the decline of feudalism and the extinction of the Hohenstaufen dynasty in the 14th cent. the art of the Minnesinger began to dwindle. Hugo von Monfort (1357-1423) whose texts were set to music by Burk Mangolt and Oswald von Wolkenstein (c. 1377-1445) represent the movement at its lowest ebb.

The rise of the middle class brought with it the *Meistersinger.* Following the example of Frauenlob, the Meistersingers started schools and formed guilds for singers at Mainz, Strassburg, Frankfort, Nuremberg and other German cities. The Meistersingers professed to follow the ideals of the Minnesingers, but their songs are extremely stilted and pedantic, the result of a meticulous observance of complex rules. The most important Meistersinger was Hans Sachs (1494-1576), the cobbler of Nuremberg, immortalized by Wagner in his great music-drama.

The Monodic Non-Liturgical Phase. The line of demarcation between religious and secular song is often times difficult to draw. Many of the troubadour-trouvère songs are religious in subject matter. Ever since the earliest times the secular and the religious inter-penetrated. The meeting of the two is to be observed in non-liturgical song. In northern Italy about the middle of the 13th cent. monodic song took the form of the *lauda spirituale,* a non-liturgical song of praise. Sung by the flagellant fraternities in the course of their pilgrimages, the *lauda* is folk-like in character and its rhythms show a remarkable kinship to those of Gregorian chant. The form of the *lauda* approaches that of the French *virelai*.

The flagellant fraternities gradually spread to the north extending as far as the Rhine provinces. During the period of the Black Death in 1349, the penitential mania reached its climax. In Germany flagellants included in their penitential rites the singing of *Geisslerlieder* (Geissler-flagellants), the verse forms of which were modelled on the Italian *lauda*.

Somewhat allied to the *lauda* is the *cantiga* some 400 of which were collected under the aegis of Alfonso X (*el Sabio*) of Castile and Leon (1252-84) famous patron to many Provençal troubadours. The *cantigas*, songs in praise of the Virgin Mary, are written in the Portuguese-Galician language and most frequently follow the melodic pattern of the French *virelai* or the *rondeau*. In the MS. containing the *cantigas* are several minatures showing various instruments, some of Arabic origin such as the lute, rebec, etc., thus implying a Moorish influence. It is fallacious, however, on this and other circumstantial evidence to jump to the conclusion that the Moorish element was the dominating influence not only in Spain but in Europe as well. Another miniature indicates that some of the *cantigas* were accompanied by dance—not an unusual fact considering the importance since the earliest times in Spain of the dance in popular religious worship.

Religious pilgrimages to famous shrines such as the monastery of Monsserrat claimed to be the legendary site of the Holy Grail account for some monodic pilgrim songs of popular origin (*Cants dels Romeus*) dating from the 14th cent. These songs dedicated to the Virgin and written partly in Latin and partly in Catalan also combine communal dancing with religious worship.

The Polyphonic Phase. The art of polyphony in its mature stages constitutes one of the great achievements of western civilization. For the first few centuries its development was mainly the work of monkish musicians, but its origin lay outside the Church. The writings of Bishop Aldhelm (c. 640-709) and Johannes Scotus Erigena (c. 815-c. 877), the Irish theologian-philosopher, indicate that part singing was practiced at least as far back as the 7th cent. in England and Ireland. In his discussion of Welsh music Giraldus Cambrensis (1147-1220) stated that the long-

standing popular practice of part singing was transplanted from Denmark. Although it is possible that some form of primitive polyphony was known elsewhere in Europe the evidence points to a northern origin. The introduction of popular polyphony into the Church was no doubt a concession to a persistent practice.

The earliest form of polyphony practiced in the Church is known as *organum* (or diaphony as it was also called). It is described in a treatise entitled *Musica Enchiriadis* of unknown authorship, though attributed by some to Hucbald (c. 880), Benedictine monk of St. Amand. Organum consisted of a Gregorian melody accompanied by another which proceeded in parallel motion at the 4th or at the 5th above. This crude form of polyphony was undoubtedly improvised.

Later the term organum became a generic one applied to various forms of primitive polyphony. In all its forms the unison, the octave, the 5th and the 4th served as consonances. An immense step forward in the direction of genuine polyphony was taken when Johannes Cotto (c. 1100) strongly advocated the principle of contrary motion. Theory usually lags behind practice, for this procedure appears to have been used at least a century before in the Winchester Troper, an English MS. written in neumes in *campo aperto*, i. e., without lines. Admitted by Johannes de Garlandia (early 13th cent.) and given complete sanction by Walter Odington in 1280 as imperfect consonances, major and minor 3rds were comparatively late comers into the family of consonances. In the final recognition of 3rds and 6ths as consonances must be considered the influence of *Fauxbourdon* and *Gymel* (qq. v.). As early as the 1st half of the 11th cent., however, Guido d'Arezzo in examples of organum from the Micrologus used the 3rd in the *occursus* (close) or coming together of the parts at the end forming the cadence—progression of 3rd to the unison. In the organum of the late 11th and early 12th cents., the 3rd was employed between consonances "in passing".

The first stage in the development of polyphony involved a note-against-note technique. Sometime prior to the 12th cent. a new procedure appeared—the practice of singing a florid melody in the upper part (*discantus*) against the sustained tones (*tenor*) of a Gregorian melody in the lower. In the development of this new art variously called *musica mensurata, ars mensurabilis,* etc., i.e., measured music, France (Abbey of St. Martial in Limoges and the school of Notre Dame de Paris), which during the 12th and 13 cents. was the intellectual center of Christendom, took the lead. The necessity for indicating the relative length of tones led at first to the adoption of the rhythmic modes (q.v.) as a means to express durational values. Later theorists among them the unknown author of *Discantus Positio Vulgaris* (c. 1230-40), Magister Lambert (13th cent.) and Franco of Cologne (2nd half of 13th cent.) devised means by which durational values could be expressed with mathematical precision. Emphasis was placed on ternary rhythm i.e. the division of durational values into threes (*tempus perfectum*), the justification for which was found in the dogma of the Holy Trinity. The much maligned duple rhythm (*tempus imperfectum*) was restricted for the most part during the 12th and 13th cents. to secular music.

Two great figures loom in the latter half of the 12th and early 13th cents., both leading lights of the great Notre Dame school at Paris who gave direction to the so-called *Ars Antiqua* of the 13th cent.—Leoninus (fl. 1160-80) *optimus organista,* composer of the *Magnus liber organi* consisting of a cycle of 2 part organa (*organa dupla*) for the ecclesiastical year, and Perotinus (fl. 1180-1236), *optimus discantor et melior quam Leoninus* who remodelled and added *clausulae* to Leoninus' *Magnus liber* which functioned as substitutes for certain individual sections of the organa. Practically nothing is known of the lives of these composers save for some information given by the English author of Anonymous IV (2nd half 13th cent.). Leonin substituted the rhythmic modes for Gregorian rhythms in the tenor (i.e. base in the modern sense) of his organa. Perotinus who went beyond his master, Leoninus, wrote not only 2 part organa but 3 part (*tripla*) and 4 part (*quadrupla*) organa. The employment of imitations and sturdy modal rhythms gave his polyphony a unity secured through specifically musical means independent of textual considerations.

Outstanding also among the forms practiced during the period of the Ars Antiqua are the *conductus* and the *motet.* The *conductus* was a musical setting of a Latin metrical poem in from 1 to 4 voices. It was unique in that the tenor or *cantus firmus* was not taken from liturgical song but was an original melody, thus enabling the composer

to give free reign to his imagination. The text which was religious or secular in content was sung by all the voices. Moving in chord-like formation, with occasional melismatic passages over one syllable the individual melodic threads of the conductus adopted a more or less uniform rhythm.

The motet which originated during the first decades of the 13th cent. was derived from the old principle of the trope. In fact the first motets were really imitations of *clausulae*, the upper part being set to an independent text. The tenor (or *pes*) upon which the entire composition was fashioned, although taken from liturgical melody, was performed on an instrument. While the tenor sustained the liturgical melody, the *motetus* the part directly above, sang the chief text— an elucidation of the text of the tenor (i.e. an extension of the *mot* of the tenor, hence the word motet). The triplum (from which is derived the word treble), third voice, and quadruplum, fourth voice, if present, were also set to independent texts. Originally religious in character the motet gradually absorbed secular elements. The presence of Latin and vernacular texts side by side, and secular texts often bearing no relation to each other, became commonplace. The art of writing motets was in reality an art of combination. The interplay between the rhythmic pattern of the tenor and that of the other parts frequently based on different rhythmic modes attained in many of the later motets an extraordinary complexity. An effective device sometimes met with in motets is the *hocket* (*hoquetus*) in which voices alternate rapidly with one another, the melody being interspersed with rests. The motet continued in vogue through the 14th cent. long after the conductus became obsolete.

Among the writers of the motet were the trouvère Adam de la Halle of the school of Arras, and Pierre de la Croix (end of 13th cent.) of Amiens who introduced fast rhythms requiring the use of the *semibrevis* for the first time.

The influence of the Notre Dame school made itself felt in Spain, Italy, as well as in England, the last country accounting for such outstanding theorists as Johannes de Garlandia, Johannes de Grocheo, and Walter Odington. These and others—Magister Lambert and Franco of Cologne, were concerned in expounding the work of the Ars Antiqua. Apparently of English origin in style and technique, however, was the celebrated Reading *Rota, Sumer is icumen in,* (c. 1240, scribe Fornsete) containing religious and secular texts. This remarkable composition is a canon for 4 voices over a 2 part tenor or *pes* forming a *basso ostinato,* the first of its kind. Far more advanced in the use of imitation than works of the Notre Dame school, and comparing favorably with 14th cent. French and Italian works of similar technique, the *Summer Canon"* stands out at an unique example of medieval polyphonic art.

The art of the 14th cent. is labelled by musicologists the *Ars Nova* after a treatise of the same name by Philippe de Vitry (1291-1361), Bishop of Meaux, and versatile counsellor to Charles IV of France, who combined diplomacy with the arts of poetry and music. A new art emerges heralding the end of the medieval outlook. For the first time the composer takes precedence over the theorist. The use of 3rds and 6ths, the prohibition of consecutive 5ths and octaves, observable tendencies treating the 4th as a disonnance, and a more expert treatment of the cadence are all features of the works of this period. Binary rhythm was favored over the ecclesiastically sanctioned ternary rhythm although the various subdivisions of durational values into threes continued to be called "perfect". The *minim* and *semiminim,* notes of small value, saw service in the prevalent musical forms. The systems of proportional notation described in the *Ars Nova* of de Vitry and in the *Pomerium* of Marchettus of Padua (14th cent.) (both written in the course of the 1st half of the cent.) although differing in details were similar in principle.

In France the Ars Nova was dominated by Guillaume de Machaut (c. 1300-77) a truly great figure. Poet, scholar, and musician, Machaut led a varied life being for many years in the service of the restless warrior King, John of Bohemia and later attached to the royal court of France. At the time of his death he was canon of Rheims. Machaut displayed far more resourcefulness as a polyphonic composer than as a trouvère. In spite of the constant employment of elaborate artifices, the clue to Machaut's music lies in his claim that the essential guide to good composition is the ear. His output mostly secular consisting of motets, rondeaux, virelais (chansons balladées), ballades, and the great 4 part Mass, supposedly composed for the coronation of Charles V in 1364, sums up the characteristics of the Ars Nova. The 3 part so-called Mass of Tournai, (1st half of 14th cent.) made up of pieces by various

anonymous composers is the only polyphonic setting of the Ordinary of the Mass, antedating that of Machaut. Written in the prevailing motet style, the Mass achieves a sense of unity through the employment of certain melodic formulas in the different sections.

In the motet, secular or religious, Machaut usually confined himself to related texts in the same language. The so-called *isorhythmic* motet featured a tenor in which lengthy elaborate rhythmic patterns called *talea* were repeated several times. Characteristic also of Machaut's motets is the repetition of the tenor in diminution (i.e. the values of the notes are halved).

The *ballade* (in from 2 to 4 parts), not to be confused with the chanson balladée, consisted of 2 lines set to the same music, the 1st forming an *ouvert* and the 2nd ending in a *clos.* The 3rd line was set to independent music. Since the leading melody was in the highest voice, it is quite likely that the lower parts were instrumentally performed.

The polyphonic rondeau was equivalent in structure to the monodic rondeau of the 13th cent. By this time, however, this form was no longer used as a dance. As in the motet, the most complex polyphonic devices were frequently used—imitations and *cancrizans,* (crab-like motion) i.e. the same melody used backwards.

The majority of Machaut's virelais are monodic. Structurally the polyphonic ones were similar in form.

The greatness of Machaut overshadowed all other French composers. Jean Cuvilier, Jacques de Senleches, and F. Andrieu are minor composers whose works bear Machaut's influence. Andrieu's 4 part musical setting of a poem in ballade form by Eustache Deschamps lamenting the death of Machaut shows the great esteem in which he was held.

The extraordinary musical activity in Italy during the 14th cent. (more precisely from c. 1325-c. 1425) is in marked contrast to the apparent inertia of the preceding century. The numerous Provençal troubadours who found refuge in Italian courts after the gloomy days of the Albigensian Crusade do not seem to have produced any imitators. No music of Pietro Casella the earliest composer of madrigales, whom Dante (1265-1321) mentions in the *Purgatorio* is extant. The early formative influences of the Italian Ars Nova, therefore, are not to be sought in Italy, but in a fusion of Provencal and

French elements. A marked preference for the conductus style is evident in the works of Giovanni da Cascia, also known as Giovanni da Firenze, and Jacopo da Bolognia (both 1st half 14th cent.), pioneers who paved the way for later composers. By the middle of the cent., however, the Italian Ars Nova assumed distinctive features of its own. A complete elimination of the *cantus firmus* i.e. the tenor, a penchant for canon, and the transference of the most important melodic line to the highest part are the pervading traits. The Italians were far more concerned with the idiocyncrasies of the voice than their French contemporaries. Nevertheless, there was actually no distinction between vocal and instrumental music, since in performance it was customary to substitute instruments when voices were lacking. Even more than the French, Italian composers reflected in the choice of their texts the new spirit of humanism. In the use of binary rhythm, the Italians appear to have preceded the French.

The dominant forms of the Italian Ars Nova were the *madrigal* (*matricale*) and caccia, both of purely Italian origin, and the *ballata*. The madrigal is made up of 2 sections, the 1st consisting of from 1 to 4 stanzas of 3 lines set to the same music and the 2nd, the refrain or *ritornello* of 2 lines set to different music. As a rule the meter changes in the 2nd section from binary to ternary or vice versa. There was frequent use of imitation and strict canon.

The *ballata* in common with the madrigal was written in 2 or 3 parts. In both forms melismatic passages typical of the *conductus* occur frequently. In structure the ballata is equivalent to the French chanson Balladée. The absence of a text in some compositions indicates that they were performed entirely with instruments.

Although not as highly favored as the madrigal, in certain respects the most unique form of the Italian Ars Nova is the *caccia* (literally hunt). Originally limited to the depiction of hunting-scenes, the *caccia* later included subject matter ranging from the picturesque to the dramatic—market scenes and street cries, fishing scenes, rural scenes, etc. The realism of these onomatopoeic texts was brought into bold relief through the use of strict canon liberally interspersed with hockets. Normally the Italian *caccia* consists of 2 sections, the 1st of which is a 2 part canon supported by a free base part performed on an instrument. The French *chace*

which omitted the independent base part is thought by some to have served as the model for the Italians. The origin of the *caccia*, however, is to be found in the canonic madrigal with which it has in common the use of canon and the presence of the final ritornello, and the Italian *frottola* from which it borrows the poetic element and the vivacious representation. The *ritornello* or second section of the caccia may or may not be in canonic imitation and in some instances is omitted altogether.

Besides the two already mentioned composers, among the exponents of the Italian Ars Nova are Ghiraldello da Firenze (c. 1368), Magister Piero (14th cent.), Lorenzo da Firenze (late 14th cent.), Vincenzo da Rimini (Vincenzo da Imola) (late 14th cent.), Niccolo da Perugia (late 14th cent.) and Zaccaria (papal singer 1420-32). The greatest of the Italians was the blind Florentine poet, composer and organist at San Lorenzo, Francesco Landini (1325-97) who together with Machaut dominated the century. Landini's fabulous reputation as a master of all instruments, and popularity as a composer and poet are well attested. In 1346 at Venice he was awarded the laurel crown by Pietro il Grande, king of Cyprus in the presence of Petrarch. Giovanni da Prato's *Il Paradiso degli Alberti* (1389), which contains pictures of Florentine life, gives a vivid description of the blind musician who performed his love verses so sweetly that "their hearts almost burst from their bosoms".

Over 150 compositions of Landini written in the forms practiced at the time are extant. In many instances the composer supplied his own text.

With the 15th cent. the medieval period may be said to have been concluded. The musical art of the English composer Dunstable (d. 1453) as well as his two great contemporaries of the Burgundian school, Dufay (d. 1474) and Binchois (d. 1460) though stemming from Italian and French sources is based on new methods which cannot be investigated here. These are the earliest composers whose polyphony is in a direct line with that of the great 16th cent. schools. The phenomenon of nationalism, the institution of royal choirs and chapels, and the 15th cent. Burgundian and Flemish schools which hold sway over Europe, are new forces leading to new destinations. See *Liber Usualis,* 1934 (contains music for Mass and Divine Service); Beck, J. B., *Le Chansonnier Cangé,* 1927; Ellinwood, Leonard,

The Works of Francesco Landini, 1939; Gennrich, F., *Rondeaux, Virelais und Balladen,* 2 vols. 1921, 1927; Gleason, H., *Examples of Music before 1400,* 1942; Hughes, H. V., *Early English Harmony,* Vol. 2, 1913; Liuzzi, F., *La Lauda e i primordi della melodia italiana,* 2 vols., 1935; Ludwig, F., *De Machaut. Musikalische Werke,* 1926-34; Marrocco, W. T., *14th Cent. Italian Cacce,* 1942; Wolf, J., *Geschichte der Mensural-Notation von 1250-1460,* 3 vols., 1904; Wooldridge, H. E., *Early English Harmony,* Vol. 1, 1897; *Scriptores;* Aita, V., Selmar, C., *Intro. to the Music of the Middle Ages* (in prep.); Apel, W., *The Notation of Polyphonic Music 900-1600,* 1942; Aubry, P., *Trouvères et Troubadours,* 1909; Beck, J., *Die Melodien der Troubadours,* 1908; Ferretti, P., *Estetica gregoriana,* 1934; Castoue, A., *L'Art grégorian,* 1911; Gennrich, F., *Grundriss einer Formenlehre des mittelalterlichen Liedes,* 1932; Lang, P., *Music in Western Civilization,* 1941; Leichtentritt, H., *Geschichte der Motette,* 1908; Mocquereau, A., *Le nombre musical Grégorian,* 1927; Reese, G., *Music in the Middle Ages,* 1940 (contains comprehensive bibliog.); Ribera y Tarragó, J., *Music in Ancient Arabia and Spain,* 1929; Wagner, P., *Intro. to the Gregorian Melodies,* 1910.   —V.A.

medium. Any adhesive material that is capable of cementing together the grains and particles of pigments used by the painter, can be called by this name. There has been occasional confusion between the word, medium, properly used, and non-adhesive materials added for purposes of thinning a paint mixture. Technically, the latter—water with aqueous mediums or turpentine with oil, should be classed as solvents or diluents rather than as binding mediums. The word, vehicle, is a synonym of medium. See ACOUSTICS.   —G.L.S.

medium relief. See relief sculpture.

megaron. See Aegean architecture.

Megilp. This name was given chiefly during the 19th cent. to a mixture of mastic resin and linseed oil which was added to commercially prepared oil paints during the painting process. With change in painting styles and painting methods, it has been largely abandoned.   —G.L.S.

mei (Ch.). Chinese word for plum, symbol of longevity.

Meiji art. See JAPANESE ART.

Meiningers, the. See MODERN STAGE SETTING.

Meissen ware. See CERAMICS II.

meistersinger. See MEDIEVAL MUSIC.

mekugi (Jap.). A wooden dowel to hold the tang of a sword in the handle.

Melanesia, art of. See OCEANIA, ARTS OF.

Meldrum, school of. The term refers to a group of Australian painters who follow the teaching and the art of the painter Duncan Max Meldrum (1875-   ) who, in 1913, established the Meldrum Art School in Melbourne. In *The Invariable Truths of Depictive Art* (1917) Max Meldrum has stated what he believes to be the principles of painting. Meldrum contends that painting is "a pure science—the science of optical analysis", and he maintains that the painter has the task of translating optical impressions in terms of his medium and in the scientific order in which these impressions come to the eye; tone being first, proportion second, and colour third.

During his teaching Meldrum exerted considerable influence and met also with strong opposition so that, for a time, the artists in Melbourne are said to have been divided into the so-called Meldrumites and anti-Meldrumites—a division which, however, has ceased to exist. Some of the followers of Meldrum are: Justus Jorgensen, Colin Colahan, Percy Leason, Archibald Colquhoun, John Farmer, Olive Frick, and others. See *Max Meldrum, his Art and Views,* edited by Colin Colahan, 1917; William Moore, *The Story of Australian Art,* 1934.   —H.H.

Melian amphora. See Ionian vases.

melisma. See MEDIEVAL MUSIC.

melodic interval. See interval.

melodic inversion. See inversion.

melodic minor scale. See scale.

melodic tetrachord. See scales and modes.

melodrama. (1) Originally the opera. (2) Later, spoken drama with musical accompaniment. (3) A sensational play. See opera.

melody. Series of tones including characteristic pitch changes by virtue of which the series has particular expressive qualities, these qualities being in most cases enhanced by corresponding rhythmic changes. —E.K.

melos. Song; the term used by Wagner for the vocal melodies in later musical dramas to exemplify vocal phrases which have not the quality of symmetry characteristic of earlier opera songs. See opera.

membrane. See ACOUSTICS.

memoria. See EARLY CHRISTIAN ART.

memorial ring. See JEWELRY.

memory picture. A representation of the most characteristic features and aspects of forms—found in primitive and early art. See fractional concept.

Mendi, art of the. See AFRICAN NEGRO ART.

menhir. A vertically standing rough stone or monolith; either alone or as one in an avenue or circle.

mensa. See altar.

mensural or measured music. See NOTATION.

mensuralists. See MEDIEVAL MUSIC.

menue verdure. See TAPESTRY.

menuki (Jap.). Ornaments or grips fastened to the handle of a sword by the cord wrapping (*itomaki,* q.v.).

Mercury. See Hermes.

meru. See INDIAN ART.

merz pictures. See Dadaism.

Mesa Verde (Span. green table land). A large mesa 15 miles long and 8 wide, in southwestern Colorado, so-called because in a generally arid land it is covered with cedar and piñon. In the cliffs of the canyons that traverse the mesa the Anasazi built hundreds of cliff houses, some of them the finest of the Great Pueblo Age. Cliff Palace, Spruce Tree House and Balcony House (the modern names were given by their discoverers) are among the most important. Cliff Palace occupies a cavern high up in a cliff wall protected from weather and enemies. It consists of about 200 round or rectangular rooms of well-laid stone and adobe with timber and adobe floors and roofs, up to four stories high, and about 20 kivas. The site is now the Mesa Verde National Park. See Pueblo art. —H.G.

MESOPOTAMIAN ART. Mesopotamia, i.e., the land of the two rivers Tigris and Euphrates, is a long and narrow strip of land bordered by the Arabian and Syrian deserts in the southwest and by the Zagros Mts. in the northeast. It is thus open to the invasions of the lowlanders of the desert who were of Mediterranean race and spoke Semitic languages, and of the highlanders who were of different ethnic stocks and spoke languages which were neither Semitic nor Indo-European; with the highlanders came occasionally intruders from father north. These immigrations began as soon as the country became inhabitable after the Ice Age; they influenced the history of the country in that they took place at different times and affected different parts of the country differently. Mesopotamia is thus a fertile field to study the emergence of a synthesis out of different elements. The material for such study still contains a number of gaps, yet the main lines of development can be drawn.

The period of Preparation: Before 2900 B.C. The beginnings of art go back into the prehistoric period, but it seems that at least southern Mesopotamia played no creative role in the earlier phases. A change took place in the first half of the 4th millenium, when Mesopotamia became the leading country of the ancient world, even surpassing Egypt. Architecture gives us a good picture of what was achieved. The temples show a surprisingly advanced and complex type and reach monumental size at the end of the period. A dual origin is discernible. The native materials of the alluvial plain are mud and reeds; the mud, shaped into bricks, became the material most frequently used; reeds used for light huts in the beginning were of secondary importance later on. Besides, there are traces of the use of wood which must have been imported from the wooded mountains by immigrants. But brick construction was soon substituted for it so that forms first created in wood survived only in decorative features, esp. in the vertical panel decoration of the surfaces of sacred buildings. The earliest rooms show two distinct types. One is the "long" room, i.e., an oblong room with the entrance in one of the short sides. We must conclude from its geographical distribution outside of Mesopotamia that it was introduced from some area north of the highlands. The other type has the entrance in one of the long walls close to the corner so that the person entering must turn to get to the altar or to the cult image which is located at the far-off short side. This type originated in the lowlands, perhaps in Syria, and may be termed the "around the corner" type. Used in ordinary houses it gives privacy, cherished by the Oriental, because a passer-by can see through the door very little of the room. **Temples** consisting of a number of rooms mingle the two types, with sometimes one type, sometimes the other, dominating. Such mingling and flexibility is characteristic of the prehistoric period as well as variety and unpreciseness; integration and fixed organization is still beyond the capacity of the builders. One type, the tripartite one, deserves special mention. It consists of a long and narrow central space which is flanked by a number of rooms on the two long sides and sometimes also on one of the short sides. It is uncertain whether the central space was covered or was a court open to the sky. A certain centripetalism is noticeable in spite of the great elongation. The origin may be looked for in **private architecture.** When the highlanders left their easily defensible mountain abodes and settled in the plain, they surrounded their huts with a wall to protect their belongings from the marauding Bedouins. When more rooms became needed, they were arranged in a row along the wall with the central space left open to the sky and reserved for animals. This "court" type would thus be of native origin. It was used also for temples, because an Oriental temple is the house of the god and should be as splendid or even more splendid than that of the king. They were decorated with wall paintings and with friezes of inlaid animals; ornamental patterns were produced by sticking into the mud walls clay cones the thick ends of which were painted with different colors; there were staircases leading to the flat roof from which the sky was observed; symmetry in the arrangement of the rooms begins to appear, an interesting feature which seems to have been introduced by highlanders. Some temples were erected on terraces; the fact that these terraces are higher than the merely utilitarian purpose required, i.e., to raise them above the inundation level, would warrant the assumption that they were meant to be artificial mountains introduced by mountaineers who believed that their gods dwelled on mountain tops.

The finds of **sculpture** are still scarce. Of the earlier phases small clay figures only are known; some represent deities, others perhaps worshippers; the execution is summary; those which are represented as draped have a columnar body and prove that this type, which is the prevailing one throughout Mesopotamian history, existed from the beginning. A life-sized head in marble and a statuette of a woman in stone coming from the end of the period show that monumental sculpture and the characteristic type of Mesopotamian statuary had been created by that time. The forms are natural and correct, but general and simplified. The statuette is in strictly frontal pose; the feet are side by side; the upper arms are vertical and not separated from the body; the lower arms are placed across the body horizontally and the hands are clasped exactly in the middle of the body. A short skirt from the waist downwards is approximately bell shaped and without folds. The proportions are heavy; the forms are round, bulging and swelling. We see a thick and impenetrable mass with a smooth surface. The figure thus shows strength and vigor and reveals the spirit of the settlers: they plant themselves on the occupied ground as firmly as possible and make themselves as strong and as unassailable as a rock. Power, not grace, is their aim. The religious meaning must not be forgotten. The statuette was set up in a temple. It did not "represent" the worshipper in the modern sense, but was considered to be alive and endowed with the magic power to remind the god of the piety of the dedicator and to assure the divine blessing.

Concerning minor arts we find objects for practical use, for the cult and for personal adornment. **Pottery** was made on the wheel and had become an industry. It shows good taste, particularly when painted, and is of great historical value, because shapes and decoration reveal a synthesis of influences brought in by lowlanders and highlanders. Equally instructive are the innumerable **seals** of stone, each with a different design, because every Mesopotamian possessed one and used it for his highly developed business transactions. Two types existed: the stamp seal and the **cylinder seal,** the latter rolled over the soft clay which was used for sealing jars and for tablets on which the transactions were inscribed. The stamp seal originated outside of Mesopotamia and was not much used there; the cylinder is a Mesopotamian invention. Its appropriate decoration is the **frieze**; figures and objects are lined up one behind the other, nearly all being represented in profile so that a flat and rather two-dimensional picture results. Human figures in front view are avoided except in special cases, because they were considered to have a magical influence on the beholder. Some friezes of the last phase in this period show a freer composition with the figures spread over the field on different levels. This type is best taken as a survival of primitive un-preciseness and looseness and no attempt at perspective should be read into it, because perspective presupposes a much higher de-velopment and was accomplished first by the Greeks; furthermore, other works in the minor arts as well as in architecture and in sculpture prove that the aim of the artist was to preserve the solidity of the surface and not to disrupt it by holes going into the depth as pictures in perspective do. A num-ber of seals show **heraldic groups.** Now, heraldic groups have a closed composition and are thus fundamentally different from the frieze which is endless and runs on as far as the available field permits. We must con-clude that the two principles were introduced by immigrants from two different regions, and this conclusion is borne out by the fact that the closed composition is especially popular with the Western highlanders and that the frieze is the most favored composi-tion of the lowlanders, the latter being a part of the Mediterranean world where the frieze is dominant; e.g., in Egypt, Greece and Spain. The Mesopotamian heraldic groups are often very ingeniously incorporated into the frieze: two rampant quadrupeds facing one another are repeated several times, but instead of being isolated, a connection between the groups is effected by having the heads of the animals turned back and their tails crossed; a synthesis of the two principles is thus achieved. The motives of the seals are ornaments, animals, and human beings in various occu-pations, and tells us much of the culture and esp. of the religion of the period. Worth noticing are representations of scenery. Con-trary to Greek classical art nature is not en-tirely subordinated to man, but a coordination is attempted although in a primitive manner. A "hunt in the mountain valley" shows two ranges of mountains flanking the valley; the hunters, the game and a tree are all shown on top of the higher range. The exuberant vitality and the creative power of the period

is well exemplified by the vigorous style, the variety of new motives and the experi-menting with techniques and materials, many of which had to be imported: clay, wood, horn, alabaster, basalt, granite, limestone, sandstone, serpentine, even paste and an arti-ficial stone made with gypsum, shell, mother of pearl, lapis lazuli, gold, silver, copper. Often a number of materials are used: wood-en figures are plated with gold; stone figures have inlay; copper wire was used for fasten-ing; casting and soldering were known; gar-ments were decorated with colored patterns.

The Early Dynastic Period. Ca. 2900-2360 *B.C.* We are now in the historical period and know that the people ruling in southern Mesopotamia were the **Sumerians.** Their eth-nic relationship and their original home are unknown, except that it is probable that they came from the highlands or from beyond. They had migrated into Mesopotamia some centuries earlier, but might have been re-inforced about 2900 by a new invasion. A number of great towns existed in the south; they were competitors in creating culture but also waged wars among themselves, uni-fied empires remaining ephemeral. The cul-ture was uniform over the whole of Meso-potamia, although further excavations may show regional differences of secondary im-portance. The decisive difference from the earlier period lies not so much in the creation of new motives as in a new style. The exuberant, but loose and sprawling vitality is disciplined; integration is achieved and a fixed organization is built up.

In temple architecture much variety still exists according to the needs of the individual temples; some consist of a single room only; for others a few rooms suffice; but also big complexes with dozens of rooms were built, because many temples owned large estates and were big business entreprises. Two main types are discernible, and in both the tendency to develop a strict organization can be fol-lowed step by step. One type consists of a block of rooms; the largest room is the cult room and is of the "around the corner" type; it is the organizing center and the other rooms are subordinated to it and grouped around it in various numbers and ar-rangements. The other type is related to the prehistoric tripartite type. Here the cult room, likewise of the "around the corner" type, is combined with a courtyard, but the courtyard is becoming the organizing center; the cult room is pushed off the center and other rooms, often likewise cult rooms, are grouped around the courtyard in the middle; the arrangement is strictly centripetal because the rooms are accessible from the court and have no outside openings—probably not even windows and certainly no large ones. Furthermore, the ground plan is not elongated as before, but often comes close to a square. The walls, all of brick, were thick; the outer ones were plain except for vertical buttresses. The impression of the beholder must have been that of compactness and concentration expressing the immovable strength and power of the deity, who gives security and prosperity to the people. Some details must be mentioned: certain temples were built on a long platform, others on a higher terrace which might be surrounded by a single or a doubled enclosure wall, probably a feature introduced from the highlands; the main entrance is flanked by two towers giving a fortress-like appearance; the cult room may have an anteroom and a clerestory in some cases; walls were lavishly decorated with colored stones and metal plaques forming decorative patterns; also figure friezes were found but their location is uncertain; if they decorated the outside at all it was exceptional; exceptional were also columns and pillars; altars, ablution basins and ovens served the cult. We do not know much of civic architecture. The towns were surrounded by strong walls which had deep buttresses; the layout was irregular except for some restricted parts where a regular plan is discernible showing the streets parallel and at right angles. Private houses display the centripetal type with an organizing central space and a ring of rooms around it. Vaulting had been developed, although most of the ceilings were flat and made of palm logs with layers of matting and clay; doors were often arched; windows were rare, small and high up in the walls to secure privacy; sun dried bricks were mostly used because the lack of fuel made baked bricks too expensive for ordinary purposes; most walls seem to have been plastered.

Our knowledge of Sumerian sculpture begins unfortunately not with the first, but with the second of the three stages of the Early Dynastic period. As in architecture a fixed organization has replaced the former unpreciseness, although the general type has remained the same: the figure stands in frontal pose with the feet side by side and with the hands clasped in front of the body. But the contour is pressed into a hard and geometric scheme: the garment reaching from the waistline downwards is prevailingly cylindrical; the body above shows straight and hard lines; the head too has sharply cut forms; long beards are divided by a number of horizontal parallels. A figure seated crosslegged is cast into a conical scheme; all parts fit in consistently; the garment covering the legs has an upward curve; the upper arms are held obliquely and give the outer contour; the forearms are not horizontal but form an angle pointing to the top of the cone; even the eyes are set slightly obliquely. All forms are simple and general, not naturalistic; the contour of the skull is a simple geometric curve, not modulated as in nature; the proportions of the face are faulty; the forehead is too low; the nose and eyes are too large; the arms and legs do not show any differentiation of muscles. Compared with the marble head of the preceding period, we almost feel compelled to assume a regress in naturalism. The skirt is of dubious interpretation, whether it is a sheep skin or more likely a textile imitation of one. It has in many examples a plain surface except for a long fringe at the bottom which emphasizes the roundness of the figure.

The following stage saw an increase in naturalism and refinement. The strictly geometric shape of the body assumes more natural forms by curving in and out; the proportions of the head become closer to those of nature; the forehead is higher; the eyes are better placed in their sockets and better balanced with the cheeks; the mouth is finer; the arms show some muscles; in exceptional cases one of the legs is slightly advanced suggesting mobility. In Egypt two persons forming a group are juxtaposed, each being strictly frontal, but in Mesopotamia a unified group is achieved by slightly turning the upper parts of the bodies toward each other, by making the body of the wife slightly overlapping and by having the arm of the wife grasped by the man. Yet the forms remain massive, and in particular the garment gives the impression of a heavy and absolutely impenetrable block; numerous parallel flounces cover the whole length of the skirt forming a solid surface and illustrating the round shape of the block. Some figures coming from the south show this massivity in the extreme; they are very short and stocky figures; the neck is very short; the body is broad; the arms are not separated from it so that the compactness is increased; the garment begins above the waistline so that the body is not articulated by it into two halves as in other figures; the stone is not cut away between the garment and the base. The figure appears firmly planted on the ground as an immovable mass and thus displays a parallel to the temple. Since these figures belong to the final stage of the development, their style must be intentional and cannot be attributed to incapacity; the failure to cut away of the stone around the legs and between the arms and the body cannot be due to the fear of weakening their actual stability, because the artists of the preceding stage were not afraid to do it. More finds are needed to prove or to refute the tentatively proffered hypothesis that this difference between the two styles is once more due to the ethnic dualism in Mesopotamia, at least in part, because different development stages likewise show different proportions. But it seems that the extreme compactness is not only characteristic of the third and 'intensified' stage, but has been increased by the specific style of the highlanders. The style of the lowlanders tends to more articulation and slenderness. The Egyptian style corroborates such opinion, because the Egyptians are related to the lowlanders; notice what was said about the frieze. Egyptian sculptures show greater slenderness and more articulation than Mesopotamian ones; on the other hand, they are not round, but tend to be rectangular with sharp edges. The round Mesopotamian statues thus show that a synthesis of the two ethnic elements has been achieved also in sculpture and that the two different ethnic styles have become secondary, slightly modifying the general style in some regions and in some stages of the development.

The extant reliefs are of varying quality; scenes of ritual and of war are represented. One, the *Stele of the Vultures* might be described more fully. It is divided into registers. The largest shows a god with a net in which captured enemies are held; others depict the king at the head of his attacking armies and vultures swooping down on the slain bodies; a heap of such bodies in marshy ground is shown in another scene. The variation and realistic rendering of the subject which includes elements of nature is remarkable; the army is represented as a compact phalanx by showing the men overlapping horizontally and vertically. Yet depth and three dimensionality is reduced as much as possible so that the relief appears as intentionally flattened and as showing a solid surface. The subject matter is disciplined. The forcing of life into an ornamental scheme is particularly well exhibited by the cylinder seals which

show symbolic battles of heroes with animals attacked by other animals. The composition is the same synthesis of the frieze and the heraldic group as in the previous period, but all looseness has disappeared. The whole field from edge to edge is thickly filled with figures. For this purpose the animals are set upright so that they cover the same space as the heroes; two are often crossed in an S pose to present an ornamental scheme.

The minor arts flourished as before. Mention might be made of granulation, fluted and incised vessels of gold and silver, a "helmet" of gold showing ornamentalized hair, an inlaid gaming board, a lyre of inlaid wood decorated with a wooden bull's head plated with gold and wearing a beard of lapis lazuli, female adornment in the form of necklaces made of beads and wreaths of leaves and of flowers. The famous "Royal Tombs" of Ur yielded especially fine specimens, although it must be admitted that neither the workmanship is so delicate nor the taste so good as that of Egyptian work.

The Akkadian Period. 2360-2180 B.C. In the following period the Semites of Akkad (central Mesopotamia) became dominant and their ruler Sargon founded a universal empire. The monuments are not numerous. In architecture the former types continued. A palace shows a number of central courtyard systems lined up side by side, not incorporated into a block as formerly, but no axiality is applied as in Egypt. Good care was taken of drainage and sanitation. In sculpture a new style is discernible. Slender proportions and articulation, the characteristics of the lowland style, are dominant. A girdle divides the upper part of the body from the lower, but the roundness and blocklike appearance is retained. On the other hand, the geometric scheme is being abandoned in a rapid development and a great step toward naturalism is being taken. The bodies appear flexible and moving freely with the muscles finely rendered; the flesh looks soft; folds, although used sparsely, render the natural texture of soft stuff. A great masterpiece, the *Stele of Naramsin,* can be compared to the stele of the Vultures to point out the differences of the two styles. It likewise glorifies victory. The former division into registers has given place to unification; the dividing lines survive as undulating and ascending ledges on which soldiers among trees are climbing up a mountain; the king is ahead of them on the top of the pass; before him his enemies are descending; this triangular arrangement excellently symbolizes the climax of the campaign; symbolic is likewise the small number of soldiers and trees; no really naturalistic stage has been reached; also the third dimension is strongly reduced; all figures seem to be in the same layer, whether they are in the lower or in the upper part. There is no foreshortening whatever; on the contrary, the king is taller than the soldiers because of his greater importance. On the other hand, the figures are not so crowded together, they are rounder and the relief is not so flat as in the preceding period.

The same greater spaciousness is seen on the seals. Some of the older ornamental types are retained, but they are taken out of the continuous chain and freely displayed. Many cult and mythological scenes are represented in a fine and delicate style; indication of scenery is restricted but not lacking.

The Neo-Sumerian Period: ca. 2070-1960 B.C. The empire collapsed under the invasion of mountaineers. After a while the Sumerians came to the fore again in the south, although they were now strongly mixed with Semites. The central court type was as popular as before; if more than one was needed, they were lined up in a row or comprised in a square. The Mausoleum of the kings of Ur has cult rooms around a central court and underground vaulted burial chambers. An increase in symmetrical arrangement is discernible: the "around the corner" room has been changed into the "broad" room in which the throne or the cult image is located in the middle of the long side and is in the axis of the entrance opposite to it; it could thus be seen from the court yard; ostentation has replaced privacy. The simple and high terrace of a special type of temple has become by now articulated by stories; it is called mountain peak **ziggurat.** The number of stories varies; their reduction in size toward the top is considerable; they are painted with different symbolic colors; the plan is oblong, later square; of three large staircases one is put vertical to the long side, the two others parallel, all meeting in the center. The striving of the Mesopotamians for massivity and solidity could find no better expression than these bulky and powerful landmarks visible from afar.

The sculptural type still shows frontality, the feet side by side and the hands clasped; the solidity and roundness are likewise the same as before; the shortness and compactness are even increased beyond that of the

Akkadian period and reach the exaggeration of the last stage of the Early Dynastic period, at least in the earlier phase. It is clearly a reversion to the highland style. On the other hand, the dress has been changed for mortals, although the garment with many flounces has been retained for the gods, an interestingly archaizing tendency for it indicates a lessening of the creative power. Men wear a mantle wrapped around the body, over the left shoulder and under the right arm; it has a short fringe forming a decorative pattern; a long line falls from the left wrist to the edge of the mantle which ends above the ankles; this line without being in the center of the body indicates the vertical dimension of the body, two horizontal lines branch at the ends, one along the lower edge of the mantle, the other produced by the upper contour of the left arm; the right arm likewise provides an almost horizontal line going in the opposite direction. An articulating frame of lines is thus produced which, however, remains on the surface of the body and leaves the compactness unaltered. We can hardly be wrong if we attribute this articulating tendency to the lowland style and see in this combination of articulation and compactness once more a successful synthesis. The style is very refined, for the mantle has large, smooth and finely polished surfaces and the fringes are delicately carved, while some small and rather ornamental folds and finely incised inscriptions enliven specific parts of the statue. The head is extremely well modelled and shows accurate and natural proportions; all its forms are conspicuously round. After a while the style became extremely hard and petrified and mannerism began, a frequent stage of development.

The Babylonian Period in central and southern Mesopotamia. Beginning of the second millenium to the Persian conquest in 539 B.C. Scarcity of monuments forces us to deal with this long period as one unit. This does not exclude a number of fluctuations in the stylistic development; moreover, the political development was full of vicissitudes and the country often under foreign rule. We are further justified by the fact that the creation of types was achieved before this time and that now only elaboration and refinement were advanced. We can term this period neo-classic and in retrospect the Early Dynastic period archaic, the Akkadian period balanced or classic and the Neo-Sumerian period intensified. The long room is used again in the second millenium; it is impossible to tell at present, whether intermediate examples will be found in the future, or whether it was reintroduced. The town of Babylon was laid out according to a scheme which showed a network of parallel streets crossing at right angles; since, however, neither completeness nor preciseness was needed or intended in the Orient, it fell short of the regularity of the Greco-Roman or modern type; moreover, in the course of time it became increasingly irregular, because many owners encroached upon the streets in a time of weak governmental control. Great building activity took place in Babylon in the last period before the Persian conquest. Enormous walls—considered one of the seven wonders of the world—surrounded this largest city of the Ancient Orient. The strongest gateway, the Ishtar Gate, and the walls of a large avenue leading to it were decorated with faïence tiles showing lions, bulls and dragons on a blue background and must have made a dazzling effect on the traveller coming from the gray and dusty plain. A straight and paved street led to the gigantic complex of the sanctuary of Bel; it consisted of a precinct which was surrounded by large caravanserais for the pilgrims and it contained the large temple and the famous tower of Babel, ca. 270 ft. square and high. The temples of that time were rather uniform in plan, all being built according to the central courtyard type with a broad cella and anteroom. The houses were of similar type and had broad reception rooms; a number were probably more than one story high. Other monumental buildings were the palaces of Nebuchadnezzar. One of them consisted of five courtyard systems which were placed side by side, but not lined upon an axis. Each contained a large courtyard in the center with a large room on one side and numerous smaller courtyards surrounded by rooms filling the rest of the space. Three courtyards were occupied by the administration, the two others belonged to the king and the queen. The throne room was a broad room with three entrances of which the central one was larger than the flanking ones; the façade was decorated with colored faïence tiles showing lions, schematized palms and ornaments; it was 51 x 156 ft. in size and perhaps had a longitudinal barrel vault. In one corner of the palace a complex of numerous vaulted rooms was found; they were built of stone, whereas all the other rooms were built of bricks; since some had wells, the excavators interpreted this com-

plex as the substructure of the famous hanging gardens.

The style of sculpture is fine and natural, but lacks vigor and strength. Large and smooth planes and delicate lines produce the appearance of elegance and technical perfection. The articulating framework of lines on the surface of the compact block is popular. The most elaborate scheme appears on a relief of the end of the second millenium. A king is clad in an embroidered garment reaching from the neck to the feet; a belt gives a strong horizontal articulation; two bands crossing from the shoulders to the hips form diagonal lines on the upper part of the body; the two arms bent at the elbows form lines parallel to these bands as does an ornamental band hanging down obliquely from the belt, whereas other ornamental stripes are parallel to the horizontal belt.

Assyrian art from the beginning of the second millenium to the end of the empire in 608 B.C. Before 2000 Assyrian art shows the same style as the art of the south except that at times it has a provincial touch. After 2000 it has a style of its own which is, however, in close connection with the south and which must therefore be considered as Mesopotamian in the comprehensive sense of the word. The popular central court type differs slightly from that in the south. Here in the south it is very regular in outline, i.e., if possible, a rectangle. The palace of Sargon II in Khorsabad which combines numerous courtyards is sprawling and has an irregular perimeter with many projections. Many courtyards are more spacious than is normal in the south. Besides the courtyard type the block type, i.e., small rooms around a large covered room, plays a great role. It is used for many temples and, in Nuzi in upper Mesopotamia, also for private houses. Some Assyrian private houses show an interesting combination: the reception room occupies on side of a forecourt and the adjacent "harem" is of the central court type. The broad room occurs, but is much rarer than in the rest of Mesopotamia. The "around the corner" type is very common in temples, houses, and is even used for throne rooms. Also the long room is often found in temples, but it is incorporated into the central courtyard type. The main part of these temples is commonly tripartite; it consists of a small anteroom and a small holy of holies divided by a large long room. Notice the same plan in the temple at Jerusalem. The appearance was one of strength and solidity as everywhere in Mesopotamia, although perhaps somewhat more softened by the use of decorative features. The walls of the rooms—at least of the palaces—were lavishly decorated with reliefs and paintings, but also some of the exterior, particularly the gateways had decoration, the latter having as guards lions and bulls with human heads and wings. Assyrian art shares these features with the arts farther west, as Assyrian kings also erected some buildings in the western style. Awnings, rugs and fine furniture decorated with figures and ivory, the latter likewise often of western origin, completed the splendor of the rooms. The extensive fortifications, irrigation works and one aqueduct across a valley, as well as formal gardens with parallel rows of trees, might be mentioned.

Of sculpture in the round only a few in stone are preserved; the cult images in precious materials are lost. They show frontality, compactness and solidity as do the figures in the South with an additional expression of fierceness and brutality. The Assyrians decided not only to preserve their own native ground, but also to rule; or, if necessary, to exterminate other nations. Often, although not always a framework of lines is marked on the surface of the block. The waistline is often slightly reduced and divides the upper part of the body from the lower one. The muscles and sinews are exaggerated and schematized. There is more variation in types than in the south and some western features appear. The body in section is not always round but also angular or flattened. In addition to the pose with clasped hands those with both forearms stretched forward and with one arm hanging down by the side and the other placed horizontally across the body are found. The garment reaches to the ground in upright figures and gives them a firm stand; it sometimes clings to the body so closely that the modelling underneath is shown; fringes around the body are fashionable.

After 2000 a strong and vigorous style is discernible; all forms are solidly modelled and sharply marked. In the second part of the second millenium a finer and more elegant style is current; even some schematization and mannerism is found but, on the other hand, a soft and delicate naturalism appears. There follows a consolidation again displaying heavier forms. The style of Assur-nasir-apli (9th cent.) shows a certain balance between the hardness and forcefulness

of the main forms and the finesse and wealth of secondary detail. A gradual softening and refinement takes place until under Assurbani-apli (7th cent.) a rich style is achieved. The figures are a little plump and well rounded; the contours are gently curved; the faces are fleshy and full; hair and beard are extremely well dressed, a feature which is found throughout the first millenium; the royal garments are lavishly embroidered.

The glory of Assyrian art is the relief. Cult scenes showing demons, etc., are in the minority in comparison with military scenes. The king is represented again and again but not as the sole victor of overwhelming height and strength as in Egypt. The whole army is rendered in great detail toiling and accomplishing all phases of their victorious campaigns. We see the footwolk, the horsemen, the war chariots; the crossing of mountains and rivers; the battles in the plains, in the mountains, in the marshes; the sieges of cities by means of beleaguering machines; their capturing, looting and burning; the torturing, impaling and abduction of prisoners; the resting in camps and the sacrificing by the king; his hunting which was not only a pleasure, often a dangerous one, but also a duty to rid the country of the beasts of prey. The rendering is realistic. We get a good knowledge of the equipment of the army, of the different species of trees and the characteristic types of buildings in foreign countries; the dying lion and lioness are famous for their lifelike representation. Natural scenery plays a much greater role than in Egyptian and classical Greek art. This characteristically Mesopotamian feature which we noticed in the earlier periods was brought to its fullest development by late Assyrian art. Great unified pictures show the human figures placed on a background of landscape, certainly not in the real proportion to it, but not so magnified and much better inserted than in foreign arts. Moreover, these pictures are isolated spots of a larger composition which consists of a number of superimposed friezes, each having the height of one figure only and becoming unified if the particular subject matter demands it. Occasional heraldic groups are likewise subordinated to the frieze composition which often goes all around the four walls of a room without being interrupted at the corners. The principle of roundness and concentration rules here, too, as in sculpture and architecture, and gives the room the appearance of a complete unit instead of consisting of four separate walls put together. The desire to keep the solid appearance of the wall, as well as the Assyrian mentality as such, prevented the artists from developing perspective. There is no foreshortening, no three-quarter view, very little overlapping. If some figures are smaller, this is due to lack of space as is clearly shown by the fact that smaller figures are introduced in the foreground; the beholder does not get the impression that figures or objects in the higher part of the relief are at a greater distance, but all, whether they are above or below, appear to be in the same vertical layer; i.e., on the surface of the solid wall. This fact as well as the frontality of the statue and the compactness of the buildings, prove that Mesopotamian art always remained "archaic" art and never reached the classical style of development. See various publications of the Oriental Institute of the University of Chicago; publications of the British Museum on Assyrian art; publications of the German Oriental Society on excavations; Musée du Louvre, *Les Antiquités Orientales* by G. Contenau; G. Contenau, *Manuel d'archéologie Orientale,* 1927-31; H. Frankfort, *Cylinder Seals,* 1939.   —V.M.

metal. See GLASS AND GLASS-MAKING.

metalwork. The art of metalwork has had a continuous history since the Bronze Age. The alloy of copper and tin or bronze has survived in the form of sculpture, arms, utensils, and furniture. Iron was widely used for architectural embellishment in the Middle Ages and the Renaissance and is being revived in modern times with a new understanding of its ductile properties. Copper and zinc, or brass, was exploited by the Romans and notably in medieval England in architectural forms. Gold and silver work, with its close relationship to jewelry-design, has been in continuous development.

The basic methods of preparing metals for craft uses have been drawing, spinning, hammering, and casting. Stamping, inlaying, damascening with threads of gold or silver, niello-work or metallic inlay on engraved gold, silver, or bronze, and repoussé work, the design being beaten from within to form a raised pattern, are more intricate techniques. The alloys, brass and bronze, and the precious metals, gold and silver, have the longest history of experiment and expression.

The characteristic method of using bronze is that of casting, the **cire perdue process** being the one favored from ancient times. In this process a fireproof core is covered with a modelled wax figure which corresponds exactly to the finished work desired. A mould s then applied connected with the core by metal rods. Molten bronze is then poured n replacing the wax, which melts and runs out. When the mould and core and metal rods are removed, and the surface tooled, the wax object reappears in bronze plate. The story of the achievement of artists in this craft is a long and distinguished one, and clearly raises questions of where craft ends and art begins. In the classical world, copper appears as early as 3500 B.C., but the bronze alloy is not widely current in Crete until 2000 B.C. Weapons and metallic pottery forms are the sole relics of the Copper Age, revealing evidences of Egyptian and Mesopotamia influence. From the late Minoan Age the bronze dagger blade found in a Mycenaean shaft grave, with a floral design running the length of the shaft in gold and niéllo, is representative of the expert craftsmanship in arms. Bronze work in utensils and statuettes were less notable. Italian and Oriental motives and techniques as well as survivals from pre-Hellenic times appear as the Classical Age reaches maturity. Tripods and bowls, mirrors and chariots are produced in cast and plated forms with decorative motifs used to cover structural joints, embellish rims, and serve as pedestals and bases. Human beings, plant forms, and mythological conceits are the motifs commonly employed. The Pourtales Vase in the British Museum with a human figure for the handle and silver inlay enrichment is an example. Etruscan bronze work, a provincial phase of the Greek, specialized in line engraving, as ' seen in the Dioscuri Mirror in the Metropolitan Museum. In the notable Monteleone chariot in the same museum, enriched by repousse, a monumental adornment of functional forms was achieved. In late Greek and Roman times bronze furniture forms embellished with conventionalized flora and fauna forms were characteristic, and statuettes might repeat famed works of masters of sculpture.

The Roman works of bronze for architectural and domestic purposes carried into medieval times. The bronze doors of the Baths of Caracalla reappeared in the Lateran Church in Rome, and a Roman curule chair with 12th cent. additions was rechristened the Chair of Dagobert. During the first

Golden Age Byzantium was the trade center for widespread traffic in bronze ware. After the Iconoclastic controversy at least technical knowledge survived and the bronze doors of Romanesque Italy were of Greek origin or of Greek workmanship on Italian soil or of Greek inspiration, combined with neo-classical tendencies. Greek refugees of the 9th cent. were welcomed by Charlemagne at Cologne and at Aix-la-Chapelle. The bronze doors at Hildesheim and Mainz and Augsburg are noteworthy for introducing Teutonic art forms, as seen in the lion heads with rings hanging from their jaws. Candlesticks, baptismal fonts, and candelabra add further examples to the rich medieval pageant of bronzeware in German lands. Perhaps Peter Vischer in Nuremberg in the Shrine of St. Sebald achieved the ultimate embellishment of a monumental form, mingling medieval and Renaissance detail. In the Tomb of Maximilian I at Innsbruck he showed equal skill as a monumental sculptor.

The Renaissance in Italy achieved great bronze monuments from the Andrea Pisano doors at the Baptistery in Florence to Ghiberti's first and second pairs, in the last blurring not only the distinction between craftsmanship and art, but even between painting and sculpture, so subtle are the plane relationships, so fluent the form, and precise the line. While all the great sculptors of the Italian Renaissance used bronze as eagerly as the Greeks had, usually preferring its sheen and clarity to marble ambiguity, the story is continued along craft lines rather than creative ones when the Venetians commission door knockers or Rovezzano carries Renaissance forms to England in the Cardinal Wolseley tomb.

Bronze work in medieval France has largely gone, save for such supposititious examples as the base of the seven-branched candlestick in the Cathedral at Milan. With the Renaissance the development of ormolu, or gilt bronze, for the adornment of furniture, as well as the quasi-monumentality of Goujon and Pilon with their interest in decorative emphases, indicates how serious has been the loss of medieval French work in bronze. Furniture in rococo forms reached heights of amazing elegance, saved from overlavishness only by the soundness of craftsmanship and the native French taste. Not a few ecclesiastical objects of medieval England are extant, marked by sobriety and technical soundness, a restraint which controls Gothic grace and helps fuse medieval

and Renaissance decorative motifs in later times. An intriguing bypath is that of bell-founding where the ponderous tone is on occasion integrated with the weight of the metal and the sobriety of the profile.

European brass as distinguished from bronze has a more distinctly ornamental appeal. Its value is largely one of embellishment, aided by its brilliant color. From medieval days cast and repoussé techniques were followed in brassware, the output of Dinant being especially popular throughout western Europe, called *"dinanderie"*. Ecclesiastical objects in this technique include such masterpieces as the font in St. Bartholomew's in Liege, and the lecterns in the English churches. Cologne was also a notable center. Symbolic figures, architectural tracery, and flat ornamentation were used richly and effectively. In the Renaissance the great chandeliers of England, Holland, and Scandanavia, the hammered work and dishes embossed with figures from Dutch craftsmen are also notable examples of brassware. Domestic utensils in brass or with brass ornament were likewise common, perhaps a water vessel in animal form with the spout extending from its mouth, and another animal form for handle. Inlay enamel designs and intricate open work, both floral and faunal in derivation, and elaborate engraving appear in the 17th and 18th centuries.

As one moves away from the European world, one finds notable and strange forms and techniques in bronze and brass. From the Near and Middle East come a bronze bowl from Nineveh, now in the British Museum, with repoussé concentric designs of animals, and the Luristan bronzes of western Iran, Scytho-Persian in origin, where animal forms are used with fluency and decorative skill. These small objects pertain to personal adornment and the needs of a horse-riding people. Of purer form is the work being recovered by the nomad peoples of north Eurasia, basically faunal in its motifs and possessing many affinities with the art of the ancient East, Sumerian and Iranian. The emphasis is always decorative rather than naturalistic. These dress accessories, arms, and horse fittings are often in gold, but also in bronze, and even in bone and wood.

In the Far East Chinese bronzes are clearly a major art, having the intricate iconography and freedom of design which underlies such a classification. Basically, they are ceremonial in purpose, and closely connected with the Chinese feeling for family and ancestor. The long inscriptions with their calligraphic decorative properties, suggest a relationship to meaning and writing which is strange but suggestive to the Occidental spectator. The *cire-perdue* process was used expertly from early times, whence come the finest of the bronzes. The vigor and dignity of the forms, the vital and unified outline, and the integration of form and mass give them a unique force. The artist was not afraid of angular shapes of weighted masses. The idea as well as the appearance could carry them. With meander bands to suggest natural elements, like thunder and lightning, triangular patterns to connote mountains, and tapering forms for the winds, the artist could serve a purpose functionally with his pattern, and decorate with poetic allusions. Sacrificial jars and libation cups, at times covered, of gilt-bronze or copper inlay, ceremonial tripods, and animal forms grand in scale rather than in size occur. Chinese bronzes are a continual inspiration to the sensitive spectator. Pantheism, continuity, vitality are given permanent form, enriched by the patina of centuries of burial or exposure to atmosphere.

Copper, brass, and bronze are widely employed in India, whose inhabitants prefer the first for images, at times gilded or even inlaid with gems, cast solid or on a fireproof core. In utensils many types of water vessels with long spouts, for religious or domestic use, are found cast by the *cire-perdue* process. Temple bells, hanging-lamps, and vases also reach high favor. Chasing, engraving, inlaying are the decorative techniques employed and the material varies from copper to bronze to brass, as the alloy consistency changes. Brass inlaid with silver and copper, copper with silver applied, brassware with engraving against a background of colored lac are skillful and sightly products. *"Bidri"* ware, of tin or zinc combined with lead and copper, is engraved and enriched with silver inlay. Polishing and darkening of the surface and conservative geometrical and floral motifs provide a choice example of minor art.

In Africa advanced knowledge of metal casting was brought to the peoples of Benin by the Portuguese; they produced noteworthy ancestor portraits surmounted by elephant tusks for use as altarpieces. The feeling for material and the sensitivity to sculptural values which marks so much of African art in materials easier to work are also seen here. A portrait of a *King* now in the University Museum Philadelphia, is an example.

The uses of bronze in contemporary art are many, as seen in the sculptural forms of Lachaise and Epstein and Kolbe or the decorative influences of Manship and Diedrich and the precious quality of Archipenko's silvered bronzes. More distinctively designed as a minor art are the cooking utensils in copper, now clearly fashioned to serve their purpose, and the ornamental gates of bronze. Brass in minor art forms is at present less favored than in days of brass chandeliers and bedsteads. Only copper seems to have continued tradition by fresh experimentation.

The uses in the crafts of gold and silver are again long-lived and notable. In the Old Kingdom in Egypt all the fundamental ways of handling gold had been developed, casting, chasing, soldering, hammering, and plaiting. A bracelet of gold and turquoise and amethyst devised with a lotus rosette as the central motive, or a masterful hawk's head in hammered gold with jasper eyes, detached from its original position in a bronze body, are examples. Nor can one omit mention of the ceremonial vase where a gold surface is inlaid with lapis lazuli and both contour and surface decoration are kept within restrained limits. The rich profusion of techniques and lavishness of effect in later Egyptian times is suggested by the cedar wood chair decorated with embossed gold and ivory claws from Tutankhamen's tomb, or the royal effigies of gold over wood inlaid with glass, faience, and lapis lazuli. Silver was less commonly used, but a wine jug in that material, engraved and with a handle in the form of a hind and a rim of gold is a surviving example.

The Sumerians were likewise masters of gold and silversmithy. A gold cup of simple flaring profile and fluted sides, a gold helmet with repoussé and engraved adornment, and a fantastic harp of gold and lapis lazuli with bull head base are all amazing in inventiveness and technical skill.

The Minoans may well exhibit the Vaphio Cups as their example. The smooth inner lining, the turned over rim, and the riveted handles, as well as the repoussé bands of humanistic art, the taming of the bull by man, provide a perfect example of art crossing the Hellespont in its westward migration. Perhaps the gold and silver electrum coins of the Greeks, where commercial needs and feeling for sculpture in the round fight a long battle with restrained design, illustrate the best work in these materials. One feels with them as with us a distinction between major

and minor arts. The goldsmith and silversmith work found at Pompeii, at Hildesheim,
and at Boscoreale show the Romans as lovers
of elegance rather than of workmanship. And
one must recall before leaving the ancient
world that the Eurasian animal art is basically an art of gold with patterns worked out
in terms of animal forms.

The cloisonné work of the Byzantine people, with thin gold strips forming the cells
and gold for background and with enamel
filling, carries this technique to a new level
of achievement. With the mosaics, ivories,
and textiles it suggests a culture where the
minor arts have replaced the major.

The book covers of the early medieval
peoples are rich in ivory, enamels and stone,
as well as with gold and silver; their ecclesiastical chalices and plates are at the same
time barbaric and decorative, with Celtic,
Teutonic and Gallic individuality appearing
now and again. In Gothic times greater
elegance occurs but still the sensuous appeals
of color and sheen are exploited, as in
the gorgeous Chalice of St. Remi, of gold,
enamel, and gems. Benvenuto Cellini's ebul-
lient craftsmanship, to the exclusion of taste,
in his famous salt-cellar in gold and enamel,
and the lavish gold and silver *custodia* for the
monstrance enriched with Spanish exuberance,
suggest the dangerous limits approached in the
Renaissance. In fact, the plateresque style in
architecture with its popularity in Spain and
the transatlantic lands under Spanish control
is basically a silversmith's decorative creation.

In pre-Columbian America the craft of
metallurgy was developed in Peru by the
Incas and their predecessors, the folk of
Tiahuanaca, and in Mexico by the Aztecs,
and their predecessors, the Mixtecs and Toltecs. Notable examples of the craft in gold
and silver have survived. Using all the techniques they fashioned personal ornaments as
well as ritual objects. Animal and human
figures were also fashioned. Jewelry from
tombs at Mt. Alban in Oaxaco, Mexico, reveal extraordinary finesse.

The long story of silverware as a household utensil cannot be more than touched
upon here. Its cleanness of surface and outline, its easy adaptability to varied forms,
and its permanence in solid or plated form
account for its wide popularity. Of especial
note is Sheffield plate where a silver surface
is applied by heavy pressure to a copper or
alloy base and which provides metal which
has beauty equal to that of sterling, or stand-

ard, silver, and durability superior to plated
ware. In early Republican America the silverwork of Paul Revere achieved a grace
and functional sobriety which while rococo
and regency in derivation has also the direct
craftsmanship and the Chinese echoes of the
colonist and wide-awake creator. In modern times the same trend toward simplification noted in the other utensil arts has been
noted in silverware. Following a "craft" period, where hammered silver was in vogue,
the clean, undecorated surfaces, forms based
directly on use, and the omission of bevelling,
or repoussé detail which are difficult to maintain in their original brilliance, have much
to recommend them. The Jensen designs,
originating in Denmark, have further reached
into new creative fields, and suggest that the
silversmith has only to exploit his material,
his tools, his purpose, to reach old, yet new,
achievements.

Ironwork demands seperate treatment. Its
structural uses are so varied and its prevalence so widespread that our age has been
named the Iron Age as distinct from the
preceding Bronze and Stone Ages. When it
is recalled that iron is basic in steel, that reinforced concrete is dependent on iron or
steel skeleton, the wonder is rather that iron
as an art medium still survives. Yet from
the days of the Egyptians to those of the
elevator door wrought iron and cast iron have
provided civilized man with a major part of
his tools, his weapons, and his utensils. It
has also provided him with decorative arts
and crafts. Wrought iron with its fiber-like
consistency can be hammered, drawn, or
twisted and still maintain its strength. By
welding parts may be completely fused. Even
in a cold state iron is soft enough to be hammered and bent. Cast iron, in its moulded
form, is too brittle for further manipulation,
but lends itself freely to the details of the
mould.

It is chiefly from medieval times that
wrought iron has been developed as a medium
of artistic expression. By collaring, or attaching separate units with strips, by riveting,
bolting, threading, and mortising the handicraft could function widely within the limits
of the exacting material. Pure form has been
the fundamental element in wrought iron design, in hinges, grilles, gates, balconies, and
so on. In England ironsmithy developed
from the bar which gave structural force to
the windows and the door hinges and to the
devices made for the protection of caskets
in the form of grilles and screens. Later

in the period the attempt was made to produce in iron stone tracery with small pieces rivetted and chiselled on a sheet background; for example, the grille over the tomb of Edward IV in St. George's Chapel, Windsor, the work of John Tresilian. The hinges of the west door of Notre Dame in Paris illustrate the controlled elaboration and grace of the medieval French craftsman.

In the Renaissance the quatre-foil grilles and lanterns for the corners of city palaces indicate the uses made by the Italian of iron. The German craftsman also in cathedral accessories and locks and chests was seldom able to pose problems he was unable to solve. In Renaissance Spain iron had a revival, notably, in the monumental screens in the churches, with vertical columns of hammered work and horizontal bands of arabesque ornamentation, the whole crowned by elaborate crests. Color and gilding produce striking effects in the dim interiors. In many cases two such screens are found in a single church, one to emphasize the altar, the other to mark the eastern end of the choir. Iron was also used for such church furniture as pulpits, and, often, with notable results, in domestic architecture, as, for example, in the nailheads. Renaissance France remained conservative in its iron-mongery until Louis XIV, with locks, knockers, and caskets, of great skill rather than originality.

With the reign of Louis XIV, however, the era of iron's greatest development arose. Great gates for parks, mansion staircases, screens for churches were produced by a succession of artist-craftsmen, as balusters yielded to scrolls without sacrificing structural clarity. St. Cloud, Fontainebleau, Chantilly, and Versailles offer notable illustrations. In the 18th cent. rococo forms remained within the possibilities of ironwork. Lamour in the gates at Nancy perhaps reached the limits of the craft as a monumental technique. Jean Tijon at Hampton Court palace carried the French manner to England, influencing but not dominating the native craftsmen. Not only for the city houses and country manors, but also in the English resident colleges there is revealed during the 17th and 18th cents. much work of admirable simplicity and feeling for material. Germany in the Renaissance did everything with iron which the ingenuity of the craftsman could devise, at times losing structural control. The manipulation of iron bars with floral or capital ends, door-knockers, and chests with elaborate iron

mountings recall the tireless energy of the south German worker.

Cast-iron was long in use in England for fire-dogs and firebacks, and the railing of St. Paul's cathedral, London, was an early example of its architectural use. In America the porches of Charleston and New Orleans, and even the entire façades, with classical detail on occasion, of business buildings, foretelling the skeleton structure of the end of the 19th cent., are further examples of architectural ironwork. This facility in the pre-fabrication of standardized ornament is now replaced by brass, and the more imaginative and native possibilities of wrought iron have reclaimed the field.

In the Middle East iron has had a long history, steel preceding it strangely enough in medieval India. Iron pillars illustrate its structural use, damascening its decorative use. In China iron has been used since 500 B.C., rapidly replacing bronze for weapons and domestic utensils. From the 9th cent. it even tended to replace bronze for sculpture. Iron pagodas and temple furniture and even iron pictures were ingenuously devised. More sensitive to the individuality of the material as a medium, the medieval Japanese craftsman in the decoration of armour, and most notably, in the embellishment of sword handles reached one of the high points in the craftsmanship of iron.

In recent times in Europe there has been a revival in the use of wrought iron. Beginning with a revival of traditional methods as seen in the Chantilly balustrade by the Moreau brothers, the modern movement progressed with Emile Robert's efforts at simplification and Edgar Brandt's efforts to combine the needs of art and of industry. While one can see the passing influence of Art Nouveau, of the Viennese Secession, and of the decorative art forms of 1925 in the output, and, let us admit, the functional abstraction of the modernist, still in our own day the art seems to have passed the dangerous period of revival, and to be ready to develop its own expressiveness neither medieval nor rococo. Samuel Yellin in America has done notable work in the field of architectural decoration and domestic furnishing, and Hans Panzer in Germany has produced such a work as the grille for a church near Munich which fairly cuts with metallic sharpness and stimulates with abstract symbolism. Stainless steel cutlery and simply designed tumblers in steel, as well as machine-made ironwork suggest further the wide possibilities in a material as human as iron. Our banks, our churches, our homes, with foliate and formal forms, are largely decorated by this stern, yet tractable, metal. See A. J. Koop, *Early Chinese Bronzes*, 1925; J. B. Butler, *Problems in Metal Work*; M. I. Rostovtsev, *The Animal Style in S. Russia and China, 1929*; H. Wilson, *Silverware and Jewelry*, 1931; N. Dawson, *Goldsmiths' and Silversmiths' Work,* 1907; C. L. Avery, *Early American Silver,* 1930; M. H. Saville, *The Goldsmith's Art in Ancient Mexico*, 1920; H. C. Smith, *Jewelry,* 1908; C. J. Ffoulkes, *Decorative Ironwork from the XIth to the XVIIIth Century,* 1914; A. Byne and M. Byne, *Spanish Ironwork.*   —W.S.R.

metaphor. See POETRY.

meter. Pattern of accents allotted to consecutive musical elements; alternation of accented and unaccented elements. Usually the term meter implies that a particular accent pattern recurs systematically. If this is not the case, the meter is called irregular. See also rhythm.   —E.K.

metezashi (Jap.). Dagger.

method of squares. See PERSPECTIVE.

methods of teaching art. See teaching art, methods of.

metope. The panel between triglyphs in a Doric frieze, usually decorated during the 5th cent. B.C. with sculptured figures, but sometimes with a rosette or shield, or left blank. How to fill this nearly square space so as to make it harmonize with the lines of the building and provide interesting surface modulation was a problem which appealed to many of the leading Greek sculptors. In the Athenian Treasury at Delphi, brisk figures were placed in dynamic diagonal, triangular and curvilinear designs; the metopes decorating the Temple of Zeus at Olympia were conceived in broader and quieter terms, with horizontal and vertical masses predominating; on the Parthenon the figures of the metopes assumed a rich variety of geometric patterns, with drapery skillfully used to bind them into a unified whole. The background of the metopes was frequently painted blue, and details on the figures were picked out in red and gold, so as to make the marble forms stand out more effectively in the bright sunlight, which would otherwise flatten them against the background. The most popular

subjects were the labors of Heracles and Theseus, and the battles of gods against giants, Greeks against Amazons, and Lapiths against Centaurs. After the 5th cent. B.C., there was no metope sculpture of importance.   —W.R.A.

metropolitan planning. See CIVIC PLANNING.

Metz, school of. See Carolingian art.

meubles. See FURNITURE.

Mexican art, ancient. The ancient art of Mexico and Middle America should be considered as a unit. In this region the early stages of primitive experiment and the transition from a hunting people to the beginning of agriculture have not yet been recovered by archaeologists. Three major phases may be distinguished: (a) small village period with rudimentary art; (b) ceremonial period where each tribal unit had a distinctive art style; and (c) the final period where ceremonial elements from central Mexico tended to break down the old regional arts.

Sculpture was confined at first to small baked clay figures, usually female, and while the general effect was crude there was considerable experiment and regional stylization. This type of art and type of life persisted up to the Conquest in outlying parts of Mexico with improvement in technique and presentation. The ceremonial art apparently took its first steps in southeastern Vera Cruz. Several distinctive features characterize this ritualistic civilization: erection of altars and altar temples on the mounds; polytheism and the ritualistic definition of divinities; the invention of a method of pictographic or hieroglyphic writing; the use of a calendar to conduct more accurately native worship. These steps seem to have been taken in several localities and in each case involved a distinctive regional style indubitably linked by transitional forms to the older Middle Cultures. The most important of these are the La Venta culture (formerly known as Olmec) in southeastern Vera Cruz; the Maya, visible in local traditions like those at Copan, the Peten area, and the highlands; the Zapotec tradition, best seen in the sequences at Monte Alban; and the Mexican sequence to be studied in the environs of Mexico City and in the State of Puebla. Further excavation will bring more of these to the fore. There was some change in each of these regional developments and some mutual interchange of elements through trade and borrowing.

About the 11th cent. a new religion based on the old and with a distinctive ritualistic definition came into being. It seems to have been spread by conquered and migrating groups often speaking Nahuatl, the Aztec language. In the Maya country one finds this impact at Chichen Itza, Peten, and the highlands of Guatemala, and influences are detected in tribes as far south as Nicaragua. In Oaxaca the old Zapotec religious culture is transformed by this Nahua influence. In the Valley of Mexico the old civilization of Teotihuacan is replaced by two major intrusions bringing in the Mixteca-Puebla cultures and lasting to the final Aztec period. To the north the effect of both of these cultures was felt in Sonora and Sinaloa, on the tribes in the Huaxteca in northern Vera Cruz, and attenuated influences affected perhaps the Mound Builders of the southeastern United States.

The general picture of Middle American art history discloses not a gradual ascent culminating in a high artistic peak, but rather a series of plateaus where given styles persist unchanged for a very long time. These are broken, perhaps by sharp transitions, and take off again on another protracted level.

The incredibly beautiful small stone sculptures of Vera Cruz are too little studied as yet to make any affirmation as to the effects of central Mexican influences. In Oaxaca the Mexican period seems to have added to rather than detracted from the earlier art. In the Maya area there was a strong local development characterized by a strong architectural development during and just prior to the period of Mexican contact.

Middle American sculpture, particularly in clay and stone, is one of the high points of American art. Although created with a Neolithic technical equipment, the range of style and expression was comparable to that in many of the Old World cultures. In studying the development of the arts from given regions in Middle America, one is conscious of a growing mastery of the mediums involved.

There is an Oriental tinge to some Middle American art, but its distribution in terms of time and space suggests that the Oriental aspects derive from the local sculptor's ability to reproduce the features of his own Mongoloid stock rather than from direct artistic affinities. —G.C.V.

Mexican painting, contemporary. Contemporary Mexican painting is distinguished from other contemporary art movements in Europe and America by. the unique combination of native subject matter, modern forms of expression, and functional integration with the cultural program of a national government. The origin of the style is found in the social, economic, political, and cultural reorientation which took place during the Mexican Revolution of 1910-20. Its subsequent development has been closely allied with the various policies toward national autonomy and international cooperation that have characterized the Mexican government since that time.

The first, formative, period might be considered the ten years between the great Exposition of Mexican Painting held in Mexico City in 1910 and the inauguration of a national art program under the Ministry of Education in 1920. In direct opposition to the prevailing European taste of the Diaz regime, this centennial exposition, largely organized by the dynamic Dr. Atl, featured Mexican art and subject matter as its tribute to the 100th anniversary of Mexico's independence.

Modern art in the European sense as a distinctive style was introduced under the revolutionary government by Alfredo Ramos Martínez in 1913, a Mexican impressionist who had been living in Paris, and who became director of the academy in 1913. Its introduction to Mexico was, therefore, exactly contemporaneous with the arrival of modern art in the United States via the Armory Show in New York. During the chaotic years of 1914-16 many of the artists and students of the academy, including Dr. Atl, Orozco, Siquieros, Goitia, and others, were engaged in propaganda activities for the Carranza forces. With the political stabilization of the country under President Obregon, a vast program for the cultural rehabilitation of the country was inaugurated by the new Minister of Education, José Vasconcelos. The employment of artists to paint Mexican subjects on the walls of public buildings was one of the most prominent features of that program.

The crystallization of the new style can be followed in the murals decorating the convent of San Pedro y San Pablo, the National Preparatory School, and the Ministry of Education through the next few years. The artists employed included Leal, Charlot, Siqueiros, de la Cueva, Alva de la Canal,

Revueltas, Dr. Atl, Montenegro, Orozco, and Mérida. In the beginning these men were organized into a "Syndicate of Technical Workers, Artists, and Sculptors", whose general program of a socialized artistic expression, based on native tradition and directed toward the aesthetic stimulation of the masses, was best expressed in a manifesto issued by Siqueiros in 1922.

The progress from revolutionary ideals to creative actuality recorded in the above mentioned murals suggests something of the vitality of the period. Experiments in the various mural techniques of encaustic, tempera, true fresco, and oil combinations resulted in the practical establishment of true fresco as the standard medium. The attempt to create a national "people's art" produced a renewed study of Mexico's artistic heritage, which included not only the transplanted styles of the official church and academy but esp. the Indian traditions of ancient Mexico and the native popular arts produced and used by the great masses of people. These indigenous traditions were studied and exploited by the artists, who at the same time were fully aware of the stylistic innovations in color, design, and aesthetic purpose developed by European modernists. The search for an adequate content capable of expressing the ideals of the new revolutionary Mexico varied from traditional mythological, historical, and religious subjects to a new type of socio-political symbolism growing out of the revolution in a form most closely related to the caricature and propaganda of the popular press.

The dynamic integration of these problems of technique, native aesthetic tradition, international modernism, and a significant content is essentially what constitutes the Mexican style and is to be found in work of Orozco, Rivera, Charlot, Leal, Siqueiros, and Montenegro before 1924. However, one factor which the movement failed to accomplish was an effective organization through which this interpretation could be maintained. The ideal of artistic cooperation envisaged by the Syndicate under the personal patronage of Vasconcelos was soon dissipated by political intrigue and personal ambition. After the removal of Vasconcelos as Minister of Education (1924), the history of modern Mexican art is largely the records of individual artists.

The most productive of these, esp. in mural decoration, have been Orozco and Rivera, whose works and activities, along with those of Siqueiros, are largely responsible for the fame and recognition of Mexican art outside Mexico's borders. The ideological content of their painting likewise has shifted from purely Mexican problems to those of larger and more universal import. Rivera's fresco for Rockefeller Center (destroyed and repainted in Mexico's Palace of Fine Arts) and the vast murals which Orozco has painted in Guadalajara and Jiquilpan are particularly important from this point of view.

The work of the other Mexican painters has followed three main directions. One group has sought to continue with scattered government commissions the ideological patterns of Vasconcelos and the original Syndicate (e.g., Leal, Montenegro). A second group composed of younger artists, most of whom had worked as assistants to Rivera, followed the general social and stylistic program developed under his tutelage (e.g. Pacheco, O'Higgins). A third group, also of younger men, repudiated, at least temporarily, the Vasconcelos program and concentrated on easel painting (e.g. Lozano, Mérida, Tamayo, Castellanos, Lazo, Diaz de Léon, Mendez). They were no less idealistic and patriotic about the achievement of a modern and distinctly Mexican style, but they also felt the need of the technical discipline and personal expression which only the easel painting affords. For a direct contact with a larger public, many of these artists have turned to the graphic arts in works dealing with social problems (Mendez). For a period before the outbreak of World War II, the government had awarded a number of mural contracts to these younger men (Tamayo, Castellanos) who produced works that suggest the possibility of a new and greater development. See Anita Brenner, *Idols Behind Altars*, 1929; Jean Charlot, *Art from the Mayans to Disney*, 1939; Justino Fernández, *El Arte Moderno en Mexico*, 1937 and *José Clemente Orozco*, 1942; MacKinley Helm, *Modern Mexican Painters*, 1941; New York, Museum of Modern Art, *Frescoes of Diego Rivera*, 1936 and *Twenty Centuries of Mexican Art*, 1940; Alma Reed, *José Clemente Orozco*, 1932; Laurence Schmeckebier, *Modern Mexican Art*, 1939; Bertram D. Wolfe and Diego Rivera, *Portrait of America*, 1934 and *Portrait of Mexico*, 1937; Bertram D. Wolfe, *Diego Rivera*, 1939. —L.S.

Mexico, post-Conquest architecture of. *16th Century.* The first buildings of the *conquista-*

dores, whether military, civil or religious, had an improvised and rather styleless character more dependent on immediate necessity, available materials and the building skills of native labor than on any memory of Spanish styles or on the impressive but unadaptable monuments of vanquished Indian civilizations. But within a generation, by 1550, when the conquerors had become colonists, the situation had changed: the City of Mexico had been rebuilt with semi-military plateresque palaces, and new towns were rising throughout the land with orderly streets and plazas dominated by huge stone fortress-monasteries, the most important monuments of the 16th cent. Their churches were usually aisleless with a polygonal or square apse to the east and a choir raised on a gallery over the western door; they were covered by barrel or traceried Gothic vaults, and buttressed by massive inert walls and salient pier buttresses; they were unroofed and elaborately battlemented, and occasionally equipped with a *chemin-de-ronde.* Towers were plain; often they were lacking entirely; in some regions bells were hung in the arches of a pierced gable, or *espadaña.*

South of the church there was usually a two-storied cloister surrounded by the various rooms of the monastic establishment. In front was a vast forecourt, or *atrio,* enclosed by a crenellated wall. Here congregated crowds of converted Indians for catechism, baptism and outdoor mass, celebrated by a priest in a special chapel connected to the monastery building but broadly open to the *atrio.* (In Yucatán an apse-like open chapel often took the place of the church.) In the corners of the *atrio* stood four small shrine buildings, or *posas,* with altars used during outdoor processions. This arrangement for congregational worship in a large walled court, with a multitude watching, in passive participation, a ritual performed in a special covered and often raised chapel may possibly be a borrowing—and the only one—from preconquest pagan religious architecture.

Many styles flourished simultaneously in the 16th cent., even side by side in the same building. Elements of Gothic design occur not only in the vaults, but also in portals, rose windows, gargoyles, the pointed arches of windows or cloisters, and in the decorative details of bases or moldings. Plateresque motives often dominate whole façade compositions and the architectural framework of the many-storied *retablos.* The façades of most of what little civil architecture survives are plateresque also. Another school of purer and more academic Renaissance architecture is to be found in a small group of Italianate basilican churches and occasional purist doorways and arcades. Mudéjar and direct Moslem influence is surprisingly strong,—in mosque-like open chapels, in *alfarje* ceilings, in *alfiz* doorways and windows. Even more exotic is the occasional *manoelino* or the vague reflections of styles already extinct in Europe, such as the romanesque. Carving in any of these different styles is subject to reinterpretation at the hands of Indian craftsmen, resulting in a unique stylistic blend, the *tequitqui.*

The great cathedrals which began to rise at the end of the century represent a less vigorously and more sophisticated or Spanish development than the monastic churches, for they were designed by imported professional architects and not by amateur monk-builders like most of the monasteries. They were begun on late Gothic plans in imitation of Seville or Salamanca, but developed with increasingly decorous Renaissance detail which submits, at the end of the century, to the severe discipline of Herrera. Decorations and additions of subsequent periods have now changed these XVI century cathedrals into historical museums of the development of Mexican architecture rather than exemplars of any one style.

17th Century. The characteristic church is no longer that of the monastery, but the parish church of the secular clergy. In one of the world's most assiduous fervors of religious building, more and more new churches were raised throughout the country (perhaps some 8,000 in this century alone). In the towns of the more prosperous agricultural regions and near the incredible mines, these were built with an opulence eclipsing contemporary work in Spain. The simple basic scheme is rarely varied: everywhere appears the same high aisleless nave (sometimes with shallow side-chapels), shallow transept and square apse; a high dome covers the crossing and its openings supply the main light for the interior. The façade is usually adorned with a frontispiece of sculptured ornament contained in an enframement of the orders; the larger compositions of more than one story recall the handsome gilded *retablos* within. (A few are even concave like apse *retablos.*) The frontispiece is flanked by one or two towers, plain below but elaborately ornamented in the open belfry section above. The whole construction is no more than a neutral background for the decoration of portal, tower and dome.

The general style is loosely known as Mexican baroque, though the only baroque elements are decorative, and are freely mixed with mannerist and occasional mudéjar forms. There is almost no baroque planning or spatial composition. The baroque character lies rather in the decoration,—an agitated profusion of twisted columns, broken pediments, cartouches, swags and brocade-like relief patterns arranged with the carefree independence of a country with no classical traditions but with an innate sense of ornamental logic and ordered exuberance. Though its sources are Spanish, the finished architecture is not.

Monasteries were still being built, and now also convents, usually in the cities where, though they had to be more restricted in plan, they became even more sumptuous in decoration than their XVI century predecessors. Their church-type is like the parish church, but generally without transept and with two decorated portals on the flank facing the street rather than one at the end of the building.

The rich colonial families built themselves stately rectangular palaces with rectangular patios, again on a simple standard plan in no way baroque, but with a wealth of baroque ornamentation on the mammoth entrance, or *saguán,* and in the arcaded patio and its fountain. The parapets which crown the walls are often animated in silhouette and pulled up at the corner to form the cresting of an *hornacina* or angle niche for the figure of the patron of the house. Town halls and the administrative buildings of the government followed the same palace type, sometimes with the addition of a tower and arcades across the main front.

Materials were more varied than in the preceding century. Glazed tile made in Puebla was freely used to cover whole walls, exterior and interior, and to make brilliant the many domes which dominated every town. In Mexico City the favorite building material was *tezontle,* a soft wine-purple lava, in Oaxaca and Guanajuato a green limestone, and in Morelia a peach-colored trachyte. Elaborate low stucco reliefs covered the walls of many palaces in Mexico City in all-over diaper patterns, half mudéjar, half baroque, and in Puebla stucco curled and sprang free of the walls in a filigree of strap-work derived from mannerist engravings of ornament but so developed and so vivified as to constitute a startlingly original baroque style.

Church interiors in this and the succeeding century were emblazoned with more gold leaf than the world has ever seen in architecture before or since.

18th Century. The building types of church and palace remain much the same, but the decorative elements become more varied and more important, advancing over the building until they efface any other major architectural interest. Ornamental interest does not smother or conflict with tectonic architectural interest: it replaces it.

The several extravagant styles of the first three-quarters of the century are usually classified together under the term *ultra-baroque.* The most important of these is the Churrigueresque, radiating from Mexico City but so widespread by 1760 as to constitute a national rather than a local style. It reaches its fullest expression in facade frontispieces and *retablos* (which seem to have influenced the façades), but has such a definite character and vocabulary that it can easily be identified as well in the details of doorways, windows or niches. Its main element is the "Churrigueresque order", made up of a pedestal with *faldoncito* (lambrequin ornament), a shaft in the form of an *estípite* (inverted obelisk) surmounted by a medallion block and a Corinthianesque foliate capital, and an entablature repeatedly broken in plan and again in elevation by openwork foliate brackets on axis with the shafts and keystones, etc. Moldings have bold deep unclassical profiles, and rarely run uninterrupted, but change their direction constantly and consistently in a typical sequence of straight and curved segments. This style is as extravagant as the Churrigueresque of Spain—possibly more so—but it is more disciplined: it uses a more standardized repertory of forms and lines, and submits to much stricter compositional laws. But this careful marshalling of many parts is the means to quite a different end, for the sensuous effect of a complete Mexican Churrigueresque interior is undeniably and purposefully overwhelming.

The tile work of Puebla extends its repertory until entire large baroque compositions in glittering and brilliant color are pieced together not only on flat surfaces and domes but also on cornices and columns, on capitals and *estípites* and almost every external architectural feature no matter how complicated its form. Palaces in Puebla are commonly of bright red tile dotted with indigo lozenges. Tile coverings for domes were made in Puebla in all colors and sizes and sent on mule-back to every part of the country, from Arizona to Campeche.

The 17th cent. stucco work of Puebla and its satellites in the States of Mexico, Tlaxcala and Oaxaca develops an even less architectural character in the 18th cent. as it comes to play a more important architectural role. Cornices are made to ripple and crinkle with rococo bravura giving rise to many legends of stucco mixed with sugar or white-of-egg. In the most extreme examples, the filigree of free-standing strap-work exhibits a really bewildering virtuoso luxuriance.

There are other important local styles identifiable in Mexico City, Querétaro, Morelia San Luis Potosí, Oaxaca, etc., and ingenuous versions of all of them in the folk-architecture of the Indian villages.

Towards the end of the century, academic influence is brought by imported architects and imported engravings imitated by Mexicans. French models supplant Spanish and correctness supplants invention. National character and originality dies with the chill *rigor mortis* of provincial international classicism.

19th and 20th Centuries. The 19th cent. was so troubled politically that there was little building before the parvenu period of Porfirio Diaz at its close: what little there was followed fashionable European models from Empire neo-classicism on down to Parisian Art Nouveau at the beginning of the 20th cent.

Since 1930 there has been more building in the modern style in Mexico City than in any other city in the world. At first it was just another importation, façades from Europe and structural methods and conveniences from the United States. Construction is unusually timid in span of beams and in structural systems chosen: reinforced concrete is ubiquitous, even in very small buildings. The surprisingly varied native materials have been little exploited, nor has serious study been made of the peculiar regional climatic conditions except in hospitals and schools. Though widely accepted in Mexico, modern architecture has not yet developed a vigorous national character comparable to the colonial styles. Some of the most recent work seems to indicate, however, a more autochthonous new movement, a worthy companion to the better known achievements in modern Mexican painting. —J.McA.

mezzanine. A low intermediate story between two higher ones.

mezzo-recitativo. See opera.

mezzo-relievo. See relief; relief sculpture.

mezzotint (an intaglio process). The process of making mezzotints is similar to making drypoints, only the process is reversed. A burr is raised over the surface of the entire plate. The plate, if printed before any work was done, would produce a solid black. All parts of the design, which should print lighter than black, must be scraped. For a pure white the original smooth surface of the copper is retained.

The process of roughening the surface of the plate is such a laborious one that only few artists have the courage to carry it through. It is accomplished by using a tool called a rocker. This is a steel chisel having a curved edge serrated with very fine teeth, the handle springing from the center of the curve. The surface has to be rocked with this tool in many directions, each time taking a definite angle, until the surface of the copper is cut all over into a minutely dotted surface, which holds the ink as does the burr of the drypoint. To overcome this laborious process, the Cleveland Print Makers roughen the surface by sand blasting; Alex Stavenitz, the American artist, uses the aquatint method, calling it "aquatint mezzotint." The carborundum prints made on the Federal Art Project in Philadelphia are obtained by grinding the plate with a lithograph levigator, using carborundum and water.

Mezzotints are outstanding for their richness of blacks. The process is one that will reward the artist who has the will to do the work and explore the subtle range of tones. See PRINTS AND PRINT PROCESSES. —K.K.

mf. See NOTATION.

Micronesia, art of. See OCEANIA, ARTS OF.

microphonograph Dussaud. See phonograph.

Middle American aboriginal art. See ABORIGINAL AMERICAN ART.

mihrab (Arab.). The prayer niche in a Mohammedan mosque which indicates the direction of Mecca, the holy city of all Mohammedans. Frequently used as a motif in the design of the antique Ghiordes prayer rug. See ISLAMIC ART; PERSIAN ART.

military sketching. The conveying of military information by means of hastily drawn maps

or landscapes. There are three chief forms:
(1) **military sketches** proper are maps made
in the field by *plane-table* surveying methods,
in which directions are ascertained by sighting
along an *alidade* or ruler or by means of a
compass, distances usually by pacing, by intersecting sight rays or by estimation, and relative elevations ordinarily by measuring vertical angles with the aid of a *clinometer* or by
sighting along the edge of a board to which
a plumb line is attached. (2) **Aerial photo
sketches** are maps made from combinations of
aerial photographs, often with the assistance
of some form of *stereoscope*. (3) **Panoramic
sketches** are simple, literal landscapes with
notes pointing out the features that are of
military importance. These latter sketches are
commonly made by holding the edge of the
drawing against the view, keeping it at a constant distance from the eye by aid of a knotted
string held in the teeth, and marking on the
edge of the paper where it cuts across important details of the scene as observed with one
eye closed. These marks are then extended to
appropriate places in the drawing by means of
faint lines parallel to the edges of the paper.
By this means soldiers with little artistic experience are often able to make drawings of
sufficient accuracy to serve well their military
purposes. See U. S. War Department. *Field
Manual 21-35. Field Service Pocketbook:
Sketching.* —T.I.C.

mille fleurs. See TAPESTRY.

Mimbres art. A unique pottery is the chief
expression of a people who lived in the Mimbres River Valley in southwestern New Mexico c. 1000-1200 A.D. It consists of somewhat
irregular food bowls of black on white ware,
decorated on the inside with figures of birds,
insects, fish, animals and human beings, drawn
with a lively naturalism but conventionalized
enough for decorative purposes. In marked
contrast to the highly abstract quality of most
ceramic decoration in the Southwest, all the
creatures seem strangely alive. An irregular
hole broken in the bottom of many of the
bowls indicates burial use; probably the spirit
of the bowl was supposed to be thereby released to be free with the spirit of the deceased. So entirely unique and so localized in
time and place is this ceramic ware that some
scholars have suggested that it is the work of
some gifted individual or school of potters.
See H. S. and C. B. Cosgrove, *The Swarts
Ruin; a Typical Mimbres Site in Southwest
New Mexico,* Peabody Museum Papers, 1932.
—H.G.

mimodrama. A pantomime, often accompanied
by music.

Minai ceramics. See ISLAMIC ART.

minbar (Ar.). Pulpit in a mosque. See IS-
LAMIC ART.

Minerva. See Athena.

Ming art. See CHINESE ARTS.

ming ch'i (Ch.). Modeled clay figurines for
burial in tombs.

Ming dynasty porcelain. See CERAMICS II.

miniature painting. See EARLY CHRIS-
TIAN ART.

minima. See NOTATION.

minium. Strictly, this is the red tetroxide of
lead made by heating litharge or white lead
for fairly long periods and at fairly high
temperatures. It is bright scarlet in color, has
good hiding power, and a smooth texture in
oil. It has been used generally in European
and Asiatic paintings since ancient times, although the word, minium, was also applied to
cinnabar or natural sulphide of mercury.
—G.L.S.

minnesinger (Ger.). German troubadours of
the 12th and 13th cent. of noble lineage who
composed both words and music of their
songs. See MEDIEVAL MUSIC.

Minoan architecture. See Aegean architecture.

Minoan art. See Aegean-Minoan art.

minor key. See key.

minor interval. See interval.

minor mode. See scales and modes.

minor scale. See NOTATION.

Minpei yaki (Jap.). Pottery made in Awaji
province.

minstrel's harp. See MUSICAL INSTRU-
MENTS.

minstrel show (Negro minstrels). A species
of musical and variety entertainment which
had its origin among the Southern Negroes
in the U.S.A. and which was popularized in
theatrical presentation by E. P. Christy, the
originator in 1842 of a troupe of imitation
Negro singers, musicians, and comedians. The
company usually includes a men's chorus in
black face, an interlocutor who announces

specialty numbers and who precipitates much of the comedy by interrogating two or more 'end men,' fantastically dressed specialty artists or comedians who sit in special chairs on the flanks of the chorus. Although minstrel shows originally employed dialect songs of Negro life, including some which Stephen Collins Foster wrote for Christy, modern performances emphasize popular music. Yet the bones, banjo, and tambourine, the latter employed by the chorus in intricate routines, still are used as accompanying instruments. Variety acts, acrobatic stunts, dramatic sketches, and other performances now are usually included with the minstrel show. Christy took his troupe to England, where this form of entertainment achieved a lasting popularity.   —H.R.W.

minuet. The minuet, which was to become the most famous of all court dances, originated among French peasants as one of many branles of Poitou. Since its music became part of the later instrumental suites, it is called a pre-classic dance form. In its original state, this branle was a gay and lively dance in ¾ meter. Its healthy vigor is reflected in the writing of a 16th cent. authority who mentioned the girls of Poitou stamping with their wooden sabots to mark the phrases. After the 18th cent. courtiers had made the dance over to reflect their own sophisticated artificiality in small, precise movements, they gave the branle a new name based on the word *menu* (small, neat). The court dance took on a great complexity of mannerisms and etiquette associated with its performance until it became and remains a symbol of foppish elegance.   —J.G.

minuscule. Small letter. See writing.

mirror canon. See canon.

mirrored color. See COLOR.

Mirror of the World. See ORIENTAL MUSIC.

misericord. A projection from the under surface of quirestall seats in Gothic churches placed so that when the seat is turned up it can be used as a support for a standing priest during a long church service. Therefore the name "misericord"-instrument of pity. Often **(England!)** profusely decorated with humorous scenes or representations from the Bestiary (q.v.).   —R.B.

Mishima yaki (Jap.). Pottery made in imitation of Korean ware having inlaid patterns.

missal. See MEDIEVAL MUSIC.

mission style. See INTERIOR ARCHITECTURE AND DECORATION.

miter point. See PERSPECTIVE.

Mithnagdic songs. See JEWISH MUSIC.

mitsuda-e (Jap.). A term generally applied to certain ancient Buddhist paintings which were thought to be a style of oil painting. It is now thought to be lacquer painting; as on the doors of the *Tamamushi* shrine in Horyu-ji, near Nara.   —J.A.M.

mitsudaso (Jap.). A litharge (q.v.) painting medium sometimes hard to distinguish from lacquer painting.

mixed method. See PERSPECTIVE.

mixolydian mode. See idiom A (2); scales and modes.

Mixtec. They were a linguistic group living in northern Oaxaca and southern Puebla in Mexico. These people were the authors of an important religious art which seems to have flourished about the 11th cent. A.D., and supplanted previous independent religious arts of Middle America. Later this art is sometimes known as Mixteca-Puebla since this area seems to have been its center of origin and it was carried both by Aztecan Nahuas as well as Mixtec speaking peoples.   —G.C.V.

mizu-e (Jap.). Water color painting.

mizusashi (Jap.). Utensil for *cha-no-yu* (q.v.). The fresh water jar, usually of pottery.

mo (Ch.). Black ink. A mixture of carbon and glue pressed into sticks or cakes. When rubbed up in water on an ink-stone, it is the common medium for painters and writers.

möbel. See FURNITURE.

mobile, a. See SCULPTURE.

mobile color. See lumia.

mobile sculpture. See SCULPTURE.

modality. See idiom A.

mode. *Mus.* Characteristic selection of tones forming the vocabulary of a musical idiom (q.v.). More specifically (pl.), the vocabulary of modality. See idiom A; scales and modes; ACOUSTICS.   —E.K.

model. See design.

modeled. See SCULPTURE.

modeling. (1) The act of forming a two or three dimensional figure in a plastic, malleable material such as clay or wax, the resulting figure being either retained as the end-product, or used as a model or form for the making of a reproduction in plaster, terracotta, bronze, marble, stone, or wood; (2) that quality of a painting, drawing, photograph, or other two-dimensional representation in which an effect or illusion of the third dimension is achieved, through the use of such means as lighting, contrast, color, and perspective, and control of dark-light values. Whitford and Winslow in *Dictionary of Education.*

model drawing theory. See PERSPECTIVE.

mode of vibration. See ACOUSTICS.

modern architecture. See international architecture.

modern copies of paintings. See FORGERIES IN PAINTING.

Modern dance is a concept—a point of view—and not a prescribed system. It is dance as it is conceived today in terms of its science, philosophy, and art. It inherits much from the past and is influenced by the scientific spirit of the present. Its study is profiting from increased knowledge of movement and rhythm. Physiological and psychological research have revealed the nature of the kinesthetic sense and its importance to motor and rhythmic perception. This research has also revealed the relation between feeling and its movement expression—revelations which are influencing the technical study of dance, as well as its theory and philosophy. As a result there has been a general agreement as to the basic meaning of dance. The emphasis today is to know and experience dance as a creative art experience, expressing and communicating the dancer's emotional reactions to his impressions, as he evaluates them. The technical necessity is to train the body to become a strong, flexible, sensitive and well-coordinated instrument capable of responding to the exigencies of the expressive mind. The quality and manner of movement are determined by the artistic integrity of the dancer rather than be a forced conformity to an externally imposed standard. Moreover, compositional form is no longer dependent upon musical forms. It emphasizes the necessity of the outward observable form (the dance) being an organized structure that meets the requirements of subject matter, in-

stead of the requirements of a pre-determined structure. Dance has proved its ability to compose independently in its own medium (movement), creating dance forms as objects of art in the same sense as a painting or musical composition is an art object. The expressive forces of dance are known to be embedded in muscle tension, and in the tensions arising from stresses inherent in structure itself. Today dance is free to choose for its accompaniment from a variety of possibilities: speech, song, sound effects, as well as music.

Modern dance is the contemporary phase of dance in its evolution toward its destined goal of greater universality.

The term "modern dance" should not be confused with the personalized dance manner of contemporary artist dancers. —M.N.H'D.

modern furniture. See FURNITURE.

modern glass. See GLASS AND GLASS-MAKING.

modern notation. See NOTATION.

MODERN STAGESETTING. The development of modern stagesetting cannot be explained by one common denominator. Any attempt in this direction would inevitably leave out some of its sources, trends, and facts. Nor can we explain the development of its artistic values by the development of its machinery or of the technique of lighting functionally.

The 19th cent., unsensual as it was, represented the poorest level of stagesetting for many centuries. The first protest against its conventional and trivial rendering was launched by the Duke George II of Saxe-Meiningen about 1874, whose group under his leadership played on many European stages. Besides his ideas as to directing, his ambition was to make the setting as "true" as possible; however, for him truth was identical with reliability of historical details. Thus he crowded the stage with an unbelievable number of individual items. This method was interesting for the historian but it was irrelevant from an artistic point of view, since the result was a collection of three-dimensional props before sidewings and backdrops painted in the old manner. Anyhow, the naturalism of the beginning 20th cent. can be followed back to the stimulus he gave to the European stage.

The first step forward in the 20th cent. was done by Constantin Stanislavski (1863-1938) with his Moscow Art Theatre. His work is characterized by the most truthful realism of the minutest details which now included besides the three-dimensional props solid side walls instead of the earlier flats. While the **Meiningers** believed that the mere addition of realistic details was already enough in itself, Stanislavski tried to organize these details in a kind of selective realism and to create in this way the mood of the scene. However, the naturalistic style of Stanislavski meant a perfection and an end and not a new beginning.

Max Reinhardt 1873-1943; started in Berlin 1905) added to the three-dimensional naturalism the lavish use of the meanwhile invented new machineries, such as the revolving stage, the cyclorama, wagon stages, etc. The artist to whom he gave the tasks of stage design like Alfred Roller, Emil Orlik, and especially the most versatile of them, Ernst Stern, combined the most contradictory trends, adding to his naturalism some elements of stylization. Because of this mixture we are not able yet to find out whether Max Reinhardt, in any case one of the most sensational theatrical genius, represents, after all, the climax of a period gone or can be considered as the pioneer for a new one. Anyhow, from a sociological viewpoint, he was at least the first in Western Europe who saw the difference of the artistic demands of the intimate theatre and the theatre of the masses which found its greatest development later in Russia. Reinhardt created *Kammerspiele* as well as an experimental theatre for the masses with his central-domed *Grosses Schauspielhaus* in Berlin, 1919, which was shaped by the tendency for the inclusion and greatest participation of the audience. In this way he continued Richard Wagner's (1813-1883) fight against class differentiation in his Festival Theatre at Bayreuth. Reinhardt's naturalism although based on the rendering of naturalistic details used, however, also elements of a movement which simultaneously fought vehemently against all kinds of realism. It was the trend for which two men were pioneers: Adolphe Appia and Edward Gordon Craig.

Adolphe Appia (1862-1928) in order to develop further the ideas of his master Richard Wagner considered the theatrical performance a *Gesamtkunstwerk* (q.v.), a combination of visual, acoustic, musical, and literary impressions, connected and united by rhythm. (*La Mise-en-Scène du Drama Wagnerien*, Paris, 1895). He concentrated mainly on the development of the three-dimensional built-up and the psychology of color and light, shaded arcording to rhythmical laws. The actor's proportion had to become the unit of measurement and the law of space had to correspond to the time law of music. These rhythmical laws which governed music, the movement of the actor, and the visual and spatial forms by a kind of orchestration of light equally, became later even still more evident in the theories of Jacques Dalcroze (b.1865) with whom he worked at Hellerau-Dresden, Germany.

Edward Gordon Craig (born 1872), not quite so revolutionary in his "purification of the stage" as he himself believed, emphasized the architectural organization of the stage by simplifying all details and reducing them into pure cubic volumes. Undisturbed by any technical inhibitions in his projects he changed the proportions of reality arbitrarily, used steps and platforms thus stimulating our feeling for space—helped by the influence of the dance, by distributing the actions on different levels. Later on he renounced even specific architectural forms, and composed the whole stage by portable folding screens in manifold combinations. He considered the "divine" movement as the basis of theatrical art and reduced even the role of the actor, demanding absolute craft, his ideal being the "inanimate" being, the super-marionette. Since he could not achieve this kind of theatre, he at least made the stage more rhythmical by introducing rhythm within a scenic unit into the stage decoration. Thus he contradicted naturalism even stronger than Appia, exercising a tremendous influence upon the theatrical world by his organ *The Mask* since 1908.

Already before World War I, while Stanislavski's and Reinhardt's naturalism still flourished, while Appia's and Gordon Craig's stylizing influence still grew, new ideas began to arise again in Russia. Vsevolod Emilievich Meyerhold (born 1873), formulating his "biomechanical" principles, tried to shape a stage entirely in correspondence with the needs of the actor's body and movements, emphasizing gymnastic displays. Thus he was lead to a stereometric subdivision of the stage by the abundant use of steps and different levels, too. Of course, the whole tendency of the Russian theatre for the "mobilization of the will of the masses" contrary to the entertainment theatres, influenced also the selection of the visual means. It was Leopold Jessner in Germany, 1919, who took over these stimuli, creating the world famous *Jessner Treppen* which were of strongest influence on the stage of the U.S.A.

Alexander Tairov (born 1885) in his "liberated theatre" went one step farther. He put scaffolds and technical constructions on the stage of the Kamerny Theatre in Moscow (already in 1914) without any ambition to have them interpreted as real localization of the respective scenes. His "Neo-Realism" insisted on the visibility of all constructive elements since his functional mind wanted to abolish all stage illusion and to show even the machinery as it really was. Since the whole world of theatre in itself is unreal and becomes real only through a tacitly accepted convention, this limited reality denies the frame of its art and must logically make the actor also a mere "instrument." In spite of this inner contradiction his main designer Alexandra Exter succeeded in creating bizarre constructivistic patterns always leaving free planes for histrionic action. Sometimes Tairov played even before the curtain, negating any kind of setting, sometimes he used the whole depth of the decorated stage.

It should not be forgotten that the so-called "mechanistic reproduction" relied on stimuli which went out from Tairov. So the *Locomotive Ballets,* the *Triadic Ballet* by Carl Schlemmer, the *Machine Ballet* by L. Lissitzky (1924, Vienna), by Slivinsky in Warsaw with their corresponding settings can be retraced to his ideas as well as the overemphasis on machine elements, which was so characteristic for the Jewish Moscow Academical Theatre.

In Western Europe, meanwhile, cubism and futurism had stimulated the stage, too. Reality was dissolved into rhythmically arranged stereometrical patterns (the Italian Francis Picabia, Antonio Bagaglia, Enrico Prampolini), settings which sometimes looked like retranslated cubistic paintings. The last step in this direction was done by the artists of the Bauhaus, Moholy-Nagy and Oscar Schlemmer who extended the abstraction not only on the stagesetting but also on costumes and even on the mechanically organized movements of the actors, partially, as mentioned above, stimulated by Tairov.

In connection with his ideas of the political epic theatre Erwin Piscator (b. 1893) in Berlin influenced also the visual means of stagesetting. He used the theatrical machinery as a medium of his ideas almost to the same degree as the actor. The **revolving stage,** invented in 1896 by Karl Lautenschläger in Munich, had been already used by Max Reinhardt but only for realistic purposes. Now it became an expression in itself like the elevator stage, originated by Alfred Linnebach, or the treadmill. In combination with the abundant use of different levels these devices revolutionized the stage into a tribune of continu-

ous three-dimensional action. These means were complemented by the lavish use of Mariano Fortuny's (1838-1874) diffused light which had been already introduced in 1909 in Berlin in combination with the **cyclorama.** Projection of still-pictures and of films helped the clarification of the political ideas which were to be propagandized as did the acoustic explanation of the narrator besides the actors. Dimensions, proportions, light and color were not any longer bound on any laws of reality. There were no visual means from Gordon Craig and Appia to Meyerhold and Tairov, to Schlemmer and Gropius (Bauhaus) which were not used in these highly dynamic settings.

The so-called **Architectural stage** as realized in the Théâtre du Vieux Colombier, Paris, by Jacques Copeau (born 1878) and Louis Jouvet (b. 1887) around 1920, the "Shakespearian" stages by William Poel of the Elizabethan Stage Society of London, and some German reconstructions like Max Reinhardt's "Redoutensaal" in Vienna, 1923, were stimulated indirectly, too, by Gordon Craig. Adapting either the Palladian or the Shakespearian stage to modern needs, the scene represented a definitely given architectural environment with permanent setting. Hints of the locale of acting were given by some realistic smaller props. Other architectural stages with permanent setting: the Théâtre DuMarais, Brussels, 1923, and two theatres at exhibitions, Van de Velde's at the Cologne Exhibition, 1914 and Auguste Perret's at the Exhibition of Decorative Arts, Paris, 1926.

The first step towards the formal architectural stage had been done already by Alfred Roller, Vienna, 1905. But in his works (as well as in those by Oscar Strnad [1880-1935] and Carl Czeschkà for Reinhardt in 1908) the Austrian exuberant sense for decorative effects smoothed the rigid scheme—as was the case in the Künstlertheater of George Fuchs (b. 1868) in Munich. Hence today we, looking backwards, appreciate much more the decorative elements of these settings than the elementary architectural idea which was so strongly emphasized in the theoretical writings of these reformers.

The permanent architectural setting, realized in this country for the first time by the Arts and Crafts Theatre, Detroit, 1917, which used also the portable screens of Edward Gordon Craig, was always connected with very definite ideas about the relation between auditorium and stage. The theoretical writings by George Fuchs (*The Future of the Theatre,* Munich, 1905), the Russian projects like the

Mass theatres at Kharkov and at Rostov-on-Don, the Grosse Schauspielhaus, Berlin, by Hans Poelzig, 1919, and the ingenious project of Walter Gropius and Erwin Piscator (where not the stage but the auditorium was rotaing), and in this country, the projects by Norman Bel Geddes (b. 1893) and William Lescaze (b. 1896), all of them stressed the desire for a closer contact between audience and stage and a stronger participation of the audience in the performance which helped create these ideas. Generally the trend from stylized realism toward the even stronger suppression of reality increased immensely after World War I. The locale of action was merely hinted, architectural forms, color and light, even directions of movements served mainly the purpose of expressing the mood of a given scene. Thus stylization brought the scheme into harmony with the essential spirit of the play. One single prop, one street lantern, one tree, one staircase, one Gothic arch became the symbol or "expression" for an environment whose further details were not shown.

In contrast with all these more or less architectural, more or less symbolic, more or less abstract tendencies, an outspoken contradictory movement developed simultaneously; the exclusive emphasis on painting and the use of stage perspective. However, now the idea is not one of illusionistic deception like in the 19th cent. On the contrary, it is a play based on disillusion, showing clearly that the make-believe of perspective and painting is just a make-believe and has to be looked at quasi, "in quotation marks". Currents of contemporary easel painting were transferred to the stage, from impressionism to cubism and futurism; it meant the negation of any spatial setting and the triumph of the consciously two-dimensional decoration. It meant a deceit which negated itself, a pattern for its own sake in which the actor, mainly the bearer of a costume, was just another element of the decoration. The chair, obviously painted on the wall, was just the ultimate step in this direction. This line to exaggerated artifciality began with Leon Bakst (1866-1924) and his formalistic Byzantinism and was taken over by the painters Fernand Léger (b. 1881), Henri Matisse (b. 1869), George Braque (b. 1881), Pablo Picasso (b. 1881) and André Dérain (b. 1880) between 1920 and 1930 in their settings for various ballets. Even those Austrian and German painters who generally worked in another direction, like Alfred Roller, Vienna; Oscar Strnad, Vienna; Ernst Stern,

Berlin; Panos Aravantinos, Berlin; and George Grosz played sometimes with these ideas.

The American theatre was fortunate in so far as all these contradictory individual trends were not fought out in this country. After the period of David Belasco's (1859-1931) substantial naturalism, American stage designers, far less dogmatic than the revolutionary pioneers of Europe and Russia, took the new ideas from wherever they found them, fresh and independent, being less bound by theories. The majority of American theatres continued in the old manner till the period between 1925 and 1930—unfortunately some of the greatest still today. Only then the new stimuli began to express themselves in the work of American stage designers. However, this delay was highly rewarded by the consequent freedom of choice. Thus it is impossible to identify leading masters with one of the above mentioned specific movements. Works by Donald Mitchell Oenslager (b. 1902), Robert Edmund Jones (b. 1887), Norman Bel Geddes (b. 1893), Cleon Throckmorton (b. 1897), Mordecai Gorelik (b. 1899), Boris Aronson (b. 1900), Joe Milziener (b. 1901), Harry Horner (b. 1911), Claude Bragdon (b. 1866) combine the colorful use of light of Adolphe Appia, the architectural attitude of Edward Gordon Craig, the expressiveness of the Germans of the 1920's with the constructivism and dynamic of the Russians. They use the artistic possibilities of the most complicated machineries but they are not ashamed to be sometimes entirely naturalistic in the way of Stanislavski and the early Reinhardt, if the conception of the specific play is asking for it. In other cases they are equally not ashamed of relying on the charm of playfullly painted settings in the line of the Russian Ballet. Small community theatres, college theatres and experimental stages are the pioneers, the commercial Broadway theatres follow quickly up. It is due to this spontaneity and entirely undogmatic attitude that the American stage today represents the highest development of stage-setting in the world, unhampered by the obliging traditions of past revolutions. See Harold Burris-Meyer and Edward C. Cole, *Scenery for the Theatre*, 1939; *Catalogue of the International Exhibition of Theatre Art*, The Museum of Modern Art, New York, 1934; Sheldon Cheney, *Stage Decoration* and *The Theatre, Three Thousand Years of Drama, Acting and Stagecraft*, New York, 1935; Edward Gordon Craig, *On the Art of the Theatre,* New York, 1925 and *The Theatre Advancing,* New York, 1928; Thomas H. Dickinson, *The Theatre in a Changing Europe,* New York, 1937; Hallie Flanagan, *Shift.ng Scenes of the Modern European Theatre,* New York, 1928; W. René Fuerst and S. G. Hume, *Twentieth Century Stage Design,* London, 1928; Freedley, George, and John A. Reeves, *A History of the Theatre,* New York, 1941; W. B. Gamble, *The Development of Scenic Art and Stage Machinery,* New York, 1928; Mordecai Gorelik, *New Theatres for Old,* New York, 1940 (contains an excellent bibliography); Edith J. Isaacs, editor, *Architecture for the New Theatre,* New York, 1935; Robert Edmond Jones, *The Dramatic Imagination*; Robert Edmond Jones and Kenneth Mac Gowen, *Continental Stagecraft,* New York, 1922; Yvonne Françoise Jossie, *Stage and Stage Settings,* Philadelphia, 1933; *Magazine of Art,* Four articles on American Theatre Designers by Edw. Reed, 1940, resp. 1941; René Fuelop Miller, *The Russian Theatre,* New York, 1930; Leon Moussinac, *The New Movement in the Theatre,* London, 1931; R. Myerscough-Walker, *Stage and Film Décor,* London, 1940; Donald Oenslager, *Scenery Then and Now,* New York, 1936; Lee Simonson, *The Stage is Set,* New York, 1932. —P.Z.

modes, ecclesiastical. The ecclesiastical modes (not to be confused with the ancient Greek modes) which form the basis of medieval music are eight in number—four authentic modes, and their derivative plagal modes. An apocryphal tradition ascribes them to St. Ambrose (c. 340-97) and Pope Gregory I (c. 540-604) respectively.

	Authentic	Plagal	Range	Dominant	Final
Dorian	I		D-d	a	D
Hypodorian		II	A-a	f	D
Phrygian	III		E-e	c	E
Hypophrygian		IV	B-b	a	E
Lydian	V		F-f	c	F
Hypolydian		VI	C-c	a	F
Mixolydian	VII		G-g	d	G
Hypomixolydian		VIII	D-d	c	G

The final for each pair of modes i.e. the authentic (composed of a pentachord and tetrachord) and its derived plagal (composed of a tetrachord and pentachord) a 4th below is the same, the difference between the two being one of range. In the authentic modes the dominant is a 5th above the final with the exception of mode III which during the 10th or 11th cent. was transferred to c. Use of the old dominant b, however, is often found. In the plagal modes the dominant is normally a 3rd above the final with the exception of mode IV a, and mode VIII c.

It is to be observed that there are no nodes with a and c as final. The former occurs in isolated cases and is known as *tonus peregrinus.* The latter known as *tonus lascivus,* although condemned by the Church, was favored by secular musicians.

The mode of a plainsong melody is indicated by its appropriate Roman numeral in chant books. It is a simple matter to ascertain the mode of a melody. The last note is the final. If the compass of the melody lies within the final and its octave, it is authentic, if it lies within the 5th above and the 4th below, it is plagal. Occasionally a melody will extend over the entire range, in which case it is considered mixed. A b flat in the signature indicates a transposed mode a 4th above. In some instances e.g. *Agnus Dei XVIII* (*Liber Usualis,* p. 63) the mode is undetermined, indicating that the melody is a very ancient one dating from a period when the theory of modes was not yet developed.

The names Dorian, Phrygian, etc., were first applied to the ecclesiastical modes by Boethius (c. 480-524) who for many centuries was considered the greatest authority on ancient Greek music. Boethius translated the Greek term *tonos* by the Latin word *modus* and as a consequence arrived at a system of nomenclature which was the reverse of that of the Greek modes. —V.A.

modes, musical. See scales and modes.

modes (of appearance of color). See COLOR.

modifications by the artist. See FORGERIES IN PAINTING.

modified fragments. See FORGERIES IN PAINTING.

modillion. An ornamental block or bracket under the corona of the cornice in the Corinthian and other orders.

Modra ware. See CZECHOSLOVAKIA, ART OF.

modulation. (1) The rise and fall of the voice in speaking or reciting. (2) *Mus.*

Any change of key or mode. See idiom B(3); key.

Moghul art. See ISLAMIC ART.

Mogollon culture. A culture of southwestern New Mexico, as yet little understood, contemporary with Developmental Pueblo and Hohokam, partaking of characteristics of both, yet with some peculiar to itself. Pit dwellings were used; a red and brown pottery was finished by the paddle and anvil method and polished. Shell gorgets suggest a connection with the East. Further evidence may prove that Mogollon was a local variation of either Anasazi or Hohokam. See Neil M. Judd, *Progress in the Southwest,* Essays in Historical Anthropology of North America, Smithsonian Miscellaneous Collections, 1940.
—H.G.

moire. Finish on silk, cotton, or acetate fabrics of plain weave, often corded. Engraved rollers, heat and pressure flatten the surface at intervals, leaving the natural roundness in other places.   —G.W.R.

Moki art. See Hopi art.

mokuga (Jap.). Literally, "wood picture"; a picture in marquetry, or wood inlay.

mokume (Jap.). A lacquer technique imitating the grain of wood.

mold. Plaster of Paris form in or on which ceramics are made. See CERAMICS I.

mold-blowing. See GLASS AND GLASS-MAKING.

moldings. Slender surfaces often compounded which depend for their decorative effect upon the gradations and contrasts of light and shade.

Momoyama art. See JAPANESE ART.

mon (Jap.). A family crest used on family possessions, and sometimes conceived as pure design. See SYMBOLISM IN FAR EASTERN ART.

monastic architecture. The building groups provided for communities of monks or nuns who take vows of poverty, chastity, and obedience, living under the rule of abbot or prior (abbess or prioress) devoting themselves to prayer and various good works. Early monks in Eastern Christendom lived separately in scattered cells, meeting ceremonially at the monastic church for their liturgy and in the refectory for their meals. Later the various accommodations for the Eastern monks were regularly built against the inside of a fortified girdle wall, leaving the church standing free in a central court with the refectory facing it. In Western Christendom the church is normally to the north of the **cloister,** an arcaded garden cour which is the center of the life of the community. A normal arrangement of the various rooms in a medieval monastery is as follows: Along the *east walk* of the cloister: 1, sacristy (adjoining the church); 2, **chapter house,** where the community met daily as a corporation to hear a chapter of the monastic Rule and to transact business; often there was a chapel extending further east, with the infirmary establishment for the old and the sick monks beyond; 3, parlor or auditorium for speaking (since silence was enjoined elsewhere for a large part of the time) and as communication to the easterly parts of the monastery; 4, camera or workroom. The dormitory extended over 1, 2, 3, and 4, with exit directly into the south transept of the church, or by stairway to the cloister. *South walk*: 5, **calefactory,** a social room, exceptional in that it was warmed; 6, refectory; 7, pantry; 8, kitchen or kitchens, with shops, bakery, stables, quarters for lay brethren and servants not far distant. *West walk*: 9, cellars and stores; 10, adjoining the church, cloister entrance. *North walk* along the church nave; scribes and the library were often installed here. The guest house was often north of the church nave, with the porter's cella in it or nearby; the hospice for poor visitors was in the vicinity, often southwest of the church.

These conventual structures have a simple and rather barn-like character until the 12th cent.; later they are often five vaulted constructions worthy to be compared with the churches. A general movement to replace the medieval monastic buildings begins in the 15th cent. Many fine monasteries date from the 18th cent., esp. in France. At this time they are assimilated to palace architecture in the prevailing mode. Monastery building, interrupted by the French Revolution, began again in the 19th cent., but these newer groups are almost universally poor and dull in design. See Curman, S., *Bidrag till Kännedomen om Cistercienserordens byggnadskonst,* 1912; Thompson, A. H., *English Monasteries,* 1913; Gasquet, H. E. Cardinal, *English Monastic Life,* 1919 (5th ed.); Enlart,

Manuel d'Archéologie française, Part II, tome 1, 1929; Evans, J., *Monastic Life at Cluny*, 1931, and *Romanesque Architecture of the Order of Cluny*, 1938.   —K.J.C.

Moncloa pottery. See SPAIN, ART OF.

monk's mound. See Cahakia mound.

monochord. An ancient instrument for measuring intervals. See MUSICAL INSTRUMENTS.

monochromatic color scheme. See COLOR.

monochromatic plus white specification. See COLOR.

monochrome painting. See CHINESE ARTS.

monody. *Mus.* Style of composition in which a melody (usually written for human voice) is presented simultaneously with an accompaniment of chords. The term is used particularly with reference to the early forms of solo cantatas and operatic arias of the 16th and 17th cents. In this sense, monody is a special case of homophony (q.v.). The term is sometimes used in the sense of monophony (q.v.). See MEDIEVAL MUSIC.   —E.K.

monolith. A stone of one piece, used to differentiate a column shaft cut from one block of stone from one built up in several drums.

monophony. *Mus.* Process of composition by which a single melodic line is presented without accompaniment. Sometimes also called monody (q.v.). The term monophony is sometimes used as a synonym of homophony (q.v.).   —E.K.

monoprint. See monotype.

monotype. A print technique usually classified among the graphic arts. The picture is painted in full color on a non-absorbent surface such as a sheet of plate glass or metal with any sufficiently slow-drying paint and transferred to paper by direct contact with it, using a rubbing pressure on the back of the paper with any smooth, hard, rounded implement. Various effects are produced by manipulating the paint before the impression is made. To make additional copies of the same subject the plate must be repainted, thus the variations in color and design cause each print to be a unique proof rather than an exact replica. See PRINTS AND PRINT PROCESSES.   —R.M.

monstrance. A *ciborium* designed as an *ostensorium* so that it will serve not only to contain but also to exhibit the consecrated host. To comply with this purpose the host is placed in a transparent glass cylinder which is put on a high foot and made conspicuous by profuse ornamentation. The introduction of monstrances in + 1300 is connected with the pronouncement by the church of the doctrine of transubstantiation according to which the host while retaining its outward appearance is miraculously transformed into the very body of Christ. To celebrate this miracle the church instituted the festival of *Corpus Christ* (1264) in the course of which a monstrance is used to carry the host in solemn procession and to exhibit it to the community.   —R.B.

montage. See RADIO DRAMA; collage.

montan wax. See wax.

monumenta musicae Byzantinae. See eastern chants.

mood effects, of music. See EXPERIMENTAL PSYCHOLOGY OF MUSIC.

Moqui art. See Hopi art.

moralities. A later form of the mysteries (medieval plays) and may be regarded as a rudimentary form of the oratorio.

Moravia, art of. See CZECHOSLAVAKIA, ART OF.

mordant. The word itself is of uncertain origin, but its common application in the art of painting is to a method of gilding. There the word, mordant, is used to indicate an adhesive film which remains tacky for a long enough period to allow metal leaf applied over it to become firmly adhered. It is distinguished from water gilding, used for large flat areas on the panels of alterpieces, and the application of shell gold or powdered gold mixed with a medium as a thin paint.   —G.L.S.

mordent. *Mus.* According to Philipp Emanuel Bach an ornament with the function to connect a note with another a second below, to increase their sound and to add splendor. Technically, the mordent consists of a quick interchange between the main note with its neighboring second below.   —F.D.

moresca. See morris dance.

moribana style. See FLOWER ARRANGEMENTS.

moroccos. *Book.* All genuine moroccos must be made from goatskins, which vary in quality according to the country from which they are imported. (Cape, French, Levant, Niger, Oasis, Persian, Swiss, Titling, Turkey.)

morris dance. This famous English national dance is of uncertain origin. Some authorities find proof of descent from the Moorish dance, the morisco, in the name "morris" and the fact that the dancers sometimes blacked their faces. In its earliest performances, the morris made use of pageantry portraying characters from the Robin Hood legends, and was danced exclusively by men. Some of the characteristic features of the dances were the wearing of bells, the use of swords, the waving of white kerchiefs, and the carrying of short sticks rapped together in complicated rhythmic patterns. The basic formation was two lines face to face. The most characteristic step is said to have been a cut—step and hop with a sharp forward kick of the free leg. Most morris dances were in 4/4 or 2/4 meter.   —J.G.

mosaic pictures. A decoration or picture made by inlaying small pieces of variously colored glass, stone or other materials. In photography, a detail photograph formed by matching a number of photographs of contiguous parts taken from the air. See EARLY CHRISTIAN ART.   —R.L.W.

Moscow, school of. See RELIGIOUS PAINTING IN RUSSIA.

Moslem art. See ISLAMIC ART.

mosque. See ISLAMIC ART.

Mossi art. See AFRICAN NEGRO ART.

motet. *Mus.* A composition in contrapuntal style, sung in Catholic and Lutheran services. See MEDIEVAL MUSIC.

motif. *Mus.* Structural unit, usually a short figure of characteristic melodic and rhythmic, sometimes also harmonic outline, susceptible of being varied extensively and of appearing in different contexts in order to ascertain structural relations between various parts of a musical form.   —E.K.

motif, of a design. See design.

MOTION PICTURE. The motion picture is the one new art of modern times, and the most popular of the arts today. Both its novelty and its popularity at first stood in the way of its acceptance by educated people whose tastes were formed on the traditional arts. For some years after 1895, the year of the invention of motion picture projection, it was felt that because a film was the product of a complex mechanical process it could have little to do with artistic creation, while the fact that "the movies" appealed greatly to the lowest classes of society soon stamped them as vulgar. Eventually it was the very novelty of the film, the absence of a binding canon or tradition, which attracted artists from many other media and led to much constructive experiment. It was not, however, the "intellectual cinema" of the experimentalists, but the genuinely popular film, which developed into what we recognize as the art of the motion picture.

It was as a recording medium that the motion picture was first consciously used for "artistic" purposes. In France and Italy, famous players appeared in literal recordings of their customary theatrical vehicles during the years 1900-1911, and the results were applauded as a (somewhat inadequate) substitute for the stage. Meanwhile the popular film was developing a more original style. From 1909 to 1924, D. W. Griffith produced a series of important films in which he gradually evolved all the formal principles of the motion picture. These films, the most notable of which were *The Birth of A Nation* and *Intolerance,* disregarded the Aristotelian unities of the theatre (and indeed the spatial and temporal laws of every-day experience) in order to exploit the emotional and intellectual effects of the joining of two or more images related to one another solely by *theme.* Griffith's discoveries were immediately absorbed by film directors everywhere, and the *cut,* with its destruction of time and space, became the chief formal instrument of film construction throughout the world, and particularly in the American film (see cutting).

The influence of the other arts on the motion picture first became evident after World War I, and chiefly in continental Europe. Influenced in Germany by the expressionist theatre and in France by advance guard painting, experimenting film-makers produced many interesting films and a few of genuine cinematic merit. Though some of these films, notably *The Cabinet of Dr.*

Caligari, became world-famous, they were not widely shown and had small effect on the style and content of the popular film, though their producers were from time to time imported by Hollywood. In Russia, on the other hand, the Soviet directors of the 1920's made important contributions to the principles of cinematography. S. M. Eisenstein and V. I. Pudovkin closely studied the disjunctive style of Griffith, and co-ordinated his sometimes capricious and always instinctive methods into a reasoned film aesthetic. Films such as *Potemkin* (1925) and *Storm Over Asia* (1928) were particularly successful in exploiting the physical and psychological effects obtainable by "rate of cutting" (see cutting).

With the arrival of the sound film, 1926-28, the motion picture momentarily returned to its early task of recording plays, but within a few years began to resume the freer, more cinematic techniques of the silent era. As early as 1928, the Soviet film-makers had produced a theory of the sound film which incorporated all the principles of silent cinematography while suggesting an imaginative (as opposed to a literally reproductive) use of the sound factor (see SOUND, below). This theory has never been successfully realized even in Russia, and other potentialities remain to be fully explored. The technique of the great majority of sound films continues to represent a compromise between the principles discovered by Griffith and the methods of the theatre. But the range of film expression is slowly widening through experiments conducted both independently (e.g., in the documentary film) and within the film industry, especially in recent years. Though it can hardly be claimed that spectators in the mass actually *create* moving pictures, there can be little doubt that the film is the most popular of the modern arts—popular in content and form as well as in terms of the box-office. The organization of the film industry itself demands that each picture appeal to a vast undifferentiated audience and that it bring quick financial returns. This situation has resulted in the rise to power of individual producers and artists who "think like" their audiences and therefore reflect popular taste as much by instinct as by calculation. It is for this reason that the most important aesthetic consequence of the introduction of sound to the screen is now seen to be the development of a lively naturalistic style which readily reflects contemporary feelings, interests, and notions, and which confirms the position of the popular film as the dominant form of the cinema. —I.B.

motor-constructive experience. (art ed.). The phase of the art experience characteristic of the crafts and of industrial arts; used in art education to designate activities requiring muscular-mental coordination and involving the planning and building of objects through the use of materials and tools, as distinguished from such activities as drawing, painting, and similar forms of art expression; for example, designing and building a coffee table. Whitford and Winslow in *Dictionary of Education.*

motto. See HERALDRY.

motu proprio. See MEDIEVAL MUSIC.

Mound Builders. The theory that the Mound Builders were one people with a single coherent culture which preceded that of the American Indian is now abandoned. It has been proven that mounds were built by many prehistoric peoples of different cultures, scattered widely over the eastern half of the U. S. A.; that in some localities the culture which produced them disappeared before the coming of the Europeans; and that in some places the builders were the ancestors of the historical Indians. See Eastern North American Aboriginal Art. —H.G.

mountain and water painting. Chinese name for landscape painting. See CHINESE ARTS.

mountain green. See malachite.

mountain-temples. See SOUTHEASTERN ASIATIC ART.

mourning ring. See JEWELRY.

mouthpiece. See ACOUSTICS.

movable altar. See altar.

movable Do. The basis of a system in which the notes represented by syllable names relate to a tonic note or tone center, called "Do". The note to which Do is applied may be shifted from one tonal center to another (see modulation) in the course of a composition, hence the term, "movable Do". The term is likewise used in contradistinction to "fixed Do" the basis of a system common in France, Belgium, etc., in which the scale names do, re, me, etc., are applied to a fixed pitch. Do equals C, re, D, me, E, etc., and inflections of these syllables are employed for the various sharps and flats.

The movable Do system dates to the time of Guido (see solmization). The basis of the system is relative pitch in which each note bears a relation to the tonic or key note as well as to a note that precedes or follows it. Several systems have appeared giving a modern dress to the earlier one of Guido. The Tonic Sol-Fa method developed by John Curwen in England dates from the mid-19th cent. The Chevé method is similar but seeks to simplify matters by using numbers. Thus 1 equals do, 2, re, etc. Mention must be made of the Fa-Sol-la system used in singing white spirituals in the South, another variant of the movable Do idea.

There has been endless debate on the subject of the value of Movable and Fixed Do. That of Hullah and Curwen is historical. Both systems have their merits and defects although it is generally admitted that for beginners and for music that adheres to the diatonic line (Gregorian Chant, polyphony, etc.) the movable-Do system is the better. The Chevé method mentioned above is the basis of the Ward method so widely used in the United States today.   —J.V.H.

movement. (1) *In dance,* movement is the medium of expression and the body is the instrumental means of its communication. By nature we are given a body constructed and designed for certain kinds of locomotion and body activity, whose combinations offer an infinite variety of postures, gestures, and actions. Its skeletal framework serves as a system of levers that not only support and give form to the body and its actions but also offers points of attachment for muscles. The joints determine the kinds of movement possible and set the mechanical limits for motor response. They depend, however, for their action upon muscle action whose potential energy is controlled and released by nerve impulse. Since a muscle is fastened to two bones it pulls them toward or away from each other or rotates them according to joint structure, thus causing a change of position producing movements of bending, stretching, twisting and the various forms of locomotion. So movement as observable behavior primarily originates in nerve and muscle action. When movement takes place, we can observe that **distance** is covered and **direction** taken. Movements may be confined to narrow limits or expanded to the fullest capacity of structure. They have

range. Direction is the course of motion that establishes a space relation directly between the point of departure and the point of arrival, that is, movements have aim or **focus.** The actual path travelled may be direct or deviating. Movement, like sound, is a succession of intervals continuing in time and marking the passage of time. Movement intervals, therefore, have **duration**—which may be of varying lengths. This actual length is determined in the hidden principle of muscle and nerve action. Neuro-muscular action is manifested in movement intervals having duration and force because muscular action itself can only take place in alternate intervals of contraction and relaxation which are characterized by their duration and force of execution. Movement intervals, therefore, are also observed to have heavy or light **stress** or **force** according to the amount of muscle tension present in their performance. And finally, movement intervals may follow in slow or rapid pulsations. Movement has **speed** or rate of execution. No movement, however large or small, strong or weak, fast or slow, can take place unless range, speed, force, and space are involved.

These factors do not explain the activity within the mental life of the dancer. Meaningfulness in movement is determined by forces of another order. We are designed to think and feel as well as to move, therefore we cannot submit to mechanical laws alone. The anatomical and physiological equipment represent the more impersonal forces that are universally shared. They are ever present and active in all activity. The important issue is the individual use made of them. It is when movement is submitted to the dictates of an individual intellect and emotion that it ceases to be mechanical and becomes a manifestation of a unique and individual ordering. This unique ordering is determined by the psychological factors. They represent the personal endowments that through knowledge and use are the only forces that lend warmth and significance to any act. Within this mental equipment resides the awareness of all sensations as well as the capacity to think, feel, create, and will. It is the equipment for interpreting movement experience and creating its art expression in dance. Action implies a desire which prompts it, a thought which shapes it, and a visible movement of the physical body to carry it out. Two of these component activities are invisible and belong to the consciousness, but are revealed by the third component which is visible and belongs to the body. As outward observable behavior, movement is an integration of the physical and mental natures. In dance, movements become the motor symbols of actions within the mental life of the dancer (see rhythm, kinesthetic sense, and tension). (2) *Mus.* (a) Tempo, rate of speed. (b) One of the 3/4 parts of a sonata or symphony (qq.v.).   —M.N. H'D.

moving sculpture. See SCULPTURE.

Mozarabic architecture. See SPAIN, ART OF.

Mozarabic chant. See MEDIEVAL MUSIC.
mp. See NOTATION.

mudejar. See Mexico, post-Conquest architecture of; SPANISH ARCHITECTURE IN THE NEW WORLD; FURNITURE.

mudrā (Skr.). A mystic gesture of the hands and fingers, of religious significance, which symbolizes certain functions of a deity. In oriental art it often identifies the deity. See abhaya mudrā; bhūmisparśa mudrā; dharmacakra mudrā; dhyāna mudra; samādhi mudrā; varada mudra; also *Buddhist Hand Symbols,* Aisaburo Akiyama, Yokohama, 1939; *The Gods of Northern Buddhism,* Alice Getty, 1928; *The Iconography of Tibetan Lamaism,* Antoinette K. Gordon, 1939.   —J.A.M.

muffle. *Cer.* Compartment for firing ware by radiation. See CERAMICS I.

Mughal art. See INDIAN ART.

mugharna (Ar.). *Arch.* A stalactite decoration. See ISLAMIC ART.

muller. Traditionally used for grinding pigments on a slab, the muller is a rounded stone, flat at the bottom and moved over the slab by hand. A pigment mixed with oil or water is laid as a paste on the slab. Usually the muller is of the same material as the grinding surface, a hard stone like porphyry being the traditional preference. Modern hand grinding in the studio is usually done on glass slabs with glass mullers. See grinding slab.   —G.L.S.

mullion (A corruption of the Fr. *munnion,* stump). A minor division-piece between window openings or window frames.

mul sulkas. See cotton.

mummy pigment. Composed largely of bitumen, this dull brown coloring material was taken from bones and bodily remains of Egyptian mummies in which bitumen or asphaltum had been used in the embalming process. It was used chiefly as an oil paint in the 17th to 19th cents.   —G.L.S.

muntin (A corruption of the Fr. *munnion,* stump). A minor division-piece between window-lights, openings, or panels within the main frame or outline of the opening.   —J.M.M.

mural painting. The decoration of walls, and by extension, of ceilings uses fresco, oil, or encaustic techniques. It excludes from consideration other forms of interior surface decoration such as relief sculpture, mosaic, marble encrustations, and panelling. Generally speaking, it is subordinated to the architectural surfaces it embellishes. However, such variant forms as the chalk drawings within incised outlines in the Pyrenees caves dating from the Reindeer Age and the frescos of the grottos of Ajanta in India, must be considered, as well as the Pompeian mode of painted architecture, Michelangelo's painted architecture and sculpturesque figures on the Sistine ceiling, and such baroque extravagances as Correggio's paintings at Parma and those of Balthasar Neumann at the Vierzehnheiligen church, light and space integrating with the major art forms.

In **fresco** the pigment mixed with water is applied to the plaster surface while it is still wet. The section completed by the time the plaster dries has become a permanent part of the wall, coated with a veil of carbonate of lime. The dried plaster still unpainted must be cut away before another day's work is begun. With the aid of full-sized cartoons the master or his apprentice transfers to the wall the section designed for that day's program, working rapidly and boldly with emphasis necessarily on only the main effects. Changes can be made only with tempera of limited permanence. The great masters of classical times and of the early Renaissance used this technique. In recent years experimentation in "true fresco" has been frequent.

In **tempera** the pigments, mixed with such binding material as white of egg, honey or gum, and water, are applied to a dry plaster surface. The chief danger of this technique is that of peeling, although it has the advantage of permitting changes during execution. It was much used in ancient times, by the

Egyptians, e.g., and frequently by modern artists.

In **encaustic** the wall surface is prepared with wax, tempera pigments are used, and after the painting is finished, the surface is covered with wax, or the pigments may be mixed with melted wax on a hot palette. The Romans used it on occasion for details, and it has been revived in modern times.

Oil painting uses linseed oil as the binding medium and turpentine as dryer. The advantages of this technique are that it permits the completion of the painting in the studio, it is suitable for wood, copper, or canvas surfaces, and it maintains lustrous color values. On the other hand, when the canvas is applied to the wall, with white lead and oil as adhesives, it may create a different effect from the one in the studio, and it has little permanence if the wall is subjected to dampness. Even when mounted on a stretcher the colors may darken with age and the canvas disintegrate. However, it was used with great success by the Venetian masters, and is the common method of modern mural painters. Leonardo's *Last Supper* used oil on a surface badly prepared for it and disastrous flaking has resulted.

The major problems of the mural painter center on whether his design shall ignore or integrate with or remain subordinate to the flat surface. The answer of history seems to be that the burden of proof is with the artist. The problem is essentially one of the character of the setting, its use, and the intention of the artist. Regardless of the "integrity of the wall" decorative force, monumental composition, and thrilling beauty may be achieved, as channels through which experience may be transferred with enriching results. Thus the Egyptian in his tomb painting followed such conventions as overlapping and superposition to indicate space, keeping his outlines incisive and his colors flat and conventional. The Greeks and the Romans moved in the direction of modelling and atmospheric gradations to suggest space, but also had a repertory of purely ornamental forms for decorative use. The medieval European mural painter kept his modelling on a front plane and by simplification or distortion often underscored its meaning in other than plastic senses, meanwhile keeping the background inactive. The frescos of the Horiuji Temple, Nara, Japan, with their Chinese-Greco-Buddhist characteristics, illustrate the use of "ideal" space in harmonic relationships with meaningful line and decorative color.

Realization of the objective world, controlled to some extent within architectural frames and on occasion re-created in a world of plastic reality, was sought by the Italian masters of the Renaissance from Giotto (with his still Gothic palette and strong feeling for structural relations of line and form) to Uccello with his use of vanishing-point perspective, Masaccio with his aerial perspective, and the Venetians with their chromatic perspective. In them all space was controlled, but expressively used. Piero della Francesco, Raphael, Titian, Veronese, and Tintoretto in Italy and Rubens in the North achieved high success in this creation of a world of decorative reality.

Throughout the baroque and rococo periods mural painting was either accompanied by or subordinated to other types of decorations and did not reach its modern development perhaps until Puvis de Chavannes in the 19th cent. applied Giottesque principals in the Pantheon in Paris. In America the revival is connected with John La Farge and his Trinity Church frescos in Boston, his notable *Ascension* lunette in the church of the same name in New York, and with the World's Fair in Chicago in 1893 where a large number of young painters had a chance to learn the technique. The Boston Public Library, with work by J. S. Sargent, E. A. Abbey, and Puvis de Chavannes, and the Library of Congress in Washington were also useful laboratories. Perhaps future generations will agree that the most significant factor in the development of mural painting in America was the government-sponsored projects in the 30's wherein both beginners and experienced artists were commissioned to decorate with murals public buildings in Washington and throughout the country. In a literal sense this movement has initiated a renaissance of interest in mural painting. Meanwhile in Mexico and in Brazil the technique of Europe and the heritage of Indian and Negro are finding brilliant expression on walls as Orozco, Rivera, and Siqueiros on the one hand, and Portinari on the other, reveal once more the fundamental power of mural painting. See J. H. Breasted, *Oriental Forerunners of Byzantine Painting,* 1924; P. Gusman, *Mural Decorations of Pompeii,* 1924; B. Kleinschmidt, *Die Wandmalereien der Basilika San Francesco in Assisi,* 1925; Bruce and Watson, *Mural Designs 1934-1936,* 1936; *Wall Decorations of Egyption Tombs,* British Museum, London, 1914; V. Goloubew, *Documents pour servir a l'etude d'Ajanta,* Les Peintures de la premiere grotte, 1927; MacK. Helm, *Modern Mexican Painters,* 1941 and *Portinari, His Life and Art,* c. 1940.   —W.S.R.

muscle sense. See kinesthetic sense.

MUSEUM. (L. *museum,* fm. the Gr. *mouseion,* temple of the Muses, fm. *Mousa,* muse). Museums are established for preservation, study, and exhibition of original objects as they come from nature and from the hand of man, the maker. To interpret the significance of these objects and to demonstrate their meaning for the education of the people, museums make use of reproductions and other representative devices, restorations, rearrangements, charts, photographs, and the spoken and written word, along with the display of the objects themselves. The objects are assembled in collections classified by various categories and obtained through acquisition by purchase, gift, and bequest and through exploration and excavation.

Quantities of study material such as might go to a museum in modern times were sent from conquered lands to Aristotle by Alexander the Great; but Aristotle apparently used them up; at any rate they were not preserved through the ages. Other early collections suffered the same fate; man has always been a collector of objects, but only in comparatively recent times have these objects been preserved in museums. Ptolemy Soter, under the inspiration of Alexander's Hellenizing policy, founded the museum at Alexandria in Egypt, but that was essentially a library and academy of advanced study. The ancient Romans showed trophies of conquest in the capital and the medieval church preserved ecclesiastical relics; but the first were ephemeral displays and the second were religious treasures to be venerated as such, not objective examples of the work of man or nature.

It was not until the 15th cent. that a continuous history of the preservation and development of collections began, leading up in subsequent periods to the establishment of the museum as an institution of public significance. The discovery of America and the rediscovery of the ancient Greek and Roman civilizations so stimulated the formation of collections that kings, princes, and nobles vied with each other in accumulating objects of classical art; and scholars and men of wealth assembled specimens of minerals, plants, and animals brought by explorers and traders from distant lands. There grew up during the next two centuries throughout Europe art collections, coin and medal collections, natural history collections, and collections in which all three of these were intermingled with mere curiosities. The materials thus assembled, many of them persisting as state collections, formed the nucleus of museums; for instance, Cosimo de Medici's collections, now in the Florentine galleries; the Kunst and Naturalien Kammer of Augustus, Elector of Saxony, that led to the formation of the muesums of Dresden; and the collections of Francis I and his successors that went into the Louvre.

The museum as a public institution was the creation of the 18th cent. The first of its kind that was called a museum, the Ashmolean Museum at Oxford University, came into being shortly before the opening of the century, in 1683. In that year the university erected a building to house the collection assembled by John Tradescent and given by Elias Ashmole, with other material of his own collecting, to the university. Between 1740 and 1745 Pope Benedict XIV founded the first Christian museum in the Vatican. In 1753 Sir Hans Sloan's collections were accepted by the Parliament of Great Britain for the establishment of the British Museum. The first American museum was organized in 1773 at Charleston, South Carolina, as the Charleston Museum. The Museo Nacional de Ciencias Naturales at Madrid, established by royal decree in 1771, was opened to the public in 1776. At Paris in 1793 the Muséum de la République (now Musée Nationale du Louvre) was constituted at the Louvre and the next year the Jardin du Roi became the Muséum National d'Histoire Naturelle. By the close of the century the museum was firmly established and was recognized by the state and the public for its service in the preservation of valuable materials. Its growth, however, was inward; its chief impulse was to attract further accumulations of material and to hold its collections subject to study by those who actively sought admittance; it made no attempt to attract visitors or to reach out beyond its walls to educate the general public.

In the 19th cent. the museum reached its maturity. The palace collection, the cabinet of the prince or scholar, the public depository, the formative stages, gave way to the modern museum, a laboratory of research and a center of public education. Before that time the pattern had been: in art museums, solid galleries of painting or sculpture; in science museums, specimens arranged in rows or cases in regular order. About mid-century, educational exhibits, as distinguished from exhibits that were only collections, were first installed in museums. In 1844, the Musée de Cluny was opened with craft work of the Middle Ages arranged by period; the first museum group in science in the U. S. A. was shown in New York in 1869 and had its origin in England a few years earlier. The Great Exhibition at the Crystal Palace in London in 1851 led to the establishment the next year of the first industrial art museum at South Kensington in which craft work was arranged by material in departments of woodwork, metal, textiles, pottery, and glass, and which became a source for design ideas for handicrafts first and later for machine articles, the early inartistic character of which had been exposed by the Crystal Palace exhibition. The Nuremberg museum in 1888 introduced period rooms with appropriate settings. Museums had begun to make a selection of their material for display and to house the rest of the collections separately in systematic order for the use of research and scholarship. They began to seek the attention of the general public by more flexible arrangements, changing exhibits, and other devices; and finally they extended their efforts outside the museum walls, to the schools and to the community as a whole.

By assembling large groups of material calculated to attract the wonder and curiosity of the people, by directing attention to scientific, artistic, and industrial developments, and by demonstrating the effectiveness of visual education, the international expositions of the time exerted a powerful influence on the museum movement of the 19th cent. and after. Besides the South Kensington museum, institutions directly attributable to the influence of expositions include the Ethnological Museum at the Trocadero, Paris exposition 1878; Field Museum of Natural History, Chicago exposition 1893; Museum of Science and Industry, Chicago exposition 1933; City Art Museum of St. Louis, St. Louis exposition 1904; San Diego Natural History Museum, exposition of 1915. The centennial exposition at Philadelphia in 1876 led to the construction of a building for the U. S. National Museum at Washington, and one of its buildings, Memorial Hall, is a part of the Philadelphia Museum of Art.

Early in the 20th cent., in the interval between World War I and World War II, museums established themselves throughout the world as recognized centers for the advancement of civilization. By the early 1930's new museums were being established in the U. S. A. at the rate of about two a week. Soviet Russia was setting up new museums in many communities not heretofore having stable cultural centers, many of these being intended as visual instruction texts for a population anxious to make up in as short a time as possible the inadequacies of schooling during the Tsarist regime. The republican government of China fostered the establishment of museums, of which some 100 or more were in operation at the time of the Japanese attack. In other parts of the world the museum influence grew more slowly but none the less steadily. Estimates during the early stages of this development put the number of museums in the U. S. A. and Germany at about 1,500 each, Great Britain and France about 600 each, Italy 400, Russia 200, Australia and New Zealand 160, Japan 160, Canada 125, China 100, South America 100, Mexico and the West Indies 75, Africa 60. The world total was somewhere in the neighborhood of 7,000.

The U. S. A., continuing to establish museums rapidly, had outstripped all other countries, with 2,500 museums of all kinds, at the time of the most recent comprehensive study, completed at the close of 1938 (L. V. Coleman, *The Museum in America*, 1939, Washington). In this study 387 museums that included art in their field were listed. Of these 224 were public museums, including 47 art centers sponsored by the Federal Government under the relief program. Since this survey several notable art museums have been opened, the most important being the National Gallery of Art at Washington, March 17, 1941. Other new art museums are the Museum of Modern Art, New York, 1939; the Fisher Art Gallery of the University of Southern California, Los Angeles, 1940; the Norton Gallery and School of Art, West Palm Beach, 1941; and the Santa Barbara Museum of Art, 1941. There are 1300 history museums, 700 science museums, 130 general museums, and 30 industry museums.

Public art museums in the U. S. A. (1866-1938) accumulated an investment of $83,154,-000 in buildings designed for museum use. College art museums added another $6,576,-000. Museum buildings of all kinds, constructed for museum use, represented an investment of $181,312,000. The largest single addition to these totals since 1938 was the construction of the National Gallery of Art, built at a cost of $15,000,000.

Early museum buildings were structures built for other purposes, mostly palaces or other abodes of the powerful and wealthy. Such persist to this day and in Europe they are still dominant in the scene of national and provincial institutions. In America most great public museums occupy buildings constructed for museum or exhibition use; old buildings converted from other uses are mostly the result of budgetary restrictions on new institutions or institutions that have not been able to accumulate the funds necessary to construct better quarters. In the U. S. A. the classical revival gave the form of ancient monuments to early buildings constructed for museum use, as it did to public buildings generally. Thus the first public museum building, Pilgrim Hall of the Pilgrim Society at Plymouth, was built in the form of a Greek temple. Palace designs in the style of the Renaissance were adopted in the middle 19th cent. and had the advantage of providing suites of rooms that opened one into another and disadvantage of ornate interiors. Even after the "architectural interior" became a thing of the past, near-Renaissance façades continued to be built. In the present century American Colonial styles, Gregorian in the East and Spanish in the West, began to be used. Functional elements increased as time went on in the interior of all these buildings—well studied arrangements of rooms for display, differentiation of parts of the building to provide for such developments as the period room and the habitat group, and provision for work space and space for the study collections. Since World War I museum buildings have begun to appear with functional requirements stressed both in exterior design and interior arrangement; e.g.,the Henry Art Gallery of the University of Washington, Seattle (1927), Colorado Springs Fine Arts Center (1936), Museum of Modern Art, New York (1939), Grand Rapids Public Museum (1940). The Grand Rapids Public Museum embodies such up-to-date ideas as street show windows, entrance and first floor at sidewalk level, complete artificial lighting of exhibit halls, air conditioning through the building, curtain partitions, radio and public address system reaching all halls, and a large central exhibit hall into which light trucks may be driven for loading and unloading material for frequent changing exhibits. Two new types of museums of the last two decades have their own special style of building: the trailside museum, which is a simple structure planned to conform to the natural site on which it is placed; and the planetarium built in the modified form of an observatory for the housing of a Zeiss projector and for related exhibits on astronomy.

Modern museums have widened their fields in many directions. The art museum, formerly confined to the graphic and plastic arts, now embraces practically all phases of creative art. The art museum of today may concern itself with decorative arts, music, the dance, the drama, and the film; the history museum with the city in which it is located, as a huge exhibit to be studied in place; the science museum, with the health of man and his heredity and psychology. Special museums are provided for the education of children, for the visitor to parks and trailsides, and for the instruction of the public in many aspects of science and technology.

Educational work is recognized in American museums as a primary activity and takes many forms: exhibitions (q.v.), of both permanent collections and changing material on loan; guidance of visitors through the halls and galleries; lectures, courses, concerts, and other performances in the museum for adults and for children; creative work; printed material; work with the schools and with other organizations in and out of the museum; special rooms, classes, and other activities for children; and prepared extension material for the use of schools, colleges, and universities and for general distribution to civilian and military organizations. Many of these activities have been on the program for a long time. They have, however, increased steadily through the past fifty years and they have been encouraged by fundamental research in museum education and exhibit problems beginning at the Art Institute of Chicago in 1925 under direction of Edward S. Robinson. These investigations, supported by grants from the Carnegie Corporation of New York to the American Association of Museums and to Yale University, were continued by Dr. Robinson and his associations until his death in 1937 and then by his associates and others. Studies in museum education were undertaken at the Philadelphia Museum of Art, Buffalo Museum of Science, New York Museum of Science and Industry, the Carnegie Institute of Pittsburgh, Newark Museum, and the 69th Street Branch of the Philadelphia Museum of Art. A separate study of work with grade school children was conducted by Margaret Bloomberg at the Cleveland Museum of Art and published in 1929. Recently a grant from the General Education Board of the Rockefeller Foundation has supported a series of studies of work with secondary schools at the Art Institute of Chicago, Museum of Modern Art, Albright Art Gallery, Milwaukee Art Institute, and Cleveland Museum of Art, begun in 1939 and just now being prepared for publication. Every large art and science museum in the country has established a departmental staff charged with carrying on and developing to its utmost the educational effort. The smaller museums give much of the time of staff members to the work. In St. Louis and Indianapolis special museums have been established by the public school systems with the direct duty of supplying the schools with opportunities for the study of museum material. Museums in New York and Boston have established intermuseum councils, the principal object of which is cooperation in extending and making more effective the educational work of museums on behalf of their communities.

The active character of the modern museum is esp. well illustrated in the manner in which it has sought out ways and means of supporting the morale of the armed forces as well as the civilian in the war crisis. Special programs for the armed forces have been organized in the museum halls, exhibitions have been sent out to the camps and recreation halls, musical material has been distributed to service musical organizations and song books to the individual soldier and sailor, facilities and material have been provided for soldier artists in camps, and the talents of American artists have been utilized through the museum for therapeutic work among disabled soldiers and sailors. On the side of civilian morale there have been exhibitions of methods of civilian camouflage, of material illustrating the war areas, of films and programs to acquaint the public with the problems and the aims of the war production effort.

A list of the important museums in America would be too long to include in this essay. A few of them are the following: For art, the National Gallery of Art, Washington; Metropolitan Museum of Art, New York; Philadelphia Museum of Art; Museum of Fine Arts, Boston; Art Institute of Chicago. For science, the U. S. National Museum, Washington; American Museum of Natural History, New York; Chicago Natural

History Museum, Chicago. For history, New York Historical Society, Chicago Historical Society, Museum of the City of New York, Edison Institute, Dearborn. For industry, Franklin Institute, Philadelphia; Museum of Science and Industry, Chicago. For general museums, U. S. National Museum, Washington; Newark Museum, Milwaukee Public Museum, Rochester Museum of the Arts and Sciences. See L. V. Coleman, *The Museum in America*, 1939, Washington; David Murray, *Museums: Their History and Their Use*, 3 vols., 1904, Glasgow; William Flower, *Essays on Museums*, 1896, London; *Handbook of American Museums*, 1932, Washington; *Directory of Museums and Art Galleries in the British Isles*, 1931, London; *Maecenas*, 1930, Berlin, *Mouseion*, International Museums Office, Paris, 1927-1940, triannually; *The Museum Journal*, London, monthly; *The Museum News*, Washington, semi-monthly.   —L.C.E.

Mushiake yaki (Jap.). Pottery made in Bizen province.

musica ancilla religiosis. See MUSICAL PERFORMANCE, MAIN TRENDS IN.

musica ficta, falsa. Literally false music, i.e., altered tones not included in the ecclesiastical modes (q.v.). In the words of the author of the early 14th cent. treatise, *Ars Contrapuncti*, "Music is called *ficta* when we make a tone to be a semi-tone, or, conversely, a semi-tone to be a tone". Composers did not indicate the chromatic alterations, since it was customary to rely on the singer's judgment. For the modern transcriber, the difficulties involved in musica ficta are sometimes almost insuperable, especially since there is considerable disparity of statement among the old theorists as to the rules of interpretation. Nevertheless, some rules were simple enough. The correction of the augmented 4th and its inversion the diminished 5th both melodically and harmonically was accomplished by alteration. Cadential progressions which engendered the feeling of the "leading tone" (q.v.) usually required an adjustment in the penultimate chord. Musica ficta was undoubtedly the greatest single factor which led to the gradual obliteration of the ecclesiastical modes. In modern editions of medieval music, transcribers usually indicate the altered tones by the appropriate accidentals over the notes. See NOTATION; scales and modes.

—V.A.

musica humana. See quadrivium.

musica instrumentis constituta. See quadrivium.

musical audience management. Adjusting the content of industrial music broadcasts to the scientifically measured music preferences of the employees. Techniques and tests for this purpose in industry were first developed by Dr. W. A. Kerr of RCA Mfg. Co. in 1942.
—W.A.K.

musical bow. See MUSICAL INSTRUMENTS.

musical drama. See opera; universal artwork.

musical form, psychology of. See PSYCHOLOGY OF MUSIC.

musical glasses. See MUSICAL INSTRUMENTS.

musical imagery. See EXPERIMENTAL PSYCHOLOGY OF MUSIC.

MUSICAL INSTRUMENTS. *I. The Development of Musical Instruments.* The evolution of musical instruments proceeds from two basic roots. One is the human tendency to express emotion through periodic motor activity. Thus most primitive instruments are to be regarded as audible reinforcements of bodily movements. Man stamped on a bark covered cavity instead of on the bare ground, made the movement of the forearm audible by waving a rattle. Another outlet was the expression of emotion by sounds of more or less definite pitch. Here the voice with its freedom of inflection was the most efficient means. Much technical skill was needed to construct instruments which would produce a series of musical tones. Primitive instruments were used to produce terrifying and supernatural sounds with magic power rather than pleasing and musical tones. Many early instruments were constructed in pairs as is shown by the strange twin pipes and trumpets. The organization of similar units of different vibrating lengths and hence different pitches marks a more advanced stage of development. Thus bamboo tubes of various lengths were bound together to become the panpipes and vibrating bars of wood were arranged in a series to become the xylophone.

Less obvious were the possibilities of a vibrating air column within a flute or horn. Players passed from the stage where the performer sang or shouted into a horn to the stage in which the lips vibrated against a mouth hole or cupped mouthpiece to produce one harsh sound, then two, and eventually the harmonic series into which a vibrating air column naturally divides. Another basic discovery was the artificial shortening of the air column by fingerholes pierced in the wall of cane flute or animal horn which could be opened or closed at will.

With stringed instruments also tones of varied pitch could be produced in various ways. Strings may be arranged in a series varying in length (and frequently in thickness as well) as in the harp or piano. The player might pull the string tighter to raise the pitch as the ānanda laharī of Bengal. A string might be effectively shortened and the pitch raised by being pressed down against a fingerboard with the finger; or, if lightly touched with finger or nail, it would produce tones of a more flute-like character called harmonics (q.v.).

The growing complexity of musical instruments eventually reached the point where a special craft developed to conserve and to practise the skills required. One result was a greater uniformity among instruments since a given workman or atélier was likely to make only certain types and sizes. The machine technics of the 19th cent. had a profound effect on the manufacture of instruments as did the principles of mass production. Even cheap violins are mass produced though the finer violins have always been made and repaired by highly skilled artist craftsmen. Such an elaborate musical machine as the Boehm flute is hardly conceivable except as a product of the machine age. As a result of the mass production of musical instruments which are sold at a moderate price, instrumental music has been brought more nearly within the reach of school children and music lovers of moderate income.

II. The Classification of Musical Instruments. The more detailed discussion of musical instruments which follows is organized according to the following plan.

   a. Sonorous substances
   b. Vibrating membranes
   c. Vibrating air columns
      1. Horns and trumpets
      2. Pipes
   d. Vibrating strings
   e. Electro-musical instruments

III. Sonorous Substances. Substances which resound when stamped, shaken, struck, scraped, or rubbed are so varied, so available and so numerous as to render more than a summary account impossible. Pounding with the end of a heavy stick is obviously similar to stamping with the feet. Thus the hollowed and longitudinally slotted instruments of wood called **slit drums** are at one stage sounded by stamping feet, at another by the end of a heavy stick and finally are played in modern style by being struck at the edge of the slot by a pair of drum sticks. In a similar fashion the **stamping tube**, a length of bamboo stopped at the upper end, is struck against the ground producing a sound of vague pitch. Two or three tubes are sometimes employed with contrasting tones.

The rattle is familiar as a baby's toy and as the **maraca** of Latin-American dance orchestras. It is a very ancient device and may be a rattling string of teeth, claws or the like, a hollow body of tortoise shell, basketry, clay, or perhaps a gourd containing small stones or similar objects, usually grasped by a handle.

Instruments which are sounded by percussion are frequently employed in pairs. Such are the percussion sticks, recent forms of which are the "**bones**" of the American negro, the *maracas* of the rhumba band, the **castanets** of the Spanish dancer. **Cymbals,** plate shaped discs of hammered bronze with a central boss, are usually clashed together as pairs but in modern practice a single cymbal is frequently struck with a drum stick. This relationship of beating stick and sonorous object is also characteristic of the **triangle** (a vibrating steel rod bent in the shape suggested by its name), the ominous sounding **gong** (a large circular bronze disc with the edges turned over), as well as the array of sonorous stone slabs, bells, and metal bars, often arranged as a series, which are so characteristic of Chinese, Javanese, and Balinese music and which reappear in the modern **glockenspiel**, the **xylophone**, the **marimba**, and the **celesta** (with keyboard).

Scraping as a method of producing sound seems to be chiefly confined to primitive rites. Notched bones, sticks or other substances are scraped by another hard object. A later offshoot of this primitive device is the carved **wooden tiger** (yü) with notched backbone which is sounded twice at the close of the Confucian rites. In a similar fashion Negroes in the southern part of the U.S.A. used to draw a key over the teeth of a horse's jawbone.

Even more specialized is the **kulepa** of New Ireland (Melanesia). A rounded wooden block is deeply cut so as to divide it into four segments varying in size which produce four corresponding tones when rubbed by the moistened hands. This principle reappears in the European **musical glasses** or **glass harmonica** which produce pure and ethereal tones when the rims are rubbed by the moistened fingers.

IV. Vibrating membranes. The **drum** consists of one or two skins stretched over a frame or the opening of a hollow body. Modern Western civilization is relatively poor in these instruments which are so varied among primitive peoples. The body of the drum may be a tree trunk hollowed by tools or fire. A drum shaped like a barrel and with two heads is frequent in the East. As drums became smaller and hence portable their forms reflect this fact. The wine glass form can easily be carried under the arm. Drums expanding above and below a central waist and provided with two handles are even more clearly designed to be carried. Somewhat similar in form are the **hourglass** and **spool drums** of the Far East. India developed sets of tuned drums, pairs, sets of three, and finally in Burma a circle of as many as twenty-four drums on which melodies were played.

In contrast to the relatively deep drums described above are the shallow drums with one or two heads stretched over a wooden rim of greater or less depth. The modern **tambourine** is a familiar example of one type. In addition to the tambourine type (with one or two heads) we may distinguish the **shaman's drum** as another type, a shallow one-headed frame drum, carried either by a handle projecting from the frame, by cords passing across the open back of the drum, or by a wooden brace passing from side to side of the frame.

In Europe the use of the drum seems to date from the 12th cent. The drum was played with the left hand and was associated with a horn or pipe played by the other hand. After the Crusades double headed **army drums** played with two sticks appeared and were associated with the fife. **Kettledrums** were imported from the Near East, the smaller forms in the 13th cent., the larger type in the 15th cent. Thus the kettle drum of the modern orchestra made an early entrance into Europe. The use of screws to adjust the heads is illustrated in Virdung (1518). The modern **snare drum** is smaller and shallower. The shell is of wood or metal and the rattling gut snares under the lower head are replaced by coiled wire springs. The heads are tightened by metal rods with adjustable screws. The **bass drum** was part of the Janissary or Turkish military music, associated with triangles and cymbals. Haydn's *Military Symphony* shows these instruments used for local color; they later become regular constituents of the orchestra.

V. Vibrating air column. 1. THE FLUTES. We must distinguish the recorder, the end blown flute, and the side blown or transverse flute.

In the flageolet or recorder the stream of air passes through a directive channel (languid) against a sharp beveled lip cut in the body of the instrument. The tube is provided with finger holes, and thumbhole in back.

In the end blown flute the stream of air is directed against the sharp outer edge of the open top of the tube which is also sometimes notched. The nose flute is similar but is blown by breath from the right nostril the left being closed.

In the side blown or transverse flute the player blows across a sharp edged mouth hole. The hole is held horizontally (or nearly so) and the upper end of the tube is closed with a cork or stopper. The previously cylindrical European flute was made with a conical bore and cylindrical head joint in the latter half of the 17th cent. During the same period a single key was added which produced d sharp. Keys for the other chromatic tones were gradually added. The body of the Boehm flute is cylindrical, the head parabolic in bore. The large circular holes are covered by large pads controlled by an elaborately devised key mechanism. The little octave flute or piccolo is the only other flute used regularly in the symphony orchestra; the alto (flute d'amour) and bass flutes are little used.

2. THE OBOES. The oboe group is played by a double reed which in the simplest instruments is merely a straw pinched together at the end and in later instruments consists of two opposing slips of cane bound together. Egyptian oboes were played in pairs (drone and melody), Greek oboes were also paired and were made in a variety of types. A leather mouth band (*phorbeia*) was employed, suggesting a rather violent manner of performance. Similar paired oboes appear in the East.

Renaissance oboes were called shawns and were built in families of seven. The bassoon (curtal) of this period was also a double reed instrument, conical in bore, with the tube doubled on itself and the reed carried on a tube extending from the body. The complete family of bassoons consisted of five

instruments. In the modern orchestra the bassoon survives only as bass together with the still lower double bassoon. Similarly the oboe family is now represented only by the oboe and its alto form, the English horn (the baritone Heckelphon has been little used) though other forms are required in the scores of Bach (oboe d'amore and oboe da caccia). The obsolete double reed instruments can only be named here; the bassanello, the sordone, the racket, the cromorne, and the Rauschpfeife.

3. THE CLARINET. The clarinet is sounded with a single reed which in the simplest forms was simply a vibrating tongue detached from the cane which also formed the tube of the instrument. The ancient Egyptian clarinet which still survives in the Mohammedan East was a twin clarinet. Both pipes were fingered at the same time, but small differences in the two tubes produced an undulating tone. The Indian snake charmer uses a similar instrument save that the player blows into a gourd which encloses the upper end of the tubes. One of the pipes of this instrument functions as a drone.

In Europe the early history of the clarinet is obscure. The *chalumeau* was the European folk clarinet which was manufactured in an improved form by J. C. Denner of Nuremberg towards the end of the 17th cent. The modern clarinet with its cylindrical bore overblows at the twelfth, unlike the oboe and flute which overblow at the octave. Its beaked mouthpiece has a flat surface pierced by an opening against which the reed is secured. Made originally in the keys of C, A, and Bb the latter form is now favored. The bass clarinet is frequently employed in the modern symphony orchestra. The alto or tenor clarinet has remained a band instrument. The older basset-horn (employed by Mozart) was also an alto with a more extended lower range and a bore of smaller diameter.

The saxophone family is a hybrid group invented by the French inventor and instrument maker Sax. It has the form of an old fashioned Dutch pipe. The instrument is of brass with a clarinet mouthpiece but overblowing at the octave and fingered like the oboe. It has become identified with the swing band though scored for in certain symphonic works.

The union of the reed pipe with an air chamber in the form of a skin bag which is blown either by the mouth or by a small bellows, forms the bagpipe. The instrument is ancient. Pipes of both oboe and clarinet type have been employed and the use of a drone is frequent.

4. THE ORGAN. The association of the keyboard with a series of pipes which are supplied with air by a bellows constitutes the **organ**. The Roman *hydraulis* which sounded pipes by air compressed by an enclosed body of water was outside the main line of development. The *portative* with flue pipes (pipes of metal or other material sounding by means of a stream of air directed against the lip as in the recorder) had a single bellows and was supported by a band. It was frequent in the Middle Ages and was pumped by the left fingered with the right hand. Pneumatic organs date from the end of the 4th cent. The pipes were first controlled by slides, later by levers, and finally by keys. All pipes connected with a given key sounded together. The Renaissance developed the possibility of selecting and combining the stops (a series of pipes, also the knob controlling that series) for a piece, the use of solo stops imitating wind instruments, and the possibility of using them singly. A limited pedal keyboard with its own stops appeared in certain cases. The **regal** was a small organ with reed pipes only.

The subsequent development of the organ has given the organist a more facile control of the keyboards (in four manual instruments called Great, Choir, Swell, Solo) through the evolution of the mechanical tracker action and the various pneumatic and electro-pneumatic actions. In the two latter types the organist simply sets in motion automatic agencies which perform the work formerly performed by the finger. The control of volume through the opening or closing of the shutters of the swell box (which encloses the pipes controlled by the swell keyboard) as well as the mechanical addition of stops by the crescendo pedal were inventions of later date as were the combinations, which made it possible to withdraw or retire selected groups of stops by merely pressing a button. The tendency toward tone of an orchestral type and towards organs of great size supplied with wind under high pressure has been countered by a recent trend towards the restoration of the **baroque organ**, a tendency which grew out of the interest in the organ works of Bach and his predecessors.

5. INSTRUMENTS WITH A FREE REED. The free reed of the **harmonium** and **reed organ** is similar to that in the Chinese *shêng,* an instrument of subdued and pleasant tone which resembles a tea pot filled with bamboo pipes of varying length. The reed here is a metal tongue

vibrating in the aperture of its frame. The reed itself, not the length of the bamboo tube, determines the pitch of the tone produced. Such keyboard instruments as the **harmonium** and **reed organ** as well as the **concertina,** and **accordion,** and the humble **mouth-organ** or **harmonica** (so amazingly exploited at the present day) are all recent derivatives of the Chinese instrument.

6. HORNS AND TRUMPETS. In the **horn** and **trumpet** group the lips of the player vibrate into the hollow cavity of the mouthpiece. In its typical development the horn is related to an actual animal's horn while the trumpet form is thinner, suggesting a tube of wood or bark often curving outwards rather abruptly at the end into the bell. Certain specimens consist of a tube terminating with a cow's horn as a bell. Other early instruments of this group were **conch shells,** end or side blown, and **clay trumpets** (sometimes imitated from the shell form). A distinctive African form was the side blown elephant's tusk or antelope horn. The *shofar,* blown in all Jewish synagogues on New Year's Day and the Day of Atonement, is esp. notable as a very ancient instrument which has survived to the present day. It is made of a ram's horn, flattened and rather sharply bent at the end. An ancient form of curved horn was the Nordic *lur,* fashioned of cast bronze. The *lur* was constructed in pairs in which the S curves are opposite, suggesting that early examples were made from mammoth tusks.

In addition to a straight trumpet (Greek *salpinx,* Roman *tuba*) which seems to have been played with considerable lip pressure to produce a terrifying sound, the Romans also had a straight trumpet with a bell turning up sharply at the end, the *lituus.* In the *cornu* the tube made almost a complete turn. A wooden rod passing from one side to the other supported the instrument high on the performer's shoulder, the bell pointing forward while the tube passed around the body. The mouthpiece was held to the lips of the player by the right hand while the left grasped the supporting rod.

Early European trumpets obviously have Eastern and Roman origins. The end blown ivory **oliphant** is similar to the African trumpets mentioned above, save that the African instruments are typically side blown. Other instruments are very similar to the Roman tuba. Trumpets developed in two models, the higher **tubecta** or **trombetta,** the lower *buisine* (Fr.) or *Busine* (Ger.).

The simple animal horn with fingerholes which appeared as early as 700 A.D. in Persia still survives as a pastoral instrument in Sweden, Norway, and elsewhere. This is the prototype of the **cornet** (in the older meaning of this word). The cornet (*cornetto curvo*) though made of wood or ivory, still mimics the contours of an animal horn. A straight form (*cornetto diritto*) existed, also the **mute cornet** (*cornetto muto*) with the mouthpiece excavated in the upper end of the body. The finger holes were six in number with an added key in later models. The cornet was capable of florid passages and of all the ornaments of the virtuoso singer, but was difficult to blow. In the 17th cent. the instrument was constructed in three sizes. The **serpent**, bent into deep curves, served as bass to the brass instruments till replaced by a form resembling the bassoon, the **Russian bassoon**, and the **ophicleide** or keyed serpent.

The special feature of the **trombone** consists of a U shaped slide which telescopes into the body of the instrument. The player can alter the sounding length of the tube by extending or retracting the slide and at each position can produce the various notes of the harmonic series. The instrument was constructed in three sizes, alto, tenor, and bass, towards the end of the 15th cent. **Contra bass** and **soprano trombones** were introduced in the 17th cent., but were never in common use. The trombone was hardly susceptible of real improvement. The military trumpet and the hunting horn, however, were limited in their early orchestral use by the fact that they could only produce the notes of the harmonic series. An attempt to bridge the gaps between the lower harmonics by applying padded keys to the body of the instrument resulted in such instruments as the **keyed bugle.** Various makers experimented with valves which added auxiliary tubes to the instrument. The imperfectly described twin trumpet with valve of Charles Clagget (described in 1793) appears to be the earliest attempt. In a modern instrument three valves, used singly or in combination, lower the pitch by a half tone, a tone or a tone and a half. These harmonic series when combined produce the complete chromatic scale. The system was not only applied to the horn and trumpet (and even the trombone) but to a new brass group, the **saxhorns.** The bass saxhorn appears in the orchestra as the tuba while the entire group forms a choir of the military band. The cornet employed by 19th cent. French

composers in place of or with the orchestral trumpet is now used only in the band.

VI. Vibrating Strings. 1. PRIMITIVE INSTRUMENTS. The most primitive stringed instruments were huge affairs in which the resonating chamber was a pit dug in the ground. A sheet of bark which covered the hole served as a sounding board. There were two methods of keeping the string taut. In the **ground harp** one end is attached to the sounding board, the other to the free end of a bent green stick the lower end of which is fixed firmly in the ground. The player can produce notes of lower pitch by bending the stick still more. Later the instrument becomes smaller and self contained so that it can be carried about. In the **ground psaltery** the main string (thirteen to fourteen feet long) is fastened horizontally between two posts. A shorter string runs from the sounding board to the longer string, dividing the latter into two vibrating segments which accordingly produce two different tones. In later versions several such units are set up side by side.

The **musical bow** resembles the hunter's bow. The feeble tone of this instrument demands a resonator of some sort which is variously provided by a bowl, basket, pot, or metal vessel on which the bow is rested, by an attached gourd, or by the variable resonance of the mouth cavity of the player. This last method of obtaining resonance is still used in playing the **jew's-harp.**

Later stringed instruments may be broadly classified as psalteries, lutes, lyres, and harps. In the psaltery the strings pass from one end to the other of the supporting body. This type not only includes the psaltery and dulcimer but leads to the harpsichord and piano.

In the lutes a more or less extended neck emerges from a hemispherical body. The strings are shortened and raised in pitch by pressing them against the neck or by touching them lightly with the finger or the finger nail. In more recent instruments the body, instead of resembling a halved pear, becomes a box with relatively shallow sides or ribs (as in the guitar or violin). When played with a bow the waist of the instrument is frequently constricted.

2. THE LYRE. The yoke, the characteristic feature of the **lyre,** consists of two arms rising from the body, often a tortoise shell or bowl, and connected by a cross piece. This instrument had already appeared in the Sumerian cultures. The Greeks employed it for less formal occasions than the *kithara.* The

strings pass over the soundboard and are fastened and adjusted at the cross bar.

The **kithara** was larger and more sturdily built than the lyre. The two arms like the body and sound board were of wood sturdily joined together and sometimes elaborately adorned. These instruments not only dominated classical antiquity but still survive in the form of the **Nubian lyre**. The lyre persisted in Europe during the early Middle Ages but eventually underwent a change of form. The arms and cross bar disappear as separate features since the instrument is now shaped from one block of wood. Pegs appear as tuning devices. This instrument was also played with a bow and was the ancestor of the **bowed harp** and the Welsh **crwth.**

3. THE HARP. The strings of the **harp** instead of running parallel to the soundboard extend from the· soundboard to the tuning pegs set in the neck. The frame of the harp may be curved at the top or the body may meet the neck to which the strings are attached at an angle. The front pillar completing the frame was evidently added to resist the increasing pull of the strings.

In Egyptian culture the harp was the most important instrument. The typical form was curved and was played upright with the body towards the player though other types existed. These instruments wɜre sometimes of great size as is evidenced by the pair of great harps taller than a man depicted on the walls of the tomb of Rameses III (1200 B.C.).

The **minstrel's harp,** esp. famous in Ireland and Scotland during the Middle Ages and later, was wire strung. The strings were plucked with the finger nails and tuned by a key which fitted over the ends of the tuning pegs.

In **Tyrolian harps** of the later 17th cent. iron hooks were employed which could be turned to stop a string, thus raising the pitch by half a tone. This was obviously unsuited to modern music in which chromatic alterations were frequent. The next step was to operate the hooks by a foot pedal. Finally in the **double action harp** of Sébastian Érard the pitch of the strings is controlled by seven pedals (each controlling a note of the diatonic scale and its octave duplications). The pedals actuate rotating discs with projecting studs which raise the strings affected a semitone with the pedal in the middle position, a tone in the low position.

4. THE PSALTERY. In China the classic instrument was a psaltery which was made in several types, each with its distinctive name but always consisting of a number of strings stretched lengthwise over a laterally arched soundboard. The *ch'in* was fretted, the *shê* possessed a series of open strings. The *koto* in its various forms is a similar Japanese instrument.

The *vīnā* was the classic instrument in Indian. Here we find a stick or cylinder as a body strung with a variable number of wire strings. Attached gourds serve as resonators. The frets, which are unusually tall and heavy, are movable, so as to adapt the instrument to the complex Indian scale system.

Finally, the psaltery type appears once more in the Arabian *qānūn,* a table psaltery in the form of a trapezoid. The strings were plucked with two plectra. In the *dulcimer* (Persian *santir*) on the other hand the strings were struck with two hammers thus employing the basic idea of the piano.

It was apparently the **monochord,** however, which was the most direct prototype of the keyboard instruments. Originally a single string stretched over a sound board, and furnished with a movable bridge, it was a scientific instrument used to measure intervals. The strings were multiplied in later examples. The **clavichord** seems to have evolved from this monochord with several strings. The keyboard operated what were in effect mechanically actuated bridges. As the finger depressed the key, a brass rod flattened at the end (tangent) rose and struck the string above, setting it in vibration and determining its sounding length as a bridge at the same time. Interwoven strips of felt acted as dampers and prevented the other segment of the string from vibrating. Early clavichords had more than one key and tangent to a string. Later instruments in which each string was sounded by one key only were called "bundfrei" in Germany.

In the **harpsichord** and in various forms related to it, the **spinet,** the **virginals,** etc., we again have a series of wire strings stretched over a sound board. Here, however, the strings are plucked by a key actuated jack, which is a plucking mechanism which functions as the jack ascends. The plectrum is mounted on a pivoted slip of wood, however, so that the jack drops quietly back in place ready for use again. The **eschequier** of the 14th cent. may have been a predecessor of the harpsichord.

The **piano** was a keyed dulcimer. (The early **dulce melos** seems to have had a striking mechanism operated by a keyboard but it does not appear to be closely related to the piano action). Cristofori is generally believed to have made the first piano (oldest surviving example dated 1720). The earliest pianos were without dampers and many had no **escapement**, the device which allows the hammer to drop back immediately though the finger remains on the key, though Cristofori did design an escapement. The gradual development of the modern piano involved an extension of the keyboard, heavier strings, and eventually, as a consequence, the cast iron frame to support the greater tension of the strings. Finally, the invention of the overstrung scale with the treble strings below and diagonally across the bass strings was the last great change in piano construction. Mass production has played a critical role in producing great numbers of these complicated mechanisms, the most important musical instruments in America and Europe. The influence of the small city apartment is shown in the recent vogue for the diminutive spinet model.

6. THE LUTE. It is convenient to divide our discussion of instruments of the **lute group** into the form with a long neck and the form in which the neck is a mere narrowing of the body of the instrument. The prototype of the first class is a stick inserted into a small resonating body such as a tortoise shell or coconut. The Egyptian lute was of this type. The more recent examples are scattered and form less of a series than do those of the other type, the **short lute.** There is, e.g., the lute of the Utrecht Psalter (c. 832 A.D.), the neck provided with six frets and furnished with a circular peg box, the pegs inserted from the rear. Several Oriental instruments are also of this type, the familiar Japanese **shamisen** (Chinese *san hsien*), the many variants of the Indian *sitar* with its wide neck, and the *tanbūr* of the Near East. A variant of this type which existed in Italy during the 17th cent. was the *colascione.*

The **short lute** appears in very ancient times and was at first made of a single block of wood. The top was flat, the back convex, and the body tapered to the short neck. In early examples there was a string to each note. (This form appears in Persia in the 8th cent. B.C., then reappears in the Indian Gandhara reliefs). In China a somewhat similar form was the *p'i p'a* and a closely related Japanese form the *biwa.* Notable

ancient examples from the year 749 A.D. are preserved in the Japanese Imperial Treasury at Nara.

The type may also be pointed out in the Near East. It had reached Italy in the 10th cent. and appears in modified form in a German psalter with a box-like body and a peg box with pegs inserted from the rear. The modern pear-shaped body appears in Spain associated with a peg box which is abruptly bent back.

We return to the Near East which possessed a lute of classic form. The neck was short but clearly differentiated, the peg box sharply bent back, the pear-shaped body built up of thin staves. The strings are in pairs, save the highest which is single. The eastern *'ud* is played with a plectrum. With little change save the addition of gut frets it became the European lute. Only with the demands for greater sonority was the neck extended to sustain additional bass strings as in the **theorbo** and **archlute.**

The **bow** apparently originated in Central Asia and was applied to instruments of the psaltery group (the *ya chêng* and *ch'in* of N. China) as well as to the characteristic Chinese fiddle with its drum-like soundbox (often a section of a large bamboo) covered in front with lizard or snake skin. The bow hair in these instruments passes between the strings (which are usually two in number). This fiddle and its variants have remained popular in China to the present day. The Mohammedan culture utilized a somewhat similar instrument with the handle piercing the body (which is often a coconut) extending below and terminating with a sharp point. The truly bizarre Indian instruments the *sarinda* and *sarangi* are hollowed out of a block of wood; the top is of skin. The *sarangi* is also provided with a second set of metal strings which vibrate in sympathy with the upper set of bowed strings, a trait which recurs in certain European instruments. The *rabâb* on the other hand which had been treated as a bowed instrument since 1000 A.D. survived in its simple form. The sound box was of skin and the sides were somewhat pinched to give the bow freer play. The peg box is short and sharply bent back. It became the **rebec** of Europe with curved peg box, wood (or wood and metal) sound board, and with the top at two different levels the higher serving also as a fingerboard. This instrument absorbed traits from the violin in the 17th cent. and became the dancing master's *pocket fiddle,* the *pochette.*

The other line of development towards European bowed instruments must begin with the strange fiddles of great size which are depicted in Spanish manuscripts of the 10th and 11th cents. These instruments seem to have been similar to the smaller *panduri* of the Caucasus. In the latter instrument the peg box has the shape of a leaf with frontal pegs, straight sides, which converge to the neck. The more important ancestor of the later violin however was the **lyra** with its shallow pear-shaped body with convex back, disc-shaped peg box, and three pegs in the rear. The middle string was a drone, the outer played in harmonics by touching them with the nails. Appearing in Europe perhaps in the 9th cent. it became the fiddle of the Middle Ages. The strings were usually four in number. The fiddle (*vièle*) of the Middle Ages assumed a confusing variety of forms. It was only the systematic spirit of the Renaissance that finally brought order into this diversity. One important trait which appeared was the construction of the body of the instrument as a box with top, bottom and sides or ribs. This characteristic also appears in several Eastern instruments the Chinese *yüeh ch'in* and the Japanese *gekkin*.

In addition to the **rebec** which continued to flourish, the *viola da gamba* and the *viola da braccio* appeared during the Renaissance. The former group had the form of the modern double bass, flat back, sloping shoulders (lateral tuning pegs) and six (or seven) strings tuned in fourths with a third between the third and fourth strings. The **viol family** consisted of treble, alto, tenor, and bass and added a high treble and a double bass on occasion. The **bass** became the favorite solo instrument. A small bass employing pizzicato effects and using special tunings which facilitated chord playing was the **lyra viol**. All the viols were played between the knees, as the term *viola da gamba* implies (leg viols). The *viola da braccio* was played on the arm as was the early violin. The *viola da braccio* was shallow in the ribs, had a convex back, round shoulders and employed heavier strings than the *viola da gamba*. The *lyra da braccio* was a curious instrument with pegs inserted in the flat peg board from the rear, body similar to the viola da braccia and with two drones as well as a variable number of bowed strings. The top of the bridge was flat, necessitating a chordal style of playing. The *lyra da gamba* was a bass instrument along the same general lines. Finally we must note the late appearance of bowed instruments with sympathetic strings: the *viola d'amore* and the lower pitched **baryton.**

The **violin** differed from the viol with its shallower ribs, rounded rather than sloping shoulders, arched back, narrow fingerboard, and four strings tuned in fifths (g d^1 a^1 e^2). The tone was more brilliant than that of the quiet viol. The classic form of the violin is indelibly associated with the name of Antonio Stradivarius (c. 1640-1737), though known violin makers date back to the middle of the 16th cent. The violin family consisted of the **treble violin**, the **alto** or **viola**, the now obsolete **tenor** and the **violincello.** A high treble violin was employed by Bach and others. The **double bass** with four strings (formerly five or three) has remained more viol-like than the other members of the group. The early **organistrum** (later *vièle à roue* or **hurdy gurdy**) was a stringed instrument in which the strings were sounded by a rosined wheel revolved by a crank. The strings were mechanically stopped by turning or pushing a rod against the string.

The **cittern,** wire strung with fretted neck, flat back and top was played with a plectrum. The **English guitar** was the name of a popular 18th cent. cittern. Similar to the cittern but lower in pitch are the wire-strung **pandora** and **orpheoreon.** The **mandolin** of the present day has doubled strings tuned in fifths like the violin. The body has the typical lute shape although a model with flat top and back is also manufactured. It is a purely melodic instrument and sustains its tones by a continuous vibrato of the pick or plectrum. The **guitar** was a more facile successor to the lute which still remains the basic instrument for the Spanish and Latin American cultures. The **banjo** is essentially a shallow single headed drum provided with a neck and a fretted fingerboard. The older American form was associated with the minstrel show. The **tenor banjo** is smaller, is tuned like the viola, and functions chiefly as a background instrument in dance orchestras.

VII. *Electro-musical instruments.* Electrical instruments are undoubtedly in a preliminary stage of development. Electricity may serve simply as a mechanical aid as in the electric action of the modern organ. It may amplify the tone of an instrument by means similar to those employed in stepping up radio signals., The player of an **electric guitar** plays like any other guitarist but he can increase the volume of tone produced at will. The **theremin** depends on varying the capacity of an oscillating circuit by introducing the hand of the player into the circuit. The **Hammond organ** and other similar instruments employ oscillating circuits of fixed pitch and is controlled externally by manual and pedal boards is a fashion similar to a pipe organ. See *Ancient European Musical Instruments,* N. Bessaraboff, 1941; *Early Keyboard Instruments,* Philip James, 1930; *The History of Musical Instruments,* Curt Sachs, cop. 1940; *The History of the Violin,* E. van der Straeten, 1933; *The Musical Instruments of the Native Races of South Africa,* P. R. Kirby, 1934; *The Music and Musical Instruments of Japan,* Francis Piggott, 2nd ed., 1909; *The Music of Hindustan,* A. H. Fox Strangways, 1914; *Music of the Bible,* Sir John Stainer (new ed. by F. W. Galpin), 1914; *Old English Instruments of Music,* F. W. Galpin, 1910; *Orchestration,* C. Forsyth, 1922; *Studies in Oriental Musical Instruments,* G. H. Farmer, 1931; *Textbook of European Musical Instruments,* F. W. Galpin, 1937; *Towards a New Music,* Carlos Chàvez, 1937.   —C.W.H.

musical mentality. See PSYCHOLOGY OF ART.

MUSICAL PERFORMANCE, MAIN TRENDS IN. *Ecclesiastical spirit.* MUSICA ANCILLA RELIGIONIS: The medieval spirit recognized and controlled the arts as well as philosophy as humble handmaids of religion. After the 16th cent. had rediscovered the human being, Humanism encouraged the growing individualism in musical creation and expression. Thus modern interpretation originated in the fresh air of artistic rejuvenation amid the violent clash between the revolutionary tenets of the Renaissance and the ecclesiastical ideals of tradition.

The name emerging as the noble symbol of ecclesiastical tradition is that of Palestrina—not only the superb composer of almost one thousand works for the sacred service but also their unmatched interpreter. Palestrina's Masses achieved the ultimate objective of ecclesiastical rendition: universality of expression in concordance with the Gregorian chant. Such interpretation, eliminating the individual aspect, was all-embracing in its true sense of the word. Although more than four centuries have elapsed since the birth of Pale-

strina, his performances have remained the permanent model in liturgy. This fact is clearly demonstrated in the *Motu proprio* given at the Vatican in 1903, when Pius X joined the procession of Popes representing the historic reforms of church music. The *Motu proprio,* written at the threshold of the 20th cent., once more conjured up, in all its ramifications, the performances of Palestrina. Just as this greatest *maestro di cappella* was himself a traditionalist, so the conservation of his interpretative style has unalterably remained the safeguard of the ecclesiastical spirit throughout the ages.

Renaissance. 1600, the turning point of the first century in modern times, was marked by a great spectacle. Spellbound with the trends of the Renaissance (the earlier phenomena of which had occurred long before), literati invented the opera. What proved to be of lasting importance in the performance of music was, paradoxically, but the art product of theoretical speculation in a circle of Florentine philosophers, artists and dilletante aristocrats. Inspired by their erudite discussion, composers turned away from the complicated tone rows of the Middle Ages, seeking to restore the classical Greek drama. From the pursuit of such old ideals originated the discovery of new ones. Guided by the humanistic respect for the word and its sense aspects, musical interpretation conquered hitherto unknown regions of emotional expression. Mere vocal display was demoted to secondary consideration. Especially t he tone language of the *Nuove Musiche* (the New Music), was to be rendered on the basis of a broad subjectivity, the text poetically leading the musical performer's imagination.

In the newly inaugurated opera the modern orchestra made its debut. Re-organized from medieval beginnings, the theatre band, kaleidoscopic in its variety, accompanied the operatic scenes with those instruments that suited best the changing dramatic situations. The first genius of the opera, Monteverdi, painted as a truly Venetian artist his tone pictures in transparent hues like Titian or Tintoretto. The growing emphasis on instruments was eventually felt in the realm of purely vocal rendition. Particularly, the so-called execution *a cappella* (chorus singing without accompaniment) yielded to hybrid forms of performances, admitting here the organ, there mixed instruments to accompany the choir. Gradually, that idealistic conception of former times, which had ranked *un concerto de voci* (interpretation through the human voice alone) higher than any combination of vocal and instrumental forces, waned. Instead, increasing interaction of vocal and instrumental styles came to the fore.

Everywhere the vocal performance exercised its influence on instrumental rendition. Frescobaldi, probably the greatest organ master of all times, attracted thousands of listeners to St. Peter's in Rome. Here they heard a magic organ playing: fantasies and toccatas rendered like the vocal madrigals, free in style and tempo, expressive as the *belcanto* voice itself. In Cremona, generations of craftsmen, the families of Amati, Guarneri and Stradivarius transformed their small town into the unchallenged metropolis of violin building. Wooden bodies of deepened tonal expression and widened range were constructed, instruments which spoke and sang, laughed and cried like human beings. For centuries to follow this new type of violin held the lead in the orchestral ensemble. This ensemble had its face changed when Lully replaced the variegated set-up of the Venetian with baroque simplicity—just as the multicolored palette of Titian was followed by Rembrandt's ingenious simplicity of contrasting light and shades. Lully's creation of what since has been recognized as the French music style made the score script more specific, i.e., he invested the script with more definite orders for the performers. Previous generalizations such as *tutti instrumenti* yielded to individually prescribed instructions for each instrument and its player. The whole orchestra at the royal court opera of Louis XIV was located between the parquet and the stage, the place it now holds in the opera houses of the world.

Baroque. A freak of nature selected the year 1685 for the birth of Bach, Handel and Scarlatti, and so marked the turning point of a new era, usually referred to as *baroque.* However, the general aesthetic meaning of the term *baroque* has caused more confusion than enlightenment in so far as the interpretation of works in this period is concerned. It has been the fate of the word baroque to lend itself to frequently changing meanings. From the original Portuguese *barrocco* (the fisherman's word for a small irregular pearl) through the characterization of features in the arts that tend to irregularity, to the final conception suggesting vastness of proportion and splendor of colors, the road is long and winding. And so are the ways of performing those masterpieces in music which today are labeled as baroque in analogy to ampleness in architecture and stateliness in sculpture and painting. Modern performances of Bach and Handel, the gigantic representatives of the musical baroque, are based on certain aesthetic traditions and on a partly hypothetical musical practice.

When Bach died in 1750 there was little realization of the spiritual wealth the Leipzig cantor at St. Thomas had bestowed on mankind. His works were hardly known until Mendelssohn reawakened the *St. Matthew Passion* in 1829. Thus there is a long void in which no real tradition in the performance of the great Bach scores could have been established and the so-called authentic German Bach tradition is in reality something hypothetical. The English Handel tradition developed into a performing routine on the grand scale. Thus, the famous *Messiah* rendition in Westminster Abbey (1784) exemplifies in its use of masses of participants, in its stolidity and rigidity, typical performing habits of the late baroque. Bach himself limited his performing apparatus to one of striking economy. Declaring his needs for the due rendering of church music, he asked the city council of Leipzig for a minimum of 18 orchestra players and three singers for each part. In Bach's own conception vocal and instrumental forces appear equal, very much in contrast to the modern Bach practice, where the size of the chorus often doubles or triples that of the accompanying orchestra. Both Bach and Handel are the favorite subjects of modern orchestra arrangements, of often rather forceful attempts to translate baroque sound ideals into the past—romantic accoustical conceptions of our time. Such endeavors lead to coloristic misrepresentations of the genuine baroque 18th cent. style, its vast horizontal planes and its organ-like orchestration.

Rococo, Dance types. The graceful rococo era brightened everything up. Its ornamental world cleared the severe counterpuntal baroque execution into a playfulness of melodic charm and serene elegancy. A lacework of grace notes, marked in notation by a clever system of musical stenography, served simultaneously to prolong the short-lived tone of keyboard instruments like the harpsichord. Thus, the seemingly only decorative performance of ornaments proved to be functional and progressed soon into the expressiveness of Romanticism.

In the periods of baroque and rococo, the performance of dance types underwent its most radical changes. The fact is due to the style transformation of courtly and popular models at their integration and absorption through the instrumental suite and orchestral symphony. Such changing performance of one and the same form type with the same unaltered name is but another instance demonstrating that the idea of musical forms is not absolute. Interpretation of any musical type is relative to time, place and function (purpose) of the respective rendition, interdependent on its style. What has been called a madrigal or minuet proves to be unlike in idea and execution with the shift of circumstances. The dance type sarabande, characterized as austere and of stately restraint in keeping with its slow and serious baroque performance was danced in the 16th cent. in Spain in a manner which made the law makers intercede; for dancing the Spanish sarabande, girls were exiled from the kingdom and men were sent to the galleys for six years. Analogously, the performance of other dances displays so drastic a metamorphosis that their story reads like an Ovidian tale.

Doctrine of Affections, Rationalism, Emotionalism. Rationalism, the back to nature watchword of the time, and its sweeping emotionalism were bound to leave their traces on the contemporary performance of music. The imprint of these ideologies is clearly marked in 18th cent. theories of interpretation. Concurring upon the fundamental approach to reading music, the theories center around the so-called *Affekten-Lehre,* the Doctrine of Affections or emotions (the German *affect* being synonymous with the English emotion). This *Affekten Lehre* is a practical aestheticism, a thorough system of performing practice. We understand best its implications by quoting some of its leading exponents: "The true aim of music is to stir emotions" states Mattheson, and Heinrichen's formulation holds the same, "The purpose of the performance is to move the affections". Bach's son Carl Philip Emanuel explains that "interpretation must realize the musical thought in accordance with its affections". Unequivocally Quantz demands that "the performer must recognize always all emotions embodied in the score". Without exception the theorists (most of them expert composers and performers) demand a conscientious scrutiny of the score's emotional content and its suitable application in the rendition.

The source of all musical truth is to be discovered by natural reason. A rational approach applies its rules and regulations according to different types of performance—in the church, the theatre, the home, the open air performance. For his discernment of the score's emotional content the performer depends also on technical features such as the tempo, the key, the phrasing. A staccato in an opera, symbolizing a slave's heart beat, was to be executed irregularly. Yet another staccato, illustrating the pulsations of sinners at the death of Christ must be played in strict time—two different emotions in two different style categories!

Classicism. With the great masters of the Vienna Classical School-Hydn, Mozart, Beethoven and Schubert—the score script becomes increasingly binding. The score text and its execution enter a new state of interdependence. As the classical score tends to exclude licenses on the part of its interpreter, it shows more frequently and in more details what the composer wanted. The *basso continuo* or figured bass, that inevitable characteristic of the previous practice, where the keyboard player improvised his part over a fixed bass line with indications for the harmony to be chosen, gradually vanishes. The classical close bond between the composer and his interpreter is tightened by a specific group of signs in the score script. These symbols of notation consist in the marks of agogics, dynamic and phrasing (the disciplines of tempo, tone volume and and musical punctuation respectively). Their employment is not new in the classical score. From the last part of the 18th cent., however, these marks are used profusely and have developed in modern music into minute directions concerning the composers' wishes, into detailed verbal information, into almost a musical scenario.

Summarizing, the classical attitude in the interpretative problem may be expressed in a dual formula: (1) the binding script and (2) the disappearance of improvisation and its chief device, the figured bass.

Romanticism. History has long linked the inception of romanticism with the end of the classical period. Yet, romanticism is an eternal factor in the performance of music. All epochs created romantic works and no period has any special claim on romantic interpretation. If romanticism stands for a more humanized way of playing music—with the emphasis on the subjective, the emotional, the phantastic and the virtuoso element—then it cannot be confined to the 19th cent. styles of composition and interpretation. The performing style of the *Ars Nova,* the stressing of the poet's word in the Renaissance, as well as the free "fantasies" of the baroque must be considered just as romantic in the sense of the definition given above. Even the classicists played quite romantically under certain artistic conditions. In short, before its gradual development into the most significant style-building principle of the post-classical era, romanticism was operative as a latent force in the musical interpretation of former periods.

In the middle of the 18th cent., however, a new style emerged, a style of a highly emotional nature which embodied the 17th cent. tendency toward a humanized performance and the 18th cent.'s interest in timbre. Interpretation of this new style employed all possible timbres, not in the service of polyphonic contrast and distinctness, but for the sake of emotional expressiveness. A new sensibility, a tender *cantabile* appeared, first with the scores of Philip Emanuel Bach, later with those of Mozart. Yet still another generation was to pass before these characteristics were fully absorbed by the forthcoming style of interpretation which dominated musical rendition throughout the entire 19th cent. The new trend romanticized not only the music of its own time but that of the past as well—the performance of the classicists became romanticized; the general style of interpretation had changed once more. Not the classical counterbalance of content and form, but the performer's subjective experience gradually rises as the driving force of the personalized 19th cent. interpretation. The interpreter no longer merely performs; he "reproduces" the art work. This word implies that the specific process of re-creation is being considered. The employment of the interpreter's mental and emotional qualities are claimed as being imperative in the rendition of a music which itself is but the manifestation of the most subjective experiences in life; a music wherein the composer has sublimated his world of dreams and visions. Even if such sublimation-music could convey a hidden meaning solely throughout the note-script, it would still be impossible for the performer to delineate with objective reserve the extravagance, buoyancy and emotionalism of such highly romantic and phantastic works, to use compass and ruler for his orientation in a truly dream world.

The classic score may lend itself to the tracing of its contours, for it is so splendidly adapted to formalistic copying on the part of the performer. But the romantic forms have been relaxed for the sake of new expressive forces. With romantic music, the aim of the performer has ceased to be abstract, as in a fugue or symmetrical sonata form. The romantic performance becomes more and more an appeal to the listener's imagination, to his subconsciousness—is more exciting than the plea of the baroque interpreter for conscious intellectual understanding. In striking contrast to the interpretive attitude of romantic freedom, there also prevails the heterogeneous thought: strict allegiance to the score. Despite the new expressive enrichment of the romantic technique, the tendency to preserve formalistic ground within the performance of music became manifest. Even in the theatre, with the gradual separation of the music drama from the opera, there reappear reformative approaches in the production of dramatic scores, leading to perfect coordination of the scene and the music. New designs for rehearsing, utmost conscientiousness in the preparation (of decors, the singers' acting, the dancing, and the orchestral part), led to renunciation of even the smallest licenses indulged in by vocal luminaries. These are the highroads to the unified art work of the future.

This trend culminated in Richard Wagner's *Gesamtkunstwerk* (see universal artwork) and its realization through the idea of *Festspiel* in Bayreuth. Historically, the reforms of Lully, Gluck, Weber and others are consummated in this 19th cent. craving for dramatic truth in opera performance. If Wagner's interpretative theory (as formulated in several splendid essays) appears as the quintessence of German Romanticism, so Hector Berlioz epitomizes the romantic ideals of French interpretation. Not only his dream of power and a colossal set up for performing masses but also his defense of the pure spirit of rendition gained lasting significance. He considered corrections of masterworks "the most enormous of crimes". At the other extreme, the corrective attitude of the interpreter towards the score may involve a multitude of deviations from the original when, e.g., for practical or aesthetic reasons, he resorts to the rendition of arrangements. As the title arrangement, revision, transcription, etc., imply, these versions differ from the prototype of the score and may, in spirit and expression, even lead to the exact opposite of what the composer wanted. Affinity between corrective approach and the virtuoso approach to performance, however, is to be found in the fact that frequently the exponents of either trend are identical. Thus the names of Liszt and Paganini live on as symbols of the triumph of the human mind and willpower over the hand and as arrangers of striking originality. Again, their style stresses the histrionic element in performing music; they accommodate their program, behavior and appearance to the desire for the spectacular of the spoiled *haute volée* in the European capitals of their time.

The Absolute Ideal. The train of thought in 19th cent. interpretation which proved most prophetic for developments in our own time emanated from the aesthetics of the greatest man in German philosophy—Imanuel Kant. It was Kant's *Critique of Judgment* on which Eduard Hanslick based his famous treatise, *The Beautiful in Music (1854)*. This revisal of musical aesthetics stood and still stands as the manifesto of objective interpretation as the defense of the absolute subject matter in music. Inspired by Kant in principle and formulation, Hanslick shows that an investigation of music must, above all, consider the art *object* and not the perceiving *subject*. Just as in the other arts, so in music, too, the objective mode of procedure must be adopted. Consequently, the interpreter's task is to realize music clearly as a self-sufficient form. This form—as proven in the *Critique of Judgment*—must always be in complete harmony with its content. Like the song of birds, music has no subject matter, it is the art of the beautiful play of sensations. With the existence of any extramusical subject in the score wholly denied, the interpreter's question, "What is to be expressed in my performance with the material at hand"? is answered categorically: "Musical ideas, nothing else!" Thus, lacking extraneous material as a premise of interpretation, the executant is obliged to think exclusively in terms of sound—as did the composer before him. Music is to be played, but is not to be played with. Interpretation deals with the *absolute* intrinsic beauty of tonal combinations as an end in itself. An aestheticism based on Kant's absolute ideas was bound to result in a conflict with Wagner's interpretative theories, esp. in the realm of absolute music, and to foster in the world of Brahms the inwardness and formal tendencies to be found in this composer's chamber music style.

New Gateways. Revolutionary inventions of electro-mechanical means have opened new gateways for the performance of old music as well as of music still to be written. Today, investigation of the mutual relationship between the artistic and technical features, must naturally consider all the seemingly extraneous factors which surround the electrical rendition. Such a factor is the time element, imposing specific conditions on both the musical and the technical executants. Again, the very existence of this performing team (the sound engineer collaborating with the performing musician) indicates the obvious departure from the past practice. Other problems, necessitating readjustments of the past ways of performance are entailed in electrical transmission. Also, a series of psychological ramifications cannot be neglected. The performer before the microphone is not stimulated by a visible audience, nor can the listener of a recorded or broadcasted rendition be influenced beyond aural sensation. Social stimulation, however, has been claimed an essential factor of performance by authorities of the stature of Schumann. The stylistic approach of the romanticists counted on the combined aural and visual reactions of their audiences. In contrast, the modern invisibility of performers reemphasizes the interpretive condition of classical formal lucidity instead of improvisatory display, the qualities of clarity and concise tonal balance rather than romantic dynamism.

Whatever can be said of the performer's or his audience's invisibility as a major factor determining the style of interpretation will, of course, be outmoded the moment television is made generally available to the public. To what degree the visual will be emphasized remains to be seen in the literal sense. If the accent is again, as in certain 19th cent. trends, on the performer's antics, then the streamlined magic box of the future will take the music lover back to the performing manner of a past long considered dead. Like all technical progress of mankind, its advancements may lend themselves to either course: to the conquest of the truly new, or to reactionary, perverse and frequently destructive employment. At any rate, an eternal law seems to emerge from the retrospective sketch of performing trends: the constant spiraling of heterogenous styles throughout the ages of musical history. (The above is based on the author's book, *The*

History of Music in Performance, W. W. Norton & Co., New York, 1943.)　　—F.D.

musical response, types of. See PSYCHOLOGY OF ART.

musical robot. A device for automatic playing of a musical instrument for the purpose of keeping the tone constant or varying it under control in scientific analysis and measurement.　　　　　　　　　　　　　—C.E.S.

musical scale. See ACOUSTICS.

musica mensurata, mensurabilis. See MEDIAEVAL MUSIC; NOTATION.

musica mundana. See quadrivium.

music appreciation (in the U. S. A.). The term *music appreciation,* which came into use early in the 20th cent. has found its way into our educational institutions as a course of study offered in most colleges and public and private schools. It may also be considered as expressing the state of music reception in communities and, according to the dictionary definition, it should express true or adequate estimation or recognition of the music of various ages and stages. To *appreciate* is "to be keenly sensible of or sensitive to",—therefore, courses in music appreciation are offered to cultivate and develop a love for and understanding of music as listener, performer and creator. *Appreciation* of music implies enthusiasm in its pursuit either active or passively, growth in understanding of its techniques and skills, and of its historical and aesthetic backgrounds.

Whether in a study course or as a measure of advancement of culture in this country, true appreciation of music should include not only a love for it, but also a recognition of styles, formal structure, instrumental color, harmonic and melodic structure, the dynamics necessary in interpretation, and a knowledge of the standards of various eras such as Classical, Romantic, Impressionistic, etc., and of historical and biographical material.

Familiarity is the keynote of music appreciation. We are living in an age when music is much more available to the masses than it was even in the last generation. Therefore, through radio, phonograph, the movies, free band concerts, symphony concerts, children's symphony concerts, community choruses, singing societies, recitals, school. orchestras, bands, and choruses, music is literally within reach of everyone. The phonograph, by means of which the same composi-

tion can be heard innumerable times, is a powerful factor in increasing music appreciation. Another important point in the development of music appreciation is the widespread growth of music organizations in the schools, giving thousands of young people opportunity to participate in the making of music, thus arousing an interest in and, frequently, increasing their love for music. Through school bands, orchestras, and choruses, larger audiences are developed for the concert halls throughout the country, in this way enlarging the scope of music appreciation. Today, the radio devotes more time to art music than it did formerly. The extent of this manner of disseminating musical culture or appreciation can hardly be measured. Beethoven symphonies, Mozart operas, Schubert songs, Bach fugues, works by contemporaries, penetrate into lumber camps, mining towns, lonely ranches, forestry look-outs, and into the home of factory workers and of shut-ins.

A love of music may be awakened through listening to popular and folk music, too. Many who have not been privileged to hear any music at all have frequently been led to listen to so-called classical music through being attracted by popular music and jazz heard over the air. While this method of leading listeners to the best through popular music and even popular classics is perfectly possible, musicians and teachers as a rule object to the idea of "swinging" the classics. At best it is not a legitimate treatment of music, and those who claim that people are drawn to listening to standard works by hearing them in swing version first, may be rationalizing or seeking to condone such maltreatment of music. Swing versions of Debussy, Mozart, Tchaikowsky, etc., must not be regarded as part of music appreciation.

The many music courses for the layman which have come into existence in the last few years may be cited as a sign of the growth of music appreciation.

While it is beyond the scope of this article to offer statistics, in a *Survey of College Entrance Credits and College Courses in Music,* published by the National Bureau for the Advancement of Music, New York, the statement is made that "over three-fourths of the 594 institutions (colleges) investigated offer. some instruction in music. . . ." Most of these colleges offer courses which partake of the nature of music appreciation.

A decade ago, Augustus D. Zanzig made a study of music conditions in the United States. His book, *Music in American Life,* reveals the musical activities of schools, playgrounds, playgrounds, settlements, homes, churches, industries, and museums. It shows the state of amateur music in 1932 and offers a working guide toward greater musical achievement. To encourage the development of musical appreciation through amateur participation is Dr. Zanzig's aim.

A phase of music appreciation which has widespread influence is the *Music Memory Contest,* an idea which originated in 1916 in the home of Mr. C. M. Tremaine, director of the National Bureau for the Advancement of Music. So successful was the experiment of playing music rolls and records for his children to learn to recognize a selected list of pieces, that the game was introduced into the schools of Westfield, N. J., where the Tremaines live. In 1928, more than 1500 school systems carried on Music Memory Contests, run according to given rules and a constitution. The Contest succeeds in its original purpose of cultivating among school children an appreciation of good music.

National Music Week, which is annually proclaimed by the President of the U. S. A., has done much to create a nation-wide interest in music in schools and communities. The number of school orchestras, bands and choral groups participating in National Music Week entertainments is unbelievably large, reaching into five figures.

No stronger proof of the growth of music appreciation in this country is necessary than to call attention to the increase in the number of great symphony orchestras in American cities. New York, Boston, Philadelphia, Chicago, Pittsburgh, Cincinnati, Washington, St. Louis, San Francisco, Los Angeles, Seattle, Baltimore, Cleveland, Minneapolis, Detroit, Kansas City, are a few cities with ranking orchestras and dozens of others are coming into prominence.

The more opportunity the public has to hear opera, the sooner will appreciation of opera increase, and with the development of taste will come the demand for more opera houses throughout the land.   —M.B.

music-culture. The aim of the liberal arts college is to develop all of our human gifts into free recourse, and through rounded training to cultivate and integrate the whole personality. To receive and store facts is a necessary part of the educational process but to this must be added the power of deducing from experience general and constructive principles. To be valid that experience must emerge from the accumulated riches of the intellect, the emotions and the spirit. Through the ever-increasing emphasis, since the Renaissance, upon analysis and specialization this triad of sources and forces has become disintegrated, losing the revealing and inspiring power they derive from active correlation. The science and art of music has suffered the most of all the seven arts by reason of its separation and academic segregation from life and general learning. But since 1927, with the formation of required and integrated courses in the humanities (architecture, sculpture, painting, poetry and music),—called by the Oriental sage: "The five fingers of God" —music as a vital element in liberal education has come into its own and its intellectual and cultural content and contribution to a general education is increasingly recognized and applied.

When the subject of music-study is mentioned the vast majority of adults or young people think of it as meaning music in one of two dimensions, i.e., applied music (learning to play or sing), or theoretical music (learning to compose and analyze). The history and tone-literature of music—folk and art music—constitutes an intimate record of man's thinking or intellectual self as well as man's feeling or emotional self. The development of races and nations is reflected in historic streams of beauty created by man. Just as in history, literature, and philosophy, so in music, it is our right and privilege to interpret, to apply and to re-live the truths recorded and expressed in its sensitive tone-literature. The tone language and message of music can only become a practical agency for cultural growth in the lives of all students, irrespective of musical tastes and tendencies, when its intellectual demands, its social and spiritual relationships are acknowledged and applied.

The teacher of the music-culture section in the conscientiously integrated humanities trunk course (running through at least two years), should be of necessity broadly equipped. He should be an able performer and a devoted lover of the best in folk and art music. Furthermore, he should be thoroughly versed in general history, literature and philosophy; in other words, a "man of culture", as the Greeks called such a human unit. Without this intellectual background convincing and stimulating integration is impossible, and the claims of music to be the mirror of men's thinking and feeling through the centuries fail to dignify the musical material or to reveal to the student its powers to interpret the society which created it. The teaching of music-history as such in a seriously integrated humanities group-course results in the loss of the high position and potential power of music-culture as an indispensable element in liberal education. Today men and women, musicologists in the best sense of the word, are available in increasing numbers. These scholars not only recognize the place and power of Music [in its three dimensions] in general education, but can constructively apply their knowledge to the interpretation-through-music of life past and present.

Music-culture as an accepted major element in general education opens the door of inspiring opportunity to educators and to the legions of students who are denied the understanding and appreciation of music through their false belief that the gods have not given them adequate tonal gifts and aptitudes. Music-culture integrated with history, literature and the arts is here to stay in the curriculum of the liberal arts college. The fundamental triad of things, thoughts, and emotions is as basic to a rich liberal education as it is to music. The understanding and application of its integrated relationships and creative possibilities truly educates(leads out) the total personality. Music, creative, applied and cultural, is fast becoming the emotional interpreter and spiritual leader of humanistic education in the liberal arts college. —H.P.E.

music, definition of See idiom B(6).

music drama. See opera.

music education. Music education, from the very nature of music itself, is designed to develop the ability to hear, the ability to understand what is heard and the ability to participate in the aural experience as a medium of expression. It involves the training of creators, performers and, in the present day, audiences.

The education of the professional and avocational musician differs only in the degree of intensity and extensity. Basic training for creators and performers includes (1) the learning of the relatively complex system of notation, consisting of a wide variety of signs and symbols; (2) the learning of terminology; (3) the acquiring of a sense of pitch

(except in the cases where the sense of absolute pitch is present); (4) the development of a definite feeling for metric and rhythmic groupings and tempos; (5) the learning of the aural and visual recognition of the components—rhythm, melody and harmony—and of the form and style into which they are cast; (6) a knowledge of the tone quality of the physical media of music, both in solo and ensemble; (7) the technical ability to perform music.

The learning of the notation and terminology is largely incidental and continues over a long period.

Lacking the sense of absolute pitch, a fairly accurate sense of pitch is acquired by constant attention. (In music schools courses in solfeggio or sight singing and dictation emphasize this.) The knowledge of pitch assists in making visual music aural and aural music visual.

To this must be added the developed physical feeling for metronomic divisions (meter), for related tones logically arranged in time relation (rhythm), and for established degrees of movement (tempos); a discriminating recognition of tone quality and a knowledge (first aural, then academic) of melody, counterpoint and harmony and their relation to form and style. The performer is then able to hear the printed page and the composer to write down what he has created.

Technical ability is merely a skill and, while necessary for a high degree of artistic performance and while definitely related to certain phases of music education, will not be taken up here.

The most advanced methods in music education approach the printed page as something to be heard before it is actually performed. As evidence of this mental hearing the student is asked to sing the music to be performed, in the case of melodic lines, and to analyze it harmonically in the case of chordal progressions, the material used being within his aural and mental experience. Having studied the phrases and larger divisions as a whole and having been instructed in the necessary technical skill, the student not only interprets the work of the composer but is able to use the music as a medium of self expression.

Creative music plays an important role in music education, just as original composition does in the study of a language. Students at all stage of advancement, even as beginners, learn to express themselves in music which they have created.

The history of music is being taught more and more against a background of world history with special attention to the philosophy of its transitions.

Courses for advanced students include the study of music in its cognate fields—acoustics, psychology and aesthetics.   —M.E.

MUSIC HISTORY, PERIODS IN. Like any other art, or any specialized activity, music may be viewed in two aspects—that of its purpose, and that of its technique. The purpose of music, aside from its sensuous appeal, is to utter (in intelligible and gratifying form) emotional appeal to, or emotional attitude toward, experience. Its technique is the adaptation of its materials (tone and rhythm) to that purpose.

The manipulation of tones and rhythms is itself a highly specialized activity, which often appears to the artist as the essential and even the only proper object of his effort. Those periods in which this view has been held are generally regarded in retrospect as periods of decadence. Those, on the other hand, in which extra-musical interest has generated new musical purposes are regarded as periods of growth. Since music thus derives in part from experience, its evolution pursues the general curve of human experience; and the great historic divisions of musical activity thus correspond to the great divisions of the history of mankind.

These divisions, however, are conveniences for thought, rather than temporal realities. The stream of musical thought, like the stream of human endeavor, is continuous; the forces which deflect the stream are often all but imperceptible at the instant of impact; and it is thus necessary to look backward as well as forward for any certainty of critical orientation at any given moment. The following is an attempt (utilizing the convenient but deceptive method of periodization) to indicate the course of the stream of musical thought from the earliest times until our own day. Other systems of music than our own, and systems so remote that their technique is unknown, obviously lie outside the scope of this survey. The aspects of purpose and technique have been differentiated up to the modern period, where such indication would be cumbrous and probably superfluous.

I. *The Ancient Period.* THE MUSIC OF ANCIENT GREECE. The purpose of Greek music was the enrichment of poetic ideas and poetic contours through the systematic organization of elements of pitch (in verbal accent) and of rhythm (in quantitative verse-structure) already existent in Greek speech. Because of the close association with language, ethical implications were embraced which are no longer perceived in modern music.

Out of the tetrachord (e.g., E D C B) was developed, by juxtaposition, our present diatonic scale. Segments of this scale (modes) were the progenitors of the Gregorian modes, and of our major and minor tonalities. Harmony, not practiced, was faintly imagined. Instrumental music, though highly perfected, remained subordinate to vocal (See Greek Music, ancient).

II. *The Medieval Period (150-1300 A.D.).* (a) MONODY (non-harmonic music), c. 150-900. The first purpose of Christian music was to find expression for the ideal of a universal brotherhood in a universally practicable form, the Hymn. Later, for the enrichment of an elaborated ritual, the stylized Gregorian chant, derived from Greek and other "classic" models, largely supersedes the "popular" hymn.

The rhythm of the hymn derived from its accentual verse; its melody, probably from popular song. The chant (set to prose texts) derived from Greek and Hebrew sources; was governed by modal law; was practicable only by the trained singers. Codified under Gregory the Great (d. 604), the chant assumed a form which has remained substantially unchanged to this day. Further musical progress is unrecorded until the 9th cent. (b) THE BEGINNINGS OF HARMONY: ORGANUM (900-1100). The chant is reduplicated at non-unisonous intervals (perfect 5th and 4th) as well as at unisonous (8ve). Through effort to avoid imperfect 5th and 4th, the 3rd occurs, and is recognized as imperfect concord. Contrary and oblique, as well as parallel motion between the voices, produce combinations of two or more *different* melodies, thus establishing the fact of *harmony*—probably the most remarkable artistic invention in recorded history. (Popular melody, still monodic, is continuous, but unrecorded, in this period.) Notation of pitch (but not of rhythm) becomes exact.

(c) DISCANT (RHYTHMICALLY MEASURED MUSIC), 1100-1300. Secular life is reflected in the poetry and song of troubadours, trouvères and the minnesinger. Popular melody is assimilated into learned music (motets).

Regular rhythm (essential to practice of harmony) is established on a basis of poetic meter (six rhythmic modes). Relation of discord to concord begins to be regulated; rhythmic periods are defined by pauses and cadences; musical form begins to show independence of poetic structure, but is hampered by a narrow rhythmic scheme (triple time, exclusively), and by failure to yield melodic interest to the advantage of harmony and general design. Notation becomes exact for triple time.

III. The Renaissance (1300-1600). (a) THE PRE-RENAISSANCE (1300-1400). Service music is greatly enriched (polyphonic settings of the Ordinary of the Mass) ; secular interests are greatly expanded; instrumental music is admitted into learned forms.

Duple rhythm is recognized, with appropriate notation. The musical sentence acquires a beginning and a middle, as well as an end. Structural devices (imitation, augmentation, diminution) are increasingly cultivated. Musical form becomes independent of poetic meter and verbal sentence. The relation of concord to discord is still indeterminate, and the forms inchoate; but liberation from modal rhythm compels attention to purely musical syntax. Chromatic alteration (*musica ficta*) begins to undermine the church modes, tending toward modern tonality.

(b) THE RENAISSANCE (1400-1500). Principles of composition are broadly determined: discord is "prepared" and "resolved" (Dunstable, d.1453); imitation becomes a principle of design, instead of a mere device (Dufay, d. 1474) ; "scientific" composition is carried to great heights (Okeghem, d. 1496) ; and the composition acquires a beginning, a middle and an end through the mastery of coherent harmonic progression underlying the whole fabric of interwoven melody (Josquin des Drés, d. 1521). Instrumental music begins to diverge from vocal (Paumann, d. 1437), and to express popular sentiment in dances and other forms. Patronage makes possible the musical career.

(c) RENAISSANCE AND REFORMATION (1500-1600). The process of polyphony is perfected, as applied to Catholic ideals (Palestrina, d. 1594) ; is expanded to reflect secular feeling (in the madrigal) ; and is abandoned to allow melody to predominate over harmony, in experiments leading directly to opera. Protestant doctrine, reasserting the individualism of early Christianity, is expressed in the hymn (chorale), sung as if monodic by the congregation; but harmonized by the choir, and embroidered by the organist, the hymn lays a foundation for a second polyphonic period. Instrumental forms are multiplied and expanded: fugue, fantasia, dance-suite, etc., and instruments are combined with choirs.

New alliance is formed between music and poetry, linking music definitely to the humanities.

IV. The Modern Period (1600-1900). (a) THE SEVENTEENTH CENTURY—THE MONODIC REVOLUTION. Opera appears (1600), is rapidly stylized (Lulli, d. 1687, and Scarlatti, d. 1725), with recitiative and A-B-A aria as principal forms. It greatly expands the musical public, becoming largely independent of aristocratic patronage, and thus generally affecting taste. Religious music adopts a secular tone, admitting brilliant instrumental accompaniment. Instrumental forms are perfected: concerto, sonata da chiesa, sonata da camera, fugue, etc. Major-minor tonality supersedes the church modes. The problem of equal temperament is solved.

(b) THE EIGHTEENTH CENTURY TO C. 1750. Opera is degraded in taste, perfected in technique of performance (singers the first virtuosi). Harmonic polyphony (as opposed to modal) is perfected (Bach, d. 1750) ; oratorio supplants opera in England (Händel, d. 1759). All musical forms greatly enriched, with wider expressive range, owing to application of equal temperament. Comedy appears in opera (the *Guerre des Bouffons* a kind of aftermath of the *Guerre des Anciens et des Modernes* in literature).

(c) THE EIGHTEENTH CENTURY, 1750-1800. Opera is "reformed" (Gluck, d. 1787), reflecting the "return to Nature"; but popular taste abandons polyphony for homophony in all forms, due to the influence of opera, the brilliance of aristocratic life, and the inclusion of lower classes in the musical public. Drama is incorporated in instrumental music (perfected sonata or symphonic form—Haydn, d. 1809, Mozart, d. 1791). Classicism declines and is overthrown by the Revolution.

(d) THE NINETEENTH CENTURY TO C. 1850—THE ROMANTIC PERIOD. High individualization in all forms, vocal and instrumental. Rise of the lied (Schubert, d. 1828) ; vast expansion of the symphony (Beethoven, d. 1827) ; romantic opera appears (Weber, d. 1826) ; sentimental opera superseded by "historic" (Meyerbeer, d. 1864). Smaller instrumental forms multiply (Chopin, d. 1849; Schumann, d. 1856) together with the song. Virtuosity, rampant (Paganini, d. 1840; Liszt, d. 1886), increases vastly the musical public, and fosters program-music ,Berlioz, d. 1869). Great freedom in the use of modulation and discord.

(e) THE NINETEENTH CENTURY, 1850-1900. Conflict between radicals and conservatives:

"expressive" vs. "absolute" music: Wagner (music-drama) and Liszt (symphonic poem) vs. Brahms (symphony). "Intellectual" criticism arises (Hanslick, et al.) in defense of absolutism. Bruckner and Mahler (symphony) and Hugo Wolf (song) continue Wagnerian tradition; Richard Strauss (symphonic poem) initiates new freedom in dissonance. Impressionism (Debussy) offers veiled threat to tonality (whole-tone scale). Reger expands Brahmsian structure on liberal harmonic lines.

V. The Twentieth Century. Absolutism becomes radical: polytonality and polyharmony (Milhaud et al.) and atonality (Schönberg) diffuse or obliterate tonality. New musical forms derive from intrinsic characteristics of the material employed, theoretically abandoning all relation either to emotional experience (as in romantic expression of mood or feeling) or to verbal syntax and rhetoric (until now, the implied bases of all musical form-patterns). From c. 1935 opposition to absolutism, although inarticulate critically and without a notable champion creatively, becomes strong. (As in many earlier periods, popular music is both affected by and absorbed into learned forms).   —D.N.F.

musicology (fm. Fr. *musicologie*). Musicology concerns the discovery and systematization of all knowledge pertaining to music as distinguished from the activities of musical composition and performance. It is the *science* of music as contrasted with the *art* of music, in that it stresses *knowing* rather than *doing.* As knowledge and understanding of music are basic to performance, so musicology underlies the art of music. But dependable knowledge requires careful study and investigation; hence musicology has come more narrowly to mean the field of musical research. A fundamental characteristic of any science is that it attempts to refine the knowledge of ordinary common sense by applying objective, scientific methods in the investigation of its subject matter. Thus the main function of musicology is the scientific description, analysis, and explanation of music in all its varied complexity. In the orderly performance of this function, musicology incorporates the findings of many auxiliary sciences, such as acoustics, physiology, psychology, aesthetics, education, ethnology, and history as they relate to music.

The fundamental philosophical concepts of *space* and *time* form the main axes in the frame of reference in terms of which musical knowledge and understanding are expressed.

Just as the understanding of a musical composition depends upon the perception of the relationships among the constitutive tones in both their simultaneous and successive aspects, so the understanding of music in part or as a whole depends upon the perception of both systematic and historical relationships. Naturally, then, the subject matter of musicology falls into two main divisions: the *systematic* and *historical.*

The main objective of **systematic musicology** is the study of music as it exists in the world today. Musicology investigates music as a physical phenomenon under the heading of *acoustics;* the nature of the responses and activities of the human organism in reaction to the physical sounds of music under the headings of *physiology* and *psychology;* certain problems of musical value under the heading of musical *aesthetics;* the problems of teaching music under the heading of *pedagogy;* folk music and the musical systems of the various peoples of the world under the heading of *comparative musicology;* and finally the tonal-rhythmic structure of music under the heading of *musical theory,* with numerous subdivisions such as *harmony, counterpart, orchestration,* and *musical form.*

Thus based upon the study of actual musical works in the light of findings in all these auxiliary sciences, musical theory, in a comprehensive sense, constitutes the chief purely musical division of systematic musicology.

The main concern of **historical musicology,** on the other hand, is the study of music as it existed in the past for the purpose of understanding or explaining how it came to be what it is today. In the attainment of its aims, historical musicology investigates the principles basic to a comprehensive and valid *philosophy of history;* it seeks to collect, classify, and preserve all pertinent source materials; and, finally, it attempts to express its findings in the manifold types of historical literature.

The systematic and historical orientations of musicology are complementary; they find their common application in innumerable characteristic musicological publications. The scientific study of music in Western civilization extends back at least to Pythagoras, in the 6th cent. B.C.; and from the time of the early Greek and Latin writers on down to the present there has been a steadily increasing volume of musicological literature. The natural seat of musicological investigation and teaching is the university. This fact has long been true in Europe and is rapidly coming to be true in America. The American Musicological Society, founded in 1934, is one of several national and international organizations devoted to the promotion of the scientific study of music. See Glen Haydon, *Introduction to Musicology: A Survey of the Fields, Systematic and Historical, of Musical Knowledge and Research*, 1941; Otto Kinkeldey, "Musicology," *The International Cyclopedia of Music and Musicians*, pp. 1218-1221; Egon Wellesz, "Musicology," *Grove's Dictionary of Music and Musicians*, Suppl. Vol., pp. 455-462.   —G.H.

music, origins of. The problem of the origin of music can scarcely be taken as a question of absolute beginnings. It is a matter, on the one hand, of discovering the historical evidence of the first known existence of music and, on the other, of studying systematically the conditions basic to the manifestation of music in the experience of the individual and of society. A comparative examination of the historical and systematic evidence affords the natural and logical, if not the only, scientific approach to the solution of a problem, which, like many problems of origins, is not susceptible to a definite answer.

Since the evidence of historical research, leading back several milleniums before the Christian era, yields little more than a few fragmentary representations of musical instruments which are indicative of the early existence of music, music historians have, in recent years, tended to cease their perhaps interesting but ultimately futile speculations as to the beginnings of music and to refer the whole matter of origins to the comparative musicologist. The latter considers not only the historical evidence but also the primitive, exotic, and folk music of today; the musical development of the individual; and the physical, physiological, psychological, and aesthetic factors that are basic to the very existence of music. From the study of various aspects of the amassed evidence he reaches many suggestive conclusions, of which a few may be cited. He concludes, for example, that the enjoyment of music is inherent in man's nature; that the physiological response to rhythmized patterns of sound is deep-seated, being based upon natural laws that may be scientifically investigated; that under emotional stress, highly inflected speech tends to merge into musical utterance; that music functions naturally in courtship as in most ceremonial occasions; that music may be partially accounted for as an overflow of

nervous energy; that in play as in work there are countless situations in which music affords a natural accompaniment to bodily movements; that the physical world affords practically unlimited possibilities for the production and control of sounds so that they may be organized into tonal-rhythmic patterns that have a profoundly moving effect upon man; and, finally, that the basis for these effects is to be found in man's psycho-physiological and aesthetic nature.

Thus, while early writers on the history of music tended to attribute a divine origin to music, and while 19th cent. evolutionary thinking tried to establish definite stages of development in the beginnings of music, such as Rowbotham's *drum, pipe,* and *lyre* stages, modern musicologists deal with the problem of origins by revealing the evidence of the existence of music in the earliest known civilizations and by pointing out the biological, social, and other factors that are indicative of the inevitability of music in the life of man. See Allen, Warren D., *Philosophies of Music History*, New York, 1939; Haydon, Glen, *Introduction to Musicology*, New York, 1941; Spencer, Herbert, "On the Origin and Function of Music," *Essays*, Vol. I, London, 1868; Stumpf, Carl, *Die Anfänge der Musik*, Leipzig, 1911; Torrefranca, Fausto, "Le Origini della musica," *Rivista musicale italiana*, Vol. XIV (1907); Wallaschek, Richard, *Anfänge der Tonkunst*, Leipzig, 1903. —G.H.

music printing and engraving. The various methods of reproducing musical notation form a development which may be considered in three broad stages: first, the manuscript; second, the early hand-press; third and last, the modern automatic press. The labor of one scribe could provide only one copy at a time. The editions of the early hand-press were relatively small and expensive. The output of a modern press is hardly limited at all save by the demand for its product. The significance of this development is implicit in these facts. The restricted output of the earlier processes is coupled with a restricted circulation of the music printed due both to the rarity of copies and their great cost. The unlimited output of later methods is inseparably associated with the spread of popular education and culture through the circulation of correct and cheap copies of the musical masterworks of all periods.

As would be anticipated, music printing lagged somewhat behind the printing of books. Thus, in the earliest works that required musical illustrations printers resorted to makeshift devices. In the earliest volume with music (*Collectiorum super Magnificat,* J. Charlier de Gerson, 1473) the notes only, not the lines are printed. The lines were to be filled in b hand, and since no special type was available for the notes, the printer employed stamps which were ordinary type reversed so that they printed a solid black rectangle.

In other cases a blank space was left, and both notes and music had to be filled in by hand. As the need for musical type began to be felt, two styles appear: the roman with a basic square note-shape and the gothic with a lozenge-shaped note. The gothic form appears first in the *Grammatica Brevis* of Franciscus Niger, Venice, 1480, printed by Theodor of Wurzburg.

Another device of the early printer was based on the technique of the wood engraver. In this method the musical notation, notes and staves as well as the surrounding border, is cut from a single wood block. The musical examples in the *Theoricum Opus* of Franchinus Gafurius were printed thus in the second edition (1492, printed by Mantegatius of Milan).

Secular music printing begins with the *Grammatica of Niger*. Another important early imprint is the *Legend of Saint Ursula* (1497, printed by Kustler of Strassburg) which is notable for the fact that it contains the melodies of secular songs.

Another type of publication peculiar to the Renaissance was the school play. The *Scenica Progymnasmata* of Reuchlin published in 1498 in two different editions deserves special mention in this group as the first published play with printed music. Wood blocks were evidently costly to produce and were preserved with care. When a book was republished the same blocks for musical examples were frequently used. The songs in praise of the Emperor Maximilian by De Opitiis (Wittenberg, 1523) shows the wood block technique used in a festival volume.

Many early ecclesiastical books were printed in two colors. The notes were printed in black on a four line staff which, together with the border and initials, was in red. This practice was probably derived from the practice in manuscripts of drawing the line of the staff indicating F or C in red so as to facilitate the reading of the music. The earliest work of this kind was the *Psalterium* of 1457 printed by the famous Gutenburg in collaboration with Fust and Schoeffer. This vol-

ume, however, shows a transition to the two color process since three of the four staff lines are printed in black, while the fourth or red line as well as the notes were left to be filled in by hand. The fully developed process necessitated two impressions, but printers had already acquired skill in this technique which had been employed in books of other kinds since approximately 1460. The exuberance and variety of the tone symbols, the neumes, was gradually reduced to a few basic types. Most volumes in red and black were those containing the music for the services of the Catholic Church: the *Psalter, Missal, Gradual,* and *Antiphonal.* The Roman style, employed first in Italy, has remained in use for liturgical books up to the present day. In the 15th cent., however, the so called Gothic style was employed with equal frequency. Here we must distinguish two types of note: the simple lozenge and the lozenge with a straight or curved stem (the horseshoe nail and horseshoe forms).

The problems involved in printing polyphonic music were somewhat different. Contrary to modern custom music in several parts for voices was printed in part books, each book containing the music for one voice. Ottaviano Petrucci da Fossombrone, the pioneer in the printing of secular part music and the inventor of a method of printing music from movable type, published his *Harmonice Musices Odhecaton A* in Venice in 1501. This publication which contains French chansons and Italian canzonets was followed by *Canti B* (1502) and *Canti C* (1503), and these by a long series of motets and masses. His later experiments in printing instrumental notation in the form of tablature have left no results which survive.

Though music which Petrucci had printed from movable type possessed both clarity and elegance of style, he nevertheless employed two or possibly three impressions to obtain this result.

It was a Frenchman, Pierre Haultin, who first printed music in a single impression by combining in a single character the note and the adjacent portions of the staff. Previously this had required two impressions, one for the staff and a second for the notes. Haultin was associated with the famous French publisher Attaignant, and the first publication printed according to his system was a collection of chansons which presumably appeared in 1527. This method spread to other parts of Europe and was employed with notable success by Antonio Gardano.

However, the method was most assiduously practiced in France and in 1552 the Ballard family obtained a patent which gave them the sole right to print according to this method, a right which they were able to retain to the end of the 18th cent. Early impressions of Haultin had retained the diamond-shaped Gothic notes. The round headed note which is currently employed first appeared in a collection of music by Elzear Ganet printed by Etienne Briard in 1532-34 (three volumes). This system of single impression printing was ill adapted to chordal music or to music which was florid in character, employing many notes of short duration.

The immediate answer to this difficulty was found in an application of an ancient art. Copper engraving had long been known as a method of reproducing designs or pictures. Its first application to music, as far as is known at present, was in the *Diletto spirituale* of Simone Verovio, published in Rome in the year 1600. The method was simply to copy the music in reverse on a copper or other soft metal sheet with the aid of the graver and other implements. The hollows thus formed were filled with printers ink and this, when run through a press, transferred the inked design to a superimposed sheet of paper.

A possible hint as to the manner in which the transition from engraved picture to engraved sheet of music was effected may perhaps be found in the so-called **picture motets** from the Low Countries in which musical performances are depicted including the part books from which the pictured singers and instrumentalists are reading. Early examples of this kind and the title pages of certain works from the Netherlands in which musical notation is incorporated into the design surely suggest a possible transition from decorative engraving to the engraving of musical notation. In engraved music note-heads were round. Groups of notes of uniform time value were connected by engraved lines instead of being represented as single notes each with its own flag. A work of the first importance among early examples of Italian music engraving is the *Toccate e Partite* of Girolamo Frescobaldi, engraved by Blancus for Borbone, Rome.

In England, though Thomas Morley had been granted a monopoly for engraving music in 1598, the first volume of music did not appear till the years 1609-10 when the *Fantasies* for viols by Orlando Gibbons were published. At a later period (1683-1720) Thomas Cross engraved almost all the music produced in England, including the works of Henry Purcell.

The tardy appearance of engraved music in France was due to the fact that the Ballard family which controlled the printing of French music found it simpler to continue printing with type. The conservative trend thus fostered was so fixed that even when a score of Lully was engraved (*Phaeton*, 1675) by H. de Baussen, the Gothic lozenge-shaped note heads characteristic of French musical typography were retained. Later, however, the round note-head was adopted

The next change in music printing was due to the English publishers Hare and Walsh. For motives of economy sheets of pewter were substituted for copper and the process was further facilitated by punching or stamping such symbols as clefs and note heads, the remainder being engraved as before. Cross, the leading English engraver of the period, was a bitter opponent of the new method, going so far as to engrave a warning on one of his own plates, "Beware of ye non-sensical puncht ones". Nevertheless, the process combining punched and engraved portions became and remained a standard method.

If the method of printing from type did not entirely disappear, this was due to improvements effected by Johann Immanuel Breitkopf, improvements which were in part paralleled by the work of Fournier Le Jeune in France. The latter could make no headway in putting his method into practice due to opposition from the holders of the Ballard monopoly. The musical symbols were divided into parts and were combined with portions of the staff. These units could be assembled as desired. Type setting was laborious, and the number of type forms required was very large: over three hundred in Breitkopf's method; so that, although it was considerably used during his own day in Holland and Germany, subsequent use has been restricted to volumes where the amount of music is rather small in proposition to the amount of text, such as hymnals, song books, and theoretical works. The first work printed by this process was an aria which appeared in 1754.

Breitkopf's work consisted in a more effective adaptation of the ancient art of printing to the special demands of music printing. Lithography, however, was based on quite a different principle. It was in the search for a cheaper medium than the copper plate that Alois Senefelder turned to the so-called Solnhofen or lithographic stone. In early attempts the music was written directly on the stone with a special ink. The remainder of the stone unprotected by this ink was attacked by an acid bath which left the characters in relief. The first example of music printed by this process was a *Feldmarsch der Churpfalzbayer'schen Truppen,* issued in 1796.

Two years later the process was improved. The stone on which the music was written in reverse was treated with a solution of gum arabic, acid and water. Printer's ink when applied to the stone was attracted only to the ink-covered portions and thus an impression could be obtained with the aid of a printing press. In spite of much prejudice on the part of musicians the new process had a powerful argument in its favor since engraved music was three or four times as expensive as lithographed music. Thus lithography became the usual mode of publication for popular songs of the early 19th cent.

Modern music printing is likely to combine elements from earlier processes. The original copper plate is prepared by punching and engraving. The text of vocal compositions may be either punched or printed in later. A proof in lithographic ink is taken from the copper plate and is transferred, not to a stone, but to a metal plate with a specially prepared surface. It is this second plate which is used in the actual printing. Copies may either be printed directly from the plate or, in the offset process, the plate transfers its impression to a rubber blanket, and the latter actually serves to print the page.

The development of music printing may be regarded as the progress of technical development and democratic education marching hand in hand. This development proceeds from the limited edition of the hand press to the limitless production of the modern press, from the costly product of the hand craftsman to the cheap mass output of the modern machine press, from an exclusive and aristocratic art to one which may become a people's art. This is a development which technological skill alone has made possible. Our admiration for the typographical beauty of the masterpieces of early music printing should not blind us to the fact that the basic function of printing is wide-spread diffusion.

—C.W.H.

music, the effects of. See PSYCHOLOGY OF ART; INDUSTRIAL MUSIC RESEARCH.

music, the meaning of See PSYCHOLOGY OF MUSIC.

music training. See training (in basic musical skills).

muslin (Fr. *mousseline,* fm. the town of Mosul in Mesopotamia which, though long famous for its cloths of gold, never specialized in fine cottons). A soft cotton fabric of plain weave. Varieties of muslins are named for their place of production; e.g., Dacca muslin, Indian muslin, Madras muslin, Swiss muslin. —G.W.R.

mutation. See solmization.

mute cornet. See MUSICAL INSTRUMENTS.

mute spectacle. See STAGESETTING.

mutule. A flat block projecting under the corona of the Doric cornice.

Mycenean architecture. See Aegean architecture.

Mycenean art. See HELLENIC ART.

myrtle. In Greek pottery, a decorative pattern having small pointed ovate leaves arranged opposite each other on the stem.

mystery play. See THEATRE.

myth. Two contrasting meanings belong to myth: legendary fiction and poetic truth. The double delusion that myth means only fiction and that all that is not science is myth has prevented multitudes from discovering the depths and the delights of mythical art.

Anthropologists regard myth-making as characteristic of human nature. Plato and Schelling proved that myth is indispensable for art. "The Platonic myth indicates how the mind necessarily completes through imagination its unfinished knowledge." (W. E. Hocking, orally.) Schelling viewed myth as the ancestral union of poetry and philosophy. Here in imagination man freely builds for himself the word-pictures needed to express his feelings about ultimate concerns, and to enjoy himself in the process.

The ancient Greeks used *mythos* and *logos* alike for speech, word, or report, without reference to truth or untruth. *Mythos* meant also unspoken thought, purpose, plot, story, or fable. Pindar would not ascribe cannibalism to the gods, but only beautiful acts, consistent with divine dignity.

Thus unexpectedly we discover that myths may be true. Indeed their artistic importance lies in their power to express a kind of truth about human values which cannot be embodied in prose or in any other art form.

Aristotle's use of myth may unlock its philosophical depths: "The *mythos* (plot) is the first principle and as it were the soul of tragedy." (*Poet.´* vi, 14). The poetic myth is a drama within the soul. But the mythical stage is the mind; the narrator himself carries forward the action in his imagination. The myth is a picturesque and personalized story designed to enhance some important feeling about natural wonders, destiny, or divine things.

This psychological-intuitive approach, coupled with a sympathetic anthropology and an earnest faith, provides the best method for interpreting myths. Historical, allegorical, and philological methods have added much to the science, but little to the artistic appreciation, of myths. **Artistic myth** means a kind of spontaneous narrative in which psychic realities, especially fears and hopes, are expressed in concrete imaginative language, usually in dramatic form.

Myth assumes four forms in art:
A. Myth proper:
   1. *Primitive myth,* the prototype of poetry.
   2. *Art myth,* perfected poetic narratives, like Plato's myths.

B. Derived myths:
   3. *Symbolical myth,* conscious purposive inventions: allegories, parables, fables.
   4. *Mythical transformations*: artistic works which incorporate original mythical materials, such as Wagner's operas or Dante's *Divine Comedy*.

Plato loved the myth, and cast his deepest insights into unique art myths, not only because they are aesthetically delightful but because no other art form could express his cosmic visions. Urban asserts in *Language and Reality* that the mythical form is indispensable for the expression of religious views because it is "a primary and unique way of apprehending reality".

As long as man wonders about his future and the mysteries of existence he will demand the "mythical supplement" to science. "Myths there must be, since all visions of the future must be clothed in imagery." (Hocking, *Fortune,* February, 1942.) Much of myth is artistically prefigured history, utopias that man deeply wishes somehow to happen, such as the Messianic Age or the Kingdom of God. See B. Malinowski, *Myth in Primitive Psychology,* 1926; F. C. Prescott, *Poetry and Myth,* 1927; J. A. Stewart, *The Myths of Plato,* 1905.   —R.F.P.

N

Nachayama yaki (Jap.). Pottery made in Tosa province.

naga (Skr.). The serpent. An important element in Oriental art, esp. in Cambodia and India.

Nagasaki school (Jap.). A school of painting originating at Nagasaki, after the Chinese manner.

Nagasaki ware. Lacquered porcelain, first produced in the vicinity of Nagasaki, Japan, thus the name. The decoration was applied to glazed porcelain blanks by lacquer artists.
—J.A.M.

nakago (Jap.). The tang, or the shaft that fits into the handle of a sword.

Nanga school (Jap.). A style of painting depicting genre subjects in an idealistic Chinese manner.

naos. See HELLENC ART; Hellenic style.

naphtha. Among the diluents for oil as a painting medium, naphtha or some kind of petroleum spirit ranks second to turpentine. There is still some confusion between petroleum naphtha and the coal-tar naphtha which is a crude distillate containing chiefly benzene and its homologues. The petroleum thinner, known also as benzine, gasoline, and mineral spirits, is prepared in a range of different evaporation rates, flash points, and densities. Active on oils while these are still in the fluid state and on waxes as a solvent, naphtha has little solvent effect on resins, except dammar. Historically, it has been known since ancient times, but seems to have had little use in painting until the 19th cent.
—G.L.S.

Naples yellow. Now rare as a painter's pigment, this lead antimoniate seems to have been known and used moderately during the Middle Ages and the Renaissance. As a glaze for ceramics, it has been familiar to potters since Babylonian and Assyrian times. It is yellow to orange in color and is made synthetically from the salts of lead and antimony—G.L.S.

narrative lyric poetry. See POETRY.

narrative poetry. See POETRY.

narrator. In the earlier passion plays and in oratorios, the singer of the narrative text. See RADIO DRAMA.

narthex. The portico of ancient churches; one side or member of the atrium or outer court surrounded by ambulatories.

nashiji (Jap.). Term applied to lacquerware when gold is sprinkled on a lacquered surface through a screen and, when dried, rubbed down, thus producing an allover gold-flake pattern.
—J.A.M.

Nashki script. See ISLAMIC ART.

Nasta 'liq script. See ISLAMIC ART.

national architecture. The architecture developed by a politically united people, such as Egyptian architecture or English architecture.

national planning. See CIVIC PLANNING.

national song. See song.

natural. In masonry: Term applied to stone as it is found in its natural form and shape.
natural dance. The school of *natural dance* arose in the U.S.A. in the last part of the 19th cent. It held that dance was an expression of nature and that all the forces

of nature and of man are revealed in movements manifesting the universal laws of rhythm. Its most enlightened advocates turned to the plastic arts of the Greeks—not so much to imitate their gestures, as to rediscover in them the expression of nature and to dance under the inspiration ·of the Greek ideal. Their dancing interpreted nature themes and natural qualities with what was considered to be natural movements. It was a return to nature, but unfortunately many of the followers were without conviction or a clear understanding· of its real meaning. As a result there was much dancing that was imitative only of the usual aspects of "nature movements" instead of being motivated by an inner and unique responsiveness to the forces revealed by movements of natural phenomena. Since natural dance defied the technical principles of the classic ballet, form was at the mercy of the spontaneous naturalistic interpretation of the dancer. With no inner logic of its own, dance was dependent upon music both for inspiration and structure. It is at this point of dance evolution that **interpretative dance** appeared, defining dance as the expression of the dancer's interpretation of moods and ideas created by music. The influence of this new theory of dance spread to Europe and was instrumental in affecting changes in the dancing of France, England, Italy, Russia, and Germany. "Natural dance" was an awakening to the further enlarged possibilities and achievements to be realized in the more mature art dance of today.

—M.N. H'D.

natural harmonica. See ACOUSTICS.

natural tones. The natural harmonics of an instrument.

naturalism. The doctrine that nature should be represented objectively, without interpretation or editorializing. The representation of the natural in the sense of that which exists apart from an uninfluenced by man.

(1) From a formal point of view naturalistic art has a minimum of decorative or expressive distortion of appearances. Naturalistic painting approximates camera vision; sculpture approximates a cast taken from the model directly; literature approximates scientific prose description. Impressionism (q.v.), however, is also a form of naturalism, since it aims to report objectively what the eye sees at a momentary glance.

So far as form is concerned, an artist may

be a naturalist though his subject matter consistently evoke sentimental, romantic, or idealistic associations, e.g. Holman Hunt, Millais, Watts, Meissonier, Rosa Bonheur, Landseer, Böcklin, and Saint-Gaudens. Other naturalists include painters Courbet, Manet, Monet, Pissarro, Sargent, Homer, Eakins, Sorolla, Zorn, Liebermann, Vermeer, Hals, and Caravaggio; sculptors Rodin, Barye, Falguière, Hildebrand, and Dallin; authors Zola, Flaubert, de Maupassant, the de Goncourts, Brecque, Sinclair Lewis, Dreiser, Hemingway, Faulkner, Stephen Crane, and James Farrell.

To use the language of philosophy, formal naturalism parallels nominalism and represents the "particular" rather than the "universal" (artistic idealism) or the "universal in the particular" (artistic realism). As might be expected, therefore, the doctrine flourished when belief in the reality of "particulars" was most current in philosophy, in the Hellenistic and Roman period of antiquity and in the late 19th cent. Sculpture of the type of the *Laocoon,* the *Borghese Warrior,* the *Old Market Woman* in the Metropolitan Museum, N. Y., and most Roman portrait busts of the Republic and first two centuries of the Empire are examples of ancient naturalism. In graphic arts, the *Odyssey Landscapes* in the Vatican Museum and the *Battle of Issus* mosaic in the Museum of Naples may be designated as naturalistic, and these are representative of the period.

19th cent. naturalism is the end product of the drive for illusionism (q.v.), which began in the early Renaissance and paralleled the rise of science and the disintegration of religion. Influenced by the development of the camera and the appearance of materialistic philosophy, it reached its apogee in the 2d half of the 19th cent.

(2) In the most complete sense, artistic naturalism is not merely a matter of form, but also of content, and implies a naturalistic philosophy. Courbet, Manet, Rodin, Zola, Flaubert, de Maupassant and other minor French artists and authors of the late 19th cent., and a number of 20th cent. American authors, exemplify this comprehensive use of the term. Their position is analogous to positivism in philosophy and may be described as the scientific method applied to literature and the graphic and plastic arts. Some of these artists were called realists (q.v.) and some of them used this term to describe their doctrine, but their meaning was the same as that here outlined. They programmatically presented with cold indifference and

detachment a literal transcript of the physical world about them, and refused to cultivate the world of imagination, to believe in anything not present to the senses, to seek any hidden meanings, to minimize the more disagreeable, vulgar, sordid, decadent, coarse, and morbid aspects of their world, or indeed to alter the physical world in any manner or for any purpose. Thus, their doctrine opposed alike the cultivation of classic beauty in the manner of the contemporary neo-classicists (q.v.) and the search for novel and emotive fragments of form and subject indulged in by the romanticists (q.v.). Rejecting academic rules of drawing, painting, modelling, and composition, they prepared the way for a new subjectivism in the several arts, which arose in the last two decades of the century under the name of post-impressionism (q.v.) in painting and symbolism in literature.

(3) Naturalism is occasionally loosely applied to all original forms of modern art since the time of Courbet and Zola, referring only to naturalistic content without consideration of form. In this vague sense it is employed as the antithesis of humanism in art and letters. Hence it includes artists and authors of such diverse style as Toulouse-Lautrec, Matisse, George Grosz, Picasso, Max Beckmann, Salvador Dali, Epstein, Belling, Gertrude Stein, John Dos Passos, Sherwood Anderson, and Jack London, all of whom, in contrast to humanists, depreciate man in dignity, nobility, and ethics, and treat the order of the universe as mechanistic or deterministic rather than anthropocentric and teleological.

(4) Naturalism is sometimes applied to a period, style, or artist in a comparative sense, as with reference to an art which precedes or follows, or by comparison to a more stylized art of another era; as when the painting of Middle Minoan III is compared to Late Minoan III, or when Latin illusionism of the 4th cent. is compared to East Christian art of the same century, when Greek sculpture is contrasted with that of Egypt, Ingres with Matisse, Western art with Oriental, or any comparatively representational art with one of symbolic ideographs. In each case the art first mentioned is said to be (comparatively) naturalistic, even though it is recognized as non-naturalistic in a more absolute sense of the term by comparison with Hellenistic and 19th cent. illusionism.

—L.D.L.

nature symbols. See PRIMITIVE ART.

Navaho art. The Navaho were Athapascan nomad hunters from northwest Canada and Alaska who began infiltrating into the Pueblo country and raiding the villages six or seven hundred years ago, and were a contributing cause to the concentration and later the migration of the Pueblo peoples. Contact with the Pueblos gave the Navaho a knowledge of corn culture, weaving, possibly the art of sand painting, and, most important, the acquisition of the horse, sheep and goat brought by the Spaniard. These were the chief transforming elements that enabled the assimilative Navaho to develop his characteristic semi-nomadic culture pattern. Though the high plateau country which he had appropriated in northern Arizona, New Mexico and southern Utah furnished sparse vegetation for grazing and the horse gave him mobility for wide ranging, still the acute need for rain colored his legends, ceremonials and symbolism. In winter the family lived in a substantial hogan (q.v.); in summer, under shelving rocks or in a loosely constructed brush shelter. The men farmed on a small scale or wandered with the flocks while the women wove at the looms set up out-of-doors near the hut.

With the introduction of sheep, weaving, from c. 1700 A.D., became one of the chief crafts which grew out of the needs of daily living: warm blankets for home, man and horse. This was entirely a woman's craft. The designs at first consisted of simple stripes limited in color to natural wools and a few hues obtained from native dyes, such as indigo, to which red was added from ravelings of English or Spanish baize, called bayeta. To these striped patterns were added simple geometric motifs such as zigzags, diamonds and terraced patterns. About the middle of the 19th cent. the so-called Chief blankets, in their weaving, texture, color and pattern, constitute some of the finest textiles of aboriginal America. Later in the century, with the introduction of Germantown yarns and aniline dyes the craft deteriorated and turned toward the making of rugs with borders, in response to trade requirements of the white man. Early in the 20th cent. occurred a revival of the older style based on stripes and more conservative color.

Silversmithing the Navaho learned from the Mexicans about 1850. He obtained his material first from Mexican and American dollars, later from sheet and ingot metal. By hammering, molding, polishing, engraving and stamping, though always with primitive tools, he fashioned buttons, bracelets, beads, pendants and mountings for belts and bridles which not only served as ornaments but revealed his economic status, judged by both quantity and quality of workmanship. Designs consisted of engraved lines or geometric shapes, or of motifs of Mexican origin, and show the same simple vigor as those in the blankets.

Probably the most unusual art characteristic of the Navaho was sand painting (q.v.), an American abstract expression that is thoroughly indigenous as well as rich in content and design. Sand painting, or dry painting, is but one element in the elaborate ceremonials of the Navaho in which are expressed by costume, drama, dance and song his rich complex mythology, significant of his relation to great cosmic forces. Much of this ritual reveals highly imaginative poetry. The function of the ceremonials, which last from two to nine days, is three-fold: to cure or prevent disease; to invoke the gods for rain, fertility and the general well-being of the tribe; and to provide a semi-nomadic people social contact with the tribe. As a unit they constitute one of the great coordinated, autochthonous art expressions of America. See Charles Amsden, *Navaho Weaving,* 1934; Washington Matthews, *Navaho Legends,* 1897 and *The Night Chant,* 1902; Arthur Woodward, *A Brief History of Navaho Silversmithing,* 1938. —H.G.

Navaho rugs. First made as robes by Navaho Indians. Now used as rugs for the trade. Quality is judged by smoothness of weave, dyeing and blending of the colors and beauty and originality of the design. —B.E.J.

nave. In basilican and cruciform churches, the part that rises higher than the aisles flanking it and has, usually, a clerestory.

nave arcade. The series of columns and vaults dividing the nave of a cruciform church from the side aisles.

naviform. Boatshaped.

Nazarenes, the (Ger. *Nazarener*). On July 7th, 1809, the painters Overbeck, Pforr, Wintergerst, Hottinger, Vogel and Sutter, students of the Vienna academy of art, formed the Order of St. Luke as an expression of their dissatisfaction with the teaching at the academy. In the fall of 1809, when the Vienna academy, which had been closed because of the war, was reopened,

Overbeck and Pforr, although not officially expelled, were refused readmission.

Overbeck and Pforr went to Rome in October 1809 and lived, beginning September 1810, in the deserted monastery San Isidoro on the Pincio, calling themselves the *Fratelli di San Isidoro.* They were joined later by Peter von Cornelius, Wilhelm von Schadow, Philipp Veit, Julius Schnorr von Carolsfeld, Johann Scheffer von Leonardshof, Joseph Ritter von Führich, Eduard von Steinle, Karl Begas and others. The name *Nazarener,* with ironic connotations, was given to the members of the group by other German artists in Rome who were somewhat annoyed with their religious zeal and with their efforts to renew art by means of ethical teaching. After the successful work of the group—the frescos in the *Casa Batholdy,* 1816; and in the *Casino Massimi,* 1817 to ca. 1830—the name gradually lost its ironic connotations; it is now used as a purely descriptive term.

The aim of the Nazarenes was a renewal of art on the basis of Christian (i.e., for them Roman Catholic) ideals and principles; they were opposed to the academies of art because, in their opinion, the teaching in the academies fostered superficiality and lacked the human and personal intimacy of the master-apprentice relationship which they considered to be a necessary basis for the teaching of the arts. The Nazarenes furthermore protested against the emphasis of purely artistic qualities and they held that art should primarily serve the expression of noble ideas (preferably religious). In order to achieve their aims the Nazarenes organized themselves into a group which was a combination of a monastic order and a medieval guild. In the beginning they took as their artistic example the works of the early German and Italian painters; later they were strongly influenced by Perugino, Raphael and Michelangelo. Stressing the collectivistic aspects of the medieval artists' guilds, they sacrificed part of their individuality in favor of the work of the group. Examples of works carried out in such a group spirit are the frescos in the *Casa Bartholdy,* 1816, since 1887 in the National Gallery, Berlin, and the frescos in the *Casino Massimi,* 1817—ca. 1830, Rome.

Many of the Nazarenes were appointed professors at German academies of art. However, their teaching met with just as much criticism as they (the Nazarenes) had once voiced against their own academic teachers. The reasons for the relatively quick decline of the Nazarene movement can be seen in the fact that the Nazarenes in their program over emphasized the moral and religious aspects of art and failed to recognize sufficiently the aesthetic and artistic aspects. The strict rules of the order of St. Luke, which were applicable to a small group of religiously inspired artists, were inapplicable to the larger institutions of the academies of art, and the Nazarenes had to compromise in their teaching in institutions which, after all, specialized in artistic training. Furthermore, the **Biedermeier** (q.v.) period was rather opposed to the romantic—heroic style of the Nazarenes and a fusion of their style with the Biedermeier art resulted in a compromise which, from the present-day point of view, was not too successful (see Düsseldorf, school of).

Ideas similar to those of the Nazarenes were taken up again by the Pre-Raphaelite Brotherhood (q.v. Pre-Raphaelite Brotherhood) and it is possible that the Pre-Raphaelites were influenced by the Nazarenes. See GERMAN ART; Margarete Howitt, *Friedrich Overbeck. Sein Leben und Schaffen,* 2 vols., 1886; Alfred Kuhn, *Peter Cornelius und die geistigen Strömungen seiner Zeit,* 1921; Fritz Herbert Lehr, *Die Blütezeit romantischer Bildkunst. Franz Pforr der Meister des Lukasbundes,* 1924.   —H.H.

Neapolitan school. See opera.

near-abstraction. See abstraction.

necking. Any small molding near the top of a column.

necklace. See JEWELRY.

negative carving (a technique in concave or sunk relief). This technique, because of its striking effects in achieving plastic form in low and very low relief, has been used since the Babylonian era. It is simply reversed carving in which the form is cut into a surface instead of projecting from a surface and may be used as a hollow relief or as the mold for a bas-relief. Especially suitable for smaller designs, it has been used successfully in the creation of medals, coins, plaques, relief portraits, sculptural jewelry and as a guide in glass engraving, to which it is related. It may be used in carving sculptural designs into ceramic molds; the technique allows the sculptor the creation of quick sketches of contemplated larger reliefs for the study of scale, composition, light and shade. It is possible to make rapid nature studies in negative carving, by working directly from the model and it could be used in certain types of illustration and commercial art through photographic reproduction. The usual material for negative carving is a smooth plaster surface of fine grain. (Harder to carve, but more precise is a slab of slate or lithographer's stone, for which hard, sharp tools are needed.) As tools on the plaster surface small plaster carving and retouching tools, gouges, scoops and rifflers may be used. Having explored this technique, the sculptor is well able to adapt some of his tools to this method by bending and filing them into more practical shapes.

The procedure is as follows: On the aforementioned plaster slab (slightly moistened) the outlines of the desired composition are traced or drawn in reverse, or mirror image. Throughout this procedure it must be remembered that design as well as form are created in reverse (by casting, the desired convex form will be attained). A design having an animal on the right side and a figure on the left, has to be traced and carved with the animal on the left and the figure on the right side; similarly, all lettering has to be reversed.

With larger sized tools one proceeds to scoop out the major parts of the figure (or figures, portrait, etc.) in their relative relief value and in order of size, so that the traced outline is not disturbed. (In a figure composition, the body, void of all detail, is scooped out, then follow arms, legs and head, all in their basically geometric form.) In order to check the relative depth of the various parts, a squeeze is made with moist clay or soft plasteline. For a clay squeeze, the plaster surface should be dry; for plasteline, it must be wet. During the procedure it is best to make as few squeezes as possible because of their tendency to smudge or grease the plaster. When satisfied with the general depth reached, or the plastic value of the crude forms, the details may be superimposed. Where arms, legs, draperies cut across a figure, the body must be well carved out before these parts can be carved. It is an important part of this technique that all forms are carved in order, according to size (for a head an egg-shaped form is scooped out, then details are cut into the egg-shape, as forehead, eyes, nose, mouth, etc.; or on a hand, the full part is carved before the fingers may be added).

When carving has progressed beyond the primitive stage, the work can be checked easily. The plaster is held up, allowing light to fall in on one side; closing one eye, the concave design will appear shortly as convex, an interesting optical illusion, which shows up errors at once. By checking in this manner it is possible to complete the work with only few squeezes.

After completion of the principal parts, final details, such as hair, draperies, clothing folds and other accessories are added. Where the edge around the design (circle, square, etc.) is to be raised, it should be carved in during early stages of the carving in order to avoid readjustments of the major parts. When the composition has been checked through a final squeeze, it can be cast like any plaster mold.

Because everything in this technique is reversed, some difficulty at first may be expected; once used to it, one can work rapidly. A clearness of form and precision of detail, difficult to obtain in other techniques, may be achieved.   —C.L.S.

negative volume. See SCULPTURE.

Neginoth. See JEWISH MUSIC.

Negro cubism. See AFRICAN NEGRO ART.

Negro Little Theatre. See AMERICAN NEGRO THEATRE.

Negro renaissance. See AMERICAN NEGRO ART.

Negro spiritual. Religious songs of American Negroes in syncopated rhythm, with naïve text.

Negro theatre movement. See AMERICAN NEGRO THEATRE.

neighborhood unit. See CIVIC PLANNING.

Neo-Bechstein piano. See electrical instruments.

Neo-classic architecture. A term applied to the revived classic architecture in Europe and the U. S. A. of the latter part of the 18th and early 19th cents. It is not to be regarded as a superficial or a reactionary manifestation, but one of profound and lasting consequences. The revelations of the archeologists of the 18th cent. in Spalato, Pompeii, Athens and elsewhere, and more particularly the publications of Stuart and Revett and the brothers Adam merely served to foster and orient the reaction against the expiring renaissance. The critical writings of Winkelmann and Lessing (1717-1768) had laid the intellectual foundation, and the actual contact with the age of Pericles established through the Elgin Marbles gave energy to the

movement, already apparent in the refined severity of the Louis XVI style and the revolutionary experiments of Ledoux and Boulee.

The earliest exponents of the neo-classic, Sir John Soane in England and Karl Schinkel in Germany were both men of very progressive ideas. Both were ardent advocates of contemporary planning for use and employed the neo-classic as a concession to the popular demand for a classical envelope. Soane's Bank of England and the Schinkel Museum in Berlin are inherent with a vitality which their exterior aspect is far from conveying.

In both England and Germany, however, the tendency swung from reality toward a purely archeological interpretation of classic forms. Smirke's British Museum and von Klenze's Pinakothek, Valhalla and Glyptothek in Munich have little to commend them other than the inevitable dignity of their classical envelope.

Nevertheless, H. L. Elmes in St. George's Hall, Liverpool, completed as late as 1854, embodies the most successful example of neo-classicism in England.

In France the neo-classic, except for Napoleon's Romanic buildings, remained free from the virus of archeology and displayed itself rather in a suave refining of lines and contrasts, the accentuation of the horizontal and the employment of the Greek orders not as a dominant note but secondary to the contemporary features of the design. Labrouste's Bibliotheque St. Genevieve and Hittorf's Gare du Nord (1863-4) bear witness to the vitality of the French neo-Grec.

But nowhere did the neo-classic find a more hospitable soil and flourish with a more genial adaptability to new conditions than it did in the 1st half of the 19th cent. in the U. S. A. In public buildings, such as the U. S. Treasury in Washington, the Patent Office, the Sub-Treasury in New York, it followed perhaps too closely the restraints of the temple form and, as in England and Germany, achieved a somewhat stilted and fortuitous dignity, but in the newly developing region from the Alleghenies to the Mississippi, from the Great Lakes to the Gulf of Mexico, the neo-Grec style was appropriated to the domestic requirements of the time. The old mansions of Natchez and such lovely examples as Berry Hill, Va., Andalusia, Philadelphia, the Boody House on Seneca Lake, the plantation houses near New Orleans, to mention but a very few, exhibit no casual affectation following a transitory fashion but constitute an expression of whole-hearted sincerity in the adoption of the canons of classic culture.

In our day we are no longer moved to embellish our homes with Greek columns, but the drift to simple forms, integrity of sur-face and continuity of line are a direct in-heritance from the refinement of taste incul-cated through the medium of the neo-classic style. See *Architecture Through the Ages,* Hamlin, 1940; *"An Outline of the Career of Sir John Soane," R. I. B. A. Journal,* Series 3, XXIX, 1921-22; *Domestic Architecture of the Early American Republic—The Greek Revival,* Howard Major, 1926.   —L.H.

Neo-classicism. A movement in painting, sculpture, and architecture, current in the last quarter of the 18th cent. and 1st half of the 19th cent., requiring the imitation of the outward form of Hellenic, Hellenistic, and Greco-Roman art and architecture. It was not truly classic in content, but on the contrary was romantic or academic. The forms were superficially analogous to those of late antiquity, however, and hence the term "pseudo-classic" is often used inter-changeably with neo-classic.

The movement was at its height during the French Revolution and the Napoleonic period. As the official and popularly ap-proved style, it fought the rise of rebellious romanticism from about 1820 to 1850, and thereafter throughout the 19th century re-mained entrenched in the academies of Eu-rope and America, opposing realism, impres-sionism, and post-impressionism as it had earlier defended itself against the heresy of romanticism.

Neo-classicism developed, in part, through the influence of 18th cent. antiquarianism and classical archeology, best personified in the German art historian Winckelmann. Politi-cally and culturally, it represented the reac-tion away from the luxury, license and aristo-cratic taste of the age of Louis XV, and was associated with the Spartan and stoical Ro-man virtues admired in the rise of the Third Estate during the French Revolution and the period of Napoleon. This admiration of an enviable era of the past was basically roman-tic, however; and in the illustrations of the heroic events and mythological incidents of antiquity, and in the imitation of ancient customs, dress, temples and triumphal arches, this romanticism of content is scarcely con-cealed by the pseudo-classic forms.

Hellenistic, Greco-Roman, and Roman pro-totypes were first used, and little distinction was made between Greek and Roman charac-teristics and qualities in art. As the 19th cent. progressed and knowledge of antiquity increased, the fashion changed gradually to an appreciation and comparatively feeble imi-tation of Hellenic forms.

Painters imitated antique sculpture since so little ancient painting was known. Extant examples at the time neo-classicism flourished were restricted almost exclusively to those paintings uncovered in partially excavated Pompeii. Some of the painters were also influenced by Italian High Renaissance and baroque artists, esp. Raphael and the Carracci. In contrast to romanticists, neo-classic paint-ers emphasized drawing and form rather than color and expression, and easily succumbed to academic formulae for success. The chief neo-classic painters were, in France, David, Ingres, Gérard, Guérin, Prud'hon, Couture, Chasseriau, Cabanel, Henner, Bouguereau; in England, Lord Leighton and Alma-Tadema; and in America, Allston, Thayer, Vedder and La Farge.

The major neo-classic sculptors include the Italian Canova, the Dane Thorwaldsen, Flax-man in England; in France, Pradier, Chau-det, Cortot, Bosio, Caldelari, David d'Angers (in part), Foyatier; in Germany, Dannecker and Schadow; in Sweden, Sergel; and in America, Powers, Greenough, Crawford, Hosmer, Palmer, Rogers and Rinehart.

In architecture, the forms of Roman tem-ples, basilicas, baths, and other public build-ings, and occasionally the forms of the Greek temple, propylaea, and stoa were adapted to all modern uses, whether for churches, banks, high schools, museums, legislative halls, town halls, railroad stations, palaces, or homes. Leading neo-classic architects include Vignon, Percier, Fontaine, Chalgrin, and Brogniard in France; Langhans, Schinkel, and Von Klenze in Germany; in England, Soane, Elmes, Hamilton, and Smirke; in Italy, Selva and Bianchi; and in America, Thomas Jeffer-son, Bullfinch, Hooker, Thornton, Hallet, and Latrobe, and even such contemporary archi-tects as Bacon and John Russell Pope. Many neo-classic architects, however, also worked in other styles on demand of the client. See FRENCH ART; FURNITURE.   —L.D.L.

neo-German school. *Mus.* Wagner and Liszt, and their followers.

neo-Gothic. See GERMAN ART; FURNI-TURE.

Neo-impressionism. A style founded by Seurat in the 1880's, involving the ultralogical and methodical use of the pointillist technique of applying paint as developed by the impressionists, and the rainbow brilliance of impressionist color, but emphasizing design and personal emotion rather than impressionist objectivity, and stressing the use of line, form, and color as a psychological science. The painting of Signac and Cross as well as of Seurat is termed neo-impressionist, but all fall under the more general classification of post-impressionism, of which neo-impressionism is one variety. See FRENCH ART.
—L.D.L.

Neo-plasticism. A Dutch geometric-abstract movement in painting, sculpture, interior decoration and poster design, founded in 1920 by Piet Mondrian as a phase of *de Stijl* (q.v.). —L.D.L.

neo-Renaissance. See POST-REVOLUTIONARY ARCHITECTURE AND DECORATIVE ARTS IN THE U. S. A.

neo-Romanesque. See POST-REVOLUTIONARY ARCHITECTURE AND DECORATIVE ARTS IN THE U. S. A.

neo-Sumerian art. See MESOPOTAMIAN ART.

neo-surrealisme. See FRENCH ART.

neo-traditionalism. See synthetism.

Neptune. See Poseidon.

Nereid. A sea-nymph, one of the many daughters of Nereus, a Greek sea-god.

Nergal. *Babyl. relig.* God of the midsummer sun.

nero-antico. A black marble thought to have come from ancient Laconia; discovered among fragments of Roman ruins.

NETHERLANDISH ART. The geographical area defined by the term Netherlands (Lowlands, Low Countries) corresponds roughly to the territory now occupied by the Kingdom of Belgium and the Kingdom of the Netherlands (also called Holland), bounded by France in the South, by Germany in the East, and by the North Sea in the West and North. Originally a more or less unified area in all essential respects, the Netherlands were politically and art-historically divided into two sharply separated countries by the end of the 16th cent., when the great revolution resulted in the final independence of the predominantly Protestant and democratic northern (Dutch) provinces from the Catholic-monarchic southern part. In art history, the latter can be largely identified with its Flemish-speaking provinces since the artistic achievements of the Latin part of its population (the Walloons) were comparatively negligible after ca. 1300. Differences of style are noticeable before that final separation of North and South but they hardly justify any strict division. Even after that, the deep racial and cultural kinship of the Dutch and the Flemish peoples (which is evidenced by their common language) resulted in a great number of affinities in their art which may also warrant their being treated under the same heading. The salient facts of the history of the two territories must be assumed to be familiar to the reader of this brief survey.

Middle Ages. In the early and high Middle Ages, the Netherlands reflected the art-historical situation of the great neighboring countries in varying measure, at the same time adding to it a small number of important features, with the southern part by far predominating. In architecture, significant contributions to various phases of the Romanesque style were made (Nivelles, Tournai). Sculpture, particularly bronze and goldsmith work, came to the fore with Renier de Huy and a number of shrines of the 12th and 13th cents. Great losses among works of the mural painters have focussed our attention on excellent book illuminations of the Romanesque period.

Greater independence was secured with the coming of the later Gothic age. The rising power and wealth of the middle classes account for a remarkable predominance of civic over religious architecture; town halls and guild halls of the southern Netherlands are the most important examples of that exuberantly decorative branch of Gothic architecture. In sculpture, a powerful synthesis of monumentality and realism was achieved in the works of Claus Sluter (late 14th cent.) altho most of them were done in Burgundy, i.e., in the homeland of the new rulers of the Netherlands. In painting, the years around 1400 saw the leadership of the Netherlandish book illuminators quickly and firmly established although here, too, the development is inextricably connected with southern (Italian and French) sources and with the patronage of French and Burgundian princes (the Brothers Limburg, Jacquemart de Hesdin).

In these works, the innate tendency of Netherlandish art toward straightforward, uncompromising observation and rendering of daily life and its implements according to their individual texture and to their varying appearance under changing conditions of light and spatial setting, emerged as the main source of modern painting of the North. In contrast to Italian Renaissance painting of the same period, this new "realism" of the 15th cent. was not supported by scientific and theoretical endeavors but remained essentially a matter of empirical approach. The southern area, more wealthy and powerful than the northern, continued to lead the way although a considerable number of its main masters immigrated from the North(and also from the East). Altar painting became the most decisive task (Ghent altar piece by the brothers van Eyck, 1432; Master of Flémalle, Rogier van der Weyden, Dirk Bouts, Hugo van der Goes, Hans Memling, Gerard David); portraiture made tremendous strides (same masters); other secular commissions increased. Book illumination continued important. Tapestries after designs of the great masters played a great role. What remains of the output of the northern provinces reveals a less homogeneous, highly individual production (Geertgen van Haarlem, Jerome Bosch). In the history of the graphic arts, Netherlandish engravings and woodcuts (particularly book illustration) hold a respectable place.

Sixteenth Century. Italian Renaissance principles proper were first introduced into Netherlandish painting by Quentin Massys whose role is comparable to Albrecht Dürer's in Germany, but much of the average production remained late-Gothic, often in indissoluble fusion with borrowings from the most recent Italian developments (Mannerism, q.v.). The tension resulting from the simultaneous influence of many Italian styles of the past and the present characterizes most of Netherlandish 16th cent. art. It took Netherlandish architecture a long time to go beyond casual assimilation of Italian Renaissance ornament and to penetrate to the principles of Renaissance architecture proper. Sculptors, too, combined northern tradition with Italian borrowings, the eventual result being something like an international mannerism after the middle of the cent. (Cornelis Floris). The development in painting was desultory. Specialization in various subjects started in the South although the North was eventually to profit most from it. Be-

sides portraiture (Massys, Mor, and the beginnings of group portraiture in the North), landscape became one of the most prominent fields (Patenier, Pieter Brueghel the Elder). Every-day-life (*genre*) painting reached great heights (Massys, Brueghel). Mythological representations became more popular. Religious painting continued important (B. van Orley, Brueghel) but in a vastly more individual spirit, even where the task remained ecclesiastical. Panel painting reigned supreme; tapestry work was still outstanding while book illumination declined. Engravings played an ever greater part. The uprising of the Protestants against the Catholic Spanish government was marked by great destruction of religious works of art, particularly in the North (1566), and when the opposition in the southern provinces weakened (after 1580), the differentiation between Dutch and Flemish painting became more obvious. In the Protestant North, altar painting was reduced to a negligible role, making room for a democratic art still controlled by guilds but primarily aiming at the edification and aesthetic satisfaction of the people while the Catholic-monarchic South largely continued the tasks set by the Church and the princes though the importance of civic enterprise should not be underrated.

Seventeenth Century. Separation into Flemish and Dutch art becomes inevitable here, at least as far as painting is concerned. Flemish architecture was overwhelmingly influenced by Italian models of the specifically baroque type, with the Jesuits playing a great role in church building; naturally, civic architecture was more outstanding in Holland, with work in brick gaining (Hendrick de Keyser), and became decidedly classicistic around 1650 (Jacob van Campen). Sculpture remained essentially of an international type everywhere (A. Quellinus, R. Verhulst), with few works exceeding average quality.

True to the monarchic-Catholic character of the southern constitution, Flemish art of the 17th cent. was dominated by the Catholic diplomat Pieter Paul Rubens whose leadership was uncontested throughout his life. Excelling in nearly every branch of painting, including altar and mural painting, absorbing the best of Italian art of the Renaissance and of the beginning baroque in a thoroughly integrated and essentially original fashion, he presents the sum total of Flemish baroque art with that robust exuberance which characterizes the national spirit but at the same time, with an aristocratic restraint, a scholarly cosmopolitanism, and, last but not least, in a synthesis of firm design and coloristic splendor entirely his own. His European reputation as well as his influence on European painting of all subsequent epochs, can hardly be overrated. Since his "best pupil", Anthony van Dyck, mainly a portraitist, lent the best efforts of his hypersensitive and elegant art to Italian and English sitters, Rubens dominated the scene in Flanders all the more effectively, and remarkable talents like Jacob Jordaens and Cornelis de Vos were hard put to it beside him. There was freer outlet for that genius of genre painting, Adriaen Brouwer, and his followers (D. Teniers), as well as for many specialists in landscape and still life painting who nevertheless did not achieve so great a distinction as did their Dutch contemporaries.

Compared with Flemish painting of the 17th cent., Dutch painting of the same period offers an infinitely more complex aspect, again in complete accordance with its different political and religious status. Our modern evaluation of a few Dutch artists (Rembrandt, Hals, Vermeer) as the greatest of their time, is a matter of historical perspective rather than of contemporary judgment. The immense variety of important artists, of distinctly differentiated art centers, and of subject matter, clearly reflects the democratic setup of the Protestant republic. The tasks of the painters were more numerous than elsewhere, calling for a host of specialists in each field. While Protestant religious painting was hardly popular enough to absorb the entire strength of any single artist, there were specialists in historical and mythological subjects, in landscape, seascape, animal, still life portrait, every-day-life, and architectural painting. There were even specialists in winter and moonlight landscapes, and specialists in painting *staffage* figures into other artists' landscapes. As to art centers, Amsterdam, Haarlem, Leiden, Delft, Utrecht vied with one another in richness and diversity of output. Mythological and historical painting found great encouragement from official sources and learned individuals, and was often desired for mural decorations (Amsterdam Town Hall). The main patronage in the other fields came from the public at large and concerned works to be hung on the walls of private homes, with the main exception of corporation portraits, a typical Dutch branch of painting fulfilling a democratic task par excellence. Undoubtedly, religious painting culminated in Rembrandt's non-sectarian profundity, with the Old Testament playing as great a role as might be expected from a representative of a nation which liked to parallel its own history to the history of the Jews, and from a man who lived in close contact with the Jewish community of Amsterdam. The beauty of their own country began to inspire Dutch landscape painters by the 2d decade of the cent. Their art passed through the diverse phases and trends of a more matter-of-fact (Jan van Goyen, Salomon van Ruysdael) and a more romantic interpretation (Rembrandt, A. Cuyp, Jacob van Ruisdael, Hobbema). After ca. 1645, interest centered more often on Italian scenery (Jan Both, N. Berchem). Portraiture ran the whole gamut between solid substantiality, the daring and often profound improvisations of Frans Hals, the great character studies of the mature Rembrandt, and the elegant flatteries of the *fin de siècle*. Genre subjects were sympathetically and simply viewed and either painstakingly or more broadly rendered by a host of great talents, with preference bestowed on the life of either the middle classes (Gerard Terborch, Vermeer van Delft, Pieter de Hooch), or of the lower classes (the brothers van Ostade), or of both, often with a touch of half mocking, half allegorical-moralistic goodnaturedness (Jan Steen). The outstanding names in seascape painting are Jan van de Cappelle and Willem van de Velde, in animal painting Paulus Potter, in architectural painting Pieter Saenredam and Emanuel de Witte. Only a word can be inserted on the formal problems and developments within this vast realm. The style of the most important masters is unmistakably Dutch, with comparatively few of the Italian reminiscences which were so characteristic of 16th cent. Netherlandish painting; it is sober without being trite or dry, usually less exuberant than the works of their Flemish contemporaries. Spatial freedom in indoor and outdoor scenes is a characteristic. The coloristic treatment varies from early multiplicity to monochrome tonality (most typical of the 2d quarter of the cent.) and to the use of Rembrandt's chiaroscuro or of more separate areas of contrasting colors (2d half), while the underlying design developed from corresponding multiplicity to greatly reduced and unified material and to a more restfully balanced composition with solid masses (mostclearly noticeable in landscape painting).

Even the shortest account of Netherlandish art of the 17th cent. must lay some emphasis on the line engravings and etchings produced at that time. Here again, Holland took the lead over Flanders where such contributions as van Dyck's *Iconography* (portraits of famous contemporaries) are rare. In the North, many landscapes (Hercules Seghers, Rembrandt, Ruisdael), as well as the religious works and the portraits by Rembrandt mark one of the greatest epochs in the history of etching. Among the works of the minor arts, Dutch ware (Delft) deserves especial praise.

Eighteenth Century. It has never been doubted that Netherlandish art suffered a wholesale decline during the 18th cent. The parallel to the political situation is again obvious. Imitation of foreign models became the rule rather than an exception. The classicistic theory and taste of the French artists of the court of Louis XIV had already made an inroad on late 17th cent. Netherlandish art (Gerard de Lairesse); it alternated with lame variations of the national heritage. This is true of architecture, sculpture, and painting, of the northern and the southern provinces alike; only a few genre painters (Cornelis Troost) and Dutch portraiture present a slightly more favorable aspect.

Nineteenth Century. Soon after the Napoleonic troubles, Belgium emerged as an independent nation (1830). Its architecture shares the defects characteristic of all European buildings of the time: eclecticism and bombast, until at its very end an important harbinger of new trends appeared in the person of Henri van de Velde. Sculpture produced nothing of outstanding merit until Constantin Meunier set the pace for greater sincerity in content and style. There was hardly more promise in painting until the advent of the painted and etched fantasies of James Ensor.

As to Holland, architecture and sculpture can be passed over in silence. But in painting, there was a more important movement which, though indebted to the national heritage of the 17th cent., produced works of unmistakable originality (Jan Bosboom, Josef Iraels, the three brothers Maris). It should not be forgotten either that the art of Vincent van Gogh belongs to his homeland at least as much as it does to his adopted country France.

Twentieth Century. While the promising developments in Belgian architecture of the late 19th cent. bore fruit outside rather than inside the boundaries of their homeland, Dutch modern architecture found its fulfillment at home in addition to making important contributions the world over. In fact, Dutch architecture, particularly in brick, has become a driving force in contemporary building but has primarily made Holland herself a "good place to live in" (Berlage, de Bazel, Dudok). In sculpture and painting, neither Holland nor Belgium have as yet excelled. See FLEMISH ART. MOST IMPORTANT SOURCES: Carel van Mander, *Het Schilder Boeck,* first ed. 1604, best modern ed. by H. Floerke, 1906, English ed. by C. van de Wall, 1936; Arnold Houbraken, *Groote Schouburgh der Nederlantsche Konstschilders en Schilderessen,* first ed. 1718-1721; see C. Hofstede de Groot, *Arnold Houbraken und seine "Groote Schouburgh" kritisch beleuchtet,* 1893; F. D. O. Obreen, *Archief voor Nederlandsche Kunstgeschiedenis,* 1877-1890; A. Bredius, *Künstler-Inventare,* 1915-1922; J. Denucé, *Bronnen voor de geschiedenis van de Vlaamsche Kunst,* 1931-1936 (also with English text); *Oud Holland* (periodical, since 1883). MOST IMPORTANT LITERATURE (comprehensive works only); A. von Wurzbach, *Niederländisches Künstlerlexikon,* 1906-1911; H. van Hall, *Repertorium voor de geschiedenis der Nederlandsche schilder-en graveerkunst sedert het begin der 12e eeuw tot het eind van 1932,* 1936; M. Rooses, *Art in Flanders,* 1914; St. Leurs e. a., *Geschiedenis van de Vlaamsche kunst,* 1936-1937; P. Fierens (ed.), *L'art en Belgique du moyen âge à nos jours,* 1939; H. E. van Gelder e. a., *Kunstgeschiedenis der Nederlanden,* 1936; J. J. van Ysendyck, *Documents classés de l'art dans les Pays-Bas,* 1880-1889; M. Laurent, *L'architecture et la sculpture en Belgique,* 1928; F. A. J. Vermeulen, *Handbook tot de geschiedenis der Nederlandsche bouwkunst,* 1928 ff., J. G. Wattjes, *Nieuw-Nederlandsche bouwkunst,* 1923-19. ; W. Vogelsang and M. van Notten, *Die Holzskulptur in den Niederlanden,* 1911-1912; D. Bierens de Haan, *Het houtsnijwerk in Nederland tijdens de Gothiek en de Renaissance,* 1921; G. Knuttel, *De Nederlandsche schilderkunst van Van Eyck tot Van Gogh,* 1938; M. J. Friedländer, *Die altniederländische Malerei,* 1924-1937; E. Heidrich, *Altniederländische Malerei,* 1910; M. Conway, *The van Eycks and their Followers,* 1921; F. Winkler, *Die altniederländische Malerei,* 1924; Fierens-Gevaert, *Histoire de la peinture flamande des origines à la fin du 15e siècle,* 1927-1929; E. Troche, *Painting in the Netherlands, 15th and 16th Centuries,* 1936; G. J. Hoogewerff, `*De Noord-Nederlandsche schil-*

derkunst (14th-16th cent.), 1936-1938; A. W. Bijvanck and G. J. Hoogewerff, *La miniature hollandaise,* 1922-1925; A. W. Bijvanck, *La miniature dans les Pays-Bas septentrionaux,* 1937; Comte P. Durrieu, *La miniature flamande au temps de la cour de Bourgogne,* 1921; F. Winkler, *Flämische Buchmalerei des 15. und 16. Jahrhunderts,* 1925; E. Fromentin, *Les maitres d'autrefois,* 1876; W. Bode, *Great Masters of Dutch and Flemish Painting,* 1909; M. J. Friedländer, *Die niederländische Malerei des 17. Jahrhunderts,* 1923; E. Heidrich, *Vlämische Malerei,* 1913; R. Oldenbourg, *Die flämische Malerei des 17. Jahrhunderts,* 1921; É. Michel, *Flemish Painting in the 17th Cent.,* 1939; C. Holstede de Groot, *Beschreibendes und kritisches Verzeichnis der Werke der hervorragendsten holländischen Maler des 17. Jahrhunderts,* 1907-1928 (English translation: *Catalogue of Dutch Painters,* contains only 8 instead of 10 vols.); F. Roh, *Holländische Malerei,* 1921; W. Martin, *De Hollandische schilderkunst in de 17e eeuw,* 1935-1936; P. Lambotte (ed.), *Histoire de la peinture et de la sculpture en Belgique 1830-1930,* 1930; G. H. Marius, *Dutch Painting in the 19th Cent.,* 1908; F. M. Hübner, *Die neue Malerei in Holland,* 1921; H. Goebel, *Tapestries of the Lowlands,* 1924; G. T. van Ysselsteyn, *Tapestry Weaving in the Northern Netherlands,* 1936; F. G. Waller, *Biografisch woordenboek van Noord-Nederlandsche graveurs,* 1938; A. J. J. Delen, *Histoire de la gravure dans les anciens Pays-Bas,* 1924-1935; M. J. Schretlen, *Dutch and Flemish Woodcuts of the 15th Cent.,* 1925; W. Nijhoff, *Nederlandsche houtsneden 1500-1550,* 1931-1935; K. Zoege von Manteuffel, *Die niederländische Radierung,* 1925; M. D. Henkel, *Le dessin hollandais des origines au 17e siècle,* 1931. F. Lugt, History of Art, in: *The Contribution of Holland to the Sciences,* 1943.   —W.S.

net pattern. A decorative pattern of lines crossing each other at regular intervals to make regular openings as in a woven mesh; used frequently on Greek pottery and in Roman mosaics.   —L.T.S.

netsuke (Jap.). Ornamented toggle fastened at the end of the cord by which the *inro* (q.v.), was suspended from the belt. The *netsuke* was slipped under, and over the top of, the belt to hold the *inro* in place at the side of the wearer.   —J.A.M.

Neudeutsche Renaissance. See New German Renaissance.

Neue Sachlichkeit. See New Objectivity.

NEW ATTITUDES FOR THE FUTURE OF ARCHITECTURE. The cataclysmic world in which we live today is of particular significance and consequence to both educators and practitioners in the field of American architecture. American society will be considerably shaken by the impact of the world-wide shock of the war and will be affected accordingly. The post-war adjustments which will be necessary in America will create certain new social patterns which will be considerably different from those to which we have become accustomed in the past. The future of American architectural education and practice is clearly related to these new patterns; they are of serious import to every one now engaged in architecture.

It is the purpose of this article to review some of the important relationships existing between architectural education, professional practice and the broad needs of society, and also to suggest a program which can be established to better train and equip those engaged in architecture for the new problem of our post-war society. It is imperative that definite action be taken now toward such ends if architecture is to survive and remain under its present leadership.

The future of American architecture rests upon the shoulders of the men of vision in education and practice wherever they may be. Their prime responsibility is to endeavor to meet the problems with broad and intelligent planning and with the promptness the situation demands. Architecture has had a useful place and purpose in society through the ages and has contributed much to the well being of society. The future of architecture, under planning, is bright, it can again be the source of great good for mankind; but to be most useful in the future it must have new curricula, new professional viewpoints and above all else "new attitudes". These are the basic tools for approaching the important new opportunities which lie ahead in a better planned American society.

A brief examination of the present conditions and the trends for the future should convince the most obdurate, that their status as educators and practitioners has been fundamentally affected. New responsibilities will be imposed upon both these closely allied groups by society; and architecture's relationship to the whole pattern will be markedly different from that of the past. The architectural educator and the practitioner must realize what the differences are, what the new responsibilities imply, and prepare those engaged in architecture to meet such obligations for the best interests of future American society and architecture.

These changes, because of their scope and nature, point toward a broad study, clear understanding, and use of the concepts underlying the social, economic, and political structure of our country. This changed direction in architectural thinking and practice is a new route to follow but it will lead to a sound basic premise for better and closer integration of the efforts of the architectural educator and the practitioner than has obtained in the past and an indispensable aid to solving their mutual problems for the future.

The ultimate objective of American architectural education has always been to train and equip the student with the knowledge and use of the essential tools required for a future professional place in architecture. Architectural curricula have always been planned for and were dependent on the broad needs of the architectural profession. Usually these curricula emphasized design and planning, and the problems of design and planning usually centered upon special types of buildings in limited fields. Varying lesser degrees of importance were given to the engineering and cultural subjects. Too often these collateral subjects were covered insufficiently, and they usually did not bear any particular relationship to the design and planning previously mentioned. One might charitably state that they satisfied the requirements for a college degree and the permission to apply for examination to the state board of registration three years after graduation. The far-reaching needs of society, if sketched at all, were only briefly presented through a study of the history of former civilizations. The study of modern society and its problems were not usually included. Consequently, the student's knowledge of architecture was specialized in design and planning. A broad knowledge of the problems of contemporary society was not obtainable in his college course, and unless he gleaned information from other sources he remained uninformed.

As the architectural curricula were dependent upon the broad needs of the architectural profession, likewise was the architectural profession dependent upon the broad needs of society. Unfortunately for architecture, society's needs were never clearly understood by the profession. The practitioner was himself a designer, planner and business man concerned primarily with highly specialized building types, and was not prepared for nor specially interested in the wider aspects of building for society. This attitude of the profession was naturally reflected in the curricula of the architectural schools.

The opportunities of the profession have not always been the same. They have varied considerably according to the stability or instability of the social, economic and political structure of the moment. Naturally when society was stable and prosperous the profession and the architectural schools were crowded with workers, at other times both groups suffered equally. Most of the hardships were caused by failure in the understanding of these social phenomena. The profession has always been unprepared to cope with change. Being technical specialists in mind and heart, with useful skills and knowledge of great merit and useful purpose, the profession has seemed content to rest upon such accomplishments and endure the periodic readjustments. That they were rather narrowly informed about the broad needs of society and what the true purposes of the profession were in relation to society seemed never to penetrate the profession's consciousness. Such a state of unpreparedness in the profession and lack of progressive educational curricula in architectural schools cannot again be tolerated for the future continuation of architecture in American society.

The United States has now entered another cycle of change which for severity, duration, scope and responsibility promises to be the greatest shock of all time to architectural education and practitioners. It is necessary that both groups understand the pending upheavals and plan for the essential adjustment, readjustment and reorientation of their course of action.

It will be necessary to prepare and equip those engaged in architecture to serve the larger needs of society first. The specialized skills which are already at hand can then be usefully employed to better advantage. The future of the architect calls for great collaboration with others in related fields. The degree of individualism which he enjoyed in the past is reduced, he will collaborate with the city planner, the engineer, landscape architect, lawyer, banker and many others. The future of architecture lies in the field of great public works of national, regional, state and city scope. Therefore the architect must prepare himself to fit into the technical groups involved. He may be the coordinator, the leader, the planner or he may serve in some other capacity. This experience will be considerably different from that of the past, where he dealt only with the problems of the specific or single building type; there will be a splendid opportunity to concentrate on the planning of the group, neighborhood, city, region or state problems.

The architectural schools can contribute much to the understanding of social concepts, in fact some of the schools have already initiated programs in that direction and others are in the process of planning such curricula. Where such planning is not under way it should be begun at once. Most colleges and universities have departments of social, economic and political science. The faculties of those sciences should become a part and be integrated with the architectural curriculum. From the time the freshman enters the architectural school to his acceptance in the professional field, eight years have elapsed. Within that long period he should not be trained in the usual architectural skills alone, but he should also learn how society functions, how to plan for the changes, so that he may emerge a thoroughly trained unit to take his place in society.

The architectural schools in conjunction with social studies faculties could make immediate plans for classes in social planning for the architect now engaged in professional practice, to put him in closer touch with the changes which are taking place. It is almost imperative that this be the first step in the planning of architectural curricula, because the practitioner is immediately confronted with the problem of gainful employment and if properly informed would be immediately available and very valuable in the planning effort for early post-war activities now undergoing nation-wide study. All curricula for the architectural schools should be planned now for the broad training which its students will require when they return from their war service. Such planning for the future and preparation for the reorientation of the practicing architect would usefully employ the architectural and social studies faculties for a long time to come. Curricula for restoration of the practitioner need not be confined to architecture alone; why not include the engineer, lawyer, landscape architect, banker and realtor? All of these are closely related to architecture and society, but have seldom been brought together in a logi-

cally planned manner for a viewing of their interrelated and common problems.

The new curricula should include plans for non-professional education along similar lines. The public has always been slow to appreciate the services of the architect. There are some difficulties involved with the proposed new curricula, but they are not insurmountable. The faculties of our architectural schools must also realize that they must be trained in the broad concepts of society. They must quickly become informed and qualified to teach the subjects in relation to the architectural aspects of social problems. The task for the faculties to learn and to prepare for such teaching must be undertaken now if they are to make such courses available for the architects in time to be useful to them. The new curricula for the architectural schools should be prepared and ready when the students return from war.

Everyone concerned with the problems of architectural education and architectural practice must realize the tremendous advances and contributions which have already been made toward greater social security. The planning of the nation's resources are not temporary measures, and are on a scale never before attempted. Naturally they set the pattern for the future. They have laid new responsibilities on all of the professions, architecture must assume its share. The obvious course is to study the new patterns. The architectural schools must include these topics in their curricula, the architect must reorient his viewpoint; both must adopt "New attitudes".   —R.A.F.

New English Art Club. See ENGLISH ART.

New German Renaissance. See GERMAN ART.

new localism, the. Vachel Lindsay, U. S. A. poet, announced under this title a program of action and aesthetics in *Vision, A Quarterly Journal of Aesthetic Appreciation of Life* (1912). Art, he declared, must become American, democratic, individualistic, and local by throwing off the influence of Europe and by using the opportunities of the growing public school system to "bring an exquisite sensibility and powerful beauty-making faculty among common men". Many of Lindsay's poems reflect this doctrine. See Edgar Lee Masters, *Vachel Lindsay*, 1935.
                                              —H.R.W.

New Music, the. See MUSICAL PER-FORMANCE, MAIN TRENDS IN.

New Negro Movement, the. See AMERI-CAN NEGRO ART; AMERICAN NE-GRO LITERATURE.

new objectivity (*Neue Sachlichkeit,* some-times also called *Magischer Realismus,* magic realism). A phase of modern German art which (ca. 1922) follows Expressionism (q.v.). The term was introduced by G. F. Hartlaub in 1923 as the name of an exhibi-tion which was planned for the fall of 1923, but which had to be postponed and which was held at the Mannheim *Kunsthalle* in 1925. The artists of the New Objectivity consid-ered themselves in strong opposition to the Expressionists whose work they believed to be too fantastic and irrational. The New-Ob-jectivists requested an "objective" (*sachlich*) approach to the world in which the modern artist lives. It has been said that New Ob-jectivism is a reactionary movement going back to the depicting of natural forms. While it is obvious that Dix, Kanoldt, or Hofer go back to nature, it must be observed that their smooth, painstakingly accurate and care-fully modelling technique is applied to a dif-ferent concept of nature. Underneath the natural forms which Alexander Kanoldt se-lects for his still-lifes, the cacti, rubber trees, flower pots, etc., there seems to be discernible the basic geometric shapes of cube, cylinder, globe, etc., to which the plants, etc., are re-ducible (and in contrast to impressionistic painting the objects are not fused with the surrounding atmosphere). To a lesser de-gree this holds true for the art of Karl Hofer, who among the German artists comes perhaps closest to the work of Cézanne. Georg Schrimpf builds up his figures in a manner similar to that of Kanoldt (e.g., *Sleeping Girls,* 1926), but in his later land-scapes he modifies his objectivism in favour of simple lyrical qualities. Otto Dix and George Grosz use a painstakingly and some-times almost microscopically correct technique to analyze and to depict mercilessly their hu-man models (e.g., Dix, *The Artist's Parents,* 1921; Grosz, *Portrait Dr. Neisse,* 1927) or they show with brutal frankness the horrors of war (Dix) ' or the wrongs of society (Grosz). Max Beckmann's work shows a change from heavy plastic and often fantastic compositions (e.g., *Balloon Acrobats,* 1925) to a style of painting more colorful and lighter in the treatment of forms (e.g., *Quappi,* 1937).

In architecture, design of furniture, etc., the New Objectivism emphasized simplicity of line and the function of useful objects as the all-important criteria. See GERMAN ART; also *Modern German Painting and Sculpture,* Museum of Modern Art, New York, 1931; F. Roh, *Nachepressionismus,* 1925; B. Taut, *Die neue Wohnung,* 1928, 5th ed.; F. Schmalenbach, "The Term *Neue Sachlichkeit*", *The Art Bulletin,* vol. XXII, No. 3, (Sep-tember 1940), pp. 161-165. —H.H.

New Year's cards. See ninshō.

niche (It. *nichhio,* shell). A recess generally within the thickness of a wall.

niello-work. See metalwork.

Niflheim. *Norse myth.* The northern region of cold and darkness.

niggling. Minute and very careful workman-ship, esp. on unimportant detail.

night piece. A picture of a scene at night.

Nigun. See JEWISH MUSIC.

nimai tsuzuki (Jap.). See diptych.

nimbus. *A. Circular nimbus or Halo*: A symbol of light and glory, surrounding the head. The term *nimbus* in the meaning of a cloud of light first occurs in Virgil, but the idea is at least as old as Homer. In classical art the nimbus and more rarely the aureole (q.v.) were sometimes attributed to divine or deified persons, particularly in paintings. Divinities connected with light, such as Helios, etc., were given the nimbus more often than others, but there was no strict rule. The oldest certain examples of round nimbi are to be found in the paintings of Apulian vases of the 4th cent. B.C. There they usu-ally consist of several concentric rings of light, with rays radiating from the periphery. Kindred attributes were circles of rays or diadems or crowns with rays. The nimbus as a simple disk first occurs in the frescoes of Pompeii; various light colors, not yellow or white only, are used, which makes it clear that it is not the sun or moon that are rep-resented, but rather an aura of light which has its source in the person whose heads its surrounds. Now it can be observed that the Roman painters gave nimbi esp. to those figures of gods or heroes who have an ar-tistically prominent role in the composition of the pictures. It seems therefore possible that the original form of the halo as a "cloud" of light, consisting of different spheres and ending in rays, was transformed into its later disk-like shape under the influence of the *clipeus* (q.v.) or round shield which was the characteristic background used by the Romans for the portraits, in color or relief, of famous men and later of ancestors, heroes and emperors, and which by the early Christians was transferred to Christ and his saints, like the nimbus itself.

The hypothesis which would derive the nimbus from circular rings around the heads of statues, meant to protect them from birds and from damage in general, need no longer be taken seriously.

In Christian art, from the 2d quarter of the 4th cent. onward, the circular nimbus was given to Christ, the Lamb of God and the Phoenix (symbol of resurrection). From the 5th cent. it was given also to angels, apostles and saints and to the Virgin. The nimbus of Christ was soon differentiated from the other nimbi, by placing a cross on the nimbus itself. From the 5th and regularly from the 6th cent. the nimbus with inscribed cross, the so-called **cross-nimbus**, became *the* attribute of Christ in art.

A short time before the adoption of the circular nimbus into Christian art it had become an attribute of the Roman emperors, and as such it appears occasionally in the 3d cent., regularly from the time of Constantine the Great. It was from the imperial images, not from the pagan gods, that the nimbus was transferred to Christ as the highest ruler. Biblical passages about the supranatural splendour of the face and head of Christ or God may however have contributed to the adoption of the nimbus by the Christians. In the Byzantine sphere of influence the nimbus remained an attribute not only of Christ and the saints, but also of emperors, and occasionally of other important persons as well as of allegorical and mythological figures.

The oldest nimbi in Indian and Iranian art are comparatively late; see for instance the nimbi of Indo-Bactrian Kings of the 1st cent. B.C., in their coins, the nimbed Buddhas of Gandhara art, and some figures in Seleucid-Parthian and in Sassanian stone reliefs. It is therefore scarcely possible to adopt the idea that the Greco-Roman or the Christian nimbus originated in India or Persia. For later examples of Persian and Indian nimbi and aureoles and their possible relation to Iranian and Indian light-worship see Ramsden, Coomaraswamy and Travenor-Perry.

B. Square Nimbus: This attribute, much more limited in scope and much rarer than the halo, is no nimbus in the proper sense of the word, as it has nothing to do with the symbolism of light. In the older examples it is either a square or rectangular full surface of blue or greenish-blue color or a dark-colored frame-line of approximately square shape. While in classical and in late-medieval and modern art the position of the round nimbus is not unfrequently adapted to that of the head, the square nimbus (like the polygonal one) always remains parallel to the background. There are no surviving examples of square nimbi in sculpture (it should however be observed that in the case of the circular nimbus it has been proved by Krücke [*Zeitschrift fur neutestamentliche Wissenschaft*] that the latter was sometimes painted on the background of reliefs).

There are two principal regions and periods in which the square nimbus occurs: (a) Rome and Monte Cassino, whence it spread to various parts of the Christian west. Its first certain appearance in this zone is around 700 A.D.; after the 13th cent. it is no longer in use. (b) Christian Egypt, where it is found in Coptic frescoes of the 6th cent. (Bawit, Saqqara). There is, however, the strong possibility of an earlier occurrence in the catacomb of Karmouz near Alexandria, in a fresco probably dating from the 3d century. This case would not be unique, as there is at least one certain instance of the square nimbus in the 3d century Synagogue frescoes of Dura-Europos on the Euphrates, where it surrounds the head of the white-haired man, to the left of the central panel on the west wall, who probably is Moses or Abraham; Alexandrian Judaism might form the link between Egypt and Dura. A late Coptic example of the square nimbus, probably dating from the 12th cent., is to be found in *Deyr Ambâ Hadra* ("St. Simeon") near Assuan.

The square nimbi of group (a) were used to distinguish contemporary, saintly and important persons, such as Popes, founders of churches, etc.; after the 9th cent. this meaning of the square nimbus was no longer always understood. The square nimbi of group (b) had their origin in rectangular set-offs of the portraits on late-antique mummy-shrouds. By at least about 200 A. D. these set-offs seem to have been connected with symbolical ideas concerning the perfection of the square and rectangle. Thus the square nimbi of Coptic art and perhaps also of early medieval Roman art were symbols of perfection. The diffusion of the symbol from Egypt to Rome occurred during a period of strong oriental influence in papal Rome. Concerning the allegedly earliest occurrence of square nimbi in Rome during the pontificates of Gregory the Great (590-604) or even Liberius (352-66) see my above mentioned article, where the untenable hypothesis that the Roman square nimbi originally were imitations of portrait-panels or super-imposed layers of stucco in fresco-portraits, is likewise discussed.

C. Polygonal Nimbi: Lozenge-shaped and hexagonal nimbi appear from the end of the 13th cent. onward, esp. in Italian painting, (but see also the reliefs of the virtues on Andrea Pisano's bronze door of the Baptistery of Florence). These nimbi are symbols of light, painted in gold like the round haloes. They are usually given either to allegorical figures such as the Franciscan virtues on the vaults of the lower church of S. Francesco at Assisi, or to persons of the Old Testament. But sometimes Christ Himself or, more frequently, God the Father has a lozenge-shaped nimbus (see for instance God the Father in Raphael's *Disputà*). Beside the lozenge-shaped and hexagonal nimbi, regarding the symbolism of which some suggestions are advanced in my article on the square nimbus, there exist also some examples of octagonal nimbi in Catalonian paintings of the 15th cent., in which some Old Testament figures are thus shown. See, CLASSICAL ART: L. Stephani, *Nimbus und Strahlenkranz in den Werken der alten Kunst, Mémoires de l'Académie Impériale des Sciences de St. Petersbourg,* Série 6, vol. 9, 1859; K. Keyssner, Pauly-Wissowa, *Real-Encyclopädie der klassischen Altertumswissenschaft. Neue Bearbeitung,* vol. 17, 1, 1936. CHRISTIAN ART: A. N. Didron, *Iconographie chrétienne. Histoire de Dieu,* 1843; A. Krücke, *Der Nimbus und verwandte Attribute in der frühchristlichen Kunst,* 1905 and in *Zeitschrift für neutestamentliche Wissenschaft* 30, 1937; J. Sauer, *Symbolik des Kirchengebäudes,* 1924; E. Weigand, *Byzantinische Zeitschrift* 30, 1930 and 32, 1932; H. Leclercq, *Dictionnaire d'archéologie chrétienne et de liturgie* 12, 1, 1935; G. B. Ladner, The So-called Square Nimbus, *Medieval Studies* 3, 1941 and 4, 1942. EASTERN ART: J. Tavenor-Perry, *The Burlington Magazine,* 12, 1907-8; E. H. Ramsden, ibid., 78, 1941; A. K.

Coomaraswamy, *History of Indian and Indonesian Art,* 1927; A. U. Pope and Ph. Ackerman, *A Survey of Persian Art,* 4, 1938, pl. 133 B, 153 A, 160 A.   —G.B.L.

ninsho (Jap.). Decorative New Year's greeting cards.

norvāna. See INDIAN ART.

nise-e (Jap.). Portrait painting.

nishiki (Jap.). Brocade.

nishiki-e (Jap.). A color print. *Nishiki*—brocade; *e*—picture, hence a brocaded (or colorful) picture.

No (Jap.). A Japanese classical dance; a lyrical drama-dance. See Nōgaku; JAPANESE ART; THEATRE.

nocturne. *Mus.* "Night piece"; the term for a composition of a dreamy or sentimental character, introduced by Field.

node. See ACOUSTICS.

Nogaku (Jap.). A Japanese classical dance; a lyrical drama-dance performed on a stage peculiar to itself by men rigidly trained in formal steps and postures and in the subtle intoning and chanting of the poetry and prose of the plays. Traditional sculptured masks are worn by the principal actors; and the costumes are of classic formality. The subject-matter of the *Nō* dramas is philosophic, religious or historical. See *A Glimpse of Japanese Ideals,* Jiro Harada, 1937, *The Nō Plays of Japan,* Arthur Waley, 1922; *Nōgaku: Japanese Nō Plays,* Beatrice Lane Suzuki, 1932.   —J.A.M.

non-conforming use. See CIVIC PLANNING.

non-objective painting (Fr. *non-figuratif*). The term "non-objective" is supposed to have been used for the first time by the Russian Alexander Rodchenko. Kasimir Malevich, another Russian, is said to have been the first to concentrate on entirely abstract, non-objective paintings (which he called suprematist) in 1913. Non-objectivity, young as it is, may easily change its name before it will have its ultimate denomination, yet for the time being the term "non-objective" has been rather generally accepted, even while many artists are opposed to a non-name which they do not consider constructive enough. Yet more significant than its name is the complete reversal of its philosophy of art in comparison to the older forms, surrealism included. Its basis is the utmost purity of pictorial means inasmuch as it wants to give a work built up entirely on its own merits and laws, to be a unique creation in its own space, not intellectually associable to anything else in the world. The non-objectivist uses his medium, line and color, not to portray any happening, historical scene, still-life, portrait or anything else, but, like the composer, to create freely following his intuition without introducing light and shadow, perspective, texture, psychological features or resemblance. Up till now three different styles can be distinguished: a free style, sample of which is Kandinsky's *The White Edge* (1913), a strongly architectural style, like Bauer's *The Holy One* (having inspired the theme center of the New York World's Fair, 1939) and very recently a lyrical style, developed also by Bauer, a sample of which is *Spirituality* (1938).

The non-objective creation can only be viewed in its oneness and is not to be compared to any other creation; it can only be taken as a work whose intentions are harmony, beauty and order. It is self-evident that the education of our eye through the centuries does not allow us to jump from our most materialistic level to non-objectivity in a day. The patient onlooker will discover how, slowly, he will derive more and more pleasure from the consummation of non-objective work and he will feel his soul getting the wave-length of it more and more, until it finally swings in the same accord.

Most of the members of the American Abstract Artists have progressed from abstraction to non-objectivity. The industrialist Solomon R. Guggenheim has endowed a Foundation of Non-objective Art in New York, incorporated under New York State laws on June 25, 1937, and has opened a museum at 24 East 54th Street in New York City devoted exclusively to the exhibition of non-objective art.

A large number of works at the Gallery of Living Art (New York University) is non-objective.

The most outstanding masters of non-objective painting are Wassily Kandinsky, who started to work "concrete" in 1911, and Rudolf Bauer, living in the U. S. A. since 1939. Other important non-objectivists are: Otto Nebel, Ladislaus Moholy-Nagy (Director of the School of Design, Chicago), Charles G. Schwab, Fernand Leger, Jean Xceron a n d Penrose Centurian. S e e

Art of tomorrow, Catalogue of the S. R. Guggenheim Foundation, N. Y., 1939; Catalogue, Gallery of Living Art (N. Y. Univ.), 1940; American Abstract Artists, Yearbook 1938, 1939; Wassily Kandinsky, *The Art of Spiritual Harmony,* Boston, 1914 and *XXe Siècle,* Paris, March, 1938; *Abstraction-creation, art non-figuratif,* Yearbook, Paris, 1932-35; Bill, Max, Über konkrete Kunst, *Das Werk,* Zurich, Aug. 1938; Armitage, Merle, *So-called Abstract Art,* N. Y., 1939; Cheney, Sheldon, *A Primer of Modern Art,* N. Y.　　　　　　　　　　　　　—H.F.K.

non-strophic song. See song.

nook. A recess, as in a wall.

Nordic style. Term used to describe the art of Teutonic, Celtic, Anglo-Saxon and other Northern barbaric peoples of the Middle Ages, characterized in style by a dynamic, linear expressionism often suggesting a chained or suppressed psychic energy, and in subject matter by a preference for animal motives. It contrasts stylistically with Latin illusionism (q.v.) and with Byzantine symmetrical design, balance, proportion, and restraint. One may cite as examples Celtic and Anglo-Irish illuminated manuscripts from the 8th to 12th cent., some French Carolingian illumination (e.g., School of Rheims), and much German Carolingian and Ottonian art.

In the broad sense the term "Nordic" may be used to describe that art of the Romanesque, Gothic, and Renaissance periods in Northern countries, in which the barbaric, dynamic, psychically-energized style dominates in the fusion with illusionism and Byzantine design, which takes place in Northern European art from the Romanesque period on. Thus, German Gothic architecture, sculpture, and painting are dominantly "Nordic", as are Dürer, Grünewald, and Altdorfer in German Renaissance painting. The term is synonymous with the original meaning of the word "Gothic", as referring to the barbarians of the North rather than as the designation of a historical period; and though the word "Gothic" did not originally have a connotation so precise as "Nordic" has today, the two words are now often used interchangeably.

In Nazi Germany the term "Nordic" has been misused in art to describe 19th cent. international naturalism and popular romanticism (qq.v.), which the Nazis erroneously consider the native idiom or racial style of their local ancestors.　　　　　　　　　—L.D.L.

normal illumination. See COLOR.

normal modes of vibration. See ACOU-STICS.

Norse art. See SCANDINAVIAN ART.

Northern school (of Chinese painting). See CHINESE ARTS.

Northwest Coast Indian art. The Northwest Coast Indians occupy the rugged, heavily timbered coastal fringe of British Columbia and southeastern Alaska. The chief tribes are the Nootka, Kwakiutl, Bella Coola, Haida, and Tsimshian in Canada, and the Tlingit and part of the Haida in Alaska. Little is known of the prehistoric era, but much may be inferred from the rich, spectacular culture attained in the 19th cent., largely through the acquisition of metal tools from the white man. The use of the new tools seems not so much to have changed the pattern of the culture as to have broadened its scope and improved its quality. On this coast nature is prolific for a hunting and fishing people. Game, plentiful on land and sea, and timber from the heavy forests of red cedar that cover the mountains, provided the materials for food, clothing, houses, and all the needs of daily and ceremonial life. Social patterns, which involved heraldic display of prestige and wealth, religious, especially Totemic, beliefs, and a vast store of legends were basic in their art expression. Thus it emphasized representation, though in highly conventionalized form, and at the same time subjected the content rigidly to the requirements of organization within a space. In design the curved line is predominant except where the medium demands angularity, as in basketry.

The woodcarving of these Northwest tribes was not only their most important art but one of the highest manifestatoins of the craft in the Americas. In neolithic times, that is, before the first appearance of the white man in 1774 A.D., stone sculpture, carved with stone tools, massive and conventional representations of totemic animals, served as a prelude to the great florescence following on the introduction of steel tools, which enabled the artist to make freer use of his abundant timber: houses with carved ports, totem poles (q.v.), carved canoes, chests, food dishes and innumerable other articles of daily living, and masks for ceremonial purposes. The style varied somewhat among the tribes; it was weaker in the south, reached

a climax of power among the Haida, and gradually merged in the north into the walrus carvings of the Eskimo. Still, it had some common characteristics. Its content derives partly from man and partly from native creatures—the killer whale and shark, the beaver, bear, wolf and frog, the raven, hawk and eagle. While some of the human figures approach naturalism, the animals and birds are represented in a unique convention that has nothing to do with the illusion of natural appearance. On the contrary, the intention is to lay out on a surface all the parts of the creature, some seen in front view and some in profile, and at the same time to organize these parts into the space to be filled. To differentiate the parts, carvings are painted and sometimes inlaid with abalone shell. Masks for purposes of ritual and entertainment and for the dramatization of legends reached a high level of imaginative power and were ingeniously contrived so that beak, eyelids and jaw were movable and could be manipulated by strings so as to create varying effects.

Another material used with skill was the horn from mountain goats and sheep, which was softened, moulded into dishes and ladles, and carved and engraved in the same general style seen in wood carving, with, however, due regard to the difference of material.

Painting served the same function as carving—to display ancestry and illustrate legends for a people with no system of writing, and to decorate; and it followed the same general style except for a greater fluidity in execution due to the medium. The rectangular wooden houses with low, sloping roofs and few openings offered large areas for painting, both outside and inside. These paintings, when on the façade of the house, together with the carved and painted totem poles set up in front, doubly emblazoned the social rank of the owner. In like manner the sides of the great canoes were carved or painted with totemic emblems.

Since no pottery was made, baskets were important as containers. They were made entirely by the women, of roots, grasses and stems, by a tight twining technique. They are cylindrical in shape and are decorated with bands of geometric patterns made of colored grasses used not structurally in the twining but like embroidery or brocading.

Another craft of the women was weaving, though on designs furnished by the men. Notable are the long fringed blankets of the Chilkat, a subdivision of the Tlingit. They were worn like capes in a ceremonial costume which included, in the case of a chief, an elaborate headdress of carved wood decorated with shell and ermine, and painted leather kilt and leggings to which were affixed bits of bone and ivory that would clink with each movement. The blankets were woven of wool and cedar bark on a loom with an upper beam only and hence a loose warp. The designs, in black, white, yellow and green, show the same kind of conventionalization as that found in the carvings and paintings. See Franz Boas, *Primitive Art*, 1927; Frederic H. Douglas, *Northwest Coast Indians,* Denver Art Museum Leaflet No. 1, 1937; *Types of Indian Masks,* Denver Art Museum Leaflet, Nos. 65-66, 1940; George T. Emmons, *The Chilkat Blanket,* American Museum of Natural History, Memoirs, vol. III, 1907; Pliny E. Goddard, *Indians of the Northwest Coast,* 1924; Museum of Modern Art, *Indian Art of the United States,* 1941; George C. Vallant, *Indian Arts in North America,* 1939.   —H.G.

Norwegian art. See SCANDINAVIAN ART.

nose flute. See MUSICAL INSTRUMENTS.

notan (Jap.). Japanese word for light and shade. See COLOR.

notation, in dance. Also known as stenochoregraphy, choregraphy or dance-script. Visual and graphic methods for recording dances, which include numerous systems, geometric, anatomical and cinematographic.   —L.K.

notch. A hollow cut or sunk in anything.

notched jamb. The side of a window or door opening, one portion, at least, of which is set back from the main vertical line of the jamb.   —J.M.M.

note. An artist's rough sketch, esp. of a detail.

NOVEL, THE. The long fictional prose narrative called the novel had forerunners in antiquity, and in the **medieval romance** of chivalry telling of knights encountering giants and monsters for love of fair ladies; in the pastoral romances of the Italian Renaissance, about shepherd's and shepherdesses in artificial outdoor scenes; and in the **picaresque stories** of the Spanish Renaissance, stringing together the escapades of rogues. The first great example of the modern novel is *Gargantua and Pantagruel* by Rabelais (1495-1553), abounding with the new surge of life and learning in a rebirth of language, and delighting in full-bodied facts of human nature. The second is *Don Quixote* by Cervantes (1547-1616). It achieved, also in gloriously adequate language, an interaction between the idealism attributed to shining knights and the realism of common men, transcending the cynicism of the picaresque attack upon anachronistic and exaggerated ideals, to arrive at a humorous and tragic sense of man trying to rise while keeping his feet on the ground. The subsequent course of the serious novel is an attempt at adjustment between fact and aspiration.

In 17th cent. France the burlesque genre represented by the *Roman Comique* of Scarron (1610-60) is important as an ancestor of realism. Of lasting interest is *La Princesse de Clèves* by Mme. de La Fayette (1634-93), from which the current of psychological fiction leads to *La Chartreuse de Parme* and *Le Rouge et le Noir* by Stendhal (1783-1842), and to Proust and Gide in our time. In 17th cent. England the gravity and excitement of events and the feeling that familiar things were charged with inner meaning, was expressed in the realistic and allegorical story of *Pilgrim's Progress* by John Bunyan (1628-88). Defoe (1659-1731) continued the effort to produce fiction which should enhance life without seeming to deviate from fact, using the sober tone of journalism and the personal note of the diary. Dropping allegory he emancipated his sense of the marvelous from the medieval background and exercised fondness for picaresque event in terms of the contemporary world, as in *Moll Flanders*. In *Robinson Crusoe* he celebrated the resourcefulness of man overcoming nature and making himself at home in it.

This self-reliance, which fostered voyages of discovery and scientific invention, brought about the rise of the middle class. Recognition of this class was carried further by Richardson (1689-1761) in *Clarissa Harlowe,* depicting domestic life and manners, with a sentimental version of bourgeois values put forward in sheer moral purpose. Like Defoe, Richardson gained the illusion of intimacy through adoption of the diary style and maintained this effect, while shifting the point of view, by the device of imaginary letters. The introspective life of the sensitive person enabled and obliged by modern conditions to be self-sufficient, alone in the civilized world, alone even in the bosom of the family, as drawn by Richardson, was the counterpart of Robinson Crusoe who was alone in nature. Robinson is a symbol of competent problem-solving enterprise, whether scientific or commercial. Clarissa symbolizes subjective isolation in the transition from the transcendent values of the medieval communal world to the self-centered Renaissance and Enlightenment. Absorbed as Richardson was in the life of feeling, he maintained logical sequence. But Sterne (1713-68), though his work was careful, flouted the conventions of order in art and life to give the freest expression of his private self. Fielding (1707-54) allowed individual feeling to be inferred, yet did not shrink within it like Sterne, nor try to uphold inherited morality by urging personal holiness like Richardson, but attacked the brutality of capitalism in objective and realistic presentation of character. Fielding also advanced the technique of the novel by abandoning the single-file events of the picaresque story for the complex structure of simultaneous progression on several fronts toward controlled results.

Novels in the 2d half of the 18th cent. in France and England were sentimentally romantic and artificial, and scarcely deserve aesthetic consideration for themselves. Their importance consists in being part of the reaction against the spreading view of the Newtonian world machine and the rationalism or empiricism which denied value to the yearnings of the individual. A curiosity of the period is the Gothic novel, such as *The Castle of Otranto* by Horace Walpole (1717-97), which accompanied the sentimental attempt in poetry and architecture to escape from a sober present into a make-believe medievalism. The same escape-motive explains the 18th cent. love of Oriental fiction and imitations of it. In Rousseau (1712-78) this romantic mood turned to idealization of nature and protest against the artificiality of contemporary life. He expressed the worsening of social conditions through technological and economic changes characterizing the development of capitalism, as well as through the inertia of anarchronistic institutions and authority. Novels like his *Nouvelle Héloïse* and *Émile* are called "novels of feeling" or "novels of purpose" according as they stress sensibility or the need of reform, and they have special interest in view of his role as philosopher of the French Revolution. The novels of George Sand (1803-76) are comparable in their sentimental and social cast.

The German novel first attracted attention outside Germany during the latter half of the 18th cent. through *The Sorrows of Young Werther* (1774), Goethe's romantic epistolary novel written under the influence of Richardson and the German "Storm and Stress"; through Goethe's more earthly *Wilhelm Meister's Apprenticeship* (1796), and his problem-novel on marital relations, *Elective Affinities* (1809). In the same age Jean Paul Friedrich Richter wrote his whimsical, formless, dreamy novels of life in the land of "poets and thinkers" in the manner of Sterne (*Titan, Years of Indiscretion*), and members of the "Romantic School" published a number of "novels of education" (*Bildungsromane*) patterned on *Wilhelm Meister* but with less realistic power (Tieck's *Franz Sternbald's Wanderings*, F. Schlegel's *Lucinde*, Novalis's *Henry of Ofterdingen*). This type, philosophical, often autobiographic and little concerned with the contemporary scene but more with the individual, is the most characteristic type from Germany. In its attempt to depict the gradual maturation of a hero it may be traced to Grimmelshausen's *Simplicissimus* (1668) as well as to Goethe. The age of realism after 1830 witnessed its rapid development (Gottfried Keller's *Green Henry* and Eduard Mörike's *Painter Nolten*). We meet it also in our own age (Wassermann's *The World's Illusion* and Mann's *Magic Mountain*). The historical novel was cultivated by Wilibald Alexis (pseud. for Wilhelm Häring) early in the 19th cent., while between 1850 and 1880 Gustav Freytag and Theodor Fontane evolved a more realistic type concerned with men confronted by the social problems of their day. After 1885 the Naturalists, headed by Hauptmann, introduced the recent French and Russian novelists, while in the early 20th cent. Schnitzler, Kolbenheyer, Ponten, Carossa and many others have contributed novels which again reveal the typical characteristics of the German genre—less interest in action and plot than in character and discursive concern for philosophical and politico-social problems.

One may say that the failure of the French Revolution warped the novel throughout Europe in the 19th cent., as in Foscolo's *Le Ultime Lettere di Jacopo Ortis* (1802), an expression of Italy's disillusion. The virtue of the novel in the 17th and early 18th cents. had been full revelation of human nature, in its actual condition and in its ideal. But 19th cent. novelists seem to have been unable or afraid to see man as he was, hence inadequate to his fundamental aspiration. Obliged to write for the bourgeoisie, if not actually in sympathy with it, they sensed that it could not solve its problems without a reconstruction of society as a whole, and that the middle class did not want to risk bringing back the Terror. So the age and its novelists hugged institutions antedating the French Revolution, and tended to keep within the shelter of gentility. Jane Austen (1775-1817), on the threshold of the period, limited herself to the local gentry, showing their foibles but not their setting. Scott (1771-1832), at a loss to handle the contemporary self in its own terms, disguised it in medieval trappings and removed it to a romanticized past. Following his lead the historical novel was carried on by Hugo (1802-85) and Dumas (1803-70) in France, Manzoni (1785-1873) in Italy, and Cooper (1789-1851) in the U. S. A.

The somberness of Hawthorne (1804-64) in *The Scarlet Letter* and the symbolistic pessimism of Melville (1819-91) in *Moby Dick* seem related to the romantic melancholy in Europe after the breakdown of the French Revolution and the disillusioning effect of natural science. Melville's very care with facts and figures pointed his determination to penetrate beyond them. Less devastating was the genteel realism of Wm. Dean Howells (1837-1920) in *The Rise of Silas Lapham*. Mark Twain (1835-1910) had a hatred of evil that went with deep love and knowledge of his country and people, but was mostly kept within the bounds of polite restrictions he could not surmount. That sex had no place in *Huckleberry Finn* is indicative.

Even Dickens (1812-70) did not attack the social system in general but particular evils, such as Yorkshire schools in *Nicholas Nickleby* and Chancery Court in *Bleak House*. Where he arrived at indictment it could pass for caricature and was blurred by sentimentality. It is unlikely, however, that he restrained himself. Perhaps he was not more critical of society because the richness of character, the kindness, sadness, folly, horror, and comedy of *Oliver Twist* and *David Copperfield* seemed too fundamental to be altered much by any reform or revolution. Thackeray (1811-63) satirized society in *Vanity Fair,* but within family relations rather than in larger aspects, approving conventional virtues which involved accepting the general scheme of things. Trollope (1815-82) in his

methodical chronicling of respectability must have reassured his readers that all was well with their world. How life and love were stifled beneath that smugness one may feel in the outcry of *Wuthering Heights* by Emily Brontë (1818-48). George Eliot (1819-80) exalted the Victorian code in her novels. Meredith (1828-1909) had the comic sense to ventilate the stuffiness of his time, as in *The Egoist*, and accepted the theory of evolution. But he considered it to mean an unfolding plan culminating in intelligence and justifying optimism, hence underestimated the struggle ahead. Hardy (1840-1928) found the world indifferent to man in *Jude the Obscure* and interpreted the philosophy of science as blighting human prospects. Samuel Butler (1835-1902) in *The Way of All Flesh* held that character is molded by heredity and environment and cynically showed the importance of money to the well-being of his hero.

Henry James (1843-1916) was one of the first writers who strove consciously to make the novel a form of art in the fullest aesthetic sense. In Paris he was in contact with Flaubert (1821-80), Turgenev (1818-83), and the Goncourt brothers (1822-96, 1833-78), who were associated with the art for art's sake movement, of which Poe (1809-49) is considered to have been the prophet through his influence on the poet Baudelaire (1821-67). This movement opposed the apparent vitiation of art by the results of science and commercialism in modern life. Yet the naturalist Zola (1840-1902) was in the circle James met in Paris, and they all inherited much of the passion of Balzac (1799-1858) for observation and documentation, as did Maupassant (1850-93). French influence in the direction of naturalism and realism was also strong upon Italian writers in the second half of the 19th cent., such as Verga, Capuana, and Matilde Serao. *Il Santo* (1906) by Fogazzaro marks a new lease of life in the 20th cent. in treating the attempt to reconcile the value of religion with full recognition of science. *Il Fuoco* by D'Annunzio, on the other hand, shows reversion to art for art's sake, and a hardness toward the ordinary concerns of humanity consonant with fascism. The Italian novelist now best known is the anti-fascist Silone whose *Bread and Wine* compares socialism and Christianity in terms of deep sympathy with the people on the soil.

It is increasingly seen that, while the novelist must be an artist, life is the stuff of his art. This was the dual position of James and Flaubert as they analyzed and formulated the technical aspects of the once unpremeditated craft of fiction: James in his *Prefaces* and Flaubert in his *Correspondance*. Their ideal was a self-contained story, objective, free of essays or asides by the author except for good reason; and a unified point of view not allowed to shift unless for a justifying effect. Pictorial or panoramic passages were to be used for preparation, information, description and generalization; scenic or dramatic passages of dialogue and action were to put the high points before the reader. Since non-dramatic parts are likely to drag, it was felt important to heighten their interest by various devices.

Stevenson (1850-94), who had considerable correspondence with James, followed him in striving for form in the novel, but diverged from him in love of overt action and in emulation of the romancing Scott and Dumas. Stevenson's cultivation of escape retained much realism, and the same was true of Hudson (1841-1922). Since Hudson was at home in South America his fancy in *Green Mansions* was scarcely more romantic to readers of English than his nature lore. Kipling (1865-1936) also practiced groundgripping romanticism, having the advantage of familiarity with India and animal life. But romance for him did not imply disapproval of the social order, as for Stevenson and Hudson. Kipling was eloquent in apology for imperialism.

To many readers concern for form and technique, or for anything less than the problem of fundamental values, began to seem as unimportant in the second decade of the 20th cent. as to the great Russian novelists then becoming familiar in English. Turgenev (1818-1883) was a consummate artist but concentrated his art upon the goal of relieving unnecessary suffering. He expressed Russia's need of reform in keeping with Western science and ideals, though he saw (*Fathers and Sons*) that the nihilist moved too destructively in that direction. Dostoievski (1822-81), concentrating upon the soul-searching of drab persons, condemned critical liberalism as well as headlong nihilism, believing that redemption for Russia lay entirely in Christian faith and love. He came to feel that this involved submission to traditional orthodoxy and authority. Tolstoy (1828-1910) gradually understood Christian brotherhood to dissolve orthodoxy, authority, nationalism, and all institutional structure which might oppress or exploit simple men, and was well on the way to this view in *War and Peace* and *Anna Karenina*.

Even Henry James and Flaubert, the technicians of fiction, are now appreciated for their social insight: for expressing the predicament of anyone sensitive to intellectual and emotional conflict in a culture perpetuating traditions and institutions incompatible with the advance of science and the rising demand for fairness to common humanity. *The Bostonians* and *The Princess Casamassima* by James, *L'Éducation Sentimentale* and *Madame Bovary* by Flaubert, considered as social philosophy have the limitations of their authors' education and experience. But it is largely owing to these men that critics now require adequate treatment of themes important to mature people, as well as formal excellence in presentation of character, in novels to be regarded as serious works of art.

In both requirements Galsworthy (1867-1933) ranks high. Yet, despite his social conscience, his imagination was so confined to the values of the middle class that, in presenting its decline in *The Forsyte Saga*, he seemed to be recording the downfall of the human race. Bennett (1867-1931) was a craftsman, though inartistic in sacrificing subtlety to thoroughness of documentation. He saw the writing on the wall for Victorian values, but did not seem to care as long as he could do a good job of reporting. Wells (1866) began writing fantastic romances based on the wonders of science, and went on to use the novel as the means of showing how adoption of scientific attitude and method was the best way of dealing with questions of sex, education, religion, and all the major difficulties besetting society. Taken to task by Henry James for slighting character analysis and the refinements of verbal texture in so-called problem novels, Wells replied, as in his *Experiment in Autobiography*, that he wanted to make the novel have effect on conduct. Feeling that the 19th cent. novel sinned by inculcating a false sense of security in the reader, he has believed the novel should give notice of general breakdown and the need of wholesale reconstruction on the basis of science. He has not seen how social purpose could be combined with the aesthetic ideal of James. Many novelists have sided with Wells in this controversy. If fewer have followed James, they have not been impressed by the numbers against them. Conrad (1857-1924) accepted with reverence the Jamesian teaching and example, dedicating himself to the novel as a self-contained form of art. He too was impressed by science, but instead of seeing hope in it for the solution of basic problems he was like Hardy in thinking science required a mechanistic view devoid of hope. Conrad was consoled, or solemnly diverted, by the spectacle of man struggling to do his duty, especially psychologically, against a grand background of nature. He was disillusioned about man's fate, yet filled with romantic admiration for defiance of it. He felt that if one had the courage to overcome fear, death would lose its sting, as in the story of *Lord Jim*.

In modern Spain social considerations have largely absorbed the novel, and have drawn the American Hemingway to write a novel about that divided country (*For Whom the Bell Tolls*), as well as the Frenchman Malraux (*Man's Hope*). Unamuno, the dean of Spanish letters until his death in the civil war, though in the end tragically disappointed by the effort to block the forward-looking hope of his people, had sought in the past for fundamental Spanish traits, in *Paz en la guerra* (1897) and *Niebla* (1914). Pío Baroja, however, tore tradition for the sake of a dynamic concept of life in his trilogy *La lucha por la vida* (1904) and in *El árbol de la ciencia* (1911). Valle Inclán, though a modernist at heart, recreated a barbaric and legendary atmosphere in his kaleidoscopic novel of Latin American tyranny, *Tirano Banderas* (1926). Ramón Pérez de Ayala has unveiled human passions with Freudian curiosity in *Troteras y danzaderas* (1913) and has shown his intellectual and aesthetic preoccupations in *Tigre Juan* (1926).

In Latin America the Chilean Eduardo Barrios has delved into the complexities of human motives in *Un perdido* (1917) and *El hermano asno* (1922), while Mariano Azuelo has impassively viewed the Mexican underdogs swept by the revolution of 1910 in *Los de abajo*. The struggle between man and monstrous tropical nature is depicted by José E. Rivera in *La vorágine*, a story of the plains and jungles of Colombia. Rómulo Gallegos of Venezuela, apostle of progress, has expressed a more hopeful view of this struggle in *Doña Bárbara* (1929); and there is a similar confrontation of man and nature in *Don Segundo Sombra* (1926) by Ricardo Güiraldes of Argentina, a poematic novel of the pampas and the gaucho.

At its best the novel everywhere has continued to express the human situation colored by imagination, with the growing skill of reflection upon experiments in technique, and the intensified quality of life in crisis. The novelist of the 20th cent. has been concerned with the impact of science and technology upon inherited institutions and habits. Joyce of Ireland (*A Portrait of the Artist as a Young Man, Ulysses, Finnegans Wake*) with all the resources of language and great technical inventiveness, tried in vain to make his art replace the religion discredited for him by science. Proust of France (*Remembrance of Things Past*) strove to preserve personal reminiscence and traditional culture from science, and succeeded in recording the decay of the civilization he cherished. Thomas Mann of Germany has worked out a dialectical mediation between cultural conservatism and scientific progress (*Buddenbrooks, The Magic Mountain,* the *Joseph* series). Kafka of Czechoslovakia (*The Trial, The Castle*) has expressed the confusion of modern life and a hunger for a faith like that of Protestant orthodoxy while finding it no longer accessible. Aldous Huxley of England, after blaming a travesty of science for the degradation of life (*Brave New World*), has turned to quietism. D. H. Lawrence of England tried to find salvation in sex (*Lady Chatterley's Lover*). The loneliness of a sensitive woman who cannot grasp or accept the contemporary world except as she can dissolve it into subjective insights, is manifest in Dorothy Richardson (*Pointed Roofs*) and Virginia Woolf (*To the Lighthouse*), both of England. Malraux of France (*Man's Fate, Man's Hope*) calls for collective action against social injustice. Mauriac (*Le Noeud de Vipères*) and Bernanos (*Diary of a Country Priest, Star of Satan*), both of France, deal in Catholic terms with the struggle between good and evil. Roger Martin du Gard (*Les Thibault*) and Jules Romains (*Men of Good Will*), also both of France, survey extensively the topics of contemporary experience. Santayana of Spain (*The Last Puritan*) ridicules the effort to be virtuous and rational in what seems to him an absurd world. Gide of France (*The Counterfeiters*) indicates that absurdity and futility may be dissipated when men proceed in the adventurous experimental fashion that transcends preconceived goals. Apparently it is because American novelists have failed to grasp Gide's essentially American point of view that they have lately been very disillusioned. But they have been welcome to people who feel the need of a new realism about the state of things, as the first condition of any fundamental improvement. Sinclair Lewis (*Main Street, Babbitt*) has handled the American scene without gloves, and indicated (*Arrowsmith*) that science, the hope of our time, tends to be corrupted by commercialism. Dreiser (*An American Tragedy*) conveys the sense that social changes accelerated by science and industry, as vitiated by capitalism, have badly damaged traditional values. Hemingway in his fashion has illustrated their depreciation, and has tried to start from scratch toward rebuilding them (*The Sun Also Rises, A Farewell to Arms*). Thomas Wolfe (*Look Homeward, Angel*) has groped for orientation, to recover with much emotion the record of his search. William Faulkner (*Light in August*) has depicted disintegration in the South since the Civil War. Erskine Caldwell (*Tobacco Road*) and Steinbeck (*Grapes of Wrath*) have been concerned with the impoverishment of land and people not only in the South. Farrell (*Studs Lonigan*) has represented the lack of horizon for the poor in the city. Dos Passos (*U. S. A.*) has shown the corrosion of rich and poor alike by shallow materialism. In the work of such novelists one may see the problems confronting the United States at home before the Second World War, presented with sociological realism and art, if not with sufficient insight.

The global character of this war, and the hope that out of it may come some progress toward a world order, make such a means of free communication as the novel freshly important. The vicarious experience it provides will help men to appreciate and enter into the cultural pluralism that is more and more the ideal. The Japanese novel *The Tale of Genji* by Lady Murasaki (about 1000) may help us to appreciate Oriental culture, as will India's *Mahabharata* and *Ramayana* which (although in verse) may be considered in the field of the novel; not to mention *The Arabian Nights* and the Bible stories which now belong to us as well as to the Near East. China is represented by *All Men Are Brothers* (14th cent.), a novel of adventure, by *The Red Chamber Dream* of Ts'ao Hsüehch-'in (17th cent.), and by *Monkey*, the adaptation of a folk legend.

Largely thanks to the Nobel Prize we have become familiar with Scandinavia through novels of Björnson, Selma Lagerlöf, Knut Hamsun, and Sigrid Undset, who received it respectively in 1903, 1909, 1920, and 1928.

The Norwegian-American O. E. Rolvaag, with his *Giants in the Earth,* belongs in their company. Dutch novelists of note in the 20th cent. are Couperus, Fabricus, and Queride. Czech contemporaries were Jaroslav Hasek who wrote *The Good Soldier Schweik,* an influential satire on regimentation, and Carl Capek who wrote novels on social problems arising through mechanization, in addition to such plays as his famous *R. U. R.* Writing in Yiddish are the Polish novelist Sholem Asch, author of *Three Cities, The Mother, The Nazarene,* and I. E. Singer who treats of Jews in Poland and Lithuania in his best known work, *The Brothers Ashkenazi.* Next to the newspaper, the radio, and the revival of Tolstoy's *War and Peace,* it is Sholokhov's novels that interest us in the Soviet Union. (NOTE: Acknowledgment for many suggestions is due Professors Edwin H. Zeydel, Merton J. Hubert, and Archimede Marni of the University of Cincinnati, Professor E. Neale-Silva of the University of Wisconsin, and Mr. John F. Matthews, and to the following bibliography.) *The Development of the English Novel,* Wilbur L. Cross, 1924; *The History of the Novel in England,* Robert Morss Lovett and Helen Sard Hughes, 1832; *The Art of the Novel,* Pelham Edgar, 1933; *The Craft of Fiction,* Percy Lubbock, 1921; *Discoveries,* J. Middleton Murry, 1924; *Russian Literature and Destiny,* R. A. Tsanoff, *The Rice Institute Pamphlet,* vol. XXXIX, No. 4, Oct. 1942; *The Technique of the Novel,* Carl H. Grabo, 1928; *The Novel and the People,* Ralph Fox, 1937; *The Novel and the Modern World,* David Daiches, 1939; *Axel's Castle,* Edmund Wilson, 1936; *The Triple Thinkers,* Edmund Wilson, 1938; *The Wound and the Bow,* Edmund Wilson, 1941; *American Fiction 1920-1940,* Joseph Warren Beach, 1941; *The Epic of Latin American Literature,* Arturo Torres-Rioseco, 1942; *Venezuelan Prose Fiction,* Dillwyn F. Ratcliff, 1933; *Movements of Thought in the 19th Cent.,* George H. Mead, 1936; *My Country and My People,* Lin Yutang, 1935.   —V.M.A.

novellette. Name given to piano compositions in free form by Schumann.

Novgorod, school of. See RELIGIOUS PAINTING IN RUSSIA.

nui-haku (Jap.). A fabric decorated with both gold-leaf painting and embroidery.

number notation. See NOTATION.

nunome (Jap.). Literally, cloth meshes. In art, a pattern of small nodules, simulating the texture of regular weaving.

Nuremberg, school of. In 1662 Joachim Nützel, a councillor of the city of Nuremberg, established a private academy of art which was directed by Jacob von Sandrart and Elias Gödeler. There were lessons in life drawing and architecture, the latter taught by Gödeler. In 1674 Joachim vom Sandrart, a painter of international reputation, became the director of the academy. During his directorship the academy was made a public institution in order that, as Doppelmayr says, the youth, especially the children of the poor people, might learn the art of drawing and that in future the arts would continue to flourish in Nuremberg. After the death of Joachim von Sandrart several reforms were instituted, such reforms, however, did not prevent the decline of the academy during the 18th cent.

Joachim von Sandrart is the author of the *Teutsche Academie der Edlen Bau—, Bild—und Malerey—Künste* (published in two parts, 1675 and 1679). Sandrart, who borrowed freely from Palladio, Vasari and others for his theoretical discourses on art, summarized in these volumes the teachings of his school as well as the aims and aspirations of the art of his time. See Joachim von Sandrart. *Teutsche Academie der Edlen Bau—, Bild—und Malerey—Künste,* new edition with commentaries by R. A. Peltzer, 1925; Johann Gabriel Doppelmayr, *Historische Nachricht von den Nürnbergischen Mathematicis und Künstlern,* etc., 1730.

—H.H.

nurimono (Jap.). Lacquerware (q.v.).

nurtunja. See AUSTRALIAN ABORIGINAL ART.

nymphaeum (L. *nymphaeum* fr. Gr. *nymphe,* a spirit of water, woods, mountains). A Roman building or room in a palace or villa on a grand scale and with luxurious decoration, provided with a fountain, plants, flowers, statues, paintings, etc. —L.T.S.

nyoi (Jap.). A short curved wand or scepter, the symbol of good wishes.

O

oban (Jap.). A large print, roughly 15 in. x 10 in.

obelisk. A four-sided, usually monolithic, pillar, tapering as it rises, and terminating in a pyramid.

obi (Jap.). Sash or belt worn with the *kimono*.

object. (Dadaist and surrealist usage.) A word adopted, alone, or in various combinations, in Dadaist and surrealist (qq.v.) usage, to designate an independent and self-contained structure or presentation consisting of a single entity, or assembled groups of entities, or parts of entities, and intended for contemplation as an aesthetic and imaginative stimulus; the distinctive feature being that the entities so used are not ordinarily regarded as artistic creations, or designedly of artistic quality, and their usual loci are not artistic contexts (e.g., wheels, sanitary fixtures, a dinner jacket, pieces of driftwood, stones, shoes, eggs, etc.). Such entities are taken from the non-artistic contexts in which they originally occurred, and are incorporated as they are, bodily, or in sections which do not impair the recognition of their original character, into some kinds of Dadaist or surrealist structures, whether paintings, *montages* (q.v.), sculptures, or other arrangements. They are sometimes treated, or "assisted", by the artist, signed, and exhibited in a manner usual for designedly artistic creations. There are many varieties of objects.

The earliest instance, in recent art practice, seems to have been that of the French artist, Marcel Duchamp, who, in 1914, exhibited a bottle-rack which he signed. Such "creations" were termed **"ready-made"** objects. (In popular French usage the term "ready-made", used as a noun, designates something factory-made, mass-produced, hence impersonal, without distinction.) The display of such entities, as Dadaist objects, served the Dadaists as a defiant, nihilistic, intellectually destructive act of mockery of traditional artistic values, forms, and substances; of contempt for contemporary artistic and social pretensions; and symbolically, of all traditional cultural values. It was calculated to shock by irreverence, plain statement and the violent dislocation of ordinary and habitual associations and relationships of daily life.

The surrealists later introduced (in the early 30's) many other varieties of objects, referred to generally as **surrealist objects** ("The surrealist object is one that is absolutely useless from the practical and rational point of view, created wholly for the purpose of materializing in a fetishistic way, with the maximum of tangible reality, ideas and fantasies having a delirious character." Salvador Dali.) Such objects include: **found objects** (e.g., driftwood, roots, volcanic remains), **found objects interpreted** or **assisted** (i.e., treated in some way by the artist), **mathematical objects** (mathematical and scientific models treated or viewed in such a way as to give them hallucinatory appearances), **objects of symbolic functioning** (e.g., fur-lined tea-cup; hair dresser's bust, crawling with ants, surmounted by a loaf of bread and an inkstand representing Millet's *Angelus*), **object-poems** (e.g., assemblages of miscellaneous things—a plaster egg, a candy butterfly, keys, etc.—arranged on a panel in conjunction with lettering and verse).

Something of the iconoclastic attitude of the Dadaists was carried over; and something of the scorn for the thoughtless assumption of a certain few materials as suitable for artistic manipulation, and not others. But primarily the surrealists were interested in objects as the occasions, and objectifications, of fantasy, particularly of the Freudian, fetishistic, and obsessional kinds. Such objects were intended to serve also in the interests of a confusion between "art" and "non-art", between illusion and fact, and between the phenomenal, cognitive, imaginary, and the symbolically fantastic aspects of the physical world. The surprise and shock resulting from the new juxtapositions, both within the thing displayed, and in the manner of its display, were calculated to force a new and active attention, a re-examination and re-appraisal of the instrumentalities and activities of daily life; to release inhibited fantasies, causing the object of attention to become the objectification of the fantasy, in much the same way as children, primitives, and psychotics find magic, wonder, and terror in their environments.

Through the handling, treatment, and contemplation of such objects the non-artist became artist, in that he could objectify his imaginings and fantasies in visible images; lack of a developed "artistic" technique would no longer hinder imaginative release. This was felt to be highly desirable, for according to Surrealist ideology, modern bourgeois life has enforced the impoverishment of the life of the imagination, a loss of the sense of wonder, a dulling of perception, fancy, imagination, and the free play of association. See S. Dali, in *Le Surrealisme au Service de la Revolution*, December, 1931; D. Gascoyne, *A Short Survey of Surrealism*, 1935; "L'Objet", *Cahiers d'Art*, nos. 1-2, 1936; A. H. Barr, Jr. (ed.), *Fantastic Art Dada Surrealism*, 1936; H. Read (ed.), *Surrealism*, 1936; G. Hugnet, *Dada and Surrealsim*, Bulletin, Museum of Modern Art, vol. 4, 1936.
—M.S.F.

object-poem. See object.

objects of symbolic functioning. See object.

oblique perspective. See PERSPECTIVE.

oboe, o. d'amore, o. da caccia. See MUSICAL INSTRUMENTS.

obscure. Lack of organization with specific reference to the formal structure of the work of art. The criterion here applied is one of craftsmanship, and judges the work of art from the point of view of technique. The term then indicates that the elements of the work are badly put together, that they hold only loosely, and that the transitions

and connections between them are weak and inadequate.   —I.J.

observed dance. See form (3).

occult balance. See balance.

occupational costume. See COSTUME ART.

occursus. See MEDIEVAL MUSIC.

OCEANIA, ARTS OF. Oceania includes the tropical and near-tropical islands often mentioned as the South Seas. The approximately 391,000 square miles of land are scattered throughout an area which is about one-eighth of the earth's surface and in 1941 was under the jurisdiction of eight nations: Australia, Chile, France, Great Britain, Holland, Japan, New Zealand, and the United States. The islands are usually divided into three groups: Melanesia, Micronesia, and Polynesia. Melanesia includes the island groups of New Guinea, New Britain, New Ireland, and as far east as Fiji, the northern limit being the Admiralty group, and the southern limit, Tasmania. Micronesia consists of many island groups extending east from southern Japan to Hawaii and south to the equator. The principal groups are the Carolines, the Gilberts, the Mariannes, and the Marshalls. Polynesia covers a huge triangular area with Hawaii, Easter Island, and New Zealand at the angles. The Australs, the Marquesas, Samoa, and Tonga are the better known islands that lie within this area.

The racial stock of each of these areas is the mixture of Negroid, Mongoloid, and Caucasian strains in greater or less proportions. In general, the Melanesians are more Negroid, the Micronesians largely Mongoloid, and the Polynesians more dominantly Caucasoid. In 1940 the indigenous peoples of Melanesia numbered about 1,400,000; those of Micronesia, about 100,000; those of Polynesia, about 330,000. Before the coming of the white man, the native population is believed to have been much more than double these numbers, but the commercial traffic of the whites brought about a depopulation trend that took its greatest toll during the last half of the 19th cent. By the beginning of the 20th cent., corrective measures had halted and reversed this population decrease so that in nearly all sections of Oceania the native population is now increasing.

Archeological evidences trace the native groups to Southeast Asia by way of the Malayan Islands. The distribution of the various peoples among the different islands took place in a series of migrations which probably covered many hundreds of years and whose movements are lost in antiquity. In many instances the arts suggest a higher level of culture than was discovered by the early white explorers, who found neolithic customs rather than the types of civilizations that must have existed in earlier centuries to have produced such works as are evidenced in the excavations in New Zealand and in the remnants of huge megalithic structures to be found throughout the islands of Oceania. The introduction of new ways of living which included new religions, new tools, and also the problems which entered with the advent of the white race, brought greater changes in a single century than the Oceanic cultures had evidenced in all their known history, so that today it is only in isolated areas that the old ways may be observed. Nevertheless, even today the natives show their characteristic resistance to change by a tenacious hold on old traditions and, esp. in their arts and crafts, follow the same stylistic limitations that distinguish them from each other.

The ethnological boundaries are not an infallible guide to the arts and crafts to be found therein, but there are certain visual distinctions in the art styles that are worthy of note. Melanesian design, in general, is conspicuous for its free and dynamic movement and the decorative interweaving of dark and light areas and color accents; Micronesian design is characterized by greater precision of arrangement and perfection of craftsmanship, while Polynesian art is primarily one of structure or mass with less attention being given to applied decoration. Throughout Oceania chronology is uncertain. This is further complicated by attempts in modern times to simulate older or imported pieces for commercial reasons. Interpretation of motifs also is largely a matter of speculation, as the original significance has faded with the ages until very few of the native artists are able even to attempt an explanation. Conjectures of writers show a good deal of disagreement and in many cases appear to be preconceived notions not based on scientific inquiry. The use of many of the design elements may now be attributed merely to the strength of tradition which is apparent throughout the islands. Varied as are the expressions within a small given area, the arts are nonetheless subject to great restriction within each area so that the artist, while expressing his creative urge, still is conscious of what he may or may not do in expressing his own individuality within his design.

Considerable variation of opinion is to be found in writings about this complex area depending on whether the author is an anthropologist, geologist, ethnologist, archeologist, missionary, or merely a traveler. The study of Oceanic arts is usually approached from a social or religious viewpoint; this is entirely reasonable since it is only in rarer instances that anything created from the so-called "fine arts" aspect is apparent. In nearly every case, the art of the islands is an everyday art finding expression in household objects, tools, personal adornment, ceremonial objects, canoes, and weapons. In presenting a brief summary of these arts, it is not the writer's purpose to enter into either the social or religious aspects involved, but to deal with the stylistic variations and characteristics in the main geographical divisions.

Melanesia. The Melanesians are masters of their tools and their chosen mediums. The high degree of ornamentation found on even the simplest articles indicates an unusual aesthetic awareness; the richness of their decorative design cannot be overemphasized. Except for the art of the Maoris in Polynesian New Zealand, there is no parallel of this design consciousness in all of Oceania. The advantageous use of color accents and the skill demonstrated in the handling of the dark and light areas give evidence of this, but it is, above all, in their linear design that they exhibit their greatest mastery. The linear phase of their art is most noticeable in the area around the southeastern section of New Guinea commonly known as the Massim district, and includes the neighboring island groups off the coast.

The native artist uses the materials at hand: wood, stone, cocoanut shells, clam and oyster shells, gourds, feathers, leaves, cowrie shells, human and animal bones, clay, and lime. The pigments obtainable include black from charcoal, white from lime, red from burnt clay, and yellow from unfired clay. Additional colors are now being used where commerce has made them available. From these materials are created household objects such as bowls, spoons, lime spatulas, lime holders, gourd water bottles, stools, neck rests, adzes, axes, arrows, spears, and hunting clubs. Items of personal adornment include hair ornaments, necklaces, arm and leg band, ear and nose inserts, belts, aprons, and tattooing, including cicatrization. Ceremonial obejcts include shields, sacred tablets, masks and supporting staves, decorated skulls, images, drums, flutes, trumpets, bull-roarers, spears, arrows, clubs, stools, and small platforms.

Wood carving takes the position of prime importance in Melanesian art. Most of the wood is very hard although some kinds such as bamboo and gourd are softer. Stone adzes or axes are used for the preliminary blocking of the form; burning is often used to hollow out canoes and bowls; stone splinters, oyster shells, boar's teeth, or sharpened bone are used to refine the shape and to execute the design. A drill is fashioned by setting a sharp stone or bone tip into a stick which is rotated rapidly between the palms or whirled with a cord. Since the introduction of metal tools, the process of carving is easier and quicker, but the results tend to be much less perfect. After the carving is complete, color may or may not be worked into the design. The smearing on of pigment is typically Melanesian; the fact that in some localities the pigment does not necessarily follow the design would indicate that its purpose is not exclusively aesthetic.

The bowls of the Admiralty Islands, the canoe prows of the Trobriandes, and the wooden portrait statuettes of northwest New Guinea indicate the breadth of variety found in wood carving. The bowls of the Admiralty Islands are of hardwood, beautifully finished, with round, elliptical, spiral, or square legs. Decorative handles are often attached, but these are too insecurely fastened to be utilitarian in purpose. The bowls are stained with a dark pigment obtained from volcanic mud and are often finished with a high polish. The canoes of the Trobriandes, like those of many others areas, are works of art upon which the owner lavishes years of labor. The prow is usually covered with incised carving that gives it a particularly fragile and lacelike appearance. The statuettes of northwestern New Guinea are highly stylized human figures. There is neither the flawless surface perfection of the Admiralty Island bowls, nor the intricate pattern of the Trobriandes canoe, but there is a startling degree of realism combined with a conscious handling of the design elements that shows the artist's aesthetic sincerity and that has caused these sculptures to be described as caricatures.

Very beautiful and intricate carving is done on tortoise shell. The usual form of this work is a type of hair ornament commonly called a *kap kap*. Circles of exquisitely incised tortoise shell are mounted on pieces of polished sea shell obtained from a giant bivalve native to the region. The size and shape of the mount in relation to the incised work, the thickness of the tortoise shell, and the delicacy of the design vary with the locality. The carving is apparently done with a small file or saw handled much in the manner of the modern jig saw. The softness of the tortoise shell as a carving medium makes the lacelike quality of the design all the more remarkable. The finest examples are to be found in New Ireland and the Solomon Islands. These kap kaps are objects of exchange as well as ornaments. The wearing of them may be a privilege of tribal initiates or an indication of bravery, but more often is merely an indication of wealth. Variations of the kap kap theme include pendant discs worn on the breast or forehead or in the nose or ears.

Pottery is found in some sections of Melanesia: on the southeast coast of New Guinea, in the Bismark Archipelago to the north, one island in the Solomons group, one in the New Hebrides group, in New Caledonia, and in Fiji. That its use is not more widespread may be explained by the lack in other areas of clay in sufficient quantities for pottery although nearly all sections use small amounts of clay for coloring, for modelling parts of masks, or for adhesive grounds into which are set tiny seeds or shells.

Weaving is found in many places and pounded bark cloth similar to Polynesian tapa is made in some sections; in Melanesia, bark cloth is more generally used for ceremonial purposes than for clothing and the abundant use of mats noticeable in Polynesia is lacking in Melanesia.

Numberless species of highly colored birds are to be found throughout the Melanesian islands, and feather mosaic as well as other forms of feather work are used for ceremonial articles and for personal adornment.

Permanent body ornamentation may take the form of either tattooing proper or scarification. One group may tattoo, another may scarify, but it is rare to find both methods in use in the same area. Whether the ornamentation is merely decorative or is symbolic depends on tribal customs. In many places the decoration of specific areas of the body is an indication of age, degree of initiation into the tribe, or heroic deeds. It is not uncommon for a successful adult to have the greater part of his body covered with this ornamentation. Tattooing lends itself to greater delicacy of design, but native ingenuity and patience have produced patterns of startling intricacy through cicatrization.

In most Melanesian art there is a noticeable refinement of line, a perfection of surface finish, and a conscious selection of the field to be decorated. The predominance of the bird motif is apparent, especially in the Massim district. It is a favorite in nearly all sections as a motif for hair ornaments. The pig, dog, crocodile, boar, cassowary, dugong, fish, and plant life are all used for decoration. The presentation may be very realistic or very stylized depending on the island area; as a rule a given section handles all its motifs in the same manner and it is unusual to find realistic ornament where there is a high degree of stylization. In the section near the Torres Straits between Australia and New Guinea the ornamentation reaches its highest degree of realism, but design consciousness is comparatively weak. Other sections of Melanesia show a comparatively high degree of stylization and a correspondingly advanced degree of design quality. In the Massim district where the art expression reaches its peak, most of the motifs are so highly stylized as to be practically unrecognizable. Geometric pattern elements are found in all areas. Much of Melanesia, especially New Guinea, employs motifs common in the late Shang period of China such as angular spirals and isolated eyes, while the Massim district in particular shows many features of the late Chou period as well as many motifs primarily associated with Indonesia such as the streamer, double spiral, and interlocking spirals. This similarity is too great to be the result of chance and is an important factor in suggesting the probable periods and directions of migrations into the Pacific area. Designs are often clan property; certain designs may be taboo in various clans. Seldom, if ever, are any two designs alike and yet the patterns of each area are distinctive and are not likely to be confused with the design treatment from another section.

Micronesia. The largest and most striking of the Pacific area megalithic structures are to be found in Micronesia on the island of Ponape in the Carolines. Huge pieces of basalt have been laid one on the other to construct miles of walls that are thirty feet high in some places and often fifteen feet thick. The streets were apparently waterways and the entire city covers about eleven square miles. The problem of their construction remains unsolved.

Aside from the puzzle of the megaliths, Micronesian art is not striking for a high degree of artistic achievement other than that of technical excellence. Utilitarian articles are carved from wood, bone, and shell, but there is usually little or no decorative design added. The Micronesian ax is a piece of the giant tridacna lashed to a wooden handle. Spears are made of shark's teeth inlaid in wood. Where fibre is used to lash together parts of implements, there is often a design worked in, but the Micronesian apparently gave his major attention to the use for which his articles were intended, placing form, durability, and perfection of finish above the more obviously decorative aspects.

The houses of the Micronesians are less pretentious than those of the rest of Oceania and for the most part are unadorned. The arts of pottery and loom weaving are known in Micronesia, but the extent to which they are practiced is uncertain. A fibre cloth with colored patterns is made and plaiting is employed throughout the area, but no tapa cloth is made. A fibre vest of unusual thickness and a snug fitting helmet serve the purposes of the war shields found elsewhere in the Pacific area. In the Gilberts, no timber of sufficient size is available for canoes so the natives must rely on driftwood and build large canoes by lashing together odd-sized planks.

Personal ornamentation consists of complex arrangements of assorted objects as shells, rings cut from shells, and teeth, a decided preference being shown for shark's teeth. Their patterns appear primitive and sometimes crude as compared to the more elaborate organizations of Melanesian and Polynesian jewelry. Tattooing and scarification are both practiced in Micronesia, the latter being most frequently used to produce rows of dots on the flesh. With very few exceptions, Micronesian designs are technomorphic in character. There is some human sculpture in wood, but these figures appear more primitive than stylized.

The poverty of information about or evaluation of Micronesian art seems reasonable in the light of their obvious preference for elaborately ingenious utilitarian devices such as their ocean charts which are narrow strips of wood formed into a lattice on which the islands are indicated and which could not be properly classified as art. Most authorities seem agreed that the exploitation of the Micronesian islands took place at a very early date. It is also the general opinion that these were the last of the island groups to be settled, and in the writer's opinion this may be an explanation for the viewpoint that Micronesian art appears to be that of a people starting anew in their art expression. Their works appear to lack tradition except in such isolated instances as pottery and weaving which obviously had a relationship to those of Indonesia. The frequent resemblance of Micronesian art to that of earlier Japan has been noted, but as yet has not been properly explained. Extremely opposing speculations exist as to the source and character of the elaborate coral reef structures on the island of Ponape for instance, and at present it seems impossible to analyze Micronesian art on any kind of a derivative basis. The people are more conglomerate than those of the other island areas and their works elude exact definition.

Polynesia. Because the islands of Polynesia are so widespread, it is not at all surprising to find that the art interest varies greatly in the different sections. The **Maoris** of New Zealand show a decided preference for carving in wood, bone, or stone. Even the Maori type of tattooing is a kind of carving. The Maoris feeling for design excels by far that of the rest of Polynesia and elaborate carving is done on the prow, hull, and tail pieces of canoes; on steering oars and water balers; on caskets, monumental sepulchers, digging implements, doors to storage pits, gourd drinking vessels, weapons, ornaments of human bone, frames of drag nets, floats of seine nets, stone sinkers for submerging the nets, musical instruments, and even the carving tools themselves. The Maori has developed the carving technique to near perfection, but carving in other parts of Polynesia fails to reveal a comparable refinement of line or such superior craftsmanship. A contrast to Maori carving is to be found on the Catham Islands nearby. Here carving is very crudely executed in pumice stone or on the smooth bark of a native tree. As there is no timber of sufficient size for canoes, bundles of leaves or stalks are bound together and a prow of wood is added and carved with very simple bird or human patterns. The greater part of Polynesian carving lies between these two extremes, but in most areas its importance is overshadowed by other arts. In the islands of the Marquesas, much wood carving is done and although it is by no means the cruder type found in the rest of Polynesia. it lacks the delicacy and sophistication of the Maori carving.

It is known that New Zealand was inhabited at the time of the Polynesian migration. Polynesian records describe the earlier people as being of an inferior culture, but it is more than possible that these people had a culture superior to that of the Polynesians. Excavations have revealed evidences of prehistoric craftwork that would indicate an even higher cultural level than that of the historical Maori.

Throughout Polynesia are to be found remnants of earlier cultures. In eastern islands these evidences are found in the megalithic ruins of the sacred places, or **marae** of the Polynesians, which were paved areas, sometimes surrounded by walls, and sometimes containing platform structures. In the islands of Hawaii and Tahiti it is not unusual to find all features in one place. Many of these sites were originally surmounted by large figures of stone or wood in conventionalized human forms. The islands of Tonga and Samoa in western Polynesia do not have the *marae,* but Samoa has numerous flat-topped mounds which appear to have been burial places, substructures for temples, or areas constructed for defensive purposes. That this megalithic style was developed by the Polynesians before they settled in their present area is indicated by the parallel forms that occur throughout many islands which had no inter-communication.

Featherwork is beautifully done in many places. The colorful plumage of native birds is fastened onto matting to produce intricate mosaic patterns. Elaborate headdresses are made in nearly all the islands. The artists on the islands of the Marquesas are noted for their beautiful feather coronets. It is interesting to note, however, that in the islands of New Zealand where such superior wood carving is done and where such emphasis is placed on pattern detail, the featherwork is less ornate than in other areas; feathers are used singly in the hair and the feather robes show little conscious arrangement.

Loom weaving is unknown in most of Polynesia; instead the art of plaiting has been highly developed. Flax is sometimes available, but more often grass or leaves are used. Mats and robes of unusually large size are made by this slow and tedious process. Colored designs are worked in and often human or dog hair is worked in to give a soft fluffy appearance. One type of mat has long fibres woven into one side and combed out when the piece is finished so that while one side is smooth, the other is covered with a shaggy fluff somewhat resembling fur. A very coarse, plaited robe which is water-repellant is in common usage throughout the islands. In New Zealand, looms are used and weaving is done with dressed or undressed flax. The use of a robe is determined by the kind of feathers or hair woven into it. Baskets, fans, bowls, and platters are also plaited with colored patterns. Where the Melanesian or the Polynesian Maori carves bowls, tool handles, and countless other objects, the average Polynesian uses his endless variety of plaitings.

Tapa cloth, the most universally known product of Polynesian craftsmen, is made from the inner bark of any of several native plants. This bark is soaked in water until the pulp is soft and starts to fall away from the fibres; then the pulp is scraped off, laid on mats, and pounded until it is a smooth sheet. Several layers are put on to insure uniform thickness and to give the desired size. An instance of the subtlety of appreciation of some natives, particularly those of Hawaii, for the technical achievement in tapa manufacture is shown in the practice of carving the pounding surface of the implement which is used to beat the fibres together; this produces what is called watermarked tapa which is considered very superior. Designs are applied freehand with brushes made from frayed twigs or, as is more frequent, the design is applied by means of pattern blocks. The motifs used on tapa display the amazing ability of the Polynesian to arrange almost purely geometric forms into an infinite variety of patterns with changes occurring even in the repetition of a single surface unit.

Tattooing is almost universally practiced and is generally a mark of rank, slaves being forbidden to tattoo. Maori tattoo takes the form of cicatrization, but the patterns are composed of very fine lines rather than the more lumpy scars generally associated with this type of ornamentation. Subtle distinctions are to be found in the tattoo patterns of Polynesia, Melanesia, and Micronesia although a similarity exists in the geometric quality of many of the designs.

Technomorphic designs predominate in most of the wood carving except where the human or animal figure is used for some special reason. The remnants of early stone sculpture show very crude, simplified, human

forms. The two great exceptions to this tendency are the works done in the islands of the Marquesas and New Zealand. Both of these areas show art developments that are unlike those of the rest of Polynesia. The spiral of the Marquesas and certain stylistic tendencies in delineating the human face show a marked resemblance to those found in China during the late Shang period. The art of New Zealand gives even stronger evidence of Chinese influence for it includes not only the motifs found in the Massim district of Melanesia which have been mentioned above, but many more purely Chinese elements such as the serpent forms and the double spiral forms of the late Chou period in China. It is evident that the two Polynesian areas mentioned were affected by waves of oriental influence which did not reach the rest of Polynesia and which account for the differences between their arts and the art of the other Polynesian islands.

The greatly intensified interest that is now centered around the islands of the Pacific area will undoubtedly produce much additional evidence to alter or substantiate existing theories in regard to these peoples and their arts. See British Museum, *Handbook to the Ethnographical Collections,* 1925; Brown, J. MacMillan, *Peoples and Problems of the Pacific,* 1927; Buck, Peter Henry, *Vikings of the Sunrise,* 1938; Edge-Partington, James, *An Album of the Weapons, Tools, Ornaments, Articles of Dress, etc., of the Natives of the Pacific Islands,* 1898; Haddon, Alfred Cort, *The Decorative Art of British New Guinea,* 1894; Heine-Geldern, Robert, *L'Art Prébouddhique de la Chine et de l'Asie du Sud-Est et Son Influence en Oceanie,* 1937; Reichard, Gladys A., *Melanesian Design,* 1933.   —M.C.G.

ochre. A wide range of colors is comprised by this term, all of them natural earths characterized by the names yellow ochre, golden ochre, red ochre, and brown ochre. All are silica and clay mixtures which owe their color to iron oxide. This is in a hydrous form in the yellow ochres and anhydrous in the red. As a painter's pigment, ochre has been known since prehistoric times. —G.L.S.

octave. See interval; ACOUSTICS.

octave instrument. See ACOUSTICS.

octavo. See book sizes.

octodecimo. See book sizes.

ode symphony. A choral symphony; e.g., Beethoven's Ninth.

Odo yaki (Jap.). Pottery made in Tosa province.

Odonic notation. See NOTATION.

Odysseus (L. Ulysses). A leading Greek hero of the Trojan War, famous for his nimble wit, wise counsel, ingenuity and endurance in overcoming the difficulties encountered during his ten years of wandering before he reached his home in Ithaca. The story of his adventures is told in Homer's *Odyssey*. His exploits were often pictured in Greek vase paintings. Postclassical sculptors who have taken him as a subject include Pradier and Eric Gill.   —W.R.A.

oeil-de-boeuf. A circular or oval window.

oenochoe. A Greek wine-jug, one of the loveliest shapes in the history of pottery, with a delicately curved handle and usually a trefoil-formed mouth. The 7th cent. B.C., Rhodian jugs are broad-bellied, with a volute handle; they are decorated with friezes of birds and animals, painted in brown on a cream slip. Athenian ones are slimmer and more delicate in shape, and often have a chaste panel of decorative painting on the side. 4th cent. B.C., Apulian ware is characterized by a thin, tapering body, tall stem, and high-curved handle.   —W.R.A.

offertory. See MEDIAEVAL MUSIC; psalmody; Mass.

offset. (1) Transferring an impression from a proof on which the ink is still wet to an unbitten plate or another paper. (2) Term applied to ink when it soils a page that has been piled upon it before the ink was dry. (3) A comparatively narrow set-back in the length of a wall, as when the face of a wall is not one continuous surface, but sets in by horizontal jogs, as the wall grows higher and thinner.

offset, soft ground. A method of transferring a chalk drawing to a copper plate for intaglio printing. The proof resembles crayon lithography somewhat more than the regular soft ground etching, which tends to resemble a pencil drawing. The masses of dark are richer and easier to handle.   —K.K.

offset soft ground (an intaglio process). The offset soft ground is a tonal process resembling lithography more than ordinary soft-

ground. As in lithography, the drawing is made with dark crayon so the artist can see the probable result instead of working blindly as in the case of etching.

The advantage over lithography is that the drawing on paper is made obverse and reverses on the plate to come back obverse in the proof, a great advantage in portraiture. One has absolute control over the most delicate passages fugitive even in experienced hands. The darks have the richness, depth, and the velvety quality of acquatint; large editions can be made without injury to the plate or loss of delicate tones. It does not take an expert to pull large editions as in the case of lithography.

In this type of soft ground the drawing is made on a piece of paper with charcoal, conte or similar type of crayon. A special soft ground is rolled on the plate. The drawing is transferred to the copper plate, coated with a special soft ground, by applying the pressure of the etching press. The plate is now dusted with asphaltum which sticks to the plate only where the crayon dust of the drawing has not already stuck. The plate is rinsed, dried, and heated, till the asphaltum becomes a very hard ground. The offset of the crayon drawing which is still imbedded in the ground is now washed out with cotton and alcohol, leaving bare copper wherever this drawing had been. The areas of bare copper are broken up with an acquatint ground and the plate is bitten with or without stopping out. The plate is now printed like any other intaglio plate. This process was invented by Alexander von Kubinyi of Munich.   —K.K.

off-street parking. See CIVIC PLANNING.

Ofuke yaki (Jap.). Pottery made in Owari province.

ogee. A molding with an S-shaped profile. See cyma recta; cyma reversa.

ogive. The arch or rib crossing a Gothic vault diagonally. A pointed arch.

oil varnish. See drying oils.

oils. Used chiefly for surface films and for painting mediums, the vegetable oils have included those from the flaxseed (linseed), poppy, walnut, and others (see also drying oils). All belong to the class of chemical compounds known as **esters**. To be capable of drying or forming a firm and hardened film on exposure to the air, they must contain a number of double bonds or points at which oxygen can combine with the fatty acid. The drying process is largely one of addition of oxygen. Historically, they have been best known from the early part of the 15th cent. but there is extensive evidence that they were used before that time in European painting. Painters of the Far East have never shown an interest in them, though rare examples like the representations on the doors of the Tamamushi shrine at Nara, Japan, indicate that the drying oils have been known to the Orient. —G.L.S.

ojime (Jap.). An ornamented slip-bead used on the cord which suspends the *inro* (q.v.) from the belt. The *ojime* is slipped down over the cord with slight pressure to keep the various parts of the *inro* together.
—J.A.M.

Old Bering Sea culture. See ESKIMO ART.

old copies of paintings. See FORGERIES OF PAINTINGS.

Old Nankin porcelain. See CERAMICS II.

oleoresin. Sometimes given to combinations of oil and resin, this name is usually applied in the fine arts to a natural balsam or soft semi-liquid which exudes from coniferous plants. Such a material has been employed as an ingredient in surface films and to a minor extent as an ingredient in painting mediums. The best known are Venice turpentine, Strasbourg turpentine, Canada balsam, and copaiba balsam. All are apt to form brittle and dark films on long standing.
—G.L.S.

oliphant. See MUSICAL INSTRUMENTS.

olive branch. In classical art, a decorative pattern with small elliptical pointed leaves opposite each other on a stem; a symbol of peace; made into a wreath a victor's prize at the Olympian games in ancient Greece.
—L.T.S.

Olmec. A term originally applied to peoples living in southeastern Vera Cruz and at one time in central Mexico. No arts and crafts have as yet been surely identified as the work of these people, but the term has tentatively been applied to highly stylized sculptures of men and tiger gods found in southern and central Mexico. —G.C.V.

olpe. A leather receptacle for oils or liquids. A wine pitcher, similar in shape to the oenochoë (q.v.), but more cylindrical in body.

omphalos. See altar.

one-point perspective. See PERSPECTIVE.

one stroke painting. See CHINESE ARTS.

one-way glass. See GLASS AND GLASS-MAKING.

Onohara yaki (Jap.). Pottery made in Tanba province.

Onto yaki (Jap.). Pottery made in Ise province.

open-air museum. See SCANDINAVIAN ART.

open chapel. An apse-like (occasionally church-like or even mosque-like) adjunct of the main church of Mexican 16th cent. monasteries where services were celebrated for large congregations of Indians standing outdoors in the *atrio* (q.v.) to which the chapel opened out broadly. (Occasionally also in Peru.) —J.Mc.

open cut. See CIVIC PLANNING.

opened. *Book.* The leaves of a book cut with a paper-knife.

OPERA. NATURE. Opera is an art form expressing life through speech, song, gesture, and picture. It is both visual and auditory, and cannot therefore be a purely musical form, in spite of the fact that it is sometimes so considered. Opera's wide-spread popularity can be traced to this broad psychological basis, which has assured its existence in the past, against much opposition, and will assure its existence in the future. In no other single art form can life or mankind be so comprehensively or directly mirrored; here we live or relive, in psychological projection, all the pleasures, pains, the ambitions, hopes and disappointments of our existence.

Among music-forms opera has been, in many ways, the least artistic. Its obvious pageantry has long lent itself to superficial, inartistic display, vocally as well as theatrically, in France under Louis XIV, in England under Charles II, and in the personality intrigue and social set-up of many of the leading opera houses today.

When an opera will be created and performed in which the textual, tonal, scenic, and histrionic elements are all of equally high artistic levels, an art-form would result superior to any thus far created. It is the wide discrepancy among its elements (excellent music, bad acting, ridiculous staging, poor libretti) that so often reduces opera to a low level.

The domain of opera falls roughly into two categories; that dealing with religion or other symbolism and ideologies (which is really the domain of oratorio) and that dealing with human emotions of love, hate, cruelty, intrigue and comedy. If we go back to the rituals of primitive peoples, to the sagas of early civilizations, and to the dances and pantomines of past eras, we can trace opera as a psychological projection of such basic urges, as those of acquisitiveness, sacrifice, cruelty and others. (A scholarly analysis of opera, on this basis, has been made by Dr. Ernst Lert in his *Opera Complex.*)

FORMS. *grand opera* (Ger. *Ernste Oper, Grosse Oper;* It. *opera* (*seria*); Fr. *grand opéra, tragédie lyrique*). Essentially a tragedy set to music with tragic dénouement, no spoken dialogue (*Iphigenie en Tauride, Tristan and Isolde, Rigoletto*). Today also, loosely, opera *in the grand manner* with famous cast, large orchestra extravagant scenery and action, high admission prices.

Opera comique (Ger. *Singspiel;* Eng. opera). (Cherubini, *Les deux journées.*) A form of opera in which either the dénouement is happy or the dialogue is spoken, or both. Not the equivalent of comic opera since it need not contain any comic element.

Opera buffa (Ger. *Komische Oper;* Eng. comic opera). A form of opera with dialogue (secco recitativo), interspersed between soli, ensembles and choruses and dealing with comic or light subject matter. This form developed from the "interludes" which had been used between the parts (acts) of the opera seria or of the spoken play. (Mozart, *Cosi fan tutte;* Rossini, *Ill Barbiere di Siviglia;* Pergolesi, *La Serva Padrona;* Cimarosa, *Matrimonio Segreto.*)

Opera bouffe. French light opera bordering on musical comedy, extravaganza or vaudeville.

Operetta (Fr. *Operette;* Ger. *Kleine Oper, Operette*). A diminutive opera in length and content, making no pretense to seriousness. A musical stage entertainment. Closely allied to opera bouffe. (Gay, *Beggars Opera* (*Ballad Opera*); Mozart, *Schauspieldirektor;* Rossini, *L'inganno felice;* and the works of Gilbert & Sullivan, Johann Strauss, Herbert.)

Music drama (It. *dramma per musica, dramma musicale;* Ger. *Musikdrama;* Fr. *drame de musique*). A form of opera in which all elements are equally conceived: plot, text, action, scenery, music. It forms the basis for the works of Monteverde, Gluck, and was brought to its highest perfection by Wagner in his *Ring des Nibelungen.*

Singspiel (Eng. song-play). A German form of opera with secco recitativo but the serious import of opera seria. Loosely used as equivalent to grand opera. (Mozart, *Entführung aus dem Serail;* Beethoven, *Fidelio;* Weber, *Freischütz.*)

Melodrama (It. *melodramma;* Ger. *Melodram;* Fr. *melodrame*). A form of opera in which spoken dialogue is used against an instrumental background as accompaniment. It is an entire work of accompanied recitative. (Beethoven, *Music to Egmont;* Schumann, *Manfred Ballads;* Mendelssohn, *Midsummer-Night's Dream.*)

Recitative and Aria. A division of the vocal parts of opera resulting from the attempt to express all phases of the libretto with pitch inflection. As a result, we have a series of gradations extending from the simple spoken word, with no fixed pitch inflection, to the **recitative secco,** a form of declamation with little or no accompaniment, but with some attempt at pitch variation; to the **accompanied recitative (recitativo strumentato)** in which the accompaniment helps to control the vocal pitch, and at the same time adds to the dramatic effect; to the **mezzo-recitativo** of Gluck in which voice and orchestra complement each other; to the **arioso** of Monteverde and the **melos** of Wagner, in which the vocal line leaves recitative and approaches melody without, however, being strictly metric; to the **aria** itself, in which beauty of melodic line replaces declamation. The aria is the opera equivalent of "song" (q.v.) but lacking the close connection between melody and text. In the opera aria, action is largely suspended and the lyric, emotional element is given free reign. The "patter" songs of Sullivan, also the famous *Largo al Factotum* are forms combining recitative and aria elements.

Recitative is essentially concerned with the narrative or descriptive elements of opera, too rapid or too prosaic to fit into the more slowly moving, emotional and essentially smooth aria. But a recitative may readily contain arioso phrases, and an aria may as readily contain elements of recitative.

HISTORY. Opera, as this is generally understood, originated as an art form at the end of the 16th cent. but its roots go back much further. Gesture and chant have accompanied life throughout antiquity. The marked development of 1600 resulted from an attempt, deliberately made, to free music from the restrictions of the previous polyphonic styles. Both poets and musicians were involved: Bardi, Corsi, Rinuccini, Peri, Caccini. Songs with lute accompaniment (hence homophonic) were already known and practiced. For the dramatic element the Greek tragedies of Sophocles, Aeschylus, and Euripides were studied. The urge to write *drammae per musica* had manifested itself in Vecchi's *Anfiparnasso* (1594), a madrigal opera; in the masques, a Renaissance form of musical entertainment; allegorical and mythical plays with music and elaborate theatre; in Poliziano's *Favola di Orfeo* (before 1500); and last, but not least, in the *laudi spirituali*. The ingredients of opera were thus already present. The development at 1600 was not an entire beginning, but rather an adaptation of these established elements to the new homophonic idiom.

The chief new elements of these early attempts (*ars nova, nuove musiche*) at opera (*Dafne* by Peri with text by Rinuccini, *Euredice* by Peri and also by Caccini) were monody with accompaniment, the juxtaposing of the horizontal, melodic element, and the vertical, harmonic element of music. But the impossibility of using melody to depict all phases of the drama, esp. the epic, soon resulted in the use of recitativo secco for the narrative parts. The *stile rappresentativo, musica parlante,* dominated the earliest versions, but the participation of singers and the need for lyric expression soon developed a more melodic style (Caccini). We find it also in the secular cantatas of that period. Nevertheless, recitative and not lyricism remained the main distinguishing feature of this first period. Interest quickly spread from Florence to other localities and the social and superficial by-products made opera a thing for only royalty and festive occasions.

The first composer to leave an indelible stamp on opera was Claudio Monteverde (1567-1643). He was first of all an excellent musician, and thoroughly in sympathy with the monodic development. His chief contributions were: a marked increase in the effective use of harmony, including, of course, dramatic effects of dissonance (dominant-seventh chord); the use of instrumental color and thematic material for scenic and histrionic description; and the introduction of a form of mezzo-recitativo (arioso), linking the earlier recitative with the later aria.

(*Orfeo*, 1609). In his works we find the first examples of Wagnerian idiom (melos as arioso).

In 1637 the first opera house was built in Venice. Further development of rhythmic melody characterized the works of Cavalli, Cesti and Legrenzi. Meanwhile the Italian fondness for the opera form spread, and many performances were held in various cities.

Alessandro Scarlatti (1659-1725) the foremost representative of the **Neapolitan School,** divided recitative into secco and strumentato and introduced the **"da capo" aria,** the A-B-A form, thus using the basic element of all musical forms: repetition. (Such repetition is a purely musical characteristic, and is opposed to the continuity demanded by the epic element.) In the meantime the theatrical element of opera began to usurp the field and the talented followers in the Neapolitan School wrote often for vocal display rather than for dramatic verity. The use of *castrati* lent impetus to this tendency, and in this form, opera spread to such widely separated points as Madrid, Copenhagen, Lisbon, St. Petersburg, Dresden, and Vienna.

Opera was introduced into France by Lully (1632-1687). To the imported Italian elements, he added the typically French "ballet" idiom. His recitative was adapted to the poetic meter, and the instrumental interludes were extended. (Cambert composed an early example of French comedy with music in the *Pastoral d'Issy,* 1669). Lully's style in music was similar to that in literature of his contemporaries Corneille and Racine. The connection between opera and dance is seen in the founding of the Academie Royale de Musique et de Danse (1672).

The Lully tradition was carried on by Rameau (1683-1764) with continued emphasis on dramatic truthfulness, refining somewhat the melodic, harmonic and rhythmic elements.

In England Purcell (1658-1695) developed English opera from the masque (equivalent of the French *masquerade*). This form, with incidental music, was distinctly English; however, Italian opera was at the time known also in England. Purcell was influenced both by Italian and French idioms but added an austere musical element which was distinctly his own (*Dido and Aeneas*), not unlike certain moods in Shakespeare.

The German form which served as a precursor to opera was the Singspiel, and German opera developed with Reinhard Keiser (1674-1739). The first singspiel opera was *Dafne*

(1627) by Schütz. Keiser is associated with Hamburg opera, where he wrote more than one hundred works for his theatre. An easy melodic gift, but little serious workmanship, makes all of them of mere passing interest.

The cosmopolitan character of opera is strikingly revealed in the works of Friedrich Händel (1685-1756), for here we find a German composer writing Italian opera in England and bringing the form to new, high levels of artistic achievement. His adaptability to the demands of particular occasions and the richness of his genius made his operas dominate the field. His early activity at Hamburg with Keiser, his trip to Italy and his acquaintance with French opera enabled him to utilize these sources and at the same time give them the stamp of his own superior talents. Rinaldo, written in 1711, combined these elements and gave opera its true international stamp. Händel's greatness as opera composer lies chiefly in the fact that he was willing to use any and all of the devices, musical and theatrical, that go into the making of the opera-form. To further his work he became associated with the Royal Academy of Music. He composed with consummate ease and his operas contain, besides their excellent music, many empty formalisms dictated by extraneous circumstances, some of the arias being actually composed by the castrati taking part.

The Händel period of operatic history was followed by the development of various subforms and various parts. Ensembles were enriched by Piccini (1728-1800) and for the first time effective finales were used as a consistent feature. But as an art form opera did not advance until the reforms of Gluck.

Gluck (1714-1787), following the principles of Monteverde, tried to overcome the fundamental conflict between the separateness of musical forms and the continuity of action. He replaced the set forms of recitative by using an accompaniment which, combined with the vocal line, produced a single artistic unit. His principles are clearly set forth in his preface to Alceste. Differences between recitative and aria diminished, and the empty vocal display disappeared. He worked chiefly in Paris. Among his operas are: Iphigenie en Aulide, Iphigenie en Tauride, Orfeo, Alceste and Armide. At the same time Piccini upheld the Italian traditions, which resulted in a famous controversy between him and Gluck.

We come to Mozart (1756-1791). He is usually not considered a reformer or innovator, yet the unsurpassed musicianship of his work, and a seldom appreciated genius for true musical portrayal of even obscure and subtle psychological problems (drama in the best sense) added operas of a very distinct character to the literature. In Cosi fan Tutte, Le Nozze di Figaro, and Il Giovanni he brought Italian opera to its highest point. Building upon the attempts of Keiser, he improved the German Singspiel form in Entführung aus dem Serail and still more so in the Zauberflöte. Accompanied recitative received new values and the operatic finale, as in the second act of Figaro and that of the Zauberflöte, has yet to be surpassed. Whereas Händel has integrated all elements of opera, Mozart does so primarily with the musical elements and his operas remain musicians' operas par excellence. Mozart, in opera, was the greatest and last "Italian" up to that period, as Palestrina was the greatest and last of the Netherlanders.

Beethoven's Fidelio is the most conspicuous example of a great work which is not essentially opera. The characteristic dramatic intensity and sincerity are there, so also the Beethoven profundity and truth, but they do not make theatre, a necessary element of opera. Apart from a non-vocal idiom (the voice is treated as an orchestral part) stage drama, as it is evidenced in the obvious finale and the aria as such, is missing. Fidelio is essentially non-theatrical. If Mozart wrote the musician's opera, Beethoven, in Fidelio, wrote the musician's tonal drama.

Opera in the 19th cent. divides into two types: pre-Wagnerian and post-Wagnerian. The former (early 19th cent.) continued along previous lines. In Germany, with Weber's Freischütz, German romantic opera was raised to a high level. This type, based upon legend or saga, characterized also the works of Spohr and Marschner. In France the serious import of Fidelio had its effects on opera seria in the works of Cherubini (Watercarrier), Meyerbeer (Robert le Diable), Halévy (La Juive), and Spontini (La Vestale) with the elaboration of a heroic element. Opera comique continued with Auber (La Muette de Portici) and Boildieu (La Dame Blanche). In the meantime a more lyric form developed with Gounod (Faust), Thomas (Mignon), Bizet (Carmen), Massenet (Le Cid, Thaïs) Saint-Saëns (Samson et Dalila). In Italy the traditional form is found in the works of Bellini (Norma) and Donizetti (Lucia di Lammermoor).

Verdi (1813-1901), next to Wagner, dominates the field. He began with insignificant traditional Italian works, but, with Ernani,

1844, we find the first attempt to lift mere agreeableness of sound to the dramatic level of tone-portrayal. At the same time the spirit of the Italian people begins to shine through. In *Rigoletto*, Verdi becomes cosmopolitan in styles, assimiliating French influences (Meyerbeer) and, in dramatic force approaching the German style. Although Wagnerian influences may be traced in Verdi's later operas, these, in their main characteristics, could have been written as a natural development of the composer's style itself, which passed from the superficial to a highly dramatic, tonally forceful, and psychologically sound style in *Aida, Othello,* and *Falstaff,* the last written when Verdi was 80 years old. Verdi's operas are true operas. With their musical richness and power, they also retain good theatre, colorful staging, effective ensemble and soli, and good stage plots in spite of some very poor libretti. A continuance of this tendency ultimately may readily have led to the Wagnerian concept.

In the meantime Wagner (1813-1883) himself finally brought the original opera concepts of the Florentine Camerata to their highest development. In his music drama he develops a complete psychological synthesis of plot, music, stage and action. The basic tonal means of securing this integration is the **Leit-motiv**, a tonal figure to symbolize objects, characters, and ideas. It is a highly developed counterpart of the "theme" idea in instrumental composition (fugue or sonata forms), or in tone poems such as *Eulenspiegel*. Musical forms as such, aria, set finale, etc., were discarded and recitative strumentato is elaborated into a "melos." Wagner was peculiarly fitted for this task—he was a music philosopher (*Oper und Drama*), and wrote the texts to his music dramas. As a result there is a unity of whole which has never been equalled. Since vocal utterance is limited, no matter what pitch line is used, it was natural that dramatic force and tonal color should be obtained through the orchestra, and this Wagner developed to its highest point. Individual characteristics of his style are text alliteration, chromaticism, certain metric patterns and complex chordal structures. Following *Rienzi, Tannhäuser, Der Fliegende Holländer, Meistersinger,* his artistic concepts reached their highest point in the *Nibelungen Tetralogy*: *Rheingold, Walküre, Siegfried, Götterdämmerung. Tristan und Isolde* is the lyric opera *par excellence*: *Parsifal* is a semi-sacred stage drama which leans toward the scenic oratorio.

The breadth and scope of the Wagnerian idea, esp. when voiced at Bayreuth (1876),

where a special theatre had been built, made further development along these lines improbable, if for no other than practical reasons: cost of equipment, personnel, etc.

In Germany, Richard Strauss (1864-) introduced a new psychological or better psychopathic element into opera, shown by his choice of Wilde and Hoffmansthal for libretti. The nature of his character delineation is not unlike that of Mozart, but the characters themselves are widely different. Excellent tonal painting and orchestral color dominate, with the vocal line an elaboration of the Wagnerian arioso (*Salomé* and *Elektra*). The cleverness of Strauss as colorist, as portrayer of Freudian complexes makes his work highly realistic. Yet this realism differs in the complex tonal structure from the cruder realism of the Italians — Mascagni (*Cavalleria Rusticana*) and Leoncavallo (*Pagliacci*). Puccini (1858-1924) carried on the lyric opera (*Manon Lescaut, Tosca, Madame Butterfly*) and introduced, for the first time, an American theme in *Girl of the Golden West.*

Although scenic opera has not entirely passed out of the picture (Kaminski; Jurg Jentsch; Milhaud; Christophe Colombe) the central trend of present day opera is toward greater subjectivity and smaller frames. Furthermore a socialistic element has been introduced and the greatly enriched tonal resources have turned the attention of composers to new musical forms such as suite, passacaglia and rhapsody (Berg: *Wozzeck*), and carries speech-song into the extra-tonality field.

Chamber opera is in the making. This is not grand opera merely reduced, but entirely conceived as a smaller form, in plot, in vocal and instrumental utterance and in theatre. Hints of this tendency are found in Hindemith, *Neues vom Tage;* Strawinski, *Oedipus;* Krenek, *Zwingburg;* Weill, *Bürgschaft.*

The emphasis on song, which is also characteristic, may lead to the development of concert opera, with stage setting reduced to a minimum. An extreme of this tendency is radio opera.

Finally, opera in America, like other music forms, has absorbed many foreign elements. (Parker, *Mona;* Damrosch, *Cyrano de Bergerac;* Taylor, *The King's Henchman, Peter Ibbetson*.) Real "American Opera" has not yet emerged. Among the most prominent younger composers is Minotti (*Amalie at the Ball*).   —O.O.

operetta. A little opera, usually of a comic or

gay text, having light and lively music. See OPERA.

ophicleide. See MUSICAL INSTRUMENTS.

opisthodomos. See HELLENIC ART.

opposition (Fr. *opposition*). A term in the academic theatrical dance for a means by which the body is rendered more plastic by contrast of its members arranged in asymmetrical balance, For example, the left arm and leg do not move together, but rather the left arm and the right leg. This opposition is also basis for the natural, unconscious human walk which effects a mechanical balance of weight whereby the body manages to remain in equilibrium despite transitional shifts of its center of gravity. From this essential principle, opposition further consciously enhances and emphasizes the normal elegance of the body. In sculpture of the Hellenistic and baroque periods the Italian term, *contrapposto,* expresses a static version of the same idea.
—L.K.

optical illusion. A term given to the phenomenon of perceiving things differently than would be normal for the visual stimulus. This may lead one to perceive one object as longer or larger than another object, when actually the two objects are the same size. It may lead one to see a pure green color as a green yellow when it is placed next to a blue green. It may lead one to see a mirage of an oasis on a desert when actually none exists.
—V.K.B.

optical pyrometry. *Cer.* Using experienced eye to determine temperature by color. See CERAMICS I.

opus Alexandrinum. See Cosmati work.

opus sectile. See Cosmati work.

or. *Her.* Gold.

oratorio (Ger. *Oratorium;* It. *oratorio;* Fr. *oratorio*). NATURE. The name oratorio refers to its place of origin and to its content. It derives from "oratory" which literally means chapel for prayer. Then it referred to the meetings held there by the oratorians; later to the music itself. Another equally plausible source are the oratorical acts of the medieval monasteries.

The art form oratorio expresses religious feeling. Therefore, it dates back in its pre-art form to the religious chants of even primitive man. Religious character remains the basic

element of oratorio and we find tonal expression of this feeling in the old Hebrew temple chants and Greek Psalmody. These are the ultimate general sources. Its more immediate musical source is found in the *laudi spirituali,* the hymns of praise of the Florentine *laudisti* (13th-16th cents.), at which time representation of sacred subjects was common through Europe. Oratorio may be epic, dramatic or lyric in nature, but, unlike opera, all light or comic elements are excluded. Some early examples, however, contained these.

Oratorio, as a music form, is difficult to define since its various elements permit many combinations and classifications. Four elements should be considered; the nature of the text, whether sacred or secular; the distribution of the parts; the presence or absence of scenery and action; the relative length and scope of the work. The interrelations among these parts determine the type of oratorio. All have in common an introspective, subjective, otherworldly character, in contrast to the extrospective, objective, this-worldly character of opera. (See also mass, requiem, cantata, anthem, Passion.)

We may define oratorio as an extended composition for soli, ensemble, chorus and orchestra, based upon a biblical, liturgical or other non-secular text, without scenery or action, and intended for concert, rather than for liturgical use. The extreme difficulty in clearly defining both the content and the field of oratorio results from its basic hybrid character; it is a music form and also a religious form. There is no inherent connection between oratorio as an art form and its liturgical application, and much oratorio music is not religious in spirit. Music itself, cannot be sacred in character beyond creating an appropriate mood. (The chorale *O Haupt voll Blut und Wunden* is a secular tune.)

Sacred oratorio remains the basic and true form. When an abstract, other-worldly theme, not necessarily religious, is used, we may speak of secular oratorio (Haydn, *The Seasons*). When scenery and action are included we have sacred opera (the early oratorios, 1600; Rubinstein's *Tower of Babel*). A sacred theme, spoken and acted is a sacred drama. If the work be short, but with oratorio content, it becomes what may be called an **oratorietto,** equivalent to the sacred cantata. If any specific part of the liturgy is used as basis modifying terms may be used: Passion Oratorio; Christmas O.; Easter O.; Requiem O. If these themes are intended for liturgical use not for concert or purely musical use, the word oratorio may be dropped and the works designated merely Passion, Christmas service, Mass, etc. If, further, any of the three elements be stressed, we have an epic, dramatic, or lyric oratorio. Thus extended from objectivity, stage and action determine opera; extended form, subjectivity, sacred theme but extra-church performance determine oratorio, and shorter forms determine sacred and secular cantata.

Recitative and aria, in oratorio, parallel their use in opera, the recitative being used essentially for the epic or narrative parts, and the aria for the lyric parts. All forms of recitative described under opera are used. Forms of aria also. (Aria differs from "song" chiefly in its loose repetition and elaboration of the text: the melodic outlines of both may be very similar.)

In the last analysis recitative and aria are phases of the same basic tonal representation: variations in pitch and in duration (with dynamic gradation). When neither pitch nor duration is fixed according to a pattern, we have speech (the recitative characteristic of certain forms of melodrama in which the words are actually spoken, not chanted, entirely independent of any musical background). Pitch, and metric inflection are free. At the other extreme is song, a series of definite pitch and metric patterns (phrases) closely correlated with the accompaniment. Between these extremes, all degrees of combination are found.

HISTORY. The close psychological similarity between oratorio and opera is seen in the common time origin of both; the development of monodic music about 1600. The precursors of the oratorio were the mysteries and miracle plays of the Middle Ages, and more specifically the laudi spirituali then in use. Both oratorio and opera are tonal expressions of life; oratorio, essentially serious, subjective, other worldly, deals with the things of the spirit, religion, truth, time, mankind in the abstract, the world; opera deals with the objective aspects; heroes, love, hate, pleasure.

The earliest oratorios are associated with Filippo Neri, founder of the congregation of Oratorians at Rome, about 1600. They were religious or moralizing compositions, in extended form, with soli, chorus, orchestra, scenery and action (*azione sacra*), written by composers who also composed opera. Cavaliere's *La Rappresentazione di Anima e di Corpo* (1600) is generally considered the first oratorio, a *dramma sacro per musica*. It was essentially dramatic, based upon the *stile rappresentativo* without a clear differentiation be-

tween recitative and aria. The epic element, which used recitative for narration in the character of narrator or historicus testo, was introduced by Giacomo Carissimi (1604-1674). This rôle replaced the scenery and action. The Carissimi tradition, musically an advance over the first attempts, was carried on by Alessandro Stradella (1645-1681) a pupil of Carissimi. But lyricism, after all, remains the most natural melodic characteristic, and the next chapter in the history of oratorio finds its introduction by Alessandro Scarlatti (1659-1725), whose improvement in both recitative and aria were common to opera as well as to oratorio. The aria (developed probably by Rossi [d. 1653]) was used for lyric, emotional parts (the equivalent of song), accompanied recitative for the dramatic parts, and recitativo secco for the narrative parts. But these procedures are also characteristic of his operas.

At the time of Scarlatti oratorio had used the three elements of epic, dramatic and lyric presentation, and as texts, heroes from the testaments, allegorical personages, saints and other sacred topics. The form was scarcely distinguishable in musical content from the opera of the period.

With its introduction into Germany, by Heinrich Schütz (1585-1672) with Gabrieli forming a link, oratorio narrowed down its field to the Passions, at the same time increasing in seriousness and appropriate musical content. The metric aria of Scarlatti was discarded and a modified, expressive type of plain chant (from the intonation of the psalms) was substituted. Later on this in turn gave way to the German Chorale, thus introducing a folk root (Sebastiani, 1622-1683). At this time, the narrator or evangelist was recited by a tenor, the part of Christ by a bass. Funke and Keiser are to be mentioned here as composers of Passion music. In the meantime the church cantata, in the hands of Buxtehude and J. C. Bach added to the serious musical forms available.

Thus far the composers of oratorio had also been composers of opera, and the two forms of music expression differed but little in musical form or substance. With Johann Sebastian Bach the separation came in striking force, and oratorio reached the highest artistic level it has ever attained. (*St. Matthew* and *St. John Passions, B minor mass.*)

(During the Middle Ages the various versions of the passion were recited with dramatic action, partly in church and partly in procession outside, leading symbolically to

Calvary and stopping for the presentation of dramatic scenes in costumes. The modern *Passion Play* at Oberammergau is a modified continuation of this).

The entire nature of Bach's genius fitted the musical and psychological problems of oratorio. Far overshadowing his predecessors in musical inspiration and technique, and thoroughly conversant with church music in its artistic and liturgical aspects, he brought all the essential creative elements to bear on this field. Moreover, his contrapuntal command enabled him to integrate the earlier polyphony, which is appropriate to some phases of oratorio, with the later homophonic style. The successors of Bach, although they produced some creditable works, fell short of the goal (Graun, Hasse, C.P.E. Bach).

The Italian style of oratorio flourished with George Friedrich Händel (1685-1756), particularly in England where Händel lived. In his oratorios, the musical, not the religious element, predominates. They are distinctly concert conceptions, even at times theatrical (some of them were designed for scenery and action). What Bach did for the German oratorio after Schütz, Händel did for Italian oratorio (lyrically in the Messiah; epically in Israel in Egypt). The influence of the English masque is also felt, and this partly accounts for the wide and enthusiastic reception which the Händelian oratorios found in England. Händel's knowledge of opera resulted in the use of a freer recitative and aria in his oratorios. At the same time he brought the chorus to a distinctly high artistic level. His greatest work is the *Messiah* (1741), which, of all oratorios ever written, is the best known. It owes this position to the fact that it combines the two basic elements. It is neither purely concert nor liturgical material. Instead it is both: it perhaps leans more toward the Protestant liturgy than his other works. Händel also introduced the three-part division of oratorio to replace the previously used two-part division.

Since music, preceding the birth of monody, was essentially vocal, it is natural that oratorio, in the first century of its history should be developed from a vocal center. The marked development of instrumental music, however, in the 17th cent., was forced to affect all forms of music creativèness. We find this instrumental development in the works of Josef Haydn (1732-1809) both in his *Creation* and in the *Seasons*. The emphasis is placed on the musical side and although the genius of Haydn invested recitative and aria with superb ar-

tistry, it also lifted the instrumental parts, whether ritornelli or accompaniment, to higher levels than before, and this in spite of poor texts. In fact the *Seasons,* with its highly developed tonal descriptions, is on the border line of oratorio; it may well be considered an extended cantata.

With Haydn and his predecessors, all tonal elements of oratorio had been developed. The period following him did not carry either the form or the content of oratorio any further. Numerous works were written but they were of secondary stature. Conspicuous exceptions were Mendelsohn's *Saint Paul* (1836) and *Elijah* (1846), works which combine the subjective and the objective elements in the light, typical Mendelssohnian style. Both Italian and German elements have been traced in them.

Oratorio, as an original art form, has never played a major part in the music history of France, for there the performance of religious and even liturgical subjects was permitted as a form of opera, and the predominating influence of the ballet (which is naturally ill adapted to the serious content of oratorio) further restricted the field. The introduction of oratorio into France is generally attributed to M. A. Charpentier, a pupil of Carissimi, but it slumbered until much later. F. Lesueur wrote a number of short biblical oratorios which preceded the *L'Enfance du Christ* (1854) of Berlioz. This is usually considered the first French oratorio; it contains some of the finest music of this composer. Other works which have retained a prominent position are Cesar Franck's *Beatitudes* and Gounod's *Redemption.*

In no other country has the oratorio found more fertile ground than in England, although its artistic creation has been entirely in the hands of non-English composers: Händel and Mendelssohn. On the other hand, the native English anthem was a form which lent itself very readily to absorption into the oratorio and the closeness of this transition resulted in the wide and enthusiastic acceptance of the extended oratorio in England. Unfortunately, although all English composers wrote oratorios, these are of but passing interest (Arne, Wesley, Bennett). A later revival owes its impetus to Parry, Stanford, Mackenzie and Elgar (*Dream of Gerontius*).

In Germany, after Mendelssohn, numerous oratorios were composed none of which contributed significantly to its history (Rubinstein, Raff, Gade, Bruch). Liszt in his legend of Saint Elizabeth and Christus has produced works which in some respects go back to the

Gregorian intonations, in others to Mendelssohn, and in yet others to his own individuality in both choruses and recitatives.

Oratorio, as an art form of large dimensions belongs primarily to the past. Its original function as a religious expression has resulted in texts the poetic value of which is small (*Messiah*). In fact much of the best music in oratorio is not liturgical, or even sacred in character. And conversely, some of the most pious moments are not accompanied by good music. But, as a music form, the oratorio must stand independent of its religious implication. Thus its length will be limited since the range of sacred contemplation cannot possibly equal that of the opera idioms. If it develops into a realistic tone-painting of earth, heaven and hell, it will enter the realm of tone poems. Moreover, modern tonal and musical idioms are better adapted to small forms than to large ones. Subject matter and form have caused oratoria to yield to shorter types and to serious but secular contata: Brahms, *Requiem;* Berlioz, *Damnation of Faust;* Debussy, *L'Enfant Prodigue;* Pierne, *Children's Crusade;* Coleridge Taylor, *Hiawatha;* Paine, *St. Peter;* Parker, *Hora Novissima;* Strawinski, *Oedipus Rex,* and the works of Hindemith, Honneger and Hass and others. —O.O.

orchesis (Gr.). Used interchangeably with *nomas* by the ancient Greeks, these terms referred to the art of expressive gesture, of human movement in genera. A name that has been adopted by many dance clubs in universities and colleges throughout the United States. It was first used by the University of Wisconsin dance club, organized in 1919.

orchestra. (1) In ancient Greece, the place in front of the stage allotted to the chorus. (2) The place occupied by the musicians in a modern theatre. (3) The musicians themselves. (4) The instruments for which the composition is written.

orchestration. See instrumentation.

orchid leaf line. See CHINESE ARTS.

order. An order in architecture is a particular treatment of a column and the entablature which its supports, as to its proportions, contour and enrichment. The Greeks developed the Doric, Ionic and Corinthian orders which were used with modifications by the Romans. To these the Romans add the Tuscan and the composite orders. See capital. —O.M.S.

ordinaries. See HERALDRY.

ordinary of Mass. See Mass; MEDIAEVAL MUSIC.

ordonnance. Placement of the elements of a composition with regard to each other and to the whole.

organ. See MUSICAL INSTRUMENTS.

organic. An organism is a coherence of related powers which is self-sufficient, and because of this self-sufficiency stands out in relief against the world around it, as an independent thing. The adjective derived from this noun applies therefore to the state of an organism. In the larger sense of the word every work of art must be organic because it is a unified world within itself, in which all parts are so closely related to each other that they form, when united, an independent whole.

The narrower sense of the word means not only a unity of form but a representation in which the natural organic essence is self-evident. The Greek artist, e.g., always tried to make his work organic, not only in the first sense, but in such a way that the meaning of the natural organism becomes obvious. The representation of men or groups of men, of plants or groups of plants was made in such a way that the figures represented form a unity in themselves, without the need of any external completion. In doing this he started with natural organic beings which he idealized in accordance with the law of eternal images to which all things are subject (see idealism). In opposition to the southern artists, the northerners tended to works of inorganic appearance. That which they represent has need of an external fulfillment, or at least is represented in such a way that it seems to need this fulfillment in order to arrive at universal unity and balance. To do this they had to strip natural organic models of their self-sufficient character in order to make them fit their purpose.

One may compare, for instance, the antique with Germanic art; or the works of such Renaissance artists as Raphael, Leonardo, Michelangelo, with those of the artists of the Netherlands such as van Eyck, van der Goes, Rembrandt. —A.J.S.

organistrum. See MUSICAL INSTRUMENTS.

organ point. One tone sustained through independent harmonies; also called **pedal-point.**

organum. (1) One of the medieval systems of harmonizing a cantus firmus by adding the octave and the 5th (or 4th); called also **diaphony.** (2) An instrument; later an organ. See MEDIEVAL MUSIC.

Orgatron. See Everett Orgatron.

Oribe yaki (Jap.). Pottery made in Owari province.

oriental loom. Made by fastening two poles perpendicularly in the ground to a sufficient depth, leaving above ground as much of each pole as equals in length the desired rug. This framework supports two horizontal rollers, the warp threads being wound around the upper, while the ends are fastened to the lower; the weaving is begun, and on it the rug is rolled while in process of construction. To the warp threads of fine linen or cotton the weavers tie the tufts of worsted that form the pile. This worsted, which has been dyed previously hangs over their heads in balls. When a row of knots is finished, it is pressed down to the underlying weft by a long and heavy comb with metal teeth. Then the tufts are clipped close with sheers, to make the pile. In the finer rugs there are seldom more than two or at the most three threads between every two rows of knots, but in coarser kinds there are more threads.   —B.E.J.

ORIENTAL MUSIC. For purposes of this brief survey of an immense and highly diversified field of musical utterance, the continent of Asia will be considered the geographical orient. From Arabia, Egypt, India and China arose originally the art cultures of the Occident and its science and art of rhythmitonal expression. Oriental music employs the universal material of sound organized by rhythm, melody and tone quality. Harmony, in its specific occidental meaning and practice, is absent. But harmony—*sui generis*—is present to the oriental inner ear in a greater extent than is realized by western minds. The distinguishing characteristics of oriental music considered *en masse* are:

I. *Monophony.* For the most part the Orientals sense and create rhythmitonal beauty through the manipulation and embellishment of a single and free tonal thread. The melodic contour and pattern, plus free decorations, possible alone to monophonic music, form the basis and beauty of Asiatic tone-art. The Occident developed polyphony; the Orient developed the beauty and expressiveness of monophony, an aesthetic practice and viewpoint

carried out in much of its visual arts and crafts. The folk and art songs of India reveal a loveliness and distinction of tone line that is unmatched in western music. This is true in part of the enduring body of Chinese and Japanese folk songs. Since oriental music submits to the same general classifications as does occidental, the spontaneous folk utterances can easily be contrasted with ritual music and conventionalized classics. Western polyphony is approximated in the Oriental's use of a variety of percussion and plucked string instruments as a simple-to-complex rhythmic background to the horizontally flowing melodic line, thus combining the physically rhythmic with the melodically aesthetic in emotional conflict. His conception and application of the rhythmic principle are extensive and subtle; measured, accented meters give bisymmetry, and measurable flowing rhythms asymmetry to his lyrical and dance forms. The rhythms in singing poetry and free verse follow rules of his prosody and the metre of national poetry. They are based on vowel lengths, not upon stress as in western song; the fixed unit in such a free song or chant being a section or group of bars which are not necessarily alike. Three rules are broadly applicable to all oriental songs of this free class: the rhythm must follow (a) the words; (b) the melody; (c) the rhythm deciding the close of sentences. The Oriental is not hampered by bar lines or chordal harmony; is free when freedom is desired; is a consummate master of a wide range of irregular rhythms (i.e. 5, 7, 11 beats to the unit), with syncopated cross rhythm in threes or fours. The interrelation of rhythmic and tonal movement, and linear relation of tones have an intimate bearing on oriental folk and classical forms.

II. *Use of the pentatonic scale common to most folk utterance.* Oriental folk music, particularly that of China and Japan, is reminiscent of Celtic folk music since the pentatonic tone-series is common to both. The ancient nomenclature of the Chinese pentatonic series reveals the close relationship existing between the State and its music. Taken in ascending order from F it is called **Emperor, Prime Minister, Loyal Subjects, Affairs of State, Mirror of the World.**

Employment of intervals smaller than half-step. Generations of conscious or unconscious manipulation and modification of melodic intervals in a musical system unfettered by fixed harmonic relationships tends to the distintegration of even the smallest intervals accepted by the Occidental as practicable. These microtonal intervals are used largely in the tonal embellishments but when heard with understanding the elaborate decorative "graces" become a structural factor in oriental improvisation and composition. Orientals have divided the 12-tone octave into fractional steps; the Arab, for example, recognizes 24 to 26 intervals within the octave. The Hindoos have further refined these intervals in theory and practice, hence a large number of traditional modes (called ragas in India) are available to the Indian musician-poet. Attributing definite ethical, social, or temporal significance to a single tone, and to a modal series is highly characteristic of Orientals, for music, qua music, did not attain its complete independence in either the classical or modern epoch. World War II will necessarily hasten its rise into that status.

III. *Melody.* Melody is the source, life and destiny of oriental song. Its fluid rhythms, illusive and prismatic pitch intonations and instrumental tone colors, when inter-fused, or when associated with words, reveal a new facet of beauty to western ears. A constant connecting of tone with tone through portamento, gives to Far Eastern song and instrumental solo a continuity of sound unknown in western music, demonstrating the importance in oriental music of the interval over the single note. The oriental singer is also a poet. His art is impersonal, reflecting emotions and experiences deeper than those of any single individual.

IV. *Musical Instruments.* The understanding and evaluation of Oriental music demands a knowledge of its ritual and secular instruments. Their types, limitations and capabilities have to a marked degree created their musical aesthetic and technical practices (see MUSICAL INSTRUMENTS).

V. *Symbolism.* Ancient oriental culture and civilizations have developed fixed and ideal conventions in spatial and temporal arts. Their ritualistic music has become in large measure an art of reviving strong associations and intensifying desired moods. Melodies and tone qualities are appreciated, not necessarily for their own aesthetic values and self-sufficient beauty, but as symbols of ideas, the elements, and spiritual states of inner experience. The Oriental's philosophic mind synthesizes his arts, seeking, and, to his satisfaction, attaining an at-one-ment with the beauty and meaning of life itself. This aesthetic philosophy penetrates his traditional and serious music and rewards him with a clearer perception of

and keener spiritual participation in the terrestrial and celestial drama of human life. See Levis, John Hazedel, *Foundations of Chinese Musical Art,* Peiping, 1936; Strangways, A. H. Fox, *Music of Hindustan,* 1914; Coomaraswamy, A. K., *Essays in National Idealism,* 1909; Sunaga, Katsumi, *Japanese Music,* Tokyo, 1936; Idelsohn, A. Z., *Jewish Music,* New York, 1929; Salvador-Daniel, *Arab Music and Musical Instruments,* Edited by Henry G. Farmer, New York, 1914; Grove, Sir George, *Dictionary of Music and Musicians,* 3rd Edition, 1935; Thornton, Philip, *The Voice of Atlas,* London, 1936. —H.P.E.

Oriental perspective. See PERSPECTIVE.

oriental rug dyes. *Cochineal* (coccuscacti) is the product of an insect which lives on a species of cactus. It yields a red dye. *Indigo* yields the deep blue dye. When the Indian indigo plant (indigofera tinctoria) is in flower, it contains the largest quantity of coloring matter. *Kermes* (Oriental origin means worm, Sanskrit form is *krmi.* In ancient Iranian it is known as *kerema* and in Lithuanian as *kirmis.* Bible furnishes oldest evidence of existence of this dye, uses Hebrew name *tola* or *tolaat,* meaning worm. Greeks and Romans believed it to be *kokkos* (berry). Crimson, *cramoisi* (French), and *Karmin* (German) are derived from same root). Grains are dried bodies of female of a species of shield-louse. Insects attach themselves firmly to branches and leaves by means of their jaws and remain motionless, gradually swelling to a round shape which explains why Greeks believed it to be a berry. Kermes is more durable than cochineal. *Madder* (q.v.) is a common dye used for red. *Saffron* yellow is often produced from Persian berries, turmeric, saffron, and sumac. Greens are obtained from various sources. The fruit of several buckthorns, or the Persian berries gives also greens and brilliant yellows. Most of the greens however are produced by the combination of indigo with yellow. Synthetic dyes for carpets were not known to the East until 1865. —B.E.J.

oriental rugs, doctoring of. A method used to paint the pile with dyes which have been dissolved in alcohol and painted on to the rug with a brush. It is done to correct inequalities and imperfections in original coloring or to give the customer the exact color desired. Color applied in this way is not permanent and can be usually detected by opening the pile. —B.E.J.

Oriental rugs, kinds of. *Afghan, Bakshi, Baku, Bectash,* Mohammendan, *Beluchistan, Bergama, Bokhara,* Chinese, Dasmascus, Dragon rug, *Feraghan, Ghiordes,* Hearth rug, *Herat,* Holbein rug, so-called, Indo-Persian, *Jushagan, Kazak, Khorossan, Kilim, Kis Ghiordes, Koula, Kuba, Kula, Lâdik, Makri, Mudjur, Oushak,* Polonaise, prayer rugs, Rhodian, Samakand, *Saraband, Shiraz, Soumak,* Syrian. See *Catalogue of Oriental Rugs in the Collection of James F. Ballard,* J. Arthur McLean and Dorothy Blair, Indianapolis, 1924.   —J.A.M.

Oriental rugs, main elements of. Border, field, guard lines, guard stripes, knots, Sehna and Ghiordes, panel, spandrels. See *Catalogue of the Oriental Rugs in the Collection of James F. Ballard,* J. Arthur McLean and Dorothy Blair, Indianapolis, 1924. —J.A.M.

Oriental rugs, methods of identifying. No one can determine with reasonable certainty the character and origin of an Oriental rug unless he understands the character and origin of the 5 or 6 groups of Asiatic rugs. Identify it by the manner in which it is made instead of by its appearance. The student will be assisted by a study of the following rules.

Rule I: (a) Caucasian and Turkoman designs are almost invariably geometric. (b) Turkish designs are frequently of floral and highly decorative character, detached motifs. (c) Persian and Indian designs are usually complete compositions. (d) Samarkand and Chinese designs employ detached motifs, animal, floral and geometric.

Rule II: By an analysis of the technique of a rug it will be found that the only rugs that are tied with the Senna knot are: Fereghan, Kirman, Khorassan, Ispahan, Seena, Bokhara, Khiva, Afghanistan, Beluchistan, Yomud, Beshire, Semarakand, and some Chinese. All other rugs are tied with the Turkish or Ghiordes knot.

Rule III: The pile of a rug is, of course, wool, but the web, consisting of the warp and the filling upon which the knots are tied, is a guide often to the character of a rug. Thus, most of the Persian rugs have cotton warp and weft; most of the Turkish Kurdistan and Turkoman have wool warp and weft. Caucasian rugs follow no rule; some being of wool warp and cotton filling. In the large carpet size rugs we distinguish grades very quickly, cotton being commonly used. The Turkish Oushake, however, have wool warp and wool filling. So also the Demirdji, mod-

ern Kulahs, Akhissars, Caesarians and Kirshehrs—all Turkish. Where the warp and filling are cotton, the rugs are Persian, with the exception of the Khorassan, which employs wool in the filling. The Samarkands may have wool or cotton; so also the Chinese.

Rule IV: Rugs showing at the ends a wide web instead of mere fringe, the web being sometimes plain and sometimes embroidered are: Bergamo, Afghan, Makri, Beshire, Beluchistan, Yomud, Bokhara, Shiraz, Niris, Ladik.

Rule V: It is a safe rule that Persian and Mosul rugs have overcast sides and Turkish, Turkoman, Turkestan and in most cases the Caucasian pieces have selvaged sides. Care should be taken, however, in determining characteristics by the side finish, that you be not deceived by an applied edge, sewed upon the rug as simply a repair job, where the original edge is frayed or ragged.

Rule VI: Where a rug is exceedingly fine, as indicated by the back, it may be any of the following, which contain one hundred or more knots to the square inch: Ispahan, Ladik, Ghiordes, Kashan, Senna, Kabistan, Antique Kulah, Kirman, Saruk, Tabriz, Kermanshah, Daghestan, Bokhara, Chichi. These are all, naturally, short pile rugs.

Rule VII: In the texture of the sides of a rug there are also distinguishing marks. Goat hair is conspicuous in the heavy selvage of the Yuruks and Beluchistans; parti-colored yarns in the sides of the Shiraz; fine silken cord is used on the Saruks; parti-colored selvage is used on the Yomuds and Genghis.

With the following rules no rule applies: Caucasian, Shirvan, Kabistan, Leshgian, Turkish, Oushak, Kaba-Karaman, Modern Kulah, Demirdji modern, Ghiordes modern, Akhissar, Karadagh.   —B.E.J.

original boards. *Book.* The boards or covers or other wrappers in which the book was published.

Ormazd. In Zoroastrianism, the chief of all the gods, the supreme deity, guardian of mankind, source of all good.

ormolu. A variety of brass made to imitate gold in appearance, much used in France in the 18th and early 19th cents. as a decorative accessory to furniture, etc. See metalwork.

ornament (L. *ornare,* to adorn) is an additional element to an otherwise merely structural form. This form may represent a building, a piece of furniture, a weapon, an instrument, etc., created in three dimensions; a lace, a fabric, a book cover or the written or printed page or a book, or even a single initial, in only two dimensions. Thus the ornament always means an accessory which may be added or taken away without changing the essential character of the ornamented subject.

Since the ornament is always something added—either as decoration of an architectural structure or as an embellishment of potteries or extiles; e.g., it follows and expresses the "style" of a certain period as accompaniment to the respective larger form, only that this ornament is not restricted by any functional needs or considerations. Therefore, changes in ornamentation usually follow each other more quickly than the stylistic changes which are expressed in the decorated works proper. Thus the knowledge of the history and development of ornament renders the best means for an exact dating of works of fine and applied arts.

Even the fact that in certain periods the form of the ornament itself is influenced by the function of the bearer of it or by the material in which it is executed, or by the technique in which it is applied, does not change the typical additive character of any ornament. The most materialistic conception of an ornament, however, can never reduce the meaning of the ornament as such to any utilitarian tendency of design.

Without attempting either to enumerate all the different ornaments throughout the ages or to give the history of the development of each single ornamental form (see arabesque, band ornament, echinus, grotesque, maeander, rocaille, etc.) it must be stated that some characteristic principles of their origin repeat themselves and can be followed through all the stylistic periods.

Generally speaking, we can distinguish between two main groups in ornamentation: geometrical-abstract forms on the one hand and naturalistic-vegetable forms on the other. This does not contradict the fact that very often originally geometrically conceived forms develop into naturalistic formations, and that vice-versa sometimes the abstract expression becomes less outspoken by leaning on similar naturalistic forms.

Examples for the geometrical-abstract principle of ornamentation can be found in most primitive civilizations. There the magic character supersedes the decorative tendency of the respective pattern (totemism). In some civilizations of the Near and Middle East within certain periods (in the archaic Greek culture, in the peasants' art of Europe, etc.) the geo-

metrically abstract principle is dominant. Motifs developed from the technique of weaving, such as knots, crossing threads, etc., elements from handicraft like the so-called *Beschlagwerk* (mounting) are taken over and translated into geometrized forms and thus applied, for instance, on pottery or engraved into metal. Sometimes, even three-dimensional motifs are translated into two-dimensional colored abstractions.

The naturalistic principle in ornamentation can be found to some extent as early as in the drawings of the cavement. In Egyptian civilization, and esp. in the realm of Cretan-Minoan culture, naturalistic motifs occur very frequently, and in the development from the archaic Greek period to the climax of Greek art in the 4th cent. and the following Hellenistic period, naturalistic ornamental forms flourish more and more, gradually superseding geometric tendencies.

Throughout history, the development oscillates between these two extremes: geometrical-abstract and naturalistic vegetable. In the decorations from the early Christian (q.v.) era to the Ottonian (q.v.) epoch the frequently used naturalistic motifs representing Christian symbols (grapes, fish, etc.) should not be misinterpreted as original ornamentation. They represent merely abbreviated depictions. The later medieval centuries develop increasingly a naturalistic treasure of ornamental forms (on capitals of pillars and columns, borders, friezes, etc.) which eventually leads to the rich naturalistic Renaissance ornamentation, a logical outgrowth of the revival of ancient forms. Since then the whole "vocabulary", so to speak, of "motifs" is fixed and relatively limited. Only occasionally a geometrical motif slips in like, e.g., in some geometrical Chinese ornaments in the 18th cent., or during the Classical Revival, archaic Greek formations. Two ornamental forms, however, can really be called creations of Renaissance and Baroque times: the scrollwork in the 16th cent. and the rocaille in the 18th cent.

The variations of ornamentation mirror most exactly the tastes and preferences of the respective countries, nations, and periods. Thus to follow up the change of a certain individual motif from its first appearance through all its stages of migration in the geographical and temporal sense would give the clearest insight of the differences in the visual and artistic conception of the respective countries and periods. See Owen Jones, *The Grammar of Ornament*, London, 1865; G. Hirth, *Der Formenschatz*, Munich, 1879 ff; O. Reynard, *Catalogue d' ornements dessinés et gravés,* Paris, 1846; Alois Riegel, *Stilfragen,* Berlin, 1893; D. Guilmard, *Les maîtres ornemanistes,* Paris, 1880; Peter Jessen, *Der Ornamentstich,* Berlin, 1920; For individual ornaments see under the respective articles.   L.P-E.

ornament engraving. While in our days photographs of former artistic expressions can be used for stimulating artisans and craftsmen in creating patterns for applied art, former times had to rely on models brought down by means of graphic art which could be reproduced.

The 15th cent. invented the so-called ornament engraving to fulfill this purpose of being model. Before that time, inventor and executor of a work of art were mostly the same person, so they did not need this link. Now woodcarvings and engravings, helped very much by the invention of printing, did their part in spreading new forms. Thus, architects, sculptors, and painters became not only leaders in their respective fields, but by the means of the ornament engraving (in the beginning mainly woodcarvings) their inventions or details of them were carried on for further use by later generations and in other fields of art.

This short explanation shows already that the word "ornament engraving" covers much more than only engravings of ornaments. We use this term for engraved models, published in single sheets or in whole series, determined for all kind of gold—and silversmith's work, for carpenters, panel painters, embroideries, details of doors and windows, pieces of furniture, iron work, etc. We know innumerable engravers who by purpose did their engravings only for model's sake. Ornament engraving was especially wide spread nearly during all the ·periods from the 16th to the 17th cent. in Italy (Zoan Andrea, Agostino Veneziano, Enea Vico, Agostino Mitelli, Bernardino Radi, Stefano della Bella, Guarino Guarini, Filippo Passarini, etc.), Germany (Hans Sebald Beham, Heinrich Aldegrever, Peter Flettner, Virgil Solis, Lucas Kilian, Christoph Jamnitzer, J. C. Bodenehr; Paul Decker, Johann Jacob Schübler, Hoppenhaupt, Jeremias Wachsmuth, Johann Esaias Nilson, etc.) and France (Jacques Androuet Ducerceau, Etienne Delaune, Jean Lepautre, Jean Vauquer, Jean Bérain, Daniel Marot, Claude Gillot, Jean Pillement, Nicolas Pineau, Charles Huquier, Jean François Forty). In the Netherlands, ornament engravings excelled in the 16th and 17th cents. (Cornelis Bos,

Johannes Vredeman de Vries, Adriaen Collaert, Peter Quentel, Artus Quellin, Philps Vingboons), while England had its highest development in the 18th cent. (Robert and James Adam, Thomas Chippendale, William and John Halfpenny, George Heppelwhite, Thomas Sheraton).

It needs no stressing that for ornament engravings no specific style can be typical; on the contrary, since they flourished through three centuries during which time they gave stimulation to artisans, they always showed clearly the typical stylistic elements of each respective artistic period. See O. Reynard, *Catalogue d'ornements dessinés et gravés,* Paris, 1846; D. Guilmard, *Les maîtres ornemanistes,* Paris, 1880; *Katalog der Berliner Ornamentstich-Sammlung,* Berlin, 1935; Peter Jessen, *Der Ornamentstich,* Berlin, 1920; Rudolph Berliner, *Ornamentale Vorlageblätter,* Leipzig, 1925-1926; Fiske Kimball, "Sources and Evolution of the Arabesque of Berain", in *The Art Bulletin,* vol. XXII, No. 4, 1941.   —L.P.E.

ornamentation, architectural. The embellishment of architectural or structural forms which is intended to enhance the appearance.

ornamentation, tongue. Any ornamentation in which a form resembling a tongue is used as a motif, such as the Greek egg and tongue molding.   —O.M.S.

Orpheus. The greatest of Greek musicians, famous for his tragic attempt to bring his wife, Eurydice, back from Hades, and the founder of the Orphic Mysteries, which promised worshippers a blessed immortality. In ancient art he was often pictured on vase paintings. Post classical sculptors who have represented him include Crawford, Rodin, Gregory, Stewart, and Carl Milles.   —W.R.A.

Orphism. Abtstract style founded in Paris in 1912, named by Apollinaire, and represented by Delaunay and Kupka. By "Orphism", Apollinaire meant an art of pure "musical" lyricism of color. See FRENCH ART.   —L.D.L.

orpiment. Known also as King's yellow, this painter's pigment was once widely used in the Far East and in Europe. It is mentioned by classical writers and has been identified on many illuminated manuscripts of the Middle Ages and the Renaissance. It is closely related to the orange-colored realgar and is a natural, crystalline, yellow sulphide of arsenic, occurring as a deposit in Hungary, Macedonia, Asia Minor, and variously in Central Asia.   —G.L.S.

orthographic projection (Gr. *'orthos,* straight; and *graphein,* to write). A projection in which the projecting lines are perpendicular to the plane of projection. In architectural drawing it is a drawing where each face of an object is seen in side elevation. The order of such drawing is prescribed as back, left, front, right; and then, above the front is the top; and below the front is the bottom.   —V.K.B.

oscillogram. See harmonic analysis.

Osiris. *Egypt. Relig.* The god of the underworld and judge of the dead; brother and husband of Isis.

Otsu school (Jap.). A crude style of painting; the beginning of the *Ukiyo-e* school (q.v.).

Ottoman art. See ISLAMIC ART.

Ottonian art. So-called from the German emperor Otto the Great of the house of Saxony, 936-973, or 963-973, respectively But it includes almost all the reigns of the German Saxon kings who ruled from 919 to 1024. The high point of the Ottonian epoch was around the year 1000. The reign of Henry I (919-936) and even part of the reign of Otto I, show elements of the style of the late Carolingian period rather than the Ottonian epoch, while under Henry II (1002-1024), there were already noticeable signs of the transition into the Salian style.

Ottonian art developed a true German national style and is noted for its extremely fruitful activity.

In the field of architecture the ground plans were designed and the foundations stones laid for many important cathedrals, such as the Cathedral of Mainz in 975, the Cathedral of Worms in 996, the Cathedral of St. Peter in Minden in 952, the Cathedral of Essen and the Cathedral of Augsburg (1915). The first building of the Ottonian epoch that still stands is St. Cyriacus in Gernode. The only large remaining building which shows, in spite of later changes, the character of an Ottonian interior is St. Michael in Hildesheim (begun after 1001 by Bishop Bernward).

In regard to painting the most important school was located on the island of **Reichenau** in Lake Constance. This school included several distinct groups. The oldest group was the **Eburnant,** which combined the late Carolingian with the Ottonian style. The **Ruodprecht group** was named after the writer of the Egbert Psalter, written between 984 and 993 at the order of the Archbishop of Trier. The **Liuthar group** was named after Liuthar who wrote the Evangeliar of Otto III, now in the Cathedral of Aix la Chapelle. The style of this group was remarkable for its dynamic and dramatic expression. Works by the same group are, among others, the Evangeliar of Otto III of the Cathedral of Bamberg (now in Munich), and the Bamberg Apocalypse. Perhaps the most important work of the whole Reichenau school was the Egbert Codex done by the brothers Kerald and Heribert at the order of the Archbishop of Trier. Besides the workshops of Reichenau there were the important and well known schools of painting of Echternach, Mainz, Cologne, Hildesheim, and Regensburg. The best known of these are the workshops of Cologne, Regensburg, and Hildesheim.

In sculpture they were especially occupied with reliefs made from ivory, metal, stone and wood. The oldest ivory reliefs of the time of Henry II still showed the characteristics of the late Carolingian style. There is the ivory cover of the famous Echternach Codex Aureus done in the famous Echternach workshop about 990. From the Hildesheim workshop came the two halves of the bronze door of St. Michael's Church created under Bishop Bernward in 1015. From the same workshop, but done by a different master, came the so-called Easter Column. 3.79m high, and 0.58m in diameter, covered with scenes from the life of Christ. Other important sculptures of the same time are the antependium of the Cathedral of Aix la Chapelle, the bronze door at the south entrance of the Cathedral of Augsburg, the antependium of Henry II of the Cathedral of Basle (now in the Cluny Museum in Paris), the gold statue of the Virgin and Child in the Cathedral of Essen. Made a little later but still belonging to the Ottonian epoch stylistically is the wooden carved door of St. Maria im Kapitol in Cologne.

Among the works of applied art are the crown of the German emperors, the most famous treasure of the Middle Ages which was remade under Konrad II (1024-1026), the portable altar of St. Andreas, done under Archbishop Egbert of Trier (975-993), and several enamelled crucifixes of Mathilde, the niece of Otto II, in the Cathedral of Essen.

See GERMAN ART; also GENERAL VIEW: G. Dehio, *Geschichte der deutschen Kunst*, Berlin, 1914; W. Pinder, *Die Kunst der deutschen Kaiserzeit*, Leipzig, 1933; Max Hauttmann, *Die Kunst des frühen Mittelalters*, Berlin, 1937. ARCHITECTURE: G. Dehio and G. von Bezold, *Die kirchliche Baukunst des Abendlandes*, Stuttgart, 1892; P. Frankl, *Die Baukunst des Mittelalters, Handbuch der Kunstwissenschaft*, Berlin, 1918. SCULPTURE: A. Goldschmidt, *Die Elfenbeinskulpturen aus der Zeit der karolingischen und sächsischen Kaiser*, Berlin, 1914; R. Hamann, A. Goldschmidt, *Die frühmittelalterlichen Bronzetüren*, Marburg, 1926; J. Baum, *Die Malerei und Plastik des Mittelalters, Handbuch der Kunstwissenschaft*, Berlin, 1930. PAINTING: Bernath, *Malerei des Mittelalters*, Leipzig, 1916; Georg Leidinger, *Meistewerke der Buchmalerei*, Munich, 1920 ff.; A. Boeckler, *Abendländische Miniaturen bis zum Ausgang der romanischen Zeit*, Leipzig, 1930; A. Goldschmidt, *Die deutsche Buchmalerei*, Munich, 1928; G. Swarzenski, *Die Regensburger Buchmalerei des 10, und 11, Jhd.*, Leipzig, 1901; Alois Schardt, *Das Initial*, Berlin, 1938. APPLIED ARTS J. Braune, *Meisterwerke der deutschen Goldschmiedekunst der vorgotischen Zeit*, Munich, 1922. —A.J.S.

overblow. To blow through the tube in wind instruments in such a manner as to produce harmonics. See ACOUSTICS.

overcast, oversewn. *Book.* A variety of forms of overcasting. The principle of all forms is that the stitch goes through the side of the section or sheaf of leaves closed flat, taken out at the other side and around the back before being re-inserted. Sometimes ordinary machine sewing—like a hem on a garment—is described as overcasting.
—H.E.S.

overglaze painting. *Cer.* Decoration applied directly to the glaze is called overglaze painting. See CERAMICS I.

over-grazing. See CIVIC PLANNING.

overpass. See CIVIC PLANNING.

overs. *Book.* Complete copies or sheets over and above the number ordered from the printer; i.e., an edition of 1,000 usually numbers 1,006. Sometimes depends upon the size of the paper and its cutting. —H.E.S.

overtone. See harmonic analysis; ACOUSTICS.

overture. Compositions called overtures (Fr. *ouverture;* Ger. *Ouvertüre, Vorspiel, Einleitung*) are in most cases introductions to operas, oratorios, cantatas, etc., or the first of a collective group of movements such as a suite (see J. S. Bach's *Orchestral Suites*) The earliest operas have commonly a short introduction, sometimes called **sinfonia** or **toccata.** The "sinfonia avanti l'opera" developed into two principal forms, the French overture, a slow-fast-slow movement, of which Lully is believed to have been the inventor, and the Italian overture, a fast-slow-fast movement, associated wtih the name of A. Scarlatti.

The French form began characteristically with a pompous, slow, dotted rhythm, the *stile alla francese,* to which succeeded a brisk fugal passage, the whole terminated either by a return to the original slow passage or in some dance rhythm. This form was used by many composers, including Händel (see the overture to *The Messiah*) and J. S. Bach (see the four *Suites for Orchestra*, the *Partita in D major,* etc.).

The Italian overture was more suggestive than the French in influencing later forms, especially the symphony, which quite generally follows in its several movements the order of fast, slow, fast.

Before Gluck the opera overture had little, if any, direct bearing on the drama which followed, though in church music the character of the introductory instrumental passages is frequently appropriate to the remainder of the piece (see J. S. Bach's church cantatas and *St. Matthew Passion*). "The overture", wrote Gluck in his Preface to *Alceste,* "ought to apprize the spectator of the action to be represented and, so to speak, constitute itself the argument". Gluck himself failed to make this connection in all cases between overture and subsequent action, but he stated an ideal generally accepted by subsequent composers, and in his *Alceste* and *Iphegénie en Tauride* he did make, in overtures, clear references to the drama. Among the notable dramatic works in which may be found an immediate relevance of overture to drama are Mozart's overtures to *Don Giovanni, The Magic Flute, The Marriage of Figaro,* Beethoven's overtures to *Fidelio,* Weber's overtures to *Euryanthe* and *Der Freischütz,* and all of Wagner' overtures (or, as they are in some cases called *Vorspiele* or *Einleitungen*).

Many forms of introduction or overture to opera and other dramatic works are to be found in the literature from Mozart to the present. Certain types may be distinguished: (1) The prelude of varying lengths, suggesting the scene or the action to follow. Wagner employs this type of prelude (*Vorspiel*) in *Das Rheingold, Die Götterdämmerung, Tristan und Isolde*. Verdi introduces both his *Otello* and *Falstaff* by short passages. Richard Strauss is similarly brief in the introduction to *Salomé* (in *Elektra* he dispenses entirely with an introduction) and uses a short, though highly suggestive introduction to *Der Rosenkavalier*. Puccini and Debussy are also brief in coming to the opening curtain. (2) The potpourri of melodies later to appear in the action. Such stringing together of melodies is found chiefly in light operas, though the overture to Rossini's *William Tell*, while intended as a tone painting of the scene of the tragedy, is little more than a series of tuneful episodes. (3) The sonata-form overture, employing the essential principles of the movement which is commonly the first in the cyclic sonata, symphony, quartet, etc. With modifications and adaptation to dramatic purposes, this form of overture is found in Mozart (*Marriage of Figaro*), Beethoven (*Leonora*), and Wagner (*Die Meistersinger*).

These categories are by no means inclusive of all overtures. Many notable examples, such as the Overture to *The Magic Flute*, which is fugal with an introduction and episodes, fall outside these classifications.

The term overture has been used (esp. in the 19th cent.) for works which were not intended as introductions to operas, oratorios, or cantatas. At times even symphonies have been so called. Certain one-movement works, commonly in sonata-form, written as preludes to plays or simply as musical counterparts of characters, scenes, or dramas and intended for concert performance, are known as concert overtures. Among the notable examples of such overtures are Beethoven's *Weihe des Hauses* and *Coriolan*, Mendelssohn's *Midsummer Night's Dream* and *Fingal's Cave*, Schumann's *Manfred*, Tchaikovsky's *Romeo and Juliet* (called a fantasy overture).

—R.D.W.

ovolo. A classical moulding of single convex curve in a form approximating an oval or half ellipse; often ornamented with the egg and dart pattern.

oxidizing flame. *Cer.* Flame in which complete combustion occurs. See CERAMICS I.

Oxyrhynchus hymn. A Christian hymn in Greek notation from the 3rd cent. found at Oxyrhynchus, Egypt in 1922. This hymn is the only extant example illustrating the transitional period from the ancient Greek music to early Christian music. See no. 1786, *Oxyrhynchus papyri*, Part XV, eds. B. P. Grenfell and A. S. Hunt, transcribed by H. Stuart Jones, 1922.

—V.A.

P

padded leather. *Book.* Leather bindings with blotting paper, cotton wool, or other padding between the leather and the boards.

pagoda (Port.). A towerlike building in a Buddhist compound. Inasmuch as it is often non-functional, and the highest building in the compound, it serves somewhat the same purpose as the spire of a cathedral; a visual focal point. —J.A.M.

p'ai lou (Ch.). An architectural form of gateway commemorating a virtuous deed or person. See CHINESE ARTS.

painted enamel. See ENAMELLING ON METAL.

painterly. (The term has entered our vocabulary through Heinrich Woelfflin's *Kunstgeschichtliche Grundbegriffe* [Munich, 1915, Eng. trans., *Principles of Art History*, 1932], in which he uses it in contrast to "linear". According to this theory, which was drawn from a small sector of art history, there is a genetic law of human optics whereas early styles must mature into painterly styles.) While the "linear" stresses the expression of forms or ideas by lines with the main accent on the contour, the "painterly" emphasizes the rendition of masses and their relation to light appearing as color, tone, shade or shadow. It is called "painterly" because it indicates more the painter's handling of color and brush than the "linear", which refers to the act of drawing and not of coloring. The painterly form is achieved by a dense network of lines (which makes it evident that lines as such do not make a style "linear") or by merely alluding unevenly rendered lines as we find those two elements in Rembrandt's etchings, or by blotches of color, blended together with their neighboring colors, which are descriptive of light sensitive surfaces as seen in Titian's later paintings.

While the linear implies usually a definite statement as to the structure of the objects and eliminates the element of change, the painterly, speaking in terms of masses, surfaces, light and shadow, tends toward an emphasis of the casual circumstances of presentation, such as illumination, motion, mood, etc. The painterly draws more directly from visual experiences under a given condition than does the linear. It becomes the ideal expression for groups, nations or individuals whose eye sensitiveness is less controlled by intellectual abstractions. This more sensuous quality of the painterly style may either be put into the service of realistic art (cf. Velasquez or French impressionism) or be used sybolically as transcendental light (cf. Rembrandt, Greco, Redon).

The term may be applied in a derivative sense to sculpture and architecture as well. Thus, the Hellenistic sculpture, the statues of Bernini, the architecture of the German Baroque, the marble of Rodin, can be termed "painterly".

By no means should painterly be confused with "picturesque" although in the final effect they may coincide. The "picturesque" refers to an arrangement of nature or art in which we can project the mood of the romantic, the extraordinary, the contrasting, while "painterly" merely describes a way of rendering visual data. For the same reason it is not identical with "pictorial" which, according to the Oxford Dictionary, means "consisting of, expressed in, or of the nature of a picture or pictures".

The interesting literature of the 18th cent. pertaining to this problem will be found under "picturesque" (q.v.).

714

The stress on the painterly function of color and line appears in art theory much more rarely than the emphasis on design (*dessin, dissegno, Zeichnung*) as the basis of art. This is due to the prevailing intellectualism of art theoreticians on the one side and to the beginning of art theory in the era of the Renaissance with its outspoken linearism on the other. Even the art theory of the Baroque era emphasized the linear much more than it was practiced in actual creation. The "painterly" comes strongly forward in the essays of Sir Josuah Reynolds, preceded by the 18th cent. theorists' discussion on the related "picturesque", and in the discussions of the French Romantic and Impressionist school (cf. Delacroix, Gautier, Baudelaire, Zola, Signac). Recently, with a "plasticity craze" (L. Venturi) in art criticism, the consideration of the painterly in theory and practice has receded again. See H e i n r i c h Woelfflin, *Kunstgeschichtliche Grundbegriffe*, Munich, 1915, 2nd ed., 1929 (Eng. trans., *Principles of Art History*, 1932); August Schmarsow, *Zur Frage nach dem Malerischen*, Leipzig, 1896.   —A.N.

PAINTING. *I. Painting materials and techniques.* To understand the achievements or effects, as well as the limitations, of painting, it is necessary to remember that every painting is an object made by a man at a particular date. The artist's effects may describe him as progressive or reactionary; but he cannot exceed his materials. There is even some doubt if he can think ahead of the materials which he already possesses. This viewpoint is most ably presented by Charles Marriott who says, "art is primarily the characteristic use of materials, and the representation of nature and the direct action of design are both incidental to that. . . ."

The three basic materials are a colored powder, a liquid adhesive and a support. The colored powder may be an inorganic (mineral) or an organic (animal, vegetable) substance. The fluid in the adhesive will be water or oil, or may be an emulsion which is a combination of the two. The support may be fabric, paper, papyrus, leather, wood, artificial board, plaster, stone, metal or glass. The accessories of the painter, such as brush, pen, palette, palette knife, model, anatomical figure, air-brush, varnish, stretcher and frame, are inconstant materials used only at certain times. Their variability and use is relatable to the effects which the artist

achieves; their *availability* is intimately related to the effect.

The present most popular method of painting is in oil; the finely grained pigment is in this case ground in linseed or poppy oil; the method was made practicable for the "fine arts" in the 14th cent., was quickly adopted both in the North and in Italy.

The next most popular method, at least till recently, is watercolor; tempera painting may be replacing it. In the former, gum arabic is usually the adhesive; in the latter, yolk of egg is customarily the binder. Italians of the 14th and 15th cents. favored tempera. Fresco, the painting on wet lime, a most arduous procedure, is likewise experiencing efforts at revival. The method of the Greeks and Romans, use of beeswax as a binder, is seldom attempted in its pure form; it did not prove durable.

The Marriott thesis, to be significant, must presume that the practicability of available materials will ultimately determine their popularity. Yet in the application of this judgment one must consider materials which the artist does not use directly. For instance, the improvement of the camera, as by its ability to register color accurately, may result in a diminished use of oil as a painting medium for artists—inasmuch as the oil technique is especially adapted to achieving the camera's effects. In this case the camera will have partially supplanted oil painting. This very process seems, indeed, to be going on today; tempera has increased in popularity at the expense both of watercolor and of oil.

Applying the thesis still further, one may judge what is apt to happen to the current attempts to revive fresco. One will note that the revival was instituted in Mexico where the thick masonry wall is an ideal support. In Western countries generally such structure is rapidly becoming outmoded. The effects peculiar to fresco would seem, accordingly, to be dated.

TECHNIQUES. More variable even than the materials which the artist may use, are the techniques by which he applies color to the support. Each technique is but primarily dependent, but most emphatically *is* dependent, upon the materials selected. For instance, a limp sable brush cannot possibly simulate the rugged effects of a stiff bristle brush; likewise, oil painting cannot achieve the color intensity of tempera; tempera, because it dries so quickly, cannot be worked into the tonal modulations of which oil is capable.

To illustrate. The especial color effects

in the Italian painter Uccello could only be achieved by a glazing of pigments, as his red over gold—a procedure which oil made possible. Or again, in modern times, the **"pointillist"** tapping with the stiff brush replaced the traditional stroking of the brush in such men as Signac, ostensibly because they wished an impersonal technique which would be analogous to, and would simulate the effects of, modern science. Yet for the pointillist technique to become popular, and to be utilized as an element in the more complex techniques of 20th cent. men, it was necessary not only that the bristle brush be invented, but that it be produced in quantity and cheaply; for nothing wears down and distorts the brush like the tapping technique.

No two artists will, however, handle watercolor, tempera or oil paint in the same way. There are, to be sure, certain general consistencies of time and place. The English, perhaps because they were the first to popularize watercolor, retain the most rigid concept of how it should be used. In Flanders, similarly, oil painting helped quickly to formulate a linear (q.v.) painting style which itself persisted long after this medium had obviously looser and broader technical possibilities. The individual artist therefore chooses his materials, then arrives at his technique; his choice and the development of his craft are dependent upon the time and locality in which he lives, the commercial availability of certain pigments, brushes, supports, the purpose he is conscious of when he paints, his intelligence, the nature of his schooling, and the character of his own temperament.

With so many factors involved, the degrees of what we term proficiency or excellence in a work of art are, of course, tremendous. But a consideration of the basic conditions for the making of every work of art revealed this to us: the object is always made at a particular time; the relationship of the object to the time in which it was made becomes a constant, even if a complex, factor which we can study.

MODERN MATERIALS AND TECHNIQUES. One of the decisive factors which in the 19th cent. conditioned the development of art—the use of materials and techniques included—was the discovery of the past by the painter. The consciousness of past styles was before this very slight; the emergence of art history from its archeological phase, and the printing of cheap reproductions, were partly responsible for the change; quickly the painter learned to distinguish authentic ancient sculpture, the Renaissance and Dutch painters, the remote and the near past. The establishment of public museums even permitted him to see the originals. One of the first results was revivalist painting. Artists like David, imbued with the ideal of a French regime founded upon Athenian principles, sought to weld a contemporary painting style from the fragments of classical sculpture with which they were familiar. The effort was abortive because the revivalists violated in several respects the time-object consistency: they often borrowed from marble Roman copies of bronze Greek sculptures, and they sought to capture in their oil medium an expression and a pictorial organization which had been formulated in carved relief. The result is the artifice of the box-like space in which the stilted actors strut and gesture in complete indifference to each other. Moreover, following the example of extant antique reliefs, from which the hand of time had picked off the pigment, the neo-classicists held color in contempt.

Only gradually did artists achieve a consciousness of the old techniques in relationship to the old expressions. This awareness resulted in the really great discovery of the 19th cent.; viz., that the past was the most effective of all teachers but that she must never be imitated.

In its negative aspects the result is a constant and aggravating search for novelties—negative because a style cannot ever really be invented. Positively, the achievement is a fixation upon qualities which have most permanence through time. The desire to be an innovator, yet to produce work which will never cease to please man, is the exclusive dual ambition of the modern artist.

One of the most positive or constant factors is, as we have said, the time-object relationship. It is the greatest wisdom of modern painting—a clear awareness by the present century—that in the period when the greatest repertoire of materials and techniques (thanks to modern science and to history) was available, emphasis turned from the decadent viewpoint of technique as a "hidden" means of expression, to technique as a part of expression. That the spectator should be conscious of materials and technique, is the new and revolutionary idea. In Paul Klee, for instance, the process of lithography rather than being a mechanical means for achieving known effects, has restored to it the flexibility of the independent craftsman; it is the lithographic *press*, the physical machine, which he views to be mechanical. The attitude of Klee may, indeed, be viewed as an acceptance of the facts which are basic to the Marriott theory. That is— accepting the limitations upon the artist, as specified by his materials, what latitude there is becomes better realized through an ability to define where the machine's province ends.

One can date this shift of emphasis with Courbet and the Impressionists, or place it later. The point is that in modern painting the finished object, to be most enjoyed, must be looked at with an understanding not only of the technique, but of the flexibility of the technique involved. From the social point of view, this is a resolution of the artist-public distinction. At the period when the artist, because he had no stable economic basis in society, retreated into his *atelier* to paint exclusively to please himself—the public is imperatively beckoned to follow him into the studio, invited in by the painting if not by the man. Never before in the history of painting had the artist spoken so professionally, and with such apt reticence.

From the psychological viewpoint the situation is as healthy, if not as unique. The spectator is deceived when he is ignorant; by the accumulation of knowledge he does not become a *raconteur*.

II. Characteristics of painting. The art of painting can be distinguished from the other arts by the diversity of its objects. The range in painting is from tremendous mural decorations made for public buildings, to tiny miniatures fashioned to please the individual owner; from the ultra-sophisticated art of a Redon, a Matisse and a Mondrian, to the commercially calculated illustrations of a McClelland Barclay. The range has been extended with the gradual democratization and industrialization of society, so that a number of crucial issues have arisen regarding the phenomenon of public taste.

The history of painting is more complete than that of any other art in the sense that it covers all ages and civilizations with fewer breaks in the continuity. Even sculpture, which shares with painting the distinction of being a mature art from prehistoric times, has more notable gaps or instances of *lag*—for example, the half dozen centuries which precede the Romanesque period. In these "dark ages" the painting of miniatures for manuscripts, usually of a religious nature, constitutes the one unbroken record of man's imaginative inclination. The portability of the manuscript can alone account for this survival.

PORTABILITY OF PAINTING. But painting is flexible and portable in a still more important sense. One does not, to comprehend a painting, need to know a language in which it is written, or need a translator; an assemblage of instruments and of musicians is not required to bring the art into being. These two factors, differentiating painting from literature and from music, make it in every epoch adapted to exportation—an agent in cultural diffusion whether the maker and owner so intend or not.

UNIVERSALIZING AND OPPOSING TENDENCIES. The portability of painting is inseparable from its tendency to become universal both in its expression and in its formal means. A large chapter in the history of painting is the story of racial and national importations and assimilations. The ancient art of Attica subsides in the incalculable glory of an Ionian Renaissance. Early Christian painting achieves its character from a blend of Eastern and Classical elements which have, faster than the sharp eye of the historian can observe, shuttled back and forth across the Mediterranean. Yet, because of the flexibility of the art, one can see a contrary effort, usually on the part of political and ecclesiastical personages, to make colloquial and specious propaganda out of art.

Prior to the modern era the Byzantine Christian rulers established an iconography, a scheme of objective details, which hampered the fluency of stylistic evolution. The Jesuits, alarmed at the success of the northern Protestant Revolt, perceived that specifications more substantial than the iconographical must enliven the calculated style of a Raphael. Men as dissimilar as Guido Reni and Rubens answered the call, with a febrile sentimentality and a pagan sensuality respectively. The Kings of France, Catholic and nationalist, accepted Rubens, accepted what there was of substance in the Italian Mannerists, and by this masterly judgment effected a four hundred year identification of universal culture with French political fortunes.

In this move the unique element was the nationalism. Louis XIV, by his simple formula of *L'état c'est moi* more concisely even than the Christian Fathers envisioned himself the representative of the Muse in the Western World. It was in large part his regal descendants who modified this splendid vision under the tutelage of the academicians Lebrun, Boucher, and finally David with his equivocal appeal to the ancients—until we are brought up sharply in the 1890's with Gauguin's by-now astonishing revelation that he is not treading and will not tread in the French Tradition—but is sailing off for Tahiti.

THE MODERN PERIOD. No example can better illustrate the connection between cultural diffusion and the art objects's portability than the celebrated peregrinations of Gauguin's curvilinear motif. It has been established that the designs on the clothing of the Polynesians in Gaughin's paintings had been simplified for purposes of cheapness in printing by Manchester (England) cotton manufacturers who were, by the date of the artist's adventures, selling back to the Tahitians these Neo-Polynesian designs. The sequel to this discovery is plain when we reflect how vast, after all, is the British domain—the figures in Gauguin's *Ta matete* being constructed upon an old Egyptian formula, and clothed in cotton presumably from India at a goodly profit: the cut of the gowns being acceptable to Queen Victoria, to the French Missionary Society—to almost all contemporary Western institutions excepting only the official French Salon.

The minds which confront art are, admittedly, as flexible and variable as the art itself. Only so can we explain how the German Library of Information publications, circulated until 1942 in the United States, were able to single out "decadent" painters by a stylistic definition, but had to name the artist when disposing of musicians and writers. Simultaneously the indigenous American publications, such as Peyton Boswell's *Art Digest*, brought to a final intensity their attacks upon these same stylistic tendencies which Hitler hated—but in this instance named individuals, all allegedly members of the "School of Paris". Clearly, most of these names, while not French, were foreign.

In both cases, but by varied tactics, the age-old universalizing tendency in the art was met by the naïve explanation that "emotional instability is racial". And yet, contrarily, it was the portability of painting which finally came in for resentment. Otherwise Hitler, for instance, might with equanimity have permitted the "inferior races" their "inferior art".

III. The usage of painting. Aristotle was among the first to insist upon the ethical character of art. He broadly states, for antiquity and for most of the Christian era, the premise which no artist questioned consistently until modern times. In the *genre* of landscape painting where an ethical purpose, blunted by a sort of pantheistic vulgarization of the Deist doctrine, first receives its *coup de grâce,* the traditional purposiveness is only gradually eliminated. Within the "French tradition", for instance, Claude is obliged to insert in his imaginative vistas tiny figures which feebly carry the titles: *Flight into Egypt,* or *Acis and Galatea.* As late as the 1860's, Corot of the Barbizon School (q.v.) commonly lapses, if not into Christian purposiveness, at least into a perfunctorily "humanistic" inclusion of the human figure. But there is this distinction by then: he introduces the human figure and intends in those same years to be a popular painter. He has accepted the limitation which Claude, two centuries earlier, had struggled against.

Parallel to the disappearance of the traditional form of the ethical purpose, comes the modern doctrine of realism—of faithfulness to nature. At first the new approach was suggested as an ethical alternative—and such a rationale still obtains among the uninitiated; but a new tendency has been noted, beginning perhaps with the naturalistic social philosophers, and typified by Zola's alleged "science", to justify the realistic approach as a natural, a sort of organic, way of making a work of art. At its lowest, its least cerebral, level, the argument is easiest to understand and becomes an assertion: "Man is amorphous, let what he makes be likewise." The logical error here seems to be that of the "undistributed middle". The tactical error is to have abandoned the really cerebral level where any man may be a dictator by taste, able to disparage the content of work which does not please him.

FANTASY AND IMAGINATION. The laborious ethics of the nineteenth century and of pioneer art historians so well coincided with what political and religious manipulators had previously demanded of the painter that it has but recently been observed that the art of all periods attains to a reasonable degree of permanence, or is pleasing at least to modern man, when it dodges or exceeds the specifications. The creative imagination of the individual flares up in Giovanni di Paolo, in Sassetta, and therefore provocatively in the very face of the cult of the Blessed Virgin in Sienna. But contemporaneously, in the city of Florence, Piero di Cosimo and della Francesca—yes, and Botticelli—give an equally charming lie to the "realistic purposiveness" which historians have, on the basis of disjointed remarks of Leonardo, fastened upon the whole three centuries of the city's history. We know today that visual representation, rather than being the aim of the Renaissance, was as much the civic predicament as the Medici were in the arriving epoch of the new nationalisms. Realism wore the art out; as Lorenzo the Magnificent, the bitter and smoldering spirit of Vasari's portrait, is too worn out to long accompany Botticelli on his pleasant sojourn with the fragile and poisonous women of Elysium.

The three painters we mention are not the whole of Florentine art. They are merely the titans who enter a distinguished protest, in the appropriate phrases of mythology, at the moment when painting is in a muddle. For the art historian who has staked his belief in evolution on the atmospheric perspective of Masaccio, the linear devices of Uccello and the antomical researches of Castagno or Pollaiuolo, all three painters are embarrassing and "episodic".

Curiously enough Sassetta, the fantastic Sienese generally, Lorenzo Monaco and others whom such an historian as Mather once alleged to be loiterers in the pleasant bypaths of reactionary tradition, come in for some attention (as even in the later works of Mather) with the observation that sometime towards the end of the fourteenth century, what may be identified as a Cosmopolitan Style represented painting in its most fluent, its most imaginative, and most portable form. Mather himself does not observe clearly that a meticulous or learned movement towards visual representation is the colloquial tendency, having largely independent histories in the North of Europe and in the South. It can be said that we view the creative impulse, natural to most who start out wielding the brush, being subjugated by those equally ardent individuals who wield the scepter and the cross. The disintegrating tendency, from Giotto to Ghirlandaio in Italian painting, or from Hubert van Eyck to Van Dyck in Flanders, bears certain marked characteristics; in both regions the patron became specific, a man rather than an institution, and the realism fitted the patron's cause like the glove fits the hand. This, in point of fact—this identification of the artist's vision with the patron's prejudices—is the only kind of realism to which we can accord an historical recognition. Secondly, and curiously, each of these subjugated realists (who are so oddly different in their styles) overshadowed in his time other painters whom subsequent generations accepted as the master realists. In the case of Rembrandt, proposed until recently as *the* realist of all time, the situation is clearest. He had the amazing ability, perhaps because he lived in the seventeenth century, to keep his simple faith and a steady brush while going about the popular nineteenth century task of photographing Jesus. The ethics and the realism, as elements perceived by the public, coincide, ironically but perhaps necessarily, when what we term the "capitalist system" saw it profitable to make this concession. Ary Scheffer and Bougereau can illustrate. They are the accepted painters at the beginning of our really unique modern age in which a popular art (supported by segments of all economic classes) supplants the main creative tradition which must henceforth be carried on by the socially *declasse* painter.

IMAGINATIVE AND FORMAL ORGANIZATION. Most people today agree that the artist creates an object to which he imparts a life which is dependent upon the character of the objective world and the character of his own vision. The varieties of opinion under this definition can be distinguished according to the elasticity with which the person uses the word "vision", and the precision with which he may apply the phrase "objective world". The individualism of the artist is registered partially in his choice of subject matter, in the technique used, in the extent to which he avoids what seems to be mere imitation. But the most baffling of all elements to define is that quality of the imagination which varies for the individual artist and will vary again for his separate paintings. It is the viewpoint, personal and temporal, which existed in the making of that painting, and which, through a process of communication of colors, lines, shapes—yes, and illusions—finds today a new, if perhaps similar existence. Obviously one cannot define any quality which varies so much. Perhaps the best one can do is to hang the painting on the wall.

But the simplest of elements to define in a painting are what we call the formal ones. Since most, if not all, of them are conceived as having only a relative existence—valid as mutually distinguishable—they have a pleasing permanence. One such element is the *linear,* as distinguished from the *pictorial,* quality in painting.

IV. Systems of classification. The educator and the research scholar in presenting their material find it necessary to use classifications. The cautious ones will acknowledge at the start that their systems of classification are somewhat arbitrary. But what has been insufficiently admitted is that the oldest systems are particularly arbitrary. The *genre* classification into landscape, portraiture, still life, historical episode, and the like, is arbitrary because it presumes a basic importance of subject matter. The historical classification, as into Italian, French, German and English, is equally misleading, and mainly for this reason: the amount of material which any historian can cover in a given work is sharply limited: and the limitation which he has imposed is, in this case, one which does not imply the excluded material. One can investigate French painting and, unless he is also a good student of Italian art, proceed oblivious to that other great body of creative production. The queer thing is then, that both national and *genre* classifications, which are deduced from the historian who is not concerned with the art object as such, fail in that they are not arbitrary enough.

The most valuable formalist classification to date is that of Heinrich Woelfflin which was advanced in his *Fundamental concepts of art history* in 1915. He outlines five fundamental concepts or "schemes of pure visibility". All these schemes are clearly considered as points of view of the same phenomenon; and in the case of each scheme, the individual work of art is placed somewhere between the plus and minus poles—i.e., regarded as linear or pictorial. One can endlessly place additional paintings within the same scheme, thus adding to an understanding of the concepts rather than impoverishing them. And again, the concepts being arbitrary, an addition to their quantity is invited. The schemes of Woelfflin are contrived with painting in mind, and here show an amazing usefulness. They are scarcely exhaustive of the formal qualities in the individual painting.

Woelfflin first considers the distinction between *linear* and *pictorial*. The former, generically, indicates the conception of objects in their tactile character of outline and plane, whereas *pictorial* indicates the abandonment of drawing as a technique to be seen, in favor of pure visual appearances. The distinction is further amplified and illustrated. Secondly, Woelfflin distinguishes between *vision of surface* and *vision of depth*; thirdly, between *closed form* and *open form*; fourthly, between *multiplicity* and *unity*; and fifthly,

between *absolute clearness* and *relative clearness*. The scheme seems to be based originally on perceived differences in the baroque and classical styles. Some day the concepts must be extended, and may perhaps embrace a distinction such as the *geometric* and *amorphous* which will be applicable to both line and shape. Color intensity, hue and tone may likewise be included. Likewise a perception of the tactile character in paint may be opposed to the illusion that materials are not used.

Resistance to the Woelfflin method comes promptly from three sources. The research historian whose main task is to gather information, as dates and iconographical evidence, finds the system too flexible—perhaps too close to the meaning of art—to help him. The college teacher of the newly popular "social nature of art" course finds the Woelfflin system, even if relevant to his own thought, a little beyond the sophomore range . . . but may sense that the fault is not with the sophomore caliber of mind as much as with his grade teachers. Finally, the partisan, academic or modern, may be irritated to see how little the scheme, when applied, offers any compliments either to traditional styles or to the revolutionary and new. Despite what seems to be Woelfflin's personal conservatism of taste, despite his omissions, it may be his failure to make much of the progress-concept that is most obnoxious to the partisan. See Marriott, Charles, "Mind and medium in art", *British Journal of psychology*, vol. XI, 1920; Mather, F. J., *A History of Italian painting*, 1923 and *Western European painting of the Renaissance*, 1939; Woelfflin, Heinrich, *Fundamental concepts of art history*, 1915; Giedion, Sigfried, *Space, time and architecture*, 1941; Mumford, Lewis, "The death of the monument", *Circle*, 1937; Venturi, Lionello, *History of art criticism*, 1936; Wilenski, R. H., *Modern French painters* and *The modern movement in art*, 1927.
—B.G.

painting, Chinese. For terms relative to Chinese painting, see the following: *cheng, chih hua, chou, chou shou, chüan, chuan chou, fang, fêng su jên wu*, glass painting, *heien, hsiang, hsieh-i, hua, hua chüan, hua hun, jên wu, k'uan, kung pi, ling mao, mo, pi, piao, piao pti, pi hua, p'ing chang,* seal, *shan mien, shan shui, tien huang, t'i pa, t'i shih, tou fang, ts'ao ch'ung, ts'ê yeh, t'ung ching, yen, yin chang, yüan chin.* See also *Some Technical Terms of Chinese Painting*, Benjamin March, 1935; *An Introduction to the Study of Chi-*

nese Painting, Arthur Waley, 1923; *An Essay on Landscape Painting,* Kuo Hsi (trans. by Shio Sakanishi), 1935; *Chinese Painting,* John C. Ferguson, 1927; *The Chinese on the Art of Painting,* Osvald Siren, 1936; *A History of Early Chinese Painting,* Osvald Siren, vols. I and II, The Medici Society, 1933; *A History of Later Chinese Painting,* Osvald Siren, vols. I and II, The Medici Society, 1938; *Guide Posts to Chinese Painting,* Louise Wallace Hackney, 1929; *Chinese Paintings in American Collections,* Osvald Siren, Annales du Musée Guimet; Bibliothéque d'art. Nouvelle Série II, Plates 1-200, G. Vanoest, Editeur, 1927.   —J.A.M.

painting, Japanese. For terms relative to Japanese painting, see the following: *ashide-e, butsu-e, byōbu, dōso, e-kotoba, e-maki, e-makimono, ezō, fude, fusuma-e, gaku, gakumen, gofun, hashira-e, hitsui, in, jiku, kabe-e, kacho, kakemono, kakihan, kirikane, koen, makimono, mandala, mandara, manga, mitsuda-e, mitsudaso, mizu-e, nise-e, nōlun, nurimono, rakkan, saku, sansui, sanzon,* seal, *sensu-e, shin-en, shohei-ga, shōzō, suiboku-e, suisaiga, sumi, sumi-e, tansai-e, tansaku-e, tengai, tsuitate, uchiwa-e.* See also *An illustrated History of Japanese Art,* H. Minamoto, 1935; *Three Essays on Oriental Painting,* Sei-ichi Taki, 1910; *Painting in the Far East, An Introduction to the History of Pictorial Art in Asia, Especially China and Japan,* Laurence Binyon, 4th ed., 1934; *On the Laws of Japanese Painting,* Henry P. Bowie, 1911; *Japanese Scroll Painting,* Kenji Toda, 1935.   —J.A.M.

painting, Japanese schools of. See *Bunjinga; Kanga; Kanō; Maruyama; Nagasaki; Nanga; Otsu; Shijō; Tosa; Ukiyo-e; Yamato-e.*

painting mediums. See drying oils.

painting without bones. See CHINESE ARTS.

paint remover. Most of the paint removers commercially prepared are made up of a number of organic solvents, usually with some addition of wax or paraffin to retard evaporation. Ammonia and other alkaline ingredients are frequently added.   —G.L.S.

pai-tsê. See SYMBOLISM IN FAR EASTERN ART.

pa'kua (Ch.). The eight mystical trigrams employed in divination. See SYMBOLISM IN FAR EASTERN ART.

Pala art. See INDIAN ART.

Palace school of Charlemagne. See Carolingian art.

palace style. See CHINESE ARTS.

palapore. Named from palanpur, India. A painted or printed bed cover or wall hanging, usually of cotton. High style in the 18th cent. Today inexpensive East Indian prints are used in large quantities.   —G.W.R.

pale. See HERALDRY.

paleography. See writing.

palerphone. See phonograph.

Palestinian folk songs. See JEWISH MUSIC.

palette. A figurative as well as a literal meaning has been given to this term. According to the former it is used to designate the system of color employed by a painter in a given work. Literally, it is a surface of any kind on which the paint is mixed in the actual process of picture making. In Europe since the early Renaissance the typical palette has been a thin piece of hardwood with a handle or with a thumb-hole providing an easy grip. The paint, ordinarily in an oil medium, is disposed in small lumps around the edge and mixtures are made towards the center.   —G.L.S.

palette knife. According to modern usage, this is a spatula with a thin, rounded, flexible blade. With it the paste-like oil paint is mixed and placed on the palette. The palette knives of the Renaissance, as shown in paintings of that period, were usually of a heavy blade and pointed. Probably they were not designed specifically for this purpose.   G.L.S.

Palissey enamel. See CERAMICS II.

pall. See HERALDRY.

Palladian style. An architectural style attributed to the Italian Renaissance architect Andrea Palladio. The principle feature, monumental in character, consisted of an arch supported on each side by a free standing column, sometimes twin columns, and a pilaster. A fine example of the style is the added arcades in 1549.   —O.M.S.

pallet. *Book.* (1) A tool used for spreading gold-leaf. (2) A tool, usually a line or ornament for lettering and decorating the

backs of books. (3) The type-holder for loose letters, etc., for tooling the covers.
—H.E.S.

palliotto. See altar.

palmette. Also called anthemion; a classical conventionalized ornament resembling a palm leaf, a vertical unit with radiating lobes arranged symmetrically and of decreasing height on either side of a central lobe which rises to the highest point. —L.T.S.

pandora, pandura. See MUSICAL INSTRUMENTS.

panel. (1) Painting supports of wood are usually designated as panels. The great bulk of European easel painting from early Christian times until well into the 17th cent. was done on such supports. Large panels were made of many pieces of wood joined together with dowels and frequently with cross battens to give them additional strength. The kinds of wood varied from one region to another, oak and pine being rather more common in the North, poplar, lime, willow, and nutwood in Italy. (2) A compartment, sunk or raised, in walls, ceilings, doors, wainscoting, etc.
—G.L.S.

panel-in-a-frame construction. See FURNITURE.

Pan-Ku. In Chinese myth., the first conscious being, who shaped the world out of chaos.

panorama. See STAGESETTING.

panoramic sketch. See military sketching.

Panpipes. See MUSICAL INSTRUMENTS.

pantheon. From the Greek *pan* all, *theios* divine—hence a temple consecrated to all the gods. Under this definition, among many ancient temples, the most famous is the Pantheon in Rome built by Hadrian (120-124 A.D.) on the site of an older temple erected by Agrippa in the year 25 B.C. This building was partially destroyed by fire in the reign of Titus, restored by Domitian and struck by lightning and again burned in the reign of Titus. The portico of granite columns and superstructures are all that survive of Agrippa's building. The great rotunda, 142 feet in diameter, with its coffered dome was the work of Hadrian, and constitutes the most perfectly preserved relic of Roman antiquity now extant.

The dome is built in a most complex system of mutually sustaining brick arches dividing the immense surface into relatively small units which could receive successively the concrete fill and obviate the use of extensive wood centering. In the modern application of the word, *Pantheon* signifies a building consecrated to famous men. This significance was first applied to Soufflot's Pantheon in Paris. The dedication reads: "Aux grands hommes la Patrie Reconnaissante." Built between 1764 and 1790, it incorporates innovations in design and construction of daring and unprecedented character. Metal reinforcements concealed within the stonework permit a tenuity of proportion of incredible lightness. In a manner, these metal devices anticipate the concealed metallic framework or reinforcements now used. See *Agrippa's Building Activities in Rome,* F. W. Shipley, Washington Univ. Studies, Aug. 1933; *Architecture of Greece and Rome,* Anderson & Spiers, 1925. —L.H.

pantograph. Made for changing the scale of a drawing or for copying with such a change of scale, this is an instrument which operates by a system of levers. One point is fixed, one arm is set with a pencil so adjusted as to be in contact with a piece of blank paper, and another arm connected with it has a pointer that is moved over the work to be copied. —G.L.S.

pantomime. A drama presented purely by mimics and bodily movement (gesticulation), without the aid of speech or song, but generally accompanied by instrumental music.

papal tiara. See tiara, papal.

paper. Known commonly as a support for drawings and prints, paper has served also to carry paintings from the earliest recorded history of the art in the Far East and from the time of the introduction of paper into the West. By the 2nd cent. A.D. the Chinese were manufacturing paper and by the 12th cent. the method coming through the Near East had become well established in Europe. It was made in Morocco in 1100 and paper factories were set up in Italy and in France by the end of that century. The Oriental paper seems to have been made directly from plant fibre. In Europe it was found that cotton and linen rags could be broken down into separate fibres and this used for paper making. Such a material still serves as the source of the best papers available. All of them were made by hand until at the very end of the 18th cent. the paper machine was developed in France by Louis Robert. Somewhat earlier than that, preliminary work had been done in the manufacture of paper from wood or plant fibres and, as these methods developed, much cheaper paper became possible and displaced the rag product for less important work. Wood-pulp paper is weaker and more apt to discolor than that made from rags, but it varies a great deal in its strength and stability according to the method of manufacture. Mechanical wood-pulp is hardly more than sawdust which has been matted into sheets. There are various methods of preparing a chemical pulp, all of which produce fibres of greater strength than those made by mechanical means.

—G.L.S.

paper heraldry. See HERALDRY.

paper mark. The handmade papers are settled or felted over a screen called a deckle. The wires of this leave fine marks in the paper, particularly visible by transmitted light because along those lines the amount of fibre is actually less. In the 13th cent. designs were put into the wires of the deckle in order to indicate the manufacturer and these came to be known as water marks or paper marks. They are found in products of the mills of Bologna and Fabriano between 1285 and 1295. By the 16th cent. not only the name or device of the maker but also the date of manufacture was frequently shown.

—G. L. S.

paper painting. See CHINESE ARTS.

papier collé. See collage.

papyrus. The forerunner of paper in the West, papyrus was an ancient writing material developed in Egypt and made largely in the Nile delta, at least from the time of the Old Kingdom. By the 10th cent. A.D. paper had displaced it. It was formed directly from the reed, *Cyperus papyrus* of Linnaeus. Strips of the cut reed were laid across each other at right angles, soaked, pounded flat, and dried in the sun. —G.L.S.

paraffin. See wax.

paragone (comparison). The question of the comparative rank of the different arts as expounded in the theoretical literature of the Italian Renaissance. First elaborated by Leonardo da Vinci the paragone became a favorite theme of literary discussion from the 16th to the 18th cent. The answers to the problem, although varying according to individual predilection, reflect the striving of artists as a class to win recognition for their profession and to raise its standing above that of a mechanical art (q.v.).   —R.B.

parallel perspective. See PERSPECTIVE.

parapet (L. *parpare*, to guard; *pectus,* breast). A low protecting wall about or near the edge of a roof, platform, or other raised or elevated area.   —J.M.M.

paraphrase. *Mus.* An arrangement or transcription of a composition; generally of a showy and florid character.

parchment. Any moderately good skin prepared without tanning and used for writing or painting has been called either parchment or vellum. As a rule, the latter term has been given to finer skins, those of newborn or still-born calves, goats, or lambs, and most parchment comes from one of these animals. It is prepared by washing, treatment with lime, removal of hair, successive scraping, paring, rubbing, and dusting. Characteristically, parchment is pale and smooth. The word itself comes from Pergamum, and the tradition is that Eumenes II (197-198 B.C.) was largely responsible for the development of its manufacture. It remained the best support for writing until comparatively modern times, although for general purposes paper had begun to displace it by the 13th cent.   —G.L.S.

parge work. A method of molding ornaments into plaster walls and ceilings. Popular during Tudor (q.v.) period. See INTERIOR ARCHITECTURE AND DECORATION.

Parian marble. Quarries on the island of Paros produced the finest marble known to the Greeks for sculpture, and from it their best statues were usually made. It has coarse crystals, which absorb and reflect the light, giving an extraordinary lively, luminous glow to the surface. Hence it is unexcelled for the representation of vitality and sensuous charm.   —W.R.A.

Parian ware. See CERAMICS II.

Paris blue. See Prussian blue.

Paris green. See emerald green.

parish planning. See CIVIC PLANNING.

park system. See CIVIC PLANNING.

parkway. See CIVIC PLANNING.

parlando. *Mus.* "Speaking"; in a declamatory or recitativic style. See OPERA.

parquetage a plat. See RESTORATION OF PAINTINGS.

parquetage de champ. See RESTORATION OF PAINTINGS.

part. *Mus.* Section of a composition; voice (in choral music); melodic line (in polyphony, also called voice); music sheet used by a performer in an ensemble; character in a play. —E.K.

parted coats. See HERALDRY.

partial. See ACOUSTICS; harmonic analysis.

participation. It has been generally recognized that the work of art is both an imitation and an expression—*similitudo expressiva,* to quote St. Bonaventura—of its theme. That the material work also *participates* in the reality of its thesis is often overlooked. "Participation" means that the formal cause (or meaning) is really *present* in the actual shape of the work of art. For example, in a statue, the form of a man is presented in a nature of stone; by that idea the statue is informed, or if not it would be a shapeless, informal mass of material. This can be completely misunderstood if it is taken to mean that the formal cause is *physically* present in the effect, adequacy then amounting to identity. On this basis Levy-Brühl (whose point of view is now generally discredited) revived the term "participation" (which he called "mystic") in connection with a supposed "primitive mentality" in which the symbol is confused with its referent (as in fetishism).

The perennial philosophy, however, has always assumed that all existences are what they are "by participation" in their principle: "et Plato posuit homo materialis est homo per participationem" (St. Thomas Aquinas, *Sum. Theol.* I.18.4); living things "participate" (*vbhaj*) in "not-dying" ,RV. I.164.21); and as Aristotle points out (*Phys.* IV.2.3) Plato in *Timaeus,* 51 A equates matter in extenso with "that which can participate" (metalambáno) in form. This necessarily involves the case of art, which is always an embodiment of form in matter; the form or idea being immaterial. In works of art, then, things participate (metécho) in the forms after which they are named, and to say that they "imitate" these is the same as to say that they "participate in" them (Aristotle, *Met.* I.6.4, cf. Plato, *Parmenides* 132 E—133 A, and *Phaedo* 78 E). Accordingly, the work of at the same time, imitates, expresses, and participates in its form. See Przyluski, J., *La participation,* Paris, 1940; Coomaraswamy, "Imitation, Expression, and Participation" in *Journ. of Aesthetics and Art Criticism,* vol. 3, 2, 1944.   —A.K.C.

partimen. See MEDIEVAL MUSIC.

partita, partie. *Mus.* A suite. A set of variations.

partition lines. See HERALDRY.

partridge breast. A term applied to a special glaze of light streaks seen on *Temmoku* ware.

part-song. A song for two or more independent voices or parts.

party per pale. See HERALDRY.

parvenu. See POST-REVOLUTIONARY ARCHITECTURE AND DECORATIVE ARTS IN THE U. S. A.

pas (Fr. step). While literally singular, *pas* usually refers to combination of steps, steps meaning not only movements of the feet but attendant conformations of arms, trunk and head. In the academic vocabulary a *pas* also denotes a dance number, a solo, *pas seul,* a duet, *pas de deux,* etc. From this, a *pas de guirlandes* refers to a number using garlands, a *pas de chale,* a shawl, etc. Individual steps have mimetic or associative conditionals, *pas de chat,* cat step, *pas de basque,* etc.   —L.K.

pas de basque. A movement in the classic academic vocabulary, ostensibly deriving from a basque folk dance of the 18th cent.

pas de bourée (Fr. *bourée* (q.v.), 18th cent. quick dance from Auvergne). Like many other terms originally used to describe social or folk dance, the *bourée* is a specific appellation for a type of stage movement in which the female dancer propels herself across the stage, on points, in an imperceptible shift of the toes, the knees scarcely bent.   —L.K.

pashim. Soft downy wool growing next to the body of a goat. In color it is white, dark gray, or drab and of this many of the finest India rugs are woven.

paspy. See passepied.

passacaglia, passecaille. One of the *pre-classic* dance forms, was probably a Spanish folk dance of ancient origin, which found its way into 16th cent. European court festivities. The little information we have indicates that it was danced as a solo, with great solemnity, in slow 3/4 meter, and resembled the chaconne. Early musical suites sometimes contained pieces bearing the name *passacaglia*, and arranged in *air on a ground bass* form. If the original dance was a solo, it seems scarcely possible that it could have been the source of the above musical form. At least two dancers would have been required—one to perform the *bass* and one the *air,* since, in music at least, the two must at some time occur simultaneously (see chaconne).   —J.G.

passage. *Mus.* (1) A short transitional section of a piece. (2) A rapid figure, as a scale passage called a "run".

passage, passageway. A way, channel, corridor, or hall affording a means of passing or communicating.

passant. See HERALDRY.

passepied. A member of the *pre-classic* group of dances, the *passepied* was borrowed from the Breton peasants by the court of Louis XV. 'In its ancient folk form, the dance was known as the *branle of Brittany* and was performed as a pantomime in 2/4 or 3/8 meter. The basic movements were a peculiar pawing action with the feet and a light, gliding step in which one foot was crossed over the other. The swinging rhythm of the dance in its 3/8 form suggests that it may have been an ancestor of the waltz. Following the usual adoption procedure, the passepied underwent over-refinement and formalization through courtly performance in simulated pastoral settings, but its characteristic steps became a legacy to the ballet, and its music appears in some of the classic instrumental suites.   —J.G.

Passion. In the Roman Catholic services during Holy week the story of Christ's sufferings and death are told in the four Gospels. Originally it was chanted · by three priests; during the 16th century harmonized passages were introduced. In Lutheran services the Passions have become complete oratorios due to the addition of chorales and reflective passages. Bach's St. Matthew Passion is considered one of the finest.

paste. Any of a group of adhesives made chiefly from flour or starch is called paste. The simplest preparation is by cooking the flour in a suitable quantity of water. The flour itself consists of a mixture of gluten and starch. A somewhat smoother paste is made from the starch alone, that from rice, wheat, corn, potatoes, and arrowroot being capable of furnishing a good adhesive. The best preparations usually contain some amount of other ingredient such as animal glue and, to be kept for any length of time, need to have a fungicide added. Their particular value is for joining together pieces of paper or similar light materials.   —G.L.S.

paste mold. See GLASS AND GLASS-MAKING.

pasteboard. *Book.* A (card) board made by pasting sheets of paper together. Also made with pulp and moulded.

pastel. A picture made with a paste of pigment mixed with gum water; frequently regarded as painting.

pastophory. See EARLY CHRISTIAN ART.

pastoral, pastourelle, pastorale. Music in rustic style, generally in 6/8 or 12/8 time. See MEDIEVAL MUSIC.

patchwork rugs. Made by applying bits of colored cloth to a foundation—usually black or very dark heavy cloth. The applied pieces were cut to resemble flowers, foliage and other motifs and were in varied colors. The ornamentation of bunches of flowers, wreaths, baskets or vases of flowers, trailing vines showed to advantage on the dark backgrounds.
—B.E.J.

patera. A circular ornament, resembling a shallow dish, often used in decorative work, esp. bas-relief.

pater noster. A beadlike ornament in moldings.

pâte sur pâte. A process with successive layers of white and colored slip applied to a dark ground—an impasto decoration. See CERAMICS II.

patine, patina. Any coating on the surface of an object that has been accumulated by aging; more specifically, the corrosion of old bronzes and other metallic objects caused by chemical reactions with ingredients of the atmosphere, earth or water with which they have been in contact. Recent works are sometimes subjected to chemical treatments which duplicate the various types of patina formed on old pieces. Although the commonest type of bronze patine is bluish green or blue, nearly every hue is to be found on ancient metallic objects depending on the composition of the object and the conditions to which it was exposed. See *Encyclopedia Britannica*, 14th ed.; *The Artists' Handbook of Materials and Techniques*, Ralph Mayer, 1940.   —R.M.

pattern. See design.

paua shell. Similar to mother-of-pearl.

paulownia. See SYMBOLISM IN FAR EASTERN ART.

pausa. See NOTATION.

pavane. One of the group of ancient dance forms now called *pre-classic*. Originally a Spanish folk dance, it early became incorporated into church ritual and was danced at the Spanish court of the Inquisition. The name was derived from the Latin *pavo* (peacock) and suggests the arrogant dignity and pomposity of the dance. The pavane became the opening dance of 16th cent. European court balls, where it assumed the manner and proportions of a processional pageant. When French composers began to write instrumental suites for court festivities, the pavane music took its place as the opening piece, and continued as such long after the suite lost its association with actual dances. The meter of the pavane was usually 2/4 or 4/4, played very slowly by wind instruments with a repeated drum figure accompaniment. In movement, the dance was fairly simple, using variations of a slow, gliding walk. It was danced by couples circling the room. Solos by the men sometimes were inserted between the advancing and retreating figures.   —J.G.

paysage (Fr.). A landscape picture.

peach loom. A type of Chinese pottery, the glaze of which resembles the bloom of a peach.

peach of immortality. See SYMBOLISM IN FAR EASTERN ART.

peacock. See pavane.

peasant art. See folk art.

pedal harp. See MUSICAL INSTRUMENTS.

pedestal. The base for a column, statue, etc.; usually circular, square, or rectangular, rarely polygonal.

pedigree. See FORGERIES IN PAINTING.

pediment. The triangular space at the end of a sloping-roofed building, or a decorative feature of that shape. The filling of this space was one of the most important problems confronting Greek architectural sculptors, since the gables at the front and back of the temples were the most conspicuous field for decoration. Their progress in making their designs contribute to both the religious and artistic effect of the building was rapid, in spite of the difficulty of adjusting a number of figures in harmonious relationship within such a difficult space. The center must be the focus of interest, with the chief accent; the angles must be adequately filled; and within the intervening space figures correct in scale must be built up in a steady, unbroken rhythm. In early temples, animals or serpents were used to help fill the space, but by the beginning of the 5th cent. B.C. at the temple of Aphaia at Aegina the sculptors succeeded in building up a pattern of reclining, kneeling, advancing, falling and standing figures in a series of interesting geometric forms; they were not, however, related by a continuous rhythm. The Olympia pediments (460 B.C.) show advance in both the monumental character of the forms and drapery and a steady rhythmic beat from corner to center; and in the Parthenon the fusion of geometric form, naturalistic modelling, and monumental power was unexcelled. There the figures were set at various angles, so that they emerged from the background in three dimensions; the weaving of drapery, lateral as well as around the figures, established a continuous rhythm; and the massive forms gave additional strength to the noble architecture. Not only in artistic design, but also in pictorial representation, they contributed to the significance of the building, picturing on the east end the birth of Athena and on the west the struggle between Athena and Poseidon for the lordship of Athens. No later pediments approached them in beauty; most, in fact, have been left empty of sculpture except for mouldings around the edges. In Hellenistic times the central space was sometimes filled with an

imposing group, but corners were left vacant. The Roman pediments, higher than the Greek, occasionally had a central group on a podium, but failed to fill the rest of the space successfully. The pedimental shape was used by the Romans as a decorative element to crown doors and windows, a device inherited and widely used during the Renaissance. Baroque buildings elaborated on this type of decoration. Pedimental sculpture was revived, more or less successfully, in modern Europe, and has been used on many American state capitol buildings. Interesting contemporary adaptations of Greek sculptured pediments are those on the Philadelphia Museum and the Supreme Court building in Washington.
—W.R.A.

Peisistradid era. See HELLENIC ART.

pen. Probably the common pen used traditionally for writing and drawing in Europe was that made from a quill cut, split, and pointed as the writer or draftsman wished it. The reed pen was not uncommon, however, and probably had been known from earlier times. It was usually made from the tubular stock of fine, hollow bamboo or of coarse grass, and was cut in much the same way as the quill. Metal pens have been known in ancient times but machine manufacture during the 19th cent. allowed them completely to displace the older implements.
—G.L.S.

pencil. A brush of hair or bristles used to lay on colors. Manner or skill of an artist, his own artistic style.

pendants, vaulting. Elongated voussoirs supported by transverse arches from which the vault ribs spring. The lower ends of the voussoirs project below the vault, forming pendants which are often elaborately carved. This type of vaulting was developed during the late English Perpendicular period of Gothic architecture.   —O.M.S.

pendentive. The transitional vaulting, usually triangular in shape springing from the corners of a structure with a square or polygonal in plan. Byzantine vaulting is a typical example.   —O.M.S.

penetrative seeing. See PHOTOGRAPHY.

Penglai-shan (Ch.). Buddhist land of eternal spring—paradise.

pen process acquatint (an intaglio process). The pen process aquatint, though it had been used most effectively by Gainsborough (1727-1788), seems to have been lost until recent times when it was rediscovered by modern artists in search of unique new mediums.

In the finished proof, the pen process is similar to a pen or brush drawing. The clean copper plate is drawn on with brush or pen using a special ink that has a high sugar content. The plate is heated and a regular hard etching ground is rolled on the plate over the ink drawing. The plate is now immersed in cold water and with the help of a piece of cotton batting the ink dissolves, leaving bare copper wherever the pen or brush drawing had been. If bitten in this state, the more open places would produce *crevé*. To overcome this, the plate is now put into the aquatint box and an aquatint ground is laid on the entire surface. This converts what had been brush or pen lines into areas of aquatint which are now bitten and printed in the same manner as any etching. Usually the pen process is followed up by subsequent tones of pure aquatint.

The pen process is quick, comparatively easy and certain. It is capable of almost as many variations and nuances as brush and pen, but with the added charm and preciousness of a print.   —K.K.

pentachord. (1) An instrument with five strings. (2) A diatonic scale of five notes.

pentacle. A certain figure formerly used as a magic symbol, as a five-pointed, or a six-pointed, star.

pentaptych. Often used in connection with a series of five prints which have been composed as a series.

pentatonic scale. The five note scale represented in its simplest forms by the symbols C-D-F-G-a, or D-F-G-a-c, or F-G-a-c-d, etc. If the series is continued, the 6th tone is in every case an octave higher than the first. The underlying structure of primitive music, Scotch music and many of the eastern exotic musics is pentatonic. See scales and modes.   —V.A.

Pentelic marble. Quarries opened late in the 6th cent. B.C. in Mt. Pentelicon, north of Athens, provided marble for the buildings of Athens and for much of the sculpture in Greece and Italy, although often heads of statues were made separately in the finer Parian marble. Pentelic marble is white, with fairly small crystals and sparkling quality.

It contains iron, the oxidation of which is responsible for the present rusty gold tints of the Parthenon.   —W.R.A.

pentimenti. Used to describe paint ridges existing under the finished surface of an oil painting. These ridges usually indicate earlier states of the picture.   —H.M.

people and things painting. Chinese name for genre painting. See CHINESE ARTS.

peplum. (Latinized form of the Greek word *peplos*). A large, full robe worn by women, generally of heavy material in contrast to the lighter and more elegant chiton (q.v.). It was a rectangular piece of wool or linen the upper part of which was doubled up. It was fastened on the shoulders by fibulae or clasps and was worn with or without a belt. For illustration, see Margarete Bieber, *Griechische Kleidung,* Berlin, 1928.   —L.L.

percussion instruments. Drums, gongs, triangle; the pianoforte may be regarded as the highest type of percussion instrument (percussion = striking together). See MUSICAL INSTRUMENTS.

percussion sticks. See MUSICAL INSTRUMENTS.

percussive movement. See quality.

perfect interval. See interval.

perforated. See SCULPTURE.

performance (musical), **theory of.** See MUSICAL PERFORMANCE, MAIN TRENDS IN.

performance score. A scientific music or speech score showing graphically exactly how each sound was rendered in a performance. The record is made by phonophotography (q.v.). The term was coined in the Iowa Psychological Laboratory and is abundantly illustrated in the publication emanating from that and similar laboratories.

"The photographic record on special moving picture films, as described for a five-minute song, may contain thousands of specific facts bearing on the tonal, dynamic, temporal, and qualitative aspects of every note of the song, each measurable and exactly definable. We were at first baffled by the accumulation of such masses of data without any simple way of sorting and representing them. A solution was found in the design of what we now call the performance score. In its simplest form it is somewhat like the ordinary musical score.

"In such a score we can see as much detail as may be significant. It is customary to record frequency, amplitude, duration, and form of sound waves—the correlates of pitch, intensity, —and time in this manner; and then, because of the great complexity of the timbre, to represent fair samplings of tone spectra separately. Having once adopted this idea of representing four elements of the song graphically, that scheme may be applied to any particular feature of music or speech sound studied in detail; for example, phrasing scores, rhythmic patterns, the vibrato, or the harmonic structure of the tone. All elements of the sound are represented graphically to the eye.

"This recognition is analogous to the fact that a picture of an object can be represented adequately in three dimensions of space and in color. The painter has the means of representing in a single picture all desired degrees of variation in these three dimensions of space and a vast variety of variants in color. Imagine for a moment how helpless we would be if it had not occurred to someone that all types of objects and situations could be represented in pictures. That would be analogous to the situation in which we found ourselves in music. The performance score is a unified picture in three of four dimensions of music as it is actually performed. Of course the reason we have not had such pictures until recently lies in the fact that the means of making them were discovered only recently through the invention of sound photography.

"Just as the recognition that every feature of a musical rendition can be represented in terms of four elements brought order out of chaos in the laboratory measurement, so now the adoption of various types of performance scores representing each of these four elements complements this by enabling us to assemble and interpret great masses of facts in terms of a fairly simple picture. Without such language and pictorial interpretation, most of the findings of the camera would have been lost. One can get some conception of the mass of material contained in a performance score if he realizes that for each note in the original musical score, there is a graph showing exactly the form of attack and release and all the minute changes in pitch and loudness during the body of a tone with the time and rhythmic value of each element of change during the tone.

Every element in the actual phrasing is shown; yet the score is so compact that it may not occupy more than twice the space occupied by the original musical score.

"To the musician, it seems almost incomprehensible that much of which we are aware, for example, media for the expression of musical feeling, can be represented in simple, accurate, and definable language and pictures. Before we realized the full significance of this, we in the laboratory were quite as helpless as is the musician in attempting to represent effectively what seems to be a chaotic mass of detail.

"It may seem like straining a point to say that the device for throwing all the hundreds of findings in a musical selection into a comparatively simple picture which we call the performance score is analogous to the adoption of terminology in the biological and physical sciences or in mathematics. But it may seem stranger still to assert that the performance score representing the world of music is to what we can hear as the painting or photographing of objects in color and relief is to what we can see in nature or art." Seashore, *Pioneering in Psychology*, University of Iowa Press, 1942. See Seashore, *Psychology of Music*, 1938; Iowa Studies in Psychology of Music, vols. 1, III and IV.

                                —C.E.S.

periaktoi. See STAGESETTING.

Periclean period. During the years 461-429 B.C., when Pericles was the leader of the Athenian democracy, Athens produced art of the highest quality in many fields. Social conditions were favorable for such expression; men worked "in the fearless confidence of freedom". The city was a democracy, with direct control of its affairs, local and international, in the hands of all the male citizens. Most officials were chosen by lot for one-year terms, so that there was a wide distribution of political office, and pay for public service insured that even the poorest citizen could afford to serve. Although political rights were denied to women, resident aliens, and slaves, all but the women had a large amount of economic and social opportunity; and regardless of their status men were encouraged to contribute what they could to the community. Many of the aliens were skilled craftsmen, encouraged to come to Athens to exercise their ability; and slaves (captives in war) were often able artists whose skill was recognized and given an opportunity to function happily. As Pericles

said, "We honor ability in every branch of achievement, not on class or sectional grounds, but on the basis of merit alone." It was therefore no leisure-class culture which produced the drama, religious, musical and athletic festivals, and plastic arts, which flourished then as in few other periods of human history; rather it was a community of men working together on a basis of greater genuine equality than has often been achieved in any time or place that created and controlled the life of the city. During this period Athens also governed an empire of some 250 states, and might properly be called the capital city of the eastern Mediterranean. The tribute money from these states was partly responsible for Pericles' great program of art projects.

In stating his ideals for Athens Pericles declared: "We have provided education and recreation for the spirit, festivals throughout the year, and beauty in our public buildings, which delight our hearts day by day as we see them and banish sadness. We love beauty without extravagance." It cannot be emphasized too strongly that art in this society was regarded as a normal and necessary expression of the common life, and was created by and for the people. Artists were commissioned by the city rather than a wealthy few, and the vitality of their art may fairly be attributed to the fact that they were employed on the basis of merit, served community purposes and needs, and were constantly criticized and appreciated by a population interested in and sensitive to their work.

The most important art project was Pericles' great building program, instituted to relieve unemployment, keep the residents happily engaged in productive work, and make Athens a cultural capital. Six major temples, the entrance hall to the Acropolis, the Hall of the Mysteries at Eleusis, and a music hall were the chief buildings erected. Pericles also brought the famous city planner, Hippodamus, from Miletus to lay out the port city of Piraeus on geometric principles. Buildings were planned cooperatively by state officials, architects, sculptors, and, it must be added, an interested and critical public. The most impressive temple was the Parthenon, dedicated to the patron goddess, Athena, with its noble logic of plan, enlivened by delicate variations and refinements and enriched by sculpture of surpassing beauty. It serves as a symbol of the fusion of power and grace which characterized this period of Athenian life.

In its sculpture Periclean Athens likewise achieved a synthesis of Doric power and Ionic grace. Myron and Phidias were the outstanding names, but a host of other sculptors also made their contribution to the city's prestige, picturing the gods, the heroes of the Greek past, and statesmen and athletic heroes of the present. This sculpture was essentially idealistic, with strong planes vigorously modeled, sensitive handling of line, and a sturdy sense of logical design. During the same period Athenian mural and vase painters were actively engaged, and demonstrated a similar breadth of design and well-disciplined power. Their subjects were also of community interest: the exploits of gods and heroes, and scenes from the gymnasium, festivals, and home life. The same educated public taste appears in the minor arts of the time, including dress, furniture, and jewelry.

Athens demonstrated how successfully art, regarded as a public service, can flourish under democratic auspices, and how great a contribution it can make to community happiness.   —W.R.A.

pericope. The Greek word for evangelistary. It was called pericope from *perikopein,* which means to cut, so called because the Gospels were cut into sections for use on the consecutive Sundays of the church year. A famous pericope was among others, the pericope of Henry II. School of Reichenau, between 1002 and 1014, now in the Munich State Library. See miniature; initial.—A.J.S.

periodic. *Cer.* Intermittent. Kiln fired not continuously. See CERAMICS I.

period of the Early Republic. See POST-REVOLUTIONARY ARCHITECTURE AND DECORATIVE ARTS IN THE U. S. A.

peripteral. With a line of columns on all sides.

peristasis. See HELLENISTIC ART.

peristyle (Gr. *peristylon* fr. *peri,* around + *stylos,* column). In Greek and Roman architecture, a covered colonade surrounding (1) the cella of a temple, or (2) an open interior court, as in a house or a gymnasium; also the whole court so surrounded by a colonnade, especially of a house.   —L.T.S.

permanent collection. See exhibition.

PERSIAN ART. In 559 B.C. Cyrus the Great assumed the leadership of the Persians, who were a subordinate Iranian tribe, and in 550 he conquered the Medes, a superior branch of Iranians, thereby laying the foundation of the Persian Empire. Throughout all Persian history the geographical boundaries have been constantly shifting, and all the peoples concerned, either near or far, have at some time exerted an influence on Persian art. The capacity of the Persians to absorb and utilize these impulses is one of the outstanding characteristics of their genius and is noted at the very outset, in the **Achaemenid Period,** 559-331 B.C. In the palaces of Darius and Xerxes at Persepolis the hypostyle hall which had already been employed by the Medes is found mounted on a limestone platform recalling Babylonian and Assyrian terraces, though it may have been a simple answer to the problem of defense. Typical of the Persians are the square rooms demanded by their obsession with symmetry and the tall, slender, widely-spaced columns with their multiple flutings and ornate bases and capitals, which convey an effect of elegance that is remarkable in all Persian art. The stone facings of the platform, stair-railings, etc., were carved with reliefs representing the king sacrificing or hunting, guards and soldiers, subject peoples bearing tribute, animal combats, etc., all tending to glorify the deity through his earthly representative, the king. On one half of the buildings are 1,000 feet of reliefs, which are repeated on the other half reversed as in a mirror. Although everything connected with the structure is subordinated to the master architectural plan, just as it was in Babylonia and Assyria, this does not mean that the sculpture, for example, is weak in itself, but only that it loses by being removed from its context. As a matter of fact, the sculpture is simple and powerful, its meaning gaining emphasis from the total absence of insignificant details; and this poignancy is not limited to work in stone, but is seen also in brick-tile reliefs and esp. in metalwork, in which ibexes, bulls, and lions of bronze, and the animals adorning gold and silver are all graced with a carefree, sprightly robustness reminiscent of archaic art. Such metal objects were either cast or beaten and were decorated by embossing, engraving, inlaying, or the setting of paste or stones in gold cloisons.

The Achaemenid Empire was conquered by Alexander the Great in 331 B.C., and for the next 5½ cents. the territory was ruled by the Seleucids or the Parthians (Arsacids),

Artistically, as far as Persia is concerned, the period is not very important.

In A.D. 226 Ardashīr, who claimed Achaemenid ancestry, usurped the Parthian throne and established the second national Persian dynasty, the Sāsānian. The unification of the country early in the period encouraged the pursuit of constructive activities, and the resultant production of architecure and works of art has been the envy and the pattern of succeeding generations. Mazdaism, the religion of Zoroaster, became for the first time the state religion, and most of the buildings and other works were designed as in Achaemenid times to impress upon the people the omnipotence of the deity and his servant, the king. Unlike the Achaemenid palaces, which were light and open, the Sāsānian structures, such as e.g. Fīrūzābād, Sarvistān, Tāq-i-Bustān, were massive, overpowering monuments with vaults and domes, built sometimes of rubble and mortar, sometimes of stone, with domes of brick and frequently decoration in stucco. The influence of the Sāsānians on later architecture can be surmised from the fact that they developed the vault and the dome and invented the squinch and the axial plan. Only one statue in the round is known: a three times life-size figure of Shāpūr I at Bishāpūr, the style of which is derived from 2nd cent. Indian statues, such as the one of Kaniska at Mathurā. Most of the extant stucco decoration is given to geometric and floral patterns and animals, but the main sculpture is relieved in the stone of the façades and is devoted to divine investitures of kings, royal triumphs, hunting scenes, etc. Although each scene is based on a particular event, either real or symbolic, the portrayal is ideal, which accounts for the supremacy of spiritual content over anatomical accuracy. The simplicity and directness of the statement, the dignity of the participants, and the skill of the modelling combine to give an effect of intellectual power that is rarely found anywhere. Typically Persian is the aristocratic grace with which even the most robust figure is imbued. These same qualities are found in the repoussé animals and hunting scenes of the silver dishes and in the heraldic beasts and birds of the silver ewers and silk textiles, which last, like contemporary Byzantine silks, show unusual strength of design for such basically delicate objects.

The constant fighting of the Sāsānians finally weakened them to such an extent that they fell an easy prey to the Arabs in A.D. 641, but the uncivilized Arabs knew little of statecraft, and thus the Caliphate, which they immediately set up, was forced to employ Persians in high administrative positions. The removal of the Caliphate from Damascus to Baghdad promoted its gradual Persianization at the same time that the Persians, though not required to adopt Islam, were becoming progressively Islamicized. Perhaps the strongest bond was forged in the northeast by the semi-independent Persian Sāmānid dynasty of Khurāsān, which substituted the Arabic script for the Pahlavī of the Sāsānians and established the modern Persian language. In 990 the Sāmānids succombed to the Ghaznavid Turks, who, in 1037, were overthrown by the Seljūq Turks. The Seljūqs took all of Persia, establishing their capital at Rayy (Rhages) and reinstating the Caliph in Baghdād, he and his immediate predecessors having been puppets of the Buwayhids.

Another Turkish dynasty, the Kwārazm-shāhs, acquired certain territories from the Seljūqs, and it was the last of their rulers who slighted Chingiz Khān, thus bringing on the Mongol conquest (1220) and destruction if large parts of Persia. The rule of the Mongol Il-Khāns lasted until 1336, after which the country was divided amongst local dynasties until, in 1369, Tīmūr (Tamerlane) inaugurated the Tīmūrid dynasty with its capital at Samarqand. In 1502 the Safavids established a national dynasty that lasted until 1736.

Architecturally the Islamic (q.v.) epoch is known for its mosques, minarets, tombs, and bridges, most of them built of brick, fired or unfired. Outstanding amongst the structural elements are the dome, the squinch, the pointed arch, and the monumental façade, all of which are found together in the mosque. Chronologically the development is one primarily of elaboration and organization, the earliest mosques having flat roofs on columns or piers, recalling their Achaemenid ancestors, whereas their successors had arcaded courtyards with domed bays. Soon the evolution of the squinch permitted the multiplication of domes and later the center of each side of the arcaded courtyard was pierced with a vaulted īvān, or three-sided room, with a mihrāb, or shrine, at its rear. The whole Islamic era is devoid of sculpture, but its place on buildings is taken by floral designs or inscriptions in stucco and geometric designs and inscriptions in brick. Although the elaboration and forceful modelling of stucco ornament under the Seljūqs (1037-1300) carried it to its height, by about the 12th cent, such strides had been made in the use of enamel tiles and faience mosaic that they were beginning to supplant all other decoration. In these buildings is found the same combination, though in different proportions, of overpowering masses and delicate detail that existed in earlier structures. Honor was done to god and king by the construction of such massive monuments, and the sensitive, sensual palate of the Persian people was pleased with the subtle ornament, the colorful mosaic. The mosque reached its culmination with the building of Shāh 'Abbās (1587-1628) of the great Masjid-i-Shāh at Isfahān, a perfect example of architectural planning and polychrome decoration.

Except for architecture, great religious art died with the Sāsānian Period, for the old tradition had run its course, and the Muslims were opposed to the representation of anything living. Thus, sculpture was supplanted by ornament, and pleasing decorative surfaces took the place of significant symbolic content.

What little is known about Sāsānian pottery points to the fact that it is far inferior to the metalwork, which is hardly the case in Islamic times. For now not only did tile and mosaic ultimately come into their own, but also the Persian love of color and decoration found an outlet in the painting of pottery. The body of the vessels was never as fine and tough as the hardier Chinese wares, since the makers were content to take the material at hand, but the coarse and friable local clays produced an impermanent, porous ware that responded readily to the craftsman's slightest pressure. The resultant output evinces an unfailing sense of ceramic modelling, with delicate curves united with straight lines in just proportion to the requirements of the object. Yet all these things were made for use, and each was suitable to its purpose. All of the early wares are of simple clay, but the finest of the later ones are of a powdered quartz often referred to as faience. As far as material is concerned, there are three main types, almost infinitely divisible: namely, a red ware with slip decoration and a usually colorless glaze; a buff ware with an opaque cream-white glaze decorated in luster or colored glazes; and a white sandy ware with either translucent or opaque glaze and with luster or under- or overglaze decoration. The dearth of material scientifically excavated makes impossible the task of pigeonholing the various kinds, but a few of the main categories follow. The wares of the 8th-9th cent. were splash-glazed in imitation of T'ang dynasty pottery of China, and in the 9th-10th cent. there were white wares painted with dark blue and others painted with

luster. From now on engraved, sgraffito carved, and relief decoration persist. The 11th-12th cent. wares heretofore called Gabri, with powerful animals and foliate designs relieved in underglaze slip, are now assigned to Aghkand and Yastkand, whereas the polychrome painted white dishes formerly known as Lakabī are still without a provenience. Also in the 11th-12th cent. luster-painted wares come again to the fore, this time at Rayy (Rhages), followed in the 12th-13th cents. by Kāshān and in the 13th-14th by Sultānābād. Both Rayy and Kāshān are famous for bowls with large, strong figures painted overglaze, and the potters of Kāshān often added gliding. Throughout the whole period inscriptions played a prominent part on most types, and many dates have been furnished by writings on tiles. The most usual types are bowls, cups, ewers, vases, and tiles. Somewhat in the 13th cent. and more in the 14th, figures and other components of the design began to be multiplied until the shape of the vessel lost its importance. It is true that there are excellent later wares with ethereal, elongated, swaying youths and ladies, but they are too few to impede the decline from the heights.

The earliest Muhammadan bronze and silver vessels made in the 9th-10th cent. were simple and unpretentious, with only slight engraved designs. In the 12th-14th cent. objects were made of bronze, brass, and silver. At first the decoration was confined to engraved Arabic inscriptions, roundels, animals, and foliage, but soon it was broadened to include copper and silver inlay, figures, hunting scenes, etc. The usual shapes for silver were fewer than those for bronze and brass, which took in mortars, ewers, stands (often pierced), trays, kettles, candlesticks, basin, and the like. Some incense burners were in the shape of birds or animals with pierced decoration, and a few of the latest brass ewers were ornamented with birds and animals in the half-round or round. As in the case of ceramics, the 14th cent. was the signal for the decline in metalwork. Subsequently a handful of fine candlesticks, basins, etc., was produced, but the elaboration of the ornament at the expense of the shape was not long in taking its toll.

Under the Muslims textiles continued to be of the utmost importance, the earliest being dated tentatively in the 10th cent. and carrying on the Sāsānian tradition of paired birds and animals, heraldic beasts, and roundels arranged in a rigid pattern. The same motives were employed by the Seljūqs, but geometric rigidity gradually gave way to all-over pattern with a broken field, resulting in an elegance admirably suited to silk textiles. In the 13th-15th cents. under the Mongols and the Tīmūrids the earlier regularity was sacrificed completely to a free arrangement of flowing arabesques and floral motives, and under the Safavids in the 16th-17th cents. figures, animals, and flowers were scattered with a luxurious profusion over the whole surface. It was at this time that the cone pattern originated, and stories of Laylā and Majnūn, Khusrau and Shīrīn were interspersed with various other motives. Sooner or later nearly everything was tried: more colors, metal threads, embroideries with animal and hunting scenes, and even a return to the earlier arrangement in stiff horizontal rows. Fine textiles were made well into the 18th cent., for since a textile has little shape to be either strong or weak, the elaboration and softening of the design is not necessarily so deleterious as in the case of metals and ceramics.

Although it is known that Khusrau I (Chosroes) had a large "garden carpet" in the 6th cent., the earliest extant carpets are from the 16th. Fine **"Persian rugs"** produced in the next two and a half centuries are too numerous to be recorded. In these the pile was usually of wool and the foundation of wool and cotton, but sometimes the pile, and sometimes both pile and foundation, were of silk. In certain types there is an admixture of gold and silver threads. The best-known are the garden carpet, with its crossed water-courses meeting in a central pool; hunting-scene carpets; medallion carpets, in which animals stalk amongst flowers and medallions; vase carpets, with flowers branching from a central vase; and the so-called Polish or Polonaise rugs, of silk pile and often with gold and silver threads.

The absence of early murals leaves obscured the origin of the art of painting in Persia. All that need be said is that the oldest dateable Persian paintings are book illustrations of the early 13th cent. and that there is definite Manichaean influence. The frowns directed towards "frivolous" painting by the Muslim fathers prevented there being a public art, and the Muhammadan prohibition against reproducing any living thing effectively precluded a great religious art. A few "miniatures" have religious subjects, and most show the influence of an undercurrent of Sufi mysticism, but there is nothing comparable to the great paintings of Buddhism and Christianity. The painters were employed by the nobles, who had no scruples against having their favorite manuscripts illustrated. The earliest of

these, like the *Kitāb-i-Samak-i-'Ayyār* and the Galen, are distinguished from their more famous Mesopotamian contemporaries by a consciously decorative arrangement of figures and other components against a solid red background. A 13th-cent. copy of the *Kalīla wa Dimna* or *Fables* of Bidpai displays a sympathetic understanding of animals that combines the Persian light-heartedness with a naturalistic approach that is unusual for Persia. In the second half of the 13th cent., after the Mongol invasion, one finds in a MS. like the *Manāfi' al-Hayawān,* Description of Animals, in the Morgan Library, pure Persian pages together with some that show strong Mongol influence and still others that seem to have been painted by Far Easterners. By 1300 the various elements had been assimilated to such an extent that the presence of Mongol features in one instance is taken as much for granted as is their absence in another. Of the former kind is Rashīd ad-Dīn's *Jāmi' at- Tawārīkh* or *History of the World,* in which Mongol types, the nomadic love of space, Chinese clouds and draughtsmanship are synthesized by the Persian decorative sense into pictures of great vigor. All Persian painting is two-dimensional, with no cast shadows and with the high horizon of "bird's eye" perspective, yet the adept use of brush- or pen-strokes to delineate contour gives an adequate suggestion of three contrasts, and the bird's-eye view is in many respects superior to photographic perspective. The subject-matter is anecdotal and legendary, having for the most part been taken from Firdausī's *Shās-Nāma,* or *Story of the Kings,* and from Nizāmī's *Khamsa,* or *Poems.* The former has to do with exploits of legendary heroes and actual kings, such as the great Sāsānian Bahrām Gūr, whose hunting feats are a constant delight, and is beautifully illustrated in a copy made in Tabriz about 1340. From late in the 14th cent. the intrinsic hedonism of the Persians becomes more and more evident through the increased interest in surface decoration at the expense of vitality, and greater elegance and refinement in place of anything actually reminiscent of realism. The most famous name in Persian painting is Bihzād, who, at the end of the of the 15th cent., rose above the prevailing interest in mere decoration and, using a line of the utmost delicacy, imbued his characters with the appearance of sustained motion. He was followed, towards the mid-16th., by a group of men who produced the greatest copy of the *Poems* of Nizāmī, now in the British Museum. The men were Mīrak,

Sultān Muhammad, etc., and the pictures illustrate the loves of Khusrau and Shīrīn, Laylā and Majnūn, and the Ascension of the Prophet Muhammad. By the 17th cent. the old tradition was all but threadbare, and it remained for Rizā 'Abbāsī to try to revivify it. His pictures of single figures such as youths, ladies, dervishes, etc., are remarkable for virtuosity of brush-stroke rather than luxurious of color, but the roots did not go deep enough for the nourishment of the tree, the death of which had been only postponed.

Calligraphy, to the Persian, is a greater art than painting and is found primarily in copies of or extracts from the Qur'ān. Not so profound as the Chinese, where each character not only is capable of being beautifully written but also symbolizes an idea, the Persian has a quality of abstract beauty that gives the effect of a perfect mathematical equation or an exceedingly melodic measure. It can be monumental or graceful, leisurely or impetuous, fluid or staccato. Whether it be the noble, regular characters of the early Kufic or the rhythmically flowing script of the later Naskhi, it epitomizes the Persian's desire for elegant expression. Stylistically and historically it kept pace with the art of painting, finally succombing to the universal appetite for prettiness. See *Ars Islamica,* ed. M. Aga-Oglu, R. Ettinghausen, v.1-9, 1934-42; *Handbook of Mohammedan Decorative Arts,* M. S. Dimand, 1930; *Iran in the Ancient East,* E. Herzfeld, 1941; *Manuel d'Art Musulman,* G. Migeon, 1927; *Persian Art,* ed. E. D. Ross, 1930; *Survey of Persian Art,* ed. A. U. Pope and P. Ackerman, 1938-9.   —Ho. H.

Persian carpet. A carpet made in one piece instead of in breadths or strips to be joined. The warp and weft are of linen or hemp and the tufts of colored wool are inserted by twisting them around the warp. A line of tufts being inserted, a shoot of the weft is made, and then beaten up close to the fabric.

Persian carpets in structure, design and color are the models on which the whole of the Eastern craft industry has been formulated and developed. Best productions of Turkey and India evince the influence of historic Persian work. The Turkoman has introduced bolder pattern forms executed in standardized red and blue coloring and the Indian craftsman decorative types of a purely national feeling and character, but in each result the design treatment and carpet make are plainly of Persian origin. Chinese and Japanese rugs are of a somewhat different category. The former employ silk yarns freely, and adhere to the art traditions of China in textural surface ornaments; and the productions of Japan are made of cotton and in design schemes largely borrowed from foreign loomwork. *Identification.* In the three kinds of weavings in oriental rugs, the Khilim, the Soumak and the rug with the pile are produced over one hundred different kinds of rugs named after the towns and districts in which they are made and after the people who made them. These are identified by innumerable details of design, material, construction and finish. See Persian Art, also A. U. Dilley, *Oriental Rugs;* W. R. Valentiner, *Early Oriental Rugs;* A. F. Kendrick and C. E. C. Tattersall, *Fine Carpets in the Victoria and Albert Museum;* J. F. Ballard, *Oriental Rugs;* C. R. Clifford, *Rugs of the Orient;* M. S. Dimond, *The Ballard Collection of Oriental Rugs;* G. G. Lewis, *Practical Book of Oriental Rugs;* M. B. Langton, *How to Know Oriental Rugs.* —B.E.J., G.W.R.

Persian knot. See ISLAMIC ART; Sehna knot.

Persian porcelain. See CERAMICS II.

personification. See allegory.

PERSPECTIVE (L. *perspectiva*). That which suggests the effects of distance upon the appearance of objects.

Aerial perspective concerns effects of distance upon the color and distinctness of objects. The air, especially when hazy, makes far objects appear bluer, grayer, less distinct in edges and with less contrast of light and shade than if seen nearby. There are no definite rules; skill depends upon experience in observation of nature, beginners tending to ignore such effects and paint the distance of a picture too much like the foreground. (See **constancy** under PSYCHOLOGY OF DRAWING AND PAINTING.)

Linear perspective pertains to effects of distance upon the appearance of size and form; e.g., in a typical view down a railroad track the rails and telegraph wires appear to converge to a **vanishing point** on the **horizon,** the successive sleepers and poles seeming to be progressively smaller and closer together as they recede into the distance. Such apparent diminution of these intervening spaces because they are seen from an acute angle is called **foreshortening.**

Perspective is chiefly used in pictures, but it sometimes occurs in three-dimensional art. In sculptured reliefs it can be employed much as in pictures. In a cyclorama (q.v.), the third dimension usually ranges in transition from full scale in the foreground through progressively reduced scales in the middle distances to a pictorial background which is practically two-dimensional in treatment even though its surface may be curved. Stage settings (q.v.) are often somewhat similarly designed. In landscape architecture (q.v.) the apparent depth of views can be increased by causing foreshortened lines on the ground which one would expect to be parallel to slightly converge, by having irregular instead of straight boundaries in masses of foliage, and by using materials in the distance which are small in size, fine in texture and bluish in color, contrasted with foreground features having opposite qualities.

It is probable that this illusory property of color is due not only to the simulated aerial perspective, but also to the psychological phenomenon of **retreating and advancing colors.** (See COLOR.) Corresponding influences also occur in architecture and interior decoration. Some artists have experimented with such colors for inducing an effect of solidity in paintings, but we are chiefly dependent on linear perspective for suggesting depth in pictures.

The basic principle by which a flat picture can represent a three-dimensional object is that of **radial or conical projection.** The artist or **spectator** is conceived as using only one eye and keeping it strictly in one position called the **station point.** He sees the object because **visual rays** of light, forming a **visual cone of rays,** pass from the various parts of the object into his eye. If **a pane of glass** (**picture plane,** theoretically of indefinite extent) were held rigidly and squarely across the approximate central **axis** of this cone, the spectator could trace lines on the glass coinciding with the edges of the object as he sees them and thus preserve a record of his view, a picture. In actual practice the equivalent of this situation is usually produced artificially by means of various geometric devices, on paper.

When a rectangular object, such as a box, is level and its receding edges seem to go toward one vanishing point which is directly in front of the spectator at his eye level, like that of the rails and wires in the previous example, while its other level edges are parallel to the bottom of the picture, it is said to be in **one point** or **parallel perspective.** This vanishing point in such a case is called the **center of vision.** If the box, though still level, is turned so that its sides are at other angles to the picture plane, they will seem to vanish at two widely separated points on the horizon, and it is described as being in **two-point** or **angular perspective.** Any vanishing point of a line representing an edge of an object can be located on the picture plane by imagining that the spectator looks in a direction parallel to the edge, and noting where his line of gaze, called a **vanishing parallel,** intersects the picture plane. The imaginary path, seemingly in the infinite distance, followed by the vanishing points of level edges as the box is turned, is represented on the picture plane by a line termed the **horizon line,** and all vanishing points of level edges, no matter how high or low, are on it. It is always at the level of the spectator's eye, practically coinciding with the visible horizon where sea or plain and sky seem to meet—the difference between them, due to the earth's curvature, being negligible at usual altitudes. In both parallel and angular perspective there is so little convergence in the vertical edges of the object that it is ignored. The picture plane is considered vertical. If a box is tipped, or is seen from such an angle that there is evident convergence in all its edges and conceived as seen through an inclined picture plane, it is said to be in **three-point** or **oblique perspective.**

If a box in parallel perspective has a partly opened lid hinged on one of the receding edges, the lid will have a special horizon line of its own, called a **vanishing line,** passing through the center of vision and tipped to the same angle as the lid. If a rectangular object, like a ruler for instance, is laid on the lid so that its long edges are foreshortened but not parallel to any edges of the lid, the ruler edges will vanish on the vanishing line at some point other than the center of vision. If the lid is hinged on the nearest top edge of the box, as the lid is opened its vanishing point will rise from the center of vision to points higher and higher directly above. Likewise, if the lid is hinged on the farthest top edge of the box, its vanishing point will go directly below the center of vision in proportion to the amount the lid is opened. Such vanishing points off the horizon line are called **accidental vanishing points.** The imaginary vertical paths followed by these points form a vanishing line for the imaginary planes generated by the right and left sides of the lid as it moves. If the lid is held in some sloping position and the ruler is laid across it, any foreshortened edges of the ruler will vanish at a horizontal vanishing line passing through the accidental vanishing point of the lid. If the box is in angular perspective, and if, for instance, its hinges are on its nearest right edge, when the lid is raised the sloping edges of the lid will vanish at an accidental vanishing point exactly above the left vanishing point. A ruler laid across the sloping lid would have its accidental vanishing points on a vanishing line which would pass slantingly through both the accidental vanishing point of the lid and the right vanishing point of the box.

Curving or irregular edges have no vanishing points, but can be put into perspective by locating points at selected places on them, then sketching freehand the parts between those points.

There are several methods of locating points in a perspective drawing. In the **direct projection** method a **plan** (q.v.) and a **side elevation** (q.v.), each showing the object, the picture plane and the spectator, are drawn, then visual rays are ruled connecting the station point with all important points on the object which would be visible to the spectator under the conditions, and the intersections of the rays with the picture plane are noted. The picture plane's plan and side elevation containing the notations of these intersections are finally combined by **orthographic projection** (q.v.) in a front elevation of the picture plane, which constitutes the picture. This method is used chiefly by architects, since they have plans and elevations of their subjects available, which usually is not true of painters. However, the most interesting views of buildings generally are in two-point or three-point perspective, and this process in such cases involves constructing oblique side elevations, each combining two façades. To avoid this labor the **mixed method** is more commonly employed, in which visual rays from the plan view only are projected to form a perspective view of the ground plan of the object, then the heights are usually measured by reference to one or more scales of heights or **height lines**, erected on the **ground line**, which is the intersection of the picture plane with the **ground plane**, the level ground on which the object is customarily assumed to be standing. (If an object is actually on sloping ground the perspective is

worked first on this artificial level plane, then the irregularities in the ground are constructed, usually like combinations of more or less wedge-shaped objects, the junctions of which are later rounded to natural forms by freehand drawing.) Two upright spaces of the same size and on the same level, like the heights of two fence posts, for instance, can be drawn the proper comparative height in a picture by imagining them to be connected by parallel lines at top and bottom and putting these lines into perspective. Addition or subtraction of heights can be done by direct measurement on vertical lines in parallel or angular perspective since upright edges are not noticeably foreshortened in such views.

There is often considerable practical difficulty in working by projection of visual rays because of inaccuracy and confusion of lines when many details are involved, so other methods less direct in theory but simpler in execution are frequently employed. Many of these depend on the general idea of relating the points whose location is required to some combination of parallel with diagonal lines which can be conveniently put into perspective, since diagonals of parallelograms function the same way in views which are foreshortened as in those which are not. The simple crossing of diagonals gives the center, and a line passing through this crossing, parallel to one of the sides, cuts the adjacent sides in halves; these divisions can themselves be divided likewise and the process continued to any degree of subdivision desired. Conversely, parallelograms can be multiplied indefinitely by extensions of their sides and diagonals, each space being treated as half the succeeding space. A line parallel to the lengthwise edges of a row of equal rectangles will cut all parallel diagonals in the series at corresponding places, then a line in each rectangle parallel to the other edges will carry the location to any desired distance across the row, these crosswise lines being cut off uniformly by another lengthwise line. This provides the same kind of unequal subdivision in all the rectangles at once and saves much time in drawing repeated details. A similar combination of lengthwise and crosswise lines when made to cut *opposite* diagonals in a single rectangle will provide a symmetrical arrangement of points within the rectangle—or of points outside the rectangle if the diagonals are extended beyond their corners.

Diagonals of squares are especially useful because they cut off equal distances on crossed lines extending in two directions perpendicular to each other. For example, if an equal border or overhang is desired around a foreshortened rectangular space, it can be made by drawing an imaginary square of fairly large size with its sides perspectively parallel to the sides of the rectangle (or perhaps in part coinciding with them), correcting its proportions until it looks fully satisfactory, then extending its more foreshortened diagonal to a vanishing point, called a **miter point** in such a case. This can be used also for the corresponding diagonal of a smaller square which can be made at each corner of the rectangle, thus making all four small squares consistent in proportion, while extensions of their sides can make them consistent in size and produce the desired border or overhang. Mouldings can be turned around corners by similar means, with perpendiculars, indicating the amount by which each important part projects from the base, placed on the diagonals and compared by means of perspectively parallel lines at the top and bottom of each perpendicular.

Irregular or curved patterns, such as might occur on a map or in a floor plan or wall elevation of a furnished room, can be put into perspective by making a network of squares over the pattern, drawing this net in perspective with corresponding diagonals vanishing at a single point, then sketching freehand the forms that fall within each square. This is called the **method of squares.** It is most easily managed if the squares are in parallel perspective, since this brings the vanishing points of their diagonals, called **points of distance** in this case, to the same distance from the center of vision as the station point.

The labor of making a complete network of squares can be saved and precision gained by arranging, in effect, that each point requiring accurate location shall be in turn at a corner of a single special imaginary square of its own, extending between the point and the picture plane. In other words, distances on the ground plane which are perpendicular to the picture plane can be measured, even though foreshortened, by setting off corresponding spaces on the ground line and transferring those lengths to the foreshortened line by means of lines vanishing at a point of distance.

Likewise, foreshortened distances in other directions can be measured by utilizing the geometrical principle that lines parallel to the base of an isosceles triangle cut off equal lengths on the opposite sides. In practice this is done by drawing a plan view of the picture plane and station point, and also the vanishing parallel and vanishing point of the line to be measured; usually this plan view is superposed on the perspective view, the line representing the picture plane being made to coincide with the horizon line, while the plan of the object is omitted. An arc with the vanishing point as center is swung from the center of vision to the horizon line, which it intersects at a point called a **measuring point.** An imaginary vanishing parallel to this latter point would complete a plan view of an isosceles triangle. A similar triangle, foreshortened, is formed on the perspective with (1) the ground line, and (2) any line drawn from the ground line to the vanishing point, as sides and (3) any line drawn from the ground line to the measuring point as base, setting off perspectively equal distances on the other two lines. Thus direct measurements on the unforeshortened ground line can be transferred to the foreshortened second line. This procedure is the basis of what is known as the **perspective plan** method.

If the line normally drawn to the measuring point is drawn instead to a point called a **half measuring point,** situated half-way between the measuring point and the vanishing point, the distance measured will be doubled. Use of a **quarter measuring point** quadruples the distance, and corresponding results ensue with other fractions and with points of distance. Thus long foreshortened distances can be measured without extending the ground line beyond convenient limits.

It frequently happens that the level of the ground at the base of an object is so near to the spectator's eye level that there is considerable danger of inaccuracy because lines in the perspective plan are crowded and intersect at very acute angles. This can be avoided by assuming an artificial base at a much lower or higher level, making a **sunken** or **raised plan,** and transferring data from one level to the other by means of vertical lines. In such a case the measuring of horizontal distances is done mostly on an artificial ground line or **picture line** beneath or above the normal ground line and parallel to it.

Distances on lines oblique to both ground and picture planes can be measured by conceiving that the line is contained within a vertical or an oblique plane, and finding by various geometric means: (1) the vanishing line of that plane; (2) the **center of the vanishing line**, the point on the vanishing line which is nearest to the eye and the center of vision, and which serves as a special center of vision for that vanishing line; (3) a special plan or elevation view of the eye or station point as related to the vanishing **line**; and (4) the trace or line marking the intersection of the vertical or oblique plane with the picture plane as represented by the ground line. This trace is always parallel with its vanishing line, and is called the "picture line" of its vertical or oblique plane. Now accidental vanishing points for the original line and for other lines in the same plane at any desired angle to the first line are located by means of vanishing parallels; and measuring points for each accidental vanishing point can be found and used in the same manner as that described in connection with angular perspective.

In practical use perspective frequently needs to be worked backwards by means of an **inverse process**. The artist makes a rough freehand sketch embodying about what he wants for a result, and his problem is to discover what minimum adjustments may be added in order to make this sketch represent a reasonably possible arrangement of real objects. Sometimes also it is necessary to learn the relative actual proportions of an object in a photograph.

The first step usually is the extension to vanishing points of any lines in the picture which clearly represent parallel receding edges. If these are evidently level their vanishing points should be on a single horizontal line. If any of the vanishing points are **conjugate** (belonging to edges obviously perpendicular to each other) a semicircle can be drawn between those vanishing points, and the station point must needs be somewhere on that semicircle, since the vanishing parallels of perpendicular lines form a right angle at the station point and only right angles can be inscribed within semicircles. A line used for such a purpose as this arc is called a **locus** (pl. **loci**). If the object is in oblique perspective there are three loci which are conceived as generating three hemispheres; the one point common to all three is the station point. This can be located for practical use by: (1) connecting the three vanishing points with their vanishing lines, thus forming a triangle which constitutes the base of an imaginary pyramid whose apex is the station point and whose sides have right angles at the apex; (2) finding a plan view of this apex by drawing a line from each vanishing point toward, and perpendicular to, the opposite side of the triangle, then noting where these perpendiculars intersect; (3) revolving the station point thus found into the plane of the picture by projecting it to a semicircular locus with any desired one of the vanishing parallels as a diameter, using for the projection a line perpendicular to that vanishing parallel. If the object is in angular perspective the station point is found by (1) drawing freehand with care a fairly large square, whose sides vanish at the vanishing points of the object; (2) extending the more foreshortened of the diagonals of this square to its miter point; (3) continuing the semicircular arc to a point directly above its center, thus making three-quarters of a circle; (4) drawing a line from the last-mentioned point through the miter point until it crosses the arc below; this intersection is the station point, since only a 45° angle can be inscribed within three-fourths of a circle and this is the only point which will at once satisfy the requirements of both lengths of arc. If a photograph instead of a sketch is being analyzed the center of the untrimmed print can be assumed to be in a vertical line with the center of vision and the station point thus derived. A sketch in parallel perspective of course reveals its center of vision directly; its distance points can be readily obtained by extending the diagonals of a carefully drawn freehand square whose foreshortened edges vanish at the center of vision.

Returning to the example given earlier of a view down a railroad track, it is clear that since the width between the rails is constantly diminishing in the picture as the track recedes, there is a choice of many possible scales at which to work in comparing that width with other distances. If a given plan or end elevation of a locomotive were to be put into perspective it would be easiest to do so by finding the place on the track in the perspective where the width between the wheels in the plan or elevation would exactly fit, and doing all measuring—i.e., erecting a **plane of measures**—at that point. In dealing with any object similar use can be made of pairs of lines receding to any vanishing point for the purpose of transferring heights, or to pairs receding to measuring points measuring spaces on lines in angular perspective. Thus a plane of measures can be assumed at any depth within a picture which is convenient, either in front, behind or passing through the midst of objects. Some writers identify this plane of measures with the picture plane; others distinguish between them and conceive the latter as being like a window through which the scene is viewed, hence always between the spectator and the nearest object.

Of more importance than this question of terms is the adaptation of the perspective in a picture to the distance from which it will be seen. Assuming that the picture plane coincides with the surface of the picture itself, the length of the **line of direction** (the line between the center of vision and the station point) should be about the distance from which the picture is most likely to be viewed. For instance, for a book or magazine illustration this should be about 14 inches—the average reading distance—, for a painting to be hung on a living room wall, considerably more. The inconvenience of using widely separated vanishing points frequently stimulates a placement of them too close together, resulting in **violent perspective**. Sometimes a certain amount of violence is justifiable for sake of expression, since it gives an effect of intimate closeness to the objects, but it should not be permitted for any less important reason. There are various aids available for obviating the difficulties of widely separated points. Among these are the **centrolinead**, a mechanical device resembling a T square for making converging lines, and the **half station point** (located at half the distance of the true station point from the center of vision) which can be used in the same way as the true station point for placing its special vanishing points and measuring points, then the distances of these points from the center of vision can be doubled and the corresponding true points obtained.

Distortion is also caused if too wide a space is included in the picture. The visual cone of rays should certainly not have at its vertex an angle larger than 60°, and results are better if it is 30° or smaller— especially if the picture contains round objects near its edges, as the distortion is particularly noticeable in such cases. Sometimes it is wise to avoid such effects by using **curvilinear perspective**, in which the picture plane is treated as if cylindrical, or, more rarely, spherical.

Freehand perspective or **model drawing theory** is usually treated as essentially an informal sort of curvilinear perspective in which each object is drawn freehand independently of the others in the picture except those to

which it is very near, the picture plane for each being perpendicular to an imaginary line drawn from the eye to the approximate center of each object or group of objects. It deals especially with the perspective of the structural relationships between the parts of each object, and gives relatively little emphasis to the comparative sizes and other relations of objects to each other and to the world at large.

Shades and Shadows. Perspective considerations apply also to the drawing of **shade** (darkness of certain areas on objects caused by those parts being faced away from the source of light) and **shadow** (darkness due to light being cut off by some intercepting material). Light travels in straight lines radiating from its source in all directions. This radiation is evident with artificial illuminants near at hand; but the sun and moon are so far away that their rays are treated as parallel, with vanishing points at either those bodies themselves or at points directly opposite them—depending on which way the spectator is facing.

The **base** of a point on a plane is at the place on that plane which is nearest to the point. The typical process of locating the shadow of a given point follows: (1) the base of the point is found on the plane which will receive the shadow; (2) the base of the light source or of the vanishing point opposite the source is found either on the plane itself if the source is artificial or on the horizon or vanishing line of the plane if the source is the sun or moon; (3) a line is drawn from the latter base through the given point's base; (4) a line representing a ray of light is drawn from the source, or from the vanishing point opposite the source, through the given point. The intersection of these two lines, or of their extensions, is the desired shadow of the given point.

It is not necessary, however, to find bases on all planes receiving shadows, since shadows are readily carried from one surface to another, and it is usually most convenient to do all the work with bases only on the ground plane. For illustration, let us suppose that a plumb line is dropped from the given point to the ground. This string, because of its interruption of the light flooding past it, might be conceived as generating in space on its side opposite the light source a plane of potential darkness which only becomes visible where some other object crosses through it, making a shadow of the string which is cast on the lighted parts of the object wherever the plane intersects those parts. The shadow of even a complex object can be found, if the perspective plan of the object is available, by thus dropping an imaginary plumb line from each important point on the object to its base on the ground or on some other horizontal plane, finding the shadow of each string, then drawing lines connecting the ends of these shadows.

The points on an object which are important for shadow projection are those which are on the boundaries between its lighted and shaded areas, where the rays of light are tangent to the surfaces of the object. These can be found by use of series of imaginary slices or **cutting planes** conceived as passing through the object.

Reflections. Perspective also occurs in reflections. Reflected light rays obey the same law as all rebounding bodies: the angle of reflection is equal to the angle of incidence. This causes the reflection of a point to seem to the spectator to be located as if on an imaginary line perpendicular to the reflecting surface, the same distance beyond its base on the surface as the point itself is from the base. This implies that the reflection of a three-dimensional object is by no means a mere replica in reverse of the appearance of the object, as many suppose, but needs to be constructed point by point. It often happens that the object reflected is not in direct contact with the reflecting surface—as, for instance, when the spire of a church in the middle distance is reflected in a pool of water in the foreground. In such case the reflecting surface should be imagined as extended to include the base, as if the intervening material were not there—although the latter may have its own reflection too, for which provision must be made. If an edge of a reflected object is parallel to the reflecting surface the reflection is parallel to the edge. Reflections in water are distorted and broken if there are waves, whose numerous facets transmit fragmentary images from many directions, often with beautiful effects of both shape and color.

Refraction. When a ray of light which has been passing through one medium, such as the air, enters obliquely a denser medium, such as water, the added resistance causes it to be somewhat bent from its course. The amount of this **refraction** in water is such that an immersed object appears to be at approximately only three-fourths of its true depth.

History of Perspective. It is difficult to say when the use of perspective began. While primitive men, like modern young children, have always preferred to represent each object in a scene as clearly separated from its neighboring objects, very early in the development of mankind artists began to show one figure as partly hidden behind another, both being in elevation, often supported by a straight line to represent the ground. More distant objects were drawn on a higher level, sometimes standing on another ground line, sometimes not. The diminution of size with distance has been of considerably later development, early artists frequently using size as an indication of relative importance rather than of distance.

Many modern oriental artists, due to a deeply subjective attitude toward art as a mode of spiritual expression in which resemblance to literal objective appearance is of slight importance, coupled with a strong reverence for tradition, have continued to the present day a use of linear perspective somewhat resembling these primitive types—although their employment of aerial perspective is often comparatively realistic.

Probably one of the first books on perspective was written by Agatharchus, an Athenian of the 5th cent. B.C., who also, according to Vitruvius, was the first to paint scenery for the drama. Paintings preserved on the walls of Pompeii reveal remarkable skill of Roman artists in the use of parallel perspective.

In the Renaissance the scientific study of perspective was rapidly developed by Paolo Uccello, Leonardo Da Vinci, Albrecht Dürer and many others. The enthusiasm which was felt in those days for producing illusions of depth is revealed by the emphasis in many pictures of that period upon architectural vistas and like subject matter, and by the admiration recorded by the contemporary writer, Vasari.

Familiarity with angular perspective was a comparatively late development, and oblique perspective later still. Indeed the latter has only recently begun to be used extensively, no doubt as a result of the advent of the skyscraper and the increase in air travel. It is probably in this field that we may expect the chief developments of the future.

Terminology. There has been an unfortunate lack of standardization in the use of perspective terms by the writers on the subject. Lists of synonyms follow in which terms employed by at least two authors are given in approximately the order of predominance of usage. Those about which there is general agreement and which already have been explained are omitted.

Station point (the spectator's position), *point of sight* (used by other writers as meaning *center of vision*), *eye, point of view*.

Line of direction (the spectator's orientation, fixed by a line from him perpendicular to the picture plane), *principal visual ray axis, line of sight, central visual ray;* (orientation fixed by a line through the station point parallel to the picture plane), *directing line*.

Distance of the picture (the spectator's distance from the picture plane).

Cone of rays (the spectator's range of view, in terms of angle), *visual angle, visual cone, scope of vision;* (in terms of diameter), *field of view, base of cone of rays*.

Picture plane (the theoretical transparent surface of the picture), *plane of delineation, plane of the picture, perspective plane*.

Ground line (the intersection of the picture plane with the ground plane), *picture line, base line*.

Picture line (the intersection of the picture plane with a plane other than the ground plane, used for measuring purposes). (There is no synonym for this general concept which has been given substantial usage. The term is mentioned here to distinguish it from its use by other writers as a synonym for *ground line*).

Horizon or horizon line (the imaginary line containing all vanishing points of level lines), *horizontal line*.

Center of vision (the vanishing point of lines perpendicular to the picture plane), *point of sight* (used by other writers as meaning *station point*), *center of view, center of picture, principal vanishing point*.

Point of distance (a measuring point for lines perpendicular to the picture plane), *distance point*.

Miter point (a vanishing point for lines at 45° to a pair of mutually perpendicular lines in angular or oblique perspective) *vanishing point of diagonals*.

See R. V. Cole, *Perspective as Applied to Pictures*, 1921; R. G. Hatton, *Perspective for Art Students*, 1910; W. P. P. Longfellow, *Applied Perspective for Architects and Painters*, 1901; F. C. Medworth, *Perspective*, 1936; J. C. Morehead, Sr., and J. C. Morehead, Jr., *Handbook of Perspective Drawing*, 1941; D. M. Norton, *Freehand Perspective and Sketching*, 1929; J. H. Spanton, *Complete*

Perspective Course, 1898; G. A. Storey, *The Theory and Practice of Perspective*, 1910; W. R. Ware, *Modern Perspective*, 1900; V. T. Wilson, *Freehand Perspective*, 1900.
—T.I.C.

perspective plan, plane. See PERSPECTIVE.

Peruvian art, aboriginal. See AMERICAN ABORIGINAL ART.

pes. See MEDIAEVAL MUSIC.

petit point. An embroidery with small stitches.

petuntse (Ch.) (*petunse, petuntze*). A true pottery clay.

phantasy. See fancy, fantasia.

phelloplastic. A figure or model in cork.

phenol-formaldehyde resins. These form a group of very strong film materials known commercially as Bakelite and used commercially as surface coatings. They have been little taken up by artists. —G.L.S.

phenomenal regression. See PSYCHOLOGY OF DRAWING AND PAINTING.

Philadelphia Chippendale style. See FURNITURE.

philosophical aesthetics. See AESTHETIC INQUIRY, CURRENT TYPES OF.

PHILOSOPHY OF ART. In order to determine the purpose of a philosophy of art, we must distinguish it from aesthetics. The relation between the two fields admits of divergent interpretations which fall into three main types. (*a*) We may deny the validity of the distinction and regard the two terms as synonymous—the view espoused, e.g., by Benedetto Croce and his numerous followers.[1] In this as in other cases Croce's bold simplification tends to cover up the complexity of the problem. (*b*) Aesthetics, the philosophical analysis of *beauty*, may be distinguished from the study, philosophical or otherwise, of *art* as a form of human productivity. In this view the two fields overlap without being coextensive. Although there is an important relationship between beauty and art, not all works of art, it is pointed out, purport to be beautiful. This dualistic notion sprang from a desire to emancipate the luxuriant growth of the modern study of art in its various aspects (sociological, anthropological, psychological, and so forth) from the tutelage of a conservative and classicistic aesthetics. It is reflected by the double-barrelled title of the most important periodical in the field, the *Zeitschrift für Ästhetik und Allgemeine Kunstwissenschaft,* founded by Max Dessoir in 1906.[2] Dessoir's contention may be countered with the remark that "beauty" should be conceived more broadly, not merely as denoting the harmony of formal organization or crystalline perfection but as encompassing the tragic, the grotesque, and the harshly realistic forms of art.[3] Once this is admitted, the strongest argument for the separation of the study of art from aesthetics loses its force. (*c*) While conceding to aesthetics the traditional privilege of covering the whole area of both beauty and art, account may be taken of the natural difference between the word "aesthetics" which indicates receptivity and "art" with its emphasis on production. Accordingly we may mark off within aesthetics a sector more specifically devoted (I) to the problems of art as a type of human productivity, (II) to the study of the relations between the multiple arts, and (III) to the location of art within human life. Labelling this triple branch of aesthetics "philosophy of art", we need not claim for our convenient distinction a more than pragmatic validity. This view was adopted for the following survey.

(I) In the mind of modern man, art as comprising the "fine arts", architecture, music, and poetry as well as the so-called minor or applied arts, is clearly set off against other forms of "making" such as manufacturing processes or craftsmanship. This way of grouping the facts has no parallel in the ancient civilizations. The Chinese classified drawing and painting as a part of calligraphy;[4] and the lists of arts found in Indian literature embrace every kind of skilled activity, from music to horsemanship and cookery, ascribing to all an angelic origin.[5] The Greek thinkers to whom we owe the fundamentals of a philosophy of art were equally unacquainted with our narrower, specificially "aesthetic" notion of art, and the same is true of the medieval philosophers. John Ruskin and William Morris forcefully recalled the abiding value of what their contemporaries considered an obsolete approach. The Arts and Crafts Movement initiated by Morris tried to counteract the deleterious consequences which attended the modern point of view. By overemphasizing the distinction

between artist and artisan, modern man bade fair to wrench art from its source in sound craftsmanship. As a result, beauty, esoteric and effete, retreated into museums, and the modern home became filled with useless gimcracks and poorly designed utensils.[6] Recently the admirers of medieval craftsmanship found an unexpected ally in John Dewey who decried the division between art and craftsmanship as the relic of an antiquated class distinction.[7]

Aristotle, elaborating on notions inherited from Socrates and Plato,[8] defined art (*techne*) as "a capacity to make, involving true reasoning".[9] It is distinguished, on the one hand, from routine activities which, though productive, are guided by instinct or ingrained habit rather than by reason. The artist knows the purpose of the object which he makes, and he is able to choose the means towards it in an "artistic", i.e., rational, fashion. On the other hand, art as making is distinguished from action. The value of artistic production resides wholly in the work; whereas the appraisal of action must reckon in the agent's motive. Action, ruled by practical wisdom, is inseparable from the acting character. Production, guided by art, issues in a work which has an independent existence of its own. These basic distinctions were bodily taken over by St. Thomas[10] and have been recently revived by the neo-Scholastics.[11]

The attempt to apply the notion of art as rational production to "aesthetic" creations, especially to poetry, encounters a peculiar difficulty. The artist in the Platonic-Aristotelian sense of the word should be able to give a rational account of his work. But the poet is not. He conceives his song in a fine frenzy. When questioned about the poetic art, there was, according to Plato, "hardly a person present who would not have talked better about their poetry than the poets did themselves".[12] An irrational type of production, it seems, does not admit of a rational explanation.

Aristotle contrived an escape from the Platonic dilemma. His *Poetics* reconciled the conflicting claims of inspiration and rationality. Thus he carved the way toward a philosophy of art in the modern sense of the word, opening a long procession of kindred works on the *ars poetica* from Horace down to Boileau and Robert Bridges, and setting a model for treatises on architecture, painting, and music.

The poem, according to Aristotle, is designed to arouse an emotive response—that particular emotion which is appropriate first to poetry in general, then to a specific *genre* of poetry such as tragedy or comedy. So the end or purpose, the corner-stone of all rationality, is clearly defined. This end is to be achieved by a representation of life through language. The maker of the linguistic image of life must have a knowledge of life, not of its historical factuality (this is the chronicler's knowledge) but of its ideal possibilities. He shows human actions as they might have happened.[13] Thus poetic rationality, conceived as an analogue to philosophical insight, is made to approach the dignity of inspiration. At the same time, divine inspiration is called down from its Platonic heaven and harmonized with reason. According to Aristotle, the talent of the poet consists in his "ecstatic" or "euplastic" nature, i.e., in his aptitude to be "outside himself" and to slip, as it were, into his characters, living their lives and feeling their emotions.[14]

The limitations of their metaphysical vision prevented the ancient philosophers from developing their studies of poetry and music and of the nature of images and imitation in general into a systematic philosophy of aesthetic creation. In Plato's *Timaeus* the universe is viewed as the work of a divine artificer. This notion of the world as made, implying as it does a dualism of a rational form or model and an irrational stuff, was supplanted in the Christian era with the idea of the world as created, called out of nothing into being by a Divine act. Only after a long and tortuous development did the new metaphysical premiss transmute the ancient theory of rational making (*techne, ars*) into a theory of human creativity, i.e., a modern philosophy of art. Its germs may be traced in St. Augustine, in St. Thomas, in the aesthetics of the Renaissance, in Vico, Shaftesbury, Dubos, Batteux, and Herder. But it reached its climax as late as at the turn of the eighteenth and nineteenth centuries in Kant, Shelling, Hegel, Schleiermacher, Schopenhauer, Coleridge, Ruskin, Carlyle, and Emerson. For these thinkers, art is the work of Imagination, the human faculty which, in Coleridge's words is "a repetition in the finite mind of the eternal act of creation in the infinite I AM".[15] Although today the majority of theorists disown all speculative or theological implications, the influence of the metaphysical idea of imagination is all-pervasive. It is clearly marked in the empathy theory, in Roger Fry's and Clive Bell's notion of the "significant form", in Samuel Alexander's "constructiveness", in Benedetto Croce's "intuition-expression", in I. A. Richards' analysis of poetry, in the functional theory of architecture, and in Jacques Maritain's aesthetic. The latter may be described as an attempt to broaden the Aristotelian-Thomistic notion of *techne* so as to cover the idealistic concept of imagination or human creativity.

Divine creation proceeds from the whole to the parts, from the prototypical forms to their particularized embodiments. Similarly the artist, instead of compounding given elements after a rational schema, unfolds a creative conception. This germinant Idea of his work reflects a vision of the totality of life. Human creativeness appears as the infinitely inferior image of the Divine fiat, holding an intermediate rank between true creation and purposive making. The artist is not a slavish imitator of the appearance of things. But in order to express their formative nisus in living images, he must first, as a faithful observer, subject himself to the factuality of appearance. Likewise, the artist's material, marble or pigments or sounds, is not a foreign matter to be subdued by the mind's tyrannical vision, but a natural affinity must link the mental concept with a material substratum. Nor, on the other hand, is the statue dormant in the slab of marble as the oak-tree is the acorn. The artist cannot substitute his work for the work of nature. But the limited creativity of the human mind has to be released by experience, that is, by the fructifying contact with both the world of created forms in nature and a malleable stuff.

While doing and knowing form two separate classes of human acts, the Divine creation is cognition irrefragably united with production. In an analogous way, artistic creation, though belonging to the active rather than to the contemplative life, involves an intuitive grasp of the essence of things. This cognitive element is so intimately entwined with its imaginative externalization that it can never be wholly segregated and expressed in concepts. The artistic intuition demands a local habitation and reaches maturity only through incarnation in a work. Art is not metaphysics expressed in sensuous forms. But it points towards metaphysical truth; in Schelling's words, it is "the organon of philosophy".[16] In the knowledge of essences, approximated but never fully attained by man, the knowing mind *is* the known object. In a corresponding fashion, the artist transfers himself into the object and, in a measure, becomes one with it. This union of the creative mind with reality, described as *Yoga* by the Indian thinkers,[17] formed the basis of the Greek *Mimesis* (or imitation) theory.[18] "Who paints a figure, if he cannot be it, cannot draw it", Dante said.[19]

As the order of the sensible world reveals the "vestiges" of the Godhead, the human creator must follow in the footprints of the universal Creator. Thus his work becomes a microcosm. But while reflecting the universal order, it transfigures it in the crucible of an individual mind. Hence the work of art is expressive in a dual sense: it expresses both a total order and the grain and fibre of the mind from which it sprang. This unique imprint with which every artist marks his work is called its style. Since the individual conceives and executes his work as the beneficiary of an artistic, religious, and intellectual tradition, the work exhibits the style not only of a personality but also of a culture, a period, a nation, or of a local artistic school. In this sense we speak of a Greek style in sculpture, of Baroque architecture, of a typically French art, or of the Umbrian style in painting. The notion of style as first developed by J. J. Winkelmann and Friedrich Schlegel gave rise to the modern conception of a history of art. It opened the eyes of historians to the fact that, aside from both the succession of schools and artists and the accumulation of technical experiences and contrivances, there existed an historical continuity which concerned the substance of art: a metamorphosis, a waxing and waning of the artistic vision. Style, expressive of the creative mind and its modifications, is to be distinguished from manner, which is a mode of procedure or treatment. One may copy Michelangelo's manner as Vasari and others did. Style is inimitable. The attempts to resurrect the Grecianor pre-Raffaelite style had to begin with reviving the Hellenic spirit or medieval piety. The desire to be primitive in mind gave rise to artistic primitivism. Before becoming *what* he represents, the artist must be *how* he represents it; in Buffon's words: "The style is the man himself".[20]

(II) The idealistic notion of imagination as human creativity revealed art as a unified realm and thereby stimulated a closer scrutiny of the interrelations between the arts. Comparative studies of arts or groups of arts had been made earlier. Lessing, developing an idea of Abbé Dubos', had distinguished between arts of temporal succession such as poetry and music on the one hand, arts of spatial simultaneity such as sculpture and painting on the other. It had seemed to him that the two different systems of signs entailed different procedures and different objects of representation, bodies forming the natural subject-matter of painting, actions, of poetry.[21] Kant had found the clue to the division of the arts in the triple nature of expression by word (arts of speech), gesture (figurative arts), and sound (music),[22] Herder in the diversity of the human sense-organs.[23] But only for the full-fledged idealistic philosophy of creation did the natural system of the arts become a central problem.

If we regard artistic creation as an analogue to cosmic creation, we may expect the realm of arts to mirror the scheme of the created world. According to Schopenhauer, architecture reveals the idea of crude matter, its gravity and rigidity, landscape gardening the stillness and growth of vegetative life, the figurative arts and poetry the spirit of humanity, and the creative world-ground itself becomes sound and rhythm in music.[24] Schelling and other idealists followed a similar pattern. At the same time they construed the history of art as the temporal companion-piece to the timeless system of the arts. Hegel taught that at the inception of art in the ancient Orient the Idea was still groping after an adequate incarnation. Architecture, uncouth and grandiose, provided the fittest language for this stage of heroic infancy. With the attainment of the Classic Grecian style the marriage of Idea and Form was consummated and gave birth to sculptural perfection. In the modern or Christian era the mind grew conscious of its spiritual nature and thereby passed beyond the classic equipoise of body and soul. The Romantic Style which now prevails has lost the flawless corporeality of Hellenic beauty and gained instead a heightened individuality and inwardness. In music the modern mind, enjoying the consciousness of its infinite freedom, feels most at home.[25]

The achievements of the idealistic philosophy of art are somewhat marred by a tendency to diminish the distance between original and analogue, i.e., to divinize artistic creation. The artist's dignity as a "genius", a seer of metaphysical truth, eclipses his terrestrial office, viz., the making of pleasing images. In a revulsion from those bold and airy constructions, later authors either reverted to the less exacting principles of classification which may be taken from the diversity of media and sense-organs, or, following Croce, they discarded the problem of a system of the arts as artificial.

Yet it is not necessary to take so radical a course. In an attempt to rehabilitate the idea of a "natural system" we may point out that the various arts are, and always have been, engaged in mutual co-operation. The pictorial arts, for instance, furnish illustrations for literature, music and poetry combine, with either of the two taking the lead, and architecture lends its help to stage-craft. Furthermore, the rules regulating this collaboration point to genetic affinities between the arts. The ease with which dancing and music, or music and poetry, unite into composite structures recalls the fact that they evolved through differentiation out of a primeval unity.[26] These observations suggest the existence of a system of essential affinities. The natural framework for the collaboration of the arts is found in the *fiesta* or celebration. Instead of erecting an abstract system of relations, we may derive them from the actual interplay of the arts as they meet on their common playground. The natural system of the arts is embodied in the "festival"—the locus of art in life. The arts are conjoined into a working community by the object of celebration, affirmed and exalted by each of them in its own language.

The basic affirmation of life is either *embodied* (drama, poetry, dancing—all requiring the human body for their performances), or *framed* (architecture), or *reflected* (painting and sculpture as the chief representative arts). The common denominator of the three modes of expression is the *voicing* of artistic praise in music which, as the medium of celebration, permeates and blends the distinct spheres of embodiment, reflection, and framing. In the normal local distribution, the arts of the first group occupy the center as the dramatic play does in a pageant or religious feast, architecture supplies the frame and shelter, sculptures and murals, placed in the middle region, reflect the central drama, while the musical sound, escaping such localization, fills the entire spatial expanse from center to periphery. The temporal mode of the arts shows a parallel diversification. The arts of embodiment, and with them music, are most intimately involved in the temporal flux. They eternalize the moment by filling it to the brim with an overpowering presence. Architecture salvages the fleeting existence by negating the flux and erecting the abiding shelter for countless reiterations. The Reflecting Arts mediate between the extremes. They endow the fluctuating now with permanence by selecting what Lessing called the "pregnant moment".[27] This

scheme of the realm of arts mirrors man's relation to his world. As man is the organizing center in his environment, so are the arts of embodiment in the realm of artistic semblance; and the "peripheral" art of building corresponds to the cosmic and terrestrial setting of human existence.[28]

(III) Art is a province within the wider compass of life. The attempt to determine its sphere of competence and its relation to the principles which rule life in its entirety gave rise to two antagonistic conceptions. On the one hand, art was viewed as subserving a purpose beyond aesthetic gratification, and the aesthetic judgment was made dependent upon a moral appraisal; on the other, an absolute aesthetic autonomy was proclaimed. The classic example of the subordination of art to non-aesthetic values is found in Plato's *Republic*, where Socrates politely ushers the poets out of his Best City.[29] Ruskin condemning Renaissance art on the ground that it is morally corrupt is another case in point.[30] The opposite thesis was advanced by the exponents of the Art for Art's Sake Movement who extolled a beauty exempt from moral censure.[31] This antithesis does not deserve to be taken seriously as a genuine philosophical alternative. The notion of an absolute autonomy flies in the face of the facts. Only on pain of disrupting life can we conceive of art, or of any other activity, as an independent domain. The real problem in hand is to fit art into the unified pattern of life without violating its innate laws. Life must be so ordered that its sovereign value, the Good, accords with the exigencies of beauty instead of curtailing and bending them by an alien rule.

This is the line of thought along which philosophy from its inception tried to solve the problem. The famous catharsis theory affords a characteristic example. In order to achieve catharsis, the pleasurable purge of emotions such as pity and fear, the tragic plot, Aristotle points out, must conform to certain moral requisites. If it shows the hero as a malefactor suffering a condign punishment, it may point a useful lesson but fails to attain its artistic purpose. Nor should it outrage reason by letting the rogue triumph or the completely innocent man suffer. The good plot must wisely observe the familiar disproportion between a relatively small guilt and the magnitude of the ensuing calamity. Thus it gives a truthful image of human affliction without disclosing the rationale of man's suffering and rivalling with philosophical theodicy. But the pity which it arouses in us is accorded to one worthy of it, and our fear well founded: *nostra res agitur*.[32]

In a kindred fashion, the play theory confers upon art a high moral significance while safeguarding it against moral servitude. This theory, the classic answer to the query concerning the place of art in life, goes back to Plato.[33] Friedrich Schiller renewed it in a modified form;[34] and modern sociologists and psychologists, following Herbert Spencer's example, re-interpreted it in the spirit of evolutionism.[35]

Play, an active pause in the serious business of life, imitates life. As its illusory duplication it is, on the one hand, inferior to life itself, "mere" play. On the other hand, its sublime playfulness is the likeness and anticipation of the most serious of all human occupations: of worship and intellectual contemplation. By releasing us from the petty cares of our workaday existence, it verges on august seriousness. Its place is in the forecourt of the adytum, both pointing forward to the sanctuary and causing us to linger. It is related to the supreme intellectual fruition as, for example, the Oberammergau Pageant is to the Mass. Both are concerned with the mystery of salvation through the incarnate Word—the pageant representing it as a play, the Mass enacting the mystery itself.

In Plato's ideal state, the imitative play (*paidiá*) is a form of education (*paideia*). Through it the mind which is not, or not yet, capable of grasping rational perfection itself becomes conformed to its image by receiving the imprint of rhythm and harmony.[36] In the same vein, Schiller conceived of the gratification of the artistic play-impulse as a high indifference and preparedness, the intermediate stage in the development of man from a sensuous into a rational being.[37] However, an ambiguity lurks in the notion of art as a playful occupation with images. The charm of the image may free us and lead us on the vision of the supersensible original. But it also may enthrall us by the subtlest of all sensuous pleasures. "All great things are perilous"[38]—and so is art. The view which allots to art the rank of an educator is, at the same time, an instrument of unrelenting criticism. But this criticism, if rightly understood, is not a moralizing censorship which fetters art with puny scruples. It rather gives voice to an urge indigenous to artistic creativity —to the "artistic conscience"—which is disdainful of facile charm and will not let us stoop to the "pandering Muse". The harsh treatment meted out by Plato the "host of imitators" is ultimately an insistence on greatness in art.

The play theory unites the manifold trends of the philosophy of art into a single focus. It completes the conception of art as a making of imitative images; it reveals the profound agreement between this conception, the matrix of all philosophy of art, on the one hand, and the modern speculative notion of creative imagination on the other; and it finally links the theory of artistic production with that of a natural system of the arts by discovering in the festival the orderly co-operation of the arts. *Art is a form of celebration.* In this formula, "celebration" signifies a type of play; and the specific difference, marking off art from other forms of celebration, is "creation of images". *Art celebrates through imaginative creation.* In Ruskin's words, it is "praise of something that we love".[39]

NOTES

[1] The identity of aesthetics and philosophy of art is tacitly assumed in all of Croce's works and in the majority of contemporary treatises in the field.

[2] Max Dessoir, *Ästhetik und allgemeine Kunstwissenschaft,* 2nd ed., 1923, p. 4.

[3] K. S. Laurila, Ästhetische Streitfragen, Helsinki, 1934, pp. 114-156; E. F. Carritt, *The Theory of Beauty,* 4th ed., 1931, p. 18.

[4] Laurence Binyon, *The Flight of the Dragon,* 1911, pp. 60-61.

[5] A. K. Coomaraswamy, *The Transformation of Nature in Art,* 1935, p. 9.

[6] John Ruskin, *Two Paths* § 73 (Works XVI 320), *Aratra Pentelici* § 6 (Works XX 203); William Morris, *The Lesser Arts,* Collected Works, 1914, XXII 4.

[7] John Dewey, Art as Experience, 1935, pp. 6-13.

[8] John Wild, "Plato's Theory of *techne.* A Phenomenological Interpretation", *Philosophy and Phenomenological Research,* I 255-293 (1941).

[9] Aristotle, *Eth. Nic.,* 1140 a 10.

[10] St. Thomas, *Summa Theol.,* I-II Qu. 57 A.3-4.

[11] Jacques Maritain, *Art and Scholasticism,* 1937.

[12] Plato, *Apology* 22b tr. Jowett.

[13] Aristotle, *Poetics* 1451 b.

[14] *Ibid.* 1455 a.

[15] S. Coleridge, *Biographia Literaria,* ch. XIII. Ed. J. Shawcross, 1907, I 202.

[16] F. W. J. Schelling, *System des transcendentalen Idealismus.* 1800 § 4. *Werke, Jubiläumsdruck,* II 351.

[17] A. K. Coomaraswamy, *op. cit.* p. 7 (*cf.* note 5).

[18] Gilbert Murray, *The Classical Tradition in Poetry,* 1927, pp. 45, 54.

[19] Dante, *Il Canzoniere,* ll 1811-1812.

[20] George Louis Leclerc de Buffon, *Discours prononcé dans l'académie française,* 25 août 1753, p. 24.

[21] G. E. Lessing, *Laokoon,* ch. XVI. *Sämmtliche Schriften,* ed. K. Lachman, 1854. VI 439.

[22] I. Kant, *Kritik of Judgment,* tr. Bernard, 1892, § 51.

[23] J. G. Herder, *Viertes Kritisches Wäldchen,* §§ 3-9. *Sämmtliche Werke,* ed. B. Suphan, 1878, pp. 61-126.

[24] A. Schopenhauer, *The World as Will and Idea,* tr. R. B. Haldane and J. Kemp, III §§ 42-52, 3d ed., I 274-346.

[25] G. F. W. Hegel, *Philosophy of Fine Art,* tr. Osmaston, 1920, III 3-13.

[26] J. E. Harrison, *Ancient Art and Ritual,* 1913.

[27] G. E. Lessing, *Laokoon,* ch. XVI (*cf.* note 21).

[28] H. Kuhn, "The System of the Arts", *Journal of Aesthetics and Art Criticism* I (1941) 66-79.

[29] Plato, *Republic* 398a.

[30] John Ruskin, *Stones of Venice,* vol. III, ch. II § 45, Works XI 46.

[31] K. E. Gilbert and H. Kuhn, *A History of Esthetics,* 1939, pp. 495-501.

[32] Aristotle, *Poetics* 1453 b—1454 a.

[33] Plato, *Republic* 425 a; *Laws* 643 b, 797-798; *cf.* M. C. Nahm, *"Some Aspects of the Play-Theory of Art",* Journal of Philosophy XXXIX, 148-160 (1942).

[34] F. Schiller, *Über die Ästhetische Erziehung des Menschen. Sämmtliche Werke,* Säkular Ausgabe, XII 3-120.

[35] H. Spencer, *The Principles of Psychology,* 1870-1872, vol. II, Part IX.

[36] Plato, *Republic* 401d.

[37] F. Schiller, *op. cit.* (*cf.* note 34) pp. 78, 83-92.

[38] Plato, *Republic* 497d.

[39] John Ruskin, *The Laws of Fésole,* Works XV 351.

Selected Bibliography (Supplement to the Bibliography under AESTHETICS).

Art, A Bryn Mawr Symposium, 1941; Collingwood, R. G., *The Principles of Art,* 1938; Flaccus, Louis W., *The Spirit and Substance of Art,* 3d ed., 1940; Fry, Roger E., *Vision and Design,* 1920; Goethe, W., *Einfache Naturnachahmung, Manier,* Stil. Jubiläumsausgabe XXXIII, 54-59; Marvin, F. S. (editor), *Art and Civilization,* 1928; Richards I. A., *Coleridge on Imagination,* 1935; Scott, Geoffrey, *Architecture of Humanism; A Study in the History of Taste,* 1914; Sayers, Dorothy L., *The Mind of the Maker,* 1941; Wölfflin, Heinrich, *Principles of Art History,* tr. M. D. Hottinger, 1932.   —H.K.

Phoebus. See Apollo.

phoenix. See *hōō* bird (Jap.). or *feng-huang* (Ch.).

phonautograph. See phonograph.

phonograph. An early dream of the human mind was the artificial reproduction of sounds, perhaps because the fleeting and impalpable nature of sound made such a feat seem doubly marvelous, so remarkable indeed as to take on the character of magic. We need to accept the earliest tales with great reserve since from the speaking heads of the column of Memnon to the talking dwarf of Roger Bacon and the talking head of Athanasius Kircher they seem to have depended on trickery. The voice of a hidden operator, transmitted through a speaking tube and resonated so as to seem mysterious in quality, seemed to issue from the lips of the image. These devices, as well as the pathetic attempts of Porta to preserve sounds in a closed lead cylinder, belong to the pre-history of phonographic devices. They are interesting only in showing the fascination that the idea held for the human mind long before the nature of sound was sufficiently well understood to permit the problem to be attacked with a reasonable prospect of success. The first steps which were to lead to the phonograph were taken by Leon Scott in the mid-19th cent. When the operator spoke into the horn of his **phonautograph,** the sound waves produced moved a parchment diaphragm back and forth. To the lower side of this diaphragm a bristle was attached. As the operator spoke into the horn, he simultaneously turned a cylinder covered with smoked paper by means of a crank. On this paper the bristle traced a sinuous wave pattern. This apparatus strikingly anticipated the Edison phonograph in its salient features, but it could not play back. It could only record the wave pattern of sounds spoken into its horn.

Even more amazing is the description by Charles Cros dated 1877 which envisaged the reproduction as well as the tracing of a wave pattern of sounds. His proposed apparatus made a tracing of the vibrations of a membrane and utilized the tracing to reproduce the same wave pattern as sound again. The tracing was to be made on a disc covered smoothly with wax. Although Cros himself called the apparatus the **parlerphone**, an article by the Abbé Lenoir used the finally accepted term *phonograph*. Not the least remarkable feature of this description is the fact that it antedates by two weeks and two days the invention of Edison.

The Edison apparatus used a stylus of steel which incised an intermittent pattern on a revolving cylinder covered with tinfoil. Edison did not develop the machine further, and his apparatus was elaborated by other workers including Bell. The stylus was modified so that it made a continuous tracing on a wax cylinder. Early models rotated the cylinder by means of a battery-operated electric motor. This was replaced in the commercial type by a clock-work motor. This machine had considerable success, although reproduction was imperfect by modern standards. The wax cylinders were fragile and it was some time before the problem of producing them in quantity was solved. At first numerous repetitions by the performing artist were necessary, and truly for such work the performer needed superlative powers of endurance. Finally, the original record was reproduced in reverse by depositing a shell of copper on it, thus producing a mould or matrix which could be used to produce a large number of reproductions.

The modern record in the form of a disc appeared in an apparatus devised by a German-American called Berliner. In these discs a core of metal was covered with a recording surface of wax. So far recordings had been made by mechanical means. An apparatus described to the French Academy by François Dussaud, the **microphongraph Dussaud**, incorporated a microphone and a telephone mouthpiece activated by a battery.

As the radio in more recent times gained a large audience, the phonograph lost popularity because of this increasingly formidable competitor, and the industry underwent a crisis. By this time, it is true, recordings had been made of music by many famous operatic and concert artists. Ethnologists had grasped the significance of the machine for the study of exotic and folk music. Little symphonic music had been recorded and most of this was available only in versions with cuts. In striving to attract a larger public very complete series of symphonic recordings were made, complete operas were recorded, as well as much chamber music. Special interests were fostered by "Society" issues which concentrated on one field, such as the works of Purcell or of Delius.

Not only were recordings made electrically, but the amplifying stage of the radio with its loudspeaker was adapted to the phonograph. The phonograph became a piece of furniture rather than a machine which sometimes suggested the laboratory of the alchemist. The horn was incorporated in the cabinet. The magnetic pick-up replaced the old sound box. The result was an apparatus which in power, fidelity, and purity was an incomparable advance. Nevertheless, perhaps nothing so attests the adaptability of human tastes and of the human ear as the fact that early phonograph records were so widely regarded as musically acceptable.

Finally, highly perfected phonographs developed for broadcasting have exerted a powerful influence on public taste by broadcasting recorded music, thus multiplying a thousand-fold the reach of a fine performance but at the same time contributing to the technological unemployment of the performing musician. Stations from the earliest experimental stages of broadcasting employed records for broadcasting purposes, and their use as cheap fillers for a program is by no means a thing of the past. Nevertheless, the daily broadcasting of symphonic records by such stations as WQXR must be considered a major force in the democratization of music.

—C.W.H.

Phonophotography. The science and art of recording and analyzing sounds for the purpose of measurement and adequate description.

"Let me describe a typical procedure in recording the performance of a singer or player, speaking in terms of the singing situation. The singer comes into the acoustically treated and musically acceptable studio laboratory. The set-up looks very much like a radio studio. The singer is alone in the room, standing before a microphone, without any surrounding disturbances, and aware of the fact that his voice is going to reach a large and critical audience. The song may be one of his first choices for artistic rendition. He sings in his best artistic mood, as it were, to the large audience over the radio. Thus he should feel that he has a large and inspiring audience not only at the time of recording but through a phonograph record and all the objective facts revealed by the camera.

"In the adjoining room, there is equipment for the recording by phonograph and camera, several of which may record simultaneously. Thus a permanent phonograph record is made and a battery of cameras simultaneously records pitch, loudness, time, and timbre for every note on moving picture films in terms of frequency, amplitude, duration and wave form. These films contain the complete and highly detailed permanent records of every significant element in the musical sounds; namely, the tonal, the dynamic, the temporal, and the qualitative which become the research material for measurement, reconstruction, and interpretation. From the data in the film, a performance score (q.v.) is constructed.

"The studio is of a character that musicians and listeners are accustomed to. The record contains not only the singer's voice—pure and simple, but is modified by various acoustic characteristics of the room and possibly from outside sources. To eliminate such room and environmental characteristics from the recorded voice, the singer may repeat as nearly as possible the same rendition in an adjoining dead room. A dead room, for this purpose, is one which has been built and treated accoustically so as to eliminate practically all reverberation from the walls, ceiling and floor of the room and any of its necessary contents. It is also proofed against sounds from outside. By repeating the original rendition in this room we have the record of the sound of the voice in a so-called musical environment for comparison with the sound of the voice by itself in the dead room.

"In all these recording devices, the human element from the experimenter must be eliminated so that all the recording is done automatically with far higher precision than could be produced through the control by eye, ear, or hand. The sound wave must speak for itself so that it can be faithfully interpreted whether it represents varieties of sound in nature or in art, regardless of how generated —through voice or instrument." C. E. Seashore, *Pioneering in Psychology*: University of Iowa Press, 1942. See University of Iowa Studies in Psychology of Music, Vols. I, III, and IV.

phorbeia. See MUSICAL INSTRUMENTS.

photocreative. See PHOTOGRAPHY.

photogenic. See PHOTOGRAPHY.

photogram. See PHOTOGRAPHY.

PHOTOGRAPHY. Generally photography is considered only as an auxiliary technical means for recording. Being mechanical it "cannot" produce art. On the other hand, if any interpretation tried to elevate photography to art, it was influenced by the aesthetic-philosophic concepts that circumscribed painting. So photography with "art" ambitions has remained in rather rigid dependence on the traditional forms of naturalistic painting; and like painting it has passed through the successive stages of all the various art "isms" though in no sense to its advantage.

Fundamentally new discoveries cannot for long be confined to the mentality and practice of bygone periods. When that happens all productive activity is arrested. This was plainly evinced in the photography of the last hundred years, which has yielded little results except in those fields where, as in scientific work, police records and reporting, it has been employed without art ambitions, but with real knowledge of the science and technology, physical optics and chemistry of photography. Here alone did it prove the pioneer of an original development, of one peculiar to itself.

Art or not? In this connection it cannot be too plainly stated that it is quite unimportant whether photography produces "art" or not. Its own basic laws, not the opinions of the art critics, will provide the valid measure of its future worth. It is sufficiently unprecedented that such a "mechanical" thing as photography, and one regarded so contemptuously in an artistic and creative sense, should have acquired the power it has, and become one of the primary objective visual forms, in barely a century of evolution. Formerly the painter impressed his outlook on his age. We have only to recall the manner in which we used to look at landscapes, and compare it with the way we perceive them now— "photographically". In analyzing photography we find that this means the incisive sharpness of the camera portraits of our contemporaries, pitted by pores and furrowed by lines; the airview of a ship at sea moving through waves that seem frozen in light; the enlargement of a woven tissue; the chiselled delicacy of an ordinary sawn block of wood; in fact, any of the whole gamut of splendid details of structure, texture and surface treatment of whatever objects we care to choose. These examples are typical of the way in which photography records the visible world.

The new experience of space. Through photography, and in even greater measure through the motion picture, we can participate in new experiences of space. With their help, we have attained an enrichment and sublimation of our appreciation of space, the comprehension of a new spatial culture. Thanks to the photographer, we have acquired the power of perceiving our surroundings with new eyes.

A genuine medium. But all these are isolated characteristics, separate achievements, not altegher dissimilar to those of naturalistic painting. In photography we must learn to seek, not the "picture", not the aesthetics of painting, but the ideal instrument of expression with the entirely new medium: light sensitive emulsion, the self-sufficient vehicle for creative work.

What is photography? Through the development of black-and-white photography, light and shadow were for the first time in their interdependence fully revealed. Through the development of reliable artificial illumination (more practically electricity), and the power of regulating it, an increasing adoption of flowing light and richly graduated shadows ensued. Through these a greater animation of surfaces, and a more delicate optical intensification was possible. This multitude of gradations is one of the fundamental "materials" of photography, a fact which holds equally good if we pass beyond the immediate sphere of black-white-gray values and learn to think and work in terms of color. When pure color is placed against pure color, flat, plain tone against tone, a hard, decorative, poster-like effect generally results. It is necessary to state here that non-objective painting tried to overcome exactly this deficiency, and this effort is one important part of its "problem area".

A classical device to dispel the poster-like effect, and create a more delicate and melting impression is to use colors in conjunction with their intermediate tones. Through the black-white-gray reproduction of all colored appearances, photography has enabled us to recognize the most subtle differentiations in both the gray and chromatic scales: differentiations that represent a new and hitherto unobtainable quality in visual expression. That, is of course, only one point among many. But it is the point where we must begin to master photography's genuine properties. The point where we start to deal more with the artistic function of expression than with the reproductive function of portrayal.

How to start to teach it. In teaching photography, one could start with portrait, still life, or landscape. But, looking at a face, e.g., one will discover how complex is the task of photographing it. To observe the multiplicity of details, the resemblance of the person, his psychological expression, the texture of his skin, the subtle relationships of the dark and light and middle values of the face, the aspects which reveal its most characteristic expression, etc. is a complicated task. How can one hope that a beginner who has never done any work in photography will be able to master all these complexities at once. Therefore the problem is to approach photography from an angle which directs attention to the fundamentals.

Photography without camera: the Photogram. The basic element of photography is the light sensitive emulsion. Exposed to light this will record the varied intensity of light sources in black and white and gray values. The student may start his experiments by utilizing this principle, without the use of any camera. The technique of the photogram is based on this preceding principle. The photogram is as old as photography itself. Fox Talbot made the first crude photogram in 1835 by laying lace on the photopaper he invented. It was re-invented in the 1920's by Man Ray and L. Moholy-Nagy.

Exploiting the unique characteristics of the photographic process—the ability to record with delicate fidelity a great range of tonal values—the photogram provides the path to basic discoveries with the interplay of light. The Photogram is the key to understanding the photographer's medium. As the painter uses color, and the composer uses tone, the photographer "paints" with light.

An almost endless range of gradations is one of the fundamental properties of photographic expression. These subtle differences are achieved most easily in this cameraless work—the photogram.

A good photogram has an infinite refinement of flowing gray values between the black and white poles. Their optional use, organized through the will of its maker, creates photographic quality.

The photogram conjures up as many interpretations as it has viewers and with new discoveries the original range of these elements can be enlarged upon. For example, a new method of recording light values may occur when material is put under mechanical stress as in painting on glass and pressing a second glass plate down upon it while the paint is still wet and ductile, flattening out the painted lines to a degree which vary with the pressure applied. This glass plate can be then used as a negative in an enlarging apparatus, as George Kepes experimented, producing photographic records of the effects of the stresses. By substituting photographic evidence for guess-work in computing the performance of materials, this method may become an important contribution to industrial progress similarly as M. Heteny's experiments with photo-elasticity developed for purely scientific reasons. The method of three-dimensional photo-elasticity is based on the experimental fact that samples of phenolic resins, such as Bakelite, Marblette and Trolon, when annealed in a loaded condition show a complete preservation of (a) the elastic deformation and (b) the accompanying bi-refringence produced by the loading of the annealing temperature as it is described in the article, "The Fundamentals of Three-Dimensional Photoelasticity" by M. Hetenyi [Research Laboratories, Westinghouse Electric & Mfg. Co.]. A similar method is used for checking the hardening of eye glasses used in industry for accident prevention. Seeing such a glass behind polaroid, through the appearance of a Maltese cross—an immediate decision can be made as to its perfect execution as the cross indicates diagrammatically equalized centered stress performance. Of course, his experiments may be used one day as elements of artistic creation.

Both types of light records, in black and white and in color lead to a new grasp of spatial relationships and spatial rendering. The receding and advancing values of the gradations, which are nothing but projections of the light tracks, can be used for space articulation. This new approach leads to the understanding of new art forms, especially architecture and the motion picture, both of which operate with light. It simultaneously gives an insight into the idea of space-time. This work does not have to be essenially for the sophisticated. Both the photographic amateur and the layman, acquiring through the photogram a deeper understanding of light and space values, will be stimulated to exploration, and afterwards to a fuller use of all the potentialities of the camera.

The lesson for camera work. The photogram teaches that the same characteristics of gradation and contrast have to be applied to the camera work too. Good photography with th camera allows us to capture the patterned interplay of light and shadow in the same way as in cameraless photography.

Light modulator. This is shown especially well with the help of a light modulator. A light modulator is a simple device; its function is to catch and reflect, to modulate light. Any object may be considered a light modulator, as it reflects the light, and the colors of the spectrum differently, depending upon its substance and the different way its surfaces are turned toward the light source. As the rays strike the object it reflects some rays, absorbs others; permits others to pass through if it is transparent, while refracting them to some degree. If the substance is translucent, it diffuses the rays that are neither reflected nor absorbed. The human face is the best-known of all light modulators, and it ranks near the top of the list in complexity. A face contains few straight lines; flat surfaces, if any, are small. Surfaces and lines are nearly all curved and the surfaces have mostly compound curvature—curving in many directions. Surface, texture and color vary with the person's age; the skin of a baby is vastly different from that of a patriarch, and there are countless degrees of differences between. Then there are the eyes, which present, in addition to their general expression of personality, specific light-modulating problems of surface, texture, shape and substance. The beard, mustache, present fine problems in light modulation; similarly the hair, the eyebrows, and the eyelashes. Finally, there are the lips and the teeth, and the ears—rich studies in light and shadow.

Simplified versions. With all the complexity of substance, surfaces, contour, color and texture, the face is a marvelous subject for study of the modulation of light. In practice, however, as already mentioned, it is a rather difficult task. It is better if the student manufacturers simple light modulators out of paper, metal sheets, plastics, or other materials which can be bent, molded or cut to produce various surfaces to modulate light, in the photographing of which he must become proficient.

Few detailed directions are necessary for the actual making of the light modulators. Each is the product of the individual's own ingenuity, dexterity and interest. The variety of modulators is endless, with various bends, cuts and folds of the paper. Adding other factors to this—another type of material, more shiny and oqaque, or more transparent; metal and glass—all these will change the modulating qualities, creating more depth and illusions of space. Photographing the modulator means to try to define it by lighting This can be accomplished from one or various angles, or with different combinations of light, to strive to reveal it to its best advantage. The photographer's task is to identify unmistakably the true shape and nature of his object, in this case the modulator, for the spectator. With some thought and practice one will be able to apply this information to any subject matter one wishes to photograph.

Creative Approach. After learning how to photograph a series of light modulators made from paper, metal, glass, the student must try to shoot more complicated objects, which include all the properties and problems of the whole series of light modulators. Having studied each problem separately, he will know what each type of modulation will mean in the finished photograph.

There is an important application of the light modulator in the field of creative photography. Its effects produce emotional reactions through the combinations of shape, contour, texture, color and lighting. Thus we may paint with light as surely as we can do this by painting with oil and pigment. This is the new frontier of photography.

Surfaces, textures, and structures can be understood as light modulators; so also macro and microscopic photographs and solarization. After such experiences there will be no difficulty in photographing any portrait, landscape or industrial scene in any required way.

There will be many shapes and types of surfaces, definite space relationships, depth, height, comparative dimensions; inter-penetrating objects; surfaces that meet and cut one another; transparencies, mirrorings, etc. Controlling the uses and effects of each individually and in relation to one another in a picture, one will be able to apply them as elements of a broad photographic concept allowing one to move surely, swiftly and efficiently about one's work.

Sublimated Technique. In photographic rendering—considered as the objective fixation of the semblance of an object—one may find just as radical advances compared with the prevailing naturalistic paintings, as in direct records of light forms produced by photograms. Such particular developments of naturalistic photography are known as the bird's, frog's and fish's eye views, partial mirrorings, reflections, penetrations, superimpositions, etc. Their systematic co-ordination opens up a new field of visual presentation in which still further progress becomes possible. It means an immense extension of visual possibilities. Photography can render speed or stop speed or register precisely objects in a hundredth, thousandth, or a millionth of a second. It can "see" through mist, even in the dark by using infra-red emulsion. It can penetrate and record the inside of opaque, solid objects with x-ray photography. Indeed, this advance in technique almost amounts to a psychological transformation of our vision, since the sharpness of the lens and its unerring accuracy have now trained our powers of observation up to a standard of visual perception which embraces ultra-rapid snapshots and million-fold magnification of dimensions employed in microscopic photography.

It is obvious that photography imparts a heightened and increased power of sight in terms of time and space. This process is only at its beginning. A plain matter-of-fact enumeration of the specific photographic materials in a purely technical sense enables the student to divine the power latent in these elements.

The eight varieties of photographic vision. (1) **Abstract seeing** by means of direct records of forms produced by light; the photogram which captures the most delicate gradations of light values, both chiaroscuro and colored. (2) **Exact seeing** by means of the normal fixation of the appearance of things: reportage. (3) **Rapid seeing** by means of the fixation of movements in the shortest possible time; snapshots; stroboscopic photography. (4) **Slow seeing** by means of the fixation of movements spread over a period of time: i.e., the luminous tracks made by the headlights of motor-cars passing along a road at night: prolonged time exposures. (5) **Intensified seeing** by means of: [a] microphotography; [b] filter-photography, which, by variation of the chemical composition of the sensitized surface, permits photographic potentialities to be augmented in various ways —ranging from the revelation of far-distant landscapes veiled in haze or fog to exposures in complete darkness: infra-red photography. (6) **Penetrative seeing** by means of x-rays: radiography. (7) **Simultaneous seeing** by means of transparent superimposition: the future process of automatic photomontage. (8) **Distorted seeing**: optical jokes that can be automatically produced by [a] exposure through a lens fitted with prisms, and the device of reflecting mirrors; or the dictograph; [b] Mechanical and chemical manipulation of the negative after exposure.

Series, image sequences. There is no more surprising, yet, in its naturalness and organic sequence, simpler form, than the photographic series. This is the logical culmination of photography. The series is no longer a "picture", and none of the canons of pictorial aesthetics can be applied to it. Here the separate picture loses its identity as such and becomes a detail of assembly, an essential structural element of the whole which is the thing itself. In this sequence of separate but inseparable parts a photographic series inspired by a definite purpose, can be either a potent weapon or tender poesy. The prerequisite for this is the realization that a knowledge of photography is just as important as that of the alphabet. The illiterate of the future will be ignorant of the use of the camera and the pen alike.

Photogenic vs. Photocreative. Peculiarly photography, which originally had been created for exact recording of the immediate reality, can become the tool of the fantastic, dreamy, super-real, and imaginary. The ardent desire to penetrate the subconscious and to reach a more governable mechanism of inspiration is most probably an eternal human component. Cameraless photography, super-imposition, prisms, photomontage, mechanical or chemical distortion, the use of negatives and solarization—are all legitimate photographic means of recording. At the same time they help to create a more complex language of photography.

Signs indicate that, with a changing intellectual attitude, the photographer of today is no longer exclusively interested in photogenic renderings, but more in situations synthetically produced. Objects, situations, persons are called **photogenic** if they have the properties of producing good photographs. These properties can be of most diverse nature: roundness, richness in texture, transparency, mirroring surface, skeleton structure, etc. His attention is focused on the control of photographic effects, rather than on the event itself. He tries to acquire not only a photogenic but a photocreative mind. He will not only select what he finds, but he will *produce* situations which for him contain the necessary qualities for photographic expression with devices so far unused and neglected.

Such a development seems to be in tune with the historic development of artistic expression. A growing control over the means usually liberates creative energies which now can be concentrated directly on the problems to be expressed. These problems are usually of a subconscious nature, determined by unconscious motivations behind which emotional forces stand. These emotional forces can be expressed by automatic actions in any medium.

Automatism. It is obvious that the more easily someone handles his medium, the easier his automatic recording in this medium will be. Automatic writings are used today as inspiration and source material for surrealist poetry. **Automatic writings** were originally psychological experiments. They were produced in a kind of self-hypnosis, writing down thoughts occurring without conscious control.

It is unimportant where the inspiration to express emotional forces comes from, whether from scientific, technological or any other layers. The main task remains that the artist must have the ability to produce artistic coherence of the means he uses. In this way photography which was formerly the technical rendering par excellence, can be used for subconscious recordings.

Realism in photography. The paradox is that our mental habit structure has been built up in the 19th cent. with exact observation and recording of the immediate reality. The problem of the subconscious had been insignificant in the 19th cent. Fantasy and emotional longing was substituted then by telescopic and microscopic miracles, x-ray and infra-red penetrations. These phenomena, motion and speed, electricity and wireless gave food enough to the imagination without introducing subconscious automatism. Even the introverts turned away from their possible psychic problems toward the more external events. Photography was the easy key, opening the doors to the miracles of this external universe, within the reach of everyone. But even the most astonishing records were *objective* representations though they went in some cases beyond the observation capacity of our eyes as in the already mentioned high speed, micro, macro, x-ray, infra-red and similar types of photography. This was the period of "naturalism" or "realism" in photography.

New directions. The new arts opposed the flattening simplicity of such a "perfect" explanation of reality, a reality based upon sensorial experience and logical derivation only, without the acknowledgment of the realm of the subconscious. The expressive character of the automatic writings, as employed by surrealist authors, with their strong, direct vision, with the new and fertile bonds between worn out words, through misspelling and recoining of idiomatic expressions, gives an analogy for a new use of the photographic means. Indeed, photographers of different countries try to enlarge the expressive content of photography by fusing the customary with the unexpected.

Photography is the translation of a light-saturated world into black and white and gray gradations. This is the basic departure of the photogram. The photogram changes the habitual way of viewing the world in its relative black and white values to its complete reversal; black becomes white and white becomes black. (Similarly **solarization** is the surprising change from positive into negative). This is not, however, the only performance of the photogram. By reversal of the values a new world arises out of the hidden: a supernatural glow with sublime magnificence—a play of mysterious light sources with radiating aura enveloping the objects, giving them fresh potentialities for new relations. This also applies to superimposition.

Superimposition. The mechanical process of printing photos over each other opens new territories for imagination and emotional experiences in simple or sophisticated manifestations. Superimposition is the best of all visual means to record a dream. It overcomes space and time fixations, it is able to unite strange and diverging subjects into new entities. Superimposition is the transfiguration of the insignificant singularities into meaningful complexities; banalities into vivid illumination. The transparent quality of the superimpositions often suggest transparency of the content as well, revealing unnoticed structural qualities of the objects used.

Photomontage. Another way of extending the means of photography—besides straight camera work—is the photomontage. It goes back to the cubist colleges but it has developed its own technique leading to a kind of witches' sabbath. The results may be weaker or stronger depending upon the temperament of the **photomonteur.** Photomontage was known to the old photographers as well, who were sometimes bound to assemble individual photographs into group pictures. In this type of patch-work-photomontage the intention was to present to the spectator a normal camera record.

Around 1920 the Dadaists (the predecessors of the Surrealists) enlarged upon the meaning of such photomontage. Their mosaics, made up of many cut-out details showed clearly single elements crudely glued together. This was a conscious part of their policy to annoy the public, demonstrating with a "childish" technique that they "didn't care" for artistic standards. But there was something more behind that. The Dadaists exhibited brutally the torn and divided photographs, the rough cut of the scissors because they had a contempt for any kind of illusion and because they wanted to produce with these means a "counter war", an emotional pandemonium with the atmosphere of fury and ridicule directed against World War I.

Artistically these photomontages are reminiscent of the first futuristic, bruitisic symphonies which combined noise and hubbub to a thundering orchestration. The photomontage came later to a more "rationally" organized form looking more graspable though with the penetration and fusion of relationships which are normally not recognized. Photomontage also attempted to formulate simultaneous presentation of events. Photomontage developed toward the recording of problems occurring on the threshold between dream and consciousness; a tumultuous collision of fantastic details from which hidden meaning flashes: the idea of visual poetry with its bitter jests, sometimes blasphemy.

Photomontage often shows the vicious side of the creature; often the plot against the insufficient; funny and witty; tragic and earnest. Most photomontages demand a concentrated gymnastic of the eye and the brain so that the speed of visual digestion and associations might grow immensely.

Color photography. One would think that color photography offers ideal means for "light creation", because colored light can be recorded today mechanically with the utmost delicacy. However, as long as we devote our efforts in color photography to the repetition of classical problems in naturalistic representation we cannot hope for creative results. Most of the problems of color photography even if they seem unusual and complicated, have been solved by the painters of the past. Color photography passes through the same stages as easel painting because of the ease of its application. Most people are quite unaware of the magnificence of old paintings, and happily consider their own discoveries as original. But color photography can only be developed by someone who understands its unique characteristics, its independent original "quality". With our present knowledge of processes we are already able to specify a number of indigenous properties of color photography and hope that a fuller knowledge will be developed as the work progresses.

Among significant properties of the color emulsion and of the photo apparatus, there is the ability to reproduce mechanically light and shadow in color, such as Goethe's complementary shadow effects, which cannot be observed exactly enough by the eye, or which cannot be represented with the same speed, exactness, and true quality by the easel painter.

There is the possibility, too, to record color values, not to create the illusion of a naturalistic scene, but to give spatial values to different colored light areas within a colored light display. There are experiments with color filters, motion diagrams of actions as moving with the camera towards colored light phenomena and—of supreme promise—color photograms.

Impressionism. It has always been one of the aims of painting to reproduce manifestations of color with the same intensity with which they appear in nature. This is nothing new to connoisseurs of impressionist painting, but few are aware that in many points the development of Impressionism has contributed to the problems of photography. Seurat and the other pointillists even anticipated the *additive* method of color photography. He set points of red and green adjacent to one another so as to produce, at a sufficient distance, the illusion of a broad field of yellow, just as in the autochromatic Lumiére photographic plate or the Dufaycolor film. The Impressionists not only created a new feeling for color but also laid the foundations of a new security in the treatment of "space". The Impressionists dared to take the first step toward objectivity in optical problems. They were the first to suppress the narrative, story telling element in painting in favor of color.

Cézanne's problem. Cézanne's artistic development most probably will for a long time to come remain the practical foundation of color photography and the color motion picture. Cézanne produced the colored phenomena of light playing on the surface of things; that is, he tried to render the most intense color effect that light in nature can produce. In order to reproduce these effects in paint, the Impressionists invented an extensive scale of new technical artifices, and Cézanne developed these techniques still further. Observed close at hand, most of his pictures consist of opalescent single strokes, points, tracks of color (basically similar to Seurat's method), only more conscious of their receding and advancing spatial values. These color spots, seen at a proper distance, resolve into a colorful unity, glowing with light. This analytical, dissective technique permitted the representation of nature and space with an intensity hitherto unknown. Once this step had been taken, Cézanne could direct his interest to the objective problems of a painter who speaks through color, namely, to the relation of colors to each other. In his late pictures he uses nature as a point of departure but he quickly overcomes the subject matter and uses it merely as a framework for the composition of color areas and space-composing color tensions.

Abstract painting. Painting continued to develop. In the 20th cent., by way of expressionism and cubism Cézanne's work had opened up a path to abstract painting. The abstract painters seized upon color as the direct medium of subconscious recordings with an intensified expression. But it has not yet been possible to create with pigments the highest intensity of color, as seen in nature through reflection or absorption of light by various bodies. Thus once more the same ancient problem of colored light rendering comes up; but no longer on a naturalistic plane. For a solution the painter has now the proper element, direct light itself, movable and multi-colored. This light can become active, not only through the differentiation of reflection, or through the power of absorption of any particular material upon which its rays are cast, but in the first instance through the vitalizing, planned action of the artist who uses it to create. It is here that the real conquest of color begins: through the efforts of the artist who is informed about the historic body of attempts to create with color, with colored light. The true *kinetic* representation of color values will bring the first great sensation of direct light creation. Through a new form of *montage* by purely optical means and not by sentimental content will continuity and composition be established. Naturally, much time will elapse before color photography and the motion picture will reach the point where color will be divorced from the former naturalistic-illusionistic meaning.

The creation of colored shapes through light, free from such content, will probably lead to the **abstract cinematograph**, the kinetic equivalent of the static color photogram, exposed without a camera.   **—L.M-N.**

photomacrographs. Direct enlargements of paintings or objects. They are enlargements of things visible to the naked eye as distinguished from photomicrographs which are enlargements of objects invisible to the naked eye. Photomacrographs made with a camera and enlarging lens are free of the grain seen in projected enlargements. Photomicrographs are photographed through a microscope. See FORGERIES IN PAINTINGS. —H.M.

photomontage. See PHOTOGRAPHY; collage.

photomonteur. See PHOTOGRAPHY.

photoxylography. Process in which a design is photographed on wood for the wood engraver.

phrase. *Mus.* Metrical unit comprising as many elements as, figuratively speaking, can be stated in one breath; i.e., can be considered being generated by one initial impulse inasmuch as they are grouped around one dominating accent. A phrase may be self-sustained, or may require another phrase for balance. Phrases may be clearly separated from each other, or overlapping, when a new impulse comes into action before the first one is exhausted. The relative metrical values of phrases are emphasized particularly by the cadences at the close of phrases. The sum total of phrase relationships in a composition is the articulation of the form of that composition. See articulation; accent; form; meter. —E.K.

phrase accent. See accent.

phrase construction. See articulation.

Phrygian mode. See scales and modes; idiom A(2).

phrygium. See tiara, papal.

phylomorphic. A detail resembling a leaf.

Physiologus. Illustrated compilation on zoology put together probably in the 3d cent. A.D. in Alexandria and supplied later with Christian moralizations. The title is due to the belief that Aristotle, the greatest physiologist-natural scientist among the ancients, was the author of the book. The source of all medieval bestiaries (q.v.). —R.B.

phytograph. A nature print.

pi (Ch.). (1) Jade disc with circular perforation in the center; it is the symbol of heaven, and is used ritually; (2) brush; (3) brush-stroke.

piano. See MUSICAL INSTRUMENTS; mechanical instruments; NOTATION.

piano camera. A camera which records photographically in minute detail the exact nature of piano performance so that it may be converted into a piano performance score.

The Iowa piano camera designed by Seashore and Tiffin "is comparatively simple and highly reliable. It operates on an ordinary piano in a sound-conditioned room where the pianist can perform under very much the same conditions as in radio broadcasting. He sees or hears nothing of the recording process; but by the time he has completed the movement of a sonata, for example, hundreds of feet of film contain an exact account of every item in the performance. The camera records the time for every element in the performance in hundredths of a second, the intensity in terms of the force delivered to the string by the hammer (which can be reduced to decibels of loudness), and the use of pedals. Each note in the succession of chords has an individual record. The record as a whole is a mine of information which can be dug out in proportion to the time, patience, and insight of the experimenter.

"Here is an example of a fundamental tool, really an automatic recording apparatus, which takes the analysis of piano performance from the field of hearing and makes the performance score objective in terms of black and white where we can measure, count, and classify in strictly scientific terms. By such means we can verify or disprove the theories of the past and discover new ones. Thus, this technique is entering upon a new stage. It gives us a new type of performance score which paves the way for an original scientific approach to the analysis of principles of piano performance.

"On the basis of this type of exact information a new type of stencil can be cut on the roll for the mechanical piano player, reproducing with extraordinary fidelity the actual interpretation given by an individual artist. In comparison with this change, the ordinary player piano roll is very crude and imperfect. The task is an endless one; but like the discovery of a new continent, it leads to wealth untold.

"Strange to say, so far as I know, this is the first and only piano camera that gives a comprehensive record of the entire performance. It opens up a new frontier in the science of musical art which will be a fascinating tramping ground for the musicologist. Let me repeat, it reveals the exact interpretation given by the pianist and by transferring this to the roll of the player piano, the mechanical player can do justice to the artist through the fidelity of the reproduction. Page the promoters of player pianos!" C. E. Seashore *Pioneering in Psychology,* University of Iowa Press, 1942. See Seashore, *Psychology of Music,* 1938.

pianoforte. See MUSICAL INSTRUMENTS.

piano quartet, quintet, trio. See chamber music.

piao (Ch.). Labels. Usually narrow strips of paper pasted to the outside of paintings on which may be written the dynasty, the artist's name and the title of the painting. —J.A.M.

piao pei (Ch.). The mount of a picture. Generally a brocaded area around the picture spaced and applied somewhat formally.

piccolo. See MUSICAL INSTRUMENTS.

picking. *Textiles.* Placing lines of weft between the divided warp threads.

pictograph. Pictography may be defined as that form of thought-writing which seeks to convey ideas by means of picture-signs or marks more or less suggestive or imitative of the object or idea in mind. —J.M.M.

pictorial. See ex libris.

pictorial elements. See PAINTING; painterly.

pictorial relief. See relief.

pictorial representation. The art of rendering the shape and character of objects with a graphic art medium.

picture dealer. See FORGERIES IN PAINTING.

picture line. See PERSPECTIVE.

picture motet. See music printing and engraving.

picture plane. See PERSPECTIVE.

picturesque village. See folly.

pier (L. *petra,* rock). (1) A plain detached mass, as of masonry, usually serving as a support. (2) A solid portion of a wall between window-openings, etc. (3) In archeological excavation: A detached mass, as of earth, preserver or retained for study of the strata. —J.M.M.

pieta. Devotional image derived from imagery in religious poetry and representing St. Mary mourning over the dead body of Christ in her lap. The motive was first introduced into art in Germany shortly before 1300 and spread from there to other parts of Europe. —R.B.

pietra dura (It.) Stones used for inlay; hence hard and valuable stones.

pigment. Although this word can be used for any kind of coloring matter, in the arts it is chiefly applied to a granular material taken up as a power and ground into a medium to form paint. Pigments have furnished subjects for the writing of numerous treatises since ancient times. The number of such coloring materials is large, hundreds of items being now listed by dealers who sell them. In the technology of paints it is common to classify pigments according to their color, although they are sometimes arranged according to their origin, natural or artificial, and some times according to their chemical composition. See COLOR; dye. —G.L.S.

pig-skin. *Book.* The skin of the pig used in binding, can usually be distinguished by the innumerable small hair holes close together but readily imitated.

pi hua (Ch.). (1) Wall painting, fresco; (2) brush stroke.

pilaster. A rectangular feature in the shape of a pillar attached to a wall from which it projects. It generally consists of a base, shaft, and capital. —J.M.M.

pile. (1) The substance of the rug projecting beyond the level of the warp and weft; the threads projecting from the knots tied around the warp strings; the body substance of the rug. Pile weaving may have been suggested by grass and shrub growth and fur of animal skins. Early Egyptian pile weaving of line was deficient in density and softness and failed to cover the foundation texture. (2) See HERALDRY. —B.E.J.

pile carpet. See carpet structures.

pillar. A firm, upright, separate support; column, pier.

pillar print. See kashira-e.

Pima-Papago art. The Pima and Papago Indians, kindred tribes, live on the desert plains and mountains of southwestern Arizona, in

small villages of mud houses. Some practice agriculture by means of irrigation as did the Hohokam (q.v.), who are thought by some to be their ancestors. Yet they depend upon game and native plants for a considerable part of their food supply. They are masters in basketry, a craft restricted, as in so many of the Indian tribes, to the women. Yucca and seed pods, and the willow, cottonwood and cattails that grow along the rivers supply the materials. The baskets serve a daily use: for preparing, serving, containing and storing food, and for general transportation. They are often smeared with pitch so that they will hold water. Shallow bowls and jars are popular shapes, and the designs, usually dark patterns against a light background, show an astonishing inventiveness in the infinite variation on a few geometric themes. Highly conventionalized bird, human and animal motifs are also used. See Frederic H. Douglas, *Pima Indian Coiled Basketry,* Denver Art Museum Leaflet No. 5 (1930); O. T. Mason, *Aboriginal Basketry,* 1902; Frank Russell, *The Pima Indians,* Bureau of American Ethnology, Annual Report No. 26 (1908).
—H.G.

pinakotheke. In ancient Greek times, a room or building in which paintings were displayed.

pine. See SYMBOLISM IN FAR EASTERN ART.

p'ing chang (Ch.). Sets of paintings to be hung together, such as a set of the four seasons.

pinnacle. *Arch.* A small, decorative, upright member on top a tower, buttress, etc.

pins. *Cer.* Burned fire clay supports for ware in glossed saggers. See CERAMICS I.

pinxit, pinx. A term added to the name or initials of an artist on a painting or printed copy of the painting. Means literally that the artist indicated painted the picture or copy.

p'i 'pa. See MUSICAL INSTRUMENTS.

pipal tree. See bodhi tree.

pipe. See MUSICAL INSTRUMENTS.

pipe clay. See ball clay; kaolin.

pique. Cotton fabric in white or colors with raised cords or welts running lengthwise. May be silk, rayon or acetate. Knit constructions may give similar effect. —G.W.R.

pir (Ar.). A monumental tomb. See ISLAMIC ART.

pirouette (Burgundian: *pirouette,* spinning top; or Fr. (?) *pied-roue,* foot wheel; It. *pirolle,* peg or pin). The complete spin or turn of the dancer's body, usually in one place, on one foot, elevated high on the half-toe, either fast, or less frequently, slow, in sequence from one to eight or more. —L.K.

Pisan architecture seems to be based on types of Byzantine basilicas with galleries and enormous cross transepts (Pisa, cathedral, 1063 ff.. In 12th cent. churches these elements are replaced by a simple basilica plan (without galleries) but the characteristic decoration remains preserved as late as the mid-13th cent.: exterior and interior are incrusted with black and white marble stripes, the façades are decorated by a series of dwarf galleries supported by marble columns, and capitals and bases go back to forms of Roman antiquity. See Salmi, *L'architettura romanica in Toscana,* 1928. —R.K.

pisarka. See CZECHOSLOVAKIA, ART OF.

pisciform. Fish-shaped.

piscinum. See EARLY CHRISTIAN ART.

pit. A natural or artificial cavity in the ground or given level.

pitch. Highness or lowness of tone, depending on the number of air-vibrations per second. See ACOUSTICS; NOTATION.

pitch vibrato. See vibrato.

pitcher. A vessel with constricted neck, a handle, and a lip for pouring.

pit-dwellings, pit houses. In the American Southwest: A term applied to designate the houses consisting of a circular, oval, or rectangular excavation roofed usually with a truncated superstructure of poles, brush, mud, and plaster, the former occupants of which belonged, at least in the main, to the group of tribes now known as the Basket Makers or Pre-Pueblo Indians. —J.M.M.

pizzicato. Plucking the string with the finger. A sound effect, originally employed for harps and lutes, later taken over by all the various stringed instruments in solo and orchestra performance. Pinching in contrast to using the bow (**coll' arco**) on the strings.   —F.D.

plagal echoi. See eastern chants.

plagal modes. See modes, ecclesiastical; idiom A(2); MEDIEVAL MUSIC.

plain armorial. See ex libris.

plain song, chant. See MEDIEVAL MUSIC; NOTATION.

Plains Indian art. The Plains Indians occupied an area from the Rocky Mountains to the Missouri River and from southern Canada to northern Texas. Of their more than 30 tribes the more important were the Arapaho, Assiniboine, Blackfoot, Cheyenne, Comanche, Crow, Gros Ventre, Kiowa, and the Western Sioux (Dakota). From a geographically restricted, semi-nomadic, agricultural pattern, dependent upon the buffalo and other animals for food, clothing and coverings, the whole group suddenly evolved a wide-ranging hunting and warrior pattern, largely because of the introduction of the horse by the Spaniard. At their climax, in the 19th cent., they were a nomadic, tipi (q.v.) dwelling people, without basketry, pottery or weaving, possessing only portable objects—even their tipis were portable—and non-breakable rawhide containers. With greater mobility and increasing wealth the Plains Indians gave expression to the art impulse in the decoration of the objects of daily life. With the exception of weapons and carved calumets, or peace-pipes, often decorated elaborately with feathers and hair, all these objects—dresses, shirts, leggings, moccasins, horse-trappings, robes, rugs, carrying bags large and small coverings of tipis and shields—were made from the skins of the buffalo, deer, elk, beaver and other animals, and decorated with quill and bead work, feathers, teeth and claws, fringes and painting. Quill work is an ancient and peculiarly American mode of decoration. Porcupine quills were colored with native dyes, flattened and sewed on the hides in simple geometric patterns. Bead work, of shell, stones and seeds before the coming of the Europeans, became more colorful and more intricate in design with the introduction of porcelain and glass beads from Europe, though still confined to simple geometric shapes adapted to the surfaces to be decorated. The best work belongs to the last quarter of the 19th cent., and styles vary somewhat among the tribes. A dash and flair for dramatic life and a pride in display of material wealth led to elaborate ceremonial costumes with feather headdress and richly ornamented garments and trappings. All this decorative art was strongly geometric except the paintings on skin robes, tipi coverings and shields. Painting was an important art practiced by both men and women but with a strict division of style. Geometric decoration on rawhide carrying bags and containers or on robes was the province of women; while a representative style—hunting and fighting scenes in a lively flat linear style—constituted that of the men. Though these tribes have suffered almost to extinction by the destruction of the buffalo and the advent of the civilization of the white man, a revival of the representative style has produced modern paintings full of characteristic movement and drama. See Denver Art Museum, Dept. of Indian Art, Bulletins: *Plains Beads and Beadwork Designs* (Leaflet 73-74, Dec., 1936), *Parfleches and Other Rawhide Articles* (Leaflet 77-78), Dec., 1936); John C. Ewers, *Plains Indian Painting*, 1939; Carrie A. Lyford, *Quill and Bead Work of the Western Sioux*, 1940; William C. Orchard, *Beads and Beadwork of the American Indian*, 1929; Clark Wissler, *North American Indians of the Plains*, 1912.   —H.G.

plain weave. See weaving.

plan. See design.

plane of delineation, of measures, of the picture. See PERSPECTIVE.

planh. See MEDIEVAL MUSIC.

planning authority, board, commission. See CIVIC PLANNING.

planographic process. See PRINTS AND PRINT PROCESSES.

plaster. A great variety of materials made up for a variety of purposes carries the name, plaster. Essentially for surfacing the walls of buildings, plaster has been used in the arts as a modelling and casting substance. For such purposes gypsum or plaster of Paris is most common. This has the advantage of recrystallizing or setting by the addition of water and of losing none of its volume in the process. Its tendency to set or harden rapidly can be modified by additions of other materials. Plaster used on walls (see also lime) has served as a ground for painting, the best known being that in the process called "true fresco". —G.L.S.

plaster of Paris. See gypsum.

plastic art. Changing malleable materials into art products through modelling or molding; generally used in connection with modelling in clay, but in recent years includes working with modern synthetic "plastics" such as celluloid or bakelite. Whiteford and Winslow in *Dictionary of Education*.

plastic clay. See ball clay.

plastic form. See architectural form.

plasticizer. Many of the film materials used as binding mediums for paint or for surfacing or varnishing have a tendency to dry too rapidly and become brittle and friable. In order to reduce this tendency, they have added to them slow-drying ingredients known as plasticizers. For the resins, drying oils and a few semi-drying or non-drying oils have served this purpose. More recently synthetic or chemical plasticizers like dibutyl phthalate and tricresol phosphate have been introduced chiefly for use with the artificial resins.
—G.L.S.

plastic orchestration. See architectural form.

plastics. See resins, synthetic.

plat, platting. See CIVIC PLANNING.

plate. (1) In construction: A horizontal member, as a timber, placed on walls, etc., usually flat-wise, to receive other members. (2) See ACOUSTICS.

plate line. See PRINTS AND PRINT PROCESSES.

plate mark. *Etch.* Impression made in the paper, on which a proof is being pulled, by the edges of the metal plate. —K.K.

plate oil. *Etch.* A light, medium or heavy burnt linseed oil varnish, used with dry pigments for making the etching ink. —K.K.

plateresque. See Mexico, post-Conquest architecture of; FURNITURE; SPAIN, ART OF.

platform. Any floor or flat surface raised above the adjacent level.

platform mound. See Eastern N. American Aboriginal art.

play-party. The play-party (at its height a generation or two ago) was a rural American social gathering for playing games, distinguished by the manner in which it was "got up", by the age of its participants, and by the character of the games played. In its typical form it was not an "invitation affair" but was open to the whole countryside. Attended by the entire family for the same reason that they attended the singing school and the literary society, because they had no other place to go, it had for its active participants the young people of high school and marriageable age and young married couples, with the old folk and the children present chiefly as spectators, although the former might serve as leaders or have their square dances (if they were not conscientious objectors) and the latter might play their own games off at one side or before the regular party began. The most important differentia, however, was the character of the games played. Play-party or party games (to give them their generic name) were, with few exceptions, singing-games, including both dramatic choosing or marching games (which may conveniently be known as "party plays") and dancing games, in which the dancers swung each other by the hands or, if permitted, by the waist, with no music save their own singing ("swinging plays"). Synonyms for the play-party include "party", which meant a play-party as distinguished from a "dance", and "bounce-around" or "frolic" to distinguish the boisterous and rollicking fun of the play-party from the milder diversions of the social or evening party, "social", or "sociable", which was for invited guests and, although it might include swinging plays, was largely restricted to parlor and school games.

Although loose usage has tended to confuse the play-party with any kind of party at which games are played and play-party games with ring-games and singing-games in general, these must be regarded as unwarranted extensions of the terms. And although one might conceivably apply the name "play-party" to picnics and birthday parties at which party games were an incidental feature and from which any or all of the three conditions laid down above might be absent, and although many play-party games have passed into the tradition of the schoolroom and playground, strict usage requires that the term be limited to country or country town gatherings of young people from the teens on up, for the sole purpose of playing games with words, tune, dance figures, and dramatic action.

With respect to origins, the play-party game was the natural outgrowth or extension of the traditional game among those who sought a more convenient, well-balanced, and self-sufficient form of rhythmic group movement than either the game or the square dance afforded, one that would combine the best features of both for those who were past the age for the one and yet not wholly content with the other, and one that could be "jumped up" on short notice without the complicated organization that the square dance required, including a good floor, a floor manager, a caller, and musicians. It must not be thought, however, that the play-party arose by any such process of rationalization. Rather, in the nature of things, with the precedent of the singing game before them and the lack of instruments and other facilities for dancing as a motive, the young people hit upon the idea, and once tried and approved, it gained headway and in competition with the dance had to take over more and more of the features of the dance, being kept alive as an independent form and prevented from passing over entirely into the square dance as much by the definite advantages it developed as by church restrictions on dancing. See Botkin, B. A., *The American Play-Party Song,* 1937.   —B.A.B.

play-party game. See American folk forms, in music.

player-piano. See mechanical instruments.

playing with ink. See CHINESE ARTS.

play theory of art. A theory of art held by Schiller and Herbert Spencer, and more recently by Karl Groos and Hans Lange, according to which fine art arises from energy not required in the struggle for existence and consists of the artificial exercise of higher human powers such as imagination independent of practical ends and for the sake of the sense of freedom (Schiller), the pleasure (Spencer), the sense of power (Groos), the opportunity for conscious self-deception (Lange) intrinsic to the exercise itself.
—D.W.G.

plaza. See CIVIC PLANNING.

pleated band. See guilloche.

plinth (L. *plinthus*). (1) The slab, block, or stone on which a column, pedestal, etc., rests. (2) The horizontal projecting course or courses of masonry built at the base of a wall. (3) A block serving as a base for a statue.

plique-a-jour. See ENAMELLING ON METAL.

plum. Symbol of longevity. See *ume* (Jap.); *mei* (Ch.).

plumberiferous. *Cer.* Containing lead or its compounds. See CERAMICS I.

plywood. Laminated boards made ordinarily with a heavy core and two faces of very thin wood attached with an adhesive have become common in building construction. Some of these plywoods have also been taken up by painters as panel supports. If well made with strong adhesives, they are less apt to warp and shrink than pieces of solid wood.   —G.L.S.

pochette. See MUSICAL INSTRUMENTS.

pocket. *Book.* (1) The receptacle usually on the inside back cover for holding loose maps, plates, etc. (2) Also for holding the card or ticket in library books, sometimes called a **corner,** as it is usually a triangular slip pasted at the corner of the inside cover.
—H.E.S.

pocket altar. See altar.

pocket reliquary. See reliquary.

podatus (pes). See neumes.

podium. See amphitheatre.

poet-cantor. See JEWISH MUSIC.

poetic insight. See POETRY.

POETRY. Definitions of poetry begin with the assumption that its subject-matter is clearly delimited and homogeneous. And the single test applied to a work's claim as poetry appears to be its promulgation in this category by the author. The poem may be a bad one, and pronounced "mere verse", but if published as poetry it will be accepted and judged as such. The extreme variety of these productions is recognized and handled by a general division of poetry into kinds, the most fundamental and common such classification being that of *narrative, dramatic,* and *lyric.* Critics, however, agree in their accounts of these types only upon a very elementary level. The drama and narrative both connote a story, plot, or course of events where there occur related and progressive actions by human beings; these types are distinguished by the mode in which the events occur: a poem is "dramatic" if the events are told as dialogue or monologue, "narrative" if the story is related by one who does not participate in it. The "lyric" is characterized in a different manner: the traits ordinarily ascribed are reducible to the definition that the lyric is a short, personal, expression of feeling. Because the drama and the narrative both refer to the same element—the form in which the events are related—these types are exclusive. The lyric, on the other hand, is differently defined and, while it may be neither dramatic or narrative, still does not exclude them. Thus we can classify Browning's *The Last Duchess* as a dramatic lyric, and Alfred Noyes's *The Highwayman* as a narrative lyric. The use of these five poetic forms (drama, narrative, lyric, dramatic lyric, narrative lyric) are perhaps adequate to organize into sub-species the complex content of poetry. It does not, however, describe the nature which these several forms, as poetry, have in common.

Definitions of poetry are generally unsatisfactory as designations of the essential trait of the various productions classified as poetry. When such definitions are not merely "literary", that is, serving as the occasion for a striking phrase rather than for serious definition, like Coleridge's remark that prose is words in their best order and poetry the best words in their best order, the characterizations offered are either too broad or too narrow to coincide with what is generally recognized as the extant body of poems. Max Eastman's conclusion that the crucial trait of poetry must be "quality or experience itself" identifies the poetic with at least all aesthetic, and perhaps with all sensuous, experience; whereas Santayana's characterization of poetry as "metrical discourse" excludes many productions usually named poems.

The common element in all of what we ordinarily call poetry is language; but language is not an adequate definition of the poetic, for poetry is distinguished from prose. Of the two elements—meter and metaphor—most generally recognized as essential to a poem, only meter belongs to poetry alone. Literature that we loosely call prose commonly has metaphor as a component. On the other hand, in certain non-metrical literature denominated "poetry", there is to justify this title only the presence of metaphor, which also appertains to "prose".

What seems to have happened is that the use as a criterion of the poetic of *either* of these elements—now meter, now metaphor, and frequently both—has led critics to throw into one category all the multi-colored, multi-shaped things we call poetry. And that for these we cannot find a single definition is precisely because more than one principle has been employed in their selection. For example, it is primarily for the recognition of the element of meter that we consider Aristotle's *Poetics* as a treatise on poetry. While he gives some attention to metaphor and "ornament", Aristotle's obvious concern is with plot structure (which of course may be narrated in prose), and meter is the only pervasive, consistent element linking with recent lyric poetry the dramas and epics which are the primary object of his discussion. On the other hand, among certain metrical lyric poetry and other non-metrical lyrics, the only common element is metaphor. Between the predominantly or exclusively metaphorical and the exclusively metrical poetry there are the poems that contain both meter and metaphor pervasively and essentially; these serve as sort of a bridge extending in either direction to literary expressions that in one case contain meter emphatically but metaphor only at intervals, and in another are essentially metaphorical and possess meter only in such a general, vague way as to have no real correspondence with the quality pertaining to the intrinsically metrical.

Analysis of our use of the term "poetic" and of the composition of what we regard as poetic, discloses that of meter and metaphor it is the latter that constitutes poetry's essence. We may not deny to a creation the adjective "poetic" wherever the metaphor is apt; we may not apply this qualification, however regular the metrical structure, wherever language is not metaphorical. The nature of poetry or metaphor is to be found in an examination of language, which forms the visible substance of poetry.

The function of language is the conveyance of meaning, and meaning therefore is the primary poetic element. But both language and its function poetry shares with prose. Since prose is the proper linguistic contrary of poetry, it is their distinction that sets the terms for the definition of poetry. This distinction resides in their presentation of different kinds of meaning or knowledge. In poetry or metaphor knowledge and meaning become identical, because the meaningful propositions by which knowledge is communicated do not in poetry refer to, or attempt to accurately describe, an externally existing object. Prose meanings refer to externally existing objects. Metaphor uses these prose meanings to compare such objects, discovering therein a *new* meaning or quality, the presentation of which is poetry. *Poetry, then, is the creation of a new quality or meaning through the manipulation of old or prosaic qualities or meanings.* This is demonstrated by a consideration of the nature of knowledge and meaning.

In relation to the world of real objects, knowledge consists in the capacity to compare and distinguish. This function is discovered in the nature of the linguistic symbols by which knowledge is conveyed, perpetuated, extended, and facilitated, if not first made possible in any complex form. All linguistic signs except proper names designate some *general* relation, quality, or kind, "general" indicating that these signs are applicable to a multiplicity and variety of concrete instances. Ultimately to indicate the meaning of a general term is to give its denotation, to point to one of its instances; and since objects are complex, containing many more traits than the one whose particular meaning we are concerned to indicate, it is necessary to point to several objects differing in all respects except in the possession of that trait symbolized. It is clear, then, that if linguistic signs refer to the world of empirical objects —to something directly experienceable—this act of comparison is implicit in the conscious use of any general meanings, and that ultimately knowledge, which is presented in terms of such meanings, is reducible to this act of comparison.

Metaphor makes explicit this to which knowledge ultimately reduces—direct comparison of concrete things, the expression of a quality by physically pointing to those entities which share it. Metaphor resorts to this primitive form of expression because the qualities it wishes to articulate, to give permanent substance to, are utterly original and therefore have not been formulated into a linguistic symbol. If, for example, one wishes to refer to the quality condensed in the established meaning "smooth" it is not necessary to refer to particular objects sharing this quality; but if one wishes to express some variation of quality for which there is no name, he must invoke objects that share the quality.

Instead of saying "smooth water-lilies", he will, with Elinor Wylie, say "water-lilies smooth as cream".

Accordingly any attempt to explain a metaphor's aptness is to proceed in the opposite direction from clear perception. As ultimately we can indicate what "smooth" is only by pointing to smooth objects, so must we either realize metaphor in the juxtaposition of the objects it presents, or fail altogether to realize its nature. Our loss to explain why smooth objects are alike in the quality of smoothness is identical with our inability to explain why water-lilies are like cream. The only provocation to look for explanation in the latter instance and not in the former is that smooth is a generally recognized, familiar, qualitative ultimate; whereas this identity between water-lilies and cream is a novel and unique one, not sufficiently recurrent to have been formulated into a word meaning, or a quality resident in, and yet isolable from, many different contexts. Our search for an explanation is really a search for, and must culminate in, a name—a name which we could then give significance only by pointing to the original objects whose identity it expresses.

In our automatic use of language this comparison of concrete entities implicit in the use of general terms and classification into kinds, and explicit in metaphor, is so suppressed that very infrequently do we become aware of the comparative origin and basis of meaning. Paradoxically the only things we are acutely aware of comparing are those that are the least conspicuously similar. We tend to take general classifications for granted, using terms without considering the particular concrete things they designate,—perhaps in the unconscious conviction that whenever the occasion arises we can lay hand to appropriate instances of the kind. But when there is implied or asserted a comparison which we are not accustomed to make and with which we are not familiar, at once we hasten to test it by calling to mind probable objects for comparison. When a term is placed in a relation or ascribed a quality with which it is not habitually associated, then it requires an explicit comparison between the objects so conjoined.

For example, we shall speak of a white house without realizing that thereby we implicitly compare a variety of concrete objects, but when we encounter the phrase "melancholy house" our minds become suddenly alert, evoking live images and vivid comparisons of houses to things not obviously similar. The comprehension of "white house" requires no fresh mental effort, for the object house as characterized is a familiar experience; we are accustomed to refer to certain objects as white houses, or to certain houses as "white". The phrase readily evokes an adequate image and the mind traces the path of previous experience. But we are not used to calling houses "melancholy", and since our mental stock does not include the requisite image, we must perform a new mental operation describable either as a putting together of our previous experiences of houses and melancholy things so as to find among the former an instance to which the adjective appropriately applies, or as a fusion of the previously segregated ideas of, and responses to, "melancholy" and "house". However the mental process be stated, the result is a new correlation in which there is presented a certain kind of house (that we have experienced, or can imagine ourselves experiencing) which is more like melancholy things than it is like anything else. Then poetic insight is realized.

This distinguishes the poetic from the prosaic. It is the nature of prosaic meanings to refer to *kinds of things*; it is the nature of poetic meanings to refer to concrete individuals. The culmination of the prosaic tendency is pure mathematics, where the abstracting process has been carried to such degree that but one kind of thing remains, there being no existing object to which the mathematical meanings do not appropriately apply. The culmination of the poetic tendency is an individual experience. In poetry meaning practices self annihilation, perfecting a unique whole relevant to nothing else, speaking to itself, and only *about* itself. The poem is a structure built of symbolic elements referring to classes of things, but which, through the relationship they attain in the poem, exchange their symbolic function of representing, for the substantial one of constituting, an experience. Thus, while in prose, meaning follows its internal bent toward development away from experience (although perhaps—as the instrumentalists insist—with the ultimate object of thereby instituting more satisfactory experiences), poetry turns the abstract back upon itself, and with symbols creates a particular quality.

By taking ordinary signs designating kinds cognitively familiar and therefore used without reference to particular instances, and conjoining them in a way cognitively unfamiliar and actually unexperienced, metaphor creates a new quality, a new experience, and a new kind—even though this "kind" may have but one instance. The comparison of physical things which is the basis for knowledge and its symbols, depends upon the perception of that common element or quality in terms of which comparison is made. In so-called "figurative" language, signs for these qualities, or for objects constituted of a complex of qualities, are so juxtaposed as to elicit a quality distinct from that meant by any component term, and experientially non-existent previously. This seems to happen in the following way: while, in a simple metaphor (as "shadow-rain") the terms employed each refer to an entity or experience in itself prosaic, since alone each would represent a kind, and, assuming no extraordinary personal exercise of imagination, would be apprehended cognitively; the bringing of these prosaic kinds into juxtaposition explicitly *identifies that which had not before been identified* (here rain and shadow), and in this identification creates a quality and kind not before known. In more detail, the process involves the recollection by the reader of experiences of shadows and rain: in the surprise of this unexpected uniting of kinds he swiftly reflects upon and attends to each kind, discovering in his experience or knowledge of these that quality which in each had escaped him until the two were presented together.

The recognition is no different in nature from the insight by which were discovered any of the familiar, general, prosaic (these standing for the same characteristic) qualities that form the substance of practical or facile discourse. We might, for example, imagine a time when there was first recognized that the blue sky and blue sea were both blue, so occurring the identification of blueness in which the quality first became a kind and a name. At such a hypothetical frontier of knowledge "sea-sky" might have served as a metaphor as effective as "shadow-rain". Now, however, "sea-sky" would only be confusing, since we have come to find so many identities in sea and sky that unless told by the context, we would not know whether to look for a new quality or to refer to a familiar, prosaic one; and, if the latter, which of the various identities is intended.

The formal poem is simply an extension of the process and phenomenon of metaphor. If the poem is successful—that is, if it achieves that indispensable condition of all art, unity, then the greater the complexity of content, the more will the number of signs (and kinds) operate to establish a vivid and unique quality. The achievement of the latter does impose limits upon the number and variety of signs (kinds) that can be used. The same sort of limitation is duplicated in the case of the ingredients available to the other arts, namely, the selection of those that can be assembled into an integral whole.

Against this view the following objection might be raised: if a metaphor perfects a unique quality, and since a poem contains several metaphors—each presumably with its unique quality, a poem must consist not of a single quality but of as many qualities as there are metaphors. The objection illuminates the way in which metaphor is embodied in a formal poem. The particular, explicit metaphors of a poem are variations of the single quality of the entire poem, and emerge only as patterns upon its background, or, more exactly, as forms of its substance. We discover how this occurs in searching among poems for metaphors to extract from the poetic body: we find that thus separated they usually lose their meaning. The poem is a whole so closely united that every phrase requires for the expression of its meaning, either all the other lines of the poem, or a certain assembly of lines which together require the remaining poem for their effect. Therefore something is inevitably lost when we lift a metaphor out of a poem, even though in isolation that metaphor may preserve a perfection beyond cavil.

The radical implication of the conception of poetry as essentially metaphor, is that such classical works as Dante' *Inferno*, Milton's *Paradise Lost*, Shakespeare's plays, Homer's *Odyssey* and *Iliad*, are not poems. This does not mean that they are not "greater" (whatever the adjective may mean) artistic works than any poems in the strict sense. To judge this one must determine in what greatness in art generally consists, and just what is the nature of the above productions. It may be that these are greater in that they contain within their non-poetical scope superlative isolated poems. It may be that they are greater as representing a higher type of art, in which poems may enter as contributing elements,—the way drama and music combine in the opera. Or, finally, it may be that they are inferior. All that is insisted is that the poem as here defined does constitute a distinct kind of art and experience, and that it is in the interest of clarity to recognize this even when it involves the reclassification of a vast outstanding body of literature. Following the latter conviction, we have drawn into the body of poetry proper its simple element—the metaphor—rather than taking the traditional path of proceeding from the formal poem to sweep into its category the more extended forms in which this already complex entity serves as a component. The method can strike as objectionable only those who read into it some kind of depreciation of the contributions of the authors enumerated. And indeed that this can occur is only another indication of the need of the term "poetry" for revision. It indicates that the term has acquired a connotation of more excellence, applying as a form of praise, rather than designating simply a type of art, which—like all art—is excellent when successful. See *The Enjoyment of Poetry*, Max Eastman, Revised Ed., 1939; *Poetry, The Renascence of Wonder*, Theodore Watts-Dunton, 1916; *The Poetic Principle*, Edgar Allen Poe, 1850; *Theory of Poetry*, Lascelles Abercrombie, 1924; *The Kinds of Poetry*, John Erskine, 1920; *A Study of Poetry*, Bliss Perry, 1920; *Poetics*, Aristotle; *Laocoon*, G. B. Lessing; *Form in Modern Poetry*, Herbert Read, 1932.

—S.Z.

pointed style. Gothic style.

pointes (Fr. extremities). The academic term for dancing on the extended toes (*sur les pointes*), supported by the rigid metatarsal arch, enclosed in satin slippers with a stiff leather shank, the point of contact with the floor strengthened by a small box of cardboard, the toes often protected by lamb's wool. —L.K.

pointillism. See PAINTING.

pointing. Reproduction in stone of a clay or plaster model by drilling holes to the proper depth in a stone block at points corresponding to points indicated on the model by the sculptor.

point of distance, of sight, of view. See PERSPECTIVE.

pole. A long slender piece of wood, commonly tapering and more or less rounded; usually five inches or less in diameter.

police power. See CIVIC PLANNING.

polichinelley. A clown-dance.

POLISH ART. *General Characteristics.* Dating from the arrival of Christianity from Rome in 966, Poland has culturally always been closely connected with Western Europe. Thus Polish art always went hand in hand with the evolution of art in Western European lands. Like there, so in Poland do we distinguish the Romanesque, Gothic, Renaissance, baroque, rococo, and classic periods, and the 19th and 20th cent. multiple art movements.

Foreign influences that reached Poland from various Western European countries were by no means limited to a single source of origin; they came from Bohemia, from Italy, from France, the Netherlands, and Germany. But in spite of the parallelism in the development of Polish art and that of the entire West, certain characteristics took root in Poland more easily than others. Moreover, guided by native predilections and inspired by the native temperament, Polish artists tended to modify the adopted forms of art.

In architecture, e.g., the local variations of the different Western European styles were brought about by climatic conditions, by the character of the landscape and that of the building materials abundant in Poland—wood or brick—, and last but not least, by the fact that the builders, even when the architectural designers were foreigners, were mostly local people accustomed to the particular features of the wooden Polish dwellings, the sources of which might be traced back to wooden architecture of prehistoric Poland, and which partly survived until the present day in the peasant's huts.

On the other hand, Polish painting, while from its inception characterized, in common with Western art, by naturalism, often shows certain decorative tendencies in respect to form, and a lyric and pensive mood as regards inner content, both features held in common with Byzantine-Russian art. One may easily understand, however, that by reason of its interest in nature, the form as well as the content of Polish art are richer than those of Byzantine-Russian art, which is essentially imaginative, refusing to model itself upon forms seen in nature.

The decorative qualities of Polish art, esp. noticeable in the applied arts, were in later centuries encouraged by the growing Islamic influences, which brought with them a wealth of ornamental designs. Particularly welcome seemed to be the floral motifs which have been fruitfully combined into new patterns with the indigenous motifs of more naturalistically conceived flowers, a most beloved element of all Polish peasant art, be it old or new.

No doubt also the general Polish fondness for clear, vivid, yet always harmoniously arranged color schemes has its roots in indigenous Polish peasant art.

In the art of Poland, native and foreign elements now exist side by side on a separate and even hostile footing, now they intertwine and mingle. At times, the decorative traits and the vivid color harmonies in Polish art generally, and the tendency toward pensiveness in painting and sculpture specifically, appear only in works of art produced away from the art centers by local artists who had only an indirect or casual contact with the great art currents of contemporary Western Europe; at times, however, they victoriously shine through the pan-European forms as created by Polish artists well acquainted with the art evolution abroad, who notwithstanding, did not lose their national individuality. Finally, let us still mention that as a rule the Polish national characteristics appear most distinctly in the decorative arts.

The Romanesque Period. To the oldest Polish architectural stone relics belongs the *St. Felix' Church,* a small rotunda, not so long ago excavated on the *Wawel Hill* in Cracow, and dating from the beginnings of the 11th cent. During this and the following century a number of monumental Romanesque cathedrals and monastic churches was erected in Poland. Among the Polish most remarkable Romanesque sculptures are the famous bronze doors (ca. 1127) of the Gniezno Cathedral. These doors are ornamented with bas-reliefs representing scenes from the life of St. Adalbert, patron of Poland. Twelfth-century chalices and other accessories used in divine worship, preserved in the treasuries of many Polish churches, are engraved with scenes closely related in style to the Gniezno doors and bear witness to French influences, then predominating in Poland.

The Gothic Period. By the middle of the 13th cent. the Gothic style was spreading throughout Poland. Soon it acquired distinctive local features. The Polish modification of the Gothic architectural style is known as the **Vistula Gothic.** Its clear formulation was achieved by the middle of the 14th cent. and its most mature representative is the *Church of Our Lady* in Cracow (1226-1442). The Vistula Gothic is characterized by the use of brick for the walls, stone being used only for the constructive and decorative parts. The brick walls, while lofty, are massive and solid. Thus the buttresses are directly in contact with the walls and are not reinforced by a second row of flying buttresses and auxiliary arches, so typical of the French Gothic. The windows, while having pointed arches, are relatively small. The churches thus often bear resemblance to fortified castles. Multi-colored bricks, arranged in decorative patterns, enliven the outdoor surfaces; frescoes the interior walls.

Polish Gothic wooden sculpture, which reached a high degree of perfection during the 14th and 15th cent., is marked by deep expressiveness. Religious in kind and destined for the churches, it developed in cities, where artists and craftsmen were organized into guilds. The attempts at realism, noticeable during the latter part of the 15th cent., received a powerful impulse by the creative work of Wit Stwosz, or Stosz (ca. 1445-1533), in German called Veit Stoss, an artist claimed both by Poland and Germany. Among the many masterpieces executed by him in Cracow, where he spent the best years of his life, at least the gigantic wooden polychromed altar piece (1477-1489) at the Church of our Lady ought to be mentioned. The influence of Wit Stwosz on Polish sculpture lasted far into the 16th cent.

Polish Gothic painting is represented by numerous altarpieces, mural decorations, as well as illuminations. It reached the peak of its evolution during the 15th cent. A gem of Polish Gothic painting is, for instance, the *"Deposition" of Chomranice* (middle of the 15th cent.), at the Tarnow Museum. In this and other Polish Gothic paintings one may observe, despite strong foreign influences, a greater emphasis upon decorative detail than in the West, a leaning to a harmonious arrangement of a few but saturated colors, a special fondness for gilding; one may further note that the faces of the human figures are, like those of Polish contemporary sculptures, strongly imbued with feeling and lyric mood.

While the names of the Polish guild painters chiefly remain anonymous, let us mention Jan Polak, painter of Polish origin, a leading master of the Bavarian school from the end of the 15th cent.

Of many highly accomplished contemporary miniatures and illuminations, those illustrating the *Codex of Baltazar Behem* (ca. 1505) are worthy of special attention, as they represent the activities of the flourishing Gothic craftsmen's guilds.

Also woodcut, copper engraving, and stained glass reached a high degree of perfection during Poland's late Gothic period.

The Period of the Renaissance. The Italian Renaissance was introduced in Poland by King Zygmunt (Sigismund) I (1506-1548) and is often referred to as the **Cracow Renaissance.** This king entrusted the rebuilding of the medieval royal castle on the Wawel Hill at Cracow to an architect known in Poland as Franciszek Wloch (*Wloch* meanng "the Italian"), who constructed a three-story colonnade of arcades around the castle's courtyard (1502-1516). Another Italian, Bartolomeo Berecci, built the much admired *Sigismund Chapel* (1517-1533), in the medieval Cracow Cathedral on the Wawel.

Following the example of the king, many Polish notables and Polish towns summoned architects from Italy to erect or rebuild castles and townhalls according to the laws of the Italian Renaissance. However, these architects soon succumbed to local influences. They enhanced the picturesqueness of their buildings by adding certain architectural details, especially placing high ornamental galleries over the top stories. These fanciful galleries soon became a typical feature of Polish Renaissance buildings throughout Poland.

Above all, dwelling houses in small towns developed a late Renaissance ornamental style of their own, still flourishing at the beginning of the 17th cent. The houses in Kazimierz-on-the-Vistula provide a good example of this style. Besides the crowning galleries, they have façades all covered with multiple linear decorations. At the same time, a modified Gothic style still was alive in small wooden country churches.

The evolution of Polish Renaissance sculpture may best be followed in sepulchral monuments. Of the Italian sculptors carving tombs in Poland, Giovani Maria Padovano, was the most influential toward the beginning of the 16th cent.; of the Polish, Jan Michalowicz of Urzedow, active from 1553 to 1582. He gained the surname of the *Polish Praxiteles* for himself.

While 16th-cent. Polish architecture and sepulchral sculpture both enjoyed the patronage of the Polish kings and notables, wooden church sculpture and painting as well as all kinds of crafts remained in the hands of the guild masters, who held more or less fast to the traditions of the Polish Gothic. Especially in provincial towns painting and sculpture became only slightly touched by the new currents. Nonetheless, the guilds produced many a true masterpiece during the first half of the 16th cent.

But by the middle of this century the guilds, deprived of the protectorate of the wealthy, began to decline. Still, for many decades to come, they created throughout the country religious works of art which, although to a certain extent primitive in character, excite our great interest as Polish art manifestations completely deprived of direct foreign influences. In this city guild art the national characteristic features were manifested more freely and more distinctly than in other, more mature but less independent trends of Polish art of the time. Thus, for instance, the Polish guild paintings of the period are marked by a decorative quality, forming a counterpart to the façades of the contemporaneous small town houses, by a naïve but refreshing sincerity of expression, and by harmoniously contrasted colors, having no half-tones but local values. A most distinctive specimen of this popular national trend in Polish art is the *St. Martin* in one of the altars of the Poznan Cathedral, painted in 1628 by Krzysztof **Boguszewski.**

Of the Polish artists of the period who attained success abroad, Jan Ziarnko of Lwow, known also as *Il Grano* or *Le Grain,* is the best known. An outstanding draughtsman and engraver, he was active toward the end of the 16th and beginning of the 17th cent.

The Baroque and Rococo Periods. Notwithstanding the traditional tendencies of Polish provincial art, the Italian baroque architecture found its way to Poland very early, which is witnessed by the *Church of SS. Peter and Paul* in Cracow, built in 1597-1619 by Gian Maria Bernardone and J. Trevano, greatly inspired by the *Il Gesù* in Rome. Italian baroque churches soon became popular in Poland. By the end of the 17th cent. and at the beginning of the 18th certain local innovations were introduced. Along with an ornamental treatment of the façade, an exuberance of sculptured interior decoration became characteristic. This style reached a particularly high level in 18th-cent. churches of Wilno and Lwow, famed for their rococo decorative sculptures.

The baroque also influenced the style of the Polish palaces. Also here it soon appeared under a polonized form, which may readily be recognized in the royal palace at Wilanow (1677-1694), the favorite residence of King Jan Sobieski, built by an Italian under the king's personal supervision. The Wilanow palace stretches wide and low like the Polish noblemen's wooden country man-sions, they themselves being an enlargement and enrichment of the simpler peasant dwellings.

From the middle of the 17th cent. until the end of the 18th the inter-European trends in sculpture and painting came to be represented almost exclusively by foreign royal court painting and that developing at the palaces of the Polish aristocracy and in some wealthier monasteries. This foreign painting acquired such an importance that it gave no chance to develop even to the more popular paintings of the guilds. Nonetheless, native art did not die out: It withdrew to the peasants' quarters.

Here must first of all be mentioned the vivid yet harmonious decorations consisting of stylized flower motifs, which often covered the walls and ceilings of the 17th-cent., and also earlier peasant wooden churches. Besides, there exist intimations that it was toward the end of the 17th cent. that the Polish peasant woodcuts, which came to full bloom more than one hundred years later, made their first appearance. These religious woodcuts, similar to the figures of saints carved in wood by the peasants to be placed in wayside shrines, combine traditional Polish Gothic elements with those of the baroque and rococo styles. Both the peasant carved figures and woodcuts, strikingly expressive, attained a high degree of beauty within their primitive forms.

Also the beginnings of the peasant **kilims** and of tapestry weaving—the latter usually executed in country manors but most often with the help of peasant craftswomen—seem to have occurred in Poland during the 17th cent. The peasant *kilims,* which flourished during the following two centuries, clearly show a merging of typically peasant, freely treated flower patterns with some geometricized Oriental designs.

It must be emphasized that it was just during the baroque and rococo periods that strong Islamic influences invaded Poland, bringing with them, besides direct Turkish, very numerous Persian elements, which left an impression on contemporary Polish textiles, the nobleman's dress and his arms and armor.

The Classic Period. The second half of the 18th cent. witnessed a flowering of Polish art comparable in kind to that during the Cracow Renaissance. The center of this flowering became Warsaw, the new capital of Poland; the great protector of the arts being the last king of Poland, Stanislaus Augustus

Poniatowski. *The Royal Palace in the Lazi-enki Park* in Warsaw, built and decorated in 1784-88 by Italians in strict co-operation with the king, is the most outstanding example of the Polish late 18th-cent. classicism, known as the **Stanislaus Augustus style**, combining French rococo reminiscences with predominating Roman Palladian elements. The famous interiors of the often reconstructed Royal Castle in Warsaw, often referred to as to *Zamek* (which means castle), were executed in the same style.

This Warsaw classicism, when reaching other Polish towns and cities, underwent through local changes. In Wilno, where one of the most eminent Polish architects of all times, Wawrzyniec (Lawrence) Gucewicz (1753-98), was active, it acquired an almost Grecian purity of style. The Wilno Cathedral may be proof of it. Many other Polish architects distinguished themselves during the Stanislaus Augustus period.

The most influential of the numerous French and Italian painters, sculptors, and interior decorators working for this king, was the Italian Marcello Bacciarelli (1731-1818), a talented portraitist and author of the large historical paintings decorating the Warsaw Castle's walls. But it was the French painter Jean Pierre Norblin (1745-1830), not employed by the king but by one of the Polish notables living outside of Warsaw, who became best known of all the foreign artists who at the time found bread and fame in Poland: He was the first to introduce Polish genre motifs into painting and thus became the forerunner of a large number of Polish 19th cent. artists devoting their talents exclusively to Polish country scenes.

On the other hand, the Pole Tadeusz Konicz, or Kuntze (1733-93), became noted for his genre scenes illustrating the life on the streets of Rome, where he spent most of his creative years. Of the many other talented Polish late 18th-cent. painters Franciszek Smuglewicz (1747-1807) was the most outstanding representative of the current inter-European pseudo-classic trends.

In the field of the decorative arts, wide silk sashes profusely interwoven with gold and silver became world famous. A striking feature of the Polish nobleman's costume, they attained a style of their own by the end of the 18th cent., thanks to a skilful merging of Near Eastern and Western elements with indigenous peasant flower motifs. Produced in workshops scattered throughout the country, these sashes are often termed the **Sluck sashes**, as the workshop in the town of Sluck was one of the most prolific.

The 19th Century. At the beginning of the 19th cent. Polish architects produced many a beautiful building reminding one of the severe classicism of the late 18th cent. Wilno school. Then, like in all Europe, so also in Poland, the different "historical" styles followed. Similar trends might have been noticed in 19th cent. sculpture, and still more in the decorative arts. It was chiefly in painting that the creative spirit of the Polish nation expressed itself freely during the past century.

The tragedy of the Polish partitions toward the end of the 18th cent. and the simultaneous development of new social ideas centered the attention and emotions of the Polish people upon their country. Thus during the entire 19th cent. the subjects of the Polish paintings were in one way or another connected with the life of the nation. Yet, while a large number of the Polish paintings from the first half of this century represented important moments from Polish history, in style they corresponded to current Western European art. With the exception of Henryk Rodakowski (1823-94), adherent of the progressive French coloristic school of his time, most of the Polish portraitists and historical painters followed the path of pseudo-classic art as already Franciszek Smuglewicz had done.

It was only during the latter part of the past century that Polish historical painting became more distinctly national in character, but even then not so much in respect to outer form as to inner content. The decisive step in this direction was made by Jan Matejko (1838-93). His historical canvases, while conceived in the style of the contemporary romantic school, are famous for their dramatic intensity, for their strength and depth of expression, for the power of feeling emanating from the figures which he created. The pensiveness of certain personages which had been here and there noticeable in the religious pictures from earlier times, or even in the historical pictures of Matejko's immediate predecessors, grew in the hands of this great master to a strength of feeling which became an integral part of his works.

A close contemporary of Matejko, Artur Grottger (1837-67), pupil of the Vienna Academy, represented the sad scenes from the Polish insurrection of 1863, the tragic life of the political prisoners, and the Polish widows and orphans, endowing his drawings with truly poetic and lyric qualities. Jacek Malczewski (1855-1929), a symbolist, was greatly inspired both by him and by Matejko. Let us add that generally in all art that followed Matejko and Grottger, even up to the invasion of Poland in 1939, i.e., in realistic, impressionistic, cubistic, formistic, and neo-classical trends—sadness, melancholy, and pensiveness come to the fore as characteristic features of the inner content of the Polish paintings. Lyric mood has become the chief ingredient even of landscapes.

Along with the development of 19th-cent. Polish historical painting, another line of evolution may be followed in the creativeness of artists who took the road opened by Norblin. First of all, Alexander Orlowski (1777-1832), world-known caricaturist of Polish types and manners, who later settled down in Petrograd, and Piotr Michalowski (1800-55), a splendid painter of horses, the *Polish Géricault*, must be mentioned. Another excellent draughtsman of horses was Juliusz Kossak (1824-99), to a large extent self-taught, who began to show the picturesque life of the Polish nobleman, at the battle, at the hunt, and on the ride. He gave inspiration to a large number of Polish artists of the end of the century, who, like himself, placed accent on the picturesque side of the life of the Polish spirited country gentleman of their own and bygone days. Jozef Brandt (1841-1915), a disciple of the realistic Munich school, was their leader.

Finally, other artists began to depict the life of the Polish peasant and the Polish landscape. Jozef Chelmonski (1849-1915), a realist and a famous painter of horses in his youth, became in his later years a poetic interpreter of the Polish lowlands. After him came numerous other landscapists led by Julian Falat (1853-1929) and Leon Wyczolkowski (1852-1937), chief representatives of the *Polish impressionism*; while Alexander Gierymski (1849-1901) and Jozef Pankiewicz (1866-1940) were ardent adherents of the French impressionism.

Of the graphic arts, lithography and etching came to full bloom during this period.

Owing to the creativeness of the Polish impressionists, the Polish national features of form once again—after a long absence—found their way into art of a general European character. Yet even in Polish impressionistic painting the native form elements came into view only sporadically and not always in full. Here and there a distinct tendency to decorativeness became visible, else-where a clear, vivid arrangement of colors appeared. But these features neither occurred simultaneously nor did they strike by their distinctiveness. They fought for existence with the more or less predominating features of current French art.

The national Polish elements of form appeared much more distinctly in Polish decorative painting of the time. Jan Mateiko—who, as has been pointed out before, introduced into his historical canvases Polish inner content but remained faithful to the Western European style as outer form was concerned—gave toward the end of his life the principal incentive to the development of a national form in modern Polish mural decoration. The beginning of a splendid evolution in this field was made by the polychromy with which Matejko, aided by Stanislaw Wyspianski (1869-1907), painter, interior decorator, as well as poet, and Jozef Mehoffer (b. 1869), decorated the vaults and walls of the famous old Gothic *Church of Our Lady* in Cracow. This decoration brought in, along with some ornamental Gothic motifs, certain floral designs and stylizations peculiar to peasant creations. These latter designs triumphed in the church polychromies and esp. stained glass windows created by Wyspianski and Mehoffer during the time of their artistic maturity. Mehoffer, who outlived Wyspianski for several decades, gained international renown thanks to his gorgeously beautiful windows designed for the Fribourg Cathedral in Switzerland. He worked on them since 1894 for thirty years.

Both these artists were, together with the Polish impressionists, members of the art society **Sztuka** (Art), which, founded in 1897, was active until the very last days of the independent Republic of Poland. This fact explains the lasting influence of all these artists on modern Polish art. Their influence was enforced through their educational activity: In 1895, two years after the death of Matejko, Julian Falat, one of the leaders of the Polish impressionists, became director of the Cracow School of Fine Arts, reorganized it into an Academy, and, inviting most of the progressive Polish artists of his time as professors, made it the most radical Academy of Fine Arts in Europe of the end of the past century.

The 20th Century. THE FINE ARTS. It was the versatile genius Stanislaw Wyspianski (cf. above) who, during a period of international eclecticism in architecture, turned his attention, and that of his generation, to the beauty of the wooden homesteads and churches built by the Polish peasants and foresaw how these peasant architectural forms could be applied to monumental buildings and could help to create a national style in modern Polish architecture. However, this great artist's efforts brought true results almost two decades after his premature death. These results could be seen in the modernistic style of architecture of the restored Polish Republic. In this modernistic Polish architecture two tendencies were distinctly apparent: one marked by strict adherence to the so-called *international* (q.v.) style, so widely adopted in France and in the Netherlands; the other characterized by an effort to combine rational modern forms and new building techniques and methods with architectural and decorative elements peculiar to Polish peasant wooden buildings. This modern national architectural style found its purest expression in the Polish Pavilion built from the plans of Jozef Czajkowski (b. 1872) for the International Exhibition of Decorative Arts in Paris in 1925. During the evolution of Polish architecture that followed, an increasing tendency toward blending of modern architectural forms with a neo-classical monumental style was to be observed. Bohdan Pniewski was one of the foremost representatives of this tendency.

Ksawery Dunikowski (b. 1876) was the strongest personality in sculpture of reborn Poland. He created works in stone for architectural decoration of a distinctly monumental character. Among his contemporaries, Stanislaw Ostrowski (b. 1878), an excellent portraitist, remained faithful to impressionistic art, while Edward Wittig (1877-1940) represented the more advanced international tendencies in modern sculpture. In contrast to Wittig, Jan Szczepkowski (b. 1878) drew his chief inspiration from the woodcarvings of the Polish highlanders of the Podhale Valley—with the village of Zakopane as its artistic center—situated on the northern slopes of the Tatra Mountains.

These artists were followed by a number of very talented younger sculptors, each of whom found an individual way of expression within the modern sculptural style. Among the many, at least Henryk Kuna (b. 1883), August Zamoyski (b. 1893), Stanislaw Szukalski (b. 1895), and Alfons Karny (b. 1901) ought to be mentioned.

In painting, the first two decades of the 20th cent. may be considered the years of triumph of the Polish impressionists. However, between 1917 and 1922 Polish artists instigated by modern anti-naturalistic trends and organized into the society of the **Formists** were passionately protesting against the art of the Polish impressionists. Tytus Czyzewski (b. 1884) was one of the leading painters of the new group, and Zamoyski, the most outstanding sculptor. The Polish formists were affiliated with the French cubists, placing, however, a stronger accent on color and its expressive qualities in their paintings. While some of the formists remained faithful to their ideals during all their creative years, in time many others returned to nature as the source of their inspiration.

Already in 1922 another artistic group, called **Rytm** (Rhythm) was formed. A rhythmically arranged composition of their paintings was the common aim of the *rhythmicists*. Tadeusz Pruszkowski (1888-1942), an outstanding colorist, was the most popular among them; Eugene Zak (1884-1926) formed the link between the modern Parisian school and the members of the group. Kuna and Wittig represented best the sculptors.

Closely related to the founders of the *Rytm* society was Ludomir Slendzinski (b. 1889) of Wilno, a decided linearist of neo-classic predilections, who was the head of the flourishing **Wilno Neo-classicist School.**

Of art societies formed by younger painters the **Komitet Paryski** (Parisian Committee), called also **K. P.**—whence its members became known as **Kapists**—is of great interest. Zygmunt Waliszewski (1897-1936) was one of the leaders of this group. Pupils of Jozef Pankiewicz—a splendid colorist who first adhered to the French impressionism and later consecutively to the more progressive Parisian movements—the *Kapists* inherited a love of color and of modern French art from their master. Thanks to these preferences they were in many ways closely related to the Polish formists.

On the other hand, both the **Brotherhood of St. Luke** and the so-called **School of Warsaw** took as a possession some of the ideals of the *rhythmicists* and the Wilno neo-classicists. The *Brotherhood* was organized in 1925 by former disciples of Tadeusz Pruszkowski, Professor at the Academy of Fine Arts in Warsaw. In accordance with their old-fashioned name the founders of the *Brotherhood,* as for instance Boleslaw Cybis (b. 1899), were zealous students of old masters, especially in so far as the technique of painting was concerned. *The School of Warsaw,* composed of somewhat younger graduates of Professor Pruszkowski's class, placed greater emphasis on color than did the others. Finally, let us add that while Zakopane was the favorite summer resort of artists grouped in the *Sztuka* society, the younger generations of Polish painters felt increasingly attracted by the old picturesque little town of Kazimierz-on-the Vistula.

Although in all the work created by the various Polish painters of independent Poland typically lyric tendencies found an adequate expression and scattered elements of national form might have been easily recognized by the eye of an art connoisseur—yet again, like several decades before, the national outer form appeared in a unified and condensed manner only in decorative painting. As time went on the followers of Mehoffer and Wyspianski began to seek national motifs in peasant art more and more consciously, realizing that this art had remained almost untouched by alien influences. This turning of the newer Polish art toward the folk primitive corresponded to analogical movements in other countries where, for instance, cubists, expressionists, futurists, infantilists—as well as the Polish formists—also sought inspiration in the simple and expressive art of the various manifestations of the primitive.

In sculpture, this development came to full flower in the decorative wooden bas-reliefes of Jan Szczepkowski; in painting, in the striking mural decorations and book illustrations of Zofia Stryjenska (b. 1894), which are Polish in line, color, and composition, Polish in their spirited vigor, not devoid of lyric and romantic notes. At the same time, her manner of stylization, her form tending to strong simplification, rejecting all detail and concerning itself only with the basic and the essential, gives her work qualities which characterize all modern progressive art. Thus Stryjenska's decorative paintings, while being distinctly Polish, are at the same time universal in character.

The initiator of a similar trend toward folk art in the Polish graphic arts was Wladyslaw Skoczylas (1883-1934), Poland's leading wood engraver, who very strongly based his art on national traditions as manifested by the Polish peasant woodcuts. In 1926 he founded a society of Polish graphic artists, mostly wood engravers, called **Ryt** (Engraving). The artists grouped in the *Ryt* were able to unite in a most masterful manner the native qualities of the Polish peasant woodcut with international so-called modernistic principles of composition and drawing. Of these ar-

tists Stanislaw Ostoja-Chrostowski (b. 1897) became best known abroad.

THE DECORATIVE ARTS. Poland participated vividly in the 20th cent. revival of handicrafts in Europe, the more so as the Polish decorative arts found an additional impulse in the peasant crafts which had not lost their integrity even in face of the 19th cent. eclectic styles and the still more threatening 19th cent. mass production.

To create a Polish style in interior decoration, Polish 20th cent. artists turned to the peasant's hut for inspiration. They learned from the peasant themselves to handle tools and were reminded by him of the golden rule of long past centuries that form must logically be related to its medium and function. In consequence they rejected the eclectic imitations of various historical styles and replaced them by forms subordinated to the material used and to the utility of the objects created. Moreover, the professional artists introduced many of the peasant's traditional ornamental motifs into their art, all in all achieving a purely national style.

The first contact of professional Polish artists with Polish peasant art occurred at least thirty years before the time of Poland's liberation, when a handful of artists and writers "discovered" Zakopane and the arts and crafts of the Podhale highlanders. As years went by, the professional artist's understanding of the Polish peasant art became deeper and his own art more mature and more convincing. A year before World War I a society was founded in Cracow, called the **Cracow Workshops**, which became a laboratory for many artists inspired by the peasant handicrafts. One of the chief promoters of the new movement in Polish decorative arts was Jerzy (George) Warchalowski (1875-1939).

When at the International Exhibition of the Decorative Arts in Paris in 1925 restored Poland had her own pavilion and participated in a number of special international expositions, the national character of the Polish exhibits was universaly recognized. They received 189 rewards, among them 36 *Grand-Prix,* 31 diplomas and 60 gold medals. The fame of Polish interior decoration and applied arts has been established since. The arrangement of the Polish section at the Paris International was under the able supervision of Warchalowski. Among the artists who bene in charge of the interior decoration of the Polish section, Jozef Czajkowski the designer of the entire Pavilion, Wojciech Jastrzebowski (b. 1884), and Karol Stryjenski

(1890-1935), all three since Poland's regained independence professors at the Warsaw Academy of Fine Arts, had been Warchlowski's collaborators already in the *Cracow Workshops* of pre-war times. So were Jan Szczepkowski, the carver of the wooden chapel at the Exhibition, Zofia Stryjenska, the painter who executed the now world-famous decorative panels for the main hall of the Pavilion, and last but not least, Jozef Mehoffer, renowned creator of stained glass windows. Among the latter artist's work for reborn Poland first of all the stained glass windows for the Wawel Cathedral in Cracow ought to be mentioned. Two of these were shown in Paris in 1925.

Along with the above-named artists many others contributed to the success of the Polish sections at the Paris Exhibition. Books, beautifully illustrated by Stryjenska, Skoczylas and a number of other prominent artists and covered in attractive book-bindings, bore witness to the high level of the art of bookmaking in modern Poland. Expressive figures carved in wood by pupils of the *State School for Wooden Industry* in Zakopane gave proof that the Polish style, based on the peasant's age-long traditions, has also captivated the Polish artistic youth.

Among the specimens of the Polish applied arts at the Paris Exhibition, embracing furniture, toys, posters, textiles, etc., it was the *kilim* which at once occupied the first place artistically. Outstanding Polish artists had been drawing their creative inspiration from the old peasant kilims. However, they treated them creatively, bending their ornamental motifs and color harmonies to modern stylistic trends and to the demands of the modern technique. The most beautiful Polish kilims were produced by Bogdan Treter and by the aforementioned Jozef Czajkowski and Wojciech Jastrzebowski.

Also members of the Warsaw co-operative society of decorative arts for the interior, called Lad, which means *order* or *harmony,* became famous for the kilims they produced. The *Lad* was founded in 1926 through the initiative of the creators of the Polish sections at the Paris Exhibition, in close co-operation with their pupils, representatives of the post-war generation of artists. The *Lad* also produced outstanding textiles made of flax, and more recently also of silk cultivated in Poland, and generally objects of great beauty in all fields of the applied arts.

During the last years of Poland's independence, a development in the field of furniture, ceramics, and metal work became noticeable. Graceful pieces of furniture, characterized by fluent and soft lines, agreeably shaped earthen vases and figurines as well as all kinds of metal adornments, such as buckles, bracelets, and belts, attracted the attention of many a visitor of the Polish Pavilion at the New York World's Fair, 1939-40.

The many handsome speciments of Polish decorative arts created during the last few years of Poland's independence and exhibited at this Fair, harmoniously blended Polish native taste with modernistic trends of present-day art, and even with those of past centuries—without, however, any detriment to the national character of the Polish arts and crafts.

The same style was the dominant feature of the interior decoration of the Polish transatlantic liners, especially of the *MS. Pilsudski,* built in 1935 and torpedoed in 1939, and of the *MS. Batory,* built in 1936. The interiors of these beautiful passenger ships perhaps represented the most mature achievements in this domain of Polish art. The decoration and furniture of the ships were designed and executed by a number of first-rate Polish artists under the able direction of Stanislaw Brukalski (b. 1894) and Lech Niemojewski (b. 1894), architects, Wojciech Jastrzebowski, the previously cited decorative artist, and Tadeusz Pruszkowski, the influential Polish painter. It is characteristic that on this as on other Polish art projects, artists of all branches of Polish art strictly co-operated, no distinction being made between those who represented the so-called fine arts and those devoting their talents to the decorative arts. In modern Poland both fields of art were considered to be of equal artistic importance.

ART EDUCATION. Although the stylistic evolution of any art follows its own, innate rules, independent of social and political happenings within the country, yet a proper care given to art by all who influence the education of the nation may contribute immeasurably to the results obtained. In modern times the responsibility for the protection of the arts chiefly rests in the hands of the governments of the countries. In subdued Poland, private individuals sponsored art schools. But as soon as Poland regained her independence, the new Polish government took art into its protection, reorganizing the existing and founding a number of new art schools.

Among the art schools, the Academy of Fine Arts in Cracow should be mentioned first, being the only one already in existence before World War I, thanks to a relative freedom that Cracow had enjoyed under the Austrian rule. The professors of the Cracow Academy belonged to the most eminent representatives of the Polish impressionistic movement; many of them were active as art educators until the last days of Poland's independence. Since 1925 the Academy of Fine Arts in Cracow had its branch in Paris with Jozef Pankiewicz as its head.

In contradistinction to Cracow, before the re-establishment of free Poland Warsaw, under sterner Russian rule, had only one school of fine arts, which was supported by donations and private contributions. But this school, reorganized and opened by the Polish government as the *School of Fine Arts in Warsaw* and soon afterwards bestowed with the title of *Academy,* became the center of the modern art movement in Poland. It may suffice to remind the reader that a number of renowned art societies—for instance, the *Brotherhood of St. Luke* and the *School of Warsaw,* both embracing painters, the *Ryt,* embracing graphic artists, the *Lad,* devoted to the decorative arts—were founded by professors and graduates of the Warsaw Academy. Other Polish art schools on an academical level in independent Poland were the *Faculty of Architecture* at the *Warsaw Polytechnic Institute* and that at the *Lwow Polytechnic Institute* and the *Faculty of Fine Arts* at the *University of Wilno.*

Along with the academical schools of fine arts, professional schools of arts and crafts were of great importance in the development of art in Poland. Of these the most significant were the schools at Cracow, Lwow, Poznan, Warsaw, Wilno, and Zakopane. It should also be noted that the Academy of Fine Arts in Warsaw, the most progressive art school in Poland, embraced important departments of the decorative arts, considered by this Academy to be as important as the departments of the fine arts. This introduction of the study of decorative arts by an academy of fine arts was logically consistent with the modern Polish principles of art education. These new education methods affected in one way or another all Polish art schools, the elementary as well as the academical, and were best evident in the professional schools of arts and crafts.

The new system of art training in Poland was based on Polish art traditions and Polish peasant art, at the same time, however, following the most progressive principles of art education in Europe. When Poland regained her political freedom after World War I, she had many artists who ror years previously had studied privately the working methods of the peasant and had learned from him to work directly in the medium used and create their designs as they fashioned the material. The most eminent among these artists became leaders of art education in modern Poland. Thus, while before the liberation of Poland in official schools of decorative arts the chief accent was placed on copying from nature and the study of historical styles, in free Poland the art students were taught how to handle tools. They were encouraged to make the style of their creations correspond to the material employed, stressing its specific properties and limitations, and they were not allowed to overstep the bounds of its inherent potentialities. All Polish art schools possessed workshops in the most important branches of the decorative arts, such as weaving, woodcarving, metal work, ceramics, commercial graphic art, bookbinding, etc. In this way the Polish schools of arts and crafts trained their pupils to be craftsmen and artists excelling in good workmanship. According to their predilections, the graduates of these schools could either devote their talents to some handicraft, find employment as designers and skilled workers in factories, or pursue their studies in art academies.

Although in Polish art schools the mere imitation of historical styles was discouraged, yet care was taken that the pupils receive a proper theoretical education in the evolution of the fine arts through the ages, and especially, that they become thoroughly acquainted with the traditions of Polish art in all its domains: architecture, sculpture, painting, the decorative arts, as well as peasant art.

Such an education was designed for encouraging young Polish artists to fuse traditional native Polish elements with the general principles of current European art, thus facilitating them to attain the goal for which many Polish artists, both of the near and distant past, were striving. See Borowy, W., "The Genius of Poland", *The Studio,* April 1934; Gotlib, H., "Art in Poland", *All about Poland,* 2nd ed., 1941; Gotlib, H., *Polish Painting,* 1942; Kuhn, A., *Die Polnische Kunst von 1800 bis zur Gegenwart,* 2nd ed., 1937; Loret, M., *Gli artisti polacchi a Roma nel Settecento,* 1929; Manning, C. A., "The Great Past of Poland"; Treter M., "The Character and Development of Polish Painting" and "The Folk Arts of Poland", *Art and Archaeology,* May

1928; Piotrowska, I., "Polish Painting—Historical Influences, Present Tendencies, and Future Possibilities", *Polish Science and Learning,* February 1943; Piotrowska, I., "Problems of Early 17th Cent. Polish Painting", *Quarterly Bull. of the Polish Institute of Arts and Sciences in America,* April 1943; Piotrowska, I. and Tarnowski, M., "Polish Religious Art," *Liturgical Arts,* May 1942; Soltynski, R., *Glimpses of Polish Architecture,* London, 1943; Walicki, M., "L'art polonais des origines au XIX-me siècle"; Starzynski, J., "L'art polonais au XIX-me et XX-me siècles"; Niemojewski, L., "Architecture contemporaine en Pologne" and "Décoration d'intérieurs en Pologne", *Catalogue officiel de la section polonaise a l'exposition internationale Art et Techniques dans la Vie Moderne, Paris,* 1937; Walicki, M., "The Art of Poland before the Partitions"; Treter M., "Modern Polish Art", Niemojewski, L., "Modern Polish Architecture"; Dziewulski, S. and Marczewski, K., "City Planning in Poland"; Grabowski, J., "Ornamentation and Peasant Art in Poland". *Poland, Official Catalogue of the Polish Pavilion at the World's Fair in New York,* 1939; Warchalowski, G., *L'art décoratif moderne en Pologne,* 1928; Werten, M., "Principles of Art Education in Poland", *The School Arts Magazine,* January 1935. —I.P.

Polish carpets. Misleading names given to Persian carpets of the 17th cent. with purely geometrical patterns; probably came from the workshop of Kashan or Ispahan. Many of these rugs came into possession of the noble families of Poland which led scholars to believe that they were made in Poland by Persian prisoners. —B.E.J.

polka. Popular Bohemian dance in lively 2/4 time. Polka-mazurka—a slower dance in tripple time with accent on the last beat.

polonaise. The polonaise is said to have originated in Poland in 1573 on the occasion of Henry of Anjou's accession to the Polish throne, when the court ladies performed a stately procession in his honor. This procession later became part of court functions in Poland and elsewhere. It scarcely merits the name "dance", since it was little more than a grand march in slow 3/4 time. Sometimes, however, the simple line of march around the room was broken by dance-like figures. —J.G.

polychromy. The artistic combining of many colors, esp. vivid ones, as in ancient sculpture-architectural decoration.

polyglot. *Book.* A collection in one volume of several translations of the same work.

polygonal nimbus. See nimbus.

polymerized methyl methacrylate. See acrylic resins.

polymerized oil. Although this term is comparatively modern, oils which could be so classed have been used from the earliest history of this material as a painting medium. They are distinguished from the common drying oils by a molecular rearrangement, smaller molecules being united to form larger molecular masses. The changes is effected by heating or, in modern commercial production, by blowing air through the thin oil. Some chemical chance occurs, also, and there is a degree of oxidation. In the older practice of painters, polymerization producing what has been called "stand oil" was brought about by heating and at times by exposure to the sun for long periods. The polymerized oil is more viscous than that which has not been treated and is apt to be more stable. —G.L.S.

polymeter, modern. See NOTATION.

Polynesia, art of. See OCEANIA ARTS OF.

polyphony. *Mus.* Process of composition by which two or more melodic lines are presented simultaneously, each of these lines being aesthetically meaningfull (at least to some extent) if considered separately from the other lines. This property is sometimes referred to as "independence" of the melodic lines involved in polyphony; the term **independence** should be used in this context only if it is understood that the melodic lines in question obey the principles of counterpoint, notwithstanding their self-sustained character.

Polophony also designates the music written by means of polyphonic technique; e.g., medieval polyphony: polyphonic technique used in the Middle Ages, or medieval music written in polyphonic technique. See MEDIEVAL MUSIC. —E.K.

polyptych. See altarpiece.

polytonality. Style of composition in which two or more melodic lines, or series of chords, are presented simultaneously, each of these elements being related to a different major or minor key. —E.K.

polyvinyl resins. These synthetic materials have had some recent use as surface films and varnishes for pictures and have been proposed also as painting mediums. They are polymerized derivatives of vinyl alcohol. The vinyl acetate is insoluable in water, is fairly flexible, colorless, and, according to tests, is stable to light. It is somewhat affected by moisture and is easily permeable. It is readily dissolved by most of the organic solvents.
—G.L.S.

pomegranate. In Greek art, an ornament in the shape of the pomegranate fruit, circular with the characteristic projecting knob with flaring end, at the blossom end. See SYMBOLISM IN FAR EASTERN ART.
—L.T.S.

Pomo art. See California Indian art.

Pompeiian blue. See Egyptian blue.

pongee. A fabric made from wild silk. Imitations are made of cotton or spun silk and rayon.

Pontic ware. See Ionian vases.

pontil. See GLASS AND GLASS-MAKING.

poppy-seed oil. Somewhat lighter in color and slower in drying than linseed oil, this has had a long use as a painting medium. It was known in classical times and was brought into rather general practice during the 17th cent. in Italy. It is still used in the preparation of some artists' oil paints. It comes from the seeds of the opium poppy, grown largely in India, Russia, France, and Asia Minor.   —G.L.S.

popular art. See folk art.

popular romanticism. A term used in the criticism of painting and sculpture to describe that kind of romanticism which is concerned with the appeal of popular. subject matter rather than, like genuine romanticism (e.g., Delacroix), with the invention of new visual or formal values. Typically the popular romanticist is a formal naturalist who chooses subjects which have a romantic appeal to the average man, e.g., subjects from the Middle Ages or the Near East, from Goethe, Shakespeare and other poets, literary illustration in general, popular subjects sentimentally stressing the appeal of childhood, motherhood, the home, the farm, adventure, courage, nationalism, hero worship, and the like. Representative popular romantic artists include Delaroche,

Breton, Bonheur, Hunt, Millais, Orchardson, Fildes, Boecklin, Hoffmann, Cole, Melchers, Chapu, Saint-Gaudens, Dallin, and Gutson Borglum.

As a historical phenomenon, it is characteristically a 19th-cent. product, but continues in the 20th cent. in popular magazine illustrations like Saturday Evening Post, Cosmopolitan, etc., and in the work of such artists as Dale Nichols, Grant Wood, Thomas Benton, Paul Sample, et al.; and was consciously revived by Nazi Germany as a healthy, normal, native, and Nordic art suitable for the "new order".   —L.D.L.

popular song. See song.

porcelain. See CERAMICS I; II.

porcelain, artificial. Soft porcelain: bones, gypsum, etc., used as ingredients. See CERAMICS I.

porcellaneous stoneware. See CERAMICS II.

porch. A covered structure forming an entrance to a building: outside and with a separate roof which is usually lower than the main roof.

port de voix (Fr.). See appogiatura.

portable altar. See altar.

portamento. A gliding transition from note to note in pitch, intensity, and timbre. Conventionally, portamento refers only to pitch but there is experimental evidence to show that the principle of a modulated transition should apply to intensity and timbre as well.
—C.E.S.

portative organ. See MUSICAL INSTRUMENTS.

portfolio. Any container for loose sheets of paper is called a portfolio. One made with covered boards hinged at one side and provided with strings or tapes for tying at the other three sides is commonly listed among artists' supplies.   —G.L.S.

portico. A covered gallery flanked on one side only by an open arcade or colonnade. Thus the term includes the exterior colonnades and *pteromae* of Greek and Roman temples, the arcaded courts of the Renaissance, and the varied cloisters of medieval times.

Porticos may be grouped into two major classifications: (a) *Trabeated.* Those using the pier and lintel or the column and lintel

In this type the construction is simple, involving vertical loads only. (b) *Arcuated.* Pier or column and arch. In this group the arcades are longitudinally in balance, except at the corners where care must be exercised to secure stability by buttressing or by tie rods.

In both classifications, when associated with vaulting, they must be reinforced laterally.

Very interesting examples of different arcaded treatment are to be seen in the Rue de Rivoli with simple pier and arch; the Doges Palace and Loggia de Lanze, illustrating cases where the use of tie rods is mandatory; the Colosseum and Court of Farnese Palace, showing pier buttressed by engaged columns; the Palazzo del Te in Mantua, where four grouped columns and arch afford both strength and lightness; the Cloisters of St. Paul's F. L. M., in which columns coupled transversely are varied in ever changing designs; the Basilica in Vicenza, with the Palladian motive in series; and in the Cloisters of Mont St. Michel, with staggered columns giving very curious effects in perspective.

Many charming examples of porticos in the more restricted sense of an entrance porch are to be seen in Colonial and Neo-classic houses throughout the eastern, southern and central U. S. A. Homeward, Md., Monticello, Va., and the old homes of Natchez, Miss., will serve as illustrations. See *Elements et Theorie de L'Architecture,* Guadet; *Dictionary of Architecture and Building,* Russell Sturgis, 1902; *Dictionnaire Raisonne de L'Architecture Francaise du XI au XVI Siècle,* Viollet-Le-Duc, 1867; *Encyclopedie de L'Architecture et de la Construction,* P. Planat; *History of Architectural Development,* F. M. Simpson, 1929. —L.H.

portrait. See ex libris.

portrait, sculptural. No single subject in the history of sculpture has been so popular as portraits, which have had an obvious appeal to the subject represented, to the time in which he was known, and to later periods as data of historical value. Sculptors have approached the problem of portrait sculpture in three broad ways, concentrating on a realistic likeness, a character study, or a work primarily of aesthetic value. The realistic likeness is obviously the easiest to produce, requiring merely careful study and measurement and adequate technical craftsmanship. The value of such portraits is chiefly as an historical record; as such, the great number of Roman portraits are important documents for the student of history. Greater sculptors have attempted to do more than simply record the actual human face; they have, in Rodin's phrase, plumbed the depths of their sitters and have brought to the surface what they found. Egyptian portraits, eliminating unnecessary detail and emphasizing the main lines and planes of character, are of this type; so are the portraits by Renaissance masters and by the French sculptor, Houdon, who came to understand the moods and thoughts of their subjects, then, omitting what was commonplace and accidental, amplified in stone and bronze the really significant elements. But the greatest portraitists have done more than this. They have made, regardless of the artistic value of their sitters, works of art. They have brought out the beauty of the material in which they worked: the luminous radiance of fine marble, the native character of various kinds of stone, the lovely textures of bronze and wood. They have made the surface interesting by skillful modulation, so that the light striking it is spread in a multitude of merging cross-currents. The Hellenistic Greeks and Rodin were especially successful in producing such tonal values. And, most important of all, they have constructed the planes and masses of the sculptured head in designs that, revealing the character of the subject, go further by creating objects so firmly coordinated and dynamically composed that the result is aesthetically moving. Hellenic portraiture was of this type. Among modern sculptors a master of such sculptural portraits is Charles Despiau. —W.R.A.

posa. Shrines or chapels in the four corners of the *atrio* of Mexican 16th cent. monasteries thus called from the pauses (*pausas*) made there in outdoor religious processions. (Occasionally also in Guatemala and Peru.) —J.Mc.

Poseidon (L. Neptune). Classical god of the sea, rivers and springs. His chief attribute was the trident, with which he rules the waves. In classical art he was usually represented as a stalwart standing figure, with a mature, bearded face. In later painting he was pictured by Giordano and Tiepolo, and in sculpture by Bologna, Bracci, Begas and Cecere. Often he has been the central figure of fountain groups, sometimes surrounded by Tritons and sea nymphs.

—W.R.A.

positions. The five traditional absolute positions of the body (usually referring to the feet, although there are less arbitrary ones for the arms), upon which the academic classic dance is founded. These positions, based on gravity and body mechanics, were codified ca. 1670-80 by Beauchamps, first director of the Royal French Dancing Academy. (1) Heels together, toes turned completely out, so that the feet, heel to heel, are in a straight line. (2) Feet in parallel line as in first position, weight evenly distributed on both, but the heels separated by about twelve inches. (3) The heel of one foot locked parallel against the instep of the other, weight evenly distributed. (4) The forefoot twelve inches in advance of the back, but parallel, weight evenly distributed. (5) The feet locked right heel to left toe, right toe to left heel.

The five positions are the net or comb through which ballet movements continually pass, serving as anatomical and stylistic substructure to the entire academic dance.
—L.K.

positive volume. See SCULPTURE.

post. An upright piece of timber or other material used as a support.

post-and-lintel. A system of architecture based on vertical members suporting horizontal beams; trabeated.

post-Colonial period. See POST-REVOLUTIONARY ARCHITECTURE AND DECORATIVE ARTS IN THE U. S. A.

post-impressionism. A term used to describe French painting following impressionism, from about 1885 to 1905, in which a subjective art of self-expression succeeds objective naturalism and impressionism (q.v.). The post-impressionists were thus expressionists (q.v.) rather than impressionists. Like all expressionists they emphasized any or all of the following: the artist's conception of the expressive structure and inner meaning of objects, pattern of line, form, and color for the sake of decorative beauty, distortion for the purpose of recording subjective emotion. Post-impressionists include Cézanne, van Gogh, Gauguin Toulouse-Lautrec, Seurat, Signac, late Renoir, late Degas. The post-impressionist were succeeded by the *Fauves* about 1905, though the latter were also expressionists, who, in contrast to the post-impressionists, were more radical in departing from objective naturalism in order to express their personal emotions.

The term is seldom applied to sculpture because it developed later than painting. When used in this connection, however, it includes 20th cent. moderate-progressive sculptors such as Maillol, Despiau, and Bourdelle, and artists of countries other than France who represent an analogous stage in the development of the art, i.e., sculptors who have given up the impressionism of Rodin, but who do not represent radical expressionist distortion or cubism and abstraction. The list of such sculptors includes Kolbe, Haller, Barlach, Zorach, Manship, Milles, Scaravaglione, Dobson, Gill, Gaudier-Brzesca, Epstein, Rosandic and Mestrovic.   —L.D.L.

POST-REVOLUTIONARY ARCHITECTURE AND DECORATIVE ARTS IN THE U. S. A. While architecture and the decorative arts do not follow exact chronological parallels in movements from 1776 to date, it is impossible to divorce the two at any time, according to traditional background, stylistic tendencies, and aesthetic and commercial considerations. The relationship started prior to this date, but at no time reached the unity and consistency of idea achieved in the late Georgian phases in all of the former colonial states, with the advent of the influences of the Adam Brothers of England.

1776-1790 (1800). Reconciliation of exterior architectural details and interior architecture with furnishings, in forms, proportions and colors, became the paramount issue in the last quarter of the 18th cent. Windows became more delicate, with less prominent mullions and larger panes; the giant order was introduced and proportions of exteriors became suggestive of increased height compatable with the slender reedings and pencillings in colonettes used in interior details; rounded or oval chambers and hallways with severely refined mouldings reflected the oval backed chairs, straight slim legged furniture, and striped fabrics. Revivals of forms discovered at Pompeii and Herculaneum appeared in reliefs of urns, wreathes and garlands in the panels under the slender mantle shelves, in complete harmony with draped fabrics at windows and festoons of crystals in the chandeliers; tinted woodwork joined in the effects of rich but soft hues of the fabrics. Outstanding architect of this period was Samuel McIntire (1757-1819) of Salem; well known examples of architecture are Woodlands (c. 1788) in Philadelphia; the Nicholls House (McIntire, c. 1779) in Salem; Monticello (Thomas Jefferson, 1796) in Charlottesville, Va. Augmenting the appearance of fine living in the social centers of the late 18th cent. were the great numbers of silverware objects, most of them reflecting the Adam Bros.' ovals and parabolic curves, urn shapes, and delicate engravings. The name of Paul Revere (Sr.) (1735-1818) ranks highest at this time—if not for outstanding merit in design, at least for greatest skill and popularity. American ceramics made their real beginnings at this time (excepting glass, which was generally finer in the period preceding 1776) in spite of English attempts to hold the American market with exportations of Wedgewood, Spode, Staffordshire, Minton, lustre ware, etc. After the war, British soldiers and German auxiliaries remained in America to work as skilled artisans in the ceramic fields, and the character of the wares developed by all at that time was determined by the nature of the locality. The best local wares were made in Philadelphia, the social center, whereas Vermont did not make fine pieces until mid-19th cent., due to land-title controversies.

According to some authorities, the finest decorative arts of America at this time were made in and for homes of more moderate circumstances, particularly in the Hudson Valley and Pennsylvania. The American market which had opened during the Revolutionary War for French *Toiles de Jouy*, not only brought to this country the fine wood-blocked prints in one color on white or cream linen, with popularized allegorical subjects and portrait groups of LaFayette and our own military and political leaders, but opened the way for American production of block-printed fabrics and papers. Embroidered samplers produced quieter color schemes with greens, yellows, blues and blacks, instead of the raw reds of earlier times, and stressed the above-mentioned subjects, just as modelled glass whiskey and rum bottles appeared with the portraits of Washington, Jefferson and La-Fayette. Perhaps the most charming decorative arts of all were those produced by the Pennsylvania Dutch, with the largest quantity and highest artistic quality of their embroideries, decorative drawings on furniture, pottery and tin, and *Fractur* paintings falling between the years 1780 and 1830, when social conditions offered more time for leisurely or spontaneous work.

By contrast to the tremendous amount of artistic production in the eastern states, chiefly English, Dutch and German in inspiration, the Spanish contributions to the country were meagre. The Cabildo, in New Orleans (1795), was a combination of French and Spanish influences (Creole), and now houses a museum of the arts of that area at that time. In 1786 the Santa Barbara Mission was founded, of typical California Spanish style, perhaps the best in design of all the California missions built from 1769 to 1823, from San Diego to Sonoma. Most missions are now restored, and serve partially as museums. Recent researches by the American Index of Design have materially aided the student in search for the arts of the California section, prior to the settlements following the gold rushes of the mid-19th cent.

1790-1815 (1800-1820). When Benjamin Latrobe was a surveyor of public buildings early in the 19th cent. he deplored the country as destitute of architects or even good workmen in any branch of architectural decoration. Certainly the odds and ends of carpenter Georgian in less pretentious structures would bear out his words. However, six strong architects, among others, rose to prominence at this time, namely, Jefferson (1743-1826), Bulfinch (1763-1844), Hoban (1762-1831), Latrobe (1764-1820), Thornton (c. 1761-c. 1828), and McComb (1763- ?). This period was transitional to that of the Greek revivals as introduced by Latrobe c. 1815, and variously has been called the **Post-Colonial Period**, the **First Federal Period**, the **First National Period**, and the **Period of the Early Republic**. The Adam phase of Georgian continued in the more pretentious domestic architecture, e.g., Homewood in Baltimore, the Shreve House in Salem, and the Dow House in Salem, but was too refined and detailed for the public buildings. The fan lights at the entrances now spanned the entire doorway; Tuscan columns, spiral stairs and new classical details made their entrance. Mansard roofs were stressed in New England; hipped roofs in the middle and southern states. Either high square three or four-storied forms were preferred for residence architecture, e.g., the President's House in Philadelphia (1792-7), or long two-storied horizontal houses with projecting bays or wings at either end, as in Homewood. Devoured were the books of Asher Benjamin, who believed that domestic styles in America should differ from the Georgian in England, and that the different materials in this country needed different handling. Stylistic foundations became increasingly classical, Jefferson among others introducing the type of Roman revivals as were expressed in France at this time, in the Virginia Capitol (1795), the University of Virginia (1818) and in the

National Capitol (c. 1790-1827, by Thornton, Latrobe and Bulfinch). Other outstanding architectural examples of this time are: Park Street Church, Boston (1809), New South Church, Boston (Bulfinch, 1814), the New York City Hall (Mangin and McComb, 1803), the White House (Hoban, 1792), Montpelier (Thornton, 1793), University Hall at Harvard (Bulfinch, 1813), and the Gore House at Waltham, Mass. (1800).

The fires in New Orleans in 1788 and 1794 gave great impetus to building in that area, and most authorities concede the best New Orleans architecture to have been done at the end of the 18th cent. and the beginning of the 19th cent. Simple adaptations of the more classical of French and Spanish Renaissance types were produced, embellished with graceful and delicate wrought iron gates, balconies and stairways still reflecting Creole character, and were to become unique in American traditions. The later structures in this area showed less taste and less grace and simplicity, with heavy cast iron forms of architectural decoration replacing those so charmingly conceived at the height of this style.

Interiors showed the introduction of Empire styles, with Duncan Phyfe's Adam-Sheraton phase (1795-1818) only gradually merging into a more Empire aspect (1818-1830), and with Latrobe's modifications of French Empire furniture. It was a time of mahogany veneers, carved mahogany beads, acanthus leaf and pineapple motifs, scenic wallpapers related to Revolutionary scenes, high studded rooms with white woodwork, Oriental rugs and other oriental importations, and brocade hangings. French influences in all of the decorative arts showed a domination of the ungainly Empire, completely lacking the dignity, grace or refinement of the Louis 14th, 15th, and 16th periods respectively. Duncan Phyfe (1768-1854) lightened his structures by combining 18th cent English with Empire designs, and John Goddard of Rhode Island designed solid block front furniture of admirable simplicity, but heaviness prevailed in general. Silver objects became swollen with Empire character; early 19th cent. hooked rug designs emerged from their 18th cent. sequences from purely goemetric designs to leaves, scrolls and flowers, and now added animals and birds to the foliage motifs. Simon Willard (Mass.) invented the Banjo clock in 1801, with all brass works—almost a prophesy of the industrial era about to be born, with its lamentable inability to express artistically our new-found freedom and principles, and its turn to inventions, establishment of factories, and the attempt to control decorative arts media solely by means of increasing skills and varieties of novel techniques which might result in a more profitable enterprise.

1815-50/60.   The Classic Revival.   The second National Period of architecture exhibited a completed break from the Georgian, with monuments of close resemblance to Greek and Roman temples in domestic, civic and ecclesiastical buildings. The classicism of Europe at this time had penetrated the States; cities were named "Troy", "Athens", "Ionia" and many other terms referring to classical times and places; travellers visited Greece, and Stuart and Revett's book *The Antiquities of Athens* with measured drawings, was a lure for many architects and designers. Interiors of these buildings reflected the bold simple space divisions of the Greek and Roman monuments, with heavy mouldings and friezes utilizing classical motifs, with skin rugs, and with furniture retaining the boldest of classical *décor*. The most typical monuments of the time were the Cathedral of Baltimore (Latrobe, 1821); the Bank of Pennsylvania (Latrobe, 1819) in Philadelphia; the Treasury Building, Washington (Mills, 1836); Girard College, Philadelphia (Walter, 1833); the Lee House, Arlington (1826); the Hermitage (1835) in Nashville; the residence at 107 Monument St., Baltimore (1835); and the Athenaeum, Portsmouth, N. H. (c. 1815). Strickland (1759-1828), Walter (1804-c. 1887) and Upjohn (1802-1878), all pupils of Latrobe, continued his teachings in their work. The latter years of the Classical Revival period, however, showed far less of the true Greek, and more of the French academic translations of classicism of such dull and pretentious monumentality as is to be seen in the wings of the National Capitol Building added by Walter in 1851-59). Buildings in and west of Ohio were begun c. 1820, in the style of the Greek revival and were generally well designed with only minor local differences in the more northern and southern areas until after the Civil War.

Silverware at first followed both Empire and Classic shapes and decorative motifs, later in the century to be influenced by porcelain and pottery forms. Silver-plated wares took the place of pewter after 1820. The first transfer-printed ceramic wares came into being at this time, also Rockingham semi-vitreous wares. In 1825 the first porcelain making in America generally attempted to follow the stylistic examples of Sevres; it was the time of the beginning of hard paste Bennington wares. The ceramics field was too busy with the establishment of factories in every locality boasting fine clay and with technical developments to show a reflection of either classical or Empire elements until the seventies, when they were more gross and lacking in taste than had they been created earlier in the century. See CERAMICS II.

Fabrics were heavy and boldly designed, following furniture tendencies in general, the best of which was Duncan Phyfe's Victorian period (1830-1847), although he was wont to call it his "butcher period" in disgust with the demands for heavy furniture. Stencilled walls continued in some cases, and printed wallpapers bore local American scenes. Heavy chandeliers carried out the preponderant weight of the *décor* of the times. Glass factories had been known to exist from the time of the 17th cent., but Deming Jarves introduced the first financially paying glass business when he incorporated in 1825, at Sandwich, Mass., following years of technical studies. A great diversity of glass types and forms of every color and usage were produced here, and while it is difficult to distinguish Sandwich glass from that of the many other houses by motif, shape or technical excellence, it has been generally admired by collectors, the most prominent being Henry Ford.

Simultaneously with the years of classical revivals in architecture and the decorative arts, a series of more romantic revivals made their appearances, not to become prevalent until the latter half of the century. Some Egyptian influences are to be seen in the Washington Monument (Mills, begun 1836), in the Old Tombs Prison, N. Y. (1836) now demolished, and in the Old Croton Reservoir, N. Y. (1837-1843) in the place now occupied by the New York Public Library. Gothic revivals joined the strong movement toward classicism in the buildings of the entire south after 1830; in the Vieux Carré, New Orleans, emblems and varied designs from the Gothic as well as from later French and Spanish prototypes appeared in heavy cast iron architectural decorations, along with invented motifs on the part of the local designers. Cast iron foundrys were started, producing balustrades, ornamental window lintels, column caps and bases, gradually more and more Gothic in character. Towers were added to white

pillared houses of classic nature; in fact Gothic came into existence in every material available but that which was most characteristically used in Gothic times, namely, stone.

With Renwick (1790-1863) as the most prominent architect, some of the outstanding monuments of early Neo-Gothic are those of Grace Church, N. Y. (Renwick, 1843); St. Patrick's Church, N. Y. (Renwick, 1850); the Smithsonian Institution in Washington (Renwick, 1846-52); the State Capital at Baton Rouge, La. (c. 1847, Weiss, Dreyfous and Seiferth); and Trinity Church, N. Y. (Upjohn, 1839-46).

Eclecticism, 1850-1893. Known by many names (**Parvenu, Roaring Eighties, Brown Decades, Age of Romanticism,** etc.) this period roughly divides itself into the type of eclecticism that prevailed prior to 1876, and that which came about between the Centennial Exposition at Philadelphia in 1876, and the World's Fair or Columbian Exposition in Chicago, in 1893. For the brief time before the Civil War there was an adaptation of the Downing Cottage style of England of western Europe's smaller domestic architecture, and the above mentioned Gothic revivals. With the boom following the Civil War, and with our westward movements taking precedence over contacts with Europe, our intellectual and artistic background was not sufficient to keep up with territorial and commercial expansions. The result was a vigorous, ostentatious movement, lacking in taste, seeking its architectural and decorative arts forms in an undisciplined trail in manifestations from the most rustic to the most exotic. Diverse styles appeared, based on Swiss chalets, castellated medieval forms, jigsaw-decorated combinations of Georgian and Gothic, Renaissance (gingerbread) villas, Eastlake styles, Hobb's architecture (an elaboration of Downing's cottage style), Queen Anne styles (an admixture of Victorian Gothic and Eastlake), Victorian Gothic either with Italian flavor, or with Third Empire French, and Chinese, Persian and other Oriental aspects. Porte-cocheres, conical roofs, wide porches, high roofs, towers, gables, and all manner of unrelated architectural forms were jumbled together. Outstanding examples of these "brown decades" are the McCormick House, Chicago (1873); Memorial Hall at Harvard (Ware and Van Brunt); The State Capitol at Hartford, Conn. (Upjohn, 1873-78); and the Philadelphia Centennial Exposition buildings of 1876. Even in the south there was an occasional echo of a Renaissance villa only in the materials available instead of the stone tile and marble of Italy, as seen at Annandale, Madison County, Miss., in 1855.

The craze for the picturesque and romantic was largely occasioned by mid-Victorian tendencies in literature, such as the writings of Sir Walter Scott, by the enthusiasms of the followers of Ruskin or Pugin, or by sudden wealth on the part of thousands throughout the country who were unprepared to announce their progress up the social ladder by other than lavish and vulgar display. Domestic interiors, like the exteriors, were of excellent workmanship, accounting for their current preservation, but of execrable taste, with panelled wainscots, golden oak beamed ceilings, profuse mill work, pictured tiles, cubby holes and mantle shelves weighted with an indiscriminate assemblage of objects ranging from Blackamoor statues and cornucopias filled with hot-house fruits, to Oriental bric-a-brac and products of taxidermy. Furnishings were eclectic, ranging from the most medievally romantic to the most heavily antiquarian with Victorian, Biedermeier and Third French Empire vogues; weighty chandeliers and lighting fixtures added to the massive conglomeration of furnitures, and the ensemble was unwholesomely lightened in appearance by billowing drapery swags and a profusion of exotic growing plants. (The Victorian furniture of black walnut and rosewood, textiles of horsehair, plush, satins and brocades, Axminster carpets of heavy floral designs predominantly red and green hues and other Victorian features have enjoyed a brief vogue in recent years due to the whims of clients who wished to dramatize their surroundings with as great a contrast to Modern as possible, or to indulge in a nostalgic escape from the pressures of a modern world).

The Industrial Revolution in England at the start of the 19th cent. had its reflections throughout the century in this country, with factory methods, machines and inventions taking the place of the hand crafts of the preceding times. During this surge of industry was imported Victorian bric-a-brac and English and French earthenware and chinaware (one French factory simulating Limoges china having been started by an American, David Haviland, formerly an importer in N. Y.). Some locally produced ceramic forms seemed to present the lowest aspects of the artistic decline during this period. Experiments to produce novel surface effects were carried out, such as a type of marbling, slip-combing or scroddle ware; romantically con-

ceived cow pitchers appeared, and ceramic sculptured grotesques for such purposes as ink wells, paper weights or door stops; cartoons and political jests became motifs for the ornamentation of utilitarian objects. Parallel with these tendencies were the pictorial embroidery contests, and hooked rugs bearing mottoes and expressions of sentiment.

In architecture between 1876 and 1893 there appeared a distinctly encouraging directive for the electicism to come, on the part of two Beaux-Arts trained architectural leaders, namely, Henry Hobson Richardson (1838-1886), and Richard Morris Hunt (1828-c. 1896). These men selected simpler and more direct traditional styles than had been evidenced in the borrowings prior to 1876. Richardson was mainly trained in a classical style, but worked in a Victorian Gothic manner in his first commissions. He soon turned to the strong and vital construction, picturesque masses and rich surface textures of the Romanesque of southern France and Spain, and worked so consistently in this manner for all buildings of domestic, civic and ecclesiastical nature that the movement became known as the **Neo-Romanesque**. The best examples of his work are: Trinity Church, Boston (1877); Sever Hall, Harvard (1878-80); the Field Warehouse, Chicago (1885); the Gratwick House, Buffalo (1886); and the Pittsburgh Courthouse and Jail (1884-87). Hunt was largely influenced by the French Renaissance, and was commissioned by prominent families in N. Y. to build homes simulating the larger French chateaux, as seen in the W. K. Vanderbilt residence in N. Y. (now demolished), and in the G. W. Vanderbilt residence "Biltmore", in N. Carolina. His civic structures suggested similar architectural features, e.g., the N. Y. Tribune Building (1874), and he designed the Administration Building at the Chicago World's Fair, at which time the significance of his particular contribution was absorbed in the work of fellow architects similarly trained.

During these years the character of the architectural schools in the country became fairly well established, and schools for training in the crafts began to appear, each following the stylistic tendencies of the men on the faculties. However, commercially produced art objects proved to be superior for this brief time, as in the instance of the manufacture of fine chinaware in Syracuse, N. Y., by the Onondaga Potteries, 1870 henceforth. to be followed by the Lenox plant at Trenton, N. J., in 1889.

Eclecticism, 1893 to the Present. All traditional styles have been utilized by architects for the past fifty years, the relative successes being governed by the good taste of the designer and the lattitude given him by the commissioner. The foremost of these stylistic selections was the Renaissance, for it had been voted to build and decorate the Exposition Buildings at the Chicago Fair of 1893 in the classical aspects of the Renaissance. Many meetings of the architects, sculptors and painters involved took place not only in Chicago but in other large cities where the offices of the designers were located, thus spreading interest and research for all possible translations of Renaissance details. Of greatest significance were the Agricultural Building (McKim, Mead and White), the Manufacture and Liberal Arts Building (Post), the Fine Arts Building (Atwood), the Horticultural Building (Jenney), and the Transportation Building by Adler and Sullivan, which was the sole departure from the stylistic manner of the Exposition. Outstanding exponents of the movement now known as the **Neo-Renaissance**, were McKim, Mead and White. C. F. McKim (1847-1909) was later the father of the American Academy of Rome, where many of our architects studied; Stanford White has been called the father of American architectural decoration. Their best known works are the Boston Public Library (1887-1895); the Old Madison Square Gardens, N. Y. (in the 90's); the old Columbia University Library, N. Y. (1895); the N. Y. Herald Building (1894); the Pennsylvania R. R. Station, N. Y. (1906-1910) and the Morgan Library, N. Y. (1906). Following the stylistic lead of these men, Carrere (1858-1911) and Hastings built the N. Y. Public Library in 1910; Chedanne added a distinctly French flavor to the Clark Mansion, N. Y.; Cass Gilbert (1859-1934) is well known for the Minnesota State Capitol Bldg. (1906), the Woolworth Building, N. Y. (1911-1913); H. Bacon (1866-1924) for the Lincoln Memorial in Washington in 1913. The other major traditional borrowing after 1893 was led by the architects C. R. Cram (1863-   , B. G. Goodhue (1869-1924) and F. W. Ferguson (1861-1926), followed by Day, Klauder, and Rogers. The spirit and plan of the buildings by these men were based on medieval architecture ranging from Gothic to Byzantine, each designer progressing as far as the function of the building and his own philosophy of beauty would permit, and following the gospels of Ruskin, or the Morris and Oxford movements. The best known monuments of these men are The United States Military Academy (Cram and Goodhue, 1903); St. Thomas's in New York (Goodhue, 1906); the First Baptist Church, Pittsburgh (Cram and Goodhue, 1909); St. Bartholomews in N. Y. (Goodhue, 1914); St. John's the Divine, N. Y. (LaFarge and Cram); the San Diego Exposition Building (Goodhue, 1915); and the Capitol Building in Lincoln, Nebraska (Goodhue, 1925). (These men were frequently called to collaborate with local architects in other parts of the country, e.g., Cram's part in the planning of the Doheny Memorial Library, University of Southern California (1931); Goodhue's Los Angeles Public Library (1925) belongs rather to the modern style into which his earlier designs merged.) Other outstanding monuments in this tradition are the Museum of the University of Pennsylvania (Day, Cope, Stewardson and Eyre); the Princeton dormitories (Day and Klauder); the Harkness Memorial Tower at Yale (Rogers); and the Cathedral of Learning (University of Pittsburgh) (Klauder).

The first skyscrapers were Romanesque in appearance, their home being in Chicago where the first architects to attack their problems were located. Skyscraper projects had been under way since 1880, dependent on inventions in metals and glass, in the fire-proofing of metal materials, and in the varied inventions of elevators. The Tacoma Building in Chicago (1887-1888) by Holabird and Roche was the first building to have the outer walls entirely supported by the interior metal skeleton; Jenney's Leiter Building in Chicago (1889-1890) was the first building in which all the walls were supported internally. Burnham and Root were occupied with further solutions, to be followed by Adler and Sullivan, in whose hands the buildings grew out of the Romanesque into their more recent Rationalistic trend. New York skyscrapers stressed the Renaissance details affected by their designers in general as seen in the New York City Administration building by McKim, Mead, and White (1908) and the Woolworth Building (1911) by Gilbert. The trend toward greater verticality stimulated Gothic details as seen in the prize-winning design by J. M. Howells and R. M. Hood in the Tribune Building Competition in Chicago (1922). Since that time the aesthetic and structural story of the skyscraper belongs mainly to the movement which has been termed **Rationalistic**, due largely to the design submitted by Eliel

Saarinen in the 1922 competition, and his successors.

The movements in decorative arts showed the influence of expositions since 1876. The pendulum swung between the extremely practical aspects at the Philadelphia Centennial, to the "art for art's sake" appearances in the World's Fair in Chicago, back to a union of arts and crafts at the St. Louis Exposition of 1904, to the practical arts at the fairs in San Diego and San Francisco in 1915, and back to the extremely decorative at the Exposition of Decorative Arts in Paris in 1925 which had such a wide-spread influence on subsequent designs. In 1881 William Morris in England started the "Honest Crafts Movement" in revolt to the poverty of design brought about by machine-made objects in the 19th cent., and stimulated his artists to turn to medieval examples of decorative arts for their inspiration in returning to hand craftsmanship. During the 1888 Arts and Crafts Exhibition in London, a society was formed which was parent to most American crafts organizations of the present century. *L'Art Nouveau* of Belgium and France at the end of the 19th cent. did not enter America's trends in design except briefly at the time of the St. Louis Exposition. The china-painting vogue climaxed at this time; so-called "art groups" of ceramic sculptures appeared, utilizing white parian wares, and not only continuing a type of mid-Victorian sentimentality, but creating an American *genre* with such well known sculptors as John Rogers and Daniel Chester French participating. For utilitarian wares, an epidemic of "jug towns" came about. Tapestry manufactories such as those of Baumgarten and of Herter were started in N. Y. in the early 20th cent., the designs ranging through all subjects from the medieval times to the present, consistent with the preferences for furniture of Florentine, Roman and Venetian Renaissance, and of all French styles of furniture of the 18th cent.

In the making of hand-forged and hand-carved iron doors, gates, grills, and other ornamental features of architecture, Samuel Yellin of Philadelphia (1886-) has achieved outstanding fame, and examples of his works are to be seen in many museums. Designers of architectural decoration stressed a style maturing about 1910 which appeared to be a combination of the ornaments of any or many historical periods, the motifs seeming to be selected from transitional times where there were no fixed forms. Contemporary with this group was another movement

on the part of men who recognized that ornament should not be the determining agent of the style of architecture. They ignored books on historic ornament and sought a study of masses, proportions, and textures destined to bring out the technical beauties of the engineering of a monument. The principles of this latter group were incorporated by the larger number of industrial designers who recommended the machine as an art tool and who were only temporarily swerved from their course by the designs introduced at the Paris Exposition of Decorative Arts. Immediately following this exposition of 1925 a brief period of "modernistic" filled the *ateliers* of designers and department stores in large cities (cf. pictured examples in Park, *New Backgrounds for a New Age*) to be dissolved in the more contemporary manner of architects and designers in a greater harmony of so-called "rationalistic" forms.

Rationalism in America, 1890 to the Present. The utterance of Louis A. Sullivan (1856-1924) to the effect that "form follows function" gave the first name of **Functionalism** to this movement in architecture as a social expression and with complete interdependence of form, function, and decoration. His transportation Building at the World's Fair in Chicago (1893) showed a marked departure from the Romanesque traditions seen in his earlier work as typified by the Auditorium building in Chicago (1886-1889). In his contributions to a more organic type of office building and in his residences of the late 19th and earlier 20th cent. in the midwest are to be seen the simple character and texture-stressing ornament that has been carried on by his outstanding pupil, Frank Lloyd Wright (1869-). The dynamic experimentations of Mr. Wright certainly establish him as America's foremost modernist, esp. in residence design, and his writings have perhaps stimulated more thought and controversy than any other. From the time of his early works in 1894 he has consistently stressed horizontality; he has indicated his worship of the machine as shown in his use of pre-cast concrete blocks and geometric motifs, and has desired to reduce all building design to the simplest possible terms, in cooperation and harmony with the natural surroundings. His predilection for projecting eaves and cantilevered units has been well known since his successful use of them in the Imperial Hotel of Tokyo which withstood the severe quakes in 1923. The early difficulties of Wright in harmonizing exterior and interior architecture with the furnishings owned by people or produced by furniture factories in general, and which he attempted to solve by actually creating furniture, lighting fixtures, and other decorative arts, are no longer major problems. Modern furniture designers such as Paul T. Frankl, Kem Weber, Donald Deskey, Gilbert Rhode, Joseph Urban (1872-1933, also a stage designer of great note) and others have produced furnishings of all categories which are compatable with the new materials and principles of modern architectural design. Among modern architects of more monumental edifices Raymond M. Hood (1881-1934), Eliel Saarinen of Finland (now at Cranbrook) and Ely J. Kahn (1884-   ) rank high. The influences on America by the Bauhaus, started in Germany early in the 20th cent., and by many of its leaders who are now in this country, are yet too indirect and too contemporary to be seen in any perspective.

The word "functionalism" is not recent in connection with the decorative arts either, for since the first of the 20th cent. arts and crafts societies have used this word to describe their designs. The modern designer, particularly since 1925, has been interested in developing an object which appears decorative in the home through fine handling of material, shape, color and texture, but which does not depend individually upon ornamentation for its decorative effects. The industrial designer of today, exemplified by the above mentioned men, and by Norman Bel Geddes, Russel Wright and Raymond Loewy among others, must not only know his art, but the machines which are to translate the designs to the finished product. Considerable variance in the interpretation of Modern has resulted in designs ranging from elegance and sumptuousness suggestive of traditional periods (especially the American Indian, Persian and far-Eastern *décor* stressed in recent exhibitions), or of modern painting to the craft viewpoint where designs of simple effectiveness are produced either by a direct shaping of materials with the hope that good design will automatically result or by working out patterns, to be translated by simple tools, e.g., the loom, rather than the commercial machine. Neither is as yet completely capable of mass production any more than is the continued creation of traditional styles in all of the decorative arts, especially in furniture. Since merchandisers have stimulated not only seasonal changes but regional styles, the great variety of so-called "Rational" forms, patterns and surface textures range from the most naïve to the most formal or effusive.

Outstanding names of the present day in the making of glass are Dorothy Thorpe of Los Angeles and the designers of the world famous Steuben glass made at the factory at Corning, N. Y.; for modern textiles—Dorothy Liebes of San Francisco, Ruth Reeves and Marguerita Mergentime of N. Y.; for modern ceramics one turns to the repeat prize winners of the annual shows of the National Ceramics Exhibition, first established as the Robineau Memorial Exhibition, of Syracuse, N. Y., in 1932. For pottery, the names of Arthur E. Baggs, Cleveland, Glen Lukens, Los Angeles, Edgar Littlefield, Ohio, and Henry Varnum Poor, N. Y., appear most frequently; for ceramic sculpture those of Waylande Gregory, Michigan, Paul Bogatay, Ohio, Russell B. Aitken, Cleveland and Victor Schreckengost, Cleveland. Special prizes were given to Edward Winter of Cleveland in the field of enamels. Most handwrought silver has been made by individual designers within large organizations, but in recent years museums such as the Cleveland Museum of Art have sponsored competitions for the independent silversmith. Hudson, B. Roysher, Los Angeles, has won many awards in such competitions. Work such as submitted by these silver craftsmen and by other designers in precious materials, demanding precision of skill and long hours of thoughtful care in handling, will no doubt serve as guide posts of sound craftsmanship and sure knowledge of good design for those who work with new synthetic or relatively inexpensive materials, or who follow an undisciplined concept of Modern as a "growing style".

Outstanding collections of American decorative arts are to be seen at the Art Institute of Chicago, the Metropolitan Museum of Art, N. Y., the Brooklyn Museum of Art, the Pennsylvania Museum of Art, the Cleveland Museum of Art, the Museum of Fine Arts, Boston, the Detroit Institute of Arts, the William Rockhill Nelson Gallery of Art in Kansas City, and the M. H. de Young Memorial Museum in San Francisco. See EARLY AMERICAN ART; also Avery, C. Louise, *Early American Silver*, 1930; Edgell, G. H., *The American Architecture of Today*, 1928; Frankl, Paul T., *New Dimensions*, 1928, and *Form and Re-Form*, 1930; Hitchcock, Henry-Russell, Jr., *The Architecture of H. H. Richardson and His Times*, 1936, and *In the Nature of Materials; the Buildings of Frank Lloyd Wright 1887-1941*, 1942; Knittle, Rhea M., *Early American Glass*, 1927; Miller, Gladys, *Decoratively Speaking*, 1941; Newcomb, Rexford, *Spanish Colonial Architecture in the U. S.*, 1937; Park, E. A., *New Backgrounds for a New Age*, 1927; Ramsay, John, *American Potters and Pottery*, 1939; Smith, J. Frazer, *White Pillars*, 1941; Stiles, Helen E., *Pottery in the United States*, 1941; Tallmadge, Thomas E., *The Story of Architecture in America*, 1927.   —A.W.M.

POST-REVOLUTIONARY PAINTING AND SCULPTURE IN THE U. S. A. The

chronological divisions below are arbitrary, for painters and sculptors elude the more exact classification that was possible in the development of architecture and the decorative arts. The type of patronage was different, and while their works were as generally reflective of the society in which they were created, each man is an individual problem. The sources of his training were usually multiple and the man may have changed the nature of his work many times as he grew older or met influences strong enough to alter his viewpoint or manner of presentation, thus lifting him from one category into another.

Scholars have found the matter of classification of painters and sculptors since 1776 like that of handling quicksilver; for instance, Homer St. Gauden's (1941) began by tying the men who worked after the Revolutionary War to those who preceded it by some years in all-inclusive group dated 1750-1828, the latter date being the year of the death of Gilbert Stuart. He followed these by a unit ending in 1876; for him there seemed to be a distinct group between the Fairs of 1876 and 1893, after which are the Contemporary men. Virgil Barker (1931) has generally followed Samuel Isham in the first of his categories, namely, the "Colonial", ending c. 1790, the "Provincial" ending in 1876 and the "Cosmopolitan" to the time of the Armory Show in New York in 1913. His last group he approached qualitatively, calling them "Contemporary", and attempting to sub-divide by style, as an aid for further study and possible reclassification. Alfred Barr in his catalogue of the American Exhibition in Paris under the auspices of the Museum of Modern Art, 1938, divided his survey arbitrarily into painting since 1776 to the time of the Civil War, thence to the year 1900, and then simply "Twentieth Century American Painting". Another 1938 exhibition of Contemporary American Painting, in London, was accompanied by a catalogue with an introduction by Henry McBride, who suggested that American painting development had followed a chronological swing of the pendulum first from the British influences, to the native tendencies exhibited in the Hudson River School, then back to influences from abroad, and finally back to America with the Contemporary men. Suzanne La Follette (1929) allowed her colonial painters to extend to 1800, after which she found two main groups, placed under the headings of "Material Expansion and Artistic Contraction", 1800-1876, and "Recommencements" after 1876. For Mellquist (1942), all painters before 1898 were the "Forerunners", to be followed by a series of men in "Revolt" until World War I; thereafter for him the men were the "Culmination".

Lorado Taft attempted even more difficult organization in the field of sculpture, there being little of importance prior to 1850, and not many more artists of relatively outstanding merit in the intermediary period to 1876. With him, as with other writers, the last division of "Contemporary" referred to the inclusive time of the types of works which are still produced today. His death prevented a newer edition of his important history of American sculpture to include men of the last two decades, and anyone seeking names of current prominence in the field of sculpture, as in painting, must go with trepidation to as unbiased and objective sources as possible, with full knowledge that some names a generation hence may prove to have been of transient worth, whereas others at this time modestly observed, may rise to greater favor with the light of perspective thrown upon them. Work such as is currently undertaken by the American Art Research Council and by other centers of similar investigation will prove to be of inestimable value in the future.

The categories here selected are simply those of fifty-year intervals, there being sufficient evidence of traditional and stylistic preferences within each to make the classifications possible when based on training, technique and style rather than on content or concept. Since 1776 there have been "revolts" in every period as to subject matter and the personal idiom; subjects which today would be called "Regional", "Provincial" or the "American Scene" abounded in the 19th cent. in *genre* paintings, in so-called "Primitives", or in Currier and Ives prints. To date, if viewed objectively, there have been no "Culminations" as such in the crucible of progresssive movements. As has been seen, a distortion of time or tendency is bound to result when a particular thesis is expounded. Therefore, no thesis is here presented, and the developmental progress in the crafts of painting and sculpture seems to be the more logical to tie to for some type of chronology, at least until the 20th cent., since biographical material herein is out of the question. Names brought forth are those which, to 1943, have been most universally accepted by scholars and critics, and in terms of museum purchases and representation in collections of reliable dealers and recognized patrons.

The First Fifty Years, 1776-1826. This period is marked by a strong adherence to the style of social paintings in England, due mainly to patronage, to familiarity with the techniques evolved prior to the Revolutionary War, and to the fact that territorial expansion until after the first quarter of the 19th cent. was not sufficient to tempt the painter's eye away from the strong cultural contact of England. After 1763, when Benjamin West (1738-1820) settled permanently in London, a large group of American painters studied with him at his school. Among them were the following men of note: Matthew Pratt (1734-1805), Charles Willson Peale (1741-1827), his son Rembrandt Peale (1778-1860), Abraham Delanoy, Jr. (c. 1740-c. 1790), Henry Benbridge (1744-1812), Edward Savage (1761-1817), Joseph Wright (1756-1792), William Dunlap (1766-1839), John Trumbull (1756-1843), Robert Fulton (1765-1815), E. G. Malbone (1777-1807), Henry Sargent (1770-1845), Thomas Sully (1783-1872), Samuel Waldo (1783-1861), Washington Allston (1779-1843), Samuel F. B. Morse (1791-1872), possibly Ralph Earl (1751-1801) who visited him and at least had his advice, and Gilbert Stuart (1755-1828). Thus while the type of painting which had been styled "Colonial" was the tradition during the early years of West's life and was based generally on Lely and Kneller, these later man reflected West's more sophisticated manner and that of Reynolds, Romney, Lawrence and Hoppner, some of the above men studying for some time with the English masters. Several continued English portrait tradition well along into the 19th cent., such as the popular Sully. Even a group of independent portrait painters uninfluenced by study abroad, such as Chester Harding (1792-1866), John Neagle (1796-1865), J. Eichholtz (1776-1842), and J. W. Jarvis (1780-c.1835), would pose their subjects similarly to the English-trained group, with the same background foils of turbulent skies or monumental architecture, although more realistically direct and less sophisticated in manner.

Miniature painting did not come into its own in America until after the Revolutionary War, and faded into obscurity some sixty years later with the introduction of photography. Malbone, Fulton, James Peale (1749-1831), Robert Field (c. 1765-1819), Walter Robertson (1765-1802), Benjamin Trott (c. 1770-1841), Charles Fraser (1782-1860), and Raphaelle Peale (1774-1825), also a painter of still-life, are among the most notable. John Ramage painted miniatures in this country from 1774-1794, among them one of George Washington; Charles St. Memmin who came to this country from France in 1796, perhaps painted the most reliable miniatures of Washington, due to his reputation as a physiognomist.

The three items of greatest single interest occurring in the latter part of the 18th cent. have probably been the paintings made of George Washington, the paintings made by Gilbert Stuart, and the paintings by Ralph Earl. Controversies over authentic portraits of Washington (1732-1799) have waxed hot. We know that C. W. Peale painted him in the uniform of a colonel in the Virginia Militia in 1772; he painted another in 1795; Robert Edge Pine came to this country in 1784 and lived here until his death in 1788, painting Washington in 1785. Edward Savage painted a portrait of the Washington family in 1789 and finished it in 1796, as well as one of Washington in uniform in 1790 and another in civilian dress. Christian Gullager (1762-1826/7) painted him in 1789. However, Gilbert Stuart's portraits are the most famous, since he not only painted Washington many times from life, but copied his paintings for ardent patrons over many years following. His so-called "Vaughan" portrait of 1795, now in the National Gallery in Washington, reveals the right side of Washington's face; the left side is shown in the full-length picture called the "Lansdowne" portrait of 1796 and in the "Athenaeum" portrait c. 1795, of which he made many copies.

Not only because of these portraits, but because of his superb handling of paint, Gilbert Stuart deserves special attention. He painted well even as a young boy, and after his return to New York in 1793 following several trips abroad, hundreds of portraits have been attributed to his swift and competent hand. His pearly flesh tones were his greatest contribution; the rest of the figure he handled with great economy of paint and effort, if at all, since his prime interest was the study of character.

The paintings of Ralph Earl, who has been listed indiscriminately under headings of sophisticated paintings, provincial paintings, and even of folk arts, are enjoying a new recognition because of our present day search for things typically American. As early as 1775 he painted a view of the town of Concord, Mass., believed to be the first historical painting by an American artist. He was an itinerant painter, but revealed a refreshingly "native" character in his paintings of the last quarter of the 18th cent., with strong design, good color, and fine pictorial sense.

Of sculpture in the first fifty years following the Revolution, there is little to say. Patience Wright, mother of the above-mentioned painter, went to London in 1772, where her modelled figures in wax became internationally famous. Other than the portraits of George Washington by the French sculptor Houdon in 1785-1788, the American yields boil down to the wood-carvings of William Rush (1756-1833) and of Hezekiah Augur (1791-1858). The stone carvings of John Frazee (1790-1852) moved into the next chronological period, with frankness and expressiveness half way between folk art and classicism. Otherwise folk arts such as polychromed ships' figureheads, cigar-store Indians, small wood sculptures of animals, birds and men, lawn figures, gravestones, weathervanes and cast-iron stoveplates, made up the larger number of plastic arts contributions, and have become increasingly important as reflectors of the social-economic aspects of the times.

Transitional to the next chronological period of painting were examples of folk arts in the craft of painting on velvet, silk, canvas and glass, exhibiting in spite of an abstract character and untutored manner the predilection for portraits, miniatures and family groups in the late 18th and early 19th cent. that marked the work of the professional painters after 1826, and for the landscapes, *genre* subjects and historical scenes which were the outstanding constributions of the men to be cited in the group dated 1826-1876. Transitional to the professional class of painters one finds listed the names of Washington Allston and John Vanderlyn (1776-1852), who went to Paris to study. The romantic leanings of these two led into a movement in painting which stressed landscape instead of figures, namely, the **Hudson River School**. William Dunlap, famous for his volumes entitled *The History of the Rise and Progress of the Arts of Design in the United States,* published in 1834, and John Trumbull contributed to the tendency towards historical scenes. The founding of the art school of the National Academy of Design (now the National Academy) in 1826 marked the end of a craft primarily taught in England, and inaugurated an era of training in America and on the continent.

1826-1876. Neo-classicism in sculpture resulting directly or indirectly from study in Italy with Canova or Thorwaldsen is to be seen in the works of Horatio Greenough (1805-1852), Hiram Powers (1805-1873), Thomas Crawford (1813-1857), Erastus D. Palmer (1817-1904), William Wetmore Story (1819-1895), Harriet Hosmer (1830-1908), Randolph Rogers (1825-1892), and William H. Rinehart (1825-1874), the founder of a scholarship fund for study abroad in sculpture. Little or no evidence of this type of pseudo-classicism based on linear and decorative compositions appeared in the works of painters. The only marked parallels in painting and sculpture were primarily the more native elements such as can be observed in the plastic works of Joel Hart of Kentucky (1810-1877), Henry Kirk Brown (1814-1886), Clark Mills (1815-1883), and the *genre* groups of John Rogers (1829-1904), and secondarily in the academically trained sculptors who went to Paris instead of to Rome in the 60's and 70's. Two outstanding men served to bridge the gap to the type of sculpture continuing through to the present day, namely, John Quincy Adams Ward (1830-1910) and Olin Levi Warner (1844-1896).

Painting took two directions during the period of 1826-1876, one a continuation of figure painting, and the other, that of landscape painting. Each presented what might be called a native (provincial) character on the one hand, and a continental aspect on the other. Figure and portrait painters who moved westward in the country were likely to reflect their new environmental conditions in a type of American *genre,* to be found in the works of George Caleb Bingham (1811-1879), David C. Blythe (1815-1865), William S. Mount (1807-1868), Richard Caton Woodville (1825-1856) and others. Those who went to Europe to study, or remained in the east to work with American masters reflected the influences from abroad more directly. These men were Emanuel Leutze (1816-

1891), Eastman Johnson (1824-1906), George Fuller (1822-1884), Charles Robert Leslie (1794-1859), William Morris Hunt (1824-1879), J. G. Brown (1831-1913), Alvan Fisher (1792-1863), and the muralists John La Farge (1835-1910), Elihu Vedder (1836-1923) and Charles Caryl Coleman (1840-1928). European influences at this time were the traditions of Hogarth and of the Dutch *genre* masters, the academies in Munich and Düsseldorf, the poetry of the Barbizon painters of France, the academic portrait and figure painters of France, and the murals of Puvis de Chavannes.

Halfway between these men and the landscapists were the works of groups of men ranging from the naturalist John James Audubon (c. 1785-1851), the whimsical John Quidor (1801-1881) and th artists of Currier and Ives lithographs (important between 1835 and 1889, at which latter date the first true chromolithography appeared in America), to the so-called "primitive" painters who combined figures and landscapes in their self-taught and semi-abstract fashion. Hundreds of names of painters of this latter category have risen from former anonymity, chiefly those of Edward Hicks (1780-1849), J. S. Ellsworth (1811-c. 1873), Eunice Pinney (1770-1849), J. W. Stock (1815-1855), Joseph H. Headley who worked c. 1840-60, and Rufus Porter (1792-1884) and Joseph Pickett (1848-1918) whose work carried on into the subsequent period.

The movement toward landscape painting has been styled the **Hudson River School**, because of its early concentration in that area. The romantic and poetic landscapes coming from the brushes of Thomas Doughty (1793-1856), Thomas Cole (1801-1848), Asher B. Durand (1796-1886), and John W. Casilear (1811-1893) were largely Italian in tradition, the exactitude of details, the formal compositions and the color formulas coming from Titian through Rubens and Claude Lorrain, who had gone to Italy to study. Attempts to secure unlimited space, and effects of air and light were to a large degree frustrated by the current demands for faithfulness and precision of representation of all things within the range of the artist's eye. The later works of Doughty and Durand bore evidences of the style of Constable, and the influences of the more atmospheric Barbizon school. J. F. Kensett's (1818-1872) works reveal marked leaning on Constable; Albert Bierstadt (1830-1902) showed that his Düsseldorf study with Lessing had made an indelible impression on him even in his more dramatic paintings of Yosemite Valley and in California, during far-west migrations in the mid-18th cent. The lyrical romance of Düsseldorf styles made intimate and sentimental by devoted care in drawing and painstaking brushwork, was in marked contract to the grandiose, sensational and sweepingly broad techniques taught at the Munich academy; few landscapists sought Munich until after 1876.

1876-1926. This period might be styled that of technical experiment for the first thirty years, and after that of experiments in interpretation as well. The two groups of the previous period began to blend by introducing landscapes as more frequent backgrounds for figure groups, or interpreting figures in out-of-doors light rather than in the constant light of the studio. First to move out of the characteristics of painting prior to 1876 were the landscapists George Inness (1825-1894) who started with Hudson River School precision, moved on to Barbizon School atmosphere, and eventually to tonalism where he began to see his compositions as emotional units; F. E. Church (1826-1900), a pupil of Cole; Thomas Moran (1837-1926), W. Whittredge (1820-1910), William Keith (1839-1911), Alexander Wyant (1836-1892) and Homer D. Martin (1836-1897). The Barbizon character of Inness, Wyant and Martin, where moods took the place of literal representations of nature, was half way between map-like photographic aspects, and the emotional qualities of light. Inness was one of the first to mix white pigment with color; from here on the problem of overcoming technical limitations in order to paint sunlight, was paramount. It was first attacked by the use of thick white paint, thus forcing light by contrast; since this lacked the life of real sunlight, small brushstrokes of broken color came next, to produce vibration. As the width and length of the brush stroke made a big difference in the quality of vibration, Frank Duveneck (1848-1919) tried the broad Munich-type strokes to effect his luminosity. Various experiments called **Tonalism** were made by a group including Inness, Keith, Albert P. Ryder (1847-1917), J. Francis Murphy (1853-1921), Henry W. Ranger (1858-1916), and Ralph A. Blakelock (1847-1899). Ranger, for example, painted his canvas entirely with white, and let it dry. Then a thin coat of golden color, or the prevailing hue of the picture, was painted over it, and the subjects painted into that hue with all the other colors. Another coat of the basic hue was then added, and subsequently a repetition of the former process, making many thin layers of color. The chief color selections of these men were raw umber, burnt sienna, raw sienna, burnt umber and yellow ochre, with the pervading hue established by underpainting with the tonal color, and at times painting the subjects into this before it was dry. Inness' method of painting the glow of the setting sun by putting a thin transparent coat of red over a dry coat of white was followed by similar attempts to secure the richness of transmitted color. A group of men who moved from these experiments to the adaptation of the high keyed colors of Monet, and pure colors placed side by side for mixing by the eye of the spectator, have been called **Luminists.** Outstanding among them were Charles H. Davis (1856-1933), Willard L. Metcalf (1858-1925), and Childe Hassam (1859-1935) whose works of opalescent beauty have also been cited under the heading of Impressionism.

The men who have been classified as "Impressionists" were primarily landscape painters who at times also used techniques other than those precisely impressionistic, and who modified the facts of the landscape to secure the mood of the setting. Rather than an exact translation of French impressionism and its subsequent movements toward pointillism, etc., the American painters depended on their own observations and experiments, as in the case of Emil Carlsen (1853-1932) who put on paint, scraped it off, put more on, with each coat thin and dry, and thus built up his composition of tumbling water and old trees with sunlight striking them. Abbott H. Thayer (1849-1921) was one of those men whose study of the physical properties of color led to the knowledge of protective coloration, or camouflage. Ben Foster (1852-1926) and Dwight Tryon (1849-1925) presented pastoral scenes showing poetic early morning, sunset or moonlight effects. Later Impressionists, as Robert Reid (1862-1929), Frank W. Benson (1862-   ), F. C. Frieseke (1874-1939), Robert Spencer (1879-1931), Edmund C. Tarbell (1862-1938), Daniel Garber (1880-   ), Ernest Lawson (1873-1939), J. W. Twachtman (1853-1902) and Maurice Prendergast (1859-1924) each presented sunlight in his own way, although unmistakably following Impressionist dictates of fleck-like strokes with no distinct outlines of forms, informal picturesqueness, no particular organization of design, and primarily pleasurable aspects of nature.

Contemporary with Impressionists and Luminists were a group of landscape painters who were impatient with vague contours, and who tried to infuse a new solidity into the forms of their subjects. Their modelling of shapes of clouds, rocks, trees and water by means of bold brush strokes, brought to them such names as **The School of Direct Painting,** the **Athletic School,** or the **Sculpturesque Painters,** by their friends and critics. It was the indirect result of Munich training, most likely instigated by Edward W. Redfield (1869-   ) and carried on by Gardner Symons (1863-1930), William Wendt (1865-   ), W. Elmer Schofield (1867-   ), Jonas Lie (1880-1940), Paul Dougherty (1877-   ), and Birge Harrison (1854-1929), among others.

The three Americans who have been most revered for their independently American styles in a period characterized by academies, obvious technical explorations, or revolts, are Thomas Eakins, Albert P. Ryder, and Winslow Homer. One places Eakins (1844-1916), with his accuracy of observation, among the objective *genre* painters, and Ryder among the tonalists, where he painted the creations of his imagination. Winslow Homer (1836-1910), evades classification. Self-trained, and with keen powers of observation, he became an excellent draughtsman, and whether he painted the sea or anecdotal subjects in oil or water color, he infused such dramatic realism, vigor, freshness or grandeur, that the stylistic experimenters appeared tedious by contrast.

The figure painters in the period of 1876-1926 continued to a degree the *genre* types of the previous years, as seen in the works of Thomas Hovenden (1840-1895), William Harnett (1848-1892) and the important Thomas Eakins, but after the World's Fair in Chicago in 1893, the tendencies of the academies of France prevailed in easel and mural painting, and in work of illustrators. F. D. Millet (1846-1912), Edwin A. Abbey (1852-1911), Kenyon Cox (1856-1919), John W. Alexander (1856-1915), Julian A. Weir (1852-1919), A. B. Frost (1851-1928), George de F. Brush (1855-1941), and Thomas Dewing (1851-1938), for example, illustrated the thorough training in drawing and design, the strong sense of form, the acquaintance with anatomy, and, in general, the dignity of subject that characterized the French academies. Similar were the results of training in the Royal Academy at Munich, only with emphasis on the handling of pigments, as seen in the works of Frank Duveneck and William Chase (1849-1816). John Singer Sargent (1856-1925), trained in the academies on the continent and in London, always maintained the freshness of his personal expression in spite óf an aristocratic patronage and large numbers of commissions: J. A. McN. Whistler (1834-1903) retained his personal sensitivity and subtlety in spite of a lifetime in London and Paris, both in his paintings and in his etchings. His temperament and his interest in the arts of the Far East, which became such a vogue late in the 19th cent., produced the combination of whimsical fancy and of simplicity, the latter being the particular result of his study of the tonal qualities of Japanese prints. Mary Cassatt (1845-1926) and Cecilia Beaux (c. 1863-1942) will never be forgotten for their fine draughtsmanship and color, unusual at that time for women, and above all for their helpfulness to American painters in Paris and their stimulation of art patronage.

A timid impressionism among figure painters started with Theodore Robinson (1852-1896), and moved primarily into the field of landscape with the above mentioned Impressionists and with such painters as Lillian Genth (1876-　) who was wont to paint nudes in wooded settings, or secondarily into figural groups wherein the interpretation suggests the most poignant moment, fleeting mood or essence of the subject for translation, such as are to be seen in the paintings of frontier life or of Indians, by Irving Couse (1866-1936), William Leigh (1866-　), Brush, and the illustrator Frederick Remington (1861-1909). Once the style of Impressionism had become established, some of its men who were superb draughtsmen and colorists became academicists in a new meaning—that of conservatism (as opposed to the revolts taking place since the formation of **The Ten**) with Gari Melchers (1860-1932), F. J. Waugh (1861-1940), Charles Hawthorne (1872-1930) and Frieseke being outstanding among them.

Rivalry came about as early as the 1880's between the National Academy, and the Society of American Artists which had sprung into existence mainly through the efforts of such men as Dewing, La Farge, Cox, Brush and Thayer due to the extreme conservatism of the Academy. They came to a common agreement in 1906 however, after the activities of **The Ten**, formed in 1898, in which Dewing, Twachtman, Tarbell, J. A. Weir, Metcalf, Hassam, Reid, Benson, J. R. De Camp (1858-1923) and E. E. Simmons (1852-1931) proclaimed their interest in individual experiments to clear their palettes, and in more progressive ideas, rather than continuing the traditions of the Academy. A series of revolts henceforth was inevitable, for painting was not yet expressing typical qualities of contemporary everyday American life. In 1908 the so-called **Ash Can School** or **The Eight** was founded, with Arthur B. Davies (1862-1928), George Luks (1867-1933), Everett Shinn (1876-　), John Sloan (1871-　), Robert Henri (1865-1929), William J. Glackens (1870-1938), M. Prendergast and E. Lawson, who portrayed realism with rich observation of emotions, humble life and picturesque types, and starting the 20th cent. movements in what has been called "regionalism" and the "American scene". In 1905 and for many years hence, another company of artists met at Alfred Stieglitz's small galleries at 291 Fifth Avenue, N. Y. At the increasingly famous "291" they exhibited photographs, experiments in which induced a new aesthetic, then etchings and prints, and finally paintings by men who were wildly enthusiastic about the Post-Impressionist manifestations in Europe. Seven men of "The Eight" were members of an Association of Painters and Sculptors which brought about an international exhibition of painting and sculpture at the Armory of the 69th Regiment, N. Y., in 1913. The **Armory Show** displayed to an unprepared American eye the 19th and early 20th cent. evolutions of European "isms" in all stages from the neoclassicism of Ingres and romanticism of Delacroix, through the structures of Cezanne to the cubistic organizations of Duchamp and Picasso, and the color and space organizations of Matisse and the "Fauves" as well as other tendencies not only by European masters but the American artists who followed them. Two Americans who lived in Paris at this time, S. MacDonald-Wright (1890-　) and Morgan Russell (1886-　), created one of the "isms" of Post-Impressionism, which they called **Synchromism**. They returned to this country and helped bring about the Forum Exhibition of Modern American Painters in N. Y. in 1916, where works by themselves and fourteen others were selected from fifty applicants to display the "new aesthetics". Ben Benn (1884-　), Thomas H. Benton (1889-　), Oscar Bluemner (1868-1938), Andrew Dasburg (1887-　), Arthur Dove (1880-　), Marsden Hartley (1877-　), John Marin (1870-　), Alfred Maurer (1868-1932), Henry L. Mc-

Fee (1886-   ), George F. Of (1876-   ), Man Ray (1890-   ), Charles Sheeler (1883-   ), A. Walkowitz (1880-   ), William Zorach (1887-   ), Morgan and Wright composed the group. Each in his own way sought a spatial organization of rhythmic lines, colors and masses abstractly achieved to suggest forms of non-objective character to the observer in the hope that his emotional response would be akin to that stimulated by music, and in many ways similar to the effects produced later by Wilfred's color organ (q.v.). These assertions of volumes composed of color and light revealed qualities of oriental sensuousness now seen as one of the indirect results of stimuli given to painting by the Mohammedan exhibitions in Europe in 1904 and 1911, and other exhibitions of exotic art, and by the study of oriental philosophies. Art movements started by these men and all revolts of one kind or another against the Academies of Europe and America, were to become in themselves kinds of Academies wherein there were varied approaches once again to the fundamental principles of form and draughtsmanship with the eventuation of more realistic representations. Several of this group have handed down through teaching and contact with other present-day painters the lessons of such dynamic experiences, where experiment in techniques, idea and interpretation became one.

Transitional to the Contemporary period, which herein has been arbitrarily dated 1926-1943, were the abstractionists Preston Dickinson (1891-1930), Allen Tucker (1866-1939), Stuart Davis (1894-   ), and Lyonel Feininger (1871-   ), and such significant realists as George Bellows (1882-1925), Leon Kroll (1884-   ), Gifford Beal (1879-   ), Eugene Speicher (1883-   ), Edward Hopper (1882-   ), Victor Higgins (1884-   ), Maynard Dixon (1875-   ), E. L. Blumenschein (1874-   ), Walter Ufer (1876-1936), Guy Pene du Bois (1884-   ), John Sloan (1871-   ), Jerome Myers (1867-1940) and the "primitive" John Kane (1860-1934).

In sculpture, Gutzon Borglum (1871-1941) might be considered transitional to the styles of the present day, in his spirited and independent handling of all subjects from equestrians to the gigantic figures on Stone Mountain, near Atlanta, Ga., and in the Mount Rushmore Memorial in the Black Hills. Before him, however, the predominating character of the sculpture of this period was first definitely academic, the majority of our sculptors working at L'Ecole des Beaux Arts in Paris, and second, also French inspired, impressionistic. Of the first group the works of Augustus St. Gaudens (1848-1907) rank high for dignity and impressiveness, with delicacy and precision due to his early cameo cutting, and yet force and factuality that the French school was unable to obliterate. Daniel Chester French (1850-1931) was popular due to his sentimentality, picturesqueness and aspect of geniality, but he lacked the depth of expression in the works of St. Gaudens. Frederick William MacMonnies (1863-1937) expressed strenuous motion in his pieces, with a Carpeaux-like intensity, but lacking in monumentality. Herbert Adams (1858-   ) displayed great charm in his early polychrome portrait busts, and still exhibits delightful works. A group of Indian sculptors were topped by Cyrus E. Dallin (1860-   ) and Herman A. MacNeil (1866-   ) and varied their efforts from highly dramatic to more contemplative interpretations. Paul W. Bartlett (1865-1925), the "American Fremiet", excelled in not only animal subjects but in romantic reverberations of Michelangelo. Other animal sculptors were Anna Vaughn Hyatt Huntington (1876-   ), Edward Kemys (1843-1907), Edward C. Potter (1857-1923), A. P. Proctor (1862-   ), Solon Borglum (1868-1922) and Paul Manship (1885-   ) whose compositions, although perfect in craftsmanship, became more decoration than sculpture. James Earle Fraser (1876-   ) popularly known for his sculptures for coins and medals, exhibits a monumental quiet in all of his sculptured pieces, large or small.

Two famous sculptors, among others, grew out of the Academy into the Impressionism of Rodin, namely, George Gray Barnard (1863-1938), the founder of the Cloisters, now a branch of the Metropolitan Museum of Art, and Lorado Taft (1860-1936). Barnard's powerful figures showed his early training as a jeweler and engraver, but displayed monumental simplicity and an emotional rather than an intellectual concept. Taft was not only a sculptor of sound figures, some of colossal scale, and of large numbers of figures so interwoven that the sculpturesque mass was not lost, but was also a beloved teacher and lecturer. Both men left the endowment of a genuinely awakened appreciation of sculpture to patrons and students alike. Many other names are worthy of mention, but regardless of merit and the fact that their efforts are far scattered in place, subject and style, they exhibit the fundamentals of the plastic art as taught in Paris, Munich or in American schools whose teachers reflected the many academic and subsequent impressionist manifestations, especially those of Bourdelle and Maillol, who were transitional to more recent tendencies.

1926 to date. The works of present-day painters and sculptors are too comparatively recent for objective analysis or classification. Many of the names were well known before 1926. Among the sculptors who have been universally accepted are the following: Gaston Lachaise (1882-1935) following the symbols and semi-abstractions of French Post-Impressionism in an energetic full-bodied style; William Zorach, already mentioned as a painter, outstanding for his primitive simplicity and his directness of stone cutting. J. B. Flannagan (1898-1942), Alfeo Faggi (1885-　　), Heinz Warneke (1895-　　), Hugo Robus (1885-　　), Jo Davidson (1883-　　), Charles Rudy (1904-　　), Richard Davis (1904-　　), Mahonri Young (1877-　　), Malvina Hoffman 1887-　　), Hunt Diederich (1884-　　), Robert Laurent (1890-　　), José de Creeft (1884-　　), Louis Slobodkin (1903), Gertrude V. Whitney (　　-1942), Chaim Gross (1904-　　), Henry Kreis (1899-　　), Ahron Ben-Schmuel (1903-　　), Concetta Scaravaglione (1900-　　), Alexander Archipenko (1887-　　), Carl Milles (1875-　　), Merrill Gage (1892-　　), Donal Hord (1902-　　), and Alexander Calder (1870-　　) are known for all aspects of modernism from the mobiles and stabiles of the latter, wherein varieties of expressions of the dynamic forces of nature appear in plastics and metals, to earthy factuality in social subjects, or the profoundly idealistic concepts of reality in the works of Gage. Carl Walters (1883-　　) deserves special mention for continued excellence in glazed ceramic sculpture.

Present-day painters follow like manifestations in expressive forms ranging from cubist organizations to social subjects, the latter prevailing in more recent years, and representing all phases of the life of the American people from those stressing social propagandas in the works of William Gropper (1897-　　), the Soyer Brothers, Nicolai Cikovsky (1894-　　), and Benjamin Kopman (1887-　　) to the intellectual literalism of Charles Sheeler and the objective panoramas of Paul Sample (1896-　　). A typically American sense of fact, prevailing optomism, poise in the craft of painting, a strong sense of design, a sense of humor which is

at times satirical, and confidence in the individual idiom appears variously and frequently unanimously in the works of the following men not already cited: Reginald Marsh (1898-　　), Georgia O'Keefe (1887-　　), John Steuart Curry (1897-　　), Maurice Sterne (1877-　　), Kenneth Hayes Miller (1876-　　), Luigi Lucioni (1900-　　), John Carroll (1892-　　), George Biddle (1885-　　), Charles Demuth (1883-1935), Jack Levine (1915-　　), Alexander Brook (1898-　　), Charles Burchfield (1893-　　), Bernard Karfiol (1886-　　), Aaron Bohrod (1907-　　), Morris Kantor (1896-　　), Bryson Burroughs (1869-1934), Glenn O. Coleman (1877-1934), Henry E. Mattson (1887-　　), George Grosz (1893-　　), Yasuo Kuniyoshi (1893-　　), Jon Corbino (1905-　　), Frederic Taubes (1900-　　), Franklin C. Watkins (1894-　　), Peter Blume (1906-　　), Gladys R. Davis (1901-　　), Vaughn Flannery (1898-　　), Lauren Ford (1891-　　), Katherine Schmidt (1898-　　), Georgina Klitgaard (1893-　　), Francis Chapin (1899-　　), Doris Lee (1905-　　), Rockwell Kent (1882-　　), Waldo Pierce (1884-　　), Henry Varnum Poor (1888-　　), Fletcher Martin (1904-　　), Ward Lockwood (1894-　　), H. E. Schnakenberg (1892-　　), Arnold Blanche (1896-　　), Julian Levi (1874-　　), Ernest Fiene (1894-　　), Charles Hopkinson (1869-　　), Lamar Dodd (1909-　　), Grant Wood (1892-1942), Millard Sheets (1907-　　), Peter Hurd (1904-　　), Dan Lutz (1906-　　), Philip Evergood (1901-　　), Emil Ganso (1895-1941), Peppino Mangravite (1896-　　), Walt Kuhn (1880-　　), Max Weber (1881-　　), Paul Cadmus (1904-　　), Isabel Bishop (1902-　　) and Ivan Le Lorraine Albright (1897-　　), winner of the first medal for the best painting at the 1943 Victory Exhibition at the Metropolitan Museum of Art. Portrait painting other than that which has been done along with other subjects by the above mentioned men, remains in the hands of a score or so of Americans, among whom the names of Louis Betts (1873-　　), Leopold Seyffert (1877-　　), J. C. Johansen (1876-　　), and Wayman Adams (1883-　　), are outstanding.

Edward Bruce (1879-　　) was selected to lead the government project in art in 1933, and a few years later Holger Cahill took over, the government commissions being chiefly mural projects. The earlier mural styles of Benton, Kroll, Poor, Barry Faulkner (1881-　　), Eugene Savage (1883-　　), Ezra

Winter (1886-   ), Hugo Ballin (1879-   ), Conrad Buff (1886-   ), and Jessie Arms Botke (1883-   ) changed into what might be called a national style with Biddle, Sterne, Marsh, Curry and Boardman Robinson (1886-   ), leading the pace. Many of the above named painters such as Marsh, Cadmus, Sloan, Benton, Marin, Kuniyoshi, Curry, Kent and F. W. Benson are also outstanding printmakers of today, and to this assemblage should be added the names of John Taylor Arms (1877-   ), Thomas Handforth (1897-   ), Howard Cook (1901-   ), Robert Riggs (1896-   ), Stow Wengenroth (1906-   ), Adolph Dehm (1895-   ), Harry Sternberg (1904-   ), Wanda Gág (1893-   ), Mabel Dwight (1876-   ), Roi Partridge (1888-   ), and Peggy Bacon (1895-   ) among others who deserve mention. Among artists of animation, growing in number yearly, Walt Disney, who opened the Disney studio in 1923 ranks highest.

The National Academy today still stresses sound craftsmanship as its basis of selection by jury. Many who would not have been recognized formerly by the Academy are now members, such as Louis M. Eilsshemius (1864-   ). In opposition are the moderns such as were selected by the staff of the Whitney Museum of American Art, the opposition not existing in the fundamentals of craftsmanship, but primarily in subject matter and interpretation. It is impossible to properly characterize present-day tendencies, since no two painters are alike, and since all the years since 1776 have been the battlegrounds of conservatism vs. liberalism subjective vs. objective and romantic vs. realistic, unless one may do so by indicating the comparative freedom from technical limitations, the catholicism of patronage, and the fusion of what might be called significant vision with significant form whether it be introspective, intuitional or representationally factual. See EARLY AMERICAN ART; also American Federation of Arts, *Painters and Sculptors of Modern America*, 1942; Boswell, Peyton, *Modern American Painting*, 1939; Cahill, Holger, Ed., for New York World's Fair Exhibition, *American Art Today*, 1939; Cheney Martha C., *Modern Art in America*, 1939; La Follette, Suzanne, *Art in America*, 1929; Lipman, Jean, *American Primitive Painting*, 1942; Mellquist, J., *The Emergence of an American Art*, 1942; Peters, Harry T., *Currier and Ives*, 1942; St. Gaudens, Homer, *The American Artist and His Times*, 1941; Taft, Lorado, *History of American Sculpture*,

1925; Wehle, Harry B., *American Miniatures, 1730-1850*, 1937.   —A.W.M.

posy ring. See JEWELRY.

pot. *Cer.* Container of clay, or production of clay articles. See CERAMICS I.

pot furnace. See GLASS AND GLASS-MAKING.

potential value. A term coined to denote whatever latent values may be developed at any point by placing a visible accent there—as at the center of a circle. Its value lies in calling attention to the fact that aesthetic values are not always *created* from nothing by putting a spot in a certain place, but that a certain number of them are generated automatically by any line or spot that is set down on paper and are merely *developed* by the addition of other spots and lines. It is a concept that can be utilized in the solution of a variety of aesthetic problems. See Carl Thurston, *The Structure of Art.*   —C.T.

potne oeron. See PRIMITIVE ART.

pot-pourri. A musical medley, a flimsy construction of a series of melodies.

potter's wheel. Wheel on which pottery is formed or thrown by hand. See CERAMICS I.

pottery. See CERAMICS II.

pottery, Chinese. See the following terms: blue and white ware; body; bulb bowl; celadon; *Chien yao*; china porcelain; *ch'ui-ying wen*; *Chün yao*; *claire de lune*; clay; crackle; crazing; earthenware; egg-shell porcelain; *famille jaune*; *famille noire*; *famille rose*; *famille verte*; *Fat-shan Chün yao*; five-color ware; *flambe*; foot; granary urn; hare's fur glaze; hawthorn design; hill jar; *ju yao*; kaolin; *Ko yao*; *Kuangtung yao*; Kuan yao; *Lung-ch'üan yao*; *ming ch'i*; overglaze painting; partridge breast; peach bloom; petuntse; porcelain; pottery; reticulated; sagger; *sang-de-boeuf*; seven-color ware; *sha t'ai*; sherd; spur marks; three-color ware; *Ting yao*; *t'zu t'ai*; *Tz'u, Chou yao*; underglaze painting; CERAMICS II; CHINESE ARTS; also *Chinese Pottery of the Han, T'ang and Sung Dynasties*, Parish-Watson and Co., Inc., 1917; *Chinese Pottery and Porcelain*, R. L. Hobson, vols. I and II, 1915; *The Wares of the Ming Dynasty*, R. L. Hobson, 1923; *The Early Ceramic Wares of China*, A. L. Hetherington and R. L. Hobson, 1923; *The Later Ceramic Wares of China,* R. L. Hobson, 1925; *The George Eumorfopoulos Collection,* vols. I-VI.   —J.A.M.

pottery. For Japanese names, see the following: *Agano yaki; Akahada yaki; Akogi yaki; Arita yaki; Awata yaki; Banko yaki; Bizen yaki;* body; clay; crackle; crazing; *doki;* earthenware; egg-shell porcelain; *Etchuseto yaki;* foot; *Gojo yaki; Hagi yaki; haniwa;* hare's fur glaze; *Himejitōzan yaki; Hinnokōgi yaki; Hirado yaki; Hizen yaki; Iga yaki; Igeta yaki; Imari yaki; Imbe yaki; ishiyaki; Iwakurayama yaki; Izumo yaki; jiki; Kakiemon* ware; kaolin; *Karatsu yaki; Kinkazan yaki; Kiyomizu yaki; Kosobe yaki; Kusuura yaki; Kutani yaki;* litherage; *Temmoku yaki; Minpei yaki; Mishima yuki; Mushiake yaki; Nachayama yaki; Nagasaki* ware; *Odo yaki; Ofuke yaki; Onohara yaki; Ontō yaki; Oribe yaki;* overglaze painting; partridge breast glaze; porcelain pottery; *Raku yaki; Rakutōzan yaki;* reticulated; *Ryumon yaki;* sagger; *Sanda yaki; Satsuma* ware; *seiji; sekki; Seto yaki;* sherd; *Shidoro yaki; Shigamine yaki; Shigaraki yaki; Shino yaki; Shōdai yaki; Soma yaki;* spur marks; *suyaki; Tachikui yaki; Takatori yaki; Tanba yaki;* thread mark; *tōki; Tokoname yaki; Utakawa yaki; Wakakusa yaki; Yanagihara yaki; Yatsushiro yaki; Yoro yaki; Zeze yaki;* also *Catalogue of the Morse Collection of Japanese Pottery,* Edward S. Morse, Museum of Fine Arts, Boston, 1901; *Japanese Pottery, with Notes describing the Thoughts and Subjects employed in Its Decoration,* James L. Bowes, 1890; *Japan Porcelain,* Egan Mew.   —J.A.M.

pottery wheel method. See terra cotta sculpture, direct method.

pounce. (1) The perforated design used in pouncing (q.v.). (2) The powder used in pouncing (q.v.).

pouncing. The technique of dusting powder through punched holes which define the outlines of a design.

pozzolana. A volcanic clay or cement has been given the name pozzolana, because of the presence of such material near Naples at Pozzuoli. It is found also in the Islands of the Greek Archipelago and along the Rhine. Such cements were probably used in the modelled figures and reliefs classified as stucco. They are made up of easily decomposable silicates formed by the action of volcanic fires. Mixed with lime, they provide a cement that is slow to harden and moderately strong.   —G.L.S.

pp. See NOTATION.

practical arts. Generic term for the following fields of study: agriculture, domestic art (syn. *homemaking*), commercial art, and industrial art, all of which are characterized by "practical" activities used in everyday life.

practical jokes. See American folk forms, in literature.

prägnanz, law of. See PSYCHOLOGY OF DRAWING AND PAINTING.

prāsāda. See INDIAN ART.

prayer modes. See JEWISH MUSIC.

prayer niche. See mihrab.

prayer rug. Used by the followers of Mohammet. Design usually includes a representation of a mosque or place of public worship, showing the mihrab which is a niche in the wall of the mosque, so located that when the worshipper prostrates himself before it he will be prostrating himself toward Mecca. See ISLAMIC ART.   —B.E.J.

pre-classic dance forms. *Pre-classic* is a contemporary term used to designate certain ancient dance forms. These dances were "pre-classic" in the sense that they antedated and influenced the growth of the classic ballet as a theatre art. They existed originally among the countless ancient dances of the common people of Europe and were performed in the villages, fields, and vineyards.

The pre-classic dances are distinguished from other folk-dance forms by the fact that they were adopted by European courts, refined and formalized until they constituted the court ball program. This new status led to their further function as basic material for the early ballet. As another result of the shift from village to palace, the music of these dances became the substance of the instrumental suite, first written for court ball accompaniment and eventually growing into the classic sonata and symphony. The dances usually included in the "pre-classic" group are *pavane, galliard, allemande, courante, sarabande, gigue, minuet, gavotte, bourrée, rigaudon, passepied, chaconne,* and *passacaglia.*   —J.G.

pre-Columbian art. See AMERICAN AB-ORIGINAL AMERICAN ART.

precentor. See JEWISH MUSIC.

precision drawing. See drawing.

predella. See altar; altarpiece.

pregnance, law of. See PSYCHOLOGY OF DRAWING AND PAINTING.

PREHISTORIC ART. In the earliest art, as in much of the art of the present, the student is frequently mystified by its significance. If in the latter, one feels that rich variations of the human mind are somehow revealed, in the former, one searches not so much for the dawn of aesthetic consciousness as for a record, and it is a brilliant one, of man's rise from savagery. Gordon Childe speaks of two great stages of development, that of a food-gathering and again of a food-producing economy. Naturally the arts reflect these activities. In a general way they correspond to the paleolithic and neolithic divisions of the anthropologist but since the rate of development as between the peoples of one part of the earth and those of another has been far from constant, varying in fact over thousands of years, a division by date is impossible.

Evidences of man's earliest activities are revealed by implements of flint which are widely distributed over the world. The beautiful leaf-shaped blades found in the rock-shelter of Solutré near Mâcon, France call for such exquisite refinement in the chipping that they might well be classified as works of art. Much earlier but cruder examples of flint chipping have been found at Chelles near Paris. This site has given the name **Chellean** to that period in the development of early man which some scholars believe extends back to 100,000 B.C. The flint industry extended into the age of metal as flint knives from Egypt and poinards from Scandinavia testify. Although there is considerable uniformity in the development of these implements, in America a peculiar type of flint-arrow was used quite unlike European or Asian examples. Those discovered at **Folsom** (q.v.), New Mexico are thought to date around 10,000 B.C.

The arts of representation seem to have had their origin with **Cro-Magnon** man probably some 25,000 years ago. Considerable credence may be given to the theory, held by Édouard Piette, that man's first attempts were made in fashioning a likeness from a free standing object. Later he turned to the more symbolic medium of drawing. Certainly the skill involved in the earliest sculptures surpasses that of the enigmatic signs painted on caves of equally early date. But the fact that from the very beginning there are various approaches to art forms gives rise to many problems. How complex are the motives which prompt man to visual expression? How dependent is any particular form of expression on qualities of race or outside influence? Is a work unskillful because it only approaches an ideal which has not yet been attained or because an indifference or decadence has set in Baldwin Brown who has made a penetrating study of the art of prehistoric times from the point of view of aesthetic theory concludes that always the initial movements in what are to become the arts are non-artistic. This element enters afterwards as a regulative agency. The various motives may spring from some instinct such as that of imitation, from pride, as in personal adornment, from some practical end to which magic and superstition have been brought or merely from the desire to convey information. As these forces each produce a result peculiar to itself and are present in the nature of man independent of each other it is futile to search for priority. In the acquisition of skill, however, and in the sharpening of the aesthetic instinct, there must be a continuity or evolution within each cultural unit.

The best work of Cro-Magnon man seems to have been largely prompted by the love of imitation but was soon modified by other forces. A female figure found at **Willendorf,** Austria, carved in the round form limestone and some three inches high, is representative of a large group in which the characteristics of sex are so exaggerated as to indicate a fertility cult. A similarly proportioned figure, but in relief and eighteen inches high, was found on the wall of a rock-shelter at Laussel in the Dordogne, France. Here she holds the horn of a bison which one is tempted to say suggests the crescent moon. Nearby was represented a male figure in profile treated with no fanciful or mystical suggestion. He wears a girdle.

But it was in the presentation of animals that this art reached full maturity. The best examples are concentrated in the Dordogne just north of the Pyrenees and also just south in Santander province at **Altamira** and Castillo in Spain. Osborn gives 16,000 B.C. as the approximate date for this art which is distinguished from the earlier work just discussed by the term **Magdalenian** from the rock-shelter of La Madeleine along the Vézère River. This art is outstanding for its realism and some three hundred specimens of animals have been identified. The polychromy has been preserved by the deposits of lime which have seeped through the rock. The position of many in low dark recesses where they could be seen only with difficulty and the fact that the animals are often represented wounded by darts, suggests a superstitious origin connected with success in the hunt. The discovery of numerous incised drawings on stag horns, for which it is difficult to find a use, has led to the belief that these also were connected with some form of magic as sceptres for ritual occasions.

Further evidences of ritual and magic occur in representations of men dressed as animals as in a mimetic dance. A well known wall painting from Cogul near Lérida, Spain, represents clothed women surrounding, as in a dance, a small figure of a nude man. Here, however, there is manifested an entirely different aesthetic approach. This gives rise to baffling questions of relationships between sites classified by Obermaier as **Capsian**, from a place in Tunis, and the shelters mentioned above. Perhaps we have in these later Spanish examples evidence of a new migration from Africa and it would seem likely that the representation of the bow in Capsian art indicates a later date. North of the Pyrenees at Mas d'Azil there are indications of decadence. Imitation no longer seems important but now rather the emphasis seems to be on a symbolic expression for information. This is the approach which would lead to picture writing, hieroglyphics and a literature. Such an advance, however, would mark the more settled conditions of neolithic times.

Researches of recent years have greatly emphasized the importance of pre-historic Africa (see AFRICAN NEGRO ART). While Northern Europe was under a layer of ice and the Pyrenees were capped with glaciers, the Sahara enjoyed abundant rainfall. Rock engravings from Kef Messioner, Algeria and in Fezzan depict with the same extraordinary skill of Cro-Magnon drawings, numerous animals requiring woods and lush meadows for grazing. Closer parallels exist between examples of Capsian art in Spain and early Bushmen paintings from Rhodesia. It will be remembered that the Bushmen are the last survivals of the earliest peoples to have inhabited Africa. It is impossible to develop an accurate chronology between racial types, nor can we now believe that all art had its origin in a single source. Certainly large migrations followed climatic changes, some races have disappeared, others have fused into a stock which gradually evolved a new culture in accordance with the advances of civilization.

Nothing is more convincing of the penetration of eastern peoples into the west than the series of huge stones for burial and ceremonial purposes which extend from Asia Minor to the British Isles. There is also evidence that the custom spread eastwards to India. Of these monuments **Stonehenge** in England is the most famous. It consists of a great circle or cromlech about an altar stone arranged so as to tell the season of the year by a cast shadow; a principle similar to that of the sun dial. Astronomers have been able to date this monument around 1600 B.C.

The earlier development of time measurement in Egypt is emphasized when we recall that the calendar is thought to have been established there in 4236 B.C. The neolithic cultures of Egypt, especially the Gerzian of the upper Nile, are of considerable interest. Childe speaks of the Egyptians as the earliest farmers. Progress in spiritual life is indicated by the graves in which numerous amulets have been found. Examples of bulls' heads and falcons indicate the firm establishment of totemic clans. Of especial interest is a tomb at Hierakonpolis containing wall paintings. These are in the style of early decorated pots but announce the sepulchral frescos of later times (see EGYPTIAN ART).

Always there is the problem of foreign influences. Mesopotamian inspiration is evident in many of the late neolithic finds of Egypt and it is likely that the use of bronze came from that source (see MESOPOTAMIAN ART). Gold was the first metal to be used by man and beads of hammered copper have been found in Egypt which must date as early as 5000 B.C. but they were not fashioned by the aid of fire.

It is the pottery, however, which is of the most importance in determining early cultural centers and their connections. The study of these objects reveals certain parallel tendencies between Egypt, Sumer and the Indus region which argue for direct contacts between these important groups. It would be risky to assume definite dates for such relationships before the third millennium. What is important is that we have the roots of three great civilizations, each with definite and individual characteristics, each a cultural unit derived from a mixed race in similar climatic conditions, and each making some contribution to the other.

From the material which has come to light up to the present time it would seem that a certain degree of priority might be given in the art of pottery, possibly even the invention of the potter's wheel, to a region in the upper reaches of the Tigris and Euphrates valleys extending westwards even to the coast of Northern Syria. Some of the finest pottery of antiquity comes from Tell Halaf. This is hand made, has thin walls fired to a considerable heat and is painted with conventional designs. One representation has been found of a man and a chariot. There also occur the winged solar disk so characteristic of Egypt and the double axe designs which are associated with Crete. There is, however, no evidence of the use of metal and the culture must belong to the fourth millennium or earlier.

The development of culture in Crete which is now thought to have been. the center of early Mediterranean art extending even to the shores of Spain would certainly have been later. Sometime perhaps scholars will be able to decipher the tablets of baked clay which survive in Crete in great numbers. One found at Phaestos is unique in that each little picture of the pictographic inscription was pressed in by its own special seal.

But to return to the earlier centers in Mesopotamia we find that of the several sites in the highlands which have come to light within the last few years those of the al-'Ubaid peoples are especially significant. It is believed that these peoples migrated south as the rich delta lands became available and formed the stock from which the great Sumerian civilization sprang. Their pottery is allied to the finds at Susa belonging to the first of the two distinct neolithic periods which have been unearthed there. This ware exhibits considerable ceramic skill and may have been turned on a slow wheel.

The ware from Susa may be slightly earlier, 4000-3500 B.C. The designs are of the greatest interest being undoubtedly magical in content. They consist of circles, wave patterns, the maltese cross, conventionalized human figures and birds. The stylizations and shapes suggest an origin in basketry. Yet they are close to the abstractions which an accomplished culture always makes in order to better reflect the essential quality of the object as a

symbol. We see in these painted pots the forerunners of the complicated symbols engraved upon seals of a later date and signs which eventually were converted into elements of writing.

If it has not been possible to distinguish precisely all the various stages which led up to the great civilizations of the Near East and the Indus Valley certainly the arts reflect definite contacts of one with the other. In the case of China and again in the Americas the problem is much more vague. Anthropologists have evidences of the existence of man in China from remote times but no art forms have been discovered prior to late neolithic times and these suggest the painted pottery of the Near East. Nevertheless the spiral and strange zigzag patterns have a distinctive quality of their own. Large quantities of such vessels have recently been unearthed in Kansu province. It is not a little bewildering to find just a hint of this ware in some of the pottery of the Americas. A small rain-god from the Pan Shan Find, Kansu province suggests the kacinas of the Hopi Indians; a burial jar from the Diaguite culture of Argentina has the same conventionalized finger ornament as a jar from the Ma Chang Find of the same province. But of these finds the unpainted tripod form alone announces the Chinese aesthetic ideal of the great Shang dynasty. The origin of the extraordinary accomplished and highly symbolic designs of this historic period, 1765-1123 B.C. are veiled in obscurity.

It is intriguing to follow some thin and disconnected parallels of these exquisite Shang motifs in the Americas but any attempt at definite conclusions as to prehistoric contacts around the Pacific area is impossible. There were probably many migrations into North America and thence down to the southern hemisphere. Unique in prehistoric sculpture are the stone seated figures found along a strip extending from Georgia to the Mississippi. They have round moon-like faces indicating a ceremonial image. There are many indications of Lunar worship among the American aborigines (see AMERICAN ABORIGINAL ART) some of the motives as the double axe (q.v.) suggest forms used elsewhere, others indicate a completely isolated evolution. It is strange that the potter's wheel so well known in China before the Shang dynasty was not used in the western hemisphere, yet bronze casting was well known among the Incas of Peru.

Whence came that art of bronze casting so magnificently developed by the Chinese? One must certainly take into consideration stylistic relationships between the bronzes of the Ordos region west of Peiping on the border of Mongolia and finds from Luristan in Western Persia or even closer connections with Scythian and earlier objects from South Russia. It can only be supposed that racial migrations carried the technique and an instinctive feeling for the designs across the steppes of Siberia into Mongolia. However, the migrations were not always to the east. We know that the Celts at one time inhabited the Black Sea region and in their turn carried this style westwards even to Ireland. Just what was added and what was lost in these migrations is impossible to say. The **Luristan** finds are not necessarily earlier than those from the Kuban in South Russia and yet it would seem likely that the art originated in Persia. In these objects we see how the old stone age interest in animals has given way to the geometric abstractions of the new stone age and then how it was rendered with all the aesthetic force of the discovery of a new medium superbly adapted to the expression of the symbolic ideas. Human headed monsters and grotesque combinations of parts of different animals are molded into masterpieces of pierced design. The further away from Persia the objects are the more intricate become the patterns.

In Europe there are two important centers connected with the progress of this animal style westwards. They are **Hallstatt** in Austria and **La Tène** in Switzerland. There are evidences that the Dorians who invaded Greece from the North before 1000 B.C. had been in contact with this culture and, of course, in historic times Greece was constantly aware of the peoples of the Danube and Black Sea region. Thus we see how complicated and uncertain becomes the problem of tracing stylistic connections.

The **Viking style** (q.v.) in Scandinavia together with the zoomorphic ornament of the Celts certainly received the basis for its peculiar forms as the result of racial migrations. Although south Russia served as a center of dissemination it is impossible to trace precisely the extent of the creative accomplishment there.

Perhaps the most remarkable pre-historic bronzes are the **Luhrs** or trumpets from Denmark. These are occasionally eight feet in length but are riveted together, precision being obtained by hammering. It is likely that they date from the iron age. Mention should be made of two gold horns discovered in Denmark but no longer extant. These were incised with designs which have been variously connected with the East. One, however, had a runic (q.v.) inscription which indicates a date of about the 5th cent.

From the above it will be seen that the student of prehistoric art is confronted with problems beyond his grasp. However, were it not for that quality, unique in man, of expressing his ideas visually, our knowledge of the rise of civilization would be more limited than it is. Every year produces some new evidence bearing on the process. When we recall that the entire subject does not antedate the 19th cent. and, one might almost say 1862 when M'sieur Lartet began his excavations in Southern France, one is impressed with the strides that have been made. Especially important have been the discoveries in the Near East and the Indus Valley since 1920. Of the enigmatic sculptures of Easter Island and other problems too numerous to mention, one may only hope that the clues may be forthcoming. But this much the arts of prehistoric times reveal; man has roamed over the surface of the earth for thousands upon thousands of years and in his evolution from a lower form of life to a civilized human being the need for art has ennobled and quickened the change. See Andersson, Johan G., *Children of the Yellow Earth,* 1934; Brown, G. Baldwin, *The Art of the Cave Dweller,* 1928; Brunton, G., and Caton-Thompson, G., *The Badarian Civilization,* 1928; Burkitt, Miles C., *Prehistory,* 1921 and *South Africa's Past in Stone and Paint,* 1928; Capitan, L., Breuil, H., and Peyrony, D., *La Caverne de Font-de-Gaume aux Eyzies (Dordogne),* 1910; Cartailhac, É., and Breuil, H., *La Caverne d'Altamira à Santillane prés Santander (Espagne),* 1906; Childe, V. Gordon, *New Light on the Most Ancient East,* 1934; Contenau, Georges, *Manuel d'Archéologique Orientale depuis les Origines jusqu'a l'Époque d'Alexandre,* 1927 ff.; Déchlette, Joseph, *Manuel d'Archéologie Préhistorique Celtique et Gallo-Romaine,* 1908-13; Ebert, Max, *Reallexikon der Vorgeschichte,* 1924-32; Frankfort, Henri, *Cylinder Seals,* 1939 and *Studies in the Early Pottery of the Near East,* 1925-27; Frobenius, Leo and Obermaier, Hugo, *Hádschra Máktuba,* 1925; Godard, André, *Les Bronzes du Luristan,* 1931; Grosse, Ernst, *The Beginnings of Art,* 1907; Hall, H. R., and Woolley, Sir C. L., *Ur Excavations, vol. I. Al-Ubaid,* 1927;

Hall, H. R., *The Civilization of Greece in the Bronze Age,* 1928; Hersfeld, Ernst E., *Die Vorgeschichtlichen Töpfereien von Samarra,* 1930; Hoernes, M., and Menghin, O., *Urgeschichte der Bildenden Kunst in Europa,* 1925; Kühn, Herbert, *Die Kunst der Primitiven,* 1923 and *Die Malerei der Eiszeit,* 1922; Lartet, É. A., and Christy, H., *Reliquiae Aquitanicae,* 1875; Marshall, Sir John Hubert, *Mohenjo-daro and the Indus Civilization,* 1931; Obermaier, Hugo, *El Hombre Fósil,* 1925; Oppenheim, Baron Max von, *Tell Halaf,* 1933; Osborn, Henry F., *Men of the Old Stone Age,* 1919; Petrie, Sir William M., *Prehistoric Egypt,* 1920; Piette, Édouard, *L'Art Pendant l'Âge du Renne,* 1907; Rostovtsev, Mikhail Ivanovich, *The Animal Style in South Russia and China,* 1929; Shetelig, Haakon, *Scandinavian Archaeology,* 1937; Speiser, E. A., *Mesopotamian Origins,* 1930; Thompson, John E., *Archeology of South America,* 1936; Wace, A. J. B., and Thompson, M. S., *Prehistoric Thessaly,* 1912; Wilson, Thomas, *Prehistoric Art,* 1898. PERIODICALS: *Anthropologie; Antiquity; Fornvännen; Ipek* (Jahrbuch für prähistorische und ethnographische Kunst) ; *Man* (Royal Anthropological Institute) ; *Prähistorische Zeitschrift; Revue archéologique; Société d'anthropologie de Paris, Bulletin,* 1873.

—W.R.H.

pre-Khmer art. See INDIAN ART.

preliminary matter. *Book.* The pages of a book or the matter on them preceding the body of the work. Usually numbered in Roman numerals. —H.E.S.

prelude. *Mus.* An overture or introduction to a musical drama; an instrumental composition such as a fugue, suite, or partita.

preparation. See PSYCHOLOGY OF ART.

Pre-Raphaelitism. A movement in late 19th cent. English art and literature, referring especially to painting. From the point of view of form, pre-Raphaelite painting was based on mutually conflicting doctrines, of which one or the other alternately prevailed. Often the artists imitated Florentine *quattrocento* (q.v.) painting, and especially such predecessors of Raphael as Gozzoli and Botticelli, and from this they derive their name. They considered art before Raphael more sincere and genuine, less artificial, mannered, and formalized than it was thereafter. More frequently, however, they merely emulated the spirit of the *quattrocento,* conceiving their forms with a naturalistic and almost photographic vision. In either case, they opposed all academic rules and conventions of drawing, composition, and color, which in England were then based upon Raphael, Reynolds, the Carracci, and antique sculpture.

From the point of view of content, the pre-Raphaelites were sentimentalists and popular-romanticists who preferred to depict moral, religious, historical, or anecdotal subjects, or literary illustrations,—especially of Shakespeare and Dante. Holman Hunt's *Light of the World* is a good example, wherein naturalistic form is employed in the service of a sentimental and popularized idealism. Hunt's *Hireling Shepherd* and *Scapegoat* and his scenes from Shakespeare are also typical. His *Finding of Christ in the Temple* and *Christ Among the Doctors* illustrate the pre-Raphaelite belief that in depicting a historical scene the artist must be true to all details of our scientific knowledge concerning the event. He went to Palestine to discover needed facts of costume and setting for such pictures.

A distinction is made between the pre-Raphaelite movement and the **Pre-Raphaelite Brotherhood** (P. R. B.). The Brotherhood was founded in 1848 by Holman Hunt, Sir John E. Millais, and Dante Gabriel Rossetti under the stimulus and inspiration of Ford Madox Brown, who was never himself a member of the Brotherhood. The founders were soon joined by two other minor painters, a sculptor of no great success, and a writer, William Michael Rossetti, brother of the more illustrious, painter-poet Dante Gabriel Rossetti. The members of the Brotherhood defined the aims of pre-Raphaelitism, held several exhibitions, were vigorously defended by Ruskin, and gradually drifted apart in the late 1850's. Individually Hunt and Brown continued the original aims of the Brotherhood throughout their lives; Millais went over to the academy, Rossetti gradually developed a very personal idealism, a little less photographic than the others and more similar to Botticelli. New followers soon began to imitate one or another of the original Brotherhood and, as representatives of the movement, continued pre-Raphaelitism to the end of the century. The most notable is Rossetti's pupil Sir Edward Burne-Jones. Others include Frederick Sandys, J. M. Strudwick, Spencer Stanhope, Evelyn de Morgan, Arthur Hughes, Bryam Shaw, William Windus, Matthew Lawless, Charles Collins, and W. S. Burton. See ENGLISH ART. —L.D.L.

pre-Romanesque art. See Ottonian art; GERMAN ART.

presbyacousis. The progressive loss of hearing in the upper register due to age. From early childhood up to about middle age a normal individual under favorable circumstances may hear tones as high as 20,000 vibrations per second. From middle age this upper limit of hearing falls progressively so that at the age of 70 under equally favorable circumstances he can not hear tones above 4,000; that is, there has been a gradual change in his hearing of tone quality by the progressive loss of four-fifths of the overtone register which he could hear in the prime of life. "This finding is of almost unbelievable significance for the hearing of music, as it is also to some extent for speech. In this loss of capacity for discrimination of tone quality, age has no respect for professional standing, training, or knowledge. It is a physical law in that the hearing curve represents the degeneration in the harp structure of the ear. This specific law is in accordance with the general biological law of degeneration; namely, that degeneration of function begins with the latest acquired and most delicate structures.

"It is comforting to know that the register which remains practically normal is the region in which the fundamental of most of our musical tones occur and within which speech sounds are most significantly differentiated. The loss comes upon us so gradually that we make corresponding adaptations in hearing and would perhaps not be aware of it in ordinary experience, radical as it is.

"I confess to feeling a little like a bull in a china shop in bringing this law to the attention of artists who are enjoying the rich musical life in old age. The greatest comfort lies in the realization that our subjective hearing, as in the case of deaf musicians, still plays a very important role." (From *Music Educators Journal*, May, 1938.) See C. C. Bunch, "Age Variations in Auditory Acuity" *Archives of Otolaryngology*, vol. 9, 1929, pp. 625-636; N. H. Kelley, "Study in Presbycousis; Auditory Loss with Increasing Age and Its Effect on Perception of Music and Speech," *Archives of Otolaryngology*, vol. 29, March, 1939, pp. 506-513; National Health Survey 1935-36, Hearing Study Series Bulletin 6, "Sex Differences and Age Variations in Hearing Loss in Relation to Stage of Deafness"; Division of Public Health Methods, National Institute of Health, U. S. Public Health Service, Washington, D. C., 1938.   —C.E.S.

presentation (L. *praesens*, that is before one, in sight or at hand). Sensory appearance; exhibiting or being exhibited to sense-perception; serving or ability to serve as a stimulus to sensory experience. One of the two modes by which works of art are transmitted to the mind of the observer or appreciator; the other being *suggestion* (q.v.). In a painting, lines, light and dark areas, and colors are *presented* or *presentative,* while associated meanings, things represented, etc., are suggested. Thus a work of art may contain both presented and suggested factors.
                                                          —T.M.

pressing. *Cer.* Process of squeezing clay in molds to form ceramics. See CERAMICS I.

Priapus. The Hellenistic god of the male generative power.

primary colors. See COLOR.

prime interval. See interval.

Prime Minister. See ORIENTAL MUSIC.

priming. See ground (1).

"primitive", American. See EARLY AMERICAN ART.

PRIMITIVE ART. It is unfortunate that the term primitive has been vulgarized into one of the vagaries of expression with which the vocabulary of art is filled. One speaks of "the primitives" to indicate a school in painting which developed just prior to the renaissance interest in space. Or again it is customary to refer to various phases of the work of the folk artist as primitive. Formerly it usually carried some note of condemnation but more recently the expression has come to convey an element of emotional sincerity. This indicates a keener understanding of the nature of art and leads to the more precise use of the term followed here. Primitive society is one in which the conventions, and individual acts dependent upon them, are based not on purely physical phenomena but rather upon superstition. This results at times in a passionate appeal to a protective spirit. Primitive art as a reflection of this society disregards physical accuracy and, although following established traditions, has an intuitive, elementary and mystical existence. As primitive man participates more than civilized man in natural phenomena so his art is instinctive rather than intellectual.

The appreciation of this quality is of recent development. Of course in the 18th cent., Europe was intrigued by the idea of the noble savage and again in the nineteenth century, the desire to escape from the artificialities of civilization made the South Sea Islands idyllic retreats of romance, but only with the 20th cent. did the mind of primitive man, and hence his art, come to have a real significance. This interest was largely aroused as a result of Bergson's philosophical writings in which he placed emphasis on instinctive reactions rather than upon factual knowledge. Again the increasing interest in psychology has produced attempts to discover parallels in the development of the child and the development of the race, which has caused primitive man to come under closer observation. As in the study of pre-historic man, whom primitive man only vaguely resembles, great progress in understanding has been made in recent years. Whether an interest in these related things has developed a taste for the art, or a realization of the art has caused these interests, is a futile question. Each is a part of the other.

But are the factors which lay at the source of primitive art still active in the mind of civilized man? Here we have a divergence of opinion among ethnologists. Lévy-Bruhl, a foremost exponent of the French school, sums up the situation. He says, "Do the collective representations of the communities in question arise out of higher mental functions identical with our own, or must they be referred to a mentality which differs from ours to an extent yet to be determined?" It is this latter supposition that he has tried to analyze, while the English scholars under the influence of Taylor, whose great work *Primitive Culture* appeared in 1871, have pursued the former. Lévy-Bruhl feels that the English school of anthropology in trying to show the relation between "savage" and "civilized" mentality, and to *explain* it, has been greatly hindered. Franz Boas, so prominent among American scholars, suffers the same criticism. Perhaps our reactions to primitive art could furnish an important clue to this question. The difficulty here lies in a lack of free spontaneous emotion which is especially characteristic of civilized peoples. But is it not significant that the modern artist has found in recent years, magnificent inspiration in the art of the savage?

Yet however varied may be the fundamental traits of the mind it must be obvious to all that different peoples react very differently to the same phenomena. The individual is certainly conditioned by the society to which he belongs and we can understand the art of any society better if we can follow its historical evolution. But this is never completely available. Obviously there are other conditions which must be taken into consideration. Environment, physiological, psychological and social factors all have an important bearing on ideas and in these there is great variation. Yet notwithstanding this, it is the general similarities in widely scattered areas and peoples which is astounding. This gives rise to the feeling of a unity in the human race but also raises the difficult question, when similar forms exist, of parallel developments or contacts through migration. Evolution of art forms has by no means followed a single formula. The study of peoples and even civilizations emphatically reveals many survivals, that is, ideas which were once of use and persist long after they have lost their usefulness, many mixtures of both retarded and advanced ideas, and many concepts which can only lead those who follow them into a blind valley. Perhaps this latter is true of primitive peoples, yet all societies seem to have passed through that stage and the solution has not yet been found.

In any event it is obvious that the aesthetic reactions of primitive man are limited by the knowledge at his disposal, and primitive man everywhere has not learned to view physical data objectively. He does not think logically, though he may have a complicated process of reasoning. His mind is made up of logical and prelogical elements which are subject to what Lévy-Bruhl has called the "law of participation". To the primitive there is a mystical element in every existing object and he, himself, is but a helpless part of a great spiritual entity. This concept suggests the much used term animism. Although the precise meaning of this word is subject to controversy it is at any rate the key to primitive art. Frazer's magnificent work the *Golden Bough* is filled with examples which illustrate this characteristic. It is perhaps inaccurate to assert that the primitive imagines in all forms of natural phenomena exactly the same elements, "souls", "spirits", "intentions", which they themselves have experienced, but there is no denying his certainty of a pervasive spirit. Many peoples believe in a multiplicity of souls and

Lévy-Bruhl feels that the concept of the "soul" appears only in peoples of a relatively advanced type. Earlier, in accordance with the principle of participation elaborated by Lévy-Bruhl, an individual felt himself mystically united with the animal or vegetable species which became his **totem**. He may have felt this kinship in many instances as a "dream-soul", a "forest-soul" and so on. This authority objects to the concept that, "One and the same soul" manifests itself as "life on the one side and phantom on the other". That, to him, is too simple an explanation and does not take into account his theory of prelogical mentality. According to his general law of participation, the primitive has no objection to contradiction, i.e., a person may be two things at once. Hence, to quote Lévy-Bruhl again, "The individual, while living participates in the *kra* that inhabits him, that is, he to a certain extent is this *kra,* and at the same time he is not ... At the moment of death, this participation comes to an end."

To the primitive there is no insuperable barrier separating the dead from the living. Everyone is aware of the great amount of attention paid to the dead by all peoples, particularly in the great ancient civilizations of Egypt and China. The persistence of basic ideas and practices in China makes a study of Chinese civilization especially illuminating. J. M. de Groot's *The Religious System of China* is a valuable document for the study of the primitive mind, yet China is recognized as producing one of the most cultured of civilizations. The belief of the mingling of the dead with the living is part of the general concept of the spirit world which must be grasped as a preliminary towards understanding the art.

This is because of the tangible quality of art in which there may at the same time exist a symbol of an intangible element, or, even more positive than that, in which the spirit may actually be embodied. To treat in detail the variations which result from the general attitude described above is beyond the scope of the present study. When, however, it is understood that the spirit of the dead may reside in a tree, in an altar, or in a statue, one begins to grasp the significance given to these things. Again when it be understood that a representation actually had the vital quality of the thing it represented, it takes on a new meaning. The chief motive in the creation of art forms was to appease the spirits, either those of the phenomena of nature or those of one's ancestors,

for man is in need of their favors. He does this by giving to each spirit a material object where it may reside, and thus, in venerating the object, he is in reality placating the spirit. This object is called a **fetish**.

The ability to partake in mystic fashion of the essence of the animal or vegetable species whose name he bears is the basis of the concept of the **totem**. Each totem is mystically bound to a strictly defined locality and becomes a powerful social force for it holds a group together. One must not believe that the ancestor of the totemic group was exactly like the appearance of the animal by the same name. They may have been mythical animals which had a mystic share of both the animal and the human nature. The feeling of unity within the social group was very strong, and this is important in so far as it did not allow the individual freedom to create an art form as a personal variation of the symbol. An awareness of the sacredness of the group, of the established ritual and symbolism of the art forms was often learned by long and arduous discipline to which each member of the tribe must be subjected.

Fertility cults, both of nature and human, are of universal importance and are connected with solar and lunar worship. All peoples have felt a kinship between man and nature which has resulted in an anthropomorphic attitude towards nature. That is, the thought arises that various spirits are the off-spring of more important deities and usually the first great union was that of Heaven and Earth. In concepts such as this involving a narrative theme folklore is peculiarly rich. The visual representation was more impressive as a specific symbol although narrative incidents of great complexity were often developed. These are sometimes so stylized that interpretation is possible only to those familiar with the theme. In any case a precise significance for any art form is an extremely risky supposition.

The oldest symbols, no doubt, represented the great forces of nature: the solar disk, the alternating light and dark cycles of the moon, the elements of air and water depicted by birds and fishes or wavy lines. Eventually came the idea of space and direction as indicated by the equal armed cross. Symbols of life, generation, and divinity were woven into textiles and baskets and painted on pottery. No doubt a feeling for greater vitality, a dynamic forcefulness, resulted in the forms of the spiral, the swastika and the so-called

Greek fret. The swastika has been spoken of as the symbol of the sun's movements. It is probably indicative of a combination of ideas, such as the cross of direction and the rays of the sun. Certainly it is one of the most universally used and enduring of symbols. There is a kinship between it and the whorl although this latter symbol was frequently shaded in alternate light and dark, suggesting the phases of the moon or, as in China and Japan, divided into one dark and one light section indicative of the *Yin* and *Yang*, or male and female principle.

The evolution and interpretation of the two basic Chinese motifs, the *lei wen* and *t'ao t'ieh* are extremely important for they represent the furthest development of two generalized primitive concepts, the one having primarily to do with the forces of nature, the other with the forces of life. They both became highly abstract cosmological symbols and perhaps furnish the basis for an understanding of the devious and mystical symbols connected with the moon. (See Hentze, Carl, *Mythes et symboles lunaires* [Chine, ancienne, civilisations anciennes de l'Asie]; also Hentze, Carl, *Objets rituels, croyances et dieux de la Chine antique de l'Amérique*). Hentze has brilliantly displayed how the well known **glutton motif** reveals the lunar cycles. In swallowing a figure it stands for night and obscurity and in ejecting it forth it stands for birth and regeneration. This motif is popular not only in the bronzes of ancient China, and in the art of pre-Columbian America but survives with perhaps a different meaning in the sculpture of the Middle Ages in Europe. Again the urge to represent disconnected parts of animals as though they had been bitten off would seem a part of this same concept. This also occurs in the motives of medieval art, a survival, no doubt, from the barbaric style of Northern Europe into which many aesthetic forms penetrated from the Near East.

It has been said that Egypt invented plant design and Mesopotamia subjected the animal kingdom to art. We have now learned that any priority of this sort is relatively unimportant since the real source is an instinctive feeling within mankind. Goodyear has brought out some surprising relationships as regards Egypt in his *Grammar of the Lotus* and Frankfort's recent work *Cylinder Seals* is revealing as to the richness of animal symbolism in Mesopotamia. Yet the source of cosmological symbols remains a mystery. Specific animals are related to certain forces, but in this there is naturally great variation probably depending for the most part on the predominance of certain animals in certain regions. One thinks of the Chinese symbols of the tortoise, red bird, dragon and tiger for the four points of the compass, the four seasons, the four elements and even four organs of the body (See SYMBOLISM IN FAR EASTERN ART). Again, one recalls the lion of Babylon or the eagle of Egypt as solar symbols, the bull in Crete as the lunar sign, though in Egypt he at times represents the sun, and the complicated symbolism of the serpent. Never in primitive thought is this considered evil. The rabbit, the bear, and the tiger have all been thought of as lunar animals. It was relationship such as these which developed the signs of the Zodiac. The imagination, no doubt, evolved fantastic creatures, chimeras, sphinxes, garudas and others, in order to combine several ideas in one symbol. The Persian esp. favored such combinations. The **hippolectryon**, a combination of cock and horse, must have been a solar sign. The **bird and serpent** is another important combination very generally used. It is esp. featured in the plumed serpent of the Mayans and is related, of course, to the Chinese dragon and the medieval basilisk. Finally, there is the symbol of the tree with its many implications.

When the superiority of man and the nobility of his form becomes recognized, primitive art is at an end, yet this has not been a gradual evolution. One of the fine examples of the human form in sculpture is the pre-historic engraving of a man from the rock-shelter of Laussel in France, and who is not aware today of the animal symbols for the evangelist! It is commonly said that the greatness of Greek civilization depends upon its relative freedom from the mystical forces of nature. This anthropomorphism was to be a great heritage for civilization, but the change from primitivism to the theosophical tendencies of the East was likewise a process of civilization and a heritage perhaps equally great.

A study of primitive Greek art is esp. fascinating in that it announces this final achievement. The exhaustive researches of Cook in his work *Zeus* reveal again and again how primitive concepts gradually fade into myth and fancy. The legend of Zeus and Europa, a survival of the early belief in the marriage of the Sun and Moon, is but one of many examples. The relationship between man and nature was often represented by a human figure between two animals. To this symbol the Greeks gave the name *Potne Oeron*. Collum, in a study of a megalithic monument of the Iron Age at Tressé, suggests that the thought of this symbol is similar to the snake-hood over the seated Buddha. But as a true primitive sign it probably had to do with a lunar cult.

The study of the gradual emergence of the primitive mind into other attitudes belongs to the study of each individual civilization. It will be of interest, however, to look briefly at the art of some of the peoples who even today have not passed beyond this stage. For the most part the vitality of their beliefs has been lost, however, and the true primitive concept is a rapidly disappearing phenomenon.

The Bushmen of South Africa are probably a unique survival of a pre-historic race. Their drawings suggest the **Capsian art of** Spain but its significance has been lost among the present survivors. They were driven at an early date from Northern Africa to the South by the negro. The finest art of the African negro was produced by the great empires of Yoruba, Dahomey, Ashanti and Benin. This region of Western Africa is agricultural and consists of a charming landscape not overwhelmed by forest. Here the great art of bronze casting was developed as early as the 15th cent. Some early examples are portrait heads showing tattooing and fine characterizations from Ifé, Nigeria. Heads of a similar type exist in terra-cotta. The Yoruba peoples had an unusually rich mythology said to contain some 600 gods and a supreme being but their art passed beyond purely religious expression and contains secular subjects. The Benin bronzes are later and not infrequently represent the Portuguese from whom they may have learned some technical improvements in their method of bronze casting. The 18th cent. marks a definite decline among these peoples even to extreme fanaticism and human sacrifice. It is noteworthy that sun and fire worship so common among primitive peoples had here completely disappeared. The gold dust weights of the Ashantis are often amusing bits of genre, but even more animated are the wood carvings from the Congo. The Batshisks are famous for their carved wooden chairs. Wooden masks for ceremonial use are common among most tribes but the Ashantis seem not to have used them. The very beautiful ones of the M'Pongine even suggest the exquisite examples of Japan. Often the figure

sculpture was not for use in a cult but rather as charms to keep away evil (see AFRICAN NEGRO ART).

The Aborigines of Australia, as a hunting people, have not a highly developed art, although their social organization is complex. Oceania (q.v.), however, offers many distinctive characteristics which differentiate the Melanesians, Micronesians and Polynesians. All possess a great love for surface ornament and utensils are richly decorated. The Maori especially exhibit great skill in carving and a delight in facial tattooing (see Maori carving). In the Marquesas Islands some of the men are completely tattooed even to lips and eyelids.

In the Americas the Indians of the northwest coast, especially the Kwakiutl (q.v.), Haida and Tlingit (q.v.) tribes developed a rich art. Totem poles are the outstanding feature and served as a sort of family crest. Sometimes a mythological story was intended by the carvings but always the ancestral animals served as a basis. The peoples of the southwest developed a distinctive culture with perhaps decorated pottery as its finest manifestation. Pottery is also distinctive of the various cultures which extended even to the tip of South America. The great civilizations of the Inca and Maya (qq.v.) deserve special treatment but they are merely outstanding among the many cultures of the Americas before the coming of the white man.

All primitive art is marked by a singular indifference to realism. Pleasure in imitation is doubtless present but soon becomes overshadowed by other qualities. An abstraction based on essential characteristics is found more forceful and appeals to the final controlling influence of pattern. The desire for symbolic expression and for decoration are the dominant characteristics. Sometimes each is quite independent of the other, sometimes the one becomes merged with the other. A pleasure in craftsmanship must have been at times the sole motivating force. There is an intuitive quality in man which delights in rhythmic relationships while at the same time he enjoys adapting those combinations of symmetry—double, inverted, or otherwise— to the exigencies of different materials. Much has been made by recent writers of the idea that art originates as a kind of byproduct of some utilitarian occupation. Man needs a basket and takes pleasure in making it beautiful. He must have a dwelling place for a spirit and he creates a form possessed with beauty. He wishes to convey a message and finds it more effective when it appeals to the aesthetic sense. He finds that by creating beauty he pleases and that, too, may have a practical end. If his peculiar aesthetic reaction is lost to the "civilized" individual it may be because the latter is too superficial to grasp it or his mind too warped by prejudice. For primitive man is still man. And though we may find the workings of his mind quite different from our own—so different that an interpretation of his art is extremely dangerous—and though his artistic expression may at times seem to have become strangely perverted as in the "disfigurement" of the body, still the quest for beauty must remain a fundamental instinct of the human race. See Adama Van Scheltema, F., *Die Altnordische Kunst*, 1923; Boas, Franz, *The Mind of Primitive Man*, 1916; Boas, F., *Primitive Art*, 1927; Catlin, George, *North American Indians*, 1903; Clawson, Hamilton P., *By Their Works*, 1941; Collum, V. C. C., *The Tressé Iron-Age Megalithic Monument*, 1935; Cook, Arthur B., *Zeus; a Study of the Ancient Religion*, 1914-25; Cushing, Frank H., "Zuñi Creation Myths," *Report of the Bureau of Ethnology of the Smithsonian Institute, Washington*, xiii; Firth, Raymond, *Art and Life in New Guinea*, 1936; Frazer, Sir James G., *The Golden Bough*, 1935; Goblet d'Alviella, Count E. F. A., *The Migration of Symbols*, 1894; Goodyear, William H., *The Grammar of the Lotus*, 1891; Groot, J. J. M. de, *The Religious System of China*, 1892-1912; Haddon, Alfred C., *Evolution in Art*, 1895; Hallowell, Alfred I., *Bear Ceremonialism in the Northern Hemisphere*, 1926; Hardy, Georges, *L'Art Nègre*, 1927; Hentze, Carl, *Mythes et Symboles Lumaires*, 1932 and *Objets rituels, croyances et dieux de la Chine antique de l'Amérique*, 1936; Hirn, Yrjö, *The Origins of Art*, 1900; Junod, Henri, *Centres de Style de la Sculpture Nègre Africaine;* Lévy-Bruhl, Lucien, *How Natives Think*, 1926; Lothrop, Samuel K., *Pottery of Costa Rica and Nicaragua*, 1926; Lumholtz, Karl S., "Symbolism of the Huichol Indians," *Memoirs, American Museum of Natural History*, v. 3. Anthropology, v. 2, pt. 1, 1900; Lumholtz, Karl S., *Unknown Mexico*, 1902; Mackenzie, Donald A., *The Migration of Symbols*, 1926; Malinowski, Bronislaw, *Argonauts of the Western Pacific*, 1922; Nassau, Robert H., *Fetichism in West Africa*, 1904; New York. Museum of Modern Art, *African Negro Art*, Ed. by James J. Sweeney, 1935; Riegl, Alois, *Stilfragen*, 1923; Roes, Anna, *Greek Geometric*

Art, 1933; Spencer, B., and Gillen, F. J., *Northern Tribes of Central Australia*, 1904; Steinen, Karl von den, *Die Marquesaner und ihre Kunst*, 1925-28; Stephan, Emil, *Südseekunst*, 1907; Teit, James Alexander, *The Thompson Indians of British Columbia*, 1900; Tylor, Sir Edward B., *Primitive Culture*, 1871; Wensinck, *Tree and Bird as Cosmological Symbols*, 1921; Wilson, Thomas, *The Swastika, the Earliest Known Symbol, and Its Migrations*, 1896.   —W.R.H.

primitive loom. In the Swiss Lakes we find warp weights judged to be perhaps 10,000 years old. The Swiss Lakes looms must have been similar to the loom pictured on the famous Grecian vase illustrating Penelope weaving the Tapestry she unravelled each night. In Scandinavia skulls are used as weights. In Iceland the same primitive loom is used today.

The primitive loom covers a span of 10,000 years. We find this same loom used by the Haida tribes of Coastal Alaska. It doubtless came into Alaska from Siberia.

The primitive loom was used by the Aztecs in Mexico probably before the birth of Christ. We have few fabric relics of the Aztec art which date before the Spanish invasion but we have evidences in their codices that weaving of cotton was of ancient date.   —G.W.R.

primitive music. The term *primitive* is used in describing the music of societies which have attained only a comparatively low cultural level, whether those societies be prehistoric, historic, or contemporary. Studies of primitive music make use of the methods of comparative musicology. The findings of such studies have value not only in the light they may shed on the music of higher cultures but in the contributions they make to such other sciences as ethnology and anthropology.

Primitive music must be studied, in the cases of prehistoric and historic cultures, from artifacts, archeological remains, occasional pictures, and verbal descriptions of musical instruments, systems, and usages. Very little actual music, either as a tradition or in notation, is available. The music of the ancient Mediterranean civilizations — Ur, Chaldea, Babylon, Egypt, the peoples of the Old Testament — have been studied in this manner.

In the case of contemporary primitive societies, the music of the African Negro and the American Indian furnish the best known and most studied examples of primitive music. Here again, the music does not exist in notation, but must be phonographically recorded for study, analysis, and transcription. Difficulties of transcription grow out of the fact that primitive scales and rhythms often fall into patterns which defy western notation, and such music cannot be reproduced on western musical instruments.   —T.M.F.

principles of design. See design.

principal vanishing point. See PERSPECTIVE.

principal visual ray. See PERSPECTIVE.

print, in. *Book.* A book that can be obtained from the publisher. A book is out of print when no copies can be so obtained.

printed notation. See NOTATION.

printers' mark. *Book.* The trademark or device of the printer, sometimes on the title page, sometimes on the last page.

printing, intaglio. Printing in which the design is formed by ink rubbed into incised lines and areas below the surface of the plate. This is the opposite of relief printing.
    —K.K.

printing, planographic. Printing from a plane surface, the design being formed by areas which have an affinity for the greasy ink on the roller.

printing, relief (or cameo). Printing from ink rolled onto a raised surface, such as type, woodblocks, etc.

PRINTS AND PRINT PROCESSES. Prints are the product of processes that permit multiple examples of a design. For all types an inked design on a plate or block is imprinted on paper, usually by means of a press, in a manner closely approximating the printing of a book page. Since the earliest time prints have been associated with book printing. Probably the first woodcuts were an effort in the early printed books, to provide by a cheap method that could be combined with type, a substitute for the miniatures which had adorned manuscripts. Later, prints were a means of reproducing drawings. Today they exist in their own right as an art form. Many of their technical charactersitics have been adapted to commercial printing processes.

In no other art expression is an understanding of processes and the peculiar opportunities and limitations of the mediums so essential to judging the final product. So true is this that print collectors and connoisseurs are sometimes inclined to judge a print more on its excellence of technique than on its purely aesthetic expression. From the art point of view, both must be taken into consideration: a fine design in a print, aesthetically speaking, would be lost if not expressed with all the richness and possibilities of its medium, and inferior, if the printing process were not well performed also. A print is, accordingly, a harmonious blend of highly exacting requirements in artistic conception and execution, and in mechanical skills and manipulations. The work of creative art is the finished print, product of all the intermediate processes, creative and mechanical, which go into turning out the finished print on paper. In that final form it must be judged as an original work of art.

Print processes are many. Those depending on pressure for the impression fall into three general classifications according to process: (1) **relief process,** in which the impression is made by a line or area that stands out from the background of the block, carries the ink and under pressure of press or rubbing transfers it to the paper (includes woodcuts, wood engraving, chiaroscuro prints, linoleum cuts, Japanese prints, and the commercial zinc cut, as examples); (2) **intaglio process,** in which the line or area that makes the impression, cut into and lower than the general surface of the metal plate, holds the ink which is drawn out on the paper in printing by the great pressure of the press (includes engraving on metal, mezzotint, etching, aquatint, drypoint, etc.); (3) **planographic process** in which there is no appreciable difference in level between the printing area and the general surface, but in which the area designed to print has been chemically treated so that it retains ink which transfers to paper under pressure (includes lithography on stone, most used in fine art prints, and on the plates of metal and other material which have wide commercial adaptation). Not dependent on pressure, but classed also as prints because producing multiple examples by a related process are silk screen prints (serigraphs) and other stencil print variants, used commercially and in applied arts, and adapted also to creative art expression in wide variety.

Chronologically, print processes have been developed and had vogue according to contemporary artistic needs and tastes approximately in the order given below. Certain types have enjoyed popularity for a time and then have fallen out of fashion. Today a variety of print processes are appreciated and employed by artists, and all methods used in the past are understood and could be used today. Preferred are lithography, block printing with wood or linoleum, etching and aquatint, engraving, probably in that order. Serigraphs have been gaining popularity among artists in the U. S. since ca. 1938 as a creative art medium.

Wodcuts, block prints. This medium, much used by early printers as book illustration, either left in black and white or colored by hand, consists in cutting away the wood (commonly cherry, pear, beech, apple or sycamore) of a block cut along the grain, leaving in relief the lines and areas which, when inked, will leave their impression on the paper. It is probably the oldest print process and dates from the 14th cent. The reverse may be done, incising the lines of the design, which remain as white outlines or areas in the printed surface. Usually a press is used, but pressure of any method, as rubbing, will suffice. Early woodcuts were predominantly outline designs. Modern woodcuts are usually arrangements of light and dark areas with great possibilities of decorative effect. The quality of the woodcut lies in the crisp contrast of dark printing on white paper.

The **linoleum cut,** printed from a wood block on which fine quality linoleum has been mounted and its surface cut exactly as in a woodcut, is a 20th cent. development and is easily worked. For fine work it is less satisfactory than a wood block.

Albrecht Dürer excelled among early artist-designers of woodcuts. Not a favorite medium in its simple form after the 16th cent., the woodcut was revived most effectively for its decorative possibilities by Paul Gaughin in the late 19th cent., and for the same reason has been generally popular among contemporary artists. Sharing popularity with lithography and etching in countries of Europe and in the U. S., the woodcut has been the principal print medium in contemporary Peru and Ecuador, and an important print process in Mexico.

The woodcut can be used with several blocks, keyed to print exactly in register, and each one inked with a separate color, to produce color prints. In the past, two important variations depended on several blocks used in printing:

Chiaroscuro. As the woodcut had been first used as an inexpensive substitute for the miniaturist's illustration, when printed books replaced manuscripts, the chiaroscuro prints, relying on tonal effects to depict form by values as the name implies (light-dark), appears also to have been a less costly substitute for the wash drawings in line and tone which the masters of the Renaissance produced and which were greatly appreciated by connoisseurs.

By multiple examples, chiaroscuros helped to satisfy the taste for drawings which there were not enough fine originals to meet, as well as allowing their enjoyment to a wider public. In some cases the chiaroscuro prints appear to have been done after celebrated drawings; in others they were apparently produced as art works in their own right. Essentially they are wood cuts, in which early examples are in line, touched up by hand after printing with white and a tone, closely approximating the drawings they resembled. Soon, however, several blocks, keyed so they would print exactly one over another, were used to print one or more tones, usually sepia, browns, greys or greens, to produce the effect of multiple values of a wash drawing. Chiaroscuros were especially popular in the 17th and 18th cents. in Italy, and were produced also in northern Europe, usually with the addition of outlines, sometimes from etched or engraved metal plates, to complete the compositions.

Japanese prints. These prints from woodcuts, which at first were limited in number of colors, developed by the height of their vogue a great range of colors, each one applied by a separate carefully keyed block printed by rubbing. They were a popular art form of the late 18th and 19th cents. in Japan, devoted principally to actors' portraits in famous roles, and a little later to scenery. Woodcuts, with multiple blocks for color, were also produced in China, probably from a very early period. Less is known about Chinese prints than about the Japanese, however. They continue to be produced in Japan. The subject matter has become more varied, the technique more adroit; but generally speaking, the art quality has deteriorated as they tend to fall into literal illustration. The elaboration of their multiple printing has seldom been rivaled in the western world, though essentially any color print produced from woodcuts is identical in process. Their design and decorative qualities have had notable influence on Western art through such painters as Van Gogh, Gauguin and Whistler.

Wood engraving. Known early, but first adapted brilliantly to delicately representing tonal effects by Thomas Bewick in the 18th cent., and by Timothy Cole in the late 19th and early 20th cent., wood engraving permits most subtle and varied effects. Essentially the process is the same as that of the woodcut in that it is a relief process. The work is done on the end of a finely grained hard wood block cut across the grain, usually of box wood, with delicate engraving tools and fine lines which give the greatest delicacy with an infinite range of tone as well as lines and solid areas. It has subtlety and delicacy where the woodcut has decorative boldness. It enjoys considerable popularity among contemporary artists.

Engraving. This method of printing from metal, incised directly with a sharp tool, used by early Italian and German print makers, probably was discovered in the shops of gold and silversmiths or armorers as a means of recording decorative motifs carried out on their handiwork. The lines of the design are drawn on a metal plate, usually copper, with a sharp triangular chisel-like tool called the **graver** or **burin.** The edge of metal turned up as the tool is pushed forward is polished off to leave a smooth surface except for the graven lines. These lines receive the ink which moist paper soaks up in the press to produce the print. It is a linear process; tone and intermediate values can be obtained by flecking or dotting the area with little holes; or by use of fine parallel or crossed lines. Great pressure is necessary and the edge of the plate leaves a mark known as the **plate line.** The quality of an engraving lies in the clear clean line well controlled. Used with mastery in Italy and Germany since the 16th cent. engraving was revived in France in the 18th cent., principally for portraits. Today it is used principally by English artists.

Etching. This process resembles engraving in being linear for both outline and tone effects, but the lines are eaten into the metal plate (most frequently copper, though zinc and iron are used) by acid instead of being cut directly with a tool. The design to be printed is traced, with a needle, through a layer of varnish or wax ground impervious to acid, down to the metal. These bared lines are eaten out on the plate by the corrosive action of a solution of nitric acid. The depth and size of the lines are controlled by the successive immersions in the acid bath. The lines to be lightly "bitten" are covered almost immediately with varnish; those to be deep and heavy are bitten more thoroughly. The acid-etched lines hold the ink, which is forced out in printing by the press at great pressure. As in all intaglio processes a "plate line" results. Additional tone effects can be obtained in printing by leaving a thin coating of ink upon the surface or portions of the plate each time it is run through the press, a procedure known as **wiping.** The quality of the line also may be manipulated to a degree by careful pulling of the ink out of the lines with a cloth (**retroussage**) at each printing. Developed in the 17th cent., notably by Anthony Van Dyck and Rembrandt, etching has been popular ever since. It was especially effectively used by English artists and the American Whistler in the 19th cent., and is popular today in Europe and America. The quality of an etching depends on the freedom of line and the varied and rich effects obtainable. It is often used in combination with aquatint, and sometimes with dry point.

Soft ground etching. Another etching process, though of less frequent use than the foregoing, is soft ground etching, which somewhat resembles in effect a pencil or soft crayon drawing. It is done by using a soft varnish or ground. A paper is then placed over the surface and a pencil drawing made. The pressure of the pencil forces the soft varnish to adhere to the paper, leaving lines, closely approximating those of the original pencil, bared to the surface of the metal which is then immersed in the acid bath and biting takes place as for a line etching.

Aquatint. As in etching, the design is eaten into the plate with acid. Aquatint, however, depends on tonal areas instead of line. The varnish or ground used to cover the metal plate is granular, usually fine rosin grains thickly sprinkled over the plate, which permits the acid to eat through the minute intervals between each grain. Successively, areas to be left white (**unprinted**) are blocked out with the regular stopping out varnish, lightly toned areas are immersed briefly, then stopped out, and so on with each part of the design until the darkest areas are reached which are velvety black in printing because the little pits eaten by the acid during the many immersions are deep and close together. Linear effects may also be added by the usual etching process or by drypoint. Aquatints, like wash drawings, build up their forms by tonal gradations and their quality is dependent on the manner in which the rich range of values from the white of the paper to the black of the most heavily bitten areas is used. Especially popular in the 19th cent., it remains a much used process today.

Stipple engraving. Used often in connection with etched processes, this method of producing tone depends on piercing the varnish ground with a multiplicity of small dots, and further adding dots or flecks directly on the plate with the special stipple engraver.

Drypoint. A process used for its own sake, but also to add richness of effect to etching, consists of scratching directly on the copper plate with a sharp-pointed needle. The thickness of the lines depends on the amount of pressure used by the artist, but the rough edge of the furrowed line is not removed as it is in engraving. In this case the little **burr** of metal turned up by the furrowing of the tool as well as the line beside it holds the ink in printing, and produces a surface richness on the print in which the ink appears to stand out in relief. As soon as the burr wears down, as it does very quickly, this effect is lost, so that the number of prints from a plate is limited. Sometimes the plate is plated with a thin steel facing for greater durability.

Mezzotint. This process gives effects of tone in mass. The copper plate is uniformly roughened or scored with a **roulette** or **rocker** so that it would print when inked an intense uniform velvety black. The design is then worked out by polishing the plate to a shiny hard surface that will not retain ink for the highlights, which are to remain of the white of the paper. The areas of intermediate tones are polished down (**burnished**) also according to their value, between the black of the plate and the polished surface of the highlight, so that all intermediate tones are obtained by removing more or less of the roughened copper surface of the plate with a **scraper** or **burnisher.** The mezzotint was much used in the 18th cent. to reproduce paintings. It is too laborious a process to have much attraction for the creative artist and has rarely been used since, or for purely creative work. In mezzotint, as for all the other processes described above using metal plates, printing is done in a press under great pressure and the plate line always shows.

All these intaglio processes can be adapted to color printing by using a number of plates, carefully keyed to print exactly one over another, each one taking care of the portions of the design in a given color. Mezzotints, etchings, and engravings in color were much used in England in the 18th and early 19th cent., in sporting and horse racing prints,

and in the reproduction of famous paintings by the popular painters of the day.

Lithography. This method was discovered by Aloys Senefelder in the late 18th cent. It produces the most autographic of prints for it offers the artist the most freedom and directness in transcribing his design, and reproduces it with great fidelity. Lithography is in part a chemical process, and is based on the principle that oil and water do not mix. The drawing is made with greasy crayon or ink upon a special type of stone as freely as if the artist were drawing on paper. By the application of gum and nitric acid the grease is driven into the stone and "fixed". This portion always thereafter attracts the greasy printer's ink rolled over it, while all other portions of the stone's surface are protected by the water which will not cover the greasy drawing. A greasy ink or wash may be used to make the drawing and the resulting print somewhat resembles in effect a wash or ink drawing and may be called a **lithotint.** It is possible to do lithography on an aluminum plate, and commercially, other materials, like a rubber mat, are used. Drawings may also be made on especially prepared paper in greasy crayon and then by pressure transferred to the stone. Best contemporary practice favors working directly on the stone. Lithographs are printed by considerable pressure in a press, but no plate line results. Lithography was much used in the 19th cent. for illustrations, and it has many important modern commercial applications. It is a favorite print medium with contemporary artists, because of its infinite possibilities and its directness and flexibility, which give full scope to personal expression and style. Technically its great qualities are its richness of effects with strong contrast of deep black to white of paper, the infinite gradation of intermediate grays between these extremes, and the wide range of texture and effect possible. By multiple stones, each carrying a different color, and keyed for perfect register, color lithographs are produced, and have had some use as a creative art medium, while elaborate developments in the commercial field are commonplace.

Color print. As indicated above, each of the standard print processes can be adapted to color printing, by the use of multiple plates or blocks, each for its own color, keyed to print exactly in register, and used successively. However, except for the Japanese print which can be said to exist only as color print, and the chiaroscuro which depended essentially on several areas of usually neutral tone, the print mediums already described are most important as an art medium in black and white. Color had been added by hand to prints from the earliest woodcuts, and some hand coloring was usually added to color prints in 18th cent. England and France as an addition to the printing in color. The contemporary development of a process for multiple production of designs used primarily for color work has depended principally upon refinement of stencil techniques. In its simplest form this technique consists of breaking a design to be reproduced into areas of different colors which are cut out of cards, which are then keyed like printing blocks, and applied one over another, the respective colors being pushed or squeezed on the paper through the holes left for the purpose. It is a somewhat slow process, and best adapted to decorative designs, dependent on flat areas of color for their effect. A more flexible and easily handled variant of the stencil print, like it first used commercially, but within the past four or five years mastered by a large number of artists in the United States as a creative art medium is the serigraph or silk screen print.

Serigraph or **silk screen print.** Used first commercially, this process was the subject of extensive experiment by artists under W. P. A. direction from about 1936, and has finally become in the hands of some experts a most flexible, expressive and varied creative medium in color, which permits a multiplication of examples and the resulting relatively low price which has always been the advantage of the print as compared with other art forms. A frame on which very fine silk mesh (or screen of other material is possible) is mounted and after mounting is placed over the paper to be printed. The design is worked out in a type of varnish which is impervious to the ink and stops out those portions not to be printed. A special ink or paint is then passed over the frame and penetrates to the paper below through those areas on the mesh unstopped out by the varnish. The drawing in varnish can be removed and the screen used again, for other portions of the design in other colors, or for other designs, as the case may be. As in other color print processes the printing must, of course, be repeated for each color, but technique and apparatus required are comparatively simple. A large group of artists in the United States are now practicing this technique with notable success, and have

made of it an independent creative medium of the most varied range, technically and expressively.

Monotype. A unique print, produced by painting on a glass or metal plate or other surface and transferring the design in color by pressure to paper, monotype is not strictly speaking a print in the sense of the others described here. As a process it dates from the 19th cent. and has considerable use among contemporary artists.

In all prints the combination of the artists' creative ability and of the technical execution is of greatest importance. In some periods, the artist has furnished the design, and artisans and craftsmen have executed it in one or another medium. In modern practice artists generally prefer to carry out the mechanical as well as the creative portions of the work themselves on the theory that only by direct knowledge of the entire process can they have the full understanding of the medium and its use and possibilities. It is true that in each step of a print-making process there are opportunities for triumph or failure. Ideally, the original design used by the artist to express himself should be fine and adapted to the print process which he chooses for it. In applying it on the block or plate or stencil he should use every resource of the process appropriate to expressing his design. In printing, the inking, the paper, the pressure all may make or mar the print even if all preceding steps have been successful. Because of their multiplicity prints have always been comparatively inexpensive, and today as in Dürer's and Rembrandt's time are an art form available to the mass of the people. It is appropriate that in our time color in a freer, richer, more creative use has been added to the resources of the multiplied original work of art, to satisfy the greater taste for color and interest in it which are the heritage of modern painting.

TECHNICAL TERMS. For a complete explanation of technical terms, see Hind, pp. 1-17, and Kistler, pp. 200-205, etc. A few important terms used in connection with prints: **Edition,** the number of prints, issued, often numbered by contemporary artists, with total number printed indicated, as 3/50, 3rd of an edition of 50. **Impression,** each print produced. **Proof** or **trial proof,** impressions printed while the artist is working on the block or plate to check progress. **State,** when, as occasionally happens, the artist prints a number of impressions, changes the plate and

prints others, the first group are said to be of the *first state,* those printed later after the addition or revision, of the *second state,* etc. **Remarque,** a sketch originally made by the artist on the margin of his plate to test his tools. In the 19th cent. such sketches came to be valued as a part of the finished print but they are not used on prints today. **Steel facing,** a thin layer or plating of steel that may be added to metal print plates for greater durability, often used for drypoint (q.v.), to assure an edition of good quality larger than the untreated plate would give. See Hind, Arthur, M., *A History of Engraving and Etching,* 1923; Kistler, Aline, *Understanding Prints,* 1936; Leighton, Clare, *Wood Engraving and Woodcuts,* 1932; Morrow, B. F., *The Art of Aquatint,* 1935; Reichel, Anton, *Die Clair-obscurschnitte des XIV., XVII., und XVIII. Jahrhunderts,* 1926; Von Seidlitz, Waldemar, *Geschichte des Japanischen Farbenholzschnitts,* 1897, 1910, 1920; Sternberg, Harry, *Silk Screen Color Printing,* 1942; Wegenroth, Stow, *Making a Lithograph,* 1936.
                                                        —G.L.M.M.

prints, Japanese. For terms, see the following: *beni; beni-e; beni-zuri-e;* broadsheet; *chūban; dai-bon; diptych; e-hon; hashira-e; hoso-e; ichi-mae-e; kakemono-e;* keyblock; *kira-e; koban;* lacquer print; *nima tsuzuki; ninshō; nishiki-e; ōban;* pentatych; pillar *sammai tsuzuki; surimono; tan; tan-e;* triptych; wood block; wood-block print; *yoko-e;* also *Modern Japanese Prints,* The Toledo Museum of Art, 1930 and 1936; *Japanese Colour Prints,* Edward F. Strange, Victoria and Albert Museum, 1923; *Block Printing and Book Illustration in Japan,* Louise Norton Brown, 1924; *Japanese Colour Prints,* Laurence Binyon and J. J. O'Brien Sexton, 1923; *Subjects Portrayed in Japanese Colour Prints,* Basil Stewart, 1922; *Japanese Woodblock Printing,* Hiroshi Yoshida, 1939; *The Ukiyo-e Primitives,* Yone Noguchi, Privately Published, 1933; *A History of Japanese Colour-Prints,* William von Seidlitz, 1910; *Chats on Japanese Prints,* Arthur Davison Ficke.
                                                        —J.A.M.

private collector. See FORGERIES IN PAINTINGS.

privately issued, printed. *Book.* It is believed that the term is not legally defined, but is usually understood to mean a book all the copies of which are subscribed for, without being offered to the public, before printing and none sold after printing.
                                                        —H.E.S.

producer. See RADIO DRAMA.

progression. *Mus.* The movement from one chord to another.

prolation. See NOTATION.

pronaos. See HELLENIC ART.

proof. *Book.* (1) The full-sized leaves of a book not cut when the rest of the book is cut to show the amount of margin that has been cut. (2) Proof copies in binding are those bound from the sheets printed in proof, to submit to the author, publisher, ect. Also proofs of type matter used for checking or "proofreading" for accuracy of composition. See PRINTS AND PRINT PROCESSES.
                                                        —H.E.S.

proof before letter. In engraving and etching, a proof impression taken before the title or inscription is engraved.

prop. See STAGESETTING.

proper. See HERALDRY.

Proper, of the Mass. See Mass; MEDIEVAL MUSIC.

proportion. This term is used in literary criticism in a sense generically similar to that of *balance* (q.v.), but is customarily restricted in application to the artist's treatment of his subject-matter. An artist—and hence, his work—is said to exhibit *proportion* when he respects and adheres to the true worth and significance of the different elements of his subject, and gives to the various aspects of this subject the emphasis that they deserve. The use of the term thus involves an assumption about comparative values in the real world, and works are praised or condemned by this criterion as they make agreeable or disagreeable judgments concerning the relative importance of these values.   —I.J.

proportional divider. See compass.

proscenium. See STAGESETTING.

prose. See MEDIEVAL MUSIC.

prosody. The science of metre, or metrics.

proto-Attic, — Corinthian, — Doric, — geometric. See HELLENISTIC ART.

proto-Renaissance. See Hohenstaufen art.

provenence. See FORGERIES IN PAINTING.

Provincial French style. See FURNITURE.

Prussian blue. The first blue pigment to be made synthetically on a large scale, this was first produced in the early years of the 18th cent. by Diebach, a dryer or color maker of Berlin. It is also called Berlin blue, Paris blue, Antwerp blue, and Chinese blue. Chemically it is complex but can be described as a ferric ferrocyanide. It is usually made by a precipitation process. Because it can be given an approximate date for entry into the arts, the analytical identification of Prussian blue has frequently been the means of placing a limiting date on picture in which it has been used.   —G.L.S.

psalm tones. Eight formulas corresponding to the eight modes to which psalms are chanted. Occasionally the *Tonus peregrinus* (strange or foreign) is employed. A Roman numeral at the beginning of its antiphon indicates the psalm tone to be used (see psalmody). The psalm tones are given in pp. 113-117 of the *Liber Usualis*. For a detailed exposition of the manner in which texts are fitted to tones see Rev. Dom. Johner, *A New School of Gregorian Chant,* pp. 65-93, 1925.
                                                  —V.A.

psalmody. The three forms of psalmody, each having its own method of delivery are (1) the responsorial psalmody, (2) the antiphonal psalmody, and (3) the direct psalmody.

(1) **Responsorial psalmody,** the oldest of these forms was taken over from the Synagogue. It was practiced in the early days of the Christian Church as follows: The psalm was chanted by a soloist in a monotone with inflections and cadences at appropriate places in the verses. At the close of each verse the congregation interjected a response—hence responsorial psalmody. Out of this primitive procedure grew the more or less elaborate type of responsorial chant in the Mass and the Divine Service. Even the most elaborate psalmody of this character clearly shows its origin, and can be analyzed on the three-fold basis of intonation, inflected monotone, and cadence.

(2) In **antiphonal psalmody,** two choirs or groups chant alternately. The structure of the psalms naturally led to this manner of chanting which also originated in the Synagogue Service. Ignatius of Antioch (d. 115) is supposed to have introduced the antiphonal method into Christian worship after having seen a vision of angels singing in alternate choirs. St. Ambrose (c. 340-97), Bishop of Milan, is credited for its introduction in the west. In the early days, a refrain or *antiphon* introduced the psalm and was repeated after each verse. Later (c. 9th cent.) in the interests of brevity the antiphon was sung at the beginning of the psalm and repeated only after the concluding *Gloria Patri* (see doxology). The antiphonal psalmody of the Office is less elaborate than that of the Mass. Although technically the Introit, Communion and in a certain sense the Offertory of the Proper of the Mass are antiphons, the word is now used to indicate the psalmody of the Breviary Offices sung in the antiphonal manner.

(3) In **direct psalmody** (*in directum*) which survives in the *Tract*, the verses of the psalms are sung without any refrain, i.e., sung from one end to the other. See Psalm tones; MEDIEVAL MUSIC; also Article, *psalmody* in Grove's *Dictionary of Music and Musicians,* 1935.   —V.A.

psaltery. See MUSICAL INSTRUMENTS.

psychoanalytic aesthetics. See AESTHETICS, RECENT TRENDS IN (2).

psychological aesthetics. See AESTHETIC INQUIRY, CURRENT TYPES OF.

PSYCHOLOGY OF ART. Psychological investigations in the realm of art have developed along two main lines, one general and the other specific. The general line includes studies and views on the nature of the creative process and the creative mind, and the nature of the aesthetic experience. The specific line consists of efforts to bring art into the sphere of experimental science.

The nature of the creative activity. It is in the main agreed upon by students of what goes on in the mind of the creative worker that the creative idea is the result of a long mental process divisible into the steps of *preparation, incubation, illumination,* and *verification.* In preparation the seed for the creative idea is planted in the soil of creative mindedness, whether consciously or unconsciously; in incubation it undergoes development until it sprouts and flowers forth in illumination, and matures and is harvested in verification.

There is also considerable agreement that what characterizes the creative mentality, as compared with ordinary practical intelligence, is a high degree of susceptibility for experience, an overwhelming inner power, and an irresistible drive for expression. Genius is said to possess, in the words of Bergson, "un élan, une initiative, une effort pour faire produire a la matière quelque chose que, d'elle même, elle ne produirait pas". This happens because of the great significance that the stuff of experience possesses for a richly endowed mind, a mind which is, so to speak, pitched an octave above that of the ordinary person. This accounts for the originality of the work of genius as compared with that of talent. The creations of genius are rooted in nature and life, while those of talent are either imitations of, or departures from, older masters.

These views on the creative process and the creative mentality find full corroboration in what creative workers with a bent for psychological introspection and analysis report about their mental adventures, and in studies on the genesis of particular art masterpieces. An example of the former is the account given by the French mathematician Poincaré of the origin of his mathematical formulas, and an illustration of the latter is Lowes's exhaustive study of the sources of Coleridge's *Kubla Khan* and The Ancient Mariner. Poincaré speaks of the appearance of a sudden illumination as a manifest sign of long, unconscious prior work. The sudden inspirations appear only after days of conscious effort which seemed quite fruitless. It is this effort, however, that set the unconscious machine agoing, and without which nothing could have been produced.

Lowe's study of the two poems by Coleridge leads him to the conclusion that "Every great imaginative conception is a vortex into which everything under the sun may be swept . . . Oral traditions—homely, fantastic, barbaric, disconnected—which had ebbed and flowed across the planet in its unlettered days, were gathered up into that marvel of constructive genius, the plot of the *Odyssey*, and out of 'a tissue of old Marchen' was fashioned a unity palpable as flesh and blood and universal as the sun itself" (4, p. 55).

The nature of the experience of beauty. The outstanding feature in the development of theories regarding the nature of aesthetic experience is the increasing recognition that what appear to be contradictions are in some instances but differences in manner of statement rather than in matter stated, and in other cases the apparent disagreements arise from the fact that each theory stresses one out of three possible approaches to a complex experience. Thus, some theories concern themselves with the nature of the experience itself, others with what the experience is

experience of, and some with what the experience does to the experient. To the first class belong the theories of *intrinsicality, disinterestedness*, and *objectification;* to the second the theories of *significant form* and *intuition;* and to the third those of *psychical distance, aesthetic repose*, and *catharsis*.

Disinterestedness, intrinsicality, and objectification belong together, because a disinterested attitude gives rise to an intrinsic experience, and in an intrinsic experience the subjective is objectified. The theories of significant form and intuition come to the same thing, each calling attention to what it is that is experienced in beauty. Bell defines significant form as the common quality in all visual art, and this common quality lies in certain forms and relations of forms that stir the aesthetic emotion. Croce contrasts intuition with intellect by calling intuition the process by which we obtain knowledge of individual things, while intellect gives knowledge of relations between things.

Of the third group of theories that of catharsis is the oldest and most widely known. Aristotle states in the *Poetics* that it is the service of tragedy to effect a proper catharsis or purgation of the emotions of pity and fear, and attributes such an effect also to music in the *Politics*. Now whereas Aristotle nowhere explains directly the nature of this purgation, we can infer what he had in mind from his definition of fear in the Rhetoric as "a species of pain or disturbance issuing from an impression of impending evil which is destructive or painful in its nature". It is clear, from this definition, that a catharsis of fear must consist of the elimination from it of the "impression of impending evil", in which case the fear becomes, in the words of Butcher, "an almost impersonal emotion, attaching itself not to this or that particular incident, as to the general course of action which is for us an image of human destiny" (4, p. 146). In other words, the emotion is stripped in imagination of its biological implications and becomes intrinsic experience. In such case, the restlessness, the drive to action, that is the dominant trait of every-day emotion, also disappears, resulting in a state of repose in tension. And this is Puffer's definition of beauty as aesthetic repose. Bullough's theory of psychical distance states the same thing in different language. If a person is psychically distanced from himself when standing on ᴗ hillside with lightning playing about him he is at repose because he is engrossed in the phenomena rather than in the thought of the danger to himself. Psychical distance is but another name for catharsis, only it explains how the catharsis is effected.

Experimental aesthetics. The most fruitful definition of experimental aesthetics is offered by Munro as "making use of all possible clues to the nature of aesthetic experience, from a variety of sources and modes of investigation. It would imply putting all these clues together, and on that basis working toward tentative generalizations through induction and the testing of hypotheses" (3, p. 24). A considerable literature on art that fits into this conception of experimental aesthetics has accumulated since the first researches were conducted along this line by Fechner (1865). We can do no more than enumerate the main problems that have been investigated in each of the arts.

Visual Forms. Fechner's purpose was to determine experimentally the degree of pleasantness of a series of simple visual forms constructed by himself, as well as of existing objects whose proportions were obviously influenced by aesthetic considerations. This procedure was also followed by Witmer (1893), Augier (1903), Legowski (1908), Thorndike (1917), and others. Chandler summarizes the results of these experiments as follows:

"Fechner had begun experimentation with simple forms in the hope of determining the one best form in each category—the best rectangle, the best cross, etc.—at least for any group homogeneous as to race, culture, and maturity. The results reached by his successors failed to show any one best form in each category; individual differences became conspicuous; the irrelevance of exact ratios like the golden section became evident; only such vague criteria as moderation, simplicity, or comprehensibility retained any validity" (1, p. 44).

Similar studies have been made by numerous investigators on the pleasantness of colors, singly and in pairs, the results showing no substantial agreement either among the subjects used in the different experiments or in the conclusions reached by the investigators.

The results of investigations on the expressiveness of lines and colors show a modicum of uniformity. Thus, big curves, downward or horizontal, are quite consistently judged to be sad, lazy, serious, weak, dead, quiet, gentle; small curves, and at times angles, upward and horizontal, are playful, merry, agitating, furious and hard. For the effect of colors it can be said that not every effect is likely to arise from every color equally, as, for instance, saturated reds are not cold, nor are the darkest colors cheerful.

Auditory forms. The experimental literature on music is vast and varied, comprising studies on its effects on animals and human beings, the classification of listeners into types, the nature of the beautiful in music, and the psychology of melody and harmony.

The Effects of music. There are numerous studies on the physiological, emotional, and mental effects of music, from single tones to complete compositions, and the feeling effects of the elements of melody, harmony, rhythm and tempo. The data from these studies indicate quite conclusively (1) that the effects of music on organic processes are quite pronounced; (2) that emotionally music creates a mood rather than specific feelings; (3) that a musical composition tends to create a uniform mood in an audience; (4) hat the intellectual effects of music vary from person to person; (5) that the most important melodic element for the expression of excitement is swift tempo; for dignity it is slow tempo, firm rhythm and lower pitches; dreamy sentimental moods call for the minor mode, slow tempo and flowing rhythm; while happiness demands faster tempo, simple harmonies, flowing rhythm and medium pitch.

The types of musical responses. Experimental data point to four classes of listeners to music. These are the *intra-subjective* type, to whom music appeals for its sensory, emotional, or conative effects; the *associative* type, which values music for the associations a critical attitude towards music and values it as an object; the *character* type, which characterizes music in terms of human traits like morbid, joyful, mystic, etc. These four types are further reducible to two classes of listeners based upon the source of the meaning of the music to the person. There are those who value music *intrinsically*, or for the music itself, and those who prize it *extrinsically*, or for the extra-musical message it conveys to them. There are grounds for believing that the intrinsic listeners are the truly musical persons.

The aesthetic hearing of music and the traits of the musical mentality. Inquiries among outstanding musicians and laymen with pronounced interest in music justify the conclusion that music is heard musically only when it is heard through and through tonally. These persons report that whenever anything it arouses; the *objective* type, which assumes extra-tonal intrudes into their consciousness while listening to music, it is an indication that the music no longer interests them or that it is trivial music. A battery of tests of auditory sensitivity and discrimination administered to these persons shows that they rank above average in these abilities, from which it may be inferred that at the basis of the aesthetic response to music is a high degree of sensitivity to the structural elements of music like pitch, dynamics, duration, tone quality, interval discrimination, tonal movement, and many others.

The psychology of successive tonal combinations. Since a melody is a succession of pitches that are experienced as an organic whole, many students have inquired into the sources of this phenomenon of tonal belonging-togetherness. Ortmann enumerates three *absolute* and five *relative* factors which account for the tonal relationships in a melody. The absolute factors are *first and last tones, highest and lowest tones,* and *tone repetition;* the relative factors include *interval, pitch direction, pitch proximity, emphasis in tone-groups,* and *interval relationship.* The first and last tones and the highest and lowest tones give the melody its temporal and pitch boundaries, and thereby become a source of unity, while tone repetition serves the same purpose through frequency of stimulation. The five relative factors serve to unite the tones through contiguity in time and pitch. Bingham investigated the phenomenon of melodic trend or finality and formulated the law that *"two melodically 'related' tones tend to establish a tonality,* and the melody is judged to end only when the final tone is one of the members of the tonic triad—preferable the tonic itself" (5, p. 42).

The psychology of simultaneous tonal combinations. A number of theories have been formulated in explanation of the fact that the intervals of the musical scale differ in degree of consonance and dissonance. The most prominent of these theories explains consonance as degree of fusion (Stumpf, 1898), and fusion is defined as the singleness of impression produced by two or more tones. The greater the fusion the greater is the consonance of the component tones. The upholders of this theory do not agree, however ,on the basis of fusion. Some hold that it depends upon vibration ratio of the tones, while others claim that numerous factors are operative. Consonance has also been accounted for on the basis of the beats of the upper partials (Helmoltz, 1870), the har-

monic series of partials (Ogden, 1920), the chord of nature (Redfield, 1928), cultural acquisition (Moore, 1914).

Language and Literature. In the realm of the verbal arts, research studies have been made on the rhythm of speech, the effects of speech sounds, and the effects of single words.

Scripture (1899) sought to determine the nature of the rhythm of verse by analyzing mechanical recordings of spoken verse, tracings on phonograph records, and other devices. He found "accent"to be a combined effect of a number of factors, and not alone of loudness or duration. This combined effect he called "energy" or "strength", and the rhythm of verse he claimed to consist of the periodic recurrence of *regions* of strength and of weakness. The midpoint of a region of strength he named the "centroid", with intervals between centroids being approximately equal. Wallin (1911) calls the interval between centroids a "sound centroid interval" when no pause occurs between the centroids, and a "composite centroid interval" when a pause does intervene. His data show no constant length of interval between centroids. Also, according to his results, loudness is the most prominent factor in accent, with duration next and pitch last. Patterson (1916) corroborates Wallin's view that rhythm is not conditioned upon mathematical regularity of recurrence of centroids, because pulses can be accelerated or retarded, or the interval between pulses can be divided into several shorter intervals, or several intervals combined into one longer interval, or the interval may be syncopated. Patterson finds three rhythmic types: the "stresser" or the person whose rhythmic experience is predominantly in terms of alternations of stress or the differences of loudness among the syllables; the "passive timer", or he who responds to the objectively given temporal regularities; and the "active timer", or the individual who sets up subjective time patterns into which he fits the presented stimuli. The difference between prose and verse, according to this investigator, lies in the way of hearing or reading a passage. "For a 'timer,'" he concludes, "the definition of prose as distinguished from verse experience depends upon a predominance of syncopation over coincidence in the coordination of the accented syllables of the text with the measuring pulses" (1, p. 259). In other words, the distinction is subjective, not objective. But Griffith (1929) finds the difference between grades of rhythm in prose and that between the most rhythmic prose and blank verse to reside in the length of pause and the length of phrase in time and in number of syllables. She reports that spaced prose is a structure of many pauses, or comparaticely short phrases balanced against one another—hence spaced. There is a greater difference in the pauses occurring *in* a sentence and at the *end* of a sentence between fluid and non-rhythmic prose than between spaced prose and blank verse. In non-rhythmic prose the pauses are fewer and shorter than in blank verse and spaced prose. The length of phrases as measured by the number of syllables they contain is relatively brief in time for blank verse and spaced prose as compared with other prose. Also, 75 per cent of the phrases in blank verse contain even numbers of syllables, while all three forms of prose predominate in phrases of odd numbers of syllables. Further, the most frequently occurring phrases found in blank verse contain four and six syllables, in spaced and fluid prose this happens with phrases of five and seven syllables, while in non-rhythmic prose there is no predominance of any particular phrase lengths. Finally there occurs a steady increase in the duration of the phrase with the number of syllables in it, up to ten syllables for blank verse, thirteen for spaced prose, twenty for fluid prose, but for non-rhythmic prose no regular relation is found whether for short or long phrases.

The feeling effect of speech sounds and words. From the results of studies on the feeling of speech sounds, there appear to be very slight differences in the degree of pleasantness of the different vowels and consonants. One investigator, however, reports that when the sounds of a poem, especially of a lyric poem, are arranged into nonsense syllables and composed into iambic lines, the sounds themselves are able to arouse a mood somewhat like the mood of the original poem.

The investigations on the effects of single words have led to a four-fold classification of responses similar to that found for tones and colors.

Sculpture and Architecture. To the knowledge of this writer no experimental studies on these arts are available at present.

REFERENCES

1. Chandler, Albert R., *Beauty and Human Nature,* New York, 1934.

2. Diserens, Charles M. and Fine, Harry, *A Psychology of Music,* 1939.

3. Munro, Thomas, *Scientific Method in Aesthetics,* New York, 1928.

4. Schoen, Max, *Art and Beauty,* New York, 1932.

5. Schoen, Max, *The Psychology of Music,* New York, 1940.

6. Seashore, Carl E., *Psychology of Music,* New York, 1938.　　　　　　—M.S.

PSYCHOLOGY OF DRAWING AND PAINTING. This article deals esp. with the processes of perception and visualization involved in the acts of drawing and painting as modes of realistic representation. Research in the psychology of the production of art is still in an early stage of development, and quantitative information on much of the following discussion has not yet been published: but no positive statements are made here which are not well substantiated by at least qualitative evidence.

PSYCHOLOGY OF FORESHORTENING AND LINEAR PERSPECTIVE. From the standpoint of *perspective* (q.v.), a picture is essentially a two-dimensional projection of three-dimensional material. If two untrained people of equal moderate ability draw a greatly foreshortened view of a long table top, A, tracing its image as it appears to him on a perpendicular pane of glass, will draw it correctly, while B, drawing on paper in the ordinary way, will make the distant and near edges too far apart. B, lacking a tangible *picture plane* for the gathering of his visual images, is unable to relate them properly; his judgment of proportions in them is influenced by his perception of the real length of the table. The new vision of adults who, born blind, have been given sight by surgical operation, is practically flat, like a picture, all objects seeming to be about equally near; and it is only after considerable experience in handling objects and moving around among them that these patients acquire normal visual perceptions of distance, size, and foreshortened form. This experience is gained by most people in early infancy; and the primitive consciousness of visual images as such has been so long neglected by the time an individual begins to draw intelligibly that he is hardly aware of them. An important part of the teaching of drawing is the reawakening of a consciousness of these visual sensations. A well-trained artist is able at will to think clearly and accurately of an object either *visually,* in terms of a flat or spherical pattern of images, or *constructively,* in terms of concepts of the real object, of three-dimensional space relationships. A less trained person drawing usually mixes those two types of thinking without realizing that he is doing so. This is the principal explanation of the traditional difficulties of foreshortening, which have troubled artists of all times, causing ancient or primitive artists to represent for instance people with shoulders in front view while heads and feet were in profile view.

The normal tendency to think of the objective real instead of the subjective sensation is called **constancy**, or **phenomenal regression**, which terms are applied to judgments of size, form and color. (The last will be discussed later).

The difficulties already mentioned arise from a confused mixing of constructional concepts with what should be, under some circumstances at least, practically pure visual images. Conversely there is a different kind of trouble that comes when visual thinking intrudes too much upon what should be mainly constructional thinking. This is illustrated by Hogarth's famous jocular drawing which shows a man on a distant hill lighting his pipe from a candle held out by a woman from an upper window of a nearby house. While no sane person ever commits so glaring an absurdity unknowingly, art students often make mistakes which though somewhat disguised are the same in principle—assuming parts to be near each other in space because they happen to be juxtaposed in the drawing, when they really belong in different planes of depth. This type of error which commonly occurs in drawings from imagination is essentially identical with another form in which adjacent parts of an object are individually drawn well but their intersections or other interrelationships are not thought out properly—as, for example, when a beamed ceiling is drawn without regard for the shapes made by the beams in penetrating the wall. All such faults appear to come from *incomplete visualization*. The student is able to conceive separately of the beams and of the wall but does not exert enough imaginative effort to bring into clear focus, as it were, the junction between them. The man and the woman, in the previous type case, are both clearly realized, but the ground between them is forgotten.

EXCESSIVE CONCENTRATION OF ATTENTION. Even when a drawing is being made from an observed model the relations between parts are frequently neglected. As has been indicated before, a drawing on paper from observation involves more than a mechanical matching of the visual images received from it

with those received from the model. Many influences come into play and modify the mental impressions made by the images. Among these *attention* is important. Any part of the object which is especially interesting tends to receive special attention, to the neglect of other parts. The result usually is that the former is refined increasingly; more and more minute details are added, space for which is robbed from the surrounding areas, with the result that the interesting part is made too large, if the drawing is of moderate size. If the drawing is unusually large in scale, however, the part is likely to be made too small. In either case the same cause is operating—too narrow a confinement of attention.

ARBITRARY SPACE UNITS. A remedy for this difficulty is a special effort to pay attention to the shapes of the comparatively empty, uninteresting areas that surround these centers of spontaneous interest. In fact it is important to go further and to conceive the whole drawing as composed of arbitrary visual units of abstract space or **masses** which are largely independent of constructional units. For example, suppose a model is seated with an elbow on a table, leaning his head on his hand. One mass might be thought of as bounded by the outer edges of the head, hand, arm, part of the edge of the table, part of the edge of a shadow which chances to fall across the body, a fold in the sleeve of the other arm, a part of the back and the edge of the neck—all combining to make an imaginary approximation to a triangle. Another mass might be conceived that omits the head but includes the knees and parts of the chair. There is great advantage in thus making units of space overlap each other, having elements in common which are used again and again in many varied relationships, like parts of letters in a monogram, since each mode of thinking about a given component thus serves as a check on the other modes; and mistakes of proportion are discovered which would otherwise escape notice. As this work proceeds, the units become gradually subdivided into smaller and smaller sub-units, until all important relationships and areas are properly adjusted, a proof of correct proportion in the larger masses being the ability of the smaller subdivisions to fit into them rightly. Considerations of structure, anatomy, and perspective furnish additional proofs; but, though important, they must needs be secondary to consideration of visual pattern if truthful representation of a specific model and pose is desired, since an infinite variety of forms can be satisfactory from the structural, anatomical or perspective standpoints while only one set of forms can represent the visual patterns of that particular arrangement. Therefore the establishing of habits of thinking in terms of arbitrary space units is one of the chief objectives in the teaching of drawing.

EXAGGERATION OF SLIGHT DIFFERENCES. Another problem concerning attention arises from the fact that it is naturally attracted to differences of direction in contours, which if slight, usually are exaggerated. Very obtuse angles tend to be drawn too acute, very gentle curves to be made more rounding, very small irregularities to be augmented. Likewise contrasts of *value, hue* and *chroma* (q.v.), occurring in adjacent areas, tend to be exaggerated. For example, a patch of reflected light slightly illuminating the shaded side of an object is frequently made by beginners as brilliant as much of the lighted side, and a half-tone on the lighted side as dark as a shadow.

NORMALIZING TENDENCY. However, there is an opposite tendency which is manifested in cases where the model is extreme in angularity or eccentricity and which tends to make the copy somewhat more conservative, generalized, compact, and symmetrical in shape than its original. Thus these two complimentary tendencies, one toward accentuation, the other toward moderation, in combination help to keep drawings from extremes of simplicity on the one hand or of irregularity on the other. The "Gestalt" school of psychologists advance as explanation of these facts the theory that there is a "law of pregnancy" which causes each form as apprehended by the mind to gravitate toward the character of a "good figure" or good example of that type of form. One writer has proposed the name "eidotropic tendency" for this trend of perception toward an ideal for each form.

There is a similar generalizing tendency in the observation of color which tends to cause untrained people to paint in pictures approximations to "local" colors of objects (the colors of a part of an object which is fully exposed to strong but diffused daylight) when they should paint the apparent "stimulus" colors (the modifications of the local color which are due to aerial perspective or to the character of the direct or reflected illumination), probably because the local colors are more typical, more often seen under average conditions. The terms "constancy" and "phenomenal regression" are applied also to this tendency.

The relation of these accentuating and minimizing tendencies to aesthetic preference has not yet been determined experimentally, but there is considerable likelihood that there is a relationship.

EFFECTS OF OPTICAL ILLUSIONS. There are so many *optical illusions* (q.v.) in almost everything we see that there is no hope of entirely escaping from their influence while drawing or painting. However, if realistic representation is desired it is reassuring to reflect that the more closely a picture is made to resemble the appearance of nature the more nearly its particular combination of illusions will come to matching the corresponding illusions in the scene depicted, and hence, the more completely the two sets of illusions will come to neutralizing each other. For this reason if maximum correctness is important it seems desirable that all areas of the paper or canvas be made to vaguely resemble the general appearance of the scene as soon as possible, then be slowly brought into focus, as it were, by a gradual sharpening of edges as the adjustments of masses make locations more certain. A model with strongly contrasting lights and darks, for instance, should be drawn or painted with approximately corresponding value relationships, beginning at a very early stage in the development of the picture, not in outline. If an outline drawing is wanted as a final result, the best procedure, from a psychological standpoint, would be to make a preliminary study in values, then derive the outline drawing from that. A similar plan can be followed in cases where a medium is used which does not lend itself to a gradually focussing treatment. Frequently the backgrounds of models are dark, perhaps complicated with forms of furniture or architecture, while the drawings of them are made with plain white paper as background; or sometimes part of a drawing is given heavy slanting strokes of technique which do not correspond with anything in the real scene. Such departures may be fully justified by aesthetic considerations, but the artist should realize that he is giving himself a psychological handicap, if he desires correct proportions, unless he makes these departures after his study of the proportions has been completed.

LAG OF PERFORMANCE BEHIND JUDGMENT. Suppose a student's vision is misled by certain illusory angles in the model and he makes a certain distance in his drawing too short.

Even if he later discovers his mistake through neutralizing the illusion by adding the corresponding angles to his drawing, he is likely to fail to make the needed correction, perhaps through lack of energy or of confidence in his own judgment. Errors due to other causes tend to be perpetuated likewise.

The resulting lag of performance behind judgment may be considerably diminished by use of a medium which permits easy alteration, such as charcoal, pastel, or oil paint, and by insistent instructions to keep the drawing vague and simple until all the important masses are correctly adjusted, after which edges can be sharpened, needed details, accents and refinements added, and the result made as clean, crisp and vigorous as may be desired for purposes of aesthetic expression.

Published data on this subject have been thus far largely confined to articles in periodicals and individual chapters in books. Most of these have been summarized in R. S. Woodworth, *Experimental Psychology,* 1938, pp. 71-91, 539-712. —T.I.C.

PSYCHOLOGY OF MUSIC. Throughout the history of aesthetics so many aspects of music have been subjected to psychological study and analysis that no adequate comprehension of the complexity of the field can be given in a brief statement. For purposes of convenience and brevity it is possible to group the various ramifications of the psychology of music under the following four headings :

(1) *The materials of music.* All musical perception begins with the materials of auditory sensation. At the present time a study of auditory sensation overlaps three fields of scientific inquiry: physics, physiology and psychology. Musical sound begins as periodic disturbances of the air which strike the ear drum, and are then transformed by various electro-chemical processes in the auditory mechanism of the ear into a wide range of pitches of varying intensities and tone-colors.

(2) *Musical form.* Auditory sensations become music only after they are grouped into sequences and patterns which vary all the way from the simplest succession of tones in a folk melody to the elaborate structures of modern choral and orchestral composition. Many varieties of musical pattern follow rather strict rules of construction and have acquired a technical nomenclature indicated by such terms as canzona, gigue, fugue, canon, minuet, courante, toccata, passacaglia,

chacono, bolero, etc., etc. Psychological studies in this field are concerned primarily with problems relating to the origin of scales, the use and perception of intervals and chords, the degree of auditory complexity to which the ear is adequate, and the analyses of rhythm and harmony.

(3) *Tests of musical talent.* The ability of performers to perceive, discriminate, and execute the materials and forms of music has been subjected to critical analysis in order to construct tests of musical capacity. The best that can be said about these tests at the present time is that they have an important negative value,—that is to say, if a person does poorly on these tests it is not likely that he will succeed as a musician. It can not be said with such assurance, however, that success on these tests will predict success as a musician.

(4) *The meaning of music.* One school of thought in music aesthetics has maintained, ever since the Greeks, that music has no meaning beyond that contained within the auditory structure itself, as contrasted, for example, with arts like painting and poetry which lead the mind into a realm of ideas far transcending the nature of the materials used in the construction of these arts. This formalistic view of music has had a tenacious hold upon aesthetic theory, but has recently been expanded to explain an oft-repeated assertion that music is the language of emotion. Music need not directly arouse emotions in the listener, and it certainly does not contain emotion within its own tonal framework; but its intrinsic tonal structure is nevertheless patterned in such a way that the listener frequently seems to be brought into direct contact with the whole range of human mood and passion. The music itself possesses no passion, nor does the listener himself necessarily feel strong emotion. He listens to tonal configurations which closely resemble in their outline the bodily reverberations which lie at the basis of real emotions. Music sounds the way emotions feel.

The literature on the psychology of music is enormous. The following books may serve merely as examples, and will furnish the interested reader with many references for further study. Haydon, G., *Introduction to Musicology,* 1941; Pratt, C. C., *The Meaning of Music,* 1931; Schoen, M., *The Psychology of Music,* 1940; Seashore, C. E., *Psychology of Music,* 1938; Stevens, S. S., and Davis, H., *Hearing.* 1938. —C.C.P.

psychology of the artist. See ARTIST, PSYCHOLOGY OF THE.

psychology of tone. Psychologically, a single tone is a permanent acoustic impression in which height, intensity and timbre remain more or less constant, the deviation from this constancy being restricted to certain limits and tolerated only if they occur regularly (vibrato, crescendo, articulation). Still, the difference between noise and tone is not principal but gradual.

In comparison with our visual capacities we must admit that a static aural impression is inferior so far as accuracy of location is concerned. It produces more a sensation in us than an image of something eternal, the source of the sound. This holds true even of daily experiences but especially of the use of a tone in music. Thus music with only a static aural impression would be unable to produce a picture. There are only moving-pictures in music. Even localization appears much stronger in motion: approaching, passing by, disappearing.

On the other hand the ear is superior to the eye with regard to the variety of color. The number of possible colors, their discrimination and combination is unlimited. This quality of color does not depend on the wave length as in optics but includes every quality of a sound except its wave length (pitch) and wave height (intensity). Thus *physically* it depends entirely on the shape of the wave and on changes within this shape. These changes account for the deviations mentioned above. They contribute especially to the warmth of a tone. Especially strong at its beginning and ending they produce definite articulation, for singing as well as instrumental rendering. The absence of such changes produces an organ-like character. Every musical instrument is characterized by a specific shape of its tonal wave. *Psychologically* we distinguish: grades of brightness and fullness that depend on the amount of overtones; a kind of vowel character if certain "formant" regions dominate among these overtones; metallic quality if the intensity reduces slowly, and wooden quality if it fades away immediately; light or darkness, smoothness or sharpness, weight, volume and penetrance of a tone. *Musically* these qualities are prescribed by the choice of a certain instrument and the manner of playing it (touch, etc.).

The limits of our capacity to hear extremely high or deep tones is somewhat connected with the limits of intensity since the extreme frequencies are intelligible only at medium loudness and vice versa. The same holds true of the threshold for the distinguishing of very small intervals. The range of audibility reaches from 16 to 16000 oscillations per second and more. For musical purposes, however, the range does not surpass 32 and 4000 oscillations respectively.

Historical and regional styles of music differ in their systems of tones selected for use in music with regard to melodic easiness as well as to the allowance of simultaneous sounding. Yet the natural relationship as given by the harmonic overtones seems to be a fairly general principle for all these systems. The pentatonic scale (d-f-g-a-c) also appears as a very general root for tonal systems throughout the world.

The theoretical fundamentals of the nature of a tone were already known to the ancient Greeks (Pythagoras). Yet the modern scientific research did not start before Helmholtz's historic publication "The Sensation of Tone" (1863). Valuable contributions were added by A. J. Ellis (*History of Musical Pitch*, 1877), C. Stumpf (*Psychology of Tone*, 1883), Th. Lipps, E. c. Hornbostel, M. Wertheimer, E. Kurth, G. Revesz, who more and more transferred the problems from physics and physiology to psychology. The modern invention of electro-acoustics equipped this research with a perfection of tools undreamed of before and promoted abundant results, esp. in the laboratories of the U. S. A.; e.g., The University of Iowa (C. E. Seashore), Carnegie Institute of Technology (M. Schoen), and Peabody Conservatory (O. Ortmann).   —H.R.

public forest. See CIVIC PLANNING.

publisher's binding. See edition binding.

pueblo (Sp. town, village). As used in the American Southwest: An agglomeration of essentially rectangular living rooms of adobe or masonry construction, generally flat-roofed and built above ground.   —J.M.M.

Pueblo art. The Pueblo (Sp. village) peoples, or the Anasazi (q.v.), inhabited southwestern Colorado, part of Utah, northern New Mexico and northeastern Arizona—a colorful, semi-arid plateau region cut by buttes and canyons. Worship of the powers of nature and supplications for rain and fertility are basic in their elaborate ceremonials and other art expressions. In contrast to the confused picture of the Eastern Indian cultures, the pueblo culture reveals a clear pattern of continuous evolution from earliest times to the present, and actual dating has been determined in certain areas by dendrochronology (q.v.). The first inhabitants, with the exception of Folsom Man (q.v.), were nomadic hunters and seed gatherers, now called the Basket Makers because of their skill in basketry; and their evolution is divided into Basket Maker I, which is hypothetical, II and III, or, according to other authorities, Basket Maker and Modified Basket Maker. These early nomads wove finely coiled baskets of osier, yucca fiber and roots for household, transportation and burial use, and decorated them with red and black designs of intricate zigzag, terrace and other geometric motifs. Closely allied to basketry was the weaving of bags and sandals of yucca fibers. The sandals in particular show intricate designs similar to those found in the baskets. Both crafts reveal a high quality of craftsmanship. They may be dated c. 500-600 A.D.

The introduction of maize, probably from the south, and later of beans and squash, led to a more sedentary life. The first structures, stone-lined storage pits, assumed a domiciliary function and were given a superstructure of poles and adobe, with a smoke hole for entrance. Pottery was invented or introduced, and decorated with motifs derived from weaving. The Basket Makers seem to have reached their climax in the area drained by the San Juan River.

With the infiltration, beginning c. 400 A.D., of a new race of unknown origin, a transitional age (Pueblo I and II, or Developmental Pueblo, c. 800-950 A.D.) led to the fullest development of the culture (Pueblo III, or Great Pueblo, c. 950-1300 A.D.). Basketry continued, and the use of wild cotton made possible the weaving of cotton cloth, enriched with embroidery. But the two chief arts were architecture and ceramics. The pit house was discarded in favor of one built entirely above ground and evolved into the single-room communal house, yet survived in the subterranean kiva (q.v.). These unit houses of stone and adobe were arranged contiguously in a long row or crescent in widely scattered villages. A trend toward concentration of population led to the building of great terraced communal houses in natural caverns and in the open. Mesa Verde (q.v.) (1073-1262 A.D.) contained one of the greatest groups of the former both as to number and variety of buildings and quality of masonry. Other important sites were the Cañon de Chelly (q.v.) with its many dwellings of various dates, of which the White House (1060-1275 A.D.) is best known; Betatakin (q.v.) (1242-1286 A.D.), Keet Seel (q.v.) (1274-1286 A.D.) and Casa Grande (q.v.) (1300-1400 A.D.). Of pueblos in the open, Chaco Canyon (q.v.) contained large, wealthy villages (at their climax c. 1200 A.D.), composed of communal houses on a rectangular or oval plan, built about a court and terraced back from the one-story rooms enclosing one side of the court to upwards of five stories at the back. Within the court were many large circular kivas with exceptionally fine masonry.

Painting was practiced by the Basket Maker—Pueblo peoples on a large scale, on the smoothed walls of canyons and on boulders. These so-called pictographs or petroglyphs show a great diversity of scale, subject matter and style. They range in size from gigantic to diminutive, depict human, animal and geometric figures, and vary in style from purely geometric to highly conventionalized to naturalistic. Recent excavations have disclosed many mural paintings in the kivas on many successive layers of adobe. At Awatovi, an ancient Hopi village, the designs are highly conventional, reminiscent of Hopi pottery and apparently ceremonial in subject; they are flat and hieratic in style. At Kawaika-a in Arizona and at Kuaua near Albuquerque are represented masked figures, animals and birds in a freer, more naturalistic style.

Pottery consisted first of a black and white ware made possible by the use of slip, with angular textile-like designs; of a unique corrugated ware in which the constructional coils were left unsmoothed (pottery in all the Southwest was coiled, not thrown); and of a polished red ware—all with many shapes for household use, such as shallow food bowls, water jars, cooking pots. Distinctive local styles developed with a trend toward polychromy. Outstanding for their shape and decoration are the Sikyatki (q.v.) bowls with red or brown decorations on a yellow or orange base.

Articles of personal adornment were plentiful—gorgets, necklaces and bracelets of shell and stone and especially of turquoise—and appear to indicate a ceremonial life comparable to that of the historic Pueblos.

For unknown reasons, probably the great drought of 1276-1299 A.D. and pressure from the invading Utes, Comanches, Navaho and Apaches, the region was abandoned and the people migrated southward, many eventually to the Rio Grande Valley to the sites now occupied by the historic Pueblo peoples. In this period of migration (Pueblo IV or Regressive Pueblo, 1300-1700 A.D.) the culture of Great Pueblo continued, though in decline, until the historic period. In 1540 A.D. came the first contact with Spanish culture, by way of Mexico, and a material change in the pueblo pattern of life through what the Spaniard brought: metal tools: sheep for wool and food; the horse for work and transportation; fruits, vegetables and cereals; and Christianity. Since the Spaniard did not find the gold and other wealth which motivated his expeditions, he did not push his attempts at conquest and colonization until after the rebellion of the Pueblos in 1680 A.D. With the subjugation of the tribes the historic or Pueblo V period (1700 A.D. to date) begins. The large number of villages known to have existed when the Spaniard arrived has dwindled to about 17 in the Rio Grande group. The more important are Acoma, Cochiti, Isleta, Laguna, San Ildefonso, San Juan, Santa Clara, Santo Domingo, Tsia, Taos, Tesuque; the Hopi group (q.v.) in Arizona; and the Zuñi in western New Mexico. In general the tribes have adapted and profited by some of the material benefits of the foreign culture. Yet they have subordinated them to the long-lived, powerful traditions of their social and religious patterns. There has been a direct continuity of the ancient arts. Building has remained the adobe communal structure, as at Taos; with modifications such as the addition of *portales* and chimneys seen at San Ildefonso.

In all the crafts the influence of the tourist trade has been banal in lowering standards of quality and taste. In the field of weaving basketry has continued, and in the making of woolen articles and cotton garments embroidered in wool a great expansion has taken place. Pottery has always flourished, and each village has developed an individual style, mostly polychrome. It is still a craft of the women. Its enduring vitality has expressed itself in an upsurge from decadence to a revival of ancient quality through the work of several gifted, understanding potters, notably Marie and Julian Martinez of San Ildefonso and Nampeyo of the Hopi First Mesa. Articles for household use and also as *objets d'art* for trade are produced in great variety.

A recent innovation is the development of a spontaneous contemporary school of watercolor painting by young Indians who are gifted and in their painting free from influence of the whites. The subject matter consists usually of costumed ceremonial figures, alone or in the dance. In style they are flat and decorative, with no backgrounds, and seem to continue the ancient traditions of the art. Important members of the group are Awa Tsira and Crescencio Martinez of San Ildefonso, and Fred Kabotie, a Hopi.

In the field of religion and ceremonial the ancient faith survives with vigor, and the old ceremonials are still enacted in the kivas and on the plazas. Christianity is superimposed upon this faith, and the Indian sees no inconsistency in going to early mass in the Christian church and then performing an ancient religious dance in front of the church in the presence of the statue of the Christian saint.

However, the further encroachments of modern civilization, especially since the development of the West through easy means of transportation and trade, poses the very difficult problem of an inevitable further adjustment. One encouraging aspect is the strong endeavor, on the part of understanding whites who are interested in the preservation of a noble indigenous culture, to assist the artists to maintain the ancient traditions in all their arts and to resist the lowering of quality in the face of quantity demands for tourist trade. See Ruth Bunzel, *The Pueblo Potter*, 1929; F. H. Douglas, *Modern Pueblo Indian Villages*, Denver Art Museum Leaflets Nos. 45-46 (1932); Exposition of Indian Tribal Arts, *Introduction to American Indian Art*, 2 vols. (1931); E. L. Hewett, *Ancient Life in the American Southwest*, 1930; E. H. Morris, *Archaeological Studies in the La Plata District*, Carnegie Institution of Washington Publications, 1939; Museum of Modern Art, *Indian Art in the United States*, 1941; F. H. H. Roberts, Jr., *A Survey of Southwestern Archeology*, Smithsonian Institution Annual Reports (1935); G. C. Vaillant, *Indian Arts in North America*, 1939.

—H.G.

pugging. *Cer.* Process of wedging clay in pug mill. See CERAMICS I.

pulvinar. See amphitheatre.

punctum. See neumes; MEDIEVAL MUSIC.

punto in aria. See lace.

Punuk art. See ESKIMO ART.

Purbeck marble. A brown limestone.

pure abstraction. See abstraction.

pure drawing. The essence of drawing with emphasis on the abstract character. See drawing.

purism. A movement of secession from cubism, founded in 1916 by Ozenfant and Charles Edouard Jeanneret (later a famous architect under the name of Le Corbusier). Flourishing until about 1925, purism emphasized semi-abstract painting in which faultless precision, clarity, and elegance of line and form, and an impersonal, mechanical cleanliness were emphasized. It was self-consciously modern and culturally technological. To a larger extent than in cubist painting, which it most closely resembles, recognizable objects appear in purist work. It is two-dimensional, frankly decorative, and constructed on the basis of an elaborate, systematic color theory. Le Corbusier, after 1921, applied the same "machine-age" aesthetic to his architecture, for which the purist paintings were decoratively well adapted. From 1920 to 1925 Ozenfant and Jeanneret edited a magazine in defense of their doctrine, called *L'Esprit Nouveau*. See FRENCH ART.   —L.D.L.

purity. This term has one general meaning in criticism: that a work pursues and exhibits the one true artistic value, and neglects all spurious values. As is to be expected, it has as many special meanings as there are special schools of criticism. Each group calls *pure* those works which seem to it to fulfill the nature and function of literary art. Recently, the term has been the most frequently used to indicate literary work in which the values of sound and structure have been emphasized, and those of meaning and reference neglected. Here, music is regarded as the most *pure* of the arts, because it can rely upon only the artistic values of the formal organization of sound, and can obtrude all extraneous values. Then, literary art is regarded as *pure* to the extent that it approaches music as a strictly formal art.   —I.J.

Purkinje effect. See COLOR.

purlin. A horizontal beam in a roof, resting on the principal rafters and supporting the common or minor rafters and roof covering.   —J.M.M.

purpose painting. See RUSSIAN ARTS.

purpure. *Her..* Purple.

putti (It.). Figures of nude Cupid-like children. Often found in Italian Renaissance painting and sculpture.

Pyramids, the. See EGYPTIAN ART.

Q

qanum. See MUSICAL INSTRUMENTS.

qaysaria (Ar.). A bazaar. See ISLAMIC ART.

qibla (Ar.). Direction toward Mecca; usual orientation of a mosque. See ISLAMIC ART.

quadrille. A dance in 5 movements or figures.

quadrivium. The *trivium*, grammar, logic and rhetoric, and the *quadrivium*, geometry, astronomy, arithmetic and music made up the 7 liberal arts in the medieval curriculum. Music, the 4th branch of the quadrivium was zealously cultivated in medieval universities. For its theory the treatise of Boethius (c. 480-524) *De Institutione Musica* was studied. Boethius' 3 divisions of music are characteristic of medieval thought and with slight variations were adopted by later writers. (1) *Musica mundana* included the music of the revolutions of celestial bodies, a concept borrowed from the Pythagorians. (2) *Musica humana*: "Human music", he states, "is that which is understood by anyone who descends into himself or enters into himself". This concept rejects the testimony of the ear ("*relicto aurium judicio*") in the investigation of music and proclaims the superiority of theory over practice. (3) *Musica instruments constituta* is sensuously perceptible and includes both that of the voice and instruments. It stands to (1) and (2) in the same relation that Plato's world of individuals does to the Ideal world. —V.A.

quadruplet. A group of 4 equal notes performed in the time of 3 or 6 of the same kind.

quail. See SYMBOLISM IN FAR EASTERN ART.

quality of a dance movement. Refers to some essential property which characterizes a dance movement and distinguishes it from other movements.

Since the essential characteristics of motor sensations by which movement is known and judged are time and stress, it follows that the source of the distinguishing qualities must lie in the particular rhythmic structure of actions and in the degree of tension present in their execution. Many of the body's actions establish their own time and stress phases by the very law of their functioning. Out of these innate motor responses have evolved a meaning and an appreciation of their characteristic forms and qualities. Especially is this true of swinging movements. Most of the large movements of the body are pendular because of the hinged character of its construction. Consequently swinging action is of necessity a structural characteristic that is dominant in all movement. Therefore its rhythmic form is by nature established in the neuro-muscular system and furnishes the source of study for all other rhythmic structures. Swinging pendular action by nature of our behavior equipment must be considered as the primary form from which all other movements are derived by a modification in its proportionate time and stress values.

On the basis of all movement being derived from an original swinging form, the following list is suggested as modifications of it: swinging, sustained, flowing, percussive, vibratory and syncopated.

The free, *swinging pendular* movements are characterized by a rhythmical to and fro action having passive acceleration and retardation as experienced when swinging in a swing. The end of each phase is marked by a momentary pause which continues until momentum is overcome by the force of gravity, permitting the return phase to be made. For this reason little fatigue accompanies such movements. They continue in an uninterrupted series of pulsations and are grouped or measured by the number of pulses required to complete the movement. Swinging movements easily fall into a one-two-three rhythm due to the placement of accent inherent in pendular action. They are very soothing in effect and their rhythm has the power to stimulate repetition to an almost hypnotic degree.

The rhythmical pendular to and fro character of swinging movement is easily changed to a to and fro "pistonlike" quality, if the moving part, such as an arm, is swung forward and pulled back before momentum is overcome. Such movements are stimulating yet fatiguing because of muscular effort necessary to check momentum and change direction.

The pendular character of the swing may also be changed to a more *sustained* quality by the introduction of tension in the support of the weight of the moving body instead of abandoning it to free pendular action. Sustained movements are executed with a steady release of energy maintaining an even tension throughout their execution. They have a feeling of restraint and are rich in associative meaning. On the other hand a slackening of tension introduces the quality of relaxation which may be present in varying degrees from the relaxation of *flowing,* undulating motion to a complete relaxation resulting in a "collapsing" either of unit parts of the body or the whole body resulting in a "fall" as in a faint. A falling movement may be executed with more tension than relaxation in which case a more sustained quality is imparted to the fall.

Contrasted with the uninterrupted flow of energy release of swinging movements is the sudden checking of movement by a vigorous muscle contraction, which produces movements of a jerky, explosive, *percussive* quality. Such movements usually have a swinging and sustained preparatory movement and are abruptly completed by an equalization of muscle tension causing the moving parts of the whole body to be steadied and held in suspension seemingly without effort. Or the contraction may occur almost without a perceptible retard imparting a puff-like accentuation like in a golf stroke and permitting the movement to continue to its full range of action. If a series of sharp muscular contractions are used to break up a movement

cycle into a series of abrupt starts and stops, there results a series of disconnected "staccatto-like" actions each one marked by a sharp emphasis. If such a series proceeds at a sufficiently rapid rate, its quality is changed to a *vibratory* effect. Tension is an essential feature for the effective execution of percussive movements.

If a muscle contraction occurs so as to place an accent in an unexpected place within a movement series, the element of *syncopation* is introduced. Syncopated movements are executed by beginning action on an unaccented interval and continuing its duration through the following accented one. They have a rhythmic structure whose sensations are experienced against those sensations of regularity of long established and customary patterns—thus destroying the monotony of regularity. Although syncopation destroys the feeling of the grouping accent of the underlying physiological beat, it does not destroy its rhythmic pull. It is only by its degree of deviation from the expected sequence of time and stress intervals that a movement is sensed as being syncopated. A syncopated muscular contraction is sensed as a sudden and unexpected delay in the progression of movement pulsations. This element of shock and surprise is highly stimulating and is most likely the reason for the delight and fascination in syncopated movement.

Any continued action will include several of these qualities, and more than one may be present in the same motor act. It is as one or the other dominates that a movement is said to be of a certain type. By changing the dynamics of an action its "feel"or quality is changed. Emphasis should not be on the movement we see as a movement, but upon what we are made to feel by the qualities revealed in its performance. For example: it is not significant that an arm executes a swinging movement. The important fact lies in what is evoked by the quality of "swingingness" projected by the swinging arm. These qualities, inherent in dynamic movement structure, are the emotive forces that arouse emotional forces as opposed to being expressive of them. Significant dance movements are emotive and not emotional. See rhythm; kinesthetic sense; tension; movement.   —M.N.H'D.

quality (of tone). See timbre.

quantitative aesthetics.   See AESTHETIC INQUIRY (4).

quarter. See HERALDRY.

quarter distance point, measuring point, point of distance. See PERSPECTIVE.

quartet. (1) A composition for 4 solo voices or instruments. (2) The 4 performers themselves.

quarto. See book sizes.

quatrefoil. *Arch.* Foliation, ornamental in nature, with four foils (q.v.).

quattrocento. See Florentine school.

quaver. See NOTATION.

qubba. A monumental tomb. See ISLAMIC ART.

Queen Anne architecture. The architecture associated with the brief reign of Queen Anne, from 1702-1714, marks the close of a century of compromise in England between the baroque, borrowed heterogeneously from Italy and Holland and championed most successfully by Inigo Jones and Sir Christopher Wren, and academism. Before the purer 18th cent. forms of Gibbs and Wood became paramount, the baroque enjoyed an impressive finale in the monumental edifice of Blenheim Palace, erected between 1705 and 1724 in honor of the Duke of Marlborough's military triumph at Blenheim. It at once represents the power, prosperity and increasing national consciousness of England and dominates the architectural output of the period. The designer was Sir John Vanbrugh (1666-1726), the leading architect of the reign, who also created the vast plan for Castle Howard. In Blenheim Palace baroque picturesqueness, spectacular compositions of masses, broken skylines, and interrelated forms are presented on a grand opera scale; and the interior, the antithesis of domestic intimacy, is overwhelmingly impressive. Yet even Vanbrugh, when he collaborated with Nicholas Hawksmoor on the Clarendon Press building at Oxford in 1710, prophesied through a strictly classical portico the academic triumph.

Less ostentatious but more enduring forces were at work in the realm of interior design. The Queen Anne style of furniture, with its graceful and elegant curves, its unprecedented modern upholstery and its fantastically gay and colorful chinoiserie lacquers—all parallel to the rising Rococo in France—inaugurated England's Golden Age of furniture design, and it remains to this day one of the favorite modes in the English-speaking world. See INTERIOR ARCHITECTURE AND DECORATION; EARLY AMERICAN ART.

—P.C.B.

quilisma. See MEDIEVAL MUSIC.

quintuplet. A group of 5 equal notes performed in the time allotted to 4, 3 or 6 of the same kind.

quodlibet. (1) A medley, pot-pourri (q.v.). (2) A humorous combination of various tunes.

quoin (Fr. *coin*, angle). A term generally applied to the corner-stones at the angle of a wall.

R

Ra. The great and chief god of ancient Egypt, god of the sun.

rabab. See MUSICAL INSTRUMENTS.

rabeschi. See arabesque.

racket. See MUSICAL INSTRUMENTS.

raden. (Jap.). A lacquer technique. Inlaid patterns of mother-of-pearl and metal in the lacquered surface. Also known as *kanagai.*

radial projection. See PERSPECTIVE.

radiance. See COLOR.

radiant emittance. See COLOR.

radiant energy. See COLOR.

radio actor. See RADIO DRAMA.

radio and music. It is impossible to overstate the importance of radio broadcasts as a factor in our musical culture. Radio transmits music to rural districts and small communities which were never visited by touring concert artists. It provides that element of repetition which is so necessary to the appreciation of symphonic music. It furnishes a point of contact with foreign cultures as well as the many diverse elements which have entered into our own musical culture.

Our own use of the radio is conditioned by the organization of the broadcasting industry in this country. It is perhaps useful to compare our own system with that of Nazi Germany and Great Britain. Germany under the Nazi regime has utilized the radio largely as an instrument of propaganda. They have thus developed the **folk-radio,** a receiving set of limited receptivity, which is only capable of reproducing broadcasts from domestic stations. In Great Britain the control of the air has been retained for the government through the agency of the British Broadcasting Corporation. In the U. S. A., however, broadcasting has been allowed to pass into the hands of powerful corporations which sell time on the air for the purpose of advertising various firms and products.

This pattern has had profound effects on the character of American broadcasting. It has in many cases resulted in musical programs at an inferior level of taste since a sponsor might feel (and possibly with reason) that a more general response might be secured in this manner. It has produced the "commercial" which, even in those cases when it is neither fulsome nor blatant in tone, is hardly a happy preliminary to the musical pleasures which follow. It has tended to foster timidity since it is undoubtedly safer to use music in a familiar style than to seek novelty in form or content.

It was, however, in pre-Nazi Germany that the possibilities of radio as a new channel of expression for the creative musician were first exploited. A work for chamber orchestra and organ commissioned from Paul Hindemith as early as 1927 was broadcast in 1928. In 1929 a monthly broadcast featured original music written esp. for the radio. Among the composers whose works were thus broadcast were Franz Schreker, Paul Graener, Max Bütting (who became a specialist in this field), and Kurt Weil. Courses in the various phases of radio music were offered by Hindemith, Butting, and others. A group of twelve north German composers also wrote music chiefly for chamber orchestra which was presented in broadcasts originating from Hamburg.

Peculiarities of scoring such as the omission of double basses and second violins, the cultivation of an open and transparent orchestral texture, the avoidance of thick and massive tutti passages, were in part concessions to the limited range and sensitivity of early broadcasting apparatus. Obviously, these very limitations made for distinctive musical qualities which have largely vanished with the special conditions which brought them into being.

In France an early competition for a radiogenic score was won (in 1927) by Florent Schmitt with his *Çançunik*. In general, however, both France and England seem to have been slower to utilize the resources of broadcasting for the various composer than was Germany.

The earliest period of broadcasting in the U. S. A. reached an audience of enthusiastic amateurs who were likely to be more concerned with the call letters of the station received than the content of the broadcast. In a remarkably short time, however, musicians and musical organizations began to realize the growing possibilities of the medium. As early as 1923 a week of Wagnerian opera was broadcast from the Manhattan Opera House over station WJZ. In that same year the Philharmonic Symphony Orchestra was broadcast from the Lewissohn Stadium and the Goldman Band from Central Park. A gala broadcast by John McCormack and Lucrezia Bori took place on New Year's Day, 1926. By 1928 the list of famous artists who had made broadcasts was impressive indeed. The very considerable prejudice against broadcasting disappeared rapidly in view of the desirable publicity and the substantial fees which rewarded such appearances. Three educational concerts conducted by Walter Damrosch in 1928 developed into a series of weekly broadcast lecture-concerts for school children which continued over the air the work which Dr. Damrosch had long carried on in his orchestral concerts for young people. By 1930 the Sunday afternoon Philharmonic Symphony Orchestra broadcasts had commenced, thus beginning a series of concerts over the air which have played so important a part in American musical life. The broadcasts of the Metropolitan Opera Company and those of the N. B. C. Symphony Orchestra remain major musical events.

In the U. S. A., though serious music was broadcast at a relatively early date, little consideration seems to have been given the American composer till 1936. In that year the Columbia Broadcasting System commissioned six American composers to write works suitable for broadcasting. The participating composers were Aaron Copland, Roy Harris, Howard Hanson, William Grant Still, Walter Piston, and Louis Gruenberg. The radio-operas which resulted from this and succeeding commissions were esp. interesting since they were composed for the ear alone without scenic adjuncts and without the intervals for the shift of scenery which break up broadcasts of actual stage performances in such an awkward fashion. Gian-Carlo Menotti's *The Old Maid and the Thief* (1939) is a cleverly realized work though not as interesting musically as others of the series. In the summer of 1938 Howard Barlow conducted a series of American works from a much larger number of manuscripts submitted at his request. Among the composers whose works were thus performed were Paul Creston and William Schuman. Mention should also be made of the broadcasts of American music by the Rochester Philharmonic Symphony Orchestra under the direction of Dr. Howard Hanson.

Very characteristic of American radio programs is the large amount of incidental music required for dramatic programs of the most varied kinds. Much of the music composed for such programs is clever, facile, effective. Much is a synthetic pseudo-romantic product of a kind which has been made only too familiar in commercial movie scores.

The list of serious works summarized far too briefly above forms only the smallest percentage of the enormous amount of music broadcast. Popular dance music dominates the broadcasting channels. Name-bands, on the strength of their air-won prestige, have become household words. Poular singers gain tremendous and fanatically devoted followings during their day before the microphone. A popular song enjoys only the briefest period of popularity before ears of the radio audience become satiated, and another must be found.

The picture presented by modern broadcasting is extremely complex. The amount of music broadcast is almost incredibly large. The dominance of popular music is pronounced; but the actual amount, if not the proportion, of serious music broadcast is substantial. For the most part, however, music on the radio has the character of a competent commercial product. This is possibly inevitable in view of the nature of the broadcasting industry. It is quite clear that a higher level of public taste would be reflected in the quality of music broadcast since the sponsor seeks to buy good will. Since, however, the radio is the most powerful educative force in the field of music, it may well be asked whether this force will not tend to hold public taste at its own level, teaching the public to accept what it offers with occasional concessions to listeners who prefer the deeper and higher forms of music.   —C.W.H.

RADIO DRAMA. One of the earliest attempts to use radio as a medium for dramatic expression occurred in 1922, when station WGY, Schenectady, N. Y.,. broadcast a performance of Eugene Walters' play, "The Wolf". Since then, radio drama has won an enormous daily audience, and has discovered and developed techniques peculiar to itself.

Limiting and defining the character of radio drama is the fact that it must work solely with the instruments provided by aural experience. Scene and state of mind alike must be conveyed by words or music or easily identifiable sounds.

Further, radio drama has an audience of individuals, widely separated by space and circumstance. Each listener stands in a peculiarly intimate relationship to the program which is unimpaired (and unfacilitated) by the crowd reactions common to the theatre. His interest or approbation cannot be stimulated by glamorous lights and furnishings, or the tense, somewhat uncritical excitement of a crowded auditorium. In the familiar surroundings of his own home, office or automobile, the auditor's sympathy and attention must be attracted by sound alone.

Finally, radio drama depends for its success upon the active (though perhaps unconscious) collaboration of each member of its audience. It is a truly "suggestive" art. The listener's imagination must translate sound into colour and costume; must identify the tone and accent of a voice with the size and nature of a man. The ease with which such translations and identifications are made is rather remarkable. Part of radio drama's astonishing popularity is probably due to the fact that every hearer is participating in the creation of his own enjoyment; lending from past experience the visual facts which fill out the "reality" of characters and places.

Production of a radio drama begins with the **script writer**, who provides plot and verbal characterization, in terms of the requirements of broadcast technique.

First, he must use some aural device to create in the public an "intention to listen". He may use a fanfare, theme song, or some sharp, attention-getting sound or sentence. But however he chooses to introduce his program, it is necessary for him to get on with the action almost immediately. The long, slow introductory scenes common to the theatre are useless on the air; the listener must be given intrinsically interesting development at the very beginning, or he will turn to another station.

Further, the radio writer must build his scenery out of words, music and sound-effects. To set the aural stage, he will frequently use a **narrator**, a commentator usually external to the plot, to whom are assigned lines introducing, partially describing, and sometimes explaining the place, action and characters of the play. Although his functions are usually somewhat similar to that of the "Chorus" of antiquity, the narrator may sometimes be used as the dominant figure in the action itself; subjective drama, told in the first person singular, is one of radio's distinctive achievements.

Having no visual stage to interfere with his fancy, the radio writer enjoys a freedom of movement unknown to the theatrical playwright. He can shift scenes rapidly in time and place, and make effective use of *"flashbacks"*, in which past events are reproduced to explain present plot-situations. To separate scene from scene, he may use a brief musical interlude, or **bridge**, a piece of narration, or a moment of complete silence. Interesting emotional effects may be achieved by using the **montage**, in which a variety of short and perhaps superficially unrelated speeches are presented by different voices, simultaneously or in rapid succession; the total impression conveying the mood or idea intended by the author. The montage can also be used to indicate the passage of time, and may include short chords of music or interludes of sound as well as alternating or intermingled voices.

In his script, the writer must indicate where all sound effects or musical passages are to be introduced, and specify their nature and duration. Finally, he usually finds it necessary to use simple plots, uncomplicated by sub-plots or non-dramatic material. Simplicity and compression are essential to any good script.

To the **radio actor** falls the task of translating the printed script into living words. With neither paint nor costume, light nor shadow to help, he must find all the equipment for producing his illusion within the range and intensity of his voice. Since his speech is "overheard by", rather than "projected at" his audience, over-acting is uncongenial to radio technique.

The radio actor does not memorize his lines; instead, he reads them from the script with only a few hours (at most) of rehearsal. Consequently, he must be able to give a subtle vocal characterization almost at sight. Sometimes he is called upon to play more than one part in a single show; to **double** successfully in a variety of roles, he must be able to use different dialects convincingly, and throw his voice into various registers.

Vocal personality and sincerity, together with expert delineation of character through tone, pace, accent and volume; these are the necessary and ultimate instruments of the radio actor.

Sound effects play an important role in strengthening the illusion of reality in the listener's imagination. The whirring screech of a lathe, for example, immediately suggests a factory scene. Many sounds have been recorded, so that they may be reproduced realistically over the air; others must be simulated by highly trained sound-technicians. Whenever used, sound effects must be easily recognizable (or carefully identified), and integrated with the dialogue in such a manner as to be unobtrusive.

Music is frequently used as a sound effect, with great success in certain types of production. In emotional scenes, a musical background can heighten the dramatic impact of the lines immeasurably. Music also serves as a transition device between scenes, and is especially useful in suggesting (or "setting") moods.

The **engineer** functions as radio's stage-manager. He controls the microphones which translate sound into radio-electrical impulses, and regulates (or "balances") the volume of broadcast sound.

Radio drama depends on the collective efforts of writer, actor, sound-effects man and engineer. But the person who collects these efforts,—the *Producer*, is ultimately responsible for the success or failure of any broadcast. The producer's function is similar to that of the director in the theatre; he must cast, rehearse and unify the show, and manage to get it off the air on time.

His first responsibility is to the clock; he must use precisely the amount of time assigned him,—no more, not a second less. In radio's early days, the "stopwatch producer" was a common phenomenon; such a person was concerned only with timing his program correctly.

But the modern radio producer realizes a much more complex task. Working with the medium of simple sound, he must weave a complicated pattern of speech and speed, of music and sound-effects, to create a radio drama. A good producer can do as much for a radio play as a Ford or an Eisenstein can do for a movie. And as in the movies, writers sometimes handle their own production; this is desirable, since it is often necessary to cut or re-write portions of the script during rehearsal.

TYPES OF RADIO DRAMA. Almost everything which can be broadcast may involve dialogue and actors, but radio drama generally falls into several loose classifications, which will be discussed in quantitative order. It must be remembered, however, that there are undoubted exceptions to every rule and judgment made below.

(1) In terms of time, the biggest thing in radio is the **serial** (often called **soap opera** because so many serials are sponsored by soap companies). More programs of this sort are heard daily than any other single dramatic type.

The **radio serial** is a continued story which is enacted either in consecutive chapters, or in a related series of independent episodes each of which is a complete playlet in itself. In the consecutive variety, each chapter begins with a climax, contains a solution of the problem situation obtaining at the beginning, and rises to a second unresolved climax near the end, so that the listener will be intrigued into tuning in for the next development. Most serials present 5 fifteen-minute chapters each week, broadcast during the daytime or early evening. Some, however, are weekly half-hour shows. The endurance of writer, audience, or sponsor constitutes the only limit to the number of chapters.

Serial characters, like almost all dramatic characters in radio, are simple, rather than complex; definite, immediately comprehended types who rely more for their identification on dialect and vocal personality than on gradual development or growth through action. Since characterization is left largely up to the actor, plot is the most important element of any serial script.

Serials differ in their quality and approach, depending on the type of audience to which they are designed to appeal. Among the most popular and prevalent are those directed exclusively at housewives,—tear-jerking tales in which emotion is at a premium, and blatant sentimentality is both permitted and preferred. The leading character is almost invariably a woman, usually one skilled in that interesting sort of platitudinousness known as "homey philosophy". This heroine is manipulated through an interminable series of emotional crises; her function is to suffer, but always to triumph because, like Lancelot, her heart is pure. The general message conveyed by such serials is one which confirms the average woman in her belief that "feminine intuition" combines with middle-class morality to make, if not the good, at least the desirable life.

It is generally agreed that these serials are of a low order, but since they continue to sell merchandise, there is no reason to believe that they will be immediately improved or withdrawn from the air. To some extent they are slowly being replaced, but at present they constitute the dominant type.

Other serials, usually presented in the late afternoon hours, are intended for a juvenile audience. They are pure adventure stores, of the "dime-novel" sort. The leading character is either a remarkable adolescent or a modern Robin Hood, and the plots usually point up some obvious moral or manly virtue.

Finally, there are a number of serials which attempt maturity either in plot, or treatment of characters, or both. These are considerably less maudlin, and often use a humorous approach. Some even attempt consideration of serious (though non-controversial) domestic problems. Most of them make amusing capital out of typical incidents of daily life; although too unvaryingly optimistic, they frequently maintain rather high standards of excellence. Such serials are usually (although not always) intended for a mixed audience of men *and* women; their success indicates that more would be appreciated.

(2) The **straight drama**, generally a half-hour playlet written especially for broadcast, is usually presented at night. Light comedy, melodrama, mystery, etc., are the popular bases for straight drama plots, although historical themes and romantic biography are sometimes utilized. Some of the best radio-writing is done for this type of show, and production is often of a very high order. The category as a whole probably includes many of radio's most entertaining dramatic programs.

(3) The **adaptation** is a form of radio drama in which a stage-play, short-story, novel or movie is re-written for broadcast purposes. The adaptive method, although the oldest of radio techniques, is not calculated to produce programs of particular excellence.

Where, as with Shakespeare or Shaw, the original version consists largely in self-sufficient dialogue, the adaptation may turn out splendidly (aside from the fact that so much must be chopped and pruned away in the process). And it is certainly true that adaptations of famous plays and novels have great educational value.

Still, the average play or book contains elements which cannot be reproduced by broadcast; moreover, at best only a scant portion of the original lines may be retained. To re-write and condense a stage-play for air-presentation is a difficult task, demanding great care and technical sympathy if it is to be done properly. Such patient skill is infrequently applied to adaptations; hence, they often lack coherence, and almost always fail to do justice to the original. It is significant that such programs usually rely more for their appeal on "big name" stars and directors, or on recent popular titles, than on the actual quality of the individual adaptation.

(4) The **comic skit**, a short, humorous sketch usually presented as part of a variety (music and drama) program, is closely related to the burlesque or vaudeville "blackout". Polished dialogue, presented with sparkle and clarity by talented comedians, often combines with intelligent satire to place the comic skit among the better examples of dramatic art on the air.

(5) **Educational drama** includes all radio plays or sketches whose intention is to instruct or propagandize. Featuring enactments of historic events, biographical material, or dramatic exemplification of ideas and modes of conduct, such programs have demonstrated their ability to perform many effective pedagogic functions. Some of radio's best writers and producers have probably done their most significant work in this field. The **aural newsreel**, in which contemporary events are "reported" in dramatic form, is an exciting member of the "educational" class which has done much to further the development of radio technique.

(6) Finally, there are the so-called **experimental productions**. These are self-conscious attempts to exploit the possibilities of aural presentation, and to create new art forms suited to the medium. Some excellent programs have resulted from these efforts to

lend the pretensions of "art" to what is at present an industry; but in general it may be said that most experimental radio plays are failures, when judged by the aesthetic criteria to which they appeal. They usually turn out to be rather badly written melodramatic fantasies, often of the psychological or "super-science" variety.

Partly responsible for this failure is the fact that writers of such programs have been too much concerned with achieving "effects", and too little with producing plays with "total" dramatic significance. A new narratorial technique, a new sound pattern; these have been sought, rather than good playwrighting. Radio drama may be said, in its more ambitious moods, to be still in its adolescence.

Of *radio drama in general,* it may be noted that beyond comedy or rare educational works, the results do not equal the means. Serious themes are seldom undertaken; the maudlin, the melodramatic or the fantastic remain the characteristic types. The production techniques are ready to accommodate significant work, but radio writers have not yet supplied the script. The reasons for this may be discovered, perhaps, in several facts.

Radio is very young, and so are most of the men who write for it.

Moreover, radio is subject to the most tyrannical censorship known to the arts (not excluding the movies). Since a wide variety of homes contain radios, and since any child capable of motor reflexes may turn the switch which floods his nursery with broadcast sound, it is argued that radio drama may not properly deal with subjects which might offend *any* listener. Considering the enormous number of subjects which might (and do) offend a portion of radio's 100,000,-000 auditors, the writer is restricted to a rather narrow range of materials. He can be entertaining, or he can be a propagandist for "respectable" opinions; beyond that, he is not expected to go. (Sometimes he may go further, but such instances are exceptional).

This censorship is closely connected with the fact that radio is a commercial medium. Radio's present function is to make profits for the owners of stations and networks. These profits come from advertising. The material produced cannot be of such a nature as to endanger profits from advertising. Listeners are to be attracted, entertained, and made receptive to selling messages. Anything which might be repugnant or uninter-

esting to a potential buyer is not likely to be produced. The level and content of radio drama is thus censored by stations and sponsors in terms of the low-average taste; occasional sops to the high-brows notwithstanding. To which it must be added that the function of most programs is to sell merchandise or services; not to be significant or serious.

Most radio programs are sold or produced in bulk. With some notable exceptions, the writer does not simply turn out one program; he turns out a series. A tremendous quantity of material must be produced to meet inflexible deadlines. The average serial writer, for example, must create an average of 60 or more pages per week; the equivalent of 14 full-length plays per year.

The writer has neither the time to polish, nor the peace to invent. In consequence, he falls back on formula-fiction; grinds out his weary stint, and is not surprised to discover that his work is not comparable (from the qualitative point of view) even to that printed in "pulp" magazines, or produced in the most tenuous Hollywood "quickie".

Moreover, since radio shows are usually aired only once, and then forgotten, there is no incentive comparable to that of the literary man who may hope to leave his printed mark on posterity. Radio is ephemeral; the writer must be content with but a single performance.

Writing under pressure, frequently interested in his medium only because of the profits it holds out; restricted by censorship and required only to fill time in a manner which will entice people to sit through the commercial announcements, the radio writer has neither the opportunity, the motive, nor frequently the ability to do much better than he does.

Despite this, programs are regularly produced which have high entertainment value; and radio drama has achieved remarkably fine results on many occasions. Although the general standard is low, the individual program is sometimes excellent. Potentially, radio drama holds great promise; its quality is gradually improving, and the future may find it taking its place among the mature and serious arts. It remains to be seen whether television will outmode the familiar form of radio broadcast before such maturity can be achieved. See *Radio Writing,* Eric Barnouw, 1942; *Radio Writing,* Max Wylie, 1939.
—J.F.M.

radio drama, transcribed. It is sometimes necessary to broadcast the same program over various stations at different times. In such instances, the show may be transcribed, i.e., recorded on an 18-inch record at 33-1/3 revolutions per minute, so that it may be "played back" whenever convenient. Auditions of radio programs are usually transcribed, so that they may be criticized at the sponsor's leisure. —J.F.M.

radiograph. X-ray "photographs". They are more correctly called shadowgraphs. A camera is not used to produce the radiograph. —H.M.

rafter. A timber or beam giving form, slope, and support, as to a roof.

raga. See ORIENTAL MUSIC.

rag rug. Woven or hand-looms. Pieces of cotton, linen or woolen cloth cut into narrow strips and woven. —B.E.J.

ragtime. See jazz; AMERICAN NEGRO MUSIC.

rain-drop stroke. In Chinese painting, the technique of shading developed by the Southern School of the T'ang dynasty, i.e., shading by small, pointed, oval strokes.

raised plan. See PERSPECTIVE.

Rajput painting. See INDIAN ART.

rakkan (Jap.). Signature on a painting. A painter's sign and seal.

Raku yaki (Jap.). A ceramic ware made by various potters in different places.

Rakutozan yaki (Jap.). Pottery made in Yamashiro province.

ramada. Wall-less wood, withe and palm shed used in place of nave before open chapels for Indians in Franciscan monasteries of 16th and 17th cents. in Yukatán. —J.M.

ramma (Jap.). Perforated decorative wooden panels placed above the inner walls of a Japanese interior to insure circulation of air.

rampant. See HERALDRY.

random or **uncoursed.** Term applied to masonry in which stone is laid without continuous horizontal joints.

random coursed. Term applied to masonry in which the heights of the courses are in no regularly recurring arrangement. (Note distinction between random coursed masonry and random masonry.) —J.M.M.

range, in dance. See movement.

ranz des vaches. A simple melody played on the Alpine horn.

rapid seeing. See PHOTOGRAPHY.

rapid-transit. See CIVIC PLANNING.

rate of pitch. See vibrato.

raten (Jap.). See raden.

rationalism. Synonymous with functionalism; modern; international style; progressive. An approach to architectural or industrial design unrelated to traditional styles, and chiefly a 20th-cent. manifestation; called a style of reason due to (1) cooperation of the artist with the engineering principles involved, with the dictates of machinery and with primary respect for function; (2) an appeal to the intellect by means of inherent relations, lines and proportions, rather than to the emotions by romantic associational aspects; (3) intelligent use of plastics and new materials; (4) a new "classicism" by virtue of emphasis on structural simplicity; (5) the affectation of mathematical systems of lines and spaces (cf. Paul T. Frankl, *Form and Re-Form*); (6) the logical awareness of new social demands, as mass-housing with problems of finance, sanitation, etc.; (7) realization of the need for horizontalism in line and form not only as functional "streamlining" in an era of speed, but as an observation of the psychological demand for repose. See POST-REVOLUTIONARY ARCHITECTURE AND DECORATIVE ARTS IN THE U. S. A.; also MUSICAL PERFORMANCE, MAIN TRENDS IN. —A.W.M.

rattle. See MUSICAL INSTRUMENTS.

rauschpfeife. See MUSICAL INSTRUMENTS.

raw sienna. See iron pigments.

raw umber, dark. See iron pigments.

rayonism. A style of abstract painting founded by Michael Larinov in Russia in 1911, and characterized by radiating rays of light. See RUSSIAN ARTS. —L.L.D.

ray pattern. In Greek art, esp. on pottery of the 8th to 6th cent. B.C., a row of upward or outward pointing rays, contiguous at the bottom or regularly spaced.   —L.T.S.

Rayy ware. See PERSIAN ART.

"ready-made" objects. See object.

realgar. The name of this painter's pigment comes from the Arabic, *Rahj al ghār,* and the use of it appears to have been largely in the eastern Mediterranean and the Far East. It has been identified on wall paintings from sites in Central Asia and is mentioned frequently in ancient and medieval treatises. Chemically, it is closely associated with the pigment, orpiment, being also a sulphide of arsenic. Its color, however, is orange-red.   —G.L.S.

realism. The depiction of the real or actual, in the sense of that which is immediately present to the senses or to the experience of men in the life of their own time and place. (1) In art, and from a formal point of view, realism differs from naturalism (q.v.) in stressing the "Universal in the Particular" while naturalism merely presents the "Particular" as the foundation of reality. While such a distinction is often difficult to make in practice, Rembrandt, Velasquez, Millet, Daumier, Brueghel, Egyptian sculpture of the Old Kingdom, Roman portrait sculpture (often), and Gothic sculpture of the fifteenth century are ordinarily termed realistic, while Hellenistic sculpture of the type of the *Barberini Satyr* or the *Torso Belvedere* in the Vatican, and the 19th cent. art of the type of Rodin's *Age of Bronze,* the sculpture of Hildebrand, and Meissonier's "photographic" painting are instances of formal naturalism.

(2) From the point of view of content, realism differs from naturalism in that it does not necessarily involve a naturalistic philosophy of life. In literature, naturalism is sometimes spoken of as an extreme form of realism. For instance, Hardy, Ibsen, and Flaubert are called realists; Zola and de Maupassant naturalists. In both art and literature realism appears more frequently, since it allows more varied opportunities for significant expression. It is likely to be a higher grade of art than naturalism, since it tends to be more complex and charged with human values, probing for some inner hidden truths or structures, and allowing the possibility of a teleological order.

(3) Realism is often used in both art and literature merely with reference to subject matter, an inaccurate connotation, since it

may then be applied to art of many diverse styles, and is very likely to be confused with expressionism, unless the emphasis on design and on personal conception which characterizes expressionism (q.v.) is clearly understood.

Realism differs from idealism (q.v.) in stressing the actual as opposed to ideal ("Universal"), often insisting upon what the layman would call "ugly" subjects as opposed to "beautiful", e.g., The *Sheik-el-Beled,* German painting and sculpture of the 15th and 16th cents., Rembrandt's nudes, Velasquez's dwarfs, Donatello's *John the Baptists* and *Mary Magdalen,* Rodin's *Burghers of Calais* and *Old Courtesan,* Millet's *Man with the Hoe.* Realism differs from romanticism (q.v.) in its insistence upon fact as opposed to imagination, upon actuality as contrasted with plausibility and desirability, upon the present rather than the distant in time and place.

The philosophic meaning of the term realism has no application in art criticism.   —L.D.L.

realism, in photography. See PHOTOGRAPHY.

realistic Manifesto. See SCULPTURE.

rebacking. See RESTORATION OF PAINTINGS.

rebeck. Primitive violin shaped like a half-pear; it had 3 strings. See MUSICAL INSTRUMENTS.

rebinding. The great bulk of hand binding practiced in the U. S. A. today consists primarily of rebinding damaged books. Our cheaper edition bindings too often have a short life in the lending library and must be rebound for further useful service. The larger libraries usually have their own facilities and smaller ones send their damaged books to trade binderies.

The damage to a trade edition usually consists of a broken back, including broken sewing plus a partially torn and loosened cover. The first step in rebinding the book is to remove the cover and either cut or sand off enough of the back to remove the original sewing. The back edge is then glued and allowed to dry. New end sheets (the fly-leaf and sheet that is applied to the inside cover) are then prepared by folding a strong sheet of paper and reinforcing the fold of the sheet with muslin. A folded end sheet is applied with paste to the first and last sheet of the book. The glued book is broken up into sections approximating the original signatures and fed one at a time into a special sewing machine that oversews each signature to the previous one until the book is completely sewn together. This method produces an exceptionally strong book that is superior to the original, but results in a book that does not open easily due to the over-sewing of about one-fourth of an inch along the back of the book. The back of the book then receives a light layer of glue.

The next step is to trim the book just enough to straighten the edges, and in this operation some binders trim so deeply that the original margins are completely destroyed. This is particularly true of old books that have been rebound more than once and have, due to the carelessness of the binder, lost about all of their margins, and with them most of the beauty and value of the original volume. The book is then rounded and smashed either by hand or machine. The smashing spreads the outer edges of the book to conform with the additional thickness of the cover and permits a better join to the cover hinge. A second layer of glue is applied and a strip of cloth (muslin, flannel, or a stiff net called super) is applied to the back and allowed to project about an inch onto the sides. Head bands, if used, will be applied at this time. A stain or stipple treatment is then applied to the top or all three edges of the book and it is ready to be cased in (the application of the cover to the book).

Marbled edges and fly-leaves were frequently used until a few years ago. Marbling consists of floating several colors upon water and combing them into a suitable pattern, then laying the edge of the book or side of the sheet on the surface of the water to transfer the pattern. Specially-made colors work best; however, ordinary oil colors diluted with linseed oil and turpentine will transfer fairly successfully and produce interesting results.

The making of the case (cover) is a simple operation. Two boards made of non-warping pasteboard are cut to fit the book plus a small fraction of an inch over-hanging on the top, bottom, and outside edges. A piece of binding cloth is cut large enough to wrap around the book and allow an over-hang of about three-fourths of an inch on all sides. Glue or paste is applied to the back side of the cloth by brush or machine and with the boards in place on the book the cloth is wrapped around the book, pressed

down, and then removed carrying the boards in proper position. A center strip of stiff paper equal to the width of the back is placed between the boards to stiffen the cloth back. The corners of the cloth are cut on a diagonal, folded in, and the edges turned and smoothed down. The completed case is allowed to dry and is ready to receive the title, which is usually hot stamped with brass type on the back with metal foil. Type metal may be used for the stamping of a very few books if the temperature is kept low enough to avoid the softening of the metal.

The casing-in operation consists of wrapping the cover around the book, gluing or pasting the top of the end sheet, and pressing down the cover. This is then repeated on the back and the book is placed between boards in a press to dry for about a day. The boards have metal edges that force the cloth of the cover down between the back and the boards to form a groove to the hinge. See EARLY BOOKBINDING AND FINE BINDING.   —H.E.S.

receding colors. See COLOR.

reciprocal pattern. A design in which the motive is repeated, but, alternately reversed top for bottom.

recital. A concert at which a single performer executes the entire program.

recitative. See opera; oratorio.

recorder. See MUSICAL INSTRUMENTS.

recto. *Book.* The page of an open book on the right-hand side. The opposite page is the **verso.**

red. See SYMBOLISM IN FAR EASTERN ART.

red bird. See SYMBOLISM IN FAR EASTERN ART.

red chalk. Red ochre, ruddle.

red-figured vases. About 525 B.C., Athenian vase-painters invented a technique far superior to the previous black-figured type (see black-figured vases). After the vase was shaped, they incised their designs with a blunt tool, painted around the incision a narrow glazed line, then painted in the details, probably with a single-bristled brush, and finally filled the entire background with black glaze. As a result the figures appeared as terra-cotta red against a black background. The advantage over the previous technique was that this allowed them much more freedom and variety in drawing than the earlier silhouette permitted. The great period of red-figured vases was from 525 to 400 B.C., in Athens. During these years hundreds of potters and painters flourished, supplying the great demand for Athenian pottery at home and for the export trade of the city. The range of their work was enormous. But certain broad periods may be distinguished, roughly dividing the 5th cent. into three parts. From 525 to 470 the paintings were distinguished by nervous, crisp, linear treatment, a fine rhythmic sense, spirited compositions, and experimentation in three-dimensional portrayal of the human body in action by the use of foreshortening and hatching. Among the leading painters were Euphronios, Euthymides, Macron, and, perhaps the greatest of all, Brygos. By the middle of the century the élan of the earlier time had generally been supplanted by a more monumental technique; the number of figures was lessened, the emphasis was on power and the amplification of forms. Polygnotus and the Penthesilea Painter are representative of this tendency. Toward the end of the century there was a vogue for the florid, ornate, and over-refined, with a consequent deterioration in linear precision and masterly design. Meidias, Aison and Aristophanes are typical of this trend. With the fall of the Athenian Empire at the close of the century the center of vase production shifted to Italiot Greece, where, during the fourth century, red-figured vases were made in Apulia, Lucania and Campania. These vases exaggerated the florid and over-refined tendencies of the final Athenian period, vulgarizing the shapes, crowding figures into chaotic compositions on various levels, profusely using polychromatic effects, and picturing melodramatic and comic scenes for popular appeal.   —W.R.A.

red lead. Like the white pigment made from metallic lead, this has been manufactured since ancient times. Writers like Pliny seem to confuse it with other bright orange-red pigments such as cinnabar, but analysis has discovered it on many ancient objects. Probably the wide spread of artificial vermilion in the later Middle Ages had something to do with the decline in the use of red lead by artist painters. It is still a common article of commerce and is much used, particularly over metal where mixed with oil it serves as a firm undercoating for whatever color is desired. Chemically, it is a tetroxide of lead.

Its color is moderately stable but has been found to darken and turn brownish with long exposure, particularly in the presence of some light and of high moisture.   —G.L.S.

reducing temperature. *Cer.* To limit use of air in burning fuel so that excess gases will rob oxygen from oxides in body or glaze. See CERAMICS I.

reed instruments. See MUSICAL INSTRUMENTS.

reed organ. See MUSICAL INSTRUMENTS.

refectory. See FURNITURE.

reflectance. See COLOR.

refinement. *Arch.* Any variation from precision or exactness of line for the purpose of increasing the beauty of a building or making it more dynamic.

reflections. See PERSPECTIVE.

refraction. See PERSPECTIVE.

refraction colors. The colors of the spectrum as obtained by a refractive prism.

refractive index. The expression of the ratio of the velocity of flight traveling in a vacuum to its velocity in another transparent medium and is an index of the amount which the light rays will be bent when obliquely entering the transparent medium.   —V.K.B.

refractory. *Cer.* Clay capable of resisting action of heat. See CERAMICS I.

regal. See MUSICAL INSTRUMENTS.

regardant. See HERALDRY.

regence style. See FURNITURE.

regeneration of varnishes. See RESTORATION OF PAINTINGS.

regionalism. The self-conscious and programmatic cultivation of a style and subject matter considered natural to the people and representative of the environment of a restricted geographic area, e.g., a state or province, to which the artist himself belongs by birth or early training. Regionalism is founded upon the following argument: (1) that an artist or author normally knows best the environment in which he was born and spent his early childhood, rather than anything he may have experienced later or elsewhere, (2) that a work of art is successful in proportion as it depicts what the artist or author knows best rather than in proportion as it embodies timeless and/or international aesthetic values, which are empty abstractions (relativism), and (3) that therefore, most of the artistic quality of the work will derive from faithfulness to the appearance of the environment and to the habits and mentality of the people of the region, rather than from aesthetic merit *per se*.

In theory, regionalism would necessitate above all a stylistic unity among the artists of the region in question. Moreover, the style must be consciously cultivated and programmatically represented as native or natural to the region. It is then spoken of as either regionalistic or regional. As used in the United States today the two terms are synonymous. Neither term could be used to describe the art of Florence or Siena in the Renaissance, where the stylistic unity is unconscious and inevitable.

Historically, a mild regionalism occurred in Spanish novel writing of the second half of the 19th cent., which was consciously provincial, and which included such authors as Caballero, Valdés, Valera, Alarcón, Bazan, Pereda, and early Ibáñez.

The term ordinarily refers, however, to a minor American movement, primarily in painting, but to a lesser degree in literature as well, which achieved public attention in newspapers and popular magazines during the 1930's, flourishing essentially in the Middle West between 1933 and 1937. It was a subsidiary phase of the main movement in art and literature in the U. S. A. during the 1930's, known as the **"American Scene"**. This movement was largely a product of the depression and the efforts of the government to solve the economic problems of the artist through W. P. A. and P. W. A. projects which could be carried on wherever he was then living, and which would be considered useful by the public at large. The results of the "American Scene" movement were (1) to reintroduce into the arts a larger interest in subject matter as such and American subject matter in particular, (2) to encourage a realistic or romantic depiction of this subject matter, (3) to give artists and authors a greater confidence in the power of America· to produce an important art independent of European influence, (4) to create an enormous public interest in art, and (5) to multiply the number of inferior but successful artists.

Within this general trend the regionalists, both by definition and historically, represented a special and narrower doctrine. The following are the chief characteristics of modern American regionalism not necessarily involved in the basic definition, but comprehended in the term as it is used in the U. S. A. today:

(1) Style was not stressed and no stylistic unity was achieved in any one state or geographic area, since, contrary to the expectations of the partisans, national and international forces, represented by such mechanisms as education, the radio, newspapers, magazines, cinema, and automobile, militated powerfully against regionalistic isolation. Moreover, each regionalist had drawn upon different European sources to form his style, so that they had nothing in common except the doctrine. Finally, they produced no converts or imitators of importance to carry on and propagate their several styles.

(2) Emphasis was placed almost entirely upon subject matter and the general attitude of the artist toward it; and the representatives of the doctrine even frowned upon the use of the word "style" as "arty".

(3) Ideationally, regionalism was the artistic counterpart and expression in America of the forces of conservative reaction in politics and culture which characterized the decade of the 1930's throughout the world, and of which the German version is the most clear and comprehensive. The regionalists themselves were in most cases unconscious rather than conscious fascists, i.e., cultural, but not necessarily political fascists. This is apparent in the following complex of characteristics of American regionalism: (a) It was antiinternational. In particular it was antiFrench. In the same sense as contemporary German art, American regionalism was "tribal", contending that blood relationship takes precedence over the international cultural forces of a given era in influencing art, and that an artist owes first allegiance to his local culture and national and racial heritage, and should reject the products and influence of contemporary, but foreign aesthetic principles and artistic styles. Regionalists stressed that an artist must "return from Bohemia" to the scenes of his childhood, renounce all foreign ways, cut off long hair and put on overalls. Like Nazi artists they painted self-conscious illustrations of the types of people in the several provinces of the country. (b) Regionalism was escapist, isolationist, and Americanist. Like isolationism in the politics

of the 1930's, it was an effort to escape to-day's cultural issues. The method employed was a flight to the farm, and a Victorian revivalism, flavored by a mildly humorous popular-romanticism, and by a nostalgic admiration of the good old horse and buggy days. The chief subjects (usually presented with catchy titles) were farm scenes glorifying happy, healthy peasants—haying, plowing, praying, eating, washing, or fighting the elements—; farm animals, barns, and back-houses; old Victorian houses and bric-a-brac; Currier and Ives subjects; river steamboats; pioneers portrayed with historic accuracy to detail; early Americana; Daughters of the Revolution; and popular illustrations of the stories of Paul Bunyan, Paul Revere, Frankie and Johnnie, Tom Sawyer, and George Washington. (c) Regionalism was anti-intellectual and anti-aesthetic. The artists opposed or attacked museums as storehouses of old cultures managed by snobs, aesthetes, and decadents. They opposed the study of aesthetics and of the history and criticism of art as the activity of effete impractical intellectuals. They opposed liberal education as dull, non-creative, and confusing. They opposed art whose whole purpose is to please the eye or elevate the mind as "art for art's sake", and hence foreign, un-American, and likely to be "Bohemian" and immoral. Regionalism was, instead, ideological, and aimed to persuade the public to its general philosophy through the choice and treatment of the subject. It sought favor primarily with the masses rather than the specialists, i.e., serious artists, critics, amateurs, and art historians. It sought attention in the public press, glorified the man of simple tastes and little formal education, and appealed to the authority of common sense as contrasted with specialized education. This point is well illustrated by an oft-repeated public statement of one of the regionalists that the only good ideas he ever had came while he was milking a cow, and by the fact that the same individual conspicuously wore overalls when painting and teaching.

The chief regionalists in painting were Thomas Benton, John S. Curry, and Grant Wood, of whom the first two are still painting; and the chief trumpeter of the movement in popular books and in manifestoes to the press was Thomas Craven. A few literary men who wrote of the local scene in the 1930's subscribed to certain aspects of the regionalistic doctrine, but of these the abler writers can not properly be called regionalists any more than the great majority of "American Scene" painters, and none designates himself by this label. Robert Frost, for instance, who might be suspected, has elaborately denied the connection, and writers like Caldwell, Steinbeck, and Farrell, though they use material from restricted areas of the country, are clearly no more regionalists than was Thomas Hardy.

—L.D.L.

regional planning. See CIVIC PLANNING.

register. (1) A set of organ pipes of the same tone quality; generally called a "stop". (2) A distinct division of the tone quality of a voice—chest r., head r., etc.—or instrument.

register, register mark. *Etch.* Little dents in multi-color acquatint plates, used as a guide to insure that the various colored impressions match in the final proof.   —K.K.

regnum. See tiara, papal.

Reichenau school. See Ottonian art.

Reims, school of. See Carolingian art.

reisner work. Wooden inlaid work of different colors.

relation. *Mus.* The degree of affinity between the keys, chords or tones of a scale.

release. In vocal music, the manner in which the musical tone ends in pitch, intensity, and timbre. It has many of the characteristics of the attack of a tone but a gliding release except in portamento is decidedly unpleasant. The extent and rate of a most acceptable attack would be musically intolerable for the release. The term release is usually applied to pitch, but there is every reason for extending it to intensity and timbre.   —C.E.S.

relief. Art (originally an adaptation of It. *rilievo*, from It. *rilevare*, to lift up, to raise; subsequent adoption of Fr. *relief*).

1. *Architecture, sculpture, and allied arts*: (a) The projection or elevation of a design from a plane or curved surface, without complete detachment, in order to give an appearance of greater solidity or depth; also the degree of the projection and the part which projects. (b) The design or composition executed in relief.

2. *Painting, drawing, etc.*: (a) The effect of solidity, depth, or detachment given to a design on a plane or curved surface by the lines, shading, or colors of which the design

is composed. (b) In a figurative sense, the vividness and sharpness of outline obtained by contrast or technical rendering, such as a figure in bold *relief* against the sky. (c) Certain processes in printing and photography.

3. *Cartography*: (a) (Attributed use) The effect of elevations and depressions of land surfaces obtained on maps by suitable coloring. (b) Relative effect of such conformations produced at suitable scale on maps or models.

4. *Physical geography*: The elevations and depressions of land surfaces.

5. *Military fortifications*: The difference in level between the top of a parapet and the bottom of trench or ditch.

The term relief *has two major meanings both derived from the same Latin root, one through the French* relever, *to lift up, to comfort; the other through the Italian* rilevare, *to lift or raise up. The first and most widely employed has come to mean the removal of pain or want, succor, release from duties by substitution, etc. The second meaning deals with measurement of the distances that one surface is raised above another or appears to be raised. It is in this sense that the term* relief *is used in art and accounts for the inclusion of subjects under 3, 4, and 5.*

Relief in the sense of the plastic arts, whether it refers to the design itself or to the distance the design projects, presupposes a solid background or surface from which the ornament rises. Relief then is essentially ornament which has projection or gives the illusion of projection (painting), and which is applied to a more basic form or surface. This form or surface may vary greatly in nature; it even may be sculpture itself; witness the designs in relief on the armor of Erasmo di Narni (Gattamelata) as represented in Donatello's equestrian statue. This admits also to the classification of relief, works in repoussé, cameo, embossing, chasing, and intaglio (qq.v.). It is evident, however, that the more monumental aspects of relief are seen as architectural sculpture applied as decoration to buildings and monuments.

Relief falls into two general classes or types: high relief, It. *alto-rilievo*; and low relief, It. *basso-rilievo*, Fr. *bas-relief*. Formerly the third classification of middle or half relief, It. *mezzo-rilievo* was used but has been merged by modern custom with low relief. The breadth of these terms not only causes confusion but makes accurate description difficult. Moreover, the type of relief is determined by the relative projection and not by the actual projection; for example,

a silver jewel box may be decorated by figures in high relief though their total projection is no more than an inch, while the Parthenon frieze, whose projection is four times as great, is low relief; but in all cases some natural attachment to the surface from which the relief rises is essential.

A design may be considered in **high relief** when the projection from its background is never less than one-half the relative thickness of the object in relief. Generally, high relief designates ornaments or figures almost wholly detached from their background. This is achieved by "undercutting", which in many cases limits the attachment to a few isolated points. Examples: Parthenon metopes, 5th cent. B.C., (British Museum, London); Retable of St. George by Jan Borreman, active ca. 1479-1522 (Musée du Cinquantenaire, Brussels); Basin of Poseidon Fountain by Carl Milles (Gothenburg, Sweden).

A special use of architectural sculpture related to relief is the practice of attaching by artificial means to the surface decorated figures or objects carved or cast "in the round". This practice gives the effect of high relief and while productive of designs of great merit is not relief but pseudo-relief. Examples are seen in the pediment figures from the Parthenon, Athens, and from the Medici tombs by Michangelo in the New Sacristy, San Lorenzo, Florence.

Low relief may be considered to be any design whose projection from its background is not more than one-half the relative thickness of the object placed in relief, and in some cases this projection may be so slight that the surface of the relief and the surface of its background almost will coincide. Low relief as we understand it was called **anaglypta** by Pliny, but he also included in this term embossing and chasing. Examples: "The Wounded Lioness" from *The Lion Hunt of Assurnasipal*, Assyrian, 8th cent. B.C. (British Museum, London); "Nymphs" by Jean Goujon, Fountain of the Innocents (Place des Innocents, Paris).

Low relief of special nature is seen in **incised** or **sunk relief**; that is, the carved or modelled surface is sunk below the surface of the ground decorated. The design, therefore, is outlined by a sharply incised groove or channel, and within this limit of figures or ornament the surface modelling takes place, but only to the degree permitted by the depth of the incised outline, no portion of the design projecting beyond the normal surface of the ground decorated. This method was used greatly but not exclusively by the Egyptians in monumental wall treatments as it lent itself both to the hardness of granite and the brilliance of light. (See relief sculpture; negative carving.) Examples: *Seti I in Battle,* Temple of Amon, Karnak; *Ramses III Overcoming his Enemies,* Temple of Ramses III, Karnak.

In architecture, three dimensional surface treatments to produce effects of greater strength or solidity are forms of low relief, such as quoins, chains and other forms of rustication. (See rusticate).

Relief, as the term is used in sculpture and architecture (see relief sculpture) in its more nearly original sense, is always associated with the decoration of a panel or frieze whose essential flatness is always impressed upon the mind of the spectator. Among the peoples of ancient Egypt, the Near East, and Pre-Columbian America this essential flatness was attained by keeping the relief of all forms in a design virtually constant. Spatial depth was indicated (a) by skillful modelling which allowed one form to be placed in front of another, as in line drawing, the relief of all forms being the same; or (b) by the convention of placing near forms at the bottom and more distant forms at the top of the panel. Examples: Details from the Mastaba of Akhuthotep (Louvre, Paris); "Naval Expedition," panel from Khorsabad (Louvre, Paris). As early as the 5th cent. B.C. in Greece and Rome the desire to create the illusion of spatial depth led to the rendering of several planes, one behind the other. This necessitated the use of several degrees of relief projection in the same design, often including both high and low relief. This practice led inevitably to a disregard for the inherent flatness and solidity of the panel. This same phenomenon may be observed in mural painting. (See mural painting.) Examples: Panels from the Altar of Peace, late 1st cent. B.C., Rome; "Triumph of Titus," Arch of Titus, Rome.

It must be remembered, however, that the use of high and low relief in the same design will not in itself destroy the inherent flatness of a panel, but only when the relief projection is used in an effort to create the illusion of atmospheric depth. In fact, the use of high and low relief combined in one design is observable in all periods and divisions of art. In Byzantine and Romanesque art as well as in the pre-classic, oriental, and pre-Columbian American cultures its use was for decorative or illustrative purposes rather than for rendering the illusion of spatial depth. Examples: Egyptian Funerary Stele, New Kingdom (Louvre, Paris); Bronze Doors, 10th-11th cent. A.D., Cathedral, Hildesheim, Germany; Maitreya Buddha, Western Caves, Yün Kang, Shansi, China). However, in Gothic and subsequent periods the rendering of one plane behind another in order to heighten the realistic effect of the scene became the accepted practice, continuing to be seen in numerous examples of contemporary work.

A phase and development of the illusionary idea is seen in the introduction of pictorial backgrounds in low relief. The resultant design is known as **pictorial relief.** This seems to have been an invention of classic times due to realistic predilections, as it is noted as early as the 1st half of the 2nd cent. B.C. in the smaller frieze of the Pergamon Altar, but reached its fullest classic development under the Roman Empire. In the Renaissance, with the added knowledge of linear perspective, pictorial relief reached its maximum development and use. Example: 2nd set of gilded bronze doors for the Baptistery at Florence, by Lorenzo Ghiberti, 15th cent. The idea of pictorial illusion is carried still further in architecture when the relief composed of architectural forms becomes part of the basic design of the structure in order to give the illusion of increased dimension. Example: Apse in relief, San Satiro, Milan, by Bramante.

Modern methods and materials have given rise to additional uses and forms of decorative relief. Panels of monumental size are now possible in moulded glass and synthetic plastic materials. Modern theory tends to abandon the use of relief to create illusion of spatial depth and to confine its use once again to its decorative and illustrative functions, at the same time expressive of the function of the surface decorated and the nature of the material used. See *Oxford Universal English Dictionary,* c. 1937; Chase and Post, *History of Sculpture,* 1924; Charles R. Morey, *Medieval Art,* 1942: *Encyclopedie Photographique de l'Art,* Musee de Louvre, Edition "TEL", 1935; Meyric R. Rogers, *Carl Milles,* 1940; A. M. Rindge, *Sculpture,* 1929.

—J.C.

relief cutting. See GLASS AND GLASS-MAKING.

relief printing. See line etching.

relief process, in prints. See PRINTS AND PRINTS PROCESSES.

relief sculpture. Is one of the oldest forms of art and was used in every cultural epoch. It originated in pre-historic caves, emanating from drawing. Relief has been carved in stone, wood, ivory; hammered into metal sheets and cast into various metals; cast in plaster, cement, metals, ceramics and plastics. It has been used on every type of building created by man for the living and the dead as well as on his places of worship, on decoration of his home, on useful or decorative articles, perhaps more than any other form of art.

The term "relief" designates the projection, in various degree, of one or several sculptural figures, animals or objects, from a surface. It derives from the Latin *rilievo* (projecting), but is also used when the sculptural design is on the same level as the surrounding surface or set back of this surface. Incised (intaglio) and hollow (concave) reliefs are not true relief forms according to established rules; however, they are generally classified as reliefs.

The primary rule of relief, high or low, is the uniform expression on a frontal plane (as many high points must be arranged in a plane so that they will give the impression of a plane). In order to achieve depth there must be a rear surface parallel to the frontal plane which is the background from which the figures are silhouetted. It follows that, if a composition is arranged along a frontal and a rear plane, all parts of the composition must conform to this rule. It is therefore wrong to flatten the bodies (as in low relief) and round out the heads (as in high relief) or allow any extremities to rise forward beyond the frontal plane. In low relief, all parts must be in relation to each other, viz., low; and in high relief, all parts must be relatively high.

Prime considerations in relief are light and shade, materials, and the distance from which it may be seen. It is most important to study the proposed location of a relief for light conditions, the distance from which it may be observed and the probable effect of light and distance on the desired material, before execution of the design. A stone relief may be more compact, emphasizing the form, whereas a bronze relief allows looser construction but demands a clear silhouette. The visibility of a relief may be increased by treating foreground and background differently: a stone relief treated smoothly on the figures may have a rough background or the latter may be colored contrastingly; on a bronze relief the foreground may be gilded or patined in contrast to the background. Ceramic reliefs are generally polychromed for better visibility and effect.

High relief (grand relief, alto-rilievo), as the name indicates, is well set off from the background and the figures may be almost or entirely in the round. It is generally used on the exterior of buildings and monuments or churches, usually at considerable distance from the spectator. We find in the Greek pediments of Aegina or the Parthenon that sculpture entirely in the round was used, yet since the figures were arranged along a frontal plane against a background, they form a true relief.

Medium relief (half or demi relief, demi or mezzo-rilievo) varies in projection between high and low relief. As the term is not definite, it is rarely used. A medium to high relief is usually called high relief and a medium to low one, bas-relief or low relief.

Low relief (bas-relief, basso-rilievo) is the common type of relief, and may create an impression of roundedness and depth, even when quite low. As it has little projection, it offers fewer difficulties in technical execution or reproduction than higher relief. This type of relief is used on low exterior and interior architecture, interior decoration, wall and other placques, on medals and coins, jewelry. As the emphasis on form decreases in low relief, line, and esp. silhouette and perspective, are of great importance. Extremely low relief may be little more than a plastic drawing.

Incised relief (intaglio) is not a true relief, inasmuch as it consists only of a frontal plane without background. It consists of incised outlines and rounded out forms cut into a flat surface. The impression of depth and roundness is created by light and shade on the rounded forms, by overlapping and foreshortening.

Intaglio (in contrast to *rilievo*: projecting) was used extensively by the Egyptians; it made its reappearance in the 20th cent. and is used largely in the decoration of architectural surfaces which do not allow projections.

Hollow relief (inverted, concave relief, cavo-rilievo) is not a true relief, having no background, but may be used as the mold for a true relief. Hollow relief creates the impression of roundness by optical illusion since its sculptural forms are not convex or plastic, but concave, hollow. As the light touches an inverted relief, light and shade are reversed. When highlighted from above, shadows form on the upper parts of the relief and light appears below, in contrast to a projecting relief, which would be lighted on top and shaded below. It is unusual to encounter the hollow relief; some examples may be seen on the walls of British and French buildings, Rockefeller Center, New York. The Greeks and Romans used it mainly on gems for sealing rings; the Babylonians carved it into stone cylinders which were then rolled over clay and left a plastic imprint. It is now used mainly in negative carving (q.v.) for bas-relief, and in modern abstract and semi-abstract relief sculpture, sometimes in connection with convex forms, also in sculptural cut glass. —C.L.S.

religion and art. *Kinships.* (1) The closest kinship between religion and art is their common endeavor to reshape the world better to satisfy man's vision and desire. Each demands a more abundant and harmonious life for man, and adds wonder and meaning to the commonplace. Both presuppose an orderly world amenable to their purposes. Both approach life with zest and enthusiasm; are adventurous and creative; require a self-forgetful devotion and concentrated striving; face the risks of failure; and result in deeper insight into reality. (2) The kinship of religion and art is emphatically proved by their inseparable blend in primitive ritual and festival; here are united at once the seeds of the fine arts and the roots of religion. (3) There is also kinship of effects. Aesthetic enjoyment and religious adoration are psychologically similar. Both spring from emotion, live in exuberant imagination, and awaken admiration, reverence, and awe. Both demand free meditation and absorbed attention, and may issue in a feeling of harmony attained, increased vitality, and a liberated and expanding self. Each experience has a kind of immediacy, self-sufficiency, and intrinsic good which one would gladly prolong; and at the heights: ineffable rapture, with a sense of finality amid an incomparable calm.

Differences. (1) The greatest difference between art and religion is that the aesthetic object is a particular thing present to the senses, whereas the religious object is the idea of a spiritual being of cosmic range. The aesthetic response is impersonal contemplation; the religious, a personal communion. (2) Religion issues in moral demands upon daily living, whereas aesthetic enjoyment remains detached from moral and practical concerns. Religion concerns one's destiny; art

is an immediate and present satisfaction. Art seeks an imaginative transformation of life; religion, an actual one. (3) Art moves in a restricted sphere of semblance, whereas religion is an orientation of man's whole self to total reality. (4) The widespread antagonism between religion and art springs basically from the religionist's fear that the sensuous art creation will monopolize attention, become an idol, and obscure the Invisible Infinite; while the artist, if he is religious, encounters fearful difficulties in representing spiritual conceptions and the Infinite in particular sensuous materials.

Interactions. The interactions of art and religion are age-long and profound. (1) "Religion is the mother of the arts" (Hocking). The principal subject-matter and the most powerful inspiration in the history of the arts has been religion. Religious contemplation of nature has produced manifold artistic creations, notably transcendental poetry. (2) The arts serve religion in endless ways. Since art enhances and joyifies human values, it is inevitable that religion should forever call upon the arts to make its values vivid, impressive, attractive, enjoyable, and immortal. To list the arts which have served religion constructively would be to name them all. (3) The religionist who has discovered the secrets of beauty knows that he needs the fine arts for perfecting his worship of the Perfect One. The artist who has discovered the secrets of religion finds himself animated by the most powerful drive to artistic creation. So long as art and religion endure they will stand in profound need of each other. See Percy Dearmer (ed.), *The Necessity of Art*, 1924; G. Arnaud D'Angel, *L'Art Religieux Moderne*, 1936; Jane E. Harrison, *Ancient Art and Ritual*, 1913; Von Ogden Vogt, *Art and Religion*, 1921. —R.F.P.

relining. The process of backing a painter's old and weakened canvas with a strong and fresh one is called relining or sometimes lining. In this treatment the original canvas is not removed from the structure but is merely given further support by the new one attached. Until the latter part of the 19th cent. some mixture of glue or glue and paste was the common adhesive for this attachment, but since that time there has been a growing tendency to fasten the canvas together with a wax or a combination of wax and resin. See RESTORATION OF PAINTINGS. —G.L.S.

reliquary. Any precious and mobile object expressly designed or merely used permanently to enshrine and thereby to honor the material remains of a person provided that the spirit of that person be regarded as immortal and as the worthy object of a religious cult. Material remains in this definition are either any parts of the person's body or objects hallowed by contact with him (her). Although not absent from other religions reliquaries are proper to Christianity, since from early times no Christian altar could be consecrated unless it contain, support or be built upon the relics of a Saint.

Outstanding forms of reliquaries are: (1) **pocket reliquaries,** imitations in precious material of the bags, in which relics were carried in the times of the geographical expansion of Christianity; (2) **shrines** or **chasses,** which in accordance with an age-old mortuary tradition usually were conceived as houses of the dead and took the forms of dwellings or churches; (3) arm, head and finger reliquaries shaped to represent the outer contour of those members of the body of which they enshrine the skeleton. In addition any capsule, box or casket can be used as a reliquary as well as any cross, cover of a sacred book, statue or statuary group. See ostensorium; depositorium; encolpion.   —R.B.

relish. An obsolete ornament of the family of shakes, used esp. in the old harpsichord music.

remarque. See PRINTS AND PRINT PROCESSES.

Renaissance (rebirth). This term is applied to the reawakening of the arts, of learning and living in Italy in the spirit of the classical past of Greece and Rome. The conception of a renewal of the arts was expressed first by Ghiberti (1378-1455), in his *Comentarii* (2d book) in which he discusses the works of the leading painters and sculptors at the end of the 13th and the beginning of the 14th cent. The architect L. B. Alberti (1404-1472), in the dedication to Brunelleschi in his *Three books on Painting* (1455), conceives the rise of a new era in Florence with Ghiberti, Brunelleschi (1377-1446), Donatello (1386-1466), Masaccio (1401-1428) and Luca della Robbia (1399-1482), in the first part of the 15th cent., thus continuing the ancestral line of Ghiberti into his own age. Finally, Giorgio Vasari (1511-1574) in the introduction of his *Life of the Painters* (1st ed. 1550) uses for the first time the actual term *"rinascità"* (Renaissance). The idea of the "revival" has also drawn elements from the religious conception of the return of a new era after a thousand year aevum (K. Burdach). The French term *"Renaissance"* has been chosen as a subtitle by Michelet for the 7th volume of his *Histoire de France* (1855), and has been made universal by Jacob Burckhardt's book *The Civilization of the Renaissance* (1860). In contrast to Burckhardt, there have been varied efforts to pre-date the period of the Renaissance to the time of the flourishing of Italian art in the High Medieval period, most notably that by Henry Thode in his *Franz von Assisi* (1885). Thode wants to stress the Christian elements in the Italian Renaissance and consequently sees in St. Francis of Assisi (1181-1226), Dante (1265-1321), Giotto (1266-1337) and Petrarch (1304-1374) the founders of the Renaissance movement. We have learned from the opponents of Burckhardt an understanding for the continuity of tradition in Italian art from the 13th cent. to the era of the classical revival in the early 15th cent. Essential contributions to our knowledge of the Renaissance have been made by Jacob Burckhardt, Arthur Symonds, Walter Pater, Heinrich von Geymüller, Adolfo Venturi, Wilhelm Bode, Bernard Berenson, Heinrich Woelfflin, Aby Warburg, Erwin Panofsky, J. Huizinga and many others.

We speak of an early Renaissance, 1420-1500, of a High Renaissance, 1500-1520 or 1530, and a late Renaissance or Mannerism, 1530-1600. This period is characterized by its effort to rationalize and systematize the steadily increasing amount of empirically gained observations and to apply them in the fine arts. The scattered observations about *perspective,* which the 14th cent. with its growing naturalism had made, were welded into a scientific system by Alberti, Piero della Francesca (about 1420-1492) and Pacioli (c. 1445-1509) and applied since the days of Masaccio (most important the "Holy Trinity", S. Maria Novella, Florence, 1427). The study of *anatomy* became based on analysis and since the end of the 15th cent. On dissecting and was translated into exact human *proportions* in the sculptures of Donatello, Ghiberti and others. The study of proportions, supported by the revival of Vitruvius' book on architecture (MS. rediscovered 1455 by Poggio in St. Gallen), was carried forward by Brunelleschi and Alberti. The inborn Mediterranean tendency for harmony, symmetry and anthropocentric thinking grew strongly and opposed medieval transcendentalism. Yet the Christian tradition remained dominant. It found a closer kinship with Plato's idealism than with Aristotle's realism.

The rebirth of the classical spirit is, in the beginning, based less on the actual knowledge of antique art than on divination, on scattered observations of the few known examples, esp. sarcophagi and triumphal arches and an occasional reference to classical literature. Antique mythology is handed out to the artists by the humanists since the days of Petrarch (therefore "Humanism"). Not until the end of the 15th cent. was a large group of antique sculpture (*Hercules Farnese, Laocoon, Apollo Belvedere, Marsyas, Venus Medici, Three Graces, Torso Belvedere,* etc.) unearthed, collected (the most important collections those of the Medici in Florence, the Gonzaga in Mantua, and the Popes in Rome), and its motifs introduced into sculpture. Roman architecture was studied by Brunelleschi and Alberti, sketched by Jacopo Bellini (c. 1400-1470) and introduced into painting by Mantegna (1431-1506) and his contemporaries.

Architecture. Gothic churches in Italy, in their façades as well as in their interiors (as we may see exemplified in the cathedrals of Siena, and Orvieto), have never conceded to the verticalism of the Northern Gothic but have maintained an even balance between the horizontal and the vertical tendencies that is traditional with Mediterranean architecture. The architects of the Renaissance had only to replace the ornamental system of the Gothic with that of the Antique but could maintain the basilica scheme and the spatial conceptions of a tradition which was to some degree continuous since Roman days. Brunelleschi was the first to force upon the traditional basilica scheme of the Gothic cathedral of Florence (1296-1462), the classical dominant of a cupola. Although in its design still using elements of Gothic construction (outside ribs), it clears the way for one of the main motives of Renaissance and baroque architecture, the fusion of the longitudinal nave and the centralizing cupola into one organic structure of half antique and half medieval derivation. Michelangelo (1475-1564), in his designs for St. Peter's (since 1547) and its cupola (finished 1590), has carried this tendency to its first climax, preparing the ingenious solutions of the baroque. The second important contribution of Brunelleschi was the harmonious decoration of classically proportioned interiors with antique columns, architraves and pediments as we see it first in small buildings in Florence such as the Pazzi Chapel (1429-43) and the old Sacristy of S. Lorenzo (1420-29) followed by the basilicas of S. Lorenzo (1421—after 1461) and St. Spirito (1436-1476). Leon Battista Alberti, introduced a more powerful, partially antique-Roman version of the new style into other parts of Italy (Rimini, S. Francesco [1446-1455]; Mantova, S. Andrea [1472-1494, side nave, choir and cupola later]). As the most ideal solution of a perfectly harmonized interior and exterior appears to the Renaissance architect the centralized building of the Pantheon type. Yet the liturgical demands of the Christian Church have successfully opposed these aesthetical conceptions. Instead of a centralized new St. Peter's as conceived in the drawings by Bramante (c. 1444-1514) and Michelangelo, only Bramante's small model church of S. Pietro in Montorio (Rome, 1499-1502) carried out the conception of the architect. Other centralized churches of exemplaric beauty are Santa Maria della Consolazione in Todi (1508-1524) and Santa Maria Carceri in Prato (1485-1491). Hospitals and monasteries humanized their exteriors in adding hospitable loggias and colonnaded courts (Florence Foundling Hospital, 1420-1451, by Brunelleschi. It is with Bramante, Michelangelo and the brothers San Gallo, that richer and more dramatic effects became introduced (Medici Chapel, Florence [1520-1524]: Choir of St. Peter's, Rome [1546-1604]), which prepared the transformation toward the baroque.

The architecture of secular buildings such as palaces, villas, and city halls found a genuine Mediterranean expression with the re-introduction of the classical column orders and of antique decorative motives. The defense character of the medieval house gave way to the comfortable and representative edifice. Harmonious and convenient groundplans, regularity and symmetry of façades, clarity of proportions, open loggias and galleries, large gardens and impressive vistas bespeak the house as the artistic shelter of the cultured owner. From the Palazzo Medici-Riccardi (1444-1452) by Michelozzo in Florence to Antonio San Gallo's (1483-1546) and Michelangelo's Palazzo Farnese in Rome (1534-1580), a continuous development of the new façade and groundplan type can be observed. With the publication of Vitruvius' books on architecture by Fra Giocondo in 1511 the tendency toward greater monumentality and ornateness found support in a closer imitation of classical examples. Rusticated stones and engaged columns dramatized the façades. Bramante's Belvedere (1486-1492), Peruzzi (1481-1536), Raffael's Villa Farnesina (1509-1511) in Rome, the Library of San Marco in Venice (since 1536) by Sansovino (1486-1570), the architecture of Vignola (1507-1573) and Palladio (1518-1580) in Northern Italy bespeak the style of secular architecture in the High and Late Renaissance.

Sculpture. The Renaissance worship of the human body as the noblest feature of creation gave sculpture a new meaning and importance. The large sculptural programs for churches in the sense of Gothic cathedral iconography came to an end with Donatello's (1386-1466) statues for the cathedral (1408-1415) and the Campanile of Florence (1416-1426) and Ghiberti's bronze doors for the Baptistry of Florence (1403-1452) and with both artists statues for Or' San Michele (since 1412). After 1450, secular and semi-secular subject matter created an art for the collector or patron, while devotional art continued for the altar shrine, the baptismal fountain or the pulpit. Monumental assignments for public squares, court yards and gardens fostered the appearance of new types of equestrian monuments (*Gattamelata,* by Donatello, in Padua, 1446-1453; and *Colleoni,* by Verrocchio [1436-1488], in Venice, 1481-1493); statues (*Judith* by Donatello, c. 1455, and *David,* c. 1430 or 1450; *David* by Verrocchio, c. 1465, and *David* by Michelangelo, 1501-1504); and fountains (Verrocchio's *Boy with Dolphin,* Florence, Palazzo Vecchio, c. 1480). The art of bronze casting became regenerated by Ghiberti and Donatello. Donatello's *David* was the first life-size bronze statue since the days of antiquity. It was also revolutionary in its full nudity, something exceptional within the Christian tradition. Themes from pagan mythology stimulated the representation of human flesh and human passion (Pollaiuolo, 1429-1498). The late A. Warburg has opened our eyes for the return of these Antique *"Pathosformeln"* (basic motives of passion), in sculpture and painting. In Michelangelo's figures for the Medici Chapel, in Florence (c. 1523-1533), the Christian and pagan currents, still harmoniously combined in his David, came to a dramatic and profoundly tragic encounter. For more popular use and in simpler interpretation, the technique of terra cotta cast (della Robbia's), helps to spread the forms of the Renaissance.

Painting. Similar characteristics apply for painting. Works of medium and small size,

created by individually appreciated masters, made paintings objects for collectors or for religious-aesthetical worship at home besides the continued use in churches. Portraits and mythological subject matters worked towards a partial secularization of the Renaissance civilization. Fresco painting continued to be a favorite with the Italian painter. Besides the Florentine masters such as Masaccio, Uccello (c. 1396/9-1475), Castagno (1423-1457), Fra Angelico (1387-1455), Fra Filippo Lippi (c. 1406-1469) and his son Filippino Lippi (c. 1457-1504), Ghirlandaio (1449-1494), Pollaiuolo, and Verrocchio, the greatest masters outside of Florence are Piero della Francesca, Giovanni Bellini (1430-1516), and Mantegna. Elements of antique architecture and sculpture form a learned framework for the Neo-Classical spirit in composition. However, the interference of the Gothic "International" style and the Christian background in the native tradition can be continuously felt as a counteracting element. The examples of Botticelli's later mystic style, the influence of northern prints, the subject matter of the **pieta** (q.v.), imported through German wood sculpture, the introduction of the new Flemish technique of oil painting, may suffice. As far as form and composition are concerned, the main problems of the Renaissance artist were: the conquest of three dimensional space (Masaccio); the achievement of plasticity by means of light and atmosphere (Masaccio); the symmetrical or harmonized composition of anatomically well built and well proportioned human figures and a mood of controlled humanity in aesthetically beautiful bodies and configurations (Botticelli, 1444 or 1445-1510, and Signorelli, 1441-1523). Expressive tendencies and realism are subordinated under the ideal of harmony.

All these endeavors, handed on and improved throughout the 15th cent., reached their culmination in the masters of the High Renaissance: Leonardo (1452-1519), Giorgione (1478-1510) and Titian (1476/-1576), but foremost in Raffael (1483-1520) and in Michelangelo. The complete application of the laws of perspective, anatomy and proportion, the Aristotelian unity of time and space in perfectly harmonized and deeply animated compositions seems achieved in Raffael's School of Athens (1510), in the *Veneration of the Holy Sacrament* (c. 1510), and in Michelangelo's Sistine Ceiling (1508-1512). However, it must be realized that the so-called High Renaissance did not last longer than from 1500 to 1530 and was quickly superseded by Mannerism and pre-baroque tendencies.

The Late Renaissance enhanced the chiaroscuro style for greater emotional effects as we discern in the later work of Titian, in Tintoretto (1518-1594) and in Correggio (1489-1534). It combined this quality with a dramatization of movement, following the all-influential example of Michelangelo's *Last Judgment* (1535-1541) and the rhetorical style of Raffael's latest works. Art tended in Florence toward Mannerism, [Rosso (1494-1541), Primaticcio (1504-1574), Pontormo (1494-1557), Bronzino (1502-1572)], in varying and paraphrasing the style created by the masters of the High Renaissance.

While Florence under the Medici was the center of the early Renaissance, Rome became the center of action under the warrior Pope Julius II (1503-1513) and the epicurean Leo X (1513-1521); Venice, Ferrara, Mantova, Verona and Milan created highly productive local types of their own. But mostly, Florentine artists were those who disseminated the germs of the new movement to smaller communities and to foreign countries. The rest of Europe accepted the forms and doctrines of the Renaissance rather from these late children of a great age, then from the style of the Early and High Renaissance.

At the beginning of the 16th cent., the northern late medieval realism and naturalism had developed to a point where it was ripe for an understanding of the doctrines and forms of the Italian Renaissance.

FRENCH RENAISSANCE: the elements of the Italian Renaissance came to France under Francois I (1515-1547) and found its application in the construction of richly decorated castles with medieval groundplan but Renaissance decoration (Blois, finished 1519; Chambord, since 1526; Fontainebleau, since 1528). The south and west wings of the old Louvre received since 1546 their Renaissance shape through Pierre Lescot (1510-1578). With Philibert De l'Orme (c. 1515-1570) France saw a master in whom theoretical knowledge and classical application came to its climax. Since 1564 he built for Catharina Medici the Tuilleries castle (destroyed 1871). In church architecture we find a continuation of the Gothic church interior cloaked into a mantle of Renaissance forms. St. Etienne du Mont (since 1517) and St. Eustache (since 1532) in Paris represent the new type. Here the foundations for the Classicism of French art, inborn as it was, were laid. Goujon (1510-1568) and Pilon (1535-1590), expressed the

new ideals in sculpture, while a host of Florentine artists such as Rosso, Primaticcio and others, including the aging Leonardo, brought classical form and content to France. Jean Clouet (c. 1485-1540) and his son Francois (1510-1572) paralleled the work of the German Renaissance painter Hans Holbein (1497-1543), in a porcelain smooth and minature-like art of portraiture. In general, French Renaissance as well as German Renaissance only slowly yielded to classical proportions and Mediterranean structure but willingly lent itself to an adaptation of the ornamental system of the Renaissance amalgamating it with the Gothic tradition.

ENGLISH RENAISSANCE: The German painter Hans Holbein brought the message of the Renaissance to the English court. It remained prevailingly an affair of the court circle, stimulated by the occasional visit of Italian sculptors and painters. Throughout the 16th cent. architecture and decorative arts clung to the "perpendicular" late Gothic style, sometimes connected with Italian ornamentation introduced by Pietro Torrigiani (1472-1526) and Benedetto Rovezzano (1474-1552). Not before the 17th cent. did it find its proudest expression in the Palladian classicism of Inigo Jones (1573-1652) and Christopher Wren (1632-1723). Jones' free usage of Palladian motives appears in the Banquet Hall of Whitehall (since 1619) or in the staircase of Ashburnham House (1650/60). (Yet in Jones' work and more so in that of Wren we recognize many baroque elements so that it might be more appropriate to deal with it under the term baroque [q.v.].) Lord Burlington's (1695-1753) Palladian revival kept the architectural language of the late Renaissance alive in the 18th cent.

GERMAN RENAISSANCE: developed under the guidance of the systematical mind of Albrecht Dürer (1471-1528). He made the graphic arts the most powerful vehicle for the new conceptions in form and thought. His striving for perspective representation, anatomical precision and humanistic subject matter, based on methodical studies, widened the scope of Northern European art for centuries. Between 1500 and 1530, most of the German painters are seized by the Renaissance current. Hans Holbein, whose name we have met already, carries the specific forms of the German Renaissance to Switzerland and England. He is the foremost portraitist of the era, a great draftsman and illustrator. Mathias Gruenewald (c. 1470-1528) may rather be considered a late medieval artist while

Lucas Cranach (1472-1553), Hans Burgkmir (1473-1531), and Albrecht Altdorfer (c. 1480-1538) show the direct influence of the Italian Renaissance, transmitted partially by Dürer himself. In sculpture and architecture, the peculiar blend of northern heaviness and love for intricate ornamental playfulness with Italian classicism becomes evident. Amongst the sculptors we notice Konrad Meit (c. 1480-1551), Peter Vischer, the Younger (1487-1528), Hans Vischer (1488-c. 1549) and Peter Floetner (c. 1490/5-1546), all of them with the exception of the first products of Nürnberg's humanism.

The "German Renaissance" in architecture, not without influence on the architecture of the neighboring countries to the Northwest and North, finds its most typical representation in secular buildings such as castles, city halls and patrician dwellings. Cities like Nürnberg, Münster, or Luebeck still furnish an idea of the German Renaissance town. Elias Holl's (1573-1646) city hall of Augsburg (1615-1620) is perhaps the greatest document of a typical German Palladianism.

FLEMISH AND DUTCH RENAISSANCE: In the Flemish countries Metsys (c. 1466-1530), Mabuse (real name Gossaert, 1478-1533/4), Van Orley (c. 1492-1542), Lucas van Leyden (1494-1533) and Scorel (1495-1562), headed the large number of Romanists (q.v.) who turned for artistic inspiration toward the South. International recognition as a portraitist fell to Antonis Mor (1519-1577) while Pieter Aertsen (1508-1575) started the long line of Dutch still-life painters. With Pieter Breughel the Elder (c. 1525-1569), the Flemish soil contributed one of the greatest interpreters of human life and of nature as a refreshing force to the aging and mannered Late Renaissance epoch.

In the field of architecture similar as in England the Gothic Style continued longer than in painting and sculpture. Painters were even instrumental in the introduction of Renaissance motives in architecture, often applied to smaller decorative units such as doors or paneled walls. Jacques Dubroencq (c. 1505-1584) must be considered the initiator of an Italianate style in Holland. In Cornelis Floris' (1514-1575) city hall of Antwerp (1561-1564) the ornate mannerism of the Late Renaissance appears in its most typical formulation. From it resulted the peculiar Flemish mannerism. Yet the spirit of the Renaissance has found its most genuine expression in the North in the growth of the sciences and to a certain extent in the religious spirit of Protestantism.

SPANISH RENAISSANCE: As in all non-Italian regions the transformation into the Renaissance appeared first in smaller monuments and merely as a decorative system. The structural qualities of Spanish art remained first unimpeded. Italian artists were instrumental in the dissemination of Renaissance forms. The combination of Renaissance forms with Spanish-Moorish-Islamic ornamentation was known as the Plateresque style (q.v.), a term taken from silverwork. Due to its exuberant ornateness it foreshadowed the baroque. Amongst the most classical, and therefore rare, solutions we may mention the sacristy of the cathedral of Sevilla and the city hall of Sevilla (since 1527) by Diego de Riaño (✠1534) and his successor Martin De Gainza (c. 1500-1555/1556). With Juan de Herrera (1530-1597) the disciplining influence of Vignola and Palladio brought true Classicism to Spain as exemplified in the Escorial (1563-1586) in Madrid or in the Court of the Bank of Sevilla (1583-1598).

Spanish sculpture did not detach itself from the church in the period of the Renaissance except in the field of pure decoration. The Italian Pietro Torrigiani (1472-1526) whose name we also find connected with the introduction of Classical art in England brought the naturalistic terra cotta style of Northern Italy to Spain and thus was instrumental in the development of the extreme realism in Spanish sculpture. Alonzo Berruguete (1480-1561) transferred the language of Michelangelo and Sansovino to his native soil.

In the field of painting Charles V's (1519-1556) taste was eclectic and Italian artists invaded the country throughout the later 16th cent. The flourishing of a genuine Spanish school can hardly be observed within our period.

The Renaissance in Spain appears rather as an alien interact between the Moorish-Gothic and the baroque era. See Giorgio Vasari, *Life of the Painters* (first ed. 1550), several English ed.; Jacob Burckhardt, *The Civilization of the Ren. in Italy* (1860), ill. ed. N. Y., 1929, Dagobert Frey, *Gotik und Renaissance als Grundlagen des modernen Weltbildes*, Augsburg, 1929; John A. Symonds, *Renaissance in Italy*, 2 vol.; Wilhelm Bode, *Die Kunst der Fruehrenaissance in Italien*, Berlin, 1926; Paul Schubring, *Die Kunst der Hochrenaissance in Italien*, Berlin, 1926; Max Dvorak, *Geschichte der Ital. Kunst im Zeitalter der Ren.*, 2 vol., Munich, 1928; Heinrich

Woelfflin, *The Art of the Ital. Ren.*, (trans.)
N. Y., 1913; Adolfo Venturi, *Storia del Arte
Italiana* (vol. 6-9), Milan, 1908/33; Julius
Baum, *Architecture and Decorative Sculpture
of the Early Ren. in Italy* (trans.) Stuttgart-
ended, N. Y., 1926; Corrado Ricci, *Architec-
ture and Decorative Sculpture of the High
Ren. in Italy*, (trans.) N. Y., 1923; W. J.
Anderson, *The Architecture of the Ren. in
Italy*, N. Y., 1927; Wilhelm Bode, *The Sculp-
tors of the Florentine Ren.* (trans.), London,
1908; Paul Schubring, *Ital. Plastik des Quat-
trocento*, Berlin, 1919; Bernard Berenson, *Ital.
Painters of the Ren.*, Oxford, 1932; Bernard
Berenson, *Ital. paintings of the Ren.* (cat.),
Oxford, 1932; Raimond van Marle, *The De-
velopment of the Ital. School of Ptg.* (vol.
8-18), The Haag, 1929-1937; Laurence
Schmeckebier, *A Handbook of Ital. Ren. Ptg.*,
N. Y., 1938; Frank J. Mather, *Western Euro-
pean Painting of the Ren.*, N. Y., 1939; C.
Enlart and C. Martin, *la Ren. en France,
Architecture et Sculpture*, Paris, since 1928;
W. H. Ward, *The Architecture of the Ren. in
France*, 2 vol., 2nd ed., 1926; P. Guiffrey and
Marcel, *la Peinture Francaise, les Primitifs*,
2 vol., Lausanne, 1925/6; L. Dimier and L.
Reau, *Histoire de la Peinture Francaise*, 4 vol.,
Paris., 1925/30; O. G. Destree, *The Ren. of
Sculpture in Belgium* (trans.), London, 1895;
F. Ewerbeck, *Die Ren. in Belgien und Holland*,
Leipzig, 1891; Gustav Glueck, *Die Kunst der
Ren. in Deutschland, den Niederlanden, Frank-
reich*, Berlin, 1928; *Karl Horst, Die Archi-
tektur der Deutschen Ren.*, Berlin, 1928; Bur-
ger-Schmitz-Beth, *Die Deutsche Malerei der
Ren.*, 3 vol., Berlin, 1913; Adolf Feulner, *Die
Deutsche Plastik des 16. Jahrhunderts*, Leipzig, 1926; R. Blomfield, *A History of Ren.
Architecture in England*, 2 vol., London, 1897;
C. Baker and W. Constable, *The Painting of
the 16. and 17. Century in England*, Florence,
1930; A. Haupt, *Geschichte der Ren. in
Spanien und Portugal*, Leipzig, 1927; A. Byne
and M. Stapley, *Spanish Architecture of the
16. Century*, N. Y., 1917; J. F. Rafols, *Arqi-
tectura de Renacimiento Espanol*, 1929; M.
Gomez-Moreno, *Spanish Ren. Sculpture*
(trans.), N. Y., 1931; Chandler Post, *A History of Spanish Painting*, Cambridge, 1930.
—A.N.

Renaissance modes. See idiom B.

rendering, architectural. See architectural
rendering.

renge (Jap.). The lotus, very commonly
used in Buddhist art as the symbol of purity.

renge-dai (Jap.). See lotus throne.

repaints. See RESTORATION OF PAINT-
INGS.

repercussion. *Mus.* (1) The constant repetition of a note or chord. (2) In a fugue the
constant recurrence of the theme. (3) The
most reiterated tone in Gregorian chant, the
dominant of the mode.

repose. See balance.

repoussage. *Etch.* When a plate is repaired
and scraping and rubbing with snakestone and
charcoal, a hollow is left which would print
a gray smudge. To prevent this, the plate
is laid on a flat steel surface and the hollow
is eliminated by gently tapping the plate on
the back with the ball pen of the retroussage
hammer. This is called retroussage. —K.K.

repoussé (Fr.). The technique of producing
a design in relief by hammering the reverse
side of a ductile material, such as silver,
etc. A common metal technique in the Orient.
See METALWORK. —J.A.M.

representation, representative (L. *repraesenta-
tio*). A mode of *composition* (q.v.) in art,
in which details are arranged in such a way
as to suggest to the imagination some concrete object, person, scene, or group of them,
in space. Some representation goes further,
and suggests a series of events in time, in
which such objects (things, persons, scenes)
move, change, and affect each other. Representation can be mimetic (based on resem
blance, as in pictures), or symbolic (based on
words or other abitrary symbols, as in literature). Representation can be highly naturalistic or abstract, altered, distorted, stylized.
It may co-exist with utility, decoration, and
exposition as a factor in the total form of a
work of art. —T.M.

reprise. See SONATA; SYMPHONY.

Requiem Mass (L. *Missa pro defunctis*). A
solemn mass (q.v.) sung in commemoration of
the dead. The Introit gives the Mass its
name: *Requiem aeternam dona eis, Domine.*
The divisions of the Requiem are similar
to those outlined under *mass* except for the
omission of the Gloria and Credo, and the
substitution of the Tract for the Allelulia.
The great sequence *Dies irae* follows the
Tract. Save for the Kyrie, *Dies irae*, and
Libera which though often included is not
an integral part of the Requiem, all of the
plainsong melodies date from the 7th cent. or

earlier. For plainsong melodies of the Requiem see *Liber Usualis* pp. 1807-15. —V.A.

requiem oratorio. See oratorio.

reredos. See altarpiece.

reservation. (1) A very large, naturalistically landscaped park; see CIVIC PLANNING. (2) The space occupied by a street railway when it is separated from other traffic by curbing. —T.I.C.

resettlement. See CIVIC PLANNING.

residential estate. See CIVIC PLANNING.

resin. Most of the varnishes used for surface coatings on works of art are made by dissolving a resin in a suitable solvent so that it can be brushed or sprayed. It is not a new practice. Egyptians of the 19th dynasty were familiar with it and it was used by the Incas of South America in their embalming practice. The general term is applied to any of a large number of hardened secretions or excretions of plants. Most resins are taken from the plant by tapping, the fluid at that stage being a balsam. Evaporation or artificial treatment removes volatile oils, leaving usually a hard, brittle, and slightly colored lump which has been dissolved by the varnish maker. It is general to classify resins for convenience as the oil-varnish resins, largely copals and spirit varnish resins, including dammar, mastic, and sandarac. The former group is made in oil, the resin being fused with the oil rather than dissolved in a solvent. —G.L.S.

resins, acrylic. Among the so-called plastics or synthetic resins, these are well known and one commercial form is produced as a molding compound under the name, *Lucite.* These have been used more in industry than in the fine arts, but recently have been employed to a limited extent as a film material like varnish. As a molding material, the *polymerized methyl methacrylate* is probably the most useful of the group. It is a hard, strong substance, somewhat thermoplastic, and works well mechanically. Its distinguishing feature among the various kinds of synthetic resins is its lack of color and its extreme clarity. Print can be read through many inches of it. —G.L.S.

resolution. *Mus.* The reduction of the degree of tension of an interval by moving one or both of its constituent tones in such a way that an interval of lesser tension is the re-

sult. In a broader sense, any procedure aiming at a reduction of tension within a group of elements (particularly chords) closely following each other. Apart from, sometimes instead of, reduction of interval tension, voice leading, metrical and dynamic arrangements etc. are effective devices of resolution.
—E.K.

resonator. See ACOUSTICS; MUSICAL INSTRUMENTS.

resources planning. See CIVIC PLANNING.

respond. See MEDIEVAL MUSIC.

responsorial psalmody. See psalmody.

responsorium. See MEDIEVAL MUSIC.

RESTORATION OF PAINTINGS. The aim of restoration as it is practiced today by reputable restorers is to preserve works of art by detecting and correcting their causes of deterioration and returning them as nearly as possible to their original state. This simple and logical end has not always been sought by restorers. Indeed more paintings have been permanently injured or destroyed by inexpert or over-zealous restorers than have been lost by years of neglect. Straightforward, intelligent restoration dates roughly from the turn of the century. Earlier literature on the subject is of little value to the student or professional. Much of it is vague, describes doubtful methods long since considered obsolete. It is only in recent years with the establishment here and abroad of technical schools and well-equipped museum laboratories that the profession of restoration has been regularized and practiced for the good of the works of art. The present discussion will attempt to deal with the subject in the light of recent generally accepted practice. It must be borne in mind that many of the answers to problems are still lacking and that there is much room for study and improvement. This advance will undoubtedly come in the wake of technical publication and wider consideration among those working in the field.

Panel paintings because of their age, their construction, and the many destructive agents to which they have been subjected, present serious problems in restoration. As a rule Italian pictures on wooden supports will have suffered to a greater degree than Flemish or other northern works of equal age. Northern artists, esp. those of the Flemish school, selected and constructed panels more carefully than did the Italian painters. Thin, clear oak panels, prepared with a minimum of *gesso* or oil ground, was the accepted practice in the north as opposed to the Italian method of using thick panels of soft woods prepared with heavier *gesso* grounds. This difference in technique accounts for the tendency of Italian panels to warp more readily than Flemish panels, thus weakening the bond between *gesso* ground and wooden support with resulting loss or damage of paint film. Extremes of moisture or absence of moisture due to overheating are the most frequent causes of such damage plus the destructive action of wood beetles in undermining the structure of the panel itself.

The cradles, much in vogue in the last century and still widely employed, is considered by many to be a harmful procedure. It has been observed that uncradled panels have survived in better state than those so harnessed. Cradling consists of applying a grillwork of wooden slats to the rear of a panel to hold it straight while allowing it freedom of movement with changes in its moisture content. This movement in wooden panels is always across the grain, the length remaining unaffected. In the early form of cradling (*parquetage a ptat*) notched slats were glued to the panel at regular intervals, the grain of the slats running with the grain of the panel. Into these stationary members, sliding slats resting on the panel were fitted. Theoretically, this method was designed to keep the panel in a simple plane and prevent buckling along the face of the painting. In practice, however, the fixed members, made of new wood, at times covered up to 75 per cent of the original panel subjecting it to new stresses. In time, too, the sliding members became locked or frozen with the result that new cracks appeared along the shearing edges of some fixed members. The face of the panel also tended to assume an undulating character similar to a washboard. To overcome these obvious objections an improved method was introduced *parquetage de champ,* in which thin stationary strips were used, placed edgewise, one narrow edge being glued. This beam-like construction covered less panel area at no sacrifice of strength. Panels so treated twenty-five years ago have given less trouble although no way has been found to assure free movement of cross slats at all times. Because of the physical properties of wood, it is improbable that a perfect harness of this type can be devised. Both

of the foregoing systems have other more serious faults. To successfully cradle a picture, it must be planed down to a thickness of ¼ in. to ⅛ in. While this facilitates straightening, it exposes a new section of wood which readily reacts to moisture and one original dimension of the picture is destroyed. In many cases the thickness of a panel furnishes important clues to the scholar in reconstructing altar-pieces or other works, parts of which have become scattered in various places. The complete character of a work of art should always be preserved.

Transposition. Wood beetles are another cause of deterioration within the fabric of wooden supports. The tunnellings of these insects are so extensive at times that panels, especially those of soft woods, are reduced to a dusty sponge-like structure of the most fragile nature. *Gesso* ground and paint film resting on such uncertain supports are in extreme danger. The traditional treatment in such cases was that of transposing or transferring them to a new panel or to a canvas support. This operation, requiring the greatest skill, consisted of protecting the paint film with paper and canvas and by working from the rear, of removing the wooden support down to the *gesso* ground. The *gesso* and paint film were then attached to a new panel and this cradled, or the whole was mounted on a stretched canvas. Neither of these systems is recommended. They both destroy the remnants of the panel and with the second method, the canvas weave in time becomes visible on the paint film transforming its character by destroying the crackle or competing with it. The most satisfactory method of treating excessively weakened panels is to bind the fibres together with some pliable water-proof agent. This has been successfully accomplished by the impregnation method, a technique which offers the only logical solution to date. This is accomplished by thoroughly protecting the paint film and floating it in a thermostatically controlled tank containing a mixture of beeswax and resin. Time of immersion will depend on the kind of wood, its thickness and condition. Panels so treated have regained up to 75 per cent of their weight and most of their original strength as supports. Furthermore, the wax, flowing through the interstices of the wood fibre, reaches the *gesso* ground and paint film furnishing a new bond with the support. The advantages of the above treatment are obvious. Wax is one of our most permanent materials and it has great adhesive power.

Fibres bound with it are protected against moisture and consequent expansion. Furthermore the original dimensions and character of the support remain unchanged. Where a panel is still structurally sound the back may be treated with liquid resins applied at room temperature or with the aid of infra-red lamps, and given additional support by attaching slotted aluminum channels of small section. These are secured by means of small aluminum screws placed in the slots and penetrating into the panel the distance of three or four threads. For small panels, a U shaped section is applied over the ends of the panels. These may be slotted and attached with screws or held in place with wax.

Most cradled pictures still thick enough to be treated with wax and metal supports benefit if their cradles are removed. Excessively thin panels, however, must be given some auxiliary support. This is best done by the use of sheet aluminum or plywood of waterproof construction. The panel is impregnated and then floated onto the support in a bed of wax. The adhesive power of wax will firmly hold the picture to the auxiliary support while permitting any slight lateral movement required.

The **cleaning of paintings** is another delicate problem of the restorer. In recent years the old notion that paintings must not be deprived of their old *patina* (q.v.) has been discarded. Protective films of varnish, especially oil varnishes deteriorate with age and become yellow. At times, because of excessive moisture, exposure to smoke, acid fumes or other agents, varnish films completely obscure an otherwise sound painting. It was also general practice during the 19th cent. to add warm brown pigments to varnishes to simulate the *patina* of age. Pictures in these states may be successfully cleaned and restored to much of their original brilliance. Two methods are generally employed, the friction method and that employing solvents. The first of these is the traditional one and is not to be recommended. It consists of rubbing with the fingers aided by an abrasive, usually powdered resin. The difficulty of controlling the degree of cleaning by this method is its chief fault. It is also very drastic where paint film has a very fine crackle, the edges of which are raised and subject to loss through abrasion. Solvents in the hands of experts furnish the safer method. Many solvents are available among which turpentine, acetone, diacetone, alcohol are the safest. The last two may be mixed with retarding agents and when so

diluted their speed of action may be regulated. They are used with neutralizing agents such as turpentine. Alcohol is a very valuable agent but its use must be left strictly to the expert. It readily dissolves varnishes and gums but its action on glazes may be disastrous. In all cleaning, small unimportant sections should be cleaned first. This will serve the dual purpose of finding the key of the original colour and of determining the resistance of the varnish films. As a rule, **repaints**, covering old losses or modifications in design painted by others than the artist, will come away with the varnish as many of these will have been executed between varnish films. At times, however, old restorations or changes will require more drastic measures, involving stronger solvents or scraping. In all cleaning operations care should be exercised when working in dark areas. Black and brown pigments are easily damaged. In tempera paintings, the use of water must be avoided as this may disturb the water soluble ground and pigments. The use of soap and water as a cleaning agent is not recommended in any case.

Regeneration of varnishes rather than cleaning is sometimes desirable. This may be accomplished by exposing the painted surface to the fumes of ethyl alcohol over a specially designed tank. The fumes will coalesce the granular particles of resin in the varnish and restore some of its transparency. Similar results may be obtained by finely spraying with diacetone alcohol. Neither of these treatments should be taken as permanent cures and they both involve certain dangers. **Retouching** of losses is a necessary evil. It is best done with water colours as these remain stable with age while oil pigments tend to darken. Losses are stippled to harmonize with surrounding areas of old paint. These repairs should be visible with a glass and not painted to appear as original although care must be taken to match the neighboring colour as closely as possible and not cover it. Where large losses are encountered the best museum practice indicates the use of a neutral tone blending with nearby original paint but not reproducing its design or form. This is esp. desirable in early works but may be more difficult to achieve in the later realistic types of painting. It should be remembered that the original work is more important than that of the ablest restorer.

Rebacking or **relining** is the operation of placing a new canvas behind an old painting. It is not to be confused with transposing or transferring the pigment of a picture to a new canvas support. Rebacking is a required treatment for all torn paintings and pictures more than 50 years of age, the maximum life of the average canvas. Due to rotting linen fibre, the weight of ground and pigment and, at times, the destructive action of mold, canvases sag, lose their strength and usually shear along the edges of the stretcher. Once so released they tend to shrink causing buckling and loss of paint film. Rebacking may be applied to paintings on single canvas supports and to those previously rebacked. The procedure is much the same in both cases. The face of the canvas must be protected with paper applied with medium strength glue. It is then removed from its stretcher and placed, face down, on a board. The new canvas is stretched on a heavy relining *châssis* and shrunk by application of water. When the canvas is dry, the operation is repeated to achieve maximum tautness. The painting may now be attached with a paste or glue adhesive or by use of wax. The aim in both operations is to achieve a strong and flexible bond. Hygroscopic and brittle glues and pastes must be avoided as well as excess of wax if this is used. In each case the use of moderate heat is required to achieve the bond although some restorers favor using a press for this purpose. Where the *impasto* is thick, however, the press is not an advisable tool, as excessive pressure will break down raised pigment and force it into the canvas. Relining of older pictures, already rebacked, follows in the above order after the old relining has been removed. In these cases, the painting is placed face down on a board and its edges fastened to prevent shrinking. The old relining canvas is removed in small strips. In stubborn cases water may be used to help this operation but it is not allowed to remain longer than necessary. When the relining canvas has been removed, the back of the original support is thoroughly cleaned. Rebacking onto wood or plywood panels for aesthetic and practical reasons is not recommended. Aesthetically, a canvas mounted on a firm support loses its character and practically, one so mounted is difficult to remove should the support move or split. Both glue and wax methods of relining on canvas may be used although in very large paintings the weight of the wax may be considered a drawback. When the relining process has been completed, the picture is removed from the heavy *châssis* and placed on a stretcher. Its protecting paper is removed and it may then be cleaned as described earlier or varnished. In all cases the edges

of relined pictures should not be trimmed but should be preserved in their original dimensions. The common practice of trimming and binding edges destroys evidence indicating whether a painting is in its original size or only a fragment of a larger work.

Varnishing or **resurfacing** a picture, is the final operation in restoration. The traditional varnishes used are **Mastic** and **Dammar** and they are still the safest protective films for this purpose. Recently synthetic resins have been employed. Advantages are claimed for these because they are water white and are stable. The conservative restorer, however, will doubtless care to learn more of their properties before using these materials exclusively. Good qualities of Mastic and Damar varnish can be purchased although each restorer has his preferred formula. They should be applied on a dry day in a dust free room maintaining a temperature of about 80 deg. F. The object in brushing varnish is to evenly spread as little as possible. It is applied in quick crisscross strokes and brushed until practically dry. Brushes and the paintings must be free from lint or other foreign substances. The excessive lustre of freshly varnished paintings may be eliminated by applying a thin coat of wax (for formula see *Technical Studies,* October 1934), and buffing with a soft brush. This also tends to reduce blooming.

Technical aids and records. The well equipped restorer's shop should own or have access to x-ray and ultra-violet ray apparatus for studying and recording the state of works before they are restored. He should have the services of a competent photographer to do the necessary technical photography required in recording all steps of any operation. In addition, written records should be assembled for future reference. The accumulation of radiographs, infra-red ray photographs and other prints will form a growing body of technical information of value in problems of restoration and study of style. The above requirements are especially important where public or museum property is concerned.

Many details of technique have been omitted because of space limitations and because many are personal choices with each restorer and achieve similar ends. The most important principle in all departments of restoration is to avoid drastic or final treatments which cannot be modified or changed if necessary. See *Restauration des Tableaux,* Charles Dalbon, Paris, 1898; *Materials and the painters Craft,*

A. P. Lawrie, Phila., 1911; *Painters' Methods and Materials,* A. P. Lawrie, Phila, 1926; *The Scientific Examination of Paintings,* A. Martin de Wilde, London, 1929; *Ultra-Violet Rays and their use, etc.,* James J. Rorimer, N. Y. 1931; *Materials of the Artist,* Max Doerner, N. Y., 1934; *l'Esame Scientifico Delle Opre d'Arte ed il Loro Restauro,* Renato Mancia, 2 vols., Milano, 1936; *Die Bedeutung der Gemäldedurchleuchtung mit Röntgenstrahlen für Kunstgeschichte,* Christian Walters, Frankfurt-am-Main, 1938; *Art Criticism from a Laboratory,* Alan Borroughs, Boston, 1938; *La Conservation des Peintures,* pub. by l'Office International des Musées, Paris, 1939; Philadeliphia Museum of Art Bulletin, Jan., 1940; Preservation versus Restoration, David Rosen, *Mag. of Art,* Nov. 1941; Brooklyn Museum Journal, 1942, pp. 71-82 and plates; *Technical Studies,* Cambridge, Mass., vols. I to date; *Mouseion,* Paris, vol. I to date.   —H.M.

restrictions, real estate. See CIVIC PLANNING.

rest stick. See mahlstick.

resurfacing. See RESTORATION OF PAINTINGS.

Resurrection. Although central to the Christian faith the Resurrection was hardly ever represented in early Christian and East Christian art, as the canonic Gospels fail to describe it directly. Instead there is in 4th cent sarcophagi symbolic reference to it in form of the labarum (q.v.) placed triumphantly above a cross surrounded by the sleeping guardsmen form the Gospel account. Other forms of indirect reference are: (1) the Anastasis (usual in Byzantine art and in phases of Western art directly or indirectly dependent on it); (2) The holy women being shown the empty tomb by an angel (both in Eastern and Western art, in Italy until 14th cent.). (3) *Noli me tangere* (q.v.).

Direct representation of the Resurrection was prepared theologically in the apocryphal Gospels of St. Peter and by the Eastern church father Ephraim Syrus, who initiated the belief of all medieval writers in the miraculous Resurrection from the closed sepulchre. Western art, which after ca. 1000 A.D. undertook the direct representation of the Resurrection, usually neglected this theological specification and showed Christ standing in the open tomb (earliest German and Italian type) setting one foot on its rim (usual German and French type) or standing beside it

(Flemish 15th cent.). Representation of the Resurrection through Christ rising above the sepulchre was initiated by Italian artists of the 14th cent. in imitation of pictures of the Ascension to heavens and spread in the 16th cent. to artists of all Europe. Sleeping or startled guards are a usual corollary of all types of direct representation.   —R.B.

retable. See altarpiece.

reticella. See lace.

reticulated. When referring to Oriental pottery, the design is a perforated weblike form, superimposed over the main body of the vessel.

retouching. See RESTORATION OF PAINTINGS.

retreating color. See receding color.

retrograde, retrograde form, retrograde inversion. See imitation; TWELVE-TONE TECHNIQUE.

retroussage. *Etch.* A method of bringing the ink up from the incised lines of an intaglio plate in order to make certain passages darker and richer, by widening the lines. This is done by dragging a soft rag gently across the ink-filled lines before printing. See PRINTS AND PROCESSES.   —K.K.

reveal. The surface at right angles to the face of a wall, at the side of an opening cut through it; known as a splay when cut diagonally.   —J.M.M.

reverberation. See ACOUSTICS.

reversible carpet. See carpet structures.

revetted architecture. See ARCHITECTURE.

revolving stage. See MODERN STAGE SETTING.

Rhages ware. Persian (Iranian) pottery from the city of Rhages. See PERSIAN ART.

Rhenish architecture. Within Romanesque architecture Rhenish churches are characterized by the clarity of their basilica plan ("square schematism"), their early monumental groin vaulting systems (Speyer cathedral, 1080 ff.; Mainz, cathedral, 1081 ff.), their picturesque silhouettes with tower groups at either end (Worms, cathedral, ca. 1180 ff.), often with tre-foil transepts (Cologne, St.

Mary in the Capitol, ca. 1065; Cologne, Holy Apostles, 1191 ff.), and by their rich decoration (Schwarzrheindorf, ca. 1151). See Frankl, *Die fruehmittelalterliche und romanische Baukunst*, 1926; Lasteyrie, *L'architecture réligieuse á l' époque romane*, 1912; Porter, *Medieval architecture*, 1909; Rave, *Romanische Baukunst am Rhein*, 1922.   —R.K.

Rhenish school. The term refers to the style of works of art, primarily reliefs, of the 12th and early 13th cent. in the Cologne region. This style presents an interesting combination of French Gothic, German Romanesque and Carolingian Renaissance; its most outstanding example is the *Dreikönigsschrein* (ca. 1200, Nicolaus of Verdun, Cologne cathedral). The figures of the prophets and apostles which decorate the shrine containing the relics are not treated with the archaic cube-like simplicity of the German Romanesque, but they are clearly and plastically developed. The softly flowing folds of their robes lack the stylized treatment of the Gothic and the faces, instead of the conventionalized Gothic beauty, show strong individual expression which is carried over into the attitudes of the bodies.

Other examples of this style are the *Viktor Schrein* in Xanten, ca. 1129, by Master Eilbertus of Cologne; the *Heribert Schrein* of Deutz (near Cologne), ca. 1170-1180, by Godefroy de Claire (born in Huy near Dinant and also known as Gottfried of Huy). —H.H.

rhinocerous cup. Made from rhinocerous horn which was supposed to detect poison. Rhinocerous horn is a material often used for glyptic art in the Orient.   —J.A.M.

Rhodian ware. See Ionian vases; ISLAMIC ART.

rhombus (Gr. *rhombos*). In Greek art, esp. pottery, an ornament of diamond shape, i.e., a four-sided figure with two opposite sides parallel and with two angles obtuse and two acute.   —L.T.S.

rhyparography. The depiction of sordid, foul or mean objects. Also refers to the painting of genre or still life pictures.

rhythm. The word rhythm is derived from the Greek *rhein* which means "to flow". Rhythm means a continuance resulting from reiteration of the same or similar component parts.

General. The importance of rhythm is based on the value of alternative tension and relaxation like working and resting, waking and sleeping, etc. Rhythm suggests, therefore, the lawful periodicity of every phase of life, whatever it may be. Without rhythm life would be chaotic and one would not be able to look back over it as a whole. The recognition of periodically recurrent signs or marks gives man the feeling that this course is necessary by law and it gives him a certain relief, calmness, and pleasure. Every human being has his particular rhythm of life. Every work created by men must reveal this rhythm. In works of art rhythm plays an especially important role because it is the main instrument for organizing and unifying the different parts, and unity is one of the main requirements of art. The rhythmical element becomes especially evident in the applied arts. Here the rhythmical periodicity is the foremost means of aesthetic expression and is perceived by the spectator as such. In each so-called independent work of art, moreover, rhythmic repetition, sometimes very complicated, is present and can be perceived. Each artist, every people, and every epoch produces a characteristic kind of rhythm. Thus the recognition of rhythmical peculiarity aids in finding the time in which, and the author or school by which a work has been created. One may distinguish between rhythm of color, line, and form. In the continuity of the three originates the whole rhythm of a work.
     —A.J.S.

Music. Pattern of time values allotted to consecutive musical elements. Usually the term rhythm implies that a particular time pattern recurs systematically. If this is not the case, the rhythm is called irregular. In the tonal idiom the time patterns are related systematically to the basic accent patterns; therefore, in the province of this idiom, frequently no strict distinction is made between rhythm and meter (see idiom).   —E.K.

Dance. Rhythm in movements of dance, apart from the rhythm of their emotional content, is the organization of the time and stress values into a united motor experience. Rhythm is a constant principle of muscular action, which is action and rest, and is the only form in which muscular action takes place (see movement). It is the particular proportioning of the time and stress elements within these periods of action and rest that determines the specific rhythmic structure of a given movement. Rhythmic responses, therefore, are based upon the rhythmic experience we gain from sensations of active muscles, for it is the organization existing in these muscle sensations that furnish the uniting element for consciousness (see kinesthetic sense). Through association, rhythmic stimulation has the power to stimulate emotional responses. It produces a fundamental and elemental response, primarily organic, secondarily intellectual and discriminating. Through the medium of these fundamental responses and their resulting stimuli of association, feeling states are aroused according to the richness of the imaginative and emotional natures. Thought and feeling also follow rhythmic pulsations. Every feeling state has its appropriate and peculiar motor concomitant. There are movements of joy, rage, sorrow, and so on through the list of feeling states, each with its own rhythmic structure. Therefore, expressive movements is of necessity rhythmical because of the influence of thought and feeling upon its form. The rhythms of song, poetry, music, and the cadences of speech are as much manifestations of organic rhythm as breathing, walking, or any other muscular action. All song forms that have grown up to stir mankind to mass action and concert the efforts of human physical power are based upon the rhythms of muscular action. They employ for their forms the measured accents, durations, and pauses of the tasks they are to stimulate and heighten. Thus rhythmic stimulation has the power to arouse emotional responses.

In its broadest meaning *rhythm* may be said to be the mold through which expressive life flows in creating its art forms. In this sense rhythm is the primary, fundamental art form. In dance, rhythm means much more than keeping time or the rhythm of skilled movements. Skilled movements as such are not art, i.e., not dance. They are unemotional. But when associated with and conditioned by the rhythms of thought and feeling, they become emotive and through the power of suggestion they call up the feeling state they are meant to portray. Technical movements that are intended to arouse feeling require the use of rhythm in its fullest meaning. Rhythm overflows into all the compartments of thinking, feeling, and acting, and produces an artistic rhythmic whole. *Rhythm of dance* is intellectual, emotional, and spiritual forces manifested in rhythmic movement.

The terms *"a rhythm"*, *"rhythms"*, and *"rhythmic pattern"* must not be confused with *rhythm*. Rhythm is the inclusive term which is the feature that all rhythms share. The other terms refer to a definite pattern embodying rhythm.   **—M.N.H'D.**

rhythmicists. See POLISH ART.

rhyton (Gr. *rhyton* fr. *rhytos,* flowing). In Greek pottery, a drinking cup originally in the shape of a horn running to a point with a small hole for drinking, later in the shape of an animal or human head, open only at the top.   **—L.T.S.**

ribat. (Ar.). Military station for the Holy War against unbelievers (of the Mohammedan faith) ; a monastery. See ISLAMIC ART.

ribbed vault. A masonry vault in which solid ribs carry a lighter, relatively thin web or vaulted surface.

ribbon and wreath. See ex libris.

ribbon development. See CIVIC PLANNING.

ribeba, ribeca, ribible. See MUSICAL INSTRUMENTS s.v. rebeck.

ricercare, ricercata. *Mus.* Instrumental composition in free fugual form.

richness. Used in criticism to refer to the artistic material that is wrought upon the formal structure of the work. It is recognized that there are two extremes beyond which works of art can not go, and between which they vary: at one end, a bare formal organization, with no matter to give this texture and content; e.g., a simple plot. At the other end, a mass of matter that obscures the art form, and so becomes incoherent and meaningless. Works become "rich" as they approach this second extreme; i.e., as they exhibit a greater wealth of detailed treatment of artistic material serving to exploit and vary the bare form.   **—I.J.**

riddle canon. See canon.

ridge. *Arch.* The upper angle of a roof; that part of a roof where the rafters meet the ridge-pole. See also drypoint (an intaglio process).

ridge-pole. A horizontal timber at the ridge of a roof, to which the rafters are nailed or attached.

rigaudon. The original name of the pre-classic dance form now known as the *rigaudon* is not recorded, but the origin of the dance has been traced to ancient Italy. Peasants of Provence knew the rigaudon at a later period. It received its present name when a 17th cent. dancing master, Rigaud, presented it to the French court, where it became very popular. In 4/4 or 2/4 meter and rhythmically similar to the *bourrée* and the *gavotte,* the rigaudon began on the last quarter-note of the measure, the beat being divided into two eighths in contrast to the single-note upbeat of the *bourrée.* The frivolous mood and brilliant steps of the dance found a permanent place in ballet vocabulary, and rigaudon music is sometimes found in the old instrumental suites.   —J.G.

right of eminent domain. See CIVIC PLANNING.

rikkwa style. See FLOWER ARRANGEMENT.

rinceau. See acanthus scroll.

ring. See JEWELRY.

riohitsu (Jap.). Two side openings in a sword guard.

ripieno. *Mus.* A part or instrument which merely rounds out the harmony; opposite *solo* or *concertante.*

riser. The vertical part of a step.

risposta. Answer or response in a fugue (q.v.).

ritornello. *Mus.* Something returned to, or repeated. (1) A burden or refrain. (2) An introductory, connective, or concluding instrumental passage in a song.

ritual costume. See COSTUME ART.

rivaq (Ar.). Roofed arcade surrounding court of a mosque. See ISLAMIC ART.

rivolgimento. *Mus.* The inversion of parts such as in double counterpoint (q.v.).

ro (Jap.). A square fire-box fitted in the floor as an appurtenance of *cha-no-yu* (q.v.).

Robineau porcelains. See CERAMICS II.

rocaille. See rococo.

rocker. See PRINTS AND PRINT PROCESSES; mezzotint.

Rockingham ware. See CERAMICS II.

rockwork. *Arch.* Stonework with a broken and rough surface.

rococo. (From *rocaille,* shell shape, a favorite motive in late Baroque ornamentation, composed of shells and stones. Term used first between 1830/40. It signifies the latest phase of the Baroque from ca. 1720 to ca. 1770/80 and is applied to all manifestations of the fine arts, although the term indicates that it originated in the decorative arts.)

As a reflection of the growing sophistication of the French court under Louis XV (1715-1774) and the increasing influence of woman's taste in its circle, the pompous and heavy forms of the Baroque take a turn now toward the light and the elegant. Undulating S-designed forms become more slender and impress their shape upon every organic and inorganic being. Composite creations, half shell, half branch, express the playful vitality of the period in a wealth of ornamental inventions. It is indeed basically an ornamental style comparable in its abundance of designed motives only with the Late Gothic and indicating in this similarity that we are dealing with a late phase in the history of styles in which static-classical composure dissolves into a dynamic and yet refined ornamental language of forms. And indeed, the Rococo is the last *genuine* art style of Europe in which architecture, sculpture, painting and the decorative arts partake of the same expression. The feminine element appears in the predilection for richly decorated silks and brocades, instead of velvets characteristic of the Baroque proper and in the choice of a lighter color scheme of silken blues, pinks and white which replace the dark colors (contrasted with light) of the 17th century. Introduction of new techniques such as the porcelain (by Boettcher 1708/9) and the pastelle (Rosalba Carriera since 1720) can be taken as an expression of the growing sophistication and daintiness of taste. The unusual, the eccentric, the irregular are chosen in order to counteract the "ennui" of a more and more formalized and rationalized civilization.

The motives peculiar to the Rococo originated in the ornamental designs of grotesques by Berain (1640-1711). Gilles Marie Oppenordt (1672-1742), Juste-Aurèle Meissonier (1695-1750) and Claude Gillot (1673-1722) excel in the new ingenious designs for the decorative arts which become exemplary for the rest of Europe. In *architecture,* the temperamental and plastical Baroque style of Filippo Juvara (1685-1736), and his predecessors Guarino Guarini (1624-1685) and Francesco Borromini (1599-1667) becomes translated into the different national idioms

and blended with the new French system of
decoration. The new rooms at Versailles decorated by J. J. Gabriel (1667-1742) and the
Hotel Soubise by G. Boffrand (1667-1754) bespeak increasingly of the change since 1720
from the majestic to the elegant and comfortable. Francois De Cuvilliès (1695-1768) brings
the Rococo to the court of Bavaria in 1725
and is thus instrumental in the distribution
of the new style over Southern Germany and
Austria which now begin to take a leading
part in the history of Rococo architecture.
Cities such as *Nancy, Potsdam, Dresden,
Prague, Wuerzburg, Munich, Salzburg* and
Vienna still appear today as the exponents of
this era. The castle of Sans-Souci at *Potsdam* (by Knobelsdorff, 1745), the Zwinger
(by Pöpelmann, 1711-24), the court church
(by Chiaveri, 1738-51) in Dresden, the Resi-
denztheatre in *Munich* (by Cuvilliès and Eff-
ner) and the palais Kinsky in Vienna (by
Hildebrand, before 1745) may well represent
the secular style of Rococo architecture while
the ecclesiastic architecture of Bavaria finds
its greatest masters in Christoph Dientzenhofer (1655-1722) and his son Kilian (1689-
1751), Balthasar Neumann (1687-1753) and
the artist family Asam (Hans Georg 1649-
1711; Cosmas Damian 1686-1739; Egid
Quirin 1692-1750). In Austria, the Rococo
flourishes in the work of Kilian Dientzenhofer
(1689-1751) in J. Lukas von Hildebrand
(1668-1745) and in Jakob Prandauer (d.
1727). In all the architectural creations
of these masters we notice a sense for
effective planning of the location in context with the surrounding nature or street
architecture, a plastical handling of ground
plan and elevation developed into complicated
and picturesque spatial organisms of the highest order and the use of painting, sculpture
and the decorative arts for the achievement
of a festive total effect.

The architectures of Spain and England do
not take any considerable part in the Rococo
style, the one expressing itself in the chirru-
queresque Baroque, the other in neo-classical
Palladianism.

In sculpture, the dynamic Baroque of Bernini and his followers turns similarly toward graciousness and even affectation. The
erotical genre replaces more and more the
heroic. Smaller sizes and more intimate expression go hand in hand with it. However,
France has expressed its Rococo phase more
in its decorative arts than in sculpture. Etienne M. Falconet (1716-1791) and Jean Baptiste Pigalle (1714-1785) direct the plastical

trend gradually from the Rococo toward the
new classicism. It is again Germany and
Austria that develop the Rococo to its most
exuberant expression. Balthasar Permoser
(1651-1732) exerts a strong influence on
the Bavarian masters such as the earlier mentioned Egid Quirin Asam, Ignaz Guenther
(1725-1775) and countless others. The typical
Rococo art of china (by J. G. Boettger (1662-
1719) found in Johann Joachim Kaendler
(1706-1775) of Meissen its greatest master.

In painting the Rococo expressed itself in
monumental fresco art as well as in the intimate entertainment genre. In both fields it
produced—shortly before the neo-classical
drought set in—a number of great masters.
Giovanni Battista Tiepolo (1696-1770) and
his sons carried the exuberant virtuoso style
of his late Baroque from the castles and palaces of Venice and Madrid to those of
Southern Germany and thus were instrumental
in the creation of a Rococo fresco style of
turbulent dynamism in the Catholic countries
of Central Europe. On the other hand
Venice produced in Francesco Guardi (1712-
1793) a landscapist of delightful spontaneity.
Francesco Goya's (1746-1828) early frescos
in Madrid also reflect Tiepolo's spirit. Yet
the very essence of the Rococo appears in
the delicate and intimate painting of the
French masters. Antoine Watteau (1684-1721)
combines his Flemish and Rubens nourished
naturalism with the subtlety of French court
art and from it springs the shepherds and
comedian genre which so deeply influences
European painting for the next generation.
In Francois Boucher (1703-1770) and in
Honoré Fragonard (1732-1806) the elegant
and the frivolous genre find their most typical
expression, appearing similarly in a most refined art of book illustrations and color prints.
In England, Thomas Gainsborough (1727-
1788), still represents in his colorism and
in his interpretation of aristocratic portraiture
the characteristics of the Rococo style.

In the Rococo painting of Europe the last
type of a pictorial art bound to a definite
architectural system and to a definite set-up
of society comes to an end. Its design and
its color scheme must be imagined within the
dynamic and elegant setting of the spatial
and plastical compositions of the late Baroque
style. See MUSICAL PERFORMANCE,
MAIN TRENDS IN; FURNITURE; also
Fiske Kimball, The Creation of the Style
Louis XV, *Art Bulletin,* March 1941, p. 1;
E. and J. De Goncourt, *L'art du XVIIIe
siècle,* 2 vol. 1881/83; M. Osborn, *Die Kunst*

des Rokoko, Propylaenkunstgeschichte, Berlin, 1929; L. Réau, *Histoire de la Peinture Francaise au XVIIIe siècle,* 2 vol., Paris, 1925/6: R. Graul, *French art from Watteau to Prudhon,* 3 vol., New York, 1906; O. Biermann, *Deutsches Barock und Rokoko,* Berlin, 1914; G. Morazzoni, *il settecento Italiano,* 2 vol., Milan, 1932; L. Feulner, *Skulptur und Malerei des 18. Jahrhunderts in Deutschland,* Potsdam, 1929; A. E. Brinckmann, *Die Baukunst des 17. und 18. Jahrhunderts in den romanischen Laendern,* 5 ed., Potsdam, 1930; M. Wackernagel, *Die Baukunst des 17. und 18. Jahrhunderts in den germanischen Laendern,* 4 ed., Potsdam, 1932; S. De Ricci, *Le style Louis XVI,* Stuttgart, 1929; Fiske Kimball, *The Creation of the Rococo,* Phila., 1943.   —A.N.

rococo style (in music). See gallant style.

rods, of the eye. See COLOR.

rogata-zome (Jap.). Word for batik.

Rogers groups. See CERAMICS II.

roiro (Jap.). Black lacquer of finest quality.

rollwerk. See scrollwork.

Roman-Arretine pottery. See CERAMICS II.

ROMAN ART begins to rise to independence in the 2nd and 3d cent. B.C. After a period of experimentation, a synthesis of Greek-Hellenistic, Classical Greek, and Romano-Etruscan traditions is achieved under the rule of Augustus (43 B.C.-14 A.D.). The art of the Roman Empire, centering in Rome, dominates the Mediterranean during the first three centuries of our era. But from ca. 100 A.D. on regional arts gain importance. Infused with Roman elements of varying strength, these arts (Eastern Hellenistic, Asiatic, Syro-Mesopotamian, Palmyrene, Gallo-Roman) become the foundations for the rise of the Byzantine, Islamic, and European medieval arts. In various transformations, the influence of Roman art reaches into Central Asia and India.

Roman art was never entirely uniform, but if we must choose its unifying aspect is political. Man is seen as a political leader, a servant of the state, and as a faithful member of his class or profession. The Emperor symbolizes the political unity of mankind, and his portraits, reliefs, and coins reflect the imperial doctrine in the provinces. In architecture, civic buildings (fora, basili-

cas, palaces, amphitheatres) represent the authority of state and constitute, in the provinces, the visible proof of Romanization. These political connotations of Roman art played an important part in its revival during the French and the American Revolutions.

Roman art is frequently defined as a continuation or a vulgarization of Greek art. Roman art had, indeed, continued the anthropomorphic conceptions of Greece and had standardized them into a vocabulary that could be comprehended by primitive provincial cultures. Greek heritage endowed the Romans with the dubious blessing of a ready-made artistic vocabulary. The Roman artist was constantly torn between the stabilizing heritage of Greece and a personal bias reflecting the visual, emotional, and spiritual reality of his own day. Thus he never experienced the continued creative struggle with the surrounding phenomena that distinguished the Greek artist. The decay of Greek forms preserved without radical visual re-interpretation and adaptation to new concepts is reminiscent of the degeneration of the Renaissance-Baroque iconography in the 18th cent. The Rococo evolved certain distinguishing aspects; so also did Roman art include new departures and creative ventures. From the beginning the adopted Greek forms had indigenous functions and aims.

Architecture must perforce preserve contact with actuality. It was the dominant Roman art. The traditional Greek architecture based on the post-lintel system was gradually replaced by a system of arch and vault that sought the abstract contrast of architectural mass and interior space. The Greek wall, a unit composed of many individual blocks, was replaced in Roman architecture by walls conceived as homogeneous masses. The change was not sudden; it began in utilitarian structures that were elevated to artistic expressions (arches of bridges, aqueducts, terraces, amphitheatres). The materials necessary for this transformation were burnt brick and concrete which the Romans were the first to exploit. The emphasis shifted from the exterior to the interior of the buildings. The façades are used as "stage decoration" often masking the true character of the walls. The interior space is rhythmically formed, as in the directed movement of a basilica or as in the restful static interior of the Pantheon (126 A.D.). Light, too, is used for rhythmic effects, but this light is diffused and impersonal, not dramatic as in the Baroque. Greek architectural elements (columns, pilasters, entablatures, friezes) are used to decorate both interiors and exteriors but they gradually lose their tectonic function and are reduced to decorative orders. The Roman art of the Republic and the Early Empire is still dominated by traditional Greek forms. The trend toward a more abstract architecture, which grows in the second and third century A.D., finds its ultimate logical expression not in the basilica of Constantine (306-312 A.D.), which is the last great pagan building of Rome, but in the Byzantine church of Sta. Sophia in Constantinoples.

With a Roman building the parts are subordinated to the total effect. In a similar way the individual building is subordinated to a strictly planned complex of buildings. An early form of strict **axial planning** appears in the designs of Roman camps and colonies (Ostia, 336 B.C.) and in temples precincts (Largo Argentina, Rome, 3d and 2nd cent. B.C.; Ostia, 1st cent. B.C.) in which several temples are set in a row. Planning of large architectural units and zones was perhaps the most enduring contribution that the Romans made to European art. Roman Imperial Fora provide examples of isolated architectural zones symmetrically planned on a long axis. The vista is often dominated by a temple on a high **podium**. Originally, the **Fora** were market places and "commons", but under the Empire they served to commemorate events or personalities and to symbolize the power of the Roman state. The greatest example of "Roman magnificence" was the Forum of Trajan (113 A.D.) a memorial of Roman victories over the Dacians. Entering through a triumphal arch the spectator saw a vast oblong enclosure bordered by porticos. A basilica stood at the end opposite the entrance. The traditional rectangular plan of the forum was changed by the architect Apollodorus with the inclusion of two semi-circular projections from the long sides. Behind the basilica the spiral column of Trajan flanked by two libraries, accentuated the main axis. The precinct climaxed monumentally with the temple of Trajan (added under Hadrian). Excepting the high wall which surrounded the whole Forum, the buildings were of marble and were profusely decorated with sculpture.

Roman temples of rectangular plan were conservative adaptations of Greek models, but they often included an apse in the cella and omitted the columns in the rear. Their interest lies in the monumental scale and in the profusion of ornament (Republican temples of Largo Argentina, Rome; Mars Ultor, Rome, 2

B.C.; "Domus Aurea", Nimes, 16 B.C.; Venus and Roma, Rome, 135 A.D.). In grandeur of conception and symmetry of planning the temple precinct of Baalbek (Syria, 1st to 3d cent.) rivals the Imperial Fora of Rome. The circular and polygonal temples (Tivoli, 1st cent. B.C. Temple by the Tiber, Rome) eventually drop the Greek colonnade and become identical with similar types of fountain houses, funeral monuments, and civic buildings (Pantheon, Rome; Fountain in the Licinian Gardens, 3d cent. A.D.; Mausoleum of Sta. Constantia, 354 A.D.). This type of central building had a persistent influence upon Early Christian and later European art (G. Rivoira, Roman Architecture, 1925). Roman palaces were at first enlarged houses (Golden House of Nero, Rome 64-69 A.D. Palace of Flavians, Rome, 92 A.D.), but later they became immense castles planned on the axial scheme of a Roman camp (Diocletion's Palaces in Spalato and Palmira, 298-305 A.D.). Roman baths based on a plan of ornamental symmetry which combined rectangular, circular and polygonal rooms, achieved in their huge vaulted halls an effect of majestic space that dwarfs human beings (Baths of Caracalla, 212-216 A.D., of Diocletian, 298-305 A.D., Baths in Trier).

The Roman basilicas which served as courts, community halls, and club houses are basically triumphal highways, bordered by one or two-storied colonnades and roofed over. Their protypes are the colonnaded streets of the Roman East (Antioch, Palmyra, Gerasa). Basilicas sometimes included apsidal chapels at the ends. Their function as community halls may have influenced the Christians to select this type for their churches (Basilicas: Pompeii, ca. 100 B.C.; Ardea, 80 B.C.; Julia, Rome, 12 A.D.; Ulpia, 112 A.D.; of Junius Bassus, 331 A.D.; and many examples in the provinces. Christian: Old St. Peter's, 326 A.D.).

Theatres (Marcellus, Rome, 11 B.C.; Orange, France, 50 A.D.; Aspendos, Asia Minor, 170-180 A.D.), amphitheatres (Colosseum, 80 A.D.), city gates (Autumn, Miletus, Treves), libraries (Timgad, Ephesus) and even bridges and fortifications were treated with the same feeling for grandeur, rhythmic decoration and perspective effects (vistas).

In sculpture, the study of the isolated human figure attracted little interest. Some new types, however, were created to express Roman ideals of service to the state; the cuirass statues comprising a long series from Augustus of Primaporta (19 B.C.) to the

Colossus of Barletta (360-370 A.D.), the toga statues which begin with the fine bronze figure of the "Orator" in Florence (100 B.C.) and continue into the Byzantine Period, and the seated statues of consuls and emperors. Most of the statues in the round were closely modelled on Greek prototypes as were the legions of decorative statues and reliefs which adorned Roman public and private building enterprises. Schools of copyists (ca. 100 B.C.-200 A.D.) supplied the majority of these commissions. Like all academies, these schools offered little incitement to originality, but contributed a certain technical competence and even virtuosity. In judging Roman sculptures we should remember that they were designed as parts of definite settings, not as isolated monuments.

The Roman conception of reality showed primarily a keen observation of an individual phenomena. There resulted a strong interest in individualistic portraiture. The earliest original achievements of Rome are the late republican portraits (100-30 B.C.), prosaic conceptions in which each feature is recorded with disarming honesty. The portraits of the civil wars (Pompey, Caesar 50-30 B.C.) show an attempt to reconcile an unrelated observation of individual traits with a dynamic, psychological conception of personality. A compromise, based on cool Classicistic dignity and aristocratic refinement, is achieved in the portraits of the Augustan age (30 B.C.-20 A.D., Augustus, Octavia, Livia). The Roman eye for human fallibility records its observations with greater formal refinement and psychological penetration in the portraits of Augustus' successors (Claudius, Vatican, Nero). An intentional return to Republican honesty under Titus and Vespassian (69-81 A.D.) yields to courtly, affected portraiture under Domitian. The sculptors now begin to exploit optic effects in their quest for subtle differentiation of sentimental moods.

The heroic period of Trajan produces magnificent portraits that summarize the commanding attitude of Imperial leadership. With the cultured dreamers of the Hadrianic era (117-138 A.D.) begins a withdrawal of the human being into reflective meditation. The hardness of structure is abandoned for surface charm and scintillating contrasts of light and dark. The startled, cautious portraits of the anarchic third century are at first rendered in loose "impressionistic" forms. After Gallien (258-268 A.D.) the disintegrating physical features petrify into patterned masks penetrated only by magnetic widened eyes. And realism in portraiture is completely supplanted by a spiritual symbolism.

Historical reliefs, derived from the poster-paintings of triumphal processions pass through similar phases. After superficial experiments with Greek formulae (frieze of "Domitius Ahenobarbus", ca. 100 B.C.), the first Imperial program in marble appears in the friezes of the Altar of Augustan Peace (13-9 B.C), which sets the pattern of idealized historical reality that continues to characterize Roman historical reliefs (Arch of Titus 81 A.D.). The most remarkable type of pictures are the "idyllic landscapes", reflecting the Roman feeling for civilized Arcadian nature, a nature interspersed with evidence of human life—villas, statues, and small groups of people. The column of Trajan (A.D.), is a continuous account of the Dacian wars with many short-hand details of armies, tribes, landscape, and architecture. These compositions stem from the same illustrative tradition that we find in a Hadrianic mosaic of Egypt from Preneste, in the Jewish wall paintings of the Synagogue in Dura (Mesopotamia, 3d cent. A.D.), and in the Christian Joshua Roll (Byzantine copy, after an original of 4th cent. A.D.).

Most of the Roman painting we know is little more than interior decoration. For over a century Roman decorators strove for a three-dimensional illusion. The trend to dissolve the surface of the wall into a sequence of receding vistas reaches its heights in the Flavian period (Fourth "Pompeian" style, ca. 80 A.D.). Although the Romans had developed a graded and varied palette and achieved considerable skill in a three-dimensional portrayal of isolated objects and groups of objects (partial perspective), this initial pictorial conquest of reality never reaches a unified visual effect. Later, the interest in problems of space, light, and atmosphere diminishes in favor of abstract symbolic forms. Abstract pattern, strong delineation, and rich colors become the prime objectives. We can trace this development in the paintings of houses and ombs in Rome, Ostia, and the provinces as well as in the mosaics produced over the entire Roman Empire (esp. in Gaul, Africa, and Antioch).

The rise of abstract compositions and formalized visual concepts under the late Roman Empire expresses the attempt to grasp a reality beyond the fleeting appearances of naturalistic vision. It emphasizes the shift from the physical and vitalistic aspect of visual reality toward a belief in a static universe of eternal, cosmic forces. This change lowered the original Roman concern for mundane realities and paved the way for expression of transcendental ideas in Early Christian and Byzantine art. See E. Strong and G. Rodenwaldt in *Cambr. Anc. Hist.* IX, XI, XII.   —G.M.A.H.

Romanesque architecture (11th and 12th cents.). Romanesque architecture presents the revival and application of Roman principles of construction, especially the use of round arch, barrel vault and cross vault. The title is therefore pertinent, for it declares the essential contribution of the style, the renewal of Roman engineering in the art of architecture.

It is true that the application was limited to ecclesiastical structures, judging from surviving material, and in this respect differs from the elaborate social usage of the Roman Empire. Civilization of Europe in the middle ages had no such requirements as are represented in Roman architecture. The knowledge and use of concrete failed entirely, and was not revived until modern times (125 years ago in Portland cement).

About the year 1000 men wearied of the barbarian experience and began to work their way out. They were specifically tired of the task of restoring such churches of the old Roman basilica style as they chanced to possess, with their unstable walls and column supports and their wooden roofs easily wrecked in times of war and disorder.

Most of the churches erected in the age of barbarian violence and adjustment had been on the Roman pattern, as the tribes received Christianity from the Roman missionaries and docilely accepted the rule of the See of Peter. There were of course many exceptions and modifications as in Saxon England, in Gothic Spain, Lombardy, Merovingian France, and many other areas, all of which invite the theories of specialists. Well known is the attempt during the Carolingian renaissance to adapt the Byzantine style with cupola (Charlemagne's minister at Aix-la-Chapelle c. 800). But the Byzantine did exert constant influence all through the Romanesque period and even resulted in the construction of domes on pendentives and squinches as in the Aquitainian group in France (Augoulême, Périgueux, Souillac). It may have stirred interest in the idea of the erection of cupolas over crossings, which had large development in Romanesque. But the core of the matter is that the style developed on the heritage of the T cross plan of the early Christian Roman bailica, with three aisles and transept.

The energizing influence in the Romanesque contest with barbarism was the Church, the depository and source of such intellectual treasure as the age possessed. All men were Christian by right of birth and accepted Christianity thankfully and with emotion. The Church likewise had been purified and was ruled by a group of reforming popes under strong monastic influence. Monasticism at the time was resolute and intelligent and very active. Christian society and its institutions were international and universal, but flexible enough to permit great variety in expression. This was also the period of the earliest and most worthy of the crusades, an exploit in history which knows no equal. Scholars likewise were originating an intellectual movement which holds an assured place in philosophic thought.

In harmony with the activity thus let loose the art of architecture began its revival. Romanesque architecture accordingly presents the contribution of many varied minds of diverse racial stocks, united in their instinctive striving for an undefined objective, but never arriving at complete expression. There is no single example which may be said to constitute the style. Romanesque style is assembled from the examination of all the existing and varied examples. The great diversity in experimental creation and expression is a reason why Romanesque architecture is of constant interest. And yet it is a true style, consistent within itself, and is easily recognized. Of course not the least reason for its significance is that its experiments led directly to the final satisfaction afforded by Gothic.

Requirements represented in the architecture consist of stable, powerful structure for the impressive and mystic presentation of the Christian liturgy (in which the function of music of the age should receive greater attention), and the ordering of space for such effects, and specifically inviting the frank outpouring of dynamic emotion which characterizes the barbarian experience, finding satisfaction in the vigor of creative energy. A special demand was that of wall decoration, esp. sculpture, which the Western Church in opposition to the Eastern had never renounced and now revived with wild emotion. The sculpture was in true association with architecture, even when not suggesting structure, and was accordingly flat. (Very revealing estimates of periods in civilization, including the present era, are implicit in the criterion of how men relate the figure to the wall. For example, in the Gothic age the figure came forth fully.) The technique of mosaic languished, but fresco painting had free expression in some areas, especially in the south where climate suggested that windows be suppressed in favor of wall. (C. Post, *History of Spanish Painting,* vols. I ff.)

The ground plan, required by the Western liturgy, is that of the three-aisled basilica focusing attention on the altar. But at once the transept began to move west, affording the plan of the Latin cross. The choir was thus made longer, and the side aisles continued around the apse, resulting in the ambulatory, from which a necklace of chapels radiated at times. The veneration of the relics was the reason for the marked increase in chapels, as for example, Cluny and the pilgrimage shrine of *Santiago de Compostela.* There was endless variation in plan. Thus in Germany there was the demand for two choirs, with transepts, at both ends of the nave, probably because of monastic usages. Examples at Cologne feature large rounding of the transepts with consequent enlargement of space from the crossing, whereas in Norman England there was a general tendency towards straight terminal walls for choir and transepts, resulting in a military effect, stern and forbidding without and secure within. Here begins the English custom of lodging the altar against the wall. In almost all cases the intersection of nave with transept marked the rise of a cupola of some sort.

In elevation marked innovations occur. There is no particular search for height (with exceptions). Height is regularly an exterior effect and is in cupolas or towers which punctuate the crossing, or towers associated with the transepts (as in Germany) or incorporated in the façades, as in Norman practice, possibly resulting from the observation of churches in Syria by the crusaders. Towers, however, never attain a true integration with the structure of the mass of the basilica. The front elevation is triple, with three portals with round arch, recessed, marking the nave and side aisles within.

The interior is normally low and heavy, as suggested by the use of the round arch. The primary supports are walls of manifest thickness and weight and piers instead of columns for the elevation of arches and vaults. The bay system is thus revived and with authority. The walls of the nave originate

the triple division of ground arcades, triforium and clerestory, but seldom with effect of height. In the vast majority of cases the wooden roof over the nave persists, but is finally supplanted by the fireproof vault.

Experiments in the construction of the vault of masonry and its support represent the essence of the Romanesque contribution. An obvious solution was that of the continuous barrel vault as used by the Romans (Cleremont-Ferrand). This required very heavy walls for the support, since the outward thrust was powerful and equal at all points. Novel construction of quarter circle vaults over the side aisles helped to absorb such thrust, but the experiment suggested further innovation, such as supporting the vault on arches thrown transversely across the nave, lodged on piers of the bay and fortified on the exterior by heavy pier buttresses attached to the wall (St. Sernin, Toulouse and *Santiago de Compostela*).

Such experiments called attention to the functions of the bay and the use of the intersecting vault, employed already in the construction of side aisles and perfected by the Romans centuries earlier. But the knowledge of the properties of concrete used by the Romans was lost, together with the sources of supply. The crowning achievement of the Romanesque builders thus lay in their bold exploit of constructing the segments of the cross vault of a bay on ribs, attaching the ribs to the mass of the four great piers involved (resulting in the compound pier) and thus visually transmitting to the ground the thrust which originated in the crown of the bay and which naturally concentrated upon the four piers (St. Ambrose at Milan). Each bay buttressed the next on the long axis of the basilica, the terminal buttress masses being the choir and the powerful end wall, often developed with narthex or porches. The thrust along the cross axis of a bay presented a more difficult problem, never solved satisfactorily in Romanesque. The obvious solution was to throw the thrust over the side aisles by further extension of the principle, as at Milan where an alternate pier created two bays in the aisle to one in the nave (but with incomplete visual expression), or by use of the quarter circle continuous vault (St. Stephen at Caen) and finally by half arches over the aisles, corresponding to the piers, but concealed by the slant of the roof (Church of the Trinity at Caen). These segments of arches were, however, true flying buttresses and all that the Gothic builders had to do was to expose them over the roof. Pier buttresses attached to the exterior side walls completed the solution of thrust.

It is clear that when the four piers of a bay mark a square and ribs describing round arches are lodged upon them the diameter of the arches of the diagonal ribs will be greater than those of the longitudinal and transverse, with consequent effect of a dome. A procession of domical vaults is very impressive and is in the spirit of Romanesque, denoting slow, stately approach to the altar, but it did not appeal to the Norman builders employed by William the Conqueror. Accordingly at Caen, seeking greater height, they employed the alternate pier of full height for the support of a third transverse rib, thus dividing the bay into six parts, and also arbitrarily broke the profile, making the ribs in part seek vertical and in part horizontal directions, with consequent elevation of the intersecting vaults to a common level. The result, however, was awkward, but it led to the Gothic solution, pointing the ribs and reducing the bays to rectangles.

Such is the general trend of the Romanesque development. It is to be remembered that there is abundant regional variation and experiment, such as the effects achieved in Lombardy (corbel string, polygonal lantern, cupolas and the very graceful Lombard porch); the marble style of Tuscany (blind arcades, gallery arcades in subtle ordering); the Norman style in Sicily, not to mention Normandy itself and Norman England; sectional variations in France, in Spain and in Germany, and that the style has vitality within itself is shown by the work of Henry Richardson in America in the 19th century, followed by Bertram Goodhue.

Romanesque architecture is of the very essence of the medieval experience. There is no swift advance on the axis of the nave. Massive piers hold the eye, and the round arches with their repeated return downward suggest by their rhythm slow and stately progress. But full consolation is afforded by the altar and its mysteries, exposed to view for man's veneration and love. It is an architecture of emotion, of faith undisturbed by question, the authentic art of an authoritative Church, and its symbol is the strength and form of the round arch. See A. W. Clapham, *Romanesque Architecture in Western Europe*, 1936; A. K. Porter, *Lombard Architecture*, 4 vols., 1917; R. de Lasteyrie, *L'Architecture réligieuse à l'époque romane*, 1929; C. Ricci, *Romanesque Architecture in*

Italy, 1925; T. G. Jackson, *Byzantine and Romanesque Architecture*, 2 vols., 1920; C. Ward, *Medieval Church Vaulting*, 1915; Robb and Garrison, *Art in the Western World*, 1942.   —C.D.L.

Romanesque style. See GERMAN ART.

Romanists. A group of Flemish painters who worked in Rome under the influence of Raphael and Michelangelo. They called themselves "Romanists" to signify their devotion to Italian art. Among these artists were Jan Gossaert (Mabuse), Van Orley and Frans Floris. They are often referred to as the Italianizers (q.v.).   —R.L.W.

Roman notation. See NOTATION.

Roman school. See mannerism.

Roman theatre. See THEATRE.

romantic ballet. The term "romantic" is not applied in ballet discussion as opposite to "classic" (or the traditional academic line), but rather as a stylistic department of it. The "romantic" division of the classic repertory originated ca. 1830, as a parallel in the lyric theatre of the movement headed by Victor Hugo and Byron in literature, Delacroix and Gericault in painting. *La Sylphide* (Phillippe Taglioni, 1832) and *Giselle* (Coralli, 1841) are two typical romantic classic ballets, costumed in gauzy white skirts (*ballets blancs*). The subject matter in both cases is an imaginative search for a vague ideal. *Les Sylphides* (Fokine, 1909) is a twentieth century pastiche of this style, without definite subject but with the poses and atmosphere derived from the earlier works.
                                                          —L.K.

Romanticism. From the French *Romance*-like. In the 17th and 18th cents. used for: strange and unusual as in a "romance". The term in this general sense can be applied to any period in which the emotional and the imaginative qualities in art and life are stressed. In this general sense, one has spoken of "Romantic" trends in Venetian painting, German art, etc. It thus becomes the expression of a basic attitude opposed to the "classical" with its stress on the rational, the definite, and the harmonious. Yet, we are here concerned with the other usage which applies the term "Romanticism" to the definite period between 1800 to 1840/50.

Through the German writers Tieck, Novalis (Friedrich von Hardenberg), the brothers

Schlegel, Schelling, and Fichte, the early Romantic School established around 1800 the philosophical and poetic foundations of the new "religion of the infinite". It represented a reaction of the European, esp. the Northern spirit, against the rationalism and classicism of the Mediterranean spirit. Its first indications appeared already in the 2d part of the 18th cent. in the English sentimental and in the Gothic novel, in garden architecture, in the German "Storm and Stress" movement, and in Rousseau and his followers. Romanticism in the German school valued emotion against reason, the subconscious against the conscious, divination against deduction, the individual against the typical, the folk against humanity, history against utopia, the demonic, night and moon against the enlightened hero, the day and sunlight, irony against bathos, the organic against the calculated, the musical against the sculptural, becoming against being. The Romantic theory appears condensed in the statement of Novalis: "The world must be romanticised. In giving the usual a noble sense, the ordinary a mysterious appearance, the well known the dignity of the unknown, the temporal a perennial aura, I am romanticising" (Fragments VI, 100).

We owe to Romanticism a new understanding of folklore and fairytale, of world-poetry, of individual psychology, of historical writing, of mythology and religion. While German Romanticism by its medieval and Christian ideals became connected with political restoration, French Romanticism showed itself politically active, joining in with ideals of a liberal progress. This later French phase of Romanticism has more similarity with the English version of it as represented by Lord Byron and Shelley. Exalted egotism clad in *Weltschmerz*, escape from the now and here into the exotic, the abnormal, the passionate have transformed the cosmic, religious, philosophical and introvert early Romanticism into a worship of the dynamic forces of "Life" as they are expressed in the subconscious, in nature, in the people, and in the nation.

In the Fine Arts accordingly a definite difference will be noticed between early and late Romanticism, between German and French Romanticism.

Germany: In Germany, Romantic painting developed in direct contact with the Dresden circle of the literary movement of Tieck and Novalis. Philipp Otto Runge (1777-1810) and Caspar David Friedrich (1774-1840) strove for a new landscape art which wanted to make nature the symbol of Christianity, thus relating the cosmic universe to historical religion. In 1810, for the first time, a landscape painting (by Friedrich) was placed over an altar of a Christian chapel. Besides Romantic landscape painting, the revival of religious art under the so-called "Nazarenes" (q.v.) which, since 1810, spread out from Rome, is esp. significant. Under its devout leader Friedrich Overbeck (1789-1869) it exerted influence on English and French religious art as may be seen in the work of some of the pre-Raphaelites and of Hippolyte Flandrin (1809-1864). The revival of historical and religious fresco painting under such artists as Peter von Cornelius (1783-1867) and Alfred Rethel (1816-1859) is an outgrowth of the Nazarene School. In the 30's the transcendental character of Romantic art changes into a simple, homely, imaginative, and story-telling art as exemplified in the paintings of Moritz von Schwind (1804-1871), the friend of Franz Schubert, Ludwig Richter (1803-1884), esp. famous for his innumerable woodcut book illustrations, and Karl Spitzweg (1808-1885), the humorist and most progressive colorist of the "Biedermeier" (q.v.) spirit. In the field of sculpture and architecture, the Romantic era continued in the neo-classical vein. Yet the imitation of medieval ecclesiastic architecture became increasingly a challenge to the neo-classical style. Carl Friedrich Schinkel (1781-1841) and Leo von Klenze (1784-1864) are the outstanding architects of the periods who built according to needs in the classical, the medieval, or the Renaissance style. Out of Romanticism grew on the one hand the sentimental "entertainment art" of the Munich and Düsseldorf School which exerted considerable influence on American art and taste; on the other hand, the art of naturalistic landscape and portrait painting, fostered by the Romantic "devotion to the minute" (*Andacht zum Kleinen*).

France: There is nothing comparable to the religious early Romanticism of Germany in French art. The heroic mood of the revolutionary and Napoleonic days had inspired the artists with a more activist feeling toward the contemporary. In the hero worship and the military paintings of Antoine Jean Gros (1771-1835), the classicist style was already tainted by romantic exaltation of form and content. A trend for *la sensation* (the sensations) of reality became combined with a new interest for the cruel, the morbid, the passionate, and the exotic. Dante,

Shakespeare, and Byron provided the fuel for the Romantic flame. Politically the Romanticists lined up with the opposition against the Bourbon restoration—classicism became identified with reaction. The influence of the liberal ideas and manners of England and of their naturalistic landscape art (Constable) was strongly felt. The sensualism of the period found new inspiration in the Orient, especially in the French colonies of Tunisia and Maroc. The realization of the new ideals asked for changed means of expression. The classicist doctrine of pure linearism (q.v.) and restrained color seemed unfit. The rehabilitation of color and the subordination of line in the work of Théodore Géricault (1791-1824) and in that of the leader of the Romantic school, Eugène Delacroix (1798-1863) represent a creative contribution to the adequate expression of the Romantic concepts. Nourished by the study of Michelangelo and Rubens, a baroque element appears in the endeavor toward dramatization of content, line, and color. As in German Romanticism, a new impulse toward naturalism can be observed. The greater flexibility of the Romantic type as compared with the doctrinary classicist, his sense for the undiscovered and the intimate made him willing and curious to look at nature with open eyes. The later naturalistic artists felt clearly that they owed much to Delacroix' naturalistic (and with it, coloristic) discoveries. In its blend of the Romantic with the naturalistic, the Barbizon School (q.v.) (or school of 1830) of landscape painting was the world's favorite by the middle of the 19th cent. The lyrical and the heroic became symbolized in moods of nature. Théodore Rousseau (1812-1867), Charles Daubigny (1817-1878), but foremost Camille Corot (1796-1875) imbued their naturalistic approach in color and design with a superimposed Romantic "idea." The "entertainment" genre of Romantic painting was skillfully provided by Ary Scheffer (1795-1850), Paul Delaroche (1797-1856), and Leopold Robert (1795-1835). The Romantic current became increasingly counteracted since the middle of the century by the realistic art of Gustave Courbet (1819-1877) and his followers.

As in Germany, Romanticism in France has not created a style of its own in the field of sculpture and architecture (with the exception of the Neo-Gothic fashion). Yet out of this Neo-Gothicism grew the way-leading contributions of Eugène E. Viollet-Le-Duc (1814-1879) in the field of restoration of medieval architecture and of medieval architectural history.

Other countries: None of the other countries has contributed essentially to the making of a Romantic fine art. Yet the sentimental or sensational features of German and French Romanticism have provided germs of corruption in the general decline of the arts in the first part of the nineteenth century. The Belgian school of history painting with its emphasis on heroic calamities as seen in the huge canvasses of Louis Gallait (1810-1887), Edouard De Bièfve (1808-1882), and Gustave Wappers (1803-1874) exerted some influence on Central European art. In England the art of William Blake (1757-1827), William Turner (1775-1851) and the pre-Raphaelites shows an intrusion of Romantic concepts in form or subject-matter without ever being fully a part of the Romantic movement. In America the half Romantic, half naturalistic style of the middle of the nineteenth century was introduced by Emanuel Leutze (1816-1868), Eastman Johnson (1824-1906), and George Inness (1825-1894).

In conclusion one may state that Romanticism has nowhere found a stylistic expression of its own in the field of architecture and sculpture. In painting it is also more a changed emotional content and a new subject-matter than a different form that we find. Only in French painting, Romanticism has expressed itself with a new, anti-classicist style of dynamic color and composition. Romanticism was more a literary movement and a universal mood than a stylistic phenomenon of the arts. See FRENCH ART; GERMAN ART; MUSICAL PERFORMANCE, MAIN TRENDS IN; also Smith, Logan P., *Four Romantic Words* (Romantic, Originality, Creation, Genius), Oxford, 1924; Neumeyer, Alfred, *Is There a Romantic Style? Parnassus*, Dec. 1937; Pauli, Gustav, *Klassizismus und Romantik*, Propyläen Kunstgeschichte, 2d ed., Berlin, 1925; Deusch, Werner, *Malerei der Deutschen Romantiker*, Berlin, 1937; Benz, Richard, *Die Deutsche Romantik*, Leipzig, 1937; Gautier, Thèophile, *Les beaux art en Europe*, Paris, 1856/57, vol. II; Baudelaire, Charles, *L'art Romantique*, Paris, 1885; Rosenthal, Léon, *La peinture Romantique en France*, 2d ed., Paris, 1906; Focillon, Henri, *La peinture du XIXe siècle à nos jours*, Paris, 1925; vol. I; Rocheblave, Samuel, *La Peinture française an XIX siècle*, Paris, 1936; Clark, Kenneth, *The Gothi- Revival*, London, 1928; La Follette, Suzanne, *Art in America*, New York, 1930;

Neuhaus, Eugen, *History and Ideals of American Painting,* Stanford, 1931; *Romanticism in America,* Catalog of Exhibition of Baltimore Museum of Art, 1940.   —A.N.

romantic novel. See NOVEL, THE.

rondo, rondeau. (1) An old dance form with alternating solos and choruses. (2) A composition in which a principal theme appears at least three times with contrasting episodes between the repetitions. See MEDIEVAL MUSIC.

rood. A cross or crucifix generally standing on the rood screen (q.v.) or attached to the vaulting of the entrance to the chancel of medieval churches.   —L.L.

rood beam. The beam supporting a rood (q.v.) in medieval churches.   —L.L.

rood screen. The partition separating the part of a medieval church reserved for the use of the clergy from that intended for the use of the public. The rood screens were often richly decorated by sculpture. A famous example is the rood screen of the West Choir of the Cathedral of Naumburg on the Saale, Germany, dating from about 1250. A late example is the Jubé or rood loft of St. Etienne du Mont in Paris.   —L.L.

roof. *Arch.* The exterior upper covering of a structure. (2) Any top covering.

root. *Mus.* The tone upon which a chord is built, i.e., the chord's fundamental bass.

rose. A circular ornament conventionalized from a full blown rose.

rose du Barry. See CERAMICS II.

rosemaling. See SCANDINAVIAN ART.

rose Pompadour. See CERAMICS II.

rosette. A circular conventionalized ornament with leaves or petals of any one of various shapes arranged regularly around a center.

rose window. A round window with ornate radiating tracery.

rosin. This name, sometimes confused with resin, is now usually given as a substitute for colophony to designate the hard residue left after spirits of turpentine has been distilled away from the balsam of pine trees.   —G.L.S.

rota, routula. See rondo.

roucou (Fr.). Salmon color.

Roudprecht group. See Ottonian art.

rouge. See Indian red.

roughing-in. Process of laying on first coat of plaster; the first coat of plaster itself.

roulette. *Etch.* A small wheel running in a socket attached to a handle, which leaves the indentations of its teeth upon the metal as it is rolled across the plate. It is used to correct mezzotint plates, as well as to make designs which take on a special character from the tool used. A roulette print can be easily distinguished by the pattern of little teeth marks on the plate. The roulette is difficult to handle and is not often used. See PRINTS AND PRINT PROCESSES.   —K.K.

roulette (an intaglio process). Prints made with a roulette are essentially the same as drypoint, with one exception. Instead of using a point to produce the burr, a small wheel, running in a socket attached to a handle, is used. This leaves the indentations of its teeth upon the metal as it is rolled up and down the plate.

The roulette is often used by mezzotinters to add darks in places that have been scraped too light. It is also used occasionally on aquatint and drypoint for corrections and additions.

The roulette is extremely difficult to control, but in the hands of an expert it can be made to yield most unusual results.   —K.K.

round. *Mus.* A special kind of "perpetual canon (q.v.) at the unison" for two or more voices.

round notation (hagiopolitan). See eastern chants.

rounded. *Book.* (1) Rounded back; a book that has had the back of the folded sections hammered or rolled until it forms the segment of a circle. (2) Rounded corners; when the front corners, either top or bottom or both, of boards are rounded to prevent the wear of friction. See EDITION BINDING.   —H.E.S.

roundelay. A song characterized by a continuously reiterated refrain.

Rowen ware. See CERAMICS II.

Roxburghe binding. *Book.* Leather back, quite plain except for lettering, cloth or paper

side, top gilt, front and bottom edges untrimmed. Sometimes half-Roxburghe to denote leather corners.

royal. See book sizes.

royal Axminster. See carpet structures.

royal canopy. See SYMBOLISM IN FAR
EASTERN ART.

rubbed. In masonry: Surface of a stone
rubbed as smooth or as regular as possible.
The work is usually accomplished by rubbing
one piece of stone with a second piece.

rubber. Although widely used in industry,
this material seems to have acquired little
place in the fine arts. It has been developed
very slightly for coatings, synthetic varnishes
being made from chlorinated rubber. This
provides a film with good protection against
smoke, salt spray, and fumes.   —G.L.S.

rubbing. An impression on thin tough paper
made by moistening the paper and patting
it into the interstices of the relief, or into
the incised parts of a carved or modelled
surface, then tapping it with an inked pad,
producing an actual-size image in ink on the
paper.   —J.A.M.

rubble. (1) Term applied to natural stratified, or broken stone which does not permit
laying with uniformly thick joints; or
dressed stone not permitting horizontal joints.
(2) Term applied to masonry construction
which is usually classified under two main
divisions: (a) Uncoursed rubble or random
rubble. — Rubble masonry laid without any
attempt at regular courses, or continuous horizontal joints. (b) Coursed rubble or range
work. — Rubble masonry laid with continuous
horizontal joints. (3) Term also applied to
a mass or fill, as the core of a wall, composed
of rubble stone generally laid in mortar, as of
mud.   —J.M.M.

rubble ashlar. Term applied to rubble stone
which has been roughly squared to permit
laying with fairly uniform and thin joints.
   —J.M.M.

Rubens school. A school of art that found
its inception in the studio of Peter Paul
Rubens at Antwerp in the early 17th cent.
Here Rubens' baroque style influenced such
artists as Van Dyck, Seghers, Snyders, and
produced a fusion of the Italian and Flemish
styles which proved a guiding influence on
the future course of painting.   —R.L.W.

rubia. See madder.

rubic. *v.* To color with red; redden.

rug. A covering for the floor, a mat usually
oblong or square and woven in one piece.
In several books rugs and carpets are referred to as identical. In fact most written
information on rugs has been catalogued under
the term carpets; and there seems to be good
reason for assuming that the terms *tapestries* and *carpets* as used in ancient times,
were synonymous with the word *rugs* of the
present day, for these were spread loosely on
the floor without the aid of fastenings.
   —B.E.J.

Rum (Ar.). Asia Minor.

run. *Mus.* A rapid scale passage.

rune (a derivation of the 17th—18th cent. from
the Icelandic *rūn*—secret, or the old-high-
German *rūna*—secret council). The name of
the characters used for writing in the Scandinavian and Teutonic cultures. The oldest
runic alphabet contained 24 signs; it was
deciphered by means of the so-called alphabet-
inscriptions found in Scandinavia, England
and the European continent. The oldest known
of these alphabet-inscriptions is the one of
Kylver (Gotland) probably of the 5th cent.
In the beginning the runes were used for
brief inscriptions, cut or scratched into bone,
metal, stone and presumably also into wood.
The two instances of runic writings generally
considered to be the oldest (ca. 250 A.D.),
inscribed respectively on a shield-buckle and
a comb, were found on the moors of Thors-
bjerg and Vimose (Denmark). However,
some findings in Styria have been interpreted
as indicating that runes were used before
the birth of Christ. The runes did not originate in Northern Europe but were developed
from Southern European alphabets. According to the theory of the Norwegian scholar
Marstrander the runes are based upon the
celtic-etruscan and celtic-latin alphabets, and
originated in Bohemia and Moravia in the
Roman border region along the Danube.
   Memorial stones erected in honour of the
dead — the Scandinavian **bautasteinar** — were
decorated with runic inscriptions and with
simple linear designs and ornaments (ca. 6th—
8th cent.); these stones are found most often
within the sphere of the Viking culture (e.g.
the stone of Krogstra, 6th cent., National
Museum, Stockholm; the stone of Snoldelev,
9th cent., National Museum, Copenhagen).
See G. Stephens, *The Old-Northern Runic*

Monuments of Scandinavia and England, 1879; Sophus Müller, *Nordische Altertumskunde,* 2 vols., 1897-98; Carl J. S. Marstrander, *"Om runene og runenavnenes oprindelse," Norsk tidskrift for sprogvidenskap,* vol. I, 1928.

—H.H.

rung. A cross-strip, generally rounded, as of a ladder or chair.

running head, title. *Book.* The short title of the book sometimes appearing at the top of both pages, sometimes only on the left hand of the two open pages.

running set. See American folk forms, in music.

RUSSIAN ARTS. *Painting.* Belonging originally to the Byzantine East, Russia did not inherit the classic tradition, which so profoundly moulded the peoples of Western Europe. The art of Russia, nurtured on Byzantine-Greek tradition and dominated by the Greek Orthodox Church, remained ecclesiastical and medieval long after the art of western Europe had become secularized and was aiming at the visual conquest of nature. But within its own framework, Russia produced a great art of icon-painting.

It was not till the end of the 17th cent. when Western ideas were introduced, that Russian art broke its bondage to the old Byzantine tradition. The Western tradition in Russian art is thus only a little over two centuries old, while the art of modern Western Europe, which began with Giotto, has had over six and a half centuries of development and is in direct continuity with classic art. Up to the late 19th cent., the history of European art could be written with practically no reference to the Russians.

Russia's weak plastic tradition has been ascribed to many causes, climatic, economic, political, and cultural. Certainly iconoclastic aversion to images, feudal peasant economy, and the comparatively late growth of large cities and modern industry kept the plastic arts from developing as freely and fully as in other countries.

The Russians, like most peoples of Northern Europe, have a literary rather than a plastic genius. From the beginner, Russian art was always the handmaiden of literature. Formal elements in painting were subordinated to ideas that could better be stated in words. Until the 20th cent., Russian artists seldom expressed themselves in a truly plastic way; they never produced a painting or sculpture of universal significance. Long before Soviet ideologues declared that "art is a weapon", Russian painting became an instrument for the propagation of social, national, political, and religious ideas of various kinds. The very essence of Russian painting throughout the 19th cent. was theme or "purpose painting"; its aim, never genuinely aesthetic, was chiefly to tell a story.

But at the beginning of this century, parallel with the basic social and political changes produced by revolution, the Russian arts broke with the Renaissance tradition and sought to create a new plastic expression for our epoch. For the first time, Russian artists appear in the vanguard art movements of Europe and exert a reciprocal effect on them. In the years prior to World War I and the Revolution of 1917, the tradition of naturalistic representation was destroyed in Russia. While this mutation in art coincided with the social and economic changes, it was not directly due to them but was part of the whole plastic revolution that occurred in Europe between 1905 and 1914.

The new plastic art came into prominence with the establishment of the Soviets in 1917. It had only a few short years of experiment and was followed by a gradual retrogression to naturalistic representation. This ended in a return to old Russian models of the 19th cent. In the decade between 1930 and 1940, painting had become a Russian national academic art in which all plastic advances had been expunged in the interest of what was termed "Soviet Realism" (see socialist realism).

The Western tradition in art was introduced into Russia by Peter the Great (1682-1725). The growth of cities and of industry stimulated an art of painting based on Western European models. This officially created art was supported by the aristocracy and the court circles. It had no roots in the life of the people. These were, for the most part, peasants, who still clung to primitive and local forms of expression.

From Peter's time on, art may be divided into two kinds: peasant handicraft arts, often religious and based on oriental and Byzantine motifs, and urban art dominated by the new capital, St. Petersburg. It took almost two centuries for the latter to develop and to produce anything indigenous and genuinely Russian in feeling.

Beginning with Peter's reign, professional art was in constant touch with France, Italy, Germany, and Holland, and closely reflected Europe's fluctuations in style. From the 18th cent. on, Russian art passed through the same style changes as in Western Europe—Baroque Rococo, Neo-Classic, Romantic, and Modern. But the tempo of these style changes was always slower due to Russia's distance from the cultural centers of Europe. Modern means of communication gradually reduced this distance until in our century, the modern art movements of Paris appeared almost simultaneously in Russia.

Peter's break with the past was so decisive and sudden that the works of art of his reign bear little or no trace of the old Russian style. For the building of St. Petersburg, his new capital on the Neva, Peter invited many foreign artists to Russia. Included were French, German, Dutch and Italians, among them the sculptors, Andreas Schleuter, Carlo Bartholmeo Rastrelli, and Pinaud; and the painters Tannhauer, Carvague, Tarsius and Pillement. The cost of maintaining these foreign visitors led Peter to the idea of educating his own artists by sending them abroad. Andrei Matvyeyev and Ivan Nikitin, two of the first painters to study in Europe, had little influence at home. Matvyeyev died shortly after his return to Holland and Nikitin, who came back in 1720, was involved in a conspiracy, knouted and sent to Siberia.

In the reign of Peter's daughter, the Empress Elizabeth (1741-1762), fantastic Rococo palaces rose on the banks of the Neva, built and decorated by foreign artists; Italians like the Grot brothers, Valeriani, Torelli, and Count Rotari, and French painters like Le Lorrain, Lagrensèe, Toqué and Develis. However, the taste of Elizabeth's reign reflected nothing of the real contemporary painters of France like Watteau, Boucher, and Chardin, but was shaped by the French Academy and its "grand art."

Elizabeth founded the Imperial Academy of St. Peterburg, which was to dominate Russian art for over 150 years. The fact that an art academy was needed in this time attests to the growing number of professional Russian artists and the necessity of providing an education for them. Among the Russian painters of this period were Ivan Argunov, born a serf; Alexei Antropov, a "master of perspective", and Makhayev, pupil of the Italian, Valeriani. Under the leadership of Count Shuvalov, the Academy turned out numerous architects, sculptors, engravers, and painters. Best known of the painters were A. Losenko, Rokotov, Sablukov, and S. Shchedrin. There also existed a large number of icon painters, who re-interpreted orthodox ideas in the

Italian Rococo style. Portrait painting flourished thanks to the court. And as the Rococo palaces under the vast Russian sky assumed more grandiose forms than their European models, so 18th cent. portraiture in Russia had a more dramatic intensity than the fragile Rococo art of France.

It was under Catherine II that this Russian school of portraiture attained its full development. The most outstanding portrait painter was Dimitri Levitsky (1735-1822), who was so well known abroad that Diderot preferred Levitsky's portrait of himself to all others. Levitsky's portraits of the Russian aristocrats were executed in the style of Greuze and also under the influence of the elder Tischbein. He was a master at handling silks, laces, and jewels, but in his later life, his style became grandiose and lost its vitality. Another contemporary, Fedor Rokotov, painted the well known portraits of Catherine II, the third of which is considered her best likeness. Equally famous was Vladimir Borovikovsky (1757-1826) whose style followed the informal tendency of the late 18th cent.

In Catherines' time, landscape painting and theatrical decoration became increasingly important. One of the best masters was Fedor Alexiev, whose *Quay of Neva* shows a sense of color and technical knowledge. Silvestre Shschedrin and M. Ivanov painted perspective views of St. Petersburg. Numerous architects practised water color painting in "the English manner". Maxim Vorobyvov, who studied under Canaletto in Venice, was considered the foremost historico-architectural painter. Galktionov was the first to depict the urban bureaucratic life of the capital in a precious style. The number of painters at this time had grown enormously but few attained to more than common-place and dilettante imitations of European masters.

Toward the close of the 18th cent., the revical of the classic spirit begun by the Enlightenment in France began to effect Russia. Roman republican ideas became fashionable and the aesthetics of Winckelman, Lessing, Mengs and David were known. A. Losenko, who studied under Vien, the teacher of David, was one of the first to bring in the classic idea. He was also the first to introduce strict art training among his pupils. Headed by Akimov, last of the epigones of the rococo, the Imperial Academy fought the neo-classic tendency, which was associated with all that was progressive and revolutionary. However, this conflict between the grand manner of the Rococo and the Neo-classic spirit ended by the Academy taking over the latter and becoming its bulwark for over a hundred years. Russian classicism, far from expressing the revolutionary ideas of David, became a vehicle for the most bureaucratic, rigid, and official ideas of the time. The Russians ceased to look to France and turned to Rome for their inspiration. The reign of Alexander I was the heydey of this academic classicism. Ugryumov, the exponent of this tendency in painting, was one of the first to essay historical subjects in his canvases *The Capture of Kazan* and the *Coronation of Mikhail Fedorovich*. His two pupils, Shebuyev and Yegorev were servile copyists of classic art. Andrei Ivanov, who had real technical knowledge, was with Ugryumov, an initiator of the "national historical genre" painting, which flourished later in the 19th cent. By the time that the Romantic movement was sweeping Europe, classicism, imprisoned in a sterile, provincial form, had been firmly incorporated in the Imperial Academy, where it exercised a deadening influence on Russian art for years.

In Russia, however, the opening years of the 19th cent. marked a period of great spiritual ferment. The invasion of Russia by Napoleon aroused a tide of national feeling that led to his decisive defeat; at the same time, the liberal, democratic ideas of the French Revolution brought by the French army, profoundly effected Russian thought. The result was the ill-fated Decembrist Revolt of 1825 led by Russian officers, first of a long series of social protests against feudalism and absolutism. At this time, Russian literature experienced a new flowering in the works of Pushkin, Gogol, and Lermontov.

In contrast to the high level of literature, the level of art was low, lower than in the 18th cent., when the influx of foreign artists had stimulated an auspicious beginning. Due to the war and the rise of national feeling, there were now few foreign artists. The great Russian literary figures were nearly all of aristocratic origin and familiar with Western culture. The new Russian artists, on the other hand, came from the middle or lower classes and had no opportunity for education abroad. Their economic condition was often bad. The landowners on the great estates frequently trained their serfs as painters and architects, even educating them in St. Petersburg, but forcing them to do menial work along with their artistic activi-

ties, and not infrequently flogging them if their art did not meet with approval.

The four best artists of the period were Kiprensky, Bryullov, Bruni, and Ivanov. Alumni of the Academy, they became its opponents and joined the Romantic movement. Kiprensky (1782-1836), a serf by origin, drew and painted the heroes of the war against Napoleon. His most successful portrait was that of his friend, the poet Pushkin. The best genre painter of the time, Tropinion (1776-1857), was also born a serf and gained his liberty only in 1823 after he had acquired a national reputation as a painter. His work prepared the way for the development of Russian realist art of the 50's and 60's.

The official leader of romantic painting was Karl Bryullov, (1799-1852), often called the "Russian Delacroix." The son of a skilled carver, he entered the Academy at an early age and was sent to Rome by the newly founded Society for the Encouragement of Artists. More ambitious than talented, he spent eight years working on a large historical canvas, *The Last Days of Pompeii,* which on his return home earned him great acclaim. His painting of *The Siege of Pskov* was one of the first of a long line of dreary national historical painting that always has been popular in Russia. Bryullov died in Rome on a second visit but his influence permeated Russian art for years. His follower Bruni (1800-1870) sought to emulate him by painting *The Brazen Serpent* in Rome. On his return, he was made rector of the Academy and held that office for sixteen years. His superficial, bombastic art was far inferior to Bryullov's work but it is the perfect example of the official taste of the period. He had countless pupils, none of whom exhibited any genuine artistic gift. By the fifties, Romanticism as a movement had become sterile and the pseudo-romanticism of Kaulbach, Delaroche and the followers of the Duesseldorf School flourished in St. Petersburg. It was the misfortune of both the neo-classic and the romantic movements in Russia that their spirit was soon smothered in official academicism and the genuine leaders in Europe were ignored for second rate epigones.

Realism in Russia grew up with the populist movement (Narodniki) and had an even stronger literary trend than in other countries. In its beginnings, realistic painting was strongly tinged with academic romanticism. This may be observed in the work of Alexander Ivanov (1805-1856), one of the most talented

Russian painters and an important early realist. Influenced by Gogol's ideas, his style was that of Oberbeck. But he showed a far more acute observation of nature than his predecessors and his work was marked by deep sincerity. His two large canvases, *Christ Showing Himself to Magdalene* and *Christ Appearing before the People* were painted in Rome, where he spent twenty-five years. His Biblical sketches rather than his large paintings sustain his reputation as a painter.

Ivanov's successor and artistic opponent was Nicolas Guë (1834-1894), who in contrast to Ivanov's idealistic treatment of religious themes, painted stories from the Gospel with gruesome naturalistic realism (cf. his *Crucifixion*). His meticulous rendition of all that was sordid and ugly in life was in its turn an inverted idealism and part of the social protest of the group around Alexander Herzen to which Guë belonged. At the height of his career, under the influence of Tolstoy's teachings, he gave up painting. His portraits of men like Tolstoy and Herzen are the best in the second half of the 19th cent.

Ivanov's true disciples included such diverse talents as Kramskoy, Vasnetzov, Nesterov and Vrubel. Nicholas Kramskoy had an important influence on painting not because of his artistic talent but because he was an organizer. While still a student at the Imperial Academy, he led thirteen students to revolt against the classical dogma and to withdraw to form their own artel. In 1872, the year of the first great Exhibition of the Impressionists in France, he organized the Russian Union of Wanderers' Exhibitions (Obachtschestwo Peredwischnych Wystawok) in direct protest against the Academy.

The program of the Wanderers was didactic and social. Realism was to them a means to an end: to bring art to the people and to inspire and enlighten them, just as the various radical parties in Russia were seeking to enlighten them politically. For this reason, the Wanderers attached far more to the moral and literary aspect of art than to aesthetics. In their outlook they were part of the whole social tendency of the time which had such a brilliant expression in literature. For twenty years they dominated the scene and exercised a great educational effect by sending exhibitions into many cities where prior to this art was unknown. The chief painters of the group were V. V. Vereschagin, Ilya Repin, Vladimir Makovsky, W. Polenov, and Lebediew.

Their tendency to realism had its forerunners in painters like Venetzianov (1770-1847), who founded the first school for the study of nature, and in portrait painters like Varneck, Terebenov, Count T. P. Tolstoy, and Peter Sokolov, who was one of the few to keep the artistic aims of painting alive between the forties and the seventies. The real father of Russian "purpose painting" was F. A. Fedotov (1815-1852) and his successor V. Perov (1833-1882) who painted the portraits of Turgenev and Destoivsky. The first marine painter in Russion was Aivasoski, (1817-1900). Realistic landscape had its first exponent in Ivan Shiskin, who born in the far north, was one of the first to paint Russian landscapes instead of ideal Italianate versions of Russia. The depiction of Russian life and Russian landscape really began with Alexander II who inaugurated a liberal era by emancipating the serfs in 1861.

The most facile propagandist in paint among the Wanderers was V. V. Vereschagin (1842-1904). He achieved the greatest popularity outside of Russia, especially with his anti-war pictures. Born a nobleman, he painted Russian scenes from the viewpoint of Western culture. His large canvases with many figures have little to recommend them on the formal side.

Ilya Repin (1844-1930) was perhaps the most gifted of the Wanderers and best expressed their spirit. A pupil of Kramskoy, his natural skill led him into pictorial journalism in which he treated contemporary ancedotes from the Russo-Japanese War and from our Spanish-American War. But in his two most famous paintings *The Zaporogian Cossacks* and *Ivan the Terrible and His Son;* he established himself as a master of literal detailed realism. Among his best work are his portraits. Another portrait painter of distinction was Vladmir Makovsky. W. Polenov and Lebedjew were the landscape painters of the group, the latter painting Russian landscape with lyric intensity.

The Wanderers were part of the progressive social movement in Russia which was directed against the growing absolutism of the Czar. But following the assassination of Alexander II by the Nihilists, his son, Alexander III inaugurated a period of reaction and repressions. Censorship put a stop to all social propaganda in art. An era of official Slavophilism and a return to orthodoxy began. The reactionary atmosphere was reflected in painting by a change of theme.

Religious subject matter, national and historical scenes and landscapes became popular.

Victor Vasnetzov, another follower of Kramskoy but never a member of the Wanderers, aspired to create a "truly Russian art". He decorated the Cathedral of St. Vladimir in Kiev in the Byzantine style, Decadent and decorative in style, even his easel paintings were for the most part on religious subjects. He was the first to introduce old Russian fairy tales as a motif for painting and was thus the precursor of the Moscow revival of "Russian National Art" that began just before World War I. Another religious painter of the time was M. Nesterov (born 1862) who painted lyric scenes of Russian landscape with churches, monks, nuns and priests in the foreground. He was still living as an Honored Artist of the People in the U. S. S. R. before the outbreak of this war.

More nationalistic than religious was Surikov (1848-1916), who broke with the sentimental, humanitarian ideals of the Wanderers and recreated scenes out of the history of Russia in brilliant but sombre peasant colors. Despite crudity of execution, his talent was greater than that of Vasnetzov and Nesterov. His harsh coloring influenced Repin and the later Moscow painters. Surikov's backgrounds of old Moscow with its crenelated skylines became the theme of later painters like Appolinaris Vasnetzov and S. Ivanov.

At this time when the Realists, the Slavophiles and the Orthodox painters were on the crest of popularity, a new movement entered Russia from France. Impressionism, with its undercurrent of scientific skepticism and internationalism, was welcomed by the younger artistic forces, who were in touch with French painting and excited by the color discoveries of Monet and Pissaro. The Slavophiles fought the new aesthetic doctrine as an "insidious French influence", but the Impressionists increasingly gained adherents.

Paralleling the two streams of Russian painting—realism and decorative National painting—Impressionism had two different facets in Russia. The work of the doctrinaire Impressionists was devoted to landscape painting of actual out-of-doors scenes and actual people; the imaginative artists depicted in Impressionist technique fantastic subject-matter, often colorfully decorative and oriental in feeling. Among the early leaders of Impressionism were W. Serov, called the "Russian Degas" and J. Levitan,

a pure landscape painter. Michael Vrubel was the best of the fantastic Impressionists.

The *fin de siècle* mood of the out-going century which gave to art throughout Europe a nostalgic, precious, and symbolic character was expressed in Russia in the work of Vrubel. In his weird landscapes overcast with gloomy blue shadows and haunted by strange demons, was embodied the metaphysical yearning for another and better world. It was in this period just prior to the Revolution of 1905 that a section of Russian art sought to escape in mysticism and dreams from the oppressive rule of Nicholas II. The work of these artists who gave up painting from nature became tenuous in plastic structure and ever more illusionary. In color and technique, Vrubel remains the best artist of this tendency. Never popular during his lifetime, he succumbed to mental disease and died in 1910.

Another phase of the fin de siècle was expressed by the magazine "**The Golden Fleece**" and the group of painters called "**The Blue Rose**" which included Lancères, N. Sapanov, and Konstantin Somov. The early work of P. Kuznetzov and B. Sudeikin was in this style.

The tradition of doctrinaire Impressionism upheld by Serov and Levitan was continued by the members of the "Union of Russian Artists", most important of whom were Maliavine and Korovin. The first had the superficial vigor of the Swedish painter Zorn carried to excess in bright compositions of lusty peasant women. Korovin was known for his stylized landscapes and he became increasingly decorative and made original theatre decor. Other impressionists included men like Vinogradsky, Schukovsky, a painter of old estates and palaces, Perepletschikov, Baron Koldt, and Brytackov and K. Yuon, genre painters of rustic scenes. More experimental was J. Grabar, originally a pointillist, and Krymov, who painted in pure colors.

Following the defeat of the 1905 Revolution, the main line of Russian Impressionism following Vrubel forsook the natural world. Painting became stylized in a decorative linearism, which without much of plastic consequence, had a revivifying influence on the theatre, particularly in the settings of the Russian ballet, which was making its first tours of Europe's capitals. Most of these painters were associated with the "**World of Art**" group (Mir Iskusstva), which was organized as a protest against the Wanderers in 1890 and originally included both the fantastic and realistic Impressionists. Its leader, Alexander Benois, as well as most of the others, had spent much time in Paris. "Art for art's sake" was the slogan of the whole group and they stood for interpretation rather than imitation of nature. The decorative artists included Leon Bakst, Somov, Golovin, Benois, Nicholas Roerich, Debuschinsky, Sudeikine, Stelletski, Remisoff. Interested in portraiture were Schoukhaev, Jacovlev, Sorine, Boris Grigoriev. In Russia this new decorative art had an important influence on the graphic arts, book illustration, mural painting, as well as on the theatre. Bilibine was one of the most talented of the illustrators.

Strangest of the anti-naturalistic painters was Nicolas Tschurlianis, first to abandon all subject-matter in his search for equivalent expressions in line and color for music. Although his work is plastically weak, it marks a real turning point. In this respect, he may be considered the ancestor of the Non-objective school of painters, who derive from Kandinsky. Tschurlianis died in 1911 but his painting had a tremendous vogue in Russia just prior to World War I.

At the beginning of the 20th cent., the great changes in modern life and thought produced a crisis in art. In Western Europe this crisis, marking the end of the Renaissance tradition, was manifested in various insurgent movements by a tendency to decompose the old color gamut, the old vision of space, and the object itself. Cezanne had sought to re-establish the grand structure of the past, but unconsciously he was moved to destroy it in the interest of the surface plane of the picture. Stimulated by his late work, the Cubists carried out a revolution in style, destroying naturalistic representation by concentrating on the plastic elements of painting. At the same time, the Italian Futurists, seeking a more dynamic expression in art, introduced simultaneous movement. The destruction of three-dimensional space illusion and of the natural appearance of objects led to plane painting.

Post-Impressionism, Fauvism, Cubism, and Futurism reached Russia almost simultaneously with their appearance in Western Europe. Many Russian artists were living in Paris and the fine collections of modern art brought to Moscow by the merchant princes Morosov and Schukin acquainted the artists at home with the new advances. Four years after Cezanne's death, his first Russian followers founded a group called "Jack of Dia-

monds", which included Kontschalovsky, Rodestvensky, Lentulov, Yakulov, Falk, Larionov ond Burliuk.

The latter two may also be included with the "Primitives". For at this time when the artists in Paris came under the influence of primitive and exotic arts, certain Russian artists went back to their own past for new sources of inspiration. Related to the Fauves and the early Expressionists in Germany, they were interested in forms and colors that did not imitate nature. Many of them later developed in divergent directions. They included Larionov, Gontscharova, Marc Chagall, Kandinsky, Gritschenko, Sheritshenko, and Sternburg.

One of the most gifted of the "Primitives" was Marc Chagall, who later attained the greatest reputation in other countries throughout the world. Both his work and that of Kandinsky had far greater influence outside of Russia and belong primarily to the modern international movement in art. Chagall, using motifs from Jewish folklore and the life of his native Vitebsk, created a fantastic dream world of lyric beauty, in which Cubist elements were mated with primitive color and expressionist mood.

David Burliuk introduced the simultaneous movement of the Futurists into a colorful painting design. He was one of the first propagandists of modern art in Russia, travelling and lecturing on the subject in many cities along with the Futurist poet, Mayakovsky. In his work, primitive, mystical, revolutionary and modern were combined in a personal symbolism of revolt.

Close to Burliuk was Filonov, a painter peculiarly Russian in his social, Messianic feeling. He declared himself opposed to the whole "Realist Fallacy", in which he included even Cubism, Expressionism and Futurism. His work, however, had elements of all these movements embodied in monumental canvases of apocalyptic revelations.

Larionov, in the light of cubism and futurism, revised Impressionism into what he called **"Rayonism"** (*lutschism*), a theory that dealt with dispersion and interpenetration of rays emanating from objects. He had no real adherents, but he and his wife, Gontscharova, had a stimulating effect on theatre decoration.

In contrast to the mystical and primitive modernists, the doctrinaire Cubists were not concerned with philosophical, social or literary ideas but only with the plastic problems of their art. Following the early Cubist work of Picasso and Braque, they devoted themselves to compositions showing simultaneous and multiple planes of vision and the dissection of the object into its component parts. In this way, perspective disappeared in their work and the natural appearance was distorted. They also experimented in textures introduced by collage and sought to achieve pictorial unity through the imposition of varied materials onto the canvas. Called "factura", this exploration of textures became so popular that a book on the subject was written by the painter Markov. Factura had its greatest effect on the Constructivists.

The outbreak of the war in 1914 brought many of the modern Russians home from the capitals of western Europe. This gave a new impetus to the modern art movement in Russia. Among the returning exiles was Vassili Kandinsky (b. 1868), who had lived abroad since 1902. One of the leaders of German abstract expressionism, he was co-founder with Franz Marc of the **Blue Riders** (*Blaue Reiter*) in Munich. The group included two other Russians, Javlensky and Burliuk. Kandinsky developed the color discoveries of the Fauves into a new plastic language of line and color without natural objects. He is credited with having made the first pure abstract painting in 1911.

In the midst of the war in 1916, Vladimir Tatlin assembled a group of artists around him; they proclaimed the death of easel painting and the birth of a new art (at first called **Tatlinism**), which found its rhythm, construction, and logic in the machine. Like the Dadaists, these artists found no material unworthy of use for art. They employed glass, wood, nails and wire constructively to create a new art language in terms of modern technique. "Tatlinism" later became Constructivism.

With the founding of the Soviet Republic in 1917, the Bolsheviks, determined to make a clean sweep of the past culturally as well as politically, made an alliance with the "Russian Futurists". These included all the extreme groups of the modern movement such as "Jack of Diamonds", the Cubists, the Primitives, the Expressionists, etc. The insurgent artists immediately discovered a parallel between the plastic revolution and the political revolution. Those who were not in agreement retired or went into exile. But to these modern artists, it seemed that the liberation of art and the artist from all traditional slavery was assured. They took a leading part in artistic reforms of sweeping consequence.

The Imperial Academy was abolished and a Free College of Arts was established in its place. Free art schools were opened and private collections were transferred to the state and opened to the public. The Morosov and Schukin collections were joined and became the State Museum of Western Art. Other museums of "Artistic Culture" were founded and the artists were employed by the new government to stage revolutionary festivals, to make posters and book illustrations. Leading modern artists like Kandinsky were invited to organize these new institutions of art.

Despite all the external disturbances that accompanied the shift from an absolutist feudal society to a new society, whose ideal was the emancipation of all men, art flourished as never before in Russia and enjoyed a brief honeymoon of experiment. Some of the experiments were bizarre and impossible of achievment, but many had a creative effect on the periphery arts. A new poster art and a new film art were born and later influenced other countries.

At this period, the modern movement in art in Russia was more direct, more logical, and more intense than anywhere else. All the various groups, to a greater or a lesser degree, moved away from the imitation of nature toward a more abstract expression. The revolution in the plastic means was characterized by the following general trends: from representing nature toward a pure plastic culture of independent works of art; from the rhythm of nature to the rhythm of the machine; from all that was timely, accidental, and subjective, toward an objective, architectonic plastic creation; and from the empirical world of appearances toward the transcendental and the purely human.

While the early Cubists, driven by the necessity of their evolution, had arrived at the surface plane of the picture, they did not carry out their discovery to its logical conclusion. Abstract art, born out of this basic change in tradition, developed outside of France, chiefly in Holland, Germany, and Russia. Of the three innovators of abstract art—Mondrian, Malevich, and Kandinsky—the latter two were Russians.

Kasimir S. Malevich (1878-1935), one of the most creative of all Russian artists, began as a Fauve, developed into a Cubist in Leger's style, and was the first in Russia to make pure geometrical abstract compositions. He created **Suprematism**, whose basic principles were economy in the plastic means, rhythm of lines and planes in universal relationships achieved through primary color and elementary geometric forms.

Suprematism aimed at the creative treatment of the surface of the picture and within its severe limitations offered great variety in the rhythm of related planes, the equilibration of pure color and the relationships of full and empty space. In Malevich's work, painting was definitely emancipated from the appearance of nature. In his book *Die Gegenstandslose Welt* (World without Objects) published by the Bauhaus in Germany in 1926, he set down his principles declaring that "the art of the past, which at least externally was in the service of religion and the state, will awaken in the pure, independent art of Suprematism to a new life and a new world—the world of constructive perceptions." Among his followers were Rosanova, Exter, Rodchenko, Drevin, Puni, and Lissitzky.

The **Constructivists**, organized by Tatlin, declared that the picture itself was dead and that the necessity for creating works of art was historically past. Constructivism sought to put artistic activity to use for new social ends. Its aesthetic derived from the precision, order, and organization of the machine was directed toward the creation of dynamic constructions of concrete materials and technical processes. The Constructivists looked to science and industry as a means of educating new artists. Their investigation into the properties and function of materials and their effort to relate these materials to specific forms had many practical results in stage decoration, typography, posters and architecture.

Tatlin, a brilliant inventor, created **"counter relief"**, a sculptural relief in volume and planes of contrasting materials. His most famous work, the model for the Third International, consisted of a huge spiral built in the form of a cube, pyramid, and cylinder, these forms to rotate according to the day, month, and year of the calendar. Never erected, the model was later destroyed.

The constructivist best known outside of Russia was El Lissitzky. He held that the function of art is not to beautify but to transform and organize life, until life and art eventually merge and works of art as objects disappear in the total environment. In both these ideas and in his work he was influenced by the ideas of De Stijl and of the German abstract movement. N. Altmann, a former member of the "World of Art" became a constructivist and one of the chief designers

of the revolutionary pageants and festivals. Other constructivists were Medunetzky, Popova, Varst, Ioganson, Mituritch, Kluitzis, G. and V. Stenburg, the sculptors Tchaikov, Gabo, and Pevsner. The latter two went abroad later and had a great influence on the development of abstract sculpture in France and England.

For a short time, the Constructivists were the leading exponents and representatives of revolutionary proletarian art. For the most part, their influence was felt outside of the creative arts—architecture, film, poster, theatre decoration. But Expressionism, the tendency opposite to Constructivism, also exercised a potent influence. In these years, Kandinsky, its personal leader in Russia, changed his art from the free colorful improvisations of his Munich period to a more somber and increasing geometric composition. In 1921, he founded the Russian Academy of Artistic Sciences in Moscow, where most of the art activity had been centered following the change of government from Leningrad to Moscow.

The first five years of the Soviet regime were the most creative period of artistic activity in the history of Russia. But the increasing difficulties resulting from the Civil War and the economic upheaval, led to the New Economic Policy of 1922 (the NEP). Private buyers and patrons reappeared and a market for traditional art was re-established. The growing demand for portraits, landscapes, and genre art brought the older schools to the fore again. The change was apparent in the public exhibitions where traditional art was again displayed.

The government, in need of funds for more vital necessities, withdrew a great deal of its support from the modern artists. Many were forced into the applied arts in order to live. Others, like Kandinsky, Gabo, Pevsner, Chagall, and Burliuk went abroad. Only a few returned to Russia like Lissitzky. The artists belonging to the extreme left were gradually pushed in the background, lost their official positions, and their work was withdrawn from public view.

By 1927, naturalistic representation was in vogue again and abstract and expressionist tendencies in art were declining rapidly. An emphasis on easel painting led to the formation of new groups such as The New Society, the Four Arts (OST) and the Society of Easel Painters (NIJ). The formation of the Artists' Association of Revolutionary Russia (AKKHR) turned the tide against all modern art. It had the largest membership of any group and embraced artists of all schools and tendencies. Many members of former groups like the *Jack of Diamonds* and the *World of Art* joined AKKHR and thereby received a yearly income for doing pictures that could be bought and reproduced by the government for wide distribution among the people. These pictures were necessarily illustrative and propagandistic.

The aesthetics of AKKHR revived that of the old Wanderers. The main difference lay in the choice of theme. This government-sponsored movement had as its program the depiction of the Revolution, its history, struggles and triumph in terms of 19th cent. naturalism. It became known as **"heroic realism"**. In further imitation of the Wanderers, the AKKHR sent exhibitions all over Russia on a great scale, attracting thousands of people who had never before visited an art gallery. The exhibitions were often dedicated to a single theme; they depicted subjects like May Day, factory workers, Red Army life, collectivisation, etc. AKKHR also arranged travelling scholarships for artists, who were commissioned to visit different parts of the country and to set down their pictorial record of contemporary life.

The initiation of the First Five Year Plan was considered of such importance that it was made the main theme for Soviet art. While some of the artists still painted in styles reminiscent of the now defunct modern movements, the main current of art rolled backward with the same swiftness as it had gone forward, recapitulating regressively the styles of Abstract Art, Cubism, Expressionism, Impressionism to a Realism in which naturalistic and romantic elements were combined. The pictures of modern artists like Malevich, Kandinsky, and Lissitszky gradually disappeared even from the state museums like the Tretyakov Gallery in Moscow.

The fight against "formalism" in the 30's was directed against the modern in all fields of culture and it expunged the last traces of new discoveries in color and form from Soviet art. In this era, the old academic art of pre-war Russia was again enshrined in popular favor and many of the old academicians who were still living in quiet retirement were restored and given government commissions and the main place in public exhibitions. Among them were the painters I. Brodsky, V. Yakovlev, the Korin brothers, and Nesterov. Brodsky, a pupil of Repin, became an important illustrator in paint of large his-

torical revolutionary subjects like his *Shooting of the Twenty-six Commissars* and his *Congress of the Third International.*

Painters once associated with the *World of Art* like Nogayevsky, Ostroumova-Lebedeva, and Lancères now sought to paint *Heroic Realism.* Followers like Pavolov and Dormidontov sought to portray the new Soviet construction "romantically". Petrov-Vodkin, Pavel Kusnetzov, and the Armenian painter M. Saryan, once primitives and Fauves, now painted Soviet subject matter. Masters of post-impressionism like Mashkov, P. Kontchalovsky, A. Lentulov, V. Rozdestvensky, Kuprin, Osmerkin and others returned to 19th cent. realistic painting. A romantic like Gerasimov and a landscape artist like Istomin followed suit. S. Sternburg, a disciple of the School of Paris and former leader of OST illustrated children's books. Old Wanderers like Kotov, Yakovlev and Krainev were in demand again as well as painters like K. Yuon and B. Johannson.

The younger Soviet painters trained since the Revolution and having little or no contact with the art outside of Russia have been from the first realist painters. A Soviet genre art akin to the old Russian genre art has grown up. It deals with anecdotes of Soviet life rendered "realistically". This realism is without pretensions to plastic quality and is often mannered and romantic. It has little of the solidity of good 19th cent. realistic painting in Europe. Among the younger men are A. Deincka and those of his direction, Antonov, Yuvalov, Zernova-Nissky. Also well known are G. Pimenov and A. Goncharov. More modern painters like P. Williams and Tischler, a talented expressionist who decorated the Jewish theatre, now essay Soviet genre subjects.

In answer to the universal demand created by the "new stress on the individual", portraiture has again become popular. There are countless portrait painters who make a living painting portraits of Soviet leaders, workers, Red Army men, Soviet heroes and even pretty Soviet girls in the style of **Soviet realism.** These portraits are often inclined toward heroic and dramatic gesture. Many of the works reveal so little knowledge of modern composition and color that they are close to American magazine illustration and have the same appeal of saccharine sweetness and ancedotal detail.

The younger Soviet artists have been given many opportunities by the government—education, scholarships, and positions. Some have been sent abroad to study. The number of artists in the USSR has consequently greatly increased since the Revolution. But the fact that all art has become official and is based on old academic realist traditions of pre-revolutionary Russia has hindered free experiment and the development of real talent. In the decade 1930-1940, Soviet art was aesthetically below the standards of Western European art and that of the U. S. A., as shown by the exhibitions sent to the Worlds Fairs in Paris and in New York. While the tendency to restore representative art and to go back to national sources for inspiration has been common to the whole of art in Europe and the U. S. A. in this period, it has been carried to an extreme in the U. S. S. R. The result has been to repudiate all the advances which the plastic arts made in the first two decades of this century. Part of the whole recrudescence of national feeling in Russia, the return to national academicism cannot be considered permanent. In 1935, Malevich, who had long since withdrawn from public view, died, and Soviet art lost its most creative exponent.

In our century, many Russian painters have achieved their reputations outside of their native land. Many became closely associated with the art movements that originated in France. Among those who went to Paris in the early years were various members of the "World of Art", including Alexander Benois, Boris Grigoriev, painters like Schoukhaieff, Jakovleff, and Sorine, and decorators like Stelletski, Soudeikine, and Remisoff.

Certain Russian-Jewish painters early attained preeminence in the modern art movement in Paris, among them Marc Chagall, Moise Kisling (born in Krakau and more properly Polish), Manne-Katz, and Chaim Soutine, whose expressive style is rich in color and vibrantly rhythmic.

Among the Russian painters who came to the United States after the First World War were Nicolas Roerich, painter of mystic and Asiatic themes, David Burliuk, Boris Anisfeld, and John D. Graham, a modernist combining strong primitive tendencies. In recent years, their number has been augmented by Chagall, Kisling, Manne-Katz, Soudeikine, and the Surrealist painter, Pavel Tchelitchew.

Sculpture. Prior to Peter the Great's reign, sculpture was virtually unknown in Russia. The Greek Orthodox Church maintained the iconoclastic prohibition of images even down to modern times. In the churches, the place of religious sculpture was taken by flat ornamentation and polychrome decoration. In the 12th and 13th cents., some churches in the Vladimir region were lavishly decorated with sculptured low-reliefs, whose motifs were derived from Byzantine textiles and ivories. Peasant wood carving was the only form of native sculpture practiced down to the end of the 18th cent. A single departure from the orthodox ban occurred in this century, when under Catholic influence emanating from Poland, crucifixes and small carved figures of saints were introduced into Russia. Owing to the lack of sculptural tradition, these works scarcely come under the heading of art.

Despite Peter's admiration for the products of Western culture, he upheld the orthodox position on sculpture. In 1724, he issued an edict banning all religious images (with the exception of plain metal crosses) from the churches. Whatever contraband religious sculpture existed now definitely came to an end. On the other hand, Peter created secular sculpture in Russia. Along with architects, artisans, and painters, he imported French and German sculptors to glorify himself and his reign. The sculptural decorations of St. Petersburg were, therefore, almost all of foreign origin.

Among the sculptors invited to Russia were Conrad Osner, who made the bas-reliefs of St. Peters (Peter and Paul Fortress); Andreas Schlueter, the builder of the Berlin Palace, and Nicolas Pineau, who came with the architect Leblond, and remained ten years. A master of the Regency style, he became the great decorator of the period. The sculptor who left the greatest impression on the new capital was Carlo Bartolomeo Rastrelli, a French-Italian, who came from Paris. His best works are the bronze statue of the Czarina Anna Ivanovna (1741) and the great equestrian statue of Peter the Great, which was modelled on Schleuter's statue of the Great Elector in Berlin.

Russian sculpture actually begins with the founding of the Imperial Academy by Elizabeth. The first teachers of the Russians were the French sculptors living in St. Petersburg. Nicolas Gillet (1707-1791) was made the first professor of sculpture at the Academy and he taught a whole generation of Russian sculptors. By the time Catherine came to the throne, these French sculptors had either returned home or had died, but she continued the tradition of inviting foreign artists, favoring the French above all others.

The most famous sculptor to accept her command was Etienne Falconet, who came to Russia in 1766 and stayed for twelve years. He brought with him his best pupil, Marie Anne Callot, who executed the busts of Falconet and Diderot now in the Hermitage Museum in St. Petersburg. Falconet's most important Russian work is the bronze equestrian statue of Peter, made famous by Pushkin's poem as the "bronze cavalier". It is considered among the most outstanding equestrian works of the century. Another French sculptor, Dominique Rachette (1744-1809) was the creator of the models for the Imperial Porcelain Manufactury. He is remembered for his small busts and medallions.

At the end of the 18th cent., Gillet's first Russian pupils were graduated from the Academy and sent to Paris to round out their studies in the studios of Pigalle, Allegrain, Bouchardon, and Pajou. The first original sculptor to emerge from this tutelage was Schubine (1740-1805), who studied with Pigalle and whose style developed close to Houdon's. On his return from Paris, Pajou was treated with contempt by the Academicians, but his busts of Catherine II and her favorite, Prince Potemkin, are considered with Levitsky's portraits the best work in the Western tradition in the 18th cent.

Other sculptors of the period included Kozlovski (1755-1802), who made the monument to General Suvorov, and Schedrine (1751-1833), who was the best decorative sculptor of the time.

The outbreak of the French Revolution temporarily dissolved the cultural ties that existed between Paris and St. Petersburg. From this time on, Rome became the artistic center for all Russian artists. Martos (1752-1833) was the first Russian sculptor to study there; he worked in the studio of Thorwaldsen, Martos' academic Classicism is exemplified in the monument of Minine and Pojarski, Russian generals decked out in Roman togas with mock heroic gestures.

In the 19th cent., Russian sculpture which had such an auspicious beginning, did not continue on the same level of accomplishment. The classical revival, which was the reflection of the French Republic and became the universal style in Europe, led to a great architectural development in Russia. But it had a stultifying effect on young sculpture. Martos, whose pseudo-classic Canovian sculpture attained great popularity, could boast of as many pupils as Gillet, but none of them exhibited any great gifts. They included sculptors like Pimenov, Orlowski, Krylov, and Sokolov.

The upsurge of national feeling aroused by Napoleon's invasion effected sculpture less than literature. But a change took place in subject matter if not in style. The first truly Russian sculptor was Mark Matveevitch Antokolski (1843-1902), in whose work the new national feeling is incarnated. He undertook a series of marble statues of the great national heroes of the past, including the *Cossack Ermak, Ivan the Terrible*, and *Peter the Great*. His innovation consisted in representing them in their national costume instead of in the draperies of antiquity. He also made a series of pagan, Jewish, and Christian martyrs, among them, *Socrates Drinking the Hemlock, Christ before his Judges*, and *Spinoza driven from the Synagogue*. The latter statue, considered his best work, had a great success at the Paris Salons. Plastically Antokolski's work was weak, his figures theatrical, but the spirit that animated them was new in Russian sculpture. He had numerous followers, among them the sculptors Bernstamm, Aronson, and Ginzburg, all of whom lived and worked in Paris. The first animal sculptor in Russia was the Baron Klodt (1805-1867) who made the equestrian statue of Nicolas I.

Until the end of the 19th cent. Russian sculpture had little development. Monumental sculpture in Russia was still practically unknown. It was only with the beginnings of the modern movement in art that new talent came to the fore. The first Impressionist was Prince Paul Petrovitch Troubetskoy, a facile portrait sculptor, who made busts and portrait statuettes of famous contemporaries like Count Witte, Rodin, and Tolstoy. Troubetskoy's one attempt at monumental sculpture, the statue of Alexander III, was not a success. The Russian sculptors of Rodin's generation were profundly influenced by him. Many of them went to Paris and remained there, among them Sondbinine, Yurievitch, and Mme. Chana Orlov.

The plastic revolution of the first decade of the 20th cent. did much to destroy the traditional conception of sculpture as a three-dimensional art of organic forms. The new analysis of plastic elements made in painting were applied to sculpture, which was purged of all literary and historical associations. From the oldest and most primitive of the arts, there emerged a new secular plastic art closely related to the realities of modern life. Russian sculptors with their primitive strength

untrammeled by tradition made a great creative contribution to this transformation. The
sculptor who best expressed the Primitive
tendency in Russian sculpture just prior to
Cubism was S. Konenkov, who began as an
Impressionist and was sometimes called the
"Russian Rodin".

Cubism itself produced three Russian sculptors, who became leaders in the modern movement. They all developed in Paris and had
little effect on Russian sculpture at home.
They were Alexander Archipenko (born
1887), Jacques Lipschitz, (born 1891) and
Ossip Zadkine (born 1890). Archipenko, who
came to Paris in 1908 from Kiev, went to
Germany after World War I and attained a
great reputation there. He was one of the
first of the modernists to settle in the U. S.
A. His Cubist work (1909-1921) in which
he used convex and concave forms had a new
rhythm and great delicacy. Jacques Lipschitz came to Paris in 1909. He applied
the plastic discoveries of Picasso and others
to sculpture, but in spirit he always remained close to African negro sculpture and
the primitives. In his later work, he returned to rounded organic forms in an original expressionist manner. Zadkine, who also
began as a Cubist, has always been a primitive in his expression. This sensitive lyricism
is combined with a strong feeling for the
material of his craft. Both Lipschitz and
Zadkine have recently come to the U. S. A.

In Russia itself, Cubist ideas either mixed
with Expressionism or led to Constructivism.
The first expressionist in sculpture was Boris
Koroliew, whose statue of Michael Bakunin
was unveiled in Moscow in 1919. In his later
work, he became more abstract and sought
to create a sculpture of pure plastic elements.

During the first years of the Soviet regime,
every effort was made by the young government to encourage sculpture along with the
other arts. In 1918, a national competition
was held to which sculptors were invited to
contribute models and designs for a series of
monuments to be erected to revolutionary
heroes past and present. About sixty models
were set up in the streets and squares of
Moscow for public criticism. Most of these
were of negligible artistic value, but one of
the best, D. Merkulov's *Dostoievsky* was
later carried out in Finland black granite and
set up on one of the boulevards.

In these years (1917-1921) traditional
sculpture was practically abandoned for new
experiments in which the interdependence of
sculpture, painting, and architecture was realized. Tatlin, who combined the talents of all
three arts, had a pre-eminent influence at this
time, and constructivist models, practically
none of which were ever completed in enduring materials, were used for revolutionary
festivals and in the theatre. His invention,
the *counter-relief*, was a new form of pure
plastic art, in which elements of painting and
sculpture were combined. In collaboration
with the sculptor Gregory Jakulov, Tatlin
made a series of these counter-reliefes for the
Moscow Cafe "The Red Rooster." Most of
the best sculptors of the time were in the
Constructivist group. They included men like
Rodchenko, Medunetzky, Tahaikov, Pevsner
and Gabo.

After 1922, the high-tide of Constructivist
experiment receded and traditional representational art was brought back. The ultra-left
artists, for the most part, lost their government positions. Rodchenko gave up art for
industrial design. Tahaikov returned to naturalistic sculpture. The two brothers Gabo
and Pevsner left Russia for good. Pevsner
(b. 1886) had been professor at the new Soviet
Academy and Gabo (born 1890) had issued
the "Realist Manifesto of Constructivism" in
1920. They had a great influence on modern
abstract sculpture in Europe. They settled
in Berlin and later in Paris. In 1933, Gabo
went to England, where he became one of
the leaders of the English abstract movement. Pevsner's work done in solid materials, frequently metal, is heavier in its forms
than that of Gabo. The latter makes use of
modern synthetic materials, including glass,
plastic, and wire. He employs new kinetic
rhythms and interpenetrating planes to create
new forms belonging exclusively to the 20th
cent. (see SCULPTURE).

The development of sculpture in Russia
after 1922 followed the same direction as
painting away from all that was abstract and
formal toward an ever-increasing naturalism.
Academic, classic, and romantic elements were
mingled in a new representational art called
Soviet realism. Detailed realistic portraiture
of heroes, officials, and important contemporaries became ever more popular. The number of sculptors increased but no work of any
great plastic value was attempted. In the
great building plans that began to be realized
in the Second Five Year Plan, architectural
sculpture became important again. A tendency toward colossal monumental figures
may be noted. This official sculpture has
been for the most part based on classical
models with realistic details. An example is

the model for the statue of Lenin for the Palace of Soviets and the completed work of Vera Mukhina, the figures of *Worker and Kolhosnitza* (Woman Collective farmer) executed in stainless steel, which surmounted the Soviet Exhibition Building in Paris in 1937. See A. Michel, *Histoire de l'art,* Tome 7 and 8; Alexander Benois, *The Russian School of Painting,* 1916; Constantin Umanski, *Neue Kunst in Russland,* 1920; Louis Lozowick, *Modern Russian Art,* 1925; Joseph Freeman, *Voices of October; The Studio;* Ed. G. Holme, *Art in the U. S. S. R.;* Elie Ehrenbourg, *L'art russe d'aujourdhui,* vol. 2, *L'amour de L'art,* Paris, 1921; C. Giedion-Welcker, *Modern Plastic Art,* 1937.

Architecture. Like painting and sculpture, architecture in Russia falls into three separate phases: 1) early architecture under Byzantine influence: 2) architecture in the western tradition of Europe, beginning with Peter the Great; 3) and the Soviet period subsquent to the Revolution of 1917.

EARLY ARCHITECTURE. From its earliest beginnings, Russian architecture reveals a unique feeling for color and form, which appears under the borrowed forms of other cultures and traditions. Ancient Russian architecture appears as a complex of various and curious tendencies rather than a unified stylistic achievement.

The surviving watch-towers of the Caucasus region are the earliest known architecture in Russia and they are akin the early watch towers of the Pyrannees. In Russia's forest covered regions in the north and central sections, wooden architecture early attained a great pre-eminence and even today the Russians exhibit a natural gift for working in wood. Northern wooden architecture, of which only few early chaurches exist, resembles the wooden church architecture of Norway. But these Russian chaurches also reveal a fusion of northern and eastern elements of design that has its own stark beauty. Domestic architecture was developed from log houses of simple strong structure in horizontal lines with steeply pitched roofs.

In the twelveth century, Byzantine influences permeated Russia and profoundly transformed its artistic style, leaving an indelible impress on architecture and all the minor decorative arts. The arts of Byzanz reached Russia from Constantinople and also indirectly from the Greek monasteries. Cities and villages throughout Russia became dotted with churches in the Byzantine style, built with central cupolas that increased in number and often assumed fanci-

ful and colorful shapes. For the most part smaller than their original models, Russian churches were modified in style by the monastic churches of Greece. Despite local variations, they were nearly all based on a universal plan: a square foundation supported by four piers, surmounted by a drum, which terminated either in a bulbous cupola or an octagonal tower ending in a blunt spire. The drum was frequently raised to great height and the church entrance marked by porches with tall flights of stairs and bell towers were often attached to the church.

Russian national architecture reached its highest development between the fourteenth and fifteenth centuries. Early centers of culture like Novgorod, Vladimir, and Suzdal built noteworthy churches and convents. In the reign of Ivan III, Moscow became the most powerful state and the center of great building activity. Italian architects and engineers were summoned to build the great walls of the Kremlin, which remains today the most famous monument of old Russia. Situated on a small hill above the Moscow River, the Kremlin (which means fortified place), consists of a group of palaces, cathedrals, and secular buildings enclosed by battlemented walls having nineteen watch towers and five gates, four of whose large towers were built by Ivan the III, the fifth, the tall Gothic tower of the Spaskiya Gate being added by an English architect (Holloway) in the seventeenth century. Within its girdle of crenelated rose-colored brick walls, there still stands the Uspensky Cathedral, rebuilt by a Bolognese architect in the fifteenth century, the Archangelski Cathedral containing the tombs of the Czars, the Blagovyeshensk Cathedral, and a complex of palaces dating from early times down to the great palace of the Romanovs' completed in the nineteenth century. Exposed to attack by arms and fire, the Kremlin has at various times undergone eleborate restorations, but it still preserves the appearance of a fortified medieval city with its fantastic skyline of golden domes and crosses.

Adjacent to the Kremlin, is the Red Square (900 yards long) with the bizarre Cathedral of Vasilli Blazhennyi, whose multicolored onion cupolas seem like a vision from the Arabian Nights. Begun by Ivan the Terrible in commemoration of his capture of Kazan from the Tartars, it was not completed until the end of the seventeenth century, and suffered exensive restorations in the second quarter of the ninetenth century.

The Byzantine influence in architecture lasted into the seventeenth century in Russia and in its decadent period became mixed with Italian Rococo motifs.

ARCHITECTURE IN THE WESTERN TRADITION. The founding of St. Petersburg in 1705 marks the change in Russia from oriental and Byzantine influences to those of Western Europe. Russian architecture now came under the dominance of the West and followed its stylistic changes with great fidelity, making only necessary variations due to climatic and social conditions. Peter planned the new capital on the Neva as a "window on Europe" and intended that it should be a "New Amsterdam". But the vastness of its size, the grandeur of its scale of building, and the unconscious influence of nameless Russian workers who built it stone by stone transformed this northern capital into a city peculiarly Russian in spirit.

The first plans and buildings of St. Petersburg were conceived in the style of the Northern Baroque of Holland and Germany. Peter's first architect, Domenico Trezzini, came from Copenhagen and was thoroughly imbued with the Dutch tradition. He was responsible for the plans of the Church of the Fortress of St. Peter and Paul, the various colleges on the isle of Vassili Ostrov (later the University) and the St. Alexander Nevsky Lavra. He also laid out the city's great boulevard, called after the early Russian hero-saint, Nevsky Prospekt. Among the German architects, who played a prominent part in the first period of building were Andreas Schlueter, architect to the King of Prussia, who built the little palace of the Summer Gardens; Theodor Schwertfeger, who completed Trezzini's work on the Alexander Nevsky Monastery, and Gottfried Schaedel, who built the Palace of Prince Menshikov, Peter's powerful favorite.

Most celebrated of the architects invited by Peter to Russia was the Frenchman, Alexander Leblond, who came from Paris in 1716, bringing with him a whole colony of artists and artisans. He drew up plans for the Summer Gardens, the Palaces of Strelna and Petershof. His work turned the tide against German and Dutch taste in Russia.

Under the regency of Empress Elizabeth, who hated the Germans, French taste was exclusively fostered at court and an architectural style developed combining the old Moscow national tradition with the extravagences of the French Rococo. Elizabeth's favorite architect was Rastrelli, the Younger, the son of the sculptor who had come with Leblond. Acting as director of construction at St. Peters-

burg, he was responsible for the building of many palaces, including the Winter Palace, the Summer Palace, the palaces at Tsarskoe-Selo, and the palaces of great princes like Strogonov and Anitckov. The Smolny Convent and the Church of St. Andrew of Kiev were also his work. His style, flamboyant and Rococo in taste, left its mark on the new capital. His best disciple, Sava Tchevakinski, built the graceful tower of the Church of St. Nicholas-of-the-Sailors.

Eighteenth century architecture in Russia was, for the most part, however, the work of foreign artists. The founding of he Imperial Academy of Fine Arts in 1758 may be considered the true beginning of Russian architecture in the Western tradition, but it was even much later toward the end of Catherine II's reign that the first generation of young Russian architects had completed their education and were entrusted with actual building.

Catherine, who began as a friend of the Enlightmen in France, took an exceptional interest in architecture and surrounded herself with French architects, who expressed the return to more sober and classical forms that was aking place in France. Under their influence, the transformation of the Baroque and Roccoco style into the grave classicism of Louis XVIth took place in Russia. The discovery of the lost city of Herculaneum in the early part of the century had initiated a classical revival in Europe that gradually embraced all countries and was to have a great efflorescence in Russia.

Catherine's first architect was Vallin de la Mothe, who became first professor of architecture at the Academy and shaped the taste of the whole first generation of Russian architects. To him are due the majestic Palace of the Academy of Fine Arts, (built from Leblond's plans), the Pavillon of the Hermitage (later the famous museum) and the Catholic Church of St. Catherine.

The graceful, restrained style of Louis XVIth found its best exponent, however, in the Italian architect, Rinaldi, who built the Park of Oranienbaum, the Chinese Pavillon, and the Palace and Chateau at Gatchina, the latter presents of the Empress to her favorite, Prince Gregory Orlov. Perhaps the most gifted of Catherine's architects was the disciple of Palladio, Quarenghi, whose style, marked by great delicacy of proportion, is the purest at the end of the eighteenth century. Among his works were the colonnade of Alexander's Palace at Tsarskoe-Selo, the portico of the English palace at Petershof, and the little theater of the Hermitage. In his old age, he was superseded by Russian architects and his plans for the Imperial Theatre and the Bourse were set aside. Starov, Russian architect was entrusted with building the Tauride Palace for Catherine's powerful minister, Potemkin. Its hall of colonnades marks the triumph of the column in Russian classical architecture.

Under Catherine, building went on not only in St. Petersburg, but in Moscow and other cities. In Kazakov, a Russian architect, who never went abroad, the Moscow style of the period was exemplified. He built the Pachkov Palace (Roumiantsov Museum) and the Razoumovski Palace in more Russian and less grandiose taste than St. Petersburg. The effect of his work was felt in many parts of Russia. Bajenov, another Russian and one of the first graduates of the Academy, spent ten years on a gigantic project for a palace which was to replace or to enclose the whole of the Kremlin.

Under Alexander I, after the great national victory of the Russians over Napoleon, building activity reached a climax. But if the French were defeated on the field of battle, they triumphed in the field of art, for the style of Napoleon, the Empire Style, became the national style of Russia and enjoyed a far greater and more widespread popularity than it did in Paris, where revolution and war confined building, for the most part, to paper projects, and brought it to a standstill with the defeat of Waterloo. In Russia what was often dry, pedantic and overladen in French Empire, became simpler, more massive, and more severly classical, and the exterior of buildings was enriched with colors of yellow, ultramarine, orange and viridian. In the work of Thomas de Thomon, foremost of Alexander's architects, the Corinthian column gave way to the Doric, and he built the St. Petersburg Stock Exchange in a style reminiscent of the archaic simplicity of the Temple of Paestum. In his period, the first important Russian architects come to the fore, among them Voroninkhine, born a serf belonging to Count Strogonov, and Zhakarov, who built the Admiralty, considered the most perfect example of the Empire Style in Russia. Last of Alexander's great architects was Richard de Montferrand, who drew the plans for the cathedral of St. Isaac, which in size and sumptuosity sought to vie with the Pantheon and St. Peter's at Rome. But despite its lavish use of precious materials, such as interior columns of malachite and lapis-lazuli, the interior appears barren and more Asiatic than classical in feeling. It was a Russian architect of Italian descent, Carlo Rossi, who created the vast architectural ensembles of St. Petersburg, such as the hemi-cycle of the Winter Palace. With his taste for over-ornate and magnificent decoration, the pure style of Empire began to disintegrate.

The political reaction which began shortly after Nicolas I ascended the throne was followed by a similar reaction in architecture which lost its grand simplicity and became more practical. Toward the end of his reign, a tendency to resuscitate the older Russian national style arose, but as little concerning its best examples were known, its most decadent period was copied. Under Nicolas II, reaction was firmly in he saddle and architecture began to decline. During the whole last half of the nineteenth century, it never regained the vigor and serenity of the Alexander period. The Church of the Savior built in Moscow by the German architect, Thon, was before its destruction by the Soviets, the most elaborate example of the garish, hollow taste of the end of the century.

The coming of the twentieth century saw new activity in Russian architecture due to the advent of industrial enterprise. Factories, commercial buildings, and enginering projects were undertaken. The newly acquired wealth of the industrial class was used in part to build elaborate residences either in the old Russian style or in the classical style. The Swedish influence and the *art nouveau* ideals of Vienna were introduced into the Russian scene, where they appeared exotic and often grotesque. The first World War in 1914 summarily put an end to all building for over a decade.

THE SOVIET PERIOD. The first years of the Soviet regime were occupied with the Civil War, the Polish War, the blockade, foreign intervention, and a great famine—events which took an enormous toll of human lives and completely disrupted the ordinary course of life. Architecture, the most stable of the arts, could not be practised under such difficult conditions.

The 1917 Revolution not only changed the political and economic structure of Russian life but it completely transformed its ideal values. New energies in all fields of endeavor were released and led to a great intellectual ferment. Architectural theory flourished as never before. The ideas of the extreme modern movement in European architecture were introduced for the first time and integrated with the new social theories. As soon as economic recovery set in, the universities re-opened; the architectural courses were thronged with students of a new type unhampered by past traditions. Leaders of the new architectural movement and heads of the architectural departments were chosen from the ultra-left wing of modern art. Parallel to the same development in Western Europe, painters who had participated in the plastic revolution, became the innovators in architecture; thus modern architecture was born out of modern painting.

From 1917 to 1920 was a period of privations and of Utopian dreams, but practically no actual building took place. In the first decade after the Revolution, three separate but related tendencies in architecture made their appearanc in the U.S.S.R.: Constructivism, Formalism, and Functionalism. The first to dominate the scene were the Constructivists, who had a creative effect on architectural theory, but achieved no concrete results except in the theatre. The Suprematist conceptions of Malevich, the projects of Lissitsky, and the experiments of Tatlin received widespread attention and influenced the younger architects and designers, who produced quantities of paper projects imaginative and daring in design but often coupled with technical ignorance. Neither the actual material means nor the skilled craftsmen for the construction of a truly modern architecture were to be found. But out of the dynamism of this first period, a dream of the future took shape, which still remains a valuable archive for coming generations to ponder over.

The first post-revolutionary building was entrusted to the more conservative architects, who in spite of themselves were forced to change their conception of architecture, for the abolition of private enterprise had destroyed the individual character of architecture. The new needs of a "collective" society demanded new solutions on a great scale in such enterprises as town-planning and social institutions. The first buildings erected in the modern style in Russia reflected the stern mood of war Communism; for the most part, like the Lenin Institute at Moscow, they are grim, colorless cubes of concrete completely at variance with the exuberant, colorful spirit of the best of the old architecture. The removal of the new government from St. Petersburg back to the ancient capital made Moscow the first center of rebuilding and among the other buildings erected were the Mossel-Prom Building (1924) and the wooden tomb of Lenin (architect Stchousev), the Izvestia Building (architect Barkhine) and a series of apartment houses in the international style (architect M. Ginsburg).

The mechanistic concepts of the Constructivists were followed by an almost mystic veneration of pure form, which the Formalists indulged in. From 1920 to 1922, the heads of the architectural faculty at the new Moscow School of Fine and Applied Arts were the architects, Ladovsky and Godosov, who envisaged an objective, absolute and universal system of form. They carried out important laboratory experiments in the study of scale, the relations of rhythm, proportion and mass, statics and dynamics termed the functions of volume, which, however led to a formal symbolism.

In 1923, a young group of architects along with painters and sculptors most of whom were students of Ladovsky organized the first association of modern architects called Asnova. Many of the formalist principles were modified by actual work, but the group as a whole adhered to the idea that new revolutionary forms could only be based on the latest scientific and technical discoveries. The Asnova group were responsible for such buildings as the Stadium at Moscow, the Soviet Pavilion at the Paris Exposition, of 1925 (designed by the brilliant architect Melnikov), the White-Russian Academy of Sciences, the Palace of Labor and it also participated in exhibitions at Bordeaux, Marseilles, and Strassburg.

The defection of some of the more radical architects from Asnova, among them the talented Vesnin brothers, Barkhine, Ginsburg, and the engineer designer, Melkoets, led to the founding of a new organization in 1928. Called SASS (Section of Architects of Socialist Construction) they represented the point of view of Functionalism. They aimed to abolish all emotional appeal of extraneous decoration in architecture in the interest of scientific functioning and spatial organization, holding that the content of a building resides in its function. For them architecture ceased to be a fine art and became a problem of engineering. The influence of modern architects in Western Europe was felt in the work of many members of SASS, such as the work of Corbusier, in France, Oud and Dietveld in Holland, Gropius and Mies van der Rohe in Germany. The members of SASS took an active part in social competitions for new buildings, among their commissions being the administrative buildings of the Turksib Railroad, the Theatre of the People at Kharkov, the apartment houses of the Commissariat of Finance in Moscow.

In 1929, Professor Ladovsky also seceded from Asnova to form the Association of Town-Planning Architects (ARU), who sought to solve the huge tasks of construction on a broader basis— theoretically in terms of spatial organization and spatial composition considered as a unity. The need for such a group was the natural outgrowth of the first Five Year Plan, which in 1928 had inaugurated the greatest building program the world has ever seen. Part of a long-term plan to completely industrialize and modernize the whole of the USSR, it brought about another epoch of foreigners in Russia. Noted engineers, architects, designers, and technicians were glad to accept contracts for work in the nation-wide building plan, which gave them greater scope for their efforts than in their home countries. On a hitherto unknown scale, plans were drawn for new cities, sea-ports, industrial centers, agricultural collectives, community and housing projects with schools, clubs, recreation parks, stadiums, new high ways, bridges, etc. New cities and sea-ports sprang into existence and building went on feverishly from the Arctic to the Black Sea, and from the Baltic to the Pacific. The first Five Year Plan was concerned primarily with vast engineering and industrial projects, the second with housing, community centers, theatres, schools etc. Out of the plan grew such stupendous works as the Dnieperstroy Dam, the electric power station at Kura, the Caucausus, the industrial cities of Magnitogorsk and Kuznetzk (now Stalinsky), the White Sea Canal and the Moscow-Volga Canal, the electrification of vast rural sections, the rebuilding of the pleasure and health resorts of the Caucausus and Black Sea Regions. The first Moscow subway was built and the plans for rebuilding the city into a modern world capital were put into execution.

The experimental period of Soviet architecteur may be said to have come to an end with the First Five Year Plan (1928) and from this time on, the whole direction of Soviet architecture changed, although many buildings were still erected in the modern international style, official directives demanded the creation of an architecture in the spirit of "Socialist Realism." This led to the founding of the All Russian Society of Proletarian Architects (WOPRA), a group which paralleled the AXHR society of painters in its aesthetic aims. While these aims were never clearly defined, WOPRA claimed priority because of its orthodox proletarian ideology, which it applied to architecture by attacking all "right" and "left" groups. Work produced by its members was eclectic, more traditional, pseudo-monumental, and in the spirit of "realism."

The conflicting trends in Soviet architecture were brought to a head and found official solution to the competition for the great Palace of Soviet in Moscow. Architects the world over and all Soviet organizations were invited to compete and over 450 designs, many of them brilliant and original, were submitted to a large Soviet commission. Competing architects included the most distinguished in the USSR and such internationally known men as Corbusier, Mendelsohn, Urbans, Hamilton, Brazini, Perret, Lebetkin, Poelzig, Gropius and others. First prize went to an American, (Hamilton) second to a Russian (Schuko) and final award to the Russian architect, Jofan, whose design, circular in shape was classical and Roman in feeling. with rich detail in ornament, painting, and sculpture.

When the second Five Year Plan went into effect, a new period began in Russian architecture. Within five years, the epoch of foreigners was over and a strong national feeling began to assert itself. Due to practical experience and the acquisition of technical knowledge which the foreign architects and engineers had bequeathed, Soviet architecture began an independent career. All the plastic and formal advances in modern architecture were rejected and efforts were made to mould a truly national style on traditional foundations. It was officially stated that the ideal peoples' architecture must be basically human, not mechanistic, and that it should appeal to the emotions through ornament, sculpture and painting. The architecture of the past which best incorporated social utility and pleasure was that of Greece and Rome. The international style, which had revealed certain practical disadvantages due to the use of large areas of glass and the flat roofs was now deemed aesthetically unsuited for Soviet life and was abandoned.

This classic trend coincided with the popular taste, which had been shaped by the classical buildings of the Alexander period. From 1932 to 1937, new building was in the hands of Russian architects who had been trained in the academic tradition. Lenin's tomb, built before the second Five Year Plan by Stchousev, was one of the few Soviet creations which fused modern and traditional elements by means of the severe polished planes of native stone in black, red, and grey. The stations of the Moscow subway also made use of polychrome decoration but were conceived in a far more ornamental and elaborate style. The classic column was again re-instated and the new buildings in Moscaw assumed an almost imperial and heavy classical style. If Soviet architecture like all the arts went backward to the sources of its inspiration, it went forward in its practical solutions of large scale collective enterprises. In its town-planning, its building of socialist cities like Autostroy and Magnitogorsk, its new forms of community living like the state farm and the collective, in its creation of new types of buildings like works clubs, rest-homes, communal restaurants, the boldest experiments have been made. New forms of social life have re-shaped a whole new conception of architecture, in which man and his physical and social environment in relation to each other are treated as the central theme. The war which put a stop to all large building projects and has destroyed much that was built in large areas of the country will necessitate a vast re-construction in the coming peace. —C.W.

Russian bassoon. See MUSICAL INSTRUMENTS.

Russian porcelain. See CERAMICS II.

RUSSIA, RELIGIOUS PAINTING IN.
Iconography. The iconography of Christian art in Russia is to all intents and purposes based on the tradition of the Byzantine Church. Certain themes are particularly favored by the icon-makers, as, for example, the representation of the Trinity as the three angels at Abraham's table, which was only replaced by the conception of the subject as God the Father, the Son, and the Dove, with the coming of western European influence in the 18th cent. The types of the Madonna, developed in Byzantine art, were introduced at an early period; various versions of the theme became identified with the locality where the earliest or reputedly miraculous example of the type was preserved: one need mention only Our Lady of Vladimir and the Madonna of the Don, by Theophanes the Great. Paintings dedicated to the legend of the Madonna were ordered in a cycle of twenty-four stations, the **Akathistos** or **Hymn to the Virgin**, corresponding roughly to the rosary of Latin origin. In addition to the archangels and the great saints of the Byzantine calendar, a host of local Russian saints completed the iconographical repertory of the icon-painter.

The icons were revered and treasured as spiritual objects rather than as works of art. By a kind of fetishism, the Russian worshippers believed the images to be actually imbued with the very presence of the sacred personages represented. As in all traditional art, the effectiveness of the icons depended on the intensity of faith of the artist who created them and the people who venerated them with a zeal surpassing anything known in the Christian world.

The Pre-Mongolian Schools of Painting. Religious painting in Russia prior to the 18th cent. has been divided into the work of various local schools where this last of the Byzantine styles continued to flourish for centuries after the fall of the Eastern Empire in 1453. The beginning of Christian art in Russia goes back to that day in 989 when Prince Vladimir of Kiev established Christianity as the state religion. Although nothing survives from the period of the Holy Vladimir, the decorations of several churches from the 11th century have survived to the present day. These include the mosaics of Hagia Sophia in Kiev which represent a transference to Russia of the style of the Second Golden Age in Byzantium, as represented by the mosaics of Daphni and Hosios Loukas in Phocis. The Pantokrator is a kind of Antique Zeus, and the plastic treatment of the draped forms marks a return to the technique of classical painting. These mosaics in Hagia Sophia are obviously the work of Greek artists, imported under the Kievian dynasty. Another important work of this so-called pre-Mongolian period are the frescoes of secular scenes, mainly of gladiatorial combats, decorating the stairway of the Bishop's Palace in the church of Hagia Sophia, Novgorod. These are perhaps the sole surviving examples of a lost tradition of secular painting in Byzantine art. It is thought that this secular style with its emphasis on the intensity of dramatic presentation exercised an influence on the so-called Neo-Hellenistic art in both Byzantium and Russia. To this tradition belongs the great cycle of frescoes of the 12th cent. in St. Demetrius at Vladimir. These pictures have been dated 1196 to 1212, and are the Russian variant of a style represented by the mosaics of Kahrie Djami in Constantinople and the 12th cent. frescoes at Nerez in Bulgaria. The highly spiritualized heads are informed with a gravity and expressiveness that is quite new in the Byzantine tradition. Gestures and poses, meaningful in their explanation of the dramatic action, replace the old language of symbol and attribute. The colors, too, in a seeming revival of the Hellenistic technique, have taken on a new clarity and brilliance, and are slashed by highlights of a strident intensity. One of the most famous icons in the history of Russian art is the very much damaged panel of Our Lady of Vladimir which, legend has it, was brought by sea from Constantinople in the middle years of the 12th cent. This painting, which survived the Mongol sack of Vladimir and was brought to Moscow at the approach of Tamerlaine's hordes, has suffered much from subsequent restorations. No less than seven layers covered the original work. The iconography of the Madonna of Tenderness must almost certainly be associated with the emphasis on emotional values, characterizing the Neo-Hellenistic manner. Although the early layers of overpainting are in a dark rich tonality, typical of the pre-Mongolian school, originally the panel was painted in that illusionistic, sparkling technique that goes back to the Antique tradition. The figures have the simplicity and monumentality of the Byzantine mosaic tradition. Although legend assigns Our Lady of Vladimir to a Byzantine origin, there is a possibility that it is one of the first panel paintings by a Russian artist. The first of the Russian icon painters, the holy Alypios Petscherski, was active in the early 12th cent. His name is sometimes associated with this icon. In the wistful melancholy of expression, in the rhythmic elegance of the lines, there is already a suggestion of the later schools of Novgorod and Moscow. Our Lady of Vladimir, the very palladium of Russia, barely escaped destruction at the hands of the Mongols who in 1209 swept like a plague of fire across the plains of Holy Russia.

However great a debacle this invasion may have been for the economic and social development of the country, no reflections of this disaster are to be seen in the new school of Russian art at Novgorod, which had survived the wave of destruction, thanks to its isolation, and now became the cultural center of Russia. It was probably due to the great geographical isolation of Novgorod from Byzantium that its artists should have been the first to display an emancipation from the earlier, completely Greek styles.

The School of Novgorod. Such indirect Mongolian control as there had been of the city of Novgorod came to an end in 1259. An entry in the city chronicle of the year 1378 mentions for the first time the name of "Theophanes the Greek", with whose work there opens the greatest era of Russian paint-

ing. The most famous works by this master are the frescoes in the cathedral of the Transfiguration at Novgorod. The painting of the figures marks the final development of the Neo-Hellenistic manner. The brownish flesh tints are outlined with thick and freely painted black lines; violently slashed highlights stab the shadows and provide almost phosphorescent accents for the salient planes in masks that suggest at once the incandescent luminosity of El Greco and the haunting gravity of the Fayum portraits. Like Theotokopoulos the Greek in Spain, so Theophanes was the wonder of his contemporaries, and was styled "the Philosopher". Like El Greco, too, this master was one of the last to re-work the coloristic technique of the Antique world. Perhaps the nearest artistic equivalents to Theophanes' work in Byzantine art are the illusionistic frescoes of Mistra.

The panel painting of the School of Novgorod in the 14th and 15th cents. are the first to show a distinctly Russian style. They have a rarefied ethereal character; and the enormously attenuated forms are perhaps the most ghostly that any religious art has produced. An abstract rhythm of lines, in which the contours of figures and landscape are antiphonal one to another, is one of the most striking features of the style. The architecture is a collection of picturesque aediculae drawn from the artist's own imagination. The mountains are conceived as fantastic explosions of prismatic forms. The sparkling highlights represent a modification of the radical illusionistic formula employed by Theophanes the Greek. It has been conjectured that this national technique may have originated in the atelier of central Russia, even before the Mongol invasion.

The School of Moscow. Famous in the annals of Russian painting is the master Andrei Rublióv, who in 1405 collaborated with Theophanes in the Church of the Virgin Annunciate in Moscow. Nothing is known of Rublióv's training, and although he was associated with Theophanes, his manner is more closely related to the so-called idealistic style of the 14th cent. at Mistra than it is to the illusionistic technique exemplified by Theophanes. Formerly associated with the School of Novgorod, Rublióv is now believed to have been one of the founders of the School of Moscow.

The most famous single work by this master is the icon of the Holy Trinity, painted for the monastery of the Trinity and St. Sergius. This picture is the most notable

Russian example of the symbolical representation of the Trinity in the form of the three angels who came mysteriously to Abraham's feast. The figures of Sarah and Abraham have been omitted, and our concentration is rivetted on the forms of the three ghostly personages. In many respects this is one of the first icons in a truly Russian style. The classic nobility of the heads and the masterfully draped bodies stem from the Byzantine tradition, but the forms are infused with a new and almost musically cadenced rhythm of line that is totally different from anything in later Greek painting. A new and tensile beauty sits on the proudly curving brows. This beautiful line is echoed in the curves of eyes and nose and mouth. The whole effectiveness of the arrangement rests largely on the wonderfully moving lines of the contours. There are subtle and indescribable rhythms between the angels with their great wings tentatively folded that make the whole composition a melodious accord of lines and silhouettes. It is this marvellous presentation of abstract ideas in moving linear terms that is perhaps the chief pictorial strength of Rublióv and his followers in the Moscow school. Adding to the feeling of unreality in these superb phantoms is a strange pictorial device of reversing completely the relative positions of dark and light areas in certain sections of the angel's draperies. Only a few traces of the illusionistic chiaroscuro of Theophanes survive. The colors, in their translucency and brilliance, suggest the work of the Italian masters of the 14th cent.

Not far from Novgorod, in a monastery founded by St. Cyril and the holy man Therapon, is preserved one of the great monuments of Russian wall-painting: the vast cycle of the Hymn to Mary, inscribed with the name of the icon painter Dionisij (Dionysios), and dated 1500 to 1501. Although the style of these frescoes recalls the 15th cent. icons of Novgorod, the painter Dionisij has been assigned to the School of Moscow. The sure and quiet contours of the forms and their rhythmic organization suggest the style of Rublióv. The figures are further distinguished by their suave feminine grace and elegance amounting almost to preciosity. The juxtaposition of colors—rose, pistachio green, and turquoise—against deep, azure backgrounds is strangely reminiscent of 'the Arena chapel at Padua. The figures have a distinct architectonic character and are set in severely simple compositions that make the paintings enormously effective as wall decorations. In this the developed style of the School of Moscow the sacred themes are presented in a style that is a fusion of the ideal Byzantine style and elements of a directness and naïveté that suggest an origin in Russian folk art.

In the course of the 14th cent. the art of icon-painting became a tradition separate from that of mural painting. This period is also marked by the development of the iconostasis, or icon-screen separating the church from the sanctuary. Such retables consisting of a single row of paintings had been used in earlier centuries, but the structure of the iconostasis now becomes a tall and wide screen with as many as five registers of painting, completely shutting off the altar from the body of the sanctuary. In the central row, or tschin, the Deesis—Christ flanked by the Madonna and John the Baptist—occupies the place of honor above the door leading to the inner shrine. On either side of the Deesis are panels representing SS. Peter and Paul and SS. Michael and Gabriel. The portals leading to the holy of holies were decorated with paintings of the Annunciation and the four Evangelists. The upper rows of the iconostasis were given over to panels of various saints, paintings of the twelve feasts of the Christian year, and representations of the great Councils of the Orthodox Church. Although it is known that Justinian's great church in Constantinople had an altar-screen set with jewels and precious metals, the enormous screens of the churches of Moscow and Novgorod are a peculiarly Russian development. This typically Russian iconostasis appears at a moment when Russian painting for the first time begins to manifest a truly national character.

The School of Moscow in the 16th century and the Stroganov School. In the year 1534 the decline of Russian art began when Ivan the Terrible assumed the triple crown of Muscovy. With the sack and burning of Novgorod in 1570 Moscow in all its tawdry splendor became the capital of Russian art. Tsar Ivan undertook to make it another Rome in an architecture which combined influences of the newly conquered Oriental provinces and of Renaissance Italy. In art there is an influence at once of western Europe and of the late Italo-Byzantine schools that had survived the fall of Constantinople. The 16th cent. icons of Moscow, although in a sense still based on earlier styles, displayed very certain and unhappy departures from the great tradition. The heavy and overladen shields of gold and silver with which the icons are all but concealed make the holy pictures appear more as objects for ecclesiastical pomp than for veneration. The compositions come to be crowded with all manner of fantastic and irrelevant details. The heads of the sacred personages are no longer ideal in their conception, but are realistic portrayals of Muscovite types. The ideal or rarefied style of the Novgorod school is replaced by a richly ornamented anecdotal manner of representation, marked by a delight in the multiplication of decorative and incidental features and exotic details in both figures and architectural setting. In place of the sensitive scale of vibrant colors used in the earlier schools these later icons are distinguished by their sooty, reddish brown tonality.

A certain group of icons of the 16th and early 17th cents. are attributed to the so-called Stroganov school, from the inscriptions on these holy pictures stating that they were made for the Stroganovs, a powerful family of Novgorod origin, particularly associated with the conquest of Siberia. The great period of the House of Stroganov, with which the florescent period of this icon school coincides, extends from the 16th cent. until the reign of Peter the Great. Members of the family, Maxim and Nikita Stroganov, were even active as icon-painters in the last decades of the 16th cent. Frequently the masters of the Stroganov school signed themselves "painter to the Tsar" or "painter of Moscow", in token of their activity in the capital. The style of Novgorod is again at the basis of the painters of the Stroganov school. A greater sharpness of contour drawing and an even more precise definition of detail differentiates these paintings from the work of the Moscow school. There is a tendency towards a miniature-like elaboration in an infinity of incidental detail that detracts largely from the monumentality the compositions might otherwise have. The color varies from an almost garish brilliance to a dull, metallic opacity. More often than not, the gold inscriptions, among the most distinguished examples of Russian chrysography, form a vital part of the composition. Although it is possible that certain icons of the Stroganov school show an influence in composition and types of Italian art of the 15th cent., their style seems in the main to be the final elaboration of the exhausted tradition of the great

period of Russian art. It is to be noted, however, that certain details from the cycle of wall-paintings devoted to the Apocalypse in the church of St. Nicholas at Jaroslavl very clearly display an adaptation of Dürer's compositions for the Book of Revelations. Leaders in the Stroganov school were Istoma Savinus and his successors. These works have the same complexity of linear organization, the harsh metallic colors, and richness of ornamentation characteristic of this last phase of the icon-maker's art.

Although icons were mechanically copied from the great works of earlier periods until comparatively recent times, the great tradition of religious painting in Russia comes to an end in the late 17th cent. The work of the painters under Tsaral patronage from the time of Peter the Great until the end of the Romanov dynasty is distinguished by an unhappy and disagreeable effort to adapt the types and techniques of Baroque painting in Western Europe to the expression of the traditional themes. See RUSSIAN ARTS; also Farbman, Michael, ed., *Masterpieces of Russian Painting*, 1930; Kondakov, N. P., *The Russian Icon*, 1927 and *The Russian Icon*, 2 vols., 1928 and 1929; Muratov, P. P., *Les Icones Russes*, 1927; Schweinfurth, Philipp, *Geschichte der Russischen Malerei*, 1930; Talbot-Rice, David, *The Beginnings of Russian Icon Painting*, 1938 and *Russian Art*, 1935.

—B.R.

rusticate. The recessing of joints between the blocks or bricks in a wall leaving the outer surfaces projecting and rough.

Ruthenia, art of. See CZECHOSLOVAKIA, ART OF.

rya. From the old Scandinavian *ry* meaning rough or shaggy. The plural form is *ryor*. The rugs or *ryor* made by the peasants were for warmth and were used generally as bed covers, cushion covers and for wraps rather than on the floors. Many ryor were made in a flat or tapestry weave.   —B.E.J.

ryo (Jap.). Volume.

ryt. See POLISH ART.

rytm. See POLISH ART.

ryū (Jap.). Dragon.

Ryumon yaki (Jap.). Pottery made in Satsuma province.

S

sabiji (Jap.). Lacquer work imitating the surface of old metal.

sable. (1) The general name for a type of small animal has become a synonym for a painter's brush. This is a fine brush from the hair of the kolinsky, one of several species of Asiatic minks. (2) *Her.* Black.
—G.L.S.

sacred cantata. See oratorio.

sacred pearl. See SYMBOLISM IN FAR EASTERN ART.

sacrificial bronzes, of China. See the following: body; *chia*; *chih*; *chüeh*; *chung*; *fu*; *ho*; *hsien*; *hu*; *i*; *ku*; *kuang*; *kuei*; *lei*; *li*; *ting*; *to*; *tou*; *tsun*; *tueh*; *tui*; *yu*; *yü*; also *Ancient Chinese Bronzes,* Toledo Museum of Art, 1941; *Early Chinese Bronzes,* Albert J. Hoop, 1924; *Catalogue of Eumorfopoulos Collection,* W. Perceval Yetts, 1932; *History of Early Chinese Art,* Osvald Siren, 1929.
—J.A.M.

sacristy. A room or chamber in or attached to a religious structure, essentially for the sacred utensils, vestments, etc., used in connection with the religious or sacred ceremonies; a vestry. —J.M.M.

saddle-stitching. *Book.* Stitching single sections on a stitching machine with the section placed "astride the saddle", i.e., the section opened with the saddle in the center.

Safavid art. See ISLAMIC ART.

saffron. An unusual coloring material, this is a dye rather than a pigment. It is extracted from the dried stigmas of the crocus flower and seems to have been a favorite— in producing a pale yellow golden color— among the painters of the Middle Ages. Prob-

ably it was more used for illumination than for larger works. —G.L.S.

sageo (Jap.). Cord by which the sword scabbard is attached to the belt. It is threaded through the *kurikata* (q.v.).

sagger. A receptacle used to protect delicate pottery while being fired in a kiln.

sahn (Ar.). Court in a mosque. See ISLAMIC ART.

saku (Jap.). When used, in painting, after a signature it means "made by".

sakura (Jap.). The cherry blossom, symbolizing the soul of Japan; also the transient aspects of human life.

Salian art. The period of the Salian style parallels the epoch of the German emperors of the Salian Frankish House (1024-1137).

The peculiarities of the Salian style in painting and sculpture began with the school of Regensburg and were already established under the Ottonian King Henry II. Salian art favored the static, linear, and symmetrical elements of style and was inclined toward a one-sided metaphysical and ascetic expression. These tendencies stand in sympathetic relationship to Byzantine art from which it derived strong suggestions and influences.

There were two events of real importance in the field of architecture; the use of the vault for the first time in the rebuilding of the Cathedral of Speyer, and the spreading of the style of the Hirsau monks. About 1030 the largest building of the pre-Gothic period, the Cathedral of Speyer, was started. The newly introduced verticalism of the walls is to be noted. About 1100 the building was vaulted, under Henry IV. About 1100 they began to rebuild the Cathedral of Mainz, following the scheme of Speyer. The cloister church of Maria Laach shows the characteristic attributes of a building in the transition from the Salian to the Hohenstaufen period. About the end of the 11th cent. the style of the Hirsun monks spread over all Germany. The cloister church in Limburg a.d. Hardt and the rebuilt cloister church of Hersfeld may be considered as a preparation for this reformed style. The Hirsau style began with a thoroughly changed ground plan. As complicated as the groundplan is, the completed work appears simple and noble. Churches constructed in this style are, among others, the churches of Alpirsbach in the Black Forest (1095 to the first half of the 12th cent.), of Paulinzella (begun 1112), the Church of Our Lady in Halberstadt, and the cloister church in Maursmünster in Alsace (after the middle of the 12th century).

Salian standards of painting were established in Regensburg and later in Salzburg. The Sacramentar made at the order of Henry II (now in Munich) and the Evangeliar of the Abbess Uta from Niedermünster (now in Munich), both done under the last Ottonian emperor, already show the peculiarities of the Salian style. The mature style can be seen in the Evangeliar of Henry III (now in Upsala) done in the School of Echternach near Trier. The characteristic style of the period, which became very stiff, can be seen in the Evangeliar of Henry III (now in Krakau) and in the Evangeliar of the Abbey of Abdinghofen. The same stylistic peculiarities are in the contemporary murals of the choir of the former Benedictine abbey in Prüfening near Regensburg (1125-68) and of the west part of the Nonnberg abbey in Salzburg, about 1145. After 1100 a certain softening and loosening of style together with sentimental influences began to appear as for instance in the "liber florum" by Theofried of Echternach, done about 1100, now in Gotha, or in the Pericope of St. Erentrud in Salzburg, painted about the middle of the 12th century and now in Munich. The same softening appears in the murals in the choir of the chapel at Hocheppau near Bozen, belonging to the middle of the 12th cent. The highest achievement of Salian mural painting is the mural in the west building of the former abbey in Knechtstedten, about 1150.

In the field of sculpture the Salian style was already forecast by the antependium of Basle done under Henry II (now in the Cluny Museum in Paris). The various periods of development of the Salian epoch can be studied in the Virgin and Child of the Liebighaus in Frankfort, done in the 2nd quarter of the 11th cent., the bronze crucifix of the former abbey in Werden, the "Imad Madonna" in Paderborn (1051-1076), the burial plate of King Rudolf of Swabia in the Cathedral of Merseburg (after 1080), the tomb of a Westfalian duke (1100), called the Wittukind tomb in Enger, and the reliquary of St. Sigismund from the Welfenschatz, done in a Hildesheim workshop. To the same Salian period belong, among other works, the so-called Saint's Tomb Chapel in Gernrode, the bronze door on the south portal of the Cathedral in Gnesen, the wooden reading desk with the four Evangelists from Alpirsbach (now in Freudenstadt), the Externsteine near Detmold, 1115, the reliefs on the chancel arcades in Gustorf, 1130, and the "Madonna" from a reredos in the Cathedral of Erfurt about 1150.

Among works of applied art those to be noted are the crown of the German emperors, remade under Konrad II, the jewelry of the Empress Gisela, the Reichs Cross of Konrad II, and the portable altar done by Roger of Helmershausen, 1100, in the Hildesheim treasury. See GENERAL VIEW: G. Dehio, *Geschichte der deutschen Kunst*, Berlin, 1914, new edition by Gall; W. Pinder, *Die Kunst der deutschen Kaiserzeit*, Leipzig, 1933; Max Hauttmann, *Die Kunst des frühen Mittelalters*. ARCHITECTURE: G. Dehio and G. V. Bezold, *Die kirchliche Baukunst des Abendlandes*, Stuttgart, 1892; Paul Frankl, *Die Baukunst des Mittelalters*, Handbuch der Kunstwissenschaft, Berlin, 1918. SCULPTURE: J. Baum, *Malerei und Plastik des Mittelalters*, Handbuch der Kunstwissenschaft, Berlin, 1930; H. Beenken, *Romanische Skulpturen in Deutschland*, Leipzig, 1924; E. Panofsky, *Deutsche Plastik des 11. bis 13. Jahrh.*; Adolf Goldschmidt, *Die Elfenbeinskulpturen*, 1914-18. PAINTING: Bernath, *Malerei des Mittelalters*, Leipzig, 1916; Georg Swarzenski, *Regensburger Buchmalerei*, Leipzig, 1901 and *Salzburger Buchmalerei*, Leipzig, 1913; Paul Clemen, *Die Romanische Monumentalmalerei in den Rheinlanden*, Düsseldorf, 1916; Josef Garber, *Die romanischen Wandgemaelde Tirols*, Vienna, 1928; Georg Leidinger, *Meisterwerke der Buchmalerei*, Munich, 1920 ff; Hans Swarzenski, *Vorgotische Miniaturen*, Koenigstein, 1927; Adolf Goldschmidt, *Die deutsche Buchmalerei*, Munich, 1928. APPLIED ART: G. v. Falke and G. Swarzenski, *Das Kunstgewerbe im Mittelalter*, part of Lehnert, Illustrierte Geschichte des Kunstgew. I;

Falke-Frauberger, *Deutsche Schmelzarbeiten des Mittelalters,* Frankfurt, 1904; Josef Braun, *Meisterwerke der deutschen Goldschmiedekunst, vorgotische Zeit,* Munich, 1922.
—A.J.S.

salpinx. See MUSICAL INSTRUMENTS.

saltarello. This Italian national dance is usually associated with the Rome district. It is danced by a couple to music in ¾ meter with an exaggerated accent of the first beat. Some of the steps are similar to those of the Tarantella with the exception that while the saltarello rhythm is uneven and skipping, that of the tarantella is even and running. The basic skipping step of the saltarello is varied at intervals by more elaborate footwork. —J.G.

saltire. See HERALDRY.

samādhi mudrā (Skr.). See dhyāna mudrā.

samé (Jap.). Skin of the ray, or of a shark, sometimes covering the wooden hilt of a sword.

samisen. See MUSICAL INSTRUMENTS.

samai tsuzuki (Jap.). See triptych.

sanctuary (*sanctus,* holy, sacred). (1) A holy or sacred place: especially a building or space devoted to sacred use. (2) Any structure devoted to worship.

sanctus. See Mass.

sandal-wod. Fragrant wood from Indo-Malaya, often the basic material for incense.

sandarac. This is little used now as a varnish material. It has been found to produce a very brittle surface film with a tendency to crazing. In ancient times it seems to have been more favorably thought of and, according to some writers, is supposed to have actually given rise to the name, varnish. Large quantities of it were exported from what is now Benghazi, then known as Berenice, and it is thought that the word, varnish, comes from a corruption of that. —G.L.S.

Sanda yaki (Jap.). Pottery made in Settsu province.

sand blasting. See GLASS AND GLASSMAKING.

sand painting. A form of expression of unknown origin, practiced by many Indian tribes but to an unrivalled degree in quality and complexity by the Navaho (q.v.). It constitutes one phase of a healing ritual and is made on the floor of a medicine lodge by young men under the direction of the medicine man or shaman. The paintings vary in size from 3 to 20 ft. in diameter. Sand is spread over the floor of the lodge to a depth of 1-3 in. and smoothed with a batten. The pigments consist of five colors of finely ground sand: white, red, yellow, black and a gray-blue, each used symbolically. Pollen and powdered corn meal are also used. The artist takes a pinch of sand with the thumb and fingers and allows it to trickle on the ground, forming a design in color on the neutral sand base. He works from the center outward and develops the design according to exact traditional rules, with opportunity for individual variations only in a few minor details. From one to a dozen artists, the number depending on the size and complexity of the design, may work upon one painting, for it is begun at dawn and finished before nightfall. The subject matter consists of highly conventionalized figures of the gods, the rainbow, lightning, mountains, clouds, animals and reptiles, all with a legendary significance. The patient is seated on the painting and pinches of sand from the painting are applied to the corresponding parts of his body, thus affecting the passage of the power of the god to the body of the ailing person. At the conclusion of the rites the shaman obliterates the picture, and the sand is removed from the lodge and thrown away. Reproductions are made from memory by white men who have been permitted to witness the rite, and are checked by sympathetic shamans. See Washington Matthews, *The Night Chant,* 1902; Laura Armer, *Sand Painting of the Navajo Indians,* 1931; Gladys Reichard and Franc J. Newcomb, *Shooting Chant; Sandpaintings of the Navaho,* 1937; Hasteen Klah, *Navajo Creation Myth,* 1942. —H.G.

sandpaper painting and drawing. A process of painting or drawing on sandpaper for reproduction. Usually a waxed crayon is used to build up an impression on the sandpaper which is then inked and printed. —R.L.W.

sandstone. A stone composed of grains of sand, united with other mineral substances, cemented together by a material of an argillaceous, calcareous, or siliceous nature.

sang-de-boeuf (Fr.). A red glaze on Oriental ceramics imitating the color of oxblood. See CERAMICS II.

sanhaja architecture. See ISLAMIC ART.

san hsien. See MUSICAL INSTRU-MENTS.

sanitary ware. See CERAMICS I.

sansui (Jap.). Mountains and water; a type of landscape painting.

santir. See MUSICAL INSTRUMENTS.

sanzon (Jap.). In religious art, a trinity.

sarabande. The *sarabande* was an ancient dance thought to have originated with the Moors and been brought by them to Spain. Since it ultimately reached 16th cent. European courts, it is included in the list of *pre-classic* dance forms. In its earliest Spanish days, the sarabande is reported to have been so wild and uninhibited that it was suppressed for a time by the moralists, to reappear in so sedate a form that it was used in religious drama. This stately and solemn dance in ¾ meter, having been adopted by the nobility, gave its name and form to the third movement of the instrumental suite. The movement of the court sarabande was limited to a slow walk by large groups of couples progressing in straight lines and large, sweeping curves.   —J.G.

sarangi. See MUSICAL INSTRUMENTS.

sarcophagus (L.). A stone coffin, grave, or chest-like tomb. See EARLY CHRISTIAN ART; ALEXANDER THE GREAT, SAR-COPHAGUS OF.

sari (Hind.). An East Indian woman's garment. A long narrow cloth wrapped around the waist covering the legs as a skirt, passing over the bosom and sometimes covering the head. See cotton.   —J.A.M.

sarinda. See MUSICAL INSTRUMENTS.

sarsenet, sarcenet. An antique fabric of plain silk weave.

Sasanian, Sassanian art. See ISLAMIC ART; PERSIAN ART.

satellite city, town or suburb. See CIVIC PLANNING.

satin. A fabric with a glossy surface and a dull back; also the weave by which this fabric is achieved. Satin weave throws filling threads to the surface. See weaving.

Satsuma yaki (Jap.). A type of pottery from Satsuma province. The most widely known has a creamy crackled glaze and is decorated with an elaborate minute pattern of figures, inserts, geometric designs, etc.   —J.A.M.

saturation. See COLOR.

Saturn. Ancient god of seed sowing.

Sauroktonos (Gr. from *sauros* + *kteino*). The Lizard slayer. Sobriquet given to a statue by Praxiteles. The original was of bronze and originated about 350-325 b.c. It is listed among the works described in Pliny's "Natural History" XXXIV, 70. There are, among others, Roman copies in marble in the Vatican and the Louvre, and a small bronze replica in the Villa Albani in Rome. All these statues represent the young Apollo as he watches a lizard creeping up a tree. He holds an arrow and evidently waits for the moment to kill the lizard. For illustration, see Gisela M. A. Richter, *The Sculpture and Sculptors of the Greeks,* New Haven, 1929, Fig. 674 and 675.   —L.L.

savonarola chair. See FURNITURE.

savonnerie. One of the most sumptuous and formal rugs in the world, was developed and perfected in a discarded soap factory in a district which is now part of Paris. "Savon" being French for soap, the rugs made there were called "savonnerie" (soap factory) rugs. Savonnerie means to us a most elegant and aristocratic floor covering of deep rich pile, woven by hand, in France. The technique is about the same as had been in use in the Orient. The loom is strung with warp threads and the pile is formed by tying in separate knots of worsted, making a row of knots or tufts across the entire width of the warp. Then two or three weft threads are woven in to bend in the knots and form the fabric before the succeeding row of knots is tied.   —B.E.J.

sawing-in, sawn-in. *Book.* When the cords or tapes are placed in grooves sawn in the back of the book. The sawing machine is the machine doing the work. In handwork it is usual to use a tenon saw.

saxhorn. See MUSICAL INSTRUMENTS.

Saxony, Saxon wool. (1) Fine, soft, wool having a short, very fine, strong and elastic staple, with excellent felting properties. (2) A worsted fabric originated in England.

saxophone. See MUSICAL INSTRU-
MENTS.

saya (Jap.). Sword scabbard.

sayydi. See ISLAMIC ART.

scabbard. Sheath for sword or dagger. See
saya.

scabble. As used in masonry: To dress or
shape roughly, as a stone.

scale pattern. In ancient Mesopotamian and
Greek art, an ornamental pattern in which
rows of pointed or round tipped scales overlap and are arranged so that the tips of one
row come over the joints of the lower row.
—L.T.S.

scales and modes. A *scale* is an abstract of
certain pitch interval relations. With reference to primitive or folk music or even to
Gregorian chant, the abstract takes into consideration all the tones of a composition, independent, however, of the specific sequence,
number, rhythm, or pitch height in which they
occur. The relevance of a scale to more
complex music is, on the other hand, as a
representation, in the same abstract way, of
only some of the tones—those which are, in
a sense, more basic or elementary to the
structure.

The formulators of such an abstract assume an identity between a tone and its octave above or below, or two octaves above
or below, and so forth. This identity is illustrated when men and women sing the same
tune, thinking they are singing in unison.
Each tone in the scale, although represented
once, is available in various octaves of the
pitch continuum.

The apprehension of a scale pattern as
basic to a conglomerate of tones exceeding
that pattern, was facilitated by the establishment of the **diatonic system** as a European standard for scales in the last part of
the period of Greek music. Such scales embodied intrinsic affinity among their constituents, so that other tones could be immediately recognized as not belonging to the
basic group. It was not, however, until recent
centuries that these possibilities were appre-
ciably realized.

Diatonic scales assume several different
forms which are known as their **modes.** Since
the 18th cent., a favoritism for the **major
mode** has made itself evident. But this mode
was not ignored by the Church composers as
it is generally thought. Thus, what was theoretically the **Lydian mode** (the white keys on

the piano from F to F) was in practice the
major, as a result of the constant improvised
interpolation of the B-flat as so-called *musica
ficta.* Major manifested itself in *musica ficta,*
moreover, in still other ways (see below).

Ancient music provides a great many types
of scales upon which it is difficult to generalize and whose authenticity is often doubtful because of the inadequacy of records. The
results of comparative musicology show, however, a prominence of the pitch intervals of
the fourth and fifth. The transition to the
diatonic system seems to have been a broaden-
ing of the role of those intervals. The result
was the achievement, after a long period of
trial and error, of a set of scales whose
plasticity was so great that it was considered
unnecessary to seek further. It would seem
justified, then, that space be devoted here
to these later scales and to a determination
of the factors which contribute to their preferred position. In the course of this approach a natural basis for one of the most
prominent of the primitive scales—the **pentatonic**—will be provided, since this was probably a link to diatonism.

There are said abstractly to be twelve tones
in the present musical system. Each is concretely available in about eight different
forms—that is to say, at eight degrees of
pitch height or depth. With the exception of
certain contemporaries among whom Schönberg is outstanding, composers have found it
expedient to select some of the twelve tones
as a basic recurrent pattern, against which
the other tones are made to stand out as a
deviation. Thus, musical composition is based
on a number of recurrent patterns along the
various dimensions of tone (pitch, duration,
loudness, timbre). These patterns are unfolded simultaneously and they allow of deviation which may or may not occur coin-
cidentally along the various dimensions.

The capacity of tones to group themselves
in the so-called diatonic manner is determined
by their intrinsic affinities. It was seen that
tones at the octave have a certain identity.
Now tones at the fifth bear similarity to one
another to such an extent that the musically
undiscriminating sometimes sing in fifths,
thinking that they are singing the same thing.
Musical theory, moreover, since the time of
the Greeks, bears witness to the fact that occidental musicians have always recognized the
fifth as embodying the highest degree of unity
or **consonance** possible in the combination of
two tones unless the two tones be related
by means of the octave identity. Stumpf

psychological experiments in which two pure tones at the interval of a fifth were often mistaken to be one tone, may also be cited. Many more illustrations of the peculiar unity of the fifth could be given but for the limit of space. It should be noted, however, that the oft-cited numerical ratio 2:3 of the vibrational frequencies by which tones at the fifth are generated, is not so much a proof of what is heard, as much as it is a verification.

There is not only an immediately recognizable simplicity in the relationship of the tones of a fifth, analogous to the simplicity of the right angle as compared with other angles, but there is also a direction in the relationship. The lower tone of the fifth is fundamental to the upper tone. This is demonstrated by the instability of the fourth, in which the two tones are inverted, so that the heavier or fundamental tone seems top-heavy appearing as it does in the higher or less dense pitch position.

It is possible to arrange the twelve available tones in a series so that their affinity to one another with respect to the unity of the fifth can be demonstrated, and in this affinity will be found a justification for diatonic scales and modes. Certain points relative to this series must be stressed in advance. It is not a historically accurate representation of how the modes were derived, but seeks rather to elucidate intrinsic relations which, directly intuited, may have guided composers in their choice. It must be understood, moreover, that this series is being constructed regardless of the exact octave position of a tone. Of the tones C and F, either one may be on top, and each may be in any of the eight possible octave ranges of the pitch continuum. The significant factor for the series is that F is fundamental to C.

Any tone may be taken as a starting point, for example, F. The series is circular, that is to say, comes back upon itself: thus, F-C-G-D-A-E-B-F#-C#-G#-D#-A#-E#, etc. For the present E# is identical with F; A# with B-flat, etc. For convenience, the tones should be imagined as arranged in a circle like the numbers of a clock. F and its counterpart E# will occupy the position of 12; C the position of 1; A#, the position of 11; B, the position of 6; etc.

If F is fundamental to C, and C is fundamental to G, then through C, G can be subordinated to F. The ear actually hears G come to rest on F, in the manner that a given element may be expected to rest upon something which is basic or fundamental to it.

It may be objected that F may be subordinated to D# (E-flat) through A# (B-flat), and then to G# (A-flat), and finally, through the intervention of nine tones in the series, may be subordinated to G, from the direction of D. It is obvious however, that a closer connection may be established through G. It still remains that F, so to speak, is more fundamental to G than G is to F. The same is true of the relation of D, A, and E, severally, to F. A difficulty arises with the diametrically opposed tone, B, which is as fundamental to F as F is to B, because it takes the same number of steps to subordinate F to B as to subordinate B to F.

The tones from F to B comprise a **diatonic scale.** Any group of seven tones which lie in an unbroken series along the circle will likewise be the same relationship, and must therefore comprise a diatonic scale in a different vicinity of the circle, or, as it is commonly said, in a different key. It is obvious that there are natural co-ordinates or natural boundaries to mark off the group of tones which comprise a scale. Tones diametrically opposite mark a difference point, because two tones in this position are the only ones which introduce an ambiguity with reference to the direction of the relation.

With F as a starting point, until B was introduced, all the tones tended to subordinate themselves directly to the first tone. If any of the tones on the right side of the circle are given with or prior to B and F, the means for subordinating the former to the latter will be provided. But B will always cast a doubt upon, and thus weaken, F. As a result, the interval F-B lacks equilibrium or center of gravity, technically known as a **fundamental.** Thus, the interval has a strong tendency to lean for support on the tones in its immediate vicinity. Within the given group of a semi-circle, these tones are C and E which are, moreover, the closest in the diatonic community whether the community is viewed in the abstract arrangement in the series of fifths, or in the concrete arrangement in the pitch continuum in which E is just below F and C just above B. Thus, B and F, by contracting or leaning upon the inner tones of the semi-circle, tend to hold them intact as an elastic binds a group of objects together.

C is the next highest to F in the hierarchy of tones arranged in a series of fifths from F as a starting point. Thus, C profits by F's inability to subordinate all the tones. C takes over, being next in the hierarchy.

The way in which the second tone of a semi-circle subordinates all the tones of the diatonic group, reflects in *minutia* the way in which composers ordinarily unify all the tones of a composition with respect to one central tone. Thus, not only a group of tones is taken as a recurrent pattern, but one tone within the group is emphasized above the others as a recurrent element. The tone thus stressed is called a **tonic**. After the tonic has been established, stress of another tone, with or without change of the diatonic group of tones, is felt obviously as a change of place.

The composer is not at all times obliged to use the intrinsic tonic (for example, C in the semi-circle under consideration). For sometimes ·he might desire the conflict of exalting the tone which is not intrinsically the principal tone, just as the poet may end a line with a word that is not, in the sense of meaning, the final word of a thought. Thus, a line pause may be slightly acknowledged in reading, but the voice is not dropped, so that there is comparatively little rest in this pause. Likewise, an intrinsic tonic may be recognized in its special quality as a certain point of rest and emphasis though the composer has not stopped dead upon it. What matters most is the composer's awareness of the conflict and thus of the intrinsic affinity of tones. But awareness of the affinity does not mean constant procedure *in accordance* with the intrinsic direction.

When a composer's tonic coincides with the intrinsic tonic, he is said to be using the **Major** mode. The use of the word major reflects the conviction of composers that this is the more unified arrangement of tones. The conviction is likewise reflected in the more frequent use of major in contrast to the other modes during more recent centuries.

When the tonic is decided, a scale is commonly represented in analysis by a series of tones rising gradually in pitch from the tonic to the octave above the tonic, for example, C-D-E-F-G-A-B-C. Any part of the concrete musical composition in which tones of the scale move in this gradual, simple pitch movement, as in the abstract (that is, mainly in whole and half steps), is said to move in **scale-wise motion**. It is curious that G and F which are nearest to C in the structural arrangement of the tones of the key in the series of fifths, are farthest from C in the reduction of the tones to a single octave range. Moreover, B and C, or F and E, which are almost the farthest apart in the circle, are closest in pitch. The ratios, however, are not completely reversed, because B and F, farthest apart on the circle, are not closest in pitch.

The use of modes other than major involves the choice of a less authoritative tonic. Thus, the **minor mode** takes as its tonic, or point of greater emphasis, the tone that stands in the relation of A to the key of C major—that is, the fifth tone down from the top (F) in its semi-circle. Its remoteness from the more final or fundamental tones is a measure of its lesser authority and consequent availability for moods in which affirmation is not the chief characteristic. Of the old **ecclesiastic modes** which some modern music revives, the **Lydian** would take F as its tonic (the characteristics of which have already been observed); the **Mixolydian, G**; the **Dorian, D**; and the **Phrygian, E**. It is significant, that the modes other than major have manifested a growing tendency to borrow from major mode ever since the greater complexity of music demanded a greater unity. Thus, the choice of modes other than major may have been determined in the period of Church polyphony, by the demands of a solemn text and a humility which regarded man presumptuous to assume the definiteness and finality of the major mode. Yet at certain points where definiteness and finality were required in *minutiae* for the sake of the form, namely, at cadences, it was customary for performers to interpolate (according to the practice known as musica ficta) the leading tone and major chord third (*tierce de picardie*) borrowed from the major. Unity was thus strengthened by showing, at certain prominent points, the subordination of the tones of a composition to more fundamental tones, with means eminently furnished by the major mode. This practice survives in the minor mode of later music where the borrowings are no longer improvised and are much more numerous. The **melodic tetrachord**, borrowed from the major, is almost inevitably used in approaching the minor tonic, so that the latter may have some of the authority of the major tonic. In Bach and Mozart, moreover, the *tierce de picardie* quite characteristically offers final major resolution to a work that has started in minor.

Just as Mozart was (perhaps only intuitively) aware of the tendency of the major tonic towards its subdominant, so Stravinsky today, reviving the ecclesiastic modes, senses their tendency towards the more authoritative major. He senses this tendency not as the ecclesiasts did, vague groping towards major, but as one who may retrospectively profit from a period of remarkable exploration of the potencies of this mode. The *Symphonie de Psaumes* commences with phrygian, Stravinsky's favorite among the older modes. It ends on a C major chord. Thus, E phrygian offers a rather bleak arrangement of the same tones with respect to C, however, places in relief the tones towards which the diatonic group tends. This tendency of E phrygian towards C is, moreover, felt throughout the first movement.

In the light of the circle of fifths, the primitive **pentatonic scale**, which is still encountered in folk music and many jazz melodies, is merely a shorter series of tones than the series which comprises a diatonic scale. Instead of moving seven tones along the circle, it stops at the fifth tone, thus: F-C-G-D-A. The same affinity of tones is provided, but there is no tritone F-B to mark the boundaries of the set of relations in a way that was found above to suggest the action of a rubber band. It is, therefore, easy to understand why there were so many pentatonic Gregorian melodies though the full diatonic scale seems to have been known; and why even when the diatonic scale was used, the extremity tones were admitted sparingly, so that the pentatonic basis sounds forth. The Church composers were intuitively confining themselves to the simpler elements of the diatonic scale and were avoiding the ambiguity of the diametrically opposite tones.

There have been numerous attempts to expand the barriers of diatonism by increased attention to the tones not directly a part of the basic pattern. This practice, which passes under the name of **chromaticism**, was observable around 1600, notably, in such composers as Gesualdo and Monteverdi. In the works of such later composers as the Scarlattis, the Bachs, Mozart and Haydn, this chromatic expansion was absorbed into a new diatonism rehabilitated by the increased possibilities of the major mode. This mode provided a higher degree of unity strong enough to control the more daring chromatic deviations. A more vigorous chromatic expansion has taken place since the middle of the 19th cent., as part of the romantic drive to break down all limitations. The increased attention to the deviation from the scale patterns has finally led to the acceptance of the deviation, paradoxically, as a norm. Thus, in Schönberg's system there is no longer a selection of tones, but all twelve tones constitute the so-called **duodecuple** scale. A tran-

sition is discernible in Debussy who is commonly said to have contributed a **whole-tone** scale which one may construct by taking every alternate key on the keyboard (black as well as white) or every alternate member of the above circle of fifths. It is purely a matter of terminology whether Debussy's predilection for movement in whole-tones is to be dignified with the rubric "scale" or not. Such works as the piano prelude, *Voiles*, in which there is only the briefest deviation from adherence to a single whole-tone scale, are, to be sure, exceptional. For the rest, there is merely a feeling of some diatonic basis, at least in the formulation of many of the chords. As in Wagner, there is frequent shift of the diatonic scale from one chord to the next. Also, there is even greater preference than in Wagner for chords which straddle diatonic scales (such as the opening chord of *Tristan*) and which thereby tend towards a whole-tone pattern.

The **twelve-tone scale** is, in a sense, a return to the concept of primitive scales as an abstract of all the available tones. It is a negation of the later European concept of the scale as a selection of tones. In more than one sense it is a negation, for twelve-tone music, while presumably encouraging the freedom of tones, distributes tones in such a way that they will avoid any accidental reference to the older concept of restriction to a diatonic scale. The twelve-tone system is more than a scale, it is a method of composition, and thus exceeds present boundaries. Twelve-tone music by its deliberate avoidance of diatonic principles, presumably sacrifices the possibilities of unity observed above in diatonic scales. Twelve-tone adherents, however, attempt to justify themselves by maintaining a genetic theory as to an acquired perception of unity in frequently associated tones. The intrinsic unity which is recognized as existing among certain tones by those who seek to revive diatonic principles today, is regarded as an illusion, and habit is substituted as a criterion of such unity. At other times the lack of this unity in the twelve-tone scale is admitted, but the unity of motive development is said to compensate for the lack (see TWELVE-TONE TECHNIQUE). See *Vergleichende Musikwissenschaft*, Curt Sachs, 1930; *The Harmonics of Aristoxenus*, H. S. Macran, 1902; *Greek Music and its relation to modern times*, J. F. Mountford in *Journal of Hellenic Studies*, vol. XL, 1920, p. 13; *Music in the Middle Ages*, Gustave Reese, 1940, chap. VI; *An Aristotelian Analysis of* *the elements, principles and causes of the art of music,* Herbert Spencer Schwartz, 1936; Problems of Harmony, Arnold Schönberg, *Modern Music,* May-June, 1934, vol. XI, no. 4, p. 167.   —A.V.B.

scale-wise motion. See scales and modes.

scale stone, stool. In sculpture, one of the pair of blocks upon which the model and the block stone are placed.

scandicus. See neumes.

SCANDINAVIAN ART in all its manifestations is singularly indigenous to the North. The virile intensity of Norwegian painting, for example, is the expression of man whose pulse beats as one with Norway's dramatically compelling nature; the note of mystic lyricism that transcends its formal plastic qualities is the communication of painter closely akin to the mood-variegated environment of scintillating septentrional light, of constraining boreal darkness. What is less generally understood, however, is that northern art both fine and applied has not been isolated from the notable historic periods and school isms of continental Europe but has followed these closely through cultural and commercial relations and electically shared and natively absorbed the familiar characteristics both good and bad. Furthermore, there is a third fundamental factor that must be primarily considered. That is that nowhere has the technology of the power age been more widely accepted and skillfully utilized than in Scandinavia. This, combined with the universal literacy, the far-reaching adult education programs and the pioneer advancement in economic reforms and social cooperation that has distinguished 20th cent. Scandinavia, has made for a highly progressive homogeneous society which is unique in its wide appreciation and developed achievement of art for the masses as evidenced in the dynamic art-in-industry movement, in the quality of public housing and the democratic state sponsorship and support of all creative talent.

Norse Art from Viking Age to Nineteenth Century. Though little is recorded of Norwegian history prior to 800 A.D., archeological studies made from graves and antiquities preserved from the Stone, Bronze, and Older Iron Age reveal that tools, weapons, ornaments, vessels, and utensils had already a beauty of form and a taste in ornamentation truly admirable. However, it was during the illustrious Viking Age, from the end of the 8th cent. to the middle of the 11th, that the foundations of Norwegian applied art were firmly laid. The Vikings had an intense interest in handicrafts and were pre-eminent in the decoration of their arms and domestic utensils. In that era the higher classes of Norway dwelt on country estates where men spent much of their time at metalwork, woodcarving, and the making of weapons while the women were devoted to needlework and the weaving of tapestries of colored wool as well as fine linens.

Unearthed in southern Norway in 1904, the 9th cent. *Oseberg* viking ship with its decoratively carved prow and contents is one revealing example of the technical ability, the artistic talent and the feeling for his material evidenced by the craftsman of the period. The University Collection of Antiquities in Oslo likewise testifies to the sensitive feeling these early Norwegians had for fashioning their every-day objects so that they were functionally and aesthetically satisfying. Further illustrating the ancient culture of the country is the *Norsk Folkemuseum* in the outskirts of Oslo (here, for example, is *Raulandsstuen,* the oldest dwelling house in the country, a chieftain's hall from about 1200) and the outdoor museum, *Maihaugen,* at Lillehammer, where have been re-erected, still housing their hand-fashioned interior furnishings, all types of early dwellings from many parts of Norway, humble crofters' huts and elaborate ancestral estates alike.

Moreover, in most towns and rural districts throughout Norway are similar museums, usually the open-air type where one can study the past cultural development of regional Norway. The period dwellings which have been thus reestablished from their original site to a similar one in the outdoor setting of natural landscape which is the museum grounds, make possible a first-hand study of art expression from the Viking era through the Middle Ages and so up to recent times. The aged buildings are characteristically of timber and it is apparent that the owner often carved the portal even as he did the furniture, wall cupboards and other fittings or, frequently, by floral brushwork, *rosemaling,* adorned walls, ceilings, furnishings, and utensils such as the wooden bowls and drinking vessels which he had so beautifully shaped. There is likewise wide evidence of the weaving of decorative textiles which found such fertile origin in the Middle Ages. Outstanding are the figured tapestries of wool in rich earth colors, characteristic of Eastern Norway valleys and the *Aaklae* weaving (wall hangings) of the West Coast with colors heraldic and patterns based on the check. Embroidery is conspicuous as a popular textile art from the 12th cent. on. It will be further noted that silversmithing in the form of bridal crowns, belts, buckles, brooches of gothic influence, and exquisite filagree jewelry romanesque in character also prospered. It is of great significance to present-day creative Norway that this many-sided inspirational material is not only to be found in the generous museum collections throughout the land but that almost every dwelling place over the countryside has at least some pieces which have come down from these rich ages past, used in the family generation upon generation.

Divided into various sections by mountains and valleys with nature favoring each section in a different way, Norwegian applied arf became regional in character. This regional development of folk handicraft reached its height from 1750 to 1850. For example, around Stavanger, where there was much wool, weaving was paramount while in the forested Budbrandsdal and Telemark the art of woodcarving, with the baroque vine serving as leading motif, reached masterly heights. This popular art expression was supplemented, at the same time, by the guild-directed crafts of the towns which flourished not only in the Middle Ages (when the church took the lead in decorative art, e.g., carved chairs) but through the baroque, rococo and classic periods, the most important production being the gold and silversmiths' art. Conspicuous also in the Norwegian art industry of the 17th and 18th cents. were the richly decorated stoves which, made by the iron works, were notable for the linear beauty expressed in their relief. The cabinet-maker's art was likewise well established. In the latter 18th cent. a distinguished faience also flourished for a short period. Furthermore, in 1744 an eminent glass works was founded whose artistic traditions have continued into the current modern production. In close touch with the evolution of style in Europe proper, a national Norwegian decorative art developed along the lines indicated in high degree of achievement until 19th cent. industrialism destroyed the age-old organic pattern of native Norse creativity and temporarily gave rise to an era of confusion and poor taste.

Closely related to the development in Norway was that of the Swedish and Danish applied arts The arrowheads and implements of the Bone Age, monumental graves, dolmens and cists of the Neolithic Age, rock engravings of the Stone Age, geometric ornaments in the Bronze Age and the characteristic Norse interlaced animal forms introduced in the Iron Age proclaim Sweden's 8000 years of prolific creativity. Already by the 7th cent. ornamental style was distinctive in the magnificent compositional use of the awesome animal forms as evidenced, for example, in a chieftain's helmet of iron and guilded bronze found in one of the Uppland mountains. The elegance of this style and great skill of craftsmanship reached unsurpassed heights with the Viking Age. Along with the arms, weapons and ornaments of exquisite conception and workmanship that the vast mounds about the Swedish countryside reveal are the rune stones, these standing above the ground, impressive and monumental, their inscriptions and highly simplified but virile decorative features incised to the memory of martial feats and peaceful pursuits alike. Again the interlaced animal forms enclosing motives of many kinds, which have since come to the symbolic of the Viking epoch, are typically employed.

With the advent of Christianity which was more or less established in Sweden by 1000 A.D., foreign influences became more and more apparent though the traditions of national art were often incidentally taken into the new forms of Christendom. Thus the adornment of the first churches in metal-work and textiles was still of Viking Age character and this transmission continued far into the Middle Ages. Medieval art in Sweden was, in fact, largely ecclesiastical but even as this bore characteristics of the Swedish popular tradition so, in turn, did the religious production inspire and influence the home creativity which persisted in its evolution of a distinctive people's art. This development of a native tradition continued, in fact, until the Industrial Revolution having survived meanwhile the Renaissance period when art entered into the service of the Swedish lords who imported their artists and craftsmen (German and Flemish ones in particular) as they did also through the 17th cent., the period of Sweden's wide political ascendency, and the brilliant French-inspired 18th which brought first a strong rococo influence, then the Louis XVI styles (in its Swedish form called Gustavian) and later the neo-classic. *Nordiska Museet* (1872), the central institute of Swedish cultural history, and its open-air section, Skansen, also founded (1891) by

Dr. Arthur Hazelius, originator of the open-air type of museum) as well as some 400 regional museums over Sweden reveal how the popular art took unto itself forms and colors from the style epochs of the higher classes, absorbed and repeated these in original variations through generations, as, the animal motifs of the Viking period, the Romanic scroll, the late Renaissance baluster and interlaced ornament. Furthermore, these variations of the same national or international motive or technique had independent modifications in one Swedish province from another and the local traditions, particularly in the textile art, became strong and independent in their own right. To be noted also is the judicious use of native materials: wood in the form-expressive and decorative utensils, drinking vessels, chests and furniture fixtures such as the cupboards, beds and benches which were often built to the walls; iron in the ornamental locks, hinges and chest bindings, in vanes and crosses; linen for textiles, and wool for the woven hangings and covers used on festive occasions. Painted wall-hangings sometimes supplemented the latter. Usually in the form of horizontal borders these were highly decorative in character with natively conceived, beautifully patterned biblical scenes as well as portrayals of daily life. The 18th and 19th cents. found local masters in the southern provinces of Smaland, Halland and Dalarna particularly adept at this art.

The cognate relationship of Denmark's development in the Scandinavian pattern is best evidenced in the Danish Collection of The National Museum in Copenhagen which includes also the Danish Folk Museum and the Open-Air Museum in Lyngby. This vivid revelation of the cultural unfoldment in Denmark through the ages is further illustrated in the art and craftsmanship of the collections in *Det National Historiske Museum Paa Frederiksborg,* a notable castle adapted as a public museum of Danish natural history. The Old Town in Aarhus, Jutland, is a unique departure in the famed Scandinavian outdoor museum technique in that here, in a town scientifically re-erected, is reproduced the background of Danish urban life before the coming of industrialization. The large burgomaster's house, for example, with rooms in the many different styles developed during its years of occupancy reflects Denmark's close cultural contact with greater Europe. From a room Renaissance in character, to others rococo and baroque, one meets

finally the Empire and early Victorian influence. More formally Copenhagen's *Kunstindustrimuseet,* typical of Scandinavia's important Museums of Applied Arts, displays the whole development of Danish applied art.

Painting in Norway. When in 1814 Norway became a more politically independent state by its separation from Denmark, artistic life had a blossoming and Norwegian painting its inception. The first movement was a vigorous national one with J. C. Dahl (1788-1847) masterfully leading the way in Norwegian landscape composition monumentally conceived while A. Tidemand (1814-1879) and Hans Gude (1825-1903) depicted the popular life amid the imposing Norwegian nature. It was to Düsseldorf that these painters and their followers travelled to study and work. In the 70's, however, Munich became the center of Norway's painters and, the challenge of vigorous new forces being recognized in French painting, romanticism here gave way to naturalism. Stimulated thereby, a group of gifted artists returned and solidly established painting in their native Norway. Notable among these was Christian Krohg (1852-1925), a key figure in the new concern in social questions, a strong colorist and figure painter. Another colorist, eminent for her interior studies with their sensitive handling of light, was Harriet Backer (1845-1932). It was, however, with Erik Werenskiold (1855-   ) that art in Norway became autonomous and organized (about 1880). Extraordinary interpreter of the Norwegian national character, Werenskiolds' gifts are uniquely manifest in the black and white illustrations for the Norwegian Fairytales and the Sagas of the Norse Kings by Snorre Sturlason, Norway's two national literary monuments. His portraits, furthermore, are among the outstanding Norwegian paintings. Another member of this galaxy and further exponent of a national revival was Gerhard Munthe (1849-1928) an excellent landscape painter but of greatest importance for his lasting influence on modern Norwegian applied art through his highly decorative compositions for which he used old Norse saga and tale as source material. Following upon the realism of the eighties was coming in fact a brief period of neo-romanticism. Its import for later developments lay in the experimented treatment of light in landscape. On the one hand were the lyricists Halfdan Egedius (1877-1899) with idyllic canvases of vibrating delicacy and Harald Sohlberg (1869-   ) whose landscapes are individualized by an enamel-like glow. The painting of Thorvald Erichsen (1869-   ) and Oluf Wold-Torne (1867-1919) on the other hand, reach eventually beyond their own group of the 90's who received technical training under Zahrtmann in Denmark and cultural expansion in Italy, and develop an advanced sense of color and form through the influence of Cezanne. While Torne came to be identified more with Norway's national movement in the decorative arts, Erichsen is celebrated for his final freeing of Norwegian art from narrative concern to an emphasis on formal design considerations, leading the way thereby to general cognizance of the great creative genius Edvard Munch (1863-1944).

Pioneer Expressionist, Munch's influence has been internationally revolutionary, his famous controversial exhibition in Berlin in 1892 causing the schism of *Berliner Künstlerverein* which led to the foundations of the *Berliner Sezession*. Munch's dynamic art likewise marks a radical change of direction in Norwegian painting with emphasis no longer on realism and illusionism but powerfully expressed individual interpretation. At once lyrical and violent, Munch has portrayed with most sentient perspicacity the profoundness of the modern psyche. His paintings are impressive in their masterly synthesis of coloristic construction, vigorous pattern and spirited intensity of execution. In his murals for the auditorium of the University of Oslo is evident also his ability to most sensitively express the Northern feeling tone and character. In the medium of graphic arts, Munch has been further prolific. Among the painters in whose work the influence of Munch began to be discernible were Ludvig Karsten (1876-1926), of outstanding coloristic talent, and Henrik Lund (1879-1935), noted for his portrait compositions and, like Karsten, for marked technical affluency. A. C. Svarstad (1869-   ) and Nicolay Astrup (1880-1928) are looked to as able colorist interpreters of urban and West Norway respectively. Arne Kavli, Bernhard Folkestad, Sören Onsager, and Torstein Torsteinson are other prominent painters of the generation characterized by a deep feeling for and a distinctive handling of color.

A galaxy of contemporary Norwegian painters has been coming to international attention in recent years. Schooled in the 1910's under Henri Matisse in Paris, they received stimulus towards simplification in style and constructive composition which considerations they later saliently incorporated into their endeavors to transcribe the pictorial possibilities of the most intimate contact with Norwegian nature. Under the leadership of Henrik Sörensen (1882-   ) they have developed a unique sense of the monumental which has taken form in huge mural decorations painted al fresco in the public buildings of Norway. Pioneers in this field are Axel Revold (1887-   ), Per Krogh (1889-   ), and Alf Rolfsen (1895-   ). Typical frescos are the ones in the Bergen Stock Exchange by Revold, those in the Oslo Navigation College by Krogh, Rolfsen's commissions for the Artisan's Auditorium and the Oslo Crematorium, and Sörensen's work in the Cathedral of Linköping, Sweden. These painters were engaged in mural decoration of Oslo's new Town Hall at the time of Norway's entry into World War II, Sörensen's fresco being the largest in Norway to date, twelve meters high and twenty-four wide. Furthermore the talents of these prominent artists had been earlier recruited in the execution of decorations for the 1937--built liner Oslofjord. Closely associated with this group is Hugo Lous Mohr, Jean Heiberg, Rudolf Thygesen, and Per Deberitz. A still younger generation, whose initial training at the State's Art Academy in Oslo (where Revold and Heiberg are professors) has been supplemented with study in Paris, have experimented in turn with the *Neue Sachlichkeit* (q.v.), cubistic abstraction and social studies. Among those who have already distinguished themselves nationally with original talents are Henrik Finne, Aage Storstein, Willi Midelfart, and Reidar Aulie. Characteristic tendencies are the use of richer color towards striking pattern and bold decorative values and a more simplified handling of form and color in landscape organization.

Supplementing the larger museums are *Kunstforeninger* in fifteen Norwegian towns which arrange excellent circulating exhibits of contemporary art, changing their local displays every two weeks. In the State's annual art exhibition held in Oslo since 1883 and open to the whole nation for participation, the new talent discovered in the fields of painting, sculpture and the graphic arts is awarded by fellowship to the State's Art Academy. Norway's recognized artists are also financially assisted by an appanage from the State treasury appropriated by the *Storting* (since 1863) on recommendation of the Department of Education. Furthermore, since 1888 the Norwegian government has recognized a committee elected by painters and sculptors consisting of seven members (at least four painters and two sculptors) as an administrative committee for state exhibitions of art and as adviser to the government in questions of art. All commissions for the decoration of public buildings and works are awarded on the basis of national open competitions sponsored by the State. The leading artists are also widely engaged on such democratic projects as illustrating the Norse fairy tales and public school readers, as in the new 1939 editions of these books, in an effort to bring the nation's best art into the widest application possible.

Sculpture in Norway. Following the Viking period of high plastic attainment in wood, the sculptural creativity evidenced in the richly carved Romanesque timber churches and the restrained but sensitively expressive crucifixes, heads and masks of 13th cent. Norwegian Gothic (notably in Trondheim Cathedral), sculpture in Norway fell into almost total eclipse until the 20th cent. brought conditions more favorable for nourishing this art. The name of Stephan Sinding (1846-1923) marks the first turn from the unsuccesses of a borrowed and artificial 19th cent. classicism to a new forthright realism. It is in Gustav Vigeland (1869-1943), however, that Norway has at last realized a sculptor with monumental gifts. Endowed with tremendous imaginative faculty and a productive energy extraordinary, Vigeland is a towering individualist whose idea-rich, form-significant sculpture is a thing apart from school or era. In an intense personal way he expresses the universal. Through those of his many compositions called simply "Man and Woman" he communicates with impassioned power the whole gamut of basal human emotion. From 1905 on the sculptor was largely absorbed in the unique "Fountain of Vigeland", a mighty epoch of life he was creating in Frogner Park, Oslo. As an integral part of his impressive architectural lay-out rise some one hundred granite groups, sixty bronze figures and sixty reliefs centering about a dominant sculptured monolith seventeen meters high symbolizing humanity struggling for freedom. In tribute to Vigeland's genius, he continuously received State support while the municipality of Oslo presented a palatial studio to the artist in 1919 which will ultimately become the Vigeland Museum.

Wilhelm Rasmussen (1879-   ) is a pupil of Vigeland who has worked with him in the execution of works for the Cathedral of Trondheim. As Professor of Sculpture at the State Academy of Art, Rasmussen has in turn had an influence on the development of two of the most talented younger sculptors, Dyre Vaa (1903-   ) and Stinius Frederickson (1902-   ). The latter have been contributing constructively to recent public sculptural works as are also a new gifted generation among whom Bast, Grimdalen, Janson, Lie and Schiöll are particularly active.

Painting in Denmark. While color gives to Norwegian painting its greatest distinction and a marked faculty for decorative synthesis characterizes Sweden's art, it is the developed sense of form that is the highest achievement of the artist Dane. Danish painting is fundamentally preoccupied with reality rather than the visionary; it is unassuming and of sterling simplicity. It is marked not by passion but integrity, by a moderation indigenous to so temperate a land. It was not, however, until the 19th cent. that a native Danish painting as such began to take root within the country itself in some independence of the archetypes set up by continental Europe which to date Danish expression had been weakly mirroring.

It was C. W. Eckersberg (1783-1853) who established the first important direction in Danish painting. Though he had early contact with the pseudo-classicism of the time through study in Paris under David and in Rome, Eckersberg was personally impelled by an entirely different drive, to paint with objective truth what he saw with his own eyes: the Dane, the Danish countryside, the Danish sea. As professor at the Academy of Art he established a school whose influence was wide, the emphasis being on truthfulness of observation and painting what lay close at hand and was thus close in meaning to the artist. Portraits and Copenhagen streets and houses particularly served as subject matter. One of Eckersberg's pupils, Christen Köbke (1810-1848) became distinguished as an outstanding observer of color affected by light and atmosphere. A master of color values, his open-air paintings, among Denmark's finest, led a new way. By the latter 30's, on the other hand, Eckersberg's followers were experimenting in Rome and once more there was a turn in direction. The painter in this group who, nevertheless, carried Danish painting far beyond the confines of Eckersberg's naturalism, Wilhelm Marstrand (1810-1873), stands as one of Denmark's most prodigious artists. His spontaneous painting of the Italian people developed in him a special feeling for the plastic possibilities of the human form and this he handled with a freshness that was notable. His Danish genre, historical and religious paintings were a marked departure from the old formalism in the vital relationship to real life with which they were conceived and the new directness and breadth of style with which they were treated. The note of humor and keen character interpretation which Marstrand also handled with masterly effectiveness is superbly exemplified in his drawings illustrating Holberg's comedies.

The new freedom which Marstrand's departures encouraged gave rise to two groups among the Danish painters in the middle 19th cent. On the one hand were those propagating the wide adoption of European influence, on the other, those advocating a national art. Among the more prominent followers of the former ideology the name of Carl Bloch (1834-1890) rose to temporary heights. His pictorial power, compositional merit and bold use of color were momentarily beneficial until exaggerations of these qualities made for decline in quality. The nationalists, on the other hand, were stimulated in their goal by the 1844 ultimatum of the art-historian Höyen who fervently urged a national art expressive of Scandinavia. A lack of technical adeptness was generally limiting in this group but the sum contribution of the following individuals was not without importance: Sonne expressively captured the moods of the Danish nature, particularly the Northern summer night; Dalsgaard in his interior genre paintings brought attention to the actual folk life as material for the artist as did in a less way Exner and Vermehren. Meanwhile, four painters discovered the Danish landscape and their deep feeling for the spirit of this nature Lunbye expressed with a rhythmic lyricism, Peter Skovgaard with penetration and plastically handled form, Kyhn and Rump with a special sensitivity to mood interpretation.

In the 1880's a new generation came forward in Danish painting who displayed to advantage the benefits of formal training. This they received in Paris, the center which now drew them because of the growing challenge of the realists and impressionists. P. S. Kröyer (1851-1909) became the dynamic center of the new interest in light and experimented widely with atmosphere primarily in relation to its pictorial effect. With Viggo Johansen (1851) impressionism was completely launched and he brought most successfully into his intimate Danish interior studies

what he had learned in the open air concerning the reaction of light upon color. It was Kristian Zahrtmann (1843-1917) who had the added faculty for color imagination and in spite of the objective analysis of color which was engaging most artists of the time he struck forward with a subjective color emphasis that fostered not only wider acceptance of color use but encouraged individuality. His school had a constructive influence on not only Danish but Norwegian proselytes. In direct contrast to Zahrtmann's brilliant color palette, Vilhelm Hammershöi (1864-1916) held to a greyed scale of rare subtlety and his sensitively handled interiors have a restraint unequalled in ascetic and refined distinctiveness.

A movement in counter tendency to naturalism began to be felt in Denmark by 1890. Now there was a going back to the great art of the past, a seeking out of whatever period or country could provide the fundamental truths that would restore to art its ancient impressiveness. Nowhere was this new direction better realized than in the monumental frescoes of Joakim Skovgaard (1856-   ) for Viborg Cathedral (1900-1906) in which from four to five hundred figures cover an area of some sixteen thousand square feet. This notable architectonic work is characterized by an influence of Greek and Italian archaism individualized by gifted artist strongly grounded in Danish tradition and genuinely inspired by the Grundtvig philosophy. Niels Skovgaard (1858-   ) shares the decorative talents of his brother.

The search for style was actively pursued under the leadership of Johan Rohde, the Slott-Möllers were also enthusiasts. Nevertheless, it was a forceful individualist who came to the fore in his own right at this time who has been of greatest significance to recent developments in Danish art. J. F. Willumsen (1863-   ), versatile in talent, independent, a bold experimenter, has been a powerful freeing force for the younger artists of modern Denmark from the tyranny of tradition and reactionary public. Furthermore, his noteworthy command of plastic form has been a particularly beneficial influence. Something of Willumsen's pantheistic symbolism is apparent in the pictorial compositions of Ejnar Nielsen (1872-   ), another individualist who occasionally attains the monumental by way of his classic drawing. On the other hand, in this same generation a group of provincial painters tended towards a new naturalism. In their painting there is a freshness and vigor as forthright as the Danish earth to which they are stating their kinship. L. A. Ring (1854-1933) is Sjaelland's master representative while the island of Fyn is ably served among other pupils of Zahrtmann by Peter Hansen (1868-1928) and their leader Fritz Syberg (1862-).

With strong impulses from France, Expressionism was introduced into Denmark between 1905 to 1907, the experimental period culminating in the latter war years. Greater color freedom, simplification in style and concern with structural composition became discernible along two major lines; a highly abstract-decorative figure approach and an abstract-decorative landscape painting. In line with the former direction, Harald Giersing (1881-1927), Edward Weie (1879-), William Scharff (1886-) and Vilhelm Lundström (1893-) were significant pioneers in their bold handling of the new formal problems. These a still younger generation have resolved further towards meeting the special monumental decoration in connection with architecture; Kraesten Iversen (1886-), Jais Nielsen (1885-), Harald Hansen (1890-), Mogens Lorentzen (1892-) and Hjalmer Kragh Pedersen (1883-). Less radical in their departure are those expressionists who followed the second direction, taking their lead in landscape motif: Sigurd Swane (1879-), close in feeling to the Fyn painters, Olaf Naur (1889-), and Olof Höst (1884-) who has developed the psychological possibilities of color in his efforts to transcribe the mysticism of nature.

Parallel with expressionism in painting the movement has most actively penetrated the field of graphic illustration. Particularly as concerns newspaper illustration, the satirical esp., there has been in latter years a distinguished handling of the formal problem by such prominent graphic artists as Valdemar Anderson, Carl Jensen and Hans Bendix. Since Denmark's involvement in World War II and the consequent cutting of news material the Danish press has given over more and more of its copy to illustrations by the country's leading contemporary artists and has developed a new method of color lithography suitable for press printing which makes possible the mass reproduction of color of unusual quality.

Sculpture in Denmark. In the period of the New-Classicism Denmark contributed its sculptor of greatest stature and artist of widest influence, Bertel Thorvaldsen (1770-1844).

At the Danish Academy, studying under Abilgaard (1743-1809), Thorvaldsen was imbued from early youth with an appreciation of the antique and thus upon arriving in Rome in 1797, just as the new classicism had triumphed over the rococo, conditions were perfect for his development. He stayed to work in Rome throughout his lifetime and became the acknowledged apostle of the antique not alone for his sculptural gifts but because his very temperament, simple, beautific, was the nearest reincarnation of the actual human spirit of antiquity that the period produced. The notable Thorvaldsen Museum, completed in Copenhagen in 1848, contains several thousand figures from his hand including the figures, busts and reliefs of the enormous production which he handled in one uniform classic style and spirit whether his subject was The Life of the Gods or Bible and Christian Allegory. Nevertheless, because Thorvaldsen also understood the importance of study of nature and, accordingly, was not restricted solely by analysis of the antique, there was a freshness in his creations, which his genius endowed with a marked linear harmony, a most sensitively felt balance and quiet restraint which gave to his handling of the human figure quality epochal in example.

H. V. Bissen (1798-1868), a pupil of Thorvaldsen, became Denmark's leading sculptor following the death of the master. Using, at first, male figures from Greek mythology that gave opportunity for more vigorous and dramatic treatment than his teacher's, he later gave his energies over to Denmark's oncoming national movement in art. To this end, his choosing of the common Danish soldier rather than a classic ideal as sculptural motif to be handled in his *Landsoldat,* a monument commemorating the Danish victory at Fredericia, was a radical departure and marked the severing from tradition. It was under Bissen's guidance that the next generation of sculptors worked and thereby it was his influence and indirectly that of Thorvaldsen that was the determining one until the present century. There has been no one strong movement since though there have been such able individuals as Ludvig Brandstrup (1861-), Carl Mortensen (1861-), Carl Bonnesen (1868-), and Anders Bundgaard (1864-) who were seriously concerned with the formal plastic problem through their main lead, naturalism. The painter J. F. Willumsen experimented briefly towards the truly monumental handling of sculptural form and in this Niels Skovgaard (1858-) was particularly successful from the time of his Magnus Stone which, with its figures of primitive vigor growing out in bold relief from the great rough slab of granite, was erected (1899) on Lyrskov Heath. However, it is the name of Kai Nielsen (1882-1925) that has held the widest attention in recent times. He is decidedly independent in his original handling of the female and child figure. At times there is, in fact, a kind of jocund informality in his style, even a sensual earthiness of conception, yet with an almost primal feeling for the plastic, his effective interplay of forms within a well-organized unit is surely handled. In the same generation, Gerhard Henning (1880) has been closest to Kai Nielsen in approach, while Utzon Frank (1888) on the other hand, with a highly decorative figure style in bronze, works according to early Renaissance sculptural formula. Jean Gauguin (1881-), Jais Nielsen (1885-) and Axel Salto (1889-) are able artists who find the medium of ceramic sculpture uniquely expressive for their talents.

Statens Museum For Kunst in Copenhagen contains the most extensive collections of Danish painting and sculpture, including contemporary works, while the provincial towns have their own galleries. Most notable of the latter is the highly modern museum in the small town of Faaborg on the island of Funen devoted entirely to representative twentieth century works.

Attracting international attention has been Copenhagen's *Kunst For Varer*, Art For Goods, a voluntary organization acting through its attractive gallery in the heart of Copenhagen. Here the working or tradesman can obtain art of the highest aesthetic quality in exchange for his services or goods. In order to insure the standard, artist membership is confined to those whose work has been shown for at least five years in recognized exhibitions. This unique barter arrangement assists not only the artist in providing his material needs but makes possible the most democratic ownership of the outstanding artists' works. Thus is extended the appreciation of contemporary art among the general population according to the educational and social ideal of the organization.

Painting in Sweden. In contrast to Norway and Denmark where the fine arts had to initially struggle for existence and final recognition in their own right, from the time of the Renaissance a culturally influential nobility introduced them eclectically into Sweden

via imported artists and subsequently fostered the thereby stimulated native talent. True, in the Romanesque and Gothic periods mural painting in churches of central and southern Sweden was common but it was not until the spirited architectural program of the Vasa kings during the Renaissance, when German and Flemish artists were brought into Sweden to decorate the newly built fortified castles, that painting gained formal recognition. With the Thirty Years' War and Sweden's gain to political eminence and wealth as one of the Great Powers, a great cultural expansion was inaugurated in the 17th cent. Again it was primarily the decoration of palace and mansion that brought the foreign painter and sculptor to Sweden but portrait painting also flourished. From France came Bourdon and Signac, Beck from Holland and Cooper from England but it was the German artist David Kloker (1628-1698) who remained in Sweden long enough to exert a wide influence and train a younger generation. Raised to Swedish peerage as von Ehrenstrahl, he is loosely categorized as the father of Swedish painting. The principal monuments to his achievement are his baroque ceiling paintings in the House of Nobles in Stockholm and a collection of historical portraits.

The 18th cent. resolved into the most notable era in Swedish art annals. The influence from France was dominant. Among the determining factors was the building and decorating of the Royal Palace in Stockholm which involved the importing of an influential assemblage of French artists and craftsmen. The school of design set up in the palace for the training of Swedish youth by the visiting French artists was the beginning of the Swedish Academy of Art. Furthermore the Parliament itself began to encourage a native Swedish art largely for the economy of avoiding importation. Young Swedish artists were materially encouraged by Sweden's ambassador to France, the art patron Carl Gustaf Tessin, who, in addition, played a powerful role in his acquisition of European art collections now in the National Museum. Meanwhile Gustav Lundberg (1695-1786) became recognized in Paris for his pastel portrait painting in the current French rococo style, Nicolas Lafrensen's (1737-1807) gouache paintings were long acclaimed, and Alexander Roslin (1718-1793), whose center was also Paris, became internationally accepted. It was Carl Gustav Pilo (1711-1793), however, director first at the Copenhagen and later at the Stockholm Academy of Art, via studies in Germany and Italy, who sounded the keynote of 18th cent. Swedish painting at home with his Coronation of Gustavus III. Pilo evidenced together with Elias Martin (1739-1818), a landscape painter in the English manner, a more distinctly Swedish expression than had been known heretofore, particularly through their color force. Actually it was during the reign of Gustav III (1771-1792) that 18th cent. Sweden reached its illustrious cultural heights. The munificent patronage of this monarch was based on an extraordinary personal interest in the arts, an understanding which had been encouraged by Tessin. "The Gustavian Period", accordingly, not only reflected the king's close contact with the prevailing European movements—the rococo had been superseded by the Louis XVI style (the Gustavian), and this, in turn, was succeeded by the Neo-Classic,—but Gustav III also encouraged any national manifestations among his young Swedish artists. In fact, art now flourished not alone in the royal domain but along with Europe's whole romantic movement, penetrated the very fastness of the entire country, enriched and in turn became diffused with the traditional.

Sweden of the 19th cent., on the other hand, more straitened economically and politically, let the arts wane grievously. A few painters surveyed the classic and romantic trends in Italy, Düsseldorf attracted another handful, Munich, in turn, some adherents. Generally, however, Swedish art was both isolated and dilettantishly static. Georg von Rosen (1843-1923), however, stands out in the quality of such historical compositions as King Erik XIV and Karin Månsdotter, and exerts lasting influence through the distinctive power of his portraits. Johan Höckert (1826-1866) painter of Swedish history and rural popular life brought color handling to new heights and is immortalized by one of Sweden's most notable paintings, The Palace Fire. Leading exponent of Old Norse in the national art efforts of the 60's, August Malmström expressed a quality essentially Scandinavian in his pictorial characterizations of the ancient sagas. Also bearing a national cast was the intimate realism of the Swedish landscape painting of Edward Bergh and Gustaf Rydberg. With the seventies, however, the younger Swedish painters journeyed en masse to Paris for a radically fresh reorientation. Alfred Wahlberg (1834-1906), who became an active representative of the Barbizon school (q.v.), had a wide initial influence and one finds for the first time the seeking to express the spiritual mood of landscape, *stämning*, to this day the most compelling characteristic of Scandinavian painting. By 1885 the new Paris group of Swedish painters, self-termed, "The Opponents" had revolted against the formalistic and stagnant policies of the Stockholm Academy and formed an independent body, *Konstnärsforbundet*, Association of Artists which for three decades played a decisive role in Swedish art. Because of their determined struggle for reform the State Art instruction as well as the National Museum were brought up to date and public opinion vitalized.

Initial leader of the new group of independents was Ernst Josephson (1851-1906), a strong colorist whose boldly approached painting generated as a liberating force for a generation to come. His celebrated *Strömkarien* (The Water Sprite) combines uniquely a northern subjective lyricism with the Manet-influenced realism he employed. Less cosmopolitan, however, were the eminent members of *Konstnärsförbundet* who, upon return from their studies in France, adapted the open-air approach and impressionist technique in a fresh and newly eager interpretation of their native Sweden. This eager contact with perspicacious observation of the intimate home scene soon brought forth a nationally Swedish art with such devoted representatives as Anders Zorn, Carl Larsson, Karl Nordström, Nils Kreuger, Carl Wilhelmsson, and Georg Pauli. Because of the essential Swedishness of his conception of the home scene, Carl Larsson (1853-1919) became the most popular national representative of his day. Basically an illustrator, there is a calligraphic quality in the water color studies of his own genial home life and glowing interiors that served as his favorite material. On the other hand, Larsson achieved something of the monumental in his depictions of Swedish history, notably his frescoes in the national museum. His joyous, humor-rich, and intimate characterizations have at once a captivating liveliness and warmth together with a handling of distinctiveness and quality unique for such informal material. He further brought the mural into school and public building, opening the way for Sweden's oncoming emphasis of art in every-day life. Pauli (1855) also produced al fresco, experimenting widely for a valid mural style and ultimately adhering to cubistic theory as evidenced in his 1913 staircase paintings in the New Elementary School in his native Jönköping. Carl Wilhelmsson (1866-1928) further demonstrated the public mural form in the decorative Stockholm Post Office Harbor-Motif. It was, however, through his salient characterizations of the Swedish west coast people in brilliant color and light effects that Wilhelmsson's deep integrity as an artist came notably to the fore. Sharing his sensitive recognition of Swedish nature were three key men in *Konstnärsförbundet* whose interpretation was at once national and richly personal. Having in common the atmospheric technique of their time and a rare feeling for expressiveness of mood in landscape, Karl Nordström (1855-1922) painted with bold intensity the northern sombreness, Nils Kreuger (1858-1930) transferred the added lyricism of wide horizon with classically handled pasture animal while Eugene Jansson (1862-1915) specialized in the nocturnal effects of Stockholm mirrored in the night waters within the city.

The capturing of the pensive mood of Northern summer night has likewise been treated with distinguished insight by Prince Eugen, whose mysticism of tone is supported by stately compositional handling. His contributions to Swedish landscape painting have resolved further into an impressive fresco type such as those for the Stockholm Town Hall. Greatest of all Swedish painters of wild animal life in relationship to this poetically understood nature, on the other hand, Bruno Lijefors (1860-) synthesizes an objective naturalist's observation with a distinctively Swedish feeling for nature and artist's discernment.

The artist who, however, among this advancing assemblage of "Opponents" received world-wide attention was Anders Zorn (1860-1920). A virtuoso and cosmopolitan in his portraits, a spirited painter notably facile in translating to canvas the phenomena of air tones, light values particularly as affecting the nude female form, the versatile Zorn was nevertheless genuinely Swedish when employing motifs from the life of his native Dalarna. Famed as an etcher, his interest in movement and the fleeting moment was brilliantly, warmly captured in the copper plate.

Around 1910 the national impression of *Konstnärsförbundet* began to be superseded by a new Swedish art pioneered by a young generation who, though their earliest studies had been at the School of the Artists' Association, developed along strikingly individual lines after the quickening experience of study under Matisse in Paris. While giving greater emphasis to formal plastic values, their work became characterized by a decorative power with color used in a bold subjective manner. Among these with color used in a bold subjective manner. Among these expressionists Nils Dardel, Leander Engström, Arvid Fougstedt, Isaac Grünewald, Einar Jolin, Carl Kylberg, Arthur C:son Percy, Gösta Sandels and Birger Simonsson have had wide influence in establishing new directions. Meanwhile, the generation successive of World War I had been more confined to the homeland, attacked the Matisse group for an overformalism, and stressed instead a return to nature and an unconventional primitive outlook. Victor Axelsson, Gideon Börje, Sven Erixon, Alf Munthe, Axel Nilsson, William Nording, Torsten Palm and Fritjof Schüldt represent this tendency with Hilding Linnquist (1891-) esp. making a continued signal contribution to modern Swedish art, not alone through his decoratively patterned paintings similar in spirit to the Swedish folk song but in addition by his more recent murals and weaving decorations for the Stockholm City Library. Concerned rather with intellectualized pure form is Otte Sköld while among the experimenters in current painting frontiers are the celebrated critics Gösta Adrian-Nelsson and Otto Carlsund. Among the outstanding schools of the Swedish provinces, on the other hand, is that of Scania with such distinguished painters of the local scene as Svant Bergh, Emil Johanson Thor, and Johan Johansson. Halland's group of young painters, *Halmstadgruppen,* have been developing their expression and technique along surrealist lines with Axel Olson, Stellan Mörner, Sven Jonson, Erik Olson, Waldemar Lorentzon and Esaias Thoren gaining recognition at their exhibitions in Stockholm's *Akademien För De Fria Kosterna* since 1932.

Among the illustrators and graphic artists of contemporary Sweden Albert Engström's masterly humor-rich drawings of distinctively Swedish types take an outstanding lead. Gustaf Isander specializes in Stockholm studies while Fridell, Johansson-Thor, Jansson, Sallberg dominate in the fields of portrait and landscape and the ilustrators Berg, Lybeck, Jungstedt and Elgström contribute vitally to such public organs as press and periodical.

Sculpture in Sweden. The earliest sculpture of note in Sweden was the Romanesque and Gothic ecclesiastical art on the island of Gothland, while the outstanding medieval work was the statue of St. Göran and the Dragon (-480) by Bernt Notke of Lübeck for *Stork-yrkan* (the Great Church) in Stockholm. During the Renaissance sculptors from the continent, particularly the German and Dutch, were commissioned to decorate the castles of royal house and nobility and in the 18th cent. French artists were imported including Larchevesque, teacher of Johan Sergel (1740-1814), Sweden's first great sculptor. Sergel's expression ran the gamut of French Rococo to Italian neo-classicism but the static forms of his time were transformed by the vigor of his genius into vitally personal statements. Reflecting his plastic power are the *Reclining Faun, Mars and Venus, Gustavus III.*

It was during the dynamic maturation of a nationally Swedish art in the 80's that a native sculpure also became grounded. John Börjesson (1835-1904), Per Hasselberg (1850-1894), Christian Eriksson (1858-1935), and carl Eldh (1873-   ), while holding primarily to an academic realism, achieved a mastery of form and an integrity of expression distinctively Swedish, corresponding to that of their fellow artist-painters in *Konstnärsförbundet.*

The most revolutionary change in plastic directin, however, was stimulated under the new leadership of Carl Milles (1875-   ), Sweden's most eminent contemporary sculptor and resident-artist since 1931 at Cranbrook Academy of Art, Bloomfield Hills, Michigan. Milles' creative genius finds impetus from the archaic Greek, also the Gothic and baroque, but is resolved powerfully into an original stylization which seeks the monumental and restrained even in the highly imaginative and decoratively vigorous forms which are so uniquely his own. Architectural, landscape and particularly fountain sculpture, involving massive figures of heroic proportions, engage his major attention. The whimsically grotesque as well as stark pagan mood come frequently into play with naiads and tritons the basis of rhythmically conceived, highly simplified organic form as in *The Meeting of the Waters Fountain,* St. Louis. The *Orpheus Fountain* for the Stockholm Concert Hall is, on the other hand, notably representative of the highly stylized anatomy, exaggerated slenderness and controlled ecstatic expressiveness of his figure designs.

Among the younger sculptors incited by Milles' departures, Ivar Johnson (1885-   ) whose austere David statue in Hälsingborg is noteworthy, Olof Ahlberg, arl Frisendal, Eric Grate, John Lundqvist, Nils Möllerberg and Nils Sjögren are in the forefront. In latter years, however, French influence has been particularly strong, Maillol and Despiau serving as favored prototypes.

In Sweden wide understanding and appreciation of the fine arts has been fostered among the masses particularly since 1930 by the traveling study exhibitions of *Riksförbundet för Bildande Konst,* The National Association for the Development of the Arts, which comprises the Swedish museums, institutions and organizations whose aims are to advance art. This highly organized cooperative activity has led to the founding of such popular movements as *Sveriges Allmänna Konstförening,* The Swedish People's Art Association. The society *Konsten i Skolan,* Art in the School, on the other hand, commissions Sweden's leading artists to execute murals for the public schools. Furthermore, through *Konstradet,* The Art Council (founded 1938), the Swedish government purchases or commissions works of art for public buildings, appointing a percentage of the cost of each building for this purpose. Most powerful of nation-wide organizing forces for bringing art to all the people through every possible educative agency of film, radio, press, pamphlets, popular courses, lectures, exhibits and expositions are The National Museum, The Röhss Museum of Arts and Crafts and the Swedish Association of Arts and Crafts (*Svenska Slöjdförening*).

There has been an extraordinary upturn in the national art consciousness since the spring of 1940 when an art crisis brought on by the war was diverted and resolved with momentous results by the timely support of the National Museum in association with other leading art organizations. In a unique exhibition, arts and crafts were introduced side by side with paintings and purchases were made both by the government and lay public. Since that successful turn the contemporary art market has flourished under the growing investments of the average citizen. Of incalculable import is the press which has been a singularly powerful ally of the nation's current art manifestations. Above all the feeling for what is essentially Swedish in art has become increasingly evident on the part of both artist and consumer. Furthermore, in spite of the evacuation of permanent collections, the National Museum alone held forty-five temporary exhibits of painting, sculpture, drawing, engraving and arts and crafts in the three year period 1940-42.

20th Century Scandinavia's Art-in-Industry Movement. Largely responsible for the high standard of contemporary production in the Scandinavian countries are those national organizations which were created to work for the advancement of art in craft and industry and for the improvement of public taste. In Sweden *Svenska Slöjdföreningen,* The Swedish Society of Arts and Crafts, has been the central clearing house through which this phase of the country's aesthetic education has been skilfully organized on a nation-wide scale. Since its founding in 1845 this association has faced systematically the problem which unguided machine production ahd brought. Subsidized by the Swedish Government, *Slöjdföreningen* was designed to arouse a nation-wide critical consciousness of the status-quo, to stimulate an awareness of the possibilities for beauty in everyday living and to serve as contactor between industry, the art world and the general public. Because of its influence producers began as early as 1914 to collaborate with artists. Initially the Society lessened the risk of manufacturers reluctant to take the artist into their ranks by lending money under very generous conditions to factory owners who were willing to experiment with the production of finer forms in glass, ceramics, metalwork, textiles and furniture. As for the artists, the younger ones were esp. willing to co-operate with *Slöjdföreningen* which, in turn, sought to establish them as designers with the various manufacturers. They worked directly in the factory where they came to understand intimately the special characteristics of the raw material and also gain first hand knowledge of technical matters. Fellowships for advanced instruction in techniques and craftsmanship were given by the Society to young artists of promise. (Today, however, artists previously distinguished in painting, sculpture or professional craft are also widely affiliated with manufacturing concerns.) In 1919 the motto *Vackrare Vardagsvara*—"More beautiful things for everyday life"—was adopted and since has been emphasized constantly by the press, periodicals, and every possible educative agency. With this aim the Society, among its wide range of activities in the campaign, has arranged for traveling exhibitions to be sent to all parts of the country, covered as wide a field as possible with lectures, issued instructive pamphlets, published *Form,* the leading organ in the north for industrial art and collaborated closely with both the industrial art and the public school. As a result of this extensive educational program, a real public demand for quality and aesthetic considerations in goods began to make itself increasingly evident. Moreover, the Society, with the assistance of the best artists and experts, worked out patterns and models which proved stimulating to both manufacturer and craftsman alike. In addition, a fine collection of illustrative material was gathered and put at the disposal of industry. As a result of this effective artist-manufacturers' union fostered by *Slöjdföreningen,* Swedish industrial art had attracted much attention from foreign countries already by 1924 and at the Paris International Exhibition of Decorative Arts in 1925 Sweden's leadership in this field was universally acknowledged. Since 1930 the Association has put special emphasis on the artist-in-industry designing for mass production methods thereby so cutting costs that home furnishings and everyday-ware of high technical and aesthetic quality have been made available at a price range within reach of the entire populace. This activity has been greatly stimulated by the social building program of the Swedish state which has provided even the lowest income groups with modern housing and stimulated democratic and spirited participation in the whole new movement for an improved home culture. *Svenska Slöjdföreningen* has reached, however, not only the individual of the nation but since 1925 has arranged on country-wide scale the remodeling or planning of office, shop and hospital along rational and modern lines exerting incidentally thereby a wide influence on the taste of the lay public. In the first three years alone thirty hospitals were redesigned and refurnished under the aegis of Sweden's leading artist craftsmen. Of further moment are the yearly competitions arranged by *Slöjdföreningen* among, e.g., the wallpaper concerns, the ceramic manufacturers, etc. to foster and reveal superior production.

With a similar, sound working program the Norwegian *Foreningen Brukskunst,* The Association of Applied Art, established in 1918, has generated throughout Norway an appreciation of fine modern forms and made them available to the people at large. Denmark, in like manner, through its *Forening for Kunsthåandvaerk,* has also been highly successful in achieving an effective working alliance between artist, producer and consumer. The Norwegian organization holds periodical exhibitions in its handsomely modern Oslo headquarters where the public may study directly the latest artist-manufacturer collaborative output and learn at which shops they may purchase the furniture, fabrics, etc., displayed. The Danish association, on the other hand, is instrumental in the running of a unique institution notably effective in encouraging uniformly high standards among producers and a forward-looking consumer emphasis. *Den Permanente,* the Permanent Exposition of Danish Art Handicraft and Industrial Art was established in 1931 with large display quarters in a central Copenhagen business locale. The exhibition represents the current production of furniture, textile, ceramic and related Danish firms as well as the work of individual professional craftsmen. All goods featured must be first approved by an advisory board (organized by the aforementioned *Forening for Kunsthaandvaerk*) as to design quality and workmanship. Constructive criticism is available to the exhibitors as well as guidance to the interested public. Furthermore, not only can the latter get a cross-view acquaintanceship with the contemporary market but also purchase on the spot.

The cooperative course now collectively followed by Swedish firms towards the policies of *Svenska Slöjdföreningen* was already well affirmed by the Stockholm exhibition of Swedish Industrial Arts and Crafts in 1930 which, as its catalog stated, was a conclusive review of "Sweden's contribution to the present day endeavor to combine sound quality and attractive appearance by the utilization of artistic resources in dwellings and objects of furniture, particularly those intended for general use." It is, in fact, in the furniture area that recent changes are particularly manifest. To this end Carl Malmsten, Sweden's leading furniture designer and craftsman is serving the two most influential firms concerned with aesthetic quality in mass production, *A.-B. Nordiska Kompaniet* and *A.-B. Svenska Möbelfabrikerna.* The wide influence of the forward-looking s m a l l e r establishments *Svenskt Tenn, Domus, Futurum, Pefta* and *Studio* is also calculable. It is, however, in Swedish glass that the rest of the world has found leadership in the creation of excellent types of domestic glass with Hald, Gate and Lindstrand of *Orrefors,* Elis Bergh of the *Kost* works and the newer firm *Strömbergshyttan* doing notable frontier experimenting. Nevertheless, it is in the two china factories of most venerable tradition, *Gustafsberg* and *Rörstand,* that a radical change away from stereotyped production is most actual. Their engaging of the artists Wilhelm Kage and Edward Hald, respectively, has resulted in

a change in technical method, ascertained to be the basis of former poor taste, and a consequent rationality, tasteful simplicity and cost as low as to bear no competition. As for pottery, the most interesting and distinctively Swedish is now produced by the small workshops, *Tobo Stengodsverkstad* under Ingrid and Erich Triller and the faience firm of *Jobs.* Among contemporary jewelers Wiwen Nilsson of Lund and C. Hallbergs *Guldsmedsaktiebolag* have met special recognition for the quality of their departures while Baron Erik Fleming and Jac. Angman are acknowledged leaders in silver. Furthermore, the present interest in textiles has made for an important output along contingent lines, home crafts, professional studio-made and machine-made fabrics. A firm of rare individuality in the face of its timely production is that of Elsa Gullberg *Textilier och Inredning.* Märta Maas-Fjetterström, modern Sweden's most eminent textile artist also expresses a unique personal quality in the markedly original *flossa* and *röllakan* rugs which are her specialty.

Basic to the success of the artist-in-industry movement in Sweden has been the recognition on the part of he manufacturing concerns to the need of opportunity for purely personal expression on the part of the artist apart from his factory affiliation. Accordingly, working hours are halved and his independence to carry on his own studio production is not only respected but fostered as a guard against any possible mechanical creation. This freedom and the versatility of commissions taken on by the artists is typified by a gifted leader among them today, Ewald Dahlskog whose table ware continuously being developed for Bobergs *Fajansfabrik* is supplemented by such projects as his intarsia panels for Stockholm's Concert House or his frescoes for the City Hall. Einar Forseth and Arthur G:son Percy, in the same way, while one day engaged at their respective porcelain works creating beauty in utilitarian ware, are the next absorbed at their own easel or at work in the decoration of bank, cinema or restaurant.

Outstanding among Norwegian industrial artists is Sverre Pettersen of Hadeland *Glasvaerk* who has brought household glass to new heights in technical and aesthetic quality as has Nora Gulprandsen of Porsfrunds *Porslaensfabrik* in the area of distinctive porcelain dinner ware for the general market. Modern stained glass has recently been an era of wide experimentation among Norwegian designers and has been handled with unusual plastic power in expressionist church windows by Fridis Haavardsholm. Leading woman artist of 20th Century Norway, she has also contributed significantly to the renaissance in design of ecclesiastical raiment, her chasubles for the Trondheim Cathedral, for example, bearing a striking modern character. Silver also is a particularly favored medium among contemporary artist-craftsmen and the notably advanced and timely treatment is evidenced in the simple, organically conceived forms typical of the national production and largely stemming from the leadership of the famed Oslo firms Tostrup and David Anderson. The artists staffing these concerns have been intensively trained at *Statens Handverks og Kunstindustriskole* which since 1934 has been under the active directorship of Jacob Prytz, himself a master goldsmith who is also manager of Tostrup's and organizer of the *Brukskunst* movement. To be further noted is the wide use of enamel in small objects and restrained ornamentation, a special feature of the Norwegian goldsmith's art.

A close collaboration between architect and craftsman has resulted in a rational furniture production suited to the needs of the modern-type interior universally built since the 1920's. An extensive use of metal in furniture manufacture is also manifest. Moreover, smart furnishing fabrics have been made available to the general consumer by joint action of the professional weaving studios and textile factories under the *Brukskunst program*. On the other hand, monumental picture tapestries distinctily modern in conception have been executed of late years by the leading textile artists Sigrid Mohn, Tora Qviller, Frida Hansen, and Ulrikke Greve for public buildings, as the new Oslo City Hall, and the recently built Norwegian passengers liners. Of the latter, the S.S. Oslofjord, the interior decoration of which was executed by the combined efforts of Norway's leading artists and craftsman, represents an excellent cross section of Norway's highest pre-War II production. This is reflected in the fresh approach not only to the Norse murals and artist-designed furniture, fabrics and rugs but in the newly handled wall-surfaces of hand-blocked linen and native woods (to the Peer Gynt designs of Per Krogh), the vigorous ceramic reliefs of Maja Refsum and free pictorial tiles by Hvalstad and Scheel decorating smoking room and bar. The library likewise bears evidence of the intimate cooperation recently developed between publisher and artist accounting for the handsomely designed

typography, illustration and binding of not only luxury volumes but particularly the popularly sold books. In the same way the embroidery, knitting, weaving and entire field of women's handwork has been profoundly affected by the tasteful and contemporary patterns executed for popular use by the country's outstanding artists who are also contributing thus to Norway's exhaustive drive for aesthetic quality in everyday living.

Denmark's modern industrial art is conspicous for its excellent craftsmanship along with an optimum feeling for material and elegant simplictiy of design. This is most evident in the famed Danish silver production which had its impetus under the organization of the pioneer genius Georg Jensen (1866-1935) but which has since his generation resolved from the elaboratively decorative to that monumental simplicity of character found in the work of the firm's present staff G. Albertus, Grundlach-Pedersen and Harald Nielsen. First to commission designs from leading Danish artists was the establishment of the court jeweller, A. Michelsen. Typical of the highly restrained contemporary conceptions are those by the architects Kay Fisker, Kaj Gottlob and Palle Svenson and the painter Stähr-Nielsen, while new departures are under constant development by the silversmith Frantz Hingelberg of Aarhus.

Among other Danish concerns distinguished by the creative production of top-ranking artists as Knud Kyhn, Jais Nielsen and Jean Gauguin are *Den kgl. Porcelainsfabrik* (The Royal Copenhagen Porcelain Manufactory) and *Bing & Grndahl A/S* (The National Factory of Porcelain). Greatest emphasis has latterly been put on quality everyday ware. Among the excellent ceramic factories in outlying Denmark is Kähler's in Naestved which has had in its employ the sculptor Kai Nielsen, the painter Svend Hammershi and now enjoys the ceramic gifts of Jens Thiirslund. Stoneware in particular is engaging the interest of most of these artists at present because of its marked plastic possibilities. To be specially noted is that of the painter Axel Salto, the ceramist Bode Willumsen and Natalie Krebs of the firm Saxpo. As for glass manufacture, newly stimulated by the Swedish, *Holmegaards Glasvaerk,* under the architect Jacob E. Bang, has most successfully initiated a tasteful production of simple glass forms for daily use. The "P. H. Lamps" designed by Architect Poul Henningsen and used widely over the Continent are a singular Danish contribution to the area of electric lamp fixtures in the industrial art industry. As for furniture, the highly skilled professional cabinet maker holds a prominent place with heavy popular demand for his individual pieces. Among the commercial firms, however, Fritz Hansens house is a typical producer of pleasingly simple and serviceable bent-wood and metal types. Smartly modern furniture and curtain fabrics, have been increasingly demanded, the relatively newly established studios, the workshops Askovhus, Gerda Henning, Marie Moos and Karen Warning being most prominent. Book-binding as an art has also made recent strides under the distinguished craftsmanship of Jacob Baden, Anker Kyster and August Sandgren. In the field of toy design too much attention has been given outside of Denmark as well to the wooden block, boat, car and similar forms developed by the silversmith Kay Bojesen.

In Denmark as in Norway and Sweden the Museums for Industrial Art have contributed in great measure to the general appreciation of modern design by their current exhibits of contemporary applied arts and active cooperation with the special organizations for fostering art-in-industry. Also the wide provision for instruction in advanced design and professional craftsmanship has provided these countries with a richly equipped talent. In addition, the creative versatility of the Scandinavian architect, whose formal training in his own field is significantly complemented by extensive study of the fine arts as well as industrial design, has been of momentous import in that he has been exceptionally well prepared to serve as coordinator of the various forces that play into the dynamic new design of art in society. To this end it will be seen that museum nad organization leaders are most often architects as are frequently the frontier designers in furniture, metal, ceramics.

Modern Scandinavia's Home Arts and Crafts Movement. In each of the Scandinavian countries there is a national organization with branches in all parts of the land, which is seeking, by means of wide adult education to promote home arts and crafts along sound contemporary lines. This movement for a renaissance in handicrafts, developing side by side with the currents in the art-in-industry program, has likewise been affected by the general improvement in taste, by the new consciousness of organically conceived functional design, by an awakened social awareness and emphasis on a creative design

for living for the masses of people. Purely decorative handwork of the old pastiche character has given way to simple, practical forms for daily use. Weaving, for example, has been popularly revived, attention being focused on the creation of a variety of attractive and substantial materials for clothing, curtains, upholstery. Thus, handicraft since the 20's has received increasing social recognition and has gained a place of respect unknown since the onslaught of industrialism because it now stands for utility, for quality, for intrinsic beauty, and because in its modern simplicity it harmonizes with and becomes part of a machine age environment.

In pre-World War II Norway the whole problem of handicrafts had been attacked afresh and translated into terms of the new needs and demands of twentieth century living by the most comprehensive, highly organized and nationally important government-subsidized system of modern times. In its educational and cultural aims it seeks to promote home handicraft and the development of good taste, individuality, and quality craftsmanship by means of instruction and propaganda. Further, in support of one of the economic objectives of this movement to make possible for below-minimum incomes to be supplemented by means of home arts and crafts, a substantial market is provided through the sales shops of member organizations over the country. Four hundred local *Husflidsforeninger* or home arts and crafts associations, under yearly state grant for their educational work, direct their energies towards providing opportunities for the training of people of all ages and all levels of society. This they have largely realized through arranging series of ambulatory courses, establishing permanent *husflid* schools, holding study exhibitions, publishing texts, working-drawings and designs and maintaining collections of patterns and models for general popular use. The State provides a central *husflid* school for women which offers advanced courses and provides teacher training. In addition are fourteen other State subsidized *husflid* schools for women and thirteen for men, four hundred *arbeidsskoler* for training young people in handwork and over seventy *arbeidsstuer* to encourage small children in creative endeavor. Supplementing these are in turn numerous craft courses now provided in the agricultural and continuation schools. Attention has been focused on building up skills and knowledge of materials as a basis for individual creativity.

Furthermore, the economic aspect of *husflid* has been developed in Norway as a relevant part of the general cultural program. This consideration has made possible the economic of many, and the self-sufficiency of many more. Besides, the organized *husflid* production for sales purposes presupposes a market which sets up standards that demand aesthetic and technical quality in goods, a market which in turn stimulates the whole native production to a higher character. Besides, the *husflid* sales shops in the Norwegian towns also act as important guidance bureaus for local producer and lay public and centers for *husflid* promotion.

In order to foster this united activity in Norway, an administrative set-up has been developed whereby the local *husflids-foreninger* gather into county units, *fylkes husfildsdag*. These in turn, together with *husflid* schools, museums, and other institutions and groups with *husflid* on their programs, become members of a national association, *Norges Husflids-og Husindustrilag*. This latter body, administered by a central office, *Husflidsstyret*, a common council of representatives, *Husflidsradet*, and a general assembly *Landsmtet*, is represented finally by a council within the Department of Agriculture, *Landsradet for Husflid, Husindustri og Smaindustrie*. *Landsmtet* is a national meeting held every third year. *Husflidsstyret* is elected by this assembly. *Husflidsrad*, on the other hand, a board of representatives to which each county *husflidslag* elects a delegate, come together with *Husflidsstyret* in yearly meeting. *Landsradet*, with permanent office in Oslo supervised by the State's *husflid*-inspector, is now the official integrating body and the authority for *husflid* activity over the country. This arrangement in organization has proved to be a practical and democratic one, as is provides for independent local initiative as well as local representation in the greater collective endeavor of planning the nation's general lines of direction. Since 1930, particularly, all classes of society have been actively participating in the movement.

The Swedish and Danish home arts and crafts systems are broadly speaking parallel to the Norwegian one though each one bears a unique individuality. In 1912 *Svenska Hemslöjdsföreningarnas Riksförbund*, a national league of all the local homecraft organizations in Sweden, was ofunded. Planned to act as a centralizing agency and provide contact between the existing local associations, according to its laws the *Riksförbund* was further designed to maintain and develop *husflid* on the basis of the old folk arts, to bring together producers and other interested persons, to discuss *husflid* matters and act on common questions, to foster a united activity for raising the level of *husflid* instruction, to facilitate exchange among the *foreninger* in regard to their experiences in promoting *husflid* and to work for the preservation and improvement of native raw materials. Joined under the *Riksförbund* are thirty-four *husflidsforeninger* representing each province of the country; also *Föreningen för Svensk Hemslöjd*, a pioneer Stockholm agency whose highly distinctive showrooms bear evidence of the highest quality contemporary craft, furniture included. Because the *Riksförbund's* aims included making known and selling *husflid* products, in 1928 it founded a marketing division, *Hemslöjdsförbundet för Sverige*, with permanent show rooms and sales shops in Stockholm. In behalf of the member *husflidsforeninger* this organization promotes their goods in Sweden and abroad and sells on consignment basis, sending a report every third month to each province. Unlike the Oslo shop the Stockholm one does not provide patterns and directions for producers but, while it offers advice and stimulus, encourages each province from Skane to Norrbotten to send in its own typical and self-determined work in order to maintain the regional integrity of the native production in regard to material, color, form, pattern and purpose.

In Denmark the home arts and crafts program, of minor importance compared with that of Norway and Sweden, is under the central authority of *Dansk Husflidsselskah*. There are no sales outlets and simple, practical men's crafts dominate in emphasis. Since 1928, however, *Selskabet til Haandarbejdts Fremme*, with sales shop in Copenhagen and Odense, has been developing a quality production of extraordinary distinctiveness.

In 1926 *Nordens Husflidsforbund*, a cooperative alliance of the home arts and crafts organizations of Norway, Sweden, Finland, Denmark, Iceland and Estonia was established. This organization then convened at the first *Nordiske Husflidsting* held in Stockholm in May 1927 and thereafter every third year, the member countries rotating as meeting places.

It has been well said that Scandinavian art not only forms a unity but a trinity as well. While Sweden stands supreme in bringing art into industry it looks to the monumental painting of contemporary Norway as a mutually completing part, to the sound craftsmanship of Denmark, "the art appreciator", as an important supplement to its own expression. In fact, while the temperament of their art is individual, there is to marked degree reciprocal recognition and interaction of those values indigeneous to the tranquil lowlands of Denmark on the one hand, to the violent heights of Norway on the other, and to Sweden where nature too runs the middle course. See (BOOKS) Laurin, G., Hannover, E., Thiis, J., *Scandinavian Art*, 1922; Stavenow, Ake, *Swedish Modern: A Movement Towards Sanity in Design*, 1939; Vreim, Halvor, *Norwegian Decorative Art*, 1937; Wettergren, Erik, *Modern Decorative Arts of Sweden*, 1926; Wilmann, Preben, *Dansk Kunst*, 1934; Wollin, Nils, *Modern Swedish Arts and Crafts*, 1937; (PERIODICALS) *Form*, Stockholm, 1929-40; *Nyt Tidsskrift for Kunstindustri*, Copenhagen, 1927-40; *The American Scandinavian Review*, New York, 1912-1943.   —M.L.

Scandinavian glass. See GLASS AND GLASS-MAKING.

scauper. A tool used in engraving.

scenae frons. See STAGE-SETTING.

scenario (or continuity, shooting script, screen play). The manuscript of the narrative expressed in terms of shots and sequences, from which the director works. It often contains, besides a complete literary description of the visual images that compose the film, plans and drawings of the sets and of the camera positions. When dialogue is added to description of the action, the manuscript is usually called a screen play.   —I.B.

Scheele's Green. The Swedish chemist, Carl Wilhelm Scheele, first prepared this painter's pigment in 1778. It is somewhat similar to emerald green, being also a compound of copper and arsenic. It shares the disadvantages of that, however, in being easily discolored by sulphides and by sulphur-bearing air. It has now been largely abandoned. —G.L.S.

scherzo. An instrumental piece of animated character. The scherzo of the symphony (q.v.) was developed by Beethoven from the minuet, (q.v.) of Haydn and Beethoven.

schizzo (It.). A sketch.

schloss, burg, festung. See castle.

schola cantorum. See NOTATION.

school art museum. See art museum, school.

schuhplatteltanz. This German national couple dance of Bavarian origin takes its name from one figure in which the man slaps his leather breeches and the soles of his shoes in a brisk rhythmic pattern. Very simple in form, the dance consists of a waltz introduction or promenade, a single major figure, and a delicately restrained conclusion suggestive of a minuet. In the dance proper, the woman whirls continuously while the man moves about her with pantomimic gestures and the rhythmic motif of slapping his breeches and shoes.   —J.G.

Schweinfurt gren. See emerald green.

sciences of signs and symbols. See AESTHETICS, RECENT TRENDS IN.

scope of vision. See PERSPECTIVE.

score. *Mus.* A systematic arrangement of all the vocal or instrumental parts of a composition placed on separate staves one above the other.

scorper. See scauper.

Scotch carpet. See ingrain carpets.

scotia (Gr. *skotia,* darkness). A classical moulding of a single concave curve of more than an approximate quarter circle or ellipse.

scraper. A three-cornered sharp tool for scraping the lithographic plate to make corrections. See PRINTS AND PRINT PROCESSES.

scratchboard. A type of chalk-covered cardboard used for drawing on with pen and ink, crayon, etc.; the board has a smooth surface with line or stipple tint and the lights desired are achieved by scratching them out with a steel tool.

scriber. See ENAMELLING ON METAL.

script writer. See RADIO DRAMA.

Scriptores. A collection of treatises on musical theory by medieval Latin writers was made available by Martin Gerbert (3 vols.) in 1784 entitled *Scriptores eclesiastical de musica.* Another collection was issued by C. E. H. Coussemaker (4 vols.) 1864-76 entitled *Scriptores de musica medii aevi.* A facsimile edition of both editions appeared in 1931.

The treatises included in these collections are indispensable for research in medieval music. For contents of both collections see article, *Scriptores,* in Grove's *Dictionary of Music and Musicians,* 1935.   —V.A.

scrollwork. An ornament which has its characteristics and main possibilities for variations on the framing parts of a plate, plane, label, etc. In contrast with the greater part of ornamental forms which developed in the course of time or which were revived in modern times from ancient forms, the scrollwork means an ornament for which—in its proper appearance—we can nearly state an actual birthdate. It is natural with the scrollwork that its main accents are developed on the framing zone of an object. Even if we consider related motifs in the rolling ends of ribbons, hat brims, etc., which we can trace during the Middle Ages, or in the ending volutes of classic capitals already—for it is obvious for any unfastened ending to get rolled—the scrollwork as such was created but in the 16th century. In the decorations of the Castle of Fontainebleau, France, in the Gallery of François I (1494-1547) we find the first genuine scrollwork, executed by Rosso Fiorentino between 1535 and 1540. Its formations show all the typical characteristics: (1) an elastic body with a plain surface, without reminding of any natural formations; (2) the framing motif, symmetrically built up; (3) the decoration built up within two layers which become evident towards the framing zone where the endings of both planes are interwoven and pierce through each other. Thus the scrollwork has an outspoken three-dimensional character.

The Italian *cartoccio*—a little plate very often used for the inscription of the artist's name or for that of the portrayed—prepared the development which was achieved in Fontainebleau by Italian artists. On the other hand, the three-dimensionality makes the scrollwork an ornament closely linked to Baroque tendencies.

The usage of the scrollwork was largely encouraged by the masters of ornament engravings. Artists like Cornelis Floris and Cornelis Bos in the Netherlands, or Virgil Solis in Germany helped a lot for its spreading, by the publication of whole series of engravings; thus they gave the model for silver and goldsmiths as well as for interior decorators, sculptors, etc. Naturally, like the grotesque or the mauresque or arabesque, forms of the scrollwork were used very fre-

quently in combinations with other ornament forms like especially the above mentioned. See Peter Jessen, *Der Ornamentstich,* Berlin, 1920; Max Deri, *Das Rollwerk in der deutschen Ornamentik,* Halle, 1905; Rudolf Berliner, *Ornamentale Vorlageblätter,* Leipzig, 1926; Robert Hedicke, *Cornelis Floris und die Florisdekoration,* Berlin, 1913; Lotte Pulvermacher, *Das Rollwerk in der süddeutschen Skulptur und seine Entwicklung bis ca. 1620,* Strassburg, 1931; Kurt Kusenberg, *Le Rosso,* Paris, 1931; *Katalog der Berliner Ornamentstichsammlung,* Berlin, 1935.   —L.P-E.

sculptural canon. See canon, sculptural.

sculptural portrait. See portrait, sculptural.

SCULPTURE. *The General Situation.* Whereas many people succeed in establishing some sort of relationship to painting mainly because of its content (the story) and its color scheme, sculptural creation stands in peculiar isolation. This is understandable as one can see usually in sculpture only a very poor "story".

Aspects of Representation. To primitive man, representation of an object meant the same thing as being able to seize it, to own it personally. It brought before his eyes in human dimensions the object which moved or overpowered him in order to put it to his service.

The incomprehensible fact of death is made more tangible by mummification. Man is changed into a doll; the dead ancestor, the root of the family, remains as a mummy in the family possession. A later stage, by death mask, sublimates this process. This may be the origin of the portrait.

The possessive point of view is extended to beings who live only in the world of imagination. There is a strong contact with ancestors, goods, personified powers of a rich pantheism. Captured within a definite form, they became—even if prayed to as deities—servants of man.

Clay, wood, stone come to life under the artist's hands. He perceives the existence of the typical, and what is *common* to different phenomena. Then one day the slightest deviations from the typical are observed. To the original observation of the typical features are added the individual characteristics.

The slightest twitchings of the muscles of the face and body are given their values in expression. The whole representation is brought down to infinitely fine gradations. The way leads from the typical to the individual. And when no further progress in this direction is possible, when the representation has reached mechanical identity, the rebound occurs: instead of tangible realism something different takes place: a neutralizing calmness, stylization, a striving for indifference toward the psychic aspects. This leads to a more conscious emphasis of the expressive and meaningful effects of material, shape, volume, and their relationships. This is a great discovery: a language of form available for expression. In the transitional period toward abstract sculpture common objects are represented, a bottle, absinthe glass, violin. There little value is placed on photographic resemblance but very much more on elements as concave-convex, curved and angular, solid and perforated, horizontal and vertical, smooth disappear. The expressive importance is condensed in the relationships of sculptural elements. Not the representation of a person, animal or object, is the real problem here, but the paramount organization of relationships of volume, of material, of mass, of shape, direction, position and light. To these elements through his biological nature everyone can have a direct, unadulterated relationship. This is the basis of a new aesthetic reality leading to abstract, non-objective sculpture.

There are a great number of other elements, mainly technological, which help to define this new type of approach. But these elements are only variations of the age-old consequences in the use of material and tools with which one creates a certain product.

Fundamental attitudes in treating materials. Sculpture can be approached from different viewpoints: tool, material, form, volume, size, proportion, balance, positive-negative, setting, expression, etc. The most natural appreciation comes from the way it is *made*.

If several people are handed a block of material to be worked on, certain fundamental tendencies will appear in all, in their way of handling the material.

At first the worker respects the homogeneity of the block. He examines it, feels it all over, estimates its weight, its dimensions. Then he starts—according to his temperament, in the passive mood of a spectator, nor in the active mood of an experimenter—to work on the block with a tool, his purpose quite clear. He knows what he would like to create but as he proceeds he may see that his tool and his material allow him only a limited freedom. He has to adapt himself to their requirements as he goes on; he unconsciously assumes the role of a meticulous artisan; he slowly becomes better acquainted with his material and his tools. He invents methods, discovers new implements, dares to proceed more drastically: to make recesses, holes; he penetrates deeper and deeper into the block. In this way **negative volumes** (hollow spaces, voids) are produced. He notes the relations between full and empty, between round and angular, dull and sharp, small and large, raised and indented. Such an articulation of the means is the basis of sculpture. But to articulate, one must thoroughly know his means.

Sculpture is volume creation. As man faces his material, experiencing it, it becomes a factor in his practical knowledge that sculpture is the best form—the original form —for taking possession of volume. Compared with volume, everything else, the kind of making, weight, structure, representational idea, likeness, expression, proportion, rhythm, consistency, color, etc., is secondary, belonging more in the sphere of mastery of details. They do not count primarily for the essential grasp of volume, and thus for the main values of plastic expression. It must be stated, however, that the most intensive method of conceiving volume, has in the course of our cultural history been more and more superseded by an intellectual conception of likeness to known objects. Thought content and illustration overrode the form, description supplanted grasp.

The five stages of development of sculpture from the standpoint of treatment of the material. In working with the material and in discovering the volume relationships, as they become more and more clear, we may set down various stages of plastic development—not alone in the individual, but as well in the history of Western, Eastern, and any other cultures. These stages are:

1. **blocked-out**
2. **modeled** (hollow-out)
3. **perforated** (bored-through) ⎫ sculpture
4. **equipoised** (suspended) ⎬
5. **kinetic** (moving) ⎭

These explanations refer in general to sculpture-in-the-round which finds its justification in fulfilling its own laws—like easel painting without architectural relationships. The legible meaning of this development may be summarized also as the path of freeing the material from its weight: from mass to motion.

Parallel phenomena. One can find close parallels to this development toward dissolution of material. There are certain processes in nature which exhibit the same tendency; e.g., water in rest, in motion, in gaseous form, liquid and solid. Water exists as tiny spherical drops, and as a smooth, plain surface stretching out far and wide. It may appear as a placid or rushing brook, as a raging sea, as plattering rainfall, spraying fountain, drifting cloud of steam. It may be frozen: as snow, ice, crystals on frosted window panes, etc. These manifold changes arise from an extraordinary variety and adaptability of its forms. One may easily feel moved to employ water as a medium of expression. In earlier periods water, as responsive to adaptations, was recognized as an important medium of creation and its natural possibilities were exploited according to the expression desired. Its form was changed from a tranquil mass to the complete dissolution of an almost ethereal form; from the calm lakes of the baroque parks to gushing fountains, or a chain of foaming cascades. All such efforts were directed to displaying water under as many aspects as possible, and dematerialization played an important part in the process.

In every cultural period a phalanx presses forward in every field of creation, in art, science, and technology. It often happens that one field pushes out from this united front, like an advancing wedge. This condition does not last long; the other lines surge onward; the phalanx is re-united, mostly even without the knowledge of the respective workers.

Thus a similar quest is made for expression by subduing or lightening the material as in sculpture: from mass to motion; in painting, from colored pigment to light (play of colored light); in architecture, from restricted closed space o free, open space articulation.

The first stage of sculptural development. The block of material which shows its mass in plain, almost untouched volume as the pyramids; dolmens, natural monuments; meteorites (the Caaba at Mecca), crystalline blocks, prisms.

The second stage. The **modeled** (hollowed-out) **block:** Small and large mass (volume) relationships of salient and sunken, positive and negative, round and angular, sharp and dull. Void can be understood as **negative volume** and it can be used as the legitimate contrast to the **positive volume.**

..*The third stage.* The **perforated** (bored-through) **block** is the third stage. After mastering the relations of all legrees of positive and negative volume, an intensive penetration follows into the material, creating polar contrasts. The completely perforated sculpture is a heightening to the very limits of hollow and full.

Succession in time. In the history of sculpture the different stages of plastic development occur successively. Each closed culture (Egyptian, Indian, Greek) shows at the beginning the barely modeled block and as a next step the more or less carefully modeled piece, penetrated to a greater or less extent. The same approach is found among the sculptural work of the pre-literary natives of the so-called "primitive peoples" (American Indian, Negro, and South Sea) where sculptural creation rests on very old traditions.

The fourth stage of sculptural development. What comes beyond the complete perforation of the third stage is a speculation that we, still deeply rooted in our yesterdays, can scarcely grasp; a bold sublimation of the material, a triumph of relations pure and simple. It is the **equipoised sculpture,** the self-contained volume. Its preparation can be traced in the consequent steps of sculptural development. In an illusionistic way they appear in baroque churches as angels suspended in the air, even earlier, in the Gothic cathedrals, sculptures hovering on cantilevered platforms. Sculpture "normally" rests on a heavy base, occupying a certain position in relation to its surroundings. It also has relationships of direction to the earth: horizontal, vertical, oblique. The equipoised sculpture, contains *theoretically* only relationships of material and volume, and all other possible elements *within its own system.*

The freedom from relationships to points eternal to the sculpture means the fourth stage of sculptural development; it means a floating volume in space freed from the complication of gravity forces. This problem is at the same time the crux of the problem of equilibrium, which is an important part of the total problem of plastic creation.

That is a long way from the Renaissance idea of appreciating sculpture from only one certain, "the best" position. This was the mechanical application of the vanishing point, the central perspective of paintings to a three-dimensional object. This of course could have been seen from any point if the canon of looking at pictures would not have had its influence upon the sculptors, too. The reaction against the dogma of viewing sculpture from one point and making it so, came up lately with the introduction of the idea to make sculpture-in-the-round.

Examples of equipoised sculpture which do not depend on illusion, namely, by the use of glass, or of almost invisible wires, on which the sculpture is hung, are very hard to find. Such a sculpture must effectively be kinetic sculpture as well, since only through the action of opposed forces can it be brought to balanced rest in equipoise. Analogous solutions could be seen in balloons, airplanes, toys. All these are, however, limited in their formal quality by unavoidable, compulsory considerations of power, which must overcome gravitation. The actual realization of equipoised sculpture will be possible only with the application of magnetic forces or remote electrical control. Such a possibility is shown in a simple way by an electromagnetically controlled metal bar floating between two glass plates.

Within the system of equipoised sculpture we can find again three former stages of sculptural form: (1) the block, (2) the modelled, (3) the perforated.

The fifth stage. In the lightening of masses the next step beyond equipoise is **kinetic equipoise,** in other words, **mobile** or **moving sculpture.** There the volume relationships are mainly virtual, i.e., resulting from movement usually of thin bodies, rings, rods, and other objects. Here the material is utilized not in its mass but as a carrier of movements. To the three dimensions of volume, the fourth —movement—(in other words the *time element*) is added. The originally heavy block of material, the solid volume, transforms itself—depending upon the speed of motion—into a kind of ethereal extension appearing without mass and heaviness. **Mobile** is a weightless poising of volume relationships and interpenetrations. With this transformation, the original phenomenon of sculpture which equaled material plus mass relationships, changes to a dematerialized, abstract formula: sculpture equals volume relationships.

The history of kinetic sculpture. The history of kinetic sculpture begins far back in the ancient ages, with the very first Greek hydro-clock, and later in the different clockwork automata with moving figures in the Middle Ages. As a step toward kinetic sculpture in our own time one may single out toys, advertising signs, fountains, fireworks and the like. These often contain interesting suggestions for experiments. Recently the futurists have came forward as conscious propagandists of the "dynamic" as a principle of artistic creation. Boccioni presented the first **dynamic sculptures** in his *Pittura, scultura*

futurista (dinanismo plastico). In 1912 he wrote: "The futurists broke down the concept of repose—the static—and put forward that of movement—the dynamic. They showed the new grasp of space by bringing into contrast the inner and the outer."

Written as a challenge to the aims of the Russian constructivists, the **Realistic Manifesto** of Gabo and Pevsner, Moscow, was published in 1920.

"Space and time are the two exclusive forms for fulfillment of life, and therefore art must be guided by these two basic forms if it is to encompass true life."

"To incorporate our experience of the world in the forms of space and time: this is the single goal of our creative art."

"In sculpture we eliminate (physical) mass as a plastic element. Every engineer knows that the static power and power of resistance of an object do not depend on mass. One example will suffice: railway tracks. Notwithstanding this fact, sculptors labor under the prejudice that mass and contour are indivisible."

"We free ourselves from the thousand-year-old error of art, originating in Egypt, that only static rhythms can be its elements. We proclaim that for present-day perceptions, the most important elements of art are the kinetic rhythms."

In 1922 L. Moholy-Nagy published, in collaboration with Alfred Kemeny, a manifesto on *The Dynamic Constructive System of Forces.* "Constructivism means the activation of space by means of a dynamic-constructive system of forces, that is, the constructing within one another of forces actually at tension in physical space, and their construction within space, also active as force (tension)."

"We must therefore put in the place of the static principle of classical art the dynamic principle of universal life. Stated practically: instead of static material construction (material and form relationships) dynamic construction (vital constructivism and force relationships) must be evolved, in which the material is employed only as the carrier of forces."

"Carrying further the unit of construction, a dynamic constructive system of force is attained, whereby man, heretofore merely receptive in his observation of works of art, experiences a heightening of his own faculties, and becomes himself an active partner with the forces unfolding themselves."

"The first projects looking toward the dynamic-constructive system of forces can be only experimental demonstration devices for the testing of the connections between man, material, power, and space. Next comes the utilization of the experimental results for the creation of freely moving (free from mechanical and technical movement) works of art."

Duality of volume? This progress obliges one to use the term "volume" in several ways, though basically they form a unity. There are the following meanings of **volume**:

(1) The clearly circumscribed mass, body of measurable weight, tangible in the three dimensions is the customary description of volume.

(2) But there exist negative volumes, too: the voids, holes and openings; they are perceived merely visually; they are—although bodiless—yet outstanding plastic elements.

(3) Then there are the volumes produced by the motions of points (smallest bodies), linear elements, or larger bodies. The results are virtual volumes, new elements of plastic creation.

To sum up, sculpture is both material—volume and its transformation into virtual volume; from tactual grasp to visual grasp.

Ability to recognize a certain stage of sculptural development does not mean necessarily an aesthetic experience. To define sculpture on the basis of technological development is far from an exhaustive treatment of the problem of sculptural creation. It means only the first steps toward a really thoroughgoing experience. The five stages of plastic development offer merely the rough differentiations of the outward technical conception. They are an introduction to the first recognition of the creative problems involved in perceiving sculptural form. The complete experience of a work in sculpture implies—along with an intuitive basic grasp— knowledge of the workings of other elements as well.

Such elements are the geometrical and **biotechnical elements of construction**. (Raoul France, the Hungarian biologist, has distinguished seven biotechnical constructional elements: crystal, sphere, cone, plate, strip, rod, and spiral [screw], and says that these are the basic technical elements of the whole world. They suffice for all its processes and are sufficient to bring them to their optimum.) Laws of light, motion, size, mass (proportion), relationships of structure, texture, surface treatment, representation, expression, etc. As is the case everywhere, it is true here that a wide and comprehensive knowledge of characteristics and elements is less important for creative work than the capacity and the courage to build up new relations among the elements of expression already at hand. What is really important is to raise them above the commonplace by giving them a new meaning through shifting their connotations.

Without this, elements, harmonious in themselves, can never grow into an organism. They remain only a series, forming perhaps a rich arabesque, but of no significance in the sense of the building up, of the biological "nourishment" of man.   —L.M-N.

sculpture, ceramic. See CERAMICS I.

sculpturesque painting. See POST-REVOLUTIONARY PAINTING AND SCULPTURE IN THE U. S. A.

seal. (1) A matrix or die engraved on metal or gem stone for making an impression in wax or other soft material placed on a document to indicate authenticity. The word is also used legally to mean the impression itself. The art of seal cutting is of great antiquity. Cylindrical seals were in use in Egypt and Babylonia and beautiful examples of gem engraving are found in the ancient seals of Greece and Rome. After the fall of the Roman Empire the use of seals in Europe declined except for the Papal bullae stamped in lead, and was not revived until the latter part of the 8th cent. In the 11th cent. Edward the Confessor introduced the pendant seal hung to the document by a parchment strip. Since his time each monarch has had his own great seal. Seal engraving reached its peak of skill and beauty in the 14th cent.

The Great Seal of the United States, well known from its reproduction on the one dollar silver certificate, was designed in 1782 and recut last in 1902. Each State has its own seal, of which some are artistic while others violate the canons of both heraldry and beauty. Colleges, corporations and other organizations have their individual seals. The dies for seals, medals and coins are now cut by machine from large models. See HERALDRY; sphragistics. See Frankfort, *Cylinder Seals*; Birch, *Seals*.   —T.E.F.

(2) An impression made with a stamp, generally accompanying the signature on East Asiatic paintings. Usually applied with vermilion pigment. See *in* (Jap.); *yin chang* (Ch.).   —J.A.M.

seal carving. See CHINESE ARTS; MESOPOTAMIAN ART.

secco recitativo. See OPERA.

Secessionists, the. See art nouveau.

secondary colors. See COLOR.

secondary highway, street, etc. See CIVIC PLANNING.

secretary. See writing; FURNITURE.

sedimentation. See expression.

seggar. See sagger.

segmental. Having the form of a part or arc of a circle; anything characterized by the use of such a segment.

seguidilla. One of the classic Iberian Spanish dances, is perhaps the one most universally performed. Each region or province has its own version, which often retains few of the original characteristics and occasionally is given another name. In general, the style of the dance places most emphasis upon movements of the arms and torso, accompanied by rapid footwork in alternation with high leg-swings. The motions of the upper body are performed with elegance, the torso at once supple and erect. The dancer accompanies himself upon castanets. Each figure is also given the support of a short verse of love-poetry called a "copla."   —J.G.

Sehna knot, Persian knot. Takes its name from a town in Persia. This technique is seldom found in European rugs. The short length of wool (or other fibre) is "wrapped around" only "one" warp thread. The ends are brought forward to the surface with a warp thread between them. This makes on the surface a tuft of wool (half the knot), then a warp thread, next another tuft or wool (the other half of the knot) and then the other warp thread.   —B.E.J.

seiji (Jap.). Celadon, or green pottery ware.

sekki (Jap.). Stoneware.

selenium cell. See electrical instruments.

Seljuq art. See ISLAMIC ART; PERSIAN ART.

selvage. The method of securing the edges of the rug so that the knots forming the pile are protected in which contiguous warp threads are included in the weaving process with weft threads, but lacking pile threads.   —B.E.J.

Semantic notation. See NOTATION.

semantics. See AESTHETICS, RECENT TRENDS IN (1).

semi-abstraction. See abstraction.

semi-breve, — c, —f, — minima, — pausa, — quaver. See NOTATION.

semi-formal script. See writing.

sendal (O. F. cendal; Gr. sindon; Skr. sindhū). (1) A thin silk fabric used in the Middle Ages. (2) A kind of linen.

Senoufo art. See AFRICAN NEGRO ART.

sensu (Jap.). Folding fans, the surfaces of which are often decorated by the best artists.

sensu-e (Jap.). Paintings for folding fans.

sepia. Both as the name of a color, a neutral brown, and as the name of a specific coloring material, this is familiar in the fine arts. The coloring material provided an ink that was known in classical times but evidently was little used in Europe until the latter part of the 18th cent. Then it was taken up for ink drawings and for water color painting. It is a secretion from the ink bag of the common cuttlefish or squid and from other related species.   —G.L.S.

seppa (Jap.). Washers placed on both sides of the sword-guard.

sepulchre (L. sepulcrum, a burial-pplace). A grave, tomb, or place of interment.

sepulchrum. See altar.

sequence. (1) Mus. (a) The chromatic or whole-tone repetition or progression of a melodic or harmonic figure. (b) In the Roman Catholic Church a kind of hymn founded on the alleluia (q.v.). The popularity of the sequence attained its height in the 12th cent. during the time of Adam of St. Victor (d. 1192), the most famous and prolific writer of sequence-texts. A great number gradually found their way into the Church services. With the exception of five, all were excluded from the official Church song by the Council of Trent (1545-63).

1. *Victimae Paschali laudes* by Wipo of Burgundy (d. 1050). For Easter Sunday.

2. *Veni sancte spiritus* variously ascribed to Robert the Pious, King of France (996-1031), Hermannus Contractus of Reichenau (1013-54), Pope Innocent III (d. 1216), and Stephen Langton, Archbishop of Canterbury (d. 1228). For Pentecost.
3. *Lauda Sion Salvotorem* by Thomas Aquinas (c. 1225-74). For Corpus Christi.
4. *Stabat Mater dolorosa* by Jacopone da Todi (c. 1306). For festival of Seven Sorrows of Mary.
5. *Dies irae* by Thomas of Celano (13th cent.). Interpolated in Requiem Mass (q.v.).

The five official sequences are to be found in the *Liber Usualis*. A complete collection of sequence texts is available in G. M. Dreves, *Analecta Hymnica* vols. 50, 53, 54 (1886-1911). For a discussion of the melodies see P. Wagner, *Einführung in die Gregorianischen Melodien*, vol. 3, 1921. See MEDIEVAL MUSIC.   —V.A.

(2) *Motion Pictures*. A series of shots developing one single phase of the narrative, and observing within them a unity of time, place and action, or a unity of theme. —I.B.

serenade. *Mus.* (1) An evening song of a quiet character. (2) An instrumental piece of such character. (3) A sort of suite (q.v.) in several movements.

serge. A fabric with a twill weave.

serial. See RADIO DRAMA.

series, photographic. See PHOTOGRAPHY.

series title. *Book.* The name of the series of a book usually found at top left hand of half-title page, but sometimes taking the place of the half-title.

serigraph. See PRINTS AND PRINT PROCESSES.

serigraphy. A name coined by Carl Zigrosser, Curator of Prints, Philadelphia Museum of Fine Arts for the silk screen process as a fine arts reproduction printing medium. The screen is prepared in the regular manner. (See *silk screen.*) A lithographic tusche (*ink, oily in nature*) is painted on the silk where the flat color is to be printed. When the tusche is dry a solution of one part glue, one part water, is lightly scraped over the entire surface of the screen. The glue fills in all the open spaces in the mesh of the silk and does not adhere to the lithographic tusche (oil and water do not mix). The tusche is removed by turpentine soaked rags, leaving the design to be printed clear and free of any tusche. Silk screen poster oil base colors which come in paste form in quart containers must be thinned to the consistency of heavy cream before using. An extender base is used to extend the color—a transparent base is added to make the color transparent when desired. Mixing varnish is used to thin the color to the right consistency. One color is applied at a time throughout the entire edition. The screen is cleaned with turpentine to remove the glue. Tusche is again applied to the screen for each additional color. The first edition is the last and can never be exactly duplicated when the design on the screen is removed. See *Silk Screen Color Printing*, Harry Sternberg; *Silk Screen Stencilling as a Fine Art*, G. I. Bregelisen, M. Cohn.
                                                        —B.E.J.

serpent. See MUSICAL INSTRUMENTS.

serpent bracelet. See JEWELRY.

serrated dovetailing. See TAPESTRY.

Set. Ancient Egyptian god of evil, brother and enemy of Osiris.

set-back. A requirement that a structure be built a certain minimum distance from a specified reference line, such as the edge of the street—applied either to the foundation or to higher parts of the structure. See CIVIC PLANNING.   —T.I.C.

Seto yaki (Jap.). Pottery made in the province of Owari.

settee. See FURNITURE.

settle. See FURNITURE.

seven color ware. Chinese porcelain with the following seven colors: red, yellow, green, blue, violet, black and aubergine.

seven gods of luck. See SYMBOLISM IN FAR EASTERN ART.

seven jumps (syvspring, sieben sprünge). This lively dance cannot be definitely assigned to one nation, since it seems equally native to Holland, Denmark, Belgium, and Germany. The music varies from country to country, but the dance is virtually identical in all four. It is a strenuous, semi-comic dance of alertness, in 2/4 meter, usually performed by two men. The "jumps" are sections of the dance. At the end of each section, the musician holds the last note indefinitely, forcing the dancers to maintain their last position for an unpredictable period and still to be ready for the first note of the next section. The seventh "jump" leaves the men down on both knees with foreheads touching the floor. Skips, jumps, stamps, and rapid whirling are characteristic of the movement.   **—J.G.**

Seven, the Group of. See CANADA, ART OF.

Sevres ware. See CERAMICS II.

sewing. *Book.* In theory there are three (at least) forms of binding the sections of a book together. (1) Sewing. (2) Stitching. (3) Stabbing. But they overlap to some extent in practice. Stabbing is stitching with wire or thread from side to side, near the back fold, but this must not be confused with over-sewing, in which the stitches are smaller and closer. Sewing and stitching are often used synonymously. But the latter describes the sewing of a single section or sections sewn singly to some other substance. Sewing is applied to the work when all the sections of a book are sewn or bound together either by machine or hand.   **—H.E.S.**

sextodecimo. See book sizes.

sfumato (It. smoked). Hazy in outline. See atmospheric perspective.

sgabello. See FURNITURE.

sgraffito (It.). A ceramic technique whereby the design is produced by scratching through an overglaze revealing a different colored ground. See CERAMICS II.

shade. See tint; PERSPECTIVE.

shading-wrinkling. See CHINESE ARTS.

shadow. See PERSPECTIVE.

shaft. In archaeology: (1) The part of a column or pier between capital and base. (2) A vertical passage or well-like excavation.

shagreen. An artificially pebbled leather, or the rough skin of the shark, or ray.

Shakespeare-theatre. See THEATRE.

shakudo (Jap.). A special black bronze finish often used on sword-guards.

shaman's drum. See MUSICAL INSTRUMENTS.

shan mien (Ch.). Fan paper or silk for fan paintings.

shan shui (Ch.). Mountains and water; a type of landscape painting.

shape. See form.

shard. See sherd.

sharkskin. The pebbled rough skin of the shark. Sometimes confused with the similar-looking skin of the ray when seen covering the handle of a Japanese sword.

sharp. *Mus.* The sign (#) which raises a note a semi-tone above its sound in the scale of C major. See NOTATION.

sha t'ai (Ch.). Stoneware; a term applied to pottery when the body, under the glaze, has a dense, stonelike quality.

shawn, shalm. See MUSICAL INSTRUMENTS.

shê. See MUSICAL INSTRUMENTS.

shedding. Raising and lowering warp threads.

sheets. *Book.* The book before it is bound or folded.

Sheffield plate. See METALWORK.

shelf. A horizontal top set into or against a wall; being at least twelve inches in width and more than three feet six inches above the floor. See CIVIC PLANNING.

shellac. Now commonly used in interior house-painting, this resin has little place as an artist's varnish. Probably one reason for its being abandoned was its rather intense orange color and its cloudiness when this is bleached out. It is also slow to dissolve and, because of that, might endanger paintings if an attempt were to be made to take it off at a later time. It is a resinous secretion of the lac insect and now comes largely from India.   **—G.L.S.**

shen. See CHINESE ARTS.

sheng. See MUSICAL INSTRUMENTS; CHINESE ARTS.

Sheraton-Directoire style. See FURNITURE.

Sheraton style. See FURNITURE.

sherd. A fragment of pottery.

shibori (Jap.). Tie-dyeing (q.v.).

shibuichi (Jap.). A special silvery bronze finish often used on sword-guards.

shibumi. See JAPANESE ART.

Shidoro yaki (Jap.). Pottery made in Tō-tōmi province.

shield. See HERALDRY.

Shigamine yaki (Jap.). Pottery made in Hizen province.

Shigaraki yaki (Jap.). Pottery made in Omi province.

shih k'o (Ch.). Stone carving.

Shijo school (Jap.). School of painting combining the naturalism of the *Maruyama* School and the idealism of the *Nanga* School.

Shikasta script. See ISLAMIC ART.

shikhara (Skt.). Turret on a medieval Indian temple. See INDIAN ART.

shikki (Jap.). Lacquerware (q.v.).

shin-en (Jap.). A term meaning "deep distance" in a painting; mountains painted as though seen through a break in a range of hills.

shinden-zukuri (Jap.). See JAPANESE ART.

Shingon sect. See JAPANESE ART.

Shino yaki (Jap.). Pottery made in Owari province.

shipapulima, shipapuyana. See sipapu.

shitodome ana (Jap.). Two holes in the pommel of a sword through which is passed the cord that fastens it to the handle.

sho-chiku-bai (Jap.). A combination of pine, bamboo and plum, symbolizing longevity, happiness and good fortune.

shodai yaki (Jap.). Pottery made in Higo province.

shofar. See MUSICAL INSTRUMENTS.

shohei-ga (Jap.). Paintings on screens and sliding doors.

shoin-zuquri (Jap.). See JAPANESE ART.
shoji (Jap.). Sliding panels covered with thin tough paper. Used, in architecture, as inner partitions where light must be admitted.
—J.A.M.

Shoso-in (Jap.). A famous 8th cent. treasure-house in Nara, Japan.

shot, the. One separate visual image on the screen, its time length being determined by thematic or rhythmical considerations (see cutting). —I.B.

shou. See SYMBOLISM IN FAR EASTERN ART.

shozo (Jap.). A portrait.

shrine. A sacred place or object, as a receptacle for relics. See reliquary.

shrinkage. *Cer.* The amount of volume lost by contraction in drying and in burning.

Siam, art of. See SOUTHEASTERN ASIATIC ART.

sibyl. A prophetess.

siccative. A material which is added to oil paints by artists in order to promote more rapid drying. Their use, particularly in excessive amounts is usually held to be detrimental to the life of the paint. —R.M.

sickle motif. Also called crescent pattern; a decorative pattern, used on Greek pottery, consisting of a row of long, vertical curves resembling a sickle or crescent. —L.T.S.

side elevation. The drawing of an object as though it were only possible to see one side (face) of its mass (volume). It is drawn at eye level.

siderography. The art of engraving on steel. The word is now used more specifically to mean the transferring of an engraving from one steel plate to another as done in banknote engraving. —T.E.F.

sienna pigments. The raw and burnt sienna are earth colors similar to the ochres but somewhat finer in grain and more translucent. In color raw sienna is comparable to yellow ochre and, burnt, it becomes a warm reddish brown. —G.L.S.

Siena, school of. Siena, city of pageants and mystics, was throughout the 14th and 15th cents. the last stronghold of medievalism in Italy. The work of its painters, too, is the final artistic expression of the spiritual intensity of the twilight of the Middle Ages.

The first Sienese master whose name is known to us is Guido da Siena (fl. ca. 1250-1270). The famous Madonna of the Palazzo Pubblico, painted in 1271, is an Hodegetria in the Italo-Byzantine manner. One of the greatest of the Sienese painters was Duccio di Buoninsegna (fl. 1278-1319), whom the Sienese regard as the precursor of Giotto in his innovations in realism. Actually, his style is a combination of classic, Byzantine, and northern Gothic elements, combined with an extraordinary intuition for dramatic expression and a realization of the sacred legend in human rather than hieratic terms. These qualities may be seen particularly well in the panels of the *Maestà*, the altarpiece for the cathedral of Siena. The straining pathos and ghostliness of his Madonnas is achieved through meaningful distortion and the employment of ecstatically moving line. The use of line as an instrument of spiritual expression was brought to its highest fulfillment in the hands of Simone Martini (d. 1344). In his masterpiece, the Sant' Ansano Annunciation of 1333, the earthward descent of Gabriel, the startled recoil of the Madonna, are shown in lines suggestive of the angel's settling to earth and the Madonna's staccato agitation. Simone's visit to the Papal court at Avignon, 1339 to 1344, was responsible for the introduction of the Sienese style to northern Europe. A no less poignant expression of the Christian legend is seen in the work of Pietro Lorenzetti (d. 1348) who adapted the Florentine idiom of monumental form to a typically Sienese emotional expression. His brother Ambrogio (d. 1348), likewise Giottesque in training, is chiefly famed for his didactic allegory of Good and Bad Government in the Palazzo Pubblico, Siena. With the frescoes of Barna in the cathedral of San Gimignano we come to the last great monumental work of the Sienese school in which the dramatic effectiveness of Duccio is combined with the more heroic manner of the Lorenzetti. The 2d half of the 14th cent. was a period of stagnation, marked by the work of such minor followers of Simone Martini as Andrea and Luca Vanni (d. 1375) and Barna's collaborator, Bartolo di Fredi (d. 1410).

Throughout the 15th cent. the artistic tradition of Siena remained essentially medieval, untouched by the scientific progress of the neighboring school of Florence. Rigorous prohibitions discouraged the work of foreign artists who might have introduced the innovations of the Renaissance. Siena drew apart from change. Sassetta (1392-1451) revived the linear tradition of Simone in a peculiarly rarefied and lyric style of his own. That strangely neurasthenic personality, Giovanni di Paolo (1403-1482), presented his dreams of the Christian story in an idiom almost surrealistic in the extravagance of its distortions. The only truly Renaissance painters of Siena were Domenico di Bartolo (fl. 1428-1447), who had learned something of Masaccio's dignity of form, and the engineer, Francesco di Giorgio (1439-1502), who rivalled Botticelli in his mastery of poignant line and the luminous beauty of his types. His imitator, Neroccio dei Landi (1447-1500), perpetuated his formula in an endless series of sentimentalized Madonnas. Vecchietta (1412-1480) in his best work was capable of evoking mystic visions still conceived in the terms of the great school of the 14th cent. Some slight suggestion of Florentine monumentality is to be found in the work of Matteo di Giovanni (1435-1495) who specialized in the production of Madonnas of a cool and aristocratic nature. By the end of the 15th cent. the Sienese school was a completely worked out and exhausted tradition. Such artists as there were engaged in the endless repetition of no longer meaningful formulae.

The only painters of any note in the 16th cent. were Sodoma (1471-1549) and Domenico Beccafumi (1486-1551). The former was an eclectic who managed to combine elements borrowed from Signorelli and Leonardo. Beccafumi was a mannerist who in his distortion of the human form and preoccupation of lurid effects of lighting produced paintings strangely suggestive of the work of El Greco. See Berenson, B., *Central Italian Painters of the Renaissance,* 1909; Brandi, C., *La Regia Pinacoteca di Siena,* 1933; Cecchi, E,. *I Trecentisti Senesi,* 1928 and *Sienese Painters of the Trecento,* 1928; Edgell, G. H., *A History of Sienese Painting,* 1932; Gielly, L., *Les Primitifs Siennois,* 1926; Van Marle, R., *The Development of the Italian Schools of Painting,* vol. I ff., 1923; Weigelt, C., *Sienese Painting of the Trecento,* 1930.

—B.R.

signature. *Book.* (1) A sheet after being folded. (2) The letters or figures at the foot of the first page of each folded sheet or section. Does not always appear when the page number is at the foot of the page commencing new chapters, etc. In large books after the alphabet has been used once it is the practice to continue AA or 2A, etc.

Sometimes both figures and letters are used at the same time.   —H.E.S.

Mus. The collection of sharps and flats (qq.v.) to indicate key (q.v.).

signatures on paintings. See FORGERIES IN PAINTING.

signet ring. See JEWELRY.

significant form. See architectural form.

sikhara. See INDIAN ART.

Sikyatki. An ancient Hopi village on First Mesa, a center of ceramic industry in the Pueblo IV period, from which Sikyatki pottery takes its name. See Hopi Art. When this ware was discovered, in the excavations made on the site in the late 19th cent., it stimulated Nampeyo, a gifted potter of Hano, to revitalize the current decadent ceramic craft and to restore to the wares of the First Mesa the high quality of the ancient product. Nampeyo's own pottery is now nationally recognized as among the finest of the Pueblo wares.   —H.G.

silenus (Gr. *seilenos*). A companion of Bacchus; the most famous of the satyrs. There was never a clear separation between the two concepts of Silenus and Satyr. In archaic times the shape of the sileni is half animal, half human. Later they resemble more human beings, though they generally retain the long pointed ears and the tail. In this shape they appear frequently in Greek vase painting and sculpture. A famous example from antiquity is the *Satyr* by Praxiteles, a lost work known only through literature. There are, however, many replicas of satyrs pouring wine which are brought in connection with Praxiteles. One of the best known is in Dresden (illustrated in *The Sculpture and Sculptors of the Greeks* by Gisela Richter, New Haven, 1929, Figs. 682-684). The picture of the old drunkard Silenus is based on the *Cyclops* by Euripides. In this shape he appears in Rubens' picture "The drunken Silenus" in the *Alte Pinakothek* at München. Rubens painted the picture at about 1616. The Baroque, with its predilection for allegory, made ample use of such mythological subjects. Another Flemish painter attracted by the motif was Jacob Jordaens. The goat-legged satyr in his picture *The Satyr and the Peasant's Family* in the Gallery of Kassel, Germany is one of the variations which Jordaens painted on the subject of the Aesopian fable.   —L.L.

silica. Well known in the arts for its importance in glass making, glazing and fired enamels, this element also provides filler or extender for the manufacture of artists' paints. This is a silicon dioxide, a natural product. Like other fillers it is mixed with pigments of high tinting strength or intense color in order to give them greater bulk and lower cost.   —G.L.S.

Silk. Silk is produced by the mulberry silk moth bombyx mori, indigenous to China. The silk industry has flourished in China from a remote period, native writings recording that the Empress Si-ling, wife of the Emperor Huang-ti, discovered the method of reeling silk from the cocoon and devoted herself personally to sericulture; she is often called the Goddess of Silk Worms. The secret of silk culture was jealously kept in China for many centuries. Korea learned the silk secret and in the 3d cent. A.D. imparted the knowledge to Japan. Tradition says that a Chinese princess carried silk worms' eggs wrapped in her hair into India but the Indians never developed silk culture to its highest point because of religious scruples which forbade the killing of the silk worms. (Cocoons pierced by the worms yielded short staple silk far inferior to the silk reeled from the cocoons. The product of this silk is coarse and rough, as in pongee or tussah silk.) Sanskrit literature states that a silk industry existed in India 1000 B.C. Persia is said to be the first country to import silk from China. The oldest known Chinese patterned textiles are those which were discovered by Sir Aurel Stein in the Lop Desert Chinese Turkestan in 1914. The site where the textiles were discovered lay on the route opened by the Chinese for silk trade with Western Asia in the 2nd cent. B.C., which leads to the belief that these textiles date from before the Han Dynasty. These fabrics show intricate weaves and designs of griffins, animals, birds, scrolls, wave patterns, cloud forms, bearing a remarkable resemblance to later Chinese work. The spinning of the threads shows an intricate technique and tapestry weaving is used (cf. *Scrindia,* Aurel Stein, 1921).

Aristotle is the first writer to describe the silk worm and its metamorphosis suggesting that the conquest of Alexander in the 3rd cent. B.C. must have disclosed the secret of silk. We read that Justinian, the great Emperor of Byzantine was struggling to discover the secret of silk in the 6th cent

A.D. There are many interesting accounts of the sensational history of silk in Rome. (See *Ciba Review*, No. 11, The Early History of Silk.)

The earliest known silks of Persia belong to the time of the Sassanian kings who ruled from 211 A.D. until the Mohammedan Conquest in the middle of the 7th cent. A.D. No silk fabrics of that time are known to exist today but rock cut reliefs show what the patterns were like. The influence of Babylonian and Assyrian designs are seen in the Persian patterns (e.g., twin griffins facing a palm tree which is between them). Sassanian influence persisted after the conquest of Persia by the Arabian hordes.

In Persia the palm had superseded the "Tree of Life", the "Horna" of Assyria and Babylon. The Sassanid weavers adopted the sea monsters, griffins and lions which the Greeks had taken from the Orient and then returned in modified form to the Orient.

In the 7th cent. identical twin motifs enclosed in a circle became the prevailing pattern. These designs reached their finest development during the reign of the last Sassanid king of Jesdegerd who was dethroned by the Arabs in 640. The endless pattern repeated on surface appealed to the ancient Persians (Sassanians) and to their Islamic conquerors. These patterns symbolize life beginning in the unknown and continuing to the unknown. They liked to have a part of a pattern appear on each salvage suggesting the infinite continuance of the design. The colors of the Sassanid silks were the wonder of the world. Vegetable, mineral and animal dyes were used and mordanting was known. The prevailing colors were deep dark blue, dark green, red, brown, purple, yellow and black.

Syrian weavers adopted the technique and the comparatively limited range of subjects of the Sassanids. The conquest of Persia by the Arabs served to increase the tendency toward geometrical designs. The Mohammedan distaste for the reproduction of nature is the same as that of the ancient Hebrews. (Neither, however, were always faithful to the commands of the Koran and the Old Testament to make no image of anything on land or sea.) Persian art was too vigorous to be quickly changed by their Islamic conquerors. The traders of Islam spread the silks of Persia far to the east and to the west. From the 7th cent. on Persian silks influenced Chinese and Indian weavers as well as Turkish weavers. The Seljuks (Turkish)

followed most closely the Persian designs and later showed the Islamic influence. In Bagdad and Samarkand great silk workshops flourished, turning out patterns of intricate weaves perfectly done which were destined to become the object lessons to the whole of Europe. These are the designs which gave the great impetus to the European Renaissance. Cufic script formed an important part of the designs developed under Mohammedan influence. In the 11th and 12th cents. silks from Tiraz workshops showed floral patterns combined with animal motifs with the same arrangement of twin motifs enclosed in roundels placed side by side. There is no question but these patterns helped to develop the Gothic style. The Byzantine silks show human figures. The Byzantine blending with the Spanish Islamic design dominated the famous textile work shops of Sicily which flourished in the 12th cent. A graceful likeness pervades all designs. Twin lions are often woven into the silks by the weavers of Bagdad and Isaphan, but there is no rigid geometrical form. A graceful lightness pervades all the work.

In the year 800 Charlemagne received gifts from Haroun Al Raschid of oriental fabrics which inspired Charlemagne to establish spinners, weavers and dyers in his own shops to emulate and equal the technique shown in the oriental fabrics. Whether or not Charlemagne's industries survived after his death is not known. There is a letter in the archives of Lyons, France, in which the Consuls in 1399 ordered 10 lengths of red satin from Avignon for the making of robes of office.

In the 14th cent. silk weavers of Lucca settled at Lyons. It is probable that these weavers gave Louis XI (1423-1483) the inspiration to start the production of fine fabrics in Lyons. Probably Italian weavers were gathered in these workshops; it is recorded that a Greek weaver wove all the metal threads used. The dyers of these fabrics were all Frenchmen. Louis XI ceased patronizing his Lyons weavers but they continued to struggle on helped by their fellow citizens. Etien Turquet, a cloth merchant of Italian descent, recognized that there was a need for silk production in Lyons so he gained the patronage of Francis I and set out to break the velvet monopoly of Genoa. Soon there were 1200 people in Lyons alone engaged in the manufacture of silks. The real prosperity of Lyons silks, however, came in the reign of Henry IV (1589-1610) when they finally outdid the Italians in color and design and quality of workmanship. Also, about this time a silk weaver, Claude Dangon, invented a silk loom on which patterned silks could be more easily woven.

Colbert, Minister to Louis XIV (1619-1683), realized the importance of the Lyons industry and reorganized the factories and regulated the output, ushering in a great creative period of the French textile industry. But the greatest prosperity of the Lyons industry occurred in the 18th cent. when Prussia, Spain, Russia (Catherine the Great), ordered silks and draperies for court use. Periods of court mourning and changes in style (as when Marie Antoinette affected muslins and plain simple silks) wrought great hardships on the silk weavers. Later, the French Revolution almost brought the Lyons industry to ruin. After the Revolution Napoleon became a great patron of the Lyons industries, ordering the women of fashion to wear Lyons silks. Wall hangings of silk became the fashion and Napoleon rewarded the weavers whose work attracted his attention. The prosperity of the French weavers of Lyons lasted through the Restoration of the Republic, the Second Empire and the Third Republic. Finally, the Jacquard loom, power driven first by steam and then electricity, took the place of much individual labor and threw thousands of weavers out of business. Adjusting itself to the machine age, Lyons became the center of the world production of creative design not only in silk but wool, cotton, linen and rayon. —G.W.R.

Besides its use as a textile fibre, silk has served in making the fabric supports for a great deal of Far Eastern painting. Except for scattered works done on linen and other fabrics and for the painting on walls, silk and paper have served to carry what is generally familiar as the painting of the Far East. Technically known for its strength as a fibre, this has a double filament and microscopically takes the appearance of a lustrous rod. —G.L.S.

silk painting. See CHINESE ARTS.

silk rugs. See ISLAMIC ART.

silk screen print. Silk screen process is a method of printing a flat color design through a piece of silk, called Swiss bolting cloth, which has previously been tightly stretched over a wooden frame firmly fastened to a table by means of hinges with removable pins. The design is transferred to the silk—all parts of the design not to be printed are stopped out by a resist medium. Silk screen printing can be applied to many surfaces such as glass, plastics, wood, metal, leather paper and cloth. The printing medium such as a lacquer, water color or oil base, is slowly pushed through the open meshes of the exposed silk by means of a long wooden-handled squeegee edged with hard rubber. Only one color can be printed at a time. The same silk and frame can be cleaned and used repeatedly for different designs.

The silk screen method of printing had its origin in the stencil, a craft process first produced by the Chinese and Japanese as a medium for decorating many of their beautiful textiles. These stencils were cut from layers of paper made from the fiber of the mulberry tree and were treated to withstand the intricate cutting of the stencil knife. Some of the Fiji Island tribes used the stencil cut from a banana leaf as a border decoraion on their bark fiber cloth. The stencil was also used in conjunction with the woodcuts in the early history of playing cards in Europe. Decorative stencilled wall papers were introduced into France by the *Dominotiers*, "makers of domino papers". Americans living in pre-revolutionary times used the stencil as a decorative device on furniture, floors, ceilings and walls. As late as 1925 many French designers were reproducing limited deluxe art book editions by the stencil method.

The discovery of attaching a stencil to a piece of silk nailed to a wooden frame is obscure. England, France and Germany played their part in the development of this new discovery. After World War I the silk screen process began its rapid development as a printing method. New materials opened up new methods which added to the scope of the silk screen process. In 1925 the Federal Art Project of New York opened up a poster division which designed and printed silk screen posters for the various departments of the project. The outgrowth of this experimentation resulted in the nation-wide recognition of the silk screen process as a fine arts medium and was accepted by the museums of the country as a medium in the same classification as etchings, wood engravings, woodcuts and lithographs. See *Silk Screen Process*, Earle Dowling; *Silk Screen Methods of Reproduction*, Bert Zahn; *Handbook of the Silk Screen Printing Process*, Harry Summer and R. M. Andrieth; *Silk Screen Printing Process*, Biegelisen & Busenbark; *Silk Screen Process Production*, Harry Hielt; *Silk Screen Color Printing*, Harry Sternberg;

Silk Screen Stencilling as a Fine Art, M. Cohn and J. I. Biegelisen; *Outline of the Silk Screen Printing Process,* American Artists Color Works, Inc.   —B.E.J.

sill. The lower horizontal side of an opening.

silver point. This as a drawing instrument was probably developed from the ancient stylus along with points of copper, lead, and gold. In order to work as a drawing instrument it has to be used on prepared paper, coated with a fine abrasive which will take off and hold small grains of the metal. The line of the silver point later corrodes to a darker, duller, and warmer tone. See also metal point.   —G.L.S.

simultaneism. The simultaneous presentation of different views of an object in the same painting, and more or less superimposed one on another. A form of cubism and futurism (qq.v.) which appeared in 1912. It was soon rejected by the cubists in favor of synthetic cubism, but became an important principle of futurism since it contributed to their expression of dynamic movement. See FRENCH ART.   —L.D.L.

simultaneous scene. See THEATRE.

simultaneous seeing. See PHOTOGRAPHY.

sincerity. See LITERARY CRITICISM.

sinfonia, sinfonie. See symphony; overture.

single fabrics. See weaving.

single-warp knot. The short length of wool is wrapped around only one thread of warp and the ends are brought forward to the surface, one on either side of the same warp thread, leaving one free warp thread between each two knots. Knots are tied on the alternate warp threads in each succeeding row. As in other weaves, after each row of knots has been tied, one or more weft threads are put in. This technique appears in early Spanish carpets which differ radically from that of the carpets of other lands.   —B.E.J.

singspiel (Ger.). The German national form of the opera established by J. A. Hiller during the second half of the 18th cent. See opera.

sinister side. See HERALDRY.

Sino-Indian art. See CENTRAL ASIAN ART.

Sioux art. See Plains Indian art.

sipapu. Term used by the Indians of the American Southwest and applied to a small hole, cavity, opening, or pit in the floor of a ceremonial chamber. There are a number of various explanations given for this feature the most common among the southwestern Indians being that it symbolizes the opening through which the first people, their ancestors, emerged on their journey from the underworld to the surface of the earth. It is the belief of the Indians also, that through this hole comes the beneficent influences of the deities. (Also known by the names *shipapulima, shipapuyana, cibobe,* and *chapap.*)
                    —J.M.M.

sirventes. See MEDIEVAL MUSIC.

sitâr. See MUSICAL INSTRUMENTS.

site planning. See CIVIC PLANNING.

Siva. One of the supreme deities of Hinduism, representing both the principle of destruction and the power of reproduction or restoration.

size. There has been a tendency to use this word for that type of animal glue which is derived from skins and bones. This makes it practically synonymous with gelatin. The word, glue, would then be applied specifically to the adhesive material obtained from cartilage and sinew. This is somewhat different because it contains chondrin. See glue.
                    —G.L.S.

sketching. The process of developing an idea through drawing (q.v.).

sketching easel. See easel.

skive. *Book.* Paring or bevelling edge of leather.

slab. In masonry: Stratified or flat oblong stone, usually not over two inches thick; natural or dressed.

slab system. See terra-cotta sculpture, direct method.

slant brush. See CHINESE ARTS.

slanting spot. See CHINESE ARTS.

slave narrative. See AMERICAN NEGRO LITERATURE.

slave secular. See AMERICAN NEGRO LITERATURE.

sleeve bands. Narrow embroidered bands sewn on to the edge of the Chinese sleeve as a kind of cuff.

slice. A scraper, apparently used in former times to pick up paint from the grinding slab, carried this name. It was made of metal or of wood and was like a putty knife, though the scraping edge was often at an irregular angle to the sides and the blade was broader.
—G.L.S.

Slicha mode. See JEWISH MUSIC.

slip case. *Book.* A case usually of cardboard to take a rare book and protect it from rubbing.

slit drum. See MUSICAL INSTRU-MENTS.

slittered arch. An elaborate arch with much vertical detail achieved by the grouping of cusps and stalactites. See ISLAMIC ART.

Slöjdförneningen. See SCANDINAVIAN ART.

Slovakia, art of. See CZECHOSLOVAKIA, ART OF.

slow seeing. See PHOTOGRAPHY.

sluck sashes. See POLISH ART.

slum clearance. See CIVIC PLANNING.

small axe stroke. In Chinese painting, the technique of shading developed by the North-ern School of the T'ang dynasty; i.e., shad-ing by small strokes resembling axe splits.

smalt. Although literally one of the cobalt pigments, this dates from a much earlier time. Like them, it is an artificial compound, a potash silicate strongly colored with cobalt oxide and ground to a powder. There is some argument that it may have been known to the ancient Egyptians. As a dark blue color on the palette of the painter, it has not been located in European pictures earlier than the 15th cent. and it was at about that time when certain cobalt minerals were discovered on the borders of Saxony in Bohemia. Like the other cobalts, it is permanent but, unlike them, has a weak tinting strength and poor hiding power. It will not keep its color with ex-tremely fine grinding. Its weakness probably led to its displacement by the much stronger Prussian blue in the 18th cent.   —G.L.S.

smashed. See edition binding.

smoking. *Etch.* A specially constructed taper is used to smoke the hard ground used in line etching. The melted hard ground combines with the lamp black from the taper to form a black surface on which the drawing is easily seen.   —K.K.

smooth calf. *Book.* A plain calf binding without decoration.

S motive. The S curve. Commonly used as a unit of design in East Asiatic art.

Smyrna morocco. *Book.* An imitation mo-rocco from a sheepskin split and grained.

Smyrna rugs. See ISLAMIC ART.

snake. See SYMBOLISM IN FAR EAST-ERN ART.

snare drum. See MUSICAL INSTRU-MENTS.

snuff bottles. Small decorated bottles of vari-ous materials. Each bottle has a stopper to which is attached a tiny spoon for dipping out the snuff.

soak. *Cer.* Soaking period. Heat is held and given time to penetrate ware. See CERAM-ICS I.

soap-rock. See CERAMICS II.

socialist realism. Theory of art developed in the Soviet Union. Art is conceived of as an aesthetic reflection of reality, good to the extent that it is faithful to the reality. To be faithful, however, is not to be photo-graphically realistic. It is held that photo-graphic realism renders things statically, as they might seem at some motionless moment if there were any such moment; it does not render the movement and development of things. Dialectical materialism is held to be a philosophic theory which directs the atten-tion of the artist and the critic to the fact that nothing is static. Hence it is necessary to deal with a given subject in such a way as to render its future implicit in its present, to see the subject as a developing entity. This development, of which the essential fac-tor is a conflict of opposing elements, is seen to involve, in social fields, the transition from capitalism to socialism and the further de-velopment of socialism into communism. The socialist element in the realism is therefore indicative of the direction in which social subject matter is considered moving. So-cialist realism, accordingly, is not essentially pessimistic, but optimistic, and involves a "revolutionary romanticism", which depicts the many-sided devotion of human beings to social ideals, and the richness of emotional and psychological content which is generated in the struggle for such ideals.

In the field of literary criticism (q.v.) socialist realism sets before itself the task of overcoming what it considers the mechanical narrowness of earlier tendencies in the Soviet Union and elsewhere; tendencies which are characterized as vulgar sociologism (q.v.). These tendencies are criticized as attempts to "explain" art by relating it to the class consciousness of the author and reducing it directly to sociological forces. Socialist realism holds that a genuine class analysis of art, which should be made, consists in investigating the relation of the objective content of the art (not the subjective consciousness of the author) to the course of the class struggle. It is considered that if the art reflects social reality faithfully (however indirectly, symbolically or fancifully) it will reflect the class struggle as a central part of that reality. The view taken is that the class significance of a work of art—in the sense of what it reflects and also how it affects the further course of class struggles—may have nothing to do with the personal class membership or consciously held social viewpoint of the author. Lenin, for example, in his essay on Tolstoy, points out, in opposition to the narrower view, that Tolstoy, himself a noble, nevertheless presented some of the best pictures of the Russian peasant in all literature and depicted with powerful reailsm the social content of his times and the forces that contributed to the revolutionary dénouement in Russia, in spite of the fact that his consciously held philosopry rejected the whole idea of the revolution. Balzac, by conscious belief a Catholic and a royalist, is likewise evaluated as an artist of great genius in virtue of his faithful portrayal of a social reality which actually led, it is considered, to results quite contradictory to his own views. Moreover, while the sociology of art, properly approached, is considered of great value, it does not exhaust the philosophy of art; the latter should include, it is held, an aesthetics of art in which the specific qualitative richness of artistic productions must be accounted for in aesthetic terms, in terms of the analysis of forms of beauty and of related problems, such as the perennial appeal of "classics." These problems are not felt to necessitate a non-historical methodology. On the contrary, it is considered that they can only be solved within the changing frame of reference of the life of social man.

socially-conscious art. A term used in contemporary American art criticism to describe painting or sculpture which consciously employs social maladjustment as a theme, e.g., poverty, unemployment, the hardships of labor, strikes, class warfare, capitalist greed, religious strife, militarism and the disasters of war, etc. Frequently it supports socialist or communist doctrine and is disillusioned, satirical, and propagandist in nature, though at the same time it is often dramatic and of high artistic quality. Orozco, Rivera, and Siqueiros in Mexico are good examples of socially-conscious art, as also, in varying degrees in the United States, William Gropper, George Grosz, Mervin Jules, Mitchell Siporin, and the various artists who were employed by *The New Masses.*

The term was used frequently in the 1930's, at first commonly in a derogatory sense. It gradually lost its precise meaning and rather deprecatory connotation, as in increasing numbers American artists were influenced in their work by social conditions. At present it has nearly lost its value as a term, since it cannot usefully be defined so broadly as to include all contemporary painters of the streets and back yards of city slums, the Louisiana bayou shacks, Georgia "jungles", and Oklahoma dust storm ruins, in most of which neither satire and irony, nor the artist's political convictions are evident.

The term has never been employed to designate socially conscious artists of fascist inclinations, or artists who, in a more casual way, are aware of and influenced by the society in which they live.   —L.D.L.

sociological aesthetics. See AESTHETIC INQUIRY, CURRENT TYPES OF.

Sociology of art. That science which investigates the interaction between art and the social life-process. It studies the dependence of the forms and subject matters of art works on the basic structure of society, just as it examines the meaning of art works for the sustaining and overthrowing of given social conditions. The social role of art varies from time to time. The same art work will take on a new meaning for each succeeding generation, in each new historical period. A Greek temple has an appearance in classical Greece wholly different from that in the Christian Middle Ages, the Renaissance or in the Counter-Reformation. The sociology of ruins is quite different from the sociology of a sanctuary.

As a distinct cultural realm art is a product of the social division of labor. Among primitive tribes rhythm, song and work constitute a continuous whole; singing is at once the expression and conciliaion of the pain of toil. The first paintings were probably made to keep away the dead, whose spirits men dreaded. Even during periods of advanced cultural development, such as the Middle Ages, art was not dissociated from ritual and secular practices. Religious paintings and cathedrals were not viewed aesthetically any more than furniture and clothes. The former served material or religious ends, not to mention social prestige.

Just as primitive artistic expressions are attempts to mitigate the pains of toil and death through their representation so does later art contain the reaction of men to the constraint of social reality. Art works mirror the world in the light of man's undiminishing claims for happiness and growth; they objectify those experiences which have not yet been set forth in everyday language or schematized. In everyday life human reactions, thoughts and feelings are oriented by practical ends; in the last analysis, by the existing modes of production. Men perceive the world in terms of concepts enforced and born of current practical needs. An art work, however, reflects reality in a way strange to and different from the practical. What appears as necessary and absolute in the practical world is revealed through art to be contingent and relative.

Not only are the critical literary works which appear some time before great historical changes antagonistic to the goals of the practical world, but even so are those works which were intended by their authors as glorifications of their own society. The tendency to be outspoken is only—and in no way the most important element of an art work on which the sociologist of art focusses his analysis. The ideality and harmony of the goals toward which a musical composition or poem seeks to transfigure the world can be judged from the intrusiveness, the determined singleness of purpose, the tender attention to the momentary, the thoughtfulness attended each minute detail, the measure of freedom given the part which is nevertheless kept bound to all the other parts,—these are ever so many tugs which signal the tension between the art work and reality. Hence the

formal elements, just as much as contents or outspoken theses of art works, have sociological relevance.

Sociology of art is to distinguished from psychology of art. Balzac, for example, was a royalist and many of his works contain an absolutistic credo. Yet his works, if for no other reason than the skill with which they portray the deep emotions of men from all walks of life, are just as liberal and democratic as the works of the republican Victor Hugo. Sociological analysis strives for insight into the objectice relationship between art works and social reality. From this point of view, the psychology and the fate of the artist constitute only aids to sociological understanding.

Likewise, the association of art works with individual social groups is one of the tasks of sociology of art. This task includes an examination of the style of art works, of its characterizing views and thoughts; it is an investigation into what past and present strata of society particular art works are in fundamenal accord with. It is possible that sometimes an upper middle class artist produces lower middle class, aristocratic or proletarian works of art. Now this gathering together of detached facts into a single confirmation has its purpose insofar that without a sociological identification of the aforementioned thoughts and views there will be neither comprehension of the art work in question nor will the social reality of the art work be fully disclosed. What is decisive, however, is that these social elements unite in each work of art into a single structure which actually throws a new light on the present.

The ultimate object sought for in sociological analyses of art works is the power of insight of the latter, the ability of art works to make society intelligible. The historical effectiveness of art objects does not lie solely within this capacity of great works of art to give insight into social processes. Sociology of art is also concerned with the negative functions of the aesthetic. It shows that the independence of art from the world of practical ends is, for the greater part, only an appearance and discloses the agreement between art and social power in all its ramifications. From the role of art as an hypnotic tool in the hands of the primitive sorcerer to its crafty use by modern authoritarian cliques constitutes, as it were, a history of the dark or sinister aspect of the aesthetic. This dark side of the aesthetic extends not merely to those instances in which art consciously serves some purpose but especially to the distortions of the world to be found in the aesthetic realm, such as are to be found in works reflecting the appearance of the world to different periods and classes. In these instances art has helped to consolidate the obsolete, to prolong injustice, and to usher in oppressions.

The social role of art is no more amenable to all-embracing principles of explanation than are other cultural phenomena. Furthermore, the boundaries between philosophy of art, aesthetics (*Kunstwissenschaft*) and sociology of art are in many instances not to be sharply drawn with any significance. Fundamental even today for sociology of art are the great philosophical treatises; e.g., all of Hegels' lectures on aesthetics, the writings of Spencer, Comte, Max Weber, and Georg Simmel. Among the few works which are exclusively devoted to sociology of art the book by M. Guyau, *L'art au point de vue sociologique,* who was a student of Durkheim, has played an important role. The works of Eduard Fuchs give extensive sociological view of art are contained in the many monographs on the history of art. Mention should be made of the works of Doorac and Alois Riegl. To these should be added all general works in the fields of sociology and anthropology. —M.H.

soda-lime glass. See GLASS AND GLASS-MAKING.

sofa. See FURNITURE.

soffit. The ceiling or underside of any architectural member.

soft ground etching. See etching, soft ground.

soft ground offset. See offset, soft ground.

soku (Jap.). Ancient name for *kanshitsu* (q.v.).

solar cult. See PRIMITIVE ART.

solarization. See PHOTOGRAPHY.

solar print. *Photog.* An enlargement made by means of daylight.

solfeggio. A vocal exercise sung to one syllable.

solid black and white. See SYMBOLISM IN FAR EASTERN ART.

solo anthem. See anthem.

solvent. Any of the volatile, fluid, organic compounds which, without chemical change, make a solid material into a usable fluid are eligible to be called a solvent. In the arts these are used largely in varnish making and in the removal of varnishes from pictures. The gums, like gum arabic used in water color painting, are dissolved in water and so are glues and size. —G.L.S.

Soma yaki (Jap.). Pottery made in Iwaki province.

sonance (*adj.* sonant). That aspect of tone quality which results from fluctuations in pitch, intensity, time and timbre from wave to wave within a tone (see acoustics, terminology in). We do not hear the quality of a single wave. It requires a succession of waves to give us the experience of tone. What we do hear is a sort of average pitch, intensity and timbre, the result of a succession of changes in the structure of a tone from wave to wave. This we call *sonance*. While timbre gives us a cross section of a tone, sonance represents the body of a tone as a whole for the period of its duration.

With laboratory instruments we can produce a complex sound in which the harmonic structure of the sound waves remains constant for any length of time. In that case the timbre for one wave furnishes a complete description of all the waves, and, therefore, of the tone as a whole, because it is uniform. But such uniformity rarely occurs in music. In practically all musical tones, both vocal and instrumental, there is a continuous flux in the structure of the tone; i.e., the spectrum (q.v.) changes from wave to wave. The result is a fusion of all these changes, a sort of average timbre, pitch and intensity, which may be represented as a toneband with fringes. As timbre represents simultaneous fashion in one spectrum, i.e., for one wave, so sonance represents successive fusion of changing timbre spectra, pitch and intensity.

The term *sonance* was coined in the University of Iowa Psychological Laboratory in the attempt to describe the phenomenon of vibrato (q.v.) which is one of the large variables in the quality of a musical tone. Since then it has proved an essential concept for the understanding and description of any musical tone and, when once understood, should be as familiar to musicians as is its companion piece, timbre.

The performance score (q.v.) shows that a musical tone is complicated and unstable in structure. When measured with precision, a graphic picture of the tone shows not only unsteadiness in pitch and intensity of the tone as a whole but also a complicated flux representing periodic and progressive, as well as erratic, changes in the pitch and intensity of each overtone as well as the coming and going of accessory and inharmonic factors. All of these changes can now be measured and expressed quantitatively. This is an important forward step in the scientific approach to music. Thanks to phonophotography (q.v.) we can now describe adequately any particular musical tone in terms of the timbre as representing a single cross section, and the sonance —the progressive changes in timbres from wave to wave throughout the tone.

Tone quality has always been a very vague and airy term for which music has dozens of ill-defined terms and only rarely any scientific concepts. With the coming in of phonophotography in the last 25 years an entirely new situation has been created in the field of musical acoustics. Musical sounds have been taken into the laboratory where they have been analyzed, measured, classified and explained in rigid scientific terminology which may have musical connotation. The result of such measurements is that in the psychology of music we can now talk about tone quality with the same sort of certainty that we could talk about the structure of the ear or the velocity of sound. The subject is approached by means of phonophotography and the result of measurements show that tone quality has two components, namely, timbre (q.v.) and sonance.

On the basis of the above considerations, I recommend that musicians scrap their whole repertoire of synonyms for tone quality. The diversity of words simply adds to the confusion. "Tone quality" is a term which is adequate and clearly defined, and has the same meaning in music and all the sciences dealing with tone. When we wish to distinguish between its two aspects, a cross section of the tone and the whole tone, we have the two adequately defined terms, timbre and sonance; but for most musical purposes in daily use, the generic term, *tone quality,* should be used in the technical sense of *sonance.* See C. E. Seashore, *Psychology of Music,* 1938; and *In Search of Beauty in Music,* Musical Quarterly, 1942.   —C.E.S.

sonata. The sonata formula, as crystallized in the 18th cent., provided a plan for greater contrast than the fugue had prescribed and for more extended development of ideas. The term is first found in the last part of the 16th cent. (e.g., in *Sacrae Symphoniae,* Joh. Gabrielis, 1597). It is believed that its early use was merely in the sense of "music to be played" as distinct from "music to be sung" or as distinct from closely related instrumental forms such as the *canzona* which retained certain vocal characteristics.

Considerable strides towards the sonata form were made by the Mannheim school. The so-called classic four-movement form, however, is that of Haydn and Mozart. In their sonatas the plan of the first movement is most characteristic. The last movement normally either conformed with the first movement plan or it was based on the rondo form which involved several simple statements of a main theme interspersed with digressions. The other movements often derived their plan, without very great alteration, from the suite. Haydn, however, had a particular attachment to the variation form as a basis for his slow movements. While the term sonata was normally confined to works for solo instrument, or for solo instrument with piano accompaniment, the sonata formula was used as well for trios, quartets, symphonies, concertos, etc.

It is possible to attach too much importance to the specific devices of the sonata pattern, and too little to the principles behind it. The first movement plan of the sonata provides a point of departure for a composer who wishes to achieve certain ends that might also be achieved with a somewhat different plan. If composers accepted the general pattern it was because it embodied a suitable principle of limitation, and limitation is important to the creative process. Limitation is not, however, an end in this process, but rather a means. The time spent inventing novel patterns would be time lost on the means, when the full absorption should be in the end.

It is commonly said that the exposition of a sonata presents two contrasting themes, motive, or ideas. Tovey, however, insisted on the recognition of the fact that the greater sonatas present many more than two ideas of more than transitional status. The ideas tend to fall into two groups, in each of which one thematic element is often primary. A brief pause often discretely separated the groups. In this aspect there is a rather significant difference from the ever-going-on-ness of the dove-tailing sections of the fugue.

If the contrasting groups, in one respect, satisfied the principle of variety, the principle of unity was maintained by means of a close key relationship: that of the fifth above the tonic (the so-called dominant) or, if the opening theme was minor, that of its relative major towards which minor intrinsically tends. (See scales and modes.) The composer then was limited in two useful ways. He was checked from over-indulgence in a single idea, and he was prevented from using up in advance, and thus weakening the impact, of the modulatory expansion of the development, or middle section. Thus, the striking impression of the middle section is not simply due to the drama of rapidly changing key suggestions and the more complex relations in general, but to the perception of certain thwarted appetences suddenly let loose towards a harmonic goal. The so-called recapitulation restores the initial state with certain modifications. It may be true, as it is often surmised, that the restatement of the second group in the main, rather than in the dominant key, is in order that the final cadence in the main key may be prepared sufficiently well in advance. The extended codas of many Mozart and Haydn movements would seem to obviate such a necessity. The limitation, however, is worthwhile, in so far as it keeps the composer from the easy way of literal repetition of the beginning. A new transition must be made between the two groups, since the relationship is somewhat different.

Characteristic of the first movement form is the rapidity with which it moves from one idea to another. This is especially true in the development section where motives, derived from the longer main themes, are mainly dealt with. But even the longer themes of the exposition move directly into transitions by means of extension, and are often immediately decomposed into transitory developments. The posthumous B-flat major sonata for piano of Schubert is weak in the way it lingers for some forty measures over the opening theme, repeated twice with meagre modification. The composer manifests a lack of control in not being able to resist his immediate infatuation with an admittedly pleasing theme. In preoccupation with the detail he loses the large view of the sonata form whose excitement lies in the rapid drive towards the development which realizes the implications of the themes. The weakness is not simply failure to adhere to a conventional requirement. For the practice of presenting a fact and immediately commenting upon it is obviously a more significant proced-

ure than the mere statement and restatement of a fact.

The contemporary use of the term sonata often derives from the earliest general historical sense of music "to be played." Even where there is a more literal adherence to the scheme, the key requirements are often adapted to a more modern tonal structure. See Chamber Music. See *Essays in Musical Analysis,* vols. I-II, Donald Tovey, 1935; *Musikalische Formenlehre,* Hugo Leichtentritt, 1927.   —A.V.B.

sonatina. A little sonata (q.v.).

SONG. NATURE. Song, basically, is melody. In music, it means a composition combining words and a melody. Although epic and dramatic songs exist, the most typical elements of song remain lyricism and relative brevity. Song seeks an aesthetic effect through pitch inflection. This, in its most primitive form, is the gliding intonation of the sounds of nature and the indefinite pitch-points of emotionalized speech. Melody must be present in all song as must also motion in the pitch range. (Texts such as the *Monotone* of Cornelius, avoid this motion.) Harmony and meter are present in practically all art-songs. Song melody, further, is characterized by a predominance of diatonic progression (the essence of melodic relationship among tones) and the relationship between diatonic and skip-progression is one detriment of a composer's song style. In song, the procedure is seldom from music to poetry; in almost all cases the poetry inspires the music, since word language is familiar to all composers. The reverse procedure, however, is artistically quite possible, provided that the poet is sufficiently trained in musical perception. (In the period preceding the Middle Ages, poets frequently were also musicians, thus, the troubadours.)

FORMS. Song may be classified in many ways, but the elements of any one class will overlap those of some other class; on the basis of musical merit (art-song, popular-song); simplicity (art-song, folk-song); application (love-song, dance-song, work-song, drinking-song); secular or sacred content (folk-song, hymn); tone-text relationship (word-song, mood-song); stanza construction (strophic, non-strophic); accompaniment (unaccompanied, accompanied, a capella).

Art-song (It. *canzone;* Ger. *Kunstlied;* Fr. *chanson*). A song meeting the requirements of musical and poetic art. Usually written by composers of note to good texts, with interesting, appropriate, and individual accompaniments and with the melodic line, except for occasional short phrases, not paralleled by the accompaniment. If the accompaniment or melody attempts to depict the meaning of individual words or phrases we have word-setting; if it projects merely the basic mood of the text (as in strophic-song) we have a mood-setting. Most art songs contain elements of both.

Folk-song (Ger. *Volks-lied*; It. *canzone folkloriana*; Fr. *chanson*). A song of and for the people, consisting of simple melodic, harmonic and metric elements. Strophic, with the melody usually duplicated in the accompaniment. Traditionally of obscure origin with composer unknown, sometimes set by composers (J. A. P. Schultz, *Lieder im Volkston,* 1782; Foster, *Swanee River*). Text expressive of obvious sentiments. Also one form of ballad. Folk-songs, in English-speaking countries, are in major keys, in Russia, Spain, Balkan countries and others, many are minor. To this class belong also the *"volkstümlich"*, *"volksmässig"*, folk-like, songs by many composers.

National song (national anthem or hymn). A song in the folk-song idiom with the text restricted to national, usually martial themes. (*Star-Spangled Banner*; France: *Marseillaise;* Germany: *Deutschland über Alles*; Austria: *Gott erhalte Franz den Kaiser*; Italy: *Marcia Reale*; Russia: *God ever Glorious.*)

Popular song (Ger. *gassenhauer* [street hit]; It. *canzone poplare*; Fr. *chanson populaire*). A song of the people, of trivial musical and poetic value, written for immediate popular consumption, usually by laymen. Similar to some of the English ballads.

Strophic-song. A song (folk—or art-song) in which each stanza is set to the same music. Such songs necessarily belong to the mood-song class. (Schubert, *Ave Maria*; Schumann, *Marienwürmchen*; Brahms, *Sonntag*; and many *Bergerettes.*)

Non-strophic song (Ger. *Durchkomponiertes Lied*). A song in which the music varies with the meaning of each verse. (Schubert, *Erlkönig;* Schumann, *Die beiden Grenadiere.*) It usually combines word and mood elements. When long dramatic texts are used it approaches a form of "ballad" or tone-poem in which the simple lyric element may be all but lost. The "ballad" song differs from the operatic aria in a closer adherence to the text.

Ballad (Ger. *Volkstümliches Lied;* Fr. *chanson*; It. *ballata*). (a) A style of song long used in England and derived from *ballata,* a song with dance. It is roughly equivalent to the popular song, sharing with this the binary-form: verse-with-refrain, or verse-with-chorus. (Such a division is characteristic also of the larger recitative-aria form.)

(b) An extended song composition of serious, usually epic content, non-strophic in character and with descriptive and detailed accompaniment. In this form the ballad becomes the highest and most complex type of song composition. (Schubert, *Erlkönig*; Wolf, *Mignon*; Loewe, *Eduard Ballade.*)

Plain song. The unisonous vocal music of the early Christian church, based upon poetic meter rather than musical meter. Not a form of "song" as this is understood in music.

HISTORY. Song, as vocal expression, originates in antiquity. Folk-song, especially in its rudimentary form, has accompanied human life as call motives, burial chants, or work-songs in even the most primitive tribes. The earliest songs were unaccompanied and in a single part. During the Middle Ages song received an impetus from the troubadours, minnesingers, and Meistersingers, and we meet such names as *pastourelle, canzona, lied, lei, spruch, romance.* Adam de la Hale's pastourelle, *Le jeu de Robin et de Marion* is a very early collection of French folk-songs. Toward the end of the 12th cent. other parts were added to the original part. The absence of a sufficiently specific system of notation necessitated oral transition of songs; as a result the original forms are obscure. However, song as we generally understand it, did not develop as an art-form until the 14th cent., with the development of instrumental accompaniment (see madrigal). Naturally, when the monodic reforms of 1600 took place they had to include song in its broad meaning, since song is in its very nature monodic. The decadence of song in the 17th cent., asserted by some authors, is merely relative. With its folk-song basis it had already spread into all countries but was then obscured by the rapid and more commanding forms of the oratorio and opera, and the simultaneous development of instrumental music. (This difference between the cultivation of one monodic form and not the other remains an interesting musicological topic.)

Caccini set a series of short poems to instrumental accompaniment in his *Nuove Musiche,* which represent early types of song. In 1570, Antoine de Boif founded an Academy of Music and Poetry in France. The aim of these early songs was to free the melody from slavish metric imitation of verse, and to lend greater expressiveness to the melody. About this time Heinrich Albert (1604-1651) published eight volumes of "arias" using the choral and dance-song as basis, and giving a hint of the later non-strophic song. In England collections of solo-songs in ballad and folk-song style appeared as early as 1600 (Morley, Byrd, Dowland, Campion). During Queen Elizabeth's reign, trade and work songs were widely used. To this general period belong also such *"volkstümliche"* songs as *The Willow Song* and *Greensleaves*. At the same time occurred a transition from the old modal system to the modern major and minor tonalities. Collections of *Ayres and Dialogues* were published. The period reached its climax in the songs of Henry Purcell (1658-1695). The English folk-song idiom continued into the early 19th cent. (*Home, Sweet Home; Blue Bells of Scotland*).

No other art form has been more closely adapted to the "Weltschmerz and Wanderlust" of Germany than the song, and the simultaneous appearance of the' great poet Goethe and the great composer Schubert in the early part of the 19th cent. formed a combination which brought the art song to one of the highest points it has ever attained. The outstanding position which Schubert (1797-1828) holds in this field results from a well-nigh perfect adaptation of his talent and personality to the song form, and to equally favorable developments (early Romanticism) in the history of music. What had happened in the field of operatic song and aria, cantata and other vocal works, together with the piano as an accompanying instrument, and the presence of excellent poetry gave rich opportunity for the expression of his genius, which embraced all song types from the folk-song to such epic ballads as the *Erlkönig* and *Gretchen am Spinnrade*. Moreover, Schubert had no contemporaries who equalled him and the more than six hundred songs he wrote, very few of which are mediocre and many of which are great, not only gathered the various preceding tendencies, but at the same time established art-song on a level which has never been actually surpassed. (The songs of Haydn, and Beethoven, although musically very valuable, did not affect the history of song.) Mozart in *Das Veilchen* wrote what is usually considered the fine art-song. The *volkstümlich* type went on with J. A. Hiller and J. A. P. Schultz. In England, the light ballad form

continued; in France, song took on a more nationalistic, patriotic hue, and in Italy, monody flourished chiefly in the operatic aria.

Robert Schumann (1810-1856) added a characteristically reflective, dreamy mysticism, or subjectivity to the song, drawing on such lyricists as Heine, and forming a link between the more clear-cut objectivity of Schubert and the complex tone-paintings of the later period of composers, H. Wolf and others. In the Schumann vein, but at lower artistic levels are the songs of Abt, Jensen and Franz. The songs of Brahms bear the stamp of his individuality and have thus further enriched the literature. In his *Vier Ernste Gesänge*, he gave to the world examples of spiritual, subjective song which have never been surpassed, if even equalled in value, and which had no predecessors in song literature.

In the meantime the "ballad" or narrative type of song had been given an initial impetus by Johann Zumsteg (1760-1807), and later served for the rich and dramatic ballads of Carl Loewe (1796-1869). This form is furthest removed from the original short, lyric content of song and actually becomes a short "tone-poem" for voice and accompaniment. It applies to song the dramatic principles of Monteverde and Gluck, and it contains elements of both recitative and aria. Such ballads are essentially non-strophic, gaining unity through thematic development by means of the leit-motiv principle. (The use of the word "ballad" is very misleading, since this originally, and even today, in its popular connotation is just the opposite. See ballad A. Song-poem would be much more appropriate.)

Once the close association of word with music was stressed, later songs frequently carried this narrative element. In the songs of Hugo Wolf (1860-1903) we find many passages resembling the speech-song of Wagner. Moreover, there is a better choice of poet, and Wolf composed entire cycles on texts by Möricke, Goethe, Eichendorff, and translations from the Spanish. In its very nature, song must be a duo between word and tone. In Italy the relative absence of lyric poetry was accompanied by a relative dearth in song composition, with the Italian fondness for melody finding expression in the operatic aria. In France the escape from the light *chanson* (latter part of the 19th cent.) came with the development of art song elsewhere (Faure, the French Schumann), and with the advent of the impressionistic poets Verlaine and Mellarmé and their contemporary composers Debussy, Duparc, Chausson. (Debussy, *Ariettes oubliée* to Verlaine, *Cinq Poemes* to Baudelaire.) Of all art forms, the short song lends itself best to the *pastelles* of the impressionists, and these French songs have contributed a charming, and colorful type of song literature. Debussy, with his whole-tone scale, began this distinctive coloration.

The poet-composer associatior is also reflected in the songs of the Scandinavian, Grieg (1843-1907), set to poems of Bjornson and Ibsen, and marked by typically national melodic and harmonic progressions.

In Russia, Glinka (1804-1857) may be credited with founding the art-song. He and his followers (Balakirev, Cui, Moussorgski, Rimsky-Korsakoff) adhere to dramatic verity, using the traditionally sombre Russian hue, and rich harmonization. Once again, the composers use the poems of the best writers, Pushkin, Turgenev, Dostoevsky, Tolstoy.

Similar nationalistic styles were developed in other countries: Spain and the Balkans. In Spain the charming lighter forms have been widely used, the art-forms much less, until recently.

At the same time, the more cosmopolitan song-style of Schubert, Schumann and Brahms continued to exist in the songs of Rubinstein, Tschaikovsky, Rachmaninoff, R. Strauss, Marx, Mahler, and others. To this style belong also the songs of English (Bantock, Delius, Quilter, Scott, Vaughan Williams) and of American composers (Stillman Kelly, Huss, Buck, Beach, Cadman, Chadwick, Hadley, Macdowell, Griffes). In the U. S. A. an original color has occasionally been added by the use of Indian and Negro tunes, but the essential characteristic remains an eclecticism, the sources of which are drawn from European origins.

Recently, in England, an attempt has been made to write unaccompanied song (Herbert Bedford). A single vocal line portrays the text, with close attention to pitch inflection and agogic freedom in the onomatopoeic aspect of the words. As an art-form this style is limited; any gain in word-tone integration and freedom of pitch outline is offset by the loss in rhythmic vitality and in harmony. Moreover, unaccompanied song places burdens of musicianship and intonation on the singer which few vocalists can carry.

Nor has the twelve-tone technique added materially to the history of song (Schönberg,

Krenek, Van Webern, and others). Some songs have been written in this idiom which are musically valuable. Their meagre acceptance is not a fault of the system itself, but rather of the vocal and musical difficulties which they impose upon ill-equipped vocalists.
—O.O.

song-form. *Mus.* A simple form of three sections, the third being a repetition of the first (a, b, a).

song play. See opera.

sonorous stone. See MUSICAL INSTRUMENTS.

sordone. See MUSICAL INSTRUMENTS.

soritsuno (Jap.). Small hook in the side of of scabbard to prevent the scabbard from being pulled through the belt when the sword-blade is drawn.

sorrowing Christ. See ecce homo.

Soumak or Cashmere rugs. An abbreviation of Shemakha, the name of the town in the Caucasus where this weaving is done. It is a rug of three members—warp, weft and stitch. The stitch is flat woven with a needle on the warp, making an oriental rug weaving with a smooth surface. The distinguishing feature of this weaving is the long loose ends of stitch yarn at the back of the rug, as at the back of Cashmere shawls. Their surfaces are compact with rows of stitches, sometimes twenty to the inch, perpendicular, and the numerous long threads at the back act as a buffer between the back and the floor.
—B.E.J.

sound. *Motion pictures.* Consists, in the film, of speech, natural sound, and music. Although speech and sound are used most frequently in conjunction with their visual sources, as in the theatre, many theorists and practitioners, such as V. I. Pudovkin, contend that speech and sound should not be used merely to duplicate and supplement the effect of the visuals, but may be removed from their visual source and superimposed upon some action to which they are related only thematically, e.g., the speech of a character may be laid over images or action which present a parallel or an ironic contrast to the sense of what is being said. This *contrapuntal* use of sound applies also to music, which may either represent literally the effect of the visuals (as is customary) or develop an independent succession of ideas and sentiments.
—I.B.

soundboard. The thin board placed below or behind the strings of musical instruments to increase their resonance.

sound effects. See RADIO DRAMA.

sounding box. In southwestern archaeology: It is believed by many that some of the subfloor vaults, as found in kivas, may have functioned, when covered, as sounding boxes or oversized drums. —J.M.

South American aboriginal art. See AMERICAN ABORIGINAL ART.

South American art. See LATIN AMERICAN ART.

SOUTHEASTERN ASIATIC ART. Burma, Siam, (Thailand), Cambodia, and Campā derived their artistic stimulus from India, both directly and indirectly, in the latter case influencing each other and being influenced by Ceylon, Sumatra, Java, Malaya, and China. All of the earliest statues were made by Indians, some of them evidently in India, and the construction of many of the buildings must have been at least supervised by Indians. Paintings are scarce and there is a paucity of inscriptions and other literary evidence. All the art is religious and communal: no artist's name is known.

Burma is on the Irawadi River. Not much is known about it before the 10th cent., except that the Pyus had their capital in the north, at Prome, and the Talaings had theirs in the south at Thaton. Markedly Indian ruins have been found near Pagān, which became the northern capital in the 9th cent., after Prome had fallen before the independent southern kingdom of Pegu.

In 1056 King Anawratā (Aniruddha) of Pagān, being displeased with the Tāntrik Mahāyāna Buddhism practiced by some of his people, requested King Manuha of Thaton to send him priests and texts for the dissemination of Hīnayāna doctrine. Manuha's refusal caused Anawratā to attack and conquer his kingdom with exceedingly important results. Hīnayāna supplanted Mahāyāna in Upper Burma, Pāli replaced Sanskrit as the scriptural language, and the people adopted the Talaing (Mon) alphabet and wrote their own language for the first time. The subsequent unification of Burma by Anawratā inaugurated two centuries of building that finally left Pagān and vicinity with remains of over 5000 religious structures, some in stone, but most in brick decorated with carved stucco.

Nearly all show Indian affinities. The Ngakye Nadaun, for example, is reminiscent of Sārnāth, the Mahābodhi is almost a copy of Bodhgaya, and even the most distinctively native types, such as the Ānanda and the Hindu Nat Hlaung Gyaung, with a high, cubical base with openings in the sides, have a precursor at Mīrpur Khās, Sind. Certain ones, like the Mingalazedi and Shwesandaw, recall the terraced temples of Cambodia and Java (Borobudur), and others refer to Ceylon and China.

At least until the 11th cent., Burmese sculpture is too Indian to require independent consideration. The reliefs of the Ānanda pagoda (1082-1090) appear more self-sustaining and are both charming and lively. They represent scenes from the life of the Buddha and, unlike reliefs at Ankor and Borobudur, are not continuous. Several temples contain glazed *Jātaka* bricks, which are closer to the Indian style.

Fresco paintings are found in various temples, some very competent, all close to India (Bengal and Nepāl).

Burmese bronze Buddhas after Bengal and Bihār models are noteworthy mainly for their influence on northern Siamese sculpture.

While the strength of the people had been sapped by such great expenditures on building and related works, Kublai Khan sacked Pagān in 1287. The subsequent incursions of Shān-Thai (true Burmese) people and the struggles between the Shān and the Talaings further vitiated the productive impulse, so that there was a rapid decline in the quality of artistic production, coincident with the diminution of direct Indian influence. By 1760 the Burmese had gained complete control, and the only significant later works are several groups of monasteries reminiscent of earlier, extinct Indian wooden buildings; the Mandalay palace of Mindon Min; and illuminated Buddhist texts prepared for him. These latter are of palm leaf, decorated in red and gold lacquer with writing in black. In soaring modern pagodas, like the Shwedagon in Rangoon, the exterior definition of the different architectural elements has been sacrificed for a sensation of aspiration, with the result that structural composition has been supplanted by rather insipid attenuation.

What has in the West been known as **Siam** and is now called **Thailand** was neither settled nor controlled by the Thai (Siamese) until the 13th cent., but different parts of the territory, under various leadership, were centers for the production of objects of art.

Most of these centers were on the Menam River or its tributaries. The earliest objects found are bronzes of the **Amarāvatī school** of India and the base of a temple that is purely Indian. Nothing is known about this period. The first historical facts come from records of Chinese pilgrims, who refer to a kingdom of Dvāravatī existing in the 6th or 7th cent. between Burma and Cambodia. The people were Mons, related to the Talaings of Lower Burma, their inscriptions were in Pallava characters analogous to those of pre-Ankorian Cambodia, and their architecture and sculpture were markedly under the influence of India of the Gupta Period. From the stupa at P'rapatom, which has been too much restored to be of historical value, come some of the earliest pieces of sculpture. They are a stone Wheel of the Law (q.v.) and deer, survivals of abstract representation of the Buddha. The statutes of Ardhānarī and the *Vaksi* from Srīdeb may be Funanese (i.e., before Mon or Khmer ascendancy) and in any case hark back to considerably pre-Gupta Indian prototypes. The main output of the Dvāravatī Period, however, was a number of Buddhas in bluish limestone having heavy curls, high arched eyebrows, and an asexual body showing through a double monastic garment. These are definitely related to the Gupta sculpture of Sārnāth.

The kingdom of Srīvijaya or Jāvaka, in the Malay Peninsula, was apparently contemporary with the kingdom of Dvāravatī and produced both Hindu and Buddhist architecture and sculpture, some of which is indistinguishable from Indian monuments of the Pāla Period, and some of which has affinities with that of Java, Dvāravatī, and even Campā. Large bronze representations of Lokeśvara and Padmapāni are among the finest pieces produced in Siam; although they are quite Indian, their material seems to indicate a Srīvijayan origin.

The **school of Lopburi (Labapurī)** came into being with the Khmer (Cambodian) dominion over Siam, from the early 11th cent. to about the middle of the 13th cent. Although Hinduism and Buddhism of both kinds existed side by side, as witnessed by the buildings, nearly all statues are Buddhist. The buildings of the period are typically Khmer with little or no local (Mon) influence, whereas the sculpture varies from pure Khmer to Mon-Khmer to Khmer-Thai. The Khmers did not take kindly to the native blue limestone, but preferred the sandstone to which they were accustomed, and bronze.

Generally speaking, the statues had eyebrows raised like ledges, acutely arched noses, jutting chins, and a decidedly marked outline to the hair. In the seated figures, an idiosyncrasy is that the distance between the knees is equal to the height.

The capture of the Mon capital of Thaton in Burma in the 11th cent. had deprived the Siamese Mons of leadership, so that they were being slowly absorbed; and when, late in the 13th cent., the southern thrust of Kublai Khan started the Shān-Thai people moving again, the Khmer power was only a fragment of what it had been. It was not difficult, therefore, for Meng Rai to conquer Northern Siam and establish a Thai capital at Chiengsen, nor for Rām K'amheng, himself a Thai, to conquer the rest of the country and set up his capital at Suk'ōt'ai. This is the beginning of what is called Siam or Thailand. Architecturally and sculpturally both sections of the country drew on Pala India (via Burma), on Burma, on Ceylon, and on China. Nearly all statues are bronze and nearly all represent the Buddha seated in the earth-touching pose. The stylistic peculiarities of these Buddhas at Chiengsen are tightly crossed legs, full body with feminine chest, oval face, high arched eyebrows, arched nose, small mouth, fleshy chin, and an *usnīsa* like a lotus bud. The bronzes of Suk'ōt'ai have *usnīsas* in the shape of a flame, as in Ceylon; otherwise, they have the same characteristics as those of Chiegsen, but all have been exaggerated: the eyebrows and the nose are more arched, the mouth is smaller, and the face is elongated. In addition, the figures appear blown up, instead of modelled and cast.

The **school of U-T'ong** in the 14th cent. continues the production of bronze Buddhas in two styles, one pure Thai and the other derived from the Bayon of Ankor Thom. The school of Ayuthia, on the foundations of the ancient Dvāravatī, accentuates the attenuation of the figures to the point of complete decadence.

At Sawank'alōk were manufactured ceramics derived from Chinese celadon, Tz'u-chou, and other Sung dynasty wares. Later, porcelain was made in China after Siamese designs and sent to Siam for decoration.

In considering **Cambodia** one must take into account the kingdom of Funan, which existed at least as early as the 3rd cent. A.D. and supported both Hīnayāna Buddhism and Brahmanism. In the 6th and 7th cents. Funan was overcome by Chen-la, which was itself divided into two parts. Early in the 9th cent. Jayavarman II, a Javanese, united the two Chen-la and founded what is referred to as Cambodia, a country on the Mekong River composed of Kâmbuja (born of Kambu) or Khmers. It cannot be said under which hegemony the art of this early period was produced, but it is known that the first temples were made of brick after Indian models and that the first sculptures were inspired by, though not copied from, Indian originals. Of these the earliest appear to be half-life-sized statues of Visnu inspired by the Kusāna sculpture of Sārnāth and Mathurā. Then come life-sized and larger figures, mostly of Harihara, and a group of Buddhist statues, all of which are close to Gupta and may have derived their impetus through Dvāravatī. The majority of the Hindu statues stand with the weight distributed equally between the two feet, whereas the Buddhist have the weight on one foot and the hip thrown slightly to the side.

About 900 A.D. Yaśovarman I moved the capital to Ankor and built over a small hill in the center of the city a "mountain-temple" known as Phnom Bakheng, which doubtless originally had at its top a shrine housing a *lingam*. This marks not only the beginning of the classical period, but also the complete independence of Khmer architects and sculptors from Indian influence. In the Roluos group there is a survival of brick construction, whereas both brick and sandstone were used at Koh Ker. From the middle of the 10th cent. to the middle of the 12th, Bantéay Srei, the Baphuon, and Ankor Wāt were built all of stone. Not only is Ankor Wat the most famous of the thousand odd temples of Cambodia, but also it is the culmination of the extraordinary architectural genius of the Khmers. Despite its size, the large number of different elements of which it is composed, and the incredible profusion of its decoration, every detail is subordinated to the whole, so that it stands—in partial ruin—as the perfect example of the concept of the "mountain-temple." These **mountain-temples** of the Khmers were always in the form of stepped pyramids symbolizing Mount Meru, the center of the Universe, and at the top was enshrined the *lingam* representing the divine energy of the god-king (**devarāja**).

The best Cambodian sculpture is unsurpassed and embodies, regardless of its date of production, a combination of the sensual and the spiritual, the human and the divine, that stirs both the emotional and the intellectual depths. The Ankorian approach was concerned more with relief, whereas the pre-

Ankorian sculpture was mostly in the round and had no relation to the architectural background. Thus, the enormous amount of energy that is confined in a single early statue is released to comprise a whole later building, sculpture and all, with a consequent decrease in immediate impact that is balanced by an increase in synthetic breadth. The reliefs of Ankor Wāt, representing episodes from two great Vaisnavite epics, the *Mahābhārata* and the *Rāmāyana,* are marvels of complex yet perfectly clear composition.

About 1200 A.D. Jayavarman VII built the walls and gates of the city of Ankor Thom and, in its exact center, the Bayon, which is a microcosmic model of the macrocosm. Sculpturally slightly decadent, it exemplifies iconographically the acceptability to the Khmers of either Buddhism or Hinduism, for each of its many towers contains four identical faces of the Buddhist Lokeśvara and yet represents the Hindu *lingam*. Since the faces were done in the likeness of the king, the building symbolizes the power (*lingam*) of the god-king (*devarāja*) and also of the god (Lokeśvara). The bas-reliefs of the Bayon are decidedly inferior, with a marked tendency towards realism and a consequent loss of form.

The bronzes of the Ankorian period are miniatures of the stone sculpture, except that the different medium has been subjected to a suitable technique. The subjects are both Hindu and Buddhist.

In the middle of the 15th cent. the Siamese (Thai) defeated the Khmers and sacked Ankor. Cambodian art since this date is insignificant.

At the height of its power Campā occupied the territory now known as **Annam.** The people were warlike and fought consistently with the Cambodians, the Chinese, and, especially, the Annamites, who began forcing them southward in the 11th cent. and finally conquered them in the 17th cent.

The dating of Cam monuments is in a state of extreme confusion. The earliest piece of sculpture found on Cam soil is a standing bronze Buddha that must have been made at Amarāvatī (India) or Anurādhapura (Ceylon) in the 3rd or 4th cent. In spite of this fact there is no early "Indian period" in Campā, architecture and sculpture bursting into full flower with obvious Cambodian, some Javanese, some Chinese, and some Annamite influence. The earliest native monuments are found at Tra-kiêu, Mi-son, and Dong-duong in the northern province of Quang-nam, and probably date between the 7th and the 11th cents. All extant buildings are of brick, those at Mi-son consisting, like most Cam structures, of disconnected towers and long rooms reminiscent of segments of Cambodian edifices. Apparently they were built at different times over a period of about three centuries, but all are remarkable for their tall pilasters and opulent decoration. The only Buddhist site in Campā, the great shrine at Dong-duong, gives evidence of a more coherent plan without any lessening in the luxuriance of the decoration. By the 11th cent. the ornament had been largely given up, but its place is taken, as at Binh-dinh, by soaring pilasters that convey an extraordinary feeling of aspiration.

Regardless of where it was made, Cam sculpture presents a paradox. Much of it is devoid of character, yet the best is notable for a concentration of rugged force and sculptural synthesis that is hardly surpassed. Most statues of females are refined, sensuous, and sometimes noble; most statues of males are coarse, sensual, and brutal. All of the finest have power, in one way or another.

When the Cams began succumbing to the Annamites in the 11th cent., their sculpture grew less interesting, so that there is little of significance from Binh-dinh. It may be mentioned that all Cam sculpture is in sandstone, usually brown, but sometimes gray, and that all is Hindu. With the exception of the early Indian bronze, even the statues found in the Buddhist buildings at Dong-duong are Saivite. See *History of Indian and Indonesian Art*, A. K. Coomaraswamy, 1927; Musée Guimet, *Cat. des Collections Indochinoises,* Pierre Dupont and others, 1934; *Les Arts de l'Indochine,* G. de Coral Rémusat, 1938; Arts Asiatica XII, *Les Collections Archéologiques du Musée National de Bangkok,* George Coedès, 1928; *Buddhist Art in Siam,* Reginald LeMay, 1938; Ars Asiatica XVI, *Les Collections Khmères du Musée Albert Sarraut à Phnom-Penh,* George Groslier, 1931; Ars Asiatica V, *Bronzes Khmèrs,* George Coedès, 1923; Ars Asiatica IV, *Les Sculptures Chames au Musée de Tourane,* H. Parmentier, 1922.   —H.Ho.

space arts. Those fine or visual arts such as painting, sculpture, and architecture that are particularly concerned with space, light, and color; those arts dealing with either the representation of forms in space (as painting, drawing, etc.), or whose products are erected or constructed in space, as are the products of sculpture and architecture; to be distin-guished from those fine arts not concerned esp. with space, such as music and poetry. Whitford and Winslow in *Dictionary of Education.*

SPAIN, ART OF (from Roman times exclusive of Mohammedan work). Unlike the other principal countries of Europe our knowledge of the role played by Spain in the various fields of art is not as yet based on definitive conclusions. Large areas still exist which demand scientific analysis although scholars both native and foreign have done much in the last twenty years toward clarification.

Lamperez y Romea wisely stated, "The art of Spain is alluvial." Numerous foreign influences have recurrently sifted on Spain to be absorbed and modified by local physical and spiritual conditions. The Spanish temper itself is best explained by acknowledging its dependence on both native Christian and absorbed Mohammedan factors. Their intensity of religious zeal, austerity, and expression mingles with certain stoic qualities, love of luxury and individualism that stems from the followers of Mohammed. This accounts for various surprising factors in their art productions such as the recurrent use of an excitingly rich motif set as a foil against a large austerely plain area (q.v. Plateresque).

In general sublety and refinement count for less in Spanish work than does boldness and vigor of conception. In architecture this is explained by the intensity of reflected light which is a product of both her atmospheric conditions and a certain harshness found in her landscape setting. This strong reflected light destroys subtle shadows on delicate form and renders them inconsequential, whereas in Greece the reverse is true and thus renders refinements in form desirable. One learns to look for drama, intensity of expression, and swift contrast in the various arts in Spain. The principal currents of her influence radiate most distinctly beginning with colonization in the Americas. The dependent cultures of the countries of South America and Mexico are now recognized as of genuine importance.

ARCHITECTURE. ROMAN PERIOD. Roman influence dates from the end of the 3d cent. B.C. when the Carthaginians were overthrown by Scipio Africanus and terminates with the invasion of the Northern tribes in the 5th cent. A.D. Rome established here the pattern of her own political and cultural system. Numerous fortifications were established, excellent highways engineered, aqueducts constructed and the growth of cities assured which were then embellished with temples, basilicas, therme, theaters, imposing urban dwellings and adjacent villas. As elsewhere in Roman possessions, the style of these as closely as possible followed those prevailing in Rome itself. They are often distinguished by their size rather than artistic merit and failed to attain the staus of a separate style. Plan types are essentially Roman as are methods of construction.

While Roman remains are not numerous in Spain they are impressive. They include the justly famous six arched bridge at Alcántara (early second century A.D.) built of granite laid without mortar or metal clamps, which rises 180 feet above the surface of the Tagus river. The bridge at Merida (reign of Augustus) exceeds a half mile in length, while various smaller bridges remain. The great aqueduct at Segovia in some respects surpasses the Pont du Gard at Nimes as an engineering achievement. Roman fortifications of importance remain at such centers as Seville and Leon. Amphitheaters are represented by the example at Santiponce and Mérida. A well-restored theater at Merida (18 B.C.) complete with *scenae,* Corinthian columns and sculpture exists; and with the theater remains at Ronda la Vieja they yield us important information. A triumphal arch 43 feet high, two temples, a well-defined circus and numerous other remains are found at Merida and indicate the colonial importance of the city. A basilica occurs at Talavera la Vieja; a small Corinthian temple at Vich; triumphal arches at Medinaceli and Caparra; and tombs of architectural importance near Tarragona, Caspe and Sádaba.

VISIGOTHIC PERIOD (mainly 6th and 7th cent.). Christianity dates from the 2d cent. in Spain although its early phase (2d to 6th cents.), prior to the Visigothic period, is evidenced by only scant remains largely represented by the basilica of S. Pereró near Manorca (on Majorca), the palace at Mérida and the baptistry of Gabia La Grande near Granada. More is known of Visigothic work. While considerable controversy exists regarding dates of buildings and parts of buildings, it is evident that constructions of high interest were achieved that warrant continued study. Both the barrel and groin vaults were employed on three aisled basilican, cross-inscribed and cross-exposed types of plans. A good sense of mass composition is felt. Decorative instinct is sound but not of high maturity. Influence from Syria and Persia

is acknowledged (q.q.v. Dieulafoy, Bevan). The slightly flattened (three-centered) horseshoe arch (q.v. Gomez Moreno) and barrel vault is used prior to the Mohammedan conquest (711) when the full circular (one-centered) horse-shoe shaped arch from Persia is introduced. The transept, low central tower, side portico, square sanctuary, rectangular *prothesis* and *diaconicon* and pierced stone window grilles are employed here. Construction is craftsman-like and enduring. Architectural sculpture is mainly linear in conception, and of only moderate merit, but some use is made of borrowed Roman details. The chief monuments include the church of S. Juan at Baños (661 A.D.); San Antolin, (late 7th cent.) under Palencia Cathedral; S. Comba de Bande at Orense (8th and 9th cent.); S. Pedro de la Nave (probably early 8th and 10th cent., q.v. Bevan) near Alcañices; S. Eulalia (6th cent.), Toledo; S. Sebastián (7th cent), Toledo; and remains of churches at Elche, near Alicante and Cabeza del Griego near Ucles.

ASTURIAN STYLE (mainly 9th cent.). This style takes its name from the small northwest corner of Spain which, with Galicia, was the only part of the country left unconquered by the Mohammedan invasion. Here in a region only forty by thirty miles in area, Christian architecture progressed from Visigothic precedent, blended with some Carolingian influence and independent solutions which by the 9th cent. permits it to be regarded as an individual style with monuments that hold their own with most contemporary western European work.

The style is marked by sturdy construction of stone with large flat brick often used for the arches (q.v. Carolingian work). Plans depend largely on the single aisle and three aisle basilica types although evidence points to the survival of the cross-inscribed-in-square plan. Several instances of the imposing two storied narthex occur with arches springing from columns with linearly enriched shafts and boldly executed capitals sometimes showing debased classic and some provincial Byzantine influences. The stilted round arch of Carolingian work is used rather than the horseshoe-shaped arch. Naves are covered with stilted round-arched barrel vaults with ribs that synchronize but do not connect, with the pier supports below. The square sanctuary is flanked by rectangular compartments which generally open to the transept instead of connecting with the sanctuary. A choir screen or *iconostasis* separates the sanctuary from the rest of the church. Effects of increased height are evident over Visigothic work. Well marked flat wall buttresses are systematically used on the exteriors. Windows are fitted with handsomely-pierced stone screens. Both double and triple arched window treatments occur.

Among the important surviving examples are the imposing church of Santullano (791 to 842 A.D.) near Oviedo; S. Maria de Naranco (mid. 9th cent.) near Oviedo, probably a royal palace originally but later a church; S. Miguel de Liño (mid. 9th cent.) adjacent to S. Maria de Naranco, near Oviedo; S. Cristina de Lena (mid. 9th cent.), between Oviedo and Leon, recently reported a war casualty; S. Salvador de Valdediós (893 A.D.) near Villaviciosa, S. Salvador (921 A.D.) at Priesca, near Villaviciosa; and S. Salvador de Fuentes, (1023 A.D.) near Villaviciosa.

MOZARABIC STYLE (mainly 9th through 11th cents.). This phase takes its name from the work of Spanish Christians who had through either necessity or choice adopted various of the customs and even the language of the Mohammedans. In their Christian architecture they blended to some extent the procedure of the conqueror with that of Visigothic and Asturian practice. Their work varies from products of definite beauty to works of moderate merit. Four separate schools of work are recognized: the Leonese basilicas, the Western hermitages, the Arogonese hermite caves, and the Catalonian churches (q.v. Bevan). In general it may be noted that single and three aisle basilica type plans occur with adaptations that betray connecion to Mosque plans (e.g. Cordova). Ribbed barrel vaults, an unusual system of barrel vaulted cupolas or even the timber truss roof may mover the nave. Apses may be horse-shoe shaped in plan on the interior or square with a barrel vault. The eastern type of single centered horse-shoe shaped arch is found recurrently supported on either columns or piers. Sculpture varies from notably fine work in S. Maria de Lebaña to work of little merit. Among the principal examples of this style are: S. Miguel de Escalado (913 A.D.) near Leon; S. Maria de Bamba (prior to 928 A.D.) near Baños and Mazote; S. Maria de Lebeña (931-937 A.D.), east of Ofiedo; Santiago de Peñalba, (prior to 919 A.D.) in the Vierzo Hills; S. Miguel de Celanova (c. 940 A.D.) south of Orense; S Maria de Marquet (last half of 10th cent.)

near Tarrasa; S. Millán de la Cogollo (c 929 A.D.) east of Burgos; and S. Baudel (probably 11th cent.) southeast of Burgos near Berlanga de Duero.

ROMANESQUE (mainly 11th and 12th cent.). The Romanesque architecture of Spain is, broadly speaking, divided into two main schools, the Catalonia and the Castilian (q.v. Bevan for separate stylistic qualities). It is now recognized that Spain played an important role in the Romanesque period. Despite her internal conflict with the Mohammedans, she achieved a kind of national unification in the North which allowed important constructions in the early decades of the 11th cent. Foreign influence first comes from Lombardy and is expressed in such examples as the great Abbey Church of Ripoll (1020-32 but largely rebuilt in 1887, after serious damage in the Carlist wars, according to original scheme) and San Vincente de Cardona (1020-1040). This is followed in the latter half of the 11th cent. by French influence (the extent and even the direction of influence is debated by Spanish and Frnch scholars) as seen in such examples as Santiago de Compostella (probably begun in 1075 and largely finished in 1128 but much altered in the 18th cent. by a baroque west facade); S. Martin de Fromista (1066); S. Isidoro at Leon (1054-1067); the Old Cathedral, Salamanca (1120-78); the Collegiate Church at Toro (12th cent); Cathedral of Zamora (1174); S. Pedro (early 12th cent.) at Avila and among the many important conventual examples are the Cistercian Abbey of Poblet (mainly late 12th and early 13th cent) and the Monastery of Veruela (last half of the 12th and early 13th cent.).

While generalizations are difficult regarding the characteristics of Spanish Romanesque architecture the following may be noted: Plans are three aisled basilicas terminating in three apses with the center one deeper, with or without transepts. An occasional use is made of the central type plan, e.g. Santa Vero Cruz (1208) Segovia. The barrel vault is employed first with round arches and then pointed arches, finally rib and panel vaulting on square bays is introduced. The triforium gallery or a clerestory is commonly met with but a combination using both is rare. Some examples use neither, having the vault spring from a line shortly above the crown of the nave arcade. Due to the practice of pulling the enclosed choir past the crossing and down into the nave (protected by stone or metal screen), naves tend to be wide and the central apse not remarkably deep except in the famous example of Santiago de Compostella which had the first apse in Spain with surrounding vaulted ambulatory aisle and radiating vaulted chapels. Roofs are rather flat in slope and protected with tile. Windows and door openings tend to be small with deep reveals. Walls are plain except for strategically placed concentrated enrichment about the doors, windows, and in the imposing lantern over the crossing. This last feature is one of the pleasant accomplishments of the period in Spain. Boldly conceived they attain fine plastic and decorative quality while effectively serving to light the choir below (e.g. Old Cathedral Salamanca and Collegiate Church, Toro). (See Hershey.)

In spite of foreign influence the style attains a national character, well suited to native climate and temper. The flat slope of the roofs testifies to a dry climate, the small openings and numerous one and two storied cloisters indicate the harsh sunlight. The vigorous sculptural forms without plastic subtleties recognize the visually destructive quality of the strong reflected light so characteristic of much of Spain, that would tend to obscure, or visually destroy, small scale refinements.

GOTHIC PERIOD (13th to mid-16th cent.). The Gothic development in Spain produced work of real distinction though unequal in quality. The unification of northern Spain under the Christians allowed commercial prosperity to develop. Catalonia, then as today, was the most progressive and built up rich trade connections which allowed her to undertake important constructions. Her initiative and justifiable pride asserted itself in her new architecture. While Aragon was indifferent and Castile subservient to French Gothic ideas, Catalonia surveyed the building procedures of the Ile de France, Languedoc and that of the Cistercian Order. She then embarked on a sensible course of adjustments that incorporated foreign ideas and yet satisfied her own special needs. The resulting general characteristics are: large, lofty, single-aisled church plans, or plans with wide nave and narrow high side aisles. Large churches terminate at the east end in a broad chevet, and small ones in triple apses. Interior buttressing is usual with aisle chapels between them. On the exterior, the buttress may or may not be expressed on the lower part of he church but projec boldly above the aisle roof and connect with the line of outward thrust of the nave vaults. In the 13th and 14th cents. four part rib- and panel-vaults are used functionally. The triforium gallery is often dispensed with or greatly curtailed in importance. The clerestory is kept small as the problem was often to limit side light and concentrate on a large richly glazed area at the altar end. Otherwise, windows are small but sharply vertical inproportion. Effects of great breadth and height were striven for and one of the prevailing characteristics of Spanish Gothic is the carefully calculated effect of spaciousness and lift. Facades often make use of triple-arched portals, great flankinv towers, imposing lanterns, and important transept porches. In common with Gothic elsewhere in Europe, the style grows richer and less vigorous in the 15th cent. with more dependence placed on decorative instead of functional expression. In line with this, window tracery changes from geometric to curvilinear designs and vaulting loses its sleek structural quadripartite system and becomes multiribbed, stellar, etc.

The cloister, as in the Romanesque period, plays an imposing role. Indeed the shaded court, patio and loggia is a recurrent theme in ecclesiastical, civil, and domestic planning to the present time due not only to climate, but also to an almost oriental love of privacy hat motivated Christian Spain which may well stem from contact with the cultivated Moors.

Important examples are: Barcelona Cathedral (mainly 1298-1339), a key church in Catalonian work; S. Maria de Mar (1328-1383), Barcelona; Collegiate Church (1328-1596), Manressa; Palma Cathedral on Mallorca (mainly 1229-1380), one of the most spectacular of all Gothic achievements with nave height exceeded only by Beauvais Cathedral in France. Gerona Cathedral (begun in 11th cent. but mainly 1316-1458 with vaults not complete until 1598), outstanding example of the great single-aisle plan with interior span of 73 ft. (widest in Europe); Burgos Cathedral (1221-1230, spires 1442-1558, choir 1497-1512, lantern finished 1568); Toledo Cathedral (1227-1493); Seville Cathedral (1402-1520) one of largest Gothic cathedrals in Europe but exterior design much obscured by Renaissance additions; New Cathedral of Salamanca (1513-1560); Segovia Cathedral (1522-1593); Monastery of Las Huelgas (1249 near Burgos; Alcazar (1352-1358), Segovia, now restored; Castle of Olite (1403-1419); The Audiencia Palace (1436) Bercelona; Casa Consistorial (1369-1378) Barcelona; and *La Lonja* or Exchange (1482-1498), Valencia.

PLATERESQUE STYLE (late 15th to last quarter of 16th cent.). The characteristics of this syle are based on decorative aspects rather than new structural principles of its own. Rightly, it should be regarded as marking the end of the Gothic period and the ushering in the Renaissance and so should be treated in two separate phases (Q. V. Bevan). Characterized by compactly massed decoration unified into large zones of ornament, it finds its basis in the decorative procedure of Mudájar work stimulated at a time when new wealth on an appreciable scale was making possible a sumptuous effect that appealed to the Spaniard at this time. Because of the richly wrought character of the decoration and its obvious relationship to the spirit of ornament prevalent in the work of native silversmiths, *plateros,* subsequent generations of critics (17th cent.) called it the "Plateresque style". According to the particular critic, the style is either regarded as marked by rich decorative insight, coupled with highly individual quality and truly expressive of the Spanish taste and temper; or held to be aesthetically inconsequenial and lacking in any true functional quality. It cannot be denied that decoration, in the main, exists wih a definite disregard of fundamental relationship to the structural core of the building, although its manipulation is often marked by a freshness and decorative insight that yields effects of undeniable charm.

No clear boundaries separate the Gothic from the Renaissance phase of the Plateresque style. In certain instances the same architect produced work in each phase. Their difference is primarily based on whether the work is applied to buildings based on Gothic or Renaissance plans and structural procedures and whether the individual elements making up the compacted areas of rich decoration are curvilinear Gothic arches, Gothic sculpture, pinnacles, tracery, etc. (Gothic phase); or freely interpreted classic elements such as pilasters, columns, entablatures, pediments, candelabra, etc. (Renaissance phase). The recurrent use of heraldic devices was common to both and indeed the devices characteristic of the separate phases are sometimes found in combination.

Some of the leading master masons, or architects, were foreigners (from France, Germany, and Flanders) whom we know primarily through the Spanish equivalent of their names such as the de Egas, Güas and de Silóee families. Other architects of importance include Alonso de Covarrubias, Francisco de Colonia, and Rodrigo Gil de Hontañón.

HIGH RENAISSANCE (last three quarters of 16th cent.). This period is relatively dry and uninspired. Definite knowledge of the principles of the High Renaissance in Italy are evidently a part of the equipment of the leading architects of the times but is applied with unequal adherence to Vitruvian theory. As heretofore variety in regional effort is discernable. In the large region around Granada, Renaissance motifs are sometimes applied to Gothic plans and may still retain medieval rib vaulting (Cathedral of Granada) but may also, as in the unfinished Palace of Charles V, reveal a close dependence on Italian Renaissance procedure. In general Andalusia in the southwest, Central Spain around Toledo, and Madrid and Northeast Spain acknowledge Italian Renaissance precedent. Upper Castille and Galicia are conservative in undertaking the new manner but continue it overly long. The Escorial, monastery-palace of Philipp II represents a streamlining of High Renaissance design principles as practiced in Italy by Michelangelo and made popular by the Spanish translation of Serlio. Coldly austere, built of gray granite, on a gigantic plan including seventeen courtyards, it is expressive of the calculated restraint of the style dogmatically established by Juan de Herrera. The architects of the time include Alonso de Covarrubias and Simon de Colonia who likewise practiced in the Plateresque manner. Juan de Herrera, Juan de Toledo, Diego de Silóee, and Pedro Machuca attain genuine importance. Of lesser note are Pedro and Andres Valdelvira, Bartolome Bustamante and Francisco de Villapaudo. Noble scale is sought in the great buildings of the times. Great attention is paid to courtyards and imposing stairways. Private palaces often make use of corner towers, and loggias in the upper stories. Convenience in planning is often sacrificed for imposing effects. Representative buildings are: Cathedral of Granada (1529- facade, 17th cent.) by Diego de Silóee; Cathedral of Valladolid (1585) by Juan de Herrera: Palace-Monastery of the Escorial (1563-1581) by Juan Bautista de Toledo and Juan de Herrera; Palace of Charles V. Granada (1527) mainly be Pedro Machuca, Tavera Hospital, Toledo (1541) by Bartolomé Bustamante; Reconstruction of the Alcazar, Toledo (mid-16th cent.) by Alonso de covarrubias, Francisco de Villalpando Enrique de Egas et al.

BAROQUE STYLE (late 17th to middle 18th cent.). The Baroque movement in Spanish architecture marks the expression of the individualistic sumptuous aspect of the native taste that had been curtailed since the plateresque style. While related to Italian baroque design, no servile following is evident. The Spanish people found evident delight in the new style and her architects moved with freedom and independence within its fertile field. Zestful invention grows into excess in the building up of fabulously enriched designs that finally reach their maximum in the work of followers of José Churriguera. Plans are complex, often involving the use of curved elements. Domes and towers are frequent but the chief characteristic is a striving for rich plastic effects in both two and three dimensions. While decoration is somewhat concentrated in early work, it expands everywhere in Churrigueresque designs (q.v. sacristy of La Cartuja, Granada). The classic elements are freely distorted, used at different scales in the same design in ways diametrically opposed to their functional nature, and are often united with plant forms constructed in stone, marble, or stucco. Serpentine columns, broken pediments, scrools, volutes, human and animal forms in sculpture are all found strangely and richly welded together. At its best, Spanish baroque architecture compares favorably with any produced in Europe, at its worst it lacks all pretension to distinction. Toward the end of the period the Bourbon rulers introduced French designs that reflect the styles of Louis XIV and Louis XV in their residences such as the Royal Palaces of Madrid, Aranjuez and La Granja but this manner never became popular. Chief among Spanish architects of the period were José Churriguera (and his extensive family), Narcisco Tomé and Fernando Casas y Novoa. As usual some foreign architects were employed as Carlo Fontant, Filippo Juvarr, Giovanni Battista Sachetti and Theodore Ardemans. Examples of buildings include the Jesuit College at Loyola (1686) by Fontana; West Facade of Santiago de Compostella (1738) by Fernando Casas y Novoa; University, Valladolid (1715) by Narcisco Tomé; Town Hall, Salamanca (1720-1733) mainly by José Churriguera; Academy of San Fernando, Madrid (early 18th cent.—former Goyeneche Palace); Royal Palace at Aranjuez (1715-78) mainly by Pedro Caro; Royal Palace, la Granja (1721-35) begun by Theo-

dore Ardemans and continued by Juvarra and Sachetti; and Royal Palace, Madrid (1734-1764) by Juvarra and Sachetti.

NEO CLASSIC PHASE (last half 18th early 19th cent.). The work of this period is dominated by the academicians who sponsored a return to restrained classic design. Attempt is made to infuse a true Vitruvian spirit in the use of the Orders and some effort of a Greek revival nature is also effected. The dominant architect of the period is Venture Rodriquez who designed innumerable structures which include: The Church of San Marcos, Madrid (1749-1753); Augustinian Convent, Valladolid (1760) and the facade of Pamplona Cathedral (1783). Sanchez Bort executed the facade of Lugo Cathedral (1784); Francisco Sabatini did the Hacienda Ministery, Madrid (1769) and Juan de Villanueva introduced Greek influence in the Prado, Madrid, (1785).

The subsequent years of the 19th cent. are given over to using earlier styles to solve the current building problems. Romanesque, Gothic and Renaissance revival types are all found. The 20th cent. concerned itself with ecclectic designs stemming from the *Institute des Beaux Arts,* in Paris to be refuted by the proponents of the International Style (q.v.) who prior to the Spanish Revolution succeeded in introducing work of a crisp functional type of considerable merit.

PAINTING. Spanish painting offers a rich field for future investigation. Except for a relatively few outstanding masters of great impotrance much is yet to be done in the accumulation and correlation of knowledge of both the lesser known personalities and the separate schools of painting. The work of Chandler Rathfon Post, in this connection, is of the highest importance.

PRE-ROMANESQUE (up to 10th cent.). Few examples survive on which to base judgment. It appears that the principal characteristics stem from interpretations based on provincial Roman painting. The technique is dependent on that of Roman Mural decoration but accomplished with little evidence of finesse. The quality of line is uninspired and esthetic conception impoverished. Remaining examples include the wall paintings from S. Miguel de Linio, S. Eulalia de la Bóveda and S. Julian de los Prados.

ROMANESQUE (10th to 13th cent.). Spain is rich in surviving examples of this period compared with other European countries. Painting is, however, almost entirely confined to the enrichment of church decoration and is found throughout much of the area covered by Christian Spain at this time. The technique is a simple one, unrelated to the true fresco process. A whitewash ground was laid and the designs applied directly on this in water-soluble pigments. Retouching was effected with the same pigments mixed with thin binders and lastly a thicker tempera was used to clarify details. The brilliant colors used have stood well the test of time.

While the work of regional schools is not clearly marked, two prevailing types of procedure are evident. The first is the most strongly native in feeling and stems from the illuminations in early Spanish manuscripts. This is marked by a grave architectonic quality, a somewhat abstract stylization and simple but vigorous color organization. Figures loom large in the compositions and are set against simply enriched backgrounds. The second bears obvious dependency on Byzantine Mosaic composition and doubtless was intended to substitute for the mosaic technique as practiced in Italian examples. In general the draughtsmanship is less rigidly stylized and acknowledges a more realistic representation. Examples of note include: Apse mural from S. María de Mur (c.1150) now in the Museum of Fine Arts, Boston; Apse mural from S. Clemente de Tahull (c. 1123) now in the Barcelona Museum; murals in the Panthéon de los Reyes in S. Isidro of Leon (last half 12th cent.); Apse decoration from Pedret (probably late 12th cent.) now in the Barcelona Museum. Panel painting as applied to alter decoration may be represented by the altar frontal from Martinet (c.1175), Worcester Art Museum and a later example, The Pantocrator with incidents in the S. Martin Cycle (c.1250), Walters Art Gallery, Baltimore.

GOTHIC (13th through 15th cent.). The achievements in painting in Spain at this time are of genuine significance. While connection with France, Italy, and Flanders are all evident, the strong impress of native taste and temper is undeniably present. The separation from Romanesque work is slowly accomplished in the 13th cent. More ease of composition, a greater degree of naturalism and a more telling quality of draughtsmanship eventually identify the new procedure as noted in surviving murals and altar panels. In the 14th cent. Italian Gothic influence competes with the French Gothic and Flemish influeces, each having practitioners largely throughout Christian Spain.

Examples of the Franco-Gothic styles are murals in S. Pablo de Casseras, Cardona;

retable of S. Andrew, Cloister Museum, N. Y.; and altar frontal with Holy Trinity and Passion Scenes, Kelikian Collection, New York; and the imposing retable of Pedro Lopez de Ayala, Art Institute, Chicago.

The Italo-Gothic style of the 14th cent. emanates largely from Siena via the papal court at Avignon. A spirit of gentle piety and mysticism, a use of rich color areas, flower-spangled fabrics, fine calligraphic flow of drapery and incised gold backgrounds characterize the work. It is likewise accompanied by a more skilled technical manipulation. Panels are well prepared with gesso for the tempera painting. Green underpainting is used for flesh areas and then thinly glazed as in Sienese work. A pioneer in this style was Ferrer Bassa (active 1324-1347) who successfully combines Sienese idealization with a Spanish tension as exemplified in his painting of the Nativity and the Pietá (c.1346) on the walls of the S. Miguel chapel in the convent of Pedralbes, Barcelona. Arnau de la Pena (active 1355-1385) is responsible for both the illumination of manuscripts and important panel paintings as The Polyptic with scenes from the Life of Christ and The Virgin (c.1375), Morgan Library, New York and the retable of S. James in the Barcelona Museum. The two Serra brothers, Jaime (active 1361-1395) and Pedro (active 1363-1400) are important both for their projection of the Italo-Gothic style in their own work and for the wide influence they exerted through their many followers. Pedro Serras retable of the Pentecost (c.1394) in Manressa Cathedral while showing a lack of facility in figure organization, incorporates landscape elements against the gold ground and infuses a psychological awereness in the faces of his personages. Jaime Serra did the Holy Sepulchre Retable, Saragossa and among other productions the panel of the Adoration of the Shepherds (c.1360) in Montillor collection, New York. In the 15th cent., Spanish artists are mainly divided between adherents to the International Style and those influenced by contemporary Flemish work.

The proponents of the International Style (15th cent.) are identified by the high decorative quality of their work based on a rich, ornamental, calligraphic quality of their work based on a rich, ornamental, calligraphic qualbased on a rich, ornamental, calligraphic quality and aristocratic stylization. Expression of third dimension is expressed in a more decorative, less vigorous way than by Hispano-Flemish artists. Color tends toward clear tonal effects with an absence of strong patterns of light and shade. Artists working in the International Style include: Luis Borrassá (1380-1424) who, working in Catolonia, achieves a heightened pictorial quality and an added sense of vigor and realism. He is mainly influenced by Sienese work of such masters as the Lorenzetti and Orcagna. He does away with the gold background and sets his figures in more realistic surroundings. An outstanding example of his work is the Retable of the Guardiola (c.1410-1420) in the Soler y March collection, Barcelona. Bernardo Mantorell or the Master of St. George (active 1427-1452) combines Italian and Franco Flemish influence and lays the foundation for the local characteristics of the Catalan School. The Art Institute of Chicago owns his important Retable of St. George (c.1430); Scenes from the Life of S. Lucy is in private hands in Barcelona; and the Vich Museum owns the Retable of the Magdalen. Jaime Jacomart (c.1410-1461) of the Valencian School worked in Naples and probably in Rome. His Italianized manner exerted appreciable influence in his native school. His retable of S. Martin (c.1447-1457) is in the Diocesian Museum of Segorbe. Jaime Huguet (active 1448-1489) brings to a focus the medieval Catalan manner and foretells Renaissance procedure. His style represents an extension of the work of Mantorell with some admixture of Flemish influence. Through commisisons from Sardinia, his work established the character of native Sardinian painting. His employment of many assistants in his numerous large retable accounts for the uneven quality of his work. Contrary to general Spanish practice, he is reported to have worked from living models which accounts for his fine breadth and simplicity in handling both the human figure and drapery. In his best works he achieves a heightened quality of individual expression and feeling. His important Retable of the Portuguese Constable (c.1465) and his S. George and the Princess are in the Barcelona Museum.

The Hispano-Flemish style in Gothic painting (14th and 15th cent.) expressed itself in most of Christian Spain. It results from contact with the work of the great Flemish artists. Is practitioners varied from a relaively close dependence on Flemish precedent, to mere assimilation of certain technical procedures to effect (at the end of the century) works thoroughly Spanish in temper. The general results of this influence resulted in use of the oil medium and a heightened sense of realism, although the Flemish appreciation for minutia of detail is seldom met with Luis Dalmau (c. 1400-1463) and Fernando Gallego (c.1440-1495) are representative of this style. Dalmau was a Castilian painter, who had worked in Flanders and came in contact with the pinting of the van Eycks, though he failed to assimiliate their old technique and continued to work in tempera. His style was personal rather than popular involving fine portraiture, elaborate architectural effects and distant landscapes. The outstanding example of his work is the Madonna of the Councilors (1445) in the Barcelona Museum. Fernando Gallego worked in Castile after study in Flanders where he came in intimate contact with the work of Dirk Bonts and the engravings of he German, Schongauer. His work is marked by an emotional, mundane quality. He was given to expressing individual detail to the sacrifice of broad compositional considerations. He executed the Pietá in Weibel collection, Madrid and the Retablo at S. Lorenzo, Toro.

RENAISSANCE PAINTING (end of 15th and 16th cent.). Two sources of influence in the main contribute to Spanish Renaissance painting. The predominant one is Italian of the Early and High Renaissance, while Flemish influence is secondary in importance. The new procedure is introduced by a group of Spaniards who traveled or worked in 0taly at the end of the 15th and early 16th cents. Their early work should rightly be regarded as Gothic and their later productions as Renaissance. At the beginning of the century greater merit is evident than at the end (with the exçeption of El Greco) when various second rate foreign painters (mainly Italian) came into positions of influence in Spain.

The Spanish founders of the Renaissance style include such masters as Bartolomé Bermejo (c.1440-1495), Pedro Berruguette (d.1504) and Rodrigo de Osona *The Elder* (active at least between 1464 and 1484). Bermejo worked in Catalonia and reveals connection with Flemish precednt. He employs the oil medium, avoids the use of gesso relief, attains a new power of expression and compositional skill that is comparable to Florentine work. He is represented by: the monumental painting of S. Domingo de Silos (c.1474), Prado Museum, Madrid; S. Engracia (c.1475), Gardner Museum, Boston;

S. Michael, formerly Ludlow collection, London and the great Pieta (finished 1490) in Barcelona Cathedral. Pedro Berruguette worked in Castile, influenced by his lengthy residence in Italy where he came in close contact. with Melozzo da Forli. In his best work he attains genuine distinction with the expression of inner feeling and well ordered space as in his S. Peter Martyr in Prayer, Prado Museum, Madrid and the Retable of the Life of Christ (c.1508), Avila Cathedral. Rodrigo de Osuna the Elder worked in Valencia after study in both Flanders and Italy. His figures often show the influence of Hugo van der Goes but his landscape elements stem from the school of Ferrara. His work is solidly conceived and is marked by gravity of expression and atmospheric perception, as in his imposing Retable of the Crucifixion (c.1476), in the Church of S. Nicholas, Valencia.

After the first quarter of the 16th cent. there is a heightening of Renaissance characteristics, through the influence of Pierre de Campaneer (Pedro Campagna). Grandeur and grace of composition are achieved, forms are more plastically and accurately realized, the human figure in action is studied and psychological aspects in a fuller sense are rendered. Portraiture is developed through the sojurn in Spain of the able Dutch painter Antonis or, and the work of his follower, Alonzo Sanchez Coello. Classical mythologies fail to interest Spanish patrons and, except for the newly popular portraits, religious painting is the chief outlet of the artists. In the later part of the century the building of the Escorial Palace-Monastery caused Phillip II to invite important foreign artists to come to Spain to enrich its decorations. However, only second rate painters came such as Frederico Zucchero, Pelegrino Tibaldi, Bartolomeo Carducho and Patricio Caxés. The work of these men proved an unwholesome influence on native painters, that was however somewhat mitigated by their access to the magnificent royal collecion with its great series of Titians and other works of genuine importance. The end of the century is glorified by the work of a foreigner, Domenikos Theotocópulos, called El Greco, who achieved the fullest expression of Spanish temperament combined with inventive genius of highest order.

A brief catalogue of important Spanish painters of the century and representative examples of their work follow: Alonzo Sanchez Coello (1515-1590) although born in Valencia, spent his professional life largely at the Spanish court in Aragon. He was largely subject to the Flemish influence of Antonis Mor. His work is somewhat conservative and linear in approach. Primarily a portrait painter of the court circle, he is proficient in painting richly dressed personages of considerable dignity and reserve. The characterizations are seldom penetrating, but from a technical standpoint the painting is highly finished and has good color sense. Examples: *The Infanta Isabella Claudia Eugenia,* Prado Museum, Madrid; *Juana of Austria and Her Niece Margaret,* Gardner Museum, Boston; *Prince Carlos,* Prado Museum, Madrid. Pedro Campagna or Pierre de Kempeneer (1503-1580), was born in Brussels and was early influenced by the work of Roger de la Pasture and Van Orley. He traveled to Italy, came under the influence of Michelangelo and Raphael and remained there for at least ten years. For twenty-three years he occupied a position of influence in Seville. The energy and grace combined with his sense of good composition and strong color sense were highly regarded in Spain and we think of him primarily as a Spanish artist. Examples: *Descent from the Cross,* Cathedral, Seville; *Purification of the Virgin,* c.1553, Cathedral, Seville. Luis de Vargas (1502-1568), an Andalusian painter who spent twenty-eight years in Italy and was influenced by Raphael or Raphael's pupil, Perino del Vaga. His work is correct, distinguished by fine, warm color, but is lacking in personal expression and depth of emotion. His knowledge of anatomy as a revelation to the Church restricted Spaniards. Example: *The Ancestors of Christ,* Cathedral, Seville. Francisco de Herrara the Elder (1576-1656), an Andalusian painter working mainly at Seville, is noted (together with Roelas and Morales) for infusing a native Spanish quality into 16th cent. painting. His style is morbid and his sense of composition crowded. His figures are anatomically observed, dignified and somewhat monumentally conceived. He painted many martyrdom and apocalyptic visions. He appears to have been the first artist to work with a heavy impasto. A feeling of unhealthy excitement is frequently present in his work. Velasquez worked for a time with him but was repelled both by his style and disagreeable temperament. Examples: *S. Bonaventura Received as a Franciscan,* Earl of Clarendon Collection, Oxford; *Vision of S. Basil,* 1639, Provincial Museum, Seville; and *S. Joseph with Infant*

Christ, 1648, José Lazaro Collection, Madrid, Puan de Roélas (1559-1625), an Andalusian artist, like Herrera and Morales, is important for the native Spanish quality of his work. He received a classical education and became a religious painter. He subsequently journeyed to Italy and worked under Tintoretto. His work is marked by warm color harmony and fine distribution of light and shade. Like Herrera, his compositions are large and complicated. Examples: *Martyrdom of S. Andres,* Cathedral, Seville; *Apotheosis of S. Hermenegied,* Chapel of the Hospital de la Sangre, Seville. Juan de Juanes or Vincente Juan Macip (1500 or 1523-1579), a Valencian artist who studied in Italy and was influenced by the early work of Raphael. He is regarded as the founder of the 16th cent. manner of the Valencian School, but his work is of only moderate importance due to his too slavish deference to Italian work and his lack of achieving a personal style. Examples: *Visitation of S. Ann to the Virgin,* Prado Museum, Madrid; *The Last Supper,* Prado Museum, Madrid. Francisco de Ribalta (1551-1628), a Valencian artist who studied in Italy but brought back Italian principles, rather than mannerisms, which he translated into Spanish expression. He was interested in effects of chiaroscuro, as first observed in Correggio and Schidone, but projected them further toward the manner of Caravaggio and his (Ribalta's) greatest pupil, Ribera. Strong dramatic feeling, force of composition, sense of plastic relief, effects of light and shadow, and reflected light characterize his work. Examples: *Vision of S. Francis,* Museum, Valencia; *The Evangelists S.S. John and Matthew,* Prado Museum, Madrid. Fernadez Navarrette, called "El Mundo", the deaf mute, (1526-1579) studied in Italy. He was the most adequate Spanish interpreter of Titian, whom he understood deeply as to color sense, plasticity and composition. Both in draughtsmanship and coloristic attainments he stood ahead of his immediate Spanish contemporaries. Examples: *Baptism of Christ,* Prado useum, Madrid; *The Nativity,* Palace-Monastery of the Escorial. Luis de Morales (1509-1586), an Andalusian artist called "El Divino" (because he painted only religious subjects), is noted for the native quality in his painting (q.v. Herrera and Róelas). There is an indirect, dilute influence from Michelangelo in his work. His style is somewhat angular with a kind of cloying sweetness present His touch is precise and rather weakly elegant;

his color is refined and delicate. He infuses an almost psychopathic quality in his faces. His early compositions are large and elaborate but his later. ones are limited to one or two personages. Examples: *Madonna and Child,* Prado Museum, Madrid; *Presentation of Child Jesus in the Temple,* Prado Museum, Madrid.

El Greco, Domenikos Theotocopulos (born in Crete in 1541, died in Toledo 1614), while a foreigner, achieved the fullest artistic expression of the underlying forces that motivated 16th cent. Spanish life and thought. The buring intensity of religious fanaticism, as expressed in the horrors of the Inquisition, find artistic expression in the flame-like contours of El Greco's canvases.

Trained in Venice in the studio of Titian, we feel him more drawn to Tintoretto. Shortly after his arrival in Spain (c.1575) he undergoes a psychological change that results in a vividly personal style of painting that causes him to be classed as one of the world's greatest innovators, the "Old Master" of our contemporary "New Masters." He evolves new worlds of form, new rules of anatomy, a more and more grandly simplified sense of composition, amazing plasticity, and intense expression of vibrant, tortured, spiritual insight.

Living in his beloved Toledo, he turns his back on the court influences and refuses to compromise his personal convictions in Art. He draws about him an enthusiastic local circle of patrons, who pay richly for his canvases. Deep scholar in philosophy, literature and the Arts, he was warmly appreciative of beauty, proud and independent.

His work may be divided into three main periods of development: *First period, (c.1570-1580).* Appreciable Venetian influence, little creative distortion, sound plasticity, naturalism, and vivid light and shade mark the work of this period. Examples: *Christ Expelling the Money Changers from the Temple* Cook Collection, Richmond; *Portrait of Guilio Clovia* (miniature painter), National Gallery Naples; *Assumption of the Virgin,* Chicago Art Institute; *Annunciation,* Prada Museum, Madrid. *Second Period, (c.1580-1604).* He invents, or carries further, his newly felt concepts of anatomy, special composition and broader, simplified color and muted tones. He achieves a new expression of linear rhythms and fluctuation of mobile forms. He aims to express spiritual ideals, rather than naturalism. The real point of departure for this and his later work is his own Byzantine background of the mosaics, frescoes, icons and manuscript illuminations of the Christian East. Without recognition of this factor, his style cannot be rationalized. Examples: *The Dream of Philip II*, Palace-Monastery, Escorial; *Martyrdom of S. Maurice and the Theban Legion*, Church of Palace-Monastery, Escorial; *Burial of Count Orgaz*, S. Tomé, Toledo; *Crucifixion with Virgin and S. John*, Prado Museum, Madrid; *Holy Family*, Hospital of S. Juan Bautista, Toledo; *Mary Magdalene*, Don Cristobal Ferriz Collection, Madrid; *Portrait of Doña Jeronima de Cuevas*, Penn Museum, Philadelphia; *S. Jerome as Cardinal*, Frick Collection, New York; *Expulsion from the Temple*, Frick Collection, New York; *Resurrection of Christ*, Prado Museum, Madrid; *Portrait of the Grand Inquisitor*, Don Fernando Nina de Guevare, Metropolitan Museum, New York. *Third Period*, (*1604-1614*). Simplification of form, color and composition is pushed to its maximum. The creative distortion is further pronounced in numerous paintings (*Sacred and Profane Love*, the *Assumption* (late version) and the *Laocoön*), but at the same time other pictures are sharply observed from a naturalistic angle (*Fray Felix Hortension Palavincina* portrait) proving that El Greco was not subject to astigmatism as had been suggested. Certain works of amazing power, linear and plastic unity grace this period (*Christ on Mount of Olives*, Csete Collection, Budapest), others are difficult for conservative critics to comprehend. Examples: *View of Toledo*, Metropolitan Mus., New York; *Self Portrait*, Metropolitan Mus., New York; *Fray Felix Hortensio Palavincina*, Museum of Fine Arts, Boston; *Christ on Mount of Olives*, Csete Collection, Budapest; *Laocoön*, formerly in the collection of Prince Paul of Jugoslavia, Belgrade; *Assumption of the Virgin*, San Vincente Mus., Toledo; *Salutation*, Dumbarton Oaks collection, Washington; *Sacred and Profane Love*, Ignacio Zuloaga collection, Zumaya, Spain.

SEVENTEENTH CENTURY. Regional distinctions, in the main cease to be of significance and painting may now be spoken of as national. This century is rich in achievement and in the eyes of many critics, painting reaches its culmination in the art of Velasquez. Portraits take on highest distinction; figure compositions achieve mastery by any European standard; handling of chiaroscuro, color organization, and movement attain the utmost significance, and both still-life and landscape are brought to a lofty point.

While numerous painters of varying degrees of excellence occur, the attainments of the century may be summarized in the work of the five following masters: Jusepe de Ribera (1590-1652), called because of his small stature "Lo Spagnoletto" by the Italians during his long residence there. He was a pupil of Ribalta and regarded as belonging to the School of Valencia although most of his professional life was spent outside Spain. His style is based on the teachings of his master and assimilations from the study of Titian, Veronese, Correggio and Caravaggio, which he fused into his own manner of working. If we grant that Caravaggio was primarily interested in shadow, we would have to accept that Ribera was interested in both light and shadow. His drawing is sound and his form sense monumental. By 1630 his style loses some of its harshness and takes on a more thoughtful and dignified quality, with an ever-increasing evidence of his study of light. Compositions bathed in a silvery light date around 1635, while those with a rich amber tonality begin around 1640. Examples: *Assumption of Mary Magdalene*, 1626, Academy of S. Fernando, Madrid; *Martyrdom of S. Bartholomew*, c. 1626, Prado Museum, Madrid; *S. Andres, Apostle*, Prado Museum, Madrid; *S. Paul, Hermit*, Louvre, Paris; *S. Sebastian*, Prado Museum, Madrid; *Adoration of the Shepherds*, 1650, Louvre, Paris; *The Club-foot*, 1652, Louvre, Paris. Francisco de Zurbaran (1598-1663), an Andalusian painter, was the pupil of Roélas and Herrera, but was later more permanently influenced by the heavy chiaroscuro of Caravaggio's manner which he acquired through Ribera. His work has a strongly pronounced Spanish flavor. Examples: *Bonaventura Refers Thomas Aquinas to the Crucifix*, 1629, Kaiser Friederich Mus., Berlin; *Apotheosis of S. Thomas Aquinas*, 1631, Provincial Museum, Seville; *S. Hugo Enters the Refectory*, 1636, Provincial Museum, Seville; *A Student of Salamanca*, Gardner Museum, Boston; *Dominican Monk*, Hispanic Society of America, New York; *S. Casilda*, Prado Museum, Madrid.

Diego Velasquez de Silva (1599-1660), born in Seville of Portuguese parents, spent the major part of his life at the Spanish court. With El Greco, he dominates Spanish art and ranks as one of the world's greatest painters. His brief study with Herrera and the subsequent work with the scholarly but relatively unimportant Sevillian painter, Pacheco, seem but minor preparation for his eventual achievement. Velasquez goes down in history as a great observer of natural appearance. Effects of enveloping atmosphere are magically caught in his later works. Always courtly and dignified, a noble restraint and reserve permeate his art and reflect a truly Spanish temper.

His work may be classified according to four major periods: *Sevillian Period (1616-1623)*. Velasquez painted his *bodegons*, a few religious pictures and several portraits. This work in general is marked by a search for, rather than assimilation of, fundaments of construction and character. He acquired his cool, silvery tonality, yet his modeling is strong with pronounced opposition of light and shade. His edges tend to be somewhat hard and his shadows lacking in transparency. He is not yet able to enfold his subjects in an embracive atmosphere although he acquires the capacity to control receding space. He displays little psychological penetration at this time. Examples: *The Maid Servant*, Chicago Art Institute; *Luis de Gongora, the Poet*, Boston Museum of Fine Arts; *Supper at Emmaus*, Metropolitan Museum, New York. *First Madrid Period (1623-1629)*— prior to first Italian journey. This is mainly a period of reorientation and search for personal expression motivated by his quest of natural appearance rather than formal schematic procedure. Friendship with the young King Philip IV grows and he makes his adjustments to court life. His works are well modeled and coldly impressive but show only the beginning of character analysis. No masterpieces result from this period. Examples: *Standing full-length Portrait of Philip IV*, Prado Museum, Madrid; *The Drinkers*, Prado Museum, Madrid. *Second Madrid Period (1630-49)*. Velasquez spent two highly useful years of study in Italy (1729-30). He wisely neglected the Caravaggio's as foreign to his point of view. The art of Venice influenced him permanently in his assimilation of the Venetian artits' "compromise between decorative and optical effects." His work grows into a harmony of silvery tonal effects. His sense of composition is greatly strengthened and a new monumentality pervades his work. Effects of distance and enveloping atmosphere are successfully achieved. His portraits are distinguished by fine penetration and magnificent, carefully observed atmospheric quality with subtle distinctions drawn between indoor and outdoor lighting. His work grows in stately effects of great aristocratic beauty highly ac-

ceptable to the Spanish royal circle. Examples: *Self Portrait*, Palazzo dei Conservatori, Rome; *Joseph's Bloody Coat*, Church, Palace-Monastery, Escorial; *Forge of Vulcan*, Prado Museum, Madrid; *Surrender of Breda*, Prado Museum, Madrid; *Infante Ferdinand of Austria as Sportsman*, Prado Museum, Madrid; *Philip IV on Horseback*, Prado Museum, Madrid; *Infante Don Balthasar Carlos on Horseback*, Prado Museum, Madrid; *Infante Don Balthasar Carlos on Horseback*, Prado Museum, Madrid; *Infante Don Balthasar Carlos with Two Dogs*, Prado Museum, Madrid; *The Sculptor, Montañes*, Prado Museum, Madrid; *Philip IV*, Frick Collection, New York; *Portrait of Little Girl*, Hispanic Society of America, New York; *Coronation of the Virgin*, Prado Museum, Madrid. *Last Madrid Period (1650-60)*.. The second journey of Velasquez to Italy (1649-51) resulted in his most magnificent and personalized achievements as a painter, growing in power and penetration until his death in 1660. A new and graver simplicity marks the triumphs of this last phase of his work, but his greatest achievement lies in his new interpretation of form built up with minute changes in lighting, that renders line almost needless and marks his works as the precursor of "Impressionism". He proves with his consummate mastery of the physical world with all its fleeting, atmospheric effects and subtleties of personal distinctions of rank and class, that he is the preëminent painter of the visible tangible things of earth, rather than of the mystical, glorified spirits of the other world.

Technically the work of this last period is built up in most economical terms. His paint is sparing, his glazes are infinitely thin, his handling is deft, sure and never hurried or impetuous. He died in 1660 at the height of his career. His life was one of calm dignity, constant security and success. Examples: *Pope Innocent X*, Doria Palace, Rome; *Calabasches*, Prado Museum, Madrid; *Aesop*, Prado Museum, Madrid; *Infanta Maria Teresse*, Boston Museum of Fine Arts; *Philip IV*, Prado Museum, Madrid; *Maids of Honor*, Prado Museum, Madrid; *The Weavers (Las Hilanderas)*. Prado Museum, Madrid; *Venus and Cupid*, National Gallery, London; *Infanta Marguerite*, Prado Museum, Madrid; *Infanta Marguerite*, (bust), Weber Collection, Hamburg.

Bartolomé Estéban Murillo (1618-1682), an Andalusian painter, first studied with the mild-mannered Sevillian painter Juan de

Castillo. The works of Roélas, Rubens, Van Dyck, Raphael and particularly Corregio influenced him. He is preëminently associated with Seville, where practically his whole professional life was spent except for a period of study of the Royal Collection at Madrid. His works in the past have been enormously admired, but now are regarded with perhaps even less interest than they deserve. His color sense is gracious as far as it goes— but it must be regarded as under-developed. His religious paintings are weakly sentimental and "pretty" rather than strong. In his portrait and narrative pictures he is seen to much greater advantage (*Prodigal Son among Harlots,* Beit Collection).

While Baroque in date, his style represents a blending of Renaissance and Baroque features. He is an exponent of the persuasive Jesuit style. His painting of flesh is often remarkably beautiful, with a fine, pearly tonality. Early pictures in general make use of a warmer palette than the later ones, which tend toward cool, silvery effects.

Examples, portrait and narrative: *Gallician Girl with Corn,* c. 1645-50, Prado Museum, Madrid; *John Tells His Dream to Liberius,* c. 1645, Prado Museum, Madrid; *Young Beggar Boy,* c. 1645-55, Louvre Museum, Paris; *Miracle of S. Diego or Angels' Kitchen,* 1646, Louvre Museum, Paris; *Old Woman Cleaning Head of Boy,* c. 1670-82, Alte Pinakothek, Munich; *Moses Striking the Rock,* c. 1674, Cathedral, Seville; *Prodigal Son among Harlots,* 1680, Alfred Beit Collection, London.

Examples, Religious: *Adoration of the Shepherds,* 1650-60, Prado Museum, Madrid; *Madonna and Child,* 1650-60, Pitti Palace, Florence; *Vision of S. Anthony of Padua,* 1656, Cathedral, Seville; *Immaculate Conception,* c. 1660, Provincial Museum, Seville; *The Child S. John with Lamb,* 1660-70, Prado Museum, Madrid; *Virgin of Seville,* c. 1670, Louvre Museum, Paris; *Soultá Immaculate Conception,* 1678, Louvre Museum, Paris.

Juan de Valdés Leal (1622-1690), an Andalusian painter, pupil of Antonia del Castillo and bitter rival of Murillo, is potentially an original and gifted artist who failed to fully express his native capacity. Often guilty of understudy in his compositions, he still has left us highly interesting works that in some instances (*Dead Bonaventura,* and *In the Twinkling of an Eye*) are consummately expressive of the Spanish temper. His color is rich, his construction solid and there is often a fine energy and dramatic quality in his pic-

tures. After Murillo's death, he ranked as the leading Sevillian painter. Examples: *Temptation of S. Jerome,* 1657, Cathedral, Seville; *Dead S. Bonaventura Finishing His Life of S. Francis,* Sir Robert Cook Collection, Richmond; *Hieroglyphic of the End of our Days,* c. 1670, Church of the Hospital de la Caridad, Seville; *In the Twinkling of an Eye,* c. 1670, Church of the Hospital de la Caridad, Seville.

EIGHTEENTH CENTURY. The principal figures of this century are foreigners with the exception of Goya (1746-1828). The native creative impulse was at low ebb and Spain imported such artists as René and Michel-Ange Housse, Giovanni Battista Tiepolo, Louis-Michel Van Loo, and Raphael Mengs. Native artists such as Luis Menéndez (1716-1780), Paret Alcázar (1746-1799), Goyas' Master, Francisc Bayeu (1734-1795), José Castillo (1737-1793), Mariano Maella (1739-1819) and Gregorio Ferro (1742-1812) were for the most part followers of either the foreigners working on Spanish soil or (at the end of the century) of Goya. The art of Goya is by far the most significant achievement in Spanish painting of the 18th and early 19th cent.

Francisco Jose Goya y Lucientes (1746-1828), an Aragonese painter, studied first under José Luzán y Martinez (1710-1785) and then under his future father-in-law, Francisco Bayeu y Subias (1734-1795). He studied in Italy in 1769-17. His early work was influenced by Raphael Mengs, Luca Giordano and Tiepolo. He was appointed Royal Academician in 1780. His own vigorously personal manner emerged (c.1785) and captivated the Spanish court to which he was appointed in 1789. Mural painting, portraits, genre, satirical and political painting, etchings, and tapestry designing all claimed his attention. His work subsequently proved an important influence on such later 19th cent. French innovators as Daumier, Manet and Cezanne.

His work may be divided into three main periods: *First Madrid Period (1772-1799).* His style is influenced by Mengs, Giordano and Tiepolo. Grey-green color schemes, thin, liquid brush work, pale, slightly modeled flesh tones predominate. Examples: Frescoes in El Pilar Cathedral, Zaragossa; Frescoes in S. Antonia de Florida, Madrid; *Don Sebastian Martinez,* Metropolitan Art Museum, New York; *Josefa Bayeu, Goya's Wife,* Prado Museum, Madrid; *Witches' Conventicle,* Collection of the Duke of Osuna, Madrid; *Duchess* of *Alba* (standing), Palace of Liria; *Maja Nude,* Prado Museum, Madrid; *Maja Clothed,* Prado Museum, Madrid; *They Cut Each Others' Nails* (etching). *Second Madrid Period (1800-1808).* This period is marked by a great coloristic advance. Warm whites, blues, crimson, gold and black sift and scintilate with wonderful, broken intensities, yielding a splendid impressionistic quality. The satirical quality grows and plays havoc with royal dignity. The brush work is forcible and a heavy impasto accumulates. Examples: *Family of Charles IV,* Prado Museum, Madrid; *Queen Maria Luisa* (standing), Prado Museum, Madrid; *Queen Maria Luisa* (three-quarters length), Prado Museum, Madrid; *Dona Isabel Corbo de Porcel,* National Gallery, London; *Isidoro Maiquez, the Comedian,* Chicago Art Institute. *Final Madrid Period (1808-c.1824).* This period is broken up by his dramatic, almost morbid reaction to the War of 1808-1814, his adjustment to the Bourbon Restoration government of Ferdinand VII (after the reign of Josef Bonaparte) and his sojourn in Bordeaux and his eventual death on French soil. Artistically this work is marked by a simplification in form, composition and color. Frequently he attains surprisingly rich effects by using only black, white, and brown. He strives for an increasing monumentality of form. Toward the end of his life he takes to painting with the palette knife. The mood is often combre or melancholy. It is this period that yielded such definite influence on 19th century French impressionism. Examples: *Scenes from the "Second of May" series—Citizens of Madrid Being Shot Down by the Troops of Murat,* Prado Museum, Madrid; *Hanging of the Monk,* Art Institute of Chicago; *Majas on Balcony,* Metropolitan Art Museum, New York; *The Forge,* Frick Collection, N. Y.; *Self Portrait,* Academy of S. Fernando, Madrid; *Frescoes from Goya Residence,* Prado Museum, Madrid.

NINETEENTH AND TWENTIETH CENTURIES. The early part of the 19th cent. is dominated by the later work of Francisco Goya (discussed under the 18th cent.). Other work roughly follows the pattern of painting in France beginning with the Classicism of David and continuing through Romanticism, Impressionism, Expressionism and the subsequent phases, inclupding Cubism, Surrealism, and Abstractionism, that motivate contemporary International Art. This long and varied cycle of developments stimulated the production of paintings of historical, literary, narrative,

landscape, still-life, and portrait subject matter. From there it went on to psychological analysis, attempts to express the underlying factors of the Old Masters in a contemporary idiom. Problems of light, form, mass, gravity, dream subject matter, and pure design are investigated in new and daring ways. Certain contemporary Spanish artists such as Picasso and Salvatore Dali have risen to positions of great importance in international art circles. The influence of Picasso must be reckoned one of the most vital art forms in the world today.

SCULPTURE. While sculptural remains such as the bronze busts from Ampurias and architectural sculpture survive from the period of Roman Occupation and interesting Byzantinesque sculptural details from such Visigothic structures as San Miguel de Lino, San Juan de Baños, San Pedro de La Nave and those at Mérida, the main stream of development begins with Romanesque work. From this time on Spanish sculpture is now recognized as of genuine importance and high aesthetic interest.

ROMANESQUE (11th to end of 13th cent.). The general character of Romanesque sculpture in Spain from the latter part of the 11th cent. relates to certain phases of corresponding French work. However, critics are still divided as to whether the influence stemmed from France or Spain (q.v. Porter). The fact remains that the Cluniac (q.v.) Order was a means for the transference between the two countries and the churches of the Pilgrimage Road tended to be a unifying factor. The Entombment and the five related panels (late 11th cent.) in the cloister of S. Domingo de Silos, in common with those of Moissac in France, show a strong linear hieratic conception probably based on Spanish Moslem ivories. The 12th cent. work in general shows a compositional advance. Drapery tends to be somewhat more naturalistic in treatment and, though still stylized, is more plastically felt as in the Descent from the Cross, S. Isidoro at Leon; the early Fuerta de Platerias and the later Puerta de Gloria both at Santiago de Compostella; S. Vincente at Avila and the Apostles from the Camera Santa at Oviedo Cathedral. While examples of original polychromy are exceedingly rare, evidence points to its widespread use in sculpture from roughly the middle of the 12th cent. on. The work of the 13th cent. shows a heightened, though still essentially restrained, sense of movement; less stylization is felt in anatomical feature

but the general spirit is still definitely Romanesque. Examples include the Deposition group
from S. Joan de las Abadesas; figures from
the South Porch of S. Vincente, Avila; a
tomb in the church of the Magdalena, Zamora;
certain of the tombs in the Cloister Chapels,
Old Cathedral, Salamanca and the Crucifixion
Group at S. Andres, Cuellar.

GOTHIC (end of the 13th to end of 15th cent.).
The Gothic spirit expressed itself tardily in
Spain and the early work here corresponds
to the 13th cent. French Gothic style, which
was introduced mainly by the Cistercians. The
new spirit is characterized by a more naturalistic though still idealized handling of features, body proportion and drapery; a growing
sense of movement in the freer postures of
figures and a new sense of grace. Examples
include the South Transept Pork at Burgos
Cathedral; the tomb of the Infanta Doña
Blanca, Cathedral of Pamplona; and the West
Porch sculptures of the Cathedral of Leon.
At about the beginning of the 15th cent. a
marked change developed in Spanish Gothic
sculpture. A richly elaborated method, akin
to contemporary northern work, marked by
flowing lines, more animated descriptive quality and a less functional, more surface character, accompanied by a markedly increased
realism identify this phase. Numerous retablos, choir stalls, chantries, and rich tombs
become popular. Sculptors from Burgundy,
Flanders, and Germany practice alongside
native sculptors frequently signing their work
and taking pride in personal expression. Examples are numerous and include: The imposing retables of La Seo, Saragossa; and that
of S. Thekla, Cathedral of Tarragona; the
tombs of Juan of Aragon in the Cathedral of
Tarragona, and Lope de Luna in aL Seo,
Saragossa; The Holy Sepulchre Group,
Church of Réal Perpignan and the Retable
of the Cartuja of Miraflores at Burgos.

RENAISSANCE (late 15th to early 17th cent.).
Early Renaissance sculpture in Spain at the
start maintains a connection with the late
Gothic and finally achieves full renaissance
expression. Both foreign and native artists
are importantly employed. The former include Miguel the Florentine, Francisco Nico-
losso Pisano and the more renowned Pietro
Torrigiano. Damian Forment (died 1535),
working in Valencia is representative of the
latter. His final style is highly Italianate and
relates to the manner of Donatello. He executed the Retable for the Pilar church at
Saragossa (c.1510) and the tomb of Marquis

Vasquez d'Arco (c.1520). With Forment may
be classed the Sevillian, Pedro Millan (active
from 1505) who shows Flemish influence in
his important Virgin del Pilar at Saragossa.
Philip Borgoña (died c.1543) although of a
Burgundian family settled in Burgos, occupies
an important place in early 16th cent. Spanish
sculpture. His style is markedly Italian, once
the Gothic survival found in his early work
is passed, as in his Retable (c.1520) for the
Royal Chapel, Granada and in his collaboration with Berruguete on the Choir Stalls in
Toledo Cathedral. The *High Renaissance* is
largely dominated by Alonzo Berruguete
(c.1486-1561), who after being strongly influenced by the style of Michelangelo during
his long study in Italy, returned to Spain as
Royal Sculptor (1520) to Charles V. He
personalizes the rich, plastic, powerful conceptions of Michelangelo by infusing a dramatic exaggeration of movement that yields a
high emotional and religious expression of
great intensity. His appeal to Spanish taste
was so marked that his style extended itself
to many of his contemporaries and is continuously felt to our own time in subsequent
work. Among the large number of sculptures
assigned him are his collaborative work with
Philip Borgoña on the Choir Stalls of Toledo
Cathedral (finished 1543); the rich tomb of
Archbishop Tavera, Toledo; the tomb of Juan
de Rojas and his wife at Valencia and the
sculptures (early) for the Monastery of S.
Benito Real, now in the Valladolid Museum.
Bartolomé Ordonez (died 1540), a Catalan
sculptor, embodies a strong Italian influence
less adjusted to Spanish taste than Berruguete's. His influence in consequence was more
limited. While difficult problems of attribution exist, the Royal tombs at Granada (c.
1522) are in the main regarded as his work as
is the Don Juan Tomb in S. Thomas, Avila.
Gaspar Becerra (1520-1571) worked for a
large part of his professional life in Italy.
Like Ordonez, he is primarily Italian in his
point of view. The influence of Michelangelo
is dominant in his style. He is noted for his
anatomical knowledge and rich plastic conceptions that are emotional in organization
but without deep religious insight as in his
S. Jerome, Cathedral of Burgos and the Retable in the Cathedral at Astorga. Juan Juni
(1507-1577) is an important follower of
Alonso Berruguete and capitalizes on strong
emotional effects and marked exaggeration
of movement to intensify his conceptions as
in his Entombment group in Segovia Cathedral.

BAROQUE (17th to middle 18th cent.). In the judgment of conflicting critics Spanish contribution to Baroque sculpture is either marked by highest national expression and accomplished individualism or by pietistic excess coupled with oppressive realism carried to the ultimate. The fact remains that the 17th cent produced works of admirable quality that compare favorably with contemporary work produced elsewhere in Europe. The latter part of the period under discussion should be identified with Rococo production and it is here that the real decline in taste manifests itself. The first outstanding sculptor of the period is the Castillian painter, Gregorio Fernandez or Hernandez (1566-1636) who achieves a fine unmannered baroque spirit. Master of form and movement, he seeks an evocative realism heightened by a more restrained use of polychromy than was current in the works of such sculptors as Juan de Juni. His use of crystal for such detailing as eyes and tears met with favor at the time and was continued by subsequent sculptors. His Retable of S. Jerome at Santiponce; his Virgin of Sorrows; and his Baptism of Christ, both at Valladolid are expressive of his style. Juan Martinez Montañes (1564-1649), the Sevillian sculptor and contemporary of Hermandez, displays an admirable technical knowledge which he dericted toward realism coupled with piety and taste. A deep religious conviction is resident in such of his works as the S. Bruno at Cadiz Cathedral, the Immaculate Conception at Seville Cathedral and various Saints in the Museum at Seville. Among the followers of this tradition which include Alonzo de Mena, Alfonso Martinez, and Juan Gomez, the most important is Alonso Cano (1601-1667). Primarily associated with Granada and Seville where he studied under Montañes, Cano's style is an extension of his master's. He achieved acclaim both as sculptor and painter. Among his achievements in sculpture are the S. Anne, the Virgine and the Infant Jesus in Granada Cathedral; the S. Bruno in the Carthesian Monastery at Granada and the Virgin in S. Ana at Granada.

The Spanish love of realism and piety at this time lead to unfortunate excesses. The use of crystal for eyes and tears to evoke life-like effects was extended to include the use of real eyebrows and, in certain instances, sculptors superseded polychromed drapery by real fabrics. In these latter instances only exposed parts as the head, hands, and feet might be sculptured, the rest being covered with stuffs. The last stage in realistic ex-pression is unpleasantly revealed in statues equipped with mechanisms that allowed hands to move, etc.

The 18th cent. was a busy period in sculptural production marked by native pietistic works alongside numerous productions of French and Italian sculptors working in Spain. The native group includes Alonso de los Rios, Juan de Villanueva, Salvator Carmona, Juan Alonso Villabeille, Uuis del Peral, and the prolific Francisco Salzillo. The foreign group was headed by Robert Michel, Director of the newly-formed (1752) Academy of S. Fernando. The predominating character was largely derived from contemporary French work with some stemmings from the style of Bernini. In general the old spirit of religious intensity is replaced by a mundane grace and charm lacking in both vitality and indigenous expression.

NINETEENTH AND TWENTIETH CENTURIES. The pattern of development in Spanish sculpture from the beginning of the 19th cent. to the present may de described as international. In the main, each of the current tendencies prevalent in France (and thence reflected to other parts of Europe) found adherents in Spain with only a few of the noted practitioners falling back to native inspiration. The first half of the 19th cent. is largely guided by the spirit of academicism. Its practitioners include José Ginés, Jose Piquer, Jose Alvarez, and Francisco Mortilla. Later in the century a more eclectic spirit prevailed that included medieval, Renaissance, Baroque, Rococo, Classic, and Romantic inspiration. Prominent sculptors include Manuel Ohms, Augustin Querol, Ricardo Bellver, Eduardo Barrón and Mélida. The end of the 19th and the early 20th cent. is marked by realism pushed almost to the photographic as in the work of Miguel Blay only to give way as the century progressed, to more subtle and impressionistic interpretations based on the influential work of Rodin as in the work of José Clará. The work of the most progressive contemporary sculptors reflects the varying important international tendencies as from such foreign masters as Bourdelle, Maillol, Mestrovíc, Brancusi, and others.

THE MINOR ARTS. Spain occupies a distinguished position in the realm of the minor arts. Her metal work at its best equals the general quality of production of any other European country. In wood working, ceramics, and textiles her evident achievements are acknowledged.

METAL WORK. Rich in mineral deposits, Spain early developed skill in manipulating golds, silver, iron, and bronze into works that are a true index of her artistic capacities. In the Roman period she was noted for her skillful produtcion of iron and bronze weapons of great strength and durability as well as domestic utensils, brooches, and buckles. Remains found at Cordova, Santisteban del Puerto, and Mogón tells us of splendid articles for silver table services with richly embossed exterior surfaces joined to plain interiors with a filling of lighter metal between the two shells as was common in Rome. In general, designs also followed Roman precedent.

In the Visigothic period there was a general rejection ot Roman designs or what elements that were retained are debased and lose their classic character. Geometric and linear floral motifs, both raised and flat, in repeated formation are current. Iron jewelry inlaid with gold and silver, and bronze buckles sometimes ornamented with gold occur. Objects of precious metal were sometimes richly worked, inlayed and mounted ith cabochon jewels massively set or hung as pendants recalling Byzantine work as in the Visigothic votive crowns from Guarrazar, now at Paris in the Cluny Museum. In the Romanesque period forged iron church grilles of repeated scroll motifs, and fine hardware elements were produced. The importance of the crafts is evidenced by the founding of the Ironsmiths Guild in Barcelona in the year 1200, a full two centuries before a similar French organization. Important doors were sheathed with bronze or iron plates enriched with die-stamped designs and mouldings as in the sacristy door of Seville Cathedral. In the Gothic period a wealth of utilitarian objects were produced. The decorative effect was enhanced by the use of a whole grammar of ornament including plant forms, pierced decoration and laminated relief work. Metal grilles became imposing architectural elements enriched with repoussé, pierced and embossed ornaments as in the early 16th cent. chapel grille at Cuenca Cathedral. Precious metals were worked into imposing architecturally designed relinquaries, custodia caskets and even thrones as the silver throne (15th cent.) of King Martin of Aragon at Barcelona Cathedral, the sumptuous silver relinquary in Jaen Cathedral, the smaller but important relquary in Pamplona Cathedral and the delicately wrought gold and jewelled so-called crown of S. Ferdinand in Seville Cathedral.

Productions of the 15th and 16th cents. mark a high point of achievement.

In the Renaissance, classic motifs begin to appear sporadically at the end of the first quarter. of the 16th cent. Grille designs increase in architectural quality and become more third dimensional with the use of classic columns, entablatures, *en ressaut* and early renaissance sculptural motifs of small flowers and arabesques (Italiante) as in the grille (c.1523) of the Condestable Chapel, Burgos Cathedral. These grilles were often built of metal plates applied to a structural wood core, because of the thickness of their individual parts. Important tomb sculpture, groups and independent figures were produced. Both cast and chiseled ornament, some polished and some unpolished, are all found in the same piece of precious metal, producing effects of great variety and beauty. Designs are complex and evidence great technical skill. As the century progresses a fuller renaissance spirit reveals itself in larger scale use of classic figures, floral swags, friut, animals, medallions and classic architectural elements. The end of the 16th cent. saw this tendency culminate in work of an austerely classic and coldly correct design quality as a result of Herrera's influence (q.v. Renaissance Architecture). The 17th cent reveals a decline in taste in the counter movement against the Academicism of Herrera. Work becomes almost oppressively rich in ornament involving the unrestrained use of naturalistic forms in great excess. The 18th cent. proved to be obviously influenced by contemporary France and followed the succeeding movements there that moved through the rococo and eventuated in the dry classicism of the style of Louis VXI. The 19th and 20th cents. were influenced by industrialization but various successful efforts have been made to maintain the crafts. Damascened work continues to thrive and the general tendency of the other crafts may now be described as marked by international tendencies.

CERAMICS. Evidence points to Spanish production of varied pottery in Roman times mainly influenced by contemporary types prevailing at Rome. The Visigothic period produced in the 8th cent. fine enamels laid on bronze recalling Byzantine precedent. Both incised and stamped decoration occurs on their pottern forms. The Mohammedan invaders executed important pottery at various noted centers in Spain. Their work is marked by rich, fine-scale ornaments based on stylized foliage and interlacing motifs sometimes incorporated inscriptions. As in the famous Alhambra Vase, red, white, green, yellow and blue are employed with varied enamels, slip glazes and metalic lustres. Important examples of Romanesque and Gothic pottery remain involving fine glazes and metalic lustres. Designs in general are marked by bold organization of large scale vigorous elements someties united with small scale motifs. Interlacing foliage, armorial devices and decoratively employed mottos occur on vessels of rich and varied shapes. Decorative tiles enriched with enamels are noteworthy, sometimes designed as single units or as interlocking designs for running motifs or as parts of larger patterns. Renaissance elements of decorations become frequent in the 16th cent. They stem from Italian Majolica sources as in the tile painting of the Tuscan, Nicoloso Francisco who worked in Seville in early years of the 16th cent. A tile painting by him depicting The Visitation to the Virgin (now in Amsterdam) shows the scene spread over a group of tiles (as one area) recording an early renaissance knowledge of pictorial composition. **Talavera** and related wares become increasingly important after the early 16th cent. They are marked by exceptional boldness and vigor of design including splendid, swiftly-indicated bird and animal forms and heraldic devices in conjunction with floral and strapwork motifs. Blue, purple and orange frequently occur. The 17th cent. work is in general marked by a loss of vigor and spontaneity. Designs become more naturalistic, are drawn in greater detail and appreciation for narrative subject matter is shown. The palette is enlarged and includes strong greens and yellows, purple, and a rather neutral blue as shown on The Bull Baiting Bowl' in the Victoria and Albert Museum. The 18th cent. ushers in French influence in the founding of the **Alcora** Potteries which employed French designers. An appreciation of fine scale ornament in elegant devices is evident following the manners respectively of the Regncy, Louis XV and Louis XVI. Blue and white ware is common as are richly polychromed work involving organizations or orange, blue, purple and green. Floral motifs and figure groups set in rococo inframements are frequent. Faïence, lead glazed ware and porcelain in variety of forms were produced as in the fine bowl and cistern in the Victoria and Albert Museum. The work of the **Buen Retiro** Porcelain Works dates from the middle of the 18th cent. and represents a continuation of the Naples Royal Porcelain works

of Capo di Monte with a concurrent influence from Meissen productions in Germany. A Spanish quality soon modified these designs in a bolder, more sparing form sense and more thooughtful use of color. In general the designs followed the trends in France through the rococo to the staid and somewhat unimaginative classicism of Louis XVI. Fine glazes and enamel work are revealed in the numberless ornamental figurines, **urns,** group pieces and moulded wall panels that were produced, involving figures of the *Fêtes Galantes* as in the Porcelain Chamber of the Royal Palace at Madrid and in the Porcelain collection at the Prado Museum in Madrid. Due to a tendency to easily fracture, the output at Buen Retiro was largely confined to pieces serving a decorative purpose. The productions of the porcelain factory of **Moncloa** were likewise of note, producing among other objects, porcelain plaques of considerable distinction as in the Hercules panel in the Prado Museum, Madrid. The 19th cent. saw the spread of commercial production with a counter movement exerting itself in the 20th cent. to restore the native craft at such centers as Segovia under the enlightened direcion of contemporary artists.

TEXTILES. *Silk Stuffs.* Our knowledge of the production of Spanish textiles prior to the coming of the Mohammedans is obscure and considerable subsequent uncertainty is acknowledged. During the period of their occupation it is difficult to separate their exceedingly important work from Christian production as the Mohammedans frequently supplied rich stuffs to the Christian nobles and even the clergy. The magnificence of their productions are evidenced in important museum collections here and abroad (q.v. Kendrich in Burlington Monograph). With the unification of Spain under the Catholic monarchs at the end of the 15th cent., Spanish textiles were influenced by the famous Italian brocades and cut velvets. Sumptuous designs with large scale motifs supported by small scale elements such as the palmette, the opening pomegranate, small scale foliage, vines, heraldic lions and other animal forms occur in well ordered arrangements. A rich color sense controls these productions utilizing combinations of red, green, yellow, blue, white, gold and silver. Church vestments attain the highest degree of richness through the use of silk brocades or velvets embroidered with gold galoon worked in high relief. Orphreys embroidered with saintly personages in multicolors and richly framed in galoon ornaments enrich the chasubles and related accessories. In some instances precious jewels were lavishly used in these embroidered ornaments as those preserved in the treasury of Toledo Cathedral. Chair backs, altar stuffs, hangings and covers of various sorts testify to the richness and beauty of these worked fabrics. *Tapestries.* Weaving of tapestries in Spain began in late Gothic times through contact with the great Flemish centers of Arras, Brussels and Bruges. Both high warp and low warp looms were employed. The general method, both technical and artistic, largely followed these great predecessors except for some departures in draughtsmanship, subject matter and color sense. The sequence of stylistic changes from late Gothic through renaissance, baroque and rococo are recorded here. Splendid examples of these are found in the famous collection of El Pilar in Saragossa, the Cathedral of Burgos, the royal and various private collections. In the 18th cent. French influence, as usual, is to be noted in the royal tapestries designed by Goya and now preserved in the Prado Museum, Madrid. *Carpets.* Rug weaving was an important craft in Spain from late Gothic times to the present. Near Eastern methods were employed with some variation as making the knot on single warp threads (q.v. Kendrick and Tattersall) to facilitate fine linear motifs. Great variety of design is met in these productions. Armorial carpets involving the Arms of the patron set on a field of small, repeated motifs were frequent in late Gothic productions but few of these have been preserved. Geometric designs and tile motifs were employed, as well as traditional near Eastern organizations and the decorative elements derived from the contemporary silks and brocades following the principal evolution in these to the present.

For GENERAL REFERENCE, see: M. Diculafoy, *Art in Spain and Portugal*, 1913; R. Tyler, *Spain*, 1907; L. Williams, *Arts and Crafts of Older Spain*, 1907; Roger Fry, A Sampler of Castile, 1923. For ARCHITECTURE, see: Bernard Bevan, *History of Spanish Architecture*, 1938; Royall Tyler, Architecture Chapter in *Spanish Art* (Burlington Monograph II), 1927; C. K. Hersey, *The Salamantine Lanterns*, 1937; V. Lamperez y Romea, *Arquitectura Civil Española de los Siglos* I al XVIII, 1922; M. Gomez-Moreno, *Iglesias Mozárabes; arte Española del siglo IX al XI*, 1919; G. G. King, *Pre-Romanesque Churches of Spain*, 1924; G. E. Street, *Gothic Architecture in Spain*, 1914. For PAINTING, see: Chandler Rathfon Post, *History of Spanish Painting*, 1930-1941; E.

Harris, *Spanish Painting*, 1937; Jose Gudiol, *Spanish Painting*, 1941; Sir Charles Holmes and H. Isherwood Kay, Painting Chapter in *Spanish Art*, (Burlington Monograph II) 1927; C. Gasquoine Hartley, *A Record of Spanish Painting*, 1904; A. L. Mayer, *Geschichte der Spanischen Malerei*, 1922; A. G. Temple, *Modern Spanish Painting*, 1908. For SCULPTURE, see: Robert West, Spanish Sculpture From 15th to 18th Cent., 1923; Geoffrey Webb, Sculpture chapter in *Spanish Art*, (Burlington Monograph II), 1927; M. Gomez Moreno, *Spanish Renaissance Sculpture*, 1931; A. K. Porter, *Spanish Romanesque Sculpture*, 1928; A. Calvert, *Sculpture in Spain*, 1912; M. Dieulafoy, *La statuaire polychrome en Espagne*, 1908; A. K. Porter, *Romanesque Sculpture of the Pilgrimage Roads*, 1923; W. W. S. Cook, *The stucco altar-frontals of Catalonia*, in Princeton "Art Studies, Mediaeval, Renaissance and Modern." 1924. For METALWORK, see: Pedro M. de Artiñano, Metalwork chapter in *Spanish Art*, (Burlington Monograph II), 1927; E. Roulin, *Orfevrerie et emaillerie. Mobilier liturgique d'Espagne.* In "Revue de l'Art chretien," 1903; J. Gudiol y Cunill, *L'orfebreria en l'Exposició Hispano-francesa de Saragosa.* In "Annuair de l'Inst. d'Estudis Catalans." 1908; A. Byne and M. Stapley, *Spanish ironwork*, New York, 1915; A. Byne and M. Stapley, *Rejeria of the Spanish Renaissance*, 1914; A. F. Calvert, *Spanish Arms and Armour: Royal Armoury at Madrid*, 1907. For CERAMICS, see: A Van de Put and Bernard Rackham, Ceramics chapter in *Spanish Art* (Burlington Monograph II), 1927; E. A. Barber, *Hispanomoresque pottery in the collection of the Hispanic* Society of America.—Spanish maiolica in the collection (etc.), 1915; P. Páramo, *La ceramica antigua de Talavera*, 1919; Conde de Casal, *Historia de la cerdmica de Alcora*, 1919; M. Pérez-Villamil, *Artes e industries del Buen Retiro*, 1904, *Catalogo de la coleccion de porcellana del Buen Retiro del* Senor D. F. de Laiglesia, 1908; E. A. Barber, *Spanish porcelains and terra cottas in the collection of the Hispanic Society of America*, 1915. For TEXTILES, see: A. F. Kendrick, Textiles chapter in *Spanish Art* (Burlington Monograph II), 1927; L. Williams, *The Arts and Crafts of Older Spain*, 1907; Marques De Valverde, Catalogo de la Exposicion de lenceria y encajes españoles, del siglo XVI al XIX, 1915; Burlington Magazine, XVIII, 100 (Nov.) 1910. Hispano Moresque carpets—by W. G. Thomson; XIX, 344 (Sept.) 1911, XX, 124 (Sept.) 1924. Some fifteenth century Spanish carpets—by A. Van de Put. A. F. Kendrick and C. E. C. Tattersall, *Hand-Woven Carpets,* 1922.   —J.G.V.

spall or **shiver.** In masonry: A chip, splinter, or flake, as from a stone, usually worked off in dressing.

span. The distance between supports, as of a roof or beam.

spandrel. The space between the top of a window or wall opening and the bottom of the one directly above it. Also the space above the springing of an arch and a horizontal line through the top of the arch.

SPANISH ARCHITECTURE IN THE NEW WORLD. As was to be expected, Renaissance Europe strongly moulded the beginnings of Spanish architecture in the New World. The Gothic renderings of the early 16th cent. in the Americas show distinct evidence of Romanesque strength. The *conquistadores* imported Moorish workmen of superb skill from a Spain glad to be rid of any Moor; as the 16th cent. advanced, these craftsmen imposed florid touches which came to be known in some places as **mudejar** (Moorish-influenced) architecture. The same century saw the development of what was called the plateresque—a Spanish term describing the practice of relieving barren medieval expanses of wall with door- and window-openings as intricately-ornamented as fine silver. In the Colonial Americas, woodworking reached its zenith in the huge carved Renaissance **retables,** or **altar pieces** (q.v.), which usually covered one end of the church by the beginning of the 17th cent.

The architecture of the Americas passed through a brief phase of classical severity in the latter years of the 17th cent., then blossomed into elaborate baroque. Painting and furniture, too, evolved baroque intricacies.

The style known as **churrigueresque** superseded baroque during the first half of the 18th cent. Here, the practice of ornamenting standard architectural forms with baroque superlatives gave way to an overwhelming play of sheer design, in which rhythm and movement dominated and the emphasis upon structural elements was smothered in decoration. Everything from churches to residential furniture was ornamented in churrigueresque style. Fundamentally and intensively a religious expression, it was employed somewhat more conservatively in secular architecture.

The emergence of ' folk arts—typified by the advances in ironworking and in the making of colored glazed tiles—was the most important architectural characteristic of the latter half of the 18th cent. in the Americas.

The true Colonial period now drew to a close, accented by an unimportant classical revival. With it ended true Spanish architecture in the New World.

Early in the 19th cent., all the arts had declined in this hemisphere, and—save for certain localized movements such as that which produced the great present-day Mexican frescoes—there have been no outstanding architectural styles employed until the current use of "modern" geometric forms, so strikingly successful in Rio de Janeiro, Brazil, and in Montevideo, Urugay.   —M.R.

Spanish leather. *Book.* A name used by many leather dressers and others for any bright straight grained leather.

Spanish tango. See tango.

spanograph (art ed.). Diagrammatic representation to illustrate graphically the comparative duration of time embraced in life spans of artists, and the elapse of time in comparative art periods. Whitford and Winslow in *Dictionary of Education.*

spatial arts. See space arts.

spatular. See ENAMELLING ON METAL.

spectator. See PERSPECTIVE.

spectral sensitivity curves. See COLOR.

spectral transmission curve. See COLOR.

spectrophotometer. See COLOR.

spectroradiometry. See COLOR.

spectrum. See COLOR.

speech vibrato. See VIBRATO.

speed, in dance. See movement.

sphinx. A being with a lion's body and a human head or the head of another animal.

sphragistics. The study of numismatic seals, their origin and design, covering ancient metal and stone signets and after the 12th cent. A.D. the wax and lead impressions of heraldic seals, on official documents, which often afford genealogists more accurate information than emblazoned arms.   —T.E.F.

spider. See SYMBOLISM IN FAR EASTERN ART.

spilled ink style. See CHINESE ARTS.

spina. See circus.

spinach-green. A very dark green color. The term is most often used in the Orient to describe a certain color of jade, as spinach-green jade.

spine. *Book.* The modern term for the back of the book.

spinet. An obsolete keyboard instrument like the harpsichord, but small and square in form. See MUSICAL INSTRUMENTS.

spiral. An ornament in which a curved line moves continuously in ever-widening circles out from the center about which it revolves; common in all artistic styles, used in single and complicated forms.   —L.T.S.

spiritual. See AMERICAN NEGRO MUSIC.

splay. A slanted surface or bevelled edge, as of the sides of a doorway or window, or of a joist. See reveal.

Spode ware. See CERAMICS II.

spool drum. See MUSICAL INSTRUMENTS.

sposalizio. Italian for "marriage". The term is the sobriquet for Raphael's famous picture in the Brera Museum at Milan, Italy. The picture relates the story of the wedding of Mary and Joseph. It was painted by Raphael in 1504 for the Church of St. Francis at Citta di Castello and remained there until the Napoleonic times (1798) when it was removed and brought to Milan. The picture is signed "Raphael Urbinas MDIIII" and was painted shortly after Raphael had left the studio of his teacher Perugino. There he had seen Perugino's picture, with the same subject, which is now in the museum at Caen, France, and by which he was undoubtedly influenced. But in Raphael's picture the subject has been infused with new life. The group of persons shows a vivacity of motion and expression quite new in the Umbrian school of that time.   —L.L.

spot zoning. See CIVIC PLANNING.

spout. A tube or trough for discharging a liquid or other flowable substance.

spreader. See ENAMELLING ON METAL.

springing line or **springing.** The point at which an arch begins to curve over; usually a horizontal line.

sprinkled. *Book.* Like "marbled" this is usually applied to edge coloring and denotes that the edges have been cut and sprinkled with color. Generally all three edges are so treated and described.

spruch. See MEDIEVAL MUSIC.

spun glass. See GLASS AND GLASS-MAKING.

spur marks. Marks on ceramic ware where the spurs or separators have adhered to the object and have been broken off after the object has been removed from the kiln.

square. See CIVIC PLANNING.

square dance. See American folk forms, in music.

square nimbus. See nimbus.

square notation. See NOTATION.

squared paper. Used as the translation of a water color sketch for a rug into a loom-pattern. Its beauty must not be marred or lost while adapting it to the little square on the loom pattern paper, which indicates each knot of worsted to be tied, and woven into the fabric.   —B.E.J.

squinch. An arch, lintel, or beam carried across the angle of a square or polygonal structure to support a superimposed mass such as a dome.

stadium, stadion. See circus.

staff (*pl.* staves). *Mus.* See NOTATION.

stage design. A phase of theatre art pertaining to the designing of curtains, scenery, properties, costumes, lighting effects and stage sets in general. Whitford and Winslow in *Dictionary of Education.*

STAGESETTING. Stagesetting comprehends the organization and the whole complex of objects which help the spectator visualize the place and environment of action. These elements consist principally of four categories: (1) the **background** (either a fixed architectural built-up, or painted background or a movable and interchangeable painted backdrop), (2) the **lateral parts** (either a continuous architectural or painted wall or a sequence of **changeable flats** which may be perspectively painted and arranged or may represent just a sequence of interrupted architectural details), (3) **props** (individual movable objects like pieces of furniture or single painted or modelled rocks, trees, etc.), (4) the **proscenium,** an architectural or painted frame which separates the stage from the audience. The importance and the treatment of these four elements of stagesetting vary through the history of the theatre. However, stagesetting in the narrower modern sense of the word was not created before the time of the High Renaissance.

The ancient Greek theatre set its stage mainly by architectural means in developing the back wall with its three doors (see THEATRE ARCHITECTURE). Nevertheless, some painted scenery has been used although probably later than Vitruvius (2nd half of the 1st cent. B.C.) and Pollux (2nd cent. A.D.), the authors on whose works our knowledge of the ancient theatre is based, assume. Surely, since the end of the 5th cent. B.C. single painted props like rocks were used and also **a kind of flat painted canvas (coulisse).** Whether these paintings were already then done in any kind of perspective, is not clear. A more complicated system was represented through the so-called **"scena ductilis"** that means an arrangement of painted canvas one behind the other in a way that when one flat was drawn back the one behind appeared. Even changeable **periaktoi** (triangular revolving prisms) were arranged in connection with the stationary architectural background—probably besides the doors. Vitruvius described standardized decorations for the three types of theatrical plays: different architectural motives for tragedy and comedy, pastoral motives for satyr-plays. It is possible that these descriptions of Vitruvius were true more for his contemporary Roman theatre than for the real ancient Greek stage.

The technique of machinery was quite far developed, a series of specific devices was generally used. The most important device was a movable platform in semi-circular or square form which was pushed through the middle door and on which were placed the individual props representing an interior like a throne, altar, etc., called **ekkyklema.**

The Roman theatre developed and specified painted scenery much farther. Here the use of real perspective is sure since murals at Pompeii and other places have come down to us which imitate these scenic effects. So we have to suppose that these painted decorations were not in any way bound to the stationary architectural background (scenae frons) but varied freely.

The development during the Middle Ages cannot be considered as a continuous unity in the same sense as the Greek and Roman theatre. There is in every respect a greater difference between the 11th and 15th cents., between Spain and Germany, than between the 5th cent. B.C. and the 2nd cent. A.D. in Graeco-Roman civilization, and than between a theatre in Greece proper and in Southern France. All varieties of the liturgical drama or mystery plays took place first inside the church corresponding to individual ecclesiastic holidays. First small movable props were used and arranged before the altar such as the crib under a straw covered roof, the sepulchre of Christ, etc. Later simultaneous small boxes or scaffolds were arranged fitting into the architectural structure of the church which represented the various localities of the Holy stories. Only to a very small degree they were characterized by visual hints except the mouth of the Hell whose frame was always literally decorated.

When during the 14th and 15th cents. the play was shifted from the interior to the square before the church or the market place, the setting became much more elaborate. The various scenes became **"mansions"** like the Paradise, the City of Jerusalem, the Limbo, the Lake of Genezareth, the Heaven, and always the most favorite—the Hell. The individual guilds which had to care for the decoration competed by the accumulation of very realistic props and more or less primitively painted canvasses. In these painted decorations perspective was never used. The diversity of the places of action substituted for the visual stimulus provided later by the perspectival built-up and the change of decorations. All kinds of complicated machinery, from the flying device to fountains and burning hell-kettles, supplemented the realistic props and painted accessories. They became almost self-purpose during the 15th and 16th cents.

This development showed different aspects in the individual European countries. The English version represented in so far an exception as the individual mansions were put on wheels as a kind of richly decorated floats, whose succession substituted for the simultaneity of action in other European countries.

The stagesetting of the Renaissance developed from three sources which finally amalgamated. The rediscovered Roman comedies, mainly plays by Seneca, Plautus and Terence, were performed on stages which showed—probably unconsciously—still a variant of the medieval mansions. We know exactly by early illustrated editions of Terence about their appearance. Generally, it was a row of pillars with curtains in between. Behind these curtains small compartments represented different localities. These pillars were arranged either in one row, or as a half octagon or square-like. This form of representation lasted till the first decade of the 16th cent. Then the influence of the second root for the Renaissance theatre began to grow gradually. It was the rediscovery of Vitruvius with his descriptions of ancient theatres (see THEATRE ARCHITECTURE), of which many editions were published. Although the reconstructions by the leading Renaissance artists were not at all reliable in the sense of modern archeology, they at least paved the way for the use of perspective on the stage which had so far developed in the painting of the 15th cent. Perspectival backgrounds for the performances of Ludovico Ariosto's (1474-1533) *Cassaria,* Ferrara, 1508; for Bernardo Dovizio's—called Bibbiena— (1470-1520) *Calandra,* between 1504 and 1513, Urbino; some perspectival stagesettings by Baldassare Peruzzi (1481-1537). This perspectival rendering substituted for the simultaneity of the medieval stage. The third influencing factor were the "trionfi", "masques", "entries", or "ballets" of the 15th cent. These were festival processions with individual floats of allegorical decorations. They were composed by painted props, costumed actors who moved on complicated machineries using technical elements of the medieval mystery stage, augmented by artificial animals, etc. (e.g., Leonardo da Vinci's *Il Paradiso,* Milan, 1489).

The balance of these various influences can be seen in the stage as it was represented in Sebastiano Serlio's (1473-1554) *Della Architecture,* Venice, 1545. Serlio referred to the three different kinds of settings by Vitruvius for tragedy, comedy, and satyr-play (see above). The background was a perspectively painted backdrop. To the right and to the left of this backdrop individual flat, perspectively painted canvas were erected. Background and flats created the frame for the action.

Andrea Palladio (1518-1580) and Vincenzo Scamozzi (1552-1616) shared in the erection of the Teatro Olimpico at Vicenza, 1580-84 (see THEATRE ARCHITECTURE). Besides its architectural importance this theatre

showed for the first time plastic stagesetting. Serlio's suggestions were now transferred from flat perspectival rendering into real three-dimensional settings. But these perspectival architectures, visible through three triumphal arches created only the background. The actors did not play within, but before them. The setting as such was not changeable.

Changeable settings at Italian theatres were achieved about the same time by the re-introduction of the ancient periaktoi, now called "telari" about which we are fully informed by the writings of the German architect Josef Furttenbach, the Elder (1591-1667) who explained carefully what he saw on the Italian stage of his time.

The final step was done in the Teatro Farnese at Parma, 1618-19 erected by Giovanni Battista Aleotti (1546-1636). Here we have only one large framing arch, the first modern "proscenium" instead of the three, resp. five arches of the Teatro Olimpico. Behind this main arch the rear part of the stage is not any longer filled by three-dimensional perspectively arranged settings but by a changeable backdrop and by two sequences of changeable painted side flats. In this way it was now possible to act there, on the rear stage, too. This invention means virtually the birth of modern stagesetting.

The following centuries, the 17th and 18th, represent the climax of stagesetting as an art for its own sake. Changeable side wings and changeable backdrops created the necessary instruments and possibilities. Stagesettings were considered so important that they were preserved in sequences of highly precious specific publications in copper engravings. In this way names and works of the leading theatre architects and stage designers came down to us. It is impossible to enumerate the names of even the most important among them. From the beginning of the century, designs by Alfonso Parigi (died 1656) and Guilio Parigi (1635), the disciples of Bernardo Buontalenti delle Girandole (1536-1608) and by Jacques Callot (1592-1635) are preserved in excellent prints. Their gift and knowledge were equally used for real plays, for the so-called *intermezzi,* for entrées, ballets and pageants. However, the greatest opportunity was given by the opera. Giacomo Torelli (1608-1678), the disciple of Aeotti, the builder of the Teatro Farnese in Parma, brought the achievements of the Italian stage to France where he worked esp. between 1650 and 1660. He was followed, among others by Carlo Vigarini (1586-1663) and by the Venetian Francesco Santurini (1627-1682) who worked in Italy and esp. in Munich. Others were the brothers Domenico, Gasparo and Pietro Mauro, Venetians too, working through all Europe, esp. in Munich, around 1680-1690. Of greatest importance for this generation were Giovanni and his son Ludovico Ottavio Burnacini (1636-1707) who worked especially for the Austrian Emperor in Vienna. The technique of their rendering and the necessary machinery used by all these artists, were based mainly on the experience and theories of Niccolò Sabbatini (1574-1654), *Pratica di fabbrica scene e machine ne' teatri,* Pesaro, 1637. Without analyzing the stylistic differences between the individual artists it may be said that the scene was always symmetrically built and the main machinery usually combined with water plays or fireworks and flying machinery was arranged in the center. If any excuse could be found, pompous architectures were shown. Typical scenes like the "forest", an arrangement of symmetrical trees and bushes; "desert" and "ocean", "village" and "prison" followed the symmetrical scheme. The result was that the 17th cent. and still the first third of the 18th cent. showed more formal restraint on the stage than did the really built simultaneous Baroque architecture.

Italian architects led through the whole of Europe. France's Comédies du Roi and their chief artist Laurent Mahelot around the middle of the 17th cent. followed still the example of Serlio, sometimes relapsing even into the medieval manner of simultaneous rendering of different localities. However, these localities in themselves were now perspectively painted. Soon, the influence of Torelli and his disciples assimilated the French stage to the Italian.

The Shakesperian stage is too well known to be analyzed here. Anyhow, already in the fourth decade of the 17th cent. changing scenery stimulated by Serlio and Palladio appeared on the English stage. Of greater importance for the history of stagesetting in England than the real theatres were the "masques", the elaborate dramatic-lyrical court plays. It were these pretentious representations for which Inigo Jones (1573-1652) created his main works at the time of Shakespeare. He used the stimuli he had received from travelling in Italy. Technically he relied on the periaktoi, later on two-sided flats and finally, under the influence of the Teatro Farnese and of Sabbatini's theories,

on changeable flats and backdrops. After the Restoration, men like Christopher Wren (1632-1723) and his assistant John Webb took over the Italian system entirely, and beyond that tried even to reform the theatre building itself (see THEATRE ARCHITECTURE).

In Germany and Austria, Italian designers produced Italian settings, sometimes richer than in Italy proper since the Emperor and the individual sovereigns spent large amounts of money on them (e.g., Vienna, Munich, Dresden). Peculiarly, there was almost no difference as to setting between the opera for the Emperor and the Intermedii on one hand and the religious plays staged by the Jesuits on the other hand, which were widely spread at this time as public amusement and propaganda.

A decisive turn was brought about after the first third of the 18th cent. by the genius of the leading stage designer of this time, Ferdinando Galli Bibiena (1657-1743). His work changed the stagesetting from its stiff architecturally organized symmetry to a loose, more spacious and principally *illusionistic appearance.* The way for him was paved by the perspectival illusionism of Andrea Pozzo (1642-1709). This virtuoso of perspective created successfully in his Teatra Sacra (large paintings for the decoration of churches for religious celebrations) and in his stagesettings the most illusionistic perspective with all refinements of Baroque deceptions. His tendency is an entirely naturalistic one and not any longer mainly defined by the desire to create symmetrical architectural views as those by earlier artists.

The last step, however, was done by Ferdinando Galli Bibiena, a member of the most famous family of stage designers Galli Bibiena who worked in four generations of the 17th and 18th cents. through the whole of Europe. This classic of stage design who did innumerable settings invented the angular perspective for the stage, *"maniera di veder le scene per angelo"* as explained in his main work *Architettura civile preparata sulla Geometria e ridotta alle prospettive,* Parma, 1711, and *Varie opere di Prospettiva,* Augsburg, 1740. The result was that from now on the spectator did not any longer look at the stage like into a room whose fourth wall is taken away but that he himself became included into the room which was represented on the stage. In this way the naturalistic illusion had gained immeasurably. The borderline between the auditorium and the stage was extinguished.

Ferdinando Galli Bibiena's principles were followed up by his sons and other relatives who exactly like he himself worked at almost any great opera house in Europe. The most important among them was Giuseppe (1696-1756) who superseded even his father in the luscious pomposity of his inventions (e.g., in his work *Architetture e prospettive dedicate alla Maestà di Carlo sesto,* 1740).

A reaction against the confusing overrichness of the new angular system started around the middle of the 18th cent., esp. in France. It was helped by the gradually development of classicist tendencies in architecture. The leading masters who worked in this direction were Filippo Juvarra (1676-1736) working mainly in Turin, and Giovanni Niccolò Servandoni (1695-1766) worked esp. in France and emphasized archeological and antiquarian moments especially. All these artists used the angular perspective by Ferdinando Galli Bibiena as well as the older type of symmetrical arrangement, however, both types always in a more academic manner than the Bibienas did in their exuberant baroque feeling. In France, Servandoni worked together with the painter François Boucher (1703-1770) who did many settings for the theatre of Mme. Pompadour and for the Opéra Comique. It should be mentioned that in the cooperation of these men Boucher painted sometimes figures on the wings done by Servandoni. This application of painted figures on architectural settings can still be found in the 1st third of the 19th cent. and Johann Wolfgang von Goethe (1749-1832) discusses intensely the aesthetic reasons for this combination. Servandoni and many other designers of this time did not only settings for operas but also arrangements for ballets, fireworks, and celebrations of the court. He even went one step farther inventing **"mute spectacles"** which showed only sequences of settings following each other through many hours, illustrating a specific story, accompanied by music. In this way he became the pioneer for the later **panoramas** and **dioramas.**

Archeological conceptions began to prevail more and more in the works of the Italian Giovanni Battista Piranesi (1720-1778) who displayed an exuberant imagination in the rendering of classical motives (*Prima Parte di Architettura e Prospettive,* Roma, 1743). His *"Carceri"* (prison scenes). Venice, 1770 typical stagesettings which he himself called "inventioni capricciosi" increased this spirit into the boldest visions. His spatial fantasy is even more audacious than that of Pozzo

or Bibiena. He makes the spectator divine the space, without showing it directly. He even adds some moments of technical romanticism showing the most complicated machineries. His French counterpart is Gabriel Pierre Martin Dumont (ca. 1720-1790), like Servandoni a connecting link between the Italian and the Parisian classicism. Antonio Basoli (active between 1800 and 1820) is another very important Italian classicist whose *Raccoltà di prospettive serie, Rustiche e di Paesaggio,* Bologna, 1810, influenced the stagesetting through whole Europe. The family of Bernardino Galliari (1707-1794), Francesco Fontanesi (1751-1795), and Pietro Gaspari (1720-1785) belong into the same orbit and show the identical preference for complicated prison scenes, fantastic staircases, and romantic ruins. Towards the end of the 18th cent. Pietro Gonzaga (1751-1831), again a Venetian, took the lead through Europe and worked esp. for the court in Russia. His work *La musique des yeux ou l'optique du théâtre,* Petersbourg, 1807, gained an international reputation.

In Germany the Neo-classicism brought forth a great number of stage reformers, among them most important the famous architect Karl Friedrich Schinkel (1781-1841). His stagesettings show exactly like those of the last mentioned French and Italian artists an increasing interest in so-called "natural" gardens enriched by ruins and beyond the usual classical architecture even in the reproduction of Gothic buildings from a typically romantic point of view.

One more fact has still to be mentioned. Towards the end of the 18th cent. people felt that the dissolution of interiors into individual side wings was not realistic enough. They wanted to see closed sidewalls, too, besides the closed third wall, represented by the backdrop. We find attempts for this **box set** sometimes on English stages during the last three decades of the century and in France during the Revolution. Simultaneously some German theorists fought for it, while Johann Wolfgang Goethe declined it considering it one more consequence of Diderot's (1713-1784) naturalism.

The Romanticism and later on the Realism of the 19th cent. abolished the visual interest in the stage which had dominated during the 17th and 18th cents. and had produced so ingenious stage designers. There is not one individual artistic personality through the whole century who could be compared with the above mentioned artists. In spite of the

progress of theatrical machinery and lightning, a dull combination of props and wings, sometimes archeologically true, sometimes not even that, gave just enough to make clear the locality of the action. Scenic design became an art again not before the beginning of the 20th cent. See MODERN STAGESETTING; also Allardyce Nicoll, *The Development of the Theatre,* London, 1937; George Freedley and John A. Reeves, *A History of the Theatre,* New York, 1941.
—P.Z.

stained edges. *Book.* Color applied to edges of book to prevent dirt showing. Used in place of gilding.

STAINED GLASS. Generally considered to be a pictorial or decorative composition made by uniting various sizes and shapes of colored, translucent glass together with strips of lead. Detail and shading in the composition are painted in afterwards. Except for a wider range of colors and textures now available, in addition to certain minor technical developments, the art of stained glass making is very much the same today as it was in the 12th cent.

Preparing the Glass. All stained glass is blown. Molten glass is dipped from the furnace on one end of a blow-pipe. The glass blower puts the other end to his mouth and blows until a bubble is formed. The bubble thereupon is usually elongated, after which the ends are cut off and a cylinder is formed. This cylinder is in turn cut down one side, and the glass is reheated so that it can be opened out as a flat sheet upon a piece of asbestos or plaster of Paris. Sometimes, on the other hand, the glass bubble is put inside a square box and blown until it fills the box. In this method, because the glass first touches the center of each side of the box, it gets thinner at these points as the glass is blown out into the corners. Thus the glass is irregular in thickness, affording unusual possibilities for the artist.

Another method for making sheets of glass is to twirl the glass bubble until it forms a flat disc. This is called **crown glass,** and here, too, the glass is irregular, being thinner towards the edges and thicker near the center.

Coloring the Glass. The colors are obtained from oxides added to the molten glass. Copper oxide, for example, produces blue or blue-green depending upon the amount used, the composition of the molten glass, the temperature of it, the length of time the batch

is heated, and so on. The variations obtainable from each oxide are infinite.

A **gather** or small amount of molten glass is obtained on the end of the blow pipe. This gather of clear glass is then dipped into another color of glass and a bubble blown. The colored glass forms a film around the clear glass bubble, and this is called **flashed glass.** The clear glass is used with the colored to prevent the colors, red and blue in particular, from appearing too dark for use in stained glass windows. Occasionally pieces of colored glass are further treated with hydrofluoric acid thereby producing glass of varying degrees of intensity, or **shaded glass.** Furthermore, two colors are sometimes stirred together slightly before being blown resulting in **streaked glass.**

Designing the Window. The artist who designs a stained glass window must continually think in terms of light. First, he should be intimately acquainted with the location of his window in the church or building under consideration. For example, there might be an adjoining building cutting off the sun from striking the window directly, or a tree located directly outside may cast shadows against it. It also makes a difference in which side of the building the window is to be, as a northern exposure where the sun never strikes, or a southern one with an abundance of sunshine. Moreover, the time of day the window is most often to be viewed is an added factor which the artist must take into consideration when he is designing in terms of light.

Because a window is part of the architecture of a building, the artist must treat it as such. Restraint in handling is thus called for. The brilliant colors have enough life in themselves to give vitality even though the window is compositionally conceived with monumental dignity rather than as a restless, quick-moving picture. In fact, to be true to the medium of glass, the artist will try to design in color areas rather than attempt to make a complete and detailed study.

As for procedure, the artist first makes a **sketch** of his window to scale, usually one inch to a foot. The plan is then enlarged to the size of the window, this drawing being called a **cartoon.** Finally an **outline** is made on the cartoon to show the position of the lead strips.

Making the Window. The **cutting** of the glass is usually done on a wheel with the outline serving as guide. The wheel cuts a crack in the top of the glass which deepens

966

when the glass cutter taps the glass from the underside. The important part of the process here is to see that the glass gets cut accurately, and does not chip or splinter. Because of the various sizes and shapes needed, about two-thirds of the colored glass cut is waste although some of it is subsequently reheated and used again.

After the required pieces of colored glass are all cut, they are arranged on a sheet of clear glass, and adhered by hot wax applied at the corners of each piece. This is called waxing-up, and when thus located, the glass is ready for the next step, that f painting. Using a pigment of one color, consisting of powdered glass melted and mixed with copper and iron oxide, desired detail and shading are now applied to the colored glass.

These painted pieces are in turn fired in an oven at a temperature between 400 and 500 degrees Centigrade, the pigment melting and becoming a permanent part of the glass. Staining comes next. Silver chloride is applied to the back of the glass, forming a yellow stain, and the glass is fired once again. After firing, the pieces are assembled on the outline and the leading takes place. The workman puts the prepared strips of lead in between the pieces of glass, bending the edges to form a flange or rim to hold the glass, and soldering the places where the lead strips meet. Finally he works in a kind of cement under the flanges, making the window watertight.

The History of Stained Glass. The exact origin of stained glass is not known. It is believed that it dates back no farther than the 9th cent. with probable origin in the Near East. The art spread to Italy and it is estimated that by the 10th cent. Venice was the center of stained glass making.

The first record of pictorial windows is a manuscript giving an account of the various stories illustrated in the windows of Rheims Cathedral rebuilt by the bishop from 969 to 988. The use of lead in stained glass windows is initially referred to in Mâlés *Miracles of Saint Benoit* in the Church of Fleury-sur-Loire.

Most of the windows of the 11th and early 12th cents. were of the one window type, consisting of one monumental figure in each window, but about the middle of the 12th cent., two or three windows were combined within one frame to represent incidents in the life of Christ or one of the saints. After this departure still larger windows developed and thus the architecture of the time was in-

fluenced in turn. Specimens of 11th cent. stained glass can be found in Augsburg Cathedral, Germany, and Le Mans, France, and of the 12th cent. at York, Canterbury, Chartres, and Bourges.

By the 13th cent., more attention was paid to the colors used in the windows, and greater detail was painted in with lines. Borders, too, were undergoing a change at this time from the simplified, classical motives to more natural, representational leaves, vines, and scrolls. Grisaille painting, or decorative painting in grey monotone, in which foliage patterns were painted in grey, black, or brown enamel on large, clear areas of glass, had developed by the latter part of the 1200's. Examples of 13th cent. stained glass may be found in some windows at Canterbury, Chartres, and Bourges, as well as at Lincoln, Sens, Cologne, Rouen, and Le Mans.

It was during the 14th cent. that a movement towards naturalism in stained glass reached its height. Instead of the earlier idealized abstractions the figures began to be individualized as if they were the friends and acquaintances of the glass designer. Flowing curves were now introduced for the eyes, hair, and lips, as well as for the folds in the garments. The clothes, in fact, bore resemblance to the contemporary fashions. By the end of the 14th cent., even perspective was employed a great deal for the natural effect it afforded.

The 15th cent., on the other hand, saw the decline of naturalism. Somewhat nondescript leaf forms replaced ivy and vine patterns. Gradually heraldic designs developed as decoration. The technique of scratching the design of a shield, for example, into the glass came into use along with the further development of symbolic designs painted with the brush. Individualism in glass treatment also came to characterize the stained glass of this era. Various local "schools" sprang up around talented artists all over Europe, each deviating slightly from the accepted and more or less standard stained glass design of the past. Also about this time, as painting became more important than architecture as an art, stained glass workers tried to make their production look like painting, thus violating the integrity of the glass medium. This resulted, therefore, in an unfortunate influence on stained glass making for an indeterminable period to follow.

During the 16th cent., windows developed as large pictures;—to be viewed as one large canvas. A master of this technique was Barnard Flower who came from the Netherlands to England to execute the windows for King Henry VII at Westminster as well as four windows for King's College chapel at Cambridge. Other important stained glass windows of this period are at Rouen, Marne, Dreux in France, Antwerp, Gouda, Amsterdam, Brussels, and Liege in the Netherlands, Augsburg, Strasbourg, Cologne, and Nuremberg in Germany, and at Rome, Florence, Milan, and Arezzo in Italy.

Switzerland reached the peak in a type of stained glass painting in the 17th cent., by the use of it in almost every home. A social art, oftentimes taking the place of a painting on the wall, the glass design became intimate, and, for viewing at close range, became fine and delicate. Here, too, the technique of stained glass became more like that of painting.

In the late 18th cent. a Gothic revival developed. Because the Gothic styles were copied without the inspiration or rationality with which they were first created, the result was stained glass produced according to formula. Revolting against this in the 19th cent. was William Morris, who encouraged once again creativeness rather than indiscriminate imitation. Working with Morris was Burne-Jones, and together they produced windows for the Christ Church, Oxford, for Salisbury Cathedral, Holy Trinity, Cathedral in Birmingham, and at Easthampstead, all in England, as well as at the window at Biarritz in France. Besides their cathedral windows based on biblical themes, they created some stained glass on romantic and literary themes for domestic use.

In the field of modern stained glass we find the artists concerned with abstractions in color and bold decorative patterns highly effective in carrying power rather than the traditional pictorial realism. Some of the modern stained glass windows are religious, others secular, but most are expressionist in interpretation. Three Germans, Gottfried Heinersdorff, Jan Thorn-Prikker, and Karl Schmidt-Rottluff, have experimented widely with religious symbolism and abstract studies in color and light, and have advanced particularly far the use of modern stained glass. Among other pioneers in the field is Fröydis Haavardsholm of Norway whose feeling for plastic treatment and structurally monumental composition has resulted in a powerfully expressive art; also, James Hogan of England whose recent designs include windows for Liverpool Cathedral and Temple Eman-

uel and St. Thomas Church in New York City.

The big problem in modern stained glass is not the handling of design, color or manufacture but rather that of a wider usage. Its potentialities as a contemporary art for use in home, commercial and public buildings are almost unlimited but to date stained glass is still more or less confined to church windows. See *Encyclopedia Brittannica,* 1942, vol. 21, pp. 291-297; Heaton, Maurice, "Progressive Steps in the Making of Stained Glass Windows," *American Architect,* Jan. 2, 1929, pp. 97-103; "Stained Glass: The Living Tradition of Religious Art," *Studio,* April, 1936, pp. 190-193; Teague, Walter Dorwin, "The Future of Stained Glass," *Architectural Forum,* August, 1940, pp. 99-100; Walker, N. W. Gregory, "How Stained Glass is Made," *Discovery,* April 1939, pp. 163-169.
—N.P.

stämning. See SCANDINAVIAN ART.

stamp. *Book.* Strictly applicable to most binders' tools, but used in a restricted sense for a metal block having a complete ornament, coat of arms, name, etc.

stamping tube. See MUSICAL INSTRUMENTS.

standard pitch. See ACOUSTICS.

stand oil. This term comes from the German word, *Standöle,* and is used for a thickened oil. Traditionally it was thickened merely by standing or by being placed in the sun in shallow vessels. It appears to have been much used in the European oil painting of the 15th to 18th cents. —G.L.S.

Stanislaus Augustus style. See POLISH ART.

starch. In the arts this is used for an adhesive made from flour and so takes a secondary place in the construction. Pastes are made from the starch of rice, wheat, corn, potatoes, or arrowroot. —G.L.S.

state. See PRINTS AND PRINT PROCESSES.

state planning. See CIVIC PLANNING.

state umbrella. See SYMBOLISM IN FAR EASTERN ART.

static. The adjective static comes from the Greek root *sta. "stand." Statikos* means "causing to stand". It pertains to bodies or forces at rest or in equilibrium. Aside from its mechanical application in architecture, it means figuratively resting, not active and denotes the reduction of all moving and changing forms to steadfast, unchangeable and unequivocal forms or combinations of forms. This figuratively static effect is accomplished in art if all parts of a whole are shown as resting elements in perfect equilibrium. In order to effect this static impression the single parts must be clearly outlined and easy to grasp, as e.g., in the Greek, Roman, or Italian architecture. It is interesting to notice how the Italian architects separated the clock-tower (campanile) from the main building in order to remain within the limits of this static effect. In painting and decorative art of a static character all parts are more or less arranged around a central point, so that the mutual center of gravity lies in the middle of the work. In the case of an oblong shape all parts are ordered about the two centers of gravity of an ellipse, as for instance in the Greek sculpture and in many Renaissance paintings. It is highly interesting to notice how the Greeks transformed agitated and therefore dynamic scenes like duels, battles, etc., into such of static characteristics. The people who had the natural feeling for static expression were the Greeks and, in fact, the whole Greco-Roman family, ·in contrast to the northern Celto-Germanic cultural family, which preferred dynamic expression.

—A.J.S.

station point. See PERSPECTIVE.

staurotheke (Gr. from *stauros theke*). A container for a part of the Holy Cross. A reliquary used for this purpose. Since the story of the finding of the Holy Cross is connected with Constantine the Great's mother, the most famous reliquaries of this type originated in the Byzantine Empire. An ancient Byzantine reliquary of this kind is in the treasure of the cathedral of Limburg an der Lahn, Germany. For illustration see Willy Burger, *Abendländische Schmelzarbeiten*, Berlin, 1930, Figs. 11 and 12.

—L.L.

St. Cloud ware. See CERAMICS II.

steel facing. *Etch.* To prevent an intaglio metal plate from wearing out in printing a large edition, it can be chromium steel faced by electroplating. Delicate plates, esp. drypoints, are protected in this way also. See PRINTS AND PRINT PROCESSES.

stele. A stone pillar, used as a gravestone or to mark a site. The earliest known stele decorated with sculpture is a Summerian one dating from 2550 B.C., representing the king leading his army to defend his country; another pictures King Urnammu pouring a libation to a god. Buddhist votive stelai in China show the Buddha seated in the center with reliefs of figures, including the donors, sculptured above. Mayan stelai have also been found, decorated with religious scenes. The most beautiful stelai, however, are those made in Athens during the 5th and 4th cents. B.C. to serve as tombstones. The earliest ones were high and narrow, with usually a single figure, but by the middle of the 5th cent. the slab was made wider, allowing for more elaborate relief. Scenes pictured were usually a characteristic episode from the life of the deceased (a knight dealing the death blow to his foe, a lad with a pet animal, a woman looking at her jewels) or the final farewell in the home. These slabs were often crowned with a pediment and framed by engaged pillars at the side, the whole being impressive alike for the poignancy of the representation and the gracious simplicity of the design. In the 4th cent. the compositions became more crowded and the relief more coarsely cut. After the decree of Demetrios of Phaleron against the display of wealth, the market in Athens for such sculpture ceased, but similar grave reliefs continued to be popular in Italiot Greece.

—W.R.A.

stencil. This is a mechanical means of applying patterns with paint. The stencil itself is cut out of metal, thin cardboard, or other firm material in such a way that paint can be put into the areas left open. —G.L.S.

stenochoreography. See notation, dance.

step pattern. A decorative pattern in which lines are arranged like a section through steps, i.e., short lines alternately vertical and horizontal are set at right angles to each other and each horizontal projects in front of the last. —L.T.S.

stereobate. A masonry foundation or basement as seen above the ground level.

stereochromy. Known also as water-glass painting, this is a method characterized largely by the medium used. Water-glass is a mineral, a thick, syrupy, clear liquid, an aqueous solution of potassium or sodium silicate. With this pigments are ground or, in some instances, a thin water-glass is used as a fixative with pigments that have been applied with water alone. It has been much advocated for mural painting.   —G.L.S.

St. Gallen, school of. See Carolingian art.

Stiegelware. See GLASS AND GLASS-MAKING.

stile. One of the vertical side-pieces in the frame of a door, sash, or panel.

still life. A picture of inanimate objects.

stilt block. See pulvin.

stilted arch. An arch, the springing of which is above its apparent impost; also **stilted vault.**

stilts. *Cer.* Fired clay supports to avoid sticking during firing. See CERAMICS I.

simulation artistic. See inspiration.

stipes. See altar.

stipple. To engrave by means of dots rather than by lines. See PRINTS AND PRINT PROCESSES.

St. John's dance. See St. Vitus dance.

stock characters. See THEATRE.

stone. Highly honored as a building material from ancient times, stone early became the substance of sculptured designs and, to a slight extent, became also a support for painting. Broadly, the kinds of stone can be defined as sedimentary, igneous, and metamorphic. The more familiar sedimentary rocks are slate, shale, sandstone, limestone, and gypsum. Igneous or primary rocks formed by solidification of molten masses from the within the earth include granite, feldspar, quartz, diorite, and basalt. Metamorphic rocks are either sedimentary or igneous in origin but have been slightly changed in character by movement of the earth's crust or by chemical action. Marble is a metamorphic condition of sedimentary limestone and chalk.   —G.L.S.

stone carving. See CHINESE ARTS.

stone-close. Term applied to a circular doorway or opening in a wall. The term is derived from the practice of closing such an opening with a stone slab shaped to fit and held in place with props.   —J.M.M.

Stonehenge. See PREHISTORIC ART.

stone pipe. See Eastern North American aboriginal art.

stop. Name for the draw-stops, or stop-knobs, of an organ.

stopping out. *Etch.* The act of stopping certain sections of a plate from further exposure to the acid bath; also protecting the back of the plate from etching. Quick-drying stopping out varnishes are used for this purpose. See PRINTS AND PRINT PROCESSES.   —K.K.

storage forms. See FURNITURE.

Storm and Stress. See GERMAN ART.

story. In architecture: The space between two floors.

straight drama. See RADIO DRAMA.

straw, artificial. A rayon specialty yarn where viscose spinning solution is forced through an "L" shaped spinnerette instead of the round hole. The viscose process is used only for this yarn in America. The yarn consists of the continuous, flat and heavy filament, which is folded during spinning. It resembles a silk-like straw and has a lustrous or dull crinkled surface. It is quite flexible and made in 100 and 150 denier sizes in America.   —G.W.R.

Strasbourg turpentine. See oleoresin.

streamlined. Originally expression for forms which were shaped in order to overcome the pressure of air or water currents, e.g., piers of bridges, bows of ships, locomotives, automobiles, airplanes. The streamline originates as result of aero-dynamic calculations. Applied to these objects it represents the true expression of their function.

During the last decade the word often has been applied and misused for any so-called modernistic forms. From architectural façades to ladies' hats and flashlights, everything became "streamlined". Virtually, that did not mean anything else than the renunciation of superfluous ornamentation. Paradoxically, even so-called modernistic architecture, supposed to be functional, became streamlined by applying the forms of swift moving objects to balconies, corner windows, roofs, etc., as if these architectural details were exposed to terrific aerial pressure. Actually, these forms were entirely unfunctional since they were not born of practical needs or technical suppositions but merely patterned by a slogan-like fashion. Leading pioneering

architects of our days did not succumb to this temptation. See functional architecture; international architecture; traffic, aesthetics of.
—P.Z.

street music. Presupposes an urban environment and consists, in its most characteristic form, of the cries of venders of various types of merchandise. To these we must add the music of ballad singers, of performers on the hurdy-gurdy, and on other instruments, who seek to induce passers-by to part with coins of small value. It is a very ancient practice, but one which has fallen into disuse in modern industrial communities where the most leather-lunged vender might call in vain without being heard against competing mechanical noises of all kinds.

A French poem of the 13th cent., the *Crieries de Paris,* represents the poet as the victim of his own lack of sales resistance, having spent his substance on the innumerable venders who swarmed the streets of old Paris: the *étuviste* who called in the streets when the water in the baths was warm, the *mercier* selling pins, needles, and even *bons flageus a pastor* (good shepherd's pipes), sellers of brooms, sausages, herrings, cheese, birds, and Noës.

In this and other works of the period we are simply informed about the various kinds of street venders. In the *Cris de Paris* of Jannequin we possess the actual music of a number of these songs woven into the polyphonic texture of a French chanson. After the four voices harmoniously invite the listener to hear the cries of Paris, we hear the soprano sing of "little warm pastries", the alto "claret wine for ten deniers", and the tenor "fried tarts", while the bass finally joins in with fine, hot "cache-museaux", the whole ensemble painting a vivid and witty genre picture.

A ballad of the period of the French Revolution draws its rather grim humor from the fact that the hero, "le franc Picard", interprets the calls of the street venders whom he hears according to his fears. Thus the oyster woman sings to a pretty air, "Oysters on the half shell" (*Huître à l'écaille*), but the uneasy Picard imagines he hears, "There is the rascal" (*v'la la canaille*), and runs off as fast as his legs will carry him.

Perhaps no more detailed account of the street cry has been published than *Les Voix de Paris* by Jean Georges Kastner who flourished in the mid-19th cent. (1857). He not only reproduces a multitude of cries, some of them (like those of the newsboys)

having a strangely modern flavor, but anticipates a scene in Charpentier's *Louise* by writing a sort of cantata in which various characters indulge in reveries to a musical background suggesting in poetic fashion the street noises appropriate to the time of day. Thus the first episode, *"Paris le matin",* introduces the Sleeper (*Le Dormeur*) who clings to his slumbers till finally roused by the cries of the street peddlers outside. Of later date and much more familiar is the opening scene of the second act of Charpentier's *Louise* where the awakening of Paris is musically portrayed by the voices of workers and itinerant venders. Thus we see the persistence and vitality of a trait which spans six centuries.

In Italy music tended in general to be courtly almost to the exclusion of popular elements which, when they do appear (as in the *frottola*), seem frequently to be treated as parodies rather than in a serious mood. Nevertheless, traces of the popular street cries can be pointed out, such as the call of the fish peddler who praises his crayfish in a *caccia* by Landino. The *Pazzia Senile* of Adriano Banchieri belongs to the 17th cent. It represents a series of scenes derived from the traditions of the *commedia dell'arte* (q.v.) which are interrupted by intermezzi, one in the guise of the song of the rag and bone men, another sung by match peddlers, the finale in the form of a peasant dance. Even Domenico Scarlatti, if we can credit the music historian Burney, employed popular motives and the songs of muleteers in his elegant and vivacious lessons for harpsichord.

The German tradition, at least as far back as the 15th cent., includes elements which are hearty, popular, robust, so that it seems quite natural to find references to street cries in German musical compositions. The *Jahrmarktsgauner* of Sebastian Knüpffer portrays such types as the rat-catcher and the scissorsgrinder. The music composed for the latter suggests the continual turning of the grindstone by a persistent *ostinato* in the bass. A *quod libet* of 1622 by Friderici is constructed on the street cries of Rostock, divided (like the more recent work by Kastner) into sections depicting morning, midday, and evening. This work begins with the call of the night watchman followed by milkmaids, cabbage venders, broom-makers, cobblers, and the quack doctor, each with appropriate music. All then join in a New Year's song. The watchman blows his horn as a warning that the town gates are about to close, and an agitated *sinfonia* suggests the rush of the market folk to get out of town before the gates close. A song of rejoicing closes the work. Finally, Johann Caspar Horn has painted a similar genre picture in his *Zum Jahrmarckt* with its broad and festive opening. His list of characters is again drawn from familiar folk types, the town crier, the rat catcher, while part two introduces the scissors-grinder and the tooth-puller. Enough has perhaps been said to show the strong popular element in this music and the part which street merchants and their cries play in such works. Bach's *Peasant Cantata* is in this same style though here we find no use of street cries. The sentimental and emotional nature of much German romantic music was not favorable to the use of folk cries though the figure of the night watchman reappears later in Wagner's *Mastersingers* intoning his reassuring "All's well".

In France the earliest use of the street cry is in the chanson. In Germany the favorite medium is the cantata. In England, however, composers employed a special form which was derived from the fancy. In these compositions the cries of the London streets are counterpointed against a polyphonic background played on the viols. Among the composers who cultivated this form were Orlando Gibbons and Richard Deering. The vogue for Italian music during the 18th cent. formed an unfavorable background for folk music though we find traces of the cries of street merchants here and there, as in a popular song published in the *Musical Miscellany* in which the singer calls on the maids to bring out their coney skins.

At the present day street music survives with difficulty in the industrial west, overcome by the competing mechanical noises and the restless motion of the great city streets. The street singer has not altogether passed from our streets, and the German band and the Italian organ grinder with his monkey are at least recent memories. The junk man in his horse-drawn wagon attracts attention by a string of jangling bells, or intones his hoarse cry. On London streets before World War II the Welsh miners sang, and in Paris an itinerant herd of goats was escorted by a goat-herd whose shrill piping announced his presence. These, however, are survivals of a very ancient past, doomed to extinction except perhaps in the East, in corners of our own South, wherever older ways of buying and selling still persist. However dubious a future street music may face it has

left a firm imprint on the musical art of the past. It was Rameau who said in his *Code de musique pratique,* "Listen to the people who sing as they cry their goods in the street."   —C.W.H.

strength. In literary criticism this term is used to indicate that a work is forthright, obvious, and definite in the statement and treatment of its material, the quality of *strength,* usually contrasted with *subtlety* or *delicacy,* denotes that a work is positive and uncompromising both in the development of its subject-matter and in its formal structure. "Strong" art is held back by no doubts springing from a consciousness of complexities, but exhibits a complete assurance and conviction.   —I.J.

stress, in dance. See movement.

stretcher. (1) This is an accessory to the canvas support of painted pictures. It is a frame of four or more pieces over which the canvas is fixed, usually by tacks. As a rule, stretchers are provided with keys or small wedges so set that they can slightly enlarge the frame and tighten the canvas if it gets slack.   —G.L.S.
(2) In masonry: A stone laid with its longer face in the surface of the wall.

stretto. (1) Coda or finale in quicker time than the rest of the piece. (2) The part of a fugue (q.v.) where subject and answer overlap.

strigil. See Apoxyomenos.

string. See ACOUSTICS.

string course. In masonry: A horizontal band of stone sometimes specially shaped and projecting, often carried at a given level to accentuate the horizontal divisions of a structure.   —J.M.M.

string quartet, quintet, trio. See chamber music.

Stroganov school. See RUSSIA, RELIGIOUS PAINTING IN.

strontium yellow. This is related to barium yellow, being a strontium chromate instead of a barium chromate. Like the barium pigment it has a lemon hue but is a little deeper in tint and has a somewhat greater hiding power.   —G.L.S.

strophic song. See song.

structure. *Mus.* Term designating the formal properties of a composition; almost a synonym of *form, structure* is used instead of *form* esp. if constructive factors are focussed.   —E.K.

Stuart period. The reign of the house of Stuart in England began with the accession of James I in 1603, was interrupted by the artistically sterile Commonwealth from 1649 to 1660, and ended with the death of Queen Anne in 1714. It began with the supremacy of a heavy baroque style imported from Flanders and Germany, but soon accepted an academic compromise inspired by Palladio and the Italians. It produced a number of native designers now famous in English architectural history, Inigo Jones, Sir Christopher Wren, and Sir John Vanbrugh, and their equally noted creations, respectively the Banqueting Hall of Whitehall Palace, St. Paul's Cathedral, and Blenheim Palace. See ENGLISH ART.   —P.C.B.

stucco. Evidently this word has been adapted to a style or type of thing rather than to a particular material. It is ordinarily applied to reliefs and similar decorations on buildings. These may be made of gypsum, of pozzalanic cement, or of lime plaster.
—G.L.S.

studio. (1) The workroom of an artist; (2) a classroom in which art work is carried on. Syn. *art room.* Whitford and Winslow in *Dictionary of Education.*

studio easel. See easel.

stuffers. Sometimes called "fillers" are extra threads laid lengthwise and crosswise of a carpet and which do not add strength, but simply increase the bulk, weight and stiffness.   —B.E.J.

stump. A small instrument used by a draftsman, this is rolled up from chamois skin or paper and serves for smoothing out the tones of crayon or charcoal drawings. A still smaller tool of the same sort, pointed at only one end, is called a **tortillon.**   —G.L.S.

stupa. The stupa or **tope** was originally a tumulus for the interment of royalty in early India. Later, such mounds were used for the interment of the relics of the Buddha and His sainted followers. By this function, the stupa, divinely animated by the quickening presence of the relics of the Tathâgata, came to be a special kind of Buddhist shrine. The principal elements of the stupa consist of one or more square or round bases surmounted by a hemispherical cupola or *aṇḍa.* This domical member is a solid mass of brick and earth. Above the *aṇḍa* is a balcony-like member or *harmikā,* and, surmounting all, a mast or *yasti,* upon which are ranged numbers of ceremonial umbrellas or *chattas.* At some time in the course of its development, a cosmological or metaphysical interpretation was assigned to the stupa and each of its elements. Thus, the base represented the earth, the cupola the enclosing dome of the sky, and the *yasti* represented the world-axis with the tiered parasols typifying the successive *devalokas* rising above the world of men. The *harmikā* symbolized the Tuṣita Heaven set on the summit of the cosmic Mt. Meru which we must imagine as enclosed in the dome of the monument. The whole could therefore be regarded as a reconstruction of the Indian concept of the cosmic scheme. The stupa is at once a symbol of the Buddha's *Nirvāna;* it is an architectural body for Him who had disappeared into the realm of invisibility; and, by derivation from its cosmic symbolism, a likeness of the Buddha as the Universe itself. Its former employment for royal burials was assimilated to the concept of the Buddha as *cakravartin* or world ruler.

In Ceylon the stupas or *dagabas* are believed to typify in hieratic fashion in their architectural form the successive stages of magical power attained by Buddha at the time of His Enlightenment.

In later stupas of Mahāyāna Buddhism the corporeal relics were replaced by written spells or *dhāraṇī.* The insertion of these magic writings was believed to be no less effective in endowing the monument with divine vitality in a form of Buddhism which regarded the Buddha's earthly appearance and *Nirvāna* as a mere illusion. The typical Indian stupa may be illustrated by the famous monument at Sāñchī and numerous examples in Gandhāra (Northwest-Frontier-Province). In Tibet and Nepal, the chief centers of esoteric Buddhism, a special type of stupa was developed in which the four mystic Buddhas of the Four Directions were represented by statues on the base, and the all-seeing eyes of the self-created primordial Adi Buddha were painted on the *harmikā.*

The final development of the stupa form is to be seen in the great monument of Barabudur in Java, in which the hemispherical profile of the structure literally encloses the terraces of the pyramidal world-mountain

Meru. Barabudur is really a *maṇḍala* in stone, and its symbolism goes far beyond that of the original stupa.

It is definitely known that elaborate geomantic ceremonies determined the orientation of the stupa, and the most precise system of proportions fixed the measurement of the whole and its every member. It is for this reason that the stupas have something of the same mathematical perfection of sheer architectural form and mass that we find in the Pyramids. The architectural effectiveness of the stupa depends on the alternation and balance of round and square shapes. The completely undynamic and static character of stupa architecture is thoroughly expressive of its function of enclosing and guarding the relic and its symbolism of the fixed cosmic structure.   —B.R.

Sturm und Drang. See GERMAN ART.

St. Vitus dance or St. John's dance (according to the patron saint who was supposed to protect the afflicted). The dancing malady that swept over Europe during and immediately after the Black Death (14th cent.). Its appearance is thought to be due to a nervous disorder akin to imitative hysteria. The depleted physical and tortured mental conditions of the wretched populace, caused by war, pestilence and famine, played a large part in conditioning their minds for the mental disorder that found relief in this demoniacal dancing epidemic. Men, women, and young boys and girls would dance in wild delirium, seemingly possessed and without any will of their own. Morbid bystanders often became infatuated and would join in the bacchanalian frenzy. In Italy the same disorder was called *tarantism,* as it was at first thought to be caused by the bite of a tarantula. It was discovered, however, that even those who were not bitten contracted the disease, and the only explanation pointed to a mental disorder. (H'Doubler, M. N., *Dance, A Creative Art Experience,* F. S. Crofts & Co., 1940.)

style (from the Gr. *stylos;* L. *stilus*). (1) A stilus was a metal writing instrument which was used to engrave letters upon small tablets covered with wax, comparable with our modern pen. In the same way that we in our time have transferred the meaning of the word pen to that which is expressed, saying he has a fluent pen, the writing instrument stilus became an expression of the manner of writing. From this the meaning became more inclusive and was transferred to the whole field of art.

Starting with this figurative sense, style means those characteristics of form which are peculiar to a certain work or a group of works, and which at the same time distinguish it or them from other works. These characteristic peculiarities must be organic, and thus are recognized as the signs of an expression of a complete unit. Take for example a work in the Gothic style. The single and separate characteristics, such as the pointed arch, the crossed vault, the aspiring pillars, etc., do not make the Gothic style, but it is the organic relationship of all these parts which forms a significant whole.

As one applies this word to the works of a single artist, so the word is applied to the works of a whole school when we speak of the style of a certain school: the style of the School of Leonardo, of Cranach, or of Rembrandt, for instance. An entire group of artists can be bound by such peculiarities of style without necessarily having a leader, as for instance the Bohemian school, the Danubian school, or the Fontainebleau school. We can continue and apply the word to whole epochs characterized by a certain coherence of style. So we speak of the Roman, Gothic, baroque styles, etc. Besides these styles of epochs, whole groups of peoples or races are distinguished by certain peculiarities of expression or style. So the style of Egyptian art is in clear contrast to that of the Greek people. In recent times research has been done on the difference of style between the northern (Germanic) and the southern (Latin) peoples. (See O. Hagen, *Deutsches Sehen.*) Principles of development have also been found within the changing style of an epoch. (See Woelfflin, *Formprobleme der Kunst.*)

Of decisive importance to the discussions of style and on the causes originating that which we call style was Gottfried Semper's work, *Der Stil.* Semper argued that the peculiarities of style in art are caused mainly by the peculiarities of the material which must be worked with: clay, metal, wood, wool, silk, etc. All materials require to be worked according to their natural characteristics. Clay, for instance, must be modelled which makes its forms appear different from those of metal which must be melted, or from those of wood which must be carved. A wool fibre demands a different treatment even in its coloring from a silk fibre, because the structure of each is very different. To these material peculiarities there must be added the purpose for which the material serves: Receptacles, for instance, result in the different shapes of a casket, a barrel, a bottle, etc., acarding to their various uses. On the basis of the peculiarities of material and purpose, that which we call style necessarily depends. The followers of Semper's theory are numerous even today.

This theory was opposed by Aloys Riegl who in his several works, esp. in his *Spätrömische Kunst-Industrie,* took the position that style originates in a subjective will-to-art lying in the human being himself. The spiritual structure of the will of man and the artist seeks an expression which is in accordance with the individual peculiarities of his own will. With every material there are several possibilities of handling, and the solutions of the purpose may be varied. One can and should choose that manner which is in accordance with these alternatives. One is reminded of the different techniques of handling stone used by the artists of the Egyptian and the Gothic epochs. Only by means of Riegl's theory is it all possible to explain the historical development of a style as it may be observed, for instance from antique times up to the Christian era. Riegl decisively opposes the so-called "Verfalls Theorie". Each period has its own style arising from its spiritual depth of will. Different styles, of course, may be compared by an analysis of the content, but the value of a style is a thing which cannot be compared with any other value. The followers of this theory were mainly historians of modern art (art from medieval times until today). Woelfflin and his circle applied Riegl's rules to special departments of art.

A compromise between these two theories had already been found in 350 B.C. by the Chinese people. In his parable of the carver of the stand for chimes, Dsuang Dsi said that the natures of the material and the man must be united before a real work of art can be created. The parable concludes with the words: "When the right tree stood before my eyes then the stand for the chimes stood finished before me, so that I had only to put my hand to it. If I had not found that tree I should have given up. Because I allowed my nature to conform to the nature of this tree, men consider it a divine work." (Dsuang Dsi, *The Right Book of the Southern Land of Blossoms,* trans. and comments by Richard Wilhelm, Jena, 1920.)   —A.J.S.

(2) *Dance.* Style is the by-product of the particular way in which the dancer selects, organizes, and manipulates all the contributing elements of his materials, physical and psychical, into a harmonious entity. In this sense every dance that is an organic solution of its problem has a style of its own, while at the same time it may erect characteristics that belong to the *style* of the creator and performer.

In the *style of* refers to a manner of performance distinctive or characteristic of an era or of another dancer.   —M.N. H'D.

(3) *Mus.* Set of idiosyncrasies characteristic of certain types of compositions (e.g., symphonic style, a cappella style); of a period (16th cent. style, baroque style); of a composer (Palestrina style, Wagner style); of a period in the life of a composer as distinguished from other periods (late Beethoven style, early Schönberg style); of a manner of interpretation (virtuoso style). Sometimes used in the sense of idiom (modal style, atonal style), the terms covers actually less than idiom (q.v.).   —E.K.

style flamboyante. See Gothic.

style mécanique. See FRENCH ART.

stylize, stylization, in dance. To *stylize* movement is to emphasize the essential phase of a movement to heighten the awareness of certain qualities. This is accomplished by checking the movement at the one point that is most suggestive of the intended meaning, as opposed to abandoning the movement to its full range of action. Stylization imparts a pictorial element of design to the body and its parts while in action, and if not sensitively and artistically employed such movements easily become manneristic and statically patterned. The result, under these conditions, is that the body is used more as a decorative unit than as a plastic expressive instrument. Stylization is artistic individual distortion.

                —M.N. H'D.

stylobate. Uppermost part of a stereobate (q.v.) or top step before a temple, on which is supported a row of columns.

stylotint. An aquatint process that resembles a dry brush drawing or a monochrome Japanese water color. Whole passages can be controlled by the stopping out.   —K.K.

stylotint (an intaglio process). Stylotint is an unexplored medium which is capable of great freedom, variation, character and sensitiveness, and a great variety of curious textures, and when it is combined with tones of aquatint it can produce results similar to a Japanese monochrome water color.

Stylotint is a method of etching in which the coating on the plate is soft and easily displaced with a stick, stump, stiff brush, rag, or steel point. If the stylus, of wood or any other material, is cut like a chisel on the end it will produce a line of variable thickness. This is the type of line which most resembles the Japanese brushline.

The parts of the plate from which the coating has been removed in this way will appear black in the finished proof. After the drawing has been made, the plate is heated and the ground becomes stronger than a regular hard ground.

This process belongs to the family which includes pen process aquatint, offset soft ground, as well as stylotint. Although each one of these processes uses a different way of producing areas of open copper on an otherwise coated plate, they all break up the open surfaces with aquatint so that they print as areas of aquatint in the shape of pen or brush lines, crayon lines, or wooden stylus lines.

The beauty of this process, invented by Alexander von Kubinyi of Munich, lies in the quality of the lines and textures, the ease with which large areas of black are produced, and in the smooth, easy resistance of the drawing tool on the surface of the copper. The interplay of the first and the last of these qualities, the way a sharpened wood stylus acts on the smooth copper plate covered with a soft ground, makes possible a control, a type of line, a kind of drawing not obtainable in any other way.   —K.K.

stylus. In the history of art a metal point used for faint marking probably has had a wide and variable use since metals were discovered. Such a point was a common writing instrument in ancient times. It marked preparatory lines on pottery and on walls where paintings were to be executed. In some cases it indicated the lines for writing in manuscripts. It turned the circles of haloes and punched the holes in paper cartoons through which drawings were pounced or transferred to another surface.   —G.L.S.

sub-arterial highway, street, etc. See CIVIC PLANNING.

subdivision. See CIVIC PLANNING.

subdominant. *Mus.* See idiom B (1).

subject. See fugue.

subjective color sensation. See COLOR.

submarginal (district). See CIVIC PLANNING.

submediant. *Mus.* See idiom B (1).

subordinaries. See HERALDRY.

subtile balance. See balance.

subtractive color mixing. See COLOR.

suggestion (L. *suggestio*). Calling to mind through the association of experiences, images, or ideas, or having the power to do so under specified conditions. One of the two modes by which works of art are transmitted to the mind of the observer or appreciator; the other being *presentation* (q.v.). Suggestions may be conveyed through arbitrary symbolism, based on conventional bonds of cultural usage; through imitation and resemblance, as in a realistic picture or statue; and through common association, as between smiling and happiness. The suggestive power of an image operates only through the previous conditioning of an individual; but similar conditioning among individuals makes possible similar apprehension of meanings, as when members of a cultural group read a poem produced therein. Suggestion and presentation operate as factors in a work of art, when part of its effect is produced by direct sense-perception, part by associated meanings.   —T.M.

sui (Ch.). Jade girdle-clasp.

Sui art. See CHINESE ARTS.

suiboku-e (Jap.). Black and white painting. *Sumi*, or ink, is used as the sole medium.

suiboku-ga (Jap.). See suiboku-e.

suibokugwa (Jap.). See JAPANESE ART.

Suiko art. See JAPANESE ART.

suisaiga (Jap.). Term for water color painting.

suite. *Mus.* A set, cycle, or series of pieces. The suite was the predecessor of the sonata (q.v.) and the symphony (q.v.). It was a succession of dance compositions, frequently introduced by a prelude. The chief dance forms employed were the allemande, courante, sarabande, gigue, gavotte, bourrée, minuet, passepied (qq.v.).

sukiya (Jap.). See chashitsu.

Sultanabad. See ISLAMIC ART; PERSIAN ART.

Sultania ware. See ISLAMIC ART.

Sumerian art. See MESOPOTAMIAN ART.

sumi (Jap.). Black in, composed of a mixture of carbon and glue moulded into sticks or cakes. When rubbed up on water on an ink-stone, it is the painter's and writer's common medium.   —J.A.M.

sumi-e (Jap.). So-called black and white paintings. See sumi.

summer canon. See MEDIEVAL MUSIC.

Sunga art. See INDIAN ART.

Sung art. See CHINESE ARTS.

Sung dynasty porcelain. See CERAMICS II.

sunken plan. See PERSPECTIVE.

sunk relief. See relief; negative carving.

suovetaurilia. A representation of a boar, a ram, and a bull together.

superhighway. See CIVIC PLANNING.

superimposition. See PHOTOGRAPHY.

super-piano. See electrical instruments.

superrealism. See surrealism.

superstructure. Any structure or any part of a structure, built upon or considered in relation to the part on which it rests; a building considered in relation to its foundation.   —J.M.M.

supertonic. See idiom B (1).

support. There has been some difference in terminology about the underlying material on which pictures are made. Frequently it has been called the ground but that word has now come to mean, almost without exception, the uniform coating or preparation which lies next underneath the paint itself. A more recent tendency has been to give the word, support, to any of these materials and it has been defined as 'the physical structure which holds or carries the ground or paint film.'   —G.L.S.

supporters. See HERALDRY.

suprematism. An abstract movement in painting founded in Moscow in 1913 by Kasimir Malevich, famous painter of the picture *White on White* (1919). Includes Alexander Rodchenko, painter of *Black on Black* (1919). Flourished during World War I and into the 1920's. Malevich defined the doctrine in the following sentence: "By Suprematism I mean the supremacy of pure feeling or perception in the pictorial arts—the experience of non-objectivity". See RUSSIAN ART.   —L.D.L.

suq. (Ar.). A bazaar. See ISLAMIC ART.

surface color. See COLOR.

surface film. This has a general definition of any outer coating material which may be used on a picture, on a piece of sculpture or on any work of art. It can include oils, varnishes, waxes, and other substances which are capable of forming such a film. —G.L.S.

suri-haku (Jap.). A fabric with the decoration painted on in gold-leaf alone.

surimono-e (Jap.). A wood-block print used as a greeting-card.

surrealism (Fr. *Surréalisme*; Ger. *Surrealismus*). A 20th cent. movement in art which finds a "super-reality" in the objects of subconscious mental activity. It is sharply opposed both to naturalism (q.v.) and to purely abstract painting (q.v.)

André Breton issued in 1924 the first "Manifesto of Surrealism." Since that time the movement has had many followers among French and Spanish artists and has spread to many parts of the world. While surrealism has been manifested chiefly in painting and poetry, it has also appeared in drama, stage settings, photography, the motion picture, architecture, and commercial art.

As to its sources, the most immediate one seems to have been dadaism (q.v.), several of the most prominent surrealists, such as Hans Arp, Tristran Tzara, Marcel Duchamp, Man Ray, André Breton, and Max Ernst, having been allied with the dada movement. Surrealism shares with dadaism such features as the latter's irrationalism, its denial of the conventional values of civilization, and its repudiation of ethical, religious, and (at least conventional) aesthetic values. In many respects surrealism is closely related to expressionism (q.v.). Furthermore, many anticipations of surrealist motives and methods may be found in the romantic school, especially in the romantic poets, though this point may have been overemphasized by some exponents of surrealist theory, such as Read.

Fantastic art which has at least an external similarity to the work of the surrealists may be found throughout the entire history of European art. Abundant pictorial evidence is given in the earlier portion of *Fantastic Art, Dada, Surrealism,* listed below. Yet we must be cautious in attributing to such artists as Giuseppe Arcimboldo, Hieronymus Bosch, Giovanni di Paolo, Giovanni Battista Bracelli, or William Blake psychological motives identical with, or even closely similar to, those of twentieth century surrealists.

Surrealists assert that their work is based upon the dialectical materialism of Karl Marx and the psychoanalysis of Sigmund Freud. In their actual products, however, they are far less obviously dependent upon Marx than upon the Freudian theories. A relatively uncontrolled imagination reigns supreme. Subconsciousness is the well from which creative activity is considered to draw its inspiration. The dream is exalted above waking thought, pathological states above the normal. Surrealists feel a close affinity with primitive art and with the spontaneous, untutored art of the child. Symbolism, to a great extent sexual in character, is prominent. The ideal method of artistic activity is held to be automatism— letting the hand of the painter move freely without conscious control or letting the poet's pen record the free flow of images which spring up from the subconscious or unconscious. At the same time, the degree of formal organization achieved in many surrealist works would seem to indicate a greater measure of conscious or rational control than is sometimes conceded.

That surrealist painting is closely bound up with poetry is evidenced in various ways. In some surrealist writings, we find that such poets as Coleridge and Blake among the English, and Lautréamont and Rimbaud among the French, are looked upon as sources of inspiration. A number of representative surrealist painters are also to be numbered with the surrealist poets, for example, André Breton, Paul Éluard, Georges Hugnet, Tristran Tzara, Francis Picabia, Georgio di Chirico, Hans Arp, and Salvador Dali. Pablo Picasso, who has contributed to surrealism as well as to so many other modern movements, is a poet as well as a painter. Again, a number of surrealist painters—for example Breton, Hugnet, and Joan Miró—have incorporated poetry, in a literal sense, in certain of their paintings.

In addition to those mentioned above, some of the artists who have figured in the surrealist movement are Eileen Agar, John Ban-

ting, Hans Bellmer, Constantin Brancusi, Victor Brauner, Edward Burra, Oscar Dominguez, Leonor Fini, Alberto Giacometti, S. W. Hayter, Valentine Hugo, René Magritte, André Masson, Reuben Mednikoff, E. L. T. Mesens, Henry Moore, Paul Nash, Richard Oelze, Erik Olson, Meret Oppenheim, W. Paalen, Roland A. Penrose, and Yves Tanguy. Of course, the activity of some of these artists has not been confined to surrealism.

See also automatism; collage; Dadaism; French Art; expressionism; frottage; object; and *Art in Our Time* (Museum of Modern Art), 1939; Alfred H. Barr, Jr., ed., *Fantastic Art, Dada, Surrealism,* essays by Georges Hugnet, 1936; Anthony Bertram, *Contemporary Painting in Europe,* 1939; Sheldon Cheney, *The Story of Modern Art,* 1941; Carl Einstein, *Die Kunst des 20. Jahrhunderts* (vol. XVI in *Propylaen-Kunstgeschichte*), 1931; Louis W. Flaccus, *The Spirit and Substance of Art,* 3d ed., 1941; James Johnson Sweeney, *Joan Miró,* 1941; *Surrealism,* Julien Levy, 1936; Herbert Read, ed., *Surrealism.* Contributions by André Breton, Hugh Sykes Davies, Paul Éluard, Georges Hugnet (n. d.); James Thrall Soby, *Salvador Dali,* 1941.   —J.R.T.

surrealist object. See object.

susan chi (Ch.). Ritualistic jade disc with coglike projections; considered as possibly an astronomical instrument.

Susa ware. See PREHISTORIC ART.

suspension movement. See quality.

sustained movement. See quality.

suyaki (Jap.). Glazed ceramic ware which has been fired before the glaze was applied.

suzuri (Jap.). A very fine-grained whetstone slab on which *sumi* (q.v.) is rubbed up with water; ink stone.

suzuri-bako (Jap.). Generally, a lacquer box holding ink-stone, writing brushes and water pot. A writing box.

swag. An architectural ornament consisting of a heavy garland of carved foliage.

swastika. In ancient Mesopotamia and Greek art, an ornament composed of an equal-armed cross with the ends of the arms bent at right angles, all four in the same direction. See PRIMITIVE ART.   —L.T.S.

Sweden, art of. See SCANDINAVIAN ART.

swinging movement. See quality.

Swiss music box. See mechanical instruments.

swivel-broché. See broché.

swivel weave. See weaving.

sword-guard. See tsuba.

swords and sword furniture. See *dai-shō; fuchi; habaki; itomake; kashira; katana; kojiri; kozuka; kurikata; mekugi; menuki; metezashi; nakago; riohitsu; sageo; same; saya;* scabbard; *seppa; shakudo;* sharkskin; *shibuichi; shitodome ana; soritsuno; tachi; tanto; tsuba; tsuka; wakizashi;* also *Japanese Sword Mounts in the Collection of the Field Museum,* Helen C. Gunsaulers, Field Museum of Natural History, 1923; *Japanese Sword Guards,* Okabe-Kakuya, Museum of Fine Arts, Boston, 1908; *The Gōda Collection of Japanese Sword Fittings,* Robert Hamilton Rucker, Metropolitan Museum of Art, 1924.   —J.A.M.

syllabic chant. See MEDIEVAL MUSIC.

symbol notation. See NOTATION.

symbolism. The purposeful or non-purposeful use of sensory intermediaries not as likenesses of objects otherwise accessible, but as means of establishing contact with objects so universal, so extended in space or time or so remote from our approach as to be partly or wholly, momentarily or always inaccessible to direct intuition. This definition, though suitable to cover all forms of artistic and religious symbolism, is not meant to cover also the symbolism of mathematics and of symbolic logic in which the term is used as equivalent to "substantial sign" and to "conventional sign".   —R.B.

SYMBOLISM IN FAR EASTERN ART.

Symbolism is all important in the arts of the Far East. What would pass in the West for an item of decoration is nearly always the picture or symbol of an idea, readily understood by the people of the culture which produced it. Consequently, without some knowledge of the meaning of the principal symbols, and of the traditions from which they rose, it is impossible for an Occidental fully to appreciate the productions of Far Eastern Art. It is not enough to enjoy symbols as mere design without knowing the reason for their presence.

This subject, at first glance discouragingly complex, becomes less so when one finds that the wealth of symbols in Eastern Asia can nearly all be traced to Chinese origins—except for the small but significant group which came from India with Buddhism. For Korea, Indo-China, and even Japan were, artistically-speaking, merely cultural provinces of China. Thus the student can restrict himself to the mastering of but one basic tradition. Furthermore, one soon finds that most of the symbols can be conveniently reduced to three general types. These are: (1) ancient Chinese symbols of religious or philosophic portent; (2) Buddhist and Taoist religious symbols; and (3) folk symbols intended to bring luck or repel demons, derived from popular beliefs. As will be seen, however, a given symbol might originally have belonged to the first or second category, only to lapse into the third at a later period.

Ancient Chinese symbolism is well represented on the sacrificial bronzes of the Shang and Chou dynasties to be seen in many of our museums. The principal motive on these vessels is a full-face monster mask, made up of prominent features from several animals, and often composed of two such faces in profile, forming a single mask. People of later ages called this face the t'ao-t'ieh or "glutton", because the conventional absence of the lower jaw gives the appearance of a wide-open mouth with vast swallowing capacities. However, the fearsome aspect of this mask, often shown looming half-formed through scroll patterns representing thunder clouds, suggests that the face was intended to represent a potent sky-god, who was to be propitiated by the offerings presented in the vessels on which it is figured. In later, less rigidly conventionalized representations the ogre is shown as either giving forth or devouring bird and plant forms. Thus it was probably either a sun god, with the power to give life and warmth, or to burn and sear; or else a storm god who—like the more recent dragon —could bring life-giving rains or cause devastating floods. In later times the t'ao-t'ieh mask was figured on armor, shields, temple friezes and incense burners, where its frightful expression was believed efficacious in scaring off evil spirits.

Also portrayed on the bronzes are more recognizable animal heads, frequently repeated, suggesting prayers for the fertility of flocks. While cicadas on burial objects, or carved in jade, symbolized the continuance of life after the death of the body. Bird forms were also popular, particularly owls, indicating that the latter had not yet come to be regarded as a creature of ill-omen, though it has been shunned as such by Chinese artists of later ages. The identity of most of these early symbols can only be conjectured, however, because with the burning of the books in 213 B.C. all exact knowledge of the tradition that produced them was swept away.

With the Han Dynasty (206 B.C.-204 A.D.) China emerged as a unified empire, and in the arts stimulated by unity and relative peace, more profound philosophic and religious concepts made their appearance. These were particularly expressed in diagrams of the universe in microcosm, which have been constantly repeated in Asiatic art, with but slight variations, until modern times.

The most abstract of these diagrams was a circle bisected by a wavy line, one half being red, the other black. The red section represents **Yang**, the male element in the universe, source of life, light, and heat, while the black, or colorless, section represents **Yin**, the female element, to which is ascribed darkness, cold, and death. The complete symbol, containing both, is known as the **t'ai-chi** or great Absolute. Around the *t'ai-chi* are usually grouped the eight trigrams (**pa-kua**) which since antiquity have served as the basis for Chinese divination. These trigrams are made up of straight, long and broken lines, each pair of which represents two of the chief contrasting phenomena which were believed to have been created by the interaction of the Yin and the Yang at the time of the origin of matter, the principal ones being Heaven (pure Yang) and Earth (pure Yin). Around these are often grouped the twelve animals of the zodiac, a group of creatures arbitrarily chosen to represent the months of the year, and the years in the Chinese cycle,—thus adding the element of Time to the basic pattern of Matter and Space. In all diagrams of the above type, however, the *t'ai-chi* is considered to be the main element, to which the other symbols are merely accessory. As will be seen below, the philosophical dualism expressed by the Yang and Yin still underlies all Chinese thought, and has had a profound effect on Chinese symbolism.

A more concrete representation of the cosmos, which first appeared in the art of the Han period, was the portrayal of the axis of the universe as a mountain (like *Sumeru* of the Hindus), standing in the midst of the waters, with sky dragons among the clouds above. This persisted through the centuries until in the last two dynasties (Ming and Ch'ing) it was eventually incorporated in the pattern on the imperial robes, to symbolize the fact that the Emperor, as the Son of Heaven, was vested in the universe.

Also popular was a flat plan of the world order, often shown on the backs of Han mirrors. In this, the circular, central boss on a square field represents the dome of Heaven above the square of Earth (q.v. stupa). On each side of the square was one of the animals of the four directions. These animals (the **black tortoise** of the North, the **azure dragon** of the East, the **red bird** of the South, and the **white tiger** of the West) have occupied a prominent place in Chinese art ever since. Particularly popular have been the **dragon** and the **tiger**, which were chosen as symbols of contrasting ideas, as well as of opposite directions. For as concrete representatives of Yang and Yin—the dragon as a celestial creature, and the tiger as a terestial—they represent the contrast between spiritual and material. One must remember, though, that symbols may change their meaning entirely in different contexts. Thus the tiger, which was probably originally chosen to signify the Yin because of its soft step and reputed guile, may be considered equally effective as a Yang symbol because of its great strength and energy, and in fact it has often been used by itself as a symbol of Yang.

The beneficial, rain-bearing dragon, apart from its other symbolic uses, has long been the symbol of China itself, and of the Emperor who was thought to confer grace to his people by acting as the Regent of Heaven. As a result the perfect, five-clawed dragon (**lung**) was reserved for the Emperor alone, the only exception being its use on religious objects. Similarly, the less perfect, four-clawed dragon (**mang**) was reserved for the sons and immediate relatives of the Emperor, until with the decline of tradition in the last dynasty its use was conferred on the highest officials as well. Popular art, denied the use of these, was forced to content itself with a sort of dragon-snake. (Dragons in Japanese art commonly have but three claws.)

Just as the dragon represented the Emperor, and was figured on his possessions, the robes and belongings of the Empress displayed a magnificent mythical bird, composed of the most resplendent characteristics of several natural birds such as the peacock and argus pheasant. (Although Western writers have generally described this as a "phoenix", it seems wiser to retain the Chinese name **fêng-huang**, since it bears no resemblance whatever to the phoenix of Occidental folklore.) Princesses living at court were allowed to have robes and hangings showing slightly less elaborate species of the same bird, under different names; but except for use in temples or on wedding gear (since the bride was figuratively queen for a day), this too was forbidden in popular art.

Among the other mythical creatures which abound in Chinese folklore, the one most frequently shown in art is probably the **ch'i-lin.** (Western writers often wrongly describe it as a unicorn, though it has two horns, and differs in every other respect from the unicorn of medieval European bestiaries, having the body of an antelope, covered with scales, a dragon-like head, and a bushy tail.) Since before the time of Confucius this creature has been considered as having vast wisdom, and being a thing of good omen. In addition, because of an allusion to it in an ancient poem, it has long been considered a symbol capable of granting an illustrious posterity.

Also to be listed among the mythological animals is the **lion** of Chinese art, a strange curly-haired creature, usually white with a blue mane, devised by artists who had never seen the living animal. It is generally a symbol of bravery, or of the power of Buddha's law. This in turn seems to have been the inspiration for still stranger creatures, such as the **horned lions,** called *hsieh-chai* and *pai-tsê,* which in imperial days symbolized the lesser nobles and the court censors.

The **crane** and **tortoise,** because of their reputed great age, were symbols of longevity, along with the **pine tree,** but during the Mongol Dynasty—when Marco Polo visited China—the **turtle** came to have lewd associations, and since that time it has been assiduously avoided in Chinese art. (In Japan, Korea, and Annam [Northern Indo-China] it has retained its original meaning, however. In fact at the court of Annam the turtle still appears as one of four sacred animals on the state robes of the highest officials.)

Other animals and birds have long been popular because of supposed desirable qualities. For example, the **mandarin duck** and the **quail** have both acquired a reputation for devotion to their mates, and for this reason they are often portrayed in pairs to symbolize domestic felicity. The **carp,** known to the

Occident as a sluggish fish, has come to be known in China as a symbol of ambition, and a carp leaping through the dragon gate (*lung-mên*), a familiar subject in all media of Chinese art, represented a successful candidate in the Imperial examinations. This was a particularly important symbol in a land where the highly-organized civil service system made success in such examinations the prerequisite for any official position.

Various trees and plants, such as the **pine, cypress,** and **tree-fungus,** have been considered as symbols of great age; while the **pine, bamboo,** and **blossoming plum,** collectively known as the "three friends in winter" because they are the only plants to display their colors against the snow, are symbols of constancy. The **Flowers of the Four Seasons** (usually **plum blossom, grass orchid, lotus,** and **chrysanthemum,** but varying with the individual artist's choice) are popular designs, esp. in paintings, on porcelain, and on rugs.

With the T'ang Dynasty (618-906 A.D.), Buddhism burst into full flower as a state religion, and Buddhist art, already highly developed in China, came into its own, under imperial patronage. Chief among the Buddhist symbols, of Indian origin, was the **lotus,** usually represented with eight petals to recall the Eight Noble Truths taught by the Buddha Gautama. Moreover, as Buddhist deities commonly shown supported above the earth on lotus-thrones, the flower was also venerated as a symbol of purity and detachment from earthly cares. Because of this, and because it was a familiar attribute of Kuanyin, "Goddess of Mercy", it became a constant symbol in Chinese art. We must admit, however, that in later centuries its symbolism became less sublime. For artists of recent times have incorporated the lotus with emblems of good fortune to symbolize continuing felicity, since the more common Chinese word for lotus (*lien*) has the same sound as the verb meaning "to continue". (The other word for lotus (*ho*) is a pun on the word harmony, so the lotus is also used in modern rebuses to mean "harmonious".)

Equally significant as a Buddhist symbol was the **Wheel of the Law,** its eight spokes also representing the eight-fold path of Buddha's teachings, and the flames which usually surround it recalling the fact that the wheel was an ancient solar symbol in India and Central Asia. Both wheel and lotus are included in the group commonly known as the **Eight Buddhist Symbols.** (The other six are the vase and **conch shell**, the **twin fish** and **endless knot**, the **royal canopy** and the **state umbrella**.) All these were Indian symbols of remote antiquity, revered long before Buddhism, and about them had gathered a long tradition. In China, however, they rapidly degenerated into mere lucky symbols, of which only the wheel and lotus retained any special significance.

A number of other esoteric symbols came to China from India by way of Buddhism, such as the **sacred pearl**, the **alms bowl**, and *vajra,* or *thunderbolt*, but these do not seem to have excited the imagination of Chinese artists. Except in the Lamaist art of the Ch'ing period in North China, they seldom occur unless as attributes in the hands of painted or sculptured deities. In fact the vajra itself is frequently replaced by a conventionalized Chinese mace.

Taoism began, some centuries before the birth of Christ, as a great philosophical religion, embodying the best of Chinese abstract thought. Even before the Han Dynasty, however, this began to degenerate into a popular faith of mumbo-jumbo and sorcery, much concerned with the pursuit of long life, to be attained by "pills of immortality", and with release from evil influences thought to have been generated by Yin elements. (By now the Yang and Yin instead of representing active and passive forces in harmonious relationship, had come to be considered as the essence of all Good and of all Evil, resp.) This form of the religion, corrupt as it was, even gained imperial favor under some of the T'ang Emperors to the extent that it replaced Buddhism for a time as the state religion. It was inevitable, then, that Taoism should also donate some symbols to Chinese art.

As popular Taoism devoted so much attention to magical methods for prolonging life, it placed great reverence on a series of persons who were believed to have achieved immortality by esoteric practices. Eight of these in particular gained a firm hold on popular imagination. Each of these men or women was identified in art by one or two attributes (flower basket, gourd and crutch, bamboo rattle, lotus, fan, flute, sword, and castanets). In time the attributes came to be painted instead of the personages they represented, and finally the Chinese people believed them to have lucky or wonder-working powers in themselves. Thus the symbols of the **Eight Taoist Immortals**, like the Eight

Buddhist symbols, degenerated into mere symbols of good fortune.

The second preoccupation of the Taoists, which lay in finding and exploiting methods of exorcism against evil forces generated by the Yin element, was also linked with the search for longevity since disease and the evil spirits who might try to shorten the span of life were also believed to be embodiments of Yin. Thus, anything associated with Yang was believed to have great power as a counteracting force, and demon-repellent. For this reason, anything colored **red** (the Yang color) was considered as "lucky" for weddings and other festivities, while colorless things, of **solid black or white**, were avoided. Certain flowers, usually red ones like the scarlet peony, and medicinal plants with real or fancied curative properties, such as **artemisia**, were thought to be esp. efficacious in repelling demons,—as were most of the spike-leafed plants, such as the **iris**. The beautiful plant designs on porcelains, rugs, and textiles, were often applied with this intent.

The evil forces of Yin were collectively expressed in art under the form of five loathsome creatures (usually the **spider, lizard, centipede, snake**, and **toad**), together known as **The Five Poisons**. Paradoxically, it was believed that if figures of these animals were displayed, they could ward off the Yin influences which they represented. Hence the five poisons are often seen portrayed in carvings of wood or jade, on textiles or in paintings, sometimes being trodden under the feet of a spirit tiger ridden by Chang Tao-ling, the father of modern Taoism, or more often alone. In this group of five any one of the animals may be exchanged for another equally detestable, but the total number must always remain the same. This peculiarity, already noted in connection with the Flowers of the Four Seasons, may also be observed in other groupings such as the **Eight Jewels** (formerly symbols of sacrifice, but now symbols of luck and wealth in their own right). It would seem that in the Far East the idea of a symbolic number of things is more important than the specific objects themselves. The number **eight** seems to be especially propitious.

Since Chinese characters are usually ideographs—concise and decorative symbols of ideas—it is only natural that they should have occupied a prominent place in Chinese symbolic art. Characters were first used as art forms in the Han Dynasty, when, in groups of four, they were cast on bronze presentation mirrors, to express wishes of good fortune for the recipient. Centuries later, by the time that painted porcelain came into favor with the Ming Dynasty (1368-1644), such expressions were largely supplanted by single characters for Happiness (fu), Longevity (shou), and Good Fortune (chi). These were ingeniously fitted into ornamental medallions, in reserves left in the principal pattern. Often these were shown in their usual printed form, but sometimes they were written in archaic styles, for variation. Another common form of Ming decoration was the symbol by association of ideas. The many-seeded pomegranate was pictured to denote Fertility; ivory tusks or a stick of coral carried hopes for wealth; while the Four Attributes of the Scholar (book, scroll, lute, and chess-board) or the Hundred Antiques, pictures of the things dear to the heart of the collector, suggested the much-desired life of a scholar-connoisseur.

Finally, with the Ch'ing Dynasty (1644-1912) when the Manchu conquerors of China managed to destroy much of what remained of the old Chinese culture, the breakdown of religious tradition began to show its effects in widespread superstition and an exaggerated reverence for lucky symbols, even among the upper classes. The former wishes for happiness and longevity were now expressed with far greater elaboration, in the form of pictorial puns, using pictures of objects with the same pronunciation as the character for the quality desired. Thus a bat, or an oddly-shaped citrus fruit called the "Buddha's hand" were both used to mean Happiness, since the chief syllable of their respective names was pronounced fu. Similarly, the butterfly came to be a symbol for Longevity, since its name, pronounced t'ieh, had the same sound as the word meaning "sixty years of age". This development had begun in Ming, but in later Ch'ing times (toward the end of the 18th cent.) these became so elaborate that whole sentences came to be expressed in pictorial patterns. For example, a halberd, a jade musical stone, and a scepter were combined in a single design which by a pun meant, "May you have as much joy and good fortune as you desire". Along with these more and more involved plays on words, the simpler symbols by association of ideas continued to be expressed, but with the late Ch'ing horror vacui they were repeated an infinite number of times on the same object, until they were no longer meaningful, but merely tiresome decorations. It was at this time that the Eight Buddhist Symbols and the Symbols of the Taoist Immortals also reached their ultimate degeneration, no longer considered even lucky, merely decorative. With the demand for constant repetition of all these, by now almost meaningless, symbols, the artists and artisans of the last two centuries were sorely tried in their efforts to produce objects with some originality. It was probably this aridity of subject, as much as the dynastic decline and the impact of Western ideas, that produced the collapse of the Chinese artistic tradition at the end of the 19th cent.

As has been said, the arts of Korea and Northern Indo-China (Annam) are basically derived from Chinese art, and are but provincial expressions of it, slightly altered by environment. Their symbols show few variations, and these tend to be alterations in style and modes of expression rather than innovations in the realm of ideas. Nearly all the familiar Chinese symbols can be found in their arts, with the exception of the more elaborate puns, since they would not be valid in other languages than Chinese. Unfortunately, however, these cultures have suffered at the hands of unappreciative alien rulers, whose colonization policies have been devoted mainly to exploiting the people, and have only favored those arts which were commercially profitable. Thus the traditional arts with all their symbols have been largely abandoned.

Japanese art has also been greatly indebted to the Chinese tradition for ideas as well as for techniques, ever since the influence of T'ang China and Sinified Korea raised the island nation from virtual barbarism. Its symbolism is highly developed and refined, but with very few exceptions the symbols are not indigenous, but have come from China, either directly or through Korea; while some few have come more or less directly from India with itinerant monks. The artistic genius of the Japanese people has not expressed itself in the invention of symbols, but rather in their application as objects of decoration—with great feeling for their secondary and poetical meanings, but often showing little evidence of any comprehension of their deeper significance. The latter statement does not apply to Buddhist symbols, however, for the Japanese, being essentially a more religious-minded people than their continental neighbors have not allowed the Buddhist symbols to degenerate into mere lucky emblems.

The Japanese have a number of lucky symbols, however, which are loosely grouped under the name of **takara-mono,** or "treasure things". These are made up of Chinese symbols of wealth, such as the Eight Jewels, and a few elements from native folklore, such as the magical **feather cloak** (*hagoromo*) and the **mallet of Daikoku,** one of the **Seven Gods of Luck.** Even these seven lucky gods, so popular in Japanese art, are with one exception of foreign origin, though the **treasure boat** (*takara-bune*) in which they are often depicted is a purely Japanese idea. The Japanese have never developed the punning symbols to the same degree as the people of China, partly because the Tokugawa Shoguns were strictly enforcing their isolation policy at the time when these symbols were gaining a vogue in Ch'ing China.

The one field in which Japanese artists are at their best is in representations of Nature. They have been especially partial to Chinese animal and plant designs, often extending the meaning of the latter. Among the plants featured in Japanese art are several which have been ignored in China, notably the **paulownia, wisteria,** and the **maple,** the first of which has been adopted as the crest and symbol of the Empress (as opposed to the Emperor's sixteen-petalled chrysanthemum). Plants and birds frequently appear in rigidly conventionalized forms as motives for the circular crests (**mon**) which are profusely emblazoned on Japanese works of art in silk, metal and lacquer. In this case the motives usually have no symbolic meaning, however, beyond their association with the clan or family entitled to bear the crest. Unfortunately, with the rapid advance of materialism since the Restoration of 1868, and the fashion for aping Occidental Art along with other modern improvements of doubtful value, the symbolic art of Japan is rapidly following that of China to eventual extinction. To the average Japanese of the last decade, the ancient symbols had become little more than pretty decorations, as meaningless to him as they would be to the Western tourist.

Tibetan culture, like the Japanese, is essentially adaptive rather than inventive, but it differs from the latter in being more strictly conservative. While its art is primarily based on Buddhist motives brought from India, and therefore should be studied primarily as an offshoot of the Indian Buddhist tradition, it has drawn almost as heavily from Chinese culture. This is due to the influence of centuries of trade, and the recent position of Tibet as an outlying portion of the Chinese Empire. In addition to the many Buddhist symbols which both countries have in common, the Tibetans have borrowed the *t'ao-t'ieh* mask, the Yin-Yang and the eight trigrams, the dragon with all its connotations, and even the symbols of the Taoist Immortals. Also popular are the simple folk symbols, such as the bat, the **peach of Immortality** (longevity), and the "Buddha's hand".

Thanks to the strong conservatism of Tibetan culture, plus the fact that its tradition is being kept relatively untainted by Western influences, owing to the Government's policy of isolation, Tibet may well remain a living storehouse for the symbols of Far Eastern culture, when the disease of modernism has robbed them of their meanings—and thus their very reason for existence—in the other lands of Eastern Asia. See CHINESE SYMBOLISM: De Groot, J. J. M., *The Religious Systems of China,* vol. V, 1904, vol. VI, 1910; Doré, Henri, *Recherches sur les Superstitions en Chine,* 1915; Chavannes, E., *De L'Expression des Voeux dans L'Art Populaire Chinois,* Journal Asiatique, 9th series, vol. XVIII, 1901; Hobson, R. L., *Chinese Pottery and Porcelain,* vol. II, 1915. JAPANESE SYMBOLISM: Joly, H. L., *Legend in Japanese Art,* 1908; Weber, V. F., *Koji Hōten,* 1923. BUDDHIST AND TIBETAN SYMBOLISM: Coomaraswamy, A. K., *Elements of Buddhist Iconography,* 1935; Waddell, L. A., *The Buddhism of Tibet,* 2nd edition, 1939; Gordon, Mrs. A. K., *Lamaist Iconography,* 1940. ANNAMITE SYMBOLS: Doumoutier, G., *Les Symbols et les Emblèmes du Culte chez les Annamites,* 1891.   —S.C.

symbols for colors. See HERALDRY.

symmetry. (1) Comes from Gr. *syn* meaning "with" and *metron* "measure", and means the distribution of the single parts of a work of art around a central point or axis in such a way that equal or similar parts on one side correspond to equal or similar parts on the other side. Comparable to this is the distribution of the parts of the human body; an almost perfect example of bilateral symmetry. In case the axis is indicated by a certain object, perhaps by a human figure, a building, etc., then there is a fixed center. But in case the center is not fixed, then there is an imaginary center. If the corresponding parts are so arranged that the parts can be or can almost be interchanged, then there is a rigid and reflected symmetry. If the corresponding parts are arranged in such way as to be symmetrical but not rigid, then an elastic symmetry results. In case the axis is fixed by an object and the corresponding parts are interchangeably arranged, then centralization will be the consequence, as for instance in the works of the late Roman Empire, in many works of early Christianity, in the Byzantine time, and in the Salian epoch of the Middle Ages. Of all the systems of order, the symmetrical system produces the greatest possible feeling of calm and security in the spectator. But it may also produce the impression of dictatorial rigidity. Generally speaking, one may say that the Greco-Romans favor the symmetrical arrangement, especially in their decorative arts. While the Romans were inclined to a more centralized symmetry, the Greeks preferred the imaginary center and the more elastic arrangement of the corresponding parts. The Renaissance follows more or less either the one or the other direction. See asymmetry. —A.J.S.

(2) *Mus.* Term borrowed from the field of visual experience to designate equal length and similar construction of corresponding phrases. —E.K.

symphony. The word symphony (*symphonia, sinfonia, sinfonie*; from the Gr. meaning "sounding together") has been used to designate a number of different kinds of instrumental and vocal compositions and also as the name of instruments on which two or more tones might be sounded together. About the middle of the 18th cent. the word rapidly came to be used chiefly, if not exclusively, for orchestral works in several movements, similar to the sonata. "A sonata for the orchestra" is the common definition of the modern symphony. The word seems not to have been in general use until the early 17th cent. (though Riemann discovered "a symphony" of the 15th cent., Riemann, *Klavierlehrer,* 1898, No. 4) when it is used to designate introductory passages or interludes in opera (Peri, *Euridice,* 1600; Conteverdi, *Orfeo,* 1603) or to distinguish harmonic from polyphonic writing (Rossi, *Third Book of Sonatas,* 1613; Marini, Op. 1, 1617). Several of the ways in which the term symphony came to be used in the 17th and early 18th cents. are found in the works of J. S. Bach, where each of the Three-Part Inventions and the opening movement of the second Partita are called Sinfonia, the introductory movement of cantata No. 54 and the movement in D major from an unknown church cantata

are likewise called "sinfonia" and a three-movement orchestral work in F is given the same title. The habit of referring to the introduction and interludes (ritornel) of arias as "symphonies" persisted into the 19th cent. It is the *sinfonia avanti l'opera* or opera overture that forms the chief ancestor of the modern symphony, esp. the 17th cent. Italian form of these overtures (of which A. Scarlatti is the chief exponent), consisting in a movement divided into three sections, fast-slow-fast. When such movements came to be played as concert music, apart from opera (first probably in the late 17th cent.) and the divisions came to be represented by separate movements and, finally, the structural principles of sonata-form were used in the first of these movements, the modern symphony emerged in all its essential features. These developments are found in the works of Stamitz, Monn, Cannabich, Gossec, Boccherini and many others, especially K. P. E. Bach. By the middle of the 18th cent. a classical norm for the symphony had been established, consisting in four movements, the first fast and in sonata-form, the second slow and song-like or in variation form, the third a minuet, and the fourth a lively movement of rondo character. It was this norm which was passed on to the Viennese school (Haydn and Mozart in first rank) with which the symphony in the modern sense of the word comes to its first complete artistic maturity.

The major musical characteristics of their periods and of their composers are to be found in the symphonies of Haydn and Mozart, their contemporaries and successors. With few (though notable) exceptions (Chopin, Mussorgsky, Debussy, *inter alia*) instrumental composers since the close of the 18th cent. have written symphonies and the form has been regarded as one demanding the highest degree of skill and mature comprehension.

In certain of Haydn's 104 authenticated symphonies and of Mozart's 39 or 40 there may be found experimental and tentative efforts toward a satisfactory form and style, whereas others, such as Haydn's last 12 (1791-1795) written for London, and Mozart's last 3, the E-flat, the F minor and the C major or "Jupiter" (1788), are the great masterpieces of the classical style. Beethoven's 9 symphonies (1797-1823) are the great source book in which may be traced the historic change from a classical to a romantic point of view. Beethoven greatly expanded the form as he inherited it and augmented the orchestra, creating a more flexible orchestration especially for wind instruments. Incisive, boisterous, tempestuous scherzi take the place formerly held by the stately or sprightly minuet. Movements are highly organic and developmental processes are present everywhere. Other forms on which Beethoven left the impress of original treatment, such as the Variation and the Fugue, are included within the framework of symphonic movements. A quartet of solo voices and a full chorus are used in the finale of the ninth. Above all else the mood and manner, personal with their composer, characterize these symphonies, seen in the epigrammatic thematic material, the vitality of expression and the dramatic quality of harmonic and contrapuntal thought. Poetic suggestion is also manifest in these works as elsewhere in Beethoven. The "Eroica" (No. 3, E-flat major, originally dedicated to Napoleon), the dramatic C minor (No. 5), the Pastoral (No. 6, F major) are but the most apparent examples of "poetic suggestion by musical means", essentially a romantic characteristic.

The most notable of Beethoven's contemporaries, Schubert (8 symphonies, 1813-1828) achieved in his C major (No. 7) and "Unfinished" (No. 8) an appropriate, sustained structure for his essentially lyric materials. The romanticists Berlioz (4, 1830-1840), Schumann (4, 1831-1850), Mendelssohn (4, 1824-1832) and Liszt (2, 1853-1861) while employing in the symphony styles highly characteristic of their several individualities, have in common a strong tendency toward the picturesque and the narrative in their thematic material, their forms and treatments. Poetic titles are common and indicative of romantic preoccupation with programmatic suggestion (Berlioz, *Fantastic Symphony;* Schumann, *Spring Symphony;* Mendelssohn, *Reformation Symphony;* Liszt, *A Faust Symphony*).

Brahms' (4, 1855-1885) symphonic thought is more akin to that of Beethoven than to that of his more romantic contemporaries. Strongly personal in idiom and massively constructed, Brahms unites in these works a classical feeling for pure music with a romantic individuality of invention. Tchaikovsky (6, 1868-1893) in his last three symphonies (the *Pathétique* is No. 6) represents an extreme of romantic expression. In the main sombre and suggestive of melancholy protest to the point of vehemence, these works are masterpieces of the decadent romanticism of the late 19th cent. César Franck's one symphony (1888) is likewise highly individual in thematic materials and treatment and non-programmatic. Dvorak (9, 1865-1880) left in his "New World" symphony one of the most successful of works in a national or racial musical idiom. Bruckner (10 finished, 1 unfinished, 1863-1894) and Mahler (9 finished, 1 unfinished, 1888-1909) wrote large-scale works, involved in structrue and crowded with materials, beside which Sibelius (7, 1898-1924) with his new interpretations of form and melodious, nationalistic thematic material and strikingly picturesque scoring seems direct and simple.

These are but the few most frequently heard composers who have contributed to the extensive literature of the symphony. Even a brief account of the history of that literature should not omit mention of Spohr (10), Strauss (3), Glazunoff (8) and Scriabine (5) among the men who have written symphonies of historical value if not of permanent interest.

With those interpretations of form and those widely different idioms that are indiscriminately grouped together as "modern" the symphony in the present century, as in the 19th, has represented most of the characteristic musical thought of the period. There are belated romanticists (Chadwick 3, Hadley 4, Vaughan Williams 4, Rachmaninoff 3), and there are men who revitalize older procedures (Bloch 3, Bax 6, Hanson 2) and others who maintain the fundamentals of accepted tradition, following them to conclusions not previously realized (Sessions 1) and there are the "radicals", Hindemith, Stravinsky, Shostakovich, again to mention but a few.

The changes that have been brought about in the form of the symphony, the offshoots of symphonic procedures (such as the symphonic poem) and the immense bearing of the constitution of the orchestra and the methods of orchestration on the symphony as a form of expression are subjects to be treated elsewhere. See *Grove's Dictionary of Music and Musicians,* article, Symphony; Grove, *Beethoven and His Nine Symphonies;* Brenet, Michael, *Histoire de la Symphonie;* Weingartner, *The Symphony since Beethoven;* Kretzschmar, *Führer durch den Konzertsaal* (I, Sinfonie und Suite) ; Tovey, *Essays in Musical Analysis,* vols. I and II.   —R.D.W.

synaesthesis. A theory of aesthetic experience propounded by C. K. Ogden, I. A. Richards, and James Wood in their book, *The Foundations of Aesthetics,* and describing the experience of beauty in terms of a coming together (*syn*-aesthesis) or an equilibrium and harmony of impulses which have been called out in contemplation by the object said to be beautiful.   —D.W.G.

synagogue music. See JEWISH MUSIC.

synagogue music in America. See JEWISH MUSIC.

synagogues. Since the Service of the synagogue consists mainly of prayer and Scripture reading the architecture of the synagogue could never have any connection with that of the Temple at Jerusalem where both Service and architecture had been based on sacrifices and on a highly developed ceremonial. Consequently the simplest examples of synagogues in Antiquity are plain rectangular rooms, sometimes with a courtyard on one side (Aegina I and II, the later one 5th cent. A.D.; Isfiyā, 6th cent. A.D.; perhaps Delos, 1st cent. B.C.). A seat, probably for the leader of the congregation (*archisynagogos*), flanked by benches (for the Elders (?)), occupies one of the short sides; the Ark of the Law, containing the Scrolls (*aron hakodesch*) and the reading platform (*bema*) may have been wooden; the Ark was brought in for Services only and placed on the side towards Jerusalem. Throughout Roman-Hellenistic Antiquity synagogues were nothing but ecclesiastical variants of Roman secular meeting house patterns such as *curiae* and *basilicae*. Consequently they are either single-naved or basilical in plan, in the latter case with aisles, rarely on four sides of the nave (perhaps Alexandria, before 2nd cent. A.D.), more frequently on three (leaving free the entrance side facing Jerusalem), and often with upper galleries for the women (Galilean type, 3rd (?) 5th cent. A.D.: Kerâze; Irbid; Capernaum-Tell-Hum). Elsewhere the plans show only two aisles flanking the nave (Meron), often with an *atrium* in front (Miletus, 4th cent. A.D.). Stable structures for the *aron* appear from the 4th cent. on (Tell-Hum, rebuilding). At Gerasa (ca. 400) a rectangular niche terminated the nave, reversing the orientation. A small niche to contain one scroll during Services had already occupied the center of one of the long walls of transverse synagogue rooms, situated within larger edifices, at Dura-Europos, I and II (200 and 245 resp.) and at Hammam-Lif (4th cent. A.D.). Later synagogues, depending on small Christian basilicas, show semicircular apses (Hammath-by Gadara, 5th

cent. (?); Tell-es-Sultan, 8th cent. and also occasionally a narthex (Beth Alpha, 518-27 or 565-78). The walls are decorated with figured frescoes (Dura), the pavements with figural or decorative mosaics (Hammam-Lif; Hammath-by-Gadara; Beth Alpha); capitals and friezes are richly sculptured (Tell-Hum). Their style like the plan conforms to the local (Syro-Palestinian, North African, Greek) variants of Roman-Hellenistic art.

Entirely different are the synagogues of the Middle Ages in Germany, Bohemia, Poland. From the 12th to the 16th cents. the prevailing type is a two-naved vaulted hall with from one (Eger, 1347-75) to three (Regensburg, 1210-27) supports along the center axis. The pattern is known from medieval secular structures, refectories and libraries; the style follows that of contemporary non-Jewish architecture with Romanesque (Worms, ca. 1175, destroyed 1938) or Gothic (Prague, ca. 1300; Cracow, 16th cent.) vaults and capitals. A richly decorated Ark occupies the short Eastern side, facing Jerusalem, a *bema* the center of the building. The decoration is purely ornamental without any figure design. In simple structures the plan is single naved (Speyer, ca. 1100; Miltenberg, late 13th cent.). Occasionally small rooms for women were added to the main building (Worms, 1213).

Like central European medieval synagogues the Spanish ones follow the local, this time the Moorish style. In plan they resemble mosques with one (Cordova, 1315; Toledo, S. Maria del Transito, 1357), three (Segovia, 13th cent. (?), destroyed 1899, rebuilt) or five aisles (Toledo, S. Maria la Blanca, ca. 1260 (?)). They all are splendidly decorated with stucco ornament and rich capitals. Yet unlike mosques their main axis is longitudinal rather than transverse, the nave is higher than the aisles and women galleries open on the entrance side. As a whole the type resembles Christian and Islamic ecclesiastical rather than secular architecture, contrary to the custom of central European Jewry.

New types appear from the 16th through the 18th century in Eastern Europe. The city synagogues are square stone buildings in Late Renaissance and Baroque forms, frequently fortified; their vaults are supported by four piers around the central *bema* (Lwow, 1632; Zolkiew, 1692; Wilna ca. second half of 17th cent.). This pattern is popularized in Russian-Polish Baroque village synagogues. They are small, square wooden structures with high peaked roofs, sometimes with low corner towers and often surrounded by deep porches. The interior shows complicated wooden vaults and lavish ornamental wall and ceiling paintings, a rich Ark of the Law and *bema* (Chodorow; Przedborz; Nasielsk, 1692; Kurnik, 1767). From Poland this type was carried to Southern Germany (Bechhofen, 1727-28; Horb). Retranslated into stone and into more sophisticated forms it appears in the Rococo synagogues of Western Czechoslovakia (Kuttenplan, 1756-9; Neuzedlisch, 1786).

In contrast to this Jewish variant of an Eastern peasant baroque and rococo, contemporaneous Western synagogues follow more modish patterns. The Italian synagogues are squarish or rectangular rooms, due to police regulations frequently on the upper floor of a house. Women galleries accompany the main room on a higher level either on one of the short or on the long sides. *Aron* and *bema* (at opposite ends of the room), chandeliers and walls are richly decorated in a splendid baroque (Venice, *Sc. Spagnuola,* rebuilt 1654/5, architect B. Longhena; Mantova, 1751) or an elegant Rococo (Venice, *Sc. ashkenasi,* rebuilt 1745; Ancona, ca. 1750; Cavaillon (Southern France), 1772/3). Vaulting is rare (Padova, *Sc. italiana,* 16th cent., rebuilt ca. 1750).

Far more important for the future development was a 17th cent. plan in which the nave is surrounded on three sides by aisles and galleries. It seems to have prevailed among the Spanish-Portuguese congregations in Italy, Holland and England, and resembles Protestant church types. At Leghorn (1591, rebuilt 1602, rococo decoration added in 1789) double galleries surmount the aisles. Dutch and English synagogues use a classicist vocabulary. The Portuguese synagogue at Amsterdam (1675) has three naves of equal height, supported by tuscan columns; the aisles are partly filled with galleries; an enormous *bema* stands near the entrance, a "classicist" Ark of the Law at the east wall. Similarly classicist, but only single naved with galleries, is Bevis Mark's synagogue in London (1699-1702); Harrison's synagogue at Newport, R. I. (1763), and the demolished synagogue at Charleston, S. C. (1792), have their naves surrounded on three sides by aisles and galleries on light classicist supports.

The simple and "functional" plan and the limpid classicist vocabulary of this Western synagogue type (cf. also Munich, 1824/5,

demolished; Buchau, ca. 1830; London, Duke's Place synagogue, 1722, rebuilt 1830) is superseded from the middle of the 19th cent. on by more intricate patterns which follow Romanesque or Gothic church plans, incompatible with the requirements of the synagogue Service, often with towers at the façade and over the crossing and with richly developed apses. The ornament is frequently "Byzantine", "Moorish", "Romanesque" or "baroque" or a fanciful mixture of all these styles (Munich, 1884/7, arch. A. Schmidt; Philadelphia, Mikveh Israel; New York City, Temple Emanuel, 1929, arch. R. D. Kohn, Chs. Butler, Cl. Stein). Occasionally a dome rises from a Greek cross structure (Florence, 1883; Augsburg, 1914, arch. F. Landauer; Buffalo, N. Y., Beth Zion, 1890, arch. Ed. A. Kent). Only recently has modern architecture penetrated into synagogue architecture (Plauen, 1929, arch. F. Landauer). See Grotte, *Deutsche, boehmische und polnische Synagogentypen,* 1915; Krautheimer, *Mittelalterliche Synagogen,* 1927; Sukenik, *Ancient synagogues in Palestine and Greece,* 1934; Lowenthal, *A World Passed By,* 1938. —R.K.

synchromism. A doctrine favoring completely abstract color designs as the proper aim of painting, founded in Paris in 1913 by the American painter, MacDonald-Wright, and the Canadian painter, Morgan Russell. See FRENCH ART; POST-REVOLUTIONARY PAINTING AND SCULPTURE IN THE U. S. A. —L.D.L.

syncopated movement. See quality.

synthetic cubism. See cubism.

synthetic resin. Hardly yet established in the fine arts, the synthetic or artificial resins are complex, amorphous, organic solids or semi-solids. They are made by chemical methods from a variety of raw materials. In appearance they resemble the natural resins but are generally less brittle, slightly less colored, and more stable. Dissolved, they are useful as film materials, and in the solid form some of them serve for molding or even for carving. —G.L.S.

synthetism. A variety of post-impressionism developed by Gauguin in the late 1880's, which challenged the analytic procedure of impressionism, supported a synthetic painting in broad, simple, flat tones of color, often with definite edges, distorted in form and color for the sake of decoration and heightened expressive power, and influenced by Japanese prints, medieval stained glass and enamels, Italian primitives, and Egyptian painting. Also called "symbolism" and "neo-traditionalism". The manifesto of synthetism was written by Maurice Dennis in 1890.

—L.D.L.

synthronos. See EARLY CHRISTIAN ARCHITECTURE.

systematic musicology. See musicology.

systematical accent. See accent.

sztuka. See POLISH ART.

T

t'a. See CHINESE ARTS.

Ta-amim. See JEWISH MUSIC.

tabby binding. See TAPESTRY.

tabernacle. See synagogues.

tablature notation. See NOTATION.

table. See FURNITURE.

tablinum (L.). A place (alcove, recess, room) for family records; between the atrium and the peristylium.

tablita. High wooden headdress of the Pueblo Indian. See COSTUME ART.

tachi (Jap.). An ancient sword, now rare.

Tachikui yaki (Jap.). Pottery made in Tanba province.

taenia. The fillet, or projecting band, separating—and at the bottom of—a Doric frieze from the architrave.

taffeta weave. See weaving.

tagasode-byoha. See JAPANESE ART.

tagelied. See MEDIEVAL MUSIC.

t'ai. See CHINESE ARTS.

taiaha (Maori). A ceremonial spear.

t'ai-chi. See SYMBOLISM IN FAR EASTERN ART.

tail. Book. The head and tail of a book are the top and bottom; the tail-piece is an illustration, etc., at the bottom of a page or the end of a chapter.

takamakie (Jap.). A style of lacquer decoration in which the design is in high relief.

The relief is produced by an under-base of composition. —J.A.M.

takaramono (Jap.). Precious things : anchor, cowrie shell, copper coin, coins in a chest, weight, purse, key, jar of valuables, fan, bridge of the harp, clove, mallet, hat of inviolability, raincoat, feather robe, rolls of manuscripts, rolls of fabric, coral, sacred gem. See SYMBOLISM IN FAR EASTERN ART. —J.A.M.

Takatori yaki (Jap.). Pottery made in province of Chikuzen by the potter, Takatori.

takya (Ar.). In the Ottoman Empire, a dervish hostel. See ISLAMIC ART.

Talavera ware. See SPAIN, ART OF.

talea. See MEDIEVAL MUSIC.

talisman. See JEWELRY.

tall tale. See American folk forms, in literature.

tall talk. See American folk forms, in literature.

tambourine. See MUSICAL INSTRUMENTS.

tambur. See MUSICAL INSTRUMENTS.

tan (Jap.). A wood-block printing color derived from red lead.

Tanagroa. One of the chief Polynesian gods.

Tanba yaki (Jap.). Pottery made in Tanba province.

tan-e (Jap.). A primitive woodblock print in which the only color, or the predominating one, was a red oxide of lead, somewhat orange in tone.

990

T'ang art. See CHINESE ARTS.

T'ang dynasty porcelain. See CERAMICS· II.

tango. The Spanish tango is one of the group of flamenco dances, distinct from the classic Iberian group in that the former embody elements of traditional gipsy dance. The flamenco dances belong to the café and theatres, rather than to rural or social gatherings, since they developed through professional dancers' appropriation of gipsy figures and manner.

The Spanish tango is danced by a woman. It is characterized by sudden dynamic changes from flowing to vigorous, percussive movement. The rhythmic pattern of the dance is accentuated by heel and toe tapping, clapping, and finger-snapping. The use of castanets belongs almost exclusively to the Iberian dances.

The **Argentine tango** bears little similarity to that of Spain, being a couple dance and quite different in style.   —J.G.

tank furnace. See GLASS AND GLASS-MAKING.

tansai-e (Jap.). Black and white painting with the addition of colored tints.

tanto (Jap.). A short daggerlike sword.

tan-ye (Jap.). See JAPANESE ART.

tanzaku-e (Jap.). Paintings on poem papers.

tao t'ieh (Ch.). A decorative motive commonly used in Chinese art. The face of an ogre or mythical animal form. See PRIMITIVE ART; SYMBOLISM IN FAR EASTERN ART.

tapa cloth. A cloth made by pounding into a thin sheet the pulp from the inner bark of certain trees found in the various islands of Oceania. See OCEANIA, THE ARTS OF.

tapes. *Book.* Tapes are used for sewing the sections to, but the term is sometimes applied generically to the strings to which the sewing is carried.

TAPESTRY permits a free non-repeating design and unlimited polychromy, for it is woven, not with a loom set to pattern for the passage of shuttles the full width of a shed, as are yard-goods, but with bobbins each used to insert its yarn only in the area where the pattern requires that color. The usual weave is simple **cloth** or **tabby binding**, over and under the warps alternately, and in the following passage under where before it was over, and so on. The interpenetrating of the differently colored areas in a mosaic, for which the design must provide, prevents the fabric from-falling apart when removed from the loom, but wherever the margin between two colors is straight and coincides with the warp direction, a slit results. These slits may be dealt with in any of five ways: (1) left open, when they may be deliberately exploited in the effect of the finished weave—a characteristic, e.g., of the Chinese silk tapestries, called, for this reason, *k'ssu* (cut silk), and of so-called *khilim* rugs; (2) sewed up after the tapestry is removed from the loom —the usual procedure in European tapestries before the 18th cent., the sewing being necessary to prevent tearing at the ends of the slits because the warps are horizontal and the considerable weight of the relatively coarse wool fabrics would otherwise drag on the slits; (3) dovetailing—passing the threads of the juxtaposed colors alternately over the common warp either (a) single—**comb dovetailing**, or (b) in groups—**serrated dovetailing**—found, often combined with unsewn slits, in Egyptian early medieval ("Coptic") tapestries; (4) interlocking—looping each weft through the weft of the adjacent color in the same line of weave—typical of the elegance of the **Gobelins tapestries** from the 18th cent.; (5) passing a fine, cloth-woven weft the full width between every two tapestry-woven wefts, which, in compacting the weave, conceal the binding weft—a peculiar variant that almost contradicts the technical definition of tapestry, found in Japan (8th cent.), East Persia (10th cent.), and Peru ("medieval").

In the simplest tapestry the warps, all on one level, are vertical in relation to the design—as in *k'ssu*, but European weavers, at least by the 14th cent., almost always rendered the design at right-angles on the loom so that the warps would run horizontally when the panel was hung, the rather marked ribbing thereby helping to bind the pattern into a continuity, instead of severing it with vertical shadows. A more definite texture is effected by warps on two levels—depressed in regular alternation—in a small group comprising the Japanese and East Persian pieces with an alternate full-width cloth-bound weft, and also slit Persian silk tapestries of the Seljuq (11th cent.) and Safavid (mid-16th cent.) periods.

In fully evolved tapestry weaving the wefts are kept strictly at right angles to the warps, as in good shuttle weaving, but in more "primitive" types (e.g., "Coptic") they may slant and curve, sometimes considerably, following the design. Persia also employed in the Safavid period—though likewise rarely— a variant dovetailing: a black weft serving as outline dovetailed (usually, perhaps always, "comb" dovetailed) between color areas where there would otherwise be a slit, and elsewhere freely curved to follow the pattern contours.

At an early period a special technical adjustment was evolved in order to employ tapestry weaving to create spaced polychrome motives in a plain cloth (typically white linen): the interruption of the shuttle weaving at each spot where pattern was desired, leaving exposed the warps, when they may be combined in groups, each treated as a single warp in the tapestry weaving. The pattern in this case may parallel the warps (i.e., warps vertical in relation to it) or—far less often but sometimes necessarily in a shaped garment design—run at right angles.

The technique first appears in Egypt in a linen cartouche of Thutmose III (1463-1451 B.C.) and another cartouche of his son, Amenhotep II (1451-1420 B.C.), but whether Egypt is to be credited with the invention of tapestry remains undetermined, probably undeterminable. It is an obvious fallacy to attribute to certain countries (e.g., Egypt, Peru) the initiation of textile techniques simply because their conditions are favorable for subsoil preservation over long periods. From the time of Thutmose III, Syrian war prisoners appear in Egyptian records and the Syrians were famous as expert weavers.

All textile material except plain cloths (chiefly linen mummy wrappings) are very scanty until about the Christian era, but a continued use of the tapestry technique is almost certain, though its diffusion in the interval cannot be even guessed.. In the Han period it appears in the Far East (Loulan fragments), and shortly thereafter in the Paracas culture in Peru where llama wool and native cotton are used. Probably other American cultures were producing comparable fabrics that have disappeared. Some anthropologists still defend the old anti-diffusionist theory of an independent invention in the Western Hemisphere of this and the numerous other techniques utilized in the pre-Columbian civilizations, but to an ever-increasing predominance of students the number and variety of points of identity between Asiatic and American cultures (notably in textile techniques), and the small margin of fundamental divergence in the latter, puts any thesis of parallel development beyond the most liberal interpretation of probability. Until, therefore—or unless—the contrary is proven, it must be assumed that tapestry weaving, like so many other processes and ideas, moved from a place of origin somewhere in the Near or Middle East, to Eastern Asia, to the Western Hemisphere. There its use, with some variations, can be traced with reasonable continuity, chiefly through specimens preserved in Peru, down into the Spanish period. The Peruvian patterns are composed from the symbolic motives common to their other textiles and also pottery and metal: human figures, often holding a staff, masks, felines, birds—all reduced to geometrical outlines. The dyes are strong and clear and fairly numerous. After the Conquest, Spanish designs, including armorial bearings, were executed by the native craftsmen who imparted thereto a hybrid quality that has its own piquant charm; and thereafter in many uses the technique persists in various parts of the Western Hemisphere to our own time.

In China, likewise, surviving examples form a reasonably continuous series from the Han period on, though the dating of specific pieces even as late as the Ming Dynasty is more often than not problematical. From the T'ang period, at least, the technique appears almost exclusively in the thin, fine-textured slit tapestry (*k'ssu*) of silk (frequently supplemented with "gold" thread made of gilt paper strips spirally wound on a silk core), common down to today, and the patterns are drawn from the characteristic Chinese repertoire: stylized flowers, symbols, naturalistic bird and flower compositions, and illustrations, including religious themes. The weave has been put there to a wide range of uses, from small rectangles to enrich the outer mountings of hand-scroll paintings, to large wall panels, and also garments, including coats and slippers, or garment trimmings— very characteristically the square which from the Manchu conquest designated rank, civil or military, on the breast and back of officials' coats.

Chinese weavers were settled in Japan at intervals in the 3rd and 4th cents. A.D. and probably brought there tapestry, as well as various shuttle weaves. Here, too, slit tapestry has been the rule, executed in silk, often with the wound gilt-paper thread, and judging from the specimens in publications and Western collections, has been used chiefly for panels of moderate size such as **gift cloths** (*fukusa*), with the typical decoratively treated figural, animal and flower motives even more familiar in Japanese embroidery.

Korea had a well-established silk-weaving industry somewhat before Japan, doubtless likewise derived from China, but the early history of tapestry there seems obscure. In recent times coarse wool slit-tapestry rugs have been made, with broad and effective conventionalized bird and flower designs and abstract motives.

Examples of Near Eastern tapestry became numerous in Egyptian burial grounds from the 4th or 5th cent. A.D., so numerous indeed that the wealth of material (unfortunately labelled as a rule "Coptic") still has not been adequately studied. The bulk of these pieces are fragments from tunics, cloaks, cushion covers, or (far less often) wall hangings, in the pre-Islamic period woven almost invariably with wool and linen wefts—occasionally with some cotton, usually white—on linen warps. A few silk pieces from this time are known, and after the Islamic conquest silk becomes common, though coarser wool types are by no means discontinued.

The pre-Islamic material falls principally into three classes: (1) Egyptian-woven indigenous patterns in either (a) silhouette, almost always violet wool of some tone (occasionally dark blue) and natural linen, or (b) polychrome; (2) Egyptian-woven copies of Near Eastern designs, almost always polychrome; (3) Near Eastern renditions of Near Eastern designs—a class almost wholly neglected in the literature. The indigenous patterns comprise, on the one-hand, strapwork and other formal compositions, and, on the other, figures—human, animal, plant—derived chiefly from the popular eschatological cults, though occasionally major Hellenic deities (e.g., Hermes, Dionysos, Orpheus) are depicted. Christian symbols, notably various forms of the cross, are fairly common, Christian figures rare.

The bichrome silhouette style, though it tends to break down in the 6th and 7th cents. into a rather ambiguous polychrome silhouette style, with details in red, green, or mustard-yellow (or combinations thereof), also continues in pure form well into the Islamic period with a corresponding change of motives, esp. fine renditions of conventional lotus

patterns being attributable to the Tulunid period (875-905).

The most usual Egyptian use of the tapestry technique in the Islamic period was for the rendition of bands, varying in width from a half inch to a foot or more, or less often medallions, in silk (rarely enriched with metal thread) in linen cloth for garments (turbans, belts, etc.). The patterns are largely stereotyped—e.g., chains of small hexagons or other units framing more or less degenerate lions or ducks between line-schemes or set in strap patterns, and calligraphy—Kufic types, some very handsome, giving way in the 12th and 13th cents. A. D. to cursive styles. The inscriptions are most often formulae of blessing or good wishes, but quite often Koranic or from prayers; not infrequently they contain parts of the protocol or even names of rulers, and there is a considerable number which indicate the place of weaving (*tirāz*), though these are even more numerous in embroidery than in tapestry weave.

The 5th and 6th cent. A. D. specimens attributable to Syria can be assigned in many instances to specific cities through internal evidence, stylistic and iconographic, but the Syrian tapestry of the following centuries seems to have practically all been destroyed. A notable exception—often arbitrarily assigned to Europe—dateable in the 10th or 11th cent., with a griffon felling an ox, in large roundels, was found in the Church of St. Gereon, Cologne, and is now divided among the Berlin Museum, the Germanisches Museum, Nuremberg, the Musée du Tissu, Lyons, and the Victoria and Albert Museum, London.

A small series of wool tapestry fragments of the 7th and perhaps 8th cents. A. D. showing bird figures, chiefly ducks, usually on a fine red ground, and a larger piece with a cock, in the Hermitage Museum, Leningrad, can be assigned to Syria, again only from internal evidence yet with a reasonable degree of probability.

A large unique wool fragment in the Moore Collection, Yale Museum, showing the forequarters of a running goat in a vigorous semi-abstract style, is characteristically Sasanian.

The weave has continued to be used in the Near and Middle East in silk and linen for towels, belts, table-covers, etc. (especially Syria), mostly with geometrical designs, and for rugs in wool (rarely silk, occasionally elaborated with metal thread), with stylized plant or conventional patterns (Persia, the Caucausus, Asia Minor, Southeast Europe).

A special variant of the technique is typical of Persia and India, with the "tabby" binding supplanted by a twill weave over-and-under-two (or "warp-and-weft-twill-over-two"). This is employed characteristically in fine goats' hair or wool for garments: shawls ("Kashmir" and "Kirman" shawls), belts, coats, etc., the most typical pattern-motive being the mis-called "palmette", a round-bodied, sharply pointed ovoid with the tip turned over, which can be traced back to a foliage origin in Syria in the 6th cent. A. D: but has been given numerous fantastic interpretations. The earliest use of a twill-tapestry weave so far noted is in Persia in the 16th cent., and this particular type was established there at least by the mid-17th cent. (examples: Metropolitan Museum; Moore Collection, Yale Museum).

European countries were certainly weaving tapestry by the 12th cent. and quite probably long before. The earliest remaining examples —notably the Halberstadt Apostle tapestry— show an imperfect control of the medium, resulting in meagreness of detail and rigidity of delineation, qualities smoetimes extolled as "primitive"; this set, however, and other isolated panels like a Norwegian fragment illustrating two of the Months in the Oslo Museum of Industrial Art, represent semiamateur work, executed in convent or castle, and may not, therefore, give a just impression of the standards of the time.

Most of the tapestry weaving of Germany and Scandinavia continued to be of this domestic type until well into the 16h cent.—small panels, for the most · part, with doll-like figures, almost always vested with a naive charm, none the less beguiling for being in large part accidental. The work of the various German provinces and towns has been systematically classified by Dr. Betty Kurth (*Die Deutschen Bildteppiche des Mittelalters,* Vienna, 1926), who also has identified the literary sources of many of the designs.

The earliest examples of a fully evolved professional European tapestry art are the remnants of the great Apocalypse series of Angers Cathedral, the Mackay King Arthur, now in the Metropolitan Museum, and a closely related unpublished and unexhibited set of the Heroes. All are the work of Paris weavers of the 14th cent. and are based on cartoons determined by the book-painting of the period. Time and circumstances have been unkind to the great Apocalypse, woven (1376-1381) by Nicolas Bataille after designs of Jean de Bruges, for the Duc d'Anjou, yet it is still aesthetically the greatest European tapestry known, combining clarity without sacrifice of content for exploration, and variety without intrusive devising, with intensity and exalted elevation. The manuscript illustration style of the time was ideally adapted to tapestry—vigorous silhouettes, with highly simplified interior modelling, and varied enrichment of accessory detail.

From the beginning of the 15th cent. the chief focus of the industry in Europe shifts from France to the Low Countries. An interest in 15th cent. tapestries was reawakening in the 1st half of the 19th cent. (A. Jubénal, *Les anciennes tapisseries . . . ,* Paris, 1838), but no really systematic scholarship was devoted to them until the 1920's, and by that time the more thoughtful art historians were transferring their emphasis away from mere attribution, whether to schools or masters, towards interpretations, in terms both of cultural history and of aesthetics. Consequently the "cataloguing" of this material is still rudimentary. Dr. Betty Kurth identified the Tournai school; the Brussels school of the end of the century is well known; and an attempt was made to establish a Touraine school, but it dissolves under critical reexamination and its components are reabsorbed into Low Country groups.

Similarly, but for somewhat different reasons, an attempt to identify individual masters —primarily cartoon designers, secondarily loom-heads—has thus far proved largely abortive. In 1904 Joseph Destrée with the aid of "signatory" inscriptions identified a "Maître Philippe", and in 1907 A. Thiéry undertook to assemble the work of Jean van Roome. The results of both included ambiguities and errors—as is inevitable in pioneer work—and progress in that direction has been checked, chiefly by two circumstances: the difficulty of the epigraphy, for which a technique has to be forged *de novo;* and the standardization of attribution methods in current art history, and resultant automatic rejection of so fundamental a revision.

The fact remains, however, that this epigraphic method, combined with a more penetrating application of stylistic analysis, provides the definition of a 15th cent. Bruges school—hitherto completely neglected and of special interest in view of the major cultural role of that city at the time—comprising a dozen nameable masters; four or five ateliers in Tournai, in which more than a score of designers can be distinguished; an Antwerp school, likewise hitherto disregarded, with a half dozen marked personalities; and in the welter of late 15th and early 16th cent. Brussels production, at least eight or ten individuals.

Such attribution does not constitute art history but it does provide classification and definition of interrelations which are preliminary to historical interpretation. Some work has been done on the literary origins of certain of the large series—notably the *Roman de Troie*—but the full discussion of this, and especially of the social setting of the Low Countries' "Gothic" tapestry is still in the making.

The Flemish 15th cent. panel-painting styles, of which the cartoons were a reflection or adaptation, depending on the subject, also were well fitted to tapestry execution: a robust objective narrative sense, energetic delineation, decoratively conventionalized modelling—esp. of drapery—and an unflagging interest in accessories: plants, animals, objects, architectural elements, dress patterns, armor details.

Particularly attractive is the *menue verdure*, now called in the trade *mille-fleurs*, type, with little flowering plants often combined with small shrubs—esp. oak, apple, or orange bushes in blossom and fruit—closely sprinkled over the entire ground (usually dark blue, very effective when light red, rarely green, in early 16th cent. sometimes beige), frequently with birds and small animals interspersed, and later degenerating into ambiguity by the addition of a band of landscape at the top. *Menues verdures* also serve as background for armorial bearings and for personnages.

The intrusion of Renaissance taste is sudden and sharp in the history of tapestry, well typified by the Apostle series designed by Raphael and first woven by Pieter van Aelst of Brussels (1515). Scale is greatly magnified; silhouette is subordinated to substantial modelling; illustrative groupings and sequences give way to compositions organized in three dimensions; accessory detail is largely eliminated in favor of space, air and light— the latter a novel element that heightens the chromatic key, thereby diluting the palette, and encourages the use of silk. Metal thread enrichment, occasional in the preceding century, also becomes more frequent, evolving in the most ostentatious examples into "basket-weave" brocading. Painting *per se* takes precedence over narrative action. All these innovations were ill adapted to the flat, flexible, thick, ridged material of tapestry, which to function most successfully should be equally

interesting near and far, and offer material for ruminative exploration without being self-assertive.

The purely decorative elements—properly a central concern in tapestry design—are now relegated largely to borders, which become proportionately larger, more complex and more varied.

Bernard van Orley compromised between the preceding Flemish style and the new trends successfully—notably in the so-called "Hunts of Maximilian." The distinctive verdure of the time (*grosse verdure*) is composed of large, scrolling foliation of acanthus inspiration, often combined with other big-scale plants, birds, sometimes butterflies, and larger animals than hitherto—hounds, lions.

In the course of the 16th cent., weavers dispersed from Brussels, the chief center of the industry, and Antwerp to many other European cities, a movement considerably stimulated by Protestant persecutions initiated by the Spanish Government, and shops were set up in England (Sheldon works—c. 1560; noted for tapestry maps), Sweden (Gripsholm, 1540; Stockholm, 1549); various German cities; Fontainebleau (c. 1540), certain Italian cities (Ferrara, 1536; Florence, 1546) and later in Paris. Each developed its own more or less distinctive variation of the common style. The monumental classicism which was the dominant ideal reached new extremes in the work of Peter Paul Rubens and his followers.

The 17th cent. saw the founding of important new shops in England and France: in England at Mortlake near London (1619), where Lowland influence remained strong; and in Soho, London (1685), distinguished for its chinoiserie panels; in France, the great state-patronized factories. In Paris the new enterprise, which was in part derivative from preceding looms manned by Netherlanders, was set up (1667), along with ateliers for other decorative crafts, in an old factory in the Faubourg St. Marcel built by the Gobelins family, which gave the whole organization its name; in Beauvais (letters patent 1664) the factory was almost of equal status; in Aubusson (royal patent 1665; previous private looms) less expensive, coarser work was for the most part done.

The French Court placed lavish orders; outstanding p a i n t e r s provided cartoons (Charles LeBrun, Claude Audran le Jeune, Antoine and Charles Coypel, J. B. Oudry, Francois Boucher, Jean Bérain, François Desportes, etc.); the rich developments in French domestic architecture and furnishing promoted corresponding accomplishments; the dyers perfected a greatly increased palette, with a large range of intermediate nuances; silk was more freely utilized; and finally in the Gobelins, interlocking was devised to obviate slits invisibly. The weaver could duplicate the work of the painter.

The discriminating decorative taste of the 18th cent. prevented this virtuosity from being unfortunate, as it subsequently became, and the skilful use of birds, flowers, urns and other decorative objects, and architectural elements—mouldings, columns, balustrades—together with grace of composition and drawing, lifts the best work of the period to a high artistic level.

Meanwhile Brussels and neighboring cities had been adjusting their repertoires to the changing taste, in general, however, with less success, though the verdures of the time—wooded landscapes with limited vistas, often showing fountains, small figures (huntsmen, peasants, by or in the style of the Teniers)—have considerable decorative merit.

The 18th cent. again saw a dispersal of weavers, both Flemish and French, for the founding of new looms abroad: Madrid (1720, royal patronage 1746), famous for renditions of cartoons by Goya; St. Petersburg (1716); Naples (1783), etc.

William Morris, as one of his efforts to revive the old hand-crafts, established the Merton Abbey looms (1877), where cartoons, by members of the pre-Raphaelite school were executed.

The craft survives in the West today for repairs (and occasionally falsifications), but while efforts have been made to restore it to a genuine creative activity, notably in the Beauvais works where cartoons were ordered from painters of the so-called "modernist" school (i.e. Paris decadent school, c. 1905-1925), the medium is probably now hopelessly anachronistic.

For a classified bibliography on European tapestry see: J. J. Marquet de Vasselot, *Bibliographie de la Tapisserie,* Paris, 1935; also extensive references in: H. Göbel, *Wandteppiche,* Berlin, 1923-1934.   —P.A.

tarantella. A mass of legend has accumulated around this famous Italian national dance. According to one tale, the bite of the tarantula spider caused nervous disorders which could be cured only if the victim performed a specified dance to a traditional melody, dance and music thus acquiring the name "tarantella." Another legend asserts that the medieval

disease, tarantism, produced spasmodic motions which became the basis for the dance. Most creditable is the account that describes the dance as originating in the region of Tarantum, from which it took its name. It is a couple dance of fast running steps and rapid turns punctuated by poses suggestive of the courtship theme. The woman carries a tambourin, with which she produces a variety of tones and rhythmic patterns in the characteristic 6/8 meter. See St. Vitus dance.   —J.G.

tarantism. See St. Vitus dance.

Tarascan. A term loosely applied to the various local cultures which flourished in western Mexico and occupied different positions in time and space. There is no evidence of their having been made by the same people.   —G.C.V.

tarsia. See intarsia.

TASTE AND ITS EDUCATION. Taste became a major technical term in western philosophy of fine art in the 17th cent. Its chief meaning in 17th and in 18th cent. theory was a sense or sentiment of good form, and its chief use was in explanation of the formal excellence of classical art. The prevailing explanation in terms of conformity to exact rules and rational laws did not satisfy. Good form was held to be irreducible to mathematical regularity and canonical exactness. It was a matter of sentiment, of feeling, of the heart, and taste was understood as a feeling for a charm, a nuance, a grace which was at once the soul of classical beauty and inexpressible by mathematical or scientific law. Shaftesbury, Hutcheson, Hume, the so-called School of Taste generally, illustrate this usage. Probably however its most rigorous formulation in general aesthetics was in the *Critique of Judgment* by Kant. Taste is defined there as a disinterested judgment whose basis is the feeling of pleasure, not concepts. Taste is the sense of beauty, but more exactly it is a feeling of the fitness of the form of objects to our perceptual powers. Taste is a feeling for the presence of "good" form, and, although this feeling is said by Kant to be universally valid because it arises from an agreeable play of cognitive powers equally shared by all, its universality and validity are denied to rest upon conformity of the object to rational concepts or to exact rules and scientific laws. In some circles to-day taste retains this 18th cent. meaning, a feeling for excellence of form. Not only formalists but nonformalists such as T. M. Greene agree that pure taste is man's response to mere formal beauty. But since the 18th cent. taste has acquired other meanings. 19th cent. romanticism insisted that content even more than form, powerful emotions even more than pleasing designs, are the properties of aesthetic excellence in the arts. As a result taste in art came to mean man's response to the qualities of emotion and expression even more than man's response to the nuances of form. Finally, in 20th cent. philosophy of art taste is often used not only in these two senses but also to designate man's response to aesthetic qualities of any type, material or formal, contentual or functional, instrumental or terminal, etc.

The topic of the education of taste brings up more immediately than this variety of meanings the famous maxim *de gustibus non est disputandum*. The 17th-18th cent. theory of taste implies that this maxim is correct. Questions of taste cannot be decided by concepts and rational laws. Tastes are nonrational, disputations regarding them cannot eventuate in objective and rational decisions. Some have taken this position to imply that education of taste in art is futile and that nothing can be done except to ridicule those who attempt to provide such education. But the problem is not so simple even after acceptance of the "de gustibus" position of 17th-18th century theory. The fact is that we feel in terms of what we discriminate in the object felt and we discriminate in terms of what experience teaches us to be there, or in terms of what we know. As a consequence there is one great and good task for education of taste even within the subjectivism of the early modern theory, *viz.* the illumination of the field of taste, the increase of our knowledge of what is there for judgment. In the fine arts this still remains an extraordinarily urgent and important undertaking. Most people today know little of what can be discerned in the arts for taste and judgment. In a painting, for example, they may observe certain obvious items such as the subject, the person or countryscene or dramatic incident being portrayed. But they are not likely to be very vividly aware of the precise properties of the color and lines and lights and darks and shapes and organization, or of the exact shadings in the expression of abstract qualities, of personal and technical qualities. Comparative analytic discussion of paintings on view can serve to bring these and other properties into clear forceful light so that persons previously unlearned in paintings be-

gin to see with some definiteness what otherwise would have remained very vague and indefinite, or not perceived at all.

In supplying knowledge about the arts, educational method may go astray into two equally objectionable extremes. It may provide merely external knowledge, such as information about the artist's life and times which is not integrated with his particular concrete creations, or descriptions of identifying tags of his art without insight into their characteristic properties as art elements. This first extreme often leads to great enlargement of the vocabulary and the verbal memory of the auditor but to only comparatively slight gain in his power of concrete discernment and judgment. On the other hand, educational method may go to the other extreme, providing merely internal knowledge, such as those imaginative recreations of works of art which are rhapsodic, diffuse, unsystematic, and emotive. This extreme may engender a pleasing mystic trance in the auditor and an illusion of widened experience. The auditor may be 'edified'. But actually he is likely to be no more enlightened than by a mirage. The ideal would seem to be a combination which avoids these extremes, e.g. a combination of exact external and imaginative aesthetic knowledge directed by some generalized method of analysis which secures system to this knowledge and trenchant applicability of it to particular works. This ideal seems possible only where historical scholarship and aesthetic power are united with and guided by philosophical insight into art, or insight into general principles. In the education of taste in the field of painting, Thomas Munro's *Great Pictures of Europe* and A. C. Barnes's *The Art in Painting* are examples of attempts in the direction of such an ideal.

It may be granted that education can widen and deepen the areas open to feeling and taste, and even that this is an important and necessary undertaking. But it may be objected that this will not change the inborn leanings and temperamental affinities which are the basis of taste. You cannot make a rosebush into an oak using the most fertile soil and the most skilful methods of cultivation. The answer is: quite true, you cannot. But often you can make a weak and runted rosebush into a very fine rosebush. And if education of taste begins early enough, it often can do likewise. Education of taste cannot delete the heredity of a person. But it can refine and expand inborn capacities. It can broaden and make more subtle both feeling and judgment. By bringing feeling and judgment into contact with the whole orbit of value possibilities theoretically open to them in the arts, it can sharpen and clarify a person's unexamined scale of values. This enrichment of individual capacity is clearly a great gain judged by any humanistic standard. Nor is it unlike the best fruits of education in any other of its fields of endeavor.

Can education of taste in art do more than open the gateway to individual improvement? Probably not, so long as it operates within the early modern definition of taste. But if taste is defined as man's response to the total set of values in the arts, the case is somewhat different. Everyone is familiar with the distinction between instrumental and terminal values. In the area of instrumental values in fine art, education seems capable of developing taste 'objectively' as well as subjectively. Is this quiet color the proper material means for getting the melodramatic effect clearly aimed at in this painting? Is this loose organization the most appropriate formal means for making this painting an effective decorative constitutent of this tiny room? Endless questions of this instrumentalist type can be asked regarding the elements of each art, the elements of sculpture, architecture, music, motion picture, literature, the dance, as well as painting, and in each instance of each art. Here education can open a field for judgment which is not only immensely large and interesting and instructive, but in which inquiry can attain results of considerable exactitude widely verifiable by competent observers. Perhaps one should call such results judgments of technique rather than judgments of taste, since they are judgments of the adequacy of certain means to certain fairly well-defined ends. But this is, as I say, a question of definition. In one sense, they are judgments of taste. They are responses to an area of the total values in art, and express discrimination and feeling and choice. The chief difference between such responses and certain other responses to values in art is that these are immediately determined not by mere subjective satisfaction but by the adequacy of one objective element (color, organization) to serve as an instrument of another objective element (melodramatic effect, decorative effect) and independent of whether this second objective element is subjectively preferred or not.

As to terminal values, such as the intrinsic satisfactoriness of quiet color or loose organization, inquiry cannot attain and educa-

tion cannot provide results as universally valid. It can supply here the widest possible basis for decision. It can illumine the relevant field vividly and provoke each person to the fullest self-examination. It can exert its great power of persuasion. But it cannot establish or divulge a set of terminal values in all cases identical for all persons or binding upon all persons, since terminal values are what an individual in his innermost individuality alone can fully approve. Education of taste in art has often seemed to ignore this. It has proceeded as if its business was to teach what everyone "should" like regardless of who he is. But this is to be false to the great personal quality of the arts. The arts are more than mere social products which reach to what is common among men. They are also personal expressions which reach to what is singular in each man. This truth should not be lost. At the same time, from a practical standpoint, there is more than mere dogmatism and error in an educative method which ignores without violently suppressing the individual differences of its clients, especially in the field of arts. First, these individual differences are rampant and ineradicable, and will operate with the strength natural to them in judgments of terminal values in any case, unless a violence foreign to all sensible educational procedure is employed. Why underline the virulently obvious, particularly when the most precious part of the common values in the arts is so difficult to experience and so easy to overlook? Second, these individual differences are by definition subjective and private. Hence, the educative clarification of the arts is not properly concerned with their emphasis. Its chief topic is something else, viz., objects or works of art. Third, the extent of the common ground in the field of terminal values has never been determined and has no definitive limits at present. It may be, as I think it is, surprisingly large. Why not explore it without reservations, particularly since the chief reservation imposed by the diversity of human nature is obvious and will receive constant reiteration? Finally, whatever agreement in terminal values education is able to gain, whatever genuine similarity of approvals education can promote by free inquiry and discussion and an aspiration for human good, is a gain in human solidarity and brotherhood.

In summary, we may say that in the present day broad sense of the term taste, the education of taste, in the fine arts has three objectives: (1) illumination of the properties of art and of works of fine art so that taste possesses the most ample and precise material for judgment, (2) instruction in the instrumental adequacies within this field of judgment, (3) promulgation within the ineradicable limits imposed by the individual differences of human beings of a set of common terminal values. See Bosanquet, B., *History of Aesthetics, London,* 1904; Croce, B., *Aesthetic,* trans. Ainslie, London, 1922; Ducasse, C. J., *Philosophy of Art,* New York, 1929; Greene, T. M., *The Arts and the Art of Criticism,* Princeton, 1940; Kant, I., *Critique of Judgment,* trans. Bernard, London, 1914; Gilbert, K. and Kuhn, H. A. *History of Esthetics,* New York, 1939; Parker, D., *The Analysis of Art,* New Haven, 1926; Pepper, S. C., *Aesthetic Quality,* New York, 1937; Spingarn, J. E. *Critical Essays of the Seventeenth Century,* 3 vols., Oxford, 1908.

—D.W.G.

tatami (Jap.). Straw mats, 3′ x 6′, and about 3″ thick, multiples of which are used to completely cover the floors of rooms in Japanese houses.

Tatlinism. See constructivism; RUSSIAN ARTS.

tattoo. The process of permanently marking the skin by pricking in pigment. Sometimes includes the producing of scars for decorative effects. See OCEANIA, THE ARTS OF; COSTUME ART.

Ta-urt. *Egypt. Relig.* Wife of Set; presided over birth of kings and gods and was an important figure in the underworld.

tea ceremony. See cha-no-yu.

teaching art, methods of. Procedures employed by teachers for guiding the various art experiences of pupils. (Methods are often characterized by the nature of pupil activity engaged in, such as *copy method, dictation method, free creative expression method;* certain art educators have devised methods of teaching which have been labelled so as to indicate their originators, for example, the *Dow* or *structure* method, the *Sargent* or *graphic vocabulary* method of teaching drawing, the *Ross* or *systematic* method of teaching design, the *Cezik* or *creative* expression method of stimulating pupil activity in the arts; other terms utilized to designate procedures of teaching art are *traditional, academic, art school,* or *studio, problem-solving,*

unit, and *progressive* methods. Often several or all of these methods may be followed by an art teacher at various times and under various circumstances.) Whitford and Winslow in *Dictionary of Education.*

tear drops. The term is applied to globules of glaze on pottery which often appear near the base of a vessel in large tear-drop formation. —J.A.M.

teatra sacra. See STAGESETTING.

technique (Gr. *technikos* fr, *technē,* an art). Expert method of executing the technical or mechanical details of an art. The most teachable aspect of an art, having to do with the development of skills in the manipulation of a given art medium, leading to virtuosity when exhaustively studied.

The development of technique in the arts is theoretically, but not practically separable from the development of expression. While facility in the use of a medium may be stressed in education and developed by practice, it can never be completely divorced from the character of an artistic statement. Thus, while virtuosity may be the theoretical aim of technical studies, "good technique" must be defined in practice as the ability to employ a medium adequately to achieve a predetermined expressive effect. —L.D.L.

technography. Description of arts and crafts; the geographic study of the occurrence of technics such as weaving, ceramics, etc.

techtiform. Hut or house shaped.

techtonic (adj.). Pertaining to building or construction.

telari. See STAGESETTING.

telamon. A male figure used like a caryatid, as a supporting column.

temmoku yaki (Jap.). Pottery of black (or very dark brown) stoneware glaze due to the presence of iron oxide.

tempera. A generic term for any one of several paint media which leaves the surface of the finished product *matte* or without shiny reflections. Strictly speaking, egg is occasionally used for the same purpose, and once in a while someone attempts to use the albumen or white of the egg, but this results in a very brittle film which checks and cracks readily. If the yolk alone is used, a pliable, firm, and completely perma-

nent film is formed with far less change of color or value than the layman would suppose possible, and complete permanence when permanent pigments are used. Acetic acid (vinegar) or formaldehyde may be used to preserve the medium while in use. Fig milk, honey, and various gums are used as tempera media, usually with other materials. The commonest modern tempera is glue (q.v.) (usually called *size* by artists). Ordinary skin glue is satisfactory, except for its tendency to swell when exposed to humidity or actual wet; casein glue is a newer development commercially, although it, too, goes back to the Middle Ages, at least for its origins. Used as a paint medium, casein is firmer but more difficult to manage than skin glue. See PAINTING; mural painting; also *Glue and Gelatin*, J. Alexander, 1923; *Animal Proteins, Bennett*, 1921, pp. 200-268; *The Materials of the Artist*, M. Doerner, 1934; *Über mikrochemische Bilduntersuchung*, Hetterich, Mikrochemie X, 1-3, 1931; *The Painters Methods and Materials*, A. P. Laurie; *Casein and its Industrial Applications*, E. Sutermeister, 1927; *The Materials of Medieval Painting*, D. V. Thompson, 1936; *The Book of the Art of Cennino Cennini*, Cennini (Il Libro dell'Arte o Trattato della Pittura di Cennino Cennini), Florence, 1869.
—R.F.H.

temperament. *Mus.* See ACOUSTICS.

tempered glass. See GLASS AND GLASS-MAKING.

template. A slab or piece of material, as of stone or wood, placed under the end of a beam or girder to distribute the weight over a greater area.

temple. A building or structure set apart for the services of religious worship.

temptation of St. Anthony. According to the legend, St. Anthony of Egypt, who was born at Alexandria in the 3rd cent., went to live in the desert. During his hermit's life he was tormented by demons and tempted by women, but he overcame all peril by prayer. The subject, with its dramatic implications, was popular during the Middle Ages and the following periods, and has been treated many times. One of the most fantastic representations is the engraving by the German artist Martin Schongauer (1445-1491) in which St. Anthony is seen as he is lifted into the air by horrible demons. The most famous of all versions on the subject is the one by the

German painter Matthias Grünewald in the Isenheim Altar in Colmar (Alsace) which he accomplished around 1515. The right inner wing of this gigantic altar piece shows, on the interior, how St. Anthony is tortured by evil spirits. The subject has recently been taken up in music by the German composer Paul Hindemith, who, inspired by Matthias Grünewald's work composed an opera called *Mathis der Maler* (Mathis the Painter) which he arranged as a symphony. One of the parts depicts the Temptation of St. Anthony. See *The Golden Legend* or Lives of the Saints as trans. by William Caxton, vol. II, pp. 224 ff., London, 1900; Anna Jameson, *Sacred and Legendary Art*, vol. II, pp. 724 ff., Boston and New York, 1895; Margaret E. Tabor, *The Saints in Art*, London, 1913, p. 7; Fitzroy Carrington, *Engravers and Etchers*, Chicago, 1917, pp. 30 and 32; Arthur Burkhard, *Matthias Grünewald*, Cambridge, Mass., 1936, pp. 37-39, plates 31-35.
—L.L.

Tempyo art. See JAPANESE ART.

tenchi-konger-m'yazukuri (Jap.). See JAPANESE ART.

Tendai sect. See JAPANESE ART.

tenebrists. Painters of darkness; international group of painters of early 17th cent. inspired by the art of Michelangelo di Caravaggio (1565-1609). Characteristic is the use of violent contrasts of light and shade reminiscent of and often derived from conditions in basements or other rooms with artificial light. Most tenebrists preferred drastic and unidealized, occasionally even vulgar treatment of subject matter, religious, mythological or genre (q.v.) and therein opposed the idealizing academic painters of Bologna.
—R.B.

tengai (Jap.). The canopy often shown above a deity represented in painting or sculpture.

tenjiku-yo (Jap.). See JAPANESE ART.

tenor. See MEDIEVAL MUSIC.

tenor banjo. See MUSICAL INSTRUMENTS.

tenor clarinet. See MUSICAL INSTRUMENTS.

tension. (1) *Mus.* Considerable stress (higher than that provided by the general metrical conditions of a structure), brought upon a musical element through the context in which it appears. More specifically applied to intervals and chords, the term *tension* designates their relatively high number of acoustical beats. See consonance. —E.K.

(2) *Dance. Tension* in movement implies force due to muscles acting against resistance. It depends upon the cooperative action of opposing muscle groups. This united action serves as a regulating device for controlling the amount of tension in the performance of motor activity. All types of movement depend upon it. Movements are strong or weak according to the amount of resistance present in their execution. It is only through proper tension that the muscles can adjust themselves to any desired intensity, or speed of execution, or the varying shades of artistic meaning. Muscle tension is the very basis of aesthetic experience and of expressive and communicative movement. The more *tensile* the movement, the deeper its physical power. Success in dance depends upon the dancer's ability to constantly readjust the proper balance between emotional demands and muscle tension. —M. N. H'D.

tenson. See MEDIEVAL MUSIC.

Ten, The. See POST-REVOLUTIONARY PAINTING AND SCULPTURE IN THE U. S. A.

Teotihuacan. The name of the great ceremonial culture made in central Mexico prior to Aztec times but having its origin in the earlier Middle Cultures with influences coming from Vera Cruz. Late authors believe this culture to be the one of the semi-legendary Toltecs. —G.C.V.

tepidarium (L.). A warm room for a bath.

tequitqui (from Aztec word meaning tributary). Used in analogy with mudéjar (q.v.), (from Arab word meaning tributary) for Mexican Christian work with strong Indian character; usually the result of actual execution by Indian hands (intro. by J. Moreno Villa in *Escultura Colonial*, Mexico, 1942).
  —J.Mc.

terrace. A raised level space; natural or artificial.

terra cotta sculpture, direct method. Direct terra cotta sculpture can be made in three techniques: (1) The coil method; (2) the slab system; (3) the pottery wheel method. In building up sculpture in any of the three methods, the sculptural forms may be reduced to their simplest geometrical form. A head, e.g., could be formed from a clay cylinder, or two smaller cylinders superimposed on each other. A clothed female figure may be worked from a tall cylinder, a group of two figures from two cylinders, a reclining figure or an animal from a half-cylinder cut lengthwise. Or a seated figure can be formed by two half-cylinders (legs) and a full cylinder (body) over a cube (seat); a kneeling figure may consist of a large cylinder (body) and a shorter half cylinder (legs). After building up the mass of the group, it can be modelled in detail. Any variety of finish may be applied: tooling with wooden or wire tools; the application of small pieces of clay; or it may be smoothed. The latter has to be done most carefully. When the smooth piece is semi-dry, it may be burnished with a smooth tool to a light gloss, which it will retain after burning in the kiln.

For guidance in building up (in all three techniques) it is advisable to use a small sketch of the proposed figure; by measuring with calipers and multiplying these measurements in the chosen ratio, errors may be avoided.

Terra cotta sculpture should be made 10 p.c. to 12 p.c. larger than desired in the final stage to allow for shrinkage, depending on the type of clay used. Information on shrinkage ratios may be obtained from the clay dealer or by experiment. Clays of fine substance usually shrink more than those containing grog. The latter are esp. suitable for larger pieces, because of greater strength. Clay must be free of foreign matter, esp. plaster particles, as plaster will release gases during burning and may cause the piece to explode. Before starting to build, the moist clay must be well kneaded to remove air bubbles. During the entire process air holes should be avoided by pressing on the clay firmly, allowing the air to escape.

The coil method is used in sculpture of small to medium size: because of its simplicity it may be used successfully by pupils, amateurs and sculptors unfamiliar with ceramic sculpture.

One rolls out on a table long rolls of clay 3/8 inch to 1/2 inch thick, according to the size of the contemplated figure; these rolls should not be too wet, yet pliable. On a board, reinforced against warping, a coat of shellac is applied; when dry, one or more holes are drilled through the center of the board, inside of the bottom outline of the proposed sculpture. This outline is then painted on the board with clay slip, which will cause the clay to adhere. The first coil is then laid along this outline. Subsequent coils are then laid on the first one; between each coil slip must be applied. As the piece develops, the outside as well as the inside have to be welded together by finger pressure so that hollows between coils are filled. During the process of building it is advisable to compare and measure constantly until the sketch may be discarded and the piece is finished. It is advantageous in direct terra cotta that the shape and form of the sculpture can be worked out from the outside as well as the inside. This results in a full, plastic form and, if carefully done, may elicinate in large measure any surface modelling. When the piece is built up completely, but still open on top, a plug of clay is pushed into the slip-treated opening. After finishing the sculpture, the highest part should be pierced in an inconspicuous spot (a knitting needle will do) to insure airflow while drying and burning. Terra cotta sculpture, like any ceramic product, must be absolutely dry for burning; any moisture remaining in the piece may cause its ruin in the fire. Drying should be gradual, not forced; it is advisable to lift the piece to allow passage of air so that it may dry evenly, as uneven drying may cause warping or cracks.

The slab system is preferable to the coil method in larger pieces and for quicker results, but proper construction, inside as well as outside, is the main problem in this technique. The larger the piece, the more it becomes an engineering construction problem, in which weight, pull and stress must be considered. For greater strength and to avoid cracking and warping, grog clay should be used. A small sketch or drawings of the design from all sides should be used as a guide. For the control of moisture (in any of the three methods of direct terra cotta) one may construct a permanent cover by nailing strips of wood together forming an open box, which then is covered with oilcloth, tacked over this frame. Damp rags (not wet) are used over the sculpture when evaporation of the clay becomes noticeable; in damp weather and while the clay is wet, covering with the oilcloth box is sufficient. A good sized board, 18 by 24 inches or larger, is covered with unbleached muslin. Two strips of wood 1/2-5/8 inch thick are laid on (or nailed) parallel, lengthwise to the board. The clay, after thorough kneading, is pounded well between the strips so that no airholes are formed. The surplus clay is then removed by running a straight, smooth strip of wood over the parallel strips until the clay surface is entirely smooth. The strips may then be removed from the clay slab, which then is allowed to dry for a few hours. When dry enough to allow handling, the clay is cut lengthwise into strips 3-6 inches wide; on the lower part of a figure wider strips may be used than on the higher parts. For large, flat surfaces, larger clay slabs may be used instead of strips (as in the plinth, or a cube-shaped seat or in parts of the inner construction). The first strip is carefully lifted from the muslin (which prevents sticking) and transferred to a narrow obard; this, in turn, is taken to the turntable on which the modelling board rests.

The modelling board should be strongly constructed and large enough to allow for air space or bulky rags between the sculpture and the oilcloth box. For large figures a board of double layers of wood, running crosswise, reinforced below by parallel strips, is screwed together so that warping will not occur. A few airholes may be drilled through the board in the center where the figure will stand. The board is then shellacked and when dry, the approximate outline of the sculpture is painted on broadly with thick slip. The clay strip is now laid along the outline, possibly around a curve or edge to prevent its falling over; when the next strip is attached to one end of the first one, it must be well pressed on. When the wall outline is completed and the first strip is firm enough, the second line of strips may be attached after covering the top of the first strip with slip. All seams must be eliminated by working the two strips together. As strips are set upon strips and the sculpture begins to rise, sustaining walls have to be built inside the piece. These inner walls should be carefully considered before starting the sculpture so that a maximum of strength may be obtained with a minimum amount of walls. They have to be pierced so that air may pass from one compartment to the other in drying and burning. In some cases one or the other wall may be eliminated when a buttress can supply enough strength. When a certain height is reached, 18 to 24 inches or more, a horizontal layer (pierced) may be established. It is obvious, that the inner walls must be well attached to the outer shape with slip and clay. As the piece rises to a height where weight becomes a factor it is good policy to allow the lower part to harden somewhat, which will increase carrying strength. When the first section is completed the piece may be shaped from the inside and the outside. Curves in the construction are made by bending the strips after they have been put in place. Should the piece harden quicker than desired, it may be moistened with a wet sponge; this is important, as otherwise any added clay will not adhere firmly. Care should be taken to enlarge the piece as accurately as possible; it is well to stay within 1/4 inch or so of the final dimension of the surface. This 1/4 inch should be added when the piece is entirely built up, for the sculptural finish; as this outer skin is usually applied in small pieces under firm pressure, it will act as a protection against possible cracks in the more porous walls of the piece, which thereby seldom penetrate the surface. The openings on the highest parts of the figure should remain open as long as possible so that the inside of the piece may dry at the same rate as the outside; the openings are finally closed with a plug set in with slip. When the surface modelling is finished, the piece should be left to dry gradually but thoroughly. In large sculpture, transportation to the kiln must be considered; it is also well to know the size of the kiln beforehand. If possible, a large piece should be built close to the kiln; if the piece is too large to fit into a good sized kiln, it may be cut while moist, in places where the cut will show least. After burning the pieces can be cemented together. When cutting is foreseen from the start, it may be made less difficult by attaching the clay on the cutting line without slip or reinforcement and by marking the line on the outside. Cutting may be done with a knife, but the best method is the use of a twisted wire, in cutting the piece from the board before drying or in cutting any part of the piece.

The **pottery wheel method** is advisable only for sculptors familiar with the wheel or to those having the services of an experienced potter at the studio. This method is esp. suitable for decorative sculpture. Practically every part is thrown on the wheel, fitted together and modelled mainly from the inside out, requiring very little surface modelling. Accessories, such as hair, draperies, foliage, flowers, etc., are modelled in hand and then applied. Work of this type usually is glazed after the bisque firing and lends itself to unique effects, such as glazing in part only; the contrast between the unglazed parts (body) and the accessories in multi-colored glazes is often very striking and decorative. Because of the rapidity of execution the relative frailty of this type of sculpture is no handicap, provided that the work is executed near the kiln, so that transportation is avoided.

Throwing clay on a wheel is not simple; a craft in itself, it requires years of practice. The clay to be used should be of fine grain and must be wetter than for modelling. It is centered on the turning pottery wheel and shaped by hand in the desired form; when sufficiently dry, it is cut from the wheel and transferred to the sculpture. Before starting, it is advisable to make full size drawings, from all directions, of the proposed figure; from these drawings the size and shape of the parts, to be thrown on the wheel, are determined. After the base is made by the slab or coil method, slender cylinders, thrown on the wheel are applied for the lower legs. Larger cylinders are used for the upper legs; a low, wide cylinder for the abdomen and a higher cylinder for the chest; a small cylinder forms the neck; and an oval shape is used for the head. Arms are formed similarly and hands and feet are made of flat forms, to which individual fingers and toes are fastened. While applying these pieces with slip, the form may be given by reaching into the hollow cylinders and pushing out the form or by pressure from the outside, starting from the lowest parts. As each piece is cut to fit and applied, it has to be braced by sticks pushed into clay balls on either end. As the piece hardens and shrinks, the braces have to be adjusted. Since the desired form is given each part as the piece is built up, the sculpture is almost finished after all parts are applied. Hair is made of clay rolls shaped into ringlets or strands and then applied; drapery is shaped from larger rolls. Leaves may be made by hand or pressed out of a mold made over a model leaf, etc. The thickness of all parts should not vary much; the larger piece should be sufficiently strong to carry itself and must be well balanced. This method is suitable for sculpture near life-size. Smaller figures may be constructed along the same principle, without the potter's wheel. In this case the various cylinders are made by shaping thin slabs of clay over rounded sticks of natural wood. When slightly hard, the cylinders are taken off the sticks, cut to fit and applied exactly as in the former method.

—C.L.S.

terra verde. See green earth.

tertiary colors. See COLOR.

tetrachord. *Mus.* (1) A scale of 4 diatonic tones. (2) A four-stringed instrument.

text. *Book.* The body-matter of a book as distinct from the preliminary matter, etc.

texture. *Mus.* Term borrowed from the field of tactile experience, used in a figurative sense to describe the character which a musical structure has by virtue of the type of relationships prevailing particularly between its simultaneously presented elements (e.g. polyphonic t., homophonic t., compact t., transparent t., etc.)   —E.K.

tezontle. Porous pumice-like red lava building stone of the Valley of Mexico.

THEATRE (Gr. showroom). The obvious and most striking characteristic of the theatre: the disparity of its sources and origins, the complexity of its contents and aspects, the variety of its manifestations and forms, indicates the quantity as well as the quality of the problems involved. An intricate composition of particular social, spiritual and psychological conditions, of customs and traditions, of subsidiary arts and contributive techniques, theatre is a collective phenomenon in foundation and principles, structure and form, i.e. the concept theatre comprises a multitude of subordinated or coördinated phenomena of essentially different nature and order. As compared to other arts, which are determined by material and aesthetic data of one single category, it is the distinctive criterion of the theatre to achieve a coherent artistic unity out of numerous constituents of divergent natures. This ultimate achievement, however, can but partly be preserved in lasting evidence. In fact, as soon as the specific theatrical creation is completed it ceases to exist as such; a process which reveals the ephemeral and illusionary quality of the theatre art-work.

Therefore any productive estimation of the theatre depends on the basic notion that this particular quality of fugitive illusion, in whatever scenic representation of play and drama, is actually the theatre's form of reality, finality and completion. Theatrical reality is not conditioned upon its relation to objective, concrete appearance in space, nor on its measurable duration in time, but on the participants' spontaneous or deliberate acceptance of its specific validity. Many discrepancies in dramatic and theatric theory can thus be explained. The conflicting views with regard to this condition are mainly due to the an-

tagonistic directions of artistic endeavor: one tended toward unrealistic fantasy, the other directed toward naturalistic resemblance. However, if the scenic reality is to have artistic relevance, such relevance depends solely upon the degree of genuine theatric perfection, not on the exactitude, probability or truthfulness obtained in one direction, nor on the quantitative effort of imagination expended in the other.

Theatre originates as well as culminates in the transient instants of the actual performance, the vital centre of which is, or at least ought to be, the actor. Nevertheless the creation of the actor, however dramatic the scenic situation, would be incomplete, if not impossible, but for the active and reactive participation of the audience. For the audience is an integral part of the theatrical process proper; between performers and spectators exist functional relations which create suspense and tension not originally resident in the presented subject. Although the position or opposition of performer and public in space have significance beyond the practical requirements of providing favorable visual and auditory conditions, any scene or decoration or architecture supporting and surrounding the performance is merely accessory, however important or artistic in itself. The predominance of overwhelming scenic display and sumptuous architecture during certain periods, in particular the Baroque, substantiates this often ignored principle.

It is also obvious that literary evidence, as contained in a dramatic text, cannot convey an accurate idea of the eventual scenic interpretation—the latter being an accomplished creative act in itself. Incidentally this condition points towards the peculiar and suggestive problem that a work of art which already constitutes an ordered artistic whole becomes the material of yet another creative process, aesthetically valid in its own right. As a legitimate artistic category, however, theatre can be directly appreciated, independent of any literary consideration. The production of literary drama in terms and with means of the theatre is a genuine artistic creation, and in no way a re-production. Consequently, despite the intrinsic interdependence, the aesthetic validity of literary drama does not depend on its actual realization on the stage; nor does a perfect scenic or histrionic performance imply literary substance of any avail. Originally the concepts of theatre and drama refer to but one phenomenon. In fact, the primitive form of drama is at the same time a rudimentary form of theatre, thus disclosing the original identity of this source.

Theatre and drama arise from early ritual. This moment marks a highly significant attempt at intentional, formal expression of primitive man, in direct emotional response to the unfathomable, fear- and awe-inspiring mysteries of nature. At all times and with all peoples, giving suggestive evidence of universality, these initial performances originate spontaneously in a collective emotion. Almost generally assuming the form of either pantomimic or ecstatic dance, these spectacles tend to prove that man possesses innate mimetic and rhythmic dispositions. Indeed, the impulse to act as well as the instinct to release physical or emotional tension in rhythmical movement antedates any permanent record of art. At this early stage of civilization the language of tangible images and material symbols is far more developed and differentiated than speech. Thus visible effigies and representative performers stand for phenomena yet beyond the grasp of human mind, or else for facts, things and experiences yet beyond the capacity of abstracted expression. Also the inadequacy of spoken language appears compensated by an extraordinary expressiveness of the bodily language.

However considerable at times the incidental aesthetical benefit, these first dramatic manifestations of creative mind are but instrumentally relevant, i.e. as means for the attainment of real and vital ends. Notwithstanding the metaphysical principle implied in worship of spirits, deities, demons and personified cosmic or physical phenomena, the primitive ritual emphasizes practical rather than spiritual issues, such as the quest for rain or game, the conjuration of plagues and disasters, etc. For this material reason no categorical distinction can yet be made between the performance of ritual proper and secular ceremonies bearing upon war, labor, hunting, birth and death, mating, initiation, etc., or even the formal routine of collectively organized pleasure and play.

The subsequent differentiation is not due to a conscious, cognitive act: it is rather an instinctive, twofold expression of the latent dualism between material and spiritual tendencies. And although they grow eventually apart, visual and visionary world still hold an identical quality of magic and fascination. This becomes particularly evident in the important rites related to natural production and fertiliy. They contribute a great

variety of subjects and forms, covering the whole range from strict rites and solemn ceremonies, through orgiastic pageants, to frankly erotical and phallic symbolism. Although the profane tendency shows unmistakably in ostensible exaggerations, comical imitations and vulgar or burlesque allusions, the majority of these performances discloses nevertheless the characteristics of their metaphysical origin. The performers, however drastic in suggestions and expressions, feel themselves as integral parts of an inspired collective or participants in a sacred service. On the other side, the practice in dealing with fearsome superhuman forces or religious mysteries requiring knowledge and involving responsibilities beyond the scope of ordinary man, it often develops into the exclusive and esoteric office. of privileged representatives: medicine man, sorcerer or priest. Supposed to be endowed with mysterious qualities they assume frequently the authority of professionals who may virtually be considered as actors.

The gradual transition from these various ceremonies to genuine drama and theatre is indicated in the significant process that dance yields its dominant position to the medium of speech. Indeed, the human experience that urges and desires, emotions, thoughts and feelings are communicable must be considered a revelation of immeasurable consequence. No longer restrained by the bodily limitations of mere physical expression, man avidly grasps and develops the almost unlimited power to convey something on the strength of spiritual effort. Thus the circle of subjects widens considerably, comprising the spontaneous narration of actual incidents and events as well as the more involved accounts of mythological and historical legends. Often the components of these simple tales already hold potential dramatic tension, i.e. a latent antagonism between opposed persons, groups or tendencies. This ever possible conflict, presented so as to form a consistent plot or story, is the very essence of drama, wether visually enacted or spiritually sublimated in poetry.

Gradually the repetition and recurrence of typical performances leads to regular and increasingly strict and ingenious conventions and traditions, with dance providing physical pattern and spatial organization, i.e. structural principles for the development of artistic form. It would be conjectural though, to determine to what extent the impressive formal stylization in so-called 'primitive art', in particular as manifested in theatrical forms and attributes: masks, costumes, make-up, pantomine, dance practice, etc., denote an original artistic quality or rather one inferred by subsequent aesthetic evaluation. The formal perfection and expressive power of theatrical masks—e.g., in the primitive ceremonial, in the ancient Greek and Roman theatre, in the performances of the Far East—may easily lead to the conclusion that they represent ends, intentionally artistic in themselves, and which are meant to be appreciated as such. However, originally they are rather scenic means, instrumental in portraying or emphasizing dramatic characters, moreover without reference to their consistency with the actor's individual capacity of interpretation or transformation.

As long as the actor wears a mask—whether it be modelled in some plastic material or painted on with heavy make-up—he is virtually an anonymous representative: his every distinctive feature points toward the accomplishment of a stylized type or character, established and admitted in advance. Subsequently this practice leads to the fixation of rigid, permanent 'stock characters', a theatrical tradition which covers the greater part of theatre history and can yet be traced in the present theatre. Stock characters dominate the ancient Greek and Roman theatre; they flourish magnificently in the Italian improvised comedy (*commedia dell'arte*), from where they spread over the European world, clearly manifest in the comedies of Gozzi, Goldoni and Molière; they are still alive on the Chinese and Japanese stage; they persist universally in the traditions of puppet- and marionette-plays.

As a specific form of histrionic characterization stock characters are in current usage on the lowest level of public performances, serving the purpose of easy appreciation for an unpretentious or uncultured audience. In the other extreme the typified characters bring to visual life the imaginary or allegorical or superhuman symbols of a homogeneous collective emotion or conception. As such they can but be conceived in a compact religious, social or ethnic unity, as e.g. in ancient Egypt and Greece, in China and Japan. Only with the differentiation, or even disintegration, of later social organisms individual traits, and finally psychological interpretations, appear in histrionism.

In the early stages of theatre history the solution of the various aesthetical and practical problems is simple and automatic. There is no conflict as yet between spiritual or emotional contents and their adequate expression, since only that is expressed which is actually experienced or only experienced that which can be adequately expressed. As long as the performance deals with subjects which are indiscriminately known to the whole assistance, performers and spectators are either identical or interchangeable or they meet on the same plane. But once the performance enters the sphere of imagination or abstraction invisible barriers first, tangible ones later, separate the initiated actors from the mere audience. At some moment during this evolution the medicine man or priest will seize the prerogative of playing, leading or directing an activity, the suggestive power of which serves his spiritual purposes, and not rarely his practical ones as well. Yet outside the realm of sacred ceremonial arises irresistably an elementary urge to play and act, directly and successfully appealing to the lower instincts of the masses. And henceforth exists a perpetual, open rivalry between the church (in the broadest sense) and popular entertainment.

In chronological or genetical order the ritual precedes any other definite form of beginning theatre, a principle which is again repeated whenever the continuity of evolution has been interrupted. Of the theatrical activities in the oldest civilizations many dramatic and literary documents have been preserved, but comparatively few reliable, specifically theatrical data are available. In particular with reference to the Egyptian theatre the specific knowledge is limited. Owing to modern research and recent authoritative investigation there were several forms of actually enacted drama (the resurrection plays and the 'Coronation Festival Plays', roughly two centuries before the well-known document of an 'Osiris Passion Play' of 2000 B.C., an activity continuing up to the beginning of the Christian era. Presumably played and directed by the priesthood these dramatic ceremonies were performed in "regularly appointed places"; sculptured masks have been in use. There are no substantial indications as to the Hebrew theatre, although the recorded forms of dramtic poetry may lead to such an assumption, and although the Bible frequeutly refers to dance and ceremonial. But the very principle of imagery and theatrical representation was contrary to the Hebrew creed; there were most certainly no theatres in Judea.

The Hindu theatre has a well established theatrical tradition. The early period, strictly religious in its origins, is lost in the dark. While there exists a flourishing, highly poetic Hindu drama, the plays are nevertheless not truly dramatic to our Western comprehension; subjects, language and representations are a refined art, requiring a high level of culture and education from both actors and spectators. Consequently the theatre, in this exclusive form, never became a wide-ranging, popular art; nor was there a necessity for special theatre buildings or stage settings. The modern theatre, under Western influences, has little distinctive character or importance. The **Javanese theatre** is literally related to the Hindu drama. It develops, however, in a curiously independent way which has no analogy whatsoever in the entire history of the theatre. It originates in the shadow-play, which leads to puppet- or marionette-plays, and further to living actors who imitate in costume, make-up and gesture the model of their artificial ancestors. Only lately independent living actors appeared on the stage. The actors are mute; their text is spoken by a reciter. Owing to the immense popularity of the Javanese theatre play houses are built all over the country. The Javanese theatre presents an extraordinary phenomenon which can be correctly and fully appreciated only upon careful analysis.

As a specific art form the **Chinese theatre** is by far the richest and most consistently developed. The literary drama, not prominent in itself, is almost meaningless for any but Eastern appreciation. Although the high standard of the theatrical art is objectively evident its intricate symbolism is scenic traditions, practised and perfected for hundreds of years, is lost to the uninitiated, and we have no means of approach to the significance of the exceedingly strict scenic and histrionic traditions. The very simple scheme of the unchangeable stage, a number of stylized properties and even the plays or dramas themselves, remain merely accesory; it is in the art of the actor alone that the Chinese theatre is represented. His artistic means are conventional, from the wearing of magnificent costumes, to the implications of his every step, movement and gesture; his interpretation is limited to unvarying stock characters which are indicated with mask-like, symbolical make-up, derived from original masks. Yet within these limitations the histrionic art develops consciously and purposefully to still valid, unequaled height of final, formalized expressiveness and utmost artistic completeness. There re many common features between Chinese

and **Japanese theatre**, the latter being imported from China by way of Korea. Two forms of theatre can be clearly distinguished: *No* and *Kabuki*, and an additional, very popular puppet theatre. Originating in the ritual, the *No* play is intellectual, refined and aristocratic, with only the slightest suggestion of a truly dramatic text. The *No* is not popular and not meant to be so. Again, the highly formalized style of the representation and the esoteric associations in word and gesture evoked to the initiated, completely escape our appreciation. There are but few actors in one play; their movements are strictly regulated and formally prescribed; they are impersonal representatives and wear masks. The stage is extremely simple; the only purely decorative element is displayed in the richness of the costumes. This old and noble tradition has been carried on faithfully for over 600 years and is still unchangeably valid. The popular theatre, '*Kabuki*', is much younger and, although secular in dramatic substance, it owes most of its formalism and pantomimic customs to the *No* form. Although no mask is used the make-up still reminds of the mask tradition. The stage however is more elaborate; in 1758 the revolving stage is introduced. In principle any survey of the Oriental theatre, whether thus brief or more explicit, will have to suffer from the fact that our understanding of its innumerable, rich and beautiful manisfestations is limited to mere aesthetical appreciation. Thus the present *No* seems far more remote than the farthest vestiges of the Western theatre world.

The theatre of all Western civilizations is inextricably determined by the powerful stimuli of the **ancient Greek theatre**, the unequaled beauty and harmony of which for long centuries set the standard of perfection for the entire theatre complex: drama, playhouse, histrionism and theory. Thus in litera ture the serious drama is under the overwhelming impression of the gigantic Greek tragedies; the dramatic theory of generations to come depended on the rules of this drama and its theorists. In the field of architecture and scenic settings innumerable formal solutions evidence the respective interpretation or mis-interpretation of the Greek scheme of stage and auditorium. And in the essentially histrionic activity the elementary impulses for true, mimetic expression are released and stimulated.

Once again this theatre originates in sacred ceremonial: the worship of Dionysus, the god of wine and fruitfulness, the great creative power which embraces the spiritual as well as the material and sensual world. At the very beginning are already revealed the two directions of human aspirations, one eventually leading to the tragedy, the other to the comedy and the Satyr-play. The unordered mass of worshippers is soon grouped and organized by a leader, and particularily gifted individuals find an opportunity to detach themselves from the performing group or 'chorus', up till then the centre of the performance and later an integrant part of it. The first who achieved this decisive innovation was Thespis (in 535 B.C.) who probably also introduced the mask. Aeschylus added the second actor, Sophocles the third; thus they created a visual opposition equivalent to the spiritual one and transposed the latent dramatic conflict in the tangible representation of tragedy.

The immediate tradition, however, does not follow the sublime ways of the tragedy, but is rather perpetuated on a considerably lower level by the actors of the comedy and the burlesque Satyr-players, by the comedians of the Roman *mimi* and *atellanae,* all of which are popular comedies or farces with simple plots and stock characters. Here generate the very ancestors of innumerable successive generations of those ever popular actors who fill not only the popular stages, but streets, markets and meeting places, who amuse and entertain the broad masses of populace, who constantly and successfully rival with the serious, elevated, literary theatre. The most important and coherent period of these actors is the era of the commedia dell'arte, the comedy of improvisation powerfully thriving in the 15th and 16th centuries. The force of their improvisations, besides true histrionic genius, is the very simplicity of their plays and plots, the transparency of their characterizations and the easy adaptability to the responsiveness of the varying audiences. Moreover they renounce on the commodities of an elaborate stage or scenic display and technical devices and are thus ever ready to start on the spur of the moment. It always was, and still is, hard for the literary theatre to compete with the spontaneity of such elementary histrionism.

The great contributions to the theatre during the Renaissance, with the revival of the ancient Greek and later Roman theatre, and the Baroque, the sumptuous scenic display of which surrounded magnificent operas or ballets or insignificant dramatic substance, are specially dealt with (see DRAMA; OPERA; STAGESETTING). One sig-nificant event, however, must be mentioned here, although it left no literary or histrionic or even decorative heritage: it is the spontaneous generation of a specific form of theatre in the Middle Ages. The center of this theatre is the Christian ritual. The first sacred dialogues and scenes, enacted by priests within the church, were so successful that they soon outgrew this restricted circle of action, to be transferred on the steps of the church or some public square. Although other sacred subjects are recorded, the main tale of these religious plays, called mystery plays, was the passion of Christ. Innumerable such mystery plays can be traced throughout the 15th, 16th and 17th cents. all over Europe and England. They are wholly undramatic, but highly suggestive and imaginative. Conceived for and played by the entire community they comprise huge masses, either as players or as spectators. There was no stagesetting in the usual sense; but since numerous scenic situations or mansions had to be suggested, the mystery play developed a unique and very characteristic form of simultaneous scene, i.e., of places arranged simultaneously one next to the other. They were often decorated with care and drastic realism. The organization of these giant plays, sometimes lasting for several consecutive days, indicates the great skill of the clerical directors and producers. Yet, despite their wide range of influence, the mystery plays disappear almost and leave no direct traces whatsoever in either the contemporary or the later theatre. Only the "Confrèrerie de la Passion", a group of professional mystery-players, survived, owing to official support and privileges. United with Molière's "troupe" they found (1680) the "Comédie Française" in Paris.

With Shakespeare's dramas and comedies a new specific problem is introduced into the theatre, independent of the flourishing contemporary court theatre. The representation of a Shakespe rean play requires first: actors, capable of differentiated individual characterization; secondly: a stage, suitable for frequent and quick shifting of the scene. The first requirement is soon, and badly, realized: English comedians go on tour on the continent, inaugurating an era of effective, but cheap, drastic, realistic play practice. And although the Elizabethan popular stage must have served its purpose, the second requirement was elsewhere not realized at all. Thus the greatest, genuine theatrical genius fades out of the world of the theatre for several centuries. But again, when he is finally re-discovered and made available in continental translation (in the late 18th cent.), the performance is met with the same two problems. However, in the meanwhile the actor has developed a far more refined art, and soon some prominent ones excel particularly in Shakespearean rôles. Yet, the scenic solution is inseparable from the actor's play. Some remarkable, so-called "Shakespeare-Theatres", accomplish more or less successfully an adaptation of the Elizabethan scheme to modern conditions, fully aware of the actor's predominant position. Up to this day there are almost as many attempted solutions as there are imaginative men at work in the theatre. Indeed, such never ending, fascinating challenge to ever better achievement preserves the theatre from stagnation.

Fundamentally new, and still essentially valid, problems enter the theatre through the medium of the naturalistic dramatic tendencies. Now the actor is to interpret characters conceived not in the sphere of imagination and artistic abstraction, but rather in the psychological climate of human completeness and verity. While, on one side, he is thus led to an overemphasis of merely descriptive detail, he acquires on the other a sensitiveness and nervousness which indicates the temporary break with the ancient mimetic tradition. The conflict is inevitable: any excess of realistic accuracy stresses the incompatibility between the almost-perfection of mere copy and the unrealistic quality of the scenic art. The capacity of physical imitation is, indeed, the very reverse of the histrionic principle. For the object of imitative characterization is reality: its ideal achievement is perfect deception; whereas the object of histrionic characterization is an artistic creation: its ideal achievement is artistic truth.

The concept *theatre* is complex and collective. An intricate composition of particular ethnic and social, spiritual and psychological conditions, of customs, institutions and traditions, of subsidiary arts and contributive crafts, the theatre is determined by a specific process of integration of all or any number of different constituents. This accounts for the infinite variety of position, function and significance of theatrical phenomena, forms and expressions within the cultural pattern of human societies. In aesthetic appreciation it appears as the distinctive characteristic of the theatre to achieve a coherent artistic unity out of numerous elements of divergent nature and order. This ultimate achievement, however, can but partly be preserved in lasting evidence. In fact the ephemeral character of the theatre art work is its specific form of finality and artistic completion. For any theatrical creation is valid and significant in progress only, i.e. in the chronological sequence of those transient instants which compose a continuous dramatic action. These fugitive moments, and only these, yield full and authentic aesthetical information.

The obvious and most striking characteristic of the theatre: the disparity of its sources and origins, the complexity of its contents and aspects, the variety of its manifestations and forms, indicates the quantity as well as the quality of the problems involved. It accounts primarily for the fact that the growing importance of accessory circumstances tends, and sometimes achieves, to obliterate the central figure of the theatre: the performer, be he dancer, mimic, actor or singer. Thus the splendor of the late Renaissance court festivals and the overwhelming scenic display of the Baroque theatre left a great heritage in state design, costume drawings and architectural documents, but only scarce and fragmentary choreographic or histrionic records. Moreover the creation of the performer—however important his individual interpretation or however dramatic the scenic situation—would be incomplete, if not impossible, but for the active and reactive participation of an audience. For the audience is an integral part of the theatrical process proper; between performers and spectators exist functional relations which create suspense and tension not originally or not necessarily resident in the presented subject. Although the position or opposition of performer and public in space has significance beyond the practical requirements of providing favorable visual and auditory conditions, any decorations, scene or architecture supporting and surrounding the performance is merely accessory, even though often artistically relevant in itself. The mise-en-scène and the various artistic elements it is composed of have no intrinsic aesthetical justification; and they give but incomplete information on the theatrical accomplishment.

For the same reasons literary evidence, as contained in a dramatic text or musical evidence, as contained in a score, cannot convey an accurate idea of the eventual scenic interpretation—the latter being a completed crative act in itself. Incidentally this condition points towards the peculiar and consequential problem that a work of art which already constitutes an ordered artistic whole becomes the material of yet another creative process, artistically valid in its own right. As a legitimate artistic category, however, theatre can and must be directly appreciated, independent of any literary or musical consideration. The production of a literary drama or a musical one in terms and with means of the theatre is a genuine artistic creation, and in no way a re-production. Despite the evident interdependence between subject matter and interpretation the validity of a literary drama or an operatic composition does not depend on their actual realization on the stage; nor does a perfect scenic performance imply literary or musical substance of any avail.

Originally the concepts of theatre and drama, danced, enacted, spoken or sung refer to but one and the same phenomenon. In fact the primitive forms of drama are at the same time rudimentary forms of theatre, thus disclosing the identity of their source. The origins of theatre-drama can be identified with those of early ritual. This holds true not only to the extent that both theatre and ritual are integral parts of a homogenous culture characteristic for a given time or people; beyond any such generalization both manifest identical elements in their origins and identical principles in their interpretation. At all times and with all peoples, giving suggestive evidence of universality, these initial spectacles originate spontaneously in a collective emotion, in direct response to the unfathomable, fear- and awe-inspiring mysteries of nature. And almost generally they soon assume the form of either pantomimic or ecstatic dance. As exhibition of a single individual or as ordered group movement, dance unfolds visibly that curious and complex urge to creative self-realization which precedes and also pervades the organized theatrical activities of developed societies. Regardless of various degrees of artistry and elaboration all of these dance spectacles tend to prove that man possesses innate mimetic and rhythmic dispositions. Indeed the impulse to act as well as the urgency to release physical or emotional tension in rhythmical movement antedates any permanent record of art.

At this early stage of civilization the language of tangible images and material symbols is far more developed and differentiated than speech. Thus visible effigies and representative performers stand for phenomena yet beyond the grasp of human comprehension, or eles for facts, observations and experiences yet beyond the capacity of abstracted expression. It also appears that the inadequacy of the spoken language is largely compensated by an extraordinary eloquence of the bodily language, far beyond its usefulness to procure physical symbols for inarticulate or inadequate speech. This language of gestures, at first wholly spontaneous, purely functional or merely useful, gradually develops into an involved system of combined technique and meaning, increasingly independent of primitive impulses or physical necessities. A striking example thereof offers the oriental theatre which developed an immense body of codified gestures and rigid play conventions. Sublimely beautiful, dispassionate and detached the oriental theatre does not permit of spontaneous improvisations, subjective interpretations or the exhibition of individual emotions. Unlike our occidental theatre experience, the pleasure both for the actor and the spectator is derived not from the moments of surprise and suspension, but from the satisfaction of being initiated; not from the immediate impact of strong passions, but from the appreciation of a perfectly controlled play of harmoniously balanced emotions. This tradition has become so integral a part of the entire cultural set-up that it stands, as it may decline, with it. In the western cultures only lately the complex meaning or symbolic signification of gestures has been critically evaluated; quite recently it has been applied purposely in modern dance and, in a less consistent way, in modern acting. However, certain codes and traditions of gestures can be traced almost everywhere; in various forms of ecclesiastical or court ceremonial, in many histrionic conventions, as well as in numeruos minor formal practices down to the curtsey and other social customs.

Despite many obvious discrepancies there appears a repetition of expressive forms and means or a correspondence in the evolution to such forms and means which permit of a schematically valid pattern of the world theatre. In the beginning ritual-dance or ritual-theatre are but instrumentally relevant, i.e. as means for the attainment of real and vital ends. And notwithstanding the metaphysical principle implied in worship of deities, spirits, demons and personified cosmic or physical phenomena, the primitive ritual emphasizes practical rather than spiritual issues; no categorical distinction can yet be made between the performance of ritual and proper secular ceremonies or even the formal routine of organized pleasure and play. The subsequent differentiation is not due to a conscious, cognitive act; it is rather an instinctive, twofold expression of the latent dualism between material and spiritual tendencies. And when eventually they grow apart, visual and visionary world still hold on identical quality of magic and fascination. This beocmes particularly evident in the important rites related to the generative powers of nature. Contributing a great variety of subjects and forms they cover a wide range, from strict ritual and solemn ceremonies, through orgiastic pageants, to phallic symbolism and frankly erotical performances. Although the profane tendency often shows in ostensible exaggerations, comical imitations and vulgar or burlesque allusions, the majority of these performances discloses nevertheless the characteristics of a metaphysical origin.

The performers, however drastic in suggestions and expressions, feel themseves as integral parts of an inspired collective or as participants in a sacred service. On the other side, the practice in dealing with fearsome superhuman forces or religious mysteries requiring knowledge and involving responsibilities beyond the scope of ordinary man, it often develops into the exclusive and esoteric office of privileged representatives: medicine man, magician, sorcerer or priest. Supposed to be endowed with mysterious qualities they assume high authority and frequently the rank of accomplished professionals in acting and experts in directing and choreography.

The gradual transition from these various ceremonies to genuine theatre-drama parallels the significant process of dance expression yielding its dominant position to the medium of speech. Indeed the human experience that urges and desires, motions, thoughts and feelings are thus communicable must be considered a revelation of immeasurable consequence. No longer restrained by the physical limitations of bodily expression and symbolic language, man avidly grasps and develops the potentialities and almost unlimited means to convey something on the strength of essentially spiritual effort. This new power of communication of the non-visible or the non-present breaks the boundaries of time and space, appropriates the past and future and the dimension of imagination. Consequently the circle presented subjects widens considerably, from the simple form of spontaneous narration of actual incidents and events, through the primitive and oriental theatre has been or historical legends, to real hopes, wishes and formulated expectations, and eventually to pure abstractions. Often the components of these

tales already hold potential dramatic tension, i.e., a latent antagonism between opposed persons, groups or tendencies. This ever possible conflict, presented so as to form a consistent plot or story, is the very essence of drama, whether visually enacted or spiritually sublimated in poetry.

It should be borne in mind, however, that representations essentially without speech, like dance, dance-drama and pantomine constitute primitive forms of the theatre only with reference to a strictly genetical order; regarding their artistic significance they may, and often do, represent the highest conceivable form of artistic accomplishment. This again applies particularly to the evaluation of tribal dance and oriental performances. In a generic appreciation the almost complete absence of intrinsically relevant dramatic literature—if dramatic at all—in primitive cultures or in the Orient as compared to the volume and consequence of dramatic literature in the Occident tends to further confuse the theatrical issue. Latest in every theatre history, the literary drama is but one of several specific forms of dramatic expression all of which are equally genuine and legitimate branches of the theatre complex. Music also parallels the evolution of the theatre, from the simple beating of time, the regular reiteration of sounds, rhythmic songs and monophonic tunes, to elaborate polyphonic accompaniment, symphonic compositions and musical drama (see opera). Although a special survey is beyond the scope of this study the increasing importance of music for the development of dance (q.v.) and any but the literary drama (q.v.) is duly emphasized.

Gradually the periodical repetition and seasonal recurrence of typical performances leads to regular and increasingly strict and ingenious conventions and traditions, with dance providing physical pattern, spatial organization and harmonious rhythm, i.e. structural elements for the development of artistic form. It would be conjectural though to determine to what extent the formal stylization in so-called 'primitive' art, as manifested in theatrical expressions and attributes: masks, costumes, make-up, dance steps, dance gestures, etc., denotes an intrinsic artistic quality or rather one inferred by subsequent aesthetic evaluation. So far our appreciation of any historical and foreign, and in particular of historical and foreign, and in particular of the primitive and oriental theatre has been largely determined by and expressed in terms of an aesthetic experience. Of necessity this approach not only lacks the spontaneousness and immediacy of response which is so essentially theatric, but also the all-inclusive completeness of understanding which is determined by the material circumstance of participation; the immediate reference to actuality, directly and strongly appealing to the contemporaries or active witnesses, is irremediably lost to later generations or detached investigators. The complex of material evidence preserved and handed down as thatrical 'form' is not only an aesthetic expression of specific dramatic contents, but just as much a function of the respective social circumstances, and often not more than accidental solution conditioned by technical facilities or concessions. These simple considerations may account for the manifest failure of various attempts at literally reviving, in substance and form, e.g. the Antique festivals, the Mystery plays, the Elizabethan stage or the ceremonies of primitive peoples.

Outside our well defined cultural circle we cannot rely on an objective test of authenticity for the appreciation of theatrical art and activity. Any theatrical creation, inasmuch as it corresponds to the particular cultural set-up wherein it occurs, carries its very own justification. For example the formal perfection and expressive power of theatrical masks may easily lead to the conclusion that they represent ends intentionally artistic in themselves, and which are meant to be appreciated as such. However originally they are conceived merely as scenic means, instrumental in portraying or emphasizing dramatic characters—for an audience which comprehends the immediate meaning and implication rather than the abstracted quality of artistic significance. Yet beyond any such usefulness, the universally recognized validity of the mask tends to prove that it is more than an ever fascinating accessory: the theatrical symbol of an anthropological principle. Thus it can safely be assumed that a thorough analysis of its origins and forms and varying significance will yield invaluable information toward the understanding of the origins and the psychological implications of theatrical phenomena in general.

Originally not the mask, but its wearer is the accessory, although the terrifying potentialities of the symbol may eventually be identified with himself. Feeling himself distinguished through the inherent power of the symbol, though arbitrarily vested with, the wearer often develops, mystically or rationally, the distinctive personality that adequately fills the given form. This holds particularly true for the representation of divine, imaginary, legendary or allegorical characters. Such symbolic validity can but be conceived in complete religious, social or ethnic integration, as e.g., in ancient Egypt and Greece, in China and Japan, in primitive cultures. But, more generally, whenever it appears first the mask stands in its own right, without necessary reference to the wearer and his individual capacity of interpretation or transformation. As long as the actor wears a mask—whether carved in wood, modelled in plastic material or painted on with heavy make-up—he remains virtually anonymous, his every distinctive feature pointing towards the accomplishment of a stylized symbol, type or character established and admitted in advance.

The continuance of this practice explains the eventual fixation of rigid, permanent characters: 'stock-characters', representing generalized human traits, features or types. By their very form of summary characterization they determine a simple form of drama, requiring little, if any, literaty substance and only the merest suggestion of costume, stage and decoration. Serving the purpose of easy appreciation for an unpretentious or uncultured audience, they are typical for all forms of popular entertainment. And regardless of the theatre's constantly varying poetic climates and scenic surroundings they are faithfully preserved and transmitted from one generation to another. Sometimes they also seem to generate spontaneously; for there are many instances when they appear without any possible or provable direct contact or chronological sequence. Thus stock-characters dominate the ancient Greek and Roman comedies; they flourish magnificently in the Commedia dell' Arte, whence they spread over the whole Western world, clearly manifest also in the comedies of Gozzi, Goldoni and Molière; they persist universally in the tradition of the puppet- and marionette-play; and they can yet be recognized on the contemporary stage.

Mask and stock-characters begin to disappear with the progress of the literary drama which opens a new histrionic era by introducing individual instead of typical characters into the theatre. As histrionic conceptions the two are mutually exclusive. The stock-character, on one side, is originally appreciated for the very condensation and stylization which prevents it from representing a dramatic character as a consistent, if not human, totality. Assembled in a cumulative process it is a schematic personage with virtually the same position and function in every dramatic constellation. It should be remembered though that in a later stage of evolution in the occidental theatre their number attained up to several hundred varieties, thereby demonstrating a symptomatic tendency toward individual discrimination. On the other side the truly individual character, as conceived by a dramatist, is not just another variation of a standard type, but a genuine creation, valid only with reference to one specific and unique drama. This condition, however, does not imply that there is but one possible, ideally 'correct' interpretation for each role. It mainly indicates a fundamental change in the histrionic attitude.

In historical perspective the change does not appear as radical as in fact it is, because it is far less obvious in the dramatic literature which is wholly preserved than in the histrionic achievement which is wholly lost. However, regarding the histrionic potentialities the artistic relevance of the drama itself is of secondary importance, for the actor is not concerned with the intrinsic quality of the dramatic subject matter, nor with the literary merit of the art work. The absolute standard of his art depends on his individual vision and accomplishment rather than on the dramatist's. More generally all histrionic efforts and energies are merely means toward a definite final effect: the direct impact upon a receptive mass. The immediate response of the audience is an infallible, in fact the only, test for the actor's achievement or failure; even though such spontaneous mass judgment is forcibly subject to endless subsequent revisions.

Notoriously the dubious and often equivocal relation between the drama as a literary product and the drama as a stage play tends to obscure the one significant fact: that the actor himself is truly creative. The identity between a literary figure and its histrionic counterpart cannot be preconceived, but has to be created in each individual instance. The actor does precisely this. Realizing the perennial human desire for transformation he creates an original personification which never existed before and admits of no duplication or imitation—not even by himself. This also accounts for an infinite variety of equally significant and convincing renditions of one and the same dramatis persona.

Primarily it is not so much important that a dramatic message be worth while to be communicated than that it be communicable at all. But it is also obvious that subject matter and form determine the interpretation to a very large extent. Involved scenic situations and complicated characters require a specific expressive technique in order to adequately cope with the increasing complexity of the task. In the early stages of theatre history there is no conflict as yet between spiritual, emotional or factual contents and their histrionic expression, since only that is expressed which is actually experienced or only experienced that which can be adequately expressed. As long as the performance deals with subject matter indiscriminately known to the entire assistance, performers and spectators are either identical or interchangeable. But once the performance enters the sphere of individual imagination and personal interpretation invisible barriers first, tangible ones later, separate the now essentially creative actor from an essentially receptive audience. At some psychologically significant moment in this evolution the medicine man or priest, on the strength of legitimate authority, seizes the prerogative of playing, leading or directing an activity, the potentialities of which serve his spiritual purposes, and not rarely his practical ones as well. Yet outside the realm of sacred ceremonial arises irresistably again the elementary urge to play and act, directly originating from or successfully appealing to the primitive instincts of the masses. And henceforth exists a perpetual, open rivalry between the representative drama of the church (in the broadest sense) and the popular theatre of the crowds. Naturally the popular forms of drama often degenerate into vulgarity and license, thus furnishing an ever valid motivation for the traditional anathema against mimes and comedians. It is certain, however, that as far as the European theatre is concerned but for this coarse mimetic activity there would hardly be any theatre at all between the disintegration of the Roman Empire and the revival of the ancient Greek and Roman theatre in the early Renaissance.

Fundamentally new, and still essentially valid problems enter the theatre with the naturalistic conception of the arts in general and of drama in particular. Here and now the actor is to interpret characters not within the open spaces of mimetic spontaneousness, nor within the wide horizons of poetic imagination, but expressly in the close perspective of physical and psychological veracity. While, on one side, he is thus lead to a confusing accumulation of artistically irrelevant, descriptive details, he acquires on the other a sensitiveness, nervous refinement and analytical knowledge which benefits him with the microscopic technique of the film. Evidently this means a clear break with countless centuries of histrionic tradition, and the beginning of a problematic era. Problematic because the aesthetic (and indirectly the psychological) conflict resulting from this artistic attitude is unavoidable: any excess of realistic accuracy stresses the incompatibility between the almost-perfection of mere copy and the unrealistic quality of the scenic atmosphere. And the capacity of imitation is indeed the very reverse of the histrionic principle. For the principle of imitative characterization is the attempt at objectively creating reality; its ideal achievement is deception. The principle of histrionic characterization is an attempt at subjectively creating illusion; its ideal achievement is art.

In conclusion it may be said that any productive investigation of the theatre depends on the basic notion that theatrical reality, in whatever representation of dance, play and drama, is not conditioned upon its relation to objective, concrete appearance in space, nor on its measurable duration in time, but on the participants' spontaneous or deliberate acceptance of its specific validity. The typical conflicting views with regard to this condition are mainly due to the antagonistic directions of artistic endeavor: one tended toward unrealistic fantasy, the other directed toward naturalistic resemblance; each corresponding to either extreme of the performer's or spectator's motional or rational approach to scenic reality. However, if the scenic reality is to have artistic relevance, such relevance depends solely upon the degree of genuine theatric perfection, not on the exactitude, probability or truthfulness obtained in one direction, nor on the quantitative effort of imagination expended in the other.

Cheney, Sheldon, *The Theatre: Three Thousand Years of Drama, Acting and Stagecraft,* New York, 1941; Freedley, George and Reeves John A., *A History of the Theatre,* New York, 1941; Hughes, Glenn, *A story of the Theatre, A Short History of Theatrical Art from its Beginnings to the Present Day,* New York, 1938; Nicoll, Allardyce, *The Development of the Theatre. A Study of Theatrical Art from The Beginning to the Present Day,* New York, 1927.   —G.A.

theatre art. Art involved in theatre or dramatic activities, as setting the stage, providing lighting, and making costumes, properties,

and scenery. Whitford and Winslow in *Dictionary of Education.*

theatre dance. A term used for a dance manner designed for the entertainment of the theatre audience. Because dance moves too swiftly for its meaning to be grasped by the average audience, it is essential that it be presented as directly and vividly as possible. To accomplish this dance calls to its aid costuming, helpful properties, music, and lighting as well as realistic and pantomimic movement. Although theatre dance, as it is known at the present writing, is not dance in its most highly developed abstract art form, nevertheless, it is a vehicle for great artistic treatment and it will continue to be an important agent in educating audiences in dance appreciation. (H'Doubler, M. N., *Dance, A Creative Art Experience,* F. S. Crofts & Co., 1940.)

theatrical costume. See COSTUME ART.

thematic development. *Mus..* The varied repetition of a theme to bring out its inherent resources.

theme (Gr. *thema,* fr.*tithenai,* to set, place). (1) An image or set of images, details, qualities, ideas or appearances capable of being repeated, varied and contrasted with others. Such repetition, variation, and contrast are the basis of *thematic* development, *design,* and *decorative* composition (q.v.). The term is used most often in music, where it is applied to a short melody which constitutes the basis of variation and development. It is also applied to the visual arts and literature, where (for example) a certain color, pattern, or idea may be taken as a subject for repetition with modification. A *design* is an aesthetic form, or a factor in one, involving relatively complex and unified thematic development.
                                                                    —T.M.

(2) *Mus.* Musical idea; subject of a composition, susceptible of being treated in many various ways, the context of these treatments forming the *raison d'être* and the logical coherence of the composition. The theme may be identical with a motif (as it is the case with many fugue themes), or it may be a composite of several, even contrasting, elements (as it is the case with many sonata themes), provided these elements are welded together into one unit.   —E.K.

(3) *Dance.* In its broadest meaning *theme* is a term used to denote subject matter or content of any nature, principal, or subsidiary. In its fullest significance, however, it applies

to the main topic to be developed into a complete dance composition. The theme may originate in any activity, rhythmic scheme, feeling state, idea, literary concept, or a dramatic plot. —M.N. H'D.

theorbo. See MUSICAL INSTRUMENTS.

theory of musical performance. See MUSICAL PERFORMANCE, MAIN TRENDS IN

Theremin. See electrical instruments; MUSICAL INSTRUMENTS.

thermionic valve. See electrical instruments.

thin ink landscape. See CHINESE ARTS.

thinner. As the word is used in the paint trades, thinner can apply to either a solvent or a diluent of a painting medium. It may also be applied to a mixture of both and designates any fluid used to reduce a film material to a consistency suitable for application. Technically, a thinner is a diluent rather than a solvent. —G.L.S.

thirty-three gods. See INDIAN ART.

Thoueris. Ta-urt.

thread mark. Marks on the bottom of Japanese pottery caused by the use of a thread to separate the object from the potter's wheel.

three-color ware. Chinese pottery, the decoration of which is in red, blue and yellow colors.

three-element tube. See electrical instruments.

three-point perspective. See PERSPECTIVE.

through. See bond-stone.

through stones. In masonry: Stones which extend through the entire thickness of a wall to tie or bond it.

throwing. *Cer.* Process of forming ware by hand on potter's wheel. See CERAMICS I.

Thule art. See Eskimo art.

Thuluth script. See ISLAMIC ART.

thumb-index. *Book.* Half circles cut from the fore-edge for different sections of a book.

thumb ring. A large Chinese ring, generally made of jade, ivory or metal, worn on the thumb. See JEWELRY.

thunderbolt. See vajra (Skr.); ko (Jap.); dorje (Tib.); see SYMBOLISM IN FAR EASTERN ART.

thyara. See tiara, papal.

thyrsus. A staff surmounted by branches or a pine cone. Carried in Egypt, in Greek and Roman Bacchic rites, in May festivals in Europe. See FLOWER ARRANGEMENT.

tiaoch'i (Ch.). Carved lacquer ware.

tiara, papal. A head-dress of the Pope, used on occasions of high solemnity, but not during liturgical functions; at least from Innocent III (1198-1216) sometimes considered as symbol of the Pope's temporal power (cf. Migne, P. L. 217, 481 and 665). The shape was originally more or less conical, but since the 16th cent. the top is rounded and the sides almost straight. The tiara is surmounted by a little globe with the cross. In its present form it is adorned by three crown-like circlets, surrounding the body of the tiara at its base, middle and top. Originally, however, these crowns were lacking, although, from an early period, a diadem-like band, surrounded the base; the so-called *caudae* or *lemnisci* or *infulae*, bands hanging from the back or from the sides of the tiara, may have developed from the ends of the "diadem-band" just mentioned. The term *tiara* occurs in Herodotus and other Greek sources to designate a well-known Persian head-gear, esp. that of the king; some of the royal tiaras on Parthian coins are surprisingly similar to papal tiaras, not of the Middle Ages, but of the Renaissance, surely an accidental similarity. The name *tiara* is also used in the *Vulgata* for the head-dress of the Jewish High Priest (along with other expressions; see *Exodus* 28, 37; 29, 6; 39, 30; *Leviticus* 8, 9). Before the 16th cent., however, the usual names for what we call the papal tiara were *camelaucum, phrygium, regnum, corona, diadema,* and finally *triregnum* after the addition of the three crowns; the term *thyara* first occurs in the life of Pope Paschal II (1099-1118) in the *Liber Pontificalis,* but remains rare to the end of the Middle Ages. There is no direct evidence of the sources that would prove that the tiara of the Jewish high priest influenced the early development of the papal tiara. In literary sources the papal tiara first appears in the life of Pope Constantine (708-715) in the *Liber Pontificalis,* and there is called *camelaucum* which is still the name of a liturgical head-dress in the Greek rites. A little later, in the forged "Donation of Constantine" the name of the papal tiara is *phrygium*. Both these names indicate origin from the east, and it is probable that hats or caps of conical shape, worn by Byzantine secular dignitaries, were used as models for the earliest papal tiara, which probably did not come into use before the wave of oriental influence swept over Rome in the 7th and early 8th cents. It is not impossible that the origin of the papal tiara had something to do with the beginnings of papal sovereignty in the nascent Papal States.

As to the first appearance of the crownless conical tiara of the Pope in surviving monuments, we have to refer to a coin of Sergius III (904-911). It is still rare in the 11th cent.; see e.g. the frescos in the lower church of *S. Clemente* in Rome. In this period the conical hat was also used by bishops outside Rome, to whom it usually had been conferred as a special honor by the pope; a clearer distinction between the tiara as a papal, non-liturgical and the mitre (q.v.) as a pontifical, liturgical head-dress took place soon afterwards; special forms of the mitre make their appearance in the monuments from around 1100 onward.

Benzo of Alba (*MG. SS.* 11, 672) says that in the coronation of Nicolas II (1059) Hildebrand caused a royal crown of two circles to be added to the tiara; perhaps he meant to say that this crown was no longer the diadem-like band, but that points or fleurons had been added like in the medieval royal crowns. Such a crown, at any rate, can be found on the base of the tiara in surviving monuments from the time of Innocent III (1198-1216). The older form with the simple band, however, still occurs in the monuments throughout the 13th century, and even longer.

A new and decisive change in the papal tiara occurred under Boniface VIII (1294-1303), as can still be seen in the extant effigies of this Pope; the change was probably made in the first Holy Year, in 1300. The height of the tiara was much increased so that it reached the extent of a cubit, which was the mystical measure used in the building of Noah's Ark, that ancient symbol of Church unity; thus the tiara's height of a cubit could serve as a symbolic indication of the Pope's leadership of the one and universal Church (see Bull *Unam Sanctam;* cf. Ladner and Schramm). Furthermore, in the tiara of Boniface, the ancient diadem-like band on the base was now combined with two crowns;

one of them found its place immediately above the diadem, the other higher up. The recumbent Sepulchral statue of Boniface VIII in the *Grotte Vaticane,* it is true, does not clearly show the three circlets, but they can be seen in the statue in the *Museo Petriano* in Rome, which was likewise part of the sepulchre, and in that of S. Giovanni in Laterano; it is therefore, misleading to call the tiara of Boniface VIII a two-crown tiara, as is usually done. Boniface VIII tiara is actually enriched by three symbols of rulership, one diadem and two crowns, a fact which is borne out by papal inventories of the early 14th cent. which speak of the tiara of this Pope as adorned with three golden circles (see F. Ehrle, in: *Archiv für Literatur und Kirchengeschichte* 4 [1888] 191 ff.). It is probable that in conformity with Boniface VIII far-reaching formulations of the papal *plenitudo potestatis*, the three circles of his tiara symbolized the highest priesthood and the imperial and royal dignities. Perhaps, at this time, the tiara of the Jewish high priest also exerted some influence upon the development of the papal one, seeing that Josephus in his *Antiquitates* (3, 7, 6), which had long been part of Christian literary tradition, had said that the Jewish tiara was adorned with three crowns; still it must be said that there is no reference to the Jewish tiara in the sources dealing with that of Boniface VIII.

It was during the pontificate of one of the Avignonese Popes, probably Benedict XII (1334-42) or Clement VI (1342-52), that the diadem on the base of the tiara was replaced by a crown, so that three real crowns were placed one above the other at equal intervals. Since then there was no further essential change in the form of the papal tiara, except that it gradually lost its sharply conical form. See M. A. Mazzaroni, *De tribus coronis Pontifici Maximi,* 1587; G. Garampi, *Illustrazione di un antico sigillo della Garfagnana,* 1759; E. Wüscher-Becchi, Ursprung der päpstlichen Tiara (regnum) und der bischöflichen Mitra, *Römische Quartalschrift,* 13, 1889, 77 ff.; E. Müntz, La tiare pontificale du 8e au 16e siècle, *Mémoires de l'Académie des Inscriptions et Belles-Lettres,* 36, 1, 1897, 235 ff.; J. Braun, *Die liturgische Gewandung im Occident und Orient,* 1907, 489 ff.; K. Burdach, *Vom Mittelalter zur Reformation,* 2, 1, 1913-28; G. B. Ladner, Die Statue Bonifaz VIII. in der Lateranbasilika und die Entstehung der dreifach gekrönten Tiara, *Römische Quartalschrift,* 42, 1934, 35 ff.; P. E. Schramm, Zur Geschichte der päpstlichen

Tiara, *Historische Zeitschrift*, 152, 1935, 307 ff.   —G.B.L.

tie. In construction: A structural member, as a timber, rod, etc., binding two bodies together, which have a tendency to separate or diverge from each other.   —J.M.M.

tie-dyeing. A textile technique whereby the stuff is gathered up in small areas and wound with a dye-resisting thread, then dipped in the dye. When dry, the thread is removed thus producing a spotted patterned fabric.
                             —J.A.M.

t'ieh. See SYMBOLISM IN FAR EASTERN ART.

t'ien huang. (Ch.). Seal.

tier. (1) To pile up in successive layers or ranges. (2) A rank or row in a series of things placed one above another.

tierce de picardie. See scales and modes.

tiger. See SYMBOLISM IN FAR EASTERN ART.

tight back. *Book.* When the back of the cover is attached to the back of the paper and bends with the book when it is opened.

timbre. That characteristic of tone which depends upon its harmonic structure, pitch level, and total intensity. The *harmonic structure* is expressed in terms of the number, the distribution, the relative intensity, and the phase relations of the partials in the tone. In a given tone this **harmonic structure usu**ally varies with the *pitch* of the fundamental and the total *intensity* of the tone. The word timbre, like the word pitch, is a psychological term referring to the mental aspect in hearing. But like pitch, it is often correctly used with reference to the physical aspect or in situations referring to both the physical and the mental. As we define pitch in terms of *frequency* of sound waves so we define timbre or, overtone structure, with reference to the *form* of the sound wave as expressed in terms of *harmonic structure* (q.v.). For certain purposes, timbre may, however, be defined in purely psychological terms giving recognition to the mental, musical, and auditory points of view.

Physically, the timbre of a tone is a cross section of tone quality for the moment represented by the duration of one vibration in the sound. It is mainly in terms of timbre that we differentiate the tonal character of

musical instruments, of voice, of vowels, and all other sounds in art and nature.

The word *timbre* is a French word meaning stamp or character. The French pronunciation seems to add mystery to the connotation. I propose, therefore, that we pronounce the word in English as approved by Webster and use it as frequently and naturally as we use the word *pitch* or *time* and with the same degree of clarity.

Aside from the names for vowels, we have no satisfactory names for the vast variety of timbres possible. But progress in modern acoustics gives promise of a progressive building of terminology for timbre in terms of characteristics of the spectrum. It is quite within bounds of possibility to define and popularize a dozen or twenty names for the timbre of musical tones in terms of the position and relative dominance of its for-**mant** or resonance-regions. For example, one beautiful voice has a dominant region composed of the lower partials. Another, a next higher group, and so forth. Each formant region may be characterized by a wide or narrow band of partials. Another tone may be characterized by the presence of three or four namable formant regions. In other words, we have the material and the exact definition of the terms which can define any musical tone and the immediate problem is to familiarize ourselves with a working number of such classes. See phonophotography; sound wave; wave form; oscillogram; tone spectrum; tone generator; training in musical skills; timbre, sense of.   —C.E.S.

timbre, sense of. A measure of talent or capacity for the hearing of the timbre (q.v.) of musical tones. Individuals may differ in capacity for hearing of timbre just as they differ in capacity for hearing pitch or rhythm. One individual may be 100 times as sensitive to timbre or tone quality as another individual of equal intelligence and training. The measurement may be made with a tone generator (q.v.) or with phonograph records as in one of Seashore's *Measures of Musical Talent* of which the following is a description.

For the purpose of building a measure of the sense of timbre we took a tone with the fundamental pitch of F sharp composed of six adjacent partials of known energy which made a rich and pleasing tone. To vary the steps of difficulty in this tone certain amounts of energy were taken from the third partial and added to the fourth with the total intensity of the tone kept constant. The problem was to measure the least perceptible change in timbre caused by such shift. Ordinarily such measurements are made by the use of actual musical instruments but here the measurement is reduced to exact laboratory procedure whether it is made directly from the tone generator or from an adequate phonograph record from it.

For music and speech, this measure furnishes an index to the natural ability that a person tested has for hearing differences in "kind of tone" such as differences between instruments, differences in the playing of a given instrument, or in voices. A full account of this measure is contained in the reference here given: Saetveit, Joseph G., Lewis, Don, and Seashore, Carl E.: The Revision of the Seashore Measures of Musical Talents, *University of Iowa Studies,* 1940.

—C.E.S.

timbre vibrato. See vibrato.

time imperfect (tempus imperfectum). See MEDIEVAL MUSIC.

time perfect (tempus perfectum). See MEDIEVAL MUSIC.

Timurid art. See ISLAMIC ART.

tinctures. See HERALDRY.

ting (Ch.). Sacrificial bronze vessel; three-legged, with two upright vertical handles and sometimes a cover. Occasionally a square form. Used to hold sacrificial food.

—J.A.M.

t'ing. See CHINESE ARTS.

ting yao (Ch.). *Ting* pottery or *ting* ware. A thin, white porcellaneous pottery, semi-translucent and sonorous.

tint. Any color tone which has more or less brilliance than it would have in its spectral hue.

tip. This is a tool used by gilders and is a very thin, flat, square brush made of long hair. The hair is mounted in a light handle, usually of cardboard. The tip is used for picking up gold leaf from the gilder's cushion and laying it on the area where it is to stay.

—G.L.S.

t'i pa (Ch.). A general annotation written on painting or on the mounting of a painting.

tipi (Dakota, dwelling). The tipi, the conical house of the Plains Indians, was well adapted to their nomad life because it is portable and easily erected. It is made of three or four poles set up like a tripod and covered, originally, with buffalo hide strongly staked down, but now with canvas. At the smoke hole left at the apex are two projections or ears held by poles, which control the draft and cover the opening in bad weather. The exterior is often decorated with geometric or representational paintings. An average tipi is 15 ft. in diameter and 15 or more ft. in height.

—H.G.

tipped-in. *Book.* When a leaf, illustration, map, etc., is pasted in without guarding it is said to be tipped in.

t'i shih (Ch.). A poem inscribed on a painting.

titanium white. The white dioxide of the metal, titanium, has been found to have good qualities as a painter's pigment. It is distinguished by its hiding power in which it is stronger than white lead and far stronger than zinc white. Although it can be used pure, titanium pigment usually contains some amount of other white, the most common being barium sulphate in the amount of about 75 per cent. This is a modern pigment. The ore has been known since the latter part of the 18th cent. but only in 1916 to 1919 was the commercial production of the white undertaken.

—G.L.S.

title-poem (Fr. *titre poème*). See collage.

Tjurunga. See AUSTRALIAN ABORIGINAL ART.

Tlingit art. See Northwest Coast Indian art.

T-motif. An art motive often seen in Oriental art resembling the capital letter T.

to (Ch.). Bell form with clapper and handle.

toad. See SYMBOLISM IN FAR EASTERN ART.

toccata. See overture.

togidashi (Jap.). A term applied to lacquerware when gold, or silver, leaf is laid on and polished flush with the surface.

togidashi-makie (Jap.). A lacquer technique whereby the raised pattern is produced by successive layers of pure lacquer, polished.

tohunga (Maori). A leader skilled in the crafts or possessing traditional lore. See Maori carving.

oiles-de-jouy. Printed curtains, popular during the time of Louis XV. See INTERIOR ARCHITECTURE AND DECORATION; POST-REVOLUTIONARY ARCHITECTURE AND DECORATIVE ARTS IN THE U. S. A.

toki (Jap.). Glazed earthenware.

Tokoname yaki (Jap.). Pottery made in Owari province.

tokonoma (Jap.). A recessed place of honor in a Japanese house in which *objets d'art* are shown. See JAPANESE ART.

Tokugawa art. See JAPANESE ART.

olerance. *Mus.* The limit beyond which attempted artistic deviation or erratic deviation from the exact score or other supposed indications of fidelity and regularity in pitch, intensity, time, or timbre ceases to be acceptable. —C.E.S.

Toltec. Master builders; the generic name given to the makers of the high cultures in central Mexico. The term is applied in two ways: one, to dynastic groups who probably introduced and spread the Mixteca-Puebla cuture; second and more vaguely, to the makers of the Teotihuacan culture in central Mexico. —G.C.V.

tomb figures. See CHINESE ARTS.

tomoe (Jap.). A comma form. Two (or three) are often arranged to form a circular area. Used as a *mon* (q.v.) or as a decorative design. Its exact origin is unknown. —J.A.M.

tonalism. See POST-REVOLUTIONARY PAINTING AND SCULPTURE IN THE U. S. A.

tonality. See idiom B.

tone. The designation of any color considered with respect to its attributes but indefinite as to the characterization of its attributes.

tone color. The *timbre* of a tone when the reference is to the tone spectrum and *tone quality,* when the reference is to the tone or selection as whole, including both timbre and sonance. It is proposed to scrap the ill-defined musical term color and adopt in the arts of music and speech the terms *quality* and *imbre,* meaning kind of tone as now defined in psychology and the physicial sciences. See tone quality. —C.E.S.

tone generator. An instrument for the generating of sounds in terms of blueprints or specifications for tonal timbre. There are now many forms of tone generators in use. For the purpose of description of the principles involved, the Iowa tone generator may serve as an example.

"This tone generator is built on the electrostatic principle and is capable of generating 16 pure tones standing in a harmonic series, thus representing 16 partials, or in music terminology, the fundamental and the first 15 overtones, if sounded together. Each of these partials can be varied in intensity. The wave phase can be kept constant. The instrument is therefore capable of producing any desired timbre of tone, generally spoken of as tone quality or color, that can be obtained from the permutations of 16 variables, which is more than a million. It therefore makes it possible for us to set up any kind (timbre) of a tone that may be desired and for each one of this enormous number of possibilities, to state exactly what the harmonic structure of the tone is in terms of the number of partials present, the amount of energy in each one, and the distribution of regions of energy. For example, the harmonic structure of any instrument, voice, or vowel within this range can be produced and reported with precision. Frankly, the performance of the instrument seems almost magical. This feeling is intensified when we submit the resulting complex tone to harmonic analysis (q.v.) and find that the tone spectrum built on the harmonic analysis corresponds exactly to the registration of the structure as set up on the tone generator.

"To put these technical statements into simpler language: here is an instrument with which we can produce any complex tone of harmonic structure that can be built from a fundamental with as many as 15 overtones varying in prominence; we know exactly what the structure of the tone is to be in scientific terms; and we can verify the accuracy of the production by comparing the harmonic analysis of it with the prediction. For example, if we have the tone spectrum for a given section of the note played by a great violinist, we can set up that tone on the generator, hear it sounded, and analyze it to see just to what extent the imitation corresponds to the original." C. E. Seashore, *Musical Educators Journal,* October, 1939. See E. B. Kurtz and M. J. Larsen, An Electrostatic Audiogenerator, *Electrical Engineer,* September, 1935. —C.E.S.

tone quality. That aspect of a tone which differentiates it from other tones in terms of timbre (q.v.) and sonance (q.v.). The most important basic attribute of all music is tone quality, meaning kind of tone. Tone quality, like harmony, volume and rhythm, is a complex in which the four elemental attributes of tone—pitch, loudness, time and timbre—function. In terms of these we can measure and describe all kinds of tone.

A musical tone has several distinct lives. It exists in the mind of the composer as image and idea; a great composer not only images the tonal structure which he is to employ, but hears out his composition realistically without recourse to any instrument. It exists in the mind of the performer, again as image and idea accompanied by musical feeling; the musical score is merely a cue which gives a basic suggestion for the artist to interpret. It exists as a physical tone consisting of sound waves. It exists in the mind of the listener, who experiences the tonal message in accordance with his capacities, musical background, and personality.

At each and all of these stages, we must consider the structure or quality; i.e., kind of tone. At the physical stage, the sound camera can intercept the tone and furnish a complete quantitative description of it in terms of sound waves. Therefore, both science and the art of music begin at this stage and work backward and forward towards the physiological, the psychological, and the musical interpretations.

It is entirely legitimate for a musician to describe his tone primarily in exact physical terms—indeed it should be demanded of him—even though he may be fully cognizant of the fact that the physical tone does not exactly correspond with what the artist intended or what the listener is to hear. Endless confusion comes into musical accounts of tones by a careless flirting between the physical and the mental facts.

Everything that is conveyed from the performer to the listener through hearing, is conveyed on the sound wave. The sound wave has four variables: frequency, which gives us pitch; amplitude, which gives us loudness; duration, which gives us time; and wave form, which gives us timbre, the crowning jewel of richness and beauty in sound structure.

Every sound wave has form. Form is absolutely as basic as frequency, intensity, and duration. This form is determined by the number, distribution, relative intensities, and phase relationships, of the partials.

In terms of the form of the wave, harmonic analysis (q.v.) enables us to describe completely the structure of a tone for that brief instant in which the single wave operates. This gives us a cross-section of the tone, revealing its basic structure. A diagram of this is called a tone spectrum (q.v.). In physics, the fundamental and its overtones are called partials, each treated as a single pure tone in the complex harmonic structure which the ear tends to integrate into a unitary tone or clang. We speak of this integration of the partials in a single complex wave as simultaneous fusion. In music this represents timbre, so far as we can symbolize the mental object by the physical object, and the tone spectrum, therefore, becomes a timbre pattern.

Exact measurements show that, almost without exception, the form of the sound wave changes from wave to wave; i.e., there is an internal flux among the partials that changes the tone from moment to moment, from wave to wave, throughout the duration of the tone. This stage, which contributes towards the quality of the tone, we call successive fusion. We have coined the term sonance (q.v.) to represent this progressive change in a tone.

The situation is analogous to that of the moving-picture film. The first frame of a series depicting, e.g., the progress of a smile, is a complete picture in itself; but each successive frame is slightly different, and the frames occur with such frequency that the pictures fuse in the eye. The successive fusion is the physical basis for our actually seeing the course of the smile. The simultaneous fusion of partials gives us a still picture; the successive fusion gives us a moving picture.

The simultaneous fusion, as in the rich tone of a violin, corresponding to the still picture, gives us the basic structure. In terms of the tone spectrum represented by a single wave, we can describe the basic tonal structure, the difference between one instrument and another, between one voice and another, and between one vowel and another. But to describe the full quality of a musical tone, we must add the progressive change which we call successive fusion or sonance. To parallel the term timbre pattern, I venture to coin the term sonance pattern to describe the progressive picture of the quality of a tone. As we do not see the individual image of a single frame in the moving-picture film, we do not hear the tone of a single vibration. However, physically both are basic structures.

We speak of the physical tone, as well as of the psychological tone, as having quality, and here is the main point of my message: Quality in a harmonic musical tone consists of two phases—*timbre and sonance*. The timbre represents a cross-section of the tone; sonance represents progressive change. But there will be distortions in the harmonic structure, and to it there may be added inharmonic partials and noises. Each of these is determinable and measurable on the principle herein set forth.

But how will knowledge of harmonic structure help the musician in dealing with tone quality? Here we strike a most serious snag. We may secure, see, and describe perfect sonance patterns for thousands of tones in nature and art; but we have no exact names for any of them except one, the pure tone. The best we can do is to point to the picture, but that is not very practical. Will future acoustics give us such names? Yes, it will give us some fairly definable concepts with names. In the first place, it enables any musician who has a clear concept of any of the conventional names for tone quality, such as light or dark, to find out and state exactly what he means by this term. Such efforts will immediately lead to house-cleaning and rejection of terms on which musicians do not agree. We have a few terms on which there is fair agreement; as when we speak, in connection with vowels, of the *ah* quality, the *ee* quality, or the *oo* quality. Twenty or more such vowel qualities are fairly distinguishable and can be defined on the same principle. Thus, when we know that "vowel" means "quality", we have fairly acceptable names for a number of qualities. Acoustics will gradually build up other names; e.g., on the basis of the number of partials present, the form and regularity of their distribution. Progress in this direction will tend to clarify our musical terminology.

But current contributions to acoustics may be of considerable immediate advantage to the musician in that they may facilitate his understanding of the exact structure of his tone, his precision in musical terminology, his ability to hear and criticize tone quality with technical discrimination, and his ability to interpret his thoughts and feelings about musical quality in terms of tonal structure. See vols. I and IV in the *University of Iowa Studies in the Psychology of Music*; C. E. Seashore, *The Psychology of Music*, ch. 6; C. E. Seashore, The Harmonic Structure of a Musical Tone, *The Musical Quarterly*, Jan., 1939.   —C.E.S.

tone row. See twelve-tone technique.

tone spectrum. A qualitative and quantitative graphic representation of the structure of a tone in cross section for the duration of one sound wave revealing the structure of the tone in terms of the number of partials present, their distribution within the tonal register, and the percentage of energy of the tone as a whole contributed by each partial. The spectrum also indicates the fundamental pitch and the total intensity of the tone as a whole. It reveals the grouping of dominant regions of the partials known as formants, if present. This is a definition of the physical spectrum. Various forms of corresponding psychological spectra are so constructed as to indicate how the physical tone is perceived.   —C.E.S.

tongue pattern. In classical art, especially in Greek architecture and pottery, a decorative pattern consisting of a row of contiguous units of long narrow shape with bottom corners rounded, each with a border around the sides and bottom.   —L.T.S.

tongue rug. Usually doormat size made of pieces of cloth about three inches wide by about five inches long, rounded at one end. Pieces were blanket stitched with woolen yarn around three edges to keep them from ravelling and sewn at their narrow straight end, to a foundation of burlap.   —B.E.J.

tonic. *Mus.* The key note of a scale, the tone on which a scale is built up and from which it takes its name. See idiom B (1); scales and modes.

tonic sol-fa. See movable do.

tonoscope. An instrument which converts sound waves into moving picture patterns on the principle of stroboscopic vision. It is designed to measure vocal and instrumental pitch performance in remedial and general training in the mastery of a musical skill and to tune standardize and measure the response of musical instruments.

"One of the first demands in our equipment for the psychology of music was for an instrument which would enable us to see ourselves sing or play in terms of all aspects of pitch; such as attack, release, and the sustaining of a tone, regarding conformity to true pitch and the possibility of artistic deviations from true pitch, each essential to the art of music. The original instrument for this purpose was the tonoscope which converted the vibrations of sound into visual pictures so that the moment you sang or played a tone you could see instantly the degree of success or failure.

"In 1893 Scripture conceived the idea of building a tonoscope on the principle of stroboscopic vision and I collaborated with him. In Iowa this conception went through a series of stages and we built one model after another; first, in the direction of making it adequate however costly, and then in the direction of simplifying models, taking advantage of new resóurces coming in from time to time. The idea was that when playing or singing a tone, the exact pitch intonation should be exhibited visually for the duration of the tone within accuracies of from .10 to .01 of a whole tone step, the degree of precision depending upon the steadiness of the registering tone.

"Music teachers generally today are in a position analogous to that of the otologist a generation or two ago who had but few and insignificant instruments for exact and convenient measurement of the character and loss of hearing, function of the vocal cords, and location of lesions. Today the up-to-date otologist's office is equipped with audiometers, oral cameras, X-ray cameras, and fluoroscopes. So the progressive music teacher of the near future will be equipped with up-to-date instruments for quick and accurate measurement of the four elements of tone, of which the measurement of pitch is the first to attract attention. Thus we paved the way for the development of a new feature in teacher-training institutions; namely, the use of instruments in the development of musical skills, and our original goal has been reached. There are now on the market a variety of tonoscopes built on the most recently developed electrical principles of stroboscopic control of which the Conn Chromatic Stroboscope is perhaps the best at present. My *Measurement of Pitch Intonation with the Tonoscope in Singing Playing* gives a general account of principles involved and serves as a manual for remedial and general training in pitch as a musical skill." C. E. Seashore, *Pioneering in Psychology: University of Iowa Press,* 1942.

tonus peregrinum. See psalm tones.

tooth ornament, dog tooth. Tooth ornament such as used in the Romanesque and early Pointed styles consisted of a series of pointed toothlike forms. Also see dogtooth.

tope (Hind.). See stupa.

topia (L.). Landscape mural decoration depicting diverse and fanciful scenes.

Topographers, The. See CANADA, ART OF.

torana (Skr.). A gateway of upright pillars with two or more transverse members, usually a part of the perambulatory surrounding a stupa (q.v.). See INDIAN ART.

torculus. See neumes.

toreutics. Sculpturing by embossing, chasing, etc., esp. in metal.

torii (Jap.). A gateway of two pillars and generally two transverse members, seen before, and erected over, the pathway to a temple.

torse. See HERALDRY.

tortillon. This is really a small stump, a spreading or smoothing tool used by draftsmen with charcoal and crayon. It is made of soft paper rolled in such a way as to give a conical point at one end. —G.L.S.

tortoise. See SYMBOLISM IN FAR EASTERN ART.

torus. A large moulding of single convex curve in the form of a half circle; used especially for bases.

Tosa school (Jap.). A school of painting depicting historic episodes after the *Yamato-e* style (q.v.), reaching its peak about the 15th cent. See JAPANESE ART.

totara (Maori). A tree, closely related to the yew. See Maori carving.

totem pole. A pole carved and painted by the Northwest Coast Indians (q.v.) to display the heraldic devices and social rank of the family, to illustrate a legend, or to honor the dead. It was set up in front of or against the house, or served as a support to the beams. Carved from red cedar, abundant and gigantic in the region, the poles vary in height from 3 to 70 ft. The carvings represent animal, bird, or mythical guardian spirits with which the family is identified and from which it draws qualities peculiar to the being. See PRIMITIVE ART; CANADA, ART OF; also Frederic H. Douglas, *Totem Poles,* Denver Art Museum Leaflet No. 79-80 (1936). —H.G.

Totonac. The name given to the linguistic group living in the present state of Vera Cruz in Mexico. This name is also given to archaeological objects found in that area. There is, however, too much stylistic variation in terms of time and space to warrant the belief that these very fine arts were all the work of the same people.   —G.C.V.

tou (Ch.). Sacrificial bronze vessel. Globular form, with cover, on a stem standard with flaring base. Supposed to hold votive meat.

tou fang (Ch.). A small album-picture, usually square.

Touraine, school of. See FRENCH ART.

tourdion, tordion. See galliard.

Tournai school. A popular school of art that developed in 15th cent. Tournai that was conventionally religious. It influenced the schools of Ghent, Haarlem and Louvain. The leaders of the school at Tournai were Robert Campin and Roger Van der Weyden.
    —R.L.W.

Tours, school of. See Carolingian art.

tower. A structure, usually very tall in proportion to its depth and width, frequently forming a part of, and generally rising above, a larger structure or building.   —J.M.M.

townless highway. See CIVIC PLANNING.

town planning. See CIVIC PLANNING.

trabeated portico. See portico.

tracery. Ornamental work with ramified lines, as in the head of a Gothic window or in some styles of vaulting.

tract. See psalmody; Mass; MEDIEVAL MUSIC.

trade binding. See edition binding; EARLY BOOKBINDING AND FINE BINDING.

traffic, aesthetics of. Means of traffic and transportation are more modified in their appearance by modern design than any other elements and utensils of daily routine. It is highly characteristic that the most technical objects of our time follow in this way most closely the trend of modern art and are influencing vice versa the visual apperception of the two last generations.

Quickly moving machines, the locomotive, the car, and the airplane, calculated and shaped by engineers, showed first no func-

tional design at all. The first locomotive looked like a richly ornamented piece of furniture, the first car like a horse-drawn coach without horses, the first airplane resembled a gigantic children's kite. Gradually technique and functional necessities, among them the need for housing the increasing driving power, for overcoming the resistance of air, the simplification of power transmission, etc., changed their forms. However, it was not before the beginning of the 20th cent. that the specific beauty of technical perfection was achieved and more generally appreciated.

During the last three decades conscious consideration of this typical technical beauty began to influence the forms of locomotive, car, and airplane. Sometimes the engineer even called voluntarily for the co-operation of an architect, or an industrial designer in launching a new model. Modern industrial design got the greater stimulus from these demands.

In the realm of architecture proper, railway stations, gas stations, garages, airplane hangars, complicated highway turnpikes, became legitimate tasks for artistic moulding, based, of course, upon functional fulfillment of the engineering needs. It is impossible to overestimate the influence of the thus created forms upon other problems of modern architecture.

Finally, modern traffic influences also generally the aesthetic conception of our time. The visual apperception of the last generation has entirely changed through the adjustment to the speed of modern traffic and the experience of large covered distances. Birds-eye view from the flying airplane, spread through the movies, became an ordinary experience. The consequences of these various influences are mirrored in architectural forms as well as in modern painting and, of course, in industrial design. The experience of speed does not allow the enjoyment of complicated ornamentation, and modern trends in painting beginning with Futurism tried to freeze the sensation of the daily experienced speed by simultaneous representation of moving objects. Post-Futuristic painting sublimized this tendency. See engineering, aesthetics of; streamlined; functional architecture; CIVIC PLANNING; also George R. Chatburn, *Highways and Highway Transportation*, 1923; Le Corbusier, *La Ville Radieuse*, 1934; N. Pevsner, *The Pioneers of the Modern Movement, from William Morris to Walter Gropius*, 1936; Lewis Mumford, *Technics and Civilization*, 1934; Cyril Bruyn Andrews,

The Railway Age, 1938; Norman Bel Geddes, *Magic Motorways,* 1940; Paul Zucker, *American Bridges and Dams,* 1941; David B. Steinman, *Bridges and Their Builders,* 1941; L. Moholy-Nagy, *The New Vision,* 1938.

—P.Z.

traffic circle, lane. See CIVIC PLANNING.

training (in basic musical skills). The basic musical skills are the control of pitch, intensity, time, and timbre. In various combinations, these appear in complex forms as in harmony, melody, rhythm, volume, and tone quality. Training in these should be the ABC of musical education and by the use of instrumental aids, this training can be vastly shortened and sharpened beyond the degree obtainable without the use of instruments. The fundamental principle involved is that the ear is trained by aid of the eye. The singer or player can *see* the tonal, the dynamic, the temporal, and the qualitative aspects in turn as he plays or sings. The visual pictures offer a measuring scale which reveals details finer than the ear can hear.

"One of the goals of the psychology of music is to apply scientific principles to methods of training which shall guarantee insight into the nature of the learning process, a shortening of the time of training, and attainment of higher precision and mastery than is ordinarily obtained. In this, it follows the universal requirement of the scientific procedure of dealing with one specific factor at a time, employing objective standards and measurements of performance.

"Training begins with the most elementary steps by setting up efficient habits which become thoroughly fixed so that they function automatically in the actual musical situation. A fundamental requirement is that the pupil shall know exactly what element in the music he is trying to master in a given assignment, shall have an objective check on his achievement in this for every trial, and shall practice until this particular control of tone is completely established as a habit.

"Instruments for such a purpose are fast coming upon the market and are reasonably priced so that, for the price of a good piano, one can equip a studio adequately. A single equipment of this kind can serve an entire large school; the cost is not prohibitive for a music school or a department of music in a public school.

"At present, the problem is to convince music teachers of the possibilities and significance of this scientific approach to musical training. The instruments are here and more are coming. The first essential is knowledge of the fundamental techniques in the psychology of music. Courses in that subject are fast developing in progressive teacher-training institutions. The range of possibilities is unlimited when we once establish confidence in the idea that it can be done.

"One of the most valuable principles involved in most of these instruments is that the sound wave is converted into a visual picture so that the moment one sings or plays a given note, he will see on a dial or some other dictator, the exact performance of the element under consideration. These visual pictures of sound waves are to the student of music what the microscope is to the student of microörganisms: every element in the tone produced is enlarged; even factors not recognized by the unaided ear become clear and conspicuous.

"A laboratory studio of this kind assumes three aspects: first, the measurement of natural talent at the beginning of practice; second, training in the acquisition and refinement of specific skills in musical performance; and third, measurement of achievement. The talent testing should include on the one hand measures of musical hearing and, on the other, measures of natural talent for motor skills." C. E. Seashore, *Pioneering in Psychology*: University of Iowa Press, 1942. See also, C. E. Seashore, *Psychology of Music,* 1938.

tram (original L. *trama* meant weft). A soft silk yarn.

transept. The part of a cruciform church which crosses at right angles to the greatest length and between the nave and apse or choir; loosely, one of the arms, or projecting ends, of a transept.

transferring. A process of printing from one surface to another. In lithography a crayon drawing is made on a specially prepared gesso paper, dampened and then printed on a stone. It is then processed and printed as a lithograph. Transfers are made by taking a print on gesso paper from one stone and printing it on another as in commercial lithography. —R.L.W

transmissance. See COLOR.

transom. A horizontal piece framed across an opening; hence, a window or opening above such a bar.

transom-bar. A horizontal construction dividing a window or opening into stages.

transpose. *Mus.* To change a composition from one key to another.

transposition. See twelve-tone technique.

transverberation. A mystic experience of Sta. Theresa: the piercing of her heart by an angel by means of a flaming arrow. Frequently represented in Baroque art, the most famous rendition being that by L. Bernini in the church of Sta. Maria della Vittoria, Rome. —R.B.

transverse flute. See MUSICAL INSTRUMENTS.

tread. The horizontal part of a step.

treasure boat. See SYMBOLISM IN FAR EASTERN ART.

treatment. See design.

treble clef. See clef.

Trecento school. See Florentine school.

tree-fungus. See SYMBOLISM IN FAR EASTERN ART.

tree of life (L. *arbor vitae,* tree of life). In classical art, a conventionalized ornament based on the arbor vitae tree, a tall narrow shape rounded at the bottom and coming to a point at the top. —L.T.S.

tree ring dating. See dendrochronology.

tremolo (in voice). A bad vibrato; a periodic pulsation or quivering in tone which does not contribute toward a pleasing flexibility, tenderness, or richness of tone. The terms vibrato and tremolo have been confused for the last 1700 years. Experimental analysis by phonophotography reveals that in the most generally accepted meanings the two terms refer to the same tonal eelments, namely, pitch, intensity, time, and timbre, singly or combined, and that they must be evaluated in relation to the same goals; namely, flexibility, tenderness, and richness of tone. The tremolo is, therefore, a vibrato and since in musical literature the tremolo is most generally regarded as undesirable, it is proposed on laboratory analysis to stabilize this terminology in vocal sonance (q.v.) by speaking of a good vibrato as a vibrato and a bad vibrato as a tremolo. For distinction between "good" and "bad" vibrato, see article on

vibrato in which it is shown that the distinction is a relative one depending upon the listener's sense of vibrator (q.v.) and many othe psychological and physical factors. Hence what is the vibrato to one person may be a tremolo to another, usually a person with a fine musical ear. In general, a vocal tremolo is excessive or irregular vibrato. The same principle applies in general to musical instruments. But in the instrumental field there has been and are yet several other meanings to features which cannot be classified as vibrato. It would be well if these could be reviewed critically and given other names. These should include only cases which may not be regarded as vibrato whether they be good or bad. See VIBRATO; also *Iowa Studies in Music,* vols. I, III, and IV. —C.E.S.

trench. A long narrow excavation in the ground or given level; a ditch.

trepak. The trepak constitute one of the four general types of Russian national dance. They are perhaps the most unrestrained, and have been called "Bacchanalian", in contrast to the romantic kamarienskaya, the dramatic kasatsk, and the ballad-dances of the chorovody. Unlimited freedom of movement, building to an almost frenzied figure of whirling and springing into the air, characterizes the trepak dances. —J.G.

tressure. See HERALDRY.

trestle table. See FURNITURE.

triad. *Mus.* A three-tone chord composed of a root, its third and fifth in ascending diatonic order.

triadic color scheme. See COLOR.

trial proof. *Etch.* An impression from a plate which is not completed. See PRINTS AND PRINT PROCESSES.

triangle. See MUSICAL INSTRUMENTS.

tribunal. See EARLY CHRISTIAN ARCHITECTURE.

triclinium. A couch reaching round three sides of a table for eating in a reclined position; a room having such a couch.

triforium. The gallery forming an upper story to the aisle of a church, often having three openings to each bay.

triglyph (Gr. *triglyphos* fr. *tri,* three + *glyphein,* to carve). In the Greek Doric order, the vertical member of the frieze which alternates with the metope, a projecting block marked by two vertical grooves on the face and a half groove at each corner. —L.T.S.

trill (Ger. *Triller*; Fr. *trille*). Same as shake (q.v.). Phillip Emanuel Bach specifies four different types of trill; viz., the trill proper, the trill from below, the trill from above and the imperfect trill, half trill, transient trill or Pralltriller.   —F.D.

trio. *Mus.* (1) A composition for three voices or instruments. (2) The middle part of a minuet or scherzo.

trionfo. See STAGESETTING.

tripartite temple. See MESOPOTAMIAN ART.

triple fugue. See fugue.

triplet, triole, triolet. Three equal notes which are to be performed in the time allotted to two of the same kind.

trippant. See HERALDRY.

triptych. (1) Three panels, generally designed as a single composition; commonly seen in Japanese wood-block prints. See also altarpiece. (2) *Book*. A tablet of three leaves hinged so that it can be folded to show a new "page".

triquetra. A triangular figure or ornament.

triregnum. See tiara, papal.

tristimulus values. See COLOR.

Triton. An ancient Greek sea demigod.

tritone. The interval from f to b, called by medieval musicians *diabolus in musica*. It was avoided in ancient liturgical melodies. Later medieval theorists asserted that the b flat was introduced in order to avoid the tritone. See musica ficta.   —V.A.

trivium. See Quadrivium.

trobar clus. See MEDIEVAL MUSIC.

trombetta. See MUSICAL INSTRUMENTS.

trombone. See MUSICAL INSTRUMENTS.

trope. See MEDIEVAL MUSIC.

troubadours, trouveres. See MEDIEVAL MUSIC.

trough. A long or narrow open receptacle or channel, as for holding or conducting food or water.

true blue. See lapis lazuli.

true porcelain. See CERAMICS II.

trumeau (Fr.). In medieval architecture, a supporting column in the center of some large doorways.

trumpet. See MUSICAL INSTRUMENTS.

trunk highway. See CIVIC PLANNING.

truss. *Arch.* A bracket.

truth. This term is frequently used in literary criticism as synonymous with sincerity (q.v.), where it means that the work is a faithful account of the artist's feelings and sentiments, with no adjustment to what might be expected or desired by the public. It is also employed in a more special sense to indicate that the work is faithful to the external environment to which it refers. The predicate "true", as used in criticism and attached to art, does not carry the meaning of correctness or correspondence that is involved in philosophical and matter-of-fact conceptions of truth. Truth in the artistic context indicates that a work illuminates some aspect of its subject that is open to normal and healthy experience. Art is here held responsible to some "real" world, and is called true when it increases our awareness of this world.
                                                —I.J.

ts'ao ch'ung (Ch.). Grasses and insects; one of the stipulated subjects in a Chinese school of painting.

tschin. See RUSSIA, RELIGIOUS PAINTING IN.

ts'e yeh (Ch.). An album (of paintings).

T-shaped fibula. See JEWELRY.

Tsimshian art. See Northwest Coast Indian art.

tsuba (Jap.). Sword-guard, located between the handle and the blade, to protect the hand.

tsuikoku (Jap.). Carved black lacquer.

tsuishu (Jap.). Carved red lacquer, whose color is due to the use of cinnabar. Often known as "cinnabar" lacquer.

tsuitate. (Jap). A solid, single-paneled screen with two low transverse feet, on the surface of which the artist paints pictures, generally of a decorative nature.

tsuka (Jap.). Handle or hilt of a sword.

tsun (Ch.). Sacrificial bronze vessel. Vase-like jar with flaring rim and a base.

ts'ung (Ch.). A jade form used in ritual, especially in burial, as the earth symbol. It combines an inner cylindrical form with an outer rectangle, the cylinder usually projecting at top and bottom.   —J.A.M.

tuba. See MUSICAL INSTRUMENTS.

tubecta. See MUSICAL INSTRUMENTS.

Tudor. The Tudor period marked the belated emergence of England from the Middle Ages into the Renaissance. Her most striking response to the new enlightenment was, perhaps, political. Henry VIII (1504-47) broke with Rome, and Elizabeth (1558-1603) crippled the feudal lords, survived the Spanish Armada, laid the foundations of an empire, and brought to her land a prosperity and tranquillity unprecedented in its history. The artistic reflections of these changes are varied: Henry VIII commissioned Holbein to do some of the world's masterpieces of portraiture, but the string of Germans, Flemings, and Italians, like Torrigiano, who crossed the Channel were, for the most part, secondraters. This fact, the natural insularity of the English, and the conservatism which clung to the picturesque Gothic skyline, rendered the classical orders quite superficial, even, in the column-chimneys of Burghley House, somewhat ridiculous. But healthy influences were at work. The predominance of churches gave way to a predominance of domestic dwellings, some of England's greatest, like Hampton Court, Burghley House, Montacute House, and Wollaton. Owing to extended peace, these abandoned the formidable Medieval fortress character for great bay windows which overlooked fine gardens and parks. Plans became more open and symmetrical, sometimes employing, as a tribute to the monarchs, the H of Henry or the E of Elizabeth. If classical motifs were at best a picturesque veneer, the brick-and-stone work of the period is among the finest of mural treatments. In the field of literature, always England's most vital form of expression, Spencer, Raleigh, and Shakespeare bowed to no contemporary on the continent.

An interesting present day evidence of Tudor influence is to be found in the architecture of many American colleges and universities. Washington University, at St. Louis, Missouri, is a particularly fine and consistent example. See GT. BRITAIN, ARCHITECTURE OF, INTERIOR ARCHITECTURE AND DECORATION; FURNITURE.   —P.C.B.

tueh (Ch.). Sacrificial bell form. Clapperless, with handle.

tufted rug or carpet. See pile.

Tughra script. See ISLAMIC ART.

tui (Ch.). Sacrificial bronze vessel. Sometimes three-legged, with two loop handles at the sides.

tumulus. An ancient grave mound.

t'ung ching (Ch.). Several hanging paintings that make up one large composition.

tung oil. Little used as a painter's medium, oil from the seeds of the *Aleurites cordata,* a tree growing principally in China and surrounding countries, has had an extensive use, particularly for surface varnish, in the heavy paint industry. It is also called Chinese wood oil.   —G.L.S.

tuotilo. See MEDIEVAL MUSIC.

turbat (Ar.). A monumental tomb. See ISLAMIC ART.

Turkestan, art of. See CENTRAL ASIAN ART.

Turkish knot. See Ghiordes knot.

Turkish rugs. Includes all those rugs that are manufactured within Turkey. They are not so finely woven as Persian; they have a longer pile and looser texture. Each rug-weaving district of Turkey seems to have a distinct and individual class of rugs. See *Persian rugs* for references of classifications of Turkish rugs.   —B.E.J.

turn. *Mus.* A grace note of extremely varied execution, defined by Philipp Emanuel Bach as a simple *manier* that makes a singing melody more pleasant and brilliant.   —F.D.

turpentine. In the Western hemisphere this term is used to define what in Britain ordinarily goes by the term, spirits of turpentine, a distillate from balsam. The crude resinous exudate may come from any of a number of pine trees, larch, and fir. Distilled turpentine is a volatile solvent for oil and for most varnishes. Although its general history reaches into the ancient world and although the distillate has been made since the 8th cent., it may not have been used in the art of painting before the Renaissance. Leonardo da Vinci speaks of it but does not specifically mention it as an oil solvent. —G.L.S.

turret. A small tower, usually rising above a larger structure.

turtle. See SYMBOLISM IN FAR EASTERN ART.

Tuscan architecture. See Romanesque architecture.

Tuscan red. See iron pigments.

Tuscan school. See Florentine school.

tussy mussy. A bunch of flowers put together to convey a message through the symbolism of the materials chosen. See FLOWER ARRANGEMENT.

tutti. *Mus.* All. Used especially in contrast to "solo".

tutu (Fr. [?] diminutive, derived from second person singular *tu*). The skirt worn by female dancers in classic ballets, usually of layers of tarletan. There are two traditional styles, the long, "romantic", bell-shaped skirt originating ca. 1832 with Taglioni, and the short, so-called "classic skirt" originating with the Italian Zucchi (1887), who clipped off the length of tarletan in the old style skirt to create a new. The term *tutu* of mysterious origin, perhaps close to *frou-frou,* etc., usually refers to the later style. —L.K.

twelfth. See ACOUSTICS.

twelve-tone scale. See scales and modes.

twelve-tone system. Current, but erroneous designation of the twelve-tone technique (q.v.).

twelve-tone technique. Technique of composition evolved by Arnold Schönberg within the idiom of atonality (see idiom, C). The basic principles of the twelve-tone technique are the following:

(1) Anyone of the 479,001,600 available different successions of twelve different tones can be made the "basic series", or "tone row", of a composition, or a comprehensive section thereof, or of a group of compositions.

(2) Within the musical area thus circumscribed, the basic series is used exclusively for the formation of all elements of the composition (melodies, chords, motifs, themes, etc.) in such a way that the area under consideration forms an unbroken chain of consecutive entrances of the basic series.

(3) Any number of tones of the series may appear simultaneously.

(4) Transposition of individual tones of the series to higher or lower octaves is admissible.

(5) The series may assume any rhythmic shape.

(6) The following derivative forms of the series are available: (a) **Inversion** (direction of the original interval progressions changed into its opposite; see inversion); (b) **Retrograde form** (original series running backward, from its last to its first tone); (c) **Retrograde inversion** (direction of the interval progressions of the retrograde form changed into its opposite); (d) The pitch level of the original series and of each of its derivative forms can be changed eleven times (**transposition**) so that each form may begin with any of the twelve tones.

(7) Any number of the 48 series forms thus obtained may be used simultaneously in the manner indicated under 2.

(8) Any series form may be divided among several voices, provided the resulting succession of tones on the whole is identical with that of the underlying series form.

(9) Repetition of tones, or of groups of tones, of the series is admissible conditionally.

The twelve-tone technique has grown out of the practice of composition in the **atonal idiom** and has shown its particular usefulness within that idiom. It is, however, not identical with, or a synonym of, atonality. **Atonal music** can be, and has been, written without the aid of the twelve-tone technique. On the other hand, selection of suitable basic series permits of composition in other idioms than the atonal by means of the twelve-tone technique. The principles outlined above, being subject to manifold modifications and further evolution in the practice of numerous contemporary composers, are of high pedagogical value as a method of counterpoint (q.v.) in making students of composition acquainted with the peculiarities of the atonal idiom.

—E.K.

twill. A weave of fabric in which a series of regularly recurrent warp threads pass in echelon over and under the weft threads two or more at a time is called a twill. Roughly, in appearance it produces an effect of diagonal ribs or of stepped patterns, depending on how the warp threads are carried. Twill was a favorite weave in painters' canvases from the 16th cent. on. It seemed to be much used by the English portrait painters of the 18th cent. and, although it has continued to the present, it is less a favorite now than formerly. See weaving. —G.L.S.

twin fish. See SYMBOLISM IN FAR EASTERN ART.

two-point perspective. See PERSPECTIVE.

two-step. A dance in 2/4 or 6/8 time with two accents to the bar.

typographic. See ex libris.

Tyrian purple. Among the few coloring materials particularly characteristic of ancient and medieval times is the so-called Tyrian purple, a rare organic dye prepared from several species of mollusk. Occasionally it has been called whelk red. Pliny said that the best quality of this dye was made at Tyre. It was the color used in togas of Roman emperors and is principally known in the arts as the purple dye used in coloring parchments. —G.L.S.

Tyrolienne. A Tirolese round dance in 3/4 time.

Tz'u Chou yao (Ch.). Chinese pottery of the *Sung dynasty*. The body is covered with a creamy white slip and decorated with impressionistic sketches.

t'zu t'ai (Ch.). *Chun-yao* (q.v.) with porcelain body.

U

uchiwa (Jap.). Round fans, the surfaces of which are often decorated by the best artists.

uchiwa-e (Jap.). Paintings for non-folding fans.

ud. See MUSICAL INSTRUMENTS.

ugly. The property ascribed to an object which disappoints painfully an aesthetic ideal.

Ukiyo-e school (Jap.). Literally, pictures of the every-day world. A school of genre painting at its peak in the 18th cent. See JAPANESE ART.

ultra-baroque. Inclusive name for several extravagant Mexican styles of the first three-quarters of the 18th cent.

ultramarine blue. Although a modern synthetic pigment goes by this name, the natural ultramarine made of powdered lapis lazuli is the one usually meant in the fine arts. When this stone began to be taken over as a pigment is not known. Apparently the ancient Egyptians did not use it. The principal source is in Afghanistan and it occurs in wall paintings of cave temples in that region as early as the 6th and 7th cents. Its presence has also been reported in Byzantine illuminated manuscripts of the 7th cent. and it continued in use in the painting of Europe until it was displaced to some extent by the blue crystalline pigment known as smalt and later by more intense artificial blues. These were much stronger in their tinting strength, easier to use particularly in oil, and far cheaper. —G.L.S.

ultra-violet ray photograph. One taken under the short wave lengths in the ultra-violet end of the spectrum. A quartz lamp and special filter produce the vibrations.

Ulysses. Odysseus.

Umayyad art. See ISLAMIC ART.

umber. A raw and burnt brown earth pigment is called umber. In color the raw material is dark and inclined to a neutral greenish brown. Burnt umber made by roasting the raw earth is redder and warmer in hue. The umbers are characterized chemically by the presence of manganese dioxide in addition to the iron oxides common to all the earth pigments. Although its name would indicate that it came from a region of Italy, it is widely distributed, and one of the best varieties known is Turkey umber, found on the island of Cyprus. —G.L.S.

Umbrian school. See ITALIAN ART.

Unakah. See CERAMICS II.

uncut. *Book.* The margins uncut as issued in rebound books. Paper full size and not cut after binding in new books.

uncut edges. *Book.* Edges that have not been cut flush.

underglaze painting. Decoration applied directly with metallic oxides to the biscuit of porcelain, and covered with transparent glaze, is called underglaze painting.

underground. See CIVIC PLANNING.

underpass. See CIVIC PLANNING.

unequal temperament. See ACOUSTICS.

ungen (Jap.). See JAPANESE ART.

unguentarium (L.). Vessel used to hold unguents.

union carpet. See carpet structures.

unison. The sounding of the same tone by two or more voices or instruments.

unity. Means that all component parts of a work of art must be combined in such a way that the final result is a whole. But there is a distinction between formal and spiritual unity. Formal unity means about the same thing as balance (q.v.) which is achieved when all single parts are counterbalanced, as a common pole unifies all the forces. Spiritual unity means that all single spiritual parts of a work of art must converge toward one concentrating spiritual pole. The final goal of the spiritual factors of a work of art cannot be for instance both God and material or both idea and accident. In such a case the consequence can only be a confusion which causes dissatisfaction. The more formal and spiritual unity are bound together and the more logical the whole unity is, the more satisfactory is the effect and the greater the psychological solution. To accomplish this result the focal point must be unequivocal, and as far as possible it must be comprehensive, which implies it should have a universal value. The best work of art is created when a chance occurrence is related to a last unifying coherence in an unambiguous way. This unity results in the feeling of a complete satisfaction which means a materially useless one. For the human will is always striving to reduce all the variations of the universe to one immaterial least common denominator. See variety in unity.   —A.J.S.

universal artwork (Ger. *Gesamtkunstwerk*). The notion (literally) that all the arts including painting, music, architecture, poetry, *et al.*, be combined into one unified art object. This conception was apparently suggested as early as Johann Mattheson, the 18th cent. composer and theorist, who saw in the opera theatre an academy of the fine arts wherein such a universal artwork could be produced. The idea of a *Gesamtkunstwerk* has been linked with 19th cent. romanticism and more particularly with Richard Wagner. With Wagner, the universal art work takes on a more specific meaning, viz., that of the tonal drama. He early conceived opera as evolving naturally from number opera to the music drama; i.e., from opera consisting of a series of occasions for singers to display

their individual excellence to a drama in which symphonic music is utilized to portray subtle and deep emotions incommunicable by words and dramatic action. (It is this theory of the use of music to convey specific emotions that Hanslick so strongly objected to in romantic theory.) In his later operas Wagner's orchestra dwarfs into insignificance his actor-singers and the stage. His actor-singers lose their songs to the orchestra, cease to be interesting as individual character-studies, and become symbols of the universal love-death (*Liebestod*) struggle in nature. These Wagnerian attempts at a universal art work were thus successful only within limitations and his last operas marked the death of the romantic conception of a universal art object. Berlioz also sought to develop a universal art work in his "drama without voices" which involved conversion of the symphony by assigning equal roles in the work to poetry and the instrumental parts. Whereas the idea of a universal artwork implies a unification of *all* the arts into one art object, the romanticists conceived of it primarily in terms of a unification of poetry and music. More often than not they left the problem of including the other arts in the universal art work to the realm of speculative theory.

Perhaps a closer approximation of a universal art work is to be found in some 20th cent. ballet productions in which music, scenery (stage included), and choreography (including mimicry and dramatic action) are brought together by contemporary masters of the arts involved. An example of this is afforded in the Monte Carlo Ballet Russe production of *Rouge et Noir* based on the novel by Stendhal and which involves the music of Shostakovich's *First Symphony*, choreography by Massine, and scenery by Matisse.

Past failures to achieve a universal art work are variously explained by aestheticians and musicologists. One of these is that any attempt to unify music with the other arts is destined to culminate in the swallowing up of the other arts by the music involved, esp. if the latter is "great" music. This is an unacceptable explanation because it presupposes a universal primacy of musical aesthetic sensitivity, for which there is at present no evidence. Another theoretical difficulty encountered in the notion of a universal art work is in discovering just what it is believed that such a work would achieve. It may be thought that the final universality of art can only be achieved by unifying the products of the various arts. But this would involve a misconception of the nature of universal art. The universality of an art object does not consist of the diversity and quantity of aesthetic sensibilities it might arouse as the result of combining it with other types of art objects, but rather, that universality is a function of the inseparable and indiscriminate integration of the form and matter of the particular art object in question. See MUSICAL PERFORMANCE, MAIN TRENDS IN.   —H.G.S.

unorganized. This term is used very broadly in literary criticism with one general meaning that varies specifically as it occurs in different contexts. Generically, the term indicates that the parts of the literary work have not been successfully combined; that is, the work lacks structure and unity, because the elements have not been well molded into a whole. For the more important specific variants of the term, cf.: episodic, inchoate, verbose, obscure.   —I.J.

unprinted. An area left "white" in a print process. See PRINTS AND PRINT PROCESSES.

unrhythmical, rhythmical chant. See JEWISH MUSIC.

unrounded. See edition binding.

upbow. *Mus.* The stroke of a bow in the direction "from point to nut".

upturned roof. See CHINESE ARTS.

uraeus. The representation of the sacred asp (in ancient Egyptian religion) on the headdress of rulers.

urceus (L.). A pitcher or jug with one handle.

urn. In Oriental art, a receptacle, varying in shape, for holding the ashes of the deceased. Applicable to a shape or form simulating a mortuary vessel, as, urn shape. See also ex libris.

ūrṇā (Skr.). Tuft of hair growing between the eyebrows; a definite mark of the Buddha. In Buddhist sculpture and painting it is usually represented as a sort of jewel on the forehead. In this form it is considered as a third, and divine, eye, indicating supernatural spiritual insight.   —J.A.M.

urushi (Jap.). Sap, from the poisonous su-

mac tree, known as lacquer. See lacquerware.

urushi-e (Jap.). "Lacquer picture." The technique of painting with lacquer as a medium. See JAPANESE ART.

U. S. A., LITERATURE OF THE. In the transplantation of Englishmen from their native middle-class environment to the wilderness of the eastern coast of North America, the rude arts of survival took precedence over aesthetic enterprise. Although Michael Drayton speeded Raleigh's Company with an ode and although George Sandys translated a portion of Ovid while in Virginia, belles lettres did not flourish. With a howling wilderness to be subdued, with savage Red Men constantly on the war path as pawns in the persistent British and French colonial chess game seeking increased territory, and with a supernatural world of evil spirits ever waiting to tempt unwary souls, these first settlers had practical problems to face before there was leisure or education for creative activity apart from the beautification of their houses and tools. Yet these pioneers, sensing their formative part in the world's onward movement, prepared maps, drawings, diaries, and histories of their enterprises. John Smith (1580-1631), swashbuckling leader of the Virginia Company in 1607, wrote several narrative-descriptive accounts, such as *A True Relation* (1608) and *Generall Historie of Virginia* (1624); William Bradford (1590-1657) recounted "in a plain stile" the Pilgrims' crusading energy in *Of Plimoth Plantation* (1856); and John Winthrop (1588-1649) in *Journal* (1790, 1908) recorded in vigorous prose the social history of Massachusetts Bay from 1629 to 1649. The gay Anglican, Thomas Morton (1590-1646), enemy of the Plymouth Pilgrims, in *The New English Canaan*, 1637), denounced by Bradford as an "infamous and scurrilous book", wove a bright thread into the otherwise colorless historical writing of the colonial era. Only occasionally does the music of noble English prose of the early 17th cent. echo through these artistically barren structures.

Religious dissent gave birth to New England and Pennsylvania; economic enterprise established New York and the Southern colonies. Learning flourished only amidst heated theological arguments. The best prose emerged in sermon and polemic literature, some of it as fascinating in its baroque crabbedness as it is ˙ pelling in its chilling dogmatism. The most memorable 17th cent. prose writings are

Roger Williams's anti-clerical and democratic *Blovdy Tenent* (1644), Nathaniel Ward's fiercely intolerant yet stylistically ornate *Simple Cobler* (1647), and Mary Rowlandson's pathetic tale of suffering during her captivity by Indians. Influential as an elementary textbook for a century was *The New-England Primer* (c. 1690), whose 64-page combination of prose tales of Protestant martyrs, Calvinist catechetical lessons, and mnemonic couplets adorned with crude woodcuts taught millions to read and spell.

Poetry in 17th cent. New England was largely elegiac and religious. Michael Wigglesworth (1631-1705) versified in jigging meters popular Calvinist dogmas in *The Day of Doom* (1662). Anne Bradstreet (c. 1612-1672) in *The Tenth Muse* (1650) echoed contemporary British poets like Sylvester and Quarles while revealing the comfort which religion afforded a sensitive person in a weary, wilderness land. Edward Taylor (c. 1660-1729), whose poems were first published in 1939, wrote notable devotional poetry in a metaphysical style.

New England's walls of religious conservatism did not prevent the infiltration of the free intellectual questing inherent in the new learning: Newtonian science, Lockean psychology, and deistic theology. In the 18th cent. Puritanism receded from its conservative Calvinist position steadily if unwillingly. Cotton Mather (1663-1728), foremost Puritan man of letters in America, reflected these new thoughts in some 400 publications which vary greatly in style: some retain the learned allusiveness and embroidered beauty of 17th cent. prose, and some imitate Addison and Steele's limpid clarity. His *Magnalia Christi Americana* (1702) is "the prose epic of New England Puritanism". Jonathan Edwards (1703-1758), often called the last great defender of Puritanism, combined a mystic's sensitiveness to spiritual beauty with a scientist's exactitude in examining, as he did at the age of 12, the web-making activities of a spider. He pictured the beauties of Heaven and the torments of Hell in sermons; one, "Sinners in the Hands of an Angry God," has been used to give an unfair, harsh interpretation to his character. *Freedom of the Will* (1754), his superbly reasoned defense of the tottering old order, remains one of America's most learned books.

One Boston boy migrated to Philadelphia in 1723, worked at the trade of printer, and by shrewd guarding of the main chance rose to be the most important citizen of Pennsylvania and one of the two or three most important in our Revolution. That lad, Benjamin Franklin (1706-1790), symbolizes the effect of the Enlightenment upon America. By escaping the repressiveness of Puritan New England and by establishing himself among freedom-loving, individualistic Quakers and German Lutherans, Franklin was able to expand intellectually as well as to grow rich and politically powerful. In youth he practiced the art of writing by imitating Addison. By becoming a master of the popular prose styles of the 18th cent.—letter writing, light essay, and satire—he gave powerful support to the colonists' protests against unwarranted invasion of their constitutional rights by Britain. A practical sociologist, Franklin initiated many civic improvements, including the establishment of a literary club, a library, and a school which later grew into the University of Pennsylvania. As a scientist he achieved world renown for experiments on electricity. In a day when "literature" meant "learning" Franklin towered above his fellows in reputation; for this reason, among others, he was received cordially in Europe and was successful as an ambassador in securing the aid of France and thus assuring victory in the Revolution. His proverbs in *Poor Richard's Almanac* (1733-1758) and the didactic, mildly self-disparaging *Autobiography* (1771-1789) inadequately represent Franklin's many-sided greatness as a man and a writer.

"Get John Woolman (1720-1772) by heart," counseled Charles Lamb, in speaking of the *Journal* of this pious Quaker tailor. More worldly was William Byrd (1674-1744), a philosophic Virginia plantation owner and author of frank records of colonial society phrased in sprightly style. Other memorable books are Sarah Kemble Knight's outspoken *Journal* (1825), an account of a trip in 1704 from Boston to New York, and Mather Byle's *Poems* (1744), unsuccessful imitations of Alexander Pope by a punning Boston parson.

In 1761 English mercantilistic colonial policy collided violently with American economic ambitions when an attempt was made to invade the privacy of business houses in a search for smuggled goods. James Otis repelled this aggression in a brilliant address; "Then and there the Revolution was born." As the British insisted upon taxing the colonists, learned constitutional lawyers, like John Dickinson and John Adams, spied in each action new threats to American self-respect.

"Taxation without representation is tyranny." Emotion replaced legalistic thinking. "Give me liberty, or give me death," declared Patrick Henry in 1775. Thomas Paine (1737-1809), an English Quaker who came to Pennsylvania in 1774, became the chief propagandist of the revolutionary party. In a pamphlet, *Common Sense* (1776), he painted King George as a bully, besmirched the concept of royalty, and affirmed the necessity for an independent nation. A prolific pamphlet warfare matched the actual cannonading. A state document, *The Declaration of Independence,* is the literary masterpiece of the era.

The problems of creating a new nation gave rise to *The Federalist* (1787-88), essays by Alexander Hamilton, James Madison, and John Jay, and to such books as Thomas Jefferson's *Notes on Virginia* (1787). The political nationalism of these volumes was matched by a cultural nationalism requiring American control of churches, and American manners, dress, language, art, printing, and literature. As early as 1770 John Trumbull, the poet, laid down the basic principle of nationality in literature. Other Connecticut men, especially Timothy Dwight in a patriotic song "Columbia" and Noah Webster in textbooks, essays, and *The American Dictionary* (1828), fostered national advancement. Philip Freneau (1752-1832), whose poetry combined harsh rabblerousing political qualities with sensitiveness to nature's beauty, asked for independence in strident verse; a few stanzas in the contemporary romantic manner make him the first memorable poet in the U. S. A. William Dunlap (1766-1839) prepared a few American plays, such as André (1789), but he suffered the common ailment of imitativeness in adapting or translating European plays. In fiction Hugh Henry Brackenridge (1748-1816) is remembered for *Modern Chivalry* (1792-1815), an amusing satiric commentary upon American aristocratic pretensions in the youthful democracy; and Charles Brockden Brown (1771-1810) still teases readers with unfulfilled promises in a half dozen melodramatic Gothic novels echoing Godwinian humanitarian sentiments.

Although the new literary theories of Wordsworth were not unknown to Americans, neo-classical conservatism marked literary efforts until 1815, when in Boston *The North American Review* was founded. The successful completion of the second war with England occasioned renewed enthusiasm for freedom, not only freedom in politics, but freedom in spiritual and artistic life. Unitarianism in Massachusetts gave further impetus to the separation of Church and State (completed in Conn. in 1817 and in Mass. in 1833); this liberal religious movement gave to the U. S. A. a whole galaxy of famous writers. Anti-slavery agitators demanded manumission of the Negroes in the United States. Philhellenists echoed Byron in requesting independence for Greece and for all small nations.

Washington Irving (1783-1859), a New Yorker, was the first American to win international praise for artistry in prose. A lover of the picturesque and marvelous, he used scanty plot materials as a framework for a heavily embroidered fabric of description and sentiment in the manner of Addison and Goldsmith. *The Sketch Book* (1819-20), written in England, contains "Rip Van Winkle" and "The Legend of Sleepy Hollow," two tales now classic. Lingering in Europe until 1832, he wrote on English, German, Italian, and Spanish themes; the best of these books is "the Spanish sketch book", *The Alhambra* (1832). Other New Yorkers, often called the Knickerbocker Group, include Fitzgreene Halleck (1790-1867), a poet; James Kirke Paulding (1778-1860), an essayist, novelist, and dramatist whose stylistic defects are compensated by bristling patriotism; and Nathaniel Parker Willis (1806-1867), gossipy essayist and traveler, poet, and dramatist. James Gates Percival (1795-1856), Connecticut poet and geologist, in 1821-23 published four voulmes of Byronic verse; for a brief moment his fame equalled Irving's. Slowly the merits of William Cullen Bryant (1794-1878) emerged; a Massachusetts man transplanted to New York as a newspaper editor, he wrote a few poems, but these maintain a uniform high quality in the Wordsworthian manner, as in "Thanatopsis" (1817-1821) with its organ-like musical reassurance that Nature bids us accept death stoically.

After a brief career at sea and as a gentleman farmer, James Fenimore Cooper (1789-1851) accepted his wife's challenge to write a novel. Following a feeble first attempt, he struck out vigorously in *The Spy* (1821), a tale of the neutral zone between the contending armies during the Revolution. With immense creative power he prepared The Leatherstocking Series, five novels tracing Natty Bumppo's career from a young scout to an old man leaving the East to retain his freedom on the western prairies. Thirty additional novels, a history of the U. S. Navy, and other volumes on politics and travel cascaded from his desk. Chiefly known as a romancer employing the technique of pursuit and surprise, he also wrote solid studies of American manners and class conflict in *Satanstoe* (1845), *The Chainbearer* (1845), and *The Redskins* (1846). These realistic novels never achieved the popularity accorded the frontier tales. Cooper's numerous defects as an artist—hastiness, generalized description, wooden dialog, inability to create women characters—are counterbalanced by gusto, unflagging excitement, plausible invention even in melodramatic situations, and the inclusion in each story of stimulating general ideas. Balzac found the basis for his vast panoramic plan for a Comédie Humaine in Cooper's Leatherstocking Series.

Two titans of U. S. literature slowly attained in critical, if not in popular estimation their proper stature. Herman Melville, (1819-1891) sailed on whaling vessels as a youth. His earliest novels, *Typee* (1846) and *Omoo* (1847), recount with some imaginative invention his experiences in a cruise to the South Seas. During ten years he wrote nine novels, none of which really succeeded. He surrendered authorship and at his death was an almost forgotten customs clerk in New York City. *Mardi* (1849) began as a romance but turned fiercely satirical of western civilization in passages beclouded by allegory or impassioned rhetoric. *Moby Dick* (1851), one of the great books of the U. S. A., recounts a monomaniac whaling captain's pursuit of a white whale; the magnificent story, carrying a heavy freight of zoological information and philosophizing, is an allegory of man's inability to overcome evil. Melville moved steadily toward an extreme pessimistic, anti-democratic, anti-clerical position. Although much of his reasoning is sophomoric, his dithyrambic sentences roll and heave with the thunderous power of ocean waves.

The antithesis of Melville was Walt Whitman (1819-1892), who in his poetry shouted optimistically an affirmative mystical faith in the individual, in democracy, in universal brotherhood; he welcomed death as the inlet to immortal life; he gloried in the noble destiny of the United States, whose leadership in world progress was inevitable. He rejected no one as unworthy; he sang the female equally with the male. His incautious ascription of goodness to every part and function of the human body led Emerson to request the omission of "Children of Adam" from *Leaves of Grass* (1855-92). Whitman clung to his principles, each few years adding a new group to the old in an expanded edition of his book. Yet Walt was no uncritical optimist; his prose writings contain searching analyses of the shortcomings of the U. S. A. *Democratic Vistas* (1871) show Whitman's untutored groping for a solution. *Specimen Days* (1882), an autobiography, sketches Whitman's career as a journalist and government clerk. Whitman's rejection in his own day resulted from the novelty of his verse pattern—a long, surging, oratorical line of irregular length; the absence of narrative or simple lyric statements and of regular meter and of traditional poetic devices; the ejaculatory, dithyrambic nature of his utterance; the use of lists or catalogs of events, persons, or places; and the inclusion of strange words. The average reader desires in poetry a narrative, or a clearly discernible moral interpretation, or a humorous twist of language enforced by rhymes. Even yet Walt is a poet's poet; such a pure gem as "When Lilacs Last in the Dooryard Bloom'd", being very intricate in its intertwining of three symbols, is more often praised than understood. Immense has been his influence on later poets; he freed verse from the shackles of meter, and he gave experimenters fruitful suggestions about symbolism and verse structure.

The South and the Old Southwest utilized the tall tale (q.v.) pattern of humor in books descriptive of local scenes and characters. A. B. Longstreet's *Georgia Scenes* (1835) described gander pulling, horse swapping, and similar rural customs. J. P. Kennedy fathered the romantic Virginia plantation tradition in *Swallow Barn* (1832). Even Edgar Allan Poe (1809-1849) in minor tales employed comic extravagances, although few of his stories are localized. Poe, born in Boston and raised by a Richmond merchant, stands apart from the main stream of American letters by his emphasis upon the purely aesthetic aspects of literature. While others were moralizing, Poe demanded "the rhythmical creation of beauty" and harangued against the "didactic heresy". He made a reputation as a critic and editor; his short stories fixed the pattern for that form of literature; and he dreamed of fame as a poet. He worked best within the narrow limits of Gothic terror in fiction and elegiac sentimentalizing in lyric poetry. A half dozen poems, a dozen stories, and three or four pieces of criticism are imperishable; he was America's first true aesthete in literature. Pride, intemperance, and instability humbled and finally killed him;

he remains a dark, enigmatic figure like the raven in his celebrated poem. In Charleston, S. C., William Gilmore Simms (1806-1870) wrote poetry, fiction, history, and political essays; his Cooperlike frontier and historical novels surge with turbulent action and boisterous humor. Henry Timrod (1829-1867) phrased eloquently in a few poems the Southern nationalist ideal in the War between the States. In this conflict numerous songs achieved high poetic beauty, such as Albert Pike's "Dixie" and J. R. Randall's "Maryland! My Maryland."

In New England dawned a Golden Day in literature, a day enriched by noble sentiments in accord with reform aspirations in every area of human endeavor. Most popular and even accorded a niche in Westminster Abbey was Henry Wadsworth Longfellow (1807-1882), whose sweet, moralizing lyricism tunefully embodied a gentle melancholy, and whose narratives of Evangeline, Miles Standish, and Paul Revere have molded U. S. concepts of certain historical events. Longfellow's seemingly fluent simplicity hides delicate artistry and sensitive perceptivity; his management of music, even if borrowed, and of figures of speech shows true poetic craftsmanship. His ideas, such as his pacifism in "The Arsenal at Springfield," reflect the best taste of his generation. The "Divina Commedia" sonnets belong with the greatest in the language. With more certitude in religion but with less artistry, John Greenleaf Whittier (1807-1892) pictured the simple, rustic beauty of New England scenery and the daily duties of common people. A Quaker, he phrased his people's humanitarian faith in terms now generally acceptable to all Christian sects. His dozens of anti-slavery poems have been forgotten, but still remembered are "Snow-Bound" (1865) and a few Burns-like pictures of New England life, as well as his religious lyrics.

The reforming zeal of New England caught up James Russell Lowell (1819-1891), whose early essays and poems questioned the necessity for human poverty, advocated abolition, and denounced the imperialistic aims apparent in the Mexican War. *The Bigelow Papers* (1847), dialect verses, gave literary sanction to this form of expression and paved the way for local color (q.v.). After the death of his wife, 1853, he turned literary critic and in studies of famous continental authors submerged his talents during the weaving of the civil crisis. In old age, as a minister to Spain and England, he became an outspoken defender of the democratic tradition. A few verses remain memorable; the heavy, essay-like odes and the elaborately jeweled prose criticism lack survival qualities. Perennially amusing are several light verses by Oliver Wendell Holmes (1809-1894), surgeon and man of letters, who typifies the finest qualities of the Brahmin caste of New England; faded now are the breakfast table conversations, the fiction directed against the enemies of the new science, and the biographical sketches of his contemporaries.

Two New England minds remain fresh and stimulating in spite of a century's changes. Ralph Waldo Emerson (1803-1882) and Henry David Thoreau (1817-1862) were fellow townsmen in Concord, Mass. The elder had come by way of Harvard College and Unitarianism to the conclusion that "The highest revelation is that God is in every man." Self-reliance, therefore, becomes God-reliance, and man's duty is to trust the Spirit of God radiant within all nature and within himself. This mystical belief informs almost every one of Emerson's writings; seldom has an author devoted so many different compositions to the elaboration of a single theme. In meditative and lyric poems Emerson's ideas are highlighted by apt imagery; the essays are prose poems employing all the artifice of verse. *Essays* (1841, 1844) is one of America's great books. Emerson's power arises from intensity of faith and verbal dexterity. Aphorisms stud his paragraphs like jewels. Short sentences, abundant figures of speech and allusions, and a public speaker's willingness to startle an audience with unexpected words—these are some of the elements of Emerson's art. As a critic be subordinated literature and art to ethical ideals, distinguished between talent and genius by discovering in the latter the always necessary God-reliance. The orotund universality of his utterance is difficult to translate into foreign tongues; yet his work is the least tarnished by time in the whole realm of American literature. Around Emerson gathered the so-called Transcendental Club, a dozen forceful Unitarian preachers and several energetic women like Margaret Fuller and Elizabeth Peabody.

Emerson's handyman and gardner, as well as Concord's pencil maker and surveyor, was Henry David Thoreau, who came into this world, he said, "not chiefly to make this a good place to live in, but to live in it." An individualist, he desired to live free and uncommitted, unhampered by any institution.

This doctrine he phrased in *Walden* (1854), one of the great books of the U. S., the discursive account of his experiences while living as a hermit, and an ethical teacher's appeal to society to return to simplicity and elevated feelings by living close to nature. Mahatma Ghandi, the Hindu nationalist leader in India, carried Thoreau's "On Civil Disobedience" (1849), a brief explanation of the political theory of non-cooperation. Unlike Emerson, Thoreau lacks constructive power in the organization and phrasing of his thoughts. Yet many aphorisms and many poetic passages adorn his several books.

The rise of the public school system after 1834 and the spread of education played its part in creating a vast reading audience. Gift books (q.v.), beautifully printed annuals, circulated in large numbers. Fiction lost something of the stigma attached to it, although novels and plays were still considered artifices of the devil. Fiction became increasingly popular; between 1789 and 1850 no fewer than 1500 novels were published. The master craftsman in fiction was the anatomist of sin-haunted minds, Nathaniel Hawthorne (1804-1864), a descendant of a witch-hanging Puritan judge. After study at Bowdoin College, he retired to his attic room to write, burn, and rewrite for a dozen years. *Fanshawe* (1827), a slight novel, was withdrawn from sale and burned. Year by year Hawthorne wrote a few stories which satisfied his high standards; in 1837 he culled a dozen for *Twice-Told Tales*, which was enlarged to 39 in 1842. Poe greeted the second collection with a review in which were laid down the laws of the short story and in which Hawthorne was pronounced "original on all points." *The Scarlet Letter* (1850) immediately was recognized as a masterpiece and still is considered America's finest piece of long fiction. This story of a woman's heroic maintenance of self-respect after being publicly punished for adultery has all the intensity and beauty of a Shakespearian tragedy. A thread of romance brightens the melodramatic *The House of the Seven Gables* (1851), which manages also to contrast the aristocrat unfavorably with the democrat in American life. Hawthorne's uniqueness lay in his ability to focus upon single incidents, such as that in "The Gray Champion," until a universal interpretation emerged. Like Poe he succumbed to contemporary taste for terror stories, but he never descended to hoaxes and extravaganzas. A uniform high seriousness, often balanced with humor, marks his concern

over the sins of mankind. Although his popular appeal is small compared with Poe's, Hawthorne's quiet artistry, as in "Rappaccini's Daughter," knew no equal before his time.

Five dramas still sparkle with vitality: J. N. Barker's *Superstition* (1828), picturing a bigoted Puritan parson's unrelenting hostility to two non-conformist strangers; R. M. Bird's *The Gladiator* (1831), based on the slave rebellion in Rome led by Spartacus; N. P. Willis's *Bianca Visconti* (1837), a story of an Italian girl's murder of her brother to enthrone her husband; Anna Cora Mowatt Ritchie's *Fashion* (1845), a comedy of manners satirizing the nouveau riche; and G. H. Boker's *Francesca da Rimini* (1855), a superb poetic version of the tragedy of Paolo and Francesca.

The conflict between the manufacturing interests of the North and the agrarians in the South seemed unimportant compared with the controversy over the manumission of Negro slaves. Statesmen like John C. Calhoun and Daniel Webster set forth the opposing sectional views in legislative debate. The issue remained doubtful in the public mind until Harriet Beecher Stowe (1812-1896) clarified the problem in a sentimental, melodramatic novel, *Uncle Tom's Cabin* (1852). With unprecedented rapidity the book circulated throughout the North; in vain a dozen fictional answers were prepared. Slavery was doomed. When conflict flared, a mood of grim determination marked both sides. Few of the writings, other than several songs and E. E. Hale's "The Man Without a Country" (1863), are as memorable as Abraham Lincoln's "Gettysburg Address" (1863), possibly the best prose-poem on democracy yet written, and "The Second Inaugural Address" (1865) with its humane last paragraph, beginning "With malice toward none, with charity for all."

The Civil War accentuated the alterations transforming the U. S. A. from an agricultural to a manufacturing nation, from a people of independent mind living on farms to industrial workers huddled together in company towns or cities. The westward migration afforded an outlet to farmers, but free land became exhausted in 1892. The frontier shifted from within to without the nation. Imperial plans led to an interest in the Pacific Ocean and the acquiring of Alaska and the Philippines, an act whose importance would be clear forty years later in Japan's attack on December 7, 1941. Possibly in no other nation had religious sanction seemed so necessary to its major policies; at home and abroad missionary societies spread a humanitarian "law of love," pictured well in C. M. Sheldon's novel *In His Steps* (1896), which sold more than 20 million copies. Public high schools in every community replaced academies, and state universities with federal support outdistanced private institutions. Government increasingly controlled business, so that by the 1930's in the depth of a depression socialistic schemes became increasingly popular.

Literature reflected these social changes, and literary theory tended to phrase social concepts rather than aesthetic principles. Pre-Civil War literature in the U. S. A. was primarily romantic and escapist; post-War writings reflected a realistic approach, which became modified after 1900 by the imposition of sectarian or social ideologies. Elbowing the older New England generation of writers from the scene were self-educated westerners. Bret Harte (1836-1902) electrified the nation with a humorous verse, "The Heathen Chinee," and short stories, "The Outcasts of Poker Flat" and "The Luck of Roaring Camp." With a new technique of realistic presentation based upon tall-tale humor Harte pictured the strange goldfields of California and their agglomeration of wicked gamblers, thieves, and prostitutes who retain a spark of goodness which lights up in a moment of stress. William Dean Howells (1837-1920) in reviews and books denounced romance and praised realism, in his case really a genteel fictional comedy of manners; in nearly a hundred volumes of novels and plays he pictured aspects of Eastern U. S. Following Harte's model and aided by Howells's criticism, dozens of authors described whimsical persons in a unique regional atmosphere in local color (q.v.) stories. Most famous of the Western writers was Samuel Langhorne Clemens, "Mark Twain" (1835-1910), whose tall-tale humor finds joyous outlet in *Roughing It* (1872), an account of the Nevada silver rush, and in three books on the Mississippi River, *The Adventures of Tom Sawyer* (1876) and *The Adventures of Huckleberry Finn* (1884), two delightful picaresque, episodic extravaganzas of boy life, and *Life on the Mississippi* (1883), an autobiography of his boyhood enthusiasms. A strain of pessimism in *The Mysterious Stranger* (1916) gave rise to the untenable theory that Clemens had suffered from repression. Clemens' exuberant anecdotal humor and perceptive descriptive skill were employed to further social justice and to secure equality for all men.

Henry James (1843-1916), born in New England but schooled in Europe, first insisted that fiction is an art; he taught dozens of writers, including Joseph Conrad and Edith Wharton, the principles of narrative structure. The inventor of the novel of international contrast, he developed psychological analysis of motive beyond that of his predecessor, Hawthorne. Hamlin Garland (1860-1940), born in Wisconsin, revolted against Eastern fictional romanticism in *Main-Travelled Roads* (1891) in an effort to improve the conditions of farmers in line with the ideas of the single taxer Henry George and of the Populist Party; his doctrine was labeled vertism (q.v.). Stephen Crane (1871-1900) in verse and prose transferred to literature the new French aesthetic theory of impressionism (q.v.); *The Red Badge of Courage* (1895), a novel, pictures a soldier's responses to war. Theodore Dreiser (1871-) in *Sister Carrie* (1900) set off a bombshell with a story of a wayward girl whose actions were excused in accord with the conclusions of materialistic naturalism (q.v.). For thirty years Dreiser's extreme frankness typified all that was hateful in the new realism. With the rise of the magazines as purveyors of advertising to millions of readers, fiction became the most important form of literary expression. William Sidney Porter, "O. Henry" (1862-1910), created brittle, slangy, ironic stories with undisguised compassion for the submerged masses, while Jack London (1876-1916) fictionized the theory of the survival of the fittest in tales and novels, many set in the Yukon. Upton Sinclair's *The Jungle* (1906) brought the stench of meat packing plants to public nostrils. With Sinclair Lewis's *Main Street* (1920) realism became enthroned, and thereafter, partly because of the mood of national self-disparagement created by World War I, dozens of novelists poked probing fingers into every area of human action. Yet as fiction increasingly became synonymous with the sociological tract, aesthetic experimentation flourished. Willa Cather (1876-) not only asked Middle Western immigrants to find happiness in a life of disciplined endeavor close to the soil, but she demanded in an essay, "The Novel Demeublé," that the novel be stripped of its unnecessary trappings of description and commentary. Edith Wharton's *The Writing of Fiction* (1925) asked, as did James, for tightness of construction in traditional methods and for attention to moral values. The new barbarism, so called by conservative critics, was popularized in the short stories and novels of Sherwood Anderson (1876-1941), an awakened dreamer who reported the crudity and yearning of people unable to express their feelings. By employing the results and some of the techniques of Freudian psychology, esp. in *Winesburg, Ohio* (1919) and *Dark Laughter* (1925), Anderson opened to fiction writers Pandora's black box of subconscious mental activity and its devastating effects upon repressed individuals. The method of stream-of-consciousness affected almost all novelists; possibly the best single novel in this form was Conrad Aiken's *Blue Voyage* (1927). Yet naturalism had new areas of degeneracy to survey in the Deep South, where are set William Faulkner's stories of rape, lust, and brutality, and Erkine Caldwell's photographic reproductions of sharecroppers' moral decay.

In Ernest Hemingway's stories of war, racketeering, and bullfighting, the method of impressionism achieved new intensity. Yet it was John R. Dos Passos whose experiments seemed most fruitful, especially in the discontinuous technique of the movie news reel in *Manhattan Transfer* (1925) and in the successful rendering of the total social and intellectual impact of a moment upon a set of fictional characters, as in *U. S. A.* (1932-1938), through the use of four types of material in alternating chapters of narration, thumb-nail biographical sketches, quotations from newspaper stories and from popular songs, and a shorthand autobiographic record of the author's emotions. New depth of character insight as supplied by realism and psychology, coupled with an awareness of folklore and folk arts, gave the fictional practitioners of the New Regionalism (q.v.) attractiveness in recording local scenes and characters. Experimental fiction in the 20th cent., in advancing from timid realism to a full representation of every aspect of life, tended to come under the influence of the dogmas of socialism, communism, and naturalistic materialism. Yet such popular authors as Booth Tarkington and Dorothy Canfield Fisher, as well as most magazine writers, surrendered reluctantly, if at all, fiction's ancient romantic subject matter and traditional form.

Poetry after the Civil War, except from 1912 to 1920, became an art studied in the schools, practiced vigorously by many writers, but seldom supported by the public. Whitman remained unrecognized while the early New England poets' verses were memorized in every school. Bayard Taylor in "Bedouin Love Song" unconsciously symbolized the romantic escapism or exoticism of U. S. poets. Bret Harte and John Hay wrote a few local color verses, and James Whitcomb Riley (1849-1916) penned Hoosier nature poems and versified common sense. Joaquin Miller (1841-1913), a Byron of the Rocky Mountains, gave a few rhetorical yet perceptive word paintings of the pioneers' westward movement. Sidney Lanier (1842-1881) combined professional musicianship with poetry; like Poe he tried to wed the two arts. A nationalist and a humanitarian, he cried out against the materialism of the raven days of Grant's Administration in a plea, especially in "The Symphony" and "Corn," for the establishment of universal brotherhood. William Vaughan Moody (1869-1910) in "Ode in a Time of Hesitation," bitterly denounced the imperialism evidenced in the taking of the Philippines, but Richard Hovey (1864-1900), poet laureate of an American college fraternity, insisted in "Unmanifest Destiny" upon the doctrine that fate guides our nation's expansion. Whitman's prophet bard had not emerged; only an occasional poem reflected the national will or duty.

In 1912 in Chicago, Harriet Monroe (1860-1936) founded *Poetry: A Magazine of Verse*, seemingly just another little magazine (q.v.). Yet in these pages appeared a startlingly new poetry, a poetry which at last had come to grips with life and with the technical problems of poetics. Amy Lowell (1874-1925), sister of Harvard University's president, flamboyantly announced the arrival of a new era in poetry, espoused Imagism (q.v.), and put discussions of poetry upon the front pages of newspapers. Free verse (q.v.), the medium of the "new poetry," became the center of a public squabble. Vachel Lindsay (1879-1931), a modern troubadour who traded rhymes for bread on cross-country walks, phrased in a raucous manner, borrowed equally from jazz and from the Salvation Army, a set of pious, moralizing, patriotic, humanitarian ideas; he created poem games, rewrote Biblical narratives, and characterized politicians and movie queens in an effort to bring chanted poetry into each person's daily experience. His utopian dreaming first took form as the New Localism (q.v.). Carl Sandburg (1878-   ) in a free verse akin to Whitman's has run the gamut of moods and experiences; his slangy word pictures of disgust, deceit, envy, and pride among poor people startled traditional critics. Yet Sandburg continued to be the people's poet, as in *The People, Yes* (1936), possibly America's best imaginative exposition of democratic principles. A symbolist and an imagist, Sandburg has had the originality to use the steel mill and industrial civilization as the setting for his commentaries upon man's struggle and as a background for his faith in human striving.

Edwin Arlington Robinson (1869-1935), drew upon his New England home community for a set of characters whom he pictured as always failing. "Laureate of failure" he was once called, but Robinson clearly demonstrates that God is always at hand to help and that men are not fools by compulsion so much as through some flaw or weakness in character. Similarly transcendental in outlook but affirmative in his characterizations, Robert Frost (1875-   ) uses New England scenes with which to universalize a sense of human brotherhood and to oppose theories or doctrines, such as materialism or self-interest, by which men are placed in hostile opposition. Both Robinson and Frost write almost solely in traditional metrical forms, yet their work differs greatly. Robinson is best in brilliant phrasing, subacid humor, ironic situation, and character delineation; Frost is supreme in conversation-like descriptions, wherein seemingly unobtrusive details supply clues to intentional allegory and a universal interpretation.

French symbolism gave direction to Thomas Stearns Eliot (1888-   ), whose *The Waste Land* (1922) aroused a furore because of its metrical novelty and its mood of despair and frustration. Eliot's radical experimentation involves the seemingly incongruous mixture of trivial and important, traditional and experimental words, figures, and statements; yet his musical lines suggest his moods even when the words, drawn in part from many foreign languages, may not be clear. Eliot's influence on later poets has been immense. Conrad Aiken (1889-   ) is heir apparent to Poe and Lanier as a musical poet; his delicate efforts to evoke rather than to portray Eliot-like moods have limited his audience. Robinson Jeffers (1887-   ), Whitman's antithesis, draws from scholarly study a negative philosophy which holds that civilization is a transient sickness and that man is doomed to defeat. His long-lined free verse differs greatly from Whitman's and Sandburg's in its failure to make the line a phrasal entity. In an epic of the Civil War, *John Brown's*

Body (1928), employing many meters and including fragments of prose, Stephen Vincent Benét (1898-1943) proved that poetry still speaks to the average reader; in other poems Benét has phrased the terror and impact of the totalitarian threat to liberty. Recent experimentation in verse has tested every possible alteration to rhythm and cadence, lineation and structure, and verbal effect through sound and suggestion.

Among the traditional poets three women have gained high place. Sara Teasdale (1884-1933) with bright clarity pictured in love poems a woman's slightly cynical or disillusioned feelings. Elinor Wylie (1887-1928) counseled an aloofness to the struggles of the marketplace; her patrician mood is found in a small collection of exquisite poems. Edna St. Vincent Millay (1892-   ) sprang to fame as a college student with "Renascence," a remarkable poem describing a mystical experience; her later work has dealt with death and love in traditional meters or has excitedly opposed tyranny and repression in free verse.

From 1865 to 1915 the American theatre suffered colonial dependency upon Europe because the theatrical chains and managers looked for financial profits rather than artistic success. After 1883 vaudeville (q.v.) and stock companies created theatres or so-called opera houses for every city; in 1910 there were 1,520 legitimate theatres in the U. S. A., but fifteen years later the number had fallen to 634 and continued to fall. Partly because of a "star system" and chain management, drama in the U. S. A. imitated French well-made plays. Occasionally the influence of Ibsen appeared: yet the more famous authors, Augustin Daly, Bronson Howard, Augustus Thomas, Clyde Fitch, and David Belasco, used rapid-fire melodramatic effects in modified comedies of manners. Dramatizations of popular fiction and adaptations of foreign plays largely filled the stage, although an occasional play, such as Clyde Fitch's *The Truth* (1907), W. V. Moody's *The Great Divide* (1909), or Margaret P. Peabody's *The Piper* (1910), hinted awareness of the new spirit rising in the European theatre. With the formation in 1912 of the 47 Workshop by G. P. Baker at Harvard University and in 1915 of The Provincetown Players and the Washington Square Players, experiment and native authorship received new impetus. The vogue of the Little Theatre movement (q.v.) gave opportunities to actors and writers who were denied expression when the commercial theatres closed.

Eugene O'Neill (1888-   ), the single internationally important figure in contemporary U. S. drama, began with Baker and the Provincetown Players. Combining realistic and romantic techniques while utilizing the results of modern psychological research, O'Neill has become notable for delineation of character through the evocation of feeling, dramatic experimentation with Strindbergian expressionistic techniques, and facility in giving universality to isolated incident. His most striking dramas include *The Emperor Jones* (1920); *The Hairy Ape* (1922); *The Great God Brown* (1926) with its experimental use of masks; *Strange Interlude* (1928) with an elaborate use of subvocal speech in stream-of-consciousness asides in a 9-act treatment of repression; and *Mourning Becomes Electra* (1931), a trilogy on the Electra theme reinterpreted with psychoanalytic insight into the effect of Puritan American attitudes. In *Lazarus Laughed* (1927) and *Days Without End* (1934) O'Neill gives affirmative answers to questions of religious faith and immortality. *Ah, Wilderness!* (1933) shows O'Neill's gifts as a comic writer.

Maxwell Anderson (1888-   ) who alone rivals O'Neill as a serious dramatist, uses social themes for purposes of tragedy; *Winterset* (1935), a study in class conflict, in spite of flaccid verse has moments of greatness. Elmer Rice in *The Adding Machine* (1923), an expressionistic drama of the effect of industrialism, and Clifford Odets in *Waiting for Lefty* (1935), on trade unionism, best represent the rise of proletarian influence in drama. Even more effective in using the drama for social discussion was the W. P. A. Federal Theatre Project (1936-1939), which created a new dramatic form, the Living Newspaper, a combination of techniques derived from the radio, moving picture, and recent theatrical experimentation. Much regional activity resulted in a few excellent plays, esp. those of Paul Green and Dubose Heyward.

Although problem and social plays were numerous, especially upon the themes of the futility of war, of class hatred, and of the need for human brotherhood, the largest production continued in the field of comedy by such skilled artisans as Rachel Crothers, Clare Kummer, George Kelly, Philip Barry, George S. Kaufman, Marc Connelly, and Robert Sherwood.

Literary criticism, practiced incidentally by such writers as Poe, Howells, and James, became an art in the 20th cent. Van Wyck Brooks enunciated the need for a continuous flow of general ideas about an author and the evaluation of his work in terms of his social thought. Irving Babbitt and P. E. More created the New Humanism (q.v.), an ethical theory requiring authors to maintain a balance between extremes. H. L. Mencken skeptically examined all theories while demanding that authors tell the truth; his eclecticism as editor of *The American Mercury* (1923-33) gave critical support to dozens of new writers of all creeds and schools. Communism became the popular ideology of the 1930's; V. F. Calverton gave the most reasoned interpretation of the value of this Marxian concept. B. A. Botkin through essays and anthologies gave clearest expression to the concept of the New Regionalism. Under John Crowe Ransom a group of young Southerners developed an agrarian economics with a metaphysical poetics and a preference for T. S. Eliot's aristocratic traditionalism. Never before had literary criticism been as controversial or so lively.

The essay maintained its traditional forms during the remainder of the 19th cent. John Burroughs and John Muir perfected the nature essay of Thoreau, and many authors vied to become genteel commentators upon nature and man. Not to the mild, conservative Samuel McChord Crothers or to the acidulous Agnes Repplier does one turn today for a record of the times, but to the journalistic prose of Upton Sinclair, Stuart Chase, Walter Lippmann, and the newspaper and magazine columnists (q.v.). Fresh breezes blew the academic dust from U. S. prose when H. L. Mencken and G. J. Nathan founded the *American Mercury* and H. R. Luce *Time* in 1923. *The New Yorker* in 1925 completed the rout of traditionalism with well-bred sophistication in satiric sallies, biographical profiles, light verse, stories, and criticism of the arts and fashions.

Biography rose into a major art after 1920, when the biographical pattern of fiction seemed less important than swiftly told yet accurate interpretations of the major figures of world and American significance. W. E. Woodward coined the word "bunk," which served to denounce falsification of fact. His *Meet General Grant* (1928) was called a "debunking" biography. Washington, Lincoln, and other persons were subject to close analyses of actions and motives; the net effect was the discovery that biography might escape funereal solemnity and achieve the sprightliness of life itself. Carl Sandburg's 6-vol. study of Lincoln and D. S. Freeman's 4-vol. description of Lee, as well as 3 supplementary vols. on Lee's generals, have already achieved the status of classics. A vogue of autobiography has led to thousands of such volumes; Henry Adam's *Education* (1907) and Ludwig Lewisohn's *Upstream* (1922 attracted attention because of their exasperation at U. S. shortcomings.

Literature in the U. S. A. is concerned more with matter than manner, more with ideas than style, more with ethics than aesthetics. Yet not only does each new technical advance or aesthetic theory in the four quarters of the globe receive immediate trial, but U. S. writers now are in the vanguard of literary experimenters. In general excellence, if Nobel prizes be considered a criterion, the U. S. A. now has come of age, for the U. S. A. has had as many winners of this distinguished honor as any other nation. See R. Blankenship, *American Literature*, 1931; *Cambridge History of Am. Lit.*, 1917-21; V. L. Parrington, *Main Currents in American Thought*, 1927-30; P. H. Boynton, *Literature and American Life*, 1936; A. H. Quinn, *A History of American Drama*, 1923-36 and *American Fiction*, 1936, C. Van Doren, *The American Novel*, 1940, F. L. Pattee, *The First Century of Am. Lit.*, 1935, *A History of Am. Lit. since 1870*, 1915, *The New Am. Lit.*, 1930, and *Development of the Am. Short Story*, 1923; W. F. Taylor, *A History of Am. Letters*, 1936; F. B. Millett, *Contemporary Am. Authors*, 1940; K. Macgowan, *Footlights across America*, 1929; A. Hornblow, *A History of the Theatre in America*, 1919; B. Smith, *Forces in American Criticism*, 1939; J. D. Hart, *Oxford Companion to American Literature*, 1941; F. L. Mott, *A History of Am. Magazines*, 1930-39. COLLECTIONS: A. H. Quinn, *Representative Am. Plays*, 1938; N. Foerster, *Am. Poetry and Prose*, 1935; M. D. Zabel, *Literary Opinion*

in America, 1937; H. R. Warfel, R. H. Gabriel, and S. T. Williams, *The American Mind*; E. C. Stedman and E. M. Hutchinson, *A Library of American Literature*, 1889-90; S. T. Williams, *The Am. Spirit in Letters*, 1925; A. Jessup, *Representative Am. Short Stories*, 1923.   —H.R.W.

use zoning. See CIVIC PLANNING.

Ushaq carpets. See ISLAMIC ART.

ushnīsha (Skr.). A protuberance or topknot on the skull of the Buddhas, always shown in painted or sculptured figures.

usnīsa. Cranial protuberance of the Buddha, signifying gnosis (knowledge of positive spiritual truth).

uta-e (Jap.). See JAPANESE ART.

Utakawa yaki (Jap.). Pottery made in province of Chikuzen.

utilitarian, utility (L. *utilis,* useful). A mode of *composition* (q.v.) in art, in which details are so organized as to be instrumental (or at least apparently or intentionally instrumental) to some end in the world of action which can be considered useful. Approximate synonyms are *functional, practical,* especially in contrast with *decorative, aesthetic,* etc. The utilitarian or functional factor in art is to be described in terms of fitness or intended fitness for some active use, beyond serving as an object for aesthetic or intellectual contemplation. In a work of art such as a chair, utilitarian or functional arrangements may coexist with decorative and other. These various factors may be merged (so that, for example, all decorative aspects are also utilitarian) or may be separate, as in applied, "non-functional" ornament.   —T.M.

U-T'ong, school of. See SOUTHEASTERN ASIATIC ART.

Ut-napishtim. Hero of the ancient Babylonian deluge myth.

V

vair. See HERALDRY.

vajra (Skr.). So-called thunderbolt, generally a short double-trident form used in Hindu and Buddhist rituals and often shown as one of the attributes of a deity. See SYMBOLISM IN FAR EASTERN ART.

Valencia ware. See CERAMICS II.

valley. *Arch.* The internal angle formed by two inclined sides of a roof.

value. The term assigned by the Optical Society of America to the designation of relative brightness. It is used in this sense in the Munsell Color System as the designation for the lightness to darkness psychological attribute of color. See COLOR.
—V.K.B.

valve. *Mus.* A device for diverting the air-current from the main tube to an additional side-tube, in certain brass wind instruments. Because of the lengthening of the air-column the pitch of the instrument's entire scale is lowered.

Van Dyke brown. A painter's pigment said to have been named for the artist who liked a brown of that hue, this is a somewhat organic material coming from earthy substances like lignite or brown coal. It is partially soluble in oil and makes a transparent film; though it fades when exposed to strong light, it is more permanent in oil than in water color. —G.L.S.

vanishing line, v. parallel, v. point, v. point of diagonals. See PERSPECTIVE.

Vaphio cup. See METALWORK.

varada mudrā (Skr.). A mystic gesture symbolizing charity in gift bestowing. Arm pendent, fingers extended, palm outward.

vargueno (Sp.). Writing desk.

variance. See CIVIC PLANNING.

variation. *Mus.* Repetition of a musical statement in which some of the characteristic features of the original statement are retained while others are omitted, or replaced by new features. —E.K.

variety. See LITERARY CRITICISM.

variety in unity. Variety in unity or unity in variety is a universal and necessary mark of a satisfying artistic work. The problem needs a psychological approach. The function of variety is to intensify the spectator's interest, and the function of unity is to increase, by skilful organization, the range of factors which attention can grasp. (Pepper)
"Variety is the mother of enjoyment." Disraeli). Artful variety comprises all the means by which the artist enhances the vividness of his creations by multiplying and altering their elements. A work of art is too simple if it summons only an instantaneous glance and it is too complex if it uses up the spectator's energy of attention before he wins compensating satisfaction. When a barren form or a bewildering chaos requires painful and fruitless effort, it precludes aesthetic enjoyment, which is both free and pleasing. An enjoyable work needs enough complexity to invite exploration and not so much as to weary our limited powers of attention. Pleasing variety is a well balanced mean between the excesses of deadening monotony and maddening chaos.

The chief means of attaining variety in works of art are: (1) *In medium*: richness and variation of appeal in sense qualities. (2) *In form*: rhythms involving wide variations; contrasts whether asymmetrical or occult (psychic). (3) *In value or meaning*: development of a theme through wide excursions; richness in imaginative suggestiveness; dramatic conflicts; specialties of personal style. (4) *In the whole*: freshness or novelty at any level.

Thus variety means creative complexity, range, richness, and variousness, perhaps charm, within a well-bounded whole. By itself, however, variety does not guarantee aesthetic satisfaction. The presentation of a conglomeration of sprawling and straggling objects without inner ties is favorable to the jitters and guarantees ugliness. Variety needs its supplement of unities. Their function is dual: to bring measured and pleasing order into the parts, and to expand thereby the range of our grasp.

The basic ways in which a work of art may be unified are: (1) *In medium*: consistency of medium and of craftsmanship. (2) *In form*: regular rhythm; symmetrical balance; proportion; the representation of familiar things; the use of well known traditional schemes and scales of organization; and, in temporal arts, lawful progression and climax. (3) *In meaning*: dominance of one emotion, theme, or personality; coherence of poetic truth. (4) *In the whole*: clarity or simplicity as excluding irrelevant or nonfunctional factors; fitness or suitableness of all parts within the whole; consummatory individuality or harmony.

The skilful combination of the modes of variety and unity in artistic works is the principal source of our enjoyment of them. Satisfying variety with unity means sufficient complexity to sustain exploration and sufficient integration to hold the parts together in a comprehensible whole. To variety and unity respectively are due the qualities of vitality and repose which distinguish aesthetic response. The harmony we call beauty is a union of variety and order; it is diversity with integration, organic unity, satisfying individuality. See T. M. Greene, *The Arts and the Art of Criticism,* 1940; D. H. Parker, *Analysis of Art,* 1926; Stephen C. Pepper, *Aesthetic Quality,* 1937.   —R.F.P.

varnish. Any protective coating laid over a paint or any film material used as a protective coating for sculpture and other objects is commonly called a varnish. As a rule, varnishes are principally resinous films with more or less oil added for strength and plasticity. Originally it is supposed that the word indicated a resin dissolved in an oil or mixed with it.   —G.L.S.

varnishing. See RESTORATION OF PAINTINGS.

vase (L. *vas,* a vessel). The term *vase* denotes a vessel of many types and materials: esp. one that is ornamental or decorative in style. It is usual to define this term as meaning a vessel without a cover, the height of which is greater than its width. Greek vases included vessels for holding or carrying oil, wine or water; for mixing wine and water; for pouring or drinking wine; and for perfumes or ointment. See SYMBOLISM IN FAR EASTERN ART.   —A.W.O.

vase carpets. See ISLAMIC ART.

vase form. Any vessel, small in size, with contracted neck and substantial foot or base.

vat dyed. Dyed with insoluble dyes formed on the fiber by oxidation.

vaudeville (from Fr. *Vau de Vire,* a locality in Normandy from which emanated in the 15th cent. popular humorous songs). A form of variety theatrical entertainment in the U. S. A. embracing songs, dances, dramatic sketches, monologues, acrobatic stunts, and specialty tricks, each of which is presented and announced as a separate performance. In England the nearest corresponding term is 'variety theatre' or 'music hall'; occasionally when a thread of plot unites the various performances the terms 'musical comedy' and 'revue' are used. Vaudeville originated in the U. S. A. in 1883 in Boston, Mass., as the Gaiety Museum, when Benjamin Franklin Keith exhibited a midget and a stuffed "mermaid." Other attractions were added, inculding the famous comedy team of Weber and Fields. By emphasizing skill and keeping the presentation morally clean, Keith attracted audiences of ladies and children. With Edward F. Albee as partner, Keith developed a chain of theatres, so that by 1911, the year of Keith's death, every important city had a vaudeville theater. Since the vogue of the motion picture, vaudeville has increasingly become a subordinate variety entertainment; many performers play in night clubs. Since 1935 the term vaudeville has seldom been used in popular speech. See E. F. Albee, *Encyclopaedia Britannica,* 1942, XXIII, 13: Douglas Gilbert, *American Vaudeville: Its Life and Times,* 1940.   —H.R.W.

vault. (1) An arched roof. (2) A subterranean compartment.

vehicle. See medium.

veil. See COSTUME ART.

velarium. See amphitheatre.

vellum. There is no technical difference between vellum and parchment (q.v.). In some instances the former term has been applied to what is called uterine vellum, skins of new-born calves, kids, or lambs. Usually it is given to any fine skin used for writing or illumination.   —G.L.S.

vellum finish. *Book.* A smooth finish on binding cloth.

velour. Any soft, napped worsted or woolen dress goods fabric heavier than flannel. Pile fabrics are often called velours.

velvet. A fabric with a thick, short, cut pile on the surface and a plain back.

velvet carpet. Velvet in the better qualities resembles Wilton in appearance, but has more possibilties in color. It does not have the structural quality of the Wilton, as there is no buried wool in the jute back and it is not made on a Jacquard loom. Only one yarn is used but this has to be of good quality and of the same grade throughout in order to take the various color dyes properly. The natural yarn is wound around a drum-like small edition of a Ferris-wheel. The strips of pattern paper are followed by a printer who watches a vertical line of square on the pattern. The first square may call for a green and the drum is set in the #1 stop on the brass rim of the drum. Then he releases a car of aniline dye, in wheat flour paste, which prints a stripe of green across all the threads on the drum. Following the pattern he prints stripes of this same color on the yarns across the drum wherever required by the little square on the paper. Changing the car for each color, he prints all the colors required for each square of the pattern.

The yarn is removed from the drum, the dye is set and the flour paste is washed out. Each yarn is wound on a separate spool and arranged in its proper order on the creel and drawn between two tapestry setters. They set the yarn every few feet and the pattern can actually be seen on the surface. The pattern as seen is elongated over three times its actual length in the finished fabric as it is shortened up by the pile wires in the weaving. Just yarn, which has been sized is used for weight and strength as a stuffer in this weave. It is also generally stained on the

back. Although this is the cheapest of the weaves it requires the use of a high quality of yarn. Velvet is a comparatively inexpensive weave but the weave itself is highly durable. It can be woven seamless to 18 feet wide.   —B.E.J.

veneer. A thin layer, as of wood or stone, upon a commoner or under surface. See plywood.

veneered (revetted) architecture. See ARCHITECTURE.

Venetian glass. See GLASS AND GLASSMAKING.

Venetian red. The differences among the red iron oxides are hard to describe. This is one of them and, although formerly the name was used for a natural pigment, it is now given to a calcined mixture of copperas and whiting.   —G.L.S.

Venetian school. See ITALIAN ART.

Venice turpentine. One of the few balsams used directly in the arts is a frequent ingredient in painters' varnishes. It has been mentioned since the time of the Renaissance and has probably been in use since varnishes were first employed. It comes from the European larch and is collected chiefly in the Tyrol.   —G.L.S.

vent. An opening, commonly small, for the passage of something, as air; hence, an outlet of any kind.

ventilator. In southwestern archeology: The term usually applied to the opening or passageway which led from the open air through or under the wall and into the chamber. The ventilator consisted usually of an exterior or outer vertical shaft, a horizontal tunnel or passage, and often an interior or inner vertical shaft. (Some archeologists believe the "ventilator" served to conduct air into the chamber while others are of the belief that the so-called "ventilator" was thought to be the entrance and exit of spirit beings.)   —J.M.M.

Venus. Aphrodite.

verbose. Lack of organization with specific reference to the presentation of material. The term indicates that a work of art is far longer and more complex than is demanded by the matter it treats and the meaning it carries. To be verbose is to give several bad reports, which repeat and perhaps obscure one another, instead of one good report which presents itself and retires.   —I.J.

verdigris. An artificial green pigment, a normal acetate or one of the basic acetates of copper, this has acquired the comparatively modern name, verdigris (*vert de Grece*). It was known in ancient times and methods of preparing it from metallic copper by exposure to mermenting grape skins in vinegar are described by Theophrastus and Pliny. It is a reactive and unstable pigment, and more permanent colors have displaced it on the artist's palette.   —G.L.S.

vergo. *Book.* The lefthand page of an open book.

verification. See PSYCHOLOGY OF ART.

veritism. A literary theory set forth by Hamlin Garland in *Crumbling Idols* (1894), demanding of western U. S. writers an individuality arising from local characteristics, freedom from past models and books, and the sincere utilization of the present experience of honest, wholesome people. In modifying the prevailing emphasis upon local color (q.v.) in literature, Garland followed the leadership of William Dean Howells in demanding a realistic treatment of life and of the new sociology emerging from the study of natural science. Since evolution or natural law had created a new science, there should be a new art. The revolt was directed largely against the literary domination of the East, where most publishing houses and magazines were then located.   —H.R.W.

vermilion. Both natural and artificial sulphides of mercury are called vermilion. The former, cinnabar, is now no longer used as an artist's pigment and probably was displaced to some extent in the Middle Ages. It is a mineral widely distributed, occurring in England, Europe, China, Japan, Peru, Mexico, and Spain. This and the artificial oxide of lead were the bright orange-red pigments of antiquity. An Arabian alchemist in the 8th or 9th cent. speaks of a red pigment produced by the union of sulphur and mercury, and from that time on recipes for such preparation are common in the literature of painting and craftsmanship. There is little difference between the artificial and the natural pigments, although the former seem to have a somewhat higher intensity of color.   —G.L.S.

verse anthem. See anthem.

vert. *Her.* Green.

vertical. *Mus.* Term used figuratively to designate the simultaneity of musical elements, particularly the formation of chords.

vesi'ca. In art a lenticular shape formed of two equal circle arcs each passing through the center of the other. Used in early Christian art as the traditional panel for a standing figure of Christ or an Apostle, in heraldry as the escutcheon of a churchman's arms. It is the usual shape of the seals of bishoprics and priories. In architecture it is known as **vesica piscis** from its original use in symbolic ornament as a cartouche holding a fish.   —T.E.F.

vestibule. A small room or antechamber, usually between the outer entrance and an interior doorway to a larger chamber.

vibrato. The vibrato is the most important of all the musical ornaments on account of the extent of its occurrence and the essential characteristic which it contributes to tone quality in the form of flexibility, tenderness and richness of tone.

There are several reasons why this aspect of music has not been understood, explained, or properly appraised by musicians. One obstacle has been that, until recently, there was no measuring instrument available for accurate recording and scientific analysis of the phenomenon. Another obstacle is the fact that the vibrato as we hear it is entirely different from the vibrato as it is performed. We now have the means by which it may be recorded and analyzed into the minutest detail.

On the basis of laboratory experiments, we are now in a position to offer a definition which is subject to critical examination and verification in the laboratory: *A good vibrato is a pulsation of pitch, usually accompanied with synchronous pulsations of loudness and timbre, of such extent and rate as to give a pleasing flexibility, tenderness and richness to the tone.* (See ACOUSTICS, TERMINOLOGY IN.)

This is a definition of a *good vibrato*; but vibratos may be good, bad, or indifferent. In general, we may say that a *bad vibrato* is any periodic pulsation of pitch, loudness, or timbre, which, singly or in combination, fails to produce pleasing flexibility, tenderness, and richness of tone. Likewise, if we desire a *generic definition of all vibratos,* we might say that the vibrato in music is a periodic pulsation of pitch, intensity, or timbre, singly or in combination.

This definition is a result of years of experimentation, and tells a long story. It identifies the media through which the vibrato may ocur, showing that there are three distinct kinds of vibrato, namely: *pitch vibrato, intensity vibrato,* and *timbre vibrato.* The first two may occur singly or in combination. On the basis of the analysis of musical tones, we are in a position to say that these three can be isolated and demonstrated, and that they are the only kinds possible because they cover all possible basic attributes of sound waves.

The second part of the definition describes its function, namely: to give a pleasing flexibility, tenderness, and richness to the tone. These three aspects are universally recognized in musical aesthetics as desirable and fundamental. Each holds a distinct and definable place in any psychological classification of the expression of feelings.

The average pulsation in pitch for all the best singers of today is about a semitone step in *extent* at the *rate* of six-and-a-half cycles per second. The *intensity vibrato* is, as a rule, present in parts of the tone, but is not conspicuous in a good tone. Where it occurs, it tends to be at the same rate as for the pitch and between two and three *decibels of intensity* in extent. The pitch vibrato is present in every good tone, long or short, and in all the transitions.

By collecting musical *performance scores* for adequate samplings of singers under all sorts of conditions, we can build a veritable *science of the vibrato,* which, when it becomes a matter of popular knowledge among musicians, will probably be treated as a common-sense knowledge. Here, we can mention only a few things about the occurrence of the vibrato and its true nature.

In singing, the pitch vibrato is practically universal. No good artist sings without it. It occurs not only in long tones, but in short tones, attack, release, and portamento. It tends to come in gradually in the voice of the child, just to the extent that the child sings with genuine feeling. It occurs in the most primitive races, wherever the intonation is of an emotional nature. It occurs in sustained and emotional *speech*; and in very hearty *laughter* of the adult. It is present in the vigorous *crying* of the newborn infant, in the singing of the *canary,* in the *bark* of the dog, in the *cooing* of the dove.

In short, it is present wherever sustained vocalization expresses genuine emotion. It is a basic phenomenon of nature, both in man and in higher animals. It rests fundamentally upon the periodic innervation of paired muscles under emotional tension. The *canary* bird in the simplest tour has a mere chatter in one pitch at the rate of six or seven pulsations per second; in fact, all the recognized tours of that bird may possibly be traced as embellishments upon this basic time pattern, through modulations of pitch and increasing complexity of rhythmic pattern in time and intensity and timbre.

The same principle applies to man. We are born with the neuro-muscular organism which has a number of natural periodicities. One of these is at the rate of from five to ten pulsations per second and is probably a phenomenon of what is known as *refractory phase*; which means that it requires a certain time after one nervous discharge into a muscle before the next discharge can become effective. The "ha-ha-ha" in a most hearty laughter at the rate of six or seven pulsations per second is a basic illustration of this phenomenon; and the corresponding chatter may be heard in vigorous crying.

On this basic time pattern the human vibrato, both of pitch and intensity, tends to take the form of a *sine curve*; partly on the ground of the natural ease of this type of pulsation, and partly because that form is most pleasing to the musical ear. The reason that the vibrato is present in that type of bodily tension which is characteristic of emotional expression is that it is actually a form of trembling. In good music this is so modulated that it lends beauty to the tone.

All instrumental vibrato is undoubtedly an imitation of the vocal. The *violinist,* for example, aims to give the tone the richness, tenderness and flexibility characteristic of the voice; but in this imitation or voluntary production of the vibrato, he improves upon the vocal because he has a better control of the tone. He is, therefore, able to make it even more pleasing to the ear, usually by holding down the extent of the pulsation to a quarter tone step as opposed to a semitone in voice. The vibrato occurs not only in the bowed stringed *instruments* but possibly in all the orchestral and band instruments, although not to the same degree of pulsation or so conspicuously. In the clarinet, for instance, it is seldom recognized in hearing but phono-photography almost invariably reveals it in beautiful clarinet tones, especially in solo parts. Sometimes it is a pitch vibrato, sometimes intensity, but usually both, and there is nearly always a timbre vibrato present.

In certain instruments a particular kind of vibrato is produced by mechanical devices; as, for example, the tremolo or the *voix celeste* in the organ. In fixed instruments, such as the piano and organ, there are various devices by which the vibrato may be produced through sympathetic vibrations and other means. The sympathetic vibration in the violin often results in a conspicuous intensity vibrato.

The significance of the conception here presented is of far-reaching consequence in music. It recognizes the organic basis for a trembling in tone production. This trembling is evidenced in the *tonal,* the *dynamic,* the *temporal* and the *qualitative* aspect of the tone. The term vibrato is generic: scores of kinds of vibrato may be designated in terms of specific characteristics for which we now have names. To the singer it is not a question as to whether or not he shall use the vibrato; the question is, What kind is to be *cultivated* and *tolerated*?

Beauty in the vibrato is found in *artistic deviation* from the precise and uniform in all the attributes of tone. It is the most systematic, natural, and essential of musical ornaments. Its beauty lies in its contribution to the flexibility, the tenderness, and the richness of the tone as opposed to the thinness, the rigidity, and the coldness of a tone. It represents the periodic changes of pitch, intensity, and timbre in *sonance.* Richness of tone results from *successive fusion* of changes of tone as distinguished from simultaneous fusion in timbre. *Flexibility* of tone results from indefiniteness of outline. Tenderness of tone results from evidence of organic trembling. The genuine vibrato is automatic and expresses the truth, like the smile and the frown. To cultivate the vibrato, one should not cultivate a sign of feeling which is not present, but cultivate the power to feel music genuinely.

In ordinary listening we hear many more bad vibratos than good ones. We find evidence for the *desirability* of the good vibrato from many sources, among which we may mention the following:

The Universality of Its Occurrence in Good Singing: No singing can be good without the vibrato except for an occasional contrasting effect. Objective measurements reveal its presence often in the most desirable form where the singer denies its use, and the musical listener has failed to hear it as such. If any recognized musician thinks he can find one exception to this rule, it is his duty to document it by making an objective recording and publishing the fact. The issue involved is a vital one for good music, but it is greatly confused in most current theory and practice.

Its Automatic Nature: The fact that the vibrato in voice occurs automatically whenever the person sings with genuine feeling indicates that it is an inherent mode of expression in the *aesthetic mood.* Like the smile and the frown, it is an organic, natural, and true expression of feeling when genuine. It can, of course, be imitated and learned, just as a smile and a frown can be acquired; and to that extent it is an imitation of feeling.

Its Use in Instrumental Performance: The fact that the violinst cultivates the vibrato at the expense of great effort and vastly increased difficulty in performance attests its desirability in the highest of instrumental arts.

Its Conflict with Precision: The fact that the vibrato is a clearly preferred alternative to precision and smoothness in tone in the face of the violence that it does to intonation, melody, and harmony testifies to its great worth.

Its Place in Tone Quality: The fact that in the best musical hearing the vibrato is not thought of distinctly as a pulsating affair but as flexibility, tenderness, and richness in tone quality, all of which are regarded as desirable, constitutes significant evidence of its place in the musical situation.

The most desirable average extent of pitch, intensity, and timbre, singly or in combination, is that which produces flexibility, tenderness, and richness of tone, *without giving undue prominence to the pulsating quality as such.* That is, the effect is good when it produces the desired tone quality, but does not make us clearly conscious of the fact that there are distinct waves.

An *extent* of the pulsation smaller than that defined in the above rule fails, in proportion to its smallness, to contribute toward the betterment of tone quality and a larger pulsation produces a bad vibrato, usually a tremolo.

Freedom from *irregularity* in extent or ratio within a given tone is essential to a good vibrato. As in all motor skills, the inceptive stages are irregular. The extent may be large or small: it may increase or decrease within a single tone or in a succession of tones, but the change must be gradual and smooth. This rule applies also to the part-time or intermittent use of the vibrato on a single tone, which is always an indication of inadequacy.

Artistic performance demands *variation in extent and rate* throughout a performance. A uniform vibrato, even in the most perfect form, becomes monotonous and fails to function in phrasing, interpretation, and expression of the individuality of the performer.

The most desirable *average rate* is that which causes the best fusion of tone quality in sonance without producing a chattering through excessive rate. The faster the rate the more completely the fusion takes place in sonance within a medium range of tolerance. High rate introduces a new element; namely, chatter, which takes the place of pitch wave. Slow rate not only fails in producing fusion, but makes the wave movement more prominent.

In vocal vibrato the pulsations in pitch should be primary and dominant. This is true primarily on the ground of its near universality in good singing, but also on the ground of its relative prominence perceptually in the most refined vibrato.

The combination of synchronous pulsations in the three media makes a larger contribution toward tone quality than its occurrence in one or two.

In instrumental music, relatively pure intensity pulsation is permissible, as in organ stops and in the use of beats within a region of tolerance for rate.

In solo parts, both vocal and instrumental, the artist has larger latitude for giving prominence to the vibrato than he has in ensemble. This rule holds particularly for instrumental performances and, more specifically, for all other than the string instruments.

The more nearly alike the timbres of the instruments within an orchestral choir, the greater may be the demand for the vibrato in that choir.

A *bad* vibrato is one which is excessive or erratic in the extent of pulsation in pitch or intensity. There is, of course, more bad vibrato than good in music on the same principle that a comedian says, "Black horses eat more than white horses because there are more of them," and also because of the relative difficulty among individual singers of producing a good vibrato. Of course we dislike a bad vibrato and should discourage it, but that is no excuse for rejecting or disliking a good vibrato.

Scarcely any two persons hear a given vibrato alike. The reason for this lies in certain facts of individual differences, among which the following are conspicuous:

The Vibrato Ear: As in pitch discrimination or hearing ability, one person may be a hundred times as keen as another person in his capacity for hearing the presence of the vibrato or vibrato differences. This presents a most embarrassing problem to the performer, and, hence, a very great confusion as to what is good and what is bad in the discussion among individuals in the audience. These gross individual differences in what we may call *vibrato ear* or *sense of vibrato* prevent us from saying that a particular vibrato is ideal, good or bad without specifying for whom it is so. Ordinarily we may aim at a particular group type; such as, the fine musical ear, the average ear, or the crooner-saxophone ear.

The Feeling-Response: One thing that is as important as the ear is the natural and temperamental feeling-response or the emotionality of the listener. So far as the arousing of feeling is concerned, the majority of persons in a normal population shed the artist's outpouring of a beautiful tone as a duck sheds water. It has no meaning to them; it does not arouse the appropriate feeling, and is, therefore, largely lost. We have the technical word, *empathy,* to designate this trait of "feeling oneself into a situation." Musical empathy is one of the most essential elements of musical appreciation.

The Attitude and Training: The effect of attitude of the musician has been demonstrated in a shocking manner by the history of the attitude toward the vibrato—the inadequate and ridiculous descriptions that have been given, the fanciful explanations, the mystical implications, the groundless musical criticisms, the ill-directed and wasteful musical pedagogy as affecting the vibrato. These musical tragedies have their common root in the absence of correct knowledge of the nature of the vibrato.

The Listener's Mood: In addition to all the above variables, we have learned to take into account the point of view of the listener, and have distinguished between the critical mood and the musical mood. Both are legitimate and essential, but each yields quite different results. The former must prevail largely in training periods and in critical activities; whereas, the latter should prevail in the normal musical situation in which the object is the derivation of pleasure.

We are dealing with aesthetics, and aesthetics is analytical and critical throughout. Therefore, in speaking of norms of beauty, indifference, or ugliness, we must confine ourselves to that which can be observed or felt in the critical mood. In view of these facts, it is clear (1) that what makes a good vibrato or a bad one is to be answered in terms of the extent to which it serves its purpose of contributing the three specifically named elements of feeling value to the tone; (2) that there can be no single standard of good— and the feeling value depend upon the listen— and the feeling value depend upon the listener's *"sense of vibrato"*; (3) that norms for best current practice are available and applicable: and (4) that there is abundant room for improvement beyond these norms in the direction of an ideal vibrato for the fine musical ear.

There are three stages in ear training for the vibrato: (1) factual information, such as musical terminology and nomenclature, analysis of the problem, demonstration of specific aspects: (2) practical exercises in the recognition, description, and evaluation of elements involved in each skill; and (3) drill exercises for the development of speed and accuracy in each operation. The mastery, appreciation, and feeling is really the ultimate goal in ear training. Only after these three stages have been pursued thoroughly can we undertake to master the rendition of the vibrato in voice or instrument.

As to a general theory for *training in the vibrato,* we may suggest the following considerations:

Wherever a student of voice has natural capacity for singing with feeling, *the vibrato has come in automatically.* Therefore, the problem with the musical student is not how to inject the vibrato but how to modulate it.

This modulation should take place not through conscious innervation of particular muscles but through the exercise of censorship of the ear which has been refined for hearing of the vibrato by exact knowledge of its nature and variables and by the acquisition of skills for the hearing, evaluation, and feeling each variable in turn.

However, a part of this orientation for the vibrato is knowledge of the musculatures and various physiological factors which determine rate and extent of vibrato. But the point here made is that the modulation of the vibrato will gradually take care of itself when the ear and the aesthetic judgment have been trained.

On the basis of cumulative experimental evidence, I would predict that an approach to an ideal vibrato for a fine musical ear may be found in the direction of enhancement of tone quality by a slight increase in the rate of the vibrato over the average rate now prevailing, and a very material reduction of the pitch and intensity extent. What would it mean to the musical world if our great singers were to reduce their vibrato to the extent now prevailing in the violin? See C. E. Seashore, *Psychology of the Vibrato in Voice and Instrument.* —C.E.S.

vibrator. See ACOUSTICS.

vibratory movement. See quality.

vicuna. Wild and smallest member of the Llama family, yielding the finest fibre classified as wool.

Viddui mode. See JEWISH MUSIC.

vièle, viele a roue. See MUSICAL INSTRUMENTS.

Vienna Secession. See art nouveau.

Viennese ware. See CERAMICS II.

viga (Sp.). A beam.

vihan (Siam.). Buddhist chapel or hall of worship.

vihāra (Skr.). Buddhist hall of learning.

Viking art. See SCANDINAVIAN ART; PREHISTORIC ART.

village baroque. See CZECHOSLOVAKIA, ART OF.

village, picturesque. See folly.

village planning. See CIVIC PLANNING.

villanella. An Italian folk song of the 16th cent. allied to the madrigal, but in rustic or humorous style. Also a dance with song, of similar character.

vīnā. See MUSICAL INSTRUMENTS.

vine. In classical art, especially in Greek pottery, a decorative motif in which leaves are set on either side of either a straight or wavy stem line; it may represent ivy, grapevine, or laurel, depending upon the shape of the leaf. —L.T.S.

vinyl resin. Among the synthetic materials that serve as coatings for works of art, the polymerized derivatives of vinyl alcohol probably have the greatest use. They form clear, transparent films with mild organic solvents, are capable of being brushed or sprayed, and can be removed safely from most types of painting. —G.L.S.

viol family (viola, viola d'amore, viola da braccio, viola da gamba). See MUSICAL INSTRUMENTS.

violent perspective. See PERSPECTIVE.

violin clef. See NOTATION.

violin family (violoncello, etc.). See MUSICAL INSTRUMENTS.

virelai. See MEDIEVAL MUSIC.

virga. See MEDIEVAL MUSIC; neumes.

Virgil practice clavier. A "dumb" piano.

virginal. A small type of harpsichord. See MUSICAL INSTRUMENTS.

virgin parchment. *Book.* Parchment made from the skins of newborn lamb, calf, kid.

virgin wool. Wool that has never been previously spun, woven, knitted, felted or otherwise made into a manufactured product.

viridian. Called also transparent oxide of chromium, verte emeraude, and Guignet's green, this pigment is a fairly modern contribution to the art of painting, having been first put on the market in 1838. It is a slightly bluish green, useful in both oil and water color, and stable under even extreme conditions of exposure to light and to chemical reagents. —G.L.S.

virtuosity. See virtuoso.

virtuoso (L. *virtu,* excellence, strength, courage, virtue). A person who excels in the technique of an art, especially a performer on the violin, the piano, or any musical instrument. Used occasionally in the graphic and plastic arts to describe one whose technical facility or skill in the use of a medium excels his conceptual power or originality of expression to such a degree as apparently to become an end in itself. Thus many Hellenistic sculptors or 17th and 18th cent. baroque and rococo painters, sculptors, and architects may be said to be characterized by "mere virtuosity." —L.D.L.

viscose rayon. The third method (historically) of producing rayon filaments and by which about 83 per cent of the world's rayon was produced in 1938. The product by this method is regenerated cellulose, which has been coagulated or solidified from a solution of cellulose xanthate. —G.W.R.

Vishnu. In Hindu religion, *the Preserver,* and second god of the triad.

Visigothic architecture. See SPAIN, ART OF.

visorium. See amphitheatre.

Vistula Gothic. See POLISH ART.

visual and space arts. A term used by artists, authors, and art educators to embrace the entire field of art variously designated as "visual arts," "space arts," fine, industrial, and related arts; introduced into the nomenclature of art education in an attempt to coin a term that would avoid the distinction implied between fine and not fine, practical and impractical, or useful and non-useful concepts of art; includes the following areas of study: art appreciation, architecture, sculpture, painting, industrial art, graphic art, advertising art, domestic or household art, civic art, theatre art, and history of art. Whitford and Winslow in *Dictionary of Education.*

visual angle, cone. See PERSPECTIVE.

visual form. See PSYCHOLOGY OF ART.

visual instruction. Instruction in which a great variety of illustrative materials may be utilized as aids in pupil understanding or appreciation, such as lantern slides, models, and specimens. Whitford and Winslow in *Dictionary of Education.*

vitreous enamelling. See ENAMELLING ON METAL.

vividness. See LITERARY CRITICISM.

Vladislav Gothic. See CZECHOSLOVAKIA, ART OF.

vocabulary, musical. See idiom A.

vocalization. The art of singing prolonged and sustained vowel sounds.

vocational art. Any art serving an occupation or means of livelihood. Whitford and Winslow in *Dictionary of Education.*

voice, leading. See idiom C (4).

voile. A transparent, clinging fabric which

is dainty and durable. May be made of any one or a combination of twisted cotton or rayon yarns.

volté. See galliard.

volume, a. *Book.* A bound book complete, or part of a whole. Generally, *but not always,* having its own title page and register.

volume color. See COLOR.

volume creation. See SCULPTURE.

volume, negative, positive. See SCULPTURE.

volutes. In Greek and Roman architecture, the spiral scrolls of the Ionic capital; also the small scrolls of the Corinthian and composite capitals.

volute-crater. See crater.

vomitorium. See amphitheatre.

Vorschlag (Ger.). See appogiatura.

votive tablets. Generally, ornamented and inscribed stone markers signifying devotion or fulfilment of a vow.

voussoir (Fr.). Any of the wedgeshaped pieces which constitute an arch or vault.

vulgar sociologism. The term now used to characterize that trend in the philosophy of art and esp. in literary criticism which predominated in the Soviet Union in the early 30's and which has been rejected in favor of the concept of socialist realism (q.v.). The older tendency was to interpret art and cultural productions generally as a reflection of the class consciousness of the author and to "explain" art mechanically in terms of sociology alone, without taking into consideration its unique qualitative richness, and without explaining why certain works of art have an appeal enduring through centuries. The older view also tended to search classic works for an expression of the personal, consciously held views of the author on social questions, and to confuse an evaluation of such views with a critique of the art. Some of the advocates even went so far as to hold that in communist society the works of even the greatest poets of the bourgeois epoch, like Shakespeare, for example, would no longer have any significance for people.

W

wainga. See AUSTRALIAN ABORIGINAL ART.

Wakakusa yaki (Jap.). Pottery made in Yamato province.

wakasnuri (Jap.). Mottled lacquer ware. Overlapping colors, black, white, gold and silver, rubbed down to produce a level surface cloudlike or mottled in effect.

wakizashi (Jap.). Short sword. A companion weapon worn with the long sword, *katana* (q.v.), by the *samurai.*

walling wax. A kind of wax used in etching to form a miniature wall or bank round the edge of a plate to hold the etching acid, etc.

wall painting. A picture painted on a wall such as fresco, oil or tempera.

walnut oil. Among the oils used as mediums for painting, this seems to have been much favored in the latter part of the Renaissance in Europe. It is mentioned by Armenini, Bisagno, Borghini, Leonardo da Vinci, Lornazzo, Vasari, Volpato, and others. It comes from walnuts which are oil to about 65 per cent. It dries rather more slowly than does linseed oil and it is less apt to discolor and to crack on drying. —G.L.S.

Wanderers, The. See RUSSIAN ARTS.

warm colors. See COLOR.

warp. Threads running lengthwise of the fabric, always in two series. In the loom, each series is connected to a heddle. The heddles work up and down, causing the warps to cross at the moment that the shuttle is thrown across the loom carrying the weft. —B.E.J.

Warsaw, school of. See POLISH ART.

washing. *Cer.* Process of purification by levigation, settling or lawning. See CERAMICS I.

water color. The art of painting on paper with a medium whose solvent is water. A process of painting with transparent or semi-transparent washes which distinguishes the medium from other types of painting. The colors are usually mixed with gum which acts as a binding medium.

Although this type of painting has developed mainly in the last hundred years, it was used by the Egyptians on papyrus rolls. In the medieval period illuminated manuscripts were painted with a water color medium.

The practice of water color as it is used today developed out of the drawings executed in various mediums from the 15th to the 17th cent. These wash drawings were usually made with pen and ink and a brown wash was used to indicate the volumes. Many drawings of this type were done by Rembrandt.

Water color painting developed rapidly in England with the work of Paul Sandby and John Cozens. The progress of development was from monochrome through neutral tints to full color. J. M. W. Turner was one of the first to employ a full range of colors in his water colors.

Since the time of Turner water color has become a separate and distinct art form employing various drawing mediums such as pencil, charcoal, ink, crayon, or pastel which are then gone over with washes ranging from transparent to opaque. The type of paintings made with opaque water color are often referred to as gouache (q.v.) drawings, esp. when a pliable adhesive is added to the binder to give the surface a soft sheeny quality. See PAINTING. —R.L.W

1053

water-glass. See stereochromy.

water-marks. (1) Patterns in paper made by wires set in designs in the screen on which the paper sheeting is formed have been called water-marks or paper-marks. These are not found in Oriental papers or in those of Arabian manufacture. They appear in European papers at the end of the 13th cent., particularly in products of the mills of Bologna and of Fabriano. Various designs have been used, at times the maker's full name. (2) *Book.* The design, etc., in the sheets of paper denoting maker, the mill at which it was made, or the size, introduced when the paper is in a pulp stage.

water-organ. See mechanical instruments.

wattle. *n.* A frame of poles and twigs platted together. *v.* To weave or twist, as twigs, into a network. (**Wattle-and-daub construction:** A wattle, or frame of poles and twigs platted together and covered or daubed, as with mud or plaster.) —J.M.M.

wattle and daub construction. See daub; wattle.

wave molding. A type of molding developed in the English decorated period consisting of adjacent convex and concave surfaces, sometimes compounded with other forms.

wave ornament. A highly conventionalized wave motive. Generally a repeat pattern of overlapping curves.

wax. Long known in the arts as both a molding and a surfacing material, wax has a variety of sources. All waxes, chemically speaking, are esters of monohydric alcohols, being different in that respect from oils which are esters of a trihydric alcohol. Paraffin, derived from shale oil, lignite, and petroleum, is similar in its source to montan wax which comes from lignite and from peat. Other common waxes are beeswax, Chinese insect wax, candelilla wax, and carnauba. These differ somewhat in hardness, plasticity, and melting point. As a coating material, wax in some form has been known since the earliest records of the arts. Sculpture and modelling in wax were common in the Renaissance, and at various times wax has been taken up as a painting medium. One such time was the early part of the Christian Era in the Fayum district of Egypt where mummy portraits were made with this as a vehicle for the pigment. —G.L.S.

wax sculpture. Owing to its pliancy and its readiness to absorb various dyes wax is particularly suited for two frequently associated purposes in art: (1) for the creation of images in the service of transitory needs, images which may or may not be destroyed after having been used. Examples: the effigies used in image magic. (2) For the creation of credible counterfeits of reality with the intention of deceiving the eye of the spectator. Examples: mannequins or Mme. Tussaud's waxworks. In order to render the illusion more complete the effect of the sculptured and properly colored parts of such an effigy may be heightened by the addition of real human hair and of human garments. The influence of wax sculpture upon art corresponds to the two extremes of its technical application. It leads either (1) to perfunctory sketchy treatment just sufficiently detained to assure recognition of the objects represented or (2) to the most meticulous realism. The latter is well attested in the case of Roman portraiture which arose from the imitation in more durable materials of the wax effigies used in family cults and in the ceremonial of funerals. —R.B.

wa-yo (Jap.). See JAPANESE ART.

weathering. The slope given to offsets, to buttresses, and to the upper surfaces of exterior features, to throw off rain.

weaving. The interlacing of the **warp and filling** (weft) to produce a fabric. In a strict technical sense only fabrics produced on a loom are called woven. All woven fabrics are composed of two or more systems of threads known as warp or ends and filling, weft or picks. The warp and filling threads are interlaced with each other at right angles. The manner in which these threads interlace with each other determines the weave.

All woven fabrics are divided into four main classes: **Single fabrics** having one warp and one filling; **compound fabrics**, having more than one warp or filling or both; **pile** or **plush** having a pile or nap of either warp or filling on the surface of a single or compound fabric; **gauze** or **leno** in which the warp thread in addition to interlacing with the filling threads is twisted with threads of its own system. **Lappet** and **swivel** weaves are sometimes classified in this fourth group, but because they both represent special methods of decorating a single or a compound fabric by means of extra threads, they may be classed as a compound fabric. All weaves are derivatives of one of the **foundation weaves** which are **plain weave, twill weave,** and the **satin weave.**

There is only one **plain weave,** and it completes itself on two ends and two picks and may be woven on a two-harness loom. It is the most closely interlaced of all weaves and is used more often than any other. In cotton goods it is called the **cotton weave,** in linen, the **linen weave,** in silk the **taffeta weave.**

Twill weaves are numerous; all produce diagonal lines on a fabric. The smallest twill weave completes itself on two ends and two picks. By the use of more ends and picks (to the capacity of the loom to reproduce them) larger and more elaborate twills are made. Twills have special names as **Prunella, Cashmere, Jean, Jeanette** and **Genoa.** Four harness filling twills are known as **Swandsdown twills, serge weave, blanket weave,** **Shallon** and **Cassimere twill** are well known names.

Satin Weaves do not have the lines found in twills. They have a smooth surface. Satin weaves are used in high textured fabrics. **Sateen** is a stout lustrious cotton fabric woven with a satin weave.

web. The continuation of the insertion of weft threads beyond the extent of the pile, to form a securely finished end of a rug, and also act as a protection for the end of the pile. —B.E.J.

Wedgewood ware. See CERAMICS II.

wedging. Process of working or kneading clay by hand. See CERAMICS I.

weft. The weft is a thread shuttled through the fabric crosswise of the loom between the warp threads. The weft serves to tie-in the yarn that forms the surface tufts or loops. The number of rows per inch is indicative of the closeness of the weave. —B.E.J.

wei. See CHINESE ARTS.

well-tempered. *Mus.* Tuned in equal temperament (see ACOUSTICS). *Well-tempered Clavichord* (*Wohltemperiertes Clavier*), title of Bach's 48 preludes and fugues.

Werkbund, Deutscher. See Deutscher Werkbund.

West-Islamic art. See ISLAMIC ART.

wheel. See GLASS AND GLASS-MAKING.

Wheel of the Law. In Buddhist art, an eight-spoked wheel symbolizing the eight-fold path of Buddha's teaching. See *cakra* (Skr.). See SYMBOLISM IN FAR EASTERN ART.

wheel window. A round window with mullions radiating from the center like the spokes of a wheel.

whelk red. See Tyrian purple.

white lead. The basic carbonate of lead, containing ordinarily about 70 per cent of lead carbonate and 30 per cent of lead hydrate, has been by far the most used white pigment in the history of the painting art. It was one of the first artificially prepared pigments, and methods for its preparation were described by Theophrastus, Pliny, and Vitruvius. Numerous medieval recipes for its manufacture are recorded. Most of these involve the exposure of strips of metallic lead to the fumes of vinegar in some way combined with vapors of fermentation to introduce carbon dioxide. Although generally stable, white lead is darkened if in a lean tempera or aqueous film when exposed to hydrogen sulphide in the air, even in low concentration. This accounts for much of the blackening of the white touches used on Renaissance drawings and probably explains why Far Eastern painters never adopted this pigment for general use. —G.L.S.

white porcelain. See CERAMICS I.

white spirituals. See American folk forms, in music.

white tiger. See SYMBOLISM IN FAR EASTERN ART.

whiting. This name is commonly given in the trade to powdered chalk, natural calcium carbonate, generally used in painting grounds and in grounds for gilding. See chalk. —G.L.S.

whole rest. See NOTATION.

whole step, whole tone scale. See scales and modes.

Wiener Keramik. See CERAMICS II.

wild flower sanctuary. A tract of land especially devoted to the propagation and protection of wild flowers under natural conditions. See CIVIC PLANNING.

wild life sanctuary. See CIVIC PLANNING.

wild man (wild folk). Representation in Western medieval art of men and women whose bodies are covered with long hair. Derived from native pre-Christian folklore wild men are conceived as dwarfs or giants, as uncivilized, as intimately allied with the life of forests and as demonds of fertility. Consequently they are used in art as symbols of lust and progeny (holding coats of arms). Frequent in drolery (q.v.) from late 13th to early 16th cent. —R.B.

Willendorf figure. See PREHISTORIC ART.

William and Mary style. See EARLY AMERICAN ART.

Wilno neo-classicist school. See POLISH ART.

Wilton carpet. A Wilton weave derives its name from the fact that it was first woven in the town of Wilton, England. This weave is the one which is generally known as having the buried or hidden values and quality and is therefore generally in the higher price range. By this is meant that a portion of the yarn used in the rug is buried in the back, adding resiliency and quality to the carpet. The Wilton weave is made in two types, the worsted Wilton and the wool Wilton. The worsted Wilton offers the greater possibilities as to fineness of design and texture, whereas the wool Wiltons is more luxurious under foot, owing to its greater depth of pile and softness.

The difference between the worsted and wool Wilton is really seen by comparing the general appearance and difference in the depth of pile in the two types of fabric. The tufts of the worsted Wilton are very resilient and stand up straight, as is easily noticeable, and give the appearance of velvet. It is on account of this stiffness that it is possible to produce a velvet-like yarn and obtain fine detail in the design.

The construction of the wool Wilton is heavier, esp. in the back, as the yarn is coarser in twist, and it is also buried in the same manner as in the worsted Wilton. A genuine Wilton must be woven by the Jacquard process. Any carpet or rug not so woven is not a Wilton. In all essentials the Wilton is still loomed by the method given to the world through the genius of Joseph Marie Jacquard, plus the addition of the power drive.

While generally in the past this weave has been made in the better qualities, it is pos-

sible to produce "Wiltons" that are less expensive than high grade axminsters and velvet weaves. —B.E.J.

wing. A side building, attached to, but usually of less importance and size than the main building.

wiping. *Etch.* In preparing an intaglio plate for printing, the etching ink is spread on the entire plate and is then wiped off the surface, leaving the ink only in the lines. Done by wiping the warm plate with a stiff tarlatan rag to produce a rage-wiped print or finishing the wiping of the plate with the palm of the hand to produce a hand-wiped print. See PRINTS AND PRINT PROCESSES. —K.K.

wire-marks. In the process of making paper by hand a wet pulp of fibre is formed into a sheet on a screen of wire, the deckle. The pulp in settling is slightly thicker in the interstices of the wires than over them and by transmitted light shows this pattern called wire-marks. These are further specified as laid lines and chain lines. —G.L.S.

wire sewing. *Book.* Stitching the sections of a book.

wisecracks. *Quip* is the older word; *gag* is the theatrical equivalent. As a "jocular smart remark", the wisecrack resembles the epigram rather than the proverb, although many wisecracks originate in parodies of proverbs, contain proverbial phrases, or pass into proverbial usage. In its ephemeralness and desire to be different the wisecrack is the rhetorical counterpart of slang. Strictly, like slang, it belongs to the popular rather than the folk level of usage; but like slang, it is constantly playing back and forth between written and unwritten tradition and between individual and group invention. The lore of the wisecrack, like that of slang, is for the most part an urban and sophisticated lore. In its instability, its pattern of formula and variation, and its creation of folk metaphor, it is, if not folklore, at least "folklore in the making."

Almost every form of wit and rhetorical device is employed in the wisecrack: puns, malapropisms, boners, and other varieties of word play and humorous mistakes. (She was so dumb she thought a subordinate clause was one of Santa's offspring; He is a big needle and thread man from So-and-So; She is not my best girl—just necks best; Lettuce is a proposition); Wellerisms (As the pencil sharpener said, "Now to get down to the point"); Irish bulls and paradoxes (I couldn't commit suicide if my life depended on it; She would be cute if it wasn't for her face); extravagant impossibilities (Yours till elephants roost on rose bushes); nonsense (More fun than I've had since the day the cow catcher had a calf); exaggeration (She was so thin that she could fall through a flute and never strike a note); the fabulous or the tall tale (It was so cold the cows gave ice cream); *reductio ad absurdum* (If steamships sold for a nickel, I couldn't buy the echo of a whistle); *non sequitur* (Let's you and him fight until I get tired).

The use of the formula is basic to the wisecrack: so dumb, so tight, you tell 'em, they call, she was only, you don't have to, you may be. Certain formulae are identified with disparaging or insulting wisecracks which may be called "slams" (They call her a toe dancer because she dances on other people's toes; You don't have to hang from a tree to be a nut; You may be bread in old Kentucky but you're just a crumb around here).

The habit of wisecracking is related to the American trait of "laughing it off" and to the love of mottoes and slogans. Many trade slogans are nothing but wisecracks: We wash everything but the baby; You can whip our cream but you can't beat our milk; You furnish the girl, we furnish the rest; Look at your hat, everyone else does; Why kill your wife? Let us do the dirty work; You wreck 'em, we fix 'em. See *The People, Yes,* by Carl Sandburg, 1936; *10,000 Jokes, Toasts & Stories,* by Lewis and Faye Copeland, 1939.
—B.A.B.

Wistar glasses. See GLASS AND GLASSMAKING.

wisteria. See SYMBOLISM IN FAR EASTERN ART.

Woelfflin method of classification. See PAINTING.

wood. The fibrous structure of trees and similar plants has had a multiplicity of use in the arts. As a solid material, it has been the substance of many sculptures and of innumerable objects. It has served as handles and as tools for designers and craftsmen, as supports for painting, and as blocks for printing. In all cases the bulk of wood fibre is cellulose and the structure is cellular, muhe like that of a honeycomb. Wood is principally characterized by its dimensional changes corresponding largely to changes in moisture content. It is this which makes it warp and, on extreme drying, check and crack. It is subject also to deterioration from the attacks of insects, beetles, and termites, and by parasitical growths such as the dry-rot fungi. Technically, woods are classified into two large groups: the hardwoods, characterized by a certain large cell called a pore or vessel; these hardwoods are further differentiated into a ring-porous group such as oak, ash, and elm, and the diffuse-porous group such as maple, black walnut, and yellow poplar. In the former the springwood pores are generally large compared to those of the summer-wood and annual rings are easily visible. Softwoods have fibre-like cells or tracheids instead of pores. The name is slightly misleading because all of the technically called softwoods are in reality soft. They come from needle—or scale-leaved trees, most of them bearing cones. —G.L.S.

wood block. A die cut from wood, used for making impressions on paper or on fabric.

wood block print. An impression from wood block on paper or on fabric. In the Orient the flat of the block is used as the surface to be cut.

woodcut. See PRINTS AND PRINT PROCESSES.

wood engraving (in woodcut). See PRINTS AND PRINT PROCESSES.

wooden tiger. See MUSICAL INSTRUMENTS.

wood-pulp. Broken up fibres of wood are used in the manufacture of cardboard and of paper and in many of the artificial building boards. All of these materials have had some use as supports for painting. In general, wood-pulp as such is either mechanical, in which the fibres are separated by grinding and soaking, or chemical, in which the fibres are separated out of chips by the action of alkali or acid solutions. See paper. —G.L.S.

wool (Skr. *urna*; L. *lana*; Gr. *lenos*). The soft curled or crisped covering or coat of the sheep.

How the knowledge of shearing wool came to our ancestors is lost in the mists of antiquity. We have account books dated 2200 B.C. telling of the weavers of Ur who were working for the priests of the temple. On clay tablets are the records of the weavers and the amount of wool each one received.

It is thought that in the Paleolithic period man plucked the tufts of wool left on the bushes by wild sheep and discovered, perhaps accidentally, that with his fingers he could twist it into a strong cord. The cord had many uses. Felt and cord were the first results of processing wool.

Mesopotamia is the country of wool production and wool weaving. The Babylonian loved the heavy luxurious folds of wool material. About 1800 B.C. heavy goat skins were worn as a skirt. From cuneform inscriptions from Asia Minor, we learn that at Assur, centre of the Assyrian Empire, the merchants were organized into Guilds, very much as the merchants of the medieval period were organized. The wool business was their major concern. There is no doubt that the raw material of the Babylonian and Assyrian textile industries was wool. (Linen was also used. Fragments of linen have been found at Susa.) Draperies and tapestries as well as clothing were made of wool. In the Assyrian period the dress seen on the stone reliefs were long tunics with short sleeves worn with a fringed shawl. Elaborate knotted fringe and tassels finished the bottom of these tunics over which leather belts were worn. These dresses were ornamented with geometric designs, rosettes, the "Tree of Life", and human figures. These patterns may have been woven or embroidered. We read of purple, blue, dark red, red yellow, and red brown fabrics.

There are many records of trading in wool with Phoenicians. Very little wool was used in Egypt until the Coptics (Egyptian Christians) wove their wonderful fabrics using linen and wool. The Doric Greek chitons (long tunics) were made of wool. The heavy folds and strong lines of the apotygma, with its overfold at the top suggesting a blouse, is seen in Greek sculptured figures. Later the Greeks used linen which gave the finer, sharper folds seen in the sculptured figures of Ionic and Corinthian sculptures.

The Romans used wool for their tunics and togas. (Linen and a very small quantity of silk were used in the *clavis*.) The Romans bred sheep for fine long staple wool, the Roman sheep being the ancestors of the Spanish merino wool bearing sheep. (The merino sheep are the parent stock of all the fine wool sheep of Europe, America and Australia.)

At the end of the 13th cent. England was the great wool producing country of Europe. They furnished the weavers of Flanders with wool to such an extent as to tend to keep the peace.

Sheep were first introduced into America at Jamestown in 1609. President George Washington imported the best breeds of sheep from England and promoted the bringing to America of the best spinners and weavers from England.

In 1801-1812 Colonel David Humphries imported merino sheep from Spain, which were sold to the Connecticut farmers.   —G.W.R.

wool, artificial. All types of cellulose and non-cellulose materials made to imitate the wool fibre and its valuable physical and chemical characteristics. Some of them are "Sniafil", "Lanusa", Casein fibre, etc.
—G.W.R.

Worcester porcelain. See CERAMICS II.

work forms. See FURNITURE.

work habit. (art ed.) Procedure in art which has been established, become semi-automatic, or automatic through repeated use. Whitford and Winslow in *Dictionary of Education*.

workmanship. Technical skill applied to the execution of a piece of art work. Whitford and Winslow in *Dictionary of Education*.

work period. (art ed.) Time provided for the carrying on of art activities, connected with an integrated unit of teaching. Whitford and Winslow in *Dictionary of Education*.

workshop. (art ed.) A place in a school building provided for carrying on art activities. Whitford and Winslow in *Dictionary of Education*.

work songs, hollers. See American folk forms, in music; AMERICAN NEGRO LITERATURE.

World of Art group. See RUSSIAN ARTS.

world planning. See CIVIC PLANNING.

worsted yarn. The long, straight fibres combed out of wool, twisted together on high speed spinning frames. A slender, hard, lustrous type.

woven felt carpet. See carpet structures.

wreath. In Roman art, an ornament consisting of an intertwined rope of flowers or leaves forming a circle. Also see HERALDRY.

"wrecks," repainted. See FORGERIES IN PAINTING.

wrinkling. See CHINESE ARTS.

writing (verbal noun of to write, Old English *writan,* to incribe). (1) The use of conventional symbols for the recording by visible means of ideas or of significant sounds; (2) the art or act of tracing by hand such symbols on paper or other material with pen and ink or other writing tool; (3) the product of the art and act of writing.

Writing of all kinds is the subject matter of the science of **paleography**, although inscriptions on, or in, hard materials, which are not writing in a strict sense (see LETTERING), are assigned to a branch discipline known as **epigraphy**, and thus the term paleography is commonly restricted to the study of writing on less durable materials. Materials used for writing have varied with time, place, and use. In western civilization the principal materials have been papyrus in the ancient world, vellum and parchment (in general use after 400 A.D.) during the Middle Ages, and paper (after the 15th Cent.) for the modern world. The chief tool for writing has always been the pen, made in ancient times from a reed and in medieval and later times from either a reed or the wing feather of a large bird. The quill pen remained in general use until superseded in the early 19th cent. by the steel pen nib.

The style of writing also has varied with the intended use. In general three classes may be distinguished: **formal scripts** used for books; **semi-formal scripts** (the **legal hands,** i.e., **chancery, charter, bastard,** and **secretary)** for documents; and **cursive scripts,** the ordinary running hands, for everyday private use. Formal writing acquires its character (1) from being done with a chisel-shaped pen, which, because of its form and not from

variation of pressure in its use, produces wide and narrow strokes; (2) from being written deliberately, each letter being composed of several separate pen-strokes, with the pen lifted from the paper after each stroke; (3) from having the heads and serifs built up of several strokes. Cursive writing on the other hand is done (1) with a pointed pen which produces the running character of the hand (2) by remaining on the paper to form an entire letter or several letters with one stroke, and (3) which frequently ties several letters together in ligatures. Semi-formal scripts show in varying degrees an intermixture of these two contrary characters. It was this interplay of **formal** and **cursive elements** which produced the great variety of scripts in use in western civilization from the 1st cent. to the present time. Probably the most notable example of the process is the change from capital **(majuscule)** to small-letter **(minuscule)** script in which the influence of cursive tendencies on the capital letter-forms produced during the 1st to the 5th cent. A.D. the first of an entirely new genus of scripts. In the modern world formal writing has to a large extent, but not entirely, been replaced by printing from type; semi-formal writing has been superseded by typewriting; and only cursive continues to fulfill its historic role.

The materials, tools, and processes of formal and semi-formal writing are discussed in detail by Edward Johnston and those of cursive writing by Alfred Fairbank in his *A Handwriting Manual,* 1932. See also Edw. Johnston, *Writing and Illuminating, and Lettering,* 1906 ff. and *Decoration and Its Uses: in the imprint,* 1913; E. M. Thompson, *An Introduction to Greek and Latin Paleography,* 1912; B. L. Ullman, *Ancient Writing and Its Influence,* 1932. —E.F.D.

Wu school. See CHINESE ARTS.

X

xoanon (Gr. from *xeo,* to carve). A carved image, a sculpture, a statue. In early archaic times the Greek artists used wood as material for sacred images which were called "xoana". None of these primitive works have been preserved. In his work *Periegesis Hellados* (Description of Greece), Pausanias, the author of the 2nd cent. A.D., still mentions several such "xoana" which were held sacred and had escaped destruction to that time.

—L.L.

xylophone. See MUSICAL INSTRUMENTS.

xystris. See apoxyomenos.

Y

ya chang (Ch.). A knifelike jade tablet, symbol of rank.

ya chêng. See MUSICAL INSTRUMENTS.

yajnoparita (Skr.). Thread worn over the left shoulder and breast of a Hindu designating a twice-born man.

yaksas, yaksis. See INDIAN ART.

Yamato-e (Jap.). Literally, pictures of old Japan. A school of painting in native style at its peak in the 12th cent. and centered largely at Kyoto. See JAPANESE ART.

Yanagihara yaki (Jap.). Pottery made in Chikugo province.

yang. See SYMBOLISM IN FAR EASTERN ART.

yarn. See American folk forms, in literature.

yasti (Skt.). See stupa.

Yastkand ware. See PERSIAN ART.

Yatsushiro yaki (Jap.). Pottery made in Higo province.

yellow ochre. See iron pigments.

yellow ware pottery. See CERAMICS II.

yen (Ch.). Ink stone on which Chinese ink is rubbed up with water.

yi (Ch.). See I.

Yiddish folk-song. See JEWISH MUSIC.

yin. See SYMBOLISM IN FAR EASTERN ART.

yin and yang. See PRIMITIVE ART.

yin chang (Ch.). An impressed seal used in connection with an artist's signature.

Ymagiers. See FRENCH ART.

yoko-e (Jap.). A large, horizontal woodblock print, approximately 10 inches high by 15 inches wide.

Yoro yaki (Jap.). Pottery made in Mino province.

Yoruba art. See AFRICAN NEGRO ART.

yu (Ch.). Sacrificial bronze vessel. Bulbous jar-form with cover and a swiveled bail. For holding sacrificial wine.

yü (Ch.). Bronze vessel, in the form of a large bowl with flaring rim and a base, and generally inscribed. See also MUSICAL INSTRUMENTS.

Yuan art. See CHINESE ARTS.

yüan chin (Ch.). Literally, far and near. Referring to perspective in landscape painting.

yüeh ch'in. See MUSICAL INSTRUMENTS.

Yugoslavia, art of. From the earliest times the Yugoslav groups were never able to achieve political unity. It was only in 1918 that the rising tide of feeling brought together the various South Slavonic lands which had started with the same fundamental inheritance in the days of paganism and had then been separated by cultural and political influences. This has not failed to have its effect upon the history of art but any attempt to separate the provinces would lead to extensive repetition of material created in various periods.

The territory of Yugoslavia, esp. the area along the Dalmatian coast, had formed an integral part of the Roman Empire. It was filled with Roman settlements and Roman remains such as the great palace of Diocletian in the city of Split. This was perhaps the largest monument of the country but it was by no means isolated.

After the Slavs appeared and took control of the country, there was a new outburst of art on Yugoslav territory which was far more advanced than was the Italian art of the same period. It may be questioned whether this new feeling was secured from Byzantium or from points east of the imperial city on the Bosporus. Perhaps it came from the original home of the Slavs and the forced creation of stone instead of wooden buildings. Yet long before the year 1000 there was a large number of church buildings on the east shore of the Adriatic, such as the Church of St. Donatus in Zadar and some of the Churches of Knin.

These buildings, of a type that may be called Byzantine, were gradually remodelled as the Slavs came more closely under the influence of Venice and the Papacy. We can begin to trace in them Romanesque and Gothic elements and in the north in Croatia Western influences, passing from the Crown of St. Stephen, joined in Italian influences of the Renaissance to produce something new. From the 12th to the 17th cent., the Adriatic cities were subjected to these Western influences which reached their height in Dubrovnik. The city was almost destroyed by an earthquake in 1667 but even after it was rebuilt, it was still one of the most perfect examples of the Renaissance with such gems of architecture as the Palace of the Ban, the Mint, and also the old churches.

Further to the north in Croatia, which was directly under the Crown of St. Stephen, and in Slovenia, which was under Hapsburg sovereignty, we find the combination of these forms with the typical Austrian forms of Gothic and it is this type that dominates the oldest buildings of Zagreb and even Lyublyana.

On the other hand in such provinces as Zeta, Rashko, etc., there was a definite preponderance of members of the Orthodox Church and the influence of Byzantine was a decisive factor in the creation of the Serb monasteries of the 12th, 13th and 14th cents., as the Monastery of Dechani and of Grachanitsa, the Monastery of the Archangel at Prilep and the Monastery of Ravanitsa which was built by Knez Lazar, the hero of Kosovo.

Perhaps in no part of Europe was there a greater development of frescos, even more than mosaics. Most of them are unfortunately in a bad state of repair and they have not yet had the careful study which they deserve. Painted in a somewhat stiff and formal style they still personalize and individualize all the leaders of the Nemanya and later dynasties, esp. St. Sava and some of the later secular rulers as Dushan.

The coming of the Turks broke down this flourishing art. The monasteries were burned and plundered and if they were restored, it was never to their former splendor and beauty. The Eastern influences in the decorating of the church and in the construction of dwellings and palaces turned largely into Turkish borrowings, while the more cultured classes were forced into exile or retreated northward across the Danube.

Thus it was not until the beginning of the 19th cent. when Serbia recovered its independence that the way was open for the introduction of a modern architecture and other arts in their modern form. In Croatia and the Roman Catholic provinces art passed through all the same phases which were found in Vienna and in Italy.

The first modern painter was undoubtedly Arsenij Todorovich (1768-1826) while the greatest artist of the period was Konstantin Daniel (1798-1873), a colorist of the first rank. The classical period was replaced about 1840 by a group of romanticists who preferred views of landscape or historical scenes. Still later they were followed by a group of realists after 1875 who became even more popular than were the earlier painters. Vlaho Bukovac and Paya Jovanovich secured a great following at this time because of their skill. Still other painters as Marko Murat began to develop in the pattern of impressionism. After 1912 all authors from all parts of the country really turned to France and the Parisian influence has been strongly felt by the younger artists. During this period there came steadily increasing relations between the Croat Roman Catholic and Orthodox Serb painters. They worked more and more on the same themes and the fundamental cultural divergence between East and West seemed on the way of being bridged.

Sculpture developed more freely in the Roman Catholic area, although there are surprising specimens of wood carvings scattered throughout the entire country. It passed through the same general phases but in the person of Ivan Mestrovich, Yugoslavia found a genius of the first rank. Whether he is picturing his mother or the Balkan hero Marko, Mestrovich has produced striking figures with an independence of technique that separates him from most of his fellows and places his achievements above those of most modern artists. A still younger generation is endeavoring to combine his influences and those of other Western masters.

The confused political situation during the last decade before World War II led to the formation of new local blocs and there were energetic attempts again to disentangle the skeins of provincial culture and to recreate a Serb art, a Croat art, etc., but there were equally strong groups continuing to work toward a large unity. This local patriotism was complicated by Fascist, Nazi, and Communistic ideologies, which seriously hampered all development and often sacrificed art to political theories and other considerations. It remains to see what the future will bring forth, but with the exception of the works of Mestrovich, it must be admitted that the modern art has not reached the level of the medieval period. See *La Yougoslavie d'aujourd'hui,* Belgrade, 1935.   —C.A.M.

yun. See CHINESE ARTS.

yung. See CHINESE ARTS.

Yunkang caves. See CHINESE ARTS.

yurok. See California Indian art.

Z

Zakopane. See POLISH ART.

zapateado. A Spanish dance in which the rhythm is marked by the stamping of the dancer's feet.

Zapotec. A linguistic group living in the valley of Oaxaca, Mexico. They were the authors of a ceremonial civilization which had a pantheon, a calendar system, a method of writing, and they built great ceremonial centers. Their art is highly stylized, yet seems to have been influenced by Maya and Olmec and was later largely supplanted by Mixtec. —G.C.V.

Zemiroth. See JEWISH MUSIC.

Zeus (L. Jupiter). The classical "father of gods and men," supreme deity and sky-god, symbolized by a thunderbolt, sceptre and eagle. In early Greek sculpture and painting he was represented as an austere divinity, brandishing the thunderbolt; later he was thought of as a more benign god, an elderly "man of the world." The most famous statue of him was Phidias' majestic chryselephantine figure at Olympia; but there is an excellent extant bronze recently recovered from the sea and now in the National Museum in Athens. In later painting he was pictured by Correggio, and in sculpture by Cellini, Thorvaldsen, Iannelli, Jennewein and Aitken. —W.R.A.

Zeze yaki (Jap.). Pottery made in Omi province.

ziggurat, zikurat. See MESOPOTAMIAN ART.

zigzag. A continuous decorative pattern in which a line or band is broken into short sharp turns in alternating directions.

zinc pigments. The chief of these is zinc white, an oxide of the metal, first suggested for use as a pigment in 1782 and available on the market as an artist's color in 1834. During the early years of its production zinc white was made largely for water colors, but improvements in the manufacture allowed it to be satisfactorily employed with oil. It is weaker in its hiding power than the white lead which had preceded it for many centuries on the palette of the artist and weaker, also, than the titanium white which has come since. A bright, clear, lemon yellow pigment is made artificially from zinc and chromium and is known as zinc yellow. It made its appearance on the market in the middle of the 19th cent. —G.L.S.

zincography. A method of printing from zinc plates similar to lithography. The drawing or decoration is made on the plate, processed and printed. Sometimes a relief plate is made by etching the zinc plate. —R.L.W.

zingaresca. A gypsy song or dance.

zo (Jap.). Sculptured deity image.

zoanon. See xoanon.

zogan (Jap.). Inlaid work of gold or silver.

zogan-nuri (Jap.). A lacquer technique imitating cloisonné.

zone, zoning. See CIVIC PLANNING.

zoophorus. In classical architecture, a frieze of relief sculptured figures of men or animals or both, continuously arranged.

1064